McDougal, Littell
LITERATURE

English Literature
American Literature
Blue Level
Orange Level
Green Level
RED LEVEL

BLUE MOU
Solomon R.

McDougal, Littell
LITERATURE

Red Level

Susan Duffy Schaffrath
Specialist in Educational Materials
for the Middle Grades, Chicago, Illinois

Lee Sternberg
Nichols Middle School
Evanston, Illinois

McDougal, Littell & Company
Evanston, Illinois
New York   Dallas   Sacramento   Raleigh

Consultants

Sister Regina Marie Alfonso, S.N.D., Assistant Professor of Education Notre Dame College of Ohio, Cleveland, Ohio

Jo Ann L. Amato, Director of Language Arts Grades 7–8, Gesu School, University Heights, Ohio

Helen Brown, Director of the Bureau of Curriculum, Inservice, and Staff Development, Louisiana Department of Education, Baton Rouge, Louisiana

Joseph L. FitzPatrick, Supervisor of Instruction, Brandywine School District, Claymont, Delaware

Saundra Bryn Harmon, Curriculum Specialist for Language Arts, Washington School District, Phoenix, Arizona

Frances L. Miles, Mentor Teacher, Serra High School, San Diego, California

Frances M. Russell, Director of English and Reading K–12, Winchester School District, Winchester, Massachusetts

Blanche M. Sandefer, Instructor of English, Louisiana State University, Baton Rouge, Louisiana

William H. Thomas, Curriculum Specialist, Mt. Diablo Unified School District, Concord, California

Acknowledgments

Arizona Quarterly: For "The Circuit" by Francisco Jiménez, from *The Arizona Quarterly,* Autumn, 1973. Isaac Asimov: For the introduction to *Fantastic Creatures,* edited by Isaac Asimov, Martin Greenberg, and Charles Waugh; copyright © 1981 by Isaac Asimov. Patricia Ayres: For " 'I,' Says the Poem," from *It Doesn't Always Have To Rhyme* by Eve Merriam; copyright © 1964 by Eve Merriam; reprinted by permission of the author. Bantam Books, Inc.: For "The Gift of Cochise" by *Continued on page 712*

ISBN: 0-8123-5900-3

Copyright © 1989 by McDougal, Littell & Company
Box 1667, Evanston, Illinois 60204
All rights reserved. Printed in the United States of America

90 91 / 15 14 13 12 11 10 9 8 7 6 5

CONTENTS

SPECIAL FEATURE

Writers on the Process of Writing   93

UNIT 2.

The Short Story   103

UNIT 3. *N*onfiction   **279**

Shape and Meaning 435

Images and Meaning 447

Ideas in Poetry 471

Vocabulary Development Lessons   633

Handbook of Literary Terms   646

Glossary   661

Suggestions for Further Reading   677

Style Manual for Capitalization, Punctuation, and Spelling   679

Index of Skills   703

Index of Fine Art   709

Index of Titles and Authors   714

Features of This Book

▲ **Great Literature.** *McDougal, Littell Literature, Red Level,* contains unadapted, uncut selections that represent the finest traditional and contemporary literature.

▲ **Organization by Genre.** The text provides a comprehensive study of literary types: myths, tales, and fables; short stories; nonfiction; poetry; drama; and the novel. Each genre is covered in a unit. Most units are divided into sections: for example, The Short Story is divided into Setting, Character, and Plot. Unit introductions and section introductions define and characterize the genres and suggest ways to read different kinds of literature.

▲ **Sustained Study of Literary Techniques.** *McDougal, Littell Literature* is the only series to offer a sustained study of literary elements and techniques. Each literary term is defined, discussed, retaught, extended, and reviewed until students understand clearly how different writers use the element or technique to achieve their purposes. (See the Index of Skills on page 703 for evidence of the breadth and depth of skills coverage.)

▲ **Logical Organization of Study Questions.** The Getting at Meaning questions following each selection are organized in order of increasing difficulty, from **RECALLING** to **INTERPRETING** to **CRITICAL THINKING.** The Developing Skills in Reading Literature exercises guide students in thinking critically about literary techniques. (See page 9 for examples.)

▲ **Integration of Reading and Writing Instruction.** The text teaches students how to write in response to what they have read. Writing assignments emphasize the process of prewriting, writing, and revision. The process is taught in depth in **Handbook: How To Write About Literature.** (See page 612.) A special feature titled **Writers on the Process of Writing** explores the craft of writing as practiced by professional writers. (See page 93.)

▲ **Comprehensive Vocabulary Study.** Each unit teaches one major vocabulary skill. **Vocabulary Development Lessons** may be used for preteaching, reinforcement, or review. (See page 633.)

▲ **Emphasis on Critical Thinking.** The study questions following the selections and the **Critical Thinking** feature at the end of each unit train students in skills such as understanding relationships and making inferences. (See page 90 for an example of a **Critical Thinking** lesson.)

Myths, Tales, and Fables

ST. GEORGE AND THE DRAGON, about 1518. *Sodoma. National Gallery of Art, Washington, D.C. Samuel H. Kress Collection.*

Introducing Myths, Tales, and Fables

What Are Myths, Tales, and Fables?

Thousands of years ago, most people could not read and write. However, they did tell stories. The stories were passed by word of mouth from one generation to the next. These stories make up what is called the oral tradition, which includes myths, folk tales, and fables.

Myths. Myths are traditional stories. They usually tell about super-human beings or unlikely events. Often myths try to explain why the world is the way it is and why things happen as they do.

Folk Tales. Folk tales include fairy tales, children's stories in which magic plays an important part. Folk tales also include tall tales, stories with exaggerated characters and events, and legends, stories based on historical fact.

Fables. Fables are brief stories, usually with animal characters. Fables teach lessons about human nature. A fable often ends in a moral, a sentence that states the lesson of the story.

Most stories from the oral tradition have things in common: There generally are several versions of each story. The stories usually begin with action. Events, descriptions, and even certain lines tend to be repeated from story to story. The stories tell what people of earlier times valued and how they viewed the world.

How To Read Myths, Tales, and Fables

The selections in this unit are modern versions of stories that originated orally. When reading these stories, imagine hearing them spoken by a master storyteller. Ask yourself, "Why would a storyteller learn and pass on this story?" Remember that myths were often told to explain happenings in nature; folk tales, to entertain; and fables, to teach moral lessons.

Previewing the Unit

Reading the Selections

The selections in this unit are presented in three sections: Myths, Tales, and Fables.

Using the Study Questions

Following each selection are exercises that will help you to develop your reading, vocabulary, and writing skills.

Getting at Meaning. This section contains questions of three types: The **RECALLING** questions will help you to remember the selection. The **INTERPRETING** questions will help you to understand the selection. The **CRITICAL THINKING** questions will help you to evaluate the selection and to relate it to your own life.

Developing Skills in Reading Literature. These exercises will introduce you to the literary techniques used in myths, tales, and fables.

Developing Vocabulary. These exercises teach vocabulary skills, such as tracing the etymologies, or origins, of words.

Developing Writing Skills. In one kind of assignment you will write about myths, tales, and fables. In another you will use the literary techniques that you have learned.

Using the Unit Study Materials

Research Skills for Writing. This feature will teach you how to find materials in a library.

Critical Thinking. The critical thinking exercises will teach you how to apply classification skills to literature.

Unit Review. The unit review will help you to recall, interpret, and think critically about the selections in the unit. The writing assignments will give you a chance to apply your writing skills.

Myths

What Is a Myth?

A myth is a traditional story, usually about a superhuman being or unlikely event. Myths often try to explain why the world is the way it is and why things in nature happen as they do. Usually, myths deal with events that happened in the past, beyond the memory of any human being.

The Origins of the Myths

Long ago, people were frightened and puzzled by the world around them. They needed explanations for the seasons, fire, and thunder. The myths were created to provide these explanations.

Myths came to be in all parts of the world. On the following pages are myths from Africa, Greece, and the American West. Among the most important are the myths from Greece. These myths have affected the languages and literatures of people throughout the Western world.

Thinking About Myths

As you read the myths in this unit, picture an early storyteller retelling the myths to a group of listeners. Ask yourself questions such as these: Why would the myth hold the interest of the listeners? What does the myth explain or teach? What do the people who created this myth think is important?

HERMES RUNNING, 470 B.C. *Attributed to the Tithonus Painter. Greek Vase. The Metropolitan Museum of Art, New York. Fletcher Fund, 1925. (25.78.2)*

Prometheus defies Zeus to bring fire to humans.

Prometheus   Greek Myth

Retold by *Bernard Evslin*

Prometheus[1] was a young Titan,[2] no great admirer of Zeus.[3] Although he knew the great lord of the sky hated explicit questions, he did not hesitate to beard[4] him when there was something he wanted to know.

One morning he came to Zeus and said, "O Thunderer, I do not understand your design. You have caused the race of humans to appear on earth, but you keep them in ignorance and darkness."

"Perhaps you had better leave the race of humans to me," said Zeus. "What you call ignorance is innocence. What you call darkness is the shadow of my decree. Humans are happy now. And they are so framed[5] that they will remain happy unless someone persuades them that they are unhappy. Let us not speak of this again."

But Prometheus said, "Look at them. Look below. They crouch in caves. They are at the mercy of beast and weather. They eat their meat raw. If you mean something by this, enlighten me with your wisdom. Tell me why you refuse to give humans the gift of fire."

Zeus answered, "Do you not know, Prometheus, that every gift brings a penalty? This is the way the Fates[6] weave destiny—by which gods also must abide. Humans do not have fire, true, nor the crafts that fire teaches. On the other hand, they do not know disease, warfare, old age, or that inward pest called worry. They are happy, I say, happy without fire. And so they shall remain."

"Happy as beasts are happy," said Prometheus. "Of what use to make a separate race called humans and endow them with little fur, some wit, and a curious charm of unpredictability? If they must live like this, why separate them from the beasts at all?"

"They have another quality," said Zeus, "the capacity for worship. An aptitude for admiring our power, being puzzled by our riddles, and amazed by our caprice.[7] That is why they were made."

---

1. **Prometheus** (prō mē′ thē əs).
2. **Titan** (tīt′'n): one of a giant race of deities.
3. **Zeus** (zo͞os): king of the gods.
4. **beard:** to face or oppose courageously.
5. **framed:** designed or built.
6. **Fates:** the three goddesses who control destiny. They spin, measure, and cut the thread of life.
7. **caprice** (kə prēs′): a sudden, apparently unmotivated change of mind or emotion.

"Would not fire, and the graces they can put on with fire, make them more interesting?"

"More interesting, perhaps, but infinitely more dangerous. For there is this in humans too: a vaunting pride that needs little sustenance[8] to make it swell to giant size. Improve their lot, and they will forget that which makes them pleasing—their sense of worship, their humility. They will grow big and poisoned with pride and fancy themselves as gods, and before we know it, we shall see them storming Olympus.[9] Enough, Prometheus! I have been patient with you, but do not try me too far. Go now and trouble me no more with your speculations."

Prometheus was not satisfied. All that night he lay awake making plans. Then he left his couch at dawn, and standing tiptoe on Olympus, stretched his arm to the eastern horizon where the first faint flames of the sun were flickering. In his hand he held a reed filled with a dry fiber; he thrust it into the sunrise until a spark smoldered. Then he put the reed into his tunic and came down from the mountain.

At first, humans were frightened by the gift. It was so hot, so quick; it bit sharply when you touched it, and for pure spite, made the shadows dance. They thanked Prometheus and asked him to take it away. But he took the haunch of a newly killed deer and held it over the fire. And when the meat began to sear and sputter, filling the cave with its rich smells, the people felt themselves melting with hunger and flung themselves on the meat and devoured it greedily, burning their tongues.

"This that I have brought you is called 'fire,'" Prometheus said. "It is an ill-natured spirit, a little brother of the sun; but if you handle it carefully, it can change your whole life. It is very greedy; you must feed it twigs, but only until it becomes a proper size. Then you must stop, or it will eat everything in sight—and you too. If it escapes, use this magic, water. It fears the water spirit, and if you touch it with water, it will fly away until you need it again."

He left the fire burning in the first cave, with children staring at it wide-eyed, and then went to every cave in the land.

Then one day Zeus looked down from the mountain and was amazed. Everything had changed. Humans had come out of their caves. Zeus saw woodmen's huts, farmhouses, villages, walled towns, even a castle or two. He saw humans cooking their food, carrying torches to light their way at night. He saw forges blazing, humans beating out ploughs, keels, swords, spears. They were making ships and raising white wings of sails and daring to use the fury of the winds for their journeys. They were wearing helmets, riding out in chariots to do battle, like the gods themselves.

Zeus was full of rage. He seized his largest thunderbolt. "So they want fire," he said to himself. "I'll give them fire—more than they can use. I'll turn their miserable little ball of earth into a cinder." But then another thought came to him, and he lowered his arm. "No," he said to himself, "I shall have vengeance—and entertainment too. Let them destroy themselves with their new skills. This will make a long, twisted game, interesting to watch. I'll attend to them later. My first business is with Prometheus."

He called his giant guards and had them seize Prometheus, drag him off to the Caucasus,[10] and there bind him to a mountain peak with great chains specially forged by

---

8. **sustenance** (sus′ ti nəns): something that feeds, nourishes, or encourages.
9. **Olympus** (ō lim′ pəs): the home of the Greek gods.
10. **Caucasus** (kô′ kə səs): mountain range in southeast Europe between the Black Sea and the Caspian Sea.

Hephaestus[11] — chains that even a Titan in agony could not break. And when the friend of humans was bound to the mountain, Zeus sent two vultures to hover about him forever, tearing at his belly and eating his liver.

Humans knew a terrible thing was happening on the mountain, but they did not know what. But the wind shrieked like a giant in torment and sometimes like fierce birds.

Many centuries he lay there — until another hero was born, brave enough to defy the gods. He climbed to the peak in the Caucasus and struck the shackles from Prometheus and killed the vultures. His name was Heracles.[12]

---

11. **Hephaestus** (hi fes' təs): god of fire and the forge.
12. **Heracles** (her' ə klēz): a son of Zeus known for his great strength.

ATLAS AND PROMETHEUS, about 555 B.C. *Attributed to the Arkesilas Painter. Laconian Cup. Vatican Museum. Scala/Art Resource, New York.*

Getting at Meaning

RECALLING

1. What points does Zeus make to show that humans are happy without fire?

2. Prometheus asks, "If they must live like this, why separate them from the beasts at all?" Later, he asks, "Would not fire . . . make them more interesting?" How does Zeus answer each question?

3. Why does Zeus think that humans should not "improve their lot"?

4. How does Prometheus bring the gift of fire to humans?

5. How does Prometheus make humans want fire?

6. What advice does Prometheus give about his gift?

7. What is Prometheus' punishment for disobeying Zeus?

INTERPRETING

8. Describe Prometheus. How is he different from Zeus?

9. How does fire change humans? What do these changes suggest about the power and importance of fire?

10. Remember Zeus' predictions about how fire would change humans. Do these predictions come true? Explain.

11. Zeus says, "I shall have vengeance — and entertainment too." What vengeance is he planning? How will he be entertained?

CRITICAL THINKING: EVALUATING/APPLYING

12. Zeus refers to a "long, twisted game, interesting to watch." What is he describing? Is this an accurate description? Give reasons for your opinion.

13. Think about human life before fire, as it is described in this myth. Then think about human life after fire. Was fire a good thing for humans? Would humans have been better off without fire? Explain your ideas.

Developing Skills in Reading Literature

1. **Myth.** A myth is a traditional story, usually about a supernatural being or unlikely event. Myths often try to explain why the world is the way it is and why things in nature happen as they do. Myths offer solutions to mysteries such as how the earth was created, how man and woman came to be, and how the stars got into the sky.

What natural phenomenon does this myth explain? Give your explanation in a few sentences.

Reread the last three paragraphs of the myth. What other natural phenomenon is explained?

2. **Personification.** Personification is the giving of human qualities to an object, animal, or idea. Find the paragraph in which Prometheus personifies fire. Notice that he calls fire "ill-natured" and a "brother of the sun." Can fire be good-natured or ill-natured? Can it have relatives? In what other words and phrases does Prometheus apply human qualities to fire?

Developing Vocabulary

Word Origins. As you know, the Greek gods and goddesses lived on Mount Olympus. Use a dictionary to find at least four other words that are based on, or derived from, the word *Olympus*. Remember that the words in a dictionary are arranged in alphabetical order. Remember also that guide words appear in the upper left-hand and upper right-hand corners. These words are the first word in the left-hand column and the last word in the right-hand column. The other words on the page fall between the guide words in alphabetical order. Once you find the word *Olympus* in the dictionary, look at the words that appear before and after it. Identify those words whose spellings and meanings are closely related to *Olympus*.

Developing Writing Skills

Using the Senses in Writing. Imagine that you are an ancient human. Prometheus has just given you and your family the gift of fire. What does it look like? How does it feel? How does it sound? What smells come from the roasting meat? from the fire itself?

Divide your prewriting notes into four columns, and head them *sight, touch, hearing,* and *smell.* In each column, list vivid words and phrases that describe fire and that appeal to that sense. Use as many of these words as you can in your draft. When you revise this draft, make sure that your topic sentence introduces your subject. Also make sure that your description will appeal to your reader's senses. If you need help in completing this paragraph, study **Using the Process of Writing** on pages 614–623.

B I O G R A P H Y

Bernard Evslin (born 1922) is a professional writer and an award-winning producer of documentary films. He has written several film scripts and many books for young people. Most of his works, such as *Heroes, Gods, and Monsters of the Greek Myths, The Adventures of Ulysses,* and *The Trojan War,* deal with Greek mythology and history. Evslin was born in Philadelphia, Pennsylvania, and attended Rutgers University.

Fire was in the sky. Could a boy bring it down?

The Origin of Fire

Nez Percé Indian Myth

Retold by *Ella E. Clark*

Long ago the Nimipu[1] had no fire. They could see fire in the sky sometimes, but it belonged to the Great Power. He kept it in great black bags in the sky. When the bags bumped into each other, there was a crashing, tearing sound; and through the hole that was made, fire sparkled.

People longed to get it. They ate fish and meat raw as the animals do. They ate roots and berries raw as the bears do. The women grieved when they saw their little ones shivering and blue with cold. The medicine men beat on their drums in their efforts to bring fire down from the sky, but no fire came.

At last a boy just beyond the age for the sacred vigil said that he would get the fire. People laughed at him. The medicine men angrily complained, "Do you think that you can do what we are not able to do?"

But the boy went on and made his plans. The first time that he saw the black fire bags drifting in the sky, he got ready. First he bathed, brushing himself with fir branches until he was entirely clean and was fragrant with the smell of fir. He looked very handsome.

With the inside bark of cedar he wrapped an arrowhead and placed it beside his best and largest bow. On the ground he placed a beautiful white shell that he often wore around his neck. Then he asked his guardian spirit to help him reach the cloud with his arrow.

All the people stood watching. The medicine men said among themselves, "Let us have him killed, lest he make the Great Power angry." But the people said, "Let him alone. Perhaps he can bring the fire down. If he does not, then we can kill him."

The boy waited until he saw that the largest fire bag was over his head, growling and rumbling. Then he raised his bow and shot the arrow straight upward. Suddenly, all the people heard a tremendous crash, and they saw a flash of fire in the sky. Then the burning arrow, like a falling star, came hurtling down among them. It struck the boy's white shell and there made a small flame.

Shouting with joy, the people rushed forward. They lighted sticks and dry bark and

---

1. **Nimipu** (nĭ' mĭ pu): one of the bands of the Nez Percé (nez' pər sā'), a tribe of Native Americans who lived in Washington and Oregon.

hurried to their tipis[2] to start fires with them. Children and old people ran around, laughing and singing.

When the excitement had died down, people asked about the boy. But he was nowhere to be seen. On the ground lay his shell, burned so that it showed the fire colors. Near it lay the boy's bow. People tried to shoot with it, but not even the strongest man and the best with bow and arrow could bend it.

The boy was never seen again. But his abalone shell[3] is still beautiful, still touched with the colors of flame. And the fire he brought from the black bag is still in the center of each tipi, the blessing of every home.

---

2. **tipis** (tē′ pēz′): alternate spelling of *tepees.*
3. **abalone** (ab′ ə lō′ nē) **shell:** a spiral-shaped shell lined with mother-of-pearl.

THE MEDICINE MAN, 1948. *Joseph Henry Sharp. The Thomas Gilcrease Institute of American History and Art, Tulsa, Oklahoma.*

Getting at Meaning

RECALLING

1. Why do the people want fire?
2. How does the boy prepare himself for his trial?
3. How does the boy bring the fire to earth?
4. What do the people do when they see the flame?
5. Tell what happens to the boy and to his belongings.

INTERPRETING

6. How do the medicine men react to the boy's plans? Why do they react this way?
7. In what ways is the boy unlike ordinary human beings?
8. What do you learn from this myth about the Nez Percé way of life?
9. In "Prometheus" fire is a gift from a god. In this myth do the gods give humans fire? Explain your answer.

CRITICAL THINKING: EVALUATING

10. Where might the boy have gone? Why? Is this a good ending for a myth? Explain.

Developing Skills in Reading Literature

Myth. A myth is a traditional story, usually about a superhuman being or unlikely event. Myths often try to explain why things in nature happen as they do. The first paragraph of this myth gives the Nez Percé explanation for a natural phenomenon. What is that phenomenon? What are the "great black bags" in the sky? What is the "cracking, tearing sound"? What is the fire that sparkled from the bags? How does the myth explain the appearance of the abalone shell? What phenomenon does the entire myth try to explain?

Developing Vocabulary

Using a Dictionary To Find Word Origins. "The Origin of Fire" is a Nez Percé Indian myth. Look up *Nez Percé* in the dictionary, and examine the entry carefully. Find the explanation of the origin of the word, which probably will be enclosed in brackets or parentheses after the pronunciation of the word. Learn the meanings of any unfamiliar symbols and abbreviations by looking them up in the front of the dictionary. Then answer these questions: Is Nez Percé an Indian name? Where does the name come from? What false belief does this name reflect?

Use a dictionary to find the origins of the following place names. Explain the origins on a sheet of paper.

1. Mississippi
2. Tennessee
3. Chicago
4. Arizona
5. Massachusetts
6. Chesapeake Bay

B I O G R A P H Y

Ella E. Clark (1896-1984) wrote many books about North American Indian folklore. Her books for young people include *Guardian Spirit Quest* and *In the Beginning*. Born in Tennessee, Clark attended Northwestern University. She taught in Illinois high schools for nine years and eventually became a professor of English. At the age of sixty-five, she retired from full-time teaching. She then wrote several books, including *Indian Legends from the Northern Rockies*.

It was a deed of great daring.

How Humans Got Fire

African Myth

Retold by **Susan Bennett**

In the beginning, Obassi Osaw made all things on earth, but he did not give fire to humans. It was very cold, and the people in the villages huddled together for warmth. Finally, one of the chiefs cried out, "It is not fair. What is the use of Obassi Osaw putting us on earth if he will not give us fire to comfort ourselves?" He grabbed his youngest son and said, "Go to Obassi Osaw; tell him we must have fire!"

The boy made the journey, but when he came to Obassi Osaw, the god shook his head angrily. "Tell your father he is a fool," he yelled, and the boy went back to earth.

"I will go myself, then, you good-for-nothing boy," the father cried. "Obassi Osaw will listen to me!" But when the chief appealed to the god, he too was sent home; and then his son laughed. "Who are you to call yourself a chief? I will go back myself, and if Obassi Osaw doesn't give me fire, this time I will steal it!"

Again the boy made the long journey; and when he came to the compound of Obassi Osaw, he went in and helped the wives get din-

ner. For many days he did not approach the god but made himself useful to all. One evening, Obassi Osaw sent for him. "You seem trustworthy and helpful. Go to my third wife and bring back a lamp." The boy did as he was told; and while he was getting the lamp, he noticed that in this house the fire was stored. The next night Obassi Osaw again sent for him. "Bring my light," he said, and the boy went forth. The wife was busy, so she told the lad to light the lamp himself. The boy was excited. He lighted the lamp with a long, slender stick. Then he carefully wrapped the burning stick in leaves so that the fire would not go out and hid it in the folds of his clothes. When he took the lamp to Obassi, he suddenly doubled over as if in pain. "May I go out?" he asked the god, "I think I am going to be sick." Then he ran to the brush and hid the stick. That night, as soon as it was dark and all were asleep, he crept to the bush; and taking out the fire, he ran and ran until he once more reached earth.

He pulled the leaves from the burning stick,

and the flame lighted his face. "Bring me wood!" he cried with excitement. "I will show you how to use fire."

Obassi Osaw woke up sneezing. He looked around his compound, but the fires were burning evenly; none of them were throwing out smoke. He looked down at the earth, and then he understood. "Akpan," he called, "Akpan Obassi, go to earth and find out if it is the boy who has stolen our fire." Obassi's eldest son nodded and traveled to earth.

The boy confessed. "I stole it, and I am not sorry; we needed the fire here. You suffer no loss."

Akpan bowed, "I bring you a message from Obassi Osaw. You walked to heaven and took the fire; you walked back to earth. From this moment forth you will walk as one burned, not straight and proud but lame."

And so it has been. Lame boy cannot walk. He brought fire to earth from the home of Obassi Osaw.

Getting at Meaning

RECALLING

1. What does the chief do when his son comes back without fire?

2. What does the boy do when his father is sent home without fire?

3. How does the boy get fire?

4. Whom does Obassi Osaw send to earth to investigate?

5. How is the boy punished for bringing fire to earth? Why does Obassi Osaw consider this a fitting punishment?

INTERPRETING

6. How does Obassi Osaw know that fire has been stolen?

7. Although Obassi Osaw is a god, he has many human qualities. He also lives like a human being. What are his human qualities? How is his life like that of a human?

8. In what ways is this myth the same as the Nez Percé myth? In what ways is it different? How is the African myth similar to the Greek myth? How are the two myths different?

CRITICAL THINKING: EVALUATING

9. You have read three myths that explain how humans got fire. Which of the three seems to you the most creative and interesting? Explain your choice.

Developing Skills in Reading Literature

Hero. A hero is the main character in a story. Usually, a hero has admirable qualities. In this myth, who is the hero? What are the hero's qualities? How is he different from other human beings?

Developing Vocabulary

Word Origins: Old English Words. The word *fire* comes from Old English, the early language that is the basis for the English spoken today. Like most words from Old English, *fire* describes something that is important and basic to life. Study the following words, which also come from Old English:

word	woman	shell
life	food	man

Add at least five words to the list that you suspect might come from Old English. Check the origins of your words in a dictionary. Which words do come from Old English? What symbol is used to mean "derived from"? What abbreviation is used for Old English?

Developing Writing Skills

Writing a Story. It is now the twentieth century and the power of fire has been replaced in part by nuclear energy. If Zeus, Obassi Osaw, or the Great Power saw what the human race was doing, how would he react? Would he try to take nuclear energy away? Would he help the humans on earth?

Write a story about what one of the gods might do. Follow the steps in **Using the Process of Writing,** which are explained on pages 614–623. In your prewriting notes, put down the events that will take place in your story. As you write your first draft, follow your prewriting notes. Be sure to tell your story simply and clearly. When you revise the story, check to be sure that you have moved smoothly from one event to the next. Also be sure that your ending fits the rest of the story.

The Fateful Contest   Greek Myth

Retold by *Olivia Coolidge*

Arachne[1] was a maiden who became famous throughout Greece though she was neither wellborn nor beautiful and came from no great city. She lived in an obscure little village, and her father was a humble dyer of wool. In this he was very skillful, producing many varied shades. Above all he was famous for the clear, bright scarlet which is made from shellfish, and which was the most glorious of all the colors used in ancient Greece.

Even more skillful than her father was Arachne. It was her task to spin the fleecy wool into a fine, soft thread and to weave it into cloth on the high-standing loom within the cottage. Arachne was small and pale from much working. Her eyes were light and her hair was a dusty brown, yet she was quick and graceful. Her fingers, roughened as they were, went so fast that it was hard to follow their flickering movements. So soft and even was her thread, so fine her cloth, so gorgeous her embroidery, that soon her products were known all over Greece. No one had ever seen the like of them before.

At last Arachne's fame became so great that people used to come from far and wide to watch her working. Even the graceful nymphs[2] would steal in from stream or forest and peep shyly through the dark doorway. They would watch in wonder the white arms of Arachne as she stood at the loom and threw the shuttle from hand to hand between the hanging threads or drew out the long wool, fine as a hair, from the distaff as she sat spinning. "Surely Athene[3] herself must have taught her," people would murmur to one another. "Who else could know the secret of such marvelous skill?"

Arachne was used to being wondered at. She was immensely proud of the skill that had brought so many to look on her. Praise was all she lived for, and it displeased her greatly that people should think anyone, even a goddess, could teach her anything. Therefore, when she heard them murmur, she would stop her work and turn round indignantly to say, "With my own ten fingers I gained this skill, and by hard practice from early morning till night. I never

---

1. **Arachne** (ə rak′ nē).
2. **nymph** (nimf): nature goddess in Greek and Roman mythology, represented as a beautiful, young maiden.
3. **Athene** (ə thē′ nē).

had time to stand looking as you people do while another maiden worked. Nor if I had, would I give Athene credit because the girl was more skillful than I. As for Athene's weaving, how could there be finer cloth or more beautiful embroidery than mine? If Athene herself were to come down and compete with me, she could do no better than I."

One day when Arachne turned round with such words, an old woman answered her. She was a gray old woman, bent and very poor. She stood leaning on a staff and peering at Arachne amid the crowd of onlookers. "Reckless girl," she said, "how dare you claim to be equal to the immortal gods themselves? I am an old woman and have seen much. Take my advice and ask pardon of Athene for your words. Rest content with your fame of being the best spinner and weaver that mortal eyes have ever beheld."

"Stupid old woman," said Arachne indignantly, "who gave you a right to speak in this way to me? It is easy to see that you were never good for anything in your day, or you would not come here in poverty and rags to gaze at my skill. If Athene resents my words, let her answer them herself. I have challenged her to a contest, but she, of course, will not come. It is easy for the gods to avoid matching their skill with that of people."

At these words the old woman threw down her staff and stood erect. The wondering onlookers saw her grow tall and fair and stand clad in long robes of dazzling white. They were terribly afraid as they realized that they stood in the presence of Athene herself.

Arachne herself flushed red for a moment. She had never really believed that the goddess would hear her. Before the group that was gathered there she would not give in. So, pressing her pale lips together in obstinacy and

pride, she led the goddess to one of the great looms and set herself before the other. Without a word, both began to thread the long woolen strands that hang from the rollers and between which the shuttle moves back and forth. Many skeins lay heaped beside them to use, bleached white, and gold, and scarlet, and other shades as varied as the rainbow. Arachne had never thought of giving credit for her success to her father's skill as a dyer, though in actual truth the colors were as remarkable as the cloth itself.

Soon there was no sound in the room but the breathing of the onlookers, the whirring of the shuttles, and the creaking of the wooden frames as each pressed the thread up into place or tightened the pegs by which the whole was held straight. The excited crowd in the doorway began to see that the skill of both in truth was very nearly equal. But, however the cloth might turn out, the goddess was the quicker of the two. A pattern of many pictures was growing on her loom. There was a border of twined branches of the olive, Athene's favorite tree, while in the middle, figures began to appear.

As they looked at the glowing colors, the spectators realized that Athene was weaving into her pattern a last warning to Arachne. The central figure in her design was the goddess herself competing with the sea god for possession of the city of Athens. In the four corners were mortals who had tried to strive with gods and pictures of the awful fate that had overtaken them. The goddess finished before Arachne did and stood back from her marvelous work to see what the maiden was doing.

Never before had Arachne been matched against anyone whose skill was equal to her own. As she stole glances from time to time at Athene and saw the goddess working swiftly, calmly, and always a little faster than herself, she became angry instead of frightened. An evil thought came into her head. Thus as Athene stepped back to watch Arachne finishing her work, she saw that the maiden had taken for her design a pattern of scenes which showed evil or unworthy actions of the gods. She showed how they had deceived fair maidens, resorted to trickery, and appeared on earth from time to time in the form of poor and humble people.

When the goddess saw this insult glowing in bright colors on Arachne's loom, she stepped forward, her gray eyes blazing with anger, and tore Arachne's work across. Then she struck Arachne across the face. Arachne stood there a moment, struggling with anger, fear, and pride. "I will not live under this insult," she cried. Seizing a rope from the wall, she made a noose and would have hanged herself.

The goddess touched the rope and touched the maiden. "Live on, wicked girl," she said. "Live on and spin, both you and your descendants. When men look at you they may remember that it is not wise to strive with Athene." At that the body of Arachne shriveled up. Her legs grew tiny, spindly, and dis-

torted. There before the eyes of the spectators hung a little dusty brown spider on a slender thread.

All spiders descend from Arachne, the legend says. And as the Greeks watched them spinning their thread wonderfully fine, they remembered the contest with Athene and thought it was not right for even the best of mortals to claim they were the equal of the gods.

Getting at Meaning

RECALLING

1. For what is Arachne famous? What does her father have to do with her fame? Does she give him credit?

2. People who watch Arachne murmur, "Surely Athene herself must have taught her." How does Arachne react? Why?

3. Who is the old woman who warns Arachne? How does Arachne respond to the woman's advice? How else does Athene warn Arachne?

4. Who issues the challenge, Athene or Arachne?

5. Who wins the weaving contest?

INTERPRETING

6. What quality of Arachne is responsible for her downfall? How does Arachne show this quality? Give several examples from the myth.

7. What design does Arachne weave? Why does she choose this design?

8. Why does Arachne want to hang herself? Why does Athene prevent her from doing so?

9. Athene is the goddess of wisdom. How does she show her wisdom in this myth?

CRITICAL THINKING: APPLYING

10. This myth teaches that mortals should not claim equality with the gods. Express this same lesson in modern terms. Do you think that the lesson still applies? Explain.

Developing Skills in Reading Literature

1. **Myth.** A myth is a traditional story, usually about a superhuman being or unlikely event. Myths often try to explain why things in nature happen as they do. What natural phenomenon does this myth explain? What does the myth reveal about the Greek gods?

2. **Conflict.** Conflict is a struggle between opposing forces. Sometimes the conflict in a story is between two characters. Who are the opponents in this myth? Who wins the struggle? What does this outcome suggest about the relation between gods and humans?

3. **Title.** The title, or name, of a story can give a clue to its ending. The title of this myth is "The Fateful Contest." What does *fateful* mean? Why is the contest fateful?

Developing Vocabulary

1. **Words from Greek Mythology.** Find the word *arachnid* in the dictionary. What does it mean? What connection exists between the word and the myth that you have just read?

2. **Using a Glossary.** Several words in this selection are defined in the Glossary on pages 661–676. The words in a glossary are arranged in alphabetical order, just as they are in a dictionary. A glossary, though, is generally much shorter than a dictionary, for it contains words that appear in only one book. Look up the meanings of the following italicized words in the Glossary. Write their meanings on a sheet of paper.

a. "She lived in an *obscure* little village."

b. "She would stop her work and turn round *indignantly.*"

c. She pressed her pale lips together in *obstinacy* and *pride*.

d. The *spectators* realized that Athene was weaving a last warning to Arachne.

e. "Her legs grew tiny, spindly, and *distorted.*"

Choose one of the italicized words and compare the Glossary entry with the dictionary entry for the word. What information is given in both entries? What information is given in the dictionary but not in the Glossary?

B I O G R A P H Y

Olivia Coolidge (born 1908) grew up in England, the daughter of a newspaper columnist. After completing her studies at Oxford University, she came to the United States and taught English for several years. Coolidge is interested in politics and history as well as in the classics of Greek and Latin literature. Her many books include *Greek Myths, Gandhi,* and *The Apprenticeship of Abraham Lincoln.*

Her daughter had been stolen and Demeter wanted her returned.

Demeter Greek Myth

Retold by *Bernard Evslin*

Demeter[1] means "Barley-mother." Another name for her is Ceres,[2] from which we get the word *cereal*. She was the goddess of the corn-field, mistress of planting and harvesting, lady of growing things. Zeus was very fond of her. He always obliged her with rain when her fields were thirsty. He gave her two children, a boy and a girl. The girl was named Persephone,[3] and Demeter loved her very much.

Persephone was raised among flowers and looked like a flower herself. Her body was as pliant as a stem, her skin soft as petals, and she had pansy eyes. She took charge of flowers for her mother. She was adept at making up new kinds and naming them.

One day she went farther than usual — across a stream, through a grove of trees, to a little glade. She carried her paint pot, for she had seen a stand of tall, waxy lilies she had decided to stripe. As she was painting their faces, she saw a bush she hadn't noticed before. She went to look at it. It was a very strange bush, with thick, green, glossy leaves and hung with large red berries that trembled on their stems like drops of blood. She stared at the bush. She didn't know whether she liked it or not. She decided she did not and seized it

by its branches and pulled. But it was toughly rooted and hard to pull. She was used to getting her own way. She set herself and gave a mighty tug. Up came the bush; its long roots dragged out of the ground, leaving a big hole. She tossed the bush aside and turned to go back to her lilies, but she heard a rumbling sound and turned back. The noise that grew louder and louder was coming from the hole. To her horror, the hole seemed to be spreading, opening like a mouth, and the rumbling grew to a jangling, crashing din.

Out of the hole leaped six black horses, dragging behind them a golden chariot. In the chariot stood a tall figure in a flowing black cape. On his head was a black crown. She had no time to scream. He reached out his long arm, snatched her into the chariot, and lashed his horses. They curvetted in the air and plunged into the hole again. When they had gone, the hole closed.

Demeter was frantic when the girl didn't come home and rushed out to search for her.

---

1. **Demeter** (di mē′ tər).
2. **Ceres** (si′ rēz).
3. **Persephone** (pər sef′ ə nē).

The tall, green-clad goddess rode in a light wicker chariot behind a swift white horse, a gift from Poseidon.[4] She sped here and there, calling, "Persephone ... Persephone...." But no one answered. All night long she searched, and as dawn broke, she came to the glade. There she saw the uprooted bush and the trampled grass. She leaped from her chariot. Then she saw something that stabbed her through—Persephone's little paint pot, overturned. She lifted her head to the sky and howled like a she-wolf. Then she fell still and listened. The sun was rising; the birds had begun to gossip. They told each other of the heedless girl and the strange bush and the hole and the chariot and the black rider and how surprised the girl was when he caught her.

Then Demeter spoke softly, questioning the birds. They told her enough for her to know who had taken her daughter. She put her face in her hands and wept. Just then a little boy came running into the meadow to pick some flowers. When he saw Demeter, he laughed. He had never seen a grownup crying before. But when she looked up, he stopped laughing. She pointed at him, whispering, and he was immediately changed into a lizard. But he hadn't learned to scuttle yet and just sat there looking at Demeter a moment too long, for a hawk swooped and caught him. He was a lizard for only a short while.

Demeter climbed back into her chariot and sped to Olympus. She charged into the throne room where Zeus sat.

"Justice!" she cried. "Justice! Your brother Hades[5] has stolen my daughter—*our* daughter."

"Peace, good sister," said Zeus. "Compose yourself. Hades' wooing has been a trifle abrupt, perhaps, but after all he is my brother — *our* brother — and is accounted a good match. Think, sweet Demeter. It is difficult for our daughter to look beyond the family without marrying far beneath her."

"Never!" cried Demeter. "It must not be! Anyone but Hades! Don't you realize this is a spring child, a flower child, a delicate unopened bud. No ray of sunlight ever pierces that dank hole he calls his kingdom. She'll wither and die."

"She is our daughter," said Zeus. "I fancy she has a talent for survival. Pray, think it over."

Then Demeter noticed that Zeus was holding a new thunderbolt, a marvelously wrought zigzag lance of lightning, volt-blue, radiant with energy. And she realized that Hades, who in his deep realms held all stores of silver and gold, had sent Zeus a special gift. It would be difficult to obtain justice.

"Once again," she said, "will you restore my daughter to me?"

"My dear," said Zeus, "when your rage cools, you will realize that this is a fine match, the very best thing for the child. Please, go back to earth and give yourself a chance to be intelligent about this."

"I will go back to earth," said Demeter, "and I will not return until you send for me."

Weeks passed. Then Zeus found his sleep being disturbed by sounds of lamentation. He looked down upon the earth and saw a grievous sight. Nothing grew. The fields were blasted and parched. Trees were stripped of leaves, standing blighted, with the blazing sun beating down. The soil was hard and cracked, covered with the shriveled brown husks of wheat and corn and barley killed in the bud. And there was no green place anywhere. The people were

---

4. **Poseidon** (pō sī′ d'n): god of the seas.
5. **Hades** (hā′ dēz): god of the underworld.

starving; the cattle had nothing to eat; the game could find nothing and had fled. And a great wailing and lamentation arose as the people lifted their faces to Olympus and prayed for Zeus to help them.

"Well," he thought to himself, fingering his new thunderbolt. "I suppose we shall have to compromise."

He sent for Demeter. When she came, he said, "I have been thinking. Perhaps I have not been quite fair to you."

"No," said Demeter.

"Do you still wish your daughter's return?"

"Yes," said Demeter. "While she is gone, no crops will grow. No tree will bear; no grass will spring. While she is gone and while I mourn, the earth will grow as dry and shriveled as my heart and will put forth no green thing."

"Very well," said Zeus. "In light of all the facts, this is my judgment. Your daughter shall be restored to you and shall remain with you. However, if any food has passed her lips during her sojourn in Tartarus,[6] then she must remain there. This is the Law of Abode, older than our decrees, and even I am powerless to revoke it."

"She will have been too sad to eat," cried Demeter. "No food will have passed her lips. She shall return to me and remain with me. You have spoken, and I hold you to your word."

Zeus whistled, and Hermes,[7] the messenger god, appeared. Zeus sent him with a message to Hades demanding Persephone's release.

"Will you ride with me to the gates of Tartarus?" cried Demeter. "I have the swiftest horse in the world, given me by Poseidon."

"Thank you, good aunt," said Hermes. "But I believe my winged shoes are even faster." And he flew out of the window.

In the meantime, Persephone was in Ere-bus[8] with the dark king. After the first few days of haste and brutality and strangeness, he began to treat her very gently and with great kindness. He gave her rubies and diamonds to play jacks with, had dresses spun for her of gold and silver thread, ordered her a throne of the finest ebony, and gave her a crown of black pearls. But she made herself very difficult to please. She tossed her head, stamped her foot, and turned from him. She would not speak to him and said she would never forgive him. She said she wanted to go home to her mother, and that she had to attend to her flowers, and that she hated him and always would. As she launched these tirades at him, he would stand and listen and frown and keep listening until she flounced away. Then he would go and get her another gift.

Secretly, though, so secretly that she didn't even tell it to herself, she was rather enjoying the change. She did miss the sunshine and the flowers, but there was much to amuse her. Secretly she gloated upon her power over this most fearsome monarch. Secretly she enjoyed his gifts and his efforts to please her ... and marveled at the way he was obeyed. Although she never forgot how he had frightened her when he came charging out of that hole in his chariot, she admired the lofty set of his black-robed figure, the majestic shoulders, the great impatient hands, and his gloomy black eyes. But she knew that part of her power over him was disdain and so kept flouting and abusing him; and, which made him gloomier than ever, refused to let a crumb of food pass her lips.

He tried every way he knew to tempt her

---

6. **Tartarus** (tär′ tər əs): Hades' kingdom; the land of the dead.
7. **Hermes** (hur′ mēz).
8. **Erebus** (er′ ə bəs): the dark place under the earth through which the dead pass before entering Tartarus.

into eating. His cook prepared the most delicious meals, and his servants bore them to her chamber. But she would pretend not to notice a thing and sit there holding her head high, not even allowing her nostrils to twitch, although the rich smells were making her wild with hunger. She swore she would not eat a mouthful until he had returned her to her mother.

He was desperate to please her. He set aside a corner of the palace grounds for a dark garden and gave her rare seeds to plant — magical blooms that did not need the sunlight. She grew a species of black orchid, and mushrooms, and nightshade, henbane, and hellebore. He gave her a little boy to help her garden, a very clever little gardener, a new spirit. He was very deft and good company too, although she noticed that his eyes were a bit lidless. She had no way of knowing that he was the same little boy her mother had turned into a lizard and fed to a hawk. But he knew who she was.

She had other amusements too. She liked to wander in the Elysian Fields[9] and dance with the happy shades. She was fascinated by the torments, particularly the funny man trying to roll the stone uphill and always having to start over again. She pitied Tantalus,[10] and when no one was looking, cupped some water in her hands and gave it to him to drink. And he thanked her in a deep, sad voice. But after she left, it was worse than ever; he knew she would not remember him again, and this one flash of hope made the ordeal worse.

Still, she liked her garden best, and that was where she spent most of her time—more time than ever, because she was so hungry she didn't know what to do, and she didn't want Hades to see how she felt. She knew he would think up more delicious things to tempt her if he thought she was weakening.

Standing in the garden one afternoon, half hidden in a clump of nightshade, she saw the little boy eating something. It was a red fruit, and he was eating it juicily. He saw her watching and came toward her smiling, his mouth stained with red juice. He held out his hand. It was a pomegranate, her favorite fruit.

"We're alone," he whispered. "No one will see you. No one will know. Quickly now — eat!"

She looked about. It was true. No one could see them. She felt her hands acting by themselves, as though she had nothing to do with them. She watched as the fingers curled savagely and ripped the fruit across. They dug in, plucked out seeds, and offered them to her lips. One . . . two . . . three . . . she thought she had never tasted anything so delicious as these tiny, tart, juicy seeds. Just as she swallowed her sixth seed, a high, glad yelling cry split the air, and the pomegranate dropped to the ground. It was a cry that any god recognized — Hermes' keen herald shout, meaning that he was coming with news, good or bad, but worthy of high attention.

She raced to the palace. The little gardener scooped up the pomegranate and raced after her. Sure enough, it was cousin Hermes, his hair tumbled from the wind, the wings on his feet still fluttering from the speed of his going.

"Good day, cousin," he said.

Hades loomed next to him, scowling blackly.

"I bring you a message from your mother. She wants you home. And your host has kindly agreed to an early departure. How are you?

_____

9. **Elysian** (i lizh′ ən) **Fields:** the dwelling place of virtuous people after death.
10. **Tantalus** (tan′ tə ləs): a king who lives in the underworld, who is doomed to stand under branches of fruit and in water up to his chin, but can reach neither the fruit nor the water.

PERSEPHONE AND PLUTO, about 500 B.C. *Relief. Archeological Museum of Taranto. Scala/Art Resource, New York.*

Haven't eaten anything here, I hope. No? Good! Let's be on our way."

He put his arm around her waist, and they rose in the air. And Persephone, looking back, saw the little gardener rush to Hades with the pomegranate in his hand.

By the time Persephone had come home to her mother, Hades had already been to Olympus and had presented his case to Zeus. Zeus pronounced his judgment. Because the girl had eaten six seeds of the pomegranate, she would have to spend six months with Hades each year.

"Never mind, Mother," said Persephone.

"Don't cry. We must be happy for the time that I am here."

"I suffer!" cried Demeter. "I suffer! Here —" She struck herself on the chest. "Here—in my mother's heart. And if I suffer, then everyone else shall suffer too. For the months that you spend with that scoundrel, no grass will grow, no flowers blow, no trees will bear. So long as you are below, there will be desolation everywhere."

That is why summer and winter are the way they are. That is why there is a time for planting and a time when the earth must sleep under frost.

Getting at Meaning

RECALLING

1. What are Demeter's responsibilities?
2. What happens when Persephone pulls the strange bush out of the ground?
3. How does Demeter find out about her daughter's abduction? How does she react?
4. Why does Zeus decide to compromise with Demeter? What is the compromise?
5. How does Hades behave toward Persephone? How does she behave toward him?
6. Why does Persephone eat the pomegranate? What happens as a result?
7. How does Demeter punish the earth?

INTERPRETING

8. Who is more powerful, Zeus or Hades? Explain your conclusion.
9. Why is Zeus reluctant to rescue Persephone? What reason does he give Demeter? What is the real reason?
10. Zeus tells Demeter that, if any food has passed Persephone's lips, she must remain with Hades. Later, though, he allows Persephone to leave Hades for half of every year. Why might he have changed his mind?
11. Demeter believes that Hades' kingdom is the worst possible place for Persephone. Does Persephone feel the same way? Explain.

Developing Skills in Reading Literature

1. **Myth.** A myth is a traditional story, usually about a superhuman being or unlikely event. Myths often try to explain why things in nature happen as they do. How does this myth explain the changes of the seasons? The myths give the gods both superhuman and human characteristics. What human qualities are shown by Zeus? Hades? Persephone? Demeter? What are their superhuman characteristics?

2. **Setting.** Setting is the time and place of the action of a story. This myth has three settings. What are they? Which settings are de-scribed in detail? Choose one setting and list words and phrases from the story that give information about this setting.

Developing Vocabulary

Words from the Myths. At the beginning of "Demeter," you are told that another name for *Demeter* is *Ceres,* from which we get the word *cereal.* Many other words in the English language are taken from mythology. Look up each of the following words in a dictionary. Find the place in each entry where the origin of the word is given. Be sure that you understand each abbreviation and symbol used. Then, on a sheet of paper, write the Greek or Latin source of the word and the definition.

1. hermetic
2. herculean
3. ambrosia
4. mercurial
5. tantalize
6. jovial
7. atlas
8. aegis

Developing Writing Skills

Writing a Myth. What is the weather like outside? Is it hot? cold? raining? sunny? Write a myth explaining why the weather is the way it is. During prewriting, decide on the characters that you will use. Will they be characters from the myths that you have read? Will you invent your own? Also decide on your basic story: what happens first, what happens second, and so on. As you write your first draft, add new details that come to mind. Be sure, though, that you stick with your basic story. As you revise your myth, reread it several times. During one rereading, pay close attention to the story itself. Does it make sense? Should any details be taken out or moved? During another rereading, check the punctuation, capitalization, and spelling. Make all corrections before making a final, neat copy. If you need help with this assign-ment, see **Using the Process of Writing** on pages 614–623.

It was always cold, and the people were hungry.

How the Seasons and the Birds Came
Native American Myth

Retold by *Princess Atalie*

Children of the Red people snuggled close in their wigwams. Winter winds were cold, and there were no changes of season. Days and nights were of unusual length, and the Red people and animals had one language. They ate only herbs, roots, and the flesh of small animals they were able to catch with their hands; so the Red people became hunters. Before they killed an animal, they would offer a prayer to the Great Spirit and apologize to the animal for taking his life because they deemed it a necessity.

A Council was called to decide upon the length of the days and nights, for the animals did not feel safe and decided to declare war on the Red people.

Rabbit, who was a peace-loving little creature, happened along just then. He was known among the animals as a clever magician.

"I will go to the Thunder Spirit," he said, "and ask him to help us." He ran to the Thunder Spirit and told him that he wanted something for the Red people to plant.

The Thunder Spirit saw that all the animals would soon disappear if the Red people did not have other food to eat. He tapped on Mother Earth with his wand of witch-hazel. Tiny little green stalks shot from the earth. Rabbit was excited and said, "May I take some of these to the Council for the Red people?"

"If you will eat a few in the presence of Owl, who is the judge, you may give these plants to the Red people," said the Thunder Spirit. Rabbit hastened to Owl, who was a very stern old judge. Although he was afraid, he hopped close to Owl's hollow tree and nibbled some of the green leaves.

Owl stared at him without blinking or closing his eyes. To this day he is known to stare with eyes open longer than any other living creature. Finally, he said, "The Red people would like to share your food."

Rabbit was so pleased that he gave one leap and returned to the mountain of the Thunder Spirit. The Thunder Spirit was expecting him and sent him back to the Council with a load of the green stalks. Wherever Rabbit hopped, an abundance of the green plants sprang up in the forest, and the Red people called it rabbit lettuce. Today lettuce is good for rabbits and people.

It was still very cold, and the Red people longed for sunshine. The animals at the Council said they would try to bring Summer. Bear, however, became very angry, as he did not wish to have warm weather. He growled, "I will continue to give my flesh for food if you will let the winter stay." No one listened to

THE FIVE SACRED COLORS OF MAIZE, 20th century. *Huichol Yarn Painting.*
The Fine Arts Museums of San Francisco. Gift of Peter F. Young.

Bear, for most of the animals were kind.

Wild Turkey strutted up, spreading his tail feathers, and gobbled, "The year shall have as many moons as there are spots on my tail."

But the members of the Council said, "No, that would make the year too long."

Then Partridge said, "Count my spots and divide your year by their number." But the council declined that suggestion too.

A tiny chattering voice then said, "I am Chipmunk, and I insist that there be as many moons as there are stripes on my back." There were six black stripes and six white stripes on his back. The Councilors said that that number was about right. The white stripes would represent the summer moons, and the black stripes the winter moons. Bear did not approve of this and jumped at Chipmunk to crush him; but Chipmunk was too swift for him and ran to safety, saying, "You are the cause of my having these stripes. Your claws scratched me when I said I was for the warm weather." Bear went away in anger, growling, "Whoever gets my flesh for food will have to catch me!" He ran away into the forest of the far North, and to this day Bear is difficult to catch.

Other wild creatures of the forest wished to help the Red people. Frog made a long trip to Ha-shootch-ga and told him that he also wished to make a gift of food to the Red people. The Thunder Spirit saw a plant with a little pointed top growing in the woods. He sent a drop of rain into Owl's eye and caused him to lessen his stare, while Frog quickly uprooted one of these plants. Frog then hopped down toward the Council, holding the plant over his head like an umbrella. Wherever he leaped, other little umbrellas grew from the earth, and in this way the first mushrooms came, giving food to people.

Wild Turkey came to Council with a plant whose roots were peas. She strutted up to Owl and said, "Thunder Spirit said for the Red people to plant these and grow many more peas." She scratched in the earth and left them there. Turkey peas grew in abundance. The Red people have been digging in the woods ever since for Turkey peas.

Now the Red people had plants for food, but Winter still covered the land. This was because O-kee, who was an evil spirit, was afraid that the Red people would climb the wall of the sky and destroy his dark and dreary days. So he turned a beautiful lake into a caldron of fat and decreed that whoever could swim across should find a land of warm sunshine. Red people and the animals all jumped into the lake. Some were swift in swimming across, and they remained very lean. Some were slow in swimming, and they became very fat. That is why some people and some animals are fat and others are lean.

Rabbit was the first to cross the lake. He came to the wall of the sky and disappeared. Red people were amazed at this. One of the young braves said, "I will follow Rabbit and see what lies beyond the sky wall. When I return I will be able to tell you many wondrous things."

The journey through the sky was dangerous. No Red person had ever entered its gardens before and returned. It was said to have birds of gorgeous plumage, golden fruits, and green grass. But one had to pass O-kee first. The brave followed Rabbit and opened four closed doors. When he opened the first, a bird of paradise flew out; then a great eagle flew out. It circled high and low and beat its wings against the other doors. They, too, opened, and vast flocks of smaller birds flew in every direction. The brave looked at them in great astonishment. He had never seen so many birds before.

He spoke to them, "Beautiful birds, fly to the earth and give my people courage and sunshine."

Eagle gathered the birds into families, all but the bird of paradise. He preferred to remain aloof and find refuge in enchanted places. Eagle directed other birds to fly in flocks. The cedar birds, the chickadees, the woodpeckers, and the snow birds gathered in one flock; they were to be winter birds. The song sparrows, meadow larks, blackbirds, and robins gathered in one flock; they were the spring birds. The crows, wild geese, sparrows, and blue jays gathered in one flock; they were the autumn birds. With a rush of wings, they flew through the hole in the sky on their way to the earth people.

O-kee knew that he was defeated. He rushed to the hole in the sky and closed it just as the young brave was climbing through.

"I will make you a prisoner of the sky. You shall look down on the earth only at noon," grumbled O-kee as he seized the brave with his long fingers. The young brave was turned into the great round sun that now fills the hole in the sky.

Today when the Red people see the sun they say, "There is the brave who took away our winter and sent us sunshine and warm days, with birds for every season."

Getting at Meaning

RECALLING

1. Why does Rabbit go to the Thunder Spirit?

2. What does the Thunder Spirit give to Rabbit? What instructions does he give Rabbit? Does Rabbit follow them?

3. How does the Council decide on the length of the year and the seasons?

4. What contribution do Frog and Wild Turkey make to the Red people?

5. Who is O-kee? Why does he turn the lake into a caldron of fat?

6. How do the birds come to earth? Who groups them into families? What are the families?

7. Into what form is the young brave changed?

8. Tell in your own words how the seasons came to be.

INTERPRETING

9. This myth describes humans as living like animals. In what other myths that you have read are humans described the same way?

10. In "Demeter" the gods are responsible for the seasons. In this myth who is responsible: the animals? a human? both?

11. How is O-kee different from the Thunder Spirit? How can you tell?

12. What makes the young brave a hero? What does he accomplish? What qualities does he show? In what other myths do young boys do great things for their people?

CRITICAL THINKING: EVALUATING

13. What might you conclude from this myth about the Native American attitude toward nature? Now, think about the Greek myth "Demeter," which also explains the seasons. What is the role of nature in this myth? What does this role suggest about the Greek

attitude toward nature? How does this attitude contrast with that of the Native Americans?

Developing Skills in Reading Literature

1. **Myth.** A myth is a traditional story, usually about a superhuman being or unlikely event. Myths often try to explain why things in nature happen as they do. This myth explains the origin of the seasons and the birds. What other natural phenomena are explained? Name at least five, and tell how each came to be, according to the myth.

2. **Personification.** Personification is the giving of human qualities to an object, animal, or idea. In the story that you have just read, what human qualities are given to the following?

a. Rabbit   d. Bear
b. Owl   e. Frog
c. Chipmunk f. Eagle

Developing Vocabulary

Using a Dictionary To Find Word Origins. The following animal names appear in this myth. Look up the origin of each name in a dictionary. As you study the entries, make a list of abbreviations used to explain the origins. Check these abbreviations in the front of the dictionary, and be prepared to explain their meanings.

rabbit   whippoorwill
owl   woodchuck

raccoon   eagle
chipmunk   chickadee

On a separate sheet of paper, answer these questions:

1. Which animal names come from a Native American language?

2. Which names describe the sounds made by an animal?

3. Which names come from European languages such as English and French?

Developing Writing Skills

Writing Dialogue. Choose an event from the myth that you have just read. You may choose, for example, Eagle gathering birds into families or Frog making a trip to Ha-shootch-ga. Write a one page dialogue, or conversation, for that event. For example, if you choose Frog's visit, you would write a conversation between Frog and the Thunder Spirit.

During prewriting, study the dialogue in the myth. Notice the way that it is capitalized and punctuated. Notice also that the writer begins a new paragraph each time the speaker changes. When you write your first draft, use your imagination. Try to make the dialogue sound real. Also be sure that each line suits its speaker. During revision, compare your dialogue with the dialogue in the myth. Have you punctuated and capitalized correctly? Have you paragraphed correctly?

SWEET-SCENTED GRASS, TWELVE-YEAR-OLD DAUGHTER OF BLOODY HAND, 1832. *George Catlin*.
National Museum of American Art, Smithsonian Institution, Washington, D.C. Gift of Mrs. Sarah Harrison.

Tales

What Is a Folk Tale?

A tale is any simple story told in prose or poetry. The tales that you will read in this section are all folk tales. A folk tale is a story that is handed down, usually by word of mouth, among the people of a region.

Kinds of Folk Tales

Fairy tales, tall tales, and legends are three kinds of folk tales. Fairy tales are children's stories in which magic plays an important part. Often fairy tales contain talking animals, elves, giants, ogres, and magical spells. Tall tales are stories with exaggerated characters and events. These tales often are based in fact but have changed through centuries of retelling. The characters in tall tales often are quite unusual and larger than life. Legends also are based on historical facts. The facts are blended with imagined details and stories.

Thinking About Folk Tales

The fairy tales, tall tales, and legends in this section came from the oral tradition. Each tale has lasted because it was interesting to thousands of people throughout the years. As you read these tales, ask yourself why they have been enjoyed for such a long time. Try to decide why these tales are so appealing.

King Midas and the Golden Touch

Greek Tale

Retold by *Bernard Evslin*

There was a king named Midas,[1] and what he loved best in the world was gold. He had plenty of his own, but he could not bear the thought of anyone else having any. Each morning he awoke very early to watch the sunrise and said, "Of all the gods, if gods there be, I like you least, Apollo.[2] How dare you ride so unthriftily in your sun-chariot, scattering golden sheaves of light on rich and poor alike — on king and peasant, on merchant, shepherd, warrior? This is an evil thing, oh wastrel god, for only kings should have gold; only the rich know what to do with it."

After a while these words of complaint, uttered each dawn, came to Apollo, and he was angry. He appeared to Midas in a dream and said, "Other gods would punish you, Midas, but I am famous for my even temper. Instead of doing you violence, I will show you how gracious I can be by granting you a wish. What is it to be?"

Midas cried, "Let everything I touch turn to gold!"

He shouted this out of his sleep in a strangling, greedy voice, and the guards in the doorway nodded to each other and said, "The king calls out. He must be dreaming of gold again."

Wearied by the dream, Midas slept past sunrise; when he awoke it was full morning. He went out into his garden. The sun was high; the sky was blue. A soft breeze played among the trees. It was a glorious morning. He was still half asleep. Tatters of the dream were in his head.

"Can it be true?" he said to himself. "They say the gods appear in dreams. That's how men know them. On the other hand, I know that dreams are false, teasing things. You can't believe them. Let us put it to the test."

He reached out his hand and touched a rose. It turned to gold — petals and stalk, it turned to gold and stood there rigid, heavy, gleaming. A bee buzzed out of its stiff folds, furious; it lit on Midas' hand to sting him. The king looked at the heavy golden bee on the

---

1. **Midas** (mī′ dəs).
2. **Apollo** (ə päl′ ō): god of the sun and music.

back of his hand and moved it to his finger.

"I shall wear it as a ring," he said.

Midas went about touching all his roses, seeing them stiffen and gleam. They lost their odor. The disappointed bees rose in swarms, and buzzed angrily away. Butterflies departed. The hard flowers tinkled like little bells when the breeze moved among them, and the king was well pleased.

His little daughter, the princess, who had been playing in the garden, ran to him and said, "Father, Father, what has happened to the roses?"

"Are they not pretty, my dear?"

"No! They're ugly! They're horrid and sharp, and I can't smell them any more. What happened?"

"A magical thing."

"Who did the magic?"

"I did."

"Unmagic it, then! I hate these roses."

She began to cry.

"Don't cry," he said, stroking her head. "Stop crying, and I will give you a golden doll with a gold-leaf dress and tiny golden shoes."

She stopped crying. He felt the hair grow spiky under his fingers. Her eyes stiffened and froze into place. The little blue vein in her neck stopped pulsing. She was a statue, a figure of pale gold standing in the garden path with lifted face. Her tears were tiny golden beads on her golden cheeks. He looked at her and said, "This is unfortunate. I'm sorry it happened. I have not time to be sad this morning. I shall be busy turning things into gold. But, when I have a moment, I shall think about this problem; I promise." He hurried out of the garden, which had become unpleasant to him.

On his way back to the castle, Midas amused himself by kicking up gravel in the path and watching it tinkle down as tiny nug-

gets. The door he opened became golden; the chair he sat upon became solid gold like his throne. The plates turned into gold, and the cups became gold cups before the amazed eyes of the servants, whom he was careful not to touch. He wanted them to continue being able to serve him; he was very hungry.

With great relish Midas picked up a piece of bread and honey. His teeth bit metal; his mouth was full of metal. He felt himself choking. He reached into his mouth and pulled out a golden slab of bread, all bloody now, and flung it through the window. Very lightly now he touched the other food to see what would happen. Meat . . . apples . . . walnuts . . . they all turned to gold even when he touched them with only the tip of his finger . . . and when he did not touch them with his fingers, when he lifted them on his fork, they became gold as soon as they touched his lips, and he had to put them back onto the plate. He was savagely hungry. Worse than hunger, when he thought about drinking, he realized that wine, or water, or milk would turn to gold in his mouth and choke him if he drank. As he thought that he could not drink, thirst began to burn in his belly. He felt himself full of hot dry sand, felt that the lining of his head was on fire.

"What good is all my gold?" he cried, "if I cannot eat and cannot drink?"

He shrieked with rage, pounded on the table, and flung the plates about. All the servants ran from the room in fright. Then Midas raced out of the castle, across the bridge that spanned the moat, along the golden gravel path into the garden where the stiff flowers chimed hatefully; and the statue of his daughter looked at him with scooped and empty eyes. There in the garden, in the blaze of the sun, he raised his arms heavenward and cried, "You, Apollo, false god, traitor! You pre-

KING MIDAS, 1981. *Kinuko Craft.*

tended to forgive me, but you punished me with a gift!"

Then it seemed to him that the sun grew brighter, that the light thickened, that the sun-god stood before him in the path, tall, stern, clad in burning gold. A voice said, "On your knees, wretch!"

He fell to his knees.

"Do you repent?"

"I repent. I will never desire gold again. I will never accuse the gods. Pray, revoke the fatal wish."

Apollo reached his hand and touched the roses. The tinkling stopped; they softened, swayed, blushed. Fragrance grew on the air. The bees returned, and the butterflies. He touched the statue's cheek. She lost her stiffness, her metallic gleam. She ran to the roses, knelt among them, and cried. "Oh, thank you, father. You've changed them back again." Then she ran off, shouting and laughing.

Apollo said, "I take back my gift. I remove the golden taint from your touch, but you are not to escape without punishment. Because you have been the most foolish of men, you shall wear always a pair of donkey's ears."

Midas touched his ears. They were long and furry. He said, "I thank you for your forgiveness, Apollo . . . even though it comes with a punishment."

"Go now," said Apollo. "Eat and drink. Enjoy the roses. Watch your child grow. Life is the only wealth, man. In your great thrift, you have been wasteful of life, and that is the sign you wear on your head. Farewell."

Midas put a tall, pointed hat on his head so that no one would see his ears. Then he went to eat and drink his fill.

For years he wore the cap so that no one would know of his disgrace. But the servant who cut his hair had to know, so Midas swore him to secrecy, warning that it would cost him his head if he spoke of the king's ears. But the servant, who was a coward, was also a gossip. He could not bear to keep a secret, especially a secret so mischievous. Although he was afraid to tell it, he felt that he would burst if he didn't.

One night he went out to the banks of the river, dug a little hole, put his mouth to it, and whispered. "Midas has donkey's ears, Midas has donkey's ears. . . ." and quickly filled up the hole again, and ran back to the castle, feeling better.

But the river-reeds heard him, and they always whisper to each other when the wind seethes among them. They were heard whispering, "Midas has donkey's ears . . . donkey's ears. . . ." Soon the whole country was whispering, "Have you heard about Midas? Have you heard about his ears?"

When the king heard, he knew who had told the secret and ordered the man's head cut off; but then he thought, "The god forgave me; perhaps I had better forgive this blabbermouth." Therefore he let the treacherous man keep his head.

Then Apollo appeared again and said, "Midas, you have learned the final lesson, mercy. As you have done, so shall you be done by."

And Midas felt his long, hairy ears dwindling back to normal.

He was an old man now. His daughter, the princess, was grown. He had grandchildren. Sometimes he tells his smallest granddaughter the story of how her mother was turned into a golden statue, and he says, "See, I'm changing you too. Look, your hair is all gold."

And she pretends to be frightened.

Getting at Meaning

RECALLING

1. Midas says, "Let everything I touch turn to gold." Who grants Midas his wish?

2. How does Midas find out that his dream has come true?

3. What happens when Midas touches his daughter? How does he react?

4. How does Apollo punish Midas for being "the most foolish of men"?

5. Why does the king's barber tell the secret to the river hole? How is the king's secret discovered?

6. What does Apollo do when he sees that Midas has learned a lesson?

INTERPRETING

7. Why does Apollo grant Midas his wish? Does Apollo accomplish his purpose? Explain.

8. What question does Midas ask when he realizes that he cannot eat? How would Midas have answered his question?

9. Midas falls on his knees and repents before Apollo. What does Midas promise, if Apollo will revoke the wish? What two lessons has Midas learned?

10. What attitude does Midas have toward Apollo before the god gives him the golden touch? How does Midas' attitude change? How do Midas' dealings with his barber show that he has learned a lesson?

11. What is Midas like in his old age? How does his granddaughter seem to feel about him? How has he changed since his own daughter was a young girl?

CRITICAL THINKING: APPLYING

12. Apollo could have explained that greed is a bad thing. Instead, he lets Midas learn for himself. Do you think that this is a good way to change someone's behavior or attitude? Can you give some other examples of learning from experience, perhaps from your own life?

Developing Skills in Reading Literature

Tale. A tale is a simple story told in prose or poetry. This tale combines two stories. Briefly tell each story. How are the two connected? Are their characters the same? Does the action of one story grow out of the other? Are the lessons they teach similar? Explain.

Developing Vocabulary

Words from Tales and Myths. Many of the words and phrases used today are originally from tales and myths. For example, if someone has a "Midas touch," it means that everything he or she does is successful. On a separate sheet of paper, explain the meanings of the following phrases. You may use a dictionary to help you learn the meanings of any unfamiliar words.

1. a Cinderella story 3. looks like an Adonis
2. a herculean task 4. a nemesis

Can you think of any other words or expressions that come from tales or myths?

Developing Writing Skills

Explaining an Idea. Write a paragraph explaining the meaning of this statement: "You have learned the final lesson, mercy. As you have done, so shall you be done by." In your prewriting notes, jot down ideas about what the statement means. Also briefly describe one or more situations that illustrate the statement. When you write your first draft, begin with a topic sentence that gives the basic meaning of the statement in your own words. Follow with supporting sentences that present one well developed example or several brief ones. During revision, make sure that your example or examples actually do illustrate the meaning of the statement. You can find more help for writing a paragraph in **Using the Process of Writing** on pages 614–623.

Baucis and Philemon   Greek Tale

Retold by *Roger L. Green*

There came a time when Zeus, the king of the gods, the father of gods and humans, felt that the men and women in the land of Phrygia[1] in Asia Minor had grown so wicked that they must be destroyed.

"But I do not wish to slay the innocent with the guilty, the good with the bad," he said. "And so I will go among them in disguise with my son Hermes, the messenger of the gods, to see if any are fit to be saved."

The two gods set out disguised as ordinary mortals, an old man and a young, clad in simple cloaks as if they were no more than farmers or shepherds. To house after house they went, asking for food and rest—but every door was barred against them, and no one paid any heed to the sacred duty of hospitality.

At last, when it seemed that every dweller in that country was indeed worthy of the punishment that Zeus had decreed, they came to a little cottage where they met with a different welcome.

In it dwelt Baucis[2] and her husband Philemon,[3] who had been married for many years and grown old together. They had always been poor, but it had made no difference to their happiness; and they dwelt as contentedly in their one room under a roof thatched with reeds as if it had been a palace.

When the disguised immortals reached this simple home and asked for hospitality, they were welcomed in at once. The old man set chairs for them and begged them to be seated and rest after their journey, while Baucis hastened to spread a piece of cloth over the wooden seats, and to pile dry chips on the smoldering fire and fan it into a blaze.

As soon as the fire was burning well, Baucis set a pot of water to boil on it. Meanwhile, Philemon brought in vegetables from his carefully watered garden, and cut pieces from the one smoked ham that hung from the rafters.

When the meal was nearly ready, Baucis took a beechwood bowl and filled it with warm water for them to wash their hands, while Philemon drew up the one couch that served also as a bed—a willow wood frame strung with

---

1. **Phrygia** (frij' ē ə): ancient country in west central Asia Minor.
2. **Baucis** (bô' sis).
3. **Philemon** (fi lē' mən).

leather thongs and set on stout legs — and shook up the sedge-stuffed mattress that lay on it. Baucis spread her finest rug of woven linen on it, poor, coarse cloth but the best she had, which was kept only for times of festival.

When Zeus and Hermes were seated, Philemon set the small round table in front of them. One of its legs was shorter than the others, but Baucis made it level by pushing a piece of broken tile underneath.

Then, having rubbed the top of the table with a handful of fresh mint, she placed the meal before her guests. First of all olives, and wild cherries pickled in the lees of wine, endives and radishes and a piece of cheese, and eggs baked lightly in the hot ashes. All these were placed on the table in clay dishes and in the midst an earthenware flagon of wine with beechwood cups well waxed inside. Then came the main course steaming out of the pot, with simple wine to wash it down, and finally for dessert, nuts and figs, plums and apples and black grapes, and a shining yellow honeycomb lest any of the fruit might prove sour.

But better than the meal itself was the eager attention that Baucis and Philemon paid their guests and the cheerfulness with which they entertained two simple strangers with a hospitality far beyond their means — a generosity that would leave themselves hungry and on short rations for many a day.

At first they thought that the two strangers were no more than poor wanderers in search of work. But as the meal drew to a close, Baucis and Philemon noticed that the flagon that they had filled with all the wine they possessed seemed always to refill whenever the last cup appeared to have been poured from it. When they found that this miracle was really happening and that the wine was richer and rarer each time the flagon refilled itself, they were overcome with awe.

They knelt before their guests, and Philemon said,

"Noble sirs, we do not know who or what you are, but I took you for simple men such as I myself am. So forgive us, we beg you, for the poor meal we have given you and the roughness of our service. If you are still hungry, we have nothing more to offer you, save perhaps the old goose who acts as guardian to our cottage and cries aloud if strangers approach in the night. He, I fear, is tough; but if we boil him long enough in the pot, maybe our old friend will still prove tasty to our guests — though unworthy of such as you must be."

"No, no, spare the poor goose!" cried Hermes, his eyes filling with tears of ready sympathy for the kind old couple.

"Listen, my friends," said Zeus, smiling at Baucis and Philemon. "We are indeed far greater than we seem. Have no fear, and I will tell you all.... We are two of the high gods come down from Olympus to visit this region of the earth. A great punishment is about to fall on all this land, for indeed the wickedness of those who dwell in it passes belief. Amongst them all, only you two have shown yourselves worthy to be saved. Therefore, leave your home and come with us up the mountainside."

Without a moment's hesitation, Baucis and Philemon flung their cloaks about them and followed Zeus and Hermes up the mountain, struggling bravely with the aid of their sticks until they came to the top of the long slope.

Just below the top, the gods halted and, turning, Baucis and Philemon cried out in terror and pity. For already the whole country beneath them had turned into a great sea of rising water, flooding the cities and villages of Phrygia and blotting out all the wicked ones who dwelt in that land.

As they watched, the flood water stopped just short of their little cottage on the mountainside below them, and began slowly to sink once more. Now they saw a new marvel. The little cottage with its walls of mud-bricks and its roof of reeds grew and changed before their astonished eyes. Marble columns took the place of the wooden supports that held up the roof. The thatch itself grew yellow until it shone as if made of gold, and the doors turned to silver, richly carved and embossed.

Then Zeus spoke, "Tell me, Philemon and Baucis, you who deserve so well at our hands, what gift shall I, the father of gods and humans, give to you?"

Baucis and Philemon consulted together for a few moments, and then Philemon said, "Kind father Zeus, our prayer is this. May we both pass what is left of our lives as priest and priestess of your temple yonder. And, since we have lived together so happily for so long,

grant that we may both die at the same instant. For we would neither wish to live without the other for a moment, even if death were ready even now to touch us with his sword."

Zeus granted their prayer and gave them also such a lease of life that no one who was born in the year of the great flood outlived them. But when their time came, which chanced as they stood hand in hand looking up at the temple that they had tended for so long, each saw that the other was changing suddenly and strangely. Their feet were growing into the ground; their legs and bodies were swiftly covering with bark; and their arms and hands were putting forth leaves.

"Goodbye, dearest love!" whispered Philemon.

"Dearest love, goodbye!" answered Baucis.

Then words failed them, and they were no more. Only where they had stood before the temple of Zeus grew two trees—an oak and a lime.

Getting at Meaning

RECALLING

1. Why do Zeus and Hermes come to earth? How are they disguised? How do they test the people of Phrygia?

2. What do Baucis and Philemon serve their guests? How do they serve them?

3. How do Baucis and Philemon realize that the strangers are not ordinary men?

4. Why do the gods take the old couple up the mountainside? What do the old people see when they look down the slope?

5. What replaces the old couple's cottage?

6. What do Baucis and Philemon ask from Zeus? Does he grant their request? How?

INTERPRETING

7. Baucis and Philemon show hospitality to their guests. What seems to be the Greek idea of hospitality?

8. The tale says that Baucis and Philemon are poor. What details in the tale emphasize their poverty?

9. How are Baucis and Philemon different from the other people of Phrygia? Why does Zeus consider them "fit to be saved"?

10. In what ways does this tale show the power of the gods? In what ways does it show their human side?

CRITICAL THINKING: APPLYING

11. The ancient Greeks who heard this tale accepted the events as natural. To them, gods could take human form and they could turn humans into trees. Most modern readers, on the other hand, would not view the events as natural. How did the events strike you as you read the tale? Did you accept the events as the ancient Greeks did? Did you feel that the events were too unreal? Explain.

Developing Skills in Reading Literature

Symbol. A symbol is a person, place, or object that stands for something beyond itself. For example, a national flag is a symbol for a country. A white dove is usually a symbol for peace.

Baucis and Philemon grow into trees that stand next to each other. What does their standing close together symbolize? What are the characteristics of an oak tree? What does the oak tree symbolize? What are the characteristics of a lime tree? What does the lime tree symbolize? To help you, another name for a lime tree is a linden tree. Which tree is probably the symbol for Baucis? for Philemon? Use a dictionary or reference book if you need help.

Developing Vocabulary

Using a Glossary. Several words in the story may be unfamiliar to you. Using the Glossary in the back of this book, find the definitions of the following italicized words. Remember that in a glossary as in a dictionary a word may have more than one definition. You must select the definition that fits the phrase or sentence in which the word appears.

1. "*sedge*-stuffed mattress"
2. "an earthenware *flagon* of wine"
3. Zeus had *decreed* punishment
4. "a roof *thatched* with reeds"
5. "*blotting* out all the wicked ones"
6. *immortal* and *mortal*

Developing Writing Skills

Describing a Place. The tale gives only a few details about the little cottage and the temple of Zeus. Choose either one and write a paragraph describing it. As you develop your prewriting notes, draw details from your imagination as well as from the tale. Arrange the details in spatial order, the order in which you would notice them. As you write your first draft, use transitional words and phrases to help the reader follow your description. Such words and phrases include *in front of, next to, above,* and *below.* During revision, make certain that the words you have used are the most vivid and precise possible. Keep in mind that your readers should be able to form a picture of the cottage or the temple in their minds.

If you need help with this assignment, see **Using the Process of Writing** on pages 614–623.

B I O G R A P H Y

Roger L. Green (born 1918) grew up in Norwich, England, and was educated at Oxford University. Before becoming a writer, he worked as an actor, rare book dealer, and schoolmaster. He particularly enjoys retelling fables, fairy tales, and folk stories. His many books include *Tellers of Tales* and *The Land of the Lord High Tiger.* Between travels, Green resides in Cheshire at an English country estate that has belonged to his family for many generations.

Axe Porridge   Russian Folk Tale

Retold by *Alexander Afanasiev*

An old soldier was once on his way home for his leave, and he was tired and hungry. He reached a village and he rapped at the first hut.

"Let a traveler in for the night," said he.

The door was opened by an old woman.

"Come in, soldier," she offered.

"Have you a bite of food for a hungry man, good dame?" the soldier asked.

Now the old woman had plenty of everything, but she was stingy and pretended to be very poor.

"Ah, me, I've had nothing to eat myself today, dear heart; there is nothing in the house," she wailed.

"Well, if you've nothing, you've nothing," the soldier said. Then noticing an axe without a handle under the bench, "If there's nothing else, we could make porridge[1] out of that axe."

The old woman raised both hands in astonishment.

"Axe porridge? Who ever heard the like!"

"I'll show you how to make it. Just give me a pot."

The old woman brought a pot, and the soldier washed the axe, put it in the pot, and filling the pot with water, placed it on the fire.

The soldier got out a spoon and stirred the water and then tasted it.

"It will soon be ready," said he. "A pity there's no salt."

"Oh, I have salt. Here, take some."

The soldier put some salt in the pot and then tried the water again.

"If we could just add a handful of groats[2] to it," said he.

The old woman brought a small bag of groats from the pantry.

"Here, add as much as you need," said she.

The soldier went on with his cooking, stirring the meal from time to time and tasting it. And the old woman watched, and could not tear her eyes away.

"Oh, how tasty this porridge is!" the soldier said, trying a spoonful. "With a bit of butter there would be nothing more delicious."

The old woman found some butter too, and they buttered the porridge.

---

1. **porridge** (pôr′ ij): a soft food made by boiling cereal in water until thick.
2. **groats:** hulled, cracked grain such as wheat, oats, or barley.

MY FATHER AT TABLE, 1925. *Marc Chagall.*
Private Collection. A.D.A.G.P., France/V.A.G.A., New York.

"Now get a spoon, good dame, and let us eat!" the soldier said.

They began eating the porridge and praising it.

"I never thought axe porridge could taste so good!" the old woman marveled.

And the soldier ate, and laughed up his sleeve.

Getting at Meaning

RECALLING

1. Why does the old woman say that she has nothing in the house?

2. What does the soldier do with the axe?

3. What ingredients does the old woman give him?

4. Why is the old woman so surprised when she eats the axe porridge?

INTERPRETING

5. What does the soldier trick the woman into doing?

6. What seems to be the soldier's most important quality? Explain your answer.

CRITICAL THINKING: EVALUATING

7. In what ways is the old woman an exaggerated character? How is the soldier exaggerated? What is the purpose of these exaggerations? Is the purpose achieved? Explain.

Developing Skills in Reading Literature

1. **Folk Tale.** A folk tale is a story that is handed down, usually by word of mouth, among the people of a region. Folk tales generally show ordinary people in everyday situations. From what region does this folk tale come? Do the people in this tale seem ordinary? What situation are they in? Might this have been a common situation in the time and place of the tale? Why do you think that this tale has lasted through the years?

2. **Theme.** The theme is the main idea of a work of literature. Often the theme is a message about human nature. What undesirable human quality does this tale portray? What character illustrates this quality? What happens to the character? What lesson does the tale teach? State this lesson in one sentence.

Developing Vocabulary

Using the Dictionary. The word *axe* also can be spelled *ax*. There is no difference in meaning between these two spellings. Following are six other words that each have two spellings. Use a dictionary to find the second spelling of each word. Then, answer this question: Does any difference in meaning go along with the difference in spelling?

advisor	catsup
enquire	draught
judgment	intrust

Developing Writing Skills

Retelling a Tale. Rewrite "Axe Porridge" in your own words, using a familiar setting and modern-sounding dialogue. During prewriting, decide on your new setting and characters. Could one character be a student hitchhiking home from college? a tourist stranded in a snowstorm? Could the porridge be a casserole? Could it be cooked in a microwave oven? Could a character refer to a closed supermarket? As you write, use the tale as a model for punctuating and capitalizing dialogue and for paragraphing correctly. When you revise your story, check to be sure that it makes some point about human nature. See **Using the Process of Writing** found on pages 614–623 for help with this assignment.

To be bold or to be cautious—that is the question.

The Two Brothers

Leo Tolstoy   Translated by *Ann Dunnigan*

Two brothers set out on a journey together. At noon they lay down in a forest to rest. When they woke up they saw a stone lying next to them. There was something written on the stone, and they tried to make out what it was.

"Whoever finds this stone," they read, "let him go straight into the forest at sunrise. In the forest a river will appear; let him swim across the river to the other side. There he will find a she-bear and her cubs. Let him take the cubs from her and run up the mountain with them without once looking back. On the top of the mountain he will see a house, and in that house will he find happiness."

When they had read what was written on the stone, the younger brother said:

"Let us go together. We can swim across the river, carry off the bear cubs, take them to the house on the mountain, and together find happiness."

"I am not going into the forest after bear cubs," said the elder brother, "and I advise you not to go. In the first place, no one can know whether what is written on this stone is the truth—perhaps it was written in jest. It is even possible that we have not read it correctly. In the second place, even if what is written here is the truth—suppose we go into the forest and night comes, and we cannot find the river. We shall be lost. And if we do find the river, how are we going to swim across it? It may be broad and swift. In the third place, even if we swim across the river, do you think it is an easy thing to take her cubs away from a she-bear? She will seize us, and, instead of finding happiness, we shall perish, and all for nothing. In the fourth place, even if we succeeded in carrying off the bear cubs, we could not run up a mountain without stopping to rest. And, most important of all, the stone does not tell us what kind of happiness we should find in that house. It may be that the happiness awaiting us there is not at all the sort of happiness we would want."

"In my opinion," said the younger brother, "you are wrong. What is written on the stone could not have been put there without reason. And it is all perfectly clear. In the first place, no harm will come to us if we try. In the second place, if we do not go, someone else will read the inscription on the stone and find happiness, and we shall have lost it all. In the third place, if you do not make an effort and try hard, nothing in the world will succeed. In the fourth place, I should not want it thought that I was afraid of anything."

The elder brother answered him by saying,

THE BEAR AND THE GARDENER, 1926–1927.
Marc Chagall. Private Collection.

"The proverb says: 'In seeking great happiness small pleasures may be lost.' And also, 'A bird in the hand is worth two in the bush.'"

The younger brother replied, "I have heard: 'He who is afraid of the leaves must not go into the forest.' And also, 'Beneath a stone no water flows.'"

Then the younger brother set off, and the elder remained behind.

No sooner had the younger brother gone into the forest than he found the river, swam across it, and there on the other side was the she-bear, fast asleep. He took her cubs, and ran up the mountain without looking back. When he reached the top of the mountain, the people came out to meet him with a carriage to take him into the city, where they made him their king.

He ruled for five years. In the sixth year, another king, who was stronger than he, waged war against him. The city was conquered, and he was driven out.

Again the younger brother became a wanderer, and he arrived one day at the house of the elder brother. The elder brother was living in a village and had grown neither rich nor poor. The two brothers rejoiced at seeing each other and at once began telling of all that had happened to them.

"You see," said the elder brother, "I was right. Here I have lived quietly and well, while you, though you may have been a king, have seen a great deal of trouble."

"I do not regret having gone into the forest and up the mountain," replied the younger brother. "I may have nothing now, but I shall always have something to remember, while you have no memories at all."

Getting at Meaning

RECALLING

1. What message is written on the stone?

2. After the two brothers read the message on the stone, the elder brother raises five objections. Summarize these objections.

3. The younger brother answers the elder brother's objections. What four things does he point out?

4. Who follows the directions on the stone? What is his reward? How long does it last?

INTERPRETING

5. What two proverbs does the elder brother cite? What do they mean? What do they suggest about him?

6. What two proverbs does the younger brother cite? What do they mean? What is he suggesting about his elder brother?

7. At the end of the tale, does either brother regret his choice? Why or why not?

CRITICAL THINKING: EVALUATING

8. Find the paragraph that ends with the words "where they made him their king." If the writer had ended the tale there, what would be his message? (Keep this answer in mind as you complete the following exercise on the theme of the tale.)

Developing Skills in Reading Literature

Theme. The theme is the main idea of a work of literature. Often the theme is a message about human nature. The theme of a tale generally is not stated directly. Rather, it is suggested through other elements such as the characters. Think about the characters in this tale. How does the elder brother's choice fit the kind of person that he is? How does the younger brother's choice suit him? Do they each make the right choice? What if the elder brother had followed the directions on the stone? What if the younger brother had stayed home? Would they have been satisfied? What is the tale saying about people and the choices that they must make in life? Do you agree with the writer's message? Give reasons for your answer.

BIOGRAPHY

Count Leo Tolstoy (1828–1910) was one of the greatest figures in the history of Russian literature. He was also an important moral thinker and social reformer. His works, including such masterpieces as the novels *War and Peace* and *Anna Karenina,* have been translated into many languages. Tolstoy admired the simple lives of Russian peasants. He is known for his statements about the virtues of the simple life and for his portrayal of Russian society in the nineteenth century.

The White Snake

Retold by *Jakob and Wilhelm Grimm*

Translated by *Margaret Hunt and James Stern*

A long time ago there lived a king who was famed for his wisdom through all the land. Nothing was hidden from him, and it seemed as if news of the most secret things was brought to him through the air. But he had a strange custom; every day after dinner, when the table was cleared, and no one else was present, a trusty servant had to bring him one more dish. It was covered, however, and even the servant did not know what was in it, neither did anyone know, for the King never took off the cover to eat of it until he was quite alone.

This had gone on for a long time, when one day the servant, who took away the dish, was overcome with such curiosity that he could not help carrying the dish into his room. When he had carefully locked the door, he lifted up the cover, and saw a white snake lying on the dish. But when he saw it he could not deny himself the pleasure of tasting it, so he cut off a little bit and put it into his mouth. No sooner had it touched his tongue than he heard a strange whispering of little voices outside his window. He went and listened, and then noticed that it was the sparrows who were chattering together and telling one another of all kinds of things which they had seen in the fields and woods. Eating the snake had given him power of understanding the language of animals.

Now it so happened that on this very day the Queen lost her most beautiful ring, and suspicion of having stolen it fell upon this trusty servant, who was allowed to go everywhere. The King ordered the man to be brought before him and threatened with angry words that unless he could before the morrow point out the thief, he himself should be looked upon as guilty and executed. In vain he declared his innocence; he was dismissed with no better answer.

In his trouble and fear he went down into the courtyard and took thought how to help himself out of his trouble. Now some ducks were sitting together quietly by a brook and taking their rest; and, whilst they were making their feathers smooth with their bills, they were having a confidential conversation together. The servant stood by and listened. They were

THE FROG PRINCE, 1912. *Maxfield Parrish.* *Cover of* Hearst's Magazine, *July, 1912. University of California, Berkeley.*

telling one another of all the places where they had been waddling about all the morning and what good food they had found; and one said in a pitiful tone: "Something lies heavy on my stomach; as I was eating in haste I swallowed a ring which lay under the Queen's window." The servant at once seized her by the neck, carried her to the kitchen, and said to the cook: "Here is a fine duck; pray, kill her." "Yes," said the cook, and weighed her in his hand;

"she has spared no trouble to fatten herself and has been waiting to be roasted long enough." So he cut off her head, and as she was being dressed for the spit, the Queen's ring was found inside her.

The servant could now easily prove his innocence; and the King, to make amends for the wrong, allowed him to ask a favor and promised him the best place in the court that he could wish for. The servant refused everything and only asked for a horse and some money for traveling, as he had a mind to see the world and go about a little. When his request was granted, he set out on his way and one day came to a pond, where he saw three fishes caught in the reeds and gasping for water. Now, though it is said that fishes are dumb, he heard them lamenting that they must perish so miserably, and, as he had a kind heart, he got off his horse and put the three prisoners back into the water. They leapt with delight, put out their heads, and cried to him: "We will remember you and repay you for saving us!"

He rode on, and after a while it seemed to him that he heard a voice in the sand at his feet. He listened and heard an ant-king complain: "Why cannot folks, with their clumsy beasts, keep off our bodies? That stupid horse, with his heavy hoofs, has been treading down my people without mercy!" So he turned on to a side path and the ant-king cried out to him: "We will remember you — one good turn deserves another!"

The path led him into a wood, and there he saw two old ravens standing by their nest and throwing out their young ones. "Out with you, you idle, good-for-nothing creatures!" cried they; "we cannot find food for you any longer; you are big enough and can provide for yourselves." But the poor young ravens lay upon the ground, flapping their wings and crying:

"Oh, what helpless chicks we are! We must shift for ourselves, and yet we cannot fly! What can we do but lie here and starve?" So the good young fellow alighted and killed his horse with his sword and gave it to them for food. Then they came hopping up to it, satisfied their hunger, and cried: "We will remember you—one good turn deserves another!"

And now he had to use his own legs, and when he had walked a long way, he came to a large city. There was a great noise and crowd in the streets, and a man rode up on horseback, crying aloud: "The King's daughter wants a husband; but whoever seeks her hand must perform a hard task, and if he does not succeed he will forfeit his life." Many had already made the attempt but in vain; nevertheless, when the youth saw the King's daughter, he was so overcome by her great beauty that he forgot all danger, went before the King, and declared himself a suitor.

So he was led out to the sea, and a gold ring was thrown into it, before his eyes. Then the King ordered him to fetch this ring up from the bottom of the sea and added: "If you come up again without it you will be thrown in again and again until you perish amid the waves." All the people grieved for the handsome youth; then they went away, leaving him alone by the sea.

He stood on the shore and considered what he should do, when suddenly he saw three fishes come swimming towards him. They were the very fishes whose lives he had saved. The one in the middle held a mussel in its mouth, which it laid on the shore at the youth's feet, and when he had taken it up and opened it, there lay the gold ring in the shell. Full of joy he took it to the King and expected that he would grant him the promised reward.

But when the proud princess perceived that

he was not her equal in birth, she scorned him and required him first to perform another task. She went down into the garden and strewed with her own hands ten sacks-full of millet seed on the grass. Then she said: "Tomorrow morning before sunrise these must be picked up and not a single grain be wanting."

The youth sat down in the garden and considered how it might be possible to perform this task, but he could think of nothing, and there he sat sorrowfully awaiting the break of day, when he should be led to death. But as soon as the first rays of the sun shone into the garden he saw all the ten sacks standing side by side, quite full, and not a single grain was missing. The ant-king had come in the night with thousands and thousands of ants, and the grateful creatures had by great industry picked up all the millet seed and gathered them into the sacks.

Presently the King's daughter herself came down into the garden, and was amazed to see that the young man had done the task she had given him. But she could not yet conquer her proud heart and said: "Although he has performed both the tasks, he shall not be my husband until he has brought me an apple from the Tree of Life." The youth did not know where the Tree of Life stood, but he set out and would have gone on forever, as long as his legs would carry him, though he had no hope of finding it. After he had wandered through three kingdoms, he came one evening to a wood and lay down under a tree to sleep. But he heard a rustling in the branches, and a golden apple fell into his hand. At the same time three ravens flew down to him, perched themselves upon his knee, and said: "We are the three young ravens whom you saved from starving. When we had grown big and heard that you were seeking the Golden Apple, we flew over the sea to the end of the world, where the Tree of Life stands, and have brought you the apple." The youth, full of joy, set out homewards and took the Golden Apple to the King's beautiful daughter, who had now no more excuses left to make. They cut the Apple of Life in two and ate it together; and then her heart became full of love for him, and they lived in undisturbed happiness to a great age.

Getting at Meaning

RECALLING

1. What power does eating from the king's dish give to the servant?

2. What crime is the servant accused of by the king?

3. How does the servant find out what happened to the queen's ring?

4. The king allows the servant to ask for a favor. What does the servant ask for?

5. What animals does the servant assist and in what ways?

6. What three tasks does the servant perform in order to win the daughter of the second king? How do the animals help him in these tasks?

7. What is the source of the first king's wisdom?

8. What effect does eating the Apple of Life have on the princess?

Developing Skills in Reading Literature

1. **Fairy Tale.** A fairy tale is a type of children's story in which magic plays a central role. What things mentioned in this story are magical?

2. **Motif.** A motif is an element that appears over and over again in a literary work or in a group of literary works. "The White Snake" contains many motifs common in fairy tales. These motifs include the following:

a. talking animals

b. wishes that are granted

c. a young man who sets out to see the world

d. tasks to be performed

e. golden apples

f. the marriage of a princess

Think of other fairy tales that contain these motifs. List the motifs and the tales that contain them.

Developing Writing Skills

Writing a Fairy Tale. Choose three of the fairy tale motifs listed in Developing Skills in Reading Literature. Write a brief fairy tale using these motifs. Make sure that your tale contains an element of magic. In your prewriting notes, list the fairy tale motifs that you plan to use. Make notes on the characters and setting of your story. Also, list the events of the story in chronological order. Once you have finished your first draft, refer to the guidelines for revision and proofreading in **Using the Process of Writing** on pages 621–622.

B I O G R A P H Y

Jakob and Wilhelm Grimm   (1785–1863; 1786–1859), known to the world as "The Brothers Grimm," were born in Hanau, Germany. Both men studied law at the University of Marburg and later held positions as librarians and as university professors. The Brothers Grimm became famous for their studies of the historical development of literature, law, and language. Outside the scholarly world, they are most widely known for *Grimm's Fairy Tales,* a collection of German folk tales and saints' legends. Among the most famous of the *Grimm's Tales* are "Hansel and Gretel," "Little Red Riding Hood," "Snow-White," "Rumpelstiltskin," "Sleeping Beauty," and "Cinderella."

A gift is a great responsibility for the giver.

Arap Sang and the Cranes

African Folk Tale

Retold by *Humphrey Harman*

Some people of Africa believe that before you give anything to anyone, you should first carefully think out what your gift will mean to the person. A gift is a great responsibility to the giver, they say; and after they have said that they may tell you the story of *Arap Sang and the Cranes.*

Arap Sang was a great chief and more than half a god, for in the days when he lived great chiefs were always a little mixed up with the gods. One day he was walking on the plain, admiring the cattle.

It was hot. The rains had not yet come. The ground was almost bare of grass and as hard as stone. The thorn trees gave no shade, for they were just made of long spines and thin twigs and tiny leaves, and the sun went straight through them.

It was hot. Only the black ants didn't feel it, and they would be happy in a furnace.

The sun beat down on Arap Sang's bald head. (He was sensitive about this and didn't like it mentioned.) And he thought, "I'm feeling things more than I used to."

And then he came across a vulture sitting in the crook of a tree, his wings hanging down and his eyes on the lookout.

"Vulture," said Arap Sang, "I'm hot, and the sun is making my head ache. You have there a fine pair of broad wings. I'd be most grateful if you'd spread them out and let me enjoy a patch of shade."

"Why?" croaked Vulture. He had indigestion. Vultures usually have indigestion; it's the things they eat.

"Why?" said Arap Sang mildly. "Now that's a question to which I'm not certain that I've got the answer. Why? Why, I suppose, because I ask you. Because it wouldn't be much trouble to you. Because it's pleasant and good to help people."

"Bah!" said Vulture.

"What's that?"

"Oh, go home, Baldy, and stop bothering people; it's hot."

Arap Sang straightened himself up, and his eyes flashed. He wasn't half a god for nothing; and when he was angry, he could be a rather terrifying person. And he was very angry now. It was that remark about his lack of hair.

The really terrifying thing was that when he spoke, he didn't shout. He spoke quietly, and the words were clear and cold and hard and all separate like hailstones.

"Vulture," he said, "you're cruel, and you're selfish. I shan't forget what you've said, and you won't either. NOW GET OUT!"

Arap Sang was so impressive that Vulture got up awkwardly and flapped off.

"Silly fool," Vulture said uncomfortably.

Presently Vulture met an acquaintance of his. (Vultures don't have friends; they just have acquaintances.) They perched together on the same bough. Vulture took a close look at his companion and then another, and what he saw was so funny that it cheered him up.

"He, he!" he giggled. "What's happened to you? Met with an accident? You're *bald*."

The other vulture looked sour, but at the same time you felt she might be pleased about something.

"That's good, coming from you," she said. "What have you been up to? You haven't got a feather on you above the shoulders."

Then they both felt their heads with consternation. It was quite true. They were bald, both of them; and so was every other vulture, the whole family, right down to this very day.

Which goes to show that if you can't be ordinarily pleasant to people, at least it's not wise to go insulting great chiefs who are half gods.

I said that he was a rather terrifying person.

Arap Sang walked on. He was feeling shaky. Losing his temper always upset him afterward. And doing the sort of magic that makes every vulture in the world bald in the wink of an eye can take it out of you.

And he *did* want a bit of shade.

Presently he met an elephant. Elephant was panting across the plain in a tearing hurry and was most reluctant to stop when Arap Sang called to her.

"Elephant," said Arap Sang weakly. "I'm tired and I'm dizzy. I want to get to the forest and into a bit of shade, but it's a long way."

"It *is* hot, isn't it?" said Elephant. "I'm off to the forest myself."

"Would you spread out your great ears and let me walk along under them?" asked Arap Sang.

"I'm sorry," said Elephant, "but you'd make my journey so slow. I must get to the forest. I've got the most terrible headache."

"Well, I've got a headache too," protested the chief.

"I'm sure," said Elephant, "and no one could be sorrier about that than I am. Is it a very big headache?"

"Shocking big," said Arap Sang.

"There now," said Elephant. "Consider how big I am compared to you and what the size of *my* headache must be."

That's elephants all over, always so logical. Arap Sang felt that there was something wrong with this argument, but he couldn't just see where. Also, he had become a little uncomfortable about all those bald vultures, and he didn't want to lose his temper with anyone else. You have to be careful what you do when you're half a god. It's so dreadfully final.

"Oh, all right," he muttered.

"Knew you'd see it that way," said Elephant. "It's just what I was saying about you the other day. You can always rely on Arap Sang, I said, to behave reasonably. Well, goodbye and good luck."

And she hurried off in the direction of the distant forest and was soon out of sight.

Poor Arap Sang was now feeling very ill

indeed. He sat on the ground, and he thought to himself, "I can't go another step unless I get some shade; and if I don't get some soon, I'm done for."

And there he was found by a flock of cranes. They came dancing through the white grass, stamping their long, delicate legs so that the insects flew up in alarm and were at once snapped up in the cranes' beaks. They gathered around Arap Sang sitting on the ground; and he looked so distressed that they hopped up and down with embarrassment, first on one leg then the other. "Korong! Korong!" they called softly, and this happens to be their name as well.

"Good birds," whispered Arap Sang, "you must help me. If I don't reach shade soon, I'll die. Help me to the forest."

"But of course," said the cranes, and they spread their great, handsome black and white wings to shade him and helped him to his feet; and together, slowly, they all crossed the plain into the trees.

Then Arap Sang sat in the shade of a fine cotton tree and felt very much better. The birds gathered round him, and he looked at them and thought that he had never seen more beautiful creatures in the whole world.

"And kind. Kind as well as beautiful," he muttered. "The two don't always go together. I must reward them."

"I shan't forget your kindness," he said, "and I'll see that no one else does. Now I want each one of you to come here."

Then the cranes came one after another and bowed before him, and Arap Sang stretched out his kindly hand and gently touched each beautiful sleek head. And where he did this, a golden crown appeared. And after the birds had gravely bowed their thanks, they all flew off to the lake, their new crowns glittering in

the evening sun.

Arap Sang felt quite recovered. He was very pleased with his gift to the cranes.

Two months later, a crane dragged herself to the door of Arap Sang's house. She was a pitiful sight, thin with hunger, feathers broken and muddy from hiding in the reeds, eyes red with lack of sleep.

Arap Sang exclaimed in pity and horror. "Great Chief," said the crane, "we beg you to take back your gift. If you don't, there'll soon be not one crane left alive, for we are hunted day and night for the sake of our golden crowns."

Arap Sang listened and nodded his head in sorrow.

"I'm foolish," he said, "and I harm my friends. I had forgotten that humans also are greedy and selfish and that they'll do anything for gold. Let me undo the wrong I have done by giving without thought. I'll make one more magic, but that'll be the last."

Then he took their golden crowns, and in their place he put a wonderful halo of feathers which they have until this day.

They still are called Crowned Cranes.

Getting at Meaning

RECALLING

1. Describe the setting of this tale.
2. Who is Arap Sang?
3. What does Arap Sang request of the vulture? What is the vulture's answer?
4. How does the vulture anger Arap Sang? How does Arap Sang punish the vulture?
5. What excuse does Elephant give for not helping Arap Sang?
6. Who finally helps Arap Sang? What is their reward?
7. Why does Arap Sang replace his first gift? What does he replace it with?

INTERPRETING

8. The animals in this tale have human qualities. What kind of person does the vulture resemble? the elephant? the cranes?
9. What lesson does Arap Sang learn from his experience with the vulture? From his experience with the cranes?
10. How is Arap Sang like a character in a myth? How else is this tale similar to a myth?

CRITICAL THINKING: EVALUATING

11. Arap Sang says that humans are "greedy and selfish" and that "they'll do anything for gold." Is this an objective view of humans? Or is it a one-sided, narrow view? Explain.

Developing Skills in Reading Literature

Sequence. Sequence is the order of events in a literary work. On a sheet of paper, number the following events in sequence.

1. Vulture and his acquaintance realize that they are bald.
2. Arap Sang asks for help from Elephant.
3. A half-starved crane drags herself to Arap Sang's house.
4. Arap Sang meets a vulture.
5. Arap Sang sits on a rock and says, "I can't go another step unless I get some shade."

6. Arap Sang touches the crane's head, and a golden crown appears.
7. The vulture insults Arap Sang.
8. Arap Sang takes the crowns away, and in their place he puts a halo of feathers.
9. Elephant refuses to help Arap Sang.
10. The cranes spread their wings and protect Arap Sang from the sun.

Speaking and Listening. Copy the events from the story in sequence on one or more note cards. Then, using your note cards as a guide, tell the story to a child or record the story.

Developing Vocabulary

Word Origins: Compounds. Sometimes a new word is formed by putting together two words to make a compound word. *Hailstone* is an example of a compound word. Look through this folk tale and find at least one other compound word. Then make a list of ten more compounds, using as many words from the selections in this unit as possible.

Developing Writing Skills

Writing About a Personal Experience. Have you ever tried to help someone, but your plan did not work out the way you intended? For example, have you ever brought a gift of candy to someone on a diet or lost a sick friend's homework when taking it to school? Write a paragraph about such an incident in your life. In your prewriting notes, list several possible topics. Choose the one that you think will make the most interesting subject. List the sequence of events that you will cover in your paragraph. As you write your first draft, follow closely your prewriting list of events. When revising your paragraph, look for straightforward ways of expressing your ideas. Take out any unnecessary details or repeated ideas. For a review of the steps involved in the process of writing, see **Using the Process of Writing** found on pages 614–623.

Popocatépetl and Ixtacihuatl

Mexican Legend   Retold by *Juliet Piggott*

There was once an Aztec emperor in Te-nochtitlan.[1] He was very powerful. Some thought he was wise as well, while others doubted his wisdom. He was born a ruler and a warrior; and he kept at bay those tribes living in and beyond the mountains surrounding the Valley of Mexico, with its huge lake called Texcoco[2] in which Tenochtitlan was built. His power was absolute, and the splendor in which he lived was very great.

It is not known for how many years the Emperor ruled Tenochtitlan, but it is known that he lived to a great age. However, it was not until he was in his middle years that his wife gave him an heir, a girl. The Emperor and Empress loved the princess very much, and she was their only child. She was a dutiful daughter and learned all she could from her father about the art of ruling, for she knew that when he died, she would reign in his stead in Tenochtitlan.

Her name was Ixtacihuatl.[3] Her parents and her friends called her Ixta. She had a pleasant disposition and, as a result, she had many friends. The great palace where she lived with the Emperor and Empress rang with their laughter when they came to the parties her parents gave for her. As well as being a delightful companion, Ixta was also very pretty, even beautiful.

Her childhood was happy, and she was content enough when she became a young woman. But by then she was fully aware of the great responsibilities which would be hers when her father died, and she became serious and studious and did not enjoy parties as much as she had done when younger.

Another reason for her being so serious was that she was in love. This in itself was a joyous thing, but the Emperor forbade her to marry. He wanted her to reign and rule alone when he died, for he trusted no one, not even his wife, to rule as he did except his much loved only child, Ixta. This was why there were some who doubted the wisdom of the Emperor; for, by not allowing his heiress to marry, he showed a selfishness and shortsightedness towards his daughter and his empire which many consid-

---

1. **Tenochtitlan** (tā nok' tē tlän').
2. **Texcoco** (täs kō' kō).
3. **Ixtacihuatl** (ēs' tä sē' wat'l).

ered was not truly wise. An emperor, they felt, who was not truly wise could not also be truly great or even truly powerful.

The man with whom Ixta was in love was also in love with her. Had they been allowed to marry, their state could have been doubly joyous. His name was Popocatépetl,[4] and Ixta and his friends all called him Popo. He was a warrior in the service of the Emperor, tall and strong, with a capacity for gentleness, and very brave. He and Ixta loved each other very much, and while they were content and even happy when they were together, true joy was not theirs because the Emperor continued to insist that Ixta should not be married when the time came for her to take on her father's responsibilities.

This unfortunate but moderately happy relationship between Ixta and Popo continued for several years, the couple pleading with the Emperor at regular intervals and the Emperor remaining constantly adamant. Popo loved Ixta no less for her father's stubbornness; and she loved him no less while she studied, as her father demanded she should do, the art of ruling in preparation for her reign.

When the Emperor became very old, he also became ill. In his feebleness, he channeled all his failing energies towards instructing Ixta in statecraft, for he was no longer able to exercise that craft himself. So it was that his enemies, the tribes who lived in the mountains and beyond, realized that the great Emperor in Tenochtitlan was great no longer, for he was only teaching his daughter to rule and not ruling himself.

The tribesmen came nearer and nearer to Tenochtitlan until the city was besieged. At last the Emperor realized himself that he was great no longer, that his power was nearly gone, and that his domain was in dire peril.

Warrior though he long had been, he was now too old and too ill to lead his fighting men into battle. At last he understood that, unless his enemies were frustrated in their efforts to enter and lay waste to Tenochtitlan, not only would he no longer be Emperor but his daughter would never be Empress.

Instead of appointing one of his warriors to lead the rest into battle on his behalf, he offered a bribe to all of them. Perhaps it was that his wisdom, if wisdom he had, had forsaken him; or perhaps he acted from fear. Or perhaps he simply changed his mind. But the bribe he offered to whichever warrior succeeded in lifting the siege of Tenochtitlan and defeating the enemies in and around the Valley

---

4. **Popocatépetl** (pō pō′ kä te′ pet′l).

CLASSIC MAYAN MURAL IN BONAMPAK, CHIAPAS (detail), 8th century. *National Museum of Anthropology, Mexico City. Photograph by Peter Furst.*

of Mexico was both the hand of his daughter and the equal right to reign and rule, with her, in Tenochtitlan. Furthermore, he decreed that directly he learned that his enemies had been defeated, he would instantly cease to be Emperor himself. Ixta would not have to wait until her father died to become Empress; and, if her father should die of his illness or old age before his enemies were vanquished, he further decreed that he who overcame the surrounding enemies should marry the princess whether he, the Emperor, lived or not.

Ixta was fearful when she heard of her father's bribe to his warriors, for the only one whom she had any wish to marry was Popo; and she wanted to marry him, and only him, very much indeed.

The warriors, however, were glad when they heard of the decree. There was not one of them who would not have been glad to have the princess as his wife, and they all relished the chance of becoming Emperor.

And so the warriors went to war at their ruler's behest, and each fought trebly hard; for each was fighting not only for the safety of Tenochtitlan and the surrounding valley, but for the delightful bride and for the right to be the Emperor himself.

Even though the warriors fought with great skill, and even though each one exhibited a courage he did not know he possessed, the war was a long one. The Emperor's enemies were firmly entrenched around Lake Texcoco and Tenochtitlan by the time the warriors were sent to war; and as battle followed battle, the final outcome was uncertain.

The warriors took a variety of weapons with them; wooden clubs edged with sharp blades of obsidian,[5] obsidian machetes,[6] javelins which they hurled at their enemies from troughed throwing boards, bows and arrows, slings and spears set with obsidian fragments, and lances, too. Many of them carried shields woven from wicker and covered in tough hide and most wore armor made of thick quilted cotton soaked in brine.

The war was long and fierce. Most of the warriors fought together and in unison, but some fought alone. As time went on, natural leaders emerged and, of these, undoubtedly Popo was the best. Finally, it was he, brandishing his club and shield, who led the great charge of running warriors across the valley, with their enemies fleeing before them to the safety of the coastal plains and jungles beyond the mountains.

The warriors acclaimed Popo as the man most responsible for the victory; and, weary though they all were, they set off for Tenochtitlan to report to the Emperor and for Popo to claim Ixta as his wife at last.

But a few of those warriors were jealous of Popo. Since they knew none of them could rightly claim the victory for himself (the decision among the Emperor's fighting men that Popo was responsible for the victory had been unanimous), they wanted to spoil for him and for Ixta the delights which the Emperor had promised.

These few men slipped away from the rest at night and made their way to Tenochtitlan ahead of all the others. They reached the capital two days later, having traveled without sleep all the way, and quickly let it be known that, although the Emperor's warriors had been successful against his enemies, the warrior Popo had been killed in battle.

It was a foolish and cruel lie which those warriors told their Emperor, and they told it for no reason other than that they were jealous of Popo.

When the Emperor heard this, he demanded that Popo's body be brought to him so that he might arrange a fitting burial. He knew the man his daughter had loved would have died courageously. The jealous warriors looked at one another and said nothing. Then one of them told the Emperor that Popo had been killed on the edge of Lake Texcoco and that his body had fallen into the water and no man had been able to retrieve it. The Emperor was saddened to hear this.

After a little while, he demanded to be told which of his warriors had been responsible for the victory; but none of the fighting men before him dared claim the successful outcome of the war for himself, for each knew the others would refute him. So they were silent. This puzzled the Emperor, and he decided to wait for the main body of his warriors to return and not to press the few who had brought the news of the victory and of Popo's death.

Then the Emperor sent for his wife and his daughter and told them their enemies had been overcome. The Empress was thoroughly excited and relieved at the news. Ixta was only apprehensive. The Emperor, seeing her anxious face, told her quickly that Popo was dead. He went on to say that the warrior's body had been lost in the waters of Lake Texcoco; and again it was as though his wisdom had left him, for he spoke at some length of his not yet being able to tell Ixta who her husband would be and who would become Emperor when the main body of warriors returned to Tenochtitlan.

---

5. **obsidian** (ob sid' ē ən): a very hard, usually black, glassy volcanic rock.
6. **machetes** (mə shet' ēz): large, heavy-bladed knives.

But Ixta heard nothing of what he told her, only that her beloved Popo was dead. She went to her room and lay down. Her mother followed her and saw at once she was very ill. Witch doctors were sent for, but they could not help the princess, and neither could her parents. Her illness had no name, unless it was the illness of a broken heart. Princess Ixtacihuatl did not wish to live if Popocatépetl was dead, and so she died herself.

The day after her death, Popo returned to Tenochtitlan with all the other surviving warriors. They went straight to the palace and, with much cheering, told the Emperor that his enemies had been routed and that Popo was the undoubted victor of the conflict.

The Emperor praised his warriors and pronounced Popo to be the new Emperor in his place. When the young man asked first to see Ixta, begging that they should be married at once before being jointly proclaimed Emperor and Empress, the Emperor had to tell Popo of Ixta's death and how it had happened.

Popo spoke not a word.

He gestured the assembled warriors to follow him, and together they sought out the few jealous men who had given the false news of his death to the Emperor. With the army of warriors watching, Popo killed each one of them in single combat with his obsidian studded club. No one tried to stop him.

That task accomplished, Popo returned to the palace and, still without speaking and still wearing his stiff cotton armor, went to Ixta's room. He gently lifted her body and carried it out of the palace and out of the city, and no one tried to stop him doing that either. All the warriors followed him in silence.

When he had walked some miles, he gestured to them again, and they built a huge pile of stones in the shape of a pyramid. They all worked together and they worked fast, while Popo stood and watched, holding the body of the princess in his arms. By sunset the mighty edifice was finished. Popo climbed it alone, carrying Ixta's corpse with him. There, at the very top, under the heap of stones, he buried the young woman he had loved so well and for so long and who had died for the love of him.

That night Popo slept alone at the top of the pyramid by Ixta's grave. In the morning he came down and spoke for the first time since the Emperor had told him the princess was dead. He told the warriors to build another pyrmid, a little to the southeast of the one which held Ixta's body, and to build it higher than the other.

He told them, too, to tell the Emperor on his behalf that he, Popocatépetl, would never reign and rule in Tenochtitlan. He would keep watch over the grave of the Princess Ixtacihuatl for the rest of his life.

The messages to the Emperor were the last words Popo ever spoke. Well before the evening, the second mighty pile of stones was built. Popo climbed it and stood at the top, taking a torch of resinous pine wood with him.

And when he reached the top, he lit the torch, and the warriors below saw the white smoke rise against the blue sky; and they watched as the sun began to set, and the smoke turned pink and then a deep red, the color of blood.

So Popocatépetl stood there, holding the torch of memory of Ixtacihuatl, for the rest of his days.

The snows came, and, as the years went by, the pyramids of stone became high, white-capped mountains. Even now the one called Popocatépetl emits smoke in memory of the princess whose body lies in the mountain which bears her name.

Getting at Meaning

RECALLING

1. Why does the Emperor forbid Ixta to marry? How do his people feel about this decision? How does Ixta feel?

2. What bribe does the Emperor offer his warriors?

3. Who becomes the strongest leader of the warriors? What does he succeed in doing?

4. What lie do the jealous men tell the Emperor?

5. How does Popo punish the jealous men who lie to the Emperor?

6. Ixta's grave is built in the form of a pyramid. What is the purpose of the second pyramid?

INTERPRETING

7. Why do the Emperor's enemies attack when they hear that he is old and ill? What is their goal? Are they successful?

8. Why does Popo choose to keep watch over Ixta's grave? What does this show about him?

9. What is the present-day form of the pyramids?

CRITICAL THINKING: EVALUATING

10. Who is responsible for Ixta's death and Popo's grief: the jealous warriors or the Emperor who created the situation? Explain your answer.

11. What does *tragic* mean? Is the story of Ixta and Popo tragic? Explain.

Developing Skills in Reading Literature

1. **Setting.** Setting is the time and place of the action of a story. Describe the setting of this folk tale. What details in the story help you "see" the setting in your mind?

Locate the mountain called Ixtacihuatl on a map of Mexico. According to the map, is the setting in the story fairly accurate?

2. **Hero and Character.** A hero is the main character in a story. Popo is the hero of this tale. What are his admirable qualities? What heroic deeds does he perform?

A character is a person or animal who takes part in the action of a work of literature. Popo is one important character in this story. Ixta is another. List several adjectives that describe Ixta. Is she as admirable a character as Popo? Explain.

3. **Conflict.** A conflict is a struggle between opposing forces. In this tale there are several conflicts between characters. What is the conflict between the Emperor and his daughter? What are two other conflicts in this tale? Who are the opposing forces in each?

Developing Vocabulary

Using a Glossary. Using the Glossary at the end of this book, write the definitions of the italicized words in the following sentences.

1. The Emperor remained *adamant*.
2. "The city was *besieged*."
3. "His domain was in *dire* peril."
4. "His enemies were *vanquished*."
5. They hurled *javelins* at their enemies.
6. The cotton was soaked in *brine*.
7. He *brandished* a club.
8. "No man had been able to *retrieve* it."
9. "The others would *refute* him."
10. "Ixta was only *apprehensive*."

When Paul was a baby, he knocked down a mile of trees just by rolling over in his sleep.

$\mathcal{P}$aul Bunyan   American Folk Tale

Retold by *Adrien Stoutenburg*

Some people say that Paul Bunyan wasn't much taller than an ordinary house. Others say he must have been a lot taller to do all the things he did, like sticking trees into his pockets and blowing birds out of the air when he sneezed. Even when he was a baby, up in Maine, he was so big he knocked down a mile of trees just by rolling over in his sleep.

Everyone was nervous about what might happen when Baby Paul grew older and started crawling. Maine wouldn't have any forests left.

Paul's father, who was an ordinary-sized man, was a bit nervous about it all himself. One night he had wakened to find his bed down on the floor. There beside it sat Baby Paul, a crosscut saw in one hand. In the other hand he held one of the sawed-off legs of the bed. He was chewing on it to help his teeth grow.

"I'll have to put him somewhere safe," Paul's father decided, "where he won't be a public nuisance."

He cut down some tall trees growing near his own cabin and built a boat shaped like a cradle. Paul's mother tucked Paul into it. Then Paul's parents put a long rope on the floating cradle and let it drift out to sea a little way.

It was a lovely, blue-green place for a cradle, with fish flashing around and the waves making small, humpbacked motions underneath. Baby Paul sucked his thumb and watched the seagulls flying over, light shaking from beneath their wings. Paul smiled, and then he hiccoughed. The hiccough started a gale that nearly blew a fishing boat all the way to the North Pole.

Finally, Paul went to sleep. He snored so loudly the gulls went flapping toward land, for they thought a thunderstorm was coming. Then young Paul had a bad dream, brought on by the extra large ham his mother had given him for breakfast. He tossed about in his sleep and started the cradle rocking. Each time the cradle rocked, it sent a wave as big as a building toward shore. Paul tossed harder, and the waves grew even larger, bigger than cities. They smashed against the shore and threatened to drown everything on land.

People scampered up church steeples. They scrambled onto rooftops. They clawed their way up into trees, and they yelled for the government to save them. The settlers for miles around put rifles on their shoulders and marched up to Paul's father.

"Get that baby out of here!" they shouted. "He's a danger to the whole state. A baby like that is against the Constitution!"

Paul's father, and his mother, too, couldn't help feeling a bit proud of how strong Paul was. But they knew that the smartest thing to do was to move away. No one seems to know exactly where they went. Wherever it was, Paul didn't cause too much trouble for the rest of the time he was growing up. His father taught him certain things that helped.

"Don't lean too hard against smallish trees or buildings, Son," his father told him. "And if there are towns or farmers' fields in your way, step around them."

And Paul's mother told him, "Never pick on anybody who isn't your own size, Son."

Since there wasn't anyone his size around, Paul never got into fights. Being taller than other boys, by about fifty feet or so, he was naturally the best hunter, fisherman, walker, runner, yeller, or mountain climber there was. And he was best of all at cutting down trees and turning them into lumber. In those days, when America was new, people had to cut down a lot of trees. They needed the lumber for houses, churches, town halls, ships, bridges, ballrooms, stores, pencils, wagons, and flag poles. Luckily, the trees were there, stretching in tall, wind-shining rows across America. The trees marched up mountains and down again. They followed rivers and creeks. They massed up together in purple canyons and shoved each other out of the way on the shores of lakes. They pushed their dark roots down into rock and their glossy branches into the clouds.

Paul liked to flash a sky-bright axe over his head. He loved the smell of wood when it was

cut and the look of its sap gleaming like honey. He didn't chop trees down in any ordinary way. With four strokes he would lop all the limbs and bark off a tree, making it a tall, square post. After he had squared up miles of forest in a half-hour, he would take an axe head and tie a long rope to it. Then he would stand straddle-legged and swing the axe in a wide circle, yelling "T-I-M-B-E-R-R-R! Look out!" With every swing and every yell, a hundred trees would come whooshing down.

The fallen trees had to be hauled down to a river so that they could be floated to a sawmill. Paul grew a bit tired of lugging bundles of trees under his arms, and he wished he had a strong friend to help him. Also, at times he felt lonely, not having anyone his size around.

About the time he was feeling loneliest, there came the Winter of the Blue Snow. Paul, who was full-grown by then, had never seen anything like the blue flakes falling from the sky. Nobody else had either, and perhaps they never will, unless it happens again. The blue snow fell softly at first, like bits of sky drifting down. The wind rose and the flakes grew thicker. The blue snow kept falling, day after day. It covered branches and roof tops, hill and valley, with blue, and Paul thought it was about as beautiful a sight as anyone could want.

One day when Paul was out walking in the blue snow, he stumbled over something the size of a mountain. The mountain made a faint mooing sound and shuddered.

"Excuse me," said Paul and looked closer.

Two huge, hairy ears stuck up above the snowdrift. The ears were as blue as the snow.

"Who are you?" Paul asked. There was no answer. Paul grabbed both of the ears and pulled.

Out of the snow came a shivering, clumsy, completely blue baby ox. Even its round, blinking eyes and its tail were blue. Only its shiny nose was black. The calf was the largest Paul had ever seen. Strong as Paul was, he felt his muscles shake under the creature's weight.

"Ah! Beautiful blue baby!" Paul said. He cradled the half-frozen calf in his great arms and carried it home. There he wrapped the baby ox in warm blankets and sat up all night taking care of it. The calf did not show much sign of life until morning. Then, as the dawn light came through the window, the ox calf stood up. The calf stretched its neck out and sloshed its wet tongue lovingly against Paul's neck.

Paul gave a roar of laughter, for his one ticklish spot was his neck.

Paul patted the baby ox and scratched his silky, blue ears. "We will be wonderful friends, eh Babe? You will be a giant of an ox and carry forests for me on your back."

That is how it happened that Babe the Blue Ox went with Paul Bunyan when Paul started out into the world to do his mighty logging work. By that time, Babe had his full growth. People never could figure out how long Babe was. They had to use field glasses even to see from one end of Babe to the other. And there were no scales large enough to weigh Babe. Paul did measure the distance between Babe's eyes, and that was exactly forty-two axe handle lengths and one plug of tobacco. Every time Babe needed new iron shoes for his hoofs, a fresh iron mine had to be opened. The shoes were so heavy that a man couldn't carry one without sinking up to his knees in solid rock.

Paul and the Blue Ox logged all over the northern timber country, from Maine to Michigan, Wisconsin, and Minnesota. Paul hired many men to help him. These lumberjacks liked working for Paul Bunyan because he was

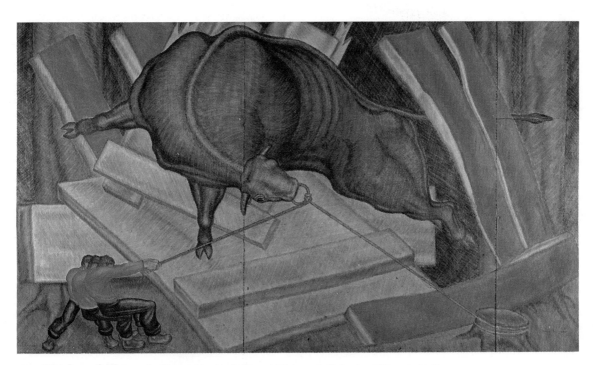

BABE, 1934. *James C. Watrous. Paul Bunyan Mural in the Memorial Union at the University of Wisconsin, Madison.*

always good to them and made sure that they had plenty of food.

The lumber crews liked pancakes best, but they would gobble up and slurp down the pancakes so fast that the camp cooks couldn't keep up with them, even when the cooks got up twenty-six hours before daylight. The main problem was that the griddles the cooks used for frying the pancakes were too small.

The winter that Paul was logging on the Big Onion River in Michigan, he decided that he had to do something about making a big enough griddle. He went down to the plow works at Moline, Illinois, and said, "I want you fellows here to make me a griddle so big I won't be able to see across it on a foggy day."

The men set to work. When they were finished, they had built a griddle so huge there was no train or wagon large enough to carry it.

"Let me think what to do," said Paul. "We'll have to turn the griddle up on end, like a silver dollar, and roll it up to Michigan." He hitched the Blue Ox to the upturned griddle, and away they went. It wasn't any job at all for Babe and Paul, though they had to hike a couple of hundred miles. A few miles from the Big Onion lumber camp, Paul unhitched Babe and let the griddle roll on by itself. When it stopped rolling, it started to spin as a penny does when it's ready to fall. It spun around and around and dug a deep hole in the ground before it flopped down like a cover over the hole.

The lumberjacks cheered and rushed off to haul a few acres of trees into the hole for a fire. The cook and a hundred and one helpers mixed tons of batter. When everything was ready, with the flames under the griddle blazing like a forest fire, Paul picked out a crew of men who could stand the heat better than others. He had them strap fat, juicy slabs of bacon on their feet.

"You men skate around on that griddle and that'll keep it well greased," he told them.

The men skated until the griddle shone with bacon fat. White batter came pouring out onto the griddle, and soon the smell of crisp, brown, steaming pancakes was drifting across the whole state. There were tons of pancakes — with plenty left over for Babe, who could eat a carload in one gulp.

There wasn't much Paul couldn't do, especially with Babe's help. But there was one job that seemed almost too hard even for him. That was in Wisconsin, on the St. Croix River. The logging road there was so crooked that it couldn't find its own way through the timber. It would start out in one direction, then turn around and go every which way until it grew so snarled up it didn't know its beginning from its end. The teamsters hauling logs over it would start home for camp and meet themselves coming back.

Maybe even Babe couldn't pull the kinks and curves out of a road as crooked as that one, Paul thought, but there was nothing to do but try.

He gave Babe several extra pats as he put the Blue Ox's pulling harness on. Then he hitched Babe to the end of the road and stood back.

Babe lowered his head and pushed his hoofs into the earth. His muscles stood out like rows of blue hills. He strained forward, pulling at the road. He stretched so hard that his hind legs spraddled out until his belly nearly scraped the ground. The road just lay there, stubborn as could be.

"You can do it, my big beautiful Babe!" Paul said.

Babe tried again. He strained so hard that his eyes nearly turned pink. He sweated so that water poured from the tips of his horns. He grunted and pulled, and his legs sank into the ground like mighty blue posts.

There was a snap, and then a loud C-R-A-C-K! Paul saw the first kink come out of the road, and he cheered. The road kept fighting back, flopping around and trying to hold on to its crooked twists and turns, but it was no match for Babe. At last, the road gave a kind of shiver and then lay still. Babe pulled it straighter than a railroad tie.

Paul Bunyan's chest swelled up so with pride that it broke one of his suspenders. The broken suspender whizzed up into the sky like a long rubber band. Just then, thousands of wild ducks were flying overhead. The suspender wrapped itself around the ducks and strangled the whole flock. Paul felt sorry for the ducks, but there was nothing to do but gather them up and hand them over to the cooks.

That night, after a wonderful duck dinner, Paul's bookkeeper, John Inkslinger, started writing down all that had happened. He was busily scratching away with his pen when he saw that he had only two barrels of ink left. He asked Paul what to do.

"That's easy," said Paul. "Don't bother to dot your i's or cross your t's. You'll save enough ink that way to get by until we can haul in another load of ink in the spring. Then you can fix up the i's and t's."

Winters could be very cold there in Wisconsin and Minnesota. One year, Lake Superior froze solid from top to bottom. In the spring, Paul had to haul all the ice out of the lake and stack it up on shore to thaw.

That same winter, men's words froze in front of their mouths and hung stiff in the air. Brimstone Bill, who was a great talker, was frozen in by a solid wall of words all turned to ice. Paul had to chip the ice from around Bill's

shoulders, tie a rope to him, and have Babe pull him out.

The greatest logging job Paul ever did was in North Dakota, where some of the trees were so tall it took a man a whole day to see up to their tops. Shortly after Paul had finished logging off most of the white pine, spruce, and hemlock in Minnesota, he received a letter from the King of Sweden. Paul's Swedish blacksmith, Ole, read the letter to Paul.

"The king says there are too many Swedes in Sweden. He wants to send a batch of them over here, but they need rich farmland without many trees, so they can raise wheat. He says he'll pay you in silver and gold if you can fix up a place for them."

Paul thought awhile, puffing on his pipe so hard that the sky began to cloud over. "North Dakota's the place," he said. "Nice and flat for farming. I'll fix it up for the Swedes, but I'm going to have to build the biggest logging camp ever built."

There never was such building, banging, tree-whacking, and hammering as went on in North Dakota when Paul started the new camp. Cook houses, bunk houses, and sheds grew up out of the ground, each building as big as a good-sized town. The dining room alone was so long that the man who brought the salt and pepper wagons around started out at one end in the morning and did not reach the other end until night.

Paul had found that it was easier to skid logs on roads made slippery with ice. There weren't many lakes in North Dakota, so Paul hauled his water for freezing from Lake Superior. He put the water into a big tank which Babe pulled. The thousands of lakes in Minnesota today were made by Babe's hoofs sinking into the ground and the holes filling up with water that leaked out of the tank. On one trip, Babe

AXEMAN, 1934. *James C. Watrous.*
Paul Bunyan Mural in the Memorial Union at the
University of Wisconsin, Madison.

slipped and the tank tipped over. All the water ran out and started the Mississippi River.

On the day that Paul had cut down the last big tree in North Dakota, he stood looking around proudly. Then he frowned. Everywhere he looked there were hundreds and thousands of stumps sticking up. The Swedish farmers weren't going to like those stumps standing in the way of the plows.

"Blast it all!" Paul said, angry at himself for not having pulled the trees up roots and all. "Blast!" he thundered again and brought his fist whistling down on the stump beside him. The stump sank a foot below ground.

Paul Bunyan stared, scratched the side of his head, and stomped off to find Ole the blacksmith. "Ole," said Paul, "I want you to make me a maul—and make it as strong as

Brimstone Bill's breath!"

The next morning, before the regular workday began, Paul went out with the new maul, which was like a giant hammer. He began knocking the stumps down into the ground. After about two weeks, working a couple of hours each morning, he had hammered every stump into the earth.

The King of Sweden was pleased when he heard about the fine job Paul had done, but one thing troubled him. He sent the Swedish ambassador to ask Paul if the soil in North Dakota was rich enough to grow fine crops.

"I'll prove that it is," said Paul. He got himself a kernel of corn, dug a hole four feet deep with a flick of his thumb, and dropped the corn in. "You come back in a week," he told the king's messenger, "and you'll see a fat stalk of corn pushing up out of the ground." He started to walk off, when he heard a rustling, whooshing sound behind him.

Paul turned. The kernel of corn had already sprouted and was rising up like a green rocket. In one minute it grew as high as Paul Bunyan's eyebrows. In two minutes more its tip struck a flying eagle and then split a cloud in two.

The Swedish ambassador's false teeth jumped out of his mouth and started biting the ground in excitement. "You'd better stop that corn growing!" he yelled at Paul. "It's apt to poke a hole in the sky and let all the air out. Besides, if I tell the king about it, he'll think it's just a tall story I made up."

Paul called to his men. "Ole," he said when all the men arrived, "you climb up there fast and cut the top off."

Ole straddled the stalk, but the thing was growing so fast it took Ole right along with it. Before Paul could think of what to do, Ole was out of sight.

"Come on down!" Paul yelled up at Ole.

Ole was almost beyond hearing then. When he answered, his voice took an hour to fall back to earth. "I can't come down! For every two feet I climb down, it carries me up ten!"

Paul bit the ends of his whiskers, rubbed his forehead, and tried to think of what to do. He ordered Shotgun Gunderson to load his rifle with doughnuts and sourdough bread and shoot it up to Ole so that Ole wouldn't starve to death while waiting for Paul to rescue him.

Finally, Paul took his biggest and brightest axe and began chopping at the base of the cornstalk. The stalk was growing so fast, he couldn't hit the same place twice with his axe. He put a chain around the stalk, planning to have Babe pull the corn out by its roots. The stalk grew out over the chain and pulled it into the air before Paul could even call Babe.

Paul remembered the iron rails that the men who had been building the Great Northern Railroad had left lying beside the tracks. He marched off a few miles, picked up an armload of the rails, and came back. He tied the rails together, wrapped them around the cornstalk, and made a tight knot. The cornstalk grew fatter and thicker. With every foot the stalk grew, the iron hoop around it sank in deeper.

"It's going to kill itself if it keeps on growing," said John Inkslinger. "It's going to cut itself in two."

That is what the cornstalk did. It gave a shudder at last and started to sway. It was so tall that it took three days to hit the ground. Just before it hit, Ole jumped off, so he fell only four feet and didn't get a scratch.

The Swedish ambassador wrote to the king that the soil seemed pretty rich, and the king sent Paul a shipload of money.

Paul began looking around for an even bigger job. Most of the land nearby had been logged over, and there weren't many large forests left. Paul decided to go west to the Pacific Ocean. There were trees there so huge, called the Big Trees, that it took a day to walk around them. There were redwood trees and Douglas fir trees so tall they were bent over from pressing against the sky.

Paul told his friends goodbye, and he and Babe started out for the West Coast. On the way, Paul happened to let his peavey, a pole with a sharp spike on the end, drag along behind him. This made a rut that is now called the Grand Canyon. Farther on, heading through Oregon and Washington, Babe trampled some hills in the way, and that made the passes in the Cascade Mountains.

When Paul Bunyan started lumbering in the West, the fir and redwoods began to fall like grass. He built one big camp after another and invented all sorts of ways to make the lumbering business go faster. When the biggest part of the job was done, he grew restless again. He would go and sit on a hill with the Blue Ox and think about the old days. Even though there was gray in his beard now—and gray mixed in with the blue hairs on Babe's coat—Paul felt almost as young as ever.

"We've had a good life, eh, Blue Babe?"

Babe's soft blue eyes would shine, and he would push his damp muzzle against Paul Bunyan's cheek.

"Yes, sir, Babe, old friend," said Paul on one of those starlit nights with the wind crooning in the sugar pines, "it's too good a life to leave. So I guess we'll just keep on going as long as there's a toothpick of a tree left anywhere."

Apparently, that is what Paul Bunyan and his blue ox did. They just kept on going. The last time anyone saw them they were up in Alaska. And people there say, when the wind is right, they can still hear Paul whirling his sky-bright axe and sending the shout of "T-I-M-B-E-R-R-R!" booming across the air.

Getting at Meaning

RECALLING

1. When Paul is a baby, why do the people of Maine want him out of the state?

2. How does Paul solve the following problems?

   a. feeding the lumber crew their favorite breakfast

   b. the crooked logging road on the St. Croix River

   c. thousands of stumps in the North Dakota fields

   d. the giant cornstalk

3. How does the tale explain the following geographical features?

   a. the lakes in Minnesota
   b. the Mississippi River
   c. the Grand Canyon
   d. the passes in the Cascade Mountains

INTERPRETING

4. Why do Paul and Babe go West?

5. How do Paul's parents feel about him? In what ways do they treat him as an ordinary child?

6. How would you describe the relationship between Paul and Babe?

7. Why is *John Inkslinger* such an appropriate name?

8. What do you learn about logging from this tale?

9. What makes Paul a good lumberman?

Developing Skills in Reading Literature

1. **Tall Tale.** A tall tale is a story with exaggerated characters and events. When the United States was being settled, the pioneers would sit around the campfire and tell stories. In the retelling of the stories, one fact and then another would be stretched. This is how many tall tales became so exaggerated.

Why do you think that tall tales were popular with the pioneers? What might have been the purpose that tall tales served in their lives?

2. **Hyperbole.** Hyperbole is exaggeration for emphasis. It can give you an instant image. It also can create humor. "Her eyes were as big as saucers" is an example of hyperbole. The girl's eyes could not possibly be as big as saucers.

At one point the narrator says, "Everyone was nervous about what might happen when Baby Paul grew older and started crawling. Maine wouldn't have any forests left." What image do you get of Paul Bunyan's size from this description? What makes this description humorous? Find at least ten other examples of hyperbole in this tall tale.

3. **Setting.** Setting is the time and place of the action of a story. What is the time of this tall tale? Using a map, find the places named in the tale.

Developing Vocabulary

Using a Dictionary To Find Word Origins. The following names of states are mentioned in this tall tale. Look up each name in a dictionary. On a separate sheet of paper, explain the origin of the name in your own words.

Maine	Wisconsin	Oregon
Dakota	Minnesota	Washington
Michigan	Illinois	Alaska

Developing Writing Skills

Writing a Tale. Write a tale about the area in which you live. Using your imagination, tell how a lake was formed or how the land became flat or mountainous. During prewriting, choose a subject and then decide whether you will treat it seriously, as in "Popocatépetl and Ixtacihuatl," or humorously, as in "Paul Bunyan." Organize your ideas in a logical order, and follow this order when writing your first draft. Reread your final tale several times and revise where necessary. Make a clean final copy. If you need help with the writing process, study the lessons in **Using the Process of Writing** on pages 614–623.

BIOGRAPHY

Adrien Stoutenburg (1916–1985) grew up in Darfur, Minnesota, and attended the Minneapolis School of Arts. She worked as a librarian, reporter, and editor. She began writing in 1941. Her work includes poetry, short stories, biographies, novels, and folk tales. Examples of her work include *Timberline Treasure, The Silver Trap,* and *Stranger on the Bay.* Although writing was her profession, Stoutenburg was also an accomplished artist, sculptor, and musician.

Fables

What Is a Fable?

The fables in this section differ from the myths and tales that you have read. First, the purpose of fables is more to teach than to entertain. Each fable clearly illustrates a lesson, or moral. Second, the main characters in fables are usually animals that talk and act like human beings. Often these animals have human faults: they are proud and lazy, overconfident and ungrateful.

The Origins of Fables

Aesop, a slave from ancient Greece, is known as the father of the fable. However, Aesop only recorded the fables. He did not create them. Like myths and tales, the fables were a part of the oral tradition. They were told for many years before they were first put into writing.

Thinking About Fables

As you read these fables, think about the lessons that they teach. Ask yourself these questions: Do human beings still have the same faults and weaknesses? Have people's values changed much since the earliest fables were written?

THE HARE AND THE TORTOISE, 1981. *Kinuko Craft.*

The Lion and the Mouse

Aesop

Once when a lion was asleep, a little mouse began running up and down upon him. This soon wakened the lion, who placed his huge paw upon him and opened his big jaws to swallow him. "Pardon, O King," cried the little mouse. "Forgive me this time; I shall never forget it. Who knows but what I may be able to do you a turn some of these days?" The lion was so tickled at the idea of the mouse being able to help him that he lifted up his paw and let him go. Some time after, the lion was caught in a trap, and the hunters, who desired to carry him alive to the king, tied him to a tree while they went in search of a wagon to carry him on. Just then the little mouse happened to pass by. Seeing the sad plight in which the lion was, he went up to him and soon gnawed away the ropes that bound the king of the beasts. "Was I not right?" said the little mouse.

"Little friends may prove great friends."

Getting at Meaning

RECALLING

1. Why does the lion let the mouse go?
2. How does the mouse repay the lion?

INTERPRETING

3. What qualities do you generally associate with lions? with mice? Do the animals in this fable show these qualities? Explain.

4. What is the lion's attitude toward mice at the beginning of the fable? Do you think that his attitude might change now? How?

CRITICAL THINKING: EVALUATING

5. Does the lion behave in the way that a human would in a similar situation? Does the mouse? Is this fable really about animal behavior or human behavior? Explain.

Developing Skills in Reading Literature

Fable and Moral. A fable teaches a lesson about human nature. This lesson is called the moral. Often, the moral appears at the end of the fable. Paraphrase, or restate in your own words, the moral of this fable.

THE LION AND THE MOUSE FROM *THE FABLES OF AESOP*, 1665.
Wenceslaus Hollar. The Metropolitan Museum of Art, New York.

B I O G R A P H Y

Aesop (620?–560 B.C.) was a Greek slave who is credited with a collection of animal fables that are still enjoyed today. Most people agree that at least some of these tales came from sources other than Aesop, and some scholars question whether Aesop ever existed. There are, however, many legends about him. It is said that he was a slave to two different masters. The second master, in appreciation of Aesop's wit and learning, gave him his freedom. Another story puts Aesop in the court of King Croesus where he used his storytelling ability to advise and instruct.

AESOP AND THE FOX, (detail) 5TH CENTURY. *Attic Cup. Photograph from the Vatican Museums.*

"Come you with me," said the Town Mouse, "and I will show you how to live."

The Town Mouse and the Country Mouse

Aesop

Now you must know that a Town Mouse once upon a time went on a visit to his cousin in the country. He was rough and ready, this cousin, but he loved his town friend and made him heartily welcome. Beans and bacon, cheese and bread, were all he had to offer, but he offered them freely.

The Town Mouse rather turned up his long nose at this country fare and said, "I cannot understand, Cousin, how you can put up with such poor food as this; but of course you cannot expect anything better in the country. Come you with me, and I will show you how to live. When you have been in town a week you will wonder how you could ever have stood a country life."

No sooner said than done. The two mice set off for the town and arrived at the Town Mouse's residence late at night. "You will want some refreshments after our long journey," said the polite Town Mouse and took his friend into the grand dining room. There they found the remains of a fine feast, and soon the two mice were eating up jellies and cakes and all that was nice. Suddenly they heard growling and barking.

"What is that?" said the Country Mouse.

"It is only the dogs of the house," answered the other.

"Only!" said the Country Mouse. "I do not like that music at my dinner."

Just at that moment the door flew open. In came two huge mastiffs,[1] and the two mice had to scamper down and run off. "Goodbye, Cousin," said the Country Mouse.

"What! Going so soon?" said the other.

"Yes," he replied:

"Better beans and bacon in peace than cakes and ale in fear."

---

1. **mastiffs:** large, powerful, smooth-coated dogs with hanging lips and drooping ears.

Getting at Meaning

RECALLING

1. How is the food offered by the Country Mouse different from that offered by the Town Mouse?

INTERPRETING

2. Why does the Town Mouse turn up his nose at the country meal? What does he value?

3. What does the Country Mouse mean when he says, "I do not like that music at my dinner"? How does the Town Mouse feel about the "music"?

4. What is the moral, or lesson, of this fable? Explain its meaning.

CRITICAL THINKING: EVALUATING

5. Most of Aesop's fables feature animal characters. Why might Aesop have used animals to teach lessons about human beings?

Developing Skills in Reading Literature

Personification. Personification is the giving of human qualities to an object, animal, or idea. The Town Mouse and the Country Mouse are personified. What are their character traits? Are these traits ones that are found in people? Explain.

The Ant and the Grasshopper

Aesop

In a field one summer's day a Grasshopper was hopping about, chirping and singing to its heart's content. An Ant passed by, bearing along with great toil an ear of corn he was taking to the nest.

"Why not come and chat with me," said the Grasshopper, "instead of toiling and moiling in that way?"

"I am helping to lay up food for the winter," said the Ant, "and recommend you to do the same."

"Why bother about winter?" said the Grasshopper; "we have got plenty of food at present."

But the Ant went on its way and continued its toil. When the winter came, the Grasshopper had no food and found itself dying of hunger, while it saw the ants distributing every day corn and grain from the stores they had collected in the summer. Then the Grasshopper knew:

It is best to prepare for the days of necessity.

THE ANTS AND THE GRASSHOPPER, 1909. *Edward Julius Detmold.*
Reprinted from *The Fantastic Creatures of Edward Julius Detmold,*
Peacock Press/Bantam Books and an earlier book, *The Fables of Aesop,*
Hodder and Stoughton, *1909.*

Getting at Meaning

RECALLING

1. This fable spans what two seasons?
2. Who says each of the following:
"Why bother about winter?"
"I am helping to lay up food for the winter...."

INTERPRETING

3. What is the moral of this fable? Which insect puts this moral into practice? Which insect realizes too late the truth of the moral?

CRITICAL THINKING: APPLYING

4. Consider these new endings for this fable:

a. The Ant has extra food and shares it with the Grasshopper.

b. The Ant shares his food with the Grasshopper, and they both starve by the end of the winter.

What new moral would fit each ending? Does either of these endings reflect human life as well as the current ending does? Explain.

5. Think of three ways that the moral of this fable might apply to your own life. Then write three sentences that describe practical ways that you might prepare for the future.

Developing Skills in Reading Literature

Symbol. As explained before, a symbol is a person, place, or object that stands for something beyond itself. You may have some symbols in your own life. For example, your grandparents' house might stand for childhood happiness or family unity.

In this fable, what kind of person does the Grasshopper symbolize? What kind of person does the Ant symbolize?

The Fox and the Crow

Aesop

A Fox once saw a Crow fly off with a piece of cheese in its beak and settle on a branch of a tree. "That's for me, as I am a Fox," said Master Reynard;[1] and he walked up to the foot of the tree.

"Good day, Mistress Crow," he cried. "How well you are looking today. How glossy your feathers; how bright your eye. I feel sure your voice must surpass that of other birds, just as your figure does. Let me hear but one song from you, that I may greet you as the Queen of Birds."

The Crow lifted up her head and began to caw her best; but the moment she opened her mouth, the piece of cheese fell to the ground, only to be snapped up by Master Fox.

"That will do," said he. "That was all I wanted. In exchange for your cheese I will give you a piece of advice for the future:

"Do not trust flatterers."

---

1. **Master Reynard** (rā′ närd): the fox in the medieval beast epic *Reynard the Fox;* therefore, a suitable name for a fox in any folk tale.

Getting at Meaning

RECALLING

1. List phrases that the Fox uses to flatter the Crow.

2. At the beginning of the fable, who has the cheese? Who ends up eating it?

INTERPRETING

3. Why does the Crow drop the cheese? What is her weakness?

4. Foxes are often thought of as sly animals. Is Master Reynard sly? Explain your answer.

5. What advice does the Fox give the Crow? What other advice might he have given her?

6. What are flatterers? Why are they not to be trusted?

CRITICAL THINKING: EVALUATING

7. Think about the following description of Aesop: "Aesop was a practical man. He cared little for social status and looked upon foolishness as the cause of most human problems." Explain how the fables of Aesop reflect these qualities.

Developing Skills in Reading Literature

Dialogue. A dialogue is a conversation between two or more characters. In many fables the characters are animals. Nonetheless, they are able to speak to each other. Their words are written as dialogue.

Who speaks the dialogue in "The Ant and the Grasshopper"? Who speaks the dialogue in "The Fox and the Crow"? On a separate sheet of paper, write one example of dialogue spoken by each animal character. Include both the actual words spoken and the tag that identifies the speaker.

Developing Writing Skills

1. **Writing a Fable.** Write a fable of your own. You may demonstrate a moral or saying that you have heard, or you may make up your own moral. During prewriting, decide on the animal characters that you will use and on the moral that you will illustrate. List the traits of each character. Decide also on your basic story. As you write your first draft, remember to model your fable on the fables of Aesop, writing the moral at the end of the fable. As part of revision, read your fable aloud to a classmate or friend. Also check carefully for correct capitalization and punctuation of dialogue. For help with this assignment and also for the one that follows, see **Using the Process of Writing** on pages 614–623.

2. **Writing About a Fable.** Write a paragraph about one of the fables that you have read. Tell what characteristics make it a fable and not just a very short story. As a prewriting activity, list the characteristics of a fable. If necessary, refer back to the unit introduction. Then tell how the fable you have chosen illustrates each characteristic. Begin your first draft with a topic sentence that introduces the fable that is your subject. When you revise your paragraph, make sure that you have covered each characteristic listed in your prewriting notes.

In this fable James Thurber teaches the same lesson as Aesop but in a different way.

The Fox and the Crow

James Thurber

A crow, perched in a tree with a piece of cheese in his beak, attracted the eye and nose of a fox. "If you can sing as prettily as you sit," said the fox, "then you are the prettiest singer within my scent and sight." The fox had read somewhere, and somewhere, and somewhere else, that praising the voice of a crow with a cheese in his beak would make him drop the cheese and sing. But this is not what happened to this particular crow in this particular case.

"They say you are sly and they say you are crazy," said the crow, having carefully removed the cheese from his beak with the claws of one foot; "but you must be nearsighted as well. Warblers wear gay hats and colored jackets and bright vests, and they are a dollar a hundred. I wear black and I am unique." He began nibbling the cheese, dropping not a single crumb.

"I am sure you are," said the fox, who was neither crazy nor nearsighted, but sly, "I recognize you, now that I look more closely, as the most famed and talented of all birds; and I fain would hear you tell about yourself, but I am hungry and must go."

"Tarry awhile," said the crow quickly, "and share my lunch with me." Whereupon he tossed the cunning fox the lion's share of the cheese and began to tell about himself. "A ship that sails without a crow's-nest[1] sails to doom," he said. "Bars may come and bars may go, but crowbars last forever. I am the pioneer of flight; I am the map maker. Last, but never least, my flight is known to scientists and engineers, geometrists and scholars, as the shortest distance between two points. Any two points," he concluded arrogantly.

"Oh, every two points, I am sure," said the fox. "And thank you for the lion's share of what I know you could not spare." And with this he trotted away into the woods, his appetite appeased, leaving the hungry crow perched forlornly in the tree.

Moral: 'Twas true in Aesop's time, and La Fontaine's,[2] and now, no one else can praise thee quite so well as thou.

---

1. **crow's-nest:** a small, partly enclosed platform close to the top of a ship's mast, used by the lookout.
2. **LaFontaine** (lä fōn ten′): a French poet and writer of fables (1621–95).

Getting at Meaning

RECALLING

1. Does the crow fall for the fox's flattery immediately? Why or why not?

2. In this version of the fable, who praises the crow?

3. Why does the crow give the fox most of his cheese?

INTERPRETING

4. The crow uses two words that contain the word *crow*. What are these words? What do they mean? Do their meanings have anything to do with crows? Why, then, does the crow use them?

5. The crow concludes his speech arrogantly. What does *arrogantly* mean? What adverb at the end of the fable shows a change in the crow's attitude?

6. Write the moral of this fable in your own words. Be prepared to explain its meaning.

CRITICAL THINKING: EVALUATING

7. Which of the two versions of "The Fox and the Crow" do you find more entertaining? Which is most effective? Give reasons for your answers.

Developing Skills in Reading Literature

1. **Fable.** A fable is a brief story, usually with animal characters, that teaches a lesson about human nature. How are Aesop's version of "The Fox and the Crow" and Thurber's version of that fable alike? How are they different? On a separate sheet of paper, list three ways in which the two versions are alike. Then divide the rest of the paper into two columns. Head the first column *Aesop* and the second *Thurber*. List at least four differences between the two versions.

2. **Allusion.** Allusion is a reference to another work of literature or to a familiar person, place, or event outside of literature. In this fable Thurber makes an allusion to two other writers of fables. Who are they? When did they live? Read the sentence that mentions these writers. What is Thurber suggesting about human nature? According to Thurber, has human nature changed much over the last two thousand years?

Developing Vocabulary

1. **Using a Dictionary: Understanding Idioms.** An idiom is an expression that means something other than the literal meaning of the words. For example, *to catch a person's eye* is an idiom meaning "to attract a person's attention." Look up the word *crow* in a dictionary. Find the part of the entry that gives idioms containing the word *crow*. In most dictionaries, this information follows the definitions of a word. Write these idioms on a sheet of paper along with their meanings. Then write a sentence using each idiom.

2. **Using a Dictionary: Parts of Speech.** Often the same word can be used as different parts of speech. The word *crow*, for example, is used as a noun to refer to a particular type of bird. However, the word also can be used as a verb. Look up the definition of the verb *crow* in a dictionary. How is this meaning appropriate to Thurber's fable? In what sense is the crow in Thurber's fable *crowing*?

B I O G R A P H Y

James Thurber (1894–1961) made a career out of laughing at humankind. His humorous stories and cartoons were filled with small, frightened people bowing under the weight of life's pressures. Sad-looking dogs and unmannerly children also lived in the Thurber world. Much of his work appeared in *The New Yorker* magazine. Among his most famous short stories is "The Secret Life of Walter Mitty." His books include *The Thurber Carnival* and the autobiographical *My Life and Hard Times*.

What Happened to Charles

James Thurber

A farm horse named Charles was led to town one day by his owner, to be shod.[1] He would have been shod and brought back home without incident if it hadn't been for Eva, a duck, who was always hanging about the kitchen door of the farmhouse, eavesdropping, and never got anything quite right. Her farmmates said of her that she had two mouths but only one ear.

On the day that Charles was led away to the smithy, Eva went quacking about the farm, excitedly telling the other animals that Charles had been taken to town to be shot.

"They're executing an innocent horse!" cried Eva. "He's a hero! He's a martyr! He died to make us free!"

"He was the greatest horse in the world," sobbed a sentimental hen.

"He just seemed like old Charley to me," said a realistic cow. "Let's not get into a moony mood."

"He was wonderful!" cried a gullible goose.

"What did he ever do?" asked a goat.

Eva, who was as inventive as she was inaccurate, turned on her lively imagination. "It was butchers who led him off to be shot!" she shrieked. "They would have cut our throats while we slept if it hadn't been for Charles!"

"I didn't see any butchers, and I can see a burnt-out firefly on a moonless night," said a barn owl. "I didn't hear any butchers, and I can hear a mouse walk across moss."

"We must build a memorial to Charles the Great, who saved our lives," quacked Eva. And all the birds and beasts in the barnyard except the wise owl, the skeptical goat, and the realistic cow set about building a memorial.

Just then the farmer appeared in the lane, leading Charles, whose new shoes glinted in the sunlight.

It was lucky that Charles was not alone, for the memorial-builders might have set upon him with clubs and stones for replacing their hero with just plain old Charley. It was lucky, too, that they could not reach the barn owl, who quickly perched upon the weather vane of the barn; for none is so exasperating as he who

---

1. **shod** (shäd): another form of *shoed;* to furnish or fit with shoes.

is right. The sentimental hen and the gullible goose were the ones who finally called attention to the true culprit—Eva, the one-eared duck with two mouths. The others set upon her and tarred and unfeathered her, for none is more unpopular than the bearer of sad tidings that turn out to be false.

Moral: Get it right or let it alone. The conclusion you jump to may be your own.

Getting at Meaning

RECALLING

1. Why does Charles's owner take him to town? What does Eva think is happening to Charles?

2. Which animals build a memorial to Charles? Which animals do not take part in the building?

INTERPRETING

3. Eva is described as having "two mouths but only one ear." What does this mean?

4. Why are the animals angry at Charles? at the barn owl? at Eva?

5. What is the moral of this fable? Explain its meaning in your own words.

CRITICAL THINKING: APPLYING

6. This fable warns against jumping to conclusions. In what real-life situations might this lesson apply?

Developing Skills in Reading Literature

Proverb. A proverb is a brief saying that expresses a truth or bit of wisdom. "A stitch in time saves nine," "The way the twig is bent, the tree grows," and "Honesty is the best policy" are proverbs.

Each of the following sentences contains a proverb. Write the proverbs on a separate sheet of paper.

a. "It was lucky, too, that they could not reach the barn owl, who quickly perched upon the weather vane of the barn; for none is so exasperating as he who is right."

b. "The others set upon her and tarred and unfeathered her, for none is more unpopular than the bearer of sad tidings that turn out to be false."

Often, the moral of a fable can stand alone as a proverb. Look carefully at the morals of the other fables in this unit. Which are familiar proverbs? Which are similar to proverbs?

Developing Vocabulary

Using a Dictionary. Each of the following phrases is made up of an adjective and a noun. On a separate sheet of paper, write the meaning of each adjective. Use a dictionary if you need help.

sentimental hen   gullible goose
realistic cow   skeptical goat

RESEARCH SKILLS FOR *WRITING*

Locating Materials in a Library

A library is a treasure house of information. Its books, magazines, newspapers, pamphlets, recordings, and cassettes and video tapes can provide a wealth of information about almost any subject.

Librarians divide books into two categories, fiction and nonfiction. Fiction deals with imaginary characters and events; nonfiction deals with real characters and events. Nonfiction works are subdivided into several categories. Two of the largest are biographies and reference works. Many libraries display recent issues of magazines and bind the past issues into annual volumes. Past issues of newspapers are sometimes stored on microfilm. Many libraries keep pamphlets and other materials about many subjects in a cabinet called the vertical file.

Developing Writing Skills

Getting To Know Your Library. Go to your school or neighborhood library and investigate where its materials are located. Then, on a sheet of paper, draw a floor plan of the library and label the following, using the abbreviations in parentheses: fiction section (FIC), magazines (MAG), reference works (REF), biographies (BIOG), vertical file (VERT), newspapers (NEWS), recordings (REC).

After you have drawn your floor plan, write a paragraph in which you give instructions for using the library. Base your instructions on your floor plan. Pretend that you are writing for someone your own age who has just moved into your neighborhood and has asked you for help.

See **Handbook: How To Write About Literature,** Lessons 1–4.

CRITICAL THINKING

Classifying

Every day you make use of your ability to classify and to understand classification systems. Classification involves grouping items according to categories. For example, you probably have sorted your clothes so that you can locate items quickly. You may have put all your socks into one drawer and all your sweaters into another. You have classified your clothes according to type.

Identifying Useful Categories. Most groups of objects can be classified in a number of ways. Not all of these ways are equally useful, however. Imagine, for example, that you decide to classify your family's shoes into two categories: right shoes and left shoes. This system would not help you find your shoes quickly.

Classifying Literature. Literary selections and elements within the selections can be classified. The selections in this unit, for instance, have been classified into three categories: myths, tales, and fables. Reread the introduction to one of the categories. What do the selections have in common?

Now examine the selections in the section titled "Tales." Suggest two different ways to classify the tales. In what situations would each classification system be useful?

Developing Critical Thinking Skills

Using Classification Systems. The following are several ways to classify materials in this unit. On a separate sheet of paper, copy the categories. Then write the titles of the selections or the names of the characters that fall into each category. You should have at least one item in each category. Be prepared to give reasons for your classifications.

Myths Classified by Subject
  myths about fire
  myths about the seasons
Mythical Characters Classified by Type
  gods
  humans
  animals
Tales Classified by Kind of Conflict
  between human beings
  between human beings and the gods
  between human beings and nature
Fables Classified by Time of Composition
  ancient fables
  contemporary fables

Understanding Myths, Tales, and Fables

RECALLING

1. Choose three selections in which gods interact with humans. Tell how the gods either reward or punish humans and why.

INTERPRETING

2. Three myths in this unit explain how humans got fire. Name the myths that deal with fire, and write a few sentences paraphrasing each story. Then answer these questions: How are the stories similar? How are they different?

3. Identify the human characteristics of the following gods and goddesses.

Zeus	Athene
Demeter	Prometheus
Hades	O-Kee

4. List the names of two characters whose strengths are to be admired and two who exhibit common faults. Beside each name write one or two words that describe the character.

5. The following are quotations from the fables. Tell who speaks each line, and explain what the line reveals about the character of the speaker.

a. "When you have been in town a week you will wonder how you could ever have stood a country life."

b. "I am the pioneer of flight; I am the map maker."

c. "They would have cut our throats while we slept if it hadn't been for Charles!"

d. "Why bother about winter? We have got plenty of food at present."

CRITICAL THINKING: EVALUATING

6. "Demeter" and "How the Seasons and the Birds Came" are about the changing seasons. How does each story explain the change? Which story better explains the changes in weather? Explain your answer.

Writing About Myths, Tales, and Fables

See **Using the Process of Writing** on pages 614–623 for help with this assignment.

Choose the myth or tale in this unit that you think is most relevant to life today. Write a paragraph explaining why you think the myth or tale still has something worthwhile to say.

Using Techniques from the Oral Tradition

See **Using the Process of Writing** on pages 614–623 for help with these assignments.

1. The following are five common proverbs:

A fool and his money are soon parted.
Look before you leap.
He who hesitates is lost.
A bird in the hand is worth two in the bush.
Nothing ventured, nothing gained.

Choose one of these proverbs, select another well known saying, or make up a proverb of your own. Then write a brief fable that illustrates the proverb. As you finish your first draft, remember to state the proverb.

2. Write a myth or tale called "Why Humans Have Happiness." Use Greek, African, American, or imaginary gods in your story.

*W*riters on the Process of Writing

TWO FIGURES AT DESK, 1944. *Milton Avery. Oil on Canvas, 48" x 32". Neuberger Museum. State University of New York, Purchase, New York. Gift of Roy R. Neuberger.*

Writers on the Process of Writing

Good writing isn't simply a matter of talent or luck. As short story writer and novelist Eudora Welty puts it, writing well "amounts to one long, sustained effort." To turn ideas into finished works, writers think and plan. They put their ideas on paper. Then they revise until they have a final product to share. This entire process is called the process of writing.

The Process of Writing

Prewriting.　Writers make plans, gather information, and organize their ideas.

Writing.　Writers put their ideas down on paper in rough form.

Revising and Sharing.　Writers rewrite and refine their work until it is ready to share.

In this unit you will learn how many professional writers adapt the process of writing to their own kinds of writing. After reading what these writers say, try some of their suggestions in your own writing. You will find that what works for some famous writers may work for you, too.

Prewriting

The first stage of any kind of writing is prewriting. Some writers say that this is the most important stage. Prewriting is a time for thinking and planning.

In one sense, prewriting can include almost everything that a writer experiences. Writers often make use of bits of knowledge and experience gathered years earlier. Carol Ryrie Brink, author of *Caddie Woodlawn,* advises young writers to "begin to make your five senses work for you. See, hear, smell, taste, and touch the things around you."

Many writers keep journals in which they record interesting ideas, striking details, and exciting events. Isaac Bashevis Singer explains his approach to collecting ideas:

> My stories are all based upon things that have come to me in life without my going out to look for them. The only notes I take are notes on an idea

for a story.... When such an idea comes to me, I put it down in a little note-book I always carry around.

When a writer wants to begin a specific project, he or she uses the prewriting stage to prepare. This stage includes these steps:

Choosing and limiting a topic. Writers often begin by thinking about areas that interest them or that make them curious. Sometimes they list experiences that they remember well. Then, with these subjects in mind, they list specific ideas for topics, look over the list of topics, and choose a favorite.

Topics come from almost anywhere. Walter Edmonds, author of *Drums Along the Mohawk,* tells how he finds a topic:

> I get ideas from all sorts of sources—old newspapers, books, or letters from readers.

Madeleine L'Engle, author of *A Wrinkle in Time,* explains how she collects ideas:

> My story ideas are somewhat like a big, old-fashioned French stove with several pots on the back keeping warm. As ideas come along, I drop them into the appropriate pot, and when one book is finished, I pull forward onto the fire whichever pot seems most ready to be written into a book. I get my ideas from everywhere, everybody, and everything.

Kurt Vonnegut, author of many best-selling science fiction books, gives this advice to other writers: "Find a subject you care about and which you in your heart feel others should care about."

Once a writer has a topic, he or she may need to limit it. A topic should be narrow enough to be handled in the form that the writer has chosen. A novelist, for example, can choose a much broader topic than a short story writer can.

Deciding on a purpose. Every writer must keep in mind a general goal. To decide upon a purpose, or goal, the writer must ask, "What do I want my writing to accomplish? Should it ask questions or answer them? Should it make the reader laugh or get the reader angry about a problem?" What and how the author writes depends on his or her purpose for writing.

Considering the audience. Some people write for children, while others write for teenagers or adults. Still others want to reach members of certain groups, such as hockey players or stamp collectors. All authors write in ways that will interest their special audiences.

Different audiences require different kinds of writing. For example, when writing for young children, a person must use simple words and clear action. When writing for older readers, the same person may use a more formal style.

Writer John Steinbeck, another winner of the Nobel Prize, thinks of his audience in this way:

> Forget . . . the nameless, faceless audience . . . it doesn't exist. In writing, your audience is one single reader. I have found that sometimes it helps to pick out one person—a real person you know or an imagined person—and write to that one.

Gathering supporting information.   Writers may need to gather information. They do this research by reading, interviewing, and observing first-hand. Most writers keep a journal, and many review it before beginning a writing project.

Best-selling novelist Irving Wallace gives advice on researching a subject:

> Read all you can about it, interview experts on it, even travel to the sites of the story to guarantee authenticity and get a feel for the background. In my case, this process takes six months to a year.

Many professional writers begin by making a list of questions that they need to answer about their topic. Then, they use all the resources they can to answer these questions. Through careful research, they make sure that their writing will be accurate as well as interesting.

Organizing ideas.   At first, organizing ideas is like cleaning a closet. The writer goes through his or her notes and sets aside what is not needed. The writer sorts into groups the ideas that are left. Sometimes, the writer discovers that more information or details are needed. If so, he or she then does more thinking and more research.

Once the writer has a list of ideas to work with, the next step may be to arrange these ideas in a logical order. For example, it is usually best to arrange the events in stories in chronological order. For writing meant to persuade or convince, it is often best to arrange reasons either from most important to least important or from least important to most important.

Stephen King, the author of many popular novels and film scripts, stresses the need for planning and organization:

> All good writing has some kind of underlying structure or framework. It must, no matter how powerful the writing might be. Without a framework, it is as useless as a mass of muscle would be without an underlying structure of bone.

Many writers use outlines of some kind to help them organize their material. Some writers use a formal outline. Others simply list their ideas in order. Some writers make complete outlines in their heads before they write. Jean Craighead George, author of *Julie of the Wolves,* compares her outline to "the pencil sketch an artist renders before he starts to paint." Its purpose, she says, "is to get the story into my head before I begin the first draft."

Writing the First Draft

The prewriting stage ends when a writer begins the first draft. How does an author know when it is time to start writing? "When it becomes more painful not to," playwright Edward Albee answers.

DESK SET, 1972. *Wayne Thiebaud. Collection of The Southland Corporation, Dallas, Texas.*

Patricia Highsmith, an author of children's books, describes a similar feeling:

> I often reach a point beyond which I cannot think, cannot make an outline, and I become impatient to see something on paper, and so I begin.

When working on a first draft, some writers try to follow an outline. Almost all writers use prewriting notes of some kind. However, few good writers stick exactly to a prearranged plan. They remain open to the ideas that occur while they are writing.

John Steinbeck believes that a writer should work quickly, that he or she should concentrate on getting ideas onto the paper, not on technical matters such as grammar, spelling, and punctuation. He says,

> Write freely and as rapidly as possible and throw the whole thing on paper. Never correct or rewrite until the whole thing is down.

After finishing a first draft, writers then take a good look at what they have written. It is time to revise.

Revising and Sharing

Revising means making changes to improve a piece of writing. Not even famous writers get everything right the first time.

> New ideas and new material are added or rejected, as the case may be. Details are changed or developed further. Most of all, each paragraph, each sentence, each word is worked over and over. This takes a long time.
> —H. A. and Margaret Rey
> I rewrite and rewrite and rewrite. My record is eight complete different drafts! —Jean Craighead George

Most writers agree that when you revise you need to stand back and look at your own work objectively. Eleanor Estes, author of many popular children's books, describes revision in this way:

> The writer must survey his work critically, coolly, and as though he were a stranger to it. . . . He must be willing to prune, expertly and hard-heartedly.

When revising, a writer must review carefully. The writer must not be afraid to cut something that does not add to his or her main idea. As Isaac Bashevis Singer says, "The wastepaper basket is a writer's best friend."

The following are some of the many questions that writers ask themselves as they revise:

1. Is the writing interesting? Will it attract readers?
2. Have I stuck to my topic? Do all the ideas and details that I have

FIRST PINK LIGHT

Jay ~~stood~~ *leaned* the last piece of cardboard against the legs

of the chair and ~~then he walked all the way around his hiding~~ *looked at it carefully*

~~place to be sure it was just right.~~

Then he crawled ~~inside.~~ *under the chair, his hiding place.* *It was almost dark →* He couldn't see his mother ~~xxx~~

doing her homework on the card table, so he knew she couldn't

see him.

"Mama," he called," you don't know where I am."

"Where *in the world* are you?" his mother said. "Are you lost?"

Jay laughed. "No, I'm not lost," he said. "Im inside

~~here.~~ *my hiding place*

~~"Okay.~~ *Oh, that's where you are, huh?*" his mother said. "But in ~~a~~ *just one* minute you have to

come outside. *your hiding place* It's time *for you* to go to bed. *Well,*"

Jay laughed again and stuck his head out. "Mama," he

said, "you forgot! Daddy's coming home! I can't go to bed,

yet."

His mother put her pencil down. "~~Of course, I didn't~~ *Now you knew I didn't*

~~forget,~~ *that, Jay* she said. "But your daddy won't be home until ~~early~~ *five o'clock early*

in the morning. ~~He'll wake us up when he comes.~~ *You have to go to bed*"

"No!" Jay said. "~~I want~~ *I just* to stay in *here* so I can surprise *him* !"

You're going to get "You'll get sleepy," his mother said. *He'll wake you up as soon as he gets here.*

His mother didn't understand. ~~He wouldn't get sleepy.~~

His daddy had been *away* ~~gone~~ *taking care of Grandma for* a whole month, and now that Grandma included belong in this piece of writing? Are any ideas or details missing?

3. Is my organization logical? Do my ideas flow together smoothly? Are the paragraphs in the clearest possible order? In each paragraph, do all the sentences stick to the main idea?

4. Have I used exact, clear words? Does my language match my audience?

Most writers mark up the draft copy. They add information and make corrections. They show changes in the order of words, sentences, and paragraphs. They also cross out parts that are unnecessary. Soon they find that their pages are crowded with notes. Eleanor Estes says, "At the end of each revision, a manuscript may look like a battered old hive, worked over, torn apart, pinned together, added to, deleted from, words changed and words changed back."

Many writers find it helpful to read their work aloud as they revise. Children's author Ruth Stiles Gannett uses this procedure:

> Now it is time to read it aloud and listen to how it sounds. Does it read smoothly, with some sense of rhythm? When it doesn't, I rearrange or substitute to avoid awkward word combinations. Have I used too many words or dull words? If so, I cut them out.

Another technique many writers use is seeking the opinion of others. Madeleine L'Engle explains how she gets feedback:

> I don't try ideas on anyone, but I do like to read bits and pieces of manuscript to people—either children or grown-ups, whoever is available.

Finally, many writers find it helpful to set aside their work for a time. When they read it again later, they often notice ways to improve it. Poet Myra Cohn Livingston explains how she gets a fresh viewpoint:

> Searching for the right form to express certain ideas takes time. I try to put poems away, once written, and take them out much later.

Proofreading. A final stage in the revising process is proofreading. Proofreading is a last check on punctuation, grammar, spelling, and capitalization. When a writer proofreads, the goal is to make the writing clear and correct. The writer marks proofreading corrections on his or her final draft.

Making a Final Copy. With the finishing touches completed, the writer is ready to make a neat, readable final copy. The final draft, with all its corrections, is copied and then proofread. At this point, the work is ready to share.

Sharing.   Many writers share their work as part of the revision process. Others wait until they have produced a finished product. Then their work may be published in a book, magazine, or newspaper. Some writers create scripts for plays. These works are shared when the plays are performed on radio, television, or the stage.

Practicing the Process of Writing

When you write, try using the techniques suggested by the writers quoted in this unit. Refer also to **Handbook: How To Write About Literature.** As you develop your own skills, you will come to understand why writers write. You too, will share in their excitement. Like the poet Gabriel Fielding, you may decide that "Writing is a voyage, an odyssey, a discovery because I'm never certain of precisely what I will find."

Stages in the Process of Writing

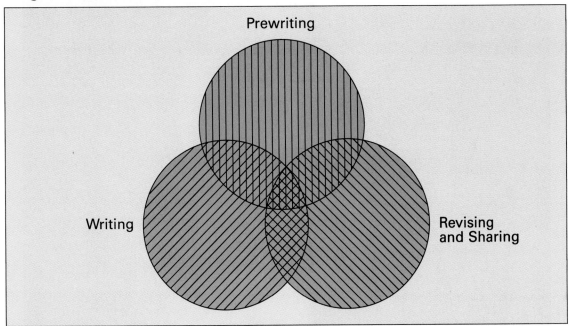

Reading a Diagram. The stages in the process of writing do not always follow an orderly step-by-step sequence. One way to understand the stages is to see them as overlapping circles. The above diagram shows how all the stages overlap. How does the diagram show the overlap between prewriting and writing? between revising and prewriting? Notice that not only do the stages overlap but also that they blend together at the center. This blending suggests that at times writers are working on all the activities at the same time.

The Short Story

BERNADITA, 1922. *Robert Henri. San Diego Museum of Art.*

Introducing the Short Story

What Is a Short Story?

A short story is a work of fiction that can be read at one sitting. Usually, a short story has one major conflict and produces a single effect on its reader. The people, places, and events in a short story are drawn from the writer's imagination. Short stories differ in many ways, but most have setting, character, and plot.

Setting.   Setting is the time and place of the action of a story. It is the background against which the events take place.

Character.   A character is a person or animal who takes part in the action of a story. Most stories have one main character and one or more minor characters. Usually, a story has a conflict, or struggle. The main character must face this conflict.

Plot.   Plot is the sequence of events in a story, the writer's plan for what happens, when, and to whom. In a typical short story, the writer introduces a conflict. The conflict builds to the climax, a high point of interest or suspense. After the climax, the events of the story move quickly to the end, or resolution, of the conflict.

How To Read a Short Story

When reading a short story, try to picture the details of setting, character, and plot. Ask yourself, "How does this setting make me feel? How would I feel if I were this character? How would I act in this situation? How do I feel about the way that the main character faced the conflict?" Most of all, enjoy reading this exciting kind of literature.

Previewing the Unit

Reading the Selections

The selections in this unit are grouped into three sections: Setting, Character, and Plot.

Using the Study Questions

Following each selection are exercises. They will help you with your reading, vocabulary, and writing skills.

Getting at Meaning.   This section contains questions of three types: The **RECALLING** questions will help you to remember the selection. The **INTERPRETING** questions will help you to understand the selection. The **CRITICAL THINKING** questions will help you to evaluate the selection and to relate it to your own life.

Developing Skills in Reading Literature.   These exercises will teach you the writing techniques used in short stories.

Developing Vocabulary.   These exercises will teach you vocabulary skills, such as using dictionaries and glossaries.

Developing Writing Skills.   In one kind of assignment you will write about the short stories that you have read. In another you will use the techniques that you have learned.

Using the Unit Study Materials

Research Skills for Writing.   This feature will teach you how to use the card catalog.

Critical Thinking.   The critical thinking exercises will teach you how to think about relationships in works of literature.

Unit Review.   The unit review will help you to recall, interpret, and think critically about the selections in the unit. The writing assignments will help you to use the writing skills that you have learned.

HOUSE BY THE RAILROAD, 1925. *Edward Hopper. Oil on canvas, 24" x 29". The Museum of Modern Art, New York.*

Setting

What Is Setting?

Every story takes place in an imaginary world created by a writer. This world, often modeled on the real one, is the setting of the story. Setting includes both time and place. The time is both the period in history and the time of day or year. The place is the location or locations in which the events of the story happen. A writer must make details such as clothing, scenery, weather, and customs fit the setting that he or she has chosen.

Thinking About Setting

As you get ready to read the stories in this section, think of yourself as an explorer starting out on adventures in new times and places. Sometimes, as in the story "Nancy," you will go no further than an ordinary town in the present-day United States. Sometimes you will go to wildly fanciful places such as a jungle on the planet Venus in the story "All Summer in a Day."

When you come across a passage that describes setting, read the lines carefully. Then, close your eyes and picture the setting in your mind. Consider the mood, or feeling, that the setting creates. Picturing the setting and thinking about the mood will add to your enjoyment of a short story. It will help you to feel, as you read, that you are present at the scene of the action. It will help to make the story come alive.

The Trout

Sean O'Faolain

One of the first places Julia always ran to when they arrived in G——was The Dark Walk. It is a laurel walk,[1] very old; almost gone wild; a lofty midnight tunnel of smooth, sinewy branches. Underfoot, the tough brown leaves are never dry enough to crackle; there is always a suggestion of damp and cool trickle.

She raced right into it. For the first few yards she always had the memory of the sun behind her; then she felt the dusk closing swiftly down on her so that she screamed with pleasure and raced on to reach the light at the far end. It was always just a little too long in coming, so that she emerged gasping, clasping her hands, laughing, drinking in the sun. When she was filled with the heat and glare, she would turn and consider the ordeal again.

This year she had the extra joy of showing it to her small brother, and of terrifying him as well as herself. And for him the fear lasted longer because his legs were so short, and she had gone out at the far end while he was still screaming and racing.

When they had done this many times, they came back to the house to tell everybody that they had done it. He boasted. She mocked. They squabbled.

"Cry baby!"

"You were afraid yourself, so there!"

"I won't take you anymore."

"You're a big pig."

"I hate you."

Tears were threatening, so somebody said, "Did you see the well?" She opened her eyes at that and held up her long lovely neck suspiciously and decided to be incredulous. She was twelve, and at that age little girls are beginning to suspect most stories. They have already found out too many, from Santa Claus to the stork. How could there be a well! In The Dark Walk? That she had visited year after year? Haughtily she said, "Nonsense."

But she went back, pretending to be going somewhere else; and she found a hole scooped in the rock at the side of the walk, choked with damp leaves, so shrouded by ferns that she uncovered it only after much searching. At the back of this little cavern, there was about a quart of water. In the water, she suddenly perceived a panting trout. She rushed for Stephen and dragged him to see; and they were both so excited that they were no longer afraid of the

---

1. **laurel walk:** evergreen trees or shrubs on both sides of a path.

darkness as they hunched down and peered in at the fish panting in his tiny prison, his silver stomach going up and down like an engine.

Nobody knew how the trout got there. Even old Martin in the kitchen garden laughed and refused to believe that it was there, or pretended not to believe, until she forced him to come down and see. Kneeling and pushing back his tattered old cap, he peered in.

"Be cripes, you're right. How did that fella get there?"

She stared at him suspiciously.

"You knew?" she accused; but he said, "The divil a' know," and reached down to lift it out. Convinced, she hauled him back. If she had found it, then it was her trout.

Her mother suggested that a bird had carried the spawn. Her father thought that in the winter a small streamlet might have carried it down there as a baby, and it had been safe until the summer came and the water began to dry up. She said, "I see," and went back to look again and consider the matter in private. Her brother remained behind, wanting to hear the whole story of the trout; not really interested in the actual trout but much interested in the story which his mummy began to make up for him on the lines of, "So one day Daddy Trout and Mammy Trout...." When he retailed it to her, she said, "Pooh."

It troubled her that the trout was always in the same position. He had no room to turn. All the time the silver belly went up and down; otherwise he was motionless. She wondered what he ate; and in between visits to Joey Pony and the boat and a bath to get cool, she thought of his hunger. She brought him down bits of dough; once she brought him a worm. He ignored the food. He just went on panting. Hunched over him, she thought how all the winter, while she was at school, he had been in there. All the winter, in The Dark Walk, all

day, all night, floating around alone. She drew the brim of her hat down around her ears and chin and stared. She was still thinking of it as she lay in bed.

It was late June, the longest day of the year. The sun had sat still for a week, burning up the world. Although it was after ten o'clock, it was still bright and still hot. She lay on her back under a single sheet, with her long legs spread, trying to keep cool. She could see the D of the moon through the fir tree—they slept on the ground floor. Before they went to bed, her mummy had told Stephen the story of the trout again; and she, in her bed, had resolutely presented her back to them and read her book. But she had kept one ear cocked.

"And so, in the end, this naughty fish who would not stay at home got bigger and bigger and bigger, and the water got smaller and smaller.... "

Passionately she had whirled and cried, "Mummy, don't make it a horrible old moral story!" Her mummy had brought in a fairy godmother then, who sent lots of rain and filled the well; and a stream poured out, and the trout floated away down to the river below. Staring at the moon, she knew that there are no such things as fairy godmothers and that the trout, down in The Dark Walk, was panting like an engine. She heard somebody unwind a fishing reel. Would the *beasts* fish him out?

She sat up. Stephen was a hot lump of sleep, lazy thing. The Dark Walk would be full of little scraps of moon. She leaped up and looked out the window, and somehow it was not so lightsome now that she saw the dim mountains far away and the black firs against the breathing land and heard a dog say *bark-bark*. Quietly she lifted the ewer[2] of water and climbed out the window and scuttled along the

_____
2. **ewer** (yoo′ ər): a large pitcher.

ANONYMOUS FRESHET, 1975. *Neil Welliver.* The Collection of Mr. and Mrs. Graham Gund/Art Resource, New York.

cool but cruel gravel down to the maw[3] of the tunnel. Her pajamas were very short, so that when she splashed water, it wet her ankles. She peered into the tunnel. Something alive rustled inside there. She raced in, and up and down she raced and flurried and cried aloud, "Oh, gosh, I can't find it," and then at last she did. Kneeling down in the damp, she put her hand into the slimy hole. When the body lashed, they were both mad with fright. But she gripped him and shoved him into the ewer and raced, with her teeth ground, out to the other end of the tunnel and down the steep paths to the river's edge.

All the time she could feel him lashing his tail against the side of the ewer. She was afraid he would jump right out. The gravel cut into her soles until she came to the cool ooze of the river's bank, where the moon mice on the water crept into her feet. She poured out,

watching until he plopped. For a second he was visible in the water. She hoped he was not dizzy. Then all she saw was the glimmer of the moon in the silent-flowing river, the dark firs, the dim mountains, and the radiant, pointed face laughing down at her out of the empty sky.

She scuttled up the hill, in the window, plonked down the ewer, and flew through the air like a bird into bed. The dog said *bark-bark*. She heard the fishing reel whirring. She hugged herself and giggled. Like a river of joy, her holiday spread before her.

In the morning Stephen rushed to her, shouting that "he" was gone and asking "where" and "how." Lifting her nose in the air, she said superciliously, "Fairy godmother, I suppose?" and strolled away, patting the palms of her hands.

_____
3. **maw:** the jaws or mouth.

Getting at Meaning

RECALLING

1. What is The Dark Walk? How does it look inside?

2. Julia's mother and father each try to explain how the trout might have gotten into the hole. What are their explanations?

3. Julia is troubled because the trout is always in the same position. What else worries her about the trout?

4. How does Julia remove the trout? What does she do with it?

INTERPRETING

5. After freeing the trout, why does Julia "fly through the air like a bird into bed"? Why does

her holiday spread before her "like a river of joy"?

6. The morning after Julia rescues the trout, her brother asks how the trout disappeared. Julia replies superciliously, saying, "Fairy god-mother, I suppose?" What does *superciliously* mean? Why does Julia reply superciliously? Does she think that she is more mature than her brother? How do you know that this is what she thinks?

CRITICAL THINKING: APPLYING

7. At the beginning of the story, the writer states that racing through The Dark Walk is ter-rifying for Julia and Stephen. How can an experi-ence be both terrifying and exciting? What experiences and places had a similar effect on you when you were a young child?

Developing Skills in Reading Literature

1. **Setting.** Setting is the time and place of the action of the story. In this story the place of the action is more important than the time. The Dark Walk is where most of the story is focused. How do Julia and her brother react to The Dark Walk at the beginning of the story? How does Julia act when she enters The Dark Walk at the end of the story? Why is she not afraid of The Dark Walk when she rescues the trout?

2. **Personification.** Personification is the giving of human qualities to an object, animal, or idea. Read the following excerpts from the story. Then, tell what is being personified in each excerpt.

a. "...she saw the dim mountains far away and the black firs against the breathing land...." (p. 109)

b. "Quietly she lifted the ewer of water and climbed out the window and scuttled along the cool but cruel gravel.... " (p. 109)

c. "Then all she saw was the glimmer of the moon in the silent-flowing river, the dark firs, the dim mountains, and the radiant, pointed face laughing down at her out of the empty sky." (p. 111)

Developing Vocabulary

Using a Dictionary. In a dictionary entry, a word that is to be defined is printed in boldface type and divided into syllables. After the word, the dictionary lists some or all of the following additional information:

a. the pronunciation, usually in parentheses

b. the part of speech

c. the etymology, or word origin, usually in brackets

d. the definition or definitions of the word

e. derived words, or words that can be made from the main entry word

f. the synonymy or list of synonyms—words that are similar in meaning to the entry word—and definitions of these synonyms

g. antonyms, or words opposite in meaning to the entry word

h. cross references, which suggest other entries that contain additional information about the word

The following dictionary entry contains all of these parts.

false (fols) *adj.* **fals′er, fals′est** [< OFr. < L. pp. of *fallere*, to deceive] **1.** not true; in error; incorrect; wrong *[a false* argu-ment*]* **2.** untruthful; lying *[to give false* testimony*]* **3.** dis-loyal; unfaithful *[a false* friend*]* **4.** deceiving; misleading *[a false* scent*]* **5.** not real; artificial; counterfeit *[false* teeth*]* **6.** not properly so named *[false* jasmine*]* **7.** based on mis-taken ideas *[false* pride*]* **8.** temporary, nonessential, or added on for protection, disguise, etc. *[a false* drawer*]* **9.** *Music* pitched inaccurately —*adv.* in a false manner—**play (a per-son) false** to deceive or betray (a person) —**false′ly** *adv.* —**false′ness** *n.*
SYN.—false refers to anything that is not basically what it seems to be and may or may not suggest something intended to deceive others *[false* teeth*]*; **sham** refers to an imitating or pretending to be something, usually with the intention of deceiving others *[sham* piety*]*; **counterfeit** and the colloquial **bogus** refer to a very careful imitation and always imply an intention of deceiving or defrauding others *[counterfeit,* or *bogus,* money*]*; **fake** is a less formal term for any person or thing that is not genuine *[a fake* doctor, *fake* tears*]* See also **SYN.** at FAITHLESS —**ANT. genuine, real**

On a sheet of paper, complete the sentences that follow. Refer to the dictionary entry for the word *false*.

1. Four synonyms for the word *false* are
_____, _____, _____, and _____.

2. This dictionary entry lists _____ different definitions for the word *false*.

3. The two derived words listed in this entry are _____ and _____.

4. The word *false* is a _____ (part of speech).

5. Two antonyms for the word *false* are _____ and _____.

6. The note "See also SYN. at FAITHLESS" is an example of a _____ _____.

7. *False* comes from the Latin word *fallere,* which means _____.

8. The word *falser* is divided into _____ syllables.

Developing Writing Skills

Writing About Characters. A foil is a character who provides a striking contrast to another character. In "The Trout," Julia's brother acts as a foil for Julia. Write a paragraph describing the differences between Julia and her brother. Scan the story, looking for passages that show differences in the ways in which the two characters understand and react to events. Copy these passages into your prewriting notes. As you write and revise your paragraph, refer to Writing About the Short Story on pages 623–625 and to **Using the Process of Writing** on pages 614–623.

B I O G R A P H Y

Sean O'Faolain (born 1900) came originally from County Cork, Ireland. He has written many short stories about Irish country life and about the period of Ireland's War of Independence from England. O'Faolain fought in the war before entering the National University of Ireland. He then took a master's degree from Harvard and stayed on briefly in the United States to lecture at Harvard and at Boston College. In addition to short stories, O'Faolain writes biographies of Irish heroes and travel books such as *An Irish Journey.* The first volume of *The Collected Stories of Sean O'Faolain* was published in 1980.

Fiona discovers a new world, one so foreign that she can hardly believe it exists just a short walk from home.

ancy

Elizabeth Enright

Fiona Farmer was seven years old. Her mother was forty-six, her father was fifty-five, her nurse was sixty-one, and her grandmother and grandfather with whom they were all spending the summer had reached such altitudes of age that no one remembered what they were. From these great heights Fiona was loved and directed.

She wore her hair as her mother had worn it in 1914, braided tight and tied back in pretzel loops with big stiff ribbons. In winter she was the only girl at school to wear a flannel petticoat and underwear with sleeves. Her mother read her all the books she had loved in her childhood: *Rebecca of Sunnybrook Farm* and *The Five Little Peppers* and *Under the Lilacs.* Her grandmother read her the books *she* had loved as a child: Macé's *Fairy Tales* and Grimm's *Fairy Tales* and *The Princess and Curdie.* On this mixed diet of decorum and brutality Fiona was rapidly turning into a "quaint little creature." She was a pensive child with large attentive eyes and rather elderly manners. All her play was quiet, accompanied at times by nothing noisier than a low continuous murmuring, so it was strange that the ranks of dolls on her nursery shelves were scalped and eyeless, like the victims of a Sioux massacre.

"What on earth does she do to them?" her mother said to Nana, the nurse. "Why, when I was little, my dollies were really like babies to me. I took such *care* of them; I *loved* them so.... "

"I honestly don't know, Mrs. Farmer," Nana said. "She'll be as quiet as a mouse in here for hours at a time, and then I'll come in and find all this—this destruction! It seems so unlike her!"

Fiona's grandmother reproached her quietly. "How would you like it if your dear mother pulled all your hair out of your head and broke your arms and legs? Your dolls are your little responsibilities, your *children* in a way.... "

Her admonishments, though frequent, were always mild. When Fiona scratched her head or picked her nose, she would say: "That's not very pretty, dear, is it? We don't do those things, do we?" She was a lofty, dignified, conventional lady; and she smelled like an old dictionary among whose pages many flowers have been dried and pressed. She taught Fiona how to make a sachet and a pomander ball and how to play Parcheesi.

Fiona liked her grandfather the best. He was a man of wonderful patience and politeness but deaf as a post. Every morning she followed him out to the vegetable garden where, in his old loose button-down-the-front sweater and his white canvas golf hat that sagged in a ruffle around his head, he worked along the rows of beets and cabbages with his hoe and rake. Fiona followed at his heels, speaking ceaselessly. It did not matter to her that he never heard a word she said. She told him everything. Now and then he would stop, resting on his hoe handle, and look down at her appreciatively. "Well," he would say. "You're a pleasant little companion, aren't you?" Then he would reach out his old parched hand (he was so old that he never sweated any more) and give her a brittle tap or two on the shoulder or head, and he and Fiona would smile at each other out of a mutual feeling of benevolence.

Sooner or later, though, Nana's voice would begin to caw, "Fee-ona! Fee-ona!" and she would have to go back to the house to pick up her toys or change her dress or eat a meal or some other dull thing.

Her grandparents' house was big and cool inside. All the rooms were full of greenish light reflected from the maple trees outdoors. The floors were dark and gleaming. The carpets had been taken up for the summer, and the furniture had linen dresses on. There was no dust anywhere, not even in the corners of the empty fireplaces, for Cora and Mary, the maids who had been there for thirty years, spent their lives seeing that there was not.

Cora had arthritis, and on Sundays when Fiona had noon dinner with the whole family,

she marveled at the extreme slowness with which the maid moved about the table, like a running-down toy. Her face looked very still and concentrated then, relaxing only when she served Fiona, whispering: "Eat it all up now, dear, every bit, so I can tell Mary."

Oh, food! People were always speaking of food to Fiona. The Sunday dinners were a trial to toil through. "Eat it all up, dear" and "Clean your plate" were phrases that were ugly in her ears.

After Sunday dinner everyone went to sleep for a while and the house droned with different pitches of snoring. Wearing nothing but a pink wrapper, Fiona would lie on the big white bed while Nana sat in an armchair by the window rattling the Sunday paper. Out of doors the cicadas sounded hot as drills. The lazy air coming in the window brought a smell of grass, and Fiona wished that Nana would fall asleep so that she could get up and find something to play with, but Nana would not fall asleep.

But once she did.

Once on Sunday after the usual slow, massive dinner, as Fiona lay in the extremity of boredom counting mosquito bites and listening to herself yawn, she heard another sound, a new one that might promise much. Quietly she raised herself to her elbows, hardly daring to believe, and saw that the impossible had happened at last. Nana lay in the armchair, abandoned, with her head thrown back and her hair coming down and her mouth wide open like that of a fish. A faint guttural sound came out of it each time she breathed.

A great light seemed to flood the room, and a voice from on high addressed Fiona: "Get up and dress, but do not put on your shoes. Carry them in your hand till you get outside, and close the front door quietly behind you."

Fiona got up at once, dressed with the

silence and speed of light, and departed. The upstairs hall hummed and trumpeted with the noises of sleeping. No one heard her running down the stairs.

Out of doors it was bright and hot. She sat on the front step and put on her sandals with her heart galloping in her chest. Though old, the members of her family were tall, their legs were long as ladders, and if they came after her they would surely catch her. Leaving the sandal straps unbuckled, Fiona ran out of the gate and down the street, terrified and exhilarated. She ran till she was giddy and breathless, but when at last she stopped and looked behind her the street on which she found herself was still and empty, steeped in Sunday.

She walked for a long time. Her heart stopped racing and her breathing became comfortable again. Her fear, too, gave way to pleasure and pride. It was a beautiful afternoon. The street was very high with elms. The light that came through their roof of leaves was green and trembling like light through water. Fiona became a little crab crawling among the roots of seaweed. The parked cars were fishes which would eat her up, danger was everywhere.... She walked sideways, made claws out of her thumbs, hid behind trees, and felt that her eyes grew out on stems. But not for long. Suddenly, as sometimes happened, the fancy collapsed, betrayed her completely. There was no danger; the cars were cars only. Nothing was any better than real. In the end somebody would catch her and take her home or she would return of her own accord, driven by hunger or conscience, and everything would be as it had always been.

The houses sat back from their green laps of lawn, silent and substantial, regarding her like people wearing glasses. There was a smell of privet and hot asphalt in the still air, a boring smell.... Intolerable boredom amounting to anguish drove Fiona to turn abruptly and kick the iron palings of a fence that she was passing, a kick that hurt right through her shoe.

The big street came to an end finally at a small Civil War monument and branched out beyond it in three roads. She chose the right-hand one because there was a dog asleep on the sidewalk there, but when she got to him, she saw the flies strolling up and down his face and he looked up at her balefully with a low ripple of sound in his throat and she hurried on.

This street had few trees; it was broader, and the houses, while farther apart, were shabbier. The afternoon sun was in her eyes, drawing her along the gilded road. The wind had sprung up, too, warm and lively, blowing from the west.

On the outskirts of the town she came upon her destination, though at first she did not realize it. For some time the wind had been bringing her great blasts of radio music, and she saw now that these had their source in a gray frame house that fairly trembled with melody. Though not small, this was the seediest of all the houses. It stood in the middle of a yard as full of tall grass as a field. There were paths through the field and bald patches where people had stamped and trampled, and many souvenirs abandoned and half grown over: a rusted little wagon with no wheels, somebody's shoe, an old tire....

The house had a queer shape, fancy, but with everything coming off or breaking. Some of the shutters hung by one hinge only; the cupola[1] on top was crooked and so was the porch from which half the palings were gone. The fence, too, had lost many of its pickets and stood propped against the tangle like a large

---

1. **cupola** (kyōo′ pə lə): a small dome or similar structure on the roof.

comb with teeth missing, but it had kept its gate and hanging onto this and swinging slowly back and forth were three little girls. Fiona walked more slowly.

One of the girls had a bandanna tied tightly around her head, but the other two regarded her from under untrimmed dusty bangs, like animals peering out from under ferns. The gate gave a long snarl of sound as they pushed it forward. "Where are you going?" said the tallest one.

Fiona could not be sure of the tone of this question. Was it a friendly or a hostile challenge? She moved still more slowly, touching each picket with her forefinger.

"No place," she said guardedly.

"What's your name?" demanded the girl with the bandanna. She smelled of kerosene.

"Fiona Farmer," said Fiona.

"That's a funny name. My name's Darlene, and hers is Pearl, and *hers* is Merle. Nancy is a nice name."

Fiona saw that all of them were wearing red nail polish and asked a question of her own.

"Are you all three sisters?"

"Yes, and there's more of us. *Them*," said Pearl, the tallest girl, jerking her head. "In the swing."

Beyond the house Fiona now saw for the first time an old double-rocker swing full of boys.

"There's Norman and Stanley and Earl," Darlene said. "And in the house we got a baby sister named Marilyn, and down to the picture theater we got a big sister named Deanna. Come on in."

"Will they let me swing in the swing?" said Fiona.

"Sure they will. *What* did you say your name was?"

"Fiona," she admitted. "Fiona Farmer."

"Gee," said Pearl.

"We'll call her Nancy," said Darlene, who, though younger, seemed to be a leader in her way. "Come on, Nancy, you wanna swing on the gate? Get off, Merle."

Merle got off obediently, sucking her thumb.

"I would like to swing in the *swing*," Fiona said.

She came into the yard, gazing up at the tipsy cupola. "Can you get up there into that kind of little tower?"

"Sure," said Darlene. "Come on up and we'll show you."

Fiona followed them through the interesting grass in which she now saw a broken doll, somebody's garter, somebody's hat, and many weathered corncobs and beer cans.

On the porch that swayed when they walked on it there were a tough-looking baby buggy, two sleds, a bent tricycle, a lot of chairs and boxes and bushel baskets and peck baskets and a baby pen and a wagon wheel and some kindling wood. The screen door was full of holes, and instead of a doorknob there was a wooden thread spool to turn.

The noise of music was stunning as they went indoors; it kept the Mason jars ringing on the shelves. They walked right into it, into the thrilling heart of noise which was the kitchen, where a woman was sitting nursing a baby and shouting random conversation at an old, old woman with a beak nose.

The music ceased with a flourish and the radio announcer's tremendous tones replaced it, but this did not stop the shouted discourse of the woman with the baby. As the girls crossed the kitchen, she turned for a moment to look at them, saw Fiona and said, "Who's she?"

"She's Nancy," called Darlene, against the radio.

"Who?"

"Nancy! She dropped in."

"That's Mom," Pearl said.

Fiona went over to the lady to shake her hand. She made her usual curtsy and said, "How do you do?"

Mom's hand felt limp and rather damp and startled. She was a big woman with a wide face and tired blue eyes.

"The old one's Gramma," Darlene said, so Fiona curtsied to the old lady too and shook her hand, which felt like a few twigs in a glove.

"And that's my father," Darlene added a few seconds later when they had gone up the loud bare stairs to the next floor. Fiona peeked in the doorway of the dim, strong-smelling room, but all she saw of *him* was the soles of his socks, and she heard him snoring.

"Just like at home," she said. "Sunday afternoon they all sleep."

"Heck, he sleeps all *day* on Sundays," Darlene said, and Fiona felt a little humiliated for her own father.

"This is Gramma's room." Pearl threw open the door. "She likes flowers."

The room was a jungle steeped in musky twilight. A vine of some kind had crawled all over the window and parts of the wall, and on the sill, the sash, the floor below, were pots and jars and coffee tins in which stout, lusty plants were growing and flowering.

"How does she open the window at night?" Fiona wondered.

"*She* don't open no windows day or night," Darlene said. "Heck, she's *old*; she's gotta stay *warm*."

They went up another flight of stairs, narrow steep ones, crowded with magazines and articles of clothing and decayed toys. "Up here's where we sleep," Darlene said. "Us girls, all of us except Marilyn. Pearl and me

and Merle sleep in the big bed, and Deanna she sleeps in the cot. This is the attic like."

The big bed was made of iron, with the post knobs missing. It dipped in the middle like a hammock; and there, Fiona knew, the little girls would lie at night, dumped together in a tangle, quarreling or giggling in whispers.

"Look at all the comic books!" she cried; and indeed they lay everywhere in tattered profusion, a drift of stained, distorted leaves.

"We got about a hundred or a thousand of 'em, I guess," Pearl said. "You want some?"

"Could I really, Pearl? Could you spare them?"

"*Atom Annie*'s a good one," Pearl said. "We got a lot about her, and here's one called *Hellray* that's real good, real scarey. Take these."

Fiona looked at them longingly.

"I don't know if my mother—she doesn't like for me to have comics."

"Heck, why not?"

"Well, maybe this time she won't mind," Fiona said, taking the books, determined that everything would be all right for once. "Thank you very, very much, Darlene and Pearl."

"Here's the stairs to the lookout," Darlene said. "Get out of the way, Merle, you wait till last."

They climbed the ladder steps in the middle of the room. Pearl pushed open the trap door, and one by one they ascended into the tiny chamber.

It was a tipped little cubicle like a ship's cabin in stiff weather, and stiflingly hot. It seemed remote, high, cozy; and its four soiled windows showed four different views of the town faded and reduced as pictures in an old book. Flies buzzed and butted at the hot glass. Fiona felt disappointed when she saw the steeple of the church that stood across the street

KATIE AND ANNE, 1955. *Fairfield Porter. Hirshhorn Museum and Sculpture Garden, Smithsonian Institution, Washington, D.C.*

from her grandfather's house. She had not thought it was so near.

"Jump!" cried Darlene. They all began to jump, and the cupola jarred and trembled under the pounding.

"Won't it break?" cried Fiona, pounding with the rest. "Won't it fall off?"

"Naw, it won't break," Darlene called back.

"It never did yet."

"But it might some day, though," shouted Pearl encouragingly.

It was fun to jump riotously and yell, as the tiny tower rocked and resounded.

There was an interruption from below.

"Get out of there!" bawled Mom up the stairs. "How many times I told you kids to stay down out of there! You want to get your backs broke? You want to get killed? You scram down!"

"Get out of the way, Merle; let Nancy go first," Pearl said.

Mom stood at the foot of the steps wearing the baby around her neck. Anxiety had made her furious. "That place ain't safe; you know that!" she cried. "How many times have I told you?" She gave Pearl a slap on the cheek and would have given one to Darlene, too, if Darlene had not bent her neck adroitly.

"You let me catch you up there one more time, and I'll get your father to lick you good!"

"Aw, climb a tree," said Darlene.

Fiona was aghast. What would happen now?

But nothing happened. Merle still quietly sucked her thumb. Darlene and Pearl seemed cool and jaunty, and as they descended through the house, Mom's anger dried up like dew.

"You kids want a snack?" she said. "You didn't eat since breakfast."

"Can Nancy stay?"

"Why sure, I guess. Why not?"

"Oh, thank you very, very much.... "

The kitchen, like the rest of the house, had a rich, bold, musty smell. It smelled of constant usage and memories of usage. It was crowded and crusted with objects: pots, pans, kettles, boxes, jars, cans, buckets, dippers. There were two alarm clocks, one lying on its side and each asserting a different hour, and four big Coca-Cola calendars on the wall, none for the current year. The radio was still thundering music; and close beside it, warming herself at the noise, sat Gramma, dark as a crow, chewing and chewing on her empty gums.

The stove was named Ebony Gem, and behind it in a cardboard box there was something alive; something moved....

"It's kittens," said Merle, removing her thumb from her mouth and speaking for the first time. "Our cat had kittens."

"Oh, let me see!" Fiona knelt by the box. There inside it lay a bland and happy group: mother cat with her yellow eyes half closed and her paws splayed out in pleasure; kittens lined up all along her, nursing.

Merle put out her little forefinger with its chipped red nail polish, stroking first one infant, then the next. "The black one's name is Blackie and the white one's name is Whitey, and we call *this* one Butch because he's so.... "

"My father usually drowns them, all but one," Darlene interrupted. She bent her kerchiefed head close to Fiona's, so that there was a blinding smell of kerosene. "Tomorrow probably," she whispered. "We don't tell Merle; it makes her feel so bad." Then she raised her voice. "She knows it's going to happen, but she don't know when, huh, Merle?"

"You could take one, Nancy," Merle said, still gazing at the kittens. "You could keep it and be good to it."

"Do you mean honestly and truly?"

Fiona's joy was suffocating.

"Any one? Any one at all?"

"Except Butch," Darlene said. "We're going to keep him to help with the rats."

"Could I have Blackie? Really for keeps?"

Merle plucked the dark little thing from the mother as if she were plucking off a burr and gave it to Fiona.

"I can feel its little tiny heart," Fiona said. "I'll give it milk all the time and brush its fur and it can sleep in the doll cradle. Oh, look at its ears. Oh, Merle, oh, thank you!"

Shamed by gratitude, Merle put her thumb back in her mouth and looked away.

"You kids get out from under my feet," Mom said. "Sit up to the table now; it's all ready. Come on, Mama; come on, *boys!*" She opened the screen door and put her head out, shouting so hard that great cords stood out on her neck.

They sat around the big table with its oilcloth cover, everything in easy reach: cereal in paper boxes, sugar, catsup.... They had cornflakes and milk, Swiss cheese sandwiches with catsup, cream soda in bottles, and little cakes out of a box with pink and green beads on them. Fiona ate everything.

"Nancy eats good, don't she, Mom?" Darlene said.

"I never had catsup before," said Fiona. "My, it certainly is delicious, isn't it?"

The table was a family battlefield. Fiona had never seen anything like it in her life. Stanley and Norman threw pieces of sandwich at each other; Earl took one of Merle's cakes and Merle cried and Mom slapped Earl. Darlene stole big swigs from Pearl's soda bottle, was loudly accused and loudly defended herself.

"You kids shut up," Mom said, eating over Marilyn's head and giving her occasional bits of cake dipped in tea. Gramma was the only quiet one. She sat bent over, all wrapped and absorbed in her old age, gazing into her cup as she drank from it with a long, purring sound. Blackie was quiet, too, asleep in Fiona's lap.

She kept one hand on his little velvet back. Mom pointed at Fiona with her spoon. "Looks like Margaret O'Brien[2] used to, don't she? The ribbons and all."

"Margaret who?" said Fiona.

"O'Brien, *you* know, the kid in the movies," Darlene said.

"Oh, I never go to movies," said Fiona. "I'm not allowed."

"Not allowed!" cried Darlene incredulously. "Heck, we go all the time, don't we, Mom? Even Deanna goes. We could take Nancy with us sometimes, couldn't we, Mom?"

"Maybe, if her folks say yes."

"Oh, if I went with *you* it would be all right, I'm sure," cried Fiona joyously. Drunk with noise, strange flavors, gifts, and new friendship, she really believed this.

Afterward, still with catsup on their upper lips, they went outdoors to play hide-and-seek.

"You be her partner, Stanley," ordered Darlene, who was "it." "You kind of look after her; she don't know our places to hide."

Then she hid her eyes with her arm, cast herself against a tree like a girl in grief, and began to count out loud.

"The cellar," hissed Stanley, grabbing Fiona's hand. He was a big eight-year-old boy, and still clutching the kitten, Fiona ran with him willingly, hesitating only for a second at sight of the dark abyss. On the steps were many cans and crates, but Stanley led her safely down among these and into the black, deep tunnel beyond. Fiona could feel that there were solid things all around them, probably more boxes, more crates, but she could see

---

2. **Margaret O'Brien:** a child movie star who was popular in the 1940's.

SUPPER CALL, 1966. *Carroll Cloar.*
Private Collection.

nothing. Stanley's hand was warm and firm. It just fitted hers, and she liked having him lead her.

"We can stop now," he said, "but keep quiet."

Darlene could still be heard, faintly. Her counting voice sounded deserted and defiant: "*Ninety*-five, *ninety*-six, *ninety*-seven. . . ." The blackness throbbed and shimmered, and the air had a dense aged smell.

"Coming, ready or not!" called the faraway defiant voice.

"We're safe here anyways," Stanley said.

"She won't come down *here;* she's scared to." He laughed silently and gave Fiona's hand a squeeze. "There's rats down here."

"Oh, no; oh, no! Oh, Stanley, let's go up again," cried Fiona, tears of panic in her voice.

But Stanley held onto her hand. "You going to be a sissy too?" he demanded. "We got the *cat,* ain't we?"

Fiona strained the tiny kitten to her chest. Her heart was banging terribly, and she wanted to cry, but she would not. All around the rats were closing in, large as dogs and smiling strangely, smiling like people. She almost sobbed when Stanley said, "Now we can go. Hurry up, and keep still!"

They were the first ones back.

For a long time they played, and Stanley always was her partner. He knew the best places to hide: up in the boughs of a pear tree, under the porch steps, in the fearful little dark privy with its different-sized "family accommodations," and flat on their stomachs under the folded-back cellar door. Darlene was "it" till she caught Merle, and Merle was "it" for hours. Fiona got spider webs in her mouth and gnats up her nose, tore her dress, scraped her knee, lost one hair ribbon, and gave the other to Merle, who had admired it.

When they were through with hide-and-seek, they all got into the rocker swing and played gangsters. The swing leapt to and fro, to and fro, screaming wildly at the joints. Surely it would break, and soon! That was the thrilling thing about this place: so many features of it—the tower, the swing, the porch—trembled at the edge of ruin, hung by a thread above the fatal plunge. Earl and Stanley and Norman leaned over the back of one of the seats, firing at the enemy. "Step on it, you guys," yelled Stanley. "They got a gat!"

"They got a rod!" yelled Norman. "They got a lotta rods!"

"What's a rod?" cried Fiona. "What's a gat?"

"Guns, he means," Darlene told her. "Rods and gats is guns."

"Shoot 'em, Stanley," yelled Fiona. "With your gat, shoot the eyes out of 'em!"

Clutching the clawing kitten to her collarbone, her hair in her open mouth, she bawled encouragement to them. The swing accelerated ever more wildly; soon it would take off entirely, depart from its hinges, fly through the air, burn a hole through the sky!...

"Fee-ona Farmer!"

The cry was loud enough to be heard above all sounds of war and wind and radio music.

Beside the swing stood Nana, so tall, so highly charged with hurry and emotion, that the children stopped their play at once.

"Who's she?" Stanley asked.

"She's my nurse," Fiona murmured.

"Your nurse! What's the matter, are you sick?"

"No . . . she just—takes care of me."

"Takes *care* of you!"

"You get out of that swing and come this instant!"

Having struck the bottom of disgrace, Fiona stepped down and slowly went to Nana. From the swing, the others watched, as still as children posing for a photograph.

"Put down that cat and come at once."

"Oh no!" Fiona said. "It's mine; they gave it to me."

"Put. Down. That. Cat."

Darlene came to stand beside Fiona. "But we did give it to her; we want for her to have it."

Nana struck the kitten from Fiona's arms. "You will not take that creature home! It's filthy; it has fleas!"

"Oh my kitty!" shrieked Fiona, diving after Blackie, but Nana caught her wrist.

"You come!"

Fiona pulled, struggled, cast a glare of anguish at all the rapt photograph-faces in the swing.

"You should be punished. You should be whipped. Whipped!" Nana whistled the cruel words—Nana, who was never cruel! Her fingers on Fiona's wrists were hard.

"Let me say goodbye to them, Nana. Let me say goodbye to their *mother!* You said I should *always* say goodbye to the mother!"

"Not this time. This time it doesn't matter,"

Nana said. "You're going straight home and into the tub. Heaven knows what you will have caught!" Upon Fiona's friends she turned a single, brilliant glance, like one cold flash from a lighthouse.

There was nothing to commend Fiona's departure; dragged by the hand, whimpering, she looked back at her friends in desperation. "Oh, Darlene!"

But it was easy to see that Darlene had detached herself. "Goodbye, Nancy," she said, not without a certain pride. She did not smile or say anything else, but her attitude showed Fiona and Nana that she had no need for either of them, could not be hurt by them, and would not think of them again. As they went out the gate, she turned her back and skipped away; and Fiona heard the rocker swing resume its screaming tempo.

Halfway home, Nana's recriminations began to modify, gradually becoming reproaches: "How could you have, Fiona, run away like that? Why, it's only by the grace of God I ever found you at all! And all the time I was half sick with worry, I never said a word to your father and mother! I didn't want *them* to worry!"

Somewhere deep inside her, Fiona understood exactly why Nana had said nothing to her parents; but she just kept on saying, "I want my kitty, I want my kitty."

Finally Nana said, "If you're a good girl, maybe we'll get you another kitten."

"I don't want another. I want that one."

"Oh, for pity's sakes, it had fleas, or worse. Anything belonging to the Fadgins would be bound to have—"

"Do you know them?"

"I know *about* them; everybody does. They're the dirtiest, the shiftlessest, the most down-at-the-heel tribe in this whole town!"

"They are not; they're nice. I love them!"

Nana relented a little. "Maybe it's hard not to be shiftless when you're that poor."

"*They* aren't poor. You should see all the things they've got! More than Grandmother's got in her whole house!"

"All right now, dearie, all right. We'll forget about it, shall we? It will be our secret, and we'll never tell anyone because we don't want them to worry, do we? But you must promise me never, never to do such a thing again. Hear?"

"I want my kitty," droned Fiona.

Her grandparents' house smelled cool and sweetish. There was a bowl of white and pink stock on the hall table, and her grandmother's green linen parasol leaned in a corner among the pearly company of her grandfather's canes.

In the shaded living room, Fiona saw her mother knitting and her grandmother at the piano playing the same kind of music she always played, with the loose rings clicking on her fingers.

"Is that my baby?" called her mother—but Nana answered hastily, "I'm getting her right into her bath, Mrs. Farmer. She's simply filthy."

Upstairs, Nana went in to run the water in the tub. Fiona kicked off one sandal, then the other. A terrible pain took hold of her; it began in her mind and spread down to her stomach. She had never been homesick before and did not know what ailed her. She knew only that she wanted to sleep at night in a big, twanging bed full of children and to eat meals at a crowded table where people threw bread at each other and drank pop. She wanted Stanley's hand to guide her and Darlene's voice to teach her and Blackie's purr to throb against her chest....

Beyond the window, she saw her grandfather's wilted golf hat bobbing among the cornstalks. She escaped again, running on bare feet down the back stairs and out of doors, across the billowing lawn, which seemed to be colliding with the trees and sky and shadows, all flooded and dazzled with tears. Blindly she flung open the garden gate and pushed her way through the green-paper corn forest to her grandfather, who dropped his hoe and held out his arms when he saw her face.

"Come here now," he said in his gentle, deaf voice. "Well, well, this won't do, no it won't, not at all. Come sit here with Grandpa; sit here in the arbor. Did you hurt yourself?"

He led her to the seat under the green grape trellis where he sometimes rested from the hot sun. He put his arm around her shoulders, offering himself as a support for grief; and Fiona howled against his waistcoat till the wet tweed chapped her cheek and there was not a tear left in her. He did not interrupt or ask questions but kept patting her shoulder in a sort of sympathetic accompaniment to her sobs, which he could not hear but which he felt. What's the cause of it all, he wondered. A broken toy? A scolding? Children's tragedies, he thought, children's little tragedies. There are bigger ones in store for you, Fiona, a world of them. The thought did not move him deeply. Everyone must suffer, but for an instant he was not sorry to be old.

Fiona leaned against him, and after a while, between the hiccups left from sobbing, she could hear the ancient heart inside his chest tick-tocking steadily, as tranquil and unhurried as he was himself. All the wild performance of her sorrow had not quickened its tempo by a single beat, and this for some reason was a comfort.

The sound of her grandmother's music, sugary and elegant, came sparkling from the house, and upstairs in the bedroom or the hall Nana began to call. "Fee-ona?" she cried. "Oh, Fee-*ona?*"

There was a hint of panic in her voice, now; but no response came from under the green trellis. Fiona's grandfather could not hear the calling; and Fiona, for the time being, did not choose to answer.

Getting at Meaning

RECALLING

1. Does Fiona have any brothers or sisters? Are there any other children in the house in which she is staying?

2. Fiona and Nancy are the same character. Who calls her Fiona? Who calls her Nancy?

3. Fiona joins in the activities of the Fadgin children. Name five things that Fiona does with them.

INTERPRETING

4. How does Fiona treat her dolls? What might be the reason for Fiona's actions toward the dolls?

5. How are the Fadgins different from Fiona's family? Why does Fiona want to live with them?

6. Fiona says of the Fadgins, *"They* aren't poor." In what ways are the Fadgins richer than the Farmers?

7. How does Fiona's grandfather help Fiona when she returns from the Fadgins'? Why is Fiona's grandfather her favorite family member?

CRITICAL THINKING: EVALUATING

8. By showing the different ways of life of the Fadgins and the Farmers, is the writer saying that one of these ways of life is better than the other? Does the writer suggest what is needed to make a child happy? Refer to the story to explain your answers.

Developing Skills in Reading Literature

1. **Setting.** Setting is the time and place of the action of a story. In "Nancy," two distinctly different settings are described—Fiona's world and Nancy's world. Read the descriptions of Fiona's world. On a sheet of paper, list at least eight phrases from the story that describe the sights, sounds, and smells of that world. Then read the descriptions of Nancy's world. On the same sheet of paper, list at least eight phrases from the story that describe that world.

2. **Metaphor.** A metaphor is a comparison of two unlike things that have something in common. Consider the statement "People are sheep." People and sheep are basically unlike. The comparison, though, makes the point that, like sheep, people can be stupid and quick to follow anyone or anything.

On the third page of the story, the writer states that "Fiona became a little crab crawling among the roots of seaweed." This sentence contains a metaphor. What does this metaphor suggest about Fiona? What two things are compared by this metaphor? The following sentence from the story contains another metaphor: "The table was a family battlefield." What two things are compared by this metaphor? What are the similarities between these two things?

3. **Style.** Style is the way in which a piece of literature is written. Style refers not to what is said, but to how it is said. What is the effect of the unusual punctuation of "Put. Down. That. Cat." on page 123? Why might the writer have chosen to punctuate the sentence in this way?

4. **Fiction.** Fiction is writing about imaginary people, places, and events. Writers of fiction try to make their imaginary subjects seem real. Did the writer of "Nancy" succeed in doing this? Is the Fadgins' home described realistically? Do characters such as Merle and Grandpa seem as though they could actually exist?

5. **Title.** The title of a selection often provides important clues about the writer's message or purpose. What did the writer emphasize by calling this selection "Nancy" instead of "Fiona"?

Developing Vocabulary

Using a Glossary. A glossary is a list of words and their definitions, usually placed toward the end of a book. The Glossary in this book, which begins on page 661, defines the most difficult words from the selections. Refer to the Glossary whenever you come across an unfamiliar word in this book.

Using the Glossary, look up the italicized words in the following sentences. Then, write these words and their definitions on a sheet of paper.

1. "She was a *pensive* child with large, attentive eyes."

2. "She was a lofty, dignified, *conventional* lady."

3. "Fiona lay in the *extremity* of boredom, counting mosquito bites and listening to herself yawn."

4. " 'Look at all the comic books!' she cried, and indeed they lay everywhere in tattered *profusion.*"

5. "It was a tipped little *cubicle* like a ship's cabin in stiff weather."

6. "Fiona was *aghast.* What would happen now?"

Developing Writing Skills

Writing About Setting. Two important parts of "Nancy" are the two settings—the Fadgins' home and Fiona's grandparents' house. If you haven't already done so, complete Developing Skills in Reading Literature, #1. Then, using your answers as your prewriting notes, write three paragraphs. In the first paragraph, describe the house in which Fiona lives. In the second, describe the Fadgins' home. In the third, tell which place Fiona prefers, and explain what Fiona's preference reveals about children in general. Use evidence from the story to support the points that you make. As you write and revise your paragraphs, refer to **Using the Process of Writing** and to Writing About the Short Story on pages 614–625.

BIOGRAPHY

Elizabeth Enright (1909–1968) was born in Chicago. Both her parents were artists, and at first she followed in their footsteps. She studied art in New York and Paris. At twenty she got her first job, doing illustrations for a fairy tale. Other work followed, and Enright decided to try writing as well. She soon preferred it to drawing. Her second book, *Thimble Summer,* was awarded the 1939 Newbery Medal. Many successful volumes followed and continue to be popular.

In this story a snake has an unusual talent.

J. P. Sousa

Adrien Stoutenburg

Lots of folks around Killdugan Creek thought Uncle Jerry was crazy. Instead of selling his rickety little farm after years of dry weather and ruined crops, he stayed on and kept preaching about how there was going to be tons of rain soon. All the rest of the people, except those who stayed, sold their farms and moved to California. Old Jerry wouldn't budge. Day after day he'd sit on his porch playing his harmonica. "Old Jerry's a harmonica-playing fool," his neighbors said. But they admitted that he was very good at it.

One hot afternoon, along about sundown, Uncle Jerry was playing a concert for his bony chickens and his two or three skinny cows. He liked to play marching tunes, especially "The Stars and Stripes Forever," by the great bandmaster, John Philip Sousa. He was blowing away at that piece when suddenly he glanced down and saw a big, black, diamondback rattler coiled up at his feet. Uncle Jerry's false teeth almost fell out and the harmonica almost fell in, but he managed to keep on playing because that seemed the sensible thing to do. He played everything he knew and then started all over again. When he swung into

"The Stars and Stripes Forever" once more, he noticed that the snake got kind of a happy look and swayed back and forth with the music.

Uncle Jerry kept playing until he ran out of breath. The sun had gone down and the moon was floating around overhead when, finally, he gave up. "You'll just have to go ahead and bite me," he told the snake, "if that's what you're hankerin' to do. I'll be blasted if I'm going to entertain you any more."

The snake seemed to nod as if it understood, and it looked completely satisfied. Then it gave its rattlers a few shakes, as if it were applauding, and crawled meekly away.

Every day after that, when Uncle Jerry came on the porch to play his harmonica, the snake showed up. It would sit there swaying in time to the music, its eyes glistening with pleasure. It wasn't long before Uncle Jerry liked that snake so much he'd play "The Stars and Stripes Forever" over and over. He even decided to call the snake J. P. Sousa, after his favorite composer. By the time a week or two had gone by, the snake had learned to shake his rattlers in time to the piece, and this made a really fine-sounding duet.

The days went on, getting hotter and dryer, and everybody said Uncle Jerry was double-crazy not to leave his farm and try raising crops somewhere else. Uncle Jerry just kept blowing his harmonica, while J. P. Sousa listened and rattled his tail in time. Then, one afternoon, the snake didn't come to the concert. He didn't show up the next day either, or the next. This shook Uncle Jerry so that he lost all his joy in music. Each day his concerts grew briefer until finally he put his harmonica away and sat silent, watching and waiting for J. P. Sousa to come back.

By July, Killdugan Creek was as dry as sandpaper, and Uncle Jerry's cows and chickens were standing around with their tongues hanging out, they were so thirsty. Then, on July 10, big, dark clouds started building up in the sky. It began to rain. It kept on raining for weeks on end. When the rain was over, the creek was full and all Uncle Jerry's crops were growing even faster than the weeds. People decided he wasn't as crazy as they thought—except for his talking about his pet snake and waiting for him to come back.

One day a neighboring farmer came along

SNAKE, about 1975. *Felipe B. Archuleta. International Folk Art Foundation Collections in the Museum of International Folk Art; the Museum of New Mexico, Santa Fe.*

and said he'd like to graze a few of his cows on Uncle Jerry's land. He offered so much money for this that Uncle Jerry agreed. Uncle Jerry hitched up his two old horses to his broken-down wagon and drove the man around his land to show him the best grazing spots. All the time he kept watching for some glimpse of the musical snake.

Well, he and the neighbor were bouncing along in the squeakly old buckboard wagon when all of a sudden Uncle Jerry heard a sound like drums rattling out a marching rhythm. The sound was coming from the top of a nearby hill. Uncle Jerry hollered "Whoa!" to the horses and jumped out of the wagon as fast as he could. He clambered up toward the top of the hill, his heart racing so fast his legs could hardly keep up with it.

There, at the top of the hill, was a large, flat rock. On the rock were three dozen fat diamondback rattlers in a circle. In the center of the circle was J. P. Sousa, his head high, his eyes shining with pride, waving his tail like the baton of an orchestra conductor. He was beating out the rhythm of "The Stars and Stripes Forever," while the rest of the snakes rattled along with him.

Fortunately, just that morning, Uncle Jerry had happened to put his harmonica in his hip pocket. Now he pulled it out and started blowing away. J. P. Sousa glanced around, stood up on the tip of his tail, and looked happy enough to faint. Then he went to work leading his snake orchestra again, and Uncle Jerry played along with them until the moon came up. The farmer who had come with him hated snakes, and he couldn't get away fast enough. He ran home and told everybody that Uncle Jerry was even crazier than they knew, that the snakes were going crazy, too, and that anybody with any sense would sell and get out of the country.

That's what everybody did, except Uncle Jerry. He stayed there with his fat cows and his green growing crops and plump chickens, and every day, around sundown, he'd go up to the hill and play his harmonica while the snake orchestra rattled time. Those were the happiest hours of his life, and the happiest for J. P. Sousa too.

Those happy days are gone now, but the big, flat rock on the hill is still there (unless somebody has carried it away), and people say that on certain summer nights, the snakes still come there and form a circle and shake their rattlers to the tune of "The Stars and Stripes Forever." The snake in the middle, they say, is so old he has a beard. Whether it's really J. P. Sousa or not, no one knows. But they do say it makes sort of a pretty sound there in the Killdugan Creek country, if you happen to like marching tunes.

Getting at Meaning

RECALLING

1. Where does this story take place? What causes some of Uncle Jerry's neighbors to move away the first time?

2. What musical instrument does Uncle Jerry play?

3. Who wrote "The Stars and Stripes Forever"? What kind of tune is this?

4. What animal is attracted to Uncle Jerry's music? What does Uncle Jerry name this animal? Why?

5. What happens on July 10?

6. What is J.P. Sousa doing with the other snakes on the large, flat rock?

7. What are the happiest hours of Uncle Jerry's life?

INTERPRETING

8. How does Uncle Jerry feel about J.P. Sousa? How do you know?

9. What kind of person is Uncle Jerry? What do his neighbors think of him?

10. Why do Uncle Jerry's neighbors all move away at the end of the story?

Developing Skills in Reading Literature

1. **Fantasy.** Fantasy is a type of fiction that contains settings, characters, or events that defy the laws of nature or of logic. What elements make "J. P. Sousa" a fantasy?

2. **Humor.** Humor is writing or speech that is funny or amusing. For example, if you describe your brother as ''a human trash compactor,'' you are using humor to highlight his tendency to eat anything and everything.

In this story the narrator says that Uncle Jerry, while playing the harmonica, ''glanced down and saw a big, black, diamondback rattler coiled up at his feet. Uncle Jerry's false teeth almost fell out and the harmonica almost fell in.'' What is humorous about this line? What other examples of humor stand out in this story?

Developing Vocabulary

1. **Compound Words.** Compound words are words that are made from two or more other words. For example, the word *rattlesnake* is a compound word made from the words *rattle* and *snake*. Other compound words that contain these word parts are *rattlebrain, rattletrap, snakebite,* and *snakeskin.* Using a dictionary, find one compound word that is formed from the word *trap.* Then, find four compound words that are formed from the word *brain.*

2. **Echoic Words.** In some dictionaries, words that imitate sounds are called *echoic,* because they sound like, or echo, the things that they describe. *Rattle* is such a word. Other echoic words include *babble, murmur,* and *thump.* Think of two more words that are echoic in origin. Look up your words in a dictionary to make sure that they are echoic.

3. **Word Families.** Word families are groups of words that share common word parts. For example, the following words all belong to a single word family:

harmonica	harmonious
harmony	harmonium
harmonize	

Look up these words in a dictionary. On a separate sheet of paper, write each word and its definition. Then, study your list of definitions. Can you find any similarity in the meanings of these words? Do these words share any part of their meanings in common?

Pranks can be harmless, but on the planet Venus, Margot's classmates play a prank on her that is unspeakable.

All Summer in a Day

Ray Bradbury

Ready?"

"Ready."

"Now?"

"Soon."

"Do the scientists really know? Will it happen today, will it?"

"Look, look; see for yourself!"

The children pressed to each other like so many roses, so many weeds, intermixed, peering out for a look at the hidden sun.

It rained.

It had been raining for seven years; thousands upon thousands of days compounded and filled from one end to the other with rain, with the drum and gush of water, with the sweet crystal fall of showers and the concussion of storms so heavy they were tidal waves come over the islands. A thousand forests had been crushed under the rain and grown up a thousand times to be crushed again. And this was the way life was forever on the planet Venus, and this was the schoolroom of the children of the rocket men and women who had come to a raining world to set up civilization and live out their lives.

"It's stopping, it's stopping!"

"Yes, yes!"

Margot stood apart from them, from these children who could never remember a time when there wasn't rain and rain and rain. They were all nine years old, and if there had been a day, seven years ago, when the sun came out for an hour and showed its face to the stunned world, they could not recall. Sometimes, at night, she heard them stir, in remembrance, and she knew they were dreaming and remembering gold or a yellow crayon or a coin large enough to buy the world with. She knew that they thought they remembered a warmness, like a blushing in the face, in the body, in the arms and legs and trembling hands. But then they always awoke to the tatting drum, the endless shaking down of clear bead necklaces upon the roof, the walk, the gardens, the forest, and their dreams were gone.

All day yesterday they had read in class about the sun. About how like a lemon it was, and how hot. And they had written small stories or essays or poems about it:

I think the sun is a flower
That blooms for just one hour.

That was Margot's poem, read in a quiet voice in the still classroom while the rain was falling outside.

"Aw, you didn't write that!" protested one of the boys.

"I did," said Margot. "I *did*."

"William!" said the teacher.

But that was yesterday. Now, the rain was slackening, and the children were crushed to the great, thick windows.

"Where's teacher?"

"She'll be back."

"She'd better hurry; we'll miss it!"

They turned on themselves, like a feverish wheel, all tumbling spokes.

Margot stood alone. She was a very frail girl who looked as if she had been lost in the rain for years, and the rain had washed out the blue from her eyes and the red from her mouth and the yellow from her hair. She was an old photograph dusted from an album, whitened away, and if she spoke at all her voice would be a ghost. Now she stood, separate, staring at the rain and the loud, wet world beyond the huge glass.

"What're *you* looking at?" said William.

Margot said nothing.

"Speak when you're spoken to." He gave her a shove. But she did not move; rather, she let herself be moved only by him and nothing else.

They edged away from her; they would not look at her. She felt them go away. And this was because she would play no games with them in the echoing tunnels of the underground city. If they tagged her and ran, she stood blinking after them and did not follow. When the class sang songs about happiness and life and games, her lips barely moved. Only when they sang about the sun and the summer did her lips move, as she watched the drenched windows.

And then, of course, the biggest crime of all was that she had come here only five years ago from Earth, and she remembered the sun and the way the sun was and the sky was when she was four, in Ohio. And they, they had been on Venus all their lives, and they had been only two years old when last the sun came out and had long since forgotten the color and heat of it and the way that it really was. But Margot remembered.

"It's like a penny," she said, once, eyes closed.

"No, it's not!" the children cried.

"It's like a fire," she said, "in the stove."

"You're lying; you don't remember!" cried the children.

But she remembered and stood quietly apart from all of them and watched the patterning windows. And once, a month ago, she had refused to shower in the school shower rooms, had clutched her hands to her ears and over her head, screaming that the water mustn't touch her head. So after that, dimly, dimly, she sensed it; she was different, and they knew her difference and kept away.

There was talk that her father and mother were taking her back to Earth next year; it seemed vital to her that they do so, though it would mean the loss of thousands of dollars to her family. And so the children hated her for all these reasons, of big and little consequence. They hated her pale, snow face, her waiting silence, her thinness, and her possible future.

"Get away!" The boy gave her another push. "What're you waiting for?"

Then, for the first time, she turned and looked at him. And what she was waiting for was in her eyes.

THE MARRIAGE OF HEAVEN AND EARTH, 1962, *Max Ernst. Collection of Georges and Lois deMenil.*

"Well, don't wait around here!" cried the boy, savagely. "You won't see nothing!"

Her lips moved.

"Nothing!" he cried. "It was all a joke, wasn't it?" He turned to the other children. "Nothing's happening today. *Is* it?"

They all blinked at him and then, understanding, laughed and shook their heads. "Nothing, nothing!"

"Oh, but," Margot whispered, her eyes helpless. "But, this is the day, the scientists predict, they say, they *know,* the sun...."

"All a joke!" said the boy, and seized her roughly. "Hey, everyone, let's put her in a closet before teacher comes!"

"No," said Margot, falling back.

They surged about her, caught her up and bore her, protesting and then pleading and then crying, back into a tunnel, a room, a closet, where they slammed and locked the door. They stood looking at the door and saw it tremble from her beating and throwing herself against it. They heard her muffled cries. Then, smiling, they turned and went out and back down the tunnel, just as the teacher arrived.

"Ready, children?" She glanced at her watch.

"Yes!" said everyone.

"Are we all here?"

"Yes!"

The rain slackened still more.

They crowded to the huge door.

The rain stopped.

It was as if, in the midst of a film concerning an avalanche, a tornado, a hurricane, a volcanic eruption, something had, first, gone wrong with the sound apparatus, thus muffling and finally cutting off all noise, all of the blasts and repercussions and thunders, and then, secondly, ripped the film from the projector and inserted in its place a peaceful tropical slide that did not move or tremor. The world ground to a standstill. The silence was so immense and unbelievable that you felt that your ears had been stuffed or you had lost your hearing altogether. The children put their hands to their ears. They stood apart. The door slid back, and the smell of the silent, waiting world came in to them.

The sun came out.

It was the color of flaming bronze, and it was very large. And the sky around it was a blazing blue tile color. And the jungle burned with sunlight as the children, released from their spell, rushed out, yelling, into the summertime.

"Now, don't go too far," called the teacher after them. "You've got only one hour, you know. You wouldn't want to get caught out!"

But they were running and turning their faces up to the sky and feeling the sun on their cheeks like a warm iron; they were taking off their jackets and letting the sun burn their arms.

"Oh, it's better than the sun lamps, isn't it?"

"Much, much better!"

They stopped running and stood in the great jungle that covered Venus, that grew and never stopped growing, tumultuously, even as you watched it. It was a nest of octopuses, clustering up great arms of fleshlike weed, wavering, flowering in this brief spring. It was the color of rubber and ash, this jungle, from the many years without sun. It was the color of stones and white cheeses and ink.

The children lay out, laughing, on the jungle mattress and heard it sigh and squeak under them, resilient and alive. They ran among the trees, they slipped and fell, they pushed each other, they played hide-and-seek and tag, but most of all they squinted at the sun until tears ran down their faces. They put their hands up at that yellowness and that amazing blueness and they breathed of the fresh air and listened and listened to the silence that suspended them in a blessed sea of no sound and no motion. They looked at everything and savored everything. Then, wildly, like animals escaped from their caves, they ran and ran in shouting circles. They ran for an hour and did not stop running.

And then—

In the midst of their running, one of the girls wailed.

Everyone stopped.

The girl, standing in the open, held out her hand.

"Oh, look, look," she said, trembling.

They came slowly to look at her opened palm.

In the center of it, cupped and huge, was a single raindrop.

She began to cry, looking at it.

They glanced quickly at the sky.

"Oh. Oh."

A few cold drops fell on their noses and their cheeks and their mouths. The sun faded behind a stir of mist. A wind blew cool around them. They turned and started to walk back toward the underground house, their hands at their sides, their smiles vanishing away.

A boom of thunder startled them, and like leaves before a new hurricane, they tumbled upon each other and ran. Lightning struck ten miles away, five miles away, a mile, a half mile. The sky darkened into midnight in a flash.

They stood in the doorway of the underground for a moment until it was raining hard. Then they closed the door and heard the gigantic sound of the rain falling in tons and avalanches everywhere and forever.

"Will it be seven more years?"

"Yes. Seven."

Then one of them gave a little cry.

"Margot!"

"What?"

"She's still in the closet where we locked her."

"Margot."

They stood as if someone had driven them, like so many stakes, into the floor. They looked at each other and then looked away. They glanced out at the world that was raining now and raining and raining steadily. They could not meet each other's glances. Their faces were solemn and pale. They looked at their hands and feet, their faces down.

"Margot."

One of the girls said, "Well...?"

No one moved.

"Go on," whispered the girl.

They walked slowly down the hall in the sound of cold rain. They turned through the doorway to the room, in the sound of the storm and thunder, lightning on their faces, blue and terrible. They walked over to the closet door slowly and stood by it.

Behind the closet door was only silence.

They unlocked the door, even more slowly, and let Margot out.

Getting at Meaning

RECALLING

1. According to this story, what is the weather usually like on the planet Venus? What does the landscape look like and why?

2. For what event are the children waiting?

3. Where was Margot born? When did she move to Venus?

4. For how long will the sun shine? When will it appear again?

5. Why does Margot miss the appearance of the sun?

INTERPRETING

6. How is Margot different from the other children? Why is it "vital" that she return to Earth?

7. What evidence is given in the story to show that Margot is sensitive and creative?

8. Why do the other children dislike Margot? Describe several ways in which they show their negative feelings toward her.

9. How do you think the other children feel about their prank at the end of the story? How do you know?

CRITICAL THINKING: EVALUATING

10. When Margot emerges from the closet, how do you think she will feel? How will this prank affect her relationships with other children?

Developing Skills in Reading Literature

1. **Science Fiction.** Science fiction is writing that is based on real or imagined scientific developments. It often presents an imaginary or fanciful view of the future or of the distant past. Is this story set in the past, the present, or the future? How do you know? What scientific developments would have to occur before events like those in this story could take place?

2. **Theme.** The theme is the main idea of a work of literature. Often the theme is a message about how people should act toward one another. What is the theme of "All Summer in a Day"? Does this theme apply equally well to life in the real world and to life in the imaginary world of the story? In other words, can a story about fantastic, improbable events have meaning for people's everyday lives? Explain.

3. **Sensory Images and Mood.** Sensory images are words and phrases that appeal to the five senses. For example, the words "perfumed like a locker room" appeals vividly to the sense of smell. "Louder than a thousand trumpeting elephants" appeals to the sense of hearing.

Mood is the feeling created by a literary work. A story might make you feel sad, amused, frightened, lighthearted, or some mixture of feelings.

Read the description of the landscape of Venus on page 135. What sensory images does Bradbury use to describe this landscape? What mood is created by these images?

4. **Figurative Language.** Figurative language is language that communicates ideas beyond the ordinary meanings of words. Two common types of figurative language are metaphors and similes.

Metaphor. You may remember that a metaphor is a direct comparison of two unlike things that have something in common. The line "I think the sun is a flower" contains a metaphor that points up some similarity between a flower and the sun, which seem quite unlike.

Simile. A simile is a comparison using *like* or *as*. If you say that a friend runs like a gazelle, you have used a simile. If you say instead that your friend is a gazelle, you have used a metaphor. In the following simile from "All Summer in a Day," the children are compared to stakes: "They stood as if someone had driven them, like so many stakes, into the floor." How would you turn this simile into a metaphor?

Metaphors and similes are used to make descriptions more concrete and vivid. Choose a person, animal, or place that you want to write about. On a sheet of paper, write one metaphor and two similes to describe your subject. Model your similes and your metaphor on those used in "All Summer in a Day."

5. **Onomatopoeia.** Onomatopoeia is the use of words to imitate sounds. Consider the following sentence from "All Summer in a Day":

"It had been raining for seven years; thousands upon thousands of days compounded and filled from one end to the other with rain, with the drum and gush of water."

Which words in this sentence sound like water hitting a hollow object or pouring quickly through an opening?

Developing Vocabulary

Using a Synonymy. A synonymy is a list of synonyms, or words that are close in meaning.

In a dictionary entry, the synonymy comes after the list of definitions. The following is a synonymy for the word *shock*:

SYN.—shock suggests a violent disturbance of the mind or emotions caused by an unexpected, overwhelming event that comes as a blow *[shocked by her sudden death]*; **startle** implies a slight shock of surprise or alarm, often one that causes a person to jump or flinch *[startled by the clap of thunder]*; **paralyze** suggests such extreme shock as to make one unable to move for a time *[paralyzed with fear]*; to **stun** is to shock with such force as to make one numb, dazed, or speechless *[stunned by the disaster]*

Study the following sentence from "All Summer in a Day":

"They were all nine years old, and if there had been a day, seven years ago, when the sun came out for an hour and showed its face to the *stunned* world, they could not recall."

Now look at the synonymy for the word *shock.* Did Bradbury use the most precise synonym for the meaning that he wanted to communicate? Should he have used *shock, startle,* or *paralyze* instead? Explain your answer.

B I O G R A P H Y

Copyright © 1986 Jill Krementz

Ray Bradbury (born 1920) writes mainly in the field of science fiction and fantasy. As a boy he was devoted to adventure books, secret code rings, comics, and Saturday at the movies. In high school he predicted the coming of the Space Age. Born in Waukegan, Illinois, Bradbury has published more than a thousand short stories, some collected into books such as *The Martian Chronicles* and *The Illustrated Man.* Several of Bradbury's works, including *Fahrenheit 451,* and *Something Wicked This Way Comes,* have been made into movies.

Humans Are Different

Alan Bloch

I'm an archaeologist, and Humans are my business. Just the same I wonder if we'll ever find out what made Humans different from us Robots—by digging around on the dead planets. You see, I lived with a Human once, and I know it isn't as simple as they told us back in school.

We have a few records, of course, and Robots like me are filling in some of the gaps; but I think now that we aren't really getting anywhere. We know, or at least the historians say we know, that Humans came from a planet called Earth. We know, too, that they rode out bravely from star to star and wherever they stopped, they left colonies—Humans, Robots, and sometimes both—against their return. But they never came back.

Those were the shining days of the world. But are we so old now? Humans had a bright flame—the old word is "divine," I think—that flung them far across the night skies, and we have lost the strands of the web they wove.

Our scientists tell us that Humans were very much like us—and the skeleton of a Human is, to be sure, almost the same as the skeleton of a Robot, except that it's made of some calcium compound instead of titanium. They

speak learnedly of "population pressure" as a "driving force toward the stars." Just the same, there are other differences.

It was on my last field trip, to one of the inner planets, that I met the Human. He must have been the Last Human in this system, and he'd forgotten how to talk—he'd been alone so long. Once he learned our language, we got along fine together, and I planned to bring him back with me. Something happened to him, though.

One day, for no reason at all, he complained of the heat. I checked his temperature and decided that his thermostat circuits were shot. I had a kit of field spares with me, and he was obviously out of order, so I went to work. I turned him off without any trouble. I pushed the needle into his neck to operate the cut-off switch, and he stopped moving, just like a Robot. But when I opened him up he wasn't the same inside. And when I put him back together I couldn't get him running again. Then he sort of weathered away—and by the time I was ready to come home, about a year later, there was nothing left of him but bones. Yes, Humans are indeed different.

Getting at Meaning

RECALLING

1. What is the storyteller's profession?

2. Where do the robot historians think that humans came from? Are they sure?

3. According to this story, in what ways were humans similar to robots?

INTERPRETING

4. The storyteller considers himself something of an expert on humans. What makes him an expert? What experiences has he had that other robots have not had?

5. According to the storyteller, some force flung humans far across the night skies. In other words, humans were driven to explore and colonize the heavens. In our time, what drives humans to explore and colonize new places? What force do you think the robot is talking about?

6. The storyteller found out through first-hand experience that "Humans Are Different." What does this title mean? Are humans different from each other? From some other form of life? In what way are they different? How did the robot find this out?

7. The storyteller uses past tense verbs such as *were* and *had* when speaking about humans. Why? What possible explanation is there for the use of such verbs?

CRITICAL THINKING: EVALUATING

8. Do you think that the future predicted in "Humans Are Different" is possible? Why or why not?

Developing Skills in Reading Literature

1. **Science Fiction.** Science fiction is writing that is based on real or imagined scientific developments. Like other science fiction stories, this one has some basis in scientific fact. What real-life scientific trends form the basis for this story?

Science fiction writers often use technical or scientific terms in order to make their stories appear to be based in scientific fact. What scientific and technical terms are used in "Humans Are Different"?

2. **Setting.** Sometimes writers of short stories describe settings in detail. At other times, the reader must infer the setting from hints given in the story. What is the time in which this story is set? How do you know? Is there anything in the story that suggests that the speaker is in a specific place? Where might the speaker be?

3. **Narrator and Point of View.** The narrator is the teller of a story. Point of view is the perspective from which a story is told. When you read a story, ask yourself the question "Who is telling this story?" If the answer is "one of the characters," then the story is an example of first-person point of view. That character is the narrator.

Who is the narrator of this story? In other words, from whose point of view is "Humans Are Different" told? To whom is the narrator speaking?

4. **Surprise Ending.** A surprise ending is an unexpected twist at the conclusion of a story. What is surprising about the ending of "Humans Are Different"?

Developing Vocabulary

Using a Glossary. According to the narrator of "Humans Are Different," "the skeleton of a Human is, to be sure, almost the same as the skeleton of a Robot, except that it's made of some calcium compound instead of titanium." Look up the words *calcium, compound,* and *titanium* in the Glossary. What do these words mean in the passage from the story? What special properties of titanium might make it useful for building machines that are meant to move about on their own?

Developing Writing Skills

Writing a Short Story. Write a brief story of three or four paragraphs based on the following situation: An extraterrestrial scientist lands on the Earth. The place where the scientist lands happens to be a section of grazing land in the middle of a cattle ranch. The scientist proceeds to study a cow, thinking that this is the most advanced form of life on the planet. Write the story in the form of a report back from the Earth. Tell the story from the point of view of the alien scientist.

List all the events of your story in your pre-writing notes. Also list any specific descriptive details that you want to use. As you write, stick to the point of view of your alien observer. When you revise, eliminate any unnecessary words and phrases, and add sensory details to make the story come alive in your readers' minds. Refer to **Using the Process of Writing** ⟨⟨ on pages 614–623 for help in completing this assignment.

B I O G R A P H Y

Alan Bloch (born 1915) has a strong background in physics and mathematics. Born in New York City, Bloch attended Swarthmore and Oberlin Colleges. Early in his career, Bloch became involved with computer development. He also worked as an engineer and physicist, eventually becoming a science consultant and writer. Bloch writes about science and related subjects such as computers and problem solving. He also writes award-winning science fiction novels and short stories.

It is May, 2157, and Tommy has a real book!

The Fun They Had

Isaac Asimov

Margie even wrote about it that night in her diary. On the page headed May 17, 2157, she wrote, "Today Tommy found a real book!"

It was a very old book. Margie's grandfather once said that when he was a little boy, *his* grandfather told him that there was a time when all stories were printed on paper.

They turned the pages, which were yellow and crinkly; and it was awfully funny to read words that stood still instead of moving the way they were supposed to—on a screen, you know. And then, when they turned back to the page before, it had the same words on it that it had had when they read it the first time.

"Gee," said Tommy, "what a waste. When you're through with the book, you just throw it away, I guess. Our television screen must have had a million books on it, and it's good for plenty more. I wouldn't throw *it* away."

"Same with mine," said Margie. She was eleven and hadn't seen as many telebooks as Tommy had. He was thirteen.

She said, "Where did you find it?"

"In my house." He pointed without looking, because he was busy reading. "In the attic."

"What's it about?"

"School."

Margie was scornful. "School? What's there to write about school? I hate school."

Margie always hated school, but now she hated it more than ever. The mechanical teacher had been giving her test after test in geography, and she had been doing worse and worse until her mother had shaken her head sorrowfully and sent for the County Inspector.

He was a round little man with a red face and a whole box of tools with dials and wires. He smiled at Margie and gave her an apple, then took the teacher apart. Margie had hoped he wouldn't know how to put it together again, but he knew how all right; and after an hour or so, there it was again, large and black and ugly, with a big screen on which all the lessons were shown and the questions were asked. That wasn't so bad. The part Margie hated most was the slot where she had to put homework and test papers. She always had to write them out in a punch code they made her learn when she was six years old, and the mechanical teacher calculated the mark in no time.

The Inspector had smiled after he was

finished and patted Margie's head. He said to her mother, "It's not the little girl's fault, Mrs. Jones. I think the geography sector was geared a little too quick. Those things happen sometimes. I've slowed it up to an average ten-year level. Actually, the overall pattern of her progress is quite satisfactory." And he patted Margie's head again.

Margie was disappointed. She had been hoping they would take the teacher away altogether. They had once taken Tommy's teacher away for nearly a month because the history sector had blanked out completely.

So she said to Tommy, "Why would anyone write about school?"

Tommy looked at her with very superior eyes. "Because it's not our kind of school, stupid. This is the old kind of school that they had hundreds and hundreds of years ago." He added loftily, pronouncing the word carefully, "*Centuries* ago."

Margie was hurt. "Well, I don't know what kind of school they had all that time ago." She read the book over his shoulder for a while, then said, "Anyway, they had a teacher."

"Sure they had a teacher, but it wasn't a *regular* teacher. It was a man."

"A man? How could a man be a teacher?"

"Well, he just told the boys and girls things and gave them homework and asked them questions."

"A man isn't smart enough."

"Sure he is. My father knows as much as my teacher."

"He can't. A man can't know as much as a teacher."

"He knows almost as much, I betcha."

Margie wasn't prepared to dispute that. She said, "I wouldn't want a strange man in my house to teach me."

Tommy screamed with laughter. "You don't know much, Margie. The teachers didn't live in the house. They had a special building, and all the kids went there."

"And all the kids learned the same things?"

"Sure, if they were the same age."

"But my mother says a teacher has to be adjusted to fit the mind of each boy and girl it teaches and that each kid has to be taught differently."

"Just the same, they didn't do it that way then. If you don't like it, you don't have to read the book."

"I didn't say I didn't like it," Margie said quickly. She wanted to read about those funny schools.

They weren't even half-finished when Margie's mother called, "Margie! School!"

Margie looked up. "Not yet, Mamma."

"Now!" said Mrs. Jones. "And it's probably time for Tommy, too."

Margie said to Tommy, "Can I read the book some more with you after school?"

"Maybe," he said nonchalantly. He walked away whistling, the dusty old book tucked beneath his arm.

Margie went into the schoolroom. It was right next to her bedroom, and the mechanical teacher was on and waiting for her. It was always on at the same time every day except Saturday and Sunday, because her mother said little girls learned better if they learned at regular hours.

The screen was lit up, and it said, "Today's arithmetic lesson is on the addition of proper fractions. Please insert yesterday's homework in the proper slot."

Margie did so with a sigh. She was thinking about the old schools they had when her grandfather's grandfather was a little boy. All the kids from the whole neighborhood came, laughing and shouting in the schoolyard, sitting together in the schoolroom, going home together at the end of the day. They learned the same things, so they could help one another with the homework and talk about it.

And the teachers were people....

The mechanical teacher was flashing on the screen, "When we add the fractions ½ and ¼—"

Margie was thinking about how the kids must have loved it in the old days. She was thinking about the fun they had.

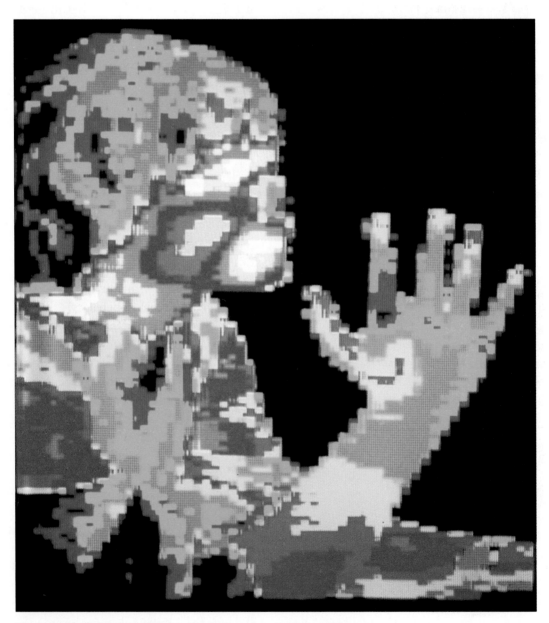

Thermographic Computerized Portrait. *Richard Lowenberg. Petaluma, California.*

Getting at Meaning

RECALLING

1. What has Tommy found in his attic?
2. What is a telebook? What are the differences between a telebook and a book?

INTERPRETING

3. How have schools and teachers changed since Margie's grandfather's grandfather was a boy?
4. Why does Margie think that kids in the old days had fun in school?

CRITICAL THINKING: APPLYING

5. What advantages does the system of schooling that exists today have over the one described in the story? What advantages does the system of schooling described in the story have over the one that exists today? Which system would you prefer? Why?

Developing Skills in Reading Literature

1. **Setting.** The setting is the time and place of the action of a story. Isaac Asimov tells his readers in the first paragraph of this story that the year is A.D. 2157. If the year were not given, would you still be able to tell that this story is set in the future? Explain your answer.

2. **Science Fiction.** Science fiction is writing that is based on real or imagined scientific developments. Many science fiction stories warn readers about possible consequences of scientific developments. What are the scientific developments on which the story "The Fun They Had" is based? What are the negative consequences of these developments?

3. **Dialogue.** A dialogue is a conversation between two or more people. What characters engage in dialogue in "The Fun They Had"?

Speaking and Listening. Find a partner and read aloud the dialogue that begins in paragraph 2, col. 1, on page 143. Notice how precisely Asimov has captured the speech of quarreling children. Also notice the indentions and punctuation marks that show which person is speaking.

Developing Writing Skills

Description: Science Fiction. In "The Fun They Had," Isaac Asimov imagines what school might be like in the future. Choose one of the following places: a zoo, a library, a museum, or a restaurant. Write a description of this place as it might appear in two hundred years.

In your prewriting notes, list sensory images that you can use to describe your place of the future. Divide your notes into groups of related ideas, and develop each of these groups into a separate paragraph. As you revise, follow the suggestions in **Using the Process of Writing.**

B I O G R A P H Y

Copyright © 1986 Jill Krementz

Isaac Asimov (born 1920) is an extremely popular writer of science fiction and nonfiction. Born in Russia, Asimov came to the United States at the age of three. He has written on a wide variety of subjects, including robotics, the Bible, Shakespeare, and nearly every branch of ancient and modern science. Among Asimov's most famous works of fiction are his series of novels, *The Foundation Trilogy*, and his short stories "Nightfall" and "The Last Question."

Lecia is forced to make some of the most important decisions of her life.

Winter Thunder   Part 1

Mari Sandoz

The snow began quietly this time, like an afterthought to the gray Sunday night. The moon almost broke through once, but toward daylight a little wind came up and started white curls, thin and lonesome, running over the old drifts left from the New Year storm. Gradually the snow thickened, until around eight-thirty the two ruts of the winding trails were covered and undisturbed except down in the Lone Tree district where an old yellow bus crawled heavily along, feeling out the ruts between the choppy sand hills.

As the wind rose, the snow whipped against the posts of a ranch fence across the trail and caked against the bus windows, shutting in the young faces pressed to the glass. The storm increased until all the air was a powdery white and every hill, every trace of road, was obliterated. The bus wavered and swayed in its direction, the tracks filling in close upon the wheels as they sought out the trail lost somewhere far back; and then finally grasped at any footing, until it looked like some great snowy, bewildered bug seen momentarily through the shifting wind. But it kept moving, hesitating here, stalling there in the deepening drifts,

bucking heavily into them, drawing back to try once more while the chains spun out white fans that were lost in the driving snow, which seemed almost as thick, as dense. Once the bus had to back down from a steep little patch that might have led into a storm-lost valley with a ranch house and warmth and shelter. It started doggedly around, slower now, but decisive, feeling cautiously for traction on the drifted hillside. Then the wheels began to slip, catch, and then slip again, the bus tipping precariously in the push of the wind, a cry inside lost under the rising noise of the storm.

For a long time it seemed that the creeping bus could not be stopped. Even when all discernible direction or purpose was finally gone, it still moved, backing, starting again, this way and that, plowing the deepened slope, swaying, leaning until it seemed momentarily very tall and held from toppling only by the thickness of the flying snow. Once more a wheel caught and held under the thunder of the red-hot smoking exhaust. It slipped and held again, but now the force of the wind was too great. For a moment the tilting bus seemed to lift. Then it pivoted into a slow skid and turned half around, broadside. Slowly it went over, almost as though without weight at all, settling lightly against a drift, to become a part of it at that thickening place where the white storm turned to snowbanks, lost except that there were frightening cries from inside and a hiss of steam and smoke from the hot engine against the snow.

In a moment the door was forced outward, the wind catching a puff of smoke as dark, muffled heads pushed up and were white in an instant. They were children, mostly in snow-suits and in sheepskin coats, thrust down over the bus side, coughing and gasping as the force of the blizzard struck them, the older ones hunching their shoulders to shield themselves and some of the other children.

Once more the engine roared out and the upper back wheel spun on its side, free and foolish in its awkward caking of snow. Then the young woman who had handed the children down followed them, her sheepskin collar up about her head, her arms full of blankets and lunch boxes.

"You'll have to give it up, Chuck," she called back into the smoking interior. "Quick! Bring the rest of the lunches—"

With Chuck, sixteen and almost as tall as a man, beside her, Lecia Terry pushed the frightened huddle of children together and hurried them away downwind into the wall of storm. Once she tried to look back through the smother of snow, wishing that they might have taken the rope and shovel from the toolbox. But there was no time to dig for them on the underside now.

Back at the bus thick smoke was sliding out the door into the snow that swept along the side. Flames began to lick up under the leaning windows, the caking of ice suddenly running from them. The glass held one moment and burst, and the flames whipped out, torn away by the storm as the whole bus was suddenly a wet, shining yellow that blistered and browned with the heat. Then there was a dull explosion above the roar of the wind, and down the slope the fleeing little group heard it and thought they saw a dark fragment fly past overhead.

"Well, I guess that was the gas tank going," Chuck shouted as he tried to peer back under his shielding cap. But there was only the blizzard closed in around them and the instinctive fear that these swift storms brought to all living creatures, particularly the young.

There was sobbing among the children now, a small one crying out, "Teacher! Teacher!" inside the thick scarf about her face, clutching for Lecia in her sudden panic.

"Sh-h, Joanie. I'm right here," the young woman soothed, drawing the six-year-old to her, looking around for the others, already so white that she could scarcely see them in the powdery storm.

"Bill, will you help Chuck pack all the lunches in two, three boxes, tight, so nothing gets lost? Maggie's big syrup bucket'll hold a lot. Throw all the empties away. We'll have to travel light—" she said, trying to make it sound a little like an old joke.

"My father will be coming for me soon—" the eight-year-old Olive said primly. "So you need not touch my lunch."

"Nobody can find us here," Chuck said shortly, and the girl did not reply, too polite to argue. But now one of the small boys began to cry. "I want my own lunch box too, Teacher," he protested, breathless from the wind. "I—I want to go home!"

His older brother slapped him across the ear muffs with a mittened hand. "Shut up, Fritz," he commanded. "You can't go home. The bus is—" Then he stopped, looking toward the teacher, almost lost only an arm's length away, and the full realization of their plight struck him. "We can't go home," he said, so quietly that he could scarcely be heard in the wind. "The bus is burned, and Chuck and Miss Lecia don't know where we are—"

"Sure we know!" Chuck shouted against him without looking up from the lunch packing, his long back stooped protectively over his task. "Don't we know, Lecia? Anyway, it won't last. Radio this morning said just light snow flurries, or Dad wouldn't have let me take the bus out 'stead of him, even sick as he was." The tall boy straightened up, the lunch boxes strung to the belt of his sheepskin to bang together in the wind until they were snow-crusted. "Baldy Stever'll be out with his plane looking for his girl friend soon's it clears a little, won't he, Lecia?" he said. "Like he came New Year's, with skis on it."

ILLUSTRATION, 1951. *Mead Schaeffer. From the original* Saturday Evening Post *publication of the story "The Lost School Bus,"* later retitled "Winter Thunder." *The Curtis Publishing Company, Indianapolis.*

But the bold talk did not quiet the sobbing, and the teacher's nod was lost in the storm as she tied scarves and mufflers across the faces of the younger children, leaving only little slits for the eyes, with the brows and lashes already furred with snow. Then she lined up the seven, mixing the ages from six-year-old Joanie to twelve-year-old Bill, who limped heavily as he moved in the deepening snow. One of the blankets she pinned around the thinly dressed Maggie, who had only a short outgrown coat, cotton stockings, and torn overshoes against the January storm. The other blanket she tied around herself, ready to carry Joanie on her back, Indian fashion, when the short little legs were worn out.

Awkwardly, one after another, Lecia pulled the left arm of each pupil from the sleeve, buttoned it inside the coat and then tied the empty sleeve to the right arm of the one ahead. She

took the lead, with little Joanie tied to her belt, where she could be helped. Chuck was at the tail end of the clumsy little queue, just behind Bill with the steel-braced ankle.

"Never risk getting separated," Lecia remembered hearing her pioneer grandfather say when he told of burying the dead from the January blizzard of 1888 here, the one still called the schoolchildren's storm. "Never get separated and never stop moving until you find shelter—"

The teacher squinted back along the line, moving like some long snowy winter-logged animal, the segmented back bowed before the sharpening blizzard wind. Just the momentary turn into the storm took her breath and frightened her for these children hunched into themselves, half of them crying softly, hopelessly, as though already lost. They must hurry. With not a rock anywhere and not a tree within miles to show the directions, they had to seek out the landmark of the ranch country—the wire fence. So the girl started downwind again, breaking the new drifts as she searched for valley ground where fences were most likely, barbed-wire fences that might lead to a ranch, or nowhere except around some hay meadow. But it was their only chance, the girl from the sand hills knew. Stumbling, floundering through the snow, she kept the awkward string moving, the eyes of the older ones straining through frozen lashes for even the top of one fence post, those of the small ones turned in upon their fear as the snow caked on the mufflers over their faces and they stumbled blindly to the pull from ahead.

Once there was a bolt of lightning, milky white in the blizzard, and a shaking of thunder, ominous winter thunder that stopped the moving feet. Almost at once the wind grew sharper, penetrating even Chuck's heavy sheepskin coat, numbing the ears and feet as panting, sobbing, the children plowed on again, the new drifts soon far above Lecia's boots, and no visibility, no way to avoid the drifts.

With their hands so awkwardly useless, someone stumbled every few steps, but the first to fall was the crippled Bill, the others, the crying ones too, standing silent in the storm, not even able to slap one frozen hand against another while the boy was helped up. After that others went down, and soon it was all that the teacher and the boy Chuck could do to keep the children moving as they pushed through the chop hills and found themselves going up what seemed a long wind-swept, wind-frozen slope, Lecia carrying Joanie on her back most of the time now. But they kept moving somehow, barely noticing even the jack rabbit that burst out among their feet and was gone into the storm. Otherwise there was nothing.

After a long, long time they reached what seemed a high ridge of hills standing across the full blast of the north wind that bent them low and blinded. Suddenly Chuck's feet slid off sideways into a hole, a deep-cupped blowout[1] hidden by the storm. Before he could stop, he had drawn the rest tumbling in after him, with an avalanche of snow. Crying, frightened, the smaller ones were set to their feet and brushed off a little. Then they all crouched together under the bank to catch their breath out of the wind, shivering, wet from the snow that had fallen inside their clothes, which were already freezing hard as board.

"With the blowouts always from the northwest to the southeast," Chuck shouted into the teacher's covered ear, "the wind's plainly from the north, so we're being pushed about due

---

1. **blowout:** a valley or depression caused by wind.

south. That direction there can't be a house for five, six miles, even if we could find it—unless we got clear out of our home country—"

The girl shivered, empty with fear. "—So that's why we haven't found a fence," she said slowly. "We're probably in the old Bar M summer range, miles and miles across. But we can't go any other direction—"

"I could alone; I could make it out alone!" Chuck shouted suddenly, angrily.

For a moment the teacher was silent, waiting, but when he added nothing more, she said: "You can't leave these little ones now, Chuck. Even if you were sure you could find a ranch—"

There was no reply, except that the crippled boy began to cry, a reddening from his ankle coming up through the snow that was packed into his overshoes around the brace. Others were sobbing too and shaking with cold, but the younger ones were very quiet now, already drowsing, and so the young teacher had to get to her feet and help lift the children out of the blowout. Slapping the muffler-covered cheeks, shaking the smaller ones so hard that the caked snow fell from them, she got the line moving again, but very slowly. She was worn out too, from the path-breaking and with Joanie in her arms to warm the child, keep her from the sleep of freezing that came upon her on Lecia's back, with only the thin blanket against the ice of the wind.

They seemed to be going down now through a long deep-drifted slope, plowing into buried yucca clumps, the sharp spears penetrating the snowsuits, even the boot tops. Here a few head of cattle passed them, less than three feet away and barely to be seen. They were running, snow-caked, blinded, bawling, and Lecia squinted anxiously back into the storm for others, for a herd that might

be upon them, trample them as surely as stampeding buffaloes. But there were no more now, and she could see that Chuck was shouting, "Little chance of its clearing up soon, with that snow thunder and those cattle already drifting so fast—all the way from the winter range!"

Yes, drifting fast with the force and terror of the storm, even hardy, thick-haired range cattle running!

Then suddenly one of the younger boys cried out something. "Teacher!" he repeated, "I saw a post!"

But it must have been a trick of the wind, for there was only the driving snow, except that the sharp-eyed Maggie saw one too, ahead and to the right—a snowy post with only the upper foot or so out of the drifts, holding up a strand of gray wire taut and humming in the cold.

For a moment Lecia could not see through the blurring of her eyes. At least this was something to follow, but which way? To her signal

Chuck lifted his arm and dropped it. He didn't recognize the fence either, and so the teacher took the easier direction, leftward, only side-face to the wind, although it might lead to the hills, to some final drift as the fleeing cattle would end.

Moving slowly along the fence, Lecia knew that it could not be much farther away. Her arms were wooden with cold and the weight of the child, her legs so weary in the deepening drifts that with each step it seemed that she could never lift a snow-caked boot again.

Then suddenly Chuck was doubling up the line. "I think I know where we are! That old split post just back there's where we made a takedown running coyotes with Dad's hounds this fall. If I'm right, this is Miller's north meadow, and there's a strip of willows down ahead there, off to the right—"

For a moment the girl set Joanie into the deep snow, panting, and even when she caught her breath, she was afraid to speak.

"How far to a house?" she finally asked, her

lips frozen.

"There's no house along this fence if it's the Miller's," Chuck had to admit. "It just goes around the meadow, three, four miles long."

"You're sure—" the teacher asked slowly, "—sure there's no cross fence to the ranch? You might get through, find help in time—"

The boy could only shake his snowy head and then, thinking that the storm hid this, he shouted the words on the wind. No, no cross fence, and the ranch was five miles south. Not even a haystack left in the valley here. Miller had had his hay balers in this fall, hauled it all out for his fancy Angus[2] herd.

Then they must take a chance on the willows, with Bill hardly able to limp along, Joanie too heavy to carry, and several others worn out. So they wallowed through the drifted fence and tried to keep parallel to its direction, but far enough in the meadow to see any willows. There must be willows now.

Suddenly Lecia went down in what must have been a deep gully, the ground gone, the girl sinking into soft powdery snow to her shoulder. Panting, choking, she managed to get Joanie and the rest back out and the frightened ones quieted a little. Then she swung off right along the barer edge of the gully, seeking a place to cross. The wind was blowing in powerful gusts now, so that she could scarcely stand up. Bent low she dragged at the line behind her, most of the children crawling in the trench she plowed for them. There was no crying now—only the slow, slow moving. Perhaps they should dig into the snow here below the gully bank. Indians and trappers had done that and survived. But they had thick-furred buffalo robes to shut out the cold and snow, and they were grown men, tough, strong—not

---

2. **Angus** (aŋ′ gəs): a breed of cattle.

helpless, worn-out children, their frozen feet heavy as stone, with only an overgrown boy and a twenty-three-year-old girl to lead them, keep them alive.

More and more often Lecia had to stop, her head down, her arms dropping the weight of the little girl. But there seemed to be a shallowing in the gully now, and so it was time she tried to break a path through it and turned back toward the fence if they were not to wander lost as so many did that other time, long ago, when a teacher and her nine pupils were lost, finally falling to die on the prairie. They must cling to the fence here, if it went no farther than around the meadow. At least it was proof that something existed on the earth except the thick, stinging blizzard, with a white, freezing, plodding little queue caught in the heart of it, surrounded.

Once when the girl looked up from the running snow it seemed there was something darkish off to the right, little farther than arm's reach away. She saw it again, something rounded, perhaps a willow clump, low, snow-filled, and possibly with more near by. Signaling to Chuck, Lecia turned down to it—a willow covered as in sleep, but with at least two more bushes just beyond, larger, darker, and standing closer together, their longer upper arms snow-weighted, entwined over the drifts. There, between the clumps, out of the worst of the storm, she left the children squatted close, the blankets held over them. With the belts of her coat and Chuck's, they tied the longer brushy tops of the two clumps together as solidly as they could. Then, fighting the grasping wind, they managed to fasten the blankets across the gap between the willows, to hold awhile. Behind this protection Lecia dug through the snow to the frozen ground while Chuck gathered dead wood. Inside a close little kneeling circle of children they built a fire pile with some dry inner bark and a piece of sandwich paper for the lighting. Awkwardly, with freezing hands the teacher and Chuck hurried, neither daring to think about matches, dry ones, in any pocket after this stumbling and falling through the snow.

The two smaller children were dropping into the heavy sleep of exhaustion and cold and had to be held in their places by the older ones while Chuck dug swiftly through his pockets, deeper, more awkwardly, then frantically, the circle of peering eyes like those of fearful young animals, cornered, winter-trapped.

Down to his shirt, Chuck found some in his pocket, six in a holder made of two rifle cartridges slipped together. Hurrying clumsily he struck one of the matches. It sputtered and went out, the flames sucked away. They had to try again, making a closer circle, with the coattails of the children thrown up over their heads to shut out the storm. This time the match caught on the waxed paper and the diamond willow began to snap and sizzle in the snow, throwing a dancing light up to the circle of crouching children.

But it seemed even colder now that they had stopped walking and Lecia thought of the night ahead, with the temperature surely down to twenty-five or thirty below zero. Beyond that she would not look now; but to get through this night they must have a great pile of wood, and they must have shelter even to hold the fire.

"We can't both go out at one time," the teacher told Chuck in their planning, somehow making it seem as for a long, long time. "It's too risky for the children. We might not get back."

The boy looked around from the fire he was

nursing, and upward, but there was still no thinning of the storm, the area of snowy visibility almost as small as the confines of their new meat-freeze room at the ranch. Even so he gave the girl no sign of agreement.

Lecia set willow poles into the snowbanks as she went to look for wood, none farther apart than the outstretched reach of her arms. She found more willows, each clump sitting alone in the isolation of the driving storm, so cold now that the green wood snapped off like glass. Each time it was only by the row of sticks in the drifts that she managed to stagger her blinded and panting way back against the wind with her load of wood.

The brushier portions she piled behind the blankets of the shelter to catch the snow and shut out the wind. Some, long as fish poles, she pushed through the willow clumps and across the opening between, in a sort of lattice inside the bellying blankets that Eddie and Calla tried to hold in place. They were the first of the children to separate themselves from the snowy composite, the enforced co-ordinate that had been the queue driven by the storm, the circle that shielded the sprouting fire. Now they were once more individuals who could move alone, hold the blankets from blowing inward, pile the dry powdery snow from the ground against and between the sticks, trying to work it like plaster, building a wall between the clumps of willows. Even Bill helped a little, as far as he could reach without moving the bad ankle. They worked slowly, clumsily, pounding their freezing hands at the fire, but returning.

By one o'clock the north wind was cut off so that the fire fattened and burned higher, softening the ice caked to the clothing until it could be knocked off and softening the face of the drift reached by the wind-blown heat. The children packed this against the north wall too

and into the willow clumps both ways, drawing the rounded wall inward toward the top along the bend of the willows, making what looked like half of an Indian snow shelter or the wickiup[3] Calla had seen at the county fair, just high enough at the center for a seven-year-old to stand up, the snow walls glistening rosy in the firelight as the wind was shut off.

"That's a good job!" Chuck shouted over the roar of the storm as he tried to rub circulation into Joanie's waxen feet. The small girl was beginning to cry out of her sleep with the first pain; others began too, their ears and hands swollen and purpling, their toes painful as their boots thawed. But it seemed that the feet of nine-year-old Maggie must be lost, the ragged old overshoes and cotton stockings so frozen that she had to cut them away with Eddie's knife. Under them her feet were like stone, dead white stone, although the girl was working hard to rub life into them. She worked silently and alone, as had become natural long ago, her thin face pinched and anxious with the pain and the alarm.

Of them all only Olive seemed untouched. She was dry in her heavy waterproofed snowsuit with attached rubber feet inside the snow boots. And she was still certain that her father would soon come for her.

"He would not care to leave me in such an unpleasant place—"

When they had the semicircular wall of the shelter drawn in as far as the snow would hold, Lecia decided to pull the blankets away from the outside and use one over the top, with the belt-tied willows sticking through a smoke hole cut in the center. But as the blankets came down, part of the loose snow wall was blown in

---

3. **wickiup** (wik′ ē up): a hut made by covering an oval-shaped frame with grass, brush, or other materials.

by the force of the blizzard, the huddle of children suddenly white again, the fire almost smothered. So the wall had to be rebuilt in discouragement, but with care, using more brush and sticks, more fire-softened snow to freeze in place as soon as it was struck by the storm. Lecia had to stop several times for her hands too, pounding them hard, holding them over the fire, the diamond sparkling. She tried to turn the ring off before the swelling became too great and then gave it up. The wall must be finished, and when it was solid, Calla came to whisper under the roar of the wind. "Bill's been eating the lunch," she said.

"Oh, Bill! That's not fair to the others, to your own little sister, Joanie!" Lecia cried. Suddenly not the good teacher, she grabbed up the containers and hung them on high branches out in plain sight for watching, for reminders and derision from the other children. "Why, it may be days before we are found!" she scolded, in her exasperation saying what should have been kept hidden in silence.

Before the boy could defend himself with a plea of hunger or his usual complaint about the crippled foot, some realization of their plight had struck the others. Even little Fritz, with the security of an older sister and brother like Calla and Eddie along, began to sob. Only the round-cheeked Olive was calm, the others angered to see it, wanting to shout against her outsider's assurance, to tell her she was too stupid and green to know that her father could not come for her in such a blizzard, that he would never find her if he could get through. But they were silent under the teacher's admonitory eye. And, as in the schoolhouse and on the playground, Bill had withdrawn, except that now it could not be more than a foot or two.

As the frozen earth between the willow humps became soggy, Calla and Eddie helped move the others around so that there was room to draw the fire first one way and then another to dry and warm the ground. Lecia watched to see that they set no one afire and then bowed her head out into the storm again. Chuck was dragging in willows for the night. They drove sticks into the hardening drifts around the front of the shelter and piled brush against them to catch the snow. It filled in as fast as they worked until there was no more than a little crawling hole left. Then Chuck laid a mat of brushy sticks on the ground and packed soft snow into them to freeze, making a handled slab big enough to close the low doorway. Now, so long as the blanket with the smoke hole stayed tied over the top, they could be as warm as they wished in the little shelter that was scarcely longer than a tall man—a close cramping for the teacher, Chuck, and the seven pupils, but easily warmed with a few fingers of wood, an Indian fire. Safe and warm so long as the shelter stood against the rising ferocity of the blizzard and the willows lasted.

By now the cold stung the nose and burned the lungs, the snow turned to sharp crystals that drew blood from the bare skin. It drove the teacher and Chuck in to the fire, shaking, unable, it seemed, ever to be warmed through again. Lecia opened her sheepskin coat, hung up her frozen scarf and cap and shook out her thick brown hair that gleamed in the firelight. Even with her tawny skin red and swollen, her gold-flecked hazel eyes bloodshot, she was still a pretty girl, and the diamond on her hand flashed as she hunted for her stick of white salve to pass around for the raw, bleeding lips. It was all she could do.

Now they tried to plan for what was to come, but here they were as blind as in the flight through the storm. There would be sickness, with the noses already running, Joanie coughing deep from her chest, and, worst of all, Maggie's feet that seemed to be dying. Besides, the fire must be kept going and the food spread over three, perhaps four, days.

Here Bill raised his complaining voice. "You ain't our boss outside of school! We'll do what we want to. There ain't enough to eat for everybody."

"You mean *isn't,* not *ain't,*" the teacher corrected firmly. "And talking like that—when you've barely missed one lunch time!"

"You ain't never my boss," Chuck said casually, "—only about the kids while in the bus, like you do with my dad when he's driving. I sure can do what I want to here, and I'll do it."

Slowly the girl looked around the ring of drowsy, firelit eyes upon her, some uneasy at this bold talk to their teacher, but some smaller ones aping the defiance of the big boys. Chuck, who sat almost a head taller than Lecia, grinned down at the pretty young teacher but with an arrogance that was intended to remind her that he saw nothing here as his responsibility, nothing this side of the bus except saving himself.

Unable to reply in words that would not frighten the children more, the teacher looked past the fire into the boy's broad, defiant face, into his unblinking, storm-red eyes, the look commanding at first, then changing to something else in spite of herself, into a sort of public test, until it seemed she dared not turn her gaze away or at that instant the sixteen-year-old boy must assert his victory by plunging out into the storm and perhaps destroy himself, perhaps bring death to all of them.

Before this silent, incomprehensible struggle the children were uneasy and afraid, even the coughing stilled, so that the storm seemed very loud outside the smoke hole. But little Fritz was too young to be held so for long. "I'm hungry!" he shouted against the restraining hand of his sister. "I want my lunch!"

As though freed, released, Chuck sat back and grinned a little at the small boy. Matter of factly the teacher washed her raw hands with snow and held them over the fire. Then she spread her napkin on her lap and set out all there was in the eight lunches now: fourteen sandwiches, most of them large, six pieces of Sunday cake, a handful of cookies, a few pieces of candy, and six apples and two oranges, frozen hard. There were two thermos bottles of milk, and these Lecia pushed away into the snow wall.

"If somebody gets sick and can't eat solid food," she said to the owners, their eyes following her hands in consternation. Even with the best management, there would be no food of any kind in a few days, but this the small owners could not yet understand.

The frozen fruit she handed to Chuck and, without meeting the girl's eyes, he set it around the coals for toasting, to be eaten now because it would not keep well, and might sicken leaner stomachs. In the meantime Lecia set one lunch box filled with snow near the fire and packed away all except four of the big sandwiches into the others, the eyes of the children following her hands here too, even as she hung the containers back above her head. Then she divided the four sandwiches into halves and passed them around.

"Eat very slowly," she cautioned. "Blizzards usually last three days, so we must make what we have here last too, probably clear to Thursday or longer."

But Bill seemed not to be listening. "Chuck's eating!" he suddenly protested. "He ain't, *isn't,* in on the lunches."

For a moment the teacher looked sternly at

the boy. "After Chuck carried them all from the bus, helped you through the bad places, and helped to make the shelter and the fire!" the girl said in astonishment. "Now we'll have no more of this bickering and complaint. Here we are equal partners, and not one of us will get out of this alive unless we keep working together. Even your comic books should have taught you that much! And don't think this is play. You remember what the storm of 1888 was called in your history book—because so many schoolchildren died in it. That storm was short, not over two days most places, nothing for length like the one we had holiday time this year, and no telling about this one. Most of the children in 1888 died because somebody got panicky, didn't think, or they didn't stick together—"

There was silence all around the fire now, the storm seeming to rise, the children edging closer to each other, glancing fearfully over their shoulders as though toward night windows with terrible things stalking outside.

"Oh, we're O.K.," Chuck said optimistically. "We can last three days easy here—" the rebellion gone from him or hidden for the moment.

Thinking of a five-day storm, the teacher looked around the frightened, sooty faces, the children coughing and sniffling, their pocket tissue gone, the few handkerchiefs hung to dry, and wondered if any, even the man-tall Chuck, would be here by then.

But Olive, the newcomer, was unconcerned. "I should like another sandwich, Miss Terry. From my own lunch, please," she said, with the formality of an old-fashioned boarding school for eight-year-olds. "I won't need the remainder. My father will come for me when it is time."

"He won't find you—" Maggie said as she rubbed at her feet, color seeping into them

now, an angry, gray-splotched purple, with pain that twisted the thin face.

"My father will come," Olive repeated, plainly meaning that he was not like the fathers of the others here, particularly Maggie's, who had done nothing since the war except make a little South Pacific bug juice, as he called it, for himself from chokecherries, wild grapes, or raisins in the way they did in the war. He had only a little piece of copper tubing and so he couldn't make more than enough for himself, yet he got into jail just the same for crashing his old truck through the window of the county assistance office. But things had not been good before that. Often this fall Maggie was at school when the bus arrived, not waiting at the stop near their crumbling old sod shack but walking the three miles. Sometimes her face was bruised, but she was silent to any questioning. If Maggie lost her feet now, it was because she had no warm snowsuit and high boots like

the others, only the short old coat above her skinny knees, the broken overshoes with the soles flopping.

But there was still a cheerful face at the fire. Although little Fritz's cheeks seemed swollen to bursting and his frosted ears stood away under the flaps of his cap, he could still show his gap-toothed grin in mischief.

"If we don't get home till Thursday, Teacher, Baldy'll be awful mad at you when he comes flying out Wednesday—"

The rest laughed a little, drowsily. "Maybe Baldy won't be flying around that soon," Eddie said and was corrected by Calla's sisterly concern. "Don't say Baldy. Say Mr. Stever."

But the teacher busied herself hanging up everything loose. Then with Chuck's knife she slit the remaining blanket down the middle and fastened half around each side against the snow wall, like a tipi lining. By the time the white blizzard darkness came, the smaller children had all been taken outside for the last time and lay in fretful, uneasy sleep. Olive had been the last, waiting stubbornly for her father until she toppled forward. Calla caught her and made room for the girl still murmuring, "Papa—"

Finally the last sob for parent and home was stilled, even Joanie asleep, her feverish head in the teacher's lap, her throat raw and swelling, with nothing except hot snow water to ease the hollow cough. There were half a dozen lozenges in Lecia's pocket but these must be saved for the worse time that would surely come.

The children were packed around the fire like little pigs or puppies on a very cold night. Chuck was at the opposite side from Lecia, the boys on his side, the girls on hers, with Calla and her brothers around the back. The older ones lay nearer the wall, their arms over the

younger to hold their restlessness from the fire.

But Bill was still up, drawn back under the willows, his head pulled into his sheepskin collar, his ankle bent to him. He watched the teacher doze in fatigue, met her guilty waking gaze sullenly. But finally he reached down into his pocket and drew out something in waxed paper.

"I didn't eat the piece you gave me—" he said, holding out his half of the sandwich.

"Bill! That was fine of you," the girl said, too worn out for more as she reached up to put it away.

"No—no, you eat it. I guess you didn't take any."

A moment Lecia looked at the boy, but he avoided her as he edged himself around Chuck closer to the fire, turning his chilled back to the coals, and so she ate the buttered bread with the thick slice of strengthening cold beef, while more snow was driven in through the smoke hole and settled in sparkling dust toward the little fire. There were white flashes, too, and the far rumble of winter thunder.

"Is—is there lots of willows left?" the crippled boy asked.

The teacher knew what he meant—how many clumps, and if so far out that someone might get lost.

"I think there are quite a few," she replied, needing to reassure the boy, but unable to make it a flat lie.

A long time he sat silent. Finally he pulled his cap off and shook the long yellowish hair back from his petulant face. "I wonder what Mother's doing—" he said slowly, looking away, his hand seeking out the tortured ankle. Lecia motioned him to hold it over to her and so she did not need to reply, to ask what all the mothers of these children must be doing, with the telephone lines still down from the other storm and surely nobody foolish enough to try bucking this one unless it might be Olive's father, the new Eastern owner of the little Box Y ranch.

With snow water heated in the lunch tin, Lecia washed the poor stick that was the boy's ankle, gently sponging the bone laid almost bare where the frozen snow and the iron brace wore through the scarred and unhealthy skin.

"It looks pretty bad, Bill, but you probably won't have to put the brace back on for days—" Lecia started to comfort, but it was too late, and she had to see fear and anger and self-pity darken the face in the firelight. Because nothing could be unsaid, the girl silently bandaged the ankle with half of the boy's handkerchief. "Now get a little sleep if you can," she said gently.

The boy crawled in next to Eddie as though Ed were the older, and for a long time the teacher felt the dark eyes staring at her out of the shadowy coat collar as though she had deliberately maneuvered this plunge into the blizzard.

Several times before midnight the girl started to doze but jerked herself awake at the frozen creak of the willow shelter to push the out-tossed arms back and replenish the fire.

Eddie's cough began to boom deep as from a barrel. He turned and moaned, digging at his chest, Calla helpless beside him, her sleep-weighted eyes anxious on the teacher. Maggie too was finally crying now. Her feet had puffed up and purpled dark as jelly bags, with the graying spots that would surely break and slough off, perhaps spread in gangrene.[4] Yet all Lecia could do was turn the girl's feet from the fire and push them behind the blanket against the snow to relieve the pain and itching a little. Perhaps only freeze them more. Lecia touched the girl's forehead to calm her but felt her stiffen and start to pull away from this unaccustomed kindly touch. Then Maggie relaxed a little, and as the teacher stroked the hot temples, she wondered how many days it might be before help could get through. Suddenly their plight here seemed so hopeless, the strength and wisdom of her twenty-three years so weak and futile, that she had to slip out into the storm for calm. And finally Maggie slept, worn out, but still tearing at her feet.

To the weary girl watching, half asleep, at the fire, the roar of the storm rose and fell like the panting of a great live thing, sometimes a little like many great planes warming up together. If only she had married Dale Stever New Year's, they would be in the Caribbean now, these children all safe at home, with probably no other teacher available so soon.

---

4. **gangrene** (gan′ grēn): decay in a bodily tissue due to an insufficient supply of blood.

Once Lecia turned her swollen hand to the fire, watching the ring catch and break the light into life, and tried to recall the fine plans Dale had made for them. He wasn't a rancher's son like those who usually took her to parties and dances—like Joe, or Wilmo, or even Ben, of the local bank. Dale had come from outside last summer and bought up the sale pavilion in town. Since then he flew all around the surrounding ranch country in a plane the color of a wild canary rising from a plum thicket, gathering stock for the sales. Fairtime he took Lecia and her friend Sallie down to the state fair and several times on long trips since to Omaha, to the ballet, and to Denver. At first it seemed he was all jolly big-talk, with windy stories of his stock in an oil company down in Dallas and in a Chicago commission house. He had a touch of gray at his temples that he thought made him look distinguished when he had his hat on, and to their fathers he called himself the Dutch uncle of the two girls. But

gradually he concentrated on Lecia, and at Christmas there was a big diamond and the plane ready to fly south. He even took her to the school board to ask for a release from her contract.

"No," the old school director told the girl. "Bill Terry was a friend of mine, brought me into the country. I can't help his granddaughter marry no man in a rush hurry."

Dale laughed confidently and put his arm about the girl's shoulder as they left, but somehow Lecia couldn't break her contract. They must wait until school was out. Dale had been angry. "This is no life for a girl as pretty as you," he said. Truly he was right. Today it was no life for any girl.

Soon after midnight Lecia was startled out of a doze by the sound of cattle bawling somewhere in the roar of the storm, like the herds that passed her home in the night of the May blizzard three years ago, when so many died in the drifts and lakes that the whole region was a stench far into the summer. Then suddenly the girl realized where she was and hurried bareheaded out into the storm. The bawling was very close; any moment hundreds of storm-blinded cattle might be running over the little willows, over their own two clumps.

Lecia dragged burning sticks from the fire, but in an instant the storm had sucked their flame away. So, with her arms up to shield her eyes from the snow that was sharp as steel dust, she stood behind the shelter shouting the "Hi-ah! Hi-ah!" she had learned when she helped the cowboys push cattle to market. It was a futile, lost little sound against cattle compelled to run by an instinct that could not be denied, compelled to flee for survival before the descent of the arctic storm, never stopping until trapped in some drift or boldly overtaken in some open fence corner to freeze on their feet, as Lecia had seen them stand.

Realizing her danger as a warmth crept over her, the girl stumbled back into the shelter and crouched at the fire. She barely noticed the sting of returning blood in her ears and face while she listened until the drifting herd was surely past, made more afraid by the knowledge of this thing that drove cattle galloping through the night, the power of it, and how easily it could overcome the little circle of children here if it were not for the handful of fire, for the walls of the storm's own snow.

Toward morning the weary girl knew that she could not keep awake. She had stirred Chuck to sit up a while, but he was unable to shake off the weight of sleep so heavy on an overgrown boy. Trying to remember how the Indians carried their fire—something about moss and damp, rotted wood—Lecia pulled old dead roots from the willow butts and laid them into the coals with the ends sticking far out. Even with waxed paper handy it would be a desperate chance. Willows burned fast as kindlings and there were only five matches, including the one from Eddie's pocket, and no telling how many spoiled by dampness.

Even so it was sweet to let herself sink into darkness, but it seemed that she awoke at once, stiff and cold from the nightmare that reached into the waking black, even the ashes of the fire spot cold. With the waxed paper held ready, the girl blew on the ends of the unburnt roots her hands found, carefully, breathless in her fear. At last a red spark glowed deep in one, and when the fire was going again, she slipped outside for calm in the cold that was like thin, sharp glass in the nose.

There was still no earth and no sky, only the white storm of late dawn blowing hard. But the wood had lasted and now Lecia put on a few extra sticks and heated water to wash the goose mush from the inflamed eyes of the children. She started a rousing song: "Get up! Get up, you sleepyhead!" but even before it was done, Joanie began to whimper, "I'm hungry—"

So the teacher laid out four sandwiches on sticks over the coals and then added another half for herself when she saw Bill watching. "There won't be anything more today except a pinch of cake unless the sun breaks through."

"If it does, we can stomp out a message on the snow," Calla said cheerfully.

"Yes, even if people can't travel for a whole week, Baldy'll come flying over to see about his girl friend," Bill said, boldly.

The younger boys laughed a little, but Chuck was more serious. "If the sky lightens at all and there's no blowing, I'll do the stomping before I leave."

"You'd run away now?" the teacher asked softly as she combed at Joanie's fine brown hair.

"Somebody's got to get help," he defended in loud words.

The children around the fire were suddenly quiet, turning their eyes to follow the tall boy as he pulled up his sheepskin collar and crawled out into the storm. And they were silent a long time afterward—all except Joanie, who sobbed softly, without understanding. Even Olive looked up once, but Maggie grated her feet hard along the snow wall and tore at their congestion as though she heard nothing.

Then suddenly there was stomping outside and Chuck came back in, snowy, thick frost all over his collar and cap, his brows and lashes in ice, the children pushing over toward him, as to one gone, lost. He brought more wood, and the teacher seemed to have forgotten that he had said anything about leaving. But the children watched him now, even when they pretended they didn't, and watched Lecia too, for suspicion had come in.

The teacher started as for a school day,

except that the arithmetic was rote learning of addition and multiplication tables and a quick run through some trick problems: "If I had a fox, a goose, and some corn to get across a river in a boat—" and then, "If I had a dollar to buy a hundred eggs—no, I should take something that won't make us hungry."

"Like a hundred pencils?"

"Well, yes, let's take pencils. I want to buy a hundred for a dollar. Some are five cents each, poor ones two-and-a-half cents, and broken ones half a cent. How many of each kind must I buy?"

In history and nature study they talked about the Indians that still roamed the sand hills when Lecia's grandfather came into the country. They lived the winter long in skin tipis something like the shelter here, and almost as crowded, but with piles of thick-furred buffalo robes for the ground and the beds. The girls sat on one side, the boys on the other.

"Like we are here—" Fritz said, his eyes

shining in the discovery. "We're Indians. Whoo-oo-oo!" he cried, slapping his mouth with his palm.

They talked about the food too, the piles of dried and pounded meat, the winter hunts, how the village and lodges were governed, and what the children did, their winter games, one almost like "button, button." The boys learned from the men—such things as arrow-making, and later bullet-making, hunting, fighting; and particularly the virtues of resourcefulness, courage, fortitude, and responsibility for all the people. A girl learned from the women—beading, tanning hides, and all the other things needed to live well with modesty, stead-fastness, and generosity; and with courage and fortitude and responsibility too, for it was thought that the future of the people lay in the palms of the women, to be cherished or thrown away.

"What does that mean, Teacher?" Fritz asked, hitting out in mischief at his brother Eddie, despite Calla and the teacher both watching, then shouting he was hungry again.

The rest tried to laugh a little as Calla whispered to her small brother, trying to make herself heard against the storm, while Lecia taught them a poem about Indians. Even Joanie repeated a few lines for her, although the child leaned weak and feverish against Calla while Bill comforted his bound ankle and Maggie tried hard to pull herself out of the curious drowsiness that had the teacher frightened.

After a while the children played "button, button" and tried to tell each other poems. When Eddie got stuck on "Snowbound," Bill nudged Fritz, and they laughed as easily at his discomfiture as at school, perhaps because Chuck was back and this was the second day of the storm, with tomorrow the third. Then it would clear up and somebody with a scoop shovel would get his horse along the barer ridges to a telephone.

"Maybe somebody'll just come running over the hills to find us," Eddie teased, looking at Olive, turning his face from the teacher.

Well, even if nobody came and Baldy couldn't find a place to land with skis on his plane, he would have sacks of food and blankets and stuff dropped like in the movies and the newspapers.

"I saw it in a movie once, I did," Joanie cried.

So they talked, pretending no one was looking up at the hanging lunch buckets or sick and afraid. But Lecia did not hear them.

"Oh-oo, Teacher's sleeping like one of those old Indian women up to Gordon, just sitting there!" Eddie exclaimed.

"Sh-h," Calla said, in her way. "Let her stretch out here," and with a polite smile Olive moved aside.

That night Joanie was delirious, and once Maggie slipped past the teacher out into the storm to relieve the fire of her feet. By midnight she couldn't stand on them, and the grayish spots were yellow under the thick skin of a barefoot summer, the swelling creeping above the girl's thin ankles, with red streaks reaching almost to the knees. Her eyes glistened, her cheeks were burning, and she talked of wild and dreadful things.

Lecia tried to remember all that she had read of frostbite, all that her grandfather had told, but she knew that the inflammation spreading past the frozen area was like the cold overtaking the fleeing cattle, and she had to make a desperate decision. She dug two holes deep into the snow wall and laid Maggie with her feet in them almost to her knees, wishing they had something waterproof for covering. The cold would probably freeze the girl more, but it would numb the nerves and perhaps slow the congestion and tissue starvation. Later, when the girl was restless again and crying, Lecia found the yellow spots spreading, painful and hard as boils. She burned the end of a safety pin and while Maggie's frightened eyes became caverns in her thin face, Lecia opened one of the spots. Bloody pus burst down over her hand. Holding the foot aside she wiped it away on the snow, from her ring too and then slipped it from her shrunken finger and hung it on a twig overhead where it swayed a little, like a morning dewdrop, while she opened the rest of the festering.

After the girl's feet were bathed and bound in the sleeves torn from Lecia's white shirt blouse, Lecia thrust them back into the snow. Then she gave Maggie half a cup of the milk, very quietly, hoping none would awaken to see, although none needed it more. Almost at once the girl was asleep, to rest until the pus gathered again. But the first time Lecia returned with firewood she saw the thermos bottle half out. She jerked it from the hole. The milk was all gone, and across the little fire Olive stared at her teacher.

"It was mine," the girl said flatly.

So the time had come when the little food left must be hidden. Now, with all but Olive sleeping, was the time. When Lecia came back in, the girl held out something—the ring that had been left hanging on the twig and forgotten.

PART 1

Getting at Meaning

RECALLING

1. Why does the driver of the school bus lose the trail? Why do the teacher and her pupils have to leave the bus?

2. How old is Lecia? How old is Chuck? How many small children must Lecia and Chuck care for?

3. What does Lecia do to keep the children from becoming separated in the blizzard?

4. How is Chuck able to determine where the group is? Where are they?

5. How much food does the group have? How long does Chuck expect the storm to last? How long does Lecia think that it might last?

6. Which of the children is in the most immediate danger? What does Lecia do to care for this child?

7. What does Lecia do on the second day to keep the children's minds off their predicament?

INTERPRETING

8. Which person has the greater commitment to the children, Chuck or Lecia? How do you know?

9. What does the shelter built by Chuck and Lecia look like? How do they build it?

10. Which two children steal some of the food when no one is watching? Why do they do this? How do these children try to make up for their actions?

CRITICAL THINKING: APPLYING

11. How do Chuck, Bill, and Olive challenge Lecia's authority? Why is it important that Lecia maintain control over the group? Why do people in emergency situations usually choose one person to act as their leader? Why can't everyone simply do what he or she wants to do?

Developing Skills in Reading Literature

1. **Conflict and Setting.** Conflict is a struggle between opposing forces. Setting is the time and place of the action of a story. What is the major conflict in this story? What role does the setting play in this conflict?

2. **Suspense.** Suspense is a feeling of growing tension and excitement felt by a reader. One way that a writer creates suspense is by raising questions in the reader's mind. The first section of "Winter Thunder" raises a number of questions. These include "Will the teacher and her children survive?" and "Will Chuck remain with the group?" What other questions are raised by the first part of the story? List these questions on a separate sheet of paper.

What happened during January of 1888? How does knowledge of this event add to the suspense of the story?

3. **Character.** A character is a person or animal who takes part in the action of a work of literature. Short story writers describe their characters with as few words as possible. They suggest what their characters are like through a few important details.

Make a list of the characters in "Winter Thunder." Beside each name, list two or three details that are used in the story to describe the character. These details may be comments made about the character by the narrator, or storyteller. They also may be the character's actions or words. Study your list. Notice how the writer has suggested what each character is like by using a few specific details.

Part 2

The next day and the next were the same, only colder, the drifts deeper and harder along the willows, the wind so sharp with snow that it froze the eyeballs. Lecia and Chuck covered their faces as they fought their way back against it, the wood dragging from their shoulders, tied by a strap of cloth cut off around the bottom of Lecia's coat. One at a time they went out and came back, a hand stretched ahead feeling for the next guide pole in the snow before the other let go of the last, the covered face turned from the storm to save the breath from being torn away by the wind.

All the third day there was watching out of the smoke hole for the sky that never appeared. When night finally came without star or stillness, even Lecia, who had tried to prepare herself for this eventuality, felt that she could not face another day of blizzard. Maggie no longer sat up now and both Joanie and Eddie were so sick—their fever high, their chests filling—that the teacher had to try something. She seemed to remember that the early settlers used willow bark to break a fever, so she steeped a handful in Maggie's tin cup until the liquid was strong and dark. She made the two children drink it, first experimentally, then more, and after a while they began to sweat. When they awoke they were wet, their hair clinging to their vulnerable young foreheads, but they seemed better all the next day, except weak. Then at night it was the same with Joanie.

The fourth day was like the rest, colder, with the same white storm outside, the children hunching silent upon themselves inside. Sometimes a small one sobbed a little in sickness and hunger, but it was no more than a soft moaning now, even when Lecia divided most of the little food that was left. The children, even Chuck, took it like animals and then sat silent again, the deep-socketed eyes watching, some slyly gnawing at willow sticks and roots hidden in the palm.

Everybody around the fire was coughing and fevered now, it seemed to Lecia, the bickering going beyond childish things to quarrels about real or fancied animosities between their families. Once even Calla spoke angrily to Bill, defending her brothers.

"At least they aren't mama babies like you!"

"Mama babies! I wouldn't talk if everybody knew that my family got a start in cattle by stealing calves—"

"You can't say such things!" Calla cried, up and reaching for Bill, caught without his brace and unable to flee into the storm, Joanie crying: "Don't! Don't hit my brother!"

When Lecia returned, Chuck was holding the two apart, shaking them both. The teacher spoke in anger and impatience too now, and Bill's face flushed with embarrassment and shame, the sudden red like fever in his hunger-grayed cheeks.

Only Maggie with her poor feet was quiet, and Olive, sitting as though stunned or somewhere far away. The teacher knew that she should do something for this girl, only eight yet apparently so self-contained. Olive never spoke of her father now, as none of the boys teased Lecia about Baldy any more. Olive was as remote about him as everything else since the night she drank the milk, and found the ring on a twig.

Too weary to think about it, and knowing she must keep awake in the night, Lecia stretched out for a nap. When she awoke Olive was sitting exactly the same, but the places of

Chuck and Eddie were empty—Eddie out in the blizzard after his night of sweating. When the boys returned with wood, weak, dragging, almost frozen, and with something that Lecia had to be told outside. There seemed only one willow clump left.

One clump? Then they must start digging at the frozen butts, or even pull down their shelter to keep the fire alive, for now the boys too were believing that the storm would blow forever. Yet toward evening there was a thinning above the smoke hole, the sun suddenly there like a thin disk of milky ice from the bottom of a cup. It was almost a promise, even though the storm swept the sun away in a few minutes, and the wind shifted around to the south, whipping in past the block the boys had in the hole of the shelter. The children shivered, restless. Once Eddie rose from his sleep and fought to get out, go home. When he finally awakened, he lay down in a chill, very close to the fire, and would not move until a stench of burning cloth helped rouse him. Then he drank the bitter willow bark tea too and finally he slept.

Friday morning the sun came out again toward ten o'clock, the same cold, pale disk, with the snow still running along the earth, running higher than the shelter or Chuck, shutting out everything except the veiled sun. The boy came in, looked around the starved, listless circle at the fire, at the teacher too, with her face that had been so pretty Monday morning, gaunt and sooty now.

He laid two red-tipped matches, half of all he had, in the girl's lap. "I'm getting out," he said, and without a protest from anyone crawled through the hole and was gone.

The children were almost past noticing his desertion now, barely replying when spoken to. If the colds got worse or pneumonia struck, it would be over in a few hours. Maggie hadn't sat up since yesterday, lying flat, staring at the white storm blowing thin above the smoke hole. If any of them wondered how Lecia could keep the fire going alone, with nothing much except the willow butts left, none spoke of it. The teacher sat with her arms hanging between her knees, hopeless.

She finally stirred and put the matches away in waxed paper in her shirt pocket where her ring lay, buttoning the flap down carefully now. Joanie started to cough again, choking, turned red and then very white under the grime and grayness of her face, lying very still. Now Bill made the first gesture toward his small sister.

"Come here, Doll," he said gently, drawing her awkwardly from Lecia's lap, the child lifting her head slowly, holding herself away, looking up at him as a baby might at a stranger, to be weighed and considered. Then she snuggled against him and in a moment she was asleep.

After a long time there seemed a dull sound outside, and then Chuck was suddenly back, crawling in almost as though he had not left, panting in his weakness from the fight against the wind that had turned north again, and colder.

"Scared an eagle off a drift out there," he finally managed to say. "And there's a critter stuck in the snow—beyond the far willows. Small spring calf. Froze hard, but it's meat—"

Then the realization that Chuck was back struck the teacher. She was not alone with the children and he too was safe for now. But there was something more. The boy who had resented them and his involvement in their plight—he had escaped and come back.

"Oh, Chuck!" the girl exclaimed. Then what he said reached her mind. "A calf? Maybe we could build a fire there so we can cut some off, if we can't get it all out." She reached for her boots. "But we'll have to go work at it one at a time—" looking around the firelit faces that were turned toward her as before, but the eyes alert, watching as though a morsel might be dropped, even thrown.

"I'll go with Chuck, Miss Lecia," Bill said softly. "He can show me and I'll show you. Save time hunting—"

The teacher looked at the crippled boy, already setting Joanie gently aside and reaching for his brace. She felt pride in him and unfortunate doubt.

"He can probably make it," Chuck said, a little condescending. "It's not over an eighth of a mile, and I found more willows farther along the way, the drifts mostly frozen hard, too. I blazed the willows[5] beyond our poles—"

"You'll be careful—mark everything," the girl pleaded.

"We've got to. It's snowing again, and the sun's gone."

It seemed hours since the boys went out and finally the teacher had to go after them, appalled that the younger ones had to be left alone, yet it must be done. She moved very carefully, feeling her way in the new storm, going sideways to it, from pole to pole. Then she came to a place where the markers were gone, probably blown down and buried by the turning wind. The boys were out there, lost, in at least fifteen, perhaps twenty, below zero. Without sticks to guide her way back, the girl dared go no farther but she crouched there, bowed before the wind, cupping her mouth with her mittens, shouting her hopeless: "Boys! Chuck! O-hoo!" the wind snatching it away. She kept calling until she was shaking and frozen and then frighteningly warm.

But now she had to keep on, for it seemed that she heard something, a vague, smothered

sound and yet a little like a reply. Tears freezing on her face she called again and again until suddenly the boys were at her feet, there before she could see them, so much like the snow, like white dragging animals, one bowed, half carrying the other. For a few minutes they crouched together in desperate relief, the snow running over them as something immovable, like an old willow butt. Then, together, they pulled themselves up and started back. When they finally reached the shelter, out of breath and frozen, they said nothing of what had happened, nor spoke at all for a while. Yet all, even little Joanie, seemed to sense that the boys had almost been lost.

As soon as the teacher was warmed a little, she started out alone, not certain that she could make it against the storm, but knowing that she must try to get meat. She took Chuck's

_____

5. **blazed the willows**: made marks on the trees with a knife.

knife, some dry bark, waxed paper, the two matches in her shirt pocket, and a bundle of poles pulled from their shelter. Moving very carefully beyond the gap in the willow markers, she set new sticks deep, and tipped carefully with the new storm. She found the farther willow clumps with Chuck's blazing and the brush pile the boys had made and beside it the ice-covered head of the calf still reaching out of the snow. The hole they had dug around the red hindquarters, was drifted in loosely but easily dug out. Lecia set a fire pile there and felt for a match with her numb fingers, fishing in the depths of her pocket, something round in the way, her ring. But she got the match and lighted the fire under her shielding sheepskin coat. For a long time she crouched protectively over the flame, the wind carrying away the stench of burning calf hair. As the skin thawed, she hacked at it the way Indians must have done here a thousand years ago, their stone knives sharper and more expertly handled.

At a sound she looked over her shoulder and saw a coyote not three feet away, gaunt-

bellied too, and apparently no more afraid than a hungry dog. But suddenly he caught the human smell, even against the wind, and was gone. He would have made a soft rug at the fire, Lecia thought, and wondered if he might not return to watch just beyond the wall of storm. But she was too busy to look. As the heat penetrated the meat, she cut off one slice after another until she had a little smoky pile, not much for nine people who had lived five days on one lunch apiece, but enough to bring tears that were not all from the storm. In this meat, perhaps three pounds, might lie the life of her pupils.

Lecia scattered the fresh ashes over the calf to keep the coyotes away and piled brush into the fire hole. Then she headed sideways into the storm, so violent that it was a good thing she had the strength of a little cautious meat inside her, for it seemed no one could face the wounding snow. Numb and frightened, she managed to hold herself, not get hurried, panicked, never move until the next broken willow, the next marker was located. So she got back to find Chuck out near the shelter, digging wood from the old clumps, watching uneasy.

It was hard for the children to wait while the thinner slices of meat roasted around the sticks. When the smell filled the little shelter, Lecia passed out toasted bits to be chewed very slowly and well. It tasted fine and none asked for bread or salt—not even Olive, still silent and alone. She accepted the meat but returned only distant gravity for the teacher's smile.

By now the white blizzard darkness was coming back, but before they slept there was a little piece of boiled veal for each and a little hot broth. It was a more cheerful sleeping time, even a confident one, although in the night they were struck by the diarrhea that Lecia had expected. But that was from the fresh meat and should not last.

By now Lecia could build a coal bed with rotten wood and ashes to hold a fire a long time, even with diamond willows, and so she dressed Maggie's feet, the girl light as a sack of bird bones, and prepared the night fire. For a while Chuck and Eddie kept each other awake with stories of coyote hunts and with plans for another morning of storm, the sixth. The two boys met the day with so much confidence that Lecia had to let them go out into the storm. Eddie, only ten, suddenly became a little old man in his seriousness as he explained their plans carefully. They would make a big brush pile so that they could settle out of the wind and work the fire until they got a whole hind-quarter of the calf hacked off. So the teacher watched them go out very full of hope, the hope of meat, one of the half blankets along to drag their prize in over the snow, like great hunters returning.

Bill had looked sadly after the disappearing boot soles, but without complaint. He helped Lecia with the smaller children, washing at the grime of their faces that would never yield except to soap, and took them out into the storm and back while the teacher soaked Maggie's great swollen feet and tried to keep the girl from knowing that the bone ends of her toes could be seen in the suppurating pits of dying flesh. There were holes on the tops of the toes too, along the edges of her feet, and up the heels as high as the ankle. But above there the swelling seemed looser, the red streaks perhaps no farther up the bony legs. Once Bill looked over the teacher's shoulder and then anxiously into her face. Others had chilblains—his own feet were swollen from yesterday—but not like this.

"Will she lose—" he started to whisper, but he could not put the rest into words, not with a crippled foot himself.

The air was thick and white with new snow whipped by a northwest wind when Lecia went out for a little wood and to watch for the boys. But they were once more within touching distance before she could see them—very cold and hacking awkwardly into the storm through the soft, new drifts, but dragging a whole hindquarter of the calf. It was a lot of meat, and surely the wind must finally blow itself out, the clouds be drained.

By the time Eddie and Chuck were warm, they knew they had eaten too much roasted veal while they worked. Next Olive became sick, and Fritz, their deprived stomachs refusing the sudden meat, accepting only the broth. During the night the nausea struck Lecia too and left her so weak that she could scarcely lift her head all the next day. That night Chuck lost his voice for a while, and Joanie was worse again, her mind full of terrors, the cough so deep, so exhausting, that Bill made a little tent over her face with the skirt of his coat to carry steam from a bucket of boiling snow water to her face. Then sometime toward morning the wind turned and cut into the southeast corner of the shelter, crumbling the whole side inward.

The boys crawled out to patch it with brush and snow softened at the fire, Lecia helping dry off the children as much as she could. Then when they were done and she laid her swimming head down, she heard a coyote's thin, high howl and realized that the wind was dying. Through the smoke hole she saw the running snow like pale windrows of cloud against the sky and between them stars shining, far pale stars. As one or another awoke, she directed sleepy eyes to look up. Awed,

Joanie looked a second time. "You mean they're really stars—?"

"Yes, and maybe there will be sunshine in the morning."

Dawn came early that eighth day, but it seemed that nothing could be left alive in the cold whiteness of the earth that was only frozen scarves of snow flung deep and layered over themselves. The trailing drifts stretched down from the high ridge of hills in the north, so deep that they made a long, sliding slope of it far over the meadow and up the wind-whipped hills beyond, with not a dark spot anywhere to the horizon—not a yucca or fence post or willow above the snow. In the first touch of the sun the frozen snow sparkled in the deep silence following a long, long storm. Then out of the hills a lone grouse came cackling over the empty meadow, gleaming silver underneath as she flew, her voice carrying loud in the cold stillness.

But the meadow was not completely empty, for out of a little white mound of drifted willows a curl of smoke rose and spread thin and blue along the hill. There was another sound too, farther, steadier than the cackle of the grouse, a sound seeming to come from all around and even under the feet.

"A plane!" Chuck shouted hoarsely, bursting out into the blinding sunlight.

Several other dark figures crept out behind him into the frosty air, their breath a cloud about them as they stood looking northward. A big plane broke from the horizon over the hills, seeming high up, and then another, flying lower. Foolishly Chuck and Eddie started to shout. "Help! Hello! Help!" they cried, waving their arms as they ran toward the planes, as though to hasten their sight, their coming.

But almost at once the sky was empty, the planes circling and gone. For a long time the boys stared into the broad, cold sky, pale, with nothing in it except wind streaks that were stirring along the ground, too, setting feather curls of snow to running.

"Quick! Let's make a big smudge!" Lecia called out, her voice loud in the unaccustomed quiet and fearful. She threw water on the fire inside, driving smoke out of the hole while the boys set the snowy woodpile to burning.

Before the smoke could climb far, there were planes up over the north hills again, coming fast. Now even Fritz got out into the stinging cold—everybody except Joanie, held back by Lecia, and Olive, who did not move from her place. Maggie was lifted up by the teacher to watch through the smoke hole as something tumbled from the higher plane, came falling down. Then it opened out like the waxy white bloom of the yucca and settled toward the snow with several other smaller chutes, bright as poppies, opening behind.

There was shouting and talk outside the shelter and while Lecia was hurrying to get the children into their caps and boots, a man came crawling into the shelter with a bag—a doctor. In the light of the fire and a flashlight he looked swiftly at Joanie and then at Olive, considered her unchanging face, lifted the lids of her eyes, smiled, and got no response. Then he examined the poor feet of Maggie, the girl like a skin-bound skeleton in this first sharp light, her eyes dark and fearful on the man's face.

The doctor nodded reassuringly to Lecia and smiled down at Maggie.

"You're a tough little girl!" he said. "Tough as the barbed wire you have out in this country. But you're lucky somebody thought to try snow against the gangrene—" He filled a little syringe and fingered cotton as he looked around to divert the child.

"All nine of you alive, the boys say. Amazing! Somebody got word to a telephone during the night, but we had no hope for any of you. Small children lost eight days without food with fifty inches of snow at thirty-eight below zero. Probably a hundred people dead through the country. The radio in the plane picked up a report that six were found frozen in a car stalled on the highway—not over five miles from town. I don't see how you managed here."

The doctor rubbed the punctured place in the child's arm a little, covered it, smiling into her fearful eyes, as men with a stretcher broke into the front of the shelter.

When they got outside, the air was loud with engine roar, several planes flying around overhead, two with skis already up toward the shelter and a helicopter, hovering like a brownish dragonfly, settling. Men in uniform were running toward the children, motioning where they should be brought.

They came along the snow trail broken by the stretcher men, but walking through it as through the storm. Lecia, suddenly trembling, shaking, her feet unsteady on the frozen snow, was still in the lead, the others behind her, and Chuck once more at the end. Bill, limping awkwardly, carried little Joanie, who clung very close to her brother. They were followed by Calla and Eddie, with Fritz between them, and then the stretcher with Maggie. Only Olive of all the children walked alone, just ahead of Chuck and brushing aside all help.

There were men running toward the bedraggled, sooty little string now, men with cameras and others, among them some who cried, joyous as children, and who must be noticed, must be acknowledged soon—Olive's father and Dale Stever of the yellow plane—

But for now, for this little journey back from the smoke-holed shelter of snow, the awkward queue stayed together.

PART 2

Getting at Meaning

RECALLING

1. What does the teacher do to treat the children's fevers?

2. What do the children bicker about on the fourth day?

3. What does Chuck leave with the teacher when he departs?

4. What does Chuck find in the snow beyond the far willows?

5. What happens to Chuck and Bill when they go out to get some meat? Who rescues them?

6. How long does the snowstorm last?

7. Who finally comes to rescue the group? Who is the first of the rescuers to enter the shelter?

INTERPRETING

8. Lecia cuts enough meat from the frozen calf "to bring tears that were not all from the storm." What is the cause of Lecia's tears?

9. What is a smudge? How do Lecia and the children signal the airplanes?

CRITICAL THINKING: APPLYING

10. Lecia makes use of survival techniques that she has learned from her grandfather and from studying how the Native Americans of previous eras lived. From reading this story, what have you learned about surviving during a blizzard?

Developing Skills in Reading Literature

1. **Character.** A character is a person or animal who takes part in the action of a work of literature. Characters often change as a result of the events of a story. Chuck is one of the characters who changes during this story. How does Chuck feel toward Lecia and the children at the beginning of their ordeal? Why does he leave the group? Why does he return? What change does his return indicate? What other characters are changed by the events of the story? In what ways do these characters change?

2. **Setting.** Setting is the time and place of the action of a story. In this story the writer has used many vivid words and phrases to describe the setting. On a separate sheet of paper, list words and phrases from the story that describe each of the following:

> the sound of the blizzard
> the feeling of the wind, snow, and cold against the skin
> the shelter built by Lecia and Chuck
> the coming of night
> the sky through the smoke hole

3. **Suspense.** Suspense is a feeling of growing tension and excitement felt by a reader. Often a writer creates suspense by raising questions that are answered by subsequent events. This makes the reader want to continue reading to find out the answers to his or her questions. Look at the list of questions that you made for the exercise on Suspense on page 164. By the end of the story, were all of your questions answered? What were the answers to your questions?

4. **Theme.** The theme is the main idea of a work of literature. Often the theme is a message about human nature. This story is about survival. What is the significance of the last sentence in the story? What has enabled the group to survive? What does the last sentence have to do with the earlier episodes in which some of the children steal food? What theme is suggested by the last sentence?

Developing Vocabulary

Using a Dictionary: The Multiple Meanings of Words. Many of the words listed in a dictionary have more than one meaning. Consider, for example, the different meanings of the word *light* in the following sentences:

1. The fire threw a dancing *light* on the faces of the children.
2. Lecia was careful as she tried to *light* the damp match.
3. Carrying Joanie on her back through the blinding snow, Lecia realized that the child was not *light* enough to be held for a long time.
4. The wind that had blown so strongly now was *light*.

The many meanings of a word are listed as separate definitions in a dictionary entry. Look up in a dictionary the italicized word in each of the following sentences. On a sheet of paper, write the definition of the word as it is used in the sentence. Then, write a second sentence that uses the word in a different way.

1. "Then she swung off right along the barer edge of the gully, seeking a place to *cross.*"
2. "This time the *match* caught on the waxed paper and the diamond willow began to snap and sizzle in the snow."
3. "The girl held out something—the *ring* that had been left hanging on the twig and forgotten."
4. "The early settlers used willow *bark* to break a fever."
5. "Maggie hadn't sat up since yesterday, lying *flat,* staring at the white storm blowing thin above the smoke hole."
6. "A big *plane* broke from the horizon over the hills, seeming high up, and then another, flying lower."

Developing Writing Skills

Writing About a Short Story. Reread the exercises on Suspense on pages 164 and 172. Write a paragraph explaining how the writer of "Winter Thunder" created suspense in her story. Use your questions about the story and your answers to these questions as your prewriting notes. Begin your paragraph with the following sentence:

> Mari Sandoz creates suspense in "Winter Thunder" by raising questions in the minds of her readers.

This will be your topic sentence—the statement that you will try to prove in the body of your paragraph. Prove the statement by giving several examples of questions that the story raises and then answers. You may present your questions chronologically, in the order in which they are raised in the story. You may also choose to present your questions in order of importance. In either case, as you write and revise your paragraph, refer to **Using the Process of Writing** and to Writing About the Short Story on pages 614–625.

B I O G R A P H Y

Mari Sandoz (1901–1966) wrote about life in the Old West. Born in the Sand Hills of northwest Nebraska, she became a leading historian of the area. Her first book, *Old Jules,* won the *Atlantic Monthly's* $5,000 prize for nonfiction. Sandoz wrote several novels, including *Battle of the Little Big Horn* and *Miss Morissa. Hostiles and Friendlies* is a collection of her short stories.

ALBERT'S SON, 1959. *Andrew Wyeth*. National Gallery, Oslo.

Character

What Is Character?

Characters are the people or animals who take part in the action of a story. Usually, a short story centers on an event in the life of one person or animal. He or she is the main character. In most stories, the main character takes part in a struggle, or conflict. This conflict is the central focus of the story. The conflict almost always tests the main character in some way. This test brings out the true nature of the main character.

Most stories have one or more minor characters. Minor characters sometimes provide part of the background for the story. More often, however, minor characters interact with the main character and with one another. Their words and actions help to advance the plot, or events of the story.

Thinking About Characters

As you read the selections in this section, ask yourself, "What makes each character speak, act, and think as he or she does? Which of the characters in each story is the main character? What conflict does this character face?" If a character changes in some way, ask yourself, "How has the character changed? Why has this change taken place? Is the change for the better or worse?" Thinking about the characters in stories may help you to understand yourself and other people.

The day is beautiful, and Tom longs for freedom, but Aunt Polly has other plans.

The Glorious Whitewasher

Mark Twain

Saturday morning was come, and all the summer world was bright and fresh and brimming with life. There was a song in every heart; and if the heart was young, the music issued at the lips. There was cheer in every face and a spring in every step. The locust trees were in bloom, and the fragrance of the blossoms filled the air. Cardiff Hill, beyond the village and above it, was green with vegetation; and it lay just far enough away to seem a Delectable Land, dreamy, reposeful, and inviting.

Tom appeared on the sidewalk with a bucket of whitewash and a long-handled brush. He surveyed the fence, and all gladness left him and a deep melancholy settled down upon his spirit. Thirty yards of board fence nine feet high. Life to him seemed hollow and existence but a burden. Sighing, he dipped his brush and passed it along the topmost plank, repeated the operation, did it again, compared the insignificant whitewashed streak with the far-reaching continent of unwhitewashed fence, and sat down on a tree-box, discouraged. Jim came skipping out at the gate with a tin pail and singing "Buffalo Gals." Bringing water from the town pump had always been hateful work in Tom's eyes before, but now it did not strike him so. He remembered that there was company at the pump. White and black boys and girls were always there waiting their turns, resting, trading playthings, quarreling, fighting, skylarking. And he remembered that although the pump was only a hundred and fifty yards off, Jim never got back with a bucket of water under an hour—and even then somebody generally had to go after him. Tom said,

"Say, Jim, I'll fetch the water if you'll whitewash some."

Jim shook his head and said,

"Can't, Mars Tom. Ole missis, she tole me I got to go an' git dis water an' not stop foolin' roun' wid anybody. She say she spec' Mars Tom gwine to ax me to whitewash, an' so she tole me go 'long an' 'tend to my own business—she 'lowed *she'd* 'tend to de whitewashin'."

"Oh, never you mind what she said, Jim. That's the way she always talks. Gimme the bucket—I won't be gone only a minute. *She* won't ever know."

"Oh, I dasn't, Mars Tom. Ole missis she'd

take an' tar de head off'n me. 'Deed she would."

"*She!* She never licks anybody—whacks 'em over the head with her thimble—and who cares for that, I'd like to know. She talks awful, but talk don't hurt—anyways it don't if she don't cry. Jim, I'll give you a marvel.[1] I'll give you a white alley!"[2]

Jim began to waver.

"White alley, Jim! And it's a bully taw."[3]

"My! Dat's a mighty gay marvel, *I* tell you! But Mars Tom I's powerful 'fraid ole missis—"

"And besides, if you will I'll show you my sore toe."

Jim was only human—this attraction was too much for him. He put down his pail, took the white alley, and bent over the toe with absorbing interest while the bandage was being unwound. In another moment he was flying down the street with his pail and a tingling rear, Tom was whitewashing with vigor, and Aunt Polly was retiring from the field with a slipper in her hand and triumph in her eye.

But Tom's energy did not last. He began to think of the fun he had planned for this day, and his sorrows multiplied. Soon the free boys would come tripping along on all sorts of delicious expeditions, and they would make a world of fun of him for having to work—the very thought of it burnt him like fire. He got out his worldly wealth and examined it—bits of toys, marbles, and trash; enough to buy an exchange of *work,* maybe, but not half enough to buy so much as half an hour of pure freedom. So he returned his straitened means to his pocket, and gave up the idea of trying to buy the boys. At this dark and hopeless moment an inspiration burst upon him! Nothing less than a great, magnificent inspiration.

He took up his brush and went tranquilly to work. Ben Rogers hove in sight presently—the very boy, of all boys, whose ridicule he had been dreading. Ben's gait was the hop-skip-and-jump—proof enough that his heart was light and his anticipations high. He was eating an apple, and giving a long, melodious whoop, at intervals, followed by a deep-toned ding-dong-dong, ding-dong-dong, for he was personating a steamboat. As he drew near, he slackened speed, took the middle of the street, leaned far over to starboard and rounded to ponderously and with laborious pomp and circumstance—for he was personating the *Big Missouri,* and considered himself to be drawing nine feet of water. He was boat and captain and engine-bells combined, so he had to imagine himself standing on his own hurricane-deck giving the orders and executing them.

"Stop her, sir! Ting-a-ling-ling!" The headway ran almost out and he drew up slowly toward the sidewalk.

"Ship up to back! Ting-a-ling-ling!" His arms straightened and stiffened down his sides.

"Set her back on the stabboard! Ting-a-ling-ling! Chow! ch-chow-wow! Chow!" His right hand, meantime, describing stately circles—for it was representing a forty-foot wheel.

"Let her go back on the labboard! Ting-a-ling-ling! Chow-ch-chow-chow!" The left hand began to describe circles.

"Stop the stabboard! Ting-a-ling-ling! Stop the labboard! Come ahead on the stabboard! Stop her! Let your outside turn over slow! Ting-a-ling-ling! Chow-ow-ow! Get out that headline; *Lively* now! Come—out with your

---

1. **marvel:** *dialect:* marble.
2. **alley:** a fine shooting marble.
3. **bully taw:** a first-rate shooting marble.

spring-line—what're you about there! Take a turn round that stump with the bight of it! Stand by that stage, now—let her go! Done with the engines, sir! Ting-a-ling-ling! *Shiv't! shiv't! shiv't!*" (trying the gauge-cocks).

Tom went on whitewashing—paid no attention to the steamboat. Ben stared a moment and then said,

"Hi-*yi! You're* up a stump, ain't you!"

No answer. Tom surveyed his last touch with the eye of an artist, then he gave his brush another gentle sweep and surveyed the result, as before. Ben ranged up alongside of him. Tom's mouth watered for the apple, but he stuck to his work. Ben said,

"Hello, old chap, you got to work, hey?"

Tom wheeled suddenly and said,

"Why, it's you, Ben! I warn't noticing."

"Say—*I'm* going in a-swimming, *I* am. Don't you wish you could? But of course you'd druther *work*—wouldn't you? Course you would!"

Tom contemplated the boy a bit, and said,

"What do you call work?"

"Why, ain't *that* work?"

Tom resumed his whitewashing, and answered carelessly,

"Well, maybe it is, and maybe it ain't. All I know, is, it suits Tom Sawyer."

"Oh come, now, you don't mean to let on that you *like* it?"

The brush continued to move.

"Like it? Well, I don't see why I oughtn't to like it. Does a boy get a chance to whitewash a fence every day?"

That put the thing in a new light. Ben stopped nibbling his apple. Tom swept his brush daintily back and forth—stepped back to note the effect—added a touch here and there—criticized the effect again—Ben watching every move and getting more and more interested, more and more absorbed. Presently he said,

"Say, Tom, let *me* whitewash a little."

Tom considered, was about to consent; but he altered his mind.

"No—no—I reckon it wouldn't hardly do, Ben. You see, Aunt Polly's awful particular about this fence—right here on the street, you know—but if it was the back fence I wouldn't mind and *she* wouldn't. Yes, she's awful particular about this fence; it's got to be done very careful. I reckon there ain't one boy in a thousand, maybe two thousand, that can do it the way it's got to be done."

"No—is that so? Oh come, now—lemme just try. Only just a little—I'd let *you*, if you was me, Tom."

"Ben, I'd like to, honest injun; but Aunt Polly—well, Jim wanted to do it, but she wouldn't let him. Sid wanted to do it, and she wouldn't let Sid. Now don't you see how I'm fixed? If you was to tackle this fence and anything was to happen to it—"

"Oh, shucks, I'll be just as careful. Now lemme try. Say—I'll give you the core of my apple."

"Well, here— No, Ben, now don't. I'm afeard—"

"I'll give you *all* of it!"

Tom gave up the brush with reluctance in his face, but alacrity in his heart. And while the late steamer *Big Missouri* worked and sweated in the sun, the retired artist sat on a barrel in the shade close by, dangled his legs, munched his apple, and planned the slaughter of more innocents. There was no lack of material; boys happened along every little while. They came to jeer, but remained to whitewash. By the time Ben was fagged out, Tom had traded the next chance to Billy Fisher for a kite, in good repair; and when *he* played out, Johnny Miller bought in for a dead rat and a string to swing it with— and so on, and so on, hour after hour. And when the middle of the afternoon came, from being a poor poverty-stricken boy in the morning, Tom was literally rolling in wealth. He had, besides the things before mentioned, twelve marbles, part of a jew's-harp, a piece of blue bottle-glass to look through, a spool cannon, a key that wouldn't unlock anything, a fragment of chalk, a glass stopper of a

BOY KNEELING, date unknown. *Winslow Homer. Addison Gallery of American Art, Phillips Academy, Andover, Massachusetts.*

decanter, a tin soldier, a couple of tadpoles, six firecrackers, a kitten with only one eye, a brass doorknob, a dog collar—but no dog—the handle of a knife, four pieces of orange peel, and a dilapidated old window-sash.

He had had a nice, good, idle time all the while—plenty of company—and the fence had three coats of whitewash on it! If he hadn't run out of whitewash, he would have bankrupted every boy in the village.

Getting at Meaning

RECALLING

1. What task did Aunt Polly give to Tom? How does Tom feel about this task?

2. Ben gives Tom an apple in exchange for the privilege of whitewashing for a while. What do the other boys give Tom?

INTERPRETING

3. How does Tom usually feel about bringing water from the town pump? How does he feel about getting water on the day of this story? Why does he feel different than he normally does?

4. Ben at first teases Tom about having to whitewash the fence. Soon, however, he begs Tom to let him take over the job. What does Tom do to make Ben change his mind?

5. At the beginning of the day, Tom has "straitened means." What are "straitened means"? How does this situation change by the end of the day?

CRITICAL THINKING: EVALUATING

6. Would Tom Sawyer make a good leader? What leadership qualities does he have? What leadership qualities does he lack?

Developing Skills in Reading Literature

1. **Character and Conflict.** A character is a person or animal who takes part in the action of a work of literature. Conflict is a struggle between opposing forces. Who is the main character in "The Glorious Whitewasher"? What is the conflict, or difficulty, faced by this character? How does the character resolve this difficulty? What does the character reveal about himself in the process?

2. **Irony.** Irony is a contrast between what is expected and what actually exists or happens. At the close of this selection, the reader is told that "when the middle of the afternoon came . . . Tom was literally rolling in wealth." The narrator, or storyteller, then gives a list of the items that Tom has collected during the day. Why is it ironic to call these items "wealth"?

Developing Vocabulary

Types of Dictionaries and Jargon. There are two main types of dictionaries—unabridged and abridged. An unabridged dictionary is as complete as its writers and editors can make it. Most unabridged dictionaries of English contain entries for over six hundred thousand words. A typical abridged dictionary is shorter, containing only about one hundred thousand words. Therefore, an abridged dictionary is easier to carry around and use. However, unabridged dictionaries are more useful for looking up the spellings and definitions of uncommon words.

Uncommon words are often used in jargon, the language of a specialized area of activity. For example, in "The Glorious Whitewasher," Mark Twain uses a number of words from the jargon of sailors when describing Ben Rogers' imitation of a riverboat. The following are some jargon words from Twain's story. Look up these words in an unabridged dictionary. Then, on a piece of paper, write a definition for each word.

> hurricane-deck
> bight
> gauge-cock

Developing Writing Skills

Writing a Paraphrase. A paraphrase restates a written passage in simpler language or in a new form. The paraphrase expresses the same ideas as the original passage. It is in the same order and has about the same number of words as the original.

On page 177 of the story is a long, difficult paragraph that begins with the sentence: "He took up his brush and went tranquilly to work." Write a paraphrase of this paragraph. Begin by making prewriting notes. Follow these guidelines.

1. Read the entire paragraph several times.
2. Look up unfamiliar words in the Glossary or in a dictionary. Try to find simpler words that have the same meanings as the unfamiliar words. Include these simpler words in your notes.
3. Rewrite the long sentences in the paragraph. Shorten each long sentence by cutting words from it or by breaking it into two or three separate sentences.

Using your prewriting notes, and beginning with the first sentence in the paragraph, rewrite each sentence, one at a time. Try to put each idea in your own words, using as few of the words and phrases of the original as possible. When you revise, check to make sure that you have not changed the meaning of Twain's paragraph.

BIOGRAPHY

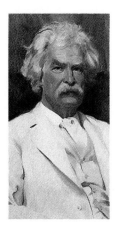

Mark Twain (1835–1910) was the pen name of Samuel Clemens, one of America's greatest humorists and storytellers. Twain grew up in Hannibal, Missouri, on the Mississippi River. His two most popular books, *The Adventures of Tom Sawyer* and *The Adventures of Huckleberry Finn,* are based upon his boyhood experiences in Hannibal. As a young man Twain worked as a printer, a riverboat pilot, and a journalist. Eventually, he began to make his living as a writer and public speaker. Twain traveled widely, lecturing and gathering materials for his novels, travel books, essays, and comic sketches. Mark Twain is known for his use of humor to draw attention to human failings and social injustice.

SAMUEL LANGHORNE CLEMENS, 1895. *Frank Edwin Larson.*
National Portrait Gallery, Smithsonian Institution, Washington, D.C.

What happens when the stingiest man in town lends his silver to the town trickster?

Shrewd Todie and Lyzer the Miser

Isaac Bashevis Singer

In a village somewhere in the Ukraine[1] there lived a poor man called Todie. Todie had a wife, Shaindel, and seven children, but he could never earn enough to feed them properly. He tried many trades and failed in all of them. It was said of Todie that if he decided to deal in candles, the sun would never set. He was nicknamed Shrewd Todie because whenever he managed to make some money, it was always by trickery.

This winter was an especially cold one. The snowfall was heavy and Todie had no money to buy wood for the stove. His seven children stayed in bed all day to keep warm. When the frost burns outside, hunger is stronger than ever; but Shaindel's larder[2] was empty. She reproached Todie bitterly, wailing, "If you can't feed your wife and children, I will go to the rabbi[3] and get a divorce."

"And what will you do with it, eat it?" Todie retorted.

In the same village there lived a rich man called Lyzer. Because of his stinginess he was known as Lyzer the Miser. He permitted his wife to bake bread only once in four weeks because he discovered that fresh bread is eaten up more quickly than stale.

Todie had more than once gone to Lyzer for a loan of a few gulden,[4] but Lyzer had always replied, "I sleep better when the money lies in my strongbox rather than in your pocket."

Lyzer had a goat, but he never fed her. The goat had learned to visit the houses of the neighbors, who pitied her and gave her potato peelings. Sometimes, when there were not enough peelings, she would gnaw on the old straw of the thatched roofs. She also had a liking for tree bark. Nevertheless, each year the goat gave birth to a kid. Lyzer milked her but, miser that he was, did not drink the milk himself. Instead he sold it to others.

---

1. **Ukraine** (yo͞o krān'): region of southwest Russia.
2. **larder:** pantry.
3. **rabbi** (rab' ī): the spiritual head and adviser of a Jewish congregation.
4. **gulden** (go͞ol' dən): unit of money.

Todie decided that he would take revenge on Lyzer and at the same time make some much-needed money for himself.

One day, as Lyzer was sitting on a box eating borscht[5] and dry bread (he used his chairs only on holidays so that the upholstery would not wear out), the door opened and Todie came in.

"Reb[6] Lyzer," he said, "I would like to ask you a favor. My oldest daughter, Basha, is already fifteen and she's about to become engaged. A young man is coming from Janev to look her over. My cutlery is tin, and my wife is ashamed to ask the young man to eat soup with a tin spoon. Would you lend me one of your silver spoons? I give you my holy word that I will return it to you tomorrow."

Lyzer knew that Todie would not dare to break a holy oath and he lent him the spoon.

No young man came to see Basha that evening. As usual, the girl walked around barefoot and in rags, and the silver spoon lay hidden under Todie's shirt. In the early years of his marriage Todie had possessed a set of silver tableware himself. He had, however, long since sold it all, with the exception of three silver teaspoons that were used only on Passover.[7]

The following day, as Lyzer, his feet bare (in order to save his shoes), sat on his box eating borscht and dry bread, Todie returned.

"Here is the spoon I borrowed yesterday," he said, placing it on the table together with one of his own teaspoons.

"What is the teaspoon for?" Lyzer asked.

And Todie said, "Your tablespoon gave birth to a teaspoon. It is her child. Since I am an honest man, I'm returning both mother and child to you."

Lyzer looked at Todie in astonishment. He had never heard of a silver spoon giving birth to another. Nevertheless, his greed overcame his doubt and he happily accepted both spoons. Such an unexpected piece of good fortune! He was overjoyed that he had loaned Todie the spoon.

A few days later, as Lyzer (without his coat, to save it) was again sitting on his box eating borscht with dry bread, the door opened and Todie appeared.

"The young man from Janev did not please Basha because he had donkey ears, but this evening another young man is coming to look her over. Shaindel is cooking soup for him, but she's ashamed to serve him with a tin spoon. Would you lend me...."

Even before Todie could finish the sentence, Lyzer interrupted. "You want to borrow a silver spoon? Take it with pleasure."

The following day Todie once more returned the spoon and with it one of his own silver teaspoons. He again explained that during the night the large spoon had given birth to a small one and in all good conscience he was bringing back the mother and newborn baby. As for the young man who had come to look Basha over, she hadn't liked him either, because his nose was so long that it reached to his chin. Needless to say that Lyzer the Miser was overjoyed.

Exactly the same thing happened a third time. Todie related that this time his daughter had rejected her suitor because he stammered. He also reported that Lyzer's silver spoon had again given birth to a baby spoon.

"Does it ever happen that a spoon has twins?" Lyzer inquired.

Todie thought it over for a moment. "Why

---

5. **borscht** (bôrsht): a Russian beet soup.
6. **Reb:** a Jewish title of respect equivalent to *Mister.*
7. **Passover:** a Jewish holiday lasting eight days.

not? I've even heard of a case where a spoon had triplets."

Almost a week passed by and Todie did not go to see Lyzer. But on Friday morning, as Lyzer (in his underdrawers to save his pants) sat on his box eating borscht and dry bread, Todie came in and said, "Good day to you, Reb Lyzer."

"A good morning and many more to you," Lyzer replied in his friendliest manner. "What good fortune brings you here? Did you perhaps come to borrow a silver spoon? If so, help yourself."

"Today I have a very special favor to ask. This evening a young man from the big city of Lublin is coming to look Basha over. He is the son of a rich man and I'm told he is clever and handsome as well. Not only do I need a silver spoon, but since he will remain with us over the Sabbath, I need a pair of silver candlesticks, because mine are brass and my wife is ashamed to place them on the Sabbath table. Would you lend me your candlesticks? Immediately after the Sabbath, I will return them to you."

Silver candlesticks are of great value and Lyzer the Miser hesitated, but only for a moment.

Remembering his good fortune with the spoons, he said, "I have eight silver candlesticks in my house. Take them all. I know you will return them to me just as you say. And if it should happen that any of them give birth, I have no doubt that you will be as honest as you have been in the past."

"Certainly," Todie said. "Let's hope for the best."

The silver spoon, Todie hid beneath his shirt as usual. But taking the candlesticks, he went directly to a merchant, sold them for a considerable sum, and brought the money to Shaindel. When Shaindel saw so much money, she demanded to know where he had gotten such a treasure.

"When I went out, a cow flew over our roof and dropped a dozen silver eggs," Todie replied. "I sold them, and here is the money."

"I have never heard of a cow flying over a roof and laying silver eggs," Shaindel said doubtingly.

"There is always a first time," Todie answered. "If you don't want the money, give it back to me."

"There'll be no talk about giving it back," Shaindel said. She knew that her husband was full of cunning and tricks—but when the children are hungry and the larder is empty, it is better not to ask too many questions. Shaindel went to the marketplace and bought meat, fish, white flour, and even some nuts and raisins for a pudding. And since a lot of money still remained, she bought shoes and clothes for the children.

It was a very gay Sabbath in Todie's house. The boys sang and the girls danced. When the children asked their father where he had gotten the money, he replied, "It is forbidden to mention money during the Sabbath."

Sunday, as Lyzer (barefoot and almost naked to save his clothes) sat on his box finishing up a dry crust of bread with borscht, Todie arrived and, handing him his silver spoon, said, "It's too bad. This time your spoon did not give birth to a baby."

"What about the candlesticks?" Lyzer inquired anxiously.

Todie sighed deeply. "The candlesticks died."

Lyzer got up from his box so hastily that he overturned his plate of borscht.

"You fool! How can candlesticks die?" he screamed.

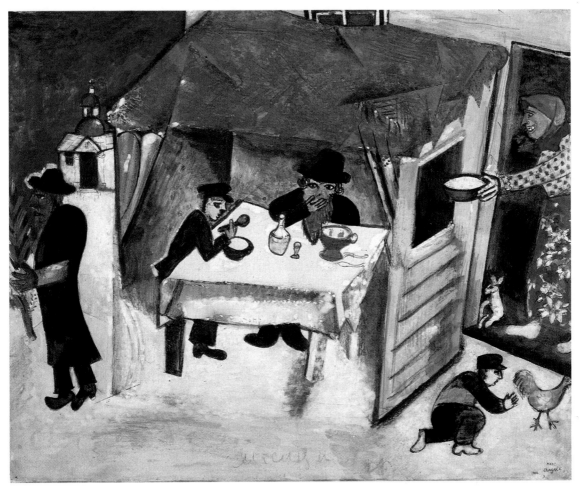

THE FEAST OF THE TABERNACLES, 1916. *Marc Chagall. Private Collection.*

"If spoons can give birth, candlesticks can die."

Lyzer raised a great hue and cry and had Todie called before the rabbi. When the rabbi heard both sides of the story, he burst out laughing. "It serves you right," he said to Lyzer. "If you hadn't chosen to believe that spoons give birth, now you would not be forced to believe that your candlesticks died."

"But it's all nonsense," Lyzer objected.

"Did you not expect the candlesticks to give birth to other candlesticks?" the rabbi said admonishingly. "If you accept nonsense when it brings you profit, you must also accept nonsense when it brings you loss." And he dismissed the case.

The following day, when Lyzer the Miser's wife brought him his borscht and dry bread, Lyzer said to her, "I will eat only the bread. Borscht is too expensive a food, even without sour cream."

The story of the silver spoons that gave birth and the candlesticks that died spread quickly through the town. All the people enjoyed Todie's victory and Lyzer the Miser's defeat. The shoemaker's and tailor's apprentices, as was their custom whenever there was an important happening, made up a song about it:

Lyzer, put your grief aside.
What if your candlesticks have died?
You're the richest man on earth
With silver spoons that can give birth

And silver eggs as living proof
Of flying cows above your roof.
Don't sit there eating crusts of bread—
To silver grandsons look ahead.

However, time passed and Lyzer's silver spoons never gave birth again.

Getting at Meaning

RECALLING

1. What are Todie's and Lyzer's nicknames? Why are they called by these names?

2. How successful has Todie been at the many trades he has tried?

3. Why does Todie hold a grudge against Lyzer?

4. What reason does Todie give Lyzer for needing to borrow the spoons? What reason does he give for needing to borrow the candlesticks?

5. What does Todie do with Lyzer's candlesticks? What explanation does he give to Lyzer for not returning them?

INTERPRETING

6. Why does Lyzer believe Todie's stories about spoons that give birth? What does this willingness to believe Todie's stories reveal about Lyzer?

7. Why does Lyzer agree to loan the candlesticks to Todie? What does Lyzer expect?

8. Does Todie's wife really believe the story about the flying cow? Why does she decide not to ask any questions? What does this reveal about her?

CRITICAL THINKING: EVALUATING

9. Despite the fact that Todie has cheated Lyzer, the Rabbi dismisses Lyzer's case. Why? Do you agree with the Rabbi's decision?

Developing Skills in Reading Literature

1. **Characterization.** Characterization is the use of literary techniques to reveal the nature of a character. There are two types of characterization, direct and indirect.

Direct characterization occurs when the narrator, or storyteller, makes direct comments about a character's appearance and personality. Find sentences in this story in which the narrator comments directly on the personalities of Todie and Lyzer.

Indirect characterization occurs when characters are revealed through their actions, words, and thoughts. What does Lyzer do or say to show that he is greedy? What does Todie do or say to show that he is shrewd?

2. **Hyperbole.** As you have learned, hyperbole is exaggeration. The line "I'm hungry enough to eat a buffalo" is hyperbole, or exaggeration to make a point. It creates a mental picture that is vivid and also humorous.

The sentence "It was said of Todie that if he decided to deal in candles, the sun would never set," is an example of hyperbole. What kind of picture do you get of Todie from this statement? Why is the statement humorous? Find two other examples of hyperbole in this story.

Developing Writing Skills

Writing Hyperbole. In "Shrewd Todie and Lyzer the Miser," Singer uses hyperbole to create humor and to paint vivid portraits of his characters. Imagine that you are writing a story for children. The characters in your story are a baker and a fox. The story tells how the hungry fox tricks the baker into leaving a pie unattended, which the fox then steals. On a sheet of paper, use hyperbole to describe the baker, the fox, and the baker's pies.

Copyright © Layle Silbert

B I O G R A P H Y

Isaac Bashevis Singer (born 1904) received the 1978 Nobel Prize in literature. Though he has lived in the United States since 1935, Singer still writes in Yiddish, the language of his birthplace, Radzymin, Poland. Singer uses simple, clear language in his folk stories, which are usually set in nineteenth century shtetls (small Jewish villages in Poland). His works include *The Manor, The Magician of Lublin,* and *The Family Moskat.*

Some secrets can be shared only between two really good friends.

A Secret for Two

Quentin Reynolds

Montreal[1] is a very large city; but, like all large cities, it has some very small streets. Streets, for instance, like Prince Edward Street, which is only four blocks long, ending in a cul-de-sac.[2] No one knew Prince Edward Street as well as did Pierre Dupin, for Pierre had delivered milk to the families on the street for thirty years now.

During the past fifteen years, the horse which drew the milk wagon used by Pierre was a large white horse named Joseph. In Montreal, especially in that part of Montreal which is very French, the animals, like children, are often given the names of saints. When the big white horse first came to the Provincale Milk Company, he didn't have a name. They told Pierre that he could use the white horse henceforth. Pierre stroked the softness of the horse's neck; he stroked the sheen of its splendid belly, and he looked into the eyes of the horse.

"This is a kind horse, a gentle and faithful horse," Pierre said, "and I can see a beautiful spirit shining out of the eyes of the horse. I will name him after good St. Joseph, who was also kind and gentle and faithful and a beautiful spirit."

Within a year, Joseph knew the milk route as well as Pierre. Pierre used to boast that he didn't need reins—he never touched them. Each morning Pierre arrived at the stables of the Provincale Milk Company at five o'clock. The wagon would be loaded and Joseph hitched to it. Pierre would call, *"Bonjour, vieil ami,"*[3] as he climbed into his seat; and Joseph would turn his head, and the other drivers would smile and say that the horse would smile at Pierre. Then Jacques, the foreman, would say, "All right, Pierre, go on," and Pierre would call softly to Joseph, *"Avance, mon ami,"*[4] and this splendid combination would stalk proudly down the street.

The wagon, without any direction from Pierre, would roll three blocks down St. Catherine Street, then turn right two blocks along Roslyn Avenue; then left, for that was Prince Edward Street. The horse would stop at the first house, allow Pierre perhaps thirty sec-

---

1. **Montreal** (män′ trē ôl′): city in Quebec, Canada.
2. **cul-de-sac** (kul′ də sak′): a passage with only one outlet.
3. *Bonjour, vieil ami* (bōn zhōōr′ vē yā′ lä mē′): *French:* Hello, old friend.
4. *Avance, mon ami* (a vôns′ mō′ nä mē′): *French:* Go ahead, my friend.

onds to get down from his seat and put a bottle of milk at the front door, and would then go on, skipping two houses and stopping at the third. So down the length of the street. Then Joseph, still without any direction from Pierre, would turn round and come back along the other side. Yes, Joseph was a smart horse.

Pierre would boast, at the stable, of Joseph's skill. "I never touch the reins. He knows just where to stop. Why, a blind man could handle my route with Joseph pulling the wagon."

So it went on for years—always the same. Pierre and Joseph both grew old together, but gradually, not suddenly. Pierre's huge walrus moustache was pure white now, and Joseph didn't lift his knees so high, or raise his head quite as much. Jacques, the foreman of the stables, never noticed that they were both getting old until Pierre appeared one morning carrying a heavy walking stick.

"Hey, Pierre," Jacques laughed. "Maybe you got the gout,[5] hey?"

"Mais oui,[6] Jacques," Pierre said a bit uncertainly. "One grows old. One's legs get tired."

"You should teach that horse to carry the milk to the front door for you," Jacques told him. "He does everything else."

He knew every one of the forty families he served on Prince Edward Street. The cooks knew that Pierre could neither read nor write; so instead of following the usual custom of leaving a note in an empty bottle if an additional quart of milk was needed, they would sing out when they heard the rumble of his wagon wheels over the cobbled street, "Bring an extra quart this morning, Pierre."

"So you have company for dinner tonight," he would call back gaily.

Pierre had a remarkable memory. When he arrived at the stable, he'd always remember to tell Jacques, "The Paquins took an extra quart this morning; the Lemoines bought a pint of cream."

Jacques would note these things in a little black book he always carried. Most of the drivers had to make out the weekly bills and collect the money; but Jacques, liking Pierre, had always excused him from this task. All Pierre had to do was to arrive at five in the morning, walk to his wagon, which was always in the same spot at the curb, and deliver his milk. He returned some two hours later, got down stiffly from his seat, called a cheery *"Au'voir"*[7] to Jacques, and then limped slowly down the street.

One morning the president of the Provincale Milk Company came to inspect the early morning deliveries. Jacques pointed Pierre out to him and said, "Watch how he talks to that horse. See how the horse listens and how he turns his head toward Pierre? See the look in that horse's eyes? You know, I think those two share a secret. I have often noticed it. It is as though they both sometimes chuckle at us as they go off on their route. Pierre is a good man, *Monsieur*[8] *Président,* but he gets old. Would it be too bold of me to suggest that he be retired and be given perhaps a small pension?" he added anxiously.

"But of course," the president laughed. "I know his record. He has been on this route now for thirty years and never once has there been a complaint. Tell him it is time he rested. His salary will go on just the same."

But Pierre refused to retire. He was panic-stricken at the thought of not driving Joseph every day. "We are two old men," he said

---

5. **gout** (gout): a disease marked by swelling and pain, especially in the hands and feet.
6. *Mais oui* (mā wē′): *French:* oh yes.
7. *Au'voir* (ō vwär′): *French:* goodbye.
8. *Monsieur* (mə syŭr′): *French:* sir; mister.

OLD MAN BY THE HORSE, 1915. *Frank Schoonover. Courtesy of Schoonover Studios, Wilmington, Delaware.*

to Jacques. "Let us wear out together. When Joseph is ready to retire—then I, too, will quit."

Jacques, who was a kind man, understood. There was something about Pierre and Joseph which made a man smile tenderly. It was as though each drew some hidden strength from the other. When Pierre was sitting in his seat, and when Joseph was hitched to the wagon, neither seemed old. But when they finished their work, then Pierre would limp down the street slowly, seeming very old indeed; and the horse's head would drop, and he would walk very wearily to his stall.

Then one morning Jacques had dreadful news for Pierre when he arrived. It was a cold morning and still pitch-dark. The air was like iced wine that morning, and the snow which had fallen during the night glistened like a million diamonds piled together.

Jacques said, "Pierre, your horse, Joseph, did not wake up this morning. He was very old, Pierre; he was twenty-five, and that is like being seventy-five for a man."

"Yes," Pierre said, slowly. "Yes. I am seventy-five. And I cannot see Joseph again."

"Of course you can," Jacques soothed. "He is over in his stall, looking very peaceful. Go over and see him."

Pierre took one step forward, then turned. "No...no...you don't understand, Jacques."

Jacques clapped him on the shoulder. "We'll find another horse just as good as Joseph. Why, in a month you'll teach him to know your route as well as Joseph did. We'll...."

The look in Pierre's eyes stopped him. For years Pierre had worn a heavy cap, the peak of which came low over his eyes, keeping the bitter morning wind out of them. Now Jacques looked into Pierre's eyes and saw something which startled him. He saw a dead, lifeless look in them. The eyes were mirroring the grief that was in Pierre's heart and his soul. It was as though his heart and soul had died.

"Take today off, Pierre," Jacques said, but already Pierre was hobbling off down the street; and had one been near, one would have seen tears streaming down his cheeks and have heard half-smothered sobs. There was a warning yell from the driver of a huge truck that was coming fast, and there was the scream of brakes; but Pierre apparently heard neither.

Five minutes later an ambulance driver said, "He's dead. Was killed instantly."

"I couldn't help it," the driver of the truck protested; "he walked right into my truck. He never saw it, I guess. Why, he walked into it as though he were blind."

The ambulance doctor bent down, "Blind? Of course the man was blind. See those cataracts?[9] This man has been blind for five years." He turned to Jacques, "You say he worked for you? Didn't you know he was blind?"

"No...no..." Jacques said softly. "None of us knew. Only one knew—a friend of his named Joseph.... It was a secret, I think, just between those two."

---

9. **cataracts** (kat′ ə rakts′): an eye disease causing partial or total blindness.

Getting at Meaning

RECALLING

1. Why does Pierre name his horse after St. Joseph?

2. Why doesn't Pierre have to touch the reins?

3. Why don't the cooks along Prince Edward Street leave notes for Pierre?

4. What suggestion does Jacques make to the president of the Provincale Milk Company?

5. What happens to Pierre immediately after he hears of Joseph's death?

6. What is Pierre's secret, and with whom does he share it?

INTERPRETING

7. What offer does the company president tell Jacques to make to Pierre? Why doesn't Pierre accept this offer?

8. What circumstances make it possible for Pierre to hide his blindness from his employer?

9. Why can't Pierre teach another horse his route?

10. What are the causes of Pierre's death?

Developing Skills in Reading Literature

1. **Character.** A character is a person or animal who takes part in the action of a story. Who is the main character in this story? Who are the minor characters? Briefly describe each character.

2. **Characterization.** Characterization is the use of literary techniques to reveal the nature of a character. Sometimes the nature of a character is revealed through his or her thoughts. How do you know that Pierre has a special feeling for horses in general and for Joseph in particular? Which of his words and actions reveal this about his character?

3. **Foreshadowing.** Foreshadowing is a writer's use of hints and clues to suggest events that will occur later. Early in this story Pierre says, "Why, a blind man could handle my route with Joseph pulling the wagon." This statement foreshadows the actual blindness that Pierre later develops.

After refusing to retire, Pierre says to Jacques, "When Joseph is ready to retire— then I, too, will quit." What event in the story does this statement foreshadow?

Developing Vocabulary

Using the Dictionary: French Words in English. The word *cul-de-sac* is a French word that has been borrowed by speakers of English. Many words in English were originally taken from French. The following is a list of some of these words. Use an English dictionary to find out what French words these words were taken from, what the original French words meant, and what the words now mean in English. Write out your findings in a simple chart, similar to the one on page 193.

prairie	debut
bureau	debris
tête-à-tête	debonair
dandelion	beau
glissade	envoy

Developing Writing Skills

Writing from a Different Point of View. This story is told from the third-person point of view. In other words, the narrator, or storyteller, is someone who stands outside the story and tells it using third-person pronouns such as *he, she,* and *it*. Write a paragraph from the first-person point of view, using first-person pronouns such as *I* and *me*. Imagine that you are Joseph, the horse, and that you have just been brought into the dairy for the first time. Pierre has come up to you and is speaking kindly. What do you think? How do you react to Pierre? What are your feelings toward this new person in your life? Explain all of these things in your paragraph.

Begin by recording in your prewriting notes the information given in the story about the first meeting between Joseph and Pierre. Also include notes about Joseph's possible thoughts, feelings, and other reactions. When revising, make sure that you have used a consistent point of view throughout. For help with this assignment, refer to **Using the Process of Writing** on pages 614–623.

Borrowing from Other Languages

English	French	Latin	Greek	Meaning
cone	cône	conus	kōnos	a geometrical figure
idol	idole	idolum	eidōlon	a likeness
myrtle	myrte	myrtillus	myrtos	a shrub
poem	poème	poema	poiēma	verse
topaz	topaze	topazus	topazus	a gem

Reading a Chart. The chart shows some English words borrowed from French. The origins of the French words go back to Latin and Greek. Read across the chart to find the origin of the word *cone*. What English word did the Latin word *topazus* become?

B I O G R A P H Y

Quentin Reynolds (1902-1965) worked as a journalist and reporter for several major newspapers. As a foreign correspondent during World War II, he covered the news from North Africa, Teheran, Palestine, and Europe. Thereafter, he wrote numerous books about the war and about famous people. Reynolds's books include *The Battle of Britain, Winston Churchill,* and *The Life of Saint Patrick.*

Luke learns more from Uncle Henry than Uncle Henry will ever know.

Luke Baldwin's Vow

Morley Callaghan

That summer when twelve-year-old Luke Baldwin came to live with his Uncle Henry in the house on the stream by the sawmill, he did not forget that he had promised his dying father he would try to learn things from his uncle; so he used to watch him very carefully.

Uncle Henry, who was the manager of the sawmill, was a big, burly man weighing more than two hundred and thirty pounds; and he had a rough-skinned, brick-colored face. He looked like a powerful man, but his health was not good. He had aches and pains in his back and shoulders which puzzled the doctor. The first thing Luke learned about Uncle Henry was that everybody had great respect for him. The four men he employed in the sawmill were always polite and attentive when he spoke to them. His wife, Luke's Aunt Helen, a kindly, plump, straightforward woman, never argued with him. "You should try and be like your Uncle Henry," she would say to Luke. "He's so wonderfully practical. He takes care of everything in a sensible, easy way."

Luke used to trail around the sawmill after Uncle Henry, not only because he liked the fresh, clean smell of the newly cut wood and the big piles of sawdust, but because he was impressed by his uncle's precise, firm tone when he spoke to the men.

Sometimes Uncle Henry would stop and explain to Luke something about a piece of lumber. "Always try and learn the essential facts, son," he would say. "If you've got the facts, you should know what's useful and what isn't useful, and no one can fool you."

He showed Luke that nothing of value was ever wasted around the mill. Luke used to listen and wonder if there was another man in the world who knew so well what was needed and what ought to be thrown away. Uncle Henry had known at once that Luke needed a bicycle to ride to his school, which was two miles away in town, and he bought him a good one. He knew that Luke needed good, serviceable clothes. He also knew exactly how much Aunt Helen needed to run the house, the price of everything, and how much should be paid for doing the family washing. In the evenings Luke used to sit in the living room watching his uncle making notations in a black notebook that he always carried in his vest pocket, and he knew that he was assessing the value of the smallest transaction that had taken place during the day.

Luke promised himself that when he grew up he, too, would be admired for his good, sound judgment. But, of course, he couldn't always be watching and learning from his Uncle Henry, for too often when he watched him he thought of his own father; then he was lonely. So he began to build up another secret life for himself around the sawmill, and his companion was the eleven-year-old collie, Dan, a dog blind in one eye and with a slight limp in his left hind leg. Dan was a fat, slow-moving old dog. He was very affectionate and his eye was the color of amber. His fur was amber, too. When Luke left for school in the morning, the old dog followed him for half a mile down the road, and when he returned in the afternoon, there was Dan waiting at the gate.

Sometimes they would play around the mill-pond or by the dam or go down the stream to the lake. Luke was never lonely when the dog was with him. There was an old rowboat that they used as a pirate ship in the stream, and they would be pirates together, with Luke shouting instructions to Captain Dan and with the dog seeming to understand and wagging his tail enthusiastically. His amber eye was alert, intelligent, and approving. Then they would plunge into the brush on the other side of the stream, pretending they were hunting tigers. Of course, the old dog was no longer much good for hunting; he was too slow and too lazy. Uncle Henry no longer used him for hunting rabbits or anything else.

When they came out of the brush, they would lie together on the cool, grassy bank being affectionate with each other, with Luke talking earnestly while the collie, as Luke believed, smiled with the good eye. Lying in the grass, Luke would say things to Dan he could not say to his uncle or his aunt. Not that what he said was important; it was just stuff about himself that he might have told to his own father or mother if they had been alive. Then they would go back to the house for dinner, and after dinner Dan would follow him down the road to Mr. Kemp's house, where they would ask old Mr. Kemp if they could go with him to round up his four cows. The old man was always glad to see them. He seemed to like watching Luke and the collie running around the cows, pretending they were riding on a vast range in the foothills of the Rockies.

Uncle Henry no longer paid much attention to the collie, though once when he tripped over him on the veranda he shook his head and said thoughtfully, "Poor old fellow, he's through. Can't use him for anything. He just eats and sleeps and gets in the way."

One Sunday during Luke's summer holidays, when they had returned from church and had had their lunch, they had all moved out to the veranda where the collie was sleeping. Luke sat down on the steps, his back against the veranda post. Uncle Henry took the rocking chair, and Aunt Helen stretched herself out in the hammock, sighing contentedly. Then Luke, eyeing the collie, tapped the step with the palm of his hand, giving three little taps like a signal; and the old collie, lifting his head, got up stiffly with a slow wagging of the tail as an acknowledgment that the signal had been heard, and began to cross the veranda to Luke. But the dog was sleepy; his bad eye was turned to the rocking chair; in passing, his left front paw went under the rocker. With a frantic yelp, the dog went bounding down the steps and hobbled around the corner of the house, where he stopped, hearing Luke coming after him. All he needed was the touch of Luke's hand. Then he began to lick the hand methodically, as if apologizing.

"Luke," Uncle Henry called sharply, "bring that dog here."

When Luke led the collie back to the veranda, Uncle Henry nodded and said, "Thanks, Luke." Then he took out a cigar, lit it, put his big hands on his knees, and began to rock in the chair while he frowned and eyed the dog steadily. Obviously he was making some kind of an important decision about the collie.

"What's the matter, Uncle Henry?" Luke asked nervously.

"That dog can't see any more," Uncle Henry said.

"Oh, yes, he can," Luke said quickly. "His bad eye got turned to the chair, that's all, Uncle Henry."

"And his teeth are gone, too," Uncle Henry went on, paying no attention to what Luke had said. Turning to the hammock, he called, "Helen, sit up a minute, will you?"

When she got up and stood beside him, he went on, "I was thinking about this old dog the other day, Helen. It's not only that he's just about blind, but did you notice that when we drove up after church he didn't even bark?"

"It's a fact he didn't, Henry."

"No, not much good even as a watchdog now."

"Poor old fellow. It's a pity, isn't it?"

"And no good for hunting either. And he eats a lot, I suppose."

"About as much as he ever did, Henry."

"The plain fact is the old dog isn't worth his keep any more. It's time we got rid of him."

"It's always so hard to know how to get rid of a dog, Henry."

"I was thinking about it the other day. Some people think it's best to shoot a dog. I haven't had any shells for that shotgun for over a year. Poisoning is a hard death for a dog. Maybe drowning is the easiest and quickest way. Well,

I'll speak to one of the mill hands and have him look after it."

Crouching on the ground, his arms around the old collie's neck, Luke cried out, "Uncle Henry, Dan's a wonderful dog! You don't know how wonderful he is!"

"He's just a very old dog, son," Uncle Henry said calmly. "The time comes when you have to get rid of any old dog. We've got to be practical about it. I'll get you a pup, son. A smart little dog that'll be worth its keep. A pup that will grow up with you."

"I don't want a pup!" Luke cried, turning his face away. Circling around him, the dog began to bark, then flick his long pink tongue at the back of Luke's neck.

Aunt Helen, catching her husband's eye, put her finger on her lips, warning him not to go on talking in front of the boy. "An old dog like that often wanders off into the brush and sort of picks a place to die when the time comes. Isn't that so, Henry?"

"Oh, sure," he agreed quickly. "In fact, when Dan didn't show up yesterday, I was sure that was what had happened." Then he yawned and seemed to forget about the dog.

But Luke was frightened, for he knew what his uncle was like. He knew that if his uncle had decided that the dog was useless and that it was sane and sensible to get rid of it, he would be ashamed of himself if he were diverted by any sentimental consideration. Luke knew in his heart that he couldn't move his uncle. All he could do, he thought, was keep the dog away from his uncle, keep him out of the house, feed him when Uncle Henry wasn't around.

Next day at noontime Luke saw his uncle walking from the mill toward the house with old Sam Carter, a mill hand. Sam Carter was a dull, stooped, slow-witted man of sixty with an

iron-gray beard, who was wearing blue over-alls and a blue shirt. He hardly ever spoke to anybody. Watching from the veranda, Luke noticed that his uncle suddenly gave Sam Carter a cigar, which Sam put in his pocket. Luke had never seen his uncle give Sam a cigar or pay much attention to him.

Then, after lunch, Uncle Henry said lazily that he would like Luke to take his bicycle and go into town and get him some cigars.

"I'll take Dan," Luke said.

"Better not, son," Uncle Henry said. "It'll take you all afternoon. I want those cigars. Get going, Luke."

His uncle's tone was so casual that Luke tried to believe they were not merely getting rid of him. Of course he had to do what he was told. He had never dared to refuse to obey an order from his uncle. But when he had taken his bicycle and had ridden down the path that followed the stream to the town road and had got about a quarter of a mile along the road, he found that all he could think of was his uncle handing old Sam Carter the cigar.

Slowing down, sick with worry now, he got off the bike and stood uncertainly on the sunlit road. Sam Carter was a gruff, aloof old man who would have no feeling for a dog. Then suddenly Luke could go no further without getting some assurance that the collie would not be harmed while he was away. Across the fields he could see the house.

Leaving the bike in the ditch, he started to cross the field, intending to get close enough to the house so Dan could hear him if he whistled softly. He got about fifty yards away from the house and whistled and waited, but there was no sign of the dog, which might be asleep at the front of the house, he knew, or over at the sawmill. With the saws whining, the dog couldn't hear the soft whistle. For a few minutes Luke couldn't make up his mind what to do; then he decided to go back to the road, get on his bike, and go back the way he had come until he got to the place where the river path joined the road. There he could leave his bike, go up the path, then into the tall grass and get close to the front of the house and the sawmill without being seen.

He had followed the river path for about a hundred yards, and when he came to the place where the river began to bend sharply toward the house, his heart fluttered and his legs felt paralyzed; for he saw the old rowboat in the one place where the river was deep, and in the rowboat was Sam Carter with the collie.

The bearded man in the blue overalls was smoking the cigar; the dog, with a rope around its neck, sat contentedly beside him, its tongue going out in a friendly lick at the hand holding the rope. It was all like a crazy dream picture to Luke; all wrong because it looked so lazy and friendly, even the curling smoke from Sam Carter's cigar. But as Luke cried out, "Dan, Dan! Come on, boy!" and the dog jumped at the water, he saw that Sam Carter's left hand was hanging deep in the water, holding a foot of rope with a heavy stone at the end. As Luke cried out wildly, "Don't! Please don't!" Carter dropped the stone, for the cry came too late; it was blurred by the screech of the big saws at the mill. But Carter was startled, and he stared stupidly at the riverbank; then he ducked his head and began to row quickly to the bank.

But Luke was watching the collie take what looked like a long, shallow dive, except that the hind legs suddenly kicked up above the surface, then shot down; and while he watched, Luke sobbed and trembled, for it was as if the happy secret part of his life around the sawmill was being torn away from him. But even while he watched, he seemed to be fol-

lowing a plan without knowing it, for he was already fumbling in his pocket for his jackknife, jerking the blade open, pulling off his pants, kicking his shoes off, while he muttered fiercely and prayed that Sam Carter would get out of sight.

It hardly took the mill hand a minute to reach the bank and go slinking furtively around the bend as if he felt that the boy was following him. But Luke hadn't taken his eyes off the exact spot in the water where Dan had disappeared. As soon as the mill hand was out of sight, Luke slid down the bank and took a leap at the water, the sun glistening on his slender body, his eyes wild with eagerness as he ran out to the deep place, then arched his back and dived, swimming under water, his open eyes getting used to the greenish-gray haze of the water, the sandy bottom, and the imbedded rocks.

His lungs began to ache; then he saw the shadow of the collie floating at the end of the taut rope, rock-held in the sand. He slashed at the rope with his knife. He couldn't get much strength in his arm because of the resistance of the water. He grabbed the rope with his left hand, hacking with his knife. The collie suddenly drifted up slowly, like a water-soaked log. Then his own head shot above the surface, and, while he was sucking in the air, he was drawing in the rope, pulling the collie toward him and treading water. In a few strokes he was away from the deep place and his feet touched the bottom.

Hoisting the collie out of the water, he scrambled toward the bank, lurching and stumbling in fright because the collie felt like a dead weight.

He went on up the bank and across the path to the tall grass, where he fell flat, hugging the dog and trying to warm him with his own body. But the collie didn't stir; the good amber eye remained closed. Then suddenly Luke wanted to act like a resourceful, competent man. Getting up on his knees, he stretched the dog out on its belly, drew him between his knees, felt with trembling hands for the soft places on the flanks just above the hipbones, and rocked back and forth, pressing with all his weight, then relaxing the pressure as he straightened up. He hoped that he was working the dog's lungs like a bellows. He had read that men who had been thought drowned had been saved in this way.

"Come on, Dan. Come on, old boy," he pleaded softly. As a little water came from the collie's mouth, Luke's heart jumped, and he muttered over and over, "You can't be dead, Dan! You can't, you can't! I won't let you die, Dan!" He rocked back and forth tirelessly, applying the pressure to the flanks. More water dribbled from the mouth. In the collie's body he felt a faint tremor. "Oh, gee, Dan, you're alive," he whispered. "Come on, boy. Keep it up."

With a cough, the collie suddenly jerked his head back, the amber eye opened, and there they were looking at each other. Then the collie, thrusting his legs out stiffly, tried to hoist himself up, staggered, tried again, then stood there in a stupor. Then he shook himself like any other wet dog, turned his head, eyed Luke, and the red tongue came out in a weak flick at Luke's cheek.

"Lie down, Dan," Luke said. As the dog lay down beside him, Luke closed his eyes, buried his head in the wet fur, and wondered why all the muscles of his arms and legs began to jerk in a nervous reaction, now that it was all over. "Stay there, Dan," he said softly, and he went back to the path, got his clothes, and came back beside Dan and put them on. "I think we'd better get away from this spot, Dan," he said. "Keep down, boy. Come on." And he crawled on through the tall grass till they were about seventy-five yards from the place where he had undressed. There they lay down together.

In a little while he heard his aunt's voice calling, "Luke. Oh, Luke! Come here, Luke!"

"Quiet, Dan," Luke whispered. A few minutes passed, and then Uncle Henry called, "Luke, Luke!" and he began to come down the path. They could see him standing there, massive and imposing, his hands on his hips as he looked down the path; then he turned and went back to the house.

As he watched the sunlight shine on the back of his uncle's neck, the exultation Luke had felt at knowing the collie was safe beside him turned to bewildered despair, for he knew that even if he should be forgiven for saving the dog when he saw it drowning, the fact was that his uncle had been thwarted. His mind was made up to get rid of Dan; and in a few days' time, in another way, he would get rid of him, as he got rid of anything around the mill that he believed to be useless or a waste of money.

As he lay back and looked up at the hardly moving clouds, he began to grow frightened. He couldn't go back to the house, nor could he take the collie into the woods and hide him and feed him there unless he tied him up. If he didn't tie him up, Dan would wander back to the house.

"I guess there's just no place to go, Dan," he whispered sadly. "Even if we start off along the road, somebody is sure to see us."

But Dan was watching a butterfly that was circling crazily above them. Raising himself a little, Luke looked through the grass at the corner of the house; then he turned and looked the other way to the wide blue lake. With a sigh he lay down again, and for hours they lay there together, until there was no sound from the saws in the mill and the sun moved low in the western sky.

"Well, we can't stay here any longer, Dan," he said at last. "We'll just have to get as far away as we can. Keep down, old boy," and he began to crawl through the grass, going farther away from the house. When he could no longer be seen, he got up and began to trot across the field toward the gravel road leading to town.

On the road, the collie would turn from time to time as if wondering why Luke shuffled along, dragging his feet wearily, head down. "I'm stumped, that's all, Dan," Luke explained. "I can't seem to think of a place to take you."

When they were passing the Kemp place, they saw the old man sitting on the veranda, and Luke stopped. All he could think of was that Mr. Kemp had liked them both, and it had been a pleasure to help him get the cows in the evening. Dan had always been with them. Staring at the figure of the old man on the veranda, he said in a worried tone, "I wish I could be sure of him, Dan. I wish he was a dumb, stupid man who wouldn't know or care whether you were worth anything.... Well, come on." He opened the gate bravely, but he felt shy and unimportant.

"Hello, son. What's on your mind?" Mr. Kemp called from the veranda. He was a thin, wiry man in a tan-colored shirt. He had a gray, untidy mustache, his skin was wrinkled and leathery, but his eyes were always friendly and amused.

"Could I speak to you, Mr. Kemp?" Luke asked when they were close to the veranda.

"Sure. Go ahead."

"It's about Dan. He's a great dog, but I guess you know that as well as I do. I was wondering if you could keep him here for me."

"Why should I keep Dan here, son?"

"Well, it's like this," Luke said, fumbling the words awkwardly. "My uncle won't let me keep him any more...says he's too old." His mouth began to tremble; then he blurted out the story.

"I see, I see," Mr. Kemp said slowly, and he got up and came over to the steps and sat down and began to stroke the collie's head. "Of course, Dan's an old dog, son," he said quietly. "And sooner or later you've got to get rid of an old dog. Your uncle knows that. Maybe it's true that Dan isn't worth his keep."

"He doesn't eat much, Mr. Kemp. Just one meal a day."

"I wouldn't want you to think your uncle was cruel and unfeeling, Luke," Mr. Kemp went on. "He's a fine man...maybe just a little bit too practical and straightforward."

"I guess that's right," Luke agreed, but he was really waiting and trusting the expression in the old man's eyes.

"Maybe you should make him a practical proposition."

"I—I don't know what you mean."

"Well, I sort of like the way you get the cows for me in the evenings," Mr. Kemp said, smiling to himself. "In fact, I don't think you need me to go along with you at all. Now, supposing I gave you seventy-five cents a week. Would you get the cows for me every night?"

"Sure I would, Mr. Kemp. I like doing it, anyway."

"All right, son. It's a deal. Now I'll tell you what to do. You go back to your uncle, and before he has a chance to open up on you, you say right out that you've come to him with a business proposition. Say it like a man, just like that. Offer to pay him the seventy-five cents a week for the dog's keep."

"But my uncle doesn't need seventy-five cents, Mr. Kemp," Luke said uneasily.

"Of course not," Mr. Kemp agreed. "It's the principle of the thing. Be confident. Remember that he's got nothing against the dog. Go to it, son. Let me know how you do," he added, with an amused smile. "If I know your uncle at all, I think it'll work."

"I'll try it, Mr. Kemp," Luke said. "Thanks very much." But he didn't have any confidence; for even though he knew that Mr. Kemp was a wise old man who would not deceive him, he couldn't believe that seventy-five cents a week would stop his uncle, who was an important man. "Come on, Dan," he called, and he went slowly and apprehensively back to the house.

When they were going up the path, his aunt cried from the open window, "Henry, Henry, in heaven's name, it's Luke with the dog!"

Ten paces from the veranda, Luke stopped and waited nervously for his uncle to come out. Uncle Henry came out in a rush, but when he saw the collie and Luke standing there, he stopped stiffly, turned pale, and his mouth hung open loosely.

"Luke," he whispered, "that dog had a stone around his neck."

"I fished him out of the stream," Luke said uneasily.

"Oh, oh, I see," Uncle Henry said, and gradually the color came back to his face. "You fished him out, eh?" he asked, still looking at the dog uneasily. "Well, you shouldn't have done that. I told Sam Carter to get rid of the dog, you know."

"Just a minute, Uncle Henry," Luke said, trying not to falter. He gained confidence as Aunt Helen came out and stood beside her husband, for her eyes seemed to be gentle, and he went on bravely, "I want to make you a practical proposition, Uncle Henry."

"A what?" Uncle Henry asked, still feeling insecure, and wishing the boy and the dog weren't confronting him.

"A practical proposition," Luke blurted out quickly. "I know Dan isn't worth his keep to you. I guess he isn't worth anything to anybody but me. So I'll pay you seventy-five cents a week for his keep."

"What's this?" Uncle Henry asked, looking bewildered. "Where would you get seventy-five cents a week, Luke?"

"I'm going to get the cows every night for Mr. Kemp."

"Oh, for heaven's sake, Henry," Aunt Helen pleaded, looking distressed, "let him keep the dog!" and she fled into the house.

"None of that kind of talk!" Uncle Henry called after her. "We've got to be sensible about this!" But he was shaken himself, and overwhelmed with a distress that destroyed all his confidence. As he sat down slowly in the rocking chair and stroked the side of his big face, he wanted to say weakly, "All right, keep the dog," but he was ashamed of being so weak and sentimental. He stubbornly refused to yield to this emotion; he was trying desperately to turn his emotion into a bit of good, useful common sense, so he could justify his distress. So he rocked and pondered. At last he smiled. "You're a smart little shaver, Luke," he said slowly. "Imagine you working it out like this. I'm tempted to accept your proposition."

"Gee, thanks, Uncle Henry."

"I'm accepting it because I think you'll learn something out of this," he went on ponderously.

"Yes, Uncle Henry."

"You'll learn that useless luxuries cost the smartest of men hard-earned money."

"I don't mind."

"Well, it's a thing you'll have to learn sometime. I think you'll learn, too, because you certainly seem to have a practical streak in you.

It's a streak I like to see in a boy. OK, son," he said, and he smiled with relief and went into the house.

Turning to Dan, Luke whispered softly, "Well, what do you know about that?"

As he sat down on the step with the collie beside him and listened to Uncle Henry talking to his wife, he began to glow with exultation. Then gradually his exultation began to change to a vast wonder that Mr. Kemp should have had such a perfect understanding of Uncle Henry. He began to dream of someday being as wise as old Mr. Kemp and knowing exactly how to handle people. It was possible, too, that he had already learned some of the things about his uncle that his father had wanted him to learn.

Putting his head down on the dog's neck, he vowed to himself fervently that he would always have some money on hand, no matter what became of him, so that he would be able to protect all that was truly valuable from the practical people in the world.

Getting at Meaning

RECALLING

1. How old is Luke?

2. With whom is Luke living? Why is he living with these people?

3. What reasons does Uncle Henry give for wanting to get rid of Dan? What does Luke do to save Dan from drowning?

4. Why does Luke go to see Mr. Kemp? What advice does Mr. Kemp give to him?

5. What vow does Luke make at the end of the story?

INTERPRETING

6. What kind of person is Uncle Henry? On what basis does he decide whether or not something is valuable?

7. When Luke watches Uncle Henry, he sometimes thinks about his father. What does Luke feel when this happens? Why, then, does Luke build up his "secret life" with Dan? What does Luke do in his secret life? What need does this secret life fulfill?

8. Uncle Henry is an exceptional person in many ways. However, there is an important side of life that Uncle Henry doesn't understand. What does Luke know about life that Uncle Henry doesn't?

Developing Skills in Reading Literature

1. **Characterization.** Characterization is the use of literary techniques to reveal the nature of a character. One way to show what a character is like is to tell how other characters react to him or her. What did Luke's father tell him concerning Uncle Henry? How is Uncle Henry treated by his employees and by Aunt Helen?

What does Mr. Kemp say to Luke about Uncle Henry? What do these other characters' reactions reveal about Uncle Henry's personality and values?

2. **Conflict.** A conflict is a struggle between opposing forces. In many stories the main character is in conflict with something outside himself or herself. Who is the main character? With what or whom is the main character in conflict? How is this conflict resolved?

3. **Theme.** The theme is the main idea of a work of literature. Often the theme is a message about human nature. What is the theme of "Luke Baldwin's Vow"?

4. **Irony.** Irony is a contrast between what is expected and what actually exists or happens. At the end of this story, Luke vows that he will always have some money on hand. Luke's vow leads the reader to think that Luke has decided to become a practical person like his uncle. However, the idea that Luke wants to be practical is contradicted by the last line of the story. What is the purpose for which Luke wants to have money? What is ironic about this?

Developing Writing Skills

Relating an Action. Reread the paragraphs on pages 198–199 that relate how Luke saved Dan from drowning. Notice the writer's use of vivid action verbs such as *dived, ache, slashed, grabbed, hacked, drifted, shot,* and *scrambled.* Also notice the use of vivid verbals, or words made from verbs, such as *glistening, treading, lurching,* and *stumbling.* These words help to make the action of the passage clear and exciting.

Write a paragraph that relates an action. Your paragraph may be about a series of events from a sporting contest, a movie, or a television program; or it may be about an action from your own experience. In your prewriting notes, list three vivid verbs and two vivid verbals that you can use to describe the action. Also list in your prewriting notes each event that you wish to include in your paragraph and place these events in chronological order. Refer to **Using**  **the Process of Writing** on pages 614–623 for help with the actual writing and revising of the paragraph.

B I O G R A P H Y

Morley Callaghan (born 1903) is a Canadian novelist and short story writer. He studied at the University of Toronto and received a law degree from Osgoode Hall Law School. During his college years he worked as a part-time journalist. When some of his stories were published, he decided to give up the idea of a law practice and try writing as a career. He has won numerous awards for his work. "The Snob" and "Luke Baldwin's Vow" are two of his most popular short stories.

It was Miss Caroline's first day in the school. Who was going to tell her about Walter Cunningham?

One of the Cunninghams

Harper Lee

Dill left us early in September, to return to Meridian. We saw him off on the five o'clock bus and I was miserable without him until it occurred to me that I would be starting to school in a week. I never looked forward more to anything in my life. Hours of wintertime had found me in the treehouse, looking over at the schoolyard, spying on multitudes of children through a two-power telescope Jem had given me, learning their games, following Jem's red jacket through wriggling circles of blind man's bluff, secretly sharing their misfortunes and minor victories. I longed to join them.

Jem condescended to take me to school the first day, a job usually done by one's parents; but Atticus had said Jem would be delighted to show me where my room was. I think some money changed hands in this transaction, for as we trotted around the corner past the Radley Place, I heard an unfamiliar jingle in Jem's pockets. When we slowed to a walk at the edge of the schoolyard, Jem was careful to explain that during school hours I was not to bother him. I was not to approach him with requests to enact a chapter of *Tarzan and the Ant Men,* to embarrass him with references to

his private life, or tag along behind him at recess and noon. I was to stick with the first grade and he would stick with the fifth. In short, I was to leave him alone.

"You mean we can't play anymore?" I asked.

"We'll do like we always do at home," he said, "but you'll see—school's different."

It certainly was. Before the first morning was over, Miss Caroline Fisher, our teacher, hauled me up to the front of the room and patted the palm of my hand with a ruler, then made me stand in the corner until noon.

Miss Caroline was no more than twenty-one. She had bright auburn hair, pink cheeks, and wore crimson fingernail polish. She also wore high-heeled pumps and a red-and-white-striped dress. She looked and smelled like a peppermint drop. She boarded across the street one door down from us in Miss Maudie Atkinson's upstairs front room, and when Miss Maudie introduced us to her, Jem was in a haze for days.

Miss Caroline printed her name on the blackboard and said, "This says I am Miss Caroline Fisher. I am from North Alabama, from Winston County." The class murmured apprehensively, should she prove to harbor[1] her share of the peculiarities indigenous to that region. (When Alabama seceded from the Union on January 11, 1861, Winston County seceded from Alabama, and every child in Maycomb County knew it.)

Miss Caroline began the day by reading us a story about cats. The cats had long conversations with one another; they wore cunning little clothes and lived in a warm house beneath a kitchen stove. By the time Mrs. Cat called the drugstore for an order of chocolate malted mice, the class was wriggling like a bucketful of catawba worms. Miss Caroline seemed unaware that the ragged, denim-shirted and floursack-skirted first grade, most of whom had chopped cotton and fed hogs from the time they were able to walk, were immune to imaginative literature. Miss Caroline came to the end of the story and said, "Oh, my, wasn't that nice?"

Then she went to the blackboard and printed the alphabet in enormous square capitals, turned to the class and asked, "Does anybody know what these are?"

Everybody did; most of the first grade had failed it last year.

I suppose she chose me because she knew my name. As I read the alphabet, a faint line appeared between her eyebrows. After making me read most of *My First Reader* and the stock-market quotations from *The Mobile Register* aloud, she discovered that I was literate and looked at me with more than faint distaste. Miss Caroline told me to tell my father not to teach me any more; it would interfere with my reading.

"Teach me?" I said in surprise. "He hasn't taught me anything, Miss Caroline. Atticus ain't got time to teach me anything," I added, when Miss Caroline smiled and shook her head. "Why, he's so tired at night he just sits in the living room and reads."

"If he didn't teach you, who did?" Miss Caroline asked good-naturedly. "Somebody did. You weren't born reading *The Mobile Register.*"

"Jem says I was. He read in a book where I was a Bullfinch instead of a Finch. Jem says my name's really Jean Louise Bullfinch, that I got swapped when I was born, and I'm really a "

Miss Caroline apparently thought I was lying. "Let's not let our imaginations run away with us, dear," she said. "Now you tell your father not to teach you any more. It's best to begin reading with a fresh mind. You tell him I'll take over from here and try to undo the damage—"

"Ma'am?"

"Your father does not know how to teach. You can have a seat now."

I mumbled that I was sorry and retired, meditating upon my crime. I never deliberately learned to read, but somehow I had been wallowing illicitly in the daily papers. In the long hours of church—was it then I learned? I could not remember not being able to read hymns. Now that I was compelled to think about it, reading was something that just came to me, as learning to fasten the seat of my union suit without looking around, or achieving two bows from a snarl of shoelaces. I could not remember when the lines above Atticus's moving finger separated into words, but I had stared at them all the evenings in my memory, listening to the news of the day, Bills To Be Enacted into Laws, the diaries of Lorenzo Dow—anything Atticus happened to be reading when I crawled into his lap every night. Until I feared I would lose it, I never loved to read. One does not love breathing.

---

1. **harbor:** cling to.

I knew I had annoyed Miss Caroline, so I let well enough alone and stared out the window until recess when Jem cut me from the covey of first-graders in the schoolyard. He asked how I was getting along. I told him.

"If I didn't have to stay, I'd leave. Jem, that lady says Atticus's been teaching me to read and for him to stop it—"

"Don't worry, Scout," Jem comforted me. "Our teacher says Miss Caroline's introducing a new way of teaching. She learned about it in college. It'll be in all the grades soon. You don't have to learn much out of books that way—it's like if you wanta learn about cows, you go milk one, see?"

"Yeah Jem, but I don't wanta study cows, I—"

"Sure you do. You hafta know about cows. They're a big part of life in Maycomb County."

I contented myself with asking Jem if he'd lost his mind.

"I'm just trying to tell you the new way they're teachin' the first grade, stubborn. It's the Dewey Decimal System."

Having never questioned Jem's pronouncements, I saw no reason to begin now. The Dewey Decimal System consisted, in part, of Miss Caroline waving cards at us on which were printed "the," "cat," "rat," "man," and "you." No comment seemed to be expected of us, and the class received these impressionistic revelations in silence. I was bored, so I began a letter to Dill. Miss Caroline caught me writing and told me to tell my father to stop teaching me. "Besides," she said. "We don't write in the first grade; we print. You won't learn to write until you're in the third grade."

Calpurnia was to blame for this. It kept me

RED OAKS, GEORGIA SCHOOLROOM, 1946. *Norman Rockwell. By permission of the Estate of Norman Rockwell. Copyright © 1946 Estate of Norman Rockwell.*

from driving her crazy on rainy days, I guess. She would set me a writing task by scrawling the alphabet firmly across the top of a tablet, then copying out a chapter of the Bible beneath. If I reproduced her penmanship satisfactorily, she rewarded me with an open-faced sandwich of bread and butter and sugar. In Calpurnia's teaching, there was no sentimentality: I seldom pleased her, and she seldom rewarded me.

"Everybody who goes home to lunch hold up your hands," said Miss Caroline, breaking into my new grudge against Calpurnia.

The town children did so, and she looked us over.

"Everybody who brings lunch put it on top of the desk."

Molasses buckets appeared from nowhere, and the ceiling danced with metallic light. Miss Caroline walked up and down the rows peering and poking into lunch containers, nodding if the contents pleased her, frowning a little at others. She stopped at Walter Cunningham's desk. "Where's yours?" she asked.

Walter Cunningham's face told everybody in the first grade he had hookworms. His absence of shoes told us how he got them. People caught hookworms going barefooted in barnyards and hog wallows. If Walter had owned any shoes he would have worn them the first day of school and then discarded them until mid-winter. He did have on a clean shirt and neatly mended overalls.

"Did you forget your lunch this morning?" asked Miss Caroline.

Walter looked straight ahead. I saw a muscle jump in his skinny jaw.

"Did you forget it this morning?" asked

Miss Caroline. Walter's jaw twitched again.

"Yeb'm," he finally mumbled.

Miss Caroline went to her desk and opened her purse. "Here's a quarter," she said to Walter. "Go and eat downtown today. You can pay me back tomorrow."

Walter shook his head. "Nome, thank you, ma'am," he drawled softly.

Impatience crept into Miss Caroline's voice: "Here Walter, come get it."

Walter shook his head again.

When Walter shook his head a third time, someone whispered, "Go on and tell her, Scout."

I turned around and saw most of the town people and the entire bus delegation looking at me. Miss Caroline and I had conferred twice already, and they were looking at me in the innocent assurance that familiarity breeds understanding.

I rose graciously on Walter's behalf: "Ah—Miss Caroline?"

"What is it, Jean Louise?"

"Miss Caroline, he's a Cunningham."

I sat back down.

"What, Jean Louise?"

I thought I had made things sufficiently clear. It was clear enough to the rest of us. Walter Cunningham was sitting there lying his head off. He didn't forget his lunch; he didn't have any. He had none today nor would he have any tomorrow or the next day. He had probably never seen three quarters together at the same time in his life.

I tried again: "Walter's one of the Cunninghams, Miss Caroline."

"I beg your pardon, Jean Louise?"

"That's okay, ma'am, you'll get to know all the county folks after a while. The Cunninghams never took anything they can't pay back —no church baskets and no scrip stamps.[2] They never took anything off of anybody; they get along on what they have. They don't have much, but they get along on it."

My special knowledge of the Cunningham tribe—one branch, that is—was gained from events of last winter. Walter's father was one of Atticus's clients. After a dreary conversation in our living room one night about his entailment,[3] before Mr. Cunningham left he said, "Mr. Finch, I don't know when I'll ever be able to pay you."

"Let that be the least of your worries, Walter," Atticus said.

When I asked Jem what entailment was, and Jem described it as a condition of having your tail in a crack, I asked Atticus if Mr. Cunningham would ever pay us.

"Not in money," Atticus said, "but before the year's out I'll have been paid. You watch."

We watched. One morning Jem and I found a load of stovewood in the back yard. Later, a sack of hickory nuts appeared on the back steps. With Christmas came a crate of smilax and holly. That spring, when we found a croker sack full of turnip greens, Atticus said Mr. Cunningham had more than paid him.

"Why does he pay you like that?" I asked.

"Because that's the only way he can pay me. He has no money."

"Are we poor, Atticus?"

Atticus nodded. "We are indeed."

Jem's nose wrinkled. "Are we as poor as the Cunninghams?"

"Not exactly. The Cunninghams are country folks, farmers, and the crash[4] hit them hardest."

---

2. **scrip stamps:** stamps allowing a person to receive food or clothing from the government.
3. **entailment:** Mr. Cunningham is having a legal problem about his inheritance of property.
4. **the crash:** the Stock Market Crash of 1929. Many people lost their homes, their farms, and their jobs as a result of this collapse in the economy.

Atticus said professional people were poor because the farmers were poor. As Maycomb County was farm country, nickels and dimes were hard to come by for doctors and dentists and lawyers. Entailment was only a part of Mr. Cunningham's vexations. The acres not entailed were mortgaged to the hilt, and the little cash he made went to interest.[5] If he held his mouth right, Mr. Cunningham could get a WPA job,[6] but his land would go to ruin if he left it, and he was willing to go hungry to keep his land and vote as he pleased. Mr. Cunningham, said Atticus, came from a set breed of men.

As the Cunninghams had no money to pay a lawyer, they simply paid us with what they had. "Did you know," said Atticus, "that Dr. Reynolds works the same way? He charges some folks a bushel of potatoes for delivery of a baby. Miss Scout, if you give me your attention, I'll tell you what entailment is. Jem's definitions are very nearly accurate sometimes."

If I could have explained these things to Miss Caroline, I would have saved myself some inconvenience and Miss Caroline subsequent mortification,[7] but it was beyond my ability to explain things as well as Atticus, so I said, "You're shamin' him, Miss Caroline. Walter hasn't got a quarter at home to bring you, and you can't use any stovewood."

Miss Caroline stood stock still, then grabbed me by the collar and hauled me back to her desk. "Jean Louise, I've had about enough of you this morning," she said. "You're starting off on the wrong foot in every way, my dear. Hold out your hand."

I thought she was going to spit in it, which was the only reason anybody in Maycomb held out his hand. It was a time-honored method of sealing oral contracts. Wondering what bargain we had made, I turned to the class for an answer, but the class looked back at me in puzzlement. Miss Caroline picked up her ruler, gave me half a dozen quick little pats, then told me to stand in the corner. A storm of laughter broke loose when it finally occurred to the class that Miss Caroline had whipped me.

When Miss Caroline threatened it with a similar fate, the first grade exploded again, becoming cold sober only when the shadow of Miss Blount fell over them. Miss Blount, a native Maycombian as yet uninitiated in the mysteries of the Decimal System, appeared at the door hands on hips and announced: "If I hear another sound from this room I'll burn up everybody in it. Miss Caroline, the sixth grade cannot concentrate on the pyramids for all this racket!"

My sojourn in the corner was a short one. Saved by the bell, Miss Caroline watched the class file out for lunch. As I was the last to leave, I saw her sink down into her chair and bury her head in her arms. Had her conduct been more friendly toward me, I would have felt sorry for her. She was a pretty little thing.

---

5. **mortgaged…interest:** Mr. Cunningham has borrowed money from the bank to pay for his land (mortgaged it) and must pay more money (interest) for the use of this loan.
6. **WPA job:** Works Progress Administration job. During the depression of the 1930's, the government created many public works jobs for the unemployed.
7. **mortification:** shame; embarrassment.

Getting at Meaning

RECALLING

1. What is Jean Louise's nickname?

2. How does Scout feel about starting school?

3. How do the children react to Miss Caroline's story about cats?

4. Who are the Cunninghams? How do they pay their debts? Why do they use this method?

5. How has Scout learned to read? How has she learned to write? What does Miss Caroline say about these accomplishments?

INTERPRETING

6. By recess on the first day, how have Scout's feelings toward school changed? Why have they changed?

7. Why does Walter Cunningham refuse the quarter offered by Miss Caroline?

8. Why does Miss Caroline punish Scout? What is the punishment? What do the children think of the punishment, and how does the reader know this?

9. Why does Miss Caroline bury her head in her arms after the students leave the classroom?

CRITICAL THINKING: APPLYING

10. What advice would you give to Miss Caroline to get her through her second day of school?

Developing Skills in Reading Literature

1. **Narrator.** The narrator is the teller of a story. Who is the narrator of "One of the Cunninghams"? How old is the narrator at the time of the story? In what ways is the narrator exceptional for someone at this age?

2. **Characterization.** Characterization is the use of literary techniques to reveal the nature of a character. In this story Walter Cunningham is characterized both directly, through comments made by the narrator, and indirectly, through his speech. What is Walter like? How does the reader know?

Someone else who is characterized both directly and indirectly is Miss Caroline. What direct comments does the narrator make about Miss Caroline's appearance and background? Which of Miss Caroline's actions show that she is unfamiliar with children like those in her class? Which of her actions show that she is confident about her new teaching methods? Which of her actions are insensitive? Which show a lack of experience? Which show that she is proud?

3. **Dialect.** A dialect is the variety of a language spoken by the people of a particular region or social group. There are four major regional dialects in the United States. Each major dialect is divided into local dialects. Every person speaks some dialect, generally that of the place in which he or she grew up.

Sometimes, when writing the dialogue, or speech, of a character, a writer will spell words as they are pronounced in the character's dialect. For example, in this story, Walter Cunningham's first answer to Miss Caroline's questions is written as *Yeb'm.* This spelling shows how Walter pronounces the words *Yes, ma'am.* Find three more examples in this story of spellings that have been changed to show the pronunciation of words in a character's dialect.

Developing Vocabulary

Using a Glossary. This story contains many difficult words. Most of these words are defined in the Glossary at the back of the book. Read the following sentences from the story. Look up the meanings of the italicized words in the Glossary. Write the words and their definitions on a separate sheet of paper.

1. "Hours of wintertime had found me in the treehouse, looking over at the schoolyard, spying on *multitudes* of children through a two-power telescope Jem had given me."

2. "Jem *condescended* to take me to school the first day."

3. "The class murmured *apprehensively,* should she prove to harbor her share of the *peculiarities indigenous* to that region."

4. "I never deliberately learned to read, but somehow I had been wallowing *illicitly* in the daily papers."

5. "I let well enough alone and stared out the window until recess when Jem cut me from the *covey* of first-graders in the schoolyard."

6. "In Calpurnia's teaching there was no *sentimentality.*"

7. "Entailment was only a part of Mr. Cunningham's *vexations.*"

8. "My *sojourn* in the corner was a short one."

Developing Writing Skills

Retelling Events from a Different Point of View. Imagine that you are Miss Caroline Fisher. Write a letter to a friend in Winston County telling what happened in your classroom on the first morning of school. Do not change any of the events of the story. However, present these events as Miss Caroline would view them. In your prewriting notes, list the events of the story in the order in which they occur. Next to each event, make a note about how Miss Caroline must have been feeling at the time. As you write and revise your letter, refer to **Using the Process of Writing** on pages 614–623 if you need help.

B I O G R A P H Y

Harper Lee (born 1926) writes slowly and carefully, generally producing only one or two pages of manuscript a day. Though it took a long time to write, her first novel, *To Kill a Mockingbird,* was a popular and critical success. It won many awards, including the 1961 Pulitzer Prize. The book has been translated into ten languages and was made into a movie starring Gregory Peck. Lee, who is related to Robert E. Lee, continues work on short stories and novels at her home in Monroeville, Alabama, the town where she was born. She attended Huntington College, spent a year at Oxford, and studied law at the University of Alabama.

The Richer, the Poorer

Dorothy West

Over the years Lottie had urged Bess to prepare for her old age. Over the years Bess had lived each day as if there were no other. Now they were both past sixty, the time for summing up. Lottie had a bank account that had never grown lean. Bess had the clothes on her back and the rest of her worldly possessions in a battered suitcase.

Lottie had hated being a child, hearing her parents' skimping and scraping. Bess had never seemed to notice. All she ever wanted was to go outside and play. She learned to skate on borrowed skates. She rode a borrowed bicycle. Lottie couldn't wait to grow up and buy herself the best of everything.

As soon as anyone would hire her, Lottie put herself to work. She minded babies; she ran errands for the old.

She never touched a penny of her money, though her child's mouth watered for ice cream and candy. But she could not bear to share with Bess, who never had anything to share with her. When the dimes began to add up to dollars, she lost her taste for sweets.

By the time she was twelve, she was clerking after school in a small variety store. Saturdays she worked as long as she was wanted. She decided to keep her money for clothes. When she entered high school, she would wear a wardrobe that neither she nor anyone else would be able to match.

But her freshman year found her unable to indulge so frivolous a whim, particularly when her admiring instructors advised her to think seriously of college. No one in her family had ever gone to college, and certainly Bess would never get there. She would show them all what she could do, if she put her mind to it. She began to bank her money, and her bank became her most private and precious possession.

In her third year in high school, she found a job in a small but expanding restaurant, where she cashiered from the busy hour until closing. In her last year in high school, the business increased so rapidly that Lottie was faced with the choice of staying in school or working full-time. She made her choice easily. A job in hand was worth two in the future.

Bess had a beau[1] in the school band, who

___

1. **beau** (bō): boyfriend, sweetheart.

had no other ambition except to play a horn. Lottie expected to be settled with a home and family while Bess was still waiting for Harry to earn enough to buy a marriage license.

That Bess married Harry straight out of high school was not surprising. That Lottie never married at all was not really surprising either. Two or three times she was halfway persuaded, but to give up a job that paid well for a homemaking job that paid nothing was a risk she was incapable of taking.

Bess's married life was nothing for Lottie to envy. She and Harry lived like gypsies, Harry playing in second-rate bands all over the country, even getting himself and Bess stranded in Europe. They were often in rags and never in riches.

Bess grieved because she had no child, not having sense enough to know she was better off without one. Lottie was certainly better off without nieces and nephews to feel sorry for. Very likely Bess would have dumped them on her doorstep.

That Lottie had a doorstep they might have been left on was only because her boss, having bought a second house, offered Lottie his first house at a price so low and terms so reasonable that it would have been like losing money to refuse.

She shut off the rooms she didn't use, letting them go to rack and ruin. Since she ate her meals out, she had no food at home and did not encourage callers, who always expected a cup of tea.

Her way of life was mean and miserly, but she did not know it. She thought she lived frugally in her middle years so that she could live in comfort and ease when she most needed peace of mind.

The years, after forty, began to race. Suddenly Lottie was sixty and retired from her job by her boss's son, who had no sentimental feeling about keeping her on until she was ready to quit.

She made several attempts to find other employment, but her dowdy appearance made her look old and inefficient. For the first time in her life Lottie would gladly have worked for nothing, to have some place to go, something to do with her day.

Harry died abroad, in a third-rate hotel, with Bess weeping as hard as if he had left her a fortune. He had left her nothing but his horn. There wasn't even money for her passage home.

Lottie, trapped by the blood tie, knew she would not only have to send for her sister but take her in when she returned. It didn't seem fair that Bess should reap the harvest of Lottie's lifetime of self-denial.

It took Lottie a week to get a bedroom ready, a week of hard work and hard cash. There was everything to do, everything to replace or paint. When she was through, the room looked so fresh and new that Lottie felt she deserved it more than Bess.

She would let Bess have her room, but the mattress was so lumpy, the carpet so worn, the curtains so threadbare that Lottie's conscience pricked her. She supposed she would have to redo that room, too, and went about doing it with an eagerness that she mistook for haste.

When she was through upstairs, she was shocked to see how dismal downstairs looked by comparison. She tried to ignore it, but with nowhere to go to escape it, the contrast grew more intolerable.

She worked her way from kitchen to parlor, persuading herself she was only putting the rooms to right to give herself something to do. At night she slept like a child after a long and happy day of playing house. She was having more fun than she had ever had in her life. She was living each hour for itself.

SUNDAY OUTING, 1974. *Reginald Gammon, Collection of Mrs. Russe Jackson, Philadelphia.*

There was only a day now before Bess would arrive. Passing her gleaming mirrors, at first with vague awareness, then with painful clarity, Lottie saw herself as others saw her and could not stand the sight. She went on a spending spree from specialty shops to beauty salon, emerging transformed into a woman who believed in miracles.

She was in the kitchen basting a turkey when Bess rang the bell. Her heart raced, and she wondered if the heat from the oven was responsible. She went to the door, and Bess stood before her. Stiffly she suffered Bess's embrace, her heart racing harder, her eyes suddenly smarting from the onrush of cold air.

"Oh, Lottie, it's good to see you," Bess said, but saying nothing about Lottie's splendid appearance. Upstairs, Bess, putting down her shabby suitcase, said, "I'll sleep like a rock tonight," without a word of praise for her lovely room. At the lavish table, top-heavy with turkey, Bess said, "I'll take light and dark both," with no marveling at the size of the bird or that there was turkey for two elderly women, one of them too poor to buy her own bread.

With the glow of good food in her stomach, Bess began to spin stories. They were rich with places and people, most of them lowly, all of them magnificent. Her face reflected her telling, the joys and sorrows of her remembering, and above all, the love she lived by that enhanced the poorest place, the humblest person.

Then it was that Lottie knew why Bess had made no mention of her finery, or the shining room, or the twelve-pound turkey. She had not even seen them. Tomorrow she would see the room as it really looked and Lottie as she really looked and the warmed-over turkey in its second-day glory. Tonight she saw only what she had come seeking, a place in her sister's home and heart.

She said, "That's enough about me. How have the years used you?"

"It was me who didn't use them," said Lottie wistfully. "I saved for them. I forgot the best of them would go without my ever spending a day or a dollar enjoying them. That's my life story in those few words, a life never lived. Now it's too near the end to try."

Bess said, "To know how much there is to know is the beginning of learning to live. Don't count the years that are left us. At our time of life it's the days that count. You've too much catching up to do to waste a minute of a waking hour feeling sorry for yourself."

Lottie grinned, a real wide-open grin, "Well, to tell the truth I felt sorry for you. Maybe, if I had any sense, I'd feel sorry for myself, after all. I know I'm too old to kick up my heels, but I'm going to let you show me how. If I land on my head, I guess it won't matter. I feel giddy already, and I like it."

Getting at Meaning

RECALLING

1. At what job does Lottie work when she is twelve? What does she save her money for?

2. When she is in high school, what becomes Lottie's most private and precious possession?

3. At what job does Lottie begin working during her third year in high school?

4. What does Bess do immediately after high school?

5. What does Bess's husband do for a living? How successful is he financially?

6. How does Lottie acquire her house?

7. How does Lottie finally lose her job? Why can't she find another one?

8. What does Lottie do to prepare for Bess's arrival? Why does Bess come to stay with her?

INTERPRETING

9. Why doesn't Lottie buy the clothes that she had planned to buy as a child? Why doesn't she go to college? Why doesn't she get married? Why does she allow some of the rooms in her house to go "to rack and ruin"? What can you conclude about her from this information?

10. How does Lottie feel at first about her sister's coming to stay with her?

11. Why does Lottie enjoy fixing up her house as much as she does?

12. Bess fails to praise Lottie's finery, the newly decorated room, and the turkey dinner. How does this make Lottie feel?

13. What change takes place in Lottie when she hears Bess's stories? What does Lottie realize about her own life? What change does she plan to make in the way she lives?

14. How do you imagine Lottie and Bess will busy themselves in the coming days?

CRITICAL THINKING: EVALUATING

15. Which of the two sisters has lived the more fulfilling life? What do you think Lottie would do differently if she had her life to live over?

Developing Skills in Reading Literature

1. **Foil.** A foil is a character who provides a striking contrast to another character. In this story, Bess acts as a foil for Lottie. Divide a sheet of paper into two columns. Label one column *Bess* and the other *Lottie.* List the contrasts between the two sisters, following this example:

Bess	Lottie
As a child, all she wanted to do was to go outside and play.	She spent her childhood wanting to grow up.

2. **Theme.** The theme is the main idea of a work of literature. Often the theme is a message about human nature. In this story the theme is the lesson about life that Bess teaches Lottie. What is this lesson? What is the meaning of the title of the story?

Developing Vocabulary

1. **Using the Dictionary: Parts of Speech.** In dictionary entries, special abbreviations are used to identify the part of speech a word is. A list of these abbreviations is given at the beginning of most dictionaries. Consider the following sample entry:

dis•mal (diz´m'l) *adj.* [ME., originally a noun, evil days < OFr. < ML. *dies mali*] **1.** causing gloom or misery *[dismal* news] **2.** dark and gloomy; bleak; dreary *[a dismal* room] **3.** depressed; miserable —**dis'mal•ly** *adv.*

The abbreviation *adj.* tells you that *dismal* is an adjective, a word that is used to modify a noun or a pronoun. Look up the following words in a dictionary and tell the part of speech for each word.

frivolous   errand
dowdy   retire

2. **Words Used as Different Parts of Speech.** Many words can be used as two or more parts of speech. Consider this sentence from "The Richer, the Poorer":

"She began to *bank* her money, and her *bank* became her most private and precious possession."

In this sentence, *bank* is used first as a verb and then as a noun.

When a word can be used as more than one part of speech, this is shown in the dictionary entry for the word. Look up the following words in a dictionary. On a separate sheet of paper, write each word and the parts of speech given for it in the dictionary entry.

risk   sum
clerk   skate

For each of these words, write two sentences, each using the word as a different part of speech.

B I O G R A P H Y

Dorothy West (born 1910) grew up in Boston. After attending Boston University and the Columbia University School of Journalism, she worked as a magazine editor. During the Depression, a period of extreme economic hardship in the 1930's, she was employed as a relief investigator in Harlem. Moved by what she saw in Harlem, West soon began to write short stories based on her experiences. These stories have been published in newspapers throughout the United States. Her novel, *The Living Is Easy,* appeared in 1948.

Do you take for granted the things you love the most?

Home

Gwendolyn Brooks

What had been wanted was this always, this always to last, the talking softly on this porch, with the snake plant in the jardiniere in the southwest corner and the obstinate slip from Aunt Eppie's magnificent Michigan fern at the left side of the friendly door. Mama, Maud Martha, and Helen rocked slowly in their rocking chairs and looked at the late afternoon light on the lawn and at the emphatic iron of the fence and at the poplar tree.

These things might soon be theirs no longer. Those shafts and pools of light, the tree, the graceful iron, might soon be viewed possessively by different eyes.

Papa was to have gone that noon, during his lunch hour, to the office of the Home Owners' Loan. If he had not succeeded in getting another extension, they would be leaving this house in which they had lived for more than fourteen years. There was little hope. The Home Owners' Loan was hard. They sat, making their plans.

"We'll be moving into a nice flat[1] somewhere," said Mama. "Somewhere on South Park, or Michigan, or in Washington Park Court." Those flats, as the girls and Mama knew well, were burdens on wages twice the size of Papa's. This was not mentioned now.

"They're much prettier than this old house," said Helen. "I have friends I'd just as soon not bring here. And I have other friends that wouldn't come down this far for anything, unless they were in a taxi."

Yesterday, Maud Martha would have attacked her. Tomorrow she might. Today she said nothing. She merely gazed at a little hopping robin in the tree, her tree, and tried to keep the fronts of her eyes dry.

"Well, I do know," said Mama, turning her hands over and over, "that I've been getting tireder and tireder of doing that firing. From October to April, there's firing to be done."

"But lately we've been helping, Harry and I," said Maud Martha. "And sometimes in March and April and in October, and even in November, we could build a little fire in the fireplace. Sometimes the weather was just right for that."

---

1. **flat:** an apartment.

JACKS, 1985. *Ethel Sanderson. Collection of the Artist, Chicago.*

She knew, from the way they looked at her, that this had been a mistake. They did not want to cry.

But she felt that the little line of white, somewhat ridged with smoked purple, and all that cream-shot saffron, would never drift across any western sky except that in back of this house. The rain would drum with as sweet a dullness nowhere but here. The birds on South Park were mechanical birds, no better than the poor caught canaries in those "rich" women's sun parlors.

"It's just going to kill Papa!" burst out Maud Martha. "He loves this house! He *lives* for this house!"

"He lives for us," said Helen. "It's us he loves. He wouldn't want the house, except for us."

"And he'll have us," added Mama, "wherever."

"You know," Helen sighed, "if you want to know the truth, this is a relief. If this hadn't come up, we would have gone on, just dragged on, hanging out here forever."

"It might," allowed Mama, "be an act of God. God may just have reached down, and picked up the reins."

"Yes," Maud Martha cracked in, "that's what you always say—that God knows best."

Her mother looked at her quickly, decided the statement was not suspect, looked away.

Helen saw Papa coming. "There's Papa," said Helen.

They could not tell a thing from the way Papa was walking. It was that same dear little staccato walk, one shoulder down, then the other, then repeat, and repeat. They watched his progress. He passed the Kennedy's, he passed the vacant lot, he passed Mrs. Blakemore's. They wanted to hurl themselves over the fence, into the street, and shake the truth out of his collar. He opened his gate—the gate—and still his stride and face told them nothing.

"Hello," he said.

Mama got up and followed him through the front door. The girls knew better than to go in too.

Presently Mama's head emerged. Her eyes were lamps turned on.

"It's all right," she exclaimed. "He got it. It's all over. Everything is all right."

The door slammed shut. Mama's footsteps hurried away.

"I think," said Helen, rocking rapidly, "I think I'll give a party. I haven't given a party since I was eleven. I'd like some of my friends to just casually see that we're homeowners."

Getting at Meaning

RECALLING

1. Where are Mama, Maud Martha, and Helen sitting at the beginning of the story? What are they looking at?

2. Where did Papa go at noon? Why did he go there? What are Mama, Maud Martha, and Helen waiting for?

3. Both Mama and Helen make statements about the advantages of moving. What are some of the advantages that they mention?

4. Maud Martha comments that Papa lives for his house. Helen contradicts this statement. What, according to Helen, does Papa live for?

5. What happens when Papa gets home? Will the family have to move?

INTERPRETING

6. Do Mama and Helen really think that the new place will be better than their old home? If not, why do they talk about the advantages of moving?

7. In the last paragraph Helen says that she will give a party. Why does she want to do this?

CRITICAL THINKING: APPLYING

8. A time of crisis sometimes helps people to appreciate more fully the things that they normally take for granted. What is the crisis in this story? What does this crisis help Mama, Maud Martha, and Helen to appreciate? Are there any things in your life that you usually take for granted but that you would miss terribly if they were taken away from you?

Developing Skills in Reading Literature

1. **Characterization.** Characterization is the use of literary techniques to reveal the nature of a character. How does Maud Martha differ from Mama and Helen in her reaction to the possibility of losing the house? What does the difference in her reaction reveal about her character? In other words, in what ways is Maud Martha different from Mama and Helen?

2. **Irony.** Irony is a contrast between what is expected and what actually exists or happens. Early in the story, Helen says that she would rather not bring her friends to her "old house." What does she say later in the story to contradict this statement? What makes her first statement ironic?

3. **Suspense.** Suspense is a feeling of growing tension and excitement felt by a reader. What is the reader of this story waiting to find out? How does the description of Papa's walk help to build suspense for the reader?

Developing Vocabulary

Using a Dictionary: The Multiple Meanings of Words. Many words have more than one meaning. The dictionary entries for such words therefore contain more than one definition. Look up the word *home* in a dictionary. For each of the following sentences, find the definition that most closely fits the meaning of the word as used in the sentence. Then, on a separate sheet of paper, write the appropriate definition of the word *home* for each sentence.

1. The pitcher tagged the runner before he reached *home*.

2. The child grew up in a *home* for orphans.

3. The bride and groom crossed the doorway into their new *home*.

4. She was born in Montgomery, but Atlanta is now her *home*.

Copyright © Layle Silbert

B I O G R A P H Y

Gwendolyn Brooks (born 1917), Poet Laureate of Illinois, grew up in a black community in Chicago. Her youthful experiences inspired much of her writing, for which she received a Guggenheim Fellowship, a Pulitzer Prize, and many other awards. She is the author of several books of poetry for adults, including *Annie Allen* and *The Bean Eaters*. She has also written a novel, *Maud Martha,* and a book of children's verse, *Bronzeville Boys and Girls.* Brooks has taught at many colleges in the Chicago area as well as at the University of Wisconsin and the City College of New York. She gives entertaining readings from her works throughout the United States.

The Apprentice

Dorothy Canfield Fisher

The day had been one of the unbearable ones, when every sound had set her teeth on edge like chalk creaking on a blackboard, when every word her father or mother said to her or did not say to her seemed an intentional injustice. And of course, it would happen as the end to such a day, that just as the sun went down back of the mountain and the long twilight began, she noticed that Rollie was not around.

Tense with exasperation at what her mother would say, she began to call him in a carefully casual tone—she would simply explode if Mother got going—"Here, Rollie! He-ere, boy! Want to go for a walk, Rollie?" Whistling to him cheerfully, her heart full of wrath at the way the world treated her, she made the rounds of his haunts; the corner of the woodshed, where he liked to curl up on the wool of Father's discarded old windbreaker; the hay barn, the cow barn, the sunny spot on the side porch—, no Rollie.

Perhaps he had sneaked upstairs to lie on her bed where he was not supposed to go—not that *she* would have minded! That rule was a part of Mother's fussiness, part too of Mother's bossiness. It was *her* bed, wasn't it? But was she allowed the say-so about it? Not

on your life. They *said* she could have things the way she wanted in her own room, now she was in her teens, but—her heart raged against unfairness as she took the stairs stormily, two steps at a time, her pigtails flopping up and down on her back. If Rollie was on her bed, she was just going to let him stay right there, and Mother could say what she wanted to.

But he was not there. The bedspread and pillow were crumpled, but not from his weight. She had flung herself down to cry there that afternoon. And then she couldn't. Every nerve in her had been twanging discordantly, but she couldn't cry. She could only lie there, her hands doubled up hard, furious that she had nothing to cry about. Not really. She was too big to cry just over Father's having said to her, severely, "I told you if I let you take the chess set, you were to put it away when you got through with it. One of the pawns was on the floor of our bedroom this morning. I stepped on it. If I'd had my shoes on, I'd have broken it."

Well, he *had* told her to be sure to put them away. And although she had forgotten and left them, he hadn't said she mustn't ever take the set again. No, the instant she thought about that, she knew she couldn't cry about it. She could be, and she was, in a rage about the way Father kept on talking, long after she'd got his point, "It's not that I care so much about the chess set," he said, just leaning with all his weight on being right, "it's because if you don't learn how to take care of things, you yourself will suffer for it, later. You'll forget or neglect something that will be really important, for *you*. We *have* to try to teach you to be responsible for what you've said you'll take care of. If we...." on and on, preaching and preaching.

She heard her mother coming down the hall, and hastily shut her door. She had a right to shut the door to her own room, hadn't she? She had *some* rights, she supposed, even if she was only thirteen and the youngest child. If her mother opened it to say, smiling, "What are you doing in here that you won't want me to see?" she'd say—she'd just say—

She stood there, dry-eyed, by the bed that Rollie had not crumpled, and thought, "I hope Mother sees the spread and says something about Rollie—I just hope she does."

But her mother did not open the door. Her feet went steadily on along the hall, and then, carefully, slowly, down the stairs. She probably had an armful of winter things she was bringing down from the attic. She was probably thinking that a tall, thirteen-year-old daughter was big enough to help with a chore like that. But she wouldn't *say* anything. She would just get out that insulting look of a grown-up silently putting up with a crazy, unreasonable kid. She had worn that expression all day; it was too much to be endured.

Up in her bedroom behind her closed door the thirteen-year-old stamped her foot in a rage, none the less savage and heartshaking because it was mysterious to her.

But she had not located Rollie. Before she would let her father and mother know she had lost sight of him, forgotten about him, she would be cut into little pieces. They would not scold her, she knew. They would do worse. They would look at her. And in their silence, she would hear droning on reproachfully what they had said when the sweet, woolly collie-puppy had first been in her arms and she had been begging to keep him for her own.

How warm he had felt! Astonishing how warm and alive a puppy was compared to a doll! She had never liked her dolls much, after she had held Rollie, feeling him warm against her breast, warm and wriggling, bursting with life, reaching up to lick her face—he had loved her from that first instant. As he felt her arms around him, his beautiful eyes had melted in trusting sweetness. As they did now, whenever he looked at her. "My dog is the only one in the whole world who *really* loves me," she thought passionately.

Even then, at the very minute when as a darling baby dog he was beginning to love her, her father and mother were saying, so cold, so reasonable—gosh! how she *hated* reasonableness!—"Now, Peg, remember that, living where we do, with sheep on the farms around us, it is a serious responsibility to have a collie dog. If you keep him, you've got to be the one to take care of him. You'll have to be the one to train him to stay at home. We're too busy with you children to start bringing up a puppy, too." Rollie, nestling in her arms, let one hind leg drop awkwardly. It must be uncomfortable. She looked down at him tenderly, tucked his dangling leg up under him and gave him a hug. He laughed up in her face—he really did laugh, his mouth stretched wide in a cheerful grin.

Her parents were saying, "If you want him, you can have him. But you must be responsible for him. If he gets to running sheep, he'll just have to be shot; you know that."

They had not said, aloud, "Like the Wilsons' collie." They never mentioned that awfulness—her racing unsuspectingly down across the fields just at the horrible moment when Mr. Wilson shot their collie caught in the very act of killing sheep. They probably thought that if they never spoke about it, she would forget it—*forget* the crack of that rifle, and the collapse of the great beautiful dog! Forget the red, red blood spurting from the hole in his head. She hadn't forgotten. She never would. She knew as well as they did, how important it was to train a collie puppy about

sheep. They didn't need to rub it in like that. They always rubbed everything in. She had told them, fervently, indignantly, that *of course* she would take care of him, be responsible for him, teach him to stay at home. Of course, of course. *She* understood!

And now, this afternoon, when he was six months old, tall, rangy, powerful, standing up far above her knee, nearly to her waist, she didn't know where he was. But of course he must be somewhere around. He always was. She composed her face to look natural and went downstairs to search the house. He was probably asleep somewhere. She looked over every room carefully. Her mother was no-

where visible. It was safe to call him again, to give the special piercing whistle which always brought him racing to her, the white-feathered plume of his tail waving in elation that she wanted him.

But he did not answer. She stood still on the front porch to think.

Could he have gone up to their special place on the edge of the field where the three young pines, their branches growing close to the ground, make a triangular, walled-in space, completely hidden from the world? Sometimes he went up there with her. When she lay down on the dried grass to dream, he too lay down quietly, his head on his paws, his beautiful eyes fixed adoringly on her. He entered into her every mood. If she wanted to be quiet, all right, he did too.

It didn't seem as though he would have gone alone there. Still—she loped up the steep slope of the field rather fast, beginning to be anxious.

No, he was not there. She stood, irresolutely, in the roofless, green-walled triangular hide-out, wondering what to do next.

Then, before she knew what thought had come into her mind, its emotional impact knocked her down. At least her knees crumpled under her. Last Wednesday the Wilsons had brought their sheep down to the home farm from the upper pasture! She herself had seen them on the way to school, and like an idiot had not thought of Rollie. She had seen them grazing on the river meadow.

She was off like a racer at the crack of the starting pistol, her long, strong legs stretched in great leaps, her pigtails flying. She took the short cut down to the upper edge of the meadow, regardless of the brambles. Their thorn-spiked, wiry stems tore at her flesh, but she did not care. She welcomed the pain. It was something she was doing for Rollie, for her Rollie.

She was tearing through the pine woods now, rushing down the steep, stony path, tripping over roots, half-falling, catching herself just in time, not slackening her speed. She burst out on the open knoll above the river meadow, calling wildly, "Rollie, here, Rollie, here, boy! here! here!" She tried to whistle, but she was crying too hard to pucker her lips. She had not, till then, known she was crying.

There was nobody to see or hear her. Twilight was falling over the bare knoll. The sunless evening wind slid down the mountain like an invisible river, engulfing her in cold. Her teeth began to chatter. "Here, Rollie, here boy, here!" She strained her eyes to look down into the meadow to see if the sheep were there. She could not be sure. She stopped calling him as if he were a dog and called out his name despairingly, as if he were her child, "Rollie! oh, *Rollie,* where are you!"

The tears ran down her cheeks in streams. She sobbed loudly, terribly. Since there was no one to hear, she did not try to control herself. "Hou! hou! hou!" she sobbed, her face contorted grotesquely. "Oh, Rollie! Rollie! Rollie!" She had wanted something to cry about. Oh, how terribly now she had something to cry about.

She saw him as clearly as if he were there beside her, his muzzle and gaping mouth all smeared with the betraying blood (like the Wilsons' collie). "But he didn't *know* it was wrong!" she screamed like a wild creature. "Nobody *told* him it was wrong. It was my fault. I should have taken better care of him. I will now. I will!"

But no matter how she screamed, she could not make herself heard. In the cold, gathering darkness, she saw him stand, poor, guiltless victim of his ignorance, who should have been protected from his own nature, his soft eyes looking at her with love, his splendid plumed tail waving gently. "It was my fault. I promised I would bring him up. I should have *made* him stay at home. I was responsible for him. It was my fault."

But she could not make his executioners hear her. The shot rang out. Rollie sank down, his beautiful liquid eyes glazed, the blood spurting from the hole in his head—like the Wilsons' collie. She gave a wild shriek, long, soul-satisfying, frantic. It was the scream at sudden, unendurable tragedy of a mature, full-blooded woman. It drained dry the girl of thirteen. She came to herself. She was standing on the knoll, trembling and quaking with cold, the darkness closing in on her.

Her breath had given out. For once in her life she had wept all the tears that were in her body. Her hands were so stiff with cold she could scarcely close them. How her nose was running! Simply streaming down her upper lip. And she had no handkerchief. She lifted her skirt, fumbled for her slip, stopped, blew her nose on it, wiped her eyes, drew a long quavering breath—and heard something! Far off in the distance, a faint sound, like a dog's muffled bark.

She whirled on her heels and bent her head to listen. The sound did not come from the meadow below the knoll. It came from back of her higher up, from the Wilsons' maple grove. She held her breath. Yes, it came from there.

She began to run again, but now she was not sobbing. She was silent, absorbed in her effort to cover ground. If she could only live to get there, to see if it really were Rollie. She ran steadily till she came to the fence and went over this in a great plunge. Her skirt caught on a nail. She impatiently pulled at it, not hearing

or not heeding the long sibilant[1] tear as it came loose. She was in the dusky maple woods, stumbling over the rocks as she ran. As she tore on up the slope, she heard the bark again, and knew it was Rollie's.

She stopped short and leaned weakly against a tree. She was sick with the breathlessness of her straining lungs, sick in the reaction of relief, sick with anger at Rollie, who had been here having a wonderful time while she had been dying, just dying in terror about him.

For she could now not only hear that it was Rollie's bark. She could hear, in the dog language she knew as well as he, what he was saying in those excited yips—that he had run a woodchuck into a hole in the tumbled stone wall, that he almost had him, that the intoxicating wild-animal smell was as close to him—almost—as if he had his jaws on his quarry. Yip! Woof! Yip! Yip!

The wildly joyful quality of the dog-talk enraged the girl. She had been trembling in exhaustion. Now it was indignation. So that was where he had been—when *she* was *killing* herself trying to take care of him. Plenty near enough if he had paid attention to hear her calling and whistling to him. Just so set on having his foolish good time, he never thought to listen for her call.

She stooped to pick up a stout stick. She would teach him. She was hot with anger. It was time he had something to make him remember to listen. She started forward on a run.

But after a few steps she stopped, stood thinking. One of the things to remember about collies, everybody knew that, was that a collie who had been beaten was never "right" again. His spirit was broken. "Anything but a

_____
1. **sibilant:** making a hissing sound.

broken-spirited collie," she had often heard a farmer say that. They were no good after that.

She threw down her stick. Anyhow, she thought, he was really too young to know that he had done wrong. He was still only a puppy. Like all puppies, he got perfectly crazy over wild-animal smells. Probably he truly hadn't heard her calling and whistling.

All the same, all the same—she stood stock-still, staring intently into the twilight—you couldn't let a puppy grow up just as he wanted to. It wouldn't be safe—for *him*. Somehow she would have to make him understand that he mustn't go off this way, by himself. He must be trained to know how to do what a good dog does—not because *she* wanted to, but for his own sake.

She walked on now, steady, purposeful, gathering her inner strength together, Olympian[2] in her understanding of the full meaning of the event.

When he heard his own special young god approaching, he turned delightedly and ran to meet her, panting, his tongue hanging out. His eyes shone. He jumped up on her in an ecstasy of welcome and licked her face.

She pushed him away. Her face and voice were grave. "No, Rollie, *no!*" she said severely, "you're *bad*. You know you're not to go off in the woods without me! You are—a—*bad—dog.*"

He was horrified. Striken into misery. He stood facing her, frozen. The gladness went out of his eyes, the waving plume of his tail slowly lowered to slinking, guilty dejection.

"I know you were all wrapped up in that woodchuck. But that's no excuse. You *could* have heard me, calling you, whistling for you, if you'd paid attention," she went on. "You've got to learn, and I've got to teach you."

With a shudder of misery he lay down, his tail stretched out limp on the ground, his head flat on his paws, his ears drooping—ears ringing with the doomsday awfulness of the voice he loved and revered. To have it speak so to him, he must have been utterly wicked. He trembled, he turned his head away from her august[3] look of blame, he groveled in remorse for whatever mysterious sin he had committed.

As miserable as he, she sat down by him. "I don't *want* to scold you. But I have to! I have to bring you up right, or you'll get shot, Rollie. You mustn't go away from the house without me, do you hear, *never.*"

His sharp ears, yearning for her approval, caught a faint over-tone of relenting affection in her voice. He lifted his eyes to her, humbly, soft in imploring fondness.

"Oh, Rollie!" she said, stooping low over him, "I *do* love you. I do. But I *have* to bring you up. I'm responsible for you, don't you see."

He did not see. Hearing sternness, or something else he did not recognize, in the beloved voice, he shut his eyes tight in sorrow, and made a little whimpering lament in his throat.

She had never heard him cry before. It was too much. She sat down by him and drew his head to her, rocking him in her arms, soothing him with inarticulate small murmurs.

He leaped in her arms and wriggled happily as he had when he was a baby; he reached up to lick her face as he had then. But he was no baby now. He was half as big as she, a great, warm, pulsing, living armful of love. She clasped him closely. Her heart was brimming full, but calmed, quiet. The blood flowed in equable gentleness all over her body. She was deli-

---

2. **Olympian** (ō lim′ pē ən): powerful and majestic, like a god.
3. **august** (ô gust′): inspiring respect.

ciously warm. Her nose was still running, a little. She sniffed and wiped it on her sleeve.

It was almost dark now. "We'll be late to
supper, Rollie," she said, responsibly. Pushing
him gently off, she stood up. "Home, Rollie,
home."

Here was a command he could understand.
At once he trotted along the path towards
home. His tail, held high, waved plumelike.
His short dog-memory had forgotten the suffering just back of him.

Her human memory was longer. His prancing gait was as carefree as a young child's. She
plodded behind him like a serious adult. Her
very shoulders seemed bowed by what she had
lived through. She felt, she thought, like an
old, old woman of thirty. But it was all right
now; she knew she had made an impression on
him.

When they came out into the open pasture,
Rollie ran back to get her to play with him. He
leaped around her in circles, barking in cheerful yawps, jumping up on her, inviting her to

run a race with him, to throw him a stick, to
come alive.

His high spirits were ridiculous, but infectious. She gave one little leap to match his.
Rollie took this as a threat, a pretend, play-
threat. He planted his forepaws low and
barked loudly at her, laughing between yips.
He was so funny, she thought, when he
grinned that way. She laughed back, and gave
another mock-threatening leap at him. Radiant
that his sky was once more clear, he sprang
high on his steel-spring muscles in an explosion of happiness, and bounded in circles
around her.

Following him, not noting in the dusk
where she was going, she felt the grassy slope
drop steeply. Oh, yes, she knew where she
was. They had come to the rolling-down hill
just back of the house. All the kids rolled down
there, even the little ones, because it was soft
grass without a stone. She had rolled down
that slope a million times—years and years
before, when she was a kid herself, six or seven

years ago. It was fun. She remembered well the whirling dizziness of the descent, all the world turning crazily over and over. And the delicious, giddy staggering when you first stood up, the earth still spinning under your feet.

"All right, Rollie, let's go," she cried, and flung herself down in the rolling position, her arms straight up over her head.

Rollie had never seen this skylarking before. It threw him into almost hysterical amusement. He capered around the rapidly rolling figure, half scared, mystified, enchanted.

His wild, frolicsome barking might have come from her own throat, so accurately did it sound the way she felt—crazy, foolish—like a little kid, no more than five years old, the age she had been when she had last rolled down that hill.

At the bottom she sprang up, on muscles as steel-strong as Rollie's. She staggered a little and laughed aloud.

The living room windows were just before them. How yellow lighted windows looked when you were in the darkness going home. How nice and yellow. Maybe Mother had waffles for supper. She was a swell cook, Mother was, and she certainly gave her family all the breaks, when it came to meals.

"Home, Rollie, home!" She burst open the door to the living room. "Hi, Mom, what you got for supper?"

From the kitchen her mother announced coolly, "I hate to break the news to you, but it's waffles."

"Oh, *Mom!*" she shouted in ecstasy.

Her mother could not see her. She did not need to. "For goodness' sake, go and wash," she called.

In the long mirror across the room she saw herself, her hair hanging wild, her long bare legs scratched, her broadly smiling face dirt-streaked, her torn skirt dangling, her dog laughing up at her. Gosh, was it a relief to feel your own age, just exactly thirteen years old.

Getting at Meaning

RECALLING

1. What reason does Peg's father give for making a major issue of such a minor matter as the chess set?

2. Under what condition is Peg allowed to keep Rollie? What is Peg supposed to teach the dog?

3. Why was the Wilsons' collie shot?

4. What realization causes Peg to go "off like a racer at the crack of the starting pistol," searching for Rollie in the meadows and woods?

5. While looking for Rollie, Peg imagines seeing him "as clearly as if he were there beside her." What does Peg imagine, at this moment, that Rollie looks like?

6. When Peg finds Rollie, what is he doing? What punishment does she start to inflict on him? Why doesn't she continue to punish Rollie in this way?

INTERPRETING

7. Why does Peg start feeling like "an old, old woman of thirty"? What does she do to make herself feel like a child again?

8. What similarities are there between Peg's relationship to Rollie and her parents' relationship to her? In caring for Rollie, what does Peg learn about being a good parent? What unpleasant but necessary task does Peg have to perform?

Developing Skills in Reading Literature

1. **Character.** A character is a person or animal who takes part in the action of a story. In many short stories, the main character is faced with some crisis that causes him or her to change. What kind of person does Peg seem to be at the beginning of this story? What is her attitude toward her parents? toward her responsibilities? What crisis faces Peg? How does she change as a result of this crisis?

2. **Theme.** The theme is the main idea of a work of literature. In many short stories, the theme is a lesson learned by the main character. What lesson does Peg learn about responsibility in this story?

3. **Title.** The title often sums up the main idea, or theme, of a short story. What does the word *apprentice* mean? In what sense is Peg an apprentice? What "work" will the events of this story prepare Peg for?

4. **Irony.** Irony is a contrast between what is expected and what actually exists or happens. What similarities are there between Peg's comments to Rollie and the lecture that Peg's father gives her about the chess set? What is ironic about Peg's behavior towards Rollie?

5. **Mood and Suspense.** Mood is the feeling created by a literary work. Suspense is a feeling of growing tension and excitement felt by a reader. What is the mood of the passage on pages 225–226 in which Peg imagines seeing Rollie? How does this passage help to increase the suspense of the story?

Developing Vocabulary

Using a Dictionary: Compound Words. A compound word is formed by combining two or more separate words into one. Compound words are sometimes spelled as one word, as in *nightfall,* sometimes with a hyphen, as in *statewide,* and sometimes as two words, as in *goal post.* The meaning of a compound word is related to the meanings of the words that form it. Although a desk-sized dictionary contains the meanings of many compound words, not all compounds are listed. To determine the meaning of a compound word that is not in the dictionary, break the word into its parts and look up each part. Then, combine the definitions to arrive at the definition of the compound word.

Examine the following list of compound words. On a separate sheet of paper, write the two words that form each compound. Then look up the compounds in a dictionary. Place a check mark beside each compound that your dictionary lists. Look up the separate words that make up the compounds that are not listed. Finally, write the definition of each compound word.

windbreaker	bedspread
doomsday	plumelike
stage manager	heartshaking
skylarking	full-blooded

Developing Writing Skills

Analyzing a Character. Write a paragraph explaining how Peg's attitude toward responsibility changes and why. As a prewriting activity, gather details that reveal Peg's attitudes. Write a strong topic sentence and organize your details in chronological order before you begin to write. As you write and revise your paragraph, refer to **Using the Process of Writing** and to Writing About the Short Story on pages 614–625 for help.

B I O G R A P H Y

Dorothy Canfield Fisher (1879–1958) was born in Lawrence, Kansas, but she spent most of her life in Vermont on a farm inherited from her great-grandfather. Many of her books have rural settings and are accurate pictures of country life and attitudes in the early 1900's. *Understood Betsy* is one of her most famous books for young people. She has also published books on education, and novels and short stories for adults.

CONVERSATIONS, 1958. *Ben Shahn. Whitney Museum of American Art, New York.*
Gift of the Friends of The Whitney Museum of American Art.

Plot

What Is Plot?

Plot is the sequence of events in a story. It is the writer's plan for what happens, when, and to whom. The events in a plot are connected. One event causes another, which causes another, and so on until the end of the story.

The Elements of Plot

The plot of a story begins with a basic situation. The writer introduces a conflict, a problem faced by the main character. The conflict leads to other events and builds to the climax, or high point of interest and intensity. At this point in the story, or shortly after, some event ends, or resolves, the conflict.

Within the plot of a story, a writer may use any or all of the following techniques.

Foreshadowing. Foreshadowing is the technique of hinting about some event that has not yet happened.

Flashback. A flashback is a part of a story that interrupts the sequence of events to tell about an earlier conversation, scene, or event.

Suspense. Suspense is a feeling of growing tension and excitement felt by a reader.

Surprise Ending. A surprise ending is an unexpected twist in the plot at the end of a story.

Thinking About Plot

When reading a short story, pay attention to the order of events. Think about how these events are connected. Ask yourself, "What event introduces the conflict? What events make the conflict more intense? What event brings the conflict to an end?"

In animals and in humans, the instinct to protect the young is strong.

How Whirlwind Saved Her Cub

Dorothy Johnson

Whirlwind was a widow now. Her hair, hacked off in mourning for White Thunder, had grown out long enough to make short, ragged braids, but she no longer cared very much how she looked. The cuts made when she had gashed her arms and her legs had healed to scars. She no longer had a lodge of her own. When White Thunder died of a wasting sickness—not in battle, as he had wished—she abandoned the lodge as was proper and let other people take away everything in it.

But she had a good home with her son, Morning Rider. She was Grandmother Whirlwind, the old-woman-who-sits-by-the-door. She worked hard and took pride in her work. She was the one who told small children the old stories about the White Buffalo Maiden and the other sacred spirits just as those stories had been told to her by Grandmother Earth Medicine when she was very small.

Her people[1] lived in the still rich hunting country along the Tongue River. . . . All over the huge encampment there was singing and drumming now, and all over people were busy.

There was much to be done, because they would move again very soon. The pony herds needed new grazing.

There was plenty of work to be done in the lodge of Morning Rider, but there were plenty of women there to do it, so Whirlwind left on a project of her own.

"I'm going to dig roots," she explained to Round Cloud Woman. "Shall I take the baby for company?"

"He has just been fed, so take him if you like," her daughter-in-law agreed. His ears had not yet been pierced, so he did not have a boy name yet; his baby name was Jumps.

Whirlwind slung her baby grandson's cradleboard onto her back with the ease of long practice and went walking at a brisk pace, answering the baby when he made small sounds. She had two things hidden under her dress: her digging stick and a soft leather bag for carrying roots. She thought she knew where biscuit root would be growing—desert

---

1. **Her people:** the Cheyenne.

parsley. The roots were good to eat raw, or she might dry and grind them to make big flat cakes. The biscuit root made good mush with a wild onion cooked in it.

As a rule she liked company when she worked, but there was no point in inviting some other busy woman to come along to dig something that might not be there.

She did tell her destination to one person, her grandson, Shoots, thirteen years old. She met him when he was returning on foot from his turn at guarding part of the vast pony herd.

"Your little brother is going to help me dig biscuit root over there," she said. "Don't tell anybody where we are. Let the other women be sharp-eyed and find their own roots."

Shoots smiled and promised. He patted his baby brother's cheek and said, "Ho, warrior, old man chief. Take care of Grandmother." The baby jumped in his buckskin wrappings and cooed.

The biscuit root was plentiful on flat ground under a cutbank,[2] just out of sight of the lodges. Whirlwind carefully propped the baby's cradleboard against a rock so the sun wouldn't shine in the child's face. Then, talking to him quietly, she began to dig skillfully, filling her buckskin bag, stooping and kneeling and rising again like a young woman. She was not young. She had lived through fifty-six winters, but she was strong and happy and healthy.

Her back was toward the baby when she heard him shriek with glee. She turned instantly—and saw a dreadful thing. Between her and the baby was another kind of baby, an awkward little bear cub, the cub of the frightfully dangerous grizzly bear. The cub itself was harmless, but the old-woman bear, its mother, must be near, and she would protect her child.

Whirlwind did not even think of danger to herself. She ran to save *her* cub. She snatched up the baby on his cradleboard and threw him, with all her strength, above her head toward the level top of the cutbank.

At that moment the old-woman bear appeared. She snarled and came running, a shambling, awkward-looking run but very fast.

Whirlwind saw with horror the cradleboard with its precious burden sliding back down the cutbank. She had been too close when she threw the baby upward. The baby was screaming. Grandmother Whirlwind ran, picked up the cradleboard, ran back a few steps, and then threw hard again. This time the bundle stayed up there.

Whirlwind ran again toward the cutbank and climbed as fast as she could, digging into the dirt frantically with clutching fingers and digging toes.

The upper part of her body was on the flat ground and she was gripping a small tree as she tried to pull up her legs. Just then the old-woman grizzly reached up and tore at the legs with curved claws as long as a big man's middle finger.

Whirlwind thought, I am dead—but my cub is safe if the sow bear does not come up here. No, I am not dead yet. I have something more to do. She screamed as hard as she could.

And her scream was heard.

Shoots was an untried boy. He had never even asked to go along with a war party to do errands for men of proved courage, to watch how a man should act. He had only thought of going on the hill to starve and thirst and lament to the Powers, praying for a powerful spirit helper. He had not yet done this thing. He believed his heart was strong. That day he found out.

He was only playing when he heard the she-bear snarl. He was practicing a stealthy

---

2. **cutbank** (kut' baŋk'): the steep bank of a stream.

approach, intending to startle Grandmother Whirlwind. He was creeping quietly through thin brush, pretending that she was an enemy. He did not really expect to surprise her; she was usually very alert. She would scold when she discovered what he was up to, and then she would laugh at him because she had caught him.

He saw a bundle fly through the air and slide down the cutbank. It happened too fast for him to see that it was the cradleboard with his baby brother. He heard fast movement in the weeds as Whirlwind ran back and threw the cradleboard again. He stood up, mouth open, just as she scrambled up the bank. With horror he saw the old-woman bear's claws rake her struggling legs.

With his heart in his mouth he did the best thing he could think of. He dropped his bow and grabbed the cub with both hands, so that it

BABY IS SLEEPING, 1968. *Allen Sapp. Collection of the Artist, Vancouver, British Columbia.*

squalled with fear and pain. Then he threw it hard—past its mother.

Hearing her child cry, the woman bear whirled away from the cutbank to protect her cub. Shoots snatched up his bow; it was a good one, as strong as he could pull, and in a quiver on his shoulder he had six hunting arrows tipped with sharpened iron. At his waist he had a good steel knife.

But his enemy was better armed, with twenty immensely long, curved, sharp, death-dealing claws and a mouthful of long, sharp teeth, and she weighed more than five times as much as he did. She was protected by thick fur. Shoots was almost naked.

He stood his ground and fired his arrows at her, fast but very carefully. Few grizzlies had ever been killed by one man alone; there were true tales of some bears killing men even after they should have been dead themselves. The woman bear yelled in pain and fury. She batted at the arrows deep in her flesh. She bit at them. But she kept coming.

Then Shoots did the last thing he could do, because it was too late to run. While the grizzly fought at the arrows, especially one that had gone into her left eye, he leaped on her back. With all his strength he sank his good steel knife into her throat, through the heavy fur and hide.

Then, as Grandmother Whirlwind had done, he clambered up the cutbank while the bear groped and swiped at him. He wondered why he could not see very well. He wondered who was screaming. He wondered if this was the day he was going to die.

Whirlwind, lying helpless with the calf of one leg torn away, screamed louder when she saw him with blood running down his face, but he did not even know blood was there.

She cried, "Take the baby and run!" in so commanding a voice that he never thought of doing otherwise. With the cradled baby under one arm, he ran toward camp, howling for help, but stumbling.

His yells were heard. Two men on horseback lashed their ponies and met him. One seized the squalling baby. The other pulled Shoots up behind him on the pony. They rode fast toward where Whirlwind lay.

They leaped off—the one with the baby hung the cradleboard on a tree branch—and Shoots tumbled off. He had just realized that there was something he ought to do to prove his valor. He did something that his people talked about for many years afterward. While the men knelt by Whirlwind, he slid down the cutbank, picked up his bow, and struck the bear with it. She was coughing and dying. He shouted, as warriors do, "I, Shoots, have killed her! I count the first coup!"[3]

Whirlwind and the men above heard him say it. They shouted in wonder and admiration. For a man to kill a grizzly without help was a very great thing indeed, and he had actually gone back into danger to count coup and claim the credit that was due him. He had counted coup against an armed enemy, after he was wounded, although he had never gone to war before that day. Now he was entitled to wear an eagle feather upright in his hair for first coup, a feather tipped with red paint because he had been wounded in battle.

He was the one who rode toward camp for more help while the two men stayed with Whirlwind and did what they could to make her comfortable. A crowd of people came hurrying after he delivered his message. There were women on horseback with poles and

---

3. **count … coup** (ko͞o): to strike or touch an enemy, an act of bravery.

hides to make a pony drag for Whirlwind, because a great chunk of the muscles in the calf of one leg had been torn out by the she-bear's claws. There were men riding and boys riding, leading horses. More women brought supplies to help the wounded, and a medicine woman came with them, carrying her bundle of magic things. Round Cloud Woman came riding, crying, and Morning Rider came at a hard gallop to see about his mother and his infant son.

Whirlwind fought them off, so keyed up and triumphant that she did not yet feel much pain. "Let me carry my grandchild!" she ordered when Round Cloud tried to take him away.

"I saved your cub," Whirlwind kept boasting, laughing and proud. "And Shoots saved us both. He is not a cub any more. He is a warrior!" She tried to make a victory trill in his honor, but as they lifted her gently onto the pony drag she fainted.

Morning Rider himself attended to the wound of his son, Shoots, who did not even remember when the old-woman bear had slashed his forehead. The boy was able to laugh as he said, "She tried to scalp me!"

Morning Rider covered the wound with clotted blood from the bear and tied the flap of skin down with a strip of buckskin around the boy's head. He remarked fondly, "You will have a big scar there. The girls will keep asking you to tell how you got it. I am very proud of you."

Now maybe Grandmother Whirlwind would stop treating him like a little boy, to be ordered around.

He heard her shouting, laughing: "Behold Shoots—he is a warrior. He fought a grizzly bear and killed her."

Shoots shouted back, "Behold Whirlwind! She is a warrior. She was wounded in battle."

He began to sing a praise song for her, although he was feeling weak all of a sudden.

She laughed hysterically. "I am a warrior who was wounded while running away! Take the hide of the enemy—it belongs to Shoots."

Women were skinning out the dead, bloody bear and fighting with a horse that reared, not wanting to carry the hide on its back. The medicine woman filled a big dish with bear blood. She washed the great wound on Whirlwind's leg with water, chanting prayers. She covered the wound with the bear's thickening blood and then cut a big piece of the bear's hide, covering the wound and the blood with the raw side of the fresh hide.

She said with pity, "My friend, I think you will have trouble walking—always, as long as you live. But nobody will ever forget how you saved your son's cub today."

They killed the great bear's cub and cut off its claws to make a necklace for the baby when he grew older. They cut off the immense claws of the woman bear; these were for Shoots. Not long afterward, when he went out to lament for a vision, his dream was a powerful one, and when he made up his protective medicine bag, one of the claws was in it. The others he wore for a necklace when he dressed up.

That night the people had a victorious kill dance over the bloody hides of the great bear and the little one. Morning Rider rode around the camp circle leading a fine horse to give away, with Shoots riding beside him. Morning Rider sang:

"A bear killed a woman long ago.
A bear killed a mother long ago.
Now the woman's son has avenged her.
The warrior son has avenged his mother!"

Morning Rider gave the fine horse to a very brave old warrior, who gave Shoots a new name. The warrior shouted, "The boy Shoots counted first coup on a grizzly bear and killed her to save two people. So I give him an honorable name. Kills Grizzly is his name!"

Grandmother Whirlwind lay on her bed, smiling as she listened to the singing and the triumphant drumming of the kill dance in honor of Shoots—no, now she must remember to call him Kills Grizzly. Her daughter was with her, and the medicine woman, who used all her spells and prayers and medicines to try to ease the pain. No matter how Whirlwind lay, with her foot propped up, the pain was very great, but her pride was greater.

"It does not hurt," she said. "It is nothing." She pretended to sleep.

Brings Horses stayed, and Morning Rider's wives came back with their sleepy children. They spoke softly but were full of talk that Whirlwind wanted to hear about how everyone was honoring Shoots for his courage and talking about how brave Whirlwind herself was.

"Everybody wants to see you," one of them remarked, smiling, "but we refused them all— all except one, who will come soon."

They were hurrying around, Whirlwind noticed, to tidy up the lodge—her work, but she could not do it now. It must be an important visitor or the women would not be so careful to have everything neat and nice this late at night, with the baby and the little girl, Reaches Far, asleep.

Men's voices came nearer, two men. One was Morning Rider; his mother did not recognize the other one. Morning Rider entered and ushered in his companion. He said, "This is Whirlwind Woman, my mother. She saved my baby son."

The other man stood looking down at her. He smiled a little and said, "I am Crazy Horse."

Whirlwind gasped. For once in her life, she had nothing to say. This was the great man, the quiet one, whose very presence made the hearts of his people big.

Morning Rider told her, "I have asked Crazy Horse to name the baby, and he agrees. When the boy is old enough, we will have the ear-piercing ceremony. But today Crazy Horse will give my youngest son a name."

Round Cloud Woman brought the sleeping infant. She was shaking with excitement.

Crazy Horse looked long at the sleeping little face. Then he touched the child's forehead

Sioux Cradle, late 19th century. *Collection of the Newark Museum.*

and said, "I give you a name that you can make great in honor of your grandmother, who saved you, and your brother, who counted first coup on the bear. I name the child She Throws Him."

A murmur of delight went up among Morning Rider's family: "Thank you, friend, thank you!"

Round Cloud Woman said to her child, "Wake up, She Throws Him, so that sometime you can say you looked on the face of Crazy Horse the day he gave you your name." The baby opened his eyes, yawned, and went to sleep again.

Now Whirlwind thought of something to say: "My son has forgotten his manners. I did not raise him right. He has not asked our visitor to sit down in the place of honor beside him."

The two men chuckled, and Morning Rider explained, "I asked him before we came, but he thought he would not stay long enough. Will the visitor sit down and smoke?"

Crazy Horse would. Morning Rider filled and lighted the sacred pipe and smoked it to the Powers of the six directions. Then he passed it to Crazy Horse, who did the same and gave back the sacred pipe.

"I wish also to speak to the warrior woman," he said. "Grandmother, how is it with you in your pain?" He used the term "grandmother" in the sense of great respect.

"Not so bad," she replied stoutly, as a warrior should.

Crazy Horse stood up, then knelt beside her and looked into her face. "I give you a name, too, Grandmother. Your name is Saved Her Cub."

Then he nodded and left the lodge, leaving Whirlwind speechless for the second time that day.

When she got her wits back, she complained happily, "But I am too old to remember another name for myself!"

Morning Rider replied, "Others will remember."

Cheyenne Homelands, 1860–1890

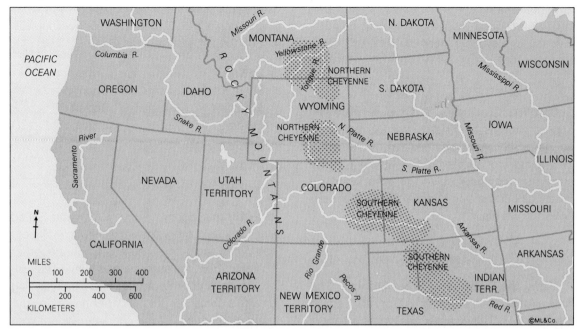

Reading a Map. This map shows where the Cheyenne tribes lived in 1860–1890. The northern and southern Cheyenne tribes are labeled on the map. Locate the Tongue River, the Platte River, the Arkansas River, and the Red River. Around which of these rivers did the northern Cheyenne live? the southern Cheyenne?

Getting at Meaning

RECALLING

1. Why does Whirlwind tell only Shoots where she is going to dig for roots?

2. When Whirlwind sees the grizzly, what is her first reaction?

3. What is Whirlwind doing when she is injured?

4. Why is Shoots close enough to hear Whirlwind's scream? What is he doing at the time?

5. How does the village celebrate the killing of the grizzly?

6. Who comes to visit Whirlwind at the end of the story? What is the purpose of this visit?

INTERPRETING

7. Shoots and his grandmother are obviously fond of one another. What actions show their mutual affection?

8. What do Whirlwind and the mother bear have in common?

9. How does Shoots manage to defeat the bear? Is he a skilled warrior?

10. Why is it considered brave for Shoots to count coup as he does?

11. What customs of the Cheyenne are mentioned in this story? What does the reader learn about the Cheyenne way of life, particularly about the passage of a boy into manhood?

12. After Whirlwind says that she is too old to remember a new name, her son says that "others will remember." What else will others remember besides her name? What function will her new name serve?

CRITICAL THINKING: EVALUATING/APPLYING

13. What characters in this story behave courageously? Why is courage such a prized virtue among the Cheyenne? What parts of

their lives require courage? How is courage rewarded among them? Is courage as important a virtue in contemporary American culture? Give reasons for your answers.

Developing Skills in Reading Literature

Conflict. Conflict is a struggle between opposing forces. In this story, a major conflict is between Shoots and his need to prove himself a grown man, or warrior. At what point in the story is this conflict resolved? In other words, at what point does Shoots prove, finally, that he is a worthy warrior?

Developing Vocabulary

Using the Dictionary: Word Origins. The Native American names in this story are English translations of Native American words meaning *white thunder, whirlwind, earth medicine, shoots,* and so on. Most people's names today also have special meanings. For example, the name *Deborah* is a Hebrew word meaning, literally, "a bee." The name *Phillip* is a combination of two Greek words meaning "lover of horses."

Look up the following names in a dictionary. Then, on a separate sheet of paper, write what each name originally meant. If your own name is not on the list, look it up as well.

Edward	Frank	David
Laurence	Susan	George
Margaret	Marcia	Robert
Dolores	Angela	Joyce

Developing Writing Skills

Writing a Story. "How Whirlwind Saved Her Cub" is a story that explains how Shoots and Whirlwind get new names. Choose another character from the story such as White Thunder or Jumps, and write a brief short story telling how this character got his or her name. In your prewriting notes, list the character whom your story will be about. Also list the events of your story in chronological order. As you write, refer to your list of events. Add details to help your reader visualize what is happening. As you revise, refer to the suggestions for revision made in **Using the Process of Writing.**

B I O G R A P H Y

Dorothy M. Johnson (1905–1984) is best known for her stories about the West. Many of her works portray what it was like to be a Native American during the days of the frontier. Johnson's books for young people include *Montana* and *Western Badmen.* Johnson attended Montana State University and was an honorary member of the Blackfeet Indian tribe of that state.

The Circuit   *Francisco Jiménez*

It was that time of year again. Ito, the strawberry sharecropper, did not smile. It was natural. The peak of the strawberry season was over, and the last few days the workers, most of them *braceros*,[1] were not picking as many boxes as they had during the months of June and July.

As the last days of August disappeared, so did the number of *braceros*. Sunday, only one—the best picker—came to work. I liked him. Sometimes we talked during our half-hour lunch break. That is how I found out he was from Jalisco,[2] the same state in Mexico my family was from. That Sunday was the last time I saw him.

When the sun had tired and sunk behind the mountains, Ito signaled us that it was time to go home. *"Ya esora,"*[3] he yelled in his broken Spanish. Those were the words I waited for twelve hours a day, every day, seven days a week, week after week. And the thought of not hearing them again saddened me.

As we drove home, Papa did not say a word. With both hands on the wheel, he stared at the dirt road. My older brother, Roberto, was also silent. He leaned his head back and closed his eyes. Once in a while he cleared from his throat the dust that blew in from outside.

Yes, it was that time of year. When I opened the front door to the shack, I stopped. Everything we owned was neatly packed in card-board boxes. Suddenly I felt even more the weight of hours, days, weeks, and months of work. I sat down on a box. The thought of having to move to Fresno and knowing what was in store for me there brought tears to my eyes.

That night I could not sleep. I lay in bed thinking about how much I hated this move.

A little before five o'clock in the morning, Papa woke everyone up. A few minutes later, the yelling and screaming of my little brothers and sisters, for whom the move was a great adventure, broke the silence of dawn. Shortly, the barking of the dogs accompanied them.

While we packed the breakfast dishes, Papa went outside to start the "Carcanchita." That was the name Papa gave his old '38 black Plymouth. He bought it in a used-car lot in Santa Rosa in the winter of 1949. Papa was very proud of his car. *"Mi Carcanchita,"* my little jalopy, he called it. He had a right to be proud of it. He spent a lot of time looking at other cars before buying this one. When he finally chose the "Carcanchita," he checked it thoroughly before driving it out of the car lot. He examined every inch of the car. He listened to the motor, tilting his head from side to side like a parrot, trying to detect any noises that

---

1. **braceros** (brä sä′ rōs): *Spanish:* Mexicans who are allowed to work on American farms.
2. **Jalisco** (hä lēs′ kō).
3. **Ya esora** (yä äs ô′ rä): *Spanish:* It's time.

spelled car trouble. After being satisfied with the looks and sounds of the car, Papa then insisted on knowing who the original owner was. He never did find out from the car salesman. But he bought the car anyway. Papa figured the original owner must have been an important man because behind the rear seat of the car he found a blue necktie.

Papa parked the car out in front and left the motor running. *"Listo"* (ready), he yelled. Without saying a word, Roberto and I began to carry the boxes out to the car. Roberto carried the two big boxes and I carried the two smaller ones. Papa then threw the mattress on top of the car roof and tied it with ropes to the front and rear bumpers.

Everything was packed except Mama's pot. It was an old, large galvanized pot she had picked up at an army surplus store in Santa Maria the year I was born. The pot was full of dents and nicks, and the more dents and nicks it had, the more Mama liked it. *"Mi olla"* (my pot), she used to say proudly.

I held the front door open as Mama carefully carried out her pot by both handles, making sure not to spill the cooked beans. When she got to the car, Papa reached out to help her with it. Roberto opened the rear car door and Papa gently placed it on the floor behind the front seat. All of us then climbed in. Papa sighed, wiped the sweat off his forehead with his sleeve, and said wearily: *"Es todo"* (that's it).

As we drove away, I felt a lump in my throat. I turned around and looked at our little shack for the last time.

At sunset we drove into a labor camp near Fresno. Since Papa did not speak English, Mama asked the camp foreman if he needed any more workers. "We don't need no more," said the foreman, scratching his head. "Check with Sullivan down the road. Can't miss him.

He lives in a big white house with a fence around it."

When we got there, Mama walked up to the house. She went through a white gate, past a row of rose bushes, up the stairs to the front door. She rang the doorbell. The porch light went on and a tall, husky man came out. They exchanged a few words. After the man went in, Mama clasped her hands and hurried back to the car. "We have work! Mr. Sullivan said we can stay there the whole season," she said, gasping and pointing to an old garage near the stables.

The garage was worn out by the years. It had no windows. The walls, eaten by termites, strained to support the roof full of holes. The loose dirt floor, populated by earthworms, looked like a gray road map.

That night, by the light of a kerosene lamp, we unpacked and cleaned our new home. Roberto swept away the loose dirt, leaving the hard ground. Papa plugged the holes in the walls with old newspapers and tin can tops. Mama fed my little brothers and sisters. Papa and Roberto then brought in the mattress and placed it in the far corner of the garage. "Mama, you and the little ones sleep on the mattress. Roberto, Panchito, and I will sleep outside under the trees," Papa said.

Early next morning Mr. Sullivan showed us where his crop was, and after breakfast, Papa, Roberto, and I headed for the vineyard to pick.

Around nine o'clock the temperature had risen to almost one hundred degrees. I was completely soaked in sweat, and my mouth felt as if I had been chewing on a handkerchief. I walked over to the end of the row, picked up the jug of water we had brought, and began drinking. "Don't drink too much; you'll get sick," Roberto shouted. No sooner had he said that than I felt sick to my stomach. I dropped to my knees and let the jug roll off my hands. I

PORTRAIT OF NITO, 1961. *Peter Hurd. Courtesy of El Prado Gallery, Sedona, Arizona.*

remained motionless with my eyes glued on the hot sandy ground. All I could hear was the drone of insects. Slowly I began to recover. I poured water over my face and neck and watched the black mud run down my arms and hit the ground.

I still felt a little dizzy when we took a break to eat lunch. It was past two o'clock, and we sat underneath a large walnut tree that was on the side of the road. While we ate, Papa jotted down the number of boxes we had picked. Roberto drew designs on the ground with a stick. Suddenly I noticed Papa's face turn pale as he looked down the road. "Here comes the school bus," he whispered loudly in alarm. Instinctively, Roberto and I ran and hid in the vineyards. We did not want to get in trouble for not going to school. The yellow bus stopped in front of Mr. Sullivan's house. Two neatly dressed boys about my age got off. They carried books under their arms. After they crossed the street, the bus drove away. Roberto and I came out from hiding and joined Papa. *"Tienen que tener cuidado"* (you have to be careful), he warned us.

After lunch we went back to work. The sun kept beating down. The buzzing insects, the wet sweat, and the hot dry dust made the afternoon seem to last forever. Finally the mountains around the valley reached out and swallowed the sun. Within an hour it was too dark to continue picking. The vines blanketed the grapes, making it difficult to see the bunches. *"Vámonos,"*[4] said Papa, signaling to us that it was time to quit work. Papa then took out a pencil and began to figure out how much we had earned our first day. He wrote down numbers, crossed some out, wrote down some more. *"Quince"* (fifteen dollars), he murmured.

When we arrived home, we took a cold shower underneath a waterhose. We then sat down to eat dinner around some wooden crates that served as a table. Mama had cooked a special meal for us. We had rice and tortillas with *carne con chile,*[5] my favorite dish.

The next morning I could hardly move. My body ached all over. I felt little control over my arms and legs. This feeling went on every morning for days until my muscles finally got used to the work.

It was Monday, the first week of November. The grape season was over, and I could now go to school. I woke up early that morning and lay in bed, looking at the stars and savoring the thought of not going to work and of starting sixth grade for the first time that year. Since I could not sleep, I decided to get up and join Papa and Roberto at breakfast. I sat at the table across from Roberto, but I kept my head down. I did not want to look up and face him. I knew he was sad. He was not going to school today. He was not going tomorrow, or next week, or next month. He would not go until the cotton season was over, and that was some-

time in February. I rubbed my hands together and watched the dry, acid-stained skin fall to the floor in little rolls.

When Papa and Roberto left for work, I felt relief. I walked to the top of a small grade next to the shack and watched the "Carcanchita" disappear in the distance in a cloud of dust.

Two hours later, around eight o'clock, I stood by the side of the road waiting for school bus number twenty. When it arrived, I climbed in. No one noticed me. Everyone was busy either talking or yelling. I sat in an empty seat in the back.

When the bus stopped in front of the school, I felt very nervous. I looked out the bus window and saw boys and girls carrying books under their arms. I felt empty. I put my hands in my pants pockets and walked to the principal's office. When I entered, I heard a woman's voice say: "May I help you?" I was startled. I had not heard English for months. For a few seconds I remained speechless. I looked at the lady who waited for an answer. My first instinct was to answer her in Spanish, but I held back. Finally, after struggling for English words, I managed to tell her that I wanted to enroll in the sixth grade. After answering many questions, I was led to the classroom.

Mr. Lema, the sixth-grade teacher, greeted me and assigned me a desk. He then introduced me to the class. I was so nervous and scared at that moment when everyone's eyes were on me that I wished I were with Papa and Roberto picking cotton. After taking roll, Mr. Lema gave the class the assignment for the first hour. "The first thing we have to do this morn-

---

4. **Vámonos** (bvä′ mō nōs): *Spanish:* Let's go.
5. **carne con chile** (kär′ nä kän chi′l ä): *Spanish:* meat with chili.

ing is finish reading the story we began yesterday," he said enthusiastically. He walked up to me, handed me an English book, and asked me to read. "We are on page 125," he said politely. When I heard this, I felt my blood rush to my head. I felt dizzy. "Would you like to read?" he asked hesitantly. I opened the book to page 125. My mouth was dry. My eyes began to water. I could not begin. "You can read later," Mr. Lema said understandingly.

For the rest of the reading period I kept getting angrier and angrier with myself. I should have read, I thought to myself.

During recess I went into the restroom and opened my English book to page 125. I began to read in a low voice, pretending I was in class. There were many words I did not know. I closed the book and headed back to the classroom.

Mr. Lema was sitting at his desk correcting papers. When I entered he looked up at me and smiled. I felt better. I walked up to him and asked if he could help me with the new words. "Gladly," he said.

The rest of the month I spent my lunch hours working on English with Mr. Lema, my best friend at school.

One Friday during lunch hour, Mr. Lema asked me to take a walk with him to the music room. "Do you like music?" he asked me as we entered the building.

"Yes, I like Mexican *corridos*,"[6] I answered. He then picked up a trumpet, blew on it and handed it to me. The sound gave me goose bumps. I knew that sound. I had heard it in many Mexican *corridos*. "How would you like to learn how to play it?" he asked. He must have read my face because before I could answer, he added: "I'll teach you how to play it during our lunch hours."

That day I could hardly wait to get home to tell Papa and Mama the great news. As I got off the bus, my little brothers and sisters ran up to meet me. They were yelling and screaming. I thought they were happy to see me, but when I opened the door to our shack, I saw that everything we owned was neatly packed in cardboard boxes.

---

6. **corridos** (kô rē' dōs): *Spanish:* ballads.

Getting at Meaning

RECALLING

1. How does the family prepare to move? At what two places in the story does this happen?

2. Who asks Mr. Sullivan for work? What is his answer?

3. How does the boy respond when Mr. Lema asks him whether he likes music? What does Mr. Lema promise to teach him?

INTERPRETING

4. Why does the family move frequently?

5. Why does the sight of the school bus alarm Papa?

6. When does the boy begin school? Why can't Roberto enter at this time?

7. What does Mr. Lema do to make the boy

feel at home in his new school? How does the boy feel about Mr. Lema?

8. How do the younger children in the family feel about moving? How does the boy probably feel? Why does he probably feel this way?

9. What is Mama's most prized possession? What is Papa's? Why might these possessions be so important to them?

CRITICAL THINKING: EVALUATING

10. What insights does this story give you into the difficulties faced by migrant children? What unique problems do these children face?

Developing Skills in Reading Literature

1. **Narrator and Point of View.** As you have learned, the narrator is the teller of a story. Point of view refers to the perspective from which a story is told. This story is told from the first-person point of view. In other words, the narrator is also one of the characters in the story. The events of the story are presented through this character's eyes. How does the narrator feel toward the following things: moving, school, Mr. Lema, his work, his mother and father, and music. In what ways are the narrator's feelings revealed to you?

2. **Conflict.** Conflict is a struggle between opposing forces. The major conflict in this story is between the narrator's desire for some sense of permanence and the necessity of moving. Is this conflict resolved in the way that the narrator would like it to be? Explain.

3. **Surprise Ending.** A surprise ending is an unexpected twist in plot at the conclusion of a story. Before reading the last paragraph of "The Circuit," did you know what was going to happen? What is the surprising twist in the plot?

4. **Title.** The title of a work of literature often provides a clue to its meaning. What does the word *circuit* mean? In what way is the family traveling in a circuit? In what way are the narrator's emotions also traveling in a circuit?

Developing Writing Skills

Description: Using All of the Senses. The writer of this story uses sensory details such as these to describe what it is like to work in the fields under the hot sun:

> hot, sandy ground (senses of touch and sight)
> the drone of insects (sense of hearing)
> wet sweat (sense of touch)

Think about the hottest place you have ever been in, and list five or six sensory details to describe this place. Choose details that appeal to at least three senses. Then use these prewriting notes to write a one paragraph description. Refer to **Using the Process of Writing** on pages 614–623 if you need help.

B I O G R A P H Y

Francisco Jiménez (born 1943) was born in Jalisco, Mexico. Although he became a United States citizen, Jiménez chose a career that enabled him to study his native culture. He is a professor at the University of Santa Clara where he specializes in Mexican-American literature. Jiménez has written articles for journals and has coauthored two textbooks, *¡Viva la Lengua!* and *Spanish Here and Now.*

I was having a grand time, having died.

Stolen Day

Sherwood Anderson

It must be that all children are actors. The whole thing started with a boy on our street named Walter, who had inflammatory rheumatism.[1] That's what they called it. He didn't have to go to school.

Still, he could walk about. He could go fishing in the creek or the waterworks pond. There was a place up at the pond where in the spring the water came tumbling over the dam and formed a deep pool. It was a good place. Sometimes you could get some big ones there.

I went down that way on my way to school one spring morning. It was out of my way but I wanted to see if Walter was there.

He was, inflammatory rheumatism and all. There he was, sitting with a fish pole in his hand. He had been able to walk down there all right.

It was then that my own legs began to hurt. My back, too. I went on to school but, at the recess time, I began to cry. I did it when the teacher, Sarah Suggett, had come out into the schoolhouse yard.

She came right over to me.

"I ache all over," I said. I did, too.

I kept on crying and it worked all right.

"You'd better go on home," she said.

So I went. I limped painfully away. I kept on limping until I got out of the schoolhouse street.

Then I felt better. I still had inflammatory rheumatism pretty bad but I could get along better.

I must have done some thinking on the way home.

"I'd better not say I have inflammatory rheumatism," I decided. "Maybe if you've got that, you swell up."

I thought I'd better go around to where Walter was and ask him about that, so I did—but he wasn't there.

"They must not be biting today," I thought.

I had a feeling that, if I said I had inflammatory rheumatism, Mother or my brothers and my sister Stella might laugh. They did laugh at me pretty often, and I didn't like it at all.

"Just the same," I said to myself, "I have got it." I began to hurt and ache again.

I went home and sat on the front steps of our house. I sat there a long time. There wasn't

---

1. **inflammatory rheumatism** (rōō′ mə tiz′m): a painful soreness and stiffness of the joints and muscles.

WHITTLING BOY, 1873. *Winslow Homer. Malden Public Library, Malden, Massachusetts.*

anyone at home but Mother and the two little ones. Ray would have been four or five then and Earl might have been three.

It was Earl who saw me there. I had got tired of sitting and was lying on the porch. Earl was always a quiet, solemn little fellow.

He must have said something to Mother, for presently she came.

"What's the matter with you? Why aren't you in school?" she asked.

I came pretty near telling her right out that I had inflammatory rheumatism, but I thought I'd better not. Mother and Father had been speaking of Walter's case at the table just the day before. "It affects the heart," Father had said. That frightened me when I thought of it. "I might die," I thought. "I might just suddenly die right here; my heart might stop beating."

On the day before, I had been running a race with my brother Irve. We were up at the fairgrounds after school, and there was a half-mile track.

"I'll bet you can't run a half mile," he said. "I bet you I could beat you running clear around the track."

And so we did it and I beat him, but afterward my heart did seem to beat pretty hard. I remembered that, lying there on the porch. "It's a wonder, with my inflammatory rheumatism and all, I didn't just drop down dead," I thought. The thought frightened me a lot. I ached worse than ever.

"I ache, Ma," I said. "I just ache."

She made me go in the house and upstairs and get into bed.

It wasn't so good. It was spring. I was up there for perhaps an hour, maybe two, and then I felt better.

I got up and went downstairs. "I feel better, Ma," I said.

Mother said she was glad. She was pretty busy that day and hadn't paid much attention to me. She had made me get into bed upstairs and then hadn't even come up to see how I was.

I didn't think much of that when I was up there; but when I got downstairs where she was, and when, after I had said I felt better and she only said she was glad and went right on with her work, I began to ache again.

I thought, "I'll bet I die of it. I bet I do."

I went out to the front porch and sat down. I was pretty sore at Mother.

"If she really knew the truth, that I have inflammatory rheumatism and I may just drop down dead any time, I'll bet she wouldn't care about that either," I thought.

I was getting more and more angry the more thinking I did.

"I know what I'm going to do," I thought; "I'm going to go fishing."

I thought that, feeling the way I did, I might be sitting on the high bank just above the deep pool where the water went over the dam, and suddenly my heart would stop beating.

And then, of course, I'd pitch forward, over the bank into the pool; and, if I wasn't dead when I hit the water, I'd drown sure.

They would all come home to supper and they'd miss me.

"But where is he?"

Then Mother would remember that I'd come home from school aching.

She'd go upstairs, and I wouldn't be there. One day during the year before, there was a child got drowned in a spring. It was one of the Wyatt children.

Right down at the end of the street there was a spring under a birch tree, and there had been a barrel sunk in the ground.

Everyone had always been saying the spring ought to be kept covered, but it wasn't.

So the Wyatt child went down there, played around alone, and fell in and got drowned.

Mother was the one who had found the drowned child. She had gone to get a pail of water, and there the child was, drowned and dead.

This had been in the evening when we were all at home, and Mother had come running up the street with the dead, dripping child in her arms. She was making for the Wyatt house as hard as she could run, and she was pale.

She had a terrible look on her face, I remembered then.

"So," I thought, "they'll miss me, and there'll be a search made. Very likely there'll be someone who has seen me sitting by the pond fishing, and there'll be a big alarm and all the town will turn out and they'll drag the pond."

I was having a grand time, having died. Maybe, after they found me and had got me out of the deep pool, Mother would grab me up in her arms and run home with me as she had run with the Wyatt child.

I got up from the porch and went around the house. I got my fishing pole and lit out for the pool below the dam. Mother was busy—she always was—and didn't see me go. When I got there, I thought I'd better not sit too near the edge of the high bank.

By this time I didn't ache hardly at all, but I thought,

"With inflammatory rheumatism you can't tell," I thought.

"It probably comes and goes," I thought.

"Walter has it and he goes fishing," I thought.

I had got my line into the pool and suddenly I got a bite. It was a regular whopper; I knew that. I'd never had a bite like that.

I knew what it was. It was one of Mr. Fenn's big carp.

Mr. Fenn was a man who had a big pond of his own. He sold ice in the summer, and the pond was to make the ice. He had bought some big carp and put them into his pond; and then, earlier in the spring when there was a freshet,[2] his dam had gone out.

So the carp had got into our creek, and one or two big ones had been caught—but none of them by a boy like me.

The carp was pulling and I was pulling and I was afraid he'd break my line, so I just tumbled down the high bank, holding onto the line and got right into the pool. We had it out, there in the pool. We struggled. We wrestled. Then I got a hand under his gills and got him out.

He was a big one all right. He was nearly half as big as I was myself. I had him on the bank and I kept one hand under his gills and I ran.

I never ran so hard in my life. He was slip-pery, and now and then he wriggled out of my arms; once I stumbled and fell on him, but I got him home.

So there it was. I was a big hero that day. Mother got a washtub and filled it with water. She put the fish in it, and all the neighbors came to look. I got into dry clothes and went down to supper—and then I made a break that spoiled my day.

There we were, all of us, at the table, and suddenly Father asked what had been the matter with me at school. He had met the teacher, Sarah Suggett, on the street, and she told him how I had become ill.

"What was the matter with you?" Father asked; and before I thought what I was saying, I let it out.

"I had the inflammatory rheumatism," I said—and a shout went up. It made me sick to hear them, the way they all laughed.

It brought back all the aching again, and like a fool I began to cry.

"Well, I *have* got it—I *have*," I cried, and I got up from the table and ran upstairs.

I stayed there until Mother came up. I knew it would be a long time before I heard the last of the inflammatory rheumatism. I was sick all right, but the aching I now had wasn't in my legs or in my back.

_____

2. **freshet** (fresh′ it): a flooding of a stream.

Getting at Meaning

RECALLING

1. Who is Walter? Why doesn't Walter go to school?

2. What disease does the boy who is telling the story begin imagining that he has?

INTERPRETING

3. Why does the boy envy Walter? Why does he want to have inflammatory rheumatism himself? How much does he know about inflammatory rheumatism? How do you know?

4. The boy implies, or suggests, that he has a large family and a very busy mother. Find evidence in the story that supports this idea.

5. Which of the boy's actions show that he is actually in fine physical condition?

6. Why do the members of the boy's family laugh so heartily when he says that he has inflammatory rheumatism?

7. At the end of the story, the boy refers to an aching that isn't in his legs or back. What kind of aching could he be referring to?

CRITICAL THINKING: EVALUATING

8. Sherwood Anderson wrote this story when he was a grown man. Did he manage to create a realistic child? What parts of the story seem the closest to the realities of a boy's life? What parts are not so realistic?

Developing Skills in Reading Literature

1. **Plot and Climax.** Plot is the sequence of events in a story. It is the writer's blueprint for what happens, when, and to whom. The climax, or turning point, is the high point of interest in a story. The events in this story are related in chronological order, building up to the climax of the day. On a separate sheet of paper, make a list of the major events in the story. Place a star by the event that is the climax, or turning point.

2. **Point of View.** Point of view refers to the perspective from which a story is told. A story is told from the first-person point of view when the narrator, or storyteller, is also a character in the story. This story is written from first-person point of view, and thus the narrator uses the pronoun *I*. The *I* narrator can tell the reader only what he or she thinks and sees and hears. He cannot tell what others are seeing or thinking or feeling. Readers must draw their own conclusions about the other characters based upon what the first-person narrator says.

Answer these questions about the other characters by drawing conclusions from the information that the narrator provides:

a. Is the boy Walter really too ill to go to school? Support your answer with facts from the story.

b. Why does Mother send her son to bed when he comes home with aches? What might have been her reason? Explain.

Developing Vocabulary

The Multiple Meanings of Words. *Pool* is one of the many words in the English language that has several definitions. Study the following sentences. Then, on a separate sheet of paper, write a definition for the word *pool* as used in each sentence.

1. I took my fishing pole and set out for the *pool* below the dam.

2. If there is a gasoline shortage, we will form a car *pool*.

3. We have a *pool* table in the basement.

4. We will *pool* our money and buy mother a present.

5. They formed a *pool* to purchase the property.

6. In the summer we go to the public swimming *pool*.

Developing Writing Skills

Writing a News Report. In "The Stolen Day" the narrator relates in vivid detail the tragic drowning of a child. Imagine that you are a newspaper reporter. Write a brief news report about the child's death. Before you begin writing, study some newspaper stories to get an idea of their style. Also reread the section of Sherwood Anderson's story in which the death is recounted, and in your prewriting notes record all the information that Anderson gives. As you write and revise your report, refer to **Using the Process of Writing** found on pages 614–623.

B I O G R A P H Y

Sherwood Anderson (1876–1941) was a novelist and short story writer from Camden, Ohio. His youth was spent moving from place to place with his family. At the age of fourteen, he left school to help support his six brothers and sisters. In 1912 he left a successful business career to begin a new life as a writer. Two years later his first novel, *Windy MacPherson's Son,* was published. Anderson is most famous for collections of short stories, such as *Winesburg, Ohio.*

Last Cover

Paul Annixter

I'm not sure I can tell you what you want to know about my brother; but everything about the pet fox is important, so I'll tell all that from the beginning.

It goes back to a winter afternoon after I'd hunted the woods all day for a sign of our lost pet. I remember the way my mother looked up as I came into the kitchen. Without my speaking, she knew what had happened. For six hours I had walked, reading signs, looking for a delicate print in the damp soil or even a hair that might have told of a red fox passing that way—but I had found nothing.

"Did you go up in the foothills?" Mom asked.

I nodded. My face was stiff from held-back tears. My brother, Colin, who was going on twelve, got it all from one look at me and went into a heartbroken, almost silent, crying.

Three weeks before, Bandit, the pet fox Colin and I had raised from a tiny kit, had disappeared, and not even a rumor had been heard of him since.

"He'd have had to go off soon anyway," Mom comforted. "A big, lolloping fellow like him, he's got to live his life same as us. But he may come back. That fox set a lot of store by you boys in spite of his wild ways."

"He set a lot of store by our food, anyway," Father said. He sat in a chair by the kitchen window, mending a piece of harness. "We'll be seeing a lot more of that fellow, never fear. That fox learned to pine for table scraps and young chickens. He was getting to be an egg thief, too, and he's not likely to forget that."

"That was only pranking when he was little," Colin said desperately.

From the first, the tame fox had made tension in the family. It was Father who said we'd better name him Bandit, after he'd made away with his first young chicken.

"Maybe you know," Father said shortly. "But when an animal turns to egg sucking, he's usually incurable. He'd better not come pranking around my chicken run again."

It was late February, and I remember the bleak, dead cold that had set in, cold that was a rare thing for our Carolina hills. Flocks of sparrows and snowbirds had appeared, to peck hungrily at all that the pigs and chickens didn't eat.

"This one's a killer," Father would say of a morning, looking out at the whitened barn roof. "This one will make the shoats[1] squeal."

A fire snapped all day in our cookstove and another in the stone fireplace in the living room, but still the farmhouse was never warm. The leafless woods were bleak and empty, and I spoke of that to Father when I came back from my search.

"It's always a sad time in the woods when the seven sleepers are under cover," he said.

"What sleepers are they?" I asked. Father was full of woods lore.

"Why, all the animals that have got sense enough to hole up and stay hid in weather like this. Let's see, how was it the old rhyme named them?

> *Surly bear and sooty bat,*
> *Brown chuck and masked coon*
> *Chippy-munk and sly skunk,*
> *And all the mouses*
> *'Cept in men's houses.*

"And man would have joined them and made it eight, Granther Yeary always said, if he'd had a little more sense."

"I was wondering if the red fox mightn't make it eight," Mom said.

Father shook his head. "Late winter's a high time for foxes. Time when they're out deviling, not sleeping."

My chest felt hollow. I wanted to cry like Colin over our lost fox, but at fourteen a boy doesn't cry. Colin had squatted down on the floor and got out his small hammer and nails to start another new frame for a new picture. Maybe then he'd make a drawing for the frame and be able to forget his misery. It had been that way with him since he was five.

I thought of the new dress Mom had brought home a few days before in a heavy cardboard box. That box cover would be fine for Colin to draw on. I spoke of it, and Mom's glance thanked me as she went to get it. She and I worried a lot about Colin. He was small for his age, delicate and blond, his hair much lighter and softer than mine, his eyes deep and wide and blue. He was often sick, and I knew the fear Mom had that he might be predestined. I'm just ordinary, like Father. I'm the sort of stuff that can take it—tough and strong—but Colin was always sort of special.

Mom lighted the lamp. Colin began cutting his white cardboard carefully, fitting it into his frame. Father's sharp glance turned on him now and again.

"There goes the boy making another frame before there's a picture for it," he said. "It's too much like cutting out a man's suit for a fellow that's say, twelve years old. Who knows whether he'll grow into it?"

Mom was into him then, quick. "Not a single frame of Colin's has ever gone to waste. The boy has real talent, Sumter, and it's time you realized it."

"Of course he has," Father said. "All kids have 'em. But they get over 'em."

"It isn't the pox we're talking of," Mom sniffed.

"In a way it is. Ever since you started talking up Colin's art, I've had an invalid for help around the place."

Father wasn't as hard as he made out, I knew, but he had to hold a balance against all Mom's frothing. For him the thing was the land and all that pertained to it. I was following in Father's footsteps, true to form, but Colin threatened to break the family tradition with his leaning toward art, with Mom "aiding and abetting him," as Father liked to put it. For the

---

1. **shoats** (shōts): young hogs.

past two years she had had dreams of my brother becoming a real artist and going away to the city to study.

It wasn't that Father had no understanding of such things. I could remember, through the years, Colin lying on his stomach in the front room making pencil sketches, and how a good drawing would catch Father's eye halfway across the room; and how he would sometimes gather up two or three of them to study, frowning and muttering, one hand in his beard, while a great pride rose in Colin, and in me too. Most of Colin's drawings were of the woods and wild things, and there Father was a master critic. He made out to scorn what seemed to him a passive "white-livered" interpretation of nature through brush and pencil instead of rod and rifle.

At supper that night, Colin could scarcely eat. Ever since he'd been able to walk, my brother had had a growing love of wild things; but Bandit had been like his very own, a gift of the woods. One afternoon a year and a half before, Father and Laban Small had been running a vixen through the hills with their dogs. With the last of her strength the she-fox had made for her den, not far from our house. The dogs had overtaken her and killed her just before she reached it. When Father and Laban came up, they'd found Colin crouched nearby holding her cub in his arms.

Father had been for killing the cub, which was still too young to shift for itself, but Colin's grief had brought Mom into it. We'd taken the young fox into the kitchen, all of us, except Father, gone a bit silly over the little thing.

FOX HUNT, 1893. *Winslow Homer. Pennsylvania Academy of the Fine Arts, Philadelphia. Temple Fund Purchase.*

Colin had held it in his arms and fed it warm milk from a spoon.

"Watch out with all your soft ways," Father had warned, standing in the doorway. "You'll make too much of him. Remember, you can't make a dog out of a fox. Half of that little critter has to love, but the other half is a wild hunter. You boys will mean a whole lot to him while he's kit, but there'll come a day when you won't mean a thing to him, and he'll leave you shorn."

For two weeks after that, Colin had nursed the cub, weaning it from milk to bits of meat. For a year they were always together. The cub grew fast. It was soon following Colin and me about the barnyard. It turned out to be a patch fox, with a saddle of darker fur across its shoulders.

I haven't the words to tell you what the fox meant to us. It was far more wonderful owning him than owning any dog. There was something rare and secret, like the spirit of the woods about him; and back of his calm, straw-gold eyes was the sense of a brain the equal of a man's. The fox became Colin's whole life.

Each day, going and coming from school, Colin and I took long side trips through the woods, looking for Bandit. Wild things' memories were short, we knew; we'd have to find him soon, or the old bond would be broken.

Ever since I was ten I'd been allowed to hunt with Father, so I was good at reading signs. But, in a way, Colin knew more about the woods and wild things than Father or me. What came to me from long observation, Colin seemed to know by instinct.

It was Colin who felt out, like an Indian, the stretch of woods where Bandit had his den, who found the first slim, small fox-print in the damp earth. And then, on an afternoon in March, we saw him. I remember the day well, the racing clouds, the wind rattling the tops of the pine trees and swaying the Spanish moss. Bandit had just come out of a clump of laurel; in the maze of leaves behind him we caught a glimpse of a slim red vixen, so we knew he had found a mate. She melted from sight like a shadow, but Bandit turned to watch us, his mouth open, his tongue lolling as he smiled his old foxy smile. On his thin chops, I saw a tell-tale chicken feather.

Colin moved silently forward, his movements so quiet and casual he seemed to be standing still. He called Bandit's name, and the fox held his ground, drawn to us with all his senses. For a few moments he let Colin actually put an arm about him. It was then I knew that he loved us still, for all of Father's warnings. He really loved us back, with a fierce, secret love no tame thing ever gave. But the urge of his life just then was toward his new mate. Suddenly, he whirled about and disappeared in the laurels.

Colin looked at me with glowing eyes. "We haven't really lost him, Stan. When he gets through with his spring sparking[2] he may come back. But we've got to show ourselves to him a lot, so he won't forget."

"It's a go," I said.

"Promise not to say a word to Father," Colin said, and I agreed. For I knew by the chicken feather that Bandit had been up to no good.

A week later the woods were budding, and the thickets were rustling with all manner of wild things scurrying on the love scent. Colin managed to get a glimpse of Bandit every few

---

2. **sparking:** courting.

days. He couldn't get close though, for the spring running was a lot more important to a fox than any human beings were.

Every now and then Colin got out his framed box cover and looked at it, but he never drew anything on it; he never even picked up his pencil. I remember wondering if what Father had said about framing a picture before you had one had spoiled something for him.

I was helping Father with the planting now, but Colin managed to be in the woods every day. By degrees, he learned Bandit's range, where he drank and rested, and where he was likely to be according to the time of day. One day he told me how he had petted Bandit again, and how they had walked together a long way in the woods. All this time we had kept his secret from Father.

As summer came on, Bandit began to live up to the prediction Father had made. Accustomed to human beings he moved without fear about the scattered farms of the region, raiding barns and hen runs that other foxes wouldn't have dared go near. And he taught his wild mate to do the same. Almost every night they got into some poultry house, and by late June, Bandit was not only killing chickens and ducks but feeding on eggs and young chicks whenever he got the chance.

Stories of his doings came to us from many sources, for he was still easily recognized by the dark patch on his shoulders. Many a farmer took a shot at him as he fled, and some of them set out on his trail with dogs, but they always returned home without even sighting him. Bandit was familiar with all the dogs in the region, and he knew a hundred tricks to confound them. He got a reputation that year beyond that of any fox our hills had known.

His confidence grew, and he gave up wild hunting altogether and lived entirely off the poultry farmers. By September, the hill farmers banded together to hunt him down.

It was Father who brought home that news one night. All time-honored rules of the fox chase were to be broken in this hunt; if the dogs couldn't bring Bandit down, he was to be shot on sight. I was stricken and furious. I remember the misery of Colin's face in the lamplight. Father, who took pride in all the ritual of the hunt, had refused to be a party to such an affair, though in justice he could do nothing but sanction any sort of hunt; for Bandit, as old Sam Wetherwax put it, had been "purely getting in the Lord's hair."

The hunt began next morning, and it was the biggest turnout our hills had known. There were at least twenty mounted men in the party and as many dogs. Father and I were working in the lower field as they passed along the river road. Most of the hunters carried rifles, and they looked ugly.

Twice during the morning I went up to the house to find Colin, but he was nowhere around. As we worked, Father and I could follow the progress of the hunt by the distant hound music on the breeze. We could tell just where the hunters first caught sight of the fox and where Bandit was leading the dogs during the first hour. We knew as well as if we'd seen it how Bandit roused another fox along Turkey Branch and forced it to run for him, and how the dogs swept after it for twenty minutes before they sensed their mistake.

Noon came, and Colin had not come in to eat. After dinner Father didn't go back to the field. He moped about, listening to the hound talk. He didn't like what was on any more than

I did, and now and again I caught his smile of satisfaction when we heard the broken, angry notes of the hunting horn, telling that the dogs had lost the trail or had run another fox.

I was restless, and I went up into the hills in midafternoon. I ranged the woods for miles, thinking all the time of Colin. Time lost all meaning for me, and the short day was nearing an end, when I heard the horn talking again, telling that the fox had put over another trick. All day he had deviled the dogs and mocked the hunters. This new trick and the coming night would work to save him. I was wildly glad, as I moved down toward Turkey Branch and stood listening for a time by the deep, shaded pool where for years we boys had gone swimming, sailed boats, and dreamed summer dreams.

Suddenly, out of the corner of my eye, I saw the sharp ears and thin, pointed mask of a fox—in the water almost beneath me. It was Bandit, craftily submerged there, all but his head, resting in the cool water of the pool and the shadow of the two big beeches that spread above it. He must have run forty miles or more since morning. And he must have hidden in this place before. His knowing, crafty mask blended perfectly with the shadows and a mass of drift and branches that had collected by the bank of the pool. He was so still that a pair of thrushes flew up from the spot as I came up, not knowing he was there.

Bandit's bright, harried eyes were looking right at me. But I did not look at him direct. Some woods instinct, swifter than thought, kept me from it. So he and I met as in another world, indirectly, with feeling but without sign or greeting.

Suddenly I saw that Colin was standing almost beside me. Silently as a water snake, he had come out of the bushes and stood there. Our eyes met, and a quick and secret smile passed between us. It was a rare moment in which I really "met" my brother, when something of his essence flowed into me, and I knew all of him. I've never lost it since.

My eyes still turned from the fox, my heart pounding, I moved quietly away, and Colin moved with me. We whistled softly as we went, pretending to busy ourselves along the bank of the stream. There was magic in it, as if by will we wove a web of protection about the fox, a ring-pass-not that none might penetrate. It was so, too, we felt, in the brain of Bandit, and that doubled the charm. To us he was still our little pet that we had carried about in our arms on countless summer afternoons.

Two hundred yards upstream, we stopped beside slim, fresh tracks in the mud where Bandit had entered the branch. The tracks angled upstream. But in the water the wily creature had turned down.

We climbed the far bank to wait, and Colin told me how Bandit's secret had been his secret ever since an afternoon three months before, when he'd watched the fox swim downstream to hide in the deep pool. Today he'd waited on the bank, feeling that Bandit, hard pressed by the dogs, might again seek the pool for sanctuary.

We looked back once as we turned homeward. He still had not moved. We didn't know until later that he was killed that same night by a chance hunter, as he crept out from his hiding place.

That evening Colin worked a long time on his framed box cover that had lain about the house untouched all summer. He kept at it all the next day too. I had never seen him work so hard. I seemed to sense in the air the feeling he was putting into it, how he was *believing* his picture into being. It was evening before he finished it. Without a word he handed it to Father. Mom and I went and looked over his shoulder.

It was a delicate and intricate pencil drawing of the deep branch pool; and there was Bandit's head and watching, fear-filled eyes hiding there amid the leaves and shadows, woven craftily into the maze of twigs and branches, as if by nature's art itself. Hardly a fox there at all, but the place where he was—or should have been. I recognized it instantly, but Mom gave a sort of incredulous sniff.

"I'll declare," she said, "it's mazy as a puzzle. It just looks like a lot of sticks and leaves to me."

Long minutes of study passed before Father's eye picked out the picture's secret, as few men's could have done. I laid that to Father's being a born hunter. That was a picture that might have been done especially for him. In fact, I guess it was.

Finally he turned to Colin with his deep, slow smile. "So that's how Bandit fooled them all," he said. He sat holding the picture with a sort of tenderness for a long time, while we glowed in the warmth of the shared secret. That was Colin's moment. Colin's art stopped being a pox to Father right there. And later, when the time came for Colin to go to art school, it was Father who was his solid backer.

Getting at Meaning

RECALLING

1. Who tells the boys to name their fox Bandit? Why does he choose this name?

2. What is Colin's talent? What does Colin's mother think of her son's talent? Early in the story, what does his father think of it?

3. How does Colin acquire Bandit?

4. What does Bandit do that Colin's father predicted?

5. Why is a hunt for Bandit organized?

6. During the hunt, how do Stan and his father follow what is going on?

7. What does Bandit do to escape the hunters?

8. What does Colin draw on the framed box cover?

INTERPRETING

9. In what ways are Colin and Stan different? In what ways are they alike? When Stan and Colin meet at the pool in which Bandit is hiding, Stan says, "It was a rare moment in which I really 'met' my brother." What does Stan mean by this?

10. What does the father warn Colin and Stan about with regard to Bandit? What does he fear will happen? What does this reveal about the father's character?

11. Why does the father refuse to participate in the hunt?

12. What secret does Colin share with his father? How does he share this secret? Why does the father come to support Colin's ambition to be an artist?

CRITICAL THINKING: APPLYING

13. In the early part of this story, the father seems to hold the opinion that art is not very important because it is not practical and useful. Do you agree with the father's opinion? Explain your answer.

Developing Skills in Reading Literature

1. **Plot.** Plot is the sequence of events in a story. It is the writer's blueprint for what happens, when, and to whom. On a separate sheet of paper, list in chronological order the major events in the plot of this story.

2. **Conflict.** Conflict is a struggle between opposing forces. In this story, there are two major conflicts. One is between Colin's father, who thinks that art is impractical and unimportant, and Colin, who is the sort of person who needs to express himself through art. How do you first learn about this conflict? How is the conflict resolved? What is the other major conflict in this story? How does this second conflict begin? How is it resolved?

3. **Suspense.** Suspense is a feeling of growing tension and excitement felt by a reader. How does the writer of this story create suspense?

4. **Character.** A character is a person or animal who takes part in the action of a work of literature. Stan says of Colin that he "was always sort of special." What makes Colin special? What is different about the way that he sees things and the way that he feels about them?

B I O G R A P H Y

Paul Annixter (born 1894) grew up in Minnesota. He staked out a Minnesota timber claim when he was young and, as he worked, made up stories about the animals and the elements around him. At nineteen, he published his first story. By the time he was fifty, he had published over five hundred stories, all under the name Paul Annixter, a pseudonym for his real name, Howard Sturtzel. Collections of his stories include *Devil of the Woods* and *Pride of Lions*.

Respect grows between an old Apache and a young homesteader.

The Gift of Cochise

Louis L'Amour

Tense, and white to the lips, Angie Lowe stood in the door of her cabin with a double-barreled shotgun in her hands. Beside the door was a Winchester '73, and on the table inside the house were two Walker Colts.

Facing the cabin were twelve Apaches on ragged calico ponies, and one of the Indians had lifted his hand palm outward. The Apache sitting the white-splashed bay pony was Cochise.

Beside Angie were her seven-year-old son Jimmy and her five-year-old daughter Jane.

Cochise sat his pony in silence. His black, unreadable eyes studied the woman, the children, the cabin, and the small garden. He looked at the two ponies in the corral and the three cows. His eyes strayed to the small stack of hay cut from the meadow and to the few steers farther up the canyon.

Three times the warriors of Cochise had attacked this solitary cabin and three times they had been turned back. In all, they had lost seven men, and three had been wounded. Four ponies had been killed. His braves reported that there was no man in the house, only a woman and two children, so Cochise had come to see for himself this woman who was so cer-

tain a shot with a rifle and who killed his fighting men.

These were some of the same fighting men who had outfought, outguessed and outrun the finest American army on record, an army outnumbering the Apaches by a hundred to one. Yet a lone woman with two small children had fought them off, and the woman was scarcely more than a girl. And she was prepared to fight now. There was a glint of admiration in the old eyes that appraised her. The Apache was a fighting man, and he respected fighting blood.

"Where is your man?"

"He has gone to El Paso." Angie's voice was steady, but she was frightened as she had never been before. She recognized Cochise from descriptions, and she knew that if he decided to kill or capture her it would be done. Until now, the sporadic attacks she had fought off had been those of casual bands of warriors who raided her in passing.

"He has been gone a long time. How long?"

Angie hesitated, but it was not in her to lie. "He has been gone four months."

Cochise considered that. No one but a fool would leave such a woman and such fine children. Only one thing could have prevented his return. "Your man is dead," he said.

Angie waited, her heart pounding with heavy, measured beats. She had guessed long ago that Ed had been killed, but the way Cochise spoke did not imply that Apaches had killed him, only that he must be dead or he would have returned.

"You fight well," Cochise said. "You have killed my young men."

"Your young men attacked me." She hesitated then added, "They stole my horses."

"Your man is gone. Why do you not leave?"

Angie looked at him with surprise. "Leave? Why, this is my home. This land is mine. This spring is mine. I shall not leave."

"This was an Apache spring," Cochise reminded her reasonably.

"The Apache lives in the mountains," Angie replied. "He does not need this spring. I have two children, and I do need it."

"But when the Apache comes this way, where shall he drink? His throat is dry and you keep him from water."

The very fact that Cochise was willing to talk raised her hopes. There had been a time when the Apache made no war on the white man. "Cochise speaks with a forked tongue," she said. "There is water yonder." She gestured toward the hills, where Ed had told her there were springs. "But if the people of Cochise come in peace, they may drink at this spring."

The Apache leader smiled faintly. Such a woman would rear a nation of warriors. He nodded at Jimmy. "The small one—does he also shoot?"

"He does," Angie said proudly, "and well, too!" She pointed at an upthrust leaf of prickly pear. "Show them, Jimmy."

The prickly pear was an easy two hundred yards away, and the Winchester was long and heavy, but he lifted it eagerly and steadied it against the doorjamb as his father had taught him, held his sight an instant, then fired. The bud on top of the prickly pear disintegrated.

There were grunts of appreciation from the dark-faced warriors. Cochise chuckled.

"The little warrior shoots well. It is well you have no man. You might raise an army of little warriors to fight my people."

"I have no wish to fight your people," Angie said quietly. "Your people have your ways, and I have mine. I live in peace when I am left in peace. I did not think," she added with dignity, "that the great Cochise made war on women!"

The Apache looked at her, then turned his pony away. "My people will trouble you no longer," he said. "You are the mother of a strong son."

"What about my two ponies?" she called after him. "Your young men took them from me."

Cochise did not turn or look back, and the little cavalcade of riders followed him away. Angie stepped back into the cabin and closed the door. Then she sat down abruptly, her face white, the muscles in her legs trembling.

When morning came, she went cautiously to the spring for water. Her ponies were back in the corral. They had been returned during the night.

Slowly, the days drew on. Angie broke a small piece of the meadow and planted it. Alone, she cut hay in the meadow and built another stack. She saw Indians several times, but they did not bother her. One morning, when she opened her door, a quarter of antelope lay on the step, but no Indian was in sight. Several times, during the weeks that followed, she saw moccasin tracks near the spring.

Once, going out at daybreak, she saw an

Indian girl dipping water from the spring. Angie called to her, and the girl turned quickly, facing her. Angie walked toward her, offering a bright red silk ribbon. Pleased at the gift, the Apache girl left.

And the following morning there was another quarter of antelope on her step—but she saw no Indian.

Ed Lowe had built the cabin in West Dog Canyon in the spring of 1871, but it was Angie who chose the spot, not Ed. In Santa Fe they would have told you that Ed Lowe was good-looking, shiftless and agreeable. He was, also, unfortunately handy with a pistol.

Angie's father had come from County Mayo to New York and from New York to the Mississippi, where he became a tough, brawling river boatman. In New Orleans, he met a beautiful Cajun girl and married her. Together, they started west for Santa Fe, and Angie was born en route. Both parents died of cholera when Angie was fourteen. She lived with an Irish family for the following three years, then married Ed Lowe when she was seventeen.

Santa Fe was not good for Ed, and Angie kept after him until they started south. It was Apache country, but they kept on until they reached the old Spanish ruin in West Dog. Here there were grass, water, and shelter from the wind.

There was fuel, and there were piñons and game. And Angie, with an Irish eye for the land, saw that it would grow crops.

The house itself was built on the ruins of the old Spanish building, using the thick walls and the floor. The location had been admirably chosen for defense. The house was built in a corner of the cliff, under the sheltering overhang, so that approach was possible from only two directions, both covered by an easy field of fire from the door and windows.

For seven months, Ed worked hard and steadily. He put in the first crop, he built the house, and proved himself a handy man with tools. He repaired the old plow they had bought, cleaned out the spring, and paved and walled it with slabs of stone. If he was lonely for the carefree companions of Santa Fe, he gave no indication of it. Provisions were low, and when he finally started off to the south, Angie watched him go with an ache in her heart.

She did not know whether she loved Ed. The first flush of enthusiasm had passed, and Ed Lowe had proved something less than she had believed. But he had tried, she admitted. And it had not been easy for him. He was an amiable soul, given to whittling and idle talk, all of which he missed in the loneliness of the Apache country. And when he rode away, she had no idea whether she would ever see him again. She never did.

Santa Fe was far and away to the north, but the growing village of El Paso was less than a hundred miles to the west, and it was there Ed Lowe rode for supplies and seed.

He had several drinks—his first in months—in one of the saloons. As the liquor warmed his stomach, Ed Lowe looked around agreeably. For a moment, his eyes clouded with worry as he thought of his wife and children back in Apache country, but it was not in Ed Lowe to worry for long. He had another drink and leaned on the bar, talking to the bartender. All Ed had ever asked of life was enough to eat, a horse to ride, an occasional drink, and companions to talk with. Not that he had anything important to say. He just liked to talk.

Suddenly a chair grated on the floor, and Ed turned. A lean, powerful man with a shock of uncut black hair and a torn, weather-faded

THE PRAIRIE IS MY GARDEN, 1950. *Harvey Dunn. South Dakota Memorial Art Center Collection, Brookings.*

shirt stood at bay. Facing him across the table were three hard-faced young men, obviously brothers.

Ches Lane did not notice Ed Lowe watching from the bar. He had eyes only for the men facing him. "You done that deliberate!" The statement was a challenge.

The broad-chested man on the left grinned through broken teeth. "That's right, Ches. I done it deliberate. You killed Dan Tolliver on the Brazos."

"He made the quarrel." Comprehension came to Ches. He was boxed, and by three of the fighting, blood-hungry Tollivers.

"Don't make no difference," the broad-chested Tolliver said. " 'Who sheds a Tolliver's blood, by a Tolliver's hand must die!' "

Ed Lowe moved suddenly from the bar.

"Three to one is long odds," he said, his voice low and friendly. "If the gent in the corner is willin', I'll side him."

Two Tollivers turned toward him. Ed Lowe was smiling easily, his hand hovering near his gun. "You stay out of this!" one of the brothers said harshly.

"I'm in," Ed replied. "Why don't you boys light a shuck?"

"No, by—!" The man's hand dropped for his gun, and the room thundered with sound.

Ed was smiling easily, unworried as always. His gun flashed up. He felt it leap in his hand, saw the nearest Tolliver smashed back, and he shot him again as he dropped. He had only time to see Ches Lane with two guns out and another Tolliver down when something struck him through the stomach and he stepped back against the bar, suddenly sick.

The sound stopped, and the room was quiet, and there was the acrid smell of powder smoke. Three Tollivers were down and dead, and Ed Lowe was dying. Ches Lane crossed to him.

"We got 'em," Ed said, "we sure did. But they got me."

Suddenly his face changed. "Oh Lord in heaven, what'll Angie do?" And then he crumpled over on the floor and lay still, the blood staining his shirt and mingling with the sawdust.

Stiff-faced, Ches looked up. "Who was Angie?" he asked.

"His wife," the bartender told him. "She's up northeast somewhere, in Apache country. He was tellin' me about her. Two kids, too."

Ches Lane stared down at the crumpled, used-up body of Ed Lowe. The man had saved his life.

One he could have beaten, two he might have beaten; three would have killed him. Ed Lowe, stepping in when he did, had saved the life of Ches Lane.

"He didn't say where?"

"No."

Ches Lane shoved his hat back on his head. "What's northeast of here?"

The bartender rested his hands on the bar. "Cochise," he said....

For more than three months, whenever he could rustle the grub, Ches Lane quartered the country over and back. The trouble was, he had no lead to the location of Ed Lowe's homestead. An examination of Ed's horse revealed nothing. Lowe had bought seed and ammunition. The seed indicated a good water supply, and the ammunition implied trouble. But in the country there was always trouble.

A man had died to save his life, and Ches

Lane had a deep sense of obligation. Somewhere that wife waited, if she was still alive, and it was up to him to find her and look out for her. He rode northeast, cutting for sign, but found none. Sandstorms had wiped out any hope of back-trailing Lowe. Actually, West Dog Canyon was more east than north, but this he had no way of knowing.

North he went, skirting the rugged San Andreas Mountains. Heat baked him hot; dry winds parched his skin. His hair grew dry and stiff and alkali-whitened. He rode north, and soon the Apaches knew of him. He fought them at a lonely water hole, and he fought them on the run. They killed his horse, and he switched his saddle to the spare and rode on. They cornered him in the rocks, and he killed two of them and escaped by night.

They trailed him through the White Sands, and he left two more for dead. He fought fiercely and bitterly and would not be turned from his quest. He turned east through the lava beds and still more east to the Pecos. He saw only two white men, and neither knew of a white woman.

The bearded man laughed harshly. "A woman alone? She wouldn't last a month! By now the Apaches got her, or she's dead. Don't be a fool! Leave this country before you die here."

Lean, wind-whipped and savage, Ches Lane pushed on. The Mescaleros[1] concerned him in Rawhide Draw and he fought them to a standstill. Grimly, the Apaches clung to his trail.

The sheer determination of the man fascinated them. Bred and born in a rugged and lonely land, the Apaches knew the difficulties of survival; they knew how a man could live,

---

1. **Mescaleros** (mesk′ ə le rōs): an Apache people of Texas and New Mexico.

how he must live. Even as they tried to kill this man, they loved him, for he was one of their own.

Lane's jeans grew ragged. Two bullet holes were added to the old black hat. The slicker was torn; the saddle, so carefully kept until now, was scratched by gravel and brush. At night he cleaned his guns and by day he scouted the trails. Three times he found lonely ranch houses burned to the ground, the buzzard- and coyote-stripped bones of their owners lying nearby.

Once he found a covered wagon, its canvas flopping in the wind, a man lying sprawled on the seat with a pistol near his hand. He was dead and his wife was dead, and their canteens rattled like empty skulls.

Leaner every day, Ches Lane pushed on. He camped one night in a canyon near some white oaks. He heard a hoof click on stone and he backed away from his tiny fire, gun in hand.

The riders were white men, and there were two of them. Joe Tompkins and Wiley Lynn were headed west, and Ches Lane could have guessed why. They were men he had known before, and he told them what he was doing.

Lynn chuckled. He was a thin-faced man with lank yellow hair and dirty fingers. "Seems a mighty strange way to get a woman. There's some as comes easier."

"This ain't for fun," Ches replied shortly. "I got to find her."

Tompkins stared at him. "Ches, you're crazy! That gent declared himself in of his own wish and desire. Far's that goes, the gal's dead. No woman could last this long in Apache country."

At daylight, the two men headed west, and Ches Lane turned south....

The lonely rider who fought so desperately and knew the desert so well soon became a subject of gossip among the Apaches. Over the fires of many a rancheria they discussed this strange rider who seemed to be going nowhere, but always riding, like a lean wolf dog on a trail. He rode across the mesas and down the canyons; he studied signs at every water hole; he looked long from every ridge. It was obvious to the Indians that he searched for something—but what?

Cochise had come again to the cabin in West Dog Canyon. "Little warrior too small," he said, "too small for hunt. You join my people. Take Apache for man."

"No." Angie shook her head. "Apache ways are good for the Apache, and the white man's ways are good for white men—and women."

They rode away and said no more, but that night, as she had on many other nights after the children were asleep, Angie cried. She wept silently, her head pillowed on her arms. She was as pretty as ever, but her face was thin, showing the worry and struggle of the months gone by, the weeks and months without hope.

The crops were small but good. Little Jimmy worked beside her. At night, Angie sat alone on the steps and watched the shadows gather down the long canyon, listening to the coyotes yapping from the rim of the Guadalupes,[2] hearing the horses blowing in the corral. She watched, still hopeful, but now she knew that Cochise was right: Ed would not return.

But even if she had been ready to give up this, the first home she had known, there could be no escape. Here she was protected by Cochise. Other Apaches from other tribes would not so willingly grant her peace.

At daylight she was up. The morning air was

---

2. **Guadalupes** (gwäd′ ə loo′ pās): a mountain range in Texas and New Mexico.

bright and balmy, but soon it would be hot again. Jimmy went to the spring for water, and when breakfast was over, the children played while Angie sat in the shade of a huge old cottonwood and sewed. It was a Sunday, warm and lovely. From time to time, she lifted her eyes to look down the canyon, half smiling at her own foolishness.

The hard-packed earth of the yard was swept clean of dust; the pans hanging on the kitchen wall were neat and shining. The children's hair had been clipped, and there was a small bouquet on the kitchen table.

After a while, Angie put aside her sewing and changed her dress. She did her hair carefully, and then, looking in her mirror, she reflected with sudden pain that she *was* pretty, and that she was only a girl.

Resolutely, she turned from the mirror and, taking up her Bible, went back to the seat under the cottonwood. The children left their playing and came to her, for this was a Sunday ritual, their only one. Opening the Bible, she read slowly,

"Though I walk through the valley of the shadow of death, I will fear no evil; for thou art with me; thy rod and thy staff, they comfort me. Thou preparest a table before me in the presence of mine enemies: thou. . . ."

"Mommy." Jimmy tugged at her sleeve. "Look!"

Ches Lane had reached a narrow canyon by midafternoon and decided to make camp. There was small possibility he would find another such spot, and he was dead tired, his muscles sodden with fatigue. The canyon was one of those unexpected gashes in the cap rock that gave no indication of its presence until you came right on it. After some searching, Ches found a route to the bottom and made camp

under a wind-hollowed overhang. There was water, and there was a small patch of grass.

After his horse had a drink and a roll on the ground, it began cropping eagerly at the rich, green grass, and Ches built a smokeless fire of some ancient driftwood in the canyon bottom. It was his first hot meal in days, and when he had finished he put out his fire, rolled a smoke, and leaned back contentedly.

Before darkness settled, he climbed to the rim and looked over the country. The sun had gone down, and the shadows were growing long. After a half-hour of study, he decided there was no living thing within miles, except for the usual desert life. Returning to the bottom, he moved his horse to fresh grass, then rolled in his blanket. For the first time in a month, he slept without fear.

He woke up suddenly in the broad daylight. The horse was listening to something, his head up. Swiftly, Ches went to the horse and led it back under the overhang. Then he drew on his boots, rolled his blankets, and saddled the horse. Still he heard no sound.

Climbing the rim again, he studied the desert and found nothing. Returning to his horse, he mounted up and rode down the canyon toward the flatland beyond. Coming out of the canyon mouth, he rode right into the middle of a war party of more than twenty Apaches— invisible until suddenly they stood up behind rocks, their rifles leveled. And he didn't have a chance.

Swiftly, they bound his wrists to the saddle horn and tied his feet. Only then did he see the man who led the party. It was Cochise.

He was a lean, wiry Indian of past fifty, his black hair streaked with gray, his features strong and clean-cut. He stared at Lane, and there was nothing in his face to reveal what he might be thinking.

Several of the younger warriors pushed forward, talking excitedly and waving their arms. Ches Lane understood some of it, but he sat straight in the saddle, his head up, waiting. Then Cochise spoke and the party turned, and, leading his horse, they rode away.

The miles grew long and the sun was hot. He was offered no water and he asked for none. The Indians ignored him. Once a young brave rode near and struck him viciously. Lane made no sound, gave no indication of pain. When they finally stopped, it was beside a huge anthill swarming with big red desert ants.

Roughly, they quickly untied him and jerked him from his horse. He dug in his heels and shouted at them in Spanish: "The Apaches are women! They tie me to the ants because they are afraid to fight me!"

An Indian struck him, and Ches glared at the man. If he must die, he would show them how it should be done. Yet he knew the unpredictable nature of the Indian, of his great respect for courage.

"Give me a knife, and I'll kill any of your warriors!"

They stared at him, and one powerfully built Apache angrily ordered them to get on with it. Cochise spoke, and the big warrior replied angrily.

Ches Lane nodded at the anthill. "Is this the death for a fighting man? I have fought your strong men and beaten them. I have left no trail for them to follow, and for months I have lived among you, and now only by accident have you captured me. Give me a knife," he added grimly, "and I will fight *him!*" He indicated the big, black-faced Apache.

The warrior's cruel mouth hardened, and he struck Ches across the face.

The white man tasted blood and fury. "Woman!" Ches said. "Coyote! You are afraid!" Ches turned on Cochise, as the Indians stood irresolute. "Free my hands and let me fight!" he demanded. "If I win, let me go free."

Cochise said something to the big Indian. Instantly, there was stillness. Then an Apache sprang forward and, with a slash of his knife, freed Lane's hands. Shaking loose the thongs, Ches Lane chafed his wrists to bring back the circulation. An Indian threw a knife at his feet. It was his own bowie knife.

Ches took off his riding boots. In sock feet, his knife gripped low in his hand, its cutting edge up, he looked at the big warrior.

"I promise you nothing," Cochise said in Spanish, "but an honorable death."

The big warrior came at him on cat feet. Warily, Ches circled. He had not only to defeat this Apache but to escape. He permitted himself a side glance toward his horse. It stood alone. No Indian held it.

The Apache closed swiftly, thrusting wickedly with the knife. Ches, who had learned knife-fighting in the bayou country of Louisiana, turned his hip sharply, and the blade slid past him. He struck swiftly, but the Apache's forward movement deflected the blade, and it failed to penetrate. However, as it swept up between the Indian's body and arm, it cut a deep gash in the warrior's left armpit.

The Indian sprang again, like a clawing cat, streaming blood. Ches moved aside, but a backhand sweep nicked him, and he felt the sharp bite of the blade. Turning, he paused on the balls of his feet.

He had had no water in hours. His lips were cracked. Yet he sweated now, and the salt of it stung his eyes. He stared into the malevolent black eyes of the Apache, then moved to meet him. The Indian lunged, and Ches sidestepped like a boxer and spun on the ball of his foot.

The sudden side step threw the Indian past him, but Ches failed to drive the knife into the Apache's kidney when his foot rolled on a stone. The point left a thin red line across the Indian's back. The Indian was quick. Before Ches could recover his balance, he grasped the white man's knife wrist. Desperately, Ches grabbed for the Indian's knife hand and got the wrist, and they stood there straining, chest to chest.

Seeing his chance, Ches suddenly let his knees buckle, then brought up his knee and fell back, throwing the Apache over his head to the sand. Instantly, he whirled and was on his feet, standing over the Apache. The warrior had lost his knife, and he lay there, staring up, his eyes black with hatred.

Coolly, Ches stepped back, picked up the Indian's knife, and tossed it to him contemptuously. There was a grunt from the watching Indians, and then his antagonist rushed. But loss of blood had weakened the warrior, and Ches stepped in swiftly, struck the blade aside, then thrust the point of his blade hard against the Indian's belly.

Black eyes glared into his without yielding. A thrust, and the man would be disemboweled, but Ches stepped back. "He is a strong man," Ches said in Spanish. "It is enough that I have won."

Deliberately, he walked to his horse and swung into the saddle. He looked around, and every rifle covered him.

So he had gained nothing. He had hoped that mercy might lead to mercy, that the Apache's respect for a fighting man would win his freedom. He had failed. Again they bound him to his horse, but they did not take his knife from him.

When they camped at last, he was given

THUNDER MOUNTAIN, 1910–1915. *William R. Leigh. Private Collection. Courtesy of Hirschl and Adler, New York.*

food and drink. He was bound again, and a blanket was thrown over him. At daylight they were again in the saddle. In Spanish he asked where they were taking him, but they gave no indication of hearing. When they stopped again, it was beside a pole corral, near a stone cabin.

When Jimmy spoke, Angie got quickly to her feet. She recognized Cochise with a start of relief, but she saw instantly that this was a war party. And then she saw the prisoner.

Their eyes met and she felt a distinct shock. He was a white man, a big, unshaven man who badly needed both a bath and a haircut, his clothes ragged and bloody. Cochise gestured at the prisoner.

"No take Apache man, you take white man. This man good for hunt, good for fight. He strong warrior. You take 'em."

Flushed and startled, Angie stared at the prisoner and caught a faint glint of humor in his dark eyes.

"Is this here the fate worse than death I hear tell of?" he inquired gently.

"Who are you?" she asked, and was immediately conscious that it was an extremely silly question.

The Apaches had drawn back and were watching curiously. She could do nothing for the present but accept the situation. Obviously they intended to do her a kindness, and it would not do to offend them. If they had not brought this man to her, he might have been killed.

"Name's Ches Lane, ma'am," he said. "Will you untie me? I'd feel a lot safer."

"Of course." Still flustered, she went to him and untied his hands. One Indian said something, and the others chuckled; then, with a whoop, they swung their horses and galloped off down the canyon.

Their departure left her suddenly helpless, the shadowy globe of her loneliness shattered by this utterly strange man standing before her, this big, bearded man brought to her out of the desert.

She smoothed her apron, suddenly pale as she realized what his delivery to her implied. What must he think of her? She turned away quickly.

"There's hot water," she said hastily, to prevent his speaking. "Dinner is almost ready."

She walked quickly into the house and stopped before the stove, her mind a blank. She looked around her as if she had suddenly waked up in a strange place. She heard water being poured into the basin by the door and heard him take Ed's razor. She had never moved the box. To have moved it would—

"Sight of work done here, ma'am."

She hesitated, then turned with determination and stepped into the doorway. "Yes, Ed—"

"You're Angie Lowe."

Surprised, she turned toward him and recognized his own startled awareness of her. As he shaved, he told her about Ed and what had happened that day in the saloon.

"He—Ed was like that. He never considered consequences until it was too late."

"Lucky for me he didn't."

He was younger looking with his beard gone. There was a certain quiet dignity in his face. She went back inside and began putting plates on the table. She was conscious that he had moved to the door and was watching her.

"You don't have to stay," she said. "You owe me nothing. Whatever Ed did, he did because he was that kind of person. You aren't responsible."

He did not answer, and when she turned

again to the stove, she glanced swiftly at him. He was looking across the valley.

There was a studied deference about him when he moved to a place at the table. The children stared, wide-eyed and silent; it had been so long since a man sat at this table.

Angie could not remember when she had felt like this. She was awkwardly conscious of her hands, which never seemed to be in the right place or doing the right things. She scarcely tasted her food, nor did the children.

Ches Lane had no such inhibitions. For the first time, he realized how hungry he was. After the half-cooked meat of lonely, trailside fires, this was tender and flavored. Hot biscuits, desert honey … Suddenly he looked up, embarrassed at his appetite.

"You were really hungry," she said.

"Man can't fix much, out on the trail."

Later, after he'd got his bedroll from his saddle and unrolled it on the hay in the barn, he walked back to the house and sat on the lowest step. The sun was gone, and they watched the cliffs stretch their red shadows across the valley. A quail called plaintively, a mellow sound of twilight.

"You needn't worry about Cochise," she said. "He'll soon be crossing into Mexico."

"I wasn't thinking about Cochise."

That left her with nothing to say, and she listened again to the quail and watched a lone bright star in the sky.

"A man could get to like it here," he said quietly.

Getting at Meaning

RECALLING

1. Why is Angie alone at the beginning of the story? Why is it dangerous for her to be alone?

2. Why doesn't Ed return to his family?

3. Why does Ches begin to search for Angie?

INTERPRETING

4. What does Cochise tell Angie about her husband? How does he know this?

5. Who brings the quarters of antelope to Angie? What does Cochise admire about her?

6. What proposal does Cochise make to Angie? What is Angie's response to this proposal? Why does Angie cry later that night?

7. Why does Ches spare the big warrior's life? How does Cochise feel toward Ches? How do you know?

8. What "gift" does Cochise make to Angie at the end of the story?

9. What similarities are there between Angie, Cochise, and Ches?

CRITICAL THINKING: EVALUATING

10. Do the characters in this story seem realistic? Explain the reasons for your opinion.

Developing Skills in Reading Literature

1. **Suspense.** Suspense is a feeling of growing tension and excitement felt by a reader. How does Louis L'Amour create suspense in the first paragraph of this story? What other events in this story are suspenseful?

2. **Flashback.** A flashback is a part of a story that interrupts the sequence of events to relate an earlier conversation, scene, or event. Reread the flashback that begins in paragraph 2 on page 265. What does this flashback explain about the situation faced by Angie?

3. **Conflict.** Conflict is a struggle between opposing forces. In most short stories a conflict arises, develops, and is then resolved. There are several conflicts in this story. However, the major one is Angie Lowe's struggle to survive on her own. What event creates the major conflict in this story? What other conflicts does the story relate?

4. **Stereotype.** A stereotype is a character who conforms to a simplified common type. What stereotypes of cowboys and Indians are presented in novels, stories, and movies about the American West? Do the cowboys and Indians in this story fit the stereotypes of cowboys and Indians? Is Ches a stereotypical character? Is Cochise?

Developing Vocabulary

Using the Dictionary: Cross References. A cross reference directs the reader to another entry for more information about synonyms or word origins. Look up the words below in a dictionary. For each word, write, on a separate sheet of paper, whether the entry in your dictionary contains a cross reference. If the entry does contain a cross reference, look up that word. Then, on your paper, tell what information the cross reference word provides about the entry word.

fang	solitary	mute
grip	canyon	secure

Developing Writing Skills

Writing About a Character. Write a paragraph describing the character of Angie Lowe. Begin by thinking of a single word that sums up Angie's most outstanding character trait. Write this word in your prewriting notes. Then, look through the story for evidence that Angie has this trait. Include this evidence in your prewriting notes. Next, write a topic sentence that identifies Angie's most outstanding character trait. In the body of your paragraph, present the evidence that you have gathered from the story. As you work on this assignment, refer to **Using the Process of Writing** and to Writing About the Short Story on pages 614–625.

BIOGRAPHY

Louis L'Amour (1908–1988) wrote more than one hundred books, most of them Westerns, which he preferred to call "stories of the frontier." He carefully researched his novels and short stories, paying special attention to historical and geographical details. Many of his books, including *How the West Was Won* and *The Broken Gun,* have been made into motion pictures. L'Amour was born in Jamestown, North Dakota.

RESEARCH SKILLS FOR *WRITING*

Using the Card Catalog

The card catalog is an alphabetical file that lists every book in a library. This file is kept in a cabinet of narrow drawers or in a computer. Each nonfiction book in the library can be located in three different ways: by title, by author, and by subject. If you look up a book's title, author, or subject, you will find the following information: title, author, publisher, and place and date of publication. You will also find a call number, which helps you to locate the book on the library shelves. Works of fiction can be located by title and by author only.

Developing Writing Skills

Finding Information in a Card Catalog. Use the card catalog in your school library to compile a list of books both by and about one of the following writers:

Isaac Asimov
Gwendolyn Brooks
Ray Bradbury
Isaac Bashevis Singer
Mark Twain

Locate the books you have listed. Browse through the books, keeping these questions in mind: How many books did you find by the author? about the author? What kinds of books did you find? When did the author live and write? Does the story you have read in this unit seem to be typical of the writer? Then write a brief paragraph in which you draw some conclusions about the author. Begin your paragraph with a topic sentence that makes an important generalization about the author.

See **Handbook: How To Write About Literature,** Lessons 1–4.

CRITICAL THINKING

Understanding Relationships

To understand a work of literature, you must think about the relationships, or connections, between its parts or elements. To understand short stories, for example, you must think about relationships between characters and between events.

Relationships Between Characters. Whenever you read a short story, note how the characters are linked. Determine whether the characters are relatives, friends, enemies, or related in some other way. For example, when reading "Home," you should notice that two of the characters are sisters.

Often, the relationships between characters invite comparisons or contrasts. For example, in "The Fun They Had," the relationship between Margie and Tommy is that of friendship. In "The Glorious Whitewasher," the relationship between Tom and the other boys is that between a con artist and his victims.

Relationships Between Events. Two kinds of relationships between events are especially important in short stories: chronological relationships and causal relationships.

A **chronological relationship** is a relationship in time. Usually, the events of a story are presented one after another, in the order that they happen. Sometimes, however, a writer will jump back in time to relate an earlier conversation, scene, or event. When reading short stories, always notice words such as *then, finally,* and *meanwhile,* which show the connections between events.

A **causal relationship** exists when one event brings about, or causes, another. Many short stories begin with some event that sets in motion or leads to the rest of the action. For example, in "Winter Thunder," the events of the story result from the bus being stranded in a blizzard.

Developing Critical Thinking Skills

Recognizing Relationships in a Story. Follow the directions and answer the questions.

1. Explain the relationships between the following characters.

   a. Julia and her brother in "The Trout"
   b. Joseph and Pierre in "A Secret for Two"
   c. Peg and Rollie in "The Apprentice"

2. Discuss the similarities and differences between Todi and Lyzer.

3. The following are some events from "The Gift of Cochise," presented in the order in which they appear in the story. Write these events in chronological order.

   a. Cochise tells Angie that her husband is probably dead.
   b. Angie gives an Apache girl a ribbon.
   c. Ed and Angie start west for Santa Fe.
   d. Ed leaves his wife alone in the cabin and goes to El Paso.
   e. Cochise brings Ches to Angie's cabin.

4. In "The Gift of Cochise," what events cause Cochise to admire Angie? In "Humans Are Different," what causes the death of the human? What does the robot fail to understand?

Understanding the Short Story

RECALLING

1. Which of the stories in this unit are set in the American West? Which are set in the future?

2. Which of the stories have major characters who are animals? Which have major characters who are children?

INTERPRETING

3. Name two stories from the unit that are told from the first-person point of view. Name two that are told from the third-person point of view.

4. Choose two stories that are particularly suspenseful. How does the writer create suspense in each of these stories?

5. Choose one story in which the setting creates a particular mood. What is this mood? What elements of the setting help to create the mood?

6. Choose two stories and explain the conflict in each. Tell how each conflict is resolved.

CRITICAL THINKING: EVALUATING

7. Choose one story from this unit that has a theme that you believe is especially important. Explain the theme of this story, and tell why you think it is important.

Writing About the Short Story

> See **Using the Process of Writing** and Writing About the Short Story on pages 614–625 for help with this assignment.

Choose one short story that has an interesting plot. Write a one paragraph plot summary of this story. Begin by listing in your prewriting notes the major events in the story. Place a star (*) next to the point at which the reader first learns of the main conflict. Place a second star next to the point at which the main conflict is resolved. Mention the title and the author of the short story in your topic sentence. In the body of the paragraph, present the events of the story in chronological order. Draw your reader's attention to the points in the story at which the conflict is introduced and resolved.

Applying Short Story Techniques

See **Using the Process of Writing** on pages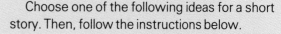
614–623 for help with this assignment.

Choose one of the following ideas for a short story. Then, follow the instructions below.

a. A new student at school turns out to be an extraterrestrial.

b. A cat runs away from home only to find that the outside world is less pleasant than the home that it left behind.

c. An IRS computer makes a mistake and sends every person in a small town a twenty-thousand-dollar tax refund.

Begin by thinking of a conflict for your story. Write a sentence describing this conflict. Then, invent two characters, and make prewriting notes describing these characters. Next, make notes describing one setting that you can use in the story. Then, write a plot summary, one that points out the events that introduce, develop, and resolve the major conflict.

*N*onfiction

DETAIL OF AN ELK HIDE. *Painted by an Unknown Native American. The Thomas Gilcrease Institute of American History and Art, Tulsa, Oklahoma.*

Introducing Nonfiction

What Is Nonfiction?

Nonfiction is writing about real people, places, and events. Often nonfiction contains elements of the short story, such as plot, setting, and character. However, nonfiction differs from the short story in one important way: nonfiction must be true.

Kinds of Nonfiction

Nonfiction is by far the most common kind of writing. The reports that you write for school are nonfiction. So are your notes, journals, and diaries. Other kinds of nonfiction include textbooks, newspaper articles, and entries in reference works such as dictionaries and encyclopedias. In addition, all books and magazine articles that deal with real-life subjects are nonfiction. This unit covers the following three kinds of nonfiction:

Autobiography.   An autobiography is the story of a person's life, written by that person.

Biography.   A biography is the story of a person's life, written by another person.

The Essay.   An essay is a brief nonfiction work that deals with one subject, often in a personal way.

How To Read Nonfiction

When reading a selection in this unit, ask yourself the following questions: "What kind of nonfiction am I reading? What is special about this kind of nonfiction? What is the writer's purpose or purposes? What elements of the short story has the writer used? What people, places, and events has the writer chosen to tell about? What does the writer say about these?"

Previewing the Unit

Reading the Selections

The selections in this unit are presented in three sections: Autobiography, Biography, and The Essay.

Using the Study Questions

Following each selection are exercises that will help you to develop your reading, vocabulary, and writing skills.

Getting at Meaning. This section contains questions of three kinds: The **RECALLING** questions will help you to remember the selection. The **INTERPRETING** questions will help you to understand the selection. The **CRITICAL THINKING** questions will help you in evaluating the selection and in relating it to your own experiences.

Developing Skills in Reading Literature. These exercises will introduce you to the literary techniques used by writers of nonfiction.

Developing Vocabulary. These exercises will introduce you to using context clues to learn the meanings of new words.

Developing Writing Skills. In the first kind of assignment you will write about the nonfiction works that you have read. In the second you will practice using the literary techniques that you have learned.

Using the Unit Study Materials

Research Skills for Writing. This feature will teach you how to use parts of books.

Critical Thinking. The critical thinking exercises will teach you the difference between facts and opinions.

Unit Review. The unit review will help you to recall, interpret, and think critically about the selections in the unit. The writing assignments will direct you to apply the writing skills that you have learned.

MAN WITH KNAPSACK, 1873. *Winslow Homer. The Cooper-Hewitt Museum, the Smithsonian Institution's National Museum of Design, Washington D.C.*

Autobiography

What Is Autobiography?

What would it be like to be a different person? to live in a different time and place? to think another person's thoughts? to feel another person's feelings? You can, in fact, enter another person's life by reading an autobiography. An autobiography is the story of a person's life, written by that person.

Short Story Elements in Autobiographies

Autobiographies are similar to short stories. Both contain plots, settings, conflicts, and characters. However, unlike short stories, autobiographies tell only what has happened. The people, places, and events are all real.

Thinking About Autobiography

The following section has eight autobiographies. Some of these are selections from longer autobiographical works. The settings range from southeastern Alaska to northern Kenya. Their authors include an explorer, an anthropologist, and a Native American leader. As you read each selection, identify the plot, setting, and characters. Ask yourself how the writer has used these short story elements to accomplish his or her purpose. Also ask yourself why the writer has chosen to tell about this experience.

*In a wild, frozen wasteland, an explorer and a dog face
a life-and-death challenge.*

from Stickeen

John Muir

In the summer of 1880, I set out from Fort Wrangel in a canoe to continue the exploration of the icy region of southeastern Alaska. After the necessary provisions had been collected and stowed away, and my Indian crew were in their places ready to start, my companion the Rev. S. H. Young came aboard, followed by a little black dog that immediately made himself at home by curling up in a hollow among the baggage. I like dogs, but this one seemed so small and worthless that I asked the missionary why he was taking him.

"Such a little, helpless creature will only be in the way," I said. "The poor, silly thing will be in rain and snow for weeks or months and will require care like a baby."

But his master assured me that he would be no trouble at all; that he was a perfect wonder of a dog, could endure cold and hunger like a bear, swim like a seal, and was wondrous wise and cunning.

Nobody could hope to unravel the lines of his ancestry. In all the wonderfully mixed and varied dog tribe, I never saw any creature very much like him, though some of his sly, soft, gliding motions brought the fox to mind. He was short-legged and bunchy-bodied, and his hair was long and silky and slightly waved. His most noticeable feature was his fine tail, which was about as airy and shady as a squirrel's and was carried curling forward almost to his nose. But his strength of character lay in his eyes. They looked as old as the hills, and as young, and as wild. I never tired of looking into them: it was like looking into a landscape, but they were small and rather deep set. Mr. Young told me that the little fellow had been presented to his wife by an Irish prospector, and that on his arrival at Fort Wrangel, he was adopted with enthusiasm by the Stickeen Indians as a sort of new good-luck totem and was named "Stickeen" for the tribe.

On our trip he soon proved himself a queer character—odd, independent, and invincibly quiet. As we sailed week after week through the long, intricate channels and inlets among the innumerable islands and mountains of the coast, he spent most of the dull days in sluggish ease, motionless, and apparently as unobserving as if in deep sleep.

Though capable of great idleness, he never failed to be ready for all sorts of adventures and excursions. The days that were too stormy for sailing I spent in the woods or on the adjacent mountains, wherever my studies called me; and Stickeen always insisted on going with me, however wild the weather, gliding like a fox through bushes and thorny tangles, wading and wallowing through snow, swimming icy streams, skipping over logs and rocks and the crevasses[1] of glaciers with the patience and endurance of a determined mountaineer, never tiring or getting discouraged.

Yet none of us was able to make out what Stickeen was really good for. He seemed to meet danger and hardships without anything like reason; insisted on having his own way, never obeyed an order, and never fetched birds the hunter shot. He reminded me of a small, squat, unshakable desert cactus. No matter what advances you might make, scarce a glance or a tail wag would you get for your pains. But though he was apparently as cold as a glacier, I tried hard to make his acquaintance, guessing there must be something worthwhile hidden beneath so much courage, endurance, and love of wild-weathery adventure.

After exploring the Sumdum and Tahkoo fjords and their glaciers, we sailed through Icy Strait into Cross Sound, searching for unexplored inlets leading toward the great fountain ice fields of the Fairweather Range. At length we made the joyful discovery of the mouth of the inlet now called "Taylor Bay" and about five o'clock reached the head of it and encamped in a spruce grove near the front of a large glacier.

On the morrow I awoke early, called not only by the glacier, which had been on my mind all night, but by a grand floodstorm. The wind was blowing a gale from the north, and the rain was flying with the clouds in a wide, horizontal flood, as if it were all passing over the country instead of falling on it. I had intended making breakfast before starting; but when I heard the storm and looked out, I made haste to join it; for many of Nature's finest lessons are to be found in her storms.

Mr. Young and the Indians were asleep, and so, I hoped, was Stickeen; but I had not gone a dozen rods before he left his bed in the tent and came boring through the blast after me. That a man should welcome storms for their exhilarating music and motion, and go forth to see God making landscapes, is reasonable enough. But what fascination could there be in such tremendous weather for a dog? Surely nothing akin to human enthusiasm for scenery or geology. I stopped and did my best to turn him back, shouting to make myself heard in the storm. "Stickeen, you must be daft. Go back to camp and keep warm. Get a good breakfast with your master, and be sensible for once. I can't carry you all day or feed you; and this storm will kill you."

I stopped again and again, shouting good warning advice, but saw that he was not to be shaken off. As well might the earth try to shake off the moon. So at last we struggled on together, and thus began the most memorable of all my wild days.

The level flood, driving hard in our faces, thrashed and washed us wildly until we got into the shelter of a grove on the east side of the glacier near the front. There we stopped awhile for breath, and to listen and look out. When the wind began to abate, I traced the east side of the glacier; and about three miles above the front of it, climbed to the surface by

_____
1. **crevasses** (krĭ văs′ əz): deep cracks, especially in a glacier.

means of ax steps made easy for Stickeen. As far as the eye could reach, the level, or nearly level, glacier stretched away indefinitely beneath the gray sky, a seemingly boundless prairie of ice. The rain continued and grew colder, which I did not mind; but a dim snowy look in the drooping clouds made me hesitate about venturing far from land. No trace of the west shore was visible; and in case the clouds should settle and give snow, or the wind again become violent, I feared getting caught in a tangle of crevasses. Snow crystals, the flowers of the mountain clouds, are frail, beautiful things, but terrible when flying on stormwinds. Watching the weather, I sauntered about on the crystal sea. For a mile or two out I found the ice remarkably safe. The marginal crevasses were mostly narrow, while the few wider ones were easily avoided by passing around them; and the clouds began to open here and there.

Thus encouraged, I at last pushed out for the other side. I took bearings occasionally with a pocket compass to enable me to find my way back more surely in case the storm should become blinding, but the structure lines of the glacier were my main guide. Toward the west side we came to a closely crevassed section in which we had to make long, narrow tacks[2] and doublings, tracing the edges of tremendous crevasses, many of which were from twenty to thirty feet wide and perhaps a thousand feet deep—beautiful and awful. In working a way through them I was severely cautious, but Stickeen came on as unhesitating as the flying clouds. The widest crevasse that I could jump, he would leap without so much as halting to take a look at it.

The weather was now making quick changes, scattering bits of dazzling brightness through the wintry gloom at rare intervals when the sun broke forth wholly free. Then suddenly all the glorious show would be darkened and blotted out.

Stickeen seemed to care for none of these things, bright or dark, nor for the crevasses, wells, moulins,[3] or swift flashing streams into which he might fall. The little adventurer was only about two years old, yet nothing seemed novel to him, nothing daunted him. He showed neither caution nor curiosity, wonder nor fear, but bravely trotted on as if glaciers were playgrounds. His courage was so unwavering that it seemed as if he were only blindly bold, and I kept warning him to be careful. For by now we had been close companions on so many wilderness trips that I had formed the habit of talking to him as if he were a boy and understood every word.

We gained the west shore in about three hours; the width of the glacier here being about seven miles. Then I pushed northward in order to see as far back as possible into the fountains of the Fairweather Mountains. The walking was easy along the margin of the forest, and I would gladly have continued my exploration; but the day was already far spent, and the threatening sky called for haste on the return trip. I decided, therefore, to go no farther, and, after taking a general view of the wonderful region, turned back. We made good speed until we had left the west shore about two miles behind us. Here we got into a difficult network of crevasses. The gathering clouds began to drop misty fringes, and soon the dreaded snow came flying thick and fast. I pushed on as best I could, jumping innumerable crevasses after cutting hollows for my feet to avoid possible slipping or any uncertainty

---

2. **tacks:** zigzag courses.
3. **moulins** (m$\overline{oo}$ lanz′): vertical shafts in a glacier, down which a stream of surface water plunges.

on the farther sides, where only one trial is granted—exercise at once frightful and inspiring. Stickeen followed seemingly without effort.

Many a mile we thus traveled, mostly doubling up and down, making but little real headway in crossing, running instead of walking, as the danger of being compelled to spend the night on the glacier became threatening. I could not see far enough through the blurring snow to judge in which general direction the least dangerous route lay. I had simply to grope my way from crevasse to crevasse, holding a general direction by the ice structure and by the wind. Again and again I was put to my mettle, but Stickeen followed easily, his nerve

apparently growing more unflinching as the danger increased. So it always is with mountaineers when hard beset.

At length our way was barred by a very wide and straight crevasse. I traced it northward a mile or so without finding a crossing, then down the glacier about as far, to where it united with another uncrossable crevasse. In all this distance there was only one place where I could possibly jump. The side I was on was about a foot higher than the other, but even with this advantage, the crevasse seemed dangerously wide. One is liable to underestimate the width of crevasses where the magnitudes in general are great. I therefore stared at this one mighty keenly, estimating its width and the shape of the edge on the farther side, until I thought that I could jump it if necessary, but that if compelled to jump back from the lower side, I might fail. Now, a cautious mountaineer seldom takes a step that he cannot retrace in case he should be stopped by unseen obstacles ahead. This is the rule of mountaineers who live long; and, though in haste, I compelled myself to sit down and calmly deliberate before I broke it.

After considering the problem from all angles, I decided to explore further. To my dismay, I discovered that we were on a narrow island about two miles long, with two barely possible ways of escape: one back by the way we came, the other ahead by an almost inaccessible[4] sliver bridge that crossed the great crevasse from near the middle of it!

After this nerve-trying discovery I ran back to the sliver bridge and cautiously examined it. Crevasses are mere cracks when they first open, so narrow as hardly to admit the blade of a pocket knife, and gradually widen according to the depth and the extent of the strain on the glacier. Now, some of these cracks are interrupted, like the cracks in wood, and in opening, a strip of ice may connect the sides, just as the two sides of a slivered crack in wood that is being split are connected. Some crevasses remain open for months or even years; and the sliver bridges, level on top at first and perfectly safe, are at length melted to thin, knife-edged blades that curve downward like the cables of suspension bridges. This one was evidently very old, for it had been weathered and wasted until it was the most dangerous and inaccessible that ever lay in my way.

The width of the crevasse was here about fifty feet, and the sliver crossing diagonally was about seventy feet long. Near the middle, its thin knife-edge was depressed twenty-five or thirty feet below the level of the glacier; and the upcurving ends were attached to the sides eight or ten feet below the brink. Getting down the nearly vertical wall to the end of the sliver and up the other side were the main difficulties, and they seemed all but insurmountable. Of the many perils encountered in my years of wandering on mountains and glaciers, none seemed so plain and stern and merciless as this. And it was presented when we were wet to the skin and hungry, the sky dark with pick-driving snow, and the night near. But we were forced to face it. It was a tremendous necessity.

Beginning a little to one side of the sunken end of the bridge, I cut a deep hollow on the brink for my knees to rest in. Then, leaning over, with my short-handled ax I cut a step sixteen or eighteen inches below. Its floor sloped slightly inward and formed a good hold for my heels. Then, slipping cautiously upon it and crouching as low as possible with my left side toward the wall, I steadied myself against the wind with my left hand in a slight notch, while with the right I cut other similar steps and notches in succession. Life and death were in every stroke and in the finish of every foothold.

After the end of the bridge was reached, I chipped it down until I had made a level platform six or eight inches wide. It was a trying thing to poise on this little slippery platform while bending over to get safely astride of the sliver. Crossing was then comparatively easy, by chipping off the sharp edge with short, careful strokes of the ax and hitching forward an inch or two at a time, keeping my balance with my knees pressed against the sides. The tremendous abyss on either hand I studiously ignored. To me, the edge of that blue sliver was

---

4. **inaccessible** (in′ ək ses′ ə b'l): impossible to reach or use.

then all the world.

But the most trying part of the adventure, after working my way across inch by inch and chipping another small platform, was to rise from the safe position astride and to cut a step-ladder in the nearly vertical face of the wall—chipping, climbing, holding on with feet and fingers in mere notches. At such times one's whole body is eye, and common skill and fortitude are replaced by power beyond our call or knowledge. Never before had I been so long under deadly strain. How I got up that cliff I never could tell. The thing seemed to have been done by somebody else.

I never have held death in contempt, though in the course of my explorations I have often-times felt that to meet one's fate on a noble mountain or in the heart of a glacier would be blessed as compared with death from disease or from some shabby lowland accident. But even the best death, quick and crystal pure, set so glaringly open before us, is hard to face.

But poor Stickeen; think of him! While I was on my knees chipping a hollow on the rounded brow above the bridge, he scanned the sliver and its approaches with his myste-rious eyes, then looked me in the face with a startled air of surprise and concern and began to mutter and whine. This was the first time I had seen him gaze deliberately into a crevasse or into my face with a speaking, troubled look.

Never before had the daring midget seemed to know that ice was slippery or that there was any such thing as danger. I talked to him in sympathy, as I would to a frightened boy, and in trying to calm his fears perhaps in some mea-sure moderated my own. "Hush, my boy," I said. "We will get across safely, though it is not going to be easy. No right way is easy in this rough world. We must risk our lives to save them. At the worst we can only slip, and then

how grand a grave we will have; and by and by our nice bones will do good in the terminal moraine."[5]

But my sermon was far from reassuring him. He began to cry, and after taking another piercing look at the tremendous gulf, ran away in desperate excitement, seeking some other crossing. By the time he got back, baffled of course, I had made a step or two. I dared not look back, but he made himself heard; and when he saw that I was certainly bent on cross-ing, he cried aloud in despair. The danger was enough to daunt anybody, but it seems won-derful that he should have been able to weigh and appreciate it so justly. No mountaineer could have seen it more quickly or judged it more wisely, discriminating between real and apparent peril.

When I gained the other side, he screamed louder than ever. Could this be the silent, philosophic Stickeen? Again and again I shouted encouragement, telling him the bridge was not so bad as it looked, that I had left it flat and safe for his feet, and he could walk it easily. But he was afraid to try. His natural com-posure and courage had vanished utterly in a tumultuous storm of fear. Had the danger been less, his distress would have seemed ridiculous. But in this dismal, merciless abyss lay the shadow of death; and his voice and ges-tures, hopes and fears, were so perfectly human that none could mistake them.

Finally, I went to the brink of the crevasse and in a severe tone of voice shouted across to him that now I must certainly leave him. I could wait no longer, and that, if he would not come, all I could promise was that I would

---

5. **terminal moraine** (mō rān'): a mass of rocks, gravel, sand, and clay, carried and deposited directly by a glacier at its lower end.

return to seek him the next day. I warned him that if he went back to the woods the wolves would kill him, and finished by urging him once more by words and gestures to come on, come on.

He knew very well what I meant; and at last, with the courage of despair, hushed and breathless, he crouched down in the hollow I had made for my knees. He pressed his body against the ice as if trying to get the advantage of the friction of every hair, gazed into the first step, put his little feet together, and slid them slowly, slowly over the edge and down into it, bunching all four in it and almost standing on his head. Then, without lifting his feet, he slowly worked them over the edge of the step and down into the next and the next in the same way, and gained the end of the bridge.

Lifting his feet with the regularity and slowness of a pendulum, as if counting and measuring *one-two-three,* holding himself steady against the gusty wind and giving separate attention to each little step, Stickeen gained the foot of the cliff. Here he halted in dead silence; and it was here I feared he might fail, for dogs are poor climbers. But he looked keenly into the series of notched steps and fingerholds I had made, as if counting them and fixing the position of each one in his mind. Then suddenly up he came in a springy rush, hooking his paws into the steps and notches so quickly that I could not see how it was done, and whizzed past me, safe at last!

And now came a scene! "Well done, well done, little boy! Brave boy!" I cried, trying to catch and caress him. But he would not be caught. He flashed and darted hither and thither as if fairly demented, screaming and shouting, swirling round and round in giddy loops and circles like a leaf in a whirlwind, lying down and rolling over and over, sidewise and heels over head. When I ran up to him to shake him, fearing he might die of joy, he flashed off two or three hundred yards, his feet in a mist of motion, then turning suddenly, came back in a wild rush and launched himself at my face, almost knocking me down, all the time screeching and screaming and shouting as if saying, "Saved! Saved! Saved!"

But there is nothing like work for toning down excessive fear or joy. So I ran ahead, calling him in as gruff a voice as I could command to come on and stop his nonsense; for we had far to go, and it would soon be dark. Neither of us feared another trial like this. Heaven would surely count one enough for a lifetime. The ice ahead was gashed by thousands of crevasses, but they were common ones. The joy of deliverance burned in us like fire, and we ran without fatigue. Stickeen flew across everything in his way, and not till dark did he settle into his normal foxlike trot. At last the cloudy mountains came in sight, and we soon felt the solid rock beneath our feet and were safe. Then came weakness. Danger had vanished, and so had our strength.

We tottered down the lateral moraine in the dark, over boulders and tree trunks, through the bushes and thickets of the grove where we had sheltered ourselves in the morning, and across the level mud slope of the terminal moraine. We reached camp about ten o'clock and found a big fire and a big supper. But we lay down, too tired to eat much, and soon fell into a troubled sleep. The man who said, "The harder the toil, the sweeter the rest," never was profoundly tired. Stickeen kept springing up and muttering in his sleep, no doubt dreaming that he was still on the brink of the crevasse; and so did I, that night and many others long afterwards, when I was overtired.

Thereafter, Stickeen was a changed dog. During the rest of the trip, instead of holding aloof, he always lay by my side. He tried to keep me constantly in sight and would hardly accept a morsel of food, however tempting, from any hand but mine. At night, when all was quiet about the campfire, he would come to me with a look of devotion and rest his head on my knee.

Nothing in after years has dimmed that Alaska storm day. As I write, it all comes rushing and roaring to mind as if I were again in the heart of it. I have known many dogs, and many a story I could tell of their wisdom and devotion, but to none do I owe so much as to Stickeen. At first the least promising and least known of my dog friends, he suddenly became the best known of them all. Our storm battle for life brought him to light, and through him, as through a window, I have ever since been looking with deeper sympathy into all my fellow mortals.

Getting at Meaning

RECALLING

1. Where does this true-life adventure story take place?

2. What makes the explorer's return to camp difficult?

3. What is a crevasse? How is a sliver bridge formed?

4. Why is crossing the sliver bridge so dangerous? Why must the explorer try?

5. How does Stickeen react to the idea of crossing the sliver bridge? Why is his behavior surprising?

6. What techniques does the explorer use to cross the sliver bridge? Does he succeed in crossing?

7. How does Stickeen change after the incident involving the sliver bridge?

INTERPRETING

8. What human qualities does Stickeen show throughout the story?

9. How does Muir's attitude toward Stickeen change? What does he realize about the dog?

10. Explain the last sentence. How has Stickeen provided Muir with a "window" into human beings?

CRITICAL THINKING: EVALUATING

11. Find the passage that states Muir's attitude toward death. Do you think that this is a common way of looking at death? Do you share Muir's view? Explain.

Developing Skills in Reading Literature

1. **Autobiography.** An autobiography is the story of a person's life, written by that person. Who is the subject of this autobiographical selection? Does the selection tell about the writer's entire life or just about a single incident?

Autobiographical writing often gives the reader insight into the writer's personality.

What kind of person is John Muir? What characteristics get him into trouble on the glacier? Do you think that he will approach exploration differently after this experience? What has he learned from the experience?

2. **Nonfiction.** Nonfiction is writing about real people, places, and events. Although this selection is nonfiction, it contains many elements commonly associated with the short story. Name several of these elements. How do these elements make the story more exciting and suspenseful?

3. **Description.** In description a writer paints a picture with words. One type of description focuses on physical appearance. The writer relies heavily on sensory images to create a word picture of a person, place, or thing. Reread John Muir's description of Stickeen, which appears on page 284 of the selection. On a separate sheet of paper, list five phrases that describe the way the dog looks.

Another type of description focuses on action. The writer relies mainly on colorful, precise verbs and verbals to create the word picture. Find the paragraph on page 291 in which Muir describes Stickeen's behavior after surviving the bridge crossing. On the same sheet of paper, list ten verbs and verbals that describe the way the dog acts.

Developing Vocabulary

Context Clues: Definition. When reading this selection, you probably came across a few words that you did not know. You might have had to consult the Glossary on pages 661–676 or a dictionary for the meanings of some of these words. In other cases you may have been able to guess the meanings of unfamiliar words based upon clues provided by the writer. These context clues, or words and sentences that surround an unfamiliar word, often make the meaning of the unknown word clear.

Sometimes a writer anticipates that a word will be new to his or her readers and so defines the word for them. John Muir defines a crevasse as follows: "Crevasses are mere cracks when they first open, so narrow as hardly to admit the blade of a pocket knife, and gradually widen according to the depth and the extent of the strain on the glacier."

Certain key words and phrases signal that a definition is coming. These words and phrases include *is, are, which is,* and *that is.* In the definition of *crevasse,* the signal word is *are.*

Copy on a separate sheet of paper the italicized words in the following sentences. Then, using the clues provided, write both the definition of each word and the key word or words that signals the definition.

1. John Muir found himself stranded on a *glacier,* which is a large mass of ice and snow.

2. One false step and Stickeen would have fallen into the *abyss.* That is, he would have fallen into the deep crack in the ice.

3. We were *fatigued;* that is, we had grown extremely tired.

4. We searched for a path through the *thicket.* A thicket is a dense growth of shrubs, brush, or small trees.

5. Norway is noted for its *fjords,* which are narrow inlets of the sea bordered by steep cliffs.

6. A mountain climber must know a great deal about *geology,* which is the study of the physical nature of the earth.

7. Explorers of a dangerous territory must be careful not to lose their *composure.* That is, they must keep their emotions under control.

Developing Writing Skills

Analyzing a Character. John Muir writes of Stickeen that "his voice and gestures, hopes and fears, were so perfectly human that none could mistake them." One human attribute that Stickeen shows is courage. Write a paragraph giving reasons for believing that Stickeen is courageous.

Begin the assignment by examining Stickeen's reactions to the storm and to the crevasse. Record Muir's statements about Stickeen's reactions in your prewriting notes. Decide which details from your notes you would like to include in your paragraph. Then decide on the order in which you would like to present these details. You might find that order of importance or chronological order works well.

Begin your first draft by writing a topic sentence. As you write, use transitional words and phrases to connect your ideas. Then, as you revise, check to make sure that all the details you have included support your main idea. Consult **Using the Process of Writing** on pages 614–623 and Writing About Nonfiction on pages 626–627 if you need help.

B I O G R A P H Y

John Muir (1838–1914) attended grade school in Dunbar, Scotland, where he was born, and then emigrated to America with his family. After attending the University of Wisconsin, Muir set out to see the world, often traveling with nothing more than a pack of tea, bread, and a hand axe. He became particularly interested in forests. He advocated the preservation of American forests and was instrumental in the establishment of national parks. Muir's books, such as *The Yosemite* and *Our National Parks,* combine autobiography with descriptions of the places he loved.

In 1947, Thor Heyerdahl, a Norwegian explorer and scientist, tried to prove that the Inca Indians of Peru had traveled by water to Polynesia and were the original settlers. Heyerdahl used Peruvian balsa wood to build a primitive raft and named it Kon-Tiki. He set sail with five other men. Heyerdahl proved his theory that the Peruvians could have made the two-thousand mile voyage across the Pacific Ocean.

from Kon-Tiki

Thor Heyerdahl

After a week or so the sea grew calmer, and we noticed that it became blue instead of green. We began to go west-northwest instead of due northwest and took this as the first faint sign that we had got out of the coastal current and had some hope of being carried out to sea.

The very first day we were left alone on the sea, we had noticed fish round the raft; but we were too much occupied with the steering to think of fishing. The second day we went right into a thick shoal of sardines; and soon afterward an eight-foot blue shark came along and rolled over with its white belly uppermost as it rubbed against the raft's stern, where Herman and Bengt stood barelegged in the seas, steering. It played round us for a while but disappeared when we got the hand harpoon ready for action.

Next day we were visited by tunnies, bonitos, and dolphins, and when a big flying fish thudded on board we used it as bait and at once pulled in two large dolphins (dorados) weighing from twenty to thirty-five pounds each. This was food for several days. On steering watch, we could see many fish we did not even know; and one day we came into a school of porpoises which seemed quite endless. The black backs tumbled about, packed close together, right in to the side of the raft, and sprang up here and there all over the sea as far as we could see from the masthead. And the nearer we came to the equator, and the farther from the coast, the commoner flying fish became. When at last we came out into the blue water where the sea rolled by majestically, sunlit and serene, ruffled by gusts of wind, we could see them glittering like a rain of projectiles which shot from the water and flew in a straight line till their power of flight was exhausted and they vanished beneath the surface.

If we set the little paraffin lamp out at night, flying fish were attracted by the light and, large and small, shot over the raft. They often struck the bamboo cabin or the sail and tumbled helpless on the deck. Unable to get a take-off by swimming through the water, they just remained lying and kicking helplessly, like large-eyed herrings with long breast fins. It sometimes happened that we heard an outburst of strong language from a man on deck when a cold flying fish came unexpectedly, at a good speed, slap into his face. They always came at a good pace and snout first, and if they caught one full in the face they made it burn and tingle. But the unprovoked attack was quickly forgiven by the injured party, for, with all its drawbacks, we were in a maritime land of enchantment where delicious fish dishes came hurling through the air. We used to fry them for breakfast, and whether it was the fish, the cook, or our appetites, they reminded us of fried troutlings once we had scraped the scales off.

The cook's first duty, when he got up in the morning, was to go out on deck and collect all the flying fish that had landed on board in the course of the night. There were usually half a dozen or more, and once we found twenty-six fat flying fish on the raft. Knut was much upset one morning because, when he was standing operating with the frying pan, a flying fish struck him on the hand instead of landing right in the cooking fat.

Our neighborly intimacy with the sea was not fully realized by Torstein till he woke one morning and found a sardine on his pillow. There was so little room in the cabin that Torstein had to lie with his head in the doorway; and if anyone inadvertently trod on his face when going out at night, he bit him in the leg. He grasped the sardine by the tail and confided to it understandingly that all sardines had his entire sympathy. We conscientiously drew in our legs so that Torstein should have more room the next night, but then something happened which caused Torstein to find himself a sleeping place on top of all the kitchen utensils in the radio corner.

It was a few nights later. It was overcast and pitch dark, and Torstein had placed the paraffin lamp close by his head, so that the night watches could see where they were treading when they crept in and out over his head. About four o'clock, Torstein was awakened by the lamp tumbling over and something cold and wet flapping about his ears. "Flying fish," he thought and felt for it in the darkness to throw it away. He caught hold of something long and wet, which wriggled like a snake, and let go as if he had burned himself. The unseen visitor twisted itself away and over to Herman, while Torstein tried to get the lamp lighted again. Herman started up, too, and this made me wake, thinking of the octopus which came up at night in these waters.

When we got the lamp lighted, Herman was sitting in triumph with his hand gripping the neck of a long, thin fish which wriggled in his hands like an eel. The fish was over three feet long, as slender as a snake, with dull black eyes and a long snout with a greedy jaw full of long, sharp teeth. The teeth were as sharp as knives and could be folded back into the roof of the mouth to make way for what was swallowed. Under Herman's grip, a large-eyed white fish, about eight inches long, was suddenly thrown up from the stomach and out of the mouth of the predatory fish, and soon after up came another like it. These were clearly two deep-water fish, much torn by the snakefish's teeth. The snakefish's thin skin was bluish violet on the back and steel blue underneath, and it came loose in flakes when we took hold of it.

Bengt, too, was awakened at last by all the noise, and we held the lamp and the long fish under his nose. He sat up drowsily in his sleeping bag and said solemnly,

"No, fish like that don't exist."

With which he turned over quietly and fell asleep again.

Bengt was not far wrong. It appeared later that we six sitting round the lamp in the bamboo cabin were the first men to have seen this fish alive. Only the skeleton of a fish like this one had been found a few times on the coast of South America and the Galapagos Islands.[1] Ichthyologists[2] called it *Gempylus,* or snake mackerel, and thought it lived at the bottom of the sea at a great depth because no one had ever seen it alive. But, if it lived at a great depth, it must have done so by day when sun blinded its big eyes. For on dark nights *Gempylus* was abroad high over the surface of the sea; we on the raft had experience of that.

A week after the rare fish had landed on Torstein's sleeping bag, we had another visit. Again it was four in the morning, and the new moon had set so that it was dark; but the stars were shining. The raft was steering easily, and when my watch was over, I took a turn along the edge of the raft to see if everything was shipshape for the new watch. I had a rope round my waist, as the watch always had, and, with the paraffin lamp in my hand, I was walking carefully along the outermost log to get round the mast. The log was wet and slippery, and I was furious when someone quite unexpectedly caught hold of the rope behind me and jerked till I nearly lost my balance. I turned round wrathfully with the lantern, but not a soul was to be seen. There came a new tug at the rope, and I saw something shiny lying writhing on the deck. It was a fresh *Gempylus,* and this time it had got its teeth so deep into the rope that several of them broke before I got the rope loose. Presumably the light of the lantern had flashed along the curving white rope, and our visitor from the depths of the sea had caught hold in the hope of jumping up and snatching an extra long and tasty tidbit. It ended its a jar of Formalin.[3]

The sea contains many surprises for him who has on a level with the surface and drifts slowly and noiselessly. A sportsman breaks his way through the woods may come back and say that no wild life is to be seen. Another may sit down on a stump and wait, and often rustlings and cracklings will begin and curious eyes peer out. So it is on the sea, too. We usually plow across it with roaring engines and piston strokes, with the water foaming round our bow. Then we come back and say that there is nothing to see far out on the ocean.

Not a day passed, but we, as we sat floating on the surface of the sea, were visited by inquisitive guests which wriggled and waggled about us; and a few of them, such as dolphins and pilot fish, grew so familiar that they accompanied the raft across the sea and kept round us day and night.

When night had fallen and the stars were twinkling in the dark tropical sky, a phosphorescence flashed around us in rivalry with the stars; and single glowing plankton[5] resembled round live coals so vividly that we involuntarily drew in our bare legs when the glowing pellets were washed up round our feet at the raft's stern. When we caught them, we saw that they were little brightly shining species of shrimp. On such nights, we were some-

---

1. **Galapagos** (gə lä′ pə gōs′) **Islands:** group of islands in the Pacific on the equator.
2. **ichthyologists** (ik′ thē äl′ ə jists): scientists who study fish.
3. **Formalin:** a solution used for preserving.
4. **phosphorescence** (fäs′ fə res′ ′ns): a sparkling light.
5. **plankton:** microscopic animal and plant life.

On this small raft, the *Kon-Tiki,* Thor Heyerdahl and his crew braved thousands of miles of open ocean.

times scared when two round, shining eyes suddenly rose out of the sea right alongside the raft and glared at us with an unblinking hypnotic stare. The visitors were often big squids, which came up and floated on the surface with their devilish green eyes shining in the dark like phosphorus. But sometimes the shining eyes were those of deep-water fish which came up only at night and lay staring, fascinated by the glimmer of light before them. Several times, when the sea was calm, the black water round the raft was suddenly full of round heads two or three feet in diameter, lying motionless and staring at us with great glowing eyes. On other nights, balls of light three feet and more in diameter would be visible down in the water, flashing at irregular intervals like electric lights turned on for a moment.

We gradually grew accustomed to having these subterranean, or submarine, creatures under the floor; but nevertheless we were just as surprised every time a new species appeared. About two o'clock on a cloudy night, when the man at the helm had difficulty in distinguishing black water from black sky, he caught sight of a faint illumination down in the water which slowly took the shape of a large animal. It was impossible to say whether it was plankton shining on its body or whether the animal itself had a phosphorescent surface; but the glimmer down in the black water gave the ghostly creature obscure, wavering outlines. Sometimes it was roundish, sometimes oval, or triangular; and suddenly it split into two parts which swam to and fro under the raft independently of each other. Finally there were three of these large shining phantoms wandering round in slow circles under us.

They were real monsters, for the visible parts alone were some five fathoms long, and we all quickly collected on deck and followed the ghost dance. It went on for hour after hour, following the course of the raft. Mysterious and noiseless, our shining companions kept a good way beneath the surface, mostly on the starboard side where the light was, but often they were right under the raft or appeared on the port side. The glimmer of light on their backs revealed that the beasts were bigger than elephants; but they were not whales, for they never came up to breathe. Were they giant ray fish which changed shape when they turned over on their sides? They took no notice at all if we held the light right down on the surface to lure them up, so that we might see what kind of creatures they were. And, like all proper goblins and ghosts, they had sunk into the depths when the dawn began to break.

We never got a proper explanation of this nocturnal visit from the three shining monsters, unless the solution was afforded by another visit we received a day and a half later in the full midday sunshine. It was May 24, and we were lying drifting on a leisurely swell in exactly 95° west by 7° south. It was about noon, and we had thrown overboard the guts of two big dolphins we had caught earlier in the morning. I was having a refreshing plunge overboard at the bow, lying in the water but keeping a good lookout and hanging on to a rope end, when I caught sight of a thick brown fish, six feet long, which came swimming inquisitively toward me through the crystal-clear sea water. I hopped quickly up on to the edge of the raft and sat in the hot sun looking at the fish as it passed quietly, when I heard a wild war whoop from Knut, who was sitting aft behind the bamboo cabin. He bellowed "Shark!" till his voice cracked in a falsetto, and, as we had sharks swimming alongside the raft almost daily without creating such excitement, we all realized that this must be something extra-special and flocked astern to Knut's assistance.

Knut had been squatting there, washing his pants in the swell, and when he looked up for a moment he was staring straight into the biggest and ugliest face any of us had ever seen in the whole of our lives. It was the head of a veritable sea monster, so huge and so hideous that, if the Old Man of the Sea himself had come up, he could not have made such an impression on us. The head was broad and flat like a frog's, with two small eyes right at the sides, and a toadlike jaw which was four or five feet wide and had long fringes drooping from the corners of the mouth. Behind the head was an enormous body ending in a long, thin tail with a pointed tail fin which stood straight up and showed that this sea monster was not any kind of whale. The body looked brownish under the water, but both head and body were thickly covered with small white spots.

The monster came quietly, lazily swimming after us from astern. It grinned like a bulldog and lashed gently with its tail. The large, round dorsal fin projected clear of the water and sometimes the tail fin as well; and, when the creature was in the trough of the swell, the water flowed about the broad back as though washing round a submerged reef. In front of the broad jaws swam a whole crowd of zebra-striped pilot fish in fan formation; and large remora fish and other parasites sat firmly attached to the huge body and traveled with it through the water, so that the whole thing looked like a curious zoological collection crowded round something that resembled a floating deep-water reef.

A twenty-five-pound dolphin, attached to six of our largest fishhooks, was hanging behind the raft as bait for sharks; and a swarm of the pilot fish shot straight off, nosed the dolphin without touching it, and then hurried back to their lord and master, the sea king. Like a mechanical monster, it set its machinery going and came gliding at leisure toward the dolphin which lay, a beggarly trifle, before its jaws. We tried to pull the dolphin in, and the sea monster followed slowly, right up to the side of the raft. It did not open its mouth but just let the dolphin bump against it, as if to throw open the whole door, for such an insignificant scrap was not worth while. When the giant came close up to the raft, it rubbed its back against the heavy steering oar, which was just lifted up out of the water; and now we had ample opportunity of studying the monster at the closest quarters — at such close quarters that I thought we had all gone mad, for we roared stupidly with laughter and shouted overexcitedly at the completely fantastic sight we saw. Walt Disney himself, with all his powers of imagination, could not have created a more hair-raising sea monster than that which thus suddenly lay with its terrific jaws along the raft's side.

The monster was a whale shark, the largest shark and the largest fish known in the world today. It is exceedingly rare, but scattered specimens are observed here and there in the tropical oceans. The whale shark has an average length of fifty feet, and according to zoologists it weighs fifteen tons. It is said that large specimens can attain a length of sixty feet; one harpooned baby had a liver weighing six hundred pounds and a collection of three thousand teeth in each of its broad jaws.

Our monster was so large that, when it began to swim in circles round us and under the raft, its head was visible on one side while the whole of its tail stuck out on the other. And so incredibly grotesque, inert, and stupid did it appear when seen full face, that we could not help shouting with laughter, although we realized that it had strength enough in its tail to smash both balsa logs and ropes to pieces if it attacked us. Again and again it described narrower and narrower circles just under the raft, while all we could do was to wait and see what might happen. When it appeared on the other side, it glided amiably under the steering oar and lifted it up in the air, while the oar blade slid along the creature's back.

We stood round the raft with hand harpoons ready for action, but they seemed to us like toothpicks in relation to the mammoth beast we had to deal with. There was no indication that the whale shark ever thought of leaving us again; it circled round us and followed like a faithful dog, close up to the raft. None of us had ever experienced or thought we should experience anything like it; the whole adventure, with the sea monster swimming behind and under the raft, seemed to us so completely unnatural that we could not really take it seriously.

In reality, the whale shark went on encircling us for barely an hour, but to us the visit seemed to last a whole day. At last it became too exciting for Erik, who was standing at a corner of the raft with an eight-foot hand harpoon, and, encouraged by ill-considered shouts, he raised the harpoon above his head. As the whale shark came gliding slowly toward him and its broad head moved right under the corner of the raft, Erik thrust the harpoon with all his giant strength down between his legs and deep into the whale shark's gristly head. It was a second or two before the giant understood properly what was happening. Then in a flash, the placid half-wit was transformed into a mountain of steel muscles.

We heard a swishing noise as the harpoon line rushed over the edge of the raft and saw a cascade of water as the giant stood on its head and plunged down into the depths. The three men who were standing nearest were flung about the place, head over heels; and two of them were flayed and burned by the line as it rushed through the air. The thick line, strong enough to hold a boat, was caught up on the side of the raft but snapped at once like a piece of twine; and a few seconds later a broken-off harpoon shaft came up to the surface two hundred yards away. A shoal of frightened pilot fish shot off through the water in a desperate attempt to keep up with their old lord and master. We waited a long time for the monster to come racing back like an infuriated submarine, but we never saw anything more of him.

A member of the *Kon-Tiki* crew holds a *Gempylus,* or snake mackerel.

Getting at Meaning

RECALLING

1. What do the men aboard the *Kon-Tiki* eat? What is the cook's first duty when he gets up in the morning?

2. Why does Torstein sleep with his head outside the cabin?

3. What happens to awaken Torstein and Herman in the middle of the night?

4. What is a *Gempylus*? What does it look like? What humorous remark does Herman make when the *Gempylus* is first shown to him?

5. What is the largest fish in the world? What does it look like? What reactions do the men in the story have to this fish?

INTERPRETING

6. How can you tell that Thor Heyerdahl knows a great deal about the sea and its creatures?

7. According to Heyerdahl, people usually plow across the sea "with roaring engines and piston strokes." What is different about Heyerdahl's method of travel? What are the advantages of this method?

8. The men aboard the *Kon-Tiki* make several observations and discoveries that are of scientific interest. What are these observations and discoveries?

9. What feeling is evoked by the passage about the "monsters" on pages 298–300? What other names does Heyerdahl use to refer to these creatures? What effect does the use of these names have on the reader?

CRITICAL THINKING: EVALUATING/APPLYING

10. What other explorers have achieved fame by voyaging into the unknown? What characteristics do these explorers have in common with Heyerdahl?

11. One purpose that Heyerdahl had for writing this selection was to arouse feelings of curiosity and wonder about the sea and its life.

How successful is Heyerdahl in achieving this purpose? Which of the sea creatures described in the selection intrigues you most? Why?

Developing Skills in Reading Literature

Fiction and Nonfiction. Fiction is writing about imaginary people, places, and events. Nonfiction is writing about real people, places, and events. Because Heyerdahl is writing nonfiction, he must report events exactly as they happened. Think about the encounter between Heyerdahl's crew and the whale shark. How did this encounter end? What prompted Erik's action? Was his action heroic? What consequences did his action have? In what ways could a writer of fiction have changed the story of Erik and the shark? What different outcomes could this story have had?

Developing Vocabulary

1. **Context Clues: Restatement.** To help you understand the meaning of an unfamiliar word, a writer will sometimes provide a complete definition. At other times a writer will restate the meaning of the new word, or say it again in a different way. A restatement usually is signaled by the word *or* or by parentheses, a dash, a pair of dashes, a comma, or a pair of commas.

Consider this example from the selection: "Ichthyologists called it *Gempylus,* or snake mackerel, and thought it lived at the bottom of the sea at a great depth because no one had ever seen it alive." When you read this sentence, you understand that a *Gempylus* is the same as a snake mackerel. The phrase "or snake mackerel" is a restatement. This restatement is signaled by a pair of commas and the word *or.*

On a separate sheet of paper, write the definition of the italicized word in each of the following sentences. Identify the key words or punctuation marks used to signal the restatement.

a. *Nocturnal* animals, those animals that are active during the night, are seldom seen during the day.

b. Sailing on a raft increases a person's *intimacy,* or closeness, with the sea.

c. *Ichthyologists* (scientists who study fish) sometimes store specimens in jars of Formalin.

d. When Knut yelled, "Shark!" the other members of the crew flocked to the *stern*—the rear of the raft—to investigate the commotion.

e. Anyone who is going to spend time on a boat must learn the terms *port,* or left side, and *starboard,* or right side.

2. **Using Restatement Clues.** Look up each of the following words in the Glossary. Then use each word in a sentence that contains a restatement. Use the word *or,* commas, dashes, or parentheses to signal the restatements in your sentences.

shoal   mammoth   predatory
tunny   falsetto

Developing Writing Skills

Using Images To Create a Mood. Sensory images are words that describe things that can be seen, heard, touched, tasted, or smelled. By choosing the right sensory images, a writer can create in his or her readers a particular emotional response, or mood.

Reread Heyerdahl's account on pages 298–300 of the three submarine creatures that follow the *Kon-Tiki* one night. Notice how Heyerdahl uses images such as "large shining phantoms" and "goblins and ghosts" to create a mood of mystery tinged with fear.

Write a paragraph in which you describe a frightening experience that you had as a child. The purpose of your paragraph will be to create a mood of mystery and fear. Start by listing in your prewriting notes all the events that you want to include. Arrange these events in chronological order. Then make a list of the sensory images you can use to create the mood.

Begin the paragraph with a topic sentence that places you, its subject, in a particular place at a particular time. As you write, use transitional words and phrases to show the order of events. Also include sensory images from your prewriting notes. As you revise, make sure that all the details you have included contribute to the mood that you want to create. Also check to make sure that the order of events in the paragraph is clear. Refer to **Using the Process of** ≪ **Writing** on pages 614–623.

B I O G R A P H Y

Thor Heyerdahl (born 1914) went on an expedition to the South Pacific, which made him curious about the origins and culture of the islands. Heyerdahl became convinced that the Pacific Islands of Polynesia could have been populated by Indians from South America. To prove the theory, he and five companions constructed a balsa wood raft and named it *Kon-Tiki.* The crew successfully sailed across 4,300 miles of ocean. His book *Kon-Tiki* describes the journey. In 1970, he led another crew across the Atlantic in a papyrus reed boat called *Ra.* He claims that this journey proves that ancient Egyptians could have traveled to the New World. *The Ra Expeditions* tells about this crossing. Heyerdahl was born in Norway.

---

from *R*ascal

Sterling North

I decided one day that Rascal was clean enough and bright enough to eat with us at the table. I went to the attic and brought down the family highchair, last used during my own infancy.

Next morning while my father was fixing eggs, toast, and coffee, I went out to get Rascal. I placed him in the highchair beside me at the table. On his tray I put a heavy earthenware bowl of warm milk.

Rascal could reach the milk easily by standing in the chair and placing his hands on the edge of the tray. He seemed to like the new arrangement and chirred and trilled his satisfaction. Except for dribbling a little milk, easily wiped from the tray of the highchair, his table manners proved excellent, much better than those of most children. My father was amused and permissive as usual, and even petted the raccoon as we finished our meal.

Breakfast-for-three became part of the daily ritual, and we had no trouble whatsoever until I had the idea of offering Rascal a sugar loaf. It is true we were at war, observing heatless, meatless, and wheatless days, and conserving sugar. But my father and I did no baking, and

used almost none of our sugar ration, save for a lump or two in coffee. So I did not feel too unpatriotic when I gave Rascal his first sugar.

Rascal felt it, sniffed it, and then began his usual washing ceremony, swishing it back and forth through his bowl of milk. In a few moments, of course, it melted entirely away, and a more surprised little raccoon you have never seen in your life. He felt all over the bottom of the bowl to see if he had dropped it, then turned over his right hand to assure himself it was empty, then examined his left hand in the same manner. Finally he looked at me and trilled a shrill question: who had stolen his sugar lump?

Recovering from my laughter, I gave him a second sugar lump, which Rascal examined minutely. He started to wash it, but hesitated. A very shrewd look came into his bright black eyes; and instead of washing away a second treat, he took it directly to his mouth, where he began to munch it with complete satisfaction. When Rascal had learned a lesson, he had learned it for life. Never again did he wash a lump of sugar.

His intelligence, however, created many

problems. For instance, he had seen the source of the sugar—the covered bowl in the middle of the table. And whereas I had previously been able to confine him to his highchair, he now insisted upon walking across the table-cloth, lifting the lid of the sugar bowl, and helping himself to a lump. From that day on, we had to keep the sugar bowl in the corner cupboard to avoid having a small raccoon constantly on the dining room table.

Another lesson he learned swiftly was how to open the back screen door. I purposely had not repaired the catch or replaced the weakened spring, because all of my cats liked to open the door and walk in, or push it from inside and let themselves out again. Rascal watched this performance several times. Obviously the trick was to hook your claws into the screen and pull. Feeling very pleased

with himself he showed the cats he was as smart as the oldest and wisest tom.

Several nights later, I was startled and delighted to hear Rascal's trill from the pillow beside me, then to feel his little hands working all over my face. My raccoon baby had climbed from his hole, opened the back screen door, and with eyes that could see in the dark had found his way to my bed.

There were no strict rules in our house, as both Rascal and I realized. My raccoon had decided that the very best place to sleep was with me. He was as clean as any cat, house-broken immediately and without training, and he thought my bed was softer and more comfortable than his own in the oak tree. So from that night on we became bedfellows, and for many months we slept together. I felt less lonesome now when my father was away.

Getting at Meaning

RECALLING

1. Describe how Rascal sits and eats at the dining room table.

2. What happens to Rascal's first lump of sugar? the second lump?

3. What does Rascal discover about the source of the sugar? What does he do with his discovery?

4. How does Rascal get in and out of the house? Who teaches him how to do it?

5. Where does Rascal decide to spend his nights?

6. How does Sterling North react to Rascal's decision?

INTERPRETING

7. What is North's attitude toward Rascal?

8. What can you infer about North's youth? Was it happy or sad? What was North's relationship with his father?

CRITICAL THINKING: EVALUATING

9. At what point do you find out that Rascal is a raccoon? What words in the beginning of the selection imply that Rascal is an animal? Why do you think that North chose to delay revealing Rascal's true identity?

Developing Skills in Reading Literature

1. **Aphorism.** An aphorism is a brief statement, often of a general truth. One widely known aphorism is, "Truth is often stranger than fiction." Explain how this aphorism relates to the story of Rascal.

2. **Point of View.** Point of view is the perspective from which a story is told. In "Rascal" the narrator is the raccoon's owner. He tells the story from his own point of view. How does the narrator feel about the raccoon eating breakfast in the dining room? about its going in and out of the house? about its sleeping in his bed? How would this story be different if it were told by a guest? by a father who did not like raccoons?

Developing Writing Skills

Writing an Anecdote. An anecdote is a brief story told to entertain or to make a point. Write an anecdote about an interesting, unusual, or amusing animal. Your subject may be a pet that you have owned or some other animal that you have encountered in a zoo or in your neighborhood. Confine your writing to one short incident and to one specific purpose.

Once you have found a topic, list in your prewriting notes the events that you want to write about. Also jot down a few phrases that describe the animal you have chosen. As you write and revise your anecdote, refer to the lessons in **Using the Process of Writing** on pages 614–623.

B I O G R A P H Y

Sterling North (1906–1974) always felt that he had been blessed with a rich childhood and tried to share it with his readers. The gentle joys of the past were described in two of his most popular books, *So Dear to My Heart* and *Rascal: A Memoir of a Better Era.* Both were made into Walt Disney movies. North also wrote poetry, articles, stories, and biographies of famous Americans.

Cub Life

Joy Adamson

For many years my home has been in the Northern Frontier Province of Kenya, that vast stretch of semi-arid thornbush, covering some hundred and twenty thousand square miles, which extends from Mount Kenya to the Abyssinian border.

Civilization has made little impact on this part of Africa. There are no settlers. The local tribes live very much as their forefathers did, and the place abounds in wildlife of every description.

My husband, George, is Senior Game Warden of this huge territory. George has many duties, such as enforcing the Game Laws, preventing poaching, and dealing with dangerous animals that have molested the tribes. His work causes him to travel over tremendous distances. These journeys we call safaris. Whenever it is possible, I accompany my husband on such trips; and in this way I have had unique opportunities of coming to grips with this wild, unchanged land, where life is tough and nature asserts her own laws.

This story has its beginning on one of these safaris. A Boran tribesman had been killed by a man-eating lion. It was reported to George

that this animal, accompanied by two lionesses, was living in some nearby hills; and so it became his duty to track them down. This was why we were camping far to the north of Isiolo among the Boran tribes.

Early on the morning of the first of February, 1956, I found myself in camp alone with Pati, a rock hyrax who had been living with us as a pet for six and a half years. She looked like a marmot or a guinea pig, though zoologists will have it that on account of the bone structure of its feet and teeth, the hyrax is most nearly related to rhinos and elephants.

Pati snuggled her soft fur against my neck and from this safe position watched all that went on. The country around us was dry with out-crops of granite and only sparse vegetation. All the same, there were animals to be seen; for there were plenty of gerenuk and other gazelles, creatures that have adapted themselves to these dry conditions and rarely, if ever, drink.

Suddenly I heard the vibrations of a car. This could only mean that George was returning much earlier than expected. Soon our Land Rover broke through the thornbush and stopped near our tents, and I heard George shout, "Joy, where are you? Quick, I have something for you. . . . "

I rushed out with Pati on my shoulder and saw the skin of a lion. But before I could ask about the hunt, George pointed to the back of the car. There were three lion cubs, tiny balls of spotted fur, each trying to hide its face from everything that went on. They were only a few days old, and their eyes were still covered with a bluish film. They could hardly crawl; nevertheless, they tried to creep away. I took them on my lap to comfort them, while George, who was most distressed, told me what had happened. Toward dawn, he and another Game Warden, Ken, had been guided near to the place where the man-eater was said to lie up. When first light broke, they were charged by a lioness who rushed out from behind some rocks. Though they had no wish to kill her, she was very close and the way back was hazardous, so George signalled to Ken to shoot. He hit and wounded her. The lioness disappeared, and when they went forward, they found a heavy trail of blood leading upward. Cautiously, step by step, they went over the crest of the hill till they came to a huge flat rock. George climbed onto it to get a better view, while Ken skirted around below. Then he saw Ken peer under the rock, pause, raise his rifle, and fire both barrels. There was a growl; the lioness appeared and came straight at Ken. George could not shoot, for Ken was in his line of fire. Fortunately, a Game Scout who was in more favorable position fired his rifle and caused the animal to swerve. Then George was able to kill her. She was a big lioness in the prime of life, her teats swollen with milk. It was only when he saw this that George realized why she had been so angry and faced them so courageously. Then he blamed himself for not having recognized earlier that her behavior showed that she was defending her litter.

Now he ordered a search to be made for the cubs. Presently he and Ken heard slight sounds coming out of a crack in the rock face. They put their arms down the crevice as far as they could reach. Loud infantile growls and snarls greeted this unsuccessful maneuver. Next they cut a long, hooked stick and after a lot of probing managed to drag the cubs out. They could not have been more than two or three days old. They were carried to the car, where the two biggest growled and spat during the whole of the journey back to camp. The third and smallest, however, offered no resistance and seemed quite unconcerned. Now the three cubs lay in my lap, and how could I resist making a fuss of them?

To my amazement Pati, who was usually very jealous of any rival, soon came to nestle among them, and obviously accepted them as desirable companions. From that day onward, the four became inseparable. During these early days Pati was the biggest of the company and also, being six years old, was very dignified compared with the clumsy little velvet bags who couldn't walk without losing their balance.

It was two days before the cubs accepted their first milk. Until then, whatever trick I tried to make them swallow diluted unsweetened canned milk only resulted in their pulling up their tiny noses and protesting: "ng-ng, ng-ng," very much as we did as children, before we had learned better manners and been taught to say, "No, thank you."

Once they had accepted the milk, they could not get enough of it. Every two hours I had to warm it and clean the flexible rubber tube, which we had taken from the wireless set to serve as a teat until we were able to get a

proper baby's bottle. We had sent at once to the nearest African market, which was about fifty miles away, not only for the teat but also for cod-liver oil, glucose, and cases of unsweetened milk. At the same time, we had sent an S.O.S. to the District Commissioner at Isiolo, about a hundred and fifty miles away, announcing the arrival there within a fortnight[1] of Three Royal Babies, asking him to be good enough to have a comfortable wooden home made in time for our return.

Within a few days the cubs had settled down and were everybody's pets. Pati, their most conscientious self-appointed nanny, remained in charge. She was devoted to them, and never minded being pulled and trodden on by the three fast-growing little bullies. All the cubs were females. Even at this age, each had a definite character. The "Big One" had a benevolent superiority and was generous toward the others. The second was a clown, always laughing and spanking her milk bottle

with both her front paws as she drank, her eyes closed in bliss. I named her Lustica, which means the "Jolly One."

The third cub was the weakling in size, but the pluckiest in spirit. She pioneered all around, and was always sent by the others to reconnoiter when something looked suspicious to them. I called her Elsa, because she reminded me of someone of that name.

In the natural course of events, Elsa would probably have been the throw-out of the pride.[2] The average number of cubs in a litter is four, of which one usually dies soon after birth, and another is often too weak to be reared. It is for this reason that one usually sees only two cubs with a lioness. Their mother looks after them till they are two years old. For the first year she provides their food. She re-

---

1. **fortnight:** two weeks.
2. **pride:** a group or family of lions.

gurgitates[3] it, thus making it acceptable to them. During the second year, the cubs are allowed to take part in the hunting, but they get severely disciplined if they lose their self-control. Since at this time they are unable to kill on their own, they have to rely for their food on what may be left over from a kill by the full-grown lions of the pride. Often very little remains for them, so they are usually in a bad, scruffy condition at this age. Sometimes they can't bear the hunger. Then either they break through the line of gorging adults and are likely to be killed, or they leave the pride, in small groups; and, because they do not yet know how to kill properly, often run into trouble. Nature's law is harsh and lions have to learn the hard way from the beginning.

The quartet — Pati and the three cubs — spent most of the day in the tent under my camp bed. This evidently seemed to them a safe place and the nearest thing they could find to their natural nursery. They were by nature house-trained and always took great care to reach the sand outside. There were a few accidents during the first days; but afterward, on the rare occasions when a little pool disgraced their home, they miaowed and made comical grimaces of disgust. In every way they were wonderfully clean and had no smell except for a very pleasant one like honey—or was it cod-liver oil? Their tongues were already as rough as sandpaper. As they grew older, we could feel them, even through our khaki clothes, when they licked us.

When, after two weeks, we returned to Isiolo, our Royal Babies had a palace awaiting them. Everyone came to see them, and they received a royal welcome. They loved Europeans and especially small children. They took a great liking to a young Somali, called Nuru. He was our garden boy. Now we appointed him guardian and lion-keeper in chief. The post pleased him, for it raised his social status. It also meant that when the cubs got tired of romping all over the house and its surroundings and preferred to sleep under some shady bush, he was able to sit near them for long hours, watching to see that no snakes or baboons molested them.

For twelve weeks we kept them on a diet of unsweetened milk mixed with cod-liver oil, glucose, bonemeal, and a little salt. Soon they showed us that they required only three-hourly feeds, and then gradually the intervals became longer.

By now their eyes were fully opened, but they could not yet judge distances and often missed their target. To help them over this difficulty, we gave them rubber balls and old inner tubes to play with—the latter were perfect for tug-of-war games. Indeed, anything made of rubber, or that was soft and flexible, fascinated them. They would try to take the inner tube from each other, the attacker rolling sideways onto the possessor, pressing her weight between the end of the tube and its owner. If no success was achieved by this method, the rivals would simply pull with all their might. Then, when the battle had been won, the victor would parade with the trophy in front of the others and provoke an attack. If this invitation was ignored, the rubber would be placed in front of their noses, while the owner pretended to be unaware that it might be stolen from her.

Surprise was the most important element in all their games. They stalked each other—and us — from the earliest age, and knew by instinct how to do it properly.

---

3. **regurgitates** (ri gur′ jə tāts′): brings partly digested food from the stomach back into the mouth.

They always attacked from the rear. Keeping under cover, they crouched. They then crept slowly toward the unsuspecting victim until the final rush was made at flying speed, and resulted in the attacker's landing with all her weight on the back of her quarry, throwing it to the ground. When we were the object of such an attack, we always pretended to be unaware of what was going on. Obligingly we crouched down and looked the other way until the final onslaught took place. This delighted the cubs.

Pati always wanted to be in the game; though, as the cubs were soon three times her size, she took good care to keep out of the way of heavy spankings and to avoid being squashed by her charges. In all other circumstances, she retained her authority by sheer character. If the cubs became too aggressive, she put them in their places by just turning around and facing them. I admired her spirit, for, small as she was, it needed a lot of courage to convince them of her fearlessness; the more so that her only defenses were her sharp teeth, quick reactions, intelligence, and pluck.

As the lions became increasingly aware of their strength, they tested it on everything they could find. For instance, a ground sheet, however large, *had* to be dragged about; and they would set to work in proper feline fashion, placing it under their bodies and pulling it between their front legs, as in later life they would drag a kill. Another favorite game was "king of the castle." A cub would jump onto a potato sack and keep her attacker at bay until she was suddenly dethroned by the other sister coming up from behind. The victor was usually Elsa, who, seeing the other two locked in combat, made the most of her opportunity.

Our few banana trees were also regarded as delightful toys, and very soon their luxuriant leaves hung in tattered fringes. Tree climbing was another favorite game. The little lions were born acrobats, but often they ventured so high that they could not turn to come down, and we were obliged to rescue them.

When at dawn Nuru let them out, they shot out of doors with a whole night's pent-up energy, and this moment could be compared to the start of a greyhound race. On one such occasion, they spotted a tent in which two men who had come to visit us were staying. Within five minutes it was a wreck. We were awakened by the cries of our guests who were vainly trying to rescue their belongings. Meanwhile the cubs, wild with excitement, dived into the wreckage and reappeared with a variety of trophies—slippers, pajamas, shreds of mosquito netting. We had to enforce discipline that time with a small stick.

Putting them to bed was also no mean task. Imagine three very naughty little girls, who like all children hated bedtime, but who could run twice as fast as those who were in charge of them and had the added advantage of being able to see in the dark.

We were often obliged to resort to subterfuge. One very successful trick was to tie an old bag to a length of rope and drag it steadily toward and then into the pen. Usually they could not resist chasing it.

Outdoor games were all very well, but the cubs also developed a fancy for books and cushions. So, to save our library and other possessions, we were eventually obliged to ban them from the house. To effect this, we made a shoulder-high door of strong wire on a wooden frame and placed it across the entrance to the veranda. The cubs resented it very much; so to compensate them for their lost playground, we hung a tire from a tree, and this proved to be grand for chewing and also as a swing. Another toy we gave them was an empty wooden honey barrel which made a resounding boom when it was pushed. But best of all was a hessian bag. We filled it with old inner tubes and tied it to a branch, from which it dangled invitingly. It had another rope attached to it; and when the cubs hung on to the bag, we pulled and swung them high up into the air. The more we laughed the better they enjoyed the game.

Yet none of these toys caused them to forget that there was at all times a barrier in front of the veranda, and they often came and rubbed their soft noses against the wire.

Late one afternoon some friends had arrived for a sundowner. Intrigued by the sounds of merriment inside, the cubs soon turned up, but that evening they behaved in a disciplined fashion. There was no nose-rubbing against the wire; all three kept a foot away from it. This exemplary conduct aroused my suspicion, so I got up to investigate its cause. To my horror, I saw a large, red spitting cobra between the cubs and the door. In spite of the presence of three lions on one side and of ourselves on the other, it wriggled determinedly across the veranda steps, and by the time we had fetched a shotgun it had disappeared.

No barricades, cobras, or prohibitions made Lustica give up her intention of entering the house. Repeatedly she tried all the doors. Pressing a handle proved easy enough. Even turning a knob could be done. Only when we quickly fitted bolts all around, was she defeated; and even so, I once caught her trying to push the bolt aside with her teeth. Thwarted in her purpose, she had her revenge upon us, for about this time she tore the laundry off the

clothesline and galloped off into the bush with it.

When the cubs were three months old, they had teeth big enough to make it possible for them to eat meat. So now I gave them raw minced meat, which was the best we could do to imitate their mother's regurgitated food. For several days they refused to touch it and pulled grimaces of disgust. Then Lustica made the experiment, and found it to her taste. The others took courage from her, and soon there was a fight at every meal. This meant that poor Elsa, who was still weaker than the others, had little chance of getting her fair share; so I kept the tidbits for her and used to take her on to my lap for her meals. She loved this. Rolling her head from side to side and closing her eyes, she showed how happy she was. At these times, she would suck my thumbs and massage my thighs with her front paws as though she were kneading her mother's belly in order to get more milk. It was during these hours that the bond between us developed. We combined playing with feeding, and my days were happily spent with these charming creatures.

They were lazy by nature, and it needed a lot of persuasion to get them to move from a comfortable position. Even the most desirable marrow bone was not worth the effort of getting up, and they would roll into position to get at it by the easiest way. But best of all, they liked me to hold their bone for them while they lay on their backs, paws in the air, and sucked at it.

When the cubs went into the bush, they often had adventures. One morning I was following them, for I had given them a worming powder and wished to see the result. I saw them a little way off, asleep. Suddenly I noticed a stream of black soldier ants approaching them. Indeed, some were already climbing up their bodies. Knowing how fiercely these ants will attack anything that lies in their path and how powerful their mandibles[4] are, I was just about to wake up the cubs when the ants changed their direction.

Soon afterwards, five donkeys approached and the cubs woke up. This was the first time they had seen such big animals, and they certainly showed the proverbial courage of a lion, for they all charged simultaneously. This put them into such good heart that when, a few days later, our forty pack donkeys and mules came near the house, the three little lions fearlessly put the whole cavalcade to flight.

At five months they were in splendid condition and getting stronger every day. They were quite free except at night, when they slept in an enclosure of rock and sand which led off from their wooden shelter. This was a necessary precaution, for wild lions, hyenas, jackals, and elephants frequently roam around our house. Any of these might have killed them.

The more we grew to know the cubs the more we loved them, so it was hard to accept the fact that we could not keep forever three fast-growing lions. Regretfully we decided that two must go and that it would be better that the two big ones, who were always together and less dependent on us than Elsa, should be the ones to leave. Our African servants agreed with our choice; when asked their opinion, they unanimously chose the smallest. Perhaps they were influenced by visions of the future and thought: "If there must be a lion in the household, then let it be as small as possible."

As to Elsa, we felt that if she had only ourselves as friends she would be easy to train, not only for life at Isiolo but also as a traveling companion on our safaris.

---

4. **mandibles** (man′ də b'lz); the biting jaws of an insect.

As a home for Lustica and the Big One, we chose the Rotterdam-Blydorp Zoo and made arrangements for them to make the journey by air.

Since they would have to leave from the Nairobi airfield, which was one hundred and eighty miles away, we decided to get them accustomed to motoring; and took them for short daily trips in my one-and-a-half-ton truck, which had a wired box body. We also began to feed them in it, so that they might get used to it and consider it as one of their play pens.

On the last day, we padded the car with soft sandbags.

When we drove off, Elsa ran a short way down the drive; and then stood with the most mournful expression in her eyes, watching the car in which her two sisters were disappearing. I traveled in the back with the cubs and had armed myself with a small first-aid kit, fully expecting to be scratched during the long journey. However, my medical precautions were put to shame; for, after an hour of restlessness, the cubs lay on the bags beside me, embracing me with their paws. We traveled like this for eleven hours, delayed by two blowouts. The lions could not have been more trusting. When we reached Nairobi, they looked at me with their large eyes, puzzled to know what to make of all the strange noises and smells. Then the plane carried them off forever from their native land.

After a few days, we received a cable announcing the safe arrival of our cubs in Holland. When I visited them, about three years later, they accepted me as a friendly person and allowed me to stroke them, but they did not recognize me. They live in splendid conditions and, on the whole, I was glad to know that almost certainly they had no recollection of a freer life.

Getting at Meaning

RECALLING

1. Where does this story take place? Describe the setting.

2. How does Joy Adamson first meet the cubs? Why are they motherless?

3. How does Pati, the hyrax, treat the cubs?

4. How are the cubs fed? What are they fed?

5. Each cub is described as having a definite character. Name the cubs and describe each one's particular characteristics.

6. Give an example of how the lions test their strength.

7. How are the cubs finally kept out of the house?

8. Why do Adamson and her husband send the two biggest lions away?

9. Where are the cubs sent? How do they travel to their destination?

INTERPRETING

10. Why does Elsa require special attention? What role does Joy Adamson play in Elsa's life? What reasons do you think the Adamsons have for keeping Elsa? Find evidence in the selection to support your answers.

11. What is the mood of the last two paragraphs of the selection? How do you think Joy Adamson feels about sending the cubs away from Africa?

CRITICAL THINKING: EVALUATING

12. What do you think is the biggest challenge involved in raising the lion cubs? What is the biggest satisfaction?

13. Are the Adamsons good substitute parents for the cubs? Explain your answer.

14. Being mature means being ready to take responsibility for the consequences of your actions. What action on George's part leaves the cubs alone in the world? What responsibility does George's action place on his own shoulders? Does he meet this responsibility?

Developing Skills in Reading Literature

1. **Nonfiction.** Nonfiction is writing about real people, places, and events. Nonfiction therefore presents factual information. What facts do you learn from this selection? What do lion cubs eat? What games do they like to play? How does their play prepare them for life as adults?

Give two examples of factual information about other wildlife in the story.

2. **Description.** Description is writing that creates a picture of a scene, event, or character. Adamson describes the cubs as "tiny balls of spotted fur" and "clumsy little velvet bags." How do these descriptions help you to visualize the cubs? What other examples of vivid description can you find in the selection?

Developing Vocabulary

Context Clues: Examples. You often can guess the meaning of an unfamiliar word from examples provided by the author. Words that signal examples will include *and, other, like, for instance, such as, for example,* and *especially.* Consider the following sentences:

The lion cubs had some prohibitions. For example, after a time, they were not allowed to enter the house.

The example is signaled by the words *for example.* You can understand from the second sentence that prohibitions are rules against doing certain things.

The following sentences illustrate three types of context clues: definitions, restatements, and examples. On a separate sheet of paper, write the meaning of each italicized word and the type of context clue that helped you determine this meaning.

1. Pati, a *rock hyrax,* had been living with the Adamsons as a pet. A rock hyrax is a small, hoofed mammal native to Africa and southwest Asia.

2. Near the Adamsons' home were plenty of

gerenuk and other gazelles.

3. The *quartet*—Pati and the three cubs—spent most of the day under the camp bed.

4. The Adamsons often resorted to *subterfuge* and other tricks to put the cubs to bed.

5. The Adamsons built *barricades* to keep the cubs out of their house. For instance, they blocked one entrance with a door of strong wire.

Developing Writing Skills

Supporting an Opinion. Do you agree or disagree with the Adamsons' decision to send two of the cubs to a zoo? In a paragraph, state your opinion and support it with reasons.

List in your prewriting notes reasons for and against the Adamsons' decision. Then, examine your notes and decide whether you agree or disagree with the decision. State your opinion in a topic sentence. Then, in the body of your paragraph, present the strongest supporting reasons from your prewriting notes. When revising your paragraph, think about other reasons that you can add to strengthen your argument. Refer to **Using the Process of Writing** on pages 614–623 and to Writing About Nonfiction on pages 626–627 if you need help.

B I O G R A P H Y

Joy Adamson (1910–1980) is best remembered for her work with wild animals in Africa. She and her husband, a game warden, raised Elsa, an orphaned lion cub. When Elsa was fully grown, the couple trained her to hunt and kill so that she could return to the jungle instead of having to be sent to a zoo. Joy Adamson wrote about Elsa's training in *Born Free*. Two subsequent books, *Living Free* and *Forever Free,* told more about Elsa and her cubs. Joy Adamson was also a talented painter and an illustrator of books on African plants and shrubs.

A chief remembers the Apache way of life.

from Geronimo: His Own Story

Geronimo

I was born in No-doyohn Cañon, Arizona, June, 1829.

In that country which lies around the headwaters of the Gila River I was reared. This range was our fatherland. Among these mountains our wigwams were hidden. The scattered valleys contained our fields. The boundless prairies, stretching away on every side, were our pastures. The rocky caverns were our burying places.

I was fourth in a family of eight children—four boys and four girls. Of that family, only myself; my brother, Porico (White Horse); and my sister, Nah-da-ste, are yet alive. We are held as prisoners of war in this Military Reservation (Fort Sill).

As a babe, I rolled on the dirt floor of my father's tepee, hung in my *tsoch* (Apache name for *cradle*) at my mother's back, or suspended from the bough of a tree. I was warmed by the sun, rocked by the winds, and sheltered by the trees as other Indian babes.

When I was a child, my mother taught me the legends of our people; taught me of the sun and sky, the moon and stars, the clouds and storms. She also taught me to kneel and pray to Usen the spirit father, for strength, health, wisdom, and protection. We never prayed against any person; but if we had aught[1] against any individual, we ourselves took vengeance. We were taught that Usen does not care for the petty quarrels of men.

My father had often told me of the brave deeds of our warriors, of the pleasures of the chase, and the glories of the warpath.

With my brothers and sisters, I played about my father's home. Sometimes we played hide-and-seek among the rocks and pines; sometimes we loitered in the shade of the cottonwood trees or sought the *shudock* (a kind of wild cherry) while our parents worked in the field. Sometimes we played that we were warriors. We would practice stealing upon some object that represented an enemy, and in our childish imitation often performed the feats of war. Sometimes we would hide away from our mother to see if she could find us, and often when thus concealed go to sleep and perhaps remain hidden for many hours.

When we were old enough to be of real service, we went to the field with our parents, not to play, but to toil. When the crops were to be

---

1. **aught** (ôt): anything whatever.

planted, we broke the ground with wooden hoes. We planted the corn in straight rows, the beans among the corn, and the melons and pumpkins in irregular order over the field. We cultivated these crops as there was need.

Our field usually contained about two acres of ground. The fields were never fenced. It was common for many families to cultivate land in the same valley and share the burden of protecting the growing crops from destruction by the ponies of the tribe, or by deer and other wild animals.

Melons were gathered as they were consumed. In the autumn, pumpkins and beans were gathered and placed in bags or baskets; ears of corn were tied together by the husks, and then the harvest was carried on the backs of ponies up to our homes. Here the corn was shelled, and all the harvest stored away in caves or other secluded places to be used in winter.

We never fed corn to our ponies; but if we kept them up in the winter time, we gave them fodder to eat. We had no cattle or other domestic animals except our dogs and ponies.

We did not cultivate tobacco, but found it growing wild. This we cut and cured in autumn; but if the supply ran out, the leaves from the stalks left standing served our purpose. All Indians smoked—men and women. No boy was allowed to smoke until he had hunted alone and killed large game—wolves and bears. Unmarried women were not prohibited from smoking, but were considered immodest if they did so. Nearly all matrons smoked.

Besides grinding the corn (by hand with stone mortars and pestles) for bread, we sometimes crushed it and soaked it; and after it had fermented made from this juice a *tiswin,* which had the power of intoxication, and was very highly prized by the Indians. This work was done by the squaws and children. When berries or nuts were to be gathered, the small children and the squaws would go in parties to hunt them, and sometimes stay all day. When they went any great distance from camp, they took ponies to carry the baskets.

I frequently went with these parties, and upon one of these excursions a woman named Cho-ko-le got lost from the party and was riding her pony through a thicket in search of her friends. Her little dog was following as she slowly made her way through the thick underbrush and pine trees. All at once a grizzly bear rose in her path and attacked the pony. She jumped off and her pony escaped, but the bear attacked her; so she fought him the best she could with her knife. Her little dog, by snapping at the bear's heels and distracting his attention from the woman, enabled her for some time to keep pretty well out of his reach. Finally the grizzly struck her over the head, tearing off almost her whole scalp. She fell, but did not lose consciousness, and while prostrate struck him four good licks with her knife; and he retreated. After he had gone, she replaced her torn scalp and bound it up as best she could. Then she turned deathly sick and had to lie down. That night her pony came into camp with his load of nuts and berries, but no rider. The Indians hunted for her, but did not find her until the second day. They carried her home, and under the treatment of their medicine man all her wounds were healed.

The Indians knew what herbs to use for medicine, how to prepare them, and how to give the medicine. This they had been taught by Usen in the beginning, and each succeeding generation had people who were skilled in the art of healing.

In gathering the herbs, in preparing them, and in administering the medicine, as much

faith was held in prayer as in the actual effect of the medicine. Usually about eight persons worked together in making medicine, and there were forms of prayer and incantations to attend each stage of the process. Four attended to the incantations, and four to the preparation of the herbs.

Some of the Indians were skilled in cutting out bullets, arrowheads, and other missiles with which warriors were wounded. I myself have done much of this, using a common dirk or butcher knife.

Small children wore very little clothing in winter and none in summer. Women usually wore a primitive skirt, which consisted of a piece of cotton cloth fastened about the waist, and extending to the knees. Men wore breech cloths and moccasins. In winter they had shirts and leggings in addition.

Frequently when the tribe was in camp, a number of boys and girls, by agreement, would steal away and meet at a place several miles distant, where they could play all day free from tasks. They were never punished for these frolics; but if their hiding places were discovered, they were ridiculed. To celebrate each noted event, a feast and dance would be given. Perhaps only our own people, perhaps neighboring tribes, would be invited. These festivities usually lasted for about four days. By day we feasted; by night, under the direction of some chief, we danced. The music for our dance was singing led by the warriors, and accompanied by beating the *esadadedne* (buckskin-on-a-hoop). No words were sung—only the tones. When the feasting and dancing were over, we would have horse races, foot races, wrestling, jumping, and all sorts of games.

Among these games, the most noted was the tribal game of *Kah* (foot). It is played as follows: Four moccasins are placed about four feet apart in holes in the ground dug in a row on one side of the camp, and on the opposite side a similar parallel row. At night a camp fire is started between these two rows of moccasins; and the players are arranged on sides, one or any number on each side. The score is kept by a bundle of sticks, from which each side takes a stick for every point won. First one side takes the bone, puts up blankets between the four moccasins and the fire so that the opposing team cannot observe their movements, and then begin to sing the legends of creation. The side having the bone represents the feathered tribe; the opposite side represents the beasts. The players representing the birds do all the singing, and while singing, hide the bone in one of the moccasins. Then the blankets are thrown down. They continue to sing; but as soon as the blankets are thrown down, the chosen player from the opposing team, armed with a war club, comes to their side of the camp fire and with his club strikes the moccasin in which he thinks the bone is hidden. If he strikes the right moccasin, his side gets the bone, and in turn represents the birds, while the opposing team must keep quiet and guess in turn. There are only four plays; three that lose and one that wins. When all the sticks are gone from the bundle, the side having the largest number of sticks is counted winner.

This game is seldom played except as a gambling game, but for that purpose it is the most popular game known to the tribe. Usually the game lasts four or five hours. It is never played in daytime.

After the games are all finished, the visitors say, "We are satisfied," and the camp is broken up. I was always glad when the dances and feasts were announced. So were all the other young people.

Our life also had a religious side. We had no churches, no religious organizations, no Sabbath day, no holidays, and yet we worshiped. Sometimes the whole tribe would assemble to sing and pray; sometimes a smaller number, perhaps only two or three. The songs had a few words, but were not formal. The singer would occasionally put in such words as he wished instead of the usual tone sound. Sometimes we prayed in silence; sometimes each one prayed aloud; sometimes an aged person prayed for all of us. At other times, one would rise and speak to us of our duties to each other and to Usen. Our services were short.

When disease or pestilence abounded, we were assembled and questioned by our leaders to ascertain what evil we had done, and how

Usen could be satisfied. Sometimes sacrifice was deemed necessary. Sometimes the offending one was punished.

If an Apache had allowed his aging parents to suffer for food or shelter, if he had neglected or abused the sick, if he had profaned our religion, or had been unfaithful, he might be banished from the tribe.

The Apaches had no prisons as white men have. Instead of sending the criminals into prison, they sent them out of their tribe. These faithless, cruel, lazy, or cowardly members of the tribe were excluded in such a manner that they could not join any other tribe. Neither could they have any protection from our unwritten tribal laws. Frequently these outlaw Indians banded together and committed depredations which were charged against the regular tribe. However, the life of an outlaw Indian was a hard lot, and their bands never became very large. Besides, these bands frequently provoked the wrath of the tribe and secured their own destruction.

When I was about eight or ten years old, I began to follow the chase; and to me this was never work.

Out on the prairies, which ran up to our mountain homes, wandered herds of deer, antelope, elk, and buffalo, to be slaughtered when we needed them.

Usually we hunted buffalo on horseback, killing them with arrows and spears. Their skins were used to make tepees and bedding; their flesh, to eat.

It required more skill to hunt the deer than any other animal. We never tried to approach a deer except against the wind. Frequently we would spend hours in stealing upon grazing deer. If they were in the open, we would crawl long distances on the ground, keeping a weed or brush before us, so that our approach would not be noticed. Often we could kill several out of one herd before the others would run away. Their flesh was dried and packed in vessels, and would keep in this condition for many months. The hide of the deer was soaked in water and ashes and the hair removed, and then the process of tanning continued until the buckskin was soft and pliable. Perhaps no other animal was more valuable to us than the deer.

In the forests and along the streams were many wild turkeys. These we would drive to the plains, then slowly ride up toward them until they were almost tired out. When they began to drop and hide, we would ride in upon them and by swinging from the sides of our horses, catch them. If one started to fly, we would ride swiftly under him and kill him with a short stick, or hunting club. In this way we could usually get as many wild turkeys as we could carry home on a horse.

There were many rabbits in our range, and we also hunted them on horseback. Our horses were trained to follow the rabbit at full speed, and as they approached them, we would swing from one side of the horse and strike the rabbit with our hunting club. If he was too far away, we would throw the stick and kill him. This was great sport when we were boys, but as warriors we seldom hunted small game.

There were many fish in the streams, but as we did not eat them, we did not try to catch or kill them. Small boys sometimes threw stones at them or shot at them for practice with their bows and arrows. Usen did not intend snakes, frogs, or fishes to be eaten. I have never eaten of them.

There are many eagles in the mountains. These we hunted for their feathers. It required great skill to steal upon an eagle; for besides having sharp eyes, he is wise and never stops at any place where he does not have a good view of the surrounding country.

I have killed many bears with a spear, but was never injured in a fight with one. I have killed several mountain lions with arrows, and one with a spear. Both bears and mountain lions are good for food and valuable for their skin. When we killed them, we carried them home on our horses. We often made quivers for our arrows from the skin of the mountain lion. These were very pretty and very durable.

During my minority, we had never seen a missionary or a priest. We had never seen a white man. Thus quietly lived the Be-don-ko-he Apaches.

Getting at Meaning

RECALLING

1. Describe the area of Arizona in which Geronimo is raised.

2. What does Geronimo's mother teach him?

3. What games do Geronimo and his brothers and sisters play?

4. What tasks are performed by the Apache children? What crops do they cultivate? What other work do they do?

5. What happens to Cho-ko-le when she gets lost?

6. Describe, in your own words, the game of Kah.

7. How do the Apaches treat criminals?

8. Which animal, according to Geronimo, requires the most skill to hunt? Why is this animal so valuable?

9. Which animals are hunted by the Apaches? Which animals are not hunted by the Apaches?

INTERPRETING

10. According to Geronimo, about eight Apaches work together to make medicine. What other activities do the Apaches do in groups? What does the emphasis on group activity tell you about Apache life?

11. How important is play to the Apaches? How can you tell? What are the other joys and rewards of Apache life?

CRITICAL THINKING: EVALUATING

12. Many people believe that we can learn much from the Native Americans of Geronimo's day about living in harmony with nature. What is the relationship between the Apaches and their natural surroundings? What seems to be Geronimo's attitude toward the creatures of the natural world? How do Geronimo's experience of and attitude toward nature differ from those of many people today?

Developing Skills in Reading Literature

Autobiography. An autobiography is the story of a person's life, written by that person. Autobiographies often contain information that is of great historical value. Why would a historian be interested in Geronimo's autobiography? What specific details does Geronimo give about Apache clothing, hunting techniques, religion, and agriculture? What use would an historian have for this information?

Developing Vocabulary

Words of Native American Origin. Many of the words and expressions used today come originally from Native American languages. Look up the following words in a dictionary. On a separate sheet of paper, write the meaning of each word.

1. squash
2. hominy
3. raccoon
4. persimmon
5. chipmunk
6. skunk
7. tepee
8. caribou
9. woodchuck
10. succotash

Notice that many of the words borrowed from Native American languages are names of plants and animals. Why might this be so?

Developing Writing Skills

Writing Directions. In this selection, Geronimo explains how to play the game of Kah. The explanation is so clear and complete that anyone who has read the selection could play the game. Imagine that you have a pen pal in a foreign country who is interested in the games played by American children. Write a letter to your pen pal containing directions for playing a simple children's game such as hopscotch or dodge ball.

Begin your prewriting notes by writing the name of the game that you want to explain. Then, list the steps in the game in chronological order. Also list any special equipment or supplies needed in order to play.

Begin the letter itself by telling what game you are going to explain. Then tell what equipment or supplies are needed. Finally, discuss the steps in the game, one at a time, in order. As you revise, remember that your paragraph is intended for someone who does not know how to play the game. Therefore, make sure that you haven't left out any steps and that all the steps are in the proper order. Consult **Using the Process of Writing** on pages 614–623 for help in completing this assignment.

B I O G R A P H Y

Geronimo (1829–1909) was an Apache who struggled but finally lost the battle between the Native American way of life and the advancing frontier. He was born in No-doyohn Canyon in Arizona and named Goyakla, "He Who Yawns." The Mexicans later called him Geronimo (Jerome). In 1858, he lost his mother, wife, and three children to Mexican bounty hunters. "I could not call back my loved ones … but I could rejoice in … revenge," he declared. For the next eighteen years, he led his Apache band through arrests, escapes, and the bitterness of broken promises. He planned hit-and-run raids from his Mexican mountain stronghold, attacking settlements on both sides of the border. In 1886 the United States sent five thousand troops to capture Geronimo and the thirty-nine members of his band. It took four months before he finally surrendered, on the condition that he could return to Arizona after two years' imprisonment. The terms were ignored. After two years at Ft. Pickens, Florida, the group was moved to Ft. Sill, Oklahoma, where they were kept as prisoners of war. Geronimo's reminiscenses, *Geronimo's Story of His Life,* were recorded by S. M. Barrett in 1906.

The coyote pack is determined to drive Sandy and her pups over the cliff.

Wild Courage

Robert Franklin Leslie

It had been a long, lazy summer vacation. Early in September I had set up a final camp at lonely Moraine Lake on the Chagoopa Plateau in Sequoia National Park. I had chosen a spot near the High Sierra Trail, a short distance from the northeast precipice of the Big Arroyo, a giant slash in the Sierras some five miles wide and a mile-and-a-half deep. Labor Day weekend had seen the last backpacker, mule train, and back-country ranger off the trails for the season. Dazzling Sierra autumn now charged the air, sharp and crisp. The lively spirit with the magic frost brush had stippled every aspen, cottonwood, and sumac leaf. Mountain passes above eleven thousand feet had already undergone their first snowstorm. Constantly shifting shadow patterns escaped from cloud clusters. Big weather changes, associated annually with the autumnal equinox,[1] were near. Massive horizons of fourteen-thousand-foot peaks along the Kings-Kern Divide looked as if winter had already crystallized them.

The vast Sequoia hinterland of pine scents, wind songs, and startling colors would belong to the wildlife and one man throughout September before the first general storm sent all of us scurrying into more temperate regions below. This was the season I loved best.

One late afternoon I was stoking a campfire and enjoying the symphony of sound which the approach of dusk always brings forth from every wild throat when suddenly all sounds ceased. Birds and squirrels sat motionless in the trees. Along the beach between campsite and Moraine Lake not a frog lisped, not a cricket whispered. Chipmunks and golden mantles peered cautiously from crevices in the rocks. I had the creepy feeling that every forest creature was silently staring at me.

Suddenly there was a sharp sound behind me. Dropping the wood I was carrying, I whirled around. Backing out of the shadows of the tall pines that ringed the camp was a female coyote — teeth bared, fur bristling. Towards her, clearly in pursuit, came a pack of seven full-grown coyotes. The female's backward progress was painfully slow because, beneath her feet, whining and stumbling as she and they moved, were four small coyote pups.

---

1. **autumnal equinox** (ô tum′ n'l ē′ kwə näks): a time when night and day are of equal length worldwide, approximately September 22.

In less than a second I realized what was happening. The pack, open-jawed and growling, was bent on driving mother and pups toward the rim of the Big Arroyo's perpendicular granite cliffs. As the female backed toward the sandy beach, the pack quickly encompassed her and the pups in a rough semicircle.

Suddenly and desperately, the mother lunged toward the pack leader, then turned to slash at her other tormentors. But she was hopelessly outnumbered. In a matter of minutes she would be destroyed and her pups forced over the edge of the cliff to certain death.

Though I'd long been taught the folly of interfering in nature's battles, this time I couldn't help myself. Brandishing a stick of firewood and letting out a cry that was a cross between a shriek and a war whoop, I leaped forward and scooped up the four cubs in my arms. The pack, startled by the wild yell and the appearance of a human on the scene, swiftly retreated into the shadows of the forest. The mother coyote, obviously as fearful of me as the others, tried to run but collapsed on the sand about twenty yards from camp.

I sat on a log near the fire pit and held the pups gently but firmly against my chest until they stopped squirming. Four wide-eyed, button-nosed little faces peered curiously into mine. As they gradually quieted down, I glanced from time to time at the mother. She lay unmoving, stretched out on her side, eyes closed. Breath vapor, caused by prolonged gasping during the fight at this high altitude, formed a cloud over her body. I thought that she was dying.

The pups began to whine and I knew that they must be hungry. Anchoring them securely under my arms, I clumsily opened a can of condensed milk and a package of raisins. Provided their parents have not yet taught them otherwise, coyote pups often run to people for handouts. With these four, the smell of food swiftly put to rest any remaining fear of me. As soon as I put them down, they wiggled, snapped and cuffed at each other, and whined for shoulder room around the aluminum pan into which I mixed the sticky milk with water and raisins.

As they ate, I looked them over more closely. They seemed to be about three months old. Each lanky pup appeared different from the next. The larger male probably weighed about four pounds. The other male was the runt of the litter, little more than half the size of his brother. The big male and the two females constantly nipped at him, muscling him out of line when I offered bits of cheese and peanut-buttered crackers. He was dark brownish-gray —really the wrong color for a coyote. The big fellow, a silky, golden tawny-yellow, was unusually light for one of his kind. One of the females was darker than her sister. The larger male's bold, aggressive attitude definitely established him as boss of the litter.

While strangely varying in color, the fur of all four pups was fluffy puppy "floss," not yet interspersed with long, coarse gray and white guard hairs typical of the coyote coat. Like other wild canine infants, the pups tottered about awkwardly on legs that seemed much too short for their bodies—legs that never quite functioned in unison. The four even haunched awkwardly and plopped down recklessly on bushy tails that got in their way, forcing them each time to try a second, more coordinated sitting.

When the pups were at last convinced that they could beg no more food from me, they scrambled over to their mother, who still lay motionless on the beach. I noticed that she was almost exactly the color of the sand. (Later I was to name her Sandy.) Suddenly, to my surprise—and equally to that of the pups—she sprang to her feet. Emitting a high-keyed growl, she bounded away toward the other end of the lake, leaving her pups behind her.

All this time I'd been wondering about the father of the litter. Coyotes mate for life and the male assumes responsibility for his offspring just as the female does. Why hadn't the father of these four been on hand to protect and defend his young as well as his mate against the marauding[2] band which had so recently tried to destroy them?

I was not allowed much time for reflection, however. The pups were apparently still hungry and, looking at me with appealing eyes, began to wail soulfully. Much against my better judgment, for I had carefully planned my meager rations to stretch over the next weeks of my stay, I began to dole out goodies—mainly peanut butter and fig newtons—to the nervy little varmints, who received them with no show of gratitude whatever.

Their bellies finally satisfied, the pups began to romp. Growling fiercely, they jumped each other, snapping, nipping, and snarling, rolling over and over on top of one another. Strangely enough, they soon demanded that I play with them. Within a short time my hands, arms, and legs were scratched and bleeding. The four scalawags couldn't have cared less that human skin has no cushion of fur to protect against needle-sharp coyote teeth!

All this while I wondered where the mother coyote had gone. Surely she would return for her pups before dark. Just possibly both parents were hunting their offspring's evening meal on the wide plateau which lay a mile and a half beyond Moraine Lake. This part of the landscape was covered by a savannah-like moor,[3] known on topo maps[4] as Skyparlor Meadow, its dense grass, watered by a creek, providing wild hunters with a wilderness supermarket of frogs, rodents, reptiles, grazers, birds, and insects. I could only hope my half-guess to be a true one.

It was beginning to grow dark and soon the amber of twilight would fade into the blackness of night, accompanied by biting cold. I kept putting aside the thought that the female might never come back, but of course I knew there was a strong possibility, particularly if some disaster had previously overtaken her mate, that she had finally succumbed to attack by the marauding pack, which would have done her in in the beginning had I not been there to intervene.

I bolted a hasty supper and decided I had better make overnight preparations for my young visitors. I fixed a bed for them inside the pup tent next to my sleeping bag. I foresaw that the little rowdies would give me a sleepless night, but it would have taken a man with a heart much harder than mine even to consider turning them out. With darkness the territory would be filled with predators. Even this early in the evening, I could glimpse now and then a few silhouettes with reflecting eyes within the perimeter of the campfire.

I decided to wait by the fire for a while before turning in. The pups were still roughhousing, though with less enthusiasm, and now they simmered down to two-by-two fights in order to determine warm snoozing positions on my lap. I found myself constantly having to

---

2. **marauding** (mə rôd′ iŋ): roaming in search of things to rob or destroy.
3. **savannah-like moor:** a vast treeless grassland.
4. **topo maps:** topographical maps — maps that show hills, rivers, and roads.

prevent the three larger cubs from shoving the runt of the litter from my lap to the ground.

It must have been about ten o'clock when I decided it was useless to wait any longer for the missing female. The pups were sound asleep and I was very near to dozing off when suddenly there came a single sharp bark from the direction of the beach. The sleeping cubs came instantly awake, their bodies rigidly alert, their ears flipped to the attention position. To my surprise, for a matter of perhaps ten minutes they sat absolutely immobile and utterly silent. The only sound came from the occasional snapping of wood as my campfire burned itself out.

The stillness, certainly to me and perhaps to the pups as well, began to be nerve-racking. The mother coyote was out there somewhere, but she gave no further sign. Perhaps she was studying me.

Then it came—a single note of command. The pups dove from my lap in sprawling belly-flops and bounded away into the darkness.

I gave a great sigh of relief. With the warm sensation that I had truly performed my good deed for the day, I windproofed the campfire embers with stones and crawled thankfully into my sleeping bag.

But I did not fall asleep at once. Instead, I found myself trying to recall what I knew of coyote behavior. My visitors of the afternoon hadn't followed any familiar behavioral pattern—or had they?

I had learned much of coyotes and their ways from my Cherokee Indian father who had had long first-hand acquaintance and a remarkable rapport with most wild creatures. Also, over the years, on my own many treks into the wilderness, I'd had hundreds of chances to observe coyote conduct at close range.

Why, I asked myself, even if an accident had befallen the father of the four pups I'd rescued, did the pack of seven seem bent on destroying this particular mother and her cubs? They had probably been harassing her for some time. There had to be a reason.

I knew that, as with other wild species, certain strict rules govern coyote behavior. One rule has to do with the matter of territory. A coyote pack may "stake out" a given stretch of wilderness—perhaps only a few yards wide but sometimes extending in length for two hundred miles or more. Other coyotes cross it at their peril. It was quite possible that the mother coyote and her pups had been unwitting trespassers, thus bringing down upon themselves the enmity of the pack I'd succeeded in driving off this afternoon.

But, whether or not this was true, why hadn't the seven killed their victims in a short, sharp battle instead of trying to drive them to the edge of the Arroyo? Seven against one, even allowing for the savagery of a mother bent on protecting her young, added up to odds that were overwhelming.

The only answer I could come up with— and not a very satisfying one at that—was that the pack had been uneasy regarding the whereabouts of the father, fearful that he might appear during the fight. A male defending his family is a creature to be reckoned with, even when badly outnumbered.

The entire puzzle was too much for me, especially at that late hour. In all probability I'd never know the answers, no matter how hard I tried to discern them. Devoutly hoping that the little coyote family would somehow solve its own problems without further assistance, I turned over and went to sleep.

The eastern sky was just beginning to turn pink when the sound of four meek little voices

woke me up. I looked out. Four haunched coyote pups, lined up in a neat row, faced the tent. When they saw that I was awake, they leaped forward in joyful recognition, whining, barking, and attempting to lick my face. Only half awake, it was still perfectly clear to me that, with daylight, the mother coyote had brought them back, not only for food but also for protection. But why? Was the pack that had so nearly done her in yesterday still on her trail? Once more I asked myself what could have become of her mate.

I was too sleepy to ponder the problem for long and the pups were growing insistent in demanding their breakfast. With something between a groan and a sigh as I thought of my dwindling food supply, I wriggled into my jeans.

As the pups gulped the food I fixed for them, shoving and snapping at each other as they did so, I was infinitely relieved to catch a glimpse of the mother. She was a wraith[5] that drifted rather than ran among the manzanita[6] shrubs behind the tent. She moved with a liquid ease and grace but her tongue hung limp from the side of her open mouth — a sign of extreme fatigue. She scrutinized every move I made.

---

5. **wraith** (rāth): a ghost.
6. **manzanita** (man′ zə nēt′ ə): a small shrub or tree found in the western United States.

As the morning wore on and I went about my usual chores, I counted seven motionless heads, seven pairs of unblinking eyes that peered from the manzanita less than forty feet from my fire pit. The pack had not given up.

Sandy, as I now called her, stayed near camp all morning. Clearly, mother instinct to preserve her brood outweighed her innate fear of humans. Also, she seemed to recognize, through some sense we do not yet understand, a person who emanated no hostility toward her kind and was somehow on her side.

From time to time she lunged viciously at members of the encircling pack. Once it appeared that they were about to finish her off. Three of them pinned her to the ground, trying to slash her throat and her soft underbelly. Had I not intervened, shouting and waving a tough branch of manzanita, they would surely have had their way.

While the seven milled about after that unusually savage attack, Sandy managed to slip through their ranks and disappear. Apparently she now felt secure that I would defend the pups during her absence.

By this time I realized that my thinking had undergone an about-face since last night. No matter how foolish, how inconvenient it might be for me, I'd already made a subconscious commitment and I was going to continue to help and protect the beleaguered family in any way I could.

Within half an hour Sandy returned with a large Sierra hare. Before the seven realized the effectiveness of her strategy, she raced into camp by way of the beach. Having dropped the hare near the fire pit where I sat holding the cubs, she quickly vanished again.

While her pursuers, at least temporarily outwitted, snarled, whined, and skittered through the underbrush at the rear of the campsite, I quartered the hare with my side-knife and fed the famished cubs, who gulped the food with such gluttony that they nearly choked.

Finally, the seven coyotes slowly drifted up to an open granite shelf a quarter mile above Skyparlor Meadow where they could sprawl in the sun and still spy on our activities. The cubs caught beetles and grasshoppers, grazed on miner's lettuce and prickly chilicothe fruit, tried to dance on the air like the butterflies they chased, but never strayed beyond a forty-foot radius of my feet.

At about noon Sandy returned to camp with a fat marmot. She approached cautiously, paced the beach for ten minutes before streaking into the camp area to drop the big rodent. Then she cantered to the lake and lapped water while I quartered the prey. During the pups' meal, she trotted in wide circles around the camp, watching us carefully. She searched through the bushes as if she still expected the hungry seven to pounce at any moment. Apparently she was unaware that they were standing as rigid as statues on the hillside shelf above.

Anxious that she regard me with unconditional trust, I sat down on the sandy beach and took her four pups on my lap. All babies fall asleep after a meal as soon as they feel an envelopment of warmth and security. I wanted Sandy to see her sleeping youngsters sprawl across my legs with complete confidence in my friendship. She lay down about thirty feet away and closed her eyes, but her nose twitched constantly as if every breath of air required sampling. She may have trusted me to the point of leaving her pups in my care, but the look in her greenish-yellow eyes, the hackled ruff and shoulder-mane,[7] her refusal to wag her tail, diminished any hope that I could overcome her instinctive distrust of me to the point of making friends.

At last Sandy fell into a deep sleep. As I sat watching her, I tried to think of a possible way to communicate that the pups would be welcome to spend nights with me, secure inside the tent. But probably the gulf between us was too wide for me to get that message across.

While mother and pups slept, the seven marauders on the shelf above us maintained their vigil, watching every movement I made.

At sundown a single distant coyote call broke the stillness. Instantly Sandy and the pups raised their heads and cocked their ears. The pups ran to their mother, who showered them with affectionate licks, nibbles, and light paw cuffs.

Could the call we had just heard have come from the coyote father? I asked myself. I wanted to believe it. But if indeed he *had* called, why wasn't he around to protect his offspring? Male coyotes never shirk rearing responsibilities, which include guarding, feeding, teaching, cleaning, and amusing.

Then a horrible thought struck me. I wondered why it hadn't occurred to me before. The U.S. Department of Interior, the Park Service, sometimes furnished trappers with number-4 steel traps to reduce coyote populations. Misinformed government officials often blame coyotes for predatory acts which are actually biologically impossible for them to commit.

Mates have been known to carry food for weeks to trapped partners, who eventually die of thirst. Coyotes have no way to bring water.

But surely the father of these pups couldn't be in a trap. Not in a national park. Or could he? As I stood there, silently cursing the blindness and cruelty of my own kind, the distant call came again — this time a series of clear, high-pitched notes. With tails between their legs, Sandy and the four pups loped toward the dusky forest and vanished from sight.

I glanced toward the shelf above me. The coyote pack had quietly disappeared. Could one coyote successfully mimic another to the point of deceiving a mate?

In the gentle glow of predawn on the third morning, a woodpecker with no consideration for sleeping neighbors tapped out his own clattery version of the Morse code on a dead aspen. The hollow trunk acted as a soundboard to transmit the monotonous "dot-dash-dot" throughout the misty forest. Sleepily, I sat up, then glanced through the tent's mosquito netting. There sat the four wide-eyed pups, lined up in a row. "You little rascals," I groaned aloud. "It's too early to get up." I lay down again, determined to sleep at least until sunup. But my young visitors thought otherwise. After a half hour of whining, cuffing, and colliding with the tent, they had their way and I emerged grumpily into the chilly morning.

While I prepared bannock hoe-cakes,[8] pemmican,[9] and coffee, the young coyotes at my feet nipped, rolled, and tumbled with extravagant sound effects. Because I thought that Sandy might arrive at any minute with their breakfast, I decided against feeding them part of mine. As a result of unwise handouts to the coyotes as well as to other wildlife, my store-bought supplies had already shrunk

---

7. **the hackled ruff and shoulder-mane:** Sandy's ruff, or collar of fur, and her shoulder-mane, the fur on her shoulders, are bristling, which shows that she is prepared to fight.

8. **bannock hoe-cakes** (ban' ək hō' kāks): thick, flat cakes made of oatmeal or barley.

9. **pemmican** (pem' i kən): dried lean meat, pounded into a paste with fat and pressed into cakes.

alarmingly. Moraine Lake billeted no fish with which to supplement human diet.

Surrender to pleading eyes and doleful wails was about to occur when Sandy trotted into camp, dropped two large rattlesnakes on the grass near the fire pit, then quickly retreated to the lake front. I cut them into short sections and fed them to the pups. Sandy stood quietly watching while I did so, but suddenly she dashed into the chaparral, whining and snarling, fangs bared. In a moment I saw two of the marauding coyotes, until now concealed from me by the thick underbrush, lope toward the beach and disappear.

Perhaps Sandy wanted me to understand that the band was still menacing her. At any rate, she then made a lightning pass into camp, stopped momentarily, looked me squarely in the eye, whined once, wagged her tail somewhat like a dog, then shot away. Vaulting the lowest shrubs in long, soaring leaps, she vanished into the forest....

On a diet of rattlesnakes and mice, Sandy grew steadily scrawnier. The pack of seven became bolder each day. Attacks occurred every time she tried to break through their lines to deliver the pups to my campsite or to bring them food.

One morning the family failed to appear.

When noontime came and went without the appearance either of Sandy and her pups or the coyote pack, I was not only worried but actually lonesome. Cub coyotes, like cub bears, know all the means of winning their way deep within your affections. It had been the keenest pleasure to sit in the warm September sunshine while the fidgety foursome crawled over my lap or engaged me in their rough and tumble play. The button-nosed pups never ran out of energy, never napped except after a meal, and never tried to run away. If they

missed their mother while they were in my camp, they kept it a well guarded secret. However, when she took charge, they responded to her commands with the immediate precision of a drill squad. From the moment of each reunion with her — and, in consequence, reinstatement in the wild kingdom — they quickly became serious creatures of the forest.

By sunset I was pretty well convinced that the overwhelming odds against Sandy had at last prevailed. All day throughout the surrounding forest I had sensed an unusual quiet. It seemed to me almost that birds and squirrels, chipmunks and rabbits actually missed the pups. I hadn't dared to leave camp for any prolonged investigation of adjacent territory. I still entertained a faint hope that the family would return. But that hope was all but extinguished when I saw a mother bear with her twin cubs establish themselves on the sunny granite shelf where the coyote pack had so recently maintained its tireless surveillance. Sadly, I began to believe that its purpose had been achieved.

With a heavy heart and little appetite, I went about preparations for a lonely supper. I was just sitting down to eat when the sounds of savage growling and snarling, not fifty yards away, broke the stillness. Grabbing a stout manzanita branch from the woodpile, I ran toward the sounds, yelling. There on the trail a battle was taking place between Sandy and four of her tormentors. Miraculously, so far, she had apparently managed to stand them off. The pups were nowhere to be seen.

At the sight and sound of me, the pack slunk away. Sandy ran to the lake, drank greedily, then disappeared into the forest. I returned to camp and my interrupted meal.

The first chilly stars had begun to blink in

the darkening sky when I heard faint but unmistakably familiar whimpers from the bush behind me. I sprang up from the log where I was sitting. Four pups rushed toward my outstretched arms. As I picked them up, I glimpsed Sandy backing away into the shadows.

There was no doubt that all day she had met with increased pressure from the hostile pack, the reason why she had been unable to bring the pups into camp before nightfall. That they had weathered a bad day was evidenced by the fact that they rejected offers of food. Instead, they curled up on my lap where they went immediately to sleep.

Sandy returned twice before midnight, once with a pine grouse, once with a hare. Obviously, she had been forced to switch to a nocturnal life style in order to outwit her tormentors. No doubt she had decided that she could defend her brood and provide meat for them more successfully after dark. I wondered if she might now leave the pups in my custody both day and night.

After each delivery of food, she lay down and waited for me to divide it equally into four parts. Each time I did so, she got up, shook herself, critically examined the quality of the air in every direction, then sprinted toward the meadow. The pack, having once more been outwitted by me, must have given up for the night and wandered away.

Ordinarily, healthier appetites than that of the pups did not exist. Always, from the moment their mother dropped game in camp until the last scrap was gulped, the only thought in their greedy little heads was to seize the ration and slink to nearby solitude in order to avoid any form of sharing. But tonight they were so thoroughly exhausted I had to coax them to eat.

For the thousandth time I wondered where they had spent their nights up to now. For the thousandth time I asked myself why Sandy continued to bring the pups to me—a human being, the coyote's traditional archenemy—instead of migrating to another range beyond the harassment of the pack. How long could the present situation continue?

September nights at 9,540 feet above sea level are bitter cold. I realized—and not for the first time—that I was completely unprepared for a lengthy bivouac in the face of seasonal weather violence that could begin any day. I had already begun to ration myself to the leanest conceivable diet on what remained of my own supplies. While I pondered the problem, beginning to feel sorry for myself, four pairs of appealing eyes pleaded a more immediate cause.

With no possible alternative, I invited the shivering pups into the tent, wrapped them in my down-lined jacket, and put them beside my sleeping bag. Within fifteen minutes I felt the touch of one cold little nose after the other as the four pups squeezed inside the bag. I pushed them halfway down inside and went to sleep.

In the chill dawn I woke from a deep sleep to a chorus of sound that was at once terrifying and beautiful. I sat bolt upright, straining to see beyond the tent flap. The seven marauding coyotes were within a few yards of the tent, muzzles pointed to the sky, chanting their morning madrigal. Had they done away with Sandy in the night and, emboldened by success, in spite of previous fear of me, come to finish off the pups?

I lay there in the sleeping bag, scarcely daring to breathe, while one by one the impudent seven strolled fearlessly through camp between fire pit and tent. I confess I began to

be increasingly fearful, not only for the safety of the pups but for my own safety as well.

I peeped inside the sleeping bag where four little bodies pressed against my stomach. The pups were wide awake but as silent as death. They seemed to gape an appeal for help, but at that moment I felt woefully helpless. I couldn't continue to lie there, that was certain. But to extricate myself quickly from the sleeping bag, grab some kind of weapon, and charge upon the pack before they were aware of what I planned to do would be no mean feat.

Just as I was tensing nerves and muscles to try it, to my utter astonishment Sandy came charging into camp. Her fur was puffed out, making her look as though she weighed eighty, not thirty, pounds. The menace of her whole body, the gleam of pure rage in her eyes, seemed to galvanize the pack into action. Without a backward look, the seven coyotes turned and raced toward the granite shelf above the plateau.

Sandy called her pups and, as always, they sprang to her command. Shivering in the nippy air, I rushed out to watch the five trot confidently down the trail. Chipmunks, squirrels, and birds began to sing. The seven on the shelf also watched but stayed where they were.

That same night, shortly after dark, Sandy returned the pups to my custody. They milled for a few moments at my feet, then headed straight for the sleeping bag. Carrying her tail low, Sandy circled camp half a dozen times before silently fading into the moon shadows of the pines. Because of an icy wind and with the idea of preventing any mischief that might develop in my bed, I decided to join the pups immediately.

When I slipped into the sleeping bag, each one whined and gurgled, nuzzled, and licked my hands, arms, and face in a mighty display of affection. Apparently all of them now regarded me as a family fixture.

During three of the next five days rain, sleet, and wind kept me inside the tent much of the time. Sandy continued to bring her children, wet and muddy, at odd times between dusk and midnight and to call for them at daylight. The belligerent pack was still much in evidence and rarely missed an opportunity to harry her or to menace the pups.

More gaunt, haggard, and weedy each day, the spindle-shanked mother was clearly starving in order to feed her family. Rodents, snakes, and insects had either crawled into deep underground hibernation or had migrated to the canyons of the Kern and Kaweah Rivers. Ground-nesting birds had flown to the San Joaquin Valley. More than a week had elapsed since the last nuts, berries, and hips of eglantine had been consumed.

On the other hand, the coyote pack now enjoyed the results of team hunting on more distant ranges. The band could travel twenty miles of an evening, gorge themselves on prey, and return to the Chagoopa by morning to resume their persecution of Sandy. They seemed now to await almost carelessly the inevitable, when hunger, weakened reflexes, and a broken spirit would make Sandy the easiest of victims.

Each evening when she arrived with the pups, her tongue seemed to hang farther from her long, panting muzzle. Her ears, so efficiently pointed earlier, now drooped. Her

foot pads had accumulated heavy clods of sticky autumn resin that she no longer bothered to chew away.

In spite of diminished rations, the pups underwent a sudden spurt of growth. Their short, stubby legs stretched out like spindly asparagus shoots. Gray guard hairs grew into their winter pelage. Rib cages expanded, but no cushion of fat padded ribs, and fluted sides stood out as alternate furrows and ridges. The soft, minklike puppy touch was soon gone, replaced by rough, saggy hide so loose on the two females that it looked as if they might inadvertently jump out of their skins or turn around in them.

Rain, sleet, and wind at last gave way to a few sparkling, sunny days, a respite before the big tempests of October. Most wildlife, however, had drifted to lower elevations.

In the chill of an early morning I crawled from the sleeping bag, built a fire, and, while the coffee boiled, tried to think how I could stretch my remaining half pound of rice for more than three days. Neither Sandy nor the pups had been near the camp for forty-eight hours. I was frightened for them and perturbed for myself, for obviously it was time for me to leave. But how could I do so without knowing their fate?...

I was lost in thought when, without a sound, the four lanky pups appeared at my side. Their unaccustomed silence and the submissive look about them made me feel certain that the worst had happened to Sandy. Hastily I zippered up my jacket and set out to look for her. The pups followed me to the trail near the beach, the route that led from Skyparlor Meadow to the Big Arroyo.

Suddenly I saw Sandy. She was standing in the middle of the trail about forty feet from me. Slowly she wagged her tail, looking straight at me. Her muzzle was closed; her ears stood erect; her body stance was proud, straight, balanced forward. The resin clods were gone from her feet.

Beside her stood a large, densely pelaged male, surely one of the handsomest specimens of his kind. At sight of me he raised his upper lip and bared his shiny-white fangs to indicate that I should come no further.

I dropped to the ground and scooped the cubs into my lap, knowing it was for the last time. I felt sure the reunited family was on its way to lower ranges where it could survive the winter.

The pups looked earnestly into my eyes, licked my face, and whined. After a minute or two Sandy gave her sharp bark of command and they bounded back to their parents.

The male turned, obviously to lead his family down the trail. As he did so, I saw that his right foot was missing just below the ankle.

The mystery was at last explained. He *had* been in a trap! How long had it taken him to gnaw through bone and muscle to secure release? Then the long days for healing, holed up in some den while his mate hunted in order to feed him and their four growing pups — while she evaded or stood off the attacks of seven predators.

The family was already headed down the trail, the pups in line, following obediently behind their parents.

I raced back to camp and grabbed up the binoculars, then ran to the rimrock where I would be able to watch the six coyotes until they disappeared into a distant canyon.

I focused the binoculars. The coyotes were well along the trail by now, in spite of the fact that their progress was slow because the male must travel on three legs instead of four. Suddenly the binocular lenses fogged up and I couldn't see them any more.

Getting at Meaning

RECALLING

1. Where do the events in this selection take place? Why are there no other people around?

2. Why does Leslie first become involved with the coyotes?

3. According to Leslie, why might the marauding pack be attempting to destroy Sandy and her pups?

4. Where do the pups stay while their mother hunts?

5. What food does Sandy bring to the pups? What other food does Leslie give to them?

6. Besides feeding them, what other services does Leslie perform for the coyote family?

7. How is the mystery of the missing coyote father finally explained? Where has the father been?

INTERPRETING

8. Coyotes are known for their intelligence and resourcefulness. Does Sandy have these qualities? Explain.

9. Reread the last paragraph of the selection. Why do Leslie's binocular lenses fog up?

CRITICAL THINKING: APPLYING

10. Leslie refers to the "blindness and cruelty" that leads people to set coyote traps. Do you agree with Leslie or disagree? Why? Did reading this selection affect your opinion in any way?

Developing Skills in Reading Literature

1. **Autobiography.** An autobiography is the story of a person's life, written by that person. In this autobiographical selection, Leslie focuses not on himself but on the struggles of a mother coyote. However, in describing these struggles, Leslie does reveal a great deal about his own personality and opinions. What sort of man is Leslie? What are his likes and dislikes? Is

he sensitive and humane? Is he a rugged individualist — someone who is self-reliant and independent? How do you know?

2. **Hero.** A hero is the main character in a story. Usually, a hero has admirable qualities. In this true story, Sandy, the mother coyote, behaves heroically. In what ways is Sandy heroic? What are her most admirable qualities? When do you feel most sympathetic toward her?

Developing Vocabulary

Context Clues. Study the following sentences from "Wild Courage." Look for clues to the meanings of the italicized words. On a separate sheet of paper, write a definition for each word. Your definition should be one that makes sense given the context in which the word appears. After you have written your definitions, check them in a dictionary. See how close you came to the dictionary definitions.

1. "The lively spirit with the magic frost brush had *stippled* every aspen, cottonwood, and sumac leaf."

2. "I knew there was a strong possibility, particularly if some disaster had previously overtaken her mate, that she had finally *succumbed* to attack by the marauding pack."

3. "*Brandishing* a stick of firewood and letting out a cry, I leapt forward."

4. "She moved with a liquid ease and grace but her tongue hung limp from the side of her open mouth—a sign of extreme *fatigue*."

5. "She *scrutinized* every move I made."

6. "I quartered the hare with my sideknife and fed the famished cubs, who gulped the food with such *gluttony* that they nearly choked."

7. "Obviously, she had been forced to switch to a *nocturnal* life style in order to outwit her tormentors. No doubt she had decided that she could defend her brood and provide meat for them more successfully after dark."

Developing Writing Skills

Writing a Report. "Wild Courage" is set in a national park. Using encyclopedia articles, magazine articles, books, and other library resources, research the topic "National Parks." Find one national park that interests you and write a report about it. Include in your prewriting notes information about the location, size, and facilities of the park you have chosen. Before you begin writing, divide your notes into groups of related ideas. Develop each of these groups of ideas into a separate paragraph. Refer to **Using the Process of Writing** on pages 621– 623 for suggestions about how to revise your report.

B I O G R A P H Y

Robert Franklin Leslie (born 1911) is a photographer as well as a writer. He has explored the wilderness areas of North America, often living in remote regions for months at a time. He has hiked thousands of miles, canoed dozens of rivers, climbed mountains, collected relics from ancient Native American cultures, and lectured about the preservation of deserts, forests, and mountains. Through such books as *High Trails West, The Bears and I,* and *Wild Pets,* Leslie has shared his interest in nature with his readers.

Biography

What Is Biography?

One of the most popular forms of literature is the biography. A biography is the story of a person's life, written by someone else. The person who writes a biography is called a biographer. The person about whom the biographer writes is called the subject.

How Biographers Work

Biographers face many challenges. Perhaps the greatest of these is getting enough information. Some biographers get their information from interviews. Some study letters, diaries, journals, and other writings by their subjects. Biographers also read the books and articles written about their subjects by other people. Like other writers of nonfiction, biographers must make sure that their facts are true.

Thinking About Biography

In this section you will read the biographies of five Americans. These biographies will help you understand the periods in which these Americans lived. As you read the biographies, look for short story elements used by the writers. Also think about why the writers look upon their subjects as interesting or important enough to write about.

FREDERICK DOUGLASS, about 1844. *Attributed to Elisha Hammond. National Portrait Gallery, Smithsonian Institution, Washington, D.C.*

Paul Revere

Esther Forbes

The voice in the dark crying the alarum,[1] the man on the horse always galloping through a moonlit night of long ago—galloping into poetry, folklore, art, legend, advertising, editorials—hardly a real man on an actual horse, more a symbol of preparedness, awareness of danger.

Although that is what Paul Revere seems to us today, it was not what he seemed to himself or to his contemporaries. To those who knew him, he was one of those men who always get things done. They were impressed with the way he could learn a new trade as fast as other men could turn around, for he was the typical "ingenious Yankee" of the period. And they called him "cool in thought, ardent in action." But he was not so cool as to be quietly thinking when the time had come for quick action, nor so ardent as to jump heedlessly into difficulties and by his carelessness get himself and everybody else into trouble. For instance, take the way he rode his horse the night before the battle of Lexington. If he had been too cool and cautious, he never would have taken that ride at all. If as "ardent" as in the poem and all known statues and pictures of him, he would have foundered the animal and been of little good as a messenger. Paul Revere had been riding that horse for some three hours before the British captured him, and it was still so fresh that the major (as Paul Revere remembered) "asked the Sarjant if his horse was tired, he said yes...he ordered him to take my horse."

It is as "bold Revere" he was sung in a song of that day in the ale houses, taverns, shops, along the wharves of Boston. So, to the men who knew him best, he was bold and ardent, but also cool and ingenious. Such men not only are ready to do things, but can do them well.

In many ways he was a typical American—even to the fact that his father was not born over here, but came as a child refugee from Europe and could not even speak English when he arrived. He was thirteen and penniless, but like many older and more important people he had come to find a different way of life and greater freedom than was possible in France during the religious persecutions of the period. His son was ready to risk everything

---

1. **alarum:** alarm.

for that way of life and that freedom. No one around Boston cared whether or not Paul Revere's father was a foreigner. They knew that being an American is not a matter of blood or race, but point of view. Then, too, Paul Revere's industry and versatility make him seem a typical American. He was an artisan and worked with his hands all his life.

As his father was a silversmith, Paul first learned this trade, beginning to work when he was thirteen or fourteen — and people then worked from sunup to sundown — sometimes for twelve hours every day but Sunday. He was still a boy when his father died and, as eldest son, it was up to him to support his mother, sisters, and younger brothers. Soon people were saying there was not a better silversmith in all Boston (now they say in all America). His ledgers show that he made silver tankards and trays, coffeepots, flagons and cups (and sometimes little things like "a baby's whistle," a chain for a pet squirrel, a dog collar) for many of the wealthiest and most important people in Boston. It was obvious that if he continued to work so hard and well and said nothing to offend his wealthy patrons, he could be sure of a good living. But first there was a war with the French and Indians. He went off on that. And he evidently liked to say what he thought. He sided with the men who believed England had no right to tax the colonies without giving them some say in the matter. The names of some of his wealthiest patrons — like the royal governor, Thomas Hutchinson — disappeared from his ledgers, but still he did very well until in 1764 there was a terrible depression in Boston.

Being an ingenious man, he taught himself a new trade. During hard times there might be more people who could pay a few pennies for a print than a few pounds for a piece of silver. If he could have sold one of these prints to a modern collector, his worries for that year would have been over. They are mostly political cartoons: British ships landing troops in Boston, political enemies hanging by the neck from Liberty Tree, the famous view of the Boston Massacre. His silverwork he loved and in that medium he is a great artist, but his copper-plate engravings seem to have been tossed off by a man more interested in the political situation and in supporting his family than in art. No one has ever called him an artist and an engraver.

There was another trade in which his training as a silversmith would be of help to him. This was setting false teeth. He did not at first advertise that you could chew with these teeth — only talk and smile. A regular doctor would pull the aching tooth, and then one went to an artisan like Paul Revere to have a false one wired in. They were usually carved out of hippopotamus teeth, or uncarved animal teeth "of not to perculiar form" were used. Paul Revere did not do this work for long. His false teeth seem to have been a stopgap both for his patients and for his purse.

Other things interested him more. In 1773 there was that Boston Tea Party. He was one of the known leaders. Boys and men worked all night, saying little except in grunts, breaking open chests of tea, throwing it into the harbor, making, as they said, "saltwater tea." Before Paul Revere had time to go home and get some sleep, he was asked to ride to New York and Philadelphia to carry word of the destruction of the tea.

At that time it must have been nearly eight hundred miles for the round trip. Paul Revere did it in eleven days. Although he may have changed horses often, to ride some seventy miles a day is a fair test of a man's endurance.

THE BOSTON MASSACRE, 1770. *Paul Revere II. Hand-Colored Engraving.* The Museum of Fine Arts, Boston. *Centennial Gift of Watson Grant Cutter.*

During the next year he took the same hard ride at least four more times and a number of shorter ones. It was not only his hardihood that made Boston choose him so often as express rider. It was necessary to send a man who, when questioned by the excited people, would say the right thing. The Tories referred to him as an "Ambassador from the Committee of Correspondence of Boston to the Congress of Philadelphia," which is as much an overstatement as to call him merely an express rider is an understatement.

When Parliament sent troops and warships to close the port of Boston to all shipping until the tea was paid for, Paul Revere began keeping a boat hidden under a wharf so that he could get to the mainland (Boston was almost an island in his day) and carry word of the British general's plans. He and some other Boston mechanics organized a spy system. They knew that sometime General Gage would move his troops out of Boston and attempt to capture the war materials the colonists were collecting in inland towns. They watched and listened and interested the small boys of Boston in watching and listening. So it was a boy working in a stable who overheard the British plans to march next day to Concord and Lexington. The child ran to tell Paul Revere. The Patriots were expecting some such sortie. Their plans were carefully made. Lanterns were to be hung in the steeple of Old North Church—one lantern if the British left Boston by land and two if by sea. And Paul Revere had promised to get out of town with a more detailed account of what the British were up to if he could slip past their guards. Billy Dawes also rode that night; but as Revere was the first to reach Lexington and had the more exciting trip, it is about him Longfellow[2] wrote the poem and he is the messenger best remembered today.

All through the eight years of the Revolution, Paul Revere did whatever seemed most necessary for carrying on the war. When paper money was needed, he printed that. When powder was short (as it usually was), he made plans for a powder mill and he worked on cannon. Much of the time he was a lieutenant colonel of the Boston Artillery Train, stationed at Castle Island. It was the most important fort protecting Boston in those days but now is part of the mainland. But it is not as a soldier but as a civilian and an artisan that he made his greatest reputation and served his country best.

After the war was over, he found out how to manufacture a great many things which before had been imported from Europe. It was then he cast those beautiful church bells which still ring in New England steeples—to the glory of God and Paul Revere. But perhaps the greatest service Paul Revere did for his young country was the prosaic, unsung setting up of a copper mill to roll sheet copper. We were waging an undeclared war with France and paying tribute to the North African pirates. England was watching with an understandably jaundiced eye, and yet (until Revere set up his rolling mill) we could not build a single warship without importing the sheet copper for sheathing the bottom of the ship. Not one man in America knew how to make a copper amalgam suitable for this work. The old gentleman (for he was sixty-five when he went into this new venture) experimented until he found out. He risked every cent he had or could borrow— and succeeded; and we read in the log of *Old Ironsides* how "the carpenters gave nine cheers, which was answered by the seamen and calkers, because they had in fourteen days

---

2. **Longfellow:** Henry Wadsworth (1807–1882), American poet who wrote "The Midnight Ride of Paul Revere."

completed coppering the ship with copper made in the United States" by Paul Revere.

When he died, in 1818, all the newspapers wrote of his enterprise, industry, generosity, ingenuity. But none of them mentioned the one thing we know best about him—that ride on the 18th of April. They, who had so recently seen the stocky, benevolent old colonel walking the streets of Boston, never guessed that he was destined to forever ride a foaming charger through the dark of a famous night until in time he hardly seemed a real man at all—only a hurry of hooves, a knock on a door, a disembodied voice crying the alarum.

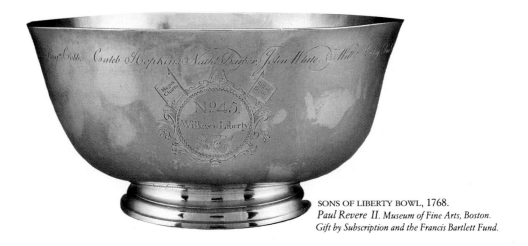

SONS OF LIBERTY BOWL, 1768.
Paul Revere II. Museum of Fine Arts, Boston. Gift by Subscription and the Francis Bartlett Fund.

Getting at Meaning

RECALLING

1. Name three occupations that Paul Revere practiced before the war with England.

2. What caused Paul Revere to give up his trade as a silversmith?

3. What two qualities made Paul Revere a good express rider and messenger?

4. Name several ways that Paul Revere helped the colonists during the Revolution.

INTERPRETING

5. What was Paul Revere's role in the Boston Tea Party? How committed was he to working for the revolution before the war?

6. The biographer describes Paul Revere as *ardent* and *ingenious*. What do these words mean? Which of Revere's actions show that he was, in fact, ardent and ingenious?

CRITICAL THINKING: EVALUATING

7. The biographer opens this selection by saying that Paul Revere seems "hardly a real man on an actual horse, more a symbol of preparedness, awareness of danger." The writer's major purpose in the selection is to make Revere seem more like a flesh-and-blood person. Has the writer succeeded in doing this? Explain.

Developing Skills in Reading Literature

Biography. A biography is the story of a person's life, written by someone else. Usually, biographers write about people whom they admire. What qualities did Paul Revere have that are worthy of admiration? Why do you think Esther Forbes considered Paul Revere interesting or important enough to write about?

Developing Vocabulary

Context Clues: Choosing the Correct Meaning. Often you can determine which of the multiple meanings of a word a writer had in mind by studying the context of the word. Use a dictionary to check the meanings of the italicized words in the following sentences. Then, on a separate sheet of paper, write each word, followed by two different definitions. Underline the definition that fits the meaning that you believe the writer intended.

1. "So, to the men who knew him best, he was bold and ardent, but also *cool* and ingenious."

2. "Then, too, Paul Revere's *industry* and versatility make him seem a typical American."

3. "As his father was a silversmith, Paul first learned this *trade,* beginning to work when he was thirteen or fourteen."

4. "But still he did very well until in 1764 there was a terrible *depression* in Boston."

5. "A regular doctor would pull the aching tooth, and then one went to an artisan like Paul Revere to have a *false* one wired in."

6. "Although he may have changed horses often, to ride some seventy miles a day is a *fair* test of a man's endurance."

7. "So it was a boy working in a *stable* who overheard the British plans to march next day to Concord and Lexington."

8. "It was then he *cast* those beautiful church bells which still ring in New England steeples."

Developing Writing Skills

Writing a Summary. The writer describes many of Paul Revere's accomplishments. In one paragraph, summarize the three or four of these accomplishments that you believe to be the most interesting or important.

List, in your prewriting notes, the accomplishments mentioned in the selection. Then, decide whether you would like to summarize the most important or the most interesting of these. Finally, choose the accomplishments that you want to include and number them in order of importance or interest.

Begin your first draft with a strong topic sentence that tells the purpose of the paragraph. Then, discuss the examples chosen from your prewriting notes. When you revise, check to make sure that all of your examples support your topic sentence. Refer to **Using the Process of Writing** on pages 614–623 for help.

B I O G R A P H Y

Esther Forbes (1891–1967) wrote historical novels. One of her best known books, *Paul Revere and the World He Lived In,* won her the Pulitzer Prize in history in 1942. Another book, *Johnny Tremain: A Novel for Young and Old,* was made into a Walt Disney movie. Forbes received honorary degrees from several major universities. Her books have been translated into many languages.

Mark Twain *Cornelia Meigs*

The morning was still early, yet the sun was already hot on the sand bar, shining up into Sam's eyes in a white glare. He pulled down his battered straw hat and stood for a minute listening to the ripples of the big river as they went hissing along the edge of the sand.

Behind him the town of Hannibal was waking up to a blazing hot summer day. Thin columns of smoke were rising from the houses crowded below the bluff, and above Cardiff Hill the sky was scorching blue.

Sam had gone to sleep last night with a strange, rather terrible idea in his head, and even this morning it would not be put out of his mind. It was filling his thoughts now, even though he was walking so carefully beside the water on an entirely different errand.

He was looking for a simple thing which all boys learned how to find if they lived beside the Mississippi River a hundred years ago. Most of the time Sam Clemens had no idea where his hat was; he only wore it this morning because he needed it for a different use than that of keeping the sun away from his mop of reddish-yellow hair.

Now he saw what he had been seeking—a line of small, scrambling footprints leading up from the water. He followed them until they turned toward the shore again, and there he threw down his hat and began digging with his hands in the warm sand. He felt something. A grin of delight crossed his face, and he brought up the first of his prize, pink, leathery, oval things—turtle eggs!

He knew, better than anyone else, how to find the tracks of the turtle where she came out to lay her eggs to be hatched by the heat of the sun. Back on the main shore the other boys were waiting under the buttonwood trees. They had built a little fire, for Sam Clemens had promised them turtle eggs for breakfast.

He filled his hat and walked slowly back with his mind full once more of that thought which had been troubling him ever since he awoke. Should he tell the other boys? Should he startle them with the news of what he meant to do? No, not quite yet, because he was not exactly certain that he was going to do it.

His three friends were waiting — John Briggs, Will Bowen, and Tom Blankenship. They were his own size, they wore torn trousers and hickory shirts just as he did, and they were barelegged and freckled like himself. Tom Blankenship was a perfect marvel of raggedness, but what did any of them care? They, none of them, had anything like Sam's mop of sandy hair, or his eager, watchful eyes, or that slow speech with which he greeted them.

"Well, I told you I was goin' to bring turtle eggs," he said. "Got some good coals to roast 'em?"

They had a wonderful breakfast there under the trees, listening to the wide river slip by. John Briggs was telling about how there had been a fight last night down at the steamboat landing, and how the *Mary Evans* had backed off in the morning, leaving a big man with a broken head on the bank.

"Someone'll take him in," Will Bowen said, "and let him lie on the hay in the barn until he gets well."

Tom Blankenship listened, digging his toe, the one with the rag on it, into the soft dirt under the tree.

"My pop got left like that, down on the Louisiana levee," he remarked carelessly. "He didn't come home for a month, and we wondered a lot where he'd got to."

Sam was scarcely paying attention. He was watching the bowing willows on the bank opposite, more than half a mile away, and staring at the current. A long raft was coming into view around the bend above them. Pushed by a dingy gray steamboat, it moved slowly downstream. It would be in sight for two hours or more before it slid beyond the next turn in the smooth, clean road of the river. It was nearly in front of them when he burst out suddenly with the thought which had been troubling him ever since he had opened his eyes that morning.

"I've got to get out of here," he said. "I've got to get away from a place like this, where nothing ever happens. I'm goin' to run away."

What did he want? He did not know himself. Knights in armor, perhaps, castles to be captured, buried treasure to be discovered?

Hannibal, with its little rude houses, its dusty streets where the pigs ran free, and ragged men like Tom Blankenship's father walked slowly past on no special business, was not the place to satisfy those strange desires which were always rising up within him. He sat looking out at the river while Will Bowen spoke sternly.

"You've been reading those books again, Sam. There never was any good in readin' so many books. Anyway, come on, now; you promised you'd go with us to the cave."

They left the rest of their breakfast and set out. The hot miles of the road were deep in dust where the road looped along the hill above the river. The little valley, when they reached it presently, looked green and shady and deliciously cool. They threw themselves down on the deep grass under the shade of the pecan trees. The mouth of the cave showed black and gaping on the slope above them.

They talked for a while, resting their weary legs, and going over the tales of adventure that hung about the cave. Indians had hidden in it; white men had taken shelter from their enemies and lain in the doorway with rifles leveled, daring anyone to come up the hill and chase them out.

Sam himself had been lost once in the winding passages of the cave and had felt that terrible instant of panic when he knew that he had missed the way. He had been wise enough simply to sit down and wait until he was found, even though his candle burned down until it was too small to hold and he was within a minute of being left in the blind dark. No one knows what real darkness is who has not seen it inside the deep hollows of a hillside cave.

One of the boys asked Sam to tell about it again, but he put the idea aside. "Oh, that wasn't anything. Anybody might get lost in a cave," he said.

Mark Twain   347

They filed in at last. They had brought a few candle ends, and Sam, the most daring, even had a handful of matches. There was every danger that they might go too far and all the candles burn out, but they did not think for a minute about that.

It was a clean, dry cave, with its low passages hung thick with stalactites (the icicle-like sticks of white limestone which hang from the roofs of caves) and with great blocks of stone here and there which had fallen from the roof. The fresh air was like late autumn, not only cool but cold. They grew tired at last of wandering and shouting to make echoes, and they came out of the dark passage into the blazing sun and the smothering heat again.

The other boys were grinning over the games inside, but Sam's face was dark and thoughtful. Tom Blankenship looked at him anxiously but did not say a word. No one ever knew what would come out of those queer moods of Sam Clemens'. Not even Sam himself could tell what he was going to do. But never before had the spirit of restlessness and discontent clutched him so firmly; never before had such wild thoughts and plans swung back and forth within him. They walked home saying little, the boys trailing after Sam.

Even his own family remarked on his silence as he sat at the supper table.

"What's got into you?" his sister Pamela asked, as she passed him his plate. She looked really worried, for Sam was hardly ever so quiet.

His mother said quickly, "Oh, don't start anything, Pamela. Just be thankful when the boy isn't in some kind of mischief."

Sam glanced at her thoughtfully, and even she began to look uneasy. "It's been pretty hot," he said at last. "I think I'll go to the top of the hill and see if there's a breeze." He was up and out of the door before anyone could say another word.

He climbed to the top of the great hill which stood so boldly above the little town. It was beginning to grow dark as he threw himself down on grass that was dry and stiff and springy. He stretched himself at full length and looked down at the world below him.

There are few places on earth where you can see such a view as is spread at the foot of Cardiff Hill. The clear, wide Mississippi turns in a great bend and, as far as the eye can see, flows away past low "bottom lands" which are dotted with clumps of willows and with cleared green meadows, with little winding streams and arms of the river twisting in and out among the trees. In the smooth water the islands look as though they are afloat, mere clusters of green, with white sand bars and a ripple of current at the head of each.

Almost below where Sam had thrown himself down, a steamboat lay with her nose against the bank, big and white, with her lights being lit as twilight fell. He knew from the bustle on board her, from the rows of lamps which beaded her sides, and from the slow drift of smoke from her great smokestacks that she was making ready to back out into the river and go downstream. Where would she go? What would she see?

Here the desire which had been gnawing at Sam's restless heart all day grew suddenly big and powerful, and he knew, not what he wanted to do but what he was going to do. There was his mother at home, and Pamela and his two brothers. He did not let himself think about them. Sam knew without being told — although he often was told — that he was a mischievous, troublesome son, a boy who brought no peace or comfort to the house.

GIANT STEAMBOATS AT THE LEVEE IN NEW ORLEANS (detail), 1853. *Hippolyte Sebron.*
Tulane University, New Orleans. Gift of D.H. Holmes Company.

He did not mean to be that. He wanted so to help them, not just by filling the woodbox, perhaps, or whitewashing the fence, but in some bigger, more splendid way.

If he could once get out into the great world, of course he would do great things; he was sure of it. Then they would all be proud of him, and people would say, "Do you remember Sam Clemens? Why, he used to live right here in Hannibal. We all knew him; he wasn't a bit proud."

Sam grinned. Even at that minute he could see the joke of it. He had more respect at that instant for Tom Blankenship, in his ragged, secondhand clothes and his scrap of a shirt, than he had for himself. Tom had certainly had adventures with his wandering, good-for-nothing father, while he, Sam—

The steamboat bell rang, very clear in the still evening air. The smoke began rolling out dark and thick above the stacks. Without one more thought, without drawing breath, Sam flung himself over the edge of the hill and ran, slid, and scrambled to the bottom. The whole company of deck helpers, with the mate who had charge of them, was on shore struggling with some last difficult pieces of freight. No one saw a small barelegged boy slip over the gangplank and lose himself in the shadows of the lower deck.

He found a pile of grain bags, from which he lifted one sack and climbed into the middle of the heap like a gopher into a hole. There was a tramping of feet, a hail of orders from the mate, and commands shouted. The slow splash of the paddle wheels and the steady beat of the engines began. They were off.

An hour passed, and Sam got very tired of hiding. There were cramps in his legs, and the sharp dust of grain husks in his hair and down his neck. Every time he began to move, heavy feet would come tramping by, and he had to lie still again. At last he heard the voices of two who had stopped beside him. By peeping out he could see that a big man, with a smaller man beside him, had stopped under a swinging lantern while the bigger one lighted his pipe.

"You better push right on, Joe," said the little man. "If the boss ketches you here, you'll git what for."

"Let him ketch me! I ain't afraid of all the mates on the whole Mississippi," answered the big one. "Let Tim Carter just try to ketch me. I've got a long knife for him; it's been ready for him this whole trip. Got it right here inside my shirt."

Sam could both hear and guess how he put his hand inside his belt and patted the handle of the knife while he whispered to it in his big, soft voice, "There now, gal, you lay quiet. Did you git tired waitin' for Tim Carter? Well, it's not so long now."

There was another sound. Someone else was coming. Sam heard the big Negro mutter something and draw closer into the shadow. The little man gave a high, shrill giggle from pure nervous terror. The voice of the mate, Tim Carter, came gruffly in the dark.

"What are you doin', you Joe? Git out of—" There was a roar from the big Negro, a leap and a struggle, the sound of a heavy blow, and a loud, thin cry from the little man.

After a second of silence Tim Carter spoke to his companion, who had come hurrying up behind him — the second mate, whom Sam had seen as he slipped on board. The assistant was a thin, very tall young man, evidently making his first trip. The first mate's voice was quite calm.

"Just let him lie there a bit, and he'll be all right. Shorty's had a good many bumps like that before, and not been the worse."

The younger man spoke unsteadily. "But it wasn't him with the knife, Mr. Carter. It was big Joe."

"Doesn't make a bit of difference," replied Carter. "Every deck man on the boat has a knife in his shirt or a razor in his pocket, and thinks he's going to get the mate with it. Whenever you see something stir in the dark and you don't know what it is, hit out or shoot; don't wait. That's one of the first things a boat's officer has to know. And always have your pistol handy in your pocket."

They moved on. If their feet had not been so loud on the planks, they might have heard a noise that was very like a boy's teeth chattering. Who would come across him first, Sam was wondering. Who would hear a rustle in the dark among the grain sacks? Would it be Joe with his knife or the mate with his gun? He hardly knew which would be the worse.

A long half-hour went by, and the boy grew a little quieter. He could peer out between the sacks and see, on the open deck, the dark shapes of men who had thrown themselves down, anywhere, to sleep the short night out. One of them began a deep humming under his breath, and another took it up until the note of music grew to a swinging, mournful song: "Gone are the days when my heart was young and gay—"

Sam moved carefully, inch by inch, leg by leg, until he had crawled from the heap of sacks and was sitting comfortably on the planks, still warm from the sun of the day but with the cool night wind blowing over him. The moon had climbed up and made a pavement of silver of the whole river, with shadows so black across the deck that they would hide anyone. It was beautiful to watch the moving water; to look up at the dark pilothouse; and to see the tall smokestacks, with the long roll of smoke drifting across the bright sky.

The mate's voice called an order, and two of the men nearest Sam got up and took, each of them, a long sounding pole. The boat was coming close to a difficult sand bar, and there was danger of getting stuck on the bottom. The first — it was Joe, as Sam could see in the moonlight — plunged his pole overboard and called the depth of the water, "No bottom!" This meant that the pole did not reach the bottom. The man opposite, whose high voice answered Joe's deep bass, sang out, in his turn, "N-o-o bottom!"

The mate repeated the call, so that the captain, up in the pilothouse, could hear. Sam felt himself trembling all over with a strange delight, with the wonder of the shining river, the cooling wind, and the music of those voices calling back and forth. Presently the water became shallower and the cry changed, "Mark twain! M-a-ark twain!"

Sounding, it may be explained, is done with a pole which can measure twelve feet (two fathoms), since every boat and ship uses the fathom as its unit of measure. The pole is painted round with black and white to show the feet, and it is plainly marked at one fathom and at two.

From long, long custom, older certainly than steamboats themselves, comes the habit of crying the depth of the river in such a way that it cannot be mistaken. "Two" sometimes sounds like some other number, but the old word "twain" can never be mistaken. "Mark twain" means two fathoms at the mark, twelve feet deep — safe water even for a steamboat.

"Quarter less twain! Half less twain!" came the cry. The water was less and less deep; the boat slowed down, nosing her way. There was a little soft shudder that ran through the whole of her great length; she had just touched the sand and was slipping down into deeper water. "M-a-ark twain!" came the comforting call; and then finally the pole plunged deep and did not touch, and once more came the cry, "No bottom!" They were over the bar.

The sounding came to an end, and quiet fell upon the great, steadily moving boat. Sam was still too much excited to sleep, but his thoughts began to move more slowly, to go back a little, and to wander. Had he done right in running away? Just where was he going? And what would become of him the next day, and the next?

They were no gentle people, any of those who were going to find him, as they were surely bound to do. He shivered a little in the cool night breeze. His mind went back to home, where they would all be asleep except his mother, perhaps lying awake and thinking about him. She would have believed, so far, that he was spending the night with Will Bowen, as he so often did. Not until tomorrow would she begin to be anxious.

Was he really someone that any mother would want to get back again, or was he just a worthless, freckled-faced, sandy-haired boy who was always making trouble? His eyes were growing heavy, for the night air was at last making him sleepy.

He did not dare lie down on the deck, even in the shadows, but crawled back among the freight and got into his old place among the sacks. It was not an easy bed, but he curled himself up as comfortably as he could. He was very tired, and there is no more sleepy lullaby than the deep, big, regular breathing of a moving steamboat.

A sudden sharp pain in his leg, and a voice exclaiming angrily in the darkness — it was these which woke him. Only then did he realize that he had not crawled all the way into the heap of sacks and that his legs remained uncovered. Somebody had stumbled over them in the dark.

"What — what's this?" Sam did not recognize the voice. Was it Joe, sleepy and angry, tugging at the knife in his shirt? Was it the mate, always ready for trickery and hidden danger? Was he pulling out his pistol? The sacks were being dragged away, and a hard hand caught him by the collar and jerked him to his feet. Sam fought, tried to cry out, and couldn't. The man who had found him pulled him over within the light of a hanging lantern.

"Why, it's Sam Clemens!" he said.

It was neither the mate nor Joe. It was "the old man" himself, the captain of the boat, going on watch again in the pilothouse after two hours of sleep, and making a tour of inspection first. One does not often find small sandy-haired boys mixed up with piles of freight. "What are you doing?" he finally asked.

"Running away." Sam tried not to let his voice sound sheepish, but he stood staring, at the planks at his feet, where the splinters showed in the orange light of the lantern.

It was possible that the captain did not know at once what to say. He stood staring at his uninvited passenger for some minutes. "Like to come up into the pilothouse?" he asked at length and, not waiting for an answer, walked away with Sam following.

It was still so dark that Sam stumbled more than once in going up the steps to the top deck to reach the high, glass-sided shelter from which the boat is steered. The great wheel was much taller than Sam, even with part of its rim disappearing below the floor.

The assistant pilot gave up his place and went away with only a word or two of where they were, "Just crossing the foot of Catfish Bar." The captain shifted the wheel a little, and Sam climbed up on the high bench behind him. For a while they sat in silence. The sky was growing faintly gray, but the water was still dark.

"So you were running away?" the captain said after a long time, but as though he had really spoken only a minute before. "And did you have any idea where you were going to run to?"

"Why — why, no, sir," Sam stammered, and then brought it all out with a rush. "Hannibal's so little! Nothing ever happens there. I want to — to see things and — do things. I think I could."

The captain nodded. "Yes, I know! That's how most people feel. But time goes by, and everyone has a chance to see plenty; yes, they see enough without having to be in a hurry about it." He broke off suddenly. "How does your ma get on?"

"Why," Sam answered in some surprise, "she gets on all right." Why wouldn't a capable woman with as much courage as his mother get on as well as anyone else?

"Do you remember," the captain was saying slowly, "do you remember about that widow who lived under the hill, not so far from you — lived there with her daughter, and how a man tried to break in and rob them, and how she had to shoot him?"

Sam trembled in the dark. He did remember. He had happened to see the shooting; had seen the man fall.

The captain went on without paying much attention to him. "Do you remember that poor woman married to the drunken Corsican, and how, when her husband was after her, trying to beat her, she ran to your ma and your ma stood in the door and ordered the man off and threatened him so that he really went? A woman like that is brave enough to meet anything," he added after a pause; "but with the kind of things she has to face, and with your father having to be away so much of the time, she kind of needs her boys to stand by her. Don't you think so, Sam?"

"Yes," answered Sam, miserably. He had not thought of that.

"You might make a good pilot some day." Captain Howard almost seemed to be thinking aloud. "You notice things and remember them; that is what a man has to do who is to learn the river mile by mile. But we do make a rule, before we take on a man to teach him steamboating, that he has to be taller than the wheel he steers by."

There was a very long silence, so long that pink streaks began to show above the dark hills, and the gray in the sky had almost turned to white.

The captain asked one more question. "You've got relatives in the town of Louisiana, haven't you—someone who would take you in until the next boat goes north to Hannibal? We'll find a way to send word to your family, and I'll speak to somebody about taking you up, and by and by we'll see about making a pilot of you. Give my good wishes to your ma. She's my idea of a brave woman."

"Yes," said Sam. "I will."

They did not talk any more, but sat together while the pink in the sky turned to red and then

to yellow sunlight. The water was growing shallow off Hickory Point, and they were sounding again.

Some day Sam, although he knew it so little then, was going to make books, great books, out of all that he was seeing then: the water dappled with silver, the bending willows, and the great, sliding river. Tom Blankenship, renamed Huck Finn, was to come into those books; so were Will Bowen and many of the things that happened in Hannibal — larger things, so Sam was to find, than they seemed to be when he lived among them.

He knew nothing of all that; he only knew that all he was seeing and learning at this moment was making him queerly happy, and that through it all there seemed to run strange music in the long ringing call, "Quarter less twain! By the mark! M-a-ark twain!"

Getting at Meaning

RECALLING

1. What does young Sam bring his friends for breakfast?

2. Who is Tom Blankenship? How is his life different from Sam's?

3. Describe Hannibal as Sam sees it.

4. What thought has been troubling Sam ever since he awoke?

5. What finally prompts Sam to run away?

6. What conversation does Sam overhear as he hides in the grain bags? How does the conversation make him feel?

7. How long is a *fathom*? What does the expression *mark twain* mean?

8. Who discovers Sam among the grain bags? What advice does this person give to Sam?

INTERPRETING

9. What does Will Bowen think is the source of Sam's restlessness? Is there any indication that Will might be right?

10. Why would a riverboat sailor consider the term *mark twain* comforting?

CRITICAL THINKING: EVALUATING

11. One theme of this selection can be summed up in the sentence, "There is a proper time for everything." Explain how this expression applies to the selection.

Developing Skills in Reading Literature

1. **Biography.** A biography is the story of a person's life, written by someone else. How much of Mark Twain's life does this selection recount? How is this time span different from the time span in Esther Forbes's biography of Paul Revere? Which of these selections contains more vivid, specific details? Why?

2. **Sensory Images.** You probably remember that sensory images are words and phrases that appeal to the five senses: sight, hearing, taste, smell, and touch. The line "The hot sun whipped the land" appeals to both the sense of sight and the sense of touch.

Writers use sensory images to create in their readers a sense of actually being in a particular time and place. List some vivid sensory images from this selection. What senses does the writer appeal to primarily?

B I O G R A P H Y

Cornelia Lynde Meigs (1884–1973) was born in Rock Island, Illinois, but grew up in Keokuk, a small town in Iowa. After attending Bryn Mawr College, she taught English in a boarding school. There she became interested in storytelling and soon began writing stories of her own. Her first collection of stories, *The Kingdom of the Winding Road*, appeared in 1915. Meigs has also written biographies, including *Jane Addams: Pioneer for Social Justice*.

Henry David Thoreau was a great American writer and naturalist. In this brief biography, Sterling North describes Thoreau's experiences at Walden Pond. The quotations are taken from Thoreau's masterpiece, Walden.

from *T*horeau of Walden Pond

Sterling North

Thoreau had always loved Walden. Having returned to Concord,[1] he now planned a cottage on its shore.

"Near the end of March, 1845, I borrowed an axe and went down to the woods by Walden Pond...and began to cut down some tall, arrowy white pines, still in their youth, for timber...It was a pleasant hillside where I worked, covered with pine woods, through which I looked out on the pond...."

Soon rain was melting the last ice. Thoreau heard a lark, then a stray wild goose groping through the mist "like the spirit of the fog."

It takes "a little Yankee shrewdness" to build a home. But if foxes have holes and birds of the air have nests, surely man can build himself a shelter with but little greater labor.

"I hewed the main timbers six inches square," says Thoreau, who was a good carpenter. These he mortised securely at each joint. "I usually carried my dinner of bread and butter, and read the newspaper in which it was wrapped, at noon, sitting amid the green pine boughs." Everything was scented with the fragrance of pine.

Where a woodchuck once had tunneled, Thoreau dug his cellar in the sandy soil. In May some friends came to help him set up the framework, making a picnic of the occasion. To this framework Thoreau nailed boards he had purchased at a bargain. Soon he had a neat cabin ten feet wide and fifteen feet long with "a garret and a closet, a large window on each side." There was a door at one end of the house and a fireplace (soon to be built) at the other. All this he acquired at a total cost of $28.12½ plus several weeks of enjoyable labor.

Thoreau had always desired a hideaway of his own. Now he could live undisturbed and write his books. He wanted no curtains at his windows to shut out the sunlight and moonlight. He wanted no rug upon his floor to cover the clean pine boards. He made (or borrowed from Concord attics) his few pieces of furniture.

He had cooking and eating utensils, plus a

---

1. **Concord** (kän′ kərd): the town in Eastern Massachusetts where Thoreau was born and where he lived for most of his life.

spade and a wheelbarrow. On his desk he kept a few books, writing paper, and an oil lamp. He never locked his door.

"Simplify, simplify, simplify" was his motto.

Food was no great problem: fish from the lake, wild berries from the woods, vegetables from his garden, rice and hoecakes! It cost him about twenty-seven cents a week for groceries. (One must remember, however, that money in those days would purchase eight or ten times what it will today.)

His cabin was not yet plastered. Nevertheless on July 4, Thoreau moved into his new dwelling. "The upright white hewn studs and freshly planed door and window casings gave it a clean and airy look, especially in the morning, when its timbers were saturated with dew." The morning sun rose clear. The morn-

ing wind came through the chinks in the unplastered wall. Thoreau was up with the dawn for his dip in Walden Pond.

Why did Thoreau go to the woods, and how did he live there? As we have seen, he hated the city. He loved silence and solitude. He wanted to be alone with the seasons, to live something like a woodchuck or a fox. He wanted to know what makes the universe tick and why man is part of that universe.

Thoreau felt lonely in the crowds of New York City. But he never felt lonely when he was by himself at Walden. All around him he heard the rustling and bustling of nature. Squirrels chattered; blue jays scolded. How could he feel lonely when he had for company the friendly stars which spangle the midnight sky, the warm moon rising through the Walden pines to pave a path across the pond? Sometimes in the evening he would play his flute. For accompaniment he had the flute's own echoes from the surrounding hills.

Thoreau liked a "broad margin" to his life. He wanted to improve each moment by enjoying it richly and fully.

He believed that luxuries are often a burden and that most men devote their lives to laboring frantically for things they do not need.

However, it must not be thought that Thoreau was lazy. Quite the contrary. Anyone who walked or talked with him soon discovered that he had an active body and an active mind. Those two years at Walden were not without accomplishment. Here are some of the things he did:

He built his excellent little house.

He planted a field of beans (of which, more later!).

He fished, picked berries, and cooked his own food.

He cleaned his cabin frequently, taking all of his furniture outdoors so that he could scrub his pine floor with sand and water.

He cut and carried his own firewood. (It warmed him twice, first when he split it and later when he burned it.)

He read books in several languages, and thought seriously about his reading.

He reported carefully in his journal on owls and woodchucks, wild ducks and muskrats, wood mice and chickadees — in fact every bird, animal, flower, or tree that he thought interesting.

Finally, he labored faithfully on the manuscripts of two books he was writing.

Because he worked efficiently when he was working, Thoreau had time to sit in his doorway in the sun; "to keep an appointment with a beech tree"; to let nature soak into his pores.

It was a pleasant life, but it was not a pointless one. He was living deeply and with a gentle rhythm. He saw no reason for the haste and waste, the hurry and the competition which he had seen in New York. He was not trying to keep up with the Joneses, even in Concord.

"This was sheer idleness to my fellow-townsmen," Thoreau realized, "but if the birds and flowers had tried me by their standard, I should not have been found wanting."

About a quarter of a mile from Thoreau's little house, near the west end of Walden Pond, ran the Fitchburg Railroad. The wind, playing on the telegraph wires, made sweeter music to Thoreau's ear than any symphony composed by man. He loved, too, the haunting sounds of the locomotive's whistle and bell rushing through the night. When the train had passed, Walden returned to even greater solitude.

Thoreau was not an accomplished musician. But deep inside him was a warm appreciation of nature's music. He enjoyed the whippoorwills, calling plaintively through the dusk, the owls, quavering mournfully, "Oh-o-o-o — that I had never been bor-r-n!" At the pond's edge, the bullfrogs rumbled *tr-r-r-oonk, tr-r-r-oonk, tr-r-r-oonk*. Thoreau was soothed by the frequent "roar and pelting" of rainstorms upon his tight roof. Hearing this wild music of the Walden Woods, he sometimes felt that he was alone on this planet, the first or the last man in the world.

It is wholesome and pleasant to be alone at least part of the time. No wonder he fell asleep easily and awoke eager for the new day.

Thoreau had three chairs in his little house: "One for solitude, two for friendship, three for society."

When visitors came he usually placed these

chairs in his "best room," which was outdoors beneath the pine trees—a room furnished by nature and always well swept by the wind. Sometimes a wood chopper came to visit him and they talked slowly and gravely together. Once he fed a "real runaway slave," whom he helped northward toward the Canadian border and freedom.

Bronson Alcott, the philosopher, and Ellery Channing, the Concord poet, were always welcome. So were the boys and girls intent upon berrying or fishing. Thoreau was not equally eager to entertain the men of affairs who came to see him: doctors, lawyers, merchants, and the rest. Nor did he welcome "uneasy housekeepers" who in his absence pried into his cupboard and looked to see if his sheets were washed as clean as theirs.

In fact Thoreau was gracious to "all honest pilgrims" who came for the sake of friendship, and not from idle curiosity or with the desire to reform him.

Sometimes it was Thoreau who went a-visiting.

"Every day or two I strolled to the village to hear some of the gossip" which, when taken in small doses, "was really as refreshing in its way as the rustle of leaves and the peeping of frogs."

Thoreau thought people were almost as interesting as his four-footed friends. "In one direction from my house there was a colony of muskrats in the river meadows; under the grove of elms and buttonwoods in the other horizon was a village of busy men, as curious to me as if they had been prairie-dogs...." In fact Thoreau was never as much of a lone wolf as he pretended to be.

Having bathed again in the pond, he would don a clean shirt and walk the mile and a half to Concord to visit friends or family and to buy a few groceries.

Occasionally he was invited to dinner by the Emersons or others. Although "well entertained," he seldom remained the entire evening.

"It was very pleasant ... to launch myself into the night, especially if it was dark and tempestuous, and set sail from some bright parlor or lecture room, with a bag of rye or Indian meal upon my shoulder, for my snug harbor in the woods...."

Thoreau was like a cat in the dark. Even when his eyes could not guide him, his feet always knew their way. At one place the path ran between two pines which were but eighteen inches apart. Yet on the darkest nights he had no trouble slipping between them.

Those who thought that Thoreau had lost his way in life should have seen him at night under the stars. He then seemed the least lost man in all of Concord.

Thoreau had planted a bean field of two and one half acres which required much hoeing to keep down the weeds and grass.

From five A.M. until noon on each early summer day of 1845 Thoreau might be seen, barefooted and moving slowly up one row and down the next, his hoe flashing in the sun as he chopped the weeds and pulled the fresh, moist soil around his plants. Worms, woodchucks, and cool weather were the enemies of these beans, the woodchucks being the worst, having nibbled a whole quarter acre to the ground.

"I came to love my rows, my beans," Thoreau said. They were honest plants, doing the best they could under difficulties.

Thoreau also loved woodchucks, but during his stay at Walden he killed one of these bean-destroyers — an act for which he was later sorry. He realized that the woodchucks had almost as much right to the beans as he had, and were certainly unaware of any evil-doing.

Thoreau enjoyed the sandy soil between his bare toes. He also enjoyed the serenade of a saucy brown thrasher who from the topmost spray of a birch tree sang gaily, "Drop it, drop it — cover it up, cover it up — pull it up, pull it up, pull it up."

Thoreau's hard season's work in the bean field netted him exactly $8.71½. But he was not discouraged. He had known the joy of his labor, and the pleasure of "making the earth say beans instead of grass."

The best thing about Thoreau's new home was Walden Pond itself — that ever-changing mirror of the sky, now swept with wind, now smoothed again as by an unseen hand.

Thoreau had always admired this little lake. One of his earliest memories was that of being brought to this beautiful pond by his grandmother when he was a very small boy. In later years he came to fish for horned pouts (bullheads). He and a companion on a dark summer night would build a fire near the water's edge and cast in their lines. When, after several happy hours, they had at last caught a good mess of fish, they would throw the burning brands of the fire high over the lake, "like sky-rockets, which, coming down into the pond, were quenched with a loud hissing." Then in the darkness, whistling a tune, they would start home for Concord.

Thoreau described Walden as "a clear and deep green well, half a mile long," containing "about sixty-one and a half acres; a perennial spring in the midst of pine and oak woods,

without any visible inlet or outlet.... "

It is so clear that one can see pickerel, perch and other fish at a depth of twenty-five to thirty feet. And it is so clean that Thoreau used it for his drinking water.

Besides its fish, this pond has other wildlife: bullfrogs, a few turtles, mink, and muskrats. Swallows skim over the water. Wild geese and ducks visit the pond during their migrations.

Often a single loon would utter its wild cry — like the laughter of an insane ghost. Thoreau once played a game which lasted for hours with one of these strange water birds, trying to follow it with his boat. But always the loon came up, laughing at Thoreau, where he least expected it.

Thoreau called Walden "a mirror which no stone can crack, whose quicksilver will never wear off.... "

The surface of this mirror reflects every change of the weather and the seasons. On clear days the lake is sometimes blue; on stormy days, a dark slate color. Near the shore the golden sand shines through. Often the water is a mysterious green over the greater depths.

Thoreau saw the flowers of spring and summer reflected in this forest mirror. Then came the russet and crimson of September and October. At last the leaves were scattered by the wind, and the mirror of Walden showed bare branches of oak and aspen, and the dark masses of the evergreens. Gone were the "bright tints of October" and in their place had come "the sombre November colors of the surrounding hills."

Throughout the summer Thoreau had cooked his food on an outdoor fire. His house had remained unplastered. Now, with cold weather setting in, he hurried to build his fireplace and to plaster his house against the autumn breezes.

He purchased bricks for his hearth, and used clean Walden sand in his mortar.

Thoreau was proud of his work, particularly when he lit his first fire and saw the firelight flickering on his walls and ceiling. He found "a couple of old fire dogs[2] to keep the wood from the hearth," and said, "it did me good to see the soot form on the back of the chimney which I had built, and I poked the fire with more right and more satisfaction than usual."

Outdoors the wind moaned through the trees, and the owls took up their sad November serenade. Abroad in the darkness were his friends the foxes and the raccoons. The wild geese came lumbering in through the dark, their great wings whispering stormy secrets. It was good to be safe indoors beside the fire, roasting chestnuts and wild apples.

On the twenty-second of December, Thoreau awoke to find that Walden had a crystal roof. He now had a skating rink of more than sixty acres in his front yard. Thoreau liked to lie on the clear ice peering down into the "parlor of the fishes." Air bubbles in the ice looked to him like silver coins. He discovered that each of these bubbles behaves like a small burning glass when the sun shines through it, melting the ice slightly where the light is focused.

Each morning Thoreau cut a hole in the ice to dip in a pail for drinking water. He enjoyed watching the bright chips fly through the frosty air. One day he had a happy thought. Why not measure the depth of Walden? For many days he chipped holes—more than 100 in all. Using a stout cod line weighted with a stone he took careful measurements of the exact depth in every part of the pond. No, it was not "bottom-

less" as some of the villagers thought! But it was remarkably deep for such a small pond— 102 feet in its deepest spot.

Thoreau had fewer visitors after winter set in. This gave him more time to enjoy the squirrels that came for the corn he put out and for the friendly chickadees and saucy blue jays that came for his crumbs. One of his best friends was a dainty wood mouse that scampered all over him, and was so unafraid that it would even sit in Thoreau's hand while eating.

Now, with the world blanketed deep in snow, the partridges went "budding," taking the only food available, the buds of the bushes and small trees. Sometimes he saw or heard a fox, followed perhaps by hounds baying eagerly and mournfully through Walden Woods. Occasionally at night the ice of Walden Pond cracked with a thunderous, rippling roar. But Thoreau loved this "great bed-fellow ... restless in its bed."

Often he walked eight or ten miles through the deepest snow and would return, chilled but happy. When the bitter wind smote him on one cheek, he followed the advice of the Bible and turned the other cheek. But Thoreau was glad on those days to return to his warm fire. More than ever he looked fondly on his pile of driftwood, old fence rails, and fallen branches. When he wanted a roaring fire he used pitch pine.

Wrote Thoreau, "I weathered some merry snowstorms, and spent some cheerful winter evenings by my fireside, while the snow whirled wildly without."

Each sunrise brought some new and satisfying adventure. "Early in the morning, while all

---

2. **fire dogs:** metal supports used to hold wood in a fireplace.

things are crisp with frost, men come with fishing reels and slender lunch, and let down their fine lines through the snowy field to take pickerel and perch."

Fishing through the ice is a chilly but exciting sport. The fishermen were soon hauling in their handsome prizes.

"Ah, the pickerel of Walden! when I see them lying on the ice ... I am always surprised by their rare beauty.... They are not green like the pines, nor gray like the stones, nor blue like the sky; but they have, to my eyes, if possible, yet rarer colors, like flowers and precious stones, as if they were pearls ... or crystals of the Walden water. They, of course, are Walden all over and all through; are themselves small Waldens.... "

While Thoreau was living in his house by the pond, a large crew of men came to harvest ice. Having cut thousands of tons of huge ice cubes, they used horses to haul the ice ashore at the west end of the pond near the railroad

track. From this point the ice was shipped to Boston where much of it was loaded on sailing ships to be taken to China, India, and other remote markets. Thoreau thought that these great azure crystals of Walden water bound for distant places must certainly take with them some memory of the sky and woods of Walden. Ice for India! It stirred Thoreau's imagination.

Some thoughts had come to Thoreau from India, by way of the Hindu classic, the Bhagavad-Gita. Eastern philosophers had taught him to be more courageous and more serene. Now the message of Walden was being returned to India as cubes of ice.

Perhaps a few drops of Walden water would soon be mingling with the water of the sacred Ganges River.[3] Such were the dreams of this busy hermit, measuring the depth and meaning of Walden Pond.

Spring came at last. By the first of April, Walden was completely free of ice. Bluebirds, song sparrows, and other messengers of spring sang of the great event. Squirrels raced madly through the trees. Grass began to flame green under the warm sun. Walden, which had been asleep all winter, now was awake again.

Thoreau felt that on a fine spring morning, all life is "pasturing freely." He wondered why on days like this the jailer does not "leave open his prison doors,—why the judge does not dismiss his case." On such a morning "all men's sins are forgiven." Thoreau himself went fishing, "standing on the quaking grass and willow roots, where the muskrats lurk," and catching a good string of fish.

And so the first year at Walden ended, and the season went rolling into high summer.

Thoreau says that his second year in this little house was very much like his first, and apparently it was equally enjoyable. However, after two years and two months at Walden he left the woods "for as good a reason" as he came there. Perhaps he had "several more lives to live."

He had learned that "life near the bone" is the sweetest; that truth alone endures; that however poor your life may seem, you must meet it and live it. Perhaps if you are out of step with mankind it is because you hear a "different drummer." Cling, however, to what you think is right. Hold to your dreams. You can have your castles in the air—all that you need to do is build foundations under them.

Thoreau thought that most people are "sound asleep" nearly half the time; that we need only to awake to find life beautiful. "Only that day dawns to which we are awake.... The sun is but a morning star."

---

3. **Ganges** (gan' jēz): a river in Northern India and Bangladesh.

Getting at Meaning

RECALLING

1. Describe Thoreau's cabin. How large is it? From what does Thoreau make it? What is special about its location?

2. Name four things that Thoreau does while living at Walden.

3. What guests are welcomed by Thoreau? What guests are not welcomed?

4. What does Thoreau grow at Walden? What else does Thoreau do for food?

5. What animals share the area of Walden Pond with Thoreau?

6. What preparations does Thoreau make for staying at Walden Pond during the winter?

7. What do the crew of men plan to do with the ice taken from Walden Pond? How does Thoreau feel about this ice harvesting?

8. How long does Thoreau live at Walden?

INTERPRETING

9. The writer hints that most people in Concord find Thoreau's way of life rather strange. Find two statements in the selection that suggest this.

10. What does life at Walden offer to Thoreau that life in Concord does not? What qualities does Thoreau have that enable him to survive on his own in the woods?

11. Thoreau speaks of helping a "real runaway slave" escape to freedom in Canada. Is it surprising that Thoreau would be opposed to slavery? How does this selection show his attitudes toward freedom?

12. The writer says that Thoreau's motto is "Simplify, simplify, simplify." Does Thoreau live by this motto? Explain.

CRITICAL THINKING: EVALUATING

13. How does the writer feel about Thoreau? How do you know? Has the writer succeeded in creating the same feelings in you?

Developing Skills in Reading Literature

Character. A character is a person or animal who takes part in the action of a work of literature. The main character in a biography is the subject. Explain in your own words what each of the following statements suggests about the main character in this selection—Henry David Thoreau.

1. "Thoreau felt lonely in the crowds of New York City. But he never felt lonely when he was by himself at Walden."

2. "He believed that luxuries are often a burden and that most men devote their lives to laboring frantically for things they do not need."

3. "Thoreau thought people were almost as interesting as his four-footed friends."

4. "He had learned that 'life near the bone' is the sweetest; that truth alone endures; that however poor your life may seem, you must meet it and live it."

5. "Thoreau thought that most people are 'sound asleep' nearly half the time; that we need only to awake to find life beautiful."

Developing Vocabulary

Context Clues. Review the five types of context clues: definition, restatement, examples, comparison, and contrast. Then, copy the following list of words onto a sheet of paper. Look up each word in the Glossary. Write a sentence that uses a context clue to explain the meaning of each word. After each sentence, tell which kind of context clue you used.

grope	idleness
simplify	quaver
solitude	tempestuous
luxury	perennial

Developing Writing Skills

Writing Biography. Choose someone you know and write a short biography of this person. The biography should be no more than five paragraphs long. It may deal in detail with a single incident or episode, or it may present highlights from throughout your subject's life. Gather material for the biography by conducting an interview. Prepare for the interview by making a list of questions to ask your subject. Record answers to these questions in your prewriting notes. As you write and revise this biography, refer to **Using the Process of Writing** on pages 614–623.

A young woman receives a precious gift—the gift of an education.

Miss Wilson's Miracle

Emma Gelders Sterne

On a back street in Denver, Colorado, Mary Crissman, a Quaker seamstress, pedaled away at her sewing machine. In the spring and fall, she went out to sew, spending a few days at a time in the homes of her neighbors, making up bolts of gingham or calico into dresses and shirts, or woolens or silks into Sunday clothes. In between times, she did plain sewing that was brought to her at home in her rented room. Sometimes she was called on to make a wedding dress of ivory brocade ordered from San Francisco or from the East. Or a hand-stitched christening dress for the newborn child of one of the wealthier mine-owners or merchants in town.

She had never married, but she loved little children. As she worked she often thought of the black children in the South, not yet brought to that full freedom that allows human beings to develop themselves in the fullness of the promise of God who made the world. Her father had gone into the South with the Army during the war. Being a Quaker, he wouldn't fight, not even for freedom of God's most forsaken children. But the Anti-Slavery Associa-

tion had sent him down, even before the Freedman's Bureau was established, to teach the slaves to read and write, to care for their bodies and their souls. He had gone away on his mission the day after Abraham Lincoln's Emancipation Proclamation[1] was signed. That was all he was waiting for. Mary Crissman had been ten years old at the time. She still had the letters he wrote home.

Miss Crissman was pious. She took great comfort in her beliefs and practiced her Christianity as best she could. She went to the little stone meetinghouse on Sundays. She "tithed," setting aside ten cents of every dollar she earned to give to the poor, the oppressed, and the heathen. For years she had given her tithe money to many good causes, a little at a time.

In August of the year 1889, when her customers were beginning to ask how soon she could come to them to outfit their children for another school year, Mary Crissman thought of a new plan of giving. There is no record of

---

1. **Emancipation Proclamation:** a document issued by President Lincoln in 1863 that freed the slaves.

how the idea came to her. The inspiration might have come from a human-interest paragraph in *Godey's Lady's Book*—a story about the struggle of the blacks to continue the education started under Lincoln's armies and under Reconstruction governments. Surprising bits of information often appeared in the fashion magazine, sandwiched between patterns of bustled skirts and shirtwaists with leg-o'-mutton sleeves. Or it may be that, at the homes of her customers, the middle-aged seamstress read in the home missions columns of the *Presbyterian Review* of the need for education in the South. The reasons for Mary Crissman's decision are buried in obscurity. Yet what she did that midsummer afternoon in Colorado changed the lives of many people over the continent and continued in its influence long after she was dead.

She sat down and wrote a letter to a small Presbyterian boarding school for daughters of freedmen, offering to send her tithe money to provide a year's schooling for some black girl —"one you are sure will make good." The letter was addressed to the principal of Scotia Seminary at Concord, North Carolina.

Since Scotia was supported almost entirely by contributions from individuals or church groups outside the South, Miss Crissman's letter was one of several in the mailbox at the Concord post office. Nevertheless, it excited the interest of Dr. Satterfield, the headmaster, and of the half-dozen former students staying at the school in vacation time. It was rare that one contributor was willing to take full responsibility for a scholar. And the seamstress from Colorado had left the choice of the new student to the school.

A week later, Miss Emma Wilson, who had, as usual, been spending her free time at her old school, boarded the railroad train for Mayesville, South Carolina. She had Mary Crissman's letter in her skirt pocket and, folded carefully inside the envelope, enough money to pay for a ticket from Mayesville back to Concord.

No one met Miss Wilson at the depot because she wasn't expected back so soon. It was cotton-picking time, and the school term would not begin until the cotton was ginned and baled. She asked the baggageman to keep her valise because she had a four-mile walk ahead of her.

As it turned out, however, the young schoolteacher got a ride for most of the way in a mule cart, so she arrived at the McLeod farm before sundown. The whole family was out in the field, bent over the rows of heavy-headed cotton. All the family, that is, who were still left at home. Sally had married and gone. And the older boys had gone, too. There wasn't much on a five-acre farm to hold them.

Mary saw Miss Wilson coming across the dusty field, stepping carefully between the cotton rows. Coming, maybe, to say the new term was beginning? But it wasn't any use. Mary prayed every night to ask God to help her find a way to finish her studies so she could go to teach His Word to her kin in Africa. But how could she? They didn't have a mule yet, any more than they had in the spring.

As her teacher's trim figure came closer, Mary's mind darted down a dozen trails of thought. Maybe Miss Wilson wasn't coming for her after all, but for one of the little children. Maybe, when the cotton was baled and sold, there'd be enough money to buy a mule. But then there was the debt to the white man at the bank, for her father, in spite of all his determination, had had to borrow. And Granny wasn't getting any younger. Mama would need help with the ironing if Granny's health failed. … It just wasn't any use for Miss Wilson to be coming around.

"Short of a miracle," Mary said to herself, with unaccustomed bitterness, "my schooling is done with."

Patsy McLeod got up off her knees and went toward the visitor; but Mary kept on picking cotton. She didn't look up from the row until she heard her mother calling her name in a voice like a jubilee.

"Mary! Your teacher chose you! The school chose my girl to get the scholarship. Come here, every last one of you, while Miss Wilson reads the letter again. Mary's going to Scotia!"

There were Miss Wilson and Mama hugging each other and laughing and crying over the news in the letter fluttering in the breeze. And her father and Granny and the girls crowding around, and the little ones hanging onto Miss Wilson's skirt with their grimy hands.

But Mary just stayed on her knees where she was in the cotton row and prayed to God in thankfulness.

Many times in the years to come, in her writings and on the lecture platform and in conversation with friends, Mary McLeod Bethune spoke about that moment in her life. To her it was proof of victory through prayer. And the faith that her teacher had that she was "one who would make good" was a talisman, a treasure, a foundation rock to be added to her family's faith in her. On this was built the faith in herself which many people believe to be the key to her character.

"I believe, first of all, in God, and next of all, in Mary McLeod Bethune," she said years later. Some thought her vain with pride, because she believed so confidently, so joyously, first in her God, then in herself. Yet her faith in herself was built upon the belief *that she was one chosen to advance the welfare of her people,* to bring nearer reality the American dream. And, as Rollins Winslow put it, "operating under this very credo, she launched and won many frontier battles in human relations."

There was no more cotton picked at the McLeods' that day. Miss Wilson stayed to supper. Granny killed one of the frying-size chickens and cooked it, crisp and golden. Patsy made up a pan of biscuits while Mary churned a fresh batch of butter. Then she went to the spring across the road for a bucket of cool water.

The short walk in the dusk alone under the still branches of the live oaks gave Mary time to think about the change that had come in her life. She was concerned about her family. How would they manage without her? Wintertime wouldn't be so bad. With her gone, there'd be one less to feed. But plowing time would come again. Maybe she oughtn't to go at all. But that was unthinkable. Her mother wouldn't let her give up the scholarship. Neither would her father, though he didn't drive for knowledge the way Mary and her mother did. Freedom was her father's driving force—the freedom that lets a human being take from life what his spirit needs. He knew that Mary wanted learning the same as he wanted to make his land yield a crop. As long as her father had his two hands, he'd plant seed and make a harvest— whether anybody was there to help or not.

Walking back with the water sloshing in the wooden pail, the girl considered her home almost with the eyes of a stranger. Or with Miss Wilson's eyes. The schoolteacher was kind and good, but she was not from this part of the country. She'd never known what it was to be poor—slave poor. She, likely, was wondering how they all managed in such a little place. Twenty souls there used to be, counting Granny, when all the McLeods were living at home.

Yet they hadn't felt very crowded. It was easy, if you didn't have many possessions. Pallets to sleep on weren't like having a lot of beds. Pallets could be rolled up in a corner of the back room in the daytime. If everybody had just two garments apiece — one on his back and one in the washtub — you didn't need wardrobe room. There wasn't room for enough chairs or benches around the table where they ate. But that was all right because they didn't have dishes enough for all the family to eat at the same time anyway. Granny had her rocker by the fireplace, and the two cane-bottom chairs were good to sit on when they weren't being used to prop up the ironing board. Outside of those, there were home-made benches and the floor. Anybody that didn't feel like sitting on the floor, could fetch a stump from the wood pile to sit on.

Looking at it piece by piece this way, Mary had to admit the McLeods didn't have much in the way of a house. But yet it was better than some the white farmers lived in. It had a floor. It was so clean that Reverend Bowen used to say Sister Sophia and Sister Patsy must have a soap factory hidden somewhere behind the cow shed.

Mary stopped to change the bucket to her other hand and noticed that the persimmon tree was loaded with a good crop this year. She'd have to remember to warn little Hattie again not to chunk the fruit down until after a frost. She'd pucker her mouth, for sure. Hattie took a lot of looking after, and lately she'd turned to Mary more than to her mother. Hattie would miss her when she went away to Scotia, and she'd miss Hattie. Hattie was

Mary McLeod at age twenty.

bright. Maybe, someday, Miss Wilson would take her in the school. Mary had never given up hope that some of the family besides herself would get an education.

When she got back to the house, her father and Granny and Miss Wilson were sitting at the table eating supper, and Miss Wilson was telling what the school would be like. The rest of the family were clustered around in silence, all except Hattie and the baby, who were gnawing the chicken wings on the back step. The rest of them would eat later. There might not be much chicken left but there'd be plenty of biscuits and gravy and buttermilk.

After family prayers were over, Sam went over to a neighbor's house to ask for the loan of his mule and cart to drive Miss Wilson out to Reverend Bowen's home, near Sumter, where she always roomed during school term.

"I'll have to stop at the depot to get my valise," Miss Wilson said. "And before I forget,

I'd like to give you Mary's railroad ticket to Concord. Though I'll see you again before she leaves."

Patsy took the ticket and laid it between two pages of the Bible up on the shelf. There it would be safe and come to no harm.

"When do you want she should go?" Patsy asked.

"A month from today," the schoolteacher said. "If you can get her ready by then."

Get Mary ready! Miss Wilson's words seemed to linger in the air long after the squeaking cart had gone down the road. Granny settled back in her rocking-chair and lit her corncob pipe. She sucked away at the stem without speaking. Patsy didn't say anything either. But, as she cleaned up the supper things, she rattled the tin pieplate dishes and her lips were pressed close together in a way she had when she was worried or anxious.

Finally, Mary spoke. "What did Miss Wilson mean 'get me ready'?"

Becky came in from milking the cow in time to hear the question. She set down the milk pail and the lantern she'd used to see by.

"You might be book smart, Mary McLeod," she said, "but you don't seem to have no common sense at all. There's more to going away to school than a railroad ticket and a letter. There's clothes to put on your back and something to carry them in. You saw all that extra ironing Mama did for little Miss Essie last week. Fluted ruffled drawers and starched petticoats and dressing-sacks with ribbons run through. Miss Essie going to Charleston to boarding school, that's why. And when I carried the basket of clothes home there was a dressmaker from Sumter stitching on a sewing machine in the back room and Mrs. Wilson scurrying around with dress goods on her arm, matching colors."

"That's white people's way," the grandmother interrupted sharply.

Patsy sat down wearily. "White people's way or not, Mary's got to have some good clothes to wear so far from home. It would shame me to let her go shabby. It comes at a bad time, too. A little later and the cotton would be sold. We'd have a little money for cloth and such, after paying the storekeeper and getting the flour and meal and sidemeat."

Mary shook her head emphatically. "Money from the cotton isn't going on my back," she said. "It's for a mule. I'm going to Scotia for learning. I can study my lessons without shoes and stockings. I can wash one dress while I've got on the other, same as always. Miss Wilson didn't choose me for pretty. She don't expect I should carry along any finery."

Stiffly, Sophia raised herself from her chair, and moved toward her little wooden chest where she kept her things. She had brought the chest along with her when she came, the day after Emancipation, to make her home with Patsy and Sam. That was more than twenty years ago and she had never let anybody see to the bottom of it. But whenever need got beyond a point, it seemed the old woman would open her chest and pull out something to help out. The blanket Mary was wrapped in when she was born had come from the treasure chest. So had the button string she had played with as a little child.

Hattie and little Maggie drew close, now, to watch the lid raised. Sophia pulled out a length of linsey-woolsey cloth, the kind the Wilson slaves always got for Christmas. She pulled out a spool of thread and four pearl buttons and handed them to Mary.

"I been saving this cloth too long as it is," she said. "It'll make a good dress and us has got plenty floursacking for underwear. The Lord means you shall have an education and He means you shall be dressed fitting for His work. You ain't pretty, but you're a good girl to look at. You fix up the best you can and respect your body as you do your soul. And all of you quit fretting. Mary's going to that school in a manner that won't disgrace her. The Lord will provide."

As Mary McLeod told about it long afterward, the Lord did provide, through the willing hands and good hearts of the neighbors. When the news got around the McLeod girl was going to North Carolina to get more schooling, neighbors knitted stockings. They sewed pretty aprons. They brought dresses they could spare—or said they could spare—for Patsy to make over. And Mr. Hawkins pulled a pair of brown high shoes with copper tips off his shelf. He'd had 'em, he said, since before the War, and they were too shopworn to sell. He wasn't like some folks. He liked to see black people trying to better themselves. Sam was welcome to the shoes for his girl if she didn't have something better.

The end of September came and the day Mary was to take the train to Concord. Everybody in the neighborhood came down to the depot to see her off. In wagons, on mules, in oxcarts and afoot, they made a regular procession through the streets of Mayesville to see Mary get on the train.

Most of them had never been on a railroad train themselves but they hadn't come out of curiosity just to see the train go by. They had come because Mary McLeod already was becoming a symbol to her people. She was moving ahead on the path of freedom. Here at last was one of their own, going off to a big school to make something of herself. Maybe a teacher, maybe a missionary....Some predicted one thing, some another. But each of them shared in her victory over almost unsurmountable obstacles. Each had a share of the miracle. Each felt renewed hope in the promise of America while they waited at the depot for the northbound train to come in.

No doubt the stationmaster was a little dismayed to see all the country carts pouring in, taking up space at the hitching posts. Was Mayesville going to be subjected to one of those mass exoduses he'd been hearing about? There'd been rumors floating about that black people were leaving the state in droves. They'd better stay where they were and not go running off to the North or to Kansas where they'd freeze to death. Had some agitator slipped into Mayesville stirring up trouble? He was scarcely less disturbed when he found out that all the hubbub was just because a black girl in a linsey-woolsey dress was going off to North Carolina to school....

He stood in the depot door and scowled. But he didn't try to order the crowd away. There were too many of them together. Anyhow, the train was due in five minutes....

As the time grew close, the neighbors drew away, leaving the family to cluster around to say goodbye. But Miss Wilson, who had come in from Summit, stayed a minute longer. She explained once more that a teacher from the school would meet the train in Concord. Mary was not to worry. She was just to take a seat in the cars, put her bundles on the floor and give her ticket to the conductor. The trip would take eight hours. She would be in Concord before dark.

Then Miss Wilson put a lovely plaid shawl around Mary's shoulders, because, she said, it got colder in Concord than down here. "You write a letter," she whispered. "I'll take it to your mother. And I'll write letters, too."

"Yes, ma'am," was all that Mary had time to

answer. But the schoolteacher's promise lifted a load from her heart.

The inability of members of loving and closeknit families to communicate with each other when they were separated by distance was one of the tragic features of slavery. Miss Wilson's thoughtfulness meant that the bond between Mary and her family need not be broken. There could be letters between them. She would know how the planting was going in the spring—how the mule her father was bargaining for worked out—whether Granny's new rheumatism medicine did any good. Above all, words could flow between herself and her mother. Someday, maybe, there'd be time for Miss Wilson to teach her mother to read!

"You heard what Miss Wilson said?" Mary held the thin, bony shoulders of her mother in her strong arms. The engine roared in with a rush of air. She had to raise her voice to be heard. "I'm going to write you all about Scotia. And about the train ride...."

The brakes screeched and groaned. The train hardly came to a stop before Mary's foot

PORTRAIT OF MARY MCLEOD BETHUNE, 1968. *Aaron Douglas. Oil 58″ × 48″. Minneapolis Public Schools. Gift of the John Cowles, Sr. Family.*

was on the car step. She remembered to wave goodbye to the crowd of friends standing at a respectful distance. Sam handed up the bundle of clothes and the lunch Granny had put up and wrapped in an old newspaper. The whistle blew and the wheels began slowly to turn. The shouting, waving, loving people at the depot disappeared from Mary's sight. An era in the life of Mary McLeod had ended. But the love she had been surrounded with went with her always.

"I was shown goodness in my childhood," she wrote. "My parents believed in me. I learned to believe in other people. To be sure I saw trouble and the way was not easy; but I have thanked God and said Glory Hallelujah!"

Getting at Meaning

RECALLING

1. Who is Mary Crissman? How does Mary Crissman's gift to Scotia Seminary differ from other contributions to the school?

2. Why does Mary McLeod believe that her schooling "is done with"? What makes it possible for Mary to go to school?

3. How does Mary react when she first hears the news about the scholarship? Why does she remain in the cotton row?

4. What two things does Mary believe in most?

5. How does Sophia help Mary get ready for school? What is her advice to Mary?

6. How do the people of Mayesville react to Mary's going to school?

7. Why is Miss Wilson's promise to write to Mary so important?

INTERPRETING

8. How is Mary's father different from Mary and her mother? What makes him able to understand her drive for education?

9. What problems does Mary's family have, even though they are now free? What helps them cope with these problems?

CRITICAL THINKING: EVALUATING

10. Even exceptionally talented and motivated people need support from others from time to time. Explain how the story of Mary McLeod Bethune illustrates the point.

Developing Skills in Reading Literature

1. **Character.** A character is a person or animal who takes part in the action of a work of literature. This short selection gives an insight into Mary McLeod Bethune, its main character. Why is education important to her? How do you know that she is a religious person? Why do her family and Miss Wilson have so much faith in her?

2. **Biography.** A biography is the story of a person's life, written by someone else. Although a biography can be written about anyone, certain people's lives and accomplishments are especially inspiring. What qualities does Mary have? How can the story of her struggle motivate the reader? How can her life serve as a model for others?

Developing Vocabulary

Context Clues. On a separate sheet of paper, copy the italicized words in the following sentences. Then use the context clues provided to determine the meanings of the words. Write the definitions opposite the words on your paper.

1. "In the spring and fall, she went out to sew, spending a few days at a time in the homes of her neighbors, making up bolts of *gingham* or calico into dresses and shirts, or woolens or silks into Sunday clothes."
2. "Miss Crissman was *pious.* She took great comfort in her beliefs and practiced her Christianity as best she could."
3. "She *tithed,* setting aside ten cents of every dollar she earned to give to the poor, the oppressed, and the heathen."
4. "She asked the baggageman to keep her *valise* because she had a four-mile walk ahead of her."
5. "*Pallets* to sleep on weren't like having a lot of beds. Pallets could be rolled up in a corner of the back room in the daytime."
6. "Was Mayesville going to be subjected to one of those mass *exoduses* he'd been hearing about? There'd been rumors floating about that black people were leaving the state in droves."

Developing Writing Skills

Writing About a Person. The life of Mary McLeod Bethune inspired a great many people. In two paragraphs, tell about someone who has inspired you. The person you choose can be someone whom you know — a relative, neighbor, friend, or acquaintance. It can also be someone whom you have only read or heard about.

Begin your prewriting notes by making a list of several people about whom you could write. Next to each name on your list, write the qualities that you admire in this person and tell how this person has inspired you. Choose the one person from your list who is the most inspiring. Make a second set of prewriting notes about this person. Include in your notes information about your subject's appearance, actions, speech, habits, and other personal qualities. Also include abstract words, such as *courageous, strong, joyful,* or *supportive,* that describe your subject.

Begin your first paragraph with a topic sentence that introduces your subject. In the body of the paragraph, describe your subject's most outstanding characteristics. In the second paragraph, tell how your subject has inspired you. As you revise your paragraphs, refer to the suggestions for revision in **Using the Process of Writing** on pages 621–623.

B I O G R A P H Y

Emma Gelders Sterne (1894–1971) was born in Birmingham, Alabama. She attended Smith College and Columbia University. A strong supporter of racial equality and world peace, she has explored topics in books such as *We Live To Be Free* and *They Took Their Stand.* She has written biographies of Mary McLeod Bethune and Benito Pablo Juárez, a political reformer and President of Mexico.

Frederick Douglass devoted his life to the cause of freedom.

Frederick Douglass: Fighter for Freedom

Langston Hughes

During the period when Ira Aldridge[1] was playing Shakespeare, another American black became famous in Europe, too. He had crossed the ocean three times, once fleeing America for his life. But he did not remain abroad. He always came home to battle for the freedom of his people. His name was Frederick Douglass. His father was white but, nevertheless, Frederick was born a slave. His grandmother cared for him, and he never remembered seeing his mother more than a half dozen times in his life. The last time he saw her, she had walked twelve miles after dusk to hold him on her knees until he went to sleep. Then she had to walk twelve miles back to a distant plantation before sunrise to be at work in the fields.

When Frederick was born in the backwoods of Maryland, his name was not Douglass. It was Bailey. About the time when he was shedding his first teeth the boy was taken from his grandmother and with a dozen other slave children, put into the care of a mean old hag on the plantation who whipped them often and

frequently sent them to sleep on a dirt floor without their suppers. Frederick was ragged, neglected, and sometimes so hungry that he would wait at the kitchen door of the mansion house for the serving girls to shake the bones and crumbs from his master's table cloth. Then he would scramble with the dogs to pick up what fell into the yard. Fortunately, however, while still a young lad, he was sent to work for his master's relatives in Baltimore as errand boy and servant to that family's little son. Seeing that he was an apt boy, his new mistress taught him his A-B-C's. But her husband soon stopped her, saying, "If you teach him how to read, he'll want to know how to write, and this accomplished, he'll be running away with himself." However, white playmates in the streets sometimes lent him their blue-backed spellers and helped him to learn the words. When he was thirteen, with fifty cents earned from shining shoes, he bought a copy of

---

1. **Ira Aldridge** (ī' rə ôl' dridj): a celebrated black actor of the nineteenth century (?–1867).

The Columbian Orator, which included the speeches of William Pitt and other great men. This was his only book so he read it over and over. Many of the speeches were about liberty and freedom—as applied to white people, of course. But young Frederick took them to heart. "I wish myself a beast, a bird, anything rather than a slave," he said.

His whole life eventually became a dedication to freedom. There was an old song he must have heard about "hard trials and deep tribulations." Such trials young Fred knew well. Meanwhile, he found comfort in religion under the guidance of a kindly old black named Lawson who could not read very well. Young Frederick taught Lawson "the letter" of the Bible; Lawson in turn taught Frederick "the spirit." Lawson strengthened his hope for freedom by assuring him, "If you want liberty, ask the Lord for it *in faith,* and He will give

A RIDE FOR LIBERTY—THE FUGITIVE SLAVES, about 1862. *Eastman Johnson. The Brooklyn Museum. Gift of Miss Gwendolyn O.L. Conkling.*

it to you." Frederick had begun to discover, too, that there were white people in America who did not believe in bondage. These were called *Abolitionists*. The Baltimore papers were always condemning them roundly as anarchists in league with the devil. But Frederick Douglass thought to himself that whatever the Abolitionists might be, they were not unfriendly to the slave, nor sympathetic to the slaveholder.

The more Frederick read the Bible and the newspapers, the more he began to realize that learning opened the way to achievement. As his master had warned, Frederick soon began to want to learn to write. In secret, at night in the loft where he slept, with a flour barrel for a table, his copy books being the Bible and a hymnal, the teen-age boy began to teach himself. When no one was at home, he sometimes borrowed his white master's pen and ink. In time he learned to write. When he was sent to work for another branch of the family in a small town, he found a Sunday school held there in the home of a free black. Frederick was asked to be one of the instructors. But on his second Sunday in this Sabbath school, a white mob rushed in armed with sticks and stones and drove everybody away. Young Fred was warned that if he kept on teaching Sunday school, he would be filled with shot. In the small community this sixteen-year-old slave who could read and write had gotten the reputation of being a "dangerous black," putting thoughts into other blacks' heads. Shortly his apprehensive master sent him away to a "black breaker" to be made a better slave—that is, to be tamed, humbled, taught to be contented with slavery—in other words, "to be broken."

The man's name was Covey. His plantation was a sort of reformatory work farm on a sandy, desolate point of Chesapeake Bay.

Covey specialized in taking unruly young slaves for a year and "cutting them down to size" so that their masters would have no more trouble with them. Three days after Frederick arrived there, Covey gave him a team of untamed oxen and sent him to the woods for a load of logs. The boy had never driven oxen before, but he dared not object to the job. The oxen ran away, overturned the wagon, and smashed a gate. For this the sixteen-year-old lad had his clothes torn from him by the "slave-breaker," and was flogged on his bare skin with ox-goads. As he described it many years later in his autobiography, "The sores from this flogging continued for weeks, for they were kept open by the rough and coarse cloth which I wore for shirting. Aching bones and a sore back were my constant companions." The scars which Covey put on Frederick's shoulders never went away.

Work from before dawn until long after sundown was a part of Covey's system. One day Frederick fainted in the broiling sun of the treading yard where the wheat was being separated from the straws. He was dizzy. His head ached violently. He was deathly ill. When Covey commanded him to rise, he could not. The slaver gave him a series of savage kicks which finally brought him to his feet. Frederick fell down again, whereupon Covey took a hickory slab and struck him in the head, leaving him bleeding beside the fence. That night Frederick in despair dragged himself seven miles through the woods to his own master's house to beg that he be taken away from the slave breaker. But his master did no such thing. Instead, he accused the boy of trying to avoid work and sent him back the next day to finish out his year with Covey. Then it was that Frederick made up his mind to defend himself and never to let anyone mistreat him so again.

He returned to the plantation but, it being the Lord's Day, Covey waited until Monday morning to flog him. To the slaver's surprise and chagrin, the tall young black had resolved to fight it out, man to man. Instead of submitting to a whipping, he flung the slave breaker on the ground each time he came near. Covey finally gave up. Frederick was not whipped again as long as he was there. But Covey almost worked him to death.

"I was a changed being after that fight," Douglass wrote in his *Life And Times.* "I was *nothing* before; I was a *man* now." On Christmas Day, 1834, his year with the slave breaker was up. But his spirit, far from being broken, had been strengthened. His hatred of the cruelties of slavery intensified. And his determination to be free grew ever stronger. When the boy was transferred to a new master, even though conditions were much more pleasant, he began to plan a break for freedom. Frederick persuaded five other slaves to run away with him. On the eve of their departure, someone betrayed them. Frederick was bound and dragged off to jail. When he was released, he was not wanted on that plantation any more. (He was a "dangerous black.") So he was sent back to Baltimore and put to work in a shipyard where he learned the caulker's trade. But the white workers objected to blacks working with them. One day a number of them ganged up on Frederick (who was certainly there through no fault of his own) and beat him almost to death. In fact, he was beaten so badly that his master, for fear of losing a valuable slave, did not send him back to the shipyards again. Instead, he allowed Frederick to hire himself out, providing that every Saturday night he turned *all* his wages in to his master. Sometimes he might let Frederick keep a

quarter for himself. Eventually, Frederick managed to save enough secretly to pay his fare to New York. Though it might mean his life if he were captured, Frederick decided to dare to try to escape from slavery again. Disguised as a sailor, and with borrowed seaman's papers, he leaped on a train just as it was leaving Baltimore. A day later, he reached New York. He was twenty-one years old when he set foot on free soil. A dream had at last come true. *He belonged to himself.*

A new world had opened for him. "I felt as one might feel upon escape from a den of hungry lions," he wrote in his first letter to a friend. But soon his money was gone. In the big city nobody paid any attention to him. He was afraid to approach anyone, since he did not know whom to trust for fear he might be returned to slave territory. As he later described his condition, "I was without home, without acquaintance, without money, without credit, without work, and without any definite knowledge as to what course to take or where to look for succor. In such an extremity, a man has something besides his new-born freedom of which to think. While wandering about the streets of New York, and lodging at least one night among the barrels on one of the wharves, I was indeed free—free from slavery—but free from food and shelter as well."

A sailor who lived near the docks took him in, gave him a place to sleep, and put him in touch with a committee whose work it was to help escaped slaves. While in hiding in New York, Frederick was married to a girl with whom he had fallen in love in Baltimore and who followed him to the big city. Together they set out for Massachusetts on the deck of a steamer, for black passengers were not allowed in the cabins. In New Bedford he found employment on the wharves. There he dropped his slave name, Bailey, and took the name of one of the characters in *The Lady of the Lake*[2] — Douglass. From then on he was known as Frederick Douglass, a name shortly to be in headlines around the world. For the young freeman was not satisfied just to be free himself. He became an Abolitionist.

In 1841, Douglass made his first talk at an Anti-Slavery Society meeting in Nantucket. There, groping for words, since he had never faced an audience before, he told the story of his childhood, his bondage, and his escape. People were deeply moved. William Lloyd Garrison,[3] who followed Douglass as a speaker, cried, "Is he a man or a thing?" And proceeded to point out how, in spite of slave owners treating Frederick as a *thing,* free people could see that here was a man, worthy of being treated as a man.

Douglass was then twenty-four years old, six feet tall, with hair like a lion, and very handsome. The more speeches he made, the more effective he became. Soon he was persuaded to quit his work on the docks and become an orator for the cause of freedom. In 1845 he made his first trip to England to tell sympathizers there about the plight of America's slave millions. When he returned he began to publish a paper in Rochester, called *The North Star.* From then on, for fifty years, Douglass was a great public figure. He spoke on platforms with many of the distinguished men and women of his times — Wendell Phillips, Harriet Beecher Stowe, Charles Sumner, and Lucretia Mott. He published his life story. He defied the Fugitive Slave Law of 1850 and sheltered runaways in his home. Mobs attacked his meetings. He was sometimes stoned. After John Brown's famous raid on Harper's Ferry,[4]

in which he had no part, the newspapers and the slave owners sought to implicate him. Douglass had to flee for his life to Canada, whence he made his second trip to England. When the War between the States broke out, he was back in this country, counseling with President Lincoln and recruiting troops for the Union Army — in which his own sons served. More than two hundred thousand blacks fought in this War for freedom and the preservation of the Union. Many were inspired to do so by the brilliant speeches of Frederick Douglass.

When the War was over, Douglass became one of the leaders of the Republican Party. He was made a United States Marshall. Later he was appointed the Recorder of Deeds for the District of Columbia. And in 1889 he was confirmed as United States Minister to the Republic of Haiti. Active not just as a leader of the black people, at the first convention for women's suffrage Douglass was the *only* man of any color to stand up on the floor and defend the right of women to the ballot equally with men. "Right is of no sex," he stated in the first issue of *The North Star.* He was active, too, in the national temperance organizations and many other movements for social betterment. After Emancipation, Douglass demanded no special privileges for blacks. For them he wanted simply the same freedom of action he felt *every* citizen should have. In a famous speech called, *What the Black Man Wants,* he

---

2. **The Lady of the Lake:** a long, romantic poem published in 1810 by the poet and novelist Sir Walter Scott.
3. **William Lloyd Garrison:** an American journalist and crusader who helped lead the campaign against slavery (1805–1879).
4. **John Brown . . . Harper's Ferry:** a militant anti-slavery crusader, who led a famous raid on a U.S. government arsenal at Harper's Ferry, Virginia.

said, "The American people have always been anxious to know what to do with us. I have had but one answer from the beginning. Do nothing with us! . . . If the Negro[5] cannot stand on his own legs, let him fall. All I ask is, give him a *chance* to stand on his own legs! Let him alone! If you see him on his way to school, let him alone—don't disturb him. If you see him going to the dinner table at a hotel, let him go! If you see him going to the ballot box, let him alone—don't disturb him! If you see him going into a workshop, just let him alone."

The only school from which Douglass was ever graduated, as he often repeated, was the school of slavery. His diploma was the scars upon his back. But he had about him a wit and wisdom that many a better educated person did not possess. His speeches moved thousands to action. As a writer he left behind him his *Life and Times,* an autobiography that is an American classic. His simple but effective use of words, tinged sometimes with wry humor, is illustrated in the final paragraph of a letter he wrote to his former master on the tenth anniversary of his escape to freedom. In this letter he listed all the wrongs this man had done him, but closed by stating:

"There is no roof under which you would be more safe than mine, and there is nothing in my house which you might need for your comfort, which I would not readily grant. Indeed, I should esteem it a privilege to set you an example as to how mankind ought to treat each other.

"I am your fellow man, but not your slave,

Frederick Douglass."

---

5. **Negro:** accepted term in Douglass's time; not considered disrespectful.

Getting at Meaning

RECALLING

1. Describe Frederick's interaction with his mother. What does his mother have to do in order to visit him?

2. Who gives Frederick his first reading lessons? Why do these lessons stop?

3. Who are the Abolitionists?

4. Why is Frederick beaten in the shipyards? What arrangement does his master make with him after that?

5. How does Frederick escape from slavery?

6. Where does Frederick work when he first comes to Massachusetts? Why does he stop doing this work?

7. What are Frederick Douglass's major activities and achievements during his years as a public figure?

INTERPRETING

8. Who is Covey? Why does Covey stop trying to whip Frederick? Does Covey succeed in breaking Frederick's spirit?

9. When does Frederick change his last name? Why does he do so?

10. What does Douglass's letter to his former master show about him?

11. This brief biography of Frederick Douglass is subtitled "Fighter for Freedom." At what points did Douglass have to "fight" in a literal sense? What other types of "fighting" did Douglass do?

CRITICAL THINKING: APPLYING

12. What did Frederick Douglass have to struggle for that most people today take for granted? Do you take these things for granted?

Developing Skills in Reading Literature

Biography. A biography is the story of a person's life, written by someone else. The writer of a biography is called a biographer. Frederick Douglass died in 1895. Langston Hughes was born in 1902. How could Hughes obtain information about someone who was already dead? In other words, what sources of information can a biographer use beyond first-hand experience? Find the quotations that appear in this selection. What were Hughes's sources for these quotations?

Developing Writing Skills

Writing an Epitaph. An epitaph is an inscription, especially on a tombstone, in memory of a person. Often an epitaph mentions the person's most important accomplishments. For instance, Thomas Jefferson's epitaph says, "Here was buried Thomas Jefferson, author of the Declaration of American Independence, of the statute of Virginia for religious freedom, and father of the University of Virginia."

Write a one sentence or two sentence epitaph for Frederick Douglass based on what you have learned about him from this selection. Begin by listing in your prewriting notes several of Douglass's accomplishments. Then choose two or three accomplishments that you believe should be mentioned in an epitaph. Model your epitaph on the one for Thomas Jefferson. Use no more than thirty words. Experiment with various ways of expressing your ideas until you have a wording that is brief, precise, and dignified. (Note: writing of this kind is most effective when the words used are short and simple.)

B I O G R A P H Y

Langston Hughes (1902–1967) lived in six different cities before he was twelve. By the time his first book was published, he had worked as a farmer, cook, waiter, sailor, and doorman. He had also traveled in many countries and had studied at Columbia and Lincoln Universities. Although he wrote novels, short stories, plays, song lyrics, and radio scripts, Hughes is best known for his poetry. His recognition as a poet began when he was a hotel busboy. He left some of his verses at the table where the poet Vachel Lindsay was dining. Lindsay was so impressed that he included Hughes's work with his own in poetry readings. In his writing, Hughes spoke about the common people whom he knew in New York. He often wrote in dialects of Black English and borrowed structures and rhythms from jazz and blues music. Much of his writing deals with racial prejudice and the struggle for equality.

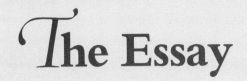
The Essay

What Is an Essay?

An essay is a brief nonfiction work that deals with a single subject, often in a personal way. Most essays are written in prose. They have one point of view and a central focus, or theme.

The Origins of the Essay

In the late 1500's, a Frenchman named Michel de Montaigne published two books of short, nonfiction writings. These writings covered many subjects. Montaigne did not try to say everything that could be said about each subject. Instead, he simply recorded a few of his thoughts and feelings. Because he did not try to be thorough, Montaigne decided to call his writings *Essais,* a word that means "attempts." This word became the name of a new kind of literature.

Thinking About the Essay

In this section you will read five essays. In two of these, "Langston Terrace" and "Mama Sewing," the writers share their own experiences and feelings. In the other three, the writers present factual information. As you read the five essays, note how they differ in purpose, style, subject matter, and tone.

SUMMER MILLINERY, 1915. *Charles Webster Hawthorne.*
Oil on Board, 58½″ × 46¾″. Chrysler Museum, Norfolk, Virginia. Gift of Walter P. Chrysler, Jr. (71.659)

Carousel Horses

Ludmilla Alexander

Visit any carnival or fairground in any town or city in this country, and you're sure to find an eager crowd gathered around the merry-go-round. Merry-go-rounds (or carousels, as they are also called) have been popular in the United States for a hundred years. In the earliest days, they consisted of a live horse and mule circling endlessly in a pit, turning a platform of happy riders above their heads. Live animals were retired when a steam-driven carousel was invented at the beginning of the century.

The steam-driven carousel, with its elegantly carved and painted wooden horses, was an instant success. Families flocked to amusement parks on weekends to ride their favorite steeds, to the accompaniment of gay organ music.

The demand for carousels and wooden horses was so great that a number of woodcarvers started companies to design and build merry-go-rounds. Each factory had its own unique style, and soon people could tell who the manufacturer was just by looking at the horse.

For example, Solomon Stein and Harry Goldstein of Brooklyn, New York, carved horses that looked as if they could carry knights from the Middle Ages. These horses had bulging muscles under carved fishscale blankets. Their wooden manes seemed to be flying in the wind, and their hooves were bent back as if galloping. Their mouths were always open, baring sharp teeth. Riders on these animals felt as if they had to hold the reins tightly, to keep their horses from galloping right off the platform.

The horses carved by Charles I. D. Looff were altogether different. Looff's horses were gentle, friendly animals that seemed to be smiling at the world. They had tails with real hair and glass jewels on their saddles and harnesses. A Looff horse could always be identified by the single rosette on its chest.

Every year when his Staten Island carousel opened for the season, Looff put a chariot and a few horses from his carousel on a float. Then he loaded up the neighborhood children, and they all rode down the street in a parade.

Looff even built a merry-go-round as a wedding present for his daughter Emma, who, with her husband Louis, operated it for years in Spokane, Washington. Looff's biggest fans were his two grandsons, Lloyd and Harold; and when Lloyd grew up, he took over the Spokane merry-go-round from his father.

The stories of old merry-go-round horses did not always end happily. With time, people grew tired of carousels and found other things to do on their holidays. One by one, merry-go-rounds lost money and had to close down.

The horses were dismantled and packed into crates. Many were in terrible shape. Layers of paint hid the fine details of the carving. Glass eyes and jeweled ornaments were lost. Tails and manes had lost their hair. Horses that once proudly rode round and round were now forgotten in dusty warehouses.

In 1968, the amusement park in Spokane, Washington, closed, and all the rides and booths were sold. The city of Spokane recognized the historic and artistic value of the old Looff carousel and wanted to buy it, but couldn't afford the price. Merry-go-round lovers from all over heard about the problem and began sending in donations. Soon a real campaign had started, and people were buying "save the carousel" buttons.

After three years in storage, three years in restoration, and six months in final preparation, Looff's old merry-go-round was installed in its new home on the Spokane River. All the horses galloped again to music played by the original organ that had come from Germany in 1907.

Today, you can still ride Looff's merry-go-round in Spokane. Several other carousels have also been saved—for example, in Central Park in New York City; Santa Cruz Boardwalk, California; Waldemeer Park in Erie, Pennsylvania; and Asbury Park, New Jersey. Many other carousel horses have been bought by collectors who lovingly restored them to their original condition. They are often exhibited in museums and galleries and are admired by thousands of visitors.

So the next time you ride a merry-go-round, see if you can find the name of the woodcarver on the back of your horse. That prancing animal might be almost one hundred years old!

Getting at Meaning

RECALLING

1. How were carousels operated before the invention of the steam engine?

2. What did the horses carved by Solomon Stein and Harry Goldstein look like? What did the horses carved by Charles Looff look like?

3. Explain why the steam-driven carousels had to close down. What happened to the carved horses?

4. In what cities are old carousels still operating?

5. How can you tell whether a horse on a merry-go-round is an old one?

6. How did the people of Spokane raise the money to save their carousel?

INTERPRETING

7. What is the writer's attitude toward carousels? Find several passages that support your answer.

CRITICAL THINKING: EVALUATING

8. Why do you think carousels lost popularity? Why do you think they are now being restored?

Developing Skills in Reading Literature

Essay. An essay is a brief nonfiction work that deals with a single subject, often in a personal way. Some essays contain a great deal of factual information. List five facts that you learn about carousels by reading this selection.

In addition to providing factual information about carousels, the writer also reveals her personal feelings about them. However, these feelings are not directly expressed. How does the reader know that the writer loves carousels?

Developing Vocabulary

Synonyms. Synonyms are words that have similar meanings. Choose the correct synonym for the italicized word in each of the following sentences. If necessary, consult a dictionary.

1. Each factory has its own *unique* style.

   old   special   beautiful

2. The horses were *dismantled* and packed into crates.

   destroyed   taken apart   repaired

3. Looff's old merry-go-round took three years to *restore.*

   buy   plan   rebuild

4. The merry-go-round was *installed* in its new home.

   placed   stopped   found

5. The horses are often *exhibited* in museums.

   stored   rebuilt   displayed

Developing Writing Skills

Writing a Description. Find something that is old in your house or in a relative's house. In an essay of three paragraphs, describe the object. Include in your prewriting notes a list of sensory images that you can use in your description. Also include any information that you can gather about the origins, history, and uses of the object. To gather this information, you may wish to interview members of your immediate family or other relatives.

Before you begin to write, organize your notes under three major headings. As you write, use vivid, descriptive words and phrases. As you revise, try to eliminate and replace words and phrases that are dull or ordinary. Refer to **Using the Process of Writing** on pages 614– 623 of this book for help in completing this assignment.

Why is it so important to have a place called "home"?

Langston Terrace

Eloise Greenfield and Lessie Jones Little

I fell in love with Langston Terrace the very first time I saw it. Our family had been living in two rooms of a three-story house when Mama and Daddy saw the newspaper article telling of the plans to build it. It was going to be a low-rent housing project in northeast Washington, and it would be named in honor of John Mercer Langston, the famous black lawyer, educator, and congressman.

So many people needed housing and wanted to live there, many more than there would be room for. They were all filling out applications, hoping to be one of the 274 families chosen. My parents filled out one, too.

I didn't want to move. I knew our house was crowded—there were eleven of us, six adults and five children—but I didn't want to leave my friends. I didn't want to go to a strange place and be the new person in a neighborhood and a school where most of the other children already knew each other. I was eight years old, and I had been to three schools. We had moved five times since we'd been in Washington, each time trying to get more space and a better place to live. But rent was high so we'd always lived in a house with relatives and friends, and shared the rent.

One of the people in our big household was Lillie, Daddy's cousin and Mama's best friend. She and her husband also applied for a place in the new project. During the months that it was being built, Lillie and Mama would sometimes walk fifteen blocks just to stand and watch the workmen digging holes and laying bricks. They'd just stand there watching and wishing. And at home, that was all they could talk about. "When we get our new place...." "If we get our new place...."

Lillie got her good news first. I can still see her and Mama standing at the bottom of the hall steps, hugging and laughing and crying, happy for Lillie, then sitting on the steps, worrying and wishing again for Mama.

Finally, one evening, a woman came to the house with our good news, and Mama and Daddy went over and picked out the house they wanted. We moved on my ninth birthday. Wilbur, Gerald, and I went to school that morning from one house, and when Daddy came to pick us up, he took us home to another one. All the furniture had been moved while we were in school.

Langston Terrace was a lovely birthday present. It was built on a hill, a group of tan brick houses and apartments with a playground as its center. The red mud surrounding the concrete walks had not yet been covered with black soil and grass seed, and the holes that would soon be homes for young trees were filled with rainwater. But it still looked beautiful to me.

We had a whole house all to ourselves. Upstairs and downstairs. Two bedrooms, and the living room would be my bedroom at night. Best of all, I wasn't the only new person. Everybody was new to this new little community. By the time school opened in the fall, we had gotten used to each other and had made friends with other children in the neighborhood, too.

I guess most of the parents thought of the new place as an in-between place. They were glad to be there, but their dream was to save enough money to pay for a house that would be their own. Saving was hard, though, and slow, because each time somebody in a family got a raise on the job, it had to be reported to the manager of the project so that the rent could be raised, too. Most people stayed years longer than they had planned to, but they didn't let that stop them from enjoying life.

They formed a resident council to look into any neighborhood problems that might come up. They started a choral group and presented music and poetry programs on Sunday evenings in the social room or on the playground. On weekends, they played horseshoes and softball and other games. They had a reading club that met once a week at the Langston branch of the public library, after it opened in the basement of one of the apartment buildings.

The library was very close to my house. I could leave by my back door and be there in two minutes. The playground was right in front of my house, and after my sister Vedie was born and we moved a few doors down to a three-bedroom house, I could just look out of my bedroom window to see if any of my friends were out playing.

There were so many games to play and things to do. We played hide-and-seek at the lamppost, paddle tennis and shuffleboard, dodge ball and jacks. We danced in fireplug showers, jumped rope to rhymes, played "Bouncy, Bouncy, Bally," swinging one leg over a bouncing ball, played baseball on a nearby field, had parties in the social room, and bus trips to the beach. In the playroom, we played Ping-Pong and pool, learned to sew and embroider and crochet.

For us, Langston Terrace wasn't an in-between place. It was a growing-up place, a good growing-up place. Neighbors who cared, family and friends, and a lot of fun. Life was good. Not perfect, but good. We knew about problems, heard about them, saw them, lived through some hard ones ourselves, but our community wrapped itself around us, put itself between us and the hard knocks, to cushion the blows.

It's been many years since I moved away, but every once in a long while I go back, just to look at things and remember. The large stone animals that decorated the playground are still there. A walrus, a hippo, a frog, and two horses. They've started to crack now, but I remember when they first came to live with us. They were friends, to climb on or to lean against, or to gather around in the evening. You could sit on the frog's head and look way out over the city at the tall trees and rooftops.

Nowadays, whenever I run into old friends, mostly at a funeral, or maybe a wedding, after we've talked about how we've been and what we've been doing, and how old our children are, we always end up talking about our child-time in our old neighborhood. And somebody will say, "One of these days we ought to have a Langston reunion." That's what we always called it, just "Langston," without the "Terrace." I guess because it sounded more homey. And that's what Langston was. It was home.

Getting at Meaning

RECALLING

1. Why do the parents want to move to Langston Terrace? Why are they worried about not getting a place there?

2. How does the narrator feel about moving? Why?

3. Name four of the adult activities at Langston Terrace.

4. Name five of the children's activities at Langston Terrace.

5. What helps the family through difficult times?

6. Find the sentence "They were friends, to climb on or to lean against, or to gather around in the evening." To what does the pronoun *they* refer?

INTERPRETING

7. How does the narrator feel about Langston Terrace? What makes Langston Terrace such a good place to grow up?

CRITICAL THINKING: EVALUATING

8. In what ways are the people of Langston Terrace wealthy even though they are poor?

Developing Skills in Reading Literature

Tone. Tone is the writer's attitude toward a subject. In this selection, the writers communi-cate their attitude toward Langston Terrace with sentences such as these:

"I fell in love with Langston Terrace."
"Langston Terrace was a lovely birthday present."

On a separate sheet of paper, copy four more phrases that convey the writers' attitude toward their former home.

Developing Writing Skills

Writing an Explanation. Langston Terrace was named after John Mercer Langston, a famous black lawyer, educator, and con-gressman. Choose something in your com-munity that was named after a person. It might be an office building, a courthouse, a school, a park, or a street. In one paragraph, explain who the person was and why he or she was honored in this way.

You may need to interview someone—a par-ent, a neighbor, or a city official—to gather information about the subject you have selected. Record the information that you gather in your prewriting notes. As you write and revise your paragraph, refer to the guide-lines presented in **Using the Process of Writing** on pages 614–623.

BIOGRAPHY

Eloise Greenfield (born 1929) was born in North Carolina, grew up in Washington, D.C., and attended Miner Teachers' College. For twelve years she worked at the U.S. Patent Office in Washington, D.C. She then joined the Black Writers' Workshop, first as co-director of adult fiction, then as director of children's literature. Greenfield's work ranges from a collection of poetry, *Honey, I Love,* to biographies of Rosa Parks, the civil rights activist, and Paul Robeson, the actor and singer. She has produced numerous picture books, novels, and short stories. She has also written about her childhood with the help of her mother, Lessie Jones Little.

Lessie Jones Little (born 1906) began writing when she was sixty-seven and a great-grandmother. With her daughter, Eloise Greenfield, she wrote *Childtimes: A Three Generation Memoir.* The book is about three children —Little, her mother, and her daughter—and tells about the similarities and differences in these three girls' lives. Little was born in Parmele, North Carolina, and attended North Carolina State Normal School. Before becoming a writer, she worked as an elementary school teacher.

Mama was patient and forgiving, and she understood the pains of growing up.

Mama Sewing

Eloise Greenfield and Lessie Jones Little

I don't know why Mama ever sewed for me. She sewed for other people, made beautiful dresses and suits and blouses, and got paid for doing it. But I don't know why she sewed for me. I was so mean.

It was all right in the days when she had to make my dresses a little longer in the front than in the back to make up for the way I stood, with my legs pushed back and my stomach stuck out. I was little then, and I trusted Mama. But when I got older, I worried.

Mama would turn the dress on the wrong side and slide it over my head, being careful not to let the pins stick me. She'd kneel on the floor with her pin cushion, fitting the dress on me, and I'd look down at that dress, at that lopsided, raw-edged, half-basted, half-pinned *thing*—and know that it was never going to look like anything. So I'd pout while Mama frowned and sighed and kept on pinning.

Sometimes she would sew all night, and in the morning I'd have a perfectly beautiful dress, just right for the school program or the party. I'd put it on, and I'd be so ashamed of the way I had acted. I'd be too ashamed to say I was sorry.

But Mama knew.

Getting at Meaning

RECALLING

1. What are the girl's thoughts as Mama fits the dress? How does she show her feelings? What does Mama do?

2. Why is the girl ashamed?

3. Why can't the girl apologize to Mama?

INTERPRETING

4. Why do you think Mama sews for her daughter?

5. What does the sentence "But Mama knew" show about Mama? Do you think that she forgives the daughter's unpleasant behavior? How do you know?

Developing Skills in Reading Literature

1. **Foil.** A foil is a character who provides a striking contrast to another character. A writer may use a foil to call attention to certain characteristics possessed by a main character or to emphasize the importance of those characteristics. In "Mama Sewing" the young girl is a foil for her mother. How does the girl react as the dress is being fitted? How does the mother react? What is the difference between their reactions? Explain how the contrast between the girl and her mother emphasizes the mother's patience and love.

2. **Point of View.** Point of view is the perspective from which a story is told. From whose point of view is this selection told? How would the selection be different if it were written from the point of view of the mother?

Speaking and Listening. Read this selection aloud changing the point of view as you read. Use *I* to refer to the mother and *she* to refer to the daughter.

from *T*antastic Creatures

Isaac Asimov

When civilization was young, what a fantastic planet we lived on. Strange creatures abounded wherever human beings looked. We've lost that wonder now, and it is hard for us even to imagine what it must have been like when even a short journey brought unbelievable sights.

Try to imagine....

Suppose you knew what cats, dogs, and various barnyard animals were like, as well as frogs, snakes, turtles, raccoons, and so on. And suppose you had never heard of anything else. Then suppose that, for the first time in your life, you saw an elephant, a giraffe, a camel, an ostrich, or even an armadillo. Could you possibly have imagined these, or any of a hundred others, if you had never seen or heard of them?

Perhaps you might have imagined a bird as large as an ostrich, but would you have thought of its long neck or imagined it scudding across the plains on its two long legs, moving as quickly as a horse? Or if you had imagined an ox ten feet high at its shoulders, would you have thought of pulling its nose into a long, snakelike appendage and making two giant fans of its ears?

It is no wonder that to early humans the earth seemed full of living wonders. It must have seemed that there was no limit to what might exist. Centaurs, sphinxes, harpies, mermaids, unicorns, winged horses, dragons, vampires, werewolves — almost anything that could entice, entrance, or affright was imagined. But then, after 1500, the world began to shrink, and step-by-step the wonders retreated. Mermaids became sea cows; unicorns became rhinoceroses and narwhals; dragons became cobras.

Yet the world did not grow entirely tame, for even though imaginary creatures dwindled, there were new real discoveries. When the French naturalist Cuvier maintained that the animals on the American continents were just small and degenerate copies of those from the Old World, Thomas Jefferson had a moose stuffed and sent to him. Cuvier had to admit that no Old-World deer could match that.

When Australia was explored, zoologists nearly went mad with wonder as whole new classes of animals — from the great red kangaroo on down — were revealed. They wouldn't believe that the duckbill platypus really existed

WINGED TIGER, 19th century. *Chinese Embroidered Textile Banner.*
The Metropolitan Museum of Art, New York.
Gift of Mrs. John H. Ballantine, 1947 (47.75.1)

when a skin was sent to them. They thought it was a practical joke, that portions of skins of several creatures had been deftly stitched together. Even older portions of the world had their surprises. As late as 1900, Europeans first spotted deep in the forests of Africa a new large mammal, a shy creature called the okapi —a shorter-necked relative of the giraffe with tentative, zebralike stripes on its hindquarters.

The sea could hide quite a bit. The giant squid was finally discovered. It was not quite as big as the legendary kraken, but it was large enough to fight desperately for its life against the sperm whale. In the 1930's an odd fish that inhabited the middle depths was discovered. This discovery was not unusual except that the fish belonged to a group of sea creatures that were ancestors to land vertebrates (like ourselves) and were thought to have been extinct since the time of the dinosaur!

We can't help but dream of still more discoveries. Sea serpents slither in our imaginations; we even look for one in the tame and constricted waters of the Scottish Loch Ness. The Yeti (or Abominable Snowman) furtively makes its way up the slopes of Mount Everest, and Sasquatch (or Big Foot) hides from us in the forests of the American Northwest.

We can't even let go of the creatures we feared and loved in ancient days. The mermaids still sit on the rocks, combing their sea-green hair; centaurs still gallop through the woods while Pegasus[1] wheels and soars up into the clouds; the dank forests of Eastern Europe still echo from the howl of the werewolf while the vast cities of the Western world lie prey to the skulking vampire. Well, why not? Surely we can have the best of both worlds. Reality may be all about us, but we can nevertheless suspend disbelief and read tales, even today, that return us to fantasy. In fact, by extending

sober reality, we can spin new fantasies that the ancients never dreamed of.

The ancients knew only one world, and though it seemed big and fearsome and unknown, it remained only one. We now know that there are other worlds circling the sun, and in the last few centuries imaginative writers have filled every one of them with strange creatures of fancy. They have been the very stuff of science fiction.

But then in the last couple of decades, fantasy withered again before the awesomeness of stark reality. There are today twelve sets of human footprints on the moon, and objects made by human hands have rested upon the rocky surfaces of Mars and Venus. Human-made space probes, hooked to human eyes, have shown us the scarred surfaces of the planet Mercury and of satellites such as Phobos, Ganymede, Callisto, Dione, Rhea, and Mimas. They have shown us the smooth, icy cover of Europa and Enceladus, the live volcanoes of Io, the thick, smoggy atmosphere of Titan, the monstrous, Earth-sized storms in the writhing atmospheres of Jupiter and Saturn, and the amazing and unexpected complexity of the structure of Saturn's rings.

All this was undreamed of when wondering eyes, unaided by technology, swept the night sky and connected the stars to form figures of animals and heroes. But all that has been revealed is inanimate. The strange life dreamed of by science fiction writers has retreated as did the strange life once dreamed of by folktale constructors. Where are the underground intelligences of the moon? Where are the wise and indomitable canal builders of Mars, wringing a despairing life out of a drying and dying world? Where is the rich, rank life

---

1. **Pegasus** (pcg′ ə səs): in Greek mythology, a winged horse.

belonging to the swamps and seas of wet and cloudy Venus?

Gone, all gone!

Well, it doesn't matter. We can cling as stubbornly to the old dreams of life in the solar system as we do to the monsters that peopled the Greek myths and the medieval European folktales. Besides, there is the still farther beyond. Our own solar system is but one small family of worlds, and within that there is certainly one richly inhabited member — Earth. But our solar system is only one of a couple hundred billion in our galaxy alone, and there are a hundred billion other galaxies—all kinds of galaxies containing all kinds of stars circled by all kinds of planets bearing on them (surely!) all kinds of amazing creatures.

We can't reach those planets yet, but we can imagine them. And we can imagine them more elaborately and better than the ancients ever could—not because we're smarter than they were, but because we now have a wider experience with a greater variety of reality than they ever had the chance to have.

Getting at Meaning

RECALLING

1. Name six fantastic creatures imagined by people before the year 1500.

2. Why did zoologists go "mad with wonder" when Australia was first explored? What was their response to the duckbill platypus?

3. What fantastic creature is supposed to live in Loch Ness? on the slopes of Mount Everest? in the forests of the American Northwest?

4. Name eight places in the solar system that have been explored for the first time in recent years.

5. Which planet in the solar system was once believed to have canals? Which was believed to have swamps and seas?

6. What planet in the solar system is "richly inhabited"?

INTERPRETING

7. Why did Thomas Jefferson send Cuvier a stuffed moose?

8. In what way did the world begin to shrink after 1500? How did this change affect people's beliefs about fantastic creatures? Is the same thing now happening with regard to the entire solar system? Explain.

CRITICAL THINKING: EVALUATING/APPLYING

9. What does Asimov mean when he writes that "mermaids still sit on the rocks"? In what sense do creatures such as mermaids and vampires actually exist?

10. What imaginary creatures can you think of that were not mentioned by Asimov? List five such creatures. What do these creatures have in common? Why might people have imagined these creatures to begin with?

Developing Skills in Reading Literature

Sequence. Sequence is the order of events in a literary work. As you know, most short stories, biographies and autobiographies are arranged in chronological order. In other words, the events in them are presented in order of occurrence, from first to last. Sometimes writers of essays also present their ideas in chronological order. This is what Isaac Asimov has done in his "Introduction" to *Fantastic Creatures.* The following are ideas from Asimov's "Introduction." Copy these ideas onto a separate sheet of paper. Then, number them in order of occurrence.

People realized that life probably does not exist on the other planets and moons in the solar system.

Increased exploration of the earth led to the realization that mermaids, centaurs, and similar imaginary creatures did not exist.

Early peoples imagined a world full of fantastic creatures, including mermaids, centaurs, and sphinxes.

People began to imagine that the solar system was populated by fantastic creatures.

Developing Vocabulary

Using the Dictionary. Many of the animals in this selection, both real and imaginary, may be new to you. Look up each of the following animals in a dictionary. Then match each animal on the left with the correct characteristic on the right. Record your answers on a separate sheet of paper.

1. armadillo
2. narwhal
3. platypus
4. unicorn
5. harpy
6. centaur

a. a man's head and trunk; a horse's body and legs
b. a single horn growing from the center of its forehead
c. the head and body of a woman; the wings, tail, and claws of a bird
d. an armorlike covering of bony plate
e. a tail like a beaver's
f. a long, spiral-shaped tusk

Developing Writing Skills

Describing an Imaginary Creature. In one paragraph describe a "fantastic creature" from your own imagination. Use language that explains what your creature looks like and that indicates the texture and feel of the animal.

Before you begin, decide what kind of creature yours will be. Will it be magical? frightening? courageous? Then, in your prewriting notes, write words and phrases that describe the creature. As you write and revise your paragraph, refer to the guidelines in **Using the Process of Writing** on pages 614–623.

The Weasel

Sally Carrighar

Night's end had come, with its interlude of peace, on the animal trails. The scents that lay like vines across the forest floor were faded now and uninteresting. Hungry eyes had ceased their watch of the moonlight splashes and the plumy, shimmering treetops. No heart had caught with fear when a twig fell or a pebble rolled, for most of the nocturnal hunters had returned to their dens or ignored one another in a truce of weariness.

From the frail defense of an oak leaf, a deer mouse stared at a passing coyote, sensing its safety by the mechanical tread of the great paws. A frog and an owl at opposite ends of the same tree closed their eyes. A black bear, trampling a new bed at the base of a cedar, broke into the burrow of a ground squirrel. With heavy eyes he saw it leap to a rock pile; then he made a last slow turn and curled himself against the trunk.

The Weasel was not tired and never joined a truce. She was stung by only a sharper fury when she saw the darkness seeping away beneath the trees. On the hillside where she hunted with her young, she suddenly pulled herself up, sweeping the slope with her nose

and eyes, trying to cup the forest in her ears, listening for the sound of a chirp, a breath, or an earth plug being pushed into a burrow. There was silence — proof that all the quick feet had been folded into furry flanks. She and her kits were alone in a deserted world.

The Weasel too was leading her family home, but she had stopped to try to stir up one more chase. She had chosen a slope that never furnished much excitement. The ground was a clear, smooth bed of pine and sequoia needles, with no underbrush where victims might be hiding. Even the odors beneath the Weasel's nose were of little help, for here no large obstructions, no fallen logs or gullies, had gathered the scent threads into strands. Still she whipped across the surface, vainly searching. It was not that she needed food after the night's good hunting. She was a squirrel's length stripped to a mouse's width and was no glutton. But she was driven by insatiable hungers of the nerves.

Now she has caught the scent of a chipmunk, redolent and sweet. Perhaps it will lead her to the chipmunk's nest. She bounds along the path of odor with her tense tail high. But

here is the trail of a second chipmunk crossing the first. The Weasel stops, confused. Now she follows one trail, now the other. Back and forth across the slope, the odors weave a record of two chipmunks chasing each other. But where are the small, warm bodies that left the tracings of delicious fragrance? The Weasel turns in her own tracks, comes to an angry stop. Her five young watch her. What will she do now? She'll forget the chipmunks. She stands erect, moving her nose through the air as she tries for a different scent.

Her nostrils trembled with her eagerness to find an animal odor in the smell of needles, loam, and cool, dank funguses. She caught the juiciness of crushed grass mixed with faint musk. Meadow mouse! Off again, she sped along the mouse's trail towards the stream

below. But the trail suddenly ended in a splash of mouse's blood and coyote scent.

The intense hope of the Weasel snapped into rage. The young ones saw her swirling over the needles like a lash. If there were another scent trail here, she'd find it. She did —the blended musk and pitchy odor left by a chickaree[1] when he jumped from the trunk of a pine. The odor line turned to a patch of cleared earth, where he had patted down a seed, and then to the base of another pine, and up. The Weasel pursued the scent to one of the higher branches and out to the tip. From there the squirrel had leapt to another tree. That was an airy trail no enemy could follow.

---

1. **chickaree** (chik′ ə rē): a reddish squirrel of the Western United States.

The Weasel came down the tree in spirals, head first, slowly. When she reached the ground, she paused, one forefoot on a root. Her eyes looked out unblinking and preoccupied. Perhaps her hungers were discouraged now—but no. Her crouched back straightened, sending her over the root in a level dash.

The Weasel young had scattered while their mother trailed the squirrel. They came flying back when a high bark told them that she had made a find at last. She was rolling over and over with the body of a chipmunk. This was not like her usual, quick death blow; again she drove her fangs through the chipmunk's fur. Then the harsh play ended. The Weasel leapt aside, allowing her kits to close in on the quiet prey.

While the brood fought over the chipmunk, their mother ran across the slope to explore the leaves beneath a dogwood thicket. By the time she returned, the shadows were thin and the chill of dawn was creeping in among the trees. Two of the young weasels munched last bites, but the others moved about slowly, only half alert, their tired legs hardly lifting their bodies above the ground. The mother bounded in among them. Her own strength still was keen, but the kits needed rest, so she called them and the little pack moved down the hill.

At the base of the slope they must cross the stream. An uprooted sugar pine leaned from one side and a silvered fir snag from the other, making a bridge with a short gap in the middle. A few times when the kits were smaller, one had missed his footing and had fallen into the water, but this time, tired though they were, all made the jump with safety.

The weasels' den was in a thicket, a few bounds off the top of Beetle Rock. To reach it they climbed the slope beyond the stream. When the Weasel approached the cliff from below, she often circled north and up through the brush at the end. Now she led the kits home the short way, over the Rock's broad, open terraces. They met no other animals until they came upon two gray mounds, strong with human scent. The Weasel dodged into a crack between the granite slabs. By connecting crevices she evaded the sleeping human forms and brought the kits to familiar ground beneath a shrubby oak. There, one by one, the six small creatures slipped into the earth.

Getting at Meaning

RECALLING

1. What is the time of day or night at the beginning of this selection?

2. The weasel is about the length of what animal? about the width of what animal?

3. What animal does the weasel attack and kill?

4. Where is the weasel's den located?

INTERPRETING

5. How does the weasel differ from other animal hunters? What does the writer mean

when she states that "The Weasel ... never joined a truce"?

6. The weasel is not hungry. However, she pauses on her way home for one last hunt. What drives her to do this?

7. How does the weasel react when she comes upon the sleeping humans? Why might she react in this way?

CRITICAL THINKING: EVALUATING

8. People who write about animals often paint sentimental portraits of their subjects. Is the portrayal of the weasel sentimental or realistic? Support your answer with evidence from the selection.

Developing Skills in Reading Literature

1. **Style.** Style is the way in which a work of literature is written. In this selection the writer presents many facts about weasels. How is this presentation of facts different from that of an encyclopedia article?

2. **Simile.** You may remember that a simile is a comparison using *like* or *as*. The following is a simile from "The Weasel":

"The scents *that lay like vines* across the forest floor were faded now."

What two things are compared in this simile? What do these two things have in common?

Developing Vocabulary

Using Context Clues. Each of the following words is taken from "The Weasel." The page number and the column where each word can be found are given in parentheses. Find each word in the selection and study the context of the word. Then, tell which of the possible defini-

tions given for each word makes the most sense in the context of the story.

1. *interlude* (page 397, column 1)
   a. a period of time between two events
   b. a special friend
   c. a crowded, bustling street
2. *nocturnal* (page 397, column 1)
   a. of or pertaining to rivers
   b. of or pertaining to the night
   c. of or pertaining to friends
3. *kits* (page 397, column 2)
   a. young trees
   b. young chipmunks
   c. young weasels
4. *redolent* (page 397, column 2)
   a. fragrant
   b. absent
   c. comical

Developing Writing Skills

Writing an Essay. Choose some animal that interests you. The animal can be a wild creature such as a fox or a muskrat or a tame one such as a horse or a cat. Write a five-paragraph essay about the animal you have chosen. During prewriting, read several encyclopedia articles and other sources of information about your animal. If possible, observe an actual animal of the kind you have chosen. Make notes about the animal's appearance, eating habits, and behavior. After you have gathered enough information, divide your notes into three groups — one for each body paragraph. Decide what you want to say in your introduction and conclusion, and jot these ideas in your prewriting notes. As you write and revise your essay, follow the directions given in **Using the Process of Writing** on pages 614–623.

BIOGRAPHY

Sally Carrighar (born 1905) spent her childhood on her grandparents' farm in Ohio. There she learned to love nature. Carrighar became a naturalist, observing and studying living things. She wrote about her observations in *One Day at Beetle Rock* and *One Day at Teton Marsh.* Carrighar also spent nine years in the Arctic. In *Wild Voice of the North* she tells the story of her association with an Eskimo sled dog.

RESEARCH SKILLS FOR *WRITING*

Using the Parts of a Book

To find the information that you need in a book, you must be familiar with its parts. These parts may include the following:

1. The title page gives the title of the book, the name of the author, the name of the publisher, and the place of publication.

2. The copyright page gives the copyright date and the Library of Congress card catalog number.

3. The foreword, preface, or introduction gives background information.

4. The table of contents lists, in order, the titles of the chapters in the book.

5. The text is the main body of the book. It may be divided into chapters or sections.

6. The appendices provide additional information such as maps, charts, tables, and graphs.

7. The glossary is a dictionary of difficult and unusual terms used in the book.

8. The index lists, alphabetically, the subjects in the book and tells the page numbers where each subject is covered.

Developing Writing Skills

Learning from a Book. Go to a library. Use the card catalog to find the call number for a book about Native Americans. Then find the book and write the following:
1. the title and the author's name
2. the publisher and the date of publication
3. the Library of Congress call number
4. the page numbers where any two of the following subjects are covered:
   a. the Pawnee
   b. hunting
   c. agriculture/farming
   d. the Iroquois Constitution
   e. Native American religions
   f. the Bureau of Indian Affairs
Choose one of these subjects and write a one-paragraph report based on the material in the book. Begin with a clear topic sentence, and present your details logically. Do not simply copy what is in the book.

See **Handbook: How To Write About Literature,** Lessons 1–4, 6.

CRITICAL THINKING

Distinguishing Facts from Opinions

Nonfiction writers make statements about the world. These statements are either facts or opinions.

A fact is a statement that can be proved true or false. The following statement is a fact:

"The average number of [lion] cubs in a litter is four." ("Cub Life")

An opinion is a statement that cannot be proved. It expresses the writer's feelings or expectations. The following statement is an opinion:

"I stood there, silently cursing the blindness and cruelty of my own kind." ("Wild Courage")

Statements of Fact.   There are two kinds of facts: definitions and observations. A definition tells what a word means:

"I named her Lustica, which means the 'Jolly One.'" ("Cub Life")

An observation tells about something that can be seen, tasted, touched, heard, or smelled:

"The marginal crevasses were mostly narrow." ("Stickeen")

Statements of Opinion. The most common kinds of opinions are judgments, statements of obligation, and predictions. A judgment is an opinion that expresses the writer's attitude toward a subject:

"There never was any good in readin' so many books." ("Mark Twain")

A statement of obligation is an opinion that tells what the writer believes should be done or should happen. Such statements usually contain words such as *should, must,* or *ought to:*

"One of these days we ought to have a Langston reunion." ("Langston Terrace")

A prediction is an opinion about what will happen in the future:

". . . we felt that if she had only ourselves as friends she would be easy to train. . . ." ("Cub Life")

Developing Critical Thinking Skills

Recognizing Facts and Opinions. The following are statements from or about the selections in the unit. On a sheet of paper, tell whether each statement is a fact or an opinion. If the statement is a fact, tell whether it is a definition or an observation. If the statement is an opinion, tell whether it is a judgment, a statement of obligation, or a prediction.

1. Rascal will continue to eat at the table for the rest of his life.
2. This dog seemed so small and worthless.
3. Frederick Douglass published a newspaper called *The North Star.*
4. Wild animals, such as coyotes, should be protected by law.
5. *Tsoch* is the Apache name for cradle.
6. The nearer we came to the Equator, the more common the flying fish became.
7. Merry-go-rounds have been popular in the United States for a hundred years.
8. "It was a pleasant hillside where I worked." ("Thoreau of Walden Pond")

UNIT 3 REVIEW

Understanding Nonfiction

RECALLING

1. Name two historical facts that a reader can learn from *Geronimo, His Own Story,* "Paul Revere," and "Carousel Horses."

INTERPRETING

2. Several of the selections in this unit deal with relationships between people and animals. Who are the human characters in the excerpts from *Stickeen, Kon-Tiki,* and *Rascal,* and "Cub Life"? What animals appear in these selections? How do the humans in these selections treat the animals? What do the humans gain from their relationships with these animals?

3. Which of the selections in this unit tell about childhood experiences? What specific childhood experiences do the writers describe? Why do you think that the writers decided to tell about these particular experiences?

4. In this unit, you have read about a number of famous people. These people include Paul Revere, Henry David Thoreau, Mary McLeod Bethune, and Frederick Douglass. What insights does the reader of these selections gain into the personal qualities of these people?

CRITICAL THINKING: EVALUATING

5. Of the people who appear in these selections, which ones do you admire most and why?

6. Which selections in this unit are similar to short stories? What specific similarities and differences exist between short stories and these nonfiction selections?

Writing About Nonfiction

Before completing this assignment, review **Using the Process of Writing** and Writing About Nonfiction starting at page 614.

Chose three people from the selections in this unit who are heroic in some way. Write a five paragraph composition defining the word *heroism* and giving as examples of heroes the people whom you have chosen. Begin by looking up the terms *hero, heroism,* and *heroic* in a dictionary. Record the definitions of these terms in your prewriting notes. Then, reread the selections about the people whom you've chosen as examples. Record their heroic actions and attributes in your notes. In the introductory paragraph of your composition, define *heroism* in your own words. In each of your body paragraphs, present one person who fulfills your definition of *hero.* In your concluding paragraph, tell why you think that it is important for people to know about the lives of heroes.

Writing Nonfiction

Before completing these assignments, review **Using the Process of Writing** on pages 614–623.

Choose one of the following subjects or one of your own and write a five paragraph essay about it. Gather information from sources such as the following: interviews, personal experience, books, magazines, newspaper articles, and television or radio programs.

  a. what a person can learn by keeping a pet
  b. the best (or worst) television programs of the current season
  c. why schools should (or should not) abolish letter grades
  d. the early life of a famous contemporary person such as a politician, a sports figure, or an entertainer.

UNIT 4

Poetry

BEASTS OF THE SEA (detail), 1950. *Henri Matisse. National Gallery of Art, Washington, D.C. Ailsa Mellon Bruce Fund.*

Introducing Poetry

What Is Poetry?

The first three units in this book are made up of works written in prose. Prose is writing in paragraphs. Poetry differs from prose in that it is presented on the page in lines. Poetry also depends more on sound devices, such as rhythm and rhyme. Finally, poetry relies more heavily on figurative language. Figurative words and phrases communicate ideas beyond the literal meanings of words.

The Elements of Poetry

Sound. Like songs, poems use rhyme, rhythm, and repetition to create special sound effects.

Shape. Poets often play with the shapes of words on a page to suggest meaning. In this unit, for example, one poet runs together the words *eddieandbill.* The new word suggests the closeness of two friends. Another poet presents her poem about a "Sidewalk Racer" in the form of a skateboard.

Image. Poets present vivid pictures through sensory images. Images are words that appeal to sight, hearing, touch, taste, and smell.

Idea. Like other works of literature, poems are written to communicate ideas. The images, shapes, and sounds of a poem work together to express the poet's meaning.

How To Read a Poem

Begin by reading a poem quickly to find any unfamiliar words. Look up these words in a dictionary, for every word in a poem is important. Then, read the poem aloud and listen to its sounds. Finally, read the poem silently. Think about how its sounds, shapes, and images suggest its meaning.

Previewing the Unit

Reading the Selections

The selections in this unit are in four sections: Sound and Meaning, Shape and Meaning, Images and Meaning, and Ideas in Poetry.

Using the Study Questions

Following each selection are exercises. They will help you to develop your reading, vocabulary, and writing skills.

Getting at Meaning.   This section has three types of questions. The **RECALLING** questions will help you to remember each selection. The **INTERPRETING** questions will help you understand the selection. The **CRITICAL THINKING** questions will help you in evaluating the selection and in relating it to your own experiences.

Developing Skills in Reading Literature.   These exercises will teach you the literary techniques used by poets.

Developing Vocabulary.   These exercises will teach you to use synonyms and antonyms and to use a thesaurus.

Developing Writing Skills.   This section has two kinds of writing assignments. In one you will write about the poetry that you have read. In the other you will use the literary techniques that you have learned.

Using the Unit Study Materials

Research Skills for Writing.   This feature will teach you how to use an encyclopedia.

Critical Thinking.   The critical thinking exercises will teach you how to make inferences about literary works.

Unit Review.   The unit review will help you to recall, interpret, and think critically about the selections. The review also will give you a chance to use the writing skills that you have learned.

Sound and Meaning

The Music of Poetry

Songs and poems are quite similar. Both are composed of words, and both depend on sound to suggest meanings and emotions. When studying a poem, always read it aloud at least once. This will help you to enjoy its musical qualities.

Sound Devices in Poetry

The music of poetry comes from the use of techniques such as rhyme, rhythm, and repetition. Rhyme is the repetition of syllable sounds at the ends of words. Rhythm is the beat of a poem—the pattern of stressed and unstressed syllables. Repetition is the use, more than once, of a sound, a word, or a phrase.

Thinking About Sound

Listen to the patterns of sound in these lines:

We'll grind and break and bind and take

and plunder ye and pound ye!

In the first line, *grind* rhymes with *bind,* and *break* rhymes with *take.* In the second line, the poet repeats the words *and* and *ye* and the *p* sound in *plunder* and *pound.* The words marked with accents (ˊ) are all stressed, creating a powerful rhythmical pattern. As you read each poem in this section, listen for patterns of sound like these.

GREEN VIOLINIST, 1918. *Marc Chagall. The Solomon R. Guggenheim Museum, New York.*

A poem is nothing without you.

"I," Says the Poem

Eve Merriam

"I," says the poem arrogantly,
"I am a cloud,
I am a tree.

I am a city,
I am the sea,   5
I am a golden
Mystery."

How can it be?

A poem is written
by some someone,   10
someone like you,
or someone like me

who blows his nose,
who breaks shoelaces,
who hates and loves,   15
who loses gloves,
who eats, who weeps,
who laughs, who sleeps,

an ordinary he or she
extraordinary as you or me   20

whose thoughts stretch high
as clouds in the sky,

whose memories
root deep as trees,

whose feelings choke   25
like city smoke,

whose fears and joys in waves redound
like the ocean's tidal sound,

who daily solves a mystery:
each hour is new, what will it be?   30

"I," says the poem matter-of-factly,
"I am a cloud,
I am a tree.

I am a city,
I am the sea,   35

I am a golden
Mystery."

But, adds the poem silently,
I cannot speak until you come.
Reader, come, come with me.   40

MEMORY, 1870. *Elihu Vedder.*
Los Angeles County Museum of Art, Mrs. William
Preston Harrison Collection.

Getting at Meaning

RECALLING

1. In the first seven lines of this poem, a poem is speaking. What, according to the first line, is the poem's attitude?

2. In line seven, the poem claims that it is a "golden Mystery." The writer then asks a question. What is this question?

3. The writer points out in lines 9–19 that poets are just ordinary people. According to the writer, what ordinary things do poets do?

4. The writer points out in lines 20–30 that poets are also extraordinary in several ways. How high, according to the writer, do a poet's thoughts stretch? What are a poet's memories compared to? A poet's feelings, fears, and joys? What mystery does a poet solve daily?

5. In lines 31–37, the poem repeats its opening comments. However, the poem's tone of voice has changed. How, according to line 31, does the poem speak these lines?

INTERPRETING

6. In lines 38–40, the poem admits that it is

dependent on readers. Why does a poem need readers?

7. Why is the poem no longer arrogant? What did the writer point out to the poem? How did the writer's comments change the poem's attitude?

CRITICAL THINKING: APPLYING

8. In line 40, the poem invites you to read poetry. Are you willing to accept this invitation? In what sense do poems need you?

Developing Skills in Reading Literature

1. **Poetry.** It is impossible to generalize about all poetry because poems vary so widely. Most poems are arranged in lines rather than in sentences or paragraphs. Many poems use figurative language and sound devices, such as rhythm and rhyme, to suggest complex feelings and thoughts in a few words. Some poems, however, do not use figurative language, and some use no more rhythm or rhyme than does ordinary speech. Although poetry itself cannot be defined once and for all, the techniques that poets use can be defined and discussed. Choose a passage from one of the selections in the nonfiction unit. Compare this nonfiction passage with Eve Merriam's "I, Says the Poem." Then, answer the following questions:

a. What difference do you notice in the ways in which the two selections are presented on the page?

b. What differences are there between the ways in which the two selections sound when read aloud?

2. **Rhyme.** Rhyme is the repetition of syllable sounds at the ends of words. For example, the word *stone* rhymes with the word *own*. Look at the first twelve lines of this poem. Which words in these lines rhyme with the word *arrogantly?*

3. **Speaker.** The speaker in a poem is the voice that talks to the reader. The speaker and the poet are not necessarily the same. In fact, a poet sometimes creates a speaker with a distinct identity. Who is the speaker of the first seven lines of this poem?

4. **Metaphor.** A metaphor is a direct comparison between two unlike things that have something in common. To what four things does the poem compare itself in the first five lines?

5. **Simile.** A simile is a comparison using *like* or *as*. What four similes does the writer use in lines 21–28 of this poem? What things are compared in each of these similes?

Developing Writing Skills

Writing a Poem. Reread the opening lines in which the poem uses metaphors to describe itself. Then, write a poem of six lines describing yourself in the same manner. Begin each line of your poem with the words *I am a* . . . . In each line, compare yourself to a person, place, or thing that is like you in some way.

Copyright © Layle Silbert

BIOGRAPHY

Eve Merriam (born 1916) loves secondhand bookstores, traveling, big cities, swimming, and most of all, writing. Although she has written advertising copy, radio scripts, and song lyrics, her favorite kind of writing is poetry. She has published many books, including *Family Circle, There Is No Rhyme for Silver,* and *Growing Up Female in America.*

Where the Sidewalk Ends

Shel Silverstein

There is a place where the sidewalk ends
And before the street begins,
And there the grass grows soft and white,
And there the sun burns crimson bright,
And there the moon-bird rests from his flight   5
To cool in the peppermint wind.

Let us leave this place where the smoke blows black
And the dark street winds and bends.
Past the pits where the asphalt flowers grow
We shall walk with a walk that is measured and slow,   10
And watch where the chalk-white arrows go
To the place where the sidewalk ends.

Yes we'll walk with a walk that is measured and slow,
And we'll go where the chalk-white arrows go,
For the children, they mark, and the children, they know   15
The place where the sidewalk ends.

EAST TWELFTH STREET, 1946. *Ben Shahn. Collection of Albert Hackett.*

Getting at Meaning

RECALLING

1. What four things from nature does the speaker name in the first stanza?

2. What three things made by people does the speaker name in the second stanza?

3. What two words in line 10 describe the walk to the place where the sidewalk ends?

4. How do children help others find the place where the sidewalk ends?

INTERPRETING

5. The first two stanzas describe two different places. Which place is associated with light? Which one with darkness?

6. What details suggest that the place where the sidewalk ends is not real but imaginary?

7. Is the speaker an adult or a child?

CRITICAL THINKING: APPLYING

8. This poem not only contrasts two different places but also suggests a larger contrast between two different worlds, that of adults and that of children. What do you think adults can gain from entering the world of children?

Developing Skills in Reading Literature

1. **Rhythm.** Rhythm is the pattern of stressed and unstressed syllables in a poem.

You hear the rhythm, or beat, when you read a poem aloud. Read each line of "Where the Sidewalk Ends" aloud. On a sheet of paper, note the number of beats in each line. Which lines have the same number of beats?

2. **Theme.** The theme is the main idea of a work of literature. Often the theme is a message about human nature. To discover the theme of this poem, first identify the speaker's attitude toward the place where the sidewalk ends. What is this attitude? What is the speaker saying about the imaginary worlds created by children?

3. **Sensory Images.** Sensory images are words and phrases that appeal to the five senses—sight, touch, taste, hearing, and smell. The following lines from the first stanza all contain sensory images:

> the grass grows soft and white
> the sun burns crimson bright
> the moon-bird rests from his flight
> the peppermint wind

Which sensory images appeal to the senses of both sight and touch? Which appeal to the senses of touch and taste? Which appeals only to the sense of sight?

Choose three images from the second stanza and write them on a sheet of paper. Then, explain the sense appeal of each image.

Developing Writing Skills

Using the Senses in Writing. Writers of children's stories often create interesting imaginary worlds such as the land of Oz in *The Wizard of Oz* and Never-Never Land in *Peter Pan.* Imagine that you are a writer of children's stories. Write a paragraph that describes an imaginary land, a place meant for children. Your paragraph should contain at least four sensory images that will help your reader form a vivid mental picture of your imaginary place. Use at least two images that appeal to the sense of sight and two that appeal to other senses.

Begin by writing the name of your imaginary land in your prewriting notes. Then, jot down some words and phrases to describe this land. Include the sensory images that you want to use in your paragraph.

Arrange your details in the order that you will present them in the paragraph. See page 617 of the writing handbook for suggestions about ways to organize your details. When you finish your first draft, revise your paragraph, following the suggestions for revision on pages 621–623 in **Using the Process of Writing.**

B I O G R A P H Y

Shel Silverstein (born 1932) draws cartoons, plays the guitar, and writes stories, poems, and songs. Many of his collections of poems and drawings, such as *A Light in the Attic,* are popular with both children and adults. He has written many books specifically for children, including *Uncle Shelby's a Giraffe and a Half* and *The Giving Tree.* Silverstein's one-act play, *The Lady or the Tiger,* was produced in New York City and starred Richard Dreyfuss. His song "A Boy Named Sue" became a hit single in a recording by Johnny Cash. When he isn't traveling around the country, Silverstein lives on a houseboat in Sausalito, California.

Macavity is a master criminal.

Macavity: The Mystery Cat

T. S. Eliot

Macavity's a Mystery Cat: he's called the Hidden Paw—
For he's the master criminal who can defy the Law.
He's the bafflement[1] of Scotland Yard,[2] the Flying Squad's despair:[3]
For when they reach the scene of crime—*Macavity's not there!*

Macavity, Macavity, there's no one like Macavity,   5
He's broken every human law, he breaks the law of gravity.
His powers of levitation[4] would make a fakir[5] stare,
And when you reach the scene of crime—*Macavity's not there!*
You may seek him in the basement, you may look up in the air—
But I tell you once and once again, *Macavity's not there!*   10

Macavity's a ginger cat, he's very tall and thin;
You would know him if you saw him, for his eyes are sunken in.
His brow is deeply lined with thought, his head is highly domed;
His coat is dusty from neglect, his whiskers are uncombed.
He sways his head from side to side, with movements like a snake;   15
And when you think he's half asleep, he's always wide awake.

---

1. **bafflement:** puzzle.
2. **Scotland Yard:** the London police department, especially the detective bureau.
3. **Flying Squad's despair:** Macavity is a problem even for the special emergency police unit.
4. **levitation** (lev′ ə tā′ shən): the illusion of being able to raise oneself into the air.
5. **fakir** (fā′ kər): a wonder worker.

Macavity, Macavity, there's no one like Macavity,
For he's a fiend in feline shape, a monster of depravity.
You may meet him in a by-street, you may see him in the square—
But when a crime's discovered, then *Macavity's not there!*   20

He's outwardly respectable. (They say he cheats at cards.)
And his footprints are not found in any file of Scotland Yard's.
And when the larder's looted, or the jewel-case is rifled,[6]
Or when the milk is missing, or another Peke's[7] been stifled,[8]
Or the greenhouse glass is broken, and the trellis past repair—   25
Ay, there's the wonder of the thing! *Macavity's not there!*

And when the Foreign Office finds a Treaty's gone astray,
Or the Admiralty lose some plans and drawings by the way,
There may be a scrap of paper in the hall or on the stair—
But it's useless to investigate—*Macavity's not there!*   30
And when the loss has been disclosed, the Secret Service say:
"It *must* have been Macavity!"—but he's a mile away.
You'll be sure to find him resting, or a-licking of his thumbs,
Or engaged in doing complicated long division sums.

Macavity, Macavity, there's no one like Macavity,   35
There never was a Cat of such deceitfulness and suavity.[9]
He always has an alibi, and one or two to spare:
At whatever time the deed took place—MACAVITY WASN'T THERE!
And they say that all the Cats whose wicked deeds are widely known
(I might mention Mungojerrie, I might mention Griddlebone)   40
Are nothing more than agents for the Cat who all the time
Just controls their operations: the Napoleon[10] of Crime!

---

6. **rifled:** ransacked or stolen.
7. **Peke:** clipped word for *Pekingese,* a small dog with long hair.
8. **stifled:** prevented from doing something.
9. **suavity** (swäv' ə tē): smooth, polished politeness.
10. **Napoleon** (nə pō' lē ən): Emperor of France (1804–15). As a military leader, Napoleon was powerful, clever, and seemed to be unconquerable.

Getting at Meaning

RECALLING

1. What does Macavity do that puzzles the police and others?

2. List six words and phrases from the poem that describe Macavity's appearance.

3. Who are Mungojerrie and Griddlebone?

INTERPRETING

4. Which of Macavity's crimes are typical of an ordinary cat? Which are not typical?

5. What do the phrases "the Hidden Paw" and "the Napoleon of Crime" suggest about Macavity?

6. Explain the meaning of this line: "His powers of levitation would make a fakir stare."

CRITICAL THINKING: EVALUATING

7. How well does the poet succeed in conveying the extraordinary qualities of Macavity?

Developing Skills in Reading Literature

1. **Rhyme.** Rhyme is the repetition of syllable sounds at the ends of words. For example, the word *stranger* rhymes with the word *danger*. In this poem, what three words rhyme with *Macavity*?

2. **Hyperbole.** Hyperbole is exaggeration for emphasis. For example, to say that someone is "as strong as an ox" exaggerates that person's strength. The speaker in this poem uses hyperbole to tell about Macavity's criminal feats. For example, the speaker says, "He's broken every human law, he breaks the law of gravity." On a sheet of paper, copy five more examples of hyperbole from the poem. Does the poet's use of hyperbole add to the humor or to the seriousness of the poem? Explain your answer.

Developing Vocabulary

Synonyms. A synonym is a word that means the same, or nearly the same, as another word. Find a synonym in the poem for each of the following words. The number of the line in which the synonym is found follows each word. Write the synonyms on a separate sheet of paper.

cellar (l.9)	search (l.30)
forehead (l.13)	revealed (l.31)
devil (l.18)	excuse (l.37)
agreement (l.27)	directs (l.42)

Developing Writing Skills

Combining Details To Make a Single Impression. Write a paragraph about a cat, real or imaginary. Choose or make up an unusual name for your subject. Before you begin your prewriting notes, decide on one impression that you want to convey. In your prewriting notes, tell what impression you want to create, and list some sensory images and other details that you can use to create this impression. Review the steps for writing a topic sentence explained on page 619 in **Using the Process of Writing.** Then, write a topic sentence that states your impression of the cat. Develop the body of your paragraph with details taken from your prewriting notes. Revise your paragraph according to the guidelines presented on pages 621–623 in the writing handbook.

HORRIBLE FIN D'UN POISSON ROUGE (detail), date unknown. *Theophile Alexandre Steinlen.*
From Des Chats: Images Sans Parole. *The Metropolitan Museum of Art, New York.*
Gift of Mrs. Edward C. Moen, 1961. (61.687.12)

BIOGRAPHY

T. S. Eliot (1888–1965) was one of this century's most influential poets. He was born in St. Louis, Missouri, and received two degrees from Harvard. In 1914, he settled in London where he became a teacher, lecturer, editor, and publisher. In 1927, he became a British citizen. His first major work, "The Love Song of J. Alfred Prufrock," was published in 1917. *The Wasteland* followed in 1922. The striking originality of these pieces caused an uproar. The literary community applauded, despised, imitated, and criticized the work as they did much of Eliot's other writing. Praise won out, however, and Eliot was awarded the 1948 Nobel Prize "for his work as a trailblazing pioneer of modern poetry." Eliot also wrote plays, literary criticism, and essays.

Macavity: The Mystery Cat   419

The dwarfs and the giants march to battle.

Narnian Suite

C. S. Lewis

1
March for Strings, Kettledrums, and Sixty-three Dwarfs

With plucking pizzicato and the prattle of the kettledrum
We're trotting into battle mid a clatter of accouterment;
Our beards are big as periwigs and trickle with opopanax,
And trinketry and treasure twinkle out on every part of us—
     (Scrape! Tap! The fiddle and the kettledrum).   5

The chuckle-headed humans think we're only pretty poppetry
And all our battle-tackle nothing more than pretty bric-a-brac;
But a little shrub has prickles, and they'll soon be in a pickle if
A scud of dwarfish archery has crippled all their cavalry—
     (Whizz! Twang! The quarrel and the javelin).   10

And when the tussle thickens we can writhe and wriggle under it;
Then dagger-point'll tickle 'em, and grab and grip'll grapple 'em.
And trap and trick'll trouble 'em and tackle 'em and topple 'em
Till they're huddled, all be-diddled, in the middle of our caperings—
     (Dodge! Jump! The wriggle and the summersault).   15

When we've scattered 'em and peppered 'em with pebbles from our catapults
We'll turn again in triumph and by crannies and by crevices
Go back to where the capitol and cradle of our people is,
Our forges and our furnaces, the caverns of the earth—
     (Gold! Fire! The anvil and the smithying).   20

2

March for Drum, Trumpet, and Twenty-one Giants

With stumping stride in pomp and pride
We come to thump and floor ye;
We'll bump your lumpish heads to-day
And tramp your ramparts into clay,
And as we stamp and romp and play   25
Our trump'll blow before us—
(crescendo)   Oh tramp it, tramp it, tramp it, trumpet, trumpet blow before us!

We'll grind and break and bind and take
And plunder ye and pound ye!
With trundled rocks and bludgeon blow,   30
You dunderheads, we'll dint ye so
You'll blunder and run blind, as though
By thunder stunned, around us—
By thunder, thunder, thunder, thunder stunned around us!

Ho! tremble town and tumble down   35
And crumble shield and saber!
Your kings will mumble and look pale,
Your horses stumble or turn tail,
Your skimble-scamble counsels fail,
So rumble drum belabored—   40
(diminuendo)   Oh rumble, rumble, rumble, rumble, rumble drum belabored!

Getting at Meaning

RECALLING

1. The poem is divided into two main parts. What is the title of the first part? the second?

2. Where are the dwarfs and the giants marching?

3. What do the dwarfs plan to do to defeat their enemy? What do the giants plan to do?

4. Where do the dwarfs live?

INTERPRETING

5. In the second stanza, the speakers state that humans do not take the dwarfs seriously. As a result, the dwarfs take what attitude toward humans?

6. What attitude do the giants take toward their enemy?

CRITICAL THINKING: EVALUATING

7. The dwarfs rely on cunning, the giants on brute force. Which do you think is the better strategy?

Developing Skills in Reading Literature

1. **Stanza.** A stanza is a group of lines that form a unit in a poem. The stanzas of a poem are usually separated on the printed page by a space. How many stanzas are there in Part 1 of "Narnian Suite"? in Part 2?

2. **Rhythm.** Rhythm is the pattern of stressed and unstressed syllables in a poem. Reread the first stanza in Part 1 of "Narnian Suite." Tap out the rhythm as you read. Next, reread the first stanza in Part 2. Again, tap out the rhythm. How do the rhythms differ? Why has the poet created a different rhythm for the dwarfs than for the giants?

Speaking and Listening. Read the entire poem aloud. Experiment with the pace, or speed, of your reading. How fast do you think Part 1 should be read? How fast should Part 2 be read? How does the rhythm of each part affect the pace with which it can be read?

3. **Alliteration.** Alliteration is the repetition of consonant sounds at the beginnings of words. In "Narnian Suite," Lewis repeats the *p* sound in *p*lucking, *p*izzicato, and *p*rattle. Find five more examples of alliteration in this poem.

4. **Repetition.** Poets often repeat vowel and consonant sounds to give their work a musical quality. The repetition of sounds at the ends of words is called rhyme. As exercise 3 explains, the repetition of consonant sounds at the beginnings of words is called alliteration. However, these are not the only kinds of repetition that poets use. Sometimes poets repeat vowel sounds within words. In "Narnian Suite," for example, Lewis repeats the *a* sound in b*a*ttle and t*a*ckle. Poets also sometimes repeat consonant sounds within words. Lewis does this in the words tro*tt*ing, ba*tt*le, and cla*tt*er. Find one more example in the poem of each of these two kinds of repetition: repetition of vowel sounds within words and repetition of consonant sounds within words.

5. **Title.** The title of a literary work often suggests its meaning and its form, or structure. *Narnia* is the name of an imaginary world created by Lewis for his series of books, *The Chronicles of Narnia*. A *suite* is a musical composition made up of several movements of dance music, each with its own characteristic rhythms. Why would Lewis have called his poem "Narnian Suite"? What does this title suggest about the content of the poem? What does it suggest about the poem's structure?

Developing Vocabulary

Using a Thesaurus. A thesaurus is a kind of dictionary that lists the synonyms of a word. Look up the following words in a thesaurus. Find three synonyms, or words that have almost the same meaning, for each. Write the words and synonyms on a sheet of paper.

tremble	clatter	plunder
tumble	writhe	

BIOGRAPHY

C. S. Lewis (1898–1963) was born in Belfast, Ireland, and spent his early years in a big house with books stacked in every possible place. "My father bought all the books he read and never got rid of any of them," Lewis once said. Lewis was an instructor at Oxford and Cambridge Universities, where he gained a reputation as a brilliant scholar. He wrote over thirty books that ranged in subject matter from science fiction to literary criticism to religion. Young people know him best for his series of seven books, *The Chronicles of Narnia*.

This story poem is about a famous American folk hero.

Johnny Appleseed

American Folk Tale

Retold by **Rosemary Carr Benét**

Of Jonathan Chapman
Two things are known
That he loved apples,
That he walked alone.

At seventy-odd   5
He was gnarled as could be,
But ruddy and sound
As a good apple tree.

For fifty years over
Of harvest and dew,   10
He planted his apples
Where no apples grew.

The winds of the prairie
Might blow through his rags,
But he carried his seeds   15
In the best deerskin bags.

From old Ashtabula
To frontier Fort Wayne,
He planted and pruned
And he planted again.   20

He had not a hat
To encumber his head.
He wore a tin pan
On his white hair instead.

He nested with owl,   25
And with bear cub and 'possum,
And knew all his orchards
Root, tendril, and blossom.

A fine old man,
As ripe as a pippin,   30
His heart still light,
And his step still skipping.

The stalking Indian,
The beast in its lair
Did no hurt   35
While he was there.

For they could tell,
As wild things can,
That Jonathan Chapman
Was God's own man.   40

Why did he do it?
We do not know.
He wished that apples
Might root and grow.

He has no statue.   45
He has no tomb.
He has his apple trees
Still in bloom.

Consider, consider,
Think well upon   50
The marvelous story
Of Appleseed John.

Getting at Meaning

RECALLING

1. For fifty years, what did Jonathan Chapman do?

2. Where did Chapman travel?

3. Why did wild things not harm Chapman?

INTERPRETING

4. Did Chapman care more for himself or for his seeds? Cite lines from the poem to support your opinion.

5. According to the poem, Johnny Appleseed doesn't have statues or a tomb to commemorate him. What, instead, serve as his monuments?

6. Why does the speaker use two names for the hero in the poem?

CRITICAL THINKING: APPLYING

7. John Chapman planted trees that bore fruit long after he was gone. In other words, he worked for the benefit of others, not for his own personal gain. What other people can you think

of who have acted so selflessly? What does a person gain from working for the benefit of others?

Developing Skills in Reading Literature

1. **Stanza.** A stanza is a group of lines that form a unit in a poem. How many stanzas are there in "Johnny Appleseed"? How many lines are there in each stanza?

2. **Rhyme Scheme.** The rhyme scheme of a poem is the pattern of rhymes at the ends of lines. Which lines rhyme in each stanza of "Johnny Appleseed"?

3. **Ballad.** A ballad is a poem, with four-line or six-line stanzas, that tells a story. Ballads usually tell about people who have had amazing adventures or who have performed outstanding deeds. Does "Johnny Appleseed" have all of the characteristics of a ballad? Explain.

4. **Folk Tale.** A folk tale is a story that is handed down, usually by word of mouth, among the people of a region. "Johnny Appleseed" is subtitled "American Folk Tale." This is because the story of Johnny Appleseed has been told and retold orally for many years.

What makes this story special or interesting enough to have become a popular folk tale? In other words, why do you think so many people have found this story worthwhile?

Developing Writing Skills

Writing a Poem. Write a poem about someone whom you admire. Use "Johnny Appleseed" as your model. Begin by jotting down details about the person in your prewriting notes. Then, write out what you want to say about the person in two or three paragraphs, each of which presents a single main idea. Next, reread two or three stanzas of "Johnny Appleseed," noting their rhyme scheme and the number of beats, or stresses, in each line. Finally, rewrite your paragraphs in three four-line stanzas that follow the rhyme scheme *a b c b*. Try to use an equal number of beats, or stresses, in each line. To rewrite the paragraphs as poetry, you will have to experiment with different ways of expressing your ideas. Try different combinations of words until you find ones that fit the rhyme scheme and rhythms that you want your poem to have.

BIOGRAPHY

Rosemary Carr Benét (1900–1962) was covering Paris for the *Chicago Tribune* and *The London Daily Mail* when she met and married a young American poet, Stephen Vincent Benét. After returning to the United States, the Benéts shared an office in New York City and a mutual interest in American history. Together they wrote *A Book of Americans,* a volume of poems about famous historical figures.

In 1775, Americans are poised on the brink of rebellion against England.

Paul Revere's Ride

Henry Wadsworth Longfellow

Listen my children, and you shall hear
Of the midnight ride of Paul Revere,
On the eighteenth of April, in seventy-five;
Hardly a man is now alive
Who remembers that famous day and year.   5

He said to his friend, "If the British march
By land or sea from the town tonight—
Hang a lantern aloft in the belfry[1] arch
Of the North Church tower as a signal light,—
One, if by land, and two, if by sea;   10
And I on the opposite shore will be,
Ready to ride and spread the alarm
Through every Middlesex village and farm,
For the country folk to be up and to arm."

Then he said, "Good night!" and with muffled oar   15
Silently rowed to the Charlestown shore,
Just as the moon rose over the bay,
Where swinging wide at her moorings lay
The *Somerset,* British man-of-war;
A phantom ship, with each mast and spar   20
Across the moon like a prison bar,
And a huge black hulk, that was magnified
By its own reflection in the tide.

---

1. **belfry** (bel′ frē): bell tower.

Meanwhile, his friend, through alley and street,
Wanders and watches with eager ears,   25
Till in the silence around him he hears
The muster of men at the barrack door,
The sound of arms, and the tramp of feet,
And the measured tread of the grenadiers,[2]
Marching down to their boats on the shore.   30

Then he climbed the tower of the old North Church,
By the wooden stairs, with stealthy tread,
To the belfry-chamber overhead,
And startled the pigeons from their perch
On the somber rafters, that round him made   35
Masses and moving shapes of shade,—
By the trembling ladder, steep and tall,
To the highest window in the wall,
Where he paused to listen and look down
A moment on the roofs of the town,   40
And the moonlight flowing over all.

Beneath, in the churchyard, lay the dead,
In their night-encampment on the hill,
Wrapped in silence so deep and still
That he could hear, like a sentinel's tread,   45
The watchful night wind, as it went
Creeping along from tent to tent,
And seeming to whisper, "All is well!"
A moment only he feels the spell
Of the place and the hour, and the secret dread   50
Of the lonely belfry and the dead;
For suddenly all his thoughts are bent
On a shadowy something far away,
Where the river widens to meet the bay,—
A line of black that bends and floats   55
On the rising tide, like a bridge of boats.

Meanwhile, impatient to mount and ride,
Booted and spurred, with a heavy stride

---

2. **grenadiers** (gren′ ə dirz): soldiers in the British Grenadier Guards.

On the opposite shore walked Paul Revere.
Now he patted his horse's side, 60
Now gazed at the landscape far and near,
Then, impetuous, stamped the earth,
And turned and tightened his saddle-girth;
But mostly he watched with eager search
The belfry-tower of the Old North Church, 65
As it rose above the graves on the hill,
Lonely and spectral and somber and still.
And lo! as he looks, on the belfry's height
A glimmer, and then a gleam of light!
He springs to the saddle, the bridle he turns, 70
But lingers and gazes, till full on his sight
A second lamp in the belfry burns!

A hurry of hoofs in a village street,
A shape in the moonlight, a bulk in the dark,
And beneath, from the pebbles, in passing, a spark 75
Struck out by a steed flying fearless and fleet:
That was all! And yet, through the gloom and the light
The fate of a nation was riding that night;
And the spark struck out by that steed, in his flight,
Kindled the land into flame with its heat. 80

He has left the village and mounted the steep,
And beneath him, tranquil and broad and deep,
Is the Mystic,[3] meeting the ocean tides;
And under the alders that skirt its edge,
Now soft on the sand, now loud on the ledge, 85
Is heard the tramp of his steed as he rides.

It was twelve by the village clock,
When he crossed the bridge into Medford town.
He heard the crowing of the cock,
And the barking of the farmer's dog, 90
And felt the damp of the river fog,
That rises after the sun goes down.
It was one by the village clock,

---

3. **Mystic:** a river.

When he galloped into Lexington.
He saw the gilded weathercock   95
Swing in the moonlight as he passed.
And the meeting-house windows, blank and bare,
Gaze at him with a spectral glare,
As if they already stood aghast
At the bloody work they would look upon.   100

MIDNIGHT RIDE OF PAUL REVERE, 1931. *Grant Wood.*
The Metropolitan Museum of Art, New York. Arthur H. Hearn Fund, 1950. © Estate of Grant Wood. (50.117)

It was two by the village clock,
When he came to the bridge in Concord town.
He heard the bleating of the flock,
And the twitter of birds among the trees,
And felt the breath of the morning breeze   105
Blowing over the meadows brown.
And one was safe and asleep in his bed
Who at the bridge would be first to fall,
Who that day would be lying dead,
Pierced by a British musket-ball.   110

You know the rest. In the books you have read,
How the British Regulars fired and fled,—
How the farmers gave them ball for ball,
From behind each fence and farmyard wall,
Chasing the red-coats down the lane,   115
Then crossing the fields to emerge again
Under the trees at the turn of the road,
And only pausing to fire and load.

So through the night rode Paul Revere;
And so through the night went his cry of alarm   120
To every Middlesex village and farm,—
A cry of defiance and not of fear,
A voice in the darkness, a knock at the door,
And a word that shall echo forevermore!

For, borne on the night-wind of the Past,   125
Through all our history, to the last,
In the hour of darkness and peril and need,
The people will waken and listen to hear
The hurrying hoof-beats of that steed,
And the midnight message of Paul Revere.   130

Paul Revere's Ride, April 18–19, 1775

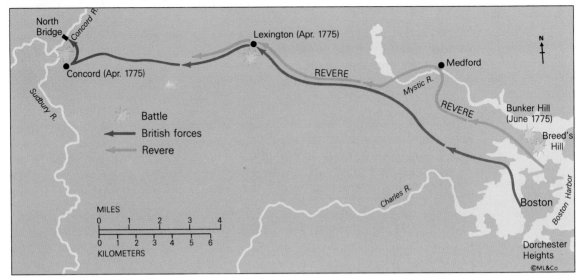

Reading a Map. The map shows Paul Revere's route as he rode westward. Notice the map scale in the lower left corner of the map. Take a piece of paper or string and place it along the scale to get a measurement of four miles. Then place your measurement along Paul Revere's route to find out how many miles he rode. Also calculate the distance in kilometers.

Getting at Meaning

RECALLING

1. On what day in 1775 did Paul Revere's "midnight ride" occur?

2. What is the *Somerset?*

3. How many lamps does Revere see in the belfry?

4. Through what villages does Revere pass? How long does it take him to get from one village to the next?

INTERPRETING

5. In what sense is Revere's "midnight message" a "cry of defiance"?

6. In line 78 the speaker says, "The fate of a nation was riding that night." What does the speaker mean?

Developing Skills in Reading Literature

1. **Rhythm.** Rhythm is the pattern of stressed and unstressed syllables in a poem. In "Paul Revere's Ride," the rhythm of the poem reflects its subject.

Speaking and Listening. Read this poem aloud, listening for the rhythm of the lines. What similarities do you notice between the rhythm and subject matter of the poem?

2. **Narrative Poem.** A narrative poem is a poem that tells a story. Like short stories, narrative poems usually contain the elements of setting, character, conflict, and plot. Are all of these elements present in "Paul Revere's Ride"? What is the setting of the poem? Who are its characters? What is its plot? What conflict does the poem tell about?

3. **Alliteration.** Alliteration is the repetition of consonant sounds at the beginnings of words. "Paul Revere's Ride" contains several examples of alliteration. For example, in line 73, Longfellow repeats the *h* sound in the words *hurry* and *hoofs*. Find two more examples of alliteration in this poem, and copy them on a sheet of paper.

4. **Personification.** Personification is the giving of human qualities to an object, animal, or idea. What does Longfellow personify in lines 45–48? in lines 97–100? What human qualities are given to nonliving things in these lines?

Developing Writing Skills

Creating a Mood. Reread lines 31–56 of the poem. These lines describe the belfry chamber of the Old North Church and the view from this chamber. Notice how Longfellow has chosen his words carefully to create a feeling, or mood, of tenseness and suspense. Revere's friend climbs with "stealthy tread." The pigeons and the rafters are "masses and moving shapes of shade." The ladder is "trembling."

The wind is "creeping along from tent to tent."

Choose a scene that you would like to describe in a paragraph. Then, choose a feeling, or mood, that you would like to create in your description. For example, you might write about a city street at night in such a way as to create a mood of fear. You might also write about a carousel in such a way as to create a mood of excitement or joy.

In your prewriting notes, list the place and the mood that you have chosen. Then, list descriptive words and phrases that will help you to create the mood. Begin your paragraph with a topic sentence that clearly identifies the place you are describing. As you write and revise your paragraph, refer to the guidelines presented in **Using the Process of Writing** found on pages 614–623.

B I O G R A P H Y

Henry Wadsworth Longfellow (1807–1882) was the most popular and respected American poet of his time. One of his long narrative poems, "The Song of Hiawatha," sold over a million copies during his life. He was the first American to have his statue placed in the Poet's Corner of London's Westminster Abbey. Longfellow was born in Portland, Maine, and graduated from Bowdoin College, where he taught for five years. Except for a few years in Europe, he spent the rest of his life in Cambridge, Massachusetts, teaching at Harvard University. His historic home, now open to the public, was George Washington's headquarters during the Revolutionary War. Some of Longfellow's best known poems are "Evangeline," "The Courtship of Miles Standish," "Paul Revere's Ride," "The Village Blacksmith," and "The Children's Hour."

APPLES, **1916**. *Henri Matisse. Oil on Canvas, 46" x 35³/₁₆". The Art Institute of Chicago.*

Shape and Meaning

How Poets Use Shape

Shape is the arrangement of words on a page. Some poets try out unusual ways of arranging words to convey meaning. Sometimes, as in "Seal" on page 441, the shape of the whole poem suggests something about the poem's subject. At other times, the poet suggests meaning through the placement of words and lines. An example is the following poem by Joy Kogawa:

Waiting

A very quiet

very quiet ticking

In the room where the child

Stays by the window

Watching

While outside innumerable snow feathers

Touch melt

touch melt

touch melt

The word "Watching" in line 5 divides this poem into two parts. Each part is four lines long. This division makes clear the contrast between the room in the first part of the poem and the outside world in the second part. Furthermore, the spacing of the words "touch" and "melt" suggests how the snow looks to the child who is watching it.

Thinking About Shape

As you read the selections in this section, remember that poets have reasons for shaping their poems as they do. Ask yourself how the shape of each poem reflects its subject and its meaning.

She sails on an asphalt sea.

The Sidewalk Racer or On the Skateboard

Lillian Morrison

Skimming
an asphalt sea
I swerve, I curve, I
sway; I speed to whirring
sound an inch above the   5
ground; I'm the sailor
and the sail, I'm the
driver and the wheel
I'm the one and only
single engine   10
human auto
mobile.

Getting at Meaning

RECALLING

1. What is the speaker riding? Where is the speaker riding?

2. What verbs describe the speaker's movements?

INTERPRETING

3. With what two things is the speaker compared in lines 6 and 7? How is the speaker like each one? What other word used earlier in the poem relates to the same general idea?

4. What comparisons does the speaker make in lines 7–12? What characteristics of riding a skateboard do these comparisons emphasize?

5. What does the word *mobile* mean? What does the prefix *auto-* mean? What idea does the poet emphasize by writing *automobile* on two lines, rather than as one word?

6. Is the speaker good at riding a skateboard? How do you know?

CRITICAL THINKING: APPLYING

7. The poet has attempted to re-create the experience of riding a skateboard. How well has she done this? What comparisons would you use to re-create the same experience?

Developing Skills in Reading Literature

1. **Concrete Poem.** A concrete poem has a shape that suggests its subject. What is the overall shape of this poem? Why do you think that the writer chose to use this shape?

2. **Sound.** This poem is one long sentence, broken only by commas and semicolons. Because the forward movement of lines is not stopped by periods, the poem suggests the continuous forward movement of a skateboard. Reread the poem, noting the alliteration, or repetition of consonant sounds at the beginnings of words. What initial consonant sound is repeated many times? Does the repetition of this sound suggest the poem's subject? What word in the poem imitates the sound of a moving skateboard?

Developing Writing Skills

Writing a Poem. Write a short poem about a favorite sport, game, or hobby, using "The Sidewalk Racer or On the Skateboard" as a model. Begin your prewriting notes by listing five vivid verbs that you can use to describe your subject. Then, think of the sounds associated with your subject, and list several words and phrases that re-create these sounds. Your first draft should be a paragraph. Revise this paragraph thoroughly, replacing any dull words or phrases with ones that are action-packed. Then, choose a shape associated with your subject, and write your sentences in this shape.

B I O G R A P H Y

Lillian Morrison (born 1917) worked for the New York Public Library, with most of her efforts aimed at services for young adults. Her interests include folk rhymes, sports, jazz, and dance. She has written *The Ghosts of Jersey City,* a book of poems, and has edited several anthologies, including *Sprints and Distances,* a collection of poems about sports.

A whistle echoes the magic of spring.

in Just-

e. e. cummings

in Just-
spring   when the world is mud-
luscious the little
lame balloonman

whistles   far   and wee   5

and eddieandbill come
running from marbles and
piracies and it's
spring

when the world is puddle-wonderful   10

the queer
old balloonman whistles
far   and   wee
and bettyandisbel come dancing

from hop-scotch and jump-rope and   15

it's
spring
and
    the
        goat-footed   20

balloonMan   whistles
far
and
wee

Getting at Meaning

RECALLING

1. What five adjectives describe the balloon-man?

2. What are the boys playing when the balloonman whistles? What are the girls playing?

3. What two made-up words describe the world in springtime?

INTERPRETING

4. Reread the first two lines of the poem. Is the subject of the poem early or late spring? How do you know?

5. What is the usual way of completing this phrase: far and _____? How does the poet vary the phrase? How does the new word tie in with the idea of whistling?

Developing Skills in Reading Literature

1. **Shape.** Shape is the way that words are arranged on a page. Notice that Cummings combines two names and a conjunction in "eddieandbill" and in "bettyandisbel." Why do you think he runs these names together? The poem has no periods or commas. What effect does Cummings achieve by not using these punctuation marks? The phrase "far and wee" occurs three times. The last time, Cummings puts one word on each line. What effect does he achieve by doing this?

2. **Sensory Images.** Sensory images are words and phrases that appeal to the five senses. On a sheet of paper, list five sensory images from the poem and tell which sense or senses each of these images appeals to.

3. **Allusion.** An allusion is a reference to another work of literature or to a familiar person, place, or event outside of literature. The adjective *goat-footed* in line 20 alludes to Pan, one of the minor gods of Greek mythology. Pan, a woodland god, half-man and half-goat, was associated with joy and rebirth. He played beautiful music on a panpipe made from reeds. What

similarities are there between the Greek god Pan and Cummings's balloonman?

Developing Vocabulary

Coined Words. A coined word is one that is newly invented for a specific purpose. In this poem, Cummings coined the words *mud-luscious* and *puddle-wonderful*. How would you define each of these words? Make up six new words of your own, two to describe each of these seasons: summer, autumn, and winter. Create your new words by combining existing ones as Cummings did. Write your new words and their definitions on a sheet of paper.

Developing Writing Skills

Writing a Poem and Avoiding Clichés. A cliché is an overused, tired expression. Two clichés about spring are *gentle breezes* and *trees heavy with blossoms*. Make up five sensory images to describe summer, autumn, or winter. Try to be as original as Cummings was in his poem. Use your five sensory images and two of the words that you coined in the vocabulary exercise to write a poem describing the coming of summer, autumn, or winter.

B I O G R A P H Y

Edward Estlin Cummings (1894–1962) signed his name e. e. cummings. This preference was typical of Cummings's unique, experimental style. Cummings revised the rules of punctuation, capitalization, and verse form to create rhythms, shapes, and sounds for his images and ideas. When his first book was published in 1923, critics could not decide whether to praise or condemn his style. From the beginning, however, young people enjoyed his fresh, original approach. Cummings was born in Cambridge, Massachusetts, and received two degrees from Harvard. During World War I, he was a volunteer ambulance driver in France. After the war, he spent several years in Paris writing and studying art. Besides being a writer, Cummings was a talented painter whose work was exhibited regularly during his lifetime.

Is anyone faster than this swimmer?

Seal

William Jay Smith

See how he dives
From the rocks with a zoom!
See how he darts
Through his watery room
Past crabs and eels   5
And green seaweed,
Past fluffs of sandy
Minnow feed!
See how he swims
With a swerve and a twist,   10
A flip of the flipper,
A flick of the wrist!
Quicksilver-quick,
Softer than spray,
Down he plunges   15
And sweeps away;
Before you can think,
Before you can utter
Words like "Dill pickle"
Or "Apple butter,"   20
Back up he swims
Past sting-ray and shark,
Out with a zoom,
A whoop, a bark;
Before you can say   25
Whatever you wish,
He plops at your side
With a mouthful of fish!

Getting at Meaning

RECALLING

1. Where does the seal begin his dive?
2. What does the seal pass on his way down? on his way up?
3. What does the seal catch during his dive?

INTERPRETING

4. How does the shape of this poem relate to its meaning?

CRITICAL THINKING: EVALUATING

5. How well has the poet depicted the underwater world in which the seal swims?

Developing Skills in Reading Literature

1. **Sensory Images.** Sensory images are words and phrases that appeal to the five senses. The poet uses many images that show how the seal dives, swims, and surfaces. Divide a sheet of paper into two columns. In the first column, write the verbs that show how the seal moves through the water. In the second, write the nouns that describe his movements.

2. **Onomatopoeia.** Onomatopoeia is the use of words to imitate sounds. Examples of onomatopoeia are *ring, croak,* and *buzz.*

On a sheet of paper, list four examples of onomatopoeia from this poem.

3. **Style.** Style is the way in which a work of literature is written. The lines in this poem are short, ranging from three to six syllables. Why are short lines better than long ones for a poem about a seal's speed?

Developing Writing Skills

Describing Action. Choose a land or sea animal such as a hippopotamus, an eagle, a turtle, a tiger, or a shark. In a paragraph, describe this animal's movements.

As a prewriting exercise, list verbs and nouns that you can use to describe the movements of the animal. Also think of a setting and list what the animal would pass as it moved along. Write a topic sentence that names the animal you have chosen. Then, using your notes, write the first draft of your paragraph.

Exchange your first draft with a classmate. Ask for suggestions on how to improve your description. See also the suggestions for revision in **Using the Process of Writing** on pages 621–623. After you have thought about these suggestions, write a final draft.

Copyright © Layle Silbert

B I O G R A P H Y

William Jay Smith (born 1918) is known for the humor in his poetry. He has published poetry, critical reviews, plays, nonfiction, and translations. Smith was born in Winnfield, Louisiana. He has studied in France, Italy, and England, where he was a Rhodes Scholar. He has had a long career as a college professor and educational consultant. From 1960 to 1962, he was a member of the Vermont House of Representatives. Among Smith's works are *The Tin Can and Other Poems,* a collection of poetry for adults, and *Puptents and Pebbles,* a book of nonsense verse for children.

Observe the world as the first man beholds it.

New World

N. Scott Momaday

1.

First Man,
behold:
the earth
glitters
with leaves;   5
the sky
glistens
with rain.
Pollen
is borne   10
on winds
that low[1]
and lean
upon
mountains.   15
Cedars
blacken
the slopes—
and pines.

2.

At dawn   20
eagles
hie[2] and
hover
above
the plain   25
where light
gathers
in pools.
Grasses
shimmer   30
and shine.
Shadows
withdraw
and lie
away   35
like smoke.

3.

At noon
turtles
enter
slowly   40
into
the warm
dark loam.
Bees hold
the swarm.   45
Meadows
recede
through planes
of heat
and pure   50
distance.

4.

At dusk
the gray
foxes
stiffen   55
in cold;
blackbirds
are fixed
in the
branches.   60
Rivers
follow
the moon,
the long
white track   65
of the
full moon.

---

1. **low:** make a mournful cry or sound.
2. **hie:** hasten.

TWILIGHT IN THE WILDERNESS, 1860. *Frederic Edwin Church. The Cleveland Museum of Art. Mr. and Mrs. William H. Marlatt Fund.*

Getting at Meaning

RECALLING

1. What times of day does the speaker describe?

2. What birds does the speaker associate with dawn? What are these birds doing? What animals does the speaker associate with noon? What are these animals doing? What animals does the speaker associate with dusk? What are these animals doing?

3. What does the light do at dawn? What do shadows do?

INTERPRETING

4. How can cedars "blacken/the slopes"?

5. Why do the turtles retreat into the "dark loam" at noon?

6. How do the blackbirds at dusk differ from the eagles at dawn?

7. In what sense can rivers "follow the moon"?

CRITICAL THINKING: APPLYING

8. Could a poem like this one be written about a city? What wonders would the poet describe?

Developing Skills in Reading Literature

1. **Alliteration.** Alliteration is the repetition of consonant sounds at the beginnings of words. An example from the poem is "*sh*immer and *sh*ine." On a sheet of paper, write as many examples of alliteration as you can find in this poem. Underline the repeated initial consonant sounds.

2. **Shape.** Shape is the way that words look on a page. In "New World," Momaday uses short lines in narrow columns rather than long lines spread out across the page. What effect does he achieve by arranging his words in this shape?

Developing Writing Skills

Using Verbs in Descriptions. Writers use specific verbs to create exact pictures. Examples from "New World" include *glitters, glistens, low, lean, blacken, hie, hover, shimmer, recede,* and *stiffen.* Write a paragraph about your favorite time of day. As a prewriting exercise, close your eyes and picture that time. Then, list several specific verbs that you can use in your paragraph. As you write your first draft, refer to your prewriting notes. When revising your draft, follow the guidelines for revision in **Using the Process of Writing** found on pages 621–623.

B I O G R A P H Y

*© LaVerne H. Clark/
Historical Pictures Service*

N. Scott Momaday (born 1934) is a Kiowa Indian who was born in Lawton, Oklahoma, and grew up on reservations in the Southwest. Although both of his parents were artists, Momaday turned to the study of literature. He graduated from the University of New Mexico and received both a master's degree and doctorate from Stanford University. He has taught at the University of California, and in 1973 he joined the faculty of Stanford. "I am an American Indian," says Momaday, "and am vitally interested in American Indian art, history, and culture." This interest is seen in his poems, stories, and novels, which tell about his people, their land, and a time gone forever. Momaday's novel, *House Made of Dawn,* won the 1969 Pulitzer Prize.

THE POOR MAN'S STORE, 1885. *John Frederick Peto. Museum of Fine Arts, Boston. Bequest of Maxim Karolik.*

Images and Meaning

What Is an Image?

An image is a word or a phrase that appeals to one or more of the five senses. A poet may appeal to the sense of sight:

A wounded wolf climbs Tolkat Ridge,
a massive spine of rock and ice.
As he limps, dawn strikes the ridge
and lights it up with sparks and stars.

A poet may appeal to the sense of hearing:

The wounded wolf whimpers softly.
A mindful raven hears.
'KONG, KONG, KONG,' he tolls....

A poet may appeal to the sense of touch:

Instantly the ravens mob him.
They scream and peck and stab his eyes.

A poet may appeal to the sense of smell:

[the wind] carries scents of thawing ice,
broken glass—and earth.

A poet may appeal to the sense of taste:

He gulps the food
And feels his strength return.
He shatters bone, flesh, and gristle.

Thinking About Images

Whenever you read a poem, pay close attention to its images. Close your eyes and imagine the things that these images describe. The poet's words will then create a vivid experience. The poem will kindle memories and move you to feeling and understanding.

A poet is a tamer of words.

Pretty Words

Elinor Wylie

Poets make pets of pretty, docile words:
I love smooth words, like gold-enameled fish
Which circle slowly with a silken swish,
And tender ones, like downy-feathered birds:
Words shy and dappled, deep-eyed deer in herds,   5
Come to my hand, and playful if I wish,
Or purring softly at a silver dish,
Blue Persian kittens, fed on cream and curds.

I love bright words, words up and singing early;
Words that are luminous in the dark, and sing;   10
Warm lazy words, white cattle under trees;
I love words opalescent, cool, and pearly,
Like midsummer moths, and honied words like bees,
Gilded and sticky, with a little sting.

RASPBERRIES AND GOLDFISH, 1981. *Janet I. Fish.*
The Metropolitan Museum of Art, New York. Purchase, The Cape Branch Foundation and Lila Acheson Wallace Gifts, 1983. (1983.17)

Getting at Meaning

RECALLING

1. According to the poem, how do poets treat words?

2. What does the word "ones" in line 4 refer to?

3. What kinds of words are like "white cattle under trees"?

4. What animals and insects are mentioned in this poem?

INTERPRETING

5. What animals are suggested but not specifically mentioned in lines 9 and 10?

6. What does the comparison between words and pets suggest about the speaker's attitude toward words?

7. How can words be "honied" and yet have "a little sting"?

CRITICAL THINKING: EVALUATING

8. This is a poem about words. " 'I,' Says the Poem," on page 410, is a poem about poetry. Why is it natural for poets to write about words and poems?

Developing Skills in Reading Literature

1. **Sensory Images.** Sensory images are words and phrases that appeal to any one of the five senses. *Smooth*, for example, appeals to the sense of touch. *Gold-enameled* appeals to sight. Identify five other sensory images in the poem and tell the sense or senses to which these images appeal.

2. **Simile and Metaphor.** A simile is a comparison using *like* or *as*. A metaphor is a comparison between two unlike things that have something in common. This poem contains similes and metaphors that compare words with animals. On a separate sheet of paper, list at least five kinds of words and the animals to which they are compared, as in the following example:

type of word   animal
smooth words   gold-enameled fish

3. **Rhyme Scheme.** The rhyme scheme of a poem is the pattern of rhymes at the ends of lines. To chart the rhyme scheme, use the letter *a* to label the sound at the end of the first line. Use a different letter for each different sound at the end of each line. For example, the rhyme scheme of the first stanza looks like this:

words	*a*
fish	*b*
swish	*b*
birds	*a*
herds	*a*
wish	*b*
dish	*b*
curds	*a*

On a sheet of paper, chart the rhyme scheme of the second stanza.

4. **Alliteration.** Alliteration is the repetition of consonant sounds at the beginnings of words. Lines 2 and 3, for example, repeat the *s* sound in *smooth, slowly, silken,* and *swish*. What do these two lines describe? How does the *s* sound fit this subject? What other examples of alliteration can you find in the poem?

Developing Vocabulary

Suffixes. A suffix is a word part added to the end of a word. The poet uses the word *opalescent*, which contains the suffix *-escent*. What does *opalescent* mean? Look up the following words, which also end with *-escent*:

incandescent
luminescent
phosphorescent

What do these words have in common? What does the suffix *-escent* mean?

B I O G R A P H Y

Elinor Wylie (1885–1928) was born into a wealthy and politically influential family. Writing and painting were hobbies until she suddenly decided to set out for Europe on her own. There, she began to write seriously. When she returned to the United States, she had a new confidence in her ability. Her first book of verse, *Nets To Catch the Wind,* was an instant success, as were the volumes that followed.

Are pigs happier than we are?

The Laughing Faces of Pigs

Fred Lape

Eight young pigs in a row look at me from the trough,
eight laughing faces waiting for their food.
Am I so funny seen from a pig's eyes?
No, they'd look the same at any stick or beam.
Nothing can make a pig look sad; his face   5
is built wrong for it; his mouth curls up;
his eyes are formed into a grin; his nose
wrinkles with laughter at every move he makes.
Is it so many centuries of good nature,
no inhibitions, no worry of neighbor opinion,   10
that leaves its stamp upon the faces of his race?
Or does it go back further?
                      I sometimes think
the soil's good humor runs inside his veins.
Maybe the earth herself had a good belly laugh   15
the era that she first gave birth to pigs.

Getting at Meaning

RECALLING

1. What word describes the pigs' faces at the trough?

2. What phrases does the speaker use to describe the mouth, eyes, and nose of a pig?

3. For what is a pig's face built wrong?

4. In this poem, is the earth referred to as a man or a woman?

INTERPRETING

5. Explain the meaning of this line: "the soil's good humor runs inside his veins."

CRITICAL THINKING: EVALUATING

6. The poet has not included unpleasant details such as the smell of pigs, their nasty eating habits, and their practice of rolling in mud. How would including these details have affected the impression that the poem conveys?

Developing Skills in Reading Literature

Tone. Tone is the writer's attitude toward a subject. What is the subject of "The Laughing Faces of Pigs"? How does the poet seem to feel about this subject? Cite words from the poem to support your answer.

Developing Vocabulary

The Multiple Meanings of Words. Each of the following words has two or more different meanings. On a sheet of paper, write all the definitions for each word. Then, underline the one that shows how the speaker used the word in the poem. Refer to a dictionary as necessary.

beam	leaves
race	row
stamp	nature

Developing Writing Skills

Writing a Poem. Write a poem about the expression on an animal's face. First, choose one animal, such as a dog, cat, hamster, fish, or rabbit, and describe its expression in a sentence. For example, you might write: "The Doberman pinscher had a menacing look." Second, make prewriting notes that describe the animal's mouth, eyes, and nose. Third, write a short poem of five or six lines that includes these details.

B I O G R A P H Y

Fred Lape (1900–1985) was a farmer for seventeen years. His interest in the land and in nature is reflected in his writing. Lape published several volumes of poetry, such as *At the Zoo, Hill Farm,* and *Poems from the Blue Beach.* His nonfiction works include *Apples and Man* and *A Farm and Village Boyhood.* Lape was born in Holland Patent, New York, and graduated from Cornell University. Before becoming a farmer, he was an instructor of English. In 1951, Lape founded the George Landis Arboretum, a place where many trees and shrubs are grown for exhibition or study, in Esperance, New York.

With an explosion of power, the jetliner roars into the sky.

Jetliner

Naoshi Koriyama

now he takes his mark
at the very farthest end of the runway
looking straight ahead, eager, intense
with his sharp eyes shining

he takes a deep, deep breath   5
with his powerful lungs
expanding his massive chest
his burning heart beating like thunders

then … after a few … tense
   moments … of pondering   10
he roars at his utmost
and slowly begins to jog
kicking the dark earth hard
and now he begins to run
kicking the dark earth harder   15
then he dashes, dashes like mad,
   like mad
howling, shouting, screaming,
   and roaring

then with a most violent kick   20
he shakes off the earth's pull
softly lifting himself into the air
soaring higher and higher and
   higher still
piercing the sea of clouds   25
up into the chandelier of stars

Getting at Meaning

RECALLING

1. What action does the speaker describe?
2. What sounds does the jetliner make?

INTERPRETING

3. What is the "burning heart" of a jetliner? What are the "sharp eyes shining"?
4. The jetliner "shakes off the earth's pull." What does this mean?
5. At what time of day does the action in the poem take place? How do you know?

CRITICAL THINKING: EVALUATING

6. How well has the poet succeeded in conveying the power of the jetliner in takeoff? Cite specific words and phrases to support your answer.

Developing Skills in Reading Literature

1. **Metaphor.** A metaphor is a direct comparison between two unlike things that have something in common. For example, in the phrase "chandelier of stars" the poet compares the stars to the lights in a chandelier. What are the clouds compared to in line 25?

2. **Extended Metaphor.** An extended metaphor is a series of comparisons between two unlike things that have several elements in common. In this poem, the poet compares the jetliner and a runner. What words and phrases does the poet use to suggest comparisons between these two things? According to the poem, what similarities exist between a jetliner and a runner?

3. **Simile.** A simile is a comparison using *like* or *as*. What is the simile in the second stanza? What do the two things being compared have in common?

Developing Vocabulary

Synonyms. Synonyms are words that are similar in meaning. The words *ponder* and *think* are synonyms. Look up these words in a dictionary. Is the meaning of *ponder* more specific than that of *think*? In line 10, why is *pondering* a better word choice than *thinking*?

Developing Writing Skills

Writing About a Literary Technique. Write a paragraph about Koriyama's use of extended metaphor in the poem "Jetliner." For your prewriting notes, jot down your answers to the questions about extended metaphor asked in Developing Skills in Reading Literature. Use the following as the topic sentence of your paragraph: *In the poem "Jetliner," Naoshi Koriyama makes use of extended metaphor.* Then, define the term *extended metaphor*. Next, present each detail from your notes, making sure that you explain how the appearance and movements of the jetliner resemble those of a runner. Follow the guidelines for writing and revision presented in Writing About Poetry on pages 628–630 and in **Using the Process of Writing** on pages 614–623.

BIOGRAPHY

Naoshi Koriyama (born 1926) is a professor of English literature in Japan who also writes poetry. Although his native tongue is Japanese, he set himself the challenge of composing his verse in English. His work can be found in anthologies, textbooks, and magazines. Koriyama was born on Kikai Island in Japan. He attended colleges in Japan and also received a degree from the New York State College for Teachers in Albany, New York. Koriyama's works include *Plum Tree of Japan and Other Poems*.

The inner city beats with a vibrant life of its own.

In the Inner City

Lucille Clifton

in the inner city
or
like we call it
home
we think a lot about uptown   5
and the silent nights
and the houses straight as
dead men
and the pastel lights
and we hang on to our no place   10
happy to be alive
and in the inner city
or
like we call it
home   15

Getting at Meaning

RECALLING

1. What do the people referred to in the poem as "we" call the inner city?

2. What part of the city besides the inner city is mentioned in the poem?

INTERPRETING

3. What word is used to describe the nights in uptown? the lights? To what are the houses in uptown compared? Given what the speaker says about uptown, how does he or she feel about this part of the city?

4. The speaker implies that some people

believe that the inner city is "no place." Would the speaker agree that "no place" is an appropriate description of the inner city? How do you know?

Developing Skills in Reading Literature

Simile. A simile is a comparison using *like* or *as*. Find the simile in this poem. What two things does this simile compare? What do these two things have in common?

Developing Writing Skills

Writing a Poem: Contrast. Lucille Clifton contrasts two parts of a city, the inner city and uptown. Choose one of the following pairs of subjects or a pair of your own, and write a short poem that presents a series of contrasts:

1. yourself and a friend or relative
2. a person and a machine
3. the present and the future
4. real life and life in the movies
5. two sports, hobbies, games, animals, or types of music

Begin your prewriting notes by making two columns on a sheet of paper. Label each column with the name of one of your subjects. Then, list several differences between the two subjects, following this model:

a bird	a jetliner
—is living	—is nonliving
—sings beautifully	—is noisy
—is covered with beautiful feathers	—is covered with cold gray or white metal
—can fly in loops and circles, plummet to earth	—flies straight ahead, cannot easily vary flight pattern

Write two similes that you can use in your poem, and add these to your prewriting notes. Also list in your notes several vivid words that describe sights and sounds associated with your subjects. Write several drafts of your poem. As you revise, replace dull words and phrases with colorful ones, and try to make the contrast between the two subjects as clear as possible.

B I O G R A P H Y

© LaVerne H. Clark/
Historical Pictures Service

Lucille Clifton (born 1936) has received many awards for her poetry and prose. She writes with love, warmth, and humor about the vitality of black life. *My Brother Fine with Me* and *Three Wishes* are two of her works for young people. She is the co-author of the television special *Free To Be You and Me*, which won a 1974 Emmy Award. Clifton grew up in DePew, New York, and attended Howard University and Fredonia State Teachers College.

Spring is the season of new life.

The Pasture

Robert Frost

I'm going out to clean the pasture spring;
I'll only stop to rake the leaves away
(And wait to watch the water clear, I may):
I shan't be gone long.—You come too.
I'm going out to fetch the little calf   5
That's standing by the mother. It's so young
It totters when she licks it with her tongue.
I shan't be gone long.—You come too.

CATTLE AT GUERNSEY, 1877. *Abbott Henderson Thayer. Private Collection.*

Getting at Meaning

RECALLING

1. What does the word *spring* mean as it is used in line 1?

2. What two reasons does the speaker give for going out to the pasture?

INTERPRETING

3. What happens when the cow licks the calf, and what does this show about the calf?

4. What details in the poem suggest that the speaker appreciates nature?

5. Why might the speaker want a companion? What might the presence of someone else add to the experience?

Developing Skills in Reading Literature

1. **Tone.** Tone is the attitude that a writer takes toward a subject. The writer of this poem views the pasture as a place of freshness and newness. The tone of this poem is therefore one of pleasant anticipation. Find four words from the poem that help create this tone.

2. **Repetition.** Repetition is the technique of using a word or a phrase again for emphasis. What words do lines 1 and 5 repeat? What idea does this repetition emphasize? How are lines 4 and 8 related? What ideas do lines 4 and 8 emphasize?

3. **Symbol.** A symbol is a person, place, or object that stands for something beyond itself. For example, the bald eagle and the stars and stripes are two symbols for the United States. In this poem, what two symbols stand for the return of new life in spring?

BIOGRAPHY

Robert Frost (1874–1963) is considered one of the world's greatest poets. Born in San Francisco, he moved to Lawrence, Massachusetts, in 1885 after the death of his father. There he worked at various jobs to help support his family. When possible, he took classes at Dartmouth and, later, at Harvard. In 1912 he moved to England, where his first book of poems, *A Boy's Will,* was published. Three years later, he returned to the United States and settled in New Hampshire. Frost won many awards for his work, including four Pulitzer Prizes and a special Congressional medal. He also received over forty honorary degrees from colleges and universities. His books of poetry include *North of Boston, A Further Range,* and *In the Clearing.*

What kind of magic lies inside a snowflake?

Winter Poem

Nikki Giovanni

once a snowflake fell
on my brow and i loved
it so much and i kissed
it and it was happy and called its cousins
and brothers and a web   5
of snow engulfed me then
i reached to love them all
and i squeezed them and they became
a spring rain and i stood perfectly
still and was a flower   10

PICKEREL WEED, 1964. *Glen Loates. Copyright © 1964 Glen Loates.*

Getting at Meaning

RECALLING

1. Where does the snowflake touch the speaker? How does the speaker react?

2. In the phrase "it was happy," what does the pronoun *it* stand for?

3. What are the snowflake's cousins and brothers? How does the speaker react to them?

4. How do the snowflakes change?

INTERPRETING

5. How does the speaker feel about snow and rain? How do you know?

6. How does a flower benefit from spring rain? Why might a person stand in the spring rain like a flower?

CRITICAL THINKING: EVALUATING

7. According to this poem, how important is it to notice a simple thing in nature? What benefit can a person gain by paying attention to such things?

Developing Skills in Reading Literature

1. **Personification.** Personification is the giving of human qualities to an object, animal, or idea. For example, in "Winter Poem," Nikki Giovanni speaks of a snowflake as happy. Find another example of personification in the poem.

2. **Sensory Images.** Sensory images are words and phrases that appeal to the five senses. What sensory images does Nikki Giovanni use in this poem? What senses do these images appeal to?

Developing Writing Skills

Writing a Poem. In "Winter Poem," Nikki Giovanni writes about an event that cannot really happen—a person becoming a flower. Poets are free to imagine, to write about impossibilities as though they were real. Write a short poem about someone becoming an object, an animal, or a plant. Begin the poem by placing your human subject in a particular place, observing the object, animal, or plant. Describe the object, animal, or plant as seen by your human subject. Then, describe the human subject's strange transformation. Write several drafts of your poem. As you revise, replace any dull language with words and phrases that will create a mood of mystery and magic.

BIOGRAPHY

Nikki Giovanni (born 1943) has written several volumes of poetry, some intended just for her younger readers. Many of these poems recall memories of a happy childhood in Knoxville, Tennessee; others view life with a more skeptical attitude. Giovanni graduated from Fisk University and also studied at the University of Pennsylvania and Columbia University. She has taught at various colleges and founded her own publishing business. Two of her books are *Black Feeling, Black Talk–Black Judgment* and *Re: Creation*. Her work has been published in many national magazines and poetry anthologies.

Beauty is never far away.

Night

Sara Teasdale

Stars over snow
    And in the west a planet
Swinging below a star—
    Look for a lovely thing and you will find it,
It is not far—   5
    It never will be far.

Getting at Meaning

RECALLING

1. According to the poem, what "never will be far"?

INTERPRETING

2. At what time of day and year does this poem take place? How do you know?

CRITICAL THINKING: APPLYING

3. Have you ever really looked at the sky at night? How did it make you feel? How does this poem make you feel?

Developing Skills in Reading Literature

Theme. The theme is the main idea of a work of literature. The theme of this poem is stated in the last three lines. What, in your own words, is this theme? Does the speaker mean, literally, that the stars are not far away? Explain.

CHRISTMAS MORNING (detail), 1946. *Rockwell Kent.*
Collection of Joseph M. Erdelac, Cleveland, Ohio.

B I O G R A P H Y

Sara Teasdale (1884–1933) was born and educated in St. Louis, Missouri. She was a shy, imaginative young woman who, after an unhappy marriage, lived in semi-seclusion for the rest of her life. Her first volume of poetry, *Sonnets to Duse,* was published in 1907 and was praised for the delicate simplicity that was typical of all of her verse.

Living Tenderly

May Swenson

My body a rounded stone
with a pattern of smooth seams.
My head a short snake,
retractive,[1] projective.[2]
My legs come out of their sleeves   5
or shrink within,
and so does my chin.
My eyelids are quick clamps.

My back is my roof.
I am always at home.   10
I travel where my house walks.
It is a smooth stone.
It floats within the lake,
or rests in the dust.
My flesh lives tenderly   15
inside its bone.

---

1. **retractive** (ri trak′ tiv): capable of drawing back.
2. **projective** (prə jek′ tiv): capable of moving forward.

Getting at Meaning

RECALLING

1. The speaker uses the word *stone* twice. What two adjectives describe the stone?

INTERPRETING

2. What animal is speaking? How do you know?

3. How are the speaker's eyelids like "quick clamps"?

4. In what sense is the speaker "always at home"? In what sense is the speaker "Living Tenderly"?

CRITICAL THINKING: EVALUATING/APPLYING

5. Your bones are inside your flesh. The speaker's flesh is "inside its bone." What advantages does having a shell of bone on the outside give to the speaker? What advantage does having bones on the inside instead give to you?

Developing Skills in Reading Literature

1. **Metaphor.** A metaphor is a direct comparison between two unlike things that have something in common. In this poem, the speaker uses a metaphor in the line "My head is a short snake." What similarity is there between a snake and the head and neck of a turtle? Find two other metaphors in the poem and explain the similarity between the two things being compared in each metaphor.

2. **Riddle.** A riddle is a puzzle, in words, that a reader or listener is invited to solve. The poem "Living Tenderly" is a riddle. The author presents the reader with a number of clues, some of them metaphors. Based upon these clues, the reader must determine the identity of the speaker. What clues to the identity of the speaker are given in the poem? Which of these clues are metaphors?

Developing Writing Skills

Writing a Riddle. Write a poem in which the speaker is an animal. Present your poem in the form of a riddle. Give clues to the identity of the speaker, but do not tell what animal the speaker is. Begin by listing the characteristics of the animal in your prewriting notes. Also list in your notes two metaphors that you can use to describe the animal. When revising your poem, make sure that your clues are specific enough to allow your readers to identify the speaker. Also make sure that none of the clues is so obvious that the reader knows immediately. what animal is speaking. Force your reader to think about the clues to determine the animal's identity.

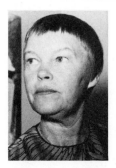

© LaVerne H. Clark/Historical Pictures Service

B I O G R A P H Y

May Swenson (born 1919) has been called an "attempter of oddities" because she likes to create new forms for her poetry. She often shapes her writing into typed pictures that present a fresh and unusual way of looking at ordinary things. She has won many prizes and awards, including a Guggenheim Fellowship. Her work has been published in many magazines and anthologies. Two collections of her poetry are *Poems to Solve* and *To Mix with Time: New and Selected Poems*.

The fog is a mysterious visitor.

Fog   *Carl Sandburg*

The fog comes
on little cat feet.

It sits looking
over harbor and city
on silent haunches   5
and then moves on.

NOCTURNE IN BLUE AND GOLD—
VALPARAISO, 1866. *James McNeill Whistler.*
*The Freer Gallery of Art, Smithsonian Institution,
Washington, D.C. (09.127)*

Getting at Meaning

RECALLING

1. Does the event described in this poem take place in the city or in the country?

INTERPRETING

2. In what sense is fog like "little cat feet"? In what senses are both the fog and the cat's haunches "silent"?

CRITICAL THINKING: EVALUATING

3. Of all the animals that Sandburg could have chosen to compare to the fog, he chose a cat. Do you think that he made the best choice? Explain.

Developing Skills in Reading Literature

1. **Sensory Images.** Sensory images are words and phrases that appeal to the five senses. To what senses does "Fog" appeal?

2. **Extended Metaphor.** An extended metaphor is a series of comparisons between two unlike things that have several elements in common. On a sheet of paper, list the similarities between fog and a cat that are mentioned or hinted at in Carl Sandburg's "Fog."

Developing Writing Skills

Writing a Poem: Extended Metaphor. Choose one of the following subjects and write a poem in which you compare between your subject and some animal:

a tornado   a train
the sea   the moon

To make prewriting notes, make two columns. Label one of the columns with the name of your subject and the other with the name of the animal to which you plan to compare your subject. Then, list the similarities in appearance, sound, and movement.

Begin your poem with a sentence that mentions both your subject and the animal to which the subject will be compared. Then, list the similarities from your prewriting notes. Write several drafts of the poem until its language is as precise and vivid as you can make it.

B I O G R A P H Y

Carl Sandburg (1878–1967) was born in Galesburg, Illinois, to Swedish immigrant parents. He did his first writing on wrapping paper that his mother saved, and he had to quit school at fourteen to help support his family. Before he was twenty, he had worked as a truckdriver, dishwasher, farmhand, floor sweeper, and potter's apprentice. After serving in the Spanish American War, he briefly attended college and then began a career as a journalist. While working in Chicago, he published *Chicago Poems* and quickly found himself famous and controversial. Critics both praised and criticized his powerful, free-form verse and his use of slang and street language. Sandburg won Pulitzer Prizes for his volume of poems, *Cornhuskers;* for his *Complete Poems;* and for *Lincoln: The War Years,* the second half of his biography of President Lincoln.

BLACK CAT ON A CHAIR, 1850–1860. *Andrew L. Von Wittkamp.*
Museum of Fine Arts, Boston. M. and M. Karolik Collection.

Ideas in Poetry

How Poets Express Ideas

In a poem, sounds, shapes, and images work together to create an imaginary experience. The ideas in the poem are the points that the poet makes about this experience. Sometimes these ideas are directly stated. At other times, they are hinted at, or implied.

Idea and Subject

When reading a poem, make sure that you know the difference between its subject and its ideas. The subject is what the poem is about. The ideas are what the poet says or implies about the subject. For example, the subject of a poem may be war. The major idea may be that war is honorable or that war is a waste of human life.

Thinking About Ideas

As you read the poems in this section, pay attention to their sounds, shapes, and images. Enter into the world of each poem. Experience what the poet describes. Then, ask yourself, "What subject does the poet speak about? What ideas does the poet state or imply about this subject?"

She was a courageous woman, a woman like a rock.

The Courage That My Mother Had

Edna St. Vincent Millay

The courage that my mother had
Went with her, and is with her still:
Rock from New England quarried;
Now granite in a granite hill.

The golden brooch my mother wore   5
She left behind for me to wear;
I have no thing I treasure more:
Yet, it is something I could spare.

Oh, if instead she'd left to me
The thing she took into the grave!—   10
That courage like a rock, which she
Has no more need of, and I have.

PRAIRIE WIFE, date unknown. *Harvey Dunn*. *Hazel L. Meyer Memorial Library, DeSmet, South Dakota.*

Getting at Meaning

RECALLING

1. What did the speaker's mother leave behind? What did she take with her to the grave?

2. Does the speaker consider herself courageous? How do you know?

INTERPRETING

3. To what is courage compared in the poem? What qualities do these two things share?

CRITICAL THINKING: APPLYING

4. What quality does the speaker of the poem wish that she had inherited from her mother? What quality would you most like to inherit from an adult whom you admire?

Developing Skills in Reading Literature

1. **Theme.** The theme is the main idea of a work of literature. How valuable is the brooch to the speaker? Does the speaker consider courage more or less valuable than the brooch?

What point is the speaker making about the value of material possessions?

2. **Rhythm.** Rhythm is the pattern of stressed and unstressed syllables in a poem. Read the following line aloud. Stress the syllables and words that are marked with accents.

Now gránite ín a gránite híll.

Can you hear the rhythm, or beat? Which other lines in the first stanza follow this pattern? Which line does not?

3. **Rhyme.** Rhyme is the repetition of syllable sounds at the ends of words. Which lines in the first stanza rhyme or nearly rhyme? Do the other stanzas have this same pattern of rhyming lines?

4. **Stanza and Quatrain.** A stanza is a group of lines that form a unit in a poem. A quatrain is a stanza of four lines. How many stanzas does this poem contain? Are these stanzas quatrains? Which stanzas are about what the speaker's mother took with her? Which one is about what she left behind?

B I O G R A P H Y

Edna St. Vincent Millay (1892–1950) graduated from Vassar in 1917 and moved to Greenwich Village where she supported herself doing translations, acting, and writing love stories under an assumed name. Her friends included other artists and writers. "Renascence," Millay's first long poem, was written when she was nineteen. In 1923, she won a Pulitzer Prize for *The Harp-Weaver.* She wrote more than twenty volumes of poetry.

Dreams must be treasured and protected.

The Dream Keeper

Langston Hughes

Bring me all of your dreams,
You dreamers,
Bring me all of your
Heart melodies
That I may wrap them   5
In a blue cloud-cloth
Away from the too-rough fingers
Of the world.

Getting at Meaning

RECALLING

1. Whom is the speaker addressing?

2. What will the speaker do with the dreams?

INTERPRETING

3. What are "heart melodies"?

CRITICAL THINKING: APPLYING

4. The speaker implies that dreams must be protected from a world that would bruise or break them. What dreams do you have? Do you think that you will be able to hang onto these dreams? What events could make you give up the dreams that you have?

Developing Skills in Reading Literature

1. **Metaphor.** A metaphor is a comparison between two unlike things that have something in common. In this poem, the speaker makes an implied comparison between dreams, or "heart melodies," and rare objects that should be

HALF DOME AND CLOUD, 1975. *Wayne Thiebaud. Courtesy of Allan Stone Gallery, New York.*

wrapped carefully and protected. What makes dreams so valuable?

2. **Symbol.** A symbol is a person, place, or thing that stands for something beyond itself. Poets often use celestial, or heavenly, objects as symbols of human aspirations, or dreams. For example, *starry-eyed* means "dreamy or unrealistic." What kinds of thoughts and feelings do people have when they watch clouds? What does the "blue cloud-cloth" symbolize?

3. **Personification.** Personification is the giving of human qualities to an object, animal, or idea. What does the poet personify in lines 7 and 8 of the poem?

Developing Writing Skills

Explaining an Idea. Everyone has dreams for the future—dreams for himself or herself, for someone else, or for the world at large. In a paragraph, explain one of your dreams for the future.

Start by narrowing your topic to one specific dream. In your prewriting notes, tell what you would like to have happen and why.

Begin your paragraph with a topic sentence that identifies your dream. Develop the paragraph with details from your prewriting notes. As you write and revise the paragraph, follow the guidelines presented in **Using the Process of Writing** on pages 614–623.

Some things cannot be fixed.

Jake Hanson

Kaye Starbird

Jake Hanson runs a fix-it shop.
He says he fixes anything
By mending what you break or drop
With wire or nails or glue or string.

I had a rose when I was small.   5
Its petals fell upon the walk.
I searched around and found them all
And, cutting off the empty stalk,

I took the shattered flower to Jake
Who turned and shouted, "Oh, it's you!   10
Did something fall? Did something break?
I'll fix it like I always do."

But when he noticed what I had
He neither helped me nor consoled me.
Speaking in level tones, not sad,   15
"I cannot mend your rose," he told me.

That was the afternoon when Jake
Shuttered his shop at two o'clock
And suddenly went off to take
His rowboat from the fishing dock.   20

Knowing Jake Hanson's skill and wit,
I lost a hero, I suppose,
The day he said he could not fit
The petals back onto my rose.

OLD MAN AND CHILD, about 1887.
*Elizabeth Nourse. Private Collection.
Courtesy of the National Museum of American
Art, Smithsonian Institution, Washington, D.C.*

Getting at Meaning

RECALLING

1. What does Jake Hanson run?
2. What does Jake say he can fix?
3. What happens to the rose?
4. When Jake sees the rose, what does he say? How does he say it?

INTERPRETING

5. Is the speaker in the poem describing a recent event or one that happened long ago? How do you know?
6. Why does Jake close his shop early?
7. How does the speaker's belief in Jake Hanson change? Why does this change occur?

8. What has the speaker lost? What has Jake Hanson lost? Who do you think has suffered the greater loss?

Developing Skills in Reading Literature

1. **Theme.** The theme is the main idea of a work of literature. In "Jake Hanson," what is the poet suggesting about human limitations?

2. **Sensory Images.** Sensory images are words and phrases that appeal to the five senses. For example, in "Jake Hanson," the poet uses the image "shattered flower." What does *shattered* mean? Can a flower shatter? Why or why not? What does the poet suggest by teaming the words *shattered* and *flower*? How does this image prepare you for what will happen to the speaker's belief in Jake Hanson?

Developing Writing Skills

Writing About a Personal Experience. The speaker in "Jake Hanson" sums up his or her experience by saying "I lost a hero." In a paragraph, write about an experience in which you lost a hero or in which someone let you down.

For your prewriting notes, jot down the name of the person about whom you plan to write. Then, give the reason why you admired him or her and the event that made you change your opinion. Begin your first draft with a topic sentence similar to this: "Sometimes, the one you look up to can hurt you." Use the details from your prewriting notes to develop your topic sentence. As you revise, follow the guidelines in **Using the Process of Writing** found on pages 614–623.

Copyright © Layle Silbert

B I O G R A P H Y

Kaye Starbird (born 1916) has written many books of poetry for young people. Her book titles, *A Snail's a Failure Socially, The Pheasant on Route Seven,* and *Don't Ever Cross a Crocodile,* offer a glimpse of the humor and imagination found in her work. Starbird was born at Fort Sill, Oklahoma, the daughter of a U.S. Army General. She attended the University of Vermont.

Seeing is an art that must be learned.

To Look at Any Thing

John Moffitt

To look at any thing,
If you would know that thing,
You must look at it long:
To look at this green and say
"I have seen spring in these   5
Woods," will not do—you must
Be the thing you see:
You must be the dark snakes of
Stems and ferny plumes of leaves,
You must enter in   10
To the small silences between
The leaves,
You must take your time
And touch the very peace
They issue from.   15

Getting at Meaning

RECALLING

1. According to line 3, how must you look at a thing in order to know it?

2. What things from nature does the poem mention?

3. To what does the word "they" in line 15 refer?

INTERPRETING

4. What do the words "you must/be the thing you see" mean? How is it possible to be what you see?

CRITICAL THINKING: APPLYING

5. The speaker points out that to look at something takes time. When was the last time that you looked at something carefully? Try this experiment: Choose some object and look at it for a full minute. Observe all of its tiny details. Imagine what it would be like to be the object that you are looking at. Then, turn away from the object and describe it to someone else. Recall as many details as you can. Does the advice given by the speaker in "To Look at Any Thing" hold true?

A FROG IN ITS POND, 1977. *Joseph Raffael. Copyright © Joseph Raffael. Courtesy of the Nancy Hoffman Gallery, New York.*

Developing Skills in Reading Literature

1. **Metaphor.** A metaphor is a direct comparison between two unlike things that have something in common. Looking at the green woods, the speaker sees "the dark snakes of/ stems and ferny plumes of leaves." What do dark snakes and stems have in common? What qualities are shared by ferns, plumes, and leaves?

2. **Theme.** The theme is the main idea of a work of literature. The theme of this poem is that real seeing requires effort. What is the reward for having taken the time to look at something carefully?

Developing Writing Skills

Writing a Descriptive Poem. Choose an object from nature—a tree, a flower, an animal, or an insect—and look at it for a long time. Then, write a brief poem about what you see.

Make prewriting notes by jotting down the details that you see. Also jot down the thoughts that cross your mind as you look at the object. What does the object remind you of? What do the parts of the object remind you of? Include in your notes two metaphors that you can use to describe parts of the object or the object as a whole.

Then, write a first draft of your poem. Ask a classmate to read your draft and to suggest ways in which the poem might be improved. Then, revise the poem and prepare a final copy.

B I O G R A P H Y

John Moffitt (1908–1988) wrote poems from the time he was eight years old. A Catholic, Moffitt spent four years as a monk. His interest in questions of a spiritual nature is often reflected in his poetry. Collections of Moffitt's work include *Escape of the Leopard* and *Signal Message.* Born in Harrisburg, Pennsylvania, Moffitt attended Princeton University and the Curtis Institute of Music. After leaving the monastic order in 1963, he worked as an editor.

Does a city devour its people?

The City Is So Big

Richard García

The city is so big
Its bridges quake with fear
I know, I have seen at night

The lights sliding from house to house
And trains pass with windows shining   5
Like a smile full of teeth

I have seen machines eating houses
And stairways walk all by themselves
And elevator doors opening and closing
And people disappear.   10

MOVEMENT, FIFTH AVENUE, 1912. *John Marin.*
Watercolor on paper, 16¹³/₁₆" x 13¾".
The Art Institute of Chicago. Alfred Stieglitz Collection.

Getting at Meaning

RECALLING

1. According to the poem, what thing quakes with fear? What things look like teeth? What things are eaten by machines? What things walk by themselves? What things open and close?

2. According to the poem, what happens to people in the city?

INTERPRETING

3. Large suspension bridges sometimes sway a bit in the wind. How is this fact interpreted by the speaker?

4. The headlights of automobiles shine on houses and then pass on. How is this fact interpreted by the speaker?

5. Is the smile in line 6 of the poem a friendly one? How do you know?

6. Earth movers are large machines with mouth-like scoops that are used to haul away debris from demolished buildings. How is this fact interpreted by the speaker?

7. What kinds of stairways "walk all by themselves"?

8. In what sense do the people described in this poem disappear? How is their disappearance connected with walking stairways and elevator doors?

9. Have you ever been in a big city? Have you ever felt dwarfed by a city's cold, impersonal machinery? Would you portray a city in the same way that Richard García did?

Developing Skills in Reading Literature

1. **Mood.** Mood is the feeling created by a literary work. What is the mood of "The City Is So Big"? What details help to create this mood?

2. **Personification.** Personification is the giving of human qualities to an object, animal, or idea. Find three examples of personification in this poem. For each, explain what human quality the speaker gives the object.

Developing Writing Skills

Writing a Poem: Personification. Choose one of the following subjects or one of your own, and write a poem that describes the subject as though it were a living creature:

a house
an automobile
a boat
an airplane
a river
a mountain
a highway
a pinball machine
a Ferris wheel
a guitar or a cello

In your prewriting notes, list your subject and the mood that you want your poem to create. Then, think of similarities between your subject and living creatures. For example, the doorway to a house might be viewed as a mouth. The headlights of an automobile might be viewed as eyes. Revise your poem until every detail helps to create the mood listed in your prewriting notes.

B I O G R A P H Y

Richard García (born 1941) has written poetry both for children and adults. His works have appeared in numerous magazines and anthologies and in a volume of *Selected Poetry.* A native Californian, he has taught children to write poetry as a participating artist in the California Poets in the Schools program. In his spare time, García is an avid fly-fisherman.

Something happens to Reggie when summer comes around.

Reggie

Eloise Greenfield

It's summertime
And Reggie doesn't live here anymore
He lives across the street
Spends his time with the round ball
Jump, turn, shoot   5
Through the hoop
Spends his time with arguments
   and sweaty friends
And not with us
He's moved away   10
Comes here just to eat and sleep
   and sometimes pat my head
Then goes back home
To run and dribble and jump and stretch
And stretch   15
And shoot
Thinks he's Kareem
And not my brother

Getting at Meaning

RECALLING

1. Where is Reggie's "new home"?
2. What does Reggie do at his "old home"?
3. How are Reggie and the speaker related?

INTERPRETING

4. What game does Reggie play?
5. What is the meaning of the line "He's moved away"?

CRITICAL THINKING: EVALUATING

6. Should Reggie spend more time with the

speaker and less time playing basketball? Explain your opinion.

Developing Skills in Reading Literature

1. **Allusion.** An allusion is a reference to another work of literature or to a familiar person, place, or event outside of literature. In the next to last line, the speaker mentions the name "Kareem." "Kareem" is a reference to a well known person. Who is Kareem? Why does Reggie identify with him?

2. **Hyperbole.** Hyperbole is exaggeration for emphasis. For example, the statement "I'm so hungry that I could eat a horse" is an example of hyperbole. The speaker in the poem says, "Reggie doesn't live here any more." Is this hyperbole? Explain.

Developing Writing Skills

Writing Hyperbole. For each of the following words, write an example of hyperbole, or exaggerated statement. Follow this model: heat—The sun melted the sidewalk.

cold	large
lazy	beautiful
tired	friendly
patient	expensive

HANDBALL, 1940–1942. *Ben Shahn. Portion of a Fresco Mural in the Department of Health and Human Services, Washington, D.C.*

Nothing is forever.

Beau

Loren Eiseley

Beau is gone now,
the huge black poodle
who, when I visited his owners,
always used to wave his yellow food dish
happily from the doorway and bark his welcome   5
or lie beside my bed in the morning.
This afternoon on the patio
his diminutive challenger the chipmunk
who used to set Beau wild
whistled dispute from the wall   10
but there was only silence.
I think even the chipmunk was abashed.
They had had a long rivalry and now silence
had fallen. A lily nodded gently
on its stem and I   15
went to my room where Beau
would never again turn three times around
and subside with a patient sigh while I wrote.
I am not a philosopher. I merely know
everything good has an end. I hope Beau   20
left without having learned this.
Yesterday his girl playmate from up the road
came by slowly, having come before.
How does one explain this to animals: that after a while
there are none of us left: no shadows, no voice, no odor. 25
One cannot even show a picture.
She goes away silently up the track.
She does not understand the world's absences.
Looking at the empty rug by my bed,
neither do I.   30

Getting at Meaning

RECALLING

1. What did Beau look like?
2. Did the speaker own Beau?
3. What fond memories of Beau does the speaker have?

INTERPRETING

4. Why does the chipmunk feel abashed?
5. To whom does the word "us" in line 25 refer?
6. The speaker says that Beau's playmate "does not understand the world's absences." What does the phrase "the world's absences" mean?

7. How does the speaker of this poem feel about Beau's absence? How do you know?

CRITICAL THINKING: EVALUATING

8. This poem is about a deeply felt loss. How well has the writer succeeded in making you feel that loss?

Developing Skills in Reading Literature

Theme. The theme is the main idea of a work of literature. Sometimes the theme of a poem is directly stated. At other times, the theme is suggested or implied. What is the theme of "Beau"? Is this theme directly stated or implied?

B I O G R A P H Y

Loren Eiseley (1907–1977) was both a writer and an anthropologist. Born in Lincoln, Nebraska, he attended the University of Nebraska. After earning his M.A. and Ph.D. at the University of Pennsylvania, he began a notable career as a professor of anthropology. Through his writings, such as *The Immense Journey* and *Firmament of Time,* he shared his knowledge of science with a wide range of readers. Eiseley also published poetry, including the collections *Another Kind of Autumn* and *All the Night Wings.*

Not everyone wants to be famous.

I'm Nobody

Emily Dickinson

I'm nobody! Who are you?
Are you nobody, too?
Then there's a pair of us—don't tell!
They'd banish us, you know.

How dreary to be somebody!   5
How public, like a frog
To tell your name the livelong day
To an admiring bog.

Getting at Meaning

RECALLING

1. What two adjectives describe what it is like "to be somebody"?

INTERPRETING

2. To whom does the word "they" in line 4 refer? Why would "they" banish the two nobodies?

3. Whom does the speaker compare to a frog? According to the speaker, what do such people and frogs have in common?

CRITICAL THINKING: EVALUATING

4. Do you think that being somebody is as dismal as the speaker maintains? Give reasons to support your opinion.

Developing Skills in Reading Literature

Simile. A simile is a comparison using *like* or *as*. What simile did Emily Dickinson use in this poem? What does the phrase "admiring bog" suggest about those who idolize important people?

MINK POND, 1891. *Winslow Homer. The Fogg Art Museum, Harvard University, Cambridge, Massachusetts. Bequest of Grenville L. Winthrop.*

B I O G R A P H Y

Emily Dickinson (1830–1886) grew up, lived, and died in Amherst, Massachusetts. During her early years, she led the typical life of an upper-class young girl in provincial New England. During her twenties, however, something happened to her that remains a mystery. At twenty-six she shut herself off from the world and was rarely seen in public again. She spent long hours in her room, secretly writing poetry on envelopes, paper bags, and other scraps of paper. Only seven of these poems were published during her life, but more than 1,700 were discovered after her death. These poems appear in such collections as *The Complete Poems of Emily Dickinson* and *Acts of Light.*

Sea-Fever

John Masefield

I must go down to the seas again, to the lonely sea and the
    sky,
And all I ask is a tall ship and a star to steer her by,
And the wheel's kick and the wind's song and the white
    sail's shaking,
And a grey mist on the sea's face and a grey dawn breaking.

I must go down to the seas again, for the call of the running
    tide   5
Is a wild call and a clear call that may not be denied;
And all I ask is a windy day with the white clouds flying,
And the flung spray and the blown spume, and the
    seagulls crying.

I must go down to the seas again to the vagrant gypsy life,
To the gull's way and the whale's way where the wind's
    like a whetted knife;   10
And all I ask is a merry yarn from a laughing fellow-rover,
And quiet sleep and a sweet dream when the long trick's
    over.

CAPTAIN'S HOUSE, 1929. *Morris Kantor.*
National Museum of American Art, Smithsonian Institution, Washington, D.C. Gift of Martha R. Kantor.

Getting at Meaning

RECALLING

1. What does the speaker need in order to steer the "tall ship"?
2. What call can the speaker not deny?
3. What does the speaker ask for "when the long trick's over"?

INTERPRETING

4. Why does the speaker say "I *must* go down to the seas again" instead of "I *would like* to go down to the seas again"?
5. What does the phrase "the vagrant gypsy life" suggest about a sailor's life on ship?
6. Does the speaker ask for simple or for splendid things? Explain your answer.
7. Explain the meaning of the poem's title.

CRITICAL THINKING: EVALUATING

8. Does the poet succeed in making the sea appear inviting to the reader? Explain.

Developing Skills in Reading Literature

1. **Alliteration.** Alliteration is the repetition of consonant sounds at the beginnings of words. One example of alliteration in "Sea-Fever" is the repetition of the *st* sound in the phrase "a *st*ar to *st*eer her by." Find in the poem an example of alliteration used to echo the sound of the wind.
2. **Simile.** A simile is a comparison using *like* or *as*. What is a "whetted knife"? To what does the speaker compare a "whetted knife"? What do these two things have in common?

Developing Vocabulary

Using a Thesaurus. A thesaurus is a dictionary of synonyms, or words that have similar meanings. Look up each of the following words in a thesaurus. Find a synonym for each word, and write the word and its synonym on a sheet of paper.

face	yarn
wild	merry
vagrant	dream

Developing Writing Skills

Writing About Poetry. In literature, the sea is often a symbol of freedom. In a paragraph, show how John Masefield presents the sea as such a symbol.

For your prewriting notes, divide your paper into three columns. Label the first column "first stanza," the second column "second stanza," and the third column "third stanza." In each column, write words and phrases that suggest freedom. For example, in the third column, you could write the phrase "gypsy life." Begin your first draft with a topic sentence that tells the title of the poem and your main idea. Then, develop the paragraph with details from your prewriting notes. As you write and revise your paragraph, refer to the guidelines in **Using the Process of Writing** on pages 614–623 and in Writing About Poetry on pages 628–630.

BIOGRAPHY

John Masefield (1878–1967) had one desire in life—to become a writer. Born in Ledbury, Herefordshire, England, Masefield had little formal education. As a child, he had a vivid imagination and loved to tell stories. At thirteen, he joined the Merchant Navy, in which he served for four years. His first collection of poems, *Salt-Water Ballads,* was published in 1902. Many volumes followed, including the prize-winning *The Bluebells and Other Verses.* In addition to poems, Masefield wrote plays, stories, novels, biographies, and literary criticism. In 1930, he became the poet laureate of England.

RESEARCH SKILLS FOR *WRITING*

Using an Encyclopedia

An encyclopedia is a reference work that contains articles on a wide variety of topics. The articles in encyclopedias are arranged alphabetically, usually in several volumes. Guide words placed at the top of each page help readers to locate particular articles. In addition, most encyclopedias contain an index, an alphabetical list of topics, along with page numbers of articles about these topics. The index usually appears in one or more separate volumes.

To look up information in an encyclopedia, first check the appropriate volume to see if there is an article on your topic. If not, look up your topic in the index to find other articles in which the topic is discussed.

Developing Writing Skills

Comparing Information in Encyclopedias. Follow the directions below.

1. Go to your school or public library and look up "Robert Frost" in an encyclopedia. Read the article. Then copy the following information onto a sheet of paper:
   a. the name of the encyclopedia
   b. the date and place of Frost's birth
   c. the titles of two books of his poetry

2. Do exactly the same thing using a second encyclopedia. Then write a paragraph in which you evaluate the different approaches taken by the two encyclopedias. How are the write-ups the same? How are they different? Which write-up of Frost do you prefer? Why?

See **Handbook: How To Write About Literature,** Lessons 1–4, 6.

CRITICAL THINKING

Making Inferences

To read a poem well, you must know how to make inferences. An inference is a conclusion reached by a process of logical reasoning. This reasoning can move from specific observations to general conclusions or from general observations to specific conclusions.

General to Specific Reasoning

Sometimes a poet makes a general observation from which you can draw specific conclusions. For example, in the poem "I'm Nobody," Emily Dickinson makes the following general observation:

"How dreary to be somebody!
How public, like a frog"

Based on this observation, you can conclude that the speaker does not long to be a famous writer, for a famous writer is a "somebody."

Specific to General Reasoning

Sometimes a poet gives specific details from which you can draw a general conclusion. For example, in "Where the Sidewalk Ends" the speaker describes a "place where the smoke blows black/And the dark street winds and bends./Past the pits where the asphalt flowers grow." Based on such details as *smoke, street,* and *asphalt,* the reader can conclude that the setting of the poem is a city.

Developing Critical Thinking Skills

1. **Reasoning from General Observations.**
Reread "Macavity: the Mystery Cat" on pages 416–417. In line 2, the speaker makes this general observation about Macavity: "For he's the master criminal who can defy the Law." What specific details about Macavity's crimes does the speaker relate to back up this general observation?

2. **Reasoning from Specific Observations.** Follow the directions below.

a. Reread "Reggie" on page 486. The speaker provides these details about Reggie: "He lives across the street/Spends his time with the roundball/Jump, turn, shoot/Through the hoop/Spends his time with arguments/and sweaty friends/And not with us." Based on these specific details, you can draw several general conclusions. Where does Reggie spend most of his day? What is the game that he plays? How much time and attention does Reggie give to his family?

b. The following are some of the poems in the unit and some general conclusions based on specific details in these poems. Reread each of the poems. Then, list on a sheet of paper two details from each poem that support each general conclusion.

"Johnny Appleseed," on pages 424–425. Johnny Appleseed did not care about such worldly matters as dress.

"In the Inner City," on page 458. Uptown is dull.

"The City Is So Big," on page 483. The city can be a frightening place.

Understanding Poetry

RECALLING

1. Which poems in this unit are about poets and poetry? Which are about famous Americans? Which are about spring?

2. Which poem compares a jetliner to a runner? houses to dead men? famous people to frogs?

INTERPRETING

3. Explain how the element listed in parentheses is used in each of these poems:

   a. (Sound) "Narnian Suite"
   b. (Shape) "The Sidewalk Racer"
   c. (Image) "Night"
   d. (Idea) "Beau"

4. Give two examples of sensory images from "Pretty Words" and two from "The Pasture."

5. Scan each of the following poems and find an example of the technique listed.

   a. (Alliteration) "Narnian Suite"
   b. (Metaphor) "Jetliner"
   c. (Simile) " 'I,' Says the Poem"
   d. (Personification) "Paul Revere's Ride"
   e. (Hyperbole) "Reggie"

6. Select two poems from this unit that express the feelings of the speaker. What feelings does the speaker express in each poem?

CRITICAL THINKING: EVALUATING

7. Select one poem from this unit that expresses an important idea. Explain what this idea is and why you consider it important.

Writing About Poetry

See **Using the Process of Writing** and Writing About Poetry, starting on page 614, for help.

Choose one poem from this unit and in a brief composition define and give examples of the literary techniques that the writer has used. Possible techniques include metaphor, extended metaphor, simile, symbol, hyperbole, personification, rhythm, rhyme, shape, alliteration, and onomatopoeia. Begin by reviewing the definitions of these terms in the **Handbook of Literary Terms** on pages 646–659. Then, choose the poem that you wish to write about. Read the poem several times. In your prewriting notes, list the literary techniques used in the poem and definitions of these techniques. List examples of the techniques from the poem.

In the introduction to your composition, name the poem and its writer. Then, name the literary techniques that the poet used. In each body paragraph define one literary technique and give an example from the poem.

Applying Poetic Techniques

See **Using the Process of Writing** on pages 614–623 for help with this assignment.

Write a poem about one of the following subjects or about a subject of your own.

1. An interesting, unusual, or exciting place, such as a carnival, a zoo, or a rock concert

2. An individual or a team sport, such as roller skating, football, volleyball, or tennis

3. A familiar place as it might appear in the future, such as a school cafeteria or a library

In your prewriting notes, include the following: five sensory images, a metaphor, a simile, and one example of hyperbole. Write several drafts of your poem.

UNIT 5

Drama

HARLEQUIN, 1901. *Pablo Picasso. The Metropolitan Museum of Art, New York. Gift of Mr. and Mrs. John L. Loeb, 1960.*

Introducing Drama

What Is Drama?

Drama is writing that tells a story through dialogue and action. Many of the same elements that are found in short stories are found in drama. These elements include setting, characters, conflict, and plot. What, then, sets drama apart from other forms of storytelling? Above all, drama is written to be performed for an audience. It can be broadcast by radio. It can be performed on a stage. It can be filmed and shown on television or in a movie theater.

The Characteristics of Drama

A drama has special characteristics, as follows:

Scenes and Acts.   Most dramas are divided into short units of action called scenes. Each scene takes place in one setting. Several scenes taken together make up an act.

Dialogue and Stage Directions.   A drama presents its story through dialogue, or words spoken by actors. The writer may include stage directions in the script. Stage directions are notes about setting, sound effects, the movements of the actors, and the ways in which lines should be spoken.

Thinking About Drama

In this unit you will read two one-act plays. Each play has several scenes. The first is a radio play. The second is a play for television. Try to imagine each play as it might be performed on the radio or on TV.

Previewing the Unit

Reading the Selections

As you read the selections in this unit, pay attention to the stage directions. Try to imagine hearing the dialogue spoken aloud.

Using the Study Questions

Following each selection are exercises. They will help you to develop your reading, vocabulary, and writing skills.

Getting at Meaning. This section has three types of questions. The **RECALLING** questions will help you to remember the selection. The **INTERPRETING** questions will help you to understand the selection. The **CRITICAL THINKING** questions will help you to evaluate the selection and to relate it to your own experiences.

Developing Skills in Reading Literature. These exercises will teach you the techniques used by the writers of drama.

Developing Vocabulary. These exercises will teach you vocabulary skills such as identifying base words, prefixes, and suffixes.

Developing Writing Skills. In one kind of assignment you will write about the dramas that you have read. In another you will use the literary techniques that you have learned.

Using the Unit Study Materials

Research Skills for Writing. This feature will teach you how to use the *Readers' Guide to Periodical Literature.*

Critical Thinking. The critical thinking exercises will teach you how to make generalizations about works of literature.

Unit Review. The unit review will help you to recall, interpret, and think critically about the selections in the unit. The writing assignments will give you a chance to use the writing skills that you have learned.

Grandpa does not believe that the statue will endure.

Grandpa and the Statue

Arthur Miller

CHARACTERS

Characters in the present time of the play:

ANNOUNCER

AUGUST

MONAGHAN (Young Monaghan, a soldier)

Characters from the past, heard in the flashback scenes which Young Monaghan remembers:

SHEEAN

MONAGHAN (Grandfather of Young Monaghan)

CHILD MONAGHAN (Young Monaghan himself, as a child)

GEORGE
CHARLEY
JACK } (neighborhood children, Child Monaghan's friends)
MIKE
JOE

ALF
GIRL } (passengers on the Statue of Liberty boat)
YOUNG MAN

MEGAPHONE VOICE

VETERAN (visitor to the Statue)

PART 1

(Music: Theme)

ANNOUNCER. The scene is the fourth floor of a giant army hospital overlooking New York Harbor. A young man sitting in a wheel chair is looking out a window — just looking. After a while another young man in another wheelchair rolls over to him and they both look.

(Music out)

AUGUST. You want to play some checkers with me, Monaghan?

MONAGHAN. Not right now.

AUGUST. Okay *(slight pause)*. You don't want to go feeling blue, Monaghan.

MONAGHAN. I'm not blue.

AUGUST. All you do most days is sit here looking out this window.

MONAGHAN. What do you want me to do, jump rope?

AUGUST. No, but what do you get out of it?

MONAGHAN. It's a beautiful view. Some companies make millions of dollars just printing that view on postcards.

AUGUST. Yeh, but nobody keeps looking at a postcard six, seven hours a day.

MONAGHAN. I come from around here. It reminds me of things. My young days.

AUGUST. That's right, you're Brooklyn, aren't you?

MONAGHAN. My house is only about a mile away.

AUGUST. That so. Tell me, are you looking at just the water all the time? I'm curious. I don't get a kick out of this view.

MONAGHAN. There's the Statue of Liberty out there. Don't you see it?

AUGUST. Oh, that's it. Yeh, that's nice to look at.

MONAGHAN. I like it. Reminds me of a lot of laughs.

AUGUST. Laughs? The Statue of Liberty?

MONAGHAN. Yeh, my grandfather. He got all twisted up with the Statue of Liberty.

AUGUST (laughs a little). That so? What happened?

MONAGHAN. Well. My grandfather was the stingiest man in Brooklyn. "Mercyless" Monaghan, they used to call him. He even used to save umbrella handles.

AUGUST. What for?

MONAGHAN. Just couldn't stand seeing any-thing go to waste. After a big windstorm there'd be a lot of broken umbrellas laying around in the streets.

AUGUST. Yeh?

MONAGHAN. He'd go around picking them up. In our house the closets were always full of umbrella handles. My grandma used to say that he would go across the Brooklyn Bridge on the trolley just because he could come back on the same nickel. See, if you stayed on the trolley they'd let you come back for the same nickel.

AUGUST. What'd he do, just go over and come back?

MONAGHAN. Yeh, it made him feel good. Savin' money. Two and a half cents.

AUGUST. So how'd he get twisted up with the Statue of Liberty?

MONAGHAN. Well, way back in 1887 around there they were living on Butler Street. Butler Street, Brooklyn, practically runs right down to the river. One day he's sitting on the front porch, reading a paper he bor-rowed from the neighbors, when along comes this man Jack Sheean who lived up the block.

(Music: Sneak into above speech, then bridge, then out)

SHEEAN (slight brogue). A good afternoon to you, Monaghan.

MONAGHAN (grandfather). How're you, Sheean, how're ya?

SHEEAN. Fair, fair. And how's Mrs. Monaghan these days?

MONAGHAN. Warm. Same as everybody else in summer.

SHEEAN. I've come to talk to you about the

fund, Monaghan.

MONAGHAN. What fund is that?

SHEEAN. The Statue of Liberty fund.

MONAGHAN. Oh, that.

SHEEAN. It's time we come to grips with the subject, Monaghan.

MONAGHAN. I'm not interested, Sheean.

SHEEAN. Now hold up on that a minute. Let me tell you the facts. This here Frenchman has gone and built a fine statue of Liberty. It costs the Lord knows how many millions to build. All they're askin' us to do is contribute enough to put up a base for the statue to stand on.

MONAGHAN. I'm not . . . !

SHEEAN. Before you answer me. People all over the whole United States are puttin' in for it. Butler Street is doin' the same. We'd like to hang up a flag on the corner saying— "Butler Street, Brooklyn, is one hundred percent behind the Statue of Liberty." And Butler Street *is* a hundred percent subscribed except for you. Now will you give us a dime, Monaghan? One dime and we can put up the flag. Now what do you say to that?

MONAGHAN. I'm not throwin' me good money away for somethin' I don't even know exists.

SHEEAN. Now what do you mean by that?

MONAGHAN. Have you seen this statue?

SHEEAN. No, but it's in a warehouse. And as soon as we get the money to build the pedestal they'll take it and put it up on that island in the river, and all the boats comin' in from the old country will see it there and it'll raise the hearts of the poor immigrants to see such a fine sight on their first look at this country.

MONAGHAN. And how do I know it's in this here warehouse at all?

SHEEAN. You read your paper, don't you? It's been in all the papers for the past year.

MONAGHAN. Ha, the papers! Last year I read in the paper that they were about to pave Butler Street and take out all the holes. Turn around and look at Butler Street, Mr. Sheean.

SHEEAN. All right. I'll do this: I'll take you to the warehouse and show you the statue. Will you give a dime then?

MONAGHAN. Well . . . I'm not sayin' I would, and I'm not sayin' I wouldn't. But I'd be more *likely* if I saw the thing large as life, I would.

SHEEAN (*peeved*). All right, then. Come along.

(*Music up and down and out*)

(*Footsteps, in warehouse . . . echo . . . they come to a halt*)

Now then. Do you see the Statue of Liberty or don't you see it?

MONAGHAN. I see it all right, but it's all broke!

SHEEAN. *Broke!* They brought it from France on a boat. They had to take it apart, didn't they?

MONAGHAN. You got a secondhand statue, that's what you got, and I'm not payin' for new when they've shipped us something that's all smashed to pieces.

SHEEAN. Now just a minute, just a minute. Visualize what I'm about to tell you, Monaghan, get the picture of it. When this statue is put together it's going to stand ten stories high. Could they get a thing ten stories high into a four-story building such as this is? Use your good sense, now Monaghan.

MONAGHAN. What's that over there?

SHEEAN. Where?

MONAGHAN. That tablet there in her hand. What's it say? July Eye Vee (IV) MDCCLXXVI...what...what's all that?

SHEEAN. That means July 4, 1776. It's in Roman numbers. Very high class.

MONAGHAN. What's the good of it? If they're going to put a sign on her they ought to put it: Welcome All. That's it. Welcome All.

SHEEAN. They decided July 4, 1776, and July 4, 1776, it's going to be!

MONAGHAN. All right, then let them get their dime from somebody else!

SHEEAN. Monaghan!

MONAGHAN. No, sir! I'll tell you something. I didn't think there was a statue but there is. She's all broke, it's true, but she's here and

HIMSELF, 1913. *Robert Henri.* Oil on canvas, 32¼″ x 28⅛″. *The Art Institute of Chicago. Walter H. Schulze Memorial Collection.*

maybe they can get her together. But even if they do, will you tell me what sort of a welcome to immigrants it'll be, to have a gigantic thing like that in the middle of the river and in her hand a July Eye Vee MCDVC... whatever it is?

SHEEAN. That's the date the country was made!

MONAGHAN. The divil with the date! A man comin' in from the sea wants a place to stay, not a date. When I come from the old country I git off at the dock and there's a feller says to me, "Would you care for a room for the night?" "I would that," I sez, and he sez, "All right then, follow me." He takes me to a rooming house. I no sooner sign me name on the register — which I was able to do even at that time — when I look around and the feller is gone clear away and took my valise[1] in the bargain. A statue anyway can't move off so fast, but if she's going to welcome let her say welcome, not this MCDC....

SHEEAN. All right, then, Monaghan. But all I can say is, you've laid a disgrace on the name of Butler Street. I'll put the dime in for ya.

MONAGHAN. Don't connect me with it! It's a swindle, is all it is. In the first place, it's broke; in the second place, if they do put it up it'll come down with the first high wind that strikes it.

SHEEAN. The engineers say it'll last forever!

MONAGHAN. And I say it'll topple into the river in a high wind! Look at the inside of her. She's all hollow!

SHEEAN. I've heard everything now, Monaghan. Just about everything. Goodbye.

MONAGHAN. What do you mean, goodbye? How am I to get back to Butler Street from here?

SHEEAN. You've got legs to walk.

MONAGHAN. I'll remind you that I come on the trolley.

SHEEAN. And I'll remind you that I paid your fare and I'm not repeating the kindness.

MONAGHAN. Sheean? You've stranded me!

(Music up and down)

YOUNG MONAGHAN. That was Grandpa. That's why I have to laugh every time I look at the statue now.

AUGUST. Did he ever put the dime in?

YOUNG MONAGHAN. Well — in a way. What happened was this: His daughters got married and finally my mom...put *me* out on Butler Street. I got to be pretty attached to Grandpa. He'd even give me an umbrella handle and made a sword out of it for me. Naturally, I wasn't very old before he began working on me about the statue.

---

1. **valise** (və lēs'): suitcase.

Part 1

Getting at Meaning

RECALLING

1. Two characters in this part of the play are called Monaghan. Who are they? Which Monaghan says each of the following:

a. "I'm not throwin' me good money away for somethin' I don't even know exists."

b. "I come from around here. It reminds me of things."

c. "I got to be pretty attached to Grandpa."

d. "You got a secondhand statue, that's what you got, and I'm not payin' for new when they've shipped us something that's all smashed to pieces."

2. Where do Monaghan and Sheean see the Statue of Liberty? In what condition is it?

3. What does this mean: July IV, MDCCLXXVI?

INTERPRETING

4. Why is Grandpa Monaghan called "Mercyless" Monaghan?

5. What does Jack Sheean want from Monaghan? Why does Monaghan refuse him?

Developing Skills in Reading Literature

1. **Setting.** Setting is the time and place of the action of a story or play. In plays that are produced on the stage, setting is indicated by means of scenery, lighting, costumes, and props. Props are small items, such as books and musical instruments, that are used by the actors.

Grandpa and the Statue is a radio play. There are two ways to indicate the setting in such a play:

a. The writer can create a narrator, or announcer, to introduce part of the play and to describe the setting.

b. The writer can have his or her characters speak to one another about the setting.

Arthur Miller uses both of these methods of indicating setting in *Grandpa and the Statue.* Reread the opening lines of the play. What does the Announcer tell the listener about the setting? Now reread the opening conversation between August and Monaghan. What further details does the listener learn about the setting from their conversation?

2. **Scene.** A scene is a unit of action that takes place in one setting. Part 1 of *Grandpa and the Statue* contains four different scenes. The first scene begins with the Announcer saying "The scene is the fourth floor of a giant army hospital" and ends with Monaghan saying "One day he's sitting on the front porch, reading a paper he borrowed from the neighbors, when along comes this man Jack Sheean who lived up the block." Where do the other three scenes in Part 1 begin and end?

3. **Stage Directions.** Stage directions are notes in plays to help readers to picture the action. Stage directions can describe setting, sound effects, or the way dialogue is spoken. Generally, stage directions are given in parentheses and printed in italics.

AUGUST *(laughs a little).* That so? What happened?

What stage direction is included in the example? What kind of information does it give?

On a sheet of paper, copy six stage directions from the play, three that tell how dialogue is spoken and three that describe sound effects. For each, note the page and column where the direction appears.

4. **Dialogue.** Dialogue is the conversation between characters in a short story or play. Plays are made up almost entirely of dialogue. When you read a play, you must imagine hearing the dialogue spoken by the characters. Study this example:

AUGUST. Okay *(slight pause)*. You don't want to go feeling blue, Monaghan.

MONAGHAN. I'm not blue.

What words are actually spoken by August? What does Monaghan say in reply?

For each of the following questions, write, on a sheet of paper, the name of the character who asks the question, the name of the character who answers, and the exact words of the answer.

a. "You want to play some checkers with me, Monaghan?"

b. "What fund is that?"

c. "And how do I know it's in this here warehouse at all?"

d. "What'd he do, just go over and come back?"

e. "What do you mean, goodbye? How am I to get back to Butler Street from here?"

5. **Flashback.** A flashback is a part of a story or play that interrupts the sequence of events to relate an earlier conversation, scene, or event. Much of *Grandpa and the Statue* is flashback. Which two scenes in the play are flashbacks? Which scenes are in the present?

The play also includes a flashback within a flashback. What early event in Grandpa Monaghan's life is recalled in a flashback? In what scene does the flashback within a flashback occur?

Developing Vocabulary

Prefixes, Suffixes, and Base Words. Some words are made up of separate parts, each of which communicates part of the meaning of the word. Three common types of word parts are prefixes, suffixes, and base words. A base word is a complete word to which one or more word parts can be added. A prefix is a word part that can be added to the beginning of a word or word part. A suffix is a word part that can be added to the end of a word or word part. The word *disrespectful,* for example, is made up of the base word *respect,* the prefix *dis–,* which means "not," and the suffix *–ful,* which means "full of." In Part 1 of *Grandpa and the Statue,* the grandfather is called "Mercyless Monaghan." What is the base word in the word *mercyless*? What suffix does this word contain? What does this suffix mean? What do the suffix and the base word mean when combined to make one word?

PART 2

(High wind)

CHILD MONAGHAN *(softly, as though Grandpa is in bed)*. Grampa?

MONAGHAN *(awakened)*. Heh? What are you doin' up?

CHILD MONAGHAN. Ssssh! Listen!

(Wind rising up and fading. Rising higher and fading)

MONAGHAN *(gleefully)*. Aaaaaaaah! Yes, yes. This'll do it, boy. This'll do it! First thing in the morning we'll go down to the docks and I'll bet you me life that Mr. Sheean's statue is smashed down and layin' on the bottom of the bay. Go to sleep now, we'll have a look first thing.

(Music up and down)

(Footsteps)

CHILD MONAGHAN. If it fell down, all the people will get their dimes back, won't they Grampa? Slow down, I can't walk so fast.

MONAGHAN. Not only will they get their dimes back, but Mr. Sheean and the whole crew that engineered the collection are going to rot in jail. Now mark my words. Here, now, we'll take a short cut around this shed....

(Footsteps continue a moment, then gradually ... disappointedly they come to a halt)

CHILD MONAGHAN. She's...she's still standing, Grampa.

MONAGHAN. She is that. *(Uncomprehending)* I don't understand it. That was a terrible wind last night. Terrible.

CHILD MONAGHAN. Maybe she's weaker though. Heh?

MONAGHAN. Why...sure, that must be it. I'll wager she's hangin' by a thread. *(Realizing)* Of course! That's why they put her out there in the water so when she falls down she won't be flattening out a lot of poor innocent people. Hey—feel that?

CHILD MONAGHAN. The wind! It's starting to blow again!

MONAGHAN. Sure, and look at the sky blackening over!

(Wind rising)

Feel it comin' up! Take your last look at the statue, boy. If I don't mistake me eyes she's takin' a small list[2] to Jersey already!

(Music up and down)

YOUNG MONAGHAN. It was getting embarrassing for me on the block. I kept promising the other kids that when the next wind came the statue would come down. We even had a game. Four or five kids would stand in a semicircle around one kid who was the statue. The statue kid had to stand on his heels and look right in our eyes. Then we'd all take a deep breath and blow in his face. He'd fall down like a stick of wood. They all believed me and Grampa...until one day. We were standing around throwing rocks at an old milk can....

(Banging of rocks against milk can)

---

2. **list:** tilt to one side.

GEORGE (*kid*). What're you doin'?

CHILD MONAGHAN. What do we look like we're doin'?

GEORGE. I'm going someplace tomorrow.

CHARLEY (*kid*). I know, church. Watch out, I'm throwin'.

(*Can being hit*)

GEORGE. I mean after church.

JACK. Where?

GEORGE. My old man's going to take me out on the Statue of Liberty boat.

(*Banging against can abruptly stops*)

CHILD MONAGHAN. You're not going out on the statue, though, are you?

GEORGE. Sure, that's where we're going.

CHILD MONAGHAN. But you're liable to get killed. Supposing there's a high wind tomorrow?

GEORGE. My old man says that statue couldn't fall down if all the wind in the world and John L. Sullivan[3] hit it at the same time.

CHILD MONAGHAN. Is that so?

GEORGE. Yeh, that's so. My old man says that the only reason your grandfather's saying that it's going to fall down is that he's ashamed he didn't put a dime in for the pedestal.

CHILD MONAGHAN. Is that so?

GEORGE. Yeh, that's so.

CHILD MONAGHAN. Well, you tell your old man that if he gets killed tomorrow not to come around to my grandfather and say he didn't warn him!

JACK. Hey, George, would your father take me along?

GEORGE. I'll ask him, maybe he—

CHILD MONAGHAN. What, are you crazy, Jack?

MIKE. Ask him if he'd take me too, will ya, George?

CHILD MONAGHAN. Mike, what's the matter with you?

JOE. Me too, George, I'll ask my mother for money.

CHILD MONAGHAN. Joe! Didn't you hear what my grampa said?

JOE. Well…I don't really believe that any more.

CHILD MONAGHAN. You don't be….

MIKE. Me neither.

JACK. I don't really think your grampa knows what he's talkin' about.

CHILD MONAGHAN. He don't, heh? (*Ready to weep*) Okay…Okay. (*Bursting out*) I just hope that wind blows tomorrow, boy! I just hope that wind blows!

(*Music up and down*)

(*Creaking of a rocking chair*)

Grampa … ?

MONAGHAN. Huh?

CHILD MONAGHAN. Can you stop rocking for a minute?

(*Rocking stops*)

Can you put down your paper?

(*Rustle of paper*)

---

3. **John L. Sullivan:** world heavyweight boxing champion in the 1880's.

I—I read the weather report for tomorrow.

MONAGHAN. The weather report....

CHILD MONAGHAN. Yeh. It says fair and cool.

MONAGHAN. What of it?

CHILD MONAGHAN. I was wondering. Supposing you and me we went on a boat tomorrow. You know, I see the water every day when I go down to the docks to play, but I never sat on it. I mean in a boat.

MONAGHAN. Oh. Well, we might take the ferry on the Jersey side. We might do that.

CHILD MONAGHAN. Yeh, but there's nothing to see in Jersey.

MONAGHAN. You can't go to Europe tomorrow.

CHILD MONAGHAN. No, but couldn't we go toward the ocean? Just...*toward* it?

MONAGHAN. Toward it. What—what is it on your mind, boy? What is it now?

CHILD MONAGHAN. Well, I....

MONAGHAN. Oh, you want to take the Staten Island ferry. Sure, that's in the direction of the sea.

CHILD MONAGHAN. No, Grampa, not the Staten Island ferry.

MONAGHAN. You don't mean — (Breaks off) Boy!

CHILD MONAGHAN. All the kids are going tomorrow with Georgie's old man.

MONAGHAN. You don't believe me any more.

CHILD MONAGHAN. I do, Grampa, but....

MONAGHAN. You don't. If you did you'd stay clear of the Statue of Liberty for love of your life!

CHILD MONAGHAN. But, Grampa, when is it going to fall down? All I do is wait and wait.

MONAGHAN (with some uncertainty). You've got to have faith.

CHILD MONAGHAN. But every kid in my class went to see it and now the ones that didn't are going tomorrow. And they all keep talking about it and all I do.... Well, I can't keep telling them it's a swindle. I—I wish we could see it, Grampa. It don't cost so much to go.

MONAGHAN. As long as you put it that way I'll have to admit I'm a bit curious meself as to how it's managed to stand upright so long. Tell you what I'll do. Barrin' wind, we'll chance it tomorrow!

CHILD MONAGHAN. Oh, Gramp!

MONAGHAN. But! If anyone should ask you where we went you'll say — Staten Island. Are y' on?

CHILD MONAGHAN. Okay, sure. Staten Island.

MONAGHAN (secretively). We'll take the early boat, then. Mum's the word, now. For if old man Sheean hears that I went out there I'll have no peace from the thief the rest of m'life.

(Music up and down)

(Boat whistles)

CHILD MONAGHAN. Gee, it's nice ridin' on a boat, ain't it, Gramp?

MONAGHAN. Never said there was anything wrong with the boat. Boat's all right. You're sure now that Georgie's father is takin' the kids in the afternoon!

CHILD MONAGHAN. Yeh, that's when they're going. Gee, look at those two sea gulls. Wee! — look at them swoop! They caught a fish!

MONAGHAN. What I can't understand is what all these people see in that statue that they'll keep a boat like this full makin' the trip, year in year out. To hear the newspapers talk, if

STATUE OF LIBERTY, 1899. *Theodore Earl Butler. Private Collection.*
Courtesy of Maxwell Galleries, San Francisco.

the statue was gone we'd be at war with the nation that stole her the followin' mornin' early. All it is is a big high pile of French copper.

CHILD MONAGHAN. The teacher says it shows us that we got liberty.

MONAGHAN. Bah! If you've got liberty you don't need a statue to tell you you got it; and if you haven't got liberty no statue's going to do you any good tellin' you you got it. It was a criminal waste of the people's money. (*Quietly*) And just to prove it to you I'll ask this feller sitting right over there what he sees in it. You'll see what a madness the whole thing was. Say, mister?

ALF. Hey?

MONAGHAN. I beg your pardon. I'm a little strange here, and curious. Could you tell me why you're going to the Statue of Liberty?

ALF. Me? Well, I tell ya. I always wanted to take an ocean voyage. This is a pretty big boat—bigger than the ferries—so on Sundays, sometimes, I take the trip. It's better than nothing.

MONAGHAN. Thank you. (*To the kid*) So much for the great meaning of that statue, me boy. We'll talk to this lady standing at the rail. I just want you to understand why I didn't give Sheean me dime. Madam, would you be good enough to....Oh pardon me. (*To kid*) Better pass her by, she don't look so good. We'll ask that girl there. Young lady, if you'll pardon the curiosity of an old man...could you tell me in a few good words what it is about that statue that brings you out here?

GIRL. What statue?

MONAGHAN. Why, the Statue of Liberty up 'head. We're coming up to it.

GIRL. Statue of Liberty! Is this the Statue of Liberty boat?

MONAGHAN. Well, what'd you think it was?

GIRL. Oh, my! I'm supposed to be on the Staten Island ferry! Where's the ticket man? (*Going away*) Ticket man! Where's the ticket man?

CHILD MONAGHAN. Gee whiz, nobody seems to want to see the statue.

MONAGHAN. Just to prove it, let's see this fellow sitting on this bench here. Young man, say....

YOUNG MAN. I can tell you in one word. For four days I haven't had a minute's peace. My kids are screaming, my wife is yelling, upstairs they play the piano all day long. The only place I can find that's quiet is a statue. That statue is my sweetheart. Every Sunday I beat it out to the island and sit next to her, and she don't talk.

CHILD MONAGHAN. I guess you were right, Grampa. Nobody seems to think it means anything.

MONAGHAN. Not only doesn't mean anything, but if they'd used the money to build an honest roomin' house on that island, the immigrants would have a place to spend the night, their valises wouldn't get robbed, and they—

MEGAPHONE VOICE. *Please keep your seats while the boat is docking. Statue of Liberty— all out in five minutes!*

CHILD MONAGHAN. Look down there, Gramp! There's a peanut stand! Could I have some?

MONAGHAN. I feel the wind comin' up. I don't think we dare take the time.

(*Music up and down*)

CHILD MONAGHAN. Sssssseuuuuuww! Look how far you can see! Look at that ship way out in the ocean!

MONAGHAN. It is, it's quite a view. Don't let go of me hand now.

CHILD MONAGHAN. I betcha we could almost see California.

MONAGHAN. It's probably that grove of trees way out over there. They do say it's beyond Jersey.

CHILD MONAGHAN. Feels funny. We're standing right inside her head. Is that what you meant...July IV, MCD...?

MONAGHAN. That's it. That tablet in her hand. Now shouldn't they have put Welcome All on it instead of that foreign language? Say! Do you feel her rockin'?

CHILD MONAGHAN. Yeah, she's moving a little bit. Listen, the wind!

(Whistling of wind)

MONAGHAN. We better get down, come on! This way!

CHILD MONAGHAN. No, the stairs are this way! Come on!

(Running in echo. Then quick stop)

MONAGHAN. No, I told you they're the other way! Come!

VETERAN. *(calm, quiet voice)*. Don't get excited, pop. She'll stand.

MONAGHAN. She's swayin' awful.

VETERAN. That's all right. I been up here thirty, forty times. She gives with the wind, flexible. Enjoy the view, go on.

MONAGHAN. Did you say you've been up here forty times?

VETERAN. About that many.

MONAGHAN. What do you find here that's so interesting?

VETERAN. It calms my nerves.

MONAGHAN. Ah. It seems to me it would make you more nervous than you were.

VETERAN. No, not me. It kinda means something to me.

MONAGHAN. Might I ask what?

VETERAN. Well...I was in the Philippine War ...back in '98. Left my brother back there.

MONAGHAN. Oh, yes. Sorry I am to hear it. Young man, I suppose, eh?

VETERAN. Yeh. We were both young. This is his birthday today.

MONAGHAN. Oh, I understand.

VETERAN. Yeh, this statue is about the only stone he's got. In my mind I feel it is anyway. This statue kinda looks like what we believe. You know what I mean?

MONAGHAN. Looks like what we believe...I ...I never thought of it that way. I...I see what you mean. It does look that way. *(Angrily)* See now, boy? If Sheean had put it that way I'd a give him me dime. *(Hurt)* Now, why do you suppose he didn't tell me that! Come down now. I'm sorry, sir, we've got to get out of here.

(Music up and down)

(Footsteps under)

Hurry now, I want to get out of here. I feel terrible. I do, boy. That Sheean, that fool. Why didn't he tell me that? You'd think....

CHILD MONAGHAN. What does this say?

(Footsteps halt)

MONAGHAN. Why, it's just a tablet, I suppose. I'll try it with me spectacles, just a minute. Why, it's a poem, I believe..."Give me your tired, your poor, your huddled masses yearning to breathe free, the wretched refuse of your teeming shore. Send these, the homeless, tempest-tost to me, I lift...my lamp beside...the golden door!" Oh, dear. *(Ready to weep)* It had Welcome All on it all the time. Why didn't Sheean tell me? I'd a given him a quarter! Boy...go over there and here's a nickel and buy yourself a bag of them peanuts.

CHILD MONAGHAN *(astonished)*. Gramp!

MONAGHAN. Go on now. I want to study this a minute. And be sure the man gives you full count.

CHILD MONAGHAN. I'll be right back.

(Footsteps running away)

MONAGHAN *(to himself)*. "Give me your tired, your poor, your huddled masses. . . ."

(Music swells from a sneak to full, then under to background)

YOUNG MONAGHAN *(soldier)*. I ran over and got my peanuts and stood there cracking them open, looking around. And I happened to glance over to Grampa. He had his nose right up to that bronze tablet, reading it. And then he reached into his pocket and kinda spied around over his eyeglasses to see if anybody was looking, and then he took out a coin and stuck it in a crack of cement over the tablet.

(Coin falling onto concrete)

It fell out and before he could pick it up I got a look at it. It was a half a buck. He picked it up and pressed it into the crack so it stuck. And then he came over to me and we went home.

(Music: Change to stronger, more forceful theme)

That's why, when I look at her now through this window, I remember that time and that poem, and she really seems to say, Whoever you are, wherever you come from, Welcome All. Welcome Home.

(Music: Flare up to finish)

PART 2

Getting at Meaning

RECALLING

1. Where does Child Monaghan ask Grandpa to go with him?

2. Where is the Statue of Liberty located? How do visitors reach it?

3. What does Grandpa expect will happen to the statue? What effect does the wind actually have on the statue?

4. Three passengers on the Statue of Liberty boat give reasons for being on the boat. What are their reasons?

5. What does Grandpa find engraved on the tablet?

INTERPRETING

6. Why have Child Monaghan's friends stopped believing Grandpa's predictions about the statue? How do they show this change in attitude? What effect does this change in attitude have on Child Monaghan?

7. What change occurs in Grandpa's feel-

ings about the statue? What causes this change?

8. Why does Grandpa stick a coin into a crack above the tablet of the statue?

9. What might be Young Monaghan's reasons for telling this story to August?

10. Who is the speaker in the poem engraved on the tablet? To whom is the poem addressed? What offer is the poem making?

Developing Skills in Reading Literature

1. **Scene and Flashback.** A scene is a unit of action that takes place in one setting. A flashback is a part of a story or play that interrupts the sequence of events to relate an earlier conversation, scene, or event. The first part of this play consists of four scenes, which you identified for Developing Skills in Reading Literature on page 507. The second part is made up of nine scenes. On a separate sheet of paper, identify each scene in the second part by place, time, characters, and action. Be prepared to tell which scenes are flashbacks.

2. **Sequence.** Sequence is the order of events in a literary work. Because this play contains flashbacks, some events are not presented in the order in which they occurred. On a sheet of paper, write these events from *Grandpa and the Statue* in the order in which they happened.

a. Child Monaghan is born.

b. Grandpa Monaghan refuses to contribute to the Statue of Liberty fund.

c. Young Monaghan points out the Statue of Liberty to a fellow patient.

d. Grandpa Monaghan and Child Monaghan visit the Statue of Liberty.

e. Grandpa Monaghan arrives in America from the old country.

3. **Climax.** The climax, or turning point, is the high point of interest or suspense in a story or play. The events lead up to the climax, at which time some important change takes place. Which of the following four events is the climax of *Grandpa and the Statue*? Write your answer on a separate sheet of paper. Be prepared to explain your choice.

a. The Statue of Liberty remains standing in the high wind.

b. Three passengers give reasons for being on the Statue of Liberty boat.

c. The veteran explains to Grandpa what the statue means to him.

d. Grandpa places a half dollar on the statue.

4. **Symbol.** A symbol is a person, place, or thing that stands for something beyond itself. For example, the American flag is a symbol of the United States. What does the Statue of Liberty symbolize to Americans? to immigrants to this country? What does the statue symbolize for Young Monaghan?

Developing Vocabulary

Word Parts: Prefixes. A prefix is a word part that can be added to the beginning of a word or word part. Each of the following words from Part 2 of *Grandpa and the Statue* is formed by adding a prefix to a complete word:

un– + *comprehending* = *uncomprehending*
semi– + *circle* = *semicircle*
im– + *migrants* = *immigrants*

Look up the meanings of the prefixes *un–*, *semi–*, and *im–* in a dictionary. Then, look up the meanings of the words *comprehending, circle,* and *migrants.* Write these definitions and the definitions of the complete words *uncomprehending, semicircle,* and *immigrants* on a sheet of paper. Notice that, if you know the meanings of the prefixes and suffixes that make up an unfamiliar word, you can often figure out what the unfamiliar word means. Study the following prefixes and their meanings:

prefix	meaning
equi–	equal, even
mal–	bad, wrong
non–	not
pre–	before
sub–	under, less than

Determine the meanings of the following words by referring to the preceding list of prefixes. Write the definitions of these words on a sheet of paper.

1. equidistant
2. maladjusted
3. nonprofit
4. preview
5. substandard

Developing Writing Skills

1. **Describing a Character.** In drama, character is revealed by dialogue and by action. List two of Grandpa's most dominant character traits as shown by what he says and does in the play. Then write two paragraphs describing these aspects of Grandpa's character. Use examples from the play as supporting details in each paragraph. Refer to **Using the Process of Writing** on pages 614–623 and to Writing About Drama on pages 630–632 for help with this assignment.

2. **Writing a Poem.** Imagine that a statue is being planned for the Miami airport to welcome immigrants who arrive from the Caribbean islands and from Central and South America. Write a poem that might be inscribed on the statue.

3. **Writing Dialogue.** Imagine that you are writing your own play. Imagine, further, that in this play two characters disagree on what course of action to take. Write a brief scene between these two characters. Remember, a scene takes place in one setting and is a single unit of action. Use stage directions and dialogue to develop your scene. Begin by describing your setting and characters in your prewriting notes. Also explain in your prewriting notes what the conflict between your characters will be about.

Speaking and Listening. As you write and revise your work, read your dialogue aloud to make sure that it sounds natural.

B I O G R A P H Y

Arthur Miller (born 1915) is one of the most popular and successful playwrights of the twentieth century. His dramas are played by amateur and professional theatre groups throughout the world. Miller graduated from the University of Michigan in 1938 and began writing radio scripts. These were soon followed by a series of Broadway plays, including *All My Sons, The Crucible,* and *A View from the Bridge.* Miller wrote the film script for *The Misfits* and has also produced many essays and short stories. He has received two Drama Critics Circle Awards and a Pulitzer Prize for *Death of a Salesman.*

On a deserted country road in a dense fog, a doctor is approached by two strangers.

In the Fog

Milton Geiger

CHARACTERS

THE DOCTOR

ZEKE

EBEN

FILLING STATION ATTENDANT

(Sets: *A signpost on Pennsylvania Route 30. A rock or stump in the fog. A gas station pump.*)

(Fade in: *Exterior. Night. At first we can only see fog drifting across a dark scene devoid of detail. Then, to weird minor music, the camera dollies in slowly so that out of the fog there emerges toward us a white roadside signpost with a number of white painted signboards pointing to right and to left. The camera continues to dolly in until it has in closeup the state route marker fastened below the signs on the post. The marker is a Pennsylvania State Route —marked characteristically "*PENNA-30.*" Now, a light as from a far headlight sweeps the signs.*)

(Sound: *Automobile approaching on road. The car pulls up close. We hear the car door open and slam and a man's footsteps approaching on the concrete. Now the signs are lit up again by a more localized, smaller source of light. The light grows stronger as the man, off-stage, approaches. The* DOCTOR *enters the shot, holding a flashlight before him. He scrutinizes the road marker. He flashes his light up at the arrows, the camera moving up with the light. We see the legends on the markers. Pointing off right there are markers that read: York, Columbia, Lancaster; pointing left the signs read: Fayetteville, McConnellsburg, Pennsylvania Turnpike.*)

(Cut to: *Another angle. We shoot into the* DOCTOR'S *perplexed and annoyed face as he turns his flashlight on a folded road map. He is a bit lost in the fog. Then his flashlight fails him. It goes out!*)

DOCTOR. Darn! (*He fumbles with the flashlight in the gloom. Then a voice is raised to him from off-scene.*)

EBEN (*off-scene, strangely*). Turn around, mister . . . (*The* DOCTOR *turns sharply to stare off-scene. His face is lit by a bobbing light from off-scene.*)

ZEKE (*off-scene*). You don't have to be afraid, mister. . . .

(*Cut to: What* DOCTOR *sees. Two men are slowly approaching out of the fog, grotesque in the distorting gloom. One carries a lantern below his knees. The other holds a heavy rifle of dim manufacture. Their features are utterly indistinct as they approach and the rifleman holds up his gun with quiet threat.*)

(*Cut to: Group shot, angling past* DOCTOR'S *shoulder, at their faces.*)

EBEN. You don't have to be afraid.

DOCTOR (*more indignant than afraid*). So you say! Who are you, man?

EBEN. We don't aim to hurt you none.

DOCTOR. That's reassuring. I'd like to know just what you mean by this? This gun business! Who *are* you?

ZEKE (*mildly*). What's your trade, mister?

DOCTOR. I . . . I'm a doctor. Why?

ZEKE (*to* EBEN). Doctor.

EBEN (*nods; then to* DOCTOR). Yer the man we want.

ZEKE. Ye'll do proper, we're thinkin'.

EBEN. So ye'd better come along, mister.

ZEKE. Aye.

DOCTOR. Why? Has—anyone been hurt?

EBEN. It's for you to say if he's been hurt nigh to the finish.

ZEKE. So we're askin' ye to come along, doctor.

(*Cut to: Another angle, favoring* DOCTOR. *He looks from one to another in indecision and puzzlement.*)

EBEN. In the name o' mercy.

ZEKE. Aye.

DOCTOR. I want you to understand—I'm not afraid of your gun! I'll go to your man all right. Naturally, I'm a doctor. But I demand to know who you are.

ZEKE (*patiently*). Why not? Raise yer lantern, Eben . . .

EBEN (*tiredly*). Aye.

(EBEN *lifts his lantern. Its light falls on their faces now and we see that they are terrifying. Matted beards, clotted with blood; crude head bandages, crusty with dirt and dry blood. Their hair, stringy and disheveled. Their faces are lean and hollow-cheeked; their eyes sunken and tragic. The* DOCTOR *is shocked for a moment—then bursts out—*)

DOCTOR. Good Lord!—

ZEKE (*impassively*). That's Eben, I'm Zeke.

DOCTOR. What's happened? Has there been an accident or . . . what?

ZEKE. Mischief's happened, stranger.

EBEN. Mischief enough.

DOCTOR (*looks at rifle at his chest*). There's been gunplay—hasn't there?

ZEKE (*mildly ironic*). Yer tellin' us there's been gunplay!

DOCTOR. And I'm telling you that I'm not at all frightened! It's my duty to report this and report it I will!

ZEKE. Aye, mister. You *do* that.

DOCTOR. You're arrogant about it now! You don't think you'll be caught and dealt with.

But people are losing patience with you men....

(Cut to: Close two-shot. ZEKE *and* EBEN.)

DOCTOR'S VOICE *(off-scene)....* You... you moonshiners![1] Running wild... a law unto yourselves... shooting up the countryside!

ZEKE. Hear that, Eben? Moonshiners.

EBEN. Mischief's happened, mister, we'll warrant that....

(Group shot, favoring DOCTOR.)

DOCTOR. And I don't like it!

ZEKE. Can't say we like it better'n you do, mister ....

EBEN *(strangely sad and remote).* What must be, must.

ZEKE. There's not changin' or goin' back and all 'at's left is the wishin' things were different.

EBEN. Aye.

DOCTOR. And while we talk your wounded man lies bleeding I suppose — worthless though he may be. Well? I'll have to get my instrument bag, you know. *(Nods off-scene.)* It's in the car.

*(*EBEN *and* ZEKE *part to let* DOCTOR *pass between them.* DOCTOR *leaves shot grimly as they watch him, off-scene.)*

(Sound: Car door opens off-scene. Pause. Slams.)

(The DOCTOR *re-enters the shot, carrying his medical bag.)*

DOCTOR. I'm ready. Lead the way.

*(*EBEN *lifts his lantern a bit and goes first.* ZEKE *prods the* DOCTOR *ever so gently and apologetically but firmly with the rifle muzzle. The* DOCTOR *leaves the shot next.* ZEKE *strides off slowly after them.)*

(Dissolve to: Exterior, night. Medium shot of a wounded man lying against a section of stone fence or a boulder or a tree trunk. He, too, is bearded though very young and wears some sort of unidentifiable tunic like the other men. His shirt is dark with blood. He breathes stertorously but never stirs otherwise. The light of

---

1. **moonshiners:** people who make and sell whiskey illegally.

EBEN'S *bull's-eye falls on him, bobbingly.* EBEN *enters the shot followed by the* DOCTOR *and* ZEKE.)

(Sound: Owl, far off, from time to time.)

ZEKE. Ain't stirred a mite since we left 'im.

DOCTOR. Let's have that lantern here! *(The* DOCTOR *tears the man's shirt for better access to the wound.)*

(Close up: DOCTOR'S *face. Appalled.)*

DOCTOR *(softly).* Dreadful! Dreadful! . . .

ZEKE'S VOICE *(off-scene).* Reckon it's bad in the chest like that, hey?

DOCTOR *(taking pulse).* His pulse is positively racing! . . .

(Tight group shot.)

DOCTOR. How long has he been this way?

ZEKE. A long time, mister. A *long* time. . . .

DOCTOR *(to* EBEN). You! Hand me my bag.

*(EBEN *puts down lantern and hands bag to* DOCTOR. *The* DOCTOR *opens bag and takes out a couple of retractors.[2]* ZEKE *holds lantern close now.)*

DOCTOR. Lend me a hand with these retractors. *(He works on man, hiding wound from camera with his body.)* All right . . . when I tell you to draw back on the retractors — draw back.

EBEN. Aye.

ZEKE. How is 'e, mister?

DOCTOR *(preoccupied).* More retraction. Pull them a bit more. Hold it. . . .

EBEN. Bad, ain't he?

DOCTOR. Bad enough. The bullet didn't touch any lung tissue far as I can see right now. There's some pneumothorax[3] though. All I can do now is plug the wound. There's some cotton and gauze wadding in my bag. Find it . . . .

*(ZEKE *probes about silently in the bag and comes up with a small dark box of gauze.)*

DOCTOR. That's it. *(Works a moment in silence.)* I've never seen anything quite like it.

EBEN. Yer young, doctor. Lots o' things you've never seen.

DOCTOR. Adhesive tape!

*(ZEKE *finds a roll of three-inch tape and hands it to the* DOCTOR *who tears off strips and, unseen to camera, slaps them on the dressing and pats and smooths them to man's chest.* EBEN *replaces equipment in* DOCTOR'S *bag and closes it with a hint of the finality to come. A preview of dismissal so to speak.)*

DOCTOR *(at length).* There. So much for that. Now then—*(Takes man's shoulders.)* Give me a hand here.

ZEKE *(quiet suspicion).* What fer?

DOCTOR. We've got to move this man.

ZEKE. What fer?

DOCTOR *(stands; indignantly).* We've got to get him to a hospital for treatment; a thorough cleansing of the wound; irrigation. I've done all I can for him here.

---

2. **retractors:** surgical instruments for drawing back part of an organ, such as the skin at the edge of an incision.

3. **pneumothorax** (noo' mō thôr' aks): the presence of air in the chest cavity as a result of a puncture in the lungs.

ZEKE. I reckon he'll be all right, 'thout no hospital.

DOCTOR. Do you realize how badly this man's hurt!

EBEN. He won't bleed to death, will he?

DOCTOR. I don't think so—not with that plug and pressure dressing. But bleeding isn't the only danger we've got to—

ZEKE *(interrupts)*. All right, then. Much obliged to you.

DOCTOR. This man's *dangerously* hurt!

ZEKE. Reckon he'll pull through now, thanks to you.

DOCTOR. I'm glad you feel that way about it! But I'm going to report this to the Pennsylvania State Police at the first telephone I reach!

ZEKE. We ain't stoppin' ye, mister.

EBEN. Fog is liftin', Zeke. Better be done with this, I say.

ZEKE *(nods, sadly)*. Aye. Ye can go now, mister . . . and thanks.

(Group shot. Another angle, favoring ZEKE, *then* EBEN.*)*

ZEKE *(continues)*. We never meant a mite o' harm, I can tell ye. If we killed, it was no wish of ours.

EBEN. What's done is done. Aye.

ZEKE. Ye can go now, stranger. . . .

*(*EBEN *hands* ZEKE *the* DOCTOR'S *bag.* ZEKE *hands it gently to the* DOCTOR.*)*

DOCTOR. Very well. You haven't heard the last of this, though!

ZEKE. That's the truth, mister. We've killed, aye; and we've been hurt for it. . . .

EBEN. Hurt bad.

(Group shot. Another angle, favoring DOCTOR *in close shot. His face puckered with doubt and strange apprehension.)*

ZEKE. We're not alone, mister. We ain't the only ones. (Sighs.) Ye can go now, doctor . . . and our thanks to ye. . . .

(The camera moves with the DOCTOR *as he leaves the other two, still gazing at them in strange enchantment and wonder and a touch of indignation. Camera takes his body from waist up as he walks against neutral, featureless background wreathed with some tendrils of fog.)*

EBEN'S VOICE *(off-scene)*. Thanks, mister. . . .

ZEKE'S VOICE. In the name o' mercy. . . . We thank you. . . .

(Cut to: Close up: ZEKE *and* EBEN, *their faces grizzled like the faces of monuments in the park in winter; their eyes unhappy and suffering. The fog drifting across them.)*

EBEN. In the name o' mercy.

ZEKE. Thanks, mister. . . .

EBEN. In the name o' kindness. . . .

(The camera pulls back for a group shot of the two men standing; their wounded comrade at their feet—like a group statue in the park . . . grizzled and time-worn. The fog thickens across the scene.)

(Music: Eerie, sad.)

(Sound: Far off the long, sad wail of a locomotive whimpers in the dark. Then fades.)

(Fade out.)

(*Fade in: The illuminated translucent glass globe atop a gasoline pump. The camera pulls back to show the young* ATTENDANT *standing in front of the pump taking a reading and recording it in a book as he prepares to close up. Lights sweep him. He turns as he hears the car approach on the gravel drive.*)

(*Sound: Car approaching. Crunches on gravel and stops. Door opens and slams shut.* DOCTOR'S *feet crunch on gravel, approaching swiftly.*)

(DOCTOR *enters shot.*)

ATTENDANT (*pleasantly*). Good evening, sir. (*Nods off at off-scene car.*) Care to pull 'er up to this pump, sir? Closing up.

DOCTOR (*impatiently*). No. Where's your telephone, please? I've just been held up!

ATTENDANT. Pay-station inside, sir. . . .

DOCTOR. Thank you! (*The* DOCTOR *starts to go past the* ATTENDANT.)

ATTENDANT. Excuse me, sir. . . .

DOCTOR (*stops*). Eh, what is it, what is it?

ATTENDANT. Uh . . . what sort of looking fellows were they?

DOCTOR. Oh . . . two big fellows with a rifle; faces and heads bandaged and smeared with dirt and blood. Friend of theirs with a gaping hole in his chest. I'm a doctor so they forced me to attend him. Why?

ATTENDANT. *Those* fellers, huh?

DOCTOR. Then you know about them!

ATTENDANT. I guess so.

DOCTOR. They're armed and they're desperate!

ATTENDANT. That was about two or three miles back, would you say?

DOCTOR (*fumbling in pocket*). Just about — I don't seem to have the change. I wonder if you'd spare me change for a quarter? . . .

ATTENDANT (*makes change from metal coin cannister at his belt*). Certainly, sir. . . .

DOCTOR. What town was that back there, now?

ATTENDANT (*dumps coins in other's hand*). There you are, sir.

DOCTOR (*impatient*). Yes, thank you. I say — what town was that back there, so I can tell the police?

(*Two shot. A new angle favoring* ATTENDANT. *His eyes are serious and candid; matter-of-fact and very steady.*)

ATTENDANT. That was . . . Gettysburg,[4] mister. . . .

(*Music: Softly, eerily poignant. "Dixie" and "Battle Hymn of the Republic" in minor counterpoint.*)

(*Camera slowly trucks around for two-shot that slowly favors* DOCTOR.)

DOCTOR Gettysburg? . . .

ATTENDANT. Gettysburg and Gettysburg battlefield . . . (*Looks off*). When it's light and the fog's gone, you can see the gravestones.

Meade's men . . . Pickett's men, Robert E. Lee's. . . .

(*The* DOCTOR *is looking off with the* ATTENDANT; *now he turns his head slowly to stare at the other man.*)

ATTENDANT (*continues*). On nights like this — well — you're not the first those men've stopped . . . or the last. (*Nods off.*) Fill 'er up, mister?

(*Camera dollies in slowly on the rapt face of the* DOCTOR.)

DOCTOR. Yes, fill 'er up. . . .

(*Fade out.*)

(*Music finishes.*)

---

4. **Gettysburg** (get′ iz burg′): town in southern Pennsylvania; site of a crucial Civil War battle, July, 1863.

Getting at Meaning

RECALLING

1. Where does this story take place? What happened there in the mid-1800's?

2. Why does the doctor get out of his car?

3. What do Zeke and Eben want from the doctor? What kind of men does the doctor take them to be?

4. How does the doctor help the wounded man?

5. Who says these words: "On nights like this—well—you're not the first those men've stopped...or the last"?

INTERPRETING

6. At the end of the play, why does the doctor turn his head slowly? Why does he stare?

7. Who does the attendant think the men met by the doctor are? How do you know?

8. What does the doctor want to do when he arrives at the filling station? What does he think he has witnessed?

CRITICAL THINKING: APPLYING

9. If you were the doctor, would you accept the explanation hinted at, or implied, by the attendant? Why, or why not?

Developing Skills in Reading Literature

1. **Stage Directions.** Stage directions are notes that are included in plays to help readers picture the action. They are usually given in parentheses and printed in italics. Find the following types of stage directions in the play and write them on a sheet of paper:

a. Two stage directions that describe how characters look.

b. Two stage directions that describe how characters act or speak.

c. Two stage directions that describe the setting, or time and place of the action of the play.

d. Two stage directions that describe music or sound effects.

In the Fog is written not to be produced on a stage but to be filmed for viewing on a television or movie screen. Therefore, the stage directions include specific suggestions for filming the action. Find five such stage directions in the play, and add these to your list.

2. **Scene and Act.** A scene is a short unit of action that takes place in one setting. An act is a major unit of action in a play; an act may have more than one setting and can include several scenes. *In the Fog* is a one-act play. How many scenes make up this act?

3. **Mood.** Mood is the feeling created by a literary work. Imagine that you are going to direct the filming of this play. What mood would you want to create? How might you go about creating this mood? Find at least five words and phrases from the first two pages of the play that help to establish the mood. Write these on a sheet of paper.

4. **Surprise Ending.** A surprise ending is an unexpected twist in the plot at the conclusion of a story. Most readers probably are somewhat surprised by the ending of this play. They are not completely surprised, however, because the play includes clues suggesting that Zeke, Eben, and the wounded man are not of this time and place. For example, these characters use old-fashioned expressions such as "Ye'll do proper" and "hurt nigh to the finish." On a sheet of paper, write at least five other clues found in the stage directions or in the dialogue.

5. **Irony.** Irony is a contrast between what is believed or expected and what actually exists or happens. What does the doctor believe about Zeke and Eben? How is the doctor's belief contradicted?

Developing Vocabulary

1. **Understanding Jargon.** Screenwriting, like many other activities, has its own special vocabulary, or jargon. The following are some words and phrases from this jargon. Each of these is used at least once in the stage direc-

tions for *In the Fog.* Look up these words in a dictionary and define them, as they are used in screenwriting, on a sheet of paper.

dolly	angle
cut to	close-up
shot	dissolve
fade in	exterior
fade out	truck

2. **Understanding Dialect.** A dialect is the variety of a language spoken by the people of a particular region or social group. Writers sometimes change the spellings of words to show how they are pronounced in a character's dialect. The following are some examples of the dialect spoken by Zeke and Eben. Rewrite each example on a sheet of paper, spelling each word in its usual way.

a. "In the name o' mercy."
b. "There's no changin' or goin' back and all 'at's left is the wishin' things were different."
c. "How is 'e, mister?"
d. "What fer?"
e. "Yer young, doctor."
f. "I reckon he'll be all right, 'thout no hospital."

Dialects differ from one another not only in pronunciation but also in vocabulary and sentence structure. Reread the examples of Zeke and Eben's dialect. How would you say these same things? What differences are there, other than in pronunciation, between Zeke and Eben's dialect and your own?

3. **Word Parts: Suffixes.** A suffix is a word part that can be added to the end of a word or word part. Some suffixes are used to make nouns into adjectives, words that modify nouns. Other suffixes are used to make adjectives into nouns. Some suffixes are used to make adjectives into adverbs, words that modify verbs. Some are used to make verbs into adjectives or nouns. Consider the following examples from *In the Fog:*

1. *worth* + *–less* = *worthless*
     noun   suffix   adj.
2. *kind* + *–ness* = *kindness*
     adj.   suffix   noun
3. *strange* + *–ly* = *strangely*
     adj.   suffix   adv.
4. *enchant* + *–ment* = *enchantment*
     verb   suffix   noun

Each of the following words from *In the Fog* is made up of a suffix added to a base word. On a separate sheet of paper, write the suffix and the base word that make up each word. Then, write one sentence using the base word alone and another sentence using the base word with the suffix added.

puzzlement
identifiable
featureless
certainly
crusty

Developing Writing Skills

1. **Writing a Plot Summary.** Plot is the sequence of events in a story. It is the writer's plan for what happens, when, and to whom. A summary is a restatement using fewer words than the original. Summarize the plot of *In the Fog.* In your prewriting notes, list the important events in the play. Make sure that the events in your list are in chronological order, that is, in order of occurrence. Using your list, write a paragraph summarizing the plot in less than 150 words. Refer to **Using the Process of Writing** « on pages 614–623 and to Writing About Drama on pages 630–632 for help.

2. **Writing Dialogue.** Imagine a conversation between the doctor and a reporter sent to interview the doctor about his strange experience. What questions might the reporter ask? What answers might the doctor give? Write this conversation as if you were writing dialogue for a play. Include at least four stage directions that tell how the dialogue is spoken and how the two characters move.

BIOGRAPHY

Milton Geiger (1907–1971) was a television playwright who often wrote about his own experiences. His work as a pharmacist and assistant drugstore manager gave him the background for a very successful TV play, *One Special for Doc.*

RESEARCH SKILLS FOR *WRITING*

Using the *Readers' Guide*

The *Readers' Guide to Periodical Literature* is an index of articles that have appeared in popular magazines. The *Readers' Guide* is published in paperback volumes twice a month from September to June and once a month in July and August. At the end of the year, the paperback volumes are bound together in a single hardcover volume. Articles are listed in the *Readers' Guide* alphabetically by subject and by author. When using the *Readers' Guide*, begin with recent volumes and work back until you find the subjects or authors that you want. An abbreviation page at the beginning of each volume explains the many abbreviations used in the entries. Consider the following example:

Drama
Study and teaching
Write a play! [Young Playwrights Festival school workshop program] G. Chapman. il *Des Arts Educ* 84:4-10 Mr/Ap '83

Under the subhead **Study and teaching** appears the title of an article, "Write a play!"

by G. Chapman. The abbreviation *il* means that the article contains one or more illustrations. The article begins on page 4 and ends on page 10 in the 84th volume of *Design for Arts in Education.* This volume was published in the March and April issue of 1983.

Developing Writing Skills

Finding Information in the *Readers' Guide.* Use the *Readers' Guide* to find two magazine articles on each of the following subjects. On a sheet of paper, write the title of each article, the name of the author, the title of the magazine in which the article appeared, and the month and year of its publication.

the Civil War   the Statue of Liberty
television dramas   stage plays

Locate one article from the eight you have listed. Read the article and write a one-paragraph summary. Include important details in a logical order.

See **Handbook: How To Write About Literature,** Lessons 1–4.

CRITICAL THINKING

Making Generalizations

To make sense of a literary work, you must sometimes observe specific facts and then draw general conclusions. A conclusion of this kind—a general statement based on specific facts—is called a generalization. For example, the statement "Plays are written in dialogue" is a generalization because it is based on specific facts and refers to plays in general.

Recognizing Overgeneralizations. An overgeneralization is a general statement that is too broad. For example, when Young Monaghan is recalling his grandfather in *Grandpa and the Statue,* he says, "My grandfather was the stingiest man in Brooklyn." This statement is an overgeneralization because Young Monaghan cannot be certain that every man in Brooklyn was less stingy than his grandfather.

Avoiding Overgeneralizations. To avoid making overgeneralizations, use qualifiers. Qualifiers are words that limit the range of things to which a generalization applies. For example, the statement "Plays are meant to be performed on the stage" is an overgeneralization. It is too broad. Some plays are radio dramas, some are meant to be filmed, and some are meant only to be read. An overgeneralization of this kind can be corrected by using a

qualifier such as *some, often, many,* or *most.* The statement "*Many* plays are meant to be performed on the stage" is not an overgeneralization.

Developing Critical Thinking Skills

1. **Making Generalizations.** Read each group of specific facts below. Then, make a generalization based on each group of facts.

a. The play *Grandpa and the Statue* is made up of dialogue and stage directions.

The play *In the Fog* is made up of dialogue and stage directions.

b. *In the Fog* is set on a foggy, almost deserted road at night.

In the Fog opens with "weird minor music."

The events in *In the Fog* are strange and mysterious.

2. **Correcting Overgeneralizations.** Add qualifiers to correct the following overgeneralizations.

a. Everyone in Brooklyn approved of the installation of the Statue of Liberty.

b. Travelers on Route 30 are always stopped by two strange men wearing ragged clothes and carrying ancient rifles.

c. All the characters in *In the Fog* speak an old-fashioned dialect.

Understanding the Drama

RECALLING

1. Which play in this unit was written to be filmed?

2. Which play does not contain flashbacks?

3. In which play must the main character react to a life-or-death crisis?

4. Do both plays deal with historical events?

INTERPRETING

5. Grandpa Monaghan is extremely stubborn. However, he is capable of changing his opinions. What action on his part demonstrates that he can change?

6. Choose one minor character from each play. Explain briefly how this character helps the audience to learn more about the main character or about the central conflict.

7. Identify the climax, or turning point, of each play in this unit.

8. What is the mood of *In the Fog*? How does the setting help to create the mood?

CRITICAL THINKING: EVALUATING

9. Which character seems to you the most developed and realistic, Grandpa Monaghan in *Grandpa and the Statue* or the doctor in *In the Fog*? Find evidence in each play to support your opinion.

10. What do you think are the characteristics of a good play? Choose the play in this unit that you like better. Explain how the play that you have chosen meets your criteria for good drama.

Writing About Drama

See **Using the Process of Writing** on pages 614–623 and Writing About Drama on pages 630–632 for help with this assignment.

Recall a favorite television drama. Identify the main and minor characters and describe the setting. Write a one-paragraph summary of the plot. Then, answer the following questions:

What conflict does the plot involve?
How is the conflict introduced?
What happens to develop the conflict even further?
When does the plot reach its climax?
How is the central conflict resolved?

Applying Dramatic Techniques

See **Using the Process of Writing** on pages 614–623 for help with this assignment.

Write two or three pages of dialogue between two characters. Begin by thinking of two characters, a setting, and a conflict. Follow this model in your prewriting notes:

characters	Bill, a running back Mike, Bill's best friend
setting	a football practice field
conflict	Bill is hiding a serious injury for fear that his coach will keep him out of tomorrow's game. Mike feels that Bill should tell the coach about his injury to avoid hurting himself even more.

The Novel

ON THE TRAIL (detail), about 1892. *Winslow Homer. National Gallery of Art, Washington, D.C.*
Gift of Ruth K. Henschel in Memory of her Husband, Charles R. Henschel.

Introducing the Novel

What Is a Novel?

A novel is a work of fiction that is longer and more complex than a short story. Like short stories, novels contain the elements of setting, character, plot, and conflict. However, in novels, all of these elements are developed in greater detail.

The Structure of a Novel

The plot of a novel includes the following:

Exposition.   Novels usually begin by providing background information and by introducing the setting and the important characters. The section of the novel that does these things is called the exposition.

Inciting Incident.   Early in a novel, an event occurs that introduces the central conflict, or struggle. This is the inciting incident.

Complications.   After the inciting incident, events occur that intensify the conflict. These events are called complications.

Climax.   The conflict builds until it reaches a high point of interest or suspense that is called the climax. The climax is usually followed by the resolution, or end, of the central conflict.

Subplots.   Novels often tell one or more less important stories. The stories are connected to the main story. These lesser stories are known as subplots.

How To Read a Novel

As you read *Old Yeller,* a gripping tale of the love between a frontier boy and his dog, think about the setting, characters, conflicts, and plot. Identify the inciting incident, the complications, and the climax. Try to determine the main idea, or theme, that the writer wishes to convey.

Previewing the Unit

Reading the Selection

In this unit you will read Fred Gipson's novel *Old Yeller* a few chapters at a time.

Using the Study Questions

Following each set of chapters are exercises that will help you to develop your reading, vocabulary, and writing skills.

Getting at Meaning. This section has three types of questions. The **RECALLING** questions will help you remember the selection. The **INTERPRETING** questions will help you to understand the selection. The **CRITICAL THINKING** questions will assist you in evaluating the selection and in relating it to your own experiences.

Developing Skills in Reading Literature. These exercises will introduce you to the literary techniques used in novels.

Developing Vocabulary. These exercises will review the vocabulary skills introduced in the first five units of this text.

Developing Writing Skills. In these assignments you will write about the novel and about your related experiences.

Using the Unit Study Materials

Following the last selection are these study materials:

Research Skills for Writing. This feature will teach you how to take notes.

Critical Thinking. The Critical Thinking exercises will teach you how to evaluate works of literature.

Unit Review. The Unit Review will help you recall, interpret, and think critically about the novel. The writing assignments will give you an opportunity to apply the writing skills that you have learned.

He's big and ugly with a stub for a tail and one ear chewed off. Why do Travis and his family love him so much?

Old Yeller

Fred Gipson

Chapter 1

We called him Old Yeller. The name had a sort of double meaning. One part meant that his short hair was a dingy yellow, a color that we called "yeller" in those days. The other meant that when he opened his head, the sound he let out came closer to being a yell than a bark.

I remember like yesterday how he strayed in out of nowhere to our log cabin on Birdsong Creek. He made me so mad at first that I wanted to kill him. Then, later, when I had to kill him, it was like having to shoot some of my own folks. That's how much I'd come to think of the big yeller dog.

He came in the late 1860's, the best I remember. Anyhow, it was the year that Papa and a bunch of other Salt Licks settlers formed a "pool herd" of their little separate bunches of steers and trailed them to the new cattle market at Abilene, Kansas.

This was to get "cash money," a thing that all Texans were short of in those years right after the Civil War. We lived then in a new country and a good one. As Papa pointed out the day the men talked over making the drive, we had plenty of grass, wood, and water. We had wild game for the killing, fertile ground for growing bread corn, and the Indians had been put onto reservations with the return of U.S. soldiers to the Texas forts.

"In fact," Papa wound up, "all we lack having a tight tail-holt on the world is a little cash money. And we can get that at Abilene."

Well, the idea sounded good, but some of the men still hesitated. Abilene was better than six hundred miles north of the Texas hill country we lived in. It would take months for the men to make the drive[1] and ride back home. And all that time the womenfolks and children of Salt Licks would be left in a wild frontier settlement to make out the best they could.

Still, they needed money, and they realized that whatever a man does, he's bound to take some risks. So they talked it over with each other and with their women and decided it was the thing to do. They told their folks what to do in case the Indians came off the reservation or the coons got to eating the corn or the bears

---

1. **make the drive:** herd the cattle to their destination.

got to killing too many hogs. Then they gathered their cattle, burned a trail brand on their hips, and pulled out on the long trail to Kansas.

I remember how it was the day Papa left. I remember his standing in front of the cabin with his horse saddled, his gun in his scabbard, and his bedroll tied on back of the cantle. I remember how tall and straight and handsome he looked, with his high-crowned hat and his black mustaches drooping in cow-horn curves past the corners of his mouth. And I remember how Mama was trying to keep from crying because he was leaving and how Little Arliss, who was only five and didn't know much, wasn't trying to keep from crying at all. In fact, he was howling his head off; not because Papa was leaving, but because he couldn't go, too.

I wasn't about to cry. I was fourteen years old, pretty near a grown man. I stood back and didn't let on for a minute that I wanted to cry.

Papa got through loving up Mama and Little Arliss and mounted his horse. I looked up at him. He motioned for me to come along. So I walked beside his horse down the trail that led under the big live oaks and past the spring.

When he'd gotten out of hearing of the house, Papa reached down and put a hand on my shoulder.

"Now, Travis," he said, "you're getting to be a big boy; and while I'm gone, you'll be the man of the family. I want you to act like one. You take care of Mama and Little Arliss. You look after the work and don't wait around for your mama to point out what needs to be done. Think you can do that?"

"Yessir," I said.

"Now, there's the cows to milk and wood to cut and young pigs to mark and fresh meat to shoot. But mainly there's the corn patch. If you don't work it right or if you let the varmints eat

up the roasting ears, we'll be without bread corn for the winter."

"Yessir," I said.

"All right, boy. I'll be seeing you this fall."

I stood there and let him ride on. There wasn't any more to say.

Suddenly I remembered and went running down the trail after him, calling for him to wait.

He pulled up his horse and twisted around in the saddle. "Yeah, boy," he said. "What is it?"

"That horse," I said.

"What horse?" he said, like he'd never heard me mention it before. "You mean you're wanting a horse?"

"Now, Papa," I complained. "You know I've been aching all over for a horse to ride. I've told you time and again."

I looked up to catch him grinning at me and felt foolish that I hadn't realized he was teasing.

"What you're needing worse than a horse is a good dog."

"Yessir," I said, "but a horse is what I'm wanting the worst."

"All right," he said. "You act a man's part while I'm gone, and I'll see that you get a man's horse to ride when I sell the cattle. I think we can shake on that deal."

He reached out his hand, and we shook. It was the first time I'd ever shaken hands like a man. It made me feel big and solemn and important in a way I'd never felt before. I knew then that I could handle whatever needed to be done while Papa was gone.

I turned and started back up the trail toward the cabin. I guessed maybe Papa was right. I guessed I could use a dog. All the other settlers had dogs. They were big fierce cur dogs that the settlers used for catching hogs and driving cattle and fighting coons out of the cornfields. They kept them as watchdogs against the depredations of loafer wolves, bears, panthers, and raiding Indians. There was no question about it: for the sort of country we lived in, a good dog around the place was sometimes worth more than two or three men. I knew this as well as anybody, because the summer before I'd had a good dog.

His name was Bell. He was nearly as old as I was. We'd had him ever since I could remember. He'd protected me from rattlesnakes and bad hogs while I was little. He'd hunted with me when I was bigger. Once he'd dragged me out of Birdsong Creek when I was about to drown and another time he'd given warning in time to keep some raiding Comanches from stealing and eating our mule, Jumper.

Then he'd had to go act a fool and get himself killed.

It was while Papa and I were cutting wild hay in a little patch of prairie back of the house. A big diamondback rattler struck at Papa and Papa chopped his head off with one quick lick of his scythe. The head dropped to the ground three or four feet away from the writhing body. It lay there, with the ugly mouth opening and shutting, still trying to bite something.

As smart as Bell was, you'd have thought he'd have better sense than to go up and nuzzle that rattler's head. But he didn't, and a second later, he was falling back, howling and slinging his own head till his ears popped. But it was too late then. That snake mouth had snapped shut on his nose, driving the fangs in so deep that it was a full minute before he could sling the bloody head loose.

He died that night, and I cried for a week. Papa tried to make me feel better by promising to get me another dog right away, but I wouldn't have it. It made me mad just to think about some other dog's trying to take Bell's place.

And I still felt the same about it. All I wanted now was a horse.

The trail I followed led along the bank of Birdsong Creek through some bee myrtle bushes. The bushes were blooming white and smelled sweet. In the top of one a mockingbird was singing. That made me recollect how Birdsong Creek had got its name. Mama had named it when she and Papa came to settle. Mama had told me about it. She said she named it the first day she and Papa got there, with Mama driving the ox cart loaded with our house plunder and with Papa driving the cows and horses. They'd meant to build closer to the other settlers, over on Salt Branch. But they'd camped there at the spring; and the bee myrtle had been blooming white that day, and seemed like in every bush there was a mockingbird, singing his fool head off. It was all so pretty and smelled so good and the singing birds made such fine music that Mama wouldn't go on.

"We'll build right here," she'd told Papa.

And that's what they'd done. Built themselves a home right here on Birdsong Creek and fought off the Indians and cleared a corn patch and raised me and Little Arliss and lost a little sister who died of a fever.

Now it was my home, too. And while Papa was gone, it was up to me to look after it.

I came to our spring that gushed clear cold water out of a split in a rock ledge. The water poured into a pothole about the size of a wagon bed. In the pothole, up to his ears in the water, stood Little Arliss. Right in our drinking water!

I said, "*Arliss!* You get out of that water."

Arliss turned and stuck out his tongue at me.

"I'll cut me a sprout!" I warned.

All he did was stick out his tongue at me again and splash water in my direction.

I got my knife out and cut a green mesquite sprout. I trimmed all the leaves and thorns off, then headed for him.

Arliss saw then that I meant business. He came lunging up out of the pool, knocking water all over his clothes lying on the bank. He lit out for the house, running naked and screaming bloody murder. To listen to him, you'd have thought the Comanches were lifting his scalp.

Mama heard him and came rushing out of the cabin. She saw Little Arliss running naked. She saw me following after him with a mesquite sprout in one hand and his clothes in the other. She called out to me.

"Travis," she said, "what on earth have you done to your little brother?"

I said, "Nothing yet. But if he doesn't keep out of our drinking water, I'm going to wear him to a frazzle."

That's what Papa always told Little Arliss when he caught him in the pool. I figured if I had to take Papa's place, I might as well talk like him.

Mama stared at me for a minute. I thought she was fixing to argue that I was getting too big for my britches. Lots of times she'd tell me that. But this time she didn't. She just smiled suddenly and grabbed Little Arliss by one ear and held on. He went to hollering and jumping up and down trying to pull away, but she held on till I got there with his clothes. She put them on him and told him, "Look here, young squirrel. You better listen to your big brother Travis if you want to keep out of trouble." Then she

made him go sit still awhile in the dog run.

The dog run was an open roofed-over space between the two rooms of our log cabin. It was a good place to eat watermelons in the hot summer or to sleep when the night breezes weren't strong enough to push through the cracks between the cabin logs. Sometimes we hung up fresh-killed meat there to cool out.

Little Arliss sat in the dog run and sulked while I packed water from the spring. I packed the water in a bucket that Papa had made out of the hide of a cow's leg. I poured the water into the ash hopper that stood beside the cabin. That was so the water could trickle down through the wood ashes and become lye water. Later Mama would mix this lye water with hog fat and boil it in an iron pot when she wanted to make soap.

When I went to cut wood for Mama, though, Little Arliss left the dog run to come watch me work. Like always, he stood in exactly the right place for the chips from my axe to fly up and maybe knock his eyeballs out. I said: "You better skin out for that house, you little scamp!" He skinned out, too. Just like I told him. Without even sticking out his tongue at me this time.

And he sat right there till Mama called us to dinner.

After dinner, I didn't wait for Mama to tell me that I needed to finish running out the corn middles.[2] I got right up from the table and went out and hooked Jumper to the double shovel. I started in plowing where Papa had left off the day before. I figured that if I got an early start, I could finish the corn patch by sundown.

---

2. **running out the corn middles:** plowing between the rows to keep down weeds.

Jumper was a dun mule with a narrow black stripe running along his backbone between his mane and tail. Papa had named him Jumper because nobody yet had ever built a fence he couldn't jump over. Papa claimed Jumper could clear the moon if he took a notion to see the other side of it.

Jumper was a pretty good mule, though. He was gentle to ride, you could pack in fresh meat on him, and he was willing about pulling a plow. Only, sometimes when I plowed him and he decided quitting time had come, he'd stop work right then. Maybe we'd be out in the middle of the field when Jumper got the notion that it was time to quit for dinner. Right then, he'd swing around and head for the cabin, dragging down corn with the plow and paying no mind whatever to my hauling back on the reins and hollering "Whoa!"

Late that evening, Jumper tried to pull that stunt on me again; but I was laying for him. With Papa gone, I knew I had to teach Jumper a good lesson. I'd been plowing all afternoon, holding a green cedar club between the plow handles.

I still lacked three or four corn rows being finished when sundown came and Jumper decided it was quitting time. He let out a long bray and started wringing his tail. He left the middle he was traveling in. He struck out through the young corn, headed for the cabin.

I didn't even holler "Whoa!" at him. I just threw the looped reins off my shoulder and ran up beside him. I drew back my green cedar club and whacked him so hard across the jawbone that I nearly dropped him in his tracks.

You never saw a worse surprised mule. He snorted, started to run, then just stood there and stared at me. Like maybe he couldn't believe that I was man enough to club him that hard.

I drew back my club again. "Jumper," I said, "if you don't get back there and finish this plowing job, you're going to get more of the same. You understand?"

I guess he understood, all right. Anyhow, from then on till we were through, he stayed right on the job. The only thing he did different from what he'd have done with Papa was to travel with his head turned sideways, watching me every step of the way.

When finally I got to the house, I found that Mama had done the milking and she and Little Arliss were waiting supper on me. Just like we generally waited for Papa when he came in late.

I crawled into bed with Little Arliss that night, feeling pretty satisfied with myself. Our bed was a cornshuck mattress laid over a couple of squared-up cowhides that had been laced together. The cowhides stood about two feet off the dirt floor, stretched tight inside a pole frame Papa had built in one corner of the room. I lay there and listened to the corn shucks squeak when I breathed and to the owls hooting in the timber along Birdsong Creek. I guessed I'd made a good start. I'd done my work without having to be told. I'd taught Little Arliss and Jumper that I wasn't to be trifled with. And Mama could already see that I was man enough to wait supper on.

I guessed that I could handle things while Papa was gone just about as good as he could.

Chapter 2

It was the next morning when the big yeller dog came.

I found him at daylight when Mama told me to step out to the dog run and cut down a side of middling meat hanging to the pole rafters.

The minute I opened the door and looked up, I saw that the meat was gone. It had been tied to the rafter with bear-grass blades braided together for string. Now nothing was left hanging to the pole but the frazzled ends of the snapped blades.

I looked down then. At the same instant, a dog rose from where he'd been curled up on the ground beside the barrel that held our cornmeal. He was a big, ugly, slick-haired yeller dog. One short ear had been chewed clear off and his tail had been bobbed so close to his rump that there was hardly stub enough left to wag. But the most noticeable thing to me about him was how thin and starved looking he was, all but for his belly. His belly was swelled up as tight and round as a pumpkin.

It wasn't hard to tell how come that belly was so full. All I had to do was look at the piece of curled-up rind lying in the dirt beside him, with all the meat gnawed off. That side of meat had been a big one, but now there wasn't enough meat left on the rind to interest a pack rat.

Well, to lose the only meat we had left from last winter's hog butchering was bad enough. But what made me even madder was the way the dog acted. He didn't even have the manners to feel ashamed of what he'd done. He rose to his feet, stretched, yawned, then came romping toward me, wiggling that stub tail and

yelling *Yow! Yow! Yow!* Just like he belonged there and I was his best friend.

"Why, you thieving rascal!" I shouted and kicked at him as hard as I could.

He ducked, just in time, so I missed him by a hair. But nobody could have told I missed, after the way he fell over on the ground and lay there, with his belly up and his four feet in the air, squawling and bellering at the top of his voice. From the racket he made, you'd have thought I had a club and was breaking every bone in his body.

Mama came running to stick her head through the door and say, "What on earth, Travis?"

"Why, this old stray dog has come and eaten our middling meat clear up," I said.

I aimed another kick at him. He was quick and rolled out of reach again, just in time, then fell back to the ground and lay there, yelling louder than ever.

Then out came Little Arliss. He was naked, like he always slept in the summer. He was hollering "A dog! A dog!" He ran past me and fell on the dog and petted him till he quit howling, then turned on me, fighting mad.

"You quit kicking my dog!" he yelled fiercely. "You kick my dog, and I'll wear you to a frazzle!"

The battling stick that Mama used to beat the dirt out of clothes when she washed stood leaning against the wall. Now, Little Arliss grabbed it up in both hands and came at me, swinging.

It was such a surprise move, Little Arliss making fight at me that way, that I just stood there with my mouth open and let him clout me a good one before I thought to move. Then Mama stepped in and took the stick away from him.

Arliss turned on her, ready to fight with his bare fists. Then he decided against it and ran and put his arms around the big dog's neck. He began to yell, "He's my dog. You can't kick him. He's my dog!"

The big dog was back up on his feet now, wagging his stub tail again and licking the tears off Arliss's face with his pink tongue.

Mama laughed. "Well, Travis," she said, "it looks like we've got us a dog."

"But Mama," I said. "You don't mean we'd keep an old ugly dog like that. One that will come in and steal meat right out of the house."

"Well, maybe we can't keep him," Mama said. "Maybe he belongs to somebody around here who'll want him back."

"He doesn't belong to anybody in the settlement," I said. "I know every dog at Salt Licks."

"Well, then," Mama said. "If he's a stray, there's no reason why Little Arliss can't claim him. And you'll have to admit he's a smart dog. Mighty few dogs have sense enough to figure out a way to reach a side of meat hanging that high. He must have climbed up on top of that meal barrel and jumped from there."

I went over and looked at the wooden lid on top of the meal barrel. Sure enough, in the thin film of dust that had settled over it were dog tracks.

"Well, all right," I admitted. "He's a smart dog. But I still don't want him."

"Now, Travis," Mama said. "You're not being fair. You had you a dog when you were little, but Arliss has never had one. He's too little for you to play with, and he gets lonely."

I didn't say any more. When Mama got her mind set a certain way, there was no use in arguing with her. But I didn't want that meat-thieving dog on the place, and I didn't aim to have him. I might have to put up with him for a day or so, but sooner or later, I'd find a way to get rid of him.

Mama must have guessed what was going on in my mind, for she kept handing me sober looks all the time she was getting breakfast.

She fed us cornmeal mush cooked in a pot swung over the fireplace. She sweetened it with wild honey that Papa and I had cut out of a bee tree last fall, and added cream skimmed off last night's milk. It was good eating, but I'd had my appetite whetted for fried middling meat to go with it.

Mama waited till I was done, then said, "Now, Travis, as soon as you've milked the cows, I think you ought to get your gun and try to kill us a fat young doe for meat. And while you're gone, I want you to do some thinking on what I said about Little Arliss and this stray dog."

Chapter 3

All right, I was willing to go make a try for a fat doe. I was generally more than willing to go hunting. And while I was gone, I might do some thinking about Little Arliss and that thieving stray dog. But I didn't much think my thinking would take the turn Mama wanted.

I went and milked the cows and brought the milk in for Mama to strain. I got my rifle and went out to the lot and caught Jumper. I tied a rope around his neck, half-hitched a noose around his nose and pitched the rest of the rope across his back. This was the rope I'd rein him with. Then I got me a second rope and tied it tight around his middle, just back of his withers. This second rope I'd use to tie my deer onto Jumper's back—if I got one.

Papa had shown me how to tie a deer's feet together and pack it home across my shoulder, and I'd done it. But to carry a deer very far like that was a sweat-popping job that I'd rather leave to Jumper. He was bigger and stronger.

I mounted Jumper bareback and rode him along Birdsong Creek and across a rocky hogback ridge. I thought how fine it would be if I was riding my own horse instead of an old mule. I rode down a long sweeping slope where a scattering of huge, ragged-topped live

oaks stood about in grass so tall that it dragged against the underside of Jumper's belly. I rode to within a quarter of a mile of the Salt Licks, then left Jumper tied in a thicket and went on afoot.

I couldn't take Jumper close to the Licks for a couple of reasons. In the first place, he'd get to swishing his tail and stomping his feet at flies and maybe scare off my game. On top of that, he was gun shy. Fire a gun close to Jumper, and he'd fall to staves.[3] He'd snort and wheel to run and fall back against his tie rope, trying to break loose. He'd bawl and paw the air and take on like he'd been shot. When it came to gunfire Jumper didn't have any more sense than a red ant in a hot skillet.

It was a fine morning for hunting, with the air still and the rising sun shining bright on the tall green grass and the greener leaves of the timber. There wasn't enough breeze blowing for me to tell the wind direction, so I licked one finger and held it up. Sure enough, the side next to me cooled first. That meant that what little push there was to the air was away from

---

3. **fall to staves** (stāvz): fall to pieces, like the strips of wood, or staves, that form the wall of a barrel or bucket.

me toward the Salt Licks. Which wouldn't do at all. No deer would come to the Licks if he caught wind of me first.

I half circled the Licks till I had the breeze moving across them toward me and took cover under a wild grapevine that hung low out of the top of a gnarled oak. I sat down with my back against the trunk of the tree. I sat with my legs crossed and my rifle cradled on my knees. Then I made myself get as still as the tree.

Papa had taught me that, 'way back when I was little, the same as he'd taught me to hunt downwind from my game. He always said: "It's not your shape that catches a deer's eye. It's your moving. If a deer can't smell you and can't see you move, he won't ever know you're there."

So I sat there, holding as still as a stump, searching the clearing around the Licks.

The Licks was a scattered outcropping of dark rocks with black streaks in them. The black streaks held the salt that Papa said had got mixed up with the rocks a jillion years ago. I don't know how he knew what had happened so far back, but the salt was there, and all the hogs and cattle and wild animals in that part of the country came there to lick it.

One time, Papa said, when he and Mama had first settled there, they'd run clean out of salt and had to beat up pieces of the rock and boil them in water. Then they'd used the salty water to season their meat and cornbread.

Wild game generally came to lick the rocks in the early mornings or late evenings, and those were the best times to come for meat. The killer animals, like bear and panther and bobcat, knew this and came to the Licks at the same time. Sometimes we'd get a shot at them. I'd killed two bobcats and a wolf there while waiting for deer; and once Papa shot a big panther right after it had leaped on a mule colt and

broken its neck with one slap of its heavy forepaw.

I hoped I'd get a shot at a bear or panther this morning. The only thing that showed up, however, was a little band of javelina hogs, and I knew better than to shoot them. Make a bad shot and wound one so that he went to squealing, and you had the whole bunch after you, ready to eat you alive. They were small animals. Their tushes weren't as long as those of the range hogs we had running wild in the woods. They couldn't cut you as deep, but once javelinas got after you, they'd keep after you for a lot longer time.

Once Jed Simpson's boy Rosal shot into a bunch of javelinas and they took after him. They treed him up a mesquite and kept him there from early morning till long after suppertime. The mesquite was a small one, and they nearly chewed the trunk of it in two trying to get to him. After that Rosal was willing to let the javelinas alone.

The javelinas moved away, and I saw some bobwhite quail feed into the opening around the Licks. Then here came three cows with young calves and a roan bull. They stood and licked at the rocks. I watched them awhile, then got to watching a couple of squirrels playing in the top of a tree close to the one I sat under.

The squirrels were running and jumping and chattering and flashing their tails in the sunlight. One would run along a tree branch, then take a flying leap to the next branch. There it would sit, fussing, and wait to see if the second one had the nerve to jump that far. When the second squirrel did, the first one would set up an excited chatter and make a run for a longer leap. Sure enough, after a while the leader tried to jump a gap that was too wide. He missed his branch, clawed at some leaves, and came tumbling to the ground. The second squirrel went to dancing up and down on his branch then, chattering louder that ever. It was plain that he was getting a big laugh out of how that showoff squirrel had made such a fool of himself.

The sight was so funny that I laughed, myself, and that's where I made my mistake.

Where the doe had come from and how she ever got so close without my seeing her, I don't know. It was like she'd suddenly lit down out of the air like a buzzard or risen right up out of the bare ground around the rocks. Anyhow, there she stood, staring straight at me, sniffing and snorting and stomping her forefeet against the ground.

She couldn't have scented me, and I hadn't moved; but I had laughed out loud a little at those squirrels. And that sound had warned her.

Well, I couldn't lift my gun then, with her staring straight at me. She'd see the motion and take a scare. And while Papa was a good enough shot to down a running deer, I'd never tried it and didn't much think I could. I figured it smarter to wait. Maybe she'd quit staring at me after a while and give me a chance to lift my gun.

But I waited and waited, and still she kept looking at me, trying to figure me out. Finally, she started coming toward me. She'd take one dancing step and then another and bob her head and flap her long ears about, then start moving toward me again.

I didn't know what to do. It made me nervous, the way she kept coming at me. Sooner or later she was bound to make out what I was. Then she'd whirl and be gone before I could draw a bead on her.

She kept doing me that way till finally my heart was flopping around inside my chest like a catfish in a wet sack. I could feel my muscles tightening up all over. I knew that I couldn't wait any longer. It was either shoot or bust wide open, so I whipped my gun up to my shoulder.

Like I'd figured, she snorted and wheeled, so fast that she was just a brown blur against my gunsights. I pressed the trigger, hoping my aim was good.

After I fired, the black powder charge in my gun threw up such a thick fog of blue smoke that I couldn't see through it. I reloaded, then leaped to my feet and went running through the smoke. What I saw when I came into the clear again made my heart drop down into my shoes.

There went the frightened, snorting cattle, stampeding through the trees with their tails in the air like it was heel-fly time. And right beside them went my doe, running all humped up and her white, pointed tail clamped tight to her rump.

Which meant that I'd hit her but hadn't made a killing shot.

I didn't like that. I never minded killing for meat. Like Papa had told me, every creature has to kill to live. But to wound an animal was something else. Especially one as pretty and harmless as a deer. It made me sick to think of the doe's escaping, maybe to hurt for days before she finally died.

I swung my gun up, hoping yet to get in a killing shot. But I couldn't fire on account of the cattle. They were too close to the deer. I might kill one of them.

Then suddenly the doe did a surprising thing. 'Way down in the flat there, nearly out of sight, she ran head on into the trunk of a tree. Like she was stone blind. I saw the flash of her light-colored belly as she went down. I waited. She didn't get up. I tore out, running

through the chin-tall grass as fast as I could.

When finally I reached the place, all out of breath, I found her lying dead, with a bullet hole through her middle, right where it had to have shattered the heart.

Suddenly I wasn't sick any more. I felt big and strong and sure of myself. I hadn't made a bad shot. I hadn't caused an animal a lot of suffering. All I'd done was get meat for the family, shooting it on the run, just like Papa did.

I rode toward the cabin, sitting behind the gutted doe that I'd tied across Jumper's back. I rode, feeling proud of myself as a hunter and a provider for the family. Making a killing shot like that on a moving deer made me feel bigger and more inportant. Too big and important, I guessed, to fuss with Little Arliss about that old yeller dog. I still didn't think much of the idea of keeping him, but I guessed that when

you are nearly a man, you have to learn to put up with a lot of aggravation from little old bitty kids. Let Arliss keep the thieving rascal. I guessed I could provide enough meat for him, too.

That's how I was feeling when I crossed Birdsong Creek and rode up to the spring under the trees below the house. Then suddenly, I felt different. That's when I found Little Arliss in the pool again. And in there with him was the big yeller dog. That dirty stinking rascal, romping around in our drinking water!

"Arliss!" I yelled at Little Arliss. "You get that nasty old dog out of the water!"

They hadn't seen me ride up, and I guess it was my sudden yell that surprised them both so bad. Arliss went tearing out of the pool on one side and the dog on the other. Arliss was screaming his head off, and here came the big dog with his wet fur rising along the ridge of his backbone, baying me like I was a panther.

I didn't give him a chance to get to me. I was too quick about jumping off the mule and grabbing up some rocks.

I was lucky. The first rock I threw caught the big dog right between the eyes, and I was throwing hard. He went down, yelling and pitching and wallowing. And just as he came to his feet again, I caught him in the ribs with another one. That was too much for him. He turned tail then and took out for the house, squawling and bawling.

But I wasn't the only good rock thrower in the family. Arliss was only five years old, but I'd spent a lot of time showing him how to throw a rock. Now I wished I hadn't. Because about then, a rock nearly tore my left ear off. I whirled around just barely in time to duck another that would have caught me square in the left eye.

I yelled, "Arliss, you quit that!" but Arliss wasn't listening. He was too scared and too mad. He bent over to pick up a rock big enough to brain me with if he'd been strong enough to throw it.

Well, when you're fourteen years old, you can't afford to mix in a rock fight with your five-year-old brother. You can't do it, even when you're in the right. You just can't explain a thing like that to your folks. All they'll do is point out how much bigger you are, how unfair it is to your little brother.

All I could do was turn tail like the yeller dog and head for the house, yelling for Mama. And right after me came Little Arliss, naked and running as fast as he could, doing his dead-level best to get close enough to hit me with the big rock he was packing.

I outran him, of course; and then here came Mama, running so fast that her long skirts were flying, and calling out: "What on earth, boys!"

I hollered, "You better catch that Arliss!" as I ran past her. And she did; but Little Arliss was so mad that I thought for a second he was going to hit her with the rock before she could get it away from him.

Well, it all wound up about like I figured. Mama switched Little Arliss for playing in our drinking water. Then she blessed me out good and proper for being so bossy with him. And the big yeller dog that had caused all the trouble got off scot free.

It didn't seem right and fair to me. How could I be the man of the family if nobody paid any attention to what I thought or said?

I went and led Jumper up to the house. I hung the doe in the live oak tree that grew beside the house and began skinning it and cutting up the meat. I thought of the fine shot I'd made and knew it was worth bragging about to Mama. But what was the use? She wouldn't pay me any mind—not until I did something she thought I shouldn't have done. Then she'd treat me like I wasn't any older than Little Arliss.

I sulked and felt sorry for myself all the time I worked with the meat. The more I thought about it, the madder I got at the big yeller dog.

I hung the fresh cuts of venison up in the dog run, right where Old Yeller had stolen the hog meat the night he came. I did it for a couple of reasons. To begin with, that was the handiest and coolest place we had for hanging fresh meat. On top of that, I was looking for a good excuse to get rid of that dog. I figured if he stole more of our meat, Mama would have to see that he was too sorry and no account to keep.

But Old Yeller was too smart for that. He gnawed around on some of the deer's leg bones that Mama threw away; but not once did he ever even act like he could smell the meat we'd hung up.

Chapter 4

A couple of days later, I had another and better reason for wanting to get rid of Old Yeller. That was when the two longhorn range bulls met at the house and pulled off their big fight.

We first heard the bulls while we were eating our dinner of cornbread, roasted venison, and green watercress gathered from below the spring. One bull came from off a high rocky ridge to the south of the cabin. We could hear his angry rumbling as he moved down through the thickets of catclaw and scrub oak.

Then he lifted his voice in a wild, brassy blare that set echoes clamoring in the draws and canyons for miles around.

"That old bull's talking fight," I told Mama and Little Arliss. "He's bragging that he's the biggest and toughest and meanest. He's telling all the other bulls that if they've got a lick of sense, they'll take to cover when he's around."

Almost before I'd finished talking, we heard the second bull. He was over about the Salt Licks somewhere. His bellering was just as loud and braggy as the first one's. He was telling the first bull that his fight talk was all bluff. He was saying that *he* was the he-bull of the range, that *he* was the biggest and meanest and toughest.

We sat and ate and listened to them. We could tell by their rumblings and bawlings that they were gradually working their way down through the brush toward each other and getting madder by the minute.

I always liked to see a fight between bulls or bears or wild boars or almost any wild animals. Now, I got so excited that I jumped up from the table and went to the door and stood listening. I'd made up my mind that if the bulls met and started a fight, I was going to see it. There

was still plenty of careless weeds and crabgrass that needed hoeing out of the corn, but I guessed I could let them go long enough to see a bullfight.

Our cabin stood on a high knoll about a hundred yards above the spring. Years ago, Papa had cleared out all the brush and trees from around it, leaving a couple of live oaks near the house for shade. That was so he could get a clear shot at any Comanche or Apache coming to scalp us. And while I stood there at the door, the first bull entered the clearing, right where Papa had one time shot a Comanche off his horse.

He was a leggy, mustard-colored bull with black freckles speckling his jaws and the underside of his belly. He had one great horn set for hooking, while the other hung down past his jaw like a tallow candle that had drooped in the heat. He was what the Mexicans called a *chongo* or "droop horn."

He trotted out a little piece into the clearing, then stopped to drop his head low. He went to snorting and shaking his horns and pawing up the dry dirt with his forefeet. He flung the dirt back over his neck and shoulders in great clouds of dust.

I couldn't see the other bull yet, but I could tell by the sound of him that he was close and coming in a trot. I hollered back to Mama and Little Arliss.

"They're fixing to fight right here, where we can all see it."

There was a split-rail fence around our cabin. I ran out and climbed up and took a seat on the top rail. Mama and Little Arliss came and climbed up to sit beside me.

Then, from the other side of the clearing

came the second bull. He was the red roan I'd seen at the Salt Licks the day I shot the doe. He wasn't as tall and long-legged as the *chongo* bull, but every bit as heavy and powerful. And while his horns were shorter, they were both curved right for hooking.

Like the first bull, he came blaring out into the clearing, then stopped to snort and sling his wicked horns and paw up clouds of dust. He made it plain that he wanted to fight just as bad as the first bull.

About that time, from somewhere behind the cabin, came Old Yeller. He charged through the rails, bristled up and roaring almost as loud as the bulls. All their bellering and snorting and dust pawing sounded like a threat to him. He'd come out to run them away from the house.

I hollered at him. "Get back there, you rascal," I shouted. "You're fixing to spoil our show."

That stopped him, but he still wasn't satisfied. He kept baying the bulls till I jumped down and picked up a rock. I didn't have to throw it. All I had to do was draw back like I was going to. That sent him flying back into the yard and around the corner of the cabin, yelling like I'd murdered him.

That also put Little Arliss on the fight.

He started screaming at me. He tried to get down where he could pick up a rock.

But Mama held him. "Hush, now, baby," she said. "Travis isn't going to hurt your dog. He just doesn't want him to scare off the bulls."

Well, it took some talking, but she finally got Little Arliss's mind off hitting me with a rock. I climbed back up on the fence. I told Mama that I was betting on Chongo. She said she was betting her money on Roany because he had two fighting horns. We sat there and watched the bulls get ready to fight and talked and laughed and had ourselves a real good time. We never once thought about being in any danger.

When we learned different, it was nearly too late.

Suddenly, Chongo quit pawing the dirt and flung his tail into the air.

"Look out!" I shouted. "Here it comes."

Sure enough, Chongo charged, pounding the hardpan with his feet and roaring his mightiest. And here came Roany to meet him, charging with his head low and his tail high in the air.

I let out an excited yell. They met head on, with a loud crash of horns and a jar so solid that it seemed like I could feel it clear up there on the fence. Roany went down. I yelled louder, thinking Chongo was winning.

A second later, though, Roany was back on his feet and charging through the cloud of dust their hoofs had churned up. He caught Chongo broadside. He slammed his sharp horns up to the hilt in the shoulder of the mustard-colored bull. He drove against him so fast and hard that Chongo couldn't wheel away. All he could do was barely keep on his feet by giving ground.

And here they came, straight for our rail fence.

"Land Sakes!" Mama cried suddenly and leaped from the fence, dragging Little Arliss down after her.

But I was too excited about the fight. I didn't see the danger in time. I was still astride the top rail when the struggling bulls crashed through the fence, splintering the posts and rails, and toppling me to the ground almost under them.

I lunged to my feet, wild with scare, and got knocked flat on my face in the dirt.

I sure thought I was a goner. The roaring of the bulls was right in my ears. The hot, reeking scent of their blood was in my nose. The bone-crushing weight of their hoofs was stomping all around and over me, churning up such a fog of dust that I couldn't see a thing.

Then suddenly Mama had me by the hand and was dragging me out from under, yelling in a scared voice, "Run, Travis, run!"

Well, she didn't have to keep hollering at me. I was running as fast as I ever hoped to run. And with her running faster and dragging me along by the hand, we scooted through the open cabin door just about a quick breath before Roany slammed Chongo against it.

They hit so hard that the whole cabin shook. I saw great big chunks of dried-mud chinking fall from between the logs. There for a second, I thought Chongo was coming through that door, right on top of us. But turned broadside like he was, he was too big to be shoved through such a small opening. Then a second later, he got off Roany's horns somehow and wheeled on him. Here they went, then, down alongside the cabin wall, roaring and stomping and slamming their heels against the logs.

I looked at Mama and Little Arliss. Mama's face was white as a bed sheet. For once, Little Arliss was so scared that he couldn't scream. Suddenly, I wasn't scared any more. I was just plain mad.

I reached for a braided rawhide whip that hung in a coil on a wooden peg driven between the logs.

That scared Mama still worse. "Oh, no, Travis," she cried. "Don't go out there!"

"They're fixing to tear down the house, Mama," I said.

"But they might run over you." Mama argued.

The bulls crashed into the cabin again. They grunted and strained and roared. Their horns and hoofs clattered against the logs.

I turned and headed for the door. Looked to me like they'd kill us all if they ever broke through those log walls.

Mama came running to grab me by the arm. "Call the dog!" she said. "Put the dog after them!"

Well, that was a real good idea. I was half aggravated with myself because I hadn't thought of it. Here was a chance for that old yeller dog to pay back for all the trouble he'd made around the place.

I stuck my head out the door. The bulls had fought away from the house. Now they were busy tearing down more of the yard fence.

I ducked out and around the corner. I ran through the dog run toward the back of the house, calling, "Here, Yeller! Here, Yeller! Get 'em, boy! Sic 'em!"

Old Yeller was back there, all right. But he didn't come and he didn't sic 'em. He took one look at me running toward him with that bull-whip in my hand and knew I'd come to kill him. He tucked his tail and lit out in a yelling run for the woods.

If there had been any way I could have done it, right then is when I would have killed him.

But there wasn't time to mess with a fool dog. I had to do something about those bulls. They were wrecking the place, and I had to stop it. Papa had left me to look after things while he was gone, and I wasn't about to let two mad bulls tear up everything we had.

I ran up to the bulls and went to work on them with the whip. It was a heavy sixteen-footer and I'd practiced with it a lot. I could crack that rawhide popper louder than a gunshot. I could cut a branch as thick as my little finger off a green mesquite with it.

But I couldn't stop those bulls from

fighting. They were too mad. They were hurting too much already; I might as well have been spitting on them. I yelled and whipped them till I gave clear out. Still they went right on with their roaring bloody battle.

I guess they would have kept on fighting till they leveled the house to the ground if it hadn't been for a freak accident.

We had a heavy two-wheeled Mexican cart that Papa used for hauling wood and hay. It happened to be standing out in front of the house, right where the ground broke away in a sharp slant toward the spring and creek.

It had just come to me that I could get my gun and shoot the bulls when Chongo crowded Roany up against the cart. He ran that long single horn clear under Roany's belly. Now he gave such a big heave that he lifted Roany's feet clear off the ground and rolled him in the air. A second later, Roany landed flat on his back inside the bed of that dump cart, with all four feet sticking up.

I thought his weight would break the cart to pieces, but I was wrong. The cart was stronger than I'd thought. All the bull's weight did was tilt it so that the wheels started rolling. And away the cart went down the hill, carrying Roany with it.

When that happened, Chongo was suddenly the silliest-looking bull you ever saw. He stood with his tail up and his head high, staring after the runaway cart. He couldn't for the life of him figure out what he'd done with the roan bull.

The rolling cart rattled and banged and careened its way down the slope till it was right beside the spring. There, one wheel struck a big boulder, bouncing that side of the cart so high that it turned over and skidded to a stop. The roan bull spilled right into the spring. Water flew in all directions.

Roany got his feet under him. He scrambled up out of the hole. But I guess that cart ride and sudden wetting had taken all the fight out of him. Anyhow, he headed for the timber, running with his tail tucked. Water streamed down out of his hair, leaving a dark wet trail in the dry dust to show which way he'd gone.

Chongo saw Roany then. He snorted and went after him. But when he got to the cart, he slid to a sudden stop. The cart, lying on its side now, still had that top wheel spinning around and around. Chongo had never seen anything like that. He stood and stared at the spinning wheel. He couldn't understand it. He lifted his nose up close to smell it. Finally he reached out a long tongue to lick and taste it.

That was a bad mistake. I guess the iron tire of the spinning wheel was roughed up pretty badly and maybe had chips of broken rock and gravel stuck to it. Anyhow, from the way Chongo acted, it must have scraped all the hide off his tongue.

Chongo bawled and went running backward. He whirled away so fast that he lost his footing and fell down. He came to his feet and took out in the opposite direction from the roan bull. He ran, slinging his head and flopping his long tongue around, bawling like he'd stuck it into a bear trap. He ran with his tail clamped just as tight as the roan bull's.

It was enough to make you laugh your head off, the way both those bad bulls had gotten the wits scared clear out of them, each one thinking he'd lost the fight.

But they sure had made a wreck of the yard fence.

Chapter 5

That Little Arliss! If he wasn't a mess! From the time he'd grown up big enough to get out of the cabin, he'd made a practice of trying to catch and keep every living thing that ran, flew, jumped, or crawled.

Every night before Mama let him go to bed, she'd make Arliss empty his pockets of whatever he'd captured during the day. Generally, it would be a tangled-up mess of grasshoppers and worms and praying bugs and little rusty tree lizards. One time he brought in a horned toad that got so mad he swelled out round and flat as a Mexican *tortilla* and bled at the eyes. Sometimes it was stuff like a young bird that had fallen out of its nest before it could fly or a green-speckled spring frog or a striped water snake. And once he turned out of his pocket a wadded-up baby copperhead that nearly threw Mama into spasms. We never did figure out why the snake hadn't bitten him, but Mama took no more chances on snakes. She switched Arliss hard for catching that snake. Then she made me spend better than a week taking him out and teaching him to throw rocks and kill snakes.

That was all right with Little Arliss. If Mama wanted him to kill his snakes first, he'd kill them. But that still didn't keep him from sticking them in his pockets along with everything else he'd captured that day. The snakes might be stinking by the time Mama called on him to empty his pockets, but they'd be dead.

Then, after the yeller dog came, Little Arliss started catching even bigger game. Like cottontail rabbits and chaparral birds and a baby possum that sulked and lay like dead for the first several hours until he finally decided that Arliss wasn't going to hurt him.

Of course, it was Old Yeller that was doing the catching. He'd run the game down and turn it over to Little Arliss. Then Little Arliss could come in and tell Mama a big fib about how he caught it himself.

I watched them one day when they caught a blue catfish out of Birdsong Creek. The fish had fed out into water so shallow that his top fin was sticking out. About the time I saw it, Old Yeller and Little Arliss did, too. They made a run at it. The fish went scooting away toward deeper water, only Yeller was too fast for him. He pounced on the fish and shut his big mouth down over it and went romping to the bank, where he dropped it down on the grass and let it flop. And here came Little Arliss to fall on it like I guess he'd been doing everything else. The minute he got his hands on it, the fish finned him and he went to crying.

But he wouldn't turn the fish loose. He just grabbed it up and went running and squawling toward the house, where he gave the fish to Mama. His hands were all bloody by then, where the fish had finned him. They swelled up and got mighty sore; not even a mesquite thorn hurts as bad as a sharp fish fin when it's run deep into your hand.

But as soon as Mama had wrapped his hands in a poultice of mashed-up prickly pear root to draw out the poison, Little Arliss forgot all about his hurt. And that night when we ate the fish for supper, he told the biggest windy I ever heard about how he'd dived 'way down into a deep hole under the rocks and dragged that fish out and nearly got drowned before he could swim to the bank with it.

But when I tried to tell Mama what really happened, she wouldn't let me. "Now, this is

Arliss's story," she said. "You let him tell it the way he wants to."

I told Mama then, I said: "Mama, that old yeller dog is going to make the biggest liar in Texas out of Little Arliss."

But Mama just laughed at me, like she always laughed at Little Arliss's big windies after she'd gotten off where he couldn't hear her. She said for me to let Little Arliss alone. She said that if he ever told a bigger whopper than the ones I used to tell, she had yet to hear it.

Well, I hushed then. If Mama wanted Little Arliss to grow up to be the biggest liar in Texas, I guessed it wasn't any of my business.

All of which, I figure, is what led up to Little Arliss's catching the bear. I think Mama had let him tell so many big yarns about his catching live game that he'd begun to believe them himself.

When it happened, I was down the creek a ways, splitting rails to fix up the yard fence where the bulls had torn it down. I'd been down there since dinner, working in a stand of tall slim post oaks. I'd chop down a tree, trim off the branches as far up as I wanted, then cut away the rest of the top. After that I'd start splitting the log.

I'd split the log by driving steel wedges into the wood. I'd start at the big end and hammer in a wedge with the back side of my axe. This would start a little split running lengthways of the log. Then I'd take a second wedge and drive it into this split. This would split the log further along and, at the same time, loosen the first wedge. I'd then knock the first wedge loose and move it up in front of the second one.

Driving one wedge ahead of the other like that, I could finally split a log in two halves.

Then I'd go to work on the halves, splitting them apart. That way, from each log, I'd come out with four rails.

Swinging that chopping axe was sure hard work. The sweat poured off me. My back muscles ached. The axe got so heavy I could hardly swing it. My breath got harder and harder to breathe.

An hour before sundown, I was worn down to a nub. It seemed like I couldn't hit another lick. Papa could have lasted till past sundown, but I didn't see how I could. I shouldered my axe and started toward the cabin, trying to think up some excuse to tell Mama to keep her from knowing I was played clear out.

That's when I heard Little Arliss scream.

Well, Little Arliss was a screamer by nature. He'd scream when he was happy and scream when he was mad and a lot of times he'd scream just to hear himself make a noise. Generally, we paid no more mind to his screaming than we did to the gobble of a wild turkey.

But this time was different. The second I heard his screaming, I felt my heart flop clear over. This time I knew Little Arliss was in real trouble.

I tore out up the trail leading toward the cabin. A minute before, I'd been so tired out with my rail splitting that I couldn't have struck a trot. But now I raced through the tall trees in that creek bottom, covering ground like a scared wolf.

Little Arliss's second scream, when it came, was louder and shriller and more frantic-sounding than the first. Mixed with it was a whimpering crying sound that I knew didn't come from him. It was a sound I'd heard before and seemed like I ought to know what it was, but right then I couldn't place it.

Then, from way off to one side came a sound that I would have recognized anywhere.

It was the coughing roar of a charging bear. I'd just heard it once in my life. That was the time Mama had shot and wounded a hog-killing bear and Papa had had to finish it off with a knife to keep it from getting her.

My heart went to pushing up into my throat, nearly choking off my wind. I strained for every lick of speed I could get out of my running legs. I didn't know what sort of fix Little Arliss had got himself into, but I knew that it had to do with a mad bear, which was enough.

The way the late sun slanted through the

trees had the trail all cross-banded with streaks of bright light and dark shade. I ran through these bright and dark patches so fast that the changing light nearly blinded me. Then suddenly, I raced out into the open where I could see ahead. And what I saw sent a chill clear through to the marrow of my bones.

There was Little Arliss, down in that spring hole again. He was lying half in and half out of the water, holding onto the hind leg of a little black bear cub no bigger than a small coon. The bear cub was out on the bank, whimpering and crying and clawing the rocks with all three of his other feet, trying to pull away. But Little Arliss was holding on for all he was worth, scared now and screaming his head off. Too scared to let go.

How come the bear cub ever came to prowl close enough for Little Arliss to grab him, I don't know. And why he didn't turn on him and bite loose, I couldn't figure out, either. Unless he was like Little Arliss, too scared to think.

But all of that didn't matter now. What mattered was the bear cub's mama. She'd heard the cries of her baby and was coming to save him. She was coming so fast that she had the brush popping and breaking as she crashed through and over it. I could see her black heavy figure piling off down the slant on the far side of Birdsong Creek. She was roaring mad and ready to kill.

And worst of all, I could see that I'd never get there in time!

Mama couldn't either. She'd heard Arliss, too, and here she came from the cabin, running down the slant toward the spring, screaming at Arliss, telling him to turn the bear cub loose. But Little Arliss wouldn't do it. All he'd do was hang with that hind leg and let out one shrill shriek after another as fast as he could suck in a breath.

Now the she-bear was charging across the shallows in the creek. She was knocking sheets of water high in the bright sun, charging with her fur up and her long teeth bared, filling the canyon with that awful coughing roar. And no matter how fast Mama ran or how fast I ran, the she-bear was going to get there first!

I think I nearly went blind then, picturing what was going to happen to Little Arliss. I know that I opened my mouth to scream and not any sound came out.

Then, just as the bear went lunging up the creek bank toward Little Arliss and her cub, a flash of yellow came streaking out of the brush.

It was that big yeller dog. He was roaring like a mad bull. He wasn't one-third as big and heavy as the she-bear, but when he piled into her from one side, he rolled her clear off her feet. They went down in a wild, roaring tangle of twisting bodies and scrambling feet and slashing fangs.

As I raced past them, I saw the bear lunge up to stand on her hind feet like a man while she clawed at the body of the yeller dog hanging to her throat. I didn't wait to see more. Without ever checking my stride, I ran in and jerked Little Arliss loose from the cub. I grabbed him by the wrist and yanked him up out of that water and slung him toward Mama like he was a half-empty sack of corn. I screamed at Mama. "Grab him, Mama! Grab him and run!" Then I swung my chopping axe high and wheeled, aiming to cave in the she-bear's head with the first lick.

But I never did strike. I didn't need to. Old Yeller hadn't let the bear get close enough. He couldn't handle her; she was too big and strong for that. She'd stand there on her hind feet, hunched over, and take a roaring swing at him with one of those big front claws. She'd slap him head over heels. She'd knock him so far that it didn't look like he could possibly get back there before she charged again, but he always did. He'd hit the ground rolling, yelling his head off with the pain of the blow; but somehow he'd always roll to his feet. And here he'd come again, ready to tie into her for another round.

I stood there with my axe raised, watching them for a long moment. Then from up toward the house, I heard Mama calling: "Come away from there, Travis. Hurry, son! Run!"

That spooked me. Up till then, I'd been ready to tie into that bear myself. Now, suddenly, I was scared out of my wits again. I ran toward the cabin.

But like it was, Old Yeller nearly beat me there. I didn't see it, of course; but Mama said that the minute Old Yeller saw we were all in the clear and out of danger, he threw the fight to that she-bear and lit out for the house. The bear chased him for a little piece, but at the rate Old Yeller was leaving her behind, Mama said it looked like the bear was backing up.

But if the big yeller dog was scared or hurt in any way when he came dashing into the house, he didn't show it. He sure didn't show it like we all did. Little Arliss had hushed his screaming, but he was trembling all over and clinging to Mama like he'd never let her go. And Mama was sitting in the middle of the floor, holding him up close and crying like she'd never stop. And me, I was close to crying, myself.

Old Yeller, though, all he did was come bounding in to jump on us and lick us in the face and bark so loud that there, inside the cabin, the noise nearly made us deaf.

The way he acted, you might have thought that bear fight hadn't been anything more than a rowdy romp that we'd all taken part in for the fun of it.

CHAPTERS 1–5

Getting at Meaning

RECALLING

1. What two meanings does the name Old Yeller have?

2. Why does Travis's father decide to drive his cattle to Abilene?

3. According to his father, what will be Travis's most important job?

4. Who was Bell? How did Bell die?

5. Why does Travis try to kick Old Yeller when he first sees him?

6. Why is Travis especially proud of himself for having killed the doe?

7. Who saves Travis when he falls near the bulls, Chongo and Roany?

8. What does Old Yeller do to save the life of Little Arliss?

INTERPRETING

9. How does Little Arliss's mother show that she understands her five-year-old boy? Does Travis understand Little Arliss as well as his mother does? Explain.

10. What are the similarities and differences between Bell and Old Yeller? What reasons does Travis have, at first, for preferring Bell?

CRITICAL THINKING: EVALUATING/APPLYING

11. In the first five chapters, does Travis act more like an adult or like a child? Explain your answer.

12. Does Travis's father seem wise, or does he seem to be asking too much of his son? Would you be willing and able to take on the responsibilities assumed by Travis? Explain.

Developing Skills in Reading Literature

1. **Narrator and Point of View.** The narrator is the teller of a story. Point of view is the perspective from which a story is told. In *Old Yeller,* the narrator is Travis. He tells the story from the first-person point of view, using pronouns such as *I* and *we.* In stories and novels written from the first-person point of view, the narrator often makes comments about his or her own feelings. Find three such comments in the first five chapters of this novel. Tell what Travis reveals about his feelings through these comments.

2. **Setting.** Setting is the time and place of the action of a story. What is the setting of *Old Yeller?* Where does the action take place? Is the story set in the present day or in the past? How do you know?

3. **Plot and Exposition.** Plot is the sequence of events in a story. It is the writer's plan for what happens, when, and to whom. Exposition is the part of the plot that provides background information and that introduces the setting and the important characters. Who are the important characters in *Old Yeller?* What background information is given about Travis's family? What background information is given about Travis's relationships with dogs? Write your answers on a sheet of paper, and save this paper until you have finished all the work in this unit.

4. **Inciting Incident.** The inciting incident is the event that introduces the central conflict and thus sets in motion the plot of the story. What event happens at the beginning of *Old Yeller* to force Travis, Arliss, and their mother to adjust to new circumstances? In other words, what is the inciting incident in this novel? Write your answers on a sheet of paper, and save this paper until you have finished all the work in this unit.

5. **Conflict.** Conflict is a struggle between opposing forces. A novel often deals with many conflicts. The central conflict in *Old Yeller* is Travis's struggle to take care of the family and the farm. This struggle is introduced when his father leaves. To meet the challenge set by his father, Travis must be responsible and mature. Is Travis responsible and mature at the beginning of the novel? What childish qualities does he have? What adult qualities does he have? Do you think that he will be able to handle his new responsibilities? Explain your answers on a sheet of paper, and save this paper until you have finished all the work in this unit.

In the first five chapters, Travis is involved in other conflicts as well. He comes into conflict with his father, his mother, Little Arliss, Old Yeller, and other animals. On a sheet of paper, list the many conflicts in the first five chapters of this novel. Again, save your paper until you have finished all the work in this unit.

6. **Flashback.** A flashback is a part of a story that interrupts the sequence of events to relate an earlier conversation, scene, or event. In the opening chapters of *Old Yeller,* Fred Gipson uses flashbacks to explain how Birdsong Creek got its name and how Travis was once saved from drowning. Find the places in the novel where these things are explained. Tell where each flashback begins and ends. Then, answer these questions:

a. Who named Birdsong Creek? Why was the creek given this name?

b. Who saved Travis from drowning? Why does Travis reject the idea of getting another dog?

7. **Stereotype.** A stereotype is a character who conforms to a simplified common type. Often, stereotypes reflect people's prejudices and misconceptions about one another. The novel *Old Yeller* was written over thirty years ago. Since then, people's attitudes about women and minorities have changed drastically. In what ways does the writer of *Old Yeller* stereotype Native Americans? Why is it silly for Travis, a boy, to be told to look after his mother,

a grown woman? What misconceptions about women does the writer of *Old Yeller* seem to hold?

Developing Vocabulary

1. **Word Origins.** Some English words were formed by combining already existing words. Others were created by imitating sounds. Still others were borrowed from other languages. Using a dictionary, answer the following questions about the origins of words used in Chapters 1–5 of *Old Yeller*.

a. From what two words was the word *cornshuck* made? the word *bobcat*? the word *cottontail*?

b. How did the words *chatter* and *bawl* originate?

c. From what languages did the word *Texas* derive? What was the original meaning of the word?

d. The word *Kansas* is the name of a state. However, it was originally the name of some-thing else. What did the word *Kansas* refer to originally?

e. From what language is the word *tortilla* derived? the word *dun*? the word *scythe*? What do these words mean? What did the words from which these words are taken mean?

2. **Understanding Dialect: Using Context Clues.** A dialect is the variety of a language spoken by the people of a particular region or social group. The following are some terms used in the American frontier dialect spoken by the characters in *Old Yeller*. The page number and column in which each word or phrase appears is given in parentheses. Study the context in which each word or phrase is used. Then, write what you think the word or phrase means.

a. tail-holt (p. 534, col. 2)
b. varmints (p. 535, col. 1)
c. lit out (p. 538, col. 1)
d. scot free (p. 546, col. 2)
e. pay me any mind (p. 546, col. 2)
f. bellering (p. 547, col. 1)
g. windy (p. 551, col. 2)

Chapter 6

Till Little Arliss got us mixed up in that bear fight, I guess I'd been looking on him about like most boys look on their little brothers. I liked him, all right, but I didn't have a lot of use for him. What with his always playing in our drinking water and getting in the way of my chopping axe and howling his head off and chunking me with rocks when he got mad, it didn't seem to me like he was hardly worth the bother of putting up with.

But that day when I saw him in the spring so helpless against the angry she-bear, I learned different. I knew then that I loved him as much as I did Mama and Papa, maybe in some ways even a little bit more.

So it was only natural for me to come to love the dog that saved him.

After that, I couldn't do enough for Old Yeller. What if he was a big ugly meat-stealing rascal? What if he did fall over and yell bloody murder every time I looked crossways at him? What if he had run off when he ought to have helped with the fighting bulls? None of that made a lick of difference now. He'd pitched in and saved Little Arliss when I couldn't possibly have done it, and that was enough for me.

I petted him and made over him till he was wiggling all over to show how happy he was. I felt mean about how I'd treated him and did everything I could to let him know. I searched his feet and pulled out a long mesquite thorn that had become embedded between his toes. I held him down and had Mama hand me a stick with a coal of fire on it, so I could burn off three big bloated ticks that I found inside one of his ears. I washed him with lye soap and water, then rubbed salty bacon grease into his hair all over to rout the fleas. And that night after dark, when he sneaked into bed with me and Little Arliss, I let him sleep there and never said a word about it to Mama.

I took him and Little Arliss squirrel hunting the next day. It was the first time I'd ever taken Little Arliss on any kind of hunt. He was such a noisy pest that I always figured he'd scare off the game.

As it turned out, he was just as noisy and pesky as I'd figured. He'd follow along, keeping quiet like I told him, till he saw maybe a pretty butterfly floating around in the air. Then he'd set up a yell you could have heard a mile off and go chasing after the butterfly. Of course, he couldn't catch it; but he would keep yelling at me to come help him. Then he'd get mad because I wouldn't and yell still louder. Or maybe he'd stop to turn over a flat rock. Then he'd stand yelling at me to come back and look at all the yellow ants and centipedes and crickets and stinging scorpions that went scurrying away, hunting new hiding places.

Once he got hung up in some briars and yelled till I came back to get him out. Another time he fell down and struck his elbow on a rock and didn't say a word about it for several minutes—until he saw blood seeping out of a cut on his arm. Then he stood and screamed like he was being burnt with a hot iron.

With that much racket going on, I knew we'd scare all the game clear out of the country. Which, I guess we did. All but the squirrels. They took to the trees where they could hide from us. But I was lucky enough to see which tree one squirrel went up; so I put some of Little Arliss's racket to use.

I sent him in a circle around the tree, beating on the grass and bushes with a stick, while I stood waiting. Sure enough, the squirrel got to watching Little Arliss and forgot me. He kept turning around the tree limb to keep it between him and Little Arliss, till he was on my side in plain sight. I shot him out of the tree the first shot.

After that, Old Yeller caught onto what game we were after. He went to work then, trailing and treeing the squirrels that Little Arliss was scaring up off the ground. From then on, with Yeller to tree the squirrels and Little Arliss to turn them on the tree limbs, we had pickings. Wasn't but a little bit till I'd shot five, more than enough to make us a good squirrel fry for supper.

A week later, Old Yeller helped me catch a wild gobbler that I'd have lost without him. We had gone up to the corn patch to pick a bait of blackeyed peas. I was packing my gun. Just as we got up to the slabrock fence that Papa had built around the corn patch, I looked over and spotted this gobbler doing our pea-picking for us. The pea pods were still green yet, most of them no further along than snapping size. This made them hard for the gobbler to shell, but he was working away at it, pecking and scratching so hard that he was raising a big dust out in the field.

"Why, that old rascal," Mama said. "He's just clawing those pea vines all to pieces."

"Hush, Mama," I said. "Don't scare him." I lifted my gun and laid the barrel across the top of the rock fence. "I'll have him ready for the pot in just a minute."

It wasn't a long shot, and I had him sighted in, dead to rights. I aimed to stick a bullet right where his wings hinged to his back. I was holding my breath and already squeezing off when Little Arliss, who'd gotten behind, came running up.

"Whatcha shootin' at, Travis?" he yelled at the top of his voice. "Whatcha shootin' at?"

Well, that made me and the gobbler both jump. The gun fired, and I saw the gobbler go down. But a second later, he was up again, streaking through the tall corn, dragging a broken wing.

For a second, I was so mad at Little Arliss I could have wrung his neck like a frying chicken's. I said, "*Arliss!* Why can't you keep your mouth shut? You've made me lose that gobbler!"

Well, little Arliss didn't have sense enough to know what I was mad about. Right away, he puckered up and went to crying and leaking tears all over the place. Some of them splattered clear down on his bare feet, making dark splotches in the dust that covered them. I always did say that when Little Arliss cried he could shed more tears faster than any crier I ever saw.

"Wait a minute!" Mama put in. "I don't think you've lost your gobbler yet. Look yonder!"

She pointed, and I looked, and there was Old Yeller jumping the rock fence and racing toward the pea patch. He ran up to where I'd knocked the gobbler down. He circled the

place one time, smelling the ground and wiggling his stub tail. Then he took off through the corn the same way the gobbler went, yelling like I was beating him with a stick.

When he barked treed[1] a couple of minutes later, it was in the woods the other side of the corn patch. We went to him. We found him jumping at the gobbler that had run up a stooping live oak and was perched there, panting, just waiting for me.

So in spite of the fact that Little Arliss had caused me to make a bad shot, we had us a real sumptuous supper that night. Roast turkey with cornbread dressing and watercress and wild onions that Little Arliss and I found growing down in the creek next to the water.

But when we tried to feed Old Yeller some of the turkey, on account of his saving us from losing it, he wouldn't eat. He'd lick the meat and wiggle his stub tail to show how grateful he was, but he didn't swallow down more than a bite or two.

That puzzled Mama and me because, when we remembered back, we realized that he hadn't been eating anything we'd fed him for the last several days. Yet he was fat and with hair as slick and shiny as a dog eating three square meals a day.

Mama shook her head. "If I didn't know better," she said, "I'd say that dog was sucking eggs. But I've got three hens setting and one with biddy chickens,[2] and I'm getting more eggs from the rest of them than I've gotten since last fall. So he can't be robbing the nests."

Well, we wondered some about what Old Yeller was living on, but didn't worry about it. That is, not until the day Bud Searcy dropped

---

1. **When he barked treed:** when he signaled by barking that the turkey had been "treed," or trapped in a tree.
2. **biddy chickens:** chicks.

by the cabin to see how we were making out.

Bud Searcy was a red-faced man with a bulging middle who liked to visit around the settlement and sit and talk hard times and spit tobacco juice all over the place and wait for somebody to ask him to dinner.

I never did have a lot of use for him and my folks didn't, either. Mama said he was shiftless. She said that was the reason the rest of the men left him at home to sort of look after the womenfolks and kids while they were gone on the cow drive. She said the men knew that if they took Bud Searcy along, they'd never get to Kansas before the steers were dead with old age. It would take Searcy that long to get through visiting and eating with everybody between Salt Licks and Abilene.

But he did have a little white-haired granddaughter that I sort of liked. She was eleven and different from most girls. She would hang around and watch what boys did, like showing how high they could climb in a tree or how far they could throw a rock or how fast they could swim or how good they could shoot. But she never wanted to mix in or try to take over and boss things. She just went along and watched and didn't say much, and the only thing I had against her was her eyes. They were big solemn brown eyes and right pretty to look at; only when she fixed them on me, it always seemed like they looked clear through me and saw everything I was thinking. That always made me sort of jumpy, so that when I could, I never would look right straight at her.

Her name was Lisbeth and she came with her grandpa the day he visited us. They came riding up on an old shad-bellied pony that didn't look like he'd had a fill of corn in a coon's age. She rode behind her grandpa's saddle, holding to his belt in the back, and her white hair was all curly and rippling in the sun.

Trotting behind them was a blue-ticked she-dog that I always figured was one of Bell's pups.

Old Yeller went out to bay them as they rode up. I noticed right off that he didn't go about it like he really meant business. His yelling bay sounded a lot more like he was just barking because he figured that's what we expected him to do. And the first time I hollered at him, telling him to dry up all that racket, he hushed. Which surprised me, as hard-headed as he generally was.

By the time Mama had come to the door and told Searcy and Lisbeth to get down and come right in, Old Yeller had started a romp with the blue-ticked she-dog.

Lisbeth slipped to the ground and stood staring at me with those big solemn eyes while her grandpa dismounted. Searcy told Mama that he believed he wouldn't come in the house. He said that as hot as the day was, he figured he'd like it better sitting in the dog run. So Mama had me bring out our four cowhide bottom chairs. Searcy picked the one I always liked to sit in best. He got out a twist of tobacco and bit off a chew big enough to bulge his cheek and went to chewing and talking and spitting juice right were we'd all be bound to step in it and pack it around on the bottoms of our feet.

First he asked Mama if we were making out all right, and Mama said we were. Then he told her that he'd been left to look after all the families while the men were gone, a mighty heavy responsibility that was nearly working him to death, but that he was glad to do it. He said for Mama to remember that if the least little thing went wrong, she was to get in touch with him right away. And Mama said she would.

Then he leaned his chair back against the cabin wall and went to telling what all was going on around in the settlement. He told about how dry the weather was and how he looked for all the corn crops to fail and the settlement folks to be scraping the bottoms of their meal barrels long before next spring. He told how the cows were going dry and the gardens were failing. He told how Jed Simpson's boy Rosal was sitting at a turkey roost, waiting for a shot, when a fox came right up and tried to jump on him, and Rosal had to club it to death with his gun butt. This sure looked like a case of hydrophobia to Searcy, as anybody knew that no fox in his right mind was going to jump on a hunter.

Which reminded him of an uncle of his that got mad-dog bit down in the piney woods of East Texas. This was 'way back when Searcy was a little boy. As soon as the dog bit him, the man knew he was bound to die; so he went and got a big log chain and tied one end around the bottom of a tree and the other end to one of his legs. And right there he stayed till the sickness got him and he lost his mind. He slobbered at the mouth and moaned and screamed and ran at his wife and children, trying to catch them and bite them. Only, of course, the chain around his leg held him back, which was the reason he'd chained himself to the tree in the first place. And right there, chained to that tree, he finally died and they buried him under the same tree.

Bud Searcy sure hoped that we wouldn't have an outbreak of hydrophobia in Salt Licks and all die before the men got back from Kansas.

Then he talked awhile about a panther that had caught and killed one of Joe Anson's colts and how the Anson boys had put their dogs on the trail. They ran the panther into the cave and Jeff Anson followed in where the dogs had more sense than to go and got pretty badly

panther-mauled for his trouble; but he did get the panther.

Searcy talked till dinnertime, said not a word all through dinner, and then went back to talking as quick as he'd swallowed down the last bite.

He told how some strange varmit that wasn't a coyote, possum, skunk, or coon had recently started robbing the settlement blind. Or maybe it was even some*body*. Nobody could tell for sure. All they knew was that they were losing meat out of their smokehouses, eggs out of their hens' nests, and sometimes even whole pans of cornbread that the womenfolks had set out to cool. Ike Fuller had been barbecuing some meat over an open pit and left it for a minute to go get a drink of water and came back to find that a three- or four-pound chunk of beef ribs had disappeared like it had gone up in smoke.

Salt Licks folks were getting pretty riled about it, Searcy said, and guessed it would go hard with whatever or whoever was doing the raiding if they ever learned what it was.

Listening to this, I got an uneasy feeling. The feeling got worse a minute later when Lisbeth motioned me to follow her off down to the spring.

We walked clear down there, with Old Yeller and the blue-tick dog following with us, before she finally looked up at me and said, "It's him."

"What do you mean?" I said.

"I mean it's your big yeller dog," she said. "I saw him."

"Do what?" I asked.

"Steal that bait of ribs," she said. "I saw him get a bunch of eggs, too. From one of our nests."

I stopped then and looked straight at her and she looked straight back at me and I

couldn't stand it and had to look down.

"But I'm not going to tell," she said.

I didn't believe her. "I bet you do," I said.

"No, I won't," she said, shaking her head. "I wouldn't, even before I knew he was your dog."

"Why?"

"Because Miss Prissy is going to have pups."

"Miss Prissy?"

"That's the name of my dog, and she's going to have pups and your dog will be their papa, and I wouldn't want their papa to get shot."

I stared at her again, and again I had to look down. I wanted to thank her, but I didn't know the right words. So I fished around in my pocket and brought out an Indian arrowhead that I'd found the day before and gave that to her.

She took it and stared at it for a little bit, with her eyes shining, then shoved it deep into a long pocket she had sewn to her dress.

"I won't never, never tell," she said, then whirled and tore out for the house, running as fast as she could.

I went down and sat by the spring awhile. It seemed like I liked Bud Searcy a lot better than I ever had before, even if he did talk too much and spit tobacco juice all over the place. But I was still bothered. If Lisbeth had caught Old Yeller stealing stuff at the settlements, then somebody else might, too. And if they did, they were sure liable to shoot him. A family might put up with one of its own dogs stealing from them if he was a good dog. But for a dog that left home to steal from everybody else—well, I didn't see much chance for him if he ever got caught.

After Bud Searcy had eaten a hearty supper and talked awhile longer, he finally rode off home, with Lisbeth riding behind him. I went then and gathered the eggs and held three back. I called Old Yeller off from the house and broke the eggs on a flat rock, right under his nose and tried to get him to eat them. But he wouldn't. He acted like he'd never heard tell that eggs were fit to eat. All he'd do was stand there and wiggle his tail and try to lick me in the face.

It made me mad. "You thievin' rascal," I said. "I ought to get a club and break your back—in fourteen different places."

But I didn't really mean it, and I didn't say it loud and ugly. I knew that if I did, he'd fall over and start yelling like he was dying. And there I'd be—in a fight with Little Arliss again.

"When they shoot you, I'm going to laugh," I told him.

But I knew that I wouldn't.

Chapter 7

I did considerable thinking on what Lisbeth Searcy had told me about Old Yeller and finally went and told Mama.

"Why, that old rogue!" she said. "We'll have to try to figure some way to keep him from prowling. Everybody in the settlement will be mad at us if we don't."

"Somebody'll shoot him," I said.

"Try tying him," she said.

So I tried tying him. But we didn't have any bailing wire in those days, and he could chew through anything else before you could turn your back. I tied him with rope and then with big thick rawhide string that I cut from a cowhide hanging across the top rail of the yard fence. It was the same thing in both cases. By the time we could get off to bed, he'd done chewed them in two and was gone.

"Let's try the corncrib," Mama said on the third night.

Which was a good idea that might have worked if it hadn't been for Little Arliss.

I took Old Yeller out and put him in the corncrib and the second that he heard the door shut on him, he set up a yelling and a howling that brought Little Arliss on the run. Mama and I both tried to explain to him why we

needed to shut the dog up, but Little Arliss was too mad to listen. You can't explain things very well to somebody who is screaming his head off and chunking you with rocks as fast as he can pick them up. So that didn't work, either.

"Well, it looks like we're stumped," Mama said.

I thought for a minute and said, "No, Mama. I believe we've got one other chance. That's to shut him up in the same room with me and Little Arliss every night."

"But he'll sleep in the bed with you boys," Mama said, "and the first thing you know, you'll both be scratching fleas and having mange and breaking out with ringworms."

"No, I'll put him a cowhide on the floor and make him sleep there," I said.

So Mama agreed and I spread a cowhide on the floor beside our bed and we shut Old Yeller in and didn't have a bit more trouble.

Of course, Old Yeller didn't sleep on the cowhide. And once, a good while later, I did break out with a little ringworm under my left arm. But I rubbed it with turpentine, just like Mama always did, and it soon went away. And after that, when we fed Old Yeller cornmeal mush or fresh meat, he ate it and did well on it and never one time bothered our chicken nests.

About that time, too, the varmints got to pestering us so much that a lot of times Old Yeller and I were kept busy nearly all night long.

It was the coons, mainly. The corn was ripening into roasting ears now, and the coons would come at night and strip the shucks back with their little hands and gnaw the milky kernels off the cob. Also, the watermelons were beginning to turn red inside and the skunks would come and open up little round holes in the rinds and reach in with their forefeet and drag out the juicy insides to eat. Sometimes the coyotes would come and eat watermelons, too; and now and then a deer would jump into the field and eat corn, melons, and peas.

So Old Yeller and I took to sleeping in the corn patch every night. We slept on the cowhide that Yeller never would sleep on at the house. That is, we did when we got to sleep. Most of the night, we'd be up fighting coons. We slept out in the middle of the patch, where Yeller could scent a coon clear to the fence on every side. We'd lie there on the cowhide and look up at the stars and listen to the warm night breeze rustling the corn blades. Sometimes I'd wonder what the stars were and what kept them hanging up there so high and bright and if Papa, 'way off up yonder in Kansas, could see the same stars I could see.

I was getting mighty lonesome to see Papa. With the help of Old Yeller, I was taking care of things all right; but I was sure beginning to wish that he'd come back home.

Then I'd think awhile about the time when I'd get big enough to go off on a cow drive myself, riding my own horse, and see all the big new country of plains and creeks and rivers and mountains and timber and new towns and Indian camps. Then, finally, just about the time I started drifting off to sleep, I'd hear Old Yeller rise to his feet and go padding off through the corn. A minute later, his yelling bay would lift from some part of the corn patch, and I'd hear the fighting squawl of some coon caught stealing corn. Then I'd jump to my feet and go running through the corn, shouting encouragement to Old Yeller.

"Git him, Yeller," I'd holler. "Tear him up!"

And that's what Old Yeller would be trying to do; but a boar coon isn't an easy thing to tear up. For one thing, he'll fight you from sundown till sunup. He's not big for size, but the longer you fight him, the bigger he seems to get. He fights you with all four feet and every tooth in his head and enough courage for an animal five times his size.

On top of that, he's fighting inside a thick hide that fills a dog's mouth like a wad of loose sacking. The dog has a hard time ever really biting him. He just squirms and twists around inside that hide and won't quit fighting even after the dog's got enough and is ready to throw the fight to him. Plenty of times, Papa and I had seen a boar coon whip Bell, run him off, then turn on us and chase us clear out of a cornfield.

It was easy for me to go running through the dark cornfields, yelling for Old Yeller to tear up a thieving coon, but it wasn't easy for Old Yeller to do it. He'd be yelling and the coon would be squawling and they'd go wallowing and clawing and threshing through the corn, popping the stalks as they broke them off, making such an uproar in the night that it sounded like murder. But, generally, when the fight was all over, the coon went one way and Old Yeller the other, both of them pretty well satisfied to call it quits.

We didn't get much sleep of a night while all this was going on, but we had us a good time and saved the corn from the coons.

The only real bad part of it was the skunks. What with all the racket we made coon fighting, the skunks didn't come often. But when one did come, we were in a mess.

Old Yeller could handle a skunk easy enough. All he had to do was rush in, grab it by the head and give it a good shaking. That would break the skunk's neck, but it wouldn't end the trouble. Because not even a hoot owl can kill a skunk without getting sprayed with his scent. And skunk scent is a smell that won't quit. After every skunk killing, Old Yeller would get so sick that he could hardly stand it. He'd snort and drool and slobber and vomit. He'd roll and wallow in the dirt and go dragging his body through tall weeds, trying to get the scent off; but he couldn't. Then finally, he'd give up and come lie down on the cowhide with me. And of course he'd smell so bad that I couldn't stand him and have to go off and try to sleep somewhere else. Then he'd follow me and get his feelings hurt because I wouldn't let him sleep with me.

Papa always said that breathing skunk scent was the best way in the world to cure a head cold. But this was summertime, when Old Yeller and I didn't have head colds. We would just as soon that the skunks stayed out of the watermelons and let us alone.

Working there, night after night, guarding our precious bread corn from the varmints, I came to see what I would have been up against if I'd had it to do without the help of Old Yeller. By myself, I'd have been run to death

and still probably wouldn't have saved the corn. Also, look at all the fun I would have missed if I'd been alone, and how lonesome I would have been. I had to admit Papa had been right when he'd told me how bad I needed a dog.

I saw that even more clearly when the spotted heifer had her first calf.

Our milk cows were all old-time longhorn cattle and didn't give a lot of milk. It was real hard to find one that would give much more than her calf could take. What we generally had to do was milk five or six cows to get enough milk for just the family.

But we had one crumpled-horn cow named Rose that gave a lot of milk, only she was getting old, and Mama kept hoping that each of her heifer calves would turn out to be as good a milker as Rose. Mama had tried two or three, but none of them proved to be any good. And then along came this spotted one that was just rawboned and ugly enough to make a good milk cow. She had the bag for it, too, and Mama was certain this time that she'd get a milk cow to replace Rose.

The only trouble was, this heifer Spot, as we called her, had been snaky wild from the day she was born. Try to drive her with the other cattle, and she'd run off and hide. Hem her up in a corner and try to get your hands on her, and she'd turn on you and make fight. Mama had been trying all along to get Spot gentled before she had her first calf, but it was no use. Spot didn't want to be friends with anybody. We knew she was going to give us a pile of trouble when we set out to milk her.

I failed to find Spot with the rest of our milk cows one evening, and when I went to drive them up the next day, she was still gone.

"It's time for her to calve," Mama said, "and

I'll bet she's got one."

So the next morning I went further back in the hills and searched all over. I finally came across her, holed up in a dense thicket of bee myrtle close to a little seep spring. I got one brief glimpse of a wobbly, long-legged calf before Spot snorted and took after me. She ran me clear to the top of the next high ridge before she turned back.

I made another try. I got to the edge of the thicket and picked me up some rocks. I went to hollering and chunking into the brush, trying to scare her and the calf out. I got her out, all right, but she wasn't scared. She came straight for me with her horns lowered, bawling her threats as she came. I had to turn tail a second time, and again she chased me clear to the top of that ridge.

I tried it one more time, then went back to the house and got Old Yeller. I didn't know if he knew anything about driving cattle or not, but I was willing to bet that he could keep her from chasing me.

And he did. I went up to the edge of the thicket and started hollering and chunking rocks into it. Here came the heifer, madder than ever, it looked like. I yelled at Old Yeller. "Get her, Yeller," I hollered. And Yeller got her. He pulled the neatest trick I ever saw a dog pull on a cow brute.

Only I didn't see it the first time. I was getting away from there too fast. I'd stumbled and fallen to my knees when I turned to run from Spot's charge, and she was too close behind for me to be looking back and watching what Old Yeller was doing. I just heard the scared bawl she let out and the crashing of the brush as Old Yeller rolled her into it.

I ran a piece further, then looked back. The heifer was scrambling to her feet in a cloud of dust and looking like she didn't know any more about what had happened than I did. Then she caught sight of Old Yeller. She snorted, stuck her tail in the air and made for him. Yeller ran like he was scared to death, then cut back around a thicket. A second later, he was coming in behind Spot.

Without making a sound, he ran up beside her, made his leap and set his teeth in her nose.

I guess it was the weight of him that did it. I saw him do it lots of times later, but never did quite understand how. Anyway, he just set his teeth in her nose, doubled himself up in a tight ball, and swung on. That turned the charging heifer a flip. Her heels went straight up in the air over her head. She landed flat on her back with all four feet sticking up. She hit the ground so hard that it sounded like she ought to bust wide open.

I guess she felt that way about it, too. Anyhow, after taking that second fall, she didn't have much fight left in her. She just scrambled to her feet and went trotting back into the thicket, lowing to her calf.

I followed her, with Old Yeller beside me, and we drove her out and across the hills to the cow lot. Not one time did she turn on us again. She did try to run off a couple of times, but all I had to do was send Old Yeller in to head her. And the second she caught sight of him, she couldn't turn fast enough to get headed back in the right direction.

It was the same when we got her into the cowpen. Her bag was all in a strut with milk that the calf couldn't hold. Mama said we needed to get that milk out. She came with a bucket and I took it, knowing I had me a big kicking fight on my hands if I ever hoped to get any milk.

The kicking fight started. The first time I

touched Spot's bag, she reached out with a flying hind foot, aiming to kick my head off and coming close to doing it. Then she wheeled on me and put me on top of the rail fence as quick as a squirrel could have made it.

Mama shook her head. "I was hoping she wouldn't be that way," she said. "I always hate to have to tie up a heifer to break her for milking. But I guess there's no other way with this one."

I thought of all the trouble it would be, having to tie up that Spot heifer, head and feet, twice a day, every day, for maybe a month or more. I looked at Old Yeller, standing just outside the pen.

"Yeller," I said, "you come in here."

Yeller came bounding through the rails.

Mama said: "Why, son, you can't teach a heifer to stand with a dog in the pen. Especially one with a young calf. She'll be fighting at him all the time, thinking he's a wolf or something trying to get her calf."

I laughed. "Maybe it won't work," I said, "but I bet you one thing. She won't be fighting Old Yeller."

She didn't, either. She lowered her horns and rolled her eyes as I brought Old Yeller up to her.

"Now, Yeller," I said, "you stand here and watch her."

Old Yeller seemed to know just what I wanted. He walked right up to where he could almost touch his nose to hers and stood there, wagging his stub tail. And she didn't charge him or run from him. All she did was stand there and sort of tremble. I went back and milked out her strutted bag and she didn't offer to kick me one time, just flinched and drew up a little when I first touched her.

"Well, that does beat all," Mama marveled. "Why, at that rate, we'll have her broke to milk in a week's time."

Mama was right. Within three days after we started, I could drive Spot into the pen, go right up and milk her, and all she'd do was stand there and stare at Old Yeller. By the end of the second week, she was standing and belching and chewing her cud — the gentlest cow I ever milked.

After all that, I guess you can see why I nearly died when a man rode up one day and claimed Old Yeller.

Chapter 8

The man's name was Burn Sanderson. He was a young man who rode a good horse and was mighty nice and polite about taking his hat off to Mama when he dismounted in front of our cabin. He told Mama who he was. He said he was a newcomer to Salt Licks. He said that he'd come from down San Antonio way with a little bunch of cattle that he was grazing over in the Devil's River country. He said he couldn't afford to hire riders, so he'd brought along a couple of dogs to help him herd his cattle. One of these dogs, the best one, had disappeared. He'd inquired around about it at Salt Licks, and Bud Searcy had told him that we had the dog.

"A big yeller dog?" Mama asked, looking sober and worried.

"Yessum," the man said, then added with a

grin. "And the worse egg sucker and camp robber you ever laid eyes on. Steal you blind, that old devil will; but there was never a better cow dog born."

Mama turned to me. "Son, call Old Yeller," she said.

I stood frozen in my tracks. I was so full of panic that I couldn't move or think.

"Go on, Son," Mama urged. "I think he and Little Arliss must be playing down about the creek somewhere."

"But Mama!" I gasped. "We can't do without Old Yeller. He's—"

"Travis!"

Mama's voice was too sharp. I knew I was whipped. I turned and went toward the creek, so mad at Bud Searcy that I couldn't see straight. Why couldn't he keep his blabber-mouth shut?

"Come on up to the house," I told Little Arliss.

I guess the way I said it let him know that something real bad was happening. He didn't argue or stick out his tongue or anything. He just got out of the water and followed me back to the house and embarrassed Mama and the young man nearly to death because he came packing his clothes in one hand instead of wearing them.

I guess Burn Sanderson had gotten an idea of how much we thought of Old Yeller, or maybe Mama had told some things about the dog while I was gone to the creek. Anyhow, he acted uncomfortable about taking the dog off. "Now, Mrs. Coates," he said to Mama, "your man is gone, and you and the boys don't have much protection here. Bad as I need that old dog, I can make out without him until your man comes."

But Mama shook her head.

"No, Mr. Sanderson," she said. "He's your dog; and the longer we keep him, the harder it'll be for us to give him up. Take him along. I can make the boys understand."

The man tied his rope around Old Yeller's neck and mounted his horse. That's when Little Arliss caught onto what was happening. He threw a walleyed fit. He screamed and he hollered. He grabbed up a bunch of rocks and went to throwing them at Burn Sanderson. One hit Sanderson's horse in the flank. The horse bogged his head and went to pitching and bawling and grunting. This excited Old Yeller. He chased after the horse, baying him at the top of his voice. And what with Mama running after Little Arliss, hollering for him to shut up and quit throwing those rocks, it was altogether the biggest and loudest commotion that had taken place around our cabin for a good long while.

When Burn Sanderson finished riding the pitch out of his scared horse, he hollered at Old Yeller. He told him he'd better hush up that racket before he got his brains beat out. Then he rode back toward us, wearing a wide grin.

His grin got wider as he saw how Mama and I were holding Little Arliss. We each had him by one wrist and were holding him clear off the ground. He couldn't get at any more rocks to throw that way, but it sure didn't keep him from dancing up and down in the air and screaming.

"Turn him loose," Sanderson said with a big laugh. "He's not going to throw any more rocks at me."

He swung down from his saddle. He came and got Little Arliss and loved him up till he hushed screaming. Then he said: "Look, boy, do you really want that thieving old dog?"

He held Little Arliss off and stared him straight in the eyes, waiting for Arliss to answer. Little Arliss stared straight back at him and didn't say a word.

"Well, do you?" he insisted.

Finally, Little Arliss nodded, then tucked his chin and looked away.

"All right," Burn Sanderson said. "We'll make a trade. Just between you and me. I'll let you keep the old rascal, but you've got to do something for me."

He waited till Little Arliss finally got up the nerve to ask what, then went on. "Well, it's like this. I've hung around over there in that cow camp, eating my own cooking till I'm so starved out, I don't hardly throw a shadow. Now, if you could talk your mama into feeding me a real jam-up meal, I think it would be worth at least a one-eared yeller dog. Don't you?"

I didn't wait to hear any more. I ran off. I was so full of relief that I was about to pop. I knew that if I didn't get out of sight in a hurry, this Burn Sanderson was going to catch me crying.

Mama cooked the best dinner that day I ever ate. We had roast venison and fried catfish and stewed squirrel and blackeyed peas and cornbread and flour gravy and butter and wild honey and hog-plum jelly and fresh buttermilk. I ate till it seemed like my eyeballs would pop out of my head and still didn't make anything like the showing that Burn Sanderson made. He was a slim man, not nearly as big as Papa, and I never could figure out where he was putting all that grub. But long before he finally sighed and shook his head at the last of the squirrel stew, I was certain of one thing: he sure wouldn't have any trouble throwing a shadow on the ground for the rest of that day. A good, black shadow.

After dinner, he sat around for a while, talking to me and Mama and making Little Arliss some toy horses out of dried cornstalks. Then he said his thank-you's to Mama and told me to come with him. I followed with him while he led his horse down to the spring for water. I remembered how Papa had led me away from the house like this the day he left and knew by that that Burn Sanderson had something he wanted to talk to me about.

At the spring, he slipped the bits out of his horse's mouth to let him drink, then turned to me.

"Now, boy," he said, "I didn't want to tell your mama this. I didn't want to worry her. But there's a plague of hydrophobia making the rounds, and I want you to be on the lookout for it."

I felt a scare run through me. I didn't know much about hydrophobia, but after what Bud Searcy had told about his uncle that died, chained to a tree, I knew it was something bad. I stared at Burn Sanderson and didn't say anything.

"And there's no mistake about it," he said. "I've done shot two wolves, a fox, and one skunk that had it. And over at Salt Licks, a woman had to kill a bunch of housecats that her younguns had been playing with. She wasn't sure, but she couldn't afford to take any chances. And you can't, either."

"But how will I know what to shoot and what not to?" I wanted to know.

"Well, you can't hardly tell at first," he said. "Not until they have already gone to foaming at the mouth and are reeling with the blind staggers. Any time you see a critter acting that way, you know for sure. But you watch for others that aren't that far along. You take a pet cat. If he takes to spitting and fighting at you for no reason, you shoot him. Same with a dog. He'll get mad at nothing and want to bite you. Take a fox or a wildcat. You know they'll run from you; when they don't run, and try to make fight at you, shoot 'em. Shoot anything that acts unnatural, and don't fool around about it. It's too late after they've already bitten or scratched you."

Talk like that made my heart jump up in my throat till I could hardly get my breath. I looked down at the ground and went to kicking around some rocks.

"You're not scared, are you, boy? I'm only telling you because I know your papa left you in charge of things. I know you can handle whatever comes up. I'm just telling you to watch close and not let anything—*anything*—get to you or your folks with hydrophobia. Think you can do it?"

I swallowed. "I can do it," I told him. "I'm not scared."

The sternness left Burn Sanderson's face. He put a hand on my shoulder, just as Papa had the day he left.

"Good boy," he said. "That's the way a man talks."

Then he gripped my shoulder real tight, mounted his horse and rode off through the brush. And I was so scared and mixed up about the danger of hydrophobia that it was clear into the next day before I even thought about thanking him for giving us Old Yeller.

CHAPTERS 6–8

Getting at Meaning

RECALLING

1. In what ways does Old Yeller help Travis with his hunting?

2. According to Travis's mother, why didn't the men take Bud Searcy with them on the cattle drive?

3. What does Lisbeth tell Travis down by the spring? Why does she choose to reveal her secret to no one but Travis?

4. How do Travis and his mother manage to keep Old Yeller from prowling at night?

5. How do Travis and Old Yeller save the corn from being eaten by raccoons?

6. What does Travis do to make Spot stand still to be milked?

7. What does Little Arliss do when he learns why Burn Sanderson has stopped by?

8. Why does Burn Sanderson lead Travis away from the house? What information does Sanderson reveal to Travis?

INTERPRETING

9. In what way do Travis's feelings about Old Yeller change after the episode with the she-bear?

10. What disturbs Travis about Lisbeth's way of looking at him?

11. What do the subjects that Bud Searcy talks about before dinner have in common?

12. Why doesn't Burn Sanderson take Old Yeller with him? What makes him agree to swapping Old Yeller for a meal?

13. Why does Travis run away after Burn Sanderson makes his offer? What does this reveal about Travis?

Developing Skills in Reading Literature

1. **Conflict and Complication.** A conflict is a struggle between opposing forces. A complication is an event that heightens, or complicates, a conflict that has already been introduced. In *Old Yeller,* Travis must struggle with many problems in an effort to look after the farm while his father is gone. Travis's struggles are complicated by several events, including the following:

a. the raccoons eating the corn
b. the discovery that Old Yeller has been stealing food
c. the disappearance of Spot

How does Travis deal with each of these complications?

At the end of Chapter 8, Burn Sanderson informs Travis of yet another complication. What is the complication? Write your answers on a sheet of paper, and save this paper until you have finished this unit.

2. **Plot and Subplot.** Plot is the sequence of events in a story. It is the writer's plan for what happens, when, and to whom. A subplot is a less important story that is closely related to the main story. In this novel, the main plot deals with Travis's attempt to take care of the farm and so prove himself to be an adult. One subplot in this novel concerns the developing relationship between Travis and his younger brother. How does Travis feel toward Little Arliss at the beginning of this novel? What conflicts take place between Travis and Little Arliss? How do Travis's feelings change after the incident with the she-bear?

3. **Episode.** An episode is a self-contained section of a longer story. Chapters 1–5 of *Old Yeller* contain episodes in which

a. Old Yeller steals the middling meat
b. Travis shoots the deer
c. Travis fights with Little Arliss over Old Yeller
d. the two longhorn bulls fight with each other
e. Little Arliss is attacked by the she-bear

Describe three episodes from Chapters 6–8. Briefly explain what happens in each.

4. **Foreshadowing.** Foreshadowing is the technique of hinting about some event that has not yet occurred. In Chapter 2 Old Yeller steals some meat. This leads Travis to fear that the dog will steal food regularly. What events in Chapter 6 are foreshadowed by the event in Chapter 2?

Developing Vocabulary

1. **Using a Dictionary.** Read the following sentence from Chapter 6. Then, read the dictionary definition for the word *rout.*

"I washed him [Old Yeller] with lye soap and water, then rubbed salty bacon grease into his hair all over to *rout* the fleas."

rout¹ (rout) *n.* [< OFr. < L. *rupta:* see ROUTE] **1.** a disorderly crowd; rabble **2.** a disorderly flight, as of defeated troops *[to be put to* rout] **3.** an overwhelming defeat **4.** [Archaic] a group of people; company —*vt.* **1.** to put to disorderly flight *[to* rout enemy troops] **2.** to defeat overwhelmingly —see **SYN.** at CONQUER

Answer these questions on a sheet of paper:

a. From what Latin word does the word *rout* derive?

b. One cross reference in this entry tells you what word to look up to find more information on the origin of *rout.* What word must you look up to find this additional information?

c. The word *rout* can function as what parts of speech? What part of speech is *rout* as it is used in the sentence from *Old Yeller?*

d. Which of the meanings of *rout* are intended in the sentence from *Old Yeller?*

e. According to the entry, what word could you look up to find a list of synonyms for the word *rout?*

2. **Roots.** Roots are word parts that cannot stand alone. The word *hydrophobia* comes from two Greek roots, *hydro,* which means "water," and *phobos,* which means "fear." People who have the disease hydrophobia, or rabies, often find it difficult or impossible to drink liquids. Look up the following words in a dictionary and write their meanings on a sheet of paper.

hydrology	claustrophobia
hydroplane	acrophobia
hydrosphere	microphobia

Developing Writing Skills

1. **Writing About Personal Experience.** In *Old Yeller,* Travis must take on many adult responsibilities. As a result, he learns and matures. Write a paragraph about a time when you took on an adult responsibility. In your paragraph, explain what you did and what you learned from your experience. As you write and revise your paragraph, refer to **Using the Process of Writing** on pages 614–623.

2. **Writing About Plot.** At the end of Chapter 8, the writer introduces a complication: Many animals near Birdsong Creek are suffering from hydrophobia. Based on this information, write a paragraph explaining what you think could happen in the rest of the novel. Do not skip ahead to find out what actually happens, since this would spoil the ending for you. Use your own imagination to come up with a possible series of events. List these events in your prewriting notes. As you write and revise your paragraph, refer to **Using the Process of Writing** on pages 614–623.

Chapter 9

A boy, before he really grows up, is pretty much like a wild animal. He can get the wits scared clear out of him today and by tomorrow have forgotten all about it.

At least, that's the way it was with me. I was plenty scared of the hydrophobia plague that Burn Sanderson told me about. I could hardly sleep that night. I kept picturing in my mind mad dogs and mad wolves reeling about with the blind staggers, drooling slobbers and snapping and biting at everything in sight. Maybe biting Mama and Little Arliss, so that they got the sickness and went mad, too. I lay in bed and shuddered and shivered and dreamed all sorts of nightmare happenings.

Then, the next day, I went to rounding up and marking hogs and forgot all about the plague.

Our hogs ran loose on the range in those days, the same as our cattle. We fenced them out of the fields, but never into a pasture; we had no pastures. We never fed them, unless maybe it was a little corn that we threw to them during a bad spell in the winter. The rest of the time, they rustled for themselves.

They slept out and ate out. In the summertime, they slept in the cool places around the water holes, sometimes in the water. In the winter, they could always tell at least a day ahead of time when a blizzard was on the way; then they'd gang up and pack tons of leaves and dry grass and sticks into some dense thicket or cave. They'd pile all this into a huge bed and sleep on until the cold spell blew over.

They ranged all over the hills and down into the canyons. In season, they fed on acorns, berries, wild plums, prickly pear apples, grass, weeds, and bulb plants which they rooted out of the ground. They especially liked the wild black persimmons that the Mexicans called *chapotes*.

Sometimes, too, they'd eat a newborn calf if the mama cow couldn't keep them horned away. Or a baby fawn that the doe had left hidden in the tall grass. Once, in a real dry time, Papa and I saw an old sow standing belly deep in a drying up pothole of water, catching and eating perch that were trapped in there and couldn't get away.

Most of these meat eaters were old hogs, however. Starvation during some bad drought or extra cold winter had forced them to eat anything they could get hold of. Papa said they generally started out by feeding on the carcass of some deer or cow that had died, then going from there to catching and killing live meat. He told a tale about how one old range hog had caught him when he was a baby and his folks got there just barely in time to save him.

It was that sort of thing, I guess, that always made Mama so afraid of wild hogs. The least little old biting shoat could make her take cover. She didn't like it a bit when I started out to catch and mark all the pigs that our sows had raised that year. She knew we had it to do, else we couldn't tell our hogs from those of the neighbors. But she didn't like the idea of my doing it alone.

"But I'm not working hogs alone, Mama," I pointed out. "I've got Old Yeller, and Burn Sanderson says he's a real good hog dog."

"That doesn't mean a thing," Mama said. "All hog dogs are good ones. A good one is the only kind that can work hogs and live. But the best dog in the world won't keep you from getting cut all to pieces if you ever make a slip."

Well, Mama was right. I'd worked with Papa enough to know that any time you messed with a wild hog, you were asking for trouble. Let him alone, and he'll generally snort and run from you on sight, the same as a deer. But once you corner him, he's the most dangerous animal that ever lived in Texas. Catch a squealing pig out of the bunch, and you've got a battle on your hands. All of them will turn on you at one time and here they'll come, roaring and popping their teeth, cutting high and fast with gleaming white tushes that they keep whetted to the sharpness of knife points. And there's no bluff to them, either. They mean business. They'll kill you if they can get to you; and if you're not fast footed and don't keep a close watch, they'll get to you.

They had to be that way to live in a country where the wolves, bobcats, panther, and bear were always after them, trying for a bait of fresh hog meat. And it was because of this that nearly all hog owners usually left four or five old barrows, or "bar' hogs," as we called them, to run with each bunch of sows. The bar' hogs weren't any more vicious than the boars, but they'd hang with the sows and help them protect the pigs and shoats, when generally the boars pulled off to range alone.

I knew all this about range hogs and plenty more; yet I still wasn't bothered about the job facing me. In fact, I sort of looked forward to it. Working wild hogs was always exciting and generally proved to be a lot of fun.

I guess the main reason I felt this way was because Papa and I had figured out a quick and nearly foolproof way of doing it. We could catch most of the pigs we needed to mark without ever getting in reach of the old hogs. It took a good hog dog to pull off the trick; but the way Burn Sanderson talked about Old Yeller, I was willing to bet that he was that good.

He was, too. He caught on right away.

We located our first bunch of hogs at a seep spring at the head of a shallow dry wash that led back toward Birdsong Creek. There were seven sows, two longtushed old bar' hogs, and fourteen small shoats.

They'd come there to drink and to wallow around in the potholes of soft cool mud.

They caught wind of us about the same time I saw them. The old hogs threw up their snouts and said "Woo-oof!" Then they all tore out for the hills, running through the rocks and brush almost as swiftly and silently as deer.

"Head 'em, Yeller," I hollered. "Go get 'em, boy!"

But it was a waste of words. Old Yeller was done gone.

He streaked down the slant, crossed the draw, and had the tail-end pig caught by the hind leg before the others knew he was after them.

The pig set up a loud squeal. Instantly, all the old hogs wheeled. They came at Old Yeller with their bristles up, roaring and popping their teeth. Yeller held onto his pig until I thought for a second they had him. Then he let go and whirled away, running toward me, but running slow. Slow enough that the old hogs kept chasing him, thinking every second that they were going to catch him the next.

When they finally saw that they couldn't, the old hogs stopped and formed a tight circle. They faced outward around the ring, their rumps to the center, where all the squealing pigs were gathered. That way, they were ready to battle anything that wanted to jump on them. That's the way they were used to fighting bear and panther off from their young, and that's the way they aimed to fight us off.

But we were too smart, Old Yeller and I. We knew better than to try to break into that tight ring of threatening tushes. Anyhow, we didn't need to. All we needed was just to move the hogs along to where we wanted them, and Old Yeller already knew how to do this.

Back he went, right up into their faces, where he pestered them with yelling bays and false rushes till they couldn't stand it. With an angry roar, one of the barrows broke the ring to charge him. Instantly, all the others charged, too.

They were right on Old Yeller again. They were just about to get him. Just let them get a few inches closer, and one of them would slam a four-inch tush into his soft belly.

The thing was, Old Yeller never would let them gain that last few inches on him. They cut and slashed at him from behind and both sides, yet he never was quite there. Always he was just a little bit beyond their reach yet still so close that they couldn't help thinking that the next try was sure to get him.

It was a blood-chilling game Old Yeller played with the hogs, but one that you could see he enjoyed by the way he went at it. Give him time, and he'd take that bunch of angry hogs clear down out of the hills and into the pens at home if that's where I wanted them— never driving them, just leading them along.

But that's where Papa and I had other hog hunters out-figured. We almost never took our hogs to the pens to work them any more. That took too much time. Also, after we got them penned, there was still the dangerous job of catching the pigs away from the old ones.

I hollered at Old Yeller. "Bring 'em on, Yeller," I said. Then I turned and headed for a big gnarled live oak tree that stood in a clear patch of ground down the draw apiece.

I'd picked out that tree because it had a huge branch that stuck out to one side. I went and looked the branch over and saw that it was just right. It was low, yet still far enough above the ground to be out of reach of the highest-cutting hog.

I climbed up the tree and squatted on the branch. I unwound my rope from where I'd packed it coiled around my waist and shook out a loop. Then I hollered for Old Yeller to bring the hogs to me.

He did what I told him. He brought the fighting hogs to the tree and rallied them in a ring around it. Then he stood back, holding them there while he cocked his head sideways at me, wanting to know what came next.

I soon showed him. I waited till one of the pigs came trotting under my limb. I dropped my loop around him, gave it a quick yank, and lifted him, squealing and kicking, up out of the shuffling and roaring mass of hogs below. I clamped him between my knees, pulled out my knife, and went to work on him. First I folded his right ear and sliced out a three-cornered gap in the top side, a mark that we called an overbit. Then, from the under side of his left ear, I slashed off a long strip that ran clear to the point. That is what we called an underslope. That had him marked for me. Our mark was overbit the right and underslope the left.

Other settlers had other marks, like crop the right and underbit the left, or two underbits in the right ear, or an overslope in the left and an overbit in the right. Everybody knew the hog mark of everybody else and we all respected them. We never butchered or sold a hog that didn't belong to us or marked a pig following a sow that didn't wear our mark.

Cutting marks in a pig's ear is bloody work, and the scared pig kicks and squeals like he's dying; but he's not really hurt. I never did like that job, but it had to be done.

The squealing of the pig and the scent of his blood made the hogs beneath me go nearly wild with anger. You never heard such roaring and teeth-popping, as they kept circling the tree and rearing up on its trunk, trying to get to me. The noise they made and the hate and anger that showed in their eyes was enough to chill your blood. Only, I was used to the feeling and didn't let it bother me. That is, not much.

Sometimes I'd let my mind slip for a minute and get to thinking how they'd slash me to pieces if I happened to fall out of the tree, and I'd feel a sort of cold shudder run all through me. But Papa had told me right from the start that fear was a right and natural feeling for anybody, and nothing to be ashamed of.

"It's a thing of your mind," he said, "and you can train your mind to handle it just like you can train your arm to throw a rock."

Put that way, it made sense to be afraid; so I hadn't bothered about that. I'd put in all my time trying to train my mind not to let fear stampede me. Sometimes it did yet, of course, but not when I was working hogs. I'd had enough experience at working hogs that now I could generally look down and laugh at them.

I finished with the first pig and dropped it to the ground. Then, one after another, I roped the others, dragged them up into the tree, and worked them over.

A couple of times, the old hogs on the ground got so mad that they broke ranks and charged Old Yeller. But right from the start, Old Yeller had caught onto what I wanted. Every time they chased him from the tree, he'd just run off a little way and circle back, then stand off far enough away that they'd rally around my tree again.

In less than an hour, I was done with the job, and the only trouble we had was getting the hogs to leave the tree after I was finished. After going to so much trouble to hold the hogs under the tree, Old Yeller had a hard time understanding that I finally wanted them out of the way. And even after I got him to leave, the hogs were so mad and so suspicious that I had to squat there in the tree for nearly an hour longer before they finally drifted away into the brush, making it safe for me to come down.

Chapter 10

With hogs ranging in the woods like that, it was hard to know for certain when you'd found them all. But I kept a piece of ear from every pig I marked. I carried the pieces home in my pockets and stuck them on a sharp-pointed stick which I kept hanging in the corn crib. When the count reached forty-six and I couldn't seem to locate any new bunches of hogs, Mama and I decided that was all the pigs the sows had raised that year. So I had left off hog hunting and started getting ready to gather corn when Bud Searcy paid us another visit. He told me about one bunch of hogs I'd missed.

"They're clear back in that bat cave country, the yonder side of Salt Branch," he said. "Rosal Simpson ran into them a couple of days ago, feeding on pear apples in them prickly pear flats. Said there was five pigs following three sows wearing your mark. Couple of old bar' hogs ranging with them."

I'd never been that far the other side of Salt Branch before, but Papa told me about the bat cave. I figured I could find the place. So early the next morning, I set out with Old Yeller, glad for the chance to hunt hogs a while longer before starting in on the corn gathering. Also, if I was lucky and found the hogs early, maybe I'd have time left to visit the cave and watch the bats come out.

Papa had told me that was a real sight, the way the bats come out in the late afternoon. I was sure anxious to go see it. I always like to go see the far places and strange sights.

Like one place on Salt Branch that I'd found. There was a high, undercut cliff there and some birds building their nests against the face of it. They were little gray, sharp-winged swallows. They gathered sticky mud out of a hog wallow and carried it up and stuck it to the bare rocks of the cliff, shaping the mud into little bulging nests with a single hole in the center of each one. The young birds hatched out there and stuck their heads out through the holes to get at the worms and bugs the grown birds brought to them. The mud nests were so thick on the face of the cliff that, from a distance, the wall looked like it was covered with honeycomb.

There was another place I liked, too. It was a wild, lonesome place, down in a deep canyon that was bent in the shape of a horseshoe. Tall trees grew down in the canyon and leaned out over a deep hole of clear water. In the trees nested hundreds of long-shanked herons, blue ones and white ones with black wing tips. The herons built huge ragged nests of sticks and trash and sat around in the trees all day long, fussing and staining the tree branches with their white droppings. And beneath them, down in the clear water, yard-long catfish lay on the sandy bottom, waiting to gobble up any young birds that happened to fall out of the nests.

The bat cave sounded like another of those wild places I liked to see. I sure hoped I could locate the hogs in time to pay it a visit while I was close by.

We located the hogs in plenty of time; but before we were done with them, I didn't want to go see a bat cave or anything else.

Old Yeller struck the hogs' trail at a water hole. He ran the scent out into a regular forest of prickly pear. Bright red apples fringed the edges of the pear pads. In places where the hogs had fed, bits of peel and black seeds and red juice stain lay on the ground.

The sight made me wonder again how a hog could be tough enough to eat prickly pear apples with their millions of little hairlike spines. I ate them, myself, sometimes, for pear apples are good eating. But even after I'd polished them clean by rubbing them in the sand, I generally wound up with several stickers in my mouth. But the hogs didn't seem to mind the stickers. Neither did the wild turkeys or the pack rats or the little big-eared ringtail cats. All of those creatures came to the pear flats when the apples started turning red.

Old Yeller's yelling bay told me that he'd caught up with the hogs. I heard their rumbling roars and ran through the pear clumps toward the sound. They were the hogs that Rosal Simpson had sent word about. There were five pigs, three sows, and a couple of bar' hogs, all but the pigs wearing our mark. Their faces bristled with long pear spines that they'd got stuck with, reaching for apples. Red juice stain was smeared all over their snouts. They stood, backed up against a big prickly pear clump. Their anger had their bristles standing in high fierce ridges along their backbones. They roared and popped their teeth and dared me or Old Yeller to try to catch one of the squealing pigs.

I looked around for the closest tree. It stood better than a quarter of a mile off. It was going to be rough on Old Yeller, trying to lead them to it. Having to duck and dodge around in those prickly pear, he was bound to come out bristling with more pear spines than the hogs had in their faces. But I couldn't see any other place to take them. I struck off toward the tree, hollering at Old Yeller to bring them along.

A deep cutbank draw[1] ran through the pear flats between me and the huge mesquite tree I was heading for, and it was down in the bottom of this draw that the hogs balked.[2] They'd found a place where the flood waters had undercut one of the dirt banks to form a shallow cave.

They'd backed up under the bank, with the pigs behind them. No amount of barking and pestering by Old Yeller could get them out. Now and then, one of the old bar' hogs would break ranks to make a quick cutting lunge at the dog. But when Yeller leaped away, the hog wouldn't follow up. He'd go right back to fill the gap he'd left in the half circle his mates had formed at the front of the cave. The hogs knew they'd found a natural spot for making a fighting stand, and they didn't aim to leave it.

I went back and stood on the bank above them, looking down, wondering what to do. Then it came to me that all I needed to do was go to work. This dirt bank would serve as well as a tree. There were the hogs right under me. They couldn't get to me from down there, not without first having to go maybe fifty yards down the draw to find a place to get out. And Old Yeller wouldn't let them do that. It wouldn't be easy to reach beneath that undercut bank and rope a pig, but I believed it could be done.

I took my rope from around my waist and shook out a loop. I moved to the lip of the cut bank. The pigs were too far back under me for a good throw. Maybe if I lay down on my stomach, I could reach them.

I did. I reached back under and picked up the first pig, slick as a whistle. I drew him up and worked him over. I dropped him back and

---

1. **cutbank draw:** a ravine or gully, with a steep bank, that water drains into or through.

2. **balked** (bôk 'd): stopped and refused to move.

watched the old hogs sniff his bloody wounds. Scent of his blood made them madder, and they roared louder.

I lay there and waited. A second pig moved out from the back part of the cave that I couldn't quite see. He still wasn't quite far enough out. I inched forward and leaned further down, to where I could see better. I could reach him with my loop now.

I made my cast, and that's when it happened. The dirt bank broke beneath my weight. A wagon load of sand caved off and spilled down over the angry hogs. I went with the sand.

I guess I screamed. I don't know. It happened too fast. All I can really remember is the wild heart-stopping scare I knew as I tumbled, head over heels, down among those killer hogs.

The crumbling sand all but buried the hogs. I guess that's what saved me, right at the start. I remember bumping into the back of one old bar' hog, then leaping to my feet in a smothering fog of dry dust. I jumped blindly to one side as far as I could. I broke to run, but I was too late. A slashing tush caught me in the calf of my right leg.

A searing pain shot up into my body. I screamed. I stumbled and went down. I screamed louder then, knowing I could never get to my feet in time to escape the rush of angry hogs roaring down upon me.

It was Old Yeller who saved me. Just like he'd saved Little Arliss from the she-bear. He came in, roaring with rage. He flung himself between me and the killer hogs. Fangs bared, he met them head on, slashing and snarling. He yelled with pain as the savage tushes ripped into him. He took the awful punishment meant for me but held his ground. He gave me that one-in-a-hundred chance to get free.

I took it. I leaped to my feet. In wild terror, I ran along the bed of that dry wash, cut right up a sloping bank. Then I took out through the forest of prickly pear. I ran till a forked stick tripped me and I fell.

It seemed like that fall, or maybe it was the long prickly pear spines that stabbed me in the hip, brought me out of my scare. I sat up, still panting for breath and with the blood hammering in my ears. But I was all right in my mind again. I yanked the spines out of my hip, then pulled up my slashed pants to look at my leg. Sight of so much blood nearly threw me into another panic. It was streaming out of the cut and clear down into my shoe.

I sat and stared at it for a moment and shivered. Then I got hold of myself again. I wiped away the blood. The gash was a bad one, clear to the bone, I could tell, and plenty long. But it didn't hurt much; not yet, that is. The main hurting would start later, I guessed, after the bleeding stopped and my leg started to get stiff. I guessed I'd better hurry and tie up the place and get home as quick as I could. Once that leg started getting stiff, I might not make it.

I took my knife and cut a strip off the tail of my shirt. I bound my leg as tight as I could. I got up to see if I could walk with the leg wrapped as tight as I had it, and I could.

But when I set out, it wasn't in the direction of home. It was back along the trail through the prickly pear.

I don't quite know what made me do it. I didn't think to myself, "Old Yeller saved my life and I can't go off and leave him. He's bound to be dead, but it would look mighty shabby to go home without finding out for sure. I have to go back, even if my hurt leg gives out on me before I can get home."

I didn't think anything like that. I just

started walking in that direction and kept walking till I found him.

He lay in the dry wash, about where I'd left it to go running through the prickly pear. He'd tried to follow me, but was too hurt to keep going. He was holed up under a broad slab of red sandstone rock that had slipped off a high bank and now lay propped up against a round boulder in such a way as to form a sort of cave. He'd taken refuge there from the hogs. The hogs were gone now, but I could see their tracks in the sand around the rocks, where they'd tried to get at him from behind. I'd have missed him, hidden there under that rock slab, if he hadn't whined as I walked past.

I knelt beside him and coaxed him out from under the rocks. He grunted and groaned as he dragged himself toward me. He sank back to the ground, his bloodsmeared body trembling while he wiggled his stub tail and tried to lick my hog-cut leg.

A big lump came up into my throat. Tears stung my eyes, blinding me. Here he was, trying to lick my wound, when he was bleeding from a dozen worse ones. And worst of all was his belly. It was ripped wide open and some of his insides were bulging out through the slit.

It was a horrible sight. It was so horrible that for a second I couldn't look at it. I wanted to run off. I didn't want to stay and look at something that filled me with such a numbing terror.

But I didn't run off. I shut my eyes and made myself run a hand over old Yeller's head. The stickiness of the blood on it made my flesh crawl, but I made myself do it. Maybe I couldn't do him any good, but I wasn't going to run off and leave him to die all by himself.

Then it came to me that he wasn't dead yet and maybe he didn't have to die. Maybe there was something that I could do to save him.

Maybe if I hurried home, I could get Mama to come back and help me. Mama'd know what to do. Mama always knew what to do when somebody got hurt.

I wiped the tears from my eyes with my shirt sleeves and made myself think what to do. I took off my shirt and tore it into strips. I used a sleeve to wipe the sand from the belly wound. Carefully, I eased his entrails back into place. Then I pulled the lips of the wound together and wound strips of my shirt around Yeller's body. I wound them tight and tied the strips together so they couldn't work loose.

All the time I worked with him, Old Yeller didn't let out a whimper. But when I shoved him back under the rock where he'd be out of the hot sun, he started whining. I guess he knew that I was fixing to leave him, and he wanted to go, too. He started crawling back out of his hole.

I stood and studied for a while. I needed something to stop up that opening so Yeller couldn't get out. It would have to be something too big and heavy for him to shove aside. I thought of a rock and went looking for one. What I found was even better. It was an uprooted and dead mesquite tree, lying on the bank of the wash.

The stump end of the dead mesquite was big and heavy. It was almost too much for me to drag in the loose sand. I heaved and sweated and started my leg to bleeding again. But I managed to get that tree stump where I wanted it.

I slid Old Yeller back under the rock slab. I scolded him and made him stay there till I could haul the tree stump into place.

Like I'd figured, the stump just about filled the opening. Maybe a strong dog could have squeezed through the narrow opening that was left, but I didn't figure Old Yeller could. I figured he'd be safe in there till I could get back.

Yeller lay back under the rock slab now, staring at me with a look in his eyes that made that choking lump come into my throat again. It was a begging look, and Old Yeller wasn't the kind to beg.

I reached in and let him lick my hand. "Yeller," I said, "I'll be back. I'm promising that I'll be back."

Then I lit out for home in a limping run. His howl followed me. It was the most mournful howl I ever heard.

Chapter 11

It looked like I'd never get back to where I'd left Old Yeller. To begin with, by the time I got home, I'd traveled too far and too fast. I was so hot and weak and played out that I was trembling all over. And that hog-cut leg was sure acting up. My leg hadn't gotten stiff like I'd figured. I'd used it too much. But I'd strained the cut muscle. It was jerking and twitching long before I got home; and after I got there, it wouldn't stop.

That threw a big scare into Mama. I argued and fussed, trying to tell her what a bad shape Old Yeller was in and how we needed to hurry back to him. But she wouldn't pay me any mind.

She told me, "We're not going anywhere

until we've cleaned up and doctored that leg. I've seen hog cuts before. Neglect them, and they can be as dangerous as snakebite. Now, you just hold still till I get through."

I saw that it wasn't any use, so I held still while she got hot water and washed out the cut. But when she poured turpentine into the place, I couldn't hold still. I jumped and hollered and screamed. It was like she'd burnt me with a red-hot iron. It hurt worse than when the hog slashed me. I hollered with hurt till Little Arliss tuned up and went to crying, too. But when the pain finally left my leg, the muscle had quit jerking.

Mama got some clean white rags and bound up the place. Then she said, "Now, you lie down on that bed and rest. I don't want to see you take another step on that leg for a week."

I was so stunned that I couldn't say a word. All I could do was stare at her. Old Yeller, lying 'way off out there in the hills, about to die if he didn't get help, and Mama telling me I couldn't walk.

I got up off the stool I'd been sitting on. I said to her, "Mama, I'm going back after Old Yeller. I promised him I'd come back, and that's what I aim to do." Then I walked through the door and out to the lot.

By the time I got Jumper caught, Mama had her bonnet on. She was ready to go, too. She looked a little flustered, like she didn't know what to do with me, but all she said was, "How'll we bring him back?"

"On Jumper," I said. "I'll ride Jumper and hold Old Yeller in my arms."

"You know better than that," she said. "He's too big and heavy. I might lift him up to you, but you can't stand to hold him in your arms that long. You'll give out."

"I'll hold him," I said. "If I give out, I'll rest. Then we'll go on again."

Mama stood tapping her foot for a minute while she gazed off across the hills. She said, like she was talking to herself, "We can't use the cart. There aren't any roads, and the country is too rough."

Suddenly she turned to me and smiled. "I know what. Get that cowhide off the fence. I'll go get some pillows."

"Cowhide?"

"Tie it across Jumper's back," she said. "I'll show you later."

I didn't know what she had in mind, but it didn't much matter. She was going with me.

I got the cowhide and slung it across Jumper's back. It rattled and spooked him so that he snorted and jumped from under it.

"You Jumper!" I shouted at him. "You hold still."

He held still the next time. Mama brought the pillows and a long coil of rope. She had me tie the cowhide to Jumper's back and bind the pillows down on top of it. Then she lifted Little Arliss up and set him down on top of the pillows.

"You ride behind him," she said to me. "I'll walk."

We could see the buzzards gathering long before we got there. We could see them wheeling black against the blue sky and dropping lower and lower with each circling. One we saw didn't waste time to circle. He came hurtling down at a long-slanted dive, his ugly head outstretched, his wings all but shut against his body. He shot past, right over our heads, and the *whooshing* sound his body made in splitting the air sent cold chills running all through me. I guessed it was all over for Old Yeller.

Mama was walking ahead of Jumper. She looked back at me. The look in her eyes told me that she figured the same thing. I got so sick that it seemed like I couldn't stand it.

But when we moved down into the prickly pear flats, my misery eased some. For suddenly, up out of a wash ahead rose a flurry of flapping wings. Something had disturbed those buzzards and I thought I knew what it was.

A second later, I was sure it was Old Yeller. His yelling bark sounded thin and weak, yet just to hear it made me want to holler and run and laugh. He was still alive. He was still able to fight back!

The frightened buzzards had settled back to the ground by the time we got there. When they caught sight of us, though, they got excited and went to trying to get off the ground again. For birds that can sail around in the air all day with hardly more than a movement of their wing tips, they sure were clumsy and awkward about getting started. Some had to keep hopping along the wash for fifty yards, beating the air with their huge wings, before they could finally take off. And then they were slow to rise. I could have shot a dozen of them before they got away if I'd thought to bring my gun along.

There was a sort of crazy light shining in Old Yeller's eyes when I looked in at him. When I reached to drag the stump away, he snarled and lunged at me with bared fangs.

I jerked my hands away just in time and shouted "Yeller!" at him. Then he knew I wasn't a buzzard. The crazy light went out of his eyes. He sank back into the hole with a loud groan like he'd just had a big load taken off his mind.

Mama helped me drag the stump away. Then we reached in and rolled his hurt body over on its back and slid him out into the light.

Without bothering to examine the blood-caked cuts that she could see all over his head and shoulders, Mama started unwinding the strips of cloth from around his body.

Then Little Arliss came crowding past me, asking in a scared voice what was the matter with Yeller.

Mama stopped. "Arliss," she said, "do you think you could go back down this sandy wash here and catch Mama a pretty green-striped lizard? I thought I saw one down there around that first bend."

Little Arliss was as pleased as I was surprised. Always before, Mama had just sort of put up with his lizard-catching. Now she was wanting him to catch one just for her. A delighted grin spread over his face. He turned and ran down the wash as hard as he could go.

Mama smiled up at me, and suddenly I understood. She was just getting Little Arliss out of the way so he wouldn't have to look at the terrible sight of Yeller's slitted belly.

She said to me, "Go jerk a long hair out of Jumper's tail, Son. But stand to one side, so he won't kick you."

I went and stood to one side of Jumper and jerked a long hair out of his tail. Sure enough, he snorted and kicked at me, but he missed. I took the hair back to Mama, wondering as much about it as I had about the green-striped lizard. But when Mama pulled a long sewing needle from her dress front and poked the small end of the tail hair through the eye, I knew then.

"Horse hair is always better than thread for sewing up a wound," she said. She didn't say why, and I never did think to ask her.

Mama asked me if any of Yeller's entrails had been cut and I told her that I didn't think so.

"Well, I won't bother them then," she said. "Anyway, if they are, I don't think I could fix them."

It was a long, slow job, sewing up Old

Yeller's belly. And the way his flesh would flinch and quiver when Mama poked the needle through, it must have hurt. But if it did, Old Yeller didn't say anything about it. He just lay there and licked my hands while I held him.

We were wrapping him up in some clean rags that Mama had brought along when here came Little Arliss. He was running as hard as he'd been when he left. He was grinning and hollering at Mama. And in his right hand he carried a green-striped lizard, too.

How on earth he'd managed to catch anything as fast running as one of those green-striped lizards, I don't know; but he sure had one.

You never saw such a proud look as he wore on his face when he handed the lizard to Mama. And I don't guess I ever saw a more helpless look on Mama's face as she took it. Mama had always been squeamish about lizards and snakes and bugs and things, and you could tell that it just made her flesh crawl to have to touch this one. But she took it and admired it and thanked Arliss. Then she asked him if he'd keep it for her till we got home. Which Little Arliss was glad to do.

"Now, Arliss," she told him, "we're going to play a game. We're playing like Old Yeller is sick and you are taking care of him. We're going to let you both ride on a cowhide, like the sick Indians do sometimes."

It always pleased Little Arliss to play any sort of game, and this was a new one that he'd never heard about before. He was so anxious to get started that we could hardly keep him out from underfoot till Mama could get things ready.

As soon as she took the cowhide off Jumper's back and spread it hair-side down upon the ground, I began to get the idea. She placed the soft pillows on top of the hide, then helped me to ease Old Yeller's hurt body onto the pillows.

"Now, Arliss," Mama said, "you sit there on the pillows with Old Yeller and help hold him on. But remember now, don't play with him or get on top of him. We're playing like he's sick, and when your dog is sick, you have to be real careful with him."

It was a fine game, and Little Arliss fell right in with it. He sat where Mama told him to. He held Old Yeller's head in his lap, waiting for the ride to start.

It didn't take long. I'd already tied a rope around Jumper's neck, leaving the loop big enough that it would pull back against his shoulders. Then, on each side of Jumper, we tied another rope into the one knotted about his shoulders and carried the ends of them back to the cowhide. I took my knife and cut two slits into the edge of the cowhide, then tied a rope into each one. We measured to get each rope the same length and made sure they were far enough back that the cowhide wouldn't touch Jumper's heels. Like most mules, Jumper was mighty fussy about anything touching his heels.

"Now, Travis, you ride him," Mama said, "and I'll lead him."

"You better let me walk," I argued. "Jumper's liable to throw a fit with that hide rattling along behind him, and you might not can hold him by yourself."

"You ride him," Mama said. "I don't want you walking on that leg any more. If Jumper acts up one time, I'll take a club to him!"

We started off, with Little Arliss crowing at what a fine ride he was getting on the dragging hide. Sure enough, at the first sound of that rattling hide, old Jumper acted up. He snorted and tried to lunge to one side. But Mama yanked down on his bridle and said, "Jumper,

you wretch!" I whacked him between the ears with a dead stick. With the two of us coming at him like that, it was more than Jumper wanted. He settled down and went to traveling as quiet as he generally pulled a plow, with just now and then bending his neck around to take a look at what he was dragging. You could tell he didn't like it, but I guess he figured he'd best put up with it.

Little Arliss never had a finer time than he did on that ride home. He enjoyed every long hour of it. And a part of the time, I don't guess it was too rough on Old Yeller. The cowhide dragged smooth and even as long as we stayed in the sandy wash. When we left the wash and took out across the flats, it still didn't look bad.

Mama led Jumper in a long roundabout way, keeping as much as she could to the openings where the tall grass grew. The grass would bend down before the hide, making a soft cushion over which the hide slipped easily. But this was a rough country, and try as hard as she could, Mama couldn't always dodge the rocky places. The hide slid over the rocks, the same as over the grass and sand, but it couldn't do it without jolting the riders pretty much.

Little Arliss would laugh when the hide raked along over the rocks and jolted him till his teeth rattled. He got as much fun out of that as the rest of the ride. But the jolting hurt Old Yeller till sometimes he couldn't hold back his whinings.

When Yeller's whimperings told us he was hurting too bad, we'd have to stop and wait for him to rest up. At other times, we stopped to give him water. Once we got water out of a little spring that trickled down through the rocks. The next time was at Birdsong Creek.

Mama'd pack water to him in my hat. He was too weak to get up and drink; so Mama would hold the water right under his nose and I'd lift him up off the pillows and hold him close enough that he could reach down and lap the water up with his tongue.

Having to travel so far and so slow and with so many halts, it looked like we'd never get him home. But we finally made it just about the time it got dark enough for the stars to show.

By then, my hurt leg was plenty stiff, stiff and numb. It was all swelled up and felt as dead as a chunk of wood. When I slid down off Jumper's back, it wouldn't hold me. I fell clear to the ground and lay in the dirt, too tired and hurt to get up.

Mama made a big to-do about how weak and hurt I was, but I didn't mind. We'd gone and brought Old Yeller home, and he was still alive. There by the starlight, I could see him licking Arliss's face.

Little Arliss was sound asleep.

CHAPTERS 9–11

Getting at Meaning

RECALLING

1. Why do Travis and his family not feed the hogs except during "a bad spell in the winter"? What do the hogs eat?

2. What, according to Travis, is "the most dangerous animal that ever lived in Texas"?

3. When Travis goes out to mark the first bunch of hogs, who helps him round them up? While Travis is marking each hog, how does he keep out of reach of the others?

4. Who tells Travis about the unmarked hogs on the other side of Salt Branch?

5. What saves Travis from being killed by the hogs at the bottom of the gully?

6. On what part of his body is Travis wounded?

7. Before going home for help, how does Travis care for Old Yeller? What does he do to make sure that Old Yeller doesn't go anywhere?

8. How does Travis's mother treat his wound?

9. Why does Travis's mother send Little Arliss to catch a lizard? Why does she ask Travis to pull a hair from Jumper's tail?

10. How do Travis, his mother, and Little Arliss manage to get Old Yeller back to the farm?

INTERPRETING

11. What keeps Travis from sleeping on the night after his talk with Burn Sanderson? What does he think about?

12. Given the hydrophobia epidemic in the

area, what danger exists in allowing the hogs to run free?

13. Why does Travis, despite his wound, insist on going back for Old Yeller? What does this reveal about Travis?

14. Travis wants to prove himself capable of taking care of the farm. As a result, he goes out to mark the hogs even though he knows that this is a dangerous task. Should Travis have taken the risk of trying to rope the hogs in the gully? In your opinion, did he take an unnecessary risk?

Developing Skills in Reading Literature

1. **Characterization.** Characterization is the use of literary techniques to reveal the nature of a character. In Chapters 9–11, the reader sees Travis changing and developing in several ways. What evidence suggests that Travis is becoming more responsible and mature? What evidence suggests that his affection for Old Yeller has increased?

As the plot progresses, Travis becomes more like Old Yeller. For example, both work hard for the family, both enjoy their work, and both are wounded. What other similarities exist between Travis and Old Yeller?

2. **Complication.** A complication is an event that heightens, or complicates, a conflict that has already been introduced. One conflict involves Travis's struggle to take care of the farm. What complication, introduced in Chapter 10, will make Travis's job much more difficult?

Developing Vocabulary

Using a Glossary. Use the Glossary at the back of this book to find the meanings of the italicized words in the following sentences.

1. "Starvation, during some bad *drought* or extra cold winter had forced them [the hogs] to eat anything they could get hold of."

2. "Papa said they [the hogs] generally started out by feeding on the *carcass* of some deer or cow that had died, then going from there to catching and killing live meat."

3. "The least little old biting *shoat* would make her [Travis's mother] take cover."

4. "All of them [the hogs] will turn on you at one time and here they'll come, roaring and popping their teeth, cutting high and fast with gleaming white *tushes* that they keep *whetted* to the sharpness of knife points."

Speaking and Listening. Use the pronunciation guide in the Glossary to learn the pronunciations of the italicized words. Then read the sentences aloud, pronouncing the words correctly.

Chapter 12

For the next couple of weeks, Old Yeller and I had a rough time of it. I lay on the bed inside the cabin and Yeller lay on the cowhide in the dog run, and we both hurt so bad that we were wallowing and groaning and whimpering all the time. Sometimes I hurt so bad that I didn't quite know what was happening. I'd hear grunts and groans and couldn't tell if they were mine or Yeller's. My leg had swelled up till it was about the size of a butter churn.[1] I had such a wild hot fever that Mama nearly ran herself to death, packing fresh cold water from the spring, which she used to bathe me all over, trying to run my fever down.

When she wasn't packing water, she was out digging prickly pear roots and hammering them to mush in a sack, then binding the mush to my leg for a poultice.

We had lots of prickly pear growing close to the house, but they were the big tall ones and their roots were no good. The kind that make a good poultice are the smaller size. They don't have much top, but lots of knotty roots, shaped sort of like sweet potatoes. That kind didn't grow close to the house. Along at the last, Mama had to go clear over to the Salt Licks to locate that kind.

When Mama wasn't waiting on me, she was taking care of Old Yeller. She waited on him just like she did me. She was getting up all hours of the night to doctor our wounds, bathe us in cold water, and feed us when she could get us to eat. On top of that, there were the cows to milk, Little Arliss to look after, clothes to wash, wood to cut, and old Jumper to worry with.

The bad drought that Bud Searcy predicted had come. The green grass all dried up till Jumper was no longer satisfied to eat it. He took to jumping the field fence and eating the corn that I'd never yet gotten around to gathering.

Mama couldn't let that go on; that was our bread corn. Without it, we'd have no bread for the winter. But it looked like for a while that there wasn't any way to save it. Mama would go to the field and run Jumper out; then before she got her back turned good, he'd jump back in and go to eating corn again.

Finally, Mama figured out a way to keep Jumper from jumping. She tied a drag to him. She got a rope and tied one end of it to his right forefoot. To the other end, she tied a big heavy chunk of wood. By pulling hard, Jumper could move his drag along enough to graze and get to water; but any time he tried to rear up for a jump, the drag held him down.

The drag on Jumper's foot saved the corn but it didn't save Mama from a lot of work. Jumper was always getting his chunk of wood hung up behind a bush or rock, so that he couldn't get away. Then he'd have himself a big scare and rear up, fighting the rope and falling down and pitching and bawling. If Mama didn't hear him right away, he'd start braying, and he'd keep it up till she went and loosened the drag.

Altogether, Mama sure had her hands full, and Little Arliss wasn't any help. He was too little to do any work. And with neither of us to play with, he got lonesome. He'd follow Mama around every step she made, getting in the way and feeling hurt because she didn't have time to pay him any mind. When he wasn't pester-

---

1. **butter churn** (churn): a container in which milk or cream is beaten to make butter. Such a container would be about one foot in diameter.

ing her, he was pestering me. A dozen times a day, he'd come in to stare at me and say, "Whatcha doin' in bed, Travis? Why doncha get up? Why doncha get up and come play with me?"

He nearly drove me crazy till the day Bud Searcy and Lisbeth came, bringing the pup.

I didn't know about the pup at first. I didn't even know that Lisbeth had come. I heard Bud Searcy's talk to Mama when they rode up, but I was hurting too bad even to roll over and look out the door. I remember just lying there, being mad at Searcy for coming. I knew what a bother he'd be to Mama. For all his talk of looking after the women and children of Salt Licks while the men were gone, I knew he'd never turn a hand to any real work. You wouldn't catch him offering to chop wood or gather in a corn crop. All he'd do was sit out under the dog run all day, talking and chewing tobacco and spitting juice all over the place. On top of that, he'd expect Mama to cook him up a good dinner and maybe a supper if he took a notion to stay that long. And Mama had ten times too much to do, like it was.

In a little bit, though, I heard a quiet step at the door. I looked up. It was Lisbeth. She stood with her hands behind her back, staring at me with her big solemn eyes.

"You hurting pretty bad?" she asked.

I was hurting a-plenty, but I wasn't admitting it to a girl. "I'm doing all right," I said.

"We didn't know you'd got hog cut, or we'd have come sooner," she said.

I didn't know what to say to that, so I didn't say anything.

"Well, anyhow," she said, "I brung you a surprise."

I was too sick and worn out to care about a surprise right then; but there was such an eager look in her eyes that I knew I had to say

"What?" or hurt her feelings, so I said "What?"

"One of Miss Prissy's pups!" she said.

She brought her hands around from behind her back. In the right one, she held a dog pup about as big as a year-old possum. It was a dirty white in color and speckled all over with blue spots about the size of cow ticks. She held it by the slack hide at the back of its neck. It hung there, half asleep, sagging in its own loose hide like it was dead.

"Born in a badger hole," she said. "Seven of them. I brung you the best one!"

I thought, if that puny-looking thing is the best one, Miss Prissy must have had a sorry litter of pups. But I didn't say so. I said, "He sure looks like a dandy."

"He is," Lisbeth said. "See how I've been holding him, all this time, and he hasn't said a word."

I'd heard that one all my life—that if a pup didn't holler when you held him up by the slack hide of his neck, he was sure to turn out to be a gritty one. I didn't think much of that sign. Papa always put more stock in what color was inside a pup's mouth. If the pup's mouth was black inside, Papa said that was the one to choose. And that's the way I felt about it.

But right now I didn't care if the pup's mouth was pea-green on the inside. All I wanted was just to quit hurting.

I said, "I guess Little Arliss will like it," then knew I'd said the wrong thing. I could tell by the look in her eyes that I'd hurt her feelings, after all.

She didn't say anything. She just got real still and quiet and kept staring at me till I couldn't stand it and had to look away. Then she turned and went out of the cabin and gave the pup to Little Arliss.

It made me mad, her looking at me like that.

What did she expect, anyhow? Here I was laid up with a bad hog cut, hurting so bad I could hardly get my breath, and her expecting me to make a big to-do over a little old puny speckled pup.

I had me a dog. Old Yeller was all cut up, worse than I was, but he was getting well. Mama had told me that. So what use did I have for a pup? Be all right for Little Arliss to play with. Keep him occupied and out from underfoot. But when Old Yeller and I got well and took to the woods again, we wouldn't have time to wait around on a fool pup, too little to follow.

I lay there in bed, mad and fretful all day, thinking how silly it was for Lisbeth to expect me to want a pup when I already had me a full-grown dog. I lay there, just waiting for a chance to tell her so, too; only she never did come back to give me a chance. She stayed outside and played with Little Arliss and the pup till her grandpa finally wound up his talking and tobacco spitting and got ready to leave. Then I saw her and Little Arliss come past the door, heading for where I could hear her grandpa saddling his horse. She looked in at me, then looked away, and suddenly I wasn't mad at her any more. I felt sort of mean. I wished now I could think of the right thing to say about the pup, so I could call her back and tell her. I didn't want her to go off home with her feelings still hurt.

But before I could think of anything, I heard her grandpa say to Mama, "Now Mrs. Coates, you all are in a sort of bind here, with your man gone and that boy crippled up. I been setting out here all evening, worrying about it. That's my responsibility, you know, seeing that everybody's taken care of while the men are gone, and I think now I've got a way figured. I'll just leave our girl Lisbeth here to help you all out."

Mama said in a surprised voice, "Why, Mr. Searcy, there's no need for that. It's mighty kind of you and all, but we'll make out all right."

"No, now, Mrs. Coates; you got too big a load to carry, all by yourself. My Lisbeth, she'll be proud to help out."

"But," Mama argued, "she's such a little girl, Mr. Searcy. She's probably never stayed away from home of a night."

"She's little," Bud Searcy said, "but she's stout and willing. She's like me; when folks are in trouble, she'll pitch right in and do her part. You just keep her here now. You'll see what a big help she'll be."

Mama tried to argue some more, but Bud Searcy wouldn't listen. He just told Lisbeth to be a good girl and help Mama out, like she was used to helping out at home. Then he mounted and rode on off.

Chapter 13

I was like Mama. I didn't think Lisbeth Searcy would be any help around the place. She was too little and too skinny. I figured she'd just be an extra bother for Mama.

But we were wrong. Just like Bud Searcy said, she was a big help. She could tote water from the spring. She could feed the chickens, pack in wood, cook cornbread, wash dishes, wash Little Arliss, and sometimes even change the prickly pear poultice on my leg.

She didn't have to be told, either. She was right there on hand all the time, just looking for something to do. She was a lot better about that than I ever was. She wasn't as big, and she couldn't do as much as I could, but she was more willing.

She didn't even back off when Mama hooked Jumper to the cart and headed for the field to gather in the corn. That was a job I always hated. It was hot work, and the corn shucks made my skin itch and sting till sometimes I'd wake up at night scratching like I'd stumbled into a patch of bull nettles.

But it didn't seem to bother Lisbeth. In fact, it looked like she and Mama and Little Arliss had a real good time gathering corn. I'd see them drive past the cabin, all three of them sitting on top of a cartload of corn. They would be laughing and talking and having such a romping big time, playing with the speckled pup, that before long I half wished I was able to gather corn too.

In a way, it sort of hurt my pride for a little old girl like Lisbeth to come in and take over my jobs. Papa had left me to look after things. But now I was laid up, and here was a girl handling my work about as good as I could. Still, she couldn't get out and mark hogs or kill meat or swing a chopping axe. . . .

Before they were finished gathering corn, however, we were faced with a trouble a whole lot too big for any of us to handle.

The first hint of it came when the Spot heifer failed to show up one evening at milking time. Mama had come in too late from the corn gathering to go look for her before dark, and the next morning she didn't need to. Spot came up, by herself; or rather, she came past the house.

I heard her first. The swelling in my leg was about gone down. I was weak as a rain-chilled chicken, but most of the hurting had stopped. I was able to sit up in bed a lot and take notice of things.

I heard a cow coming toward the house. She was bawling like cows do when they've lost a calf or when their bags are stretched too tight with milk. I recognized Spot's voice.

Spot's calf recognized it, too. It had stood hungry in the pen all night and now it was nearly crazy for a bait of milk. I could hear it blatting and racing around in the cowpen, so starved it could hardly wait.

I called to Mama. "Mama," I said, "you better go let old Spot in to her calf. I hear her coming."

"That pesky Spot," I heard her say impatiently. "I don't know what's got into her, staying out all night like that and letting her calf go hungry."

I heard Mama calling to Spot as she went out to the cowpen. A little later, I heard Spot beller like a fighting bull, then Mama's voice rising high and sharp. Then here came Mama,

running into the cabin, calling for Lisbeth to hurry and bring in Little Arliss. There was scare in Mama's voice. I sat up in bed as Lisbeth came running in, dragging Little Arliss after her.

Mama slammed the door shut, then turned to me. "Spot made fight at me," she said. "I can't understand it. It was like I was some varmint that she'd never seen before."

Mama turned and opened the door a crack. She looked out, then threw the door wide open and stood staring toward the cowpen.

"Why, look at her now," she said. "She's not paying one bit of attention to her calf. She's just going on past the cowpen like her calf wasn't there. She's acting as crazy as if she'd got hold of a bait of pea vine."

There was a little pea vine that grew wild all over the hills during wet winters and bloomed pale lavender in the spring. Cattle and horses could eat it, mixed with grass, and get fat on it. But sometimes when they got too big a bait of it alone, it poisoned them. Generally, they'd stumble around with the blind staggers for a while, then gradually get well. Sometimes, though, the pea vine killed them.

I sat there for a moment, listening to Spot. She was bawling again, like when I first heard her. But now she was heading off into the brush again, leaving her calf to starve. I wondered where she'd gotten enough pea vine to hurt her.

"But Mama," I said, "she couldn't have eaten pea vine. The pea vine is all dead and gone this time of year."

Mama turned and looked at me, then looked away. "I know," she said. "That's what's got me so worried."

I thought of what Burn Sanderson had told me about animals that didn't act right. I said,

"Cows don't ever get hydrophobia, do they?"

I saw Lisbeth start at the word. She stared at me with big solemn eyes.

"I don't know," Mama said. "I've seen dogs with it, but I've never heard of a cow brute having it. I just don't know."

In the next fews days, while Old Yeller and I healed fast, we all worried and watched.

All day and all night, Spot kept right on doing what she did from the start: she walked and she bawled. She walked mostly in a wide circle that brought her pretty close to the house about twice a day and then carried her so far out into the hills that we could just barely hear her. She walked with her head down. She walked slower and her bawling got weaker as she got weaker; but she never stopped walking and bawling.

When the bull came, he was worse, and a lot more dangerous. He came two or three days later. I was sitting out under the dog run at the time. I'd hobbled out to sit in a chair beside Old Yeller, where I could scratch him under his chewed-off ear. That's where he liked to be scratched best. Mama was in the kitchen, cooking dinner. Lisbeth and Little Arliss had gone off to the creek below the spring to play with the pup and to fish for catfish. I could see them running and laughing along the bank, chasing after grasshoppers for bait.

Then I heard this moaning sound and turned to watch a bull come out of the brush. He was the roan bull, the one that the droopy-horned *chongo* had dumped into the Mexican cart the day of the fight. But he didn't walk like any bull I'd ever seen before. He walked with his head hung low and wobbling. He reeled and staggered like he couldn't see where he was going. He walked head on into a mesquite tree like it wasn't there, and fell to his knees when he hit it. He scrambled to his feet and came on, grunting and staggering and moaning, heading toward the spring.

Right then, for the first time since we'd brought him home, Old Yeller came up off his cowhide bed. He'd been lying there beside me, paying no attention to sight or sound of the bull. Then, I guess the wind must have shifted and brought him the bull's scent; and evidently that scent told him for certain what I was only beginning to suspect.

He rose, with a savage growl. He moved out toward the bull, so trembly weak that he could hardly stand. His loose lips were lifted in an ugly snarl, baring his white fangs. His hackles stood up in a ragged ridge along the back of his neck and shoulders.

Watching him, I felt a prickling at the back of my own neck. I'd seen him act like that before, but only when there was the greatest danger. Never while just facing a bull.

Suddenly, I knew that Mama and I had been fooling ourselves. Up till now, we'd been putting off facing up to facts. We'd kept hoping that the heifer Spot would get over whatever was wrong with her. Mama and Lisbeth had kept Spot's calf from starving by letting it suck another cow. They'd had to tie the cow's hind legs together to keep her from kicking the calf off; but they'd kept it alive, hoping Spot would get well and come back to it.

Now, I knew that Spot wouldn't get well, and this bull wouldn't, either. I knew they were both deathly sick with hydrophobia. Old Yeller had scented that sickness in this bull and somehow sensed how fearfully dangerous it was.

I thought of Lisbeth and Little Arliss down past the spring. I came up out of my chair, calling for Mama. "Mama!" I said. "Bring me my gun, Mama!"

Mama came hurrying to the door. "What is it, Travis?" she wanted to know.

"That bull!" I said, pointing. "He's mad with hydrophobia and he's heading straight for Lisbeth and Little Arliss."

Mama took one look, said "Oh, my Lord!" in almost a whisper. She didn't wait to get me my gun or anything else. She just tore out for the creek, hollering for Lisbeth and Little Arliss to run, to climb a tree, to do anything to get away from the bull.

I called after her, telling her to wait, to give me a chance to shoot the bull. I don't guess she ever heard me. But the bull heard her. He tried to turn on her, stumbled and went to his knees. Then he was back on his feet again as Mama went flying past. He charged straight for her. He'd have gotten her, too, only the sickness had his legs too wobbly. This time, when he fell, he rooted his nose into the ground and just lay there, moaning, too weak even to try to get up again.

By this time, Old Yeller was there, baying the bull, keeping out of his reach, but ready to eat him alive if he ever came to his feet again.

I didn't wait to see more. I went and got my gun. I hobbled down to where I couldn't miss and shot the roan bull between the eyes.

Chapter 14

We couldn't leave the dead bull to lie there that close to the cabin. In a few days, the scent of rotting flesh would drive us out. Also, the carcass lay too close to the spring. Mama was afraid it would foul up our drinking water.

"We'll have to try to drag it further from the cabin and burn it," she said.

"Burn it?" I said in surprise. "Why can't we just leave it for the buzzards and varmints to clean up?"

"Because that might spread the sickness," Mama said. "If the varmints eat it, they might get the sickness too."

Mama went to put the harness on Jumper. I sent Lisbeth to bring me a rope. I doubled the rope and tied it in a loop around the bull's horns. Mama brought Jumper, who snorted and shied away at the sight of the dead animal. Jumper had smelled deer blood plenty of times, so I guess it was the size of the bull that scared him. Or maybe like Yeller, Jumper could scent the dead bull's sickness. I had to talk mean and threaten him with a club before we could get him close enough for Mama to hook the singletree over the loop of rope I'd tied around the bull's horns.

Then the weight of the bull was too much for him. Jumper couldn't drag it. He leaned into his collar and dug in with his hoofs. He grunted and strained. He pulled till I saw the big muscles of his haunches flatten and start quivering. But the best he could do was slide the bull carcass along the ground for about a foot before he gave up.

I knew he wasn't throwing off. Jumper was full of a lot of pesky, aggravating mule tricks; but when you called on him to move a load, he'd move it or bust something.

I called on him again. I drove him at a different angle from the load, hoping he'd have better luck. He didn't. He threw everything he had into the collar, and all he did was pop a link out of his right trace chain. The flying link whistled past my ear with the speed of a bullet. It would have killed me just as dead if it had hit me.

Well, that was it. There was no moving the dead bull now. We could patch up that broken trace chain for pulling an ordinary load. But it would never be strong enough to pull this one. Even if Jumper was.

I looked at Mama. She shook her head. "I guess there's nothing we can do but burn it here," she said. "But it's going to take a sight of wood gathering."

It did, too. We'd lived there long enough to use up all the dead wood close to the cabin. Now, Mama and Lisbeth had to go 'way out into the brush for it. I got a piece of rawhide string and patched up the trace chain, and Mama and Lisbeth used Jumper to drag up big dead logs. I helped them pile the logs on top of the bull. We piled them up till we had the carcass completely covered, then set fire to them.

In a little bit, the fire was roaring. Sheets of hot flame shot high into the air. The heat and the stench of burnt hair and scorching hide drove us back.

It was the biggest fire I'd ever seen. I thought there was fire enough there to burn three bulls. But when it began to die down a couple of hours later, the bull carcass wasn't half burnt up. Mama and Lisbeth went back to dragging up more wood.

It took two days and nights to burn up that bull. We worked all day long each day, with

Mama and Lisbeth dragging up the wood and me feeding the stinking fire. Then at night, we could hardly sleep. This was because of the howling and snarling and fighting of the wolves lured to the place by the scent of the roasting meat. The wolves didn't get any of it; they were too afraid of the hot fire. But that didn't keep them from gathering for miles around and making the nights hideous with their howlings and snarlings.

And all night long, both nights, Old Yeller crippled back and forth between the fire and the cabin, baying savagely, warning the wolves to keep away.

Both nights, I lay there, watching the eyes of the shifting wolves glow like live mesquite coals in the firelight, and listening to the weak moaning bawl of old Spot still traveling in a circle. I lay there, feeling shivery with a fearful dread that brought up pictures in my mind of Bud Searcy's uncle.

I sure did wish Papa would come home.

As soon as the job of burning the bull was over, Mama told us we had to do the same for the Spot heifer. That was all Mama said about it, but I could tell by the look in her eyes how much she hated to give up. She'd had great hopes for Spot's making us a real milk cow, especially after Old Yeller had gentled her so fast; but that was all gone now.

Mama looked tired and more worried than I think I'd ever seen her. I guess she couldn't help thinking what I was thinking — that if hydrophobia had sickened one of our cows, it just might get them all.

"I'll do the shooting," I told her. "But I'm going to follow her out a ways from the house to do it. Closer to some wood."

"How about your leg?" Mama asked.

"That leg's getting all right," I told her. "Think it'll do it some good to be walked on."

"Well, try to kill her on bare ground," Mama cautioned. "As dry as it is now, we'll be running a risk of setting the woods afire if there's much old grass around the place."

I waited till Spot circled past the cabin again, then took my gun and followed her, keeping a safe distance behind.

By now, Spot was so sick and starved I could hardly stand to look at her. She didn't look like a cow; she looked more like the skeleton of one. She was just skin and bones. She was so weak that she stumbled as she walked. Half a dozen times she went to her knees and each time I'd think she'd taken her last step. But she'd always get up and go on again — and keep bawling.

I kept waiting for her to cross a bare patch of ground where it would be safe to build a fire. She didn't; and I couldn't drive her, of course. She was too crazy mad to be driven anywhere. I was afraid to mess with her. She might be like the bull. If I ever let her know I was anywhere about, she might go on the fight.

I guess she was a mile from the cabin before I saw that she was about to cross a dry sandy wash, something like the one where Yeller and I had got mixed up with the hogs. That would be a good place, I knew. It was pretty far for us to have to come to burn her, but there was plenty of dry wood around. And if I could drop her out there in that wide sandy wash, there'd be no danger of a fire getting away from us.

I hurried around and got ahead of her. I hid behind a turkey-pear bush on the far side of the wash. But as sick and blind as she was, I think I could have stood out in the broad open without her ever seeing me. I waited till she came stumbling across the sandy bed of the wash, then fired, dropping her in the middle of it.

I'd used up more of my strength than I knew, following Spot so far from the cabin. By the time I got back, I was dead beat. The sweat was pouring off me and I was trembling all over.

Mama took one look at me and told me to get to bed. "We'll go start the burning," she said. "You stay on that leg any longer, and it'll start swelling again."

I didn't argue. I knew I was too weak and tired to take another walk that far without rest. So I told Mama where to find Spot and told her to leave Little Arliss with me and watched her and Lisbeth head out, both mounted on Jumper. Mama was carrying a panful of live coals to start the fire with.

At the last minute, Yeller got up off his cowhide. He stood watching them a minute, like he was trying to make up his mind about something; then he went trotting after them. He was still thin and rough looking and crippling pretty badly in one leg. But I figured he knew better than I did whether or not he was able to travel. I didn't call him back.

As it turned out, it's a good thing I didn't. Only, afterward, I wished a thousand times that I could have had some way of looking ahead to what was going to happen. Then I would have done everything I could to keep all of them from going.

With Little Arliss to look after, I sure didn't mean to drop off to sleep. But I did and slept till sundown, when suddenly I jerked awake, feeling guilty about leaving him alone so long.

I needn't have worried. Little Arliss was right out there in the yard, playing with the speckled pup. They had themselves a game

going. Arliss was racing around the cabin, dragging a short piece of frayed rope. The pup was chasing the rope. Now and then he'd get close enough to pounce on it. Then he'd let out a growl and set teeth into it and try to shake it and hang on at the same time. Generally, he got jerked off his feet and turned a couple of somersets, but that didn't seem to bother him. The next time Arliss came racing past, the pup would tie into the rope again.

I wondered if he wouldn't get some of his baby teeth jerked out at such rough play, but guessed it wouldn't matter. He'd soon be shedding them, anyhow.

I wondered, too, what was keeping Mama and Lisbeth so long. Then I thought how far it was to where the dead cow lay and how long it would take for just the two of them to drag up enough wood and get a fire started and figured they'd be lucky if they got back before dark.

I went off to the spring after a bucket of fresh water and wondered when Papa would come back. Mama had said a couple of days ago that it was about that time, and I hoped so. For one thing, I could hardly wait to see what sort of horse Papa was going to bring me. But mainly, this hydrophobia plague had me scared. I'd handled things pretty well until that came along. Of course, I'd gotten a pretty bad hog cut, but that could have happened to anybody, even a grown man. And I was about to get well of that. But if the sickness got more of our cattle, I wouldn't know what to do.

Chapter 15

It wasn't until dark came that I really began to get uneasy about Mama and Lisbeth. Then I could hardly stand it because they hadn't come home. I knew in my own mind why they hadn't. It had been late when they'd started out. They'd had a good long piece to go; and even with wood handy, it took considerable time to drag up enough for the size fire they needed.

And I couldn't think of any real danger to them. They weren't far enough away from the cabin to be lost. And if they were, Jumper knew the way home. Also, Jumper was gentle; there wasn't much chance that he'd scare and throw them off. On top of all that, they had Old Yeller along. Old Yeller might be pretty weak and crippled yet, but he'd protect them from just about anything that might come their way.

Still, I was uneasy. I couldn't help having the feeling that something was wrong. I'd have gone to see about them if it hadn't been for Little Arliss. It was past his suppertime; he was getting hungry and sleepy and fussy.

I took him and the speckled pup inside the kitchen and lit a candle. I settled them on the floor and gave them each a bowl of sweet milk into which I'd crumbled cold cornbread. In a little bit, both were eating out of the same bowl. Little Arliss knew better than that and I ought to have paddled him for doing it. But I didn't. I didn't say a word; I was too worried.

I'd just about made up my mind to put Little Arliss and the pup to bed and go look for Mama and Lisbeth when I heard a sound that took me to the door in a hurry. It was the sound of dogs fighting. The sound came from 'way out there in the dark; but the minute I stepped outside, I could tell that the fight was moving toward the cabin. Also, I recognized the voice of Old Yeller.

It was the sort of raging yell he let out when he was in a fight to the finish. It was the same savage roaring and snarling and squawling that he'd done the day he fought the killer hogs off me.

The sound of it chilled my blood. I stood, rooted to the ground, trying to think what it could be, what I ought to do.

Then I heard Jumper snorting keenly and Mama calling in a frightened voice. "Travis! Travis! Make a light, Son, and get your gun. And hurry!"

I came alive then. I hollered back at her, to let her know that I'd heard. I ran back into the cabin and got my gun. I couldn't think at first what would make the sort of light I needed, then recollected a clump of bear grass that Mama'd recently grubbed out, where she wanted to start a new fall garden. Bear grass has an oily sap that makes it burn bright and fierce for a long time. A pile of it burning would make a big light.

I ran and snatched up four bunches of the half-dried bear grass. The sharp ends of the stiff blades stabbed and stung my arms and chest as I grabbed them up. But I had no time to bother about that. I ran and dumped the bunches in a pile on the bare ground outside the yard fence, then hurried to bring a live coal from the fireplace to start them burning.

I fanned fast with my hat. The bear-grass blades started to smoking, giving off their foul smell. A little flame started, flickered and wavered for a moment, then bloomed suddenly and leaped high with a roar.

I jumped back, gun held ready, and caught my first glimpse of the screaming, howling battle that came wheeling into the circle of light. It was Old Yeller, all right, tangled with some animal as big and savage as he was.

Mama called from outside the light's rim. "Careful, Son. And take close aim; it's a big loafer wolf, gone mad."

My heart nearly quit on me. There weren't many of the gray loafer wolves in our part of the country, but I knew about them. They were big and savage enough to hamstring a horse or drag down a full-grown cow. And here was Old Yeller, weak and crippled, trying to fight a mad one!

I brought up my gun, then held fire while I hollered at Mama. "Y'all get in the cabin," I yelled. "I'm scared to shoot till I know you're out of the line of fire!"

I heard Mama whacking Jumper with a stick to make him go. I heard Jumper snort and the clatter of his hoofs as he went galloping in a wide circle to come up behind the cabin. But even after Mama called from the door behind me, I still couldn't fire. Not without taking a chance on killing Old Yeller.

I waited, my nerves on edge, while Old Yeller and the big wolf fought there in the firelight, whirling and leaping and snarling and slashing, their bared fangs gleaming white, their eyes burning green in the half light.

Then they went down in a tumbling roll that stopped with the big wolf on top, his huge jaws shut tight on Yeller's throat. That was my chance, and one that I'd better make good. As weak as Old Yeller was, he'd never break that throat hold.

There in the wavering light, I couldn't get a true bead on the wolf. I couldn't see my sights well enough. All I could do was guess-aim and hope for a hit.

I squeezed the trigger. The gunstock slammed back against my shoulder, and such a long streak of fire spouted from the gun barrel that it blinded me for a second; I couldn't see a thing.

Then I realized that all the growling and snarling had hushed. A second later, I was running toward the two still gray forms lying side by side.

For a second, I just knew that I'd killed Old Yeller, too. Then, about the time I bent over him, he heaved a big sort of sigh and struggled up to start licking my hands and wagging that stub tail.

I was so relieved that it seemed like all the strength went out of me. I slumped to the ground and was sitting there, shivering, when Mama came and sat down beside me.

She put one arm across my shoulders and held it there while she told me what had happened.

Like I'd figured, it had taken her and Lisbeth till dark to get the wood dragged up and the fire to going around the dead cow. Then they'd mounted old Jumper and headed for home. They'd been without water all this time and were thirsty. When they came to the crossing on Birdsong Creek, they'd dismounted to get a drink. And while they were lying down, drinking, the wolf came.

He was right on them before they knew it. Mama happened to look up and see the dark hulk of him come bounding toward them across a little clearing. He was snarling as he came, and Mama just barely had time to come to her feet and grab up a dead chinaberry pole before he sprang. She whacked him hard across the head, knocking him to the ground. Then Old Yeller was there, tying into him.

Mama and Lisbeth got back on Jumper and tore out for the house. Right after them came the wolf, like he had his mind fixed on catching them, and nothing else. But Old Yeller fought him too hard and too fast. Yeller wasn't big and strong enough to stop him, but he kept him slowed down and fought away from Jumper and Mama and Lisbeth.

"He had to've been mad, son," Mama wound up. "You know that no wolf in his right senses would have acted that way. Not even a big loafer wolf."

"Yessum," I said, "and it's sure a good thing that Old Yeller was along to keep him fought off." I shuddered at the thought of what could have happened without Old Yeller.

Mama waited a little bit, then said in a quiet voice: "It was a good thing for us, son; but it wasn't good for Old Yeller."

The way she said that gave me a cold feeling in the pit of my stomach. I sat up straighter. "What do you mean?" I said. "Old Yeller's all right. He's maybe chewed up some, but he can't be bad hurt. See, he's done trotting off toward the house."

Then it hit me what Mama was getting at. All my insides froze. I couldn't get my breath.

I jumped to my feet, wild with hurt and scare. "But Mama!" I cried out. "Old Yeller's just saved your life! He's saved my life. He's saved Little Arliss's life! We can't—"

Mama got up and put her arms across my shoulder again. "I know, son," she said. "But he's been bitten by a mad wolf."

I started off into the blackness of the night while my mind wheeled and darted this way and that, like a scared rat trying to find its way out of a trap.

"But Mama," I said. "We don't know for certain. We could wait and see. We could tie him or shut him up in the corncrib or some place till we know for sure!"

Mama broke down and went to crying then. She put her head on my shoulder and held me so tight that she nearly choked off my breath.

"We can't take a chance, Son," she sobbed. "It would be you or me or Little Arliss or Lisbeth next. I'll shoot him if you can't, but either way, we've got it to do. We just can't take the chance!"

It came clear to me then that Mama was right. We couldn't take the risk. And from everything I had heard, I knew that there was very little chance of Old Yeller's escaping the sickness. It was going to kill something inside me to do it, but I knew then that I had to shoot my big yeller dog.

Once I knew for sure I had it to do, I don't think I really felt anything. I was just numb all over, like a dead man walking.

Quickly, I left Mama and went to stand in the light of the burning bear grass. I reloaded my gun and called Old Yeller back from the house. I stuck the muzzle of the gun against his head and pulled the trigger.

Chapter 16

Days went by, and I couldn't seem to get over it. I couldn't eat. I couldn't sleep. I couldn't cry. I was all empty inside, but hurting. Hurting worse than I'd ever hurt in my life. Hurting with a sickness there didn't seem to be any cure for. Thinking every minute of my big yeller dog, how we'd worked together and romped together, how he'd fought the she-bear off Little Arliss, how he'd saved me from the killer hogs, how he'd fought the mad wolf off Mama and Lisbeth. Thinking that after all this, I'd had to shoot him the same as I'd done the roan bull and the Spot heifer.

Mama tried to talk to me about it, and I let her. But while everything she said made sense, it didn't do a thing to that dead feeling I had.

Lisbeth talked to me. She didn't say much; she was too shy. But she pointed out that I had another dog, the speckled pup.

"He's part Old Yeller," she said. "And he was the best one of the bunch."

But that didn't help any either. The speckled pup might be part Old Yeller, but he wasn't Old Yeller. He hadn't saved all our lives and then been shot down like he was nothing.

Then one night it clouded up and rained till daylight. That seemed to wash away the hydrophobia plague. At least, pretty soon afterward, it died out completely.

But we didn't know that then. What seemed important to us about the rain was that the next morning after it fell, Papa came riding home through the mud.

The long ride to Kansas and back had Papa drawn down till he was as thin and knotty as a fence rail. But he had money in his pockets, a big shouting laugh for everybody, and a saddle horse for me.

The horse was a cat-stepping blue roan with a black mane and tail. Papa put me on him the first thing and made me gallop him in the clearing around the house. The roan had all the pride and fire any grown man would want in his best horse, yet was as gentle as a pet.

"Now, isn't he a dandy?" Papa asked.

I said "Yessir!" and knew that Papa was right and that I ought to be proud and thankful. But I wasn't. I didn't feel one way or another about the horse.

Papa saw something was wrong. I saw him look a question at Mama and saw Mama shake her head. Then late that evening, just before supper, he called me off down to the spring, where we sat and he talked.

"Your mama told me about the dog," he said.

I said "Yessir," but didn't add anything.

"That was rough," he said. "That was as rough a thing as I ever heard tell of happening to a boy. And I'm mighty proud to learn how my boy stood up to it. You couldn't ask any more of a grown man."

He stopped for a minute. He picked up some little pebbles and thumped them into the water, scattering a bunch of hairy-legged water bugs. The bugs darted across the water in all directions.

"Now the thing to do," he went on, "is to try to forget it and go on being a man."

"How?" I asked. "How can you forget a thing like that?"

He studied me for a moment, then shook his head. "I guess I don't quite mean that," he said. "It's not a thing you can forget. I don't guess it's a thing that you ought to forget. What I mean is, things like that happen. They

may seem mighty cruel and unfair, but that's how life is a part of the time.

"But that isn't the only way life is. A part of the time, it's mighty good. And a man can't afford to waste all the good part, worrying about the bad parts. That makes it all bad. . . . You understand?"

"Yessir," I said. And I did understand. Only, it still didn't do me any good. I still felt just as dead and empty.

That went on for a week or better, I guess, before a thing happened that brought me alive again.

It was right at dinnertime. Papa had sent me out to the lot to feed Jumper and the horses. I'd just started back when I heard a commotion in the house. I heard Mama's voice lifted high and sharp. "Why, you thieving little whelp!" she cried out. Then I heard a shrieking yelp, and out the kitchen door came the speckled pup with a big chunk of cornbread clutched in his mouth. He raced around the house, running with his tail clamped. He was yelling and squawling like somebody was beating him to death. But that still didn't keep him from hanging onto that piece of cornbread that he'd stolen from Mama.

Inside the house, I heard Little Arliss. He was fighting and screaming his head off at Mama for hitting his dog. And above it all, I could hear Papa's roaring laughter.

Right then, I began to feel better. Sight of that little old pup, tearing out for the brush with the piece of cornbread seemed to loosen something inside me.

I felt better all day. I went back and rode my horse and enjoyed it. I rode 'way off out in the brush, not going anywhere especially, just riding and looking and beginning to feel proud of owning a real horse of my own.

Then along about sundown, I rode down into Birdsong Creek, headed for the house. Up at the spring, I heard a splashing and hollering. I looked ahead. Sure enough, it was Little Arliss. He was stripped naked and romping in our drinking water again. And right in there, romping with him, was that bread-stealing speckled pup.

I started to holler at them. I started to say, "*Arliss!* You get that nasty old pup out of our drinking water."

Then I didn't. Instead, I went to laughing. I sat there and laughed till I cried. When all the time I knew that I ought to go beat them to a frazzle for messing up our drinking water.

When finally I couldn't laugh and cry another bit, I rode on up to the lot and turned my horse in. Tomorrow, I thought, I'll take Arliss and that pup out for a squirrel hunt. The pup was still mighty little. But the way I figured it, if he was big enough to act like Old Yeller, he was big enough to start learning to earn his keep.

CHAPTERS 12–16

Getting at Meaning

RECALLING

1. How does Travis's mother prevent Jumper from eating the corn?

2. How does Travis hurt Lisbeth's feelings?

3. Why does Bud Searcy leave Lisbeth with Travis's family?

4. How does Spot react to her hungry calf? Why?

5. What does the family do to the roan bull's carcass?

6. Where does Travis kill Spot? Why does he shoot her in this place?

7. How does Old Yeller help Travis's mother and Lisbeth escape from the wolf?

8. How does Travis feel after he has killed Old Yeller?

9. What present does Travis's father bring to him?

INTERPRETING

10. On pages 589–590, Travis gets mad at Lisbeth for expecting him, even though he is badly hurt, "to make a big to-do over a little old puny speckled pup." What has Travis just told Lisbeth about his pain? Why is it unfair for Travis to be upset with Lisbeth?

11. How does Lisbeth's attitude toward work differ from Travis's? Why is Travis's pride hurt by Lisbeth's actions?

12. Why does Old Yeller have to be killed? What do Travis's mother and father say to help Travis accept the dog's death?

13. What indication does Travis's father give that Travis is nearing manhood?

14. What incident helps Travis to "come alive again"? What details suggest that the speckled pup will turn out to be like Old Yeller?

CRITICAL THINKING: EVALUATING

15. Does Travis do the right thing when he shoots Old Yeller? Explain your opinion.

Developing Skills in Reading Literature

1. **Suspense.** Suspense is a feeling of growing tension and excitement felt by a reader. The author of *Old Yeller,* Fred Gipson, creates suspense by raising questions in his readers' minds. For example, after Travis's mother leaves to burn Spot's carcass, Gipson has Travis think the following:

"Only, afterward, I wished a thousand times that I could have had some way of looking ahead to what was going to happen. Then I would have done everything I could to keep all of them from going."

What is Travis referring to? What question does reading this passage raise in your mind?

2. **Conflict.** Conflict is a struggle between opposing forces. The central conflict in this novel is Travis's struggle to take care of the family farm. This conflict involves several minor conflicts, including the following struggles:

a. to provide enough food for the family
b. to protect Arliss from the she-bear
c. to mark the hogs
d. to protect the family from animals with hydrophobia, or rabies

How does Old Yeller help Travis in these struggles?

Perhaps the most difficult of Travis's struggles occurs after he kills the wolf. What decision must he make? Why is this decision so difficult? Does Travis's decision show that he is mature and responsible? Explain your answer.

3. **Plot.** Plot is the sequence of events in a story. It is the writer's plan for what happens,

when, and to whom. Parts of the plot of a novel include the following:

a. **Exposition.** Exposition is the part of a plot that provides background information and that introduces the setting and the important characters.

b. **Inciting Incident.** The inciting incident is the event that introduces the central conflict and thus sets in motion the plot of the story.

c. **Complications.** Complications are events that heighten, or complicate, a conflict that has already been introduced.

d. **Climax.** The climax, or turning point, is the high point of interest or suspense in a story.

e. **Resolution.** The resolution is the point at which the conflict in a literary work ends.

Review your answers to the Developing Skills in Reading Literature exercises on Plot and Exposition (page 556), Inciting Incident (page 556), Conflict (page 566), and Conflict and Complication (page 571). On a sheet of paper, answer the following questions:

a. In the exposition of *Old Yeller,* the reader is introduced to the setting and to the main characters. What is the setting of this novel? Who are the main characters?

b. What is the inciting incident in *Old Yeller?* What conflict does this inciting incident introduce?

c. Describe three complications that arise after the inciting incident.

d. What is the climax of *Old Yeller?*

e. What happens at the end of *Old Yeller* to bring an end to the central conflict?

4. **Theme.** The theme is the main idea of a work of literature. Often the theme is a message about human nature. The theme of *Old Yeller* is directly stated in the following passage by Travis's father:

" 'What I mean is, things like that happen. They may seem mighty cruel and unfair, but that's how life is a part of the time.

" 'But that isn't the only way life is. A part of the time, it's mighty good. And a man can't afford to waste all the good part, worrying about the bad parts. That makes it all bad.' "

What cruel and unfair thing happens to Travis and Old Yeller? What good parts of the experience with Old Yeller will Travis be able to remember? How will having Old Yeller's pup help Travis to remember these good parts?

Developing Vocabulary

Dialect. A dialect is a variety of a language spoken by the people of one region or social group. Sometimes dialects differ in grammar and in vocabulary, or word choice. For example, Travis thinks, "And Mama had ten times too much to do, *like it was.*" In some dialects, people would say *as it was* instead. Read the following sentences from *Old Yeller,* all of which are written in the frontier dialect of the characters in this novel. Rewrite these sentences in standard English, the formal variety of English appropriate to a classroom.

1. "I was hurting *a-plenty.*"
2. "I *brung* you a surprise."
3. "But now I was *laid up,* and here was a girl handling my work."
4. "Spot *made fight* at me."

Developing Writing Skills

1. **Writing About Theme.** Write a paragraph explaining the theme of *Old Yeller.* Include in your prewriting notes your answers to Developing Skills in Reading Literature, number 4. Also include a statement of the theme in your own words. As you write and

revise your paragraph, refer to the guidelines presented in **Using the Process of Writing** on pages 614–623.

2. **Writing About Characters.** Choose any two of the following characters. Write a paragraph describing how the relationship between the two characters changes in the course of the novel.

Travis and Old Yeller

Travis and Little Arliss

Travis and his mother

As you write and revise your paragraph, refer to the guidelines in **Using the Process of Writing** on pages 614–623.

B I O G R A P H Y

Fred Gipson (1908–1973) was born in Mason, Texas. After high school, Gipson spent eight years working as a farm and ranch hand until he could afford to attend the University of Texas in Austin. He worked as a journalist and editor for several years. Finally he devoted all of his time to working his farm and to writing western adventure stories. *Old Yeller* and *Savage Sam,* two of his best-known works, were made into Walt Disney movies.

RESEARCH SKILLS FOR *WRITING*

Taking Notes

When doing research for a report, you will need to take notes to record the information you plan to use. Follow these steps:

1. Locate books, magazines, and reference works that contain information on your subject. These are your sources.

2. Take notes on 3" × 5" index cards. On each card, record one item of information. The information may be quoted or rewritten in your own words. If the information is directly quoted, be sure to use quotation marks.

3. For books, give the author, title, copyright date, and page number of the information.

4. For magazines, give the author, title of the article, name and date of the magazine, and page numbers of the article.

5. For encyclopedias, give the title of the article, name of the encyclopedia, and year of publication.

The following note cards are for a report on pioneer life. The first card contains rewritten information from a book. The second contains quoted information from an encyclopedia.

Edwin Tunis, Frontier Living, 1961, p. 154.

After the Civil War, many pioneers headed west to Kansas, Nebraska, the Dakotas, Colorado, and Oklahoma.

"Pioneer Life in America," The World Book Encyclopedia, 1984.

"The pioneers usually traveled on trails that had been blazed by explorers or fur traders."

Developing Writing Skills

Gathering Information on Note Cards. Go to your school or public library and take notes for a report on how dogs help people. Record your notes on index cards. Use at least one book, one magazine article, and one encyclopedia article. Take at least ten notes. Record one item of information on each card. If you need help finding materials in the library, refer to the following lessons: Locating Materials in a Library (p. 89), Using the Card Catalog (p. 275), Using an Encyclopedia (p. 495), and Using the *Readers' Guide* (p. 527).

After you have gathered your information, write your report. The report should be three or four paragraphs long, with a clear focus for each paragraph. Be sure to name your sources, both for information that you quote and for information that you put in your own words. If you like, include personal experiences and observations as well.

See **Handbook: How To Write About Literature**, Lessons 1–4.

CRITICAL THINKING

Making Evaluations

Your teachers often will ask you to evaluate, or judge, literary works. An evaluation is a statement that tells how you feel about some part of the work or about the work as a whole. The following are some evaluations of *Old Yeller:*

1. *Old Yeller* is a gripping, suspenseful novel.
2. Bud Searcy, one of the minor characters in *Old Yeller,* is lazy and self-serving.
3. Old Yeller is a courageous and loving dog.

Making Evaluations Specific. Whenever you evaluate a literary work, make sure that your evaluation is specific. The following evaluations are too general and vague:

1. *Old Yeller* is great!
2. I hated the ending.
3. It's a good book.

One way to make your evaluations specific is to refer to one aspect of the work, such as the suspensefulness of the plot or the realism of the setting. Another way to make your evaluations specific is to use precise judgment words. Such words include the following: *realistic, exaggerated, unbelievable, lively, contrived, surprising, inappropriate,* and *imaginative.* Look up in a dictionary any of these words that you do not know.

Supporting Evaluations with Facts. An evaluation should be supported by facts. In other words, you should be able to find evi-

dence to back up your evaluation. For example, the statement "*Old Yeller* is a gripping, suspenseful novel" can be supported by these facts:

1. Early in the novel, Gipson leads the reader to wonder whether Travis will be able to take care of the farm. The reader wants to continue reading to find out whether Travis is successful.
2. In Chapter 4, the reader wonders whether the bulls will destroy the house.
3. In Chapters 10, 11, and 12, the reader wonders whether Old Yeller will live.
4. In the last few chapters, the reader wonders whether the family will be safe during the hydrophobia epidemic.

Developing Critical Thinking Skills

Evaluating a Novel. Pretend that you are taking an essay test on *Old Yeller.* Below are some questions from the test. Answer each of these questions in writing. First, write a one-sentence evaluation, or judgment, that sums up your answer to the question. In your sentence, use specific judgment words. Then, list three facts from the novel to support your evaluation.

1. Is Old Yeller a good cow-herding dog?
2. At the end of the novel, has Travis become a mature, responsible person?
3. Is the plot of *Old Yeller* believable?
4. Is the plot of *Old Yeller* surprising, or is it predictable?
5. Does the reader of *Old Yeller* learn any important lessons?

Understanding the Novel

RECALLING

1. In what part of the country is this novel set? Is the novel set in the present or in the past?

2. Who are the two main characters in the novel?

3. Name six minor characters in the novel and describe each one.

INTERPRETING

4. What responsibility is placed on Travis at the beginning of the novel? How well does he live up to this responsibility?

5. Describe three struggles that Travis faces.

CRITICAL THINKING: APPLYING

6. According to Travis's father, life contains both good parts and bad parts, and a person must try not to dwell on the bad. Is this sound advice? How might it apply in your own life?

Writing About the Novel

See **Using the Process of Writing** on pages 614–623 for help with this assignment.

Write a composition describing the plot structure of *Old Yeller*. In your prewriting notes, include definitions of the terms *plot, exposition, inciting incident, conflict, complication, climax,* and *resolution.* Also include your answers to Developing Skills in Reading Literature, number 3, on pages 604–605.

Begin with a paragraph that names the book and its author. In this paragraph, state your topic and define the word *plot.* In your second paragraph, define the term *exposition* and tell what the reader learns in the exposition of *Old Yeller.* In your third paragraph, define the terms *inciting incident* and *conflict.* Then, describe the inciting incident and the main conflict in the novel. In your fourth paragraph, define the term *complication* and describe three complications that arise after the inciting incident. In your fifth and final paragraph, define the terms *climax* and *resolution.* Then, describe the climax and resolution of this novel.

Applying Techniques from the Novel

See **Using the Process of Writing** on pages 614–623 for help with this assignment.

An epilogue is a section that comes after the end of a literary work. Writers often include epilogues in order to tie up loose ends. Write an epilogue for *Old Yeller* in which you describe what becomes of Travis, Lisbeth, and Old Yeller's pup.

≫ *H*andbook:
How To Write About Literature

INTRODUCTION

Introduction

Can you remember the first word that you wrote? Perhaps it was your own name. Think of how far you have come from struggling to form your first words to writing sentences, paragraphs, and longer compositions. How much you have learned!

Kinds of Writing

Your writing skills make it possible for you to write in a variety of forms for many different purposes. You most likely have written short notes to friends, and maybe you have written longer letters or have kept a diary. Perhaps in school you have been asked to express an opinion in writing or to create a short story or poem. All of these kinds of writing are based on your own experiences and imagination. The success of your writing is judged by how well you communicate with your readers.

Another kind of writing is called analytical writing. This kind may be new to you. Analytical writing involves two skills. The first is reading and understanding what someone else has written. The second is explaining in a clear and logical way what you have understood. Some of the writing assignments in this book introduce you to analytical writing. Essay questions also require analytical writing.

The Writing Process

No matter what kind of writing you are doing, you can and should follow the same basic process of writing. This process makes writing easier because it divides the task of writing into stages. The first stage is called prewriting. The activities in this stage start you thinking and gathering data before you actually write. Then comes writing a draft. The next stage is revision, which includes proofreading. The final stage is sharing what you have written with an audience.

The Writing Handbook

This handbook is divided into two sections: Using the Process of Writing (Lessons 1-4) and Writing About Literature (Lessons 5-8). Lessons 1-4 introduce you to the writing process. You will find these lessons helpful for all kinds of writing. As you work through the lessons, you will study a writing assignment in progress. You also will complete your own assignment. Lessons 5-8 deal with writing about different kinds of literature. You may work through these sections when you complete assignments analyzing short stories, nonfiction selections, poems, and plays.

The handbook is both a guide and a reference manual. You can refer to it when you are given an assignment that deals with analyzing literature or that calls for another kind of writing. You also can review parts of lessons when you need help with certain aspects of the writing process.

LESSON 1 Prewriting: Setting a Clear Direction

The job of writing can seem overwhelming when you are faced with a blank sheet of paper and an assignment. However, if you approach the task as a process, it becomes easier. This process can be divided into four stages: **prewriting, writing a draft, revising,** and **sharing.** During the first stage, you set up a plan for writing. You decide what you are going to say as well as how you are going to say it. During the other three stages, you put your plan into action.

With the help of your teacher, choose a writing assignment from this book. Use this assignment as you work through this lesson and the following three lessons on the process of writing.

Studying the Assignment

When you are given a writing assignment, study it to be sure that you understand what is expected. First, read the assignment several times. The first time get a general idea of what the assignment is asking. As you reread, identify the key words in the assignment. Key words include the following:

discuss   describe   explain   show
tell   state   define   demonstrate

Other key words include the question words *how, why, who,* and *where;* nouns such as *effect, example,* and *opinion;* and literary terms such as *rhyme, character, setting,* and *flashback.* If you are unsure of the meanings of any words in the assignment, be sure to look them up in a dictionary or in the Handbook of Literary Terms in this book.

Most assignments in this book specify a length. Note this length when you study the assignment.

Choosing a Topic

Some assignments are very specific. For example, an assignment might tell you to examine one element in a particular short story. Other assignments allow you to select your own topic. For instance, an assignment might ask you to choose an experience from your own life to write about. Although deciding on a topic will be a little different for each of these assignments, you will find the following steps helpful.

Steps in Choosing a Topic

1. List several possible topics. This list will be the beginning of your prewriting notes, your plan for writing. Remember to write down any topic that comes to mind, even though it seems unlikely that you will use the topic.

2. Identify the topic that seems to be the most appealing and workable.

3. Examine the assignment for any mention of length. If the assignment does not specify length, try to estimate a length. Consider what you know about your topic and how much time you have to complete the assignment.

4. Adjust the topic to the length. If the topic seems too general, make it more specific. If it seems too narrow, broaden the topic. You might combine topics to form a new one or choose an entirely new topic.

5. Record your final topic in your prewriting notes.

Knowing Your Purpose

Readers find some writing difficult to understand because it wanders off the subject. Such writing shows that the writer does not have a clear purpose in mind. When you are the writer, be sure that you understand what you want to communicate. Your writing then will be easy for your readers to follow.

Often, the key words in an assignment will help you determine your purpose. Does the assignment ask you to describe an incident? Then your purpose will be to describe the incident so that your readers can share your experience. Does the assignment ask you to discuss a character in a short story? Then your purpose will be to communicate what you have concluded about the character.

When you have your purpose clearly in mind, write this purpose in your prewriting notes under your topic. Your entry might read:

The purpose of this paragraph is to discuss the attitude of the Greek gods toward the mortals on earth.

Sample Writing Assignment

The following assignment concerns the myth "Prometheus," which begins on page 6.

Prometheus wants humans to have the gift of fire. In one paragraph discuss why Prometheus believes that humans should be given this gift. Include one or more quotations from the myth to support your explanation.

EXERCISES   Applying the Process: Prewriting

1. Study the sample writing assignment. Then answer these questions:

What are the key words? Do you understand their meanings?

Is the topic given, or must you think of your own topic?

What length is specified?

What is your purpose for writing?

Finally, read or reread "Prometheus."

2. Choose another selection in the book that is followed by a writing assignment. (The selection does not have to be one that you have read.) Study this assignment, answering the same questions as you did for Exercise 1.

3. Study the writing assignment that you selected with the help of your teacher. Identify the key words, and note any mention of length. If necessary, choose a topic by following the suggestions listed under Steps in Choosing a Topic. Finally, write your purpose in your prewriting notes.

LESSON 2 Prewriting: Gathering and Organizing Ideas

For some assignments you will draw details from your own experience to make your topic come alive for your readers. For other assignments you will go back to a literary selection. Writing about a work of literature is quite different from recalling or imagining experiences or discussing your own observations. You must base all your ideas and opinions on the literary work. You must also make sure that you can prove your points.

Gathering Details

If you were collecting stamps from the United States, you would not bother with a stamp from Germany, even though it was an interesting stamp. Similarly, when you are gathering details, you should focus only on those that explain your topic and suit your purpose. Remember, however, that your writing probably will be stronger if you collect more details than you need. Then, while writing the first draft, you can omit the weakest ones. As you collect your details, add them to your prewriting notes, under your topic and purpose.

Gathering Details from Literature

If your assignment is to write about a poem, short story, or nonfiction selection, it is probably wise to reread the entire selection to gather your details. If you are writing about a longer selection, such as a novel, you probably will not have time to reread the entire work. Instead, find those passages that relate to your topic and reread them carefully. Your notes from class discussion and possibly your teacher can help you to find these important passages.

As you reread, take clear and accurate notes, keeping the following guidelines in mind.

Three Ways To Record Ideas

Copy. Copy short passages, sentences, or phrases when you think that the writer's own words are especially important, as when a writer is describing a person, place, or object. Be sure to copy quotations accurately, to use quotation marks, and to give a page or line number for each.

Paraphrase. Paraphrasing is putting a passage into your own words. Paraphrase when the passage is not too long and when the writer's ideas, not exact words, are important.

Summarize. Summarize, or state briefly, the meaning of long passages. Sometimes you may wish to summarize plot events that relate to your topic.

As you read, you may get ideas that will help you complete the assignment. Record these ideas in your prewriting notes.

Grouping Details

If your gathering of details has been successful, you probably will have a long list of them, more than you can possibly use.

Look over these details, and try to classify them into groups. Different assignments suggest different ways of grouping. For instance, an assignment might ask you to describe character traits. You might group the details for this assignment into desirable and undesirable traits. If you are discussing two characters, you might group together all of the information on each character.

Now is the time to cross out ideas that do not seem to fit into your groupings. Remember that these ideas are not necessarily wrong. They just do not fit the focus of the assignment.

You may find that your details cannot be classified into several groups. If so, identify the focus of most of the details, and then eliminate the details unrelated to this focus.

Organizing Details

Once you have gathered and grouped your details, your next step is to put these details into some type of order. The order is determined by the assignment. Three common ways of ordering details are described here.

Ways To Order Details

Chronological Order. When you present details in the order in which they occur, you are using chronological order. Generally, you use this order when you tell a story. When you analyze plot or character, you also might consider using this type of organization.

Spatial Order. In this method, details are ordered in the way that the viewer might notice them. For instance, you could begin describing those things nearest you and work back to what is farthest away. This type of order is most commonly used in describing settings and the appearance of characters.

Order of Importance. Often, it is useful to give the least important details first and work up to the most important ones. At other times you may want to discuss the most important details first and the least important ones last. Both your purpose and the assignment are factors in determining the best order.

Once you decide on an order, number your details to show this order.

Sample Prewriting Notes

After careful rereading of "Prometheus," one writer took these prewriting notes.

The purpose of this paragraph is to explain why Prometheus believes that humans should have fire.

① Prometheus believes that Zeus is keeping the humans "in ignorance and darkness." (p. 6)
"They crouch in caves. They are at the mercy of beast and weather. They eat their meat raw." (p. 6)
(Humans living like beasts)

~~Prometheus asks Zeus to explain the meaning of his actions.~~

② Prometheus believes that humans are happy only "as beasts are happy." (p. 6)
"If they must live like this, why separate them from the beasts at all?" (p. 6)

④ Prometheus says "Would not fire, and the graces they can put on with fire, make them more interesting?" (p. 7)
(Humans would be more interesting)

~~Prometheus is not satisfied with Zeus's answers.~~

When Prometheus roasts the deer, the humans " devoured it greedily." (p. 7) Humans had been hungry— no more; they would be less like beasts.
(<u>Humans living like beasts</u>)

~~Prometheus warns humans of the dangers of fire.~~

~~After humans receive the gift of fire, Zeus sees that the world has changed.~~

EXERCISES   Applying the Process: Prewriting

1.   Study the prewriting notes, including the statement of purpose. Now examine the details that have been crossed out. What reasons can you think of for omitting these details? Note the order in which the details will be presented. What type of order is this?

2.   Gather ideas for the writing assignment on which you are working. Be sure that your details will help you accomplish your purpose. When your prewriting notes are complete, cross out unnecessary details. Then choose an organizational pattern. Finally, number the details the way that they will appear in your paragraph or composition.

LESSON 3   Writing the First Draft

With good prewriting notes, you have a map before you, and you are ready to write a first draft. In this stage of the writing process, focus on getting your ideas on paper; do not be afraid of making mistakes. Later, you will have a chance to revise your writing to produce a correct final copy.

The first step in writing a first draft is to write an opening sentence. To do this, you need to know the difference between specific and general statements.

Understanding Specific and General

Words, ideas, and statements that are specific are exact. Those that are general are less exact. If you tell someone that you live in the United States, for example, you are making a general statement. If you add the name of a state, such as Illinois, you are being more specific. If you name a town in Illinois, a street, and then a street number, you are being even more specific.

Additional examples of general to specific order include the following:
food, fruit, grapes, green grapes, Thompson
   seedless green grapes
athlete, baseball player, Chicago Cub, Cub
   second baseman, Ryne Sandberg

Knowing the difference between specific and general is important in writing paragraphs and compositions. As you write, you often will need to structure your writing so that you begin with a general statement and then follow with specific details to back up the general statement.

Writing a Topic Sentence

The sentence that contains your general statement is the topic sentence. Usually, the topic sentence is the first one in a paragraph or composition. This sentence provides the reader with a sense of the writer's purpose.

As you examine your prewriting notes, you will discover that your statement of purpose contains a general idea and that the rest of the notes are more specific. Your topic sentence will state an idea similar to the one in the statement of purpose. The body of the paragraph or composition will give the more specific details.

Sample Topic Sentence

The following topic sentence is based on the prewriting notes in Lesson 2. Remember that this is only a first draft. The writer may change the wording of the sentence later.

Prometheus disagrees with Zeus, for Prometheus believes that humans should be given the gift of fire.

Compare the sample topic sentence with the sample writing assignment in Lesson 1. Notice that the topic sentence picks up key words such as *Prometheus*, *humans*, and *gift of fire*. The rest of the paragraph will explain why Prometheus believes in sharing the gift of fire.

When you must write a topic sentence, follow these steps.

Steps in Writing a Topic Sentence

1. Study your prewriting notes.
2. Identify the main idea contained in your statement of purpose.
3. Review the writing assignment to be sure that the main idea fits the assignment.
4. Check your prewriting notes to be sure that you can support your main idea.
5. Write a sentence that states the main idea.

Completing the First Draft

Once you have written a topic sentence, you are ready to explain, extend, or prove your idea through supporting sentences. When you are writing a composition, these sentences are grouped into paragraphs. Each paragraph has its own topic sentence. This sentence relates in some way to the main topic sentence that opens the composition.

As you begin writing your supporting sentences, go back to your prewriting notes. Since these notes are already grouped and ordered, you need only to follow the plan you have set down. Do not be afraid to add, rearrange, or eliminate details, however, if you believe that the change will produce a better paragraph or composition. When making changes, check your topic sentence to be sure that each change is consistent with your general statement.

One of the most common mistakes that students make in writing about literature is retelling the story rather than answering the question or discussing the assigned topic. In most cases, your readers—your teacher, classmates, and maybe your parents—are familiar with the story. There is no need, therefore, to retell the plot. Sticking to your prewriting plan will prevent you from including any unnecessary plot summary.

As you write, you should skip lines to give yourself enough space for revision. Also, do not be concerned about spelling and fine points of grammar. You can fix these things as you revise and proofread.

Sample First Draft

This sample first draft begins with the sample topic sentence given earlier in this lesson. The draft is based on the prewriting notes included in Lesson 2.

Prometheus disagrees with Zeus, for Prometheus believes that humans should be given the gift of fire. Prometheus feels that the mortels are living like beasts "in ignorance and darkness." (p. 6) He says "They crouch in caves. They are at the mercy of beast and weather. They eat their meat raw." He says that they are "happy only as beasts are happy." (p. 6) He says "If they must live like this, why separate them from the beasts at all?" (p. 6) Fire would give humans a way to cook their food, like roasted deer. They would be less like beasts. Fire would "make them more interesting." (p. 7) Prometheus feels that he is right, and so he goes against Zeus and gives humans fire.

EXERCISES   Applying the Process: Writing the First Draft

1.   Study the sample first draft, and answer these questions: Which sentence is the topic sentence? Does the topic sentence make a general statement? Are the supporting sentences specific? How are the supporting sentences related to the prewriting notes? How are they related to the topic sentence? What problems need to be corrected?

2.   Write the first draft of the writing assignment on which you are working. Begin by writing a topic sentence, using the Steps in Writing a Topic Sentence. Then add supporting sentences, using your prewriting notes as a guide.

Revising and Sharing

Revision is the third stage in the writing process. During this stage, you will look at the development of your ideas and at the correctness of your writing.

Begin revising by reading your first draft several times. Each time check for different ways to improve your writing. The following guidelines will help you during revision.

Guidelines for Revision

1. Check your topic sentence. Does it connect directly with the assignment? Is it consistent with the purpose stated in the prewriting notes? Is the sentence clearly stated?

2. Look for unnecessary details. Are some details repeated? Are some unrelated to the main idea stated in the topic sentence?

3. Add details if necessary. Would more details make your writing clearer? more persuasive? precise? vivid?

4. Examine your organization. Is the pattern logical and clear? Would a different organization of ideas be better? Does your writing have a clear beginning, middle, and end?

5. Read your writing aloud. Does it sound choppy? Do you overuse some words? Could you substitute more precise or vivid words?

Making Writing Smoother

You may find that your writing seems choppy, that it sounds like separate state-ments rather than one thought unit. If your paragraph or composition is organized chronologically, you may need to use time words such as *first, next,* and *finally.* These words help your readers understand the time order. A time word does not have to be the first word in a sentence; it can appear in the middle. For descriptions, direction words such as *behind, near, right, left, top,* and *bottom* are useful. In explanations, *however, therefore, also,* and other similar words can help to clarify connections among ideas.

Another way to fix choppy writing is to combine short sentences into longer ones. If two ideas are equally important, you can join them with a conjunction such as *and, but, or,* or *nor.*

Example:

Prometheus argued with Zeus. He could not convince him.

Prometheus argued with Zeus, but he could not convince him.

If one idea is more important than another, you can express the less important idea in a subordinate clause. Words such as *because, since, who, which,* and *that* introduce subordinate clauses.

Example:

Prometheus thought he was right. He gave humans the gift of fire.

Because Prometheus thought he was right, he gave humans the gift of fire.

Combined sentences, as well as the others in your paragraph or composition, may have unnecessary words that should be deleted. Example:

Prometheus gave humans the gift of fire that changed the lives of the human race.

Prometheus gave humans the gift of fire that changed their lives.

Finalizing Your Writing

After revising the content of your paragraph or composition, proofread your writing for errors in grammar and usage, spelling, punctuation, and capitalization. Use a language arts textbook or a dictionary for help in making corrections. Also use the following checklist as a guide to identifying problems.

Checklist for Proofreading

1. Have you spelled all words correctly? Check the dictionary when in doubt of any spelling.

2. Have you used correct sentence structure? Common errors include sentence fragments and run-on sentences.

3. Have you capitalized the first word and every important word in the titles of books, short stories, essays, and poems? For example: "The Origin of Fire."

4. Have you used quotation marks to enclose the titles of short stories, poems, and nonfiction selections? For example: "Prometheus."

5. Have you underlined the titles of books and plays? For example: *Grandpa and the Statue.*

6. Have you used quotation marks to enclose the exact words of a writer? For example: "Prometheus was a young Titan, no great admirer of Zeus." (page 6)

After carefully proofreading your work, make a final copy. Write neatly and use the proper heading and margins.

Sample Revised Paragraph

In the Greek myth "Prometheus," Prometheus ~~disagrees with Zeus, for~~ *argues* ~~Prometheus believes~~ that humans should be given the gift of fire. Prometheus *believes* ~~feels~~ that the mort*a*els are living like beasts "in *age* ignorance and darkness." (p. 6) He says , "They crouch in caves. They are at the mercy of beast and weather. They eat their *points out   humans* meat raw." He ~~says~~ that ~~they~~ are "happy *and asks,* only as beasts are happy." (p. 6) ~~He says~~ "If they must live like this, why separate *age With* them from the beasts at all?" (p. 6) Fire *could protect themselves, keep warm, and* ~~would give~~ humans ~~a way to~~ cook their *Therefore,* food, ~~like roasted deer,~~ They would be less *Also, they   be* like beasts. ~~Fire~~ would "~~make them~~ more *to the gods. For these reasons,* interesting." (p. 7) Prometheus feels ~~that~~ *justified in giving* ~~he is right, and so he goes against Zeus and~~ ~~gives~~ humans fire.

622   *Handbook: How To Write About Literature*

Sharing Your Writing

Most of your finished writing is shared with your teacher and classmates. You may read your work aloud or post it on a bulletin board. You may put your work into a booklet with the work of others in your class, or submit your writing to a school magazine or newspaper.

EXERCISES   **Applying the Process: Revising and Sharing.**

1. Study the sample revised paragraph: Which ideas have been deleted? Added? Why?

Which sentences have been combined? How have some ideas been clarified? Which changes were made to correct errors?

2. Revise the draft of the writing assignment on which you are working. Proofread, make a final copy, and share it with the class.

3. Complete the following assignment, working through the process of writing.

Zeus believes that humans should not have the gift of fire. In one paragraph, explain why. Include quotations from the myth to support your explanation.

LESSON 5   Writing About the Short Story

As you probably know, a short story is a work of literature short enough to be read in one sitting. Its three basic elements are character, plot, and setting. Although every short story contains these elements, the elements are not equally important in each story. Understanding a short story means understanding how each element works alone and how all the elements work together.

Here are some points to keep in mind as you study the individual elements of a short story.

Setting. The setting of a short story is both where and when the story takes place. Sometimes the writer uses detailed description to create a setting unfamiliar to the reader. At other times, the setting is so familiar that little description is needed.

Character. Short stories usually deal with

one main character and one or two minor characters. When preparing to write about a character, locate any passages describing the character. Think about the words and actions of the character, the comments of others about the character, and any changes in the character.

Plot. The action or story line in a work of literature is the plot. If a story keeps you reading, wondering what will happen next, and builds to an exciting climax, plot is an important element. The flashback and the surprise ending are also techniques of plot development used by writers.

The novel contains the same basic elements as the short story. However, in the novel, these elements are more complicated. Novels often have several settings that are described in detail. Most novels also have more than one major character and many minor ones. Finally, the plots of novels are more complex. Subplots, or less important story lines, are common.

For more information on **Setting**, **Character**, and **Plot**, look up these terms in the Handbook of Literary Terms.

Considering the Assignment

Sometimes you will be able to choose which short story you will write about. In this case, you should certainly write about a story you enjoyed. However, try also to choose a story whose basic elements are clear to you.

Some assignments are quite specific. They tell you which story and which element within the story to write about. Other assignments ask you to discuss your reaction to a story or to show your understanding of a story by using it as a model for your own writing.

.

Following the Writing Process

As you answer a question or complete an assignment dealing with a short story, follow the steps in the process of writing described on pages 614-622. As you work through each stage—prewriting, writing a draft, revising, and sharing—keep the following in mind.

Prewriting

You most likely will need to read the story at least three times. After the first reading, reread, keeping the key words of the question or assignment in mind. Read the story a third time to take your prewriting notes.

Writing the First Draft

Examine your prewriting notes, and write a strong topic sentence. Be sure that this sentence reflects your purpose. When you use examples and quotations from the story, be sure that they develop the topic sentence.

Revising

Check to be sure that you have followed the guidelines given in the assignment. Make sure that each detail develops the idea in the topic sentence. Finally, be certain that your sentences flow logically and smoothly.

Sample Writing Assignment

The story that is the subject of this sample begins on page 108.

An important aspect of "The Trout" is the characterization of Julia, a twelve year old who is changing from a child into a young adult. In one paragraph, explain how Julia's actions show a shift from childish to more grown-up behavior.

Sample Prewriting Notes

Following are one writer's prewriting notes.

The purpose of this paragraph is to explain how Julia's actions show that she is changing from a child into an adult.

Childish

Finds The Dark Walk wildly exciting; "she screamed with pleasure and raced on to reach the light at the far end." (p. 108)

Julia shares her experience with her brother, "terrifying him as well as herself." (p. 108)

After the run through the walk, they squabble.

Grown-up

Seeing the trout, "they were no longer afraid of the darkness." (p. 108-109)

The condition of the trout troubles Julia; she brings it food.

Julia goes to free the trout even though it is after ten o'clock.

Childish

After Julia frees the trout, she "hugged herself and giggled." (p. 111)

Childish/grown-up

Stephen asks what has happened to the trout. Julia acts smug, but she does not tease or brag.

Studying the Prewriting Notes

Examining the prewriting notes, the writer saw three possible ways of organizing the paragraph. She could present the details chronologically, in the order that they appear in the story. She could discuss first Julia's attitude toward the walk and the trout, then her behavior toward her brother. She could describe Julia's childish behavior, then her grown-up behavior. The writer chose the second way of ordering the details.

Sample First Draft

Following is the beginning of the writer's first draft.

Julia's actions show that she is growing from childhood into adulthood. The reader can see this growth in her reaction to The Dark Walk and the trout. When they first arrive at The Dark Walk, Julia and her brother race through the place, wildly excited yet frightened too. When she finds the trout, Julia loses her childish fear of the dark. The trout's condition troubles Julia so much that she sets out to free the fish, even though it is after ten o'clock. She thinks of the trout rather than herself, acting more like an adult than a child. Julia's attitude toward her brother shows the change in her as well.

Studying the First Draft

The writer has introduced the paragraph with a topic sentence. Notice that this sentence picks up the idea in the prewriting statement of purpose. The details that follow support the topic sentence with examples from the story.

EXERCISES   Writing About Short Stories

1.   Read or reread "The Trout." Then complete the sample first draft. Use the prewriting notes as a guide. Revise and proofread the entire paragraph before making a final copy.

2.   Using the sample topic sentence, write another paragraph on the same topic. This time, present the details in another order.

3.   Complete your writing assignment about a short story, and share it with the class.

LESSON 6 Writing About Nonfiction

Writing that deals with real people, places, and events is called nonfiction. Nonfiction can be written in many forms. Autobiography, biography, and the essay are just three.

Because nonfiction takes so many different forms, it is sometimes difficult to know how to begin analyzing this type of literature. Perhaps the best way to begin is by identifying the writer's purpose. Ask yourself: Is the purpose to inform? to entertain? to share a personal experience? to praise a subject? Next, decide whether the writer has developed the elements of setting, plot, and character. These elements are described in Lesson 5, **Writing About the Short Story**. Finally, ask yourself: What form has the writer chosen? Why does this form suit the writer's purpose? For help in identifying form, read **Nonfiction** in the Handbook of Literary Terms.

Considering the Assignment

An assignment or essay question dealing with nonfiction may ask you to describe a setting or a character or to discuss the importance of an event. An assignment may ask you to explain the writer's purpose or to offer your opinion on the writer's ideas.

Following the Writing Process

For all writing assignments dealing with nonfiction, follow the process of writing, described on pages 614–622. The process—prewriting, writing a draft, revising, and sharing—is your guide to clear expression. As you work through the process, keep the following in mind.

Prewriting

Read the assignment carefully, making sure you understand what is expected. Reread or skim the selection to form a general idea of what you will write about. Then reread all or parts of the selection to collect your prewriting notes. Finally, review your notes to be sure you can accomplish your purpose.

Writing the First Draft

You need a strong topic sentence to give your paragraph or composition direction. Be sure to follow the organizational plan in your prewriting notes. Add details that logically belong. Beware, though, of straying from the topic and purpose of the assignment.

Revising

Look for a smooth progression of ideas. Ask yourself: Does one point lead into another? Do sentences flow smoothly from one to another? If necessary, use the sentence combining techniques on pages 621–622.

Sample Writing Assignment

This writing assignment is based on "Stickeen," found on page 284.

John Muir was an explorer who had many adventures. In "Stickeen" he writes of the dog who shared one of his greatest challenges. In one paragraph describe a lesson that Muir learns from Stickeen. In the topic sentence name the lesson. In the supporting sentences give examples from the story to show how Muir learns the lesson.

Sample Prewriting Notes

Here are one writer's prewriting notes.

The purpose of this paragraph is to describe one lesson that John Muir learns from Stickeen.
Lesson: Don't make hasty judgments.

Muir views Stickeen as a "little, helpless creature" (p. 284); a possible burden
Finds Stickeen a "queer character" and "capable of great idleness" (p. 284–285)
Stickeen is "ready for all sorts of adventures" (p. 285); insists on going everywhere with Muir; a true mountaineer
Stickeen "seemed to meet danger and hardships without anything like reason; insisted on having his own way, never obeyed an order. . . ." (p. 285); he is aloof, "cold as a glacier" (p. 285)
"The widest crevasse that I could jump, he would leap without so much as halting to take a look at it." (p. 286)
Stickeen realizes that the bridge is dangerous; almost does not cross
Stickeen successfully navigates the bridge; runs wild with joy
"At first the least promising and least known of my dog friends, he suddenly became the best known of them all." (p. 291)

Studying the Prewriting Notes

Note that the statement of purpose recalls the assignment directions. After rereading the selection, the writer chose a specific lesson to discuss. He wrote down this lesson to use as a guide when taking the prewriting notes.

Sample First Draft

Using his prewriting notes, the writer completed the following first draft.

From Stickeen, John Muir learns a lesson about judging too hastily. Stickeen seems idle, but Muir learns that he is always ready for adventures. Stickeen seems helpless and useless, but Muir later finds him very capable. Stickeen seems to fear nothing, but Muir learns that he recognizes danger. Stickeen seems to lack emotion and feeling, but Muir later learns that the dog can feel great joy and has great love for those who earn his respect. Stickeen teaches Muir not to make hasty judgments.

Studying the First Draft

The writer's first draft states several conclusions about Stickeen. However, the paragraph has two main weaknesses. It contains no examples or quotations from the selection to illustrate the conclusions. Also, most of the sentences begin the same way. They lack the variety that makes for an interesting paragraph.

EXERCISES Writing About Nonfiction

1. Revise the sample first draft, using the prewriting notes. Support the conclusions in the paragraph with at least three quotations or specific examples. Vary the sentences.

2. In one paragraph discuss Muir's purpose in writing about Stickeen. In your topic sentence state this purpose. In three or four supporting sentences, give reasons for your conclusion.

3. Complete your writing assignment on nonfiction, and share it with the class.

Writing About Poetry

Just as the short story contains the elements of character, setting, and plot, so poetry has certain basic elements. Three of these elements are sound, shape, and images. All three combine to communicate the meaning of a poem.

Because poetry is meant to be heard, your first step in analyzing a poem might be to read it aloud. As you read, listen for the sounds of the poem. Do lines and words within lines rhyme? Is there a regular rhythm? Do the words together form any sound patterns?

Look at the poem. Is the arrangement of lines somewhat regular? Does the poem look like an object, such as a snake, a wave, or a tree? When reading, did you pause at the end of every line, or did you naturally go on to the next line?

The language of poetry is one of suggestion. Think about the language and its effect on you. How does the poem make you feel? What pictures does it bring to mind? How does the language appeal to your five senses? Does the poem use any figurative language such as simile, metaphor, hyperbole, or personification? Consult the Handbook of Literary Terms if these terms are unfamiliar.

After examining the individual elements, think about the meaning of the poem. Ask: What is the subject? What is the poet saying about the subject?

Considering the Assignment

Sometimes you will be allowed to choose a poem to write about. You may be asked to analyze its elements or to examine how these elements function separately and together. You may be asked to look at the same element in two different poems. A more specific assignment may give you not only a poem to write about but also the exact elements within the poem.

Following the Writing Process

The same process of writing that you used in writing about the short story and nonfiction applies to writing about poetry. You will work through the stages of prewriting, writing a draft, revising, and sharing, which are discussed in Lessons 1–4 on pages 614–622. As you work, keep these points in mind.

Prewriting

After reading the assignment carefully, be sure that you understand all of the key words. Use a dictionary or the Handbook of Literary Terms to define any unfamiliar words.

Because a poem is usually short, you can read it several times. Try to look at the poem differently each time you read. For instance, one time read for sound, another time read for poetic language. Also, be sure to look up unfamiliar words in the poem and to note any figurative language that you do not understand.

Writing the First Draft

Follow the order of details shown in your prewriting notes. If you are not satisfied with the way that your paragraph or composition reads, write another draft. This time try a different organizational pattern.

Revising

Check your writing for a clear topic sentence and a logical sequence of supporting details. Remember that your paragraph or composition should catch your reader's attention and move smoothly from one point to the next. Your writing should leave your reader satisfied that you have covered your topic carefully and thoroughly.

Sample Writing Assignment

This writing assignment is based on "'I,' Says the Poem" on page 410.

"'I,' Says the Poem" describes both poetry and poets. Explain in one paragraph what this poem says about poets.

Sample First Draft

The following first draft is based on prewriting notes not shown here.

The poem "'I,' Says the Poem" tells about poets. Lines 11 and 12 state that a poet is "someone like you,/or someone like me." Line 19 calls a poet "ordinary." Line 20 calls a poet "extraordinary." The ordinary poet does ordinary things such as lose his gloves and blow his nose. The extraordinary poet does exaggerated things. His "thoughts stretch high/as clouds in the sky" (lines 21-22) and he has memories that "root deep as trees." (line 24)

Studying the First Draft

The writer of this paragraph used her prewriting notes, which are arranged chronologically. As she examined her first draft she realized that the poem really makes a contradictory statement: a poet is both ordinary and extraordinary. She rewrote her first draft to show her new understanding.

Sample Revised Paragraph

Following is the final version of the second draft.

The poem "'I,' Says the Poem" describes a poet in a way that seems contradictory. Lines 11 and 12 state that a poet is "someone like you,/or someone like me." Line 19 calls a poet "ordinary." As an ordinary person a poet does ordinary things such as lose his gloves and blow his nose. Line 20 introduces the idea that a poet is also "extraordinary." This extraordinary person's "thoughts stretch high/as clouds in the sky" (lines 21-22), and he has memories that "root deep as trees." (line 24) The real poet then is a blend of both ordinary and extraordinary. He is a real human being who is able to imagine, feel, and understand the meaning of life.

Studying the Revised Paragraph

The writer changed the topic sentence so that it now expresses her new understanding of the poem. She grouped all of the details about the poet as an ordinary person together and then followed with the details about the poet as an extraordinary person. Finally, she added two sentences at the end to reinforce the main idea of the paragraph.

Note that when the writer quotes two lines of poetry she has used a slash mark to show where the first line ends.

EXERCISES Writing About Poetry

1. " 'I,' Says the Poem" is divided into three parts. In one paragraph identify the three parts.

Then explain what each part adds to the meaning of the poem.

2. Choose a poem and write one paragraph about its sound, shape, language, or meaning. Be sure to apply the process of writing as you choose a topic, then present your ideas.

3. Complete your writing assignment dealing with poetry, and share it with the class.

LESSON 8 Writing About Drama

Drama contains the same elements of character, setting, and plot that are found in the short story. As in the short story, drama develops a conflict, and the action of the play builds toward a turning point. However, drama differs from the short story in several important ways. Although people can and do read plays, plays are meant to be performed. Also, the form of a play is different from that of a short story, for a play contains only dialogue and stage directions. Unlike the short story writer, the playwright cannot comment directly on characters or events. Before writing about a play, think about each element that it has in common with a short story. Use the guidance in Lesson 5, **Writing About the Short Story**. Then examine the way that the play unfolds. Ask yourself questions such as these: Is the play divided into parts? What happens in each part? What do you learn from the stage directions? What passages of dialogue seem especially important?

Considering the Assignment

An essay question or writing assignment dealing with a play may ask you to examine an element such as plot, setting, or a major or minor character or to discuss the conflict. An assignment may ask you to look at how the play is divided into acts and scenes and to explain the reasons for the divisions. Writing assignments also can ask for comments on material in the stage directions, such as descriptions of sound effects and music.

Following the Writing Process

As you complete a writing assignment on a play, follow the process of writing discussed on pages 614–622. Work carefully through prewriting, writing a draft, revising, and sharing. Keep the following points in mind.

Prewriting

As you read a play, try to imagine how it might look and sound. Be sure to read carefully the stage directions, which are the italicized words in parentheses. These words help readers, as well as actors and directors, to visualize and interpret the play.

For longer plays, you may not be able to reread the entire play before writing an assignment. In these cases, skim the play to find the parts that relate to your purpose. Take detailed prewriting notes on these parts.

You may end up with too many details for the length of the assignment. One solution is to narrow the focus of your topic, then eliminate the details that do not develop the new topic. Another solution is to increase the length of the assignment with your teacher's permission.

Writing the First Draft

Even though no quotation marks set off dialogue in a play, you will need to use these marks when you quote from the play. If you wish to quote a long speech, indent the lines about seven spaces from each margin. The lines will then stand out from the rest of the paragraph or composition.

Revising

When revising, check to be sure that the main idea is fully developed. If it is not, consider narrowing the focus of your topic sentence. Another possibility is to add more details to your paragraph or composition.

Sample Writing Assignment

Grandpa and the Statue, the play that is the subject of this assignment, begins on page 502.

When the veteran expresses his feelings about the statue, Grandpa becomes angry. He says, "I never thought of it that way . . . . If Sheean had put it that way I'd a give him me dime." In two paragraphs contrast Sheean's arguments with the veteran's description of the statue. Begin with a general statement about the difference between the two men's views of the statue. Follow with details that support this generalization.

Sample Prewriting Notes

The purpose of these paragraphs is to show how Sheean's arguments are different from the veteran's description of the statue.

Sheean: statue as status symbol
Veteran: statue as symbol of freedom and hope

Sheean

"It costs the Lord knows how many millions to build. All they're askin' us to do is contribute enough to put up a base for the statue to stand on." (p. 504)

"We'd like to hang up a flag on the corner saying—'Butler Street, Brooklyn, is one hundred percent behind the Statue of Liberty.' " (p. 504)

"It's in Roman numbers. Very high class." (p. 505)

"But all I can say is, you've laid a disgrace on the name of Butler Street." (p. 506)

Sheean never mentions the poem at the base.

Veteran

Veteran's brother was killed in the war; no gravestone in the U.S.

"Yeh, this statue is about the only stone he's got. In my mind I feel it is anyway. This statue kinda looks like what we believe." (p. 514)

" 'Give me your tired, your poor . . . .' " (p. 515)

The writer first skimmed the play. She looked for three things: the quotation in the assignment, Sheean's arguments, and the veteran's conversation with Grandpa. Then, under her statement of purpose, she noted the basic difference between the views of the two men.

Sample First Draft

Using her prewriting notes, the writer began the following first draft.

In "Grandpa and the Statue" Sheean views the statue as a status symbol while the veteran views it as a symbol of freedom and hope. Sheean argues that the statue is worth millions and is "very high class." (p. 505) Sheean also seems more interested in the flag showing that Butler Street is "one hundred percent behind the Statue of Liberty" (p. 504) than in the statue itself. He does not even mention the poem to be inscribed on the base.

The veteran, on the other hand, understands why the Statue of Liberty is so important.

Studying the First Draft

You will notice that the first sentence of the sample presents the contrast that is set up in the statement of purpose and then further refined in the prewriting notes. The rest of the paragraph develops the first idea, Sheean's view of the statue as a status symbol. The second idea, the view of the veteran, is picked up again in the topic sentence of the second paragraph. The words "on the other hand" show that the main idea of this paragraph contrasts with that of the preceding paragraph.

EXERCISES   Writing About Drama

1.   Using the prewriting notes, complete the first draft for the sample writing assignment. Revise your paragraph and make any changes you wish in the sample first draft. Then make a final copy of the two paragraphs.

2.   Complete your writing assignment dealing with drama, and share it with the class.

Vocabulary Development Lessons

Each of the first five lessons on the following pages deals with one vocabulary skill. That skill is the same skill taught in the unit. The sixth lesson reviews the five skills. As you work through the lessons, study the explanation of the skill or skills. Then complete the exercises, writing your answers on a sheet of paper.

Vocabulary Development

Word Origins

The Sources of Words

English words come from many different sources. The following are some of the ways in which words have entered our language.

Words from Old and Middle English.   Modern English contains many words derived from older forms of the language. For example, the word *daisy* comes from two Old English words, *daeges eage,* meaning "day's eye."

Words from Other Languages.   Most of the hundreds of thousands of words in English have been borrowed from other languages. The following are examples of borrowed words.

Latin: author, candle   French: liberty, literature
Greek: drama, myth   Spanish: stampede, canyon

Words from Names.   Some words are based on the names of people or places. The word *titanic,* for example, comes from *Titan.* In Greek mythology, the Titans were a race of giant gods. *Titanic* means "of great size, strength, or power."

Clipped Words.   Some words are clipped, or shortened, forms of longer words. The word *teen,* for example, is a clipped form of *teen-ager. Gym* is a clipped form of *gymnasium.*

Combined Words.   Compounds and blends are formed by combining two words. A compound word is made by combining two existing words to form a new word. *Sawmill* and *milkmaid* are examples of compound words. If letters are dropped when two words are combined, the resulting word is called a blend. The word *laundromat* is a blend of two words, *laundry* and *automatic.*

Echoic Words.   Words that imitate sounds are called echoic words. Examples include *chirp, slurp, quack,* and *buzz.*

Dictionary Etymologies

Study the dictionary entry for the word *fable.* Inside the brackets is the etymology, or history, of the word. The symbols and abbreviations *<OFr. <L.* tell you that *fable* comes from an Old French word that was based on the Latin word *fabula,* meaning "a story." The rest of the etymology, *<fari:* see BAN[1], tells you that *fabula* came from the word *fari.* BAN[1] is a cross-reference. If you turned to the first entry for the word *ban,* you would learn that the Latin word *fari* means "to speak."

> **fa·ble** (fā′b'l) *n.* [< OFr. < L. *fabula,* a story < *fari:* see BAN[1]]
> **1.** a fictitious story meant to teach a moral lesson: the characters are usually talking animals **2.** a myth or legend **3.** a story that is not true; a falsehood or fiction —*vi., vt.* **-bled, -bling** to write or tell (fables) —**fa′bler** *n.*

Identifying Word Origins

A. Words from Myths.   The following words are based on names of people and places in mythology. Look up each word in a dictionary to find the name on which the word is based. Then, write a definition for the word.

mentor	atlas	calliope	cereal
martial	museum	panic	jovial

B. Borrowed Words.   Use a dictionary to identify the language or languages from which each of the following words was borrowed. Refer to the abbreviations key in your dictionary as necessary.

labor	volcano	alligator	geography
moccasin	algebra	skeleton	kindergarten
haiku	ski	courage	frankfurter

C. Words Formed from Other Words.   Decide whether each of the following words is a compound, a blend, or a clipped word. Use a dictionary, if necessary. Then write the words or words from which each one was made.

bus	smog	thunderstorm	grasshopper
sitcom	spacesuit	phone	plane
doorway	lab	baseball	gasohol

D. Echoic Words.   Write a dictionary definition for each of the following echoic words. Then on a sheet of paper write five echoic words that you can add to the list.

caw	hiccup	jingle	squawk
thump	gargle	sizzle	boom

Vocabulary Development UNIT 2

Dictionaries and Glossaries

Dictionaries

Types of Dictionaries.   There are two main types of general dictionaries: unabridged and abridged. An unabridged dictionary contains detailed information about hundreds of thousands of words. An abridged dictionary is much shorter and more convenient to use. For most of your work, you will use an abridged dictionary.

The Parts of a Dictionary Entry.   Look at the following dictionary entry for the word *previous.*

> **pre·vi·ous** (prē′vē əs) *adj.* [< L. < *prae-*, before + *via*, a way]
> **1.** occurring before in time or order; earlier [at a *previous* meeting; on the *previous* page] ☆**2.** [Colloq.] too soon; premature
> —**previous to** before —**pre′vi·ous·ly** *adv.*
> **SYN.—previous** generally implies a coming before in time or order [a *previous* meeting]; **prior** adds to this the idea of greater importance or claim as a result of being first [a *prior* obligation]; **preceding,** esp. when used with the definite article, implies a coming just before [the *preceding* night]; **antecedent** adds to the meaning of **previous** the idea of directly causing what follows [events *antecedent* to the war]; **foregoing** applies specif. to something previously said or written [the *foregoing* examples]; **former** always implies comparison between the first and the last (called *latter*) of two persons or things just mentioned —**ANT. following**

Notice that the entry word is printed in dark type and is divided into syllables. The pronunciation of the word is given in parentheses. Next, the entry lists the abbreviation for the part of speech of the word. The abbreviation **adj.** tells you that *previous* is an adjective.

The word's etymology, or history, is given in dark brackets. Following the etymology are the definitions of the word. Notice the abbreviation Colloq. in light brackets. This abbreviation indicates that the second definition defines the word as it is used in informal speech and writing. Next, a phrase in which the entry word appears (*previous to*) and a word derived from the entry word (*previously*) are listed in dark letters.

The abbreviation SYN. stands for synonymy. A synonymy is a list of words that are similar in meaning to the entry word. This synonymy explains the differences in the meanings of *previous, prior, preceding, antecedent, foregoing,* and *former.* The abbreviation ANT., which stands for antonym, follows the synonymy. This entry lists one antonym, or word that means the opposite of the entry word.

Glossaries

At the back of many books is a glossary. A glossary, like a dictionary, is an alphabetical listing of words and their definitions. A glossary, however, defines only the difficult or unusual words in the book. In addition to definitions, many glossaries also give the pronunciations and parts of speech of entry words. A pronunciation key explains the symbols used.

Using Dictionaries and Glossaries

A. Identifying the Parts of a Dictionary Entry. Answer the questions using the sample dictionary entry on the opposite page.
1. What is the history of the word *previous*?
2. What word is derived from the entry word?
3. Is *previous* a noun or an adjective?
4. How many definitions are given for the entry word?
5. What is an antonym for *previous*?
6. How many synonyms are listed in the synonymy?
7. How many syllables are there in *previous*?

B. Using a Glossary. Read each of the following sentences from stories in Unit 2. Look up the italicized word in each sentence in the Glossary of this book. Write a definition for each word.
1. "It was an old, large *galvanized* pot she had picked up at an army surplus store in Santa Maria the year I was born."
2. "I turned around and saw most of the town people and the entire bus *delegation* looking at me."
3. "She opened her eyes at that and held up her long lovely neck suspiciously and decided to be *incredulous.*"
4. "Fiona was *aghast.* What would happen now?"
5. "He surveyed the fence, and all gladness left him and a deep *melancholy* settled down upon his spirit."

Context Clues

The context of a word is the sentence or group of sentences in which the word appears. You often can find clues to a word's meaning in its context.

Types of Context Clues

Several types of context clues can help you figure out the meanings of unfamiliar words. These include:

Definition.   A writer sometimes will define an unfamiliar word.

A *shoal* is a large school of fish.

Restatement.   Another kind of context clue restates an idea in another way.

This shirt is made of *khaki,* a strong cloth that is yellow-brown in color.

Example.   Writers sometimes give one or more examples.

The campers packed *provisions* such as cornmeal, bacon, beans, powdered milk, and dried fruits.

Comparison.   In comparison a writer compares an unfamiliar word with other, more familiar words or ideas.

The *cavern* looked similar to the cave we had explored the day before.

Contrast.   A writer may contrast an unfamiliar word with other, more familiar words or ideas.

My brother often loses his *composure.* My sister, on the other hand, rarely gets upset.

Inferring Word Meanings

Sometimes a sentence or passage will not have obvious context clues to help you discover the meaning of an unfamiliar word. Instead, you may have to figure out the meaning by using inference. Inference is the process of drawing conclusions from known facts. You can use inference to figure out the meaning of the italicized word in the following passage.

Ms. Adams has just published a collection of *essays.* Some of the essays give her opinions about events in the news. Others describe events in everyday life from a humorous point of view. In some of her essays, Ms. Adams tries to persuade the reader to accept her point of view on a particular subject.

From the details in the paragraph, you can infer the following: An essay is a kind of nonfiction writing. It may express the writer's opinion on a subject. An essay also may try to persuade the reader to accept the writer's point of view. Some essays are written to amuse the reader.

Learning Word Meaning from Context

A. Using Context Clues.   Choose the best meaning for the italicized word in each of the following sentences.

1. When we were old enough to be of real service, we went to the field with our parents, not to play, but to *toil.*
   a. sleep   b. work   c. sing   d. eat
2. His work in East Africa requires him to travel over tremendous distances. These journeys are called *safaris.*
   a. short trips   c. picnics
   b. vacations   d. long journeys
3. A *moral* is a lesson taught through a story.
   a. fable   c. lesson
   b. opinion   d. idea
4. At the zoo the children saw several *mammoth* animals, including an elephant, a hippopotamus, a polar bear, and a rhinoceros.
   a. huge   c. fierce
   b. hairy   d. hungry

B. Inferring Word Meanings.   Determine the meaning of the underlined word in each passage. Identify the clues that led to your conclusion.

1. "The steam-driven *carousel,* with its elegantly carved and painted wooden horses, was an instant success. Families flocked to amusement parks on weekends to ride their favorite steeds, to the accompaniment of gay organ music."
2. "I stopped and did my best to turn him back, shouting to make myself heard in the storm. 'Stickeen, you must be *daft.* Go back to camp and keep warm. Get a good breakfast with your master, and be sensible for once. I can't carry you all day or feed you; and this storm will kill you.'"

Synonyms and Antonyms

Writers sometimes use synonyms and antonyms to clarify the meanings of difficult words. By choosing synonyms and antonyms carefully, writers also make their language more precise.

Synonyms.   Synonyms are words that have similar meanings. For example, the words *steal, rob,* and *burglarize* all share the general meaning of "to take another person's property." However, each word has a more exact definition.

steal—to take property dishonestly, especially in a secret manner
rob—to take personal property by using or threatening force
burglarize—to break into a house in order to steal

When choosing among synonyms, writers select the word with the precise meaning that they wish to convey. Many dictionary entries contain lists of synonyms.

Antonyms.   Antonyms are words that have opposite meanings. The following pairs of words are antonyms: *joyous* and *sad, simple* and *complex, night* and *day.*

Antonyms sometimes reveal the meanings of difficult words, as in the following example:

Jane thought that the play was *enthralling,* but I thought that it was boring.

Enthralling and *boring* are antonyms, or opposites.
Antonyms are listed at the end of many dictionary entries.
For more information on synonyms and antonyms, refer to the vocabulary development lesson on dictionaries and glossaries.

The Thesaurus. A thesaurus is a listing of words and related words. These related words may be synonyms, words derived from the entry word, or antonyms. Before you use a synonym or an antonym that you find in a thesaurus, be sure to check the complete definition of the word in a dictionary.

Here is an entry from a thesaurus:

> **humorous** *adj. The play was so humorous that the audience laughed all through it:* funny, comic, comical, full of humor, witty, droll, mirthful, laughable, amusing, sidesplitting, rib-tickling, facetious, waggish, whimsical, sportive, jocular, jocose, farcical, satirical; ludicrous, ridiculous, nonsensical.
> ***Ant.*** unfunny, grave, serious, solemn, sober; sad, melancholy; earnest, matter-of-fact.

Using Synonyms and Antonyms

A. Synonyms. Use a dictionary or a thesaurus to find two synonyms for each of the following words. Write a definition for each word and for each of its synonyms.

alibi   engulf   alight   encumber   lair

B. Antonyms. Use the antonym given in each sentence to figure out the meaning of the italicized word. Write a definition for the italicized word. Check your definition in a dictionary.

1. Although I had promised not to *disclose* the secret, I found that I couldn't hide it any longer.
2. Daniel did his best to *console* his sister, but his words seemed to upset her even more.
3. Patrick is a very *arrogant* person, while Pam is quite humble.
4. The cowboy's face was so *ruddy* that everyone else looked pale by comparison.

C. The Thesaurus. Answer the questions using the sample entry.

1. What part of speech is the entry word?
2. How many synonyms are given for the entry word?
3. What are six synonyms for the word *humorous*?
4. How many antonyms are given for *humorous*?
5. What are three antonyms for *humorous*?

Vocabulary Development   UNIT 5

Word Parts

All English words are made up of one or more word parts. The four kinds of word parts are base words, prefixes, suffixes, and roots. You often can determine the meaning of an unfamiliar word by studying its parts.

Base Words.   A base word is a complete word to which other word parts may be added. For example, the base word *use* can become *useful, reuse, misuse,* and *useless.*

Prefixes.   A prefix is a word part added to the beginning of a base word or root to change the meaning of that word. For example:

Prefix	Prefix Meaning	Example	Word Meaning
pre-	before	prepay	to pay beforehand
in-	not	incomplete	not complete
un-	not; the opposite of	untidy	not tidy
semi-	half; partly	semiprivate	partly private

Suffixes.   A suffix is a word part added to the end of a base word or root to form a new word. For example:

Suffix	Suffix Meaning	Example	Word Meaning
-ic	like; pertaining to	angelic	like an angel
-ful	full of	joyful	full of joy
-able, -ible	able to	adjustable	able to be adjusted

Roots.   A root is the part of a word that contains its basic meaning. Unlike base words, roots cannot stand alone as complete words.
   Many of the roots used in English originally came from Greek or Latin. For example:

Greek or Latin	Meaning	Example	Word Meaning
cede	go	recede	to go back
stat	stand, put in a place	status	position, rank, standing
vis	see	vision	the act of seeing

Identifying Word Parts

A. Prefixes and Base Words. Choose the best definition for the italicized word in each sentence.

1. The features of the soldiers are utterly *indistinct.*
   a. very clear
   b. not clear
   c. clearer
   d. clear again

2. Monaghan responds with some *uncertainty.*
   a. completely certain
   b. beyond certainty
   c. lack of certainty
   d. full of certainty

3. Grandpa's fears *predate* his first visit to the Statue of Liberty.
   a. come before
   b. come above
   c. come after
   d. come under

B. Suffixes and Base Words. Choose the best definition for the italicized word in each sentence.

1. The setting of the play is a *peaceful* battlefield.
   a. like peace
   b. able to be at peace
   c. full of peace
   d. without peace

2. Child Monaghan made an *enjoyable* visit to the Statue of Liberty.
   a. pertaining to enjoyment
   b. able to be enjoyed
   c. without enjoyment
   d. not able to be enjoyed

3. The actor's first *dramatic* performance was a portrayal of Zeke.
   a. not like drama
   b. the opposite of drama
   c. before drama
   d. pertaining to drama

C. Prefixes, Suffixes, and Roots. The italicized word in each of the following sentences contains one Latin or Greek root plus a prefix or a suffix. Choose the best definition for each italicized word.

1. The Statue is *visible* from the deck of the ferry.
   a. pertaining to seeing
   b. able to be seen
   c. not seen
   d. partly seen

2. One director suggested that a conversation between the doctor and the attendant should *precede* the doctor's experience with the wounded men.
   a. go before
   b. not go
   c. able to go
   d. go after

3. The statue is a *static* piece of scenery.
   a. able to stand
   b. pertaining to standing
   c. stand before
   d. one who stands

Vocabulary Development   UNIT 6

Review

The vocabulary exercises in this book deal with a number of skills, including the following:

Identifying Word Origins. Words in the English language come from many different sources. These sources include Old and Middle English, languages other than English, and the names of people and places. New words can be formed by clipping longer words, by combining two words, and by imitating sounds.

Using Dictionaries and Glossaries. Dictionaries and glossaries are both alphabetical lists of words and their definitions. A dictionary contains more words and more complete information on each word. A glossary contains only those words used in one book.

Learning Word Meaning from Context. Sentences and paragraphs often include clues to the meanings of unfamiliar words. Types of context clues include definition, restatement, example, comparison, and contrast. More general clues also may suggest the meanings of unfamiliar words.

Using Synonyms and Antonyms. Synonyms are words that have similar meanings. Antonyms are words that have opposite meanings. A thesaurus includes synonyms and antonyms.

Identifying Word Parts. The four kinds of word parts are base words, prefixes, suffixes, and roots. A base word is a complete word to which other word parts may be added. These other word parts may be prefixes or suffixes. Word parts also may be added to roots. A root contains the basic meaning of a word.

Applying Vocabulary Skills

A. Word Origins. Explain the origin of each word. Use the information given in a dictionary.

novel	coon	cricket
dog	hydrophobia	possum
outcropping	animal	San Antonio

B. Dictionaries and Glossaries. Read the following sentences. Look up the italicized words in the Glossary in this book. Write definitions for the words. Then, look up the same words in a dictionary. What new information do you learn from the dictionary entry?

1. "They kept them as watchdogs against the *depredations* of loafer wolves, bears, panthers, and raiding Indians."
2. "But as soon as Mama had wrapped his hands in a *poultice* of mashed-up prickly pear root to draw out the poison, Little Arliss forgot all about his hurt."
3. "I got my knife out and cut a green *mesquite* sprout."

C. Context Clues. Determine the meanings of the italicized words.

1. "The corn was ripening into roasting ears now, and the coons would come at night and strip the *shucks* back with their little hands, and gnaw the milky kernels off the cob."
2. "And I don't guess I ever saw a more helpless look on Mama's face as she took it. Mama had always been *squeamish* about lizards and snakes and bugs and things, and you could tell that it just made her flesh crawl to have to touch this one."

D. Synonyms and Antonyms. Use a dictionary or a thesaurus to find two synonyms for each of the following words.

rage	stout	solemn	rascal	inquire

E. Word Parts. Choose the best definition for the italicized word in each of the following sentences.

1. "Travis admired Old Yeller for his *heroic* actions in the face of great danger."
   a. able to be a hero   c. like a hero
   b. not a hero   d. the opposite of a hero
2. "They may seem mighty cruel and *unfair,* but that's how life is a part of the time."
   a. partly fair   c. full of fairness
   b. able to be fair d. the opposite of fair
3. "I lay there in bed, mad and *fretful* all day, thinking how silly it was for Lisbeth to expect me to want a pup when I already had me a full-grown dog."
   a. full of irritation   c. not irritated
   b. able to be irritated   d. partly irritated

$\mathcal{H}$andbook of Literary Terms

Act. An act is a major unit of action in a play. It may have more than one setting and can include several scenes. Each of the plays in this book contains one act.

See *Scene.*

Alliteration. Alliteration is the repetition of consonant sounds at the beginnings of words. The technique is found in all types of prose and poetry, as well as in everyday speech. Many tongue twisters, such as "*P*eter *P*iper *p*icked a *p*eck of *p*ickled *p*eppers," contain alliteration. Writers use alliteration to give their work a musical quality and to emphasize certain words. Notice the use of alliteration in the following lines.

Look for a *l*ovely thing and you will *f*ind it,
It is not *f*ar—
                    SARA TEASDALE
                    "Night"

See *Repetition.*

Allusion. An allusion is a reference to another work of literature or to a familiar person, place, or event outside of literature. Usually the reader must understand the allusion before he or she can understand the selection. The poem "in Just—," by e.e. cummings, contains an allusion to Pan, a minor god from Greek mythology.

it's
spring
and
        the
            goat-footed

balloonMan   whistles
far
and
wee

Cumming's balloonMan reminds the reader of Pan because of the similarities between the two. Both Pan and the balloonMan are associated with spring. The balloonMan is "goat-footed." Pan was half man and half goat. The balloonMan whistles. Pan played a pipe made of reeds.

Anecdote. An anecdote is a brief story told to entertain or to make a point. The following anecdote is from John Steinbeck's *Travels with Charley.*

I was reminded of a time in Pacific
Grove when I was painting the inside of
a cottage my father had built there
before I was born. My hired helper worked
beside me, and neither of us being expert,
we were well splattered. Suddenly we
found ourselves out of paint. I said
"Neal, run up to Holman's and get a half
gallon of paint and a quart of thinner."
    "I'll have to clean up and change my
clothes," he said.

    "Nuts! Go as you are."
    "I can't do it."
    "Why not? I would."
    Then he said a wise and memorable thing.
"You got to be awful rich to dress as bad
as you do," he said.

Aphorism. An aphorism is a brief statement, often of a general truth. The following are some famous aphorisms:

Life is short; art, long.
HIPPOCRATES

Beauty is in the eye of the beholder.
MARGARET WOLFE HUNGERFORD

The more things change, the more they remain the same.
ALPHONSE KARR

The only way to have a friend is to be one.
RALPH WALDO EMERSON

Autobiography. An autobiography is the story of a person's life, written by that person. It is a form of nonfiction. It does, however, have many of the same elements as fiction. Characterization, setting, plot, suspense, conflict, mood, and tone may all be part of an autobiography. An autobiography can tell a person's whole life story or just an episode from his or her life. The following was written by opera singer Marian Anderson. She tells about trying to enroll in music school. This autobiography, like most autobiographies, is written in the first person.

> There was a young girl behind a cage who answered questions and gave out application blanks to be filled out. When my turn came, she looked past me and called on the person standing beside me. This went on until there was no one else in line. Then she spoke to me, and her voice was not friendly. "What do you want?"
> I tried to ignore her manner and replied that I had come to make inquiries regarding an application for entry to the school.
> She looked at me coldly and said, "We don't take colored."
> MARIAN ANDERSON
> "Shock"

See *Biography*.

Ballad. A ballad is a poem that tells a story in four-line or six-line stanzas. In the past, ballads were written to be sung. Ballads usually tell about people who have had amazing adventures or have performed daring deeds.

Most ballads follow a standard form. Each stanza has the same rhythm, rhyme, and number of lines. Sometimes, ballads have a refrain at the end of each stanza. "Johnny Appleseed," on page 424, is a ballad by the American poet Rosemary Carr Benét. The following is an American version of an English ballad, "Barbara Allen":

> 'Twas in the merry month of May
> When the green buds were swelling.
> Sweet William on his deathbed lay
> For the love of Barbara Allen.
>
> "O, father, father, dig my grave.
> O, dig it deep and narrow.
> Sweet William died for me today.
> I shall die for him tomorrow."
>
> They buried her by the old church tower,
> And William, he was buried nigh her,
> And from her grave grew a red, red rose,
> And from his grave, a briar.
>
> They twined and twined above the ground
> To the very top of the steeple's spire,
> And there they met in a true love's knot,
> The red, red rose and the briar.

See *Narrative Poem.*

Biography. A biography is the story of a person's life, written by another person. It is a form of nonfiction. A biography has many of the same elements as fiction. Characterization, setting, plot, suspense, conflict, mood, and tone may all be part of a biography. The following excerpt is from a biography of Marc Chagall, a twentieth-century painter.

> One day Marc felt the time had come to bring up the subject of art. It was morning. His mother was alone, putting the bread in the oven. Marc watched her nervously; then, sud-

denly, he went up to her, took her by her flour-smeared elbow, and said: "Mama, I want to be a painter."

HOWARD GREENFIELD
Marc Chagall

See *Autobiography.*

Character. A character is a person or animal who takes part in the action of a work of literature. Generally, the plot of a short story focuses on one character, the main character. A story may also have one or more minor characters. In Sean O'Faolain's "The Trout," on page 108, the main character is Julia. The other characters in the story are minor characters. Minor characters keep the action moving forward and help the reader learn more about the main character.

Characterization. Characterization is the use of literary techniques to reveal the nature of a character. A writer may reveal character in many different ways. In the following excerpt from the short story "Nancy," Elizabeth Enright uses a physical description to give the reader information about a character named Fiona.

> She [Fiona] wore her hair as her mother had worn it in 1914, braided tight and tied back in pretzel loops with big stiff ribbons. In winter she was the only girl at school to wear a flannel petticoat and underwear with sleeves.... She was a pensive child with large attentive eyes and rather elderly manners.

Elizabeth Enright also uses a narrator to make direct comments about Fiona. For example, the narrator calls Fiona a "quaint little creature." Through the narrator, the reader learns that Fiona pulls the eyes and hair from her dolls; that she lives in a dull, dustless house; and that all the people in her life are older than she is.

A writer also may describe what a character says, thinks, feels, and does. For example, Fiona says that she loves the Fadgins, the people whose home she visits when she runs away. Later in the story, Fiona feels homesick for the Fadgin household.

Often writers reveal a character through the comments, actions, and feelings of other characters. In "Nancy," Mother and Grandmother call Fiona "my baby." This suggests to the reader just how sheltered Fiona has been.

Climax. The climax, or turning point, is the high point of interest or suspense in a story or play. It is the moment when the outcome of the story suddenly becomes clear. Sometimes, the climax and resolution of a story are the same. In "Winter Thunder," the climax comes when the plane arrives to rescue Lecia and the children.

See *Resolution.*

Complication. A complication is an event that heightens, or complicates, a conflict that has already been introduced. In the novel *Old Yeller,* the central conflict is a struggle between a boy and the natural world. A complication is the breaking away of a dirt bank on which the boy is lying while marking some hogs. When this bank breaks, the boy is plunged into the midst of the hogs. The conflict is therefore complicated, or intensified.

Concrete Poem. A concrete poem visually presents something important about the poem's meaning. William Jay Smith's "Seal," on page 441, is a concrete poem. The shape of the poem suggests the body and motion of a seal.

See *Shape.*

Conflict. Conflict is a struggle between opposing forces. It creates tension and suspense and is an essential ingredient in every play or story. There are two major types of conflict: internal and external.

An internal conflict takes place inside the mind of a character. For example, in the novel *Old Yeller,* Travis has an internal conflict when he must choose between killing Old Yeller and risking the lives of his family.

An external conflict takes place between a character and some outside person or force. Sometimes an external conflict is a struggle between characters. In the play *Grandpa and the Statue,* on page 502, for example, Sheean and Monaghan are in conflict. At other times the struggle is between one or more characters and the forces of nature, as in John Muir's *Stickeen,* on page 284. Yet another kind of external conflict is the struggle between a character and society. For example, in "Frederick Douglass: Fighter for Freedom" on page 373, Frederick struggles against a society that favors slavery.

Description. Description is writing that creates a picture of a scene, event, or character. Writers choose their words carefully and use vivid adjectives and verbs to create exact descriptions. Notice how the italicized words in the following passage help to create a clear picture of the character being described.

> Out of the dimness a figure approached: a *small, thin old* lady. The first thing they noticed about her was the *queerness* of her clothes; they seemed like *fancy-dress* clothes, so *old-fashioned* and *long* and *sweeping.* Her *white* hair, *curled in multitudes of little pleaty ridges,* was *dressed in a pompadour,* and on top, *like a small vessel on a choppy sea,* a *red velvet* bow was riding. Now she smiled: a whole *lacy* set of *smiling* wrinkles came into view.
>
> ELIZABETH ENRIGHT
> *Gone-Away Lake*

See *Mood* and *Setting.*

Dialect. A dialect is the variety of a language spoken by the people of a region or social group. Four major regional dialects are spoken in the United States. One is the Southern dialect; another is the Western. Writers often use dialect to make their characters seem more real. Mark Twain, for example, uses dialect in "The Glorious Whitewasher," on page 176. Here is another example of dialect in a story.

> "Do you aim to tell 'em where the dog is?" Skeeter asked.
> Cash looked at Jesse, then at the ground. "It ain't none of my business."
> "How 'bout you, Uncle Jess?"
> "I ain't telling nobody nothin'."
> "I know she's the same dog," Skeeter said. "On account of I just know it. But she's mine now." His voice rose and trembled. "And ain't nobody gonna take her away from me."
>
> JAMES STREET
> "Weep No More, My Lady"

Dialogue. A dialogue is a conversation between two or more characters. When people "talk" in a story, they seem more real. They also give hints about their own personalities and about other characters.

Dialogue is used in almost all forms of writing. It is most important in a play, in which it is the only way a writer can tell the story. No quotation marks are used for dialogue in plays. In other writing, dialogue is set apart with special punctuation, as in the following example.

Daddy didn't miss a detail of the preparations as she [Jade Snow] dashed from room to room. He waited until she was finished before he demanded, "Jade Snow, where are you going?"

"I am going out into the street," she answered.

"Did you ask my permission to go out into the street?"

"No, Daddy."

"Do you have your mother's permission to go out into the street?"

"No, Daddy."

A sudden silence from the kitchen indicated that Mama was listening.

JADE SNOW WONG
"A Measure of Freedom"

Drama. Drama is writing that tells a story through dialogue and action. Drama is meant to be performed by actors and actresses who take the parts of the characters in the story.

Playwrights usually give stage directions. These directions tell actors how to move and how to read certain lines. Stage directions also include suggestions for sound effects and music and information about the lighting and design of the stage set.

A play is made up of one or more acts. Each act may have several scenes that represent changes in time or place. Each act builds toward an emotional peak. The final act contains the climax of the entire play.

See *Act, Dialogue, Scene,* and *Stage Directions.*

Episode. An episode is a self-contained section of a longer story. In "Demeter," on page 21, the section that begins with Persephone picking flowers and ends with her being taken into the earth is an episode.

See *Scene.*

Essay. An essay is a brief nonfiction work that deals with one subject, often in a personal way. For example, "Langston Terrace," on page 386, is an essay. It tells about life in a Washington, D.C. housing project from the point of view of someone who lived there.

Exposition. Exposition is the part of a plot that provides background information and that introduces the setting and the important characters. The following is the exposition from "How Humans Got Fire," on page 14.

In the beginning, Obassi Osaw made all things on earth, but he did not give fire to humans. It was very cold, and the people in the villages huddled together for warmth. Finally, one of the chiefs cried out, "It is not fair. What is the use of Obassi Osaw putting us on earth if he will not give us fire to comfort ourselves?" He grabbed his youngest son and said, "Go to Obassi Osaw; tell him we must have fire!"

Extended Metaphor. An extended metaphor is a series of comparisons between two unlike things that have several elements in common. For example, in "Jetliner," on page 455, Naoshi Koriyama makes several comparisons between the jetliner and a human runner.

See *Metaphor* and *Simile.*

Fable. A fable is a brief story, usually with animal characters, that teaches a lesson about human nature. The animals in fables usually speak and act like humans.

The most widely known fables are those said to have been told by a Greek slave named Aesop. He is supposed to have lived in the sixth century B.C. "The Hare and the Tortoise" is one popular fable by Aesop. The moral, or lesson, of this fable is "Slow and steady wins the race."

See *Moral.*

Fairy Tale. A fairy tale is a type of children's story in which magic plays a central role. In "The White Snake," on page 50, the flesh of the snake is magical. Anyone who eats it becomes able to understand the speech of animals. "The White Snake" is one of many fairy tales collected by Jakob and Wilhelm Grimm. Other famous Grimm's tales include "Rapunzel" and "Cinderella."

Fiction. Fiction is writing about imaginary people, places, and events. Some stories are entirely fictional. In these stories, everything comes from the writers' imaginations. Other stories are only partly fictional. Such stories include some real and some imaginary people, places, and events.

See *Anecdote, Nonfiction, Novel,* and *Short Story.*

Figurative Language. Figurative language is language that communicates ideas beyond the literal meanings of the words. Some common types of figurative language are hyperbole, metaphor, personification, and simile.

See *Hyperbole, Metaphor, Personification,* and *Simile.*

Flashback. A flashback is a part of a story that interrupts the sequence of events to relate an earlier conversation, scene, or event. Generally, a plot moves forward in time. However, a writer may interrupt this forward movement to give the reader information from the past. The play *Grandpa and the Statue* is almost all flashback. The play begins with a young man looking at the Statue of Liberty from a hospital window. The statue brings back memories of the young man's grandfather. The playwright then uses a long flashback to show these memories to the audience.

Foil. A foil is a character who provides a striking contrast to another character. In "Shrewd Todie and Lyzer the Miser," on page 182, the wealthy but gullible Lyzer is a foil for the poor but clever Todie.

Folk Tale. A folk tale is a story that is handed down, usually by word of mouth, among the people of a region. Folk tales include fairy tales—children's stories in which magic plays a central role—and tall tales—stories with exaggerated characters and events. Folk tales also include legends, which are based on historical fact.

See *Fairy Tale, Tale,* and *Tall Tale.*

Foreshadowing. Foreshadowing is the technique of hinting about something that has not yet happened. Foreshadowing creates suspense and makes the reader want to find out what is going to happen. Here is an example of foreshadowing:

> The morning it happened—the end of my lovely world—I did not water the lilac bush outside my father's study.
> ESTHER HAUTZIG
> *The Endless Steppe*

Hero. A hero is the main character in a story. Usually a hero has admirable qualities. In older literary works, heroes tend to be better than ordinary human beings. They are courageous, strong, honorable, and intelligent. They are protectors of society who hold back the forces of evil and fight to make the world a better place. Ulysses, King Arthur, and Robin Hood are examples of such heroic figures.

In modern literature, the hero is simply the most important character in a story. Such heroes are often ordinary people with ordinary problems. The hero of a modern work may have unheroic traits such as greed, jealousy, or fear. For example, Grandpa, the hero of *Grandpa and the Statue,* is stingy and stubborn.

Hyperbole.   Hyperbole is an exaggeration for emphasis. In everyday speech, people use hyperbole when they say, "I'm dying of thirst" or "That sweater cost a fortune." Often hyperbole is used for humorous effect. The following example from a tall tale tells how the cowboy Pecos Bill rode a cyclone.

> What Bill planned to do was leap from his horse and grab the cyclone by the neck. But as he came near and saw how high the top of the whirling tower was, he knew he would have to do something better than that. Just as he and his horse came close enough to the cyclone to feel its hot breath, a knife of lightning streaked down into the ground. It stuck there, quivering, just long enough for Bill to reach out and grab it. As the lightning bolt whipped back up into the sky, Bill held on. When he was as high as the top of the cyclone, he jumped and landed astraddle its black, spinning shoulders.
>   ADRIEN STOUTENBURG

Imagery.   See *Sensory Images.*

Inciting Incident.   The inciting incident is the event that introduces the central conflict and sets in motion the plot of the story. For example, the inciting incident in "Demeter," on page 21, is Hades' kidnapping of Persephone.

Irony.   Irony is a contrast between what is expected and what actually exists or happens. When people say one thing and mean another, they are being ironic. Someone who oversleeps, misses the bus, and forgets his or her lunch might say, "This has been a great morning."

Situations can have irony, too. Suppose you overhear friends planning a party. Many people receive invitations, but you are not invited. On the day of the party, you feel miserable. Your mother makes matters worse by demanding that you run some errands. When you return home and open the door, twenty smiling faces shout, "Surprise!" It is ironic that after all your anger the party is for you.

In "Humans Are Different," on page 139, it is ironic that the archaeologists's attempt to "repair" the human causes the human's death.

Legend.   See *Folk Tale.*

Metaphor.   Metaphor is a direct comparison between two unlike things that have something in common. The poet Rowena Bastin Bennett used metaphor in the line, "A train is a dragon that runs through the dark." In other words, a train thundering through the night has certain things in common with a dragon. The metaphor helps the reader to visualize the train and creates a mood of awe.

Carl Sandburg's poem "Fog," on page 468, uses metaphor to compare fog to a cat.

See *Extended Metaphor* and *Simile.*

Mood.   Mood is the feeling created by a literary work. Sensory images, word choice, dialogue, and setting help to create mood.

The narrator in the following selection is a young American girl of Japanese descent. When the United States went to war with Japan, her family was sent to an internment camp. Notice how the narrator uses sensory images to create a mood of sadness and desolation.

> I looked around my empty room. The clothes that Mama always told me to hang up in the closet, the junk piled on my dresser, the old rag doll I could never bear to part with; they were all gone. There was nothing left in my room, and there was nothing left in the rest of the house. The rugs and furniture were gone, the pictures and drapes were down, and the closets and cupboards were empty. The house was like a gift box after the nice thing inside was gone; just a lot of nothingness.
> YOSHIKO UCHIDA
> "The Bracelet"

Moral. A moral is the lesson taught by a story. It is meant to be a basic guideline for living. All fables end with a moral, but other stories can have morals as well. The following are some familiar morals.

> Don't count your chickens before they're hatched.
> A rolling stone gathers no moss.
> Honesty is the best policy.

See *Aphorism, Fable,* and *Proverb.*

Motif. A motif is an element that appears over and over again in a literary work or in a group of literary works. Magic is a common motif in fairy tales such as "The White Snake," on page 50. The gunfight is a common motif in Westerns such as "The Gift of Cochise," on page 263.

Myth. A myth is a traditional story, usually about a superhuman being or unlikely event. Myths often try to explain why the world is the way it is and why things in nature happen as they do.

Many societies have created myths. Some of the most important myths are those from ancient Greece and Rome. Also interesting are myths from African and Native American cultures.

Narrative. A narrative is any writing that tells a story. The events in a narrative may be real or imaginary. Myths, anecdotes, short stories, novels, narrative poems, autobiographies, and biographies are all narratives.

Narrative Poem. A narrative poem is one that tells a story. "Paul Revere's Ride" is a famous narrative poem by Henry Wadsworth Longfellow.

See *Ballad.*

Narrator. The narrator is the teller of a story. The narrator may be a character in the story or an outside voice created by the writer.

See *Point of View.*

Nonfiction. Nonfiction is writing about real people, places, and events. Nonfiction presents factual information. Biographies, autobiographies, and essays are nonfiction. So are most newspaper and magazine articles, textbooks, and personal journals and diaries. Writers of nonfiction use many of the same techniques used by writers of fiction. Conflict, setting, mood, and imagery can all be part of nonfiction.

See *Fiction*.

Novel. A novel is a work of fiction that is longer and more complex than a short story. In a novel, setting, character, conflict, and plot are developed in detail. This book contains one novel, *Old Yeller.*

See *Fiction.*

Onomatopoeia. Onomatopoeia is the use of words to imitate sounds. Children use onomatopoeia when they call dogs "bow-wows" or trains "choo-choos." *Bow-wow* sounds like a dog barking, and *choo-choo* sounds like a puffing locomotive. Other onomatopoetic words are *bang, growl, pop,* and *screech.*

Writers use onomatopoeia to give their intended meaning double emphasis. A reader gets meaning from what the printed word stands for and from the sound of the word. Notice the effect of onomatopoeia in these lines from C. S. Lewis's "Narnian Suite."

We'll grind and break and bind and take
And plunder ye and pound ye!

Personification. Personification is the giving of human qualities to an object, animal, or idea. In "'I,' Says the Poem," on page 410, for example, Eve Merriam has a poem speak as though it were a person. In "Macavity: The Mystery Cat," on page 416, T. S. Eliot speaks of a cat who is a master criminal.

Plot. Plot is the sequence of events in a story. It is the writer's blueprint, or plan, for what happens, when, and to whom. The plot

of a story begins with a basic situation. The writer introduces a conflict—a problem or struggle faced by the main character. The conflict leads to other events and builds to the climax, or high point of interest and intensity. At this point in the story, or shortly after, some event ends, or resolves, the conflict.

See *Climax, Conflict, Resolution,* and *Subplot.*

Poetry. Poetry is an expression of ideas and feelings in compact, imaginative, and musical language. Most poems are presented in lines rather than in paragraphs. Many poems depend heavily on sensory images, figurative language, and sound devices such as rhythm and rhyme.

See *Stanza.*

Point of View. Point of view is the perspective from which a story is told. A writer may choose to tell the story from the first-person point of view or from the third-person point of view.

In stories told from the first-person point of view, the narrator is a character in the story. He or she uses pronouns such as *I, me,* and *we.*

In stories told from the third-person point of view, the narrator is not a character in the story. This kind of narrator uses pronouns such as *he* and *she.*

See *Narrator.*

Prose. Prose is writing organized into paragraphs. All fiction and nonfiction writing, except for poetry and drama, is prose.

See *Fiction* and *Nonfiction.*

Proverb.   A proverb is a brief saying that expresses a truth or a bit of wisdom. The following are examples of proverbs.

Beauty is only skin deep.
You can lead a horse to water, but you can't make it drink.

Repetition.   Repetition is the technique of using a sound, a word, a phrase, or a line again for emphasis. In the opening lines of "Paul Revere's Ride," Henry Wadsworth Longfellow uses several types of repetition to achieve a musical effect:

Listen my children and you shall hear
Of the midnight ride of Paul Revere.

Longfellow repeats the short *i* sound in the words "L*i*sten," "ch*i*ldren," and "m*i*dnight." He repeats the long *i* sound in "midn*i*ght" and "r*i*de." He also uses two special kinds of repetition—alliteration and rhyme. Alliteration, the repetition of consonant sounds at the beginnings of words, occurs in the words "*m*y" and "*m*idnight" and again in the words "*r*ide" and "*R*evere." Rhyme, the repetition of sounds at the ends of lines, occurs in the words "*hear*" and "Rev*ere*."

Resolution.   The resolution is the point at which the conflict in a literary work ends. In Mark Twain's "The Glorious Whitewasher," on page 176, the resolution occurs when Tom gives up the paintbrush to Ben. At that point, Tom's difficulties are resolved. He simply sits in the shade, planning "the slaughter of more innocents."

Rhyme.   Rhyme is the repetition of syllable sounds at the ends of words. In the following stanza from Kaye Starbird's "Jake Hanson," the first line rhymes with the third, and the second line rhymes with the fourth.

Jake Hanson runs a fix-it shop.
He says he fixes anything
By mending what you break or drop
With wire or nails or glue or string.

Rhyme Scheme.   The rhyme scheme of a poem is the pattern of rhymes at the ends of lines. This pattern is charted by using letters of the alphabet to show which lines end with the same sounds. Notice the rhyme scheme of the following stanza from Edna St. Vincent Millay's "The Courage That My Mother Had."

The courage that my mother had	a
Went with her, and is with her still:	b
Rock from New England quarried;	c
Now granite in a granite hill.	b

Rhythm.   Rhythm is the pattern of stressed and unstressed syllables in a poem. Much of the musical quality of poetry is due to its rhythm. Rhythm also helps to create mood and may suggest movement. In the first part of C. S. Lewis's "Narnian Suite," the rhythm combines with other sounds to suggest frenzied activity.

˘ / ˘ / ˘ / ˘ /
And when the tussle thickens we
˘ / ˘ / ˘ / ˘ /
can writhe and wriggle under it;
˘ / ˘ / ˘ / ˘ /
Then dagger—point'll tickle 'em,
˘ / ˘ / ˘ / ˘ /
and grab and grip'll grapple 'em.

In the second part of "Narnian Suite," the rhythm combines with other sounds to suggest the marching of heavy feet:

With stumping stride in pomp and pride
We come to thump and floor ye;

Scene.   A scene is a unit of action that takes place in one setting. Most plays are divided into several scenes. In *Grandpa and the Statue,* for example, the first scene takes place in a hospital room, the second on a front porch in Brooklyn, and the third in a warehouse.

See *Act* and *Episode.*

Science Fiction.   Science fiction is fiction based on real or imagined scientific developments. Science fiction often presents an imaginary or fantastical view of the future or of the distant past. Examples of science fiction in this book include Ray Bradbury's "All Summer in a Day," on page 132; Alan Bloch's "Humans Are Different," on page 139; and Isaac Asimov's "The Fun They Had," on page 142.

Sensory Images.   Sensory images are words and phrases that appeal to the five senses: sight, hearing, touch, taste, and smell. The following passage contains many sensory images:

Platero is a small donkey, a soft, hairy donkey so soft to the touch that he might be said to be made of cotton, with no bones. Only the jet mirrors of his eyes are hard, like two black crystal scarabs.
I turn him loose, and he goes to the meadow, and, with his nose, he gently caresses the little flowers of rose and blue and gold. I call him softly, "Platero?" and he comes to me at a gay little trot that is like laughter of a vague, idyllic tinkling sound.
He eats whatever I give him. He likes mandarin oranges, amber-hued muscatel grapes, purple figs tipped with crystalline drops of honey.
He is as loving and tender as a child, but strong and sturdy as a rock. Steel and moon silver at the same time.

> JUAN RAMÓN JIMÉNEZ
> *Platero and I*
> translated by Eloise Roach

Sequence.   Sequence is the order of events in a literary work. The most common sequence is chronological order, the order in which events occur in time.

See *Flashback* and *Foreshadowing.*

Setting.   Setting is the time and place of the action of a story. Customs, manners, clothing, scenery, weather, geography, buildings, rooms, furnishings, and methods of transportation are all part of setting.

To create a setting, a writer uses sensory images—words and phrases that appeal to the five senses. The importance of setting differs from story to story. Sometimes setting is fairly unimportant. For example, one folktale by Isaac Bashevis Singer begins, "Somewhere, sometime there lived a rich man." Singer does not tell where or when the action occurs. In other stories, setting is important. In Mari Sandoz's "Winter Thunder," on page 146, the setting—a range during a blizzard—creates the central conflict, or struggle.

Shape.   Shape is the way that words look on the page. Sometimes writers arrange words to suggest the shapes of their subjects. For example, Lillian Morrison's poem "The Sidewalk Racer or On the Skateboard," on page 436, is shaped like a skateboard.

See *Concrete Poem.*

Short Story. A short story is a work of fiction that can be read in one sitting. Usually, a short story develops one major conflict and produces a single effect on its reader. "Nancy," on page 114, and "The Gift of Cochise," on page 263, are both short stories.

See *Fiction.*

Simile. A simile is a comparison using *like* or *as.* "Neat as a pin," "quiet as a mouse," and "strong as an ox" are examples of familiar similes. The last line of the following stanza is a simile used to describe a star.

Twinkle, twinkle little star,
How I wonder what you are!
Up above the world so high,
Like a diamond in the sky!

See *Figurative Language* and *Metaphor.*

Speaker. The speaker in a poem is the voice that talks to the reader. The speaker is not the same as the poet. In Robert Frost's "The Pasture," on page 460, the speaker is someone who lives on a farm and raises cattle.

Stage Directions. Stage directions are notes included in plays to help readers picture the action. Stage directions can describe setting, lighting, sound effects, the movements of actors, and the way in which dialogue is spoken. Generally, stage directions are given in parentheses and printed in italics. The opening of *In the Fog,* on page 518, contains many stage directions.

Stanza. A stanza is a group of lines that form a unit in a poem. Stanzas are like paragraphs in prose selections. Each one develops an idea that relates to the main idea, or theme, of the poem.

In most traditional poems, all the stanzas have the same number of lines and the same rhyme scheme and rhythm. In modern poems, stanzas are often less regular.

Stanzas range from two lines to eight lines or more. Emily Dickinson's poem "I'm Nobody" contains two four-line stanzas:

I'm nobody! Who are you?
Are you nobody, too?
Then there's a pair of us—don't tell!
They'd banish us, you know.
How dreary to be somebody!
How public, like a frog
To tell your name the livelong day
To an admiring bog.

See *Rhyme Scheme* and *Rhythm.*

Stereotype. A stereotype is a character who conforms to a simplified common type. In the story "Shrewd Todie and Lyzer the Miser," on page 182, Lyzer is a stereotypical miser.

Structure. Structure refers to the way in which a story, poem, or play is put together. The poem "Jake Hanson," on page 477, for example, is organized into six stanzas that relate a series of events. The final stanza summarizes the meaning of the experience as a whole.

See *Act, Plot,* and *Scene.*

Style. Style is the way in which a piece of literature is written.

Style refers not to what is said but to how it is said. Many elements go into creating a writer's style: for example, the length of the sentences used, the difficulty of the vocabulary, the tone, the amount of sensory imagery, and the amount of figurative language. To get a sense of differences in style, compare Adrien Stoutenburg's story "J. P. Sousa," on page 128, with the selection from John Muir's *Stickeen,* on page 284. Stoutenburg's style is informal. She uses short, simple sentences and words. She also has her main character speak in a nonstandard dialect. Muir's style, on the other hand, is formal. He uses longer sentences and a more sophisticated vocabulary. Note that one of these writers' styles is not better or worse than the other. Each writer's style fits his or her material and purpose.

Subplot. A subplot is a less important story that is woven into the fabric of the main story. Usually, subplots are found only in long works such as novels and full-length plays. In the novel *Old Yeller,* one subplot concerns the relationship between the main character, Travis, and his younger brother, Arliss.

See *Plot.*

Surprise Ending. A surprise ending is an unexpected twist at the end of a story. The ending is not what the reader anticipates. In Quentin Reynolds's "A Secret for Two," on page 188, the surprise comes when the reader learns that the main character has for a long time been blind. In Francisco Jiménez's "The Circuit," on page 243, the surprise comes when the reader learns that the boy's family is moving once again.

See *Climax* and *Resolution.*

Suspense. Suspense is a feeling of growing tension and excitement felt by a reader. A writer creates suspense by raising questions in the reader's mind. In "The Gift of Cochise," on page 263, Louis L'Amour creates suspense by making the reader wonder whether Angie Lowe can survive on her own. In *In the Fog,* on page 518, Milton Geiger creates suspense by making the reader wonder who the two strange men are, why they are carrying guns, and whether they will harm the main character.

Symbol. A symbol is a person, place, or object that stands for something beyond itself. Many symbols are used in everyday life. The bald eagle is a symbol for the United States. A red cross symbolizes first aid. A skull and crossbones symbolizes poison.

Symbols are a form of shorthand. They can take the place of a long explanation. For example, when a character in a cartoon gets a bright idea, the cartoonist can symbolize this by drawing a lightbulb over the character's head.

In literature, many symbols are drawn from the natural world. Roses are traditional symbols of love and beauty. A dove is a traditional symbol of peace. The moon is a symbol of the fickleness of love. In Sara Teasdale's "Night," a planet symbolizes loveliness:

> Stars over snow
>   And in the west a planet
> Swinging below a star—
>   Look for a lovely thing and you will find it.
> It is not far—
>   It never will be far.

Tale. A tale is a simple story told in prose or poetry. Types of tales include folk tales, fairy tales, tall tales, and legends. Many tales were passed down orally from generation to generation.

Some early storytellers moved from place to place, telling stories in exchange for money or food. They spread their tales throughout their countries and even to neighboring lands. Of course, the tales changed with each retelling. For this reason, the same tale can often be found in many different versions.

See *Fairy Tale, Folk Tale, Myth,* and *Tall Tale.*

Tall Tale. A tall tale is a story with exaggerated characters and events. The more a tall tale is told, the more exaggerated it becomes. "Paul Bunyan," on page 65, is a typical tall tale.

Theme. The theme is the main idea of a work of literature. Often the theme is a message about human nature.

Some literary works are written purely for entertainment. In these, the writer often does not try to convey an important message. However, most writing does attempt to communicate a theme. Sometimes the theme is stated directly. At other times, careful reading and thought may be necessary to uncover the theme.

One theme of the tale "King Midas and the Golden Touch," on page 34, is that greed can bring misery. The theme of Robert Frost's "The Pasture," on page 460, is that the simple joys of nature can be even more pleasurable if they are shared.

Glossary

The Glossary is an alphabetical listing of words from the selections, along with their meanings. Whenever you encounter an unfamiliar word in your reading, look it up in the Glossary.

The Glossary gives the following information:

1. **The pronunciation of each word.** For example, **turbulent** (tur′byə lənt). If there is more than one way to pronounce a word, the most common pronunciation is listed first. For example, **status** (stā′təs, stat′əs).

   A primary accent (′) is placed after the syllable that is stressed the most when the word is spoken. A **secondary accent** (′) is placed after a syllable that has a lighter stress. For example, **imitation** (im′ə tā′shən). The Pronunciation Key below shows the symbols for the sounds of letters, and key words that contain those sounds. Also, there is a short pronunciation key at the bottom of each right-hand page in the Glossary.

2. **The part of speech of the word.** The following abbreviations are used:

adj. adjective	*conj.* conjunction	*pro.* pronoun
adv. adverb	*n.* noun	*v.* verb

3. **The meaning of the word.** The definitions listed in the Glossary are the ones that apply to the way a word is used in these selections.

4. **Related forms.** Words with suffixes such as *-ing, -ed, -ness,* and *-ly* are listed under the base word. For example, **decisive** *adj. . . .* **decisively** *adv.,* **decisiveness** *n.*

Pronunciation Key

Symbol	Key Words	Symbol	Key Words	Symbol	Key Words	Symbol	Key Words
a	ask, fat, parrot	oi	oil, point, toy	b	bed, fable, dub	t	top, cattle, hat
ā	ape, date, play	ou	out, crowd, plow	d	dip, beadle, had	v	vat, hovel, have
ä	ah, car, father	u	up, cut, color	f	fall, after, off	w	will, always, swear
e	elf, ten, berry	ur	urn, fur, deter	g	get, haggle, dog	y	yet, onion, yard
ē	even, meet, money			h	he, ahead, hotel	z	zebra, dazzle, haze
		ə	a in ago	j	joy, agile, badge		
i	is, hit, mirror		e in agent	k	kill, tackle, bake	ch	chin, catcher, arch
ī	ice, bite, high		i in sanity	l	let, yellow, ball	sh	she, cushion, dash
			o in comply	m	met, camel, trim	th	thin, nothing, truth
ō	open, tone, go		u in focus	n	not, flannel, ton	*th*	then, father, lathe
ô	all, horn, law			p	put, apple, tap	zh	azure, leisure
o͞o	ooze, tool, crew	ər	perhaps, murder	r	red, port, dear	ŋ	ring, anger, drink
o͝o	look, pull, moor			s	sell, castle, pass	′	able (ā′b'l)
yo͞o	use, cute, few						
yo͝o	united, cure, globule						

This pronunciation key is from *Webster's New World Dictionary, Students Edition.*
Copyright © 1981, 1976 by Simon & Schuster. Used by permission.

A

abash (ə bash′) *v.* To make ashamed and ill at ease.

abate (ə bāt′) *v.* To become less; subside.

abode (ə bōd′) *n.* Residence; home.

abound (ə bound′) *v.* To be plentiful; to exist in large numbers.

abrupt (ə brupt′) *adj.* Happening suddenly.—**abruptly** *adv.*

abyss (ə bis′) *n.* **1.** A deep or bottomless hole. **2.** A deep crack in the earth; chasm.

access (ak′ses) *n.* Being able to get at or approach.

accommodations (ə käm′ə dā′shənz) *n.* Lodgings.

accomplished (ə käm′plisht) *adj.* Skilled.

acknowledgment (ək näl′ij mənt) *n.* Recognition.

acrid (ak′rid) *adj.* Sharp, bitter.

adamant (ad′ə mənt) *adj.* Not giving in.

adept (ə dept′) *adj.* Highly skilled; expert.

adjacent (ə jā′ sənt) *adj.* Near or close; adjoining.

admire (əd mīr′) *v.* To regard with wonder, delight, and approval.

admonish (əd män′ish) *v.* To criticize mildly.—**admonishingly** *adv.*—**admonishment** *n.*

admonitor (əd män′ə tər) *n.* A person who reminds or warns.—**admonitory** *adj.*

adroit (ə droit′) *adj.* Skillful; clever.—**adroitly** *adv.*

aggravate (ag′rə vāt′) *v.* [Colloq.] To exasperate; annoy.—**aggravation** *n.*

aggressive (ə gres′iv) *adj.* Bold and active; full of energy.

aghast (ə gast′) *adj.* Horrified; terrified.

agitator (aj′ə tāt′ər) *n.* A person who tries to stir up people in support of a social or political cause: often used in disapproval.

alacrity (ə lak′rə tē) *n.* Eager willingness or readiness often shown by quick, lively action.

alder (ôl′dər) *n.* A tree of the birch family.

alibi (al′ə bī′) *n.* An excuse.

alight (ə līt′) *v.* Dismount.

alkali (al′kə lī′) *n.* Any soluble mineral salt found in desert soils.

aloof (ə lōōf′) *adj., adv.* Distant; apart.

amalgam (ə mal′gəm) *n.* Mixture or blend.

amber (am′bər) *n.* A yellowish or brownish-yellow translucent fossil resin used in jewelry. *adj.* Yellow or brownish-yellow.

ambition (am bi′shən) *n.* A thing strongly desired; a goal.

amends (ə mendz′) *n. pl.* Something given to make up for injury that one has caused.

amiable (ā′mē ə b′l) *adj.* Pleasant; friendly; good-natured.—**amiably** *adv.*

anarchist (an′ər kist) *n.* A person who believes that all forms of government interfere unjustly with individual liberty.

ancestry (an′ses′trē) *n.* Family descent or lineage.

anguish (aŋ′gwish) *n.* Great suffering.

animosity (an′ə mäs′ə tē) *n., pl.* **-ties.** Strong dislike; ill will.

anxiety (aŋ zī′ə tē) *n.* A state of being worried about what might happen.

appall (ə pôl′) *v.* To fill with dismay; to fill with horror; shock.

apparent (ə per′ənt) *adj.* Appearing to be real or true; seeming.

appeal (ə pēl′) *v.* To make a request to a higher power for a decision.

appease (ə pēz′) *v.* To satisfy or relieve.

appendage (ə pen′dij) *n.* Anything appended or attached.

appraise (ə prāz′) *v.* To estimate the quality of.

apprehension (ap′ rə hen′shən) *n.* An anxious feeling or dread.

apprehensive (ap′rə hen′siv) *adj.* Uneasy or fearful about the future.—**apprehensively** *adv.*

apprentice (ə pren′tis) *n.* A person who works for a master craftsman in return for instruction.

apt (apt) *adj.* Quick to learn or understand.

aptitude (ap′tə tōōd′) *n.* An ability.

archaeologist (är′kē äl′ə jist) *n.* One who studies the life and culture of ancient peoples.

ardent (är′d′nt) *adj.* Very enthusiastic; zealous.

arm (ärm) *v.* To equip oneself with weapons.

arrogance (ar′ə gəns) *n.* A feeling of too great self-importance.

arrogant (ar′ə gənt) *adj.* Full of too much pride and self-importance.—**arrogantly** *adv.*

arthritis (är thrīt′əs) *n.* Inflammation of a joint.

artisan (är′tə z′n) *n.* A skilled workman; craftsman.

assess (ə ses′) *v.* To set the amount of.

assurance (ə shoor′əns) *n.* Self-confidence.

astern (ə stʉrn′) *adv.* Behind a ship.

awe (ô) *n.* Deep respect mixed with fear and wonder.

azure (azh′ər) *adj.* Sky-blue.

B

baleful (bāl′fəl) *adj.* Harmful or evil.—**balefully** *adv.*

balmy (bäm′ē) *adj.* Mild, pleasant.

bandanna (ban dan′ə) *n.* A large, colored handkerchief, usually with a printed pattern.

banish (ban′ish) *v.* To send away; get rid of.

bass (bās) *n.* The lowest range of the male voice.

baste (bāst) *v.* To moisten meat with melted butter or drippings during roasting.

bathe (bā*th*) *n.* A swim or dip.

bay[1] (bā) *v.* To bark at.—**at bay** Held off; unable to advance; cornered.

bay[2] (bā) *adj.* Reddish-brown.

bedraggle (bi drag''l) *v.* To make wet, limp, and dirty, as by dragging through mud.—**bedraggled** *adj.*

behest (bi hest') *n.* Order, command, request.

beleaguer (bi lē'gər) *v.* To surround with enemies; harass.

belligerent (bə lij'ər ənt) *adj.* Showing readiness to fight or quarrel.

benevolence (bə nev'ə ləns) *n.* A feeling of kindliness or wanting to do good.—**benevolent** *adj.*

beset (bi set') *adj.* Attacked from all sides; harassed.

besiege (bi sēj') *v.* To close in on, especially with armed forces.

bewilder (bi wil'dər) *v.* To confuse hopelessly.—**bewildered** *adj.*

bicker (bik'ər) *v.* To have a petty quarrel; squabble.

billet (bil'it) *v.* To assign lodgings to.

bivouac (biv'wak, -ᴏᴏ wak') *n.* Camp in the open.

bloat (blōt) *v.* To swell.

blot (blät) *v.* To erase or get rid of.—**blot out** To kill or destroy.

bog (bäg, bôg) *n.* A small marsh or swamp.

bolt (bōlt) *n.* A roll of cloth.

bondage (bän'dij) *n.* Slavery.

bough (bou) *n.* A branch of a tree.

brandish (bran'dish) *v.* To wave or shake in a threatening way.

brine (brīn) *n.* Salt water.

bristle (bris''l) *v.* To have the hair or fur bristles become erect.

broadside (brôd'sīd') *adv.* Directly in the side.

brocade (brō kād') *n.* A rich cloth with a raised design.

brogue (brōg) *n.* A dialect or accent.

brooch (brōch) *n.* A large ornamental pin with a clasp.

brood (brᴏᴏd) *n.* All the children in a family.

burden (bʉrd''n) *n.* A heavy load, as of work, responsibility, or sorrow.

burly (bʉr'lē) *adj.* Heavy and muscular.

C

calcium (kal'sē əm) *n.* A soft, silver-white chemical element found in limestone, marble, and chalk.

calculate (kal'kyə lāt') *v.* To figure out by using mathematics; to compute.

caldron (kôl'drən) *n.* A large kettle.

calico (kal'ə kō') *adj.* Spotted.

calk (kôk) *v.* To make a boat watertight by filling seams or cracks.—**calker** *n.*

candid (kan'did) *adj.* Very honest.

cantle (kan't'l) *n.* The upward-curving rear part of a saddle.

capable (kā'pə b'l) *adj.* Having ability; able; skilled.

caper (kā'pər) *v.* To skip about in a playful manner.

carcass (kär'kəs) *n.* The dead body of an animal.

careen (kə ren') *v.* To lurch from side to side, esp. while moving rapidly.

carousel (kar'ə sel') *n.* Merry-go-round.

casual (kazh'ᴏᴏ wəl) *adj.* Nonchalant; relaxed.

cavalcade (kav''l kād') *n.* A procession of horsemen.

cavern (kav'ərn) *n.* A very large cave.

centaur (sen'tôr) *n.* A creature with a man's head, trunk, and arms and a horse's body and legs.

chafe (chāf) *v.* To rub.

chagrin (shə grin') *n.* A feeling of embarrassment and annoyance because one has failed or has been disappointed.

chandelier (shan'də lir') *n.* A lighting fixture hanging from a ceiling, with branches for candles or bulbs.

Cherokee (cher'ə kē) *n.* A member of a tribe of Iroquoian Indians.

chilblain (chil'blān') *n.* A painful swelling or sore on the foot or hand, caused by exposure to cold.

chinking (chiŋk'iŋ) *n.* Material used to fill narrow cracks.

chops (chäps) *n. pl.* Jaws.

christen (kris''n) *v.* To give a name to at baptism.

clamber (klam'bər) *v.* To climb clumsily or with effort, using both hands and feet.

clamor (klam'ər) *v.* To make a loud, sustained noise.

clarity (klar'ə tē) *n.* Clearness.

coax (kōks) *v.* To persuade or urge by soothing words.

cobble (käb''l) *v.* To pave with rounded stones.

---

fat, āpe, cär; ten, ēven; is, bīte; gō, hôrn, tᴏᴏl, lᴏᴏk; ᴏil, ᴏut; up, fʉr; get; joy; yet; chin; she; thin, *th*en; zh, leisure; ŋ, ring; ə for *a* in *ago*, *e* in *agent*, *i* in *sanity*, *o* in *comply*, *u* in *focus*; ' as in *able* (ā'b'l)

commend (kə mend′) v. To mention as worthy; recommend.

compel (kəm pel′) v. To force to do something.

compensate (käm′pən sāt′) v. To make up for.

competent (käm′pə tənt) adj. Capable.

composite (kəm päz′it) n. A thing formed of distinct parts.

composure (kəm pō′zhər) n. Self-control; calmness.

compound[1] (käm pound′) v. Combine.

compound[2] (käm′pound) n. A substance containing two or more elements chemically combined.

concussion (kən kush′ən) n. Violent shaking.

condescend (kän′də send′) v. 1. To do something thought to be beneath one's dignity. 2. To deal with others in a patronizing manner.—**condescending** adj.

confer (kən fur′) v. To meet for a discussion.

confide (kən fīd′) v. To tell or talk about as a secret.

confidential (kän′fə den′shəl) adj. Private.

confound (kən found′) v. To make feel confused; bewilder.

congest (kən jest′) v. To cause too much blood to collect in the vessels of a part of the body.—**congestion** (-jes′chən) n.

conscientious (kän′shē en′shəs) adj. Showing care and exactness.—**conscientiously** adv.

consent (kən sent′) v. To agree to.

consequence (kän′sə kwens′, -kwəns) n. Importance.

console (kən sōl′) v. To comfort; to make feel less sad or disappointed.

consternation (kän′stər nā′shən) n. Shock or fear that makes one feel helpless or bewildered.

contemplate (kän′təm plāt) v. To look at intently; gaze at.

contempt (kən tempt′) n. The feeling that a person or thing is worthless or beneath notice.—**contemptuous** adj., **contemptuously** adv.

contort (kən tôrt′) v. To twist out of a usual form.

conventional (kən ven′shən′l) adj. Conforming to accepted rules or standards.

co-ordinate (kō ôr′d′n it) n. A person or thing of equal importance.

counterpoint (koun′tər point′) n. The art of combining two separate melodies.

courtyard (kôrt′yärd′) n. An open space surrounded by buildings or walls.

covey (kuv′ē) n. A small group of people or things.

coyote (kī ōt′ē) n. A small wolf of western North America.

crafty (kraf′tē) adj. Sly; cunning.—**craftily** adv.

credo (krē′dō) n. Any statement of belief or opinion.

crest (krest) n. The highest point.

crevice (krev′is) n. A narrow opening caused by a crack or split.

crowbar (krō′bär′) n. A long metal bar used as a lever for prying.

cubicle (kyoo′bi k′l) n. A small room or compartment.

cuff (kuf) v. To strike or hit.

culprit (kul′prit) n. One guilty of a crime.

cunning (kun′iŋ) n. Slyness; craftiness.

cur (kur) n. Mongrel.

curd (kurd) n. The thick, clotted part of soured milk.

curvet (kər vet′) v. For a horse to leap by raising its hind legs just before its forelegs come down again.

custody (kus′tə dē) n. Care; safekeeping.

D

daft (daft) adj. Insane; crazy.

dank (daŋk) adj. Disagreeably damp; moist and chilly.

dapple (dap′′l) v. To cover or become covered with spots.

daunt (dônt) v. To discourage; intimidate.

declare (di kler′) v. To say emphatically.

decorum (di kôr′əm) n. Proper and dignified behavior.

decree (di krē′) v. To give an official order or decision.

deference (def′ər əns) n. Courteous regard or respect for the wishes or opinions of others.

defiance (di fī′əns) n. The act of boldly opposing a powerful person or thing.—**defiant** adj.

deft (deft) adj. Skillful in a quick, sure, and easy way.—**deftly** adv.

degenerate (di jen′ər it) adj. Having sunk below a former condition; deteriorated.

delegation (del′ə gā′shən) n. A group of people representing certain interests or ideas.

deliberate (di lib′ər āt) v. To think and consider carefully.

delirious (di lir′ē əs) adj. Having confused speech and hallucinations.

deliverance (di liv′ər əns) n. A freeing or being freed.

demented (di ment′id) adj. Mad; mentally ill.

depravity (di prav′ə tē) n. Wickedness.

depredation (dep′rə dā′shən) n. A robbing, plundering, or laying waste.

derision (di rizh′ən) *n.* Contempt or ridicule.

desolate (des′ə lit) *adj.* Lonely; uninhabited.

despair (di sper′) *n.* A loss of hope.

despise (di spīz′) *v.* To look down on with hatred.

detach (di tach′) *v.* Separate; remove.

devoid (di void′) *adj.* Empty; completely without.

devout (di vout′) *adj.* Sincere; earnest.—**devoutly** *adv.*

diminish (də min′ish) *v.* To make seem smaller; reduce in size or importance.

diminutive (də min′yoo tiv) *adj.* Very small; tiny.

dimity (dim′ə tē) *n.* A thin cotton cloth.

dingy (din′jē) *adj.* Dirty-colored.

dire (dīr) *adj.* Dreadful; terrible.

dirk (dʉrk) *n.* A short, straight dagger.

discern (di sʉrn′, -zʉrn′) *v.* To recognize; make out clearly.—**discernible** *adj.*

disclose (dis klōz′) *v.* To make known.

discomfit (dis kum′fit) *v.* To make uneasy; embarrass.—**discomfiture** *n.*

discordant (dis kôr′d′nt) *adj.* Conflicting; not in harmony.—**discordantly** *adv.*

discourse (dis′kôrs) *n.* Conversation; talk.

discriminate (dis krim′ə nāt′) *v.* To make or see the difference between; distinguish.

disdain (dis dān′) *n.* Aloof contempt or scorn.

disembody (dis′im bäd′ē) *v.* To separate from the body.—**disembodied** *adj.*

disembowel (dis′im bou′əl) *v.* To take out the bowels, or entrails, of.

disheveled (di shev′′ld) *adj.* Rumpled; untidy.

dismal (diz′m′l) *adj.* Dark and gloomy; dreary.

dismantle (dis man′t′l) *v.* To take apart.

dismiss (dis mis′) *v.* To send away.

dispute (dis pyoot′) *v.* To argue; debate.—*n.* Argument; debate; quarrel.

distaff (dis′ taf) *n.* A staff on which flax or wool is wound for use in spinning.

distort (dis tôrt′) *v.* To twist out of its usual shape or look.

divert (də vʉrt′) *v.* To distract the attention of.

docile (däs′′l) *adj.* Easy to manage or discipline.

dogged (dôg′id, däg′-) *adj.* Persistent; stubborn.—**doggedly** *adv.*

doleful (dōl′fəl) *adj.* Mournful; full of sorrow.

dolly (däl′ē) *v.* To move a camera on a wheeled platform forward or backward as in televising.

doomsday (doomz′dā′) *n.* Judgment day.

dorsal (dôr′s′l) *n.* A fin on the back of a fish.—*adj.* Of, on, or near the back.

dowdy (dou′dē) *adj.* Not stylish in looks or dress.

downy (doun′ē) *adj.* Soft and fluffy, like down.

drawers (drôrz) *n.pl.* An undergarment.

dreary (drir′ē) *adj.* Dull; depressing.

drench (drench) *v.* To make wet all over.

drought (drout) *n.* A long period of dry weather.

dumb (dum) *adj.* Lacking the power of speech.

dun (dun) *adj.* Dull grayish-brown.

E

earthenware (ʉr′thən wer′) *n.* Containers made of baked clay.

eavesdrop (ēvz′dräp′) *v.* To listen secretly to a private conversation.

ecstasy (ek′stə sē) *n.* An overpowering feeling of joy or delight.

edifice (ed′ə fis) *n.* A building, especially one that is large or looks important.

eglantine (eg′lən tīn′,-tēn′) *n.* Rose; sweetbrier.

elation (i lā′shən) *n.* High spirits.

emanate (em′ə nāt′) *v.* To send forth; emit.

embed (im bed′) *v.* To set or fix firmly in a surrounding mass.

emboss (im bôs′) *v.* To decorate with raised designs.

emit (i mit′) *v.* To send out; give forth.

emphatic (im fat′ik) *adj.* Strong; forceful.

enamel (i nam′′l) *v.* To decorate with a smooth, hard, glossy surface, as if with enamel.

encompass (in kum′pəs) *v.* To surround.

encumber (in kum′bər) *v.* To load or weigh down.

endure (in door′) *v.* **1.** To put up with; tolerate. **2.** To last; remain.

engulf (in gulf′) *v.* To swallow up; overwhelm.

enhance (in hans′) *v.* To make greater; heighten.

enlighten (in līt′′n) *v.* To inform; clarify the facts.

entice (in tīs′) *v.* To attract; tempt.

entrails (en′trālz) *n.* The intestines.

entwine (in twīn′) *v.* To twist together or around.

equable (ek′wə b′l) *adj.* Even; serene.

era (ir′ə) *n.* A period of time measured from an important date or event.

essential (ə sen′shəl) *adj.* Basic; absolutely necessary.

esteem (ə stēm′) *v.* To hold to be; consider.

evade (i vād′) *v.* To avoid or escape.

eventuality (i ven′choo wal′ə tē) *n.* A possible outcome.

---

fat, āpe, cär; ten, ēven; is, bīte; gō, hôrn, tool, look; oil, out; up, fʉr; get; joy; yet; chin; she; thin, *th*en; zh, leisure; ŋ, ring; ə for *a* in *ago*, *e* in *agent*, *i* in *sanity*, *o* in *comply*, *u* in *focus*; ′ as in *able* (ā′b′l)

exasperating (ig zas′pə rāt′iŋ) *adj.* Irritating; annoying.—**exasperatingly** *adv.*

execute (ek′sə kyo͞ot′) *v.* To put to death.

exemplary (ig zem′plə rē) *adj.* Model; worth imitating.

exhibit (ig zib′it) *v.* To show; display.

exhilarate (ig zil′ə rāt′) *v.* To make merry or lively.

exodus (ek′ sə dəs) *n.* A going out or forth, especially in a large group.

extinguish (ik stiŋ′gwish) *v.* To put an end to; destroy.

extravagance (ik strav′ə gəns) *n.* An instance of excess in spending, behavior, or speech.—**extravagant** *adj.*

extremity (ik strem′ə tē) *n.* The greatest degree.

extricate (eks′trə kāt′) *v.* To set free; disentangle.

exult (ig zult′) *v.* To rejoice greatly.—**exultation** *n.*

F

fain (fān) *adv.* Gladly or willingly.

falsetto (fôl set′ō) *n.* A voice that is much higher than one's natural voice.

fancy (fan′sē) *v.* To imagine or suppose.

fatigue (fə tēg′) *n.* Physical exhaustion; weariness.

feline (fē′līn) *adj.* Catlike.

ferocity (fə räs′ə tē) *n.* Wild force or cruelty.

fervent (fur′vənt) *adj.* Hot; intensely earnest.—**fervently** *adv.*

fester (fes′tər) *n.* A small sore filled with pus.

feverish (fē′vər ish) *adj.* Greatly excited.

fjord (fyôrd) *n.* A narrow inlet of the sea bordered by steep cliffs.

flagon (flag′ən) *n.* A container for liquids, with a handle, a spout, and, often, a lid.

flank (flaŋk) *n.* The fleshy part of the side of a person or animal between the ribs and hip.

flatterer (flat′ər ər) *n.* One who gives insincere praise in order to win favor.

fleet (flēt) *adj.* Swift.

flounce (flouns) *v.* To move with quick, flinging motions of the body, as in anger.

flounder (floun′dər) *v.* To struggle or plunge about awkwardly.

flute (flo͞ot) *v.* To make ornamental grooves.

fodder (fäd′ər) *n.* Coarse food for animals, such as cornstalks, hay, and straw.

folly (fäl′ē) *n.* Foolishness; lack of sense.

foreman (fôr′mən) *n.* A person in charge of a group of workers.

forlorn (fər lôrn′) *adj.* **1.** abandoned; deserted. **2.** miserable; pitiful.—**forlornly** *adv.*

formality (fôr mal′ə tē) *n.* Ceremony; propriety; careful attention to convention.

fortitude (fôr′tə to͞od′) *n.* The strength to bear misfortune or pain calmly and patiently; courage.

founder (foun′dər) *v.* To cause to stumble, fall, or go lame.

fowl (foul) *n.* A bird used as food, as the chicken, duck, or turkey.

frantic (fran′tik) *adj.* Wild with worry; frenzied.—**frantically** *adv.*

freak (frēk) *adj.* Oddly different from what is normal; queer.

freedman (frēd′mən) *n.* A man legally freed from slavery.

fret (fret) *v.* To worry.

friction (frik′shən) *n.* A rubbing of one object or substance against another.

frivolous (friv′ə ləs) *adj.* Trifling; trivial.

frock (fräk) *n.* A dress.

froth (frôth) *v.* To utter light, trifling talk.

frugal (fro͞o′g'l) *adj.* Not wasteful; thrifty.—**frugally** *adv.*

furrow (fur′ō) *n.* Groove.

furtive (fur′tiv) *adj.* Done or acting in a sly, sneaky way.—**furtively** *adv.*

futile (fyo͞o t′'l) *adj.* Useless; ineffective.

G

galvanize (gal′və nīz′) *v.* **1.** To make someone do something as if by giving an electric shock; excite. **2.** To coat with a layer of zinc.—**galvanized** *adj.*

gape (gāp) *v.* To open wide.

garret (gar′it) *n.* Attic.

gasp (gasp) *v.* Choke.

gaunt (gônt) *adj.* Hollow-eyed and haggard, as from hunger or illness; thin and bony.

geology (jē äl′ə jē) *n.* The science dealing with the physical nature of the earth.

geometrist (jē äm′ə trist) *n.* One who studies geometry, a branch of mathematics.

giddy (gid′ē) *adj.* Not serious in purpose; frivolous.

gilded (gild′id) *adj.* Coated with a gold color.

gin (jin) *v.* To remove seeds from cotton.

gingham (giŋ′əm) *n.* A cotton cloth, usually woven in stripes, checks, or plaids.

glacier (glā′shər) *n.* A large mass of ice and snow that moves slowly down a mountain valley.

glade (glād) *n.* An open space in a forest.

gloat (glōt) *v.* To gaze or think with evil pleasure.

glucose (gloo'kōs) *n.* Sugar syrup.

glutton (glut''n) *n.* A person who greedily eats too much.

gnaw (nô) *v.* To bite repeatedly; consume.

gorge (gôrj) *v.* To stuff oneself with food.

granite (gran'it) *n.* A very hard rock consisting chiefly of feldspar and quartz.

grave (grāv) *adj.* Dignified and solemn.—**gravely** *adv.*

gravity (grav'ə tē) *n.* Solemnness; seriousness.

grieve (grēv) *v.* To feel deep sorrow or distress.

grievous (grē'vəs) *adj.* **1.** Showing or characterized by grief **2.** severe **3.** deplorable.

grim (grim) *adj.* Stern; hard.—**grimly** *adv.*

grimace (gri mās', grim'əs) *n.* A twisting of the face in fun or in a look of pain.

gritty (grit'ē) *adj.* Brave; plucky.

grizzled (griz''ld) *adj.* Gray or streaked with gray.

grope (grōp) *v.* To feel or search about blindly or uncertainly.

grotesque (grō tesk') *adj.* Having a twisted, strange appearance.—**grotesquely** *adv.*

grouse (grous) *n.* A game bird with a round, plump body.

gulf (gulf) *n.* A wide gap or separation that cannot be crossed.

gullible (gul'ə b'l) *adj.* Easily tricked or cheated.

gully (gul'ē) *n.* A channel or hollow worn by running water.

guttural (gut'ər əl) *adj.* Harsh, rasping.

H

hag (hag) *n.* An ugly old woman, especially one who is mean.

haggard (hag'ərd) *adj.* Having a wasted, worn look.

hamstring (ham'striŋ') *v.* To disable by cutting the great tendon at the back of the hock of a four-legged animal.

harass (hə ras') *v.* To trouble by repeated raids or attacks.—**harassment** *n.*

hardpan (härd'pan') *n.* A layer of hard, clayey soil.

harpy (här'pē) *n.* A monster with the head and body of a woman and the wings, tail, and claws of a bird.

harry (har'ē) *v.* To worry or trouble; harass.

haughty (hôt'ē) *adj.* With great pride in oneself and scorn for others; arrogant.—**haughtily** *adv.*

haunch (hônch) *n.* The hindquarter of an animal.

haunt (hônt) *n.* A place often visited.

hearty (härt'ē) *adj.* Sincere; friendly.—**heartily** *adv.*

heathen (hē'thən) *n.* A person regarded as uncivilized, irreligious.

heed (hēd) *n.* Close attention; careful notice.

hellebore (hel'ə bôr') *n.* A plant with poisonous roots used in medicine.

henbane (hen'bān') *n.* A poisonous plant used in medicine.

henceforth (hens fôrth') *adv.* From this time on; after this.

hesitate (hez'ə tāt') *v.* To be reluctant; not be sure that one should.

hessian (hesh'ən) *adj.* Made from a coarse cloth, often used for bags.

hilt (hilt) *n.* **up to the hilt** Thoroughly; entirely.

hinterland (hin'tər land') *n.* An area far from big cities and towns; back country.

hydrophobia (hī'drə fō'bē ə) *n.* Rabies.

I

idle (ī'd'l) *adj.* Not wanting to work; lazy.—**idleness** *n.*

illicit (i lis'it) *adj.* Not allowed; improper.—**illicitly.** *adv.*

immobile (i mō'b'l) *adj.* Not moving; motionless.

immodest (i mäd'ist) *adj.* Improper; bold.

immortal (i môr't'l) *n.* One who never dies, specifically the ancient Greek and Roman gods.

immune (i myoon') *adj.* Protected against something harmful.

impact (im pakt') *n.* **1.** Collision; a striking together. **2.** The power of an event or idea to produce changes.

impassive (im pas'iv) *adj.* Not showing emotion.—**impassively** *adv.*

impetuous (im pech'oo wəs) *adj.* Acting or done suddenly with little thought; impulsive.

implicate (im'plə kāt') *v.* To show to have a connection with a crime; involve.

implore (im plôr') *v.* To ask for with much feeling.

imply (im plī') *v.* To suggest; hint.

imposing (im pō'ziŋ) *adj.* Impressive in manner.

impressionistic (im presh'ən is'tik) *adj.* Based on vague ideas or feelings.

impudent (im'pyoo dənt) *adj.* Bold; disrespectful.

---

fat, āpe, cär; ten, ēven; is, bīte; gō, hôrn;
tool, look; oil, out; up, fur; get; joy; yet;
chin; she; thin, then; zh, leisure; ŋ, ring;
ə for *a* in *ago, e* in *agent, i* in *sanity,*
o in *comply, u* in *focus;* ' as in *able* (ā'b'l)

inadvertent (in′əd vʉr′tənt) *adj.* Unintentional; due to oversight.—**inadvertently** *adv.*

inanimate (in an′ə mit) *adj.* Without life.

inarticulate (in′är tik′yə lit) *adj.* Produced without the clearness of normal speech.

incantation (in′kan tā′shən) *n.* The chanting of special words in magic spells or rites.

incomprehensible (in′käm pri hen′sə b'l, in käm′-) *adj.* That cannot be understood.

incredulous (in krej′ oo ləs) *adj.* Showing disbelief or doubt.—**incredulously** *adv.*

indigenous (in dij′ə nəs) *adj.* Existing, growing, or produced naturally in a particular region.

indignant (in dig′nənt) *adj.* Being angry about something that seems unjust, unfair, or mean.—**indignantly** *adv.*

indignation (in′dig nā′shən) *n.* Anger at something that seems unjust, unfair, mean, etc.

indistinct (in′dis tiŋkt′) *adj.* Not clearly seen or heard.

indomitable (in däm′it ə b'l) *adj.* Not easily discouraged or defeated.

indulge (in dulj′) *v.* To yield to or satisfy.

industry (in′dəs trē) *n.* Earnest, steady effort.

inefficient (in′ə fish′ənt) *adj.* Lacking the necessary ability or skill; incapable.

inert (in ʉrt′) *adj.* Inactive; dull; slow.

inevitable (in ev′ə tə b'l) *n.* Something that is unavoidable.

inflammation (in′flə mā′shən) *n.* Redness, pain, heat, and swelling of some part of the body.

ingenious (in jēn′yəs) *adj.* Clever, resourceful, and inventive.

inhibition (in′hi bish′ən) *n.* Something that holds one back from some action or feeling.

innate (i nāt′) *adj.* Existing naturally rather than learned.

innumerable (i noo′mər ə b'l) *adj.* Too numerous to be counted; countless.

insatiable (in sā′shə b'l) *adj.* Constantly wanting more; that cannot be satisfied.

inspiration (in′spə rā′shen) *n.* Something that inspires creative thought or action.

instinct (in′stiŋkt) *n.* An inborn tendency to behave in a certain way.

instinctive (in stiŋk′tiv) *adj.* Caused by a natural, inborn response.—**instinctively** *adv.*

insurmountable (in′sər moun′tə b'l) *adj.* That which cannot be overcome.

intensify (in ten′sə fī′) *v.* To increase; strengthen.

interlude (in′tər lood′) *n.* Anything that fills time between two events.

interpretation (in tʉr′prə tā′shən) *n.* The expression of a person's understanding of a subject.

intersperse (in′tər spʉrs′) *v.* To vary with things scattered here and there.

intervene (in′tər vēn′) *v.* To come in so as to help stop.

intolerable (in täl′ər ə b'l) *adj.* Unbearable.

intoxicate (in täk′sə kāt′) *v.* To make wild with excitement.

intoxication (in täk′sə kā′shən) *n.* Making or becoming drunk.

intricate (in′tri kit) *adj.* Complex; puzzling.

invincible (in vin′sə b'l) *adj.* Unconquerable; unable to be defeated.—**invincibly** *adv.*

ironic (ī rän′ik) *adj.* Meaning the opposite of what is said.

irresolute (i rez′ə loot′) *adj.* Not able to decide; hesitating.—**irresolutely** *adv.*

irrigation (ir′ə gā′shən) *n.* The cleaning of a wound with water or other fluid.

J

jardiniere (jär′d'n ir′) *n.* An ornamental bowl, pot, or stand for flowers or plants.

jaundice (jôn′dis) *v.* To make bitter or prejudiced through jealousy or hate.

jaunty (jôn′tē) *adj.* Gay, carefree; perky.

javelin (jav′lin) *n.* A light spear for throwing.

jest (jest) *n.* Fun; playfulness.

jubilee (joo′bə lē′) *n.* A time or occasion of rejoicing.

K

keel (kēl) *n.* The main wooden or steel piece along the bottom of a ship.

keen (kēn) *adj.* Strong or intense.

khaki (kak′ē) *n.* A strong, twilled cloth of a dull yellow-brown color.

kindle (kin′d'l) *v.* To set on fire; ignite.

kit (kit) *n.* The young of a small animal.

knoll (nōl) *n.* A small, rounded hill.

kraken (krä′k'n) *n.* A legendary sea monster of northern seas.

L

laborious (lə bôr′ē əs) *adj.* Industrious; hardworking.

lair (ler) *n.* Den; the resting place of a wild animal.

lament (lə ment′) *v.* To express deep sorrow.

lamentation (lam′ən tā′shən) *n.* Wailing or crying because of grief.

lanky (laŋ′ kē) *adj.* Awkwardly tall and lean or long and slender.

lateral (lat'ər əl) *adj.* Of, at, from, or toward the side.

lavish (lav'ish) *adj.* Very generous; more than enough.

ledger (lej'ər) *n.* A book in which a record of money transactions is kept.

lees (lēz) *n.* Sediment or dregs, as of wine.

levee (lev'ē) *n.* A bank built alongside a river to prevent high water from flooding bordering land.

listless (list'lis) *adj.* Having no interest in what is going on, as because of illness or weariness.

literal (lit'ər əl) *adj.* Actual; in fact.—**literally** *adv.*

literate (lit'ər it) *adj.* Able to read and write.

loam (lōm) *n.* A dark, rich soil.

logical (läj'i k'l) *adj.* Using correct reasoning.

loiter (loit'ər) *v.* To spend time idly; linger.

loll (läl) *v.* To hang down; droop.

lollop (läl'əp) *v.* To lounge about; loll.

lope (lōp) *v.* To move with a long, swinging stride.

lozenge (läz''nj) *n.* A cough drop or piece of hard candy.

lumber (lum'bər) *v.* To move heavily, clumsily, and, often, noisily.

luminous (lōō'mə nəs) *adj.* Glowing.

lusty (lus'tē) *adj.* Full of vigor and strength.

luxury (luk'shə rē) *n.* Something considered unnecessary to life and health.

M

madrigal (mad'ri gəl) *n.* A song with parts for several voices.

magnitude (mag'nə tōōd') *n.* Size.

malevolent (mə lev'ə lənt) *adj.* Showing ill-will; malicious.

mammoth (mam'əth) *adj.* Very big; huge.

maneuver (mə nōō'vər, -nyōō'-) *n.* Any move or action meant as a skillful step toward some goal. *v.* To plan; scheme.

mange (mānj) *n.* A skin disease of mammals caused by mites, with itching, loss of hair, etc.

maraud (mə rôd') *v.* To roam about and raid in search of loot or plunder.—**marauder** *n.*

marginal (mär'jən'l) *adj.* At, on, or close to the edge.

maritime (mar'ə tīm') *adj.* On, near, or of the sea.

market (mär'kit) *n.* A place for buying and selling things.

marmot (mär'mət) *n.* A gnawing and burrowing rodent.

martyr (mär'tər) *n.* A person tortured or killed because of his beliefs.

Mason jar (mā's'n jär) *n.* Wide-mouthed glass jar used for home canning of food.

massive (mas'iv) *adj.* Large and imposing or impressive.

matted (mat'id) *adj.* Thickly tangled.

mean (mēn) *adj.* Small; low in importance or value.

mechanical (mə kan'i k'l) *adj.* Produced or operated by machinery.

meditate (med'ə tāt') *v.* To think quietly; reflect.

melancholy (mel'ən käl'ē) *n.* Sadness and depression.

menace (men'is) *v.* To threaten or be a danger.—*n.* Threat.

merciless (mʉr'si lis) *adj.* Pitiless; cruel.

mesquite (mes kēt') *n.* A thorny tree or shrub common in the southwestern U.S. and in Mexico.

methodical (mə thäd'i k'l) *adj.* Systematic; orderly. —**methodically** *adv.*

minority (mə nôr'ə tē) *n.* The period of being under full legal age.

mischievous (mis'chi vəs) *adj.* Inclined to annoy with playful tricks; naughty.

moderate (mäd'ə rāt') *v.* To bring within limits; to make milder, less violent.

moiling (moil'iŋ) *n.* Hard work.

molest (mə lest') *v.* To annoy or meddle with so as to trouble or harm.

morrow (mär'ō) *n.* The next day.

Morse code (môrs kōd) *n.* An alphabet made up of a system of dots and dashes, or long and short sounds, used for sending radio telegraphs.

morsel (môr's'l) *n.* A small bite or portion of food.

mortal (môr't'l) *n.* A human as a being who must eventually die.

mortar (môr'tər) *n.* A mixture of cement or lime with sand and water, used between bricks.

mortar and pestle (môr'tər and pes''l) *n.* A very hard bowl (mortar) in which substances are ground or pounded to a powder with a long, narrow, blunt tool (pestle).

mortise (môr'tis) *v.* To join or fasten securely by fitting a part of one piece of wood into a notch cut in another.

muffle (muf''l) *v.* **1.** To deaden a sound. **2.** To stifle.

multitude (mul'tə tōōd') *n.* A very large number of persons or things.

---

fat, āpe, cär; ten, ēven; is, bīte; gō, hôrn, tōōl, look; oil, out; up, fʉr; get; joy; yet; chin; she; thin, *th*en; zh, leisure; ŋ, ring; ə for *a* in *ago*, *e* in *agent*, *i* in *sanity*, *o* in *comply*, *u* in *focus*; ' as in *able* (ā'b'l)

musk (musk) *n.* A substance with a strong, penetrating odor.

musket-ball (mus'kit bôl') *n.* The solid missile shot from a long-barreled firearm, used before the invention of the rifle.

musky (mus'kē) *adj.* With a strong perfumed scent.

muster (mus'tər) *n.* An assembling, as of troops.

muzzle (muz''l) *n.* **1.** The front end of the barrel of a firearm. **2.** Part of the head of a dog, including the mouth, nose, and jaws.

N

narwhal (när'wəl) *n.* An arctic sea mammal related to the whale: the male has a long, spiral tusk extending from the upper jaw.

naturalist (nach'ər əl ist) *n.* A person who studies animals and plants.

nausea (nô'shə, -sē ə, -zē ə, -zhə) *n.* A feeling of sickness at the stomach, with an urge to vomit.

necessity (nə ses'ə tē) *n.* Great need.

nightshade (nīt'shād') *n.* Flowering plants, some poisonous, some not.

nocturnal (näk tʉr'n'l) *adj.* Happening in the night.

nonchalant (nän'shə länt') *adj.* Without worry or concern; casual.—**nonchalantly** *adv.*

novel (näv''l) *adj.* New and unusual.

nub (nub) *n.* A knob or lump; a small piece.

nymph (nimf) *n.* Any of a group of minor nature goddesses, thought of as beautiful maidens living in rivers, trees, etc.

O

obligation (äb'lə gā'shən) *n.* A feeling of indebtedness for a favor done for one.

oblige (ə blīj') *v.* To do a favor or service.—**obliging** *adj.,* **obligingly** *adv.*

obliterate (ə blit'ə rāt', ō-) *v.* To blot out, leaving no traces.

obscure (əb skyoor') *adj.* Not famous or well-known.

obscurity (əb skyoor'ə tē) *n.* The condition of not being easily understood.

obstinate (äb' stə nit) *adj.* Unreasonably determined to have one's own way; stubborn.—**obstinacy** (äb'stə nə sē) *n.*

obstruction (əb struk'shən) *n.* Anything that hinders or blocks; hindrance.

ominous (äm'ə nəs) *adj.* Threatening; sinister.

onslaught (än'slôt') *n.* A violent, intense attack.

opalescent (ō'pə les''nt) *adj.* Showing shifting changes of color, like opal.

optimism (äp'tə miz'm) *n.* The tendency to take the most hopeful or cheerful view of matters.—**optimistically** *adv.*

orator (ôr'ət ər) *n.* A skillful public speaker.

ordeal (ôr dēl') *n.* A painful or severe test.

out-crop (out'kräp') *n.* An exposed area of rock or mineral that has broken through the earth's surface.

overwhelm (ō'vər hwelm') *v.* Crush; overpower.

P

pallet (pal'it) *n.* A small mattress filled with straw and used on the floor.

panic (pan'ik) *v.* To show sudden or wild fear.—**panicky** *adj.*

parasol (par'ə sôl') *n.* A light umbrella carried as a sunshade.

parch (pärch) *v.* To dry up; shrivel.

parson (pär's'n) *n.* A clergyman.

pastel (pas tel') *adj.* Soft and pale: said of colors.

patron (pā'trən) *n.* A regular customer.

pavilion (pə vil'yən) *n.* A building, often partly open, for exhibits.

pawn (pôn) *n.* A chessman of the lowest value.

peculiarity (pi kyoo'lē ar'ə tē) *n.* Something that is strange or odd, as a habit.

pedestal (ped'is t'l) *n.* The base or bottom support of a column, statue, etc.

pelage (pel'ij) *n.* The coat of a mammal.

pendulum (pen'joo ləm) *n.* A weight hung from a fixed point so as to swing to and fro under gravity and momentum.

pension (pen'shən) *n.* A payment to one who has worked a certain number of years.

pensive (pen'siv) *adj.* Expressing deep thoughtfulness, often with some sadness.

perceive (pər sēv') *v.* To become aware of.

perennial (pə ren'ē əl) *adj.* Lasting or active throughout the whole year.

peril (per'əl) *n.* Danger.

perimeter (pə rim'ə tər) *n.* The outer boundary of a figure or area.

permissive (pər mis'iv) *adj.* Tolerant; allowing freedom.

perplexed (pər plekst') *adj.* Confused; uncertain.

pestilence (pes't'l əns) *n.* Any fatal disease that spreads rapidly.

petulant (pech'oo lənt) *adj.* Showing anger or annoyance over little things; peevish.

philosopher (fi läs'ə fər) *n.* A person who studies or is an expert in conduct, thought, experience, and reality.

philosophic (fil'ə säf'ik) *adj.* Calm, as in a difficult situation; reasonable.

pine (pīn) *v.* To have a strong longing.

piñon (pin'yən) *n.* A small pine found in western North America.

pious (pī'əs) *adj.* Having or showing religious devotion.

pivot (piv'ət) *v.* To turn as on a pivot.

plague (plāg) *n.* An infectious disease that has become widespread.

plaintive (plān'tiv) *adj.* Expressing sorrow or melancholy; mournful.—**plaintively** *adv.*

plateau (pla tō') *n.* An elevated area of level land.

pliant (plī'ənt) *adj.* Easily bent.

plight (plīt) *n.* Sad or dangerous situation.

pluck (pluk) *n.* Courage to meet danger or difficulty.—**plucky** *adj.*

plumage (plōō'mij) *n.* A bird's feathers.

plumy (plōō'mē) *adj.* Like a plume; feathery.

plunder (plun'dər) *n.* Furnishings.

poach (pōch) *v.* To trespass on private property, especially for hunting or fishing.

poignant (poin'yənt) *adj.* Haunting; painful to the feelings.

poise (poiz) *v.* To balance; keep steady.

pomander ball (pō'man dər bôl) *n.* A hollow, perforated ball for holding aromatic herbs, hung in closets to scent clothes and linens.

pomegranate (päm'gran' it) *n.* A round, red fruit with edible juicy seeds.

ponder (pän'dər) *v.* To think deeply; consider carefully.

ponderous (pän'dər əs) *adj.* Heavy; in a clumsy way.—**ponderously** *adv.*

poultice (pōl'tis) *n.* A hot, soft, wet mass applied to a sore part of the body.

precarious (pri ker'ē əs) *adj.* Unsafe; dangerous.—**precariously** *adv.*

precipice (pres'ə pis) *n.* Steep cliff.

precise (pri sīs') *adj.* Speaking definitely or distinctly.

predator (pred'ə tər) *n.* A person or animal that lives by killing and feeding upon other animals.—**predatory** *adj.*

presently (prez''nt lē) *adv.* In a little while; soon.

pride (prīd) *n.* An overhigh opinion of oneself; exaggerated self-esteem.

prim (prim) *adj.* Stiffly formal; proper.—**primly** *adv.*

privet (priv'it) *n.* Shrub often used for hedges.

privy (priv'ē) *n.* An outhouse.

profane (prə fān', prō fān') *v.* To treat sacred things with disrespect.

profound (prə found') *adj.* Deep; intensely felt.—**profoundly** *adv.*

profusion (prə fyōō'zhən) *n.* Abundance; a rich or lavish supply.

prohibit (prō hib'it) *v.* To forbid; to refuse to permit.—**prohibition** *n.*

prolong (prə lôŋ') *v.* To lengthen in time or space; extend.

proposition (präp'ə zish'ən) *n.* A proposed deal, as in business.

prosaic (prō zā'ik) *adj.* Commonplace; dull.

prostrate (präs'trāt) *adj.* Lying flat.

proverbial (prə vʉr'bē əl) *adj.* Well-known because it is commonly referred to.

provisions (prə vizh'ənz) *n.* A stock of food.

provoke (prə vōk') *v.* To stir up action or feeling.

public (pub'lik) *adj.* Known by all or most people.

puny (pyōō'nē) *adj.* Weak; of inferior size.

Q

quake (kwāk) *v.* To tremble or shake.

quarry[1] (kwôr'ē) *n.* An animal that is being hunted down.

quarry[2] (kwôr'ē) *v.* To excavate stone, marble, or slate.

quaver (kwā'vər) *v.* **1.** To make a trill in singing. **2.** To shake or tremble.

queue (kyōō) *n.* A line.

quicksilver (kwik'sil'vər) *n.* The liquid metal, mercury.

quiver (kwiv'ər) *v.* To shake or tremble. *n.* A case for holding arrows.

quotation (kwō tā'shən) *n.* The current quoted price of a stock, bond, or commodity.

R

radius (rā'dē əs) *n.* Any limited extent.

random (ran'dəm) *adj.* Unplanned; haphazard.

rangy (rān'jē) *adj.* Long-limbed and slender.

rank (raŋk) *adj.* Growing vigorously and coarsely.

rapport (ra pôr') *n.* Sympathetic relationship; harmony.

---

fat, āpe, cär; ten, ēven; is, bīte; gō, hôrn, tōol, look; oil, out; up, fʉr; get; joy; yet; chin; she; thin, then; zh, leisure; ŋ, ring; ə for a in ago, e in agent, i in sanity, o in comply, u in focus; ' as in able (ā'b'l)

rapt (rapt) *adj.* Completely absorbed in thought, study, etc.

rations (rash′enz) *n.* Food or food supply.

recede (ri sēd′) *v.* To go or move back or to appear to do so.

reckon (rek′ən) *v.* [Colloq.] To think; suppose.—**reckon with** To take into consideration.

recollection (rek′ə lek′shən) *n.* What is remembered.

reconnoiter (rē′kə noit′ər) *v.* To make a survey or examination of.

recrimination (ri krim′ə nā′shən) *n.* Accusation.

redolent (red′′l ənt) *adj.* Sweet-smelling.

redound (ri dound′) *v.* To come back.

reformatory (ri fôr′mə tôr′ē) *n.* An institution where young lawbreakers are sent for training and discipline intended to reform them.

refuge (ref′yo͞oj) *n.* Shelter or protection from danger or difficulty.

refugee (ref′yo͞o jē′) *n.* A person who flees from his country to seek refuge elsewhere.

refuse (ref′yo͞os) *n.* Anything thrown away as worthless or useless.

refute (ri fyo͞ot′) *v.* To argue against.

relent (ri lent′) *v.* To become less harsh; soften.

reluctance (ri luk′təns) *n.* Unwillingness; not wanting to do something.

remorse (ri môrs′) *n.* A deep, torturing sense of guilt over a wrong one has done.

remote (ri mōt′) *adj.* Far off and hidden; distant.

repercussion (rē′pər kush′ən, rep′ər-) *n.* Reflection, as of sound.

replenish (ri plen′ish) *v.* To refuel.

reposeful (ri pōz′fəl) *adj.* Restful, peaceful.

reproach (ri prōch′) *n.* A blaming so as to cause shame.—*v.* To accuse or blame someone.

reproachful (ri prōch′fəl) *adj.* Blaming.—**reproachfully** *adv.*

resent (ri zent′) *v.* To feel or show bitter hurt or anger.

resilient (ri zil′yənt, -ē ənt) *adj.* Springing back into shape after being bent.

resin (rez′′n) *n.* A sticky substance that comes out of various plants and trees, such as pines.—**resinous** *adj.*

resistance (ri zis′təns) *n.* Opposition.

resolute (rez′ə lo͞ot′) *adj.* Determined; unwavering.—**resolutely** *adv.*

resound (ri zound′) *v.* To be filled with sound; echo; reverberate.

resourceful (ri sôrs′fəl, -zôrs′-) *adj.* Skillful at solving problems or getting out of trouble.—**re-**

sourcefulness *n.*

respite (res′pit) *n.* A period of temporary relief.

restoration (res′tə rā′shən) *n.* Repair; putting something back in its original condition.

retail (rē′tāl) *v.* To repeat or pass on.

retrieve (ri trēv′) *v.* To get back; recover.

revelation (rev′ə lā′shən) *n.* Something revealed or made known.

revere (ri vir′) *v.* To regard with deep respect, love, and awe.

rile (rīl) *v.* To make angry; irritate.

rimrock (rim′räk′) *n.* A rock forming the rim or upper part of a steep slope.

ringworm (riŋ′wurm′) *n.* A skin disease caused by a fungus that produces itchy, ring-shaped patches.

ritual (rich′o͞o wəl) *n.* The observance of set forms or rites, as in worship.

rivalry (rī′v′l rē) *n.* Competition.

roan (rōn) *adj.* Of a solid color with a thick sprinkling of white hairs.

romp (rämp) *v.* To play in a rough, lively way; frolic.

rosette (rō zet′) *n.* An ornament resembling a rose.

rout (rout) *v.* To put to disorderly flight.

rove (rōv) *v.* To wander about; roam.—**rover** *n.*

ruddy (rud′ē) *adj.* Having a healthy red color.

rude (ro͞od) *adj.* Simple or primitive.

runt (runt) *n.* The smallest animal of a litter.

russet (rus′it) *adj.* Yellowish-brown or reddish-brown.

rut (rut) *n.* A track or furrow.

S

Sabbath (sab′əth) *n.* The seventh day of the week, regarded as a day of rest and worship.

sachet (sa shā′) *n.* A small bag filled with perfumed powder or herbs and put in drawers to make clothing smell sweet.

sacred (sā′krid) *adj.* Having to do with religion or religious rites.

safari (sə fär′ē) *n.* A journey or hunting expedition.

saffron (saf′rən) *adj.* Orange-yellow.

sanction (saŋk′shən) *v.* To give official approval to; to allow or permit.

sanctuary (saŋk′cho͞o wer′ē) *n.* A place of refuge or protection.

sand bar (sand′ bär′) *n.* A ridge of sand formed in a river by the action of currents.

saturate (sach′ə rāt′) *n.* To cause to be thoroughly soaked.

savor (sā′vər) *v.* To dwell on with delight; relish.

sawmill (sô′mil′) *n.* A place where logs are sawed into boards.

scabbard (skab′ərd) *n.* A sheath or case.

scalawag (skal′ə wag′) *n.* A person full of tricks; rascal.

scarlet (skär′lit) *n.* Very bright red with a slightly orange tinge.

scornful (skôrn′fəl) *adj.* Showing contempt; looking down on another.

scoundrel (skoun′drəl) *n.* Villain; rascal.

scrawny (skrô′nē) *adj.* Thin; bony; skinny.

scrutinize (skrōōt′′n īz′) *v.* To look at carefully or examine closely.

scud (skud) *v.* To move swiftly.

scuttle (skut′′l) *v.* To scurry or scamper; to run quickly, especially from danger.

scythe (sīth) *n.* A tool with a long curved blade used for cutting tall grass or grain.

sear (sir) *v.* **1.** To make hard or unfeeling. **2.** To scorch or burn the surface of.

secluded (se klōōd′id) *adj.* Hidden from view.

sector (sek′tər) *n.* A distinct part.

sedge (sej) *n.* A coarse, grasslike plant.

segment (seg′mənt) *v.* To divide into sections.

sentimental (sen′tə men′t′l) *adj.* Having tender, gentle feelings, often in a weak or foolish way.— **sentimentality** *n.*

sentinel (sen′ti n′l) *n.* A guard; sentry.

serenade (ser′ə nād′) *n.* The act of playing or singing music outdoors at night.

serene (sə rēn′) *adj.* Calm; peaceful.

serviceable (sur′vis ə b′l) *adj.* Durable.

shamble (sham′b′l) *v.* To walk in a clumsy manner, barely lifting the feet.

sharecropper (sher′kräp′ər) *n.* Tenant farmer; one who works another's land for a share of the crop.

sheathe (shēth) *v.* To enclose in or protect with a case or covering.

sheepish (shēp′ish) *adj.* Feeling or showing embarrassment when one is caught in a mistake or lie.

shift (shift) *v.* To get along; manage.

shiftless (shift′lis) *adj.* Lazy or careless.

shirk (shurk) *v.* To get out of doing or leave undone.

shoal (shōl) *n.* A large school of fish.

shoat (shōt) *n.* A young hog.

shrewd (shrōōd) *adj.* Clever; sharp.—**shrewdness** *n.*

shroud (shroud) *v.* To cover; screen.

shuttle (shut′′l) *n.* A device used to pass the woof thread back and forth between the warp threads that go up and down in weaving.

silhouette (sil′ōō wet′) *n.* The outline of a figure; contour.

simplify (sim′plə fī′) *v.* To make simpler or less complex.

simultaneous (sī m′l tā′nē əs) *adj.* At the same time.—**simultaneously** *adv.*

sinewy (sin′yōō wē) *adj.* Tough.

skein (skān) *n.* A quantity of thread or yarn wound in a coil.

skeptical (skep′ti k′l) *adj.* Not easily convinced; doubting; questioning.

skulk (skulk) *v.* To move about or hide in a sneaky, cowardly, or threatening way.

slacken (slak′′n) *v.* To become less active or intense.

slough (sluf) *v.* To shed.

slow-witted (slō′wit′id) *adj.* Not bright or alert; dull.

smilax (smī′laks) *n.* A twining vine with bright green leaves.

smite (smīt) *v.* **smote, smitten.** To hit or strike hard.

smithy (smith′ē) *n.* A blacksmith.

smudge (smuj) *n.* A fire made to produce dense smoke.

sober (sō′bər) *adj.* Serious, solemn.

sodden (säd′′n) *adj.* Dull or stupefied.

sojourn (sō′jurn) *n.* A brief stay; visit.

solemn (säl′əm) *adj.* Serious.

solitary (säl′ə ter′ē) *adj.* Single; being alone.

solitude (säl′ə tōōd′) *n.* **1.** Being alone; seclusion. **2.** A lonely or secluded place.

sombre (säm′bər) *adj.* Dark and gloomy or dull.

sortie (sôr′tē) *n.* A sudden attack.

sound (sound) *adj.* Normal and healthy.

spangle (spaŋ′g′l) *v.* To cover with any small, glittering objects.

spawn (spôn) *n.* The eggs or young produced by fish.

species (spē′shēz) *n.* **1.** Kind; sort; type. **2.** A group of highly similar plants or animals.

spectator (spek′tāt ər) *n.* A person who watches something without taking part; onlooker.

spectral (spek′trəl) *adj.* Ghostly.

---

fat, āpe, cär; ten, ēven; is, bīte; gō, hôrn, tōōl, look; oil, out; up, fur; get; joy; yet; chin; she; thin, *th*en; zh, leisure; ŋ, ring; ə for *a* in *ago*, *e* in *agent*, *i* in *sanity*, *o* in *comply*, *u* in *focus*; ′ as in *able* (ā′b′l)

speculation (spek′yə lā′shən) *n.* Guessing; thinking about.

speller (spel′ər) *n.* An exercise book used to teach spelling.

sphinx (sfiŋks) *n.* A winged monster with a lion's body and a woman's head.

spindle-shanked (spin′d'l shaŋkt′) *adj.* Having thin legs.

spit (spit) *n.* A thin rod on which meat is roasted over a fire.

spite (spīt) *n.* A mean feeling that makes one want to hurt or annoy another.

splay (splā) *v.* To spread out or apart.

sporadic (spô rad′ik) *adj.* Happening from time to time; not regular.

spume (spyo͞om) *n.* Foam, froth, or scum.

squall (skwôl) *v.* To cry or scream loudly or harshly.

squeamish (skwēm′ish) *adj.* Queasy; easily nauseated or made ill.

squint (skwint) *v.* To look with the eyes partly closed, as in too strong light.

staccato (stə kät′ō) *adj.* Made up of short, sharp movements or sounds.

stalk (stôk) *v.* **1.** To walk in a quiet, cautious way to pursue game. **2.** To walk in a stiff, proud manner.

steadfast (sted′fast′, -fəst) *adj.* Constant.—**steadfastness** *n.*

stealthy (stel′thē) *adj.* Secret, sneaky, or quiet.

stench (stench) *n.* An offensive smell; stink.

stertorous (stur′tə rəs) *adj.* With loud, labored breathing.—**stertorously** *adv.*

stipple (stip′'l) *v.* To mark with dots.

stopgap (stäp′gap′) *n.* A thing serving as a temporary substitute.

stout (stout) *adj.* Courageous; brave; strong.—**stoutly** *adv.*

straightforward (strāt′fôr′wərd) *adj.* Honest; frank.

strand (strand) *v.* To leave or be put in a difficult, helpless position.

strive (strīv) *v.* To make great efforts; try very hard.

stun (stun) *v.* To shock deeply; astound.

stupor (sto͞o′pər) *n.* Mental dullness or lack of interest.

subconscious (sub kän′ shəs) *adj.* Occurring with little or no awareness on the part of the individual.

submissive (səb mis′ iv) *adj.* Willing to give in to or obey another; obedient.

subsequent (sub′si kwənt) *adj.* Following.

subside (səb sīd′) *v.* To become quieter or less active.

subterfuge (sub′tər fyo͞oj′) *n.* A plan to hide one's true purpose.

succession (sək sesh′ən) *n.* One after another.

succor (suk′ər) *n.* Aid; help.

suffrage (suf′rij) *n.* The right to vote in political elections.

sullen (sul′ən) *adj.* Silent and keeping to oneself because one feels angry or hurt.—**sullenly** *adv.*

sumptuous (sump′cho͞o wəs) *adj.* Lavish; magnificent.

supercilious (so͞o′ pər sil′ē əs) *adj.* Scornful; proud; looking down on others.—**superciliously** *adv.*

supplement (sup′lə ment′) *v.* To add to.

suppurate (sup′yo͞o rāt′) *v.* To discharge pus; fester, as a wound.

surpass (sər pas′) *v.* To be better or greater than.

surveillance (sər vā′ləns) *n.* Watch kept over a person or thing.

swindle (swin′d'l) *v.* To cheat or trick another out of money or property.—**swindler** *n.*

swish (swish) *n.* A hissing or rustling sound.

T

talisman (tal′is mən) *n.* Anything supposed to have magic power; a charm.

tallow (tal′ō) *n.* The pale-yellow fat from cattle, sheep, etc., used in making candles.

tankard (taŋ′kərd) *n.* A large drinking cup with a handle and, often, a hinged lid.

tanning (tan′iŋ) *n.* The process of turning hide into leather by soaking in tannin.

tarry (tar′ē) *v.* To stay for a time, especially longer than intended.

tawny (tô′nē) *adj.* Brownish-yellow; tan.

teeming (tēm′iŋ) *adj.* Being full of or crowded with.

temperance (tem′pər əns) *n.* The drinking of little or no alcoholic liquor.

tempest (tem′pist) *n.* A violent storm with high winds.

tempestuous (tem pes′cho͞o wəs) *adj.* Stormy.

temple (tem′p'l) *n.* The flat area at either side of the forehead, above and behind the eye.

tendril (ten′drəl) *n.* A threadlike vine that clings, twists, and curls.

tentative (ten′tə tiv) *adj.* Not definite or final.

thatch (thach) *n.* Straw or palm leaves used for roofing.

thermostat (thur′mə stat′) *n.* A device for regulating temperature.

thong (thôŋ) *n.* A narrow strip of leather.

thwart (thwôrt) *v.* To block or hinder.

tide (tīd) *n.* The rise and fall of the surface of the oceans caused by the pull of the sun and moon.

tirade (tī′rād) *n.* A long, angry, or scolding speech.

titanium (tī tā′nē əm) *n.* A silvery or dark-gray, shiny, metallic chemical element.

tormentor (tôr men′tər) *n.* One who causes pain, anxiety, or annoyance for another.

totem (tōt′əm) *n.* An animal used as a symbol or mascot.

traction (trak′shən) *n.* The power to hold to a surface while moving, without slipping.

tranquil (traŋ′ kwəl) *adj.* Calm, quiet, peaceful.—**tranquility** *n.* —**tranquilly** *adv.*

transaction (tran sak′shən, -zak′-) *n.* A business deal.

transform (trans fôrm′) *v.* To change the appearance of.

translucent (trans lo͞o′s'nt) *adj.* Letting light pass through but spreading it so that objects on the other side cannot be clearly seen, as frosted glass.

trebly (treb′lē) *adv.* Three times as much.

trellis (trel′is) *n.* A structure of thin, crossed strips on which vines are trained to grow.

trespasser (tres′pas ər) *n.* One who goes on another's property without permission.

trial (trī′əl) *n.* Suffering, hardship, trouble.

tribulation (trib′yə lā′shən) *n.* A great misery or distress; deep sorrow.

trick (trik) *n.* A turn at work; shift.

trifle (trī′f'l) *n.* A little bit. *v.* To play or toy.

trill (tril) *n.* A moving rapidly back and forth between one tone and another just above it in singing.

trolley (träl′ē) *n.* A streetcar.

troughed (trôft) *adj.* Grooved; made with a long, narrow hollow.

tumultuous (to͞o mul′cho͞o wəs) *adj.* Wild and noisy.—**tumultuously** *adv.*

tunnies (tun′ēz) *n.* Tuna.

tush (tush) *n.* Tusk; a very long, pointed tooth, usually one of a pair, that sticks out of the mouth.

U

unaccustomed (un ə kus′təmd) *adj.* Unusual; not used to.

unanimous (yo͞o nan′ə məs) *adj.* Based on complete agreement.—**unanimously** *adv.*

unconditional (un kən dish′ən'l) *adj.* Absolute; not depending on any conditions.

unflinching (un flin′chiŋ) *adj.* Steadfast; unyielding.

uninitiated (un′i nish′ē ā tid) *adj.* Without the knowlege or experience of some subject.

unique (yo͞o nēk′) *adj.* Unlike any other.

unpredictability (un′pri dikt′ə bil′ə tē) *n.* Inability to tell what one will do; uncertainty.

unsurmountable (un′sər mount′ə b'l) *adj.* Unable to be overcome.

unsuspecting (un′sə spekt′iŋ) *adj.* Trusting; being unaware of what is to come.

untried (un trīd′) *adj.* Not tested or proved.

unwitting (un wit′iŋ) *adj.* Unaware; not knowing.

V

vagrant (vā′grənt) *adj.* Wandering from place to place; roaming.

valise (və lēs′) *n.* A piece of hand luggage.

valor (val′ər) *n.* Great courage or bravery.

vanquish (vaŋ′ kwish) *v.* To conquer; defeat.

varmint (vär′mənt) *n.* An animal regarded as troublesome.

vaulting (vôl′tiŋ) *adj.* Leaping; jumping over.

vaunt (vônt) *v.* To boast; brag.

vengeance (ven′jəns) *n.* Revenge; the return of an injury for an injury.

venison (ven′is'n) *n.* The flesh of deer, used as food.

veranda (və ran′də) *n.* An open porch, usually roofed.

veritable (ver′i tə b'l) *adj.* Actual; true.

versatile (vʉr′sə t'l) *adj.* Able to turn easily from one subject or occupation to another.—**versatility.** *n.*

vertebrate (vʉr′tə brit, -brāt′) *n.* Any of a large group of animals that have a backbone and a brain and cranium.

vex (veks) *v.* To annoy; irritate.

vexation (vek sā′shən) *n.* Cause of annoyance or distress.

vigil (vij′əl) *n.* The act of staying awake to keep watch over or guard something.

vital (vīt′'l) *adj.* Very important.

vixen (vik′s'n) *n.* A female fox.

vulnerable (vul′nər ə b'l) *adj.* Easily wounded or injured.

---

fat, āpe, cär; ten, ēven; is, bīte; gō, hôrn, to͞ol, lo͝ok; oil, out; up, fʉr; get; joy; yet; chin; she; thin, then; zh, leisure; ŋ, ring; ə for a in *ago*, e in *agent*, i in *sanity*, o in *comply*, u in *focus*; ' as in *able* (ā′b'l)

W

wail (wāl) *v.* To make a sad, crying sound.

waistcoat (wes′kət, wāst′kōt′) *n.* A vest.

walleyed (wôl′īd′) *adj.* Having large, staring eyes.

wallow (wäl′ō, wôl′-) *v.* To roll about.

warbler (wôr′blər) *n.* Brightly-colored songbird.

wastrel (wās′trəl) *n.* A spend-thrift.

waxen (wak′s′n) *adj.* Pale.

weathercock (we*th*′ər käk′) *n.* A weather vane in the form of a rooster.

welfare (wel′fer′) *n.* Condition of health, happiness, and comfort; well-being.

whet (hwet, wet) *v.* To make stronger; stimulate; to sharpen by rubbing or grinding.

whim (wim) *n.* An idle and passing notion.

wholesome (hōl′səm) *adj.* Healthful.

wicker (wik′ər) *adj.* Made of twigs or long wooden strips woven together.

widow (wid′ō) *n.* A woman whose husband has died and who has not remarried.

wiry (wīr′ē) *adj.* Lean, sinewy, and strong.

wistful (wist′fəl) *adj.* Showing longing or a vague yearning or sadness.—**wistfully** *adv.*

withers (wi*th*′ərz) *n.* The highest part of the back of a horse or similar animal, between the shoulder blades.

woo (wo͞o) *v.* To court; try to get the love of.

wrath (rath) *n.* Intense anger; rage.

writhe (rī*th*) *v.* To twist and turn; squirm.

wry (rī) *adj.* Ironic or bitter.

Y

yarn (yärn) *n.* A tale or story, especially one that seems exaggerated.

yucca (yuk′ə) *n.* A plant with stiff, sword-shaped leaves.

Z

zoologist (zō äl′ə jist) *n.* One who studies animals, their life, growth, and classification.

Suggestions for Further Reading

Unit 1. Myths, Tales, and Fables

Andersen, Hans Christian. *Fairy Tales.* Cleveland: Williams Collins and World Publishing, 1946.

Bulfinch, Thomas. *A Book of Myths.* New York: Macmillan, 1942.

Courlander, Harold, and Wolf Leslau. *The Fire on the Mountain and Other Ethiopian Stories.* New York: Holt, Rinehart and Winston, 1950.

Graves, Robert. *Greek Gods and Heroes.* Garden City, New York: Doubleday, 1960.

Hamilton, Edith. *Mythology.* Boston: Little, Brown and Co., 1942.

Hamilton, Virginia. *The People Could Fly: American Black Folktales.* New York: Alfred A. Knopf, 1985.

Rouse, W. H. D. *Gods, Heroes, and Men of Ancient Greece.* New York: New American Library, 1957.

Thurber, James. *Fables for Our Time.* New York: Harcourt Brace Jovanovich, 1940.

Unit 2. The Short Story

Aiken, Joan. *The Far Forests.* New York: The Viking Press, 1977.

_____. *The Green Flash and Other Tales of Horror, Suspense, and Fantasy.* New York: Holt, Rinehart and Winston, 1971.

Ainsworth, Ruth. *The Phantom Carousel and Other Ghostly Tales.* Chicago: Follett, 1977.

Asimov, Isaac. *Asimov's Mysteries.* New York: Dell, 1968.

Nash, Ogden, ed. *I Couldn't Help Laughing.* Philadelphia: J. B. Lippincott, 1957.

Sandburg, Carl. *Rootabaga Stories.* New York: Harcourt Brace Jovanovich, 1936.

Singer, Isaac Bashevis. *Zlateh the Goat and Other Stories.* New York: Harper and Row, 1971.

The Stories of Ray Bradbury. New York: Alfred A. Knopf, 1980.

Yolen, Jane, editor. *Zoo 2000: Twelve Stories of Science Fiction and Fantasy Beasts.* New York: The Seabury Press, 1973.

Unit 3. Nonfiction

Adamson, Joy. *Forever Free.* New York: Pantheon Books, 1962.

Brenner, Barbara. *Beware! These Animals Are Poisonous.* New York: Coward, McCann and Geoghegan, 1979.

Brooks, Gwendolyn. *Report from Part One.* Detroit: Broadside Press, 1972.

Burgess, Robert F. *The Sharks.* Garden City, New York: Doubleday, 1971.

Burt, Olive. *Sacajawea: A Visual Biography.* New York. Franklin Watts, 1978.

Douglas, William O. *Exploring the Himalaya.* New York: Random House, 1958.

Heyerdahl, Thor. *The Ra Expeditions.* Garden City, New York: Doubleday, 1971.

Leslie, Robert Franklin. *The Bears and I.* New York: E. P. Dutton, 1968.

Mowat, Farley. *Owls in the Family.* Boston: Little, Brown and Company, 1961.

Trapp, Maria August. *The Story of the Trapp Family Singers*. Philadelphia: J. B. Lippincott, 1949.

Wilson, Charles M. *Geronimo*. Minneapolis: Dillon Press, 1973.

Unit 4. Poetry

Adoff, Arnold. *I Am the Darker Brother: An Anthology of Modern Poems by Negro Americans*. New York: Macmillan, 1968.

Ciardi, John. *Reason for the Pelican*. Philadelphia: J. B. Lippincott, 1954.

Cummings, E. E. *Ninety-Five Poems*. New York: Harcourt Brace Jovanovich, 1958.

Frost, Robert. *Selected Poems of Robert Frost*. New York: Holt, Rinehart and Winston, 1963.

Giovanni, Nikki. *Ego Tripping and Other Poems for Young People*. Westport, Connecticut: Lawrence Hill, 1973.

Greenfield, Eloise. *Honey, I Love and Other Love Poems*. New York: Thomas Y. Crowell, 1972.

Starbird, Kaye. *A Snail's a Failure Socially*. Philadelphia: J. B. Lippincott, 1979.

Worth, Valerie. *Still More Small Poems*. New York: Farrar, Straus and Giroux, 1978.

Unit 5. Drama

Aiken, Joan. *The Mooncusser's Daughter*. New York: The Viking Press, 1974.

Hughes, Ted. *The Tiger's Bones and Other Plays for Children*. New York: The Viking Press, 1974.

Jennings, Coleman A., and Aurand Harris. *Plays*

Children Love: A Treasury of Contemporary and Classic Plays for Children. Garden City, New York: Doubleday, 1981.

Korty, Carol. *Plays from African Folktales with Ideas for Acting, Dance, Costumes, and Music*. New York: Charles Scribner's Sons, 1969.

Murray, John. *Mystery Plays for Young Actors*. Boston: Plays Inc., 1984.

Rockwell, Thomas. *How to Eat Fried Worms and Other Plays*. New York: Delacorte, 1980.

Unit 6. The Novel

Armstrong, William. *Sounder*. New York: Harper and Row, 1972.

Capps, Mary Joyce. *Yellow Leaf*. St. Louis: Concordia, 1974.

Corcoran, Barbara. *Sam*. New York: Atheneum, 1967.

Freedman, Benedict, and Nancy Freedman. *Mrs. Mike*. New York: Berkley Publishing, 1947.

George, Jean Craighead. *Julie of the Wolves*. New York: Harper and Row, 1972.

Gipson, Fred. *Savage Sam*. New York: Harper and Row, 1962.

Neville, Emily. *It's Like This, Cat*. New York: Harper and Row, 1963.

Rawlings, Marjorie Kinnan. *The Yearling*. Totawa, New Jersey: Charles Scribner's Sons, 1962.

Sperry, Armstrong. *Frozen Fire*. New York: Doubleday, 1956.

Stuart, Jessie. *Old Ben*. New York: Hill Book, 1970.

Style Manual
for Capitalization, Punctuation, and Spelling

Guidelines for Capitalization

Guidelines for Punctuation

Guidelines for Spelling

Guidelines for Capitalization

Proper Nouns and Proper Adjectives

■ A **common noun** is a general name of a person, place, thing, or idea.

> apple   city   ship   honesty

■ Capitalize proper nouns. A **proper noun** names a particular person, place, or thing.

> Princess Diana   Tulsa   *Titanic*

A proper noun can be made up of one or more words. Capitalize all important words in a proper noun.

> New Year's Day   Kalamazoo River   Anne Frank

■ Capitalize proper adjectives. A **proper adjective** is made from a proper noun.

> Danish—Denmark   Portuguese—Portugal

Proper adjectives are often used with common nouns. Do not capitalize the common noun.

> French dressing   Greek alphabet   Siamese cat

■ Capitalize the names of people and pets.

Begin every word in a name with a capital letter. An initial stands for a name. Write initials as capital letters. Put a period after an initial.

> Susan B. Anthony   A. J. Foyt   Muggins

Often, a word for a family relation is used as the name of a particular person, or as part of the name. *Mom* and *Grandpa Lewis* are two examples. Capitalize a word used in this way.

■ **Capitalize a title used with a person's name.**

A **title** is a term of respect used in front of a name. Many titles have short forms called **abbreviations.** Capitalize abbreviations of titles. Follow an abbreviation with a period.

    Mister—Mr.   Mistress—Mrs.   Doctor—Dr.

The title *Miss* has no abbreviated form. Do not use a period after this title. *Ms.* has no long form.

    Did Mr. Lee interview Dr. Smith or Mayor Gentry?

■ **Capitalize the word *I.***

Margaret and I walked to the library.

Key to Writing

Take special care when capitalizing unusual names such as MacDonald or Vincent Van Gogh.

More Proper Nouns

■ **Capitalize the names of particular places and things.**

1. Capitalize cities, states, and countries.

    Laredo, Texas, is near Mexico.

2. Capitalize streets, bridges, parks, and buildings.

    The tour guide showed us the Empire State Building, the Brooklyn Bridge, Wall Street, and Central Park.

3. Capitalize geographical names. Do not capitalize *north, south, east,* or *west* when they refer to directions. Capitalize these words only when they refer to a particular section of the country or world.

> The Millers turned south and drove to Death Valley.
> In the United States, the Mississippi River is the dividing line between the East and West.
> The Blue Ridge Mountains extend from the North to the South.

■ **Capitalize the names of months, days, and holidays.**

Do not capitalize the seasons: spring, summer, winter, and fall.

> We celebrate Father's Day and the first day of summer in June.

■ **Capitalize the names of races, religions, nationalities, and languages.**

> Modern American Indian artists often use traditional designs.
> Judaism, Christianity, and the Muslim religion share a belief in one God.
> The Russians and the Chinese have a common border.
> Does this junior high school offer French?

■ **Capitalize words referring to God and to religious scriptures.**

the Lord	the Bible	the Book of Genesis
Allah	the Talmud	the New Testament

■ **Capitalize the names of clubs, organizations, and business firms.**

> Carolyn's collie is registered with the American Kennel Club.
>   Have you heard of the International Kitefliers Association?
> Don's father works for American Plastics, Incorporated.

Key to Writing

Carefully follow capitalization rules. Incorrect capitalization can confuse meaning in your writing.

Little Rock (Arkansas)	I am going out west. (direction)
little rock (pebble)	I am going out West. (area of country)

Outlines and Titles

■ **Capitalize the first word of each line of an outline.**

Notice that the divisions of an outline are marked with Roman numerals (I., II.). The next most important divisions are identified with capital letters (A., B.). After that, numerals mark the divisions.

Capitalization and Punctuation
 I. Use of capital letters
    A. Proper nouns and adjectives
    B. First words
      1. Sentences
      2. Poetry
      3. Outlines
      4. Titles
 II. Use of periods

■ **Capitalize the first word, last word, and all important words in a title.**

Do not capitalize an article (*the, a, an*), or a short preposition (*in, for, from, by*), unless it comes first or last.

    Raiders of the Lost Ark (movie title)
    Anne Morrow Lindbergh, *Gift from the Sea* (book)
    Lewis Carroll, "The Walrus and the Carpenter" (poem)

Titles are also underlined or enclosed in quotation marks. Follow this general rule for punctuating titles. Place quotation marks around titles of short works such as stories, poems, newspaper articles, and reports. Underline the titles of longer works such as books, movies, magazines, newspapers, and television series. In printed works, these titles are in italics instead of underlined.

Guidelines for Punctuation

The Period

■ Use a period at the end of a declarative sentence and most imperative sentences.

Declarative: The next clue is hidden under that rock.
Imperative: Look under that rock for the next clue.

■ Use a period after an abbreviation. To save time and space we often use words in a shortened form. These forms are called **abbreviations.**

The names of states, days, and months are often abbreviated. Except for such abbreviations as *Mr., Mrs., Ms.,* A.M., and P.M., avoid using abbreviations when you write sentences. Look at these abbreviations.

P.O.	Post Office	in.	inch
U.S.A.	United States of America	doz.	dozen
St.	Street	ht.	height
Mt.	Mountain	wt.	weight
R.R.	Railroad	lb.	pound
D.C.	District of Columbia	oz.	ounce

Some special abbreviations are written without periods.

FM	frequency modulation	PBS	Public Broadcasting System
CB	citizens' band	USAF	United States Air Force
M	meter	ml	milliliter

The two-letter state abbreviations such as IL, OH, and CA are written with capital letters and no periods. If you are not sure whether an abbreviation is written with periods, look in a dictionary.

■ Use a period after an initial. We often shorten a name to its first letter, which is called an initial. Always use a period after an initial.

P. Travers—Pamela Travers
J. C. Penny—James Cash Penny

■ Use a period after each number or letter that shows a division of an outline or that precedes an item in a list.

Punctuation (an outline)
I. End marks
   A. The period
      1. Sentences
      2. Abbreviations and initials
      3. Outlines and lists
   B. The question mark
   C. The exclamation point

Talent Show Act (a list)
1. tumblers
2. tap dancer
3. singer
4. band

The Question Mark and the Exclamation Point

■ Use a question mark at the end of an interrogative sentence. An **interrogative sentence** is a sentence that asks a question.

Where are we?   When do the geese migrate?

■ Use an exclamation point at the end of an exclamatory sentence and some imperative sentences. An **exclamatory sentence** is a sentence that expresses strong feelings.

Jackie struck out!   It's a home run!

Use an exclamation point at the end of an imperative sentence that shows surprise or other strong emotion.

Look out!   Hurry!

■ Use an exclamation point after an interjection. An **interjection** is a word or group of words used to express strong feeling.

Oh! How beautiful!   Wow! What an ending!

Key to Writing and Speaking

When you write dialogue, use question marks and exclamation points to show how words and sentences are spoken.

The Comma

Commas signal the reader to pause. This pause keeps the reader from running together words or ideas that should be separate.

■ **Use commas to separate the items in the series. There are always three or more words in a series.**

> The Jungle Pet Store sells mynah birds, lizards, turtles, and tropical fish.

In a series, place commas after each word except the last. It is important to insert commas carefully when you write a series. Notice how the meaning of this sentence changes when the commas are removed.

> The grocery clerk packed Anna's bag with soda crackers, broccoli soup, cream cheese, and peanut butter.

■ **If *yes, no,* or *well* begin a sentence, use a comma after them.**

> Yes, we're walking.   Well, we'll meet you there.

■ **When you use *and, but,* or *or* to combine two sentences, put a comma before these words.**

> We ran fast. We nearly missed the bus.
> We ran fast, but we nearly missed the bus.

■ **Use commas to set off the name of a person spoken to.**

One comma is needed when the name starts or ends the sentence. A comma is needed before and after a name in the middle of the sentence. Look at the way commas are used in these sentences.

Peter, what is your favorite movie?
Mail this letter please, Joseph.
I think, Abigail, that you are taller than Sara.

■ **Use commas to set off an appositive. An appositive follows a noun and renames the noun. It is used to give more information. Notice how commas set off the appositive in this sentence.**

Mr. Lopez, our swim coach, retired last week.

■ **Use commas to separate the parts of a date. If a date is in the middle of a sentence, use a comma after the last part.**

Our field trip to the Brookfield Zoo is on Friday, May 13.
On November 7, 1962, Eleanor Roosevelt died.

■ **Use a comma to separate the name of a city from the name of a state or country.**

We once lived near Trenton, New Jersey.
My parents traveled to Zurich, Switzerland, last year.

Key to Writing

Do not overuse commas. Too many commas make a sentence harder to read instead of easier.

Other Uses for Commas

■ Use a comma to set off the explanatory words of a direct quotation.

Notice where the comma is placed in this direct quotation.

Courtney announced, "The movie will begin in ten minutes."

The explanatory words *Courtney announced* come before the quotation. A comma is placed after the last explanatory word. Now read this quotation.

"I want to go home," moaned Lisa.

The explanatory words come after the quotation. A comma is placed inside the quotation marks and after the last word of the quotation. Sometimes the quotation is separated into two parts.

"One of the people in this room," the detective said, "is the murderer."

A comma is used after the last word of the first part. Another comma is used after the last explanatory word. You will learn more about punctuating quotations in part 7 of this guide.

■ Use a comma after the greeting of a friendly letter and after the closing of any letter.

Dear Agnes,   Sincerely yours,

■ Use a comma whenever the reader might be confused.

Some sentences can be very confusing if commas are not used.

Going up the elevator lost power.
In the grocery bags were in demand.

Notice how much clearer a sentence is when a comma is used.

Going up, the elevator lost power.
In the grocery, bags were in demand.

The Apostrophe and the Hyphen

■ Use an apostrophe to show possession. To form the possessive of a singular noun, add an apostrophe and *s* after the apostrophe.

city + 's = city's   Carlos + 's = Carlos's

To form the possessive of a plural noun that does not end in *s,* add an apostrophe and an *s* after the apostrophe.

gentlemen + 's = gentlemen's   geese + 's = geese's

To form the possessive of a plural noun that ends in *s,* add only an apostrophe.

birds + ' = birds'   cities + ' = cities'

■ Use an apostrophe in a contraction. A **contraction** is a word made by joining two words and omitting one or more letters. An apostrophe replaces the missing letters.

can + not = can't   we + are = we're
will + not = won't   does + not = doesn't
you + will = you'll   he + had = he'd
they + are = they're   she + would = she'd
are + not = aren't

■ Use a hyphen after the first part of a word at the end of a line. When you write, you sometimes run out of room at the end of a line. Then you may have to split the word. Put a hyphen at the end of a syllable. Then write the second part of the word on the next line.

Before you choose a career, investigate many fields.

Never divide words of one syllable, such as *slight* or *bounce.* If you are in doubt about dividing a word, look it up in a dictionary.
Do not write a single letter at the end or beginning of a line. For example, these divisions would be wrong: *a- mong, inventor- y.*

■ Use a hyphen in compound numbers from twenty-one through ninety-nine.

seventy-six trombones   Twenty-third Psalm

The Colon and the Semicolon

■ Use a colon after the greeting in a business letter.

Dear Mrs. Winter: Dear Sir:

■ Use a colon between the numerals that tell hours and minutes.

8:30 A.M.   3:30 P.M.

Remember to capitalize the letters and to use periods after each letter in the abbreviations A.M. and P.M.

■ Use a semicolon to combine two related sentences.

There are two ways to combine two related sentences into one. The first way is to use a conjunction such as *and, but,* or *or* to connect the sentences. When you write this kind of sentence, use a comma before the conjunction.

Judge Marino announced her decision, and the courtroom emptied quickly.

The second way to combine two related sentences is to use a semicolon (;). The semicolon takes the place of both the comma and the conjunction.

Judge Marino announced her decision; the courtroom emptied quickly.

Key to Writing

Correct use of the semicolon will help you avoid writing run-on sentences.

Incorrect: The conductor raised her baton the concert began.
Correct: The conductor raised her baton; the concert began.

Quotation Marks

When you write what a person has said, you are writing a quotation. When you write the person's exact words, you write a direct quotation. If you do not write the exact words, you are writing an indirect quotation. Study these sentences.

Direct quotation: Steven whispered, "I'm not feeling well."
Indirect quotation: Steven said that he was not feeling well.

■ Put quotation marks before and after the words of a direct quotation.

Notice that Steven's exact words are set apart by quotation marks in the first sentence.
Quotation marks (" ") are two pairs of small marks that look like apostrophes. They tell the reader that the exact words of the speaker or writer are being quoted.

■ Separate the words of a direct quotation from the rest of the sentence with a comma or end mark in addition to quotation marks.

Julie exclaimed, "The band is marching!"
"The band is marching!" Julie exclaimed.

Notice that, in the first sentence above, the comma comes *before* the quotation marks. The second sentence starts with the quoted words. Here the end mark is placed *inside* the quotation marks.

■ Place question marks and exclamation points inside quotation marks if they belong to the quotation itself.

> Michael asked, "Did the bird's wing heal?"
> "It's perfect!" answered Marianne.

In the first sentence, the question is quoted. Therefore, the question mark is placed inside the quotation marks. In the second sentence, the speaker is showing strong emotion. The exclamation point is also placed inside the quotation marks.

■ Place question marks and exclamation points outside quotation marks if they do not belong to the quotation. Remember to capitalize the first word of a direct quotation.

> Did Dad say, "Come home at seven o'clock"?
> I was shocked to hear her say, "I'll go"!

Sometimes a quotation is divided. Explanatory words, like *she said* or *he asked,* are in the middle of the quotation.

> "My favorite movie," Lewis said, "is the original *King Kong.*"

Notice that two sets of quotation marks are used in this quotation. The explanatory words are followed by a comma. This sentence has a comma after the explanatory words because the second part of the quotation does not begin a new sentence. Use a period after the explanatory words if the second part of the quotation is a sentence.

> "We wrote that," said the students. "It is a group poem."

Key to Writing

Said is a common explanatory word used in writing. Try to use a variety of explanatory words when you write. Try some of these.

explained	announced	exclaimed	requested
commented	expressed	asked	noted

Punctuating Titles

■ Put quotation marks around the titles of stories, poems, reports, articles, and chapters of a book.

"Spring Song" (poem)   "The Ransom of Red Chief" (story)

■ Underline the title of a book, magazine, play, motion picture, or TV series. When these titles are printed, they are in italics.

Mary Jane by Dorothy Sterling   *Mary Jane* by Dorothy Sterling

■ Underline the title of a painting or the name of a ship.

Washington Crossing the Delaware (painting)
Queen Elizabeth II (ship)

Guidelines for Spelling

How To Become a Better Speller

■ **Make a habit of looking at words carefully.**

When you come to a new word, be sure you know its meaning. If you are not certain, look up the word in a dictionary.

Practice seeing every letter. Many people see a word again and again but don't really look at it. When you see a new word or a tricky word, like *government,* look at all the letters. To help you remember them, write the word several times.

■ **When you speak, pronounce words carefully.**

Sometimes people misspell words because they say them wrong. Be sure that you are not blending syllables together. For example, you may write *probly* for *probably* if you are mispronouncing it.

■ **Find out your own spelling enemies and attack them.**

Look over your papers and make a list of the misspelled words. Also keep a list of new words that are difficult for you. Study these words until you can spell them correctly and easily.

■ **Find memory devices to help with problem spellings.**

Some words are difficult to remember. In these cases, a memory device may help you. A memory device is a trick, or a catchy sentence, that you can remember easily. The device tells you how to spell the word. Here are three examples:

principal	The princi*pal* is my *pal.*
tragedy	Every *age* has its tra*ge*dy.
embarrass	I turned *really red* and felt *so silly.*

■ Proofread what you write.

To make sure that you have spelled all words correctly, reread your work. Examine it carefully, word for word. Don't let your eyes race over the page and miss incorrectly spelled words.

■ Use a dictionary.

You don't have to know how to spell every word. No one spells everything correctly all the time. A good dictionary can help you to be a better speller. Use a dictionary whenever you need help with spelling.

Mastering Specific Words

When you notice that you are having trouble with a certain word, take a few minutes to study it carefully. Give it all your attention. If you spend the time and energy to learn it correctly once, you will save yourself all the trouble of correcting it many times.
Follow these steps to master a specific word.

1 Look at the word and say it to yourself.

Pronounce it carefully. If it has two or more syllables, say it again, one syllable at a time. Look at each syllable as you say it.

2 Look at the letters. Spell the word aloud.

If the word has two or more syllables, pause between syllables as you say the letters.

3 Without looking at the word, write it.

Be sure to form each letter properly. Take your time.

4 Now look at your book or list to see if you have spelled the word correctly.

If you have, write it once more. Compare it with the correct spelling again. For best results, repeat the process once more.

5 If you have misspelled the word, notice where the error was.

Then repeat steps 3 and 4 until you have spelled the word correctly three times in a row.

Rules for Spelling

Adding Prefixes and Suffixes

Prefixes

A prefix is a word part added to the beginning of a word to change its meaning. When a prefix is added to a word, the spelling of the word stays the same.

Prefix	Base Word	New Word
un- (not)	+ named	= unnamed (not named)
re- (again)	+ enter	= reenter (enter again)
dis- (not)	+ appear	= disappear (not appear)
il- (not)	+ legible	= illegible (not legible)
pre- (before)	+ set	= preset (set before)
im- (not)	+ mature	= immature (not mature)
mis- (incorrectly)	+ state	= misstate (state incorrectly)
in- (not)	+ formal	= informal (not formal)

■ The Suffixes -*ly* and -*ness*

A suffix is a word part added to the end of a word to change its meaning. When the suffix -*ly* is added to a word ending with *l*, both *l*'s are kept. When -*ness* is added to a word ending in *n*, both *n*'s are kept.

Base Word	Suffix	New Word
mean	+ **-ness**	= meanness
practical	+ **-ly**	= practically

■ The Final Silent *e*

When a suffix beginning with a vowel is added to a word ending with a silent *e,* the *e* is usually dropped.

make + ing = making   advise + or = advisor
confuse + ion = confusion   believe + able = believable
expense + ive = expensive   fame + ous = famous

When a suffix beginning with a consonant is added to a word ending with a silent *e,* the *e* is usually kept.

hate + ful = hateful   hope + less = hopeless
bore + dom = boredom   sure + ly = surely
safe + ty = safety   move + ment = movement

The following words are exceptions:

truly   argument   ninth   wholly   judgment

■ Words Ending in *y*

When a suffix is added to a word that ends with *y* following a consonant, the *y* is usually changed to *i.*

noisy + ly = noisily   fifty + eth = fiftieth
happy + est = happiest   heavy + ness = heaviness

Note this exception: When -*ing* is added, the *y* remains.

bury + ing = burying   cry + ing = crying
deny + ing = denying   apply + ing = applying

When a suffix is added to a word that ends with *y* following a vowel, the *y* usually is not changed.

joy + ful = joyful   pay + ment = payment
stay + ing = staying   annoy + ed = annoyed

The following words are exceptions: paid, said.

Words with *ie* or *ei*

When the sound is long *e* (ē), the word is spelled *ie* except after *c*. The following rhyme provides some rules which will help you.

I before *e*
Except after *c,*
Or when sounded like *a*
As in n*ei*ghbor or w*ei*gh.

Before E
belief   relieve   yield   fierce   achieve
niece   brief   field   chief   shield

Except after C
receive   ceiling   perceive   deceit
conceive   conceited   receipt

Or when sounded like A
weight   eight   neigh

These words are exceptions:

either   weird   species
neither   seize   leisure

Doubling the Final Consonant

Words of one syllable, ending with one consonant following one vowel, double the final consonant before adding *-ing, ed,* or *-er.*

sit + ing = sitting   sad + er = sadder
hop + ed = hopped   stop + ing = stopping
shop + er = shopper   let + ing = letting

The final consonant is **not** doubled when it follows two vowels.

meet + ing = meeting   loan + ed = loaned
break + ing = breaking   train + er = trainer

■ Words with the "Seed" Sound

Only one English word ends in *sede: supersede.*
Three words end in *ceed: exceed, proceed, succeed.*
All other words ending in the sound of "seed" are spelled *cede.*

concede   precede   recede   secede

Words Often Confused

Sometimes your problems in spelling are caused by the language itself.
In English there are many words that are easily confused. These words
sound the same, or nearly the same, but are spelled differently and
have different meanings. Words of this type are called **homophones.**
Here are some examples of homophones.

horse—hoarse   pare—pear—pair   tail—tale   do—dew—due

When you have problems with homophones, general spelling rules
won't help you. The only solution is to memorize which spelling goes
with which meaning.

Here is a list of homophones and other words frequently used and
frequently confused in writing. Study the sets of words, and try to
connect each word with its correct meaning.

accept means to agree to something or to receive something willingly.
except means to keep out or leave out. As a preposition, *except* means
"but" or "leaving out."

My brother will *accept* the job the grocer offered him.
Michelle likes every flavor of ice cream *except* pistachio.

capital means chief, important, or excellent. It also means the city or town that is the official seat of government of a state or nation.
capitol is the building where a state legislature meets.
the Capitol is the building in Washington, D.C., in which the United States Congress meets.

> The *capital* of Illinois is the city of Springfield.
> The *capitol* of Illinois is a stately building in Springfield.
> The senators arrived at the *Capitol* in time to vote.

hear means to listen to.
here means in this place.

> Every time I *hear* this song, I feel happy.
> Reference books are found *here* in the library.

it's is the contraction for *it is* or *it has.*
its shows ownership or possession.

> *It's* nearly midnight.
> The boat lost *its* sail during the storm.

lead (lĕd) is a heavy, gray metal.
lead (lēd) means to go first, to guide.
led (lĕd) is the past tense of *lead* (lēd).

> Water pipes are often made of *lead.*
> These signs will *lead* us to the hiking trail.
> Bloodhounds *led* the detectives to the scene of the crime.

loose means free or not tight.
lose means to mislay or suffer the loss of something.

> The rider kept the horse's reins *loose.*
> If you *lose* your book, report the loss to the library as soon as
>   possible.

peace is calm or stillness or the absence of disagreement.
piece means a portion or part.

> After two years of war, *peace* was finally achieved.
> This statue was carved from a *piece* of jade.

principal means first or most important. It also refers to the head of a school.
principle is a rule, truth, or belief.

> A *principal* export of Brazil is coffee.
> Our school *principal* organized a safety council.
> One *principle* of science is that all matter occupies space.

quiet means free from noise or disturbance.
quite means truly or almost completely.

> The only time our classroom is *quiet* is when it's empty.
> The aquarium tank is *quite* full.

their means belonging to them.
there means at that place.
they're is the contraction for *they are.*

> Our neighbors sold *their* house and moved to a farm.
> Please take the squirt guns over *there.*
> My sisters have never skied, but *they're* willing to try.

to means in the direction of.
too means also or very.
two is the whole number between one and three.

> The surgeon rushed *to* the operating room.
> The lights went off, and then the heat went off, *too.*
> Only *two* of the four mountaineers reached the peak.

weather is the state of the atmosphere referring to wind, moisture, temperature, etc.
whether indicates a choice or alternative.

> Australia has summer *weather* when the United States has winter.
> *Whether* we drive or take the train, we will arrive in three hours.

who's is the contraction for *who is* or *who has.*
whose is the possessive form of *who.*

> *Who's* been chosen to be a crossing guard?
> *Whose* skateboard was left on the sidewalk?

you're is the contraction for *you are.*
your is the possessive form of *you.*

> *You're* going to the costume party, aren't you?
> Please bring *your* sheet music to choir practice.

Index of Skills

Critical Thinking Skills

Alternatives 49, 81, 193, 305, 391, 426, 444, 625
Analysis. *See* **Literary Skills Index**
Application
  of Ideas to Selections, 16, 54, 64, 83, 137, 277, 336, 354
  of Literature to Life, 38, 81, 88, 112, 172, 211, 220, 305, 322, 354, 371, 379, 479, 481, 485, 525, 555, 609
Cause and Effect 9, 20, 26, 38, 54, 81, 112, 131, 137, 145, 164, 172, 192, 210, 230, 274, 276, 301, 314, 371, 384, 422, 432, 445, 475, 478, 515, 571, 587
Classification 26, 90, 91, 180 277, 400, 426, 432, 474, 497
Comparison and Contrast 9, 13, 16, 26, 30, 31, 38, 42, 58, 79, 85, 91, 112, 126, 131, 140, 145, 164, 216, 221, 241, 261, 274, 276, 301, 322, 354, 363, 371, 399, 403, 412, 414, 437, 444, 456, 459, 467, 469, 473, 479, 490, 494, 529, 555, 587, 604
Conclusions. *See also* **Inference**
  Drawing Conclusions, 30, 216, 467
Evaluation 42, 46, 85, 91, 126, 138, 140, 230, 253, 262, 274, 277, 292, 301, 305, 344, 384, 400, 418, 437, 439, 442, 456, 469, 489, 494, 529, 608. *See also* **Literary Skills Index**
Fact and Fiction 314
Fact and Opinion 336, 402
Generalizations 528. *See also* **Inference**
Inference 13, 16, 19–20, 26, 38, 42, 46, 49, 64, 73, 79, 83, 91, 112, 126, 131, 137, 164, 180, 186, 192, 203, 210, 216, 220, 241, 247, 248, 253, 261, 292, 305, 314, 321, 336, 344, 354, 363, 371, 378, 388, 391, 395, 412, 444, 458, 461, 463, 464, 475, 478, 481, 482, 485, 486, 489, 494, 496, 515–16, 525, 529, 555, 571, 586, 587, 604
Opinions. *See* **Fact and Opinion; Supporting Opinions**
Relationships. *See also* **Cause and Effect; Comparison and Contrast**
  Between Characters, 9, 19, 20, 26, 38, 49, 64, 72, 83, 137, 164, 172, 180, 202, 216, 230, 241, 248, 261, 262, 276, 378, 391, 403, 473, 555, 556
  Chronological, 58, 253, 262, 274, 276, 322, 395, 508, 571, 605
  of Parts to the Whole, 131, 164, 277, 422, 426, 442, 444, 461, 474, 507, 620, 630
Summarizing 13, 20, 38, 49, 277, 345, 526, 529
Supporting Opinions 49, 76, 140, 145, 180, 186, 210, 241, 261, 274, 277, 292, 314, 315, 422, 479, 487, 490, 529, 587, 604

Literary Skills

Acts 500, 525
Alliteration 422, 432, 445, 450, 494
Allusion 85, 439–440, 487
Anecdote 305
Aphorism 305
Autobiography 280, 283, 292, 322, 336
Ballad 426
Biography 280, 339, 344–345, 354, 371
  Characters, 363, 371
  Information Sources, 339, 379
Characterization 192, 202–203, 221, 587
  Direct, 186, 210
  Indirect, 186, 210
Characters
  in Biography, 339, 363, 371
  Foils, 113, 216, 391
  in Folk Tales, 64
  Hero/Heroine, 16, 64, 336
  in Literary Work, 262
  in Short Story, 104, 164, 172, 175, 180, 192, 230
  Stereotypes, 274, 556–557
Chronological Order 395–396
Climax
  in Drama, 516
  in Novel, 532, 605
  in Short Story, 253
Complications 532, 571, 587, 605
Concrete Poems 437
Conflict
  in Folk Tales, 64
  in Myths, 20
  in Novel, 556, 571, 604
  in Short Story, 164, 180, 203, 241, 248, 262, 274
Description 292, 314
Dialect 210
Dialogue
  in Drama, 500, 507–508
  in Fable, 83
  in Short Story, 145
Drama 500
  Acts and Scenes, 500, 525
  Climax, 516
  Dialogue, 500, 507–508
  Flashback, 508, 516
  Irony, 525
  Mood, 525
  Setting, 507
  Stage Directions, 500, 507, 525
  Surprise Ending, 525

in a Novel, 556
in a Short Story, 104, 107, 112, 126, 140, 145, 164, 172
in a Tall Tale, 73
Shape 406, 435, 439, 445
Short Stories 104
    Characters, 104, 164, 172, 175, 180, 192, 230, 262
    Climax, 253
    Conflict, 164, 180, 203, 241, 248, 262, 274
    Dialogue, 145
    Flashback, 233, 274
    Foreshadowing, 192, 233
    Personification, 112
    Plot, 104, 233, 253, 262
    Point of View, 140, 248, 253
    Setting, 104, 107, 112, 126, 140, 145, 164, 172
    Surprise Ending, 140, 233, 248
    Theme, 137, 172, 203, 216, 230
    Title, 126, 130, 248
Simile 137, 400, 412, 450, 456, 459, 490, 494
Sound 406, 409, 437
Speaker 412. *See also* **Point of View**
Speaking and Listening 58, 145, 422, 432
Stage Directions
    in Drama, 500, 507, 525
Stanza 422, 426, 474
Stereotype 274, 556–557
Style 126, 400, 442
Subplots 532, 571
Surprise Ending
    in Drama, 525
    in Short Story, 140, 233, 248
Suspense
    in Novel, 604
    in Short Story, 164, 172, 221, 230, 233, 262, 274
Symbols
    in Drama, 516
    in Fable, 81
    in Folk Tale, 42
    in Poetry, 461, 476
Tales 2, 38
Tall Tales 2, 73
    Setting, 73
Theme
    in Folk Tale, 46, 49
    in Novel, 605
    in Poetry, 415, 464, 473–474, 479, 489
    in Short Story, 137, 172, 203, 216, 230
Title
    in Myth, 20
    in Poetry, 422
    in Short Story, 126, 230, 248
Tone
    in Nonfiction, 388
    in Poetry, 453, 461

Maps, Charts, and Diagrams

Borrowing from Other Languages 193
Cheyenne Homelands, 1860–1890 241
Paul Revere's Ride, April 18–19, 1775 432
Stages in the Process of Writing 101

Reading Skills

Author's Point of View 58, 126, 336, 363, 384, 388, 411, 450, 485. *See also* **Purpose**
Author's Purpose. *See* **Purpose**
Cause and Effect 9, 20, 26, 38, 54, 81, 112, 131, 137, 145, 164, 172, 192, 210, 230, 274, 276, 301, 314, 371, 384, 422, 432, 445, 475, 478, 515, 571, 587. *See also* "Interpreting" questions
Comparison and Contrast
    of Characters, 9, 13, 26, 30, 42, 79, 126, 140, 164, 216, 221, 241, 261, 274, 276, 301, 354, 371, 399, 444, 555, 587, 604
    of Ideas, 31, 112, 145, 322, 363, 414, 437, 456, 459, 467, 469, 473, 479, 490, 494
    of Selections, 16, 30, 38, 58, 85, 91, 403, 412, 529
Conclusions 30, 42, 88, 172, 253, 322, 587. *See also* **Inference**
Connotation 42, 230
Context Clues 42, 85, 112, 292–93, 301, 314, 336, 345, 363, 372, 400, 461, 557, 638–39
Denotation. *See* **Connotation; Vocabulary and Language Skills Index**
Description 111, 126, 127, 137, 164, 221, 292, 314
Details 26, 42, 43, 64, 126, 141, 164, 231, 248, 293, 322, 354, 414, 461, 507, 618. *See also* "Recalling" questions
Evaluation 608
    of Author's Style, 126, 138, 140, 230, 262, 277, 292, 437, 439, 442, 469
    of Author's Effectiveness and Purpose, 46, 85, 91, 126, 301, 305, 344, 363, 384, 418, 456, 489, 494
    of Believability, 42, 126, 253, 274, 400
    of Literary Genre, 529. *See also* **Literary Skills Index**
Exposition 314
Fact and Opinion 336, 402, 608. *See also* **Opinion;** "Critical Thinking" questions
Figurative Language 9, 31, 38, 42, 73, 79, 81, 85, 112, 126, 131, 137, 186, 400, 412, 418, 432, 439, 442, 450, 456, 459, 461, 463, 467, 469, 475, 476, 482, 484, 485, 487, 490, 494, 516
Foreshadowing 192. *See also* **Predictions; Sequence**

Research Skills

Vocabulary and Language Skills

Writing Skills

Index of Fine Art

*A*rt Credits

Cover

Black, Ochre, Red Over Red, 1957. Mark Rothko. Collection of the Museum of Contemporary Art, Los Angeles. The Panza Collection. Photograph by Squidds & Nunns. Copyright © 1978 by Christopher Rothko and Kate Rothko Prizel.

Photographs

Photograph by David Heald, ii; Washington State University, Pullman, Washington, 13; Photograph by James H. Vaughn, 15; Photo Researchers, New York: copyright © 1983 Rod Planck, National Audubon Society Collection, 19; copyright © 1976 M. P. Kahl, the National Audubon Society Collection, 57; copyright © C. E. Mohr, 304; copyright © Peter B. Kaplan, 308; copyright © R. D. Estes, 313; copyright © Susan McCartney, 311; copyright © Dick Davis, 385; Houghton Mifflin and Company, 20; copyright © 1972 Douglas R. Gilbert, 43; Historical Pictures Service, Chicago, 49, 54, 425; Photograph by Stephen Mason Gray, 68, 70; Magnum Photos, Inc., New York: Photograph by Henri Cartier-Bresson, 86; Photograph copyright © Inge Morath, 517; Heinemann/Camera Press/Photo Trends, Freeport, New York, 113; Photograph by John Tennant, 119; Photograph by Sally Andersen-Bruce, 129; AP/Wide World Photos, New York, 173, 193, 203, 211, 274, 302, 305, 401, 415, Photograph by Henri Cartier-Bresson, 379; Library of Congress, Washington, D.C., 318; H. Armstrong Roberts, Philadelphia: Photograph by Charles Phelps Cushing, 321; Photograph by D. Corson, 453; Photograph courtesy of Michael Johnson, 217; Culver Pictures, Inc., New York, 231, 254, 293, 315, 323, 419, 451, 461, 469, 474, 491; Mansfield Library, University of Minnesota, 242; Santa Clara University, copyright © 1984 Glenn Matsumura, 248; High and Wild Photography, Albany, California, Photograph by Galen Rowell, 287; Kon-Tiki Museum, Oslo, 300; Photograph by Randolph Photography 337; The Bettmann Archive, Inc., New York, 290, 345, 353, 433, 465, 489; UPI/Bettmann, New York, 297; Bryn Mawr College Library, Bryn Mawr, Pennsylvania, 354; Stock Boston, Photograph by Owen Franken, 356, 361; Smith College Archives, Smith College, Northampton, Massachusetts, 372; Moorland-Spingarn Research Center, Howard University, Washington, D.C., 389 top; Photograph by David Jones, 389 bottom; Animals Animals, New York, copyright © Brian Milne, 398; Photograph by Robert E. Mates, 408; Marion E. Wade Collection, Wheaton College Library, Wheaton, Illinois, 423; Photograph by Elyre de Lanux, 437; Harvard College Library, Harvard University, Cambridge, Massachusetts, 440; Estate of Fred Lape, 454; William Morrow Company, copyright © Nancy Crampton, 463; Photograph by Antony di Gesu, 482; Photograph by Kathleen Culbert-Aguilar, 484; Harris and Ewing/Photo Trends, Freeport, New York, 495; McKnight Studio, Mason, Texas, 606.

Illustrations

Robert Borja, 41; Steven Schindler, 79; James Thurber, 84, 85, 88; Troy Thomas, 151, 152, 157, 159, 160, 162, 167, 168, 171; James Watling, 197; Karen Lidbeck, 224, 228; Arvis Stewart, 328; 333; Diana Magnuson, 421, 423; Clifford Timm, 436; Lydia Halverson, 439, 537, 540, 545, 553, 562, 569, 575, 580, 585, 587, 590, 593, 602; Robert Masheris, 457; Konrad Hack, 520, 523.

Acknowledgments *Continued from copyright page*

Louis L'Amour, from *War Party* by Louis L'Amour; copyright © 1975 by Bantam Books, Inc., from *Collier's,* July 5, 1952, copyright 1952 by The Crowell-Collier Publishing Company. Alan Bloch: For "Men Are Different" by Alan Bloch, first appeared in *50 Short Science Fiction Tales,* edited by Isaac Asimov and Groff Conklin; copyright 1954 by Groff Conklin. Brandt & Brandt Literary Agents, Inc.: For "Johnny Appleseed" by Rosemary & Stephen Vincent Benét, from *A Book of Americans* by Rosemary & Stephen Vincent Benét; copyright 1933 by Rosemary & Stephen Vincent Benét, copyright renewed © 1961 by Rosemary Carr Benét. Curtis Brown Ltd.: For "Arap Sang and the Cranes" by Humphrey Harman, from *Tales Told Near a Crocodile*; copyright 1962 by Humphrey Harman. Childrens Press: For "Wild Courage" by Robert Franklin Leslie, from an adaptation published by Golden Gate Junior Books Division of Childrens Press, © 1974. Don Congdon Associates, Inc.: For "Luke Baldwin's Vow" by Morley Callaghan; copyright 1948 by Morley Callaghan, renewed 1975 by Morley Callaghan. For "All Summer In a Day" by Ray Bradbury, published in *Magazine of Fantasy and Science Fiction,* March, 1954; copyright 1954 by Ray Bradbury, renewed 1982 by Ray Bradbury. Thomas Y. Crowell: For "Reggie," from *Honey, I Love and Other Love Poems* by Eloise Greenfield; copyright © 1978 by Eloise Greenfield. For "Langston Terrace" and "Mama Sewing," from *Childtimes: A Three-Generation Memoir* by Eloise Greenfield and Lessie Jones Little; copyright © 1979 by Eloise Greenfield and Lessie Jones Little. The Devin-Adair Company, Inc.: For "The Trout," from *The Man Who Invented Sin* by Sean O'Faolain; copyright 1948 by The Devin-Adair Company, renewed 1976. Delacorte Press/Seymour Lawrence: For "Seal" excerpted from *Laughing Time* by William Jay Smith; copyright © 1953, 1955, 1956, 1957, 1959, 1968, 1974, 1977, 1980 by William Jay Smith. Dodd, Mead & Company, Inc.: For "Frederick Douglass," from *Famous American Negroes* by Langston Hughes; copyright 1954 by Langston Hughes, copyright renewed 1982 by George Houston Bass. For an excerpt from "How Whirlwind Saved Her Cub," from *Buffalo Woman* by Dorothy M. Johnson; copyright © 1977 by Dorothy M. Johnson. Doubleday & Company, Inc.: For "The Fun They Had," from *Earth Is Room Enough* by Isaac Asimov; copyright © 1957 by Isaac Asimov, reprinted by permission of Doubleday & Company, Inc. and NEA Service, Inc. Norma Millay Ellis: For "The Courage That My Mother Had" by Edna St. Vincent Millay, from *Collected Poems,* Harper & Row; copyright 1923, 1951, 1954 by Edna St. Vincent Millay and Norma Millay Ellis. Elsevier-Dutton Publishing Co., Inc.: For a selection from *Rascal* by Sterling North; copyright © 1963 by Sterling North. For "Geronimo: His Own Story," from *Geronimo: His Own Story* edited by S. M. Barrett. Farrar, Straus & Giroux, Inc.: For "Shrewd Todie and Lyzer the Miser," from *When Shlemiel Went to Warsaw* by Isaac Bashevis Singer; copyright © 1968 by Isaac Bashevis Singer. Richard Garcia: For "The City Is So Big" by Richard Garcia, from *Selected Poetry* by Richard Garcia; copyright © 1973. Ginn and Company: For "Mark Twain," from *Young Americans* by Cornelia Meigs; copyright 1936 by Cornelia Meigs, adapted and used by permission of the publisher, Ginn and Company (Xerox Corporation). Harcourt Brace Jovanovich, Inc.: For "To Look At Anything," from *The Living Seed* by John Moffitt; copyright © 1961 by John Moffitt. For "Nancy," from *The Moment Before the Rain* by Elizabeth Enright; copyright 1948 by Elizabeth Enright; copyright © 1976 by Nicholas Gillham, Robert Gillham, and Oliver Gillham. For "Macavity: The Mystery Cat," from *Old Possum's Book of Practical Cats* by T. S. Eliot; copyright 1939 by T. S. Eliot; copyright 1967 by Esme Valerie Eliot; Faber and Faber Ltd. For "Narnian Suite," from *Poems* by C. S. Lewis, edited by Walter Hooper; copyright © 1964 by Executors of the Estate of C. S. Lewis; Collins Publishers, London. For "Fog" by Carl Sandburg, from *Chicago Poems*; copyright 1916 by Holt, Rinehart & Winston, Inc., renewed 1944 by Carl Sandburg. For "The Apprentice" by Dorothy Canfield Fisher, from *Four-Square*; copyright 1947 by Curtis Publishing Company, renewed 1975 by Downe Publishing, Inc. Harper & Row, Publishers, Inc.: For entire text and illustrations of *Old Yeller* by Fred Gipson, drawings by Carl Burger; copyright © 1956 by Fred Gipson. For excerpts from *The Wounded Wolf* by Jean Craighead George. For "Home," from *The World of Gwendolyn Brooks* by Gwendolyn Brooks; copyright 1951 by The Curtis Publishing Company; copyright 1953 by Gwendolyn Brooks Blakely. For "The Laughing Faces of Pigs" in *Barnyard Year* by Fred Lape; copyright 1949, 1950 by Fred Lape. For "Where the Sidewalk Ends," from *Where the Sidewalk Ends: The Poems and Drawings of Shel Silverstein*; copyright © 1974 by Shel Silverstein. For "New World," from *The Gourd Dancer* by N. Scott Momaday; copyright © 1976. For "The Glorious Whitewasher," from *The Adventures of Tom Sawyer* by Mark Twain. Lawrence Hill & Co., Inc.: For "Last Cover" by Paul Annixter, by permission of the author. Holt, Rinehart and Winston, Publishers: For "Paul Revere" by Esther Forbes, from *There Were Giants in the Land: Twenty-Eight Historic Americans as Seen by Twenty-Eight Contemporary Americans*; copyright 1942, © 1970 by Holt, Rinehart and Winston, Publishers. For "The Pasture" by Robert Frost from *The Poetry of Robert Frost,* edited by Edward Connery Lathem; copyright 1939, © 1967, 1969 by Holt, Rinehart and Winston. Houghton Mifflin Company: For an adaptation from *Stickeen* by John Muir; copyright 1909 by John Muir; copyright 1937 by Wanda Muir Hanna, as it appeared in Cricket, June 1978. For "Arachne" (The Fateful Contest), from *Greek Myths* by Olivia Coolidge; copyright 1949 and copyright © renewed 1977 by Olivia E. Coolidge. For an excerpt from *Thoreau of Walden Pond* by Sterling North; copyright © 1959 by Sterling North. International Creative Management: For *Grandpa and the Statue* by Arthur Miller; copyright © 1945, 1973 by Arthur Miller. Bertha Klausner International Literary Agency, Inc.: For "The Richer, the Poorer" by Dorothy West, from *The Best Short Stories by Negro Writers,* by permission of Dorothy West. Alfred A. Knopf, Inc.: For "The White Snake," from *The Complete Grimm's Fairy Tales* by Jakob Ludwig Karl and Wilhelm Karl Grimm, translated by Margaret Hunt and James Stern; copyright 1944 by Pantheon Books, Inc., renewed 1972 by Random House, reprinted by permission of Pantheon Books, a division of Random House, Inc. For "Pretty Words," from *Collected Poems* of Elinor Wylie; copyright 1932 by Alfred A. Knopf, Inc., renewed 1960 by Edwina C. Rubenstein. For "The Dream Keeper," from *The Dream Keeper and Other Poems* by Langston Hughes; copyright 1932, renewed 1960 by Langston Hughes. For "The Weasel" and specified two illustrations, from *One Day on Beetle Rock* by Sally Carrighar, illustrated by Henry B. Kane; copyright 1944, renewed 1972 by Sally Carrighar, copyright 1943, 1944 by The Curtis Publishing Co. For "Miss Wilson's Miracle," from *Mary McLeod Bethune* by Emma Gelders Sterne; copyright © 1957 by Emma Gelders Sterne. Joy Kogawa: For "Waiting" by Joy Kogawa, from *A Choice of Dreams.* J. B. Lippincott Co.: For "Jake Hanson," from *The Pheasant on Route 7* by Kaye Starbird; copyright © 1968 by Kaye Starbird. For specified material (One of the Cunninghams) pp. 21–28 in *To Kill a Mockingbird* by Harper Lee; copyright © 1960 by Harper Lee. Little, Brown and Company: For "Living Tenderly," from *New and Selected Things Taking Place* by May Swenson; copyright © 1963 by May Swenson. Liveright Publishing Corp.: For "in Just–" from *Tulips & Chimneys* by E. E. Cummings; copyright 1923, 1925 and renewed 1951, 1953 by E. E. Cummings; copyright © 1973, 1976 by Nancy T. Andrews; copyright © 1973, 1976 by George James Firmage. Macmillan Publishing Co.: For "Night," from *Collected Poems* by Sara Teasdale; copyright 1930 by Sara Teasdale Filsinger, renewed 1958 Guaranty Trust Co. of N. Y., Executor. For "The Lion and the Mouse," "The Town Mouse and the Country Mouse," "The Ant and the Grasshopper," and "The Fox and the Crow," from *Aesop's Fables,* edited by Joseph Jacobs; copyright 1950, renewed 1978, Macmillan Publishing Co. For "Sea-Fever," from *Poems* by John Masefield (New York: Macmillan, 1953). William Morrow & Company, Inc. (Lothrop, Lee & Shepard Books): For "The Sidewalk Racer or On the Skateboard," from *The Sidewalk Racer and Other Poems of Sports and Motion* by Lillian Morrison; copyright © 1977 by Lillian Morrison. For "Winter Poem (3 Feb. '72)," from *My House* by Nikki Giovanni; copyright © 1972 by Nikki Giovanni. Harold Ober Associates: For "Stolen Day" by Sherwood Anderson, from *This Week*; copyright © 1941 by the United Newspapers Magazine Corp., renewed 1968 by Eleanor Copenhaver Anderson. Pantheon Books and Collins Publishers: For "Cub Life," from *Born Free* by Joy Adamson; copyright © 1960 by Joy Adamson. Rand McNally & Company and George Allen & Unwin: For "Across the Pacific by Raft," from *Kon-Tiki* by Thor Heyerdahl; copyright 1950 by Thor Heyerdahl. Fleming H. Revell Company: For "How the Seasons and the Birds Came" by Princess Atalie Unkalunt from *The Earth Speaks.* Frederick H. Rohlfs: For "A Secret for Two" by Quentin Reynolds. Scholastic Magazines, Inc.: For "Demeter," from *Heroes, Gods and Monsters of Greek Myths* by Bernard Evslin, Dorothy Evslin, & Ned Hoopes; copyright © 1967 by Scholastic, Inc. For "Midas," from *Heroes and Monsters of Greek Myths* by Bernard Evslin, Dorothy Evslin, & Ned Hoopes; copyright © 1967 by Scholastic, Inc. For "Prometheus," from *Heroes, Gods and Monsters of the Greek Myths* by Bernard Evslin; (Four Winds Press) copyright © 1966 by Scholastic, Inc. Charles Scribner's Sons: For "Beau," from *Another Kind of Autumn* by Loren Eiseley; copyright © 1977 the Estate of Loren Eiseley, copyright © 1976 Loren Eiseley. Simon

& Schuster New World Dictionaries: For entries from *Webster's New World Dictionary,* Student Edition; copyright © 1981 by Simon & Schuster, Inc. Mrs. James Thurber: For text and drawings for "The Fox and the Crow" and "What Happened to Charles," from *Further Fables for Our Time;* copyright © 1956 by James Thurber, published by Simon & Schuster, Inc. University of Oklahoma Press: For "The Origin of Fire" by Ella E. Clark, from *Indian Legends from the Northern Rockies;* copyright © 1966. Viking Penguin, Inc.: For "Paul Bunyan," from *American Tall Tales* by Adrien Stoutenberg; copyright © 1966. For "J. P. Sousa," from *American Tall Tale Animals* by Adrien Stoutenberg; copyright © 1968. The Westminster Press: For *Winter Thunder* by Mari Sandoz; copyright © MCMLI by The Curtis Publishing Company, copyright © MCMLIV by Mari Sandoz. The authors and editors have made every effort to trace the ownership of all copyrighted selections in this book and to make full acknowledgment for their use.

Staff Credits

Susan Schaffrath	Executive Editor, Literature
Sherry Stansbury	Senior Editor
Dennis Ryan	Associate Editor
Linda Williams	Associate Editor
Robert St. Clair	Production Coordinator
Mary Schafer	Production Coordinator
Zana Courser	Production Editor
Ronald Rutkowski	Production Editor
Ronald Worman	Production Editor
Roslyn Weinstein	Associate Production Editor
Kenneth Izzi	Designer
The Quarasan Group	Design and Production

Index of Titles and Authors

CARGILL

Published by UNIVERSITY PRESS OF NEW ENGLAND

WAYNE G. BROEHL, JR.

CARGILL

Trading the World's Grain

Hanover & London   DARTMOUTH COLLEGE

DARTMOUTH COLLEGE

Published by University Press of New England, Hanover,

New Hampshire 03755

© 1992 by Wayne G. Broehl, Jr.

Printed in the United States of America   5 4 3 2 1

CIP data appear at the end of the book

Unless otherwise noted, illustrations are courtesy of Cargill, Inc.

Title page illustration, overleaf: Green Bay, Wisconsin, c. 1904.

Contents

PART THREE.
FREE TO GROW, 1916 – 1930

PART FOUR. IDEAS AND
INNOVATIONS — THE 1930s

PART FIVE. WAR ONCE MORE; NEW
FEED AND OIL DIVISIONS

Acknowledgments

This is the fifth book written by me in a series of business histories under the auspices of the research program of the Amos Tuck School of Business Administration of Dartmouth College, done under the College's requirement of full scholarly independence. Cargill recognized from the start the wisdom of engaging an outside scholar and allowing this person to view the Company at arm's length, with no editorial constraints by anyone. In order to assure this independence, it was agreed that there would be no financial relationship between myself and the Company. Instead, Cargill made a grant to Dartmouth College, to cover only my regular salary. This very private company in a very secretive industry allowed me full access to all records and all employees and imposed no constraints. For their perception of and enthusiasm for these basic principles of sound business history, I owe thanks both to the members of both families and to senior management.

Five senior members of the family have provided major input: Whitney MacMillan, James R. Cargill, Cargill MacMillan, Jr., W. Duncan Mac-Millan and John Hugh MacMillan III. Pauline Whitney MacMillan (now deceased) gave me insight into the role of her husband, Cargill MacMillan, Sr. Pauline MacMillan Keinath, their daughter, also was helpful. Marion MacMillan helped me understand her father, John MacMillan, Jr. I was privileged to attend a number of the "family meetings" described in chapter 19, and these measurably advanced my understanding of the dynamics of a family company.

Cargill's senior professional management played a significant role in my research. I especially want to thank William R. Pearce, Cargill's vice-chairman, who was my colleague and advisor throughout the project. I also wish to acknowledge the important input of the late James Spicola and of Heinz Hutter, James Howard, Gerald Mitchell, Robert Lumpkins, Leonard Alderson, Peter Von Eschen and Marleen Kurschner. John F. McGrory,

Cargill's general counsel, carried out that role so critical to sound business history with great sensitivity and unwavering support. Cheryl Pederson, his archival assistant, aided measurably in this process.

Retired Cargill senior management provided a major resource for my knowledge of the Company. I had in-depth interviews with some 85 of these people and met with several score more—in total a number too large to enumerate here. However, I would like to mention a few especially faithful people. Clifford M. Roberts, Jr., longtime lecturer for me in my Dartmouth classes, originally persuaded me to consider the project, then read with great understanding everything I wrote. Jim Cargill also did the same, with a particularly discriminating eye for editorial style. Both of these wonderful colleagues knew how to be analytical and constructive while at the same time preserving my full independence to make my own judgments. Robert Diercks and Walter B. Saunders also read most of the manuscript, and I have prized their thoughtful comments. Tom Totushek, now deceased, shared unique information on the early days. Walter Gage and Brewster Hanson were particularly helpful in assessing the role of Tradax, Cargill's European entity. M. D. Wyard was helpful on the commodity markets and Calvin Smith on a number of accounting and control matters. Erwin Kelm, retired chief executive officer, and M. D. McVay gave me many insights.

The members of the Cargill Public Affairs Department all have been supportive friends; Robbin Johnson, Garland West, Jean Spielman Housh, Jon Yeager, Lisa Vickstrom and former member Newell Searle were particularly involved in the project. Again, the entire Cargill Information Center under Julia Peterson has been a major contributor; Margaret Drews and Peter Sidney were particularly helpful. The Corporate Secretary's office is central to a business history; Marleen Kurschner's staff of Anne Carlson, Allison Gunlock and Cheryl Nikko and former members Anne Moore and Kathleen Steinmetz were all involved in the research. John Keefe's records management skills were also called upon many times. Jean Lawe has edited a number of my books and did so here with her usual grace and professionalism. Patricia Condon Johnston and James Sazevich were helpful at several points. Finally, Cargill's archivist, Rosemary Palmer, was engaged by the project at every stage, and her judgment and insight are especially appreciated.

I had major contacts with a number of members of the grain trade and the Twin Cities business community. Particularly helpful were Dwayne Andreas, the late Max Goldberg, Ralph Bagley and a number of his colleagues at the Minneapolis grain exchange. William Barney pointed the way in my understanding of the La Crosse, Wisconsin, business community. Professor Owen Gregory was an important contributor to my understanding of the Chicago Board of Trade archives. These are housed in the

Special Collections of the University of Illinois, Chicago campus, under the direction of the helpful archivist, Gretchen Lagana. Other members of the Minneapolis and Saint Paul communities provided further insights into the life of these two vibrant cities; Mrs. Dewalt Ankeny, Sr., and Marvin Borman were particularly helpful. Former Cargill executive Ben Jaffray was a thoughtful respondent throughout.

My academic colleagues have given me, as always, superb analytical feedback. I particularly wish to thank Mira Wilkins, Morton Rothstein and Ray Goldberg, each of whom read the entire manuscript with great care. This book simply would not be what it is without their very special input. I have expressed in my introduction to this book my longtime debt to Alfred D. Chandler, Jr. The two Tuck School deans spanning this long project, Colin Blaydon and Edward Fox, have given me the strong institutional support of Dartmouth College. My longtime friend, former dean John W. Hennessey, Jr., has once more provided for me that special evaluative perception he has exercised so well with my previous books.

Librarians are faculty favorites, and I have a legion of them to appreciate. Tuck School librarian James Fries and his colleagues are marvels; Bette Snyder, Jonathan Brown and Tom Labruna were particularly helpful. The Baker Library of Dartmouth is the equal of Tuck on these matters; Robert Jaccuad, Virginia Close, Patricia Carter, Joan Adams and Marilyn Curphey all were drawn into the research on many occasions.

I would also like to acknowledge the help given me by the staffs of the following institutions: Minnesota Historical Society, Division of Library and Archives; Minneapolis Public Library; University of Minnesota Libraries; Fort Worth Public Library; University of Texas, Arlington, Libraries; Amon Carter Museum, Fort Worth; State Historical Society of Texas, Austin; Iowa Historical Society; La Crosse County Historical Society; Area Research Center, University of Wisconsin, La Crosse; La Crosse Public Library Archives; Rock County Historical Society, Janesville, Wisconsin; Freeborn County Historical Society, Albert Lea, Minnesota; Rockefeller Archive Center, North Tarrytown, New York; Luther College Archives, Decorah, Iowa; Institute for Great Lakes Research, Perrysburg, Ohio; Green Bay Public Library; Manuscript Division, Baker Library; Harvard Business School; and James J. Hill Library, Saint Paul, Minnesota. I especially wish to acknowledge the research help of Robert Frame III, a member of the last-named organization, as well as that of Barnaby Conrad of the Pondera History Association, Conrad, Montana; John Gruber, University of Wisconsin, Madison; and Duane Fenstermann, archivist at Luther College.

My last acknowledgments are in many ways the most important. I have been blessed in this project with two superb secretaries, Suzanne Sweet at Dartmouth and Bonnie Meyer at Cargill. One could not ask for more wonderful friends and colleagues. Their faithfulness and diligence simply cannot be measured. Finally, my love and profound appreciation go to my wife, Jean, who was my research assistant throughout the project and whose judgment and perspective I trust above all!

Hanover, New Hampshire   W.G.B., Jr.
August 1991

Introduction

Cargill is one of the largest corporations in the United States, with annual sales of over $44 billion. It is the largest privately held company in the country. The Cargill and MacMillan families still retain essentially all of the equity in the corporation. Cargill is best known as one of the world's great multinational commodity trading companies but also has been involved more recently in a number of other agribusiness and industrial endeavors.

Private ownership has been the rule in the grain-trading industry, which is an industry with a passion for secrecy. This will be the first full-scale analytical business history of any of the "Big Five" of this industry. "Big Five," a term used widely in the 1970s, when all of the major grain companies were involved in massive sales to the Soviet Union, is no longer accurate—one of these, Cook Industries, fell on difficult days in the 1980s and was sold piecemeal. Of the other four, Cargill is the largest, followed by Continental Grain, Louis Dreyfus and Bunge y Born. All are privately held, with dominant family ownership. Only Cargill has been a United States company from its inception.

Cargill is now 125 years old and in this period has had just five chief executive officers. This book centers on the tenure of the first three, William W. Cargill, John H. MacMillan, Sr., and John H. MacMillan, Jr., who in combination held the reins for almost 100 of these years. A briefer section in the concluding chapter discusses the leadership of the last two, Erwin E. Kelm and Whitney MacMillan.

"W. W." was an early entrepreneur on the trans-Mississippi frontier, and his growth from a small-town grain buyer to the owner (with his brothers) of two large "line" elevator companies along the railroads out of La Crosse, Wisconsin, and Minneapolis, Minnesota, gives a revealing view of those hurly-burly days. Son-in-law John H. MacMillan was brought in to head the Minneapolis operations in 1903. Careful and cautious, his business values contrast sharply with those of his father-in-law. W. W. died suddenly in 1909, leaving John Sr. the task of picking up the scattered financial pieces of a business empire that was on shaky ground. His thoughtful leadership rebuilt the organization solidly and carried it through the agricultural tensions of World War I and the farmer discontents afterward.

The entry of John MacMillan, Jr., into Cargill after World War I was marked by his strong will and fresh ideas and by antagonisms toward him on the part of senior executives. He became the general manager in 1932, and his charge-ahead philosophy and militant competitiveness brought new Cargill initiatives in transportation and company facilities but also exacerbated tensions with the Chicago Board of Trade. There were several skirmishes before a famous case occurred involving the corn futures market in September 1937, in which the Chicago Board of Trade alleged that John Jr. was attempting a "corner." The outcome was traumatic for Cargill and for John Jr.

In the late 1930s, Cargill had begun to build ships, and in World War II, the Company turned major energies toward shipbuilding for the armed services. Grain trading continued during the war, and new initiatives were taken in feed and oilseed processing. Further skirmishes also occurred with the Chicago Board of Trade, both during the war, with an acrimonious disagreement about rye trading, and after the war, when government price controls were removed and the Exchange made decisions that Cargill felt were detrimental to its own interests.

In the post–World War II period, John Jr. remained a dominating chief executive officer, and his ideas held sway. Many were highly successful, particularly the pioneering in inland waterway transportation and the building of unique commodity handling terminals. One of the most important moves was the self-standing European operation, Tradax. Other ideas were less successful.

Suddenly, however, three of the Company's leaders were gone. First, Austen Cargill, the younger son of the founder, died in 1957. Then, early in 1960 the brother of John Jr., Cargill MacMillan, had a disabling stroke. A few months later John Jr. himself died.

The critically important transition into the next generation of leadership, now temporarily to be nonfamily, was harmonious, but there were troubling business problems in a number of the Company's divisions. An incisive management consulting report by Cargill's lead bank helped to refocus management energies.

Because these first three chief executive officers were so inextricably linked with both family and company, this book is necessarily both business history and business biography. Alfred D. Chandler, Jr., the respected business historian, has aided me in developing my model for this study, both in my many personal discussions with him and in his own model: his book (with Stephen Salsbury), *Pierre S. du Pont and the Making of the Modern Corporation*. In his introduction to his book, Professor Chandler stated why a combination of history and biography is so productive in analyzing a complex modern corporation: "This approach permits a careful review of the relationship of the individual to the enterprise. Such an analysis has become particularly significant in the history of the modern corporation where, as was rarely true before in the history of business, the individual must work closely with many other men in the management of a single enterprise. Such a focus, for example, makes possible a detailed analysis of the inevitable conflict between personal goals and ambitions and the impersonal demands of large-scale business organization." My debt to Professor Chandler for these specific ideas and his always-helpful thoughts is substantial.

A particularly important feature of my Cargill study is the availability of a rich set of business and personal correspondence between and among the family members over many years. This has allowed me to make a detailed analysis of the decision-making process in a family corporation and will, I believe, provide significant insights into a widespread but less understood form of corporate ownership. The Cargill philosophy of management, too, has lessons for all corporations. More broadly, this book is a vivid testimony to the growth of the country from its frontier days to the complex environments of today. Cargill traditions give us many clues to our American traditions.

The Chicago Board of Trade archives, too, have given me a unique window on the industry from the inside, and this has been particularly helpful in the compellingly fascinating corn and rye cases. However, there were significant gaps in the records of the La Crosse side of W. W.'s 19th-century organization. John Sr.'s correspondence told why. A 1916 letter detailed how W. W.'s office manager planned to burn all of the letterbooks of the defunct company, stored under the stairs of the empty Cargill mansion in La Crosse—and he did. Truly the historian's worst nightmare! Fortunately, other corroborative information has been found, so the total set of documentation available to me has been superb. As a felicitous companion to this, the Company has made available to me *all* of its records for this period and given me the full independence of judgment that is the critical ingredient of sound business history.

My enthusiasm for this research project of my institution of 37 years, Dartmouth College, comes from almost four decades of writing business history and my long-term business school teaching in the fields of agribusiness and commodity markets. The central thread for this book is corporate values, both those of the individuals involved and of that collective entity called "Cargill." The fact that a number of the key individuals were family adds a special dimension. Through these first years, a unique Cargill "corporate culture" was evolving, and by the time of John Jr.'s death a strongly held set of values and beliefs were evident, a tradition marked by independence, competitiveness, professionalism in management and an underlying ethical commitment. These remain strongly in place in the Cargill of today.

CARGILL'S ROOTS, 1865-1889

Main Street, La Crosse, Wisconsin, c. 1885–1886 (courtesy Area Research Center, UW–La Crosse).

CHAPTER ONE

Frontier Entrepreneur

When Will Cargill stepped down from the McGregor Western railroad car at the tiny end-of-the-line village of Conover, Iowa, he was reenacting once again a great American tradition. It likely was sometime in late 1865, just after the close of the great Civil War. The railroad had just been built into Conover, and the town was new. It was the frontier continued, not in this case via the wagon trains of prairie schooners but by the Iron Horse. Ex-soldiers swarmed the streets. "The people were young," wrote a local historian, "there were no gray heads or stooped shoulders in the community. Life was roseate, and fortune was on the way."[1]

The trans-Mississippi west was preeminently a farming frontier. Railroad extensions beyond the Mississippi River, haltingly initiated before the war, now burgeoned like fingers of many hands out from the formidable river to the newly established farmlands of Missouri, Iowa and Minnesota (and, of course, on westward). No longer would non-local shipping be limited to lands near navigable rivers; as these railroads expanded and multiplied, a whole mosaic of farmland opened to use. Agricultural historian Allen Bogue wrote evocatively: "Between 1850 and the 1880's . . . railroads gridded the midwestern states so thoroughly that there could have been few prairie farmers living beyond earshot of the locomotive's whistle in 1885." Further, while the railroad became the preeminent carrier of agricultural goods, the lake, canal and river continued to compete well, particularly in the period from early spring to late fall each year.

The McGregor Western Railroad Company had been organized in January 1863, taking its name from the busy Mississippi River town of McGregor, Iowa, in the northeastern tip of that state, just across the river from Prairie du Chien, Wisconsin (McGregor "averages two fights per hour and ten trades per minute," one editor trumpeted). The La Crosse and Milwaukee Rail Road Company* had arrived at Prairie du Chien,

---

*Railroads, in this early, formative period, went through many changes in names, as new branches were consolidated, bankrupt lines picked up, etc. The original name in the sequence

across the river from McGregor, in 1857, connecting from Milwaukee. No bridge was in place yet, but it was not an absolute necessity—as the line was built on westward, four rail cars at a time were ferried to and from McGregor and Prairie du Chien, on a barge positioned between two steamboats. An influx of settlers to the town's nearby farmlands further enhanced McGregor's position as a marketing entrepôt. When the federal Land Grant Act was passed in 1856, the intention of Congress was to encourage transcontinental railroads; large tracts of land alongside newly constructed tracks (essentially every other section) would be granted to individual lines, which would then sell these lands to settlers to recover their construction costs. Given the nation's preoccupation with a transcontinental rail link, the direction most often mandated in these grants of farmland was "West."

The McGregor Western, picking up some deeds from the defunct Northern Iowa Railroad Company (which had never begun construction), now obtained such a land grant and began building west from McGregor in 1863. By March 1864, trains were running into Monona, 15 miles to the west, then to Postville, Castalia, and Ossian later that year, and finally into Calmar and on to Conover (some 46 miles from McGregor) in August 1865. It was at this point that Will Cargill chose to take the trip to Conover.[2]

William Wallace Cargill—"Will"—had been born on December 15, 1844, so was just at his majority when he began his Conover experience. He was the second oldest of four sons of a sea captain, William Dick Cargill. Captain Cargill, born in the Orkney Islands of Scotland in 1812, had gone to sea in 1830, first out of the Orkneys and then in the western Atlantic after he moved to Setauket, Long Island, sometime before 1839. In that year, he married a Long Islander, Edna E. Davis, who was a niece of two well-known American painters named Mount. Edna was reputed to have hated the sea, "determined that her sons were to be brought up as far as possible from tidewater" (so said a 1945 Cargill company history). At any rate, Captain Cargill retired in 1856 (at age 44) to a farm in Janesville, Wisconsin, with his wife, his daughter Margaret, and his sons Thomas, Will, Sam, Sylvester, and James. Just why the Captain and his wife chose Janesville is lost in history. Some sources suggest that the Barkers, nearby neighbors in Janesville with family links to East Coast shipping, may have been an influence (later, in 1867, Margaret married George Barker). But it may have been also the blandishments of New York papers about the wonderful lands in Wisconsin, Iowa, and Minnesota, "such good value."

---

that brought the La Crosse and Milwaukee to Prairie du Chien was the Milwaukee & Mississippi Rail Road Company; later these lines and many others were consolidated into what eventually became the Chicago, Milwaukee, St. Paul and Pacific Railroad Company—the "Milwaukee Road."

William Wallace Cargill, c. 1885.

When the Civil War came, Thomas enlisted, but suddenly died of typhoid fever in a Union army camp before seeing any hostilities. Whether second son, Will, then went into the Union army provides the first of several questions about his early life. In the well-known (but not completely dependable) *Columbian Biographical Dictionary and Portrait Gallery of the Representative Men of the United States,* Wisconsin volume, published in 1895, Will Cargill was included, presumably with his blessing (and perhaps a monetary contribution). In it, the editors stated as fact: "When nineteen years of age, he entered the army and served in the Quartermaster's department at Duval's Bluff, Arkansas until the close of the Rebellion." John Work, in a 1965 history of Cargill, believed that the family had kept Will home—had "reverted to dedicated isolationism" after the death of the oldest son. None of Will Cargill's obituaries many years later mentioned the army service, nor does his name turn up in the lists of such veterans maintained by the National Archives. Yet it is curious that there was such a specific mention—place, unit, etc.—in the biographical profile presumably based on information from Cargill himself. It is possible he did go there but in a civilian capacity.[3]

Conover, New Prairie Town

As railroads moved out into these newer territories beyond the Mississippi, hosts of both agricultural and business opportunities for exploiting the land surfaced. As surveyors sought the best (usually cheapest) path for the railroads, existing towns perhaps thriving until then might be bypassed, to their great detriment. This happened with the McGregor Western; the county seat of Decorah was bypassed for a route eight miles or so south and west—through Conover. Indeed, another town suffered more. Calmar was the logical temporary terminus for the construction team, for it had been in existence since 1854 and was, at this time, the second largest municipality in Winneshiek county. To the absolute consternation of Calmar's citizenry, the railroad was built straight through their town, to Conover, some four miles north and west, and the switching tracks and the railroad depot were put in Conover. "Calmar is to be 'left out in the cold' . . . the cars are not to stop . . . but only leave the screeches of the steam whistle to edify the people—to remind them that they did not 'shell out' when asked to" (it was typical for local citizenry to be importuned for substantial dollar advances for construction). So Conover, rather than Calmar, became the rendezvous for the railroad operatives and the place where further construction materials were concentrated. As a writer of that day put it, Conover "bid fair to become the 'boss town' of the county . . . like a Pacific Coast mining camp."

This was an impressive appellation—Conover had not even existed a year previous, being "born of hope" (as another local historian put it) in the fall of 1864. And what a hope! By September 1865, the McGregor newspaper began to chronicle the huge influx of people into Conover. "Conley's addition" began land sale in the third week of October, "Peterson's addition" a few days later. Municipal fever was raging among the local landowners. "What a future is in store for this young town," the McGregor newspaper reported glowingly. A week later the editor had some second thoughts: "Lots change hands at fabulous advances, and the devil is to pay there generally." The newspaper also reported defections from its own business community: "Dan Kirwan, late of Big Andy's Saloon, has removed to Counover" (the original pre-incorporation spelling, after Sam Counover, an officer in the railroad for whom the town was named; a petition for incorporation as "Conover" was drawn on July 5, 1866, with W. W. Cargill as one of its 62 incorporators). Decorah, too, began to lose key businesses; it was "Counover on the brain," carped the town's editor.

Captain William Dick Cargill, father of the Cargill brothers, c. 1885.

By early November 1866, the McGregor editor estimated that the new town had nearly 800 people, including "fourteen army Captains, one Colonel and three Majors." With Conover's business pace stepping up, in early December the "Proprietors" (handling the land sales) took a huge advertisement in the McGregor paper, pushing the remaining unsold lots. "In June last it had not a house," the advertisement began, "in September 100 good business and dwelling houses were built, and NOW THERE ARE 200 HOUSES AND NEARLY 1200 INHABITANTS." Oil miners of Pennsylvania, Californians, and Colorados (*sic*) had visited Conover "and they unite in saying that it exceeds all they ever saw in rapidity of advancement. Hotels, unrivaled in the west—Lumber Yards by the acre—Business Houses selling from $300 to $1000 worth of goods a day—Streets filled with 400 produce and freight teams per day—Everybody at work at building, improving, buying or selling." With the land around Conover "rich as the Nile" (once again, the hyperbole of the McGregor editor), the future of the little village—rather, town—seemed assured. This is what Will Cargill saw when he stepped off that train—and likely what had drawn him there.[4]

The focus of Conover was business. Already there were three hotels, a dozen stores, some 32 saloons—and "a whole street of warehouses." It was not the saloons but the warehouses that drew Will Cargill. Sometime early on, perhaps in late 1865, Will Cargill made connections with H. C. Marsh, and later a partnership was formed, "Marsh & Cargill," sometimes called by the newspapers "Marsh & Carghill." The project: to run one of those grain warehouses. These were simple structures—"flathouses"—where grain could be stored under lock, safe from the elements. There was no doubt that wheat was the crop of choice on the Midwest frontier at this time. In the two decades before the Civil War this had been mostly winter wheat, preferred for its superior milling qualities.* But winter-kill occurred over and over in the upper part of this region—Western Illinois, Iowa, Southern Minnesota, and Wisconsin—and by the time of Conover and Cresco, the hardy spring wheat predominated. There were all sorts of varieties sown, including Mediterranean, Red Chaff Bald, White Chaff Bald,

---

*By the turn of the nineteenth century, there were essentially five types of wheat grown in the United States. Prior to 1860, most wheat was either (1) soft-red winter wheat, grown in a band from Delaware, Maryland, northern Virginia, and southern Illinois and through Missouri to the eastern part of Kansas, or (2) white wheat, grown in the Genesee Valley region of New York, and especially on the Pacific Coast. The other three, later adoptions, are (3) hard-red winter wheat, grown in the central states from Illinois westward through the Great Plains area, sometimes called "Kansas wheat," as the chief producing area extends from Nebraska and Iowa southward into Texas and New Mexico, with Kansas as the center; (4) hard-red spring wheat, grown in an area stretching from Maine to Washington, with the main producing areas Minnesota, the Dakotas, and Eastern Montana (areas where winters are too severe for winter wheat production); and (5) durum, grown chiefly in North Dakota and contiguous states. The hard-reds are the chief bread wheats, the soft-reds for cookies and pastries, durum for macaroni, and most white varieties for pastries and breakfast foods (Charles B. Kuhlmann, *The Development of the Flour Milling Industry* [see chap. 1, n. 5]).

Red Chaff Bearded, Black Sea, Yellow Lamas, Soft Siberian, White Flint, Canada Flint, China, Early May and Golden Chaff. Corn was also widely grown (often interspersed with wheat) and later became Iowa's preeminent grain.

Because there was no elevating of the grain in bulk, where gravity might have drawn upon it, the grain, sometimes bagged, more often in bulk, had to be hand-carted to the various parts of the building to be stacked (one old-timer, A. V. Huff, who had begun work in one of these flathouses in the 1880s, remembered "all grain . . . was loaded with a wheelbarrow that held 7 bushels. Sometimes it would take all night to load a car"). A typical flathouse might have six or so bins, each bin holding a carload.

Prior to the 1850s almost all grain was marketed by wagon or water. Bagged grain predominated then; each bag was identifiable, and selling was done by samples from specific sets of bags. But with the advent of the rail car, grain could be carried in bulk, and then it was no longer possible to identify specific lots. Weight became the measure—sixty pounds of wheat, for example, was defined as a bushel. Early on, this anonymous grain, in effect, a "commodity," often turned out to be lower quality—the farmer or middleman had little incentive to keep out dirt and chaff. The Chicago Board of Trade met this problem in the late 1850s by establishing grades, with city inspectors overseeing the process. By the time of Will Cargill's days in Conover, there were three grades of spring wheat, as well as a fourth category, "rejected."

A rail car then was a 25- to 30-foot wooden boxcar, likely of 9 to 10 tons capacity, so about 300 bushels at 60 pounds per bushel (if barley, at 48 pounds per bushel, this would be considerably more, about 375 bushels). The boxcar had an inner half door, so that grain could be shoveled in over the top until the capacity was reached, or it could be filled with bagged grain by wheelbarrow or on one's back (today special hopper cars carry some 95 to 99 tons).

The receiving of the grain was decidedly seasonal, coming at harvest. Although selling could go on through much of the year, the warehouse-man would hope that rail cars in quantity would be available at harvest time lest his flathouse or elevator fill up completely—be "plugged." He did receive storage charges if storing for an individual owner, but most of his income was made by purchasing and selling for himself. The more rapid the turnover, the greater his revenues. Most of the warehousemen bought and sold coal, salt (for preservation of meat), hides and other commodities, too.

Warehousemen like Marsh and Cargill dealt with the farmer in essentially two ways. The farmer could consign his grain to the warehouse, keeping ownership of the grain himself (if he had enough to fill a bin), paying the warehouseman a commission for the storage time and insurance coverage and then he himself making the decision when and where to sell, at the time he felt the price was right. Prices were typically lowest at harvest, with peak supply, and highest when this supply "disappearance" (the term used) brought shortages, before the next crop. This is the concept of a "carrying charge" market—the price rise approximating those storage and insurance costs.

The other route for the warehouseman was to buy the farmer's output outright at harvest. Most small farmers were on such a shoestring in these times that they often assumed chattel mortgages on future crops at planting, gambling on a good harvest and then being forced to sell at harvest. Often they would become antagonized by the low price they received, particularly when their grain was graded on the spot by the warehouseman (who, of course, had to meet a grade standard when the grain arrived at Chicago or another major consuming city). Farmers often thought they were taken advantage of in this grading process, a subject for further analysis later in this chapter. Almost all of the time warehousemen wanted to minimize price risk, for they essentially saw themselves as middlemen, taking a regularized commission for this service. Thus they established relationships with railroads, or more often with commission houses in the great trading centers (for these Iowa, Wisconsin, and Minnesota operators, the commission houses were in Chicago and Milwaukee). The telegraph had paralleled the railroad rights of way; this communication was necessary for the line's own traffic control but also critically important as a purveyor of up-to-date market information between office and field. So Marsh & Cargill and other businesses like it were utilizing a hedging concept—sell the grain in a market even before the grain arrived. In turn, these commission merchants would formally hedge this grain by buying a "futures" contract and then reversing this by a separate offsetting contract when the actual grain was sold on arrival. (By the end of the Civil War, a futures market for grain was widely available on exchanges both in the Midwest and in Europe.)

The farmers choosing to hold title to their own grain, incidentally, seemed not to understand futures very well (or chose not to understand) and rather than hedge would most often assume the price risk themselves—in effect, to speculate on their grain. But warehousemen universally were not speculators. As Frank Peavey, one of the Minneapolis pioneers in the elevator group, put it, "hedge or sell all grain as soon as it is bought; take in the hedge instantly when the grain is sold."

The farmer did have one other alternative—he could sell to a "track buyer," more colorfully called a "scooper" or "scoop shoveler," who eliminated the country elevator altogether. These people were rather more transient and had to depend on the railroad to allocate cars for their purpose. They were strongly discriminated against by the railroads, who questioned their reliability. "They did not provide a regular market," business historian Henrietta Larson wrote, in her definitive book, *The Wheat Market and the Farmer in Minnesota, 1858–1900,* "and they were often deliberately dishonest." But the scoopers provided a competitive spur for the regular warehouseman.

H. C. Marsh, Will Cargill's first partner, was an older, more experienced businessman, age about 40 and involved in hardware and lumber in addition to grain warehousing, his "character, habits and capacity good," said another R. G. Dun & Co. credit correspondent (who abbreviated each of these words in the mode of his profession). The Dun agents, usually lawyers in the local or surrounding communities (and whose role was not public), made personal observations and consulted public records such as tax books. Each would send his few sentences in the terse shorthand of the day to the nearest branch of the New York City firm, where all were transcribed to credit ledgers, county by county. The New York office monitored these reports carefully (often having two agents rate the same group of firms for comparison). There was great incentive on the part of the agents to hold onto the Dun post, for it led to lucrative business in helping to resolve the multitude of bankruptcies in the tenuous business environment of those days.

The records of businessmen on the frontier were generally skimpy, and with fires, bankruptcies and intentional disposal, few written chronicles of these Conover businesses have survived. Fortunately, however, the Dun entries for Conover and the surrounding towns were saved and in combination with local court records give some revealing glimpses of life in a boomtown on the midwestern frontier. There were intricate, often short-lived sets of partnerships between and among the businessmen; Marsh was in business with a Knowlton in hardware, with Lambert in lumber. The diminutive grain warehousing companies, generally partnerships and reasonably inexpensive to establish, were highly competitive yet often had linked ownership. In particular, a strong, long-standing McGregor business group known as Bassett & Huntting had established grain warehouses all through the towns and villages west of McGregor. William Huntting, prominent in McGregor, led the firm; they were "old operators," "large dealers," and "good and reliable," reported the Dun correspondent. They were "wide awake businessmen and deserve confidence," particularly so because they had a third, silent partner who was one of the Midwest's most prominent business tycoons. He was Joseph Reynolds, who lived and worked out of McGregor but also had offices in Chicago. His particular moneymaker was his packet boat operation on the Mississippi, the "Diamond Jo Line." Having been discriminated against by other packet boat operators in shipping his grain in the early 1860s, he had purchased the line and had become a major steamboat magnate by the time of Conover's

A "Diamond Jo" Mississippi River packet boat and barge loaded with bagged grain, c. 1875
(courtesy Area Research Center, UW–La Crosse).

birth. Reynolds was a "prudent businessman," his wealth "variously estimated at from 200 to 500M" ($200,000 to $500,000). Although the Reynolds group "speculate largely," they still "stand high." Will Cargill soon had substantial links with Bassett, Huntting and Reynolds, and later direct partnership ties.[5]

Through Dun's Conover correspondents, we gain some revealing glimpses of that hurly-burly town. G. Y. Conley & Bro. handled both drugs and liquor, "worth from 15 to 20c$" ($1,500 to $2,000). I. C. Baker had a dry goods store, but "have some doubt on him . . . a rather mixed concern . . . difficult to say who are the responsible partners." Within months, the correspondent reported that Baker "has sold out . . . is a swindle, a large one, too." A grocery partnership, Jacobs & McCartney, seemed doubtful: "Jacobs is man that has no experience in mercantile business . . . not dishonest but not careful in selling." H. L. Porter had started a hotel, a small one as he was only "worth $1000." G. A. Purdey's hardware store was valued at about the same figure; H. B. Lawrence sold stoves and some furniture, "owes but little, is of good habits, industrious and I think honest." The various saloon keepers—Pat Burns, Charles Brown, H. H. Wright, E. A. Miller, William Unbehaun, Charles Melby and others—seemed to be remarkably good credit risks (although the stringent Iowa state liquor laws persuaded Unbehaun to obtain his credit from out of the state and Melby to put his firm in his wife's name). The credit correspondent felt saloon operators needed to be watched constantly: "All liquor dealers should be dealt with carefully, even when buying other articles, as they are liable to leave at any time."

A particular Conover business had special meaning to Will Cargill—one of its partners became his father-in-law in 1868. William Austen Stowell (apparently known by his middle name) lived in Ossian, the next town east from Calmar on the McGregor Western line, about a dozen miles east of Conover. His firm was the Mississippi Valley Insurance Company, located at Decorah. The Dun correspondent approvingly noted that Stowell was "a regular rattling insurance man . . . a large business, good character . . . good business capacity & is honest." Stowell, excited by the fast-paced business scene of Conover, formed a partnership with one Williams for a dry goods and grocery store there. Williams lasted only a few months, to be replaced by a Mr. Washburn, "a new man . . . from Wisconsin, said to have considerable property there." Washburn apparently became the man on the scene, with Stowell keeping a room above the store but apparently continuing his insurance business out of Ossian. The latter town had been founded in 1855 but had not grown much until the railroad came. The *Iowa State Gazetteer* noted that it had only "a Baptist Church, three general stores and one grocery."[6]

As the Conover residents basked in their good fortune over the winter of 1865–1866 (perhaps a few in a state of intoxication, what with the 32 taverns!), dark clouds were on the horizon. Already, plans were afoot for building a new, separate railroad west from Calmar toward Charles City, some 35 miles distant. The Calmar citizenry, sensing recovery, worked together to help erect a large "depot hotel," and within months the

In 1977 this railroad outbuilding and a few houses were the last remaining evidence of the town Conover, Iowa (courtesy Duane W. Fenstermann).

McGregor Western decided to take down its depot in Conover piece by piece and move it to Calmar. To Conoverites, the railroad was double villain, for the mild winter of 1865–1866 also had allowed continued McGregor Western building north and west. By the spring of 1866, a newer town, Cresco, 18 miles northwest of Conover, had been founded (by Augustus Beadle), and the railroad decided to put a depot there. With railroad construction costs quite reasonable because of the topography of northeastern Iowa (the original 35 miles from McGregor to Conover had cost an average of only $3,500 per mile), the McGregor Western made rapid progress in a direction toward the Minnesota line. The McGregor Western was required to complete at least 20 miles of its road every year from the date of its acceptance of its land grant, although there was beginning to be some doubt about whether the land grants would even be honored now that the route had turned northward.

Conover fell like a rock. By the summer of 1866 there began to be business failures, and these mushroomed through spring 1867. Soon the disparaging name "Goneover" began to be used—and the name stuck. Conley's Drugs and Liquor failed, as did Rogers, Gardner the grocer, and Jacobs & McCartney of the same business. Porter's hotel, according to the Dun correspondent, was "not making money . . . in a dead town." Fire added another push to Conover's rollercoaster ride when a whole block that included the City Hotel burned to the ground in December 1867. Purdey, the hardware man, moved to the new boomtown Cresco, and he was followed by others. Austen Stowell's partnership in the dry goods store was in trouble. It was mortgaged in April 1867 and failed just one month later. The stock was sold, and the Dun correspondent reported, "We think we have evidence to show that the sale is fraudulent. We shall attach tomorrow." Creditors who filed civil law suits against Stowell and Washburn also expressed the same sentiments in court petitions.

The buyer was none other than H. C. Marsh, Will Cargill's partner in Conover. No Dun's record remains of how Marsh made out in his Conover dry goods business or how long he stayed, but civil court records show that Stowell's creditors attempted to recover the value of their claim from Marsh. A new newspaper was started in Cresco in early 1867, and one of its first issues confirmed that Marsh had built a warehouse there. Probably Will Cargill was still with him, as an early September 1867 issue notes that "Marsh & Carghill of Conover" were building a warehouse at Lime Springs, a tiny town 10 miles or so northwest of Cresco on the railroad. "They are No. 1 men," the editor stated, "and those who deal with them will soon come to the same conclusion." Will Cargill had another partnership in Lime Springs, joining T. W. Clapp in a lumberyard there.

So, with droves of people leaving Conover for Calmar to the southeast and Cresco to the northwest, Will Cargill and his partner Marsh chose the

Above, Sylvester S. Cargill, c. 1882;
top right, Samuel D. Cargill, c. 1885;
bottom right, James F. Cargill, c. 1881.

northerly direction (today Cresco and Calmar are bustling small towns, but in Conover there is no evidence of the town except for a few houses).

Will's two younger brothers, Sam and Sylvester, now joined their older brother, apparently traveling directly to Lime Springs. Sam was age 20, Sylvester 19. The two younger Cargills provided just what Will needed, trustworthy manpower for his Iowa operations. One family member remembered their first months as follows: "They didn't take rooms, but saved money by living in the flathouse, sleeping on cots in the room used as an office. They cooked there, on a pot-bellied heater with one stove lid. Mother [Margaret Anne Cargill Barker, Will Cargill's older sister] told that one would handle the frying pan and do the cooking while the other held his hat over the open pan to protect the food from chaff and grain dust sifting down . . ."[7]

Business Life in Cresco and Lime Springs

The Cresco and Lime Springs business communities, covered by another Dun correspondent, provided even more pungent analysis. Isaac Gregory, one of the other grain dealers was "speculating" and was "hard-pressed." B. Bank was "an Israelite of 23 yrs, single, has 100 or 150 $ worth of confectionaries . . . his first experience in business." In the proprietorship of Strother & Conklin, agricultural machinery dealers, the former was "responsible," the latter "is not & at times drinks hard." John J. Sturgess, who had an innovative combination of a hardware store and billiard saloon, also was "intemperate." A. Swanson, the jeweler, "monopolizes the business here." D. Beam had a "good reputation" as a harness maker but later "ran away in debt from Cresco." Eli J. Bertram, a sewing machine salesman, was a "worthless scallawag."

One of the grain buyers of the area, C. E. Brown, was listed as "clergyman and speculator," a "rather doubtful character." J. G. Carter sold agricultural implements and insurance; earlier, he had been "unfortunate in investing in Connover" (sic). Will Cargill's partner, Marsh, was "not doing much but well off." Doan & Kepp was a "very poor" mercantile business, "liable to break up at any time." On the other hand, Mrs. J. T. Donohugh, one of the dressmakers, "has a nice little shop & is doing well." T. H. Dunn had been clerking in one of the hotels, now started a small cigar store with a total stock of $150 and was "managing fair." W. G. Gardner, who sold hats and caps, was "one of the safest of our businessmen," although "sometimes a little slow." There were some enigmatic comments, too; William Gibby, who owned a combination hotel and saloon, "keeps his contraband in this state" and was "rather reckless." The correspondent recommended that people "would be entirely cautious about crediting" with him. There were several itinerant peddlers; E. W. Allard had a wagon and a span of horses, "not much of a man—would not like to trust him . . . he is one of those cheap men who do not set a high estimate on his word."

And so it went. Some firms did well, others faded quickly. George A. Lamb, a printer in the area, had been burned out and owed over $1,200 for his press; although "industrious," with "active habits," he had to quit and returned to his original home in New York. The saloon keepers were in and out of business constantly. Anthony Lee, "a hard old fellow," quit. Thomas Leonard, "a deadbeat, keeps a hard place" but was in trouble for liquor violations; "his family sell the rest . . . and make business for the public courts." The professional group—the doctors, dentists, and others generally seemed stable; Mrs. H. H. Jewitt, an artist, was "doing a good business and has a good reputation . . . takes a good many pictures."

Another business in Cresco provided Will Cargill with a future link by marriage. G. M. Hanchette and George A. Purdey had opened a hardware store in late 1867. Purdey, from Conover, was "a perfectly honest man" and a "very good businessman." Hanchette, who had come from Janesville, Wisconsin (perhaps having known the Cargill family there), was "married and does a good trade." In sum, it was a responsible firm. The *Cresco Times* plumped, "Hanchette brings experience and ability, and is fortunate in having obtained an interest in one of the best business stands in Northern Iowa." Will Cargill's youngest daughter, Emma, married Hanchette's son Fred in 1897.

In early 1868, Purdey & Hanchette suspended business when an injunction was obtained, which shut the store down for 10 days. The cause was not noted by the newspaper. The suit subsequently was dismissed at a hearing in the United States Court at Dubuque, and the newspaper added, "It has been the means of doing great damage to Mr. H's business, but with his cheap goods and fair dealing he will soon regain his usual trade." The editor added, "don't forget to give him a call when in town."[8]

The breezy huckstering of the *Cresco Times* editors (there were two during this period) was counterpoint to the sober, often scathing comments of the Dun correspondents. Cresco was rather "wild and wooly" (frankly admitted the paper), with fights, shootings, wife beatings, and other miscellaneous scrapes gleefully reported by the editors. With its large share of saloons (a number inherited from Conover), incidents abounded. "Three prominent businessmen were out serenading Sunday night," noted an entry in early 1868. "The hope is expressed that they feel no inconvenience as a result of their efforts to be amusing." A few months later, "the streets were so crowded with passersby that at one place the sidewalk was completely blockaded by a crowd of 'target shooters' so that ladies were obliged to turn out into the street to get by. We also heard one or two 'inebriated individuals' talking loudly and obscenely. As we are now a 'city,' it is to be hoped that the 'city officials' will look to these matters."

Marital spats were editorial favorites—a doctor, for example, had "skedaddled, taking with him his goods, and leaving his wife." Generally, the cultural activities were confined mainly to sports (on April 23, 1868, the "Silver Grays" baseball team of Cresco beat New Oregon, 52 to 19). There were constant stories about runaway horses and several references to a new form of calamity, the train wreck. A special train excursion from Cresco to Conover was planned on July 4, 1867; it was a great success, with 1,400 people on the train, "the largest load of passengers that has ever been over the road." The editors nostalgically reported that many had "envious feelings," watching the "innocent caresses of some of the young couples in the darkness, coming home on the train that night." Two months later, the mayor of Conover resigned and relocated in Cresco, and the editors could not resist a gleeful comment: "We don't know how the change from Metropolitan honors to the rural districts will affect him."[9]

These alarums and distractions aside, the dominating issue for Cresco and Lime Springs, as it had been for Conover, remained agriculture. Everything was built on its foundation; the farmer's success or lack thereof set the tone for everyone else. To fully appreciate this, an understanding of the "farming frontier" of this period immediately after the Civil War period is needed.

Farmers, Middlemen, and Others

In so many respects, the Civil War served as a watershed for American agriculture, particularly so for the plains states west of the Mississippi River. Until about 1900, an unfailing rule, at least for agriculturalists, was that the greatest percentage of population growth was on the newest lands but generally those closest to the older regions. Fred Shannon, in his book *The Farmer's Last Frontier*, noted the "astonishing degree of regularity" in the increase of populations in the western band of the North Central states (Missouri to Minnesota and Kansas to North Dakota), with somewhat lower but still impressive growth in the same band of the South Central states (Louisiana, Arkansas, Texas, and Oklahoma). Iowa's population, in 1860 just 675,000, almost doubled in 10 years to 1,194,000. Minnesota had the same pattern, although the numbers were smaller, 172,000 in 1860, 440,000 in 1870. In turn, many of the more easterly Midwest states, which had grown so rapidly in the early part of the 19th century, now began to be net losers, Illinois taking the largest drop.

So as the Will Cargills of the country poured across the Mississippi in record numbers, almost all were destined to be farmers or farm-related businessmen. The railroads had bridged the wide river, starting with the first in 1856, which linked Rock Island, Illinois, and Davenport, Iowa.[10]

Wheat culture seemed to be rather careless and hasty on many Iowa farms. One Iowa farmer reported that as late as 1865 the usual mode was "to 'hog in' and 'hog over' . . . at a half hammon gait or a hop, step and jump, and trust to Providence for the result." But after the Civil War agriculture posted enormous gains in productivity, due particularly to a veritable explosion of new farm technology. The steel plows of John Deere and others, the Van Brunt seeders so widely advertised in the Cresco papers at this time, the onrush of harvesting technology brought by the vigorous competition between Manny, McCormick and others—these and others offered a chance for farming improvements. The sulky plow allowed the farmer to work sitting down, and soon there were more complicated gang-plows. Efforts were made at this time to use steam plows to subdue the prairie, but the earlier models were not successful. Later in the 19th century, better versions had some success in California and in the so-called bonanza farms of the Red River Valley areas of Northern Minnesota and North Dakota.[11]

Farming in the Conover/Cresco area in those first few years after the Civil War was representative of most Iowa and southern Minnesota farming. The wartime period had witnessed high wheat prices, but the influx of new settlers and higher productivity combined to vastly stimulate output, soon bringing generally falling prices. The Cresco paper's crop column reported wheat at $2.50 a bushel in late April 1867. The editor exhorted farmers to "do their work well, and *then* trust in Providence." It turned out to be "a grand crop," but then prices began to sag; "stand from under," the editor warned. By September, the prices were down to $1.45 and had dropped to 90¢ by the fall of the following year. Potato bugs had hit some of the farmers' crops in this second year, but the quantity of grain coming into the warehouses was still enormous. There had been 170 million bushels of wheat produced in the country in 1866; by 1869 the figure was 290 million bushels. Exact figures for Winneshiek County (Calmar and Conover) and Howard County (Cresco) are not available, but the amount of grain coming into the elevators mirrored this rapid growth in output. Beadle & Slee had erected an elevator at Cresco, at a cost exceeding $12,000, that was capable of holding 30,000 bushels. Steam power operated the simple elevating conveyors. With the nine warehouses that also were in place for the 1867 crop, some 40,000 bushels of wheat came in to Cresco per month in the four months of the harvest, and over 12 million pounds of freight were shipped from the depot. "If there is a station on the road prepared to beat these figures, we should be pleased to hear from them . . . until then we shall believe that Cresco is ahead of all."

The supreme confidence of the Cresco editor *was* vindicated and Cresco did stay strong (perhaps to be expected, as the Latin derivation of its name means "I grow"). Cresco's growth was aided by an exciting new development on the railroad. In the spring and summer of 1867, builders had continued northward from Cresco toward Austin, Minnesota, some 40 miles north and west. Meanwhile, the Minnesota Central Railway Company had been building southward from St. Paul toward Austin. Their link-up would, in one move, connect the Twin Cities of St. Paul and Minneapolis with Milwaukee, Chicago and the East. By June 1867, the southern construction crew was only 23 miles from Austin; the Minnesota Central counterpart was already below Owatonna and closing on Austin. On October 10, they were only four miles apart, and the Cresco editor chortled, "Then hurrah for St. Paul, Red River of the North, Our Russian Possessions and the North Pole." They met the next week.

In the process, the towns north and west of Cresco picked up steam. Lime Springs, a few miles farther on from Cresco, where Will Cargill had located the lumberyard in partnership with Clapp and his warehouse with Marsh, now begged for lumber. By October 1867, over 200,000 feet of lumber had been shipped above that used by the railroad. Clapp & Cargill took out an advertisement for their "pine lumber, lath and shingles—best quality of Minneapolis," and the newspaper editor obligingly shilled in

Arrival of the Milwaukee train, Austin, Minnesota, 1874 (Minnesota Historical Society).

LUMBER YARD

LIME SPRINGS.

Best quality of Minneapolis
Pine Lumber,
Lath, and
Shingles.

13tf   CLAPP & CARGILL

One of the earliest W. W. Cargill advertisements, Cresco [Iowa] Times, *April 2, 1868.*

his news column, "They are selling lots of lumber of the best quality and at the lowest rates." Will Cargill's grain partner Marsh came with him to Lime Springs, and their new warehouse (and two more that Marsh built with others) were soon joined by four more competitors.

Marsh & Cargill now made the important decision to jump over the Minnesota line and build a warehouse at Austin. The editor of the *Cresco Times* was intrigued enough to run a short article on it as a lead piece on November 21, 1867, commenting " 'Billy' Cargill runs the machine. They have our best wishes for good luck." It is not clear just what kind of a machine this was, as the editor implied it was to be in a flathouse, not an elevator with power machinery for elevating, like the large Cresco operation of Beadle & Slee. By this time, however, elevating mechanisms were more widespread, sometimes simple "cup and belt" devices run by a horse led in a circle, a "blind horse" elevator, so-called. An old-timer recounted how one elevator "had a whip attached above the horse, and there was a hole in the wall where the men . . . could holler down at the horse . . . and a string attached to the whip so they could pull and hit the horse." Soon horses were replaced by power machinery. Alternatively, "Billy" could have been running a corn sheller or perhaps a grain cleaner.

On October 1, 1868, Will Cargill married Ellen ("Ella") Theresa Stowell, the wedding taking place at Ossian (where her father maintained his insurance business). Will was 24 years old, Ellen 15. Henry Toye, an Ossian schoolteacher (later superintendent of schools) was their witness. Shortly after, the young couple established their home in Austin; their first son, William Samuel, was born there on October 2, 1869.

Austin was a more substantial town and already had an elevator, owned by B. J. Van Valkenburgh in partnership with his brother E. P. The senior member, B. J., later became linked with Will Cargill in further elevator and warehouse acquisitions. The Dun correspondent assessed his record: "Character good . . . attentive to business & economical . . . prompt in business matters . . . all right."[12]

Communication between Will in Austin and his two brothers out in the field was effected by telegraph wire and mail, and this seemed to work well. Sometime in the early 1870s, three new warehouses were either built or acquired by Will Cargill in quite another area of Iowa, some 55 miles west of Cresco and on a different railroad, the Chicago, Rock Island and Pacific (its later name). Two of the new warehouses, at Northwood and at Kensett, were just below the Minnesota border (the railroad then ran on northward to Albert Lea); the other was at Sheffield, almost 20 miles below Mason City (and therefore over 30 miles from Kensett, 40 from North-wood). Sylvester Cargill, who had been running the Cargills' elevator at Winnebago, now became their manager for what seems to have been a separate operation from its early days. A cash book that begins on August 1, 1875 (the earliest extant financial record of any of the Cargill involve-ments), shows the operation as a going concern, headed by Sylvester but under the overall umbrella of "W.W. Cargill." This cash book chronicles innumerable trades in wheat, barley, corn, hides, salt, wool and pork. Sylvester, semiautonomous at this point, later became wholly independent of the other Cargill brothers, forming his own firm, the Victoria Elevator Company, which expanded into Minnesota and the Eastern Dakotas. Victoria grew to substantial size and from its Minneapolis headquarters became a well-known, middle-level grain firm.[13]

Albert Lea Becomes Headquarters

Austin had been a busy location for railroads, for not only was the McGregor–St. Paul north-south route in full operation, but the Southern Minnesota railroad had also begun building in 1865 straight west from LaCrescent, Minnesota, directly across the river from La Crosse, Wiscon-sin; this had reached Rushford by 1867 and onward to Lanesboro in 1868. Meanwhile, another crew was building eastward from Albert Lea, reaching Ramsey, just north of Austin, in 1869. None of the little towns along this route had tempted Will, but when the railroad's "western" and "eastern" lines were linked in 1870, giving a through line, Will Cargill followed the sun and moved twenty miles west to Albert Lea. L. W. Spicer, an Albert Lea resident, recounted in a letter in October 1945: "He must have been about 24 years old when he came here, for he joined the Masonic Lodge in 1871 (age 26), and was Lodge Secretary in 1873."

Will Cargill kept his small warehouse near Austin, in the town of Ram-sey, a mile or so north, but now began to make major commitments for new operations, beginning with Albert Lea. In May 1870, he bought two lots in the "railroad addition" and constructed a small warehouse (only the deeds for the land are extant, nowhere noting its size). "The small original warehouse collapsed after a couple of years by overloading," the

Albert Lea letter-writer recounted, and Will Cargill subsequently erected a substantial 18,000-bushel elevator on the site, with an eight-horsepower engine for elevating.

The Spicer letter continued with a surprise: "He was elected Freeborn County coroner in 1872." Here is an early example of a trait exhibited so many times over Will Cargill's lifetime, of involving himself in widely scattered endeavors that were not near his chosen field. A coroner in those days usually was not a medical doctor but performed a judicial role in criminal matters by conducting an inquest, an investigative hearing where evidence was reviewed to determine if a prosecution should be initiated. The fact that Will Cargill was not yet 30 years old attests to his credibility with his townspeople; he kept the job until 1874.

The Albert Lea resident also noted that Will Cargill "built a fine home on Grove Street in 1871." An accompanying photograph showed the home to be very substantial. The letter also noted that "on the next block south was the S. S. Cargill home"; Sylvester moved there in 1882. Will's house may have been "fine," but his well was not; a survey of the town wells classified the water from the 85-foot Cargill well as "not good."

In September 1871, Will and Ella's first daughter, Edna, was born in Albert Lea. After Edna's birth, Ella and the baby went to stay with her family in Ossian. William Stowell, Ella's father, wrote Will, "Edna is very smart . . . Willie [first son William S.] is all over the baby and thinks it is his and you have nothing to say about it." Will wrote his father in Janesville, late in 1871, "I have not seen Sam or Ves in some time but hear from them every day." In this same letter, he added plaintively, "Ella is still at home & I feel tonight rather lonesome . . . tell Jimmie [his youngest brother] I have a horse & buggy & cutter [and a] pretty mare."

A history of Freeborn County, written in 1882, has an interesting addition to Will Cargill's Albert Lea days: "An elevator with a capacity of 30,000 bushels was put up by Henry Rowell in 1876. He owned and operated it for about three years, when it was disposed of to Cargill Bros., who took it to Sherman and it has since burned. It had a 10-horse-power engine." This story is illustrative of two features of the grain trade in those days: first, how easy it was to dismantle and move one of the old wooden warehouses and, second, how vulnerable these wooden buildings were to the "fire-fiend" (as an Albert Lea newspaper editor called it). Will Cargill lost several warehouses to fire in this period, and there would be many more in the future, too.[14]

Two questions now need to be addressed. First, in what combination of people under what partnership and company names was Will Cargill operating? Second, how did he get his money? Early in his Albert Lea tenure, Will Cargill had established a downtown office for his operations in a building on Front Street owned by Bassett & Huntting, the McGregor

"A Scene on a Western Canal and Railway," Frank Leslie's Illustrated Newspaper, *October 11, 1873.*

grain dealers. He began buying land all along the Southern Minnesota Railroad (purchasing a substantial amount from W. G. Kellar, the field agent for the railroad's unused land, "which contains 400,000 acres of choice farming and grasslands"). By this time, these railroad lands were primarily west of Albert Lea, along the Southern Minnesota Railroad right-of-way (the railroad had continued building beyond Albert Lea toward Winnebago City, some 40 miles due west). At many of these locations, Will Cargill built warehouses; there were structures at Alden, Wells, and Winnebago, which was the momentary end of the line. Will also made his first purchase east of Austin on the railroad line at Grand Meadow and by 1876 also was moving up the state to towns along the Minnesota Central railroad, in the environs of Mankato.

His letterhead stated "Office of W. W. Cargill—Dealer in grain, pork, hides, wool, salt, & C." This seemed to be the parent company. But, additionally, Will also was involved in new partnership combinations. The Clapp and Marsh connections had not followed him to Albert Lea, and different names now surface. To begin with, there was a separate family entity, "W.W. Cargill & Bro.," a combination just of Will and second brother Sam; later, the entity "Cargill Brothers" appears, after youngest brother Jim (born 1852) joined the operations. A separate agreement with B. J. McGinnis in 1871 provided that Will would "furnish all the capital used excepting $200" but that they would "share alike in profit and loss." McGinnis was to do the buying and handling of grain, in this case in Albert Lea. In another agreement, with J. Edward in 1874 (apparently a more short-lived one), 31 hogs were to be butchered, "as will make good merchantable pork . . . excepting the heads and feet, to be made into sausage." All this work was to be done, presumably by Edward, "in a good workmanlike manner." Not all of Will's partnerships were profitable; in April 1874, he lost a $700 advance given to another butcher, who was going to Iowa to buy "fat cattle" but who never came back. The newspaper gave the "confidence game" quite a play.

This particular spring of 1874 produced a string of bad luck for Will Cargill; in May, his Albert Lea warehouse collapsed, spilling some 2000 bushels of grain. It had hardly been cleaned up when reports reached Will that another warehouse, at Ridgeway, Iowa, had burned to the ground, "the only piece of property which he had neglected to insure," reported the newspaper. The editor then commented on a personal quality increasingly heard about Will—his eternal optimism: "the misfortune, however, does not seem to disturb Mr. Cargill's good nature."

There was a puzzling codicil relating to a partnership agreement between Will Cargill and J. M. Flowers. Mrs. Flowers agreed to "make up any loss that my husband may make in the purchase of grain or any article that he may agree to buy in the co-partnership." Further, she agreed to "make up or pay all deficiencies made by my husband . . . in all transactions as above mentioned." Dun correspondents also were active in Albert Lea and Austin, as outspoken as in Iowa; the Austin respondent commented about Mr. Flowers, "Like all speculators, sometimes up and sometimes down."

Will Cargill's most substantial business partner in this Albert Lea period of 1870–1875 was S. Y. Hyde. Hyde had been proprietor of a Lanesboro, Minnesota, grain trading firm but had now moved his office to Albert Lea. The Dun correspondent for Albert Lea had entries in February 1875, for both W. W. Cargill alone and for "Hyde, Cargill Co." For Will, he stated, "Has an interest in 27 different towns along the line of this road . . . has commercial interest in some 40 warehouses in these 27 towns. The business is buying and shipping grain and selling salt and perhaps other goods on commission. Cargill claims to be worth 50M [$50,000] himself . . . think it a reasonable estimate." An entry a few months later introduced the partnership: "Is also of Hyde & Cargill who own and operate 47 warehouses in 27 different points . . . regarded honest . . . a good business & considered safe for any reason." The correspondent seemed confused about the interlocking nature of the relationship and whether there really were two sets of warehouses (there were not). The McGregor firm of Bassett, Huntting and Reynolds also held some interest—several legal cases in this period list them as co-partners. The partnership agreement itself has not survived, so the precise ownership percentages cannot be determined.[15]

The other enigma concerning Will Cargill's operations at this time centers on financing—just how had he been able to grow so rapidly and engage in so many commercial transactions, not only land for warehouses and the construction of these but other land purchases—farms, etc. A young man of just 21 years had come to Iowa in 1865 with what seemed to be little money in his pockets, yet was one of the more substantial businessmen of the Southern Minnesota/Northern Iowa area just a half dozen years later, despite a burgeoning depression from the Panic of 1873. A number of Will Cargill's expenditures at this time were quite large. For example, in 1873 he decided to increase his operations along the McGregor Western tracks and contracted for a large elevator at Cresco. Its total cost eventually came to over $12,000.

Scraps of information give clues to his connections. First, Will Cargill began in Albert Lea to have some substantial financial links to Jason C. Easton, who was one of the most important private bankers in southern Minnesota—"a pioneer of modern banking practices in the area," states the Minnesota Historical Society in its introduction to his collected papers. He did not seem so benign at the time—one La Crosse newspaper

A railroad grading crew, c. 1907 (Minnesota Historical Society; photograph by Henry A. Byrd).

"Railroad Building on the Great Plains" (The Bettmann Archive).

called him "the well known money Lord." Born in 1823 in New York, Easton had come to Minnesota in 1856. By the early 1870s, from his office at the Root River Bank in the tiny town of Chatfield, Minnesota, he owned or held stock in banks in Austin, Caledonia, Chatfield, Grand Meadow, Lanesboro, Owatonna, Spring Valley, and Winnebago, Minnesota, and a partnership in a Chicago commission merchant house named Holley, Easton & Allen.

Easton had become a particularly dominant figure on the Southern Minnesota Railroad line. Different from a number of other lines, this railroad at first had been more liberal in its policies toward its patrons in not tying up the warehousing itself (a great many warehouses were owned outright by the railroads). However, in 1872, the railroad changed its policy by contracting with Easton to maintain warehouses and buy produce at a number of stations along its lines. Easton was to buy at a price directed by the railroad (the Milwaukee price minus freight and the railroad's margin) and from the proceeds to deduct his expenses and a commission. The effect was to create a potential monopoly, for Easton's position was favored over that of his competitors—he was the first to get cars, the railroad assumed many risks which his competitors had to carry, and he paid only a percentage of the actual freight charge collected from other warehousemen. Easton was not the only buyer, but he was able in the process to maintain a high degree of control.

Easton tried to mollify the disgruntled sellers by proposing a more rigorous system of weighing grain at all the warehouses and elevators, but their proprietors would have none of it. Instead, they pressed for an investigation, and such an inquiry was made by a Minnesota Senate committee in 1874. The committee reported that Easton had unfairly profited to the tune of $44,000 with his preferential rebates. However, they voted "to not recommend any further action at the present time." The newspapers all through southern Minnesota immediately took up the cudgel. As one put it, Easton should " 'own up the corn' or disprove the statements made."

The year 1873 witnessed a severe economic shock to the country. The "Panic of 1873" had been building for several years. Railroads, expanding greatly after the Civil War, had pushed new construction in unprecedented amounts. The annual increase in railroad mileage had averaged about 1,300 miles in the years right after the war, rose to about 5,000 in 1869, and during the years 1871 and 1872 over 13,000 miles were built. Too much of this construction was built on a financial house of cards; a similar huge expansion in new business firms was all too often also on shaky financial ground. Exports lagged behind imports, and the trade deficit began to drain the United States Treasury. On September 8, 1973, the New York Warehouse and Securities Company failed; less than two weeks later, the powerful banking firm of Jay Cooke and Company closed its doors (sending the Northern Pacific Railroad and the Southern Minnesota railroad, among others, into bankruptcy in the process). Trade on the New York Stock Exchange was suspended for 10 days, but nothing could prevent the cumulative effect of the collapse. By the end of the year, there had been over 5,000 business failures, and almost a hundred railroads had defaulted on their bonds. It was not just a short-lived depression, either. Business failures increased precipitously in the 1876–1877 period; mills and factories closed all over, and unemployment rose. Not until 1878 was there a glimmer of recovery.

B. J. Van Valkenburgh and his partner Leonard Brieser immediately sued the Southern Minnesota railroad (in March 1874) for the overcharges, and in September of the same year, Will Cargill instituted two more suits, also against the railroad, one for $5,518 in his own name and a $12,789 figure for W. W. Cargill & Brother, to "recover excessive freights . . . between La Crosse and Milwaukee . . . a secret conspiracy between railroads to defraud shippers." Both plaintiffs won their claims when the railroad was ordered to set aside funds as part of its receivership proceedings.

CHAS. A. TENNEY, 115 Center Street, WINONA, MINN.

Minnesota Snow View Series of 1881.

"*Drawing snow blocks out, following blockade on Southern Minnesota Division,*" *Chicago, Milwaukee & St. Paul Railroad, stereopticon slide, 1881* (Minnesota Historical Society; photograph by Charles A. Tenney).

Easton then was forced by public pressure to sell a number of his warehouse properties, and several went to Will Cargill. In the process, Jason Easton seemed quite taken with Cargill and later became as close to being a mentor as Will Cargill had had in business. For example, in November 1875, Easton urged Cargill to buy into a warehouse company in Wells, Minnesota, for "I think this new stock will be . . . valuable & as I told you will render you eligible as a director of the Co."

The many bankruptcies from the depression brought opportunities for those with money to pick up these defunct organizations. Apparently, Will Cargill had enough confidence—and money—to engage in substantial amounts of this distress buying, and Easton seemed willing to furnish additional capital for someone in whom he had trust. It is even possible that Will was acting as a surrogate for some Easton purchases that could not be made directly because of the investigative pressure. In July 1876, Easton wrote Cargill a long, chatty letter, both about new deals and about the grain trade in general. Cargill had sold a considerable amount of wheat in anticipation of a drop in price, and Easton wrote, approvingly, "Edy told me yesterday that you had had the 'lambs to the slaughter' lately & were not very long on rotten wheat. I was glad as I feel sure the price will 'go to the dogs' . . . certainly below 90¢ . . . *believe wheat will not average cash in Milwaukee over 90 during the fall & winter.*" With the bad times, there were more individuals welshing on contracts; in this letter, Easton approvingly noted Cargill's efforts to "catch a wheat thief . . . I think there is nothing worse" and then invited Will to accompany him on a business trip to Milwaukee.

Later, a more important financier for Will Cargill's various partnerships and other operations was Robert Eliot, who owned a prominent Milwaukee commission house of the same name (founded in 1855). He and his partner, John P. Dibble, were almost canonized by the Milwaukee Dun correspondent: "good habits, character . . . men of integrity . . . one, all esteem . . . continually making $ . . . worth upwards of 700M [$700,000] . . . Eliot a shrewd businessman of energy and ability . . . not what are known here as speculators." Over many years, Eliot carried on an extensive commercial business with Will Cargill, buying his grain and, in the process, extending large amounts of credit to the partnerships. The cash book of Sylvester Cargill's branch, one of the earliest surviving records of any Cargill enterprise, has extensive journal entries involving credit from Eliot and subsequent payments in return from the Cargill group. An internal Cargill history, written in 1945, put the relationship this way: "It is doubtful if there was ever in the grain trade any man with a greater capacity for inspiring confidence than W. W. Cargill. His spectacular early success was in large measure made possible by the friendship of a great Milwaukee banker, Mr. Robert Elliott [sic], not once, but again and again, to their mutual profit."[16]

Finally, there was Will's father, the sea captain, William Dick Cargill. When the family had settled near Janesville in 1856, it was on a rather small farm of some 70 acres (later increased to just over 100), certainly not a prepossessing situation that would place them among the city's elite. Yet John Work cites a contribution by the Captain of $3,000 toward construction of a Janesville church, which "made Captain Cargill a 'major contributor,' " so the family did have substantial resources. Captain Cargill sent sums to his boys, perhaps not very much at the start but certainly greater amounts in the early 1870s. One financial notation shows a sum of $6,652 sent to Will over the years 1874–1877; there may have been other amounts in this same period. In the early 1880s another scrap of paper shows a running credit balance over the period 1883–1888 of some $6,000 each year. This could not finance a major portion of Will Cargill's empire (for that was what it was beginning to be), but Captain Cargill had a financial interest in his sons' business careers for quite a few years.

As if Will Cargill did not have enough to do—or perhaps he felt he needed more money—he made a contract in June 1873 to become an insurance agent for a Minneapolis company, the National Life Insurance Company of the United States of America. Will's territory was to be "Albert Lea and vicinity," and he was to sell both "ordinary life and endowment

"Closing the Doors of the Stock Exchange on its Members," the Panic of *1873,* Frank Leslie's Illustrated Newspaper, *October 4, 1873.*

policies." There was a sliding scale of commissions on the first year's premiums, running from 10 percent to 25 percent and an additional commission of 2½ percent "on all second and subsequent premiums."[17]

Grasshoppers Complicate the Panic

The farming frontier, already suffering severely from the effects of the Panic of 1873, had to endure one additional calamity, the grasshoppers. From the first days of this frontier, there had been plenty of pests (the potato bugs reported by the *Cresco Times* were an example), but few farmers had ever experienced a real plague. Yet their very cultivation practices had scared away some of the 'hoppers' natural enemies, such as insect-eating birds like the prairie chicken and the upland plover. In horror, one Iowa farmer recalled, "A large black cloud suddenly appeared high in the west from which came an ominous sound. The apparition moved directly toward us, its dark appearance became more and more terrifying and the sound changed to a deep hum. . . . We heard the buzzing; we saw the shining wings, the long bodies, the legs. The grasshoppers—the scourge of the prairie—were upon us." The northern Iowa and southern Minnesota territory of Will Cargill was one of the regions most profoundly affected. The grasshoppers ate everything in sight except potatoes. Their onslaught was random; carried by the wind, they would drop down on a particular area and wreak ruin, not touching other farms nearby. The 1873 wave left a legacy of eggs for the following year. Herculean efforts were instituted

"Grasshoppers Stopping a Western-bound Train" (The Bettmann Archive).

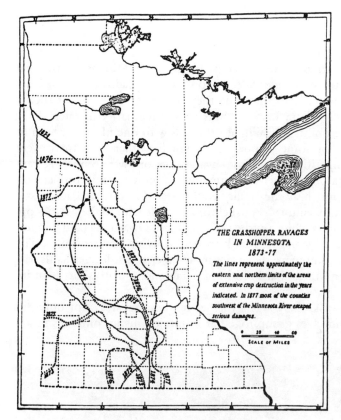

THE GRASSHOPPER RAVAGES
IN MINNESOTA
1873-77
The lines represent approximately the
eastern and northern limits of the areas
of extensive crop destruction in the years
indicated. In 1877 most of the counties
southwest of the Minnesota River escaped
serious damages.

SCALE OF MILES

(Reprinted from
William W. Folwell, *A
History of Minnesota*,
vol. 3, published by the
Minnesota Historical
Society; used with
permission)

to collect and destroy these eggs or the progeny of them if hatched. In the
four counties just north of Albert Lea, 2,500 bushels of grasshoppers had
been collected in the spring of 1875. "A careful estimate," said the newspaper, "figures 300,000 to the bushel, which would make about
750,000,000 disposed of." The Albert Lea newspaper, which had reported
in June 1873 a "constant tide of travel" westward of the wagon trains, wrote
in June 1874, "a large number of emigrants have passed through here eastward, fleeing from the grasshopper country." Severe crop losses from the
voracious insects were experienced through the year 1877. The county commissioners and the governor of the state, overwhelmed by the relief needs,
struggled to keep the farmers in the devastated areas from complete ruin.
The total quantity of grain in southern Minnesota continued to rise in the
years of the Panic, but there were disturbing signs of a deterioration in
quality due to impoverishment of the soil from the one-crop economy.
Prices had dropped through the floor. The Panic and the grasshoppers had
combined to bring agricultural expansion to a grinding halt.[18]

The Grangers Take on the Railroads

The railroads, boon to the farmers, now became their opponents in controversies over transportation rates. In Iowa and Minnesota, the zeal of communities to encourage railroad construction had often caused the roads to extend faster than the trade they served. "The result of such a system," noted Henrietta Larson, "was great irregularity in rates. They were low at some points . . . high at others, low to one place . . . high to another . . . low for some shippers . . . high for others." If there were alternatives—competition, say, from waterways or two competing railroads—discriminatory rates were rare; places enjoying no competition were charged as much as the traffic would bear. Larson cited Rochester shippers in 1870 as paying 15¢ a bushel for a 45-mile haul to the Mississippi River port of Winona while, on the same railroad, Owatonna paid just 10¢ for a 92-mile trip to Winona; Mankato paid only 13¢ for 150 miles. The railroad managers, knowing they were more efficient for longer hauls, developed "through" rates that bred innumerable long haul–short haul inequities.

By the early 1870s, there was a further irritant—rebates. Not only did the railroads themselves group together in monopolistic combines to ap-

"The Farmers' Movement in the West." A meeting of the Grangers, Frank Leslie's Illustrated Newspaper, *August 30, 1873.*

portion freight, they also rebated to favored warehousemen and elevator operators (as with Jason Easton), again with the intent of restricting competition. There was much grumbling about this by the farmers. Scattered complaints had surfaced even back in the early euphoric days when the McGregor Western was first moving out to the Conover–Cresco area. In October 1867, the *Cresco Times* reported that farmers were complaining of the " 'elevator nuisance' here at Cresco" (this was not Will Cargill's, incidentally). The newspaper editor took the side of the elevator: "It is to be presumed that some farmers do complain and they would were they given 62 pounds for every bushel of wheat, oats, smut &c., mixed in equal quantities, which they might bring. We'll venture the assertion that no farmer who has brought clean wheat here will ever complain of grade of wheat. Those running the Elevator are endeavoring to run it on 'the square.' "

When the depression hit in 1873, the farmers' discontent turned to fury. Back in late 1867, Minnesota farmer Oliver H. Kelley and six associates had formed a farmers' organization called the Order of Patrons of Husbandry, soon known as the "Grange." At that time it was a low-profile organization, espousing beliefs in cooperation and mutual aid for the "social improvement and enlightenment of the agricultural classes." Once depression settled on the farm, however, the Grange leaders turned the organization to more aggressive, indeed, militant goals. Now the railroads were lambasted as "monopolists," and the wheat dealers were the subject of special vitriol. Robert Eliot called it "the Granger tornado." In a convention of Grangers at Albert Lea, in July 1873, a ringing resolution was passed that decried the "high tariffs extorted by the railroad companies, and the robberies to which we are subjected by wheat buyers." Such combinations "are not justified by any principle of fair dealing, but are dictated by a spirit of oppression and greedy gain." The farmer members threatened not to sell their produce at all, but this was difficult to effect at such a dismal time, the farmers' resources being so strapped.

The agriculturalists of southern Minnesota were particularly hostile toward what they called "the Wheat Ring." This term was used in many locations around the country; in this particular instance, it was addressed to a combine of Joseph Reynolds, the McGregor mogul who was a silent partner of Bassett and Huntting, and two other men on the Winona and St. Peter Railroad, the rail line just north of the Southern Minnesota. In testimony before a "Special Joint Railroad Investigating Committee" of the Minnesota legislature in 1871, the railroad's discriminatory rebating to Reynolds and his colleagues was laid on the record, as well as their selective buying. Yet, as Henrietta Larson noted,

The ring was in a position to pay higher for wheat than small scalpers or independents could. Its rebates cut transportation costs considerably. By the consolidation of buying on the whole road under one management, expenses could be cut further. The ring was also able to avoid risks which had to be carried by others, because its close relations with central markets gave it an advantage in regard to market information, storage and sales. It also had more capital and could secure loans more easily. . . . Lastly, the ring was given special elevator privileges by the railroad.

The farmers were unconvinced by the arguments, particularly so because they felt that the grading methods of both the wheat buyers and the millers (the "wheat ring" and the "millers' trust," according to the farmers) were being used to downgrade the farmers' wheat—"cinching" was the term farmers applied to this.

Most small grain coming in from the field (barley, wheat, rye, etc.) did need to be cleaned to separate out bits of twigs, straw, stones, dirt, etc., that inevitably were a part of a harvest, as well as to cull the weed seeds and other miscellaneous vegetation present in most crops. The term for this is "dockage," for the farmer's price was, and is today, docked for its presence. A series of screens could allow a grain-handling company to "clean" the grain. Screening also made it possible to separate by size of grain, one of the key elements in establishing grades. This allowed an elevator or terminal to "mix to grade," in other words, to calibrate right down to grade level by mixing premium and average qualities—producing "skin grades," to use the vernacular of the trade. This was (and is) a legitimate and profitable component of grain handling, one of the necessary functions a grain company must perform. Farmers, however, usually complained about this, arguing that they were held to the lowest grade of a lot of grain, yet the grain company could then mix and gain an advantage from that extracted part which was premium. The logic of this argument was suspect—the farmer was not in a position to screen effectively. Nevertheless, grading has been for many years a source of considerable dissension within the trade.

Allegedly discriminatory grading practices became a focus in Minnesota in the infamous "Brass Kettle Campaign" of 1878. Wheat buyers used a weighing device, a two-quart brass kettle that could be manipulated by underfilling so that its total weight altered the "quality" of the wheat as much as two grades (top grades weighed more). The "lying little kettle" became the symbol of "wheat ring" and "millers' trust" dishonesty.

The farmers' Messiah, one of the Midwest's most important political and literary leaders at this time, was the famous Ignatius Donnelly. He was a large-scale farmer and was also a writer of great persuasiveness. In 1874, he founded a newspaper, the *Anti-Monopolist*, which a Litchfield, Minnesota, newspaper that year called "brimful of fight and fun, and bristles all over with invective . . . as dangerous a plaything as a porcupine." Donnelly led the battles for Minnesota railroad legislation, beginning in 1871, when the state's first law—a weak one—was passed, and was nominated as the Democratic candidate for Congress in the campaign of 1878, of which the "brass kettle" formed the centerpiece. He lost this election, contested its results, and lost on the protest as well. In the process, however, he had become a potent force for the farmers against "the monopolists."[19]

Wisconsin's "Potter Law"

In neighboring Wisconsin, meanwhile, farmers were equally hostile toward the railroads and had precipitated this state's own restrictive legislation, much more far-reaching than Minnesota's. Even before the Civil War, Wisconsin dwellers had agitated for state laws to control the railroads; a weak law had been passed in 1864, with further efforts over the next several years to tighten its ineffectual provisions. Most often this was despite opposition from the northern part of the state, which had few lines and wanted more and did not wish to antagonize the railroad builders.

In 1872, rumors flew that the state's two powerful lines, the Milwaukee and the Chicago & North Western, were contemplating a secret arrangement to pool freight. The Wisconsin governor, Cadwallader Washburn, immediately voiced vigorous opposition, and the embryonic pool was never consummated. But now the fury of the Wisconsin Grangers had been aroused, and they mounted a huge convention in September 1873. Railroads in general and their leaders in particular were lambasted, especially the excesses of Commodore Cornelius Vanderbilt, Jay Gould, "Jubilee Jim" Fisk, and Daniel Drew in the East, and the principals of the infamous "Crédit Mobilier" scandal in the Union Pacific Railroad, where high public officials, including Vice President Schuyler Colfax, had been given stock in return for political favors. Wisconsin lines were accused of "absentee ownership" (the Milwaukee, indeed, did have heavy stockholdings in the East and in Europe), their manipulation of rates was decried, and their favoring of large-scale warehousemen condemned.

The railroad companies, in a fit of ill-timed arrogance, announced new, higher rates in September 1873, right at the time of a Panic-bred rapid fall in prices. The Wisconsin state legislature rose to the challenge and, despite the railroads' contention that they were not subject to state regulation (the lines relied on the landmark Dartmouth College case, which disallowed state intervention against federal charters), passed stringent legislation in March 1874—the soon-famous "Potter Law."

This was no watered-down statute. It placed railroads in three classes, and the freight they carried in four classes. Maximum rates were established for these freight categories for all three groups. Passenger rates were also mandated (at 3 cents, 3½ cents and 4 cents a mile for the three groups). A commission was established to enforce all this, empowered in the process to gain access to all books and papers of the lines.

The law made headlines around the country; the *New York Times* had a front-page story on "the considerable excitement . . . brewing in Wisconsin." The railroads had immediately responded that, on advice of counsel, who held that the law was patently unconstitutional, they would ignore it; Alexander Mitchell, the president of the Milwaukee, even publicly announcing that if it was enforced he would take off every train on the road.

In La Crosse, the papers quickly filled with letters condemning the "contumacious roads," who used "the worst species of political bummerism" in "dodges for evading the law." It was clear that a judicial determination was needed, and it came quickly. The Attorney General of the state asked for an injunction against the higher rates, and in September 1874, the Wisconsin Supreme Court, in a "historic decision" hailed by the press all over the state as "the most important ever delivered by the Supreme Court," upheld the Potter Law.

The railroads ever so grudgingly allowed that they would comply with the law but immediately set in motion a full-scale political campaign for repeal. Extensive memoranda were laid before the legislature, picturing the financial ruin that would be wreaked by the rate regulations. A wide publicity campaign also was mounted with the general public, playing on the latter's fears of diminished service. By 1876, enough sentiment had been aroused to scuttle the law. Over the vehement opposition of the Grangers, new legislation was voted in 1876 that grandfathered rates to the 1872 tariffs, which were high enough to be more than acceptable to the lines. It was to be many more years before Wisconsin returned to stringent regulation of its railroads.

Despite the legislative turnarounds in Minnesota and Wisconsin, the concept of state regulation of railroads and warehouses subsequently was upheld by the United States Supreme Court in a series of key decisions in 1877 that have come to be known as "the Granger Cases." Several of these were railroad rate cases; the central one upon which the doctrine was established concerned an Illinois law regulating rates charged by warehousemen. In the decision, *Munn* v. *Illinois*, the Court upheld the law as a legitimate expression of the state's police power in regulating businesses "affected with the public interest." In the process, the justices did not accept the claim that due process had been denied or that state regulation impaired the unilateral control of Congress over interstate commerce.

In 1886, in another Illinois case where legislation had prohibited long haul–short haul railroad determinations, the Supreme Court invalidated the law as an infringement on Congress exclusivity in interstate commerce regulation, and the "Granger" rulings were gravely weakened. The Interstate Commerce Act was then passed by Congress in 1887, giving the Interstate Commerce Commission wide powers to regulate every railroad crossing a state line and in the process mandating a federal supremacy for railroad regulation, an effective power that has provided the basic control mechanisms down to the present day.[20]

"Minnesota Grades"

Minnesota finally enacted a railroad and warehouse law with teeth in 1885. The warehouse provisions became particularly important, for the legislators provided explicit regulation of the grading and weighing of grain. State grain inspectors were established, and grading distinctions of considerable clarity were established. Soon "Minnesota Grades" became known and recognized not only all over the United States but in foreign markets as well. Terminal warehouse owners were now to be licensed (and country elevators, too, after 1893). The commissioners who administered the law concluded, in their first report in 1888, "the grain law at once revolutionized the whole grain business of the Northwest."

The Grangers were not much involved in these frays in the 1880s and 1890s. Its members seemed to lose most of their political fervor, and the Grange became more oriented toward cooperative endeavors at the local level. Other regional farmers' groups took their place on the political scene.[21]

La Crosse Beckons

Will and Ella Cargill made a decisive business and personal decision in 1875—to move to La Crosse, Wisconsin. Existing records do not reveal any specific reasons. Most likely, business opportunities motivated Will Cargill's move, for La Crosse was a geographical node for regional commerce. This set his grain-trading sights eastward to Milwaukee and Chicago, more than north to the Twin Cities. The *Freeborn County Standard* editor gave major space to their move and ended, "While we are sorry to lose such worthy men and women, we congratulate the people of La Crosse on the acquisition of such strength to their business interests, as well as to their social system." Not to be outdone in encomiums, the La Crosse *Republican and Leader's* editor gushed, "La Crosse is always ready to extend the hand of welcome to men of pluck, brains, enterprise and capital." Will Cargill, incidentally, kept his loyalties to Albert Lea, exhibiting the same streak of generosity shown by his parents, who had contributed significantly to the Janesville Methodist Church. Twenty-five years later Will gave a substantial sum of money to Albert Lea College, a now-defunct Methodist women's school, for a science hall which was named after him.

La Crosse was to be home for Will and Ella for the rest of their lives and home office for all of Will's business endeavors. What was this town like in the mid-1870s? Certainly it was more worldly than Conover, consid-

Bird's-eye view of La Crosse, Wisconsin, 1887. Elevator to the right in foreground is the Cargill elevator (courtesy Area Research Center, UW–La Crosse).

erably larger than Albert Lea (La Crosse County had over 23,000 people on June 1, 1875, the city itself just over 11,000). As a river town that was served also by railroads direct from both Chicago and Milwaukee to the east and St. Paul to the north, it saw itself as "in the not very distant future one of the largest cities on the east bank of the Mississippi between Cairo and St. Paul" and as a preeminent grain trading mart (although its primary industry still remained lumber).

The Panic seemed not to have damaged La Crosse as much as some of its sister cities in the area; it was, in effect, "a fine business town." There *were* problems—nagging concerns about the area's wheat quality had come to the attention of Milwaukee and Chicago merchants, making some wary of purchasing. There were also concerns about the city's port facilities and the efficacy of the river channel itself.

Although La Crosse was considerably more cosmopolitan than Albert Lea, agriculture still dominated its thinking. W. R. Finch, the editor of the *Republican and Leader*, noted the near-completion of the harvest in September 1876: "The grain buyers make it lively for each other, now that the new crop is coming in, and farmers rejoice." Labor in quantity was the precious commodity during harvest, but now "the harvest is over and the servant girls begin to return with their wardrobe done up in a handkerchief only to go home again in ten months with large trunks full." It had not been an easy endeavor; there were many evidences: "The effect of the late harvest begins to be seen on the streets in the shape of maimed and wounded men, victims of the relentless reaper." Business would heighten now; editor Finch (and the business community) waited anxiously: "The streets are exceedingly quiet these days and it will be a relief to all when the farmers once more begin to come in and fill them up. At present a few hay teams are all that are to be seen, and business is dull."

And business did preoccupy the busy riverport. Finch unashamedly shilled for businessmen in his news column (provided they were advertisers) but was not above poking fun at them, too: "The numerous buttons on ladies dresses give rise to some funny things . . . one of our leading merchants was walking down the street behind a young lady who had a very large supply and thinking over some business transaction said 'One hundred and forty.' The lady overheard the remark, turned and said, 'Oh no, Mr. Blank, there are one hundred and fifty, for I sewed them on myself.' The gentleman stared, bowed and walked on wondering what she knew about his business."

La Crosse was still a small town on the prairie; animals coexisted alongside humans—sometimes too close alongside: "Cows are very domestic, and a nice thing to have around, but there is one in this city that is entirely too familiar, and we are tired of climbing over fences to escape her attentions. If the nuisance is not abated we will have to hire a small boy to take her to Uncle John's pound, where she can exercise her talent on the stone pile."

Fire department, La Crosse, Wisconsin, early 1870s (courtesy Area Research Center, UW–La Crosse).

Agricultural fair, La Crosse, Wisconsin, c. 1875 (La Crosse County Historical Society).

All in all, the La Crosse of the centennial year of the country was a lively, busy, excitable environment, ripe for business and still full of the verve of the railroad frontier that W. W. Cargill had experienced a decade earlier in Conover, Iowa. The two prairie schooners that "sailed down State Street Monday bound for Minnesota, where the passengers propose to furnish food for the grasshoppers" seemed to epitomize the tension between the excitement of the unknown and the security of the settled community. Both of these features were in La Crosse, and likely both still in W. W. Cargill.[22]

New Partners

Although the actual relocation of the W. W. Cargill business to La Crosse occurred in early 1875, Hyde, Cargill remained in business until August 1877 and kept an office in Albert Lea for this period. "W. W. Cargill & Bro." was now the La Crosse name; Sam Cargill remained Will's full partner, with youngest brother Jim, now 23 years old, also joining the firm at this time. During Will Cargill's first full year in La Crosse, the new firm (already "the largest dealers in this section," according to the newspaper) found itself facing a sensitive situation. The month of June, 1876 had been extremely hot. This not only damaged the new crop but caused much "hot wheat" in farmers' grain storage, some even catching fire from spontaneous combustion. Wanting to get their wheat off their hands, the farmers loaded up and headed for town. "There's such a crowd of farmers' teams waiting to unload at Hyde, Cargill & Co. . . . all men who can work conveniently are taking it in." But it was soon evident that much of the grain was out of condition, some so bad that it could not be accepted even for the lowest grade. Hyde, Cargill was forced to make unpopular decisions in turning some of this grain away. The newspaper admonished, "farmers who have any hot wheat had better not take the time and trouble to get it to town, as it is a glut in the market, and meets with poor sale."

But for Hyde, Cargill it was a good year, and the following spring Will and Ella, together with the B. J. Van Valkenburghs and the S. Y. Hydes took a pleasure trip to Chicago, whereupon the La Crosse *Liberal Democrat*, living up to both of its names as a critic of the wealthy, commented: "They have been making so much money on wheat that they'll buy Chicago if they feel like it."

R. G. Dun & Co., the credit reporting agency, had opened a branch office in La Crosse in 1876, and Hyde, Cargill was evaluated anew. The Dun correspondent was, if anything, more confused about Will's far-flung operations than had been his counterparts in Iowa and Minnesota—the parties "stand well . . . doing a good business . . . active & energetic young men . . . perfectly safe, but cannot obtain estimate of means." The correspondent explained, "On account of the character of the property in which

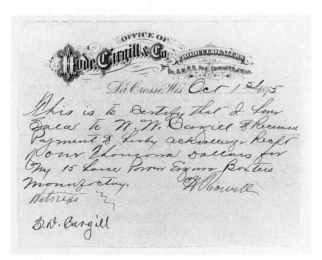

Hyde, Cargill
letterhead, *1875.*

HYDE, CARGILL & CO.,

DEALERS IN

PRODUCE.

Agents for ◇ JO ◇ LINE,

LEVY'S BLOCK,

Foot of Pearl Street.

apr9dly8m

Hyde, Cargill advertisement, April 1875, the first advertisement of the firm after its move to La Crosse, Wisconsin.

their means are invested, it is almost an impossibility to accurately estimate their worth." He worried, "in case of disaster, the opinion prevails that [the property would] not be realized upon unless at a heavy sacrifice."

The distinction between the "Office of W.W. Cargill" and "Hyde, Cargill & Co.," a relationship that had puzzled the Dun correspondent in Albert Lea, became academic in 1877, when the Hyde, Cargill relationship was phased out and the firm name eliminated. Hyde first went into a brief partnership with one Bonner, then formed a new warehouse and elevator company in La Crosse with L. F. Hodges, a general commission merchant residing in Milwaukee. The latter appeared to be a man of considerable wealth, for the Dun correspondent noted that he owned property in three states, including 59 lots in St. Paul, also a "large tract . . . of marsh land." While the new firm, Hodges & Hyde, "stand high with the trade," the Dun correspondent did worry that they "speculate more or less all of the time." Hyde was regarded "as a fair businessman . . . not understood to be worth much . . . the impression prevails that he cannot be worth the amount he claims."

Hodges & Hyde proceeded to purchase a number of elevators and warehouses along the Southern Minnesota line, ostensibly in direct competition with Will Cargill at several points. There is some evidence that Hyde was attempting to distance himself from Will Cargill, although an amicable letter from Hodges to Cargill in August 1875 belies any ill feeling.

Any posture of vigorous competition was disputed, however, by Henrietta Larson: "Hyde and Cargill had been buying together earlier, but even after they had formed different companies it appeared to the farmers that they did not seriously compete [and] tended to prevent competition on the part of other buyers. . . . Several buyers or agents jumped onto the farmers' wagons to bid for the grain, but their attempts to keep up the appearance of competition were often so ill-concealed as to make the farmer suspicious."

Will Cargill now formed new links with powerful colleagues. While keeping his firm, "W. W. Cargill & Bro." in place, Will Cargill established another partnership in 1877, "Cargill & Van," with B. J. Van Valkenburgh, who also had moved to La Crosse in 1875, the same year that Will Cargill had relocated there. The firm's first letterhead announced that it was in "Grain and Produce—on Southern and Central Railroads of Minn.," a signal that Will Cargill also continued to look north and west. Another part of the letterhead announced another important formal relationship— Bassett, Huntting & Co., the old McGregor, Iowa, firm was listed as a principal. This latter relationship may have been a formal partnership agreement, although none can be found in extant records. Still, it is likely that there were varying ad hoc arrangements for individual elevators and other projects. In one such agreement (to acquire a 1280-acre plat in an unnamed town), Bassett, Huntting had "6/12"; Will Cargill, "4/12"; and Van Valkenburgh, "2/12."

It seems clear that Will was "close and attentive" as far as repayment of debts, as this young man already commanded wide respect from his peers and was accorded ready access to money. As early as the Hyde, Cargill days, there was increasing evidence of his inattention to details. In June 1876, H. D. Brown, a banker in Albert Lea, failed to include certain pro-

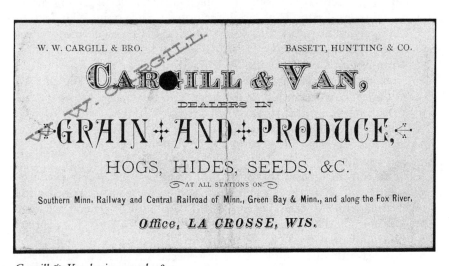

Cargill & Van business card, 1879.

visions that Will Cargill wanted in a mortgage Brown was drawing for him; Brown responded, "I would have done it if I had known in time that you so desired it." A lawyer, S. D. Abbott, in Winnebago City at the end of the Southern Minnesota line, was attempting to collect a note held by Hyde, Cargill, with a wagon as collateral. The contract was "poorly drawn, but I think I can get the wagon back, if I cannot collect." In January 1877, John Kaercher, the owner of the "Clear Grit Mills," chastised Hyde, Cargill: "The most fault I found with your letters was that I could not understand what you did propose to do, whether on a certain basis or not—it looked to me that it might be construed either way."

Some of this may have been due to Will's handwriting, as both he and Sam "had the disconcerting habit of trailing upward or downward, and the tendency to swish the pen on words that were hard to spell." In 1883 they hired a newly trained "stenographer" (male in those days), one I. C. Cuvellier, who brought with him his big box-like "Caligraph" typewriter, and the correspondence became much more readable.

Another customer of Hyde, Cargill noted, "Armstrong writes that he notified you but has heard nothing from you and he is afraid there is 'something wrong.' Please let him know that it is all right." A Hyde, Cargill assistant in Albert Lea, pushed by a fellow employee at Lanesboro for money to buy, wrote, "would send it today but Cargill went to Mankato yesterday and neglected to leave any drafts signed." Jason Easton himself wrote a detailed three-page letter to one of his branch banks, detailing exactly how monies tendered to Hyde, Cargill should be accounted for: "They must keep you notified . . . you want to insist."

Will Cargill centralized control in his hands, not vesting authority in his assistants. An Easton bank employee noted, at one point, "Hyde, Cargill & Co. say in the future they don't want you to furnish currency to any station except on orders from Headquarters, so that Hobart must get orders from H.C.& Co. before you let him have any."[23]

A July 1875 contract with a Whalan, Minnesota, firm, to buy and sell wheat, barley, oats, corn, hides, and hogs, also included a provision that "said Downing & Brother agree to make reports to Hyde Cargill & Co. at La Crosse, Wisconsin every day . . . so often as said Hyde Cargill & Co. may deem it necessary, the expense of . . . stationery and insurance to be paid for equally."

The agreements generally provided for commission charges, usually 3¢ per bushel for wheat on consignment. Some contracts contained additional constraints; for example, a Chatfield, Minnesota, "general merchandise" dealer, C. M. Lovell, wanted Hyde, Cargill "to keep this contract strictly confidential & in no way give farmers or others any information that will leave them to think I have any special advantages in buying or storing grain."

Hyde, Cargill apparently was large enough to justify rebates from the Southern Minnesota Railroad. In turn, Hyde, Cargill itself gave rebates to some farmers north of the Southern Minnesota line, presumably to draw business from the area where the Southern Minnesota and the Winona and St. Peter railroads competed. One such contract stated, "this arrangement is made with the distinct understanding that the entire rebate is to be used in paying an increased price for wheat from 4 miles north of the line."

The large number of warehouses and elevators acquired by both Cargill and Hodges & Hyde illustrate well what came to be known as "the line," a group of country elevators, sometimes with storage at primary points, under one central management. Henrietta Larson dated this development from 1876 and described it this way: "The buyers at the individual elevators receive definite instructions from the central office, where all matters of policy, price, grading, weighing, charges for storage and handling, shipping and selling in the primary markets are determined. The local buyers are merely agents of the line and as such are obliged to follow instructions." This became characteristic of elevator operation in the country wheat trade, both then and later.

The two "competitor" firms were very strong on the Southern Minnesota. Larson cited "a sale which they made in 1878 of 80,000 bushels of no. 1 wheat to a Liverpool buyer, which was said to be 'one of the heaviest wheat sales ever made in the Northwest,' and which was probably the first important sale for direct export from Minnesota." (Likely this was done through a representative or correspondent of a Liverpool firm residing in New York City.) Cargill's most common route for export wheat was by lake-shipping to Buffalo (from either Milwaukee or Green Bay), then by rail through to New York City, where the New York Central & Hudson River Railroad maintained two huge waterside terminals, one holding 2 million bushels, the other 1 1/2 million. Shipping by rail from Chicago eastward also was a common route. Robert Eliot handled most of W. W.'s business for this but complained that "certain very wealthy and influential dealers" in the East maintained control of the rates and "had an advantage at first of about 3 cents a bushel [but] we could not prove it."

La Crosse was still in the depths of the depression, and foreclosures were common. Some lawyers specialized in peddling notes, almost as if they were money. Eugene E. Snow, in Spencer, Iowa, operated a "law, loan & collection office"; J. H. Parker, in a law firm in Albert Lea, offered a note to Will Cargill for his personal purchase in April 1876. Will was assiduous in following up on these; he wrote one of these collectors, "Don't leave a thing undone or a stone unturned necessary to the collection of these notes. We must have the money . . ." It was always best to write in the contract some physical pledge; for example, a contract drawn in April 1874 provided "two spring colts" as security.[24]

"The Western Grain Movement—at the Hudson River Elevator in New York," Frank Leslie's Illustrated Newspaper, *November 10, 1877.*

In the harsh business climate of the Panic, it was the survival of the fittest. It was not just the Dun correspondents who were blunt—Will Cargill's business papers are full of similar comments. People with whom he dealt were quickly sorted out, and those unable to pay were noted as "no good" (or even "D.B.," a deadbeat). One person owing Cargill & Van a considerable sum had some land, but Will Cargill asked his collector, "Is it all exempt by law? . . . Better have him make a property statement to you & if there is anything not exempt . . . sue him and get it into a judgment." In another case, difficulties on a mortgage were blamed on a "dishonest wife." One debtor "skipped the country" in February 1880. He was traced to Centralia, Wisconsin, but the correspondent noted, "He is just making a living and a very poor one at that . . . constitutionally lazy." There is no record that Will Cargill ever got his money.[25]

Will Cargill's entrepreneurial interests kept turning him in any direction where he seemed to see opportunity for profit. Invention itself was not his bent, but he was quick to recognize the value of new, innovative machinery. Most of these were patented, so Will Cargill purchased several rights for such equipment. One, for example, was for grain-cleaning machinery. As early as 1879 he was also experimenting with seed propagation. In 1880, he obtained rights from the Southern Minnesota Railroad to put a "cleaning elevator" at Hokah, Minnesota, five miles south of La Crescent, just across the river from La Crosse, Wisconsin, in this case using some of the new technology. The railroad allowed Cargill to "clean in transit," the line giving Cargill a 10-year contract. Relations with the Southern Minnesota had not always been as amicable. For example, in October 1876, the old firm of Hyde, Cargill had acquired a warehouse from Hodges at Albert Lea. The railroad wrote, "This is contrary to our understanding and if you retain it, we will want possession of the Easton's elevator at that point." The records show, however, that Cargill & Van was a preferred shipper entitled to continuing rebates. Most of these were from the Milwaukee railroad, but some were from the independent Green Bay & Minnesota line (later called the Green Bay & Western).[26]

Will Cargill also recognized early the critical importance of a good communications network. By July 1879, the *La Crosse Chronicle* reported a telephone network connecting "Cargill & Van's office, Gund's brewery,

"Farm machinery dealers displaying their wares," Rush City, Minnesota, c. *1892* (Minnesota Historical Society).

the Green Bay depot and Segelike, Kohlaus & Co.'s factory" (this was just three years after its invention by Alexander Graham Bell).

In October 1880, W. W. Cargill and Bro. began constructing an elevator at La Crosse. A contemporary report described it as some 30 by 60 feet in dimensions, 85 feet in height, with a separate building some 30 by 100 feet, the latter containing a 60-horsepower engine for the lifting. The elevator, according to the account, had a capacity of some 50,000 bushels. This legitimately could be considered Will Cargill's first owned "terminal" elevator, an elevator (generally of substantial size) placed at the head of the line, where grain could be funneled to it for storage and further shipment. Cargill's delivery to the east was much facilitated by this addition.

In the early 1880s, Will Cargill also entered flour milling on a small scale, purchasing two moderate-sized mills, one at Hokah, Minnesota, and the other at Houston, some 12 miles farther west. The two mills were operated under a separate partnership, Cargill & Fall (James Fall was the other member); they called their flour "Diamond Dust." The two men also bought into an existing mill at Whalan, Minnesota, some 18 miles west of Houston. They improved it with a modern rolling mill, but shortly after, in 1884, the mill burned to the ground. Unfazed, the partners rebuilt the next year.

These were nothing like the giant mills in Minneapolis, but the machinery was more complex than an elevator and the investment relatively substantial. Further, it was a conscious effort to integrate forward into the end-use of grain. Cargill now often pressed vigorously to sidetrack "through" wheat destined for Chicago in order to keep a steady flow for the mills, always a dominant factor in a process-oriented business. He wrote a St. Paul commission house in May 1882, for example, "if you have 2 cars at Litchfield, you could send from there, sell to us for Chicago, to be *milled at Hokah*."

A turn eastward to Green Bay next was taken, a critically important move. Green Bay had long been a lake shipping point secondary to Chicago, Milwaukee, and Duluth and had been connected in the early 1870s with La Crosse through the building of the Green Bay & Minnesota Railroad (later called the Green Bay & Western) westward from Green Bay to the Mississippi River at Marshland (with connection across the river to Winona, Minnesota, and the Winona & St. Paul Railroad and with further connections southward to La Crosse).

In 1878, Cargill & Van began buying property along the Green Bay & Minnesota, using J. B. Canterbury as its agent. By 1880, Cargill & Van had warehouse operations at nine locations on the western reaches of this railroad, at Dodge, Arcadia, Independence, Whitehall, Blair, Taylor, Hixton, Alma Center and Circleville, Wisconsin. In Green Bay, Cargill & Van in 1878 acquired a warehouse (capacity 30,000 bushels) and leased from the

Early Cargill shipbuilding on the Black River in La Crosse, Wisconsin, 1890s.

Chicago & North Western railroad a 250,000-bushel terminal, formerly the Elmore and Kelly operation, also taking over the latter's commission business. It had been built in 1862 at a cost of $80,000 and stood 100 feet high, a landmark for the Green Bay shoreline. The company also owned "a small tug for handling local freights," once again a small step toward vertical integration and a portent of the future. Cargill & Van also was trading in salted fish in 1880, out of an office in Green Bay. The amounts were substantial—the inventory at this point included 103 half barrels of flat herring, 110 of white fish, 130 of trout, and 5 of red herring.

The Green Bay location, on the bay, linked the Company to lake shipping—grain could be sent by lakes all the way to Buffalo or sent across Lake Michigan to the port of Ludington, Michigan for eastward shipment by rail to, for example, the export terminals of New York City. Rail and inland waterway companies often have great volume going in one direction and always try to run loaded in both directions—not "deadhead" back on a return. Midwest grain for eastern milling centers and for export had both large west-to-east and north-to-south volume. The grain lakers that came to Green Bay found an important backhaul for their voyage coming in, anthracite coal from Pennsylvania. This intrigued W. W. Cargill, for his elevators sold coal as a sideline, both anthracite from the east and bituminous from midwestern mines. By the mid-1880s, a Cargill coal business was in being in La Crosse. So W. W. became keenly interested in the lakers, both as a possible forward integration and as a backhaul for his coal. The firm became an agent for the Union Transportation Company steamers, which connected with Buffalo, and W. W. also himself invested in two Great Lakes steamers, the *America* and the *Brazil*, as a minority partner in the Wisconsin Transportation Company. But his name does not appear as a "managing owner" in remaining records of any Great Lakes ship of those times.

W. W. was also a stockholder and booster for the Kewaunee, Green Bay & Western Railroad, a feeder line just over 30 miles in length that was built in 1891. It cut across the Green Bay peninsula, connecting the Green Bay & Western Railroad at Green Bay with the Lake Michigan port of Kewaunee. This port was more apt to be ice-free than Green Bay in the winter. The connections on the Michigan side included, in addition to Ludington, the ports of Manistee and Frankfort, also served by rail.

In 1881, Will and Ella Cargill began the construction of a massive, three-story home in a prestigious part of La Crosse. Added to and embellished in subsequent years and lavishly remodeled in 1906, it became a showpiece for the town. Clearly, the W. W. Cargills had "arrived," both economically

W. W. Cargill home, La Crosse, Wisconsin, mid-1880s.

and socially. A major two-column article appeared in the *Republican and Leader* in October 1880, entitled "Crop Movers: Past and Present of the Cargill Brothers." The editor complimented the organization that had "brought their business down to a system as perfect as that which regulates the movements of the corps, divisions and regiments of a grand army. . . . The firm handle[s] from 2,500,000 to 3,000,000 bushels of wheat annually . . . and keep[s] an army of clerks and buyers . . . they are live business men, a valuable acquisition to the business and social forces of La Crosse, where they have resided . . . in the quiet enjoyment of a rapidly increasing income."

Perhaps Will and Sam Cargill still sensed an unease on the part of the Dun correspondent, for in January 1882, they invited the correspondent to the offices and laid before him the books of the firm. The assets totaled $358,745; the liabilities, $186,062, "of which amt 159m is to R. Eliot & Co." The correspondent seemed surprised by the fact that over $33,000 of the inventory was in wool but was positive about the fact that the profit of the year was "some 40m." He worried that the Cargills were overvaluing their property, "that to any one else it would not be worth near that sum. . . . The R/E [real estate] item will stand a cutdown from their valuation." Just after this cautionary comment, the correspondent noted, "W.W.C. is building a very handsome home which will cost 20-30m." Even with his skepticism he still concluded that they were "live, energetic, good businessmen, close and attentive."

All of this success seemed hard to manage for Will Cargill. The flurry of activities in this 1880–1881 period apparently exhausted him—the La Crosse *Chronicle* editor reported, in August 1881, "Mr. W. W. Cargill is in Chicago and contemplates a visit to the sea coast. He is somewhat out of health from overwork and needs a season of complete rest."[27]

The Mule Farm

Another new venture of Cargill & Van occurred in the late 1870s and early 1880s, a foray into farming itself. When the economy began to come out of the doldrums in 1878, railroad construction began again all over the Midwest. One such company was the Southern Minnesota Extension Company, headed by Jason Easton as president. It was absorbed by the Southern Minnesota Division of the Milwaukee road in 1880, which began in that year to build westward from Winnebago (where the Southern Minnesota had stopped in the early 1870s) toward the border of the Dakota Territory. By June 1878, it was already through Martin County, Minnesota, and moving westward. Once again, Will Cargill followed the frontier and began buying properties at several points along the new stretches of the line in areas often not yet even platted as towns. One of these was in the western reaches of Martin County, where a new town, Sherburn, was being formed. Cargill & Van owned substantial amounts of the whole area, including most of the Sherburn townsite and a 5,760-acre piece south and west of the rail line, known variously as the Big Farm, The Mule Farm, and Muletown. Here Cargill & Van proposed to integrate backward into farming and on a consequential scale, too. The Martin County *Sentinel* picked up the development in its issue of June 27, 1879. The farm had opened the previous summer, with some 2,300 acres broken at that time; 1,900 of these were now in small grain, the remainder in "corn, potatoes, roots, etc., the greater portion of which looks promising, indeed." An additional 2,000 acres was to be broken in 1879. A move was already underway to have the farm incorporated officially as "Muletown." A "long shed," nearly 900 feet in length, was built for what was expected to be a herd of over 500 cattle.

Meanwhile, Cargill & Van had built an elevator back at Sherburn itself, one of relatively small size costing about $3,500 but with modern elevating equipment. It had been up no more than a year when, in November 1879, fire took it down to the ground, burning in the process 3,000 bushels of wheat, 2,000 of which came from the Mule Farm. Will Cargill and his partners, undaunted, rebuilt with a 6,000-bushel building, this time only a warehouse.

In 1880, B. J. Van Valkenburgh, unwell, decided to retire. Apparently he owed Will Cargill some $6,120. As a result, in June 1882, an agreement was struck between the two men, giving Will Cargill the Van Valkenburgh share of a number of the terminals, as well as the latter's rights in the Cargill operations at Green Bay. This took care of some $3,673 worth of the debt, with the remainder to be paid on a new note, at 8 percent (a lower rate than usual, since most contracts in this period were calling for either 10 percent or 12 percent). In the process, Van Valkenburgh's involvement in Mule Farm was terminated, Will Cargill then becoming, according to the newspaper, "the principal owner."

It was a dubious distinction, as the farm had begun doing badly. The first resident manager, according to the newspaper, had "run things with a lavish hand and when he left he was careful to take away everything that belonged to him." (The editor seemed a bit ashamed of having been so harsh and wrote in the next week's paper, "Rather hard on 'old Harv' in last week's *Sentinel*.") The new manager, H. N. Swarthourt, was more efficient, and the farm began to recover some, but it was a losing struggle. In 1886, the entire operation was put up for sale. Sickness in the stock and bad weather had been contributing causes, but it seems more likely that trying to run an operation of this size on an absentee basis was not effective. As a local historian put it, "The owners soon found that the more land they broke up the more money they lost." Will Cargill was 170 miles to the east and seldom saw the property. Further, he had had little experience in farming since his boyhood and was not attuned to the signals that farm records might give of impending difficulty. Swarthourt subsequently was given a job in the Cargill organization. Muletown, "now but a memory and a ghost town, with no trace of anything to prove it even existed," said a later newspaper article, was Will Cargill's last venture in large-scale, corporate farming.[28]

Will Cargill had another, smaller farm near Alden, just west of Albert Lea. Here, too, there was a resident manager, and apparently he also experienced difficulty in getting instructions from Will Cargill (writing in January 1879, "What do you want to do with your oats?"). Two months later, the manager precipitated a large argument about the measurement and grading of the wheat crop; "Eckert writes you that I took advantage of circumstances through threshing. I say that it is all false and I can back every word that I say . . . I asked one of your wheat buyers at elevator to look this matter up . . . he said he knew better without looking and would tell you when you came to Alden." Once again, Will Cargill's lack of attention had caused ill feeling.

Another farm manager had to be handled more sensitively, however. W. A. Stowell, Will Cargill's father-in-law had sold his interest in the dry goods business in Conover and had moved to Charles City, Iowa, 40 or so miles west of Conover. Here he was managing a farm owned by Will Cargill. Once again, there were letters back and forth about how to handle the marketing of the crops; Stowell had not had much luck on the farm. He had continued selling insurance and had provided some policies for Will Cargill's operation. When Will had another substantial fire loss, at the Grand Meadow, Minnesota, elevator, Stowell wrote that the company was uneasy about its exposure and wanted an additional premium. He added, "We are all well and ma & Clarra are buisey in makeing up some things for Christmass for the little fellows" (his misspellings).[29]

But neither of these farms was on the scale of the Mule Farm, where Will Cargill really had contemplated an integrated operation that would supply his grain business. It was not until the first decade of the 20th century that this notion of integrating backward into farming once again appealed to him. The location was Montana—and the results disastrous.

The Red River Valley

When the railroads commenced building anew after 1878, Minnesota's agriculture and railroad situations changed radically (Henrietta Larson regarded the year 1880 as the watershed). The wheat crops in the southeastern and southwestern regions of the state had tailed off in the late 1870s, in terms of both quality and yield. Fortunately for the farmers, livestock had become a profitable substitution. This did not bode well, however, for the shippers of grain along those southern routes.

The grain traders' sagging fortunes in southern Minnesota were more than made up, however, by a dramatic development in the northwestern part of the state, in the region bordering on the Red River. Here the rich virgin soil produced excellent wheat in large yields; the region's spring wheat was of the highest quality. The heightened importance of the Red River Valley wheat was much enhanced by the fact that the railroads rapidly built into this area. During the year 1879, not only did the Southern Minnesota line reach the Dakota Territory's border, but in the north, the St. Paul, Minneapolis and Manitoba (later the St. Paul and Pacific) and the Northern Pacific separately linked both Duluth and Minneapolis with this important new wheat-growing area on the Minnesota-Dakota line.

The combination of the new wheat fields and the extended railroads brought a phenomenal rise in the importance of Minneapolis and Duluth as wheat markets. Minneapolis had been a modest flour milling center since shortly after the Civil War. Then, with the development of the so-called New Process way of milling after 1871, the hard spring wheat of the Red River Valley could be readily converted to flour. That hardness had caused problems earlier, but the New Process approach allowed the middlings from the first grinding to be purified and reground and saved the discoloration that had come from earlier methods. This innovation, originally developed in France, was introduced with great success (and profits)

Arrival of harvesting machinery, Red River Valley, c. 1895 (Minnesota Historical Society).

·St Paul·Minneapolis &.Manitoba·R'y·

RED RIVER VALLEY LINE

RED RIVER VALLEY LINE

St.P.M.&M.R'y.
Double Track Stone Arch Bridge
Minneapolis, Minn.

·Through the Park Region *to the* New Northwest·

W. S. ALEXANDER,
General Traffic Manager,
ST. PAUL, MINN.

C. H. WARREN,
General Passenger Agent.

JAS. J. HILL,
President,
ST. PAUL, MINN.

A. MANVEL,
General Manager.

D. W. H. MORELAND, Traveling Agent, 153 Jefferson Avenue, Detroit, Mich.

MATTHEWS, NORTHRUP & CO., ART-PRINTING WORKS, BUFFALO, N. Y.

Promotional brochure for Red River Valley, picturing the "Double Track Stone Arch Bridge," Minneapolis, 1885 (Minnesota Historical Society).

in the huge Washburn "B" mill, the largest in Minneapolis, and soon was being used by other major millers in the city. Most of these were large-scale operations, an apparent requisite. Out of this milling development in Minneapolis grew a very important new organization, operating as the Minneapolis Millers' Association from 1876. This powerful buying organization was the famous (or infamous to the farmers) "Millers' Trust." In 1881, a group of Minneapolis grain traders formed the Minneapolis Chamber of Commerce, a name that continued to confuse many people, for it actually was the grain exchange. This group incurred the ill will of the millers, who felt that their own organization's monopoly's position would be challenged. Subsequently, the Millers' Association faded away, and the grain trade was centered in the Chamber of Commerce.

Duluth, too, had had a stunning rise in importance as a wheat market after 1880, jumping from an annual average of 1.6 million bushels in the 1876–1880 period to an average of 9.2 million from 1881 to 1885. The wheat was sold on Duluth's own grain exchange, its "Board of Trade," and almost all of the traded grain was then shipped via the Great Lakes eastward to flour milling cities like Buffalo, New York. While the primary markets for northern Iowa and southern Minnesota wheat continued to be Milwaukee and Chicago, the developments in Minneapolis and Duluth, and in their Red River Valley suppliers, changed a whole set of equations for the upper Midwest grain trade. This phenomenon was not lost on the Cargills.[30]

Jim Cargill in Dakota Territory

The La Crosse "W.W. Cargill & Bro." had always been Will Cargill and his brother Sam, just two years his junior. Next brother Sylvester had worked for Will for a half dozen years, but had been in his own grain business independently from the mid-1870s.

This left youngest brother James Flett Cargill, born in 1852 and therefore eight years Will's junior. Jim had begun working for Will and Sam shortly after they moved to La Crosse. Sometime in the early 1880s, Jim left the security of working for the two older brothers to strike out on his own, first with John D. McMillan (as "Cargill & McMillan"), and then in a partnership with Will and Sam, appropriately called "Cargill Brothers." Jim was headquartered at his "general offices" in Wahpeton, Dakota Territory, on the Red River in the southeast corner of what is now North Dakota.

Jim did not have enough money to accomplish this completely on his own. Some part of the capital came from McMillan (to distinguish this spelling from that of the John MacMillans, also La Crosse relatives, the former's side of the family was often called "Mick"Millan). John McMillan was born in 1860 in La Crosse, so was eight years younger than Jim. Both McMillan and Edward Osborne had been working for Will Cargill in the La Crosse office; in 1887, the separate Osborne-McMillan Elevator Company was formed by these two in Minneapolis.

Given John McMillan's age, it is probable that most of the capital for the Red River Valley effort was supplied by W. W. Cargill & Bro. General ledgers of "J. F. Cargill" for the years 1883 and 1884 show substantial drawing accounts on W. W. Cargill & Bro. and list a significant number of elevators and warehouses in the Valley during those two years, at 17 locations.

Jim Cargill had been in charge of some of the firm's elevator construction when he worked for his older brothers; now he did the same with his

"The Big Farm," Red River Valley, Frank Leslie's Illustrated Newspaper, *October 19, 1878.*

own elevators. At about this time in the industry, a new form of construction—the "cribbed" elevator—began to be the norm. "In this construction," a 1907 engineering book on grain elevators stated, "2″ x 4″, 2″ x 6″, or 2″ x 8″ are laid flatwise, so as to break joints and bind the structure together and are spiked firmly." This "log cabin" approach could resist the great fluid-like pressure on the sides, so made a strong form of construction, "one very cheap with the former low price of timber." The 1945 Cargill history claimed the cribbed elevator as an innovation of Jim Cargill, but no corroboration appears in any of the records—it may have been like the steel plow, where a number of inventors came up with the idea at about the same time.

When the 1885 railroad law was passed in the state of Minnesota, one very helpful feature of the *Annual Report of the Railroad and Warehouse Commissioners* for that year was a complete listing of every elevator in the entire state of Minnesota; the *Saint Paul and Minneapolis Pioneer Press* (the name at that time) picked this up and added all of the Dakota Territory warehouses, too. For the first time, we have a definitive list of all of the Cargill elevators in both areas. It shows both the size of the individual warehouses or elevators and the numbers of competitors and their sizes at the same locations. For the W. W. Cargill & Bro. list, in the "Southern Minnesota District" of the Chicago, Milwaukee & St. Paul Railroad, Will and Sam had elevators or warehouses at 39 locations, a total of 62 separate buildings (of these, 36 were classified only as "warehouses"). At only four of these locations did the company own the only elevator; at 22 of the 39 locations, one of the competitors (often the only one) was Hodges & Hyde. The capacities of all of the southern Minnesota buildings were relatively small—only 16 of these had a capacity of 10,000 bushels or over. Alden, Minnesota, and Howard, South Dakota, had 25,000-bushel elevators. Several of the other South Dakota operations had capacities above 15,000 bushels. The rest, all along the Southern Minnesota line, were very small (and so, too, were the Hodges & Hyde competitor operations).

In contrast, the J. F. Cargill buildings, all in the North Dakota section of the Dakota Territory, were much larger. There were a total of 26 locations by this time, each with one elevator or warehouse (actually, only four were considered to be warehouses). Another 4 of the 26 were below 25,000-bushel capacity; 3 had a capacity of 45,000 bushels, 1 was 40,000 bushels, 5 were 35,000 bushels, and 10 were 30,000 bushels. There were competitors at every location except two, and they also had large capacities. In sum, although Jim Cargill's branch of the business had only started a few years before the published Commission report, he already had a huge capacity, far greater per station than the Southern Minnesota/South Dakota part of the Dakota Territories.[31]

Partnerships with George Bagley

There was a separate Cargill set of entries on this list, under the partnership of "Bagley & Cargill." George C. Bagley was a member of a grain-trading family in eastern Wisconsin; he had lived at Eden, managing that part of the family line running from Milwaukee into Fond du Lac. By 1883, with the Wisconsin farmers' shift out of wheat into livestock, the Bagley grain business was not doing well, either. Robert Eliot, the Milwaukee financier who was bankrolling Will Cargill, also was a friend of the Bagley group; he advised George to sell his line of elevators and buy a line in South Dakota. Bagley did so, moving to Canton, South Dakota, and forming a partnership there, about 1885, with Sylvester Cargill. The firm name was Bagley & Cargill, "Dealers in Grain, Flax Seed, Livestock, Etc." Most of the Bagley & Cargill operations were in that part of the Dakota Territory

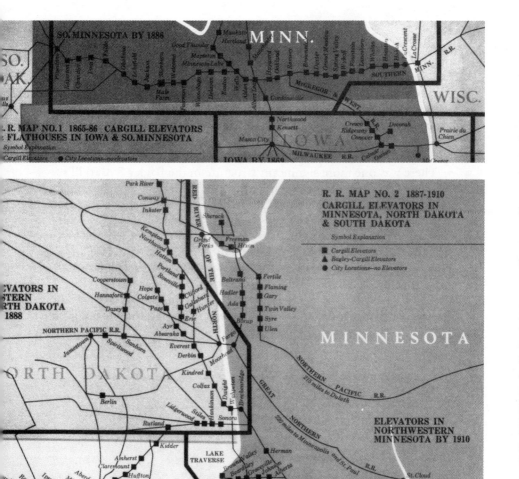

Two railroad maps; John Work, Cargill Beginnings.

that later became the northeastern section of South Dakota. Similar to Jim Cargill's larger-capacity operations in the Red River Valley, the Bagley & Cargill's 13 structures at the firm's 10 locations were more substantial (although only one was classified as an elevator). This elevator, at Aberdeen, had a capacity of 25,000 bushels; the Andover warehouse had the same; the Groton operation had an 18,000-bushel capacity and the Bath warehouse, 15,000.

There was one more significant structure in the Bagley & Cargill set—a terminal elevator at Minneapolis, with 100,000-bushel capacity (enlarged in 1886 to 250,000). This was not the largest in Minneapolis—a 1923 history of the city stated that the largest elevator "west of Chicago" was built in 1879 by the Minneapolis Elevator Company "with a capacity of 780,000 bushels and at a cost of $150,000." The 1885 Railroad and Warehouse Report listed total capacity in Minneapolis as 9,834,500 bushels, with an additional 1,560,000 in St. Paul.

To recapitulate: the three Cargill brothers (minus Sylvester by now) owned or controlled some 102 structures in 1885 in Minnesota and Dakota territory, many just warehouses and only one, the Minneapolis operation,

GEO. C. BAGLEY

Little grains of number one
With a little rain and sun
Mean a lot of grains and, lo,
Bagley turns 'em into "dough."

E. R. Buell, Just for Fun: A Port-folio of Cartoons 1915.

a true terminal. The total capacity was just over 1.6 million bushels. In addition, the Cargill group controlled a half dozen small elevators in Wisconsin (including the substantial La Crosse terminal and the leased terminal at Green Bay) and a couple of warehouses in Iowa. The total number of elevators and warehouses in Minnesota and the Dakota Territory was 1,513; total capacity in the country system was 33.5 million bushels. With the Minneapolis and St. Paul totals noted above, plus the 9.4 million bushels at Duluth, the grand total storage capacity of this upper Midwest area was 54,448,900 bushels.

Large numbers of these 1,513 elevators and warehouses were owned by one or another of the nine railroad systems involved, but there were a host of private companies, most smaller than the Cargill group. G. W. Van Dusen & Co. was larger, with almost all of its operations on Chicago & Northwestern trackage (George Van Dusen had started trading grain in 1852, had opened an office in St. Paul in 1881, then moved to Minneapolis in 1887; in 1889, C. M. Harrington and Van Dusen formed Van Dusen-Harrington Co.).

Another firm of size—if one added its operation in other states, it was larger than Cargill—was F. H. Peavey & Company. Frank Peavey started in 1874 in Iowa, and he too moved his headquarters to Minneapolis, in 1884. Many years later (in 1928) Peavey and Van Dusen-Harrington merged, to become the largest grain trading company at that time.

At this point, an important decision about organization structure was made that would turn out to be critical almost three decades later. The three brothers—Will, Sam, and Jim—decided in 1884 to cleanly separate the operations of Will and Sam in Wisconsin and southern Minnesota from the operations of the three of them together in central and northern Minnesota and the Dakota Territory. This was to be accomplished by establishing a separate entity in Minneapolis called "Cargill Brothers." Money moving back and forth between the two entities would be duly recorded in drawing accounts in the requisite set of books, and each of the three would maintain its own accounts in the La Crosse books. While the names of the two companies were quite similar and perhaps confused some people, the grain trade clearly understood that the two were separate legal entities.

The Sylvester Cargill–George Bagley duo lasted only a short time, when Bagley dissociated himself, apparently not amicably, at least according to his wife's memoirs; she wrote, "Ves Cargill [Sylvester] was a partner but George could not put up with his suspicion of all deals and bought him out." No records exist at this point of Sylvester's side of the issue. The separation left Sylvester with the elevators he had before joining Bagley; in October 1889, he organized the Victoria Elevator Company and was its president until his death in 1913.

Again, Robert Eliot intervened, writing Bagley that an opportunity was presenting itself to join the "J. F. Cargill group" (Jim, financed by Will and Sam). This led to the continuation of "Bagley & Cargill." Once again, the Bagley relationship did not stay in place. Jim Cargill, already working in the northern part of the company, became the managing officer for all of the Cargill Bros. efforts, including the relationship to the partnership of Bagley & Cargill. The chemistry between George Bagley and Jim Cargill apparently was not right. In the absence of Jim Cargill's version, we fall back once again on Bagley's wife for her interpretation of the story: "He [Jim Cargill] was put in charge but not very competent. He annoyed George by being suspicious and couldn't trust anyone, even the bookkeeping, without close inspection, so George bought out his interest in the business and the firm was changed to George C. Bagley Elevator Company. He certainly was a happy person when this was taken over."[32]

Just before or just after the termination of the partnership, a serious event occurred involving Jim Cargill. Whether from the pressures of the rapid expansion of the northern businesses or for some other reason, Jim Cargill suffered a nervous breakdown and was forced to step away from management (as the 1945 Cargill history put it, "he was never again strong enough to assume heavy responsibility"). A formal document was drawn on June 17, 1887, buying out Jim's share of Cargill Bros. For the consideration of $41,821, less a set of debts of approximately $6,000, the firm W. W. Cargill & Bro. agreed to assume "all debts of the firm of Cargill Bros." and to take over the operation of the latter. Jim did continue to work for the firm (and to draw a $5,000 salary). The need for a competent chief executive officer for the Minneapolis operations was critical; the decision was made that Sam Cargill would move to Minneapolis to assume this role, which he did in 1887.[33]

In January 1889, a "Bradstreet Co. credit correspondent" stationed in Minneapolis (this was the John M. Bradstreet firm, which merged with Dun in 1933), approached Sam Cargill for information about the La Crosse branch. In response to Sam's query, Will wrote a quick note, summarizing the "permanent accounts, without any encumbrance." Will calculated "about $100,000 cash in the business" and estimated the unencumbered accounts at $517,000.

Apparently something more specific was needed, for later that year, a careful statement of all of the unencumbered accounts at La Crosse was constructed, a rather more conservative figure than Will's off-the-cuff estimate. It read as follows:[34]

54 Elevators & Warehouses in Minn & Dakota	$147,597.16
16 Elevators & Warehouses in Wisc, G Bay RR	18,479.29
Houston Flour Mill & Water Power	40,128.54
Hokah Flour Mill & Water Power	29,384.51

Farm Lands in Minn & Dakota Cost Value	23,112.28
La Crosse City Property (Exclusive of Dwellings)	11,300.00
La Crosse Milling Co. Stock	4,500.00
La Crosse National Bank Stock	12,000.00
La Crosse Abittior [*sic*] Co. Stock	5,000.00
La Crosse Street Car Co. Stock	31,000.00
La Crosse Opera House Stock	2,000.00
Sault Ste. Marie Land Co. Stock	42,500.00
Sault Ste. Marie Water Power Co. Stock	44,000.00
Sault Ste. Marie Water Power Co. Bonds	14,000.00
Long Prairie Warehouse & Fixtures	2,294.93
	$427,296.71

This was just the La Crosse operations, not a consolidated statement. The Minneapolis operations would have totaled close to this figure, too, although we cannot be certain, as no records survive for that period. Nor did this cover W. W.'s own personal investments, which included cattle operations, a coal mine, gold mine stocks, and many other non-grain endeavors. Even discounting Will Cargill's optimistic, often-inflated financial dreams, this is an impressive total for a man in his mid-forties, in business for just 25 years, many of which were not propitious for economic development. At 1889 prices, Will Cargill and his brothers had amassed quite a fortune and in the process had become significant change agents in the grain trade of the Northwest.

GENESIS OF THE MODERN CORPORATION, 1890-1915

A yard crew of the Minneapolis-based Liberty Lumber Company, c. 1910.

Green Bay, Wisconsin
(courtesy of Manitowoc Maritime Museum)

CHAPTER TWO

Two
Families Link

M anagement and organization became critically important for
W. W. Cargill in the 1890s and early 1900s, not only for his La Crosse and
Minneapolis businesses but also for a totally different endeavor, a lumbering operation. As the key managers were to come from the families, an
understanding of these familial groupings will be helpful to the reader.

Marriages often bring about business partnerships. This happened for
W. W. Cargill. The other family name, McMillan (later MacMillan) has
been linked with Cargill in the grain trade down to the present, a lasting
bond through five generations. This relationship is the central story of this
book.

Like the Cargills, the McMillans were Scots. Alexander McMillan and
his older brother John, 2 of 12 children of Duncan Ban McMillan, had
come to La Crosse in 1852 by way of Canada, where the family had emigrated from Scotland. The two brothers formed a lumbering business that
later produced highly satisfactory returns. Alexander also set himself up as
a blacksmith. After three years the logging enterprise began to grow, and
he went with John full-time. Another brother, Ewen Hugh, joined them
in 1856 and a fourth, Duncan D., in 1859.

The business success of these four brothers and their public-spiritedness
soon put them among the leaders of the town of La Crosse. All four were
involved in their logging business, but Hugh (as he was known) and Duncan also became lawyers. Alexander and John were central figures in the
Black River Logging Association, an industry entity particularly involved
in policing the annual log drive. Both also took roles with Duncan in the
Black River Improvement Company, a group concerned with upgrading
that river and its environs. John died in 1865; and Alexander and Duncan
carried on the family logging business. These two expanded into other
major La Crosse businesses. In a particularly important step, they bought
controlling interest in the La Crosse Gas Light Company in 1869, just at

the point when gaslights were first used in the city for street illumination. The firm also sold "coke, coal, tar, lime and tar sidewalks." John had been an alderman in La Crosse and Hugh its district attorney. Alexander had moved through alderman and county board of supervision to mayor in 1871 and then to the state legislature a year later. Alexander and Duncan were directors of the First National Bank of La Crosse, and a large flour mill was also controlled by Alexander. By the time the Dun correspondent picked them up in 1873 (as controlling owners of the gas company), he was full of praise. Noting that they were also in the logging business, he considered them "flourishing . . . strong . . . all right," conducting "money making institutions" and even having "elegant homesteads." There was no doubt where R. G. Dun & Co. stood in regard to the brothers and, for that matter, how the town felt about them.

Duncan McMillan's "elegant homestead" provided a key locational impetus for a matrimonial link, for it lay across the street from the equally elegant home of Will and Ellen Cargill. The latter's children—William, Edna, Emma and Austen—grew up and played together with Duncan and Mary Jane (McCrea) McMillan's children—brothers John Hugh, William Duncan and Daniel D., and sisters Mary Isabella, Janet and Elizabeth. So it was not surprising that Edna Cargill, second child and oldest daughter (born 1871) of Will and Ellen, and John MacMillan (he and his brothers began to spell their last names with the "Mac"), oldest son (born 1869) of Duncan and Mary Jane, would later marry (February 6, 1895). Before this event, on May 26, 1892, William Samuel Cargill married a McMillan cousin, May, daughter of Duncan's nephew, George McMillan, providing the first Cargill/MacMillan tie.[1]

It will be helpful for the reader to note here the members of these two families who continued to be involved in this grain-trading saga first instituted by W. W. Cargill in 1865. This book centers on two groups within these two extensive families:

1. W. W. Cargill, *three* of his brothers (Sam D., Sylvester S. and James F.) and *all* of his four children (William S., Edna, Emma and Austen S.). W. W.'s firstborn was called Will, as his father had been (the latter was also "Billy" back in Conover, and some of his friends continued this nickname). To prevent confusion for the reader, we will from this point call William Wallace Cargill (the founder) W. W., and his son William will be Will.

2. John H. MacMillan ("John Sr."), his two adult brothers (Daniel D. and William D.), his wife Edna Cargill MacMillan, *both* of their two sons, John H., Jr. and Cargill, and his cousin, John D. McMillan.

The two young men who had married into the other family, Will Cargill and John H. MacMillan, were the same age (both born in 1869) and were destined to have a close and eventually rancorous relationship when the W. W. Cargill business empire began to pull apart in 1909. Our interests for the moment, however, are with the budding business career of John H. MacMillan, Sr.

John Sr. began working at age 15 as a trainee in his father's State Bank of La Crosse and received a thorough grounding in finance. In his own words, "I had to give up school but I kept on studying and I think I have the equal of a college education finally." These words "had to" seem to imply some constraint against John's going on to college, but his next younger brother William did become a college graduate (at Fort Worth University). The first tie to John Sr.'s business career that can be linked to contemporary documents is in a letter from his father to MacMillan in August 1888. John Sr. had gone to Minneapolis in 1884 at age 15 for a clerk's job with his first cousin, John D. McMillan, of the grain firm of Osborne McMillan (again, the "Mc" spelling). After John Sr. had been there for a few weeks, his father wrote him an important letter, elaborating in considerable detail his (the father's) philosophy of business. He particularly stressed two requirements, accuracy and rapid work, to be accomplished with careful penmanship: "I have no idea that you will have any trouble with your book keeping—always keep in view to do your work rapidly and accurately. Both will come to you with practice if you keep the fact in mind and work as rapidly as possible." John Sr. was urged to watch his colleagues: "The great thing is to get the idea of how rapidly it ought to be done, then you will soon work up to it. It is like counting money in the Bank." Later the father came back to the theme of rapidity: "Your work will always be easier on you if you do it rapidly, and when you are first starting in learn to work rapidly and accurately and you will give better satisfaction, but above all let your work be thorough & accurate, but that is not inconsistent with speed."

The father then turned to the question of penmanship and the need to "keep your book tidy and clean." He recommended to the younger MacMillan that the latter use a special pen, the "Gillotts 303"—"your book will look nicer and cleaner than with any other pen . . . if you get acquainted with a boy that is an extra good penman practice penmanship with him, you have no idea how quickly you will improve in that way."

In June 1891, a fateful venture was initiated: John Sr. and his two brothers, William D. and Daniel D., went to Fort Worth, Texas, to go into the grain business for themselves, particularly to trade in the winter wheat of the region. John was just 22, William was 20, and Daniel was 18. Already, William had had a year of experience with the Union Pacific Railroad at its Omaha office, and Dan had worked for W. W. Cargill for two years. The three had been set up in this business by their father; the name of the firm was D. D. McMillan & Sons (the printed letterhead for this period still using the spelling "Mc").[2] The *Fort Worth Gazette*, in June 1891, noted the firm's "strong financial backing," mentioned Duncan McMillan's banking position in La Crosse, and commented: "all the gentlemen are experienced wheat men."

The magnet that had drawn them was the promise of the Texas Panhandle. The Fort Worth & Denver City Railroad (FW&DC), which headed northwest from Fort Worth, had completed its link through the Panhandle in 1888 and had begun to push colonization with every possible public relations tool. The Panhandle was "a new agricultural empire of vast extent" and was the only large area of unoccupied lands with "unquestioned fertility." Credit was so easy, said a railroad brochure, that land was within reach of "the humblest son of toil." Jason Easton, for one, was already engaged by 1890 in cattle ranching near Amarillo.

The champion booster of Fort Worth and the Panhandle, however, was B. B. Paddock. Earlier, he had been editor of the *Fort Worth Democrat* (1873–1884). He then began promoting new railroads and subsequently became president of the Texas Spring Palace (built in 1889 as a fairgrounds for touting immigration). The gaudy Palace burned the next year, but Paddock, unfazed, continued to push Fort Worth as the first president of the Board of Trade, set up in 1889 specifically to search nationally for new businesses for Fort Worth. He was a four-term mayor of Fort Worth, from 1892 to 1900. One of Paddock's preferred cities for this effort was Chicago, and he set up excursions to bring men from that city to Fort Worth, to sell them on the spot. The midwestern business community, indeed the whole country's, was small enough that men of influence tended to know each other quite well. They met one other at the spas, in the financial centers and in their travels. Early contacts between W. W. Cargill and Paddock subsequently led them into joint ventures on another proposed Texas railroad. So they likely had met in the time of Paddock's Board of Trade term; perhaps W.W. even had gone to Fort Worth on one of the excursions. A reasonable guess as to why the MacMillans became interested in Fort Worth is the link through W. W. back to Paddock.

The MacMillans, caught up in the enthusiasm, began to establish elevators in 1891 and 1892 along the right-of-way of the FW & DC as well as the Wichita Valley (WV) railroad, and also obtained leased space in the "Mark Evans" terminal in Fort Worth. The FW&DC headed northwest from Fort Worth through Wichita Falls and on to the New Mexico line. The WV was a feeder from Seymour, Texas, northward to Wichita Falls. A huge crop was expected in 1891, and the newspaper commented, "D. D. McMillan & Sons of La Crosse, Wis., have appointed their wheat buyers and agents at points along the Denver, and will be ready to begin operations here as soon as wheat begins to move. They find that it is impossible to get adequate storage facilities anywhere in Texas, . . . will have to ship their wheat to St. Louis or Chicago to the great elevators there until several ship loads have accumulated . . . they will be buying continually."[3]

As this project was being mounted, major changes also were occurring in the grain-trading world. The following is necessary background for further analysis of the MacMillans' Texas venture.

Wheat Prices Sag

After the general rise in wheat prices in the late 1870s and on into 1881, there was a steady decline from 1882 through 1887, a slight rally in 1888 and 1889, a fall in 1890, another small blip upward in 1891, and then a sharp decrease over the next half dozen years. All of this came in the face of rising farmer expectations about the quality of their lives. With considerable quantities of United States wheat destined for export (for example, some 157 million bushels of American wheat was exported in 1892, up from an average 64 million in the five years previous), the country now felt the breath of competition from the "fellahs of Egypt," the "ryots of India,"

Texas Spring Palace invitation, May–June 1889 (courtesy Special Collections Division, The University of Texas at Arlington Libraries, Arlington, Texas).

and the "peasants of Russia" (so wrote the militant St. Paul newspaper, *Great West*). Argentina, which had not even appeared in a government survey of wheat-exporting countries in 1884, became a significant force in the 1890s. In spite of declining yields in many places because of monoculture, poor cultivation, "intemperance and laziness," etc., the farmer strove for larger total production. Yet it seemed to many that the only way to change the equation was through political power.

In the early 1890s, a second strong wave of agrarian discontent emerged, this time far more class-conscious than the Grangers had been in the 1870s. By that time the whole country had awakened to the threat of the "trusts." There were oil trusts, sugar trusts, beef trusts, lead trusts, barbed-wire trusts—and wheat trusts. New federal legislation also was in place—the Interstate Commerce Act in 1887, the Sherman Antitrust Act in 1890, neither, however, yet well tested in the courts.

The newspaper *Great West* was particularly exercised about the spread between producer and consumer prices in wheat. In 1890, the editors stirred up a vitriolic controversy about the difference between the price at Crookston, Minnesota, in the Red River Valley and at Liverpool, England. They alleged that this difference was 54 cents per bushel, with transportation costs only 20 cents of this. Henrietta Larson concluded that while the Duluth–Liverpool leg appeared very close to actual marketing cost, in the Crookston–Duluth arm "there was a considerable difference which cannot be accounted for by legitimate costs."[4]

The farmers contended that there was collusion in the countryside and that railroads and large line elevator companies had "sweetheart" arrangements that precluded smaller warehousemen and cooperatives, let alone the "scoopers," from having any entry and exerting any competitive thrust. The latter, very mobile, were difficult to counter. W. W. Cargill, when asked in a 1906 hearing before the Interstate Commerce Commission (ICC), "Do you try to keep them from finding a market?" replied, "No, that can not be done."

There were ample reasons why the larger warehousemen became so powerful. Henrietta Larson explained: "The wheat men of Minneapolis were highly selected . . . their ability was unusually high . . . having established their reputation for business integrity, they were able to get loans on low terms . . . to carry on an enormous business on relatively small capital." This gave them a certain measure of monopoly, "of which they were willing to avail themselves, *after the manner of the time*" (my emphasis). W. W. Cargill, asked at the same 1906 ICC hearing why two railroads in Wisconsin were willing to lease him elevators at a nominal cost, replied, "to have an elevator operated by a reliable party." It was an answer that most larger-scale businessmen would have understood.[5]

The revolution in agricultural machinery in the second half of the nineteenth century had brought increased elevator and terminal innovation: effective cleaning equipment, more rapid loading and unloading devices, and stronger fireproof structures. Insurance costs had been driven up with the larger wooden structures, so Frank Peavey decided in 1899 to try concrete (warehousemen in Denmark and Romania already had used concrete with success). In Minneapolis, he built a huge cylindrical tank, some 80 feet high, with steel hoops for reinforcement. "We have filled it full," Peavey wrote a friend, "and it stands like a rock. The pressure don't require over 200 lbs. to the square inch, while we have tested the cement and it will stand 600 lbs." Most grain men felt wood was a necessity because of its "give," and the newfangled monster was dubbed "Peavey's Folly." But the unusual experiment worked very well, leading even the *New York Times* to comment favorably on it. Concrete soon began to rival wood, and fire dangers were greatly lessened.

With improved equipment and facilities, storage itself became more important to warehousemen, merchandising profits from trading less so. Margins dropped sharply in the 1890s; Frank Peavey reported in 1901 that, while his margins for buying wheat had been 4¹/₂ to 5 cents 15 years before, it was "today a scant 2¹/₂ cents per bushel." Also, 15 years earlier "we were charging 1¹/₂ cents per bushel for handling grain through our house in Duluth, and 1 cent per bushel per month for storage." In 1901, he continued, handling charges were ¹/₂ cent, and storage costs the same (per month).

Margins were indeed small, but a warehouseman holding millions of bushels could make a considerable return despite falling grain prices. *Great West* editors and others constantly stressed the high profits of the warehousemen. One of the leaders of the Minneapolis elevator community had written a French banking concern in 1889 that the largest terminal organization in the city had averaged 30 percent on its capital for six years, that another had made 40 percent for several years, and that the prominent trader G. W. Van Dusen had made even more. *Great West* somehow obtained copies of that correspondence in February 1891 and laid all of it over the pages of that newspaper. Cargill, Peavey, and Van Dusen were among the 13 companies listed in the article (most of the other elevators were owned by railroads). The editors admitted that "even one of the largest Mercantile Agencies in the world cannot determine the profits." But the warehousemen, they alleged, were making huge profits.

By this time the "evils" of speculation on the commodity exchanges, especially the Chicago Board of Trade, were also incessantly criticized. *Great West* ran a series of articles in the summer of 1891 on what they called "options gambling." Speculators were accused of driving down prices by using futures markets to sell short, then manipulating bad news for a drop in price. Farmers said the speculators were selling only "wind" wheat. By this time, as agricultural historian Morton Rothstein wrote, "most of the men who headed grain marketing firms made it a cardinal rule to avoid speculation or risk on price changes whenever possible." The speculator, as a market maker, was said to be providing, by his high volume of trades, a liquidity for the other users of the market, especially the hedgers. But in order to make effective hedging possible, a liquid market *was* a necessity.

Were the exchanges just promoting "gambling"? The Supreme Court chose to adjudicate this critical question, in two key decisions in 1905. In one, a "bucket shop"* proprietor had been denied quotations from the Chicago Board of Trade and had sued, alleging that because many of the trades on the exchange were not for business purposes (i.e., for physical delivery of product), the exchange was in reality just allowing gambling. The lower court essentially bought this argument, but the Supreme Court disagreed. In a famous majority opinion, Justice Oliver Wendell Holmes noted that, while "success of the strong induces imitation by the weak" and incompetent traders often brought themselves "to ruin" by speculation, nevertheless, this speculation was "the self-adjustment of society to the probable." Indeed, delivery was not an essential ingredient, for "the set off has all the effects of delivery." Thus, the Supreme Court not only dismissed the gambling accusation but also affirmed specifically that futures trading itself was legitimate.

Farmer groups in the late 1880s provided the raw material for the People's Party, the "Populists," who came on the scene all over the South and West, preaching free coinage of silver, government ownership of transportation, and a host of other changes. Ignatius Donnelly was their candidate—unsucessful—for governor of Minnesota in 1892, and they also put forth a third-party candidate for president in that year (he came in third). By 1893, the tide of protest out of the farming areas of the country was substantial.[6]

It was at this high tide of hostility that *Great West* chose to attack Cargill directly. In a long front-page article in its July 23, 1893, issue, the editors featured "another interesting exposure of the way the thing is done by the grain ring . . . startling letters brought to light . . . secured by the mail of a wheat buyer going astray and falling into the hands [of *Great West*]." In fulsome detail, the paper reprinted four Cargill Commission Company letters to a South Dakota agent. (That company was the trading arm of the

---

*A bucket shop was a private "commission" house, buying and selling futures on a margin for gamblers, where there was no intention of actual future delivery and no purchase or sale on any exchange (i.e., "bucket" the transaction). See *Report of the Federal Trade Commission on the Grain Trade*, vol. 2, (September 15, 1920), pp. 332–33. Longer hours were kept, and small lots could be purchased. "Any person with a few dollars to spend . . . could patronize them [using] the quotations purely in a gambling sense" (Jonathan Lurie, *The Chicago Board of Trade, 1859–1905: The Dynamics of Self-Regulation* [Urbana: University of Illinois Press, 1979], p. 76).

W. W. Cargill organization.) Two of the letters laid out instructions for the agent, while the other two reported on the condition of the grain in several carload shipments of wheat. "Am sorry you are not going to have good grade to handle," the Cargill employee wrote the dealer, "the boys will have to mix and can make grades and good money on such a crop if can get them started right so as not to give it all away." The *Great West* editors insinuated from the shipping letters that Cargill was buying at "#1 Northern," a second grade, and selling at "#1 Hard," the top grade. However, this seemed mostly to reflect that elevators could use the mixing process to upgrade shipments, certainly not a novel conclusion. Nothing further ensued on the story, but Cargill received some notoriety.

Cargill Incorporates

After having run his businesses as partnerships for 25 years, W. W. Cargill decided to incorporate. Limited liability would have made this attractive, and he may have wished to draw in additional capital. In March 1890, the Minneapolis operations under brother Sam, Cargill Bros., was incorporated as "Cargill Elevator Company," and in July 1892, plans were made for incorporating the La Crosse business, W. W. Cargill & Bro., as "W. W. Cargill Company." Each had capital stock of $350,000. An appendix in the Elevator Company's Articles of Incorporation lists 71 elevators and 28 coal sheds (up substantially from the 1885 list mentioned in chapter 1). The total elevator capacity was just over 1.7 million bushels; the small 250,000-bushel terminal in Minneapolis gave at least a foothold in that important market. For the La Crosse operation, there were 16 elevators and 50-odd warehouses (depending on how one measured a "double warehouse"); in addition, there were the Hokah and Houston flour mills. The La Crosse elevator and the two mills accounted for 40 percent of the total capitalization.

For the La Crosse operation, the records for the decade of the 1890s are skimpy. A few letters of Sam Cargill are extant from the Minneapolis operation and help to paint a picture of a personality sharply different from that of his older brother. If W. W. Cargill was often vague, Sam was a marvel of exactness. In an interesting letter in 1891, he explained the concept of hedging to a North Dakota dealer: "Whatever cash wheat you deliver . . . No. 2 or No. 3 or No. 1, we will if you wish apply the wheat on this sale, but give you the premium that cash brings before the December option. This is just the same as selling the wheat at a higher price for cash. The hedges or protection are just the same. Whatever the cash wheat brings over the December option we give you the benefit of."

In another S. D. Cargill letter in 1891 he described the shifting ("rolling over") of hedges from one contract period to another: "they had quite a

Elevator T, Minneapolis, c. 1905, prior to purchase by Cargill.

blockade of vessels at the 'Soo'—there has been a vessel across the channel for a week blockading navigation. These vessels will be in Duluth the middle or last of this week and they may bid up pretty strong for cash wheat . . . it would be well for us to get our October wheat out of Duluth and get it into Dec. so we would not be compelled, if we had to buy our October in, to pay any premium just on account of this blockade." There was a problem with high moisture in wheat at this time, and Sam urged the dealer, "wrestle it over in the elevator two or three times, clean it if necessary, flow it through the mill . . . see if he cannot make it a little better."

In 1892, Sam Cargill opened an office in Duluth, establishing at that time a new entity under the umbrella of the Cargill Elevator Company, called the Cargill Commission Company, to trade grain on the Duluth exchange. Fred Lindahl was sent there as its head. Times were good for both the Minneapolis and Duluth operations. Cargill Elevator declared a healthy 37 percent dividend (on the capital stock) in 1892 and used additional resources to construct a terminal in Duluth. Again another separate company was formed to manage it, the Superior Terminal Elevator Company, with W. W. Cargill taking a two-thirds interest and Sam one-third. The 1945 Cargill history told the story that Sam "went to Barnett and

Elevators K and M, Duluth-Superior, before the Cargill purchase of M in 1914.

Cargill's Elevator T, c. 1929.

Main Street, Fort Worth, Texas, c. 1889 (photographer unknown; 73.93/9; courtesy Amon Carter Museum, Forth Worth, Texas).

Record [who] had recently completed an elevator for Mr. Harrington [of the Van Dusen-Harrington Co.] on the site adjoining Cargill . . . when they asked what kind of an elevator he wanted, he told them that what was good enough for Albert Harrington was good enough for him, and to go ahead and build . . . exactly like the one they just completed." In 1893, Ed McManus was named its superintendent and became the dean of company terminal managers over a career that continued into the early 1930s. Years later (in 1914), Cargill bought the Harrington elevator too, and they became known as Elevators K and M.

The importance of the town of Sault Sainte Marie, known as the Soo, was already well known in the grain trade for its locks between Lake Superior and Lake Huron. The first was built in 1855, with improvements in 1881, 1895, 1914, 1943 and 1969. The town and the locks got a big boost in the mid-1880s when the Minneapolis, Sault Ste. Marie & Atlantic Railway—the Soo line—connected Minneapolis with the Soo and met a Canadian Pacific branch built east from Sudbury, Ontario. Now grain could be shipped directly to lakers (vessels plying only the Great Lakes), standing ready on Lake Huron, or sent by rail eastward through Canada.

With the town a linchpin for all of this transportation activity, W. W. Cargill was persuaded to invest in property there. In 1887, he formed a consortium of businessmen, most of them from La Crosse but including, in a major way, Robert Eliot from Milwaukee; they joined together as the

Sault Ste. Marie Land Co., known widely as the La Crosse Syndicate. The operation had indifferent success, however, and was later liquidated, some parts of their property not being sold until the 1930s.[7]

Doom for the MacMillans' Texas Endeavor

One of the century's most painful depressions, rivaling that of 1873–1878, began with the "Panic of 1893." The British banking house of Baring Bros. had failed in late 1890. Fears among British investors pushed them to unload a number of their American securities holdings, causing an ensuing gold drain from the United States. This became severe in the first part of 1893. On May 5, the stocks on the New York Stock Exchange dropped suddenly, and there was an enormous crash in late June. By the end of that year some 491 banks and over 15,000 other businesses had failed. The depression that followed was severe and lasted through 1897. It was a time when fledgling businesses like that of the three young MacMillan brothers would experience great danger.

D. D. McMillan & Sons had had a good start in 1891, for that year had seen a crop failure in Europe causing good West Texas and other United States wheat prices. But the same visitation came to Texas the next year, with low rainfall and persisting dry winds bringing severe drought. The

Land agency, corner of Lancaster and Main streets, Fort Worth, Texas, n.d. (photographer unknown; 73.67/15; courtesy Amon Carter Museum, Fort Worth, Texas).

farmers responded once again with renewed efforts to heighten production. The 1893 harvest appeared to be promising, as reported in the MacMillan family history, *MacGhillemhaoil*: "Conservative estimates pegged the coming crop at 7,500,000 bushels, worth at least $3,750,000 to the growers and $300,000 to the commission men." The firm now had "not less than twelve elevators," said the *Fort Worth Gazette*, and were building two new structures, at Henrietta and Seymour. A Galveston office had been opened for expected large export shipments. Already, Will MacMillan told the *Gazette* in November, the firm had shipped 100,000 bushels into export channels. But, he complained, "the Panhandle wheat is above the exporting grade, and we cannot afford to pay prices that mills pay."

Then the Panic hit. Money became extremely short, and businesses in the Panhandle began to fail. The FW & DC railroad itself was thrown into receivership. Then came the grasshoppers, "as far as the eye could see." Finally, the heavens turned against the region, for an unremitting drought at the key moments for the remaining plants resulted in an almost total failure of the 1893 wheat crop.

The MacMillan brothers held on, with considerable financial aid from the La Crosse firm, Hixon & Warner. (Frank Hixon, one of the members of this firm, was later to be very influential as an outside board member of Cargill Elevator Company.) The brothers were buying mainly wheat and oats and a smattering of corn and were finding business very slow. Consignment wheat was also handled, and they began to mix to the export grade. (They paid the Hixon firm 1/4 cent a bushel commission on all of their sales.) Although John Sr. reported that their own business had not perked up very much, he felt it necessary to justify to his backers his hand-to-mouth borrowing: "We cannot afford, as you can easily see, to carry a big balance as well as to pay you a commission on all we buy. In fact the great advantage to a grain man in making this kind of an arrangement is to use money just as he may need it and you will find that we have been no different than any other grain firm would have been."

To make matters worse, John Sr. had indications that his future father-in-law, W. W. Cargill, was not himself weathering the depression very well. Indeed, had MacMillan been privy to some "private & confidential" letters that Robert Eliot was writing to W. W., he would have been even more disturbed. W. W. owed Eliot money, and in late 1894, Eliot wrote him about his precarious financial condition. He worried about W. W.'s bullishness at this sensitive time: "You carry too much at stations & eat yourself up with interest." Eliot commented, tartly, "It seems to us that you must be self-delusive as to the profits you claim to be making."[8]

By December 1894, there were further signs of trouble for the Mac-Millans. The 1894 crop once more was drought-damaged, the third year

"A Flurry in Wheat," Harper's Weekly, *October 1880* (courtesy Historical Pictures Service).

running. Again there were grasshoppers infesting the fields. Finally, the National Bank of Merrill, Wisconsin, one of the Wisconsin banks Hixon had used in the financing, refused to renew the line of credit until the MacMillans cleared up some of their notes (the bank pleading "home demand" for funds as the reason for its adamant stand).

Meanwhile, John Sr. and Edna's plans advanced. The wedding was to be in February 1895 (despite the worsening depression), and John's letters were filled with plans and waxing enthusiastic about the dwelling that he was having built in Fort Worth as their home: "I can't, though, get over the house that seems too elegant for any use. That parlor will be a perfect picture and our library will be just simply perfection. How we will enjoy living in that room . . . you will find it hard work ever to drag me out of it." The wedding took place on schedule on February 6, 1895, and the two moved into their home in Fort Worth. At the end of that year, Edna gave birth to their first child, John H., Jr.

By the year 1896, the effects of the Panic had taken full hold on D. D. McMillan & Sons. The firm had tendered Hixon a rudimentary profit-and-loss statement back on March 1, 1895, covering the previous nine months. They had bought some 364,000 bushels of wheat in the range of 50 cents a bushel, an outlay of $182,000; oat purchases totaled 320,000 bushels at a cost of $52,000. However, they had sold only $64,000 of their holdings. MacMillan figured they had made $27,000 "net profit," but this was an oversimplified single-entry calculation. Their inventory of stored grain was hard to move, because of both sagging prices and difficulties in obtaining rail cars. There was little grain to buy in Texas, yet the visible supply nationally had risen to 46.7 million bushels by August 1896, up from 38.5 million at the same time the previous year. Wheat prices were about 64 cents at this point. The depression of 1893–1897 was then at its worst, with the wholesale price index for farm products at its lowest ebb—lower, relatively, than it would be even many years later in the Great Depression of the 1930s. Soon they were in an impossible cash flow bind and fell more and more behind with Hixon.

Edna had returned to La Crosse after the birth of John, Jr., and was still there because the baby was ill. John Sr. wrote in September 1896, morosely: "If it were not for our baby, I would begin to think our marriage a snare and a delusion. I don't see that I get a bit of good out of you now, more than two years ago. I got your letters then, I get them now. I didn't see anything of you then, I see nothing of you now." Evidently father-in-law W. W. Cargill had talked of the possibility of a Green Bay job for John, who wrote Edna, "one moment I long to be able to take it, the next I will hope it won't be necessary, but on the whole I guess I really want to take it, though, of course, I don't want to give this up down here and I am afraid I can't take that position without us giving up."

Edna must have chastised John Sr. in an earlier letter, for he continued,

I never intended what you evidently understood. I don't think there is anything degrading in working for another. What hurt was the idea of failure—failure to make a success of what I managed and the idea that would almost necessarily follow, that I was unworthy of the position I had occupied and that henceforth I would find my level in carrying out what others directed instead of others carrying out what I directed. Don't for a moment think I think that of myself. Thank goodness I have too much conceit and self-respect—I don't know which—to rate myself in that class, but it is galling to have others feel that way and to feel that it will take years of hard work to again command the respect and confidence that I had or will have lost.

He continued about the business itself:

I dread the idea of having nothing to do—to see business dropping off day by day is awful. We have quit running the elevator here at night and I suppose it is only a question of time until we will have to quit daytimes too. To see this all coming on and knowing so well what comes after makes one wish he had never seen Texas or ever heard of finances and business etc. I can see plainly enough why Will [John

Sr.'s brother, not W. S. Cargill] wants to give up business life and become a student and a scholar. Very often I wish I could do the same. For five years and over, we have known nothing but failure. Never have we experienced the joys of independence but all the time this dark and dismal cloud has been hanging around us, sometimes apparently retreating but all the time gaining steadily in power until once more it seems about to strike and to shatter and to level to earth all our fond hopes, all our proud desires, all our ambitions.

Yet John Sr. knew that he had the instincts for business:

I am different from Will . . . I am conscious of or at least have a feeling that I have financial and business ability . . . my character is broadening and hardening under such a stress of experience . . . my judgment is growing keener and my powers of observation and reason stronger and that the day will yet come when all I have suffered will prove a powerful lever to aid in ultimate success. Someone I believe has said that the ultimate road to success is through failure and I am now ready to believe it. My former ideas were based on what I was taught and what I observed during periods of unbounded prosperity but they had not experienced the disasters of panics and financial depression. I see now the ideas were wrong. I see principles that I never dreamed of before and moreover principles I never heard of in all that I have read and all that I have experienced before.

Now skeptical about the grain trade, his remarks were prescient:

Do you know, Edna, it makes me feel perfectly awful that you are so dependent for happiness on the wheat market. It seems to me your father's actions in holding on to so much is really frightful. To me it dictates certain ruin in the end, for I believe that one of these days and that too very shortly we are going to see another big slump . . . the market cannot stay where it is. It will either advance or it will drop and with the Spring crop about to move I cannot see how it can advance with money in such fearful shape. I don't want to preach pessimism but I do want to preach safety. Why doesn't your father sell off enough to be able to margin down to 50 cents if necessary.

In his letter two days later (which is the last view of this period), John Sr. continued in the same vein:

I am almost getting afraid of myself. For the past ten days or two weeks it has just seemed as though I was standing all I could bear and a little more. I think it is your father's troubles that are responsible for the present state of my mind . . . your father has so many notes he can't meet. . . . His affairs worry me as much as our own. I don't know why, but they do. I seem to be getting to a point where I can't throw worry off my mind. I have felt all day that horrid choking feeling that one does at times. I have really lost for the time being the power of feeling any enjoyment and I am so nervous and irritable that I am ashamed of myself.

(Medical records in 1932 suggest that John Sr. had "several" nervous breakdowns at this point.)

The business situation had continued to deteriorate, with money very short. To make matters worse—if that were possible—the 1895 crop had failed entirely. Richard Overton, the historian of the FW&DC railroad commented, "farmers in many counties, relying on a normal harvest, had neglected to raise seed." John Sr. wrote Edna:

What worries me the most just now is that we have $10,000 due in Chicago the latter part of this month and first of next. I feel certain they will demand payment and then we will have nothing. That is all the money we have. Business has fallen off to nothing. We are buying no wheat and consequently making nothing and putting everything together grinds the very life out of one. I have lost all hope. I can see nothing bright ahead. Everything has turned out as I predicted to father a year ago, unless he could then arrange for money. We not only got none but had had to continually pay up ever since. I can't see any promise for money.

The only hope that John Sr. saw was "trying to work up a cement business," but he worried that it would "mean nothing but expense for some time to come." This poignant letter continued with long passages of homesickness: he missed his wife and needed her there.[9]

"It was almost inconceivable," Richard Overton continued, "that the spring of 1896 could bring a repetition of the hard times . . . yet such was the case. Up until three weeks before harvest time, prospects were unusually bright. Then dry, hot winds cut down wheat yields to under five bushels per acre and completely burned up corn and oats." By late 1896, the MacMillan Texas operation was defunct. All of the brothers left Texas to return to La Crosse. Their father, heavily in debt from the losses, gave up his presidency and directorship of the State Bank and moved out of his splendid home across the street from W. W. Cargill and into the much more modest La Crosse dwelling of his son-in-law, John Rowles, on 6th Street. Will Cargill, W. W.'s son and John Sr.'s contemporary, later moved into the vacated house. In an agreement signed by D. D. McMillan and his three sons on December 1, 1896, with three trustees representing their creditors (one of those trustees was W. W. Cargill), all of the Texas property of D. D. McMillan & Sons, plus properties in La Crosse owned personally by Duncan D. and his brother Alexander, were deeded to the trustees for the debts. Only this agreement itself survives; we do not know what monies the MacMillans, father and sons, were able to reserve for themselves. The family history, *MacGhillemhaoil*, puts it starkly: "Personally, Duncan D. and his brother Alexander McMillan were utterly and completely ruined." While there was no formal bankruptcy, the story is clear— the MacMillans had gone under with their grain business.[10]

There is an important, puzzling dimension of this Texas story. According to the Cargill history written in 1945, the three brothers had left Texas "after the Leiter corner, at which time their hedges were in the Chicago market." (In fact, it was an *aborted* corner). Actually, they were gone by the time of this famous futures market scandal in 1897. Still, there may have been a cause–effect relationship present in 1896, in the early stages of

The McMillan Building,
La Crosse, Wisconsin, 1888
(courtesy Area Research Center,
UW–La Crosse).

the corner. John Sr.'s brief mention of the bill that was "due in Chicago" gives credence to an inference that they were utilizing the commodity futures market in Chicago. Whatever the relationship, the distance from Texas and the time lag were baffling. The Leiter corner was indeed a spot where a number of unknowing people were badly hurt, and it seems evident that the MacMillans were somehow caught in its web, too.

The corner always has been one of the most spectacular of the grain trade's many flamboyant competitive maneuvers. If holders of grain commanded enough of the available supply to permit manipulation of the price, they could force the price up for buyers needing that grain. A formal futures market came into being at the Chicago Board of Trade in 1865, making cornering at the same time more complex and in certain ways easier to accomplish. Under uniform provisions prescribed by the CBOT, futures contracts could be made between buyers (the "longs") and sellers (the "shorts"). These contracts were defined as a required amount of standardized grades of grain (for example, 5,000 bushels of a certain grade of wheat). Each contract would have a termination date (for example, there was a May wheat contract, a separate July wheat contract, etc.). These were traded independently of actual physical grain; as William Cronon put it, "The futures market was a market not in grain but in the *price* of grain." Thus came the well-known euphemism "paper-wheat." Indeed, many more contracts than the actual supply of the grain typically would be traded in the contract period, some by hedgers and many more by speculators. Morton Rothstein captured this apparent anomaly well: The futures market was a place where "men who don't own something are selling that something to men who don't really want it."

For each "buy" contract there was always a "sell" contract, although this would not be done privately but would be accomplished in a trading pit by CBOT members as brokers by open outcry. For each contract agreed to in the pit, there would be two separate parties, a long holding a "buy" at the price and a short holding a "sell" at that price—but these were independent, not between Mr. "A" and Mr. "B."

On the day the particular contract terminated, most of these contracts would be canceled out without any reference to actual grain by buyers and sellers agreeing to exchange the differeence between the contracted price and the market price on that termination day. However, if the long wished to obtain the actual grain, he could hold his contract beyond this date. Processors of grain frequently used a long futures contract to obtain their supply. There were always equal numbers of shorts, so there automatically was a short remaining, and he had to deliver the grain—or come to an agreement with the long *on the long's terms* (for the latter could otherwise insist on the actual grain). If longs held contracts beyond the termination date at the same time as there was a shortage of actual grain that shorts need to acquire as their side of the bargain, the shorts were at the mercy of the longs—there either had been a "natural corner," caused by special supply factors, or the longs themselves had cornered the market by directly buying up cash grain in addition to the futures. Thus the presence of a futures market, with its speculators, enhanced the possibility of the corner. The speculators also brought positive inputs, providing the markets with liquidity and an enhanced process of "price discovery" through efficient supply-demand interactions. (The system elaborated here essentially describes today's futures markets, too.)

The Leiter episode is well worth recounting here, for its lessons had a major long-term impact on John MacMillan's grain trade beliefs. The man was Joseph Leiter of Chicago, "a beardless, strapping youth of twenty-nine years [who] wrote two checks for $1 million each on two successive days" as "Chicago's youthful wheat king—a Harvard graduate corners the market" (so trumpeted *Leslie's Illustrated Weekly* in January 1898). Leiter had been buying wheat in such a torrent that he was "the largest wheat-owner in the world," accomplished without "a rumor, nor a story of a rumor, or cruel tactics with small traders, nor the suspicion of mean tricks in handling the giants who six months ago were beginning to congratulate themselves over the great fortune which the green horn in wheat announced he was bringing into the pit." The MacMillans were some of those "small traders." Leiter was a young man of wealth, "born of exceedingly rich and very honorable parents"; his father was Levi Leiter, a partner of Marshall Field in the great merchandising empire the two had built in Chicago. With such a combination of "honor, breeding and money" how *could* one lose?

The crescendo, though, was vintage soap opera, a monumental debacle for an enthusiastic neophyte who had taken on the giants of the speculative grain trade in an attempted corner—and failed. Leiter's opponent in what one analyst called "the keenest speculative duel in the history of the grain market" was the famous Philip Danforth Armour ("P. D."), the scion of the packing house of his name and also one of the most memorable speculators on the Chicago Board of Trade.

P. D. had had many clashes on the CBOT, particularly those speculative lessons taught him by the greatest of the 19th-century grain plungers, Benjamin P. Hutchinson. This crafty, calculating speculator, "old Hutch," had ranged over the Board of Trade floors in Chicago on many a devious plan, the most spectacular of which was his famous corner of the December wheat contract in 1888. Hutch was a "bull" then, long on wheat as a buyer, so long that the "bears" (the shorts) suddenly came to the realization that there was simply no wheat in the whole country that was available to fulfill their contracts with "old Hutch." P. D. was one of the bears and had no way to escape. Armour's biographer put it succinctly: "All they could do was pay up on Hutchinson's terms. They paid, and through the nose."

A decade later an older and much wiser Armour deviously put the same clamp on Leiter. "J. L." was being led right down the same path that Armour had trod 10 years earlier. Leiter's crowd, the "wheat syndicate," were bulls—and thought they had the market cornered. It was rumored that Leiter controlled some 47 million bushels of wheat at one point. The news splashed over the national press; even William Jennings Bryan, then a presidential candidate, was forced to put out a statement that the soaring prices were not caused by his "free silver" campaign. He need not have bothered. To Leiter's misfortune, not only had the war scare with Spain subsided but 1898 was a banner year for wheat production, and the shortages that Leiter had depended upon evaporated. Armour closed the trap, and Leiter—or we should say, his father, Levi—dropped something in the neighborhood of $9,750,000, a widely quoted but much disputed figure.

The experience so colored the MacMillan brothers' view of the wheat market that for years they were still referring to it. However, the depression itself was likely to have been the real culprit. The authors of the 1945 Cargill history stated that the brothers "made a serious miscalculation—they had entered a territory that was not as yet sufficiently developed. The undertaking was ten or fifteen years too early." This might have been true. Yet, taking into account the devastating panic and equally damaging drought, that judgment seems too simplistic.

The three brothers took their failure very hard. Perhaps the most crushed was the youngest, Daniel, who went back to La Crosse to work for W. W., where he had been employed prior to going to Texas. In March 1899, in a poignant letter to John Sr., he poured out his dismay: "I never have a nickle [sic] from one end of the month to the other and I am strapped all of the time. I am willing to endure this for a season if we can but prosper. I am eternally anxious to know how I am to meet the next bill. My present position is more worrying than when we were in business. For the past month or so I have been so worried that I am getting frightfully nervous again. . . . My past life has embittered and made a melancholy man of me." However, he ended the letter on a more hopeful note, "For a year or so at least we should save everything possible and make every kind of a sacrifice for our future welfare. There is a duty that you owe Will and I and there is a duty that Will and I owe you. Let's all be faithful in discharging that duty." The brothers had committed themselves to contribute funds to their father and sisters and to their Uncle Alexander.

Middle brother Will MacMillan chose to go into cattle raising on a piece of land near Lubbock, Texas, that the family had purchased earlier. The property was originally four sections and later became considerably larger. It was encumbered with debt (the three brothers owed $5,000 to W. W. Cargill among others), and the going was slow at the start. They lost 24 head of cattle in 1900, the first year Will was there, and even the mule died: "He ate too much green kaffir corn and busted." But things went better in 1901—enough so to buy more land—and by April 1903, the family owned five sections and were grazing an additional three. Will had quadrupled the herd, and although they still had the debts, the outlook was much brighter. Will was utilizing scientific breeding; he wrote, "In 3 or 4 years the good cattle will have entirely displaced the common sort, leaving the ranch in an ideal condition."

The legacy of the grain disaster stayed with the brothers for a long time. All three had to live as modestly as possible. When Daniel was to move to Minneapolis in 1903 on a new assignment for W.W., he asked the bank to

William Duncan MacMillan (left), John H. MacMillan (center), Daniel D. MacMillan (right), c. 1914.

Binder parade, Grapevine, Texas, 1899 (photographer unknown; Misc. Tarrant County Collections #34; courtesy Amon Carter Museum, Forth Worth, Texas).

lend him $400; he wrote John Sr. of the results: "He turned me down cold. I assured him that the money would not be spent faster than my account accumulated, but it seemed to make no difference to him. Evidently we have no standing in that direction . . . he glared at me with a banker's pitiless stare, he addressed me in a banker's heartless manner."

Will MacMillan worried about his isolation in Texas, "that there was considerable danger of a man getting countrified and rough." Later, he renounced the business world altogether and enrolled at the University of Chicago (earlier, he had graduated from Fort Worth University). In 1908, he obtained a Ph.D. in mathematics and astronomy. He wrote John Sr. at that time, just after his oral examination, "In the department of mathematics and astronomy this grade of Ph.D. has been given not more than 5 or 6 times (including myself) since the University started." His degree was *summa cum laude*. "Dan [MacMillan] is always aiming at the very top," he continued, "Well, here it is, and I know that he will be very glad to see it a reality—not a dream." His father, mother, and two sisters later joined him in Chicago, and Will stayed at the University of Chicago for a lifetime of teaching and research (the latter including a number of successful inventions).[11]

Despite the unease John Sr. stated about "working for others," which he had expressed in that discouraged letter to Edna from Texas in September 1896, he also went back to La Crosse to work for W. W. Cargill, managing one of the firm's lines of country elevators. Robert Eliot's concerns to the contrary, John found W. W.'s empire reasonably intact, not fatally damaged by the Panic. We cannot be precise, for there are practically no remaining financial or operations records for the La Crosse side of the business in the 1890s. There *is* a legal story that is fully documented, for W. W. and Sam fought a case all the way to the United States Supreme Court.

Minnesota passed a law in 1895 requiring that all warehouses that received, stored and shipped grain and were situated along railroad right-of-ways had to obtain a license from the state (cost, $1) and be subject to state regulation regarding investigation of complaints. Pooling of freight by competitors specifically was prohibited. This was the so-called Country Warehouse Act, an extension of a similar law passed in 1893. There had already been stringent control of terminals by the state, but matters out in the countryside still remained full of alleged irregularities—misweighing and misgrading, control by the large lines to the detriment of independents, and a general lack of competition. The 1895 law addressed this.

The W. W. Cargill Company, the La Crosse organization, challenged the law, building its case on its Lanesboro warehouse, a tiny 8,000-bushel operation with minimal mechanization; all incoming wheat was bagged or shoveled out of farm wagons. Lanesboro might have looked the same as the first warehouse of W. W. in Conover back in 1865.

The Company argued that all grain that came in was owned only by Cargill and was shipped out on the Milwaukee Railroad directly to La Crosse and on eastward to Milwaukee, Green Bay, Chicago and the Atlantic Coast. Cargill averred that the act was unconstitutional and discriminatory in that it treated warehouses on railroads as a special case. The case finally wove its way through the legal channels to the Minnesota Supreme Court, which flatly turned down the Company's challenge. Where "the warehouse is sort of a public place," the majority opinion stated, "where farmers come with their grain . . . and the purchaser . . . acts as marketmaster, weighmaster, inspector, and grader of the grain . . . surely such a business is of a public character" and could be regulated.

Upon receipt of the state supreme court ruling, Cargill's lawyer wrote Sam Cargill, "it was certainly a very favorable decision for us if we care to get the opinion of the Supreme Court of the United States on this . . . we had a great streak of Cleveland luck when our Supreme Court decided the case against us" (an apparent reference to Grover Cleveland's presidential victory in 1892). The lawyer soon persuaded the Cargill brothers to press the case forward.

But the lawyer had miscalculated. The U.S. Supreme Court (with Justice John Harlan writing the opinion) affirmed the Minnesota court in a long decision that carefully elaborated the reasoning of the lower court. It was a landmark case, clearly establishing that country elevators and warehouses were to be treated under the law essentially the same as their big-city terminal counterparts. Cargill complied—there was no further basis on which to fight.[12]

Sam Cargill's Management Style

By the 1890s, La Crosse had several newspapers, and it was apparent that both the D. D. and Alexander McMillan families, as well as the W. W. Cargill family, were prominent citizens whose daily activities, outings and trips were worth reporting. The McMillan families, of longer residence and wider involvement, were most often mentioned. W. W. Cargill, running such a wide-ranging regional business, was also quoted on economic tidbits. After a trip to the Black Hills in 1898, he was queried about crop prospects, "Well, the outlook is too good—I'm getting scared. I begin to fear this year is to be a duplicate of '78. Then the early prospects promised a record-breaking crop, and along came July rains that sent all our hopes to the 'demnition-bow-wows.' " (The 1898 harvest proved to be excellent.)

The editor of one of the papers, the *Morning Chronicle*, so bothered the business community with his favoritism toward the Democrats at the time William Jennings Bryan was running for president (on his 16-to-1 silver campaign) that a group of prominent townspeople, W. W. Cargill and Frank Hixon included, bought the paper in 1899 and substituted their own views. The editor agreed to stay, and did so for two years![13]

In Minneapolis, Sam Cargill had come into his own as a chief executive officer after replacing his brother Jim in 1888. The mid-1890s had not been very profitable for the Cargill Elevator Company, but by 1899 a dividend again was declared, a modest one of 9 percent of capital stock. In 1901, a substantial surplus of over $600,000 was divided among the shareholders, and the future of the Company (and of the times) seemed much more promising.

Testimony confirms that S. D. Cargill built a strong organization during his leadership of the Cargill Elevator Company. Contemporary sources note, in particular, his ability to draw around him outstanding men—names such as Lindahl, Chilton, Cooper, Owen, Prime, Hoople, and others—who will appear in later pages of this chapter. Salaries for these men were certainly not munificent, even for those days—in the Minneap-

Samuel D. Cargill, c. 1895.

olis office, Fred Gillett, William Young, E. S. Mooers and J. B. Cooper drew $125 per month in 1900 (Cooper was a key man, the barley trader, and did get a bonus that year of $1,000), and the rest of the salaries ranged downward to Fred Young's $25 and Martin Wilco's $30. There were 2 women in the total of 14 in the office, Miss L. J. Dew, drawing $75; and Miss H. F. Allen, small, varying amounts (perhaps she worked part-time). Sam Cargill took a salary of $7,500 per year (before he claimed his shareholder dividends), and Jim Cargill, with his reduced management role, drew $5,000 per year. Yet these disparities in income seemed not to reduce effort, for the loyalties of this group became legendary.

Some of this certainly was due to the leadership of Sam Cargill himself. The 1945 Cargill history captured his personality: "S. D. was just as hard-boiled as W. W. Cargill was gentle, and although his associates in the business were scared to death of him and stories still abound of the awe in which he was held by employees, they loved him to a man" (perhaps too fulsome a compliment!). F. E. Lindahl, head of the Duluth office, often told the story of how Mr. Cargill "yelled at him to get his hat and coat and go over to St. Paul; how he was on the streetcar and well on the way before it dawned on him that in his haste to carry out orders he had forgotten to find out what he was going for."

Sam Cargill indeed had an intense loyalty to his people. In 1900, for example, a bad crop in the Northwest brought widespread layoffs in the Minneapolis grain companies, but Sam told the *Minneapolis Journal* that he would lay no one off—"this may cost us $50,000 . . . but what if it does? I shall feel a great deal better to pay them their income." In appearance, said the history, Sam Cargill was "different from his older brother, although both bore a decided family resemblance. He was a handsome, if not a striking looking man, except for one defect—he was wall-eyed." The authors continued, "There is a famous story in the trade about the time he rushed up to the telegraph counter in the Chamber of Commerce [now called the Minneapolis grain exchange] where wire operators were lined up one to each market. He gave a verbal order to sell ten December wheat to one of the operators, and a few seconds later executions came from both Chicago and Duluth."

Sam Cargill, too, was preoccupied with the Leiter corner, writing one of his shippers in early 1899, "the price of wheat is too low . . . [it] should never have sold in Chicago under 75 or 80¢ . . . but the collapse of the Leiter corner hurt so many in the trade that like a sick man, it had no power to recover" (cash wheat in Chicago had dropped from $1.85 in May 1899 to 62 cents in October).

Sam himself had had difficulty with the Chicago Board of Trade in mid-1897 when a Cargill barley shipment to Buffalo was disputed by the buyer. "We have no way of bringing the matter before the Board of Trade at Chicago," he wrote, "but I shall put it in the hands of a Chicago lawyer the coming week, and shall sue the contract in the courts." The Cargills had found that their lack of a clearinghouse membership in the CBOT put them at a disadvantage.

In the decade of the 1890s, the grain trade of the country had gone through one of the most significant changes in its history. Morton Rothstein commented on this:

By 1905 . . . every stage in the movement of the wheat surplus from the Mississippi Valley basin to the Eastern centers and export markets had undergone a transformation. Most of the string of intermediaries between the country dealers and the seaboard docks had been eliminated or reduced to relatively minor functions. New, large firms in both the Midwest and the East dominated the internal trade and were reaching beyond the seaports to [make] direct contact with foreign markets, though they continued to share that trade with British and continental companies. There were still imperfections in the market, disputes about the grading systems, conflict between various elements of the trade. But the elevator system had maintained its flexibility while imposing uniformity, the entrepreneurial leadership had responded successfully to the continued changes in transportation and to the dynamism of the wheat frontiers east of the Rocky mountains.[14]

John MacMillan, Sr.'s involvement in the grain trade was now to change, for W. W. Cargill's wide-ranging interests had brought a new, non-grain endeavor—and he wanted John to head it.

Away from Grain: The Sawyer & Austin Lumber Company

Lumbering had been the first-rank corporate endeavor in La Crosse and elsewhere in Wisconsin in the 19th century. The MacMillans were among its leaders, but W. W. Cargill had never participated in it on a large scale. This changed with his involvement in the Sawyer & Austin Lumber Company, originally a Black River Falls, Wisconsin, firm, then based in La Crosse with the trade name Red Star Mills. The firm had been in operation in Wisconsin for about 30 years. In 1899, catastrophe struck, first with the death in a railroad accident of E. L. Arnold, who was co-general manager with W. E. Sawyer, then one month later, with the demise of the other partner, David Austin. Sawyer & Austin had purchased extensive lands in Pine Bluff, Arkansas, just before Austin had died, and now Sawyer, faced with settling the estates of the two men, found himself inadequately financed for the Arkansas venture. W. W. was his close friend and soon an appeal brought Cargill into the lumber operation despite (according to the 1945 Cargill history) "the opposition of his life-long friend, Mr. F. P. Hixon, of the lumber firm of Shevlin & Hixon." Hixon also had been one of the financiers of the ill-fated Texas grain endeavor of the MacMillans.

Construction had begun for a mill in Pine Bluff, but before much had been accomplished, Sawyer himself died of malaria in November 1899. The 1945 Cargill history chronicled (and embellished) the next step: "Since there was no one in the Sawyer & Austin Lumber Company of high enough caliber to carry on, Mr. Cargill was faced with the prospect of kissing his investment good-bye or launching forth on a new enterprise. With characteristic courage, he decided to see it through, and put J. H. MacMillan in charge, although he had no lumber experience." W. W. had acquired operating control through a majority of the stock, and a year later (1901) he picked up most of the rest. In 1900 he also acquired a 75 percent (later 100 percent) interest in the Banner Lumber Company, the St. Louis retail outlet for Sawyer and Austin.[15]

Instead of the simpler management skills needed in running country elevators, John MacMillan now would face the greater responsibility for a full-scale company and would need to become truly a chief executive officer. Right away, he became involved in an incident that demonstrated to the organization—and to him—his strong sense of his own authority. It was mid-1900, the firm's lumber operations in Wisconsin had been closed (although the home office stayed at W. W.'s offices in La Crosse), and the company was just getting started at Pine Bluff. John Sr., at this time just over 30 years old, arrived as general manager (at an annual salary of $3,600); W. W. earlier had also sent along a cadre of his key employees from La Crosse. One man from there, senior to MacMillan in age, had come into the office demanding that he be given a vacation. In John Sr.'s exultant letter back home to his wife, Edna, in July 1900, he told of the next moments: "I cut him off by saying 'I cannot let you take a vacation now. There is too much to be done.' I wish I could tell you of the interview. You would die laughing." The employee proceeded to give John Sr. half a dozen reasons why he needed to go, culminating with "W. W. promised me." MacMillan recounted his next response: "I simply told him 'We had to attend to business before pleasure—I had intended being away in August myself but when I found out business demanded that I stay that I gave up the idea.' "

John then confided his tactics to Edna: "I was mild but determined with him and his effrontery did him no good. To most of his thinnest remarks I made no answer—simply sat and looked at him, and it embarrassed him considerably." MacMillan closed his letter with a surprisingly imperious comment: "Russell does not know his place, he seems to think he is about on an equality though today's conversation ought to thoroughly disabuse his mind. . . . I think he expected to ride over me from the rather independent way he started out and from the expression on his face. He evidently thought I would not dare to refuse him."[16] John Sr.'s implicit trust of Edna MacMillan and his concern for duty and responsibility stands out in this vignette. The tactic of stony silence in the face of a demand was to be repeated again and again in succeeding challenges to his authority.

John Sr. was as meticulous and careful as W. W. Cargill was not. He saved every scrap of company records. Fortunately, the bulk of these have survived, a remarkable set of firsthand documentation of those early days that gives this book a richness of documentation seldom available for similar firms. John received many dozens of letters from W. W while he was in Pine Bluff, and these give us, for the first time, a closeup of both W. W.'s and John Sr.'s day-to-day business thinking.

It was a challenging time for W. W., for the new lumber operation demanded ongoing financing. W. W. wanted to add to his timberlands by

John and Edna MacMillan, 1904.

purchasing as much as 40,000 to 50,000 additional acres. With this, he needed to construct a feeder railroad to get his lumber out to the main line. Complicating matters, there were payments due to the widows of the three original owners. By the summer of 1900, as seasonal buying in the grain business rose, cash flow problems began to trouble him. He wrote John Sr. in early June, "have got to pay $200,000 this month, and while we have got $600,000 in stuff at Green Bay, we do not seem to be able to sell any and realize the money." His local bankers seemed chary of lending too much, one of them cutting a request almost in half, "which is, I thought, rather one horse."

By August, W. W. admitted to John, "it is a little pinching with us . . . our scary time." A few days later, he asked John how much was needed at Pine Bluff: "Make it as small as possible." Yet W. W.'s pervasive optimism still held sway: "It will all work out, and all I am afraid of is that there may be a pinch between now and the time it works out."

With the La Crosse banks exhibiting caution, it was necessary to obtain financing elsewhere. W. W. wrote John: "We could probably see Head . . . as a broker for us and get a little money from banks down in that country, say, Little Rock, Kansas City and other places . . . banks that won't inter-

Downtown Pine Bluff, Arkansas, at the time of a Mississippi River flood, December 1908.

fere with our own territory." This produced a dilemma, however, as these southwestern bankers demanded details on the business that W. W. was not used to giving. He wrote John, in early 1901: "I suppose if these gentlemen wish to do business, we will show up, but we don't care to unless they do . . . they could raise the whole country up asking about me and nothing come of it." In particular, he feared the effects of a rebuff: "If you get turned down once, it is hard to get it back again."

By this time, the constant short-term, hand-to-mouth financing was just not providing the lumber operations with enough capital, so W. W. wanted to float a bond issue: "If could get a bond . . . for a million dollars and build the railroad and buy additional land . . . would be on velvet." A Boston broker had provided some short-term help at interest rates above what W. W. felt he should pay but gave no encouragement on the bonds, nor did others, in Chicago, New York and elsewhere. W. W. decided to go ahead anyway, modifying the Sawyer & Austin capital structure by establishing the bonds and then peddling them later, in the meantime going ahead with the railroad construction and at least part of the land purchases. W. W. felt the balance sheet of the company was stronger than outsiders thought it was; he wrote a Chicago financier: "the Sawyer & Austin balance sheet is very conservative. . . . I can see many millions in addition to what it shows." He enumerated the pine lands, "which are put in at $3.00 per M, easily worth $5.00" and cited also some untapped bauxite deposits that lay under their land, "ten million tons, government estimate . . . at their estimated value of $3 per ton, it is quite an item."

Despite the drains of Pine Bluff, W. W. found the time to visit a new gold mine in Colorado and subsequently to invest in it. He seemed naively optimistic about many of these outside distractions, and this troubled his brother Sam, who began sending W. W. warnings about what he (Sam) perceived as omens of another panic. "An upheaval is due in about 1904," he wrote in December 1901, "and one wants to get in shape to withstand it." Four days later, he made his admonition more direct: "I see by the paper that you are going into the threshing machine business. It is expanding all the time instead of pulling in. That is not the way to get ready for 1904. That is no anchor out to windward . . . gather in, recoup, gather up the end and be ready."

Not only Sam but W. W.'s old friend, financier, and counselor, Robert Eliot in Milwaukee, expressed open disagreement with his policies. This made W. W. feel isolated, and he confided to John Sr., "I have not got many friends to consult, as Sam and Mr. Eliot are both opposed to the lumber business and rather turned me down." But he added, "it has gone so far now that it must go through in some way."

John Sr. began to fill the void as W. W.'s confidant and was learning rapidly. W. W.'s handling of his personnel was paternal and easygoing. Another of the La Crosse employees sent to Pine Bluff by W. W. complained to him about how John Sr. had made work assignments, and W. W. wrote John afterward, "If he is doing more work than his share it should be divided up or get more help. We do not want any man to work for us and do more than he can do reasonably."

Yet W. W. would not tolerate some faults, drinking being one. One employee had been a salesman, traveling, and now was assigned to Pine Bluff. W. W. wrote John: "at Green Bay he got into a rut and did not do well . . . he has been spoiled traveling around too much . . . shall bar whisky and his absence from the business . . . at least in long spaces." When black employees out in the yard refused to work in the rain, W. W. wrote, "Young's 20th on hand and notice big storm and the non-appearance of the niggers. They have got to be educated that they must get out if it does rain, especially if under shelter."

W. W.'s disorganization and forgetfulness shows up often in the correspondence. "We are anxiously looking for your letter" [he had lost it]. "Received the paper this morning and did not look at it very close until come to date it and then found it made to the order of Fogg Bros. & Co., which is not correct." "Please accept our thanks for the correction and in future guess will have to look over the statements myself." "If I could remember when 2000 due." "John, I forgot my papers—the stock you put away & those security callables." Even Robert Eliot needled W. W. on his slipshod approach and sloppy handwriting: "Try to answer all these points & dictate it to your stenographer so anybody can read it."

One memory lapse produced a minor in-family difference. W. W. had lost track of a safe that had been in Winona and that John Sr. was supposed to send to Green Bay. W. W. asked his son Will about it and then wrote John Sr., "W.S.C. says the safe was never shipped to Green Bay as you supposed it was, and it looks as though you were the fellow that neglected to ship it, and we are out just that safe." But John Sr. *had* sent the safe—it was in the Green Bay manager's office—and W. W. had to send a letter of apology.

In 1902, Sawyer & Austin, under John Sr.'s supervision, began building the Pine Bluff & Western Railroad for shipment of both its logs and finished lumber. It was to connect with the St. Louis, Iron Mountain and Southern Railway at Benton, Arkansas. At Pine Bluff, John MacMillan moved quickly. Land was purchased, equipment contracted for, and men employed for the lumbering and processing. The railroad was first built to the town of Sheridan, then, a few months later, on to the town of Benton, a total distance of 45 miles. By November 1903, the line was in operation, with traffic arrangements made with the connecting railroad, and John Sr. promptly sold the railroad to them for $1 million. The latter promised, as one of the arrangements with Sawyer & Austin, to pay the lumber company 2 cents for every 100 pounds shipped; but when the Hepburn Act went into effect in 1906, prohibiting rebates, the St. Louis, Iron Mountain and Southern refused to pay the 2 cents, holding that they themselves had been giving an illegal payment!

In 1904, W. W. also became involved with a railroad project in La Crosse—the La Crosse & Southeastern Railway Company. It was under construction by another management, with W. W. Cargill an investor. When the railroad "found themselves in financial straits," as a 1909 article on W. W. Cargill noted, Cargill himself took over the fledgling line and began to see the railroad construction through to completion, with son Will the overseer. The line ran between the small town of Viroqua, Wisconsin, and La Crosse. The authors waxed eloquent about its success: "Today its trains are daily bringing hundreds of shoppers to La Crosse and carrying immense quantities of freight both ways, the road having become one of the city's most valuable trade avenues." The line offered at least one perquisite—the whole Cargill family was able to get free railroad passes on other railroads all over the country. This was a paltry benefit to counter the line's difficulties, for it fell on very hard times with the advent of the automobile. The 1945 Cargill history, with the benefit of hindsight, was considerably less gracious in its analysis: "There was no possible excuse for its construction; it started nowhere and ended nowhere."[17]

Tragedy Strikes the Family

With the ferment in the La Crosse–Pine Bluff side of the Cargill brothers' business, the Minneapolis–Duluth side had remained steady and profitable under the tutelage of Sam Cargill. But Sam was to be denied the fruits of his endeavors. In March 1903, he died suddenly, at age 56. He had been stricken on board a train, returning from a vacation trip to the West Indies with his wife, Lydia. W. W. rushed to West Baden, Indiana, where Sam had been taken. Assured that Sam was recovering, W. W. left, only to be called back a few days later by Sam's death. Given his dominating personality, his death truly had to be the "staggering blow" that the 1945 Cargill history lamented. Brother Jim was called upon to assume responsibility for the company and was duly elected president. Six months later, though, his second breakdown caused his sudden resignation. "Jim Cargill's health could not stand the strain," noted the history, "and in the fall of 1903 he had a complete breakdown. Something had to be done."

The "something" turned out to be John MacMillan, Sr. In October 1903, John was abruptly transferred back north by W. W. Cargill, to take over the Minneapolis grain operation. His new title was vice president and general manager. W. W. Cargill was president, James Cargill held another vice president's post, John Sr.'s brother Daniel was secretary, and E. S. Mooers was treasurer. John Sr. was to be given only the token one share of stock to qualify as an officer, but the stockholder structure had been fundamentally altered by Sam's death. Up until 1897, Sam and W. W. owned the elevator company equally. In 1901, Jim Cargill was given an additional 100 shares of unissued stock over his own one share for qualification as an officer. Then, when Sam died without children, leaving an estate valued at over $872,000, his will provided that his shares in the Company would be divided equally among the five members of his immediate family—older brother W. W.; brothers Jim and Sylvester; sister, Margaret Barker; and widow, Lydia. (John D. McMillan was executor of the estate and charged a fee that outraged W. W. and his wife). By Sam's will, W. W. Cargill gained majority ownership of Cargill Elevator Company. He increased his holdings in 1905 when he obtained the shares held by brother Jim, but the record does not show why this happened—just that it did. After this transaction, W. W. owned 2,509 of the 3,500 shares in the Company. Thus, all of the owners were a combination of Cargills by birth and S. D.'s widow, Lydia (John Sr.'s one share excepted).

There was yet one further calamity in the Cargill family. In August 1904, W. W. Cargill suffered a stroke. It was a serious, although not life-threatening one. For some months, W. W. had some paralysis on his side, and his speech was also affected. Fortunately, these symptoms disappeared over time, and he was able to resume a full business and personal life. One result of this scare, however, was the turning over of more of the La Crosse decisions to his eldest son, Will. As far back as 1892, Will (at age 23) had been made a vice president of the W. W. Cargill Company; now he was given the title of general manager and began assuming more of the strategic decisions of the family, particularly those relating to new investments.

The 1945 Cargill history faulted this decision: "A forceful personality, intelligence, and boundless energy characterized W. S. Cargill, and yet, with all these attributes he was not a successful business man. This paradox was due to a combination of circumstances. In the first place he was the eldest child of a wealthy father and a doting mother. As a result, his early environment had spoiled him, and by the time he had reached maturity he had become accustomed to having his own way." Some of these traits had begun to surface in the public press in 1904. In April 1904, a rival newspaper with several former *Chronicle* employees—the *La Crosse Tribune*—began publishing. This was at the height of the muckraking period, and the *Tribune* was in its mode, taking on the *Chronicle* in general and Will Cargill in particular. Will owned one of La Crosse's first automobiles, a red roadster that the *Tribune* dubbed the "Red Devil," and was an "automobile scorcher" by his speed. In early July 1904, a small boy on a bicycle had to jump off just before Will's auto crushed the cycle. Will gave the boy $10 for repairs, but when the charge came to $12, Will refused to pay, telling the newspaper that he could have had the boy arrested for running into his auto. The *Tribune* editorialized, "Must the heads of families see their children run down by weatherbrained snobs while well-paid officials blink drowsily and fail to do their duty?"

The 1945 Cargill history particularly faulted Will on his business acumen: "Circumstances had not forced him to learn the fundamentals of business through the 'school of hard knocks.' Though lacking in business judgment, his great energy led him to plunge into business enterprises which caution, learned by experience, would have told him to avoid. He was not a grain merchant, and, therefore, the enterprises he rushed into had no logical connection with Cargill's principal business—grain. Unfortunately, he often became involved on a large scale before anyone knew what he was doing, and in order to protect the Cargill name his father had to 'bail him out.' "

There was a particular issue, concerning the La Crosse Gas & Electric Company, over which the *Tribune* severely criticized Will. A number of prominent La Crosse businessmen, Will included, owned the firm after they consolidated their earlier companies. A convoluted set of events then occurred, essentially coming down to the fact that the electric company promptly proceeded to act like a monopolist by kiting its charges, to the consternation of the populace as there was as yet no regulation of these

William S. Cargill, c. 1900.

May (Mary S.) Cargill, wife of William S. Cargill.

W. S. Cargill's roadster, the "Red Devil," in the W. W. Cargill garage, c. 1905.

"The Charge of the Light Brigade," La Crosse Tribune, *May 16, 1905.*

charges by the state or city. Will's father-in-law, George McMillan, was president, with Will as secretary, and both were roundly and continually castigated by the *Tribune*. Finally, a competitor company, the Wisconsin Light and Power Company, was formed in December 1904 and began competing for customers. It was at this point that the *Tribune* targeted Will and his group with a series of cartoons featuring Will. Although W. W. Cargill had furnished the money for his son's stake in the electric company, the editor of the *Tribune* seemed to mirror the town's feeling when he wrote in an editorial in July 1905: "The people of La Crosse have never connected W. W. Cargill with the . . . deal; they associated W. S. Cargill with it as the consenting party . . . W. W. Cargill was an esteemed man before the . . . deal. He still is." Shortly after this, the state began to regulate rates. In 1907, the two competing companies were merged, and the issue of the "light trust octupus" faded away. Also in December of that year, Will's runabout was destroyed in a fire in W. W.'s coach house (the blaze also incinerating W. W.'s Packard and his Stearns).[18]

The New Chief Executive Takes Over

It must have been intimidating for John MacMillan, Sr., in 1903 to be thrust suddenly into the leadership of a going organization, following in the footsteps of a striking personality like S. D. Cargill. Sam indeed had

"The Light Brigade—After the Charge!" La Crosse Tribune, *May 16, 1905.*

had an "ability to gather around him strong and able executives—men who could develop as the business developed," and his legacy to John Mac-Millan was particularly this group of men who made up the Cargill Elevator Company. It was now MacMillan's challenge to become their leader. This Minneapolis organization had been in place for 19 years. The "floor force," the traders in the Minneapolis cash and futures pits were led by J. B. Cooper, an eminent barley buyer on the Minneapolis Exchange, the self-styled "King of Barley." He was assisted by A. F. "Hub" Owen, a sample boy who would later head the Company's cash grain purchases on the Minneapolis Exchange floor. The finances of the Minneapolis office were well regularized under the new cashier, E. S. Mooers, who also had just become treasurer. He was the brother of Jim Cargill's wife, Mattie Mooers. The country elevators, although many in number, operated in a simple fashion, taking most of their orders from Minneapolis for both purchases and shipments. William Young was their superintendent (B. A. "Bert" Young, his son, was an office boy who later became office manager). The two assistant superintendents of the line operations were A. S. Boult and George H. Chilton. Boult then became head of the Company's seed operations. Chilton later was superintendent of all of the country elevators farther out in the system, with George Turner handling those nearest Minneapolis. There are many legends about these two, Chilton and Turner, who sat across from each other at one large desk for years but would never speak to one another. This was one among several of the legendary feuds the Company knew in those days.

John Sr. also inherited the strongly held precepts of S. D. Cargill. While Sam had left a solid, conservative organization, he had not documented his management very well—"in those days, monthly statements were unheard of in the grain trade. Annual or at most semi-annual cutoffs and balance sheets were the rule." This latter accounting practice, common in the industry at that time, troubled John Sr. enough for him to make some decisive moves early in his management. First, he persuaded the head of the Duluth office, F. E. Lindahl, to release Roy N. Hoople, office manager at Duluth, to become the counterpart in Minneapolis. The 1945 Cargill history sketched his personality: "Mr. Hoople had not only the temperament but also the unyielding strength of character, stubbornness and stick-to-itiveness which, combined with a love for figures and statistics, makes for a great accountant and auditor." Hoople and John Sr. together devised a considerably more sophisticated accounting system for the Company, one that reportedly "was to set a model for the grain trade."

We gather a further image of Hoople in a later *Cargill News* story: "When there was work to be accomplished, time did not matter, and he was in the office early and late, Sundays included, especially during the annual closing periods. His stamina was amazing and we often wondered how he could keep going at such a pace. His intense interest in the work and his willing attitude was an incentive to everyone who worked with him to keep on and do the best they could to keep up with him." A later article reiterated the same thought: "Time means nothing to him—when a job is to be done it must be done and done well. . . . His stamina and concentration were unbelievable." Long hours for employees became the rule from about this time.[19]

The Thorpe Elevator Purchase

Within a year, John Sr. took a major step toward expansion. The owners of the Thorpe Elevator Company, a Minneapolis line elevator concern owning 52 country elevators, mostly in Minnesota and North Dakota, decided to sell their entire organization to Cargill Elevator. The Thorpe group had added elevators in 1902 but had had desultory results just before being sold to Cargill Elevator, making a profit of only $3,600 on gross sales of just over $60,000. The Thorpe minute book, telegraphically short like most in the industry, does not tell us how much Cargill Elevator paid for this significant addition.

There is no record of the reasons for the purchase of Thorpe, but they probably relate to W. W.'s purchasing of timberland in British Columbia during this period. James F. Cargill had bought a small holding in Thorpe just after the turn of the century. At this point, in 1904, apparently it was W. W. Cargill's money being used. The Thorpe elevators continued to be carried separately on Cargill's books as a separate entry for several more years.[20]

Another addition came in 1905, inconsequential at the time but later a key piece in the total Cargill map—Elevator "T," in Minneapolis (see pp. 78–79). Cargill people can readily picture in their minds the more modern monolith of cylindrical concrete stacks that Elevator T has become. It would be hard for them to imagine the puny structure acquired by Cargill Elevator in 1905—a wooden structure that was essentially a workhouse, known in the vernacular of the grain trade as a "hospital." It had no storage of any significance and could be utilized only as an in-transit processing facility, receiving grain, mixing, and reshipping. Cargill acquired this unprepossessing asset in partial settlement of an acrimonious dispute with Spencer Grain Company. Cargill had made an investment in Spencer preferred stock but found that the assets were in fact not what had been portrayed. John Sr.'s and Hoople's sense of figures soon proved to them that one could not make an elevator pay when it was purely a grain hospital. A substantial annex was added in 1908, and within a few years a series of additions of cylindrical concrete bins for storage began to be added, the first in 1911, with a capacity of about 800,000 bushels.

In 1907 the company also opened a seed company at this Dight Avenue location (it was first under the Terminal Elevator Company, a Cargill subsidiary, but became the Minneapolis Seed Company in 1912). Later, the Grain Laboratory was brought to this site, too.[21]

Management Styles

In Minneapolis, John Sr. had minute-by-minute access to his key people—J. B. Cooper, Hub Owen, Roy Hoople, E. S. Mooers and the others. Information from these people and cues to them were personal, oral, and direct, with little written record of the interchanges. This Minneapolis position was more straightforward, more strongly centered in MacMillan's hands than was his more subtle role with the executives out in the field.

Field links were particularly critical, for the state of communications then required substantial delegation of independent decision-making. Yet if MacMillan (or any other chief executive of a far-flung grain company like Cargill) wanted a strong, integrated firm and overall control, he had to provide leadership throughout the system. This tension—the interface between centralized decision-making and decentralized loci of authority—is inherently one of the most important in *any* company. A firm's strength often lies in its ability to develop the aggressiveness, independence, and autonomy of decentralization, with each individual decision-maker feeling that he is running his own show. In the grain business the traders in particular were constitutionally independent. At the same time, top management in a company needed to retain enough centralized coordination and control for the organization as a whole to be the strongest entity. Cargill's success would depend on how well John Sr. could grapple with this sophisticated concept.

He was fortunate in having two confidants who understood the nuances of management and in whom he implicitly trusted. First was his brother Daniel, who had gone with John to Minneapolis to assume an important role as an officer of the company and especially to forecast field operations—crop conditions, operations of the Company's country elevators, tracing the attitudes of the farming community, etc. Dan MacMillan stayed in this position for 36 years, until he died in 1939. The second confidant was Fred Lindahl, the head of the Duluth branch of the business. This was the most critical office for John Sr. to understand, for at the Head-of-the-Lakes were Cargill's big terminals, across the inlet at Superior, Wisconsin, and the Cargill Commission Company in Duluth, at the Duluth Exchange.

There were two pivotal people at Duluth. Arthur M. Prime, a barley trader and self-styled "barley king of Duluth," and Lindahl, then the dean of the Cargill management. Lindahl had started with James F. Cargill in 1884 at age 24 to run country elevator operations at Hope, North Dakota. After a season as manager, he had become line superintendent for two years. He then went to Minneapolis to work with S. D. Cargill on the Exchange floor. In 1891, Lindahl was sent to Duluth, where a year later he headed the newly formed Cargill Commission Company, and in 1893 he helped establish the Superior Terminal Elevator Company.

Lindahl and Prime had combined to make the Duluth segment of the business quite a success, giving the Minneapolis operations much more flexibility in purchasing, transporting and storing grain. Prime and J. B. Cooper, Cargill's Minneapolis barley trader, continued to dovetail barley purchases from the two locations as well as with the office at Green Bay, and all three offices dealt with an agent in Buffalo, Dudley Irwin. MacMillan and Lindahl together worked the remainder of the grains through the floor traders—Hub Owen, John Tresise, and Nathan Clark. Incidentally, Duluth also provided the backdrop for a second "great feud," for Prime and Lindahl at a later period would not even speak to each other.[22]

John Sr., 34 years old when he went to Minneapolis, took with him approximately a decade of experience in the grain trade. Lindahl, nine years older than MacMillan, had been in the grain trade for almost 20 years. Their interaction provides real insight into both men's management abilities. Fortunately, a wealth of written correspondence between these two remains, allowing not only a revealing view of the two men's personalities but also an early picture of an evolving Cargill corporate ethic that continues to today. They wrote detailed letters on the grain trade to each other just about every day, often appending personal postscripts with private feelings. These chronicle a warm and thoughtful relationship between two intelligent, cautious men, in an often ambiguous positioning of Lindahl as teacher and mentor and MacMillan as leader, the person responsible for the strategic and long-term decision-making that would shape the overall Cargill Elevator Company for future decades.

Lindahl's Duluth

Around the turn of the century, Duluth gained a unique role in the grain trade of the Upper Midwest. Its hinterland was preeminently a spring wheat area—grain from Minnesota, the Dakotas, Montana. When this wheat moved East, there were two important routes: the Duluth–Great Lakes route and the Chicago rail or lake–rail route. Henrietta Larson analyzed the sharply shifting trade patterns that were occurring in the decade just prior to John Sr.'s entry into Minneapolis in 1903. The Duluth–lake route had vastly improved its boats and transfer facilities. Earlier lake boats had carried only about 30,000 bushels of wheat and had taken a day to load. By 1901, claimed the trade newspaper *Commercial West*, the boats of Peavey, Cargill's great rival, were loading 250,000-bushel boats in two hours. The railroads had been strengthened in this period by better trackage, more effective switching and their aggressive rate making. Over the decade of the 1890s, Chicago had been dwindling in importance in actual physical handling, although the Chicago Board of Trade still dominated trading. Duluth had gained, and Minneapolis, especially, had jumped in importance due to the growing demand of the Minneapolis flour milling industry. In the earlier period, Milwaukee and Chicago had been the kingpins of flour milling in the Upper Midwest, but before the turn of the century, Minneapolis millers had been accorded the "milling-in-transit" privilege, allowing a rate eastward for processed flour that was competitive with unprocessed grain itself. Milwaukee and Chicago had earlier had this rate advantage, but even this could not hold off the surge of Minneapolis as a flour milling center and Duluth as a highly efficient route for shipping grain on to the East.[23]

By the turn of the century, Milwaukee and Green Bay had faded as primary ports and Cargill's terminals at these two locations decreased in importance. It was the interaction among the other three, each directly competing for wheat, that brought about aggressive efforts to rationalize and cut marketing costs and to press for preferential rates from the various federal and state agencies. In this milieu, the Company had to be alert and sophisticated in positioning itself. A number of different grains were in-

Minneapolis office staff, c. 1894.

volved—wheat was the largest in volume, but barley was a great money-maker when the situation was right, and oats, rye, flax, and durum wheat also were widely traded. It became a chess-like set of decisions. The Minneapolis office managed the purchases of grain at the country elevators, which would be filled at harvest. The goal was to load and hold it there until it was sold and transportation arranged. Some grain also came directly to the processing cities, especially Minneapolis. Much of the grain purchased for the East at harvesttime also came straight through to the Superior elevator. Great quantities were stored pending shipment by lake boat upon sale. The frantic filling of lake steamers just before the inevitable winter freeze made terminal management a delicate balancing act—ship out as much as possible, yet "top" the terminal (fill to capacity) after the last grain carrier had left in anticipation of renewed shipping in the spring. Indeed, lake shipping itself was typically used as a storage vehicle as boats filled with grain were often docked in Buffalo for the winter (usually with lower insurance rates than their counterpart terminals on land).

Lindahl's dozen years of management prior to the arrival of John MacMillan on the scene, in a period of great ferment and change, had given him a fund of experience. Further, the Duluth operation was apparently a "great money maker practically from the beginning" (here depending upon the 1945 Cargill history, for few financial records remain for this period before the turn of the century). The denominator for the whole system was competition: fierce battles among rugged individualists, each looking for the moment of vantage over the others to buy, store, and sell advantageously.

John Sr. knew how to contest his rivals. There were widespread practices of quid pro quo, insisting on business houses reciprocating with business for that done through them. MacMillan, for example, wrote Lindahl in August 1909 about two separate New York exporters, "If we are going to continue to do business with them, they have got to throw us some of their option business . . . if they were not going to reciprocate in this way, we will have to do our own shipping . . . it will do no harm for you to put the matter to them in just this way." In the previous year, the reciprocity had been in the other direction, for then he had urged Lindahl to "throw as much business as you can to McDonald & Wyman, to even up their business they are giving you."[24]

Both Lindahl and MacMillan were willing to compromise on reciprocal business but, when pushed, were vigorous competitors. In one of the periods of sharp practices, Lindahl wrote MacMillan, "There seems to be another fight, one like we had last Fall and it rather looks as though it is here to stay, and it is rather disgusting and ridiculous to think that a small bunch of men can't work somewhere near together and buy grain on a margin." John Sr. wrote Lindahl later that month, "We have decided that we are going to create a little disturbance in the country and see if we cannot come to some kind of conclusion with John Miller as to the action they have taken at our stations. We propose to retaliate on the Amenia Elevator Co. for all the injury the John Miller Co. has done at our stations this year, and we shall make up, in volume, at their points, what they have caused us to lose at some others."

Sometimes there were joint efforts with competitors to quote the same prices, but such price fixing was tenuous and always subject to the threat of legal action by the government. Arrangements to notify competitors of price changes often fell apart. For example, MacMillan wrote a Minneapolis competitor, H. F. Douglas, in 1907, "You stated you have always consulted us before making any change in price [but] your company and the Monarch Elevator Co. sent out an advance of $3^{1}/2$¢ per bushel over list without consulting us in any way . . . we had no intention whatever at any time of taking any unusual action [but] in this instance we felt this was the case."

Yet John Sr. and Lindahl were generally cautious in taking on industry adversaries—much more so than W. W. Cargill. In a 1909 price-cutting case involving the mammoth Van Dusen–Harrington organization, W. W.

wrote MacMillan, "The worst thing that struck me was that Van Dusen matter . . . they are mighty hoggish, when they have a chance to make a little money they go and break up everybody else . . . it looks to me as though you ought to go in and fight them, as our interests and capacity are so much smaller than theirs, and knock them out." But precisely because Cargill was smaller, John Sr. decided not to challenge Van Dusen.[25]

John Sr.'s instincts were particularly conciliatory toward customers, wanting to motivate them in positive ways. Some of this undoubtedly came from Lindahl, who had a natural instinct on these kinds of things. Lindahl wrote, for example, in mid-1909: "I am going to make it a point to go and visit with our customers more this year. . . . There is nothing like showing up once in awhile and having a little talk even if nothing is accomplished. But if a person never goes near their customers for awhile they begin to think we do not care much about their business anyhow and it gradually grows away from us."[26]

"Being competitive," to John Sr., did not normally include any speculation of consequence. The exigencies of the market sometimes left the Company temporarily with a net position on one side, but this was the exception. Hedging these positions in a futures market if hedges were available or trying to find a surrogate for hedging in those cases where there was no formal futures contract, for example, in barley, was John Sr.'s dominating policy. He sought to dampen price volatility to the maximum degree possible. The Texas experience had turned him in this direction; the 1945 Cargill history characterized this as follows: "The Cargills had not understood fully the principles of hedging and the carrying charge, and the Company had developed as a merchandising rather than a warehousing operation. There are, of course, distinct benefits to both types, but they tend to have good earnings under opposite sets of circumstances. The merchant tends to starve when there is a surplus of grain, but comes into his own in times of shortage, while it is just the reverse with the warehousemen."

The reasons for this were expanded upon by the authors:

When there is more grain on hand than is needed for current consumption the speculator naturally tends to buy a distant future. . . . He does this because he does not want to take delivery . . . if there is a grain shortage there is a crying need for the grain immediately and the tendency is to buy the nearby future. Thus . . . in times of surplus the demand, being in the distant future, rises in price as compared with the nearby future—[the] "carrying charge." In times of shortage the demand is more crying for the nearby future, and hence it rises to a premium over the distant future . . . an "inverse carrying charge." If a merchant can buy grain at a stipulated price today and can immediately turn around and sell it for delivery several months hence at a higher price, he will earn the difference in price by holding the grain from today until the future date. Thus the fundamental principle is that in times of surplus a grain warehouseman earns money. In times of shortage he loses money on every bushel that he carries. This is, of course, exactly as it should be. In times of surplus his services are needed. In times of shortage his services are not needed and for any grain he is withholding he is accordingly penalized.

John Sr.'s resolute desire to stay fully hedged was based not only on price safety but on profitability. The authors of the 1945 history noted why:

Futures contracts for hedging meant that relatively little capital was needed to start a merchandising organization. [In] the growing competition that was to result in increasingly narrow margins and smaller profits . . . [John Sr.] was determined not to leave the field of merchandising, but wanted as evenly distributed earnings as possible. He spent the better part of an energetic life in bringing about a balanced organization, one that would function profitably under conditions of surplus and shortage . . . the "First Generation" in the grain trade did not understand this fundamental principle, with the brilliant exception of Mr. F. H. Peavey . . . the Peavey organization was primarily designed as a warehousing organization.

John Sr. had to remind his traders often about price speculation. For example, he wrote Prime in early 1908, "We are grain merchants and not speculators, so of course we want to sell what barley we have down there and keep in the business, and buy and sell more of it . . . while I do not doubt at all that prices will go to the figure you mention ultimately, yet we want to take the stand that we are perfectly willing the other party should have some of the profit." Prime ignored MacMillan, and so the latter forcefully clamped down, describing it to W. W.: "I did not approve of his getting long on barley the way he did while I was South, and called him off on it as soon as I got back. Of course this is the first time in the history of the business that he has been pulled out of the market at this time of the year."

Prime had long arguments with MacMillan on this. The previous fall he had written, "There is no way of hedging barley. . . . It is up to the man that handles barley to use his best judgment." Having been "forced to sort of speculate on the bull side," Prime had been caught and "dumped a million or two" bushels. "I don't call it speculating myself," he concluded, "as it's the only correct method of handling barley; however, I take it for granted that the idea that you wish to convey is to try and keep sold up as well as possible . . . but we have simply been forced to accumulate this stuff up here and wait until the Eastern maltster . . . got into the market."

Barley was a different grain in this respect, for despite sporadic efforts in both Chicago and Minneapolis to develop a formal futures contract, it had not taken hold. Winnipeg had had such a market, but its volume was low. Because of the sharp price difference between high-quality malting barley and feed barley, the establishment of grade, so necessary for a futures contract, was difficult. As Prime reiterated many times, "the only way to hedge barley is to sell it."

Cargill elevator manager, Waverly, Minnesota, n.d.

The inability to hedge barley effectively caused the Company difficulties more than once. For example, T. F. Baxter, a Boston banker who had been involved in the Company's financing since about the turn of the century, wrote John Sr.: "Some of the banks who formerly purchased your paper, in re-checking it through their own channels, have decided to pass it up this year on account of your dealings in barley . . . that as this grain cannot be hedged, they are advised by their correspondents . . . that it is in the nature of speculative business." John Sr. immediately wrote back:

It is true that barley cannot be hedged in the ordinary sense, but, if handled rightly, it is not a speculative business. . . . Ours is purely a merchandising business. We have a very large Eastern trade. . . . When conditions get such that we cannot sell this trade we simply drop out of the market. We are able, under normal conditions, to make sales for future delivery and frequently have it sold for shipment several months later. . . . If there is any one thing that this company has always prided itself upon it is that it does not do a speculative business and on no account will it go into speculative transactions.[27]

Lindahl, too, sometimes was tempted to keep an open position. Yet he always knew that MacMillan would be uneasy. Lindahl wrote, for example, in a 1908 letter, "I presume that you will feel a little alarmed when you see our Long and Short Account on wheat tomorrow morning. We were about 100,000 Long this morning and we let it set, as the market was pretty soft

. . . the market began reacting and got pretty strong temporarily, is the reason we did not throw a hedge out against this and thought would let it run over until tomorrow morning."[28]

Although John Sr. did not argue with Lindahl on this particular "naked" (exposed) position, there were frequent examples where he explicitly admonished him. In early March 1909, he wrote Lindahl, "I am very much disappointed at the way you handled that changing over from Chicago September to New York . . . you have got to limit your orders in New York. If you make a change like you did yesterday, you will, every time, get the worst of it . . . you trade in Chicago first and New York later, you will always get the worst of it . . . if others can do it . . . we ought to be able to."[29]

Tactfully, Lindahl usually did not refer in any way in his next letter to a previous admonition. He took the order and acted upon it without comment, then replied good-naturedly back to John Sr. Indeed, with the genial nature of Lindahl's letters, it is easy to understand how positive was his impact on MacMillan. Lindahl seemed to have an instinctive feeling for the personal equation in the business. Often he would obliquely answer John Sr. but then gently lead him toward his own position. For example: "Note your letter this morning about Chicago Sept. being the best hedge, and I believe that you are right, either to sell Chicago Sept. or Chicago Dec. Of course if we have weak, declining market that would easily narrow up considerably, but at the same time if we have a declining market the difference between May and July would narrow up."[30]

A few days later, Lindahl chose to be more passive: "We note your letter that your idea in hedging in Chicago Sept. was only as a hedge against Durum, and we will be governing accordingly." Receiving another exhortation from MacMillan, he responded in a wonderfully ebullient way: "I note your letter fully this morning, and it is a mighty good letter, and is considerable help to us, and I realize that we have got to hustle here in order to get grain and keep the house going . . . we are hustling for wheat and flax-seed. . . . We can wiggle around some way, undoubtedly, between now and Spring to make some money on them." Answering a query about a barley trade, Lindahl pictured his own innate conservativeness: "Now there is no question at all but what we are all anxious to get a benefit of this advance if it is possible to do so. However I have always found it the best policy not to be a hog and try to get the last 1/8 of a cent, for when you do this, in most instances, you find that some other fellow will step in and get the business."[31]

Lindahl had a strong sense of his own ego, however, and occasionally would put this into perspective for John Sr. One of the most revealing letters of this time came from Lindahl to John Sr. over the issue of to whom mail should be addressed. MacMillan, perhaps conscious already of building differences between Lindahl and A. M. Prime, the barley trader, was addressing separate letters to the two people, and Lindahl exploded: "I have noticed lately that your office are sending mail in envelopes addressed to me, to Prime, and occasionally to Mr. Clark. This is *dead wrong*. This business belongs to Cargill Com. Co. and all mail envelopes should be addressed to same and any letters enclosed addressed to me. . . . Only strictly private personal letters should be sent in envelopes addressed to that person, but *all letters* addressed to me, Nate [N. C. Clark, Lindahl's assistant] or Prime or in fact anyone in your employ here that pertains to your business should be sent in envelopes addressed to Cargill Commission Co. . . . It's alright for Cooper to write Prime direct about barley, so he will be sure to get it quickly, but all other messages should be addressed to Cargill."[32]

On occasion, John Sr. would suggest that a hedge be effected in the Chicago Board of Trade, at that time, as now, by far the most extensive and therefore the most liquid of all grain futures markets. Here, however, there were many complications and hidden threats and it is clear that John Sr. did not trust "the Chicago crowd"—he seemed always worried about market manipulation there. The Company had a membership in the CBOT all through this period in the name of "Cargill Elevator Company," but had continuing difficulty with reciprocity on commissions when using brokers in other commission houses there. The Chicago houses took the position in 1908 that the Cargill Commission Company was a separate organization, and therefore, if it did not have its own membership, should be charged full commission rates when it traded. While this matter was cleared up later, there were recurrent fears of being unknowingly manipulated by the Chicago commission houses and by the Board governing bodies themselves.[33]

John Sr. particularly dreaded the Armour Grain Company, still led by the strong-willed Philip Armour. MacMillan wrote Lindahl in 1909, "I think there is no doubt but what the manipulation in January wheat at Winnipeg is due to Armour. He took delivery of a large amount of December up there, but no one seems to have any idea why or what he expects to do with it." Yet at the same time, John Sr. knew he had to work with Armour, and he wrote Lindahl, "I think you are right about doing considerable hedging business with Armour. It might be a convenient connection, and you would get back all that you gave them, without question, and they are certainly as well posted as to what is going on as any other firm in Chicago."[34]

Armour was not the only one suspected of cornering. Lindahl wrote John Sr. in this same period about another effort: "While Patton had May cornered now, no question . . . sometime between now and the first of May Patton would unload." MacMillan wrote in return, "Millers tell me they are getting no demand whatever for flour and if we get a materially heavier movement in the country, it might appear to Patton [*sic*] to be a favorable time to shake out his following. I think you had better watch this pretty closely and run if there is any tendency of this kind." A few months later John Sr. wrote Lindahl, "I should be very glad, indeed, when you get your wheat sold so as to get out of those Chicago options as I am decidedly anxious about them. Of course I presume they are safer in Minneapolis, but at the same time, we will not feel easy as long as there is so much of this manipulation going on . . . we have been badly fooled on this thing right along and I will not feel easy until we are cleaned up."[35]

Lindahl and John Sr. had misspelled their villain's name, but otherwise had their facts straight—it was the famous speculator, "Wheat King" James A. Patten, who was just in the process of effecting a corner on wheat, using code words for crop conditions in both the United States and Argentina. The courts later caught up with Patten on another corner in 1909 (in cotton), and he was prosecuted under the Sherman Antitrust Act and found guilty. Eventually the decision was upheld by the U.S. Supreme Court in a celebrated case in 1913.[36]

Another tenet of John Sr.'s philosophy was to take profits frequently, rather than "riding" a futures market position in the hope of a large gain. For example, "give some business to Armour, in Chicago, and give Commons the Minneapolis end of it, and just as soon as it shows a slight profit, take it immediately—even if it would not figure out better than an even thing . . . if you would attempt to work large profits, it would not make the business active enough. . . . I think you would want to limit losses so as not to get stuck for any big amounts . . . in this way you could make an enormous amount of business which would help to hold the accounts of such people as Commons."[37]

The relationship between Prime and MacMillan was vastly different from that with Lindahl and MacMillan. Prime was first, last, and always a trader and seemed to have little interest in overall organizational relationships, either at Duluth or for the Company as a whole. He was the prototypal hard-driving, speculatively inclined operator. The 1945 Cargill history put this delicately: "Mr. Prime, too, was a great money maker and though neither an executive nor administrator, his trading ability was such that in 1916 he became one of the seven directors of the Company."

It was not just Prime's bent toward speculation that worried John Sr., for Prime also tended to antagonize customers on occasion. His relationship with Cargill's Buffalo barley agent, Dudley Irwin, was often rocky. Prime accused Irwin of "stringing us" on a set of sales in late 1908, and after Irwin wrote a conciliatory letter in return, Prime commented to John Sr., "Of course, all this sounds very nice, but you know what our experience in the past has been." It did not help Prime's case that he had sent a blunt letter demanding a raise, considered a cardinal sin by John Sr., who felt such demands signified disloyalty, especially if accompanied by a threat to go elsewhere.[38]

Ingredients of Leadership

John Sr.'s qualities of leadership blossomed during the half-dozen years of 1903–1909. His innate conservatism and his desire to keep the business on the least cyclical track was balanced by his keen sense for business opportunities and his ability to think strategically about the overall organization. A substantial part of this ability undoubtedly stemmed from MacMillan's great attention to detail. No part of the business escaped his notice, and the volume of correspondence from him to other members of management in the field each day was staggering.

He understood the trader's rationale—his interaction with Prime is an apt illustration of this. Yet he also insisted on basing decisions on facts and underscored that his organization give him these facts promptly and accurately. He even wrote N. C. Clark about "the bad state of the tissue copies" of the accounts sales. "In this instance," he continued in his meticulous way, "you had better arrange for someone to look over these tissue copies every day, and if there are any of them in such shape that they cannot be read, have a new copy of the account-sale made and copied." As in so many instances, he softened the message with an additional sentence, "If this is watched every day, there will be no trouble, you will find—whoever is doing the copying will soon get it down to a science." He wrote to a lumber company employee, "I have noticed . . . that you do not seem to realize the importance of time. No business can stand it to have the bookkeeping end always behind . . . things must be kept thoroughly up to date all the time. . . . I want to warn you about it so we will not have reason to refer to it again." Then he added, "I write you this in a kindly spirit, because I believe it's for your own good."[39]

It was not just that John Sr. wanted accuracy, he also realized that statistical comparisons could mislead if they were not done in a consistent fashion. For example, he wrote brother-in-law Will Cargill in 1908 of a worsening problem at Sawyer & Austin: "The great trouble with these comparisons is that the figures for last year did not pan out at all. You understand, I presume, that the feet are estimates and based on the usual percentage of over-run, while last year there was a shortage, so that the comparison at the plant this year with last year is not correct." He continued, "I am not satisfied at all with this form they have of figuring . . . we will try to get this figured out so that the monthly cost will balance at the end of the year with the yearly cost."[40]

John Sr. was vitriolic with a manager at one of his country elevators who had not kept him informed about the buying at the elevator:

On your report received here I find you bought and paid for over 1500 bushels of wheat and 1900 bushels of flax, which shows us a net loss of $92.00; this in spite of the fact that all agents have had iron clad instructions not to take anything over list . . . this office wrote you some time ago asking if you had any special deals, and you did not even reply. We cannot stand in the gap this way. We have got to be able to protect ourselves. The markets have gone off sharply and your careless, slipshod way of handling this has probably cost us $300 or $400.[41]

Sometimes, John Sr. was found not to have been assiduous enough in his own record keeping, but when this happened, he was open in admitting a mistake. Cargill Elevator Company had gone into the seed business in 1907 (originally it carried the name of the Terminal Elevator Company, but the name was changed to the Minneapolis Seed Company in 1912 because "independents and Farmer's Elevators are very strongly prejudiced on the subject of selling seeds to a line company or to any middle man"). The business had done poorly in the summer of 1909, and MacMillan wrote W. W. Cargill of "a loss of about $4500. I do not think, however, there is any reason to be discouraged as this is purely a case of paying for experience. This next year I will try to follow it a little closer and see if we cannot make it show up very much better. Boult supposed he was doing business on a margin, but, as a matter of fact, he did not realize what the expense of doing business amounted to."

John Sr. always was ready to forgive a mistake openly admitted and with steps in place not to repeat. It was the glossing-over of slips that particularly irritated him. In a case involving poor performance in the lumber operation, MacMillan wrote Will Cargill about the manager, "He shows that he is 'sore' and that he is weak by not coming out 'flatfooted' and admitting the bad showing and assuming the responsibility of it." The 1945 Cargill history commented about this strongly held MacMillan prejudice: "If something had been covered up, his attitude was extraordinarily intolerant."[42]

Employee Relations

It was in the arena of line employee relations that John Sr. and Lindahl showed particular sensitivity and compassion, each seeming to draw on the best side of the other and by mutual encouragement transmitting their own values to the people working with them. Lindahl subtly urged MacMillan, both by example and suggestion, to mirror his own positive motivation toward employees. Lindahl's letters often contained examples like this one, in November 1909, "Our man Ramstad, over at the elevator, is doing good work. I am very highly pleased [with] the way he has handled it down there this year. He has worked like a tiger."

John Sr. was an able energizer, too. For example, he used a bonus system with his top management people. In mid-1909, when he surprised Lindahl with a $2,000 bonus, the latter responded, "I did not expect it this year as our balance was not as good as should have been, but will struggle hard to make a nice balance this coming year." Earlier that same year there had been a necessity for a seasonal layoff, and Lindahl wrote MacMillan on this, "I think the lowest we ever cut down before was about 13 or 14 men, and Mr. McManus [the terminal superintendent at Superior] can tell you that 12 men is practically shutting down the plant." John Sr. replied, "I think you want to let what few men you have there try to get the house in good shape for the fall business. They will not have much to do excepting something of this sort, from now on."

John Sr. was charitable when slips did occur; a letter to W. W. Cargill is typical: "I enclose you a couple of letters from Will [an employee out in the lumber yards, not otherwise identified], which are rather pitiful. Personally, I feel that Will has not had a square deal there in any sense of the word, and while I will admit he was foolish yet the aggravation certainly was very great. If you could use Will around the place in any way, I am sure he would make you a good man. Of course, as you know, he owes the store over $300 and unless something is done for him, he never will be able to pay it up in the world."[43]

A Sawyer & Austin employee who had worked for the firm for 12 years had been laid off as the fortunes of the firm declined; he had purchased a small piece of land from the Company, and in July 1911 had fallen behind on his payments. He wrote John Sr. (who was still sharing supervision of S&A at a distance) to intercede for him, that he would "catch it up" within the next three months. He continued, with halting spelling, "You is the only one that I have ever got a favor out of and so I don't know how to ast ini one Else. Mr. J. H. I have work for you near 12 years & I would like for you to give me a pen to remember you." MacMillan wrote back that he had interceded on the loan, "and I am also sending you a pen which I will be glad to have you keep in remembrance of the twelve years service which you had under the company." The man immediately wrote back, "In regards of that pen . . . i am looking for it on al trains northbound southbound & hand cars, street buses & boats." The pen soon arrived, and a much more legible letter came back a few days later, "You can see from the hand write on the wall that I have my pen but no one can tell how glad I am. Many a thanks to you. I am rely so glad I can't express myself."[44]

In a particularly poignant case, a Sawyer & Austin supervisor had become quite ill. His brother wrote John Sr., who responded, "I will appreciate very greatly any information which you can give me from time to time, as I assure you I am very anxious." A few days later MacMillan wrote once again: "I am very anxious, indeed, to be kept informed and will appreciate very much if you will kindly continue to write me daily, until you feel that all danger is past." After an operation, the employee seemed to be better but rather suddenly turned worse and died. MacMillan penned a sympathetic letter back to the man's brother, offering any services that he or the Sawyer & Austin Company could do.[45]

In turn, John Sr. asked the same high standards of others as he demanded of himself—openness, frankness, loyalty, and above all, honesty. MacMillan's personal example was impeccable. He would tolerate no shadings of truth or honesty in any dealings, business or personal, on the part of his employees. For example, in an incident in 1906 at Sawyer & Austin involving a defalcation, the man was forced to pay back the shortage and was also summarily fired. His brother, who was also a company employee, pressed MacMillan to change his mind. John Sr. replied:

We hired your brother solely on your account and he did not make good. I do not think you need to feel any responsibility about it at all. However, simply because he was your brother we could not make an exception of your case. We have to make rigid rules about such matters as this and live up to them. If you had been working in his place we should have made you pay just the same, as it is the only way we can run a large business of this kind. We must hold everyone responsible for their own results. If they make any mistakes they must stand it. We do not pretend to say where the shortage came in, but simply know it exists.

In the 1907–1908 period, there were further troubles involving Sawyer & Austin and its subsidiary in St. Louis, the Banner Lumber Company. John Sr. wrote W. W. Cargill, "One thing above everything else that I dislike about the business down there is the apparent spirit of disloyalty. As near as I can get at the undercurrent down there, they all feel it is preposterous to think of my attempting to keep track of what is going on, and in fact, all resent it. It looks to me as though everybody down there is running his own end of it and does not want to be interfered with by anybody."

In another Sawyer & Austin instance, in December 1907, a local manager had backed out of an order from Detroit, apparently when he determined that he was going to lose money if the order was filled. John Sr. wrote W. W. Cargill about this: "I think Mr. [D. A.] Kendall himself is as much to blame in this matter as John [Kendall] was for he accepted the order when it was sent in and then did not want to fill it when he found out it did not work out as he figured it would. I have always felt decidedly ashamed of this deal, as I do not believe in doing business that way. If we make a mistake, I think we ought to stand up for it."[46]

Another characteristic prized by John Sr. was an employee's ability to keep a confidence. The grain trade was a secretive business—the competitive nature of the business dictated this. At one point in 1911, MacMillan sensed a leak in the system and wrote J. B. Taylor, the secretary of the La Crosse operation, "I was very much surprised today to learn that Wallie Hyde [a partner of W. W.] seemed to know all about our Profit & Loss Account in our Seed Department last year. Now, if he knew it in our Seed Department he undoubtedly knew it in our other departments and I cannot imagine where the leak came in. . . . I certainly want to stop any leaks if there is any in our business. . . . I feel very much chagrined to think that our business is being talked about so freely."[47]

In those days, frankness also was a respected virtue when possible. Even in recommendations for people, John Sr. practiced this belief. An estimator who had once worked for MacMillan in the lumber business wanted to move to another such job in Tennessee, and the prospective employer wrote John Sr., who responded, "He is rather of a sanguine disposition and is inclined to make promises to the trade which later experience showed could not be carried out, especially in the way of deliveries, but no doubt with your organization you could correct faults of this kind. He is also inclined to figure too close on large jobs but on residence work we always found his work very satisfactory, indeed."[48]

Not all employee relations of that faraway period of pre–World War I would fit today's precepts. Employer paternalism was very strong at that time, a positive factor in many cases, an overly heavy hand in others. There were widespread prejudices, too, that would make today's equal employment program administrators anticipate legal actions. John Sr. fell into this trap occasionally, as witnessed by this excerpt from a letter in August 1909 to a female employee in the Arkansas lumber operation:

I have just heard in a very round-about way that you have been a little bit indiscrete [sic] about being out late in the evening and associating with some of the young men among the Jews. Now I don't know whether you realize it or not, but it is sure to cause unfavorable talk for you to be among the Jews, and you cannot be too careful about staying in in the evening. You must realize that no young woman can afford to be talked about, and I sincerely hope that you will take this exactly as I mean it, and be very much more discrete [sic] hereafter. You will soon find that if you are being talked about, neither Mrs. Moore nor any other lady in Pine Bluff would want you living with her and it certainly would hurt your chances for a business position as well. I sincerely hope that you will be overly careful from now on.[49]

There are other places in the John MacMillan, Sr., and James Taylor sets of correspondence mentioning "the Jews." For example, MacMillan wrote a Chicago bank at a later date when asked for a reference, "The parties referred to, as you can infer from the name, are Jews, and we understand at one time settled for twenty-five cents on the dollar. There seems to be a

Logging at Sawyer & Austin, Pine Bluff, Arkansas, n.d.

feeling that they might not be any too scrupulous along these lines should conditions at anytime put them in difficulties." He continued, "We do not know any of the parties ourselves and have had no dealings with them, but the above is the best information we have been able to secure." James Taylor also denominated a person "the Jew" more than once.

In 1906, when there had been intimations that unions might try to organize the lumber companies of the South, an employer trade organization wanted to mount a campaign against the movement. John Sr. balked at the idea, writing the manager in Pine Bluff, "I don't like to take a stand that is antagonistic to our employees. They have never given us any reason for worry along these lines. I believe, most thoroughly, in the idea of treating our employees right." He continued in a paternalistic vein:

These Louisiana operators use white labor, exclusively, while we depend almost entirely upon negroes. Negroes have never shown the ability for organization. . . . They never have any money and are forced to live, and the only way they can do it is by trading at a company store. We tried this weekly pay day system without a store, and you know the results . . . we were forced into our present method. As no employee of ours is compelled to trade at the store and can buy where he pleases, they certainly cannot claim any grievance on this account with us.[50]

Yet John Sr. was not eager to intrude into employees' lives. One of the

Cargill Elevator employees, working for one of the implement branch houses, wrote MacMillan in early 1910 that the manager of the implement house had "broken my family up by winning my wife from her home and me." He alleged that the manager had taken the wife to Minneapolis, to one of the well-known hotels, and asked MacMillan to check on this. MacMillan replied, "I am taking considerable pains to investigate the situation. There is absolutely nothing to indicate that Mr. —— [I have omitted the name] met your wife here in Minneapolis at all. She certainly was not at the Nicollet with him, and it may be your suspicions are entirely unfounded, so far as this recent trip is concerned. I do not know that I can offer you any advice in a matter of this kind. It is something you must decide for yourself."[51]

Early Public Relations

From the beginning, John Sr. concerned himself with the broader needs of the communities in which Cargill operated. Even in difficult times, he evidenced generosity about fund-raising appeals made to him or to the Company by educational and charitable organizations. Here, though, his core belief in loyalty often made him apply conditions for such donations. A group in Hatton, North Dakota, in March 1908, wanted MacMillan to help support a new high school building. He wrote:

I think you know how very bitterly the people at Hatton have fought the elevator companies there, and I cannot see the slightest grounds on which they can ask us to help them build a high school. There is no more prosperous section of the country than yours, and it certainly seems to me that if your people do not care enough, under these conditions, to pay for their own high school, that they can hardly expect to secure aid on the outside. If the people at Hatton had shown a disposition to be fair with the elevator companies and had worked for us as hard as they have worked against us, I should feel very much inclined, as far as this Company is concerned, to give a donation. We have always made it a rule to be liberal with new communities where the people are just getting a start, but certainly these conditions do not apply at Hatton.[52]

When the industry, or even worse, Cargill itself was faulted by newspapers or politicians, John Sr. became outraged. For example, a local newspaper in Ada, Minnesota, attacked "the grain companies" in that town for what the editor felt was an unprincipled spread between the local price paid by the elevators and the Minneapolis price. The editor penned that the margin was "unjust, unfair and unreasonable." MacMillan responded immediately to his own agent in the town: "We take it for granted the editor of this paper is an honest, honorable man who does not wish to misrepresent nor distort the facts, but his statement is so utterly at variance with the truth that you are at perfect liberty to show him this letter . . .

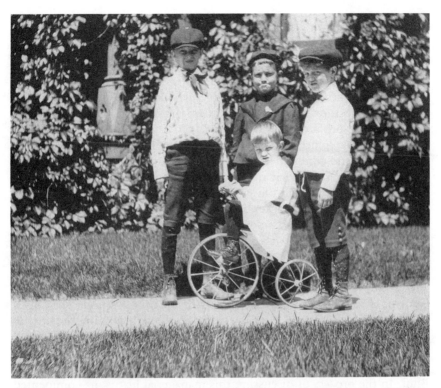

Standing, left and right, William and George Cargill (sons of William S. Cargill); standing, center, John H. MacMillan, Jr.; seated, Cargill MacMillan, younger son of John H. MacMillan.

although we do not want it published, nor do we want to enter into any controversy; we merely want to set him right." MacMillan averred that "the present basis we are buying on at Ada does not allow us a profit of over three cents a bushel . . . our investment at Ada has not been a profitable one for a good many years." Then MacMillan turned to the editor himself: "We will venture the assertion that the *Herald* makes more money out of one 'ad' that takes perhaps two minutes to set up than we could make on handling a carload of grain . . . an investigation of his profits, as compared to ours for the last several years, will show that he has made relatively much more on his investment than we have." MacMillan ended by lecturing his agent: "It certainly does not do your town any good, and it does a great deal of harm for the newspaper, to single out the various industries of the town and abuse them. The spirit of harmony and good will between all the various business interests will do very much more towards building up a town than abuse of any kind."[53]

Managing Centrally

One of the most noteworthy of John MacMillan, Sr.'s qualities was already in evidence in these early years—his singular ability to sense the overall strategic positioning of the Company. MacMillan seemed able to comprehend, without articulating it in such words, the tension between centralizing decision making and pushing out authority into the field for decentralized "profit center" operation.

John Sr.'s preference was toward the centralizing mode. His great attention to detail and comprehensive approach to everything that went on in his organization favored having one final authority—himself. In his mind, Minneapolis *was* the head office, the hub of the wheel, where the action lay. He wrote Charles Quackenbush, the Green Bay manager, in 1908, "I hope you will decide to come over here once in awhile and keep in touch with market conditions. I am sure you realize how necessary that is, and how rusty you are apt to get in a place like Green Bay, where you do not come in close touch with the trade."

Even more revealing of this belief was a long letter to W. W. Cargill in September 1908, concerning the Sawyer & Austin operation. There they had lost the manager and were trying to get by with running the organization more directly from La Crosse. Although brother-in-law Will Cargill had been named president and had the authority, John Sr. himself was pushed into continuing many contacts, given his prior assignment at Pine Bluff. In the process of discussing this managerial hiatus, he commented to W. W.:

I want to emphasize the point which I have been making for years past, namely, that the management of your business ought to be centralized in Minneapolis, and Will's office ought to be here with me; then we could work out all these problems that would come up, together, without the slightest hitch. It is absolutely impossible for me to be of any assistance in running Pine Bluff if the correspondence and everything of that sort goes to La Crosse. The only way to check up on errors is at first hand and not to find out about it after some one else has passed on what is being done. . . . In a large center like this, it is possible to know what is going on all the time, while in a place like La Crosse, it is impossible to keep posted.

Yet the very nature of the business itself would not allow full-scale centralization. Positions and prices changed rapidly out in the field, and individual direction often was demanded. John Sr. trusted others when he was certain they were honest, conservative on handling of monies, and had a wide vision that would recognize which decision was likely to involve a new policy and therefore should be referred back to him. Once the facts were in his possession, John Sr. readily put trust into employees—he did so at Sawyer & Austin, once a sound manager was identified. At that time he wrote James B. Taylor, "Mr. McGehee knows these lands much better than any other person and is much better qualified to handle them. He is absolutely honest . . . he is a native of that country and is absolutely trusted by everyone. I would be perfectly satisfied to give him a very free hand. . . . He is a man of good, safe judgment."

Some people in the organization, particularly the traders, literally demanded a high degree of independence; Prime in Duluth was a good example. N. C. Clark was being considered as a barley trader for the Green Bay operation in early 1908, and John Sr. wrote W. W. Cargill that Prime "says Nate is a fellow who will absolutely obey orders but that he does not believe he has enough initiative to act on barley matters."

John Sr. seemed particularly comfortable in so trusting Lindahl. For example, he wrote Lindahl in the fall of 1908 about Lindahl's position in October wheat: "We will always expect you to look out for such things as this. You will not need to write us if we have anything of this kind open, but change it over yourselves, as you can figure out from what we are doing, just what should be done, and very often better than we can here, as we do not know the amount of grain you have on track." But with Prime and some others, John Sr. was more leery of independence. Prime's decisions, for example, were typically narrowly barley-oriented and often speculative, overly so sometimes. Therefore, the locus of authority for decision-making would continue to pose perplexing dilemmas. Indeed, it continues to do so to the present day.[54]

The first few years of John MacMillan Sr.'s tenure as the head of the Cargill Elevator Company were as auspicious as a new, young, relatively untried chief executive could reasonably expect. Few formal financial records survive for the period prior to the Company's first outside audit in 1910. Someone did keep a running ledger of profitability, and although there is not much documentation to back this up, the qualitative correspondence appears to corroborate the figures. During this early tenure of John Sr. as chief executive, the Company was quite profitable. Earnings hovered just under $300,000 for the first three years and rose to over $400,000 in the 1906–1907 crop year. A healthy stock dividend had been declared in August 1905; the capital stock was raised to $2 million, with a total of $1 million issued to shareholders, made up of the original stock owned ($350,000), an additional $450,000 from the Superior Terminal Elevator Company, and the stock dividend itself, $200,000. In the process, the stockholder mix remained the same (W. W. Cargill still holding just under 72%).[55]

More important for the longer run, John Sr. had garnered the loyalty of his colleagues and the respect of the outside community, the financial houses conspicuous with their praise. But all of this goodwill was to be sorely tested, for a business storm was gathering, "the Panic of 1907."

CHAPTER THREE

A Panic and Its Aftermath

The country's stock markets had dropped early in 1907, and business failures began to mushroom in the middle of the year. Then came a significant tightening of credit and resulting unemployment. On October 22, the Knickerbocker Trust Company in New York suspended its operations, and there was consternation throughout the country. At this critical moment, J. Pierpont Morgan and other financial leaders intervened (thus the name "Bankers' Panic") and finally were able to restore a modicum of confidence by advancing massive loans to businesses. As the new year began, the situation moderated. It had been primarily a severe but short-term liquidity squeeze and was not followed by a depression. Still, we remember this panic as one of the classic ones, along with 1873, 1893 and 1929.

Weaknesses within an organization often surface in times of crisis. This now happened in W. W.'s La Crosse Cargill grain operation, and the firm came close to losing its internal control system. In the process, marked differences in business practice between John MacMillan, Sr., and his father-in-law became even more evident.

The Panic highlighted the problem, but it was W. W.'s stroke back in 1904 and his basic personality that were at the root. As he became sicker, his business activities slowed, and he seemed to lose his touch. He began to resort to old remembered days of glory, when he had arranged banking with Jason Easton and local friends in La Crosse, and he became more conscious of his own health. Earlier his brother Sam had held him in check on some of his most grandiose ideas, but Sam had died in 1903. He had allowed his son Will's enthusiasms to push him into efforts that were physically too much for him. His wife wrote daughter Edna MacMillan in May, 1907, "he has aged so this winter. I think he will pick up now if he does not overdo."

Despite the stroke, however, he had retained some of the verve for business and his ebullient and affectionate personality that had endeared him to those around him and brought seemingly unshakable loyalties. Word portraits of him chronicle his "sympathetic and generous" nature, his gentleness and his courage. "Perhaps if anything, he had too much courage," said the 1945 Cargill history. Although W. W. had "a shrewd intelligence," he sometimes was overtrusting of his fellow man. Indeed, "one of his most serious business faults arose from the sympathetic nature of his character. It was nearly impossible for him to say no . . . he was forever getting into deals which his intelligence told him he had no business being in . . . being imposed upon by worthless hangers-on whom he simply did not have the heart to fire."[1]

This combination of virtues and faults made for a fine, patriarchal figure for both his sons and sons-in-law. But it also made for an uneasy business situation.

The Panic Spreads

By September 1907, John Sr.'s letters chronicled widespread business bankruptcies around him. Many were "weak concerns that are speculating and will fail," he wrote W. W., but even strong firms like the Cargill Elevator Company were faced with severe problems, particularly from lack of credit. Also, MacMillan found it difficult to slow down buying by his traders—even Lindahl, who understood matters the best, could not resist holding more barley: "at no time . . . have I felt as strong on good barley as I do today. . . . I don't think we want to worry, John."

John Sr.'s fears about the Panic were exacerbated when one of the great millers of Minneapolis, Pillsbury-Washburn Flour Milling Company, Limited (owned in part by one of the Washburn brothers and an intense rival of Washburn Crosby Company), had "found it necessary to the conservation of the interests of its creditors and shareholders, to place this property temporarily in the hands of the Court." In other words, Pillsbury had gone into receivership. John Sr. wrote one of his financiers in Boston, "the general gossip is that there have been severe losses due to speculation, and . . . a good many rumors that there has been considerable graft going on among the employees . . . also general incompetency in the management . . . various leading employees holding their positions entirely from influence rather than merit." The owners had not been dishonest but too trusting. John Sr.'s comments were surprising, not in keeping with his usual cautiousness, although he was essentially accurate in his observations.[2]

The advent of the Panic had made John Sr. very uneasy about all expenses. Line employee wages at the terminals tended to fluctuate according to supply and demand. In Duluth, in September 1907, the employees of Peavey at their Belt Line Elevator had demanded 25 cents an hour; both

Peavey and Cargill were paying 22½ cents an hour at that time. MacMillan wrote back, "There is no use of having any trouble with our men at this time of the year and if you have to pay them 25 cents an hour to meet what the others are paying you better do it and keep things working smoothly. Our entire profits will have to be made in the next two or three months, so we cannot afford to get tied up now. Then, after the first of January, if conditions are different, we can reduce wages." By early December, Lindahl had suggested that the wages might be cut back to 22½ cents; now John Sr. wrote back, "It seems to me that is still too high and you should not pay over 20 cents per hour. In fact, I think you could get all the men you want for 7½ cents for the balance of the crop year."[3]

Fall was always a critical season, with enormous amounts of grain coming forward that had to be paid for by the grain company. Short-term credit and/or working capital were essential to merchandising grain. John Sr. was shocked in the fall of 1907 to be turned down by several credit sources in Minneapolis, and he wrote W. W. Cargill, worriedly, as to whether the latter could get money back at La Crosse. "No problem," wrote back Cargill, who then described a folksy walk downtown in La Crosse, stopping at the National Bank, and then "continued my walk down to the Batavian National Bank" and then "went along to The State Bank." In all cases, Cargill got substantial funds—to his manifest personal satisfaction and emblematic of his strong public reputation at that time. Cargill's euphoria about his ability to borrow money from his local friends evaporated two weeks later, when he reported to John Sr. that the Batavian National Bank had called to cancel the agreement it had made.

Still, W. W.'s rooted optimism and his isolation in a small town often made him gloss over threatening situations. On September 18, 1907, he wrote John Sr. about operational and financial storm signals at Pine Bluff: "I will be very careful and not hurry anything down there if things don't get too hot for me . . . when they get too hot . . . I will clean up the whole business, but I don't think it will come to that."

Nationally, the situation worsened with the shock of the suspension at Knickerbocker Trust. W. W., suddenly aware, wrote John Sr. the next day, "This scare in New York may shut things up tighter than a clam." At this point, the grain traders of Duluth took an unprecedented step that seems unimaginable in light of today's stringent antitrust climate. They decided, in concert, to buy no grain from the farmers until the credit stringency slacked off. John Sr. wrote W. W. that day, "The salvation of the country depends on the movement of its crop and it seems a pity the movement should be interfered with, but at present it would seem . . . the farmers were better able to carry the load than anyone else . . . it is a necessity to force them to hold the grain until conditions become more settled." A farmer short of cash might have considered this a self-serving statement.[4]

John H. MacMillan, c. 1905–1910.

Notably, although John Sr. remained cautious about the business situation, he still was open-minded about W. W.'s interest in new opportunities. He wrote W. W. on October 9, 1907, a few days before the Knickerbocker Trust suspension, when W. W. was thinking of investing in a copper mine, "there's no question in the world but what good copper mines have been the most profitable undertakings of recent times . . . there is a possibility you might lose everything you put into it, but I am not sure but what it is worthwhile to send someone down there and look into it."[5]

The combination of W. W.'s stroke and the aggressive involvement of son Will in the business seemed to bring an increasingly hands-off approach by W. W. to his managers, a dangerous policy in a crisis such as this panic. The manager at the Green Bay terminal, Walter Gueinzius, continued to buy, in the process using up cash and credit resources at that location. John Sr. was aghast and penned a worried letter to W. W.: "There is no use whatever in taking any such arbitrary stand as Walter seems to have taken. I do not care what security a man has in these days, he cannot borrow money; no matter what arrangements he has made at the banks they would not carry them out." To MacMillan this independent action seemed blatantly excessive, misplaced decentralization—his already-strong beliefs in holding authority in his own hands were definitely reinforced during the Panic.

The Green Bay office had appeared often in the past to be trading without reference to Minneapolis, and John Sr. wrote Gueinzius in late 1906, "Now it seems to me it would be a pretty good plan for us to work very closely with you, and through the same brokers, so we will not be making competition between ourselves." Gueinzius, in turn, complained that W. W. and Will in La Crosse had countermanded some of his hedging decisions and vowed that "the past two years have been handled entirely against my better judgement." W. W. had his own complaints, accusing Dudley M. Irwin, the Buffalo agent handling both Cargill–Minneapolis and Cargill–La Crosse barley of "paying you [Minneapolis] too fast" and that "La Crosse was taking the 'hind teat.' " So W. W. seemed unsure of how much autonomy to give field offices.

This no-man's-land of organizational confusion was further illustrated by another W. W. Cargill letter plaintively complaining to John Sr. that several of his own country elevator buyers (especially those at Wentworth and Stewartsville) were continuing to buy and, when they did, giving price breaks to the farmers. Having such a limited control system, Cargill envisioned the farmers and agents bleeding him with no way for him to know what was happening: "I think nearly every town is practicing the scheme of holding stuff back and if the market goes up the stuff is someone else's and if it goes down, it is ours . . . whether it is our Agents that are giving it to the farmers or have a farmer partner in the deal, I don't know how it

Grain elevators (Cargill's and two others) destroyed by fire, Flandreau, South Dakota, September 3, 1908 (courtesy *Flandreau* [South Dakota] *Enterprise*; E. O. Hover, photographer; photo courtesy of Greg's Photo Emporium, Flandreau, South Dakota).

is worked, . . . places where our houses were plump full so we could not take in a bushel, we had $6,000 drafts come in this morning." MacMillan wrote right back about the way *he* did it, describing his men's "absolute instructions" about issuing specific storage tickets every time they took in grain, and his other control devices, based on the detailed records that W. W. found so onerous. "We have only one man on our whole system," John Sr. bragged, "that we found had anything constructed in the manner you speak of . . ."[6]

W. W. had long caused concern about his own record-keeping system, such as it was. About this time, both John Sr. and J. B. Taylor were trying to pin down the details of one of W. W.'s timberland purchases in Canada, and Taylor wrote MacMillan, in frustration, "I have never had a list from this Macfarlane on any of his purchases up there and I am as much at sea as you are about the holdings we have. I have asked Mr. Cargill to get these records from him and he tells me that this man is to look after the thing and we need not bother our heads about it, but . . . if I am going to keep the records down here I would like to know something about our holdings." With this same vagueness, W. W. wrote MacMillan about another of his investments, "I don't know anything about the stock or Company, only that I own about $100,000 worth of it, as I remember." In the instance where the Cargill seed group had asked for a name change to "something like North Western Seed Company," W. W.'s answer was a typical one: "Don't allow too much bureaucracy . . . you need not have a corporation . . . just have the name and change the heading and sign on the building . . . and you have got it and I guess it will be just as well to sell that way."[7]

Trouble in Lumber

The Panic of 1907 deeply affected the lumber business, and Sawyer & Austin began to falter. The operation in Pine Bluff had been difficult to control since John Sr. had left in 1903. Both W. W. and Will Cargill in La Crosse and John Sr. in Minneapolis were trying to oversee it in a loose amalgam of undefined authority and responsibility. Worse, all three were managing it from their own separate offices. Will Cargill was handling most of the correspondence although he already was preoccupied with Montana, where he was in the first stages of a massive land and water development project at Valier, an effort that would become much more extensive in later months. In early 1906 W. W. had purchased a large tract of timberland in the state of Chihuahua in Mexico, some 542,000 acres, but plans to exploit this were still incomplete.

Just as the national business situation began to look truly ominous in early September 1907, an internal problem surfaced at Sawyer & Austin's St. Louis processing and selling unit, the Banner Lumber Company. D. A. Kendall, the Sawyer & Austin manager, had four of his sons working in the organization. One of them, stationed at Banner, had allowed the yard foremen there to become slipshod in their accounting for cash taken from customers. John Sr. knew the Kendalls and the foremen well from his earlier on-site management at Sawyer & Austin. The son, realizing that he was in trouble, queried MacMillan about accepting an outside job offer that had just been tendered him. MacMillan replied, "You had better not refuse any good chance to get a good position. . . . There is no question in the world but what, if this was anybody else than you, we would have discharged them—not that there was any proven dishonesty, but there is proven carelessness, and in order to keep up the efficiency of our employees it is necessary to make an example of any such case as yours."

John Sr. also asked the son for a full audit because "the cash at St. Louis has been mixed up with the working fund and your personal account." A consultant from Cargill's bonding company, a skilled accountant and "public auditor," H. R. Hayden, now was hired by MacMillan, to be assigned to Banner. W. W. Cargill gave lukewarm acquiescence, but wrote MacMillan, "I told Hayden I wanted some different accounting but I did not want too much red tape, that things had to be practical rather than system . . . the verification of the accounts I told him to drop and call it collecting, and to get around and collect the accounts and not have a whole lot of red tape about verification and two or three bookkeepers and collectors."[8]

Tribulations of an Outside Auditor

With Hayden now ready to leave for the Banner operations in St. Louis, the delicate question arose of how to explain his mission to that office, especially to George Funck, who was the manager there. John Sr. pressed W. W. Cargill to state bluntly that the accountant was "Acting for the President." This bothered Cargill, and he wrote back, "I have cut out the title of 'Acting for the President' as this is a little too high sounding for those lad[d]y bucks down there in the country."

On the surface, W. W. expressed commitment to Hayden's project and, in a manner not his usual style, wrote Funck, "This [accounting] has never been done right and now I am going to try and get it right if I can and I have been talking with Mr. Hayden about going down there and putting in a perfect system both for the St. Louis yard and the outside yards so that the accounting end will be done correctly."

Yet on that very day he also wrote John Sr. complaining that Hayden was being *too* perfect. Hayden had been looking at W. W.'s La Crosse books to assess how Sawyer & Austin fit in and apparently had concluded that W. W. was inflating the figures. W. W. bristled: "He shows that he cuts our surplus from $2,000,000 to less than $1,000,000 and that the profit & loss last year was $16,000. Now the details I have not gone through, but I do not like this way of doing. Our surplus is $2,000,000 and I don't think we have to wait until the property is exhausted to show what profit we have got. . . . I prefer our way to this." Once again, with his need to have his optimism reinforced, W. W. could not resist overstating his performance.[9]

The mountain of uncollected bills at St. Louis was the major problem. It was not just that the stock records themselves were poor; there was the additional complication of many "deadbeats" (using W. W.'s terminology). Funck seemed incapable of accurately verifying those behind, and was unwilling to press anyone.

John Sr., always a stickler for promptness, became very exercised when Funck's record keeping fell behind. The Panic was at its height, and Cargill Elevator Co. was finding new credit unobtainable, yet Banner Lumber was allowing almost unlimited credit. He chided the office manager: "It makes more work to allow things to get behind than it does to keep them up . . . push the office work and keep it up to date . . . it is impossible for anybody to keep up with the business properly if the information is not at hand when it is needed."

Funck was not responsible directly to John Sr. but to W. W. Cargill.

Funck's continued recalcitrance exasperated MacMillan no end. John Sr. no longer had the authority but still felt the responsibility keenly. He finally wrote a resolute letter to W. W. Cargill that the latter should tell Funck that "this is done for your protection and that you absolutely insist that it must be carried out." In another letter John Sr. fell back on his own experience in the lumbering business: "You can see it is the same old excuse from the woods. First it is one thing and then it is another, but always, the woods seem to be lame."[10]

John Sr. believed that "both Mr. Funck and Mr. Kendall are the old type of businessmen, and anything in the way of modern accounting is to them that much useless expense and trouble."[11] Finally, MacMillan sat down and penned a five-page letter to W. W., developing in the process a remarkably articulate concept of modern accounting (the state of the art in managerial accounting was somewhat primitive at that time):

In reference to the verification of the accounts . . . we can call it what we please, but until we know whether or not the accounts are owing us, we cannot get the Bond Company to bond the men, and that is all a verification means. . . . I do not see how you can call it red tape to get needed information . . .

Under the old system, we have never been able to locate where these differences come in. One yard would be a large amount over, and another a large amount short, and you could not tell whether the man short was stealing from you or whether it was due to an error in reporting, or in the accounting end of it.

John Sr. then described to W. W. his personal beliefs about organization structure, beyond simple record keeping and accounting to the essence of decision making. He was solidly for centralization under a powerful chief executive officer:

There are only two ways I know of, of doing business; one is to trust your men and let them run everything as they please and turn you out what results they please, and the other is to put in an accounting system that keeps you informed as to what is going on everywhere. The latter system is certainly the up to date way of doing, and the only way I can keep track of things. We got a pretty good taste of what it amounts to, to let things drift when we had Mink there, and we also had a taste of it in the Kirkwood yard. The great trouble has been there always—that they do not enter into the spirit of what modern accounting means.[12]

W. W. continued to apologize about his own employees, although he did admit, in responding to MacMillan, "I think we have never had a book-keeper in that office that amounted to a roll of pins. . . . Mr. Spencer, while he may be a good book-keeper is so slow that the ink will stop running on his pen and the boys are figuring out that he is a doper or dreamer as he stands and looks at a piece of paper for 5, 10 or 15 minutes at a time—and they say at Pine Bluff as long as an hour—so there is something wrong with him."[13]

Hayden, the auditor, earnestly moved ahead with his assignment. First, he hired a team of bookkeepers and bill collectors. "I tell the applicants that we required willing workers and only those who could accomplish a good day's work as it was a case of 'the survival of the fittest.' This expression seemed to please Mr. Cargill when I told him of these plans." His instructions to the collectors were equally candid: "If a customer promises to pay on a certain date, be sure to be 'Johnnie on the Spot' when the promise is due. Do not accept any indefinite promises, but make the debtor state when he will pay. . . . Never for a moment forget that your position is one of a hustling nature. . . . Results are what we want, and we shall expect you to get them."

The St. Louis personnel bucked the accountant at every turn. They liked their system and wanted to keep it and felt they could get by with it under easygoing W. W. In fact, Funck objected strongly to having Hayden around at all. He wrote John Sr. in November, 1907, "As a letter-writer he [Hayden] has not been successful in getting money or even replies to his series of lackluster demands. . . . He at once put an extra man on the Stock System and to this day they are not complete. . . . The fact is, our office is systematized to death. . . . Hayden has a mania for employing men and to everyone who comes he tells his life history from the cradle to the present, gives the Banner's complete history and then when he gets through it's up to Spencer [the Banner bookkeeper] to repeat." But Spencer was considered too slow by Kendall, the Sawyer & Austin manager: "a man has to be up and dressed [to] keep everything up to date."[14]

At every turn, Hayden met suspicion. He wrote John Sr. that even the office stenographer "is not to be trusted . . . he holds too many conversations with Mr. Funck in an undertone voice." Hayden was reduced to typing his own letters. Finally, his digging turned up a startling disclosure—that one of Funck's sons was buying lumber from Banner at cost, then undercutting Banner by selling to Banner's own customers at preferential prices.[15]

Meanwhile, the virulence of the Panic in the Midwest worsened daily. In early January 1908, the National Bank of Commerce in St. Louis, in a search for liquidity typical of difficult times, insisted that Banner immediately pay up on a $50,000 note (Banner owed it a total of $100,000). Hayden pleaded the distress of the panic and told John Sr. that he had "explained to him [the bank officer] our grain business in the North, and the $1,000,000 worth of grain in Buffalo sold and that the buyers could not take it." The adamant banker finally agreed to give Hayden a few more days. Subsequently, collections from customers allowed a partial payment, temporarily satisfying the banker.

The final straw was the fire in the same month, January 1908. The Maplewood, Missouri, yard of Banner was virtually destroyed—buildings, stacked lumber, even six mules, a home and two automobiles. Funck assured W. W. that insurance would cover almost everything, estimating only a small out-of-pocket loss: "It may be one, two and possibly three thousand . . . it will not exceed $3,000." A few days later, Hayden wrote again, with the final figure—the loss was going to be $15,100. John Sr. sent an exasperated letter back to W. W.: "This seems to be about in line with the rest of the management there at St. Louis."[16]

John Sr. then gave up on Funck and, with W. W.'s acquiescence, brought a man in over him. Hayden had gone on to his next "public auditor" assignment at another company. MacMillan chose a man from Liberty Lumber Company, R. M. Johnston. In characteristic style, John Sr. wrote a long, diplomatic letter to Funck:

We have decided to put Mr. R. M. Johnston, from this office, in St. Louis, in immediate charge of the business, with title of 'vice-president' and 'manager.' We will continue your title of 'treasurer' and make you 'assistant manager,' . . . of course, entirely under Mr. Johnston's instructions, as he will be absolutely in charge of everything. I feel very certain that you will show to him the same loyalty that you have always shown, and that together, you can make a great success of the business, as I feel sure he is strong in the points that you are weak, and with your general knowledge of the business, that together, you can make a great success of it.[17]

Given Funck's performance, this was a generous offer. Funck resigned in April.

Will's Intervention

After W. W.'s stroke in 1904, Will Cargill had assumed a central role in La Crosse in the grain operations, in Sawyer & Austin and in the La Crosse & Southeastern railroad. W. W. wanted his son to succeed to management, yet he seemed constitutionally unable to make Will start at the bottom and work his way up (nor did Will's mother want him to, either). W. W. saw Will as being his kind of person—charging ahead in new, exciting endeavors—and Will had developed a forceful personality as a result. Now this headstrong behavior was directed at John Sr. In March 1908, Will wrote John Sr. of his displeasure with Kendall, the Sawyer & Austin manager. There was none of John Sr.'s diplomacy in Will's approach; having just received a Kendall letter, Will railed to MacMillan, "I do not like the tone of it . . . upon a second reading; maybe I was wrong in forming my first opinion, but this petty work of jacking a good man up everytime you think he gets wrong or discharges the wrong man is not right and we cannot stand for it." A gratuitous aside in the same letter also criticized MacMillan: "Information came to me today that the maltsters and brewers are out after the Cargill interests in the barley business on account of your refusing to send out circulars. . . . Now if the writer understands what the circular proposition was it would not be any detriment to send it out. May be I don't know the whole of it and I wish you would let me know what stands you have taken on the matter and why there should be any such talk as the above."[18]

This query related to brewing industry efforts to pressure the grain trade into joining in opposition to some proposed prohibition legislation. John Sr. wrote back, "I simply took the stand that we were not going to take part in any political matter . . . that we would handle no literature for either side. If the brewers are fools enough to take up this kind of stand, they will bring prohibition to a dead certainty, in very short order." The brewers' trade association was singularly blatant with arm-twisting. The president wrote MacMillan:

. . . your Minneapolis barley people have been put down as exceptionally firm . . . to lean more toward the Anti-Saloon League than toward our industry . . . you Minneapolis people are understood as having refused to do anything. . . . This is a serious fight. We have to do with a thoroughly organized enemy supplied with barrels of money to fight us all over the country. They are working in Minneapolis right now, but not with a Brass Band, so maybe that is why you don't realize it. That crowd works a gum-shoe campaign. . . . We can knock them out on any phase of the issue, whether it be the economic, moral, physiological, religious, or any other.

As might be expected, the Cargill barley people, especially Prime and Dudley Irwin, Cargill's Buffalo agent, sided with their prized customers, but MacMillan could not be budged.[19]

On the Kendall matter, John Sr. continued to push Will Cargill to "get down there and have a good talk with the whole crowd." Will finally did go down to Arkansas but turned around and came right back. He wrote MacMillan, "I returned yesterday after staying at Pine Bluff as long as I could with the feeling that existed without losing temper, judgment and everything else, and in any event it was raining and very disagreeable weather." In this whirlwind visit, Will made a number of personnel changes, but no headway apparently had been made on the problems themselves. John Sr. once again exhorted Will to go back to Pine Bluff: "Not having this practical knowledge yourself, unless you were willing to stay right there and learn it thoroughly, I do not believe you can work it out."

At this point, Kendall gave up his effort to run the organization and offered to sell his own stock in Sawyer & Austin to W. W. Cargill. W. W. wrote John Sr. about the conversation: "Among the things he said in his letter was how much I would give him for his stock. I forgot to answer it yesterday but if I had I would have told him that I did not know what it was worth. You sort of figure it out and make calculations so when he comes up we can talk to him about it." MacMillan worked out the price and then made a suggestion to W. W. that certainly was a progressive view of ownership: "It might not be a bad plan if some of your better men down at Pine Bluff had some [stock] distributed among them at whatever price you paid for it. In this way it would not load you up in any way, excepting, perhaps with a guarantee. . . . I believe myself that it will be much better to have this stock in the hands of those who are friendly rather than one who might possibly become hostile." Later that summer, Kendall sold his stock back, but W. W. did nothing about selling stock to the employees.[20]

John Sr. was assiduous in tightening up on excess labor. The Sawyer & Austin and Banner Lumber companies were particularly ripe for cutbacks with the Panic-forced downturn in business there. MacMillan wrote Johnston, the new Banner manager, in March 1908: "The trouble is when there is a rush of business, they take on extra men but do not cut them off the moment they are not needed. In a large city like St. Louis, there should be no difficulty getting labor, and there is no need of carrying a lot of extra men that are not needed. . . . I think you had better continue to drop men."[21]

Each incident at Pine Bluff and St. Louis pointedly reiterated the differences in management style between W. W. Cargill and John Sr. Underlying these were two quite different philosophies. In one, management was so decentralized as almost to lack any accountability, while in the other it was highly centralized. It is simplistic, however, to stereotype these differences, for there were evident leadership qualities in W. W. Cargill that earned him great loyalty from his people. On the other hand, John Sr. was no autocratic martinet issuing orders from the top but rather a man of strong opinions and beliefs, willing to share them with his colleagues and ready to give some of his people wide latitude in effecting plans. He trusted Lindahl and now trusted Johnston.

Even at the height of the 1907 panic, John Sr. sustained his wide network of personal relationships with employees and friends, reaching out to them with affable, lengthy personal communications. He wrote half a dozen letters in this two-month period of high tension to a retired Pine Bluff employee who had moved to Michigan to farm. Just days after the Knickerbocker crash, for example, MacMillan thanked the former employee for a shipment of apples. "I want to acknowledge receipt of those apples which you sent," he started, "and tell you how very much we appreciate them. They are delicious and seem especially good coming, as they do, from your orchard." MacMillan continued for three paragraphs more, giving the retiree the latest news from the Pine Bluff operation.[22]

Barley for Malting or Feed?

The high drama of the 1907 panic faded more quickly than had earlier panics. But the better business climate still left John Sr. with some per-

A. M. Prime.   *F. E. Lindahl.*

plexing issues. First, the 1908–1910 period brought problems in barley—both tensions in trading and personal pressures on Prime. The spillover from the 1907 panic had made John Sr. ever more cautious. Prime, on the other hand, exhibited once again his dominant charge-ahead trading philosophy. As the crop year of 1908 headed into September, Prime was long in barley, in anticipation of substantial purchases by "those eastern Dutchmen," his favorite term for the brewing and distilling industry executives, most of whom were of German extraction.[23]

MacMillan began to exhort Prime to stop buying and to push the selling: "It seems to me . . . that if you cannot make sales to go East it is much better to go very slow while I am away. We do not want to be put in a position of 'holding the bag' for the Eastern Maltster." John Sr. urged a personal trip by Prime to Buffalo, but the latter responded the next day, "I do not believe a trip down there will amount to anything . . . they are simply buying from hand to mouth . . . no amount of talk or persuasion can make them buy heavily until the brewer begins to buy malt heavily."[24] Under John Sr.'s urging, Prime sold 70,000 bushels, with almost no profit; Prime carped, "There is nothing in it at this price, simply taking a new dollar for an old one, that's all, which is mighty poor business." MacMillan wrote back immediately, "The market continues so very sick that I think, by all means, you do not want to lose any chances to sell at figures that will bring you out even." He wrote Lindahl that same day, "I do not feel bullish on anything in the whole list, as long as arrivals at the terminal are so heavy, and as you know, it takes some time to clean up the grain that is in transit and that has accumulated in country houses."[25]

The company's agent in Buffalo, Dudley Irwin, was a wholesale and retail grain broker serving a number of clients. He was *not* a Cargill employee. The correspondence concerning this relationship between Irwin and the Cargill men (several, in several different locations) illustrates the substantial problems in not having one's own office in an important field location, particularly, in this case, far to the east in Buffalo, where travel to and from Minneapolis for on-the-scene follow-up was considerably more difficult.

John Sr. and Lindahl began to consider the purchase of a terminal elevator in Buffalo, which would have led to a trading office in that important city. In early 1909 a terminal building came available, but MacMillan turned it down because it was not fireproof.[26] So, having made the decision to remain with Irwin, MacMillan, Lindahl and Prime found themselves with serious misgivings about Irwin's loyalty. They were irritated by the low prices Prime was receiving for Cargill barley orders and fearful that Irwin was giving preferential bids to other customers. Prime complained, "Irwin does not seem to be able to do anything for us and he is constantly advising us to accept bids that would show a loss." From previous experiences, John Sr. had acquired a lasting mistrust of the Armour Grain Co. and its flamboyant head, Philip Armour. Irwin was not only handling Armour grain, which he was entitled to do, but he was also reported to be giving the old Nemesis all the best deals.[27]

Prime continued to be antagonistic toward Irwin about Cargill being given off-the-market bids; he superstitiously commented to John Sr., "there's a Hoodoo somewhere, and I guess it's this new office" (Duluth had just refurbished its quarters).[28] Irwin, however, had a telling riposte each time for Cargill. It concerned one of the most critical judgments in the grain trade, grain quality. Cargill barley was the culprit.

As Cargill's barley went forward to the Buffalo markets, Irwin said he had difficulty in selling it, writing Prime, "We are losing our trade every day just as I told you we would, and for the simple reason that we are shipping dirty barley. . . . It is all right to say you will ship your barley in the dirt and sell it for feed . . . that is your own business, but if you are going to sell to maltsters you have got to ship them barley as clean as our competitors will furnish them, or fall down." Irwin had just received a sharp letter from Prime about his alleged lethargy in selling, and immediately wrote Prime in return, "It certainly makes me hot under the collar after writing you as I have of the situation here and the condition of our barley as compared with others."[29]

John Sr.'s solution was to immediately admonish Prime to "put in a good deal of your time down to the elevators. . . . You used to do this and we did not get this kind of complaint. Your own man down there probably is careless and easy, and unless you get down there every day, yourself, to keep a check on things, they are undoubtedly going to continue this. I wish you would make it a point to go to the elevator every afternoon from now on . . . there is no harm in having the barley cleaned hard."

The problem was deeper than just the cleaning; it was a lack of ability to do needling. In malting, barley must germinate. Even a small percentage of skinned or broken kernels make the process unfit. Further, the maltsters were quite selective about the size of the kernels, large, fat kernels being much preferred. The more unsatisfactory long, narrow kernels, called "needles," could be separated from the fatter kernels by a device appropriately called a needling machine. Cargill did not have this machine.

The machines represented a substantial capital expenditure. John Sr., always cautious about spending money on equipment or buildings, seemed reluctant to buy them. Cargill's barley cleaning was being done in part by others on a contract basis, and MacMillan told Prime, "There is no one that can look after the cleaning of it so well as you can, yourself . . . if you go down to the Consolidated and watch their cleaning, and talk with them, and let them know just what you expect, you will be able to get better results than you will merely depending upon your man."

Prime wanted no part of such tepid solutions. He began to push W. W. to take a bolder step:

Now the Nye-Jenks people [a large Baltimore grain trading firm] have the Omaha elevator here . . . chuck full of machinery including a lot of needle machines. . . . Now, you know, it takes years to build up a business and it only takes a short time to tear it down through poor work. . . . The only solution to this barley problem is that next year we get in shape to handle this barley properly. If you cannot buy an elevator, build a small one, an up-to-date barley elevator. If you do this, we can win back all the trade that we have lost East through poor work in cleaning our barley at this end.[30]

The times seemed too hazardous to John Sr. for any such move, but later in the month, MacMillan finally agreed to the purchase of "two or three" needling machines, and they were in place by the following crop season. But by that time the price differential between needled and unneedled barley had closed, and to MacMillan's dismay, it did not even pay to use the needling machines.[31]

Prime wanted the last word on the matter and wrote MacMillan a month later about a check that he himself had made at Cargill's Superior terminal a few days earlier: "I had Louis make an estimate of the barley left in the house so as to see if he had been cleaning our barley as we have ordered . . . at the present time he only has four cars of all kinds of screenings on hand, so I have just had to add 40,000 bushels to our long barley which we supposed was in screenings in the elevator. Now you can readily see that this accounts for all our trouble East earlier. It simply illustrates that 'Murder will out' sooner or later." In other words, Prime was not to blame![32]

With Irwin's continuing criticism of Minneapolis grain, Prime then advocated a clean break from Irwin: "It is very noticeable that Gibbs' bids are anywhere from 1/2 to one cent above Irwin's all the time now. This being the case, I am especially anxious to give Gibbs some business." He added further venom in a second letter: "Irwin is submitting to us the same prices that he was two or three weeks ago when barley was 4 to 5 cents lower than at present time, and he seems to think it strange that we cannot sell so that he can please his maltster friends. . . . I never was so sick of anything in my life." A few weeks later, Prime reported that his pressures on Irwin seemed to have brought him around: "Just had a wire from Irwin to the effect that he was working on our different grades. . . . I think the fact that Gibbs is working on our barley is having a pressing effect on Irwin. I know that Irwin don't like it a little bit that Gibbs is working on our barley."[33]

Others in Cargill also had become disenchanted with Irwin. Walter Gueinzius, the Green Bay manager, wrote an opinionated letter to W. W. Cargill about the loss of business to the Nye-Jenks organization: "Now excuse me for being plain, but your house has been asleep down there for six months . . . somebody has not been working for you. . . . I have been telling you for the past two years . . . that I do not think Irwin is up to snuff or works to get the business. . . . Irwin is not trying to get the outside price for Western grain and his excuses sometimes are mighty poor." Even W. W. himself, unwilling as he so often was to make any personnel changes, seemed prepared to sack Irwin.

Despite all these polemics, John Sr., unlike Prime and the others, was able to be more analytical about the barley situation in Buffalo, to put personalities aside and also be more honest about Cargill Elevator Company's own shortcomings. He wrote W. W. Cargill, in December 1908, "While Nye-Jenks have sold 1,000,000 bushels in Buffalo, we have sold 2,000,000 bushels so that while they have cut into our trade to that extent, yet I do not feel Irwin is to blame as they were to furnish a better cleaned barley than we could."[34]

The difference in approach to Irwin, both in substance and style, between John Sr. and Prime remained striking throughout. An issue of communication will illustrate this. Prime, feeling that he was not getting enough information from Irwin, wrote an angry letter:

Lately we have only been getting letters from you about every other day, and then all that these letters contain is simply confirmation of sales. Now, this is not satisfactory. We have got to be kept well posted on what is going on down there at that end. You used to do this and there is no reason why you should not continue to do so. . . . Just look at the difference between the letters we have been writing you on the crop up to date, and the letters we have been receiving from you. . . . Just take it home to yourself, for there is no use talking, we have got to be kept well informed at all times from the Buffalo end.

A few days later John Sr. wrote Irwin on the same subject in a different vein, "There is no reason in the world why yourself and myself should not work together and get along splendidly the same as we have in past years. However, you must realize that we have got to be kept well informed."

Guarding the Integrity of the Elevator Company

By the fall of 1908, the drain on La Crosse resources from W. W. Cargill's own projects, especially the La Crosse & Southeastern railroad, the Mexican and British Columbia timberlands and the land development project at Valier, Montana, was beginning to surface. John Sr. received a discouraging letter from J. B. Taylor in September about the level of bills payable, at that time $1.6 million. MacMillan earlier had warned W. W. that his own Minneapolis credit needs were going to be substantial in the fall of 1908 and that "I feel a little bit anxious to extend our financial arrangements in the East." W. W. responded with what he believed would be a reassuring message: "Received your letter this morning in regard to credit, etc., which of course I knew and would like to have a reserve on hand and if the Conrad Investment Co. [the Valier, Montana project being pushed by Will] comes out half the way I think it will, we will have it, and if I could sell off the Railroad or the Mexican property, we would not have to question it. I am not going into anything new on any account." He ended in a now-typical W. W. way: "I intend to write more length about this but it is 5 o'clock and time to go home."

The results at Minneapolis for the crop year 1908–1909 were disappointing. The previous year's profit had been over $332,000; this figure dropped to $208,000. Even more unsettling, events at the W. W. Cargill enterprises threatened to encroach on the Cargill Elevator Company operations in ways that were threatening to John Sr. Pine Bluff lumber, for example, still begged for better management.[35]

While R. M. Johnston had proved to be a more able manager than George Funck, it had been exceedingly difficult to keep track of that isolated organization. W. W. Cargill and MacMillan had tried to muddle through, both managing the operation from La Crosse and Minneapolis. Will Cargill was living in Montana and devoting almost all of his time to that project, so W. W. then urged John Sr. to assume more responsibility: "You or I will have to take charge of the Pine Bluff business, and as I have done about my share of work, if you can, do not wait for my advice, but go ahead and manage it as though it was your own. Get what papers you want and go ahead with it."

Yet even this clear-cut assignment turned into equivocation, for W. W. seemed always ready to be further importuned by employees, customers and others. John Sr., as requested, did begin to take a more incisive role in Sawyer & Austin, at the same time assiduously trying to maintain separation between his position as head of Cargill Elevator Company and that of the lumber company. W. W. wanted MacMillan to ask for some credit for the lumber company from one of the elevator company bankers. But John Sr. demurred: "I do not believe the Security Bank would want to take Sawyer & Austin paper on the same basis as Cargill Elevator company. . . . They look on this entirely as outside paper and feel that as the money you are getting through brokers costs you 5%, they ought to get this on that basis." MacMillan subsequently arranged for some additional credit for the lumber company from a St. Paul bank. When J. B. Taylor, the head of the office in La Crosse, wanted to send Sawyer & Austin financial reports to the banks and other credit agencies used by the elevator company, MacMillan also objected.

Lunch break during harvest time, Lafayette, Minnesota, 1907 (Minnesota Historical Society).

A Cargill elevator for the Valier project.

More disturbing was the increasing tendency of W. W. to intrude into Cargill Elevator Company business itself, in an idiosyncratic way. He still was the majority stockholder, but it was not major policy decisions into which he injected himself—he seemed perfectly satisfied with John Sr.'s leadership. Rather it was insignificant, sometimes embarrassing examples of tinkering. More than once, W. W. would make commitments for the elevator company that John Sr. did not want to honor. For example, W. W. wrote, in June 1909, about a conversation he had had with a banker: "If you want to take advantage of cheap money now, they would allow you 3% interest on open a/c. You have a talk with them. I kind of half promised they could have Cargill Elevator Company a/c anyway."[36]

W. W. listened to his son-in-law most of the time. When W. W., pressed for cash, wanted to sell some of his Arkansas land, John Sr. pointed out that the bauxite deposits under the Sawyer & Austin lands were potentially lucrative, and he exhorted Cargill, "As I have told you a good many times I think it is one of the most valuable things you own, if not the most valuable . . . the only way to get the real value out of it is to . . . wait for a few years until the use of the aluminum becomes more general and the effects of this panic are worn away." Cargill took this to heart and wrote a friend a few days later, "I don't care much about selling it, and as Mr. MacMillan says, it is the best property I have got and it don't cost anything to carry, it's in the ground."[37]

On another occasion, a Chicago timber company wanted to visit Cargill's Mexican properties, and W. W. wrote John Sr., "I was very much taken with Mr. Lacey and he is a square fellow in every way." John Sr. investigated and reported back that the Lacey group was itself searching for timber tracts with merchantable trees: "I have not the slightest idea that examination of Jas. D. Lacey & Co. will amount to anything. They will be very glad to send their estimators in there and get posted so that when the conditions are right, they will have a chance at that property."[38] In other words, in trusting too much, one can give away the store!

Yet son Will seemed more and more to dazzle his father. Pushed by Will, W. W. had moved into large-scale promotions, most of them involving acquisition and development of land (including several new mines) and large-scale engineering projects. W. W. seemed to have returned to a "manifest destiny" view about some of these ventures. He wrote John Sr., in January 1908, about his Mexican timber property, "The plantation is a winner and in 5 years it will pay a dividend on an amount equal to 10 times its cost (or call it 5). Did not see the timber although had the time had we known it."[39]

By this time, John Sr. began to speak more frankly about his reservations concerning a number of W. W.'s expansive plans. The two men seemed to have that kind of a mutual regard and affection that allowed each to be plain-spoken with the other. For example: "I note what you say about that ranch proposition out near Denver. It does not seem to me you want to be doing anything of this sort. You have enough to look after without being worried with anything of that sort" (March 1909). On the copper mining property in which W. W. had wanted to invest in 1907 and John Sr. had warned "you might lose everything" (it had nevertheless been purchased), John Sr. had to write in May 1909, "I think you can look on the whole proposition, as far as you are concerned, as perfectly worthless and that the less thought and time put on this subject now, the better."[40]

The Valier Project

It was the Montana venture that occupied center stage in W. W.'s thinking—one that put John Sr. in an ambivalent position. Since early 1908, Will had been in Montana putting together the massive, sprawling project at Valier—by this point not only land development, including colonization to people the plains with new settlers, but also a collateral irrigation project (which included a very expensive dam construction) and an ambitious railroad link, called the Montana Western Railway Co., from Valier to the

The sale of the Montana land to W. S. Cargill (fourth from left) and W. W. Withee (third from left), 1908.

main railroad just under 20 miles away, part of this to be financed by the purchase and sale of cattle. This conglomeration of projects, each with different individual names, came to be known among the family as "the Valier project." Peter Valier, who had been the manager of W. W.'s La Crosse & Southeastern Railroad since 1905, had been sent to Montana from La Crosse early in the project to build the new railroad; the town that grew up around this project was named for him. Each of these endeavors had a complicated story—in several there were mistaken judgments, even chicanery by some of the individuals with whom the Cargills were dealing. The next chapter will describe these.

W. W. Cargill himself was fascinated by this operation from the start, but it was Will who was on the scene, acting rapidly in a whole set of his fast-changing activities and making substantial financial commitments. The conventional wisdom of earlier Cargill histories, namely, that W. W. was ill and "out of it," unknowing about Will's activities and uninvolved, is incorrect. W. W. and John Sr. exchanged many letters about this project, and both personally went out to Montana in this period. Yet it is also correct to say that Will was leading his father along, step by step. In the

Cargill archives is a draft in Will's handwriting defending the large expenditures, which was later sent out to bankers under his father's name.

Will Cargill wrote John Sr. again in November 1908 about the project, enthusiastically reporting on the dam-building operation and considerable cattle sales. He had contracted with a Boise, Idaho, company to be the sales agent for the lands and described the latter's methods: "They do not do so much advertizing [*sic*] but they put the men out in the field themselves and get to a farmer and get him to make an application for the lands and in this way they get right to the root of the matter without advertizing broadcast, but they keep posted from the different papers." Will assured MacMillan that he expected to sell 40,000 to 50,000 acres of land, and if they did, "we certainly will be in a clover field." If the irrigation project had to precede these sales, "it would take a little bit more money but not much."

By the time Will Cargill came back at Christmas 1908, he had succeeded

WHAT SOME FARMERS HAVE PRODUCED

John Leys produced 90 bushels of barley per acre.

Charley Sill produced 61 bushels of wheat per acre.

Frank Bazell produces every year, 5 tons of alfalfa per acre, in three cuttings.

Neil Vermullen, 100 bushels of oats per acre.

Manuel Schlepp produced beets that averaged better than 20 tons per acre.

Wm. and Theodore Anderson produced and sold 250 sacks of potatoes per acre.

REMEMBER

Good beet and potato farms are being sold for $65 per on terms that beat renting.

That the water supply is ample even in the driest years

That the soil is now producing; no long development p before you begin to get returns.

That you are locating in a partly developed country good roads, school and churches.

That the terms being given to experienced men make land cheaper than homesteading in a new country waiting for development.

THE GREAT NORTHERN RAILWAY CO.

Promotional literature for the Valier project, Pondera County, Montana, c. 1926.

in thoroughly infusing his father with the excitement of the project. John Sr., too, was positive, writing W. W., "I have great confidence in Montana after seeing it, and I believe that it is going to be the coming grain country. I am very much interested in that contract and I sincerely hope those people can do all they expect. It certainly will be great if they can, but I can hardly believe it possible such a large amount of land could be cleaned up so quickly." MacMillan's interest was in the end result—the agricultural produce that would be marketed. As he put it in another letter, "it would only be a few years before Montana and Western North Dakota will be shipping an enormous amount of grain."

In late January 1909, the Boston bankers who handled W. W. Cargill Company paper became uneasy that W. W. was getting involved in other large investments, and he attempted to allay their fears. W. W. wrote a friend in the Boston financial community, E. S. Bristol, who had talked with some of the bankers: "Note the Bankers' comment on being interested in irrigation and other large schemes, which is not true, as I have no schemes on hand more than usual, and I have all the property that I want, my ambition is satisfied and I shall probably not take on any schemes of any nature hereafter." W. W. then elaborated the Montana scheme in detail to Bristol with evident enthusiasm. He provided a glowing set of figures, ending his report with a prediction that "it is dead sure that the whole property will be paid for by sales of lands by June."[41]

A Crisis Builds

By spring 1909, things were in high gear in Montana. In April 1909, W. W. wrote his brother Jim, "if we sell 26,000 acres this Summer we pay for the whole shooting match and the rest is all velvet." Another letter a few weeks later to John Sr. gave more details: "the Montana proposition . . . is a great big proposition. They have 105 teams at work and about 250 men and Will is starting the Railroad . . . after the dam is complete the teams on the dam will go on to the ditching work and get that so they can furnish water in July to all the deeded land." W. W. had complained several times that spring and summer about minor illnesses but continued his high level of zeal, writing MacMillan in August, "I had a couple of men in here today from Conrad and they are all very enthusiastic and I am getting so full of enthusiasm that I am beginning to run over. With the likelihood of selling the bonds if we can sell the land, the thing is a bird." In August 1909, C. T. Jaffray, a well-known Minneapolis bank president, offered to help with the financing, putting a further stamp of approval on the endeavor.[42]

John Sr. had become persuaded of the logic of extending the elevator system of the Cargill Elevator Company westward, along the Great North-

Ellen (Ella) Cargill, wife of W. W. Cargill, 1880s.

ern Railroad right-of-way. There was a great potential for wheat in Montana, so MacMillan acted quickly, beginning construction of elevators at Valier and Williams. The state of Montana required that foreign corporations file Articles of Incorporation in every county, and inasmuch as this would cost Cargill Elevator about $385 for each county, MacMillan made the decision to incorporate a Montana entity—the Montana Central Elevator Company, as a wholly owned subsidiary. He wrote W. W. Cargill in early September 1909: "We will commence buying out there at once."[43]

On one of Will's lightning visits back to La Crosse, in late July 1909, he involved himself again in the La Crosse firm's decision making. Green Bay had continued to muddle along under Walter Gueinzius, and this so irritated Will that he summarily fired him, giving him little notice. Even W. W. was shocked, for not only was Walter a long-service employee but his father had been with W. W. in the early La Crosse days in the mid-1870s. W. W. wrote his son, "Walter will be over next week and I shall talk to him in a different spirit from which you wrote him. A man that has been with us 25 years is entitled to some consideration and there is [*sic*] two sides to every question." John Sr. was more diplomatic with Will: "I do not know anything about the situation and of course am not going to advise taking Walter on. His showing for several years past would justify making a change . . . although it would have been only courtesy on account of his long association with your Company to have given him more notice." John Sr. seemed to want to avoid annoying Will but also to distance Cargill Elevator Company from Green Bay, which was Will's and his father's management responsibility. Will's decision was not remanded, but Gueinzius subsequently was given a less demanding post in the organization, with the Reiss Coal Company, formerly the Cargill coal operation.

When all of the Montana activities were combined, there began to be intimations of deleterious effects on the financial statements of W. W. Cargill. Finally, concern began to surface in the correspondence about the extent of these liabilities and about whether there were adequate controls at the operations themselves. W. W. wrote one of his Chicago financial contacts in August, "it has taken considerable more money than we expected." The Boston bankers also seemed increasingly concerned; W. W.'s intermediary there wrote, "they asked me about the irrigation schemes and said you had gone into it largely and quite likely had or would contract large liabilities, etc. etc.". W. W. was not particularly well in this period; he had written John Sr. in late August, "We are figuring to go down to Madison Friday, play golf there Saturday. . . ." He was to be in Green Bay on the following Monday, but added a plea in his letter, "If I should be sick and could not attend to it you could do it, as Will is out of the question now as he has got more than he can do."[44]

A Problem with Prime

As if John Sr.'s worries about W. W.'s finances were not enough, new problems arose with Prime. The tensions around the Irwin relationship already had soured as the fall of 1909 began and were greatly exacerbated by the complications from a serious problem in Prime's personal life.

To start with, Irwin had begun to allege that the barley that arrived in Buffalo as a given grade was sometimes not what Prime had promised it to be. MacMillan again urged Prime to take the time personally to go to the terminal: "You will simply have to take the time to get over and know that they are in good shape." MacMillan continued, in a vein often repeated: "We want to do exactly as we agree. There is one thing we have always been proud of and that is—our word is as good as our bond."[45]

Prime immediately sent back a combative reply: "Now about going to the elevator to look after things—I have served my time in the elevator, put in years at it, and I can tell you frankly it is more than I want to do to

W. W. Cargill, c. 1905.

go out of a warm office building here and go over to an elevator and stay in the draft to load out barley. My health is worth more to me than my job is when it comes to this." Then Prime used a curious set of words, prophetic in light of the events of the next few weeks: "I know the game from A to Z—know all about it. If you would drink in all they say and all Irwin tells you you would be in a dippy house inside of three weeks."[46]

Prime's belligerency alarmed John Sr., and he wrote immediately, "We have got to treat our customers East, and Mr. Irwin also, courteously. It does not pay to get them riled up by sending disagreeable telegrams or writing disagreeable letters. We can always get the same results, hold them firmly, and do it pleasantly." Apparently MacMillan felt his own letter was a bit harsh, for he wrote again the same day, with praise for Prime: "I certainly feel that you made a very good deal in selling your screenings and needles. That was a fine deal and will show you a mighty good profit."

Prime remained unrepentant:

Now, I admit that diplomacy as a rule is a mighty good weapon, however, in this particular case I thought it was best to call a spade, a spade. . . . I don't care what kind of a man you have here at this point, he is practically helpless unless . . . you can work confidentially with him. . . . I would just as soon jump into the middle of Lake Superior and trust to my swimming to the shore, as I would of wiring him this, because he would go right to his maltster friends and tell them what Prime wanted to do, and advise them to hold off for a few days because barley would be lower. . . . A man at that end, selling our goods, has no right to have an opinion on the market.[47]

Just a few days after, John Sr. asked for and received physical samples of barley being shipped and found that there indeed *was* a quality difference from that stated to Irwin. MacMillan now asked Prime to send a larger sample of a shipment, called "X," and continued, "You will notice I have written Irwin to send me a sample of your X that he is selling and I want to do this so as to compare the two samples."[48]

Two days later, John Sr. received the overnight position report from Duluth and was surprised to see that Prime was again buying. He immediately wrote Lindahl, "I have written Prime a good, stiff letter about selling barley. We have either got to sell barley or quit buying . . . wish you would talk this matter over with Prime."

To complicate the situation, by mid-1909 the tension between Prime and Lindahl had intensified. John Sr. wrote W. W., "Prime is here. I wrote for him to come down just as soon as I got back. There has been some friction up there but I guess everything is straightened out. I have had a good, straight talk with him."[49]

It was just at this point, with matters quite up in the air in terms of the long barley position, the relationships in Buffalo on the selling side, and the animosities in Duluth, that John Sr. received word from Lindahl of Prime's personal incapacity. In those days just after the turn of the century the pace of the trading pits was often ferocious, rather more primitive than today's markets, and this subjected its participants to continuing high tension. A pattern had developed among the traders, especially among barley traders, of substantial business drinking. There had been intimations earlier in the year that Prime had allowed this to interfere with his work; now Lindahl reported that Prime had called in that "he had fallen from grace and was very sorry and wanted me to stay by him. He was in bad shape, I could tell from his talk."

Lindahl attributed Prime's drinking to job pressures; his letter to

MacMillan was rather unsympathetic: "it shows the weakness of the man that can't withhold in the middle of the season unless getting drunk . . . he has lost the confidence of his trade and I presume of his customers at Duluth." Two days later, Prime suddenly resigned.

This put the issue directly to John Sr., and his response was quite supportive but decisive in its action. He wrote Prime, "I was informed by Mr. Lindahl . . . that you tendered your resignation. Under the circumstances, there is nothing else to do but accept it." In this letter, he urged Prime to come to Minneapolis to talk the issue through with him. On the same day, he wrote Lindahl, "It seems too bad to let a man as valuable as he has been go completely to the dogs, and if there is anything we can do to save him, I want to do it. Of course we cannot let things go, though, the way they have been lately." At this point, MacMillan felt it wise to inform W. W. and wrote the same day, "I am sending you a copy of a letter which I've written Prime. This puts the matter in such shape that if he wants to get back, he has got to come down here and make some kind of arrangements. . . . If he will take the Keeley cure and give us his word of honor that he will not touch liquor, I would like to give him one more chance." W. W. immediately replied, "It is all right and the proper thing to do and the only thing to do."[50]

Fortunately, Prime accepted the invitation. John Sr. encouraged Prime to seek professional help, and Prime agreed. MacMillan made it clear, however, that this was the "one chance." Within a few days Prime was back on the job. MacMillan wrote W. W., "Prime came down last Saturday and I had a long talk with him and told him we absolutely have nothing whatever to do with him further unless he took some cure . . . that we could not trust him and he could not trust himself, and that we could not be worried again like we have been twice within the last six months. . . . He realized it was imperative he do something, both on his own account, our account and his family's account . . . he, of course, realized this is absolutely his last chance." Lindahl agreed with all of this but wanted to take the occasion to tighten a number of Duluth office procedures; he wrote MacMillan, "If you take Prime back you also ought to insist on return to you of the Bly [barley] statements which I believe he has copies of for years back which he *has no right to*."[51]

John Sr.'s letter to W. W. Cargill was dated October 12, 1909, a letter that MacMillan must have been happy to have written, after a summer and fall of high tension with the Irwin matter and Prime's personal problems. W. W. had gone to Montana in late September to participate in a dedication of the Valier project, had fallen ill there (reported by the newspapers then as some form of acute gastrointestinal attack), and was recuperating at home in La Crosse. There were still nagging worries over the financial soundness of W. W.'s decisions and his siphoning off of assets to Montana

(Will Cargill being so persuasive). Cargill Elevator Company business, however, was beginning to look more optimistic in total—the 1909–1910 crop year, when it was finally concluded would show a profit of over $343,000.

Five days later, on October 17, 1909, W. W. Cargill suddenly died of pneumonia.

CHAPTER FOUR

W. W.'s Business Collapses

The death of the patriarch of the Cargill empire was not only a personal loss to both the Cargill and MacMillan families but also a business debacle. W. W. Cargill's name carried great confidence in credit circles. Had he lived, perhaps he, son Will and son-in-law John MacMillan, Sr., might have brought everything to a successful conclusion. As it was, snarls in his firm's affairs not clearly seen before his death became all too evident.

Cargill died at 64 years of age. He did not leave a will, so Wisconsin law applied.* The entire estate was to be passed on to his widow, Ellen ("Ella") Stowell Cargill. However, on March 23, 1910, Ellen Cargill also died (she was 56). The probate process for the W. W. Cargill estate was just beginning; the succession passed the estate to the four children. They were (in order of birth and with spouses):

> William Samuel Cargill (Will), whose wife was Mary McMillan Cargill (married 1892)
> Edna Cargill MacMillan, whose husband was John H. MacMillan, Sr. (married 1895)
> Emma Cargill Hanchette, whose husband was Fred M. Hanchette (married 1897)
> Austen Stowell Cargill, whose wife was Anne Ray Cargill (married 1913)

John Sr. was to join with Will Cargill and Frank P. Hixon (W. W.'s La Crosse lumberman friend) to serve as administrators of the estate. The three took their first look at the situation, as described in a certified statement by outside accountants as of November 1, 1909. It valued total assets of all of the W. W. Cargill enterprises at $6.7 million. But the future was not promising. The La Crosse & Southeastern Railway, though operating,

---

*There is a story that there *was* a will but that it was secretly destroyed by three of the four heirs. Since this undocumented event is given some credence in the John Work history of the Company, Work's text is reprinted in the appendix to this chapter. I found no other documentation for the story.

was producing only marginal revenues, and the ambitious Montana project was still under construction. In the Sawyer & Austin and Banner Lumber operations (carried by the accountants at $3 million of assets, "which amount we have been instructed to use for the present occasion"), there had been lower earnings after 1907, due partially to the Panic but more to inept on-site management. There was political unrest in Mexico; the Mexican representative reported "outbreaks . . . instigated by a class seeking chances to rob and plunder." This unrest made the Cargill timberland in the State of Chihuahua virtually unsalable for the moment. Extensive tracts of fir, spruce and hemlock in British Columbia in W. W.'s portfolio were potentially valuable, but access roads and on-site organization would be needed. So that, too, was another case of short-term illiquidity. Further, W. W. Cargill's own La Crosse grain company was limping, primarily because of drains from these other businesses and also because grain was no longer as profitable in southern Minnesota and Wisconsin.

Finally, the estate held one presently profitable asset which promised high expectations for the future. W. W. Cargill Company owned a dominant share (some 8,362 shares out of a total of 10,000) of the Cargill Elevator Company, W. W.'s Minneapolis-based organization.

Against all of these assets, whether realizable or not, was a mountain of debts. W. W. Cargill had borrowed right and left to finance these new projects—he had paper out everywhere. On the balance sheet, there was over $3.9 million in notes payable to outsiders in addition to those owed to Cargill Elevator Company. Further, the accountants attached a separate sheet listing additional contingent liabilities for endorsement of notes for over $1 million, two-thirds of which were for the Montana project. The extent of this side of W. W.'s balance sheet dumbfounded MacMillan. He wrote a friend in early November, "I knew nothing about the finances of La Crosse until about two weeks after Mr. Cargill's death . . . [he] used those companies as though they were personal matters."

One fact jumped out at the three administrators right away—W. W. Cargill Company could not promptly meet its obligations. The 1945 Cargill history, emphasizing the dramatic, indulged in a time-worn cliche: "It was, indeed, a shock—the name of Cargill had stood like the Rock of Gibraltar, and suddenly doubt was raised as to whether it could meet its obligations."

Essentially, there appeared to be two alternatives: (1) try to pay off all of the debts by liquidation of existing assets, manifestly a fire-sale alternative in that many of these assets would be difficult to force-sell; or (2) call the creditors together, explain the situation fully and ask for sufficient time to solve the host of dilemmas, thus not forcing liquidation upon the estate.

The estate administrators, under the aegis of the court, quickly approached the various creditors about the second alternative. To John Sr.'s great relief, they agreed, in November 1909, to put their Cargill interests into the hands of a "Creditors' Committee," composed of Frank Hixon (the La Crosse lumberman who had arranged credit for the Texas endeavor of the MacMillan brothers),C. T. Jaffray (who was president of the prestigious First National Bank of Minneapolis) and Thomas F. Baxter (a member of the Boston firm of notebrokers, Bond & Goodwin, and a longtime friend of W. W. Cargill). Jaffray was elected chairman. Writing in his reminiscences in 1956, he recalled those first days of the Committee: "it was discovered that the Grain Firm of W. W. Cargill Company . . . was in trouble. Its President had been borrowing money through brokers and banks and did not enter it in the books. He was also buying properties in all sections of the country, including Mexico, British Columbia, Montana and Arkansas. Unfortunately for the company, this borrowed money was not shown as a liability until it reached a point where a showdown was inevitable."

Hixon became the most involved and was soon a powerful influence on John Sr. He later joined the board of Cargill Elevator Company and took a position as the vice president of the firm, although he remained in La Crosse and acted more as an advisor to John Sr.; he was not deeply immersed in the grain trading operations.

Will the Elevator Company Be Sacrificed?

The key to a positive outcome would have to lie in the one highly successful unit—the Cargill Elevator Company. John Sr. began to realize the extent of the threat to the Minneapolis enterprise, for not only were the debts of the estate daunting, but a further disturbing complication also began to surface. John Sr. learned that the agenda of one of the other administrators, son Will Cargill, would be a different one, likely continuing to draw money for the struggling Montana projects at the expense of Cargill Elevator. MacMillan told Fred Hanchette later, "the sincere sympathy everybody had for Mrs. Cargill, and her very strong and urgent requests for matters to be handled the way Will wanted them influenced the situation so very strongly . . . with the very kindliest of motives, the one serious mistake . . . was made right on the start." John Sr. sensed trouble, for since early December 1909, Mrs. Cargill had been telling other members of the Cargill family that "John was trying to get everything in his own hands." This had caused a cooling in the relationship between Edna MacMillan and her mother; the latter wrote Edna, "Your letter came to me this morning . . . you sent me no love for the first time in your life. My heart is breaking, breaking. Do you mean it? Tell me—oh God, what have I done." In early January 1910, John Sr. wrote in his diary of seeing family letters in which Ellen Cargill had said negative things about him.

J. H. MacMILLAN

MacMillan is "some pertaters"
He runs a string of elevators.
It matters not how high his rating
His work in life is elevating.

From E. R. Buell, Just for Fun: A Port-folio of Cartoons 1915.

Timing was important in any case, for if creditors pulled their financing away from the elevator company, it would fail. The indispensable ingredient of the grain trade was extensive credit during that part of the "crop year" in the fall and winter when the merchant must accumulate inventory. Such funds were tendered on trust in the soundness of the Company's management and were to be paid back by receipts from sales later in the year. There could be unpleasant adverse effects if outsiders became fully apprised of the sea of red ink.[1]

It was fortuitous yet ironic that John Sr. had just expanded his credit sources beyond the Upper Midwest. Two months before, in early August 1909, MacMillan had consummated a credit arrangement with a New York City bank, the National Park Bank. An officer there had written John Sr. at that time, "We do not think you will find us niggardly in the amount of accommodation we shall be willing to extend to you during the crop moving period."

Terribly preoccupied in those first few weeks after W. W.'s death, MacMillan knew he had to keep his organization going, and he wrote Lindahl, "I have so much on my mind right now that I do not want to think of anything more than I absolutely have to . . . you look after your end of it up there." Staying in character, he added, "I think you want to run along as conservatively as you can so as to keep us all feeling easy all the time." On the same day, he also wrote Prime, about whom he did not feel as confident: "I wish you would continue to keep me posted every day, as to what you are doing. Of course I want to be kept advised."

Lindahl sensed MacMillan's desperation and in his usual optimistic way responded, "I know you must be terribly busy now, and please do not worry about us, we will push this business along some how or other and come out all right in the end." Prime, his confidence apparently now restored by his treatment for alcohol abuse, wanted to forge ahead in barley. MacMillan knew that Prime's love of buying good barley often made him bullish and unable to see the larger picture—thus the cautionary letter. Prime replied brusquely: "Just have your letter about pulling out of the market. Don't do this. Just let me carry out my plans. I can stand the strain and I will not lose a penny for us . . . keep your nerve."[2]

With the Creditors' Committee in place, John Sr. wrote all of the credit sources of the Cargill Elevator Company. The letter to the National Park Bank, for example, first explained the committee, then provided a few details on the financial health of Cargill Elevator Company. He ended, "I should be very glad, indeed, to have you assure yourself of this point by asking any of the bankers of this city or St. Paul—who are thoroughly advised of the whole situation." A letter came back three days later that confirmed John Sr.'s suspicion that many people would view all of the Cargill companies as one:

We are glad to know that the condition of the Cargill Elevator Co. is so strong and that it is not in need of any financing; for the close association, the similarity of names and well known connections between the various companies will very naturally attract attention, and of course to your disadvantage. If you will permit me to offer a little unsolicited advice, I would suggest that the Cargill Elevator Co. send to its banking friends a very detailed signed statement of its condition. I would leave no item unexplained, nothing for any bank to write back and ask as to what is under this or that heading, and as soon as such a paper is sent out the better I think for all concerned.[3]

Right after the news of W. W. Cargill's death, MacMillan also contacted a number of Cargill Elevator Company debtors, urging them to be prompt on their payments. As he put it to an Iowa customer, "I am sure you will appreciate that, under the circumstances, your assurance that everything will be cleaned up by December 1st is a great favor to me, personally."[4]

As if notoriety among the financial community was not enough, a major news story came out in a Minneapolis paper in late December 1909 about John MacMillan, Sr., an event that under other circumstances would have had only positive implications, but in light of the W. W. Cargill disaster it was a revelation of mixed blessing. This related to a $500,000 insurance policy issued to Cargill Elevator Company on the life of John Sr. The Northwestern National Life Insurance Company of Minneapolis had just begun writing policies for "insuring capital against losses in practical men" (a news article's wording). The president of Northwestern had written MacMillan at this time about the new concept, mentioning that eight other insurance companies were part of the reinsurance provision of the policy. His wording in the MacMillan letter gave a clue to the insurance industry enthusiasm for new business: "The Metropolitan has been primarily an Industrial Company and, as nearly as I can analyze the situation, is utilizing this special competitive contract to butt in more strongly in what is known as ordinary business." Usually the fact that a corporation was enlightened enough to utilize the concept of insurance on key men would have been positive public relations. However, given the focus on the death of W. W. Cargill, a person certainly in that "practical man" category—but without such coverage—it was not a public announcement that MacMillan savored.[5]

John Sr. was not the only grain trader, incidentally, to utilize the new concept of "key-man" life insurance in favor of the company. According to Don Larson's book, *Land of the Giants*, Frank Peavey had taken such a policy in 1900 for $1 million, with the grain company as beneficiary. Larson reported that Peavey had paid only the first premium, $48,390, when he died (on December 1, 1901); "at the time it was issued there was only one in the country of a larger amount, and that belonged to the Eastern financier, George Vanderbilt."[6]

MacMillan fretted about the effect of the crisis on his own organization and wrote Lindahl a long letter on the same day that he had written the various banks. After spelling out the role of the Creditors' Committee, he ended with a poignant paragraph that scarcely hid his own apprehension: "This is not going to affect our Company at all. All the banks here and St. Paul and Duluth, understand the situation fully and are absolutely satisfied in every respect, as to our condition here. I want you to feel absolutely assured as to our own concern and have no uneasiness of any kind, as everything is absolutely all right and you can assure everybody to this effect. All our customers here have been seen and understand the situation so that I think it will make no difference whatever, as far as your business is concerned."[7]

In Duluth, business was good, and Lindahl wrote John Sr. a few days later, "I told Prime that he could cut loose and buy all the barley he wanted to and we would see that there was room in the elevator to do it." Prime likely confirmed MacMillan's preconceptions when he wrote, "We are working under peculiar conditions at this point and of course you realize as well as I do it is impossible to be 'in and outers,' and conduct a successful business. We have got started in on this little game and we've got to see it through, but mark my words, we are going to come out all right. . . . If we could buy this stuff and turn around and sell it readily it would be a nice pretty business, but of course if it were possible to do this it would be nothing but child's play." One of Lindahl's favorite expressions fit again: "You can never make any money with bare floors."

Things did work out for Prime, and he exulted to MacMillan a few weeks later, "We have got all of our competitors here skinned to a frazzle." He repeated similar phraseology a week later:"We have our competitors whipped to a standstill." Although Prime's combative language may have disconcerted John Sr., the promise of results surely did not. Lindahl guessed that MacMillan might be worried about Prime's stability in this situation and penned a separate note: "Don't let this barley business here worry you one bit. All we have to do is to keep a stiff upper lip and we will come out alright."[8]

In those dark days for the Company in the early spring of 1910, even one of the employees stepped forward with help. N. C. Clark, who was Lindahl's office assistant (and later secretary for the Superior Terminal Elevator Company), wrote John MacMillan, "I have $2500 to loan for six months. If you can use it, please let me know what rate you would be willing to pay." MacMillan wrote back immediately, "We can use the $2500" and offered 5 percent interest. Clark accepted and paid the money in cash into the Cargill Commission Company account the following day.[9]

Although praising Prime's sharp trading, John Sr. still felt it necessary to write a few weeks later, "I want to continue the policy . . . of following the market rather than trying to force it. When we can make sales, then of course we want to do all the business we can, but when we find it impossible to make sales, it seems to me the part of wisdom to let the market sag off and let the other fellow take the loss." MacMillan also continued to urge Prime to "complete the treatment." Prime wrote back that he would do so "in late January" and meanwhile wanted to go down to Buffalo. MacMillan wrote back that such a trip was "a good plan" but added, "the only thing I feared was the kind of a crowd you have to mix with down there and the tremendous temptation you would necessarily get." Prime's alcohol treatment must have been effective, for there is no further evidence in any of the written records of continuing problems.[10]

It was ironic that Cargill Elevator Company continued to have routine requests from bankers about the credit-worthiness of other companies. For example, a New York banker wrote in late February 1910 about a milling company in Minneapolis, suggesting that if Cargill Elevator Company desired, it could use a code number for the reply. Instead, MacMillan used the name of the milling company and frankly stated his beliefs, which were positive.[11]

Selling Off Assets

The Creditors' Committee moved with alacrity on the properties. First, it canceled the W. W. Cargill debts to the Elevator Company, some $234,000, when the directors of the Elevator Company agreed to take over from the W. W. Cargill estate the latter's 34 remaining elevators and other miscellaneous warehouses and coal sheds. An option to do this had been given on November 1, 1909, just days after the death, and was officially accepted by the directors on August 9, 1910, after the Creditors' Committee had studied the proposal. Minority holdings in two lakers, the *America* and the *Brazil*, owned by the Reiss Coal Company of Sheboygan, Wisconsin, were also sold. In La Crosse, James B. Taylor took over the routine business for the rest of W. W.'s interests, under direction of John Sr. and the Creditors' Committee.[12]

Its second step was to sell the Sawyer & Austin Lumber Company's Pine Bluff, Arkansas, properties. This was a situation John MacMillan knew well. The 1945 Cargill history perhaps overstated one fact when it said, "a master stroke was Mr. MacMillan's decision to build a logging railroad [at a] location of such strategic importance that two great railway systems later found themselves in the position of having to bid for it." It *had* been sold for a tidy sum, but this occurred back in 1905. However, it did turn out that the Sawyer & Austin properties in Pine Bluff were worth considerable amounts, too, and these were sold in June 1911 to the Long-Bell Lumber Company, a Kansas City, Missouri organization, for $1.1 million. Substantial amounts of land already logged had been retained by Cargill and contracts began to be made to sell sections to individuals. The main St. Louis yards of the Banner Lumber Company were sold in October 1911 for $105,000. The Maplewood yard was retained to serve as a shell organization for collection of delinquent accounts.

John Sr., knowing of the bauxite on the property, also had the foresight to reserve the mineral rights. In early 1912, MacMillan negotiated a small bauxite mining contract with Superior Chemical Company and the following year a much larger contract with American Bauxite Company, an arrangement guaranteed by its parent, Aluminum Company of America. A highly favorable longer-term contract was negotiated, extending to 1922. The estate received $1.00 a ton, and American Bauxite agreed to take 15,000 tons in the first year, 50,000 for the second, 75,000 for the third and

Bauxite mining on Sawyer & Austin lands, Pine Bluff, Arkansas, 1913.

Log wagons on W. W. Cargill's Mexican timber property, Guageneachis, Chihuahua State, Mexico.

then 100,000 tons per year to the end of the contract. This arrangement later was a significant component in the final settlement of the W. W. Cargill affairs.[13]

It was too bad that W.W. Cargill was not alive to see this final chapter in the lumber company; "Mr. Cargill had invested in the lumber business despite the opposition of his life-long friend, Mr. F. P. Hixon," noted the 1945 history, and the lack of profitability after that initial involvement seemed to corroborate Hixon's view. Now there was vindication!

The Valier Morass

Meanwhile there was turbulence at Valier, which had become the most troublesome piece of the estate puzzle in terms of both financial demands and family stress. The 70,000 acres made available to potential settlers under the Carey Act provisions in October 1909 had seemed quite attractive to potential farmer-settlers, and W. M. Wayman, manager of the Conrad-Montana Land Company, the sales company for the land, wrote John MacMillan a few weeks later, "the land hunger is on and there is a great tendency of back to the farm." Indeed, there seemed at this point to be no problem in selling either the original tract of deeded land or a new, larger addition. Further, a sizable portion of the bonds already had been sold to finance these developments.

However, the W. W. Cargill death had occurred between the offering and Wayman's euphoric letter about land hunger. W. W., with his son Will, had been deeply immersed in these Valier plans, and large debts had been incurred in Will Cargill's own company set up for the construction, the Conrad Land & Water Company (CL&W), a partnership with his close friend, W. W. Withee. The contractor was owed large amounts, the Conrad family was due money for the original deeded land, and the partners were behind on payment of commissions to the sales company. The Creditors' Committee had some inklings of this as early as December 4, 1909, when John Sr. wrote one of the lawyers handling estate matters, "of course the . . . Committee realizes the mix-up in the affairs out there and are now going to insist on getting to the bottom"

By February 1910, with an inspection visit by a representative of the Creditors' Committee, the extent of the problem became evident. First, the amount of cash in the operation was almost depleted, despite the fact that proceeds of some $475,000 from the bonds showed on the books. "Money is apparently not considered," wrote the inspector, who particularly faulted Will's purchase of seven automobiles for the project. Next, a most startling fact came to light: Will and his partner, Withee, despite the worsening financial situation and without the knowledge of anyone in La

Crosse or Minneapolis, apparently had declared themselves a "dividend" of some of the land, in the town of Valier itself and along the railroad right-of-way. The exact details were not clear to the Creditors' Committee. While the estate's records on Valier were excellent, there seemed to be no records of the Cargill & Withee partnership, nor any personal or company letters to the family from Will Cargill himself on any of this.

The Creditors' Committee insisted on a meeting with Will Cargill and W. W. Withee in Chicago. It took place on March 3, 1910, and the two men were severed from involvement in the Conrad Land & Water Co.; the day-by-day management was then vested in W. C. Winton, the secretary-treasurer. John Sr. wrote in his diary of a surprising agreement that had been reached at this meeting, that "Withee should be paid a pension of $200 per month to keep away from Montana."

Further, the work of the contractor appeared to be faulty—the dam had sprung a leak in June 1910, and the ditches, too small and crooked to carry water and not carefully edged, were falling in. Worst of all, the water promised to come down those ditches to the farmers had not arrived. Not only was much of the construction work unfinished, but the rains, which had been ample in 1909, did not come in 1910. Nor were the farmers, under the terms of their land purchases, obligated to pay if water to their property was not forthcoming.

Winton was left to face the residual ill will of the settlers. He wrote MacMillan in early July that they were "demanding money back and damages on account of undelivery . . . of water . . . immediate steps [must] be taken, otherwise useless to try to make further land sales or collect any payments of interest or principal . . . either raise funds for completion or decide on terms upon which others may take it over . . . local sentiment bad, getting worse daily." A few days later he wrote again: "Our bank balances are practically nothing, and I am standing off creditors the best I can." The contractor, even though inept, pressed the receivers to liquidate so that he might be paid; the seller of the land expressed the same sentiments.[14]

However, there *were* substantial assets, although still to be proven profitable, just as in other parts of the W. W. Cargill estate. John MacMillan had seen a Valier potential from the start, and wrote Winton in May 1910, "it looks to me as though there would be at least $1,000,000 profit in the deal to a syndicate who would take hold of it and complete it." But the risk worried him; he wrote the Creditors' Committee in mid-June, "the land contracts and town sites, while perfectly good if the work is completed, are of very doubtful value should the Company fail to put water on these lands." John Sr. rushed out to Montana in early July in a renewed effort to forestall bankruptcy, in the process meeting Will. John Sr. wrote Edna: "At first he turned his head. . . . I stuck my hand directly in front of him and he finally very gingerly shook it. He would only answer in monosyllables." Despite John Sr.'s pleadings, the contractor was adamant, and the company had to file for bankruptcy.

Even with this worsening scenario, MacMillan still wanted to keep the project alive and proposed to the receivers that they petition the court to permit the issuance of Receivers' Certificates, which were to have first lien on all property except the existing contracts for the bonds. A syndicate would presumably buy these, and the proceeds would be used to finish the project.

At a critical moment the project got an unexpected boost from the Carey Land Act Board of the state of Montana, which gave the project an extension to May 1, 1911, for finishing the irrigation and delivering water. Winton's letters showed visible relief. If the Board had not extended the time (thereby keeping in place the sellers' payment schedules), "the bondsmen would have been called upon to pay back a great deal of money . . . it will assist in easing the settlers' minds."

Will Cargill and W. W. Withee, meanwhile, had started another land development project some 250 miles southeast of Valier, near Billings (presumably Withee was endangering his "pension" by this act). Winton, warning MacMillan to "treat this as *strictly confidential*," reported that "Cargill figures on putting his teams to work down there" and that Will was apparently again short of money, mortgaging some of his own property in Valier for funds for that new effort. No record remains of this second project; it seems probable that with the cash problems of the partners it was soon aborted.

By late fall 1910, at the request of the Creditors' Committee, an independent engineering report was completed for the Conrad Land & Water Company. A new developer/contractor had been hired, and the engineers gave him a positive recommendation—there could be success if their "legal, business, engineering and financial details" were carried out. They added, justifiably, "the past record of this Company in all these particulars has been very discreditable."

So a syndicate was proposed, with the W. W. Cargill Creditors' Committee (after personal urging by John Sr.) agreeing to provide $150,000 of the $600,000 estimated to be needed.[15] There was a momentary crisis at the last minute, when Will Cargill and Withee claimed a piece of the syndicate, holding that the property they had originally taken as a "dividend," returned when the receivers insisted, had been turned back "without consideration." There was no ground for a Cargill & Withee claim, and within a few weeks both had signed the necessary papers for the syndicate, without, for the moment, making any additional demands. Of course, Will Cargill personally retained his one-quarter interest in the W. W. Cargill estate, so kept a link to Valier through this more indirect means. Steps were taken to move the syndicate to completion, and work on the Valier properties continued.

By then, the other heirs in the W. W. Cargill estate, Edna MacMillan, Emma Hanchette and Austen Cargill, had become quite incensed about Will's various actions, including what they felt were blemishes in Will's personal life at this time. They believed that Will was involved with Mrs. Withee. Clarence Stowell, a nephew of Ella Cargill, who earlier had inherited some of the land in Valier from the Ella Cargill estate along with Fred Hanchette, wrote of Will "hanging around" the Withee house and taking Mrs. Withee and her son for rides. "It simply makes a fellow want to use a gun." This feeling was mirrored in John Sr.'s furious words in a letter to Whelan, the Creditors' Committee lawyer: "All those of the heirs would be so angry over any such proceedings that they would not tolerate it a moment . . . eliminate absolutely Cargill & Withee from any rights which they now claim." Fred Hanchette expressed the same thought in an earlier letter about Will: "It is easy to forgive a damned fool or even a repentant son of a B. but it is foolish to shower sympathy on one who persists on being both." He called them "Cargill, Withee, Devil & Co."

The more hopeful turn of events with plans for the syndicate also persuaded John MacMillan to intensify the Cargill Elevator Company's plans for more elevators in the Valier area. The Williams elevator was put up during the latter part of this year and the Valier property rebuilt (a small elevator erected there in 1909 had burned down).

Although the dam and ditches had been repaired, they still were not functioning. However, a lucky star now settled over the project, momentarily, at least. Heavy rain came just when it was needed for the crops (June 1911), bringing the hope of a fecund harvest. Valier had been tendered a welcome reprieve.[16]

Frank Hixon, instrumental in putting the Montana situation into shape, then proposed a plan, in August 1911, to ensure that the remainder of the debts would not be loaded directly into the Cargill Elevator Company books. A new company would be incorporated; Hixon initially called it the "Cargill trust," but later, the name Cargill Securities Company was chosen (decades later, in October 1965, it became Waycrosse, Inc.). Its specific and only purpose would be to take over the indebtedness of the estate. Some 8,354 of the 10,000 shares of Cargill Elevator stock were trusteed to this new company to serve as assets behind the issue of new notes. These were to be called "Gold Notes," in total about $2,500,000, enough to pay off all of the creditors (thus easing the minds of a group of small creditors who earlier feared they might be shut out). The notes were to be redeemed within five years. The remainder of the shares, the holdings of the two widows, Aunt Maggie Cargill Barker, widow of George Barker, and Aunt Lydia, widow of Sam Cargill, would be left as shareholder obligations of the elevator company itself.

Hixon's analytical sense impressed James Taylor; he wrote admiringly to John Sr., "I think, myself, Frank has done pretty well for sitting down and in a few hours whipping this thing into what seems to me workable shape. . . . Austen seemed to agree with its contents and thought that it was gotten up in pretty good shape." At first, John Sr. was not so certain. Feeling that Hixon was more concerned about creditors than heirs, he wrote, "I realize fully that the Creditors' Committee have the kindliest feeling toward the heirs but . . . they must be as strongly biased in their feelings on the side of the creditors as I am naturally on the side of the heirs . . . we would be depending entirely upon the personal standpoint and not upon legal right, which it seemed to me the present arrangement affords." Hixon remonstrated at this point that "we must frame up a proposition that will clearly appeal to the creditors," and his reassurances of his own independence finally calmed MacMillan's fears.

But another irritant soon intruded and became a saga of frustration for many months. Will Cargill had suddenly appeared at one of the key meetings, on September 22, 1911. MacMillan wrote the Hanchettes about it a few minutes after the meeting broke up: "Will did not offer to shake hands, and, of course, I did not offer to with him. We barely spoke. Austen was in the room—Will shook hands with him but has made no effort to see him since."

Will made it plain over the next days that he wanted to be indemnified against any of his own debts from the Montana project and to be given his proper share of the proposed new company. Many weeks of acrimony ensued, with Will on one side, John and Edna MacMillan (with the Hanchettes) on the other, and Austen Cargill, although agreeing with the latter group, stepping into the middle in a peacemaker role. During this period, Austen had been taking increasing responsibility in the seed division of the Cargill Elevator Company in Minneapolis. John Sr. wrote Fred Hanchette about this: "I think it a fine experience for him and one that he needs particularly badly as he has been so painfully shy." Austen, at 23 years of age, was put in a difficult position in dealing with his older brother, now age 42.

Eventually, an arbitrator was proposed as a mechanism to resolve the differences between Will and the other heirs, and with much argument Will accepted the original plan (after meeting with Austen one night until 5 A.M.). John Sr., still bitter about Will's actions, wrote a draft letter to Baxter, the Boston member of the Creditors' Committee, that the heirs "feel that if he gets anything out of it, it will go to the benefit of the woman who has been the cause of these disasters." But he must have thought better of this last comment, for scrawled across the top in his hand were the words "not sent."[17]

This was not to be the last argument. The Hixon plan, ready to be effected, finally brought the administrators' work in the estate to a close, in early 1912. A fee for such services was provided in the statutes of the state of Wisconsin, 1 percent of the value of the estate. The three administrators were MacMillan, Hixon and Will Cargill.

The thought of paying part of these fees to Will Cargill was galling to the MacMillans, Austen Cargill and the Hanchettes—there was too much "water over the dam" (a Valier project pun of that time). It turned out that Will was not only demanding his share but also wanting to increase its amount. He had left Montana altogether and had settled in Benton Harbor, Michigan, without his wife, who was left in La Crosse with little funds. He was raising chickens, but this new endeavor was not doing well and he was in need of money. Withee was reported to be in South America.

MacMillan and Hixon did not want to keep any fees personally but, because of Will's demands, decided not to turn any back, as a portion would then eventually work its way around to Will. "There is no doubt that the other three heirs are going to feel very much worked up over Will being allowed the $5,000 fee," MacMillan wrote Hixon on March 1, 1912 (it is not clear whether Austen Cargill would have agreed on this). In this same letter, John Sr. proposed a plan: "I have been wondering if it would not be well to accept it, and turn it over to Fred and Emma [Hanchette], as their money is getting down very low, and I feel we must do something to protect them."

This was what was finally done, although to say it so straightforwardly simplifies a long, tortuous set of negotiations and a further worsening of intra- and interfamily relationships. It finally took a judge's decision to throw out Will's proposal for higher fees. MacMillan wrote Fred Hanchette, "Will afterwards told George Burton he guessed he had made a mistake in making the fight . . . which rather added to our amusement."[18]

Hixon's proposal became the final plan. The Cargill Securities Company was put into place, and John Sr. went to New York in April 1912 to explore the marketing of the Gold Notes and to push further on the financing of the Montana project. Unfortunately, his timing for the trip was bad, as he reported to C. T. Jaffray: "I did not complete as fully as I hoped to the investigation of above matters owing to the fact that it was very difficult to secure the attention of men on matters of business in New York last week on account of the condition of the public mind over the accident to the Steamship Titantic [sic]."

But New York City's preoccupation with the *Titanic* disaster soon passed. The Cargill Securities Company authorized $2,550,000 of the Gold

Notes ($2,525,000 were actually issued), which were to mature on or before January 1, 1917. All of the property of this new corporation was to be pledged for the benefit of the note holders. With the acceptance by the probate court, the plan let the viable organization, the Cargill Elevator Company, remain on its successful track, using proceeds from its success to pay off the Gold Notes, at which point the Cargill Securities Company perhaps could cease to exist. The heirs of W. W. Cargill surrendered to the trustees (the Minneapolis Trust Company) all of their right and title to the assets until such time as the debts were paid. In turn, John MacMillan was free to operate independently as chief executive officer of the Cargill Elevator Company.[19]

Thus, the one strong entity, the Cargill Elevator Company, would see through the dismemberment of the rest of W. W. Cargill's fallen empire on as favorable terms as possible, retiring some or perhaps even all of the Gold Notes at the end of the appointed year, 1916. It behooved John Sr. to manage the elevator company as profitably as possible, at the same time following up on the myriad details of the remaining bankrupt companies. The families Cargill and MacMillan, Will Cargill the one exception, had closed ranks and worked together to resolve the crisis generated by W. W. Cargill's death, just as had happened in the 1890s with the Texas grain bankruptcy of the MacMillans.

Prudence Holds Sway

Understandably, these events made John Sr. even more cautious than his usual conservative posture. He became obsessive about having enough credit to carry the Cargill Elevator Company through the crop season, and his almost reflexive guardedness in this period evidenced itself all through the business. When Mary Barker, daughter of Aunt Maggie, wrote John Sr. in the summer of 1912, at her mother's request, to draw on some of their balances inherited from Sam Cargill's estate, John Sr. pushed hard to persuade them to keep as much as possible in the Company: "Of course I want you to feel that you have a perfect right to all the money if you have any real need for it, but . . . we would be glad to use all the money possible in the business this Fall . . . it [is] an unusual time . . . we ought to conserve all the money we could to take care of the business." A year later, he wrote again to Mary: "I do not think you ought to draw out this money unless it is absolutely needed . . . our own stockholders ought to help out all they can . . . not draw their money out at the very time when it could be used to the best advantage." He closed with an unvarnished reproach: "The stockholders should be of every assistance they can to the business instead of pulling on the business just at a critical time like this."

Perhaps John Sr. felt he needed outward evidence of Cargill Elevator's responsible finance, for in 1910 he decided for the first time ever to initiate an outside audit. A prestigious firm, the Audit Company of New York, was employed and soon gave MacMillan more than he expected. Its report, in July 1910, was laced with caution—indeed, outright skepticism. The analysts did not like the way "in which the books of several companies have been intertwined" (the Cargill Elevator Company subsidiaries, not the W. W. Cargill enterprises) and recommended common closing dates and precise accounting between and among these. "We did not find all the vouchers and other supporting papers," they continued, and added, "we believe that greater care should be taken in the filing of such records." The Green Bay accounts were particularly criticized, "owing to the very peculiar assumption on the part of the Green Bay cashier." They found at least one instance where an advance had gone unreported for almost a month. The auditors had not been able to verify all of the physical assets either, so were unsure of "the Income of your Company for the past year with respect to maintenance and depreciation of plant."

One could palpably feel the auditors sniffing down their noses about the "careless books." This must have disturbed John Sr. a great deal. He had prided himself on his grasp of accounting principles and his meticulousness in their application and earlier had voiced some of the same criticisms about Funk and the Banner Lumber Company. To no one's surprise, the Audit Company of New York was not invited back the next year. Marwick, Mitchell & Co. (predecessor of today's KPMG Peat Marwick) replaced it, and this began a relationship that extends down to the present.

Yet John Sr. should not have been upset, for the report showed a company of considerable strength. The profit for the crop year 1909–1910 was $343,943, and the firm had a surplus of almost $1.4 million. There was only a contingent liability: a $152,000 liability to Liberty Lumber Co., partially balanced by $37,500 of Liberty's stock. (Liberty was a Minneapolis subsidiary of Cargill Elevator Company, started by John, Sr. in 1904 to serve as a retail outlet for W. W. Cargill's British Columbia timber). All of the usual accounting ratios showed conservative positions. Country elevator capacity was just under 4 million bushels; Duluth had 2.5 million; Minneapolis, 875,000. Cargill Elevator Company was in sound shape.

Precisely because of this strength, John Sr. was importuned often in this period to make loans to small commission houses out in the country with whom Cargill Elevator Company was dealing. John Sr. worried constantly that these commission houses were borrowing from the firm, then using some of this money to extend credit to farmers, who borrowed early in the crop season and paid back at the end—provided crops were good. "This is something we are not willing to do . . . we do not want any commission accounts that do not clean up at the end of the grain season," he wrote one house. "We do not do a banking business," he wrote another. When a small flour mill asked for a loan, he replied, "this is purely a banking proposition . . . one which the . . . company could not consistently go into."

Despite solid economic conditions in the grain 'trade, one of its stalwarts faltered in 1911. The giant Peavey empire had seemed so strong, but one of its officers had been speculating with company assets, unknown to top management. The losses were reported to be so severe that John Sr. wrote T. F. Baxter, the Boston financier, that it might be necessary "to trustee F. H. Peavey & Company." Baxter wrote back, "There has been a good deal of talk about the matter in the East, and I somewhat fear that it will affect the sale of milling paper for the present." The Peavey group moved quickly to provide restitution. Baxter wrote, "People forget pretty readily . . . after a month or two, it will probably make little difference in the market."

The travails of the W. W. Cargill collapse seemed to sap any entrepreneurial bent that John Sr. might have harbored. There *were* some tantalizing opportunities. For example, Lindahl, seeing the export business becoming more important, urged MacMillan to put a man in New York "who is familiar with the foreign markets and methods of doing business abroad," as Peavey had done. In 1913 one of the international brokers, A. D. Thompson Co., had given Lindahl a revealing set of figures about the costs of transportation across the Atlantic; in July and August one could ship from Duluth to Liverpool "as cheaply as 9¢ a bushel . . . this charge will gradually widen within three months to as high as 22¢ a bushel." Most of this variation was accounted for by the ocean segment— the Duluth-to-Buffalo and Duluth-to-Montreal legs were relatively more stable. Lindahl asked about the profits of the exporters; the broker replied that there was "plenty of competition among exporters and quite a bit of speculation." In sum, there were significant profit opportunities if a grain company wanted to integrate forward into trading ocean freight*—but also possibilities for large losses. The latter prospect scared MacMillan, and he told Lindahl, "I'm not sure the time is yet ripe."[20]

Inspecting Grain

The mistrust between Buffalo and the offices in Minnesota surfaced again in the 1911–1912 period, this time over the issue of grain standards

---

*In effect, a "C.I.F." contract, where the seller assumed the "cost," the "insurance" and the "freight," the buyer purchasing at the seller's total asking price, as against the seller using an "F.O.B." arrangement ("free on board") where the buyer arranged transportation and insurance. Under C.I.F., the seller himself would bargain or trade for the transportation and insurance, with the potential for a profit on these if the amounts were less than his total asking price to the seller.

and inspection procedures. In that period a new technique of testing grain was applied to barley: "chemical" analysis. Once again it was A. M. Prime and Dudley Irwin who were at the center of the controversy. Irwin had alleged that Prime was sending him "badly stained barley," that it "was very unsatisfactory, over 30 percent not germinating." John Sr. mistrusted the Easterners' inspection methods, writing Irwin, "The point you make about percentage of waste is something that we will not admit for a moment. If they are going into that kind of a proposition we certainly are going to insist on state inspection so that we have got a record that is official. . . . If the maltsters want to establish a system of inspection . . . it has got to be an official inspection at Duluth just as on other grains. . . . We certainly are not going to get into any hair-splitting arguments."[21]

Within a few days, fresh problems surfaced with Prime's barley. Irwin sent samples from this particular shipment and told MacMillan he thought he could settle it for a penalty of about 2 cents per bushel.[22] MacMillan equivocated. Irwin, still dissatisfied, sent back an almost insulting letter to Duluth: "While your kindergarten learning of years ago, namely never to guarantee germinating, is all right in a way, yet where we sell on a sample and the sample grows within 8 to 10% and we deliver barley on that sample which does not grow within 20 to 25% the buyers take the position that this barley is not like sample. . . . [It is] poor policy to endeavor to crowd this poor germinating barley on the trade."[23]

This got John Sr.'s back up, and he pointedly replied, "This seems to be an old game whenever the market goes off . . . now that the barley market has taken a radical change the other way . . . you will find the growing qualities of that barley have improved wonderfully. If your maltsters down there want any barley they better take what they get and not try any games of this sort."

Irwin considered this a direct challenge and had the controversial grain studied by a New York chemist "who analizes [sic] the barley and malt for the Eastern trade and who stands very high. . . . It looks to me as though there was some Canadian barley mixed through it by someone." Mac-Millan shot back, "I beg to say you are absolutely wrong. There is not a pound of Canadian barley in anything we have handled at Duluth to the best of our knowledge and belief."

The "chemical" part of the analysis was quite rudimentary at that time—primarily moisture and germination tests. MacMillan adamantly opposed this: "Whether we get any more business from Jones or not we cannot recognize in any way any chemical analysis. He is, of course, at liberty to have all of this class of work done that he wishes but as far as we are concerned we must continue to do business as we have always done it—on the appearance of the grain."[24]

To put his feelings more emphatically, MacMillan penned a second letter on the same day: "as grain men it would be absolutely impossible for us to pay any attention to chemical analysis. . . . While I do not in the slightest doubt the careful methods used . . . it is quite evident that there could scarcely be such a difference in two cars from the same shipment of barley. . . . We might just as well quit business if we would attempt to establish a precedent of this sort."

Actually, the barley buyers were ahead of their time in their "chemical" analysis. All through this period, the federal government had been pushed by Congressmen from agricultural states to take the initiative for federal grading and inspection. Extensive hearings were held in 1906, again in 1910, 1912, 1914 and 1916. In this last year a federal Grain Standards Act was finally enacted, which provided for official standards for the common grains and instituted a system of federal licensing and supervision of grain inspectors. But the grading provisions still involved qualitative judgments of physical appearance, along with the weighing. Grading of barley was a pointed example of this subjectivity. In the 1914 hearings in the Committee on Agriculture of the House of Representatives, the chief of the Bureau of Chemistry of the Department of Agriculture was asked about the Bureau's work on barley. He could only report that their analysts had handled some complaints of weed seed in barley shipments but that the inspectors only "saw the weed seed." The Bureau's chemical analysis was nonexistent for barley (they were limited to determining "if it contains filthy or decomposed animal or vegetable matter").[25]

Pitting Offices against Each Other?

The malaise at Green Bay spotted by the Audit Company of New York report continued for several more years. Charles Quackenbush, who had been appointed as manager there after Will Cargill fired Walter Gueinzius (in 1909), seemed to have a talent for irritating his colleagues, competing with the Minneapolis office and otherwise marching to a different drummer. He even had been selling barley in Buffalo to another broker, thereby antagonizing Dudley Irwin. Further, Quackenbush apparently had not been settling accounts as quickly as Irwin expected. The issue itself was a minor one, involving willingness on the part of the grain shipper to pay the insurance and interest on a shipment after its arrival in Buffalo for the short period before inspection took place. Duluth had been willing to foot this small charge, but Quackenbush would not. Irwin wrote John Sr. in February 1912, "My patience is pretty well exhausted with the Green Bay outfit. . . . They have not paid our commissions and some little odds and ends of insurance and interest. . . . It seems too small and piccaune [*sic*] on his part and I don't think you would sanction it."

MacMillan, although not countenancing Quackenbush's stubbornness, defended the Green Bay practice: "What we are really doing is accepting 'in store' terms on C.I.F. sales. I distinctly told both Mr. Prime and Mr. Quackenbush at the beginning of this season that I wanted them to have it understood with you that there would be no such thing thereafter." In a letter a few days later MacMillan put the matter even more bluntly: "there is no question but what the principle we have established there [Prime's acquiescence in the charge] is utterly vicious, and cannot be justified."[26]

There was a larger issue here for John Sr. He had expressed several times earlier his concern about whether Irwin was playing Duluth against Green Bay in his selling efforts. John Sr. wrote once more, "I certainly object to your using one office against the other on these transactions. If anybody wants Duluth barley let them buy it on its merits and the same way with Green Bay but do not try and force either of them to make a trade because the other office is underselling."

Irwin indignantly wrote back, "There is one thing I have always worked hard to avoid and it is just this one thing . . . competition between Green Bay and Duluth branches. . . . I think you will admit that I have fairly well succeeded." Irwin continued to be upset about Quackenbush: "He seems to have a short memory and a disagreeable tendency to impute bad faith where he has no legitimate reason for doing so. . . . These insinuations from Quackenbush . . . are certainly most disagreeable and unfair to me."[27]

A further checking of the facts now led John Sr. to "see the thing from quite a little different point of view," and he wrote Irwin a conciliatory note. He still warned Irwin, however, "I wish you would be particularly careful hereafter in any exchange of telegrams with either Duluth or Green Bay not to put either in the attitude where they think they are competing with the other office."[28]

The issue of grain quality just would not go away, and in the fall of 1912, Irwin again was complaining of Cargill's unclean "black barley," once again a shipment from Prime. Irwin wanted John Sr. to intervene and discipline Prime. John Sr. supported Prime again: "This is Mr. Prime's department . . . he has always shown himself capable of handling it efficiently and well, and I should not be willing to take any action in the matter without that it was a matter of last resort . . . and then, certainly not without Mr. Prime being present. . . . It would have an extremely bad effect all around."[29]

Interestingly, a number of years later, MacMillan did take the earlier advice to have Cargill's own agent—and chose Irwin! The latter had liquidated his own business in 1921. Reputedly at that time he was the largest dealer in malt and barley in the state and known widely as "the barley king of the East." Irwin then joined Cargill as the Company's full-time agent and stayed with the firm until his retirement in 1939 after 62 years in the grain industry. His obituary put it well: "In business, Mr. Irwin was known as a 'gentleman of the old school,' the acme of courtesy, politeness and dignity."[30]

The Annual "Outings"

In 1912, John Sr. instituted what became a great Cargill tradition, the summer "outing." From this date it became an annual affair, most often in July but sometimes in August. Details on the "Fourth," on July 10, 1915, have survived and give a vivid picture. It was held on Lake Minnetonka, west of the city. There was a trolley trip to Excelsior, then a boat ride to the St. Alban's Bay Hotel. Nineteen different "afternoon sports" were listed on the printed program—a tug-of-war between the "Salesmen" and the "Office Men," a relay race with both "Ladies and Gentlemen," a ball-throwing contest just for the ladies, and even a "Fat Men's Race." A baseball game topped it off, and there was ample "candy to keep sweet" and "smokes to keep cool." The meal featured both a fish and a chicken course; Roy Hoople wrote the manager, "think you ought to add canary tongues and fried butterfly wings." The mandatory group picture was taken and, fortunately, survives for us today. Hoople totaled the costs for the 67 participants at just over $200, including $15 for cigars, $.45 for ribbon for the prizes and $4.50 for the piano player. It was a vintage day, to be often repeated.[31]

Deepening the Board

Changes in company boards of directors often are of interest only to those directly involved and have little substantive importance. Now, however, on the Cargill Elevator Company board some basic conceptual changes were made. Outside members were appointed to the board, the first ever in any Cargill company. C. T. Jaffray had replaced W. W. Cargill at the latter's death in 1909. The next year Frank B. Hixon, one of the members of the Creditors' Committee, and M. B. Koon, a prominent Minneapolis lawyer, joined Jaffray on the board. In August 1910, two nonfamily Company employees were added, Lindahl and the barley trader at Minneapolis, J. B. Cooper. John Sr. and his cousin John D. McMillan, the head of the Osborne-McMillan grain firm, completed the seven-member board. The following year, 1911, two members of the Cargill family were added; the first was James F. Cargill, whom John Sr. had replaced as general manager of the Company in 1903; the second was Austen Cargill. Will Cargill was not on the board, nor on the board of either the lumber company or the railroad. By this time, the tensions attendant to Will's actions prior to

Fourth annual Cargill employees' outing, St. Albans Bay, Minnetonka, Minnesota, 1915.

and after the death of W. W. Cargill finally had led to an intractable split within the family; Austen remained the only family member with whom he had a relationship.

Cousin John D. McMillan's actual participation in day-to-day operations was not great, although he remained on the board until 1934. It was a different case with the other family newcomer, Austen Cargill. Austen had left Cornell University on the death of his father to work on the estate problems. In May 1910, John MacMillan asked for Austen in Minneapolis, and he began work there, first as a clerk in the accounting department, then as a salesman on the trading floor and an assistant in the Seed Division.

Austen Cargill was married in September 1913 to Anne Ray, daughter of a La Crosse banker, and the empty W. W. Cargill family home in La Crosse was reopened for the reception. J. B. Taylor recorded the modest circumstances of the honeymoon: "Austen was married Saturday, the hottest day of the three, and he had a very pretty wedding. He left Saturday night for Chicago where he spent Sunday, and left for Green Bay Monday morning, so you can see that he did not take much of a trip. Austen has been made assistant to Charley, and I hope he is going to make good."[32]

Shortly before the marriage, John Sr. had asked Austen to take this assignment in Green Bay, working with Charles Quackenbush, the man-

ager there. Inasmuch as Will Cargill had engineered the forced resignation of the then-manager at Green Bay, Walter Gueinzius, it was little wonder that Quackenbush, the next manager, was sensitive about his position. Earlier, he had been unhappy about his transfer to Minneapolis, and MacMillan, concerned about his feelings, had agreed to move him back. By 1913, Quackenbush again seemed off stride as a result of Austen Cargill's assignment there. John Sr. wanted Austen to have "the responsibility of one department [placed] onto you and give you a chance to develop yourself in an executive way" and assigned him the Seed Department (earlier he had worked in the seed operation in Minneapolis). This seemed to threaten to Quackenbush, for Austen wrote back:

Perhaps I misunderstood you, but the impression I got from the talk I had with you was that I was to have charge of all matters concerning mdse. & seeds, including the buying & selling even to the buying of seed at the stations. . . . I also understood that I should consult with Charley on matters of importance and work with him. . . I don't want to give the idea that I had any intention of going ahead and doing things regardless of Charley. Well, Charley objected very strongly. So strongly in fact that I dropped the matter by suggesting that we both go up to Mpls. and talk with you about it. Since then I have thought it would be better to stay here as I wouldn't care to say anything one way or the other. . . I did ask Charley what he had in mind for me to do . . . and he said he thought I could check reports and call his attention to anything wrong, such as too low prices, etc. I was very much surprised at Charley's attitude as he seemed to consider it a personal affair.

Once again there was evidence of Austen Cargill's personality as peace-maker—he did not like to raise his own profile by pushing himself into the middle of a situation. John Sr. wrote back, "Of course my idea has been for you to handle your department just exactly as everybody handles their department here. You would of course be carrying out Charley's instructions, and consult with him on all matters of policy [but] I want to see Green Bay make a showing that is worthwhile."[33]

Ed Grimes and Austen Cargill Join Forces

The Green Bay operation continued to limp along under Quackenbush, and in 1914, John Sr. decided to move the office to Milwaukee. He explained the rationale to a Milwaukee businessman: "There are many times when the Eastern trade are filled up, and we think we can consign our grain to the Milwaukee market to much better advantage than we could to Green Bay."[34] Quackenbush's performance was not good enough to warrant the Milwaukee post, and MacMillan chose instead to move Edward J. Grimes there.

Grimes had started with the Company in 1904 at Green Bay and was soon transferred to the Minneapolis office, where he became John Sr.'s personal stenographer. He had a natural interest in traffic, and this led him into merchandising. He became a trader on the floor, working as an assistant to J. B. Cooper and later as Cooper's equal. Grimes became one of the Company's best traders. When he was appointed to the new post in Milwaukee, he was made a vice president of the Cargill Grain Company, the corporate name given to the commission merchant arm of the parent company there.

Grimes also was assigned supervision of Green Bay and tried to work with Quackenbush, but this created mounting tensions. "A rather nasty situation developed in regard to Charley," wrote Grimes, shortly after his new job had started. "He resented this and showed his teeth yesterday afternoon." Quackenbush continued to be recalcitrant, and after several of his decisions were remanded by Grimes, he "resigned" from the job. "This of course was duly suggested to him would be the proper thing to do," John Sr. wrote Fred Hanchette. Quackenbush remained in Green Bay, and leased a competitor elevator. Grimes felt badly about his first management assignment and wrote MacMillan, "I am very sorry for the trouble I had with Mr. Quackenbush but assure you it was absolutely unavoidable. I tried to handle it without any friction but his idea was to want to do more exactly the opposite of what I intended to do and of course matters came to a head."[35]

Austen Cargill went to Milwaukee with Grimes, and the two began a

Andrew Jacobs (left), Ed Grimes (center), and Austen Cargill (right) in the Milwaukee office, c. 1915.

three-year association that became very close. In effect, Austen was the management trainee under Grimes while at the same time Grimes was the management trainee of John Sr. Grimes and Cargill hit it off right from the start. Grimes allowed Austen a free hand in just about all office matters, and it was clear that Austen was the second-in-command. A. L. Jacobs had been the commission agent in charge of the Milwaukee office prior to this enlargement of activity, and Grimes seemed to have no entry difficulties— apparently Jacobs did not feel threatened, as had Quackenbush at Green Bay.

From his first days in the Company, Austen Cargill had shown keen interest in the "country," the rural feeder part of the business consisting of the country elevators, the commission men and track buyers and also the farmers themselves. In the summer of 1914, just before joining Grimes, he had made an extensive trip through Minnesota, Iowa and South Dakota, visiting a number of other small elevators outside the Company's orbit, from which he hoped to secure shipping relationships through Cargill Elevator Company. He classified the individual firms into "likely" and "unlikely" sets. There were 25 names in the former, and "I am writing all these people a personal letter reminding them of our visit and any promises they may have given us when we called on them." Eleven subsequently contracted with Cargill.[36]

At the start of his Milwaukee assignment, Austen also had a revealing experience concerning ways of doing business in Chicago in a situation involving shipments of Green Bay rye to the Chicago Board of Trade. There seems to have been no record made of this story at the time it happened, but it was resurrected in the late 1920s, when Cargill was involved in a major disagreement with the Chicago Board of Trade. It provided an example of the Company's burgeoning mistrust of that institution. The incident itself, in 1913, began with the vice president of the Van Dusen-Harrington Company coming to John Sr. for some of the latter's "fancy Wisconsin No. 1 rye." MacMillan sold it to him and, in due time, 40 cars were on their way to Chicago. The first two cars to arrive there were graded No. 2 rye, but when the remaining 38 cars came in, the buyer reported back to Cargill that they had become No. 3 rye. Austen Cargill was sent down to Chicago to investigate; there he contacted the head of the sampling department at the commission house Logan & Bryan, which was handling cash transactions for Cargill in the Chicago market in those days. He asked for a sample of No. 2 rye, and the inspector, as the story was retold, "pulled out a sample and said 'there is real No. 2 rye.' " Fortunately, Austen had a list of every one of the cars that had been sent down from the Green Bay terminal and, by comparison, soon proved that the rye that had been graded lower really had come from the same batch. "The inspector immediately said, 'well, there must be some mistake.' Logan & Bryan's representative said 'I think it will be straightened out all right,' and that afternoon the grade on the entire shipment of rye was changed to contract grade. In explaining this queer experience, Logan & Bryan's representative told Mr. Cargill that the rye in question was going to 'an important miller' who 'practically ran' the Chicago market at that time."[37]

Grimes, while often commenting favorably on Austen Cargill's efforts, was not unwilling to discipline him. Grimes wrote John Sr., in July 1915, about a year after taking the post, "I think that Austen has spent a great deal of time in pushing sales, improving the system of reporting and has made wonderful strides along that line but has been just a little bit lax in handling of collections and of course this statement of outstanding accounts bears this out."

MacMillan recognized that this was a commentary, too, on the management of Grimes, and he wrote back the next day, "You want to train your customers to make their obligations good as they agree to. . . . There is nothing so disastrous as past due accounts. . . . When you figure up the expense of interest and the cost of collection, you will find that there is mighty little profit in any account that you have to run after . . . you are giving credit to 'dead beats.' "[38] This had been apt warning in 1907–1908 with the Sawyer-Austin and Banner lumber companies, and it was equally apt here.

Austen Cargill sometimes passed information to John Sr. directly rather than through Grimes. For example, MacMillan wrote Grimes in April, 1915, "Austen arrived here this noon, and I have had a chance to talk matters over a little. I was quite surprised to hear about your clover. I did not know you were attempting to handle that or I would have insisted on your keeping in close touch with me so that I would know what was going on. It is exactly this kind of policy on seeds that made so much trouble with Boult. It is altogether the wrong policy to play."[39] Yet Grimes did not seem to resent instances like this, as he understood that Austen Cargill and John MacMillan had a closeness in their relationship that inevitably led to these kinds of confidences. It did not appear to any of the three that Austen had gone over Grimes's head.

On the other hand, Grimes did bristle at competition from traders in other offices. More than once, Grimes felt that Minneapolis was trading unfairly against him. One of these cases involved his old boss, J. B. Cooper. The matter involved a disadvantageous transfer price from Cooper on some oats. "I dislike to complain but it is a tremendous handicap for me to overcome in competing with Minneapolis people in the East who are willing to work and to sell our oats on the basis of 1/2 to 3/4 cent profit out of Minneapolis," Grimes wrote John Sr. Still having a great regard for his mentor Cooper, Grimes continued, "I do not want you to say anything about this to Mr. Cooper, until you think it over yourself and write me further regarding it." MacMillan wrote back, "I think it is up to you to buy your oats and such grains direct instead of attempting to get them in this market. . . . I understand just as well as you do the disadvantage you are working under there, but I am also equally sure that you have got to somehow pick up the great bulk of your grain direct from the country if you are going to be able to compete . . . with Minneapolis . . . I am more and more convinced that you have got to work up your country trade." MacMillan thus encouraged Grimes to stand on his own and to establish his own profit center, as well as his independent supply, rather than leaning on Minneapolis.

On another occasion Austen Cargill, too, complained about Minneapolis treatment of a carload of durum wheat, which Austen felt had been sold by Cooper for an independent country elevator at a giveaway price. Cargill wrote MacMillan, "I believe I can say in all fairness that if I was a country shipper this would have been the last car you would have received from me." In this case, MacMillan felt that the fault lay in Cooper's decision, and wrote Austen, "I have had this matter up vigorously and I think that there will be no more of this sort of thing. I have, in fact, made considerable change in the plan of handling our floor business hereafter. Mr. Cooper is to stay right at the table and give his personal attention to all sales, fix the basis for each car and be there to consult in case any different basis is necessary than that which he originally fixed." These cases provide interesting examples of MacMillan's continuing concerns about both keeping control in his own hands and at the same time giving responsibility to the strong individuals he had gathered around him—in other words, to build independence and the feeling of "ownership" of one's own profit-center on the part of individual managers.[40]

The meticulous MacMillan attention to detail surfaced frequently in the Grimes correspondence. For example, John Sr. wrote Grimes in September, 1914, "I hope you have got your mailing department straightened out by this time, so there will be no further careless addressing of envelopes. It seems to me these envelopes should be addressed by the stenographers instead of being written out in lead pencil by an office boy." MacMillan was still concerned about collections. In one instance where Grimes had extended credit to a firm who had then reneged, MacMillan wrote, "Of course you may work out of this without any loss, only I was wondering how it was you happened to take chances on a firm that I never had heard of before."

Yet even here John Sr. also wanted to encourage Grimes:

You do not want to worry over the fact that you have been caught two or three times lately as I have noticed that this sort of thing has a very peculiar way of bunching up at times. You may not have another similar experience in the next two years, but at the same time, I think you want to make it a point to do business with people that have a recognized standing, just as much as possible, and leave the doubtful concerns alone. Of course, where you can get an extra 5 cents per bushel like this, it is very tempting." Again John Sr. was saying in effect, "It's all right to make a mistake if you learn from it."[41]

John Sr. was just as careful on small details of finance in his personal life. In the fall of 1910, John Jr. began his first year at Phillips Academy in Andover, Massachusetts, and when the room-and-board charges arrived, John Sr. questioned the bill; the amount was over what had been quoted him the previous spring. The principal, Alfred Stearns, sent a long letter in return, explaining that the building was a new one and the trustees had decided to charge at a rate of $250 per year: "This rate is higher than any charge in our other houses, but is made necessary by the increased supervision and care which will be given the boys, and by other attractions which will be offered them, such as a common reading room, study room, playroom, etc." John Sr. agreed to the new charges in a return letter.

The following summer, John Sr. and Edna traveled to New York, checking two bags through. But he was assessed two separate charges for the two bags, instead of the correct practice of one ticket covering both. This bothered his sense of fairness, and he made a claim to the Pennsylvania Lines. Five weeks later a refund check for $1.20 was sent to him, "for the reason that one passenger only instead of two was credited to the baggage at time of checking."[42]

The position that John Sr. probably disliked most was when he himself had to make a decision without the full facts. In May 1915, he wrote a particularly strong letter to Grimes about sales of wheat. Apparently Grimes had not fully reported some of the transactions on the standard "long and short card." MacMillan wrote Grimes:

I feel very much displeased to think that a matter of this kind has been buried instead of being kept before me on your long and short card . . . everybody can make a mistake, but it seems to me you should have consulted us up here in reference to the handling of wheat. Milwaukee is not a wheat market and you are entirely out of touch with wheat conditions. . . . I want to be kept thoroughly advised as to what is going on, so that everything can be talked over and met as the conditions arise and not leave it to me to find out about after things have gone wrong . . . you are bound to make some mistakes. I make them, and everybody else does, but there is a check on yourself as well as on me to talk these things over . . . instead of allowing matters to drift by keeping them buried.

Grimes, shocked by this attack, immediately responded, "I must say that I cannot help but resent this. I do not think that it is a just criticism. I have at no time attempted to bury anything, or deceive you in any transaction I have made." John Sr. answered immediately: "What I was criticizing was the fact that your office does not seem to comprehend our system of accounting well enough to see that complete information is given in reference to all character of trades. . . . There is nothing that I dislike so much as revelations. . . . I want the privilege of knowing all about these matters, so that if I want to criticize, I will have the opportunity of doing so in time, and not have to do it after it is too late."

Grimes was still disturbed and said so in his return letter. This time, John Sr. responded, on May 14, 1915, with an articulate exposition of his overall management philosophy, perhaps one of the clearest statements in all of this period of MacMillan's view of his role as chief executive officer:

I have no idea whatever that you or anyone else was intentionally covering up anything, but I found that that was the way it worked out, and that was why I was objecting, so that that sort of thing would not happen again. . . . I have been extremely anxious to see that the business is run in such a way that there is nothing important going on but what I will have a chance to pass on it.

I have been very much pleased with the general manner you have handled your business . . . the mere fact that I am going to criticize you from time to time must not leave any sting in your mind. . . . I have the whole responsibility of the affairs and it is up to me to see that the business is handled throughout in accordance with the principles which I lay down and if at any time, I don't agree with you, or I find that you are varying from the ideas which I think are sound, you can rest assured that I am going to bring the matter up very promptly. At the same time, I am thoroughly satisfied with the way you have handled matters and am very much gratified over the showing that you have made.[43]

Selling Elevators

This six-year period 1910–1916 witnessed major changes in the physical assets of the Cargill Elevator Company. To begin with, the last remnants of the La Crosse operation were terminated, the railroad excepted. With the closing of the La Crosse office in mid-1913, J. B. Taylor moved to Minneapolis. All estate matters were concentrated in the Minneapolis office. Cargill Elevator Company had taken over the 34 W. W. Cargill Company country elevators in 1910; several of these ringed Green Bay on three sides, and the others stretched along the Chicago and North Western Railroad that traversed the state southwestward to La Crosse. The performance of all of these country elevators had "suffered from sheer neglect," stated the 1945 Cargill history. By 1910, they were not producing any income, so John Sr. decided to phase out the entire Wisconsin country elevator operations. Some were sold almost immediately. Alma Center, for example, was peddled in the first year, along with Viroqua, at the southern end of the ill-fated Cargill-built railroad. The next year, Gillett and Mondovi were sold. By the beginning of the crop year 1916–1917, only Bear Creek and Blair (together with the terminal at Green Bay) were left in Wisconsin; two years later, only the Green Bay terminal remained.

Austen Cargill, under Grimes in Milwaukee, took charge of most of these sales, negotiating with the purchasers and clearing his various moves with John Sr. He wrote MacMillan in October 1915, "I am pleased to note that you sanction the sale of the Osseo House for one thousand dollars. Up to the present time our superintendent has not been able to locate the party who made us this bid but I am in hopes of closing the deal tomorrow. . . . I certainly agree with your statement that we can buy grain from Green Bay on a cheaper basis than we can at this station."[44]

While traveling in the field, Austen Cargill became adept in solving the problems inherent in country elevator operation. For example, the Bear Creek elevator had a serious defalcation by its local manager, an embezzlement that had extended over some 10 years and that had cumulated to over $3,000. Austen Cargill's investigation pointed to slipshod control at the Green Bay end of the accounting chain, where Jacobs was nominally in charge, but Austen blamed this on the fact that earlier Quackenbush would not permit sufficient help and "that Charley insisted on doing things according to plans that he laid down himself."

In this same letter, Grimes reported to MacMillan that Austen Cargill "has been working for some time on a system that will be a big improvement on the old system and that, together with a rigid supervision from this office by him through his traveling men, should prevent a recurrence of anything of this kind again." (The case at hand was a difficult one, for the guilty man had a family of eight children, the youngest of which was two months old. There is no remaining correspondence that documents what happened in this case.) Again Grimes worried about Austen Cargill's fortitude for difficult collections: "I have repeatedly told Austen that he must do something to insure the collection of these accounts and also to verify them even if it had to be done at the expense of personal solicitation of the verifications."[45]

Cargill Securities Company began to make substantial real estate purchases from Sawyer & Austin lands near Pine Bluff, Arkansas, in addition to lands that had come to the Company as part of the earlier settlement. These purchases were made nominally under Austen Cargill's name, but were, as James Taylor stated, "the absolute property of the Cargill Securities Co." First in a series of purchases in March 1912 and then with another substantial acquisition in 1914, the Cargill Securities Company purchased a number of sections of land near the small towns of Junet, Sheridan and

A homesteader loading his horse and equipment into a Great Northern Railroad boxcar, c. 1910–1915 (Minnesota Historical Society).

Cherry Grove, all in central Arkansas. Some of these plats were rural, part cut-over timberland; others were within the town environs. These acquisitions totaled nearly 100 sections of land, a very significant real estate acquisition. Over the succeeding years Cargill Securities Company sold much of this land, sometimes in full sections but in many cases down to parcels as little as 40-acre lots.[46]

Adding Terminals

Despite the fact that the Cargill Elevator Company had to be extremely cautious on its finances, given the weight of the debts from the W. W. Cargill operations, the elevator company did make a major terminal acquisition in January 1914. This was the twin to Elevator K, known as Elevator M, in Superior, Wisconsin. "M" had been sold to F. H. Peavey & Company (then the dominant firm in the industry) in 1896. In early 1914, Peavey offered the elevator to Cargill. The Cargill Elevator Company's subsidiary, the Superior Terminal Elevator Company, was the purchaser for a sum of $250,000. In one of those flukes of history, a large section of it burned on April 26, just three months after it was acquired. The directors met in a special meeting on May 6; the urgency of the matter was evident, for instead of the usual stereotyped wording of minutes, the record read, "In order to be prepared to handle the 1914–15 crop, it would be necessary to rebuild at once." The sum involved was to be in the neighborhood of $150,000 to $175,000—all, of course, covered by insurance. Nevertheless, the shock to the grain storage plans for the fall was major. However, the rebuilding proceeded, and with the twin terminals in operation later that year, Cargill then had a total storage capacity at Superior of some 3.1 million bushels.[47]

One other change in physical surroundings also occurred in this period, one that was considerably less earth shaking: In 1915, the Minneapolis corporate headquarters, John Sr.'s offices included, moved from the Security Bank Building (later known as the Midland Bank) to the First National Soo Line Building.

Glut

The year 1915 *was* eventful for the grain trade as a whole, however. The first two years of the four-year grace period given to Cargill by the Gold Notes arrangement were prewar. When World War I began in Europe in August 1914, the life of most of the world assumed a new dimension, including the grain trade. World grain production had stayed remarkably stable for the four years just before the war: world wheat "ex-Russia" (Russia excluded), had stood at 2.6 billion bushels in 1910, then stabilized at just over 2.9 billion for the next 3 years. Russia's statistics were not as dependable, so the "ex-Russia" statistical artifact typically was used. Nevertheless, in this pre-World War I period, that great wheat-producing country also had significant exports to the rest of the world until it was attacked by Germany on August 1, 1914. Once the war began, Russia dropped out of the international grain markets, and all through the war there were just five major overseas exporting countries—the United States, Canada, Argentina, Australia and India.

Now this stability was challenged by a huge bulge upward in world production. Record United States and Canadian yields were harvested, and Argentina and Australia experienced the same pattern. In the other exporting country, India, yields declined over previous years, but total production was still on an upward path. Felicitous rainfall around the world pushed yields to new highs. In short, the crop of 1915 was enormous—a record in North America for the decade ending in 1918.[48]

John Sr. wrote Grimes in April 1915 that he expected "brilliant" prospects for the crop but warned that price volatility from such a large crop might make it difficult in the months ahead: "It is a very unusual situation; no one's judgment is worth anything and the only safe thing to do is to clean up and work on the most cautious, conservative cash basis during the balance of the crop." MacMillan was especially concerned that Grimes and the others not take any open position on either side of the market in regard to rye and barley.

MacMillan also wrote Fred Hanchette about the volatility of the situation:

We have had all kinds of wild markets since last I wrote you. The markets dropped about 30 cents per bu. and are now working back again and it is certainly a fierce matter to know what to do with hedges under such conditions. . . . We certainly never have been up against anything like this year. But unless we get some disaster at the tail-end of the year, I think we are going to have a very satisfactory year. We have always found in the end that it is the years of unusual conditions that we have been able to do the best . . . our experience is able to guide us through such situations . . . while it frightens a great many of our competitors out of the market.

Writing in that same period to Austen Cargill about the "wild markets," MacMillan concluded, "It is a very trying situation, but I am afraid next year will be just as bad as I do not see any probability that this war will be finished up during this next year."[49]

In this same year (1915), John Sr. became skittish once more about what was happening in the Chicago wheat market. Grimes had been doing considerable trading there, and MacMillan wrote him, "I think it is an extremely dangerous matter now to play with Chicago May wheat. . . . Chicago May is liable to corner itself and we cannot afford to take any chances on it."[50] MacMillan's old memories of the "Leiter corner" had been exacerbated in 1909 when speculator James Patten pulled off another famous corner, on Chicago Board of Trade May wheat. The May wheat contract was always a prime candidate for such an effort, either a deliberate one or a "natural corner" from the particular circumstances surrounding the May contract, before the new crop of spring wheat was harvested. When another "Patten corner" had been attempted in 1913 in the December corn contract at the Chicago Board of Trade, everyone's guard was up. In 1915 there were again rumors of Patten moves. It turned out that there was, after all, no corner in this May 1915 contract, and John Sr.'s forebodings about the crop year 1914–1915 did not become a reality; quite to the contrary, net profits from the Superior terminal grain account, a nice $155,000 the previous year, now jumped to $460,000. The line grain account almost doubled, too. On total revenues of just over $22.6 million, the Cargill Elevator Company had made over $680,000 net profit—only a 2.9% margin but an outstanding record in the grain business, in which rapid turnover and very small margins on very large transactions generally prevailed.[51]

This excellent performance, satisfying in its own right, still left in abeyance the overriding debt of the Cargill Elevator Company, the $2.5 million Gold Notes, issued under the aegis of the Noteholders Protective Committee and due "on or before January 1st, 1917." Caution was still very much the byword, and the directors of the Company declared only a 19% dividend (on capital stock), plowing the remaining profits back into the business. John MacMillan, Sr., knew that sometime over the 1915–1916 crop year he had to meet this ominous obligation—and do it in a way that would not upset the credit lines he would need for that year.

APPENDIX

An Alternate View of the Will

(John Work, *Cargill Beginnings*, pp. 146–148)

No public mention was made at the time of Will's death, quite naturally, of his will or of other provisions to dispose of his estate. Shortly after the funeral, however, it was discovered that he had died intestate—that no will had been forthcoming from his attorneys, survivors or from among his effects. His estate, therefore, was required to be put in the hands of a court, for division "share and share alike" among four heirs, William S. Cargill, Edna MacMillan, Emma Hanchette and Austen Cargill. It was surprising, but not unique, that a man of Will's age and business responsibility should have failed to anticipate his own death with a properly constituted will; especially in view of one younger brother's death six years before, of the earlier incapacitation of an even younger brother and of Will's own declining health since his stroke. Yet the principal legatees and the courts agreed that such was the case, and so the estate was divided.

Nevertheless, a different version is obtained from descendants of one of the principals. This story, rightly or wrongly, has it that the old man did leave a will, but one which had been written antipathetically to one of his four children, Emma, and her husband, Fred Hanchette, ostensibly because the husband had not shown what Will considered "proper businesslike energy" and "was little likely to change."

According to Ellen Hanchette Gleason: "Three months after my mother and father were married, my mother was asked by a doctor at a hotel where they were staying, 'Mrs. Hanchette, do you know that your husband has tuberculosis?' It proved to be true, and from that time until 1911 or 1912, my father literally was fighting for his life. They were not 'traveling' in Switzerland as the La Crosse newspaper said (at the time of Will Cargill's death) but were at the sanatorium in Davos-Dorf. Later, in 1912 or '13, my father . . . had a severe chest operation. Shortly after that we moved to California, in those days considered mainly a health resort."

Mrs. Gleason also said: "My father had what now would be known as a periodic drinking problem, and in the context of that turn-of-the century time, it might have been embarrassing. But I cannot credit that W. W. Cargill would have slighted my mother in his will for father's not having 'proper businesslike energy,' when he was fighting with all he had to lick T.B. and live. It simply is not in character for him to have done so. I know my mother adored her father. She always spoke of him as the dearest man that ever lived and the most generous man in the world. Over and over she told me he would give money to anyone who asked for it or needed it."

In any case, an alternative version is advanced. The story has it that a will was discovered at Will's home in La Crosse by the three heirs present for the funeral—William S. Cargill, Austen and their sister, Edna MacMillan. It instructed that one-half of the estate go to the elder son, William S., and that one-fourth each go to Austen and Edna. It provided that Emma Hanchette receive the income from a $100,000 trust, to be established separately. However, according to our informant, the three heirs agreed among themselves that Emma and her family would be treated too harshly if the will were to stand; that the father's instructions reflected some ill-considered, short-term disgruntlement or pique; that his deeper intentions would best be served if the document in hand were destroyed—and that it was destroyed.

If the story is true, surely destruction of the will had decisive meaning for later Cargill history. The crux of that history, for more than a decade after Will Cargill's death, was exclusion of William S. and his advocates from company management, and the installation as head of the organization of John H. MacMillan. This was difficult enough when four heirs each controlled one-fourth of the estate. It probably would have been impossible if William S. had owned one-half.

As to whether the story is true indeed, we do not know, nor can proof be found. Along with Ellen Gleason, we agree that the will, as described, seems "out of character," inconsistent with our picture of Will Cargill's generosity. We agree with her, also, when she says: "I can scarcely credit that, if he left a will, the sole copy would have been sitting around the house where it could be found and destroyed, or that his attorney would not have known of its existence and had a copy." However, Mrs. Gleason herself has suggested one possible justification for the will's provisions.

After stating her disbelief that Will Cargill could have discriminated against her father in that way because he had not shown "businesslike energy," she said: "Perhaps my father was 'unemployable;' I don't know. The fact is, he was the only one of the sons or sons-in-law that did not have a job with the company." Perhaps, then, such provisions as are claimed for the will might not have been meant to discriminate, but to assure his own son's take-over of management of the Cargill organization; to provide the company with a working ownership throughout and, perhaps, to relieve his daughter Emma and her husband of the need for managerial responsibility while also providing them with a guaranteed income, separate from the vicissitudes of such businesses as grain, small railroads or large ranches in Montana.

So much for the story of the disappearing will. The facts, as agreed to by the courts, as recalled by most present descendants and as never officially contested by any of the heirs, must stand as initially stated: Will Cargill died intestate, and a four-way division of his estate followed, necessarily.

PART THREE

FREE TO GROW, 1916-1930

A farmers' club unloading a car of coal, Beardsley, Minnesota.

CHAPTER FIVE

Reorganization, the Great War

Both of John MacMillan, Sr.'s sons went into the Company, each to spend his full business career with Cargill. After John Sr. stepped away from major responsibilities in the firm in the early 1930s, John Jr. and his younger brother, Cargill MacMillan, joined with Austen Cargill to become a triumvirate of family at the center of the Company's management and to provide leadership for some 30 subsequent years.

The personalities of these three men influenced the Company markedly. Austen Cargill's relationship to his father and brother and to his Company mentors, John Sr. and Ed Grimes, has been described earlier. John Jr.'s role became particularly important, for he developed into an intense and controversial chief executive officer of the firm. Cargill MacMillan and Austen also had significant responsibilities, and the Company in these earlier years cannot fully be understood without assessing the sum contribution of this interesting family threesome—three young men so different from one another. The business and personal values given to these three by, especially, their fathers provide many insights in understanding the Company.

John Jr. was born in 1895, five years before his brother, Cargill MacMillan, and seven years after Austen Cargill. In September 1910, John Sr. and Edna decided to send John Jr., then not quite 15, east to preparatory school at the prestigious Phillips Academy (or "Andover") in Andover, Massachusetts. Earlier, both Edna and her sister Emma had gone to a New York "finishing school," the Granger Place School in Canandaigua, New York.

Informative letters from the young prep schooler to his mother and father and a set of encouraging yet strict replies from father to son reveal glimpses into the shaping of family values from generation to generation. At the start, John Jr. did very well in his mathematics and science courses but quite poorly in Latin. In that first fall semester he failed a number of recitations in Latin but confided to his father, "of course I won't use a pony. I think it is much better to fail them than to do that." He decided to go out for football "because I don't know how to play socker [*sic*] and I am poor at everything on the track—I can't even run a quarter mile without getting a terrific stinging pain in my chest."[1]

His father required him to report via a full-scale single-entry accounting system exactly what he had spent, and in the first two years John Jr. apparently lived within his budget. His father wrote, "I am glad to see you figure out as you go along just what you can afford and hold yourself rigidly in. It is the only way you ever can make a success. . . . I do want you also to try to *save*. No matter what your income . . . figure out some way to save something—otherwise you never will get ahead." The matter was black-and-white to John Sr.: "You must either make progress or you are going backward. There is no half way . . . fix your habits now in the right way, for you are now fixing them for life."[2]

By early 1913, John Jr.'s budget was in the red, and his father wrote, "I dislike tremendously to have you run behind this way, for it shows that you are not living within your income. . . . I do not approve of your running so close that you cannot take care of yourself for anything unexpected. It is a bad habit. . . . Sometimes it seems hard to deprive yourself when you see others spending more . . . never allow yourself merely to drift along."

A few weeks later, he wrote more bluntly, "You have got to make your own way in the world. Don't ever get thinking that I am rich, for I am not. It is all I can to educate you boys and live in comfort ourselves, and any calamity like my health breaking down, business reverses and the like might make it necessary at any time for you to earn your own living."[3] (The years 1909–1916 were tenuous for John Sr. as he attempted to reorganize the Company in the face of the W. W. Cargill estate's huge debts—he did not know what was in store for the Cargill Elevator Company.)

In December 1912, just prior to the budget problems, John Jr. was involved in an escapade. In the course of a roughhouse, he broke down a door. Right afterward, he obtained an agreement that his friends would reimburse him for the cost of a new door. The school declined to look on the matter as something that could be corrected by payment and suspended John Jr. and several of his friends from the building in which they had been living, although not expelling them from the school itself. His father, outraged at John Jr.'s behavior, minced no words. Breaking things with impunity just because one could pay for them was a cardinal offense in his mind.

John Jr.'s letter explaining the affair must have fallen short of what his father expected. John Sr. wrote, "Now one does not improve his own character and sense of proportion by playing the baby. The spirit you show in your letter is beneath you. It is the spirit of the boy who says 'I won't play' because he cannot have his own way." John Jr. confessed he had flunked a chemistry examination just before the incident, and his father railed, "You are heedless and careless . . . allowing yourself to drift with the current instead of making the most of your opportunities in the right way, struggling with difficulties and hardening and toughening your will and moral fiber—in other words, developing character." His father urged John Jr. to apologize to the faculty members, "then forget the incident. Don't talk about it, and if the incident is talked about in your presence so that you cannot ignore it, admit cheerfully that you only got what you deserved, that it was a silly, foolish thing you did and you will soon have the respect and good wishes of both the boys and faculty."[4]

Caviling about Schoolboy Discipline

John Sr. firmly backed the acting principal, Charles H. Forbes (Alfred E. Stearns, the principal, was abroad for the year) in the penalties exacted on John Jr. Forbes, in his return letter, responded that he was "especially grateful to you for the way in which you upheld the discipline which we have felt necessary to inflict." He expressed confidence in John Jr.—that his indiscretion was "merely an outburst of animal spirits, which does not indicate any trouble with his character."

Within weeks, however, John Sr. and Forbes had a confrontation over another disciplinary matter, not one directly involving John Jr., occurring just after Christmas vacation. Andover's adamant policy requiring its students to be back strictly on time from vacation periods had involved another Minneapolis boy, who had been late returning from Christmas break after having been sick. He presented no medical excuse for his tardiness, and the school had suspended the young man for a term.

John Sr., incensed, wrote a stinging letter to Forbes: "When you undertake to discipline parents because of their deliberate decisions, I believe you are jeopardizing your influence with your boys. . . . The home is a more fundamental institution than the school. The authority of the parent is paramount to that of any school faculty."

MacMillan then fell into a chauvinistic comparison:

You are creating a feeling of hostility against the school in the communities to which the boys belong. I have talked with a great many people in Minneapolis over your action in this case, and in every instance your action has been condemned most vigorously . . . it may be that Phillips Academy does not care particularly to have Western boys. If so, your action in this matter will perhaps be sufficient notice in this community, but if you do want the Western boy then you must respect family rights and treat both the boys and parents with justice and courtesy.

Forbes wrote back immediately. Absence policy had been set by the "Absence Committee" of 40 members—the president of the board of trustees, "a Boston banker, heartily supports us." Forbes curtly addressed the issue of school versus parent: "I must regretfully inform you that this school differs with you on your statement of the paramount authority of the parent in school management. Not for *fifty* years, at least, has any parent been suffered to oppose his will successfully to that of the Academy authorities, in matters pertaining to school regulations. No self-respecting school could be conducted on any other terms." As to "the Western boys," Forbes dismissed the MacMillan allegation out of hand: "You were not, of course, serious in suggesting that we do not wish Western boys. It is our pride that the school covers the country, and it does this because we try to run a good, strong school that pays attention to the business of education."

John Sr. remained extremely irate, arguing that "parents have a still greater authority and have the unquestionable right of selection of school their boy shall attend." He could not seem to drop his concern that the Minneapolis boys were being discriminated against: "If your pupils look upon this in the same light that Minneapolis people do, it cannot help putting a decided check."

Forbes gave not an inch.

We must continue to sit on opposite ends of the log. We do not question the right of the parent in the 'selection of the school his boy shall attend,' but when he sends him to us to be cared for in body, mind, and character, we do not accept the grave responsibility without undisputed control while under our charge. Would you accept the job on any other terms? . . . There never was a school that ever was seriously injured, or that lost standing amongst intelligent people, by insisting on promptness, attention to duty, freedom from special privilege, and one law for all.

This last phrase was targeted to John Sr.'s allegations of discrimination against Minneapolis boys. There the matter rested—Forbes had not acquiesced in any way; John Sr.'s fulminations had gone nowhere.

When John Jr. and his friends persisted in agitating about the case, John Sr. came down hard: "I notice . . . a growing disposition to insubordination—now you must cut that out. . . . You are certainly getting yourself in bad and there can only be one end to that sort of thing. Discipline is an absolute necessity in school business, as in all other affairs in life . . . you are not trying to help the management."[5]

John Sr. apparently felt this was the occasion to urge John Jr. to take a job the following summer: "I want you always to feel that work is a great privilege—not a penalty, and you want to earn the right to work, as you would prize any other right. . . . If you succeed you are fitting yourself more especially for intellectual work, to make your mind instead of your muscles the governing force."

John Jr. hinted that he might leave school, for he was still smarting from the incident of the door and angry about the suspension of his Minneapolis classmate. His father responded, "To quit school because you feel hurt would no more develop your mind than to sulk would develop your muscles. The worst feature would be that it would weaken your character by running away from an unpleasant experience. . . . I don't want you to think that I am scolding. Everyone makes mistakes. I only want that you learn from your experiences in life. Make every experience teach you its lesson and you will then continue to grow in character and understanding." Once again, John Sr. had expressed his strongly held tenet about the recoverability of a mistake, provided one learned from it.

John Sr. chose, too, to mention another parameter of John Jr.'s life that worried him. John Jr. needed to develop a network of friends, not only for their good companionship and help in enjoying life but also because "it increases tremendously your influence and that makes wonderfully for success. Many a man with little brain capacity makes a great success in life because he has a great capacity for making friends. These friends advise with him and help him over many hard places and frequently into good fortune because they like to benefit a friend." This seemed not a concept of "using" friends but drawing mutually upon friends for support and nurture. "You are naturally weak there," his father went on, "and it is all the more necessary that you should exert yourself so as to overcome this tendency. Make yourself one of the crowd and *be a leader*."[6]

Nor was John Sr. happy with his son's expressed career objectives. By this time, John Jr. was doing honors work in algebra and stood well in chemistry and physics, yet he still recorded an E in Latin in the spring of 1913. John Jr. had indicated interest in engineering, and his father was not enthusiastic. Engineers were out in the field too much of the time, John Sr. felt, and were never near the power center: "To get ahead in the world, from a financial sense at any rate, it is quite essential to be able to mix with those who are leading the various lines of business. It is much better for example to be the stenographer of a man like J. J. Hill, Mr. Dunwoody, and men of that type if one has a genuine ability than to occupy a fairly good position in a city like La Crosse. Big men are always looking for men of ability but naturally are confined to men they know of through their associates. . . . That is why it pays to be where you can know the big men." It was the rule rather than the exception in grain trading companies in those days to have mostly male stenographers; that was how Ed Grimes, for example, got his start in Cargill.[7]

But John Sr. was not a reflexive patrician, interested only in associating with men of money and power. At one point, John Jr. was doing some classroom field work in a working-class neighborhood in Lawrence, Massachusetts, and his father wrote:

I am much pleased at the experience you are getting in Lawrence. It puts you in touch with a class that ordinarily you could never see and it broadens one tremendously to keep in touch with business life in every strata of society. You will find people just as true and generous in the lower walks of life as in the upper and I am sure you will more and more be impressed with the fact that people are pretty much the same wherever you find them. Differences in social strata are more differences in opportunity than in intrinsic merit and it is intrinsic merit that is worthwhile—not because one man has had a little more money than another or that his father had before him.[8]

John Jr. graduated from Andover in the spring of 1914 and worked for the summer on the MacMillan ranch near Lubbock, Texas. He enjoyed this enormously and vowed, almost facetiously, that "the chief objection to farming is that you apparently have to get up before daylight and work until after dark."[9]

He entered Yale University in the fall of 1914 and found its academics more appealing to him. He wrote his father about the senior faculty members: "The older ones . . . mark easy, are only too glad to go over a paper with you in which the mark doesn't suit you and in classroom are able to make the courses interesting as possible. They discuss everything under the sun." In his second year at Yale he was able to enroll in a course with the famous economist Irving Fisher, who was teaching a course on "national efficiency." While mathematics and science had heretofore been John Jr.'s favorite subjects, he found this social science course "very good," for "in it he explains all his pet theories, etc. I really believe that is the only reason why they have it at all—just to give him a chance to teach the things that he has evolved."

Yale was a good fit for John Jr. His social skills had broadened measurably. He became an officer in his own fraternity house and led his brothers in planning a new building. Still not a student, he developed several moneymaking ventures and also enjoyed Yale's perennial poker games. He began to show a sense of his fellow man that his father had pushed him toward at an earlier point. He and a few of his friends, for example, befriended a young Irishman who had come across the Atlantic with practically no money and was peddling on the Yale campus. The young man said he was a graduate of the Royal University of Ireland and had been a teacher until his health had broken. A doctor had urged him to "take a sea voyage," and that had led him finally to New Haven. John Jr. helped the Irish visitor to find employment and wrote at length to his father about the experience.[10]

Thus emerges once again the lasting set of personal standards held by John Sr., espoused through business decisions but representing almost visceral internal beliefs, then to be passed along to his children. Over and over come forth his qualities of honesty, perseverance, and thrift, almost a 20th-century reiteration of Benjamin Franklin's "poor Richard." In John

Jr.'s adulthood his father developed an almost boundless admiration of his son's unique intelligence and an uncritical acceptance of anything that John Jr. then espoused. But in these teen years he exhorted, encouraged and shaped his son's goals. John Sr. must have found it sometimes difficult to fit this into his analytical mind—not stifle John Jr., not cause enormous rebellion, yet put bounds around him. John Sr. had a quality of acceptance and empathy for others' views, whatever their social class, but John Jr. found this difficult to emulate.

Perhaps the single best example of this credo of John Sr. is found in his letter written to John Jr. on the occasion of the latter's 21st birthday on December 1, 1916. The letter begins:

It is hard to realize that you have become a man . . . responsible for your own destiny. Your days from now on will be filled with care, with sorrow and I hope also of joy. Whether your life will be a failure or a glorious success depends entirely upon your own efforts. If you show dogged perseverance and determination and rugged honesty, there can be no question of the outcome. The greatest thing in the world to my mind is character and that is attained only by rigid self-analysis as well as honesty, courage and determination and hard work. . . . The happiest are those who do their full share of hard work. A little play is necessary for relaxation and good health and I hope you will never forget how to play. That will keep you youthful but that should be only an incident of life—not the main purpose.

Next telling his son that he had made him a small gift of Cargill Elevator stock, John Sr. then propounded a Spartan piece of advice about saving: "I hope this will be an incentive to you to begin saving as soon as you begin work so as to increase your capital rapidly. You want to make it an infallible rule to save at least 1/3 of your income to add to your capital each year. No matter how small it seems, the discipline and training are worth many times the money involved. One of the most disastrous things in human experience is extravagance, and it leads to most awful temptations."

By the time John Jr. had reached his majority, John Sr. seemed increasingly concerned about the health of his oldest son. As early as 1913, he had been commenting on John Jr.'s "poor physical condition." By 1916, John Jr.'s smoking seemed to his father to loom as the biggest threat. John Jr. visited his brother Cargill at Andover in November of that year and was seen smoking as he walked the streets there. His father immediately fired off an incensed letter: "I was very much disappointed that you should give way to such a silly notion as to smoke cigarettes going down Main Street at Andover. I wonder if you realize how much your influence is over Cargill and his young friends. Seems to me that you are old enough now to feel a personal sense of responsibility."

Then, in March 1917, John Jr. had an operation on his tonsils, and his father once again came back to the smoking: "Any one secretly holds in contempt one who becomes a slave to any vice and I fear you have gotten to the point where you have lost control. If so, you can be very certain you will pay a fearful penalty. If you cannot control your habits, you cannot long keep self-respect."

The close of the letter contained a curious warning: "You are of an extremely nervous temperament and it is of the utmost importance that you control yourself absolutely or you will break down under any heavy strain. You cannot stand excesses of any kind and it will be necessary for the next few years to do nothing that you know is keeping your nerves at high tension. . . . I am convinced that if you do not take proper care of yourself that you will become neurotic and a sort of semi-invalid." The last sentence of this paragraph seemed almost an order: "I should like to have you prove your will power to do things in such a normal fashion that there can be no question about building up your strength, health and general constitution."[11]

The sum of all of this advice and admonition gave John Jr. an unparalleled view of John Sr.'s values. John MacMillan, Sr., had consistent beliefs; he articulated these frequently and effectively, and they represented a set of personal axioms that already had become the business objectives of the Cargill Elevator Company. The legacy to the Cargill of today cannot be overemphasized.

Freeing the Debts

The "Gold Notes" of Cargill Securities Company hanging over the entire Cargill Elevator Company organization had conditioned so many moves. Perhaps the situation was not as restrictive as pictured in the 1945 Cargill history, which intoned; "the aggressive merchandising and warehousing policies were replaced by conservative operations . . . the Company could no longer assume substantial business risks." After all, in this interim, Peavey's "Belt Line" terminal (later Elevator M) had been purchased in Superior, Wisconsin, and there had been major construction at Elevator T in Minneapolis. Still, John Sr. had had to be careful.

There had been five profitable years in the Elevator Company since the shock of W. W. Cargill's death in 1909, with dividends paid for all of those years. Finally, however, the Gold Note deadline—due on or before January 1, 1917—had to be faced, either by reorganizing the debt into new securities or by eliminating it altogether. There were three critical dimensions.

First, resolving the problem was to be a public matter, as the notes were common knowledge among the financial community and traded therein, and the establishment of the Cargill Securities Company and the subsequent issue of its Gold Notes had been widely reported in the press. John Sr. had a thoroughgoing dislike of publicity generally but had no choice.

Unfortunately, the public image of the Gold Notes was ambiguous. Indeed, John Sr. had had to face periodic queries about "just how strong those notes really are." For example, rumor had reached John Sr. early in 1916 through a Boston notebroker that the notes were being offered at a discount—an implication that there was weakness in them. MacMillan immediately wrote back: "Now these notes are worth par and there's no reason why anyone should sell them for less. . . . In fact, if anyone wants to throw off the accrued interest, I can find a purchaser for the notes. . . . I hope you will advise all of the holders of these notes not to sell them as there is no reason why they should not bring the full value . . . there is no question whatever about their being paid at maturity." The correspondent wrote back an unsettling letter: "It would seem as if the inquiry that springs up on these notes, from time to time, probably originates from some source in Minneapolis, who feeling that they know something about the situation, may be endeavoring to make a little money out of it" [presumably by selling short]. This comment must have upset John Sr. even more, for he hated having anyone talking about him behind his back.[12]

The second set of issues loomed larger, indeed dominated John Sr.'s thinking: how could the Elevator Company get through this period while at the same time preserving its own economic health. By early July 1915, it was clear that Cargill's just-completed crop year, war-stimulated, had been considerably more successful than anyone had anticipated. John Sr. wrote T. F. Baxter, the Boston member of the Noteholders Protective Committee, about the good news. John Sr. had begun to see a way through the maze, utilizing once more the excellent earnings of the Elevator Company to pay off at least a large portion of the Gold Note obligations. He told Baxter, "Of course, we have no intention, as you can judge from the above, of giving out our earnings, as I do not want to show them as large as they are."

He amplified to Baxter a few days later: "After consulting with Mr. Jaffray and Mr. Hixon [the other two members of the Committee], we have decided to increase our concealed assets account by $100,000.00. . . . When it comes to making a final large dividend to meet the Cargill Securities notes it will help out our statement very much if we can have a large account of this kind, which does not show up in a statement, for it will not show such a tremendous cut in the surplus account of the company." (He also chatted with Baxter on the telephone at this time, apparently the first instance that direct connections had been made for MacMillan between Minneapolis and Boston. "It was quite a novel experience," he said afterward.)[13]

The third set of issues undoubtedly was the most draining. These were the often-knotty family tensions. A substantial circle of MacMillans and Cargills had lived close for many years, with all of the personal links and affections that family can give—but also with the misunderstandings, hurt feelings and personal attacks that can occur in such a close relationship. In this case, the effect on the W. W. Cargill estate of the expansive plans in the West, particularly those at Valier, Montana, had brought strong passions to the fore relating to the role of son William S. Cargill and his partners. The questionable activities of some of Will's cohorts and their antics had disgusted the remaining principals.

The other heirs most immediately involved were W. W. Cargill's sister, Margaret Barker ("Aunt Maggie"), the widow of George R. Barker, and S. D. Cargill's widow, Lydia Ellen ("Aunt Lydia"), together with the other direct descendants of W. W. Cargill: daughter Emma Hanchette, daughter Edna MacMillan (John's wife), and son Austen S. Cargill. By the time the Cargill Securities Company was established in 1912 and the reorganization process under way, severe antagonisms had surfaced between Will Cargill on the one side and all of these heirs on the other.

John Jr. chose, perhaps unwisely, to reopen old wounds, writing a thesis in his Yale corporation finance course in the spring of 1916 about the Valier project. His judgments were harsh:

> The manner in which the endorsement of W. W. Cargill was obtained by his son cannot be easily passed over. The number of misrepresentations and exaggerations is such that they can scarcely be called mistakes, particularly when W. S. Cargill had the deeds and bills of sale right before him. . . . Furthermore the conduct of affairs by Cargill and Withee could not bear inspection. They made contracts which they must have known they could not live up to. Their books are full of errors and misstatements, although the books themselves are few in number: No satisfactory accounting was ever made for large sums of money . . . the elimination of these two gentlemen was imperative, once the true state of affairs had been uncovered.

John Sr.'s correspondence at the time expressed the same feelings.[14]

There had been practically no contact between Will and the MacMillans, John and Edna, nor with the Hanchettes; the only link to Will was through Austen. In no way was Will to be allowed to continue the indulged position he held before his father's death, and this changed fortune must have been a terrible shock to him. He had been furious in 1912. Now, four years later, his animus again surfaced. Manifestly, Will was going to be a difficult person to deal with in any debt reorganization.

A Fresh Blueprint for Action

Acutely aware of these tensions, John Sr. wrote Fred Hanchette, Emma's husband, in March 1916, about a draft he had given Austen of a possible plan: "This is written primarily to give him the necessary data to take this refinancing matter up with Will Cargill to find out what his attitude is going to be. I think Austen rather shrinks from undertaking anything of the kind, but I do not know any other way to reach him, as Austen is the only one on speaking terms with him that I would dare trust to handle anything of this sort."[15]

John Sr. amplified his unease in a letter to Hanchette a few weeks later, in April: "Edna and I are planning to leave here Monday night and spend Tuesday with Austen and Anne in Milwaukee and it is possible by that time Austen may be able to throw some new light on Will's attitude. . . . I am inclined to believe that we will probably have to go ahead . . . none of the rest of us are willing to allow Will to dictate the policy of the Cargill Securities Company, and say what shall be sold and what shall not."

He elaborated his plan: "The way the thing stands . . . Emma, Edna and Austen will have to pool their stock in some kind of a voting trust and in this way, we could keep the present directors in charge and I think could refinance whatever will be necessary without coming to any final agreement with Will." Having the matter "be unanimous with Will, too, would be better," John Sr. concluded, "but one of the advantages of a corporation is that the majority of the stockholders can control its policy, while, when the estate was in Probate Court, it required unanimous consent."[16]

By mid-May 1916, family discord had worsened. When Austen Cargill met with Will, the latter "practically threatened to make trouble if his demands for being bought out were not complied with." Soon John Sr. fleshed out a more sophisticated version of his plan to F. P. Hixon, who was influential in this whole set of events as not only one of the three members of the Noteholders Protective Committee but also as a nonoperating vice president of the Cargill Elevator Company.[17] The situation was this: The Cargill Securities Company was owned in one-quarter shares each by Will Cargill, Austen Cargill, Emma Cargill Hanchette and Edna Cargill MacMillan, as the four heirs of W. W.'s estate. Their shares had been trusteed to the bank during the term of the Gold Notes. The estate had a number of illiquid assets, including the British Columbia timberlands; the cutover lands in Arkansas and, after the Sawyer & Austin sale, some miscellaneous yards of Sawyer & Austin and Banner Lumber Co.; the Mexican land (which could not even be visited because of the Mexican revolution); the Valier project in Montana and the La Crosse & Southeastern Railway. There was a set of debts totaling $2,651,000, made up of the $2,499,000 of Gold Notes, together with some accrued interest owed and a note of Sawyer & Austin due the Cargill Elevator Co. Finally, the estate had some income from the bauxite leases on the former Sawyer & Austin lands.

The Cargill Elevator Company continued to be the one strong link in the situation. It had been successful over the past five years and had a healthy surplus built up. About one-sixth of its stock still was held outright by "Aunt Maggie" and "Aunt Lydia," the remainder was trusteed to the Noteholders Protective Committee by Austen and Will Cargill, Emma Hanchette and Edna MacMillan as security for the Gold Notes.

John Sr. now proposed a plan to resolve the issues. Its outline was as follows:

1. The Cargill Elevator Company articles of incorporation would be amended to increase the authorized capital stock to $2,400,000 (from $2 million); $1.6 million of this would be common stock; $800,000 would be 7 percent preferred stock.

2. The *present* stockholders (i.e., the two widows and the bank as trustee) would then receive $800,000 of the common—one-half—and $800,000 of the preferred, all of it.

3. A cash dividend of $240 per share would then be paid to the widows and the trustee, with the following effect on the Cargill Elevator Company, using rounded figures:

Capital	$1,000,000
Surplus	3,000,000
Total	$4,000,000
Less dividend	2,400,000
Remaining capital and surplus	$1,600,000

Inasmuch as this $1.6 million was just about the value of the company's actual capital assets, there would be essentially *no* surplus left. If the Cargill Elevator Company was left in this situation, it would be a precarious position, especially because a zero surplus would be a conspicuous red flag for lenders to a grain business. Therefore, additional capital would be drawn in by selling the remaining $800,000 of the common stock.

The Gold Notes, together with the accrued interest owed and the small Sawyer & Austin debt, totaled $2,651,000. The cash dividend would yield just about $2 million for the Noteholders Protective Committee, its five-sixths share (the one-sixth share of the dividend going to "Aunt Maggie" and "Aunt Lydia"). If about $700,000 additional could be added to the Committee's $2 million, the Gold Notes could be totally retired. So C. T. Jaffray, the banker member of the Committee, formed a syndicate of banks for a $700,000 loan to Cargill Securities Company, with the security to be the income stream from the bauxite contract (which would retire the principal of the new loan) and the Cargill Elevator Company preferred stock dividends (which would pay the interest). These pieces were put in place, and the Gold Notes were retired forthwith.

John Sr.'s letters expressed his relief. He wrote T. F. Baxter, the note-broker member of the Committee (which disbanded itself, of course), "In financing this reorganization the . . . Elevator Co. did not have to borrow a dollar. . . . I feel very much pleased over that, as I have been very doubtful of our ability to get our grain sold and turned into money by July 1st."

He shared his pride with "Aunt Maggie:" "We have been receiving the heartiest congratulations of our banking friends."[18]

It remained only to close one more loop. It was important to acquire immediately the further working capital by the sale of the 8,000 shares ($800,000) of common stock. The purchasers became a combination of (a) members of the board of directors and other key top management people, (b) a set of other trusted Cargill employees, some fairly far down in the organization and (c) a few outsiders, close friends of the owners. The sale to employees fulfilled a wish John Sr. had expressed to W. W. Cargill, as far back as 1906, of "taking in the boys." W. W. had responded positively then but had never done anything.

Inasmuch as the second group—the lower-level employees—would not likely have much cash to put into such a scheme, an ingenious alternative was constructed for them. The two heirs, Aunt Maggie and Aunt Lydia, having received substantial cash from the dividends noted earlier, agreed to use considerable portions of that cash as loans to the employees. The 1945 Cargill history put this candidly: "Thus, by indirection, some of the dividend money found its way back into the grain company."

Despite the attractiveness of the plan, C. T. Jaffray was uneasy about it. John Sr. reported to Hixon:

His [Jaffray's] first impression was that we were asking a good deal of Mrs. Cargill and Mrs. Barker and made a suggestion that perhaps it would be better to offer them some of the preferred stock . . . and let the Cargill Securities Co. then loan the money to the employees. I did not take very well to this suggestion . . . it would make a very difficult situation to explain to the Cargill heirs [here John Sr. likely was thinking particularly of the Hanchettes]. They would naturally think that if any of the estate stock was sold for cash it should go to pay debts instead of being used to allow employees to buy common stock.

Apparently Jaffray's misgivings were resolved, for the loan plan involving the two women became the final basis for settlement.

John Sr. had no trouble in selling the stock. "I have been overwhelmed with requests from various people." Some was to go to Hixon, "who has been associated with us through all these difficulties" and some "to the Osborne McMillan people, who are altogether our largest customers at Duluth, and to a very few of our closest banking friends who have done so much for the credit of the company."

The remaining stock went to the employees. Even here there were allocation problems, as John Sr. lamented: "I did not have enough to take care of all . . . that I felt were entitled to some. . . . We must take care of the men at the top first, as it has been their ability and long and faithful service that has put the . . . Co. in such remarkably strong condition."

Strong it was. With the sale of the remainder of the common stock, the complete plan was now a reality. In their final report, on June 15, 1916, Hixon, Jaffray and Baxter, the members of the Noteholders Protective Committee, ready to disband themselves, succinctly summed up the accomplishment: "It is apparent that the creditors could not have been paid in full had an immediate liquidation been demanded. The wisdom of the plan entered into at that time is proven by the results, the creditors are to be paid in full with 6% interest and the estate to be returned to the Cargill heirs is a very substantial one."[19]

Settling with Will Cargill

As the plan moved to fulfillment, Will Cargill finally decided to capitulate to the other heirs. John Sr. had written Hixon on June 7, 1916, that the trust officers had approved the plan, though "a little fearful of Will Cargill in any plan which might be adopted, as he has openly threatened, as you know, to make trouble." John Sr. was even willing to make concessions to Will about income, but told Baxter that if Will would not agree, he would "put the plan thru rough shod without his consent." Six days later, John Sr. triumphantly reported to T. F. Baxter that "Austen had a long deal with Will Cargill Saturday and made a trade with him for his stock which is perfectly satisfactory all around. . . . This is going to eliminate Will entirely and, of course, it is a source of great satisfaction to all of us." John Sr., still fearing a last-minute recalcitrance, added, "knowing Will Cargill as we do, however, we do not dare consider the trade closed until it is actually consummated." When Austen wrote him a few weeks later that "I am having one grand time getting my papers back from Will. . . . I have already written him half a dozen times and he has promised to send them each time, but up to date I have not seen anything of them," John Sr.'s perturbation increased.

Haggling with Will ran into mid-August. By this point, the shares of the Cargill Securities Company were back in the hands of the four family owners, Austen, Will, Edna MacMillan and Emma Hanchette (5,000 shares each). The W. W. Cargill estate at that time had a book value of approximately $2 million; Will Cargill now accepted an offer of $500,000 for his share. John Sr. spelled out the details to Baxter: "$50,000.00 cash, $200,000.00 of the La Crosse & Southeastern Ry. Co. bonds, to be guaranteed by the Cargill Securities Co., and his [Austen's] note for $250,000.00 without interest for five years and then interest to run at the rate of 5% for another five years." The arrangement was to be between Austen and Will alone; the latter had made this a condition. Afterward, John Sr. joined with Austen in sharing the ownership of this stock. There is only a partial record of how John Sr. and Austen worked this out; it involved both cash outlays and further financial commitments by both. The Hanchettes did not participate. Austen then owned 7,496 shares of common stock in Cargill Securities Company; John Sr., 2,500; Edna MacMillan, 5,000; and Emma Hanchette, 5,000 (the other four shares were held as qualifying shares by other directors).[20]

The Employee Stock

The sale of Cargill Elevator Co. common stock to employees and outsiders had one important feature, and it is necessary to understand this in order to anticipate a stockholder crisis that occurred later, in 1925. The full effect of this sale could be seen in the "Shareholders and Their Holdings" section of the June 30, 1917, Cargill Elevator audit report. Aunt Maggie and Aunt Lydia still had their holdings, 655 shares each; John and Edna MacMillan controlled some 4,008 shares; brother Daniel MacMillan, another 500; Austen Cargill and his wife Anne had an additional 2,508 shares, Emma Hanchette (Edna's and Austen's sister) controlled 1,672 shares; and there were small holdings by other family cumulating to 300 shares. If one adds up all of the shares just described, the Cargill and MacMillan holdings, the total was 10,298. There were 16,000 shares outstanding in that June 30, 1917, listing.

The remaining 5,702 shares were those put in the hands of employees and close friends. Two members of the Creditors' Committee, Hixon and Jaffray, each took shares (Hixon took 500, while Jaffray took only 50). Two of the Osbornes and J. D. McMillan, all members of the Osborne-McMillan Grain Co., took shares, and several other close friends had small holdings. The remainder was divided among some 25 employees, some of them in top management—names we already know—and others far down in the organization, including cashiers, office boys, and so on. Several holdings were rather large. Frederick Lindahl and his wife had 1,000 shares; J. B. Taylor and A. M. Prime, 500 each; and J. B. Cooper and Ed Grimes, 250 each. The holdings ranged downward from there: several at 200, one at 175, another at 150, several more in the 50-to-100 range and even four people at 25 and three more at 20 shares. It was a sharing of the Company among its employees in the broader sense of the word, in contrast, for example, to a plan with shares rewarding only those in senior positions. Thus, roughly one-third of the Company was owned by Cargill family members, another one-third by MacMillan family members and an additional one-third by this group of outsiders and employees.[21]

The minutes of the Board of Directors authorized special provisions for the stock of the officers, agents and employees of Cargill. They were sold stock designated "employee stock," stamped right on the shares, and were required to execute an agreement that the stock would be sold back to the Company if they left the organization or died. They could not transfer the stock. The stock could be redeemed only at the Company's discretion, and the redemption price was to be the book value at time of redemption. The contract itself made clear that the stock was "for the purpose of increasing his [the employee's] interest in, and securing his hearty cooperation . . ."

In all other respects, however, employee stock carried full rights—for dividends, if declared, and with full voting rights. The stock of Hixon, the Osborne-McMillan people and the bankers did not have the "employee stock" provision, as their shares were unrestricted common.

This was a complex plan. One can imagine how easy it would have been at that time for persons untutored in arcane financial matters to become confused about the nuances of such intricate matters. Each of the two aunts had her own family advisors, who worked closely with John Sr. in a friendly but legitimately arms-length manner. The other "amateur" voices (in terms of financial understanding) were those of Emma Hanchette and her husband Fred. Fred had not worked for years; he had sporadically been ill with tuberculosis since his marriage to Emma, and their living and medical costs had demanded substantial resources. Emma's stake in the Cargill Elevator Company provided this. There appears to have been an affable relationship through the years between John Sr. and Fred Hanchette. The two men had corresponded every week or two, and these letters, most of them extant, chronicle an interactive and friendly association. Still, the fact remained that Emma had been "carried" by her father for many years; in W. W.'s account books are many payments just "to Emma," with no similar payments to the others.

Emma Hanchette Demurs

The reorganization plan had *not* been clear to Fred and Emma Hanchette, and after it was consummated, there were angry statements by Emma about some of the details, particularly as they related back to the settlement of the original W. W. Cargill estate and the executors' fees that had been paid at that time (1912). Also drawn into the misunderstanding were Austen Cargill and J. B. Taylor, who as secretary of Cargill Securities, had kept up an extensive correspondence with Austen and Anne Cargill and the Hanchettes.

Once the parameters of the reorganization plan were clear, in mid-June 1916, Frank Hixon wrote Emma about it, stating that the situation was "in splendid shape . . . of great advantage to the Cargill heirs" and that "I don't see any reason why you should not be provided with a reasonable income at least double the amount you have had available of late." Austen would come out to California to give her "details" on the plan, "as it would be very hard for you to understand it by reading it over."

Austen seemed the ideal person to do this. He understood finance. He also was a generous, open person—he loved everyone and everyone loved him. His relationship with Fred and Emma was close. However, he sometimes also found it difficult to tell anyone "no."

Austen went to California and after his return wrote Emma a somewhat abstruse letter to the effect that he had been "thinking of ways and means whereby I could secure for you an income of a thousand a month . . . at the start I realized that John [MacMillan, Sr.] would be the biggest obstacle, so I tried to think of some way that he would be placed in a position where he couldn't refuse my request. I . . . talked the matter over with Jim [J. B. Taylor] . . . as soon as I saw Jim felt as I did regarding your income, I told him what I was trying to do." The particular proposal Austen had in mind would have incorporated adjustments into the plan compensating for several advances that had been given to Fred and Emma earlier by John Sr., at the same time formalizing further payments to the Hanchettes. Austen continued, "after talking the matter over with John, this was finally done but it does not in any way affect you, as no interest will be charged and you will have all the time you wish to pay for it."

Independently, John Sr. had sent his own letter to Fred and Emma, outlining how *he* would handle the Hanchette advances. This plan was considerably more complex than Austen's, the major difference lying in MacMillan's desire to reconcile the advances through a set of dividends, rather than having the advances go through the Cargill Securities Company books.

Austen also wrote J. B. Taylor about this and in the process revealed his misgivings about Emma's handling of money: "You are incorrect in thinking that we were to send her $1000 the 15th of July and another $1000 on the first of August. It was both John's idea and my own that we send her $1000 six weeks apart . . . our object in doing this was to avoid her getting an impression that she was going to receive $1000 monthly." He added, in a handwritten aside, "I did not want her to know we gave John the cash [the amount in the proposed settlement] as she has some funny ideas regarding this matter."

The details of these two plans are not germane here; the response of Emma Hanchette is. Part of these advances, some $5,000, was straightforward. The remainder, just over $10,000, came from settling the W. W. Cargill estate, when Hixon and John Sr. agreed not to keep their one-third fee for executor but, rather, send this amount along to the Hanchettes. Will Cargill already had taken his one-third of the fee. Both John Sr. and Austen Cargill assumed that Emma and Fred knew that the monies she had received from John Sr. were advances. Now, in a letter Emma wrote John Sr., she registered new doubts: "You and Mr. Hixon gave me that money with no stipulations that I ever heard of . . . when Fred went to thank [Hixon] he said we would someday repay it and he said he didn't want us to." Further, Emma averred, the way the debt was originally calculated was faulty—inasmuch as Will Cargill had taken himself out of the situation back in 1912, the credits for the debt should now be split three ways (Emma, Austen, John) rather than including Will as a fourth. The amount here was very small, but because Austen and John now held equally the one-fourth that had come from Will, each would be getting slightly more credit. Emma seemed particularly to feel that John Sr. "squeezed too hard" (words she had used before and would again).

Both John Sr. and Austen Cargill now replied to Emma, on the same day and in the same vein. Emma simply did not understand the rationale of the $10,000 payment, they both stated. She was incorrect about the minor discrepancy and, further, interest was only fair inasmuch as the employees had to pay such on the notes owed for the stock. Both John Sr. and Austen now decided that the best plan would be to take the whole process through the books of the Company, in the process reducing the Hanchette holdings of Cargill Securities Company assets (specifically, some of the railway bonds) in amounts that could reconcile the whole matter. Austen was diplomatic in his exhortations to the Hanchettes: "Now, I realize that you are perfectly right in figuring as you do, since it was our intention at the time this money was advanced to handle it in such a way that Will would not share in its division. However, now that Will has been eliminated I think you are making a big mistake if you insist that we treat this advance as originally planned, and I earnestly urge you to overlook the difference and drop the matter."

Austen and John Sr. did not have long to wait, for Fred fired back an antagonistic letter to John Sr., recounting how he and Emma were having to sell assets to pay some of their own bills—"upon my word, I think it is 'no fair' to ask us to dispose of these bonds to pay these debts," he added piously. "It never entered the heads of either one of us that there would be any hurry about paying you the . . . loan." He ended the letter with a challenge: "Now you sit down and answer this letter and be just as candid and frank as if you were writing to yourself."

Fred Hanchette had his request answered in a way he likely little expected. John Sr. wrote back a caustic letter:

I am afraid, judging from your letter, that neither you nor Emma realize that we have, all of us, been seeing that you were furnished with money as needed and that without any interest, and this interest would amount to several times the difference between the one-quarter or one-third of those fees that you refer to. . . . The plan which you suggest is simply a continuation of what has gone on in the past, viz:

that you shall continue to be favored and carried along without interest, while Austen and I are both staggering under a heavy load of indebtedness which is costing us interest. . . . You have asked me to be candid and frank and I have been just as candid and frank I think as you have asked me to be, and I write this kind of a letter with a good deal of reluctance. . . . I think it is perfectly safe to say that you can figure that your average dividends on your proportion of the Cargill Elevator Company stock will average $25,000.00 a year, so if you will stop and figure these things out, there is no need to look at anything from a petty point of view.

John Sr. was being conservative on this figure as the dividends over the four years just past had averaged 21.5 percent—Emma and Fred's dividends had averaged over $53,000 a year for these four years.

Hanchette, chastened, responded with a placating letter:

It is just the kind of letter I wanted you to write, that is as to the frankness, and you are right and we are wrong. I am mighty glad to acknowledge it. We were not looking at the matter right and I am sorry we took such a narrow view of things. Years ago I remember you and I were talking and we agreed we should never have any difference—we would work out the right and that would go—now it has been done and I hope this acknowledgement may end the matter for all time. . . . To sum up—it was not until we read your letter that we thought that you were in the right and now that we see that you are, we want to come to the front, say so and apologize.

Hanchette ended on a note of appreciation for the instrumental role that John Sr. had taken in their overall financial planning: "You have done everything for us and I am telling you now that I understand it and do appreciate it." There the matter apparently rested.[22]

As one carefully reads this absorbing correspondence, a few discordant threads seem to remain. Emma and Fred Hanchette had a narrow agenda built single-mindedly around their need for income, and the Company's business was not very real to them. In truth, they continued to harbor festering discontents that would become the centerpiece of a major inter-family stockholder squabble nine years later. Austen Cargill and J. B. Taylor had held themselves forward to the Hanchettes as being somehow "with" them and having to push John Sr. to be more forthcoming with Company money. Yet, when the repair to the rupture was determined, Austen stood as one with John Sr. and, while perhaps more equivocal than the latter, nevertheless was just about as frank.

Balancing those tensions, the friendship of all of the members of the two families (with the single exception of the universal disenchantment concerning Will Cargill) permeates the correspondence. Aunt Maggie and Aunt Lydia, the Hanchettes and Austen Cargill essentially trusted the judgment and leadership of John Sr., and John Sr. reciprocated with just what he demanded of others, namely, the full set of facts tendered by him to others and received, in turn, by him in a frank and timely way.

The retiring of the Gold Notes in June 1916 and the payment of the $2,651,000 debt of the estate now freed the Cargill Elevator Company from any entanglement with the remaining businesses still held by the family's Cargill Securities Company. There were a number of these still limping along in various stages of difficulty. These go out of our story at this point, not being really related to the Cargill companies' histories. The various Cargill Securities businesses subsequently did demand much time and money—and worry—on the part of family members. In the cases of John Sr. and Austen Cargill and later John Jr. and Cargill MacMillan, the Cargill Securities businesses were a drain on their Elevator Company time and must have had some effect on their business lives.

For the readers of this book, here in brief outline is what subsequently happened to the more important of the Cargill Securities businesses. Valier, nowhere near being finished at this point, continued to command major attention. The irrigation and settlement projects experienced repeated financial problems, passing through several reorganizations. Engineering problems, a lengthy drought and the post–World War I farm depression led to an exodus of bankrupt farmers. In 1926, John Sr. had to assume management control when the previous manager died. Actual construction was not completed until 1948. The project was finally accepted by the Carey Board in 1953, and ownership was turned over to the Settlers Corporation. The Valier Company (the Conrad Land and Water Company's final name after the several reorganizations) was dissolved in 1955.

The La Crosse and Southeastern Railroad began to face automobile and truck competition for its passenger and freight business, particularly after World War I. "Motorcars"—combined passenger-freight rail cars—were tried, but it was a losing battle. The Great Depression spelled the line's death knell. The I.C.C. allowed a segment to be abandoned in 1933, and other abandonments followed. A portion ran as a branch out of Sparta until the 1970s. But that was the end.

The timberland in British Columbia seemed so promising during World War I, with war needs for lumber high (there were large contracts from Europe for use in trenches). But post–World War I demand was soft. At various times in the early and mid-1920s, Austen Cargill and John Jr. worked there on the grounds, trying to make production pay (a story in later chapters). In 1926 there was a disastrous fire, with significant damage to equipment and felled logs. Even the effort to tow the equipment to Vancouver failed. The tow came apart, some of the equipment sank and the rest was beached. The insurance did not apply because the Cargill agent had put additional equipment (his own) on the tow. The salvage company sued, the tow company sued, there were legal fees and Cargill Securities lost the value of everything. The Company ceased timber production but kept the property until it was sold in the 1960s.

The Mexican timberland had been worked briefly when the revolution intruded in 1916. (John Jr. was affected tangentially by this, a story later in this chapter.) The Cargill Securities Company could not even get on the property until 1920. In the 1930s the land was expropriated by the Mexican government under President Lazaro Cardenas, and again access was lost. When the Mexican Claims Act, mostly concerning confiscation of oil lands, was passed in 1941, Cargill Securities Company filed a claim, and to the surpise of all, in 1943 the families were notified that the Company had been awarded $642,722 (it was valued by the Company, including interest, at $1,375,000). The final amount received, however, turned out to be $300,000.

So the W. W. Cargill investments did not prove to be the bonanza that W. W. exulted about in 1909. The businesses suffered cyclical downturns after World War I, and the returns on all were minuscule. It might have been better had all been sold in 1916, when the upswing from the war would have made this possible (except for the Mexican land, of course). But John Sr. hated to sell any asset, a point of view often seen in later Cargill Elevator Company instances.

Grain and War

The outbreak of hostilities in August 1914 escalated quickly into the Great War, and it increasingly intruded into everyone's lives. The "preparedness movement" had picked up steam in 1915 despite the star-crossed pacifist effort of Henry Ford, who chartered his "peace ship" in December of that year. In January 1916, President Woodrow Wilson began a tour of the country to urge preparedness. The United States stressed its neutral rights, particularly on the seas. In early May 1915, the Germans had issued a warning that the waters around the British Isles were to be a war zone and that shipping would be there at its own risk. Within days, the British steamer *Lusitania* was sunk off the Irish Coast (without any warning), and 1,198 lives were lost, including 124 Americans. As the land war continued into 1916, there were German peace overtures that year, as well as efforts by President Wilson for a conference to end the war. None of these came to maturation, however, and the war continued. Eventually the United States entered the war in April 1917. War and famine, two of the Four Horsemen of the Apocalypse are so often linked together because war almost always involves shattering of the logistics of getting food into people's mouths. There was no doubt that the hostilities would deeply affect the grain trade.

There had been a 13-million-acre expansion in wheat acreage in the United States between 1910 and 1915. Good weather had produced record wheat stocks in the first two years of the war. Equally abundant harvests by most of the world's other key wheat producers had allowed the various belligerents to meet their wartime needs without fundamentally affecting the supply–demand equations. Thus, the stepped-up purchasing had been accomplished without skyrocketing prices.

However, any euphoria evaporated quickly with the crop year of 1916. Russia's grain exports, always an important factor in pre–World War I days, simply dried up as that country was drawn into the conflict and suffered a series of defeats. In addition, in 1916 there was damaging winter weather and subsequent serious crop disease in the United States. The 1916 harvest of wheat in the country fell from 1.009 billion bushels to 635 million, and total world wheat fell from 3.36 billion to 2.57 billion.[23]

Tremendous maritime losses from the German U-boats (amounting, by December 1916, to some 2.4 million tons) had forced the Allies to turn from Australian grain to that from North America. The British were extraordinarily sensitive to this drop in supply inasmuch as almost all of their bread stocks were imported, some 60 percent from the United States. In October 1916, they established the Royal Commission on Wheat Supplies (RCWS), which also began acting as agent for all of the Allies and became known as the Allied Wheat Executive. One of the historians of wheat noted the implications of this: The RCWS "eventually decided, for practically all of 'open' Europe, how much to buy, where to buy it, how to transport it, and where to send it. Neutrals were 'rationed.' . . . With its enormous resources and powers of bargaining and negotiation, it was a large factor in eliminating normal interplay of supply and demand, and hence normal registration of price, in the world wheat market."[24] Under the Wheat Executive Agreement, the Allies began to pool both their grain needs and their shipping.

The RCWS purchased as many long futures contracts on May 1917 wheat as it could obtain. Indeed, it bought more than needed, and since it wanted actual delivery, the supply out in the field was not enough to fulfill the demand. In short, the Allies inadvertently had worked a corner on May wheat! When dealers scrambled in April and early May to fulfill these contracts, prices for No. 2 red winter cash wheat on the Chicago market shot up from $1.03 (in June 1916) to $3.25. The following day, the Chicago Board of Trade suspended operations in the May futures contract and forced the settlement of outstanding contracts at a mandated price ($3.18).[25]

The Food Riots, February 1917

In mid-February 1917, a series of incidents involving attacks on food peddlers occurred in New York City. Pushcarts were overturned, and some were even burned. The press had a dramatic issue to embroider and wasted no time in escalating the rhetoric. The New York *Evening Post*, reporting on the riots, wrote: "Every face in the mob that was gathered around City Hall steps looked as hungry as the cries asserted. Old women with their shawls and straggling gray hair half falling down raised thin, weak voices; sunken-cheeked women cried; great flabby women had that gray-blue cast that needed but a touch of the biting wind around City Hall to make a picture of starvation." The *New York Times* added, "Women in strike riot cry 'we're starving.' " It was headlines in Minneapolis, too; the *Minneapolis Morning Tribune* began its major article, "Food Riot in East; Women Mob Dealers."[26]

The headlines in the country's newspapers were almost unbelievable. Food riots here in America! By the fourth week of February, distraught groups of housewives were rioting all over New York City, and within a few days the same unruliness broke out in Philadelphia (where the police killed one man and wounded six other people during a food clash on February 22). Angry people in Boston held mass meetings, while others in St. Louis formed a "Feed America First" committee.

One of the historians of that time warned that these were just "highly colored press accounts," that they were "much exaggerated . . . not 'hunger riots.' " Yet it was disconcerting to the grain trade, for much of the venom seemed directed not at the Germans and the war dislocations but at the grain trade itself. The pushcart dealers whose carts had been overturned by the women in those first few days were quick to point out that *they* were not the cause of high prices—it was the "unscrupulous middlemen." The chairman of the St. Louis "Feed America First" committee railed, "There will soon be a revolution in this country. The railroads and trusts are back of these high prices."[27]

Attacks on the middleman had been widespread from far back in history. It was in food marketing—most especially, grain marketing—that these attacks had become so hostile. Farmers had often viewed the middleman (as Henrietta Larson put it) as "a sort of a usurper who was displacing the farmer and destroying the cornerstone of society . . . living in comfort and luxury . . . usually the local grain buyer, with fur gloves and cigarettes, but at times . . . a mythical person who symbolized the heartless monopolies and soulless corporations, the wheat rings and the railroads."[28] Now, with the 1917 food riots, the allegations of the late 19th century were raised once again by the reformers, only this time looking backward from the retail side at this same grain trade middleman. It was a wasteful distribution system, they said, that contained too many intermediate steps, and "marketing reform" was needed to bring down the prices. A number of states instituted investigations of the food marketing system, and there were strong pressures for a "Federal food commission" to advise President

Woodrow Wilson about general food policy, particularly as related to the war effort, and to include as an agenda item "marketing reform."

Back in 1914, Wilson had asked the Justice Department to carry out inquiries into food prices and the food trades, but at that time, no evidence was found of conspiracy to manipulate food prices. In a Justice Department study in December 1916, a nationwide investigation was conducted to determine whether individuals had conspired to boost food prices. Then in February 1917, as the carts were toppling, Wilson had the investigatory role shifted to the Federal Trade Commission (FTC), which began an exhaustive study of the grain trade. A monumental set of volumes was eventually put out by the FTC in the early 1920s, minutely documenting just about every aspect of grain marketing. The FTC investigation could not, however, provide immediate amelioration of the "food riot" problem, nor was it to be completed rapidly enough to identify what should be the Allied food policy in the face of the now-evident shortfall in world grain supply.

The Grain Trade, Wartime Version

The Council of National Defense (CND), established in August 1916 under the Army Appropriation Act of Congress as an arm of the preparedness movement, turned its attention to the food crisis in March 1917. The United States was to enter the war just a few weeks later. Speed was of the essence by this time. Desperately needing an administrative head, President Wilson called upon Herbert Hoover, the famous and highly successful chairman of the Commission for Relief of Belgium, established back in 1914. Hoover returned to the United States in early May 1917 and began drafting proposals for an independent food agency with sweeping powers over procurement and distribution of all food. Enabling legislation was needed to establish the actual War Food Administration; this process became bogged down in an involved set of hearings over several months.[29]

Immediately, there were widespread demands around the country for an embargo on any wheat going out of the country. The users of grain—the millers, the consumer, etc.—were in favor of the embargo. The farmers, naturally, were opposed, as they wanted to keep the escalation in price that shortages at home would bring about. The grain traders should have been indifferent to the embargo on its face inasmuch as their income ostensibly came from handling charges, being "fully hedged." In reality, of course, this was a tempting time to take a position, and a price run-up would have tended to make this more profitable.

With the country's grain marketing in disarray, Herbert Hoover decided to meet publicly with grain trade executives. In April 1917, the Council of Grain Exchanges had sent representatives to Washington to confer with the Secretary of Agriculture, and out of this meeting came the Committee of Grain Exchanges in Aid of National Defense. Julius Barnes, the chief executive of Barnes-Ames Company, one of the major grain exporting firms, headed this committee. On May 17, 1917, the Committee held an emergency meeting with Hoover in Washington. John MacMillan, Sr., was one of the eight people at this meeting, as the representative for the Minneapolis Chamber of Commerce, the Minneapolis grain exchange.

John Sr. was a good choice for this assignment, for he had a strong moral sense of the need for a patriotic response by the American business community to the daunting challenges of the war. He had written John Jr. just a few weeks before, "These are critical days. The outlook is not very clear and it looks more and more serious, and it is a time when no one should allow any personal wishes to interfere with any duty to our country."

At the emergency meeting, Hoover emphasized that he wanted the control of the industry to be accomplished, as far as possible, on a voluntary basis, "showing that business men were as willing to make sacrifices as others." The committee agreed with Hoover that government control of the transportation of food was absolutely necessary and also that it was essential that the government take control of both prices and distribution. Under the "present extraordinary circumstances," the committee continued, a price for wheat should be fixed for the year, and rye should also have a control. The committee felt that corn and oats could probably safely be left to established trading patterns. Finally, the committee agreed that a temporary ban on futures contracts should be extended for as long as the war was in being.

John Sr. wrote a personal letter to Hoover after the May trip and told T. F. Baxter the same day, "We found Mr. Hoover a wonderful man in every respect, having a very broad vision and big enough to know that it is a problem he could not solve by himself." John Sr. expressed to Baxter once more his belief that government control was the only salvation, given the "concentrated character of foreign buying . . . to leave it to competitive methods under existing conditions would put prices so high as to cause social unrest throughout the whole country."

The sentiments of other members of the trade were not so public-minded. Just before he left for the meeting with Hoover, John Sr. himself received a telegram from one influential grain trade executive that read as follows, "Sentiment here strongly favors normal activities of grain exchanges, including speculative futures markets being continued. Prominent members consider Federal Government should immediately assure the people that export of food products will be limited to such surplus as can be spared after caring for domestic requirements. All exports to be based on government permits. No further government action seems necessary to relieve present situation. Present highly organized and efficient machinery of distribution will thus be preserved."[30]

But such a marketplace view did not hold sway. Hoover subsequently embraced the recommendations of the committee by highly centralizing the logistics of procurement and transportation. And futures trading was banned for the duration of the war.

"War Profits"

For the first several months after the entrance of the United States into the war on April 6, 1917, over the spring and summer of 1917, chaos continued all through the American food industries. The enabling legislation that would put in place Herbert Hoover's recommendations was stuck in political logrolling, and the grain trade, among others, was thrown into a chaos of indecision. The harvest of 1917 was proceeding on schedule, yet the movement to market of this grain was painfully slow, held in abeyance by farmers not wanting to sell and grain merchants not wanting to commit until a price structure seemed more certain. With futures markets already suspended, the rest of the organized markets were in turmoil.

The crux of the argument was whether Congress would mandate both minimum and maximum prices for grain. In the extended battle over these prices, there were rumors that Hoover had backed down on setting a maximum price. John Sr. wrote Barnes, urging the ceiling: "It is quite evident to me that if we should . . . merely have a minimum price and no option trade, that a few large concerns must dominate the grain and milling business of the country; that we will have speculation, not in the way of futures, but in the form of concentrated cash holdings, which will be a greater menace even than the unlimited trading in futures."[31]

John Sr. also wrote to a grain industry economist with additional concerns:

If Mr. Hoover and the Senate are agreed upon cutting out . . . maximum prices I do not see how it is going to be possible to control prices on grain and keep them within the limits which Mr. Hoover seemed to think so very necessary when we met him in Washington. If there are minimum prices and no maximum prices, I can see no escape from the opening up of the futures markets again, in order to provide some means of hedging both for the grain men and the millers. This would undoubtedly give an opening for the foreigners [the Wheat Export Corporation of the Royal Wheat Commission] to acquire enormous holdings again of futures, with all the possible disturbances which we have witnessed this spring. . . . [With] futures trading stopped a few very strong concerns would control the cash grain markets . . . the future looks rather disturbing.

Although the militant farmers were demanding that no maximum price

be set and some members of the grain trade were echoing the same sentiments, John Sr. and others recognized that the specter of runaway prices
was so threatening as to make such a price control mechanism a necessity.
Consumers simply would not stand for a lack of ceilings on prices.[32]

The farmers, to their surprise, now became targets of hostility from the
public, who had come to believe that farmers were profiteering from the
war. For example, the intellectual, Stephen Leacock, looking westward
from the East Coast, called the prairie farmer a "war drone," amassing his
profits for "pianos, victrolas, trotting buggies, moving pictures, pleasure
cars, and so on."[33]

In truth, the farmers themselves had not received the benefit of the
precipitous price rise that had occurred in the early spring of 1917. Back in
March 1917, some 570 million bushels out of a total crop of some 620
million already had left the farms. Thus, nearly 92 percent of the wheat
crop had been marketed before the jump in prices. At that point, a speculative fever had seized the markets, fueled by news of a smaller crop, frenetic buying in American markets by the Allies and America's entry into
the war in April 1917. The profits from the speculation went to the various
units along the chain of marketing beyond the farmer, up to and including
the flour miller. As one analyst put it, "It is probably conservative to say
that the consumers of the United States paid $200,000,000 more for flour
during this first six months of 1917 than would be justified by reasonable
margins above the price which the farmers obtained for their 1916–17 wheat
crop."[34]

This brought renewed attacks on "the speculators." When the United
States senator from Minnesota, Knute Nelson, made a ringing speech
along these lines, John Sr. wrote a lengthy letter on May 23, 1917, defending
the grain exchanges. Nelson answered right back, brusquely:

> The speculative price of wheat that prevailed on the grain exchanges during the
> month of April and this month has convinced me that the seed of the difficulty is
> in those exchanges. Nearly all the wheat was out of the hands of the farmers by the
> first of April and was in the hands of the middlemen somewhere, either in terminals
> or in country elevators owned by someone other than the farmer. . . . I wish the
> exchanges would attempt to control the matter themselves . . . but if the grain
> exchange will not help, we shall have to find some way to reach the evil.

The senator added an aside, "Instead of writing a letter and giving all
manner of excuses, I should be very glad if you and all the other grain men
would suggest some proper way to remedy the evil" (he also accused the
grain men of "hollering" and "kicking").

Nelson's letter jarred John Sr., and he wrote a four-page answer defending the speculator, without whom "it would be impossible for the grain
dealers of the country to finance their purchases of the crop." Nor was the

Representatives of farming interests at a wartime conference in Washington, D.C., 1918. Left to right: G. N. Tittemore, president of the American Society of Equity; E. T. Meredith, publisher of Successful Farming; *T. C. Atkinson, Washington representative of the National Grange; and C. S. Barrett, president of the National Farmers' Union* (courtesy Historical Pictures Service; © Harris & Ewing, 1918).

speculator to blame for the high prices. It was "this enormous demand from the exporters" that was the root problem.[35] Despite John Sr.'s avowal that grain traders like Cargill were just passive recipients of the heightened margins, the facts were unassailable—great profits had been made in the process. When Cargill closed its books at the end of the crop year 1916–1917 on June 30, 1917, the profit of $1,099,292 had broken the $1 million mark, by far the largest profit the Company had ever made.

The audited statements show exactly how this had happened. The outstanding difference was in the trading account, particularly for the Superior terminals, where most of the grain always had been held. The Superior books showed a profit of almost $1.3 million, with two grains accounting for most of this. First, as one might expect, given the Allies' buying spree, the wheat account had done very well, showing a profit of almost $399,000. The largest profit, however, was in barley, where the figure was $812,000.

The reasons for the profit in barley lay in a peculiar situation that emerged because of the war. Wheat was so much the overwhelming favorite of consumers for bread that it became the grain of first choice among the Allies. The most favored of all World War I slogans in respect to food was not that "food will win the war" or even that "grains will win the war" but that "wheat will win the war." But wheat was in shorter and shorter supply, particularly as the U-boat packs began sinking boatloads of grain. By the crop year 1917–1918, one expert wrote that the population of wheat consumers ex-Russia "may be said to have fallen short one loaf of bread in every five of what would probably have been eaten with peace continuing."

Because of this, a number of European governments, and finally the United States too, began urging (none too politely) that millers make a portion of each loaf of bread out of another grain. This could be rye or, particularly, barley. For most of the war, "barley bread" was one of the facts of life and not a very popular one. J. B. Taylor complained at length to Lindahl about the mix: "Barley bread is a failure. The bakers are not using the flour here, their mixture being wheat, white corn flour and rice flour. We have been living on a barley and white flour mixture at home made by our cook, but it is a poor substitute for bread. I used to eat considerable bread, but am not eating one-quarter of what I normally eat, on account of the barley bread tasting like sawdust." Cargill had been adroit enough as a company to recognize early this elevation of barley to its temporarily exalted position as a bread grain of choice, and through the efforts of Prime in Duluth and Cooper in Minneapolis had acquired substantial stocks of barley—thus the large trading profit, far greater than ever before.[36]

The question now arose as to what to do with this profit. A special meeting of the directors was called on June 15, 1917, and at this meeting the regular 7 percent dividend on the preferred stock was declared, together with an extraordinarily large dividend of 45 percent on the common stock outstanding. A small contingency reserve of $52,000 was established, and the remainder, just over $268,000, was transferred to surplus. The net worth of the Company had risen in this year from just over $2.4 million to a total of $2,668,000.

There is little documentation that would give clues as to the reasons for the large dividend. Perhaps it was linked to the 1916 reorganization. For years the Company had had a conservative policy on dividends, had believed strongly in plowing back profits, which Cargill executives felt demonstrated success to the banks. John Sr. long had been cautious about bankers, always concerned that the Company maintain its solid credit rating. For this reason, he always hated to pay a cash dividend in midyear, when credit demands were high. But this year a majority of the large profits were paid out in dividends—and in June, no less. John Sr. wrote Fred Hanchette:

Now, of course, I presume you understand that this is an abnormal year, something that we have never had anything like before, and probably never will have again. . . . I do not believe that the government is going to force us to do business for nothing or at a loss, but they might put us on a basis where it will not be possible to pay over somewhere between 5 and 6% and I merely mention this so you can take it into account. . . . I am inclined to think that you want to figure to keep a good portion of this dividend in such liquid assets that you could realize on them in case of a condition arising whereby we could not pay any dividends at all.

It was around this time that Fred and Emma bought an expensive house and a prestige car.[37]

The farmers all through the United States were manifestly perturbed that they themselves had not been the beneficiaries of that price spiral of the first six months of 1917, so the hostility of farmer organizations and their press rose markedly. Cargill soon took the brunt of some of these attacks. A Dawson, North Dakota, newspaper published an article in early June 1917 about "why the farmers should have an elevator." The article highlighted eight elevators in North Dakota, "showing how much MORE grain they SOLD than they bought" for the year July 31, 1915, through July 31, 1916 (presumably, inasmuch as the editor had taken the data from the Commissioner of Agriculture and Labor of the state, he had been forced to use the previous year's figures!). Cargill had two of these eight elevators, and their figures showed a large balance on the side of what the newspaper called "SOLD." The implication was that Cargill had profiteered on these sales, perhaps even cheated on inbound weights.

John Sr. immediately demanded a retraction, inasmuch as the newspaper had falsely stated that the report showed bushels sold, whereas the actual report was merely bushels purchased and bushels shipped. John Sr. sent the editor a copy of the report itself, but nothing appeared in the way of a retraction. Finally, late in the month, the editor did agree to make the correction "insofar as the word 'sold' was used in the place of 'shipped.' " Weeks had passed by this time, however, and the thrust of the initial article probably was not much blunted by the tiny retraction.[38]

At least John Sr. had the satisfaction that his interchange with Senator Nelson had not fallen on deaf ears. When a new food bill was being debated in the Senate, Nelson took a central role. Now his vituperation seemed more directed at the milling industry, rather than the grain trade itself. In the hearings on July 9, 1917, he first took a few shots at the millers:

I have no doubt the millers will be satisfied, for they will get their wheat, compared with what the market price would be under ordinary conditions, cheaper than ever . . . it will turn out as it did in the days of the Civil War. We had a lot of contractors who took advantage of our dire straits to bleed the government during that war.

So today there are a lot of these quasi-patriotic citizens who are trying to manipulate the government. . . . I trust that the pirates who are now seeking to bleed the Federal Government and trying to make money in every way they can will find that the future has in store for them something akin to what happened to the contractors of the Civil War.

Later in the day, when asked by a Senate colleague about the grain exchanges themselves, he answered, "While I have sometimes felt very hostile to the grain exchanges, on the whole I see that they are an absolute necessity if they are kept within proper bounds. It is the only public marketplace you have."[39]

The Government Controls Wheat Prices

On August 10, 1917, the Food Control Act was finally passed. Hoover was now officially the Food Administrator, a role he had been playing for five months. The Food Administration Grain Corporation was constituted as the administering agency for grain control, and Julius Barnes was appointed as its head.

The first order of business was a ticklish one, to set the price at which the government would buy the 1917 crop. An independent 12-person "fair price" committee was appointed by President Wilson, and after much acrimonious debate, on August 30 recommended a $2.20 price for No. 1 northern spring wheat at Chicago (with all of the other wheat prices adjusted accordingly). The farmers continued to be outraged with this price over the succeeding months and began castigating Hoover as favoring business interests in his decisions, particularly those of the millers.

Hoover proved to be a master tactician in these constant special-interest battles. At the beginning the millers held considerable bargaining power and used this to demand their own self-regulation. They wanted a separate office in the Grain Corporation, a "milling executive," staffed by appointees out of the industry itself. Hoover, in exchange, exacted a set of buying conditions under which the millers would operate, utilizing the mandated government price. Similar agreements were reached with the elevator operators in a set of conferences between August 15 and mid-September. Hoover wanted absolute control over the movement of grain from the country across the Atlantic to the Allies and also wanted to be able to use the country elevators as storage. He gained the cooperation of the elevator group with a promise of storage charges of 2 cents a bushel per month (technically, $1/15$ cent per bushel per day), combined with constraints on direct shipments by farmers. Later in the war, Hoover cut back on the independent power of the millers' representatives in the Grain Corporation.[40]

With these milling and elevator agreements in place, Hoover turned to

There's a man at the door with a package.

Ding Darling, January 27, 1919 (by permission of the University of Iowa Libraries [Iowa City]).

the crucial question, the control of wheat exports. By clever use of a newly established export license system, Hoover assured that no wheat could leave the country without his permission. He adroitly played a sophisticated hand of economic nationalism, balancing the critical needs in Europe for the war (which became even more severe as 1918 began) with the desire to maintain such adequate domestic supplies as would prevent price increases at home. Hoover wanted to free the import of Canadian grain into the United States but at the United States control price, so that the Wheat Export Corporation (the buying arm of the British Royal Wheat Commission) would continue to buy grain from the United States in the quantities that Hoover himself had determined would best align the supply–demand factors within the United States. In a set of obdurate negotiations with the British and Canadians, in which he made it plain to the

British that they would not be allowed to use money they had obtained by loans from the United States to buy outside the United States, Hoover was able to free the Canadian grain on his own terms.

He also mandated that Australian wheat coming into the United States would be purchased only by the Grain Corporation. Some Australian wheat actually was making that 12,000-mile trip, although the distance involved and the shortage of shipping made this an unattractive alternative. On the other hand, Argentina was only 6,500 miles from Europe. Here the problem was complicated by the fact that some Argentine grain in the market at this time seemed to be ending up in neutral countries (the so-called Northern Neutrals). The Allies wanted to restrict these Neutrals to approximately their own food needs as there was always the possibility that grain would be shipped through the Neutrals into the granaries of the Central Powers. Again, Hoover won the battle on essentially his own terms, with a masterful combination of promises and threats.[41]

With priority demands for the army and navy and the logistics of the food pipeline from the hinterlands to the export points, the winter of 1917–1918 produced severe traffic congestion. At the end of December 1917, Wilson directed the government to take over the management of all of the railroads, appointing William G. McAdoo as director general. During that winter there was a marked shortage of rail cars, with embargoes placed on many users. Here Hoover did not have full control, and accusations were made back and forth between him and McAdoo about who was to receive the blame for the embargoes. By March, the situation had begun to improve.[42]

Cargill's Crop Year 1917–1918

After the huge profits of the previous crop year, it was to be expected that the crop year 1917–1918, all of which was under wartime conditions, would be considerably more constrained. The regulations imposed on the grain trade by Hoover, under the aegis of the Grain Corporation, permitted only small returns on profitability. The overall net income for the company was $125,302, down from $1.1 million the previous year. The net trading income of the Superior terminal grain operation had dropped from $741,000 to $4,133, and so it was all along the line of the various accounts. John Sr. had continued his role as one of the key spokesman for the industry, and in January 1918 was elected national president of the Council of Grain Exchanges, the central organization for the 15 major grain exchanges of the country. His work with the industry gave the Company national recognition and set the stage for later successes. His brother Will, the Chicago professor, also had been called to Washington, in June 1918, to be a member of a scientific commission of mathematical experts who would confer with counterparts in England and France on theoretical work in reference to artillery and airplane manufacture; later he was commissioned a major in the Ordnance Corps.

The new crop year 1918–1919 looked promising, but John Sr. wrote Fred Hanchette in June 1918, "I am not very optimistic about the future . . . about the best that I think we can hope for during the period of the war is to hold our organization together. If we are able to do that we will be extremely fortunate. Profits in the meantime will be purely a matter of incident, . . . but we will try to get them if we can." The Hanchettes were the most importunate of the shareholders about dividends, and he added, "I have it in contemplation now that we will pay a dividend of 1% on the 30th of June and then possibly another 1% on the 31st of December, if it is absolutely necessary, although I should much prefer to pay no dividends if you do not need the money . . . I wonder if . . . your other income would not be enough to carry you through the year."

John Sr. also wrote Austen Cargill, in July 1918, about the results of the year, "the most unsatisfactory year we have ever known since I have had anything to do with the business." He asked Austen, in the service since January of that year, for far more of a sacrifice than that of the Hanchettes: "I rather think that whatever surplus money you have had better be loaned to the Cargill Elevator Company until the next Liberty Loan comes out, and then take bonds at that time (the proceeds to come from the two percent dividend to be paid at this time by the Cargill Securities Company)." The responses of Fred Hanchette and Austen Cargill to these markedly different proposals from John Sr. are not known; when the directors met on July 8, 1918, they voted the regular cash dividend on the preferred stock (7 percent) and a 5 percent dividend on the common stock, "payment to be made in U.S.A. 4 percent Liberty Bonds." The total of these two drew down the Company's surplus account from just over $268,000 to $205,895.[43]

John Jr. and Austen Go to War

Several junior Cargill employees joined the service at the time of America's entry into the war on April 6, 1917. None of the members of senior nonfamily management actually went into the service itself, although many of them carried important war production responsibilities in their roles as Cargill employees.

Two younger members of the families, on the other hand, saw extensive service in World War I—John MacMillan, Jr., and Austen Cargill. Both took major executive roles in the Company after the war, and the experiences they had during the war affected both measurably.

In the case of John Jr., the experience of being thrown at the age of 22 into a position of central responsibility and the lessons he learned from this assignment fundamentally influenced his own thinking in regard to how organizations should be run. After the war, these experiences were frequently recounted by John Jr. to other executives in the Company, and what he felt were their lessons served as rationale for a number of major changes in Cargill. Especially in this sense, perhaps more so than all of the grain trade implications of the war and John Sr.'s involvement in it, the hostilities in Europe had a seminal influence on the Company in the post–World War I period. For this reason, the story of John Jr.'s wartime experiences needs to be analyzed in some detail here.

The armed services had intrigued John Jr. in childhood. Once the hostilities in Europe began in 1914, he decided while at Yale to enlist part-time in the Connecticut National Guard, training with them over the following winter and spring while attending regular classes. It was a field artillery regiment, and John Jr. enjoyed its technical ballistic challenges. In June 1916, he was promoted to corporal and made "battery agent."

The summer of 1916 was a tense one for the various National Guard units. Just after the beginning of the year 1916, Pancho Villa, a revolutionary freebooting chieftain in opposition to Venustiano Carranza's Mexican government, had been responsible for raids and consequent deaths of Americans on both sides of the border. The particularly brutal murders of 18 American engineers, who were in Mexico to open some abandoned Mexican mines for Carranza, pushed Wilson out of his posture of "watchful waiting," and he ordered a punitive expedition of some 15,000 men to pursue Villa into Mexico. As an additional standby, Wilson called out some 150,000 militia from around the country, stationing them near the border. John Jr. was called to summer service at New Haven in early June, and for a while all the young men in the unit thought they would be heading toward the Mexican border. In the end, they were not sent. Villa was captured, and the expeditionary force was withdrawn at the end of the year. In January 1917, a new Mexican constitution was proclaimed, and Carranza was elected president.[44]

John Jr. returned to Yale in the fall of 1916, and his father began for the first time to write to his son about specific details of Cargill operations. In August, a spectacular fire had destroyed the Company's leased Green Bay elevator (in the process threatening the whole town). Historian John Gruber wrote, "Explosions threw burning timbers and sheet metal in all directions. Tons of grain spilled into the river. The loss was estimated at $345,000." Management immediately pressed the owners to rebuild, and John Sr. wrote John Jr. on November 13 about the financing of the new elevator, warning that "of course you must not repeat that." In 1917 the elevator was again in operation; with later additions in 1924, its capacity grew to 700,000 bushels.

In February 1917, resumption of unrestricted submarine warfare finally forced Wilson to break with Germany, and it seemed as if war was imminent. "The President did the right thing," wrote John Sr. to John Jr. In this same letter, he began to raise the question of possible war service by John Jr., who was still at Yale. He felt that John Jr., with the education and military training he had already had, should be qualified for a commission. "You can be very certain that I will never advise you in any way that would cause you any feeling of shame or lack of patriotic duty," he continued, "but if there is occasion for an army it is equally necessary that men of education and military training should be used to command instead of merely enlisting as privates. Any sound, healthy boy can become a private soldier, but there will be a fearful lack of competent officers."

Within days, John Jr. reported that a "Yale training battery" had been formed at the University and that he had joined it. In April 1917, after war had been declared by the United States, it was announced that a new Reserve Officer's Training Corps camp was to be instituted at Fort Snelling, Minnesota, and John Sr. immediately wrote John Jr. about applying. He called a number of his acquaintances connected with the new endeavor, attempting to move John Jr.'s application along, but he was assured by one of them that "there is nothing in fact I could do that would help you in the slightest degree."

Indeed, John Jr.'s credentials were outstanding—he did not need his father's influence. A first sergeant in the Yale Battalion, he was obviously just the kind of person the armed forces were seeking for officers' training. In May, he joined the initial officers' training class at Fort Snelling and in August 1917 was graduated as a captain in the field artillery. In November 1917, he attended the field artillery's Fort Sill, Oklahoma, "School of Fire," finishing there in late January 1918. The mathematics of artillery continued to appeal to his analytical sense, and while at Fort Sill, he shared several letters with his Uncle Will, the University of Chicago professor, on some of the complexities of firing a shell, particularly as affected by temperature and relative air density.

He next was assigned to the headquarters of the 163rd Artillery Brigade of the 88th Division, under the command of Brigadier General S. M. Foote. He was appointed acting adjutant for the brigade, a position of vast responsibility. His experiences in this position, under the leadership of Foote, were to give him those memorable lessons that he was to take away from the war.[45]

Austen Cargill, meanwhile, also was anxious to get into the fight, and in the early part of 1918, he enlisted in the navy. He was seven years older than John Jr., already in a position of responsibility at Cargill and was married. Austen's enlistment had considerable impact on the organization. F. E. Lindahl, for example, wrote J. B. Taylor at the Minneapolis

A spectacular Cargill elevator fire, Green Bay, 1916 (Neville Public Museum of Brown County).

office, "I certainly admire him tremendously. It is mighty fine of a man in his position, a young married man, to volunteer to go before he is called." Austen, however, did not have the same opportunity for officership that was extended to John Jr., having left college early at the time of his father's death in 1909.[46]

John Jr. Joins the Expeditionary Force

The war excited and exhilarated John MacMillan, Jr. Posted to Camp Dodge, Iowa, where the brigade was in training, he was promoted to adjutant within weeks. He was adept—sometimes devious—in getting things done by skirting the regular channels of the chain of command. For example, having been given the task of searching the ranks for "experts of one kind or another," he approached a colonel in another unit, who "swore that they had no telegraphers or electricians or anything of the sort and that he had no men which he could spare for us." John Jr., not believing the colonel, went to the personnel clerk and, using General Foote's name without permission, perused the colonel's files. "I found out that he had countless former telegraph operators and telephone experts, most of them R.R. men who had worked in Dakota, precisely the kind I was looking for. I at once came back and reported what I had found out to the General who was very much relieved because he had been afraid that no such men were available. Incidentally he was quite peeved at Col. Honeycutt for his unwillingness to comply with our request for men."

Naturally, the colonel was upset at being shown up and "in a quite

The 163rd Field Artillery Brigade, Camp Dodge, Iowa, 1918. John MacMillan, Jr., belonged to this unit.

*Major John MacMillan, Jr.,
c. 1918.*

heated manner" demanded that John Jr. go through channels. John Jr. called his bluff: "All I could do was to ask him to step in and see the General with me and make any complaint he had to make through 'the proper channels,' and of course the General backed me up splendidly and quite sharply told the Col. to cease covering up his sins by adopting a policy of secrecy, and that I had standing orders to find out all I could about the personnel of this brigade 'in view of the fact that some of the organization commanders were unwilling to cooperate with him.' "

John Jr. knew he had made an enemy; later he went to see the colonel and "apologized in my nicest manner for my seeming lack of tact, etc., etc. so it seems to have been fixed up splendidly to my advantage. The General later thanked me for my alertness and said that it was the kind of spirit he liked to see, etc."

Late in August 1918, Foote recommended him for promotion to major, which was the army's "table of organization" rank for a brigade adjutant. The rank was confirmed in September, making John Jr. reportedly the youngest major in the United States Army at that time. He was just over 23.[47]

By mid-September, the 88th Division had crossed the Atlantic, and John

Jr. began writing back about his experiences with the Expeditionary Force. The crossing was rough but "have really enjoyed every minute of it," he wrote. His duties were light, but his smattering of Portuguese was useful with the Portuguese crew. "They are decidedly incompetent," he told his mother and father, "their navigation seems to be all right, but they are neither mechanics nor good executives." There were about a dozen officers on board, "three of them are really very nice, the rest are former enlisted men, and quite typical." John Jr., throughout his life and in spite of his father's advice, remained an elitist.

In France the division was billeted near the town of Clermont-Ferrand, in the Departement of Puy-de-Dôme, in the south central part of the country. On one of the first afternoons, John Jr. accompanied General Foote on an inspection tour, stopping also at a chateau overlooking the town. "The C.O., Major Omstad, had been put up at a magnificent chateau owned by the Baron and Baroness of something or other." Later that week, he and General Foote had dinner in Paris, and John Jr. described the trip: "That evening we had a rather amusing incident. Someone said that we must have dinner at Ciros, but we thought we would check up by asking our driver. He replied, 'Why it must be some place, 'cause I take any number of General officers there.' It was some place, as you doubtless know."

A few days later, General Foote, with MacMillan, visited another colonel's unit; in this case, the colonel and his immediate staff were housed in a chateau. John Jr. described this chateau in admiring detail: it was perched on "a strategic promontory, projecting out over a deep gorge, perhaps 200 feet deep and three or four hundred feet wide at the top, so that on three sides there is the gorge with almost perpendicular sides, and on the third side the deep hillside sloping away from the chateau. . . . A deep dry moat has been constructed between the castle and the village." He continued, "It is a tremendous affair . . . the view from it is magnificent . . . the whole effect was remarkable in the extreme . . . you had the feeling that the castle guarded the approaches to the plain from the dark mysterious region above." He then described the organizational configuration effected by the colonel: "One wing of the castle was inhabited, in fact the officers had their quarters with the family who lived there. . . . The rest of the castle was entirely abandoned, and had been so for many many years. It was in this part that the men were quartered. . . . In this case, the men were quite fortunate, being all together where they can be kept under close supervision."

It was not just the beauty and grace of these chateaus (and the life there) that appealed to John Jr.; it was particularly their quality as an organizational billet for troops that engaged him. In later years, John Jr. recalled these experiences often, reiterating the view that General Foote had expressed a number of times, namely, that if he had his small staff around him, in isolation from all of the pressures around, he could lead most effectively. This indelible memory of John Jr, later became an important influence on the Company.

The rather giddy social whirl of the headquarters group continued. In early October 1918, John Jr. elaborated the week's schedule:

Sunday afternoon: Tea at the Chateau Villeneuve
    "   evening: Theatre with Madame Dumont
Monday afternoon: Tea with the Countess de Choiseul
Tuesday evening: Dinner and theatre with Miss Oglesby
Wednesday afternoon: Official visit to Nevers returning late at night.
Thursday afternoon: Bridge at Mme. Chaffers
Friday evening: Dinner with Mme de Villetre
Saturday 3 P.M. Dedication of a cemetery followed by tea with a French General
Sunday: Tea at Chateau de something or other.

John Jr.'s indelible memory of these chateaus later became an important influence on the Company when the executive officers were moved to the Rand estate (Lake Office) in 1946.

In late October, John Jr. accompanied General Foote on a ten-day inspection trip to the front. Peace notes were being exchanged; John Jr. commented on the response of the men: "I am proud . . . that the general sentiment among officers and men was . . . that they one and all hoped that the war would not end until we were able to carry it into Germany proper. To let the Germans off so easily as to stop the war now would be nothing short of criminal, horrible as the war is." At one point on this mission, John Jr. had the privilege of meeting John J. Pershing, the commander in chief of the American troops, in the process of hearing briefings for Pershing by corps, division and brigade commanders (including Foote). "To say it was interesting would be putting it mildly," John Jr. wrote; "It was the opportunity of a lifetime and I treated it as such, except that I took no notes out of regard to regulations."

John Jr. continued to voice restlessness about the division itself not getting into action: "We are fast rounding into shape, but are just a bit worried over these peace offers. It may be that we never will get to the front . . . of course we are anxious for the war to be over, but I would like to get one good crack at the Germans with our brigade before that time."

In that late October trip to the front with General Foote, he did see some action; in this case, he wrote his Uncle Dan about the details, rather than the family. There were two instances, both involving trips with the general to inspect advanced positions:

One wet muddy afternoon, (it is always wet and always muddy at the front) we were going forward in the General's car to visit an advanced battery . . . when without the usual warning, which consists in a preliminary noise like the ripping of a huge sheet of silk, a 150mm (about 6 inch) shell burst not fifteen yards in front of us and just off the road. As it was, the ground was very muddy, which partially suffocated or rather smothered it, and our car was merely covered with mud, not a splinter hitting it. . . . the rare luck of it was that the shell had not hit five feet farther on, in which case it would have been the end of us and our car, and of course, it was the road at which they were aiming . . . they do not throw over shells singly, but the rest were fortunately quite a bit over . . .

Another time we were going thru a little village, I say village, it was what had formerly been a village, but was now as flat as the rest of the country when a couple of 77s fell about 200 meters to our right. The corporal, our chauffeur showed a tendency to slow up to watch them, and I was later joshed about my request to him to make haste, but it was fortunate I did so for the next two landed right where we had been not five seconds before. As it was, we did get some of the splinters from them but they merely took the paint off the rear fenders.

In this same letter to Daniel MacMillan, John Jr. commented on his fellow officers and enlisted men:

I am tremendously impressed with the differences between the American soldier and those of these other countries. He is superior in every way (I do not refer to fighting ability, although he is by no means inferior in that). He is far more intelligent, more reliable, cleaner, both physically and morally, and unfailingly cheerful. Our officers on the other hand, although superior in many ways do not have the education, the general education that is, that the European officers have . . . we have exceptions, all of our higher officers are equal to them, but the junior officers are not, and the reason lies I think in our relatively small leisured class. Most of their officers come either from what we would term the leisured class, or else from wealthy manufacturing or banking families, and they are splendidly educated. . . . What it amounts to is that they have a much larger upper class from which to draw than we do . . . we have a much higher average, with relatively few extremes. The Europeans, though, have the extremes far more pronounced than do we.[48]

John Jr. continued to express an amalgam of meritocracy and noblesse oblige—ability and intelligence, enhanced by fine education, should, and will, rise to the top, but this small cadre at the top was likely to come mainly from the upper, "leisured" class, who had an obligation to lead. In his writings in this period, refined more in his later pieces at the time of World War II, John Jr. mirrored a substantial body of thinking of that time about eugenics and the science of human genetics. One of the directions this lively debate had taken just before World War I was over the question of whether peoples' "intelligence quotients" could be measured scientifically. The armed forces answered "yes" and had instituted a massive IQ testing of recruits in 1917–1918, "not primarily for the exclusion of intellectual defectives," said its sponsors, "but rather for the classification of men in order that they may be properly placed in the military service." John Jr. was given the test (scoring in the top levels) but felt "the thing is decidedly bunkum when considering any particular case." He noted that the engineers had the top average, with the artillery next, the infantry and quartermasters following, and doctors and "niggers" at the bottom.[49]

As to the privileges of rank, it was evident that John Jr. was enjoying his field grade: "This being a field officer is great stuff, as it enabled me to get a [railway] compartment all to myself. . . . I have by no means gotten used to my promotion yet, and whenever anyone calls 'Captain' I jump and answer, 'here, sir.' At —— [name censored in letter], which is full of captains and lieutenants of about father's age, I couldn't manage to enter an office with quite the dignity and assurance that my rank demanded, but I am fast learning and by the time I get home trust that I will be able to act as though the world belonged to me."

Several times he wrote of the weight of his responsibilities, "particularly when I realize how exceedingly limited has been my experience in prior military training." He continued, "After all, what is required for my position is not great technical knowledge, but rather balance, judgment and common sense. Judgment, however, is mostly common sense plus experience, so that I must make up in common sense and thought what I lack in experience." He ended another letter: "It is really quite staggering but I have enough of the MacMillan conceit against which Aunt Emma once warned me, to feel confident of my ability to handle it."

His selection by General Foote was a significant independent validation of his intellectual qualities and organizational abilities by this influential outsider. "General Foote must indeed have great confidence in me," he wrote his mother and father, "and I can't tell you how flattered I am each time I think of it. However, I am too busy to do much thinking of it, and it is fortunate that it is that way."

In his last letter from France, just before the Armistice, he wrote of having received a letter from the Yale class secretary detailing the death in action of several of his close friends. Unhappy over this news, he responded in anger and bias: "It seems too sad for words that it couldn't have been some of the Jews who have commissions in the Q.M. and Ordnance instead. By the way, H.Q. of the Service of Supply has three kinds of officers, the busted regulars who are the higher ranking ones, officers who have been wounded and are unfit for service at the front and Jews, particularly the latter. Of course there are exceptions but they are few and far between."[50]

John Jr. returned by troop ship to the United States in early January and soon was mustered out. John Sr. still seemed to harbor concerns about John Jr.'s stability and wrote with a strong word of caution:

I want you to be extra careful not to let down in any way in your morale because you are now leaving the service. You will regret it all your life if you do not hold up the same high standard of work that you have been doing since entering the army. It is causing a great deal of comment in the newspapers because of the lowered morale that our army officers and men have shown since the armistice was declared,—so I am just passing along a word of caution, as sometimes a steadying hand in a crisis helps one pass over the critical period and I want to be sure that your army record will always stand so high to the very end that you can point to it all your life with the greatest of pride.[51]

Austen Cargill had a somewhat less rarefied service rank. With his natural bent for mechanical devices of any kind, he rose quickly through the ranks to chief petty officer as an enlisted man in the navy. When John Jr. was promoted to major, Austen wrote to him, "needless to say I am proud as punch to know a Major—we gobs aren't used to associating with officers of such a high rank and I don't lose a single opportunity of bragging about it."

Austen had been sent to Columbia University to study the Liberty airplane engine and now was in France. He described his work to John Jr. as "organizing and superintending the operation of a repair shop . . . up to the present we have rebuilt and placed in commission all the aviation motors used by the Navy on this side." It was an assignment he enjoyed very much. He too had been "fortunate enough to seize an opportunity of going up to the front with the Marines." He was now "out of my sailor clothes" and wearing a civilian suit with brass buttons "which causes everyone to take me for a policeman . . . whenever I get to Bordeaux." His wife Anne, writing J. B. Taylor about one of those Bordeaux visits, commented that Austen "had been to dinner at a splendid cafe (trust him!) and to a musical comedy . . . didn't know the name or anything said, but the music was good."

Austen had more difficulty than John Jr. persuading the armed forces to let him out after the Armistice because he had enlisted for four years. John Sr. helped by contacting several officials about the need for him back with the Company. Finally, in mid-1919, he returned.[52]

Cargill MacMillan, too, was away from home during these war years, first at Andover and then at Yale in the fall of 1918. His letters home are in marked contrast to his older brother's—they picture a naive, sweet and obedient younger son, considerably less self-confident than John Jr. He was much more cautious with his money, and in spending his allowance, he was more concerned about his father's disapproval. He provided his father with detailed account books, a tedious task that consumed several hours each time he updated them. Once he mildly complained about the time lost but worried, "Father will think I am lazy." He described an intricate maneuver, carried out with a friend, whereby Cargill could save the 10-cent charge for cashing a check by endorsing it to the friend, who had a no-charge account.

Cargill was superb in his mathematics classes, even tutoring several of

Cargill MacMillan, 1922.

his classmates. One was captain of the (unofficial) military unit that had been formed at Andover in 1917 and rewarded Cargill by arranging his appointment as a corporal, the head of a squad. Later the friend was promoted to acting major, and Cargill wrote, "I want to be his orderly. . . . I could get the job just as easily as not, for if he refused I would tell him that I would not do his trig for him and then I surely would be appointed."

As with John Jr., his father began writing him about the news of Minneapolis. Cargill wrote back, "Your last letter was the most interesting I have received from you yet. You didn't spend the greater part . . . in telling me how to behave." Yet even with this mild response, he felt it necessary to add, "Don't think that I'm objecting to your letters, for I know it is your duty to tell me how to behave."

There is less evidence, however, of serious mentoring letters from John Sr. to Cargill, such as those he had sent to John Jr. Rather, this role began to be assumed by John Jr. For example, in the fall of 1917, Cargill was aspiring for a post on the editorial board of the Andover school newspaper, *The Phillipian*, but had come up against stiff competition from several classmates. Discouraged, he wrote his older brother of his fears. John Jr.'s return letter of advice is revealing, both of Cargill and himself:

I don't want you [to] take the frame of mind that your [*sic*] licked before you're started. If that is the way you go at it you'll never get on . . . force those upperclassmen and men that are on the inside to sit up and take notice of you . . . they don't dislike you or anything of that sort. They just ignore you until you are able to prove that you have something in you . . . if you quit or fail to make the *Phillipian* as I did, largely because I loafed on the job, secure in the conviction that I never had a chance because I wasn't on the inside and up against a stacked deck, it will merely confirm them in the feeling that you are not worth bothering with. I know in making a society just how it works out. You must have one of two things, either be an awfully popular sort, one of the kind whom everybody likes on first sight, or else someone with a lot of ability and push. Now if you once get on the inside they think that you are of the first kind too. . . . I know in these prep school societies they pick men largely on what they think he will do when he gets to college, and you have to show the stuff somewhere. So whatever you do keep on the job.

John Jr. followed with nine specific suggestions for stories for Cargill to write and ended with a characteristic warning, one that he was to apply to himself later in his business life: "Make sure that your managing editor would have use for these . . . but spring them gradually on him . . . ask him to keep secret anything which you might be telling him. Incidentally, keep your standing in the competition a deep dark secret. Never admit how many inches you got in any one issue or what articles were yours, or what your total credit amounts to."

Privately, John Jr. appeared not to have full confidence in Cargill's writing; he wrote his mother, "Just how they can expect to make an editor out of such an illiterate editorial writer as the enclosed editorial makes him out to be, I don't quite see." But he did allow as how Cargill "has the hustle" and ended with a prediction that Cargill would make the board (which he did).

In the fall of 1918, Cargill followed in his brother's footsteps, enrolling in Yale University. By this time, the whole University was on a war footing, with military training dominating. Cargill was excited and proud about his service and wrote John Jr. in October:

We are in the army now . . . Army discipline and all that . . . Y.M.C.A.'s, Red Cross, canteens . . . the hardest to get along with is the discipline. This morning the whole battery spent 2 hours of the hardest scrubbing and cleaning they ever did in their lives. There was not a thing which was not scrubbed or gone over with a damp rag, and Wright Hall was about three times cleaner than it had ever been in its life before. We mopped our floor twice and swept it out four times, washed our windows and about a hundred other things, and then after inspection our battery commander got out in front of the battery and naively informed us that he had to wash his hands after the inspection was over, and if we did not have our rooms cleaner he would confine us to quarters.

His father was tickled, and wrote John Jr., "He is very enthusiastic . . . they have the '*best company*,' the '*best captain*' and 'the *best* drilled' etc. etc. We enjoy his enthusiasm very much."[53]

The Grain Trade at the End of the War

For both Food Administrator Herbert Hoover and the grain trade, the last six months of the war, May–November 1917, were considerably different from the previous year. The problem now was surplus rather than shortage. The 1917–1918 wheat crop was large. At 917 million bushels, it was 44 percent larger than the short crop in the previous year. Hoover saw that he was going to be left with about a 300-million-bushel surplus. The huge crop clogged the terminals and put tremendous financial pressure on the Grain Corporation to purchase all of it at the agreed price of $2.20, which President Wilson had extended in February 1918 to the 1918 crop.

Hoover now engaged in delicate negotiations with England's John Maynard Keynes to persuade the British to take 100 million bushels of imported grain over and above the approximately 100 million bushels already sent abroad from the 1918–1919 crop year. This complicated maneuver, again vintage Hoover economic nationalism, was finally made to work, and Hoover was able to persuade the Allies to pay for their storage costs in the United States even before the grain was shipped. Hoover combined this with a new version of "war bread," which he now persuaded the Allies to redefine as an "80-20 loaf"—in other words, 80 percent wheat and 20 percent other grains. Hoover's war bread was a great improvement over the existing Allied loaf, and the food czars of the various nations readily agreed. In November, by the time the Armistice was declared, the crush on grain storage space had been partially alleviated, and Hoover had gone a long way toward taking care of the huge crop, to everyone's reasonable satisfaction.

The Armistice caught the United States with immense stores of not only grain but of pork, oils and dairy products. These would have to be marketed overseas, in one way or another, if domestic prices were not to collapse. Keynes noted at one point: "The underlying motive of the whole thing is Mr. Hoover's abundant stocks of low-grade pig products at high prices which must at all costs be unloaded on someone, enemies failing allies. When Mr. Hoover sleeps at night, visions of pigs float across his bed clothes and he frankly admits that at all hazards the nightmare must be dissipated."[54]

Thus, the shift to peacetime came to be as sensitive and touchy as was the wartime food buildup; the next chapter will recount this interesting story. For all concerned, though, the Great War was, thank God, over.

CHAPTER SIX

Farmer Discontent, Regulatory Concerns

Reconversion from war is difficult—people want to get back to normal, to forget the heartaches and memories of the hostilities and begin again from the position they held prior to the war. Herbert Hoover's War Food Administration (WFA) was a case in point. Hoover left his post just after the Armistice, going to Europe to work with Woodrow Wilson on the peace plans. By January 1919, only residual constraints remained on most commodities; by March, only wheat and sugar were still controlled. Wheat was the big food supply story, for it continued to be regulated over the 18 months after hostilities ceased, agitating a wide array of interest groups—producers, grain traders, millers and, especially, consumers of wheat as bread. These conflicting views generated tensions in agriculture that persisted through the 1920s and into the 1930s.

Farmer hostility against the ceiling price on the 1918 wheat crop ($2.20 per bushel for No. 1 Northern Spring wheat) had pressured Wilson to push for a higher price for the 1919 crop. Under equally sharp pressure to hold the price *down* by labor and consumer groups, he deferred again to his agricultural advisory committee. After more political infighting, Wilson issued a proclamation in September 1918, extending the guaranteed price, a base of $2.26 for No. 1 Northern Spring, to all wheat harvested in 1919. This was just a few cents over the previous year's price. The announcement came just before fall seeding, and the farmers reacted predictably—they planted more. For the five prewar years, 1909–1913, the average area sown to winter wheat had been about 32 million acres; for the 1918 crop this had been increased to 42.3 million acres, and in 1919 over 51 million acres were planted. Spring wheat plantings increased commensurately. As late as June 1919, the estimated yield for the 1919 crop of wheat in the United States was 1.236 billion bushels.

During the next few months, however, the weather turned sour, and the eventual crop was reduced to only 968 million bushels, still the second largest crop ever harvested in the United States. With the imminent demise of the WFA, Wilson formed the United States Grain Corporation. He persuaded Julius Barnes, the New York grain exporter who had headed the Food Administration Grain Corporation of the WFA under Hoover, to become its wheat director to handle this huge crop.[1]

Barnes brought his own personal opinions to this new task. Both Hoover and Barnes believed the 1919 guarantee was a "positive obligation" of the government (Hoover's words), but Barnes differed by interpreting this solely to maintain minimum prices. His guarantee did not obligate the government to prevent prices rising above $2.26. Inasmuch as the conventional wisdom had predicted a surfeit of wheat in 1919, a drop in prices was perceived as the greatest threat; the floor would keep the farmers happy under such circumstances (even though costing many millions of dollars in government subsidy money). The partisans of cheap bread would not be satisfied, but, wanting to keep grain trading stabilized, Barnes was willing to take the expected criticism from this group. With futures trading still banned, the Wheat Director's ability to prevent prices from dropping below the guarantee did allow the grain trade to regularize its financing without widening their margins unduly.

A successor agency to the War Industries Board was instituted in February 1919: the government's Industrial Board. George N. Peek, a former farm machinery company executive became chairman and joined the side pressing for the lowering of agricultural prices. Barnes won this argument—the floor on prices stayed at $2.26. But within two years Peek surprised everyone by changing from the consumers' to the farmers' side and becoming one of the great protagonists of farm support legislation in the early 1920s.

John MacMillan, Sr., also entered the fray, representing the desire of most of the grain trade for free-market prices when he wrote Barnes in April 1919, "I notice that already vast pressure is being brought to bear upon you . . . but I personally believe it would be a very great mistake to burden the taxpayers of this country unnecessarily by fixing an arbitrarily low price on bread in this country. The country is very prosperous on the whole and I can see no reason why we should have cheaper bread in this country than the world's basis of prices."[2]

As it turned out, the combination of the somewhat smaller crop and the clever management of the export embargo by Barnes kept prices above the $2.26 floor for the remainder of 1919. These high prices were supported by Wilson's Democratic administration. With the approaching presidential campaign of 1920 already on Republicans' minds, however, it seemed to them good politics to defend the consumers by advocating lower prices. Given the historical bias of the GOP toward business, it was incongruous to have one Republican congressman state, "It is an unequal fight between the rich producers . . . and the weak little woman in calico who is trying to get bread . . . for her little children. As far as the Republican party is concerned, it will be found fighting for the weak little woman in calico."[3]

The GOP indeed had hit a sensitive nerve among the public, and a general uproar in the press ensued at this point about "excessive" food prices. Just at this point, the Federal Trade Commission issued its report on price-fixing activities in the meat packing industry. The packers countered accusations of price manipulation by charging that the administration's wheat program really caused the higher price level. Wilson, caught once more in a cross fire, ended by backing Barnes on the Grain Corporation's mandated floor, then reverting to a device he had often used earlier—appointing investigators to "ferret out price gougers." This assignment went to the Justice Department, and Attorney General A. Mitchell Palmer hastened to expose wholesale grocers who were hoarding food. Later that fall, the country's preoccupation with the League of Nations debate left the food question in abeyance although not resolved. Prices rose sharply in the spring of 1920—wheat moved from around $2.30 a bushel in November 1919 to as high as $2.97 in May 1920.

The Wheat Guarantee Act (March 1919) had provided for the termination of the government's purchasing by June 1920. The Grain Corporation began removing many of its restrictions on free trade around the first of that year, and in May the wheat director called a meeting of key grain trade officials to discuss the measures to be taken for the resumption of futures trading. This critical mechanism of the grain trade, not available for over three years, was reinstituted on July 15, 1920. By the fall of 1920, the grain trade had returned to its prewar mode, including the trading of futures.

The record of the War Food Administration and the United States Grain Corporation during the war and immediate postwar period was, in the main, quite positive. Hoover had had an ability to balance the many partisan groups within the United States and then trade these off against the Allies' self-interested demands, all the while maintaining his political capital with President Wilson. His eminently successful act was followed by an equally able effort on the part of Julius Barnes. However, there were lasting legacies from this World War I wheat management program. Most important, the farmers of the United States had had a vivid lesson in the political management of wheat prices. They saw that price management could act as a fulcrum for overall control of the entire wheat picture. Further, the concept of "parity," whereby farm prices would be adjusted to maintain their "equality of purchasing power" relative to overall price levels, began to be espoused as one of the rubrics of agricultural price policy. This notion gained particular currency in 1922 with the publishing of *Equality for Agriculture* by George Peek and General Hugh S. Johnson (see below).

The farmers also came through the war with an intractable hostility toward Hoover, believing he had deprived them of their due from high prices. They saw again the need for an organization as a source of effective political clout, and the American Farm Bureau Federation gained substantial strength out of World War I. Henry C. Wallace, the Secretary of Agriculture from 1921 through 1924, wrote in March 1920, "Mr. Hoover's deceit in dealing with the farmers was in fact the impelling motive for the organization of the Farm Bureau in its later and stronger form. It was Mr. Hoover's efforts to bamboozle the farmers that brought them to see at last that if they were to secure economic justice . . . at the hands of the government, it would have to come through an organization of their own." Farm problems and farmer agitation was now to be a prominent feature of agricultural policy, providing a ringing prelude through the 1920s for the watershed "farm problem" of the New Deal days. Farmers felt a deep

What is sauce for the goose is sauce for the gander.

Ding Darling, October 28, 1920 (by permission of the University of Iowa Libraries [Iowa City]).

resentment at this juncture, yet at the same time they held an underlying psychological mindset that persuaded them that high wheat prices were "here to stay." Historian Tom Gibson Hall, Jr., concluded that "if Barnes was willing to take credit for $3.00 wheat, he must also take credit for creating the false optimism that left farmers unprepared for the farm crisis of succeeding years."[4]

Cargill Elevator Company's War Reconversion

Cargill's performance in the postwar crop year 1918–1919 was adequate, certainly better than in 1917–1918 (in those days the crop years at the Company began on July 1, so part of this year was still within the war period). The Company registered a $578,000 profit, and total sales, all units included, was $55,303,872. Most of these sales and most of the profits came from three units of the organization: the Line Department had sales of just over $12 million, reporting an income of $188,198; the Elevator T account (the Minneapolis terminal) also had sales just over $12 million with profits of $101,280; and the Duluth units (the Superior Terminal Grain Company) had sales of just over $25 million and a profit of $112,452. Special Grains (which traded regular grains separately from the terminals) accounted for just under $3 million in sales, with profits of $17,618. The Seed Division had sold a total of $1.6 million with profits of $13,045, and the physical elevator operations in Elevators K and M in Superior had handling revenues of $403,000, with profits of $173,940. The commission houses and the administrative units accounted for the remainder. The overall Company margin on all of this business was just 1 percent.

The combination of all of the terminals (Duluth, Minneapolis and the leased terminal at Green Bay) had handled 24,948,000 bushels in the crop year 1918–1919, approximately the amount of 1915–1916 (the two intervening years were considerably lower). A chart recording the "average expense per bushel handled" showed about the same figures for the years 1915–1916 and 1918–1919 (1.93 cents versus 1.99 cents), with the two intervening years' figures much heightened by the logistic difficulties of the war period: 1916–1917 was 2.89 cents per bushel; 1917–1918 was 3.11 cents per bushel.

The total number of country elevators had dropped to 140 from the record figure of 189 in 1910–1911. There were no more Wisconsin elevators—the last one, at Bear Creek, was sold in 1916 (only the leased Green Bay terminal remained). North Dakota had the most, with 59 elevators; then Minnesota, with 43; and Montana, with 27 after more additions around Valier. There was a scattering of additional elevators in South Dakota and Iowa. As one reads down the names of these elevators, they present a chronicle of small-town and village America along the railroads at that time. Here we see Hoving, Gwinner, Jud, Colfax, Aneta, Dazey, Forfar, all in North Dakota; Minnesota towns included Dassel, Hawick, Judge, Airlie, Ada, Syre. Among the Montana towns were, of course, Conrad and Valier, also Manson, Merino, Ledger, Pablo. South Dakota towns included Willow Lake, Claremont, Huffton, Iona, McIntire and Struble. Most of these were tiny enclaves, a few were county seats, and all had strong roots in the agricultural regions around them. Today, several of these no longer even exist as towns, as with Conover. The elevators, standing like spires in those scattered, often-isolated towns and villages, gave a permanence and an identifying physical sign, almost as if someone had moved out through the plains to put a "mark" as a signpost along the way. John C. Hudson, describing these in his book *Plains Country Towns*, wrote of the sameness of such centers:

A grain elevator rises predictably against the horizon, followed by a church steeple or school poking up above the canopy of cottonwoods. Up close, a small cluster of false-front store buildings lines Main Street, with perpendicular rows of white frame houses on one side of the highway and a railroad depot on the other. . . . The geometry is more regular when viewed from the air: individual structures are lost, but the regular spacing of towns along a railroad line that cuts across the rectangular grid of farms and fields is all the more remarkable. It is the dominant settlement pattern in a broad region beginning with the Grand Prairie of Illinois on the east, stretching northwest to the Canadian prairies, south through Texas, and west to the Rocky Mountain front.

The total assets of the Company at this time were over $4.8 million, up from $2.8 million the previous year. The increases came from postwartime inflation in the price level, from the substantial addition to surplus from the year's profits, and from increases in notes payable and accounts payable due to the more active trade of this first postwar year. A 7 percent dividend on the preferred stock had been declared, as well as a 20 percent dividend on the common stock (13 percent of it in Liberty bonds, 7 percent in cash). After the $376,000 dividend payments had been taken from the earnings for this year, the net worth stood at just over $3 million.

All in all, given the arduous period through which the Company had just passed, the 1919 audit report pictured a healthy enterprise. Figures for the 1919–1920 crop year gave much the same picture—there were profits of some $431,000; the preferred stock dividend was paid, and a 10 percent dividend on the common was also included; the net worth was up now to over $3.2 million.

A Peace Treaty, Prohibition, a "Red Scare"

As "regular" as these two years might have seemed to the grain trade, it was not so for the country as a whole, which experienced some national issues of more than passing concern. Internationally, the years 1919 and

1920 were frustrating for the United States. The Versailles Peace Conference led to the establishment of the League of Nations in 1920, but in a stunning repudiation of President Wilson, the Senate turned down America's membership. The Russian Revolution was followed by a civil war during both of these years. There was massive famine in Eastern Europe at this time, and Herbert Hoover again took a central role in Europe as director-general of the American Relief Organization.

At home, the year 1919 opened with an attempted social reform by the electorate. An alcohol prohibition amendment, the 18th to the United States Constitution, was ratified, its passage due in part to anti-German feeling (the brewers were heavily German). Its effect on the nation and on the grain trade as a provider of the ingredients of alcohol was, for the moment, unpredictable. High consumer prices continued throughout 1919 and into 1920, and there was a great amount of industrial tension during these two years. A steel strike spanned both of the years; the New York dock workers went out on strike in 1919; there was even a full-scale bitter general strike in Winnipeg, Canada.

Related to the labor strife but quickly finding a life of its own was the so-called Red scare. As an aftermath of the Bolshevik revolution in Russia, the Soviets had instituted an intensive propaganda campaign against the Western nations. The forerunner of the American Communist Party was founded in 1919, and its campaign and those of other organizations with seemingly similar messages (particularly the Industrial Workers of the World—the I.W.W., or "Wobblies") produced a torrent of left-oriented diatribes. The country was in no mood for any new "ism," having just expressed itself by a bitter anti-German outpouring and now was harboring fears of the sudden violence that had overtaken conservative Russia. So the reaction to these leftist actions was quick and harsh. Attorney General A. Mitchell Palmer in the Wilson administration was given the charge to, in his words, "tear out the radical seeds that have entangled American ideas . . . the IWW's, the most radical socialists, the misguided anarchists, . . . the moral perverts and the hysterical neurasthenic women who abound in communism." In a series of raids all over the country in early January 1920, large numbers of political and labor agitators were arrested. Later, a number were deported to Russia, including anarchists Emma Goldman and Alexander Berkman.

This ferment had pointed implications for agriculture. The *Northwestern Miller* felt it had recognized a link between the Bolsheviks and agriculture right from the start. In an editorial in April 1919, its indefatigable editor, William Edgar, commented: "The forces of Bolshevism . . . do not exist according to geographical units but are scattered wherever discontent, and above all, hunger are found. The weapon with which Bolshevism and its kindred forms of anarchy can best be overcome is bread." Edgar also highlighted with banner headlines "Winnipeg's Bolshevik strike."[5] Closer to home in the Midwest grain belt, another organization was achieving a high profile for agitation. This was the already-famous Nonpartisan League.

A. C. Townley and the Nonpartisan League

Arthur Townley had been such a successful farmer in North Dakota in 1912 that he was dubbed by railroad land agents "the flax king of the Northwest." But the combination of an early frost and a subsequent unprecedented snow that year, together with a speculative crash in flax prices, wiped him out. His bitterness over this soon led him into political action on the side of the farmers and the formation of the Farmers' Nonpartisan Political League of North Dakota.

The platform was socialist, and as might be expected, the conservative press lambasted the group. The *Grand Forks Herald* railed, "while it would be untrue to say that every socialist is a free lover, we know of no advocate of free love who is not an avowed socialist. Most of the men who are of the inner circle in . . . the Nonpartisan League . . . appear to have drifted into socialism through failure in every other line of activity. . . . They are socialists not of the conservative, but of the destructive class. . . . Among them are men who are advocates of almost every wild vagary ever put forth under the name of socialism."

But the League cleverly turned the tables by noting that it was the farmers themselves who were being called "free lovers," "failures," and worse. In 1916, the League ran its own candidates in the state elections in North Dakota and, to the amazement of establishment politicians, captured the North Dakota House of Representatives and garnered a respectable minority in the Senate. The business community in the Northwest, aghast at the results, likely shared the sentiments of a businessman quoted in a St. Paul paper: "The Nonpartisan League is a band of Socialists, led by an anarchist, bent on the destruction of the country. It will set the state back twenty years, plunge it into an overwhelming debt, and make it the laughing stock of the nation. If it stays in power past the next election most of the businessmen will leave the state and let the damned anarchists run it to suit themselves."[6]

When the United States entered the World War in 1917, the Nonpartisan League became entangled in the acrimonious debates about pacifism. While the group formally backed the war effort, it did so with enough hesitation to get it enmeshed in controversy. The League had encountered particular hostility in Minnesota. Finally, in February 1918, Townley was indicted in Martin County, the complaint charging that his actions and writings had discouraged enlistments in Minnesota, which was considered sedition under Minnesota's statute. The case quickly went to the state supreme court, and in July 1918, the League and Townley were exonerated. However, in the process, they lost the public relations battle. Press attacks continued, and Townley was painted as "guilty" all through the area.

Still, the postwar Nonpartisan League appeared threatening to John MacMillan, Sr. He wrote L. F. Gates, the president of the Chicago Board of Trade, in September 1919, that the grain trade had "made a mistake in paying no attention to the charges made by various politicians and agitators" and continued, "I think all of us in the Northwest are quite alarmed over the . . . League. They are spending unlimited money apparently to teach the farmers that they are very badly abused . . . preaching Socialistic doctrines, viz: that the State should take over all the mills and elevators. You can see that if their program succeeds, there will soon be no occasion for grain exchanges or grain merchants." MacMillan apparently had been influenced by his public efforts in Washington with the War Food Administration and now advocated to Gates and others that grain trade people become more involved in public life, particularly in educational efforts aimed at countering the hostile press of the farmer dissidents.

John Sr. also envisaged links between this protest pattern and that of his own labor relations at the terminals. The high cost of living after the war had increased the militancy of the unions around the country, and the Longshore & Marine Workers Union, the predecessor on the Great Lakes of the International Longshoremen's Association, was active in Duluth, particularly among the coal dock employees. No formal contract had yet been signed for grain handlers inside the terminals (a different union, an A.F.L. federal labor union called the American Federation of Grain Processors, finally accomplished this in 1933). Cargill had no direct contractual relationships with any union in Duluth at this time, but Lindahl confided to MacMillan that "Haley [superintendent in a competitor terminal] tells me practically all of his men belong to the union, I think probably three-fourths of ours do, and other plants probably in the same proportion." According to Lindahl, Edward McManus, the superintendent at the Superior terminals, wanted to know "if we said we were going to declare for open shop." Lindahl reported his own reply: "I told him we certainly were and that your instructions to me were that you would not stand for anything but open shop." McManus had said he would resign if Cargill gave a closed shop, because he would "have no powers . . . the Labor Union would dictate and we would never know where we were at."

MacMillan still perceived links between these labor concerns and the overall reform tension, all with financial implications to the firm. He wrote Lindahl later in the year, "We are liable to see riots in any city of the country and in case of a riot starting a conflagration of any kind, no property is insured under an ordinary fire policy." Incidentally, he also told

Lindahl in the same letter that he had just taken out "dust explosion insurance," noting that "this hazard is a much greater one than we had supposed, and I do not feel under the circumstances that we can afford to be without this kind of insurance."[7]

The issue of Townley's alleged disloyalty persisted, and in 1919 he again was indicted, this time in Jackson County, Minnesota, accused of a conspiracy through disloyal statements. When he and another League organizer, Joseph Gilbert, subsequently were found guilty, they took the case to the Minnesota Supreme Court. In 1921, that court upheld the conviction, and Townley was required to serve a 90-day sentence. By this time, the League's fortunes had begun to ebb both politically and publicly with the farmer and the general public—it was no longer a force in the Northwest. However, in the years 1916–1922, the League was a vigorous regional agent for reform in agriculture, and its efforts coalesced with others to bring the farmer through the controls during World War I and into the reconversion days with a strong sense of solidarity and a acute sensitivity to "the farm problem." Others were now ready to pick up the cudgel for the farmer in the early 1920s.

John MacMillan, Jr., Joins the Company

War had taken a toll on 23-year-old John MacMillan, Jr.; he had written his father in December 1918 that he wanted "three or four months' rest" when he came home. The tremendous responsibility at the brigade had weighed heavily on him. Not until April 1919 did he declare himself rested; at this point, he made the decision to join the Cargill Elevator Company. Every evidence points to his enthusiasm for doing this—not since his early Yale days had he mentioned any alternative. Indeed, his aptness for and involvement in his economics courses were strong, positive signs. This must have been a most satisfying moment for John Sr.

John Jr. began working directly on the trading floor of the Minneapolis Chamber of Commerce, mentoring under Hub Owen and taking a long trip into the winter wheat areas of Kansas, Nebraska and Oklahoma with Owen in late May 1919. His assignment was to learn actual *trading* of grain, in its literal sense of taking a position in the market and being responsible for carrying it through to fruition at a profit or loss, subject to the vagaries of the market and the skill of the trader's "feel." This could be a speculative ("naked") position on either side of the market or a form of hedging; in either case, there was a final balance sheet for the trader, a report card that could be explicitly assigned to the individual. Trading had become the sine qua non of the grain trade. Traders were felt to be at the center, to be the most important single group in the grain trade and, typically, receiving salaries and perquisites commensurate with this. John Sr. held this as an article of faith, and so did the rest of the Cargill organization. And this belief has continued to the present. To be considered "not good at trading" was and still is clearly a negative in the business, although the success of grain trading companies, just like other companies, depends on a wide range of other employee skills, too.

John Jr. made a nostalgic visit back to Yale for his reunion in late June. Unfortunately, he picked up a serious case of ptomaine poison complicated by a severe cold and, John Sr. confided to Fred Hanchette, was "a wreck when he reached home." He recovered and in September was sent to Duluth to work directly with Fred Lindahl.

After John Jr. had been there for a few days, he complained to his father that he did not have enough to do to keep himself busy. His father wrote Prime, "I have decided, therefore, to turn over the rye account to him and let him handle that."

Lindahl had handled rye up to this point, and John Sr. hastened to explain to Lindahl just exactly what this meant: "Of course, I will expect you to really take charge of the serious matters in connection with the handling of it, so that you will understand you have the full responsibility, but at the same time, I would like to have him do the real work, for it will be very helpful to him and tend to give him self-confidence. . . . I think John will understand that . . . it is your responsibility just the same, but in order that there may be no doubt about it, I am quite willing you should show him this letter if you so desire."

Apparently this worked well, for Lindahl wrote in early November, "Junior has been doing all right in switching hedges around." Later that month, however, John Sr. became upset about some of his son's trades and wrote directly to him, "I was somewhat startled to read in your letter that you are offering rye on basis of 3½¢ over your Dec. in store." John Sr. then outlined his own strategy and continued, "You can see that there is every advantage in holding onto the grain as long as we can earn the carrying cost. I had the matter up with Mr. Lindahl over the telephone this morning." There is no indication in the correspondence in this period that John Jr. resented this intervention by his father; indeed, letters back and forth between the two seemed from the start business-like and free of rancor.

The focus that John Sr. put here on revenues from storage—the carrying charges—is yet another example of his appreciation of the warehousing function in the grain trade. This had been emphasized in the 1945 history, where comparisons were made with the earlier W. W. Cargill organization—"the Cargills had not understood fully the principles of hedging and the carrying charge, and this company had developed as a merchandising rather than a warehousing organization." John Sr.'s prescience resulted in a strong dedication to the latter function that was to prove so important in later periods.

Just at this time, a new development surfaced relating to the East. The postwar period had brought heightened trade with Argentina, mostly out of the commodity markets in New York City. Cargill finally had decided to send one of its Duluth men, Duncan Frick, to New York City to gain information about the New York Produce Exchange, possibly as an initial move toward opening a full-scale office there. Lindahl had written, "I wish we had a man at Buenos Ayres [*sic*], just at this particular time." Lindahl had been in favor of sending Frick, although he pushed also for consideration of a Winnipeg office as an alternative. Lindahl now proposed that John Jr. be sent to New York to assess Frick's work and to learn for himself about how the market functioned there. His father was dubious about sending him with so little experience and wrote Lindahl, "It is a little early yet to do anything of this sort." Finally, John Sr. did agree.

All of this had to be put aside, however, when John Jr. became ill. He had come home to Minneapolis for the Christmas holidays, in the process picking up a bad cold. He returned to Duluth in late January 1920 but quickly became much worse and returned to Minneapolis. He was subsequently diagnosed as having a full-scale influenza attack.

The great "influenza crisis" is believed to have begun in the final days of World War I in Spain. It soon became one of those pandemic plagues that occur occasionally, in this case rivaling the worst of these, the "Black Death" medieval cataclysm. It swept over the whole world during the winter of 1918–1919 and returned again the following winter, leaving in its wake vast numbers of deaths. A noted United States epidemiologist recently estimated, with perhaps an unwarranted exactitude, that there was a total worldwide mortality of 21,647,274. The numbers were, of course, impossible to ascertain precisely; accurate estimates for the United States held that something over half a million people in the United States alone had died during those scourge-ridden four months in 1918–1919.

John Jr. took many weeks to recover. By mid-February 1920, he "walked out a few steps," but later that month he had a severe setback in his convalescence with complications to his heart, and a scheduled trip to California had to be canceled. By mid-March he was better, and the California trip (to see the Hanchettes) again was scheduled.

This particular virulent variety of the flu left many people with severe aftereffects. As the complications ran their own course, John Sr. wrote Fred Hanchette of the "strong after-effect" experienced by John Jr. It was evident that he was suffering from lingering emotional problems as he departed for California in early March. In mid-June 1920, he left California for the lumber operation in Vancouver, arriving there, as his father wrote

Fred, "a little bit tired out and depressed. He said he did not feel able to call up his friends and was taking his meals in his room." (Will Cargill, W. W.'s eldest son, also had been taken seriously ill in 1920. He died in late July; John Sr. had visited him at his bedside and wrote Lindahl, "He seemed delighted to see us. . . . I was very glad that we went down.")

John Jr. worked all that summer at the lumber camp alongside the manager, R. M. Johnston, the old Banner Lumber employee who, after the sale of all but one of the yards for Cargill Securities Company, had been moved to British Columbia. During World War I the Allies had used millions of board feet of lumber for the trenches and prices had gained famously. This had persuaded John Sr. to attempt commercial exploration of the Cargill Securities property in British Columbia. In the fall, Johnston developed serious inner-ear problems, and it seemed as if John Jr. was going to be pressed into taking greater responsibility for the operation in the Vancouver office. John Sr. wrote Austen, "This disturbs me greatly. . . . I do not want to put responsibility onto John until he has had a chance to entirely regain his health . . . any nervous disorder, such as he has been having for the past six or eight months, usually takes a long time to become entirely normal . . . the most important thing . . . is to get in thoroughly good physical condition." Johnston finally had to leave his job altogether, and Austen Cargill came from La Crosse to replace him. Austen's postwar assignment had been an effort to put the La Crosse & Southeastern Railroad on a paying basis, and he was already on the West Coast searching for a new type of rail car. Fortunately, things finally improved for John Jr., and John Sr. wrote Fred Hanchette, in early December, "It seems remarkable how well that kind of life agrees with him."

The remnants of the illness lasted for John Jr. through 1920. His father wrote him in late December, when John Jr. was thinking of a trip to England, "Just as long as you are a little fearful of your condition, you can be rather sure that you are not entirely well, but I should think that perhaps a little later you will begin to crave seeing people and that will be a pretty good symptom that your system will stand it." John Sr. was recognizing here that the isolation inherent in the lumber camp seemed to be an integral ingredient in John Jr.'s recovery. By the spring of 1921, John Jr. was back in Minneapolis and began to work short shifts at the Company. By May 1922, in a letter to Fred Hanchette, John Sr. reported, "He seems practically well now. . . . I believe he will be quite himself by the time the crop begins to move this fall."

The causes of John Jr.'s malady were likely quite complex and impossible to ascertain fully now. Some of John Jr.'s nervousness had been recognized by his father back in the Andover days. The flu epidemic may also have contributed. The result of his difficulties left John Jr. with a lifetime legacy of nervousness and concern about his own health, especially during times of stress and tension in his business life.[9]

Peacetime Problems, Once More

In many ways, the crop year 1919–1920 was a reprise of the previous year. We have no sales figures, but profits were $431,000, down from the previous year but still respectable. The grain trade had begun the return to a competitive mode by January 1920, and John MacMillan, Sr., was again worried that A. M. Prime was taking too many exposed, speculative positions in Duluth. He wrote Prime, "Of course I will be very glad to have you work on cash barley all you like, but I am not willing to go into pure speculation on our May here. . . . I have no objection to your taking on a moderate amount which you will figure to sell out as you buy the cash barley. . . . I want to do a regular, legitimate business. . . . You can protect yourself against sales of cash by buying the futures, but just merely to buy a line of Mpls. May and stand on it as a speculation is entirely against all my theories as to the proper conduct of the grain business." However, John Sr. had retreated from this purely hedged view before, when short-term opportunities for profit surfaced, and that is just what happened again. He wrote Prime six weeks later, "Just at the moment I am inclined to keep away from hedges entirely, we are just about to the time of year when the farmers' marketings drop off altogether so that it would seem to me we can afford to take a little chance, especially as the amount of barley that you are long all told is not such an amount as to give us any particular concern."

The year revived other old concerns. The Chicago Board of Trade once more was trying to bring the various exchanges together, and their president wrote MacMillan, "I assure you that Chicago would not wish to dominate in connection with any such campaign if it were possible to bring the trade together." John Sr. would have no part of it, as he was still uneasy about the Chicago crowd. He wrote Prime, "It is much better for you to trade in this market where we know what we are doing and we would get mixed up in Chicago, where we do not understand the factors. . . . We have found, however, . . . that it is difficult to get in and out, while in Minneapolis we seem to be able to trade freely at all times." In the same vein, he wrote John Jr. a few months later, "I haven't the slightest faith in the Railroad Administration giving any recognition either to Duluth or Minneapolis where the Chicago interests are concerned."

John Sr.'s national stature in the industry had risen markedly during World War I. He was beginning to speak out publicly on many issues relating to the grain trade. In mid-1919, he had written a major letter to the *New York World* about "the causes for the high cost of living." This was a sophisticated economic analysis. He first discussed the imbalances in the supply/demand equation during World War I, relating them to increases in wages under pressure for the "utmost output." While there had been "some unwarranted profiteering," it was a negligible amount, largely due to greater risks in business. He argued strongly for more production itself, rather than placing export embargoes on America's goods. It was a cogent defense of free trade. In 1920, he was elected second vice president of the Minneapolis Chamber of Commerce, and the following year he assumed the presidency.[10]

The Crash of 1920–1921

The farmers' halfdozen years of prosperity took a turn for the worse, along with the whole economy, in late 1920, a drop so sudden and so severe that thousands of businesses were forced into bankruptcy. One of the most important stories (and far-reaching on patterns of corporate organization in the 1920s) was in the effects of the crash on the automobile industry, where two sharply differing stories occurred at Ford and General Motors, the two giants of the industry. Henry Ford weathered the crisis by ruthlessly pushing out automobiles on sight draft to dealers, abruptly severing supplier contracts, and laying off numbers of management and employees. At General Motors, William Durant was ineptly failing to resolve the same set of difficulties, and his temporizing soon brought General Motors to the brink of bankruptcy. This resulted in the takeover of the corporation by outsiders, led by Pierre DuPont. These people, in turn, called upon Alfred P. Sloan, Jr., and Donaldson Brown to reconstruct the General Motors management philosophy.

Ford continued to run his organization tightly from the top, and eventually this led to great loss of market by that company in the late 1920s. At General Motors, in contrast, Sloan developed the sophisticated, fine-tuned "decentralized operation and coordinated control" that made his organization a model for American industry. Cargill was going through just this same transition all through the 1920s, a subject to be examined in detail in the next chapter.

The farmer was severely hurt in this 1920–1921 downturn. Agricultural wholesale prices sagged sharply from an index figure of 148 in 1918 to 88 in 1921 (1926 = 100). The farmers' return on total investment, almost 11 percent in 1918, dropped to 2.88 percent in 1920, and their relative share of the national income dropped to just over 10 percent in 1921 from more than 21 percent in 1918. The number of farm bankruptcies began to mount, with an upward pattern over the following three years. This rapid deflation for agriculture after World War I drove many farmers out of business, and for the first time in the history of the United States, in 1919 cropping acreage in the country began to decline. By 1924, 13 million acres had reverted by default to grasslands, scrub brush and woodland. In this context, one can understand the farmers' discontent.

John MacMillan, Sr., had seen this coming as early as November 1920, when he wrote John Jr. in British Columbia: "There is no doubt we are in the midst of a business panic and how long it will last I do not know. The only thing that is preventing an entire collapse of business is our Federal Reserve System" (some governmental controls were acceptable to John Sr.!). His forebodings heightened in 1921 when a serious national railroad strike occurred. The results of the 1920–1921 crop year were all too evident. For the first time in the history of the Cargill Elevator Company, since its beginning in 1890, the Company had a loss, a substantial one of over $116,000. The contrast with the profit of over $1 million in the halcyon year of 1916–1917 was not lost on anyone.

Messages of concern from John Sr. went out to all parts of the business. For example, he wrote A. L. Jacobs in Milwaukee, "Make it a point to find out as to the solvency and good standing of every customer that you have." He wrote Fred Hanchette in July 1921, "The banks are very much alarmed over the bad losses the grain trade have sustained this year." He was also worried about the overall situation, and wrote Knute Nelson, a United States senator from Minnesota, "It is an unfortunate fact that professional agitators are out among the farmers attempting to work out all kinds of fantastic schemes." His next comment to Nelson, however, seemed to underestimate the farmers' concerns: "There is no actual demand for this sort of thing from the farmers and they have . . . no means of checking up on the very false information which these agitators are giving."[11]

Austen Cargill had stayed at work in British Columbia after John Jr. left. By the fall of 1921, Austen and his wife had a new baby, and John Sr. wrote Fred Hanchette of their life out there: "He is taking Anne and the baby up to camp for a month. I am afraid they will find it a pretty dreary existence, for the camp now is on floats and they will have no way of getting ashore unless they are rowed ashore, but I do not know that it would help any if they could get ashore, as you will remember from the character of the country." Austen later alluded to this unconventional interlude as an important influence on his life. One story he repeated many times in management training sessions related to the singular influence of the "breaks" or fate on a person's career: "I played pinochle with my wife one time for four months (we were on a raft and never got off it) and I never won a game. I claim that she is lucky at cards. I can't conceive of anybody in a game of pinochle being so much better that in fourteen or fifteen weeks of almost constant playing every night, I could not win a game. I think that's plain luck, but it might not be."[12]

This period seemed to deeply discourage John Sr., as he wrote Fred Hanchette, in February 1922: "These times are so abnormal that I am just as much at sea as you are. We have only had one fair crop in the last six years and I am beginning to wonder if there is not something radically

If anybody gets hungry they'll have to blame it on somebody
besides the farmer.

Ding Darling, August 27, 1920 (by permission of the University of Iowa Libraries [Iowa City]).

wrong with the farming situation and whether or not it is going to be
possible to continue raising grain."[13]

The FTC Reports on the Grain Trade

A splendid addition to the fund of knowledge about the grain trade
occurred in September 1920, with the publication of the first three volumes
of the monumental Federal Trade Commission study of the grain trade.
Over the next four years, six more volumes were issued. It was an ency-
clopedic effort by the FTC. The nine volumes totaled some 2,826 pages;
given the government's predilection for small print, this was a massive
accumulation of words and statistics.[14]

The study had originated in the second half of 1916, when wheat prices had run up alarmingly. President Wilson waited until after the 1916 elections, then announced that the Justice Department would institute an immediate nationwide investigation to see if "speculators" were involved and whether any remedial legislation was needed. At first, the FTC looked narrowly at the meat packing industry, then broadened the scope to cover all foodstuffs, to see if there were possible violations of the antitrust acts, "particularly upon the question of whether there are manipulations, controls, trusts, combinations, conspiracies, or restraints of trade out of harmony with the law or the public interest."

This emphasis on market conspiracies and the focus on the middleman mirrored Wilson's conviction that "at the root of society's social and economic ills was the corrupt individual." The public seemed to approve— "the country is in the mood for an investigation that will be long and deep and thorough," noted the *Chicago Herald*. The FTC was a prestigious agency, and the industry itself, while certainly not welcoming the study, was hopeful that it would, in the words of William Edgar, the omnipresent editor of *Northwestern Miller*, "dispose of the ignorant and silly talk about a 'bread trust.' "

When that first FTC report came out in late 1920, the authors reached a number of conclusions about price spreads, profitability and competitive practices. While they believed that these sometimes had resulted in unfair advantage, in the main the authors were measured in their judgments about any "conspiracies, trusts, etc." Futures trading came in for particular scrutiny, with a number of modest recommendations. The grain futures trading act passed in 1921 appears to have resulted directly from the FTC study; this act was invalidated by the Supreme Court in 1922 and was superseded by a second act in that same year.

A consideration of the specifics of the FTC study will be enormously helpful in gaining a better understanding of grain trading in the 1920s. A section-by-section analysis follows.

The FTC Looks at Country Grain Marketing

The Woodrow Wilson charge to the FTC for this study naturally slanted its interests in certain directions. Farmers had long believed that they had too little control over their marketing, that they had to sell at certain times of the year (which they believed were the worst) because of limited finances, and that they had too few choices on where to take their grain (perhaps only one). The FTC investigators were inevitably preoccupied with matters relating to these questions.

The first volume of the FTC study viewed the start of grain processing, out in the country. The investigators had asked for detailed information from the grain companies; they eventually had returns from some 9,906 elevators and warehouses, over one-third of all those in the country. These returns gave the government a storehouse of information. One can see here geographical distributions, growth patterns, average capacities, even details about the number of bins per elevator or warehouse, the construction methods used, the advantages and disadvantages of bulk versus sack storage, and so on. There were detailed statistics for all the types of country houses—the line operations, the independents and the cooperatives.

The voluminous statistics that had been accumulated helped to depict more accurately some of these parameters. Some key figures shown in tables 1, 2, and 3 (simplified from the FTC's compendious approach to include primarily the states in which Cargill operated) offer examples.

It was price, of course, that was the focus for any discussion of competition or the lack of it. The FTC particularly scrutinized price information services (the "daily price cards," market telephone and private wire services, etc.). Many farmers believed that some mastermind back at the point of generation of these services was dictating price. Farmers remained concerned about whether they were getting the benefit of the "full" price that

TABLE I

Elevator Capacities, by Types of Elevators

	Average Capacity (bu)	Cooperatives (%)	Independents (%)	Line (%)	Mill (%)
Iowa	24,428	26	43	29	2
Montana	29,602	24	13	50	11*
North Dakota	33,046	24	15	54	7
South Dakota	25,421	23	26	44	7
Minnesota	26,305	22	19	47	12
Wisconsin	17,119	6	49	14	21*

*FTC error on total.

TABLE 2

Average and Most Frequently Recurring Number of Elevators Per Station

	Average	Model figure
Iowa	1.97	2
Montana	2.38	1
North Dakota	3.28	3
South Dakota	3.30	3
Minnesota	2.62	2
Wisconsin	2.10	2

TABLE 3

Average Distance Between Stations

Number of elevators at station	Average distance
1	8.80
2	9.47
3	10.16
4	10.91
5	11.11
6	11.09
7	11.19
8	12.16
9	11.33
10	—
11	11.00
12	—
13 and over	4.00
AVERAGE	9.70[15]

TABLE 4

Average Buying Margins

(difference between average daily prices paid by country elevators and the terminal market price, less freight)

	No. 1 northern wheat			No. 3 northern wheat		
	Average price for year in cents per bushel	Average margins in cents per bushel	Average margins as % of average yearly price	Average price for year in cents per bushel	Average margins in cents per bushel	Average margins as % of average yearly price
1912–13	90.50	4.64	5.1	85.86	5.83	6.8
1913–14	89.16	3.24	3.6	85.18	3.52	4.1
1914–15	129.79	5.99	4.6	123.61	8.70	7.0
1915–16	118.71	5.50	4.6	112.23	7.26	6.5
1916–17	199.15	11.55	5.8	186.63	15.03	8.1

their grain should bring or whether some middleman was making inordinate profits in getting the grain from the countryside to the central market. Naturally, the average buying margin was of major interest. There are numerous tables of statistics on these matters throughout these FTC reports; one among many, table 4, gives patterns over time.[16]

Statistics, even detailed ones like these, can provide only an incomplete picture of reality. The FTC investigators also amassed vast quantities of qualitative information; particularly useful were the letters and reports gathered rather grudgingly from the individual companies. In the "country elevator" sections of the FTC report, some 70 pages of these letters were reproduced, a number of them from Cargill. Here are found revealing letters to and from many companies about competition between towns, bargaining between and among companies on price, actual price wars, and a whole range of letters about grading and dockage, elevation and cleaning charges and the special role of the price bulletins. Local elevator managers built agreements and understandings among themselves, and complex linkages existed between the country elevator and the head offices and terminals. At Northwood, North Dakota, there were six elevators; Cargill ran one of them. One of the managers wrote another about all of them "coming down to list at once" and worried "but the Farmers man [the Farmers Cooperative] may not come down . . . at once but I think he will before long." One of the managers of another company back in Minneapolis wrote Cargill about a third company competing unfairly, that "no storage would be charged in a particular situation. Our agent, learning beyond question that this was true, took a few loads from Mr. Bussee on that plan and wrote us the circumstances." Another manager accused Cargill of doing something of the same: "He began hauling to you, and he presumes you are storing free of charge or at a reduced compensation at Ada."

There were widespread allegations of price shading; one president of a competitor company wrote Cargill, "Another conversation between your agent and a farmer was about to this effect: the farmer asked your agent if he had sold his (the farmer's) wheat, your man said yes, whereupon the farmer remarked: 'then it went down, did it?' So it looks as tho he undertook to sell the farmer's grain at the price before the drop when there is a drop."

There is considerable material on the competitiveness, or lack thereof, among the cooperative elevators. One of the latter instances is noted in an interesting letter from a competitor of a cooperative in Charbonneau, North Dakota, a Victoria Elevator Company man:

GENTLEMEN: Yours of the 22 instant at hand and note what you say about the Farmers getting most all the wheat.

Please dont think that I am pleased and contented with the way business goes here, there is nothing harder on my nerves and gives me more werreau [sic] then when I have to sit around and cant do anything If the future wont turn out any better than the past Then I am sorrow [sic] that we ever built here. I have got about $1300 invested in a house I wish both house and Elev. was somewhere else, You may do better by sending some one else here but as long as them Farmers stock holders think they will clear about $100 on a $25 share it is hard to get them to go pass the Farmers Elev.

Sometimes a company, challenged by a competitor for overzealous competitive pressure, would agree to back off. There was a Cargill Elevator Company example of this in the report, when the Company responded to the Northwestern Elevator Company, "We have written our South Shore agent to be particularly careful not to be aggressive with your trade, but to confine his aggressive efforts to the Farmers, more especially." A few months later, Northwestern, in turn, apologized to Cargill: "The trouble at Johnson comes largely from the fact that the two agents do not get along well. . . . I have ordered our men to buy strictly at the arranged price." Part of the problem in this second instance came from a common occurrence—the farmer playing one agent against another: "He takes the next load around to another house and claims that he has been getting the top price and unless the buyer stands pat or is suspicious of his competitor, he justifies himself by paying up. It is the case of the farmer farming the buyer."[17]

While the bargaining power still lay mostly on the buyer's side, the nuances of this competition out in the field were so complicated that the FTC came to no sharply defined conclusions in regard to the country elevators. In a small section, buried in the middle of the report, they made a "general statement" about competitive conditions. "The summary of the massive information," this section began, "indicates that at the average country marketing station, especially in the northwestern grain States, there is a considerable amount of competition. On the other hand, there are frequently stations or points at which competition is either insignificant or nonexistent on account of local or other agreements among purchasing elevators or other factors." The authors maintained that their "hundreds of letters" on the subject from the files of line elevator companies and independents showed evidence of "either agreements as to country prices, grades, dockages, etc. or else such harmonious and cooperative action with reference to these matters as would bring about practically the same elimination of competition as could be secured by more specific agreements." Even here, "it should not be hastily concluded that these methods are in any way peculiar to line elevator companies."[18]

In sum, in country buying there was plenty of competition and also many constraints. The line companies were responsible for some of this, but so were the others. The extensive section on margins was confined to what these margins were and how they were affected by various practices (dockage, etc.). The FTC chose not to make any strong concluding statement in regard to the question of whether margins were too great, or greater than competition should allow.

Volume 4 of the study, which came out in 1923, included further information on the country elevators, particularly relating to questions of profitability. Here the FTC tendered some general conclusions about both the country elevators and the terminals. The authors were judicious in weighing the various arguments on margins; they appeared almost to feel themselves caught in the middle, as they wrote:

The size of the spreads of terminal, as well as country middlemen and of those for transportation, suggest that a reduction at all points would be desirable.

A considerable spread to remunerate the country elevator for handling the grain is probably unavoidable. . . . The gross profit or spread required by the country elevator is dependent chiefly on the volume of business, and . . . it decreases with increases in volume. By increasing the volume of business . . . the country elevator spread per bushel could be decreased without making such operations unprofitable.

On the other hand, unless grain production is increased, the volume of grain handled per elevator can scarcely be enlarged without a reduction in the number of elevators. At non-competitive points, where there is only a single elevator . . . a decrease in elevators would involve longer hauls for the farmer by wagon or motor truck, thus increasing his cost of bringing the grain to the elevator.

At competitive points . . . a reduction in the number of elevators would have serious drawbacks, especially where elevators are operated for private profit, as it would result in decreased competition and in lower prices being paid to the grain grower. In the case of the patronage-dividend cooperative elevator, however, competition is of less importance, though desirable, in order to promote efficiency of operation, since these elevators ultimately return everything to their patrons over and above operating expenses.[19]

The FTC Looks at Terminal Management

Two very large volumes on terminal markets were included in the FTC study and again provided a varied compilation of data. Here are superb materials on the development of the primary markets—how each competed against the others for supremacy, what kinds of grain came to each (with detailed statistical summaries) and how such crucial factors as rate setting influenced this development. A long section described the history of the Chicago Board of Trade—the evolution of its rule-making capacities, various controversies and developments over the years in warehouse law, and how the Board policed itself. Other major exchanges were described in some detail—Milwaukee, Minneapolis, Duluth, Kansas City, Omaha, St. Louis, Buffalo and a half dozen others. The structure of the commissions was elaborated; the inspection and weighing mechanisms at the terminals were described in depth, including the relationship between federal and state laws and prevailing practice.

An entire volume dealt with marketing patterns. It explained the carlot movement of grain for each of the major grains, described the operating methods of the commission houses and clarified the merchandising and shipping side of the business. Finally, it noted the financing of this whole complex and described the "grain bulletin" devices, mentioned throughout their country grain analysis. Each of the major bulletins was analyzed, with the relationship of their managers to the industry.

The FTC had access to the papers and books of the corporations involved here as most firms had been forthcoming in providing materials.

The FTC promised that statistics on prices and profitability of individual firms, however, would be held in confidence, and this makes it difficult at this late date to assess the firms' relative strengths.

An excellent section on the Minneapolis and Duluth dealers noted the major firms and their various subsidiaries, with names of the individuals who were in charge. The following people were listed under the Cargill Commission Company: Lindahl, Prime, Austen Cargill, Grimes, John MacMillan, Sr., Harold J. Bates, J. B. Cooper, Fred W. Drum, N. C. Clark and John C. Tresise; under the Cargill Elevator Company were four more, A. F. "Hub" Owen, George Feetham, Robert M. Johnston and John Sr.; the Minneapolis Seed Company had only Daniel MacMillan; finally, the Victoria Elevator Company was mentioned as part of the Cargill interests, an incorrect designation (Robert G. Cargill, its head, was related to the W. W. Cargill family through Sylvester Cargill, W. W. Cargill's brother).

Fortunately, capacity figures for individual companies throughout the entire country and the Minneapolis and Duluth figures shown in table 5 help once again to put Cargill Elevator Company in context.

The total capacity at Buffalo, incidentally, was 24,993,000 bushels; Chicago, 42,783,000; Kansas City, 21,902,000 (no other city had as much as 10 million bushels of capacity; Milwaukee, for example, had just over 7 million bushels).

The FTC described the rivalry among Chicago, Milwaukee, Minneapolis and Duluth for the top post in grain marketing, and the "through rate" structure of railroad and lake rates was also chronicled. The FTC summary of the latter is excellent:

Out of this chaos of preferential competitive rates evolved the present system of proportionals or specifics, combination rates, reshipping rates, transit privileges and export rates . . . determining factors in the establishment of grain markets and channels of grain traffic.

Where markets became "rate breaking points"—such as Chicago and St. Louis— their interest lay in securing a favorable combination of the inbound and outbound rates. Where markets lay in the middle of classification territory—e.g., Minneapolis and Duluth—they were allowed proportional rates and transit privileges in order to compete as forwarding centers for eastern consumption. It has been possible to make or unmake markets by the allowance or withdrawal of what is known as "transit"—that is, the privilege of reshipping grain or its equivalent in grain products on a through rate calculated from producing to consuming territory or to export points.

The "proportional rate" was devised to equalize rates for shipment via one gateway as compared with existing through rates via another gateway. It also provided a through rate basis for certain interior points which were formerly restricted to local rates or a combination thereof.

It enabled shippers already enjoying a through rate via one route to consuming territory to obtain a similar rate via a different junction point or terminal market. It also enabled shippers in producing territory who had never been allowed a through rate to obtain such a rate by combination via a given gateway or basing point. The existing local rate was replaced by a so-called "proportional" into the junction point, and this proportional was combined with another proportional out of that junction point so as to provide a through-billing. The intermediate gateways or junctions in this rate structure were known as "basing points."

The report was frank about the tension between Minneapolis and Chi-

TABLE 5

Capacity Figures for Companies in Minneapolis and Duluth

Operator	Rated Capacity (bu.)
MINNEAPOLIS	
Public Elevators	
Electric Steel Elevator Co.	4,000,000
St. Anthony Elevator Co.	3,608,000
Monarch Elevator Co.	3,000,000
Bartlett Frazier Co.	2,275,000
Pioneer Steel Elevator Co.	2,000,000
G. W. Van Dusen & Co.	1,800,000
Cargill Elevator Co.	1,800,000
Sheffield Elevator Co.	1,600,000
Union Terminal Elevator Co.	1,500,000
Crescent Elevator Co.	1,500,000
Concrete Elevator Co.	1,250,000
Twin City Trading Co.	1,136,000
Hales & Hunter Co.	1,000,000
Empire Elevator Co.	1,000,000
Other smaller companies	9,012,000
TOTAL	36,481,000
Private Elevators	
G. W. Van Dusen & Co.	2,000,000
Nye, Jenks & Co.	600,000
Other smaller companies	3,694,000
TOTAL	6,294,000
GRAND TOTAL for Minneapolis	42,775,000
DULUTH	
Public Elevator	
Spencer Kellogg & Sons	300,000
Private Elevators	
Consolidated Elevator Co.	11,000,000
Peavey interests	9,000,000
A. D. Thompson & Co.	7,500,000
Cargill interests	4,250,000
Capitol Elevator Co.	2,500,000
Itasca Elevator Co. (later Cargill)	1,300,000
TOTAL Privates	35,550,000
GRAND TOTAL for Duluth	35,850,000

cago traders on rate making. That Minneapolis "demands transit and 'proportional' privileges such as are enjoyed by Chicago, St. Louis, Kansas City and other large reshipping centers and . . . the Minneapolis–Duluth rate in relation to the Minneapolis–Chicago rate is of direct interest to Chicago, and the Minneapolis–Chicago proportional is of direct interest to Duluth." The authors reported that this whole rate structure of the Northwest "is at present in a highly controversial state as a result of readjustments during the period of federal control of the railroads . . . the general increase in rates on June 25, 1918 [due to the war] had materially disturbed the relationship of rates . . . especially in the Northwest." The Minneapolis grain people were particularly disturbed that the Interstate Commerce Commission had altered the "in-transit" rate (the one that allowed intermediate milling to be done in Minneapolis, with the product sent through on the straight rate). There was great turmoil among the grain people of the Northwest about these changes; later, the former in-transit rates were reinstated.[20]

One of the most interesting discussions in the report related to "grain bulletins." These price information publications were issued on a daily basis by a number of market report agencies; their critics alleged that they were used for mandating prices and for blunting competition. "The Commission is in possession of hundreds of letters," the authors wrote, "which clearly evidence either agreements as to country prices, grades, dockages, etc., or else such harmonious and cooperative action with reference to these matters as would bring about practically the same elimination of competition as could be secured by more specific agreements."

There were several Cargill letters among these, and they were duly printed in the report. They depicted a strong link between the publishers and the companies, with the companies bringing prices into line between and among themselves. For example, in September 1915, the Minneapolis office of Cargill wrote the *Grain Bulletin* (the most important of the services) as follows: "Dear Sir: Herewith, letter from Mr. Nelson, agent, Farmers Elev. Co., Litchfield, Minnesota, giving you basis of price he wants the Litchfield list made on." Another letter two years later, also to the *Grain Bulletin*, listed prices for all of the individual units on the North Dakota part of the line; for example, "Stirum, N.D.—2¢ over everything, account the Farmers" and "Dresden—2¢ over on wheat and oats and 3¢ over on durum, account the Independent and Dresden Elev. Co."[21]

Due to John Sr.'s growing public involvement, he wrote frequently to the FTC and a wide range of people in the grain trade. For example, the authors of the report had elaborated on the iniquities of the private wire system, particularly when it was used by speculative customers: "The gravamen of the complaint against the private wires is that they open offices in a small town, and that the moral effect upon the small town is bad. . . .

It is clear that their presence does stimulate speculation." MacMillan agreed that this was a misuse of the wire system, but wanted to be certain that legitimate uses would still be maintained. He wrote one of the members of the industry on February 21, 1921: "It is entirely unnecessary for the Minneapolis market to defend the private wirehouse evil. These private wirehouses are practically all owned and controlled from Chicago and operate in the interest of that market. This market has always felt that that was an evil which should be eliminated. There is no reason why these small towns require such service and it does induce speculation by an incompetent class of people." Firms with their own private wire systems had a significant competitive advantage—they could make decisions more quickly. The FTC report did suggest that the Chicago Board of Trade develop a "public" system but recognized that the private systems were a legitimate competitive mechanism.

Most of the time, John Sr. appeared skeptical of the FTC as an agency. For example, he wrote one of the agricultural publishing company executives: "I have seen something of the workings of the Federal Trade Commission. . . . I know from observation and experience that it is human nature when placed in a position of power to attempt to carry out preconceived ideas and when making investigations to try to make the facts which they observe conform to these theories even at the expense of distorting the facts or neglecting to observe them at all."

His experience with World War I controls had strengthened his belief that government intrusion was bad. "I am very fearful of government control or government management in any form and I would rather see these problems work themselves out thru excessive competition rather than to attempt to work them out by means of government control, for I know of nothing that is so deadening to the spirit of initiative."[22]

Futures and Speculation

John Sr. was especially critical of the most controversial of all of the sections of the FTC report, that relating to futures trading. Hostility toward futures trading continued unabated during the war. Futures contracts, banned during the hostilities, were reintroduced after the Armistice. There was just as much vitriol against them as previously. Both their critics and their defenders were prone to excessive and misleading arguments; the respected economist (and outspoken critic of business) Samuel Untermyer captured this anomaly in a widely quoted speech given at the American Economic Association meetings in 1914:

There had been so much of honest misunderstanding, senseless hysteria, and ignorant, demagogic denunciation of the Stock Exchanges on the one hand, and on the other such a long, unbroken record of intemperate and misleading propaganda by the interested champions of the Exchange to justify the abuses of the system and its irresponsible form of organization, and such persistent misrepresentation of its critics, that it is a positive relief to find oneself in an atmosphere where the subject will receive the judicial treatment that its commanding public importance demands.[23]

So it was inevitable that the FTC report would allocate significant coverage to this subject. Three full volumes (the first published in 1920, the second in 1924 and the third in 1926) were devoted almost completely to this subject, some 1,140 pages of meticulous detail.

The FTC authors began with a thoroughgoing historical description of futures; in the process, they made a careful distinction, one that was not always adhered to in practice, between the broader word "futures" as a generic term and the narrower "options," relating specifically to the "put-and-call" mechanism. The latter was, and is, considered a more speculative instrument; indeed, from the mid-1930s until the early 1980s, the option contract in agricultural commodities was not allowed to be traded in the exchanges. Most people discussing the issue in the 1920s used the term "options" in its broader futures-contract sense.

When the FTC authors began to address the futures-trading techniques of the early 1920s, they put strong emphasis on the potential for corners and the central role of futures contracts in these. In the report, the corner of "Old Hutch" in 1885, the famous Leiter corner of 1897–1898 and the Patten corner of 1913 were resurrected, and a litany of "more recent" cases (September corn, 1920; May wheat, 1921; July rye, 1921; May wheat, 1922) was elaborated.[24]

The May 1922 case involved the renowned speculator Arthur Cutten. As a long, he was almost at the point of accomplishing a corner when he was defeated by executives of Armour Grain Company (the biggest shorts), who persuaded the Chicago Board of Trade to allow delivery of wheat in rail cars on track. Cutten had counted on the limited amount of storage in the "regular" terminals in Chicago (these had to be officially so designated by the CBOT) as the cornerstone of his plan; now the CBOT failed him by declaring the rail cars "regular," too.

The FTC examiners spent many hours researching Cutten's aborted effort, so fresh in everyone's mind. Yet when it came time for the FTC to make judgments about futures contracts and their alleged influence on corners, the authors were able to say only that "the Commission draws no conclusions and makes no recommendations."[25]

Congress had taken a more proactive attitude, however, and in mid-1921 had begun to debate a futures-trading proposal, popularly known as the Capper-Tincher bill (its promoters were both strongly pro-farmer Congressmen from Kansas, Senator Arthur Capper and Representative J. M. Tincher). Their bill proposed to discourage speculative transactions by a tax on grain sold for future delivery, except under certain constraints. The Secretary of Agriculture was to enforce it.

John Sr. was thrust right into the middle of this debate, having just been elected president of the Minneapolis Chamber of Commerce. The involvement of the Secretary troubled John Sr. very much; he wrote John Jr. in June 1921, "With all the power granted the Secretary of Agriculture and the entire lack of power granted the Grain Exchanges themselves, you will see that this bill would be quite unworkable." All futures transactions were to be reported to the Secretary of Agriculture. Not only would this be expensive, John Sr. averred, but "these records then become available to any employee of the Department of Agriculture or the Department of Justice, who could make public any of these facts at any time they may see fit. You can scarcely imagine any speculator wanting his transactions made public. . . . Speculation in grain would become so distasteful that all speculatively inclined people will turn their attention to other things. . . . This would be bound to narrow the market."

John Sr. began writing congressmen, senators and members of the industry that the Capper-Tincher proposals were unsound. His diplomacy in these endeavors was impressive; for example, he wrote Representative Tincher a detailed, seven-page, single-spaced letter delineating the grounds for his opposition, then ended with a conciliatory paragraph, "I have been very much impressed with the understanding which you have shown of the general problem covered in the Bill and particularly in reference to the changes as compared to previous bills which you have introduced. I am quite sure that you now have in your mind a Bill which, if it could be interpreted—as I believe you expect it to be interpreted—would be entirely workable and agreeable to practically all of the conservative and substantial members of the grain exchanges."

The bill as it evolved did not contain many of the changes that the grain traders wanted. It passed through Congress, and the President signed it in late summer of 1921. The Grain Futures Trading Act did indeed contain the provision appointing the Secretary of Agriculture as watchdog. There was such an outcry about this that the then-Secretary, Henry Cantwell Wallace, felt it wise to put out a bulletin, under the title "Legitimate Trading and Speculation Not Interfered With," that explicitly affirmed that "futures trading can be continued without interruption."

The Chicago Board of Trade challenged the Act in the courts, and in May 1922, the Supreme Court ruled that the section of the Act that levied the tax was unconstitutional. Capper immediately instituted new provisions ("precipitating the grain trade from the frying pan into the fire," lamented the *Northwestern Miller*), and in September 1922, the amended Grain Futures Act was passed. The Chicago Board of Trade tested this second effort in the courts, too, but this time the legislation cleared the

To avoid becoming public charges.

Ding Darling, September 21, 1923 (by permission of the University of Iowa Libraries [Iowa City]).

Supreme Court with no change. The CBOT, making the best of the situation, promised that "every provision of the Act will be strictly conformed to," and with bluff optimism continued, "American grain exchanges have now been given the stamp of approval. We feel that this action will tend to encourage the grain trade into great use of the future trading system for hedging and for commercial price insurance purposes." The *Northwestern Miller*, realist as always, noted, "President John J. Stream, of the Chicago Board of Trade, has shown that he takes defeat with the cheerfulness of a sportsman, and that he is wise enough to recognize the good features of a difficult situation. . . . This is the only rational way to face the situation, and the grain trade as a whole may well profit by Mr. Stream's wise example."[26]

That was more or less the way it turned out. The law did not decimate the exchanges, nor did it constrain the regular uses of the futures markets for hedging purposes, which would have been a very severe blow to the industry. The law did require stringent reporting procedures on the part of both the exchanges and their individual members on a wide range of trading practices. Individual positions of traders, in particular, were to be reported. If the Secretary of Agriculture's surveillance disclosed practices that threatened the stability of the market, especially by control or manipulation of prices, action could be taken to forestall them.

Secretary Wallace administered the law judiciously, despite John Sr.'s apprehension of letting trading secrets out. Wallace's biographers noted: "While the Agriculture Department's regulation of the grain trade failed measurably to improve the agricultural situation, it at least served to repudiate the conspiracy theory. . . . Manipulation proved to be much less widespread than excited grain farmers had imagined, and, as the few offenders were ferreted out, there was no noticeable effect on prices. Like other popular analyses of the agricultural crisis, the conspiracy theory merely clouded the issue and prevented farmers from seeing the real causes of their difficulties."

There remained a pronounced hostility within the industry against any form of governmental regulation—in truth, it was accepted only grudgingly. Yet just seven years later, in October 1930, there was renewed tension when the Russians entered the Chicago Board of Trade with large short selling of over 7.7 million bushels of wheat as hedges against sales of cash wheat in Europe. The industry feared the Russians were close to "dumping" and destabilizing the market. The Soviets were attempting at the time to sell their surplus wheat to gain foreign exchange. Then there was a demand for futures market regulations to prevent, as the *Northwestern Miller* put it, the "financial, political and economic outlaw" from using "devious means to break down the governments of other nations." Some people saw the inconsistency of the free-traders advocating controls![27]

Public Roles, Private Philanthropy

John MacMillan, Sr.'s involvement in national issues continued. The National Association of Grain Dealers held its annual convention in October 1923, in the midst of all of this legislative ferment. There were a number of speeches at the meetings, affirming the role of the middlemen, decrying the "class legislation" and questioning the role of the cooperatives. In the previous year another Arthur Capper effort, the Cooperative Marketing Act (popularly known as the Capper-Volstead Act) had exempted cooperatives from the operations of the antitrust laws and given them other special benefits. John Sr. made a major address at this session, a piece he called "Grain Financing in the Northwest." Written in an educational mode, it contrasted with the other speeches in containing few polemics and gained John Sr. much recognition.

John Sr. also was a delegate to the National Wheat Conference, held in mid-1923, representing the Minneapolis Chamber of Commerce (the grain exchange). The governors of seven states, two United States senators and a number of agricultural leaders had jointly mounted this effort. John Sr. wrote John Jr. upon his return in late June 1923, "The meeting adopted a set of resolutions, which of course endorsed cooperative marketing, but were quite harmless as far as any permanent result is concerned." John Sr. still did not seem to grasp the burgeoning importance of the cooperatives.

All of this was part of a heightened ferment in agriculture. The farmers, in particular, remembering their rewards under government-mandated prices in World War I, continued to want more direct intervention by the government in the price process. Commissions investigated "the wheat problem," papers were written on "orderly marketing" and, inevitably, more legislation was proposed.

The most striking of all legislative proposals in the early 1920s were the several bills proposed by Senator Charles L. McNary of Oregon and Representative Gilbert N. Haugen of Iowa. These bills had been inspired by the earlier George Peek–Hugh S. Johnson book on "equality in agriculture," which emphasized protective tariffs and diversion of surplus to a subsidized export market. McNary and Haugen first put their new version forward in 1924; it was defeated in the House of Representatives when Western farm interests failed to muster adequate support. It was reintroduced and defeated in 1926, then passed by both Senate and House in 1927 but vetoed by President Calvin Coolidge later that year.[28]

Along with these public activities of John Sr. and the Cargill Elevator Company, generally involving partisan grain trade positions, there also were moderate philanthropic efforts both by John Sr. as an individual and by the Company. Back in 1911, when the building campaign was mounted for an art museum, a banquet for 175 guests produced "$335,500 in 90 minutes," the *Minneapolis Tribune* reported. The pledges were sparked by William H. Dunwoody's gift of $100,000. John MacMillan was there too and pledged $1,000. Most local nonprofit groups received token amounts from the Company, but the YMCA and the Minneapolis Society of Fine Arts were more substantially supported. There were contributions to national efforts, too. In 1914, Belgian Relief received $100; in 1917 the American Red Cross "War Fund," $5,000; and in 1920 the European Relief Fund, $500 (but when the Company was asked in 1928 to support the Mount Rushmore Foundation, just beginning the collosi heads of the four presidents, John Sr. declined with vehemence: "I am entirely out of sympathy . . . a desecration of the national scenic beauty of the Black Hills . . .

only a starting point for other similar schemes"). Just after World War I a number of new patriotic organizations to combat "the Red peril" emerged. The American Defense Society was one of these and asked the Company for $50. MacMillan wrote back, "We have contributed very large sums of money the past few months to the American Committee of Minneapolis, who are carrying on the same character of work in this section of the country." Indeed, just prior to receiving this letter, the Company had contributed $1,000 to the local group.

John Sr. was open-minded about philanthropy, raising his own contributions on occasion when asked. On the other hand, he disliked having charitable groups press employees for money. The Associated Charities of Minneapolis had asked the Company to allow solicitation among the employees as a whole. MacMillan wrote back:

I am absolutely opposed to the plan which the Committee presents. If anyone is appointed Captain to solicit for this purpose among our employees, there is no doubt that many of them will feel they are obligated to give because their employers have shown themselves favorable to this plan . . . others no doubt will give because they might feel that they would be looked upon askant by their fellow employees should they not contribute. . . . I have no objection whatever to anyone approaching our executive force, but when it comes to our bookkeepers and stenographers, who are receiving only living wages, I do not feel that they should be expected or be called upon to make any donations whatever.

Tension about radicals was strong in this period, and when John Sr. was asked by the Community Fund Campaign in 1922 about publicizing Cargill's subscription, he wrote back, "This same information can be used in a confidential way in appealing to any who are apparently not doing their part, but the information, if made public will be used by the radical element of the city in a way that will be unpleasant . . . it would do more harm than good . . . you have a difficult problem to solve, but I do not believe that any possible good could come out of this coercive method."

John Sr. also was generous with his time in cases where there was no direct business or personal relationship. For example, a graduate student at the University of Pennsylvania doing a thesis on the Grain Futures Act wrote MacMillan, asking if "this Act has in any way served to help your business or on the contrary if it has in any way injured it." John Sr. sent back an informative three-page letter, detailing a description of the hedging process, particularly as it was affected by the Act, taking a few potshots in the process at the Chicago Board of Trade and stating MacMillan's own hostility toward government regulation. Although he turned down the student's request for "specific instances," the letter nevertheless was supportive and friendly, certainly a letter to buoy up the young man. In the letter he noted that he had asked the Minneapolis Chamber of Commerce executive director to send additional information.[29]

"We Are Not Engaged in the Export Trade"

There were two remaining volumes in the superb nine-volume Federal Trade Commission report on the grain trade. These were on the grain export trade and were published in May 1922. In 1915 the FTC had also been asked to explore issues related to the "methods and operations of grain exporters." Once again, Cargill Elevator Company was requested to be one of the respondents. The Company duly answered all of the questions, most of them with a sentence worded exactly the same in each case: "As we are not engaged in the export trade, we have no direct information in reference to the above question."

One readily can understand what John Sr. was thinking here—the Company did not have any agents abroad (although, as noted earlier, this already had been discussed), nor did it involve itself on a direct one-to-one relationship with foreign buyers as such. On the other hand, it had long been apparent that a substantial volume of Cargill-initiated grain headed directly overseas. All through the correspondence, for many years, detailed references had been made on Argentine, Australian, European and Canadian grain trade links. As a matter of fact, at this particular important moment of grain trade history (1922–1923) Cargill was making a first step toward direct international involvement. By the end of the 1920s, Cargill was selling on the East Coast, even beginning to think about jumping across the water to Europe.[30]

Red Lake Falls, Minnesota

CHAPTER SEVEN

Expanding
Eastward, a Revolt

Rapid communication had always been a tremendous problem for companies like Cargill that depended upon the telephone, supplemented by the telegraph for interoffice contacts. At an earlier point, Lindahl had commented on the two methods: "The wire service between here and Buffalo is simply frightful; it takes anywhere from three to five hours to get a reply from Buffalo, under present existing conditions. . . . Irwin called me upon the 'phone the other day from Buffalo, and I could hear him very distinctly. This is the first time that I have ever been able to hear him distinctly from Buffalo; he tried to talk with me several times last Fall, but neither of us could hear each other." The rapidity and privacy of these wire systems were particularly fitted to the grain trade. Organizations possessing them at this early point (few did in the early 1920s) had a tremendous competitive advantage. In the time of the FTC investigation, John Sr. had roundly condemned the "abuses" of the private wire system—he did not have it in his company.

But a momentous communications change was about to happen to Cargill in the spring of 1923. It had not seemed a propitious time for the Cargill Elevator Company. John, Sr. had worried throughout the crop year 1922–1923, writing Fred Hanchette in October, "Matters in our own business are the worst I have ever seen at this time of year . . . so bad I really do not know which way to turn, as we are so peculiarly helpless. The enormous crop in Canada has simply flooded all the Eastern ports with grain, so it is impossible for Duluth to get boats unless they can guarantee prompt unloading in Buffalo and that we cannot do." Canadian grain marketers had their own postwar depression. Finally, they began to experiment with a new method of trading: almost-complete cooperative marketing via province-wide entities (the Alberta, Saskatchewan and Manitoba pools) and a central selling agency, the equivalent of a state trading agency.[1]

The economic situation had not improved by spring. John Sr. wrote

Austen Cargill, still in British Columbia, in mid-April: "Ever since the close of navigation we have found it impossible to sell our wheat; we have two cargoes still unsold in Buffalo and we have all the Winter's accumulation in Duluth and do not seem to be able to get any bids at all. It is a most peculiar situation and I cannot figure it out." Cargill MacMillan, in England doing postgraduate work at Cambridge University, even wrote his father, "I was scared to death that I have been spending too much money." The dearth of sales quickly affected profitability, and the year's figures showed a profit of only $34,000, down from $442,000 the previous year.[2]

The 1945 Cargill history assessed the reasons for this malaise in Cargill's business with this interesting analysis:

A revolution was . . . taking place in the method of sales into the Eastern consuming market. Up to this time Northwesterners offered their grain through brokers in Buffalo and New York basis c.i.f. Eastern lake ports. They chartered the vessels, insured the grain, and drew on the buyers with documents (invoices, bills of lading, insurance certificates) attached. Not a single firm in this neighborhood made a practice of carrying grain in Buffalo or of offering direct to Eastern consuming clientele. Nor did the Eastern concerns carry any grain stored in the West prior to 1919.

In the postwar era, however, the largest Buffalo wheat broker formed his own company to lease space in Duluth and buy spring wheat on the tables in the Minneapolis and Duluth exchanges. This was a beachhead of invasion. Also, two of the important exporting firms in New York began buying spot grain in the Northwest, particularly barley, rye and durum wheat, and in turn selling to other exporters f.o.b. Montreal, New York and other Atlantic ports. Offers to the old established New York brokers such as Knight & Company, Parker & Graff, and others, drew replies such as 'No interest in offers c.i.f. Buffalo or Montreal. Buyers want f.o.b.' Messrs. Lindahl and Prime, the company's star traders, found their offers to Buffalo brokers brought unworkably low counter bids.

This was a disquieting development for the Company; John MacMillan, Jr., later recalled of their dilemma that:

one . . . fine day the large European importers—and they are still large European importers—Dreyfus, Continental, Mooney—decided that . . . they were paying tolls to a lot of brokers and people along the line that weren't necessary. Why shouldn't they move into North America, open offices in the interior and buy their grain direct . . . overnight you suddenly discovered that . . . you didn't know of any business. You never had a bid. The grain just went right on by. It didn't take any genius to figure out that either we set ourselves up to compete with that or they would just take us over piecemeal.

John Jr.'s key words here were "open[ing] offices in the interior." Prominent British and European firms had had offices in New York City from the late 1870s. At this point, however, the most competitive of these firms had sent men to the interior points, challenging Cargill and the others on their home grounds.[3]

Opportunity sometimes knocks at an inopportune moment. Just after John Sr.'s discouraged letter to Austen Cargill in April 1923, an unexpected proposal came to the Company, one that offered relief from this predicament. It was an opportunity to take over an important Milwaukee grain concern, Taylor & Bournique Co.

The Taylor & Bournique Acquisition

Cargill was well acquainted with this firm—it was a major competitor. Indeed, Cargill had taken two separate cases against T&B to arbitration in 1920. But by early 1923, with the combination of the depression and its own speculations, T&B was in difficulty. John Sr. described this to Austen Cargill: "Those deals of Armour's in Sept., and Dec., futures paralyzed the whole grain business, for he had to get rid of the deliveries by selling to the Eastern trade at whatever prices were necessary in order to move the grain."[4] As a result of being on Philip Armour's bandwagon, T&B was forced to liquidate, and A. R. Taylor, the firm's vice president, approached MacMillan as a possible savior. Lyman Bournique, the president, wanted to retire anyway, although Taylor hoped to stay in the business.[4]

Taylor & Bournique had been active in the Chicago markets; the firm's own small terminal elevator was there, and they leased another. In November 1922, John Sr. had been offered an opportunity by the Erie Railroad to take over the railroad's elevator in Chicago but had demurred. "For us to enter the Chicago market," he wrote to the Erie president, "means developing a character of organization in which we have had no experience, and while I have no doubt we can develop such an organization, I am not particularly anxious to do so. . . . I am very loathe to enter the Chicago market."

Only if he could get a satisfactory arrangement in Buffalo, John Sr. continued, would he even consider Chicago. "As you know, we have even kept out of Buffalo during all these past years, but . . . we cannot function very well under conditions such as have confronted us this Fall. . . . With the rapid development of the Canadian Northwest . . . I am anxious to have our own facilities at Buffalo so that we can move grain freely through that port at all times and not be in a position where the Canadian grain can absorb all the facilities there at the expense of the Northwest." MacMillan had even warned A. L. Jacobs, the manager of Cargill's Milwaukee commission house, not to accept any speculative business "on the ground that we have no office in Chicago. . . . I prefer to handle only business of a legitimate character."[5]

So it was not the Chicago operations of Taylor & Bournique that attracted John Sr. The firm also had substantial branch offices, not only in long-sought Buffalo but also in New York and a further presence in Boston,

Philadelphia and Pittsburgh. It was an opportunity MacMillan could not resist. The price tag was small—in effect, Cargill would take over the T&B organizations at Milwaukee, Buffalo and New York, purchasing in the process the office furniture and equipment and assuming the leases for the offices. The T&B terminal in Chicago would be sold off to others, as John Sr. still did not want to take on a Chicago initiative. A large T&B terminal in Milwaukee, a 1,650,000-bushel unit leased from the Chicago, Milwaukee & St. Paul Railroad would have its lease transferred to Cargill, as would the lease on a small terminal at Ogdensburg, New York. In turn, both Lyman Bournique and A. R. Taylor would indemnify Cargill from any of their other debts.

So only the name had changed; even A. R. Taylor was to stay as head of the Milwaukee office. Thus, for the cost of some office furniture and assumption of leases, John Sr. had consummated a major organizational addition. The arrangements were concluded amazingly fast, and by early June, T&B was a full-fledged part of the Cargill Elevator Company.[6]

One special feature of the T&B organization that came with the deal was absolutely unique for Cargill—T&B had a private wire system. The Clement-Curtis system had linked the Milwaukee home office of T&B with both Buffalo and New York. At an earlier point, T&B had a private wire to Iowa but had given it up. John Sr. immediately had the system extended to Minneapolis, "so Ed Grimes expects to be in instantaneous communication with Al Taylor at all times and also with the Buffalo and New York offices."[7]

John MacMillan, Sr., enthusiastically wrote: "The wire service is a wonderful thing; it keeps us posted in a way that we never have been posted in the past."[8] Foundations for the great Cargill communications system of recent years were put in place at this point, and the T&B wire address designations for New York ("AX"), for Chicago ("GX") and others stayed in the system into the 1980s.

John Sr. wrote Austen Cargill about T&B, and Austen endorsed the plan "since it doesn't require any investment in property." Austen continued: "While the policies under which it has been run in the past are not our policies it should under normal conditions and with careful management prove a profitable venture without requiring excessive risks. . . . Al Taylor has been one of my best friends ever since I went to Milwaukee so I am naturally pleased to have him join our organization." But he concluded with the comment: "He is more or less inclined to wear his responsibilities lightly."[9]

John Sr. also wrote Fred Hanchette, and here he was not quite so sanguine: "There will be no business there for the next two months but I thought it well to get the organization in hand and get them trained in accordance with our ideas before the new crop movement even if we could have delayed the deal until August 1st . . . everything is going to depend on the outcome of the crop as to whether or not it will prove to be a good thing . . . there will not be very much profit there for some years but when conditions are right it ought to be a good money-maker . . . in the end it should average out."[10]

Ed Grimes was dispatched to Milwaukee in May 1923 to survey the office force there. Grimes reported back: "I am very sure that the two office forces are going to work together with very little friction, at least in the beginning." Grimes and John Sr. decided that the secretary of T&B, John W. Rank, would not be retained. MacMillan explained this to Lyman Bournique: "We desire to put the office in charge of one of *our own force* who has been *trained under our ideas*" [my emphasis; these were strongly held beliefs in the Cargill organization]. Bournique asked if Rank could stay just until the end of the month, but MacMillan replied, "It seems to me . . . that it would be very much less embarrassing all around for us not to take Mr. Rank on at all, as I cannot see how he could do other than complicate matters." Bournique then acquiesced.[11]

For the Cargill organization, the Taylor & Bournique acquisition was truly momentous. In one single, decisive act, the Taylor & Bournique acquisition had metamorphosed the heretofore-regional Cargill into a national organization. Within days, John Sr. had sent Ed Grimes and John Jr. eastward; they visited prospective customers in Buffalo, New York, Philadelphia, Baltimore and Washington in preparation for the upcoming crop season. It would not be an exaggeration to say that one can trace the modern Cargill's world focus directly to this single management decision.

John Jr. had returned for a time from British Columbia and was beginning to have a major influence on the Company as a whole and especially on his father, who seemed almost dazzled by his son's intellect and fresh ideas. John Sr. had had several earlier periods of adversity that had made him cautious—risk-averse in a risk-filled business. He took vicarious pleasure in the verve and unrestrained enthusiasms exhibited by his son. At this early stage of his Cargill career, John Jr. was already espousing his concept of "the endless belt": that Cargill should have control of the movement of grain from the time it left the farmer until it reached the final buyer. In other words, he recommended that Cargill should maintain mastery over transportation and insurance as well as the physical handling and storage of grain. Only later, at the beginning of World War II, did Cargill extend this concept in any significant way to processing, although it owned a few small feed and seed operations prior to this. The Taylor & Bournique acquisition was an important first step toward the endless belt.

Further, in John Jr.'s mind, the endless belt could best be effected by maintaining centralized control over every activity. Earlier, John Sr. had evolved a particular combination of centralization and decentralization of authority. John Sr. wanted all of the facts and insisted on his own input, but he seemed willing to vest authority down in the organization to individuals who demonstrated capability in assuming this responsibility. John Jr. had a more "take charge" mentality, more of a centralizing mode. This tendency became more pronounced in the mid-1920s, although there were frequent hints of it in this earlier part of the decade.

John Sr. was the prime negotiator for the purchase of T&B. Yet in some respects the deal did not mesh well with some of his own instincts—his focus had always been on the Northwest. Acquiring T&B would signal a new direction. However, the new arrangements bypassed Chicago, and this fit John Sr.'s predilections. John Jr., now his trusted aide, a young man full of new ideas, must have had a major input in the T&B acquisition.

Not everyone was happy with the acquisition. One can readily guess who was resistant—in particular, Dudley Irwin in Buffalo. Within days, MacMillan had two letters and a wire from Irwin, inquiring about future relationships with Cargill. Taylor & Bournique had its own office in Buffalo, which was one of the attractions of the acquisition. In charge was Harold Tweeden, a brother-in-law of A. R. Taylor. Irwin wanted an immediate personal conference with John Sr., Lindahl and Prime. MacMillan wrote back that "unavoidably there is considerable confusion in taking over any large business such as that of Taylor-Bournique's . . . it would be quite out of the question to discuss any problem of this kind until some time after the transfer is arranged and business is working along in a normal way." John Sr., worried about preserving harmony in the organization, explained, "It would not be good business for me to arbitrarily make an arrangement and tell them they had to make the best of it."[12]

John Sr. had heard from Franklyn Crosby of the Washburn Crosby Company, a well-known Minneapolis miller (later General Mills), about allegations of sharp practices in the Milwaukee elevator scene at earlier periods. So MacMillan took this occasion to make a frank statement to the T&B people about Company policy. He wrote A. R. Taylor and, without impugning any motives of the latter, detailed to him exactly what Cargill Elevator's ethics were: "It seems to me that in connection with a statement of this kind [the Crosby comment] it might be well that I tell you the policy on which our business has always been conducted, viz: that we do not permit any sharp practices of any character and that our word is just as good as our bond. We want to be absolutely fair always and while I do not mean by that that we expect to be imposed upon, yet, it always pays to be absolutely just under all circumstances."[13]

Over the following months, John Sr. sent a steady flow of memoranda to A. R. Taylor, outlining in precise detail exactly how he wanted the business run. It must have been a new experience for Taylor who, after all, had been running his own firm for a number of years. But John Sr. was a strict taskmaster and commented to Fred Hanchette later in the year, "We are having rather a hard time to get Taylor broken in properly. He has not been trained in our ways of doing and does not seem to know how to figure. . . . He has a mania for doing a volume of business but hasn't the faculty of being able to follow the trades so as to know just how he is coming out on them. . . . He has a lot of very valuable qualities but he has been badly trained and of course, does not realize it."

Taylor still bulled ahead, and MacMillan wrote Austen Cargill in November 1923: "Taylor managed to make some very bad deals in corn. There have been frightful premiums prevailing with very rapid shifts and changes and in the mix-up Taylor got caught pretty badly and it was almost impossible to tell it from here because the premiums were entirely a matter of shipping dates. His figures show a loss of about $18,000.00." John Sr.'s solution, mirroring his passion for facts, was predictable: "We have put in a new system which I think will give us detailed data from now on that will make it possible to watch his operations much closer."

By May 1924, Taylor's losses in the Milwaukee operation finally led John Sr. to action, and he wrote Taylor, "I regret exceedingly to have to ask your resignation, but I do not see how we can do otherwise. . . . In justice to the organization, we will have to allow someone else to try the management."[14]

In early June 1924, Cargill's Milwaukee terminal, the one leased from the Chicago, Milwaukee & St. Paul Railroad, burned to the ground. A repair crew had been changing the wiring after a recommendation from the insurance company, a short had occurred, and then the insurance company had to cover the whole loss. The Company's grain was protected completely, with the loss estimated at approximately $225,000. The railroad was in financial difficulty and procrastinated about rebuilding. The president, H. E. Byram, wrote John Sr. a few days after the Milwaukee fire, "We have been so thoroughly 'floored' by the loss of this elevator that we have not been able to reach any conclusion in regard to rebuilding it."[15] By late 1925, MacMillan, getting by with temporary storage, was becoming increasingly impatient with the delay, although not willing himself to lay out Cargill money for a Milwaukee terminal (as he put it to the chief traffic officer of the railroad, "the fact that the Milwaukee market of recent years has been so inactive, and that it may be difficult to bring it back, makes us a little more cautious than we would be under other circumstances"). Finally, in early 1927, Cargill was able to negotiate the lease of another of the railroad's terminals in Milwaukee, formerly operated by the Armour Grain Company, which was in liquidation. This was a larger terminal than the previous one, with a capacity of 2.8 million bushels, and what became known as Elevator E now took a major position in Cargill's Midwestern sphere.[16]

A First in Publications—the Cargill Chaff

The early 1920s was one of ferment in many aspects of transportation. Not only was Milwaukee competing with Chicago for business, but Minneapolis was competing with Duluth and vice versa. The railroad rate structure in this period went through considerable disquiet with a substantial rail labor strike in 1922, pressures for downward revision of wage rates on the railroads and significant reductions in some of the overall freight rates themselves. The 1922 battle between Duluth and Minneapolis over the rail rate between the two cities (mentioned in the previous chapter) and the further competitive battles on lake shipment rates eastward to Buffalo became very acrimonious. Both cases were prime examples of the perennial "proportional rate" arguments that had filled the Interstate Commerce Commission dockets and shippers' files since far back into the 19th century. So this was a period of high tension about shipping.[17]

Given this muddle, with shippers confused about just what were the most effective traffic decisions, it seemed to make sense for organizations like Cargill to develop a formal traffic department to provide in-house expertise. Otto Mortenson emerged as the key person here.

Just after World War I, Cargill made a decision to publish its first company bulletin for the public—the *Cargill Chaff*. It was designed particularly for the shippers of grain. The style of the small pocket-sized publication was jaunty, with drawings, jokes, etc. Mortenson wrote frequently for the *Chaff*, with simple but specific advice to Cargill shippers. The *Chaff* was low-key. One could not accuse Cargill of excessive advertising hyperbole in its slogan during this period: "Ship to Cargill—you can't do better, you might do worse." When competitors starting reversing it—"you can't do worse, you might do better"—the slogan was changed to "Cargill Service," and the Company began to manifest its concern about customer relations. Over and over in the *Chaff* the editor emphasized that Cargill was "your service station," an analogy to the then-emerging auto service stations.

Mortenson—the editor called him the "go-getter"—filled the *Chaff* with timely suggestions, often listing the numbers of freight claims that he had been able to settle for his customers. For example, in the July 1921 issue, Mortenson boasted that he had settled 67 claims for the New London Milling Company of Willmar, Minnesota; 46 for Rippe Grain & Milling Company in Fairmont, Minnesota; and sundry smaller numbers of claims for a dozen other elevator companies.

The masthead of the *Chaff* featured the officers of the company first but included in each issue a short, breezy paragraph on other Cargill employees. In February 1920, it was Hub Owen, "who could borrow ten dollars from any bushel of wheat in the country—he knows them all so well. Do

Cargill Chaff

"Somehow, dearest, I feel that we are soon to be divided."

May 1921 VOL. 2 NO. 10

CARGILL COMMISSION COMPANY

"You can't do better; you might do worse," early Cargill advertising copy, c. 1915.

We Have Handled Grain For

Half a Century

"Ship to Cargill—
You can't do better;
You might do worse"

Cargill Commission Company

Duluth   Minneapolis   Milwaukee

you want to know what grade your wheat will be given? Send in your samples to Hub; the proper grading will come back toot sweet." A few months later it was Johnnie Tresise, "Coop's right-hand floor man in the barley game. Johnnie made some slight reputation a few years ago as a singer and entertainer in sundry vaudeville acts put on by the Elks. Maybe this early training in eloquence was a help. Maybe it wasn't. Anyhow, Johnnie Tresise is rated as one of the best barley salesmen on the floor. For satisfying prices on your barley, let Johnnie sell it for you." A. L. Jacobs, the Milwaukee commission house head, "finds the grain business such an absorbing game that he can't even get interested in a toy like an automobile. So Mrs. Jacobs drives the Dodge while Andy steers the grain business." J. B. Cooper, the veteran barley trader in the Minneapolis office, "wishes it announced that his information does not extend to barley malt, and he has positively no home brew recipes for sale or rent." (The *Chaff* carried a number of jokes about national prohibition, and also about the "flappers" of that period). In a few months, after the *Chaff* had run out of key Cargill people to feature, repeats were resorted to: "J. C. Tresise, barley specialist, the burr in his voice is genuine Scotch, 100 proof. J. C. has Scotch thoroughness likewise—if you want to know anything about barley, you can bank on what Tresise tells you."[18]

The Grain Laboratory

The *Chaff* of August 1922 introduced a new Cargill man and a new Cargill function, each to become of major importance to Cargill over many years into the future. The man was, to use the *Chaff*'s nomenclature,

"Julius Hendel, Scientist." The article that followed introduced the new Cargill Laboratory. The editor began, "An 'all wool' suit (so-called) may contain almost 50 percent cotton or 'shoddy' without the fact being apparent to the naked eye. You may pay for genuine gold and get something that merely looks like gold. Chemistry has come to the rescue of the clothier and the jeweler—assuring each of getting exactly that he pays for. Now the same science becomes prominently identified with the grain business."

The article then explained how chemistry could judge wheat far more accurately than the practiced eye, all to be accomplished by the new laboratory. Wheat would be cleaned and milled and, after being thoroughly dried, made into dough. The dough would then be washed out in water of certain temperature until all of the starch was removed, leaving only the gluten. The gluten itself was first dried, then weighed, giving the percentage of gluten in the flour. All of this would be done in the laboratory, "in charge of a very pleasant and mighty keen young man named Julius Hendel. He wears about half the alphabet after his name, officially, but he is too busy, so he says, to tell you about it. He has full rein in his department—unhampered by anything save a single-track idea to Get the FACTS." The article concluded with a promise that any shipper could have a sample of his wheat tested in the laboratory "for a very nominal fee—one dollar." John Jr. had succeeded in changing his father's aversion to chemical analysis, where Dudley Irwin earlier had not.

Later the laboratory took on other functions, but this first charge, to measure gluten content, was its most important assignment throughout. Now wheat could be sold much more explicitly and believably for its high-gluten content, backed up by "FACTS." Hendel developed a nomenclature, "Cargill 1," "2" and "3" for grades based on this gluten content, and the company gained a step on its competitors in being able to mix to grade more effectively and to use this as a selling tool.

Over the next several issues, the *Chaff* discussed the laboratory, both its technical attributes and its commercial implications. The laboratory was reputed to be the second in-house laboratory in the industry; the testing of gluten theretofore had almost always been done by commercial laboratories. The *Chaff* commented: "Without in the least disparaging the work of these conscientious and no doubt careful organizations, the Cargill Commission Company prefers to be doubly certain of accurate results by maintaining its own laboratory." There seems little doubt that with this step Cargill established for itself a preeminent position in the industry in regard to quality.

This appeared to be confirmed a few months later when Hendel was able to place an article he had written as a lead story in the *Northwestern Miller* issue of December 26, 1923. The article was long, spread over three full pages of the publication, and had three pictures (two of Cargill's lab) and a "gluten map of North Dakota." Hendel covered the chemistry of gluten, the process of testing and the impact of moisture in the wheat on these efforts. It was a literate and reasoned piece, putting Cargill's laboratory on the map.

Not everyone, incidentally, was enthusiastic about testing wheat. In another major article in the *Northwestern Miller*, a year before Julius Hendel's, fun was poked at what the author called "the newest trade fad." He continued:

Today a load of wheat is more like a prescription for something the matter with your liver. Instead of just weighing fifty-nine pounds and being graded with a number from one up to four, and being smelled and chewed to see if it is musty or not, a record on what's in it is now as complicated as how to make gin. . . . Getting a sample of wheat tested is for all the world like setting out for the North Pole, or trading for a Ford or ordering hash or voting the Democratic ticket. You know it is certain to come out someway, but you can't for the life of you guess just which way."

"Julius Hendel, Scientist"

Julius Hendel was not only a gifted scientist but was soon to become a grain trader par excellence and Cargill's preeminent grain-trading teacher. Hendel was a "rare bird," according to a *Cargill News* biography many years later, on the occasion of Hendel's 70th birthday. The editor continued, "His rarity aroused in some a kind of instant antagonism, and in some others a mixture of anxiety and awe." At the same time, he was "gracious and sympathetic, active and filled with ideas, and . . . optimistic."

Julius Hendeliowitz was born in 1895 and thus was the same age as John MacMillan, Jr. The backgrounds of these two, however, could not have been more different. Hendeliowitz was born in Czarist White Russia, in the great wheat-growing region bordering both Poland and the Russian Ukraine. He was of Jewish ancestry. Four generations of his family had been grain merchants in a village near Slutzk. In 1905, as the Russian Revolution began to engulf this area, the family decided it was too risky for Julius to remain at home and sent the ten-year-old boy to an older brother, a grain merchant, in Koenigsberg, Germany. Julius did his lower-school education there and later in Copenhagen, Denmark, then migrated to New York in early 1914, "speaking English very little and that very badly."

Hendeliowitz found that his name was hard for Americans to pronounce or remember, so he shortened it, to use his words, "by cutting it precisely in two." He had been sponsored in his immigration by his cousin, Maurice Hindus, a young man about the same age as Julius, also with very little money. From the start, Hendel was on his own. Two families in New

York became further sponsors for Hendel and made it possible for him first to finish high school and then to enter Cornell University. He was able to get only part of his college work in hand before the war intruded. Though he was not yet a United States citizen, he joined the United States Army and served as a noncommissioned officer in five major campaigns in Europe.

After the war he returned to the United States. "My plan . . . was to finish my studies near the Midwestern farmlands, then to take a homestead somewhere in North Dakota and raise wheat," said Hendel. Needing advice, he went to a biochemistry professor at the University of Minnesota College of Agriculture. The latter urged him to finish his degree at Cornell, which Hendel accomplished in 1921. He returned to Minnesota to enroll for advanced work at the College of Agriculture, attempting to finance his education by working on a nearby farm. Wanting to get closer to the grain trade, Hendel applied to an elevator operator for work and, when told that there was none, said, "I'll work for you for nothing for two weeks." At the end of two months, the grain elevator operator was so pleased that he did not want Hendel to leave.

The commuting from farming country to the classroom in St. Paul was too exhausting, however, and in 1922 he applied to Cargill for a job (and to continue his schooling at night). After meeting John MacMillan, Sr., he was also introduced to John Jr., and the two young men hit it off well. The result was that Hendel was hired to institute the new laboratory. Meanwhile, Hendel continued his academic work at the University of Minnesota and in 1927 was awarded a Ph.D. degree in agricultural economics and biochemistry, thus becoming one of the first persons in the grain trade with an advanced academic degree.[19]

It had been the grain trade itself that so intrigued Hendel. His doctoral studies centered directly on the trading function, and he developed a thorough understanding of the process. Yet this was still theory, and he itched to test this theory in the actual trading pit. An opportunity soon presented itself, under the aegis of John MacMillan, Jr.

John Jr.'s "Account 38"

John MacMillan, Jr., had spent just over a year, 1920–1921, in British Columbia with the logging operation. His younger brother, Cargill, had joined him there for the summer of 1921, and both returned to Minneapolis in August (Austen Cargill remained in British Columbia). John Sr. wrote Fred Hanchette, "Jr. is doing pretty well here, but he's not up to par as yet, and I doubt if he will be for a year or two to come." He ended the letter: "He will no doubt go to Duluth before very long." The Duluth assignment did not materialize; however, Cargill MacMillan joined the company "keeping the books out in the office," and John Sr. wrote Hanchette, "It seems fine to have the entire family together again."

In 1923, John MacMillan, Sr., made a portentous decision about his eldest son. Ed Grimes had been supervising the overall trading policy for the Company for all grains out of the Minneapolis office. John Sr. now split the responsibilities, leaving the coarse grains with Grimes (oats, flax, corn, barley) and giving wheat and rye (which were assigned a new title, "Account 38") to John Jr. This division was critically important for the Company and a great challenge to John Jr., involving as it did the strategic trading policy for two of the most important grains.[20]

Within a few months, John Jr. had co-opted Julius Hendel. While Hendel still continued his overall supervision of the grain laboratory, the day-by-day activities of sampling gluten content were turned over to William Glasgow and his assistant, a young office boy, Tom Totushek. John Jr. again was showing evidence of his inquisitive, wide-ranging mind. He put Hendel to work on an extensive set of weather data that he (John Jr.) had been collecting, trying to find correlation with the ups and downs of crop yields (John Sr. was skeptical and wrote John Jr., "I have no confidence in this theory . . . unless there is some correlation in the weather conditions for June and July as compared to April"). An accurate weather forecast would be a tremendous tool for trading futures. Hendel continued to work on such spot assignments for John Jr. through the remainder of that year, the most important relating to scientific grading of spring wheat. In March 1924, John Jr. published (in *Cereal Chemistry*) an extensive analytical article on this.[21]

In early 1924, John Jr. again evidenced patterns of his previous illness, and, compelled to step away from the pressures of grain trading, he returned to the British Columbia logging site. It had been an unprofitable and difficult operation there, and Austen Cargill had been laying men off. Now Austen and John Jr. assessed together the prospects of the limping endeavor. They were just about ready to call John Sr. and Fred Hanchette to come up to discuss alternatives when John Jr. severely injured his hand with an axe and had to return to Minneapolis. John Sr. had planned a European vacation at about this time but postponed his plans because of John Jr.'s injury. The hand took a number of weeks to heal but by early summer John Jr. was ready to return to British Columbia, taking with him his younger brother, Cargill.[22]

John Sr., meanwhile, had continued to act as his son's surrogate for the overall direction of Account 38. It had been a complicated time. In June 1924, the Milwaukee terminal fire occurred. At the end of that same month, Lindahl in Duluth asked for another person to work on the Duluth trading floor. Cargill MacMillan had been learning the trading business in Minneapolis, but his father did not feel he was ready for the Duluth assignment and suggested to John Jr. that Harley Flood be sent there and that Julius Hendel replace Flood on the floor of the Minneapolis Grain Exchange (at that time called the Chamber of Commerce). This idea pleased John Jr. Flood left for Duluth, and a membership was obtained for Hendel (one of 11 at that time), who immediately began trading.

Within just a few days, John MacMillan, Sr., wrote a worried letter to John Jr. as follows:

> We have had a peculiar situation develop regarding Hendel, which has bothered me a good deal, and I do not know just how to handle it. A good many of the best buyers on the floor have told Hub and others in the organization that they resented our putting Hendel down there and they absolutely would not trade with him unless they were forced to. Hendel unfortunately has not a very good personality, but I am inclined to think that the prejudice is also to a certain extent due to the fact that he is a Jew, but in any event, the character of the protests is such that we cannot ignore them.
>
> I have had some talk with Hub about it yesterday and as a result, I told him to hold up the membership transfer until I had had time to think it over. I feel very sorry about this, because Hendel has ability but it would seem to me that we can use this ability to better advantage by keeping him away from the place where he is not welcome.[23]

John Jr.'s letter in reply is no longer extant, but his father's in return gave the essence of the final decision, namely, that Flood would be left in Duluth and that a new man, Wilson by name, would be assigned a trading role under the eye of Hub Owen. As if to reinforce the gravity of the challenge, John Sr. added, "I think there is no question about the seriousness of the feeling on change, and I get the same thing from Johnnie [Tresise], Ed Grimes and from Hub [Owen]." In other words, the feeling against Hendel's trading was corroborated (and perhaps shared) by the three senior Cargill executives.

This story, with its pointed implications about anti-Semitic prejudice, has been retold in Cargill lore over the years and was frankly discussed in the *Cargill News* in a long biographical article on Julius Hendel written after his retirement in 1955. However, with such events, stories can become garbled over time, significant pieces turning into Company legends. There is just such a problem here in the article about Hendel in the *Cargill News*. The author stated:

> One story has it that, as early as 1924, a strong show of resistance was made by half a dozen company executives. John MacMillan, Sr., had proposed that membership in the Minneapolis Grain Exchange be bought for Dr. Hendel. His opponents presented themselves as a group before Cargill's president and announced that, if the plan were not dropped, they would resign en masse.
>
> Mr. MacMillan, it is said, neither argued the professional need for a full-time grain merchant to hold such a membership nor explained the particular talents and qualifications of Julius Hendel. Instead, he took six sheets of stationery from his

desk, slid them toward his visitors and sat back in the chair. All were given time and complete silence in which to write their resignations on the spot. They looked at each other, at the sheets of blank paper, at the determined face of John Mac-Millan, Sr., then turned all together and went back to their offices.[24]

The author had part of the encounter correct. It seems from John Sr.'s letter that at least four of Cargill's own executives had corroborated the prejudice against Hendel and may have shared the view themselves. The remainder of the story—the confrontation involving the ultimatum and the icy response—does not seem as likely to have happened on this occasion, although, as no person living today was there, we cannot be certain. We might dismiss this fascinating vignette of the slips of paper were it not for a set of events (discussed in a later section of this chapter) that rings truer. The most credible hypothesis about this story is that Hendel's assignment to the floor was rescinded in part because of Cargill executives' protestations. His Chamber of Commerce membership, however, was not in the end "held up"—Hendel was a member from 1924 until well after World War II.

In the days prior to World War II, there was evidence of anti-Semitism all through the Midwest, indeed, in all of the United States. Without gainsaying the tolerance of today's Minneapolis, it is fair to say that such bias was substantial there in the earlier days (but less so in St. Paul, reported John Higham in his book *Send These to Me: Jews and Other Immigrants in Urban America*). In a widely reported article in October 1946 in the magazine *Common Ground*, the well-known writer Cary McWilliams wrote: "One might even say, with a measure of justification, that Minneapolis is the capital of anti-Semitism in the United States. In almost every walk of life, an 'iron curtain' separates Jews from non-Jews in Minneapolis. It seems to have always existed." This article brought a flood of reaction, and the citizens of Minneapolis, under the leadership of Mayor Hubert Humphrey (who established the Mayor's Committee on Human Relations), moved rapidly to break down many of the barriers.

A full analysis of this broader Minneapolis pattern is beyond the scope of this study. It is important, however, to put in careful context exactly what John MacMillan, Sr., was saying in the two letters quoted above. First, he recognized frankly that the attack on Hendel was in part based on bias. Second, he explicitly deplored this. Finally, his instincts as a businessman needing to live in the real world seemed to dictate to him that those who objected were too powerful to oppose. Hendel was taken off the floor.

In subsequent years, however, there was little or no overt or covert bias against Hendel within Cargill itself. His own innate ability, enthusiasm and judgment soon carried him into the higher levels of Cargill management. Indeed, John Jr. had been instrumental in hiring him and thus seemed able to move beyond his own blanket statement, made at the end of World War I, about "the Jews in the headquarters companies." And as with other things John Jr. wanted, John Sr. waived his own caution.[25]

Clashing Management

The timber operations in British Columbia had been unprofitable after the collapse at the end of World War I, despite the enormous efforts put into the project by Austen Cargill. He and his wife had pushed themselves to the limit to make it a success, with help, off and on, from John MacMillan, Jr. The earlier relationship between Austen and John Jr. had seemed amicable enough, but by 1924 there was evidence of a cooling on the part of both. John Jr. seemed to fancy himself as an engineer and had been putting forth a considerable volume of suggestions to Austen, for example, arguing with Austen about how to lay track for a railroad on the property (Austen was right). These seemed always to find their way directly to John Sr., too, and Austen may have felt he was being "spied upon." Overwhelmed with a deteriorating business situation and frustrated in dealing with the rugged terrain and the cold, damp climate, Austen was not ready to take such advice in such quantities. In turn, this caution irritated John Jr., and he wrote his father in April 1924 that Austen seemed

Cargill's British Columbia lumber camp, c. early 1920s.

Austen and Anne Cargill with daughter Margaret, c. 1922.

unwilling to adopt his (John Jr.'s) "standard" ideas: "He could only ridicule it, as he does everything that is put up, but this time the ground for ridicule was that it would be five years before he would venture an operation of that kind, and that he was very fearful of bungling it." John Jr. concluded: "Frank Neilson [the superintendent under Austen] sums things up very well. He says that you can't drive Austen to make a decision relating to things more than a few days distant, and when he does decide, everything must be done right off the bat, a very expensive and nerve racking process."

Austen's resentment with what he saw as gratuitous meddling spilled over a few weeks later, when John Jr. submitted his personal travel bill to the logging operation for payment for a trip back East. John Jr. had said the trip was for "lumber sales," and Austen exploded to James Taylor (who handled the finances of Cargill Securities Company), "I consider it entirely unnecessary at the present time, and so long as I am responsible for the operation of this business, I shall refuse to sanction this charge. . . . In taking this attitude, I realize it is petty but . . . I have just about reached the limit of my ability to continue under existing conditions, so that such petty things aggravate me beyond reason."

John Jr. returned to Minneapolis in early May 1924, after incurring the severe axe cut on his hand. The profitability of the timber operation continued to sag, and Frank Hixon began exhorting John Sr. to cut the losses and get out of the operation. John Sr. demurred and wrote Hixon why:

Austen has taken an intense interest in the problem. . . . His tastes are entirely along mechanical lines. I do not think that he ever will fit well into the grain business or ever be happy in it. The business was well organized . . . but when the slump in log prices came, Austen fully realized that the methods which he was using could not possibly succeed, so he got further back from the water's edge. . . . I am very anxious to see him make a success. . . . Austen has an excellent knowledge of accounting. He does not fool himself in the slightest as to his operating costs, so that all told I feel it would be a grave mistake not to give him this . . . chance.

(When John Sr. spoke of "fitting into the grain business," he was speaking narrowly of the trading function itself, for Austen's other grain business skills—country elevators, seeds—were significant. Once again, a reinforcement of the belief system that assigned a transcendent role to trading.)

John Sr. had further unease about the project in the spring of 1924 and made a personal trip to British Columbia; he came back reasonably satisfied with the planning (though very uncertain of the potential in the log market itself). Later in the fall, James Taylor and Roy Hoople were there, but no further actions were taken in regard to the logging operation.[26]

"Feeling Safe" `

After the severe drop in earnings in the crop year 1922–1923, the next crop year looked considerably more promising. Earnings were up to $325,000, and after the two years of accrued preferred dividends were paid, the net addition to the surplus was over $163,000. An analysis done for John MacMillan, Sr., on the "property values" of the Company showed that there were now 140 country elevators with a total capacity of 4.8 million bushels. The terminals in Minneapolis had 1.95 million bushels in capacity; Duluth, another 4.5 million. In sum, Cargill Elevator Company owned 11,270,000 bushels of its own capacity, with additional leased space at Green Bay, Ogdensburg and Buffalo and a promising crop year ahead. John Sr. wrote Austen Cargill: "This puts us in a position where I can feel safe. It was all together too much strain to attempt to work with no surplus."[27]

In this period, John Sr. increasingly leaned on John Jr. for advice and counsel, as John Jr. was full of ideas, new plans, aggressive moves in the business. Buffalo particularly concerned both men, and although Cargill now had its own man there, Harold Tweeden, the Company still did not have its own facility. With Cargill's volume of shipments into Buffalo, it had considerable bargaining power and now began an intricate set of negotiations with two different Buffalo terminal owners, with the intent to make firm contracts at favorable prices for additional storage. John Jr. wrote his father, "Since I have been away I have been getting a somewhat less biased view of that Buffalo situation—and I am not at all certain that it would be good business for us to commit ourselves heavily in Buffalo. . . . I am just as certain as can be that property there will have relatively little value once the St. Lawrence is opened to large lake vessels" (he called this the "Great Lakes-to-the-Sea project").

The question of charges for elevation from ships into the terminal was one of the sticking points and John Jr. continued, "It does irritate me most decidedly to pay a cent elevation there with the volume of business we are doing, nor do I think it is necessary." John Jr. made efforts to lease the Kellogg terminal, where he could elevate grain for 1/2 cent per bushel. Even so, he still expressed reluctance to go to a full-lease relationship. Finally, John Jr. overcame the Kellogg owners' objections, Cargill leased their 1-million-bushel facility and gained a substantial presence in the East.

John Sr. also solicited John Jr.'s views on some complex hedges that the Company had initiated late in 1924: "I wish you would make a thorough study of the export situation as it affects our spring wheat. I frankly confess I do not know what to do about the hedges. Whenever Chicago breaks sharply we do not go down quite as fast, but on the other hand we lag frightfully when it comes to the advancing market. . . . I think it is very important to make a very thorough analysis of the eastern situation while you are there."

Yet six weeks later, John Sr. wrote John Jr. in a vein that seemed almost as if he had had about as much advice and new ideas as he could take: "I have noticed the two factors which you referred to—namely—Chicago July, and Minneapolis July and I entirely agree with what you have to say, but I do not want any more spreads on my mind than the one we have got. In fact, the more I see of these spreads the less I like them. They rarely work out the way you expect."[28]

In December 1924, John Jr. and George Cargill (Will's son) left for a week's vacation in Cuba, to be followed by a return to Florida for further rest. John Sr. wrote a friend: "He is pretty well tired out of late and I felt it was quite necessary for him to get away for a little while."[29] At this same time, a felicitous new arrangement was made for financing with Goldman Sachs & Company, a relationship that would continue for many more years.[30]

John Jr. returned from Cuba because of another assault on his health—the Cuban food had brought renewed stomach problems. He went to Chicago for treatment, and his close friend, Jack Hawley (whose father was a friend of John Sr. from the Texas days), wrote John Sr. late in February: "I saw Jr. when I was in Chicago. . . . The doctor says he must forget everything pertaining to business, until he has a complete relaxation, and then he must work only a few hours a day for a long time. The doctor indicates that his trouble is mainly nervous. The doctor also says he shouldn't see visitors or talk business." John Sr. then wrote John Jr.: "I do not know what to think of Dr. Brown finding the same trouble that Dr. Fulton found five years ago . . . it seems to me there is something more . . . possibly this would account for all of your trouble. Let him take all the time that is needed to find out exactly what your condition is so that you will know what to do. It is much better to take the necessary time off now than to continue in the poor health you have been in for so many years."[31]

It was disheartening to John Sr. to have his son again incapacitated. John Sr. wrote: "I want you to entirely forget business. Do not allow these outside offices or business connections of any kind to follow up business." Even at this point, though, John Jr.'s mind was working on some of his plans. He asked Hendel, for example, to check some new correlations between specific gravity and test weight of grain. Hendel had sent back word that "there is a very decided correlation in moisture also."[32] Once again, John Sr. had found it necessary to postpone a vacation trip.

John Jr.'s health rapidly improved, and by early March he was back on the job full-time. Later that month, John Sr. and Edna left for Europe; he wrote a friend: "We have suddenly made up our minds to go abroad again. I have been quite badly tired out of late and Dr. Bell is insistent that I go away and get far enough so I will forget about business, so we are sailing Saturday morning on the S.S. Minnetonka from New York and will go direct . . . to the Riviera. We do not expect to do any sight-seeing, but just loaf around until we get ready to come back, which will probably be in about two months."[33]

A Surprise for John MacMillan, Sr.

If John MacMillan, Sr., had left on this trip to Europe in March 1925 "feeling safe," as he had said to Austen Cargill six months earlier, he was indeed living in a fool's paradise. For while he was gone, an internal revolt by some of his key employees, probably brewing for many months, came to a head. This set of events of 1925 lay at the heart of the issue of ownership and control of the Cargill Elevator Company and therefore deeply affected the firm's management fabric and, in turn, redefined some of its basic corporate goals and objectives.

John Sr. and Edna returned to New York and checked into the Plaza Hotel in the third week of July 1925, only then learning of shocking developments back at the Company. Younger son Cargill MacMillan was there to tell them about it personally. Family lore reports that Cargill and John Jr. flipped a coin to determine who would go to New York for this disconcerting encounter. A Jack Hawley letter also awaited them, and we depend on it as the only written evidence of that first shock.

Hawley wrote, "I hope you are much better now because even a man in perfect health would be greatly disturbed to learn the things that have transpired." Hawley then sketched an unsettling set of events: six days earlier, Austen Cargill had demanded John Jr.'s resignation "or his positive assurance that he would take orders from you only thru Austen and not discuss business with you except thru Austen . . . also that he (Austen) had control of a majority of the Stock of the Elevators Company, etc. etc." Hawley had gone to Austen Cargill to corroborate this. Austen had told Hawley that he, Austen, was in a position of control. While he would do nothing "except with Mr. Hixon's approval" and wanted John Sr. to remain head of the Company, nevertheless, "if you refused this then the directors would demand your resignation."

Hawley continued, paraphrasing Austen Cargill's words: "For three years, you [John Sr.] have not been yourself, having acted through Jr.'s advice . . . John, Junior would 'go along' with all of the Company's Assets if he [John Jr.] were in the position, and if he wanted to." Therefore, John Jr. was considered a "most dangerous character." Austen added a rather enigmatic comment (to again use Hawley's words), that "Jr.'s resignation would probably not remove the trouble as it is more deep-seated (no explanation to enlighten me [Hawley] on this)." In sum, concluded Austen Cargill, again according to Hawley's secondhand report, "The whole business management must come back to 'the old order of things.' "[34]

Hawley's letter quickly was followed by another, from John Jr. to his father, on July 26. In this remarkable, lengthy document, John Jr. was quite candid about his own role. It was clear that the revolt was not just that of Austen Cargill, but most of the senior management in the Company had joined in the effort. John Jr. specifically mentioned Roy Hoople ("I am quite sure that he always blamed me for that interference with the line bookkeeping two years ago, as well as the office changes and the printing press") and James Taylor, who "resented very bitterly my marine insurance activities making it more difficult for him with Marsh McLennon." Later in the letter, John Jr. admitted that probably all of the senior employees "with the possible exception of Tweeden or Lindahl . . . believes me to be a menace to the business of the very worst kind."

John Jr. continued, "The executives have been told of how I hope to deprive them of all authority and initiative, in brief of how disastrous are my policies." Apparently this widely shared negative feeling toward him surprised John Jr. greatly, for he stated in the letter, "up to that time I do not believe that I had any more ill will from the organization generally than would normally be expected to accrue to any executive who was apparently advancing rapidly." Yet, he now learned, "the executives have

been told things about me by one or the other which would be corroborated by another, and I can truthfully say that if one-half of the representations about me had been true, I would be a d.f. of the worst variety."*

John Jr. attached what he called "a resume" of his own conversation
with Austen Cargill, which had occurred on July 18. He too paraphrased
Austen's own words:

Until three years ago, or roughly at the period when you came into the company,
I had had no reason for complaint of any kind on the conduct of the affairs of the
C.E. Co. At the time of our family quarrel I had decided that it was for the best
interests of the family to leave things in your father's hands, in spite of considerable
opposition from the other members of the family. Until three years ago, I had had
no reason to regret my decision. Up to that time your father's management of this
company has been perfect. His decisions had been almost infallible . . . during the
past three years I have not been satisfied with the course of events. The old tried
and proven policies, your father's own policies, were abandoned, especially those
parts which related to the creation of separate departments, and of non-interference
with their respective heads. In fact this interference has been so bad that it has been
only by the most strenuous efforts on my part that many of the leading executives
have been kept from quitting. . . . It is generally agreed, by all those with whom I
have talked, that you are the cause of this change that has taken place within the
past three years, and I also feel that you are the real cause of your father's breakdown
in health, this last being due to your having never given him a moment's rest from
business. You are naturally intelligent and highly original, so that you propose one
idea after another to him, which does not give him the proper rest after business
hours.

In the résumé, Austen expressed antagonism at the "great department
. . . created especially for you" and intimated that this department (John
Jr.'s "Account 38" wheat account) had been kept profitable only by claiming profits from other operations in the business.

Austen Cargill, according to John Jr.'s words, had in this meeting developed on paper a new organization structure that would allow John Jr.
to stay in the business. But he would take orders through Austen: "I feel
that your father must be relieved of your influence. . . . From this diagram
you will see that any orders to you will have to go through me. Now in
case you agree to this, it is by no means my intention to shelve you. In case
you make good, and after years of experience seem to develop, you will, if
conditions warrant it, succeed your father whenever he retires, and it is my
wish, for I realize that I do not know enough nor have I capacity enough
to run this business myself, it is my wish that you may develop to that
extent." If John Jr. refused this arrangement, Austen Cargill wanted him
out but was willing to finance him "dollar for dollar whatever your father
wishes to put up to start you in business." There were already plans afoot

---

*"Damm fool." (Lester V. Berrey and Melvin Van Den Bark, *American Thesarus of Slang*,
2nd ed. [New York: Thomas Y. Crowell, 1952], p. 353).

for Jack Hawley Jr. and John Jr. to join together in a research and development business, presumably with the latter still keeping his Cargill Elevator Company assignment.

Although John Jr., in this amazing letter to his father, had made a few gratuitous statements about Austen Cargill earlier in the letter, at the end he was honest in not overstating what Austen was demanding. Again he paraphrased Austen's words: "If you decide to oppose me, I am so fearful of your influence over your father, that I must take steps to oppose him, and in case you agree to neither of these alternatives, and if your father declines to discharge you, then I will have to have someone else selected to run this business."[35]

John Jr.'s relationship to the other men in top management *was* mixed— he was a strong-willed person and had not been backward about holding sway over other departments. There were several such examples in earlier months, John Jr.'s reference to his rift with Hoople being a prominent one. There had also been a major realignment of tasks in the merchandising department, again under his aegis.

In March 1925, just before Austen Cargill's challenge, there had been another case of John Jr.'s assertion of authority, one that was not quite settled yet but that certainly challenged traditional organizational patterns. This involved the chartering and insuring of Cargill Elevator shipments from Duluth. Each department head had done this independently as almost completely decentralized decisions. Lindahl and Prime in Duluth were involved, but so were the department heads in Minneapolis— Grimes, Owen, Cooper. Over the years, these people had developed longstanding linkages with insurance brokers of each one's own choice, an entrenched relationship that sometimes was less than cost effective.

John Jr. was proposing that this function of chartering and insuring be done centrally. Moreover, this function was to be given to one insurance company, chosen by John Jr. Harley Flood, the man assigned to Duluth at the time of the Julius Hendel unpleasantness at the grain exchange, was to be given the responsibility. The new plan was to be yet another link in the evolving "endless belt" concept that John Jr. was formulating.[36] Understandably, the proposal met with, at best, a lukewarm response from the department heads affected. A final decision on the plan was to be made after John Sr. returned from Europe.

As John Sr. sat in the Plaza Hotel, sifting through John Jr.'s letter, a telegram from John Jr. to his younger brother, Cargill, arrived: "Austen claims to have purchased Aunt Lydia's and Maggie's stock. Unable to confirm. Emma still undecided on proxy situation. Critical rush Father home." Presented with this further eye-opener, MacMillan returned forthwith to Minneapolis, the news so distressing to him that he visited his doctor on arrival (his diary noted, "Saw Dr. Bell—blood pressure 182").

The exact details of what happened next are not certain. A legend concerning this moment (many such abound about this whole saga) held that John Sr. went to all of the credit sources of the Cargill Elevator Company and persuaded them to refuse credit to the rebels. Almost immediately after learning of the challenge from Austen, John Sr. did send each bank the year-end financial statement of June 20, 1925; the probing replies of some seemed to infer that they had learned at least something about the stockholder dissidence. In truth, one can make just as good a case that the credit sources would have come *to* John Sr.—that they would have been so upset by the possibility of a young, untried management taking over that they themselves would have insisted on John Sr. remaining. One need only look at the record of the Company under John Sr.'s leadership to see that this might have been the case.[37]

In his meeting with Jack Hawley, Austen Cargill had alluded to the role that Frank Hixon might play. John Jr. had said in his first letter to his father, "The deciding factor will be the attitude of Mr. Hixon and cousin John D. [John D. McMillan], as several of the largest stockholders have agreed that they will let Mr. Hixon decide the issue for them. . . . Howard tells me that in his opinion his Father [John McMillan] will support Father [John Sr.] but not me, and if such is the case this would probably be Mr. Hixon's attitude." We are not privy to Hixon's views at this moment, as none of his letters remain. Indeed, he and John Sr. probably would have discussed this orally. Later in this momentous year for the Company, Hixon played another important role concerning Austen Cargill, as will become clear below.

No record remains of just how John Sr. got the disaffected senior executives back on board. One can speculate that his manifest affection for this group of people who were involved with him for years must have been tempered by his concern about their loyalty. Certainly, it was not a time to mince words. Although there is today no way of being certain of it, this seems to be the time when John Sr. would have sat stonily across the table and tendered blank sheets for resignation or loyalty. Two years earlier, on the occasion of the men's reluctance to let Julius Hendel trade on the floor, the situation apparently did not warrant this stand.

Whatever did happen right after John Sr.'s return, the result, known throughout the Company almost immediately afterward, was quite straightforward. John MacMillan, Sr., was to remain as head of the Cargill Elevator Company. John Jr. was to remain in the business, was to continue his control of the wheat account, and was to report directly to his father. There was no shareholder vote on any of this—it was as if the status quo had remained right in place.

Austen Cargill wrote Frank Hixon on August 7, first thanking him for intervening, then continuing, "My principal complaint, the internal friction, has been eliminated in a manner that not only wins my enthusiastic approval, but goes a long way toward removing a secondary complaint, that John Junior rather than his father is running this business. Any doubts that I still have on that point are minor and the future will, I am sure, eliminate them entirely."

All directors attended the annual meeting of the Company on August 11, 1925. The directors approved the minutes and reelected the previous year's officers. Austen Cargill made a motion for a 7 percent dividend, which was approved, and "there being no further business, a motion to adjourn was duly made, seconded and unanimously carried."

A Controversial Sale of Stock

There were critically important sequels to this, however, and in several respects these were even more important than the incipient revolt. The first action was taken immediately; at the stockholders meeting on that same August 11, 1925, the shareholders agreed to establish a voting trust for all of the common stock (23,476 shares of the total of 24,000 were represented at the meeting; all voted in favor).[38] Hixon, together with E. W. Decker and F. M. Prince (both of Minneapolis), were the designated trustees. The term of the voting trust agreement was five years.

In writing Fred Hanchette a few days later about the meeting, John Sr. noted that Frank Hixon had "stated that he had been called in conference by some of the bankers here just before the meeting" and that Hixon then made the motion for the trust. John Sr. implied that the bankers recommended the trust. It could also have been John Sr.'s own idea, but it is probable that the Company's bankers *would* have approved—the trust certainly would give stability (the $859,000 profit for 1924–1925 was a vivid buttress for this conclusion).

"It seems to me and to Austen as well," John Sr. continued, "that this is a peculiarly happy solution, maintaining complete harmony between the stockholders, employees, and management of the Company." Hanchette gave Emma's proxy for the trust—halfheartedly—but expressed at the same time the classic passive stockholders' lament: "The vital interest with us is a matter of income, and I know your policy is to cut them [the dividends] as low as possible in order to build up a surplus. I understand the wisdom of that . . . but if we wait until you accumulate 4 or 5 million, we must live pretty close for a long time."[39]

John Sr. responded immediately to Hanchette, with a reassuring comment about his goal, "which I have always had in mind," to pay an annual 7 percent dividend, and more "if justified."

John Sr. was frank with Hanchette about the chain of events that had just transpired:

I cannot tell you how sorry I am that you did not come to our annual meeting.
... The curious feature of the situation is that everything evaporated as soon as it
was known that I was home. ... I think I can say beyond any question or doubt,
that if the plan that was attempted had been put over, you, nor I, nor any of us
would have had any income for a considerable period ahead ... this business could
not have gone on. This business is absolutely dependent on borrowing vast sums
of money, and no bank will loan money where there is known to be a fight for
control within the organization.

I was sorry, more sorry than I can tell you, that Austen was so misled. Having
been out of the business for five years [in British Columbia], I can see how he might
have listened to gossip originating from jealousy and similar motives, not realizing
the real situation. However, I am sure that you will be glad to know that he is quite
straightened out, and he and Anne, and Edna and I had a very delightful time up
at Spooner last week and the first of this week.

Finally, he spoke directly of the Hanchettes' involvement: "You too
evidently, have been told a lot of idle gossip, for which there was no foundation. I cannot tell you how much I appreciate your assurance of entire

Fred and Emma Hanchette, c. 1909.

confidence. Incidentally, I have believed this right along, but the effort that was made to mislead so many of our stockholders is bound to have a bad effect, and to cost all of us a great deal of money. I cannot emphasize too strongly that unless you and I and Austen stand together, always, and are absolutely loyal to one another, the result is sure to mean disaster." It was clear in this letter that John Sr. had been aggrieved by the events, and he concluded: "There was so much misrepresentation of the whole affairs . . . such a vicious look that I cannot forget."[40]

It would be surprising if the families had gone through this experience without some residual tension and ill feeling. John Sr. soon began to believe that Emma Hanchette had been making negative references about him and about John Jr. behind his back. John Sr. reacted in his usual blunt manner, penning a long letter to Fred Hanchette that meticulously went over details of what he thought had been "settled" earlier.

Emma responded to John Sr. with an apologetic letter. She first mentioned a promise she had made to Austen Cargill "years ago" to support Austen with her own stock if ever it were necessary. "When he asked me to fulfill it," she continued, "I had to do so. I felt it so keenly that I felt we ought not to be staying in your house" [the Hanchettes were in Minneapolis at the time of the stockholder challenge]. . . . I spoke to Jr. about it. He was wonderful then & I told him in confidence why I was in such a position. [Later], from a most unsatisfactory letter from him I learned he betrayed that confidence. . . . Austen gave me his word that whatever Mr. Hixon said would be final with him and I believed him but Jr. had his doubts."

She continued about John Jr.'s relationship to the executives in the organization: "The men in the office talked very freely with Fred & they certainly gave him the impression of trouble ahead, but it was all against Jr., not you . . . in spite of all we heard, we felt Jr.'s only fault in the office was lack of tact!" She closed the letter with a long "vote of confidence" in John Sr.[41]

John Sr. wrote back, immediately turning to the allegation of John Jr.'s alleged perfidy: "About John Jr. betraying your confidence, there could not possibly be anything of that sort. You made certain definite charges against his Father, and he could not rest without knowing whether they were true or not, and it would have been rank disloyalty to me if he had done otherwise. Unfortunately, too, I heard in La Crosse after your previous visit there, that you had been saying somewhat similar things, and I felt that under the circumstances I must set you straight."

John Sr. then defended John Jr.'s business experience:

I want you to know that we have two very wonderful boys. Both of them are of very high character and of very great ability. . . . I wonder if you realize that my two boys are the only grandsons of your father who could possibly ever succeed to the management of this company? Don't you think it preferable to have competent members of the family engage in the management rather than have it run by entire strangers. I have always looked on this company as a family affair and if you, Fred, Austen, Edna and I always hold together, I do not think any of us need ever worry about the future.

(John Sr. was, of course, conveniently forgetting the Cargill side, not only Austen but others, such as William Wallace Cargill, son of W. S., who later became the successful chief executive officer of Ray-O-Vac Corporation, in Madison, Wisconsin.)[42]

Apparently there *had* been some accusatory statements made within the two families, including remarks that "John was trying to get everything into his own hands." So John Sr. wrote several other letters at this time to key people, for example, to "Aunt Maggie" (Mrs. George Barker), whom he told that Emma "has attempted to influence my own boys against me."[43] John Sr. also accumulated in his files a set of statements allegedly made by several of the individuals involved. Some of these he actually had notarized, "to whom it may concern" statements.

The gist of these statements collected by John Sr. seemed to point a finger at James B. Taylor as the mastermind behind the abortive takeover plot. One of the sworn statements held that Taylor had said he "HATED John MacMillan's God Damned Guts" and that he himself was "the brains of the Cargill organization . . . that John MacMillan was 'only a figurehead and a poor one at that.' " There is no corroboration or defense by Taylor of these allegations still remaining in the records; one result of the coup attempt, however, was J. B. Taylor's resignation from the Company at the end of the year 1925. Cargill MacMillan took over Taylor's administration of Cargill Securities Company. Incidentally, despite his severance from the Company as an operating executive, Taylor continued to hold and vote his stock.[44]

The Hanchettes Sell

There was one more very significant event. Sometime during the fall of 1925, Fred and Emma Hanchette sold their two blocks of stock in the Cargill Securities Company (a total of 5,000 shares) to John Sr. The sequence of events leading to this sale began with the telegram quoted earlier, sent by John Jr. in late July to his brother Cargill, stating in part: "Austen claims to have purchased Aunt Lydia and Maggie's stock . . . Emma still undecided on proxy situation." There is no way to reconstruct from the evidence still remaining whether the first two women had agreed to sell to Austen or whether Austen even made this claim to John Jr. There *is* support for the second part of the statement, that Austen Cargill did make an offer for the stock owned by Emma and Fred Hanchette in both

Cargill Elevator and Cargill Securities.⁴⁵ On December 5, long after the event, Fred Hanchette finally told John Sr. some of the details.

Apparently the Hanchettes were interested in selling their stock right from the beginning of the plot: "Pem [Emma Hanchette] wrote Austen to know if he and you could not buy it with the elev. stock. Austen came back with two or three impossible plans." There is evidence, in a document, "Tentative plan no. 2, purchase of Hanchette interests, Cargill companies," that a detailed plan was developed by Austen Cargill for the Hanchette sale of their interests in the two companies (the Securities Company and the Elevator Company) for just under $900,000.

Then, several weeks after this "tentative plan" apparently fell through, further events occurred, beginning with a letter from Jack Hawley (John Jr.'s close friend and contemporary), written to Fred Hanchette on September 30, 1925. Hawley also discussed a possible sale, in this case only of the Hanchette Cargill Securities Company stock, with Hawley himself as the intermediary. In this letter, Hawley stated:

I still feel that if I could get you, say, $400,000 cash and you get the dividend (proposed) of say $25,000 making a total of $425,000 net to you, that you would have a lot more pleasure out of the return from bonds than you will get standing in the position of arbiter between Austen and John Sr. . . . This is a very fine time to sell as you have all the available cash and dividends and it is unlikely you will get another for some time, unless things change a lot. . . . I will make about four or five percent on the sale over and above the price I think I can get for you.

He also alluded to the other Hanchette stock, the Cargill Elevator block: "There is of course no sale on the Elevator stock the way it looks now. The stock has just been trusteed, the large dividend declared, the grain situation good but the Elevator profits shrunk to a minimum for this first part of the season when they normally should be greatest. There is also a high book value placed on this stock."⁴⁶

After this letter was written, Hawley made a personal trip to California to see the Hanchettes. He was attracted to the Hanchette daughter, Ellen (whose nickname was Budley), and had stayed with the family a number of times previously. Apparently, Hawley obtained from the Hanchettes the option to buy their Cargill Securities stock. Then, sometime in October 1925, John Sr. purchased these 5,000 shares at a cost of $410,000 and made a gift of this stock to his two sons, John Jr. and Cargill; each received 2,500 shares.⁴⁷

In retrospect, Fred Hanchette expressed unease to John Sr. about the way the option was exercised; "We are glad to have made the sale but are simply flabbergasted at the deceit practiced by the one who made it [Hawley]. . . . That one whom we wholeheartedly loved and trusted deceived us as I cannot imagine a white man doing." Hanchette admitted to John Sr.

that he and Emma had wanted to "get out of the whole business." He continued, "If Austen knew we intended selling to you before the deal was made, we would have been perfectly satisfied. . . . Your owning it makes no difference in any way except that without his consent we could not give you absolute control over him. . . . Our one worry is that Austen, who has shown us the greatest generosity, will think we have double-crossed him." Hanchette referred again to the Summer's "revolt," mentioning again that "Junior was the subject of it all," that "Junior knew this and offered to get out," and that "then Austen declared he had not wanted him, Junior, out." Hanchette resurrected the story that had been going through the employee group at that time, "that you were both influenced and harassed by his (Jr.'s) ever occurrent schemes. The slogan was, manage as you managed before Junior's time." Hanchette ended this important letter with this paragraph: "I know something you could do that would win my applause. That is, offer to sell Austen one-half the stock we sold. I do not think for a minute he would buy it, but it would show a wonderful spirit on your part."[48]

The Hanchettes had fallen on difficult circumstances through the half dozen years since World War I. The business downturn and inflation had hit them hard, dependent as they were on Cargill Elevator Company common and preferred stock dividends. They had purchased an expensive house and an expensive car; both were sick in this period, and they had large doctor bills. Fred had attempted a loan from the Company in 1921, but John Sr. was opposed (writing Fred, "we have always made it a practice to have our statement go out showing no loans to employees, officers or stockholders. Banks are getting more and more particular about these matters all the time"). The times were not good for Cargill Elevator in this period, and John Sr.'s conservative dividend policy had been reinforced. After the 15 percent dividend on the common stock in 1919, there was only one more dividend paid in cash in the period 1920–1924, 10 percent in 1922. The Hanchettes seemed to feel a loss of control—and of influence. John Sr. had needed them in 1912 and 1916 but now, preoccupied about business, seemed no longer to need them.

Obviously, the Hanchettes felt caught in the middle and were desperately trying to stay on the good side of everyone, for on the same day that Fred Hanchette wrote John Sr., December 5, he also wrote Austen Cargill. Here the story was considerably different:

. . . about this deal. Jack came out here when I was sick enough to have a nurse. He had a friend, an oil man (I think his name was John Herbert) who had so much money that he wanted something, just such as the C.S. Co. was—no dividends, but with a big future prospect.

On that understanding, we signed our stock over to him. I had told Jack that I would not sell mine to John to give him a voting control if only for the reason that you had been so fine and generous toward us, and I want to add emphasis to the generous. The sale was made and the money deposited in the First National Bank of Ft. Worth, Texas.

Then, after some weeks after, we had a letter from Jack that he had sold it to John, we were so dumbfounded, so utterly and completely confounded that we were literally sick.

I wrote to John to this effect too. It wasn't because John had the stock. The monetary arrangement was satisfactory to us. Altho, as for me, I was not well enough to analyze it. But we would not knowingly have made that sale without your consent. That we owed to you.

Even as great a blow was, that this fellow whom we trusted and truly loved as a wonderful all-around and unusually human boy, should deceive us—we whom he claimed to like better than his own aunts and uncles.

Well this is the story and it only goes to show that one should use his head more and his heart less.

In John Sr.'s reply to Hanchette, he made no mention of the latter's suggestion of selling some of the stock to Austen. John Sr. did, however, strongly defend Hawley, asking Hanchette "to reserve judgment till you know all the facts in the case. . . . I think Jack is all that you have previously thought him to be, and he would do anything under heaven to be of service to you or to us."

John Sr. then referred to the option:

It happens that I did not know anything whatever about his having an option on your C.S. Co. stock, until Cargill and Junior came to me with it, and I decided to help the boys buy it, just as I previously helped Austen to finance the purchase of his share of Will's stock. You are quite wrong in saying that you wrote me after my return that you would like to get out of the whole business. If I had the slightest idea of that, I would gladly have cooperated with Austen in arranging some kind of deal. It did happen, however, that Austen attempted to buy you out without in any way consulting with me, and when I learned this, I did feel that it was a protection to the boys, and thought it would prevent any possibility of a recurrence of what happened last Summer. . . . I am quite sure that the only thought that has ever been in Jack's mind has been to see that the stock fell in hands that would be friendly to Junior and Cargill, whom he looks upon as his two most intimate and dearest friends. . . .[49]

The purchase now gave the John MacMillan family majority ownership of Cargill Securities Company for the first time—12,500 of the 20,000 shares, with Austen Cargill still holding 7,499. The immediate effect on the ownership structure of the common stock of Cargill Elevator Company seemed not to be too dramatic. Cargill Securities Company owned only 507 shares of the 24,000 outstanding in the Elevator Company; all of the shares were trusteed in the voting trust anyway. However, the reality of this purchase of the Hanchette Cargill Securities stock was profound. Along with this purchase perhaps came some understanding between the Hanchettes and John Jr. and Cargill MacMillan as purchasers, either tacit or written, that the Hanchettes would also sell their Cargill Elevator stock at a later date. Given John Sr.'s mistrust (certainly reasonable after the surprising events of the summer), there could have been a written agreement, although there is no documentation of this in extant records.

The proof is in the results, however—in May 1927, Cargill Securities Company purchased the common stock in the Elevator Company owned by the Hanchettes, in exchange for their receiving 7 percent preferred stock in the same company.[50] Now the combination of the MacMillan shares (John Sr., Edna, John Jr. and Cargill), when combined with the shares now owned by the Securities Company, comprised a much more substantial total of Cargill Elevator, over 43 percent. The stockholder structure after the 1916 reorganization gave roughly one-third of the holdings to "Cargill interests" and another one-third to "MacMillan interests," with the remaining one-third in the hands of the employees and other friends; it was, as Austen Cargill was quoted by Hanchette, "with the control in the hands of the employees." While the statement still was true, the finely set 1916 balance of one-third of the stock in each of those three key interest groups had been significantly altered. The five-year voting trust gave protection to all holders of common stock that no faction would be able to vote separately or attempt a takeover. In 1930, when this voting trust expired, Cargill Elevator Company was reorganized, and Cargill, Incorporated came in to being. In the process, the sale of the Hanchette stock in the two companies (Cargill Elevator and Cargill Securities) allowed the John MacMillan, Sr., family to gain outright majority control.

The most enigmatic role of any in the events was that of James Taylor. He had been centrally involved in family business affairs since the 1890s, managing most of the routine Cargill Securities Company business, handling Austen Cargill's business affairs while Austen was at war and in British Columbia and voting the proxies of the Hanchettes at stockholder meetings. In late November 1925, John Sr. dictated—and had notarized—further statements about Taylor during the course of this most recent set of events. The first involved an apparent discrepancy between what Taylor had told John D. McMillan, namely, that "we have decided to drop John H. MacMillan from the management of the Cargill Elevator Company," and what Taylor later told John Sr. himself, that "if a contest arose for control that he would of course support me." When John Sr. queried McMillan about this, the latter was quoted as saying, "He never said anything of the kind. He said just what I previously told you."

John Sr. also excerpted part of a letter to Edna from Emma Hanchette, back in early November, and personally "notarized" it. Emma said at that time, "If Jim Taylor has told you anything, I ask you to discredit it absolutely. He is no friend of ours or yours and a bitter enemy of Jrs. I have known he was two faced for years and if he is friendly with John—well it is too much for me. I can almost hear him tell John how hard he tried to keep peace in the office, etc., while John was away."[51] We do not have any Taylor response to these allegations; although there are a number of routine Taylor letters in the correspondence, none relate to these incidents.

The role of Jack Hawley, at least to the extent it is known, seems ambiguous, too: what happened with that option is still not clear, nor is it clear just what Hawley had meant by the statement, "I will make about four or five percent on the sale." Hawley remained in the good graces of the entire MacMillan family. Indeed, he was being married that fall, and many of the festivities were held under the auspices of the MacMillans. However, future events would mar this relationship once again.

There remains one more important ingredient to complete the story. This was the question of just what Austen Cargill's role in the Company was now to be. Frank Hixon played a strong hand in this matter as, indeed, he had done at so many critical points of tension—the 1909–1910 events, the 1912 formation of the Cargill Securities Company, the reorganization in 1916, and now the 1925 imbroglio caused by fear of John Jr.'s actions in the Company. John Sr. then decided to immediately ask for the resignation of James Taylor and forthwith wrote Hixon about this. Hixon cautioned, "I want to advise you very strongly to acquaint Austen with your intention of asking for Jim's resignation at least several days in advance of taking the action. It could do no harm, while if sprung as a surprise it would very likely have an unfortunate effect. He would naturally feel that he was not in the least in your confidence." Apparently John Sr. did this.

Hixon then wrote John Sr. again four days later:

You are in a position where you are absolutely protected . . . consequently I feel that, beyond letting Taylor out, you should await developments rather than try to anticipate them, when by doing so you might unnecessarily alienate Austen's goodwill and possibly instill an atmosphere of fear and uncertainty into your organization. . . . I think that he made a mistake which he will not repeat again, and if I am wrong in my estimate of him you still are taking no chances in dealing with him on the assumption that he is going to be loyal and friendly in the future . . . you can afford to be generous as well as just . . .[52]

There was still be a question between John Sr. and Austen about just what this role should be. Austen's skills with motors learned during World War I had already been drawn upon by the La Crosse & Southeastern Railway, and, of course, he had had substantial experience prior to the war at Green Bay and then at Milwaukee under Grimes. Again Hixon took a decisive role in ameliorating the tension. He wrote John Sr. in late January 1926:

I think that Austen's demands are absurd. If he comes into the organization, his future in it should rest on merit alone, and if he does not come in I do not see on what basis he can expect assurance that you will buy him out whenever he wants to sell. I received and answered a letter from him before yours came, which I quote as follows: '. . . I do not know just what John's proposition is, but, unless you want to keep yourself free from business duties and responsibilities, I wish you could see your way clear to accept it and at least give it a trial. You could thus keep in touch with the business, and what is just as important, meet John part way in what I believe to be an earnest effort on his part to establish and maintain pleasant relations . . .' I think that the best thing in the world that could happen to him and all concerned would be for him to take on a real job and occupy his time and mind with his duties.[53]

Apparently this incisive comment by Hixon, made as forcefully to John Sr. as to Austen Cargill, succeeded in breaking the log jam of feelings between the two. Austen Cargill did come into the business at this point; he first took an assignment in La Crosse to set up a new bus line to supplement the limping La Crosse & Southeastern Railway, then came to Cargill Elevator Company, in July 1926, in an important and responsible role—he became executive head of the Commission Department, working closely and coming to know very well the country elevators, the commission customers and the others out in the field. The department's first annual report, in 1927, noted this new development: "Credit facilities were extended to customers, the branch offices then numbering five were added to the Department, solicitors were engaged and serious efforts were made to develop the business." John Sr. wrote John Jr. of this assignment, "I think now that everything from a family viewpoint is just as agreeable as we could make it." John Jr.'s authority had now been reinforced openly by his father and the MacMillan stockholdings.[54]

And so the whole matter rested. It seems evident from extensive correspondence that Austen Cargill and John MacMillan, Sr., continued to have a friendly and supportive relationship. George Cargill and Austen Cargill, John Sr. and John Jr. took a long vacation together in January 1926, fishing off the Florida keys. There were further mentions of social engagements that involved Austen and Anne Cargill paired with Edna and John MacMillan. The threatening events of that summer and fall of 1925 seemed to have dissipated.

Stories still surface from time to time about these events. Perhaps the best epitaph for the families today is that it happened over 60 years ago, ended in at least surface harmony and can be put down here as interesting, worthwhile family history. At least that is what Frank Hixon concluded, writing to John MacMillan after the Company's "first stockholders luncheon," in August 1926: "While the flareup of your organization seemed a most deplorable mess at the time, I am now convinced that it served a most useful purpose in bringing about a better understanding all along the line and paving the way for the new spirit of team-work which now seems to be well established."[55]

CHAPTER EIGHT

Centralization and the "Endless Belt"

Frank Hixon had said that there was now a renewed "spirit of team-work" in Cargill. It was led by a more cautious chief executive. Indeed, there is a noticeable change in John MacMillan, Sr.'s letters in this postre-volt period of late 1925 and 1926. Evidence remained of the pervasive kindness and goodwill that John Sr. seemed intuitively to hold toward his employees, and he continued the positive motivation and encouragement so characteristic of his earlier approach. However, there was a sharper tone of criticism, a willingness to assert a more authoritarian, centralizing posture. He had worked very hard to achieve consensus. Now John Sr. was centralizing. Before, he would have been concerned about employee feelings. But now, with their disloyalty, he did not feel he need worry about it. The lesson of the revolt was to tighten the reins, sharpen control of organizational differences, and less of "all of you work it out yourselves in the field."

How much of this change stemmed from John Jr. is difficult to assess. Certainly John Jr.'s personal precepts of organization were more strongly centralizing than were his father's. World War I also significantly shaped his thinking. First, there was his commander's (General Foote's) belief that if the brigade's central staff could operate in isolation, it would be more efficient. John Jr. saw this practiced in the chateau in France, and he too found it effective. Second, the basic organization form espoused by the armed services, the "line and staff" structure, made a great impression on him. He referred to these concepts often in conversation, speeches and writings.

From 1925, John Jr. had preached—and practiced—that strong centralization was the best form of organization. He coupled this with his "endless belt" concept to form a tightly knit, multifunctional organization, peaking up through line commands to the top. The link between the military and business was particularly evident in his 1946 speech (which he had set in print), "The Theory and Practice of Organization." Interestingly, he spoke shortly after his father's death in 1944, and in this important piece he claimed virtually complete credit for the organizational changes.

He began with an armed services analogy:

I myself had the rare good fortune at the age of 21 of becoming adjutant (or Chief-of-Staff—although today I rather imagine it would be called Executive Officer), to a Brigadier-General of Field Artillery. I had previously had experience as an enlisted man in the Connecticut National Guard, where I had the fullest opportunity to see the set-up for the so-called line theory of organization. Now the Brigade was the smallest military unit which had the functional scheme of organization. It was a tactical rather than an administrative organization. I therefore had the incredible good fortune of acquiring a first-hand knowledge of the practice and theory of organization at a very early age. Most men who acquire this rarely do so until they reach advanced middle age. My associates in Cargill were intelligent enough to appreciate the value of this experience, and had enough confidence largely to give me a free hand in arranging our own organization, which had really grown in a hit or miss fashion. Consequently you will be more and more impressed with the parallel between our own set-up and that of the Army or Navy.[1]

The writings of Alfred Chandler, the highly regarded business historian, on "strategy and structure" are useful here in understanding the importance of John Jr.'s organizational thinking.[2] Chandler believes history has shown that businesses are governed by inertia, that they change their overall direction (Chandler's "strategy") mostly when forced to do so by competitive pressures, and that a change in strategy is likely to be successful only if accompanied by a decisive change in organizational structure. John Jr. now entered into a process of changing the Company's direction; his expressed reason for doing so was to counter moves by competitors. This happened to mesh with those beliefs assimilated back in his army days. In turn, he did make decisive changes in Cargill's structure.

Underlying this was the question of efficiency. Did Cargill's forward integration bring economies of scale? Just what *was* the requisite volume to bring the corporation above a "minimum efficient size?" Chandler points out that integration, both horizontal and vertical, generally must be followed by extension of more coordinated administrative efforts. However, this does not necessarily imply a full-scale, top-down centralization, John Jr.'s instinct. The successful General Motors model in the 1920s under Pierre du Pont and Alfred P. Sloan was decentralized. These judgment questions about proper organizational balance have recurred throughout Cargill's history, and have been debated anew at each stage of development.

Marine Insurance and Chartering Changes

Just after the 1925 internal revolt in the firm, John Jr. put into full effect a plan for centralizing lake freight chartering and the purchase of insurance, heretofore decentralized into the hands of the four department heads, with the Duluth heads, Lindahl and Prime, having the strongest role. He had first broached the plan in early 1925, before the revolt, as he negotiated with a close friend, vessel broker R. M. Knox, about the possibilities of Knox joining Cargill as the head of a new "marine department." It was to be a major job, for the proposed salary was $6,000, an amount that would rank with senior officers of the Company at that time. The negotiations with Knox had not set well with some members of the organization, and this patent move toward centralizing was a contributing factor in the revolt. Despite the attractive offer and his close friendship with John Jr., Knox turned Cargill down. John Jr. expressed his great disappointment but asked Knox "to do what you can to help me out in perfecting my arrangements for next year, especially with Jim [J. B. Taylor]."[3]

Then, on August 22, 1925, just days after the revolt, John Jr. revealed a detailed plan on vessel chartering and insurance to his father. John Jr. had demanded from several vessel brokers in Duluth that they allow Cargill to place its own insurance. John Jr. estimated that the Company could cut its marine insurance costs from 30 cents to 18 cents per $100 valuation. When the brokers initially refused, "I countered by stating that unless they would consent to our using whatever insurance we wished, that we would open our own chartering office in Cleveland and engage in vessel chartering business." This loosened most of the brokers' positions, although two continued their refusal to deal with Cargill on this new basis.

Inherent in John Jr.'s plan was his decision to centralize the whole process rather than allow it to be done by the individual department heads as in the past: "I asked Lindahl and Prime to turn their charters over to [Harley] Flood. . . . Each declined on the ground that they did not wish to 'submerge their individualities in a large organization,' but both agreed to tell Flood of their requirements so that we could possibly get together and use one boat whenever possible."[4]

Although there was grudging acceptance of the general plan by Prime and Lindahl, they did not follow through on it. John Sr. wrote remarkably strong letters within days to both. In his letter to Prime he wrote:

I had John Junior particularly consult with you and Lindahl so that there would be complete harmony and agreement before entering into the agreement, and I am somewhat puzzled to find that you are chartering your boats through Dinham and Stocking, and giving them the insurance at the old rate basis. For some time, I have been conscious that we have been allowing these brokers to use our various departments in a competitive way against one another. This is bad business . . . and this work of chartering boats must be done through one man so as to avoid this competition between departments.

Then John Sr. continued in an uncharacteristically severe mode: "That, however, is not the most serious feature of it. When the word of this organization is given, at any time, with my authority, as to any arrangement, our word is just as good as a written contract. . . . I must keep our word good in this case." He cautioned Prime: "This effort is therefore the result of your own theory, and yet somehow I find you are one of the department heads that insists on paying the old rates."

Lindahl responded immediately to his letter: "I . . . could not do the business I did yesterday with Montreal unless I have the boats in hand. No matter who I get them from, I have got to get them through an agency that has them or else stop doing business. Now this may not seem to your liking, but I wish you would come up and talk matters over, then you can thrash it out here any way you wanted, but to favor certain boats is going to stop business."

John Sr., adamant, wrote back: "I told you over the telephone how much money this kind of foolishness has cost us, and I hope you will see that no charters are made hereafter excepting through the three agencies with whom we discussed the matter yesterday, unless they cannot furnish the tonnage under the conditions we require." To Prime, he stressed "the absolute importance" of dealing in the way John Jr. had decided. The Duluth executives clearly were given no choice.

Other organizational moves tightened reporting relationships in the

Cargill Print Shop, December 1930.

Minneapolis office. The accounting function under Roy Hoople was re-aligned much more explicitly along John Jr.'s "line" concept. Similarly, the print shop had been given a more centralized relationship, reporting directly to John Jr.[5]

It became evident now that John Sr. had given his son major responsibility for overall company policy and would back him when John Jr. stepped on the toes of those in the organization who liked to do it "their own way." John Jr. was not tactful. Impatient with persuading those who could not see at a glance the total picture, he saw no benefit in old habits unless they fitted his ideas. He was intolerant of the time necessary to effect change. He also was a man of strong opinions, action-oriented and always thinking of new ways to put together old ideas. He was an innovative, creative person, with vision about the future. At the same time, however, he was widely perceived as authoritarian in his approach.

Lindahl Declines

It had become painfully apparent that there had been some significant changes in John Sr.'s relationship with Lindahl, poignant for the latter. The long-standing role of Lindahl as a mentor for John Sr. now seemed ended. The cooling of feelings on the part of John Sr. may have begun in 1922, when the Company voted a stock dividend. Special arrangements were made with the two widows, Aunt Maggie and Aunt Lydia, so that the employees who had borrowed money from them to buy their stock in the 1916 settlement could also participate in this new dividend. Lindahl, however, wanted no part of additional stock; indeed, he shocked John Sr. by announcing that he wished to sell all of his stock back to the Company for cash.

This had been a right explicitly stated in the contracts from the start, so John Sr. acceded to the request and tendered cash for all of Lindahl's stock. Privately, however, the action irked John Sr. considerably. He always resisted any request to remove capital from the Company, and this was probably more than just his concern for maintaining financial strength—it was as if he felt the person was expressing a lack of confidence in him as chief executive officer. He wrote Austen Cargill that "ever since he has owned that stock, he has been as nervous as could be. . . . I think his actions have at times reacted rather badly on the organization . . . this will entirely remove any anxieties he may have had in connection with ownership of this stock. . . . Of course, I have written him nicely so he will have no possible occasion to feel offended but I feel rather hurt over his lack of appreciation for what has been done for him."

Austen Cargill, too, was disenchanted with Lindahl at this time. In a report to MacMillan on Duluth's poor results in the crop year 1922–1923, he observed, "I have always felt that Duluth's showings were largely due to successful manipulation of hedges and spreads rather than a strict merchandising business. If true, a change in methods would seem to be in order and I don't believe Lindahl can bring it about as he has only been trained in the one way of doing business."[6]

This disaffection should not be overstated. John Sr. continued to be "exceedingly fond" of Lindahl (MacMillan's own words). Lindahl was certainly not one of the dissidents in the 1925 revolt—perhaps he did not even know the challenge was imminent. But Austen Cargill probably had a point in calling Lindahl "old fashioned." John Sr. worried that both Lindahl and Prime seemed unable to see the larger picture—to "make the most money" for the Company as a whole.

This difference in thinking was aptly illustrated in Austen Cargill's example, the accounting issue. In September 1926, John Sr. wrote Lindahl that he and a group of the Minneapolis Cargill executives (his brother Dan, John Jr., Ed Grimes and Roy Hoople) had decided to change the basis of profit-center charges. An expensing on the basis of allocated storage space was proposed, using an average of the past five years of expense as a basic charge. Onto this would be added a handling charge of 5 cents a bushel, and the screenings would be allotted to the grain account that was claiming the space.

Lindahl immediately demurred. He particularly wanted to keep the old traditional practice of the elevator being able to claim the screenings, irrespective of who had the grain in the bins: "I think you were wrong and making a bad mistake if you allow any of the accounts credit for screening. They belong to the elevator—always have and always should." John Sr. wrote more diplomatically, promising that "it was not my intention to change anything except the accounting, and that only to the extent that one department will not be penalized in doing business which shows a profit for some other department." He explained his rationale: "I am so anxious to work out some accounting method that will make everybody try their utmost to draw trade, and not look at it from the narrow point of view of whether his transaction is going to show a profit for his immediate department, but rather if it is going to make money for the organization as a whole."

John Sr. also was exasperated with Duluth at this time about the apparent lack of quality control. In 1925 and 1926, the federal inspectors were being particularly stringent. So it seemed at least to Lindahl (who commented, at one point, "I think Mr. Carroll, the Federal traveling superintendent, is a very bad egg"). Whether this pejorative was earned, the Duluth shippings increasingly were rejected by buyers as having too high a percentage of dockage. John Sr. wrote Lindahl in September 1926: "In looking over the inspection of your grain shipped, I notice that so far, spring wheat shows an average dockage of 1.89%, durum 1.79%, and rye 2%."

John Sr. objected to the Duluth inspection record on two scores. First, if they would do additional cleaning, it would allow some grain to be graded higher, and second, Cargill grain now was being singled out by the trade as not clean enough. As he put it to Lindahl, "There is no question about the seriousness of this situation . . . most of the trouble we have had of late in trying to get bids from the East has been due to the fact that the trade is suspicious of us, and are not willing to buy from us when they can secure so much better quality from our competitors." Lindahl was apologetic; "I had the matter up with McManus [the superintendent at the Superior elevator] and he maintains now as always that it does not pay from a money standpoint to clean grain down to 1%."

Once again, both Lindahl and McManus were using a narrow focus, comparing only the screenings obtained against the fuel costs, and shrinkage against the screenings' value, forgetting completely about the issue of quality in a competitive environment. John Sr. put the issue candidly to McManus: "I do not believe either you or Carlson [another executive at the terminals] appreciate the character of wheat that our competitors are furnishing these eastern millers, and it is a most serious loss to the organization as a whole to have a situation develop whereby we have lost the prestige that we formerly had with the eastern milling trade. The net result is that we are now unable to sell them anything."

After receiving this letter, Lindahl penned an apology: "I am very sorry that the wheat was disappointing down east, as of course it makes it bad for you and your Buffalo office" but rationalized: "It is barely possible that those complaints were received from wheat that ran down to the side of the boat that contained a little more dirt, or possibly got the last of a bin when it was loaded out from Buffalo into cars which is apt to be a little more dirty. . . . Jr. told me that they wanted it down to 1% and McManus said it was an utter impossibility."[7]

John Sr.'s new aggressiveness in addressing his colleagues began to cause friction. For example, he wrote L. N. Cote, the terminal manager at Milwaukee, "I find in talking with Mr. Hawley today that you have been disconnecting your static condenser at times, using your own judgment as to when to use it. This entirely destroys the theory on which the condenser was put in. . . . I do not know on what theory you have been disconnecting it, but in any event please see to it that this never happens again without my permission." The manager, taken aback by this, wrote John Sr. about his injured feelings. John Sr. then had to apologize: "I understand you felt somewhat hurt over the letter which I wrote you on November 9, and, if so, you have taken it in a spirit I did not intend at all. It was not intended in any sense as a reflection, but merely as an explanation. . . .

No one appreciates more than I do your keen effort to operate at the minimum cost."

Yet John Sr. still responded to his employees with respect; for example, when one employee asked if he could buy stock, MacMillan agreed, adding an indirect compliment: "I am sure you realize that we reserve it only for those who we consider key men in the organization." When A. L. Jacobs, the manager at Milwaukee, asked for a raise, MacMillan responded, "In looking at the facts of the case, I feel that this is quite proper." MacMillan asked for some reports from an auditor in one of the company's subsidiaries and, after spelling out the facts he desired, continued, "I wish you to understand the purpose of the information, and if there occurs to you anything that you think may be of interest, I would be very glad to have you include it." When a report came in from Rudy Semsch, a Company auditor, MacMillan responded, "I want to congratulate you on making this up in such a comprehensive way. It gives me just the kind of information which I wanted." He wrote Semsch at a later date, "I am very glad indeed to have this data, and I appreciate very much the care you have taken and the splendid arrangements of the various items, all of which will make it very easy for me to think over the problems we now have in hand."[8]

The various organizational adjustments during this mid-1920s period mirrored a much larger set of forces operating on the business as a whole. The center of focus for the Company was now shifting sharply eastward, with Buffalo in the vortex of this change. In turn, this brought important changes back in Minneapolis.[9]

The Enigma of Buffalo

Buffalo had been the "foot" of the Great Lakes since the end of the eighteenth century, when the first Soo lock connecting Lakes Superior and Huron was constructed by the Canadians in 1797. There is a 23-foot differential in elevation between the lakes (Superior the higher). At the Soo, the 60-mile long St. Marys River formed a rapids and falls, dropping the level of the river 20 feet in one mile. The Americans rebuilt the locks in 1853 and 1881, the Canadians again in 1883. Improvements also were made in 1914 and 1919. Cargill had been shipping from Duluth to Buffalo since the 1890s. After the fundamental shift in the early 1920s, when companies from Europe opened offices in Duluth, Western grain companies, in turn, reached eastward. Cargill's Taylor & Bournique acquisition was an example of this. The question was, for Cargill (and others), should they purchase a Buffalo terminal or build anew?

John Jr., holding tenaciously to his concept of the endless belt, was convinced that terminal facilities in Buffalo would make the process even more manageable. Indeed, to carry out the new concept (new at least for the Westerners) of export "fobbing," where the Company kept ownership and arranged transportation and insurance to the port of export and sold FOB (free-on-board) there, facilities at an important eastern terminus would be a signal asset. But plans were underway to enlarge the Welland Canal, and if such a route was developed, Montreal would become the preferred port. Perhaps even some new terminal development farther down the St. Lawrence River might be needed.

This seemed to come as a complete revelation to Lindahl, for he wrote John Sr. in June 1926: "It surprised me very much and shows how ignorant we are sometimes about large improvements that are going on. . . . It will be possible to load the largest freighter on the Great Lakes with wheat and send it on to Lake Ontario, as for instance, Oswego or any of the Ontario ports." John Sr. wrote back brusquely, "We are quite familiar here with the Welland Canal situation for some time."

As early as 1920, John Sr. had lobbied for a St. Lawrence project, concluding in a letter at that time, "The early completion of this Deep-Water-way-to-the-Sea project is essential to business throughout the Northwest and the Southwest." In 1925, he had asked John Jr. to make a study of what the Welland improvement would mean to the Company. John Sr. wrote, "I do not believe there will be a deep water way to Montreal in less than ten years' time, but with the completion of the Welland Canal it might be that the large lake boats will run to Oswego and transfer export grain there, so you can see the Buffalo situation is not a simple problem." John Sr. wrote this letter to John Jr. in early 1925, just before the revolt, and added a telling promise: "Think the matter over carefully after you get away and discuss it a little bit with the organization here. You need not fear but what I would back you up. I would not for the world have you ignored."

It was becoming increasingly arduous to get adequate storage space in Buffalo on a year-by-year lease basis (such as Cargill had been doing with the Kellogg terminal). So extensive negotiations were conducted in the period 1925–1927 looking toward the purchase of existing Buffalo terminals—the Superior Terminal and the Dakota Terminal as possibilities. John Sr. continued his antipathy toward the Chicago route. He wrote a vice president of the Chicago and North Western Railway, when offered their terminal in 1927: "It is quite unnecessary to point out to you the uncertainty that exists in Chicago at present, due to . . . the trial of the officials of the Armour Grain Company and possible new regulations of the Chicago Board of Trade. No one can foresee at this time what the operating conditions of an elevator might be in Chicago." From the early 1920s, the Company had maintained the small leased operation at Ogdensburg, New York (not a popular port to the Great Lakes shipping operators because of its difficult berths). In August 1928, John Sr. wrote Harold Tweeden, the Buffalo manager, who was also in charge of Ogdensburg: "I do not know what Mr. Grimes has in mind for the elevator [Ogdensburg] this year but it would seem to me self-evident from results of last year that we cannot afford to maintain a crew at that place. . . . I do not see any other plan on which we can afford to operate until completion of the Welland Canal."

Oswego, New York, remained an alternative possibility; the Welland Canal would be used there too, and the berths were better. In 1929, the Interstate Commerce Commission gave Oswego the right to charge a preferential rate to New York and Boston, lower than the Buffalo rate for both domestic and export, and John Jr. wrote his father, "This . . . will establish a precedent for demanding similar rates out of Ogdensburg and it seems to all of us here that it will definitely mark the end of Buffalo as an important transfer point." There was even some discussion in this period of shipping out of Churchill, Canada, via the Hudson Bay route. While this route was not competitive with the St. Lawrence, it was believed to be marginally competitive for Western grain (Montana, for example) and therefore had implications for all of the eastward movements.[10]

As puzzling as were these logistics and transportation questions, the effects of this "Buffalo-and-eastward" pressure on the Cargill organization itself was even more momentous. Heightening centralization all through the mid-1920s under the influence of John Jr.'s ideas brought tensions among department heads, both before and after the 1925 revolt. John Jr.'s Account 38 and the coarse grains accounts of Ed Grimes (since 1924 a vice president of the Cargill Elevator Company) had gained at the expense of the Duluth accounts. Although Lindahl still bought some wheat, especially durum, more trading was done under the direction of Minneapolis. Ed Grimes was making many of the decisions in filling the Superior bins and asking the Superior superintendent for mixing according to his own customer needs.

In one case, in May 1926, Grimes wanted to substitute No. 2 White oats for No. 3 Whites, to meet a Buffalo demand. John Sr. ordered this done, assuring Lindahl that he would "guarantee the Duluth account against any loss caused by the narrowing up." By return mail, Lindahl sent forth the good soldier's reply, that he would comply, but ended plaintively, "We would prefer to keep our 3W oats at 1½¢ less than 2W price but will keep the 2W as per your letter today."[11]

There was a notable difference in entrepreneurial style between Grimes and Lindahl. For example, in regard to oats, Grimes was pricing No. 2 Whites at a 1½-cent premium. Lindahl had priced his at only a 1-cent premium. Lindahl stated: "My idea of making only 1 cent difference was to have our oats invoiced at a safe price so that we would have something to go on in case the oat demand should come slow later on. This is the policy I have always pursued in making up statements, to have them on the safe side as much as possible."[12] There were also several instances where

Grimes actually purchased grain from Lindahl, in turn selling it at a profit for his own coarse grains account. In a case in late 1926, Grimes bought some of Lindahl's oats, and John Sr. commented to Lindahl: "Ed is taking a pure gamble on them, but I am sure he can work them out all right in the end as long as he has the space at Buffalo. . . . I am glad you have that off your mind now, and that you will have some room to take care of business properly."[13]

The centralization of chartering and insurance also continued to cause irritations. At first, these activity was under Harley Flood, working out of Duluth. Flood seemed too timid to John Jr. At heart, Flood was a trader, not relishing administration. Then a younger man, F. J. Hays, was given the assignment. John Jr. explained this to Harold Tweeden, the Buffalo manager: "He has actually been doing this for some little time but in the future we are turning it over to him entirely. . . . I wish you would pass the word along to the boys in your office that they should look to him for instructions relating to this end of our business." Hays wasted no time in informing John Jr. that there was "not very good teamwork between Mr. Irwin and Brown [the assistant manager of the Buffalo office] . . . that one or the other frequently fails to notify the other one either of directions he has received or of the orders given and this results in confusion and at times considerable embarrassment."

Hays was a strong-willed administrator. An iconoclast, this taciturn man soon established himself as the "dean of transportation." Stories abound about his inarticulateness. If one were meeting Hays for an interview, Hays would sit absolutely silent waiting for the visitor to make the first move. Then Hays would often answer in monosyllables. Yet the qualities that Hays exemplified suited the complex, abstruse world of ship chartering and insurance brokerage.[14]

John Sr. was meticulous in making certain that each of the departments assumed its full expense charges: when the cleaning machinery was used on wheat, there was less dockage to credit to whatever account was to receive it. John Sr. at first indicated to Lindahl that the spring wheat account itself would have to stand the difference; Lindahl worried that John Sr. was intending "to take the screenings and give it to the Spring Wheat account, which would not be fair because the elevator certainly is entitled to the screenings. It has always been the custom at all elevators at the head of the Lakes that the screenings belong to the plant and are necessary as a cost of the operation. On short crop years especially the 1½¢ elevation does not pay the cost of operation." John Sr. decided to back off: "They will be figured as always."[15]

It was space allocation, however, that most galled Lindahl. This was particularly exacerbated in 1926, when several of the elevator bins in Superior were being repaired and were temporarily out of business. Grimes had put over 7 million bushels of oats through Duluth in the earlier part of that year. Lindahl complained about both the volume and the handling and elevation charges he was being asked to absorb.

John Sr. wrote a trenchant letter in return:

You are quite wrong about this. . . . On account of the reconstruction work going on at Superior, you had to handle them the way you did, which, of course, was all right. But we cannot afford to handicap Mr. Grimes or put him out of business merely because our plant there is undergoing reconstruction. Mr. Grimes has handled through Duluth this year between six and seven million bushels of oats and that has been the most profitable business we could get. . . . The main point is this: I do not want arbitrary charges of this kind put through, as long as they do not represent a profit to the organization as a whole, and particularly when the charge merely represents a rehandling made necessary by the building of the new storage. . . . I want to encourage business and not discourage it by letting it down with charges which really represent nothing.[16]

Lindahl's lowered status, imposed from above, did not diminish John Sr.'s interest in Lindahl's personal welfare. Each thoughtfully concerned himself with the other's personal problems. In 1927, Lindahl had considerable difficulty with his legs from attacks of phlebitis (Lindahl then was 67 years old, nine years older than John Sr.). Lindahl had been with the Company for 41 years and had acquired a reputation for never missing a day at the office, always on the job. With the attacks of phlebitis, his doctor ordered him to stay off his feet. Yet he still wanted to go into the office.

Finally, Mrs. Lindahl wrote John Sr.: "Your advice is the *only* advice that counts with Mr. L. . . . Of course he *will* go to the office every day . . . he will not admit any of these ailments—call it what you will, Christian Science or stubbornness . . . if there is wheat in the country, he must be in it." The next day, MacMillan wrote Lindahl a wonderfully diplomatic letter, not alluding to his wife's remonstrances but instead urging Lindahl to take a vacation. He framed it personally: "I know how impossible it is for me to take care of myself at home, and I do not believe you are any different in this respect. There is only one safe thing for you to do, and that is to get away from temptation." Lindahl agreed to take the vacation— but shorter than John Sr. and Mrs. Lindahl had hoped.[17]

More Storage in the East

Finally, in late 1927, arrangements were concluded for extensive leased space—1.5 million bushels—at the Superior elevator in Buffalo. This decision was dictated not only by the desire to shift operations eastward—to expand both local Buffalo trade and the evolving fobbing trade—but also to heighten storage itself, to take advantage of carrying charges. With a significant short-term lease of 2.4 million bushels capacity at Port Mc-

Nicoll, Canada, at the foot of Georgian Bay, and with other small additions elsewhere, the Company's total terminal capacity jumped dramatically:

Bushel Capacities

Plants	1926	1927
Owned	10,750,000	11,450,000
Leased	4,600,000	10,700,000

Total grain purchases for the crop year 1927–1928 nearly doubled, from 33.8 million to 63.4 million bushels. Winter and spring wheat, rye, corn and barley had the largest percentage gains; durum, flax and oats were stagnant.[18]

Harold Tweeden, the Buffalo manager, had assumed that it was his prerogative to plan the use of Buffalo's additional space. But John Sr. disabused him of that idea:

I think you have somewhat the wrong theory of why that elevator was taken on. It was taken on for the benefit of the business as a whole . . . from the point of view of what will make the most money for the business as a whole. Friction and a loss result when one department begins to haggle with another and I want to discourage that sort of thing. Whenever you can make more money with a space in Buffalo than any other department, I expect them to give way to you cheerfully; on the other hand, when we need those facilities to keep our elevators and lake ports open, it will make the business more money to keep moving the grain to its ultimate destination, than by letting the plants become plugged. . . . All I am trying to preach is good teamwork . . . not to look at any of these problems from the narrow and selfish viewpoint.

John Sr.'s words were an articulate description of John Jr.'s endless belt.

This was different from the past. Managers at individual locations previously had the motivation of success shown by their own individual accounts. Now they were being asked to merge their own results into the overall Company profit. Whether they would continue to feel the individual responsibility that so characterized the past was a moot question.

Tweeden then complained about the slowness of Duluth in responding to suggested Cargill offers in Buffalo, writing John Sr.: "Mr. Heywood of James Richardson & Son of Montreal called me up the other day and I will try to give you his words as nearly as possible. He stated, 'I like you fellows at Buffalo and would like to trade with you very much, but it is almost impossible to do so. When I call you on the phone and ask for bids, part of the time you don't know what you have to sell and have no idea at what price you will sell it. . . . When I do give you a bid, I do not hear from you for several hours and sometimes not until the next day.' " Tweeden suggested a process by which Duluth would give Buffalo some limits but then a free hand to trade. He continued: "We note from your letter that they find it irritating to have offers come in that do not represent the market. It is still more irritating to us to call up our trade and not have any limits or prices."[19]

Tweeden's evident abilities in managing the Buffalo office already had been rewarded in 1926 by his appointment as a vice president in the Cargill Grain Company, one of the subsidiaries of the Elevator Company. This was somewhat surprising in that the previous year Tweeden had made a major mistake; he had been unaware that an elevator in Lockport, New York, was going into bankruptcy, and his inattention had resulted in Cargill having considerable grain tied up in the bankruptcy process. The incident happened while John Sr. was in Europe, and Daniel MacMillan, John Sr.'s brother, responded to Tweeden about the "humiliation you feel in relation to this event." Daniel continued, in words reminiscent of his brother:

The truth is, at one time or another, in one form or another, this had to happen, to round out your experience and season your judgment. . . . I am the last man to condone carelessness, or encourage lack of ceaseless vigilance, but nevertheless I realize that misadventures do happen . . . in the careers of the best of men. . . . Ponder well the circumstances, and then apply the measure of your increased experience and knowledge to future emergencies—forget the balance. That you should keenly feel your trouble is natural, but in reality it is no more than to say that you take honest pride in your efforts to accomplish results, and this is the best that can be said of any man . . . don't brood on what has happened.

Daniel could not resist a caution: "One word more: Don't do anything away from the usual during J. H.'s absence without consulting us."[20]

National Farm Issues—Glut Again?

For agriculture, the first half of the decade of the 1920s had been unsettled and filled with acrimony. The "farm problem" continued on through the decade but with a considerably lower profile. Surplus-control legislative proposals along the lines of the original McNary-Haugen bill continued to come forward; the 1924 version came within 36 votes of passage in the House of Representatives. This close outcome brought into being a number of new national agricultural policy organizations. In November 1924, President Coolidge convened a National Agricultural Conference, but no direct legislation came out of this. An alternative plan for surplus disposal, a scheme to use customs debentures to subsidize agricultural exports, was suggested in 1926. When the plan got to Congress, it failed, as did similar versions in 1928 and 1929. Another version of the McNary-Haugen bill also failed, vetoed by President Coolidge.

The grain trade itself remained reasonably stable during the mid-1920s in terms of production and price, both nationally and worldwide. Of course, substantial internal disparities can occur within a stable trend line,

Some folks don't know how to appreciate good news.

Ding Darling, September 16, 1927 (by permission of the University of Iowa Libraries [Iowa City]).

and there were these anomalies in regional and local patterns all over the world. For example, there was a serious rust problem in parts of the United States wheat crop in 1926 and 1927, yet the totals were not seriously affected.

In 1928, however, there was an event in world grain trade so momentous that it would affect world agriculture well into the next decade. In that year the world wheat crop turned out to be stunning, by far the largest in history. The United States Department of Agriculture estimated it to be 4,760 million bushels, an increase of more than 8 percent over the next-highest postwar crop, which was, importantly, the previous year, 1927. The 1928 total was even 10 percent over the largest prewar crop, that of 1915.

The reasons for this huge crop were largely fortuitous. Acreage had increased but only modestly. Yields also rose, helped greatly by widespread good weather. Not only was United States production up, so was that of

Somebody's likely to have a pig to pay for!

Ding Darling, February 17, 1928 (by permission of the University of Iowa Libraries [Iowa City]).

Canada, Australia and Argentina, as well as of Hungary, Bulgaria, Yugoslavia, Romania and the Soviet Union in Eastern Europe, together with that of France and Germany, the two largest producers in Western Europe. The yield in India, a major producer, was down, but most of the rest of the world's producers added to the surplus.

Demand for wheat was good in 1928 but could not prevent a massive carryover. Analysts at Stanford University's Food Research Institute concluded, gloomily: "While consumption was undeniably heavy, it was not heavy enough to prevent a striking upbuilding of stocks . . . particularly in the United States and Canada . . . one of the outstanding features of the crop year. It assumes special importance because, thus far in the crop year 1929–30, a short world wheat crop in 1929 has not resulted in as high a level of wheat prices as many have anticipated; and the exceptionally large carryover out of 1928–29 has undoubtedly contributed to this situation."[21]

In sum, though production totals were down in 1929, the surplus remained huge. The Great Depression was just around the corner. That the world was absorbing a glut of wheat boded ill for world agriculture in the 1930s.

Overall, Cargill Elevator Company performance was adequate all through the second half of the 1920s. In the four crop years 1925–1926 through 1928–1929, the Company averaged just over half a million dollars in net earnings, and with the conservative dividend policy, net worth grew modestly from just over $4 million in the first of these crop years to $4.8 million in the last. In that last crop year of 1928–1929, just before the crash, the Company had continued to purchase at the 1927–1928 level (61.8 million bushels of all grains), but there were portents embedded in this overall figure. Perhaps most striking was the tremendous jump in durum pur-

But the patient is desperate enough to try anything once.

Ding Darling, May 24, 1928 (by permission of the University of Iowa Libraries [Iowa City]).

chases of 15.6 million bushels, up from 3.4 million the previous year. Sales of durum were also strong, emblematic, of course, of the stronger export demand, especially from Italy and other pasta-consuming countries.

Another figure of importance, particularly given the imminence of the depression, was the level of credit required to finance these larger purchases (and longer-term storage). For the crop year 1928–1929, Cargill's yearly average of notes payable was over $12 million, by far the largest to date; the maximum that calendar year, and also the highest ever, was $16.7 million (on October 31).[22] A banking crisis was coming with this depression; Cargill's relation to its outside financiers would be crucial.

Changes in Personnel

There were important personnel developments in the late 1920s; the first involved John B. Hawley. In the story of the internal revolt in the preceding chapter, Jack Hawley's name was prominent. He was John Jr.'s close friend; the two actually had formed a company, Hawley Inventions, of which John Jr. was president and director. Further, there appeared to be a MacMillan involvement in another Jack Hawley company, an operating company called Northern Pump.

The doubts about Hawley's role in the 1925 revolt and his initiation of Fred and Emma Hanchette's sale of their Cargill Securities stock had long since dissipated. Since then, Hawley had been doing consulting for Cargill Elevator on washer pumps at Elevator K in Superior; Lindahl had written to John Sr. in March 1928: "The more I see of Mr. Hawley, the more I think he is a mighty fine man, and knows his business thoroughly." Lindahl particularly praised his diplomacy.

But later that year, diplomacy failed. In late November 1928, John Sr. noted in his diary: "Hawley makes demand for settlement." A few days before, Hawley had been invited to the Spooner, Wisconsin, fishing camp of the MacMillans. Both John Sr. and John Jr. were there too. John Sr. had helped to finance the Hawley companies and now did not agree with the reconciliation suggested by Hawley, nor with some of Hawley's tactics in the business. In John Sr.'s early December diary entry, the result of the conversation was put bluntly: "Made settlement with Jack Hawley. Haven't words strong enough to express my contempt of him."

Given John Sr.'s support of Hawley until then, these were severe words. John Sr. followed this with a memorandum to all members of the Cargill Elevator management, stating that Hawley had been "dismissed" as consulting engineer and that Cargill employees were to "have no further communications of any kind with him, nor allow any of your employees to do so." Hawley was not even permitted to enter the premises. John Jr. resigned his positions in Hawley Inventions that same day. From that moment, the two MacMillans remained distant from Hawley.[23]

A further sad event relating to the principals in the 1925 events happened in late August 1929, when Fred Hanchette died of angina. (George Cargill, the son of Will, also had died, in 1927, at 32 years of age). Within the organization, A. W. Prime retired from the Company in 1929; his hearing acuity had deteriorated, enough to make it difficult for him to hear the trading signals in the pit. John Sr. diplomatically suggested that Prime step down, and he readily accepted, the Board voting him half pay (there was no formal retirement plan for employees at that time.)[24]

Meanwhile, in a further centralizing step, John Jr. brought his and Austen's colleague from the British Columbia timber operation, Frank Neilson, to La Crosse in 1926 (after a disastrous fire had destroyed the logging camp and nearby timber), to work with the bus operation that had been mounted to supplement the La Crosse & Southeastern Railway. Then, in 1929, John Jr. moved Neilson to Minneapolis to assume a newly created post: superintendent of all terminals. This was at the time when terminal capacity was expanding. It should be noted, too, that Neilson's post was a line assignment, reporting directly to John Sr. In the process, the traditional role of the branch manager with the terminal(s) in his area (e.g., Lindahl with Ed McManus at the Superior, Wisconsin, terminals) was lessened.[25]

John Jr. expanded his own duties in 1928 with the assumption of responsibility for all grains. Julius Hendel was more involved with him than ever as his alter ego. With the major upward movement of grain buying in 1928 and 1929, John Jr. was complimented in the Board minutes of August 13, 1929, for "the brilliant showing of the wheat account" (such encomiums had never been laid upon the record like this) and promoted to vice president.

Export Fobbing, International Thrust

The most striking feature of the 1920s for Cargill was its heightened interest in export fobbing. In late 1927, John Jr. made another extensive trip, which included both New York and Montreal, and came back more enthusiastic than ever about the potentials of fobbing. John Sr. told of this in a long letter to Lindahl:

... he [John Jr.] found that it was possible to sell winter wheat fob. Montreal when we could not make sales cif., and he sold a small amount that way. Also he learned that the grain merchants of Chicago and Milwaukee are selling fob., as in that way they can get a better price, which more than compensates for the bother. The main point is that there are many exporters who cannot tie up their capital in cif. grain, but in buying it fob, they can turn their money over at once, and it rather broadens your market, and gives you a chance to do business, whereas the other way there would be nothing doing at all . . . it may broaden your opportunities, and it will tend to lessen your competition, and give you the field more and more to yourself at the Head of the Lakes.

The reasons for this important trend lay in part in the residual effects on the grain trade from World War I; Charles Kuhlmann analyzed this in 1929 in his well-known book *The Development of the Flour Milling Industry in the United States*. Before the war, shipments to Europe, for example, were CIF, with credit for two or three months. The shipper obtained a through bill of lading from the transporter, took his draft to the bank and sold it. He then had his money. The war disrupted the equation from both sides. The European buyer was not willing to take his chances buying for a long time ahead. And his credit sometimes was not as good, so the shipper was not certain the draft would be paid. While some old, established firms in England and Scandinavia were still sold CIF, now shipments went forward only on bank credits with a guarantee. This, in time, led to concentration of export business in New York (and in Montreal to a lesser degree); the through bill of lading was dropped, and fobbing became a preferred mechanism.

John Sr., in his letter to Lindahl, also commented on another related move by several of Cargill's arch-competitors: "There is one other factor in this situation. Some of these larger concerns are opening offices in the west, as a result of having to tie up their money. You have the Continental now in Duluth, and you are quite apt to have Dreyfus. By refusing to sell these people grain the way they prefer to buy it, you are quite apt to intensify your local competition . . . the main point is to be able to reach the exporters who cannot finance these cif. trades, and in this way be able to sell where otherwise you would find no market at all."

The same approximate letter had gone forth to Prime; now both he and Lindahl responded—negatively. A particular trade on rye had been suggested to Lindahl; he rejected the notion: "I do not think we need it at all on this rye. We can make just as much money, keep your transactions and get it all cleaned up when the boat leaves port, and we have no trouble making sales of all the rye we can get a hold of." To paraphrase Lindahl, take your profit at your own location—do not move down the chain and take further responsibilities. Prime had much the same philosophy: "There might be a little something in this for us. However, we have always figured and figure today that the way to do business here at the head of the lakes is cif Buffalo, Lake Ports or Bay Ports. That is about as far as we want to see our barley."

Only after many months of prompting did either Lindahl or Prime begin to look favorably on the fobbing concept. John Jr. wrote his father in early 1929: "I have been very much gratified at the interest Lindahl has been taking in our fobbing business. The last few days he has done nothing but bombard me as to what our costs are and how we figure this and figure that. I am very much in hopes that we can get him started on his rye."[26]

By this time, the reciprocal response of the European competitors—integration backward into the Middle West—had heightened John Jr.'s concerns, which he elaborated in a long letter to his father, in March 1929: "These tremendous surplus stocks are all very well for the carrying charge," he began, "but they certainly kill all merchandising." The single positive exception was export durum (the 15.5 million bushels of purchases, up from 3.4 million the previous year, was noted earlier). But here a startling new inroad had been made. John Jr. continued:

I secured some very interesting figures from Bolan [B. J. Bolan, manager of the Cargill Grain Co. Ltd. office in Montreal, which opened in September 1928]. I asked him to make an estimate of the durum shipments from Canadian ports for this year by firms, and his results are as follows:

Continental	35%
Dreyfuss	28%
Bunge	22%
All Others	15%
TOTAL	100% (About 32 million bushels to date)

This certainly provides food for thought and it shows what has been happening to Barnes, Malden, Bodman, Norris and miscellaneous exporters without European organizations. The discouraging feature of it is that the three firms in question are showing less and less of a tendency to buy from us. The Continental will buy from us only when we are several cents under the price at which they can make it, while Bunge has his own man in Duluth and has not bought a pound of us this winter and Dreyfuss bids us in full cargo lots, so that trading with him is worse than with Hecker. The only really satisfactory trades we make are with all others and you can see that they are fast dwindling in importance.

It looks to me as if we have got to find some way of competing with Continental, Bunge and Dreyfuss on more liberal terms. One feature that worries me is that the Continental have never hesitated to go into the elevator business. They operate an elevator in St. Louis . . . and I am very much worried lest if we let them continue in Duluth that they will enter the elevator business there and if they do Dreyfuss and Bunge will have to follow.[27]

This concern first had been identified earlier in the decade, at the time of the Taylor & Bournique acquisition; now, these figures confirmed a *major* inroad by the competitors. So it was not just the Cargill fobbing itself that was so striking—it was the downstream movement in general. And it was not only the forward integration that John Jr. was engaging in with his endless-belt applications but an equally potent backward integration in the *other* direction, to compete with the Europeans as they moved into inland United States and Canada.

Cargill had begun the decade looking eastward, but its definition of eastward at that time had been primarily looking to Buffalo, with some tangential interest in the other cities that had been brought into this sphere by the Taylor & Bournique acquisition. John Sr. had continued his mistrust of Chicago and unwillingness to have the Company go there, although John Jr. had had desultory discussions with Armour about a terminal as early as 1927. In a sense, Cargill had bypassed Chicago and gone directly to the East, in the process making itself much more of a national concern.

The next logical move was to extend the export fobbing one further step by making contacts abroad (and perhaps follow with a physical presence there). John Jr. had made an extensive trip to Latin America in 1926. In June 1929, he left for Europe with a lengthy agenda of contacts (and "raced" through the trip, according to his mother, "without stopping to see any of the beauties of it"). Julius Hendel would make his own trip later in the year, hoping to include Russia.[28]

A Transition Begins

These tentative steps Cargill had taken to move abroad turned out to be irreversible. An important conceptual move had been made in the 1920s. Cargill had metamorphosed from an essentially Midwest company, operating regionally and with its people holding regional perspectives, to, first, a national organization (through the Taylor & Bournique acquisition and its attendant features) and then to an international company. Collaterally, a sharp change had taken place in the leadership of the company, which was going through its own generational transition. A new, younger group had taken over, with the rise to major responsibility of Ed Grimes, the important management role at the country elevators of Austen Cargill, the strong technical base brought by Frank Nielson, the unique statistical and financial contributions of Cargill MacMillan, the trading skills of Julius Hendel, the shipping network of F. J. Hays, and, most important, the general management role increasingly being assumed by John MacMillan, Jr. The goals and values of the Company had been self-consciously developed and articulated by its chief executive officer, John MacMillan, Sr. He had made the Company a reality of what he, John MacMillan, defined it to be. Now, John MacMillan, Jr., already was redefining this in his own personal image.

PART FOUR

IDEAS AND INNOVATIONS— THE 1930s

The wheat pit, Minneapolis grain exchange, c. 1942.

Location unknown

CHAPTER NINE

Hoover's Farm Board

O n November 6, 1928, Herbert C. Hoover was elected President of the United States. Hoover captured 444 electoral votes, and Alfred E. Smith could claim only 87. The Republicans also maintained control of both houses of Congress. To achieve this impressive victory, Hoover had made promises during the presidential campaign that he needed to fulfill. Some were to farmers.

Agriculture had commanded attention all through the 1920s, ever since the farmers realized that they could not continue the halcyon days under the special conditions of World War I and the immediate postwar period. The deflation in the 1920–1921 downturn had been especially severe for agriculture. However, based on the terms of trade (the ratio of prices received by farmers to the prices paid by them), by 1925, farmers were about where they were at the end of the war. This index fell back, but even in 1928 it was still not far from the level of the prosperous prewar years.

The several McNary-Haugen bills of that decade contemplated using the power of the federal government to dump enough domestic agricultural surplus abroad to raise prices in the domestic market, with the loss on the exports being paid by farmers themselves through an "equalization" fee. Other bills proposed to use tariff receipts to pay subsidies on agricultural exports; these came to be known as "export debenture" plans. Laced throughout these debates were new concepts of "parity." It was argued that agriculture was *entitled* to its fair share of the national income by keeping the farmers in parity with the prices that had prevailed in the years 1910–1914.

Herbert Hoover fundamentally opposed these proposals; he had stumped in the 1928 presidential campaign for the traditional American way of free competition and private initiative. His "rugged individualism" speech just before the election had become famous. Throughout the campaign, Hoover pictured agriculture as organizationally backward, a sick industry, because it had gone to the extreme of individualism. He felt this bred destructive competition, abetted by a wasteful and inefficient marketing system. Farmers needed effective forms of collective action, he believed, and this led him to emphasize cooperatives. If the existing cooperative system could be strengthened, he concluded, it would lead to "orderly marketing," a term popularized in this period.

In the 1928 election campaign, agricultural issues were pressed, and Hoover responded by proposing a federal Farm Board, an institution that he felt would strengthen cooperative marketing while at the same time rejecting, as he put it, the "statist" approaches of the supporters of the McNary-Haughen bills and others. Shortly after his inauguration in March 1929, Hoover convened a special session of the 71st Congress to deal with farm relief and to consider some substantial changes in the tariff. The export debenture plan was advanced once more by the farm bloc but, faced with Hoover's hostility toward it, was finally rejected. On June 15, 1929, Congress passed and the President signed the Agricultural Marketing Act that was to provide the basic agricultural policy of the Hoover regime.

The Act eliminated the subsidy and price-fixing principles of the McNary-Haugen and the export debenture plans, but its provisions were even more significant in terms of a basic shift in United States agricultural policy. The federal Farm Board was charged with promoting the marketing of farm commodities primarily through agricultural cooperatives and certain government-established stabilization corporations. A revolving fund of $500 million was put in the hands of the Board, to be used for low-interest loans to the cooperatives and cooperative-owned stabilization corporations for the "orderly" purchasing, handling and selling of surpluses. Not only grains but cotton and some livestock were included as well. Underlying this was Hoover's belief that if cooperatives controlled a large share of the crop, they *could* influence prices.[1] If, indeed, Hoover was dedicated to "rugged individualism," the Agricultural Marketing Act version of this seemed destined to be a hybrid variety, collective rather than individual and, with the ruggedness dampened on any downside price risk by the use of the revolving fund to buy and hold grain, in the process hoping to hold prices up.

The crop season of 1929–1930 had barely begun when the the Act was passed. So the distressing events of the Great Crash in October 1929 were not yet anticipated. To the farmers, it appeared that they had realized most of their wishes—much of the language of the new legislation was similar to the old McNary-Haugen bill. One agrarian leader said it was "like sprinkling the stall with straw to make the old cow feel at home."[2]

It did not look this way to the grain trade. Although Hoover had condemned the Democratic platform as state socialism, having the Farm Board turn to the cooperative movement seemed to the private grain trade to be a stab in the back. Hoover's new Secretary of Agriculture, Arthur M. Hyde, seemed to be a reasonable choice. The *Northwestern Miller* admitted that he "was not associated as a partisan with a radical farm relief crowd." Hyde was an ex-governor of Missouri with little past involvement in farm policy. John Jr. wrote his father that the secretary-designate "could not be expected to be anything like as friendly to the grain exchanges as was Wallace, which does not sound any too good." This was Henry A. Wallace, a Republican aspirant to the post who later switched to the Democrats; he was a son of Henry C. Wallace, the Secretary of Agriculture in the early 1920s. However, Hoover's appointments to the Farm Board were felt to be more positive—"little nourishment to any of the pink tinted farm relief leaders," said the *Northwestern Miller*, which believed that Alexander Legge, former president of the International Harvester Company and named as head of the Farm Board, was "a man of the highest business standing, capable, honest and possessing the confidence of business."[3]

Still, the grain trade felt itself threatened by the Act. John Sr. captured the prevailing mood of the industry in a letter to J. Morris Barker (the son of Margaret "Aunt Maggie" Barker), who was then administrative assistant to William E. Hull, United States representative from Illinois: "I have realized ever since the Republican party and Mr. Hoover put themselves on record for this character of legislation that we could not expect anything better than this bill. . . . It is economic folly. . . . I feel it is going to bring the country to the verge of disaster in the end." Cargill MacMillan verged on alarmist; the Act, he felt, "presents a menace to the whole structure of American political philosophy of the very gravest nature" and to the "Anglo-Saxon code of law."

Barker, closer to Cargill's generation than to John Sr.'s, tactfully downplayed their views, writing John Sr.: "I can remember Uncle Sam [Sam Cargill] saying in 1895 that there was absolutely no future for the grain business, but there have been prosperous times since then . . . although business may be done in an entirely different way. . . . John Jr. and Cargill, who are young enough to adjust themselves to new conditions, will live to see prosperity crown the efforts of those who are intelligently sticking to the business. It is possible that the wish is Father of the idea."[4]

The 1928–1929 crop year reinforced John Sr.'s more pessimistic view. Despite a drought and lowered United States production, the impact of the stunningly large 1928 wheat crop kept the surplus high. Wide publicity given to the Agricultural Marketing Act had the effect of holding off buyers, both domestic and foreign, who anticipated a possible price drop. John Sr. wrote T. F. Baxter, his Boston banking friend, "instead of attempting to clean up this year, we will keep our terminal elevators filled . . . we will show an enormous inventory and corresponding enormous bills payable. This is, of course, thoroughly understood by our bankers."

The call of the community welfare doctors.

Ding Darling, December 11, 1930 (by permission of the University of Iowa Libraries [Iowa City]).

Cargill's June 30, 1929, year-end closing figures corroborated this: inventories had been $3.5 million on the same date the previous year and now were $12.6 million; the notes payable had been $2.3 million the year before and now were $11.5 million. The "plugged" terminals brought the Company large carrying charges, which earlier John Sr. had told A. M. Prime were "wonderful" but now just made him nervous. Soon he began to push John Jr. to cut back on fobbing: "I have limited Julius in net increase . . . of the wheat account . . . to just such business as represents turnover. The sales which he made yesterday were all c.i.f. Buffalo, so that turns itself into money promptly and I prefer to sell that way unless we can get a profit."[5]

The private grain trade distrusted the new law, especially because the apparent guarantee to the farmers of no price declines would artificially preclude price fluctuations—no longer would prices in the United States be subject to normal supply and demand fundamentals (although no similar constraints could, of course, be imposed on foreign markets). For hedgers, this warped the very concept itself, for if prices only moved upward or even remained frozen at the existing level, normal patterns would be distorted.

The early actions of the Farm Board allayed some of these fears. John Sr. wrote John Jr. on July 30 about Alexander Legge's first meeting with a group of 32 farmer-owned grain cooperatives: "There was no abuse to the grain trade at the meeting and . . . I do not believe that they could have adopted any program that would have been any less radical. . . . Mr. Legge made it very clear that the Farm Board have no intention of loaning money except on a basis that will be safe to the government . . . did not intend to go into competition with bankers and others loaning money . . . each corporation would have to utilize all its avenues of credit before it could get any relief from the Farm Board . . . this was a very great shock to existing pools." One of these pools soon came to dominate the cooperatives.

The Birth of "Farmers National"

The Farmers National Grain Corporation was formed in October 1929, a new central organization to bring together existing cooperatively owned elevators, terminals and wheat pools and farmer-directed sales agencies into a single unified marketing organization. In early 1930 centralized units also were formed for cotton and livestock, and later, similar national associations were established for wool, beans, pecans, sugar beets, fruits and vegetables.

Prices began to slide, despite predictions earlier in the year 1929 of an upward trend. Particularly disturbing was a full 8-cent decline in wheat on October 24. When the stock market crash came, on October 29, it fundamentally changed everything. The Senate Committee on Agriculture held hearings, struggling to understand the situation in agriculture. In the process, as *Nation's Business* reported, it inflicted "several days of torture upon Mr. Legge . . . those inquisitors examined all of Mr. Legge's mental and financial joints and expressed contempt and insult for each of them in turn." The Committee urged Legge to be more lenient toward the cooperatives, indeed, to concentrate on them. Legge capitulated.

Now the private grain trade became really worried. Were they to be bypassed in the government price-support efforts? John Sr. issued a widely publicized statement that the Farm Board "price fixing . . . is in utter violation of their pledge" and that "it threatens to destroy all existing agencies and markets." His words were featured on the front page of the November 17, 1929, *Minneapolis Journal*. The Minneapolis Grain Commission Merchants Association contacted Legge four days later: "Any price basis established through the use of government funds should be made free to all farmers, whether or not in the exercise of their individual judgment they decide their interests were best served by membership in a cooperative organization"; otherwise, "all independent elevators together with line elevators cannot operate as grain merchants."

Legge *had* changed his views, for his response was discouragingly cool: "You gave your support to the passage of the Agricultural Marketing Act, therefore it is fair to assume that you knew what the Act contained. However, your telegram might lead to another conclusion. I am, therefore, sending you a copy of the Act, from which you will note that the building up and encouraging of cooperatives is especially enjoined on us." John Sr., shocked by this rejoinder, immediately left for Washington to see Legge personally. He telegraphed John Jr. after the meeting: "Legge very much surprised that the grain trade are excited and worried. Says Farm Board have no thought of injuring those having property interests. Admits their plans might injure commission merchants and speculators as they expect to prevent violent price changes. . . . The radical senators are making it very difficult."

This was cold comfort for MacMillan and his private-sector colleagues. A few weeks later, the Minneapolis private elevator operators complained to Legge that William Kellogg, the head of Farmers National, "intimidated" them, trying to get preferential rates. Legge lashed back, "Some of those chaps up there seem to think that the Lord gave them a special right or franchise to trade or speculate in the farmer's products."

The industry was most galled about the allegation that the private middlemen were somehow less efficient, indeed, even dishonest "monopolists." John Sr. wrote a friend that the trade was "in the remarkable condition of being the most efficient industry probably in America and at the same time the most discredited." Stanford University's *Wheat Studies* analysts agreed about efficiency: "The world over, the wheat trade has operated on a narrow margin of profit under sharp competition . . . the middleman objects to being displaced with the use of government money at a low rate of interest, outside of a competitive determination on the basis of service and efficiency." Yet the producer had a "native right" to market his grain; indeed, he "has the aspiration to market his product even if he does so less efficiently than middlemen."

Alexander Legge did have to live with farm-state senators' hostility toward the private grain trader. Gerald P. Nye, the vocal senator from North Dakota, was quoted widely in the public press on a speech he had made in the Senate that the "grain men were out to wreck the U.S. farm aid program." According to one paper, Nye accused "one company, operating in Minneapolis, Milwaukee and Duluth, of trying to frighten farmers' elevators out of participation in the cooperative efforts undertaken by the Federal Farm Board." This was a reference to a statement made by John Sr. in the Minneapolis paper on November 17, in which he had said, "I am utterly astounded that our Administration should permit so unsound a system to be fastened upon this country. It means that all farmers shall be forced into cooperative concerns, which could only mean pools and monopoly. . . . Monopoly always means waste and inefficiency."

Hostile letters against John Sr. from farmers began appearing in the press. One letter writer asked, "How much grain does Mr. MacMillan produce?" Others complained of the profits of the grain trade. John Sr. reacted defensively, citing the Company's small wheat project at Valier, Montana, and quoting secondhand an elaborate argument that the farm machinery manufacturers were the real culprits, that four of these had combined profits of over $97 million, whereas the grain trade, if it handled one-half of the 1929–1930 wheat crop, would net only about $2 million. John Sr. added, "If the grain trade contributed their services and worked for nothing, the farmer would never know the difference." This was a curious assault by John Sr., for it was an invidious attack on another industry, not in keeping with John Sr.'s usual decorum. He did agree that the mushrooming growth of automobile, truck, tractor and other power machinery on the farm was "a complete revolution" but felt the farm problem could not be solved by political action. Rather, "each farmer must work out his own problem in his own way . . . that is the only safe and sound way of going at it." He defended his own industry by adding: "Unfortunately it has been a popular pastime to chase the grain trade and yet they have been, and still are, the best friends the farmer has ever had. They have given him the most perfect marketing system that has ever been devised." In light of instances over the years where farmers had been taken advantage of by grain traders (see earlier chapters), the word "perfect" seems excessive![6]

Pressures on Legge now became very strong. When the United States Chamber of Commerce condemned "the employment of public funds for the purpose of participation in business in competition with established agencies," Legge felt compelled to make a public statement. In this, he pointed out that "the Board did not alter its policies as a result of a hearing given to the grain trade, nor has the Board agreed to submit its policies to the grain trade before action."

The Legge rejoinder stung the grain trade. Barker wrote John Sr., "The radical farm bunch is not going to be satisfied with anything but the complete annihilation of the old order of carrying on the grain business." Sumner B. "Ted" Young, a friend of the MacMillans and later counsel for Cargill, told Cargill MacMillan, "I have a kind of gloomy foreboding that . . . the grain men will find themselves alone, just as the railroads, the utilities, the packers, and the livestock commission men found themselves all alone when it came their turn to take it on the chin. . . . Congress and the Public have become pretty hard-boiled about putting people out of business."[7]

The messy argument about the Farm Board in Congress, in the press and in the general public now had sharp repercussions in the industry. In late December 1929, a holder of some of Cargill's notes refused to take more from one of Cargill's investment banking intermediaries, Goldman, Sachs & Company: "You may be surprised at our returning . . . the paper. . . . I understand that Mr. MacMillan, who endorsed the paper, is a very high type of person and does exactly as he says he will. However . . . even though they may have hedged a lot of the grain which they have in inventory, their loans are very heavy. . . . If Mr. Legge agrees to make government loans at a considerably lower rate than the market rate which independent concerns must pay, the independents will be competing with the government—possibly to such an extent that they will succumb."

A worried John Sr. quickly suggested a text for the investment bankers', reply: "Loans thru the Farm Board to co-operative farm organizations . . . are not competitive with the grain concerns at all at the present time, and could in no event be a factor until the Farm Board have made their plans and have announced what their purposes will be. This could not possibly apply until the crop which will be marketed in the fall of 1930." John Sr.'s protestations notwithstanding, the loan was denied.[8]

The Farm Board "Bulls the Market"

When the crash occurred in October 1929, the Farm Board extended the loan program on wheat so that growers could hold their own grain to avoid congested grain storage. The large crop carryover had created shortages of storage space in the Midwest and Southwest regions. When vociferous members of the farm bloc advocated that the cooperatives step up their ownership of elevator and terminal space, John Sr. led a group of his industry colleagues in the Northwestern states, in January 1930, to make a publicity-grabbing "tender" to Alexander Legge, the Farm Board chairman, to sell a string of country elevators to the cooperatives: some 275 in Minnesota, 698 in North Dakota, 163 in South Dakota, 173 in Montana, 17 in Iowa and 1 in Nebraska. "The offer is made in good faith," they wrote Legge. "The control of the properties . . . will enable the Farm Board to make a fair trial of its proposed experiment in orderly marketing."

Essentially the same offer had been made by this group to the American Farm Bureau Federation back in 1924, when the Federation was proposing that cooperatives own more elevator space. At that time, too, there had been no intention of following through. Legge saw through the guile of this replay, penning a sarcastic return: "Except for your statement . . . that

"Concerned crowd gathered outside New York Stock Exchange during the 1929 Wall Street Crash" (The Bettmann Archive).

the offer was made in good faith, I would certainly not have taken it seriously. . . . What is there for you to worry about in competition with a bunch of poor farmers who have had but little in the way of a background of experience to support them?" The crocodile-teared offer had backfired. As David Miller, a chronicler of Farm Board history put it, "by February, 1930, the Farm Board and the grain trade were at war."[9]

At this point, another new organization was formed by the government under the aegis of the Agricultural Marketing Act: the Grain Stabilization Corporation. It was to work with the Farmers National Grain Corporation to "stabilize" prices. The Stabilization Corporation was to relieve the farmer cooperatives of their heavy inventories of grain. It was nominally owned by the participating cooperatives, but in reality the Farm Board called all the shots. These two units began to buy aggressively, beginning in mid-February 1930. By late March, they held about 25 million bushels of grain. By the close of the crop year, this was 60 million bushels.

Yet this competition might not have been too severe for the private grain trade—there was still much grain to be purchased from outside the cooperative group—had not some of the Farm Board policies for buying distorted the whole market. An early series of mistakes tarnished the Farm Board's reputation such that it never fully recovered. It announced that it would buy only "country run" wheat at country points under an assumption that the farmers and country elevators needed surcease from their own "glut." However, there was less wheat out there than the Board assumed, and the country prices quickly rose to 10 or 12 cents above terminal prices. The trade immediately responded by shipping grain back to the country, an illogical, ludicrous reversal of the pipeline. Ridiculed for this, the Board soon reversed itself.

The Board then decided to supplement its cash buying by purchasing long futures contracts. Once more, myopia took over—the Board made the inexplicable decision to buy only March and May 1930 wheat futures and only on the Chicago Board of Trade. This contradicted a long-standing pattern in futures markets. In a normal or surplus crop year a "carrying charge" price structure is expected—purchases of grain early in the crop year can be hedged in futures later in the year that carry a higher price. This makes intuitive sense. Physically holding the grain for this part of the crop season involves costs—unloading, storing and outloading costs, as well as insurance—but these costs can be recovered through the "carrying cost" relationship of future prices.

The Farm Board, however, proceeded to act with an apparent belief that its only concern was current price. When it found that its purchases of physical grain were not supporting price, it entered the futures markets in just those two contract months. The *Northwestern Miller* captured the grain traders' fears about this new tactic:

The Federal Farm Board put on its ceremonial hat, took its speculative fortune in its hands and boldly entered the Chicago pit in a belated campaign to bull the wheat market. It did not enter in the fashion of its distinguished predecessors, "Old Hutch," Armour, Leiter, et al, with no incentive but that of personal fortune [but] came down into the pit of iniquity clothed in the mantle of liberty, protected by the shield of equality and waving the sword of fraternity shouting "back to your dens, bears, the co-ops are coming!" It plunged into the fray up to its bureaucratic neck. And it bulled wheat.

The *Wheat Studies* editors were harshly critical: "It is evidently the policy of the Stabilization Corporation to support the price of wheat futures . . . during the trading months of the current crop year, allowing the futures of a new crop to go unsupported. This has the effect of basing the price of futures during the current crop on domestic conditions. . . . leaving the futures of the new crop to be based largely on world conditions . . . In effect, the Grain Stabilization Corporation tries to improve the current price of wheat, allowing the price on the new crop to be determined by developments."[10]

Thus, the Farm Board strategy was short-term. The effect on existing prices was ruinous. The private grain trade had purchased large quantities of grain under the assumption of a carrying cost basis between the early part of the year 1930 and the futures prices of July 1930 and later. When the May price was pushed upward by the Farm Board support efforts, the carrying cost relationship disappeared.

The Farm Board created further consternation by its avowed aim to hold its March wheat contracts until the contract terminated, then take actual grain. Thus, physical grain had to be delivered to Chicago by the shorts to fulfill these contracts. Most of these short contracts were held by private-sector grain traders, but a substantial amount of their physical stock of grain already had been moved forward in the pipeline to eastern terminals. Cargill, its Midwest storage already glutted, had shipped large amounts of grain through the Lakes to the Buffalo and Ogdensburg, New York terminals, paying transportation costs to get it there. If this eastern grain had to be used to fulfill the short contracts, either by physical movement back to Chicago or some compensating trade, the grain traders wanted to recover the transportation costs they had already expended on it. The Farm Board refused to allow this.

The *Wheat Studies* authors called the Farm Board "a cold-blooded super-speculator," a surprisingly subjective comment from the eminent Stanford University group. The press also took up the cudgel for what had been dubbed by many as the Stabilization Corporation's "May Squeeze." It was "a first class way of throwing good money into a bottomless pit," complained *The Nation* on March 26. John Sr., outraged, fired off missives to everyone in Washington about the Farm Board "squeeze." In a telegram to Walter H. Newton, secretary to President Hoover, he compared the Farm Board efforts to "those employed by the Armour Grain Co. in their spectacular, if disreputable, career." In another telegram to Secretary of Agriculture Arthur Hyde, he fumed, "We are astonished that your Board could be a party to such a flagrant manipulation."

John Sr. had been attempting to run this public relations campaign from his vacation hotel in California, where he went every winter. Now John Jr. joined the effort. Clearly, he was more combative in his approach. In the thick of the battle, on February 3, 1930, he telegraphed his father about a grain trade lobbyist's admonition that they should be more temperate lest they "needlessly irritate the Board." John Jr. vehemently disagreed with the lobbyist: "This would be a serious mistake . . . now that the Board is showing signs of being embarrassed this is the proper time of making public our statement. Suggest you wire these gentlemen to stiffen them up." In Bozeman, Montana, the next day, a John Jr. speech harshly denounced the Farm Board, so much so that the press in that area began "giving unfortunate type publicity" about John Jr., according to one of his friends.

Others were concerned not to alienate the government; the Chicago Board of Trade had even decided against forming a regular standing committee on the issue because, according to B. H. Woodworth (one of the two signers with John Sr. of the country elevator proposal), "it would become known and would be assumed that the committee was formed for the purpose of antagonizing the Farm Board." John Jr. believed this was temporizing, and it infuriated him. He wrote his father of his irritation with the Minneapolis Chamber of Commerce: "Our Publicity Committee here has completely reversed itself and is now refusing to give out anything which in any way looks like criticism of the Farm Board or its policies. I am completely disgusted with the conduct of our Anti-Farm Board Campaign . . . we are getting nowhere. I still suspect that Mr. Jaffray and the President must have come to some agreement to the effect that the Farm Board would leave us alone if we would leave them alone, altho everyone denies it."

With criticism mounting, the Farm Board began to ease off on its purchases. John Sr. urged Walter Newton, secretary and administrative assistant to President Hoover, to suggest to Legge "a formal announcement by the Board that it is not their intention to run a corner in any market or any month and that they intend to do their utmost to see that relationships approximate normal." Legge responded, "I do not see how we can undertake to restore the parity between May and July contracts, as July is to all intents and purposes a new crop month. What the Stabilization Corporation is doing at the present time is removing the surplus of the 1929 crop only." John Jr. immediately went to Washington to see Legge about what Cargill felt were his negative responses. It did not work. Legge made it plain that he felt Cargill was exerting untoward pressure on the Farm Board by persuading outsiders to write critical letters. John Jr. wrote Legge on his return to Minneapolis: "Both Mr. Lindahl and I were very much concerned with your statement that on our advice our customers and friends had been wiring the President and other officials. . . . Attached hereto is a copy of the message sent to these people. You can see that our advice was to wire Mr. Barnes as chairman of the United States Chamber of Commerce rather than to any government official." John Jr.'s statement, however, was not really in line with the facts. Legge, apparently wanting to cool the rhetoric, answered, "While we cannot agree with some of your criticisms and suggestions, yet we are always glad to have the opinion of experienced people in the trade like yourself."[11]

The rapprochement did not last. At the United States Chamber of Congress annual meeting, April 30–May 2, both Legge and President Hoover addressed the gathering. A dramatic confrontation resulted. Between the time of Legge's speech defending the Farm Board and Hoover's address, the Chamber membership body passed a resolution, introduced by Minneapolis grain traders, calling for the Board to halt loans to the cooperatives and to cease their buying and selling for "stabilization." Reporters besieged Legge for a reaction, and he responded that the Chamber was "for something to help the farmer only until they find out it works." Legge also acknowledged that it was "much easier to deal with an enemy who is squarely against you than one who pretends to be friendly but fights behind your back." Hoover's speech played down the Chamber's repudiation of Legge, but damage had been done.

The farmers, however, were delighted with Legge's tweaking of the businessmen's noses, and farm organizations and the farm press responded enthusiastically. Charles Hurst, president of the Iowa Farm Bureau Federation, even introduced some midwestern chauvinism, calling the Chamber resolution a "direct affront" to the farmers of Iowa and further evidence that that organization was willing to subjugate agriculture "to the personal interests of the industrialists east of the Mississippi River."[12]

By midspring, rumors surfaced of an incipient drought, and the resultant scare boosted wheat prices for a while, easing some of the differentials. By July 1930, the Farm Board buying had been cut back, and its influence on the market was reduced. Morris Barker wrote John Sr. on July 2: "I doubt if you will ever have a repetition of what happened last year . . . they are pretty well inclined to let the grain trade function through the regular channel. Another case of the burnt child fearing the fire."[13]

"Delivery" at the Chicago Board of Trade

The Farm Board concerns were momentarily supplanted by another issue in the fall of 1930, this time relating to the Chicago Board of Trade. Although not momentous in the overall scheme of things, it led to mounting antagonism by Cargill toward the CBOT.

When it was rumored that the CBOT was planning a tightening of delivery rules for grain being tendered in Chicago in fulfillment of futures contracts—a plan that would disadvantage companies like Cargill, still with no Chicago office—John Sr. made a decision to go over the head of the CBOT to the federal government itself. He sent the complaint to Dr. J. W. T. Duvel, who was chief of the Grain Futures Administration in the United States Department of Agriculture. After urging Duvel that "nothing should be done that would in any way make it more difficult to deliver grain on hedging contracts," John Sr. mounted a biting attack: "There is an element in Chicago that has always been opposed to the existing rule because they are interested purely in manipulative tactics on the theory that the hedger had to hedge off-grades of grain and has grain hedged that they cannot afford to deliver in Chicago, and therefore under conditions of small stocks that they can squeeze the hedger by buying up a greater line of futures than is possible to deliver."

The proposed new rule *was* meant to narrow delivery possibilities; "grain in cars" deliveries during the last three days of a particular contract would have to go to a "regular" warehouse. The CBOT required bonds to be posted, and the warehouse had to be on water as well as rail, "approachable by vessels of ordinary draft." John Sr. pointed out to Duvel, "there are only about fifteen million bushels of 'regular' storage in Chicago. At one time last year there were over 240 million bushels of open wheat contracts alone, to say nothing of oats, corn and rye . . . if the hedger is not properly protected . . . there is always the possibility of squeezing him and without permanent benefit to anyone." He concluded: "If you will talk with the bankers of this country you will find that the whole basis of credit operations for the movement of the crops is based upon the theory that hedging contracts represent really price insurance . . . if anything is done to break down the present theory of hedging contracts . . . it might demoralize the credit on which the crop movement is dependent."

A few days later John Sr. sent the same letter to a number of bankers and also to Arthur Hyde, the Secretary of Agriculture. Hyde asked the CBOT to postpone of the vote. The Exchange leadership ignored Hyde and voted the more restrictive changes on October 6. The day after, John Sr. wrote J. M. Barker: "The Chicago Board of Trade yesterday passed two drastic changes in the rules which are giving us a great deal of concern, as it stops the possibility of making deliveries in Chicago excepting in store in public elevators . . . we are fearful of continued efforts to manipulate there . . . it simply kills Chicago as a hedging market."

John Sr.'s dire predictions about damage to hedging in Chicago did not prove well-founded, and trading continued more or less as in the past. But the fact that the CBOT was willing to push its own agenda, ignoring out-of-town interests and despite exhortations from the Secretary of Agriculture, seemed to the Cargill group a cautionary portent of future relationships with the Exchange.[14]

International Complications

The Farm Board's domestically oriented policy troubled John Sr. on another score. He wrote George Roberts, a banking friend in New York City: "We have created untold ill feeling in Europe . . . they have . . . enlarged their own grain acreage . . . to take care of home requirements . . . [and] have developed trade relations with Argentina and Australia to get such surpluses they must from those countries."

There also was a surprising new international entrant into the United States grain trading scene—the Soviet Union. In Josef Stalin's Russia, the First Five-Year Plan had required purchase of great volumes of machinery and machine tools from other countries; the only ready currency the Soviet Union had at that time for payment was its wheat. Despite a devastating famine in the Ukraine involving wide starvation, Stalin made the calculated decision to send great volumes of the country's grain abroad. The need for hard currency for machinery led the Russians to throw more and more wheat into the market, causing prices to sag more and more. This brought outrage and opprobrium from the rest of the world's wheat sellers. But Stalin was quoted in the *New York Times*, in an interview with the newspaper *Nichi Nichi*, as responding: "We can afford to supply wheat to foreign countries at lower prices than rival countries because we do away with all speculators and brokers. It is ridiculous to accuse us of dumping, since we do not sell our wheat any lower than production cost."

As part of their strategy, the Russians began to make short sales on the Chicago Board of Trade. In a four-day period, September 8–11 (1930), they quietly sold some 7.5 million bushels of wheat futures, apparently as hedges for extensive cash sales they were contracting for in Europe. While the totals were themselves not great, when it became known that the Russians were the shorts, a hue and cry arose. Herbert Hoover decided to make an issue of it and instructed Secretary of Agriculture Hyde to condemn the sales as an "injury" to the American farmer and to press the CBOT to abolish Russian use of the futures markets. The CBOT diplomatically sidestepped a confrontation with Russia by passing a resolution (on September 27, 1930) condemning short sales by *any* foreign government.

Many in the grain trade disagreed with this, arguing that the Russians had just as much right to trade in the futures market as the International Harvester Company had to sell farm machinery to the Soviets, a poorly disguised allusion to Alexander Legge's old company. In both cases, the purpose was producing grain in competition with United States farmers. The *Northwestern Miller* remained intransigent about the Soviets, holding that "what applies to Russia applies to no other nation or people . . . its purpose is to destroy all order, as we understand order. . . . It has repudiated its country's debts, sought by devious means to break down the governments of other nations and openly boasts of its purpose to wreck the scheme of capitalism upon which the economics of the rest of world are founded."

The Russians stopped using the CBOT, but they continued to disrupt the European grain markets. The Five-Year Plan was immutable in terms of needs, and grain was to be the mechanism—it was one of the few concrete assets the country had at this time. Art was another; at the same time,

Andrew Mellon bought some of Russia's great treasures for the new National Gallery he was sponsoring in Washington, D.C.

Julius Hendel left for Europe in January 1930. He wanted to see his relatives in Russia during the trip and had gone through considerable trouble in Washington to obtain a visa, not an easy thing for an American citizen with Russian relatives. John Sr. wrote Hendel in mid-February that "this Russian business is paralyzing" and asked Hendel: "If you go to Russia, try to find out what the prospects are, for they are really putting this program across, but be sure you do not go unless you get guarantees that you will be able to come back."

Once in Europe, Hendel received further warnings about the threat of not being able to get back out of Russia and finally decided not to cross the Russian border. It was a sad decision—his mother and father were still living there. He had not seen them since he came to the United States prior to World War I (Hendel and his wife finally did make a trip to Russia in the early 1960s, but by this time both of his parents had died).[15]

The Bogey of Drought

In the early 1930s, drought baked the land, making a "dust bowl" out of whole sections of midwestern and southwestern United States. Well remembered are the troubling pictures of farms with no vegetation, blowing dust encircling everything, the "Okies" heading west in their ramshackle vehicles. The years so indelibly imprinted as "dust bowl" years were 1934 and 1936; history does not as readily recall the "Great Drought of 1930." Yet it was almost as serious.

In the summer of 1930 there was an intense heat wave, coupled with a widespread lack of rain. The Weather Bureau called it "the most severe . . . in the climatological history of the United States." Arkansas was the worst hit, but the central states in the Mississippi and Ohio river valleys were also deeply affected. Rivers were depleted—the Mississippi River (without today's lock and dam system) had become "a comparative trickle"—and by late summer, wells were drying up and farmers were panicking about water for their stock.

Drought relief was imperative. Fortunately, or so it was believed, the country had one of the greatest humanitarian "food relief" managers in the world—its President, Herbert Hoover. Hoover acted quickly, calling a conference of the governors of the afflicted states to establish a relief organization. However, Hoover wanted to minimize the role of the federal government. He chose instead to "mobilize and organize" state and local entities and, particularly, to depend on private agencies.

The Red Cross was asked to take a central role. Already efforts had been made to reduce freight rates for the counties most affected, and the Red

Cross attempted to provide intermediate credit for the strapped farmers. But the needs outstripped the resources under this approach. Red Cross efforts to feed the needy were rapidly being overwhelmed. Hoover then asked for a federal appropriation for the Red Cross, but at this point he committed a serious blunder. Rather than directing that the appropriation could be used for all needs, Hoover stipulated that none of the money could be spent for food for the needy, to avoid the appearance of a federally funded "dole." Over the next several months, there was a tremendous political backlash about Hoover's approach. One could use relief funds, for example, to feed rabbits—"Hoover's hogs"—while people were starving.

So the crop year 1930–1931 was a disastrous one in terms of human suffering, and Hoover came in for harsh criticism. David E. Hamilton, a historian of the Hoover period, wrote: "The damage to his reputation was in part the product of his inflexibility, his refusal to admit failure, and his lack of political acumen. His arguments that Red Cross handouts were not charity and that government loans for food were tantamount to a dole made little sense and were wholly unconvincing. . . . His obsession with the supposed benefits of proper organization blinded him to the desperate plight of thousands of Americans."[16] It was especially incongruous in light of his feeding of the hungry in Europe during World War I.

This situation might have helped the agricultural surplus: the drought would cut agricultural production and therefore the oversupply. The drought damaged the corn, the cotton and the hay and to a lesser degree the wheat; but the wheat carryover had actually increased and been supplemented, both by a good United States crop in other regions (the total was 857 million bushels) and by a very good world harvest of 3.8 billion bushels. Even this figure was "ex-Russia" (and the Russian crop was being peddled on world markets in great quantities in this period). Faced with frantic calls for relief measures for stricken farmers, the Farm Board and the Secretary of Agriculture were forced at the same time to deal with deteriorating grain prices and management of a continuing surplus. During the summer of 1930, Farm Board head Alexander Legge and Secretary of Agriculture Arthur Hyde both concluded that only by reduction in grain acreage could the problem be solved.

The two federal executives then decided to take a joint barnstorming trip to the winter wheat belt—what the *Northwestern Miller* irreverently dubbed the "Art an' Alec skit"—personally to push such an acreage reduction program. For six days they traveled throughout Kansas, Nebraska, Colorado, Oklahoma and Texas, in that sweltering summer, to persuade audiences of farmers and reporters of the need to cut production voluntarily. The farmers would have none of this; the well-publicized trip was greeted with widespread hostility at almost every stop.

It was to the advantage of an individual farmer to continue to produce as large a crop as he could on his own land, hoping that "others" would cut production. Then it was called the "free rider" dilemma; today this has been given a more striking term, "the tragedy of the commons." Just as farmers in the early days in England had overgrazed the commons because it was in everyone's individual self-interest to have as many animals as possible there, with subsequent devastation of the grasslands themselves (also a pattern in the 1980s with the Tuareg and other herdsmen of Africa's Sahel), the same thinking doomed the voluntary acreage reduction proposals. Even in the face of drought damage and the small acreage reduction achieved, prices for agricultural commodities, particularly wheat, continued to sag throughout the summer and fall of 1930.

Price declines also threatened rural banks and small businesses as well as many of the cooperatives the Farm Board was dedicated to support. Once again, pressures built for intervention by the Board to "stabilize" prices. On November 15, after obtaining Hoover's personal approval, the Grain Stabilization Corporation (GSC) entered the market once more, just as it had early in the year 1930. George Milnor, its president, strode personally onto the floor of the Chicago Board of Trade to initiate the new move, calculating that the drama of his personal appearance would turn the market—just as Richard Whitney, then president of the New York Stock Exchange, had tried to do back at the time of the stock market crash in October 1929.

Stabilization this time seemed to work—for a time. Milnor had set a goal of keeping the Chicago price of the May future at a minimum of 80 cents a bushel, and for a number of weeks the heavy government buying seemed to produce results. The Farm Board even garnered some accolades from normally hostile farm groups. The success of this stabilization, however, depended on being able to maintain prices over time without exhausting governmental funds in the process.

Since wheat prices started so low, the Farm Board pushed using wheat as feed on farms because of low supplies of alternative feed due to the drought. Some farmers did this, but most of the new crop was stored. The amount of wheat owned by the GSC increased precipitously. Legge wrote Milnor on December 31, chastising the latter because the GSC had bought more than four times the amount that Milnor had earlier estimated; Legge warned him that he was purchasing wheat as if he "were buying a cheap cigar."[17]

Had the Farm Board really divorced American grain prices from those of the world? In the short term, Milnor's efforts had held prices in the range he had set: 80 cents for wheat. However, prices of the May future that was being supported by Milnor in Chicago topped Liverpool by 20 cents and exceeded Winnipeg by almost 24 cents. Normally, Liverpool and Winnipeg prices were 15 to 20 cents higher than Chicago prices. Thus, the world price pattern had been inverted.

John Jr.'s irritation rose some more at what he perceived as continuing timidity on the part of business in speaking out against the Hoover programs. The millers particularly raised his dander. He wrote his father, "I had a long talk with Mr. Franklyn Crosby [of General Mills] on Friday, the gist of which was that the mills do not wish to make any joint representations whatever with the grain trade. It is quite apparent in my estimation that they think the grain trade have a bad name and under no conditions will they allow themselves to be linked with them." Bank presidents also drew his displeasure: "The apathy of our bankers and other leaders in New York in the face of this price-fixing program of Mr. Hoover's is almost unbelievable . . . it will take the actual advent of the calamity which we see in prospect to bring about a general realization of the folly of the present procedures."[18]

John Sr., much more cautious about taking any public position, seemed even more apprehensive about developments. He wrote Morris Barker: "The Farm Board have got into their heads that the failure of their program has been due to the Chamber of Commerce of Minneapolis and the grain trade up here . . . nothing has been done whatever except to make some protests at times on very silly and foolish policies which were self-evidently wrong to begin with . . . the Farm Board has now got into the frame of mind where they . . . are going to smash the grain trade."

By March 1931, the Farm Board was in turmoil. Alexander Legge, "isolated and alone," said Morris Barker, now resigned. Forrest Crissey, Legge's biographer, reported that "his niece . . . felt that his Farm Board experience had broken him physically." Shortly thereafter, two other members of the Board, Charles C. Teague and Samuel McKelvie, announced they would leave the Board in June. Staff members also were defecting. Hoover, upset by this erosion, ordered a full-scale media program "to save the Farm Board." But exhortations were not going to work. Arthur Hyde saw this as yet another example of Hoover's "childlike faith in the efficacy of mere statements." By the end of March, the Board announced in a news release that it was terminating its stabilization efforts and setting in motion the disposition of the huge holdings of the GSC.[19]

Immediately an outcry arose against *any* sale of the grain, prices being so low. Hoover, unwilling to listen to those demanding "impoundment," asked the Board only to set a deliberate policy for the liquidation. It did so, announcing on June 30, 1931, that it would limit its domestic sales over the following 12 months to 5 million bushels a month. The Board also hoped to make special deals with foreign governments, but the United States was not in good graces with its European competitors. Only under great pressure had it attended the International Conference of Wheat Exporting Nations in London in May 1931, where it then rejected a majority plan for a quota system advanced by a group of European countries. At the conference, the United States had pushed hard for acreage reduction, but the other ten nations involved needed their wheat exports to balance their international payments and rejected the proposal. The fact that the United States had just enacted the Smoot-Hawley tariff measures, one of the highest tariffs the country had ever had, further annoyed the export-oriented European allies.

A surprising rumor surfaced in mid-February 1931, that Cargill itself was going to take over the liquidation process for the Farm Board; the story even had appeared in a United Press wire dispatch. John Jr. quickly spiked the story and wrote his father: "I can imagine nothing more unlikely" than Cargill taking such responsibility.[20]

Over the spring of 1931, the Farm Board engaged in a delicate balancing operation. It continued to buy both cash grain and futures, having committed itself to stabilize prices to the end of the old crop. Stabilization measures were *not* to be taken on the 1931 crop. The warehouse situation was tight, and there was hard bargaining between private operators and the Board about the terms of the latter's storage. The Board's ownership of enormous amounts of futures at the Chicago Board of Trade complicated matters. As the date for the termination of the May contract approached, the grain trade once more had a problem of "out of position" grain. If the Farm Board insisted on physical delivery in Chicago, there was going to be substantial transshipment from out-of-the-way points, perhaps even reshipment backward through the normally west-to-east pipeline.

Cargill found itself in the middle of this controversy. While it had tried to reduce its stocks, it still had substantial amounts farther east than Chicago. As John Sr. put it, "Our grain is not out of position with reference to consuming centers. It is merely out of position with reference to Chicago hedges." Fortunately for the private grain trade, the Board took a more conciliatory posture than it had the previous year in the same circumstances and now allowed deliveries at points other than Chicago (in the case of Cargill, at Duluth and Milwaukee). Arguments still arose over the terms, but a new spirit of compromise on the part of the Board led to early resolution. Cargill, too, decided to swallow its antipathy to the Farm Board and conduct its negotiations diplomatically. John Sr. wrote C. V. Essroger, a Chicago bank officer: "The grain trade felt that they should have had 1½¢ per bushel instead of 1¢ per bushel but recognize just the same that Mr. Milnor and Mr. Chilton were trying to look at the problem in a big way and be fair. Personally I feel very much gratified over the outcome."

John Jr., who had conducted Cargill's negotiations personally, wrote the GSC executive in charge: "We are keenly appreciative of the sincerity of your intentions . . . and we are sure you welcome discussion on such points where we believe we have a fair and just contention." He could not resist a final homily: "Incidentally, may I emphasize that we are not seeking any selfish advantage and that we would expect that all others in the same position should have equal treatment."

Thus, the private grain trade dodged the bullet. With the April bargaining turning in their favor, the private companies now came out of the 1930–1931 crop year far better than expected. However, fatal damage had been done to the Farm Board; by the summer of 1931, it was, according to historian David Hamilton, "the most vilified agency of the Federal government since the Freedman's Bureau of the 1860s and 70s."[21]

Two Good Years for Cargill

Despite the effects of the Farm Board action, Cargill's crop year 1929–1930 had been a record one, with profits of over $1.2 million, only the second time in the history of the Company that earnings had exceeded $1 million. But Frank Hixon passed along a warning of C. T. Jaffray that "grain paper is under very severe scrutiny in the east" and that John Sr. should keep the Company "in such a liquid position that your statement would be above criticism." Now the 1930–1931 results were in, and John Sr. exulted to Frank Hixon about a second record year: "We came through this past year with again the best year in our history. Our earnings, after depreciation and federal taxes, were $1,302,469 . . . we have no bills payable to banks and brokers and show cash in banks of $2,037,000 so that I think we will have a very nice looking statement this year."

Indeed, that balance sheet was remarkable in light of the tense period. A zero figure for notes payable was unprecedented, and the low $1.7 million in inventory was comparable to those back in the early 1920s. Total assets had dropped from $17.2 million in 1929 to $7.3 million, about comparable to 1928. It was about as safe a position as a company could be in, particularly taking into account the severity of the depression, which by this time had devastated hundreds of thousands of other American businesses.

Still, there was little euphoria in the industry. World wheat stocks in August 1931 were still 300 to 350 million bushels above normal. Strong bear pressures by the summer of 1931 forced prices to a new low. The average farm price of wheat dropped to about 36 cents in July and then slightly lower in August and September. With federal farm policy already apparently bankrupt, the agricultural outlook was daunting.[22]

The star-crossed Farm Board entered its last-gasp year with vast stocks of grain, and with its dwindling resources there was a temptation to realize some cash proceeds by selling into the market. That it might do this precipitously worried the grain trade. Secretary of Agriculture Hyde proposed in mid-March 1932 to lend $200 million to foreign governments so that they could buy Farm Board wheat and cotton. But the Hyde proposal never came into being. Later that month, John Jr. wrote: "The truth of the matter, in my opinion, is that the Farm Board are in no shape to resist a declining market and they are throwing overboard whatever long futures they have in all markets." The Farm Board had tried to do the impossible: to take the dual roles of efficient merchandiser and market stabilizer, all to be accomplished in the face of both a greatly increased supply and deteriorating domestic and world economic levels. Postmortem analyses on the Farm Board were in the main highly critical—as were those on Herbert Hoover's efforts during the depression years.

The Birth of Cargill, Incorporated

Perhaps the most important outcome of the Cargill stockholder dissidence in 1925 had been John Sr.'s and Austen Cargill's joint agreement that some method would always be in place to prevent such a factional battle from ever occurring again. Shortly after the 1925 events, they established a voting trust, to last for five years, whereby the controlling family shareholders (the MacMillan and Cargill shares) would be voted as one. On September 1, 1930, this voting trust would expire. John Sr. told Frank Hixon of a new plan: "Austen and I . . . are both agreed that it is highly desirable from the family point of view that we make it impossible to have any possible conflict . . . with a corporation of our character, which borrows such enormous sums of money, we all realized that there should be no fear on the part of the banks of any shifting of the management or control of stock ownership." A new corporation was to be formed to hold the families' common stock in the Cargill Elevator Company, including that held by the Cargill Securities Company. The name chosen was "Cargill, Incorporated," registered as a Delaware corporation on July 18, 1930. Although the final steps in organization did not occur until 1936, Cargill, Incorporated, has continued to today as the parent organization for the Company's many subsidiaries.

The effectiveness of this new corporation as replacement for the expiring five-year voting trust was established by the following steps:

A. All of the shares of the Cargill Elevator Company owned by John MacMillan, Sr., John MacMillan, Jr., Edna MacMillan and Cargill MacMillan, those owned by Austen and Anne Cargill and the shares of Cargill Elevator owned by Cargill Securities Company (a total of 13,379 of the 24,000) were exchanged for common and preferred stock in Cargill, Incorporated. A total of 20,000 shares of this new corporation had been established for each of these two classes of stock; now these 13,379 shares were exchanged for a similar number of common stock shares and also a similar number of preferred stock shares in Cargill, Incorporated (the remaining 6,621 shares remained unissued for the moment).

The rest of the 24,000 shares of Cargill Elevator Company remained in the hands of employees and other close friends of the Company (Frank Hixon, etc.)

B. Voting control of Cargill Elevator Company now was held by Cargill, Incorporated; however, at this time, all the properties and operations remained with the Cargill Elevator Company.

Thus, voting control of Cargill, Incorporated, at this time was held by a combination of the various MacMillan shares and the shares of the Cargill Securities Company, 9,617 shares of the total common stock issued of 13,379. Inasmuch as a majority of Cargill Securities Company stock was held by the various MacMillans (as described in Chapter 7), the four MacMillan owners had majority control.

C. Then, on July 13, 1931, Cargill, Incorporated, exchanged all of the outstanding common stock of the Cargill Securities Company, on a pro rata basis (Cargill, Incorporated, exchanging 21 shares of its preferred and 21 shares of its common for each 50 shares of the Cargill Securities Company). Although Cargill Securities stayed in being after this (there were still a number of holdings from the old W. W. Cargill estate—timberland properties in Valier, Montana, in Mexico, etc.), no longer did Cargill Securities as such hold any Cargill Elevator stock.

At this point (July 13, 1931), the four MacMillans (John Sr., John Jr., Edna and Cargill) owned together just over 63 percent of the stock of Cargill, Incorporated. In turn, Cargill, Incorporated, owned a majority of the Cargill Elevator Company.

D. Finally, in successive steps in the early 1930s, several blocks of the Cargill, Incorporated, common stock were put in irrevocable trusts for other members of the two families, particularly to provide the women members of the family with adequate means of support in the event of the death of their husbands.

There remained in place the sizable minority block of common stock of Cargill Elevator Company held by employees (as "employee stock," carrying voting rights but required to be sold back to the Company on death or severance of the employee) and by close friends (also carrying voting rights but having no further restrictions). Just over 10,000 of the total of 24,000 shares were in this group. Other members of the families had some of this; for example, Daniel MacMillan held 750 shares, Mary Barker and her son held almost 400 shares, daughter Margaret Wisner held 194 shares. The largest single holding was that of J. B. Taylor, who held 1,001 shares, with his wife having another 37 shares. Taylor, a more distant relative by marriage on the MacMillan side, was no longer an employee—he had been asked to resign at the time of the stockholder dissidence in 1925.

Employee holdings also were significant. A. M. Prime held the largest amount, 750 shares (his colleague F. W. Lindahl had sold all of his shares back in the early 1920s). Ed Grimes held 500 shares, E. S. Mooers (related to the Cargill family by marriage) held 350, and the amounts ranged down from there to very small holdings—Eileen Lewis, for example, holding 7 shares.

The shareholder structure of Cargill Elevator still remained the same: about one-third to employees and friends and the other two-thirds split between the MacMillans and the Cargills. The changes noted above, however, had shifted the mix. The concept of a "check and balance" relationship among three groups of holders had not been in effect during the voting trust, nor was it included in the latest arrangement. The MacMillan segment of the family management group held an absolute majority in Cargill, Incorporated, the entity that also held control of the rest of the organization. Emma Hanchette's sale of her Cargill Securities Company stock to John Sr. in 1925 and her exchange of Cargill Elevator common stock for preferred stock in that company in 1927 had made this possible.[23]

Phasing Out the Employee Common Stock

On August 11, 1931, the annual meeting of Cargill Elevator was held, with its main subject the phasing out of employee common stock. John Sr. described at the meeting the reasons for this: "Due to the limited supply of stock available for employees [and] the fact that the dividend rate on the Common Stock was not sufficient to pay the interest on the cost thereof . . . it was practically impossible for any of the younger employees to obtain stock in the Company . . . therefore, the Company was not in a position to reward employees for any brilliant work that might be performed." Further, there was concern that retiring large blocks of stock owned by employees might overly deplete the Company's working capital at a time when the Company was "expanding at a rate which made it advisable to increase working capital as fast as possible."

John Sr. proposed that Cargill Elevator Company issue a 5 percent cumulative second preferred stock, one purpose being "to pay bonuses to those employees that were not common stockholders. In this way, all employees showing particular merit would be included as stockholders." The new plan also allowed an existing employee shareholder to exchange holdings of common stock for the new second preferred stock at book value if the employee so chose, and then he or she would be eligible for the bonus.

To effect this plan, a special meeting of the shareholders was called for August 28, 1931, to amend the Articles of Incorporation to raise the capital stock of the Company to $6 million. The capital structure would be (1) 32,000 shares of common stock, (2) 8,000 shares of preferred stock and (3) 20,000 shares of the new second preferred stock. The preferred stock would still remain senior to the new issue and would still have its fixed annual dividend of 7 percent; the second preferred stock would carry a fixed annual dividend of 5 percent. Neither of the preferred issues had voting rights.

The plan was discussed openly in a lengthy article in *Cargill News*, the new employee publication started in July 1930. There was special focus on the merit feature. Employees already owning common stock and who elected to retain it were reminded that they would *not* be entitled to receive a bonus. The bonus itself would not depend on the level of management, either. Younger men, said the editor, "who expect to go ahead with the Company" should exchange their stock for the new preferred.

A personal memorandum in John Sr.'s files stressed the stock bonus feature, adding, "Cash bonuses are bad." John Sr. expanded on this in a letter to Frank Hixon: "Years ago . . . we found that that did not work out well. Each employee immediately assumed that it was a permanent increase in pay, and when conditions in his department shifted and he could not make a big showing he still expected a large bonus regardless of the outcome. In addition, we found it created a great deal of jealousy among the employees."

Thus, the plan held out a carrot—a bonus for merit, payable in the new preferred stock. Built into this was an encouragement to convert—employees could get bonuses too if they exchanged. It seemed at this time to be perfectly agreeable if they did not convert. Indeed, when J. B. Taylor, who resigned in 1925 (after the squabble over ownership), requested to transfer his common stock to the new preferred, he was denied. The plan apparently contemplated the transfer only of employee stock, not stock of outsiders (like Frank Hixon and Taylor).

In the first year, some 2,578 shares of employee stock, with book value of $601,000, had been retired: $463,000 paid in second preferred stock and $138,000 in cash. The number of common shareholders continued to drop over the succeeding years. At a subsequent point, John Jr. put increasing pressure on the common shareholders to make the exchange, a point to be discussed in detail later.[24]

Training Younger Management

An organization's stability and growth over time depend fundamentally on having continuing good leadership. Fresh younger executives must always be available to replace older managers lest the organization deteriorate. In its earlier years, Cargill's management development had been hit-or-miss. The Company's positive experience over the years was in part a testimony to the judgment of its management, in part sheer luck. As Cargill Elevator Company headed into the 1930s, its management team was excellent but certainly not altogether preplanned. At this point, a more self-conscious approach was adopted with establishment of the Cargill Training Program. Since then, this has been one of the unique hallmarks of Cargill. Were Cargillites asked today what has made the Company successful, the training program likely would be high in the responses.

The program was born in part out of a negative experience. In late 1929, John Jr. and Harold Tweeden, the Buffalo manager, were negotiating to lease terminal space at Oswego, New York. They hired an outsider for on-the-spot negotiations; when he reported failure, Tweeden suggested that the man be sent to the Cleveland office for another assignment. John Jr. wrote his father what then happened: "We discovered that he had left the Leamington without paying his bill or checking out. An investigation showed that he was thoroly [sic] irresponsible . . . we called him on the telephone before he reached Cleveland and discharged him." This made a profound impression on John Jr.; he continued: "Our first loss is the smallest. . . . This has left me with a conviction that only in most extreme cases do we ever want to go outside our own organization in filling positions."

This experience led to a conscious decision to carefully screen and hire young college graduates, mostly agriculture or business majors, and then train them in a new Cargill-managed training program where Cargill values, principles and tactics would be taught. The driving force for the training program right from the start was Julius Hendel. In the summer of 1930, Hendel set up a formal evening training program, conducted by himself, with his own curriculum based on his extensive practical experience in the commodity markets, and backed by his lengthy academic training in the same fields. Soon Julius's "boys" were sitting at the foot of the teacher in the classroom—one can almost hear him say "my boys" in his Russian accent, for this is one of the great memories of Julius. The classes met every Tuesday and Thursday evening, with a well-directed focus on the grain business.

The first year's class was a small one; the record is not clear how they were picked or whether the class comprised only new college-graduate trainees. By the time of the second class in 1931, the size had greatly expanded; *Cargill News* called it "an opportunity that one cannot afford to miss. . . . These classes are open to all in the organization and are not just confined to any particular group." By this time, Tom Totushek, earlier Hendel's assistant in the grain laboratory, took responsibility for the liaison between the trainee's newly assigned department and the classroom preparation just finished. "Tommy . . . helped Julius in his kindergarten," John Jr. commented.

In the summer of 1931, Hendel developed a more advanced class for those trainees having particular promise. Often this latter group met at Julius's large farm home near Lake Minnetonka. At other times both the basic group and the advanced group met at the Cargill headquarters in the Grain Exchange building. The room that was used had some rather ornate decorations on the walls, of gold color—perhaps this was the origin of the term "Gold Room boys." Later, as this term became widely used in the Company (often enviously) as a sobriquet for the college-graduate trainees, the connotation was more invidious, sometimes seeming to imply the "gold spoon in the mouth." When management became more selective in choosing candidates, that "Gold Room boys" term began to carry a certain implication of elitism, and those not chosen for the role (for example, those without a college degree) more than occasionally expressed envy about the small favored group.

Hendel alternated his own teaching sessions with those of others in the Company, including the trainees themselves. In December 1931, John Jr. took the subject of cotton and "gave a very interesting talk on the raising, handling and marketing of this valuable crop." Several trainees also made presentations that evening, and later that month there were sessions on sugar and molasses. Wallace W. Hyde and James W. Ringwald, both trainees in the first class in 1930, had their presentations, "Why the Price of Wheat Is So Low" and "Development of Western Canada," published in a subsequent issue of the *Cargill News*. Several of the Cargill senior executives taking particular sessions put their speeches in *Cargill News*, too, including Donald L. Williams, who gave a paper on the exporting of grain, and Frank Neilson who conducted several sessions. Trainees in those first few years included names that subsequently became famous in the Company—Ralph G. Golseth, Fred Seed, Erwin E. (Erv) Kelm and others. So, from the start of John Jr.'s ascendancy, the Cargill training program produced an outstanding group of young college graduates for management roles in the Company.

Recruiting Biases

Maurice R. Smith, a college friend, wrote John Jr. in January 1934: "I have been telling a friend of mine of the success you have had in employing young college men in the top 10% test bracket, and he wants to start infiltrating a few such men in his organization." Smith solicited John Jr.'s views; he responded articulately on the underlying philosophy of Cargill's approach:

We get our men from the various Bureaus of Appointments of the different universities. So far we have had the best cooperation from our own university here, although I have secured a few men from Stu Clement [the placement officer] at Yale, with only indifferent success however . . . the men at Yale who have to work their way through are no better than the same type at any other university, and we have placed so many men from the local university that their cooperation has been excellent.

We have a committee of executives who pass on these men and our rule is that the committee must be unanimous in its choice. We pay more attention to our own impressions than to the records, but we restrict our choices to men whom we consider to be in the top 5% or 10% as far as intelligence goes.

Scholastic standing, we find, means very little, but if the scholastic standing is poor there must be a reason for it, such as extra-curriculum activities . . . the Binet tests are of substantial help, not necessarily as a guide to good men but to assist us in rejecting the slow ones who might otherwise get by on account of unusually fine presence.[25]

With John Jr.'s and Cargill MacMillan's Ivy League background, it was natural that graduates from Yale and some of the other schools in that group would seek Cargill posts. Early on, Cargill did take a Yale man, Almon Greenman, with success, but John Jr. began to build a prejudice against the Yale graduates, feeling that most of them came from family fortunes and eventually would return to the family businesses. In 1936, John Jr. wrote Stuart H. Clement at Yale: "Quite frankly our experience with Yale men has been so unsatisfactory that unless some outstanding man comes to our attention we think it would be better not to try them for a while at least. We have tried approximately six Yale men since I have been in the business, and of the six only one has worked out [Greenman]. . . . The only thing that occurs to me is that we are unable to hire the type of men that made Yale famous." Perhaps John Jr. was enough of a snob to feel that those who had to work their way through Yale were not quite of his caliber. Clement wrote back: "I have no explanation to offer beyond the fact that the salary which you pay to college graduates during the first year or two is considerably below the market and undoubtedly has some bearing on the situation."

John Jr. was espousing here his thoroughgoing belief in meritocracy. A first requisite for this merit was the achievement of a college degree. Further, these people would likely come from families of breeding. In a speech to a senior management group in May 1946, he stressed three points as being paramount in picking managers. The first of these was stated as follows: "As far as possible draw your executive talent from men of good background. Avoid the diamond in the rough type and men who have a chip on their shoulders." (The second point emphasized patience in finding the right person; the third related to the ability to delegate.)

Yet John Jr. was strongly opposed to hiring relatives of business friends. At one point, Ed Grimes had thought it might be wise for Cargill to hire the son of a business connection. John Jr. rejected this notion: "We have had one or two conspicuously successful cases of hiring sons of our friends in business life—the most recent one I can think of is Juneau [Herbert Juneau, one of the trainees in the first program] and . . . we have few men in the organization any better. However, unless you think that the son would compare favorably with the other college graduates we are hiring for executive positions, I would prefer very much not to take him. I also think you might incur ill will if we had the boy make an application and then did not take him."

There was not unanimity within the Company about the focus on college graduates, however. Few of the older employees, even those in top management, had come to Cargill with a college diploma; many of them vehemently believed that the "school of experience" was the best preparation for the grain trade, indeed, that a college degree often gave people "airs" that got in the way of being a successful employee. Frank Neilson, for one, was vocal in his opposition, at one point telling a young man who was working in the Terminal Department part-time and going to college that he (Neilson) "wanted no college boys in my organization—I'm a self made man, and that's what I want. College people expect too much." The young man wanted a job with Neilson badly and actually gave up further college education to obtain the job. Perhaps this was a partial explanation for Neilson's antagonism toward Julius Hendel, Hendel holding not only an undergraduate degree but a doctorate as well.

For recruitment, Cargill gravitated toward the midwestern universities, focusing particularly on the University of Minnesota. This and other constraints tended to cast the net somewhat narrowly. John Jr., for example, had a strong aversion to graduate business school candidates. On the plus side, the Company gained a cadre over the years of tractable young management men whom the management knew very well and whose subsequent performance with Cargill was often outstanding.

There were risks in such a narrow focus to recruiting and promotion. The same type of person and thinking was replicated over and over. The rubbing together of disparate personalities often was lacking in a selection process that concentrated on one subset. Cargill's strong promotion-from-within policy produced highly loyal people, well trained in the individual corporate culture and methods; however, there was the risk of too much similarity with too little shaking of the conventional wisdoms. Later events would put this dilemma in sharper focus.

John Jr. was fiercely protective about his cadre of younger executives and seemed to resent personally any defections. In this period, one of the Company's arch competitors, Bunge North American Grain Corporation, persuaded a Cargill buyer to come with them. John Jr. wrote the Bunge president a blunt letter:

In view of the well established custom in American business to the effect that an employee of a friendly business organization is never hired away without first discussing the matter with his employer, you can well imagine our astonishment at being informed by one of our buyers that he was leaving us to accept a position with your office here. Inasmuch as none of us had any recollection of any discussion of this matter either with you or any of your associates it is very difficult indeed for us to construe this as other than an evidence of extreme unfriendliness.

The Bunge president took umbrage at this; he delegated the response to a vice president, and the latter's reply was curt: the Cargill employee concerned had approached Bunge "several times," and "we felt that the young man was dissatisfied." There the matter rested.[26]

With the new training program in place, the Company then decided to make a public statement of its overall personnel policy, choosing a memorandum for the banking community in February 1933 as the medium:

The Company has been expanding vigorously but along conservative lines and has adopted a policy of promotion entirely from within, which makes necessary the hiring of a small group of high grade men each year. The men so selected are put through a rigorous training course, which could only be compared with a Post Graduate college course. . . . The salaries paid are very low for the first three years. After that they average materially higher than is ordinarily the case under similar conditions. Promotion is entirely by capacity and not by seniority, with a result that many of the highest paid executives are very young men. In exceptional cases, salaries as high as $300 and $400 per month are earned after the third or fourth year. . . . The wide scope of the Company's activities make it possible to find places for almost all types with a single exception that a very high level of intelligence is necessary in the first place, as the business changes with kaleidoscopic rapidity and it requires considerable mental agility to be able to adapt one's self to the changes.

The last sentence of the memorandum singled out Yale with an interesting, rather gratuitous statement: "Our greatest objection to Yale men in the past has been that they become discouraged just about the time that they have acquired enough knowledge to place them in directly executive positions."

Later, John Jr. mellowed about Yale. In 1946, when his eldest son, John Hugh III, was preparing to go to an eastern preparatory school, John Jr. wrote an official there: "I have a marked preference for his going to Yale, largely because of the intense competitive spirit which is peculiarly developed at Yale. My reason for this is that we have a fairly large family-owned business and one in which we hire each year about a dozen university graduates who compete among themselves for our higher executive positions. Naturally we cannot play favorites and I am extremely anxious to have [him] enter our business imbued with this competitive spirit, which is all too often lacking in small universities."[27]

Tightening Cargill Centralization

Two events in early 1931 combined with John Jr.'s increasing management role to bring a significant restructuring of the Cargill organization. The first came out of a tragedy. On February 27, Julius Hendel was involved in a terrible train crash, when the crack Milwaukee Railroad "Olympian" ran into a Minneapolis-bound Omaha mail train near Camp Douglas, Wisconsin. He received a severe blow to the head that threatened complications (he began running a fever after returning to Minneapolis). Fortunately, he recovered quickly, but it was a sobering event for the Company. "Julius . . . really has very few competent assistants on merchandising right now," John Jr. wrote his father afterward; Hendel truly was an indispensable member of the organization.

Another seemingly isolated event occurred two months later. Julius Hendel and Ed Grimes had had several heated arguments over a shipment of corn. John Sr., learning of the rift, wrote an angry letter to both, one of the harshest in all of his extant correspondence: "I am greatly annoyed and displeased to find that there is friction between you over a sale of corn. I cannot have anything but the best of team-work between departments and I must insist that you each treat with the other from the point of view of what is best for the business as a whole. If you cannot work this problem out between yourselves I shall have to take charge of it in person, and in this case I will take over all of the handling of corn thru the Buffalo office for the balance of the crop." After detailing exactly the way he wanted the corn to be handled, John Sr. concluded: "Any disturbance of this kind affects the morale of the entire organization. . . . I want you again to try to get together in the spirit of what is best for the organization as a whole and work out between you how you can get on without any friction in the future." His concluding sentence minced no words: "I want it distinctly understood that if at any time there is any point on which you cannot agree that it must be referred to me for settlement."

The Hendel–Grimes disagreement apparently signaled to John Sr. that further central control was needed. In July 1931, he wrote Frederick Lindahl at Duluth about his decision to centralize the handling of rye out of the Minneapolis office (Lindahl had earlier lost the Wheat Account). "We will be governed accordingly," Lindahl plaintively responded, but it was clear that those halcyon days of earlier years when Lindahl's operations were at the center of the Company were over.

Just a couple of months later, in August 1931, centralization was again tightened. The instance involved Lewis Crosby, the new head of the Omaha operations. John Sr. wrote to him: "I have just learned accidentally that you were buying wheat and offering it on the outside. Under no circumstances whatever are you to do any wheat merchandising. Any wheat of any character to be handled at Omaha must be for the Wheat Account . . . you cannot possibly understand all the factors in the situation and they must come through this office" (the Wheat Account was handled by John Jr. and Hendel). John Sr. must have felt he was too abrupt, for he added, "I do not want you to think that we do not want you to be looking around for every opportunity. What I am trying to impress upon you is that if we are trying to do the same thing from two or three different directions, we are in each other's way."

Another memorandum from John Sr. at this time, in this case to a dozen of the management in Minneapolis, spoke to the same desire for control: "On numerous occasions petitions are circulated on the floor asking for

Cargill Terminal Elevator Superintendents' Convention, December 1930. Standing, left to right, Julius Hendel, Cargill MacMillan, Elmer Grant, P. G. Oszusick, George Carlson, Marcus Marshall, Frank Neilson; seated, Lew Crosby, Adolph Swendson, Ed McManus, L. N. Cote, C. R. Reed.

signatures. Hereafter I wish you would always refuse to sign any petitions until the matter has been referred to me, as you might be interfering with some business policy of the company by so signing."

A few months later, in early 1932, another health problem intruded, and this time it was a major one. The tensions surrounding the Farm Board problem had sapped John Sr.'s strength ("I am tired out," he wrote Morris Barker). Never the healthiest of people, John Sr. now suffered a serious heart attack. Although it was not life-threatening, the doctors prescribed a long rest, and he was not in the office again until May 1932. Despite telling John Jr. and Cargill that he was "cured," he adopted a restricted regimen at the office from that time forward.[28]

John Jr., General Manager

While John Sr. was recovering from his heart attack in California, John Jr. wrote a long letter to him about restructuring the organization. C. C. Boden, who had been the Company's first resident representative abroad (assigned to Rotterdam, Holland, in 1930 and then to London in 1932), returned to the United States. John Jr. first thought to bring him to Minneapolis, to supervise all exports, including purchases in the West that were moving down the Lakes to be "fobbed" at the seaboard, but then decided to assign him instead to New York City, with some but not all of the export responsibility. The remainder would be held by Don Williams, who already was head of the export department in Minneapolis. There was also the possibility of moving Harley Flood to Minneapolis: "We always considered that Harley was available to relieve Mr. Lindahl in case of need, but we are moving so many of the functions of the Duluth office to Minneapolis that we really do not need as high grade a man as Harley in Duluth, particularly as we plan to handle all lake charters from now on here in Minneapolis rather than in Duluth." Flood spent only a few months in Minneapolis, then was transferred to the newly expanded Winnipeg office. The reassignments of both Boden and Flood resulted in more direct control by John Jr.

In July 1931, another step toward centralization was taken when T. R. Shaw, the editor of the *Cargill News*, was also given responsibility for coordinating all Company advertising. The next month, the Company stenographers were asked to regularize their handling of the mail; in an unintended slip, the authors of the memorandum (H. B. Juneau and Eileen Lewis) ended the sentence about the letters with "after they have been signed by the dictator."

Economic depressions often bring opportunities for innovation, provided resources are available, factor costs generally being lower than normal. Cargill did take advantage of the times to build, buy and lease new terminals, many of striking configuration. Feed costs were at that time very low, and in 1931, the Company received several suggestions from the outside about entering the feed business. But generally speaking, the more highly centralized a company is, the less likely it is to search for new patterns of diversification. This was true of Cargill; Ed Grimes mirrored Company thinking in his reply to a Chicago feed operator: "Several times we have considered the advisability of going into the feed business . . . each time we have decided that we would confine our operations entirely to grain, and I do not see anything new in the situation to cause us to change that policy." A molasses project also was considered—Cargill would trade molasses, itself arranging the transportation in special rail cars. Nothing came of that idea, however.

In July 1932, another move toward centralization was made, in this case one of great importance. Responsibility for the marketing operations of all of the terminal departments in the western operations (those of Minneapolis, Duluth, Omaha and Milwaukee) were consolidated under John Jr. and Julius Hendel, with F. J. Hays as their assistant in charge of accounting. This put even greater focus on the functional distinctions that John Jr. had brought to the company from his experience as an army officer in World War I. For the huge terminals in the West, Julius Hendel was now to be the functional head for all of their marketing. But the management of the terminals themselves was under Frank Neilson, who had been appointed superintendent of the warehouse companies.

Even under the best of circumstances, such a sharp functional split within the confines of such a crucial physical property would be difficult. As it was, there already was considerable acrimony between Julius Hendel and Frank Neilson, ill feeling that had continued to grow over the years. Indeed, during the time that Neilson was head of the terminal elevator operations, orders had gone out from him that Julius Hendel was not to be allowed in the terminals proper. Even if Hendel and Neilson had worked compatibly, the narrow functional bifurcation at these locations would have been difficult to manage; the personal tensions exacerbated the problem.

In these Hendel–Grimes and Hendel–Neilson spats, the correspondence points to Hendel as the more contentious. Given John Sr.'s instinct for compatibility in the organization, one could wonder how Hendel fit in. However, Hendel was John Jr.'s protégé and colleague, and the two got along very well, having many similar attributes. Further, Hendel's acuity in trading had made Cargill much money in this period.

In July 1933, John Jr. added to Frank Neilson's duties, making him the head of a new "personnel department." John Jr. sent a memorandum to all executives in the company, noting that "there has not been complete coordination in the past between the various departments in the hiring and discharging of employees." Neilson's office was to be used as "a clearing house," and the arrangement was to apply to all employees except the country line elevator agents.

Harold Tweeden, being groomed as a top management prospect, was put in charge of all domestic sales in the East, which included the Toledo, Montreal, Buffalo and New York offices. John Sr. sent a memorandum to the four office managers affected, confirming this, but added an inexplicable, ambiguous caveat: "Any time you feel that you are not getting full cooperation with him please take the matter up direct with us here in Minneapolis."

Just a year before, in late May 1931, John Sr. had severely chastised Tweeden over a difference the latter had had with Hendel over intracompany pricing of corn: "[The] basis you mention I do not feel is fact . . . corn is worth more than that. . . . I put this up to you expecting you to be fair but apparently I have to make these decisions myself and I do not like that kind of business. One department cannot figure to make its profit at the expense of another. It is the welfare of the entire business I want considered above all."

Tweeden was disconcerted by some of the centralizing changes and by John Sr.'s memorandum. John Jr. wrote him early in May 1932: "Ed tells me that you are very much perturbed lest the changes in administration which we are making might result in making it impossible for you to make the showing to which you are fairly entitled, and I am just writing to reassure you on this very point." John Jr. noted that the new centralizing would "result in a very heavy saving in overhead" but pointed out that "there should be no curtailment of initiative anywhere as a result." He spoke specifically of Tweeden's role: "In your case we are really in a quandary, as we would like to have you here in Minneapolis . . . but in order to do so we would have to sacrifice the local knowledge which you have, together with such standing and prestige as you have acquired in the East as a result of your long residence there."

Then John Jr. tried to spell out a rather perplexing reporting relationship: "We are going to try to continue just as we have in the past except that for administrative reasons we will have to carry all merchandising records here in Minneapolis and have your own activities come in the form of recommendations and advice to the merchandising staff here." Tweeden would still get credit for all of the trades done out of the Eastern offices, but the real control was now vested in Minneapolis.

Tweeden seemed destined for higher responsibilities at a later point, but then a tragic development cut short his career. After an illness of months, he died in July 1933. Once more, the result was a move toward further centralization; the major responsibilities that Tweeden had held were assumed by the Minneapolis office.

These developments came about during John Sr.'s recuperation from his heart attack. Now came the final result. In August 1932, the board of directors of the Company elected John Jr. as its new general manager. An article in the *Cargill News* made it clear that the change was a fundamental one: "We are all very sorry to see this part of the work drop from the hands of our President, but are pleased to know that he can be relieved from some of his many duties. Mr. MacMillan has always managed the affairs of the Company in a most efficient manner and has successfully brought it through many depressions and trying business periods. His thoughtful kindness and interest in the welfare of his employees is one of his great characteristics that has endeared him to us all and brought forth the highest loyalty of everyone to himself and the company." The article continued about "his sterling qualities" and pointed out that John Sr. "will continue to have our loyal support and the company will still have his guiding influence." In a poignantly characteristic swan song, John Sr. sent a long memorandum on September 7, 1932, to "all executives" on the continuing need for "absolute secrecy," lest information be divulged "detrimental to our interests." Privacy had dominated John Sr.'s thinking for many years— as it had for all of the grain trade. By the very nature of trading, where bargaining strategies were kept guarded, where timing (often almost instantaneous timing) mattered a great deal, where margins were so slim, where one's private knowledge of fresh information could be invaluable, privacy became ingrained. It was the competitor that dominated each company's thinking. It was the competitor that might steal an innovation. The grain trade companies worried about government, were concerned about what farmers thought of them—indeed, what the general public believed about the industry. They read their press accounts assiduously. The same undoubtedly could be said for almost all industries. But for grain traders it was always the competition that preoccupied them. The frenzy of the trading pit truly symbolized the industry; secrecy was its watchword. The fact that most of the industry's companies were closely held was instrumental in making this possible.

John Sr. truly felt he was the watchdog on maintaining secrecy, and he would continue to play this role. But it was crystal clear that John Jr. was now running the Company.

The organization already had been sharply restructured by John Jr. over the years that he had been involved with his father in the management. His changes back in 1925 had been the trigger for the stockholder and employee dissidence at that time. Nevertheless, these changes had endured, and John Jr. had built the Wheat Department and then the entire grain operation into a dynamic unit, centralized in his and Hendel's hands. He also had put his mark on accounting and office procedures, had restructured the transportation functions of the Company and had taken a central role with Neilson in the construction of new terminals. By the time he became general manager, the organization already had been shaped largely in the image of John Jr.'s concept of management.[29]

CHAPTER TEN

New Elevators, Cargill's Bank Crisis

From far back in its history, Cargill had dealt with commission merchants. Yet there were problems in this. Loyalties of commission merchant were not as strong as those of Cargill's own employees, whose devotion to the Company was by now legendary.

Omaha, a feeder city for the Company's Duluth terminals, was a case in point. Commission merchants had been used there since the early and mid-1920s, and the arrangement was not working well. John Jr. described the difficulties: "We were unable to buy grain of reasonable quality for ourselves. . . . The elevators in Omaha gave us wheat which made grade under federal standards and yet was not warehouseable grain. We . . . needed [to] select our own grain." So an office was opened there in 1927; Lewis L. Crosby was posted there as the buyer.

Soon John Jr., so immersed by this time in wheat trading, began to consider an actual terminal in Omaha. Heightened volume alone could have justified it, but tactical reasons made it even more desirable. There was a natural west-to-east movement of grain, from growers to users, and a heightening movement from Kansas and its neighbors to Gulf ports. It would be a safeguard to be able to store substantial amounts of grain at the beginning of this pipeline; places like Omaha or Sioux City, Iowa, would be natural collection points. By late 1929, John Jr. began to look for sites, aided by Frank L. Neilson, his colleague from the British Columbia logging days.

By March 1930, Omaha had emerged as the best site. John Jr.'s and Neilson's choice was a piece of land outside the Omaha–Council Bluffs switching district. When they asked the Omaha Grain Exchange to allow this to be an "Omaha terminal," the Exchange officials initially said no; they would allow a terminal only in Omaha proper. John Jr., a consummate bargainer, played his hand strongly and won out: "As soon as Mr. Fenton said we would then go to Sioux City, they showed signs of weakening."

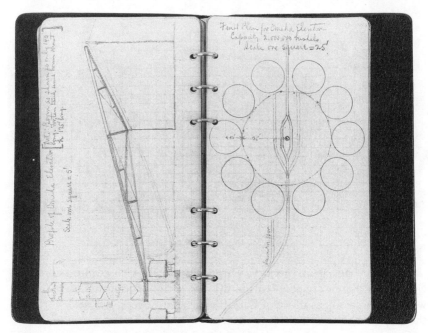

Early sketch by John MacMillan, Jr., for Cargill's proposed Omaha terminal elevator, c. 1929, showing a circular configuration.

Building the Omaha terminal elevator, July 7, 1930.

Omaha grain car dumper unloading the first car of grain, August 1930.

This Omaha bargaining in late 1929 and early 1930 coincided with the most unsettled period in Farm Board policy. With storage at a premium in the Omaha area, John Jr. felt he could use the potential new Cargill terminal as a bargaining wedge with the Farm Board to encourage them to reverse some of their unpalatable positions. So he wrote Alexander Legge a long letter on March 1, 1930 about his new elevator plan—that it would be a 5½-million-bushel elevator that "would be a material factor in relieving the pressure of new crop winter wheat." Then he outlined his opposition to the Farm Board policies concerning the May futures contract, and ended: "Unless the Farm Board reverses its policy and restores the carrying charge from May to July, or unless we have assurances from your Board that it is not the policy of the Farm Board to manipulate futures with such a result in view," Cargill would not proceed.

The heavy hand did not work here—John Jr. had overestimated his clout. Legge penned a terse letter in response: "I cannot advise you as to the building of storage beyond saying that it is quite evident that more storage is needed in that section of the country, and we certainly hope the present abnormal conditions will prove to be of short duration."[1]

The terminal still was needed, of course, so John Jr. swallowed his pride and proceeded forthwith on construction. On May 24, 1930, the Fegles Construction Company broke ground with an amazing promise that they were, in the words of the *Cargill News*, "to have the structure ready in time to take care of the new crop." It was a challenging task inasmuch as it was to be a 5-million-bushel terminal and a highly innovative new configuration.

John Jr. and Neilson proceeded on two basic premises, that large bins were cheaper per bushel than small ones and that the plant would be arranged so that only one operation could be performed at a time, but at high speed. At track-side was an elevator workhouse with attached car shed; an enormous Richardson rail car unloader was located there. The rail car was lifted up in its entirety, turned sideways, then moved up and down so that the grain was unloaded in a very short time. Cleaning the car took "less than four minutes from the time it is placed in the dumper, and . . . the car dumper could handle ten cars an hour, or some 200 to 240 cars per day."

The storage area had a set of storage tanks in two lines built as a cross. On one axis, straight from the workhouse, there were five 90-foot concrete storage tanks, open at the top. On the other axis were a set of four tanks on each side, scaled down in size to the two on the outside at a height of 30 feet. The outer points in each direction were completed as a square; the exterior walls, consisting of numerous small semicircular tanks, were 30 feet high. The large open areas in the four quadrants then became Bins A, B, C and D, each able to store—in flat storage—1 million bushels. The suspended corrugated-sheet-iron roof that enclosed the whole structure sloped down from the north-south roofline, starting at a point just over the 90-foot tank tops. From the outside, the whole structure looked like an enormous rectangular circus tent.

John Jr. produced a practical design for the precise angle of this roof configuration. His intricate calculations balanced all of the engineering concerns (stress, weight, etc.) and calculated the angle of repose to allow grain to be stored right up into the very top of the V-shaped inside angle but also to flow readily out from that high corner when needed for loading out. Unfortunately, John Jr.'s mathematics for this did not quite work; the grain peak in the high corner would stick, and several Cargill old-timers recall having to climb up on top of the grain, supporting themselves on long 2-by-10-foot planks laid on top of the grain, to dislodge the grain at the top.

The construction company had kept hundreds of men busy working night and day without relief, and the entire structure was completed in under 55 days. Indeed, on July 16 ("at 1:30 p.m.") the first carload of grain was taken into the elevator, just over six weeks from the time the whole project had started. The construction itself was a tour de force. The total cost was estimated by John Jr. (in a letter to Frank Hixon) at just about $500,000; with the total capacity of 5 million bushels, this was a cost of about 10 cents a bushel. At that time, it cost up to $1.50 per bushel to build conventional elevators. The Omaha terminal, John Jr. told Hixon, "is of the cheapest possible fireproof construction."

It was not just the outside appearance, with its strange suspended-roof topping, that was unique. Inside, in the four enormous open flat-storage areas, Frank Neilson had devised a grain-moving device that had never been tried before in such circumstances. Given that the grain in these four "bins" was really just dumped in huge piles of flat storage, the key question became how to move it to the floor conveyors. Presumably one could use bulldozers with either front-loaders or scrapers, but the required back-and-forth travel seemed to Neilson to be inefficient. So Neilson and his colleagues developed a new "secret," a shovel machine run from afar by a man on the high gallery overlooking the bins. A scoop shaped like the peel of a quarter-orange was developed. Made of steel, the gadget stood just higher than a man's waist. Cables were attached to it from fasteners located all along the wall, and the operator could set the pulling cables into a particular set of fasteners that activated the scoop in a certain path along the floor. Resetting the cables into other fasteners would change the path, and a skilled operator could so reposition the cables that the huge pile could be cut away in safety and with speed.

The flat-storage arrangement of this Omaha terminal was so different as to raise problems of nomenclature. The four large flat-storage areas began to be called vats by Company employees, but this violated John Sr.'s sense of order, and he wrote a sharp note to John Jr., Neilson, Crosby, Julius Hendel and F. J. Hays: "I notice that those having to do with the handling of grain in the Omaha elevator refer to the large bins as 'vats.' I want this practice stopped. Have these bins called 'bins' and you can differentiate if necessary by using letters for the large units and numbers for the small units. Will you please give the necessary instructions to your subordinates so that hereafter these units will be called 'bins.' " Subsequently, this Omaha configuration and others like it later became known as the "big bin" approach, and John Jr. and others (but not everyone) at Cargill became great boosters. John Jr. was particularly enamored of the "big bin" cost savings and enjoyed pointing out the huge expanse of surfaces (with attendant wear) that 100 bins of 10,000 bushels would have against a single bin of 1 million bushels.

There were concerns about the Omaha terminal. First, the concept of flat storage itself was controversial within the Company and the industry. There were substantial handling costs associated with this type of storage, to be balanced against the inexpensive fixed costs of the construction. Further, an inspector from the Nebraska Inspection Bureau was concerned about the lack of venting of the bins and the suspended dust in the air above the open storage tanks, which "can be removed only by a natural ventilation." Bert Lang, John Jr.'s bank officer friend in St. Louis, queried him in late September 1930 about turning the grain in the large bins for ventilation: "Naturally my grain man's mind runs to the thought of how this house could be safely operated in a year of high moisture content . . . how you would be able to detect a warm spot in these bins before it has progressed to a point that involved a large percentage of the contents."

John Jr. assured Lang that there was no problem, that Neilson had developed a new type of long probe. In another letter to Lang, John Jr. added, "We are more than delighted with the economy of the plant, as it is by all odds the most economical in operation of any grain elevator that we know anything about . . . in fact, some of our most practical men prefer this type of storage from results shown to date." Both John Sr. and John Jr. were extremely proud of their Omaha operation. They made a joint visit there in mid-August, and John Sr. wrote Cargill MacMillan: "Junior and I had a wonderful day in Omaha . . . the new elevator is working perfectly." The rapid construction and the unique appearance made the terminal a tourist site in Omaha.

Many people asked for a closer look, but John Sr. wrote Lewis Crosby, the manager: "Under no circumstances do we want anyone taken thru our elevator at Omaha without instructions from this office . . . we want them shown only the ground floor of the workhouse, including the operation of the car dump. . . . Under no circumstances is anyone to be allowed to see our bin plan, and we are instructing Mr. Neilson to see that there is a door with a lock provided for each one of these so no one entering these offices casually can see the plant." The Omaha terminal was a truly proprietary Cargill innovation—and to be protected! A number of Cargill men later to become senior management trained in this innovative terminal, among them Roy Gretzer and Ed McCoy.[2]

In the summer of 1931, the Omaha terminal was doubled in size to a 10-million-bushel capacity by finishing the roof and tanks on the other side as a duplicate of the first. The total construction cost for this huge terminal was astoundingly low by industry standards; John Jr., in a later memorandum to the Russian government, estimated the total cost at $1,050,000: approximately $600,000 for the first unit of 5 million bushels (which included the workhouse) and $300,000 for the second 5- million-bushel unit, with another $150,000 for cleaning tanks. Thus, the total cost of the operation, assuming these were accurate figures, was just 10½ cents per bushel.

At a later point, after John Jr. had built other versions of this terminal, a rail president queried him, wondering if the railroad could use such a building for grain storage. John Jr. answered, "In practice we are able to secure approximately four times as much for the same expenditure as with conventional design." He did not encourage the rail president, however; John Jr. truly felt that only Cargill knew the special ways of such an unconventional elevator: "If you should decide to go ahead with additional elevator construction we would be glad to talk with you further about our type of structure, although as I told you the other evening, it is very doubtful if this type could be used by any firm other than ourselves."[3]

Farm Board Fallout

The intrusions into the cash and futures markets by the Farm Board now encouraged some further Cargill changes. The Omaha terminal would have the immediate effect of keeping more grain at the western end of the west-to-east marketing movement. The Milwaukee Railroad now built 1.7 million bushels of new capacity in Milwaukee and leased it to Cargill. Beyond this, a major new addition to Elevator T in Minneapolis accommodated 2 million more bushels.

There were storage changes in the East, too. The lease to Cargill of the Superior terminal at Buffalo was relinquished at the end of the crop year 1929–1930, after three years, and the leases of four smaller terminals—at Owen Sound, Ontario; Sleepy Eye and Union, Minnesota; and LaCrosse, Wisconsin, totaling 2.5 million bushels—were not to be renewed. However, the large additions led to a net increase in total Company capacity—from 15,220,000 bushels in 1929 to 21,420,000 in 1930.

A planning memorandum on July 2, 1930, noted that "taking into account the lower price of grains now as compared with a year ago, it is probable that even with the addition of the space . . . our working capital requirements will be LOWER by from $2,000,000 to $6,000,000 than was the case last year . . . unless a large fobbing business is done at the seaboard." The report also emphasized the change in the "pipeline" concept brought about by the Farm Board's actions with that May 1930 wheat futures contract at the Chicago Board of Trade: "Special attention is directed to the much greater security in our position in carrying unsold stocks in the West in our present plants and in the new elevators rather than in the East where they are subjected to a considerable hedging hazard."[4]

Early in 1931, a large terminal elevator in Superior, Wisconsin, the Itasca, became available for purchase. Cargill wanted it, but the restrictions in the Company's certificate of incorporation relating to the mortgaging of property while preferred stock was outstanding would have made direct purchase difficult. Thus, it was decided to establish a separate corporation, with the stock subscription to be offered to the holders of the Cargill Elevator common stock, on a basis of 1 share of Itasca for each 24 shares of Cargill. The subscription price was $120 per share. Most, but not all, of the common stockholders accepted, and the 2.4-million-bushel terminal was added to Cargill's Duluth/Superior capacity, which now stood at 7.2 million.

Later, this device of offering physical properties (not just terminal buildings but also shipping) to holders of common stock as separate, personal holdings was frequently utilized by Cargill.

"The World's Largest Grain Elevator"

In the summer of 1931, a fresh proposal surfaced, one that was to be spectacular in its final form. This involved the new Albany deep-water port, where just-completed dredging had allowed a 27-foot depth, adequate for many oceangoing ships.

At the beginning, the story had a dash of drama to it. While on an inspection trip of the Erie Canal, John Jr. and Neilson learned that the Albany Port Commission was contemplating construction of a new terminal and was about to promise the lease to a Canadian syndicate. The two Cargill executives went immediately to the office of Peter G. Ten Eyck, the Commission's chairman. Ten Eyck had in mind a capacity of some 3½ million bushels and wanted to spend about $1.5 million for it. But, Ten Eyck told them, it seemed that building costs would be closer to $1 per bushel, similar to such costs at Buffalo and Montreal.

The two Cargill executives asked for a ten-minute recess, and returned with an offer: Cargill could, for $1.5 million, give the Commission at least a 12-million-bushel terminal, this in steel and concrete with pneumatic unloading, a car dump, and all of the equipment that ordinarily went into a first-class seaboard elevator.

Ten Eyck's reply was equally prompt. "If you gentlemen can return here in ten days' time with an offer from a responsible builder, I will break off negotiations with the syndicate and lease the plant to you." John Jr. once

Cargill's Albany terminal elevator, 1930s.

more had shown a high degree of entrepreneurship, making a decision to proceed without even a check back to Minneapolis and the Cargill board of directors—quick decision-making, bordering on impulsiveness, a trait likely encouraged by his father's unwavering support. The decision was all the more remarkable in that the Omaha terminal had been built under the belief that the Company's storage capacity needed to be moved west. In the two years of the Farm Board's management of the nation's grain supplies, very little grain export had been possible due to the artificially elevated United States price as against that of Europe. There was both vision and blind hope in John Jr.'s pursuit of Albany as an alternative deep-water port to that of Montreal.

He spelled out this vision in a memorandum to the Port Commission written on August 18, 1931. Using a small chart, he first showed the volume of business that Cargill did all over the Great Lakes. For the previous three years, the total had been just at 30 million bushels each year. The estimate of Cargill's lake shipments for export, however, had dropped substantially over these three years, from over 10 million bushels in 1928 and an even larger 12.1 million in 1929 to a figure of 7.3 million in 1930 (the 1931 figures, when the year ended, would be even smaller). John Jr. asserted that Cargill was the largest shipper from the Great Lakes, exclusive of the Canadian Pool shipments, and that "this shipping business would render it a very simple matter each Fall to fill a large elevator at Albany with view of supplying its foreign trade in grain while the Port of Montreal is closed."

This could be matched equally with a backhaul: "As this grain is shipped out, the space so rendered available could be filled with cotton, rubber, sugar or coffee which would be ready to go West via the Erie Canal when navigation opens in the Spring." Thus, John Jr.'s underlying strategy contemplated that most of the Company's grain shipments would be from the Lakes through a newly improved Welland Canal (finished in 1932, with only eight locks, taking 30-foot draft vessels) to Oswego and thence by the Erie Canal to Albany (or, alternatively, from Buffalo straight through to Albany via the Canal). Later this would lead John Jr. to another set of innovations, these relating specifically to the Erie Canal itself.

Within days, Cargill had contacted the James Stewart Corporation, at that time the world's largest builder of grain elevators. Their bid came forward at the target price of $1.5 million, even adding an additional 1½ million bushels of capacity—now the total would be 13½ million bushels. The layout was similar to that at Omaha, with the four huge flat-storage areas; in this case the workhouse was located in the center. The Albany Port District Commission accepted the proposal forthwith; the Commission was to be the owner of the properties, with a long-term lease being tendered to Cargill.

Construction commenced immediately, and the entire operation was finished in the spring of 1932. The dedication of the Port of Albany in early June was attended by dignitaries from all over the state of New York, including Governor Franklin D. Roosevelt. The Cargill terminal was in full operation a few weeks later. At the start, the availability of tugs and barges held them back; John Jr. wrote Ten Eyck: "The only difficulty we have encountered has been the limited capacity of the Erie Canal. We have chartered all available equipment . . . but it has been entirely inadequate to take care of the volume which we would like to have moved."

Once again the banking community seemed skittish about the new configuration. C. V. Essroger, an officer at the First National Bank of Chicago, wrote John Sr. in July 1932: "There has been considerable gossip in the grain circles about these elevators . . . some of our friends think that there is considerable potential danger in loading up bins with 750,000 bushels, particularly if there be a wet harvest. They also think that there is a great risk of grain getting out of condition when stored in such large units, and that no real test has yet been made, as you have been handling mostly dry wheat."

John Sr. chose to sidestep the question, saying only, "We have found that by using the proper precautions this large type of bin is even safer than the old type." As to damp grain, "we would not think for a moment of using this type of construction for damp grain . . . using the precautions which we do, with the technical staff which we have developed for our type of business, we consider these bins altogether superior to the old type, all factors considered." This exchange must have been unsettling to the Cargill board, however: this time the writer was not Bert Lang, an old St. Louis banker friend, but an officer in one of Chicago's most prestigious financial institutions.[5]

Was the Omaha Terminal Safe?

Ever since the disastrous explosion at the Armour Grain Company in Chicago in 1921, in which four employees had been killed and the huge terminal and its 7.5 million tons of stored grain virtually destroyed, the grain and milling industries had become extremely safety conscious. Grain is highly combustible, grain dust particularly so; grain in piles sometimes does allow excessive heat buildup inside the pile, always with the possibility of spontaneous combustion. Fire is the companion of explosions, and grain burns readily. So it is often necessary to turn or to actually unload and refill a suspect grain bin.

The configuration of the new terminal at Omaha, with its four enormous bins, had raised questions of fire protection right from the start. However, the first safety problem at Omaha did not involve fire. In February 1931, two employees were standing on one of the enormous 1,250,000-bushel bins, helping to shovel it toward the loading mechanisms. Packed wheat can be walked upon, but it is treacherous. If the grain itself starts moving, it creates a suction power similar to quicksand. Suddenly, the wheat under the two employees did just that. Both were supposed to be wearing safety ropes, attached to the ceiling, but one of the employees (who had been at the company only a week) was not. He was sucked into the wheat, and despite frantic efforts to extract him it was too late; he was smothered to death.

John Jr. wrote his father about the incident: "We had the misfortune to have a man smothered to death in one of the large vats [the name "vat" had persisted despite John Sr.'s earlier admonition against it!]. Frank [Neilson] has investigated it fully and we were exonerated in every particular as it was a clear case of gross negligence on the part of the man who was killed. Of course we were all very much upset and intend to do everything possible to prevent a recurrence of such a thing."

Just a few months later, on July 31, 1931, another accident happened at the Omaha terminal: a tremendous grain dust explosion tore out one of the sides and part of the roof of the structure. The roof was first hurled upward, then sagged back. Several grain bins burst outward, scattering huge concrete slabs over a wide area. Forty men were at work at the time; amazingly, not one of them was injured.

Nevertheless, the fact that an explosion took place led Neilson to even more stringent supervision. Accurate temperature measurements were an absolute necessity. When one supervisor there failed to keep steady measurements, Neilson wrote:

I consider this one of the most serious offenses that you could commit, especially in the face of your knowledge that the grain you had stored in these bins was of high moisture content and of poor keeping quality. This offense is so serious that I have been very much undecided as to what action I should take in the matter. However, I believe that this experience should teach you a valuable lesson and that you should profit from it to the extent that there will never be a recurrence of it. If it does happen again, drastic steps will be taken . . . they will not be to my liking or yours, either.

This second incident now prompted Bert Lang to write from St. Louis once again about the safety concerns. "In all frankness," he wrote, "men continue to whisper of the hazard that you folks, according to their version, have undertaken in the new storage construction which you have followed at Omaha, and as it comes to me, at Albany as well." Lang urged that Cargill make public its methods of turning the grain.

John Sr. invited Lang to visit both the Omaha and Albany plants, especially the latter, "as the Albany plant represents all of the improvements that our experience at Omaha has suggested." Cargill's methods of measuring temperature and turning the grain were its own, and John Sr. felt quite proprietary about the information. "Of course I would want to ask that you would hold in confidence everything you would learn," he added.

Lang did visit Omaha and satisfied himself on the turning capacities. However, he was still unclear about the temperature measurement: "As I gathered it from Mr. Onstadt, you use the roof openings, or hatches as I call them, through which were inserted some kind of a plunger device which encased thermometers. . . . If you will just tell me how this is accomplished I will appreciate it. Please do not hesitate for fear of insulting my intelligence, to go into this in the greatest detail." John Sr. balked at putting the details in writing but urged Lang to meet with him personally about Cargill's new innovation.

As Lang had also mentioned the possibility of a dust explosion, John Sr. added, "Mr. Brown, assistant to Dr. Price who is the head of the Dust Explosion Hazard Committee for the National Fire Protection Association, has examined the Omaha plant in person and passed on the plans of the Albany plant before it was built. His conclusion was that these plants were in his estimation the finest grain handling facilities in the United States . . . we do not believe that a serious dust explosion is possible in these plants."

Unfortunately, a second terrible explosion, this time involving loss of life, did occur at Omaha in November 1934; that story is in the next chapter.[6]

Breaking into Chicago

Although Cargill had traded commodities in Chicago for many decades, the Company had never had an office in that city. In a surprising move, the Company now decided to open one. A subsidiary, the Cargill Grain Company of Illinois, was formed in June 1931, and Philip C. Sayles was put in charge of its office there, in the downtown Board of Trade building. An exception to the promotion-from-within policy, Sayles had just come with Cargill the previous year from a partnership in an Ohio grain company.

For years, Chicago had fascinated people. With a growing flamboyancy in the nineteenth century, its strategic position at the lower end of Lake Michigan had made it a hub. Railroads from the Upper Midwest were forced to go around Lake Michigan via Chicago. When the Illinois and Michigan Canal was first opened in 1848, there also became a water route to the Mississippi River and on to the Gulf of Mexico. Chicago had become a magnet for all of the Upper Midwest.

Midwesterners seemed to hold a "love-hate" view of the Windy City. Although Chicago contained some of the country's strongest economic institutions, as well as a measure of great artistic and cultural endeavors, it was the "big, bad city" to many, particularly in the early 1930s. The Chicago office loved to regale the rest of the Cargill family with tales of the crime spree in the big city; in May 1932, the *Cargill News* posting from Chicago reported: "Chicago's public enemy No. 1, has finally been put away . . . the anticipated war for the control of Chicago's gangland has not yet taken place." Later that year, the *News* correspondent reported with a straight face about one of the members of the Chicago office "dodging gangster bullets."

Grain traders had ambivalent feelings about Chicago. Its strategic position made the city an inevitable shipping link for grain. Further, Chicago housed the Chicago Board of Trade, critically important since the Civil War (founded in 1848). Vocally partisan opinions came from just about everyone involved with the CBOT. Flamboyancy was certainly a feature of the CBOT past, with the likes of "Old Hutch," the speculator, and the wealthy young lamb, Joseph Leiter, shorn of some $10 million by floor traders under the leadership of P. D. Armour. The venerable institution had continued to witness wild trading and swinging prices into the 1930s, often accompanied by the breath of scandal associated with some form of market manipulation. The "corner" was probably the most feared, but there was an almost infinite variety of tricks that could be called upon. Always, there had been an uneasy alliance among the various traders. Some were speculators; others traded more cautiously by "spreading" between market contracts; still others were using the commodity markets primarily to facilitate purchasing, processing and selling of the underlying agricultural commodities. For them, hedging was the key.

By the 1930s, Cargill was one of the major grain merchants in the country and a heavy user of the CBOT cash and futures markets. Both were fundamental to Cargill. John Sr. and John Jr. held unwavering beliefs about the CBOT, mostly negative. This hostility did not stem just from the delivery rule flap in 1930; it lay rooted in long-standing Cargill history. When John Sr. and his brothers (and father) had gone bankrupt in Texas before the turn of the century, their own situation likely had been affected by happenings in the CBOT, far away in Chicago. In the World War I days,

Chicago's "tabernacle" terminal elevator, c. 1935.

John Sr., as president of the Minneapolis Chamber of Commerce (the comparable grain trading exchange in Minneapolis) and at the national level participating in Herbert Hoover's food production efforts, had found dealing with the Exchange difficult and had formed a pervading distrust concerning the motives and operations of CBOT members. He passed these beliefs along to John Jr. John Jr. added further charges, alleging that the CBOT had been hostile about the Company's "several innovations in the grain trade," especially the grain laboratory.

In 1932, Cargill began the construction of a new "transfer" terminal in Chicago, adjacent to the huge Rosenbaum Brothers' 10-million-bushel elevator at lakeside. Cargill's capacity was just 1.3 million bushels (the *Daily Calumet* had touted it as 16 million bushels). Yet its small capacity belied its importance. The design was unorthodox, having some similarities to the Omaha terminal. The long rectangular building had the same roof configuration—the low inverted V—and Cargill people began calling it "the Tabernacle."

The Cargill operation was largely transfer. Grain cars would come in from the Chicago & North Western Railway to be switched, eight cars at a time, by a small Cargill locomotive. Grain was transferred out of these cars by electric power shovels onto an endless belt conveyor that carried the grain up an incline to a tripper tower, where it was dumped directly into the Rosenbaum elevator's marine gallery, feeding the loading spouts of the boats lying at the shipping docks. Some storage also was possible in flat storage areas, as in Omaha.

In its first full year of operation, the Chicago transfer house handled 12 million bushels; the following two years' totals were considerably less, about a quarter of that first amazing performance. An earlier Cargill history explained this: "The device was a makeshift with severe limitations, and . . . provoked an adverse psychological reaction on the part of competitors. Its operation was made possible largely because this was the bottom of the depression, and lake vessels were plentiful and willing to risk a long stay in port."

With the lowered volume of the 1934 and 1935 crop years from the Dust Bowl, the costs of unloading, transferring and loading rose to figures among the highest in the Company. Yet comparative cost figures like these are often misleading. Far more important was the fact that Cargill now had its own terminal entrée in the tightly knit, highly important Chicago grain market.[7]

Wage Cuts

Over the spring and summer of 1931, the employment situation in Minneapolis had deteriorated severely. By September, the Minneapolis Industrial Committee, a prestigious group of the city's business leadership, conforming to national efforts, began urging employers to exert every effort to keep their present employees on the job and to divide employment among as many family units as possible. The committee had a number of suggestions for specific actions, including part-time employment, rotating employees for alternate weeks, and so on. They urged that employers "maintain normal buying of needed merchandise and materials" and "advocate your employees doing likewise."

In late December 1931, there was another public admonition to employers, this time a long-awaited report of the National Technological Employment Committee, appointed earlier in the year by the Secretary of Labor to investigate the country's deteriorating employment situation. Its chairman was Dr. C. A. Prosser, the head of the Dunwoody Institute in Minneapolis. The report earned a first-page headline in the *Minneapolis Journal* when it was released on December 23: "Drastic Industry Changes Urged . . . Prosser Group Survey Declares Job Must Be Assured All." The committee had urged industrialists to maintain employees in their jobs at their existing wage scales to as wide a degree as possible, and if this could not be done, to institute a scheme of unemployment payments. To Prosser and his colleagues, the need to maintain purchasing power dictated such an effort.

The article gained wide attention. John Sr. saw it and immediately sent a lengthy letter to Prosser, taking issue with a number of the committee's ideas. "There are a limited number of industries who could possibly work out such a solution," he began. He then recounted some chats he had had with workmen building his new home near Lake Minnetonka: "While they did not like to see the possibility of unemployment, yet I found they were quite cheerful about it because they said they could exist . . . on the home places that they owned." With the automobile and rapid transit, John Sr. felt it "entirely possible for a workman to own a home and live on it for a distance at least 15 miles away from his place of employment." He concluded: "If a worker had his own home, his own garden, cow and chickens, he might not have money for luxuries but at least could maintain his independence and his existence."

Prosser dismissed John Sr.'s concern about "distribution of the working class on the land" as a panacea, emphasized that his committee too felt that the dole system "is the worst of all remedies—more deplorable than poor relief," but he again emphasized that they believed the remedy for unemployment was a job "at wages sufficient to maintain a decent standard of living." He concluded: "The truth is I fear paternalism as much at least as you do. But I fear also the failure of American businessmen to realize fully the existing conditions and problems and the need for the definite planning of new economic policies and methods for prompt action."

John Sr. had been expressing cautionary, essentially pessimistic views of Cargill's situation as early as August 1931, when he wrote Lindahl in Duluth concerning an impending retirement there. Company policy put people on the retired list at half pay, subject to change if the board of directors deemed it necessary. John Sr. wrote: "There is, of course, always the possibility that changed business conditions might make it impossible to maintain the pension system . . . the political situation and crop failures together make me feel unusually cautious at the present time."

By October 1931, Lindahl was indeed putting employees on part-time work. John Sr. asked for a full listing of all company employee salaries, years in service and marital status. Certain people on the list were flagged as possible candidates for further layoffs; the listing of the "wheat account employees," for example concluded that "employees marked (X) will be dropped very shortly. If necessary, 'A' to 'E,' inclusive, in order named." Monthly salaries ranged from $60 to $100 for clerks and stenographers, $135 to $250 for traders and minor managers, and up to $583 for senior traders and department managers. John Sr. topped the executive salaries at $4,166 per month; John Jr. received $1,500; Daniel MacMillan, Ed Grimes, Lindahl and Hendel were at $1,250; Austen Cargill, $1,000; and Cargill MacMillan, $600.[8]

The exchange of letters with Dr. Prosser occurred over the Christmas season, and John Sr.'s Christmas greeting to the employees in the *Cargill News* also mirrored his heightening concern. "It has been a year of trial and tribulation but I hope we are all the better for the experience." There were two supreme tests of character, he stated—great prosperity and disaster. As a nation, great prosperity was proving demoralizing. "We needed the chastening effect of trial and tribulation." The letter ended with a ringing denunciation of "government interference in purely personal and business affairs."

Over the winter and early spring of 1932, John Sr. became more pessimistic about the business, heightened by his serious illness in that period. In spite of the excellent earnings of the previous year, in late April 1932, he decided to make an across-the-board wage cut at the Company. No written record remains of how John Sr. arrived at this decision. In past years, on a decision of this importance, he undoubtedly would have talked it over with Frank Hixon. But early in April 1932, just before the wage-cut decision, Frank Hixon died. Julius Hendel was elected to the board of directors in his place at the next meeting.

John Sr. felt very deeply about the loss of Frank Hixon. From back in the days of the MacMillan bankruptcy, from the difficulties following the death of W. W. Cargill (when Hixon was one of the administrators of the estate) through the reorganization under the Creditors Committee (Hixon was one of the three), through the innovative reorganization in 1916, involving sales of common stock to employees, through the traumas of the 1925 interfamily squabble, this truly outside board member had made unique inputs to the Company. John Sr. came to Hixon at each of these crises and at other times of lesser importance throughout their long association. In a very real sense, Hixon's death marked "a passing of the guard," particularly because it coincided with John Sr.'s heart attack and his resulting disengagement from Cargill affairs. Frank Hixon was the most important member of the board of directors to die since W. W. Cargill.

John Sr. announced the 20 percent wage reduction in a letter to all employees on April 29, 1932. "This is the first general cut in salaries in the history of the Cargill Companies and is due to causes entirely beyond control," he explained. The "primary cause" was attributed to "the crop failure in our Northwestern grain growing states this past year," although the year-end figures on these grains two months later showed only a small drop from the previous excellent year. "The continued political interference with the grain business has been a close second," John Sr. continued; "the volume of business has decreased to a pitifully small amount." (Again, this was a substantial, deliberate understatement of the actual results.) While he ended the letter on a positive note—"I feel sure you will all accept this cut with the best of good feeling, realizing that . . . we are trying to make more permanent your positions"—the general tone indicated a feeling that events now seemed beyond his control. His heart attack certainly must have added to his pessimism.

The next issue of *Cargill News*, in May, carried a lengthy unsigned editorial on the wage cut, probably written by the editor, T. R. Shaw. Entitled "Ruts," the piece seemed to place some of the responsibility directly on the shoulders of the employees:

Some of life's habits lead us into ruts from which only a severe jolt can release us. It is very easy to settle down to routine work and become so familiar with it that it does not require any special mental or physical effort. We become mentally lazy, taking everything for granted, do not bother to analyze or study out a proposition or new idea—just drift through life in the easiest and simplest manner possible. Many of us have been drifting along in a very comfortable and contented rut, not realizing how fortunate we were, but the 20% jolt this month has certainly pushed us out of this rut.

The editorial then reiterated the "getting back to basics" views of John Sr.: "We will have to do without some of the comforts and luxuries that we thought were indispensable. Getting back to the simple life may be one of the best things that ever happened to us, and we should all be thankful that we are still on an 80% basis." The writer, closing with a homily about "economy in everything," ended:"This is the time to get out of our Ruts and at least try to keep up with the progress of the House of Cargill."

Despite those substantial earnings for the crop year 1931–1932, the dividend on the common stock also was passed over; the general letter to the common stockholders, on July 1, 1932, referred directly to the crop failures, then continued: "We have more than earned dividend requirements. However, on account of the unusual business conditions, together with uncertainty as to the Northwest crop conditions, the Directors deem it wise to defer action . . . until such time as the future outlook is favorable."

John Sr. received an unexpected response to the passing of the dividend; Robert Hixon was the administrator of Frank Hixon's estate and wrote John Sr. a week later:

I have to look forward to the payment of a considerable inheritance tax, and also a sufficient amount of funds to distribute as dividends to the stockholders of Pioneer Investment Company. In looking over your statement of the previous year I note that you had $2,000,000 in cash on hand, and if it is anything like this amount, it is difficult to understand why the dividend has been withheld, particularly in view of the fact that from all the advices which I have received from St. Paul and Minneapolis it would appear that the Northwest is almost certain of a fine crop.

John Sr. responded immediately, promising that it was likely that the dividend would be paid before the end of the current year. The principal reason for the decision, John Sr. stated, "was the retiring of 2578 shares of employee stock and the issuing to them of 4636 shares of par 5% Second Preferred. . . . As this involved a heavy charge against our surplus account we did not feel it advisable to show a decrease in our capital structure."

In the corporate minutes, these reasons were stated in a different way: some $138,000 in cash had been paid out to those employees who had cashed in their common stock. "The cash payment was found to be necessary due to the fact that many of the employees had loans against their stock, for which they needed cash." An additional $280,000 of accounts receivable also had been written down, and for these reasons, "the Directors had deemed it advisable to defer action on the dividend on the Common stock."

The economic situation, for the Company at least, was not as grim as John Sr. had pictured it earlier in the year, so by mid-July 1932, some but not all of the wage cuts were rescinded. John Sr. spelled this out in a letter to Harold Tweeden on July 18: "We have been waiting for crop news before deciding that we would dare to restore to their former basis the salaries of those executives who had really produced last year." At this point in the letter, John Sr. restored Tweeden's own cut, then continued with an essentially "meritocracy" rationale: "The theory of this is that those executives who initiated and executed money saving or money making plans should not be cut, if possible, but that those who were engaged in practically routine work and whose services could be replaced without too great inconvenience, should follow the market downward."

Tweeden himself was to be given some discretion for his own people: "This leaves us with an intermediate group which is hard to assign to either one or the other . . . such men as Frank Schonhart, Mr. Irwin and possibly Brown . . . we are leaving it up to you to decide whether they should be restored to their former rate or only partially restored or left where they are." Apparently this became overall company policy—to restore the wage cuts on a selective basis, based upon individual merit and productivity (the senior executives put themselves last on this). The passed dividend for common stockholders also was restored, on December 8, 1932; it was $7 per share, just as in the previous year.[9]

John Sr.'s Christmas greeting in the December 1932 *Cargill News* sent a more buoyant message, although he was still cautious: "There is a growing tendency to look at the future from a fearful point of view. Fear does not beget clear thinking . . . we must . . . think fearlessly, clearly and honestly." Perhaps this was also a sermon to himself; nevertheless, he was not willing to let all barriers fall: "We must not fool ourselves by hoping and thereby assuming that conditions are better than they really are. . . . Let us then face the new year squarely and honestly, accept our losses with the good grace of a good loser, and rebuild on foundations that have truly sound footings."

John Jr. Takes on the University of Chicago

Ever since Britain had reestablished a gold standard for its currency in 1925, it had had recurring problems of gold outflow (Winston Churchill, then Chancellor of the Exchequer, had adopted the prewar exchange parity that overvalued the pound sterling). This gold standard, which the rest of the major financial powers also had adopted, came under severe pressure in the Great Depression. Britain was the first major country to cut the link, the Bank of England going off the standard on September 21, 1931. The British Commonwealth countries then had their own currencies suffer comparatively; Canadian exchange rapidly dropped from close to par to a 15 percent discount against the dollar by early 1932.

By March 1932, there was widespread discussion of the possibility that the United States itself would go off the gold standard. John Jr. was highly disquieted about this, and it took only another event, two months later, to send him through the roof. In late April 1932, the University of Chicago had sponsored a series of discussions, "Gold and Monetary Stabilization," and several university economists advocated extensive governmental intervention via emergency governmental expenditures, despite any untoward effects on the price of gold. Indeed, the economists noted that it might be necessary to "abandon gold for a time."

John Jr. became highly incensed and wrote a long letter to his Uncle Will, a University of Chicago mathematician, accusing the economists of "repudiating our debts by inflation" and revealing "a childish ignorance of . . . the law of supply and demand." He ended questioning "the honesty of their motives."

Perhaps if John Jr. had left the matter there, nothing much would have come of it. After all, a great many businessmen—and college professors— had just as strong feelings about governmental intervention as did John Jr. But he chose to carry it further: he wrote a captious letter to Robert Maynard Hutchins, the president of the University of Chicago, that ended: "It is my sincere hope that you and your trustees will take immediate steps to purge your faculty of these and other irresponsible and dishonest agitators."

Had the economists been a group of young, untried scholars, criticism of this personal sort might have been understandable. To the contrary, the 12 University of Chicago professors involved were all nationally known economists, several of them of world-class level—Paul H. Douglas, Frank H. Knight, Harry A. Millis, Lloyd Mints and Jacob Viner, among others. Hutchins acknowledged the letter with a curt, one-sentence reply that he was referring John Jr.'s letter to the chairman of the department. No record of any reply from the latter remains in the records.

Uncle Will saw the letter of John Jr. and angrily wrote John Sr.: "The sentiments and ideas expressed in Junior's letter are thoroughly bad. They are intolerant and bigoted and will not produce the desired effect upon a University president. They might be all right for a politician, but a thoughtful man will dismiss them immediately." Clearly, Will MacMillan was quite embarrassed by John Jr.'s letter to Hutchins.

John Sr. shared Will's letter with John Jr., but the latter was still unconvinced and unbending, telling Will, "I do not agree with you in your statement that economics is not an exact science. It is exact except insofar as price relationships can be temporarily controlled artificially . . . the intent of the proposal of your economists then is either dishonest repudiation of debt or else reveals a childish ignorance of the fact that the law of supply and demand applies to gold just as it does to other commodities . . . in my opinion your economists cannot be called too hard for advocating any scheme to try to fix the price of gold . . . they should be called sharply for openly advocating dishonesty in an institution of learning."[10]

Burned on Argentine Pesos

Early in 1932, Cargill had contracted with the Buenos Aires, Argentina, branch of Louis Dreyfus & Company for purchase of a large amount of linseed oil. The contract called for Dreyfus to be paid in Argentine pesos, in Argentina. Cargill went to the Foreign Department of New York's National City Bank and purchased 200,000 pesos for July delivery in Buenos Aires, at 25¾ (a total of $51,500). In July, when Cargill tendered its pesos at the Dreyfus office, the latter informed Cargill that the pesos it had purchased from National City were restricted only for domestic use in Argentina, rather than being in a separate category of "external" pesos that were eligible for free use domestically or in foreign exchange. Cargill would have to apply to the Argentine government for permission to have their pesos made applicable for foreign exchange. The process was known to be extremely difficult.

This came as a complete surprise to Cargill senior management. Not having a company employee on the spot in Argentina, they had assumed that National City Bank would provide the correct type of pesos. Cargill then went to the bank to have the matter rectified, but the latter refused to exchange the limited pesos for the freely exchanged pesos. John Jr. sent a telegram to the bank, alleging that "this whole transaction seems to me to reflect on the good faith of your foreign exchange department."

The bank officer, a senior vice president, replied: "Your original telegram gave no indication that you wanted pesos available for export purposes. Your people must have known that there were export restrictions and were the only ones who would know that the pesos were to be used for this particular purpose. . . . It is true that pesos have declined in price . . . this is part of the risk inherent in a forward purchase just as it might be in a commodity market. . . . I am sorry that you will suffer a loss if you sell the pesos in today's market . . . but what you have are good sound pesos, which cannot be questioned."

Cargill MacMillan, attempting to pour oil on the troubled waters, wrote the officer handling Cargill's domestic business with the bank: "I did not wish to argue with Mr. Simonson, because he had told me that he had rather taken offense at a message my brother had sent to you, and I, therefore, felt that if I argued further he might take further offense. . . . We believe that inasmuch as you handle our account and know us that you will appreciate that we most earnestly and sincerely feel that we have a grievance and are not simply yelling because we have been hurt." This effort did not produce any further results, and finally, in late September, John Jr. proposed that the whole matter be settled "by informal arbitration."

The bank, however, refused to entertain any such notions. John Sr. entered the fray, sending a long letter to Cargill's domestic link at the bank:

My first impression was that our organization must have been at fault, and the fact that it was our first transaction in Argentine pesos made it altogether likely that in our ignorance on this subject we must have blundered. However, I have checked up with other bankers who are familiar with such problems, and in no instance have we found one who thought that we had blundered or that we are under any obligation to accept anything but the official pesos. I greatly regret that someone in Mr. Shaw's department blundered and took it upon himself to assume that because you had customers who could use this type of pesos that it was reasonable to assume that we could use them also. Even granting that whoever handled this may have felt this way, at the same time it was clearly his duty to give us the facts so that we could determine for ourselves whether this character of transaction would be acceptable to us.

The bank responded with an offer to make up the difference between the rate of the freely traded pesos and the restricted pesos. However, it flatly refused to exchange the limited pesos for a new set of free pesos. John Sr. rejected this proposal: "We cannot come to any other belief but that we paid for official government pesos and we, therefore, must insist that such should have been delivered." This letter finally brought action from the bank, and the vice president of the Foreign Department agreed to cancel completely the Cargill contract. John Sr. responded, "We are glad to note your conclusion of this controversy, which I can assure you has been most distasteful to this organization."

Then John Sr. received a shock: The officer at the bank who was Cargill's regular domestic contact wrote back that the situation had "created a condition which leads me to suggest that I am very doubtful that your active relationship with this institution will be one of mutual satisfaction in the future, so I suggest that it be terminated." John Sr. replied: "I had supposed that Mr. Shaw's last letter was an acknowledgement that he was finally convinced of the correctness of our position in the matter of the Argentine pesos and I am very much surprised to learn the contrary. It is of course useless to maintain business relations except where there is mutual confidence and trust."

John Sr. seemed unable to let the matter rest (a trait he was to show more of later), and sent another long letter back to the officer. He first outlined Cargill's view of the situation itself, then continued: "The transaction referred to, we think, was one of exceedingly sharp practice . . . to our great surprise neither of you would investigate. We then took what appears to us the reasonable procedure of asking for a friendly and informal arbitration . . . and again were refused." He ended the letter: "I can only say that I have treated The National City Bank exactly as I would want one of our customers to do with us under similar circumstances, for I do not believe that either one of us will stand for sharp practices at all. That is why I feel so confident that some day you will see fit to express regret at the stand that was taken and admit that our position was right and just."

This brought an outraged letter from the bank officer: "You speak of apology due you. To this I cannot agree, but frankly if there is one due it is due us from you by reason of the accusation of sharp practices contained in the last paragraph of your letter. Even though you wrote me personally, I cannot help but resent any such reflection on my institution or my associates." This closed the matter as far as any direct relations between Cargill and the National City Bank. John Sr. instructed all company personnel to cease relations with the bank and forthwith reduced the account to a balance of 1 cent.

Probably for reasons of both prudence and pride, John Sr. decided to put together a packet of all of the materials in the controversy—the letters and telegrams to and from the bank—and then circulate these packets among several of his contacts in other banks in the Cargill orbit. One of these went to his long-time friend, Bert Lang, at the First National Bank of St. Louis. Lang expressed surprise at the set of events, asked for "the privilege of retaining your enclosures for our permanent file, thus putting us in a position to quote facts should a sincere and legitimate inquiry come to us." John Sr. must have worried that the termination of Cargill's relationship with the National City Bank would become known by other banks and result in prejudice against Cargill. Lang assured him that he did not believe this would happen: "After going through the file very carefully, I can assure you in all candor that we see nothing in the whole transaction that could possibly create any prejudice on our part against the good name of 'Cargill.' "

In John Sr.'s file on this incident, there is an unsigned fragment, apparently sent to the National City Bank from an officer in a Minneapolis bank. The letter noted that John Sr. had asked this bank to review the dossier; the bank officer continued:

I selected our Vice President, Mr. J. G. Byam, who is at the head of our Foreign Exchange Department, to do this. Mr Byam tells me that he undertook this with a strong feeling that the Cargill Elevator Company through some misunderstanding must be in the wrong, but very greatly to his surprise finds that their position has been entirely correct and that he does not see how they could possibly have done differently. He agrees with Mr. MacMillan that the internal evidence shows conclusively that neither you nor Mr. Simonson had ever checked into this affair and I strongly urge that you do so for, unfortunately, anyone going through this file carefully cannot but impugn the good faith of your Foreign Exchange Department.

Whether this letter was, indeed, sent cannot now be reconstructed from the remaining records.

By this time, in late 1932, Cargill's banking crisis of March 1933 was just around the corner. Whether this National City Bank incident had any influence on this is not clear. At any rate, even before Cargill's drawn-out difficulties at that time with the Guaranty Trust (discussed later in this chapter), a relationship had been severed with another New York bank.[11]

The Election of FDR

By 1932, the country was in dire straits. The unemployed numbered upward of 13 million, with impoverished families in cities and rural areas alike eking out a living under dispiriting prospects. William Leuchtenburg estimated that as many as 2 million people "were wandering the country in a fruitless quest for work, or adventure or just a sense of movement." Hobo jungles had sprung up all across the land. On the outskirts of many big cities, the homeless had thrown up makeshift shacks, soon known as "Hoovervilles." Those lucky people still employed, most likely already working part-time, quaked for fear that they too would be laid off. Clearly, the country had lost faith in Herbert Hoover. "As the party in power during hard times," William Leuchtenburg commented, "the Republicans faced almost certain defeat in the 1932 elections."[12]

The outlook for the farmer was, if anything, even more dismal. The crop year 1930–1931 had been excellent, so world wheat stocks on August 1, 1931, were some 300 to 350 million bushels above normal—"a persisting super abundance of wheat in the midst of intensified economic depression," wrote the *Wheat Studies* editors. Once the Farm Board had ceased its stabilization purchases, there was a sickening sag in wheat prices. From about 60 cents in May 1931, the average farm price dropped to 36 cents in

Franklin D. Roosevelt campaigning for president (Minnesota Historical Society).

July and even lower in August and September. There was a small recovery in the fall, but the trend continued downward into 1932. With the weighted average for the crop year some 37.9 cents, the farm value of the crop, including that held for seed, came only to $282 million, the lowest since the crop year 1894–1895.[13]

By the end of 1931, many farmers had given up on the Farm Board, which by this time was moribund. In the depths of their desperation, some farmers tried to take matters into their own hands. In Iowa, a group under Milo Reno, a bombastic National Farmers Union leader, banded together to declare a "farm holiday" during the spring and summer of 1932. They espoused an essentially nihilist thesis: "Stay at home—buy nothing, sell nothing." The movement spread to neighboring states. In truth, they did more than "stay at home," for angry mobs soon traveled the farm roads, not infrequently dumping milk wagons and parading the streets of the farm towns with placards such as "In Hoover We Trusted, Now We Are Busted."[14]

These were isolated events, but later there were more. The main battles fought in the spring of 1932 were by those once again searching for remedial legislation from the federal government for the "farm problem." The McNary-Haugenites resurrected their oft-rejected plan involving the

"*Pickets dumping milk,*" *Wisconsin, c. 1937* (The Bettmann Archive).

equalization fee; the export debenture plan still was the favorite of the Grange. The National Farmers Union, more radical than the Grange or the Farm Bureau, came forward strongly for outright price fixing by the government, with a built-in guarantee to the farmer of his "cost of production" plus a profit.

By the spring of 1932, it seemed highly likely that Franklin D. Roosevelt, the governor of New York, would be the standard-bearer for the Democrats. Advocates of the various farm plans beat a path to his door, hoping to have him commit to them. Roosevelt adroitly parried all of their remonstrances; by the summer of 1932, he seemed to be leaning toward a fourth way out of the farmer's dilemma that came to be called the "voluntary domestic allotment" plan. Rather than subsidizing or encouraging exports from a surplus domestic crop, this plan aimed at reducing production as the essential remedy for agricultural ills. The plan, with its avowed purpose of constraining supply (and therefore, by definition, constricting "free" markets), was an instant anathema to the grain trade industry and much of the business community.

Roosevelt handily captured the nomination at the Democratic National Convention in early July and in his acceptance speech outlined his thinking on the farm problem in terms of the voluntary domestic allotment plan. Already the master politician (although many had not yet recognized this), he continued to keep everyone guessing about his thoughts on policy initiatives.

To the grain traders, it was a Hobson's choice between Hoover and Roosevelt—the former had botched the agricultural situation with his ill-fated Farm Board, and the latter professed market-constraining approaches to the same problems. John Sr. probably mirrored the majority feeling in the trade when he wrote Morris Barker: "I have no sympathy whatever with the Democratic candidate nor his machine. As far as I can make out he is very much the same type as Mr. Hoover, and I am afraid equally dangerous. When it comes to a choice of whether Northern Bureaucrats or Southern Bureaucrats are going to run the country, as far as I can make out they are all equally dangerous."

On the other hand, Ed Grimes saw the Roosevelt nomination as a potential plus for Cargill, given that the governor had been present at the inauguration of the Albany deep-sea port the previous June. Grimes wrote a fellow member of a Chicago Board of Trade political action committee about the great amount of grain that was being shipped through Cargill's unit: "Just what appeal this would have to Governor Roosevelt in his capacity as nominee for President, I do not know, but I do think that the design of this plant, together with other improvements and refinements . . . have been of great benefit not only to the farmer but to the consumer . . . most of the economies are not retained by us but are passed on to our patrons." Grimes was unclear about how to get this notion in front of Roosevelt without sounding self-serving.[15]

Despite forebodings, the grain trade had remained surprisingly profitable during this preelection period. With the Farm Board out of the picture (except for its own sales of grain into the market on a staged basis), the industry was free to trade in its pre–Farm Board mode. Cargill had another good year, although not quite as successful as the previous one. When the books were closed on the crop year in June 1932, the Company posted a gross profit in the Wheat Account of some $794,000, down just a shade from the previous year. Coarse grains were not nearly as successful, showing a net loss of $169,000. The net income for the crop year 1931–1932 was $482,000 a considerable fall from the record previous year's profits of $1,302,000, but nevertheless a satisfying showing.

Cargill's "Economic Analysis"

On November 8, 1932, the country registered its view of the Hoover presidency. Franklin D. Roosevelt achieved an overwhelming victory over the incumbent; the popular vote of 22,822,000 to 15,762,000 gave FDR an electoral margin of 472 to 59. The Democrats also gained substantial majorities in both houses of Congress. At the top of the agenda for the new President was the sickness of the country's economy.

Four days after the election, Cargill decided to make public its own economic views in a remarkable nine-page printed document marked "strictly confidential" but given wide distribution among the business community and state and national politicians. No author is noted, although internal evidence shows considerable portions were written directly by John Jr. Certainly, it represented his own thinking.

The foreword began by reiterating John Jr.'s view that the grain trade was at the center of all business. In the past, people had not appreciated "the controlling importance of grains in the economic order. . . . There has been an ever-awakening consciousness of the role played by the price of grains."

The rest of the document ranged over a whole set of economic criticisms, highlighting Cargill's alternatives to existing policies. A central thesis involved price levels, for it was Cargill's "studied conclusion" that "determined efforts be made to bring the price of everything, especially labor and freights, down to this level, rather than to try to bring the levels of grain and other raw materials up." The high tariff—the Hawley-Smoot tariff bill—"was a blunder of the first magnitude." Efforts to prevent wage reductions "could only result in prolonged unemployment." The attempts by the government's Reconstruction Finance Corporation to forestall railroad receiverships "has prevented necessary rate readjustments."

Further, "the public works program at 1928 wage levels was a squandering of the public money."

All of this was related directly to gold, for "gold differs but slightly from any other commodity. It *obeys the law of supply and demand, just as does every other commodity*" (emphasis in the document). The paper had a chart of "the value of gold" from 1798 to 1932, designed to show that gold prices produced swings from the business cycle just like other commodities. Cargill's belief in the "quantity theory" of money, the very set of ideas propounded by Irving Fisher at Yale University when John Jr. took that eminent economist's course, was reiterated, the ending sentence of that section emphasized with capitals: "IT IS OUR BELIEF THAT THE QUANTITY THEORY OF MONEY IS PERFECTLY SOUND AND DECIDEDLY APPLICABLE TO THE PRESENT SITUATION."

What was needed for recovery was to restore public credit "by drastic economies," making sharp reductions in taxes, "which today threaten property confiscation." Efforts at class legislation "destroy the basic idea that has made this country great, namely, the idea of individual responsibility and accountability." Finally, "relief measures, if any, should be directed toward agriculture, which . . . has borne the brunt of the deflation—not labor." The paper throughout was vintage free market thinking; indeed, a sentence set apart from the others for emphasis stated explicitly: "What is needed by economists and politicians today is a close study of the principles first clearly enunciated by Adam Smith."

Austen Cargill, drawing on this document, gave a simplified version of the thesis on a popular radio program, the "Farm and Home Hour" of the National Broadcasting System; John Sr. reported to Emma Hanchette, "Austen's speech over WGY made a wonderful hit." But would this Cargill economic manifesto be that of the new administration?[16]

Cargill's Crisis with the Banks

There was a long interregnum between Roosevelt's election and his inauguration on March 4, 1932 (this date was changed to January 20 in 1933 by the Twentieth Amendment to the Constitution). The extended "lame duck" period succeeded in heightening uncertainty. It was not just that the economic situation itself was deteriorating daily; there also seemed to be a burgeoning fear in the country, breeding more and more pessimism. Bankers were among the most pessimistic.

Just after 1933 began, John Jr. and wife Marion MacMillan took a sea vacation to Cuba and its environs aboard a United Fruit Company steamship. John Jr. wrote his father and mother on January 5: "This is one of the first rests I can remember. The boat is practically deserted." Yet he could not help worrying about the situation back in the country; most of the letter concerned broader issues—inflation, the new domestic allotment proposal and so forth. Ex-President Calvin Coolidge had just died, and John Jr. commented: "It is a great loss to the country, as he was almost the only possible prospective leader for the Republican party." He ended the letter: "I know we came away to forget business, but it's pretty hard to do so in trying times like these."

Within a month of his return, a crisis of enormous import occurred at Cargill, involving the very bankers who were so pessimistic. John Sr. was still recuperating in California from his heart attack of the previous winter. John Jr., the new general manager, was clearly in charge. With all of the broader issues facing the Company, it probably had not occurred to John Jr. just how potentially serious a banker's loss of confidence in Cargill could be. John Sr. knew this to the roots of his heart—fear of losing credit had always been a great concern, given the large amounts essential to all commodity traders at the peak of the buying season.

On January 7, 1933, the Continental Illinois National Bank and Trust Company of Chicago wrote to Cargill's treasurer, asking for information on the Company's current position and the total amount of bank indebtedness, including where this was owed. John Jr., considerably less diplomatic than his father, wrote back a rather sharp refusal:

It must be evident to you that for a grain merchant to disclose his inside information where there might be the possibility of competitors knowing and taking advantage of such information is something that we are entirely unwilling to do. If you understand the grain business at all you know that there has been a very satisfactory carrying charge to May. . . . As far as our profits go I am only willing to put in writing the statement that they are perfectly satisfactory and materially better than what we told you in November, and our bank indebtedness less.

John Jr. did not even realize how untrusting his conclusion must have sounded: "I think you will quite understand if you will think this over that any letter which would give the character of information which you have asked for could leak, not only in our own office but in yours as well."[17]

Over the years since John Sr. had extricated the Company from its Creditors Committee period prior to 1916, Cargill had been able to borrow money on unsecured notes payable. In truth, they were loans on John Sr.'s own personal integrity—it was as if John Sr. had signed every note. On that January 7, 1933, when John Jr. sent the sharp note to the Chicago banker, Cargill had $12,750,000 in notes payable to 19 different banks. There was a $2,000,000 note at the Chase National in New York and a similar amount at the Guaranty Trust in New York; three other New York banks and the First National Bank of Chicago had taken $1,000,000 each. There were two Minneapolis banks and one St. Paul bank with smaller amounts, as well at Boston, Buffalo, Albany, Duluth and Omaha accounts.

In November 1930, John Sr. had written John Jr. about the possibility of using "bankers' acceptances," drafts that were issued by companies, backed in this case by inventory; these drafts were "accepted," or guaranteed, by the bank and could be further sold in the financial markets. The process of a bank utilizing acceptances was regulated by the Federal Reserve Board. John Sr. had talked with the Guaranty Trust at that time, but the officer there "says they would surely reduce our line of credit if we should adopt a policy of borrowing on stocks in our own elevators. Further, if such a system were to be used with one bank, the opportunity would need to be spread around among all the banks." John Sr. had written a bank officer at Irving Trust Company in August 1930 about this very point: "We have never used Bankers' Acceptances as against warehouse receipts in our own elevator, but perhaps someday we can work out that problem so that we would find it advantageous. However, we never like to start a new policy in the midst of our fiscal year. We would want to start it out in advance so that everyone we were dealing with would understand it."[18]

In late January 1933, John Jr. went to New York City, where Brown Brothers Harriman & Co. had offered Cargill bankers' acceptance borrowing. He wrote his father: "They know a lot about us and I am rather anxious for the account." There were complications: the grain used as collateral had to be housed in either a federal- or state-licensed warehouse. "Our acceptance credit," John Jr. wrote, "is going to end up by our being able to place all of our Western houses, except Milwaukee and Chicago, under State regulation. Milwaukee and Chicago, Albany and Ogdensburg will have to come under a field warehouse company, and we will probably use the same one as do General Mills. . . . We are all dead set against making use of the federal Licensing system" (later, the Company's preference *was* for the Federal system).

When John Jr. returned to Minneapolis the next day, an ominous missive awaited him, the first harbinger of trouble. It was from the First National Bank of Chicago, dated January 31, 1933, asking about Cargill's position vis-à-vis notes due over the next four months. The bank officer continued: "However, I have to advise you that our loan committee still has a question mark in mind as regards your new construction and would prefer that you give us terminal receipts of your other houses in the event that you desire to renew your paper" (in other words, to revert to "secured" borrowing).

Once again, John Jr. wrote a rather negative reply: "Our inventories are liquidating in a normal manner and there would be very little inconvenience to us in meeting your views. In fact, if you would prefer that you took up our paper now, please do not hesitate to let us know. As long as there is the slightest question in your minds as to our warehousing being on a sound basis, we think your position is entirely proper." John Jr. then asked for a date to talk with the officer personally, "when I sincerely hope you will tell me which features are now causing you uneasiness." When John Jr. did visit the Chicago bank a few days later, the conversation ended with the bank withdrawing any further credit on an unsecured basis.

John Jr., feeling tremendous personal responsibility for the credit situation in regard to his father, who was not well and slowly recovering in California, fell into panic. His Uncle Daniel later wrote John Sr. that he had "so positively reassured him on the general situation that he gave up the idea of special blame attaching to him for the loss of that source of credit." Daniel then cautioned John Jr. "that he would have to look for further demands of the same kind. Likewise, I told him pretty sharply that he would have to stop worrying; that there was nothing in this situation for which he was to blame or that in any way reflected discredit upon us, and that therefore he must hold himself in leash. Inside of twenty minutes he was as happy as an infant in its mother's arms."[19]

John Jr. did not himself report the First National problem to his father but did tell him of some similar unease from another Chicago bank and a Wisconsin bank, although he remonstrated that it only "reflects a combination of competitors' insinuations . . . as well as reflecting the general strain in the banking world."

The situation worsened by the day, however, with other banks communicating skittishness about Cargill. John Jr. wrote his father on February 7: "I think you can definitely count out all our Western banks as sources of credit, except our local Northwestern banks. I ascribe this entirely to the continued hammering of competitors and also to the fact that the banking situation in the West is very critical." He also reported that a Continental Illinois Bank officer had spent three days at the Cargill offices, "making the most comprehensive study of our business ever made by an outsider." While Cargill appeared to pass muster with this unexpected visitor, "he did state that our business was not conducted in what the Chicago banks considered an orthodox manner." Finally, in this letter, John Jr. enclosed the unsettling communication of January 31 from the First National Bank of Chicago, which he had chosen not to send previously.[20]

This, incidentally, was the second time in a matter of months that John Jr. had alluded to competitor machinations with Cargill bankers. Running down a competitor with customers and bankers was not unheard of in the industry, and John Jr. appeared to believe that this was indeed happening.

That same day, a letter was on its way to John Jr. from the Irving Trust Company, also asking for detailed information on Cargill finances. Fifteen separate items were requested, a disturbing list. Detailed breakdowns of profit and loss figures for all of the Cargill companies were requested, all of the borrowings were asked for, the list even to include "surplus analysis (full and complete)."[21]

The situation could not have been more ominous. Cargill had large amounts of grain already in storage at its various locations (there were good carrying charge potentials in this period), but if credit was now to be seriously restricted, at least from several of the key banks, much of these grain stocks would have to be liquidated. John Jr. wrote his father on February 14:

I have not heard further from the First National here. . . . I discussed liquidating at some length with Wakefield last week and he agreed with me that we should not liquidate if we could arrange our acceptance credit, but otherwise he felt it was necessary. We are going on the assumption now that our Eastern stocks must be liquidated and that our Western stocks can be liquidated after the opening of navigation if need be. . . . It would be decidedly to our advantage not to liquidate certain substantial portions. However, we are selling as though everything had to go.

Cargill's efforts to work out the bankers' acceptances soon bore fruit in the West: arrangements were made enabling every terminal except Milwaukee to put its stocks under state-based warehouse receipts. It was a complicated process because the individual banks each demanded to have the strongest, most liquid paper. John Jr. wrote his father on February 15: "I then went over to the Northwestern . . . and was very much surprised about Mr. Decker's reaction, which . . . was that we were allowing our Eastern bankers our most liquid paper and leaving that paper for which there would be a narrower market with our local banks. He did not like the idea at all and wanted to know if I had discussed it with Mr. Jaffray." This was C. T. Jaffray, at that time president of the Minneapolis, St. Paul & Sault St. Marie Railway Company and one of the three Creditor Committee trustees who had been so helpful to John Sr. in the 1909–1916 period.

It seemed urgent for John Jr. to speak personally with Jaffray, and he made an appointment for February 21. He wrote his father: "I spent an hour with Mr. Jaffray this morning and was unable to get a single expression of opinion. I did all the talking, and although he was obviously interested, I was unable to gather anything at all as to what he felt."

Jaffray Suggests an Outsider

This meeting between C. T. Jaffray and John Jr. (followed by several others in the succeeding weeks) apparently was quite a revelation to Jaffray, and he decided to write John Sr. It was an extremely frank letter. After noting that he had wanted to talk with John Sr. personally "about your financial matters," Jaffray first observed that Cargill had, in his view, "outgrown your financial department." Then Jaffray advanced his main thesis; it centered on John Jr.:

I know you will take what I say in the way it is meant . . . you know my keen interest in all matters pertaining to the Cargill Company and so I want to say to you that you must get someone with you who can give your finances proper care, who can put you right with your bankers, who is strong enough to say no, and who will accept a place of importance in your organization and at all times be consulted. . . . John Jr. has not the faculty of dealing with banks. His very success in the grain end prevents this and it rather antagonizes the banks, so that he must not be your financial man—and in justice to himself, he should not be required to.

Jaffray urged that there should be "a department of your business in one man's hands." Knowing John Sr. so well, Jaffray apparently suspected that John Sr. might try to fill this position with a lower-salaried man so added that "he must not be a cheap man—but one who will grow into your business as years go on."

The bankers' acceptance efforts ran into further trouble when the Federal Reserve Board raised additional technical questions about application of the regulations to Cargill. Complicating the matter was the fact that in the East there was not as wide a use of "regular" warehouses issuing warehouse receipts. John Jr. immediately approached the New York Produce Exchange as a warehousing agent; however, several of the banks in New

C. T. JAFFRAY

With dog and gun he sallies forth
To shoot things up for all he's worth
When not engaged with large amounts
Or hunting for new bank accounts.

E. R. Buell, Just for Fun: A Port-folio of Cartoons 1915.

York City seemed wary of any such arrangement. There were seven banks involved with Cargill there, and they had held almost two-thirds of Cargill's debt before the troubles started. The Guaranty Trust Company of New York, one of the most important, began to raise further concerns about Cargill at this point. In a letter on February 21, 1933, an officer there wrote John Jr.: "In our opinion the arrangement . . . would not comply with the intention of the Federal Reserve Act. . . . We would prefer not to enter into arrangements for a participating credit unless letter as well as spirit of law is complied with. . . . I question very seriously that the Federal here would sanction the operation as proposed by you."

This letter upset John Jr. terribly; he wrote lengthy replies to Guaranty, attempting to persuade them. The bank situation in the country (indeed, the whole economic situation) had become unsettled. In the 2½-year period since the stock market crash, over 5,500 banks with total deposits of some $3.4 billion had shut down. Several states had already declared brief "bank holidays." John Jr. wrote his father: "The tension in the banking world increases daily . . . the Continental Bank stock in Chicago has taken a big crash in the last two or three days. . . . We are seriously considering moving about a million dollars of cash up to the Royal Bank [in Canada] until this crisis blows over. I would not at all be surprised to see a general banking moratorium throughout the United States within the next week, which might make it very difficult for us unless we had some outside cash." On March 1, John Jr. had seen Jaffray again, who was "obviously laboring under a terrific strain . . . we could not possibly have picked a more inopportune time to have discussed the matter than yesterday."[22]

Endangered Country Elevators

In this letter of March 1, 1933, John Jr. also discussed a serious internal finance problem, the question of what to do about the "frozen accounts" (the arrears) in Cargill's independent elevators. A great many of these independents had been through very difficult times, and a number were on the verge of bankruptcy. John Jr. wrote: "I have been going over Austen's frozen accounts and I find that if we foreclosed it would give us country elevators on an astonishingly cheap basis . . . the thing for us to do is to close out every frozen account and turn the houses over to the line for operation."

This was Austen Cargill's area of the business, and John Jr. continued:

I have been discussing this with Austen for the past hour and he is, of course, vigorously opposed on the ground that if we did foreclose we would receive such a black eye in the country as Shylocks that the line itself would never be able to buy any grain. What he wants to do is foreclose with the assurance to the people you close out that any earnings from that particular point will be applied against the indebtedness, and whenever the station works itself out then the point [the elevator] will be handed back to them. I cannot see this at all and I think now it is imperative that we take over these houses and operate them for our own account.

Six days later, he wrote again on the same issue: "I am decidedly opposed to Austen's scheme. . . . I don't fear the political effect of closing them out, as does Uncle Dan." To John Jr., the bottom line of profit was dominant; acquiring money was a personal validation. With Cargill's own banking crisis so prominent, the matter remained unresolved for the moment.[23]

The Bank Crisis Worsens

"Let me assert my firm belief," stated Franklin Delano Roosevelt in his inaugural speech on March 4, 1933, "that the only thing we have to fear is fear itself—nameless, unreasoning, unjustified terror." This sentence, the most famous of that noteworthy speech, has been considered by many people the turning point of the depression. Such a belief oversimplifies, of course; there were to be eight years of New Deal tinkering with the economy before the pre–World War II buildup brought back some economic growth.

Roosevelt moved quickly. Just one day later, March 5, he prepared a proclamation, to be effective March 6, declaring a four-day national banking holiday and suspending all transactions for banks, trust companies, credit unions and building and loan associations. Only scrip was to be allowed during the holiday. This galvanized John Jr. immediately to send detailed letters to each of the seven New York banks, elaborating his plans for the bankers' acceptances, once they were instituted, and pleading with the banks to work with Cargill in the interim. Guaranty Trust had continued to do so, granting Cargill some short-term credit. The key question, of course, was the longer-term relationship, and on March 7 Guaranty sent John Jr. a bombshell. It was a one-sentence telegram: "We are not agreeable your suggestions" (i.e., those involving the use of bankers' acceptances).

John Sr., notified of this development, immediately sent a telegram to John Jr.: "Am greatly startled at rapid developments. Would you suggest that I return home?" John Jr. demurred on his father's return but continued: "We are disturbed because Rawls [the Guaranty officer] in New York did not think much of our suggestion." Edna MacMillan then wrote John Jr., and the latter replied to both of his parents: "Mother's letter yesterday was wonderfully helpful at a very critical moment, as I was nearly frantic waiting to find the bank's reaction to the information we gave them Saturday."

The Chicago Board of Trade itself had closed until the bank holiday could be resolved. Overall, however, the situation in the country seemed to be more optimistic—Roosevelt's rapid-fire actions in those first few days had allayed many fears. Unfortunately, Cargill's own situation with the banks had worsened. On March 10 the Irving Trust Company sent John Jr. a letter asking for a perturbing number of details about Cargill's overall financial position at that moment. John Jr. wrote his father of his decision: "We had a request from the Irving for specific information about our position, which indicates they are uneasy about us, so I am going to New York at once to give them the information they want in person. It is also probable that if they are uneasy the other New York banks are also, and they certainly should be called upon before the markets open."

On the surface, the situation had seemed somewhat calmer; John Jr. wrote on March 11: "Austen and Anne came over to dinner last night and we had a very pleasant evening at bridge. We had one rubber where we finished exactly even, and where Marion and I attempted five small slams and failed each time."

But this surface jocularity belied John Jr.'s real feelings. Daniel Mac-Millan wrote John Sr. in more detail on March 14 about what had happened when the letter was received:

Leo [Sheehan, John Jr.'s secretary] tells me that Junior wrote you as to the cause of his going to New York. Probably it was the wise thing to do. In any event, I think it was a good thing for him to get away from the office for he was cracking under the strain. . . . The fact that he had to face the Irving Trust Company and go over the situation in general with them seemed to unnerve him and again he went to pieces badly. He retched and vomited greatly for a few moments. As soon as I was wise to what was going on . . . I went out and read over the letter and came back and positively assured him that there was nothing in the letter that was not ordinary good prudence in times such as these, but necessarily the banks had very largely lost their capital in the debacle and it was only natural for them under present conditions to take a survey for the strong and weak features of each individual situation. I was able to get his mind switched over onto other subjects and in twenty minutes again I had him laughing and joking and feeling as well as ever. . . . It is unfortunate that Junior has these tailspins occasionally, but if I am around to reassure him he straightens right out. . . . As you know, he has a tendency to keep himself under high tension all the time, and these vomiting spells are merely warnings to him that he has been overdoing the situation.[24]

The New York visit was sobering for John Jr. His brother Cargill accompanied him, as did James Dorsey, the Company's outside counsel. Cargill MacMillan visited some of the smaller accounts, but John Jr. and Dorsey went immediately to the Guaranty Trust (which John Sr. had always considered as Cargill's "first bank of account"). John G. Peterson, then a Chase National Bank vice president and later a Cargill employee, subsequently recounted the Guaranty visit: "Apparently there was a new VP handling Cargill's a/c, and at that time he was allegedly involved in a bad situation in Detroit. The result was that John Jr. & Dorsey cooled their heels around the Guaranty for several days without result. . . . John Jr. &

Dorsey felt they were getting the run-around. John Jr. decided to go to their next bank, Chase, and make an appointment for next morning."

This meeting at the Chase the next day was critical, for it not only brought Cargill into a new relationship with the Chase National Bank but also introduced John Jr. for the first time to Peterson. The latter was one of Chase's younger vice presidents, a contemporary of John Jr. and like him an Ivy League graduate (Brown University). He was Chase's specialist in commodity financing and a member of the bank's Foreign Department.

Peterson was called into that first meeting by one of the senior vice presidents, Hugo E. Scheuermann, who asked for his advice. Peterson described his answer: "I suggested the company's method of borrowing was obsolete. I told him about a not unusual plan which appealed to him. I suggested that since I needed a lot of information about location of their elevators . . . they go with me to my room and get right to work."

It turned out that what Peterson had in mind was the bankers' acceptance idea, but he was so persuasive and knowledgeable about the issues that he made an instant impression on John Jr. and Dorsey. While the use of the acceptances for grain in public-warehouse storage seemed quite straightforward, there were other issues that troubled Peterson. In particular, grain in transit on the Great Lakes and grain left on board ships for winter storage could not be handled by the public-warehouse vehicle. Peterson continued:

I asked John how they handled their shipments . . . he answered that they had a wholly-owned subsidiary, Cargo Carriers [CCI]. I suggested that they could trustee the stock to officers in their local banks that handled their account. Cargo Carriers would exchange its custodian receipts for warehouse receipts in the West and re-exchange warehouse receipts in the East for its custodian receipts—bushel for bushel basis. . . . In the case of winter storage, Cargo Carriers would give to the bank the corresponding lake bill of lading to be attached to its custodian receipt and when the grain was to be unloaded, Cargo Carriers get them from the bank on trust receipt.

Peterson, in his memoirs, also claimed that he suggested the New York Produce Exchange to John Jr.; we know, of course, that John Jr. had already thought of this possibility. Peterson seemed to have a penchant for claiming most successful financial ideas as his!

Peterson next suggested that a consortium of banks be put together, with Chase as lead bank, for a large-scale revolving credit—Peterson suggested a figure of $20 million. Peterson took the whole proposal to Scheuermann: "I believe Hugo consulted with Irving [a Chase senior officer], who wanted a higher rate, commission being the same at all banks. Hugo told me the slightly higher rate and the substitution of a cash deposit of 15% for the elimination of the AE [accommodation endorsement], and while the upper limit of the credit was set for $20,000,000 there was to be a clause to the effect that when total borrowing reached $13,000,000 the manager was to be consulted."

This is just what happened. Peterson was able quickly to put together a small group of banks, a combination of, as Peterson put it, "my banking friends." John Jr. was also to offer participation additionally "to their regular banks of account." By this time, John Sr. was there to corroborate the plans, as he had crossed the country by train to lend support. Peterson relished the process:

Among my friends, Ruth, vice president of the Philadelphia National Bank, took $1,000,000 and my friend Hwoskinsty [spelling unclear from handwritten manuscript], VP of Central Hanover, took $1,000,000—took sight unseen. I offered a part to my old friend Chet Johnson in the Chemical but he made the mistake of giving the agreement to a young lawyer to read, who came to see me with copious notes of what he wanted to see in the agreement. I told him the practice among banks was to accept agreements drawn by known law firms. I didn't intend to open the door, so I withdrew my invitation. I had to go to Kansas City and I got the Bank of Commerce to participate for $800,000, which came out of Chase's part of the $5,000,000. Irving Trust was shaky and came in only after sending a certified public accountant to check the books. But the most shock came when John Jr. telephoned Hugo [Scheuermann] that he was having trouble with his local banks.

Scheuermann volunteered to help on the Twin Cities banks by going personally to meet with their executives on their home ground. A few days later a whole group of Minneapolis and St. Paul bank presidents assembled in a meeting chaired by C. T. Jaffray. Peterson was there too and described Jaffray as "a big, strong, athletic type, accustomed to being the boss in all gatherings, even of his peers, and perhaps good reason, for nearly every business in Minneapolis owed him gratitude, especially Cargill. . . . He was an imposing man, accustomed to obeisance." The meeting went well, and after a full accounting by Scheuermann, the local banks each seemed willing to take a piece of Cargill's consortium.

By the second week in June, the whole arrangement was in place. A total of $13,500,000 was established. For a while, this fixed upper limit constrained John Jr. more than he wished, the previous approach of unsecured credit being considerably more free-wheeling. To establish an independent entity for the borrowing and for providing independent bonding capability, Cargill Elevator Company was legally separated from two of its subsidiaries (Cargill Grain Company and Cargill Grain Company of Nebraska), and a voting trust of four outsiders, headed by John Peterson, was put in place for both of the latter. Cargo Carriers, the Cargill entity established in 1930 for lake freight and insurance purchases, then was used as the independent entity necessary for the bonding of in-transit shipments.

The participation of the various banks had to be worked out, not without some difficulties inasmuch as each had its own competitive concerns. A "commitment commission" of 0.25 percent was to go to each bank, plus interest on loans at 1.5 percent over prime bankers bills or 0.5 percent over the New York Federal Reserve Bank rediscount rate, whichever was higher. Cargill agreed to maintain a 10 percent frozen cash margin, together with a further cash balance of another 10 percent. As custodian, Chase was to be paid an additional "custodian's fee" of 0.25 percent. The arrangement was called the Chase Syndicate by the various participants.[25]

A number of banks not in Cargill's previous network agreed to join the syndicate (for example, the Omaha National Bank and the National Commercial Bank & Trust Company of Albany), as well as the full set of Minneapolis and St. Paul banks, together with the group in New York City that the Chase, through Peterson, had involved. Among the latter, however, the Guaranty Trust was conspicuous by its absence.

This hurt John Sr., for he had always considered the Guaranty as Cargill's senior bank. Now he began to brood about what he felt was a slight. His hostility toward Guaranty began to grow, later to surface.

Austen Cargill Prevails

With the Chase agreement in place, the problem of the close-to-bankrupt independent country elevators needed to be resolved. Rather than foreclosing "on an astonishingly cheap basis" (John Jr.'s earlier proposal), the final decision adopted was Austen Cargill's. He proposed that these country elevator owners sell their inventories to Cargill and, after applying the proceeds to their existing account, transfer the balance due into demand notes secured by the elevator facility. Then the elevator would be leased to Cargill, with the duration of the lease to continue until the notes were paid off. Part of the net profits would revert to Cargill as a rental; the remainder would be applied to the indebtedness. On full repayment the elevator would be returned to its original owner.

Some 79 of the independent country elevator operators immediately accepted the proposal, just about all of the endangered group. The elevators themselves were variously renamed as "community elevators," generally with the name of the town also in the title. As *Cargill News* put it in its November 1933 issue, "the former manager . . . now acts as our agent and is a part of the Cargill organization." In this same issue, the entire group of 79 were listed, and the editor commented: "We are pleased to introduce the following." A preponderance of these were small elevators (in the 20,000–30,000-bushel range), and many were quite antiquated. This set of elevators was placed in a separate unit in the Cargill organization, the Leased Line Department, with Austen Cargill in charge. The Company subsequently reaped many accolades from the farming communities involved for its temperate approach with the independent country elevators and enormous loyalties from their owners.[26]

Assessing Cargill's "Bank Crisis"

The remainder of the year 1933 was calm in the firm's banking relations. Once the Chase syndicate had been put in place, credit was not itself a significant issue. The agreement was renewed the following May (1934) on similar terms, including Chase's 0.25 percent payment.

In the final analysis, perhaps the single most important feature of Cargill's banking crisis in early 1933 was not the loss of banking relationships with the First National Bank of Chicago, the First National Bank of Boston, the Bank of Manhattan and Guaranty Trust, nor even the Chase National syndicate agreement itself. In terms of the longer run, the summer of 1933 brought a new person to the Cargill top management group, none other than John Peterson himself. The C. T. Jaffray letter to John Sr. concerning John Jr.'s shortcomings in dealing with bankers must have made a powerful impression on John Sr. and excited memories of Will Cargill's financial ineptitude. There is no evidence in the records of exactly how the Peterson relationship was originally conceived. At first, Peterson had sat with Cargill as Chase's employee—for the Chase demanded such representation. By August 2, 1933, Peterson had resigned from Chase National (with its blessing) and had accepted a position as vice president of finance for Cargill. The appointment to a post of vice president from the outside was unprecedented in Cargill history. Charles S. McCain, the chairman of Chase, wrote John Jr.: "Frankly I do not know where you could have gotten a better man for what you have in mind than he is. We did not feel that we should stand in his way and it was only that which actuated us in consenting to his going."

Peterson made it a quick break and was on the job at Cargill by late August. He brought to the Company a number of precious skills, some not present in the organization before. First, he had an intimate knowledge of and friendship with the banking community, a fact that he seldom allowed to go unmentioned. His early letters back to the Chase were masterpieces in allaying any concerns on the part of the New York bankers. Late in September he wrote: "From my viewpoint you do not need to have any worries about this Cargill credit and if at any time you would like to know about it when you are discussing your central liability babies I will be very happy to show you that everything is all right." He ended the letter with a self-conscious facetiousness that he often adopted with members of the banking community (but not otherwise characteristic of him): "Everybody is trying his best to make life here very agreeable and pleasant for me. Even the gangsters of St. Paul put on a big show to make me feel that I was right at home."

A few days later, the Chase officer apparently became worried about margins on deposit with some of the futures brokers through whom Cargill was dealing, and Peterson wrote back: "Now I do not want you to be disturbed about the money we have up with these brokers. The names are all good names, and the net amount in any one case is not sufficiently large to cause us to lose sleep at nights or to give you concern as to the goodness of your loan. . . . I want to reiterate that we are not trying any 'monkey business.' "

John Peterson was not only a clever representative of Cargill with the bankers but was also an excellent finance man (fulfilling the C. T. Jaffray hope), innovative in his approach to things, positive and direct, certainly willing to speak his mind with both John Sr. and John Jr. His eastern Ivy League background brought respect from both of them. His past experience—and his ego—allowed him to speak with authority. As his memoirs indicate, he claimed much as his own doing; he believed he had had a singular part in "saving Cargill," although something like the Chase syndicate was already in the wind and probably would have eventuated, Peterson or not.[27]

The country's banking crisis, at least in its narrower sense, ended quickly. The Emergency Banking Relief Act was introduced, passed and approved by Congress in a single day, March 9, 1933; this quick action by Roosevelt succeeded in checking the money panic. Later that spring, Congress added a more permanent piece of legislation with the Banking Act of 1933 (the Glass-Steagall Act). This gave heightened power to the Federal Reserve Board to intervene in the markets to prevent speculation and established for the investor (and the banks) the respected Federal Bank Deposit Insurance Corporation—the FDIC.

Cargill's own banking crisis had largely been resolved by the Chase syndicate arrangements. In truth, once the momentary country-wide banking panic had been ameliorated, Cargill's substantial strengths would have rapidly made it again attractive for bank credit. The Company was in a strong position in its fundamentals. Despite the tension of the period, the business results for the crop year 1932–1933 were outstanding. Net profit was again over $1 million ($1,056,000). Cash reserves had jumped from $1.3 million the previous year to $4.1 million, of which $3.6 million was required by the syndicate agreement. As John Jr. put it to Bert Lang, "we . . . consider it the most successful year in the history of the business."

The firm paid dividends on the two preferred stock issues but, surprisingly, held back the common stock dividends "due to the unforeseeable outcome of political experiments and to the disastrous condition of the new crop." The dividend was finally voted on December 28, 1933. In sum, Cargill's own inherent strength saved it during the bank crisis of February and March 1933.

That was not the Company conventional wisdom in subsequent years, however, for Peterson never let anyone forget that it was *he* who had saved the company. Julius Hendel expressed some of the complex feelings that the organization had about John Peterson when he (Hendel) was interviewed in the late 1950s in preparation for a 1960 Cargill history. Hendel indicated that "John G. was a hard man to work with. His attitude was that he did Cargill a favor in forming the syndicate. It took him a long time to become a member of the team. He pressured me, my grain merchandisers and even the MacMillans by acting as though he represented the banks, rather than Cargill. He was hired to give the Company a banking attitude similar to that of John Sr.'s and he did that job well. But, thanks to John G., we lost a lot of good men, who felt that life was just too short to take that kind of pressure." Hendel also spoke to the relationship between Peterson and John Jr., which became so close: "Peterson helped hold down John Jr., who was quick, resourceful, intelligent and ahead of everybody else but who was also too impetuous. Peterson was a buffer between the banks and the operating people but he hurt morale."[28]

From the start Chase kept a tight rein on Cargill. The constraints of segregating a percentage of the Company's cash proved a severe limitation in the summer of 1933. Cargill MacMillan wrote to his brother on June 13: "We are somewhat disturbed here by the attitude taken on our collateral by the Chase Bank. It seems now that the agreement has gone into effect, they are taking an unnecessary technical attitude which may imperil the purpose of the entire agreement. . . . We are relying on you to talk them out of this super-technical attitude, for I understand that their action leaves us with very little free cash."

The Cargill officers, not used to having *anyone* from the outside tell them they could not do something, fretted under the syndicate restrictions all through the summer and fall of 1933. Their self-consciousness was not diminished when Charles S. McCain, the chairman of Chase, wrote in late September: "While on the subject I want to give you the benefit of some rumblings that have come to my ears from other participants in the credit. It is claimed that in some quarters your bank account with these fellows is worked pretty hard. There was comment over the fact that the company was drawing on them against uncollected funds. You will understand I am giving you this in the spirit of helpfulness."[29]

The 0.25% surcharge that Chase had insisted upon also rankled Cargill people. Many felt that although the fee was legitimate right at the start of the agreement because of the tensions of the moment, it had less relevance after that point. Indeed, one of the continuing stories in the Company about Chase's and John Peterson's role was that Peterson had given Chase a special advantage in the agreement and had added the fee in perpetuity, due, according to at least some detractors, to his overweening friendship with Chase. This allegation seems questionable. The notion of a small surcharge for syndicate management is not uncommon; given Peterson's extremely important role in interacting with the rest of top management at the Company, Cargill, on balance, got a bargain in Peterson.

The "bank crisis" made a lasting impression on Cargill management, most especially on John Jr. As late as 1949, he was referring to it: "My Great-uncle, Sam Cargill, had a saying that 'credit is as delicate as the pupil of your eye.' From my own long experience I know this to be true." In 1925, Cargill's internal revolt had been fed by senior employees of the Company. They were uneasy about John Jr.'s penchant for centralizing management decisions without consultation because he was convinced of the correctness of his decisions. His father had supported him in this.[30]

In 1933, the group of bankers seemed to react in the same way, for several reasons. John Jr. had pioneered with Frank Neilson a revolutionary terminal construction, but neither man had the authority of an engineering degree. The banks expressed uneasiness; he insisted he was right. He, with Julius Hendel, had begun to trade widely in spreads, without the caution that John Sr. would have exhibited. He was interested in internationalizing the Company but had shown naïveté in international currency and had insisted on being bailed out when the agreement was not to his satisfaction. He had refused to give the banks financial details when requested. He had published an economic treatise that was not in the mainstream of thinking. He had shown stubborn belief that he was always right, and he reacted with anger when questioned. In the excitement of the quest he often seemed not to take into account the possibility of failure and potential financial loss. His ego would not allow it. It was this impulsivity, almost a repeat of his uncle Will Cargill, which alarmed the banks in this time of financial stress.

With his father ill and less able to provide a constraining hand on John Jr., the arrival of John Peterson to exert a strong, sometimes heavy-handed financial constraint was quite fortuitous for Cargill. The Company had survived its most serious financial crisis since 1909–1910 and in the process also had gained a new, strong member of senior management.

CHAPTER ELEVEN

International Interests: Poland, Argentina, Russia

The specifics in Franklin Roosevelt's inaugural speech on March 4, 1933, were vague, but they contained clues to Roosevelt's thinking. "Plenty is at our doorstep," Roosevelt stated, but the use of this plenty "languishes . . . because rulers of the exchange of mankind's goods have failed through their own stubbornness and their own incompetence." In this, he likely was reflecting the mood of the majority of the country—that much of the ills the country faced had been brought about by the business community's shortsightedness.[1]

FDR's first moves, however, allayed fears of a radical restructuring of the country's economic apparatus. Following upon the "bank holiday" of March 6 in rapid order, a whole panoply of legislation was passed. By the time the congressional session had finished, on June 16, a comprehensive set of new laws had been put in place. A Civilian Conservation Corps was formed to create jobs for the unemployed, the Tennessee Valley Authority was born, a national employment system was established. There was emergency railroad legislation, further banking legislation (including deposit insurance), a wages and hours bill; even beer and wine were made legal. Full repeal of Prohibition (the Twenty-first Amendment to the Constitution) followed in December 1933. The far-reaching National Industrial Recovery Act, with its National Recovery Administration (NRA), also was passed just before the recess. Included also was the Public Works Administration, a pump-priming effort to increase employment and business activity.

There was one further piece of legislation in this incisive three months-plus period that was to become one of the centerpieces for the first two Roosevelt terms—the Agricultural Adjustment Act (AAA), passed on May 12, 1933. Farm legislation had been debated raucously prior to the inauguration in a special session of the previous Congress in January and February 1933, and the "domestic allotment" proposal had stayed in the forefront.

The House had passed the "Jones Bill" in late January 1933, its central feature being production control. At this point only cotton, wheat, tobacco and hogs were to be so treated. Quickly, the dairy organizations, the rice and peanut growers and others lined up to have their commodities also included. Roosevelt, it was said, was in favor of the allotment principle but thought it might be confined just to wheat. By late February, the Senate had first cut back many of the provisions, then failed to pass the plan, and it died in the session.

Meanwhile, there was intricate maneuvering by many who wanted to become Roosevelt's Secretary of Agriculture. Henry A. Wallace, the Iowa farmer and farm publisher, son of Henry C. Wallace, the Secretary of Agriculture in the early 1920s, was named by the President. Wallace left no doubt of his preference for the domestic allotment plan, particularly the

Speaking of crop control.

Ding Darling, May 11, 1933 (by permission of the University of Iowa Libraries [Iowa City]).

version advocated by two economists, John D. Black of Harvard and Milburn L. Wilson of Montana State Agricultural College. Acreage was to be restricted, a tax was to be levied on the processors of agricultural commodities and farmers would be given parity payments to provide them the equivalent purchasing power held before World War I in exchange for their agreement to limit production. When the Senate seemed to be temporizing on these provisions, a renewed "farm strike" in Iowa and a call for a national farmers' strike, coupled with pressure from the Farm Bureau, quickly brought the passage of the bill. Attached to the Act was a nonagricultural amendment of great portent; this allowed the President to inflate the currency by devaluing the gold content of the dollar and/or to allow the free coinage of silver.

The new farm legislation was indeed revolutionary, the most far-reaching federal effort in the history of the country until then. Predictably, it satisfied some segments of agriculture while bringing howls of outrage from others. Most farmers were delighted, although several farm groups gave only grudging acceptance after their own plans had been shunted aside. Agricultural processors (the millers, for example) vehemently opposed the processing tax that was to pay for much of this program. The grain trade saw the legislation as a constraint on supply and upbraided the administration for what they saw as an attack on free enterprise. In the main, however, the farmers, who had seen the purchasing power of farm products dropping to about 50 percent of pre–World War I levels and who also faced the "persisting superabundance" (as the editors of *Wheat Studies* put it) of wheat and other farm products, gave widespread support to the AAA.

Wallace perceived a need to move rapidly. Staffing was first priority, and he made a controversial appointment for the first administrator of the AAA. It was none other than George N. Peek, the former Moline Plow Company executive who had written the book *Equality for Agriculture* (with Hugh S. Johnson) and who had become the foremost advocate for the McNary-Haugen legislative efforts all through the 1920s.[2] Peek was combative and autocratic and lasted in the post only seven months. During this period, the major thrust of the AAA program was put in place. Seven commodities were covered in the legislation: wheat, corn, cotton, tobacco, rice, hogs and hog products, and milk. These were the farm products in the most severe economic straits. Further, their prices influenced most other agricultural markets.

The AAA efforts in cotton, wheat, corn and hogs were most important, but some of their production control features were highly controversial. The wheat program was the first to be announced, with the White House itself elaborating its broad outline on June 16. The wheat grower could receive three years of a direct "benefit," or adjustment payment, at a figure

Off to the Economic War

Ding Darling, August 23, 1933 (by permission of the University of Iowa Libraries [Iowa City]).

approaching 30 cents a bushel on that amount of his land that was needed to produce 54 percent of the average amount of wheat he had produced during the years 1928–1932. To qualify for these payments, the grower had to agree not to plant more wheat in 1934 and 1935 than a specified percentage of his plantings in the base period. This figure could be as low as 80 percent but was actually put at 85 percent in 1934 and 90 percent in 1935. With yields high in this period, the restriction was not going to be great enough to bring production in either 1934 or 1935 below the amount needed for domestic use. Thus, the amount of actual curtailment in wheat was not expected to be very large.

In contrast to the wheat program, there were to be drastic curtailments of acreage and production for cotton. In return for "rental" payments in cash, the growers had to commit themselves to actually plow up before harvest from 25 percent to 50 percent of their acreage. The equivalent of more than 4 million bales of cotton had been plowed under by the end of the year. Even so, production was still above the previous year; if the plowing under had not taken place, it would have been a record crop.

The decision to physically plow up—destroy—whole fields of cotton antagonized many people. A similar approach for hogs brought even more vociferous outrage. Here the AAA program covered corn and hogs together. First, an emergency institution of 45-cent loans on corn on the cob stored on farms under seal was designed to facilitate a prompt flow of cash into the Corn Belt. As with cotton, such loans were without risk to the borrower, who had the option of paying off the loan and feeding or selling the corn or letting a newly established Commodity Credit Corporation take the corn over in satisfaction of the farmer's debt.

The second provision, one that brought widespread hostility both inside agriculture and out, involved pig slaughter. In the months of August and September 1933, an emergency pig (shoat) and sow slaughter was carried out, both to reduce production and to provide immediate cash help to hog producers. There were graduated bonuses per head for young pigs and premium prices for sows about to farrow. Some 6.2 million pigs and 222,000 sows were killed; about 100 million pounds of edible pork were distributed for relief, with the remaining product going to packers.

Somehow, the vision of a huge, monolithic alphabet agency, the Agricultural Adjustment Administration, murdering tiny little pigs seemed

A farmer slaughters pigs and calves to keep them off the market, c. 1933 (Minnesota Historical Society; photograph by Geppert Studio, Des Moines, Iowa).

inherently wrong to many people. William Leuchtenburg told of the consequences: "The country was horrified by the mass matricide and infanticide. When the piglets overran the stockyards and scampered squealing through the streets of Chicago and Omaha, the nation rallied to the side of the victims of oppression, seeking to flee their dreadful fate." Henry Wallace was rather nonplussed by the widespread attacks and commented: "They contended that every little pig has the right to attain before slaughter the full pigginess of his pigness. To hear them talk, you would have thought that pigs are raised for pets."[3]

The Market Break of July 19–20

The National Recovery Administration (NRA), the showcase of the New Deal plans in 1933, was built on the cornerstone of industry self-regulation. Each industry was to have its own separate "code," with specific regulations on "fair competition" to be constructed by industry leaders themselves. This was to be done under federal guidelines; for example, there were stipulations on maximum hours and minimum wages and a controversial provision enhancing labor's rights to collective bargaining.

For the agricultural industries, the NRA retained jurisdiction over the labor provisions, but the Agricultural Adjustment Administration was to shepherd the specific codes relating to the grain trade (especially the grain exchanges) and the flour-milling industry. Both groups were self-willed bastions of "free enterprise" and militant advocates of self-regulation. The NRA provisions were in place in mid-June, and over the following months the grain traders prepared for the code negotiations, dedicated wholly to preserving the maximum of independent prerogatives for the industry.

Unfortunately, any complacency that these people might have had about being able to mandate their own conditions was put awry by a sudden, severe market break in wheat on July 19–20, 1933. The rapid-fire Roosevelt initiatives in those first Hundred Days generated a substantial inflationary momentum. One of the many places where this was evident was the wheat futures market. On July 19, the *Northwestern Miller* headlined: "Public Buying on Large Scale Whirls Market Upward at Rapid Pace." The article continued: "A flood of small orders from the general public absorbed the light offerings and brought about a runaway market, which paid little attention to anything but its own advance." This speculative interest by the public had also been matched by heightened industry buying, particularly to beat the processing tax, which became effective on July 9. However, on July 18, Secretary Wallace made a speech implying that the situation was less bullish than the active speculators were entertaining. With other bearish signals too, the market all at once lost its heart. In two days of trading, July 19 and 20, wheat futures prices plummeted, some of the contracts by as much as 31 cents.

The sharp advance, followed by the precipitous decline, came at a sensitive moment for the industry. Instantly, there was a huge outcry about "speculative excesses," and the Chicago Board of Trade (followed by other exchanges) suspended trading for two days. When the market reopened, the CBOT established limits on daily fluctuations and prices (wheat could move only 8 cents; corn and barley, 5 cents; oats, 4 cents).

Even this step, taken by the exchanges themselves under their own self-regulation rules, antagonized many free enterprisers in the industry, Cargill included. In the September *Cargill News*, a set of articles appeared about the events of July 19–20. The "sensational advances and declines" were caused by "the tendency of the general public, (outside of the regular grain trade) to speculate and try to get something for nothing . . . endeavoring to make their own fortune from the misfortune of others." The professional speculator would never let such a severe situation occur, the article averred. The editor then commented on the CBOT action on limits. It was "merely building a dam in the stream," and "unless the law makes it illegal to sell above or below a certain figure you cannot compel a man from following his judgment." As to the newly imposed CBOT restrictions on limits, "it is not the function of an exchange to attempt to arbitrarily suspend every individual's judgment and prescribe his actions for him."

Clearly, the momentum was in the other direction—for more rigorous constraints on the exchanges. On July 22, George Peek, as AAA administrator, called an emergency national grain conference, to convene just two days later. Noting that the AAA was going to "get the farmers' prices up to parity and . . . keep them from falling below that point," Peek warned that unless the industry found mechanisms to constrain such serious speculative drops in price, "you will face legislation next winter which may make what we are talking about now fade into insignificance compared with the restrictive provisions that will be placed upon you." His ending left no doubt as to his feelings: "I urge you with all the sincerity I have in my heart to undertake to do whatever is necessary to clean your own house and justify your existence as the market for the farmers' grain. That's all."

The New Deal had put industry very much on the defensive, and the velvet glove now seemed to many to be more appropriate. Cargill, for one, made a significant shift in its public relations function. Rather than John Jr.'s impatient and impulsive, sometimes even confrontational approach of the Farm Board days, when he advocated that his industry colleagues ought to "stiffen up," the post was assumed by Ed Grimes. The past experience of Grimes was wide, for he had acted as overall watchdog of wages and hours practices within the Company, the physical layout of offices and terminals had interested him, and he had maintained an intimate knowledge of the overall position of trading in the Company—in all of these functions as advisor to other department heads. His special forte was his ability to sort out implications and relationships, then to send along proposed solutions to John Sr., John Jr. and others for final decision. Grimes had an intimate relationship with the older employees, often acting as an intermediary between the men of John Sr.'s generation and those such as John Jr., Julius Hendel, Frank Neilson and the others. Beyond this, by the late 1920s, Grimes was involved substantially in the broader implications of traffic and rate making and was one of the key contacts with the two exchanges that Cargill had most involvement with: the Minneapolis Chamber of Commerce and the Chicago Board of Trade.

In April 1932, Grimes was elected a vice president of the Company. In July of that year, he was elected vice chairman of the Grain Committee on National Affairs, the key public relations and lobbying entity for the exchanges and the grain trade. This committee included members from 13 exchanges around the country, as well as from the Grain and Feed Dealers National Association. Grimes believed in building consensus, working behind the scenes, using personal contacts rather than high-profile public pronouncements. He was an articulate writer and speaker, often publishing his views in trade journals and elsewhere. When it seemed appropriate to testify in some tribunal, he did so with aplomb, and often his words came to be those of the industry as a whole. While there was a circumspection about his approach that sometimes must have nettled John Jr., the two MacMillans seemed most pleased to leave a great deal of Cargill's public relations in the manifestly capable hands of Grimes.

After the shock of the market break on July 20–21, 1933, the diplomacy of Grimes was never more needed. With pressure on the industry to come up with a code that would satisfy George Peek and Henry Wallace, the Grain Committee on National Affairs strove to draw all of the exchanges into a compromise agreement that would placate the hardliners among the grain traders yet satisfy the equally rigid Department of Agriculture officials. There was foot dragging on the part of the Chicago Board of Trade, particularly by those in the CBOT who vigorously objected to the proposed elimination of options (called then "indemnities," or "puts" and "calls"). George Peek continued an unbending position throughout and at one point in early October seemed to be planning to go ahead without any approvals from Chicago. Grimes felt this unwise and wrote the Washington representative of his Committee: "It is unfair and unjust to Chicago, after the good sportsmanship and splendid cooperation that they have shown in this situation, to exclude them from the conference, and my wire to Mr. Peek was merely an appeal to him to permit them to be represented. . . . I am anxious to maintain harmony in all groups of the industry, believing that by working together we can achieve the best results." Fortunately, Chicago finally agreed to the provisions.

The shocked industry, knowing that it was under the gun to come up with an NRA code that would satisfy a legion of critics, still argued vehemently to retain as high a degree of self-government as possible. When the final version was agreed upon, on March 20, 1934, the changes were far less drastic than had been expected. Trading in indemnities was barred, and requirements were placed on margins. However, administration of the code was left in the hands of the industry, through a code authority of seven members to be appointed by the Grain Committee on National Affairs (the industry trade and lobbying group).

The constraints were low key, but many in the industry were hostile toward even this degree of control. Peter Carey, the president of the CBOT, said, "It is so drastic that many of our people honestly believe its provisions will not permit the market sufficient facility of operation to distribute the grain to the farmers' advantage." The organized farmer groups were generally unsympathetic to the code; the American Farm Bureau Federation passed a resolution condemning it for failing to reduce speculation in grains. However, as Joseph S. Davis, one of the respected chroniclers of the wheat story of the 1930s, put it, "fears that the Code might prove so onerous a burden on markets as to reduce sharply the trading and futures appear to have been unfounded." The constraints on daily fluctuations remained in the hands of the exchanges and were called upon only infrequently after the code was promulgated. It seemed that the exchanges had engineered a miraculous escape, and an only slightly fettered free enterprise was to continue apace.[4]

In late December 1933, Ed Grimes wrote a widely acclaimed article in *The Magazine of Wall Street*, entitled "Which Way for Wheat Prices?" It was diplomatic and temperate, making a strong case that farmers were finding the production limitations onerous and that the higher prices that had been experienced through the year for wheat were also provoking consumer resistance. John Sr. wrote Grimes immediately: "I think it is excellent and yet it is written in a spirit that should not in any way offend any of the politicians." He ended: "What you have been doing has been simply beyond words and I believe the entire grain trade are going to feel the benefits for years to come."[5]

Organizational Tensions

Cargill's board of directors, at the annual meeting on August 14, 1934, made an important decision relating to employee relations: the establishment of the Cargill Pension Plan. It was a program developed with the Metropolitan Life Insurance Company, by which the employees could accumulate retirement annuities from amounts contributed annually by the Company and with contributions by the employees, too. Every eligible employee could secure an annuity, regardless of physical condition, and the *Cargill News* stated: "It is the intention of the Cargill Companies to make equitable adjustments on all employees whose retirement annuities will not equal 50% of average pay." This proved to be a somewhat over-optimistic goal, for the Company could not sustain financially the 50 percent figure, and some small cutbacks were made later. Even with these, however, Cargill's pension system rated as one of the best in the industry.

Perhaps reflecting his own illness, John Sr. wrote John Jr. in January 1934: "I could . . . see that several of our executives were tired and I hope you can arrange vacations for them." In another letter, to Ed Grimes, John Jr. wrote: "Some way must be found to lighten the burden, particularly on the work of Hays, Neilson and Hendel." He suggested one possible problem, that the Company had no person active as sales manager: "We have not had any one person here through which all of the petty problems growing out of our various problems could clear, so that we were having more or less constant friction between men already tired out from a strenuous year." Harold Tweeden was being groomed for such a role until the idea disappeared with his untimely death in July 1933. So John Jr. recommended appointment of Fred W. Drum, who had first come with the Company in 1906 to head Cargill's new implement department (the Tristate Implement Co.) and later headed the commission department as sales manager. Drum began the new job on February 1.

Yet there was something deeper involved here, for it was apparent that the interpersonal relationships among a number of the top management people were not good. John Jr. had himself fostered some of this competition. He enjoyed argument and encouraged it in others—to a point. Now he took steps to meet the immediate problem. Cargill MacMillan wrote his father: "We decided that the way to correct the lack of coordination between the key executives was not by formal conference. John said he has tried that and that it did not work very well. He suggested that these conferences be informal and that they be held during the lunch hour, so we are going to see if we cannot provide a small lunch room for the key executives, where they will have to meet at lunch every day. We all think . . . that it will cut out a lot of trouble that has arisen from one department head not knowing what another department head was doing."

John Sr. was then on a long ocean voyage to the Far East. He penned a letter from the first port: "I do hope your lunch room will solve the organizational problems that bother. It might be well to include Roy Hoople, for as you know, he and Hays do not hitch together too well." Soon a small separate dining room was established in the Cargill offices, with its capacity only about ten people. It was a useful arrangement and went a long way toward easing some of the tensions of this difficult period. In the process, it became the forerunner of the morning coffee get-together of top management of more recent periods, again informal and highly informative, one of the more important of Cargill management tools.[6]

This was, incidentally, a time of tension more broadly for Minneapolis, too. The Lindbergh kidnapping in 1933 had been followed by the same kind of threats in the Twin Cities. The Company's long-held desire for privacy seemed now to John Jr. to be an asset against this threat, too: "It is certainly mighty consoling to know that we are not worth while being molested and I am also thankful that we have avoided publicity."[7]

There was also heightened labor unrest in this period. Minneapolis had experienced substantial tensions after the NRA codes came into effect, particularly over the NRA provision relating to collective bargaining. An employer organization, the Citizens Alliance of Minneapolis, fought vehemently for provisions to be attached to the so-called blanket code, making it clear that an employer could operate an open shop that would allow "the selection, retention and advancement of employees on the basis of their merit." Arguments over these and related issues continued to fester in this period.[8]

The business community blamed much of this tension on Franklin D. Roosevelt. John Sr. was temperate about the man himself: "He is an exceptionally likable man and honest, but he has no fundamental sense of economics and human nature. He has taken over a lot of theoretical university men as advisors who are not even considered sound by those university men who are outstanding in ability and reputation." John Sr. blamed most of the difficulties on labor, who "got entirely out of hand and demanded the maintenance of the highest labor scale plus reducing the number of hours worked to forty hours a week. It is making the cost of everything so great that neither the farmer nor anyone else can live."[9]

Overseas Travails

In the early 1930s, Cargill had moved perceptibly away from the dicta of John Sr., who wrote in 1927 about international involvement, "We have never engaged in the export trade, and do not expect to do so at present." Before the crash in 1929, John Jr. returned from traveling in Europe enthusiastic about the possibilities of both export and import trading. His first plans involved exporting rye and barley in a small way, "without stirring up the big three exporters, such as we would do if we started in Italy on durum." At this time, the well-established international grain traders Bunge y Born, Louis Dreyfus, and Continental Grain had major trading operations through most of Europe.

In November 1929, John Jr. posted the first Cargill employee abroad, sending Leonard L. Corlett to Genoa, Italy. John Jr. cautioned Corlett to move slowly, "to absorb the atmosphere, perfect your Italian," and act as an on-the-scene listening post for the Company. In June 1930, Cecil C. Boden from the Omaha office was assigned to a newly opened Cargill branch in Rotterdam, Holland. John Jr. told him: "While ultimately we expect to have you doing a very large business for us . . . we wish caution to be the keynote." He also reiterated the long-standing company credo relating to ethical conduct: "We wish particularly to stress the fact that our future success abroad will depend entirely on our standing in the trade. The motto of our Buffalo office 'We deliver what we sell' is an excellent one to remember. . . . If through some error of ours we fail to deliver the quality guaranteed on a contract . . . we do not wish to try to cover up that failure but instead treat our customer in such a way that he is satisfied that we have treated him fairly. Our firm has always had a reputation for fair dealing and we regard it as our most valuable asset in business."

Finally, in January 1932, Cargill representation in Europe expanded to a triumvirate when Wallace W. Hyde was assigned to a newly established London office, to work there under Boden, who had transferred the Rotterdam operation over to London at this time. Later, Corlett was moved to Rotterdam.

John Jr.'s purpose in getting Cargill moving on these international efforts stemmed in part from his concern, expressed in the late 1920s, that some of the large international grain trading companies were moving in on United States companies. The president of Seaboard-Great Lakes Corporation, Horace J. W. Phillips, wrote John Jr. in April 1932: "Bunge and Dreyfus are daily getting more powerful, so much so that today they almost completely control the world's grain markets . . . as far as their influence in [the United States] is concerned we know that they have *not yet* gone into the interior." John Jr. knew, however, that both Bunge and Dreyfus were already in Duluth. "There can be no question," John Jr. answered, "about the desirability of our making connections that can offset some of these advantages."

Unfortunately, during the period of the federal Farm Board the opportunities for international trade diminished considerably. The United States pegged its prices well over world prices, which precluded much trading other than concessional selling by the Farm Board itself. John Jr., worried that the three Cargill men abroad would become disheartened, sent optimistic letters to them, but then decided to upgrade the New York office and brought Boden back from Rotterdam. Wallace Hyde took over for him, settling in London.

It was the opening of the Albany terminal, however, that finally galvanized Cargill to push exporting. This terminal was uniquely positioned for export/import business. Fortuitously, the opportunities for such trading stepped up in late 1932 and 1933. Yet John Sr., more conservative than John Jr. and growing continuously more so, still admonished everyone to move slowly. When Boden began to contact New York banks about financing international operations, John Sr. wrote one of the lead banks that "we look upon the consigning of grain abroad as a most hazardous operation in the grain business and we have no intention of making a practice of this excepting for such limited amounts as are necessary for the immediate requirements of our trade. . . . We look upon our Export Department as being valuable chiefly for the information we secure from it, and with the present state of disturbed world conditions, are decidedly anxious to minimize the volume of our business outside of North America."[10]

Polish Rye

When the banking crisis of the spring and summer of 1933 had been resolved and the surprisingly good showing of the Company for the crop year 1932–1933 had been confirmed, Cargill executives returned once more to exploiting the competitive potentials in the trade. One exciting possibility, thought John Jr. and Hendel, lay in trading rye—in particular, importing rye. Rye, domestic and foreign, had been a modest part of Cargill's business for a number of years. In the crop year 1931–1932, some 4.2 million bushels had been traded, and this had risen to 5.9 million in 1932–1933. In late fall 1933, Julius Hendel began buying rye to import into the United States, some from Hungary and some from Argentina but the largest amount from Poland. John Jr. bragged to his father, "We are buying them [the rye cargoes] at such a price that we can move them to Chicago via Montreal and still make 5¢ per bushel profit."

Brokers in the various exchanges, seeing the heavy trading in rye, were anxious to identify the source of the new action. One of Cargill's close broker friends wired Cargill: "Can you intimate to me without violating confidence, character or source selling in rye." Grimes wired back, guardedly, "I do not know the source of the trading in rye." The broker answered, "The reason I wired you on the rye is because I suppose on at least ten different occasions in the past ten days some of the boys in the rye pit have come over to me and said that Cargill was selling rye persistently in large quantities through Pierce and Lamson. Judging by your wire they have been making a bum guess on this. I cannot for the life of me figure out just what this selling is against in view of the hazards of contracting rye for importation, if the President should use his embargo authority under the NRA."

The President could indeed shut off these importations under his extraordinary powers given by the NRA legislation. However, despite pressures from domestic rye producers to embargo foreign rye, the administration had not yet done so. Hendel and John Jr. continued trading the rye at profits upward of 5 cents per bushel all through this period, taking the chance that the importations would not be shut down. Grimes, in Washington ready to lobby against such actions, was nervous: "I think so far we have gotten away marvelously well, much to the chagrin of some of the rest of the trade." Nevertheless, he anticipated trouble if large amounts of foreign rye kept coming in the country. John Jr. replied, "The trade likes our foreign rye so I see no reason why we should not continue to import."

This profitable business continued through February 1934, and John Jr. wrote his father at the end of that month: "We have at last encountered competition on our foreign rye at the Atlantic seaboard, but that was to be expected and I really am amazed that we have had the field to ourselves as long as we have." At the end of February, the first problem surfaced. The United States customs held up the entry of a steamer with Polish rye already docked in New York "on suspicion that Poles are paying an export bounty which would bring the imports under the anti-dumping and export bounty provisions of the tariff laws." John Jr. quickly contacted Wallace Hyde in Rotterdam, who responded that it was the Polish government itself that was the seller and that no sales had been made under cost (a necessary fact to establish "dumping"). Ed Grimes immediately made this case to the Secretary of the Treasury, Henry Morgenthau, Jr., who was to be the final arbiter of the question. After a few weeks of worry for Cargill, Morgenthau ruled on April 10 in favor of the Cargill position.

But the opposition was not finished. Four days later, on April 14, one of the major New York papers sent out a wire story falsely reporting that some Polish rye in bond at the Cargill elevator in Albany had been quarantined because it contained some rodent poison pellets—if true, this would require it to be declared unfit for human consumption. Cargill immediately wrote the paper, asking for a retraction and threatening a libel suit. The newspaper promised to help Cargill trace the origin of the rumor, but such efforts are always exceedingly difficult, and nothing surfaced. Cargill sold the rest of its rye, the maligned shipment included, at a profit; but the pressures from domestic rye producers remained strong, and the Company pulled back from further importations. In early June 1934, the Rye Millers Association of America alleged a $10 million loss for domestic farmers on their rye and advocated new constraints on importations. In October 1935 the Treasury Department finally ruled that the Polish rye that Cargill had so effectively imported in 1934 was in violation of the United States antidumping legislation, and a countervailing duty of 37 cents per bushel was assessed in addition to the normal tariff of 15 cents. This was not retroactive, however.

While the Polish imports made anxious moments for Cargill, the profits were spectacular. For the crop year 1933–1934, the total amount of rye traded jumped from 5.9 million bushels to over 11 million bushels. Inasmuch as the wheat volume was substantially down from the previous year and had been traded at a net loss of some $122,000, the large gross profit on rye (up from $298,000 to $1.4 million) gave the overall profit-and-loss statement of the company a great boost. Added to this was an equally spectacular increase in the trading of corn. Some 32.7 million bushels had been traded (from 20 million the previous year), and the gross profit jumped from $245,000 to $1.4 million. For the company as a whole, the gross income was $3.5 million, and the net earnings for the year $1,995,000, the largest in the entire history of Cargill to then.[11]

The Drought of 1934

Despite these stunning successes, both John Sr. and John Jr. remained unbendingly pessimistic about the overall economic situation. The former wrote a friend in July 1934: "I am seriously worried over the future of our country. The Constitution and all that it has meant in the development of the theory of personal liberty seems to be thrown into the discard." John Jr. had been asked whether the Company would again put out its economic forecast. He wrote one of Cargill's investment banking contacts in New York: "Last fall we had one all prepared as usual but inasmuch as no discussion could be complete without a full examination of the political situation we were afraid to distribute it. The present administration has such power, especially over those engaged in the distribution of agricultural produce, that we do not dare in justice to our stockholders make the criticism which any such discussion necessarily involves . . . the outlook for the United States is unbelievably dark until there is a return to political and economic sanity."[12]

There was room for further pessimism in the spring of 1934, for the country witnessed one of the most unforeseen agricultural turnarounds in its history. Through the winter and early spring, both feed and forage crops promised to be excellent. There had been some drought in 1933, but stocks of grain had remained high; and the Agricultural Adjustment Administration, now in its second crop year, assiduously encouraged farmers to sign up for acreage restrictions. These sign-ups were not as large as hoped, and expectations into April 1934 were for a substantial crop, lower prices and increased benefit payments in 1934–1935, with the likelihood of even more stringent acreage curtailment for 1935.

Soon, however, there were warnings of drought, and from late April onward, the threat loomed larger and larger. Worst hit were wheat crops in the Great Plains states and corn in the Corn Belt; both of these areas had the higher percentages of sign-ups for acreage restrictions. "Never before, in the weather history of the United States," Dr. J. B. Kincer of the National Weather Bureau was quoted as saying, "has so little rain fallen over so wide a territory throughout the growing season as this year." An evocative recent *New Yorker* article captured well the drama of that spring: "In February, the wind began to blow, and the dust began to fly. In mid-April, a giant dust cloud, black at the bottom and tan at the top, rose from the fields of eastern Colorado and western Kansas and began to move south. . . . The storm left . . . drifts of dust six feet deep against the sides of houses. On May 10th, another dust storm came up, on a wind from the west. This one blew all the way to the Eastern Seaboard, and blocked out the sun in New York City for five hours."

Typically, drought does not hit winter and spring wheat in the same year, but this time it did. Corn and most other food and feed crops all were short. As Joseph Davis put it, "As far back as statistical estimates extend, we have no previous indication of comparable reductions in two successive years, or of such severe curtailment in a single year. In our previous history, very short crops of wheat and corn had never occurred in the same year."

The Agricultural Adjustment Administration now relaxed many of its restrictions, first by designating certain "drought counties," in which the restricted acreage could be put into pasture, then by a further set of steps that ended by removing all restrictions of any kind on the use of these acres for production of forage or pasture crops.

The devastation affected a wide area, from Texas to the Dakotas, converting formerly green agricultural lands into a huge "dust bowl." William Leuchtenburg painted a graphic picture: "The dry death scorched pastures and corn fields and turned plowed land into sand dunes. Farmers watched helplessly as cattle fell in their tracks and died. In Vinita, Oklahoma, in 1934, the sun topped 100° for thirty-five straight days; on the thirty-sixth, it climbed to 117°." Soon a veritable army of displaced small farmers and their families, called "Okies" because many of them came from Oklahoma where the drought had struck so heavily, were on the road traveling "somewhere" trying to find a new beginning.

The drought of 1934 brought home as no earlier experience had the critical importance of maintaining adequate reserves of actual physical grain in the Great Plains and other regions subject to the hazards of weather. Henry Wallace had long advocated such plans. He now revived his idea of an "ever-normal granary" in a speech given in June 1935. In this same period, special focus was also put on soil conservation; an act establishing the Soil Conservation Service was passed in April 1935.[13]

Most of the efforts under the Soil Conservation Act were noncontroversial. One plan, to build "shelterbelts" in the Plains farming areas to prevent wind erosion was criticized by professional foresters, one of whom called the plan's proponents "rattle-brained theorists." In truth, the shelterbelts worked quite well.

It was quite another thing with the ever-normal granary. Such a plan would involve managing supply in one way or another. Any deviation from "free enterprise" always brought hostile criticism from the grain trade. A number of respected economists, the Brookings Institution team of Edwin Nourse, Joseph S. Davis and John D. Black included, also were skeptical. Previous efforts of this kind, the critics held, had resulted in deterioration of the stocks and heavy financial charges. Wallace had compared the plan with the biblical story of Joseph in the land of the pharaohs, but the Brookings group felt this was an oversimplification, indeed a naive notion. Pointing out that the world's supply of food was accumulated over many countries with many agricultural systems, the Brookings authors averred that world production tended not to fluctuate as widely as the Wallace advocates assumed.[14] These were only the first exchanges of the long and acrimonious debate over the ever-normal granary, for subsequent developments under the AAA program kept the issue alive all through the second half of the decade.

Renewed International Interest

The success of the Polish rye trading, combined with the effectiveness of the Albany terminal, brought renewed enthusiasm from John Jr. about both importing and exporting. He wanted to use the Liverpool, Buenos Aires and Rotterdam futures markets as well as increase Cargill's merchandising of grain abroad. With this in view, the Company decided to incorporate companies in Argentina, England and Holland (it also considered Italy). John Jr. sent James Ringwald to Argentina. In England, John Jr. wanted offices both in London for making charters and in Liverpool for handling futures, but the futures trading in Rotterdam was to be handled by Al Greenman, who was already there. Italy was not as urgent, he felt, "as the Milan futures do not amount to much."

In this same letter, John Jr. mentioned a new idea, one of portent: "We also wish to buy our foreign grain such as our Argentine flax, South African corn, etc., f.o.b. steamer and charter the steamers ourselves, as in that way we can avoid telling the whole world about our every move." Once again, secrecy dominated.

Cargill's overall goals abroad and particularly the Company's basic ethical posture were set out by John Jr. in a communication to Ringwald in June 1934, shortly before the latter left for Argentina: "The first principle of our firm is that we decline positively to do business by bribery or any other irregular means, and as in Latin countries most business is done this way you will be at a most distinct handicap, which however cannot be helped. . . . The people with whom you will deal in general are high grade and exceedingly courteous in every respect. However, their standards of business conduct are substantially different from ours and they have not the same respect for faithful performance of contract that we have."

John Jr. had some strong feelings about the business system there: "They are going to want either a government interest in the new company or participation by influential natives in the new company. This is impractical because of the impossibility of unscrambling the hedges on grain which must be owned by the operating company." Rather, John Jr. felt that the most logical idea was the formation of an Argentine corporation with both common and preferred stock, with the preferred "to allow the leading natives of both parties" a chance at participation. All of the common would be held by Cargill.

Ringwald also began purchasing wheat for shipment to Albany. John Jr. was concerned that Cargill buy the best quality: "Buy f.o.b. steamer at those ports which serve the territory which happen to raise the best quality this year. In other words, we wish to resort to 'map buying.'" John Jr. himself made plans for traveling to Buenos Aires in late December 1934, to spend the month of January with Ringwald.

Meanwhile, over the late spring and early summer of 1934, Ed Grimes made an extensive trip to Europe to set up the new European offices. He reported back: "Switzerland, Holland, Belgium and France and, of course, Italy are tightening up regulations on trade day by day. . . . A responsible organization that can handle a two-way traffic . . . stands a grand chance of making orderly progress in all of this present disorder." Much of this "disorder" was caused by the tensions in Germany. Grimes reported on his own impressions: "Saw a lot of Hitler demonstrations. . . . Hitler is determined to reduce imports . . . has this 'self-sufficiency' idea in mind. . . . The young people of Germany are undoubtedly behind [him]. You can see them in great groups marching and singing—along highways and in the streets. . . . The people in Italy, Germany and even in this republic [he was writing from France] with its slogan 'Vivre libre ou mourir' (live free or die) seem to be surrendering their freedom and liberty to a group of politicians . . . as completely controlled as the tyrants of old."[15]

John Jr., on the other hand, was far off the mark in his understanding of what was happening in Germany; he wrote his father on March 25, 1935: "The war scare in Europe has had us all anxious, but I personally cannot see any possibility of serious trouble . . . it seems to me that Germany is in such a weak position that she would be forced to give in on any act of a strong stand on the part of France alone. . . . Hitler has overplayed his hand . . . the French will probably insist upon his retirement."

The Omaha Explosion

There had been "considerable criticism" (John Jr.'s words) by the bankers of the unorthodox design of the Omaha and Albany terminals, particularly concerning safety. In an industry where there were potentially serious safety hazards, particularly from dust explosions, Cargill had remained remarkably free of problems with its country elevators and terminals. There had been serious fires in the past; Elevator T in Minneapolis, for example, had been severely damaged in early June 1933. But there was no explosion in that case and no loss of life.

Unfortunately, on November 23, 1934, the unthinkable did happen—a tremendous dust explosion tore apart the Omaha terminal. *Cargill News* told what had happened in a long article that spared no details. "Reports from eye witnesses near the elevator state that they saw the immense roof rise and fall, and then a hole was blown through the roof, followed by flames and smoke and a terrific noise. The Fire Department and ambulances were summoned at once, and after a few hours' work, extinguished the fire."

Three men were dead, suffocated in the wheat, and several injured, largely from burns. When one of the New York bankers in the Chase syndicate wrote John Jr., "I know how badly you will feel about the deaths of your employees," John Jr. replied, "It was a terrible thing . . . the bright spot . . . is that the Bureau of Mines Experts on Explosions have commended us for our precautionary measures and assure us that had it not been for the peculiar design of our elevator it would have been one of the worst dust explosions on record with probably not a man surviving, as was the case in the Northwestern [Armour] elevator explosion in Chicago 15 years ago."

The insurance company conducted an exhaustive study of the whole set of events. The explosion apparently had originated in the tunnel in the floor that was used to load the grain out. This is one of the most vulnerable parts of an elevator. The source of the spark was never fully determined. The insurance inspector's report made further suggestions about venting and raised the question of building cut-offs in the gallery and the tunnels. The inspector did indeed conclude that "this disaster has proved conclusively the advantages of this type of construction over the conventional elevator. Had this building been constructed with concrete covered bins and concrete roof, there is no question but that the loss to life and property would have been materially greater."

It took most of the winter and early spring of 1934 to repair the elevator, as it was damaged so seriously in the explosion. Cargill had estimated that the total damages came to some $1.5 million; there were some disputes on this figure with the insurance company, but the matter was finally settled.[16]

Once Again, Health Problems

In December 1934, John Jr. left with his wife on a long sea voyage to Brazil and Argentina. At the same time, John Sr. and his wife left for what was to be a three-month sea voyage to Asia. Cargill MacMillan was left in charge of the office (it was the custom that at least one of the three MacMillans always would be available at the Minneapolis office).

The currency markets, both domestic and foreign, were in considerable turmoil due to a knotty issue before the United States Supreme Court: whether the Government could repudiate the gold clause in government bonds. "When it was first announced that the case was before the Court," Cargill wrote his father, "there was an enormous amount of speculation in foreign exchange." This speculation directly affected Cargill Elevator, for the Company had a number of its hedges in foreign markets, denominated in currencies other than the United States dollars. Some Winnipeg wheat was in Canadian dollars; some Argentine wheat purchases had been contracted for in British sterling; some 4.5 million bushels had been hedged in Liverpool futures, also in sterling; and some contracts for rye were denominated in Dutch guilders and French francs. Cargill MacMillan felt himself on the spot—the decision on what to do was his, but any changes in the foreign hedges affected Julius Hendel's grain accounts. He described his dilemma to his brother: "The remote possibility that Congress might revalue the dollar downward has caused me to instruct Julius that I did not want an exchange position, which position should include foreign hedges in excess of our working capital. This means that Julius will probably have to unwind one of his spreads . . . which he hates like sin to do."

Cargill MacMillan stood his ground despite substantial internal opposition from the Company's grain traders. He wrote John Jr.: "Everyone, and particularly Julius, feels that I am making a mistake in reducing this position because they feel that all that is going to happen is that we will be whipsawed. I think they are right, but I don't see how I could justify leaving ourselves in a position where even a remote contingency might give us such a staggering loss. . . . They simply think that what we are doing will cost us a lot of money and that naturally burns them up. The worst part of it is that I cannot help but feel that they are right."

When the Supreme Court decision was handed down in mid-February, it was a compromise. The Court found the government's repudiation of the gold clause unconstitutional yet ruled that bondholders were not entitled to sue for reimbursement. The markets steadied, and the "gold repudiation crisis" was over. Cargill MacMillan gratefully wrote his father: "We went short a large amount of foreign exchange to protect our position. We are now in the process of covering this and instead of doing it at a loss, as I expected, we are covering at a profit." John Jr., returning in early March, wrote his father: "Cargill certainly had a rough time while I was away. . . . I cannot tell you how gratified I am at the judgment and skill he showed in the handling both of our foreign exchange and our hedges in the light of the uncertainties prevailing in the gold case. He showed great determination and initiative. . . . I am sure none of us need ever have any uneasiness about going away with him in charge in the future."[17]

Far more worrisome was another situation that faced Cargill Mac-Millan, in this case relating to John Jr.'s health risk as a "key executive" on the Company insurance policy. Initially, the problem was described as being the insurance company's unwillingness to write such large amounts of insurance. But there was an unexpected complication: "This is due . . . to something that Louie Daniel [not otherwise identified] did at nobody's request. He took upon himself to write a letter addressed 'To Whom It May Concern' and sent it to each of the eleven companies that were applied to. In this letter he gave a resume of your blood pressures over a yearly period extending from 1930 to 1934." Cargill MacMillan warned his brother, "When you are passing through New York on your way home you will be examined again, so watch your weight, etc."

But there was more to it than this, as John Peterson discovered on a trip he took to New York in order to talk with one of the insurance executives involved. He learned that while they felt that the policy was a proper insurable risk, that the amount was not excessive and that "the moral risk is of the highest grade," nevertheless there were, in Peterson's words, " 'outs' on John's physical condition. They had a file with a great deal of information—with a fairly extensive medical report including his case of influenza after the War, his years spent in the lumber camps, his periodic checking with doctors and his complaints at times." Peterson ended: "Coming to the point, it's a physical hazard, as they see it, not sufficiently attractive to warrant going ahead with a larger amount. . . . It did not look very encouraging." There is nothing in the remaining record to show precisely how much insurance finally was tendered by the companies.[18]

To complicate matters, in early June 1935, John Sr. became ill again. John Jr. wrote his brother, now on his own European vacation: "The worst bit of news I have for you is that father had a severe setback following his burst of activity at the office, and the doctors put him to bed for a period of four to six weeks. We are having a hard time keeping him there as he is showing great restlessness. . . . The exact cause is unknown but the doctors thought it was a combination of overwork, too much food (party), too much exercise, and the heat, but it has given us all a bad fright. . . . It is very clear that he tried to do too much during June at the office."[19]

John Sr. Scolds Guaranty Trust

The year-end figures for the crop year 1934–1935 had been more than adequate. Given the trying agricultural times, it would have been hard to have duplicated the previous year's $1,995,000 net earnings. For this year it was $944,000. Net worth, too, was again up—it was a satisfying year, given the substantial difficulties of the times.

Yet this did not lift the pall of pessimism that John Sr. now evidenced. One incident in particular epitomized this changed personality. Undoubtedly preoccupied by his own health, John Sr. once again chose to reopen the wounds he felt he had suffered from the withdrawal of Guaranty Trust back in the bank crisis of 1933. John Sr.'s poor health seemed to combine with the memory of that trauma to make him querulous and self-pitying, accusatory and loose with the facts—traits so antithetical to his past behavior as to seem almost unbelievable.

In John Sr.'s records are two long letters, dated September 26, 1935, and addressed to the two officers at the Guaranty involved at the time. In these John Sr. poured out his bitter feelings about the episode.

The longer letter was sent to E. H. Rawls, the Guaranty vice president personally involved in the aborted 1933 relationship. John Sr. began with a lengthy description of how he had been "hastily summoned" to New York, despite the fact that he was "convalescing in Southern California from a prolonged illness." Rawls, "the first person that I went to see," had insisted that specific collateral for loans from each bank should be provided. But because of difficulties "with our many elevators located in so many places, handling so many kinds of grain," the other banks felt that the only acceptable way was pooling all the collateral. When John Sr. went back to Rawls, he found him "inflexible" and "the only banker" who felt specific collateral was the correct approach. "Your mind had become poisoned against us," John Sr. averred, and the Guaranty's opposition had "created" a most difficult problem. The ensuing three months "of about the hardest and most worrying work of my life" had thrown him into "a worse physical condition than ever," one that had just kept him away from work for three additional months. Along with the letter, John Sr. sent figures corroborating the two good years for the Company, to be "placed in your credit file of our name." Otherwise, "the letter itself requires no answer."

The second letter was addressed to W. P. Conway, the president of Guaranty Trust; its tone was more diplomatic, yet still quite defensive: "There never was a time when we could not easily have paid all we owed, but . . . we felt it would be poor policy to liquidate our stocks at the time stated. . . . I am proud of our record, of our organization and their achievements, and of my two sons. . . . I've always valued your high opinion of us and I want particularly that you know the facts. . . . I was never so astonished and hurt in my entire business career."

There was no contrition in the replies. Rawls reminded John Sr. that "the circumstances as you state them are so incomplete and in instances contrary to the facts as now set forth in our file, that I cannot allow your letter to go unanswered." The actual crisis, Rawls stated, was on March 16, 1933, shortly after the opening of the exchanges following the bank holiday. On that evening, Rawls had helped John Jr. by providing and arranging loans with which to take care of Cargill margin calls. John Sr. had approved of and appreciated this and had written an associate of Rawls in April 1933, after the problems had been solved, "May I express to you and Mr. Rawls my very grateful appreciation of your exceedingly courteous and loyal support during very trying times." Rawls expressed sympathy that John Sr.'s health had been impaired but continued, "I am unwilling to assume any responsibility therefore, as seems to be implied in your letter, for the actual crisis in your business and the necessity for your return . . . was the result of your company's own financial policies with which we had no part in making."

Rawls was, of course, correct in his dates. John Sr. had stayed in California until well after the crisis had subsided, only coming to New York to learn of the details of the new Chase syndicate put together by John Peterson. John Sr. still seemed unable to accept the statement of Rawls and penned a short, one-sentence reply: "No one could have been finer than you were up to the time referred to in my previous letter and your subsequent complete shift in your treatment of us has been a constant wonder to us and we have been utterly unable to figure the cause."

The letter from Conway, the bank president, was considerably more diplomatic. He insisted that "we had gone out of our way to be of assistance to you in every way we properly could," and stated, "I am exceedingly sorry that you apparently feel the way you do in regard to this matter."

John Sr. never forgave the Guaranty Trust. As long as he lived, Company officers were not allowed to make any further inquiries about possible business with them. John Peterson, in talking within the Company about this, would state publicly (as he did in several of the Cargill executive training sessions) that it was Guaranty's choice not to resume relations; as he put it in 1949, after John Sr.'s death, "I might add a bit of interesting history here by saying that as the years have gone by, all of those banks that would not come into our picture in 1933 have seen the error of their way and re-solicited our business—but not the Guaranty Trust . . . the Guaranty Trust Company made a mistake and sits there like a colossus, silent as the Sphinx! We are perfectly happy to let them sit." He ended this with the implication that it had been up to him alone as to whether Cargill would deal with a bank: "It has suited our convenience to have our former friends back in the fold." But in the case of Guaranty Trust, it surely was not John Peterson's choice; it was John Sr.'s—even after the latter's death.[20]

The Soil Conservation and Domestic Allotment Act

FDR was not to have his "breathing spell"—the Supreme Court saw to this. On January 6, 1936, the Court invalidated key provisions of the AAA and threw into panic its administering agency, the Agricultural Adjustment Administration. The heart of the Act, the processing tax, was declared unconstitutional. In one stroke, the Supreme Court had taken away a major fiscal source by which Roosevelt intended to pay for the agricultural allotments. Not only was the government deprived of upcoming revenues from future processing taxes, but it was ordered to return $200 million already collected. Needed at once was a way whereby the government could dispense continuing funds to the farmer while staying within the constraints mandated by the Supreme Court. By late February 1936, Congress had rushed the Soil Conservation and Domestic Allotment Act (SCDAA) into shape, and Roosevelt quickly signed it.

The central thrust of the government's aid to the farmers also changed. Rather than continued restriction of agricultural output on the crop-by-crop basis of the original AAA, the focus was on soil conservation. The great dust storms of the terrible 1934 drought, a pattern that continued through 1935, had stressed as perhaps nothing previously the need for saving the country's topsoil. The new program provided for benefit payments to farmers who practiced soil conservation in cooperation with the government. Now the involvement was based on the farmer's whole farm—one single decision, made in conjunction with county agricultural officials, in which the farmer agreed to withdraw from use certain percentages of the farm's "soil-depleting crops," such as corn, cotton, tobacco, wheat and oats. In return, the farmer was to receive compensation for efforts to check wastage of fertility and soil erosion. Provision was also made for sharecroppers and tenants to receive payments. The SCDAA was tailored to individual regions and, in the process, more directly to farmer participation. The administration had been upset by previous charges that the government's farm programs were authoritarian.

Because the SCDAA focus was on conservation rather than management of a physical quantity of output, Henry Wallace's ever-normal granary seemed put aside for the moment. In September 1936, however, Roosevelt wrote to Wallace that it was time to work out a permanent plan for such a granary so that surpluses of fat years could be carried over for use in lean years. What the President seemed to want was a system to protect consumers against shortages of food and skyrocketing prices while assuring good prices to the farmer. If another good year for agriculture occurred, yielding surpluses, the problem of sagging prices for the farmer would quickly come back—1937 turned out to be a year like that.[21]

Elevators for Argentina? For Russia?

In January 1935, when John Jr. traveled to Brazil and Argentina, a number of important bankers were on board his ship, including the head of the Buenos Aires branch of the First National Bank of Boston. "These bankers are certainly sold on the Argentine," John Jr. wrote his brother. By the time John Jr. had finished this visit, that enthusiasm had captured him. Cargill's James Ringwald, who had been posted to Buenos Aires the year before, was cautious about the Company's prospects, given the stranglehold on grain marketing held by the three private grain companies, Bunge y Born, Louis Dreyfus y Cia and Louis de Ridder. Bunge was the dominant firm, with some 43 percent of the total in the early 1930s. Nick Butler, in his book *The International Grain Trade*, wrote of this: "It is said in Brazil and Argentina that 'Bunge gives the farmer his credit, sells him his seed and buys his grain. And when the crops are in, Bunge sells the farmer the rope to hang himself.' " The whole scene seemed outmoded; as one observer put it, "The Argentine marketing system—or more correctly, the lack of system—make the nation an 'unsupervised playground' for three or four private grain companies. . . . The individual pampa farmer stood at the bottom of a financial pyramid over which he had very little if any control."

In the 1920s, the Argentine government had encouraged the building of country elevators, but the rather inefficient system of bagging grain at the railhead persisted. Indeed, just before harvest one could see huge piles of burlap bags, often 50 or 60 feet high, awaiting their use in the harvest.

Both Bunge and Dreyfus helped Ringwald when he arrived, but they made it clear that he was not to upset any prior arrangements by outbidding them. John Jr., however, suggested a new angle, namely, the possibility of actually constructing terminals in Argentina. He proposed that the Argentine government would be the owners, with Cargill making arrangements with a contractor under specifications from the government. These would be of the Omaha/Albany configuration; the Argentinians seemed quite interested and asked to have detailed plans and drawings of the Albany plant sent to them.

Ringwald estimated that the Albany plant could be duplicated in Buenos Aires for a cost of less than 45 cents per bushel, and he even had a contracting company standing by to build it. Unfortunately, he could neither get an answer from the government nor get the plans back. John Jr., suspecting that the Argentinians might go ahead on their own with the

Albany configuration, warned them (as he wrote Grimes) that "they did not [understand] well enough how to get the grain in and out of the large bins with a speed necessary for safety in case any of the grain started to heat. . . . It is doubtful if any firm other than ourselves could handle the grain at a cost low enough to make it attractive." John Jr. gave an ultimatum: "Either work with us in good faith or abandon entirely any thought of a structure similar to the Albany elevator."

Cargill's contractor blamed the Argentine obstinacy on a preoccupation with the country's hosting of an upcoming Pan-American Congress and additional time spent on settling the war between Paraguay and Bolivia. Whatever the reason, the Argentinians were not willing to make an agreement. John Jr. suspected a more sinister reason, writing his brother, "I think that Bunge's opposition was too much for us."

Ed Grimes had intimated as much in a letter to John Jr. shortly after a visit with the Argentine ambassador in Washington. "Matta said he did not see how Argentina could lease the property to us without inviting criticism from other grain merchants such as Bunge, Dreyfus, etc. . . . Bunge and Dreyfus methods were unpopular with farmers and also with many government people but they were very powerful and influential nevertheless in certain circles and undoubtedly could block any attempt to turn this property over to us for operation."

Cargill also had a long-standing commercial relationship with Bunge through its North American office in New York City, both selling to and buying from them. Now there were intimations that Bunge was undercutting Cargill in the United States on some of its bids. C. C. Boden contacted a Bunge officer, only to be told that Bunge was "only making small sales and not spoiling market and will continue. . . . If we discriminate against them or threaten retaliation, he will cut wide open everywhere."

Cargill at this same time was attempting to break into one or another of the North Atlantic ports, and once more had encountered what John Jr. felt were Bunge machinations. He wrote Ed Grimes in July 1935: "We have had quite a little trouble with Bunge lately over their financing some few fly-by-night concerns on the coast. I am inclined to think that we will have to stop buying from them for a while to bring them to time." John Jr. appeared increasingly harassed by these competitor inroads and ended the letter to Grimes: "It seems to me we never cease having a row with someone, but I suppose that is inherent in business." At this point, John Jr. gave up on the Argentine elevator proposal, recalled Ringwald and sent a new man, Don Williams, head of the Export Department in the Minneapolis office, to staff the operation in Buenos Aires.[22]

A few months later, in May 1936, a Russian commission visited the United States to investigate possibilities of Western elevators being built in the Soviet Union. Late in that month, the director of the "Grain Elevators, Flour and Grit Mills Trust" of the Soviet Union visited Cargill's Albany plant. The delegation expressed considerable interest and invited a proposal from Cargill.

By July 1936, John Jr. and Frank Neilson had developed a four-page proposal for the possible construction of 100 terminal elevators in Russia, each of 3-million-bushel capacity, and an additional 1,000 country elevators, each with 375,000 bushels of capacity. The total cost of these, John Jr. estimated in his letter, would be $255 million; however, "we are inclined to believe that introducing the economics which we can effect by our methods of design, and after making allowance for our own engineering fees, we can reduce the cost of this program to you by approximately $100,000,000, making the total cost $155,000,000."

John Jr. illustrated the cost savings of the Cargill elevators by an example:

The Cargill Albany and Omaha plants [should be compared] with the one Cargill also operates belonging to the Chicago & North Western Railway at Chicago, Illinois, of 10,000,000 bushels capacity, costing originally nearly $6,000,000 [Cargill's acquisition of this is discussed in the next chapter]. This plant was not of Cargill design. The Chicago & North Western elevator requires 182 men for full operation and the minimum crew which can be used and still do any business at all is 63 men. At Omaha, in an elevator of the same size, the maximum number of men required is 20 and the minimum crew 8. At Albany, the largest plant of them all, the normal crew is 20 and the largest number ever required has been 44.

The power requirements were cut by 50 percent in the Albany and Omaha elevators, John Jr. also asserted. "In no other elevator in the world of which knowledge is available," he ended his argument, "is it possible to turn a million bushels of grain in a single night."

The actual comparative figures for Cargill costs, terminal by terminal, were considerably less striking than John Jr. stated. It was true that in the previous crop year Omaha did have the lowest cost per bushel handled of all 12 of the Company's major terminals for both unloading and loading grain. But Albany's was the highest for unloading and ninth for loading.

Whether because of John Jr.'s bargaining strategy or because of the startlingly large total cost figures, or perhaps for some other reason, the Russians did not follow up on the proposal, and the whole project died.

These two unconventional proposals, juxtaposed as they were within months of each other in 1935–1936, did give the Company a chance to bid on actual overseas operating proposals (up to this point, the Company offices abroad had been used only to gather commercial intelligence and to do some trading). Early, firsthand market information from Cargill's own people abroad was proving to be a major competitive tool. John Jr. wrote his father of one of these cases: "Our Buenos Aires office proved its value yesterday . . . they advised us of tremendous strength in their markets after our markets had closed. We immediately told the Pacific Coast to be very aggressive in picking up cash grain . . . we accumulated 100,000 bushels at only a shade over the current price yesterday, and of course the market opened up 2¢ high this morning. There is no question but . . . that the broader your contacts the better off you are in the grain business."

Later, after World War II, full-scale operations were begun in Europe, and there was another Argentine proposal in the early 1950s. Nothing more was heard from the Russians about any kind of an on-site operating relationship until the late 1980s.[23]

Innovating with Alfalfa

The restless mind of John Jr. often seemed to work best while on vacation; this seemed particularly true when he was at sea. If there was a strong personality aboard with whom John Jr. could interact, this often stimulated the juices of innovation. Just this combination of stimulating people and isolated location occurred on John Jr.'s trip to Jamaica in January 1936. Aboard ship he met a senior officer of Imperial Chemical Industries Limited (ICI). From him, John Jr. learned of "the most revolutionary thing in agriculture since the invention of the binder," that grass, if cut before it jointed and dried to under 3 percent moisture within 6 hours, "is twice as good an animal food as corn, and takes the place entirely of high protein concentrates, such as oil cake, fish scraps, etc."

Alfalfa was widely grown in Montana. Excited about the possibilities of building a large alfalfa drying plant, John Jr. wrote his brother: "Please ask Julius to have his boys get all the available material on the protein content of grasses 6 to 10 inches high and ask Frank or Hayhoe to dig up all available literature on grass dryers in the U.S." (John Jr. was a bit lost in his terminology here—alfalfa is a leguminous plant.)

Overall, Cargill business was not good in the early part of 1936. Nevertheless, when John Jr. returned to Minneapolis, he immediately made plans for an extended visit to Valier, Montana, to arrange the establishment of an experimental plant for the alfalfa project, the trip also to include a visit to Seattle for arranging sales of the resultant alfalfa meal. This contact proved promising, and John Jr. wrote the local Valier manager: "There is therefore no question of our market. It is purely a matter of the price at which we can produce it. This being the case, I think we are quite safe in pushing boldly our acreage to be available a year from now."

By mid-1936, John Jr. had hired a graduate chemist to work in the just-completed Valier alfalfa drying plant. John Jr.'s letters during this period were full of plans about the project, not just the overall concept but all of the details. The first alfalfa crop was available before the dryer was finished, and John Jr. personally managed its testing: "Run a small sample of your ground alfalfa through the hand rolls about four times and then dry this within an hour or so after running it through in the oven at your home, then fill one of these cans with this dried stuff, label it so we will know which it is and we will have it analyzed here for vitamin content." John Jr. was worried that "all of the valuable vitamins might be in the juice."

By the end of the season, the experimental plant had been developed well enough to send off over 800 tons of dehydrated alfalfa, and the operation in its first year showed a small profit. While the Valier operation continued modestly successful, it was a small part of the larger Cargill picture. In the broader sense, however, it was a major conceptual step for the Company, soon leading to a significant line of feed.[24]

The Soybean Arrives

In mid-1936, the Chicago Board of Trade initiated a soybean futures contract. In his annual report Robert P. Boylan, the president of the CBOT, was frank in stating that the soybean contract "has been put forth to find new sources of revenue" for the Exchange but was also "another justification of futures markets which in general measure values over a considerable period of time rather than with respect to the day by day changes." "Soybeans have tremendous income possibilities," *Northwestern Miller* had predicted early that year. The editors pointed out that soybeans ranked fifth among grains in farm value in 1935, exceeding for the first time the sums received by farmers for rye, for flaxseed and for rice. Corn, wheat, oats and barley, the "big four" of that period, had higher totals.

Cargill first purchased and stored some soybeans in 1935 and continued the same small effort in 1936, although none remained in the inventory at the end of the year. John Peterson wrote a Chase National Bank officer: "This year we have bought and sold some, more from the point of getting an education and a feel of the business than as a means of moneymaking. From the standpoint of storage experience, ours is practically nil."

Peterson was not optimistic about Cargill's future in this trade. He continued: "I understand . . . that the principal market for the soy bean is in the hands of big fellows like Archer-Daniels-Midland, A. E. Staley Manufacturing Company, Allied Mills, the Glidden Company and Spencer-Kellogg." There seemed little doubt, however, that the soybean was to be a major crop, and Cargill needed to become further "educated" about its possibilities.[25]

The Drought of 1936

The 1935 wheat crop had been only a little larger than that of the drought year of 1934. North American spring wheat had had rust, and the winter wheat harvest east of the Rockies also was much below average. Thus, the wheat supplies for 1935–1936 were the smallest since 1927–1928 although still much above the normal level. The corn crop then was also a little larger than in 1934 but otherwise the shortest since 1881. The average supply of all feed grains per grain-consuming animal unit on the farms was only .691 ton, barely three-fourths of the average of the surplus years 1928–1932.

Cargill MacMillan predicted that the last four months of this 1935–1936 crop year could turn things in either direction. Unfortunately, the outcome was discouragingly negative. The firm's terminal grain accounts had lost almost $1.3 million; the country lines, an additional $132,000. There were offsets, but the final accounting was a loss of over $972,000. However, the regular common stock dividend of 7 percent was paid. With later adjustments, the firm's net worth dropped about $498,000, leaving it at just over $8 million.

Bert Lang, when sent the financial statements, wrote John Peterson:

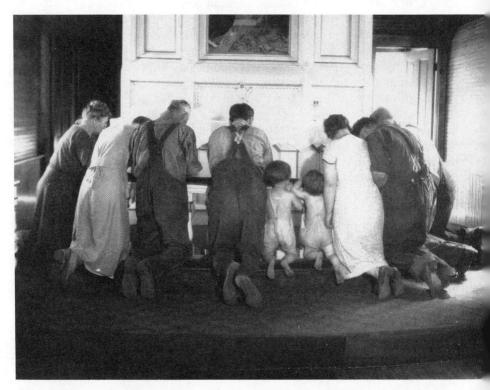

"Farmers praying for rain, July 14, 1936." Shown are members of the Holden, Minnesota, congregation of the Norwegian Lutheran Church (Minnesota Historical Society).

"Frankly I should not have been surprised had your losses been doubled, for with all of the vicissitudes which surrounded the grain market during the entire period under review, losses were almost inevitable." Peterson wrote a Chase National officer: "I suppose of all of the depression years we ought to experience one if for no other reason than that of giving us the proper degree of humility in the face of the forces over which we don't have any control." While humility was neither Peterson's nor John Jr.'s forte, the sobering results calmed some of the expansionist mentality, particularly that of John Jr. Indeed, there were cutbacks. For example, the Montreal office was closed altogether, a move dictated in part also by the increased use of the Erie Canal for Company grain shipments abroad.[26]

Early prospects for the 1936 harvests suggested a crop of moderate size, roughly the average for the five preceding years. Then, suddenly, the situation changed. The *Wheat Studies* editors captured the unfolding drama: "In June–July 1936 . . . the crop outlook changed radically for the worse. Scorching heat and drought wreaked havoc in the North American spring wheat belt, and made certain that crops would be very short almost throughout this region. In Southern Europe and French North Africa, crops continued to deteriorate, with excessive rainfall. . . . The summer weather in most of Europe was not such as to favor good yields . . . in the USSR, following retarded sowings because of the late spring, drought devastated spring-sown wheat. Excessive rainfall curtailed sowings and promoted weed growth in Argentina, while the Australian crop suffered from prolonged drought."

With wheat prospects so poor, Cargill was particularly interested in what would happen to corn. Beginning in early July, Daniel MacMillan began to travel the cornfields all through the Middle West, sending daily telegrams to John Jr. For years, Uncle Dan had been undisputedly the best of Cargill's crop observers; his telegrams chronicled a rapidly deteriorating situation: (July 17, Illinois) "Would not be surprised if a large proportion of fields . . . would not ear at all." (July 30, Iowa) "state a washout." (August 12, Illinois) "Immediate rain necessary to save anything at all." (August 18, Iowa) "From Burlington to Oskaloosa corn crops virtual failure." (August 20, Iowa) "Two fields of early sown this afternoon . . . not over five bushels for each." In sum, the 1936 drought was as severe and as devastating as that of its 1934 predecessor.[27]

Back in that earlier year, first priority was relief for distressed cattle farmers, whose animals were starving to death. In June 1934, the government had offered a buy-out plan that allowed the farmers to keep their foundation herds and to tender the remainder to the government for slaughter. By the end of 1934, the number of cattle on farms had been reduced from 74.4 million to 68.8 million head.

It seems we eat only at the second table.

Ding Darling, August 10, 1937 (by permission of the University of Iowa Libraries [Iowa City]).

For the animals remaining in 1935, the same danger arose—lack of feed. Feed grain supplies had been so decimated by the drought that it was inevitable that some imported feed grain would be needed. This flew in the face of farmer and governmental fears about foreign competition. Already there had been renewed restrictions, for example, the government ruling on Polish rye.

In 1936, feed grains were still desperately needed, but the government remained concerned that imports would compete with domestic grains. Low-grade (often frost-damaged) wheat could still be imported as feed grain, at a lower tariff. These had to be designated "unfit for human consumption," but the government worried that this would be mixed in with good wheat and be sold for milling purposes.

Grimes personally attempted to move Secretary Wallace from his fixed position on limiting feed grain imports. In the skillful Grimes manner, he

Oh, what will the harvest be?

Ding Darling, July 31, 1936 (by permission of the University of Iowa Libraries [Iowa City]).

ended his letter: "Knowing your keen interest in the feed situation in the United States, we are bringing this to your attention and respectfully request an expression of opinion from you." Wallace replied two weeks later that he "would hardly be warranted in attempting to classify this wheat," that it was up to the Commissioner of Customs.

To Grimes, this was passing the buck, and he once more urged Wallace to reconsider. The Secretary, in a blunt letter on November 27, 1936, denied the request once again and added that if Grimes was still dissatisfied, "you file a protest . . . against the liquidation of the duties and thus have the question reviewed by the Customs Court." Grimes dropped the matter as a lost cause. After a few months, the government relaxed its constraints, and more than half of the imports came in as feed wheat on a 10 percent duty (the regular duty was 42 cents per bushel).[28]

These arguments on the feed program paled in comparison to an acerbic argument in 1936 relating to seed. The spring wheat disaster due to the drought had been followed by the equally severe blow to corn. Farmers all through the drought belt simply had no seed corn for planting for 1937. The government then decided upon a federal program to relieve this distress. The Reconstruction Finance Corporation provided a $10 million grant, the Commodity Credit Corporation was to handle loans to the farmers, and the Agricultural Adjustment Administration was to administer the program.

The role of the Agricultural Adjustment Administration quickly drew resentful opposition. Notwithstanding heated remonstrances to Henry Wallace by the private grain trade, the Secretary decided that the entire program would be administered by Farmers National, the very same cooperative that had been given the inside track in the federal Farm Board program of 1930–1931. Farmers National had gone through distressed times since the demise of the Farm Board; in effect, it had gone bankrupt in 1935. Bailed out by the government, it was operating under the supervision of the Farm Credit Administration. The Grain Committee on National Affairs, speaking for the trade in August 1936, railed: "This is the rankest kind of favoritism against independent cooperatives and the private grain trade . . . outrageous favoritism . . . a complete breech of faith."

Despite lobbying by the industry, Secretary Wallace stood fast. Announcing the program on September 16, 1936, he seemed unwilling to admit publicly that Farmers National was to be the selling agency, dodging the issue in the press release by saying only that "field work in connection with the program will be supervised by the AAA." Subsequently, the administration did purchase some of its seed corn from the private sector, but most of the business went to Farmers National.[29]

Notwithstanding the industry's lost battles with the government, the overall grain trade picked up during the fall of 1936, and the crop year 1936–1937 later turned out to be excellent. Early in the fall of 1936, John Peterson pushed the bankers from the Chase consortium to increase the total amount of credit. An additional $5.4 million was granted by a subgroup of some of the banks in the consortium. Peterson sent letters to all of the banks granting increases, giving his version as to why the others did not join, masterfully implying that they had not really turned Cargill down but that other "circumstances" had precluded their increasing the amount. Later, when a Baltimore bank wanted to join the consortium, Peterson turned them down: "I wish that I could see my way clear to put you folks in the credit. It is, however, very doubtful whether I can. Old loyalties, like old names, old homes and old splendors, have their call upon whatever business we have to offer. . . . Right-of-way must be given to the banks already in our picture."[30]

The 1936 Consolidations of Cargill, Incorporated

There had been a substantial constellation of Cargill companies for many years past—separate corporate entities in states or countries requiring them, separate companies to hold terminal properties, the Cargo Carriers Incorporated (CCI) for transportation, and so on. Most of their transactions were consolidated into one financial statement at the end of each year. A few (such as the Itasca elevator corporation in Superior, Wisconsin) were separate corporations even for closing statements and therefore for income tax purposes. Losses from the parent company could not be applied against these unconsolidated, wholly independent operating companies. Beyond tax considerations, there were other reasons for simplifying the corporate structure. For example, the existence of separate companies within the overall parent made for some confusion in qualifying for such things as membership in exchanges.

In January 1935, some initial consolidations and dissolutions were made. The Cargill Commission Company was dissolved, and its business was taken over by the Cargill Grain Company, a new entity. The Cargill Warehouse Company was established (and became the parent for Cargo Carriers), and there were other minor name changes. Yet to outsiders, and sometimes to insiders, there remained confusion about the relationship between and among all of these units.

This issue gained a higher profile in February 1936, when the Federal Trade Commission (FTC) stepped into the scene. The FTC at that time was conducting a very extensive investigation of a number of industries, the grain trade among them. The lawyers of the Commission approached Cargill for information with the hope that this would be tendered by the Company voluntarily. John Jr. wrote his father: "The Federal Trade Commission has come in, pursuant to a resolution of Congress, and asked for all kinds of information as to earnings, salaries, etc., which obviously can be used for mudraking [*sic*] purposes. I am urging that we take the position that we will exhaust every legal recourse before complying, and Dorsey has promised us an opinion as to our rights sometime today."

The Dorsey law firm, however, urged John Jr. to comply. Subsequently, in doing so, a question came up as to whether the FTC wanted just the parent-company data or information on some of the less directly grain-trade companies, such as Cargo Carriers. The FTC did indeed request these statistics, and Cargill reluctantly tendered them. But this interchange pointed up once more the difficulties caused by the complexity of Cargill's organizational structure. The passage of the Wealth Tax Act of 1935, the "anti-business" tax law of Roosevelt (or so business felt, at least), had exacerbated concerns on the part of the business community, and Cargill in turn, about corporate taxation. Cargill MacMillan, for example, had continued to explore his notion of a wholly independent foreign corporation. Concerned about both state and federal taxation, he wrote outside counsel James Dorsey: "If we are forced to move from Minnesota, it may be only a short time before we may be forced again to move from the United States." Guernsey in the Channel Islands still intrigued him, and he made a personal visit there in November 1936, but no decision ensued at that time.

So, for these and other reasons, the Cargill executives finally made the decision in mid-1936 to fundamentally reorganize the entire Company. The details of this reorganization were complex; its essence can be stated as follows:

1. The Cargill Warehouse Company, titular holder of several of the Company's elevators, was liquidated, the Cargill Elevator Company now becoming their owner.

2. The Cargill Elevator Company, the Cargill Grain Company, Cargill Elevators Incorporated, Cargill Sales Company and the Itasca Corporation were merged into one entity, the Cargill Elevator Company.

3. Cargill, Incorporated, a Delaware corporation, would then have its Articles of Incorporation amended so as to bring the share structure into congruence with Cargill Elevator Company; at this point Cargill Elevator Company and Cargill, Incorporated, would be reorganized so that Cargill, Incorporated, would assume all of the liabilities and assets of the Elevator Company.

The reorganization essentially left the ownership structure almost as before. There was a small shift in that the owners of Itasca (somewhat fewer than held Cargill Elevator stock) had to first be given additional shares, as some Cargill Elevator shareholders had not chosen to subscribe to Itasca at the time it was formed.

The Company had not really changed structurally—the business was the same and the ownership interests essentially the same. From a tax standpoint, all entities were now under a common umbrella. It was clear, too, that the parent company was now Cargill, Incorporated. The Cargill Elevator Company, that name so well known and so central to all of the Cargill interests, was now reduced to a nonoperative subsidiary of Cargill, Incorporated. Indeed, it was needed only long enough to take care of necessary transfers of authority. An important one was to shift the entire Chase consortium arrangements to Cargill, Incorporated. There were also many lesser transfers—even the stationery needed to be changed. Nothing could obscure the fact, however, that a psychological milestone had been passed with the operational demise of Cargill Elevator Company, the guiding entity for Cargill since 1890.

There was one other major outgrowth of the 1936 reorganization. On December 1, 1936, John MacMillan, Sr., tendered his resignation as president of Cargill, although he did retain the title of chairman of the board. At the same time, John Jr. took over the post of president. The role of treasurer, held to this point by John Jr., was assumed by Roy Hoople. With Cargill Elevator no longer the actual operating company, the cadre of vice presidents had to be transferred to Cargill, Incorporated. The list included Cargill MacMillan, Ed Grimes, Daniel MacMillan, Frederick Lindahl, John Peterson, Julius Hendel, Austen Cargill, Frank Neilson, and C. C. Boden.

Of all of these shifts in organizational titles, John Jr.'s was by far the most important. In the role of vice president and general manager, he had been the day-to-day operating head for a several years. Yet in terms of relationships with outsiders (banks, governmental agencies, etc.), the fact that there was one further step to the president was probably an important element. The reality of command had been John Jr.'s for many months. John Sr. wrote a friend on December 7, 1936, about the change in jobs and confirmed this: "The fact that Junior was made President of Cargill, Incorporated was merely a recognition of what has been an actual fact for a long time. There is really no change in the situation, although I do think it will make it a lot easier for me to have him have the title as well as the responsibility."[31]

Borup, Minnesota

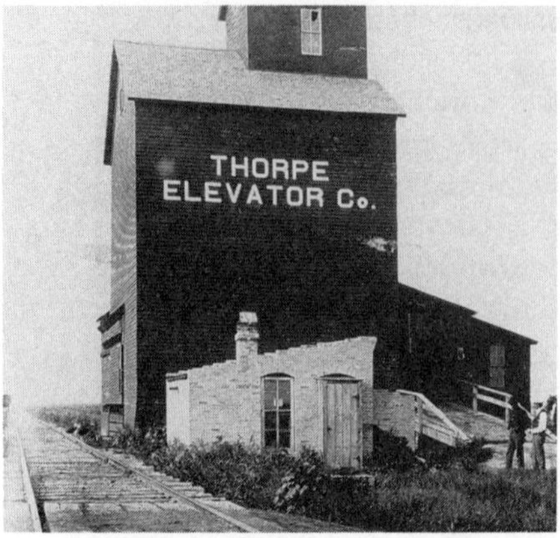

CHAPTER TWELVE

The Great Battle with the Chicago Board of Trade

A string of related clashes between Cargill and the Chicago Board of Trade in the second half of 1936 came together as a backdrop for even more serious confrontations between Cargill and the CBOT in the three years that followed. Eventually, two landmark Commodity Exchange Authority (CEA) cases were tried on the issues involved. These events, consuming four years of Company energies, came to be known as "the Corn Case." It was Cargill's most renowned litigation—indeed, also one of the two or three most famous cases for the CBOT in its own long history.

After Cargill had gained a physical foothold in Chicago in 1931 with its terminal, CBOT officialdom became more inquisitive about Cargill's operations. In July 1932, it made inquiries about grain stocks in the new terminal at Albany. Grimes answered at that time: "This elevator will not be a public house and it is not our plan at the present time to give publicity to the stocks of grain that we are carrying." In November of that year, a more serious issue arose, and this time Cargill chose to contest a CBOT ruling. The CBOT directors had ordered members holding a net short position exceeding 500,000 bushels in any one future in wheat, corn or oats (200,000 bushels for rye) to indicate whether the short position was a hedge, a spread or a speculative short sale. If it was a spread, the name of the market and the future in which the long position was carried also was to be reported.

This distinction between hedging and spreading was an important one. While a hedge with offsetting positions was designed strictly for price movement protection, the spread had speculation built into it, with the hope that the relationship would change in such a way as to make a speculative profit *on the spread*. This involved less risk than a "naked" speculative position on one side of the market. Nevertheless, spreading typically involved motives different from those for hedging. At this time, John Jr. and Julius Hendel were taking many spreads, trading on them for profit. Disclosure would have been detrimental to such an effort.

Cargill argued that as it dealt through a wide number of member firms, with the limit amounts not reached at any, it did not need to report. This argument immediately was rejected by the CBOT. This irritated John Jr., and he wired Grimes: "It is none of their business whether our short Chgo position is against cash and contracts for future delivery on which we intend to take delivery, or against cash only . . . we must decline positively to disclose as a matter of routine any detailed analysis of our position."

The CBOT officials then threatened to take action against Cargill, and John Jr. wired Grimes again: "The Secretary of Agriculture [Henry A. Wallace] has no authority to ask for [this] information . . . we cannot see any legal or moral right on part of B of T to ask for more than the Secretary can do. We suggest as a compromise that we submit the matter to the Secretary of Agriculture." The Exchange officers decided not to call John Jr.'s bluff and on January 4, 1933, rescinded the whole proposition—only the net short position would have to be reported.[1]

Although John Sr., as an individual, had held a membership at the CBOT since 1909, and Philip C. Sayles (the Company's Chicago manager) had held one since 1931, Cargill as a corporation was precluded from certain important membership privileges under CBOT Rule 313, which covered the critical Clearing House function (the reconciliation of all of the activity on the trading floor during the day). Rule 313 was particularly galling. In early November 1929, just after the crash, the CBOT had amended its membership criteria to exclude corporations from membership in the Clearing House unless they had already been members of the Clearing House on April 2, 1929. The stated reason for this change was that corporations had limited liability, and in the case of bankruptcy (then more of a threat, perhaps, because of the depression), full restitution of the creditors might not be easy. Cargill disputed this assertion, quoting the CBOT's own statistics that of the total of 50 failures that had occurred at the CBOT from 1880 to the April 2, 1929, date, only 4 of these had been corporations. Cargill officials believed, rather, that it was simply a case of the CBOT members disliking to give up the commissions paid by corporations, and in the case of Cargill, these amounts were large by this time.

So Cargill had to clear all of its trades through one of the CBOT's member companies (all individually owned or partnerships). Cargill paid full commissions to them for this service. Nor were these commission costs the only irritant. Both Clearing House functions and many other operations in the Exchange involved highly competitive interactions among all of the traders, which depended on confidentiality at all stages. The integrity of the trading process had to be accepted absolutely by everyone, or the system rapidly would break down. With their passion for secrecy, both John Sr. and John Jr. truly believed that their competitors were being given Cargill proprietary information, to be used for unfair competitive trading purposes.

Trading in the corn pit, Chicago Board of Trade.

The trading floor of the Chicago Board of Trade.

Early in 1934, the Farmers National Grain Corporation (the govern-ment-financed cooperative marketing association of farmers) challenged Rule 313, enlisting the aid of Secretary of Agriculture Wallace and suing the CBOT. When the case finally appeared to be going against them, the CBOT membership voted to allow Farmers National and other coopera-tives to be members of the Clearing House. It was a shotgun wedding, said one newspaper, "forced upon the Exchange against its will by the action of the government and a decision of the federal district Circuit Court of Appeals."

Cargill immediately petitioned the CBOT in January 1934, demanding its own membership. The CBOT directors decided to put the issue to the membership for a vote. Sayles and his friends on the Exchange lobbied hard over the next weeks. At first there seemed little opposition, but later, strong antagonistic forces began to surface. The most disturbing devel-opment came just before the vote. Now it seemed that the campaign was not being seen as a decision on all "corporations" but on Cargill itself. Sayles wired Grimes: "Certainly heard a lot of rotten talk today as to why amendment should be voted down, or rather Cargill defeated."

When the vote was tabulated on September 26, 1934, Cargill's petition had lost 412 to 202. One of the Chicago newspapers reported the next day: "The denial of clearing rights to the corporations is certain to be resented. . . . The Cargill Grain Company, Minneapolis, which has in recent years expanded operations in the Chicago market materially, is the most directly affected by the decision of the members."[2]

Bird's-eye view of the east half of the trading floor at the Chicago Board of Trade, with the corn pit at the lower left.

Another Avenue toward Membership

In early 1935, the National Recovery Administration (NRA) code provisions relating to the grain trading industry (including the grain exchanges) were due for revision (the Department of Agriculture administered these; their representatives were to conduct the hearings). One of these regulations related to membership restrictions by exchanges.

Cargill used the code hearings as a medium to bring up its own membership case. Fortuitously, Ed Grimes was a member of the Code Authority for Grain Exchanges, the hearing body, and he moved that Cargill be allowed in the Clearing House. The final vote was 4–3 in favor of Cargill's position, Grimes casting the deciding positive vote. The CBOT cried foul to Secretary Wallace about "individuals having a personal interest sitting on committees." But the Cargill lawyer pointed out that two of the three "no's" were CBOT members and would need to be excluded too. Wallace temporized, calling for further hearings, with the issue broadened to include all nonmember corporations. The CBOT officers worried privately that they unnecessarily had antagonized the Secretary.[3]

A second set of hearings was held in mid-May 1935, with wide-ranging testimony by many parties. Cargill testified, attacking the membership rule. Farmers National also made an appearance. The newspapers picked up the membership battle and featured it. The *Chicago Tribune*, in its article on May 16, 1935, headlined its story "Grain Trade Fight Begins" and discussed the "bitter struggle" that had "flared into the open" involving "a three-cornered fight" between the CBOT, Farmers National and Cargill. The Cargill 32-page brief was well reasoned and, remarkably, kept its statements temperate. But C. E. Huff, the Farmers National president, kindled the rhetoric when he called the exchanges "nothing more than social clubs or fraternities." The battle lines were clear when the CBOT attorney flatly stated that neither the Secretary of Agriculture nor any other government official had the power under the NRA Code "to take any action whatsoever regarding Rule 313." Before any final decision could be made, however, the whole issue became moot, at least in terms of the NRA Code. On May 27, 1935, the Supreme Court ruled the National Industrial Recovery Act unconstitutional in the famous case involving the Schechter Poultry Corporation (popularly called the "sick chicken" case). Cargill was back at the starting gate.[4]

Cargill earlier had developed good personal relations with influential administrators in the Federal Trade Commission, so John Jr. decided to approach the FTC about instituting an antitrust case against the CBOT because of their membership restrictions. John Jr. had to assure a worried John Sr. that by doing this "we have an excellent chance of getting in the Clearing House." The Cargill exhortations to the FTC seemed threatening enough to the CBOT for it to act on its own about Rule 313. A significant faction among its members began to support Cargill and succeeded in bringing the issue before the entire membership for a second time. The vote itself was to take place on July 17, 1935.

As the change was opposed by another large coalition, John Jr. seriously considered an aggressive public relations campaign with the membership, lobbying for a positive vote for change, the arguments also to imply once more that Cargill was going to the FTC. But Grimes wrote John Jr.: "I do not think it is advisable to make any threats down there . . . the effect on this broker group who have apparently gone over to our side strong would have a bad effect." Grimes also alerted John Jr. about a meeting with J. M. Mehl (the assistant chief of the Grain Futures Administration). "I told him we had approached the Federal Trade. . . . While he was reserved in expressing an opinion, he seemed pleased that we were showing a little spunk and he remarked that he thought we would lick the Board of Trade before the Commission." John Jr. grudgingly agreed to the softer posture before the vote, leaving any lobbying to the already converted members. July 17 arrived, the vote was taken and Cargill's position won handily. Cargill as a corporation now could become a member of the Clearing House of the Exchange.[5]

A New Grain Futures Act

Taking a cue from the 1929 crash and its "Black Thursday," FDR apologists began to call May 27, the day the NRA was declared unconstitutional, "Black Monday." But Roosevelt returned to his irrepressible optimism. The administration entered upon another three-month whirl of legislative action, a remarkable period that came to be known as "the Second Hundred Days," also often referred to as the "little NRA." Congress passed and the President signed the National Labor Relations Act (popularized as "the Wagner Act"), the far-reaching Social Security Act, the Public Utility Holding Company Act and several other important pieces of legislation affecting banking, the coal industry and others. The Works Progress Administration (WPA, later the Works Projects Administration) came into being, as did the Rural Electrification Administration (REA), the National Youth Administration (NYA) and the Civilian Conservation Corps (CCC).

In addition, Roosevelt forced through, under vehement opposition, the Revenue Act of 1935, the so-called Wealth Tax Act. Grimes wrote John Sr. about its progress through Congress: "Roosevelt is in a vicious mood, as you have probably surmised from the dispatches coming out of Washington. He is going to try and get several radical measures through Congress."

It was at this time that Congress decided to completely revise the long-standing legislation regulating grain trading on formal exchanges, the "second" Grain Futures Act, passed in 1922. Over its 13-year history the 1922 Act had been ineffectual in holding in check a set of very strong exchanges, 14 in number for the grain trade. The congressional legislators now decided to concentrate particularly on two objectives: (1) regulating margins on trading and segregating margin money from the rest of the commission merchants' assets and (2) limiting the total number of futures contracts that could be held by any given trader—what came to be known as the "limits" issue. Cargill, strongly believing in individual enterprise, decided to take a high profile in the congressional hearings. On April 20, 1935, Ed Grimes gave a ringing affirmation of speculation and argued that spreaders and hedgers like Cargill should not be unduly constrained by any regulation of limits. Swallowing his antipathy toward the CBOT, Grimes also praised the "record of achievement" of the exchanges: "Don't strangle [them] with unnecessary red tape."

A few days later, John Jr. reiterated the same theme in a letter to J. M. Mehl, the assistant chief of the Grain Futures Administration:

... the bad social effects of unrestricted speculation in commodities ... may not be nearly as serious as thought by many people. ... While we discourage participation in the market by those with an urge to speculate or gamble ... all we have done is to drive this class into economically unproductive gambling such as horse racing, the policy racket, cards, dice, etc. The tremendous prosperity of race tracks, gambling joints, etc., during the past year might conceivably be the result of the restriction of speculative facilities in securities and commodities as a result of recent legislation.

He ended on a self-righteous note: "Inasmuch as our own firm does not accept speculative business, we can speak philosophically and without bias."[6]

Henry Wallace, the Secretary of Agriculture, in his press release on a draft of the Grain Futures bill in August 1935, praised it, noting that "it would abolish the bucket shop and puts and calls and make illegal wash sales and other fictitious transactions."* Concerned about "the power of large speculators to demoralize the market," Wallace cited a particular case that "only recently came to light" where a speculator sold over 100 million bushels of wheat futures on the short side of the market "from 70 to 80 percent of the time ... by means of false reports concealing his true position on the market, he endeavored to manipulate the market for his own ends."[7]

---

*A bucket shop was a private "commission" house, buying and selling futures on a margin for gamblers, where there was no intention of actual future delivery and no purchase or sale on any exchange (i.e., "bucket" the transaction); puts and calls were options to sell and to buy, sometimes called indemnities or privileges; wash sales were simultaneously buying and selling a commodity, generally done to build fictitious figures in open interest. See *Report of the Federal Trade Commission on the Grain Trade*, Vol. 2 (September 15, 1920), pp. 332–33.

As the various exchanges attempted to coordinate positions on the new proposals for the federal legislation, it became clear that the CBOT was going to take an unbending, adamant position on *any* limitation of *any* kind. Once again, the Chicago exchange argued to preserve the use of "indemnities" (puts and calls) and wanted much-relaxed margin requirements on speculative accounts. The Minneapolis Chamber of Commerce and the Kansas City Board of Trade still felt that a more conciliatory approach was wiser. Ed Grimes, speaking for the former, wrote C. D. Sturtevant, one of the officers of the Chicago exchange, in late September 1935: "This market will be extremely reluctant to relax margin requirements at this time. [This] is an inopportune time to open the gate. . . . Resumption in trading in privileges . . . is not essential enough to warrant a defiance of Washington." Sturtevant fired back: "Chicago should be permitted to change these rules without necessarily affecting the action of the other markets. . . . We should be permitted to make this experiment without interference."

Sturtevant also was chairman of the Grain Committee on National Affairs, the industry's Washington lobbying group, and a few days later he called a meeting of this organization without inviting Grimes, its Minneapolis representative. When Grimes learned of the slight, he fired back: "Do you think suppression of the Minneapolis viewpoint on important issues of this kind by the National Committee will accomplish any good purpose?" Sturtevant was unbending: "If you had been with us to express the divergent viewpoint of the Northwest markets, the entire object of the meeting would have been defeated." Sturtevant did allow that "I told the government representative that you were not in accord with our views," but he gave Grimes no specifics. Grimes demanded the right to file a minority report.

This CBOT intransigence continued through the fall and winter, and other members of the Grain Committee on National Affairs began to balk. The hostility toward the CBOT heightened in February 1936, when the CBOT made a unilateral decision on their hours of trading. John Jr. described this to his father: "Effective tomorrow Chicago goes on Eastern time. Our directors met this morning and decided that we would not change our trading time to conform with Chicago . . . our opening and close both will be one hour later than Chicago. No one here really believes that we can continue permanently with different trading hours from Chicago, but it is sure to embarrass Chicago more than it does us and we are hoping that they can be persuaded to compromise. . . . Winnipeg meets this afternoon and probably will follow Minneapolis' lead."

A game of wait-and-see began. John Jr. wrote John Sr. about the finale:

Everyone is chuckling mildly over the Chicago Board of Trade having to reverse itself on the matter of hours . . . there was a big game of bluff going on between the various exchanges. [Finally] the Directors of the Chicago Board met and invoked the Emergency rule and, contrary to the vote of the membership, elected to change their hours so they would open at 10:30 Chicago time instead of 9:30, which means that the exchanges once more are all on simultaneous schedules. If Chicago had not reversed itself, Minneapolis and Winnipeg would have had to, but, as someone remarked here "This is almost the first time in history that the tail has wagged the dog."[8]

The proposed new grain futures act finally passed in June 1936, and the CEA came into being. The law represented the more cautious philosophy of the Minneapolis and Kansas City exchanges. Customer margin regulations were constrained, reporting requirements were tightened, indemnities (options) were eliminated. Additional futures exchanges came under regulation—those in cotton, rice, millfeeds, butter and eggs. The CEA's three-member final tribunal was a rather surprising combination: the secretaries of Agriculture and Commerce and the Attorney General.[9]

Both Dr. J. W. T. Duvel (as head) and J. M. Mehl (assistant) had moved over from their identical responsibilities at the Grain Futures Administration and now had to establish new regulations. Apparently John Jr. and Grimes had garnered a reputation over the previous months as "moderates" on the legislation, and Grimes wired John Jr. just after the Act's passage, "I understand Mehl and Duvel are very much worried over their new responsibilities and believe you should work with them." Once more, John Jr. had moved to exploit a personal relationship that he and Grimes had enjoyed with both Duvel and Mehl.[10]

By the early fall of 1936, many grain trade executives began advocating a new organization to replace the splintered Grain Committee on National Affairs. At first, many of the old Committee members reacted cautiously. Finally, a new organization was instituted, the National Grain Trade Council. The old Grain Committee became a "non-assessment organization," in other words, it would no longer have income. By November, the Council was in operation, with Edgar Markham as its Washington representative, and its membership included all of the previous group with the single exception of the CBOT.[11]

Cargill Fights for the Rosenbaum Terminal in Chicago

At the height of the tension about Cargill's CBOT membership, another portentous development had occurred in Chicago with the sudden announcement on April 27, 1935, that the Rosenbaum grain trading organization was bankrupt. This firm was one of the leaders in the CBOT, and there was great consternation about the effects there. Trading on the Exchange was suspended for a day just to sort out some of the early implications.

It was Cargill that alerted the business world to the impending bankruptcy. John Jr. wrote his father: "We were about to put a cargo of rye there and deliver it when I discovered this and, of course, we diverted it elsewhere, and at the same time we were compelled to report our findings to others, so that we have the whole Chicago market in an uproar and everyone greatly incensed at us for being the ones who unearthed a grave irregularity. The banks, however, I think were quite appreciative of our posting them." The messenger with bad news is seldom very popular![12]

The prize in the bankruptcy was control of the huge Rosenbaum terminal. Terminal space was desperately short in Chicago at that time. The Rosenbaum terminal, by its sheer size (9,500,000 bushels), was a linchpin. The terminal was leased from its owner, the Chicago and North Western Railroad (C&NW); now several eager competitors battled to persuade the C&NW to lease to them.

John Jr. desperately wanted it, for it would not only give Cargill major new space in a fundamentally important market but also serve as a further lever in the CBOT on the Clearing House matter. Fred Sargent, the president of the C&NW, had known the MacMillans since the early 1920s, when Cargill leased the former Taylor & Bournique terminal owned by the railroad at Milwaukee. Just the previous year, Sargent had invited John Jr. to join the C&NW board. John Jr. had declined but did accept in 1937, only to resign abruptly several years later, when he felt his advice was being ignored.

Any lease would have to satisfy the creditors, too, as well as the bank-

The Rosenbaum terminal in Chicago, leased by Cargill in 1935.

ruptcy courts. The situation invited behind-the-scenes maneuvering, and Cargill soon learned that Farmers National, the Norris Grain Company and the Continental Grain Company all were avidly pursuing the terminal. John Jr., suspicious of the others, wrote Grimes on June 4 that he thought a bondholders group that had been formed was "acting as a dummy for Continental or Farmers National." Grimes suspected a plot against Cargill: "Someone evidently is working hard on the C&NW in an effort to prevent the road leasing the plant to us. . . . There is certainly something going on behind the scenes."

Finally, the convoluted negotiations shifted to the bankruptcy court in Chicago. Federal Judge William H. Holly would have to accept any final plan. John Jr. made three separate "final offers" but reported to his brother Cargill that "every time on one pretext or the other, the Judge has continued the hearing to a later date." Judge Holly's reluctance stemmed from strong stockholder disagreement about the size of the Cargill offer. "Finally on Monday July 22nd I felt it advisable for me to go down and tell the court that they had to fish or cut bait," John Jr. recounted, and "the Judge signed the order to accept our proposition."

Cargill agreed to pay a lump sum of $70,000 for immediate possession, at the same time allowing an arbitrator to set a price on Cargill purchase of the 2,500,000 bushels of grain, mostly rye, that still remained in the elevator. Grimes reported the decision: "We . . . were soaked 4½ over September for the 2 million rye. We are not very happy about it except to say that it was a fair arbitration." Still, this was minor, for Cargill had consummated a major boost to its total elevator capacity (particularly after a number of improvements were made by Milt Bondus, later a senior executive in terminal management). In combination with the Company's role on the CBOT Clearing House, the new terminal gave a greatly enhanced position in the Chicago market, reflecting the reality of Cargill's trading power there.[13]

Making an Enemy

Cargill's first year as a full-fledged member of the CBOT's Clearing House had been marred in December 1935 by a dispute with the Illinois State Warehouse Commission about the "public warehouse" responsibilities of Cargill at its newly acquired Chicago terminal. The Company had delivered some wheat as "#2 Red," but a state inspector had rejected this, and the wheat had to be unloaded back into the warehouse, remixed, regraded and reloaded out once again. Cargill officials, still suspicious about Exchange members' attitudes toward them, felt that some were still opposing them behind the scenes and had put the Warehouse Commission up to the stricter posture. Because all of this took considerable time, deliveries to be made were significantly delayed, antagonizing some of the holders of the warehouse receipts on Cargill "public warehouse" grain. Two of these were Daniel F. Rice, the principal of the firm bearing his name and a CBOT member since 1920, and the Farmers National Grain Corporation.

Cargill had had several dealings with Rice, beginning in 1931. Rice had executed trades for Cargill in Winnipeg, and Cargill did the same for Rice in Minneapolis, both at members' commission rates ("reciprocals" had been widely practiced in the industry for many years). Now, protesting that his deliveries were delayed and that Cargill had deliberately put some extra-hard Canadian "garnet" wheat in the shipment, Rice took his case to the CBOT. The two parties finally settled privately, but both Rice and Cargill executives remained annoyed and mistrusting.[14]

The September 1936 Corn Contract—Harbinger of Trouble?

Daniel MacMillan had thoroughly surveyed the corn crop in July 1936 to anticipate supply over the following months. The results had been revealing. With another burgeoning drought in the summer, assessments of the "visible supply" pointed to a markedly low total for the crop, the third year in a row for wheat and corn. The existing international situation also had an impact. Revolution in Spain had broken out in mid-July; General Franco now received important economic and military aid from Nazi Germany and Fascist Italy, and the left-wing Loyalists were aided by Soviet Russia. Nationalistic concerns for controlling food supply arose worldwide.[15]

In anticipation of this, Cargill began buying large quantities of domestic cash corn and also placing substantial orders to Argentina for shipment of its corn crop, already in hand there. By this time, the Company was a major force in American agriculture. Company lawyers in later briefs estimated that in 1936 Cargill distributed in volume approximately 2 percent of all of the grain raised by American farmers—indeed, between 10 and 12 percent of the grain actually marketed. In the mid-1930s, Cargill was distributing throughout the United States and abroad 100 million bushels or more of grain annually and had actually handled as much as 150 million bushels in one year.

The logistics of those Argentine purchases complicated the matter significantly. The elapsed time between time of charter and time of arrival, according to a later Cargill legal brief, was substantial: 35 days alone for the trip from Argentina to United States ports, an additional 10 days to Chicago. This time lag seemed to make it more urgent that the Company make heavy purchases of September corn futures. By August 12, some 4,200,000 bushels had been acquired.

This long position was substantial enough to catch the attention of a group within the CBOT with which Cargill had had no previous direct dealings—its Business Conduct Committee. This was the group within the Exchange committee structure given the task of being the "policeman" for member firms. Its powers were wide; it could recommend to the board of directors severe discipline for a member, including as a last resort actual expulsion. By this time, Cargill's interest represented approximately 50 percent of the total open interest in the contract, so the chief accountant of the Committee queried John Jr. on August 11, 1936: "[Is] your position . . . hedging or [is] part of it of a speculative nature?" John Jr. replied with uncharacteristic diplomacy, "It is really very reassuring to us to know that your Committee is on the job," then pointed out that Cargill's short position was just about exactly what the Company's books showed as "open sales."

By the end of August, the Company began to exchange a portion of its September futures for cash corn and transferred some of its September futures forward to Chicago December corn futures. Nevertheless, it still held substantial amounts of September futures, for which the Company planned to "stand for delivery" (to use the futures contract at expiration to obtain actual physical grain by delivery).

On several occasions during September, Cargill was summoned before the Committee, where its members expressed increasing concern that Cargill's holdings of September corn were speculative. They urged liquidation of part of the line, even if it was necessary for Cargill to make some sacrifices—to be willing to forgo profit-taking that might stem from a price rise in the contract due to a shortage of actual corn for delivery. Finally, on September 25, John Jr. met personally with the Committee and (as recounted by the Committee secretary) "repeated statements which he had made over the telephone to the effect that Cargill's long position . . . would not be allowed to cause any unreasonable fluctuations . . . that Cargill would have corn for sale at prices within the maximum range." This mild statement by John Jr. apparently mollified the Business Conduct Committee. Cargill subsequently liquidated enough of its holdings not to upset the market, and prices on the contract held quite steady through the expiration date at the end of the month (futures contracts then expired later in the month than at present).

There remained one nagging doubt for Cargill. This related to an action by the board of directors of the Exchange on September 29. The new Commodity Exchange Act provisions were to come into effect on September 13, 1936. September futures contracts around the country would be the first to be governed by that Act. One of the features of the Act required that any person making delivery of any commodity be obligated to give a one-day written notice of the date of delivery, at least one business day prior to such day of delivery. At the expiration of a contract, this introduced a certain amount of rigidity for the "short" who was going to deliver.

This worried many Exchange officers, so the board held a special meeting on September 29, at which time delivery on a less rigid schedule (in other words, less notice to the "long") was allowed. Cargill, as the principal long in the September corn contract, was most affected by this last-minute change; John Jr., quite surprised, wired the secretary of the Exchange of Cargill's displeasure, alleging that they had lost money—cash corn had dropped on the last day, with missed opportunities for profit-taking. Further, the shorts had been able to obtain enough cash corn to meet their obligations, whereas Cargill purchases might have made some of the shorts default, at which point Cargill would be in a bargaining position to accept a more favorable settlement. No response came from the Exchange officers.[16]

The issue troubled John Jr. enough to send a detailed, four-page letter to Dr. J. W. T. Duvel, the head of the CEA. He poured forth a litany of complaints against the Exchange: "We are the largest buyers of cash grain in the market, the largest sellers of cash grain in the market, do the largest warehousing in the market, and are also the largest users of futures, yet we are not represented on any one of the three most important Board of Trade governing bodies, namely the Directorate, the Board of Governors of the Clearing House or the Business Conduct Committee . . . we feel compelled to resist with every means at our disposal any invasion of our rights by this body, however slight."

John Jr. ended with a ringing disavowal of any speculative intent by Cargill:

Lest the suspicion may arise that our trades were speculative, let me state that there has been no departure from the established policy of the firm, namely, that our net long and short position must be as nearly even as is practicable. I have been in the business approximately 17 years, and although our inventory each year reaches a peak of somewhere between 40 and 50 million bushels of grain, yet at no time during these 17 years have we ever been more than 2 million bushels out of balance, and then only for brief periods when we were engaged in handling some commodity where special conditions made it impracticable to secure a safe hedge, and for which we knew from contact with our usual trade that there were ready buyers at a relatively small sacrifice in price.

His closing sentence was confrontational: "If the futures trading facilities of the Chicago Board of Trade are not intended to serve such situations as we had ourselves during the past three months, then we can see little or no economic justification for their continued existence." It was probably too much to expect the cumulative hostilities of many years on the part of John Jr., his father, and others at Cargill to have dissipated with the grudging acceptance of Cargill into the Clearing House of the CBOT.

To complicate matters just at this time, there was another skirmish with Dan Rice. Argentine corn had been imported by Cargill and others over the early fall of 1936; this was mainly flint corn, harder than the usual domestic dent (dent commanded a premium over flint, for the flint required special processing). Federal regulations allowed only 5 percent flint when the two were mixed; now the CBOT advocated that the Commodity Exchange Authority allow 25 percent flint for fulfilling the December, 1936, corn contract. Rice objected vociferously, and urged the CEA to make it "obligatory that native Corn be delivered on contract." Rice lost this argument—the 25 percent figure was adopted—and, with much of his corn coming from Cargill, this increased his antipathy toward the Company.[17]

Double Jeopardy—December Wheat, December Corn

As the next set of corn contracts approached their closing dates, at the end of December 1936, there was another major hassle, with Cargill on one side and the Business Conduct Committee of the CBOT (and many of its individual members) on the other. One could see the problem coming. The United States corn crop for the crop year 1936–1937 totaled just over 1.5 billion bushels, one of the shortest crops on record. Only some 1.25 billion bushels of this were harvested as grain. On October 1, 1936, the visible supply of corn for the country was just 3,773,000 bushels, as compared with the average over the previous 10 years on the same date: 18,754,300 bushels.

Meanwhile, Cargill had estimated, from information received from its customers, that orders in the neighborhood of 15 million bushels and possibly as much as 25 million would be required by them. Anticipating this, Cargill became an increasingly aggressive purchaser of cash corn; by December 26 the Company had acquired 5,955,000 bushels. Foreign cash corn also had been purchased, mostly from Argentina. In total, Cargill held 14,128,895 bushels of foreign corn. In addition, before the close of the September contract, Cargill had sold September corn futures and bought December corn futures (at that time a cheaper source of supply) amounting to some 2.5 million additional bushels by October 1. Further purchases of December futures were made all through the fall, and Cargill's percentage of the total open interest in the contract rose steadily. Even though Cargill began to liquidate some of its contracts by December 1, this liquidation was not as rapid as the drop in the total open interest. Cargill's percentage continued to rise, from 27.3 percent on November 2 to 52.8 percent on December 14.

Cargill also purchased December 1936 wheat futures in volume. Supplies of wheat always are more difficult to ascertain, inasmuch as demand for the various varieties interact in often complex ways. In the late summer of 1936, Cargill executives decided that there would be a shortage of soft red winter wheat (traded on the CBOT), even though the total production of this variety was actually up from the previous year and well above the 10-year average. Their reasoning for this gives an excellent example of the subtlies of grain supply prediction: "moderate production of Hard Winter Wheat, complete failure of the Durum Wheat crop, the existence of import regulations, a small crop of wheat in Canada of high quality, which will tend to make importation of lightweight Canadian wheat for feeding purposes impracticable, and the scarcity and high price of corn [will bring] a distinct shortage of Red Winter Wheat . . . within a few months, although this development is not yet generally recognized as probable by the trade." Cargill began buying some cash wheat but particularly purchased December wheat futures. Again a similar pattern of dominance of the open interest ensued. The Company's percentage of open interest, only 15.5 percent on November 2, had risen to 57.2 percent by December 15.

The combination of Cargill's two long positions now raised a further complication. Most of the trade recognized that Cargill used long positions in futures markets for actual delivery, and the Company had formally notified the Business Conduct Committee of the CBOT of this intent. Now the question became, if all of this grain was to physically arrive at the Chicago markets in fulfillment of Cargill's long positions, was there enough warehouse space to take care of it? Only a percentage of the warehouses in Chicago were classified by the CBOT as "regular" for delivery, fulfilling Exchange regulations that allowed warehouse receipts. The total deliverable elevator capacity in Chicago was just over 16 million bushels out of a total of over 55 million bushels of total capacity. Cargill argued that the CBOT could have made these nondeliverable warehouses "regular," but the CEA replied that most of them were private houses owned by processors, most were not on water (which was an essential for "regular" delivery purposes), and furthermore, the CEA could not force any given warehouse to go through the extensive procedures to become "regular."

Cargill then argued that, inasmuch as the CBOT regulations stated that physical deliveries could be made in the last three days of a delivery month "on track," much of their "long" purchases could be handled this way. An expert witness at one of the later CEA hearings had testified that he had never heard of track deliveries as large as 7 million bushels, although other evidence did point to an occasional exception. It was true that a day's total inbound freight in Chicago was some 75,000 rail cars, but this included cars for all purposes, not just track deliveries of grain. The CEA pointed out, additionally, that track deliveries would have to be inspected and that in this particular month, December 1936 the corn was of such high moisture content that it could not be delivered officially without being dried, a process that had to be done within the elevator as such. The sum of this was that physical delivery of the two grains in Chicago to fulfill the delivery provisions of the December 1936 contract was going to cause a formidable problem.

On November 4, 1936, the Business Conduct Committee deputed the CBOT chief auditor to make a special trip to Minneapolis to ascertain from Cargill's records just what Cargill's positions really were. On November 23, the auditor reported more intransigence on the part of Cargill. The Company intended to take delivery on much of its longs, and John Jr. "declined to state at just what price the December corn futures would be liquidated." Further, "in MacMillan's opinion, the recent price advance was due to the activities of the Business Conduct Committee."

A few days later, on November 30, John Jr. and Grimes were asked to appear personally before the Committee. They told the members that "just a modest price advance" would cause Cargill to sell but that since Cargill "did not know where the corn was coming from to meet our requirements, we decided to buy futures and let someone else worry where it was coming from." Nevertheless, John Jr.'s tone, as in September, remained conciliatory, and he ended: "We assure you there will be no manipulation. We would never do anything . . . contrary to the best interests of the grain trade. You can count on our complete cooperation at all times."

On December 7, the Committee found that Cargill's position still had not much changed, and at this point it took a decisive step. Invoking a formal order against Cargill, it found that "your conduct in accumulating and maintaining these lines under prevailing conditions is detrimental to the best interests of the association; that it is unfair and unjust." In essence, they accused Cargill of holding a disguised speculative position. Cargill was directed to cease and desist from its existing position and within seven calendar days to reduce its position in both grains to 60 percent of where it had been; three days later, this was tempered by the Committee to 70 percent.

Cargill's executives were outraged by this, and on December 12 they forwarded a long, highly formal letter to the Business Conduct Committee, taking issue with its findings and flatly refusing to liquidate the Company's long positions in the percentages required by the Committee. Cargill now decided to take a different tack, urging the Committee join with it in requesting J. W. T. Duvel, the chief of the CEA, to "arbitrate the differences between us and to determine what action, if any, is required on our part" John Jr. had wired his father, on December 10, that "Dr. Duvel assured us just now by phone that we had his moral support." The

Business Conduct Committee turned aside this suggestion and continued its exhortations to Cargill to reduce its positions in both grains.

By this time, the public press had picked up the events. The *Chicago Tribune* wrote, on December 19: "While it has been known for some time that a tense situation might develop, the Committee's action served to emphasize the gravity of the market's condition. Never in past history of the Exchange has a similar warning been given."

The question of price was critical to any solution, Cargill at this point intimating to the Committee that it would be "a willing seller when the price of the Chicago December wheat futures reached a 9¢ premium over the price of wheat in the Southwest." The situation now seemed to ease, the Committee apparently concluding that the wheat situation would resolve itself and that "the Committee need not have further concern over December wheat futures." Corn prices, surprisingly, had stayed quite steady during December. Both the wheat contract and the corn contract now proceeded to expire without too much tension.

Although the situation seemed resolved, Cargill officials remained highly incensed. While they took issue with many of the actions of both the Business Conduct Committee and the Commodity Exchange Authority, there were two overriding irritants. First, the widely reported pressures on Cargill to reduce its positions had succeeded in artificially holding the price down for the two grains, and, second, the shorts were allowed in the process to wriggle out of delivering actual product. A Cargill memorandum reiterated earlier charges that "the Order obviously tended to encourage the tendency of the Board of Trade officials to permit speculative 'shorts' to operate without taking conscientious steps to fulfill their obligations. . . . It even encourages outright gambling by speculative 'shorts' who in many instances . . . have no real intent to deliver."

This same brief frankly stated that Cargill obeyed the order only because it feared it would lose its membership in the CBOT if it did not comply; and if this happened, it "would be forced to pay full commissions on all 'futures' transactions there (double the members' rates), as well as exorbitant brokerage on all cash grain transactions which would be made on the floor of the Exchange." Cargill felt that it had been cheated out of its full share of profits, "some 15¢ per bushel less than the factors of supply and demand warrant." If the Business Conduct Committee had not intervened, the December corn contract would have risen, in Cargill's words, "to the proper level and would have carried with it the price of real corn." Cargill was being penalized, its executives felt, because it had had the foresight to anticipate the direction of prices.

Beyond this, there was still a further grievance—some individual members of the Business Conduct Committee had actually themselves been shorts, and Cargill officials believed that several had personally profited in their short selling due to insider knowledge as members of the Committee. The Company's outrage had been so strong that John Jr. had even wired his father on December 11: "We should all consider advisability of withdrawing from Board of Trade after this is all over."

The CEA's own viewpoint on these Cargill allegations was not clear at this time. Cargill gained an inkling of the CEA attitude toward it in the annual report for 1937 by Dr. Duvel, the head of the CEA, who said that "one firm had an *excessively* large position in both wheat and corn" (my emphasis). In later CEA cases involving Cargill, the CEA rejected almost all of Cargill's 1936 accusations, including that of personal profiteering by members of the Business Conduct Committee (the CEA held that neither the members themselves, nor "the wives and children of the members nor even the partners had any position as such").

So Cargill came through those December 1936 incidents not only with renewed hostility toward the CBOT but also increased concern about the Commodity Exchange Authority, which seemed markedly more skeptical of Cargill actions—and Cargill motives—than the Company had ever believed. Somehow, Cargill earlier had felt that the CEA was "on their side." Given the CEA's necessary role as the adjudicator for any industry altercation, this was too naive an expectation.[18]

Cargill MacMillan's Decisions

The Board of Trade elections for director posts, held in the first week in January 1937, served to remind Cargill that its role in the CBOT was still precarious. Philip Sayles had been nominated as Cargill's candidate for a directorship. There were 12 candidates for the five board posts, and the lobbying was intense; Sayles wired Grimes: "Conditions looking better every minute unless all my friends are wearing Landon buttons."

His optimism was misplaced—he lost, and he wired Grimes about how "the machine worked to elect their crowd . . . directors are card and pencil men, and men representing big investments and those responsible for bulk of business were defeated." To add to Cargill's frustration, when the committee assignments for 1937 were announced by the new president (Kenneth S. Templeton), there was no Cargill representative on any of the 21 separate committees (in a later CEA case, the Exchange explained this away by the fact that Cargill's headquarters was out of town and said that the CEA agreed that this was "explicable").[19]

John Jr. had gone off on vacation in early January, 1937, leaving instructions that he wanted the Company to build itself into a position where it was short 10 million bushels in oats, using this as a hedge against long positions in barley and Argentine corn (an oats/corn hedge was generally considered logical; a barley/corn hedge was thought to be a speculative cross-hedge). John Sr. was also out of the office, and decisions on how to effect these hedges were left with the traders under Julius Hendel, with overall supervision in the hands of Cargill MacMillan. Ed Grimes decided to write J. W. T. Duvel at the CEA, elaborating the Company's futures strategy. Duvel responded, on January 19: "It seems rather an unusual hedge, but until such time as some limits are fixed on different classes of operations I see no reason why you should not place your hedge in that way if you care to do so." Then Duvel added a caution: "Of course if it should subsequently develop that your large short holdings in oats were handled in such a way as to seriously affect the oats market, it might be necessary for us to take some different view. . . . Your short position in May oats . . . represents approximately 35 percent of the total contracts. . . . This could easily develop into a situation which might be an undue burden on interstate commerce."

The Duvel warning gave Cargill MacMillan pause, and he wrote his father, "The boys here are frankly worried over our oats position. . . . Even Julius has furrows in his brow." Cargill also sent a copy to John Jr., apprehensive about his brother's response: "I rather expected contradictory replies and the problem of how to please you both had not at that time occurred to me." In the absence of his older brother and father, Cargill now himself made the decision to cut back on selling oats futures. "I think this is the sanest thing to do for, after all, you would not leave me here unless you had some confidence in my judgment, and my own judgment is to do just what we are doing."[20]

The total of these hedges and the other trading in the month of January 1937 resulted in a surprising $300,000 loss for the month, and Cargill MacMillan once more reported to his brother: "I went through the usual routine, had the boys in on the carpet and tried to imitate father's best manner. . . . The boys say they realized, but I think they only realized theoretically, what inverse carrying charges do to one. . . . These revelations . . . take the gimp right out of the organization."[21] Cargill MacMillan was coming into his own as another Company fiscal watchdog (along with John Peterson)—and as a leaven on his brother's expansionist, often "bull-ahead" philosophy.

Further Dan Rice Irritations—in Both Directions

In May 1937, Cargill once more had difficulties in meeting grading requirements and being prompt in loading May oats out of the Chicago warehouse. The person on the other end of this transaction was, again,

Dan Rice. He alleged that Cargill was taking care of itself first—there were 7.8 million bushels in Cargill's "public warehouse" section (including 2,308,000 bushels of Dan Rice oats), but Cargill had appropriated Rice-ordered railroad cars (there was a boxcar shortage) and shipped its own oats out of the remaining "private" section of the warehouse. "Cargill could promote and protect the merchandising of its own oats," Rice complained, "by delaying the shipping out . . . of our oats."

Rice immediately complained to the CBOT and also to the Illinois State Warehouse Commission. He got his oats but then contested Cargill's elevation and storage charges and refused to pay some $14,751. Cargill countered by bringing its own formal charge before the CBOT on July 20, 1937. A week later, Cargill withdrew the complaint; Rice had contacted the Company, expressing a desire to settle it directly as a "private business controversy" (Cargill's words). But the mutual mistrust that had developed between Rice and Cargill remained.

Earlier that spring, John Jr. had made a trip to Washington, where he had had an hourlong session with Dr. Duvel at the CEA offices. He wrote John Sr.: "Dr. Duvel . . . felt that our position on May futures was entirely correct and he spoke in very condemnatory terms of the speculative commitments in May." Once again, John Jr. seemed heartened by what he perceived as CEA support, especially welcome in relation to Dan Rice.

Nevertheless, John Jr. felt that rumormongers were running Cargill down. In early May, he wrote directly to Kenneth S. Templeton, the CBOT president, denying whisperings that Cargill was delivering wheat "of such inferior quality that the grading under the Federal standards is in doubt." He defended the quality Cargill was delivering from its Chicago terminal and bluntly stated: "There has been no mixing or degradation of this grain since it has been loaded into our house." The letter did not ask for any action by Templeton, nor was any taken.[22]

It was clear, however, that by this time John Jr.'s fuse was getting shorter. Worse was to come.

Summer 1937: Cargill Assesses Corn Supply

The corn crop for the year 1936–1937 was the second smallest on record; only the Dust Bowl year 1934–1935 had been smaller. Inasmuch as the intervening year was only average, the actual stocks of corn on farms, as of July 1, 1937, were the lowest ever recorded. The total United States visible supply of corn as of that date was just over 5.3 million bushels; the average for the same date for the years 1932–1936 was almost 22.5 million bushels. Even the availability of the corn on farms was questionable; the 1936–1937 crop was of lower merchantable quality than usual, and the best of this had to be kept for seed corn. Already, corn prices in the spring of 1937 had been high (up to $1.40 per bushel in May), and most surplus corn had been attracted into the markets.[23]

By early summer, Cargill had assumed extensive long positions, at first in July futures but then, in the second half of June, shifted to the September contract. The July price had advanced to a point where it had been advisable to take a profit on these contracts and replace them with the cheaper September contracts. This strategy continued until, by July 30, some 8,075,000 bushels of long September corn futures had been accumulated.

In late May, Julius Hendel had received a wire from Chicago that Daniel F. Rice "is selling Sept. wheat and doesn't expect to cover it for years and make the carrying charge." By about August 1, Company officials, listening to gossip in the CBOT pits, thought they began to detect concerted efforts to drive prices lower on the September corn contract—that there was an incipient "bear" raid on corn. Further, the Chicago Cargill traders thought they knew who the key shorts were—once again Cargill's old protagonists, Daniel F. Rice and the Farmers National Grain Corporation.

During the period between August 1 and September 4, according to later Cargill testimony, three separate price rallies in September corn had been checked, either by trade rumors or newspaper stories: "We believe some of these are pure propaganda, emanating from persons interested in beating down the price of corn." First, on August 4, Cargill heard rumors that Rice planned to bring in 3 million to 4 million bushels of Texas corn, yet Cargill's field sources in Texas remonstrated that the corn supply there was in quite short supply. Another rally in prices, later in the month of August, also seemed forestalled (in Cargill eyes) by a news article syndicated in the *Associated Press* that talked of "burdensome deliveries" and suggested that "with no aggressive buying demands in evidence, the markets were bowled over in rapid succession, with but little rallying power manifest."[24]

Cargill alleged that this story had been planted by the shorts as a "clever, though unscrupulous" maneuver. Later, in one of the ensuing CEA cases, the Company amassed a whole set of wires sent at this time by Cargill's Chicago office to the Minneapolis headquarters, some 920 in all, that seemed to document at least Cargill's view of a conspiracy. Here are the most telling of the wires:

August 4, 1937: "Understand Rice, Hollman big shorts Sept Corn. They remarked could bring in 3 to 4 million Texas YC [yellow corn] to deliver in Sept."

August 10, 1937: "Bache selling CU [September corn]. Rice offering it all the way down."

August 11, 1937: "Rice is in Pit waving arms and selling CU. Putting on a show."

August 12, 1937: "Rice forcing the Sep. Corn down. Offered 200 at 93¾ when market was 99¼."

August 12, 1937: "Here is a funny one. The short Corn fellow [Dan Rice] say

Cargill long Sep. Corn and he will give them a belly full this time and break them. How's that?"

August 19, 1937: "Rice and his crowd seem to be offering CU. Looks like a show as not selling much but sure making lots noise."

August 20, 1937: "I have a good hunch Uhlmann corn broker is buying CU for Rice as a friend told me he was giving Rice's clerk several trades."

August 30, 1937: "Rice just went in corn pit after long conversation with Farmers Natl."

In one of the subsequent CEA cases, a CBOT member (serving on a subcommittee of the CBOT's Business Conduct Committee, called the McDonald Committee, set up to investigate Cargill's role in this September 1937 corn contract) stated: "These messages show absolutely no evidence of bear raids . . . they are silly, unfounded and unreliable, and just idle gossip and rumor." In truth, when the McDonald Committee had taken its testimony, several of the interviewed floor traders also confirmed that something different from usual had been happening on the shorts' side. Albert E. Williams, who traded for his own account, when queried about the shorts, replied, "Well, I saw quite a few people who were supposed to be bearish . . . force the market down severely . . . I have seen the local boys going to the market and offering it down." When asked about Rice's activities, he responded, "I'm not saying that the man hasn't any right to sell the corn at any price he likes, but that was an unusual situation."

Alex Moore, a cash grain trader for John E. Bastien Grain Co., was an even more reluctant witness. Asked about the Rice activities he answered, "I refuse to answer that or rather I prefer not to answer." But he was willing to talk about raids in general: "They would offer 100 or 200 thousand at probably a quarter of a cent below the market," and when he was asked, "As a rule isn't there sufficient buying to correct that condition?," he replied, "Those offerings should never be made in that manner." Asked if he would testify that there were such raids, he replied, "I am a cash man and I would rather have you get that testimony from men in the pit."

Moore was pressed about what he did observe with the September corn contract; he reiterated his belief that the shorts "should not have offered that way" and continued: "These gentlemen are pit traders. They know if they are fulfilling an order they don't go in and offer a large quantity below the market. . . . I would say from the method used and the individual using it that it resembled more of a raid than an attempt to get a quantity of corn off at reasonably near the market." Moore's concluding words emphasized just how hard it was to determine exactly what was going on in the pit in a rapidly moving market situation: "It is difficult to explain what a raid might be unless you are suspicious that people are trying unduly to affect the market."

Harold E. Spinney, a floor trader for Lamson Bros. & Co., when asked about Rice, said: "It wasn't necessarily raiding if the broker offers the market down a bit." He corrected himself: "I really shouldn't use that term. . . . I had better say they offered it down." The Committee, too, vocally expressed unease about the term "raid." Chairman McDonald commented after the Spinney testimony, "It's a vicious term . . . if it is a term that was coined by the trade we as members [should try] to eliminate it . . . when it gets into testimony, it sounds like the devil."[25]

Two Ambiguous Contracts

John Jr. and his colleagues were, naturally, not privy to this later testimony at the time the shorts allegedly were carrying out their effort. Given Cargill's tenuous relations with the CBOT officialdom, few traders would likely have been willing to testify at the time for Cargill. Sometime in early August, having convinced themselves that a bear raid was in progress and acting on their information, Cargill officers made a fateful decision, one that later was to haunt them. With the Company's long position in September corn now over 8 million bushels, and remembering that large reported positions that seemed to dominate markets had caused Cargill trouble in two previous corn contracts in 1936, the Company decided to reduce this reported amount drastically. The operational word here is "reported," for Cargill was able to persuade two other grain companies (neither of which knew that the other was involved) to assume a great bulk of Cargill's long positions. Beginning on August 13, Cargill sold some 3,460,000 bushels of September corn futures to Continental Grain Company, the transactions completed by August 31; in approximately the same period, Cargill sold 3,675,000 bushels to the Uhlmann Grain Company.

In turn, Cargill drew a contract with each to sell back to Cargill equal amounts of cash corn at the end of September or in early October, at the seller's option. Neither Continental nor Uhlmann bought any cash corn to cover this; they planned to use the physical deliveries at the termination of the September contract to fulfill Cargill's requirements. For this effort by the two companies, Cargill promised to pay each a quarter of a cent per bushel for being the "temporary holders." Cargill's reported net long position in the September contract now dropped dramatically, from 8,745,000 bushels on August 13 to 2,237,000 on August 31, 1937. Julius Hendel was the effector of these contracts, under the direction of John Jr. and Ed Grimes.[26]

John Jr. had some unease about the plan, and he and Grimes made a special trip to Washington on August 11, two days before the actual buying was to begin, to talk with Dr. Duvel at the CEA. The exact events of that meeting were later subject to much argument among Cargill, the CEA and the Business Conduct Committee of the CBOT. According to Cargill notes on this meeting, John Jr. and Grimes first elaborated on the tight market situation in corn and explained why Cargill had accumulated its "long" line. They told Duvel and his assistant, J. M. Mehl, who also attended, about Cargill's concern that a "bear" raid was underway. John Jr. then reminded the two CEA officials of the Business Conduct Committee's earlier decision to press Cargill to sell large quantities of the December 1936 corn and wheat futures at prices detrimental to the Company and said that they feared the same treatment once again.

At this point in the meeting, John Jr. and Grimes described to Duvel and Mehl the Cargill plan to convert much of Cargill's long futures into cash purchases. However, they did not mention specifics and left the impression that Cargill was going to enter into contracts with grain merchants who, at the time of contracting, had on hand the actual cash corn, without relying upon futures transferred to them by Cargill as sources of this actual corn. The Cargill memorandum reporting on the meeting stated that both Duvel and Mehl then said they saw nothing wrong with the procedure. Cargill, however, at no time claimed explicitly that John Jr. and Grimes had actually mentioned the Uhlmann and Continental contracts. Cargill left the meeting with Duvel and Mehl, as Grimes put it in a Cargill memorandum, "with the impression that our operations to date and our contemplated operations of standing pat on our September position have their blessing and approval."

The Business Conduct Committee Acts

Whatever the perceptions of the parties to the August 11 meeting in Washington, it is clear that the Uhlmann and Continental contracts did not become known until the end of August. At this point, the Business Conduct Committee of the Exchange called executives of the three companies, Cargill, Continental and Uhlmann into committee hearings. John Jr. was there and stated that "he was willing to talk in generalities but that he felt that both in September and December of last year . . . he had made a very grievous mistake in making a statement [prematurely] . . . it was not fair for the Committee to grasp the picture piecemeal." John Jr. denied any subterfuge with the two contracts, refused any more information and ended: "They cannot see why they should be coerced as they were last December."

It took the Business Conduct Committee only a few more minutes to rule that the Cargill long position in the September corn futures would have to be amended to include both the Uhlmann and the Continental amounts. On September 1, the combined position became 9,392,000 bushels, 50.8 percent of the total open interest of 18,502,000 bushels. Thus, by September 1, 1937, Cargill's involvement in the expiring corn futures contracts looked even more dominant than in December 1936.[27]

Fighting the "Shorts"

Convinced of a continuing conspiracy by the shorts to drive down prices (in the process obtaining enough cash corn to meet their obligations), Cargill now, in the words of the CEA, "entered upon a campaign of aggressive buying of cash corn." In early September its efforts were concentrated mostly in the Midwest; later, about September 17, the buying campaign was extended to Texas and Oklahoma.

The subsequent CEA case testimony highlighted 70 wires from Cargill offices to field representatives, giving orders about these purchases. Cargill's intent, according to the CEA, was "to keep corn away from Farmers National, Rice, and other supposed shorts." The following wires appeared in the final CEA decision:

September, 8 1937: "Want to keep the corn from Fanny [Farmers National] so suggest go back up to four over if necessary."

September 9, 1937: "Pls continue taking spot corn and want to pay just enough to take away from Fanny."

September 14, 1937: "On the old corn . . . we want to take it away from Fanny so if have to make out discounts less Pls do so. We want to get the preference over Fanny so do what it takes."

September 16, 1937: "Our St. Louis office advises that Vehon is now out thru central Illinois bidding for Rice on old 2 Yel at 2 over . . . suggest go to 2½ over if have to take this away there."

September 16, 1937: "Crosby offering couple cars old two YC, do think we should sell to some other party and then buy back ourselves, it can be done, otherwise must sell to Rice."

September 21, 1937: "Rice bidding 105¾ for corn overnight we are bidding 106."

Other messages dealt with the Company's efforts to sell their cash corn only to feed companies or processors and to be assured that the corn would not be placed on the market again "so that the shorts might obtain it for delivery" (the CEA's words):

September 9, 1937: "If the feed men are taking the spot corn let them have it but want to be sure they are the ones taking."

September 16, 1937: "Any of the corn we have billed to CP [Corn Products Company] regardless of where it came from, want to know if they reshipping any of it to Farmers Natl."

The Texas corn was a particular threat to Cargill, as the supply there was rather substantial. The Company assiduously sought out this market, and by September 17 a wire from one of the field personnel, tabulating his purchases, ended with a quotation that became famous in the subsequent case: "If I have overlooked a bushel of corn it is surely out in the forks of the creek." By September 20, John Jr. wired his father: "Looks like the country is about out of cash corn."

The Company's policy in this critical period in early and mid-September was to buy cash corn, then purchase September futures as it sold the cash corn, which, according to the CEA, "had the effect of causing the shorts in the September corn future to cover in the pit rather than to buy cash corn and make delivery." The CEA continued: "The policy 'tightened' rather than 'loosened' the situation. . . . In times of shortage . . . the price of the future tends to go up to the cash and the aggressive buying of cash by complainant tended to keep the cash at a premium over the future." This then made it "financially inadvisable for a short to buy cash corn and deliver it; it was more profitable for a short to buy in his contract in the pit."

The CEA felt this to be Cargill's underlying strategy: buy up available physical supply, forcing the shorts to remain in the futures market until such time as they were willing to get out by buying their contracts back. If this went beyond expiration, there would have to be a settlement price established with the longs, primarily Cargill. To the degree that the shorts could themselves buy up remaining cash corn, the Cargill tactics could be countered. It always had been possible to entice away considerable farmer-held grain if the price was right. A St. Louis dealer wrote Dan Rice in late August: "Fellows on whom we can rely told us old corn is scarce . . . but it would certainly surprise one how much could come out on any tight situation. We tried to pin them down . . . if there were a squeeze the consensus of opinion is that every elevator up there could pick up at least 10,000 and there are a lot of elevators up there . . . a half million corn on a conservative estimate."

Frank A. Jost, the key assistant to Dan Rice, now was dispatched to the Southwest by airplane (not widely used at that time) to "smoke out" (his term) any possible corn supplies. He was asked at the McDonald Committee hearing about these Rice efforts to buy: "Every time we would try to buy cash corn, Cargill would step in and bid a higher price than we were bidding." Jost was trying to buy corn for as high as $117 1/4$ and yet was being outbid.

Cargill was using a commission house in Texas named Transit Grain & Commission Company, but, Jost reported, they "covered their tracks in Ft. Worth pretty completely." Jost further bemoaned that everywhere he found the dealers reluctant to talk—most "don't want to do anything to hurt their possible future dealings with Cargill."[28]

By September 16, Cargill's share of the total open interest in the September corn futures contract stood at almost 65 percent. The Business Conduct Committee had met the day before and at that time had begun to worry about rye, too. It had been pointed out to the Committee that Cargill "held the same relative position in September rye as in corn." On September 16, John Jr., Grimes and Sayles met with the Committee. The letter that they presented at that time stated: "We have no desire to 'punish' anybody, even short sellers, and we are, therefore, willing to consider any solution of the problem . . . which will not unduly depress the price of corn to the producers generally." John Jr. was cagey about price, saying only that "at any given moment we have a price which we consider the economic price. At certain prices we will dispose of our line." The CEA stated that John Jr. "was reluctant to reveal Cargill's full intention to the entire Committee."

The Business Conduct Committee rejected Cargill's allegation that there was a bear raid. On the contrary, "the Committee finds there is not now, nor has there been, short line or lines in the market even nearly comparable to the combined long line of Cargill, Incorporated, Uhlmann Grain Company and Continental Grain Company." Despite the Committee's seeming nonchalance about the shorts, they did decide, on September 15, to warn the shorts that, under Exchange rules, they faced expulsion if they defaulted. The press now picked up the issue, sensing a "grudge fight" (as a *Journal of Commerce* reporter called it on September 16). The press did seem skeptical of the Business Conduct Committee's real dedication on disciplining the shorts; the *Chicago Daily News* commented on September 18, after the warning became public, "those long of the market expressed the opinion that the shorts were being 'babied.' They cited numerous occasions . . . where gamblers in grain who had guessed wrong had called for help . . . charging manipulation and other unfair practices."

On September 17, the price on the September contract rose sharply, at one point standing at $1.16¾. The closing price was $1.13¼ (the December 1937 corn contract, in contrast, had stayed almost steady, closing at $.63). The Business Conduct Committee convened a special meeting after the market closed that day and soon learned that there were now misgivings in the Uhlmann group. Fred Uhlmann, its president, appeared in person and stated: "Cargill knows that we are very anxious to get out of the mess. I have never been interested in a corner. As hedgers, they have always hurt us. Cargill has promised me that as quickly as he [*sic*] sees his way clear, he will start evening up Uhlmann's line as fast as possible—no matter what Cargill will do. The Board of Trade will not need to worry about me."

Interestingly, Richard Uhlmann, his son, was one of the five members of the Business Conduct Committee who would adjudicate the Uhlmann role. This was too great a potential conflict of interest, and he resigned. Later in that year, the younger Uhlmann wrote Kenneth Templeton of the difficulties of serving on the Committee: "It has been stated that if a person served on this committee and had a personal trade, he might consider himself continually under suspicion. . . . I do not subscribe to that theory." He noted in this letter that three others of the five members had large amounts of wheat hedged "and naturally had some personal interest" but that "none of us has been criticized for having abused the information that has come to us in confidence, and rightly so, because any decent member . . . does not betray a real trust."

Simon Mayer, the Chicago head of Continental (holder of the other contract with Cargill), was asked to appear at the September 17 meeting, too, but he stood pat: "I am satisfied that Mr. MacMillan made that promise for me. As our futures are liquidated, our cash will be liquidated to the same extent." The Committee also called in Dan Rice, who was quite hostile toward Cargill: "If they persist in going through with their corner, I will get an indictment against everybody that had anything to do with it." When one of the Committee members asked if he had been buying some cash corn, Rice replied: "I've been selling September against it. I started out to buy corn at one over. Cargill bids ½ over my bid, so I told them not to buy anymore cash corn today. Yesterday I bought 150 cash corn. They paid 6 over for warehouse receipts, then turned around and sold corn to go to Indianapolis at 3 over."

The following day, September 18, was Saturday. The markets were open a half day on Saturday in those days. Late in the morning, prices on the September contract suddenly broke, falling to $1.04¾. The *Wall Street Journal* reported that "confident longs rushed to liquidate their positions influenced by relatively large tenders of the seemingly light supply of the grain." The same article noted that large supplies of corn from Texas "would arrive here early next week."

Cargill interpreted this sudden price break differently. The Company's internal memorandum noted that "around 11:20 a.m. Dr. J. W. T. Duvel, Chief of the Commodity Exchange Administration, talks on the telephone from Washington with CBOT President Templeton. Within a few minutes thereafter, Chicago September corn begins a precipitate drop in price and the 'bottom peg' is quickly reached. . . . This change of circumstances is capable of scandalous interpretation, and political interference in Washington, coupled with 'leakage' of 'confidential' news in Chicago, probably lie at the bottom of these events. Cargill does not do the selling which causes the sensational drop. . . . This selling is probably the work of existing 'shorts.' "

This was just a surmise by John Jr., but a Templeton private memorandum to his fellow directors seemed to corroborate some CEA pressure. Templeton had made careful notes of the conversation and reported that Duvel had said, "We don't like the action of the market and especially today's action. We think the market has gotten out of hand and manipulation is taking place. . . . Outsiders will think you are just running a gambling house. . . . We won't tolerate another run-up in the market such as you had today. . . . Your rules allow you to close the market and fix a price. If you don't take action, you can rest assured that action will be taken for you, if you have another run-up such as you had today."

On the next business day (Monday, September 20), Ed Grimes met with Dr. Duvel at the CEA offices in Washington. As Grimes recalled this meeting, Duvel had told him, "The Secretary, Mr. Wallace, had become interested in the matter and he had had some talks with him on it." (Cargill suspected, but was never able to prove, that Farmers National had mounted a telegraph protest from farmers charging a "squeeze or corner.")

Then the conversation began to center on price. Earlier, Cargill had intimated that the September corn contract justified an optimum price of about $1.30. Incidentally, when this came up in one of the later CEA cases, the Board of Trade lawyer vowed that the price mentioned by Cargill at that time had been $1.40. Now Grimes tested the water again with the $1.30 figure and got an immediate, tart reply: "Forget it." Duvel, however, now found *himself* in a ticklish position, as a presumably independent government administrator not wanting to appear to be dictating price. In his letter to the McDonald committee, Duvel described how he had handled this dilemma:

He asked me what was the right price. I told him that I was not naming any figure but that I wanted to see the September future liquidated in an orderly manner. I also mentioned that the September future had sold at a high of $1.16¾ on September 17, with a low price of 89¾ cents made on July 30; that I did not want to see any new high prices in the September future, neither did I want to see any new low prices. In fact, that I did not want to see either the old highs or the old lows reached again before the future expired . . . if September corn went out in orderly fashion I would expect it to go out somewhere between $1.05 and $1.15. Mr. Grimes then asked: "About $1.15," and I said "No, I don't mean $1.15, either," but that I would expect to see the September corn liquidated orderly somewhere within a reasonable range without wide daily price fluctuations, and certainly below $1.15, unless fundamental conditions should change materially before the end of the month.[28]

By Wednesday, September 22, corn again rose sharply, closing at $1.12½. During that day, Cargill had sold just 820,000 bushels; its percentage of the open interest had risen to 74.1. After the close, the Business Conduct Committee forcefully communicated its disappointment with Cargill's position that day. Sayles responded that "we had orders in the pit to sell over two and one-half million bushels, but we were unable to dispose of it, as the shorts were not eager to buy."

Sayles then went home, exhausted, only to be summoned back later that evening. Morris R. Glaser, the Business Conduct Committee chairman, called him at 11:00 P.M., insisting that he return downtown to meet with the Committee.

Sayles arrived at the Union League Club about midnight, only to find no one there. After waiting several minutes, he received a call from Glaser—they were at the University Club but had forgotten to tell Sayles. After a cab ride, Sayles finally appeared before the committee.

Mr. Glaser insisted that I promise to put market selling orders in the pit the next day and said that he would not want to put the words in my mouth to make a promise but that is what they really wanted. I told them that I would have selling orders in the pit the next day at a price but we were not going to dump our line or any part of it on a declining market, while they allowed the bears continually to offer the market down. . . . Mr. Sturtevant [another member of the Committee] asked me to leave the orders in the pit that were not filled that day. I told him that would be impossible and no one, to my knowledge, did business that way. Every order that was in the pit was a day order and at the opening the next day they would start over again and that was what Cargill intended to do. . . . Mr. Lindley asked me if we did not intend to cooperate with them in this situation. . . . I told him we would keep our promise but we had never promised to cooperate to the extent of selling out our long corn regardless of price. . . . They tried to extract a promise from me to have big orders in the pit to sell September corn at around $1.12½ the next day and I told them that would all depend on what the market did the next day and we would not make any decision until then. . . . Then Mr. English, who had driven downtown and who lives in Evanston, drove me home at about 3:00 A.M.

The Cargill brief reporting this meeting editorialized: "One cannot refrain from thinking that the Business Conduct Committee had a bad case of nerves. . . . Certain it is, however, that they gave Mr. Sayles a very bad time of it, and the results of their 'third degree' methods were peculiarly barren." The brief ended, rather piously, "The shorts were allowed to have a good night's rest; and doubtlessly Mr. Sayles felt, around 3:00 or 3:30 A.M., a twinge or two of envy."

The Business Conduct Committee minutes of this evening meeting have also survived intact; these meticulous and vivid notes conflict in some of their major particulars with the Sayles version.

Their meeting had begun at 9:00 P.M., with all Committee members present, as well as Kenneth Templeton, the CBOT president, and Howard Ellis, the chief outside counsel for the Exchange. Ellis clearly was worried about the legal implications of what he thought might be seen as Exchange inaction on the corn contract. Already one Exchange member had queried, "If farmers knew situation, wouldn't B of T be criticized?" Ellis warned: "If the Committee remains silent, Cargill is entitled to presume that liquidation to date is considered satisfactory by the Committee. . . . Wednesday the market went up. Why didn't they liquidate more? You men, as experts, say that they liquidated enough, but before an investigating committee you cannot justify scale liquidation upward. An investigating agency would say that you are letting Cargill take advantage of a squeeze."

This harsh statement galvanized the Committee to call Sayles downtown. The Committee's minutes pictured Sayles as much more compliant and deferential. In answer to Glaser's question, "Will you have an order in, at or near today's closing price?" Sayles was said to reply, "We will have an order in. How does the action suit you? If it is satisfactory to you we will do the same tomorrow; keep on selling on the way up." When Lindley stated, "It would be to the best interests of everybody concerned for you to liquidate regardless of price," Sayles answered, "I agree with you. We'll liquidate when we can." Lindley pressed for a more specific promise: "If I understand you correctly, you are a seller of corn within the limit of the market to absorb sales, and whether the price is up or down you will be selling." The minutes recorded Sayles as replying, "Yes, we will be a good seller of corn."

At this point, Theodore E. Cunningham summed up: "It seems to me that Mr. Sayles has relieved all of us considerably." Templeton added, "We'll all sleep better." Glaser, still uncertain, asked again, "You are going to be putting in corn at the market tomorrow?" Sayles replied, "We are going to be sellers of corn. We will be liquidating tomorrow." Thus ended the Business Conduct Committee version of the meeting.

The next morning (September 23), Sayles went to the pit with several orders to sell at $1.14⁷/₈. The results were not what he had hoped: "I stood in the pit next to Mr. Sturtevant and watched Mr. Rice continually offer September corn at $1.14³/₄ and lower but did not see him make any sales." At the end of the day, Sayles was called once more to the offices of the Business Conduct Committee; the members pressed Sayles as to why Cargill had not sold a big portion of its line. Sayles answered, "We had orders in the pit to sell several million bushels at a point ¹/₈¢ above where the bears raided the market."

Once more, Sayles was ordered by the Committee to stay downtown and wait for a call. Summoning him at about 11:00 P.M., the Committee insisted that Cargill liquidate a majority of its line the next day and objected strenuously to the Sayles accusation of an alleged bear raid. Sayles replied that Richard Uhlmann had told him that "they considered a raid was when any member stood in the pit and continually offered corn down in big round lots without making sales and offering it down for several cents." Apparently Uhlmann was asked to prefer charges against the Rice group but refused. "There was plenty of proof, everyone in the pit knew about it," Uhlmann stated, "if they wanted to prefer charges they would have no trouble to prove that this pit trader was putting on a bear raid."

The Committee then gave Sayles an ultimatum, insisting that he sign a statement promising to dispose of a majority of Cargill's line the following day. "I refused to do it . . . we could not tell what the market would do the next day. . . . He remarked that prices did not mean anything to the Committee . . . and I told him that price might not mean anything to the Business Conduct Committee but it meant a lot to the Cargill interests. We were not dumping our corn just to satisfy the short sellers."

The following day, September 24, Cargill's net long position had declined by only 9,000 bushels, and the Committee ordered Cargill to bring its position down to 5,400,000 bushels by the close of the business day. John Jr. fired off both a telegram and a letter, each with the same blunt message: "We categorically deny each and every charge of misconduct contained in your letter. We further deny your jurisdiction to tell us when and at what price to cancel our contracts. . . . We have no intention of being coerced by any bear raids."

This finally seemed to galvanize the Exchange to action. Kenneth Templeton, the president of the Exchange, put in a call to Dr. Duvel at the CEA. Templeton's first remembrance of this call when queried about it many months later was that Duvel had said, "I think the market should be closed." Later, Templeton modified this—that Duvel had only asked, "Do you *think* the market should be closed?" (emphasis mine). Whoever said what, the action was definitive: the Business Conduct Committee forthwith ordered trading in September corn futures stopped at the close of that day (September 24) and mandated a settlement price of $1.10½ per bushel.[29]

Uhlmann Bails Out

Early on that pivotal day of September 24, before the decision by the Business Conduct Committee to mandate a settlement price, the executives of Uhlmann Grain Company, having been named with Cargill and Continental in that morning's order by the Committee, insisted to Cargill that it be let out of the agreement.

Ed Grimes elaborated Cargill's explanation for the Uhlmann decision: "This . . . was done as a matter of grace, not of right. The Uhlmann Company told Cargill that Mr. Fred Uhlmann, a man of advanced age, was in poor health; and said that the mental and physical strain caused by the terrific pressure put upon him by the activities of the Business Conduct Committee was having a very serious effect on him." The Continental executives had made no such representations, for that company had "stood its ground when the Order of the 23rd was issued to it."

The Uhlmann version of this was signally different. On the night before (September 23), Fred Uhlmann had met with the Business Conduct Committee and the Committee's minutes quoted him:

We had orders from Cargill today to sell our whole line. . . . I called up Cargill yesterday and told him [*sic*] I was in a terrible mess, and said when I made a trade with you I did not know you had previously made a trade with Continental Grain Company and consequently as the Continental Grain Company are the first to receive the corn from the Clearing House, they are the oldest in the Clearing House, they probably got all their corn, probably enough to satisfy them and if it is not sold or there is any disagreement, I will be the victim and I don't like it. . . . I am willing to cooperate to any extent. . . . I could clear myself if I would go to Cargill and say I would not let any dollars and cents stand in my way. I want to get out. I want to do this straight, make your own terms.

Fred Uhlmann had had enough; the contract with Cargill had blown up in his face: "As far as I am concerned, I want to go to Europe. I don't want to appear as a guilty party. . . . I want to undo this trade. I have a right to do that. I could go to them and I would not let anything stand in the way."[30]

Cargill Cleans Up the September Contracts

Once the mandated price of $1.10½ had been established, the liquidation of the September corn futures contract proceeded expeditiously. Cargill continued to purchase cash corn, both because it "feared the Business Conduct Committee might prevent its obtaining much needed cash corn" and "because it wished to cooperate with the Committee." During the remainder of the month, Cargill liquidated its long September corn futures as it purchased this cash corn but did worry that it was being stuck with poorer quality in the process, "undesirable mixtures of white and yellow corn and new and old corn."

The price of cash corn, after the September 24 mandating decision, began to drop substantially. By early October it was in the neighborhood of 83 cents and later that month dropped as low as 61 cents. Cargill had been paying well over $1.00 for the cash corn it purchased to raise the price of cash corn during September. Obviously, in order to effect its overall plan, the Company had been willing to stand a substantial loss on this cash corn—to use the macabre expression common in the industry, to "bury the corpse."

The McDonald Committee, in its later public report, described the Company's strategy:

Cargill had a short position in December corn futures which exceeded its long position in September corn futures. . . . Thus, whatever effect Cargill's long September position may have had on September prices, it was offset by Cargill's short position in December corn futures. . . . Cargill's purpose in maintaining such an overwhelming short December position was to enable it (Cargill) to make a speculative profit . . . at the close of the September corn futures, at which time it (Cargill) anticipated it would undoubtedly suffer a loss on its stock of cash corn accumulated by it to sustain its September long position. The activities of Cargill in outbidding shorts for cash corn in this and other markets, under all the circumstances, were designed to strengthen Cargill's long position in the September corn futures.

Thus, the view of Cargill's motives held by both the CEA and the CBOT was that the Company was attempting to hold up the price of September corn futures until the termination of the contract, when they estimated it would be in the range of $1.40. The potential profit on this would have been huge; for example, if the Company had averaged $1.10 on its purchases, say, for the 9,372,000 bushels it held on August 31, a $1.40 sale

TABLE I

	1937–38 Crop year	Five–year average (1932–33 through 1936–37)
Total bushels		
(all grains)	126,284,000	85,352,000
Spring wheat (bu)	12,542,000	18,807,000
Winter wheat (bu)	27,597,000	5,569,000
Corn (bu)	47,542,000	22,014,000
All other (bu)	38,603,000	38,962,000

would have netted $2,811,600 profit. At no point in the record did Cargill agree that this was the Company's motive, but it does seem reasonable that some scenario close to this likely would have occurred had not the CBOT mandated a settlement price of $1.10½.

Cargill's efforts to profit on the liquidation process of the September contract were, of course, frustrated. With the major loss on cash corn sales—the "corpse had to be buried"—it was now ordained that Cargill was going to incur substantial net losses, as the September and December contracts would liquidate without positive effect.

The total bushels traded by the Company in this crop year June 1, 1937, to May 31, 1938, was strikingly larger than the average of the previous five years, a significant part attributable to the heavy Company buying in September 1937. Table 1 presents the figures for the year and for the previous five-year average.

The full implications of the trades involved in the September 1937, contract were not apparent right away, inasmuch as hedges were rolled over to later months, and the full liquidation of the 1936–1937 old-crop physical corn, to be accomplished over the fall and winter of 1937–1938, would not affect the financial statements until the end of the fiscal year, on May 31, 1938.* In the Company's closing statements at the end of the calendar year 1937, covering a seven-month period of the crop year 1937–1938, the Grains Account on the profit-and-loss statement showed a profit of $120,000 (with the net income for the Company at that point being $426,000). This was illusory, of course, for by the time the fiscal year of the Company had been reached, on May 31, 1938, the Grains Account showed a loss of $1,479,000. Indeed, the loss in the Grains Account for the United States alone was even higher, at $1,763,000. Fortunately, Canadian trading showed a profit. The net loss for the Company as a whole was shown on that closing statement, May 31, 1938, as $998,000; later, accounting revisions put this loss figure as $1,136,000. It was the largest loss that the Company had ever endured—indeed, one of only three loss years in the

*The Company's ending month for the crop year had been changed to May 31 in 1936.

entire history of the Company (the other two years were 1935–1936 and 1920–1921).

It would be misleading to blame this huge loss only on the events surrounding the September 1937 corn futures incident. For the country, there was a brief but acute depression that began in August 1937 and extended into 1938. This was a difficult time in general for the grain trade, as for other industries. Nevertheless, the root of the large Company loss reported on May 31, 1938, was the aftereffect of the September 1937 corn contract.

At the point of the mandated settlement in late September, Cargill attempted to forestall any further action by the Business Conduct Committee by planting stories in the press of its unfair treatment: "Irving [Goldsmith, Cargill's outside lawyer] is now loading newspaper boys with information re unfair trial methods of Board of Trade just in case Board of Trade decides to take action. He has pointed out no counsel allowed, no record kept, no appeal, etc. and has drawn analogy with labor board, beside which Board of Trade is a star chamber." Cargill officials truly felt that most of the membership of the Exchange were really on their side; as Sayles put it, "the majority members on floor very indignant because directors took such drastic action and all are in sympathy with Cargill."

But this presumed support proved illusory—the incident was by no means over at this point. A long saga of postcontract events now transpired.[31]

Who Were the Shorts?

Although later Cargill briefs in these cases accused Dan Rice and the Farmers National Grain Corporation of being the culprits behind the bear raid, John Jr. apparently was still unsure just what kind of a "conspiracy" (his word) had taken place. He wrote to a family member: "We are immensely puzzled in our own organization as to the identity of the shorts, who were short about 6,500,000 bushels over and above the supplies of corn which they had for delivery."

John Jr. later alleged that Thomas Howell was bankrolling the shorts (Howell, a well-known speculator, already had been censured by the Secretary of Agriculture for his activity in the July 1931 corn contract and had been barred from trading for two years). In the later CEA case, John Jr. was pressed by the CBOT lawyer to produce evidence on this allegation. John Jr. replied: "We thought, because the amounts were excessive and from an examination of the known figures and the speculative world, of which we had knowledge, that only one person possessed the means, the resources and the capacity, together with the wish to manipulate, and that was Mr. Howell." This was the extent of John Jr.'s "evidence," and Howell's name disappeared from the case.

At the time of his own testimony in the CEA case, John Jr. had composed a long, handwritten private memorandum, mentioning another of his suppositions about the shorts: "Nearly one third of the open short interest in September corn during the time of the big bear raid was allegedly of foreign origin. In fact, one short line amounting to ¼ of the entire open interest, or 4,500,000 bushels was reported to be of Chinese origin, while another large line was of English origin." Again, however, John Jr. was not able to back up his guesses, and nothing further was heard about this unsubstantiated rumor.

Cargill continued to maintain in the later CEA cases that there *was* a bear raid but never was able definitively to identify a conspiracy among the short sellers. One cannot conclude, however, because Cargill could not prove such a conspiracy, that it did not exist. Indeed, the Cargill evidence (for example, the telegrams noted earlier in this chapter) and the brokers' testimony before the Business Conduct Committee both made such suspicions more than just inferential.[32]

The Business Conduct Committee Pursues Cargill

John MacMillan, Jr., had not expected the Business Conduct Committee to take any additional steps beyond the mandating of the settlement price. On September 29, he wrote a Cargill employee in the Los Angeles office: "It looks very much to me as though stopping trading was the only way the gang could pull themselves out of a hole, particularly when we refused to sell our contracts. We do not anticipate any disciplinary action on the part of the Board, as their hands are certainly not clean."

Once again, John, Jr.'s conviction that Cargill was right led to another miscalculation. Clean hands or not, the Business Conduct Committee *did* choose to act. On October 14, 1937, a three-person committee (the so-called Wood Committee) was constituted to investigate whether Cargill, Continental Grain and Uhlmann Grain had violated the Business Conduct Committee's order on September 24 to reduce its position to 5,400,000 bushels. There seemed little argument in actual fact that Cargill had deliberately refused this order, so this subcommittee came to a preordained conclusion about Cargill. The Committee exonerated Continental and Uhlmann in its report on November 16, 1937.

On October 15, 1937, another committee, the McDonald Committee, was constituted. This was a five-person group, charged by the Business Conduct Committee to perform a wide-ranging investigation of the entire September 1937 corn futures contract. Sayles wrote Grimes the day the McDonald Committee was announced, detailing information about the five people. The chairman, William H. McDonald, "might have been put on the committee to save the scalp of the Businesss Conduct Committee." Another member, Rowland McHenry, "is a rather weak sister and has no love for Cargill . . . he made the remark on the trading floor only a couple of months ago that he would get even with Cargill the first chance he had." A third member, E. T. Maynard, a floor speculator, was close to the Uhlmann group; Sayles could not figure why he was appointed, inasmuch as the Uhlmann group was linked with Cargill. The other two men, according to Sayles, were Daniel Rice supporters—one, Edwin A. Boerner, "would follow Rice's advice in anything that comes up," and the other, E. A. Green, was a "staunch Catholic and one of the Irish Village so he is sure to do anything that Rice and that crowd demand."

Cargill had prepared a substantial brief for the Wood Committee rejecting all of the allegations and denying that the Business Conduct Committee had any jurisdiction over Cargill's cash sales. This was Cargill's only response to Wood and his two colleagues.

The McDonald Committee was another matter altogether, for this group now demanded to "examine Cargill's books." Sayles agreed to a preliminary "audit," but when the time came, Cargill had second thoughts. McDonald, the committee chairman, wired John Jr. on November 23 that he wanted to send auditors to Minneapolis. John Jr. wired back: "Courtesy does not require the corporation to meet demands for information that may be in the nature of a fishing expedition."

Despite John Jr.'s adamancy, the auditor, Earle W. English, was dispatched to Minneapolis. When he arrived, he found John Jr., Julius Hendel, and Ed and Weston Grimes "out of town"—the receptionist did not even know who English was or why he was there. Finally, after cooling his heels in the outer office for a while, Cargill MacMillan did meet "graciously" with him but would share only information on Cargill's Chicago office, not on the parent company. English wired McDonald that the materials he was given "are decidedly inadequate for Committee purposes."

McDonald testily told John Jr. that "the Committee will not concede any limitation on the scope of its examination." John Jr. responded by calling the Cargill board into special session (on December 6, 1937), where it formally voted to "decline to comply with the aforesaid demand of the Board of Directors of the Chicago Board of Trade."[33]

The CEA Considers a "Limits" Regulation

Right in the middle of this tension between Cargill and the two committees, an awkward event intruded. In early November 1937, the CEA decided to hold special hearings about the question of whether it should mandate certain maximum limits on positions that individuals and firms might take for futures in wheat, corn, oats, barley, rye and flaxseed. There had been a "gentlemen's agreement"—first applied in 1926 against the two speculators Arthur Cutten and Jesse Livermore and then regularized during the time of the Grain Futures Administration in 1932—that everyone trading in futures would keep speculative positions below 5 million bushels. Now the CEA wondered if the time had come to make this a matter of formal CEA regulation.

Cargill was asked if it wished to present testimony at the CEA hearings, a potentially ambiguous situation for the Company inasmuch as its very large position in the September contract was one of the key issues being debated by the McDonald Committee. Nevertheless, the Company decided it had too much at stake not to make its own appearance.

Some dozen or more members of the industry, together with Duvel and Mehl of the CEA, testified. C. D. Sturtevant of the Bartlett Frazier Company represented the CBOT and in the process of taking a strong stand against any further limitations made some disparaging remarks about John Jr. Noting that "Cargill is now under investigation for its activities in September corn," he added, "I will not cooperate with Cargill in their attempt to try this alleged violation of the Board of Trade Rules before this tribunal."

To a man, the industry representatives from the various exchanges were intransigently against any form of a limits rule. Cargill, however, saw these hearings as a vehicle to continue its argument with the CBOT. Its brief prepared for these ostensibly unrelated hearings referred right back to the September corn incident: "Cargill does not welcome Government regulation of the Grain Trade; but after contrasting the treatment which it might expect to receive from the Commodity Exchange Administration [sic] with the treatment which it had actually received from the Business Conduct Committee of the Board of Trade of the City of Chicago and from the Directors of that institution . . . the Company decided to support the proposal."

This ringing support of the CEA's proposed limits surprised everyone. John Jr. first stated that the early gentlemen's agreement "surely did not cover non-speculative spreading or cash transactions such as Cargill's" and ended: "We repeat we favor fixing of lines because by doing so everyone knows where he stands, and whenever anyone, we repeat *anyone*, tries to undermine that stand, the matter can then be brought into the courts, where recognized rules of law and justice prevail." It was clear from this testimony that John Jr. felt that Cargill would not be affected in any way.

Dr. Duvel pushed him on this at the hearings, asking bluntly, "Is it possible for you to state at this time, Mr. MacMillan, or give us some idea as to your views on the limitation?" John Jr. did not want to be pinned down to a specific limits figure and ducked this by stating that he would send forth a brief from the Company at a later point.

John Jr.'s confrontational testimony was not what his lawyers had wanted him to present. Just a few days before the hearings, Weston B. Grimes, son of Ed Grimes and the in-house Company lawyer handling part of the Corn Case, wired Sayles: "Consensus of opinion here is that it would be unwise to chastise the Board of Trade in the press and otherwise since it is felt here that there is a very good chance that either the Wood Committee or the directors will pass the question of violation of the order over without disciplinary action." John Jr.'s outrage apparently was so strong, however, that he made the decision to testify in the hearings, not only about the narrower issue of the limits but also the behavior of the Business Conduct Committee itself.

In addition, John Jr. asked Sayles to set up an extensive publicity campaign, to be held as a contingency in case the Business Conduct Committee did act: "Please go to the advertising dept. of the *Tribune* and the *News* and explain to them in great detail how we thought of buying advertising in case we parted company with the Board and get quotations on a space in the same place for every day in the year. . . . I think we should start off with a fairly large ad."

Although John Jr. believed he had taken Cargill and other hedgers and spreaders outside the purview of the hearing's concerns, it was evident from the testimony that both the two CEA officials and other witnesses were talking about potential limits on *all* users of the Exchange. When the CEA released its report on these hearings many months later, on June 14, 1938, there were indeed newly mandated limits for everyone. A 2-million-bushel limit was placed on all net long or short positions in all futures combined or in any one future, of any one grain on any one contract market. In the delivery month itself, the limit would be 1 million bushels. Spreads were also constrained: spread positions were permitted up to 3 million bushels, subject to the same 1-million-bushel limit in a current delivery month.

Duvel wrote John Jr. a few days later, restating the CEA's desire to have Cargill differentiate between its hedges and spreads. It was a conciliatory letter, Duvel ending, "You may have some other designation that you prefer to apply to such of your transactions that do not come within bona fide hedges or spreads." John Jr. wrote back his grudging acceptance, but continued, "I wish to point out . . . that such a breakdown is almost meaningless as it can be accomplished in an almost unlimited number of ways." (John Jr. felt strongly that none of Cargill's spreads could be considered speculative.) Not content to let the matter rest there, John Jr. included a rather arrogant addendum: "I have heard various comments, especially in

Chicago, which seem to indicate to me that your office does not fully understand the nature of some of our operations."

While the CEA limitations were not particularly onerous in most situations, they were much more restrictive than Cargill had expected. Indeed, Cargill would have substantially exceeded these limits in both the September and December 1936 incidents and the traumatic September 1937 events.

Some 18 years later, in September 1955, a CBOT symposium on the futures markets was held; John Jr. was invited. To the delight of many people, he presented a sophisticated analytical speech on futures markets in general, complete with specific reference to the September 1937 situation and the subsequent CEA case. By this time, John Jr. had had second thoughts about his one-person support of the CEA on the limits regulations. He stated in this speech: "As a matter of interest, I was the only witness (apart from employees of the federal government), who testified in favor of Regulations restricting the size of speculative lines. . . . My reasons for so doing were totally different from those put forth by the government witnesses; and they arose from the hope that they would restrict (or eliminate) certain practices which . . . were plaguing all of us."

Then he continued: "After 17 years' experience under these restrictions, I am now quite frank in saying that I was wrong. In practice, the limitations have bothered only the honest merchant. I suspect that the manipulator has found ways to evade the restrictions. . . . Limitations on speculative lines have been vastly overrated. . . . These restrictions are having a disastrous result."[34]

Cargill Charges the Chicago Board of Trade

The CEA limits hearings both boosted the morale and heightened the aggressiveness of John Jr. John Peterson counseled caution: "There is now considerable sympathy for our cause but I feel that common advice would be in the direction of amicable settlement, which may be good for business. . . . We ought to have a case that can stand up without calling anybody names. Avoid compounding the offense. . . . Any story emanating directly or indirectly from us burning up the B of T would be unwise and poor business."

Despite Peterson's admonitions, John Jr. decided to press a formal case against the CBOT. First, he thought of the Federal Trade Commission and wired Weston Grimes on December 9: "Ask Irving [Goldsmith] what he thinks of our . . . alleging Board constitutes conspiracy in restraint of trade. We can cite the Call rule, the Vessel Broker Rule, the Pit Broker Rule and attempt to exercise jurisdiction over actions of members outside City of Chicago. We can also allege attempts in price manipulation in December

1934 wheat and December 1936 wheat as well as in corn." After talking with Goldsmith, Grimes wired back: "We will not demand suspension or revocation of license. . . . A good, broad cease and desist order coupled with new regulations . . . will button the B of T up once and for all." In early January, Cargill officials met with CEA officials in Washington, the final step toward a formal charge before the CEA (rather than the FTC).

Meanwhile, the McDonald Committee had been conducting its hearings during December and into early January. John Jr. was asked to testify and did so, only to reiterate once again his beliefs about the "bear raid." The rest of the Committee's questions he parried with generalities, referring the Committee members to the earlier Cargill brief, submitted to the Business Conduct Committee on September 4.

Fred Uhlmann, testifying a few days later, commented about John Jr.: "He was absolutely sure of the justness of his position . . . he acted all the time as an injured party." Uhlmann alleged that John Jr. had not been straightforward with him: "For one reason or another, he tried to conceal his trades from us." Later, Richard Uhlmann, Fred's son, spoke of the fear that many brokers felt about losing Cargill's business: "Ever since he became a member of the Clearing House, it has surprised me that he has used other brokers so much. . . . I know the power the man has in giving up houses."[35]

What Was Dr. Duvel Told?

Both J. W. T. Duvel and J. M. Mehl testified at the McDonald Committee hearings. Mehl spoke of that fateful September meeting with John Jr. when the Uhlmann and Continental arrangements were first discussed.

At the close of that conference Mr. MacMillan said to Dr. Duvel "I wonder if maybe the best thing we can do is exchange our September futures for cash corn." That statement challenged my attention and I recall distinctly that I asked "Well, can you get the cash corn?" to which Mr. MacMillan replied "Yes, I think so." I am sure that I said then . . . a complete liquidation of the September contracts held by Cargill. . . . Nothing was said about the terms of the suggested exchange of cash for futures. . . . Uhlmann Grain Company or Continental Grain Company was not mentioned. I did not know, and I am sure that Dr. Duvel did not know until sometime later, that those firms were involved. He assumed, as I did, that the contemplated exchange of cash for futures meant an actual exchange.

At the end of his testimony Mehl asked permission to make a further statement and said, "I am a little at a loss to know just why Mr. Grimes . . . should emphasize so strongly his numerous conferences with Dr. Duvel in Washington . . . if Cargill, Incorporated was violating the Commodity Exchange Act or was violating the rules of the Chicago Board of Trade, nothing that was said in Washington could change the facts. Neither Dr. Duvel nor myself, or anyone in Washington that I know of, is in the business of selling indulgences or giving them away."

The CBOT lawyer responded that Grimes did this so that Cargill could receive "the 'blessing' as Mr. Grimes put it." Mehl then responded: "That expression and others to the effect that everything was fixed up in Washington shocks me. They carry implications that are distasteful to me, and I am sure they will be to Dr. Duvel. . . . If Cargill's operations were of a nature to constitute manipulation, or attempted manipulation, it is idiotic nonsense to say that they had the 'blessings' of the Commodity Exchange Administration."

A few days later, when Duvel wrote the McDonald Committee, he was more equivocal:

Mr. Grimes . . . indicated that I approved the transactions between Cargill and the Continental Grain Company. . . . While this is not correct, please be assured that in no sense do I question Mr. Grimes' sincerity in making the statement. Mr. Grimes . . . apparently reached this conclusion as a result of my conversation with Mr. Fitz [the Chicago supervisor of the CEA] regarding the transactions involving the exchange of futures for cash, during the course of which conversation I am reported as having said to Mr. Fitz, "I don't see anything wrong with that, do you, Fitz?" The quotation is correct. However, this conversation with Mr. Fitz took place shortly after August 11, at which time the exchange of futures for cash was first mentioned by Mr. MacMillan. At the time . . . I had no knowledge of any of the parties involved and I do not believe Mr. Fitz had any knowledge thereof.

The McDonald Committee ruling on February 1, 1938, about this incident quoted the testimony of Fred Uhlmann, the president of Uhlmann Grain Company: "He was suspicious of the above mentioned transactions [but] . . . his suspicions were allayed by representations made to him by one Julius Hendel, an employee of Cargill and a non-member of this Exchange, who stated to him, to induce him to enter into the transaction, that 'Washington has been posted about the whole deal and that there were absolutely no objections.' "

Richard F. Uhlmann, Fred's son, said his misgivings had been lulled because Hendel asserted to him that "Washington preferred to have it split up among three or four persons" and that "Edward J. Grimes had handled the whole matter in Washington." The McDonald Committee lawyer editorialized that "the above mentioned arrangements were false in substance and in fact" and had not "in any way altered or palliated Cargill's preponderant position in September 1937 corn futures and cash corn."[36]

Finally, the McDonald Committee completed its taking of testimony and on January 31, 1938, made its report to the board of directors of the CBOT. McDonald told them that the Committee's case was "proved beyond reasonable doubt and to a moral certainty" and concluded, "it is with a feeling of great solemnity that I leave this case in your hands."

The charges themselves were well documented, covering some 16 pages and detailing Cargill actions during and just after the September 1937 contract expiration. The Committee also spelled out in specific terms its beliefs about Cargill's motives in attempting to make a "speculative profit on its short December position." The Uhlmann and Continental contracts were rehashed, and the report concluded with the Committee's judgment that there were "just grounds for suspicion" that Cargill attempted to manipulate prices and had "been guilty of conduct inconsistent with just and equitable principles of trade."

John Peterson, still urging that Cargill be diplomatic and conciliatory, on January 31 wrote Kenneth Templeton, the Exchange president: "We greatly appreciate the cordial spirit of your interest, as well as that of your associates, and I am still hopeful that mutually we can find some moderate and reasonable meeting ground as a solution of the problem in which we are all interested." Subsequently, Peterson and Cargill MacMillan did visit the CBOT offices for what was described by one of the members at that meeting as an effort to "wave the olive branch." Peterson was told at this meeting that Cargill needed to make its peace with the CEA, that the CEA official in charge could not be influenced "from the straight line of duty and integrity, and if it was necessary," that the official "probably would go through 100% and like a good Japanese general who did not like his job, would probably shoot the victim with a smile."

But Peterson's hat-in-hand approach was not John Jr.'s choice. He wrote his brother: "The time for pussy-footing is past." His mother and father were in New York, ready to embark on a South American cruise. Apprised of the MacDonald findings, John Sr. wrote of his "horror and indignation" over the "mockery" of the Committee's deliberations; it was a "conspiracy . . . to drive us out of Chicago by hook or crook." His conclusion was surprisingly combative: "We cannot withdraw under fire. . . . I am going to advocate a fight to the finish . . . even if it should involve their destruction." (John Sr. might not have been as confident in this approach had he been privy to John Jr.'s letter to his brother at this same time, in which John Jr. spoke of his "feeling of despondency.")

The first public clue to Cargill's response came on February 2, when a Company public release began: "In view of the closed social club style in which the affairs of the Chicago Board of Trade have been administered for many years" and then described "our efforts to clean house" at the Exchange. John Jr. suggested to Goldsmith even harsher wording for a press release a few days later, suggesting that the CBOT was "mulcting the trade and the public" to "protect the predatory interests."

On February 10, 1938, Cargill finally took an irrevocable step, one the consequences of which its executives could hardly have anticipated. The

Company now instituted a formal complaint against the CBOT under the Commodity Exchange Act; the case was designated CEA Docket No. 6, destined to be one of the CEA's most famous. Cargill's statement of particulars alleged that the Exchange violated the Act by not requiring notice of at least one business day prior to delivery and "not providing for the prevention of manipulation of prices and . . . permitting its Business Conduct Committee to aid and abet manipulation of prices." In this, Cargill had made the decision to incorporate the September 1936 corn futures events and the December 1936 corn and wheat futures cases, both to accompany the frontal attack on the Exchange for its handling of the September 1937 saga.[37]

Unexpected Complications

The battle was now beginning to have effects elsewhere in the business. Cargill MacMillan wrote Irving Goldsmith, of "an annoying repercussion from the McDonald Report"—the Bureau of Internal Revenue was check-

The Minneapolis grain exchange, the "Chamber of Commerce," c. 1942.

Posting prices, Minneapolis grain exchange, c. 1942.

ing Cargill's 1936 return, alleging that the Company's reported hedging loss of $4 million "might be speculative losses." Apparently, according to MacMillan, "the McDonald Report has made this auditor hedging conscious and he is casting around to find out what hedging means." The record does not show whether this Bureau auditor did, indeed, find an answer that satisfied him.

Cargill also was being threatened with lawsuits by other holders of the September corn contract. Many shorts had lost money then, not only from the CBOT-mandated $1.10½ settling price but also as a result of other trades made under speculative assumptions growing out of the case. One grain company executive wrote John Jr.:

I admire your nerve but I still think you are wrong and wish to know if you will arbitrate a loss caused by the corner on corn during September, 1937. My contention for selling September corn at that time and buying December was that no one would have the nerve to violate the statutes of the United States as well as the rules of the Chicago Board of Trade. As I understand it, at this time, you have not been convicted but that your trial will be March 1st, therefore, we would like to hear from you as to whether you would agree to an arbitration covering contracts on September corn and December corn.

No answer to this letter appears in the record.

CBOT officials earlier had questioned Cargill's financial shape. On February 28, John Peterson replied. He noted that Cargill's audited report of

December 31, 1937, had shown a consolidated working capital "in excess of $7,100,000 and net worth in excess of $9,500,000." Peterson continued: "When you consider such net worth and working capital in comparison with . . . your other members of the Exchange, we do not see that you have any grounds to be unduly disturbed about the working capital of the subsidiary Cargill Grain Company of Illinois." In the process of stating this, however, Peterson had vitiated John Jr.'s earlier refusal to provide figures on Cargill, Incorporated, the parent company (although tendering Cargill Grain Company of Illinois data).[38]

The board of directors of the Exchange now became the hearing tribunal for the charges placed before it by the McDonald Committee. Kenneth Templeton immediately contacted Cargill about an appearance. John Jr. rejected this request, holding that Cargill's charges before the CEA were now pending and that "this alone, without reference to past experience, should make it apparent that your Board of Directors is disqualified to conduct this proposed hearing." The CBOT group continued, however, to meet on the matter almost every day during the first two weeks of March. On March 18, John Jr. wrote his father: "I understand they have traced so far as they could the history of every car of corn we bought from sometime in July until December." John Jr. felt optimistic that the board would eventually drop the matter. The papers had been full of a major scandal involving the president of the New York Stock Exchange, and John Jr. wrote: "It is inconceivable to me that they would risk doing anything in the face of this Richard Whitney scandal" (Whitney, the head of the New York Stock Exchange prominent at the time of the Great Crash, had been indicted in early March 1938 for fraudulent stock dealings).

Expelled!

John MacMillan, Jr.'s conviction that the CBOT would in the end take no action against Cargill proved to be totally wrong. On March 25, 1938, the board of directors of the Exchange voted to expel Cargill from the CBOT (technically, to expel the Cargill Grain Company of Illinois) and also to expel three individuals: John Jr., Ed Grimes and Philip Sayles.

The directors of the Exchange were quite self-congratulatory about their decision. President Templeton wrote to the membership about the "difficult and disagreeable task" and declared that "your Directors have acted fearlessly and without partisanship . . . governed only by the evidence presented to them." There were dissenters among the membership, but Templeton argued that "those who criticized the Board's action against Cargill should remember that every opportunity was given the Cargill interests to appear and offer such testimony and present such rebuttal as they saw fit."

He concluded that "there probably has never been a case in Board of Trade history that has reached so closely to the heart and integrity of the functions of the Exchange as did the Cargill case."

This public bravado masked some serious misgivings on the part of CBOT officials about the ultimate implications of the Cargill decision. One of the officers wrote Howard Ellis, the chief CBOT lawyer, on March 10, 1938, about a conversation with J. M. Mehl, the assistant director of the CEA: "Mehl is quite disturbed for fear that Cargill will do everything within their power to regulate futures trading before they get through. Just what they will do, he, of course, does not know." He then added a bombshell: "He [Mehl] is considering filing a complaint against Cargill." The letter ended: "I think you can definitely assume that the Commodity Exchange Administration will do everything in its power to aid you, although I expect Duvel would take the first avenue of escape which presented itself, irrespective of who got hurt by his so doing."

Cargill's public utterances on the expulsion were equally sanctimonious. The Company's news release, on March 28, began with a direct quote from John Jr., to the effect that "the Chicago Board of Trade has completed the trial of the Chicago Board of Trade and has found itself not guilty." The news release castigated the "private hearings behind closed doors" and charged that the Exchange was "attempting to dodge responsibility for the 'bear' raids it permitted and aided during July, August and September 1937." The upcoming CEA case that Cargill had brought was noted and was given as the reason Cargill had refused to testify in the Exchange hearings. The release ended: "We expect to carry on our business as usual notwithstanding the fact we have been arbitrarily deprived."

Privately, however, John Jr. and his colleagues were troubled. Most threatening was the potential effect on Cargill's bank credit. John Peterson immediately was dispatched to New York to soothe any concerns. John Jr. wrote him on March 28: "Father suggests that when you call on the banks that we do not treat the matter lightly, which of course I agree with him, but I am nevertheless of the opinion that this development is constructive, will seriously prejudice the Board's case in Washington, and will mean important earnings for ourselves for the future. I think you are warranted in taking an optimistic view of our earnings prospects."

A few days later, John Jr. reported to his father about Peterson's efforts: "He said he had talked at length with Hugo [Hugo Scheuermann, the Chase National Bank executive] on the phone from Washington and that Hugo was in nowise disturbed by our expulsion. John certainly was not disturbed and said that our balance sheet is what is going to control our credit, which is precisely the view I take." Nevertheless, John Jr. noted to Peterson that John Sr. continued to "caution me on the possibility of malicious attacks on our credit and I think he is undoubtedly correct for, as you know, in the past expulsion or suspension from the Board of Trade has been tantamount to a death sentence for the ordinary grain man."

Concerns about Supply

The other internal fear was whether Cargill could maintain its ready access to the purchasing and marketing of grain. Had Cargill given up its best avenue for obtaining its supply of grain? To almost everyone's surprise, both in the Company and in the grain trade generally, this proved to be no problem. Cargill immediately began buying grain out in the country with the help of a number of regional grain companies (like Stotler Grain Company, of Champaign, Illinois) and also began trading in a major way on other exchanges. "Julius had an immense amount of fun today," John Jr. wrote Peterson, "in re-establishing future trading in corn in Minneapolis. If we are successful, it will save us quite a little in commissions." (Later, Cargill got into further trouble with the CEA over the methods used in these 1938 Minneapolis corn futures trades.)

There appeared to be a widespread sympathy out in the field toward the Cargill position and a practical willingness to deal with a long-standing large buyer. The Company had had a practice for years of buying substantial quantities of its Chicago grain through other commission houses, particularly cash grain, and had always paid commissions, usually gaining some reciprocity so that something was saved from the full commission. Now, working directly in the field, the Company was not only saving much of these commission costs but having ready, even closer access to the sellers of grain.

The reasons for this saving lay in the CBOT's "Call Rule," a device originally established by the Exchange in 1906 and subsequently validated in a famous U.S. Supreme Court case in 1918 (with Justice Louis D. Brandeis writing the opinion). It prohibited Exchange members from purchasing "to arrive" grain (i.e., grain out in the field or on its way to the Exchange) at any price different from that of the closing price of grain traded on the Exchange that day (at "the call"). Full commissions also applied. In effect, it was a Court-approved mechanism for constraining competition, thereby protecting the Exchange members from price-cutting out in the field while preserving their commissions.

The *Chicago Daily News*, writing at this time about Cargill's new inroads in country buying, described its effects:

As the result of a 'clothesline squabble' . . . the Board of Trade lost its temper with Cargill . . . and expelled it from membership. Cargill went on buying grain, and has been bidding 1/8 to 1/4 above the closing quotations on the Board of Trade. . . .

Since in the interest of orderly trading, fair compeititon, etc., the members of the Board of Trade are barred from going out into the country and bidding more for grain than they were willing to pay on the floor . . . all Cargill has to do is to look at the last quotation, raise the ante—and take the pot. One can understand why the Board of Trade members are not pleased.

Even this was not the whole story; the newspaper continued: "But this means in turn that, day by day, country grain elevators have been getting more for their grain than the published quotations, and indirectly it means that the farmers have also tended to get more for their grain. Since this seems to be the chief purpose of a large and lusty government agency, it would be rather difficult to keep the development from being mentioned in farmer conversation, or in political oratory. Without meeting itself coming back, the CEA would find it hard to oppose Cargill." It seemed that Cargill's undercutting of the Call Rule benefited everyone but the CBOT members!

The new efforts posed a challenge to the transportation people in the Company. It was not only that Cargill would use the Chicago futures market less often, but the Company also would be bypassing Chicago on substantial amounts of actual grain shipped. By March 30, just three days after the precipitate Exchange action, a Cargill staff employee had plotted on his hand-drawn map of the East and the Midwest the new routes that this grain would take. For grain coming from the Southwest, Milwaukee and Green Bay would be used more heavily, as well as Cincinnati, as a gathering point for shipment on to Toledo and the Lakes. Some of these new routes could be used as cheaply or even more cheaply than the previously existing focal use of Chicago. It took a while, however, for most of these ideas to become practicable—the established routes (and their intricate rate structures) were far too institutionalized.

The expulsion caught the public interest. Not only were the business pages full of comments on the Exchange's dramatic step, but the national press picked it up. *Time* magazine had a two-page article on it on April 4, complete with a large and somewhat unflattering picture of John Jr. Entitled "Gentlemen's Disagreement," the article cast the event as "only the first round of the best knock down & dragout speculator's battle that has taken place behind the U.S. farmer's barn in many a harvest moon." *Time* characterized the Exchange as "an exclusive club with a divine right not only to deal in grain but also to speculate in it." The "limits" issue was described at some length, with Cargill's sole advocacy of the CEA limitation due at least in part to "the strict Scotch Presbyterianism of its bosses." The difficulties that Cargill and Farmers National had had in gaining membership were mentioned as a prelude to the story about Farmers National besting Cargill the previous July (1936): "Cargill then held the long interest

John MacMillan, Jr., in a
TIME *magazine*
photograph, April 4, 1938.

in corn and Farmers the short, but at the last minute Farmers dumped 500,000 bu. of previously invisible corn on the market, gave Cargill a real trimming as the price fell 27¢. Last September Cargill got even." Noting that in the September 1937 corn contract Cargill had bought "almost twice as much as there was available," *Time* described the "mad forage for corn by shorts." When the Board of Trade stepped in and "told Cargill to sell 1,000,000 bu. in four hours," John Jr. termed the action "confiscation of the worst order." When Cargill had refused to bring its holdings down, and the Board of Trade had mandated a settlement price, the *Time* writer noted that Cargill had refused to make any defense before the McDonald Committee, and had "since maintained a wounded silence in its head offices in Minneapolis." The article ended with a Weston Grimes quote, in which *Time* characterized him as having "sniffed" that "it is not surprising that a committee of our competitors should find our purchases of September corn to be offensive."[39]

In the process, of course, *Time* had put Cargill on the national map.

Challenge to the "Call Rule"

Cargill's effort to buy grains out in the field, an instantaneous success, had a snowballing effect on the whole grain trading scene. John Jr. wrote his father on April 1: "The boys are all talking about our having got rid of our . . . hoodoo," and he added, a few days later:

It is very clear that our heavy buying of cash corn, which we are purposely pushing, has gotten under the skin of the receivers in Chicago. . . . There is a rumor this morning in Chicago that the Directors are considering some way of inviting us back. It is my personal belief that the larger commission houses like Lamson and Bennett will have to abolish half of their offices unless the Board makes peace with us. . . . Their volume of future trading has fallen to about 40% of normal. . . . It has been their cash receiving business which has been carrying them. . . . If the Call Rule is out, this cash business is gone. If the Call Rule is not out, it is also gone because we will do the business.

John Jr. noted Cargill's evolving strategy: "We will naturally move heaven and earth to keep on buying heavily, and I anticipate no trouble in keeping sufficient sales ahead. The only limit will be the handling capacity of Milwaukee and Chicago."

On April 1, 1938, the press headlined a new development—the directors of the CBOT, in a special meeting, had suddenly reversed their position in regard to Cargill and announced that they had voided the Cargill expulsion order. An invitation to Cargill and its three ousted officials was forwarded immediately by the president, Kenneth Templeton. One of the Chicago papers noted: "Traders were at a loss to understand this unexpected turn in events. . . . Among the guesses suggested by astounded grain merchants was that the Board feared loss of importance to its corn trade, which Cargill hoped to shift to Minneapolis."

Cargill rejected the overture, refusing to return, and the attrition of the Exchange business continued. By early June, there were pressures on the board of directors from its own membership to eliminate the Call Rule. Petitions to rescind came forward, and an election was ordered for July 7. Over the several weeks before the vote, there was intensive lobbying on the part of both those wishing to do away with the rule (the elevator operators and some of the individual members) and those wanting to retain it (the commission houses and many individual pit traders). Sayles reported to Grimes that he thought the rule would be "kicked out," that "the receivers . . . will win out by at least 7 to 5." Sayles wired John Jr. on the same day "sentiment swinging back to receivers—[the rule] will be beaten better than two to one."

Once more, Cargill's assessment was not accurate. When the totals were tabulated, the vote was 513 to retain the Call Rule and only 190 against. The matter was, after all, rather academic for Cargill, for it was going to continue buying out in the field one way or the other—paying slightly below the Exchange members' total price (this latter, of course, heightened by their commission). The Call Rule, however, had withstood the challenge, at least for the time being.[40]

Farmers National Goes Under

The fallout from the September 1937 events not only adversely affected the longs (Cargill especially) but had also had a sharp effect on many of the shorts. In particular, Farmers National had sustained substantial losses, even with the Board of Trade's mandated settlement figure of $1.10½, for its short sales were considerably below that settlement amount. *Time* magazine's story, back in its issue of October 4, 1937, talked of the "corn corner" but did not mention any of the longs (even Cargill) by name. Rather, the article focused particularly on Farmers National. *Time*'s story continued: "Farmers National Grain Corp., leading U.S. grain co-operative and a leading short, formally complained to the Commodity Exchange Administration, charging 'major manipulation.' C.E.A. Chief J. W. T. Duvel, cracked back with a stinging rebuke: 'Every time there is a price rise or fall there is an outcry from those who lose money.' " It is not clear how *Time* obtained this quotation from Duvel, but the embarrassment to Farmers National was substantial.

This was a particularly bad time for Farmers National to take such a financial bump. The big cooperative conglomerate (it was then the holding entity for 10 regional cooperatives in the Midwest and West) had been in existence for eight years, helped at every stage by the federal government but, as a later *Time* article stated, "has always been sickly." It had sold a great deal of grain in 1937 (*Time* gave a figure of 66 million bushels), but its only profitable year came in 1931, when it had a privileged arrangement with the Grain Stabilization Corporation. There had been even an investigation of Farmers National by the United States Senate. Inklings of financial trouble had already surfaced prior to the September 1937 incidents. Now the cooperative's losses in the corn debacle brought its board of directors to the point in early February 1938, where a decision was made to dissolve the central organization (the regional cooperatives would continue on their own). At least one of John Jr.'s antagonists in the ongoing legal battles would not be around to castigate him.[41]

Corn Case Skirmishes

Cargill's complaint against the CBOT under the Commodity Exchange Act, filed on February 10, 1938, as CEA Docket No. 6, now began its convoluted movement through the agency's process. The final arbiters in the case would be the Commodity Exchange Commission, a three-person tribunal composed of the Secretary of Agriculture, the Secretary of Commerce and the Attorney General of the United States (at that time, respectively, Henry A. Wallace, Daniel C. Roper and Homer S. Cummings).

The CBOT had entered a motion to quash the entire Cargill matter, and on May 10, 1938, the Commission met to hear the preliminary arguments. By this time, Cargill had its own brief in final form, and John Sr. wanted badly to get it into the hands of Secretary Roper before Cargill's testimony was given. Apparently John Sr. had some intimation that Roper would be sympathetic. Through the ministrations of John Sr.'s relative by marriage, Morris Barker ("Aunt Maggie" Barker's son), Judge J. Harry Covington, the head of a famous law firm in Washington, agreed personally to approach Roper. Successful in the assignment, Covington reported back to Barker on Roper's words: "I know a good deal about this firm, Cargill, Incorporated. They are a very reputable, high grade firm dealing in grain commodities and are world-wide in their operations. I sat personally on the hearings in this case and I am of the opinion that if the rules of the Department of Agriculture can be used to discriminate against a firm like Cargill, Incorporated, then the Secretary of Agriculture ought to change the rules." The Roper comments, surprisingly critical of Wallace, were only passed along secondhand. Nevertheless, they encouraged John Jr. and his colleagues.[42]

On September 27, 1938, the three-man tribunal ruled against the CBOT effort to quash Cargill's case. A hearing was set for November 28 in Washington, D.C., to be chaired by a referee, S. Abbot Maginnis, appointed for this purpose by the Commission.

After the opening two days, John Jr. was put on the stand. In preparation, John Jr. had written out in longhand 53 pages of notes, to which he planned to refer as he testified. This manuscript, fortunately preserved, is a unique amalgam of facts and opinions, the latter most revealing of John Jr.'s personal prejudices and precepts about both the case itself and grain trading in general. He pictured the case in apocalyptic terms—"as dramatic a struggle as can be . . . it is entirely possible that it may mark the end of futures trading in grain and cotton, and possibly mark the end of the private system of distribution. . . . One thing is increasingly evident, that it is a struggle to the death . . . one or the other [Cargill or the Exchange] must go. Compromise seems impossible." Cargill, on the one side "is a relatively small and obscure firm when contrasted with such giants . . . as General Mills, Corn Products, Quaker Oats, Louis Dreyfus and Co. and Standard Brands." Cargill's management "has been hard working, conscientious, and above all, thrifty." The family "are Scotch Presbyterians" and had always been looked upon as "builders, as being constructive to a fault"; their "integrity has never been questioned," and while "it cannot be said that the family lack courage . . . yet they certainly never speculate." The Company "has shunned publicity and tended to its knitting."

On the other hand, the CBOT's history had been "replete with drama, sometimes lurid . . . the public has always heard of its corners and squeezes, and many an individual has used its facilities for a flutter in wheat

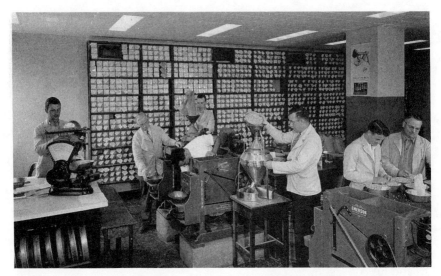

Testing for grade in Cargill's sample room, Minneapolis grain exchange, c. 1942.

or corn." The Business Conduct Committee had been given the power by Exchange members "to do everything but beget children." The Committee, protecting the shorts in the Cargill case, had issued an order "compelling Cargill to sell regardless of price," despite "countless complaints from farmers." The Exchange "has been engaged in manipulating prices downward . . . favoring short sellers and bear raiders . . . at the expense of the producer and the distributor."

This set of arguments was now laid before Maginnis, who from time to time pushed John Jr. to cut short some of his editorializing. Nevertheless, John Jr. was optimistic about Cargill's initial arguments, telegraphing his father on November 29: "We are getting all the breaks. Atmosphere of Department and referee most sympathetic." John Jr.'s testimony had made all of the national papers; John Sr. exultingly wrote Ted Young, on December 2, that "we finally made the front page of the *Wall Street Journal*, too."

Each day, full reports on John Jr.'s testimony were sent back to his father, who responded at several points with corrections of some of John Jr.'s statements. Ted Young reported back to Minneapolis that John Jr. was "particularly effective" and that "we gave the Chicago Board of Trade a real bust in the nose." Young wrote John Sr., a few days later, after John Jr. had been on the stand for about a week, still under direct examination by the Cargill lawyers, that "Jr. is making a fine witness, and it is a great pleasure to listen to him on the stand. . . . He explains things very clearly and makes the story interesting."

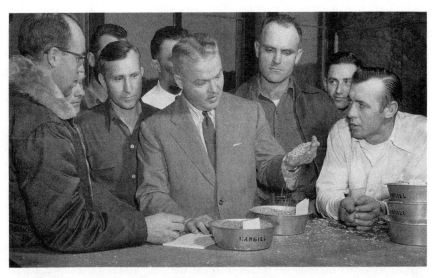

A barley buyer explains grading to members of a Cargill training class, c. 1954.

John Sr. seemed uneasy, however: "Of course I am delighted that Jr. is making a good witness, but I'm afraid he is under a pretty heavy strain, which must be tiring him badly." He was even more frank in a letter to Ed Grimes: "So far as I know the case has been going along very well, but Jr. is not in good shape and I am just fearful that he may not be able to stand up under such a long, constant strain—so it will be a great relief to me to know that you will be there to carry on." John Sr.'s remembrances of John Jr.'s nervousness in the Company's "banking crisis" in early 1933, and the earlier incidents in the period after 1920, when John Jr. was sent to the lumber camp in British Colombia, still must have been vivid.

Finally, the time came for the CBOT cross-examination. Howard Ellis, the Exchange lawyer, had already set a confrontational mode in his earlier challenges of some of John Jr.'s statements. Early on, John Jr. had shown his antipathy toward the Chicago exchange: "I also wish to place myself on record as saying that I do not wish any of the statements that I may make here or that any of my associates might make, or that our side might make, to reflect in any way on futures trading as conducted in the outside grain exchanges. By 'outside exchanges,' I refer to grain exchanges other than Chicago." At the point in John Jr.'s testimony on Cargill's first entry into Chicago, he had averred that "we opened the office with fear and trepidation." Maginnis, the referee, immediately responded: "I would suggest now, Mr. Grimes [Weston Grimes], that you warn Mr. MacMillan about the use of such opinions as 'fear and trepidation.'" Howard Ellis picked up this skepticism on the part of Maginnis, and a few hours later made a strong rejoinder against what he called Cargill's "constant slurs."

By December 13, John Jr. began to worry that the proceedings were not going to his liking; he telegraphed his father: "Hearings only moderately satisfactory and proceeding so slowly." His father immediately responded: "I take it that it must mean a lot of sharp passages between the opposing counsel and that you have been getting the worst of the Referee's decisions." In another telegram at about the same time, John Jr. told his father, "Ted is here smorning. Says we got very ruff treatment yesterday. Both him and Covington think the cards are stacked against us."

The most revealing exchanges between Ellis and John Jr. involved the distinctions between hedging, spreading and speculation, and the definition of a "corner." John Jr. first drew a distinction between "logical" hedging and "illogical" hedging; the former was a purchase in the same grain or a cross hedge in a related grain, where the effect on price would be minor, whereas illogical hedging was "a case where the purchase of the inventory bears little or no relation to the hedge." In the latter case, there might be a tendency to "move the price of a future in the direction in which the sale is being made." Ellis then pushed John Jr. to define the September 1937 hedges in these terms, but John Jr. answered that it depended "entirely on the purpose—the connection in which it is used. It may be thoroughly logical under one set of circumstances and thoroughly illogical under another set of circumstances. No categorical answer can be given to the question."

There were also lengthy interchanges between the two men on the distinction between a "squeeze" and a "corner." A squeeze, according to Ellis, was a situation where there was "no intention to acquire a monopolistic control . . . the high price may come about without there being any such intention and there may be little or no desire to exploit the situation when it transpires that there is a shortage of grain." The corner, on the other hand, was a deliberate attempt to use a monopoly position to extract profits.

John Jr., in responding to the Ellis definitions, edged the conversation toward blaming the shorts: "Where the shorts have neglected to move supplies into deliverable position, I have seen many situations which I would define as squeezes, but I have yet to see a single situation which I consider a true corner, certainly in the American grain trade." A few moments later, John Jr. further attacked the shorts: "The trade is very properly open to criticism on that score, but the corrective measure in my opinion, is to have short sellers understand they may be called upon to perform. In my opinion, the greater frequency of this type of disturbance in the United States markets in recent years has been almost exclusively due to this philosophy that a short has an unqualified right to cancel his contract by offset rather than by performance." Despite John Jr.'s efforts, by the time he was excused from the stand on December 19 the insinuation that there had been a Cargill corner had been planted firmly by Ellis.[43]

The CEA Accuses

There was to be no rest in the Christmas recess. To the absolute shock of all of the Cargill group, on December 22, 1938, the Commodity Exchange Authority, acting for Secretary of Agriculture Wallace as complainant, brought charges in a completely separate CEA complaint (subsequently CEA Docket No. 11), alleging that Cargill as a company and John Jr., Ed Grimes, Julius Hendel and Philip Sayles had manipulated the price of the September 1937 and December 1937 corn futures and had also engaged in fictitious sales of corn futures on the Minneapolis Chamber of Commerce toward the end of March 1938. The four men had engaged "in a conspiracy with each other and with others" to do this, and not only had they conspired to manipulate price but they had "made, and caused to be made, fictitious and washed sales in corn futures on the Minneapolis Chamber of Commerce, thereby causing to be reported a volume of trading greatly in excess of the volume of actual bona fide transactions. . . . Cargill, Inc., was both buyer and seller."

It was a shocking development. The implacable tenor of the CEA charge took John Jr. and his colleagues aback, particularly because the Dow Jones ticker tape story ended with an ominous sentence: "Specifically, the order said the respondent will be required to show cause why an order should not be made directing that all contract markets until further notice of the Sec. of Agriculture refuse all trade privileges and suspending or revoking the registrations as futures commission merchants of the corporate respondents." Sayles telexed Ed Grimes on the day of the announcement (December 27, 1938): "Jack Wheeler says everyone on floor think Cargill are through—isn't that funny."

If, indeed, the Exchange was exulting publicly, its private views (as expressed in records of the board of directors) were considerably more subdued. The Exchange long had held a latent fear of the CEA, despite apparently now being on the "right" side in the Cargill matter. At the December 1937 "limits" hearings with the CEA, the Exchange had stonewalled against any of the CEA's proposed charges (which were passed nevertheless). At that time, an Exchange lawyer had written, in a private memorandum to a colleague: "It looks to me as if the CEA was attempting to put the Chicago Board of Trade behind the 8-ball." CEA action against Cargill still seemed potentially able to enmesh the CBOT, too.

The press reported the second case in banner headlines, but many of the writers implied a "pox on both houses." The *Chicago Daily News* of

December 28 called the case "sensational news to the grain trade," noted the "social club" allegation against the Exchange and called the latter "complacent," a "sort of monastic organization, cloistered behind the walls." With some irony, the writer continued: "the members . . . deal with each other on terms of absolute good faith . . . with such invariable integrity that they tend to be even a little gullible when they go outside the trading floor to take the chances of trickery in ordinary business."

What particularly upset the Exchange leaders was part of the headline itself: "Integrity of Templeton is Outstanding Part of Case." Templeton was the president of the CBOT—it seemed that in the process of Cargill being called to account, so too was the Exchange. Pencilled at the top of a copy of the article in Fred Clutton's file (he was secretary of the Exchange) was a comment from a colleague: "I do not like this article."[44]

The testimony on the case resumed once more on January 3, 1939, with John Jr. scheduled to be on the stand again. However, Irving Goldsmith, the trial lawyer for the Company, had been taken ill, and Ted Young took over. He chose to put Hayes H. Miller, a member of Cargill's Administrative Division, on the stand. Young wrote John Sr. on January 7 that Miller had "taken the brunt of Ellis' cross-examination and so-called 'smart tricks.' "

At the top of Cargill's agenda at this moment was its desire to separate the two cases—their case against the Exchange and the CEA's case against Cargill (Docket No. 11). The Company wanted to keep its case single-mindedly attacking the Exchange. As Young put it, in a letter to John Sr., if the cases could be separated, "we won't have Ellis on our necks in that proceeding—only the 2nd-rate lawyers in the Dept. of Agriculture. A consolidation of [the two cases] would have meant Ellis *plus* these other 'legal lights.' "

To the relief of Cargill, Referee Maginnis ruled that the two cases were separable; later, the CEA was granted an indefinite postponement of its own case until the Cargill case against the Exchange was completed. The hearings in the latter continued for some 10 days, with John Jr. once again on the stand, much of the time subject to cross-examination.[45]

On January 16, Kenneth S. Templeton, immediate past president of the CBOT, made a striking public statement, one that appeared on the Dow Jones ticker tape and was subsequently disseminated widely through the public press. The tape stated: "In his review of the Cargill matter, Mr. Templeton declared there probably has never been a case in Board of Trade history that has reached so closely to the heart and integrity of the functions of the Exchange. The unfortunate circumstances which resulted in the expulsion . . . have certainly not been constructive insofar as the welfare of the grain trade as a whole is concerned." Templeton was also quoted as saying that "offers of compromise were made to your officials" [the CBOT leadership] but that these had been refused by the Exchange "because they did not reach the fundamentals involved." The fact that the Secretary of Agriculture had just preferred charges against Cargill "must give us all courage to renew our faith and belief in the essential soundness of our policy of self-government."

Templeton then had alluded to "adverse" statements to the public by Cargill, alleging that the case itself was "an attempt to confuse the public and to interject new issues into the picture." He had concluded the statement ominously: "If the charges filed by the Secretary of Agriculture against the Cargill interests are sustained and Cargill is unable to hedge its inventories in any of the contract markets of the United States then perhaps Cargill will not be able to cut commissions on country business in such a way as to make unfair competition for our members." Obviously, the Exchange members continued to resent the lack of "Call Rule" control over Cargill's purchases.

The Cargill group, upset by this public attack, wondered how to retaliate. John Peterson advocated caution: "I do not exactly see how these short jabs are getting us anywhere . . . every time any publicity is made now, the papers recite the fact that we were kicked off the Chicago Board of Trade and that now the Secretary of Agriculture has made out a complaint against us. . . . My own reaction is to let the thing temporarily slip until we get some more real juicy scandal on the Board of Trade . . . with colorful revelations of the workings of the Board of Trade, and shoot such a story."

A Mistake in the Crop Bulletin

John Jr. received this letter but did not take Peterson's advice. Instead, he decided to respond in kind, using the *Cargill Crop Bulletin* as his vehicle. The *Bulletin* had become a major farm publication, with circulation of many thousands among farmers all over the country. They looked forward to the handout; it had detailed summaries of world and national crop conditions and specific coverage of crop and livestock situations all over the country. Along with the agricultural statistics were broader articles on national and world agriculture. John Jr. decided to use this respected periodical to state his views of "the trial of the Board of Trade of the City of Chicago."

The idea for the *Crop Bulletin* article had been supported strongly by John Sr. at the start, but when he saw John Jr.'s text, he was disturbed by its cast. Some of it was quite antagonistic, and John Sr. wrote back to John Jr., "Bert Egermayer and John Peterson both believe that it might perhaps injure our standing in Washington and think it a doubtful wisdom to publish it." It did not occur to either John Sr. or John Jr. that publishing such self-serving material also might compromise the integrity and independence of the *Bulletin*, built up so carefully over the previous decade. Nevertheless, John Jr. insisted that there be no change, and his original draft became the final wording.

The article, appearing in early February 1939, spoke of how the shorts depressed the price "at a cost of many millions of dollars to farmers and a severe loss to distributors" and contained a special "message to our subscribers" over John Sr.'s signature, stating that "one friendly competitor compared Cargill's action to a case of 'burning down the barn in order to kill a few rats,' " and continued: "Cargill was and is very mindful of this hazard but is of the opinion that dishonest future trading is not of economic or social usefulness, and if future trading cannot be continued on an honest and proper basis that it would be better to abolish it entirely."

Not content to let it stand at this, the article continued with a several-sentence discussion of the alleged conversation between CEA chief J. W. T. Duvel and Templeton on the critical day in September 1937 when prices had dropped precipitously. The call had been made, of course, as the private CBOT records showed, but Cargill could not prove it. It had remained a hearsay story, although one that manifestly was embarrassing to the CEA and to Duvel. Ed Grimes, in his CEA testimony at this time, also had mentioned the Duvel telephone call. With this information in the record, Cargill decided not to call Duvel or Mehl as Company witnesses. Howard Ellis objected, for he desired their personal testimony, and Referee Maginnis remonstrated that both Duvel and Mehl wanted to testify on the matter. Maginnis also asked "if we were trying to make the CEA a defendant in this hearing."

The Exchange lawyers bided their time on the *Crop Bulletin* article until finishing their cross-examination of John Jr. Then, on March 2, Howard Ellis, the Exchange's trial lawyer, made a motion to the referee that Cargill be reprimanded for the article. Cargill countered that the Exchange should itself be reprimanded for its own publicity.

The Ellis side of the argument fell on receptive ears. Maginnis responded that the Board of Trade publicity that he had seen to that point did not seem prejudicial; rather, as Hayes Miller reported to John Sr., "he said that the evidence did not warrant our summation of the 'phone call between Duvel and Templeton and the resulting price break. He said that this casts a reflection on Duvel's integrity and was not fair."

The Cargill lawyers, realizing their tactical error, replied that "had Cargill known the Referee would disapprove they never would have written that article." Maginnis lectured both parties that it was never proper to try their cases in the papers. But even this statement was widely reported in the press. That day, for example, the *Chicago Daily News* headlined its column-long article: "Maginnis Orders Attorneys in Cargill Case to Stop

Propaganda." The article added further color about that day's proceedings: "On one side is Howard Ellis, attorney for the Board of Trade, belligerent and forceful, occasionally sarcastic at the expense of a witness.
Near him is dignified Fred Clutton, Secretary of the Board of Trade. . . .
Across the table is F. W. Sullivan, at the moment spokesman for Cargill,
and his fellow attorney, the alert, freckle-faced and luminously intelligent
Irving B. Goldsmith. In the background, and for once not in the witness
chair, John H. MacMillan, Jr., president of Cargill, smiles benignantly at
the proceedings."

The *Daily News* writer continued: "We have said before, and will say
again, that Kenneth S. Templeton, then president of the Board of Trade,
acted from the highest and most honorable motives throughout. . . . On
the other hand, MacMillan also impresses us as a very honorable businessman, who is obviously honest and straightforward and who wouldn't take
an unethical step for any amount of money. He is just an ordinary citizen,
looking very much like a grocer, or any other type of substantial small
businessman."

Another forum that both parties assiduously cultivated was that of Congress itself. Back on February 2, Weston Grimes wired John Jr. that the
case had been discussed in the House of Representatives that afternoon,
with "speculative short selling . . . condemned." Goldsmith pushed hard
for these speeches in Congress, especially wanting some in the Senate, and
John Jr. wrote Weston Grimes: "Irving is wild over our lack of speeches
in Congress, and especially in the Senate, so for heaven's sake do all you
can along this line, although I am not altogether in sympathy with some
of the steps he wants taken to bring about such speeches."[46]

John Jr. then wrote Goldsmith: "Both Weston and his father assured
me that they had to promise secrecy to their friends in the House, but Ed
assured me that I would be completely satisfied. . . . I am also suggesting
to him that he try to make use of the Republican Publicity Department
and I am inclined to think that can be arranged for." John Jr. spelled out
his own thinking in a letter to Weston Grimes: that the latter approach
"the Republican Publicity men . . . to arrange a daily press release linking
up Secretary Wallace with the Board of Trade."[47]

As the hearings continued through February 1939, the third month of
the testimony, John Jr. felt more optimistic about Cargill's case. He wrote
to his father, on February 17: "In Chicago I learned a great deal about the
precarious condition of the Board of Trade, financially speaking. . . . All
these so-called 'mergers' of course mean nothing but the retirement of
these people from business, and I was informed . . . that unless something
was done within the next 30 days that the whole Board would collapse like
a deck of cards." He continued: "I have a decided feeling that a proposition of some kind will be made to us within the next two weeks to a month.

We will of course refuse to talk unless we have to, but if Henry Wallace would be the one to want to discuss it with us, it would be very difficult to refuse him."

Something like this now happened, for John Jr. wrote his father three days later, on February 20: "This morning a *minor official* of the Board approached Miller, being very anxious to see Ed and claiming that the whole dispute with the Board can be settled instantly. . . . Mayer Meyer [Cargill's Chicago law firm] feel that it is probably a feeler from the Board, just as I do." John Jr. perceived broader political implications in what was going on: "Wallace has the Presidential Bee very badly . . . his scheme had been to pay the farmers' benefit checks and to secure votes in the cities by offering people on relief agricultural produce at prices less than the grocery store prices. . . . The reason for the many resignations in the department is that the more conservative people there cannot go along with him on abusing his power for this purpose." John Jr. concluded: "This all fits," for it reinforced his opinion that Wallace was dickering for a settlement.[48]

The toll on John Jr.'s energies now seemed to be affecting his span of attention. His brother wrote their mother and father on March 22: "John . . . feels that if he were at the office we would be doing considerably more business than we are. I don't doubt this, but both Julius and I feel . . . that the risks involved in doing what John would like to do seem out of proportion to the possible benefits . . . so we are keeping him home and not paying much attention to him. He is so wrapped up in the Board of Trade case that I would not want to trust his judgment as opposed to Julius' in ordinary trading matters until he has become more familiar with the grain situation." John Sr., worried about John Jr., too, responded: "John . . . is apt to disturb things without having the necessary background . . . this is no time to take unnecessary chances. . . . I insist that we play as conservative a policy as possible."[49]

Dr. Duvel on the Stand

When the hearings resumed on March 27, 1939, after a short recess, J. W. T. Duvel, the head of the CEA took the stand. Over the next four days, Duvel was questioned at length about several controversial aspects of the case, particularly those discussed earlier in this chapter concerning the contacts with Ed Grimes (Grimes had just testified on these) and with the CBOT officials. Duvel's testimony corroborated some of the testimony of Grimes, although Duvel differed sharply with Cargill's version on several key points.

The Cargill group felt heartened by this testimony; John Jr. wrote his father on April 1 that "the Board of Trade were very much put out over Doc's testimony and Miller confirms this by saying that the large delegation from Chicago who are in Washington looked very gloomy indeed while Doc was testifying. . . . Miller also added that Doc was obviously an unwilling witness . . . my regard for him has risen appreciably as a result of his testimony." A *Chicago Daily News* article, headlined "Cargill Kept CEA Informed on Moves—Duvel," was generally positive for the Cargill position.[50]

The key testimony in the case having been given, the hearings seemed to slide downhill. John Jr. wrote on April 10: "The thing has degenerated into a debate between Ellis and Goldsmith, with the Referee siding with Ellis on most occasions." Cargill had contracted for the services of an expert witness, Professor Roland S. Vaile, a University of Minnesota marketing expert. As so often true with expert witnesses, the questioning soon turned to esoteric hypotheses about theoretical features of grain trading and futures contracts. Vaile reinforced most of Cargill's theses about the futures market (these being particularly John Jr.'s philosophies) but occasionally was caught in a contradiction, his testimony momentarily eroding the Company's case. Later, when the case had been recessed, Howard Ellis, the Exchange lawyer, moved that the Vaile testimony not be included in the record of the hearings (his reason: that the testimony was "incomplete and misleading"). The referee rejected this, and it was printed in full.

By this time, many people seemed to have become tired of the case. One of the newspapers in early May headlined an article "Drama of Corn Is Assured of Long Run Here: 1,600,600 Words Spoken and First Act Is Still Uncompleted." The article began sarcastically: " 'Bull Meets Bear,' or 'Whose Shoe Pinched the Corn?' A thrilling melodrama with the grain pit of the Chicago Board of Trade as its setting—is here for an indefinite run." The article continued with further tongue-in-cheek comments: "In ye olde tyme melodrama, the villain was prone to tie the beautiful gal upon a railroad track and chuckle with glee as the fast express approached, only to be foiled by the dashing hero. In 'Bull Meets Bear,' the idea is changed somewhat. The hero (Cargill, Inc.) is depicted as doing well by his gal (the farmer), only to be foiled by the villain (the Chicago Board of Trade).[51]

The whole issue received a shot in the arm, however, in late spring 1939 with yet another alleged "corner" at the CBOT, this time in May 1939 wheat. The situation once again involved an open interest far in excess of the supply. The CEA intervened to obtain information; the shorts were allegedly imperiled by a reputed "squeeze." Although the squeeze eased at the end of the contract, prices did shoot up at the point of liquidation. This time, the shorts took a drubbing. One of the Chicago papers headlined: "Shorts Facing Tightest 'Play' Since Cargill Corn Incident of 1937," and the article mentioned Cargill prominently as possibly being one of the longs. But after the whole matter was settled, no facts leaked out as to the positions on either of the sides. The shorts did have to pay; and this led

Business Week, in its lengthy article on the story, to repeat again one of the enduring clichés of the industry, "He who sells what is not his'n must pay up or go to prison."

As June 1 arrived, it was apparent that almost everyone involved in Cargill's case against the CBOT was exhausted. One of the papers that day, sensing a termination, headlined its article "At Last!" On June 5, a recess was called; one paper reported that by this time there had been "4,000,000 words fired," and it predicted a "torrid summer" as both sides jockeyed with posthearing briefs and motions to dismiss.

John Jr. realized now that Cargill's efforts at public relations might have been counterproductive. Rather than changing the message, he killed it altogether. On June 5, 1939, he sent a memorandum to all offices in the Company: "It has come to our attention that press releases have been made from our outside offices which have caused us considerable embarrassment. In order to prevent any further such embarrassment all members of outside offices will please consult the Minneapolis office before issuing any statements for public consumption." Even a request from *Grain and Feed Journal* for information about the Company's new Erie Canal barges was turned down by John Jr. himself.

John Jr. had felt thankful enough for the efforts of Ted Young and Hayes Miller that he tendered each a substantial block of second preferred stock; these were "the only two that we have shown this recognition to, due to the very serious condition of the grain trade during this past year."[52]

Dan Rice Speaks Out Again

Meanwhile, there was a disconcerting development relating to the Corn Case. Daniel Rice had fumed for months that Cargill's huge Northwestern warehouse in Chicago had remained open as a public warehouse, even though the CBOT rules presumably allowed the Exchange to take this privilege away. The fact that Cargill's CEA case against the CBOT was still in progress might well have been a legal obstacle. "It seems rather paradoxical, to say the least," a June 20, 1939, letter from Daniel F. Rice and Company to the Exchange's president stated; "the expulsion of the Cargill Grain Company should be made effective . . . it should be expelled in reality as well as in name . . . the privileges that this expelled firm enjoys . . . are being so ostentatiously and brazenly flaunted that it has created in the public mind the idea that Cargill . . . was wrongly expelled and that the Board of Trade dare not make its expulsion a reality." Rice was probably right—the Exchange officials still felt cautious about their own position with the CEA and declined to face the heat of closing down public warehouse rights at the largest terminal in the whole area.

Within days of this Rice query, rumors began to circulate on the floor of the CBOT that (according to H. S. Yohe, the CEA official in charge of the U.S. Warehouse Act) "considerable stocks of corn in the Chicago & Northwestern Terminal Elevator which is operated by Cargill, Inc. . . . were out of condition and that there was some talk of posting the elevator." Yohe dispatched a "corps of examiners" to the elevator on July 1 and was able to report to the CBOT secretary that this was not the case. Yohe, even-handed, continued: "Since it appears these rumors were bandied about quite a little among some of the members of the Chicago Board of Trade . . . it is felt that in the interests of protecting the Chicago market as well as in justice to the elevator man in question our findings should be given due publicity in the trade and on the floor of the Board." Such a statement was made, but it was after the fact. Although John Jr. exulted, "Strikes me we can capitalize on this in a large way if we handle it skillfully," the overall effect was one further negative slash at Cargill.[53]

Two Decisions

On August 10, the CEA finished taking all of the addenda; the testimony now totaled 14,199 pages. Howard Ellis, as chief Exchange trial lawyer closed the last day, and Hayes Miller grudgingly admitted to John Sr. that the final argument by Ellis "was a beautiful thing to watch." He used his "fine display of dramatic ability," said Miller, to sprinkle the record with clever one-liners. He called Cargill's allegation "poppycock," said that the Company's findings of fact had given play to many "wild suspicions" by John Jr. and concluded that Cargill displayed an "egocentric line of reasoning." Thus ended testimony on "the great Corn Case."

The CEA now felt free to bring its own case against Cargill (CEA Docket No. 11). Hearings began in Washington in early September 1939, then were moved to Minneapolis later that month, continuing there through October and November. A great deal of time was taken up in stipulations concerning the facts already on the record in Cargill's case against the Exchange (CEA Docket No. 6). But new facts were introduced, too, relating to the allegations by the CEA of the presence of Cargill "wash sales" in corn futures on the Minneapolis Chamber of Commerce (May, July and September 1938 contracts). There was no doubt that Cargill actually had simultaneously bought and sold futures in each of these contracts—the facts established this. Further, these were not traditional spreads between and among contract months. The CEA called these "wash sales" and, despite Cargill objections that they were not, included this term in their final order.

There is always an underlying reason for such simultaneous trades, for on their face there simply would be no rationale for them. In this case, the CEA alleged that Cargill did this to increase the reported open-interest figures and therefore enhance the appearance of liquidity in the Minneapolis exchange, making it a viable alternative to the CBOT for marketing of corn. The open-interest totals for the three contracts in corn (May, July and September) went from 2,600,000 bushels on March 28, 1938, when Julius Hendel first bought for Cargill, to a high of 10,325,000 bushels on April 25; they then declined rapidly to 2,955,000 on June 1. The Minneapolis corn contracts had been dormant for several months; March 28 was the first day of renewed trading.

More than two dozen Minneapolis brokers were subpoenaed. Each was asked the exact details of Cargill's purchases or sales (there were more or less equal amounts of both). In a long document defending the Minneapolis trades that Julius Hendel prepared for possible later Cargill testimony, he argued that the trades were not fictitious wash sales because "no trade of Cargill's had any malice aforethought with intention to defraud, as every trade was a bona fide trade executed in the pit and had a definite relationship to the market." Of course this begged the question of *what* "definite relationship."

Increasingly, it began to look to Cargill as if the whole case was lost. The "tentative findings of fact" of the referee in Cargill's own case against the CBOT had been made public on January 11, 1940; these had laid out the entire record of Cargill's involvements in the September and December 1936 and September 1937 corn futures. The referee had also issued a proposed order to dismiss Cargill's case against the CBOT, and this had to be confirmed by the Commodity Exchange Authority (the three Cabinet secretaries). But at this point it seemed a matter of course. The case had visibly affected the fortunes of all of the participants. The CBOT officials, continuing to be concerned about how the CEA viewed them, breathed a collective sigh of relief. One official telegraphed: "McGinnis tentative findings reported today. No barbs or sideslaps in decision to dismiss." The Cargill group was quite downhearted, both about the damning record and the proposed decision to dismiss.

The hearings had been recessed for December and January. Upcoming testimony on the second case (CEA No. 11) was to center on Cargill's trading in the December 1937 corn contract; here Cargill was a short, and it had been to the Company's advantage to have the prices drop so that the Company could unwind more favorably. When these hearings resumed in early February 1940, further testimony was taken from the Uhlmanns and from a number of new witnesses, most of them brokers at the CBOT. When one of the government witnesses, W. T. Buster, became ill and could not return to the stand for further examination, the CEA attorneys asked for a recess. The Cargill attorneys immediately queried if the government intended to rest after the reexamination of Buster. The chief CEA attorney replied, "Well, I can't say. I don't know what may develop on Mr. Buster's cross-examination." This was an uneasy answer for the Cargill group.

At this point, Cargill was brought to one of the most wrenching decisions it had had to face in all of this set of events, namely, whether to continue to fight the CEA complaint. Irving Goldsmith, Cargill's chief trial lawyer in both CEA cases again was ill (he died in July 1941, at 39 years of age). Perhaps this influenced Cargill's decision. Cargill also had realized that its case in defending itself against the CEA allegations was not strong.

An internal memorandum in early February 1940 spelled out the pros and cons of Cargill stipulating on this (i.e., agreeing not to continue and accepting the CEA referee's judgment). One of the telling arguments for acceding to the stipulation was concern about this further testimony. The memorandum put it this way: "Given the testimony of sixty brokers, some may make harmful statements, e.g., 'I knew that filling Cargill's large order forthwith would depress the price, but I had no choice, since they insisted they be filled immediately rather than gradually. I do not know their reasons, but I can say that this certainly was not the best way to sell to get the best possible price.' "

John Sr. initially opposed any backing off. He felt that John Jr. was being "singled out," that "the honor of the family as that of the business was at stake" and that Cargill might "stand enough better . . . to fight to the bitter end even if the cost is frightful." But John Jr. had had enough. In Jamaica for his vacation, he wrote his brother: "If we can settle this . . . with me being the goat, it is well worthwhile." He left no doubt about his personal discouragement: "It will go a long way toward making for peace of mind for me."

Cargill now decided to capitulate. In a meeting in late February that included John MacMillan, Sr., Cargill MacMillan and James E. Dorsey, a tentative decision was made to negotiate a settlement with the CEA. Cargill MacMillan cabled his brother at his hotel in Jamaica: "What is your reaction to settling basis; no slap at company except suspended suspension [*sic*] of license as future commission merchants but you take indefinite personal suspension. Peterson's judgment is this will not affect our credit."

John Jr. responded with a one-word telegram: "Splendid." A day later, Cargill cabled again: "Negotiations have boiled down to what we consider better basis, namely you and Cargill Grain Illinois take indefinite suspension everyone else including Cargill, Incorporated goes scott free. Father approves this; do you?" John Jr. did, and this became the final basis for settlement. In an order dated March 6, 1940, signed by Henry Wallace, the CEA ruled that Cargill had "waived further hearing in this cause" and had consented to the final CEA order. This order closing the case was quite draconian, and read as follows:

> IT IS HEREBY ORDERED that all contract markets, until further notice by the Secretary of Agriculture, shall refuse all trading privileges thereon to John H. MacMillan, Jr. and to Cargill Grain Company of Illinois, and to each of them.
>
> IT IS FURTHER ORDERED that the complaint herein be, and the same hereby is dismissed with prejudice to the commencement of any new action for the causes, stated in said complaint as to respondents E. J. Grimes, Julius Hendel, Philip C. Sayles and the corporate respondent, Cargill, Inc.

Dorsey wrote John Sr.: "I am satisfied (a) that this settlement cannot reasonably bear the implication of an admission by anyone of any offense tainted with moral turpitude and (b) from the interviews John Peterson has had with the Chase, National City, and First National here, that the credit of the Company will not be adversely affected." But John Sr., unforgiving, called the CEA itself "vicious."

The banners in the newspapers were vivid; the *Chicago Tribune* headlined its story: "Bar MacMillan from Trade in Grain Markets," and the *Minneapolis Tribune* used the word "blacklisted" in its lead. Most of the rest of the articles, while using the words "bar" in various ways, at least only used the word Cargill as a company, rather than MacMillan as an individual. The case was "finished," said another.

Cargill, worried that its customers would think that it truly was "finished" (rumors were already circulating that Cargill was going to "reorganize"), now persuaded the CEA to clarify their order, making clear that while John Jr. and the Cargill Grain Company of Illinois were barred, Cargill, Incorporated, continued to have trading privileges on contract markets. "Mr. MacMillan himself cannot trade, but the Company may," clarified the *Chicago Journal of Commerce*. It was an embarrassing moment for the Company. The final insult to John Jr. was his expulsion two days later from the Minneapolis grain exchange; it was required, of course, by the CEA order, but being named in person in his home exchange must have hurt.

No mention whatsoever was made in the *Cargill Crop Bulletin*, nor was there anything in the *Cargill News*. The Company did put out an internal memorandum to all of its managers, under Cargill MacMillan's signature, enclosing a copy of the CEA's order. The memorandum continued: "We are doing this purely for your personal information. May we emphasize that under no circumstances are we or you to give out any publicity to the press in connection with this matter." The memorandum assured that "there is no foundation in the accounts that have been given in many of the papers that John H. MacMillan, Jr. will have to divorce himself from the management of Cargill, Incorporated, nor is there any contemplation of any reorganization within the Cargill companies."

Perhaps Cargill MacMillan felt that his brother's image indeed had been tarnished, for he closed: "Moreover, the order denying trading privileges to John H. MacMillan, Jr. applies only to his trading personally and has no application whatsoever to the present unrestricted trading privileges of Cargill, Incorporated on the various exchanges. . . . the Cargill management does not tolerate personal speculation. . . . John H. MacMillan, Jr. has never had any personal trades in grain futures in his life."

It remained now only to learn of the final decision in the other case, Cargill's suit against the CBOT. The settlement of the CEA's own case and the January "tentative findings of fact" in Cargill's case telegraphed the answer even before it came. On August 25, 1940, the CEA ruled against Cargill in its case and dismissed the action. The *Chicago Tribune*, in its major article, summed up the public reaction: "Board of Trade Wins Long Corn 'Corner' Fight."[54]

Late in the year 1940, it seemed that at least some of the influential CBOT members wanted Cargill back. Most surprising was the reaction of Kenneth Templeton himself, who wrote to John Jr. in November: "It would take too much time for me to write and too much of your time to read what I could write . . . of the 'misunderstanding' which took place between Cargill and the Board of Trade. Some day I would like to sit down and talk to you about it and tell you what a pack of damn fools we all were to allow such a 'misunderstanding' to take place." Templeton offered his good offices to "heal all wounds."

John Jr., taking this as a sign of weakness on the part of the CBOT, wrote Weston Grimes that he did indeed want "to get out of jail" (the game "Monopoly" had become the craze in the late 1930s, and this term had moved into everyday vocabulary). But he insisted that the CEA come to him, rather than having it appear that *he* had taken the initiative. The Cargill lawyers continued their private efforts toward a reconciliation, however.

The CEA now agreed to restore John Jr.'s privileges, but the order effecting this was another jolt to the Cargill group. The reinstatement order read in part:

On June 18, 1942, the Agricultural Marketing Administration filed a statement containing its views on the application. The statement relates that after extended hearings, the length of which was due largely to respondents' dilatory tactics, respondents stipulated that John H. MacMillan, Jr. had directed the activities which were the subject of the complaint. . . . The statement also expresses the opinion that the seriousness of the offenses resulting from the respondents' activities has been impressed upon the respondents and that the public interest does not require the trading privileges of John H. MacMillan, Jr. be longer denied.

Weston Grimes wrote Cargill MacMillan his views: "While I am not exactly enthusiastic about this order, as finally entered, I do think, on the whole, it is not too bad. It is quite apparent Joel Mehl felt it necessary to go into some detail about 'dilatory tactics' etc. . . . but at least there is nothing very specific stated such as a particular reference to 'corners' and considering the point at which the hearing ended, I think it might be fair to infer that violations if any, occurred in connection with corn operations in Minneapolis."

This latter judgment by Weston Grimes—that only the Minneapolis "wash sales" in the March 1938 corn contract were in question—seems simplistic. After all, this Minneapolis incident was merely a vignette in relation to the CBOT corn contract issues. At any rate, John Jr. himself apparently did not feel that this CEA order vindicated him and wrote the CEA: "As my position has always been, and still is, that I did not violate that Act, I am compelled to take exception to this statement." He continued to refuse a return of the Company or himself to the CBOT, holding this view to his death in 1960.[55]

Did Cargill Attempt a Corner?

Fortune magazine said yes. In a trenchant article on the grain trade, written in August 1949, a decade later, the Corn Case was still featured. By then, with the benefit of that decade of hindsight, the case had assumed its historic role as one of the bellwether battles of grain trading.

The *Fortune* article highlighted the competitive aberrations that had been present. This was "extreme manipulation," according to the author. It was "the squeeze absolute." If the long was able to control the supply, the short could not get out, and therefore the long dictated the price: "During famous corners in the past, the long sat in his office and granted audiences to the poor bedraggled shorts."

Then the article recounted the Cargill Corn Case: "The last big corner was run by Cargill in corn in September, 1937. But the Chicago Board of Trade stepped in near the end of the futures month, suspended trading, and let the shorts out, though not without considerable loss to them." The author featured John MacMillan, Jr.'s role in this: "The greatest feud in the grain market today is between the fast-talking, fast-moving John MacMillan of Cargill in Minneapolis—the largest grain merchant in the U.S.—and the shrewd, laconic commission man, Dan Rice, head of Daniel F. Rice & Co. of Chicago. . . . It is generally understood that when one of them is on one side of the market, the other will be found on the other side." The article featured two large line-drawing likenesses of the two men, with short biographical sketches juxtaposed.

This was indeed a battle of personal egos. Both the principals were unabashedly their own bosses; they were CEOs in the literal sense, un-

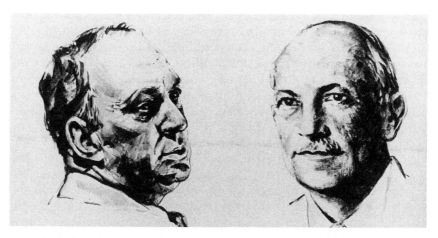

The two adversaries, Daniel F. Rice (left) and John H. MacMillan, Jr. (right), FORTUNE
magazine, August 1949 (Raymond Breinin, FORTUNE Magazine. Reprinted by permission).

questionably authoritative and, more often than not, authoritarian. Both
were brilliant, obstinate, self-willed.

Just a few months before the *Fortune* article appeared, *Business Week*
had featured Cargill in a major article and had put John Jr. on the cover.
By the 1940s, John Jr. had become a nationally renowned personage, his
fame spreading beyond the grain trade itself; indeed, many people believed
that the lyrics "Mister Thorne . . . once corner'd corn and that ain't hay"
in the Cole Porter song, "Always True to You in My Fashion" referred to
the Corn Case, perhaps even to John Jr. himself.

John Jr. had managed the entire case—this is quite evident. Ed Grimes,
Julius Hendel, John Peterson, Cargill MacMillan, Philip Sayles and Austen
Cargill all had roles. John MacMillan, Sr., was available throughout the
cases as the conservative, elderly oracle, though he always defended adamantly John Jr's morals, his ethics and his honesty. The lawyers too had
their own inputs, especially Irving Goldsmith and Sumner "Ted" Young.
Yet John Jr. was all-pervasive. It was *his* strategy, *his* tactics, *his* underlying
motives that dominated the entire story. Whatever the strengths and weaknesses for Cargill resulting from the Corn Case, they can be attributed
directly to John Jr.

A highly intelligent person, John Jr. depended on sophisticated analysis, his and others, for his decision making. He fervently believed that if
Cargill used good foresight and understood the market better than others,
this advantage would be rewarded with profitable trades. Fred Uhlmann
commented on this intense John Jr. conviction: "They really thought the

corn was worth a great deal more. . . . He had charts made showing how much corn would be wanted in September and October." John Jr. stubbornly believed in himself, almost to a fault. His reasoning was that he had assessed the corn situation better than others, knew which side of the market to be on, and had made binding commitments as a long with others whom he felt also had made binding contracts to him. He was driving a hard bargain, to be sure, but a bargain that was perfectly legal. As the *Wall Street Journal* put it on September 4, 1937, right in the middle of the purported squeeze, "it is simply a natural corner . . . buyers are well within their rights in standing pat for delivery." A Julius Hendel aphorism, often repeated by John Jr., held that "the cure for high prices is high prices"—in other words, pure, rugged, supply-and-demand competition. On the supply side, production would be stimulated by the high prices, bringing greater supply and downward pressure on prices. At the same time, substitutions would be made whenever possible, also decreasing demand. If John Jr. had miscalculated, been on the other side of the market, he would have taken his losses in stride.

Two questions need to be raised about this reasoning. First, if the September 1937 corn contract had been allowed to expire under the original provisions of the contract, John Jr.'s very large holding of long contracts likely would have forced many shorts either to bargain with him on a settlement price after the contract had expired or to bid up the price by open outcry in the pit, prior to expiration. This is, of course, the essence of a corner—one side attempting to dictate price. The fact that the shorts stayed silent is a telling commentary; it tends to support an inference that the shorts assumed they would be bailed out by CBOT intervention.

There seems little doubt in the September and December 1936 corn cases, and even less in the September 1937 case, that one of John Jr.'s several goals was to be the long who "granted audiences to the poor bedraggled shorts." Another of his stated goals, as he repeated over and over, was to obtain physical product for purchasers of Cargill grain to whom the Company was already committed. However, he was never able to make a credible case on this. If he had, he possibly would have won the case.

It is equally clear that John Jr. sincerely felt that the price of September 1937 corn futures should be in the neighborhood of $1.40—his analysis from his charts told him so. In effect, he was saying that this was the "competitive" price, set by supply and demand. Yet this was circular reasoning—he had the ability by the size of his purchases to fundamentally affect supply itself, at least temporarily, right around the close of the contract. John Jr.'s intersection point for supply and demand became a self-fulfilling prophecy.

This leads to the second concern, one that John Jr. apparently failed to acknowledge. Cargill's dominant size in the industry—it was by 1940 one of the largest traders in the country—gave it enormous market weight. If Cargill coughed, the grain trade got a cold (to use the venerable analogy). John Jr. did not admit this. He refused to see that Cargill per se could distort the market just by its normal commercial purchases, or at least it had the potential to do so, a potential that constantly would have to be monitored by regulating agencies, the two most important being the CBOT and the CEA.

In May 1939, in an impending ICC barge rate case, John Jr. again wanted to take a high profile, and Ed Grimes warned him: "There is a general knowledge here in Washington that we are a big outfit and, whether you know it or not, there is a definite prejudice against bigness. . . . I do not think it is good policy to antagonize people at this time. We are fighting now for our very existence in this CEA case—I think it is plenty as it is . . . we should be cautious about going out of our way to make more enemies." But John Jr. seemed not to see this.

John Jr. was totally correct about the sanctity of the contracts themselves. The grain trade absolutely depended on everyone's word being good. The frenetic pace of the pits, where thousands, even millions of bushels could be traded in a matter of minutes by eye contact alone (in the "open outcry" milieu) would be unworkable without implicit trust. Indeed, the whole edifice of an exchange like the CBOT would collapse instantly if this were not so. If its Business Conduct Committee did allow the shorts an "out," which it seems it did, then the sanctity of contract truly had been bent. The leaders of the CBOT, despite their solemn statements about the great portent of the case and their "deep concern" for its ethical dimensions, probably did not fully realize just how consequential this case was. If the notion had been planted that shorts (or in some other situation, the longs) could in later cases have their losses mitigated by action of the Business Conduct Committee, a fundamental tenet of the Exchange would be threatened. The Business Conduct Committee was on a higher tightrope than it realized.

The tactics of both sides in the case left something to be desired in terms of these deeper facets of market trust. John Jr. had been calculating and had resorted to subterfuge at many points in the saga. Cargill had traded with the Uhlmann Grain Company for some 49 years. Still Richard Uhlmann testified in the McDonald hearings that John Jr. "would never confide in me."[56]

Yet the record also shows that these Cargill tactics were matched step-by-step by those on the other side. Dan Rice was a master at these. For many years before this case and for many years after, the stratagems and the wiles of these traders have been the sine qua non of speculation in the exchange pits around the country. At stake here was the very validity of speculation.

Mistrusting the Speculator

Those who understand the grain trade believe almost universally that the continuity, liquidity and balance of the grain exchanges is fundamentally provided by the speculator. An overwhelming percentage of the trades on the CBOT was speculative. *Fortune*, in its 1949 article, estimated the figure at 90 percent of the trading in wheat and corn. This tremendous volume, typically far greater than the actual product available, provides, through the interaction of supply and demand, that key feature of liquidity. Yet the notion that all of these people were trading "paper" corn or "paper" wheat has bothered the layman for years. If short-term bullish or bearish excesses appeared to be present, the mistrust by the public heightened.

Shorts always had come in for particular opprobrium. If speculators in general are "traffickers in human misery" (*Fortune's* term), then the shorts were thought to be a particularly heinous group. The prediction of a short is that prices will drop. Thus, a short seems to be trading on the misery of farmers and others. Alonzo Taylor, one of the respected writers about the grain trade in the 1930s, put it this way: "Lower prices for farm products are taken to mean lower wages, lower standards of living, and lower land values. . . . Higher prices come to be looked upon as a social improvement, while lower prices spell social deterioration. To forecast a higher price has become praiseworthy . . . a lower price blameworthy." Writers in the earlier muckraking period often stereotyped the two—the longs were "active, gregarious, bold, clever" and shorts were "sly, ascetic, cryptic, aloof, cynical." (One would need to add that higher grain prices meant higher bread prices for the consumer.) It is easy to see why short selling was so heated an issue and the subject of much legislative concern in the New Deal period. Lost in that argument was the fact that the longs could be equally speculative in their guessing that the market would go up. The *Fortune* article emphasized this point: "Although the public (along with the farmer) is believed to be generally a bull in the market, the professional speculator rides the market both ways and includes the public trend in its calculation."[57]

Sometimes lost in discussions, too, is the fact that spreaders also are taking positions, though usually in total exposures carrying somewhat less risk than the speculator's one-side-of-the-market "naked" position. Futures prices for different contract months seldom move in absolute lockstep. They do move in *similar* patterns, and this partial predictability is the glue that makes hedging a good mechanism for price-movement protection. Cash markets, too, have these patterns, again almost always with variations. The widening and narrowing of these spreads provide a significant opportunity for profit for a grain trading company like Cargill. John Jr. and Julius Hendel prided themselves on predicting this. The Company might always be "fully hedged"—John Jr. stated this as Cargill policy over and over in the Corn Case, just as John Sr. had so often in previous periods. But John Sr. meant it more literally—yes, an evolving favorable spread might be followed for a short while, but his rock-solid caution would pull him back, sooner rather than later.

A strong case can be made, however, that as John Jr. and Julius Hendel took central responsibility first for wheat and then for all grains, this thoroughgoing hedging philosophy began to change, first subtly, then more openly in the mid-1930s. Trading profits, made on the spreads, became more of the game; perhaps the strictly service concepts of storing and moving grain became relatively less important, although this seems an overgeneralization, too, for John Jr. had great interest in new terminals and new ways of moving grain as part of his overall strategic planning. Still, the trading motif of the 1930s did evolve toward hard-nosed bargaining. Julius Hendel often repeated an old industry adage: "If he's yours today, tomorrow he's mine for a 1/4" (i.e., loyalty can be bought for a quarter of a cent on a bid). The heightened importance of spreading in John Jr.'s and Julius Hendel's minds mirrored this changed mentality. The payoffs had been high, with excellent Company profitability; any reservations John Sr. might have had likely were allayed by this fact.

John Jr., when asked in his testimony in the CEA case about the difference between hedging and spreading, vowed that the latter was not "a speculative transaction." When pressed on this, he facilely replied: "We are unable to see that there is any material difference . . . because *the moment the nearby contract matures* it becomes a hedge" (my emphasis). But this begged the real question—before that point, a speculative position had been taken predicting how the price of that nearby future would move up to maturity. John Jr.'s rhetoric on this issue throughout the case was not straightforward, nor was Rice's!

The CEA Assesses Speculation

The arbiter of the limits of speculation since the mid-1930s has been the Commodity Exchange Authority (renamed in the mid-1970s the Commodity Futures Trading Commission). One of the revealing aspects of the Cargill Corn Case is seen in the tentative early efforts of the CEA officials (and Henry Wallace, the Secretary of Agriculture) to define the type of competitive environment for the exchanges. The roles of Dr. Duvel and his assistant, J. M. Mehl, were particularly ambivalent—they had extensive contacts with both sides of the case, their very actions and words influenced the case and they were developing heretofore uncharted public policy piecemeal as events progressed.

The CEA was not a strong agency in 1937–1938; it was seen by many as the handmaiden of the exchanges. Even in recent years, rejuvenated as the Commodity Futures Trading Commission, the agency has never been the counterpart of the Securities and Exchange Commission, the regulator of the securities side of the "trading" industry. The *Fortune* author, writing in 1949, at a time when the grain trade was again under public attack, faulted the CEA as having a limited and constraining view of competition: "In the abstract the CEA's position in the market is uncontested . . . it 'seeks to make price a reflection of supply and demand, a result rather than a reason for exchange transactions.' To this end, the CEA seems to want to create a market that is 'dull' but liquid. This has been the ideal of classical economists, but it is questionable whether it is realistic. Traders trade and the speculator may not stay in a dull market."

In the Corn Case, the CBOT of that period saw itself as a bastion of rugged free enterprise, rigorously defending its prerogatives and emphasizing the values of speculation. By the 1940s, according to *Fortune*, the CBOT had become more timid, had "committed themselves to church-supper public relations." At the time of the Corn Case, however, the CBOT advocated the least amount of outside regulation—its ruling powers believed implicitly in "self regulation." The "old boy" domination of the Exchange was supreme. There had long been a belief that one could not become president of the CBOT unless one's father had been. John Jr. had accused the CBOT officers of being a "social club," but it had become more than that, perhaps something on the order of a medieval guild. The CBOT seemed sublimely confident that it was *the* Exchange, which irritated the members of other exchanges. In particular, the Minneapolis Chamber of Commerce and the Kansas City Board of Trade both felt that they had become major forces in the grain trade and should be accorded their due. The CBOT consistently held that they themselves were the dominant force, entitled at that time, for example, to an automatic presidency of the Grain Committee on National Affairs, the overall group set up by the industry to represent all of the member exchanges.

Whether these exchanges, and particularly the CBOT, could be self-regulating remained a concern throughout the 1930s. Later, circumstances in the 1940s, 1950s and 1960s conspired to limit somewhat the role of the grain exchanges—first World War II, then nagging surpluses and postwar government domination of the national and international grain situation gave the exchanges a somewhat lesser role. To be sure, the development of soybeans as a major crop and the availability of exciting, volatile soybean futures contracts added a new dimension. But not until the burgeoning trading of the early 1970s (particularly intensified by Russian grain purchases) did the vitality shown by the exchanges in the time of the Cargill Corn Case return.

The Industry Loner

John Jr. rigidly held to his vow at the end of the case that Cargill would never return to the CBOT; not until after John Jr. died in 1960 was any consideration given to a return (which the Company did in 1962). Was this decision to stay out of the CBOT, and the case itself, costly to Cargill? The Company had lost a great deal of money in the crop year 1937–1938; the following crop year saw profits of only $211,000, but the 1939–1940 crop year produced substantial earnings of well over $1.1 million. John Jr. remained innovative and forceful in his ideas and decisions during this period. The case preempted substantial management time all through the 1937–1939 period, a significant cost. The Company accountants compiled the "combined expenses" of the two cases and this figure came to a total of $234,740. But this only marginally accounted for the preoccupations that had worried Cargill MacMillan so much, and the lost opportunities were immeasurable. In the accountants' statement, John Jr.'s time was estimated at only $6,068 for over three years of his energies, devoted so single-mindedly to the case—definitely not a reasonable figure.

There were corresponding compensations. The Cargill attack on the Call Rule had been so strong that while the rule itself momentarily remained in place, a great many people in the industry then followed Cargill's lead out into the field to buy direct. John Jr.'s personal reputation seemed not sullied; indeed, he himself and Cargill as a company were probably taken even more seriously.

The Corn Case was a true milestone, not only for the broader concerns of Exchange regulation and governmental control, but also for Cargill's philosophy of management. Ed Grimes had proved to be a master at "networking" (the somewhat overworked term of the 1970s). His reputation in Washington was excellent, the linkages he had built with brokers, commission houses and others throughout the industry had given the Company a model for better public relations. He had come to the Company in 1904 as John Sr.'s secretary, and his values mirrored those of John Sr. He was of John Sr.'s generation, more than of John Jr.'s.

The Company seemed to change—to be more watchful, less trusting, more willing to "go it alone." One negative effect of the case was to constrain the use of the Company's private wire system—many Cargill people became fearful about leaving a record that might be subject to a subpoena at a later date. In the process, Company people sometimes were denied information that was needed, perhaps even already public knowledge. Secrecy was pervasive in the industry; one of the canons of the grain trade is taciturnity. Yet it seems likely that John Jr., already with more than an industry portion of this "loner" independence, had had this trait exacerbated in the corn case.

In moving into any business or social group, John Jr. was used to becoming the natural leader because of his brains, verve and strategic thinking. He expected this obeisance and sometimes seemed almost to look down upon those around him as less brilliant. There is more than a passing reminder of Teddy Roosevelt in John Jr. When he became involved with the CBOT, the expected role did not come to him right away—it *was* a tightly constrained closed circle. Perhaps he eventually would have been able to breach this wall, but it would have taken time—he would have had to "pay his dues." A pecking order was not in John Jr.'s style.

This was a loss for John Jr., both personally and professionally. It would have been a chance for him to have his rough edges rubbed off by the actions of the group. This might have had a tendency to stifle some of his initiative temporarily, but it might also have constrained some of his more eccentric projects and saved him some embarrassment. He had not had to deal with a group of independent peers and their restraints since college. Even in the army he had his authority direct from the general. With the CBOT, he did not possess an automatic authority, and in anger, he was not willing to deal with the approval or disapproval of these outside counterparts. With Cargill so prominent in the industry and with much to gain for *both* sides from industry interactions, this unwavering opposition to the CBOT seems, in retrospect, to be a somewhat star-crossed decision, one that probably did substantially hurt the Company over the succeeding years. It also hurt the CBOT.

Balanced against this were a number of positive outcomes. For Cargill, the need to go it alone seemed to add impetus to Company innovation, to an attitude that always questioned, "Why can't we do this a more efficient, more creative, more effective way" rather than "You can't do this—it isn't in the tradition." The attack on the Call Rule is a case in point—there certainly were elements of monopoly inherent in this arrant effort by the brokers to preserve the status quo in the name of "orderliness." Cargill's decision helped to "deregulate" the industry (to use another term of today), at least for key aspects of cash grain trading. The Company's challenge of old methodologies and conventional wisdoms seemed to grow faster after the Corn Case.

However, this attitude can also lead to arrogance—"We know how to do it, don't question us." John Sr. had always striven to gain consensus. There was less of this in John Jr.'s makeup. The Corn Case seemed to increase John Jr.'s stubbornness. His friends sensed this; one of those ubiquitous poems was read at a private party on his 50th birthday in 1945; it included these stanzas on the Corn Case and its aftereffects:

But trees, grain, marriage, golf and tennis,
Lost excitement in time as sport—
Said John, rubbing his palms in anticipation,
"I'm going to wrestle with the boys who are short."

So, in due course, he turned to Chicago,
A village located in the Middle West;
While John was involved in a corner,
They tried to steal his pants, coat and vest.

But you can't say John isn't a fighter,
He doesn't quit as easy as you might think;
Armed with Marian and fourteen attorneys,
He caused the Exchange in Chi quite a stink!

The battle ground was shifted to Washington,
Both sides argued long before the bar;
But at that bar John couldn't get Martinis,
Said John, "Another fault of F.D.R."

. . . .

But quick-on-the-trigger MacMillan,
Some hair lost butting against a stone wall,
Returned to Minneapolis and Cargill,
Still admitting he had a lot on the ball.[58]

Thus, for a host of reasons, the Corn Case was paradoxical for Cargill—and for John MacMillan, Jr. It was a massive learning experience for a great many people, including most of Cargill's top management. Whether this included John Jr. is conjectural.

CHAPTER THIRTEEN

Transportation in the 1930s

Franklin Roosevelt, while still governor of New York, personally dedicated the new Albany deep-water port on June 7, 1932. Although Cargill's new terminal was not quite finished, Company officials were invited for "their" opening, too. John Jr. was urged to come but could not. In a coincidence probably not overlooked by some people, B. J. Bolan, the manager of Cargill's Montreal office, was the senior Company representative present.

Many people connected with Montreal shipping felt quite threatened by the new Albany deep-water port. So too did other communities along the water route to the St. Lawrence, particularly Buffalo. It was noteworthy that Governor Roosevelt had chosen to be present. Undoubtedly he must have been influenced by the immediate economic situation, as his speech particularly emphasized the employment-enhancing features of the port. It was "well planned and properly financed," he averred—and it used no tax monies, either! As to its "warehouses and elevators," he continued, "instead of being an annual expense to the State Government [they would] be paid for by the actual users . . . and paid for over a period of years, as is wholly proper."

The momentousness of a new deep-water port on the Eastern Seaboard was not lost on anyone. As a final ceremony, a "wedding of the waters" was carried out when separate flasks of water from an even 100 different ports of the world were mixed with the water of the new port, as the *New York Times* put it, "to symbolize its link with the seven seas."[1]

In the following days, the effect of the Albany development became more evident. The *Montreal Gazette* noted that many worried that this might mean "the beginning of the end of Montreal's leadership as an ocean port, particularly as a grain port, on this continent," but the editor downplayed these views as "florid speeches." After all, Montreal was nearer to Liverpool than New York by 382 statute miles, and Albany was an additional 525 statute miles farther away. The channel to Montreal up the St. Lawrence had a depth of 35 feet; Albany had a depth of just 27 feet. Further,

. . . we have more water in our canals than has the Erie Canal, either from Buffalo or Oswego; the Canadian canals have a depth of 14 feet, Erie Canal but 12 feet. We have less actual canal mileage and lockage. Erie Canal is 357 miles from Buffalo to Troy with 35 locks; Oswego section is 188.5 miles to Troy, with 30 locks while St. Lawrence canals, Welland Canal being already deepened and therefore excluded, are 45.49 miles, with 22 locks. Ocean steamers of small size can make use of our waterway while only barges, and then limited, can use the Erie and Oswego canals.[2]

The old Erie Canal had been quite limited; at the turn of the century it had fallen into disuse because of its shallow draft and small lock size. In 1899, Theodore Roosevelt, then governor of New York, appointed a commission to upgrade the whole canal. It took two decades for action, but in 1918 a new "New York State Barge Canal" was opened, utilizing most but not all of the old Erie Canal route. It had three branches from Troy/ Albany—one to Buffalo, another northward to Lake Champlain and a third branching off to Oswego, on Lake Ontario. While still "limited" (accord-

Locks 4, 5 and 6 on the Welland Ship Canal, 1931.

ing to the Montreal editor), it could accommodate barge and towboat combinations up to 300 feet, and there was a 12-foot draft throughout. From that time, the system was officially the New York State Barge Canal, but the whole system still was called by most people simply "the Erie Canal" (and in this book I will do the same).

By the 1920s, an increasing volume of grain moved through the Erie Canal down to New York—over 20 million bushels in 1923 rising to 40 million bushels in 1928. The grain moving through the St. Lawrence canals in this same period was considerably greater—over 89 million bushels in 1923 and up to 184 million in 1928 (the highest year until then for both the Erie and the St. Lawrence canals).[3]

In 1932, the same year that Cargill's Albany terminal opened, there was another important change in canal transportation in the Great Lakes arena: the renovated Welland Canal opened. It brought an order-of-magnitude difference, as now there were only eight Welland locks and the draft throughout had been deepened to 30 feet.

Still, large lakers could not ply all the way to Montreal because there were rapids upstream from Montreal (in the Thousand Islands section) that still provided a bottleneck for the large ships. This was to be the last link to be completed for a "St. Lawrence Seaway." As early as 1895, the project had been discussed jointly between Canada and the United States, yet it was still in limbo, mostly due to the hostility of certain Atlantic port interests in the United States. In 1932, at least, the St. Lawrence Seaway was still only a dream.

The Welland Canal improvement did have a vital effect, however, for it allowed larger lakers to go through the Canal, traverse Lake Ontario and move into the St. Lawrence to ports connected to rail lines for shipment to Montreal and Boston (Kingston and Prescott, Ontario, and Ogdensburg, New York, being the most important). Offloading into smaller boats at these ports was also a possibility.

Oswego, New York, on the southern shore of Lake Ontario, long had been a port connected by the Erie Canal to the Hudson River and on to New York City. Barging via this route before the upgrading of Welland was not as attractive. However, with larger lakers calling, the situation changed markedly, for Oswego was only some 188 miles from the Hudson at Albany, and oceangoing ships could now proceed to Albany. The Erie barge canal also extended westward all the way to Buffalo, although this was 357 miles. So it was not just Montreal that felt uneasy; so did Buffalo.

The Harbor Commissioner of Montreal, visiting the Albany port facilities after the inauguration, felt otherwise: "It will be a threat to New York," he stated. "Albany has laid claim to a grain elevator of 13,000,000 bushels capacity," he continued, "but we discovered that she has bin storage for no more than 5,000,000 bushels. The remaining space, capable of accommodating 8,000,000 bushels, is ordinary storage for any commodity whatsoever, . . . it might even be used for cattle, sheep, goats or pigs." In other words, he concluded, "it was just an ordinary warehouse."[4] The Harbor Commissioner was wrong. He was misled by John Jr.'s new terminal configuration with flat storage—the "big bins"—which would indeed hold 13,000,000 bushels.

Right from the opening of its Albany terminal, Cargill funneled most of its eastward shipments in the ice-free months through the Erie Canal, rather than by rail. The slowness of the barge movement was offset by the lower rate. By November 1932, there were as many as 33 barges arriving per day to be unloaded at the terminal. Incidentally, high water from heavy rains in the previous month had made shipping difficult because the water was so high that barges could not get under the many bridges that crossed the canal. Barge unloading at the Albany terminal was facilitated by an innovative adaptation by Frank Neilson of a European version of a pneumatic unloading device. The sucking nozzles were arranged in such a fashion that alternate use could keep a boat or barge on an even keel while unloading.

Grain Transportation Patterns

In the vast system of grain flow that had been developed in the United States and Canada by this time, an incredible array of choices was available. To begin with, grain could go either east, south or west. By the early 1930s, Canada had a highly developed westward-moving flow by rail to its British Columbia terminals and typically on to Asian ports (although grain also could be shipped through the Panama Canal to the Atlantic and the Gulf). Westward movement of United States grains was not quite as well developed, because the traditional movement had been eastward to the Atlantic, with some also going south to the Gulf.

Eastward and southward, the matrix of alternative choices was considerably more complicated. Here, by the 1920s, combinations of rail, river, lake, canal and a newcomer, the truck, could be used in a variety of combinations. The linchpin was cost—an "opportunity cost" calculation of a freight rate and the time that the transportation took. Weather, too—droughts, winter ice and floods especially—often was a further complication. The rate was the key because each competing transporter quoted separate rates that the shipper could choose.

There was a complicating factor for these rates, inasmuch as the rails had been highly regulated by the Interstate Commerce Commission (ICC) since 1887, while the other three were largely unregulated. (All three *were* under the purview of the Federal Trade Commission for any collusive behavior). Later the Motor Carrier Act of 1935 and the Transportation Act of 1940 brought regulation to truckers and the domestic water carriers.

Ed Grimes acknowledged the frustration of the railroaders about their regulated status in a speech he gave at a convention of the New York State Waterways Association in September 1932. After extolling the virtues of waterways, particularly the Erie system, he ended: "I have only sympathy for the railroads . . . shackled by regulation, threatened and intimidated by competing markets and localities." John Sr. took a more active posture, writing his old friend C. T. Jaffray, then president of the "Soo Line" Railroad: "Railroad rates must come down to a pre-war basis because commodity prices are back to that basis. Railroad rates are subject to the same laws and economic law will in the end govern. I hope the railroads will see the handwriting on the wall . . . so that they can conform to economic law rather than attempt to fight it."[5]

Because the potential for having one's commercial advantage destroyed—one shipping point (a town) losing out to another because a rate elsewhere was lower—the ICC long had adhered to the concept of "proportional rates." The Federal Trade Commission had put this succinctly in 1923 in the "grain trade" hearings: "The 'proportional rate' was devised to equalize rates for shipment via one gateway as compared with existing through rates via another gateway."[6] Railroad rates, evolved through a labyrinthine process and changed frequently, were then pitted against the

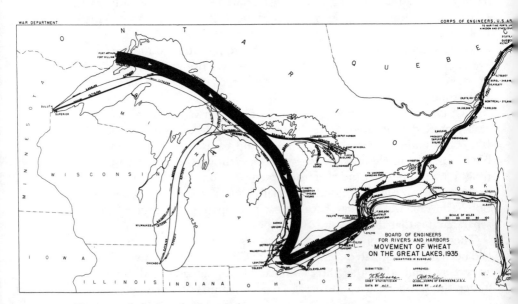

Movement of wheat on the Great Lakes, 1935.

other three, in a flurry of highly competitive parries and thrusts by the other three, less-regulated groups.

Even a brief review of the key combinations for alternative routing immediately turns up some knotty competitive questions. To begin with, there are two countries involved, the United States and Canada. There always has been a certain amount of chauvinism between these two friendly neighbors. Many people on both sides of the national boundary advocated keeping maximum control within their own borders. Better "all-American" said the Statesiders; better "all-Canadian" replied their counterparts to the north.

Take the case of Canadian grain first. Most of its eastward grain would be put on a laker at the Canadian ports of Fort William and Port Arthur on Thunder Bay on the north shore of Lake Superior. Some of this grain might be unloaded at Canadian ports on Georgian Bay or Lake Huron, to go forward by rail to Montreal. Most of the grain, however, would continue on through the Great Lakes and would stay all-Canadian all the way by being loaded on smaller boats adapted to navigation through the Welland Canal, itself on Canadian soil, and then sent through to Montreal either by the smaller boat or by a Canadian rail line. Another frequently used routing for Canadian grain was through a Lake Erie port, typically Buffalo, where it might be milled into flour. If the flour was for United States consumption, a duty of 42 cents per bushel of wheat had to be paid. If it was for international sale it could be reloaded under "milling-in-transit" privileges and escape the duty. Alternatively, it could go forward as wheat into the international chain by way of a United States or Canadian rail or canal route; foreign grain at this time could escape duty if it was stored in bond and reexported within 10 months.[7]

Eastward-moving United States grain, in turn, might move from its point of origin in the Midwest to the end-user by rail or go to one of the Lake Michigan or Lake Superior ports (particularly, Chicago, Milwaukee and Duluth/Superior). If by water, the laker might drop its grain at a western Lake Erie port or, more likely, at Buffalo. Or, as in the Canadian example, there might be transshipment by smaller boats through the Welland Canal to a Lake Ontario port such as Oswego or even the St. Lawrence River American-side port of Ogdensburg. Still, this was not "all-American," inasmuch as the Welland Canal was Canadian. In past years, there had been efforts toward an all-American route to tidewater for laker-size shipping, generally proposed to follow the Oswego–Hudson River route. However, from Lake Ontario to the highest point of the canal is a climb of 174 feet, with a drop then of 420 feet to the sea. Large, numerous locks would have been required, not to mention the many bridge relocations necessary in this populated area. The *Wheat Studies* editors reported in 1932: "According to engineering estimates, the cost of construction would be heavier than that of the St. Lawrence Seaway and would be carried by the United States alone, and not offset by any considerable power earnings. The sentimental argument that it would be an all-American waterway may be dismissed as irrelevant; in any event, if the Welland Canal were used to pass from Lake Erie to Lake Ontario, there would still be a Canadian part of the route. . . . It is therefore proper to say that the all-American canal is of historic interest only."[8]

In the late summer of 1932, an unexpected new development intruded into the Canadian–American trade relationship. Canada's farmers had been hard hit by the depression, and they began agitating as early as the Imperial Conference in 1930 for special privilege for Commonwealth countries in their exporting to the United Kingdom. They failed to get it in 1930, but when Canadian premier R. B. Bennett invited the members of the Commonwealth to an economic conference in Ottawa in the summer of 1932, Great Britain surprised many people by agreeing to a levy of two shillings per "quarter" (480 pounds, or eight bushels) for any grain imported from a non-Commonwealth country. It was a "radical extension," said the *Wheat Studies* editors, and was a particular shock to the United States grain trade. Canada gained a major preference, approximately 6

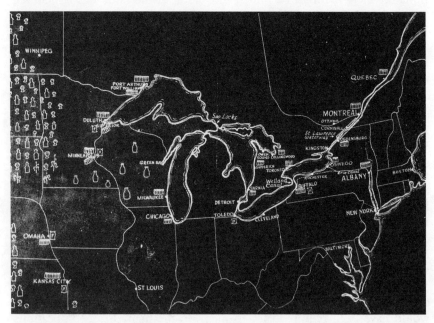

The *Cargill system for Great Lakes shipment of grain, including non-Cargill Canadian connections, mid-1930s.*

TABLE I
Exports of Grain in Millions of Bushels, 1929–35[10]

	1929	1930	1931	1932	1933	1934	1935
American grain							
Via north Atlantic ports	9	5	18	32	2	0.2	0
Via St. Lawrence ports	38	19	8	10	2	0.4	0
TOTAL	47	24	26	42	4	0.6	0
Canadian grain							
Via north Atlantic ports	87	66	62	32	25	30.8	21
Via St. Lawrence ports	72	66	94	121	87	60.6	60
TOTAL	159	132	156	153	112	91.4	81
Total American and Canadian grain							
Via north Atlantic ports	96	71	80	64	27	31	21
Via St. Lawrence ports	110	85	102	131	89	61	60
GRAIN TOTAL	206	156	182	195	116	92	81

cents per bushel, over the United States for its hard wheat, and Australia gained the same for its soft wheat.

Canada's preference remained in force for only six years. In 1938, it was removed in a major trade agreement between the United States and Canada. But for those half dozen years, the effect was substantial. Far less Canadian grain came through American ports, for to gain the preference the grain had to move from the country of origin to Great Britain by direct voyage. The volume of American exports declined precipitously (there were other causes, too—for example, the drought in the period 1934–1936).[9]

To put the quantities involved in perspective, the shipments during the seven years 1929–1935 were as shown in table 1.

Rate Battles—Oswego and Ogdensburg

The improvements at the Welland Canal allowed either offloading at Oswego for barge shipment by the Erie Canal to Albany, or sending the laker on to Ogdensburg for rail shipment into New England. Now the availability of Cargill's huge 13.5-million-bushel Albany terminal for storage altered the rate system. John Jr. commented to B. J. Bolan, the Cargill Montreal manager: "The opening of the Welland Canal and the deepening of the Hudson River to Albany have thrown the Eastern rail rate structure into a turmoil and it is hard to see what the ultimate outcome will be." Certainly, John Jr. sensed trouble when he read a Buffalo paper's story on this: "The Cargill Grain Company by going to Albany has aroused intense opposition . . . threats have been made that everything possible will be done to check this development."

John Jr. and Ed Grimes then began a delicate bargaining act that pitted existing rates against the exploitation of alternative choices for physically moving and storing grain. Cargill wanted, first, to enhance the water route to Albany via the Erie Canal and the Hudson River water route to New York. Rates quoted by the bargers on the Canal had fallen substantially in the period since the Great Crash. Grain in 1932 went from the Head-of-the-Lakes and from Chicago and Milwaukee all the way to Montreal at rates as low as 3 cents per bushel and to New York for as low as 3½ cents per bushel. Indeed, in early 1932, Grimes had been offered a boat from Lake Michigan to Oswego at 1¾ cents per bushel. Rates did have a strong seasonal pattern, however; in times of port congestion, say at Buffalo, when turnaround times were longer, rates tended to rise. In one of Cargill's ICC cases, the commissioners chronicled the pattern of wheat rates per bushel from Fort William and Port Arthur, Canada (the Canadian Head-of-the-Lakes), to St. Lawrence ports from 1929 through 1933. In that five-year period, overall rates had dropped from a weighted average for the 1929 season of 8.6 cents to 3.9 cents in 1933 (the lowest quotation that year was 2.25 cents).[11]

With competition among bargers for business so keen, Cargill ostensibly had no worries about shipping costs. Yet it was also important to keep the bargers going. If the rates deteriorated too much, these small operators would be driven out of business. In contrast to railroads, "abandonment" would be at their own (or their banks') discretion. The railroads had to petition the ICC if they wished to abandon a particular line because of unprofitable business.

Not all of Cargill's shipping needs could be met by the canal. Weather problems or congestion could intrude, and the Company needed rail rates from Buffalo into New York City that would also match costs on other routes used by Cargill's competitors. As there was no Erie Canal connection from Ogdensburg—"the 'Burg," as it was fondly called—favorable rail rates eastward into New England also would be necessary, since the Welland Canal improvement now allowed larger boats to dock at Cargill's terminal there.

A first step was getting a competitive rail rate to New York City from both Buffalo and Oswego. The New York Central Railroad served both cities, and Cargill proceeded to press for lower rates. The initial proposal by the New York Central, as described to the Albany Port District Commission chairman by John Jr., was "one of the most outrageous and iniquitous proposals which we have ever experienced." John Jr. talked with a New York City barge company about the New York Central:

They [the railroad] have intimated that they did not care to develop Oswego and Albany unless they figured that there was a chance of their competing with the Erie Canal. . . . Our analysis indicates to us that if the New York Central did so and endeavored actively to compete with the Canal, the Hudson River outlet would have a boom which would be almost inconceivably great. In fact we estimate that instead of shipping 75 million to 150 million bushels per year from the Hudson River it is possible that this amount could be increased to 500 million, practically all of which would be handled through Albany.

Inasmuch as the Delaware & Hudson Railroad also served the same two areas, John Jr. and Ed Grimes set one road against the other. The Delaware & Hudson seemed receptive but made no rate concession. Then Grimes wrote the head of traffic at the New York Central: "I am extremely discouraged about this whole matter of trying to work out rates with your railroad and I have just about come to the conclusion that probably the best thing for us to do is to immediately file a case with the Interstate Commerce Commission." The Company already had decided to use trucks for some of its deliveries to New York and New England customers. Trucks were, of course, anathema to the railroads. Grimes knew this and sent a moderately worded warning to the New York Central officer, citing a long list of customers receiving grain from Cargill via truck and ending his letter: "I believe you could reclaim most of this truck business out of Albany on your line if you published local rates similar to the rates you have out of Buffalo on a mileage basis."[12]

The problem with the Ogdensburg rates into New England seemed equally intractable. The Rutland Railroad, the owner of Cargill's leased Ogdensburg terminal, had the first small railroad leg into New England, but most of the trackage was that of the Central of Vermont, the Boston & Maine and the old foe, the New York Central. Here too, Cargill felt that it had to have lower rates to be competitive and inveighed against all three of these railroads—but to no avail. John Jr., quite upset by this, wrote his father once again about an appeal to the ICC, and ended: "It seems obvious that we have got to fight and fight vigorously unless we are to lose our commanding position in New England."

John Jr. was particularly adept at notions involving the positioning of the Company in a geographic context. Now he thought of an unconventional solution to the New England problem, elaborating a plan to his father that would "embarrass the railroads to a point where I think we can drive them into line." He had found some idle Portland, Maine, warehouses and also located ocean boats "in good running condition at unbelievably low figures . . . we had one offer on a boat which would carry 175,000 bushels of corn for $10,000, and it looks as though $7,500 would buy it." The plan involved filling the boat with grain at Albany and sending it to Portland, "where we would discharge the crew, and peddle our grain by truck. Whenever the boat was empty we would pick up a crew at Portland for a round trip to Albany and back, and be ready again for business in a week." John Jr. estimated that "we could deliver to Portland bakeries at 5¢ a bushel under what it costs them today by rail."[13]

Weeks went by with no results on the Albany–Oswego–Buffalo rate battle; Ed Grimes even wrote the New York Central traffic manager once more about the trucks: "If you cannot see your way clear to make anything better than a 3¢ differential and that is your final decision, we will have to meet the situation the best we can . . . if there is a diversion of freight from the railroads because of the seemingly unsound difference, I hope that the railroads will not take me to task because of this loss of traffic."

The Delaware & Hudson then edged forward with some compromise proposals. These leaked into the public press, with the *Albany Evening News* carrying a banner headline, "Grain Rates Cut to Boom Port," adding that it was "expected to be followed by similar action by the Central." The Delaware & Hudson traffic manager, outraged at the leak, wrote Grimes: "It seems to me very undesirable to have rates that we established featured in this manner in the public press. We have already received wires from the

Cargill's Ogdensburg, New York, elevator.

Buffalo grain interests, no doubt prompted by the newspaper articles in question."

The culprit on the news leak was Grimes himself. He wrote back: "The reporter that I talked to was from the *Times Union* and I was much surprised to note that night an article on the rates, which was so badly garbled as to the facts that I thought probably it would do very little harm. . . . I am exceedingly sorry if my talking to these reporters has resulted in any embarrassment to you." Grimes probably did this deliberately to prevent Delaware & Hudson from changing its mind—this letter certainly implies such a strategy.[14]

Eventually, the New York Central made grudging adjustments, matching the Delaware & Hudson offer. For the moment, Cargill decided to live with the rates, shelving the unusual Portland, Maine, proposal John Jr. had suggested to his father. Ed Grimes now did a turnabout, writing the Delaware & Hudson traffic head: "I want to assure you that the Albany office has very definite instructions to promote movement by rail over your line in every single instance where there is any possible chance for the use of rail facilities, and there will be no deviation from this policy."[15]

The Ogdensburg case was not so readily resolved, and the situation dragged on into 1934. Railroads throughout the country had difficulty in the depression maintaining even minimum profitability and in January 1932 had entered into agreements, country-wide, bringing about a wage reduction of 10 percent. These were to be phased out, beginning in mid-1934, with full restoration of the original wage scale by April 1, 1935. Faced with these heightened costs of operation, the railroads in many sections of the country now petitioned the ICC for rate increases. One of these was on the Ogdensburg–New England rate. Cargill earlier had succeeded in getting a favorable rail rate out of "the 'Burg" on the grounds that its port was more difficult to use. So its rate was 4.69 cents per bushel below the rate from Buffalo, while Oswego had a rate only 1½ cents below Buffalo. The railroads into New England also lowered the Ogdensburg differential to 1½ cents, contending that the two towns, Oswego and Ogdensburg, were essentially equivalent and the port at Ogdensburg had been improved. In March 1935, the ICC commissioners sided with the railroads.[16]

Taking heart from a dissenting opinion in this case, the Company decided to ask for a rehearing. To the surprise of almost everyone, the ICC Commission on Reargument reversed the commissioners, setting forth new reasoning. The Commission pointed out that the 1½-cent Oswego differential, established in a case back in 1926, was only for corn to be exported; inasmuch as Cargill's shipments into New England were all domestic, a 2½-cent differential for Ogdensburg was more proper. It was half-a-loaf for Cargill but certainly a welcome competitive gain.

Once more, there was a vigorous dissent, by Commissioner B. H.

Meyer. He asked, "If we make a shift at Oswego, how can we stop there and not do something as between Buffalo and Erie, and in that manner continue indefinitely up the Great Lakes?"[17]

Seaways and Canals

The St. Lawrence Seaway debate meanwhile became heated. The remaining constraint, a serious one, was in the "international rapids" section of the St. Lawrence. In 1895, the United States Congress had authorized a Deep Waterways Commission, and Presidents Theodore Roosevelt and William Howard Taft also pushed strongly in the first decade of the twentieth century for completion of the Seaway. Despite good intentions, however, the notion was very much in limbo in the early 1930s. The equivocating—mostly on the United States side—came from the competitive rate-making battle described above. If one's route was competitively effective, any dabbling in this by introducing new equations like the Albany Deepwater Port was threatening.

Cargill itself had a change in heart about the Seaway. Earlier, John MacMillan Sr. had ardently supported the plan. For example, in October 1920, he had written a Minneapolis business friend: "The early completion of this Deep-Waterway-to-the-Sea project is essential to business throughout the Northwest and Southwest." At that time, John Sr. saw the waterway as a chance to hold down rail rates.

While John Sr.'s optimism about railroad cooperation was misplaced, it was easy to see why he would support the St. Lawrence Seaway at that time, given the high transportation rates then in effect. By the early 1930s, with the precipitous fall in rates, many people, Cargill executives included, felt that the major cost of a Seaway project was not warranted. John Jr. wrote the chairman of the Albany Port: "We are now chartering space for Western Lake Ports to Montreal for the record breaking price of 4¢ per bushel. . . . It would not warrant any capital expenditures by the government to cheapen further the cost of moving grain from the Great Lakes to the sea." John Sr., writing a friend later in that year, estimated that "the St. Lawrence Seaway cannot possibly be justified . . . the total saving . . . would not exceed more than 1¢ or 2¢ per bushel." (Actually, this would be a substantial saving; as the Corps of Engineers' book *Transportation on the Great Lakes* (1937) put it, "It is well known that a saving of as little as one-fourth cent per bushel will serve to divert substantial movements of grain.")

It was not just the economics of Seaway construction that motivated Cargill to oppose it so vehemently, for now there was the presence of John Jr.'s brainchild, the Albany terminal. So the Company had a much-heightened vested interest in the flow of export grain through the Atlantic ports,

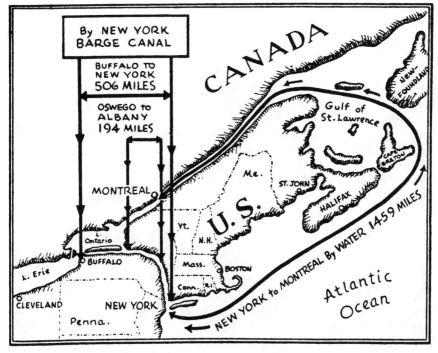

A pro–Erie Canal (and anti–St. Lawrence Seaway) map, mid-1930s (Francis P. Kimball, *New York–the Canal State*).

in particular the Albany–Hudson River–New York City route. The shipments by laker to Oswego and then by canalers from Oswego to Albany enhanced Cargill's use of the Albany terminal and was quite cost-effective for ocean shipping. If the St. Lawrence Seaway were to become a reality, Albany would be less desirable, and a Cargill terminal point beyond Ogdensburg might be necessary. Indeed, when the Seaway did open in 1958, Cargill built a huge terminal at Baie Comeau, Quebec, far out in the mouth of the St. Lawrence.

John Jr. skirted Cargill's self-interest when he discussed the St. Lawrence proposal with Marcus Marshall, the Albany manager:

New York and other North Atlantic states have aggressively opposed the construction of the greater St. Lawrence seaway, while the Middle West, generally, has supported the project. Some mid-Western people, like ourselves, have conscientiously opposed the St. Lawrence seaway in the sincere belief that in the interest of national unity and in the interest of procuring dependable low-cost transportation between the Middle West and the East, support should go toward the development of an all-American waterway, composed of the Great Lakes and connected Eastern United States waterways.[18]

The refurbishing of the Welland Canal in 1932 also stimulated other efforts on waterways in the country, notably those relating to the Mississippi River system. Bills had already been introduced into Congress for spending large sums on deepening the upper Mississippi channel. Cargill opposed this, as it did other expenditures for the Mississippi. This was succinctly put by Ed Grimes in May 1932, when he wrote a Minneapolis businessman: "In my opinion the River never will be able to successfully compete with the Great Lakes on grain. At the present time the rate Duluth to Montreal on wheat is 4¢ per bu., less than one-half the river rate Minneapolis to New Orleans." Grimes concluded with a prediction that subsequently turned out to be quite mistaken: "Grain and flour tonnage for export or domestic shipment will never be available in volume for the River, should it be completed."[19]

Trucking, and Backhaul Problems

The ferment in Cargill's eastern markets, exacerbated by what the Company felt were unfairly high transportation rates to New England out of Ogdensburg, had continued unrelieved. Throughout the war with the railroads in 1933 and 1934, Cargill had utilized common-carrier trucking to supplement its rail shipments. Then, when the adverse decision of the ICC on the Company's Ogdensburg rate case was announced in March 1935, Cargill moved to establish its own trucking fleet. Trucks were a new feature for grain companies, as they provided flexible delivery patterns that not only served customers well but also put great pressure on railroads for rate concessions. Yet the truck also gave the farmer more choices in delivering his grain to market. Formerly, farmers were limited in the area they could draw upon for delivery of their grain to elevators. Historically, with the horse and buggy this was just a few miles. By the 1930s farmers were buying the larger grain trucks for their own use and could deliver their grain efficiently and at low cost to any number of elevators all around them.

Early trucking efforts at Cargill's Albany terminal, late 1930s.

Thus, the grain companies faced some difficult decisions about elevator size and their geographic placement. Instead of a string of country elevators along railway lines, in many areas of grain country it soon made more sense for grain-trading organizations to build larger subterminals at strategic locations, both to have farmers' trucks come to them and for themselves to truck to rail, water or mill.[20]

At the start Cargill confined its new truck fleet to Albany, for shipment to other New York and New England locations. There were difficult backhaul problems here, for the natural movement of trade was from Albany and Ogdensburg to the east, and westbound loads were difficult to find. Traffic managers for rail, barge, truck, boat and air shipments alike always strive to have their carriers fully loaded at all times. In many cases this was difficult to do, as the natural flow for the goods being moved often leans strongly in one direction (e.g., grain shipments from the Midwest to eastern ports or the eastward flow of transatlantic air flights from the United States at the beginning of the summer tourist season). Hence, finding return loads for the transporting vehicle—its backhaul—becomes a challenge. For example, Cargill tried to develop westbound traffic with a Chicopee Falls, Massachusetts, rubber tire manufacturing company; this was difficult freight on which to develop long-term contracts. Backhaul continued to plague the Company. The central purpose of the trucking, however, to move Cargill's freight eastward, was a considerable success.[21]

Terminals—Albany and Other Sites

John Jr., seeking new ways of physically and geographically improving the Company, soon broached other innovative approaches to his colleagues. After the adverse ICC decision in the Ogdensburg case in March 1935, the impetus for an East Coast terminal increased. John Jr. cleverly linked this to a set of bargaining chips with the Albany Port District group. The Albany Port District's success began to persuade other businesses to look at properties in the Commission's port areas. One such property was next to Cargill. Back in 1932, John Jr. had stalled a Commission effort to bring in a competitive elevator by stating to its chairman: "Within a very short time we will wish to double the storage capacity of this plant. . . . If we are unable to build alongside it would then be necessary to duplicate the handling facilities elsewhere." In April 1935, John Jr. again tried to forestall competition, threatening the chairman about his Atlantic terminal plan: "We are well aware that you are under constant pressure to allocate . . . space to other industries. By so doing, however, you would definitely block further expansion of the elevator and we would probably be forced to build our storage at some other port, probably Newark, which would be undesirable both for us and for you."[22]

The truth was, of course, that John Jr. already was actively contemplating terminals at other locations, Newark most especially but also Providence, New Haven and Hartford. He wrote Grimes: "Frank has designed a very inexpensive house, not unlike a country elevator, which promises very cheap operation." John Jr. spelled this out in a letter to his father: "Studies indicate 18 plants could probably do about 36 million bushels of business by truck distribution along the seaboard, and I think we will need each and every one of these 18 plants before very long. It will require some 70 odd trucks to distribute this volume of business." He warned: "We really are in a very precarious situation . . . if someone else went in with these plants we would lose a very large part of our eastern business." Many rumors were circulating at that time that Continental Grain was planning further East Coast expansion. The very mention that "Continental might beat us to ———" (fill in almost any logical choice) seemed always to generate an instant response. Indeed, some Cargill people thought that John Jr. deliberately was using Continental as a bogeyman on occasion.[23]

John Jr.'s strategy was a complicated one: If Cargill's Albany terminal could not get competitive rail rates for delivery to customers in New England and the Middle Atlantic states, then these customers could be served by truck out of several smaller terminals at various East Coast ports. Cargill's own shipping (and other charters) could then supply these subterminals by going down the Hudson and into the Atlantic to the ports from which Cargill's trucks at the subterminals would deliver. In effect, the plan was another logical extension of John Jr.'s notion of the endless belt.

The movement of wheat and corn through the St. Lawrence and Erie canals for the years 1932–1935 are show in table 2.[24]

A comparison of the major North Atlantic ports compared in total receipts of grain in 1935 is outlined in table 3.[25]

Any such Cargill expansion would require financing, and John Jr. explained this to one of the Company's New York bankers: "The grain handling facilities that we have in mind would be elevators of a type larger than a country elevator but smaller than a terminal elevator. . . . Each would cost, we believe, in the neighborhood of $50,000." Further, not

TABLE 2

| | Via St. Lawrence Canals (in 1,000 bu.) | | Via the Erie Canal to New York (in 1,000 bu.) | |
	Wheat	Corn	Wheat	Corn
1932	90,363	4,974	22,840	2,367
1933	89,347	2,369	15,240	2,850
1934	53,101	2,746	15,290	2,823
1935	49,160	7,487	12,353	24

TABLE 3

| | Receipts (in 1,000 bu.) | | |
	By rail	By water	Total
Baltimore	4,938	3,739	8,677
Philadelphia	3,913	4,324	8,237
New York City*	6,529	22,403	28,932
Boston	1,299	3,097	4,396
Portland, Maine	N.A.	N.A.	6,961
St. John	6,362	245	6,607
Quebec	63	3,401	3,464
Montreal	6,481	61,894	68,375

*Includes Albany shipments.

just terminals alone would be needed: "The establishment of such units would materially increase the traffic on the Barge Canal and Cargill would need to acquire additional canal equipment." John Jr. asked for "satisfactory financing arrangements," somewhere between $1 million and $2 million.[26]

On a broad front, the Company entered complex negotiations with the port authorities at various possible sites. Fred Drum, Weston Grimes, Frank Neilson and John Jr. fanned out to Boston, Providence, New Haven, Hartford, Newark and Weehawken, to Philadelphia and to Pittsburgh, seeking deals favorable to the Company. Cargill was willing to own some of the possible properties but preferred the port authorities to build, with a long-term lease to Cargill as in Albany.

Newark was the key. John Jr. explained to his brother Cargill: "If we are to make a success of our other seaboard plants, we need enough storage in Newark so that we can in a pinch supply them during January and February in case of ice." John Jr. contemplated a 2-million-bushel terminal there. For the other locations, he planned smaller operations, four-bin structures, each bin holding 100,000 bushels.

The Boston notion foundered early, since new terminals had been built there by the railroads. The largest elevator served Continental Grain Company. Negotiations in Newark did produce a serious proposal, but construction costs would have been high because substantial pilings had to be placed, so the Newark proposal also was scrubbed. There were similar difficulties at the other locations. Thus the ambitious plan to plaster a whole set of New England and Middle Atlantic ports with Cargill-owned or -leased subterminals, with a larger feeder terminal at Newark, completely fell through, and the other tentative proposals were dropped. Once more, Cargill was thrown back to fighting rail rate battles as a mechanism for its distribution in the East.[27]

While the eventual favorable decision in the Ogdensburg rate case in July 1935 did provide Cargill a reasonable way to bring its grain into New England by rail, the competition from the two arch-rival grain trading companies, Louis Dreyfus and Continental Grain, required that the Company be alert to any innovations they might make. The aborted efforts to get an Atlantic port terminal left John Jr. with the urge to explore further intercoastal shipping.

There was one other terminal development in the East that came to fruition. Cargill already had its own terminal in Buffalo, having taken over the lease of the Canadian Pool elevator in 1932, when the changes that came out of the Ottawa conference made it less attractive for Canadian shippers to use Buffalo. Cargill had improved this property, and by the time of the negotiations with Newark and other East Coast centers, the Buffalo Pool terminal capacity was 1,900,000 bushels. Then, in 1936, the Company bought another Buffalo terminal, the "Great Eastern," acquiring an additional 1,900,000 bushels of capacity. Later in the 1930s, the Company purchased additional terminals in Buffalo, and the total Company capacity in Buffalo rose to over 11 million bushels. Buffalo proved to be an excellent location for training future senior management, Gordon Alexander and Irv Hyland, among others, being good examples.[28]

Ed Grimes had stated flatly in 1932 that the Mississippi River route was not going to be a realistic one for the grain trade. Perhaps he meant this merely as a bargaining gambit to puff up Albany, as the Mississippi was one of the great trade routes of the country and would be increasingly so for grain. Back as far as 1931, John Jr. had discussed a St. Louis terminal, and in early 1934 he revived this proposal. Public Works Administration funds were then available to cities for construction of new publicly owned terminals, and John Jr. conducted extensive negotiations with the mayor of St. Louis about a terminal there. John Jr. also contacted his longtime banking friend in St. Louis, Bert Lang. John Jr. proposed a plan modeled on the Omaha facility. The St. Louis version would have eight large bins of 1 million bushels each, together with some 75 small bins aggregating an additional 2 million bushels.

In the spring of 1935, the Memphis Harbor Commission also contacted John Jr. about a terminal. As Cargill already was involved in convoluted negotiations about a new Chicago terminal, John Jr. tried to hold off both the St. Louis and Memphis contingents. The Memphis group was more aggressive and soon pushed Cargill enough to persuade John Jr. that he needed to develop a proposal forthwith.

Perhaps it was the "squeaky wheel" principle, for the Memphis proposal moved to completion, and the St. Louis plan did not. The Memphis terminal, built by the Commission with Public Works Administration funds—Cargill's aversion to big government notwithstanding—was con-

Cargill's Electric Terminal Elevator, Buffalo.

Cargill's Great Eastern Terminal Elevator, Buffalo.

Cargill's Memphis terminal elevator, c. 1953.

siderably smaller than the Omaha terminal, although similar in function and appearance. The concept of the large bin was there, and its profile looked like the Omaha terminal. The location was ideal for water, rail and truck handling, and the terminal had a storage capacity of 1,650,000 bushels. In 1937, Cargill leased it on a long-term basis and put it in full operation.

Again, however, Cargill ran into competitive problems. Grimes described this to a colleague in Memphis: "I have started some discussions with the railroads with the objective [of] less of a penalty for water inbound grain. . . . I am hopeful of proving to the rail carriers that they will handle a very much larger volume of tonnage and receive substantially greater revenue if they will abandon the obsession that they have for discriminating against grain that moves into the port by water."

Although this Memphis terminal was small in terms of capacity, compared to other Company operations, it was critical in that it gave Cargill access to the South (the Memphis terminal was built primarily for domestic, not export business). This Mississippi River–Gulf route for waterway shipment of grain later became much more important. In the 1960s, Cargill established "unit train" rail shipments southward to Gulf ports and these became a dominant feature of grain shipment abroad. The importance of the Memphis terminal for Cargill was far more than just its volume of shipment.[29]

Western Markets

Cargill was ambitious for a global reach but had not yet shipped much grain westward. Canada had increased shipments from its British Columbia ports since the late 1920s and from the crop year 1927–1928 through the crop year 1932–1933 sent an average of almost 80 million bushels of wheat per year through these ports. West Coast export shipments of United States–grown grain were considerably smaller by comparison. For example, the largest West Coast port for wheat exports was Portland, Oregon, which averaged only 12.6 million bushels per year for the years 1929–1933. San Francisco exported considerably less wheat but averaged 7.8 million bushels per year of barley sent abroad in this same time span.[30]

While there was not a strong increase in the shipments from the West Coast of the United States in the early 1930s, the Asian markets were becoming relatively more important. Further, in the mid-1930s, the Dust Bowl began to affect production in the Great Plains wheat fields, and shipping from the West Coast began to move through the Panama Canal for delivery to Gulf and Atlantic ports and to Europe. Western wheat could be delivered to some of the eastern states by ocean shipping at a price comparable to the wheat grown in the East.

Pushed by this development, Cargill opened a West Coast office at Portland in the spring of 1934. Prospects for wheat exports seemed good; and in April 1935, John Jr. wrote E. T. Pettersen, the Portland manager, of his interest in finding a West Coast terminal: "What we are seeking is a cheap way. . . . The idea of leases appeals to us because if our experience is not favorable . . . we can drop them and then build plants which our experience tells us would be suitable to our requirements." Pettersen turned up the possibility of leasing a West Seattle terminal, an old-style flat-storage building in which wheat had been bagged for export shipment. Substantial bagging of grain was still done at this time on the West Coast (indeed, a huge western crop just before World War II had brought a shortage of bags, and wheat had to be stored on the ground). Although this was not the ideal solution to Cargill's problem, the Company signed a lease and added the 770,000-bushel terminal. Cargill had also opened a San Francisco office in December 1934, first staffed by Fred Seed, who later rose to senior management in the Company. The two offices at Portland and San

Francisco, along with the West Seattle terminal, gave Cargill a more permanent West Coast presence in the trade.

Asian Markets

Once on the West Coast, Cargill made a series of new contacts, many with firms and countries with which the Company had had little experience. John Peterson helped with some of these, particularly those involving Japanese trading companies. He wrote Pettersen:

In your dealings with these Japanese you must be very careful not to make any slip as to their authority. Out of my great experience with the Japanese I have found them to be a very loyal, friendly people, and these gentlemen that are sent to America to represent those great concerns like Mitsui & Company, Mitsubishi, etc., are all very high-class men. . . . In your dealings with them you will be safe in going ahead on the principle that anything you do with Mitsui & Company or Mitsubishi will be with very high grade people and entitled to high consideration. . . . They are in a way a formal lot, these Japanese, what with their bowing and scraping and the like of that. By all means be friendly with them, and if you act that way I am sure you will get into their good graces. Once established with them it is easy to work with them.[31]

Towboats, Barges, Boats

John Jr. and Cargill MacMillan had been "crazy about boats" since their early childhood. When Edna MacMillan took the two youngsters to Geneva in 1907, John Sr. wrote her: "Tell John I enjoyed his drawings so much. I hope both he and Cargill will keep it up. I would like to have them try other things than merely boats." Apparently this advice was not taken, for a few weeks later he wrote again: "This boat is very good. But I should like him to draw something else. Have him draw from real life— trees, houses, or anything that strikes his fancy and also from pictures. But I don't want them to confine themselves to boats."[32]

Once John Jr. began taking a major role at Cargill in the mid-1920s, his thoughts always had included the possibility that the Company would own and operate shipping. There was an important rationale for this, explained Cargill MacMillan in a letter in February 1937: "Hays and Julius are convinced that . . . we are going to be crucified on some of our charters . . . we must have some boats of our own to keep the boat owners honest."

As early as 1931, just a year after Cargo Carriers Incorporated (CCI) was formed as the transportation arm of the Company, John Jr. was dickering for "one, possibly two" boats for Great Lakes shipping, in the 200,000- to 250,000-bushel capacity. Nothing happened until 1935 when the steamer *Mayan* became available. Built in Toledo, Ohio, in 1919, it was just over

248 feet in length, with a beam of 44 feet and gross tonnage of 2,571. Cargill paid its owner, the Mitchell Steamship Corporation, $30,000 for the vessel. The *Mayan* was to be used as an intercoastal ship to move grain and other products, like coal, to and from Albany and Atlantic ports. In late September 1935, John Jr. personally inspected the vessel and wired Cargill MacMillan: "I think she is exactly what we require altho not much to look at. . . . They tell me the *Mayan* has a bad name account her former owners were deadbeats so we will have to change her name before we commission her. Think one up for us." But he couldn't, and the name stuck.

In December 1935, the *Mayan* made its maiden voyage under CCI. *Cargill News* reported: "Amid cheers of farewell and bon voyage from the Albany staff en-masse, and many prominent Cargill officials, accompanied by whistles from the many harbor craft, the SS *Mayan* cast off her lines from the Albany pier and with flags flying, proudly set her course for Norfolk." In January, when Marcus Marshall, the head of the Albany terminal went aboard, *Cargill News* proudly called it a "palatial liner." Some expenditures were made on the vessel in Norfolk, and it returned to Albany in the spring of 1936. For the first months in 1936, the *Mayan* made 14 round trips between Hampton Roads, Virginia, and "Down-East" ports (as *Cargill News* put it); all cargoes were coal.

However, there were difficulties with the *Mayan*. First, the whole intercoastal plan had fallen through. Second, there were problems with its deep draft, over 20 feet. Some of the harbors where Cargill had hoped to find

The tug Protector *partially sunk in a Hudson River flood, late 1930s.*

dockside terminal space had less than a 20-foot draft. The inner harbor at Baltimore, for example, had to be rejected as too shallow. Finally, John Jr. reluctantly came to the conclusion that the *Mayan* was not going to work well for the Company, and it was disposed of in November 1936 at a profit of $15,319.[33]

In 1935, Cargill acquired another vessel, again a first for the Company—the tug *Protector*. It was a diesel-powered, wooden-hulled vessel, powered by a 220-hp engine, to be used as the Company's own Erie Canal towboat. The boat was some 70 feet long, had an 18-foot beam, and accommodated nine people aboard. Originally, it had been a light ice-breaking vessel and often had been used as a reception tug in Boston Harbor. As it had not been built originally as a towboat, there was a problem, as Marcus Marshall described it: "The barges are 15 feet high. . . . 'Protector' at its highest point is 14 1/2 feet above the water line, and the barges, light, are about 13 1/2 high . . . how could we see to steer, as the tug is lashed absolutely rigid to the stern of the barge. So, we cut a hole through the roof of the Pilot house so that the Captain could stand up through the roof, thereby giving him clear vision ahead."

But now the problem was how to control the steering of the towboat from on top of the roof, for the *Protector* had a hand steering wheel. After trying several devices, the towboat was finally equipped with a hydraulic steering device, with controls added on the top of the roof. Marshall described further problems: "As the clearance under some of the bridges was so low that the barge and tug just barely cleared . . . it was necessary to make three steering points—one in the pilot house which can be used when the barge is loaded; one on top of the roof when the barge is light, this wheel being removable and a third, located in the ceiling of the pilot house, so that when the barge is light and clearance is very close, the Captain has to remove his wheel from the roof, duck down into the hole and use the steering wheel in the ceiling of the pilot house." For John Jr., necessity in this case truly was the mother of invention!

In this mid-1930s period, barges for charter on the Erie Canal were often in short supply. All were made of wood then, most of them of limited capacity (holding about 23,000 to 26,000 bushels). Once Cargill had its own towboat, purchase of barges was the logical next step. Cargill began buying these old-style wooden barges in early 1937, eventually acquiring six. Their condition was so shabby that they were carried on the books at a sum of $215 each.

The excitement of barging with these old units—and their inefficiency—was evocatively described by Captain O'Brien of the towboat *Protector* in the June 1937 issue of *Cargill News*. Lack of speed by the ancient combination caused problems on the Hudson River: "It is a surprise if we proceed six miles in six hours of tide bucking." Slow speed also meant slow maneuver, and as the Hudson had many cross-overs (where the channel crossed from one side of the river to the other), care had to be taken when another boat came downstream moving much faster with the current and rushing toward the *Protector*.

At Troy, the first government lock allowed only a two-barge length— the minimum size of the Erie locks was 300 feet in length, 44.5 feet in width. Seven barges were in the *Protector*'s tow, each 100 feet by 20 feet, and since the *Protector* was an additional 70 feet, some of the barges had to be temporarily "parked." At the Head of the Flight, the highest point of the canal (near Waterford), there was a series of five locks, each only a quarter of a mile apart. Four barges were taken up through all five locks, then parked, allowing the *Protector* to return to Waterford for the other three barges. Each of these locks had approximately a 25-foot lift and had been hewn through rock some 50 feet high on each side.

From the Head of the Flight to Little Falls, there were 11 more locks, ranging from 3 to 11 miles apart. After leaving Utica and Rome, the Canal became Lake Oneida. As it was a treacherous lake in a windstorm (the shallowness of the lake making the waves short and choppy and therefore more dangerous), the captain would always stop at Lock 22 for a weather report; if the wind was blowing from the northwest at more than 15 miles an hour, a tow generally did not go on the lake.

Near Rochester, the Genesee River crossed the canal, and the currents could be quite swift if there had been heavy rain in its upper reaches. When it was fast, tow captains would take only half their tow across at one time. O'Brien told of problems on *Protector*'s first trip: "Soon after we started across the river we could see by our barges that the river was plenty fast. They started to swing down the river. We had to give the tug more power to break the boats and when they did the head boat headed for one shore and the fourth boat whipped around and was part way down the river."

The rest of the trip onward to Buffalo generally was uneventful, although sometimes a current had to be contended with in the Niagara River. Adventure notwithstanding, the negative message conveyed by this process of barging with outmoded equipment was not lost on John Jr. In the winter of 1938, he made an important decision about the Company's barging equipment, a move that was to bring about a major innovation.[34]

The "Carneida Type"

The antiquated wooden barges were now phased out—by two steps. First, in the winter of 1938–1939, before the shipping season, the Company bought six modern wooden barges, at a substantial total cost of $50,000. These would be the units handled by the towboat *Protector*. Second, Cargill entered the shipbuilding business itself for the very first time. The reasons Cargill itself became the builder, rather than using an outsider specializing in towboats, are interesting.

John Jr. not only was substantially involved in shipping but also was an amateur boat designer, although up to this time only on paper. In observing the Erie Canal shipments of the Company, he came to hold three strong views. First, Cargill's towboat-barge combination was too slow, the O'Brien story of bucking the tide on the Hudson a vivid example. Second, he saw that when the towboat and barges went through the locks, there was much space around the combination—front, back and sides—that could be filled by a larger barge. Third, if a towboat-barge unit could be somehow made into one rigid unit, it would be safer in winding its way through the twists and turns of the river and canal and much of the time spent in detaching and reattaching the various barges at each lock, so well documented by O'Brien, might be completely eliminated.

Thus, John Jr. evolved in his mind a wholly new way to construct both towboats and barges, a configuration that later was named the "*Carneida* type." It was to be an integrated unit, wide enough to fill the locks almost completely. There would be four sections, and these would be held together by two steel cables fastened on each side of the first section, an-

The Carneida *filling an Erie Canal lock, late 1930s.*

chored on each side of the last section and running along the decks of the four sections. The cables were to be tightened or slackened by means of a winch. The barge itself was to be made of steel, single-skin, with no bilge, that is, no false bottom. However, the Company could not find any outside contractors who would build such a barge. The notion of the less sturdy single skin and the huge size that seemed to squeeze the locks apparently made the conventional builders back off.

At this point John Jr. made the decision that the Company would be the builder. He hired a new man, Chris Jensen, soon to be known as "the Wild Dane," who went to Albany from Minneapolis to set up a shipbuilding operation from scratch. Over the winter and early spring of 1938–1939, a four-barge steel unit was completed. It consisted of three sections, each 60 feet long, and one 45 feet long, all with beams of 43 feet and each divided into 15-foot compartments. With the *Protector* behind it, the total came to 295 feet, just 5 feet short of the length of the smallest lock. The day that Chris Jensen launched the four, one started to sink. It was soon learned that the problem was only a seacock that had been left open, and all four were determined to be seaworthy.

Now the question came, would the unorthodox combination work? The nagging concern was whether the barge was perhaps too wide to be able to go through the locks successfully—the theoretical clearances were there, but would it work practically? The *Cargill News* reported on the first trip:

We left the Elevator and started up the Hudson River. Everything progressed as planned. Mr. Neilson, Chris Jensen and myself [Marcus Marshall, the Albany superintendent] were with the crew. We went through the three bridges at Albany O.K., and everything ran fine until we came to the first lock located at Troy, N.Y., called the Government Lock. Chris, Frank and myself all stood on the bow as we neared the lock, and I think the same question was in all our minds.

We were all sizing up the entrance into the lock with the width of the barge and the question was "Will she go in?" When Captain O'Brien had it lined up and we were only 100 feet from the lock, the Captain called out, "It's too late now, Chris, if you made any mistakes in your measurements." Chris turned to me and said, 'I'm afraid she won't go,' and believe me that cigar caught hell until that barge entered the lock. With the rub-rails on the barge, we had only 1½ feet clearance in the lock. In other words, 9 inches on each side.

With the success of this unit, Cargill was now able to persuade a New York City contractor, J. K. Welding Company, to build a second similar unit. This four-section unit was 265 feet long. A new towboat was specially built to Cargill dimensions, powered with a 240-hp engine, and only 49 feet long—an unusual combination of short length and large horsepower (the *Protector*, at 70 feet, was powered with a 220-hp engine).

There was another innovation, too. The maximum lock length was 300 feet, the barge was 265 feet, and the towboat was 49 feet; simple addition shows that the total unit was 314 feet long. The Cargill plan solved this by creating a large 15-foot V-notch into the back of the rear barge unit, exactly congruent with the extended V of the front of the new towboat (called the *Carbany*, a combination of "Cargill" and "Albany"). Thus, the total length was 299 feet, just 1 foot short of the total size of the lock. Now there would be just 9 inches space on each side, only 6 inches on each end.

Once again, the new *Carbany* and its four barges went through the locks with aplomb. As the new units, now designated CCI No. 2 and CCI No. 3, respectively, began to ply the Erie/Hudson waterways, the Company took quite a ribbing for their operation. *Cargill News* reported on this:

It was quite interesting, as we entered the different locks, to hear the comments of the people standing on the locks. They would run something like this. "There is a lot of money spent for tin cans that will never work. Wait until they get high water and then see what happens." We heard one lock tender call the other saying, "That bunch of tin cans with an outboard motor behind it is going towards you," and then when the second unit, or CCI No. 3 came out with even a shorter tug, one lock tender says, "My God, they got the outboard motor in the back end of the barge."

John Jr. crowed to Ed Grimes, "the 'sardine fleet' as the boys call our new unit . . . is very successful . . . performing better than we ever expected."

The difference in capacities and speeds between the wooden units and the steel units was astounding. The six modern wooden barges of the Company could carry 120,000 bushels of wheat, but the unit would take a total of 11 days to make a round trip between Albany and Oswego, using a crew of 13 men. The new steel barges would make that same round trip, carrying 96,500 bushels in as short a time as eight days, using a crew only of nine. The locking time of the wooden fleet was about one hour. The new barges could be locked in about 10 minutes. The wooden fleet could make about 3 mph loaded and about 5 mph light; the steel units could make 5.6 mph loaded and 7.5 mph light. These speeds were based on a draft of 10 feet, used at that time because of the 12-foot draft of the Canal. This draft was going to be deepened to 14 feet; if this happened, Cargill could load to a deeper draft of approximately 11 1/2 feet, thus increasing the carrying capacity of the steel units another 20 percent.

In sum, Cargill—particularly, John Jr.—had successfully put into effect a major waterways innovation, one that would have far-reaching consequences all over the country.[35]

A Cargill Towboat Fleet

The success of Cargill's Erie Canal towboats and steel barges encouraged John Jr. to develop new ideas. The *Carbany* and its companion notched-barge unit (CCI No. 3) became the models. The smaller length of

The Carbany *in 1938, with Captain Praeger steering through a hole in the roof.*

the *Carbany* and the 15-foot notch in the rear towboat gave the maximum capacity for the Erie Canal lock system. Now John Jr. wanted more and would order five new complete towboat/barge units by the end of the year 1939.

The first and second of the new towboats, to be identical to the *Carbany*, were to be built by Bethlehem Steel Corporation at its Leetsdale yards near Pittsburgh. Some steel barges would continue to be built by Cargill itself at its new "shipyard" at Albany, and others would be purchased from outside builders. The cost for four of the towboats was in the range of $70,000 each (one, lower-powered, was in the $50,000 range), and the steel barge units each cost just over $50,000. Thus, John Jr. had made the decision to expend over $600,000, Cargill to own all the units outright.[36]

The first two towboats to be delivered in the summer of 1940 were the *Carswego* (Oswego) and the *Carneida* (Oneida). The next three to be completed by the summer of 1940, were the *Carchester* (Rochester), the *Carnectady* (Schenectady) and the *Carnesee* (Genesee). The financing of the latter three towboats, a substantial sum, concerned John Jr. Once again, he argued for an "opportunity cost" decision, writing John Peterson in December 1939:

I realize perfectly that our general credit is not going to be good until the Board of Trade case is settled. . . . The trouble with waiting for that, however, is that if we delay we will not be able to get our equipment for the opening of navigation. . . . If the war continues through next summer we will have a very brisk and continuous export demand all summer, with high freight rates both on the Canal and the St. Lawrence River. . . . If this is the case, we might conceivably pay for them the first year, although in peacetime . . . it would take about three years to pay out.

Despite the general unease in the Company about the financial effects of the Corn Case, Peterson readily agreed to the financing arrangements, and the contracts for the entire set of five units were now in place.[37]

The Sinking of the Carneida

With the towboat *Carbany* delivered and in service on the Erie Canal by late 1939, Company officials eagerly awaited the arrival of the additional towboats and steel-barge units ordered from the shipyards of Bethlehem. The first unit, the towboat *Carneida* and three steel barges, was to be delivered in the early summer of 1940. All had been built at the Pittsburgh location, but were to be used on the Erie Canal, so a substantial trip lay ahead for the units—down the Ohio River, up the Mississippi and Illinois rivers and the Illinois-Michigan Canal and then through Lakes Michigan, Huron and Erie to Buffalo. This would be a major test of the seaworthiness of the units.

Frank Neilson had argued that the towboat should be sent separately from the barges, but John Jr. telegraphed back: "It looks to me as though it is out of question not to bring our fleets around as units. We need the experience of all of them on the lakes and also as much river experience as possible which we would not be getting the other way."

So in the third week of July, the *Carneida*, lashed together with its three barges began the trip down the Ohio River. Captain O'Brien was on board and sent John Jr. a telegram on July 29: "Going fine. Lost lot of time in fog. Lights on bow not working. Making seven miles per hour. Engine running fine." John Jr. was excited about his new vessel and decided to fly to Cairo, Illinois; there he went aboard for the trip up the Mississippi and Illinois rivers. He wired his father and brother on August 8: "Expect to make Chicago in three days running time . . . against a rising river and 4 miles current. The *Carneida* fully up to expectations. Urge Cargill to join us enroute."

Immediately upon arrival at Cargill's Chicago terminal, the barges were loaded with 1,900 tons of bagged corn. On August 15, the publication *Modern Miller* sent a telegram to John Jr., asking details for what was, to use their words, a "first trip of its kind." John Jr. wired the full story and ended: "She was designed to fit as closely as possible in the locks of the Erie Canal and it is hoped that she will carry more cargo than any single locking unit theretofore to transit the Erie Canal."

Neilson himself would be on board, and he wired John Jr. of the imminent departure into Lake Michigan. John Jr. replied: "What is the weather like and was the radio phone working when they left?" John Jr. himself had been predicting weather for the earlier part of the *Carneida* trip; he had been so accurate that Philip Sayles had wired Cargill MacMillan: "What will that fellow do next. Better get him on the payroll."

Later on that day, August 17, another telegram arrived: "She is in sight now about half way between Chicago and So. Chicago and has been for some time this morning. Would assume from the maneuvering they are adjusting compass."

It was more than just maneuvering—there was trouble. The day was windy and the seas high. On August 22, 1940, those seas swamped the towboat and two of the three barges, which promptly sank in 70-foot waters. The third broke lose and floated away. Eleven of the twelve men escaped in the lifeboat. One man, the radio technician, was washed overboard and remained in the water 90 minutes before the lifeboat was able to pick him up. Unfortunately, the lifeboat itself began to split its seams and was just about to swamp when the Coast Guard (who had been summoned by radio from the towboat before it sank) appeared and found the men "crowded in a small lifeboat which was shipping water fast." All were rescued and brought ashore.

John Jr.'s telegram to John Peterson on August 23 confirmed the loss: "You have undoubtedly read the gossip about loss of the *Carneida*. We do not know yet what happened but fortunately no one was injured. Hays says we are fully insured but we may yet have a dispute with the insurance companies as there is some kind of joker in their confirmations to us." The towboat and the two lost barges lay in about 78 feet of water some eight miles off the shoreline near Wilmette, Illinois.

By the first week in September, the Company had a diver on the site; Neilson reported to John Jr.: "Diver on towboat yesterday. The units are still connected. Resting right side up and on a coarse gravel bottom. He reports large holes in forward end and a pile of corn outside that end. Am trying to get someone to bid on corn removal. He brought up some corn and it looked okay." Later, substantial amounts of the corn were brought up, but efforts to raise the towboat over the following weeks were unsuccessful.

The conventional way to salvage a boat of this size was by using huge inflatable pontoons. Neilson wanted to try another, cheaper way—to winch the towboat and the barges to the surface. The weather was bad that fall, and he could not make his system work. Finally, in May of the following year (1941), the towboat was raised by Neilson's method. He reported to John Jr. on the vessel's condition: "Both main engines and aux[iliaries] have been run and there is no apparent damage. Celotex and floor covering in good shape. No hull damage. Beds and furniture about gone. Reconditioning of towboat should be very reasonable." One of the two barges also was brought up at that time, once more using Neilson's winch method, and a few weeks later the other barge also was hoisted to the surface.[38]

It was an expensive accident for the Company. When the *Carneida* and its barges went down in August 1940, their entire cost had to be moved from the CCI property register to the Cargill, Incorporated, books—a sum of some $116,000. Fortunately, with the Neilson salvage efforts finally successful, both the towboat and the barges were put right back into service, so only a small portion of this amount had to be written off as a loss: Neilson's salvage costs turned out to be relatively small. It was a costly endeavor in human terms, however, for Neilson got wet and overtired, possibly a factor in his ill health that began in early World War II.

The next towboat/barge combination (the *Carchester* and its steel barges) was brought down the Ohio and up the Illinois and through the Great Lakes without incident; the other units were delivered over the later months of 1940 in the same fashion. Only minimum loads were put on the barges while on the lakes, however, so as not to repeat the *Carneida* disaster.

More Transportation Battles

A momentous confrontation took place on the domestic transportation scene in the period 1939–1941 that provided a window on some profound changes taking place in the country's basic transportation patterns. The issue involved a rate battle between barge lines and railroads.

The 1930s had witnessed slowly increasing use of the Illinois and Michigan Canal, particularly after the building of the so-called Illinois Waterway section in 1933 allowing larger barges entry into Chicago from the Illinois River. The grain traders and the barge companies took quick advantage of this, the former group building new terminals along the Illinois River (Continental Grain and Norris being the largest) and the barge companies providing the service.

Shipments of grain by barge now skyrocketed. In 1933, when the Illinois Waterway was originally opened, some 38,000 bushels of corn were shipped

Loading by truck to barge, Missouri River, c. 1947.

by barge into Chicago—but rail shipments were 91,432,000 bushels, some 2,400 times as much. By 1939, over 13 million bushels of corn came by barge, with rail down slightly to 65 million, so rail was now just five times as much. Truck shipments of grain into Chicago, incidentally, had almost quadrupled in this same period. Barge shipments of wheat, oats and soybeans were also increasing but not at the rate of corn. Inasmuch as downstate Illinois was "corn country," those escalating corn shipments were really a critical loss for the railroads.

They began to use their potent rate-making power to fight back. Late in 1939, the railroads published rates for shipment of grain eastward from Chicago that explicitly excluded "ex-barge" grains (those that had come into Chicago by barge) from sharing in the more favorable "proportional rates" on the eastward rail leg. Inasmuch as a large amount of this grain did go through Chicago and on eastward either directly or after being stored, this was a severe competitive disadvantage for shippers by barge. Immediately, a case was brought forward to the ICC by a group of protestants, which included several barge companies along with the key grain companies involved. In the latter group, Continental Grain and Norris took the major role, but Cargill joined with them in the protest even though the Company did not yet have terminals along the Illinois River. Other organizations intervened and/or filed briefs.

The situation presented the Chicago Board of Trade with an interesting dilemma. Many of its members were large grain-trading companies interested in the lowest possible rates and so joined with the barge companies. A number of other smaller CBOT commission houses, trading from central Illinois points other than along the Illinois River, favored the discrimination against barge shippers. At that time, the CBOT leadership was dominated by the commission houses. Expectedly, the board of the Exchange voted to intervene on the side of the railroads. Later, as the case progressed, a change in the leadership at the Exchange increased representation for terminal merchants, and the CBOT shifted to a neutral position in the case. Another intervener, a surprising one, was the United States Department of Agriculture. While the USDA was not willing to take a position favoring either rail or barge, it entered the case on the limited premise of protecting the farmer to ensure the lowest possible shipping cost.

The case progressed through the administrative maze of the ICC and was finally decided by the commissioners on July 31, 1941. In a complex opinion, covering some 46 pages, a majority favored the rail argument and ordered that the proportional rates of grain going east could not be shared in by "ex-barge" grain. There was a strong dissenting opinion by one of the commissioners.

Given the great importance of the case, the protestants promptly carried the case to the appeal group, the full ICC commissioners, acting as a Commission on Reconsideration. Once again, the railroads won the case, but this time there was a lengthy, telling dissent by Joseph B. Eastman, the renowned chairman of the Commission. Eastman was just about to be appointed Roosevelt's director of the Office of Defense Transportation, and this was his last major case before leaving the ICC.

Eastman's was a sophisticated analysis, with the kind of documentation that dissenting lawyers hope always to have for future cases. He was blunt in his feelings that farmers would be hurt by the pricing pattern established by the case. Further, Eastman chose not to soft-pedal the issue of the basic competition between rail and barge; his brief said in part: "It is significant that a witness for respondents testified that the schedules under suspension were proposed 'with a hope that we could drive this business off the water and back onto the rails where it belongs.' In the final analysis," said Eastman, "this is a case where it is proposed to charge persons shipping ex-barge grain a greater compensation than is charged other persons shipping ex-rail or ex-lake grain for a 'like and contemporaneous service.' " This violated the law, Eastman averred. An Eastman opinion was always one of importance; this lengthy, analytical effort would be used by both protestants and respondents many times in the future.[39]

This time the barge shippers lost the battle—but their war against the railroads was to continue almost unabated. In 1940, the United States Congress passed a new Transportation Act, designed explicitly to bring motor carrier and barge line companies under the jurisdiction of the ICC. While the Act did just that, in the case of the barge lines the exemptions made the regulation of that industry almost minimal. In particular, if a barge line transported no more than three commodities in bulk or if the cargo was liquid in bulk, no regulation could be imposed. Inasmuch as grain shipments made up a huge percentage of the barge lines' traffic, this was a critically important constraint on regulation. There would be many more chapters to the rail–barge battle (indeed, it became a three-way battle between rail, barge and truck). Round one, however, was over.

CHAPTER FOURTEEN

The Late 1930s

When Franklin Delano Roosevelt was reelected to the presidency in November 1936, it was by a landslide; he carried every state but Maine and Vermont. With an overwhelming majority in both the Senate and the House, the outlook seemed euphoric for the Democrats. FDR's inaugural speech on January 20, 1937, stressed "social justice," and he followed with a plan to counter the invalidation of his programs by the Supreme Court. He proposed to reorganize that body, a notion that soon was dubbed by the press as "packing the Supreme Court." Outraged debates on this plan lasted over the spring. Roosevelt lost this battle, but the issue inflamed the business community perhaps more than any other single Roosevelt initiative.

An incipient "prosperity" in early 1937 had proved false. Mass unemployment continued, and industry remained sluggish. Only government deficit spending kept things moving. Inflation now threatened, and Roosevelt answered with severe budget cuts. This triggered a recession that soon became pronounced.

Once again Roosevelt appeared indecisive, not able to choose between that cadre in the administration who advocated governmental intervention (many influenced by the 1936 book of John Maynard Keynes, *The General Theory of Employment, Interest and Money*) and his conservative advisors who were preaching a balanced budget and who believed that the administration needed to cater to business to persuade it to invest. The President aligned himself with the former. Harold Ickes wrote: "The President feels that the big money interests are in an 'unconscious conspiracy.'" Yet Roosevelt let the conservatives hold sway for the rest of 1937. The liberals countered by stepping up their rhetoric against business. Assistant Attorney General Robert Jackson spoke of the "strike of capital against reform," and Ickes charged that "America's Sixty Families" had once again renewed "the old struggle between the power of money and the power of the Democratic instinct." William Leuchtenburg, writing of Roosevelt's dilemma, likened him to Hoover, "the victim of his own hubris."[1]

The Farm Bloc rushed into this vacuum, advancing its plans for a second AAA. Despite short-term scarcities bred by the drought in 1936, Secretary of Agriculture Henry Wallace had continued to push the ever-normal granary, returning over and over to the Old Testament story of Joseph in Egypt. In a speech in August 1936, he even characterized his plan as "the Joseph Idea."

If scarcity had seemed the pattern after the 1936 drought, the crop year 1937–1938 brought back surpluses. Crops around the world were excellent, a combination of record sown acreage and high yields, due, said the editors of *Wheat Studies*, "principally . . . to nature." Grain prices had been sagging all through this crop year. Chicago cash wheat, for example, had drifted downward from more than $1.25 in July 1937, to a point below 70 cents one year later. Farm groups all over the world insisted that prices be held steady. A *Wheat Studies* editorial decried this insistence on "super-economic prices" as "palpably uneconomic." The *Wheat Studies* experts particularly took aim at Wallace's Joseph Idea: "Wheat growers have been increasingly led to expect that if a big crop came, it would be welcome to fill an 'ever-normal granary,' and that their financial interests would be assiduously safeguarded."

In the face of such surpluses, high prices could be accomplished only by governmental intervention. Thus was born the "second AAA." Faced with a seething farm rebellion, Congress passed a statute that provided a concept of "parity" for the five principal crops, coupled with acreage allotments for these. The soil conservation plan of the 1936 legislation was continued. Commodity loans would be provided to farmers for storing surpluses in big crop years. Producers of corn, wheat, cotton, tobacco and rice could obtain storage loans to put a floor under prices, which would allow them to finance the holding of surplus supplies. Each farm would be given a marketing quota after a positive referendum on the quota by producers in that area. If the loans and quotas were still too low in light of the goals of "parity," the Secretary of Agriculture was authorized to make direct subsidy payments. There was also a crop insurance plan for wheat.

A threat to any subsidy program is the possibility that a country might price itself out of the world market. This time the United States government made certain it did not repeat its ill-starred blunder of the 1930 Farm Board period. After three years as a net importer of wheat (1934, 1935 and 1936, the first years this had ever happened), the United States became the second largest wheat exporter in 1937–1938, only Australia being larger. Some of this increase was accounted for by the removal in early 1938 of the Dominion preference provisions in the United Kingdom.

Cargill itself had had spotty and relatively small foreign sales through the early and mid-1930s. However, in this 1937–1938 crop year, 28 million bushels were sold abroad, much through brokers contacted by C. C. Boden, manager of the New York office. This constituted almost 25 percent of the entire Company's sales.

The crop year 1938–1939 once again was very prolific. There was a "super abundance of wheat," said *Wheat Studies*, and cotton, too, was nearing a glut. The United States government dumped over 128 million bushels of wheat abroad in the crop year 1938–1939, losing some 29 cents on each bushel. Similar export subsidies were needed for cotton.[2]

Once Roosevelt had initiated more government intervention in the spring of 1938, the antimonopoly attack was stepped up. On April 29, the President asked Congress for funds to investigate "the concentration of economic power." This led to the establishment of the Temporary National Economic Committee (TNEC). Businessmen around the country worried as the TNEC began to schedule hearings, which ultimately lasted almost three years. Earlier, the grain trade had been investigated by the Federal Trade Commission; the former wondered if they would again be put under the microscope.[3]

The shift by the Roosevelt administration toward harsher policies regarding the business community once again raised questions in the minds of Cargill's owners about the advisability of moving part of the Company operations abroad. Cargill MacMillan proposed "to remove 10% of our working capital from the jurisdiction of the United States," and John Jr. had a more radical notion: "We would . . . be well advised to liquidate entirely our business in the United States. There seems very little real understanding in Washington of the nature of the problem, let alone with the disposition to work out a solution along rational lines." Again, however, no specifics were proposed, and the idea lay dormant.[4]

Retrenchment

John Jr. had predicted solid company performance for the crop year 1937–1938. He was wrong, and the results were dreadful. The Grain Account lost over $1.4 million and the net loss for the Company was over $1.1 million. The Corn Case had been costly. Working capital had been pushed down almost $800,000. The Company paid its preferred stock dividend and a modest 3 percent dividend on the common stock. Operating losses for this year were $998,000, and the federal and Dominion taxes were another $122,000, so a sum of over $570,000 had to be moved from the contingent reserve account just to hold the working capital drain to that $800,000 figure. Despite the sale of over 116 million bushels of grain (including exports of over 24 million bushels), John Jr.'s zealous purchasing, governed not so much by the market itself as by the dictates of the Corn Case, had left a huge 23.7 million bushels still in inventory. The year before, it had been only 6.8 million bushels.

Cutbacks seemed imperative, particularly so to John Sr., who had been pessimistic for several years. In August 1938, six offices of the Company were closed. The operations at Spokane, Washington, and Lewiston, Idaho, were taken over by the Portland, Oregon, office, their former managers now acting as brokers. Similarly, the small Boston office was closed, and the manager there became a broker, "representing ourselves and other firms." The Memphis, Tennessee, office (but not the terminal itself) was closed, with the St. Louis office handling its business. The offices in San Francisco and Los Angeles were closed outright, "as there does not seem to be enough business at the present time to warrant their continuance" (so reported *Cargill News*).

At the St. Louis office a surprise occurred in management. Merle Grover, its manager, and two of his key employees were persuaded to join the Fox Grain Company of New Orleans, a Cargill competitor. E. T. Pettersen, the Portland manager for a number of years was transferred in to take charge of the St. Louis office. This was a major defection, unsettling to the Company. Raiding of competitor personnel by grain companies was not uncommon in the industry, although Cargill, with its promotion-from-within policy, did less of this than most. Grain trading was highly confidential, and any loss of a key management person was viewed with apprehension.

These cutbacks were only initial steps. Later that year salary cuts were considered. John Sr. wrote John Jr.: "I have been thinking seriously of getting all our executives together and putting this up to them straight—that we have to trim our expenses terribly, and that while I do not want to cut salaries I do believe in the idea of trimming off all the inefficient ones in the organization." John Sr. had a study made of all management salaries, estimating the amount that would be saved if a sliding scale cut, from 20 percent down to 5 percent, were applied. The 133 people in this group made a total of $61,735 per month; the salary cut would take this down by $9,047 (the list, incidentally, gives further evidence about views on the relative worth of individuals: John Sr. and John Jr. were at $50,000 per year; Cargill MacMillan, Austen Cargill, John Peterson and Julius Hendel were paid $20,000; Ed Grimes, Dan MacMillan and Frank Neilson were at $15,000, and the rest ranged downward to 19 men paid $2,400 per year).

John Sr. primarily blamed the government for Cargill's bad year (conveniently forgetting about the losses from the abortive Corn Case). When R. E. Wisner, the son-in-law of "Aunt Maggie" Barker, wrote John Sr. about a possible further common stock dividend, John Sr. replied, "We cannot pay it and show red ink figures." Earlier in 1938, Wisner had written

John Sr. requesting a loan on his wife, Margaret's, Cargill stock. His Janes-ville bank would not allow stock in a privately held company to be used as collateral. John Sr. replied by telegram: "Dislike intensely making family loans but if necessary will do so in your case for not to exceed 14 months." He followed with a letter of elaboration: "I do not know of anything that is so unpleasant as to get mixed up in family financial matters. It almost always results in hard feeling, and that is the last thing in the world that I ever want." He grudgingly made arrangements for granting the loan but added, "I will have to ask you 4½% interest, however, as Cargill, Incor-porated pay 4% to those depositing money with it."

Family members continued to see John Sr. as the patriarch, the one to write to regarding such important matters as dividends, loans, and so on. But for the business, it was evident by this time that John Sr.'s counsel on grain trade matters was considered less relevant. Indeed, in January 1937, John Jr. had wired Cargill MacMillan a rather pointed message: "Please ask father to defer to Julius on hedges at least until I get home. We were in complete agreement when I left and I am confident that any deviation from our program is sure to be very expensive."

John Sr.'s Christmas message in the December 1938 *Cargill News* re-ferred, as it so often did, to the economics of the Company: "Business conditions generally are bad. Many are thinking of discontinuing business completely, for no concern can continue to lose money indefinitely. Heavy curtailment of expenses is inevitable." John Sr. seemed to be laying the groundwork for possible future cutbacks in offices and salaries; his ending sentence left little cheer: "This, however, is not intended as a message of gloom but merely one of warning."

The rest of this Christmas message was devoted to another subject al-together, one that, if anything, was even more upsetting to John Sr. It involved disloyalty by three Cargill employees.[5]

An "Insider Trading" Transgression

Being a grain trader—actually *trading* grain—is an incredibly demand-ing profession. Split-second timing is needed, and a tremendous amount of responsibility rests on the shoulders of traders, particularly those who trade for someone else, be they company traders or outside brokers. Cargill grain men were required to trade exclusively and only for the Company. In turn, the Company vested a high degree of autonomy in its traders—gave them wide latitude to decide when to trade, at what price and in what quantities. Over the years, actual trading of grain had become the pinnacle for a Cargill employee; one was not quite a fully successful manager until he had actually traded grain—and made money doing it. There were no female traders at that time.

One of the persistent problems of the grain exchanges was the possibility of "insider trading." If a broker was trading both for himself and for others, there was always the temptation to direct the best trades toward himself and let others absorb any losses. The temptation was particularly strong if certain inside information happened to be known. In such a case, the holder of the privileged information had a jump on those having only public knowledge.

Generally, grain-trading companies had strict rules requiring their employees to trade only for the company and never for themselves personally. Some firms were signal exceptions, and grain trade veterans recount many anecdotes of striking individual-employee profits and losses. Prohibition of individual trading, however, was Cargill's unwavering rule.

Now, in early 1938, at the worst point of the Corn Case (just before Cargill's expulsion from the CBOT) and with the recession in full bloom, an audit by R. J. Semsch showed that three employees had been trading on their own, in addition to trading for the Company. All three were key Minneapolis traders. One of them, an outstanding performer for the Company, even had been allowed a substantial amount of employee common stock. But this man had been trading on his own account since mid-1933, and the amounts involved were substantial. It was a clever arrangement, involving the use of friends' names for the trading. Losses had been hidden in Company accounts. This discovery was made just after the first of the year 1938, with the investigation extending into the spring. The result was dismissal of the three men, each agreeing to reimburse the Company for its losses. In two cases, the bonding company had to stand the loss.

John Sr. decided to devote the editorial page of the *Cargill News* to the matter in that same December 1938 issue carrying the Christmas "message of gloom." The editorial read as follows:

VALUE OF A GOOD NAME

One of the saddest things that can happen to any of us is the loss of our good name and reputation. As you know, it is an outstanding rule of this organization that no employee is allowed to speculate on his own account in Grain, Stocks or Commodities or to manage any such account for others.

This year, however, we uncovered activities of three of our prominent and outstanding employees who were speculating on their own account . . . trying to cover it up by falsifying the books. When the inevitable discovery was made we could do nothing but dismiss them all . . . we could never trust them again where money in a substantial way was involved.

. . . It is hard to believe that anyone would be so foolish as to risk his position and his reputation for so foolish an undertaking, and the reputation of these men is gone probably for good . . . so often the men who are brightest and keenest . . . get themselves trapped in this way. They feel that they are just a little brighter than the general run and can beat out the game, and I sincerely hope that every member of this organization will take warning.[6]

A Brother and a Sister Lost

A personal family tragedy occurred at this time—the death of Daniel MacMillan, John Sr.'s loyal brother. He had taken ill in mid-February and died on March 25, 1939, at age 66. John Jr. wrote his father, who was on vacation in California, that "Uncle Dan's death . . . was a very great shock to all of us, and especially to me. . . . I had planned to see him yesterday." Daniel MacMillan had been a significant force in the Company since before the turn of the century and was probably the most important single influence on his older brother, John Sr., in the earlier years before John Jr. joined the Company. Daniel also had exerted a special impact on John Jr. For both John Sr. and John Jr., it was his unique ability to be a trusted listener and advisor. His loss was sorely felt by all of the Cargill group. John Sr., in ill health himself, was not able to make the trip from California for the funeral.

This was the second death of an immediate family member within a year for John and Edna MacMillan. Emma Hanchette, Edna's sister, had died in June 1938 at age 64.

Holding in Place

By May 31, 1939, the balance sheet looked much better than that of the previous year. There was a modest profit of $218,000, and working capital stayed almost constant, after preferred stock dividends and some small additions to reserves. However, no common stock dividend was voted. The reasons for this lay in the heightened pessimism felt by John MacMillan, Sr.

The Corn Case appeared to have daunted John Sr. far more than John Jr. Although consistently backing up his son, John Sr. more and more preached prudence with both the CBOT and the government. He seemed to have a lingering unease about John Jr.'s continuing aggressive posture. As the situation in the Corn Case turned against Cargill after the first of the year 1939, John Sr. wrote John Jr.: "It is awfully hard for me to understand your point of view exactly in connection with these orders of the C.E.A. . . . I did not intend to take any chances."

John Sr. had been left in charge of the office during the absence of John Jr. for the Corn Case, and he reiterated in this letter a view he increasingly espoused: "There will be nothing done here in the organization in any way excepting to cut out unnecessary help—help that we ordinarily would carry along but under these circumstances [i.e., the Corn Case] that we can curtail. I think you will agree that that is advisable because it gives us a chance to cut out the dead wood in the organization." He wrote Cargill MacMillan in the same vein: "We are thinking seriously of cutting the organization to the bone . . . for the simple reason that we may be in for a fight extending over years, and nobody can know what the expense will be."

Ed Grimes, knowing John Sr.'s concern for holding salaries down, diplomatically wrote him about raises that were needed in the traffic department to hold exceptional men and pointed out that "the young men Flag [Flagler Flinchbaugh] has trained have been a little dissatisfied with their salaries. Being able to go out and get positions of responsibility at good increases in salary seems to indicate there was merit in the requests for more money." John Sr. was not interested in hearing this; he was preparing lists of people to lay off (one list included: "watchmen—drop one; traffic department, ——— not satisfactory; Margaret ———, understand n.g.; sample room release ———; ———, unnecessary at present; financial department, ———, poor and bad influence, ———, should only get $125; accounting and terminal—drop 14") [names were given on memorandum but I have omitted them here].[7]

World grain production remained very high in the crop year 1938–1939. Corn was about the same as the previous year and wheat was down somewhat in the United States. But a bumper crop in Argentina and an excellent harvest in Canada helped to keep the total world wheat crop very high. A huge wheat carryover of more than 500 million bushels still remained. Prices in the year were very low, with cash wheat at Chicago averaging 69 cents. A "super abundance of wheat," the *Wheat Studies* editors once again put it. The second half of their sentence telegraphed an increasingly urgent dimension of food policy: "in a world teetering between limited, insecure peace and widespread warfare." Government controls or intervention were in vogue practically everywhere, they stated, with developments deeply affected by the protracted hostilities in China and by the Spanish civil war. "Even more influential," they continued, "were successive crises caused by Germany's aggressive diplomacy backed by her armed might." There was an "eagerness" to establish increased food reserves against the growing danger of a major European war. Austria had been annexed by Germany in March 1938; the Munich Conference in September of that year had ceded the Sudetenland and vital Czechoslovakian fortresses to them. By March 1939, Germany had gained Memel and was pressing for Danzig and the Polish corridor. In April, Italy had invaded Albania. The Italians then agreed to a military alliance with Germany. Then, on August 23, a Russo-German pact was signed in Moscow. John Sr. wrote his son Cargill on August 25: "We have had tremendous war excitement this past week and it has been an enormous strain on the organization."

Hostilities did indeed break out a week later, for Germany invaded Poland on September 1, 1939. Great Britain and France declared war two days afterward. World War II had begun. The grain trade, like all other institutions of the world, was now to change overnight.[8]

War Footing

From September 1939, when Great Britain and France declared war on Germany, to December 7, 1941, and the Japanese attack on Pearl Harbor, preparedness was the watchword for the United States. Just how much the country should support the Allies' war effort was fervidly debated for most of this time. There was a strong current of isolationism running in the country, particularly in the Midwest and the Plains states—a "business as usual" approach that put heavy emphasis on preserving existing domestic positions.

This was illustrated by the farm policy of the United States in the two years immediately preceding World War II. Since the first initiatives of the New Deal in 1933, national programs had sought to hold down the production of key commodities, especially cotton, wheat, corn and tobacco in order that "parity" could be tendered to the farmers. Under the first Agricultural Adjustment Act (AAA) of 1933, the focus was on parity prices. After the 1938 AAA legislation, farm prices were related to nonfarm prices and the rates between per capita farm and per capita nonfarm income debated. In effect, an "income parity" concept had been introduced. For income and parity price determinations, the presumably "typical" years 1910–1914 were used as the base period, and government efforts were designed so that farmers would have purchasing power equivalent to what they had enjoyed then. The experience in the decade of the 1930s is shown in fig. 1.

Price parity seemed always to fall far short of the goal. For example, in August 1939, wheat was 54 cents a bushel, just 50 percent of parity. Corn was selling at that time for 46 cents a bushel, a mere 59 percent of parity. Cotton was at 66 percent of parity, while hogs were at 60 percent. Of the major commodities, only the beef cattle price was at 100 percent.

The problem was that this parity effort had flown in the face of a burgeoning supply of those commodities that had created a volume of agricultural production in 1940 some 10 percent higher than when the New Deal programs had begun and a full 16 percent greater than at the close of World War I. New technology was a large force in this bounty. Crop yields had increased, and there were other improvements that had allowed the 10 percent increase, despite the fact that the number of acres harvested had declined by 38 million. Also there still were large numbers of underemployed people on the farms, because nonfarm employment was not strong enough to take up the slack. The excess of manpower tended to force more intensive use of land, rather than less.

The continuing bounty of these basic commodities (except in the two drought years midway in the decade) edged prices downward, widening the gap between price and parity. Thus, the government, dedicated to

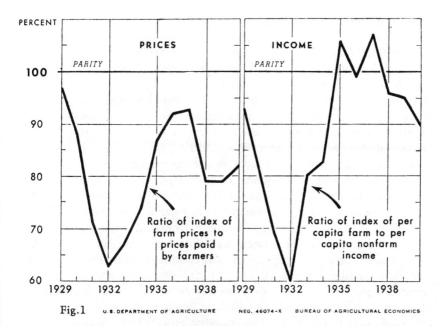

Fig.1   U.S. DEPARTMENT OF AGRICULTURE   NEG. 46074-X   BUREAU OF AGRICULTURAL ECONOMICS

holding prices and incomes up, was forced to purchase increasing amounts of these commodities for government storage. As long as it was peacetime, these purchases had been readily accomplished, although with huge subsidies and heightened government-owned surpluses in expensive storage. Suddenly, however, as the country entered World War II, with its necessity for tight controls and objective standards on all prices, the weaknesses of the parity system became more apparent.

With chronic problems of overproduction and underemployment, low farm incomes and an administration willing to pick up the slack by subsidies, it was not surprising that American agriculturalists entered the period of war preparedness and the eventual war itself wishing to hold intact the farm policy objectives of the 1930s New Deal. Their transition to wartime values and goals did not come easily. As agricultural economist Walter W. Wilcox put it, "The 'defense' period from May, 1940, to December 7, 1941 [i.e., from Dunkirk to Pearl Harbor], was a difficult period for agricultural leaders. Their peacetime objectives seemed inadequate when the rest of the economy was mobilizing for defense. For the most part, agriculture had no new goals."[9]

Still, there had been a few interesting new programs. For example, in May 1939, a revolutionary "stamp" plan was developed for the distribution of surplus supplies of food through regular commercial channels, the forerunner of what later came to be known as the Food Stamp program.

By May 1940, the National Defense Advisory Commission gained an agricultural representative, Chester C. Davis, but there was no comparable position established that would resemble the "food czar" post held by Herbert Hoover in World War I. In September 1940, Claude R. Wickard was chosen by President Roosevelt to become Secretary of Agriculture. Henry Wallace, a puzzle to the grain traders since his appointment in 1933, became FDR's vice-presidential running mate in the November elections. "Party regulars were aghast" about the choice of Wallace, wrote William Leuchtenburg, "an ex-Republican with little political savvy and a reputation for mysticism." But, of course, Roosevelt's ticket won.

In December 1940, a war-generated shift in policy was taken for the hog program by Secretary of Agriculture Wickard. He had become convinced that pork demands from the war required expanded production, despite the fact that the large number of animals already on the farms seemed to suggest a reduction. In late March 1941, the Lend-Lease Act was passed by Congress, and arrangements rapidly were mounted to ship increased quantities of pork, dairy products, eggs, canned vegetables and dry beans to Great Britain. With the exception of wheat, which remained in excess supply both in North America and Europe, most of the major commodity programs were stepped up to provide for expected increases in demand because of the war. In May 1941, Congress passed legislation that mandated loans at 85 percent of parity on five basic commodities—corn, wheat, cotton, tobacco and rice. Writing later of this development, Walter Wilcox stated: "This was the first step in the mistakenly mechanical use of the parity formula by the Congress and others, which caused so much difficulty in . . . equitable and economically desirable price supports and price ceilings during the war."[10]

Because of changing agricultural supplies and regimented prices, the period was a challenging one for grain trading companies like Cargill. Continued surpluses heightened the importance of governmental and private grain storage. The government already was building some of its own storage at country points, using steel bins (a forerunner of similar structures built by farmers on their own farms at a later date). The grain trade was annoyed by this, alleging governmental encroachment on private enterprise.

So Cargill too moved once more to increase its own storage capacity, as it had done in its large expansion from 14.7 million bushels in 1929 to 40.7 million in 1932. Now Company totals jumped from just over 51 million bushels in 1938 to more than 63½ million by 1940. The capacities at Buffalo had been vastly expanded—an addition to the Electric Elevator there increased this one terminal from 1.75 million to over 5.2 million bushels; with the Great Eastern and the Superior, the Company now had over 12.4 million bushels just at that one location. A larger Milwaukee railroad elevator at Kansas City was leased (the leased Missouri Pacific Railroad terminal was relinquished), and the rebuilding of the damaged section of Cargill's own Omaha terminal in 1939 almost doubled capacity there, to over 9 million bushels. Smaller terminals also were added at LaCrosse, Wisconsin, and Sleepy Eye, Minnesota. The increased capacities allowed a much larger total for grain receipts in these years. In the crop year 1938–1939, the Company had combined receipts of over 148 million bushels at its terminals and its country and "leased line" elevators. For the next two crop years, 1939–1940 and 1940–1941, the combined totals were just at 125 million bushels each year.

Prices had been stronger in the first of these two years, and the Company had shown a healthy net profit of over $1,117,000. In the crop year 1940–1941, governmental confusion about the wartime effects on the farm programs and other related factors depressed prices and made profits more difficult to attain. The Company earned just $105,000 that year.[11]

Contrasting Management Styles

Except for John Sr., there was little looking backward at the Corn Case around the executive offices of the Company—at least openly. One early effect of the case, however, was a tightening of centralization in management, particularly into the hands of John Jr. The injured silence after the Company had agreed to the guilty stipulation that ended the case in March 1940, and Cargill MacMillan's memorandum to management explaining John Jr.'s role were unmistakable. Nothing was to be said about the case except through John Jr.'s personal decision.

In May 1940, John Jr. issued a memorandum to all branch office managers once again enunciating the essence of his philosophy of organization. As he put it, "a clearcut understanding of our theory of organization is necessary." At this point, he seemed subtly to shift his earlier definition of the "line and staff" organization, the version that he had carried with him since his work with General Foote in the field artillery unit in World War I. For the first time, the organization was characterized as "the staff type . . . as distinguished from the line type, the difference being that our Minneapolis executives specialize in certain functions rather than attempting supervision over many different functions as would be necessary under the line type." Inasmuch as there was potential for confusion under the "staff type," John Jr. continued, "it is my duty, or in my absence, that of Cargill MacMillan, to effect the co-ordination which is necessary, and to *establish responsibility in doubtful cases*" (emphasis John Jr.'s).

The branch managers were to be "responsible for the actions of *everyone* in their respective offices" (his emphasis), and on "all ordinary routine matters they and their subordinates should correspond directly with the proper individual in charge of that routine in the Minneapolis office." The memorandum then listed the heads of those Minneapolis functions, but the memorandum ended with a blunt statement that in cases where there was a "twilight zone, when a doubt exists as to which department has jurisdiction," John Jr. himself would be the arbiter.

Not only did this memorandum telegraph additional evidence that John Jr. was centralizing Cargill's managerial decision making in his hands, but it also left in place some of the ambiguities and tensions that this system had bred since its inception in the mid-1920s. While branch managers were responsible "for the actions of everyone" in the branch office, this did not include any authority over the terminals in most of these locations. Indeed, the acute antagonism between Julius Hendel and Frank Neilson had perpetuated the sharp split between terminal management and branch management.

The portfolio of Ed Grimes was still varied, but now was concentrated on national affairs. This included grain pricing under wartime price controls and the allocation of railroad cars in the Northwest. At Cargill, new, younger men had entered the picture. Two were particularly important: Ralph Golseth, who was the only younger member of management mentioned in the memorandum (as assistant to John Jr. and Hendel), and Fred Seed, also a Hendel prodigy, soon to become the general manager of a new feed operation (and, in 1946, the first member of the Cargill board in his management generation).

There was an interesting contrast in management styles at this point when Austen Cargill came forward to the Commitment Committee in March 1940 with a set of proposals that would fundamentally shift the management of the country elevator system. The committee had had two years of experience by this time and already was assuming a major role as a policymaking entity. It had a critically important function in attempting to constrain a very strong chief executive officer, John Jr., a role it sometimes was unwilling or unable to meet.

The country elevator business had "changed materially," Austen began. "Competition is now largely confined to stations, rather than elevators at the same station. Normal trading areas of a station no longer exist . . . the trade will, for some reason or another, select a certain station for its trade center. Once that trend starts, many of the surrounding stations for a distance of 20 to 30 miles are seriously affected." Farmers had selected approximately 24 of Cargill's country elevators as their favored trading point, what Austen called "trade centers."

Here Austen was espousing a practical version of what geographers call "central place theory." Austen's proposal was to upgrade the facilities at these key points, with a particular focus on seven of the trade centers already owned by the Company. He wanted eventually a sum of $84,000 for these improvements and now asked for $40,000, which was promptly granted.

As a result of concentration on key "trade centers," important changes were made in the way that the country elevator operations were to be managed. In the past, said Austen, all of the line and leased elevators were in charge of agents, "whose activities were controlled in detail from the main office." With the changes out in the field—the diversified farming, the improved roads, the impact of trucks—the "old line elevator principle is no longer adequate to meet the situation. Management can no longer be centralized in the main office . . . it must be moved right into the elevator if that elevator is to survive." Each elevator would be in charge of a local manager instead of an agent, and the manager would be wholly responsible for the successful operation of the elevator. There would be a superintendent over these, but "the General Office . . . will provide the finances, do the accounting work and, except for special cases, confine its activities to an advisory capacity." In sum, each elevator was to be operated as a separate "profit center" unit.

Austen Cargill was anticipating here the decentralized system of authority and responsibility that later became a hallmark of American industry. This contrasted sharply with the view held by John Jr., that authority in the Company needed to be centralized, particularly in the hands of the chief executive officer. However, the country operations were different enough in their administrative demands from the rest of the Company to keep this contrast in management philosophies from becoming a sensitive issue at this time, particularly as John Jr. had never been interested enough in these to object.[12]

Education for Management

Into the early 1940s the Company's management training program had continued to serve it well. Not only Ralph Golseth and Fred Seed but others of their generation—for example, Erwin E. (Erv) Kelm, later to become the chief executive officer of Cargill—had moved into top management. John Jr. kept a strong personal hand in selecting new college graduate trainees. When James Ford Bell, the chairman of General Mills, who was advising the University of Minnesota on placement of its graduates, asked John Jr. for advice, he responded:

The inescapable conclusion . . . is that the overwhelming majority of these boys—certainly 60% and possibly 75%—should never go to the university [emphasis his]. These boys are usually sent to the university at great sacrifice on the part of their parents, while their capacity is such that they are utterly unable to benefit. *The four years are not only wasted but worse than wasted* [John Jr.'s emphasis] because the only result has been to introduce these boys to a standard of living which is higher than they can possibly hope to maintain in later life. The contrast between the relatively high standard of living which they experienced at the university and that which they must perforce accept in later life is such as to make them disgruntled citizens with a feeling that something is wrong about our entire social and economic system. These men, in our opinion, constitute a grave menace to our institutions, traditions and ideals.

Most college students should be in vocational schools, he felt, thus making "a university education a privilege and not a right." The majority of the young men who had come to Cargill, according to John Jr., while having a "high order of native intelligence," were "completely lacking in the rudiments of a liberal education." He decried the "vast multitude of alleged economic and business courses" and advocated a strong set of "cultural subjects." Eastern universities offered this liberal education, which had allowed its graduates "an immense advantage in the competitive struggle in executive talent." Yet he emphasized that

this is not intended as a brief for the Eastern universities . . . our own experience with Harvard, Yale and Princeton graduates has been extremely unsatisfactory . . . the personnel bureaus of these schools have passed on to me . . . men who looked upon a degree from Yale, Harvard or Princeton as a guarantee against their ever being forced at any time to work hard. We do not want this type at Minnesota. We do want to continue the traditions of a willingness for hard work which, in our opinion, is the greatest asset of the Western universities, and especially Minnesota.

These views once again seemed to contain a combination of admiration for privilege and the development of a meritocracy among those chosen few who had the intellect *and* connections to graduate from one of the culturally oriented universities, at the same time closing the avenue to those who were uppity.[13]

A First Venture in Ocean Shipping

John MacMillan, Jr.'s creativity surged once again in the late 1930s and early 1940s. It was a singular period for Cargill innovations—and John Jr. was the prime mover in most of these. Despite misgivings in most of the organization, John Jr. himself now carried the Company into a dimension of the grain trade not yet attempted by Cargill—ocean shipping.

The opening of hostilities in Europe early in September 1939 inevitably changed the equations on world trade, grain trading included. The *Wheat Studies* editors reported: "Only one anxious month of the season had elapsed before Germany launched her *Blitzkrieg* in Poland. This precipitated a widening involvement that strained and eventually racked all of Europe and much of the outside world. The seas were unsafe from September onward."

Grain carrier being sunk by German U boat, c. 1942 (The Bettmann Archive).

It was this latter dimension that particularly caught the eye of John Jr. There were going to be heavy shipping losses in the future and a great need for replacement shipping. Could the supplier of this be a totally new entrant? John Jr. thought so. Over the fall and winter of 1939–1940, Cargill developed a set of proposals for ocean shipping, the units to be planned *and* built by Cargill despite the fact that the Company had never constructed *any* oceangoing vessel. The evolution of this idea is clearer when the special role of Michael R. "Mickey" Cross and his British group, Ross T. Smyth & Co. Ltd., is examined.

Mickey Cross had been both a personal and a business friend of the MacMillans for a number of years. Since the early 1930s, when Cargill began to develop its "listening posts" in Europe, the Smyth group had acted as informal British representative for Cargill.

The relationship had sometimes been clouded by potential conflicts of interest. For example, in Argentina, Smyth represented other grain companies in direct competition with Cargill. Despite this, however, Cross had strongly influenced Cargill to get more involved in Europe. As he put it to Cargill MacMillan in January 1938, "you were selling to Bunge, Dreyfus and the Continental on the assumption that you would not be able to compete in the export business against them. . . . If you could bring yourselves to take the first step, at any rate on corn, you might find that you could compete and compete satisfactorily." Cross urged the Company to change its basis for competition in Europe: "This business of selling f.o.b. to your competitors is no doubt very attractive to you on many occasions, but . . . you get rid of the good at a time when the market is good, and leave yourselves with the bad to be disposed of at a time when the market is bad."

By mid-1939, with war imminent, England had instituted special arrangements to import grain from the United States. At this point, Cross pushed Cargill to become involved with the Norris Grain Company in a joint endeavor to solicit British purchases. While Cargill always had resisted any form of joint effort ("our dislike of joint deals," as Cargill MacMillan put it), the two companies did come together for some corn sales in June 1939. Cross then suggested a bolder step—that Norris and Cargill link at least some of their efforts more formally. Ed Grimes resisted this: "If it was strictly a joint account transaction . . . we would have to merge our export departments and operate as one organization. . . . We have always been very independent—I think the same can be said of Norris and my association with him has shown him to be just that. I do not know how two very individualistically minded outfits would work together."

Grimes spelled out some of the practical difficulties: "It came out pretty clear that we [had] different viewpoints when it came to putting out a hedge on the last purchase of wheat from the FSCC [the United States governmental selling agency for grain to England]. We wanted to hedge and Jim did not." Grimes also pointed out, that in the main, Norris operated through Canada in moving grain for export, while Cargill moved its export grain through Albany, "and these two routes are intensely competitive. . . . Jim has a lot of money invested in Canadian boats and I just can't see where he will ever look favorably on the U.S. route."[14] The Cargill/Norris arrangements continued but only on a desultory basis.

Instead, the Ross T. Smyth link was now exploited for a wholly Cargill plan. The Allied shipping losses in the fall of 1939 and the scramble by ocean shippers to increase their fleets encouraged John Jr. Quickly, as was the style of John Jr., the proposal grew startlingly large: that Cargill would design, build and own three oceangoing grain-carrying vessels, each to be some 400 feet long and each having the capacity for 13,000 tons of grain. This idea would be so demanding of both Company and family capital, as well as time, that John Jr. decided that he needed to provide a full-scale elaboration of his thinking, in writing and in detail. In September 1939, he issued a noteworthy document to Cargill management entitled "Ocean Transportation and Its Relation to Cargill, Inc."

He first described Cargill's export experiences of the 1920s and early 1930s, when Cargill management "became greatly alarmed by the incursions being made in the West by European importers and New York exporters, who began opening offices in the West, leasing elevator facilities and crowding Cargill out of the handling of all export grain. . . . Accordingly, a 'drang nach Oesten' [literally, 'the urge to go East'] was initiated." Here he recognized the opening of the European offices, the building of the Albany terminal and the other Atlantic Coast efforts.

He continued: "The situation . . . as of August, 1939 was as follows: Three firms were doing the bulk of the North American export business with Cargill in fourth or fifth place, and steadily losing ground." Dreyfus was the largest, next was Continental and in third place was Norris Grain (Bunge y Born was considered by John Jr. to be vying with Cargill for the fourth place). Cargill was obliged to distribute to destinations undesirable for the vessels of Dreyfus and Continental. Thus, Cargill was "unable to compete in such important ports as Rotterdam, Antwerp, London and Genoa, but was very strong in Scotland and Scandinavia." As to Norris, "Cargill could compete . . . from the Gulf and Pacific, Norris having no ocean steamers, but had difficulty competing with Norris from North Atlantic ports . . . long ocean hauls from the Gulf and Pacific ports to Europe had great appeal to Continental and Dreyfus, so Cargill had great difficulty even then." In brief, Cargill had to do something innovative or find itself in the same predicament as in the 1920s.

One successful step had been taken by Cargill, John Jr. pointed out, with the acquisition of the six towboat/barge units for the Erie Canal. In these endeavors, Cargill had become a specialist at efficient barging and efficient self-loading and unloading of grain. As John Jr. put it, "the Cargill organization prides itself more on its ability to adapt engineering principles to result in cheaper and better grain storage and handling than in any respect." What was needed, he felt, were oceangoing vessels devoted exclusively to the handling of grain and containing self-loading and unloading devices.

The memorandum then spelled out John Jr.'s vision of these ships. Their "extreme simplification of design" would allow a "remarkable cheapening of cost without being in any way at the cost of safety or efficiency." This set of tenets was characteristic of all of John Jr.'s projects. He consistently strove for the simplest ways of conducting every segment of the business, and there was no doubt of his desire to do this at bedrock cost. Generally, he took safety very seriously; it was on the score of efficiency that he was sometimes faulted. John Jr. informally had checked with the American Bureau of Shipping (the agency for certification of seaworthiness) and reported that "they have approved the design for classification to their highest rating" despite the fact that "it has less steel in the hull per ton of deadweight than any vessel which has ever been approved by them." John Jr. estimated the cost of the vessels to be $650,000 each—$50 per deadweight ton. The memorandum concluded: "On the twelve million bushels which the three grain carriers should transport yearly, this gross revenue would amount to something like $500,000. A large part of this could reasonably be expected to be net."[15]

To put it simply, because Cargill had built several steel grain barges at its yards at Albany, therefore it could build three huge, full-scale, ocean-going ships. The cocky audacity of this must have seemed to many people to be outright self-delusion. But Cargill did have special expertise on several scores that made the Company a credible and attractive prospect for being included in the huge shipbuilding effort now dictated by the war. In addition to its specialized loading and unloading devices, the Cargill-built steel barges were themselves innovations—the single-skin steel hull, adapted to a large-size barge design, as well as the innovative device of the V-notch rear of a barge to fit into the tug. While many of Cargill's ideas were not applicable to an oceangoing ship, these amateurs—John Jr., Frank Neilson, Chris Jensen and their colleagues—already had gained an expertise that made their new ideas not completely outlandish. The stated driving force for all this was the emergency shipbuiding program itself, spurred by the Maritime Commission and the armed services, along with their counterparts in England (with the unstated additional benefit to Cargill of gaining further privacy for its plans by serving as its own ocean shipper).

Although American shipping had stayed out of the war zones of the North Atlantic and environs, the attrition on the world's maritime fleet already was significant. Substantial shipbuilding subsidies were available from the Maritime Commission that would provide about 45 percent of the cost of construction. A would-be bidder had to meet certain specifications. For example, the speed of a merchant ship could vary quite widely, depending upon the horsepower of its engines and the configuration of the hull. The English were particularly concerned that shipping have enough speed to be able to keep up with the convoys now increasingly required. Insurance rates skyrocketed if speeds were so low that a ship had to travel on its own.

To join this fast-breaking game, it was imperative that Cargill develop a workable design quickly to meet the deadlines for the subsidies. John Jr. engaged a first-rank naval architect, George Sharp; he and Neilson, too, were deeply involved in the detailed design phase. John Jr. stated his broad beliefs in a wire to Neilson on October 9, 1939, for transmittal to Sharp's head of design: "Tell him . . . we want a unit which will work a good share of time especially in winter at 40 feet and that it must be economically sound at that draft, which means maximum carrying capacity. . . . We want to exceed 40 ft. of draft only by as much as he and Sharp are willing to go along without increasing arbitrarily the usual stresses and horsepowers. . . . On this basis it strikes me we should get by with 10 to 12 thousand tons of steel and 6 thousand h.p." (The American Bureau of Shipping had a required set of ratios and stress figures, whatever the final configuration.)[16]

Cargill MacMillan explained to Ed Grimes the concern about deep draft:

John's idea has been that if we could provide our boats with self-loading and unloading equipment, the draft would not be the factor that it is with the ordinary general cargo boat. . . . We could increase draft and cut down our length, thereby saving enormously in the quantity of steel required. . . . Speed is not an essential requirement for a grain carrier. . . . In normal times the slower the carrier, the better [he was assuming here that the Company would earn carrying costs for each day of the voyage].

This is not true for general cargo. . . . If we are willing to accept a speed of about eight knots, the h.p. requirements would be, roughly, 1500, whereas if we wanted a boat for general cargo purposes, we would want a speed of somewhere around 14 knots, which would require somewhere in the neighborhood of some 5000 h.p. Saving in initial cost is obvious, when you consider that the rule of thumb is that each h.p. costs approximately $100.00.[17]

As the proposed ship began to take a more specific form, it turned out to be huge. The plan was to build at 700 feet in length, 108 feet in width and 95 feet in depth, with a draft of some 70 feet and a gross tonnage of about 52,500 tons. John Jr. estimated that this would give a grain capacity of approximately 5 million cubic feet, divided into 26 separate holds. For power, there would be twin screws and rudders, each screw to be propelled by twin diesel engines of 1500 hp each. Given this size and power, the ship's sustained sea speed at the designed draft would be about 8½ knots.

John Jr. also began contemplating ways of providing for self-unloading onto floating elevators. He thought these could be placed in a neutral port, possibly Lisbon, Portugal or the Azores, so that grain could be sent from North America to these intermediate unloading facilities, with British ships providing the rest of the route to the war zone. The Neutrality Act had been passed by the U.S. Congress on November 4, 1939, and grain shipments abroad were subject to control, lest they fall into the hands of Germany. Neutral ports often were suspect.[18]

What Size Ship to Build?

With George Sharp's ship on the drawing board and plans worked out with Frank Neilson for transshipping, John Jr. now needed a firm contract to avoid being forced to go ahead alone. The costs of the latter alternative being heavy, the search for a buyer was a high priority.

As the British were one of the major purchasers of new shipping, John Jr. once more enlisted Mickey Cross. Cross learned that authorities at the British Control Board had already discarded a transshipping port at Lisbon because Australian wheat already had been offloaded there with poor results. He also stated that the British were interested in smaller ships, 8,000- to 9,000-ton vessels, and wanted the speeds to be higher than the original Cargill proposal (the presumed convoy speed being 9½ knots).

The chance to sell ships to Britain might be a lucrative one, for the British at one point intimated that they might order 10 vessels from Cargill. The detail involved in these proposals was massive, and the process was complicated by the fact that all negotiations had to be conducted by cable. At one point, in March 1940, it appeared that Cargill would get a firm bid on four vessels 300 feet in length and 40 feet in depth, with a 50-foot beam. At a draft of 30 feet, this vessel could hold 8,900 tons of cargo. The British seemed uneasy about Cargill's design, for John Jr. had proposed some variations in conventional practice in order to be able to use the Albany shipyard. Cross wrote: "I have of course been asked why the design follows lines which are entirely unusual. . . . All that I have vouchsafed is that I think you are translating into shipbuilding the experience you have gained in elevator construction [which] . . . were scoffed at by the conservative element when first put into operation but had proved to be successful [so] there was no reason why the same principle should not work satisfactorily when applied to ocean-going vessels."

All through these negotiations, Cargill management had assumed that it could subcontract substantial parts of the boats to existing shipbuilders but in early April found that the yards of these companies already were tied up. Further, the British made it clear that they needed the vessels earlier than Cargill could guarantee. Finally, the whole project fell through.[19]

The same frustrating set of events happened with the Company's proposals to the United States Maritime Commission. Again there was complex bargaining on details, and a firm proposal could not be agreed upon. Costs were very difficult to pin down. For example, insurance on ships had to include "war risk," and it was uncertain what price these premiums would command in the future. Once again Cargill was seen as too new in the business and too unconventional in its proposed building methods. John Jr. blamed the naval architects in a long letter to his father in late March 1940: "They are unwilling to consider anything which is beyond their experience, regardless of whether it is sound engineering or not. This makes it extremely difficult, as of course we are trying to work out a design suited for our own particular requirements, which are not those within their experience. . . . It was either a case of taking the whole design on which they insist or we could not take ships at all as we are in the awkward position of not being able to use Lloyds registry on account of the delays in sending plans back and forth to London, etc."

However true this was, the unpleasant conclusion of the negotiations of late 1939 and early 1940 was that Cargill did not get a single firm contract for building ocean shipping. At this point, Cargill MacMillan wired Neilson: "Junior thinks looks as tho would have to build ourselves in which case thinks would be better if you came home."[20]

John Jr.'s plans for going ahead on his own were quite ambitious. As these progressed, the numbers of ships in his proposal grew to eight. This upset his brother Cargill, and he wired John Jr.: "Pete [John Peterson] and I very much worried. . . . We are not impressed with Chris' [Chris Jensen] record to date and without further evidence we would not be willing commit ourselves to 8 ships in 20 mos. Neither of us, however, wish to put spoke in machinery and are willing to defer to your judgment providing it is judgment and not wishful thinking. We want to lend every encouragement but wish proceed cautiously."[21]

Finally, it was decided (by the group overruling John Jr.) that there would be just one vessel—but a large one. The final configuration was to be a ship of some 437 feet in length; beam, 60 feet; depth, 37 feet; and draft (loaded), 28 feet 3 inches; deadweight tonnage, 12,500; cargo capacity, 12,200 tons. Already, the Company had much of the requisite steel on order, and Chris Jensen's work force could be readily expanded. So the building began.

The method of construction developed by Frank Neilson and Chris Jensen was unorthodox, so much so that John Jr. actually had his patent attorney inquire as to the possibility of a "method" patent. In writing the patent attorney, John Jr. elaborated these differences:

The present method of shipbuilding involves the use of an extremely expensive way in which the hull is assembled and riveted or welded. After assembly (a period which requires ordinarily from 8 to 16 months) the hull is launched and the ship is fitted out afloat . . . a fabulously expensive way, requiring the use of a very slow moving gantry . . . the pre-fabricated sections are brought to the work.

The technique which we are employing eliminates entirely the need for a gantry or expensive way and consists essentially in bringing the point of assembly to the material.

. . . the hull is erected to the point where it will float (requiring about ¼ the amount of steel in the finished hull) . . . the work is done either in a very simple and inexpensive way or in a floating drydock, or even on barges.

After being afloat the sections are lowered into place by the use of an ordinary stationary crane (not a gantry). Sections weighing from 5 to 25 tons are swung into place, fastened temporarily, and then welded at their convenience by welders who remain on the floating hull. The hull may be moved forward and back or turned end for end in order to keep it on an even keel. The fabrication of panels can always be kept at one point, where automatic welders enable it to be done in the cheapest possible way, while the cost of moving the hull itself is trifling as compared with the cost of manipulating a slow moving gantry, as is done in the standard shipyards.[22]

The costs, John Jr. vowed, were "not more than one-fourth those customarily found in a shipyard . . . .This technique was worked out by our organization as a result of long experience in the maneuvering of floating rafts of logs and in the handling of heavy logs and timbers in our lumbering operations" (devised by John Jr., Austen Cargill and Frank Neilson in the British Columbia woods in the early 1920s). John Jr. left no doubt about his pride in "the Cargill method". "Beyond any question [it] represents an important revolutionary method in the art of shipbuilding."

The welded bow and stern were unique and had not been tested in practice before. Rather than large curved plates, giving the conventional rounded bow and stern, the Cargill method had sections welded together in a knuckle joint, so that the bow and stern had a series of straight plates, each changing direction slightly (i.e., looking like a knuckle). After this boat was launched, in late 1941, the head of the David Taylor Model Basin, a Bureau of Ships, Navy Department, testing laboratory for boat hulls, commented that Cargill's hull configuration "is most unusual . . . apparently adopted to simplify bending of the hull plates." Later the testing agency ran model tests on it. Fairbanks, Morse & Co. (suppliers of the engines) in their *F-M News* called the shipbuilding process "revolutionary," despite the fact that, according to their editors, "there was a great deal of speculation as to whether an inexperienced firm could successfully overcome the handicaps."[23]

Should the Carlantic Be Sold?

Under the innovative construction strategy of Frank Neilson and Chris Jensen, the Company's new oceangoing grain carrier began to take shape rapidly over the fall of 1940. It seemed natural to continue the Cargill protocol for boat names—the new boat promptly was named the *Carlantic*. The Company, not willingly, was itself financing the entire operation. Frank Neilson had written John Jr. in late October 1940 of the possibility of getting a governmental subsidy, but he pointed out that "it would be necessary to maintain ownership of the vessel until after it was in service, then it must be replaced by a vessel having a speed at least 12 knots . . . or a vessel . . . approved by the Maritime Commission as being valuable for National defense purposes." Neilson doubted that the Company could meet these requirements.

John Jr. now began to consider selling the boat, rather than putting it into service as Cargill's own grain carrier. He put the reasons cogently to Hugo Scheuermann, the Chase National Bank vice president, in a letter on December 11, 1940: "They are quoting such high prices for [purchase of] ocean shipping at the moment that I do not think we can afford to own the boat . . . we should sell it for a tanker instead of finishing it as a grain carrier." At this point in its construction, the boat readily could be con-

The Carlantic *on its maiden voyage, November 1941.*

verted to an oil tanker, and it was on this basis that John Jr. now began to approach potential buyers. "Our minimum upset price for sale as a Tanker," he wrote in late December, "should be $1,300,000 and it is believed highly probable that we can secure $1,500,000 sometime during the next six months."

Earlier in 1938, Cargill had acquired a 42-year-old laker, the *W. D. Rees*, a 396-foot vessel rated at 3,760 gross tons. With such extraordinary sales prices for ocean shipping, the Company now considered selling it as an oceangoing vessel, most likely also converted to a gasoline tanker (one bidder wanted it for a Trinidad–Montreal route). It would be necessary to get the *Rees* out of the Great Lakes and through the St. Lawrence. After that, considerable refurbishing would be required to make it qualify for ocean travel. The *Rees*, however, could not squeeze through the Lachine Locks, upriver from Montreal, so John Jr. suggested to Neilson that the vessel could be sawed in half and moved through as two units. When Neilson seemed skeptical, John Jr. wrote back: "It seems the *Rees* is 3 inches too wide to be floated out on her bottom. But in the last war at least one was cut in two and floated out on her side. Seems to me the only expense involved in doing so would be cost of welding hatch covers for eight or ten feet of length and of fastening pig iron to the rail sufficient to make her float on her side." Neilson agreed that, technically, this might be accomplished, but after a detailed evaluation, the transporting and refurbishing costs seemed inordinately high, and the project was abandoned.[24]

When the calendar-year financial statements became available, the enormous effect on Company resources from the costs of building the *Carlantic* were more evident. John Sr. wrote John Jr.: "We are in a quandary as to what to do about the boat. . . . We have spent so much money we don't dare take any further chances."

Elevator Problems

The situation was made worse by two other unexpected financial drains at that time: the addition to the Buffalo elevator and the building of the East St. Louis elevator. Buffalo had cost much more than expected (labor costs had risen sharply there). At East St. Louis part of the newly constructed elevator was sinking into the ground, resulting in an unanticipated need for additional, expensive pilings (and John Jr. hated putting *any* money into pilings). Cargill MacMillan wrote John Jr. on February 4: "The Buffalo elevator finally cost nearly 50% more than we anticipated, and as for the St. Louis elevator, there just literally isn't any bottom in sight" (he meant the money, not the pilings!).

John Jr. pulled Frank Neilson from shipping to assess the piling problem at East St. Louis. Cargill MacMillan wrote John Jr. after Neilson had returned that the total cost of the elevator had escalated to something over $1.3 million. The total of all these costs "would indicate an out-of-pocket loss to working capital of $1,826,000. . . . I am considerably concerned that this excess in cost might rock our very foundations were we to run into some heavy losses." John Jr. was contrite in his return letter: "The figures on Buffalo and St. Louis horrify me beyond belief. The error, which of course was mine, was in attempting too much at once and then trying to hurry it."

The difficulties in East St. Louis soon brought concern from outsiders. Bert Lang, the longtime banking friend of the Company from St. Louis, wrote John Peterson, " 'Just between us girls,' there seem to be rumors in the air down here that the new elevator may not be a howling success from a construction standpoint. . . . Some fear that it may not stand up under a load." Peterson quickly responded, attempting to allay any fears: "Apparently a not too serious engineering mistake was made with respect to the building of the first half of the elevator, the practical effect of which is that we shall not be able to load that section of the house to full capacity

Cargill's East St. Louis terminal elevator, 1940s.

as originally contemplated. The mistake, however, is being corrected in the second half of the house, so that when it is completed it will support a full load."[25]

A New Ship?

However, John Jr. did not really mean it when he told his brother that he was "attempting too much at once," for now he began yearning for and pursuing the construction of another vessel. The financial situation in those first months of 1941 had improved—the grain business had picked up greatly. Beyond this, there was a frenzy about construction of shipping that affected everyone, the Cargill group included. There had been huge losses in Allied merchant shipping from U-boat attacks; in the week of November 17, 1940, some 22 ships, totaling 187,975 tons had gone down, thus "maintaining the weekly average . . . at the dangerous level of approximately 100,000 tons," reported the *New York Herald*.

With this attrition, the British decided to send a high-level Purchasing Commission to the United States, hoping to book some 60 freighters for construction at United States shipyards. The Company immediately wrote Mickey Cross for help. Cross reported that his firm now had a temporary office out in the countryside, "as London became rather noisy and bits of old iron flew about." Cargill seemed willing to construct almost anything the British might want. Building for a government, British or United States, would provide priority for materials, particularly steel. John Jr. had heard that the greatest need of the British was for destroyers for convoy purposes and proposed to Neilson that they could make just such a vessel. Neilson wrote back: "I doubt our ability to sell the idea. The boats used now in this service are built with super speed because in case of attack they have to be able to circle their convoy and outmaneuver the attacking vessels. I am very much afraid the British would think our boats would not offer enough protection."

John Jr. then decided to contact the Purchasing Commission directly. The visit was not at all pleasant. Cargill MacMillan wrote Cross: "We have been given two of the coldest receptions (if you could call them receptions at all) by the British Purchasing Commission that it has ever been our lot to encounter. We are mentioning this to you because we are desperately anxious to see you win the war." Apparently John Jr. was particularly miffed, for Cargill noted, "My brother John has pointed out to me that, in his opinion, a single tactless representative can easily cost more than the loss of a battle."

Early in the British negotiations, Cargill made the proposal that some of its towboats and barges might be sent across the ocean, either for use in Britain for harbor and shallow intercoastal work or perhaps even for the eastern Mediterranean or Red Sea. This idea did not seem to appeal to the British at all.

Still not ready to give up, John Jr. wrote C. C. Boden, who was helping in the negotiations: "What do you think of our offering two to four tankers for 1941 delivery, any speed up to sixteen knots, provided buyers will go along . . . on what we can build and will take our present boat." The Commission quickly disabused Cargill of this idea. John Jr. admitted to Weston Grimes, "They would not dicker with us." Cargill MacMillan poured out his unhappiness about the negotiations to Mickey Cross, who replied: "I am very sorry that you have had such a cold reception . . . it is very sad to see that the bureaucratic tinge seems to spread over people who in ordinary life are ordinary business people the moment they get absorbed in Government departments." Cross promised to make representations in London for Cargill, but this produced nothing.

The rebuff very much antagonized John Jr. He wrote Weston Grimes: "We get a terrific propaganda from the British to the effect that they are all but starving," yet the Company could not get them interested in any of its proposals. "It seems to me as if they are using their propaganda machinery in an effort to play us for suckers, i.e., they want us to go to the expense and take the risk of building boats against a possible shortage, and are trying to put this over by making us believe that the shortage is now acute."

The Company still was concerned that its unusual method of vessel construction and the resulting "different" bow and stern might be a factor in failing to obtain a contract. John Jr. wrote George Sharp, the naval architect, on December 11, 1940: "We are very anxious to agree on the next hull on which we will start work. Both Neilson and I are very insistent on building something which can be erected in the shortest possible time, and with the absolute minimum of fabrication, even at the expense of hull efficiency."

John Jr. himself made copious technical suggestions about the new knuckle form of construction, and he elaborated its theory to Sharp, impressively using the vernacular of Sharp's own world:

If I remember my dynamics correctly, the most efficient form moving through a fluid is a prolate spheroid with the maximum diameter at a point one-third from the length. A close approximation of the prolate spheroid is one terminating in two ellipsoids with the after ellipsoid having the same lesser semi-axes but with the greater semi-axis twice that of the shorter ellipsoid. I have had two ellipses with these semi-axis drawn up to the same scale as my pencil sketch. May I suggest that you super-impose the ellipses on my pencil sketch and note how close the correspondence is, considering that the pencil design has the maximum possible of straight lines?[26]

An unexpected event occurred on January 23, 1941, just as the British possibility seemed to be slipping away, when Company officials were surprised by a visit from the United States Navy. John Jr. hurriedly wrote his father: "Yesterday the Navy came in and indicated some interest in our yard; or, at least, we think they did, for they wanted all the information they could get about it, and only gave us 24 hours in which to supply it." The Company rapidly put together a memorandum describing the history of the Company, its "financial set-up," its organization structure and its shipbuilding facilities at Albany. The navy queried Cargill about availability of the site and asked about the time required to start shipbuilding. John Jr. replied, "None, provided materials are available."

Once more there were nagging questions about Cargill's unorthodox methods and bow/stern configurations. These were yet unproven—the

Carlantic was still in the yards with its fittings just being completed, not yet tested under real conditions. Cargill MacMillan wrote John Jr. about some of the other government contracts just awarded: "The 200 boats . . . were of a knuckle form which we could not handle. As far as I can make out, this is the position we are in: No one is interested in the type of boat we can build, which gives us one of two alternatives; either (1) interest someone in what we can do; or (2) fix our yard so we can handle curved plates."

It was possible that the Company might get the government to finance the more expensive curved plate equipment, but Frank Neilson worried that the inexperienced Cargill workmen would not be able to handle this more sophisticated method. What the Company needed was some way to get the Maritime Commission and the navy to notice it, so in mid-January it asked to see the Commission plans that were just being opened for bid for a set of tuna fishing boats. Cargill MacMillan wrote John Jr.: "We were greatly amused yesterday when we heard from some engine company that we were the only people who had asked for the plans of this boat." Incidentally, nothing further came of the tuna boat project.[27]

Another force was at work that was to save the situation. In early 1941, the navy was looking for new locations somewhere in the Great Lakes area for construction of shipping. Weston Grimes explained the navy's reason: "There has been considerable debate on the floor of the House to the effect that shipyards on the Great Lakes should be given some of the Defense business." Back in May 1940, Julius Barnes, John Sr.'s disputant in the Farm Board days in 1930, had queried John Sr. about the possibility that Cargill might join him to build ships in Duluth. Barnes had done this in World War I and wanted to do so again. John Sr. replied at that time, "The increased cost of construction on the Great Lakes as compared with elsewhere, added to the time expense of getting the boats out, makes it extremely improbable that any Great Lakes yard could compete."

But six months later, Frank Neilson became surprisingly bullish about this very idea, telegraphing back: "Could easily move our yard facility to Great Lakes or Mississippi areas." Cargill MacMillan asked him for specifics, and Neilson suggested Memphis; Superior, Wisconsin; and Chicago (St. Louis was discarded for lack of land and its tight labor situation). Weston Grimes added the possibilities of LaCrosse, Wisconsin, and Buffalo, but Neilson rejected these. John Jr. was by this time in Jamaica on vacation, exhausted and suffering from high blood pressure. Cargill MacMillan telegraphed Neilson: "In John's absence I hate to leave any stone unturned because I know he is relying on us to do everything he would do to make a success of our shipbuilding program."[28]

In April 1941, John Jr. was able to return to the job, and now the pace of Cargill's search for new contracts stepped up. John Jr. flirted at this time (and later, too) with the notion of a huge vessel able to carry a large number of barges, loaded through side openings. George Sharp, the naval architect, had proposed a 750-foot vessel, with four deck levels, able to carry 56 barges (36,300 tons). John Jr.'s version was 470 feet long to take 12 larger barges. Neither version progressed to specific plans.

By June 1941, a huge merchant shipbuilding program was under way in the country, linked to the national defense effort. With materials and equipment in critically short supply, a priority system had been established that made it imperative that a company have some link to this national defense work in order to get materials and supplies. This was precisely the problem facing Cargill.

On June 20, 1941, John Jr. submitted preliminary plans to the Maritime Commission for the construction of eight tankers of 15,000 tons dead-weight, all of them to be capable of 16 knots. As the Company began to formulate specific details, both Frank Neilson and Chris Jensen objected to some of the Commission's terminology. As John Jr. put it to Weston Grimes, "Frank and Chris are adamant in that they will not tolerate the constant use of such words as 'straight,' 'plumb' and 'true.' . . . Neither Frank nor Chris are temperamentally qualified to stand for the arbitrary whims of inspectors." Weston Grimes worried about this: "If we take some arbitrary position and refuse to build except on our terms, we are not going to be in good graces . . . it is difficult enough to get the Commission to award any contracts to unestablished shipbuilders without injecting any special qualifications." In truth, the Company was not yet ready to follow through with specific plans and drawings, and in August the offer had to be withdrawn.[29]

The Carlantic Becomes the Victoria

Neilson and Jensen had continued to oversee the completion of the *Carlantic*. The hull was launched on April 11, 1941. John Jr. was there, and he wrote his brother: "The boat hit the water simultaneously bow with stern, with the result that there was no damage whatever. . . . Not a leak of any kind—not even a pin-hole leak." John Jr., still sensitive about the Cargill method of construction, continued: "In the water its appearance is not in the least freakish." He estimated the total cost when finished to be somewhere near $1 million, "although we may run somewhat above this in an effort to speed things up to cash in on these high spot freights."

Company executives still were ambivalent about whether to finish the boat as a grain carrier or as a gasoline tanker. The latter would cost an additional $50,000. With either scenario, the Company still seriously considered holding onto the boat, either for its own use or for charter. The same oil company with the Trinidad–Montreal run, earlier interested in the *Rees*, now queried about chartering the *Carlantic*. However, if Cargill kept ownership, its working capital position, despite a good spring in the grain trade itself, would continue precarious. By early July, the decision was made to put the boat in the hands of a ship agent, Collin & Gissel, for possible sale. Several oil companies were approached, but none seemed interested enough to make a bid. A problem mentioned by the British at the beginning of the year, that the vessel was "too large and too slow to operate in convoy," seemed to make for reluctant bidders. The best candidate seemed to be a Portuguese Company, but the Maritime Commission apparently was reluctant to grant permission to change the flag from a United States carrier to a Portuguese carrier.

In August, another foreign bidder, Compania Argentina Navigation Ultramar of Buenos Airies, Argentina, came into the picture. Intricate negotiations, sometimes almost resembling a Keystone Kops plot, soon took place. At several points, the Company negotiators had the distinct feeling that the Argentine agents were just exploring to find out information. C. C. Boden, the head of Cargill's New York office, wired John Jr. about one of them: "He sounds like a screwball. Do not think at all serious but will keep working. Apparently he has just heard of the boat and thinks he can scalp."

But Boden was wrong. The Argentine organization made Cargill a firm bid, offering $1,600,000. With some additional costs after the contract was signed, the Argentine group eventually paid Cargill a total of $1,665,708. The Company added up its own costs, and they came, not to $1 million, but $1,600,682. After all of the difficulties related to the construction and sale of the *Carlantic*, the Company's profit on the effort was $65,026.

But this small profit did not reflect the real values for the Company. In terms of pride of workmanship and credibility for the Cargill shipbuilding group, the completion and sale of the *Carlantic* was of great importance. With the boat finished in October 1941, it seemed wrong to continue to call it the *Carlantic*, now that Cargill was not to be its owner. Shortly before the formal dedication, the ship was renamed the M. V. *Victoria*. On November 10, a formal visitation aboard the vessel was held for federal, state and city officials, Albany dignitaries and other important members of Cargill's public. John Sr., John Jr. and Cargill MacMillan all were present for the festivities; Austen Cargill was the toastmaster for the banquet. The next day the vessel sailed down the Hudson, headed for sea trials off New York Harbor, preparatory to certification from the American Bureau of Shipping. These were a complete success, and on November 18, 1941, the Bureau gave its formal blessing.[30]

The Company received wide acclaim for the *Victoria*, not only in the public press but in a number of the more technically minded shipping

The Carlantic, *now renamed the* Victoria, *prepares to sail to South America, December 1941.*

magazines. Perhaps the rhetoric at the banquet was overblown, that "most of the established principals [*sic*] of shipbuilding and the orthodox methods of proceeding were ignominiously dunked into the waste paper basket and Cargill, Inc. proceeded with pioneer spirit into their own channels of ship construction." The banquet speakers also boasted that the boat had been "the object of more wild speculation than would attend the building of a gross of similar craft under ordinary circumstances" and that "a great many people today are eating a great many words."

Indeed, the Company could be proud of its rather astounding success—to have built an oceangoing vessel at an upstate port that had never had such a project, utilizing unconventional methods and designs. When the *Victoria* set sail on its maiden voyage for Argentina on December 11, 1941, just four days after Pearl Harbor, John Jr. and his colleagues felt that they had accomplished a miracle.[31]

A Diversification Study Falters

It was not just ocean transport that interested John Jr.; over the period August to December 1939, an extensive study was conducted on another possible Cargill diversification. Herbert Warden, Jr., a family friend living at that time in Philadelphia was commissioned to help with this.

Dubbed by Warden the "Distributing Plan," it contemplated using Cargill towboats and barges on the Mississippi River, including its upper reaches. (After years of agitation, the "nine foot channel" project of locks and dams between St. Louis and Minneapolis had been completed in 1939). Second, the development would be two-way, grain downriver and a backhaul from the Gulf all the way to Minneapolis, where on a piece of land to be acquired by the Company a distribution yard would be established. A 70-acre site had been identified in an area of South St. Paul, alongside the river.

The backhauls would include several basic commodities not already handled by the Company—coal, oil and lumber. These were not new ideas, for bulk coal had been carried from time to time on contract. Even back in the W. W. Cargill days in LaCrosse prior to the turn of the century there had been retail coal operations, and one of the backhauls of those days was coal from Pennsylvania. Further, the Cargills and MacMillans had shared ownership in lumber operations, both in the earlier W. W. Cargill days and, after the establishment of the Cargill Securities Company, with their continuing ownership of British Columbian and Mexican timberlands. Yet it was a new departure to consider being a wholesale distributor for these three commodities.

This was not all—there was a fourth component of the backhaul that was unique indeed to those in the Company who were used to dealing in commodities in their more literal sense. The Distributing Plan also proposed that Cargill become a wholesale purveyor of "groceries and food products" (Warden earlier had had experience in Jamaica tying together marketing of canned goods and trucking). As a component of Warden's plan for Cargill, the Company would need to establish a trucking operation, which it had been doing at Albany from the mid-1930s.

The Company made clear to Warden that it did not wish to have its participation known to anyone. This applied not only to those in the Minneapolis area who might be interested but also to the many companies to be contacted by Warden for information. Warden persuaded John Jr. to allow him to use Hugo Scheuermann's name (the Chase National Bank executive) as reference, while maintaining the confidentiality of Cargill itself. In these letters, the property itself was identified only as being in South St. Paul and along the Mississippi River. A crude schematic drawing of the 70-acre site showed it paralleling a double rail track, and the storage area was described in Warden's words as being "at the top of a perpendicular bank . . . about 50 feet high." An incline car hoist would have to be developed, as well as unloading equipment.

By October, Warden had contacted gasoline distributors, lumber mills and coal distributors, as well as several leaders among the wholesale grocery trade. Unfortunately for Warden, the incredibly fast pace of world events from the beginning of September, with the declaration of war against Germany by England and France, had quickly changed some of the financial equations upon which the project depended. Cargill Mac-Millan wrote Warden a diplomatic letter on October 10, 1939. It began: "John and I are both agreed that we want to go ahead with the plans we outlined with you right up to the point where it comes to putting up the money." Noting that "we must know *just* how good our scheme is," he pointed to the impact of the outbreak of war on commodity markets; there had been a precipitous rise in prices that had cost the Company more to finance its fall buying. Also, as Cargill MacMillan put it, "the spectacular rise in ocean freights has made this field look substantially more attractive than river freights, which have advanced very little, if at all." The Company wanted Warden to finish the study, "for we feel quite sure that eventually we are going to want to get into the river transportation field," but there is no evidence that the Company intended to "go ahead and buy the property."

Warden pressed on with his analysis through the rest of 1939, at one point even suggesting special ways of unloading barge freight. Nevertheless, it was clear that building of ocean shipping now consumed John Jr.'s thinking and the Distributing Plan had been put on hold. However, the concept of exploiting a backhaul, already considered in the Company's Erie Canal operations, once again had captured management's attention. In later years, Cargill was more substantially involved in coal, salt and gasoline, but the lumber and grocery wholesaling idea never came to pass.[32]

Diversification in Reality: The Feed Business

John Jr. was not alone in thinking of diversification. On June 12, 1939, Austen Cargill brought a proposal to the Commitment Committee to develop a modern elevator and feed plant at Lennox, South Dakota at a cost of $26,000. In justifying a move into feed, he once again drew on historical contrast. Whereas the grain-producing areas had been monoculture (and therefore grain trading companies could run their line elevators simply, by centralized control), now there was widespread diversified farming. As Austen put it, "While the line of demarcation is indefinite, it follows a north and south course which moves in a westerly direction. In 1917 that line was within one hundred miles of Green Bay; today it is in the Red River Valley. It is impossible for a line elevator operation with centralized control to operate successfully in the area east of that line for any length of time."

To solve this problem, Austen wanted to develop "a highgrade type of local management," who would have the ability to carry out for the Company "the intelligent merchandising of side lines." He suggested coal, building material, flour and feed. The last, he felt, had the greatest promise: "Farmers have recently changed their feeding methods . . . they have found the most efficient and economical feed consists of grinding their own grain and mixing therein approximately twenty per cent of the mixture called concentrates. Of all the numerous schemes to increase the efficiency of a country elevator . . . the manufacture and mixing of these concentrates into the ground grain of the farmer furnish the best solution."

Austen then sketched his plan for how the Company might position a modern feed operation. In the center of an area having substantial potential, a "Type A" plant would be located, one that could receive and store in car lots the ingredients for the concentrate, with facilities to maintain uniform quality control in its manufacture. There would then be a set of six or so "Type B" elevators/feed operations, with a grain grinder and a mixer to grind customers' grain and then mix it with the concentrates and with a warehouse for inventory. The Lennox facility, where the Company had leased a line elevator for a number of years, could be upgraded to a Type A operation.

The Commitment Committee agreed, and the new buildings were constructed without delay, culminating on November 8, 1939, with a "grand opening." The Lennox plant was renamed the "Farm Commodity Exchange," to sell (again a new name) "Blue Square Feed." This operation that Austen Cargill called his "Air Castles" was a noteworthy success for the Company. Soon other plants were built at key points—at Scotland, South Dakota; at Litchfield, Minneota, Alfa, LaFayette, and Milroy, Minnesota; and at Rembrandt, Iowa. All of these marketed Blue Square feeds.[33]

W. W. Cargill had sold feed at LaCrosse in the nineteenth century, perhaps as early as 1884. The Conrad, Montana, operation, started by John Jr. in the mid-1930s continued to manufacture feeds, not only poultry and hog feed but pelletized cattle and sheep feed (in spite of a setback due to a fire in 1937). In Montana, however, "Cargill" was used as the trade name. Later, Conrad too adopted the Blue Square label. Blue Square marked a truly significant milestone for the Company, one that put Cargill into the feed business, although in a relatively small geographic area.

Julius Hendel also had been interested in scientific feeds. On his own farm near Lake Minnetonka he had experimented with feeding poultry using his own formulas. In March 1941, a property became available in Minneapolis, one owned by the Chicago, St. Paul, Minneapolis & Omaha Railroad Company and leased to the International Sugar Feed Corporation. The latter had lost its lease (having failed to pay the taxes), and Hendel now proposed to Cargill management that the Company pick up the lease for its own feed operation. Hendel began to put together an organization of men to develop what came to be known as Cargill Feeds. At this time, just before the beginning of World War II, the two feeds—

Blue Square Feeds and Cargill Feeds (also marketing a small line called Du-All Feed)—were being produced and marketed by two quite separate groups within the Company. These were sometimes in competition with each other in certain sales territories. This important story will be discussed further in the next chapter.

Hendel, incidentally, had dabbled in some other interesting endeavors; he wired Cargill MacMillan in February 1940: "Just sold Kan 50,000 used Cuban sugar bags at profit 3 cents." In this same wire he referred again to a notion he had at this time—that Cargill might become a trader in ingots of forged chromium nickel steel, serving the machine tool industry. This idea did not become a live project, however.[34]

The TNEC Study: A Paper Tiger

The feared Temporary National Economic Committee, the special congressional investigating committee set up in June 1938, held extensive hearings all through 1939, involving some 775 hours and calling 552 witnesses. Its reports were eventually released—31 volumes, 6 supplements and 43 monographs. Cargill and the rest of the grain trade had been apprehensive about these investigations, remembering the vast amounts of time spent in the early 1920s with the many-volume Federal Trade Commission study of the industry. In 1936, Cargill grudgingly had complied with the FTC request for data linked to a related study, its "agricultural income inquiry." This investigation had not required any grain trade appearances at the hearings. Now the TNEC bypassed the grain trade, too.

There were two parts of the TNEC hearings that discussed the agricultural and food industries. Once again, no grain trade officials were called. Only an assistant chief economist of the FTC, Colonel William H. England, appeared to testify about what had been learned in the 1936 inquiry about the grain trade. A small part of this earlier effort had referred to terminal grain markets, and the FTC had spoken only in generalities "that many of the practices which were the subject of criticism by the Commission's earlier investigations . . . still existed." The focus of the FTC at that time primarily had been on railroad-owned terminals, "leased by large merchandisers of grain at low rentals, giving the lessees an undue competitive advantage . . . such large merchandisers practically dominate both the cash and future markets." Their conclusions and recommendations, however, did not propose any significant change in existing ownership and management practices in the terminal grain industry.

In the final report of the TNEC on "Agriculture and the National Economy," the Committee returned to the belief held so strongly by the Farm Board in 1930 that cooperative marketing was a way of building more effective competition. Still, no specific recommendations were made, and it seemed as if the TNEC had lost interest in the long-standing use of grain traders as scapegoats for farmer disgruntlements.

Indeed, the entire TNEC effort came to be considered ineffectual. As historian William E. Leuchtenburg put it, "the TNEC's shelf of studies brought knowledge of business operations up to date, but the total yield of the investigation proved disappointing . . . unwilling either to tackle the more difficult problems or to make recommendations which might disturb vested interests, the committee expressed the wistful hope that if it assembled enough facts, someone would be able to use them to solve the enigma of persistent unemployment."[35]

Cargill and War Preparedness

The European war had permeated most peoples' lives since its institution in early September 1939. But it was the invasion of Denmark and Norway in early April 1940 that seemed to signal a full-scale world war was at hand. The Netherlands and Belgium fell to the Nazis in May, and the Anglo-French expeditionary force was forced to withdraw to England in the valiant evacuation from Dunkirk from May 28 to June 4, 1940. When France fell in June, the situation looked grim indeed for the Allies.

Cargill had been doing a substantial amount of its European grain trade from an office in Copenhagen, Denmark, with Almon Greenman as the local head. He wrote in *Cargill News* of his trials in bringing himself and his wife and child out of the war zone:

After considerable delay in obtaining German visas we started out for home via Germany and Italy. It wasn't until Denmark was invaded that we were fully aware that Copenhagen was located on an island. Then the sinking of ferries between Seeland and Fyn or Germany brought the geography clearly to our attention. It was reliably estimated by Danish and American observers that between 40,000 and 50,000 German soldiers lost their lives in the waters between Denmark, Sweden, and Norway. Danish fishermen found it more profitable to go after German dead at $1.00 a piece than to fish, and many Danes remarked that they would not eat mackerel this year. Many Danish country homes were opened forcibly and filled with German dead to be shipped back to Germany by the trainload at night . . .

We took a ferry from Gedser in Denmark to Warnemunde in Germany. The route was marked by buoys every 100/150 yards and presumably mine-swept. But on nearing Warnemunde we could make out a big ship that could have been a transport lying down at one end.

Our trip through Germany was uneventful. We had 24 hours in Berlin. There were not many fine looking men nor noticeable business activity: the frightful attack on Holland and Belgium was underway. . . . There is an attempt to impress travelers, particularly Americans, in this respect.

We went on to Italy. . . . Two days each in Genoa and Florence before embarking on an honest to gosh American boat in Naples . . . Back in Genoa on the 'Manhattan' we heard that the sailing of the 'Rex' to New York had been cancelled indicating that Italian entry into the war was more likely. Friends who had secured excellent bookings on that Italian ship were immediately looking frantically for accommodations on our boat or smaller U.S. ships.

Our trip across was uneventful. We were not stopped at Gibraltar, and Italy did not come into the war until the day we docked in New York. But many of us were disturbed at the high percentage of people, German by birth, in the ship's crew. The radio news programs received on board were heard by large crowds with keen interest.

Meanwhile, Leonard L. Corlett, the Cargill representative in Rotterdam, was attempting to leave the Netherlands. He described the problem:

We discovered that immediate departure was no simple matter. Special permits or visas were required to cross all frontiers. Crowds were excitedly besieging the Belgian and French consular employees for application forms and photographers were working overtime taking passport size pictures. We needed fifteen of them for each of us. In normal times visas are ordinarily obtained in a few moments, but war time conditions necessitated the filling in of lengthy questionnaires. It required almost an entire day to get these papers prepared in a presentable fashion.

Fortunately, the American Consul General intervened in our behalf so it was not necessary for us to be delayed ten days or two weeks for a favorable consideration by the foreign departments in Brussels and Paris. After three days of waiting in stuffy offices, we were able to start for Antwerp, where our first visit was to police headquarters to obtain permission to remain in the city for more than 48 hours.[36]

Back at the Company, there were numerous efforts at war preparedness. An interesting decision was taken by the Company's board of directors on June 20, 1941, regarding employment of female personnel. The depression had led many companies, Cargill included, to allow the hiring of only one member of a family, and this was nearly always a man. Single women kept jobs (like men) if they were the only source of family income, but married women were not hired. The document explained a new policy as follows:

TO ALL DEPARTMENT MANAGERS

Because it is becoming more and more difficult for us to find suitable new employees the Directors feel that we should suspend the rule regarding married women. Until further notice, therefore, it will not be necessary for us to replace, within six months, women who marry while in our employ.

We do ask you to explain to these girls . . . that the rule has only been suspended, and that the day may come when we decide to re-instate it. In some instances it may also be advisable to point out to a girl who marries that it is going to be pretty much up to her to show us that her new responsibilities are not interfering in any way with her work, as so often happens.

We will also now be free to employ a woman who is already married, where that seems the best thing to do, but we would like to confine such employment to temporary positions, and we ask that before you hire any married woman for a permanent position you clear the matter thru Mr. Ralph Golseth or the Personnel Department.[37]

All through this period, significant segments of the country were fundamentally opposed to the preparedness efforts of the administration. Bob

Jaccard, the Company's Grain Department crop reporter (successor to Daniel MacMillan), commented on this in the August 1940 *Cargill News*: "The United States is at war, that is, East of the Wabash River. You leave the Middle West, Missouri and Illinois feeling fairly secure, then start crossing Indiana and by the time you reach Central Ohio you look in hotel closets and under the beds for 5th, 6th or 7th columners. . . . Maybe I'm wrong but I thought all portions of the U.S. were one and the same country. We'd better wake up out West before we find this war is all over with and we missed out on the fun, because it's sure hot and heavy in the East."

John Jr. wrote his brother Cargill, on April 29, 1941, of one of the Minneapolis manifestations of this dissent:

[Charles A. Lindbergh] has this section of the country by the ears, and of course we are the center of the isolationist movement. I think at least half of our friends are Lindberg [*sic*] sympathizers and he will have a tremendous outturn at the dinner to be given for him here next week [Lindbergh had grown up in Little Falls, Minnesota, and his father had been in the U.S. House of Representatives from Minnesota's Sixth District]. . . . The Palm Beach crowd are returning, talking nothing but defeatism. The whole thing perturbs me not a little but I think the President can be counted on to control the situation.

John Jr.'s support of President Roosevelt stood in considerable contrast to his earlier hostility. When some of the Minnesota congressmen voted against the administration's proposal to arm merchant vessels, John Jr. spoke out strongly against their actions, writing Weston Grimes, "The most important thing in the world today is the defeat of Hitler . . . our personal affairs and interests must be wholly subordinated until such time as he is disposed of."

John Jr. certainly had not lost all of his vitriol against FDR, however, for he ended this letter: "Then and not until then, can we resume our fight against domination from the bottom, i.e. the New Deal." But on preparedness, John Jr. supported Roosevelt unswervingly. In a letter in late September 1940, during the height of the presidential campaign, he wrote his friend John Cowles, publisher of the *Minneapolis Star-Journal and Tribune*: "With conditions as they are I think the Republican leaders are making a great mistake in endeavoring to hamper the President in any way, and I think it would be exceedingly sound politics for Mr. Willkie to say that war may well be inevitable but that if it comes it is better to have a man of proven executive capacity at the helm rather than a bungler of the type of Roosevelt." He continued: "It may well be that I take a much more grave view of world affairs than do you or Willkie."

John Jr. seemed always to opt for action; he went on: "It seems very plain to me that if the English are defeated we are next on the list. . . . Under present world conditions it is vastly better to meet the situation by our own efforts than it is to have the situation confront us later. 'A stitch in time saves nine.' " In this letter, John Jr. also argued for a total ban on all exports "which might conceivably have any war value to Japan." Noting that this would probably drive the Japanese to attack the Dutch East Indies, he also advocated that Roosevelt, "as Commander-in-Chief of the Navy," send the fleet immediately to Singapore. This, he felt, would force a peaceful solution rather than triggering war. John Jr.'s sense of overall strategic thinking was again in evidence.

John Sr., if anything, was even more opposed to the isolationists. When Richard P. Gale, a Minnesota Republican in the U.S. House of Representatives, took a position against renewing the Selective Service legislation, John Sr. wrote him a stinging letter of rebuke that ended: "The way the majority of the Republicans have voted and acted during this crisis makes it very doubtful if I will ever support the Republican ticket again." John Sr. exploded when he learned of the Republican National Committee decision to oppose the appointments of two longtime Republicans, Henry L. Stimson and Frank Knox, as the secretaries of War and Navy in the Roosevelt administration. John Jr. then wrote the chairman of the committee: "From the enclosed letter of my Father you can see he feels strongly on this matter—and when he feels strongly he feels *strongly*."

John Jr.'s views on war preparedness—and on the state of the country, too—can best be seen in a major document he wrote and had set professionally in print in July 1940, entitled "A National Program to Ensure the Defense of the Nation, the Improvement of the Race, the Maintenance of Liberty and a Higher Standard of Living." In this he laid out four "national objectives." One involved national defense, another spoke of liberty, and a third emphasized high standards of living; all three were reasonably noncontroversial.

The fourth *was* controversial. He called for "the improvement of the race, by insisting on a higher birth rate at the top of society than at the bottom." Here he returned to his views on the value of an intellectual elite that he espoused so vividly during and just after World War I. His wording for this argument was couched in military terms:

Every Sociologist will freely testify that in almost every country on earth, but especially in the United States, the birth rate is far higher at the bottom than at the top. Carried forward a few generations and the inevitable result is such a low quality that a complex civilization cannot function at all, for lack of enough brains to furnish the Sergeants, and Corporals, which keep the wheels moving. Every business executive knows what happens if he cannot find the officials, petty and important, which he needs. Without them his organization disintegrates. It is believed probable that the disappearance of all previous civilization has been due to this biological phenomenon . . . we have done nothing whatever to cope with the problem. It should be treated as our most important national problem, next to Defense.

His solution was to "encourage large families at the top" by using the taxing power, especially by manipulation of inheritance taxes. Although he did not want concentration of power in the few—fortunes would be split up at death into "at least five parts"—he still wanted to "insist on a high birth rate at the top of society, where we presumably find the brightest and strongest."

Once again, John Jr. had returned to his scrutiny of eugenics and the science of human heredity, emphasizing the statistical concepts of Francis Galton, who had strongly advocated "positive eugenics"—that one should foster more prolific breeding among the socially meritorious. Galton had used a Gaussian bell-shaped curve to segment racial characteristics among a total population. Later Karl Pearson developed what he called "the law of ancestral heredity," in which he seemed to advance the thesis that heredity might be programmed for the betterment of the race by careful selection. The use of the so-called I.Q. test by the armed forces in World War I (and in World War II also) involved a massive intelligence testing of recruits, "not primarily for the exclusion of intellectual defectives," said its sponsors back in the World War I days, "but rather for the classification of men in order that they may be properly placed in the military service." John Jr. appeared to espouse many of these notions.

John Jr. circulated this surprising pamphlet among his close friends and received a number of responses. One, an eight-page letter from Loring M. Staples, a prominent Minneapolis lawyer and Yale friend of John Jr. remains in his files. Staples came down hard on the pamphlet's thesis on racial improvement:

I cannot agree with you that the ability to accumulate wealth is the sole criterion of intelligence . . . men of the caliber of, say, Professor Einstein (who probably has accumulated very little wealth) should be preferred as parents of large families to those of the type of Moe Annenberg (who until his recent trouble with the government was considered one of the country's wealthiest citizens) [Moses L. Annenberg, a Philadelphia publisher of racetrack "tip sheets," was reputed to have had the highest income in the country at the time he was indicted for income-tax evasion; he was given a three-year sentence for this.] . . . Adolph Hitler . . . is also of the opinion that the race should be selectively improved, although he goes about it in a somewhat different although equally dogmatic method than you would employ. You would encourage Moe Annenberg to have a large family because he happens to be wealthy, whereas Adolf would discourage Moe from having a large family because he happens to be a Jew. I regard both methods as distasteful.

Daniel Kevles, in his book *In the Name of Eugenics*, pointed out that the eugenics enthusiasts of this period were "largely middle to upper class, white, Anglo-Saxon, predominantly Protestant and educated . . . well-to-do rather than rich."

Staples seemed to be putting some words in John Jr.'s mouth, for nowhere did John Jr. ever support Annenberg. Yet the Staples point was timely, given the ghastly definition of "improvement of the race" being carried out by Hitler at this particular time.

In a second letter, in October 1940, Staples also criticized John Jr.'s "two-ocean" view of national defense. John Jr. answered:

I have not in any way changed my opinion that the United States should seek only to defend what we can defend by ourselves, i.e. the Western Hemisphere north of the Equator. However in view of the certainty of the Germans, Italians and Japanese ganging up on us in the event of an English defeat next summer, I am very strongly of the opinion that sound national policy requires our polishing off the Japanese now that we might then be able to cope by ourselves with the Germans and Italians a year from now, which we could not do with the Japanese thrown into the scale on their side.

These were two good friends, used to bantering back and forth; John Jr. closed this letter "argumentatively yours."[38]

Twelve Years of Portent

The dozen years from the Great Crash of 1929 to Pearl Harbor had transformed Cargill from a medium-sized regional grain company to a large national corporation with many links abroad. In the process, it had spread into many more functions in the industry itself, particularly inland waterway transportation, ocean shipping, truck transport and animal feed. The Company's financial results for this period were satisfactory, although certainly not outstanding. The net worth of the company had risen from $5.6 million at the end of the crop year 1929–1930 to $9.3 million on May 31, 1941. Net earnings during this span had been excellent for a few of the years, average for others, and included two loss years. The mean for the 12 years was just over $719,000 (the return on net worth averaging 9.6 percent).

Nevertheless, in terms of impact on the industry, Cargill had moved from a little-known midwestern company to a respected and often feared major national force. Indeed, particularly because of the Corn Case, the name Cargill and that of its chief executive officer, John MacMillan, Jr., were well known much beyond the confines of the grain trade itself. Now the upcoming war would test Cargill.

PART FIVE

WAR ONCE MORE; NEW FEED AND OIL DIVISIONS

John MacMillan, Sr. (foreground, in light hat), laying keel for the first AOG, September 1942.

CHAPTER FIFTEEN

Cargill in World War II

Pearl Harbor changed the world for everyone. The near-catastrophic attack there by the Japanese, followed by their landings in the Philippines and capture of Guam, Wake Island and Hong Kong in the month of December 1941, accompanied by severe British naval losses in the South China Sea and Japan's invasion of Thailand and Malaya (December 8), were a great shock to the Allies. The now-combatant United States entered upon a frenzied period. The country was not ready for war before Pearl Harbor, less so after that disaster. Those remaining weeks in December and the uneasy days in the first four months of the new year seemed so grave. The Battle of the Coral Sea (May 7–8) and the Battle of Midway (June 3–6) provided the first substantial stiffening of Allied resistance in the Pacific. Japanese naval losses in these two great battles were severe, as were those of the Allies. In this same six-month period in the European theater, Germany chose not to move across the channel, and its advances in North Africa were finally checked in June 1942. The Russians had also counter-attacked on the Eastern Front. Huge raids, with 1,000 bombers, were carried out by the Allies on Cologne, Bremen and other German cities. Major General James H. Doolittle led carrier-based American B-25 army bombers in a raid on Tokyo. The first six months of full-scale world war after Pearl Harbor were incredibly intense.

The Grain Trade, Wartime Conditions

Demands on key sectors of the country during those six months were awesome. Support of the armed forces was paramount. They needed a united country backing them, agriculture and industry in particular. Both were caught off guard, neither ready for the instant buildup demanded by an all-out, global war.

It was not an easy transition for American agriculture. Soon a fundamental disagreement surfaced in regard to agricultural prices. Agricultural interests pushed hard to maintain the parity concept, abetted by a large Congressional voting bloc from the farm states. The administration, led conspiciously by President Roosevelt himself, succeeded in persuading Congress to pass price-control legislation, creating the powerful OPA, the Office of Price Administration. The President also used his power through executive orders to effect other controls. In the enabling legislation for the OPA, the farm bloc had succeeded in establishing parity at 110 percent. In the ensuing debates over the administration-sponsored Economic Stabilization Act, Roosevelt pushed to have this reduced to 100 percent. The agricultural interests agreed but forced a fateful trade-off by securing the Steagall Amendment, which required government support of prices with a floor of 90 percent parity for two years following the close of the war. Agricultural economist Walter Wilcox called this "the most important single action taken during the war period" in regard to agriculture. He prophetically commented: "This legislation . . . may well set the pattern for government programs in the field of agriculture for many years."[1]

The battle between farm legislation and price control was played out over a number of specific wartime agricultural concerns. The period right before Pearl Harbor had been agriculturally productive, and there were surpluses of wheat and adequate quantities of other agricultural crops. Fortunately, too, the almost four years of World War II were to witness fecund agriculture in most of the food-producing nations. Countering this, however, was a massive disruption of world transportation, and significant areas of war-torn countries experienced severe food deprivation. In particular, ocean shipping was traumatized by U-boat attacks over great reaches of the world's shipping lanes.

In the United States, wheat surpluses continued through the first years of the war. The OPA put stringent controls on flour prices, and there were many battles over the margins exacted by the farmers, by the middlemen grain traders and by the flour millers. Meat and poultry increasingly were in short supply. So feed grains rather than food grains became the priority. Significant surplus wheat was put to use as feed; corn was particularly in great demand. While by 1944–1945 food grain acreage (wheat, rye, rice and buckwheat) had risen only 2.9 percent higher than in 1939–1940, in this same period, feed grain acreage had increased 6.7 percent. Even more striking was the 42.6 percent increase in acreage for oil-bearing crops (soybeans, peanuts, flaxseed).

Productivity also increased throughout the war. Labor shortages in agriculture brought more mechanization, and fertilizer use rose phenomenally. "Though the over-all record of farm production during the war is excellent," Wilcox concluded, "a critical appraisal indicates several places where full mobilization for war production was not achieved." He particularly criticized growers of vegetables and especially cotton producers, who seemed unwilling to shift out of their less needed products. He also faulted planning in the feed grain arena, where an overly cyclical pattern persisted.

Grain traders had their own wartime problems along with everyone else. To start with, they believed that there was an inherent conflict between price control and the free market. Always desiring rigorous competition, they were willing to accept in the process the accompanying wide swings of supply and demand. The futures market epitomized this freedom to them. In World War I, the government had closed the futures markets altogether (John MacMillan, Sr., himself had acquiesced as the grain trade representative for the Minneapolis exchange). In debating the initial emergency Price Control Act in late January 1942, which established the OPA, its officials had wanted the futures markets closed again, for they saw fluctuating prices as a threat to tight control of agricultural prices. But the futures advocates had succeeded in inserting a proviso that futures markets would not be closed. After the OPA clamped down on wheat and flour pricing in October 1942, there were concerns that, as *Northwestern Miller* put it, there would be "a gradual decline of futures trading to the zero mark, as price fluctuations become narrower and narrower." One faction in the grain trade wanted to fight these constraints vigorously and faulted others for not supporting them. They thought Cargill was "apathetic toward the Futures, thinking they can operate without them," and Ed Grimes was accused of believing in "appeasement." Grimes, it was true, always searched for consensus in dealing with the government. Not so for Julius Hendel, however, for he put his activist colleagues' fears to rest when he circulated widely a statement that argued strongly against the OPA ceilings. Hendel felt that the OPA was moving too hastily, tampering with machinery already "perfected to such a degree that the wheat price registered by it is very sensitive to influences extremely minute and widespread in nature." Price controls, he felt, might bring serious repercussions.

Lobbying efforts by the industry against the price control legislation itself were unsuccessful. Cargill kept a low profile, as Ed Grimes's recommendations prevailed. Leon Henderson, the prickly head of OPA, made a speech shortly after an argument about wheat price controls in which he said, according to Weston Grimes, that "all the opposition to the Administration . . . was coming from the grain trade, which are more interested in maintaining market fluctuations for speculative purposes than anything else."[2]

The knottiest problem of the grain trade in that first year after Pearl Harbor was logistics—how to transport and store grain. Every arm of domestic transportation was being severely strained by war production demands. The grain trade learned this quickly, for in May 1942, the Office of Defense Transportation appropriated most Great Lakes shipping for exclusive transport of iron ore, so critically needed for armaments. This threw grain shipments back to the railroads, and with their already swollen loadings, the movement of grain through domestic channels was made extremely difficult. In the fall of 1941, Ed Grimes had headed a move by shippers in the Northwest to use a permit system—a queuing process providing a priority system. Now he led a similar effort, this time to be applied all over the country in the succeeding months of 1942. *Time* magazine praised the industry's "hard-headed cooperation . . . headed by E. J. Grimes (Cargill, Inc.)." Late in the fall of 1942, a small amount of Great Lakes shipping was released for grain trade use, but the demand for ore shipping continued for most of the war.

Grain storage capacity became short as terminals rapidly filled. The government storage facilities that had been built up in the previous two years were not enough of a supplement to privately owned facilities, even with the on-farm storage of the farmers themselves, much of it rather makeshift, although generally functional. The Grimes-initiated permit system allowed a better allocation of storage, but the logistics of grain transportation remained tense throughout the war.[3]

In spite of the momentousness of these wartime decisions, everyday competition in the industry continued its time-honored patterns. For example, a General Mills executive took the time in June 1942 to write Cargill about what he thought was an infringement on the General Mills registered trade mark, "farm-tested." In an issue of *Feedstuffs,* Cargill had placed a feed advertisement that used this same term, "featured quite prominently," the General Mills executive alleged. Ed Grimes passed the complaint along to Fred Seed in the Company's feed group, who agreed that Cargill instead would use "production tested" for the Cargill message.[4]

Cargill's Two Outstanding Crop Years

In the face of price controls, transportation bottlenecks and other frustrations in those days after Pearl Harbor, the Company's crop years 1941–1942 and 1942–1943 were excellent. These years saw rising commodity prices and tight storage, precisely the "carrying charge" market that rewarded those organizations with good storage facilities. John Jr.'s strategic planning—the building, leasing and buying of additional terminal capacity—now proved to be quite prescient. The Company's total capacity had been just over 54 million bushels in 1939; in the first year after Pearl Harbor, it rose to 69.6 million bushels (and was up another 2 million the following year). Further, it was the clever positioning of these terminals—John Jr.'s ideas—that made so much difference. The substantial terminal at Kansas City and the huge operation at Omaha (the repaired section was now in operation) provided a Western base. The East St. Louis terminal, completed just as the war started (after its problems with pilings had been overcome), became the accumulation point for Upper Mississippi, Missouri and Illinois river grain. It subsequently handled millions of bushels of inbound truck grain and also was the interchange point for both major north/south and east/west railroads, giving Cargill important transit privileges. Memphis continued its effectiveness for lower Mississippi shipping, both downstream and upstream. Storage in the Duluth/Superior area and Minneapolis remained available; the large Buffalo combination (the Electric, the Great Eastern and the Superior) and the huge Albany terminal offered a vast capacity in the East. In addition, a major terminal, with 3.1 million bushels of storage, had been leased at Maumee, Ohio (a suburb of Toledo). There were other additions, too, the total giving the Company enviable grain storage facilities, certainly among the best in the country.

As the Company purchased grain in each of those good crop years, stored some of it under its own name and some for others, and sold into the expanding wartime market, major profits ensued. Cargill's net profit in the crop year ending May 31, 1942, was $2,749,000, the highest in its history; the profit for the crop year 1942–1943 was close—$2,044,000.

The Grain Department accounted for most of this profitability. In that first war year, the gross profit for the grains was $3.4 million; in the second, $3.1 million. Feed was not a profitable operation yet. The country line, the commission division and the futures business had made small contributions, as had seed. Shipbuilding had had a net loss in the first of those two years and a modest $140,000 profit in the second. Cargo Carriers had made a significant contribution in the first year, less in the second. In sum, it was grains that provided the underpinnings of the Company's tremendous success in those two years.

As expected, grain inventories had jumped sharply during that two-year period. The total holdings for grain on May 31, 1941, was just over 22 million bushels. One year later, this figure stood at almost 33 million bushels and was at the same figure the following year. The reason for the striking figures lay in the changing mix of grain over this period. On May 31, 1941, wheat represented almost 50 percent of the total inventory. For the following year, this was down to 15 percent. Corn, the feed grain, showed the largest increase. There had been just 6.5 million bushels in inventory on May 31, 1941, and one year later it was 15.1 million bushels. Rye, too, took a tremendous jump, from 6.5 million in 1941 to 12.2 million in 1942 and just under 12 million in 1943 (the reasons for this huge increase in rye will become apparent later in this chapter). War curtailed the export of all grains, so the high Cargill sales during the first two years of the war were overwhelmingly for domestic use and storage.

Shipbuilding—in the Cornfields

A successful professional in the grain trade, Cargill now had an "amateur" foothold in shipbuilding. Before Pearl Harbor, Cargill had committed itself to the building of another major ship the size of *Victoria* at Albany. Despite many hopes, no governmental contract had been forthcoming, but the Company had made a decision to go ahead anyway. Some steel and other materials already were on hand, and further orders had been entered (although no priority status could be claimed for such a company-owned ship).

Three days after Pearl Harbor, Weston Grimes, in Washington again, contacted the navy officers, reminding them that the Company was "beginning to construct another large tanker of about 14,000 dwt" but that the Company was willing to shift over to build the Navy's "Sea Otters" (much smaller, faster craft, about 250 feet long with a 1,200-ton cargo capacity and a speed of about 12 knots). Ten of these could be made by Cargill as an alternative to building the large tanker. John Jr., always optimistic about the Albany shipyard, vowed that "we should come very close . . . in eight months" for either venture. Privately, he had been critical of some of the planning for the *Victoria*, alleging that the Company had paid "fantastic premiums" for quick delivery of unanticipated materials and that the new venture should be a "work boat and not a luxury liner like the last one."[5]

On December 30, 1941, John Jr. left for Florida for his vacation, worn out and half-sick. On January 9, 1942, an unexpected call came to Cargill MacMillan, left in charge in Minneapolis in the absence of John Jr. and John Sr. (who was in California). It was from a Navy Department commander with a surprising proposal—the navy was planning to contract for 300 ATLs, tank lighters (oil barges), each of substantial size. Inasmuch as the Navy did not want to build ATLs near the ocean, would Cargill be interested in building them in the Midwest, say, at Memphis?

Just why Cargill was approached seemed unclear at that time. A year or so later, John Jr. was given a reason by one of the naval officers: "The Navy was embarrassed by the offer of an obscure shipyard in Brooklyn, to whom they did not wish to give the contract." Apparently this undesirable firm had only a primitive outdoor facility; picking Cargill, whose Albany yard also was quite rudimentary, gave the Navy an excuse—or at least so John Jr. reasoned.

John Jr. immediately left his vacation quarters to meet his brother and Chris Jensen (the Albany shipbuilding superintendent) in Washington.

"One More River to Cross," Saint Paul Pioneer Press, *November 28, 1942.*

Overnight, the three worked out on paper a system of how a shipyard might be laid out to construct all 300 of these vessels. However, when they reached the Navy Department offices, it became clear that the officers were talking of Cargill being involved in considerably less than the total number. John Jr. made an articulate case as to why Cargill should build in Minneapolis, rather than a downriver town on the Mississippi. Their contact, Commander Philip Lemler, a Bureau of Ships officer in the Navy Department quickly negated this notion, making clear that the navy did not want Cargill to build these on the Upper Mississippi "because of ice conditions." Lemler also indicated that "his idea of the number of vessels Cargill should build will undergo a further reduction." At the end of the meeting, the number 80 was mentioned as a possible Cargill component of the 300 vessels. Even this was an exciting prospect for a company that had built just one oceangoing vessel and which had not been able to get any other governmental contracts.

The three Cargill officers returned to Minneapolis, feeling undaunted by the negative view of Minneapolis as a site. John Jr. and Jensen, in haste, worked out a detailed proposal for the construction of these 80 boats, pricing the contract on the basis of the number of ships to be delivered per day that the navy might desire: if one ship each day, the cost would be $8 million; if every two days, the price dropped to $5 million; if every eight days, $3 million. In his cover letter to Lemler on January 21, John Jr. reported that "we are especially pleased at having found an absolutely ideal site . . . served by two railroads." As to the Northern climes, "there would be no problem whatever in keeping the river open." John Jr. added a gratuitous postscript, "It was . . . a source of great gratification to discover that there is at least one agency of the government which is on its toes."[6]

The "ideal site" was on the Minnesota River, not the Mississippi. It was near the town of Savage, a "beautiful site," John Jr. reported to his mother and father. "This would involve about 13 miles of dredging of the Minnesota River," he continued, "the cost of which would probably be somewhere between $150,000 and $250,000, which however is a small matter in view of the excellence of the site." Options were now taken for possible purchase. The proposed location was made up of a number of contiguous properties (one of these was where the famous trotter, "Dan Patch" trained, and the old horse barn and training track were still there).

This notion of using the Minnesota River as a viable commercial waterway related to a long-standing effort to persuade the United States Congress that it should mandate (to the Corps of Engineers) a nine-foot channel all the way to Minneapolis. Since before 1917 (when the "Twin City Lock and Dam" was completed) a vocal group had argued that this upper waterway of the Mississippi River should be deepened to a full nine feet. Opposing a deeper channel were environmentalists; railroad interests also viewed increased barge traffic as a threat to the well-being of the rail industry. Despite their efforts, a major dam at Hastings was completed in 1930. In that same year, Congress actually went on record as approving the channel—but no funds were authorized. Later in the 1930s, money became available, and the nine-foot channel project was completed in 1939.[7]

The Minnesota River, which entered the Mississippi just above St. Paul, at the suburb of Mendota, had not been part of this project. Instead of a nine-foot channel, it was more like four-feet, at least in several spots; thus John Jr.'s report that considerable dredging (including the removal of several rock ledges) would be necessary to make the Minnesota navigable.

The new navy proposal threw Cargill's Albany planning into limbo, for the navy intimated that it wished Cargill to cease production altogether on its own vessel at Albany. Cargill acquiesced on February 6, 1942. The reason for this ultimatum was made clear on February 9, when Commander Lemler made a completely fresh proposal, that Cargill build six naval vessels called AOGs, auxiliary oil and gasoline carriers just over 300 feet long, with a 48-foot beam and a capacity of 15,000 barrels. The vessels would have a displacement of about 4,335 tons and a draft of 15 feet when fully loaded. Each had accommodations for about 10 officers and 125 enlisted men.

Ten days later, Lemler notified the Company that "the War Compensation Board has advised him that they prefer Minneapolis to Albany" and that therefore permission was given to locate Cargill's yard there. John Jr. wrote his father of the decision, noting that the navy still felt that "the draft of the boats we had under discussion is too large for us, although we know positively that this is not the case, but, like all Bureaucrats, they are so pig-headed one cannot talk with them." The navy estimated the mean draft of the AOGs at 7.34 feet; when the boat was trimmed (motor, deck trim, guns, etc.), they estimated the draft would be over 9 feet. Cargill felt that if the vessel was kept on even keel, with some of the trimming eliminated (guns, for example), the draft could be maintained at the figure of 7.34 feet.[8]

To ensure that the completed vessel did not dip at one end and thereby deepen the draft, John Jr. wired: "Chris says we can move all portable material forward to trim ship and if not sufficient we can use the stern 100 feet of *Carneida* [the Company's towboat built in 1939] as combined tug and pontoon at stern of ship. We have had extensive experience in this very thing in the *Carneida* salvage operations." The navy, however, would have no part of the Chris Jensen proposal and wanted "to float the finished ships to the ocean without 'crutches.' " John Jr. wrote his father: "I am completely disgusted with the Navy and was disposed last night to tell them that we would not work with them under any circumstances, but both Weston and Cargill were agreed that it was merely a case of necessary red tape, so we are still going along." The navy then insisted that the finishing be done (in particular, adding the main propulsion engines) at a point below St. Louis, perhaps Baton Rouge or New Orleans. John Jr. was additionally irritated by this but had no choice but to dispatch a representative to survey sites in those towns, and arrangements were made subsequently with the port commission at New Orleans.

Pricing constraints imposed by the Navy Department presented some challenging dilemmas. The government preferred fixed-cost contracts, although already it was apparent that wartime brought wholly unexpected problems that could escalate costs tremendously. Thus, the concept of a "cost-plus" contract began to be used in a great many government contracts. The Navy Department seemed to be insisting on the former basis, however, for Cargill. The sum for just one ship was to be well over $1.5 million. John Jr., fearful of damaging the Company's credit arrangements, pushed hard for a cost-plus arrangement. The navy acquiesced, but only partially, agreeing to a cost and fixed-fee basis—in other words, a lump sum for completing each ship.

Cargill's plan to have the shipyard built under a "facility" basis, with the government paying for the construction and owning it, was rejected. Cargill once again agreed to build the shipyard itself. John Jr. had a longer-term goal there, for he had had intimations that the government might be contracting for river barges in the postwar period. Cargill MacMillan had mentioned a visit of a navy official to the Savage site: "He complimented us by stating that we were the first shipyard that he had seen that would fit into a post-war program." The Company had not yet decided at this point to use the Mississippi River waterway for its own towboats and barges, although this had interested John Jr. since before Pearl Harbor.

The dredging stirred up another pricing battle. At the start, John Jr. had felt that Cargill itself could readily take on this cost, that it would be "trifling." As the plans got more specific and a more detailed underwater study was made, it was evident that the removal of the underwater rock ledge was going to be a major task. A compromise emerged: the Corps of Engineers would pay for the first four feet of dredging and Cargill for the remaining five feet, all of the work to be done by Corps of Engineers crews.

On March 19, the formal "letter of intent" arrived, and the Company had its first wartime shipbuilding contract. Six AOGs were to be built (the navy's numbers 6 to 11; the first five were being built in another firm's Seattle shipyard). The estimated cost of each vessel was $1,583,000, and Cargill's fixed fee was to be a flat $94,980 per vessel. A bonus could be earned for early delivery and cost savings, in an amount not to exceed 1 percent of estimated cost (just over $15,000). Thus, the total amount to come to Cargill was to be $569,880, a "pain in the neck," said Cargill MacMillan. "The taxing authorities will get in the neighborhood of $250,000 leaving us with $350,000." Cargill MacMillan, in describing the contract to the board was even more pessimistic, warning that the contract "offered no prospective profit to the Company, and that a certain amount of loss would probably result, instead." But, he continued, "the Company desired to aid the national war effort in every possible way . . . that the management of this corporation has always been of the opinion that in war-time those who knew how to build ships should place their knowledge and facilities at the disposal of the Government when requested to do so." This was not idle talk. It seems clear from the project's voluminous correspondence that, in addition to John Jr.'s enthusiasm for ships, patriotic reasons had weighed heavily for the Cargill officials throughout.[9]

The first two vessels were to be delivered within 13 months and the last four within 19. No facilities monies were to be involved beyond usual depreciation rates "for normal wear and tear." The letter of intent also authorized Cargill to order materials but did not assure highest priority for these. Construction methods were to be left up to Cargill, subject, of course, to Navy Department oversight. In sum, Cargill had a government contract that its executives felt they could live with.

The mold loft, Port Cargill, c. 1942.

There seemed no further reason for withholding information on the project from the Twin Cities public. On March 29 an article appeared in the *Minneapolis Star-Journal and Tribune* about the "$10,000,000 project," one that would "employ State workmen." It was a laudatory story, stressing the patriotism of Cargill, and seemed a fitting cap to the difficult negotiations. At least so it seemed at that moment.

Any euphoria about the kudos that Cargill might reap for its civic-mindedness, however, was punctured a week later when a series of critical articles came out in St. Paul newspapers, vehemently disputing the project. Critics alleged that it was a "flood-ridden and God forsaken location" and would "spoil some swell duckshooting." They asked why the government had been willing to grant the project for a location many miles up the Minnesota River, requiring a significant amount of dredging by the United States Corps of Engineers, rather than locating a similar project along the Mississippi River, which already had a nine-foot channel. Preferably, of course, the site would be located in St. Paul!

Commander Lemler, for one, was disturbed by this criticism and asked that Cargill give him more specific answers to some of the queries raised in the press articles. It seemed important to stress to Lemler (and to the public) that the government was not going to pay for all of the dredging, just that done down to the four-foot level, a level that the Corps of Engineers already had promised to maintain. Weston Grimes, preparing the letter for the Navy Department, believed that the unfavorable publicity would dissipate once the facts were known. There was one other complication, however. This involved the railroad connections to Savage.[10]

A Railroad Is Purchased

When Cargill first assembled its involved project proposal on Port Cargill for the Navy Department in late February 1942, the rail service to Savage was touted as excellent. It was on the main line of the Chicago, St. Paul, Minneapolis & Omaha Railroad and also was served by the Minneapolis, Northfield & Southern Railroad, a belt line connecting with many railroads coming into Minneapolis. Within days, however, John Jr. had a severe shock on this matter, as he described to his father: "The Omaha has flatly refused to put Savage within the Twin City switching district, which would seriously hamper its use as a grain loading and coal unloading point. The Minneapolis, Northfield & Southern are equally reluctant to do so because they would lose revenue from their stations intermediate between Savage and Minneapolis."

A suggestion now surfaced that seemed to solve this problem: If Cargill would purchase the small Minnesota Western Railway Company, which ran from Minneapolis to a point six miles west of Clara City, Minnesota (a distance of 115 miles), the Minneapolis, Northfield & Southern would give the little railroad switching rights. "This would leave us in the position," John Jr. continued, "of paying only the actual transportation costs plus a nominal profit to the Minneapolis, Northfield & Southern. . . . It would also put us in a magnificent competitive position in Central Minnesota as we could then afford to buy grain aggressively at Clara City and do an elaborate business consisting of trucking grain into Clara City and coal and gasoline out."

The Minnesota Western was just about breaking even conducting a semiweekly freight and passenger service; the other five days it sent a motor coach to take care of "the trifling passenger business" (John Jr.'s words). John Jr. thought he could get the line for $100,000; he and Cargill MacMillan would buy it themselves, inasmuch as Interstate Commerce Commission regulations would not allow Cargill to own two transportation companies (Cargill's subsidiary, CCI, was so classified). John Sr. again was uneasy, "a little fearful of tying up our assets in fixed property." Nevertheless, the deal was consummated almost immediately, for it solved the Company's problems of freight service in and out of Savage.

John Jr. was a realist on the public relations effects of this, writing his father a few days later: "The purchase by us of the Minnesota Western is certain to cause a great deal of comment and uneasiness on the part of the grain trade and the other railroads." Indeed, the public announcement in late March regarding the railroad purchase fueled St. Paul's animosity toward Cargill's Savage plans. Weston Grimes wrote Cargill MacMillan, "Someone has . . . given the Navy the seed of an idea that we purchased the railroad in order to reap some extra profit on the shipbuilding operation." The facts were that the railroad was purchased only for Savage service and for potential grain handling, and the hostile press seemed to die away when Cargill officials explained these circumstances both to the Navy Department and the St. Paul critics.[11]

The Ore Project Backfires

"We have had a lot of fun with our [Minnesota Western] railroad," John Jr. wrote Frank Neilson in early August 1942. "We receive delivery of our 660 H.P. Diesel Locomotive the last of this month. . . . Inasmuch as it will be the railroad's only locomotive we are all looking forward to it with anticipation."

If John Jr. indeed was "thinking small" at this point, not the usual posture for him, the "little railroad" all at once began to loom very large. With steel being so critical for war production, the movement of iron ore to the steel mills became a serious concern for the War Production Board and the Office of Defense Transportation.

Minnesota contained much of the country's key iron ore sources. The ore from both the Mesabi and Vermillion ranges in Northern Minnesota was shipped by rail to Duluth and by ore boat to the large steel mills of the lower Great Lakes. The third iron ore range, the Cuyuna was farther south and west in Minnesota. Here, the logical route for the ore was by rail south through the Twin Cities area and then onward to steel mills in Illinois and elsewhere. One of the largest users of ore was the Koppers United Company, with a plant in Granite City, Illinois. With the wartime crunch on the railroads, the idea occurred to many people that this ore from the Cuyuna range could travel from the Twin Cities to the St. Louis area by barge. After all, large quantities of coal came *up* the Mississippi by barge, all the way to the Twin Cities and to intermediate destinations.

John Jr. had felt from the start that Cargill's Savage location could be used for origination of barge movement of iron ore. The fortuitous acquisition by John Jr. and Cargill MacMillan of the Minnesota Western Railway Company became the key. As so often in this crisis period of the first year of the war, the iron ore barging project leaped ahead at a dizzying pace. John Jr. contacted the War Production Board, and within days, Jerome D. Beeler, who was the chief of Inland Waterways in the WPB's transportation arm, had surveyed the entire Twin Cities area, reporting back to the WPB on October 24, 1942.

Beeler saw three final possibilities for ore transfer from rail to barge: (1) a St. Paul location (owned by its Port Authority), 11.6 miles down from the "head of navigation" of the Mississippi; (2) a location on the St. Croix River, at Stillwater, 20.8 miles from this river's confluence with the Mississippi; and (3) Savage. He wrote: "Both St. Paul and Stillwater have ideal locations, and . . . from the standpoint of convenience and efficiency, St. Paul would be more attractive to the barge lines. . . . The barge lines object to Stillwater because of the necessity of moving empty barges from St. Paul and/or Minneapolis downstream 25.3 miles to the mouth of the St. Croix, thence upstream 20.8 miles on the St. Croix to Stillwater."

Against these first two locations was the cost of needed but as yet non-existent facilities, which would require critical materials. Beeler went on: "it appears that when all factors are taken into consideration, the use of the facility at Savage offers the most feasible plan under present conditions." Cargill's facility was going to be built there, whether or not they gained the ore project, and (as Beeler put it) "the facility will be an all-purpose use facility versus single-purpose facilities proposed at St. Paul and Stillwater." Beeler recommended Savage.

The proposal brought an instant reaction from the railroads involved in the southern leg, for the barge would replace rail (whichever of the three sites was chosen). The WPB could readily justify the change to barging, however, in view of the truly critical demands already being put on the railroads.

A much more telling opponent was on the horizon, as Minneapolis looked eastward to its twin city and (usually) friendly rival, St. Paul. The Stillwater alternative seemed to fade back at this point, but St. Paul interests rose up in full wrath to attack just about every aspect of the plan. The lead was taken by the *St. Paul Pioneer Press* in a vehement editorial on "The Ore Dock Mystery" on November 25, 1942. Calling the choice of Savage "one of the prize stupidities . . . of the war effort," the editors castigated "the Cargill interests," who would come out of the war with "a channel built by government to serve the large grain terminal it is evidently planning at Savage." A clever cartoon appeared a few days later, showing an ore ship, with steam up, mired in a pasture, trying to get up a narrow, twisting creek; a farmer with a shovel in hand had yelled to the captain: "Hold it, skipper, I'll dig y' out." Another editorial on December 1 ended: "the war is building a post-war river terminal for private industry at Savage." Even the motives of the WPB officials were called into question: "Here is a situation surrounded with an atmosphere of mystery. The conduct of the war ought to be above suspicion."

Even more threatening, the St. Paul town fathers now made angry representations to several of the Minnesota members of Congress, with particular heat applied to Representative Richard Gale and Senator Henrik Shipstead. At first, Cargill did not take the attack very seriously; when the Congressmen were contacted, Weston Grimes wired John Jr.: "I am perfectly sure the politicians won't intercede for them when they learn about Savage, which they apparently haven't learned about so far."

To make matters more complex, it was not just the Savage side of the equation that was at stake but also a project at the proposed southern terminus of the barges, in the East St. Louis/Granite City area. If necessary, existing facilities could have been used there, those of the Federal Barge Lines at East St. Louis. However, Koppers made it clear that it would prefer a new unloading facility, directly contiguous to the rail line of the Alton and Southern Railroad, which ran right into its mill.

Out of this preference came a new proposal, led by John Jr., that Cargill, the two barge lines involved (Federal and the Central Barge Company), the railroad and Koppers would join together as a syndicate to build a major unloading terminal. The group felt that the best sponsor for this facility would be the Defense Plant Corporation (DPC), and John Jr. was authorized to be the "syndicate manager" to negotiate with the DPC. It was to be of significant size, costing somewhere near $500,000. Participation would be split among the five, 20 percent each.

But the East St. Louis proposal was tied to the Twin Cities proposal (wherever the latter might be located), and final approval of the DPC project would likely not be made—would not even be needed—unless the Twin Cities ore shipment by barge became a reality.

The Twin Cities segment definitely was not in place. Indeed, the opposition had stepped up its attacks. The St. Paul antagonists concentrated their fire on the several government agencies involved. The *St. Paul Dispatch* headlined: "U.S. Spends $20,000 to Deepen Minnesota River to Savage," with the imputation that a private "sweetheart" deal had been perpetrated between a private company and the federal government, the private company enriching itself in the process. At this point, the Minneapolis Civic & Commerce Association came to the defense of Cargill. Colonel J. W. Moreland, the United States engineer for the St. Paul district, clarified the arrangement, noting that the government was to dredge only to the four-foot depth that had been authorized by Congress in 1892. The Minneapolis group also defended Cargill's arrangements through the Minnesota Western Railway for trackage rights for the ore project. Beeler, the WPB official, additionally was quoted in the newspapers as writing Mayor John J. McDonough of St. Paul that "premature publicity on the proposed ore docks . . . may result in the cancellation of the entire idea. . . . Such a result would be a serious blow to a constructive effort to conserve transportation."

But this did not stem the tide of criticism. Later in December, Minnesota Congressman Melvin J. Maas invited the Senate Special Committee Investigating the National Defense Program (but widely known as the Truman Investigative Committee for its head, Senator Harry S. Truman) to look into the Savage plan. The committee had a particular focus on fraud and waste. Although the committee did review both mines and mining and the iron and steel industry, Savage itself never came up for scrutiny.

On December 31, 1942, another issue was added to the argument when Frank W. Matson, the chairman of the Minnesota State Railroad and Warehouse Commission, stated that a number of bridges would become obstructions along the Minnesota River route if the Savage project became a reality. A newspaper article alleged that "six bridges, totaling 958 feet, would have to be rebuilt to make the line safe for ore traffic." Perhaps most unsettling, Weston Grimes reported to his father: "The Washington Merry Go Round [a popular nationally syndicated column] is digging into the ore deal." There was a real horror of having the well-known investigative reporter Drew Pearson looking into Cargill's business.

Cargill executives, increasingly frustrated, felt they had a right to clarification from the government agencies involved. Weston Grimes suggested: "Re-state our stand that we will abide by any decision supported by facts and reiterate our only interest is to ensure movement of ore in furtherance of war effort, but firmly demand that both ODT and WPB clarify their position and clear us of all of the STP [St. Paul] charges." Grimes wired John Jr.: "Unless we stick to this ore thing and see it thru to something like a dignified and fair decision, we are going to have a long fight on our hands ever to get any new rail river rates via SV [Savage]. . . . I think carriers could use the record in the post-war future to support an argument that SV should take a penalty over STP [St. Paul] on any new rail-water or water-rail rates. . . . I feel this decision cannot be left this way."

From the government side, there were arguments within the interagency power structure about who should take jurisdiction—the whole thing had become a political hot potato. Finally, the matter was referred back to the Office of Defense Transportation (ODT). It took many weeks for the ODT to make its decision. Finally, on March 31, 1943, Joseph B. Eastman, the ODT director (and later chairman of the Interstate Commerce Commission), made his recommendation: "That the establishment of a rail-water route for the movement of iron ore from Northern Minnesota to Southern Illinois is inadvisable at this time."

Eastman pointed out in his long memorandum that, "when this diversion was first proposed, it was looked on with much favor by the Office of Defense Transportation" because of the "ample supply of idle open-top barges on the rivers." However, by March 1943, "the loading of 350,000 tons of iron ore southbound would have the effect of materially impairing the ability of the barge lines to handle coal northward. This would make it necessary for the rail lines to have more coal northbound, with further strain on their open-top equipment, manpower and motive power." Eastman concluded that "the net effect of the diversion would be additional use, rather than a saving in the use of rail equipment." In sum, the whole notion of barging ore southward from the Twin Cities was a dead issue— for Savage, for St. Paul, for Stillwater. The syndicate for the construction of the unloading facility in East St. Louis fell through immediately, of course. The great ore project was finished. John Jr. and Cargill MacMillan maintained their ownership of the Minnesota Western Railway, however.[12]

The Savage Shipyard

The Savage shipyard took shape with a rapidity so characteristic of that early wartime period. John Jr., dissatisfied with the purchasing function at the Albany shipyard, brought a new person into the picture, Arthur L. Wheeler. He was John Sr.'s brother-in-law and had been president of the Eberhardt Manufacturing Company, a steel company in Cleveland. The firm had had a serious strike and concurrent financial difficulties. Wheeler left and opened a small steel brokerage firm. John Sr. generously lent him $25,000 for this, writing "I do not even want a note." When Cargill finally obtained the navy authorization in March 1942, John Sr. contacted Wheeler for a possible purchasing agent role at the shipyard. Wheeler accepted and was on the job within weeks.

To round out the management team, Wallace Hyde was brought in to take the sensitive liaison role with the Navy Department. Rudy Semsch became the chief accountant for the project. Cargill MacMillan recovered from a hospital stay for a severe case of kidney stones and began to take an increasingly hands-on overseer's role. John Jr. too was ill at the same time; having lost most of his vacation to the intense negotiations effort, he suffered another rise in blood pressure, and his doctor forced him to take most of the month of May off.

Those materials already on hand at Albany were either disposed of or sent to Savage. Early in April 1942, Marcus Marshall, the superintendent at Albany, was asked to release one of his key men, Kermit Wilson, to become storekeeper at Savage. Marshall wrote back: "It does not seem right to me to ask for Kermit, who I have spent two years training, and put him in a job like tool room when a man can be trained for that job in a few days. It certainly is putting me in a tough spot and everybody cannot do the job." Cargill MacMillan replied that the job was really more im-

Part of the Port Cargill shipbuilding crew, c. 1943.

portant than just a storekeeper, and Marshall grudgingly responded, "If you feel he is needed more there than Albany just let me know. . . . I have been in plenty of tough spots before."

The six AOGs were to be built simultaneously on two sets of ways constructed parallel to the river. When the two hulls on the ways nearest the water were completed, the next hulls would be jacked onto the ways closest to the water. A large administration building was built and railroad spurs into the property put in place. By the summer of 1942, the shipyard was a reality, the men and women working there already looking forward to laying the keel on Labor Day.[13]

The Victoria a "Jonah"?

Meanwhile, an unexpected new chapter in Cargill shipping occurred. It involved the *Victoria* (the former *Carlantic*), which had been sold to an Argentine company. The ship had left New York Harbor just nine days after Pearl Harbor, arriving in Curacao on Christmas Eve. C. C. Boden wired John Jr.: "Vic averaged about nine miles." Fred K. Troughton, a Fairbanks-Morse engineer sent by that company on the first voyage, reported just a few minor problems on this leg.

The second part of the trip, from Curacao to Montevideo, Uruguay, likewise was reasonably uneventful, although Troughton did report, "There seems to be something wrong with the port electric slip coupling. . . . The 'outer member' of this coupling runs true for about 45 seconds and then it runs out of true for about 2 minutes." The destination was Buenos Aires, Argentina, and after staying there for a few days, the *Victoria* set sail for the return voyage to New York.

After about four hours on the ocean, the alignment problem again became severe. Troughton persuaded the captain to turn the ship around and to return to Buenos Aires. Troughton reported back at that time: "As I see the situation, the owners don't care a damn what happens after we get out to sea, for they have repeatedly told me that all of the equipment is under guarantee . . . 6,600 miles is a long way to go, and I know that we would not make it without serious trouble, with conditions as they are."

After many arguments with the shipping company owners and some repairs, the ship once again set sail. Off the coast of Brazil, further trouble developed, and finally the vessel had to put into the port of Pernambuco, Brazil. A diver who was sent down reported that the propeller nut was loose and the propeller shaft possibly bent. Once again, repairs were made, and the ship set sail under reduced speed.

Earlier, Troughton had reported that "there might be some difficulty with the crew, for none of them wished to go beyond Curacao" (for fear of a German U-boat attack), and he added, "I am not so sure that I do not feel the same way about it." Their forebodings were realized. On April 21, 1942, just a few days away from New York, the *Victoria* was observed by a U-boat. *Time* magazine, always quick to spot a good story, described the next sequence of events:

Just before sundown one day, a torpedo smacked into her 30 feet aft of amid-ships. Deck plates buckled, but her all-welded Albany hull stood up: the bulkheads of the tanks were unbreached. Captain Salomone broke out complete identification flags and proceeded. Fifty minutes later a second torpedo smashed into the portside. Believing her doomed, her unhurt 39-man crew pulled off, beefing at her as a Jonah (on this her maiden northbound voyage—motors dead off Punta del Este; motor repairs at Rio; propeller trouble at Recife; 41 days for a 16-day run). The captain and part of his crew were mildly embarrassed when a U.S. man-of-war picked them up after two nights and a day, informed them that cranky, stubborn Victoria had refused to sink and was drifting derelict, and put them back aboard her. There they found the rest of the crew, calmly awaiting their arrival. Under her own steam the $1,000,000 Jonah limped into New York, berthed in Edgewater. "Miraculous," said the crew.

It was Argentina's "unyieldingly neutral" posture toward Germany that especially intrigued *Time*. The Argentine Foreign Office, according to the editors, "stiffly suggested that the matter was not serious because: (l) the ship had not sunk; (2) no one was killed. . . . From Germany, usually prompt with glib explanations, came only thick, embarrassed silence."

Once the *Victoria* was in port, the full extent of the damage by the two torpedoes became clear. C. C. Boden wired Cargill MacMillan: "Victoria in dry dock. Hole about about 20 by 30 in six and seven with deck bulged over a foot. Number one about same." Amazingly, however, the welded hull that Cargill had developed had not come apart at any place. Cargill MacMillan wrote Michael Cross a few weeks later: "Her being torpedoed twice and then coming in under her own power made up for our feelings over the poor return voyage."

The attack was widely reported and soon engaged both the U.S. Congress and Argentina's Chamber of Deputies. Meanwhile, Germany proclaimed its submarine zone now to include the whole United States coast. There also were many mutual recriminations about the problems with the propeller, and both Cargill and the supplier of the engines were pressed by the Argentine company to pay for all repairs. Compromises finally were reached. Late in July, the tanker was taken over by the United States government, having been reclaimed under a clause in the original purchase contract. By early the next year, she had made a trip to Murmansk, Russia, and two to Liverpool; when John Jr. next made contact, she was headquartered in Iceland; "she has been doing 9 to 10 knots in convoy service . . . you may remember that the English assured us that never by any stretch of the imagination could she function in the North Atlantic in winter because of her low speed." The tanker continued to ply the dangerous seas for the rest of World War II.[14]

More Shipbuilding

Keels were laid for all six of Cargill's AOGs during September 1942. The first two were made the centerpiece for a Labor Day celebration at the shipyards, and in a well-received gesture, John MacMillan, Sr., laid the keel of AOG-6, and Charles Horak, a boilermaker's helper, representing labor, laid the keel for AOG-7. Construction of all six of the ships was now well underway, ahead of schedule (despite continuing, frustrating difficulties in procurement of raw material, especially steel).

Sometime in the late fall of 1942, the name "Port Cargill" was given to the Savage operation; just when the term was first used is not clear, but it was a perfectly logical choice. In the second week of November 1942, the naval officer in charge of priorities for the Bureau of Ships visited Port Cargill. Cargill MacMillan soon learned that the Bureau "was contemplating additional work for us." The navy was interested in contracting for a new type of small escort ship, about 220 ft. long, one that would be capable of carrying some of the armed forces' new amphibian tanks. In addition to this new ship, the officer also wanted additional AOGs. Cargill Mac-Millan responded that the Company could likely take on about 20 of either one of the vessels but that "the problem of building the AOG would be much simpler because we were familiar with the work." If the navy wanted them to turn to the other vessel, "we would be very glad to do the best we knew how in building them."

This first contact opened up another round of negotiations, this time less harried than the early-1942 sessions. The navy continued to check Cargill's progress on the first set of six ships. Launchings were planned for the period March 15–July 15, 1943, the dates dictated by assumptions about the ice on the river. Actual delivery dates were later that same year.

John Jr. had never given up his enthusiasm for the large oceangoing barge carrier, and in early January 1943, he also presented this notion to the navy. The idea was quickly shunted aside, however, by a wholly new proposal, this time involving the Defense Plant Corporation. The DPC had become concerned about towboat capacity in the lower Mississippi, where currents were strong and more powerful boats were needed. The DPC had contacted George Sharp, the naval architect employed earlier by Cargill, and Sharp had developed a new model. Now the DPC was anxious to move ahead and began making arrangements for 21 of these advanced towboats. Several shipbuilders were to build these; Cargill was one of the possible choices.

The Company attempted to juggle the various possibilities, hoping to come out with *some* contract if not the best. There was urgency, for Cargill wanted to hold its work force together. First, John Jr. tried to bargain the Company's lake steamer *Rees* as a down payment on a barge carrier contract. However, the Maritime Commission preferred that Cargill refurbish the *Rees* (it was getting quite decrepit) rather than turning it over to the government. It *was* subsequently rebuilt for Cargill and continued to transport iron ore on the Lakes, so badly needed at this time.

Early in February, Weston Grimes, who was handling the negotiations on the Washington side, wired John Jr.: "In my opinion it would be a serious mistake to let the BC [the barge carrier] interfere with our thinking on the towboats. . . . We should take as many towboats as we can get." This is what finally happened, in spite of the navy's concern that Cargill not take on work for any other agency. "The Navy is so fearful that it will interfere with their program," John Jr. wrote John Sr. Cargill's towboat contract was for four of the vessels, at $750,000 each.

By late March, fabrication had begun on two of the towboats. Gone was the orderliness of the shipyard. Now the two sets of contracts seemed to compete with each other, particularly so because the Army Corps of En-

Minnesota River at flood stage, Port Cargill yards, April 1943.

gineers was monitoring the towboat contract. As one of the historians of the Savage effort put it, "We guess the Army and Navy really hit it off together when they're at home, but connubial bliss is not considered outside, and we found out that neither one wanted to allow any of the other spouse's material to be stored on his lot." It was imperative to get the first AOGs launched as soon as possible.

The issue was taken out of mortal hands, for Mother Nature intruded with a huge flood of the Minnesota River. John Jr. wrote his father, on April 1, 1943: "The flood unfortunately is paralyzing everything. The water this morning was within about 2 feet of where we will have to stop work. The actual flood stage is a little more than 12 feet and we figure that at about 14 feet the boats will be entirely surrounded by water. However, it will have to go to 15 feet before we reach the floor of the office building. . . . The Army engineers are quite discouraging and say the flood actually is worse than they thought a day or two ago." Four days later, John Jr. wrote again: "As of this morning the water was 22 inches below the office floor and we finally had to let water into all the boats to keep them from floating away . . . the entire yard is submerged except for the panel shop and some of the railroad tracks. . . . Nevertheless, the welding, wiring and plumbing work is continuing the same as usual."

Floods eventually recede. On Thursday, May 6, 1943, the first of Cargill's AOGs—the *Agawam*—was launched. The launching was to be sideways, and Cargill shipyard officials awaited the event with concern. "It doesn't require a great imagination," wrote Alan Clegg, one of the Savage historians, "to construe the results of an error or two which would result in that great hulk slewing in an oblique angle to the ways, capsizing and snuggling down on her side on dry land, or going over the ends of ways into the pool and crushing in her bottom." Cargill was using its same set of ways originally used in Albany, "considered very crude by people 'in the business,'" wrote the historian.

The *Agawam* in fact slid gracefully down into the water, amid great cheers from among the shipyard employees all assembled. On May 15, the second ship, the *Elkhorn* was launched. On July 24, the *Kishwaukee*, the third of the AOGs slid down the ways, and the yards lost their cramped appearance. Additional fitting had to be done on the three vessels before they could be sent down the river, but this could then be done aboard ship. The navy now followed through on its desire to give Cargill additional contracts. This time it was for 12 AOGs, each to cost some $1,675,000, with a provision for a fixed fee of 3 percent for the Company.

The navy had urged that the launchings not be made major events. Cargill officials followed this request but brought themselves some singular goodwill by their choice of people to launch the ships. For the fourth launching, that of the *Genesee*, Mrs. Helen Rae Clark, a farm wife from Norwalk, Iowa, did the honors. The *Minneapolis Tribune* commented:

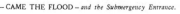
— CAME THE FLOOD — *and the Submergency Entrance.*

The Port Cargill flood, April 1943, in cartoons.

"*A Tanker for the Navy Nears the Launching Stage at Savage Shipbuilding Yards,*" Minneapolis Sunday Tribune, *November 11, 1943.*

By all the ordinary standards of selection, she is probably one of the most unassuming and obscure of ship sponsors. But listen; Mrs. Clark manages a 120-acre dairy farm while all the other grown-up Clarks are preoccupied, in civilian or military capacity, with the war effort. In addition she is raising four young Clarks and has opened her home to an orphan boy and to two children whose dad is serving in the Army. . . . There are uncounted women who are carrying on unselfishly and competently in the necessary tasks and duties of the farm home. There will never be enough ship-launchings, we fear, to honor all of them.

For the *Kishwaukee* launching in July, the sponsor was another farm wife, Mrs. John Shipp of Hay Springs, Nebraska. Mrs. Shipp had three navy sons, with service records dating back prior to Pearl Harbor. One had been on Guam and was a Japanese prisoner of war.

When the Company launched its first towboat—the *Bataan*—in early September 1943, it received almost the ultimate accolade with a three-page story in *Time* magazine, "The Farmer Goes to Sea." The article began with *Time*'s usual jaunty prose:

Farmers in the grain-growing north know Cargill, Inc. as one of the world's biggest, most audacious grain companies with a hankering as big as its elevators for taking on unconventional jobs, rushing them through by unconventional tricks. But when Cargill began buying farm and meadowland along the tree-shaded Minnesota River near Savage, Minn. little over a year ago, even Cargill-wise farmers hooted at the fantastic reason: Cargill was going to set up a shipyard to build ocean-going vessels. They had some excuse for hooting. Savage is 14 water miles from the Mississippi. For most of those 14 winding miles, the Minnesota was barely 3½ ft. deep.

The editors continued: "Last week, folks along the Minnesota were too busy to laugh. Into the Minnesota at new Port Cargill they triumphantly plopped a 180-ft. Army towboat, the *Bataan* (cost $1,000,000), moored it snugly alongside three 300-ft. ocean tankers they have launched in the last four months, [and] are now fitting out. Without wasting a moment, they jumped to work on the first of a new batch of Navy tankers Cargill contracted to build a fortnight ago."

The *Time* story would have been such a grand, crowning recognition for Cargill had not the editors also put a small footnote after the word "audacious." Here they wrote again of the 1937 corn contract, stating that Cargill "squeezed short sellers so tightly" that the CBOT forced Cargill's expulsion from the Board "for its price manipulations in the corner fight." This addendum outraged John Jr., who wrote Frank Neilson the next day:

The launching of the Nemasket, *1943 (reprinted with permission of the* Star Tribune *[Minneapolis/St. Paul]).*

"I think we got pretty rough treatment. The article was scandalously in-accurate . . . and the foot-note was quite unnecessary. I took it up with Dorsey [a Cargill lawyer] but he said there was nothing we could do about it." What could have been a moment of great acclaim for the Company and for John Jr. was overshadowed by his wounded pride. Even a glowing comment about Port Cargill by movie star Mickey Rooney, at a War Bond rally in Minneapolis Auditorium later that month, did not make up for *Time*'s "slur."[15]

Completing the Government's Ships

The first of the Cargill-built AOGs, the USS *Agawam*, was launched, fitted and ready to navigate the Mississippi River to New Orleans in early November 1943. This vessel was not just a 40-foot towboat with its own power, like the company towboat *Cartasca*—this was a 310-foot vessel that did not yet have its own power. On November 4, 1943, the *Agawam* was moved into the Minnesota River from its berth. A log kept by George Van Den Houten, the foreman in the carpenter shop, chronicled that uneasy day:

The hull was pushed from slip by small tug and straightened out in river by river towboat *Demopolis*. A line run from mid section to west shore was used for the hull to pivot [and] swing stern upstream as it moved into river. The *Demopolis* was too slow in moving against portside of hull near stern to swing stern upstream. The hull thus was caught by current as it came into river and drifted until it rested crosswise of river, with bow against east bank of slip. A bow line to west shore of slip was used to pull bow of hull from bank, while *Demopolis* pushed stern upstream . . . mooring of the hull at the derrick dock was completed at 6:30 p.m., 2½ hours after moving operation was started.

Ahead was the first trip of an AOG down the Minnesota River. On Friday, November 5, the *Agawam* began the voyage, propelled by the tow-boat *Demopolis*. The towboat was so low that the pilot could not see for-ward around the stern of the *Agawam*. Other riverboat pilots on the *Aga-wam* bridge communicated with the pilot of the *Demopolis* by telephone and loudspeakers, instructing him which way to steer to keep the big ship in the channel. In addition, there were men on shore at strategic points with cables and heavy trucks, ready to give whatever assistance might be necessary.

There are a number of twists and turns in the Minnesota River, but the *Agawam* was snaked through without a problem. The *St. Paul Pioneer Press*, earlier so incensed about the presumption of building a shipyard up the Minnesota River, reported on the event in good grace: "A sleek, gray ship, whose cavernous insides may carry fuel for planes to blast Germany or Japan, arrived in St. Paul Friday afternoon after a trip down the Min-

Launching a Defense Plant Corporation towboat, c. 1944.

Edna MacMillan (Mrs. John H. MacMillan, Sr.) sponsors the launching of the Chehalis, *April 1944; Seaman Second Class Frank E. Junkin represents Chehalis, Washington.*

nesota and Mississippi rivers, which failed to justify suspicions that the craft could not navigate the two streams." There was a huge crowd of Twin Cities residents along the shores as the vessel passed through the southern environs of Minneapolis and St. Paul. It only took an hour for the vessel combination to travel from Port Cargill to a point safely past the Mendota bridge.

The *Agawam's* trip down the Mississippi was not quite as uneventful. John Jr. wrote his son on the subsequent problems: "The *Agawam* is almost in New Orleans, although the Inland Waterways Corporation did ground her once or twice on the way down and the Navy is very fearful that some damage was done to the rudders or propeller. The towboat *'Huck Finn'* was handling her at the time." But there was little damage, and the *Agawam* was turned over to the Navy as a completed project.

Over the succeeding months of World War II, Cargill sent 17 more AOGs down the Minnesota and Mississippi, most often without event (there were occasional momentary groundings but no real problems). The navy continued to name the vessels after various United States rivers, most of them with Indian names (for example, *Chewaucan, Mattabesset, Natchaug, Noxubee* and *Wacissa*). The four towboats built for the army under DPC auspices also were delivered as planned; these were named after areas in the Pacific Theater of Operations—the *Bataan*, the *Coral Sea*, the *Milne Bay* and the *Bou Arada*. Launchings of these various ships were accomplished in the same manner as the earlier ones, with service wives and mothers and Company people as sponsors. In a well-received event in March 1944, Edna MacMillan launched the AOG vessel *Chehalis*.

The shipyard workers were anxious to hear how the first of the AOGs did in actual sea trials, and in a special memorandum to them from the U.S. Navy Supervisor of Shipbuilding in early April 1944, they learned about both the *Agawam* and the *Elkhorn*. One of the crew of the former reported: "Aside from being able to fry eggs on deck, everything is 'jake.'" The *Agawam* chief engineer reported: "This ship is o.k.—it'll maneuver better than any I've ever seen . . . but damn it, you've never seen anything roll like this ship will over nothing—especially when we're light." The crew of the *Elkhorn* reported: "The ship has all new war paint and looks like a million. . . . People like you in Minneapolis are the symbols of what we are really fighting for and, I must add, worth fighting for." It seemed to make all of the difficulties worthwhile.

At a 1969 reunion of the navy men who had crewed the *Chehalis* during the war, one of the men reminisced about that first trip down the Mississippi, where "we'd (sometimes) hear the hull scrape against the bottom of the banks . . . and at night we tied it up to trees along the riverbank." Its destination was the Pacific, and the sailors recalled fondly their vessel that "took to the water like a duck . . . a comparatively smooth-riding craft."

The Agawam *passes under St. Paul's Mendota Bridge, November 1943.*

One of the AOGs at dockside, St. Paul.

The AOGs' wartime camouflage.

The U.S.S. Tombigbee *in Antarctica, 1963.*

Austen Cargill chairs a Works Manager dinner for Port Cargill leadmen and foremen, August 1943.

Though menaced by kamikaze planes toward the end of the war, the *Chehalis* made it through, only to catch fire and sink off Tutnila, American Samoa, in 1949.

Great adventures and tragedies were common features in the lives of the 18 ships. Several stayed under military command long enough to participate in the Korean War; the *Kishwaukee* even survived the Vietnam War. *Namakagon* was transferred to New Zealand in 1962, her hull strengthened for polar operations in the Antarctic. *Nespelen* and *Tombigbee* also served in Antarctica in 1963 for the United States exercise "Operation Deep Freeze." *Chestakee* became a World War II casualty, striking a mine in the straits south of Balabac Island, in Philippine waters. Eight others in addition to *Namakagon* finally sailed under foreign flags (with new names); three went to Taiwan, two to Greece and one each to Colombia, Chile and Canada. (The record for each is set out in the Appendix to this chapter.)

The shipyard continued to be a focus for Cargill all through the rest of the war. In total employees, it was the dominant part of the business. In terms of profitability, with the small fixed-fee amount the Company received for each vessel, the results were very modest. The Company reported a loss of $477,000 on Port Cargill in 1942, made a profit of $140,000 in 1943 and $147,000 in 1944, then lost another $40,000 in 1945. This was in the same period when the Grain Department had made $3.4 million in 1942, $3.1 million in 1943, $766,000 in 1944 and $2.6 million in 1945. John Jr. had told the Company's employees in September 1943 that operation of the shipyard was going to involve considerable sacrifice, including low profitability. He continued: "The reward which we obtain for this effort lies solely in the feeling of pride we have in making sacrifices for the war effort. Whether these sacrifices are worthwhile lies wholly in your hands." When, on January 2, 1945, Cargill was awarded its first Army-Navy "E" for production excellence, Austen Cargill reiterated the same thought in accepting the flag accompanying the award (a second "E" came that summer, adding a star on the flag).

Awards like this enhanced the already high morale of the Cargill employees. The Company had enjoyed excellent labor relations through the whole war period; there had been just two short strikes at Port Cargill, both involving internal leadership and jurisdictional issues within the union. Cargill employees had performed superbly in their share of the war effort.[16]

A Surprise at Green Bay

Another railroad disappointment also occurred in this period, involving Green Bay, Wisconsin. Cargill had had a grain trade presence there since 1878. W. W. Cargill had then persuaded the two railroads serving Green Bay, the Green Bay & Western and the Chicago and North Western, to share in the cost of constructing a terminal elevator there. The original Green Bay terminal had burned in 1916. This was rebuilt by the Green Bay & Western and again leased to Cargill (as terminal A). A second terminal (B), which the Company leased from the Chicago and North Western Railroad, had also been constructed. The capacity of A was 645,000 bushels, and B could handle 400,000 bushels.

Terminal storage space was at a premium in the early part of the war. In April 1942, the Green Bay & Western abruptly sent notice that when the lease on the terminal expired on June 30, it was going take its elevator facilities back. Ed Grimes wrote the president of the railroad, Homer E. McGee, noting the substantial business that had been done with the railroad over many years; he decried the fact that Cargill "should be subjected to such peremptory treatment in view of the longstanding association."

The railroad president rejected this reasoning and wrote: "With us it is a matter of business. We have plans which we think will produce more revenue." There was no changing his mind. Cargill lost the terminal that June (and its manager, who stayed with the terminal).

Cargill's other Green Bay terminal was not in good physical shape and was standing idle at the time. Indeed, the U.S. Coast Guard wrote in early May 1942, worrying that the building, directly on the shore of the main channel, "leans three to seven feet out over the water with imminent possibility of collapse." The officer contacting the Company, mirroring the tension of that early war period, noted that the area "is frequented by hobos . . . who might be inclined to engage in subversive or saboteur activities." Later, the railroad precluded Cargill from using the dangerous side, and its usable capacity dropped to 256,000 bushels.

Now a hasty effort was needed to try to regain some comparable terminal space, not necessarily at Green Bay. Out of this small crisis, the Company was able, on short notice, to find alternative property—an elevator in Minneapolis owned by Continental Grain Company, with capacity of 1.1 million bushels. The elevator had been managed by Robert C. Woodworth, a vice president of that firm. It was a relatively new elevator; the initial building had been constructed in 1922 and additions made in 1929. The purchase solved the Green Bay problem quite well. Beyond this, it brought a collateral benefit of increasing value, inasmuch as Woodworth chose to stay with Cargill as an employee. Soon he was taking a major role in Cargill's public relations efforts.[17]

An Old Enemy

The Corn Case presumably had been settled in March 1940 by the CEA's guilty verdict for John Jr. and Cargill Grain Company of Illinois, with both barred from trading for one year. But it wasn't over. Indeed, now the situation was to take an unexpected turn. On October 25, 1940, the Farmers National Grain Corporation entered a suit in United States District Court, charging that it had suffered large losses in its market operations in 1937 as a result of illegal manipulation of prices by the Cargill interests and asking treble damages. Farmers National had been in the process of liquidation since shortly after the Corn Case, all of its assets having been turned over to the Farm Credit Administration. The cooperative had had a stormy record since its founding back in the Farm Board days in the 1930s and was heavily in debt. The actual loss alleged from the Corn Case was listed at $630,000, and with court costs, attorneys' fees and interest at 6 percent, the total damages claimed approached $2 million.

Cargill had known of the possibility of the suit since late August 1940, when Howard Ellis contacted the Company, stating that he represented Farmers National and that he intended to enter the suit. John Jr. worried about possible reactions from the banking community. John Peterson did talk privately with Hugo Scheuermann at the Chase Bank, who advised that if any of the banks in the syndicate were uneasy about the suit, they should be taken out of the group. Otherwise, "he isn't particularly disturbed."

Still, it must have been an unpleasant revelation to John Jr. and his colleagues when they discovered that the lawyer handling the suit was Howard Ellis. The Chicago Board of Trade had retained him all through the Corn Case; it was Ellis who determined the CBOT strategy even before the final days of the September 1937 contract and who had prosecuted the case for the Exchange. If anyone knew of all of the private strategies and secret maneuverings, the sensitive spots for the CBOT to guard against—in other words, all of the other side's confidential, privileged information—it was Howard Ellis. He was privy to all of the CBOT's links with the "shorts" in the case. One was, of course, Daniel Rice. The other dominant short was Farmers National. By today's legal standards of ethics, all of this would likely be a conflict of interest.

That Cargill did not immediately object about Ellis probably can be attributed to one significant fact: Irving Goldsmith, Cargill's trial lawyer and chief strategist in the Corn Case, once had been legal counsel for Farmers National before Cargill hired him away. Goldsmith, now ill (he died in July 1941), was no longer Cargill's counsel; Clark R. Fletcher, the senior partner of the law firm of Fletcher, Dorsey, Barker, Coleman and Barber, took over the case for the Company. Irving Goldsmith, too, had privileged information about Farmers National. Indeed, in the Cargill files were some Farmers National board minutes, put there by Irving Goldsmith. It would have been sophistry to have claimed conflict of interest for Ellis. Nevertheless, having Ellis as the opposing lawyer was threatening.

Cargill uniformly had ignored threats from parties who alleged they had been injured by its actions in the Corn Case. The Farmers National case was a different order of magnitude, however—much more was at stake in terms of possible damages, and the precedent for other suits that might follow made the total risk very substantial.

All through the year 1941 the team of Cargill lawyers pored over the old Corn Case, took depositions from those they wanted as defense witnesses and tried to reconstruct the happenings of that fall of 1937, now four years back. The Farmers National files were in disarray, given its near-bankrupt status, and many of its trading records created during those frenzied days had long since been destroyed. It was a nightmare to try once again to reconstruct the case. By the beginning of the United States entry into the war after Pearl Harbor, the case was nowhere near trial but had consumed enormous amounts of management time and lawyers' involvement.

When the Navy Department contacted Cargill about the potential shipbuilding program, in that first week of January 1942, the specter of trying to conduct a demanding wartime effort in the face of the drains of the Farmers National case troubled John Jr. very much, and he now made an unorthodox proposal to Weston Grimes.

Grimes wired Cargill MacMillan: "Mac. Jr. . . . feels no use even talking to Navy unless they or we can in some way postpone F N case for duration and wants me talk to Navy re this idea." The implied quid pro quo in this troubled Grimes: "I just don't know about propriety of such action . . . it was of course John's idea that any postponement wouldn't stick if we didn't consummate a big contract with Navy . . . it may be that Agriculture should be talked to re this rather than Navy but again I don't know how far I can go in intimating we have been drafted into Navy production." He concluded: "Will do anything you suggest is proper." The Company's outside counsel, however, opposed any such representation to the navy, and the case proceeded at its time-consuming pace, adding further management involvement.[18]

Settling with Farmers National

Preparation for the Farmers National suit against Cargill dragged on all through the year 1942, crowding further the already full agenda of that critical period. Memories had dimmed considerably about the exact sequence of events in September 1937. The brokerage houses did not keep most records for any length of time, and the memories of the pit brokers working in that accelerated hothouse environment inevitably were quite short-term. Farmers National's government receivership had not helped their recordkeeping, either. At one point, Cargill lawyers wanted a copy of a fundamental IRS form (No. 1099), but Farmers National officers could not even produce this. Even the Chicago Board of Trade seemed not to have kept some of the key records. John Jr. wired his brother in late 1941: "I spent half hour with ——— [I have omitted the name] but we are going to get little or no help there. His records were very recently destroyed, illegally of course."

Leavitt Barker, one of the senior lawyers with the Cargill trial team, wrote Douglas Bagnell, the head of the CEA's division of investigations: "We have encountered repeated instances in which . . . all or a portion of the records required by law to be kept were not available because of loss or destruction, or because such records were never made. In the case of the Pit Brokers . . . the impression seemed to prevail that the provisions of the law and the regulations were not applicable to them." Barker urged Bagnell to intervene "to correct any existing misapprehension as to the scope of the law."

Bad luck plagued the Cargill legal team, too. In late 1941, Leavitt Barker was seriously injured in an automobile accident. Clark Fletcher, the head of Cargill's legal team, wrote: "This accident will of course have a serious effect on preparation for trial of the Cargill case." Fletcher then took over most of Barker's duties personally.

By late 1942, Fletcher had painstakingly assembled a mountain of materials that seemed to build Cargill's defense well. He elaborated his strategy in a long series of memoranda in late November and early December 1942. Judge William J. Campbell, before whom the case was to be tried, had suggested in mid-December 1942 that the Company waive a jury trial and agree upon a Special Master before whom the case would be tried. Cargill lawyers presented this suggestion to the board of directors on December 30, 1942, advising the board that the Company had a constitutional right to trial by jury but that "while the issues were comparatively simple, the fact situation was so complex, complicated as it is by the special terminology of the grain trade, that it is quite probable that the average jury will have difficulty in understanding the case fully." The board balked, however, and unanimously recommended to the lawyers "that the Company will not waive a jury trial."

But it was not to be. As a final disastrous event in the star-crossed case, in late January 1943, Clark Fletcher himself suddenly died. In the first week of February, John Jr. and his colleagues decided to settle out of court with Farmers National. In negotiations with Ellis and his group of lawyers, kept confidential at Cargill's insistence, the Company agreed to settle by paying the sum of $137,500. As a condition of the settlement, Farmers National agreed not to give any publicity to the settlement.

This secrecy seemed a legitimate request by Cargill, inasmuch as its well-prepared case had never been made a matter of public record, and further suits by other shorts had always been a concern. John Jr. wrote Ted Young that day: "I did not want to settle and I am ashamed of the fact that we did, but the prospect of having to educate another set of lawyers was just more than I could stand, especially as it looks as though Henry Morganthau [Secretary of the Treasury] is going to pay 90% of the settlement cost." (The Company's earnings at this point had put it in that percentage level with the excess profits tax of the federal government.) Young continued with a prescient observation that John Jr. would remember later, in another bout with Dan Rice: "What will happen when some astute 'long' acquires a large 'long' line of futures contracts as a hedge against *actual* (as distinguished from anticipated) customer demands, and a 'tight' situation develops, will be interesting to see. Probably, even then, the 'long' will be made to suffer. . . . The motives of the 'long' will be under very close and cynical scrutiny."[19]

Daniel Rice and Rye Marketing

In the grain business in this period, traders generally found little excitement in trading rye. The harvested acreage of rye in the late 1930s and early 1940s was only a little larger than in Civil War days. For a few years after

World War I the acreage under rye did expand, with the United States producing its first 100-million-bushel crop. But around the time of Pearl Harbor production was less than half of that, and the price per bushel had stayed low all through this period, too. Some of the rye output was used as a food, rye flour being mixed with wheat flour for the American version of "rye bread." ("Black bread" in Europe had a much larger rye content.) Some additional percentage of the crop was used in distilling industrial alcohol and rye whiskey, and lesser grades of rye were used as livestock feed. Most of North America's production was in the Northern Plains states and in Canada; Europe also had a substantial harvest. By usual standards, trading rye was not a central concern in the feed industry.

Therefore, it was all the more surprising that one of the great grain-trading battles that occurred during World War II involved rye and pitted in opposition those old adversaries, John MacMillan, Jr., and Daniel Rice. Sometime in 1941, just before the war started, Cargill began buying much more rye than ever before. In May 1941, the rye inventory in the Grain Division stood at 6.5 million bushels; in December 1941, this had almost doubled, to 13.4 million bushels. The reasons for this decision, most likely that of Julius Hendel and Erv Kelm (the chief trader of rye), are not completely clear from remaining records. Julius Hendel, following his instincts, sensed that rye had price appreciation potential. John Jr. seconded this belief, explaining his own rationale to a Merrill Lynch executive in a wire in November, 1942: "As we see it, a speculation in rye is nothing but one on the termination date of the war. We are all agreed that with advent of peace rye in Europe will sell even money or a premium over wheat."

Another participant in this wartime rye drama had the same instincts. Charles W. Metcalf, executive vice president of General Foods Corporation and its senior trader (he himself a member on the Chicago Board of Trade), also began to buy rye for General Foods. That company had been experimenting with technology for using rye as a raw material for making syrup. The industry had been skeptical of this; corn was a better raw material, yielding a better quality of starch for conversion into syrup, at a lesser cost. At best, General Foods would doubtless use only a small amount of rye for this venture.

Yet Metcalf went into the rye market in a huge way in 1942, just after the beginning of the war, and on into 1943. General Foods holdings of cash rye kept rising, and Metcalf also brought the company to a net long position in rye futures of 2 million bushels, the maximum speculative position that it could legally attain (the Commodity Exchange Administration said of General Foods buying: "General Foods was not a user of rye and had no need for it. Its holdings of rye and rye futures were speculative, not being offset by sales of or needs for rye"). Metcalf continued to use his long positions on through 1943 as a device for acquiring physical product.

By September 1943, General Foods had acquired 5,350,000 bushels of rye futures and actual bushels of grain, or 66 percent of all deliverable rye in Chicago. As its buying continued in October and November, this amount began to rise further. Finally, on November 29, 1943, the Business Conduct Committee of the Chicago Board of Trade, assessing the "commanding position" of General Foods in rye, called Metcalf before the committee. The committee ruled that his holdings "might tend to create a corner and be in a position to dominate price movements." At the meeting, Metcalf agreed to curtail his purchases. But a few weeks later, on January 4, 1944, he abruptly changed his mind and notified the committee that he would no longer be bound by the agreement.

At this point, Daniel Rice entered the picture. Metcalf employed Rice and his company to merchandise the General Foods rye. Rice had been a short in rye up to this point but then joined with Metcalf in becoming a substantial long. He too began to convert his long futures contracts at the CBOT to actual grain holdings and did so too in Winnipeg, where rye also was traded. During this same period, Rice had been given authority by 23 of his other customers unilaterally to conduct their trading. There were additional purchases of rye futures and rye products for this group, too. At the peak of General Foods buying, their holdings were estimated by *Business Week* at some 12 million bushels, roughly one-third of the entire crop of that year. *Business Week* titled its article "Mystery in Rye," a testimony to the perplexity that the grain trade felt about the huge General Foods purchases. John Peterson warned John Sr. on February 8, 1944: "It looks to me like they have a first rate 'corner' and the good Lord help them if somebody should decide to sue them."

Rye trading on the CBOT was a "notorious center for speculative abuse," noted Jerry W. Markham in his book *History of Commodity Futures Trading and Its Regulation*. "The market was controlled by a small group of clubby traders, and it was said 'one had to be of the right religion to trade rye.' The rye crop was small, and the market was, therefore, susceptible to manipulation." Daniel Rice and many of his colleagues were Catholic; Philip Sayles called them "the Irish Village."

There had to be shorts, of course, to take the opposite side of the Metcalf/Rice long futures. Inasmuch as the latter desired delivery of physical product, the shorts had to produce actual rye and deliver it in Chicago. Cargill was by far the dominant short—most of the physical rye being delivered in Chicago came from Cargill. Could Cargill continue to supply physical product to these seemingly insatiable groups of longs?

As the Metcalf/Rice holdings of rye and rye futures continued to build up in those first months of 1944, the answer to this question became increasingly important. During the first five months of 1944, Metcalf began to trade in rye and rye futures for his own account, for his wife, his daughter and one other person. Metcalf did not notify the CEA about these new positions.

The May 1944 rye futures contract proved to be the climax. The events incidental to this contract later convinced the CEA officials that Metcalf and Rice had violated the law. The CEA brought a case that alleged the respondents "acted together . . . in concert" to acquire rye and May 1944 rye futures that exceeded deliverable supplies of rye in Chicago, that "they caused the Chicago May 1944 rye futures prices to be artificial, manipulated prices." In sum, the CEA accused Metcalf and Rice (and two of their colleagues included in the case) of attempting a corner.

The corner was not successful, however, for Cargill did indeed provide all of the quantities of rye necessary for delivery under that May 1944 contract, in addition to all of the physical product already delivered to General Foods over many previous months. The ways that Cargill accomplished this once again brought the Company into a bitter confrontation with Daniel Rice.

Rice knew that it was Cargill that had been able, by divers methods, to bring enough rye into Chicago to forestall the apparent Metcalf/Rice strategy of cornering rye at the end of the delivery period of that May 1944 futures contract. Rice felt very strongly about this; indeed, his lawyer, Lee A. Freeman, pushed very hard to make Cargill a party to the CEA proceedings. Freeman testified: "We are of the opinion that Cargill delivered as much as eleven million bushels of rye during the 1943–44 May futures and we believe that that is a fantastic figure . . . who is forcing deliveries? We are accused of having taken delivery and by that action of having manipulated the market, when Cargill made deliveries, extensive deliveries over a period of years . . . for purposes of demoralization and manipulation of the market." Freeman continued with some startlingly belligerent language: "We are accused of having forced somebody. Suppose we received a punch in the nose, are we guilty of being attacked?" When the CEA referee, Jack W. Bain, decried his language, Freeman shot back, "I propose to show that it is."

Rice's anger was understandable, for Cargill had been quite innovative in its efforts to provide rye for delivery. First, there was the issue of bringing Canadian grain into Chicago. From the start, both Rice and the Cargill group had perceived the importance of the Winnipeg market. Rice had gone long in Winnipeg futures and had taken physical delivery of as much as he could obtain there. Cargill, too, had bought extensive amounts of cash grain.

If physical grain was to be brought across the border, the issue of customs duties had to be addressed. A United States law, the Reed-Murray Bill, allowed Canadian grain to be brought into the United States in a bonded warehouse and held there without payment of duty. If the grain later was delivered for food use, duty then had to be paid. But if held for feed grain, the bill allowed cancellation of the duty. Cargill had contacted the Collector of Customs in Chicago on April 28, 1944, asking if the Company might send a certified check for the possible duty, with the check to be cashed only if the grain was delivered. The Company was importing 3 million bushels, and the duty was 12 cents per bushel. In effect, the Company was asking that this check for $264,000 be held in escrow by the Collector of Customs. Apparently the latter agreed to this.

In a subsequent federal circuit court case (discussed later in this section) the presiding judge faulted Cargill as "a large speculator" who held "a commanding position in short May futures." While both Cargill and Continental had imported a large amount of Canadian rye to Chicago, Continental had "unconditionally paid the duty," amounting to 12 cents per bushel. Cargill, on the other hand, had only "constructively paid the duty" by depositing a certified check with the Customs Department but retaining the right for one year to demonstrate that this rye was used for feed purposes, thus permitting the recovery of the duty deposit. So, while duty money had been provided to the Customs Office, it was "with strings attached."

On the same day that Cargill had written the Collector of Customs, Rice had appeared before the directors of the CBOT, urging them to pass a regulation that would prevent delivery on Chicago futures contracts of rye and other grain imported into the United States unless the import duty had been explicitly paid. Many members of the board favored such a notion, but the legal counsel for the CBOT advised the board that such a provision should be made a matter of federal law rather than CBOT rule.

The circuit court judge in the later case was quite skeptical of the CEA imputation that this effort at the CBOT by Rice was to reduce the amount of deliverable rye. The judge stated that "all were in favor of the proposal" and continued: "We suspect that the opinion expressed in the decision comes nearer representing the view of the Judicial Officer than his finding. . . . That Rice did so is an arbitrary presumption on the part of the Judicial Officer."

Rice also alleged that Cargill was misusing its ability to mix better-quality plump rye with higher-moisture "tuf" rye—that Cargill was needling the rye to take out the plumps, selling those at a premium to customers, and delivering absolutely *at* grade for the accounts of Rice and Metcalf. As part of Cargill's documentation for its possible involvement in the case, the Company lawyers assembled an extensive set of "mixing wires" from the files. These examples elaborated the practice well:

5-5-43—On the rye for Chgo. going to use it in mixing there so want lowest damage, lowest ergot count. Presume bin 1 straight. Don't care what grades tho might help if grades 2 rye.

5–13–43—If moisture on that rye mix goes slightly higher than figures still want to use the 2 rye WHR but if other factors go over the line don't want.

6–20–44—I haven't the remotest idea how we stand on feed rye as everything but the cook's breakfast goes into the mix. Will see if can find out how much duty free rye we have left if that will help.

7–11–44—Yes we could get rid of more duty free rye if we upped the ergot. However that would mean many ergoty cars and involve the Corn Exchange in picking all our rye for ergot which might be a little embarrassing . . . now using 40% of the duty free rye to our mix which makes the ergot content theoretically 5/10 and . . . not running into any trouble . . . might be best to stay as we are. What think.

In effect, Rice accused Cargill of bringing in grain for (as Rice's lawyer put it) "the sole and only purpose of breaking and demoralizing the Chicago rye market by means of a simulated movement of rye into and through Chicago." As *Fortune* magazine put it, in a later major article on grain trading, "The two positions could not have been more opposite: the government charging a corner, the defendant counter-charging a bear raid, or inverse corner."

Rice's caviling about mixing to delivery-grade level was just that, for it was universal and legitimate grain-trading practice. The grades in lots of grain delivered were subject to independent check by government inspectors. It was just good business practice to mix down to grade, particularly so for rye (and also barley), where the premium plumps could command higher prices from specialty buyers.

Before the CEA case even could get started, a raucous story broke out in the public press. Representative Frank B. Keefe of Wisconsin charged in July 1945 that "a group of manipulators . . . with tentacles reaching into Washington . . . has obtained a corner on the rye market" and that they were continuing it "right up to the present hour." He alleged "a national scandal." By late in that month, the Senate Agriculture Committee reportedly was going to look into the matter. Beyond this, Drew Pearson had entered the fray. In his breezy "Washington Merry-Go-Round," he commented on the General Foods side: "General Foods, owned in part by Mrs. Joe Davies, wife of Roosevelt's former Ambassador to Belgium and to Russia . . . after buying 89 per cent of all the deliverable supply of rye, and being stuck with it, then performed a beautiful salesmanship job in persuading the Belgium government to take a million bushels off its hand—paid for by U.S. taxpayers through lend-lease."

Pearson also came close to a public accusation about some members of Congress: "If Congress should ever dig deep enough, it will unearth one of the juiciest stories of riding the grain market the country has heard for a long time, including some of President Truman's close supporters, chiefly Ed Pauley, former treasurer of the Democratic National Committee. Other Democrats active in rye were Senator 'Pappy' O'Daniel of Texas, Senator 'Happy' Chandler of Kentucky, Attorney General Bob Kenny of California and Senator Scott Lucas of Illinois." As often was true of Pearson's column, the particulars of the Senators' involvement were not detailed.[20]

Despite great concern by Cargill, Rice did not succeed in drawing the Company into the CEA case, nor was Cargill a direct party to the subsequent circuit court case. The Company had prepared assiduously for this possibility, putting together dossiers of relevant wires and statistics (the "mixing wires" an example) and had developed strategies for testimony, if demanded. The lawyers had concluded that by far the best witness would be John Jr. himself, so he prepared carefully, particularly reviewing his own testimony in the Corn Case. However, although Cargill was mentioned at length in both the CEA and the circuit court decisions, no company person was required to testify. On April 28, 1947, the CEA ruled against Metcalf and Rice.

The latter were not ready to concede, however, and immediately took the case to the courts. The circuit court decision, in October 1948, was a landmark. Judge J. Earl Major, who was chief justice of the Seventh Circuit Court, flatly reversed the CEA's decision that Metcalf and Rice had attempted a corner and therefore were guilty on the key allegation of "manipulation." Major stated: "We are favored with numerous definitions of the word . . . perhaps as good as any is one of the definitions which appears in the government's brief, wherein it is defined as 'the creation of an artificial price by planned action, whether by one man or a group of men.' It is rather obvious that this definition does not cover the instant situation . . . there was not any purpose to create an artificial price but to preserve an existing price resulting from natural forces." Major concluded that "self-preservation has oftentimes been referred to as the first law of nature, and we suppose it applies to traders as well as others. We see no reason why the seller respondents as well as General Foods and Metcalf should not under the circumstances make an effort to protect their own interests."

The 1949 *Fortune* article concluded that "the CEA made a poor case against Rice and revealed a weakness in theory with respect to what a corner is." The editors continued: "The broader issue of what constitutes manipulation is still being debated. In the rub between merchant and speculator, the government appears to have a strong bias in favor of the merchant hedger and against the speculator, without an adequate reconciliation of their mutual dependence in the futures market . . . in politics, of course, the speculator is vulnerable because it is easy to arouse the Puritan spirit against the out-and-out chance taker."[21]

It was an astounding decision to the grain trade. This was the first major case to be brought by the CEA concerning market manipulation since John Jr. had endured the travails of the Corn Case. In essence, a decision that had a great many parallels to the Corn Case had been ruled by the courts *not* to be manipulation. There were some key differences between the two cases, however. As Judge Major stated, "the facts concerning the sale were not secret." In the Corn Case there had been some subterfuge about Cargill's long purchases. It would only be conjecture to wonder whether Major would have reached the same decision in the Cargill case had it been tried in October 1948. There seemed no doubt, however, that the grain trade took Major's decision to suggest a more open view toward the use of market power by individual speculators.

As the Rye Case advanced through the CEA hearings and the eventual circuit court case, it remained to see how the large amounts of rye that had come into Chicago eventually would be digested. Exactly how General Foods came out on the rye buying was buried in overall Company financial statements, and the particulars of the involvement of the Senators also never became publicly known. Cargill made out well on the rye trading. The Company had bought huge quantities of rye during this period: inventories had jumped to as high as 15.7 million bushels in December 1942; they were 12.0 million in May 1943 and 10.8 million in December 1943. One year later, in December 1944, levels had dropped to 3.6 million. They were down to 1.9 million in May 1945, with only 670,000 bushels in inventory in December, 1945 (Cargill's Chicago elevator still held several million bushels of rye owned by others). Cargill had sold vast quantities of its own rye at generally favorable margins. A very substantial part of the Company's large Grain Department profits in the crop years 1941–1942 and 1942–1943 ($3.4 million in the former, $3.1 million in the latter) were attributable to rye trading as such (the Company annual reports at this time did not break down individual grain contributions in the department). In 1943–1944, Cargill posted a much smaller Grain Department profit figure, only $766,000.

Prices of rye had risen during this period. In December 1941, Cargill's average was priced for inventory purposes at 74 cents per bushel. This had risen to only 87 cents in May 1943 and finally to $1.01 in May 1944. Rye parity prices had stayed well above the average farm prices for rye, whereas wheat, corn and barley prices had moved much closer to parity, with soybeans substantially over parity in this period. By mid-1943, oats and barley price ceilings were established by the Office of Price Administration, as wheat and corn had been just at the start of the war. The low rye prices never did justify price ceilings all through the war.

Perhaps if Charles Metcalf and Daniel Rice had been able to corner the May 1944 rye futures contract (whether intentionally or not) the price situation might have been different. As it was, the rather steady rye production, coupled with the equally steady demand for rye had kept that grain the most stable during the war.

Looking ahead, the story on rye *after* World War II was quite another matter, for rye prices took a major upsurge in a wild period in mid-1946. In January of that year, cash rye was selling for under $2.00. By June it was up to $2.85. At this point, the Chicago Board of Trade closed out rye futures trading, suspending them until 1948. Rye futures continued to be traded in Winnipeg, and cash rye bounded upward until it reached a high of $4.83 in the spring of 1948. Although some of this amazing price rise could be attributed to the tail end of the Daniel Rice efforts of 1944 to push up price, most was due to the fundamentals of grain in the rush of reconversion.

In December 1947, a fascinating complication hit the press. The race for presidential nominations for the 1948 elections was quickening as the year drew to a close, and in early December 1947, Harold E. Stassen, a Republican aspirant from Minnesota, escalated rhetoric with public pronouncements that "Administration insiders" were profiting from alleged "insider" speculation in food commodities, especially rye. Stassen demanded that the Commodity Exchange Authority disclose names of *all* of the individuals who had taken speculative positions in the market. When the list was released by the CEA on December 22, there were 711 large traders on it. Cargill was mentioned as a hedger for corn but as both a hedger and a "speculative or spreading" holder in wheat.

This worried John Jr. so much that he wrote a detailed letter to Hugo Scheuermann at the Chase National, explaining that the CEA designation of "speculative" was being applied incorrectly to Cargill's cross-hedges. Scheuermann replied right away to reassure John Jr.: "I was really surprised by the way in which the published information was accepted here at the Bank and the lack of comment from the outside." He considered this "a further indication of the confidence which the banks have in your organization."

Companies were not the target of Stassen, however, for he was looking for public officials on the list. Only one actually appeared there, a special assistant to the Secretary of the Army who had been trading oats and cottonseed oil. Stassen called the list irrelevant and demanded information on other involvements of administration officials. A special subcommittee was formed in the Senate, with Republican Senator William F. Knowland of California as its chair, and a wide-ranging probe ensued. In the process, the grain trade once again was painted with the brush of "gambling," "speculation," and even "trafficking in human misery." The *New York Times* tried to point out that "the activities of the speculators, if they are private persons without access to advanced information on government buying plans, are wholly legitimate," and the *Chicago Journal of Commerce* worried that the exposé would "deprive markets of lawful risktakers." By this time, the whole thing had become a political quagmire and was seen as a potentially pivotal factor in the 1948 elections. When the hearings finally were completed, the charges sounded less a reality than had been first supposed; and the issue died away, not, however, without giving the grain trade—accused once more of "speculating"—many uneasy moments.

Rice fired one additional salvo, also affecting Cargill. When he had tried to persuade the CBOT to put additional limits on deliveries of physical rye in Chicago, in December 1943, the CBOT officials seemed to support him. However, when he decided to test his beliefs on this matter in court, he found that the CBOT took a stand opposing him. He had filed a complaint before the Illinois Commerce Commission alleging violations of the Illinois Grain Warehouse Act. In effect, Rice was making a statement that state law, which was more restrictive, applied in the Rye Case.

A number of warehousemen (Cargill included) and the CBOT objected to this interpretation and counterfiled a case in federal district court. The latter ruled in favor of Rice (and with the state of Illinois). The warehousemen and the CBOT took the case to the federal circuit court of appeals, and in June 1946, the same circuit court judge, J. Earl Major, reversed the district court, siding once again with the view that the federal warehouse law was governing, even when state law was more restrictive.

Rice would not give up, and filed an appeal with the United States Supreme Court. The latter looked at the case in great detail and gave its decision on May 5, 1947—against Rice. Justice William O. Douglas wrote a lengthy majority opinion: Justice Felix Frankfurter dissented with another substantial opinion. The majority of the Court agreed that federal law was preeminent in the matters brought by Rice. "In more ambiguous situations than this," the Court majority opinion ended, "we have refused to hold that State regulation was superseded by a Federal law."[22]

Where Was the Corn?

A crisis had begun to build in 1942 relating to meat supply and the feed grains necessary to feed the animals. Already there had been a substantial black market in meat; in early 1943, mounting shortages of corn caused a similar black market in this crucial grain. Temporary price ceilings on corn had been announced in January 1943, and when these were made permanent in March (pegged to a price of $1.02 per bushel for No. 2 yellow corn at Chicago), there was widespread outcry from farmers and grain traders that the freeze had been put at a figure too low to bring corn to the market.

Farmers were holding their grain on the farm in anticipation of later price rises. Yet the government, deeply concerned about inflation, stringently held the price line.

In the marketplace, traders began to shade prices under the complex regulations. Buyers would interpret a particular rule at a slightly higher figure in order to make a sale, hoping that their bending of the rule would not be picked up by OPA regulators. This frustrated Cargill merchants. Julius Hendel, for example, apparently made public accusations of competitor price gouging. John Jr. wrote Weston Grimes: "I am distressed at hearing of Julius running down our competitors publicly, and I can only hope that he did not mention any by individual name." However, John Jr. later sided with the traders when Weston Grimes urged staying strictly within the price ceiling ranges: "I called in Art and Bert Egermayer and told them that I agreed with you in attaching great importance to this matter of ceiling prices. However, if the two of them agreed as to the legality of any sales they were not to bother me, but if they disagreed I wished to know all about it." A few weeks later, he added, "Occasional instances might arise where the boys here might disagree with you as to legality and like to take a chance."

Despite government exhortations to both farmers and the grain trade, the supply of corn to its users fell painfully short of needs. In June 1943, the War Food Administration (WFA) put out a special bulletin to farmers, urging them to market their corn and pointing out the number of products made from corn that were essential to war industries: "Among these uses are: corn, core binders for foundries; special molds for castings of aluminum, steel, iron, magnesium, bronze, and copper for airplane engines, tanks and other implements of war; nitrous starch for explosives; fibrous glass cloth used for bomber brake linings; adhesives for making containers for shipping ammunition and other war products; starch for the manufacturer of textiles and also for all paper products used in shipping containers." Some 11 million bushels were needed, said the agency.

Finally, when stocks still were falling short, the WFA took the unprecedented step of seizing all of the corn in some 96 midwestern terminal elevators. The WFA would now be the allocater, rather than the market. Cargill elevators in Omaha and Kansas City were affected. The Company had a particular problem in Omaha, for a serious flood had occurred just at this time, and the terminal had had to close from June 2 until June 21. In the process, Cargill and Hermitage Feed Mills in Nashville, Tennessee, exchanged harsh words over Hermitage's corn stored at Omaha. With the government intruding and arbitrarily allocating corn supplies, Cargill also incurred the wrath of Senator Styles Bridges of New Hampshire, who alleged that Cargill was refusing to sell corn to Merrimack, New Hampshire, farmers.

The shortages and government allocations continued into 1944. In January of that year, John Jr. complained about how empty the Company's elevators were: "We ourselves have 4,700,000 bushels of space in the country. We have 129 elevators located at 88 points." He continued: "These various OPA restrictions are driving us all crazy, as we are faced with wholesale violations by competitors, and of course we have to live up to the letter of the law." One problem, he pointed out a few weeks later, was that "the customers are showing a decided tendency to go around us and go direct to the country [which, of course, Cargill itself had done in challenging the Call Rule after the Corn Case]. This situation with fixed ceilings prevents us from obtaining any advantages from our superior efficiency and business is being done today on a friendship basis, which has never been one of our theories."

This cautiousness escalated the irritations of the Company traders. As Austen Cargill put it in a letter to John Jr. on March 31, 1944, "The boys in the Merchandising Department were terribly discouraged and resentful of the fact they could not do things everybody else was doing." The fact that the Legal Department seemed to be establishing basic company policy troubled Austen, and at this point he made a decision to "establish a buffer between the members of the organization that are working on Federal regulations and the boys in the Merchandising Department. . . . Hereafter all information pertaining to regulations, or interpretation of regulations, are to be sent to Bob Woodworth, and I have told the men in the Operating Department that they need not pay any attention to any information concerning those regulations until it comes to them from Bob and that they are to report to Bob the practices our competitors are following in all cases where those activities are injurious to us." Woodworth was a seasoned trader, and the assignment of this sensitive role was a recognition of his importance in the organization.[23]

Two New Diversifications

With the great interest in corn and other feed grains, Cargill saw opportunities in two new areas, each related to the other. Only one was a true success. The first involved dog food; the second, soybean processing.

In July 1941, Cargill MacMillan was contacted by a college friend whom he had not seen for many years, Newell H. Schooley. He headed a family firm that had been manufacturing animal foods since 1870. Schooley had become fascinated by the science of dog nutrition. After testing 61 different formulas (so he stated in his advertising), he had produced in the 62nd a dog ration of "26 choice ingredients for a balanced diet." He had named the product "Blue Streak" and was marketing it in the East from his Luzerne, Pennsylvania, headquarters. His letter to Cargill MacMillan suggested that the Company become sales agent for Blue Streak in the Midwest.

To the amazement of many Cargill people, the project was accepted, pushed along by Fred Seed, who was now heading the Cargill feed group. Seed assigned James Sheehan to handle the effort, and by September 1942, *Cargill News* devoted a half page to its new Cargill Dog Food. It was "a tasty dish for any dog," said the October *Cargill News* advertisement— "your dog will thank you." Early in the marketing, it was decided to continue the Blue Streak label, rather than calling it "Cargill." There was a full-page advertisement in the March 1943 issue, including a picture of a dog and having all of the accoutrements of full-scale advertising. Blue Streak was only marginally successful, staying on the retail shelves through the rest of the war. After the Japanese capitulation in August 1945, Cargill continued with further dog food efforts but not with Schooley.

In late 1942, Schooley was asked to visit John Jr. in Minneapolis, ostensibly for further discussions on dog food. John Jr. spent a whole morning with him and by the end of that meeting had sketched out a whole new idea, namely, development of a human balanced-diet formula, a highly nutritional, simple-to-eat food. John Jr. even had a name for it—"man food."

Schooley was fascinated and returned to his organization for a new round of testing, hoping to develop a product that would be palatable as well as nutritional. Seed and Julius Hendel also became intrigued by the notion, even taking a special trip to Peoria, Illinois, together to visit the U.S. Department of Agriculture testing laboratory there. John Jr., once again exuberant about a new project, wrote Schooley in February 1943: "I am immensely interested in your suggestions and approve whole-heartedly of your trying to develop just the product you described. If any trips seem necessary, I want you to take them, and any reasonable experimental expense is perfectly all right."

As experimentation continued, various formulas were considered. An early one had 24 percent malt powder, 17 percent bread flour, 16 percent yeast, 10 percent rice flour, 10 percent sugar and other ingredients in smaller quantities. Later, the formula evolved to higher percentages of corn flakes, wheat, rye and barley flours, rolled oats and soybean grits, again with other ingredients in smaller quantities.

One of the ingredients of great interest was the soybean. Widespread testing of soybean products (both meal and oil) was being conducted all over the country, in an effort to remove the objectionable taste of the bean. One promising approach at that time was to soak the bean in an alcohol base, then boil the alcohol off. John Jr. thought that it might be possible "to educate the people up to liking the soybean taste by gradually increasing the amount they eat." He even suggested that one could "start out with babies and build up their taste for soybeans from the start." John Jr.

enthused to Schooley that "I am confident that it is only a matter of a fairly short time before this is licked," but he was forced to admit that "for the time being I'm afraid that the soya bean is out."

The "man food" project continued into 1945, with further formulations and further cost calculations. The cost always seemed too high for ready salability of the product, and the Schooley project finally died away, once again an idea of John Jr.'s that was realistic but ahead of its time.[24]

If the soybean was not yet ready for "man food," it had come into its own as a key ingredient for animal feed. With the tremendous emphasis on feed during World War II, the soybean had become a major oilseed, crushed both for its meal and oil. Cargill had done some soybean trading in the mid-1930s. With the escalation of feed requirements, the Company now began purchasing in larger quantities (although still tiny in comparison to the major grains that Cargill traditionally purchased—wheat, barley, oats, rye and corn). Nevertheless, with soybeans in short supply, the feed division had difficulties in obtaining adequate quantities for feed mixing purposes. The OPA ceilings were so low on soybean meal that it was much more profitable for crushers to put their meal into their own feeds, rather than sell it. This was doubly frustrating, for some major new markets were evolving for both soybean meal and soybean oil.

In January 1943, the Company, with the initial push coming from Julius Hendel, announced the purchase of a soybean mill and feed plant, the Iowa Milling Company in Cedar Rapids, Iowa. The price was $300,000. Then, in October 1943, additional soybean milling capacity was acquired through the purchase of the Plymouth Processing Mills of Fort Dodge, Iowa. Later in that same month, another processing plant was purchased, in Springfield, Illinois, the Illinois Soy Products Company. The Fort Dodge plant had a capacity of 75 tons of soybean meal per day; the Springfield operation could crush approximately 3,900 bushels of soybeans per day. The November 1943 *Cargill News* commented: "Oh dem golden soybeans!"

These were all small facilities. Yet this was a beginning; unlike the dog food and "man food" projects, it had great promise, for soybean crushing became a major arm of the Company, from the later part of World War II on to the present. John Jr. visited the Cedar Rapids plant and wrote his father an ebullient letter: "I sat next to Guy Thomas at luncheon, who was extremely frank in saying that . . . he would have bought it himself at any price if he had known it was for sale. After that day spent there I readily understand this. The plant right now is grossing about $1500 a day and our expenses are relatively small. I now understand perfectly where Archer's [Archer-Daniels-Midland Company, a soybean crusher with its head office at that time in Minneapolis] enormous earnings are coming from . . . 50¢ a bushel . . . at their new Decatur plant . . . largest in the world." Archer, however, was using the diffusion method (solvent extraction, utilizing chemicals), whereas Cargill's three plants used the expeller method at that time, which was not as technologically advanced a process.[25]

Should Cargill Advertise?

An outgrowth of both the feed and dog food projects little noticed and not grasped by most Cargill people was the advent of Cargill retail advertising. As early as the summer of 1941, the Company conducted feed advertising at state fairs. By August 1942, radio advertising was being used for the Company's hybrid seed corn; the Blue Streak dog ration advertisements also began at this time. From November 1942, Cargill Feeds was broadcasting a barn dance every Saturday night over a Minneapolis station, featuring the popular Red River Valley Gang. Commercials on the program linked the Cargill name not only to "the red-striped feed sacks" but also to Cargill's overall war effort and "its folks who are giving, as you are, their BEST efforts for victory."

John Jr. gave his personal blessings to the barn dance script but wrote his father a quizzical letter a few months later, "I was talking with Fred Seed this afternoon and discovered to my astonishment that the Feed Department alone is spending no less than $25,000 a month on advertising. The largest single item is in radio. In addition to our Minneapolis program, we have one on the Cowles station in Des Moines . . . we are also advertising very heavily in the 'Farmer' and 'Wallace's Farmer.' "

John Jr. seemed not to comprehend fully this retail mentality. He continued: "The interesting part, though, is that in spite of this heavy advertising expense, we made $36,000 for the three feed mills in January and about the same in February. I was also astonished to discover that we are selling four times as much feed in Iowa as we are in Minnesota." As good as he was in making connections and seeing the larger picture, John Jr. was unable to make the link between advertising and larger sales. It was difficult for *most* of the Cargill group to think of the Company in anything but commodity terms, for the merchant (trading) mentality continued to dominate.[26]

The Barge Case Reaches the Supreme Court

In late 1941, Cargill and several of its grain trade colleagues (Norris Grain, Santa Fe Elevator, Continental Grain and Rosenbaum Brothers), encouraged by the strong dissent of Joseph Eastman in the Chicago barge case (see chapter 13), took this adverse ICC case to the federal district court for the Northern District of Illinois. They were joined in this by the Inland Waterways Corporation and the A. L. Mechling Barge Lines (as an intervenor).

Here they sought an injunction to require the railroads to grant grain arriving at Chicago by barge over the Illinois Waterways the privilege of moving out of Chicago by rail on "proportional" rates applicable to competing grain arriving at Chicago by lake steamer or rail. The railroads (the Baltimore & Ohio, the New York Central, the New York, Chicago and St. Louis, the Pennsylvania, the Erie and the Chesapeake & Ohio) were willing only to give such barged grain "local" rates, which were in all cases higher. To the surprise and delight of the plaintiffs, the three-judge panel decided on April 16, 1942, that this was unfair and granted the injunction. Pointing out that there would be less incentive to ship by barge if the higher "local" rate was required, Judge Charles E. Woodward held that this would be "a nullification of a consistent national policy to further the improvement of inland waterways in order to provide economical transportation," that this was "in practical effect, an attempt to bring about a cartelization of barge and rail transportation, which, if consummated, would destroy competition between these two means of transportation."

Strong words, these! The railroads were not daunted, however, and persuaded the United States Supreme Court itself to hear the case. That Court reversed the district court ruling in a 5–3 decision handed down on June 14, 1943, denying the injunction and awarding the case back to the railroads. The majority decision was a complex one, and there was a lengthy, involved dissent.

The majority opinion, written by Justice Robert H. Jackson, agreed with the original ICC statement that the railroads' rates were "just and reasonable," for "long hauls have generally been thought entitled to move at a rate less than the sum of the rates for local or short hauls between intermediate points." If an injunction were to be sustained, grain "originating 60 miles from Chicago" would gain proportionals "fixed with reference to grain from the Northwest Territory, embracing points in Canada and as far west in the United States as Washington and the Dakotas."

Justice Hugo L. Black, writing the dissenting opinion, reiterated the district court belief that this was unfair competition by the railroads. He quoted a rail lawyer's statement made at the original ICC hearing, that "we made this proposal, as I have stated several times, and filed these tariffs with the hope that we could drive this business off of the water and back onto the rails where it belongs. . . . We are not in love with water transportation . . . and we believe that we are entitled to that grain business." Black emphasized that the Transportation Act of 1940 provided for "fair and impartial regulation" but that "Congress, fearful, in the words of several members, that the Commission was 'essentially a railroad-minded body,' took every precaution to prevent discrimination against water carriers." He quoted Joseph Eastman's words in the same vein, in the latter's dissent in the original ICC case, and chastised the railroads for their delaying tactics.

Often a Supreme Court ruling becomes the final word, to last over many years. In this case, however, the central issue—just how railroads were to compete with a new strong entrant in transportation, the inland waterway barge—was so fundamental to the country's long-held concepts of free enterprise that it was inevitable that a further test would come in the courts.

It did, once again involving the A. L. Mechling Barge Lines. Essentially the same issue came through the courts once more, in 1946. It had been won by the railroads in the U.S. District Court and appealed to the Supreme Court. The petitioner this time was Mechling, one of the intervenors in the earlier case. The case was decided on March 31, 1947, with Justice Black now writing the majority opinion. Black found that "the basic error of the Commission here is . . . that the Congressional prohibitions of railroad rate discriminations against water carriers were not applicable to such discriminations if accomplished by through rates. But this assumption would permit the destruction or curtailment of the advantages to shippers of cheap barge transportation whenever the transported goods were carried beyond the end of the barge line." Inasmuch as Congress had forbidden such discrimination, Black and the majority held for Mechling—the barge companies had prevailed. There was a dissenting opinion by Justice Robert Jackson, with Felix Frankfurter joining. The decision was a tremendous shot in the arm for the inland waterway users. For Cargill, it had special impact in Chicago (shipping from Illinois River terminals) and in Memphis, which suddenly came alive.[27]

Guntersville: An Opening to the Southeast

In early June 1943, Austen Cargill and John Jr. and his brother Cargill were invited by A. L. Mechling, the head of the barge line involved in the Supreme Court case, to accompany him on an inspection trip up the Tennessee River. The Tennessee Valley Authority (TVA) had upgraded navigation on that river in a major way in the 1930s. A well-fitted inspection vessel was owned by the Mechling organization, and the trip was a fascinating one for the three Cargill executives. As soon as he returned, John Jr. wrote Frank Neilson: "Our trip on the Tennessee was a tremendous success and I am hoping we can have a barge line and some houses [grain elevators] going there soon. It reminded me very much of the famous junket in 1923 [in regard to lumber] when Roy [Wisner] and father went to British Columbia. We certainly had a good time and learned a great deal. . . . Austen snores just as formerly but Cargill is now running him a close second."

Out of this informative and enjoyable river trip came two new ideas. First, John Jr. proceeded immediately to obtain elevator capacity on the

Tennessee. On August 15, 1943, Cargill purchased the elevator properties and grain business of the O. J. Walls Company at Guntersville, Alabama. (Cargill failed to get a "non-compete" agreement from Walls, and O. J. promptly built another small elevator and set himself up in competition!)

By size standards, the Guntersville elevator was almost a fly speck in the Cargill terminal family—it had only a 100,000-bushel capacity. Yet in terms of concept and potential, this elevator had a tremendous impact on Company business. The southeastern part of the United States was expanding its agricultural and related businesses in a significant way even at this time (and certainly more so in later years). In particular, the poultry business, with its substantial demands for feed, was a promising business prospect. Using the Tennessee River as a stepping-off point for this whole area (utilizing trucking beyond Guntersville) proved to be a very effective way of reaching this important market area.

The second effect of Guntersville was on Cargill inland waterway equipment. Cargill had not only been building ocean shipping for the navy but also was now involved in the construction of the inland-waterway towboats for the Defense Plant Corporation. These were not of the size that John Jr. believed were most effective. Indeed, the huge length of the DPC boats made for limited use in areas where there were significant numbers of locks. These huge towboats were therefore most effective in the lower Mississippi.

John Jr. now began an extensive correspondence with TVA executives, particularly with David Lilienthal, its chairman. John Jr. wanted to build a Cargill-owned towboat to the Company's own specifications (i.e., much shorter, as with the Erie Canal "*Carneida* type" towboats). He also wanted to construct large, 200-foot steel barges. The total length was such that this configuration could navigate the Tennessee River upstream only as far as the Hales Bar lock.

The TVA officials responded to John Jr.'s question about whether this lock was going to be improved by outlining the Authority's ultimate objective of having twin locks in parallel at each site, each new lock to be some 600 feet in length. However, this plan was not to be implemented until after World War II. John Jr. wrote C. T. Barker, the head of TVA's river transportation division: "I do not think we will change the contemplated length of our new equipment but I somehow think we will be able to dig up enough small equipment to take care of what business we have above this lock."

Out of this TVA initiative came John Jr.'s decision to open a shipbuilding facility, separate from Port Cargill, to begin construction on the barges. A location on the Minnesota River a few miles upstream from Savage at Chaska was chosen for this work. Separate crews were assembled, and work proceeded quickly toward construction of two barges, each of 2,500-ton capacity. Both barges were to be 278 feet in length, with a 43-

foot, 6-inch beam. Each would have one end molded but would be square on the other end—this latter to fit John Jr.'s new concept, a square towboat that could be put between the two barges as one long integrated unit. Underneath the towboat, four propellers would be running, each in its own tunnel, to keep down the draft of the towboat. John Jr. had a ¹/₁₂ scale version of this built for practice on Lake Minnetonka, near his home, and "to our absolute amazement the mid-ship propulsion turned out to be just as good as the stern propulsion." The midship design also was tested with the *Carneida* (one of Cargill's Erie Canal towboats) by Marcus Marshal, the Albany superintendent. The results here also were promising. At one point, John Jr. even hoped that he could interest the Office of Defense of Transportation in helping to finance the new towboat/barge design as "experimental."

The towboat itself was to be built by a subcontractor, the Dingle Boat Works in St. Paul. As the planning of this towboat/barge combination continued, the midbarge positioning of the towboat seemed not to be the best idea after all, and the Company changed its plans for the towboat to a small-boat version built in early World War II called the *Sea Mule*. The final version was just over 40 feet in length and 33 feet wide; it had a draft of about 6 feet 6 inches. There were to be eight Chrysler marine engines with a total theoretical capacity of 1160 horsepower.

The towboat was completed right on schedule and launched in September 1944 as the *Cartasca* (a combination of "Cargill" and "Itasca," the lake at the headwaters of the Mississippi River). John Jr.'s 11-year-old daughter Marion was the christener, assisted by Cargill MacMillan's daughter Paula. By mid-November, the vessel was fully equipped, and John Jr., Cargill MacMillan and Austen Cargill all went, together with the towboat, down the Mississippi as far as Hastings, Minnesota. John Jr. wrote his son about the day:

The captain is a very competent man but, like any new piece of equipment, it takes time to learn how to handle it and, unfortunately, just below Saint Paul while going under the Terminal Railroad bridge, we struck a rock with a starboard propeller, which did a great deal of damage. It not only bent one propeller but ruined the reduction gears on three of the other engines, so while we were able to make Hastings all right, the damage showed up when we got down the river later on and it took them until 6:00 o'clock Wednesday night to go under the bridge at La-Crosse, a distance of only 150 miles. After we get organized, they should make this distance in one day.[28]

The Beginnings of the Carmacs

There was yet another outgrowth of that inspection trip that John Jr., Cargill MacMillan and Austen Cargill took with the Mechling group on the latter's inspection vessel. The idea of having one's own inspection vessel/private yacht appealed to the three very much. The following spring (1945), John Jr. gave C. C. Boden, the head of the New York office, the assignment of looking for just such a vessel. He spelled out to Boden his views on this craft: "We heard that the Navy is now returning yachts to their owners and that most of them were in pretty bad condition . . . it struck us that the larger yachts might be selling fairly reasonable. . . . If we could pick up a suitable boat for this purpose we would be very much interested, especially as we would view it more as a workboat than as a yacht." John Jr. wanted sleeping quarters for eight or ten people in a vessel large enough for use on the Great Lakes and for use "coast-wise in selected weather" yet low enough to go under the bridges of the New York State Barge Canal and the Chicago River. Cargill itself would do the overhauling, so condition was not a particular criterion.

The yacht broker indeed had a number of such boats listed, and in early 1945, Cargill purchased a 115-foot craft, originally built in 1929 by a reputable shipbuilder, George Lawley & Sons, and most recently used for submarine-chasing work in the North Sea. The purchase price (from the War Shipping Administration) was $16,150. The repairs and overhaul cost an additional $35,925. For just over $52,000 the Company had a quite adequate "inspection vessel" (John Jr. remonstrated, "We are very careful not to describe it as a Yacht"). It was given the name *Carmac*, a natural combination of the two family names, Cargill and MacMillan.[29]

Personnel and Wartime Tensions

That first year of the American involvement in the war (1942) brought great pressures on work life all over the country as more and more young men in their peak years of productivity were drafted into the armed forces. Attrition in the Cargill work force began to tell. It was easier to persuade draft boards of the essential nature of key jobs at the shipyard than it was for the grain trade jobs. "It seems," John Jr. wrote to his father, "that the name 'Merchant' is an anathema to a draft board as it denotes a profit motive in buying and selling." The Company had to redefine these jobs as "in Charge of Procurement and Distribution of Grain."

One pronounced effect was the increasing role of women in industry. By the very traditions of the grain trade, Cargill had been a male bastion. The heart of the business, merchandising and trading, had always been staffed by men. Now women took a number of these positions. When one young trader was drafted, his boss wired Ed Grimes: "I was thinking of putting a girl on in his place, as any young man we could get would probably be subject to call also." He queried Grimes, "If this meets with your approval" (it did).

In the terminology of that day, these women were considered "girls" (but so were male employees often called "boys"). To the surprise of many of the old-timers, a number of these women became excellent traders. The *Cargill News* reporter, commenting on four women who were being trained as merchants, noted: "It is certainly strange to enter some of the departments that have always been strictly masculine and see the pleasant surprise of a comely feminine countenance." A longer article on one of these four, Jane Spaulding, was headlined "Cargill Girl First to Enter Buffalo Grain Market." The focus of the article was on her professional qualifications.[30]

Despite attrition from the draft, the figures for total employment at Cargill skyrocketed. In 1940, the Company employed, in all of its divisions, 1,086 people; this became 1,696 in 1942, 3,488 in 1943 and a wartime high of 3,822 in 1944. Both Cargill, Incorporated, and Cargo Carriers had had small increases in numbers, but the major jump had been in the Shipbuilding Division. From a zero position in 1941 the numbers at Savage had climbed to 339 in 1940 and to 2,067 in 1944.

By October 1944, some 516 Cargill men were in the service; 7 had been killed in the war. *Cargill News* editor T. R. Shaw assigned Georgina Hamilton (later Georgina McGillivray) to the task of following all of these service people. In July 1942, she began a column, "Gems of Service," filled with news and personal reminiscences of Cargill's men in uniform. When Shaw retired as editor of the *Cargill News*, to be replaced by Tom Totushek, Hamilton became an assistant editor for the house newsletter. Memories of the effectiveness of this wartime column have extended down to the present. Well remembered, too, were the many humorous exchanges in the *News* between "Weary Willie" (Norman Williams) and "the Buzzard" (Buzz Larabee), extending over many issues in the late 1930s and early 1940s.[31]

Older men had to take over many tasks in this period. There were some devastating losses in this group. Frank Neilson had had serious heart problems since the beginning of the war and was off on an extended sick leave, with no assurance that he could get back to the job (he never did). Then, in November 1942, both company and family were shocked by the sudden death of Arthur Wheeler. He had been visiting his brother-in-law, Will MacMillan, the University of Chicago mathematician, and had a sudden fatal heart attack. He had held the purchasing job that had been arranged by John Sr. for just six months.

Three months later, Ross B. Wilson, the chief engineer of the shipyard (who had been brought from Albany), also suffered a sudden fatal heart attack. John Jr. wrote his father: "His death is a terrific shock, as he had become immensely popular within the organization and, as you know, we had come to lean on him very heavily." Health was already on John Jr.'s mind (his own hypertension had continued more or less unabated), and he confided to John Sr.: "His and Arthur's death had made me wonder if we should not institute some system of physical check-up on those of our executives who are, say, 50 and over. An occasional visit to a first-class clinic . . . should prevent this sort of thing in the future."

In January 1944, John Jr. had seen his own doctor, who "made a very careful check of the arteries and blood vessels in both eyes and told me that they revealed a shocking state of hyper-tension . . . he thought I should be in a hospital instead of the office." Austen Cargill, worried about John Jr.'s health, finally wrote a doctor friend of his, in July 1944: "John Jr. is having serious difficulty controlling his own blood pressure. . . . Roy Hoople told John Jr. that he was under the impression you had tried out the so-called 'rice diet' for high blood pressure." John Jr. asked Austen to find out the results, for "he is under the impression that a doctor at Duke University has reported some very wonderful results from the so-called 'oriental diet.' " Only after the war, however, was John Jr. able to follow up on this lead of Austen's. Cargill MacMillan's correspondence evidences his real worry at this time about his brother's health. Subjected also to the heightened tensions of his unfamilar Port Cargill assignment, he experienced the personal trial of dealing with an occasionally recurring drinking problem.

The relationship between Austen Cargill and John Jr. apparently had improved during this period. Cargill MacMillan's absence at Port Cargill had forced Austen and John Jr. to depend more on each other. John Jr. wrote his mother and father in March 1944:

I cannot tell you how I have enjoyed working with Austen this last year. It has been impossible to get a more co-operative executive. . . . I cannot see that we disagree on a single issue. Another most satisfactory thing about him is his tremendous capacity for detail . . . he can grind out more work than almost anyone around here. On top of this he has developed a capacity of a very high order in picking men and has surrounded himself with only the best. He has grown in stature beyond belief these last few years and I consider him today an enormously valuable asset to the business.

Given the truly precarious state of John Jr.'s health, it was fortunate that Austen's role had become so strong. He was the second-highest officer in the Company as executive vice president and in all probability would have been the first choice as chief executive if John Jr. were incapacitated.[32]

Employee relations practices changed markedly during the war because of wage constraints mandated by the government. These limitations led to an important new Cargill compensation supplement, the "Profit Sharing–Stock Bonus Plan." This allowed the Company to pass along to its employees a portion of its earnings in profitable years (the earlier wartime years were) without violating the federal wage stabilization laws. A trust was established, funded by an allocation of Cargill second preferred stock. Each employee had an interest in the trust based upon the proportion that his or her total compensation in 1942 bore to the total compensation earned by all eligible employees. When dividends were declared on the stock, the proceeds of the trust-held stock were then allocated to each employee on the above basis, not taxable until the money was actually distributed to the beneficiary. The trustee of the trust was given the right to decide upon the method of distribution. The amounts accruing to individual employee accounts was not very large, but the "shared" concept behind the plan made an important contribution to employee morale.[33]

The Weather Bureau Tells John Jr. "No"

John Jr. had continued his infatuation with weather forecasting, his central hypothesis being that the earth's atmosphere responded to gravitational forces of the moon and planets. Early in the war he claimed to have predicted a tornado that hit Florida. He also continued his work for a book on weather prediction. As concerns built up about the Allied invasion, in June 1944, John Jr. made a set of specific predictions about the weather off the English coast and sent drawings for the period June 6-June 14 to the chief of the Weather Bureau, Commander F. W. Reichelderfer, who turned over John Jr.'s materials to his statistical staff for serious study. On August 4, 1944, Reichelderfer wrote John Jr.:

We believe that it [John Jr.'s theory] is not in accord with observed physical facts . . . the number of cases where the conditions turned out as forecast does not appear to be greater than those which can be obtained by random methods, the successful cases are not in themselves evidence of sound principles of forecasting. . . . We must examine with care those methods of long range forecasting which rest primarily upon reference to a number of "successful" cases. . . . The record must show a significantly greater percentage of successes than can be attained by random methods or other unscientific systems. . . . Many well-known long range forecasters . . . point to their successes as evidence of the soundness of their theories and methods but when examined by impartial statistical methods, it is found that these successes must rest almost entirely on chance. A significant thing is that these various long range forecasting methods are usually quite irreconcilable, one with the other in theory, and the particular weather conditions forecast by use of the various methods are frequently contradictory.

After noting that he "would offer a number of standard references by outside, disinterested authorities which present what we believe are sound physical principles," Reichelderfer ended: "We should be glad to hear from you if you desire further discussion, but we do not believe that your present approach to long range forecasting offers a solution." The record does not show any reply by John Jr.—Reichelderfer's letter must have been very deflating to him. Yet he kept his interest and continued to add to his own book manuscript on weather.[34]

Cargill's Wartime Organization Changes

Deaths of key people and new Cargill activities early in World War II brought significant reassessment of organizational relationships. Shipbuilding was made a wholly separate profit center (necessarily, as all activities were for government contracts). John Jr. had assigned his brother Cargill executive responsibility for the shipbuilding operation—indeed, to be there almost every day. This forced many of his brother's existing responsibilities back on John Jr. himself, who missed his brother's involvement and complained often of the demands by the armed services ("our shipbuilding . . . has put an awful burden on the rest of us"). Frank Neilson, continuing on sick leave, also was sorely missed. John Jr. kept Neilson well informed of Cargill activities, particularly those under Neilson's responsibility. When John Jr. proposed appointing Wallace Hyde acting head of shipbuilding, Neilson felt that this was preempting his own assistants, James Hayhoe and Joe Bailey. John Jr.'s view prevailed on this one.

The difference of opinion here pointed up once again some intraorganizational friction (the words that Neilson chose to use in his comments about the Hyde role). Over the next several weeks, John Sr. and John Jr. worked on a written statement about coordination and interaction for the senior executives of the Company. Circulated on May 18, 1942, it began this way: "There have been several instances that have resulted in serious consequences to the Company which have been caused solely by information being unwittingly withheld from executives who had a vital interest in this information. . . . This lack of coordination, which was brought about principally by carelessness, may be overcome by our executives making use of a system similar to that we use in the case of Weston Grimes's Washington letters" (these automatically had been circulated to all 12 top executives). The memorandum exhorted each key person to make written records of trips and conferences, then pass these around to all other interested parties, each of whom would initial it. This was being treated as more than just a routine proposal—some of the jealousies and backbiting had become too pronounced. This "solution" was too tentative, too tepid, given the evident organizational stress. The stress continued, apparently unabated.

The Company's predilection toward independence continued strong. The Corn Case had had lasting effects. In mid-1943 the Balfour-Guthrie grain-trading organization made overtures to Cargill about a joint sales office in Europe. It was an intriguing proposal, said John Jr., as "they would put up the money (on which they claim themselves . . . very long) and we would put up organization (on which they seem to think we are very long)." Balfour-Guthrie was probably correct in its assessment of Cargill organizational strength (despite the stress). Nevertheless, John Jr. was lukewarm to the idea: "As, you know, we are not especially good co-operators." Nothing came of the proposal.

The Cargill organization *was* deepening, in good part because of the highly successful training program of Julius Hendel all through the 1930s. In addition to Hyde at the shipyard, several other younger men were being placed in increasingly major roles. One was Ralph Golseth, who was now appointed vice president in his position as direct assistant to John Jr. In March 1943, Frank Neilson finally was told by his doctor not to return to work, and Hayhoe and Bailey were formally appointed to Neilson's grain terminal responsibilities (Hayhoe for the physical properties, Bailey for the grain). Fred Seed (in feed) and Erv Kelm (in grain), also members of the early training programs, were taking increased responsibilities in the Minneapolis office, as was Ford Ferguson, now head of the Chicago office.

In August 1943, the board formally established separate divisions for the Company (grain, warehouse, sales, country elevator, shipbuilding, seed, administrative and financial), in the process assigning the various vice presidents as heads of these divisions and formally establishing the position of assistant vice president, as well as new positions of assistant secretary and assistant comptroller. Several new sales branches were also established at this point, at Guntersville, at Tampa, Florida (where Philip Sayles had moved from his Chicago responsibilities), at Cedar Rapids and at Maumee, Ohio.

Another new, smaller terminal had been constructed in a key spot on the Illinois River at Ottawa. It had only a 100,000-bushel capacity, but its importance went far beyond this, for it was set up to be served primarily by trucks. Highly efficient state-of-the-art unloading and loading equipment made it one of the most effective terminals, just at the time when such trucking links had become very promising. The total terminal capacity for the Company was now over 71 million bushels.

John Jr. was concerned about overlaps between rail and water transport, and in January 1944 he asked an internal study committee to look into the matter. Cargo Carriers Incorporated (CCI) seemed a logical organization to handle both of these functions, and later both were consolidated under it. A more serious concern was the overlap between merchandising grains and merchandising feed and feed ingredients, now that the Feed Group had the oilseed crushing operation, too. Ralph Golseth, the chair of the Study Committee, reported a few weeks later (in February 1944) the committee's view that all trading should be split away from Feed, that Feed was to do no trading. A Grain Department person was assigned the task for this trading, one who had as his "main job . . . to supply the Feed Mills with ingredients and whose secondary job is to make money trading in these and other feed ingredients." This put an ambiguous dual responsibility on the Grain Division, which was now to act both as trader and initiator of procurement in the case of feed ingredients.

Highly centralized organizational concepts continued. Control from the top was further enhanced with initiation of the Company's first formal budget in July 1944. In November 1944, department heads received another memorandum that public statements were to come out *only* over the signature of Ed Grimes, "in order to avoid any possibility of conflicting, contradictory or undesirable press releases." The functionally determined organization structure also stayed in place. In early 1945, Julius Hendel was put in charge of all merchandising activities of Cargill, including terminal merchandising, the Country Division, the Seed Division and the Oil and Feed Division. The *Cargill News* announcement of Hendel's new role stated once more: "Cargill has long been set up on a functional scheme of organization as distinguished from the line plan. The distinction, of course, is that Cargill has one man in charge of each function, e.g., finance, plant administration, merchandising, etc." Then the article frankly stated what had long been known: "The great weakness of the functional organization is that after a concern reaches a certain size the co-ordination between departments tends to become inadequate. . . . It is hoped that these changes will result in much closer co-operation between the four departments." Hope did not become reality—the long-standing feuding among some of the principals continued.

There also were problems once again with the issue of conflict of interest, for John Jr. put out a fresh memorandum on the subject on December 31, 1943. This time a new issue arose over employee-owned mortgaged real estate. John Jr. stated:

The Company has long made it a practice not to permit officers or employees to deal on margin in stocks, bonds or commodities, nor to permit the engagement in business in activities on any scale which might in any way detract from the undivided attention of the employees. Dealing in mortgaged real estate is considered in the same category as dealing in commodities on margin, although the prohibition has never been held to apply if the real estate is used as a personal residence. The Company has no wish to control in any way the investment by its employees of their savings, but it does want the undivided attention of its employees in behalf of its own activities.

What seemed here to be a stringent prohibition on employees holding mortgaged real estate was not followed at a later date, for several senior executives became substantially involved in outside real estate endeavors.[35]

Death Takes a Further Toll on the Organization

Unexpected deaths continued during the rest of the war. In addition to the deaths of seven Cargill servicemen, senior members of management also were lost to illness. Rudy Semsch, the controller, who had been so importantly involved in the insider trading incident in the late 1930s and in the sensitive negotiations with the government officials on the Savage shipyard arrangements, had suffered a serious brain tumor that had taken him off the job in mid-1943; he died on February 28, 1944. Two months later, in May 1944, George Turner, the general superintendent of the Country Division, died on the job. Early 1945 brought additional deaths of management veterans. Fred W. Drum, a vice president and Cargill's sales manager, died in February; he had retired in 1939. Dudley M. Irwin, the "grand old man of Buffalo," once known as the "barley king of the East," also died in February 1945; he had retired in 1940 after 40 years with Cargill.

In that same month of February 1945, Frederick E. Lindahl, the dean of Cargill's veterans, died. He had started working for James F. Cargill in 1884 and had been centrally involved as the head of the Duluth operations from 1891 to his death. He had retired from active service in 1940 (at age 80), after 55 years of Cargill employment but still went into the office every day. At retirement he obtained his first driver's license and celebrated by driving from Duluth to the Twin Cities and return (he had used a chauffeur previously).

On March 6, 1945, Frank Neilson died. After his serious heart attack early in World War II, he had continued to correspond with John Sr. and John Jr. about management decisions in his area, covering not only the terminals but the important Savage shipbuilding operation. Unfortunately, his health never allowed him to return to work, and he retired in 1943. He had worked closely with John Jr., who felt his loss deeply.

These deaths of key senior management officials occurred in the context of another death right at this time. John Sr. suffered a renewed series of heart problems in the fall of 1944 and died on October 18, 1944. No one could equal the contribution that John Sr. had made to Cargill business development and values. His philosophy permeated the entire organization, leaving a lasting imprint on John Jr., Cargill MacMillan and Austen Cargill. John Jr. had been the chief executive officer in fact since the early 1930s, when John Sr. had had his first serious heart attack. Yet the counsel of this uncommon man had continued to exert major influence on the Company through the rest of that decade. By the beginning of World War II, John Sr. had removed himself from the mainstream of Company decision making, although his sons, Austen Cargill and others kept him fully informed. The Company's senior management paid homage to his manifold contributions, as he joined the "innumerable caravan," the William Cullen Bryant poetic phrase that Ed Grimes used in the major board of directors' statement, composed in December 1944 and published in the *Cargill News* of June 1945.

It bears repeating that the values and belief systems of present-day Cargill can be traced back to John Sr. In this sense, the occasion for the family was not a sad one in its usual sense—John Sr. had contributed his full being to his family, his friends and his organization and now was at rest with a task fully accomplished. John Jr. wrote a relative shortly after his death: "We are really extremely thankful that we had him with us as long as we did because in 1933 the doctors in Johns-Hopkins took me aside and told me that he only had a very few months to live." That the doctors were wrong was a great blessing.[36]

The "Lake Office"

John Jr.'s increased interest in the armed services and their role in the war led him back to his memories of his own tour of duty in France in World War I. Then, he had become fascinated by the notion of his commander, General Foote, that the top command unit of an organization could run best if it segregated itself into quarters that allowed close interaction among the key people and minimum disturbances from the outside. General Foote particularly had been enthusiastic about the quartering of his unit in a French chateau—John Jr. had written about this in detail to his family.

In August 1944, the Company made a move influenced by his World War I experience: the Company purchased a country home, a smaller version of a French chateau, on the shores of Lake Minnetonka, west of Minneapolis. Built in 1931, it had been a private home for a prominent Minneapolis man, Rufus Rand, Jr. (a grandson of the founder of the Minneapolis Gas Light Company). "The building was copied from a chateau in France," a Cargill brochure states, "which had attracted Mr. Rand when he was stationed there as a flyer in World War I." Rand, his wife and six daughters had lived in the spacious home until 1941, when the family decided to move out because of personal financial reversals. No one had lived in the building during the first two years or so of the war, and it already was becoming rundown. In the summer of 1944, John Jr. contacted Mrs. Rand about the Rand Company selling the property to Cargill, and in September 1944, a sale was consummated, the title to be held by Cargill Securities Company (the family company).

With the wartime shortages of building materials, the Company had to leave the property idle until the end of the war. The empty building *was* used to store lifeboats being built by the Minnetonka Boat Works for the armed services . Each carried a full emergency gasoline tank, and some of the then-teenage members of the families owned up many years later to sneaking in and "borrowing" gas to supplement their small "A" ration card allotments. But plans were made almost from the start for converting the building to a corporate headquarters complex, to house about 125 people in total. Only a small group would move out from the downtown Minneapolis location; a large number of additional Cargill employees would remain downtown. John Jr. had returned again to the General Foote notion that if 60 or so key people would surround themselves with secretarial and professional help in a segregated environment, they could accomplish their work more effectively. John Jr. himself always functioned better shielded from large groups, with interchange only with one or a few trusted associates. Whether this also was true of others in senior management was not clear.

The purchase was made public in December 1944, and local journalists were given a tour of the property. Cedric Adams, a respected columnist at the *Minneapolis Sunday Tribune* reported enthusiastically: "I visited the 200-acre Rand estate with its 17-bathroom mansion, its 1,200,000-gallon swimming pool, its 23 fireplaces . . . there is probably no other estate in these parts quite as elegant, quite as elaborate." After taking his readers on a detailed room-by-room tour, he ended: "All in all, it's a daring project, but one that may be the forerunner of a brand new type of office quartering. Personally, I can't imagine how working conditions could be made any more ideal."

Moving corporate headquarters to rural settings was a fresh idea recognized already by the national press. *Business Week*, in its issue of January 6, 1945, had an illustrated article entitled "Moving to Mansions—a Trend" that highlighted the Cargill building and a similar large estate purchased by Reynolds Metals Company, an estate of the late F. W. Woolworth at Glen Cove, New York. The article also mentioned earlier moves by Pennsylvania Salt Manufacturing Company, North American Phillips Company and the Produc-Trol organization. It was "a desire for suburban quiet" and a "novel housing trend." The Cargill Rand property was indeed suburban, quiet and certainly novel for Minneapolis. Whether it would prove to be what John Jr. felt was a more effective management headquarters remained to be answered after the termination of the war.

The editor of *Northwestern Miller*, Robert E. Sterling, commented on Cargill's purchase in a long editorial: "We distinctly approve of it. The consensus of the dinner table was that too much high-priced and high-powered executive ability—when there is any—is frittered away by the attrition of office details." The editorial commented on a Mayo Clinic doctor's speech, in which he had advised executives to slow down, to conserve strength and energy for their greater responsibilities under the pressure of wartime work. "The mortality of executives and other overburdened brain workers, and the incidence of serious degenerative diseases among them, appear to be considerably higher than they are among men who work with their hands. Nervous breakdowns among executives are common because such men not only work too long hours in the office but most of their time outside is taken up with talking shop and making contacts which will be helpful in their business."[37]

Preparing for Postwar

In most companies, Cargill included, there was understandable concern by employees toward the end of World War II about just how their organizations would face the major reconversion problems that would come at the end of hostilities. Under the leadership of Julius Hendel, Cargill began to look at these issues as early as 1943. On December 16, 1943, Hendel asked the senior department heads to meet with him for an evening session at a conference room in Freddy's Cafe in downtown Minneapolis to replicate once more the sessions that he had held all through the 1930s with the college graduate trainees. Most of this group were in the room that evening, many of them already quite far along on the management ladder. The subject was "post-war plans."

In his sometimes professorial manner, Hendel first discussed a number of his own views about merchandising, price trends, the farmers' production and the recurrent surplus problem and the outlook for international trade. It was easy to sell during the war, Hendel noted, but he warned that "after the war, those who have not studied are going to be left by the wayside." The wartime grain trade was in "a nervous topsy-turvy state," and it behooved Cargill to be prepared. During the question-and-answer session, the issue of diversification came up frequently and with it the need for research and experimentation (for example, the pros and cons of developing a more complicated soybean-crushing process using the solvent method). It was a wide-ranging evening, one with a sense of excitement about the future and an awareness of the need for positioning Cargill to meet whatever was going to be ahead.

Hendel acknowledged that he himself had pushed the Company into soybean crushing, admitting that "I have probably been a little bit too ambitious. I have done a few things which possibly I should not have done but, like a nagging small boy—if he nags long enough and strong enough, the parents give in! . . . But finally I have nagged out the management . . . and we have those three plants." If Hendel was being properly self-deprecating about his advocacy of feed and soybean crushing, in reality he had

had the backing of John Jr., Cargill MacMillan and Austen Cargill in his efforts to diversify the Company in these directions.

Hendel was anxious to reinstitute the college graduate training program. In the same month of the Freddy's meeting he visited a number of East Coast grain companies and wired John Jr. enroute: "The more I visit houses with foreign connections the more I come to the conclusion that we will need more of our own trained men for postwar trade." The war would have to end first, however, for the pool of talent was still preoccupied with its winning.

In May 1945, Hendel succeeded in bringing an important new group into the Cargill organization. The Company purchased the Honeymead Products Company at Cedar Rapids, Iowa. It included a feed plant with capacity to produce approximately 300 tons of feed per day and a soybean extraction plant designed by Allis-Chalmers Company. The extraction plant originally had a 50-ton-per-day capacity, which had been boosted to 130 tons (4,300 bushels) of beans per day. As Cargill already had a Cedar Rapids feed plant, the new group was renamed the West Side Plant. The Andreas family had held the property, and Dwayne Andreas, a younger member of the family, agreed to join Cargill. John Jr.'s report on his first visit to the Cedar Rapids plant noted: "Andreas is highly intelligent and has much initiative. I don't think we will be able to hold him unless we broaden his responsibilities. Hope we can." Soon Andreas became a vice president of Cargill, the youngest in all of Cargill history.

Dwayne Andreas, c. 1950.

Interestingly, as with the Guntersville purchase, where Cargill bought a terminal but forgot to specify that the seller then not compete with the Company (which he did), Cargill left some loose ends in its negotiations for Honeymead. Julius Hendel, like the rest of the organization not particularly attuned to retail marketing, did not ask the Andreas group to include the copyright of the Honeymead name itself. Dwayne Andreas was quite surprised that he did not. Later, other members of the Andreas family resurrected the name for their new oilseed crushing plant in Mankato, Minnesota.

One of the key questions for the Company in its postwar planning was what would happen to Cargill shipbuilding in general and Port Cargill in particular. In October 1944, John Jr. was interviewed by a Minneapolis paper about Cargill's postwar plans (it was the thirteenth article in a series on Twin Cities industries). Asked about possible civilian uses of Port Cargill, John Jr. replied, "We would like very much to get our shipyard back to build for ourselves. We'll probably be building vessels for our own use at Port Cargill for some years to come."

The article mentioned once again the possibility of Port Cargill as a river terminal for grain "and possibly other products, including iron ore." John Jr. warned that any discussion of this was premature, inasmuch as "political considerations make extremely problematical any talk of development of the river as a terminal." Nevertheless, the Company would probably continue shipbuilding, more likely some form of grain carrier. It was clear that the Company intended to use Port Cargill beyond the end of the government shipbuilding contracts.[38]

APPENDIX

Service Records of Cargill's 18 AOGs

AOG 6 *Agawam* (commissioned December 18, 1943)
Served in Pacific operations during World War II. Main area of operations was in the Philippines. Placed out of commission in reserve at San Diego on January 31, 1957.

AOG 7 *Elkhorn* (commissioned February 14, 1944)
Served as station tanker in May 1944. Active in Pacific Fleet until 1962. Transferred to Taiwan on July 1, 1972, and renamed *Hsin Lung* AOG 517.

AOG 8 *Genesee* (commissioned May 27, 1944)
Served in South Pacific during the war, then delivered gas and oil to Japanese ports until December 1945. Decommissioned December 14, 1949, and recommis-

sioned on July 28, 1950, to serve in Korean War. Also took part in Vietnam. Transferred to Chile and renamed *Beagle* (54).

AOG 9 *Kishwaukee* (commissioned May 27, 1944)
Served in Pacific operations during the war. Decommissioned April 2, 1958. Transferred to Maritime Administration Reserve Fleet (MARAD) until November 1965. Recommissioned on September 1, 1966, and served in Vietnam.

AOG 10 *Nemasket* (commissioned October 20, 1943)
Operated in Pacific Islands until May 1947. Decommissioned into reserve September 22, 1960. Stricken on July 1, 1960, and scrapped in 1961.

AOG 11 *Tombigbee* (commissioned November 18, 1943)
Used to carry fresh water in lieu of gasoline or oil in the Pacific. Placed out of commission December 12, 1949. Recommissioned July 28, 1950, for Korean War. Participated in Operation Deep Freeze in 1963. On July 1, 1973, decommissioned and transferred to Greece (renamed *Airadni* A-414).

AOG 48 *Chehalis* (commissioned December 5, 1944)
Refueling operations in Hawaiian Islands and Canton Island. October 7, 1949, at Tutnila, American Samoa, ship exploded in flames, killing six crewmen, then capsized and sank. Stricken October 27, 1949. Salvaged hulk later sold to government of American Samoa.

AOG 49 *Chestatee* (commissioned December 14, 1944)
Served in Philippines. On July 27, 1945, struck mine in straits south of Balabac Island (5 crew killed and 8 injured). Repaired at Puerto Princesa, Palawan and Samoa, and returned to Philippines in November 1945. Decommissioned on April 8, 1946, and transferred to Maritime Commission on June 30, 1946. Returned to navy and placed in reserve, out of commission, August 1948. Reactivated and assigned to Military Sea Transport Service (MSTS) in March 1952. Operated by civilian crew until May 1954, at which time the vessel was placed back into the reserve fleet. Second tour of service from April 1956 until September 1957, when she was lent to the air force.

AOG 50 *Chewaucan* (commissioned February 19, 1945)
Served around Hawaiian Islands from May 1945 until June 1946 then homeported in Seattle, serving the Alaskan coast. Converted to combination oiler/tanker at Philadelphia Naval Shipyard in February 1948. Assigned to Sixth Fleet to Commander, Naval Activities, Italy, for operational control. Transferred to Colombia in 1975.

AOG 51 *Maquoketa* (commissioned August 12, 1944)
Served in Pacific and 14 months with occupational forces. Decommissioned on February 21, 1947, and transferred to MARAD on June 18, 1947. Reacquired by the navy in August 1948 and assigned to MSTS in March 1952. Deactivated on May 18, 1954, to reserve and assigned to MARAD on October 9, 1957.

AOG 52 *Mattabesset* (commissioned November, 11, 1944)
Limited Pacific involvement, then served along Atlantic coast for 4 years from June 1947. Also served with Sixth Fleet in the Mediterranean. Decommissioned on October 1, 1968, and transferred to MARAD.

AOG 53 *Namakagon* (commissioned November 4, 1944)
Served in Pacific and then along Alaskan coast out of Seattle. Decommissioned

on September 20, 1957. On June 27, 1962, was activated and transferred to Commandant, 12th Naval District, to transfer to New Zealand on October 5, 1962 (renamed HMNZS *Endeavour* A-184). Hull strengthened for polar operations in the Antarctic. Returned to U.S. Navy on June 29, 1971, and transferred to Taiwan on the same date.

AOG 54 *Natchaug* (commissioned July 16, 1945)
Operated in Pacific until February 1948, assigned to SERVRON 3 to support Tsingtao and Yohosuka. Decommissioned July 24, 1959, and transferred to Greece (Renamed *Arethousa* A-377).

AOG 55 *Nespelen* (commissioned April 10, 1945)
Operated in the Atlantic area and with the Sixth Fleet in the Mediterranean until 1955. Participated in Operation Deep Freeze in supplying scientists with stores and fuel in Antarctica.

AOG 56 *Noxubee* (commissioned April 3, 1945)
Served in Atlantic, Gulf, and Mediterranean. Decommissioned March 6, 1959. Transferred to MARAD in July 1960. Rejoined navy in 1965.

AOG 57 *Pecatonica* (commissioned March 17, 1945)
Assigned to Norfolk, Virginia. Decommissioned on February 7, 1946. Recommissioned April 24, 1948, and served along Eastern Seaboard. Decommissioned April 24, 1961, and transferred same date to Taiwan (renamed *Chang Pei* AOG-307).

AOG 58 *Pinnebog* (commissioned May 12, 1945)
Served 3½ years as gasoline tanker. Placed out of commission May 2, 1949. Reactivated March 1952 and assigned to MSTS with civilian crew until July 1954. Transferred to MARAD on April 20, 1956, and then to MSTS on April 23, 1956, until July 1957. September 1957 transferred to air force.

AOG 59 *Wacissa* (commissioned May 20, 1946)
April 23, 1947, transferred to MARAD and on February 18, 1952, transferred to MSTS. Placed out of service on May 25, 1954. May 24, 1956, returned to MSTS and on September 16, 1957, transferred to air force. Turned over to Canadian government until returned to U.S. Navy in 1963. Stricken December 1, 1963, transferred to MARAD, May 1964, and sold for scrap.

Source: Captain A. E. Becker, Naval Sea Systems Command, Department of the Navy, to Sen. David Durenberger, November 29, 1989, Cargill Archives.

Hunter, North Dakota

CHAPTER SIXTEEN

Rocky Reconversion

When the Axis powers surrendered in May and Japan in August 1945, the world entered an uncharted new period of reconversion. With the difficulties immediately after World War I still vividly remembered, there was widespread trepidation. The farmer had fared badly after that earlier Great War, and the grain trade too had faced unexpected difficulties. As World War II began to wind down, there were many predictions of huge food surpluses and sagging prices, like those which had occurred in 1919–1921. James F. Byrnes, the director of the Office of War Mobilization, reported to President Roosevelt in 1944 that, while domestic food consumption would rise, the amazing productivity of agriculture that had marked the period of the war would still produce surpluses. Hopefully, Byrnes continued, exports could take up this slack, "but we must realize there are difficulties." He was concerned about America's high price levels, compared with prices in Europe. The agricultural community, hypersensitive to threats of a price decline, prepared for political battles.[1]

Cargill's rapid growth just before and during World War II had positioned it well for the postwar period. Hugo Scheuermann, the Chase National Bank contact for Cargill, complimented the Company in the spring of 1945 on its strong financial position: "The working capital has been more than doubled since May of 1941—a real accomplishment from which you should derive much satisfaction." John Jr., however, worried about telling too much about this success. When the *Minneapolis Star Journal* reported in December 1945 that Cargill was "the world's largest grain merchant," the Company immediately ran an editorial in *Cargill News*, commenting that, while "Cargill is probably the world's largest warehouseman," there were two other grain merchants still thought to be larger than Cargill, the Bunge organization in Argentina and the Louis Dreyfus group in Paris. Vigorous competition lay ahead with these two and others, such as Continental Grain. A *Cargill News* editorial in August 1945 posed the question, "Where do we go from here?" Whatever the route, it could be successfully negotiated "only by efficient production, and rigid budget control." Later events confirmed this prognosis.[2]

Honeymead: New Company, New Faces

The functional form of Cargill's organizational structure, long espoused so resolutely by John MacMillan, Jr., continued to show weakness. Burgeoning size and increased complexity of the Company put a premium on coordination among the various functions—and this was not working well. A first step toward another form of organization had been taken in January 1945 with the decision to put Julius Hendel in charge of all merchandising activities of Cargill.

One of Hendel's first concerns was staffing the newly acquired Honeymead operation, the Cedar Rapids soybean meal and oil plant. Active management there had rested in the hands of 27-year-old Dwayne Andreas. At that time he was classified 1-A in the draft (the highest priority for being called), and it was anticipation of this that caused the family to sell the business. Cargill asked his draft board for and received a three-month deferral. At the end of the deferral, with the Pacific war now over, Andreas was permanently released from any further obligation. John Jr. then asked Andreas to join Cargill, promising that he would become an assistant vice president ("this will give you equal rank with Fred Seed").

Because Andreas had been in full charge of all aspects of Honeymead when his family owned it, Cargill's functional setup now complicated matters. Austen Cargill wrote Andreas about this in late November 1945, in the process unwittingly telegraphing the complicated, conflicting nature of the functional system:

Insofar as the feed and oil business is concerned, we have Fred Seed as the administrative head of that division. We also have a mechanical division . . . which is in charge of the mechanical operation of all our plants. One of the departments of that division is the mechanical operation of the feed and oil plants, over which Dunc Watson is in charge . . . you and Dunc Watson are the two men directly responsible for the administration and operation of the four plants we have in Iowa. While you will work direct with the Manager of each plant, Dunc, through the Manager, has most of his contacts with the Superintendent.

Austen Cargill then made a curious distinction between Andreas and Watson:

I have, however, stressed the necessity for him always to work through the Manager, so that the Manager is always acquainted with Dunc's activities in regard to the operation of each individual plant . . . while it is not necessary for Dunc to be thoroughly posted as to your administrative activities it is essential that you are thoroughly familiar with his activities, and I am sure you will find that he will cooperate with you to the limit of his ability. Should cases arise, however, where you do not feel that the mechanical operation is being properly handled, your procedure would be to take the matter up with Fred Seed, who in turn will take it up with me, and between the four of us we will iron out any difficulties of that kind.

This arrangement not only contradicted John Jr.'s original promise, that Andreas would be co-equal with Fred Seed but also pointed up the anomalies of the functional system. Fred Seed worried about what seemed to be dual authority between Andreas and Watson, but Austen Cargill stood fast on the assignments, implying that any change in the functional system "will entirely destroy the basis for managing our entire business." Within nine months, however, major changes in these assignments had to be instituted, pushed along in no small part by another major Cargill acquisition.[3]

Cargill Buys Nutrena

One striking agricultural development in World War II was the much increased interest in the scientific raising of livestock, utilizing nutritionally sound feeds rather than just grass, grain and water. Feed of all kinds was in short supply, and the major manufacturers developed scientifically mixed feeds. Cargill's Blue Square feed operation had not been offering this in its earlier days; now the Company moved to bring improvements in this profitable business. In October 1945, Cargill purchased (for $1.6 million) the entire capital stock of Nutrena Mills, Incorporated. Nutrena was a leading Midwest feed producer with a combined capacity in its three mills (Kansas City, Kansas; Coffeeville, Kansas; and Sioux City, Iowa) of some 23,000 tons per month. A complete line of poultry, dairy and hog feeds had been developed by the 25-year-old company, and specialties such as rabbit food and dog food also were in the product line. For a number of years the Company had owned and operated an experimental farm at Pleasant Hill, Missouri, near Kansas City, where Nutrena's increasingly complex feeds were tested under everyday farm conditions. Nutrena had a total of 430 employees. This company was one of the industry pioneers in its feeds and in its feed sacks, too. Nutrena, along with several leading companies, had begun using special print bags called, enticingly, "pretty prints" which had captured farm housewives' enthusiasm as material for clothing, tablecloths, and the like.

In at least two respects, Nutrena was very different from Cargill. First, Nutrena saw itself as a "retail" operation, directly serving a set of customers—farmers. Advertising and sales promotion were vital to Nutrena's merchandising, and the company had used the media (particularly radio) effectively in reaching its customers. Television was in its infancy, but Nutrena also bought into it at an early point for advertising its dog food. In Kansas City, it contracted for 15 minutes of time for a 13-week span. The program was called "The Monkeys" and featured antics of a group of live monkeys. About seven weeks into the program, a flash fire at the trainer's establishment killed all of the monkeys. Nutrena had to improvise by repeating the old shows on film and quickly received many wrathful calls from viewers, so much so that they had to hire two women to answer the telephones. The account executive, in good P. T. Barnum fashion, reminded the Nutrena executives, "After all, they *are* viewing our program!" Nutrena was a knowledgeable advertiser, its sophistication in that area far beyond that of Cargill's personnel, still wedded to a "futures market" mentality of trading basic commodities.

Second, in reaching these customers, Nutrena had fundamentally decentralized its operations into six sales territories, headed by semiautonomous managers. This, of course, was contradictory to Cargill's conventional wisdom about organization structure. For the moment, Cargill chose to let Nutrena alone, free to run itself as it had in the past from its own corporate headquarters in Kansas City, Kansas.

A persistent dilemma was the presence of some duplication of cus-

A costume party version of "pretty prints" worn by Jack Wilson and his "wife," H. E. (Hank) Schroeder, April 1947.

"Used for regular sales work," Nutrena, 1928.

tomers between Cargill's Blue Square and Nutrena. A reasonable solution
for all of these potential conflicts eventually had to be found—but what?
Many months were needed to accomplish this; later in this chapter the
resolution of this problem will be analyzed.[4]

Port Cargill in the Postwar Era

Another dilemma for the Company in its postwar planning was what to
do with Cargill shipbuilding in general and Port Cargill in particular. Management seemed enthusiastic about continuing to build boats, probably
for grain carrying. Likely these would be inland-waterway barges and towboats, possibly even an oceangoing barge. John Jr. already had been filling
his study at his home with drawings for all of these. The Commitment
Committee, however, had become uneasy about the heavy capital expenditures needed for governmental shipbuilding. Its profitability was low, and
the Company "cannot improve or even maintain the working capital position if its investment in fixed property and plant becomes excessive."
Shipbuilding on any scale was likely to be capital-intensive.

If Cargill did not build, another possibility was to buy shipping. Ocean
vessels had long intrigued John Jr., and now World War II Liberty ships
were becoming available in quantity. Further, Cargill's old *Carlantic/Vic-
toria* (now renamed the *Culpepper*) had completed its wartime work and
might be available for purchase. John Jr. was very tempted but finally wrote

Weston Grimes (who was conducting the negotiations): "We are not interested in buying any ocean tonnage until . . . prices have hit bottom. Earlier sales are sure to be high." Here John Jr. exhibited once again his ambivalence about spending money. So often he was intensely opportunity-minded, impatient to be first in any new idea. Yet, as this instance shows, he also had his father's instinct for spending as little as possible, making do or sometimes even forgoing an opportunity because of its initial cost.

There were many other possibilities for Port Cargill. An internal memorandum, undated but written sometime in July 1945, listed possible additions, including special coal-unloading rigs; a trucking center for food, feed and seed deliveries; a feed manufacturing unit; oil, gas, linseed and soybean oil and molasses storage; a fertilizer plant; and even lumber storage and sales. Port Cargill seemed destined for use beyond the life of the wartime contracts.[5]

The "Shepherd of the Hills," Bill Wilhite, accompanied by the Kaw Valley Boys, on the Nutrena radio program, station WIBW, Topeka, Kansas, December 1941.

Southeast, South, Southwest: Towboats and Barges

Cargill's adventure-filled experience in building and delivering the AOGs heightened its consciousness of the power and deceptiveness of the Mississippi. Indeed, it was the delivery of the AOGs down this river that was to leave the most lasting impression from the Port Cargill government shipbuilding episode. By the end of the war, Cargill already was taking steps to involve itself in the inland waterways. The Guntersville, Alabama, and Ottawa, Illinois, terminals each had shown major promise. The barge-truck combination for the Southeast already was significant, and as the Tennessee Valley Authority began its postwar efforts at upgrading its river, this newly developing area became even more attractive.

In January 1945, John Jr. complained to an Army Corps of Engineers officer about the channel in the upper Mississippi and Minnesota rivers. Austen Cargill had made a voyage on company equipment from St. Paul to St. Louis and "he reports to us that in long stretches of the river the controlling depths of the channel posted on the locks are surprisingly below the 9 foot channel authorized by law . . . in some cases, even as low as 6 feet." As to the Minnesota, "we are furthermore severely critical of the tortuosity of the channel . . . in marked contrast to what has been done down on the Tennessee River." The American Beet Sugar Company, which had a plant at Chaska, upriver from Cargill, joined Cargill in applying pressure about the Minnesota River's draft. A conciliatory reply from the Corps of Engineers officer gave John Jr. hope (if not full assurance) that this river was not to be foresaken after the war.

In 1945–1946, Cargill was not strong in the South and Southwest. The Kansas City terminal provided an outpost, but, as Harold Johnson, one of the key executives in the Grain Division, noted in his session on wheat with the Cargill trainees, in May 1946, "when we work through the export department we have to lease space in the Gulf [of Mexico] and work through brokers. We have some very tough competition . . . people like Uhlmann and Continental having elevator facilities . . . operated with their own men. . . . This year we are going to try to get into that territory . . . because we know we are going to have a big export demand."

A necessary first step was to become more involved in Mississippi River barging. For this, John Jr. now initiated Cargill's own fleet. The *Cartasca*, the Company's first Midwest-built towboat, already had been launched and was being outfitted at Port Cargill for its first shakedown trip on the Minnesota and Mississippi rivers. The barges that the *Cartasca* was to push on this trip were two being built by the Company in the summer and fall of 1944 at Chaska. Completing the barges and finishing the towboat took longer than expected, so it was late November 1944, before the units could

The towboat Cartasca.

begin the voyage south from Port Cargill. It was an early winter, and already the Minnesota River and the Upper Mississippi had substantial ice.

The *Cartasca* trial voyage was an unmitigated disaster. As he weighed cost versus function and safety, John Jr. made some fundamental miscalculations about both the towboat and the barges. John Jr. strongly believed that Cargill's Erie Canal towboats and barges should be replicated exactly for the Mississippi River. Cargill had had little experience in navigating the Mississippi, was used to "duck water" like that of the Erie—water with little or no current and therefore favored by duckhunters. The Mississippi was nothing like that—it had strong currents, many eddies, shifting channels and countless other navigational hazards. Cargill had had the *Cartasca* built somewhat underpowered. John Jr.'s choice of power, the Chrysler Sea Mule motor (the unit that Cargill earlier had proposed to build for the government), had been a compromise, but as he wrote Frank Neilson, "we can build three of these for the price of one of the others." There was a further complication with the Sea Mule of that day, as it was a gasoline engine, located far down in the *Cartasca* hull, a difficult place to service and potentially dangerous because of the gasoline fuel. This also complicated the work of the cooling system. Wrong assumptions had been made about the barges, too. John Jr. wanted to duplicate the inexpensive, single-skin Erie Canal version that had worked so well for him there.

The trial voyage started out badly when the *Cartasca* struck a rock just below St. Paul. Damage was done to the starboard propeller, in the process ruining the reduction gears on three of the other engines. Further down the river, the towboat-barge unit was almost uncontrollable at times, the ice floes pushing the unit all over the river. There were groundings, several serious, that uncovered the weaknesses of the single-skin version. Finally, the Coast Guard vessel *Lantana* had to help the unit through the more difficult spots. A final complication came with a gasoline leak, which made the Coast Guard apprehensive about having the unit tied up for unloading. All in all, the trip was a revealing and particularly embarrassing episode for the Company and for John Jr.

Never one to brood over a failed project, John Jr. immediately dispatched the two barges to the Erie Canal, where they gave good service over a number of years. The *Cartasca* stayed in service (with leased barges) for the 1945 season, then was brought back up to Port Cargill late in the season for substantial alteration to provide a great deal more power (over 900 hp). In the process the engines could be adjusted down from the original 400 rpm to about 200 rpm, much better from the standpoint of wear and tear on the engine units.

One further ignominious episode happened in the first week of December 1945, when the vessel accidentally slipped off its winter drydock, fell back into the Minnesota River and sank in 10 feet of water. Fortunately, little damage was done, and by the time the *Cartasca* was back in service in the latter part of the 1946 season, with three new Cargill-built barges and an upgraded power plant with Detroit diesel engines, the Company had its first viable unit on the Mississippi.

One signal innovation came out of all of this: a bow steering unit. The idea originally had come from Austen Cargill, from a similar adaptation often used by loggers. Loggers often tie a boat crosswise on the front of a log raft and used its outboard motor to move the raft right or left. Cargill's version was equally makeshift—a large-version outboard motor was mounted in the front of the barge, its propeller protected by a grating. Long cables extended back across the barges to the towboat pilot house, and the outboard was moved manually. (In the 1960s the Company developed a radio-controlled version, the "Pathfinder," and later a television camera for visual sighting). John Jr. described the Rube Goldberg device to his mother as "a revolutionary form of steering, having an engine and propeller in the bow, so that one can steer in exactly the same way that the old log rafts on the Mississippi were steered." He commented in another letter about the new unit's maiden voyage: "It certainly saved us from several collisions." The bow unit gave the pilot much greater control—no more being pushed around by the current as the first *Cartasca* unit had been.

By 1947, the *Cartasca*'s barges included a fore barge unit, an aft barge unit and three center barge units (each of the center barges holding 1,100 tons, the equivalent of about 37,000 bushels of wheat, slightly more if corn). Within two years, the Company had added a second set of three center barge units, giving the *Cartasca* great flexibility. These barges were not the standard size (195 by 35 feet) and did not fit well with other tows. This was particularly true because John Jr. had made the barges box-shaped rather than single or double rakes (sloping fronts for the single, sloping fronts and rears for the double). While he obtained more capacity this way, the unconventional configuration was not popular with other towboat pilots because it was difficult to mix them with conventional barges. Later, Cargill changed over to conventional barges.

The most frequent route was the run from Illinois River points or St. Louis up the Ohio and Tennessee to Guntersville with grain, to return with coal. But the *Cartasca* and its barges soon became known all over the Mississippi River. When the president of the Inland Waterways Corporation announced in early 1948 its own "integrated tow," with nine barges and the towboat *Harry Truman*, John Jr. was asked to come along on its maiden voyage. His schedule would not allow acceptance, but he wrote the president, not hiding his pride, "I would like nothing better than to see my original idea of 12 years ago carried to its ultimate and logical conclusion, as you will be doing."[6]

In spite of the evident need for downstream Mississippi River terminal space, the Company did not increase capacity in this immediate postwar period. Cargill had only the Memphis terminal, which had been built with WPA funds and was not used as much by this time. The total Company terminal capacity in 1942 had been just over 66 million bushels. This rose to almost 73 million in 1945, but the 1949 figure was still at this same point. Major terminal expansion was to be a development of the 1950s.

World Hunger, Once Again

The all-out production in agriculture during World War II had seen gross farm output in the United States jumping from 108 to 123 (1935–1939 output, 100). Corn and wheat production was up substantially. Oilseed totals had risen even higher; the soybean had "arrived," with total production increasing from 78 million bushels in 1941 to 193 million bushels in

1945. All of this had been accomplished with many fewer people on the farms, as farm productivity had increased dramatically. "While it was only clear in historical perspective," Gilbert C. Fite, an agricultural historian, put it, "by the end of World War II, the basis of traditional American agriculture was being drastically altered . . . technology, science and new farm organization patterns were combining to destroy the old production practices . . . developing a new farm built more on the industrial model." The rural transformation that had happened in just the four years of the war "may have been a watershed in American history."

Would this engine of productivity generate a huge postwar glut? The ideal, as one analyst put it, would be that "the last GI potato, the last GI pat of butter and the last GI slice of bread was eaten just as the last shot was fired." The reality was quite the opposite. By the end of the European war (V-E Day, in May 1945), famine had a grip on much of the war-ravaged sections of the Continent. The winter of 1945–1946 was particularly wrenching. President Truman went on national radio on April 20, 1946, to tell the nation that "millions will starve unless we eat less." Fiorello LaGuardia, the mayor of New York City, appealed to the people "desperately." Herbert Hoover, once again enlisted by the government in the food-relief battle, warned, "It is now 11:59 on the clock of starvation."

Huge amounts of American aid were promised. Under the umbrella of the United Nations Relief and Rehabilitation Administration (UNRRA), aid was sent to Eastern Europe and both direct aid and commercial sales went to the liberated countries in Western Europe. In 1947 the Marshall Plan, Secretary of State George C. Marshall's farsighted design (1947), and the European Recovery Program (ERP), also would provide aid.

But there was the unanswered question of whether the United States could produce this aid, particularly agricultural goods, quickly enough. In addition to United States consumers being exhorted to use less meat and wheat, farmers were urged to bring these things to market right away. Yet farmers were not convinced. They already had a store of cash from their substantial wartime production, and with price controls still in effect they were in no hurry to let go of their precious hoard. Price controls, a necessary ingredient of a wartime controlled economy, had succeeded in distorting normal supply–demand equations, as indicated by this farmer reluctance in 1945–1946 to sell.[7]

Cargill, among many others, had great difficulty in obtaining soybeans for its Oil Division plants. As one executive put it, "We are unable to use the price incentive. Our ability to buy beans revolves largely around a matter of personal contacts and good will." Barter arrangements became widespread industry practice. John Peterson, noting in January 1946 that Cargill had set up a trading department for swaps (under the direction of

Walter Gage), described the situation: "Right now, for instance, one car of coal will buy 5 cars of corn. We have also discovered a warehouse full of Nylon stockings in the South and 4 pairs of Nylon, invoiced at the O.P.A. ceiling of course, will enable us to buy one car of corn. However, in order to buy the Nylons we have to trade one car of corn for 6 pair of nylons. Of course this is an infernal mission, but we get full mark-ups on all transactions, so the sum total is profitable enough." This was not, of course, real barter—all sales were made at regular ceiling prices—but the nylons and other swap goods acted as the grease to bring about the trade.

John Jr. abhorred swapping. It led, he believed, to "the general corruption of the public from black markets." He wrote a lengthy public piece on the issue in February 1946, circulating it widely. Calling his essay "Plain Talk," he decried the piecemeal approach, where "everyone seems to be in favor of removing ceilings in his own field of activity but in leaving them on in the other fellow's." Instead he argued for a blanket removal of all ceilings on all grain and soybeans. This would bring a price rise, of course, but John Jr. strongly agreed with Julius Hendel's oft-recounted aphorism, "The cure for high prices is high prices" (in other words, the allure of the higher prices would bring forth supply and decrease consumption, thus, the plenty combined with decreased demand would bring the prices back down).

Despite enormous pressures on them, government price administrators were extremely reluctant to loosen controls. The case of rye was a salient reminder to them. Rye was the only grain among the major food and feed grains not to be price-controlled. By 1945 cash rye prices had shot up like a skyrocket. Prices that had stayed in the range of 55–70 cents during most of the wartime period had ballooned to over $1.50 by June 1945 (and would go much higher later). The volume of trading in rye futures had risen even faster. In the crop year 1941–1942, only 790 million bushels were traded; for the year 1944–1945, some 3,979,000,000 had been traded, including 467 million in April 1945 alone. These changes had led to the raucous disagreement relating to rye that broke out in the public press, discussed in the preceding chapter.[8]

Pressure on the government to loosen controls on grains and soybeans heightened during the early spring of 1946, fueled by continuing farmer unwillingness to sell. John Jr. was in the forefront on this pressure, wiring Ed Grimes in late February: "Please leave no stone unturned to get these price ceilings removed, if not a great increase in the ceiling . . . this is so important that it over-shadows everything else in our picture today." In April the government began offering bonuses of 30 cents to farmers on wheat and corn; even this did not seem to help. Finally, on May 9, 1946, the government partially capitulated, raising the ceiling price on corn by

The Lake Office, mid-1950s.

25 cents a bushel, on wheat by 15 cents and on the other grains and protein feeds by similar amounts. This finally persuaded the farmers, and supply for overseas shipments began to step up.[9]

Cargill Takes the CBOT to Court

The biggest controversy in the May 1946 government decision to loosen controls developed over the issue of what to do about existing futures contracts. John Jr. had been uneasy about this since early in the year, wiring Grimes in late February: "This bunch of cookies have a habit of doing something first and telling us about it later. I think now is the time to enter a vigorous protest against any idea of first wiping out corn futures and then raising the ceiling. Our long corn futures are not enough to balance out our short flat price cash sales."

But that was just what happened: the government asked all three major futures exchanges to restrict trading in old futures of all grains outstanding on May 11 and to trade for liquidation at the ceiling prices prevailing before the 25-cent and 15-cent increases. The Minneapolis exchange refused to do so, but the Chicago Board of Trade and the Kansas City exchange acquiesced. The CBOT then added a puzzling and soon damaging codicil—

that it would give no consideration to increases in ceiling prices in considering any penalties on defaults arising through refusal of sellers to deliver on contracts. An FTC report commented: "This publicly served notice that there would be no penalties for defaults. Naturally, no short would deliver cash grain that was worth 5 to 25 cents more . . . the result was heavy defaults." At a later congressional investigation, Representative August H. Andresen (Minnesota) sarcastically castigated J. O. McClintoch, the CBOT president, in the process resurrecting the same old saw: "The Board of Trade, in order to help the short seller, set aside that old rule . . . he that sells what he does not own [Andresen meant "what is not hizzen"] must deliver or go to prison."

Cargill still had a large exposure as a long at the CBOT, and John Jr. wrote his brother: "The effect is to nick us for between $750,000 and a million dollars." The Chicago *Journal of Commerce* put the issue frankly in its headline: "Board Closes Out 50 Million in Futures—Acts to Save Grain Shorts as Runaway Price Rise Looms." In discussing the "plight" of the shorts, the writer commented that there was "the danger that the removal of ceilings suddenly would set grain free to seek its natural level." The shorts certainly did not agree that the cure for high prices was high prices!

Now John Jr.'s dander was really up. Once again the CBOT had taken sides with the shorts to the detriment of the longs, with Cargill very prominent among these. Cargill officials put all of the pressure they could muster on the CBOT officials, even threatening personal lawsuits against individual directors. Julius Hendel, sent to Chicago to survey the situation, wired John Jr.: "Any move to allow futures prices to follow ceiling increase will be defeated by a wide margin . . . any threat of suits against directors will be a red flag and only increase the margin of defeat." Even a long telegram from John Jr. to Clinton P. Anderson, the Secretary of Agriculture, failed to bring any help.

John Jr. now began considering an unorthodox and potentially very expensive tactic: Cargill would institute a suit in the federal courts, alleging that the CBOT, the Board of Trade Clearing Corporation and 23 officers were in "restraint of trade," under the Sherman Antitrust Act. The Company could then seek treble damages, as the Sherman Act allowed.

The Company lawyers demurred, feeling that a Sherman Act case would be hard to win, but John Jr. wrote his brother: "I earnestly hope we don't drop our suit against the B.O. Trade [this was at the height of the Lifebuoy soap 'B.O.' campaign; John Jr. seems to have meant the term here!]. I like this triple damages proposition, and feel confident we can use the threat not only to get our money but also get a consent decree . . . that for the future these contracts mean performance." So the suit went forward.

The action made headlines all over the country. The *New York Times*, noted in a lengthy article that the treble damages were estimated at "more than $1,000,000." Even the venerable *Times* had underestimated here, for by the time John Jr. had added what he felt were all of the costs, an amended complaint was filed for $10,624,867.50.

The suit received not only an outpouring of interest in the press but widespread support from many groups of the grain trade, particularly processors and others who usually found themselves on the long side of the market. Peavey Heffelfinger, John Jr.'s Minneapolis friend and competitor, sent a telegram: "You have done grain trade a real service. Please don't ever sue me."

If John Jr. reaped kudos from his colleagues among the longs, he struck out time and again in the federal courts. The case first came before District Judge Elwin R. Shaw in Chicago; after hearing the issues Shaw flatly dismissed Cargill's case. In effect, he ruled that the CBOT directors had not unlawfully engaged in price fixing, that the action of the directors was merely to determine the amount of settlement to be made on grain futures contracts already terminated under Exchange regulations. Pointing to the fact that the Exchange had in place Rule No. 251, authorizing its directors to declare any day a holiday, close the Exchange, stop trading in any futures contract, or make other regulations concerning deliveries and settlement prices deemed proper because of an emergency, this instance legitimately met the criteria of the rule.

Cargill immediately carried its case to the federal circuit court of appeals; it disposed of the matter on December 23, 1947, again ruling against Cargill. Judge Sherman Minton, writing the opinion for the three justices, held that only "bad faith of the defendants in the discharge of their duties under the emergency" could vitiate the defendants' action. No claim of bad faith, Minton noted, had been made. As to the Sherman Act terminology about trade restraints, "the acts of the defendants, rather than being in restraint of commerce, were in aid of commerce in facilitating future trading on the market." In sum, in the absence of "bad faith amounting to fraud," all parties were bound by the Exchange regulations.

John Jr., still aggrieved by the CBOT action and smarting under some financial hurt from the case (although far short of the alleged damages), insisted that the case be carried to the United States Supreme Court. Cargill's lawyers petitioned for a rehearing. Once again, the Company was denied (on April 26, 1948). The court did not even grant a writ of certiorari. The lawyers felt they had further arguments to persuade the Court to take the case and petitioned for a second rehearing on June 1, 1948. The Court again denied the petition. The case was truly lost.

In retrospect, the effects of the case were certainly mixed. On the one hand, Cargill heightened the image that it would fight for its rights to the last ditch. John Jr. had had to capitulate in the Farmers National case four years earlier, when the lawyer Clark Fletcher had died in its midst. Now John Jr. had the satisfaction of carrying the case as far as he could.

The uniformly negative feedback from the courts made this somewhat of a Pyrrhic victory. The freezing of those May futures prices initially did hurt Cargill, although a lengthy, highly analytical report by the FTC on the whole set of circumstances found that the total possible damages to *all* parties concerned was short of Cargill's self-determined amount and that, with the complexity of both speculators' and hedgers' accounts, offsetting actions made it extremely difficult to assess who won and who lost what.

To make the story more like a comic opera, the CBOT began vacillating about its May 11 decision, finally reversing itself on June 13, ordering the reopening for settlement at the new, higher ceiling prices. For those contracts not already terminated, the roles were reversed—the longs now had the advantage. Cargill had closed its books on the usual May 31 date with heavy losses recorded for the Grain Division. Later, F. J. Hays asked for a reevaluation of this loss, "affected as little as possible by the views of those who handled . . . the transactions originally." Hays maintained that the Division had been saddled with nonexistent losses. Cargill's court case went forward anyway, as it was the principle that counted—that the CBOT had arbitrarily restrained trade.

The FTC analysts did draw strong invidious distinctions between the actions of the Minneapolis and Chicago exchanges:

The difference between what happened in Minneapolis and in Chicago lies essentially in the difference in attitude shown respecting the maintenance of the integrity of contracts and the personal responsibilities of traders thereunder. In Chicago, by these actions neither the integrity of contracts nor the responsibilities of contracting parties were preserved. The prestige of the Chicago market suffered heavily and the exchange laid itself open to legal attack by aggrieved parties.

By contrast, the Minneapolis Chamber of Commerce deliberately chose to maintain the validity of its contracts so far as possible and to insist that its traders, both speculators and hedgers, cooperate and participate in mutual settlements whereby the interests of both parties would be safeguarded so far as equitably possible under the circumstances over which neither the traders nor the Chamber of Commerce had control.

Whether this statement was some solace to John Jr. was not recorded.[10]

Would Prices Run Amok?

The vacillation of the Chicago Board of Trade on the government's order to close out the futures contracts was just a small part of larger controversies about whether price controls themselves should be continued. To put simply a complicated pattern of conflicting bargaining positions, the Truman administration felt that price controls had to be contin-

Officer, arrest that man! Which man?

Ding Darling, July 4, 1946 (by permission of the University of Iowa Libraries [Iowa City]).

ued until supply and demand began to equate, lest there be runaway inflation. Congress, on the other hand, exhorted by vocal segments of the economy (farmers and the grain trade prominent among these), pushed for controls to be eliminated forthwith. Congress passed a weak price control bill not to President Truman's liking, and he vetoed it on June 30, 1946. For a few weeks, there were no controls. A strong upward surge in prices instantly followed. Another weakened bill came forward from Congress; this time Truman signed it, "reluctantly." The bill allowed the President to reinstitute price controls on commodities at a point where prices threatened too much inflation. Farmer groups and the grain trade lobbied vigorously to keep any such controls away from farm products.

On August 21, the newly established Price Decontrol Board ordered ceilings restored on meat, cottonseed and soybeans but left in place the decontrols for dairy products and all grains except flaxseed. The previous May, the deputy price administrator in charge of enforcement had told a

Congressional committee that the "blackest markets" included grain, in the "Northern part of the Middle West." Apparently grain markets had now become whiter!

Grain prices also rose with ceilings removed, some considerably more than others. Wheat had been at $1.91 in May 1946; it was up to $2.22 by December (cash prices in Chicago). Rye (Minneapolis cash) had begun this same period at $2.84 and was down to $2.79 in December. Corn (Chicago cash) had been at $1.45 in May, had jumped to $2.17 in July but was back down to $1.34 in December, in the face of a huge new crop just harvested (it was a record—over 3.2 billion bushels). Flax, on the other hand, had stood at $3.27 in May 1946 (roughly where its price had been throughout the war) but had skyrocketed to $7.27 by the end of the year (and reached a high of $8.51 in March 1947).[11]

Trading Flax, Processing Flax

The first postwar Port Cargill project, one conceived just as the war wound down, was a flaxseed crushing plant. By the summer of 1946, a new plant was in place; the first flax was crushed on August 11. Plant size was modest, with capacity to process 3,000 bushels of flax a day—an output of about 2 tank cars of linseed oil every three days and 1½ carloads of linseed meal every 24 hours.

Cargill had traded small amounts of flax over the years, but it was not considered a central concern of the Grain Division. Now, with the new Oil Division, flax buying and flax processing became more important. The Grain Division did the buying; the Oil Division was the processor.

Flaxseed production had risen during World War II, but the acreage had been cut by more than one-half at the end of the war, when farmers turned to other crops. The country's production had been over 51 million bushels in the 1943–1944 crop season. The following year it had dropped to just 23 million bushels. Yet there was great demand for linseed oil from the paint industry and other users, particularly heightened by the housing boom that began at the end of the war.

Ceiling prices had been kept in place on flaxseed (and also soybeans) beyond the August 20 date when all other grains were freed (not being taken off until October 17, when the major price rise occurred). Cargill had argued strongly back in August for removing the controls, that the only way that the huge needs for the burgeoning housing market could be met would be by greater imports and "the only way to insure these necessary imports is by means of a high price." (Hendel's "cure for high prices" once again.)

The short flax supply and the heavy demand came to a crisis point in the fall of 1946, when the price jumped to the $7.10–$8.00 range. Dwayne Andreas, the new face in the Oil Division, had persuaded Julius Hendel early in that year to begin buying flax in the Minneapolis Exchange, where most of the trading was done. One of the long-standing stories in Cargill lore, probably not far from the truth, was that Julius Hendel left a set of "buy" orders with his traders there and went out for a haircut. During the time he was gone, the beginnings of the bull market in flax had begun, and by the time Julius returned, the Company had a huge exposure in flax, necessitating an apologetic visit "on the carpet" with John Jr., who reportedly was appalled by the amounts. Whether or not this beloved tale was exactly true, by the end of the year 1946, Cargill owned over 1.6 million bushels of flax, a good deal purchased in the $3.00 range and now worth almost $8.5 million.

This mammoth quantity posed some problems, for it was such a large amount that to put it into the market to sell would probably bring about a precipitous decline in price. Cargill had only the tiny crushing capacity of its new Port Cargill operation and the small Minneapolis plant; it could not possibly crush that much.

At this point, Dwayne Andreas proposed an innovative solution, suggesting that Cargill approach one or another of the large processors to see if the processing could be done on a contract basis. He had heard that Spencer Kellogg Company had such capacity. Two quick telephone calls brought their agreement to do the crushing for 40 cents per bushel. In the course of those few minutes, Cargill had laid the groundwork for an enormous profit. When the year-end figures of May 31, 1947, came out, the Oil Division had posted a profit of $7.7 million, the bulk of it from these flax product sales. It was fortunate, for with the capricious price controls affecting the other grains, the Grain Division had posted almost a $2 million loss. The net earnings for the Company as a whole for that crop year 1946–1947 was $4,484,000, by far the largest the Company had ever had.

John Jr. was so tickled (and relieved) about the coup in flaxseed that he gave Andreas a $10,000 bonus (three others in the division received smaller ones). There is nothing in the record about a bonus for anyone in the Grain Division for that year; John Jr. did write its key people, congratulating them "for the remarkable support which you gave the Oil Division in the recent purchases of flaxseed." The fact that the Grain Division had done the purchasing but the Oil Division received credit for the profits and received bonuses rankled some of the executives in the former group.[12]

By October 1946, the flax price rise had become (as the *St. Paul Pioneer Press* put it) the "flax price scandal." Irate flax farmers blamed the government for maintaining price ceilings through the marketing season, after which the price rose more than $3.00. Fortunately for Cargill, a number of newspapers picked up the Company's earlier championing of the farmers' side. The *Minneapolis Morning Tribune* spoke for a number of editors when it stated in late October: "Any blame which is attached to the lifting of price controls . . . should be registered against the federal government which dallied from Aug. 20 until Oct. 17 in releasing the price controls. The grain firms which received the blame actually did a remarkably fair job of protecting the producers."

Some of the farmers' flax sales contracts contained an escalator provision under which they would benefit by the price rise; most did not, however. Actually, the farmers took a double loss from this situation, for when they came to buy linseed meal for feed, the price of this too had risen. The farmers clamored for a federal government refund on the flax "steal," and when this did not come, they demanded a congressional probe. The government responded by promising the farmers a guaranteed price of $6.00 for the coming year's flax, and the farmer hostility temporarily subsided.[13]

Executive Health

The rapid-fire events of the summer and fall of 1946 added a frenetic pace to the grain business for this already fast-track industry. Interpersonal tensions at Cargill were exacerbated in this period, despite the fact that the move of the executive group out to Lake Minnetonka and the new French country house "Lake Office" had been made in early June 1946. John Jr., who originally had wanted to call the new headquarters "Cargill House," nevertheless was highly pleased with the "quiet surroundings." If it was a bit isolated, John Jr. defended the choice: "We have about 65 executives and an equal number of supporting cast. None of these individuals deal with the public. They merely direct the efforts of those who do deal with the public."

A small discordant note was struck, however, when an anonymous letter was sent to the *Cargill News* that read: "Here is a true one for the book. After going through the Rand Estate a wife said to her husband, 'Now I know why we didn't get a Christmas bonus nor a raise in pay since VJ Day.' " The author signed the note "Anonymous" and ended, "Dare you print this?"

Tom Totushek, the editor of the *News* did indeed "dare" and defended the costs as being "far from exorbitant, and have had not the slightest effect on salary increases." After commenting that the president's desk was purchased from a secondhand dealer in 1934 and that most of the carpet was bought in 1928, he then enumerated the wages paid to employees in the three calendar years, 1943, 1944, 1945. These totaled some $5.5 million. The contributions to the Servicemen's Trust, the profit-sharing trust and the dividends on preferred stock, all taken out of net profits, totaled $388,000.

Lake Office tranquility aside, the pressures of that fall brought health problems once again to John Jr. He had taken a major step in June 1946, when he visited the Kempner clinic in Durham, North Carolina, for an initial appraisal of his health by Dr. Walter Kempner. This was the institution first recommended to him by Austen Cargill two years previously. Kempner's clinic had pioneered low-cholesterol, salt-free diets and had become particularly known for the prominent role of rice as a central ingredient.

John Jr. long had suffered a weight problem. Perhaps some of this began when he was at Yale, just before his service in World War I. At that time, he was on a swimming team (it is not clear whether it was the Yale varsity team) and was a self-styled "plunger" (a term he did not explain). He told his mother and father: "The prime requisite of a plunger is great weight. Accordingly I have special food, consisting of just about everything that the other members of the team are not allowed to eat. I get milk and cream galore, as much butter as I can get, and in general everything that would tend to make me fat. The Association even offered me a weekly allowance of $3.00 for beer but as it would be a physical impossibility for me to drink that much (10 beers a day), I declined with thanks."

The Yale experience must have had effect, for John Jr.'s weight climbed over the years. Kempner, seeing the history of high blood pressure and overweight, immediately put John Jr. on the clinic's diet. John Jr. was asked to monitor his own blood pressure and report back to Kempner on a regular basis. Within months, he had reduced his weight by about 100 pounds. John Jr. quickly became a Kempner enthusiast, indeed, almost an acolyte. Already introspective about his health, John Jr. now became single-minded about his food, his blood pressure and his general well-being. His meals at home were prepared by the family's housekeeper, Martha Norris, and on board the *Carmac* by the boat's chef (one of the reasons John Jr. preferred traveling whenever possible by the inspection vessel). Later, he joined the Kempner Foundation board, helped the organization in its fund raising, wrote long bulletins about the success of the program and buttonholed his friends and almost anyone who would listen to the advantages of the Kempner diet and the efficacy of the clinic itself. He carried this interest over to the Cargill organization, too, instituting an annual cholesterol checkup for all senior executives. He was assiduous in following up on these, leading some of the more heavyset, cholesterol-prone people sometimes to cover up their poor test scores.

John Jr.'s diet had not had time to take effect back in 1946 before the fall flax excitement occurred. It was a highly stimulating period for all of the executives in the Company—great profits were made in a few short days. As John Jr. put it, in a letter to his sons on November 1: "Our big business has been in soybeans and flax . . . we have done a normal year's business in both articles [in one week] . . . Our dollar volume has unquestionably been the greatest in the 81-year history of the business. It is very nice to be doing a big business, but it also takes a good deal out of one and I am really tired this week-end." He commented similarly to his mother, adding that the Oil Division was "a relatively new field with us, so that there is an unusual strain connected with doing business there." His aplomb was further shaken when John Peterson sent him a pessimistic wire about all of the negative economic signals Peterson saw; "My memory goes back irresistibly to 33 [1933] . . . buttoning up of everything was never as important."

By late November, John Jr. was staying home frequently, "still way below par." In January 1947, he wrote his brother from his vacation of further troubles, this time with ulcers. The tensions of the business had taken their toll on John Jr.[14]

Organizational Discontinuities

Month by month in this difficult period immediately after the war the differences between the traditional Cargill organization, dominated by the grain traders, and the two new organizations, Nutrena and Honeymead, became increasingly apparent. The disjuncture was particularly striking with Nutrena, which had a corporate culture totally different from that of Cargill. In the case of Honeymead, it was the presence of the dynamic, charismatic young Dwayne Andreas that began to set the Oil Division apart from the existing Cargill organization. The nexus of both these sets of differences could be seen most clearly in the renewed tensions concerning organizational structure.

In May 1946, John Jr. decided to write his views about the "Theory and Practice of Organization," and subsequently had them set in print and bound, to be distributed widely, beyond just the Company. His long-continuing belief in the superiority of the functional type of organization permeated the paper. He referred to his "rare good fortune at the age of 21 of becoming adjutant (or Chief-of-Staff)" in the field artillery and continued: "My associates in Cargill were intelligent enough to appreciate the value of this experience, and had enough confidence largely to give me a free hand in rearranging our own organization." Ample evidence of this "free hand" has been noted in earlier chapters of this book.

John Jr. reiterated the duties of each of the heads of the functional units, referring again to the appointment of Julius Hendel to head all merchandising operations. "On a military staff he would be called Chief of Operations," John Jr. explained. He contrasted Cargill's philosophy with that of Nutrena, where decentralization had been the watchword. Commenting on the autonomy of the managers at Nutrena, John Jr. continued:

"Now there is nothing wrong with this scheme of things up to a certain point in size—this is the best and simplest scheme of organization, and I am sure that it was exactly right for Nutrena, although even here, the management was on the verge of setting up a functional type, and in fact had already taken one or two of the first steps in this direction." R. E. Whitworth, who headed Nutrena, was asked by John Jr. to read this new paper on organization and commented noncommittally, "I particularly appreciate the manner in which you present the necessity for teamwork and good manners."

Nutrena wanted to maintain its separate culture, including keeping itself centrally located in Kansas City. This culture had been an enduringly strong one—it reflected dedication, integrity, long hours and an appetite for hard work. Senior managers such as Al Fuller mirrored this culture. However, on their hope to remain in Kansas City they were to be disappointed. Although maintaining its legal entity as a separate company, within a month its executives were pressed by Cargill top management to shift the corporate headquarters to Minneapolis. In the process, Whitworth and his key assistants also reluctantly gave up their test farm, which had a small, primitive golf course attached. When the week came for the move, a *Cargill News* editor unintentionally captured the anguish of those moving when she called it an "evacuation."

The Cargill Feed Division then was folded into the Nutrena organization, Whitworth taking over from Fred Seed. The "Blue Square" organization also was integrated into Nutrena, and the brand itself disappeared. Whitworth continued to run his organization in the decentralized pattern and fought to preserve the integrity of the Nutrena culture. Some other Nutrena people did not embrace their Cargill status with enthusiasm, seeming to go out of their way not to buy grain from Cargill. The Grain Division appeared to think that Nutrena was a captive group and expected preference—but often did not get it. At one point, an executive told a Nutrena employee, "You *do* work for Cargill." The man replied, "The hell I do, I work for Nutrena—my paycheck says Nutrena Mills, Inc." Later, the Nutrena checks were changed to "Cargill." This insularity of Nutrena continued over time (although, interestingly, David Wentzell was appointed to a senior management position in Feed in 1957 after a number of years as an executive in the Grain Division).

The Oil Division also began to differentiate itself under the leadership of the assured Andreas. In September 1946, Andreas had his title changed from assistant vice president to vice president in charge of the Vegetable Oil Division. In the process, he gained autonomy over the entire oilseed operation, remedying the potential for conflict many had predicted between himself and Duncan Watson.

Through these changes, Andreas was strongly backed by John Jr., who saw Andreas as prime material for senior management (he told Andreas at this time, "You think like an owner, and most of my senior executives do not"). In 1947, Andreas was offered preferred stock in the Company. Most of the Cargill executives with "employee" common stock had already been persuaded to exchange it for preferred stock. Andreas rejected the offer and proposed that he be given regular common stock, writing an articulate letter about why he believed that "employee" common stock was "unattractive as an investment." He continued: "In fact, since the company wants to retain important rights of repossession, etc., I do not see how alterations can be made which would make it attractive as an investment."

While this was not what John Jr. wanted to hear—he already was moving to eliminate as much nonfamily common stock as possible—he and the other members of the family finally agreed to sell Andreas 5,000 shares of regular common stock. At the same time, Julius Hendel was offered 8,000 shares, and a like amount was allotted to John Peterson. Fred Seed also was offered 5,000. The only other active executive with substantial holdings was Ed Grimes; he had held his 5,210 shares for a number of years. The right of Company buy-back remained, but the terms were softened along the lines Andreas had suggested.

There were inherent differences between the Grain Division and the Oil Division by the nature of their operations. The Oil Division managed large, continuous-process plants, where the watchword always was to have a steady inventory of raw materials (soybeans, flaxseed, etc.) and to balance these on a day-by-day basis with flexibility. Andreas and John Peterson developed a sharp difference of opinion about budgets, Peterson wanting Andreas to commit to a three-year plan and Andreas believing that this would make his organization think too much in financial rather than operational terms. When Peterson said, "The banks are insisting," a threat that Peterson often used (sometimes without basis), Andreas told him, "You had better go to the bank and explain—we can't project flat prices when the market may go up or down." In this argument, John Jr. sided with Andreas.

There also was a conflict between the Grain Division and the Oil Division on soybean purchasing. This was articulated frankly by Andreas in an October 1947 meeting of all the Company division heads: "The accumulation of beans for processing presents a different problem from straight merchandising. With only four large processors dominating the market, it sometimes would be wrong to keep in the market when the other large buyers are out." Yet we "realize the difficulty the present bean buying method causes the branch offices . . . everything possible should be done by next year to work out a system by which we can continually buy beans for merchandising, even though we may not be able to use them for our crush." It took many more months to work out this relationship; it was never fully solved.

These events with Nutrena and the Oil Division highlighted the fact that not only the cultures of the two organizations but the very management mentality that was needed differed substantially from that of the existing Cargill organization. The latter had been built on the solid rock of grain trading, with the merchants and traders as kingpins. John Jr. put this bluntly in his May 1946 organizational booklet: "The most important division, both in volume and in money making is, of course, our terminal grain division . . . men in charge of their respective service departments are there for the definite purpose of serving Messrs. Lundgren and Kelm. If they cannot give them the kind of support which these two latter have a right to expect, then other men will be found for these posts. Everyone in Cargill serves the traders and merchants."

Trading had always been the way to the top at Cargill, yet here were two new organizations, feed and oil, that had separate ways of looking at the management process. These differences have stayed in place down to the present, causing many more "turf" battles over the years and constant need for coordination and control.[15]

Increasing pressures on John Jr.'s functional system brought changes— and they came quickly. In July 1947, Julius Hendel instituted a major decentralization in the terminal merchandising group. Some of the hedging responsibility was to be decentralized (although Minneapolis still was to control overall positions), and regional sales managers were established. Traffic was to be decentralized as soon as feasible and accounting, too.

The decentralizing of accounting became a sticky point. A management consulting firm, Booz, Allen & Hamilton (BAH), had been hired to develop its specifics and to find Cargill a comptroller who could effect it. Robert Harrigan was persuaded to leave General Mills for this post. As the draft BAH report came forward, Grain Division executives found much fault with it. Erv Kelm, now head of the division, was the most vocal critic. He felt that the consultants' work on the "basic hedge" analysis (the establishment of firm hedge prices for month-end accounting) was "hardly to the test tube stage" and that the consultants "had been learning the grain trade at Cargill's expense." ("It is recognized," Kelm diplomatically put it, "that the BAH crew members have acquired considerable knowledge of Cargill accounting and operations during the past year.") Harrigan recommended that "in order to prevent a fiasco," the accounting decentralization be postponed.

Finally, in August 1949, the final BAH report was ready, and it received mixed praise and skepticism. Clyde Hegman, one of the key accounting supervisors called it "superbly done." He continued: "While it is unduly lengthy, full of repetition and severely critical, yet it is so constructively critical, full of food for thought, and so easily readable that we just can't help making good use of it." This was Cargill's first experience with an outside consultant, and the "severe" criticism was not appreciated by many. The messenger was not popular!

Probably the most important single step in the decentralization—one addressed only indirectly by the consultant—was the proposal to have the local branch managers work more closely with the superintendents of the elevators. This last relationship had been spelled out in a December 1947 Hendel memorandum, written jointly with Fred Seed; both recommended that the "elevator operations manager" be "brought under the Grain Division." The memorandum continued: "However, the present personnel is not ready for it yet. This step is an ultimate goal."

This reluctance to give the branch manager full responsibility for terminal management stemmed in part from the old hostility between the two divisions, present for so many years with the antagonisms between Julius Hendel and Frank Neilson. Adding to the reluctance to change in 1947 was an additional complication—a new person had just been appointed as head of the newly established Mechanical Division, which included the terminals. This was H. T. (Terry) Morrison.

Terry Morrison had come to Cargill in August 1946 to assume a post directly in senior management. He thus became only the second direct hire into senior management (John Peterson was the first); those such as Andreas, Bob Woodworth and others had come along with Cargill acquisitions. This exception to the promotion-from-within policy, so rigidly adhered to, is all the more surprising in that Morrison literally had *no* experience in the grain trade. Before the war he had been a stockbroker and during World War II had been an officer in the air force, leaving as a full colonel (a few years later, in 1949, he was given a promotion in the reserves to brigadier general and, with his own blessing, was called "General Morrison" by everyone). Morrison was an old social friend of John Jr., and he was related by marriage to the Heffelfinger family that operated Cargill's rival, Peavey.

Morrison's first assignment was as head of the Mechanical Division, but he soon became centrally involved in the general administration of the Company. He shared many of the views of John Jr., Cargill MacMillan and John Peterson about the values of a general education, preferably from one of the eastern schools (he himself had graduated from the respected Virginia Military Institute). He became a strong advocate of the notion that the Company should promote "generalists" into upper management and let the specialists stay within their own functions. Morrison's views, therefore, had weight in the move toward decentralization that was occurring just as he came. Interestingly, John Jr. put an article in *Cargill News* just at this time entitled "Problems of Management" and included a strong reinforcement of the promotion-from-within system ("It is rare indeed that Cargill hires an executive from the outside").

Apparently feeling the need to defend the new decentralized system, John Jr. wrote, in a May 1949 memorandum to key top management personnel, "There seems to be some confusion as to the scheme of organization under which we are now operating." Now John Jr. seemed to have come full circle, for he continued: "It is our goal to make these divisions as autonomous as the quality of their management will permit. We hope that in the not too distant future each division will operate as though it were an independent company."

The memorandum stressed the need for coordination and ended: "This is exactly the form of organization which is used by substantially all large companies" (a valid statement, inasmuch as the Alfred P. Sloan system of decentralized management at General Motors Corporation had given tremendous impetus to the decentralized pattern throughout American industry). There still remained a few unbelievers among Cargill management, John Peterson being in the forefront. But by the early 1950s, Cargill was a decentralized company. In the process, the branch manager–warehouse manager tension finally had been overcome, with the branch manager being given full responsibility for *both* operations.[16]

Recruiting and Training, the Cargill Way

A decade of experience with the formal program of hiring, training and promoting college graduates already had gone by when World War II broke out; now it was time to start up again. The 1930s effort had been a program designed by Julius Hendel, but it incorporated a set of ideas and prejudices of John MacMillan, Jr. Cargill's centralized organization structure, with its need for functional specialists, underlay this. Hands-on training within a particular functional specialty became the dominant pattern; few people were accorded the opportunity to rotate widely in jobs after the initial training program itself (which, by its nature, *did* involve rotation). Training was done internally, in the Cargill way, with dedication to the way things had been done. An overall loyalty to the Company was inculcated deeply. Perhaps without realizing it, the Company had opted for a reinforcement of its conventional wisdom as articulated by the senior management.

Cargill paid modest salaries, and there was occasional grousing about this. Nevertheless, the system had served the Company very well. Of the

66 university graduates hired in the decade 1930–1940, 12 had resigned, 9 had been released and the rest were still with the Company, most with significant middle management responsibilities. Eleven had gone into the service but had returned, and 1945 found the Company with a cadre of highly trained, highly motivated younger executives.

There were now some 3,000 employees in total, with evidence that this figure would grow with the major new postwar initiatives. So there was a felt, immediate need for a second generation of recruiting and training of new college graduates.

An extra-large group of college graduate trainees was hired in the 1946–1947 period, many of them having been through the war, which raised the average age. Austen Cargill evaluated this in a speech in October 1945, commenting: "Our past efforts to train the young men coming into the business, while successful, were developed comprehensively but not extensively. . . . They served us well for the positions they covered, but failed in the scope of positions covered by the program. That experience . . . offers but little guidance in the present." He then spoke to the age issue: "Men coming to us are relatively much older than formerly. If we are to make full use of their services, their training period must be shortened by a concentrated course that will make them available to us at the earliest possible date."

Out of this set of meetings and the Austen Cargill views came an important decision, that key company management—the best—would be asked to be instructors. This "adds greatly to your already over-burdened duties," Austen Cargill told them, but the Company was in the same position "as that of an army occupying newly-won positions which it will not be able to hold unless it can consolidate . . . against future attack . . . survive the competition of well-organized smaller firms."

Ten men were in that first postwar class, and John Savage, the professional head of the training effort, formalized its stages on a more organized basis than in the prewar program. The most important ingredient of the program was the superb set of individual sessions by the executive teaching group. There were 44 of these in the period 1945–1948, with formal presentations by all of the top management, including John Jr., Hendel, Austen Cargill, John Peterson, Dwayne Andreas, Ed Grimes and others. A 570-page compendium of all of these speeches, "Cargill's Business," was printed and used as the basic document for a number of succeeding classes. The best of Cargill's own wisdom was there, a lucid exposition of where the Company stood at that point. In the decade after World War II, the training program graduated a solidly trained group of men, many of whom later became key senior executives, among them Clifford Roberts, Jr., Addison Douglass, Melvin Middents, Gerald Mitchell, Ben Jaffray, William

Pearce and Don Leavenworth. From the family, James Cargill, Cargill MacMillan, Jr., Whitney MacMillan and W. Duncan MacMillan also had the benefit of the program.

Thus, the college graduate training program continued on the prewar model as a wholly in-house effort. Whether this was broad enough to avoid perpetuating any stereotypes coming out of the past and to reach out to the future depended in considerable part on the quality and breadth of the trainee group. Breadth was crucial for upper management, too—any wholly inside board of directors tends to suffer from the lack of outsider challenges to points of view and actions. Given the authoritarian nature of John Jr.'s leadership as chief executive officer, there was (despite the counsel of Cargill MacMillan, Austen Cargill, John Peterson and a few others) a paucity of such challenges.

One of the most widely remembered tales about John Jr. aptly illustrates this. At one point in this period, the board was meeting on the Company's inspection yacht, the *Carmac*. The issue of an employee pension plan was before them, avidly supported by the other board members but not by John Jr. A vote was taken. John Jr. was the only one opposed, all of the rest saying "aye." At this point, James Dorsey, the lawyer-member acting as secretary, stated solemnly, "The nay's have it." This broke the tension, and John Jr. backed off, at least partially, from his lone position.

The need for an outsider view of management was recognized early in this postwar period with the establishment of a weeklong "management conference" in a campus environment at an inn in Stillwater, Minnesota, in February 1949. It was led by a respected outsider, Professor Kenneth Andrews of Harvard Business School. There were 14 senior management participants. A half dozen more of these sessions were held at Stillwater during the 1950s. Interestingly, though, none of the board members (John Jr., Cargill MacMillan and the others) ever attended as participants. It did not seem to occur to them that they too might find outside points of view helpful.

Concerned to keep its breadth, the Company made a study in 1953 of what colleges had been drawn upon for trainees. Eighty-four men had gone through the program in the period 1948–1953. Just over half had come from the midwestern state university system. But most of the remaining colleges were prominent liberal arts institutions (the "Ivy League" universities alone having 10 representatives). These were the types of institutions presumably espousing the general-education approach often mentioned by John Jr. and John Peterson and now by Terry Morrison.

John Jr.'s views on college recruiting had long dominated the hiring decision. As his own sons approached college age, he maintained his enthusiasm about Yale. He wrote a headmaster of a preparatory school in

1946 that he preferred Yale "because of the intense competitive spirit which is peculiarly developed at Yale . . . which is all too often lacking in small universities." Neither of his sons attended Yale, and John Jr. then seemed to turn against the institution, writing one of his Yale classmates: "Our experience with Yale men has been a disappointment, and I think our best ones today are coming from Williams, Princeton and Brown. . . . I am greatly distressed over the trend of things at Yale. . . . My overall enthusiasm has waned considerably" (his younger son graduated from Brown). Cargill MacMillan apparently did not feel the same; both of his sons, Cargill Jr. and Whitney, attended and graduated from Yale.

John Jr. continued to prefer the eastern schools, spelling out his reasoning to one of his sons:

. . . half of your success in life will depend on controlling your emotions . . . that is the great advantage which the graduates of Eastern schools have over the Western schools. Eight years in the East teaches you to control yourself . . . the result is that these men in the business world are much sought after because they simply do not quarrel with people around them. One of the best examples of this I have ever seen has been the success with which Colonel Morrison has moved into our organization. Ordinarily a man coming in at the top as he did would have the jealousy and ill will of many of the other senior executives. However, his manners are so perfect and his self-control so great that no-one could possibly think of quarreling with him, with the result that he is proving to be of extraordinary value to us as a harmonizer or co-ordinator.

John Jr. elaborated further on the importance of self-control in a letter to a college professor:

. . . we must limit ourselves to one type of man. He must first be of a background which would furnish him with excellent manners. This is because in his future role as a co-ordinator he will have to get along with other men. He must also possess iron self-discipline to the end that when irritated he will not show his irritation. We can only find this type in men of excellent family. This does not mean a family of wealth. It means a family of culture and the sons of educators, ministers, etc., are just as welcome as are the sons of wealthy fathers.

In this same letter, the liberal arts graduate once again was touted: "We must have a certain percentage of our young men with a liberal arts education, and these are the hard ones to find . . . only in liberal arts educations do the students have the flexibility of mind which enables them to switch their thoughts quickly and their power of concentration quickly from one field to another. This is in marked contrast to the specialist who can perhaps attain a higher degree on his specialty but can never act as a co-ordinator because he has never been trained in this flexibility of thought."

John Jr. himself wrote a college recruitment brochure for the Company in early 1946. There was no direct mention of the preference for liberal arts graduates or for eastern-school graduates. At the end of the brochure, however, John Jr. listed ten special features of Cargill that gave the Company what he believed was its great stability. It was one of the most explicit public statements of Cargill beliefs ever put in writing. It read as follows:

> Owner management.
> Very conservative dividend policy.
> No public pressure on management.
> The integration of the businesses.
> Fact that all activities are germane to the grain field.
> The vital and fundamental nature of the commodities and products dealt in. Man, beast and bird must eat!
> Heavy commercial borrowings mean that its management must be conservative if credit is to be maintained.
> The companies do not speculate.
> The care taken in the selection and training of prospective executives.
> An enviable record for fair dealing and of integrity both as to contracts and the quality of its products and merchandise.[17]

There is no question that this special Cargill mentality had bred a highly motivated, loyal group of executives. When John Jr. commented in his President's Report to the Shareholders on August 9, 1949, that "the morale and general efficiency of the business are at an all-time peak . . . we have never to my knowledge had better teamwork nor smoother and more efficient overall operation," he seemed not to be overstating the Company's esprit.

In spite of this, there were resignations in this period, and several were those of key people. Ralph Golseth's departure to the Glidden Company was a particularly felt loss. The real reasons for these departures were known only in the private discussions held between the Company and man before departure. However, there is some evidence that the main sticking point usually concerned salary, rather than the job itself. The men in the training program were given major responsibilities almost immediately—in comparison to many other companies, startingly so—and they reveled in this. Cargill MacMillan articulated this in a letter to his older son: "Your grandfather [John Sr.] showed us the way in believing in a 'young organization' and, as a result we aren't afraid of giving young men real responsibility, and I think we will always have a 'young organization.' " Probably the half dozen serious resignations in this period were caused primarily by Cargill's modest salary structure for younger management, the very product of the financial conservatism preached so long by John Sr. and perpetuated by John Jr. and his colleagues.

John Jr. seemed to become quite antagonized when the threat of leaving was used as a salary bargaining chip. One of the enduring legends of the Company suggests that just this had happened in the Golseth resignation—that Golseth had implied that a higher salary would hold him but that

John Jr. had replied summarily, "Good luck with your new company."

By the early 1950s, Cargill had lost four management-level people to Glidden. When the last of these (Willard Lighter) occurred, John Jr. wrote Glidden president Dwight P. Joyce a testy letter: "This is the fourth employee of executive stature hired by your organization from Cargill without, in a single instance, Cargill's having been accorded the courtesy of any advance discussion by Glidden." He continued: "Inasmuch as the practice of proselytizing personnel in an industry can only lead to disastrous retaliation [and is] so ruinously expensive. . . . I could not help but wonder if you were cognizant of all the circumstances." Joyce returned with an equally irritated response, noting that "we definitely believe that our employees are not commodities or chattels and they are free agents to do with their lives what they wish."

In this same period, John Jr. wrote a somewhat more friendly letter to A. E. Staley, president of the Decatur, Illinois, oilseed crushing company of the same name, nevertheless chiding Staley too about not checking with Cargill before taking one of the latter's young executives. Commenting that Cargill had a "*very large* investment" in the man, he mentioned again the "friction" that such raiding brought.[18]

Incentive Pay

As the issue of possibly too modest pay seemed to be surfacing more frequently, the Company turned, in the immediate postwar period, to several new compensation devices designed to increase employee incentive and satisfaction. The profit-sharing plan instituted in 1942 had stayed in place, although some reduction in the allocated percentages was made after the war. This, however, was never designed to be a full-scale individual incentive program. So, in August 1948, a major new program was voted by the board—the Incentive Pay Plan.

It had two components. First was the profit-sharing segment, for heads of divisions and "their assistants next in line who would be top ranking officers if the division were a separate corporation." Second was a compensation component called "adjusted compensation," for the middle levels of the salary range (so-called Group X) and also for certain managers and supervisors of individual plants, departments or territories. This time there was a true incentive factor built in, in that for each individual operating division profitability targets were set as minimums, with compensation to be paid only if the division exceeded the target (for this first year, for example, the Grain Division had to make $2 million in net income before the bonus took effect; Vegetable Oil, $1.75 million; Nutrena, $650,000, etc.). Adjusted compensation could not exceed 50 percent of the recipient's salary; profit sharing could not exceed 100 percent of those recipients' salaries. Also built into the plan was provision for "special compensation," which could be paid beyond the amounts of the two components. Now the divisions had much-heightened motivation to bring in profits for their own units and to guard against any other division usurping anything.

The heads of each division made the recommendations for the split-up among eligible employees. Particularly in the case of the profit-sharing group, this became quite selective, explicitly on the basis of individual performance. The Incentive Pay Plan was a major addition to compensation, and with the excellent years in the immediate postwar period, the amounts that individuals received were very substantial.

The plan was followed in the mid-1950s by another compensation device that was to be even more incentive-oriented—an employee stock ownership plan that at the time it was instituted became the major upper-management compensation package for the Company, and it has continued so up to the present. This important addition will be discussed in the next chapter.[19]

John Jr.'s assumptions about his own compensation clearly colored his views about these Company compensation patterns. He elaborated on this theme in a letter to his old preparatory school, Andover, explaining his minimal giving to them:

I have very little property of my own. The inheritance tax laws forced us to place the family fortune in a series of trusts, of which I receive only the income. Although the principal amount of these trusts is substantial, the income is modest because our business needs its earnings to strengthen its competitive position in a fiercely competitive field, and also because more than 90% of any dividends paid out would be taken by the State and Federal income taxes. Again, for inheritance tax purposes, I have been forced to buy securities from my Father's estate and have had to go heavily into debt in order to do so. I do have an excellent salary and it might seem that my income is large (as indeed it is before payment of income taxes). However since 1939 the amount remaining to me after taxes is less than half what it was at that time, while my living expenses have more than doubled with no change in my scale of living. The net result is that I have no margin between income and expenses, and I am disinclined to go further into debt in order to make charitable contributions.

Apparently John Jr. pleaded this case so strongly that it led his mother, Edna, to believe that the family was so low on money as not to be able to afford the kind of medical care that she was obtaining at the Duke Clinic, under Dr. Kempner. John Jr. wrote urging that she must "stop worrying about the cost of medical care" and continued: "I hate to be crass about this matter of expenses, but you simply must stop thinking about it or talking about it. You are anything but poor. . . . you do not have to worry about building up a large estate in order to take care of Cargill and myself. We both have excellent jobs and you and father took care of our children in the form of Trusts."[20]

New Initiatives

Although Hendel had the entire terminal merchandising under him, he became more and more associated with the feed and oil groups (he had been the prime mover in the 1945 acquisitions in both of these areas). With Andreas, he also had begun negotiations for Cargill to buy a half-interest in a Pittsburgh concern, Falk & Company, a chemical company that produced linseed oil (thus another flax involvement) and also industrial resins and other chemical products. Dwayne Andreas was a particularly strong advocate of the proposed purchase, a substantial one if consummated (the asking price was $1,850,000). There were sharp differences of opinion among Cargill management about whether the purchase should be made, with John Peterson especially strongly against it. Finally, the decision was made to accept the plan, which involved the purchase of a 50 percent interest in Falk's common stock.

The Falk acquisition got off to a rocky start. Willard Lighter, who had been with Cargill's feed group, first with the alfalfa operation in Valier, Montana, and then with the Blue Square organization, was deputed to Falk as executive vice president (he was also one of the four men later "pirated" by Glidden). The previous executives, however, were left in place, with Lighter told "not to interfere with the management."

At the time that Cargill acquired its 50 percent interest, Falk had a plant located at Carnegie, Pennsylvania, where it had manufactured synthetic resins since the mid-1930s. *Cargill News* praised these: "Falkyd Resins, or their equivalent, were established as a standard of quality for the Armed Forces, and many of the olive drab finishes of World War II were made of Falk resins." The company also had some linseed oil business (it was one of the raw materials they used), but it was "only on the fringes" in this market.

So it was decided in July 1948 that Falk would acquire a lease on the Northwest Linseed Company plant in Minneapolis. Now Cargill became a substantial purchaser of flax and seller of both linseed oil and linseed meal. A complicated contract was negotiated with the Commodity Credit Corporation, by which the CCC sold flax to Falk and purchased linseed oil, Falk keeping the meal. By mid-1949, this contract was not working well, a particular problem being inventory imbalances. Further, there had been technical difficulties in the resin department, where the head of research had been trying to solve a problem of the drying of a new resin (as he put it, "If it won't dry, we are a paint company and we're dead"). Altogether, the operation was limping, with little real control by Cargill.

Worse still, the Falk operation had complicated other Oil Division efforts. The flaxseed crushing plant at Port Cargill, one of the jewels of the Company's postwar reconversion, had had to shift its operations to the crushing of soybeans for needed soybean oil contracts that Falk had incurred. At this point (spring 1949), Dwayne Andreas advocated that Cargill purchase the other 50 percent of the ownership and realign the Falk operation to be a better fit with the rest of the Oil Division. John Peterson was unalterably opposed; to his mind, the original investment was sour, and "if half the apple is bad, my logic tells me that the situation is not improved by our owning the whole apple." After much agonizing, the Cargill board sided with Andreas and decided to purchase the rest of the Falk stock. Only time would tell whether Andreas or Peterson was right.[21]

The wartime and early postwar worldwide shortage of vegetable oils now brought a new product—new at least to Cargill—into the picture. In the summer of 1947, Cargill opened a San Francisco office and at the same time made arrangements with a California company, Valianos, Inc., for the latter to crush copra for Cargill on a contract basis. Cargill would buy the copra from the Philippines and sell the copra meal and the coconut oil

Cargill copra plant, San Francisco, 1954.

to consumers. The meal had a strong market among West Coast dairymen, and the soap manufacturing industry was the principal purchaser of coconut oil. Cargill sent Howard Boone to the San Francisco office to manage the contract relationship.

Copra was not a well-understood product for the Cargill group, so Boone wrote a lengthy article in *Cargill News* in December 1948 to explain it. He took the reader from the original coconut tree cultivation through the harvesting and decorticating of the husks for the meat and its bagging by the Filipino farmer. Copra did not suffer from a seasonal shortage—it could be harvested at any point in the year. However, collecting the copra from the widely scattered plantations was done by primitive transport methods, losing efficiency. Once the meat had crossed the Pacific to the San Francisco operation, the crushing process was quite similar to that for soybeans, with plants using similar expellers.

With Cargill's expertise in similar collecting processes in the grain business, Company officials saw many opportunities for more efficient copra processing. The Philippine side particularly needed help. An assured supply was critical for a line-process operation like this, and eventually Cargill had to solve the supply-side difficulties themselves. Further, the Valianos organization did not have expertise in coconut crushing, and Cargill finally established its own operation, right at Pier 84 in San Francisco Harbor.

It was an interesting business and intrigued John Jr. very much. By this time, John Jr. owned substantial property in Jamaica, where the family vacationed each year. He investigated the possibile raising of coconuts and doing copra processing at Greencastle, the central plantation there. Thus, both the Company and John Jr. personally were increasingly intrigued with coconut oil as a worthwhile endeavor.[22]

There were two other sources of vegetable oil, both very minor in terms of quantity, that attracted Cargill's attention right after World War II. These were safflower and sunflowers. *Cargill News* ran articles on both in the fall of 1947—"the lowly sunflower" and the safflower that "most people . . . call a thistle." Both long had been important sources of vegetable oil in Asia and South America, and both were quite unpopular with American farmers. Sunflowers, which grew very tall, were difficult to cultivate with a combine harvester. Safflower had such a low volume of production that it was difficult to find buyers.

None of this deterred John Jr. He had become intrigued with both plants and encouraged the Company's involvement. In 1947, Cargill found that there were some 160 growers planting a total 7,689 acres of sunflowers in northwestern Minnesota, eastern and northern North Dakota and northeastern South Dakota. Cargill purchased a considerable amount, and made contracts with farmers for production for the following year. Similarly, the Company had been signing contracts with farmers for safflower, mostly in Montana, Idaho, Washington and Oregon. The Company's operation at Valier/Conrad, Montana, where the alfalfa project was located, was the collecting point for the seed. Some of this was cleaned and sold as seed; the remainder was crushed into oil. The acreages involved here were minuscule, and the total profits the same. Yet it was an interesting addition to the Oil Division, one with a future. Sunflower production was particularly enhanced later when Cargill's Sam Aronoff persuaded the Oil Division to test high-yield Bulgarian sunflower seed; after further experimentation, better American hybrids were developed.[23]

A Partnership with Nelson Rockefeller

Argentina had been one of Cargill's arenas since the early efforts of Jim Ringwald in the 1930s. Various Cargill people had been sent there on and off during the succeeding years, deal-making in grain when they could, operating as listening posts when they could not. Bunge y Born was the dominant group in grain there, but Cargill always had wanted to be a force. Cargill MacMillan told Michael Cross in July 1947, "Inasmuch as the European situation is in such a mess, we thought we should look into South America." By this time, Al Greenman had been sent to Buenos Aires; George Martin to São Paulo, Brazil; and Duncan Watson to Puerto Rico (where a grain storage complex was to be built with a government subsidy; the project was announced in January 1948 but was abandoned by the end of the year).

Greenman, experienced in overseas work, soon made government contacts for fobbing export sales. It was difficult to do business in Argentina without a formal presence, so Cargill, S.A. Comercial e Industrial was established in April 1948. The most promising project was in hybrid corn, and by 1949 viable hybrids had been developed and were ready to be marketed. The Company's Commitment Committee authorized an additional $30,000 in 1949, to underwrite further expenses "until self-supporting."

By far the most exciting possibility in South America occurred when Nelson Rockefeller approached Cargill about possible interest in a joint project in Brazil to market grain. Rockefeller had just formed a unique company, the International Basic Economy Corporation (IBEC), a Rockefeller family company operating for profit but with the stated purpose of playing a role in developing countries. Rockefeller's assumption was that U.S. management, capital and technical knowledge could be focused in those countries on lowering food prices and other aspects of the "basic economy." He wanted to demonstrate that private capital organized as a for-profit enterprise could also upgrade the economies of less-developed countries. The Rockefeller family had long been involved in Venezuela and Brazil; many of IBEC's first projects would be located in those two countries.

In Brazil, IBEC already was planning a hybrid seed corn company (a competitor to Cargill), a hog production company, a helicopter crop-dusting company and a contract plowing organization. In addition, IBEC wanted to move into grain storage. Nelson Rockefeller went to Minneapolis in March 1947 to see John Jr. and his colleagues—would Cargill be interested in a joint venture with IBEC for these grain operations? Out of this initial contact came one of Cargill's most interesting postwar efforts. John Jr.'s answer to Rockefeller's question was a tentative yes. After many further exchanges, Cargill decided to go ahead.

IBEC had had a philosophy of putting half of the ownership of each of its companies in the hands of nationals of the country involved. In this case a different pattern was used. Cargill and IBEC split the common stock equally for the new company, to be called Cargill Agricola e Comercial, S.A.—the natural acronym was "CACSA." IBEC took a block of preferred stock for the same amount it subscribed for the common, contemplating that these shares would eventually be sold to Brazilians. Cargill was to furnish the technical know-how and the on-the-spot management; IBEC had policy control through its majority membership on the board.

The company began operating in 1948 in rented warehouse space, temporarily buying corn in bags. Permanent elevator space was needed, but the question of where to locate this puzzled everyone. Credit was tight, and building costs were high, so two elevators were decided upon. Should the elevators be out in the country, near the source of supply (the farmer), or should they be in the city, near the source of demand (the local customer or exporter)?

Rather than a compromise of "one each," the company took a considered risk and decided to build two country elevators. One was to be at Ourinhos, in the western part of the state of São Paulo, about 250 miles from the city of São Paulo. Ourinhos was a rail junction for the Sorocabana Railroad, owned by the state of São Paulo, and the Northern Paraná Railroad, owned by the federal government and administered by the state of Paraná. Unfortunately, each of the railroads was jealous of giving up its equipment to the other, so interlining of cars was not practiced—there was a frustrating amount of lost motion in unloading and reloading.

The other elevator was to be farther out in the country, at Arapongas, about 120 miles west of Ourinhos. The capacities of the elevators were small; the facility at Ourinhos held 100,000 bushels and that at Arapongas, 50,000. Both had bulk handling and drying machinery and were prepared for grading, a concept little used in Brazil up to that time. Most of the grain would be corn, although soybeans, rice and peanuts also were grown in the area.

Once built, the physical plants worked very well. Local management was good, and the corn could be readily purchased at expected prices. On October 30, 1949, the first carload of corn, not bagged but in bulk, was loaded at Ourinhos. Unfortunately, it had to be unloaded by hand at the receiving end, which took double the time for bulk corn than for bags (later this too was mechanized). Bagging was still required for local buyers. CACSA was off to a promising start.

When Nelson Rockefeller returned to Minneapolis for a visit with John Jr. in early March 1949, both parties were pleased with CACSA and were looking for new joint endeavors. IBEC wanted to set up a Venezuelan elevator company—Rockefeller talked about 12 elevators. The company would also handle farm machinery and produce and distribute seeds. "I think the chances are we will go along with him on this one," John Jr. wrote his brother.

Rockefeller also wanted to have Cargill join with him in a farming program in Venezuela. This was precisely what John Jr. was already investigating in Panama. John Jr. had just made a visit to Panama, using the *Carmac* to touch in at a number of unexplored areas in the Darien Gap

Left and right, a Cargill and International Basic Economy Corporation (IBEC) joint venture; the country elevator at Ourinhos, State of São Paulo, Brazil, 1959 (courtesy of the Rockefeller Archive Center).

area. John Jr. often mentioned the importance of being able to study a new port by actually sailing into it; the *Carmac* was excellent for this. It also allowed John Jr. to have his own meals prepared aboard, since his rigid salt-free rice diet was difficult to obtain in a commercial restaurant. He had visited with Panamanian officials on this trip, and possibilities of a very large concession of unexplored, untouched land in the Darien area were mentioned. Already, IBEC was doing the same in Venezuela. "They are cutting jungle," John Jr. reported, "just as we discussed for Darien, and burning the logs. Now they are trying to find a market for their lumber." The Cargill–IBEC partnership seemed to be spawning many exciting new ideas (at least in 1949 terms, for today the clear-cutting of South American forests is decried by most environmentalists).[24]

A Misplayed Trade

Julius Hendel, at this time spread so widely among various pieces of the business, still maintained close contact with his first interest, trading of grain, and now decided to engineer a major trade in wheat. He sensed a tightness in the supply of red wheat late in 1947 and felt that there would be a "natural squeeze" in the December 1947 contract on the Chicago Board of Trade. In order to help this process along, he had Cargill purchase as much soft red Chicago wheat as possible, in both cash and the December futures. The price had risen rapidly (it had been at $2.41 in August and rose to $3.09 in early December).

Unfortunately, Hendel got caught in a trap similar to that of Daniel Rice with the rye during World War II. Hendel had been particularly focusing on the price of the Chicago December wheat (the soft red). But the Kansas City December futures price (hard red) also had a direct influence, inasmuch as hard red could be delivered interchangeably with soft for the Chicago contract. Soon the price of Chicago rose more over Kansas City than the cost of transporting the wheat physically to Chicago. A group of Kansas City shorts, led by Henry Cate, the head of Flour Mills of America, began inundating Chicago with rail shipments of hard red. As the contract came closer to its end, the price began to drop as Cate and his friends continued to deliver. By February 1948, the price of wheat in Chicago was down to $2.45. There was a very sharp break downward in all commodities in that month; John Peterson called it "one of the sharpest, most sudden and wicked declines . . . ever." So the squeeze never came off. Further, Cargill was left with a huge amount of hard red to sell. But having hard red in Chicago really put it out of position—most of the Midwest buyers of hard (the flour mills) were in Kansas City and further South. The soft was more readily sold in the Chicago area and the East for the cookie and biscuit makers. Unfortunately, Cargill owned mostly hard!

Hendel's failed trade cost the Company many thousands of dollars. Company earnings for the 1947–1948 crop year had been very large, not as spectacular as the previous year but the second best that the Company had ever had (the net profit was $3,008,000). All of these profits, however, were attributed to other parts of the organization, the Oil Division alone posted a gross income of some $5 million. The Grain Division lost some $584,000. John Jr. wrote Hendel a letter after the year's results were available that praised him for the overall earnings but continued: "It is true that we made one or two costly errors, but the recovery has been so dramatic that I think we have every reason to think that we should have success in all divisions for this coming year." Clearly, Hendel's effort to move back into grain trading had proved abortive.[25]

The Albany Dock Strike, September–October 1947

Cargill's labor relations had been relatively peaceful over its history. The occasional strike had been short and relatively unimportant. Now, however, the Company got a taste of frustration from the International Longshoremen's Association (ILA), the first of a number of problems with this union. This one hurt.

On September 23, 1947, the Albany local of the ILA had called a port-wide strike. It immediately affected Cargill, as a bystander in the ILA local's interunion jurisdictional battle with the International Brotherhood of Teamsters. A month earlier, the Teamsters had refused to bring trailer trucks to the docks for a new organization called Trailerships, Inc., which was using two converted naval landing craft to bring truck trailers by water from Albany to New York City. The ILA alleged that its members were being deprived of work. Cargill, not involved in any way with the Trailerships issue, nevertheless had its operations shut down, not only at Albany but all the way through the Erie Canal to Oswego.

Nationally, a new labor law had been passed earlier in the year as a response to the huge number of labor relations tensions in 1946. The law was popularly called the Taft-Hartley Act after its sponsors in the Senate and House, Senator Robert Taft and Representative Fred Hartley. The Act had a provision against secondary boycotts, and Cargill felt this was happening here. The law allowed a company to go into court for an injunction in such cases, and Cargill did so. In the first-in-the-country temporary restraining order under the new act, the ILA was ordered to call off the strike, now 10 days old. When the port reopened, the National Labor Relations Board dissolved the injunction proceedings (on October 22). The muddy issues between the two unions and the trailer-carrying barge line eventually were settled amicably. Cargill had no part in these negotiations. Indeed, Cargill had no particular position on the interunion squabble, nor even on the trailer-carrying barge line. What mattered was that the port was opened and that grain shipments, so critical for Europe, could continue.

The unsettling events here motivated Cargill to collect all of its labor relations policies in a pamphlet, which was mailed to all employees. It was entitled *Mr. Taft, Mr. Hartley and You: Job Policies.*[26]

The Telegraphers Strike

In late 1946, the Commercial Telegraphers Union, the bargaining agent for the Company's Morse telegraph operators, pressed the Company for substantial wage increases, in keeping with the demands from employees all over the country for postwar adjustments. The telegraphers had an interesting bargaining position—they believed that any increase should be based on the volume of work a particular employee did, with higher ratings for "heavy circuits." It was true that there were heavy-volume periods in the crop year, particularly at harvest, with some telegraphers even bringing

*New teletype
communications
equipment, 1946.*

cots in to sleep in the office. The Company countered that it paid salaries "comparable to what is being paid for similar work in this or other areas" and that, further, "the relative number of messages handled by a qualified operator has no bearing on what he would receive in wages."

The first Cargill wire system came with the Taylor & Bournique acquisition in 1923. By the 1930s, most of the Company's offices were connected by private Morse lines. By the end of World War II, new teletype technology predominated. It no longer required Morse code, and most of the Morse operators had become redundant, the Company transferring them to the typewriter-based teletype. James A. Brooks, Cargill's labor relations director, pointed out that "the operation of our private wire system is definitely a luxury, and if the excessive increased cost of operation necessitated by exorbitant wage demands makes the continuation of the wire room no longer feasible in our business, we shall have no hesitancy in removing it and using public facilities as we once did and as many other companies in this or related industries still do."

A short-lived strike occurred, but the Company was unwilling to change its long-standing wage policy. Over the succeeding months, the Company upgraded the teletype system with new "torn tape" machines—messages were received on perforating machines, which simultaneously printed a copy and punched the message on tape. The latter then could be used to send the same message to any number of other people in the Company. This made for very rapid communication all through the system. Most of the remainder of the Morse work soon was phased out. Samuel Mahoney was assigned as head of the wire unit and given the responsibility to hire new employees to replace those Morse operators unwilling to make the shift.[27]

Truman's "Give-'em-Hell"

The Steagall Amendment of 1942, that perplexing wartime provision that required 90 percent parity for "two years after the war," came to an end in 1947. So 1948 was to be a pivotal year for agriculture, particularly because of the raucous presidential campaign. The record-breaking wheat crop in 1947 had filled the bins of the country (indeed, had to be piled in the streets in some places). When the 1948 crop in both wheat and corn also promised to be huge, the papers were full again of fears of overprod-uction. *U.S. News and World Report*, in a major article on agriculture in late July 1948, called it "Return of the Big Crop Problem."

Harry Truman, thrust into office by the death of Franklin D. Roosevelt, had not been given much of a chance against Governor Thomas E. Dewey. But Truman moved out into the hustings with his soon-famous "give-'em-hell" style and flayed the Republicans for causing the storage problem, implying also that they were the instigators of weakening prices (the February 1948 price collapse had raised great fears of a repeat). In one of his most famous speeches, on September 18, 1948, at an Iowa plowing contest, he said, "The Republicans gave you that greatest of all depressions, when hogs went down to three cents and corn was so cheap that you burnt it up." If the farmers had thought of forsaking the Democrats, Truman won them over by arguing that the Republicans had "stuck a pitchfork in the farmer's back."

Cargill executives grudgingly supported the Republicans, although not enthusiastic about either party. John Jr. put the Company's view succinctly in a letter to a Minneapolis friend: "I disapprove heartily of any candidate, Republican or Democrat, who supports or advocates a managed economy." To John Jr., even the very name of the Committee for Economic Development (CED), the eminent business group, suggested "the philosophy of a managed economy." Any hint of government control raised the ire of John Jr.

The year 1948 seemed to be a time when John Jr. was especially vocal in his views. In February of that year his outspoken behavior got him into trouble with R. L. Williams, the president of the Chicago and North Western Railway System. Williams had recommended to the board of directors (one of whom was John Jr.) that a dividend be declared on common stock, despite low earnings. John Jr. vociferously objected without letup, and Williams finally asked for his resignation from the board. John Jr. complied, "herewith," and wrote to Williams: "My rather extensive experience in merchandising, manufacturing and banking leads me to believe that the dividend policy . . . is neither in the best interests of the stockholders nor of the railroad. I also wish to be on record . . . that the treatment by the railroad of its shippers during the past two or three years is short-sighted and can only end in the permanent loss of very large quantities of revenue tonnage." The abrupt ending of this 11-year relationship seemed to be a shock to John Jr.[28]

When Truman astounded everyone by winning the election (the famous *Chicago Tribune* headline to the contrary notwithstanding), John Jr. wrote a position paper and circulated it widely. He attributed the Republicans' loss to being "cocky" and also to the damage done by the primary campaign of Harold Stassen (who had railed against the commodity traders). Truman's campaign, John Jr. continued, "aroused the admiration and sympathy of vast numbers of people, myself included." As for the consequences of the election, "I am not nearly as disturbed as are most Conservatives." His reasoning here was more tactical than philosophical. He was "anxious to see a rather permanent swing of power to the Conservative side," and because of the economic situation in 1948, it was wiser to let the other party have to face the music. John Jr. was prophetic about one point (although off a few years): "Note the really magnificent campaigning done by [Hubert] Humphrey. It would not surprise me in the least if he were the Democratic nominee for president four years hence."

Truman appointed a Denver lawyer, Charles F. Brannan, as his Secretary of Agriculture. Sagging farm prices had brought renewed demands for fixed supports at 90 percent or 100 percent of parity. Brannan came forward with a proposal for a new agricultural plan, and it was a startling one. It "burst like a bomb" (said economists Willard Cochrane and Mary Ryan); it "sent shock waves throughout the country" (Gilbert Fite's words). Brannan proposed to maintain the support at 90 percent to 100 percent of parity on storable commodities, but for perishable commodities (livestock, fruits and vegetables, etc.) the farmer would be free to produce whatever he chose to, and prices would be free to move wherever the supply–demand equations took them. For these producers, the guarantee of parity would be achieved by a direct payment—in effect, an income subsidy rather than a price subsidy.

Brannan's manifold critics accused him of introducing a federal handout system, and conservatives in both parties linked their disapproval to a number of other social causes being pushed in proposed legislation at this time. The American Farm Bureau Federation came out in opposition, and the plan was dead. When Congress finally adopted legislation in the fall of 1949, the 90 percent parity principle was continued for one more year for the "basic commodities," with a sliding scale below the 90 percent figure for a number of other commodities. The notions of the 1930s about farm policy had remained frozen in place.

"We disapprove heartily of any farm legislation," John Jr. wrote an economist friend during the debate over the Brannan plan; "it is the first step toward a Totalitarian form of government." Nevertheless, John Jr.

supported Brannan's ideas as "less of a drain on the nation than is the idea of parity. . . . The Brannan plan brings all costs right out into the open." National or international control of price was anathema to John Jr. An International Wheat Agreement was also being put together at this time, involving a system of quotas among wheat-producing countries and controlled export policies. Cargill was unalterably opposed to the agreement. However, it was ratified by Congress in October 1949. It specified annual minimum and maximum levels for price, with the Commodity Credit Corporation (CCC) allowed to pay subsidies to exporters or to absorb losses when selling its own stocks. "Managed" farm policy continued to prevail.[29]

The CCC and May 1949 Wheat

The CCC was heavily in the wheat market in the first months of 1949, presumably for export under the Marshall Plan and for the army and other foreign governments. The national export quota was about 100 million bushels, of which 25 million were to be purchased by the Minneapolis-area director.

Over the period January–May 1949, Cargill sold the CCC about 11.7 million bushels of this amount. The terms of this relationship became the target of a massive congressional investigation in 1952, in which it came out that the CCC had purchased this grain in the cash market and had entered into contracts with Cargill to deliver the Cargill wheat to Albany under a Cargill transportation contract. (Thanks to the foresight of John Jr. and his colleagues, Cargill was the only integrated grain company that could offer such a transportation contract.) In making these purchases, the CCC had insisted on using the cash market, despite the fact that their most effective move would have been to use the futures market, where prices at that time were considerably below cash prices. Don Stevens, a vice president of General Mills, was quoted in a Minneapolis paper at the time of the congressional hearing: "It is ridiculous to think that a grain man in private trade would pay a cash premium for grain not required immediately in a situation when futures are quoted at a substantially lower price. If I did it personally, I would lose my position."

The reasons why the CCC officials chose to stay in the cash markets were not clear. The same Minneapolis newspaper quoted the General Accounting Office (which did the investigation for Congress) as "hinting that the CCC was trying to keep farm prices high by market manipulation." Given the administration's predilection for support of the farmer and, further, that this was a presidential election year, the hypothesis makes some sense.

Whatever the CCC's rationale, the contract with Cargill was a windfall for the Company. In the later congressional investigation, Erv Kelm was brought before Congress to testify; he described the difference in the cash and futures price at the time and (to quote the subsequent congressional report) "further stated that his Company took advantage of this price differential through the new contracts to make substantial profits . . . that, under the new contracts and the transportation agreement with deferred delivery dates and change in place of delivery, his company had a real profit deal and could not lose."

Cargill had done nothing wrong here—it had negotiated a very favorable contract with the CCC and had reaped large profits. Congress and the press, however, were not as kind to the Company. The Minneapolis paper had a headline reading "Cargill Again Accused of Excessive Profits," and much the same view was expressed in the congressional report. A number of other grain trade men were brought before the Senate committee to testify, most of them decrying the Cargill contract (any one of them probably would have been delighted to have had the contract himself!). The Company had made its money legally here, but it had lost in the forum of public opinion. The case was not over, either, as the next chapter will chronicle.

Not all facts in the case accrued to Cargill's financial benefit, however, for the Company encountered problems with its own futures-market trading in that exciting month of May 1949. Cargill was short a great deal of wheat in the Chicago futures market and had taken a considered risk in making most of these sales in the May futures, rather than those of a later month. In the process, it had, according to a *Fortune* story, "maintained a large short position well into the month, while delivering considerable wheat at a loss and feigning further deliveries from ships at Duluth." The article continued:

The calculation here concerned chiefly what the U.S. Commodity Credit Corporation would do with its controlling interest in the old crop and what its buying policy would be during the delivery month. . . . The short [Cargill] evidently figured that the CCC would get out of the market and the longs would be driven to sell by the threat of delivery. . . . But then the CCC stayed in the market on the buying side apparently with light purchases—enough to give the longs courage to stick it out. The risk of the longs was great, for the next futures (July), representing the new crop, was selling far below the May—old crop—future. Delivery in this case might have entailed a carry-over into the lower-priced period with large losses. The shorts, however, failed to get the longs out of the market, and, judging by the moderate price rise near the end of the month, apparently took a beating. This contest was watched with some amusement by all the traders in Chicago.

Thus, although Cargill earlier had made and would continue to make a great deal of money on the CCC contracts during this year, it did lose a considerable amount of this by the misplaced futures decision. In normal

John MacMillan, Jr., left, views Cargill's artwork for Business Week *cover; E. J. Grimes, center, and James Sutherland, right.*

circumstances, a wide old crop–new crop inverse tends to collapse in the delivery month. As it turned out, if the initial short sales had been in the July contract, the Company's loss would have been mitigated.

Both of the two crop years that spanned these events were highly profitable for the Grain Division; in 1948–1949 it had contributed just under $2 million of the Company's $2.3 million profits that year. In 1950, the division had contributed $3.6 million, when the Company had a record year of profits, $5.3 million. The Grain Division was back at center stage in importance. Yet the events of that May wheat contract disturbed John Jr. enough to write Julius Hendel a long letter, summarizing his views on hedging policy. It was a sobering chastisement:

The purpose of this policy is to reduce to the absolute minimum consistent with continuing to do business, all hazards incidental to hedging. . . . This means that we will have no net long or short position, in excess of the out-of-balance limit, and no cross hedges, nor any unsold grain out-of-position. Any unsold stocks on January first will be inventoried at delivery prices, less freight and carrying costs, for delivery on whatever future is being used as a hedge [a practice seldom, if ever practiced in the past]. . . . If such an inventory price involves a substantial loss from either market or the December first price, then the amount to be carried will be held to such a low figure that there can be no question whatever of their liquidity in the normal course of business by April first. . . . Keeping our powder dry will permit us . . . to profit substantially during these winter months from the error of the speculative and manipulative fraternity.

Although Erv Kelm was in charge of the Grain Division, Julius apparently was being held responsible, as merchandising manager, for the failed trade.

The *Fortune* article mentioned above came out in August 1949. It included long sections devoted to John Jr. himself, with stories of his relationship to Daniel Rice and tales of the 1937 Corn Case. While the article was not derogatory, the continuing references to past events were embarrassing to John Jr.

In contrast was the article that came out in April 1949 in *Business Week*, a lengthy piece on the "mighty business" built on "little grains of wheat." The six-page article also mentioned the Corn Case at some length but called it "little more than a gentle slap on the wrist." Cargill was not allowed to see the *Fortune* article prior to publication but did receive a draft of the *Business Week* article. John Jr. asked for several changes and was accommodated (for example, when the initial article talked of the Lake Office as "lavish," he changed it to "lavishly efficient"). John Jr. thanked the editor: "I also want you to know how appreciative we are of your willingness to change it around to take care of possible damage that certain statements might have caused."

In the main, the *Business Week* article was laudatory. Perhaps most important, John Jr. himself appeared on the cover, always a trophy for corporate chief executive officers. Pictures of Austen Cargill, Cargill MacMillan and Ed Grimes also graced the article. Cargill truly had arrived as a major American corporation. With those record profits for the 1949–1950 year, it was a heady time for the Company. Cargill's organizational hubris was at high tide.[30]

PART SIX

ASSESSING THE JOHN MACMILLAN, JR., YEARS

Baie Comeau, Quebec, terminal elevator, 1960.

CHAPTER SEVENTEEN

Korean War, Tradax Beginnings

The cold war followed rapidly upon World War II. By November 1946, the Soviet foreign minister was attacking United States foreign policy in the United Nations Assembly. In March 1947, the President enunciated the Truman Doctrine to contain Russian imperialism in Europe and to protect Turkey and Greece from any such threats. A Soviet spokesman called the United States "warmongers," and the cold war was exacerbated. In April 1949, the North Atlantic Treaty Organization (NATO) was instituted by Western European countries, the United States and Canada. From June 1948 to the summer of 1949, Russia blockaded Berlin.

In Asia, the United States confronted North Korea over the latter's territorial demands and the South Korean people's demands for independence. In August 1948, the Republic of Korea was established, and most United States military personnel were withdrawn. Then, in June 1950, the peninsula erupted into hostilities when the North Korean Communist forces invaded South Korea. The United Nations Security Council authorized a United Nations military force to repel the attack and to restore international peace and security. The United States furnished an overwhelming bulk of the forces, with the unified United Nations under command of General Douglas MacArthur.

For once, John Jr. was wrong about a military matter—he wrote Terry Morrison at the end of July 1950: "I myself think this Korean scare will be over in two weeks . . . the Russians do not want a general war at this time as the crop in the Ukraine was in 10 days ago and they would need every day of dry weather until the Autumn rains come to move their armies around. . . . The Russians will intervene for peace." But he ended the letter: "Wishful thinking perhaps!"[1]

The truth was that a major war had begun, and it was complicated late in 1950 when the Chinese Communists joined the fighting on the side of the North Koreans. The United States again was at war after only five years of peace.

The state of agriculture is always important in wartime. The country entered this conflict with its farms and farmers in excellent shape. There had been a record wheat crop of 1.36 billion bushels in 1947 and a record corn crop of 3.6 billion bushels in 1948. The other four "basic crops" and their many companion farm products all had done well. Indeed, in 1950, government authorities once again were worrying about price-depressing surpluses. Most farmers slept quite well, however, for in 1949 Congress had extended provisions for 90 percent parity prices on the basic crops for an additional year, through 1950. The New Deal policies of the 1930s had continued essentially unchanged.

With the outbreak of war, demand for farm products heightened, and prices rose. Production was not as good in 1950 and 1951; the wheat crop of 1950 was only 1.02 billion bushels, and it dropped below 1 billion the next year. The corn crop, too, had decreased in both years. Surpluses eased in the face of these developments. At the same time, the grain trade, along with the rest of agriculture, once again was energized by war.

Cargill employees left for the armed forces, and John Jr. took a special page in the *Cargill News* of September 1950 to assure them that Company personnel policies would protect them while they were gone and provide a job for them when they returned. Cargill's business boomed, and there were record profits for the crop year 1949–1950: $4.3 million. A second record was set for 1950–1951: an astounding figure of $5.9 million. Sales for those years were $423.6 million and $543.8 million, respectively, with year-end net worth $27.8 million and $34.0 million. The Grain Division starred in both years, and the Feed Division also had good results. The Oil Division contribution came up from a small figure in 1950 to a respectable level in 1951. The new Falk Division (the company now owned completely by Cargill) contributed $1.1 million in that year. Only the small Seed Division had losses for both years.

The individual grains each did well. In the record year of 1950–1951 the Company had traded over 253 million bushels, with the two feed grains, corn and oats, comprising almost 55 percent of this. Feed sales had hovered at 360,000 tons in both years; the Oil Division had crushed 379,000 tons of product in 1950, and this rose to 630,000 in 1951. Falk's major sales had been linseed oil and meal, with soybean oil and meal also substantial. The resins business and the specialty oils were still moderate.

With this stepped-up activity, there were significant changes all through the divisions. An outline of these will be helpful, before some of the major stories of this period are analyzed.

A. New Grain Elevators and Terminals

The terminal elevator capacity of the Company had stayed steady from early in World War II through mid-1949, at just over 70 million bushels.

By 1950, the capacity had risen to just under 100 million bushels. Licensed terminal capacities had been boosted at several locations: Chicago was up to over 17 million bushels; the "Electric" at Buffalo was up (but the "Great Eastern" had been razed, so total capacity there was less). Of the new terminals, most were of moderate size, but their strategic importance far outweighed this. Three were on the Illinois River: Savannah (450,000 bushels), Morris (220,000 bushels) and Lockport (110,000 bushels). The astounding earlier success of Cargill's first subterminal on the Illinois, at Ottawa (100,000-bushel capacity), where truck unloading had been used so effectively, promised that these three additions would be highly significant to the Company's use of truck-barge shipping. A Richmond, Virginia, terminal with 770,000-bushel capacity had been leased, to heighten Cargill's intercoastal and ocean shipping. An additional East Coast terminal was leased at Mt. Clare (Baltimore), Maryland, with 220,000-bushel capacity.

Another strategic area, the Southeast, now had its own permanent facility, a 500,000-bushel terminal at Wilson, North Carolina. This facility was another big-bin "tabernacle" (the tent roof configuration). The Wilson plant represented a very adventurous step in taking high-technology midwestern grain-handling concepts into an area of the United States where a substantial amount of grain was still bagged rather than being handled in bulk. The move was a risky step, but the result was very successful.

Then there were the three tank farms. John Jr. believed that steel oil-storage tanks could be used effectively for grain. Many of these had been built during World War II and, with the hostilities over, were going begging. Smaller versions of oil-storage tanks had already been tried for grain, one of them in Big Bend City, Minnesota. Cargill MacMillan visited there on a Minnesota Western Railway inspection trip and wrote John Jr.: "I thought I had seen everything in grain elevators but Big Bend City taught me differently. . . . It is known as the 'Rocket' for obvious reasons." Now John Jr. persuaded Cargill's board to buy a large group of these in Mexia, Texas, to hold in total 8,800,000 bushels. Mexia is in central Texas and was not at that time a strategic grain transportation location. There was no water transportation, and trucks would have to be used. However, the tanks *could* be used for long-term storage, and at a time when the Commodity Credit Corporation needed to locate its surpluses somewhere, storage was a major part of Cargill's business. John Jr. called it, in a letter to the stockholders in August 1950, "typically a Cargill contribution to carrying grain surpluses in good condition for long periods . . . [and] in line with our willingness to introduce innovations."

Two other, smaller tank farms were purchased, at Marietta, Pennsylvania (1,060,000 bushels), and at Norris City, Illinois (3,500,000 bushels). The question of whether grain could be maintained in condition in these tight quarters (a question previously raised by the banks about the Albany and Omaha operations) was again asked. The answers were not all positive. The problems encountered at Norris City are reported later in this chapter.

In 1951, land was purchased at Corpus Christi, Texas, for a possible Gulf-side terminal. However, extensive dredging was required before this project was practicable, so it was slow in coming to fruition. Yet Gulf terminal facilities remained in short supply. Cargill was even experimenting with an unloading device on board the barge itself to facilitate midriver unloading directly into an oceangoing vessel.

These terminal additions combined to stimulate business for the Grain Division, particularly so because of parallel innovations in the Company's inland-waterways transport component.[2]

B. Expanding the Waterways Fleet

In 1949, John Jr. had turned his attention to specialized waterways equipment. With both the Oil Division and Falk dealing in vegetable oils, the transport of this product became important. He soon developed plans and drawings for a specialized vegetable oil towboat and barge (a two-unit combination) that would be able to traverse both the Great Lakes and the Erie Canal. The Oil Division was skeptical about this; Cargill MacMillan wrote his brother: "They are not transportation minded and . . . have pretty much convinced Austen that they can buy transportation cheaper." Despite this lack of confidence, contracts were let in early 1950 for what became the *Carport*. A jumbo barge/jumbo tow combination capable of carrying approximately 2,000 tons of liquid or dry cargo, it was double-skinned. By using the extra side tanks, its capacity could almost be doubled (in which case the draft was deeper, of course). The towboat and barge each cost approximately $350,000, the most expensive by far of any of the units in the Company fleet. The two units entered service in 1951.[3]

In that same year, John Jr. developed plans for an intercoastal vessel, again a towboat–single barge unit. Construction began in 1952 on the *Carpeake*. A separate corporation was formed under this name; again stock was offered to all of the holders of common stock. The *Carpeake* towboat was 66 feet long and just over 17 feet wide; the barge (H-1) was 243 1/2 by 38 by 18 feet. This unit began operation in the Chesapeake Bay area in August 1952.

New towboat and barge units also were needed for the midwestern inland waterways. Once again, separate shareholder ownership was decided upon, and another company, the Minnesota River Corporation, was formed in January 1951. Contracts were let for two more towboats, the *Carpolis* and the *Carpaul*, named after Minnea*polis* and St. *Paul*. These two new towboats were each 40 feet in length, with diesel engines of 1100

The Carpeake.

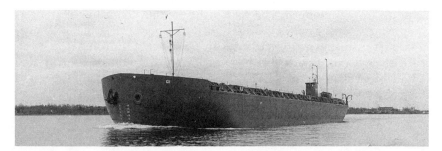

The Carport.

Moving the Carport *into the V notch on a barge.*

horsepower. The 12 barges, J-1 through J-12, were each 176 by 43½ by 12 feet. The *Carpolis* began operations in May 1952 and the *Carpaul* one year later. With the volume of grain going down the Mississippi on Company barges—clearly a one-direction movement—backhauls became increasingly important. Ray King, who had come with Cargo Carriers Incorporated (CCI) in 1952, was given the assignment to aggressively pursue new options. Coal was an early cargo, as well as salt. Because the Mississippi was frozen in its upper reaches in winter, King developed warehouses and yards and a distribution network so that the barges would be freed and not be out of position. His work had important implications for balancing operations. To help matters along, Port Cargill itself was upgraded in July 1950 with a major waterside truck-unloading rig and a set of loading galleries for the barges. In 1952, the Minnesota River Corporation acquired the Carpeake Corporation, thus becoming the holding company for all of its equipment and its leases to CCI, Cargill's transportation arm.

Important changes also were made in the status of the Minnesota Western Railway Company. It had been purchased outright by John Jr. and Cargill MacMillan in 1942, when Port Cargill was first established. The Interstate Commerce Commission would not allow Cargill as a corporation to own both a railroad and a shipping company (CCI). This purchase

The Carpolis.

was not unambiguous, and it illustrates the potential pitfalls of having outside companies owned by individuals who also work for the company. The goal was to keep an arms-length relationship: the Company should be free to buy services from others at market rates if it wished. For example, if a particular division was required to buy an internal Cargill service, this might affect the calculations for the Incentive Pay Plan relative to others who did not have to buy the same service. Indeed, if there was too much of an anomaly here, the tax authorities might begin to look askance at the arrangement. It was quite legitimate to set up such arrangements for tax avoidance; and in this case, it allowed the common stockholders to accrue capital gains in the separate company, rather than having dividends from the parent company taxed at a high rate. Yet the terms of this arrangement had to be such as to avoid the appearance of tax evasion. In a private memorandum, Cargill MacMillan noted that his and John Jr.'s ownership of the railroad was "disliked by Cargill top executives" because they were not free to seek other alternative, perhaps more competitive arrangements and because of a fear of being found in violation of the law. There was also concern about possible retaliation from commission merchants and others because of accusations of excessive shipping charges by the railroad. Further, it was "disliked by other executives because of Incentive Pay Plan." On the other side, it was "disliked by Mac Jr. and CMac because (1) attitude of Cargill organization made it virtually impossible properly to exploit the situation (2) the return was incommensurate with the risk and possible criticism."

At the time the two MacMillans had bought the railroad, an option for the railroad stock had been given to Cargill Securities Company (the family company). In December 1949, the option was exercised in the following way. A new company, the Minnesota Western Company, was formed, the common stock of which was offered to the group of common shareholders who had participated in the terminals and the Carpeake Corporation. There was also preferred stock, the largest block to go to Cargill Securities Company, with a smaller amount to the Cargill, Inc., salaried employees' pension trust. The combination of these various holders helped to meet most of the objections to the earlier arrangement. Both family and key management now participated, and there was a stake also for the employees through the Trust.

The railroad had been only a moderate performer during the ownership of John Jr. and Cargill MacMillan. However, most of management felt that there was a potential for more grain trade over the line, particularly if trackside facilities were upgraded. Accordingly, a separate corporation, the Wesota Company, was set up to own the elevators. This company was a member of the Chicago Board of Trade and cleared futures for Cargill. The Minnesota Western Company was the owner of Wesota.

The Carcrosse.

The effect of all of these moves—and the complicated set of new companies—was to separate much of the activity at Port Cargill from Cargill, Inc. Cargill MacMillan felt strongly that, in his words,

Cargill's operating heads should not be loaded down with having to . . . administer a rather complicated transportation business if we expect them to do a good job as merchants and processors . . . inasmuch as Cargill, Inc. is a large borrower, the propriety of investing a fairly substantial amount . . . in a foreign field might be open to question and harmful criticism might result. Much better that the owners of Cargill, Inc. risk their own funds rather than create any question that they are not showing every precaution in safeguarding the funds for which they are in a sense trustees.

These arrangements now made arms-length relationships more believable, with the trustees of the pension trust hopefully acting as an independent check.[4]

C. Staf-O-Life Feeds Joins Cargill

In June 1951, a major acquisition was made in the feed side of the business when the Company bought a majority holding in the Royal Feed and Milling Company of Memphis, Tennessee. Its brand name, "Staf-O-Life," was well known throughout the South. The owner, W. R. Smith-Vaniz, was retiring but kept a minority ownership in the company. The 300 people in Royal joined Cargill, and Nutrena and Royal were merged. Royal served the territory from the Mississippi to the Atlantic below the Mason-Dixon Line and included Florida in its area. It was a good match for

Nutrena, which had a primary focus in the middle and upper Midwest. Royal had been in business since 1912 and still had a number of people from the early company. This long-service cadre gave Royal a strong corporate culture of its own, one that meshed reasonably well with Nutrena's.

The most upsetting news about Nutrena during this period was the massive flood in Kansas City on that town's own "Black Friday," July 13, 1951. For weeks, the paper had been full of news about extremely high waters on the Kaw, the Marais des Cygnes and other Kansas rivers. By July 13, Kansas City faced a major flood. Dikes had broken upriver; and although Nutrena had not expected too much impact on its plant, when the high water did arrive, it inundated the entire plant. Teddi Tetherow, the Feed reporter for the *Cargill News* told what happened: "By ten o'clock Friday morning, when the word came to evacuate, we were optimistic enough to think that we had everything that could be moved on such short notice above the flood level, but as it turned out the water rose much higher than anyone had anticipated, reaching a height of four and one-half feet on the second floor of the pellet building, and about the same height in the bag room." The bulk of the accounting records were moved in time, but almost the entire inventory was a total loss.[5]

D. A Dip in Oil Division Performance

After its spectacular years of trading in 1947 and 1948, reality struck the Oil Division in 1949, when it posted a $640,000 loss. The following year it had a compensating profit of just about the same amount, but not until 1951 did the unit (now called the Vegetable Oil Division) really get back on track. Falk, the chemical products company, now a separate division, had 1951 profits of $1.1 million, and the Vegetable Oil Division registered $1.3 million.

An impetus for the division was the addition in 1950 of a new oilseed processing plant in Chicago to complement the construction at the same time of the large 6.5-million-bushel grain storage annex to the existing Cargill terminal. It was an ideal location for processing. Soybeans could be loaded on barge at Ottawa and Spring Valley, stored in the new elevator until needed and then processed by the efficient solvent process in the new plant.

The total cost of these two Chicago additions was large. The soybean plant came to over $2 million, and the new terminal space (the "annex") was about $1.8 million. Hugo Scheuermann, at Chase National Bank, agreed that the reasons for the plant "appear to be excellent" but added a caution: "I hope you can keep the cost within the figure mentioned." But there were cost overruns. Nevertheless, the operational value of these two projects was outstanding. Cargill's presence in Chicago was no longer minor—it owned the largest terminal, with a licensed capacity of 18 million bushels, and had a 700-ton soybean plant in an ideal location and with the most modern of processing equipment. The Grain Division was not as certain about the wisdom of crushing a bean inventory that could be held for carrying charges.[6]

E. Tradition in Seeds

Seeds had been sold under the Cargill name since 1907, when the forerunner of the Minneapolis Seed Company was founded. Over the years it had been a minor but dependable contributor to Cargill sales. Under the name "Crystal Brand," a whole set of field seed varieties had been sold: timothy, red clover, alsike, alfalfa, white blossom sweet clover, millets and others. In the reorganization of 1936, the Minneapolis Seed Company was phased out and a Seed Division begun, just at the time that the group began to sell lawn grass seed. At first, this new product was marketed locally to the various members of the Minneapolis grain exchange; later there were small regional sales.

In the early 1940s, Cargill entered the hybrid corn field, marketing under the Crystal Brand name from seeds originally developed by the Universities of Minnesota and Wisconsin. Soon the division was developing its own hybrids at its breeding plots at St. Peter, Minnesota; these were marketed under the trade name "Gold Seal." Just after World War II the hybrid side of the seed business was augmented by the purchase of the Nicollet Hybrid Seed Company of St. Peter, Minnesota, and a separate division was created for hybrids. Then, in July 1948, another acquisition added to Cargill's depth in hybrid corn production: the Ahrens Hybrid Seed Corn Company of Grinnell, Iowa, was purchased. Generally, it takes a number of years for hybrid seed corn projects to develop marketable strains, and the Hybrid Corn Department absorbed a series of losses during the late 1940s.

Just after World War II, the Company also sold farm supply goods of many kinds, including even "Cargill Tires," in its Farm Supply Department. This endeavor was not profitable and was closed in 1949.

In November 1950, the Seed Division announced an exciting new product—a new variety of treated lawn seed with its own scientific blending of chemicals to destroy the soil diseases, fungus and bacteria that cool, damp soil often bred. It was given the name "Miracle Green." Unfortunately, enthusiasm about the new seed carried the seed executives a bit too far in their claims. In one advertisement in the *Milwaukee Journal*, the ad writers said that the product was "treated to make up to twice as many seeds live and grow in damp, spring weather (compared to any untreated seed regardless of price)." The Bureau of Antideceptive Practices of the Federal Trade Commission saw the advertisement and wrote the Company, admonishing it about its hyperbole. Tom T. Hale, the head of the division, defended the efficacy of his seed but handled the subsequent advertising more sedately. John Jr. took Hale to task on another statement, when the latter claimed that Cargill was the "world's largest name in grain." The chastened Hale wrote back promising immediate deletion and that "all boasting will be limited to the merits of the product itself or services that can be rendered." It had never been John Jr.'s style to "boast" about the Company.[7]

The Cargill Foundation

Cargill had shown major growth in the five years after the end of World War II. Not only had those been profitable years, but the longtime policy of returning earnings back into the Company had been continued. The net worth of $16.6 million at the end of the 1944–1945 crop season had grown to almost $28 million by May 1950. There were more shareholders, too; several key nonfamily senior management had been allocated significant numbers of shares. The three family members, John Jr., Cargill MacMillan and Austen Cargill had been in management with the Company for many years. Their sons now had joined the business. As Austen Cargill was a generation ahead of the two MacMillans, his son James R. was a generation ahead of the four MacMillan sons (Cargill, Jr., John H. III, Whitney and W. Duncan); all five, however, had been born within a seven-year time span.

A decision was made to change the corporate structure by amending the Articles of Incorporation to institute a new category of shares, "special preferred stock." The board memorandum to the shareholders stated: "From the studies of many other corporations, we must recognize that changes in stock ownership and in management membership inevitably occurring with the passage of time may lead to dissension or to hasty, ill-advised corporate action." Albert Egermayer in a later memorandum elaborated on the issues in these other companies:

The roots of such problems apparently lay in the proliferation over a number of generations of descendants who (a) owned stock but (b) were not employed by the family-owned corporation and, therefore, received no compensation, and (c) to increase their incomes, voted their stock for Directors who would liberalize the corporation's dividend policy. All of this the gentlemen above-mentioned [John Jr., Cargill MacMillan and Austen Cargill] wished to avoid, along with possible intra-family discord. They preferred reinvestment of a major portion of the net profits of Cargill, Incorporated in assets which could be productive of more earnings.

The special preferred stock would be nonredeemable, and would have the power of veto on any sale of assets, on consolidations or mergers, on liquidation of the corporation and on any future amendments to the Certificate of Incorporation. Further, the special preferred stockholders would have the right to elect the largest minority of the directors of the corporation. All of this special preferred stock would be held by the existing Cargill Charitable Trust, and as soon as the mechanics could be taken care of, the shares of the Trust would be transferred to a new entity, a nonprofit "Cargill Foundation." The first set of trustees for the Foundation was to be the three family members, plus lawyer James Dorsey and relative Howard McMillan.

By these actions, the families had put certain veto powers in the hands of the Foundation trustees. The memorandum spelled this out:

The persons who from time to time are the preferred and common stockholders will continue to control the ordinary business activities of the company through the election of a majority of the directors. At the same time, the minority directors will be elected by action of the trustees of the Foundation, thus resulting in a permanence and continuity that could not otherwise be assured. . . . Veto power will reside in a group of men who it is believed, both originally and through their selection of successor trustees, will consist of persons well qualified to perpetuate the business policies and ideals of the present ownership and management.

Beyond these issues of shareholder control, the Cargill Foundation also was seen as a more independent and effective vehicle for channeling company gifts and contributions and would shield individual family members from direct monetary requests. The original Cargill Charitable Trust was essentially an internal tool for holding funds destined for employees. The new Foundation, with grants of monies from Cargill, Incorporated, each year, could become a true foundation for eleemosynary activities. Later there would be other unforeseen special roles to be played by the Foundation.[8]

1952—a Testing Year

Any Cargillite euphorically believing that the record year of 1951 would continue endlessly was disabused of this notion by the events of 1952. To begin with, although the Grain Division handled considerably more tonnage than it had in the previous year, up to 6.4 million from 5.8 million tons (tons rather than bushels were reported in the closing statements this one year), business had not been very profitable. The Feed Division had done almost as well as it had the previous year, making the largest divisional contribution for 1951–1952. On the other hand, the Vegetable Oil Division lost over $1 million, and the Falk Division alone lost $2.1 million. Even the usually modest losses of the Seed Division now ballooned to almost $580,000. In terms of overall results, the year was a bitter disappointment, profits down from the $5.9 million of the previous year to just $673,000. This figure was by far the lowest in the postwar period. If the Company's and John Jr.'s organizational hubris were both high at the end of the previous year, any arrogance about the Company's performance should now have been dissipated.

In truth, the cause of the low profits was more serious than just poor operational performance. The crop year 1951–1952 witnessed three traumatic Cargill brushes with governmental authorities, each bringing major repercussions for the Company. The first came in September 1951, when the federal government accused Cargill of violating the federal Seed Act by adulterating its alfalfa seed from Montana. Then, in March 1952, the federal government again brought Cargill into court, alleging that the Company had let some of the Commodity Credit Corporation corn in the Albany, New York, terminal and in the Norris City, Illinois, "tank" terminals go out of condition. The third case, certainly the most serious in terms of its public effects on the Company, involved a Commodity Exchange Authority allegation that Cargill had violated CEA regulations on limits for speculative positions in oats for future delivery. Here is what happened in these three stories.

Seed Adulteration

This case was a blow to top management in the Company. The seed operation was one of the oldest in the Company. The people of the division had always prided themselves on the quality of their seeds; an article in the *Cargill News* of January 1933 spoke of the "purity" of Crystal Brand and warned of the ill results from planting seeds of "unknown" provenance. Another article noted the dangers of importing seed "shipped from long distances [which] may carry disease of some kind foreign to the new locality." Yet in 1951 the Company was accused of adulterating high-grade Montana alfalfa seed with lower-grade Arizona alfalfa.

The facts were undisputed: four Cargill employees had indeed adulterated seed and sold it under false pretenses. The Company threw itself on the mercy of the Court, the judge accepting a plea of nolo contendere. Shortly before the hearings were to take place (in March 1953), Cargill's board made the decision to stop all of its field seed production and leave the business altogether (the hybrid corn group was a completely separate endeavor and would be continued). This decision was laid on the record, and Cargill's lawyer continued:

We have quit the field seed, the alfalfa and clover and the rest. In view of the loss of prestige that has certainly attended this, from our viewpoint, very unfortunate and unhappy matter . . . and in view of the fact that we took all steps and were successful in actually preventing any injury to farmers or dealers by getting back every pound of that seed, it's respectfully submitted that any fine here other than a nominal amount with its implications of criminal intent and moral turpitude will have such repercussions as to inflict enormous and unjust penalties on this corporation and its credit, its standing and its future operations.

He ended: "We know when this is over there is this black mark against Cargill which may extend to a considerable extent." District Court Judge Gunnar H. Nordbye agreed, noting that "I am satisfied that none of the officials of Cargill, that is the officers or directors, were aware of what was going on." He did criticize Cargill for lack of supervision of the lower-level management but ended by levying only a $500 fine for each of the 10 counts that were at issue.

It was a humiliating turn of events for the Company. In all of the Company's previous legal cases, serious as they were, the issues were differences of opinion about interpretation of laws, regulations and actions, such as those of the Chicago Board of Trade in the Corn Case and the Price Control Case of 1946. Cargill may have been found guilty in the Corn Case of attempting a corner, but in no sense of the word was this or the others an instance of outright flaunting or deliberately violating a law. The seed adulteration case *was*. Probably Cargill did not suffer major negative public relations from it, and it was only a minor part of the Company's business, yet the stigma of having been discovered allowing a criminal act was felt throughout the Company.

Ordinarily, there would have been high comic relief from another story that broke that fall of 1951—a vice raid on the Cargill Hotel in Des Moines, Iowa, a seedy old building that never had any connection with the Company. The proprietress had hidden the seven women involved in a secret room on the third floor, about 2 feet wide and 8 feet long. The officers discovered the seven after a search of about six hours. It was a juicy story, a natural for big headlines, and the *Des Moines Register* obliged with one that had some ambiguity:"$500,000 Tax Lien on Cargill" (the hotel, not the company). Company officials took some good-natured jibes from their friends, one of them commenting, "Your luck getting all this front page publicity."9

Continuing CCC Tensions: The Albany Corn Case

By 1952, with the Korean War subsiding (armistice negotiations had begun in October 1951 at Panmunjom), the United States economy softened. In agriculture one of the immediate effects was the increase of surpluses. Faced with the need to maintain parity at 90 percent for the six basic commodities (Congress had passed a three-year extension in 1949), the Commodity Credit Corporation (CCC) had to store vast amounts of grain, reportedly "totalling anywhere from $2,000,000,000 to as much as $4,000,000,000," said the *New York Times*. All sorts of storage was called into use, including such unconventional receptacles as gasoline storage tanks like Cargill's Mexia and Norris City operations.

This was an election year, and the Republicans had not claimed the presidency since Herbert Hoover's days. With the weaknesses in the economy, they sensed a real opportunity to turn the Democrats out. What was needed were some issues. Slippages in this huge grain storage effort provided a ready-made opportunity. By early 1952, several congressional committees were investigating what soon became dubbed the "grain storage fraud." Cheating by warehouse concerns operating on a shoestring was reported, and shady and illegal practices were laid before the public in the hearings. The Comptroller General of the United States reported on cases of what the *New York Times* called "the existing epidemic of what are euphemistically referred to as 'conversions' . . . the action of a warehouseman who, when called upon for commodities that he is being paid to hold for the Government, is unable to produce them, usually because he has lost them through speculation or through some other preventable misadventure." There were many such cases, and the problem offered a field day for investigators from both parties (Senator Allan J. Ellender, a Democrat from Louisiana, in the forefront, as chairman of the Senate Agriculture Committee).

Cargill, along with a number of other major grain-trading companies, was caught up in this web. It was shortly before this that the Company's wheat sales to the CCC in 1949 had been called into question, when Erv Kelm had testified before a congressional committee (the story discussed at the end of the preceding chapter). The publicity over the Wheat Case had barely died away when Cargill found itself defending two other controversial situations.

In two of the locations where Cargill had stored CCC corn in 1951, Albany and Norris City, Illinois, the grain was alleged to be "going out of condition." In early March 1952, the Company received a registered letter from the government that the CCC had suffered a "quantitative loss of 10,917.97 bushels as well as qualitative deficiencies resulting in a net loss of $377,916.32" when the grain at Albany was taken out by the CCC. The CCC held back $400,000 from other payments due Cargill, pending settlement of this claim.

Meanwhile, Senator Ellender focused his attention on Cargill's contract with the CCC at Norris City. He alleged that Cargill had collected some $37,000 for "work it had never done." In truth, the contract called for storage charges for holding some 5 million bushels of corn, and $37,000 for removing the grain after it had been stored for a year. When the CCC did not take the grain, Cargill charged the fee that the contract provided.

Weston Grimes was called before the committee and was quoted in a story in the *New York Times* the next day as saying, "I don't say it was a good contract for the Government but under the terms of the contract Cargill was entitled to both collections for loading out." Ellender's committee went on to another case, and the issue was dropped for the moment.

On the Albany matter, Cargill had only a few weeks to decide whether, using John Peterson's words, "to settle the matter, or else." Peterson's instinct at that time was "to see whether the thing can't be nicely cleaned up without too much damage to anybody and without pursuing the matter in the law courts." But the facts themselves spoke loudly for Cargill's not making any such compromise, for it was clear (and never disputed by the government at any later point) that the CCC had been notified by Cargill more than once that the grain was going out of condition; yet it still chose not to take its corn out of the elevator. Cargill MacMillan described the situation to his older son:

Our Chgo. office acted as their own lawyers . . . the original contract they made . . . was an impossible contract in that . . . it was stipulated that the corn should be "identity preserved." The government was, of course, just as much to blame as we for getting tangled up in an I.P. contract when the intent was otherwise. The next colossal boner took place in our New York office. The government surrendered to us their warehouse receipts, which, in grain trade practices, was tantamount to a loading out notice. I suppose our office took it for granted that the corn was going to be moved right out. Anyway they gave the New York office of the C.C.C. a guarantee that the corn would load out as 2 Yellow Corn. They forgot to put any time limit on the guarantee. The government loaded out a few cargoes and then stopped. The corn sat in the elevator for months and months and then began to get out of condition. We informed the gov't. of the state of affairs, but they did nothing. Finally we got Washington to take a hand and eventually the corn was shipped, but by this time hundreds of thousands of bushels graded sample grade and, of course, the Gov't. took an awful licking.

The Company now put out a memorandum to all of its branch offices that began: "Recently we have seen instances where dealings with Commodity Credit Corporation have been unsatisfactory for various reasons unnecessary to enumerate here." The memorandum then announced the appointment of Maitland D. ("Hap") Wyard as coordinator for all relations with the CCC. As John Peterson put it to Kelm the next day, "Thou shalt not be your own lawyer, especially when we have about five of such distinguished members of the Bar under the roof."

As the newspapers were full of the congressional investigation by this time, including Cargill's testimony, the Company decided to discuss the negative publicity with all of its employees. The key parts of the statement read as follows: "In the first place and most important of all, Cargill officials know of nothing in the cases cited for which the Company needs to apologize or feel ashamed. Quite the contrary. . . . Had the Commodity

Credit Corporation not availed itself of Cargill's facilities and services at the time the publicized contracts were entered into, it would have cost the Government more than it did." The memorandum ended with a gratuitous addendum: "Add to that the fact that this is an election year and that investigations, innuendos and unsubstantiated charges seem to be the order of the day, and you have the picture as the management sees it."

By this time, as Cargill MacMillan put it, so much "fear has been instilled into these various government agencies" that no private mediation of the difficulties seemed possible. The government investigators had turned the matter over to the Solicitor General's office, and the Albany personnel had been subpoenaed by the grand jury. On December 17, formal indictments were handed down against Marcus Marshall (the superintendent), his chief grain assistant and another Cargill employee. Cargill was appalled to find these not just civil but criminal charges. Already at a number of other companies there had been criminal cases leading to several convictions and jail sentences.

There were many months of stress before the case went to trial in November 1954. It was to be tried before a jury. When the facts were laid before the jury, on November 9, a "not guilty" verdict was returned for both the Company and for the Albany employees concerned. Cargill had been exonerated of any alleged misdeeds in the case.

Cargill now sued for the money the CCC held back through all of these months, claiming damages of some $552,000, a portion of which represented unpaid storage charges at Norris City. The CCC, still believing it was right, filed a countersuit. The Company's case was to be tried first, before United States District Judge Stephen W. Brennan. When Brennan finally rendered his decision, on September 15, 1958, Cargill won every one of its claims. The judge held that "it was not the absence of due care which caused the loss at Albany but rather the failure of Commodity to heed the notice given by Cargill that the corn was in danger of going out of condition." As to Norris City, both parties had recognized that the use of the gasoline tanks "was more or less of an experiment." The contract had noted that there was no modern equipment for turning, drying and conditioning; "day to day care [was] exercised by Cargill in the attempted maintenance of the corn stored in the tanks." Brennan awarded the full amount of damages asked by Cargill. The government's countersuit was now moot, and it decided not to test Cargill's winning decision in a higher court.

There were signal misjudgments by both parties in these two cases—the Norris City tanks and the Albany big bin were not ideal for storage of corn over long periods. Albany was at the end of the grain pipeline, at a location with a decreasing throughput of grain; the big bin was more effective at the beginning of the "continuous belt," such as at Omaha. Yet Company officials received the eventual satisfaction of knowing that they had done no wrong at either terminal.[10]

The Oats Case

Trading oats had long been a Cargill strength. The Company had become a major participant, if not the dominant marketing force, in oats. This was not a major business in comparison to the other feed grain (corn) and certainly of much less importance than the wheats. Just like flax in the year 1946, however, oats assumed a prominent position in the Grain Division in the period 1951–1953. In 1950, the Company traded some 31 million bushels of oats, which was roughly 16 percent of Cargill's total grain trades. By 1952, the oats traded had climbed to 66.6 million bushels, more than a quarter of all of the grain traded by the Company; and in 1953, the oats total of 86 million bushels actually exceeded the total of corn traded—a surprising 32 percent of all Cargill grain. Commensurately, the profitability of trading oats had increased impressively. The trading profit in 1950 had been just $880,000; for both 1952 and 1953 the figure was well over $3 million each year. What were the reasons for this change? The complicated method of trading in this period will give some clues. This particularly involved the interaction between Canadian oats and American oats.

Cargill's role in oats trading first became public knowledge in 1951, when Senator William F. Jenner, Republican of Indiana, protested that Cargill had imported Canadian oats to force down domestic prices. This was during the highly politicized grain situation of the 1952 presidential campaign, and it took little time for the Commodity Exchange Authority to begin an investigation of Jenner's allegations.

Cargill MacMillan described the Company's oats trading in a letter to his older son in early November 1952: "[Canada in 1951] had an embarrassingly large crop . . . so large that much grain couldn't be harvested before winter set in and had to remain in the fields all winter." Inasmuch as the United States crop was not large, the Company began buying Winnipeg oats and selling Chicago oats futures. He then outlined their innovative but controversial "rolling" purchase program:

First we would buy Wpg. and sell Chgo until we had done nearly three million bushels (the limit set by the C.E.A. regulations for spreading transactions of this nature) . . . then we would liquidate our Wpg. futures position by entering into a cash purchase with Cargill Grain Co., Ltd. This would leave Limited long the Wpg. futures and a cash sale to Incorporated against them, and it left Incorporated long cash purchases from Limited and short Chicago futures. . . . This technique has turned out to be a mistake. What we should have done was to enter into cash purchases with the Canadian Wheat Board and other Canadian grain companies, which we could have easily done only we saw no sense in paying a toll to outsiders when, by using Limited, we could keep it in the family.

The CEA now contended that Cargill controlled its Canadian subsidiary and that the purchases from Limited were not bona fide, that in reality they were spreads in violation of the law. It was not just a limits violation, either, said the agency. The Cargill futures position on the Chicago exchange began to build larger and larger, reaching 31 million bushels in late October 1951 (with cash oats purchases rising rapidly in Winnipeg, too). Cargill MacMillan continued: "The C.E.A. Investigating Section, stirred up I think, by political forces who are trying to make hay with their agricultural constituents, have recommended . . . that we be cited . . . not only [for] spreading, but also that we are guilty of manipulation on perhaps two grounds: One, that when we entered into these Canadian oat transactions, there was no visible profit and that therefore we must have been manipulatively minded and two, that we were trying to force carrying charges in Chicago by strong arm or manipulative methods."

The manipulation charge did not seem to trouble John Jr. and his brother, but the spreading charge did. Yet they felt that there was nothing in the pattern of their operations that would indicate a spreading pattern. The way they had covered their exchange, chartered their boats and reserved their biggest bin in Chicago all seemed to point to a plan of buying actual oats in Canada, importing them into the United States and selling them there to the best possible advantage. "The course that we are presently trying to pursue," wrote Cargill MacMillan, "is to talk the C.E.A. into the state of mind that they haven't a Chinaman's chance in pinning manipulation on us; so why not forget the whole thing, and we in turn, will promise that we will not make further cash purchases from Limited. We will simply buy from other Canadian firms. I don't know whether or not this sort of a proposal will get anywhere. I rather doubt it." Still, "in these cases we never feel too sure of what may turn up. You will remember how damaging those flippant wires were in the September 1937 corn case . . . every time we get into one of these big importations we are in for a peck of trouble. There was the Polish rye, the Argentine corn, and now the Canadian oats."

The issue had stayed alive in Congress, too. In May 1953, Senator Milton R. Young, Republican of North Dakota (the Dakotas and Minnesota were large producers of oats), called CEA officials before a Senate Appropriations Subcommittee to report on their actions in relation to Cargill. The politics of the situation became more evident at these hearings. Young stated that Cargill "broke the market" in oats and that Cargill had cost the government money by pushing prices 10 cents to 15 cents a bushel below federal price-support levels. Also prominently discussed was the fact that prices received by farmers had dropped from about 95 cents in December 1951 to just over 78 cents in June 1952.

It took just a month for the CEA to finish its investigations and issue a

complaint against Cargill; hearings were set for the third week in August
1953. In the complaint, the CEA elaborated the details of the trading between Cargill Limited and Cargill Incorporated, noting in the process the
huge total position that Cargill had taken in oats. The complaint alleged
that the various transactions "caused prices of cash oats and oats futures
in the United States to be lower than they would have been otherwise, and
brought about unwarranted changes in the spread or differential between
their prices of different futures in the United States, and between prices in
the United States and prices in Canada." Because of this, the CEA concluded, both the Company and Kelm as an individual had "attempted to
manipulate and did in fact manipulate the price."

Further, they felt that Cargill had misused the limits rule: "In its daily
reports, Cargill, Incorporated classified almost all of its net short positions
in oats futures on the Chicago Board of Trade as hedging, whereas in truth
and in fact, during most of this period a substantial part of such positions
consisted of spreading in the same grain between markets and was speculative in nature." This constituted false reporting, according to CEA rules.

The charges seemed so completely documented and the implications so
ominous that it was decided to make a lengthy statement on the matter to
the entire Cargill organization. It was printed in the June 1953 *Cargill News*
on special gray paper and signed by Austen Cargill, who since August 1950
had been chairman of the board of directors. It read in part as follows:

> . . . at no time in the 87 years of Cargill's history has there been any just reason to
> question the company's honesty and integrity. There is none now. I can tell you
> without reservation that no difficulties which we now face are the result of any
> management policies encouraging or condoning unlawful or unscrupulous ac-
> tions. Our policy is just the opposite.
>
> I want you to know that Cargill has not willfully violated any laws or contracts.
> It would be ridiculous to say that we have made no mistakes in our long business
> lifetime. We have made many. More will probably be made in spite of all precau-
> tions and controls. That by no means indicates, however, that by intention or
> design we either flout the law or short-change the customer.
>
> We are a large company and an aggressive one. We live in a goldfish bowl. We
> are a natural target for those who are suspicious of largeness and for those who find
> in progressive companies a threat to their personal interests . . . there is always a
> temptation to make political hay by loudly attacking such businesses. Remember
> that these unproven attacks reach the front pages while later refutation usually is
> given little or no prominence.
>
> We intend to continue our growth and do so by being aggressive. Only in that
> way are we sure that we can protect our job and yours. Rest assured, however, that
> in the process we will take no steps which will impair, let alone destroy, our good
> name. Without it Cargill could not have lived since 1865 as a successful and re-
> spected citizen of the business community.

In preparing for the CEA proceedings, John Jr. wrote a fact-filled analytical memorandum, detailing the Cargill sales over the time period con-

cerning the CEA. It emphasized the grain trade aspects of the case, that the grain was being imported for real needs, that there were customers buying Cargill's grain, both in Chicago and in Buffalo—"all went into consumption through various forms of merchandising." The memorandum noted that speculators were also trading at the same time and that Cargill took advantage of opportunities to buy back grain for less than the speculators had originally paid. A diagram of the sales showed all of this precisely. The memorandum ended: "This foresight made super-service possible to customers and resulted in the building up of much valuable good will." The memorandum made no mention, however, of the fact that Cargill had been using its own Canadian subsidiary as one side of the trades.

Julius Hendel also prepared an extensive paper on the Oats Case. Its title, "A Short Story of the Grain Market," belied its 54 pages. His conclusion was that Cargill had been "ahead of competition in analyzing the trend" and that the Company's large position was not taken with "manipulative intent" but because "Cargill, Incorporated is progressive."

The Canadians felt threatened by this case, for it seemed to pit Canadian farmers against American farmers. In November 1953, the Winnipeg Grain Exchange published a detailed booklet on Canadian–American grain imports. American importation of rye and wheat was discussed, although Cargill was not mentioned. The pamphlet concluded that not only would it be "unfortunate to create additional artificial barriers to the exchange of services, goods and commodities," but in the narrower sense the importation of Canadian grain was "largely beneficial to the U.S.A. and . . . not detrimental to the interests of producers . . . in the U.S.A."

Senator Jenner was not convinced. He was quoted in the *Wall Street Journal* in early November 1953 as believing that Congress was then ready to take action to "halt record-breaking imports of Canadian oats, barley and rye." Farmers were "losing millions of dollars on the grains which they sell on the open market." Senator Paul Douglas added his view, alleging that Cargill alone had cost American farmers $600,000,000. Further, the government was buying large supplies to maintain the price support program. Jenner concluded that prices were "manipulated" and that this "constitutes market manipulation of the worst type." He said he was prepared to introduce a bill that would make it unlawful to deliver not only Canadian oats but any foreign wheat, corn, cotton, rye, barley, flaxseed, soybeans, grain sorghums, cottonseed oil or soybean oil in fulfillment of any futures contract in the United States. Jenner was very protectionist across a wide range of agricultural products.[11]

In the face of such heavy political attack, the conclusion to the Cargill case seemed preordained. John Jr. asked for a personal meeting with Secretary of Agriculture Ezra Taft Benson, a meeting set up for him by Peavey

Grain executive Peavey Heffelfinger, who at that time also was chairman of the Republican National Finance Committee. The 45-minute meeting with Benson was used mostly for pleasantries; this seemed not the place for partisan pleading. Benson wrote Heffelfinger afterward: "I have just had a most profitable and revealing conversation with John H. MacMillan, Jr."

By the end of the year, it became evident that the Attorney General of the United States was considering recommending a criminal indictment of both Kelm as an individual and Cargill as a company. In late February 1954, the United States District Court in Minnesota instituted formal proceedings that would bar trading between Cargill and its Canadian subsidiary and also would enjoin both of the defendants from exercising trading privileges in oats futures on contract markets for a time period that would be set by the federal judge. No criminal charges were contained in the complaint.[12]

John Peterson felt he might be able to resolve the case privately and went to Washington to see the CEA. Cargill MacMillan wrote his brother: "One good thing may come out of it . . . Pete is getting a first class education in what it means to be immeshed in Bureaucracy . . . he is fast learning 'Put not faith in Princes.' " The Company's statements to the public contained some rationalization, but it was plain that Cargill executives, in talking with each other, truly believed their case to be strong—and right. In this same letter, Cargill MacMillan continued: "The Government, though willing to concede (off the record) that they did not think they could make the charge of manipulation stick, did not feel that they could drop the charge because of fear of Congressional inquiry." If a Cargill capitulation seemed wise, Cargill MacMillan still felt "we are not getting justice and it makes me so mad I want to fight; on the other hand, this Oats Case has our business absolutely tied up in knots." In this same letter, he mentioned the difficulties in their overall hedging policy caused by the case. The Cargill lawyers were being extremely cautious and were urging the Company never to "contemplate buying futures of the same month that we have delivered in."

Peterson, unsuccessful in Washington, now joined the side of caution, and John Jr. wrote, in a joint letter to Austen Cargill and Cargill Mac-Millan in early March: "We . . . have some trouble with John Peterson's interfering with the plans of the Grain Division boys for March deliveries. Dorsey [James Dorsey, the Company's outside counsel] thought Pete was needlessly alarmed about it. In any event, the effect was that Pete would not let the boys deliver and the cost was very considerable to us."

Partly because of the case itself and partly because of this internal cautionary pressure, John Jr. decided to again review the Company's basic concepts in regard to hedging. In an internal memorandum, he reiterated that Cargill "is not willing to carry overall or spread positions merely for the sake of a possible speculative profit. Any spreads entered into must be of a nature which will directly facilitate business." In this same memorandum, he also stated that, because of the CEA restrictions, all of Cargill's subsidiaries had to be considered as one total position, "so to eliminate any possibility of exceeding legal limits."

Austen Cargill, for one, was not in favor of a negotiated settlement. He wrote Cargill MacMillan: "I was in hopes we could use the Oats Case as a means of restoring the damage which has occurred to our integrity these past years, for I firmly believed we were either innocent of manipulation or it was time we learned where we stood on the matter. A settlement of the case won't do that . . . being denied trading privileges . . . won't help our integrity very much." Austen attributed the pressure for settlement to the lawyers, but ended, "If there are no definite facts that our legal position is weak, I believe our moral position is strong enough to go through with the case, even though it's going to cost some real money and serious intangible losses."

John Jr. apparently believed Cargill would lose the fight, however, and finally made the wrenching decision to accept the findings of the court about Cargill's past trading in oats—there seemed no doubt about the facts—and to abide by all of the remedies asked by the federal lawyers. The disruption to the organization weighed heavily in this decision. John Jr. wrote his brother: "This litigation has been the very devil, with the real cost the loss of time of our executives. It has put an impossible burden on you and of course all progress has stopped."[13]

On May 3, 1954, Cargill agreed to a stipulation from George E. Mac-Kinnon, the United States Attorney for Minnesota to accept the court's final judgment without a trial, with this final judgment not to be considered as admission that the defendants had violated any law. On the same day, the CEA issued a decision and an order barring Kelm and the Company from trading in oats futures on any contract market for the remaining seven months of the year 1954. The complaint against Kelm as an individual was dismissed. The consent decree also specified that, for the purposes of any Cargill futures transactions, the grain stocks of all subsidiaries would be treated as though they were the stocks of Cargill, Incorporated. Shortly afterward, an antitrust suit brought against Cargill by two CBOT traders, alleging "losses of income and profits" caused by Cargill's oats imports, was dismissed.

The CEA had been a reluctant antagonist. John Jr. wrote his brother after the settlement was reached that both the Justice Department and the CEA "have said that we could write the language of the stipulation ourselves and make our denials of guilt as vigorous and all-embracing as we desired. All they insisted upon was that they have an order to which we agree which they can show to those people who are putting pressure on them—something which makes it look very much as though they had been very tough with us. . . . It is very plain that neither Justice nor the C.E.A. really believe we have done anything wrong, but it is equally plain that they have been under very heavy pressure from those rascally senators."

The day after the CEA order, the Company put out a special announcement to its employees, which comprised mostly a long and rather legalistic letter from James Dorsey to John Jr. There was a two-sentence conclusion: "The fore-going summarizes the technical aspects of the case. All employees are authorized in their conversations with others to state that the Company is not convicted of any wrong-doing, and to repeat and emphasize our denial of any such wrong-doing."

John Jr. was unchastened. He wrote a friend three days later: "The government knew they had no case, but they had had so much publicity about the thing that again they had to have some outcome that would look as though they had won a great victory. We therefore agreed voluntarily not to trade in oats futures for the balance of this year. In view of the short crop coming up, this means very little to us." When the *Minneapolis Star* wrote a front-page story with a headline "City Firm Barred from Trading in Oats This Year," John Jr. wrote a long, huffy letter to the editor pointing out that it was only oats *futures* that Cargill had been barred from and that it still was free to trade cash oats. The editor responded with a long *mea culpa*, effusively apologizing for "this regrettable matter." The fact remained, of course, that Cargill *had* backed down and accepted a disciplinary penalty by the government.[14]

John Peterson penned a more diplomatic letter at this same time to "our banking friends." It was a long letter, emphasizing the political nature of the charges and the preoccupation and expense of fighting the case. "The management of the principal contract market and the Commodity Exchange representative in said market evidently did not see any manipulation of oats prices . . . and we think their eyesight was good." He continued: "People who know us know that Cargill is not a speculator as the term is understood in the trade . . . that we are not manipulators."

Once again, Cargill made the pages of *Time* magazine. In its May 17, 1954, issue, under the title "Wild Oats," the editors covered the specifics of the Oats Case, noted the consent decree barring the Company from trading oats futures and referred again not only to the 1937 Corn Case but also to the fact that the Company was "indicted for converting to its own and its customers' use 80,000 bushels of corn stored for the Commodity Credit Corporation." This was the Albany CCC storage case, which had not at that time yet been settled in Cargill's favor. The *Time* piece was negative throughout; it certainly hurt the Company's public image.

Two of its well-respected neighbor firms in Minneapolis also had serious legal problems with the federal government at this same time. In October 1954, Archer-Daniels-Midland Company had entered a plea of guilty to a number of counts brought by the CCC relating to statements to the agency under the International Wheat Agreement concerning export subsidies. Pillsbury Mills, Incorporated, was indicted the next month on a similar case involving the agreement.

The Cargill Oats Case was not to be readily forgotten. Ten years later, in 1965, *Fortune* magazine referred to it at length as an example of "Cargill's aggressiveness as a speculator" (in a long and otherwise complimentary article on the Company with the interesting title "The Two-Billion-Dollar Company That Lives by the Cent."[15]

John Jr. had mellowed some about the case by 1955, when, to the surprise of many people, he accepted the assignment mentioned in chapter 12, to make an address before a Chicago Board of Trade symposium. He prepared a hard-hitting speech, full of factual material about grain trading. Once more, he took strong exception to the way the CBOT viewed performance responsibilities for futures contracts but couched this in a more conciliatory and friendly way. He reserved most of his venom for the government, reciting briefly the price control problem in 1946 and then giving a long discourse on what he called a "case history" of the Oats Case. He appealed to the CBOT members' pocketbooks by showing in a series of charts that oats futures trading had declined measurably since Cargill had been barred from futures trading. "Cargill's oat merchants," he stated, "had learned how to offset cash purchases by cash sales, which resulted in a great reduction in the cost of hedging." He built a picture right before the attendees' eyes of futures-trading commissions disappearing into thin air. The speech was a great success; the parallel to Daniel having the courage to enter the lions' den was not lost on most people.[16]

With no ability to trade in oats futures, the question of how Cargill was to hedge cash oats was not easy to solve. Julius Hendel favored not hedging the oats inventory at all when cash oats were bought—in effect, taking a position on one side of the market, an outright speculation. Bob Diercks, who had just returned to Minneapolis from St. Louis as merchandising manager for the Grain Division, suggested corn, inasmuch as oats and corn were feed grains and there was some relative pricing ratio between the two. John Jr. felt strongly that selling soybean futures against the cash oats was the best choice. When Hendel suggested they compromise on the corn suggestion of Diercks, John Jr., exercised, insisted on the soybean choice.

As it turned out, the Hendel choice would have been best. Corn went up a small amount, but this also would have given some protection. John Jr.'s soybean choice, the one actually made, was not successful, for soybean prices had gone in the wrong direction. At one point, the oats account was down some $2 million. Finally, the prices turned, and the account came back almost to even. The Company was able to get out of its position with only some loss but it was a nerve-wracking experience. It must have been somewhat embarrassing to Hendel when he turned out to have been right and John Jr. wrong, for John Jr. was known not to enjoy being flatly shown as incorrect.

One effect of the case was to raise Diercks to a higher role in the Grain Division. Erv Kelm had been temporarily assigned to John Peterson as a tactical measure to get him away from the case. He was to spend the time familiarizing himself with Nutrena and the Oil Division. John Jr. wrote Austen Cargill and Cargill MacMillan: "I regard this as constructive no matter how you look at it . . . it will give us one more man from whom to draw in case we need someone familiar with all phases of the business. . . . I am satisfied now that we have a completely competent understudy should Kelm have to be used for other purposes."[17]

This was the denouement of the Oats Case, one of Cargill's most painful litigations. Now we return to the beginning year of the Oats Case, 1952, for another important event.

The Dwayne Andreas "Resignation"

In March 1952, at the height of the development of the three legal cases just described, Dwayne Andreas received an invitation to go to a trade conference in Moscow, which was to be held on April 10, 1952. He would not be a formal delegate but would accompany a French group that included members of the Goldschmidt firm, Cargill's agents in France. This was a tempting prospect, for the Oil Division guessed that there was a substantial vegetable oil marketing possibility in the Soviet Union.

Telling no one, Andreas went to Washington, where (with the help of political contacts) he was able to get a visa, a not inconsiderable step at the height of the cold war. It was made clear to him there, however, that he was not to assume a public profile in making the trip—a private overture on trade was not governmental policy at this time.

Returning to Cargill, he told Julius Hendel that he was leaving in a few days, that he had the Goldschmidt connection, which would be ideal for Cargill if anything came of it, and that he had to stay "out of sight" during the time he was gone. John Jr. was on vacation and could not be reached. Hendel worried a great deal about the Andreas decision, feeling he himself might be blamed for allowing it. Unfortunately for Andreas, Hendel told John Peterson. Peterson hit the roof, stating as he had often in the past, "The banks will cut off our credit" (this may not have been an idle concern this time—the Joseph McCarthy/Patrick McCarran legacy was still strong, and being "soft on communism" was just about the worst of epithets).

Andreas promised that he would visit David Rockefeller at the Chase National to explain as soon as he got back.

The next day, Hendel begged Andreas not to go and ended by saying, "I am *ordering* you not to go." Andreas responded, "Now, Julius, you know you don't mean that." Later that day, Andreas had a note on his desk to call John Peterson but ignored it and left for the trip.

The Soviet visit was an eye-opening experience for Andreas, and he brought back vast amounts of information useful to Cargill about the country and the specifics of trading prospects. John Jr. was back in the office now and called in Andreas. John Jr. reported that John Peterson worried that the banks would take a poor view of the visit and that, further, the fact that Andreas left without approval of top management was "insubordination." After saying this, John Jr. admitted that he was being urged by Peterson and Terry Morrison to take action; it did not seem to be John Jr.'s decision (Andreas remembered): John Jr. told Andreas, in effect, "Sometimes these things blow over—let's sit tight for a week."

Unfortunately, hints of the disagreement had seeped out to other members of top management. Andreas talked again with John Jr.; earlier he had offered to resign if John Jr. felt it best, and now John Jr. asked that Andreas do so. "I *have* to accept your resignation," Andreas remembered John Jr. saying—it seemed clear to Andreas that John Jr. was a reluctant partner to Peterson and Morrison on the matter. Nevertheless, Andreas stepped down as head of the Oil Division and left the Company at this point. His common stock in Cargill was redeemed, at a substantial profit to him, according to a formula established earlier. He also terminated his ownership in the family transportation companies of which he had been a common stockholder with other top management people.

It is impossible to judge objectively the impact of the loss of Andreas to Cargill. He went on to an outstanding career, first with his own family company in the vegetable oil business, then as an executive with the company that bought it, the Grain Terminal Association (later called the Farmers Union Grain Terminal Association), and finally as majority owner and chief executive officer of Archer-Daniels-Midland Company. It is not possible to know whether Andreas would have attained this outstanding success had he stayed at Cargill. John Jr.'s comment to Andreas at the time that he joined Cargill that he "thought like an owner" seemed a perceptive statement. The Andreas personality had not been truly congruent with the other executives. His élan seemed particularly to antagonize John Peterson. The year 1952 had not been a good one for the Oil Division, in part because of long delays after fires in San Francisco and Cedar Rapids and also some trading in soybean oil that backfired. John Peterson wrote a private letter to John Jr. about these trades, putting his feelings in a deliberately negative way: "Quite frankly, I am shocked—deeply shocked—by the decisions that were made appertaining to the operations. . . . Apparently these poor decisions were too many, too often, too costly. I never would have believed they could have happened under Cargill's roof."

John Jr.'s subsequent report to the shareholders was more moderate, but he too commented: "Hindsight shows such early sales to have been a mistake. . . . Doubtless, too, in the daily operations a great many mistakes were made." The bad year for the Company had seemed to heighten the rhetoric considerably, and this may have contributed to the irretrievable step taken in regard to Andreas.[18]

Tightening the Organization

Even before the incident of the Andreas "insubordination," Cargill MacMillan had written Austen Cargill: "Our bad record this year is going to be a Godsend. It is going to enable us to reinstate discipline before it is too late." John Jr. used the same theme in a blunt letter to all division heads in June 1952. He asked for "some fresh, constructive thinking . . . with respect to income and expense in your division" and added, "the past 8 to 10 years have led many of us to lose sight of the hard-nosed principles of sound business judgment."

The replacement for Andreas as acting head of the Oil Division was M. D. "Pete" McVay; he was a tough-minded, no-nonsense manager who fitted well John Jr.'s desire for "hard-nosed business judgment." Under McVay the Oil Division became known for its dedicated group of senior managers, men such as Harvey Marxhausen and John Mogush. There had been continuing tension between the Oil Division and the Grain Division, particularly over soybean purchasing—when and how much. Just a few months earlier, in November 1951, John Jr. wrote John Peterson that these two divisions were again in confrontation. The Oil Division wanted to buy beans; "however, anything they do buy is at the expense of the Grain Division turnover volume, so Julius is faced with quite a problem." Shortly after McVay took over the division, he had a long bargaining session with Kelm, and out of this came a written agreement about purchasing policy and how to handle the interdivision brokerage charges. There still remained a problem about how much allocation of space in the Chicago terminal to give the Oil Division—McVay wanted 2 million bushels; Kelm wanted to hold it to 1 million bushels. The executive committee was forced to adjudicate the situation, and McVay won.

Fortunately, the crop year 1952–1953 was excellent for the Company. The overall profits were over $4.4 million, with the Grain Division contributing almost $2.4 million; Feed, $1.4 million; and the Oil Division, almost $970,000 (this included the Falk Division, which now had been folded into the Oil Division).

In the midst of all of the legal problems, the shortfalls in profitability and the organizational infighting, E. J. Grimes died, on September 16, 1952. He had retired from active work in the Company in 1950 but had remained on the Cargill board of directors, although not particularly active. His death marked the end of an era, for he was the oldest senior management person remaining from the generation of John Sr. Born in La Crosse, Grimes had begun working for the Company at 19 years of age in 1904, just a few months after John Sr. had come to the Cargill Elevator Company. A director of the Company since 1926, he had been a major force in the Company for many years. His assignments were truly "myriad" (so said *Cargill News*), with a wide range of responsibilities in the Company and major assignments in the industry. He had been president of the Minneapolis Grain Exchange, the Minneapolis Traffic Club and the Minneapolis Chamber of Commerce and had been involved widely in national industrial and political work. During World War II his work nationally in developing priority systems for railroad freight was acclaimed. Terry Morrison stepped into the empty position on the board, and John Peterson, board member since 1936, became vice chairman.

In August 1953, a major retirement took place when Austen Cargill chose to step back from active involvement in the business. Austen, too, was of John Sr.'s generation (although not of his age). He had come to the Company in 1909 and at one time or another had taken major responsibility for a great many functions in the business. He, more than Grimes, who in 1909 was just a secretary, carried memories of his father and the 1909 struggles to redeem the W. W. Cargill estate's debts. Austen also carried the remembrance of the 1925 revolt. His particular interests were in the country elevator system and in transportation. But his influence in the Company extended far beyond individual operations, for he had been a moderating force on John Jr. through many years. Fortunately for the Company, he decided to continue his active involvement on the board of directors, although relinquishing its chairmanship (John Peterson assumed this position, John Jr., of course, continuing as president and chief executive officer).

The country elevator system had continued to flourish and contribute to operations, almost unnoticed. By May 1952, the number of country elevators was reduced to 49, at just 36 locations, from the 100 plus of the 1930s (and more before that). Yet the division was doing more business than it ever had. There were several reasons for its continuing efficiency. Trucking had wrought a revolutionary change for the farmer, who could take his grain many dozens (or even hundreds) of miles to market it. Over the years the division had consolidated its operations into many strong regional subterminals. In the year 1952, two substantial new country elevators had been purchased, one at Grandin, North Dakota, and the other at Milbank, South Dakota; and surveys were underway at this time for more of these larger houses. In October 1951, Erv Kelm had developed a new regional organization for the division, with regional managers for the Northwest, Central states, Southwest, South, and West Coast. A set of branch offices in each of these regions allowed a more effective devolution of responsibility, in keeping with the general pattern of decentralization taking place in the Company at this time.[19]

Rededicating the Company: John Jr.'s Stillwater Speech

The demoralizing year of 1952 had jolted Cargill's top management. Even the self-confident ebullience and unbounded optimism of John Jr. seemed shaken. Organizational moves had been taken to recapture that "discipline" that Cargill MacMillan had spoken of, that "hard-nosed" attitude that John Jr. had recommended to the division heads. Yet these steps, important as they were, did not get at the heart of the matter: the recapturing of the actual Cargill management philosophy itself.

John Jr. now took an occasion to attempt just this. In March 1953, he was asked to address one of the Company's Stillwater management conferences. Here he made a long speech that was subsequently published. It was blunt, frank and self-critical about the Company and its management in a manner seldom heard from John Jr. in the past. Now there was no bombast and little of the self-justification that had marked his writings during the course of those previous years. The period from World War II to 1952 "got away from us," he began; "perhaps we were biting off more than we could chew." He added, surprisingly, "In retrospect, I think we were. At any rate, our discipline within the organization was non-existent." These cumulated to bring the 1952 problems that "all hit us in one year. . . . We haven't dug out yet, and the consequences of them were so serious that I shudder to think of them."

Blame was spread out "in all divisions," although less in the Feed Division. However, "the Grain Division and the Oil Division were terrible." He then recited chapter and verse, first mentioning a wide range of laxness, poor reporting, and so on and then devoting himself to the legal cases at hand. The Albany Corn Case, with its many criminal indictments, was still not over. "Probably all but one or two of them have no merit whatever," John Jr. continued, "but even the fact that one or two could have any merit is an appalling situation. There was no intent to defraud. Great Scott! We are not out to defraud anyone. That's the last thing in the world we are thinking of." However, "our negligence . . . has exposed us to these charges. And there's no use kidding ourselves."

John Jr. spent several minutes discussing the Seed Adulteration Case.

While it was due to several people shading the facts and rationalizing illegal acts by calling them "trade practice," it was management's responsibility (as the judge pointed out in the case) to be alert about this—"He felt that Cargill should be fined, not because of the lack of integrity of people at the top, but because of their negligence in placing in positions of importance men of such low character. And I agree with him absolutely. I think he was just as right as right could be." (The Oats Case was not far enough along in the courts at this date to feature in John Jr.'s speech.)

The bulk of the speech was devoted to more basic questions of ethics and values. Cargill always had hired people of ability who wanted to work. "But that's not enough," John Jr. continued; "we've got to watch out for these character points." There were specific ways to identify a man's character. First, Cargill watched expense accounts closely—"how scrupulously honest are they?" Critically important was the matter of self-discipline. Cargill had had many extraordinarily brilliant people who should have gone places, but "weaknesses turned up—alcohol, women, finances, or perhaps they were just too fat" (John Jr.'s single-minded allegiance to the rice diet had made him a zealot about fat). John Jr. would not tolerate dishonesty—it was subject to immediate dismissal—and he had just let go one of the Company's top administrative executives for being inebriated on the job.

There were other key character defects: a man who "won't admit he has made a mistake," the lack of loyalty and "always thinking of himself" (here he specifically alluded to defectors who played competitor salary offers against Cargill's). The argument that "my competitor's doing these things and we have to meet competition" was pure rationalization, and Cargill must have men who are "willing to make important nearby sacrifices for the sake of a principle."

John Jr. then returned to a theme he had stressed earlier, the importance of temperament and "manners." He made clear that he was not speaking of the "superficial aspects of manners—ability to handle a knife and fork" but those qualities that allowed a person to get along with his fellow man. One had to have much human contact to develop this, he continued, so that one found the poorest manners on the farm "because, after all, the human contacts are fewest." He then generalized on this point, that the farther east one goes in the country, the more manners improved. However, "as we go East, the willingness to work also decreases, so these two important qualities meet in about the right proportions here in Minneapolis." John Jr. stressed again the quality of self-control, "that you conceal your emotions." Grain trading brought intense pressures, and John Jr. wanted to be certain that those "nervous, highly-strung types" were identified and that the Company "not push them too hard and too far. . . . If you crowded it on them, they would have a nervous breakdown . . . you have to gauge your promotions within the physical capacity of the men you are promoting. Don't be misled because he has great ability."

Predictably, John Jr. devoted a few sentences to one of his own personal peeves—the Yale men. For good manners, "you do the utmost possible to be as smooth as oil. The models of that are the Princeton men. I feel, that of all the colleges in the East, they somehow at Princeton have succeeded in getting a tradition of manners there. They have certainly done far better than they did at Yale." The Princeton men, on the other hand, "are always in demand for posts that require that type of thing. They are magnificent diplomats."

Throughout the speech, John Jr. stressed the quality of balance. He used the relationship between himself, Cargill MacMillan and Austen Cargill as his example. "None of us are very well rounded," he admitted. Brother Cargill "has critical powers that I think are the best in Cargill. . . . He is simply magnificent." On the other hand, Austen Cargill "can do things in the field of morale and human relations that neither my brother nor I can do. . . . Austen can come in and he'll say, 'well, here's a situation we're handling that's terrible. This would demoralize any outfit.' He's always right. I'd never sense it nor see it until he points it out." It was this type of balance that "keeps an organization clicking and pulling together and getting results."

In the final analysis, the most important single thought that seemed to permeate the long speech was the importance of integrity. Indeed, in the small handwritten outline that he used to make the speech, he had printed the word *integrity* at the bottom in capital letters and underlined it. John Jr. saw this moment as a time to stress once again, and deeply, the very values and root beliefs that the Company had stood for over the years from back in the days of the founder, W. W. Cargill, and the exemplary leader, John MacMillan, Sr. Most organizations have that "moment of truth" when everything they stand for is on the line and can only be recaptured by an incisive act. John Jr. truly felt this to be so and said so, explicitly, in the speech: "It would not have taken many more of these things—I'll say this quite frankly—to compel the liquidation of Cargill, Inc." The speech was in all respects a tour de force.[20]

The Beginnings of Tradax

"It had taken nearly a century for Cargill to move out into the world dominated for so long by the Europeans" (so said Dan Morgan in his book *Merchants of Grain*); "but when John Junior and his brother Cargill MacMillan finally ordered it done, they took two steps that put them ahead of all of their competitors. They organized an overseas subsidiary in Geneva, and they built an enormous grain elevator at Baie-Comeau, Quebec, a remote, ice-free port at the mouth of the St. Lawrence River." The Geneva project began now; Baie Comeau is discussed in the next chapter.

The three family members in the Company—John Jr., Cargill MacMillan and Austen Cargill—long had been interested in an offshore company. To be precise, Cargill MacMillan had the abiding drive for it. He had been particularly upset by the New Deal period, with its steeply rising corporate and personal taxation. All through the 1930s, he had proposed various plans, had had Cargill's lawyers search out legal ramifications, and had even visited some likely locations (Guernsey, in the Channel Islands, for example). The demanding World War II years and the hurly-burly period right after the war had shunted these plans aside. By the late 1940s, however, the idea surfaced once again, and this time the impetus was from a John Jr. memorandum to the other two. The prevailing political climate in the country now seemed to preoccupy John Jr., and he wrote: "I see breakers ahead for the near future (3 to 10) years and utter disaster for us and our children during the next generation." Still, he continued, "I do not think we need fold our hands and say 'So be it.' " He then outlined some tentative ideas for a new approach to overseas endeavors. Donald Levin, a young Company lawyer, was given the responsibility to flesh out this proposal.

In December 1951, Levin presented a lengthy memorandum on a "Proposed Foreign Trading and Shipping Operations." Whereas Cargill MacMillan's efforts in the 1930s had emphasized tax avoidance (and even John Jr.'s rough draft had this focus), now the issue was put more clearly in terms of the operational advantages of a foreign effort. Levin pointed out that the Company had spent "some twenty years of attempts to gain a foothold in international and foreign trade . . . with foreign offices . . . contacts with foreign business agents . . . three ex-North American subsidiary companies . . . and diligent efforts . . . made to compete effectively in world trade." Yet, with all of this, Cargill had had only limited success. There were several telling reasons:

1. Cargill's competitors, especially the large European and Argentine grain trading companies, "have much lower costs . . . since they are organized under political jurisdictions favoring such businesses through much lower tax policies and the granting of greater freedom in business organization and practices." Foreign transactions of large magnitude "can be efficiently developed only if segregated from domestic U.S. business." Foreign trade was essentially different, and "only by organizing it on an independent basis under people with special background and training can full returns be achieved. Language problems, shipping and warehousing matters, currency questions, local trade customs and practically every phase of such business is sharply different from domestic transactions."

2. Cargill did not wish to "subject its entire financial resources to turbulent

conditions in foreign countries . . . which inherently involve a great deal more financial risk than does its North American business."

3. Although Cargill's holdings outside of North America were negligible (Levin estimated less than 1 percent of its net assets), their administration "has required an excessive and disproportionate amount of the time and effort of the Cargill management."

4. A local corporation "has an important and distinct political advantage over an American company."

In sum, Cargill was finding itself under increasing competitive disadvantage in respect to its arch-rivals, particularly Dreyfus, Continental, Bunge, Garnac and the other large international trading houses. Erv Kelm, in a later memorandum, likened it to the "endless belt theory" of John Jr.:

Entering into all phases of the business (that is, from primary source to ultimate consumer) . . . there would be little increments along the line which in total amount to substantial margins. Each factor by itself . . . is not important, when they're all added up they are very important. This has been Cargill's theory . . . domestically from the western country elevator to western terminals—to Buffalo terminals—to the export function in New York. [The international company] now is to pick up small increments from F.O.B. United States ports . . . brokerages on freight and sales brokerages formerly paid to others, exchange margin, freight position profits. In addition . . . there usually is an over-all trading margin—both domestic and foreign. If either party to this team . . . tries to extract too large a fee for any of these functions . . . it interrupts this endless belt and these increments stop—Continental does the business. I am sure Continental effectively operates on this endless belt theory.

By late 1951, the basic plan was in place. The lawyers briefly considered Nassau, Lichtenstein, Monaco, Tangiers, Liberia and Macao, then settled on Panama as the country of incorporation for a new company, Cargill Internacional, S.A. This Panamanian entity would be empowered to hold shares in foreign corporations and to invest in subsidiary companies that, in Cargill MacMillan's words, "would do any and all *intra* national business . . . to support the primary purpose of the parent company." He defined "intra" as "domestic business, that is, business which, under the laws of the country in question, is considered to be 'doing business within the country.' " In turn, the Panamanian company would be "so clearly managed and directed from outside of the United States that the taxing authorities of the United States could not lay claim to any taxes on its profits." Both voting control and management would reside outside the United States. The Company's external counsel made this even more specific: Cargill, Incorporated, could not "supervise and analyze" the Panamanian company, for "any evidence of direct control of Internacional's everyday affairs by Cargill, Incorporated's officers or employees would seriously jeopardize the former's chances of defending its status as a non-

Walter F. Gage.

resident corporation for United States tax purposes." Putting it simply, the Panamanian operation had to be absolutely separate.

The ownership structure for the new company was similar to that of the Minnesota Western Company and the Minnesota River Company, in that the three family members, the other minority family holders and key top management people could participate. The main difference in the case of the Panamanian company was that Cargill, Incorporated, was to have *no* relationship to it. There were to be two classes of preferred stock. The first preferred stock was to be held by the Cargill Foundation. The funds from the Foundation's purchase would provide the main capital infusion, some $300,000. The second preferred stock would be held by the three family members and offered to all of the Cargill, Incorporated, minority stockholders (other family and key management). About $50,000 was expected from this source. There also were two classes of common stock. The Class A stock was to be noncallable, and holders would elect the majority of the board of directors. This stock was to be held by the Salevia Foundation, a Swiss entity that had been formed in September 1952 by the three families. The Class B stock was to be offered to any of the subscribers to the second preferred—the three family members and the other Cargill, Incorporated, minority stockholders, in proportion to their holdings of Cargill, Incorporated, common stock.

Thus, this ownership structure for Cargill Internacional (a) vested control in the three family members but gave representation in both preferred and common stock to the minority stockholders in proportion to their holdings and (b) satisfied the requirement that the entire organization be completely separate from Cargill, Incorporated.

These organizational details took many months to complete, but by 1954 Cargill Internacional was an operating company (the office in Panama first headed by C. C. Boden and later by John Shenard). The initial impetus for an international trading company had come in 1951, when the Oil Division had proposed to charter or buy a vessel to transport copra from the Philippines to the United States. Indeed, the Philippines originally had been thought of as a possible Asian base for the Company. So when Cargill Internacional was established, one of its first interests was copra. Management companies were needed in various countries of the world to accomplish this and other trades; now Internacional established these new units. An operating company called Coprax was set up to emphasize the copra-trading aspect.

Panama was not a good location for actual trading; its communication links to the rest of the world were too primitive. So a new entity was established in Winnipeg, Manitoba. As more than copra would be traded, the name Coprax was changed to EMCO, Ltd. Initially, Winnipeg seemed to be a good central location, but it soon became apparent that the center of world grain trading from Canada was in Montreal, so in mid-1954 the management company was moved there.

Concurrent with the Montreal move came a new European trading company for Cargill Internacional. At first, the lawyers thought that Cargill Internacional might be able to use a Dutch company, Cargill Handel Maatschappij, which had been set up in the 1930s by Cargill Grain Company, Ltd. Handel had done some trading in the 1930s but had become completely dormant during and after World War II. The possibility of reactivating Handel was explored, but the potential tax implications and memories of World War II difficulties with Leonard Corlett's exodus seemed to make a Dutch base unwise. This led to the eventual formation of the trading company in Antwerp. Belgium had been the first to start up private grain trade after World War II (while most of its neighbors still were dealing government-to-government) and had been a funnel for grain to and from the Hanseatic states since the 18th century. Almon Greenman was to be the new company's head (resigning his longtime position with Cargill). He suggested the name: since the Company was to "trade," Greenman added an "AX," and the firm name became Tradax Belgique.

At the same time, a presence in England was developed, to be handled through the office of Ross T. Smyth, Cargill's British link. Michael Cross, the families' longtime friend, handled this with B. B. "Stu" Hanson, a young Cargill man, as his assistant (Hanson resigning from Cargill, too). It also was intended that within a short time Cargill's Argentine and Brazilian operations would be separated from the Company and become part of Cargill Internacional.

The new name for the Montreal operation was Cargan, but then it was changed to Kerrgill Company, Ltd. While this name, too, lasted only a few months, the "Kerr" in that name is an important story.[21]

The Purchase of Kerr Gifford

Cargill never had been strong on the West Coast. The Portland terminal was a modest performer, the San Francisco copra operation rather specialized. More important, the Company had little expertise or contacts with the huge trading area of the Pacific that now is known popularly as the Pacific Rim. By the early 1950s, with the settling of the Korean War and the increasing prosperity of Japan, Taiwan, Hong Kong and other Asian and Pacific countries, it became evident that any company wishing to be engaged in the world grain trade needed roots in the Pacific Rim.

In early 1953 just such an opportunity surfaced for Cargill. A major West Coast grain-trading company, Kerr Gifford & Co., Inc., became available for purchase. It had been founded in 1893 and now was run by two second-generation Kerrs, Thomas and Andrew (the Gifford of the original firm had returned to his native Scotland). Kerr Gifford long had been a grain-trading company and even had been a large flour miller. At this time, in the early 1950's, it held owned or leased terminals in Seattle, Portland, Vancouver, San Francisco and Sacramento and a number of country elevators on the Columbia River in the Klamath Falls area. In addition, it had an important subsidiary in New York City, Smith-Murphy Co. Inc., a grain trading office for Atlantic Coast and European business as well as for most of Kerr Gifford's Pacific Rim business. The Kerr family's offer to sell was a unique opportunity for Cargill to make a quantum jump in its international trading. John Peterson commented about the fit between Cargill and the new companies: "We ought to be able to carry a lot of our own trades with Smith Murphy and with Kerr Gifford . . . keeping under the combined roofs a lot of money that goes out as surplus to others, for which we receive no adequate return."

In June 1953, Cargill's board agreed to pay the Kerr Gifford owners $4,250,000 for purchase of all of the stock. Thomas Kerr stayed with the Company, but this did not work out well, and he stepped away from Cargill in 1955. John Cole, one of the senior managers at Kerr Gifford, stayed with Cargill for the rest of his career. On November 1, 1954, Kerr Gifford was merged into Cargill as the Kerr Gifford Division. The Smith-Murphy people also stayed with Cargill, and the head of the New York office, C. J. Stuart Allan was posted to Winnipeg for the new unit there, still at this time called Kerrgill.[22]

The Move to Montreal—and to Europe

The move to Montreal of Cargill Internacional's subsidiary, Kerrgill, signaled the beginnings of actual international trading. Stuart Allan was president, assisted at the start by Robert M. Hatch; later, Addison Douglass, Michael Sladek and W. Duncan MacMillan (John Jr.'s younger son) joined them. A Vancouver office was also to be maintained, headed by R. L. Mikkelson. All had been required formally to resign from Cargill.

The name of the Montreal group still bothered a number of people, Cargill MacMillan's younger son, Whitney, for one. It was just too close to Cargill. A natural extension was to adopt "Tradax," and the Montreal operation was officially renamed Tradax, Canada, Ltd.

With skilled people in all of its offices, Internacional now began trading. By the end of 1954, with only three months of operation, it had made over $300,000. This was a promising start, for its total capitalization was just $310,000. Its annual report of May 31, 1955, noted extensive wheat trading from Commodity Credit Corporation tenders, a number of corn sales to the United Kingdom and to Japan, and some less effective sales of oats. Substantial barley had been traded, and a large United States soybean crop had resulted in substantial Tradax sales to Japan (with the help of an agent there, Andrew Weir & Co.). There also had been some interesting barter arrangements—for example, Czechoslovakian cement for wheat.

Another function of Tradax in which Cargill had had only minimal experience was trading ocean freight. In his annual report, Stuart Allan commented on this: "In today's international markets, where competition is keenest, freights are a decisive factor. . . . Many times we have lost business merely because our judgment on the freight market was not sufficiently keen. . . . The freight factor has become more and more paramount in our calculations." While the Tradax group did reasonably well here, they miscalculated when severe Atlantic weather delayed some of their charters. A particularly "cruel blow" (Allan's words) occurred when one ship, the *Transnorthern*, suffered a cracked piston and arrived many days after it was expected. They had chartered the *Clintonia* for several consecutive trips and found this longer-term commitment not sufficiently flexible. Allan ended: "It is our belief that ultimately we must either own or time charter tonnage [chartering shipping for a given period of time, rather than a 'trip charter,' for a particular voyage] to fill our requirements, so important has the freight factor become."

While the first year of Tradax was a success on many fronts, there were lingering problems. The Cargill lawyers continued to chide Tradax people for not maintaining their separation from Cargill Internacional. Don Levin wrote Cargill MacMillan about this in November 1954. Not only was Tradax drawing on Cargill's expertise in a number of fields—law, finance and accounting, insurance—but "actual trading decisions and basic underlying studies on which trading conclusions are reached, are almost completely being done in Wayzata" (the Lake Office, Cargill's headquarters, was in Minnetonka, Minnesota, bordering Wayzata). On freight, the Tradax interaction with Cargo Carriers Incorporated (CCI) was substantial. In banking, it was clear that the bankers looked upon Cargill, Incorporated, as a backup for Cargill Internacional. Under pressure from Levin and the other lawyers, the Tradax operation moved away from Cargill, Incorporated; the second year of Tradax operation was much more independent than the first.

In early 1955, the CEA had a series of contacts with Cargill as to whether Cargill, Incorporated, needed to include the futures trading of Cargill Internacional in the Company's reports to the agency. In the settlement of the Oats Case, just a few months before, the CEA had ruled that the Company's Canadian subsidiary (Cargill Grain Company, Ltd.) could not be treated as a self-standing, independent unit and that the limits rules for the Company had to include the subsidiaries. It was generally known, too, that the CEA was disturbed by its difficulty in tracing ultimate ownership of foreign-held positions for all companies on contract markets in the United States. In October 1954, the CEA passed a new regulation concerning this. As a result, the CEA pressed hard for the Cargill, Incorporated, limits report to include Cargill Internacional. Cargill executives maintained that the companies were two separate entities but "nevertheless agreed to indicate by footnotes on its weekly cash grain reports the amount of its purchases and sales commitments with Cargill Internacional." The effect of the exchange of letters spelling this out "is simply a truce," an internal memorandum noted, but it did represent a "substantial concession from the rigid and uncompromising attitude adopted by the CEA at the beginning of discussions." Nevertheless, the CEA query added concern regarding the issue of Internacional's independence.

A half dozen years later, Tradax was brought into Cargill, Incorporated, and when this occurred there were real difficulties in integrating the two, given the high degree of Tradax independence and self-guidance. Many seeds of discord had been sown between the two organizations over this first period of independent operation. The Tradax merchants were considerably more free-wheeling than their counterparts in Minneapolis. Limits policies at Tradax were less tight, and traders more than once took flat positions on one side of the market. Sometimes Cargill management became quite upset by this. In March 1955, for example, the acting head at Montreal, Wallace Hyde (Allan had had a heart attack), left the office apparently without giving careful instructions on positions. John Jr. was furious: "The result is they are long a staggering amount of grain at a time when we are all bearish as can be." John Jr. ruled that subsequently Cargill MacMillan was to be involved in all telephone calls between Montreal and Minneapolis. Still conscious of the requirement for separation, John Jr. continued: "He will be a liaison man in the true sense of the word . . . under no circumstances do we ever try to issue any orders but at the same time if they ask for advice I think we should see they get the best information possible *just as we would do for any other customer*" (emphasis mine).

It was evident even in that first year that Montreal was not the right place to have the main international trading office. The center of the internationally based grain trade was in Europe—in such centers as Amsterdam, Antwerp, and particularly Switzerland. In many ways Montreal had not forced Tradax personnel to really become "international." Montreal at that time was a bilingual city, with strong links to the United States. Communication between Montreal and the main areas of business in Europe was not nearly as good as if the Company had been on the spot. By mid-1955 the decision had been made that Tradax Canada should move to Europe. As Erv Kelm put it, "We will pull grain over, not push it from the U.S."[23]

Eisenhower and Republican Farm Policy

The World War II hero, General Dwight D. Eisenhower, was elected President in November 1952, as a Republican. It was the first time that the GOP had taken the presidency since the inauguration of Herbert Hoover in 1928. His first challenge was the settlement of the Korean War. The armistice that was signed on July 27, 1953, fulfilled one of his campaign pledges. In the period April–June 1954, Senate hearings were held which considerably defused Senator Joseph McCarthy's Communist-conspiracy charges. Eisenhower's first two years in office achieved considerable domestic economic success, with no major threats on the international front.

There was another Eisenhower initiative that was portentous for the grain trade. On May 13, 1954, he signed into law the St. Lawrence Seaway bill, authorizing construction of a joint United States–Canada waterway. A few weeks later he named Secretary of Defense Charles E. Wilson the director of the new St. Lawrence Seaway Development Corporation. There had been tremendous political pressures on the bill, and the final product was very much a compromise between those opposing the Seaway altogether (particularly the Atlantic Coast shipping interests) and the Canadians and Midwest Americans pressing for it. The final figure for the Seaway's draft (depth) was the key to the act. It was 27 feet (as against the Panama Canal's 38 feet), thus not allowing the larger ocean vessels to utilize the upgraded Seaway. The implications of this will be discussed in the next chapter.

The grain trade watched over its own arena, of course. The administration's Secretary of Agriculture, Ezra Taft Benson, was a strong believer in the farmers' ability to handle their own affairs. The resulting Republican farm policy was a sharp break from the past. The long-standing concept of parity at 90 percent had been maintained for two years, starting in 1952, when the presidential campaign had made Congress timid about any change. Now, however, Benson advocated return to a free market, a flexible price support that would move downward over the years.

Even Benson did not go far enough for John Jr. In July 1953, John Jr.'s friend Harry A. Bullis, who was chairman of General Mills, had a letter published in the *New York Times* that strongly encouraged Benson as "a courageous and sound public official." Bullis seemed to support the Benson parity concept. John Jr. wrote Bullis: "I quite agree with you that the Farm Program is being very badly handled. However, I disagree with you completely on your concept that it is a function of government to try to support the general price level. . . . We will never have a sound economy until there is wide realization that a managed economy simply will not work."

Later that year, John Jr. wrote a brusque letter to Arthur F. Burns, who was chairman of the administration's Council of Economic Advisers, taking exception to three government grain trades (carried out by the Commodity Credit Corporation) with Pakistan, Egypt and South Africa. John Jr. wrote: "The Democrats wisely returned the international trade in grain back to the private trade." Now the government was back into private business, "handicapped by a political price structure and incompetent carry-over Democrats who would like nothing better than to throw a monkey wrench in the present administration." John Jr. advocated leaving the effective distribution of international grain trade to the private sector: "We don't want socialism, collectivism or cooperativism as a scheme under which we and our children are to live."

The White House was disturbed enough by John Jr.'s letter to invite him to Washington to talk personally with Sherman Adams, Eisenhower's chief of staff. Later, a long letter from Gabriel Hauge, an administrative assistant to Eisenhower, noted that the three cases were "special circumstances" and that the administration was in full accord with John Jr.'s principle of private sector trade. But John Jr. remained militantly against anything smacking of control. In May 1954, he wrote Paul S. Gerot, president of Pillsbury, refusing to make a contribution to the prestigious Committee for Economic Development. To John Jr.'s mind, the CED was "the extreme left wing organization of American business . . . the only difference between the men sponsoring this organization and the New Dealers is that while both believed in a managed economy, the Committee for Economic Development want to do the managing. I am of the opinion this organization has done, and is doing, a great deal of harm."[24]

The end of the Korean War had brought the surplus problem back with a vengeance. There were huge stocks of dairy products, some 800 million bushels of wheat, even more corn. Agricultural historian Gilbert Fite estimated the cost to taxpayers of storage charges alone at $800,000 a day. Surplus crops were being stored "in ships, airplane hangars, and anywhere else that space could be found." Prices of most farm products sagged during Eisenhower's first two years. The farmers' heightened discontent at their increasing cost–price squeeze and irritation at being blamed for high food prices brought further political heat. Congress passed new legislation in 1954 that provided a flexible support, but the amount of flexibility was quite limited because Congress feared farmer retaliation.

Along with the farm legislation itself came another congressional effort, one with profound implications for international grain-trading organizations like Cargill. This was the "Food for Peace" legislation (its full name was the Agricultural Trade Development and Assistance Act) passed by Congress in July 1954. It became known popularly as P.L. 480. The Act combined and extended the use of surplus agricultural products for the furtherance of foreign policy goals. Considerable amounts of these products were to be used for famine relief. Agricultural goods also could be sold to "friendly populations" in any country undergoing a food emergency. The countries would pay in their own currency (most often these were "soft" currencies), and the United States could draw on these funds in the countries to purchase strategic materials, buy military supplies and purchase goods and services in the countries where the funds were held. The funds could also be used to develop new markets for United States farm goods. P.L. 480 was a rousing success right from the start and became a long-term fixture of American farm and foreign policy. That it was a boon to the American grain traders goes without saying.

Cargill's profits in the two crop years 1952–1953 and 1953–1954 were excellent: $4.4 million and just under $4.0 million. Year-end net worth increased to $37.3 million and then to $39.8 million. Apparently the exhortations for sharpened internal "discipline" had been successful. Evidence of better internal control was attested by the fact that total gross sales in 1952–1953 were almost exactly the same as in 1952 ($643 million in 1953 and $642 in 1952). Grain tonnage was up slightly between 1952 and 1953 (from 7.7 million to 8.1 million). Sales did rise more in 1954, at $776 million, and tonnage was up to over 10 million. The Feed Division had continued its solid performance, but the Oil Division posted only small profits in both the years. The stellar contributor for both years was the Grain Division. Feed grain trading profits had continued excellent (oats taking a somewhat lesser role), and winter wheat trading had been outstanding in both years. If 1952 was the Company's "year of discontent," 1953 and 1954 provided a rousing turnaround.

With the John Jr. "charge ahead" mentality back in place, it was to be expected that the physical plant of the Company would expand in those two crop years 1953 and 1954. Delivery of the towboat *Carpolis* had been taken in mid-1952; the *Carpaul* went into service in 1954. The Kerr Gifford acquisition had brought in a number of West Coast terminals. A huge elevator had been built at Port Cargill, too, with a 14-million-bushel capacity. It opened in late 1953. At the same time, the Company began a new backhaul up the Mississippi, making stops when necessary and also going all the way to Port Cargill, with the returning barges carrying blackstrap molasses. The Company's new barges were well suited for this. They were double-compartmented, and the liquid molasses could be put in the lower compartment, with dry cargo above. Coal also continued as a backhaul freight. Later, salt became another major commodity carried back up the rivers.[25]

Farther down the river, a 4.8-million-bushel addition had been constructed at East St. Louis, Illinois. Perhaps most galvanizing of all, a new 2.5-million-bushel terminal being built to Cargill specifications by the Greater Baton Rouge [Louisiana] Port Commission was leased by Cargill, to be opened in July 1955. Gulf shipping had been a problem in this period, with tremendous storage congestion. This would provide Cargill a long-term solution. All around the Gulf ports there were only public terminals, operating on a permit system. Cargill's Baton Rouge facility would be the first private-company location, a tremendous advantage in terms of continuity. With great temerity, the Grain Division had promised the Commitment Committee a throughput of 1.5 million tons a month—18 million tons a year. It seemed like such a mammoth amount then, but almost from the start the terminal exceeded this figure, soon by many times.

Fires disrupted business in other parts of the system. The Wesota, Minnesota, country elevator was seriously damaged in January 1953, and the elevator at Hankinson, North Dakota, was wiped out completely (it had been built about 1910 and had a capacity of 30,000 bushels). The most serious disaster occurred in the next crop year, when, on February 14, 1955, the Minneapolis flax plant exploded. "The shock," said *Cargill News*, "has hit the entire Cargill organization a staggering blow—the worst in our history." Four men were killed outright and 10 others seriously injured. "We have no idea what caused the explosion," wrote Cargill MacMillan, "and we probably never will know." He was terribly upset by "this . . . second big explosion that has occurred in one of our plants during my lifetime." John Jr. wrote his brother a few weeks later: "We have had some comments from the Fire Marshal which might be construed as criticism but they look more political than real to me. However, the trade certainly are not critical."[26]

There was more excitement in September 1953: a serious incident involving the *Carmac*. The Company's inspection vessel was en route up the Atlantic Coast on its way to the wedding of John Jr.'s younger son, Duncan. John Peterson and his wife were aboard. On the way toward Providence, Rhode Island, the vessel hit Watchhill Reef and promptly sank. John Peterson and the crew were uninjured, but Peterson's wife suffered a broken collar bone. A new inspection vessel, *Carmac II*, a 116-foot craft, was subsequently purchased. It was not altogether seaworthy, particularly for deep-water use and especially after the installation of a heavy air conditioner on its top deck. The vessel was sold, and *Carmac III*, a 142-foot vessel was bought in 1955. The *Carmac III* had its share of trouble, too, for it was hit by a Japanese freighter in fog-shrouded San Francisco Bay in November 1955. The blow was glancing, but the damage was substantial. Repairs were made, and the *Carmac* continued to serve well as the Company's seaborne inspection vessel.[27]

The Company's relations with the government were calm in this period, although after the storage tensions stemming from the Albany and Norris City episodes, the CCC seemed to be chary of putting its grain into storage

Cargill's inspection vessel, Carmac III.

Rear passenger deck, Carmac III.

in Cargill's "big bins." After lengthy meetings in October 1953, relating to the use of the two new terminals at Port Cargill and at East St. Louis, the government officials concluded "that the size of the proposed bins would make it difficult, if not impossible, to turn grain in the event its condition became doubtful." The CCC was further concerned about the inability to segregate two different lots in one large bin.

John Jr., speaking for Cargill, replied that "the 24-year Cargill experience . . . with large bins [showed that] grain kept better in large bins than in small bins. . . . At no time in the past had Cargill ever failed to turn grain belonging to the government or others . . . when such conditioning was indicated." The issue remained unresolved, and John Jr. finally wrote Secretary Benson, arguing that the Cargill experience had shown the Company how to "safely deal with any particular section of a large bin that begins to show a condition problem." He asked for Benson's "good offices," but a subsequent letter from the CCC made it clear that its "Minimum General Specifications" required that bins allow "the turning in full of the largest bin." Cargill's bins did not satisfy this requirement, and the government officials remained unmoved.[28]

Julius Hendel Retires

The year 1955 was not as successful as the immediately preceding years. Although the gross sales (at $764 million) just about repeated 1954, and the tonnage handled was almost exactly the same, profitability was off considerably. The final net earnings figure was $2.5 million, down almost $1.5 million. The Feed and Oil divisions were somewhat lower, but most of the drop was in the Grain Division—its $2.2 million contribution to profits in 1954 had sagged to $429,000. John Jr. wrote Austen Cargill in March 1955: "The problem came entirely in the Grain Division . . . this is the time to cry 'wolf' and we are doing so in no uncertain terms. I have just come from a meeting of the Regional Heads and I had a chance to lay it on thick." In the same week, he wrote his brother that the Grain Division "reflects too much complacency." John Peterson seconded this view, commenting to Austen Cargill, "they have shown very little, if any capacity to control the expenses of their outside offices, a number of which are . . . run on the Hollywood style."

John Jr. seemed especially jumpy about bad news at this particular time. He had just finished (in February 1955) dealing with a difficult situation in the Company's Chicago office involving a competitor allegedly pirating Cargill trading secrets. The case involved a broker who had been dealing with Cargill over the previous half dozen years. John Jr. even asked John Savage, Cargill's training director, to develop a program for "indoctrination in withholding from competitors vital trading information." Over the summer, John Jr. several times recorded in his diary being extremely fatigued, and at one point he wrote to himself, "Had a run-in with J.G.P. [Peterson] over his trying [to] write my Board of Trade speech for me at this late date. Quite ashamed of myself for my lack of self-discipline." He constantly tried to reduce his weight even more and in mid-July reported, "Hit a new low in weight" (134 3/4 lbs). Even his relationships with his brother Cargill seemed off center. He reported in his diary in November 1955: "His European conclusions are certainly at variance from ours here. Disturbed me greatly."

In 1952, when the Grain Division had had another bad period, Julius Hendel had attempted a more direct role with the division. His effort probably had a good deal to do with the better results over the following two years. But Hendel had paid a price for this in heightened antagonism from some in the Grain Division about his incursion. In August 1953, he wrote John Jr. about this: "The attitude of the personnel in the Grain Division, which started on the defensive, repelling the intrusion of top management, softened to a compulsory acquiescence, and at present is tending toward voluntary cooperation. . . . It is natural for line personnel to be promoted to staff positions, but whenever men from top management are put in a line position to make decisions and give orders, it is bitterly resented by the younger executives." Perhaps it was not just Hendel who was resented but John Jr. too, for Hendel continued: "To promote loyalty and impart the feeling that employment . . . is a way of life rather than mere gaining of a livelihood, it appears advisable formally to restore full autonomy to the Grain Division. However, informally the president and Mr. Hendel should continue to assist the Grain Division as a temporary and special assignment. . . . Unsolicited advice is unwelcome, but if made difficult to get, it is sought."

Julius Hendel already had had an instance of moving back into the Grain Division in a line capacity, unsuccessfully, to make trades that he himself wanted to manage (the December 1947 wheat futures contracts, mentioned in the preceding chapter). There were other instances in suceeding years where Hendel reversed trades that others under him had made. Hendel also seemed to have been caught in the middle of the differences resulting from the Dwayne Andreas visit to Russia in 1952. Increasingly over the late 1940s and the early 1950s, John Peterson and Terry Morrison had thought and acted in concert. Apparently it was they who had pushed for the Andreas resignation. Hendel also had had a serious

Taking down Elevator E, Duluth, June 1974.

disagreement with John Peterson after the poor performance of the Grain Division in 1952, when Peterson wanted to constrain limits and trading positions more than Hendel did.

Apparently the cumulative effect of all of this caused John Jr. himself to lose confidence in Hendel's leadership of the merchandising activities of the Company. Over the summer of 1955, he and Hendel had a number of discussions about this, and Hendel offered to resign. John Jr. accepted. The record seems clear that the impetus for this was John Jr.'s and that Hendel really did not want to leave. Hendel seemed ambivalent about staying on as a director: "I want to be of continuing service, if I can. . . . I want you to tell me if you want me to continue on as a director. I will be glad to do so, unless certain contingencies arise with which you are familiar, which would make it impossible. However, I would prefer not to unless you think it would be in the better interests of the company for me to continue to serve." Subsequently, Hendel did relinquish his directorship, when he retired on September 1, 1955. He was five years short of the retirement age of 65 but was given full retirement benefits.

Recollections of this early retirement of Julius Hendel sometimes include the inference that Hendel's being Jewish had something to do with it. There was latent anti-Semitism still in Minneapolis at that time (as with many other cities in the country). John Jr. was not totally immune to this. Julius Hendel had been slurred by outsiders more than once in this regard (the story of his entry into the Minneapolis grain exchange being an earlier example). In September 1947, John Jr. had received a two-line "thank you" from a prominent Minneapolis executive, head of one of the city's most important companies. It read as follows: "Thanks for the snapshots of the trip on the *Carmac*. Am delighted to have these even though there was apparently a 'Jewish' gentleman aboard." Although these kinds of remarks were not uncommon, it seems unlikely that John Jr. harbored any such feelings directly about Hendel. The two had grown up in the business together, had participated in hundreds of key decisions and had taught each other a great deal. Indeed, each had mentored the other—Julius on trading, John Jr. on strategy.

After Hendel retired, almost immediately he received an offer from a rival trading house. He came back to the Company to tell John Jr. of the proposal. John Jr. said, in effect, "Fine, but not with my blessing unless it is as a director, not a trader." John Jr. apparently felt that having Hendel as a competitor on the trading side could be detrimental to Cargill. When Hendel went back to the trading house with only a partial agreement from Cargill—to be a director—he was turned down. A year later, another firm in the industry, a farm services cooperative, offered Hendel a post on a part-time basis as an economic consultant. In this case, John Jr. approved, writing Hendel: "We have always looked upon G.L.F. as a friendly customer rather than as a competitor and we regard it as a great compliment, not only to yourself, but to us as well that they would like to engage you on this basis."

The retirement of Hendel marked the end of a special era. Hendel was considered to be the "dean of grain trading" and was seen as this even after his retirement. He had pioneered in Cargill's grain laboratory in the 1920s and had introduced scientific feed mixing in the 1940s. The renowned Cargill training program had been introduced by him and was nurtured by him for many years. According to a later observation by Harvard's Professor Ray Goldberg, Hendel's classes had "Cargillized the industry." The president of the Federal Reserve Bank of Minneapolis, Oliver S. Powell, wrote John Jr. after the latter's banquet for Hendel in September 1955 that it was "a real thrill" to hear of Hendel's impressive career. Probably everyone at Cargill would have echoed Powell's closing comment: "I am sure that Julius has made a real contribution to the success of your firm."[29]

Corporate Leadership, Management Losses

The second half of the decade of the 1950s, roughly coinciding with Dwight Eisenhower's second term in office (1956–1960), had been good for the country and for the grain trade but not as positive for the farmer. There had been a sharp business recession in the first half of 1958 but a recovery by the end of that year. Excluding this, the years 1955–1959 had produced solid economic growth for the nation. It was in this period that the Russians sent up Sputnik I, the first earth satellite. Americans were stunned by the Soviets' technological progress, and a massive new U.S. initiative was mounted to regain superiority in space technology. The decade ended on a strong note.

Agriculture's unabated bout with surpluses continued. Greater productivity set records in corn and soybean production, and wheat also was having a series of bountiful crops. There was a heroic attempt to insulate some of this production from commercial channels through the P.L. 480 "Food For Peace" shipments, which amounted to a total value of over $1 billion each year from 1956 into the next decade. Added to this was the "soil bank" plan in the Agricultural Act of 1956, which sought to cut supplies of the six basic crops by substantial reductions in acres planted. However, as economist Ross Robertson put it, "the plan made use of a phony conservation handle and at the same time tried to avoid the appearance of controlling farm decisions. The results were unbelievably bad. Carry-overs went right on mounting, reaching astronomic heights in 1961. . . . Ezra Taft Benson put all his Mormon zeal into an effort to become the most unpopular Secretary of Agriculture in history."[1]

So despite every effort, farm prices sagged for many commodities. Soybean prices fell some, wheat and corn prices more substantially. Farmers found themselves once again attacked for high food prices, "getting fat on the public dole," while at the same time receiving less for their product and paying more for their inputs. The political clout of the farm bloc seemed to lessen as its constituent pieces began to splinter.

For the grain trade, however, this was a satisfying period. Storage of CCC grain remained high (the value of the commodities owned by the CCC stayed above $4.5 billion all through the period 1955–1959 and was up to $6 billion in 1960). The P.L. 480 shipments were substantial, and the overall international grain trade stayed strong. Cargill prospered during this time, indeed, doing very well in the year 1959 (when it set sales and income records). This second half of the 1950s also saw significant Company expansion. The prestigious "*Fortune* Five Hundred" directory did not list privately held companies. If it had, Cargill's sales in 1959 ($1.089 billion) would have put it in place number 34 for all listed companies, just after American Can Company. The Company's assets ($185.4 million) would have followed Granite City Steel at position 186. In invested capital, Cargill would have been number 315; in profitability, 243; and in number of employees, 375. Perhaps *Fortune*'s "Fifty Largest Merchandising Firms" would have been more comparable for measuring Cargill; if so, the Company would have ranked 7th in sales, 19th in assets, 32nd in invested capital. Cargill's figure for the important comparative measure of return on invested capital was 16.4 percent that year (the Company had recorded double figures in six years of the decade); with four other companies, it would have ranked at 69 in the *Fortune* Five Hundred and would have been in fifth place among the merchandising firms.[2] This chapter analyzes the six-year period 1955–1960.

How to Expand?

By January 1956, a major rebound in Company fortunes had taken place. The Grain Division, which had faltered so badly in profitability in the previous year, had traded over 10.3 million tons of grain by the end of the crop year and contributed almost $2.6 million in profits, a full half million dollars over its budget. The Feed Division and Vegetable Oil Division had both done reasonably well, and the combined profits for the Company were over $5.5 million, the third best in the Company's history. The total merchandised grains had risen from 8.7 million tons to 9.7 million. This increase, however, had produced approximately the same sales figure as in the crop year ending May 31, 1955, so the dollar revenue per ton had fallen. Nevertheless, the healthy profitability boded well for the future.

There were some unfulfilled opportunities, however, and these troubled top management. John Jr. wrote in April 1956: "We are all terribly upset over missing out on the big volume export business." He saw the problem particularly as inadequate ocean transportation, "which means we have to step on the gas as far as marine equipment is concerned . . . we have some 13 million dollars worth of work we would like to undertake as soon as possible." Inasmuch as this seemed too much for the Company to absorb all at once, "it may be that we can finance some marine construction outside of Cargill." Here he was thinking of a family-owned business, similar to the Minnesota River Company. However, the amounts now were much larger, and there was not as much enthusiasm for this form of ownership among family and senior management as before.

The international side of the business obsessed John Jr. at this time. For one, he thought the Caribbean had great potential. His longtime ownership of land in Jamaica had led him into some commercial production of copra and sugarcane there. Further, he had become convinced that Cuban sugarcane could be brought to the United States for processing at a profit, and he had already sent a personal representative there to search out supplies, perhaps also to buy sugarcane land. The *Carport* and its barge already had been used for coastal shipping, in both the Gulf of Mexico and the Atlantic. On one of these voyages, in September 1956, the *Carport* was caught in Hurricane Flossie. One man was washed overboard, and a second, who attempted a rescue, also was lost. If the *Carport* was to be used for the Cuban trade on a regular basis, new, larger (6,000-ton) barges would be needed. Indeed, John Jr. advocated a 17,500-ton barge as even more productive.

Norfolk, the St. Lawrence Seaway

For intercoastal shipping and especially for any export shipping to Europe, an Atlantic Coast terminal of substantial size, much larger than the

Dedication of the St. Lawrence River Project by New York Governor Thomas E. Dewey (left) and Canadian Premier Louis St. Laurent, Cornwall, Ontario, August 1954 (The Bettmann Archive).

250,000-bushel leased facility at Mt. Clare (Baltimore) would be needed. In March 1956, a 2,250,000-bushel elevator at Norfolk was authorized by the board at a cost estimated to be just over $3 million. At the dedication in July 1957, John Jr. gave the welcoming speech and in the process took some swipes at government policy for intruding into the private grain trade: "I am a fourth-generation grain merchant [a slight exaggeration—his was the third!] and those of us in the grain trade for a long time fail to see how these newcomers in the field, such as these bureaucrats, can hope to do as well as we" (later, Hubert H. Humphrey, the senator from Minnesota had the speech reprinted in the *Congressional Record*). John Jr., in his diary, called the new terminal, "impressive but expensive," as it had overrun budget.[3]

One rationale for the Norfolk decision was the anticipatory belief, expressed in an April 1956 memorandum, that the Albany terminal "will be through in 3 years except as to its value as pure storage" because of the scheduled opening of the St. Lawrence Seaway in 1959. The Seaway *was* going to change everything. It was true that its 27-foot draft would not let larger ocean shipping through, but this draft would allow the lakers to go all the way out to the mouth of the St. Lawrence. In August 1955, Cargill purchased (at a total cost of $310,000) three of these lakers—all older bottoms—the *Harry R. Jones*, the *Hemlock* and the *Calumet*, each with a capacity of about 7,000 tons. Their age and basic construction did not make them eligible as oceangoing vessels, but they would be able to move right through the new Seaway to the St. Lawrence mouth.

The inference was clear—if Cargill had a transshipment point near the mouth of the St. Lawrence, a very efficient transfer could be made to oceangoing vessels calling at such a port (i.e., it would obviate the past practice of a smaller "canaler" for movement from the Great Lakes to Montreal and the mouth). Preliminary studies in early 1956 centered on a location at Seven Islands, on the Quebec North Shore, and the Cargill board of directors made an inspection trip on *Carmac III*, from Montreal to the Seven Islands vicinity, to observe firsthand possible port sites. A linking point was being sought both for the oceangoing vessels and for a backhaul by the lakers, to carry iron ore back to the steel companies at Great Lakes ports. New deposits of iron ore were being tapped by the steel companies in northern Quebec and Labrador, and Seven Islands was to become a shipping point. Cargill made contact with one of these corporations, the M. A. Hanna Company. Its ore shipping plans called for shipment of 12 million tons back up the St. Lawrence, with the existing facilities capable of loading 8,000 tons of ore per hour, dumping two 100-ton cars every five seconds. It was a particularly exciting idea for Cargill. Not only would there be a ready backhaul, but, as John Jr. reported, "savings in transportation [on outgoing grain] should be 5¢ a bushel." The choice of Hanna seemed particularly propitious, inasmuch as the steel company also had property in Rotterdam and was contemplating developing a port there for the use of very large ore carriers (30,000 to 40,000 tons) out of the St. Lawrence. There could be dock space there for Cargill, too.

As Cargill's analysis continued through 1957, an alternative site for the grain facility was preferred; this was at Baie Comeau, also on the Quebec North Shore, a little over 100 miles upriver from Seven Islands. This port had been brought into being earlier to ship wood pulp for newsprint, specifically for the *Chicago Tribune*. The urgency engendered by the scheduled Seaway opening in 1958 now brought Cargill to a commitment to build an 11,860,000-bushel elevator at Baie Comeau at an estimated cost of over $13 million. By all measures this was the largest single financial commitment ever made by the Company and one of its most important management decisions ever.[4]

The imminent Seaway opening triggered other moves by the Company. In early 1956 it decided to build five identical large-bin, million-bushel subterminals at Breckenridge and Crookston, Minnesota, and at Minot,

The Cargill Board of Directors visit to Seven Islands, Quebec, on M.V. Carmac III, 1956. Seated, left to right, Austen Cargill, John MacMillan, Jr., John Peterson, Cargill Mac-Millan; standing, Bert Egermayer, Erv Kelm, Fred Seed, Jim Dorsey, Bob Woodworth; kneeling, Jim North, Terry Morrison.

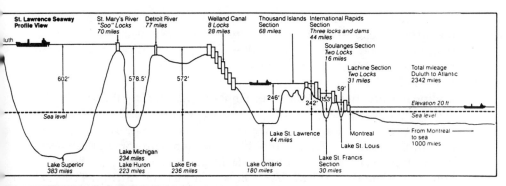

Schematic diagram of the St. Lawrence Seaway.

Carrington and Dickinson, North Dakota. These would be erected as quickly as possible and in time to handle the 1956 crop. "As a consolidation proposition," an internal memorandum commented, "it strengthens our Duluth-Superior setup and builds for the day when the St. Lawrence Seaway is a reality." At the same time, a small new lakeside elevator was built at Michigan City, Indiana, also to be operational for the 1956 crop. Its capacity was only 100,000 bushels; but just as the size of the river terminals at Ottawa and Havana, Illinois, had belied their importance, so too would this one, for it was designed particularly to serve trucks from that area, which had been going into Chicago to competitor terminals.[5]

Thus, the St. Lawrence Seaway was to be a linchpin for a new era in ocean shipments from North America. Huge oceangoing ships would now be able to dock at Baie Comeau to load efficiently and quickly with the grain that had been sent out to Baie Comeau by fleets of lakers.

Expanding to Europe

It was this strategic prospect that so excited John Jr. and turned him single-mindedly toward increasing Company ocean-shipping capacity. A critical part of the equation was the unloading of the grain in Europe and its subsequent merchandising there. Substantial amounts of grain also were going to Asia, particularly the P.L. 480 concessionary shipments to India, Pakistan and other developing countries. Cargill had little past presence in Asia and now decided to purchase for the account of Tradax the commodities department of its longtime agent, Andrew Weir & Co. (Tokyo) Ltd. (in the process inheriting some remunerative long-term coal-shipping contracts).

Europe, however, was the real focus. The great centers of grain trading were well established there, and the aggressive, strong European grain trading companies had already challenged Cargill into competing on their own ground. The establishment of Cargill Internacional had been the first step, but its trading operation in Montreal had proved out of the mainstream. So the Montreal office was transferred to Europe in the spring of 1956. Tradax Belgique was already in Antwerp and was momentarily a possibility as a site, but then the three families (Austen Cargill and John Jr. and Cargill MacMillan) decided upon Switzerland. Already there were links there, both with the newly established family Salevia Foundation (one of the owners of Cargill Internacional) and with some private residence property, purchased for Edna MacMillan at an earlier date. Both the Foundation and the residences were situated in Geneva. After brief consideration of Zurich as a possible alternative site, Geneva was chosen for what became Tradax Geneve S.A. The Cargill lawyer handling the negotiations, Donald Levin, had visited the Swiss federal and cantonal tax authorities in February 1956 to work out an agreement as to just how Tradax Geneve would be taxed, given its relationship to the Panamanian parent company, Cargill Internacional. From these sessions, Tradax was able to accurately measure its expected tax burden in Switzerland. For the immediate period, it was to be SFR 50,000 per year, but both Swiss agencies left open the question of later review if Tradax business changed.

Tradax Geneve promised to be a complex and demanding management task, and the choice of its two leaders now had to be made. The chief executive officer was to be Walter Gage. In one sense, this was a surprising choice inasmuch as he had *no* international experience. Gage was highly regarded among senior management. He had joined the Company in 1936 as a merchant and had also worked for Ed Grimes in the Washington office and been a branch manager (at Buffalo). Then he had gone to Minneapolis to assume various posts in the Grain Division, finally taking the important coordinating post as head of all of the branch operations. His choice as head of Tradax Geneve was seen by people around the Company as putting a "first-stringer" into the job.

The other member of the two-person top management cadre was an even greater surprise. It was none other than John Peterson. Although not yet retired from Cargill, Incorporated, Peterson was 65 years old. A pullback from active management was going to be required. He had talked of early retirement. With Tradex Geneve in a financial situation that was going to be tenuous at best, it would need a wise and diplomatic emissary to the European banks. The operations of Tradax Montreal had been marginally successful in its 18 months of operation (John Peterson criticized it, however, "on the sense that the net profit in relation to volume has been ridiculously small"). Even after adding in its small profit, it was bringing a painfully small amount of working capital with it to Geneva. Peterson had a deserved reputation at Cargill of being a master at cajoling bankers, and his involvement in the Swiss company was seen as a stroke of genius by some observers. He soon moved to Geneva as chairman of the board of Tradax.

Gage's role was ambiguous. He was to be an independent, entrepreneurial chief executive officer, freewheeling in a complex multinational business environment, yet was to fit himself and the trades of his group into the overall policy and specific trading plans of Cargill, Incorporated. Gage wanted decision making centralized in his hands, and this sometimes led to strained feelings between the Geneva office and the London office. Mickey Cross, for example, had many years of experience in trading ocean freight. Yet the Geneva traders more than once took issue with Cross and proceeded independently, which led to some mutual antagonism.

In October 1956, Israeli forces suddenly invaded Egypt, soon overrunning the Suez Canal and effectively shutting off shipping through that vital artery. Tradax, showing more evidence of its willingness to speculate, earlier had developed a substantial long position in freight. After the hostilities began, freight charter prices skyrocketed, and Tradax made substantial profits. These were mainly Geneva contracts rather than London contracts of Mickey Cross. While Cross might not have objected to the Geneva positions, nevertheless the success of the charter contracts seemed to make the Geneva group even more imperious about their own abilities in trading ocean freight.

John Peterson's place in the Geneva spectrum was also ambiguous. He performed essentially the same catalytic role as he had for Cargill in 1933, when he engineered the banking arrangements that brought the Company through its "banking crisis." Cargill Internacional had been given that pitifully small capital bankroll to perform the huge task the Geneva operation faced. Cargill Securities Company had put in a small additional amount, but the Tradax Geneve balance sheet would not have impressed even a small-town banker in rural Minnesota. Yet Tradax needed major working capital funds to engage in the type of broad-ranging trading it contemplated.

Peterson seemed to have a knack with banks in situations like this and was successful once again. With Gage, he made visits to a selected list of important banking institutions. They particularly focused on two key banks, one in Switzerland and one in Germany. In these contacts his approach was that one must not view the Tradax balance sheet literally but as a piece of a larger picture, one backed by the reputation and financial strength of Cargill, Incorporated. This was a delicate balancing act, for it also had to be made clear that Tradax was an independent entity, at arm's length from Minneapolis. Using his most gracious and expansive banker skills, Peterson was able to insinuate into the conversations that "Cargill had never let a subsidiary go bankrupt, and while Tradax was not a subsidiary, Cargill had never allowed a related company to go bad." Both the Swiss and German bankers understood this veiled distinction, and to the surprise of no one Tradax got its lines of credit from both.

Peterson did not disavow the subsequent stories of another "Peterson coup with the bankers." He seemed unable to resist calling attention to his self-appointed role as "savior" of Cargill. As he retired from Cargill, Incorporated, he wrote Austen Cargill: "If I bow myself completely out of Cargill, I don't know what the repercussions of that might be among our banking friends, and I feel sure some of them may not be too happy."

The Montreal office was now closed down in stages, with most of the personnel moving to Geneva and several being assigned to a new Tradax Geneve office in New York City, headed by Tom Connoly. By the end of the year, Gage and Peterson had with them in Geneva Bob Hatch from Montreal; Pearsall Helms (who had been the manager at the Wilson, North Carolina, operations); W. Duncan MacMillan, John Jr.'s younger son; and several other young men. The latter included three young British graduates, all from major universities in England: Leonard Alderson, Kenneth Spence and, later, Allen Blair. They became known as the "English Mafia." In addition, Peter Brees, a Belgian national, joined the management cadre, working out of Antwerp. A number of years later, when Tradax had a heavy influx of Dutch, the term became the "Dutch Mafia." Gage also established a Hamburg, Germany, office, assigning Charles Bachman there. The Antwerp office was headed by Brewster (Stu) Hanson, with Brees soon moving there. In London, Michael Cross had left the Ross T. Smyth Group to become Cargill's British head. With this cadre and others hired in the early months, Gage and Peterson had their own independent management team in place.[6]

Relationship Tensions

"Independent" was the operative term in those days, in order to establish the critically important legal separation of Cargill Internacional and the Tradaxes from Cargill, Incorporated. In the Montreal operation, independence had been difficult to achieve. John Peterson wrote just after Tradax Geneve opened: "Montreal and Minneapolis were just too near together by telephone. . . . Montreal, instead of operating under a contract it had with its parent company, was operating as if it were a management company—thus confusing the entire set-up."

An important memorandum in May 1956 attempted to spell out this relationship more explicitly: "It is emphasized that the Tradax companies are organizationally and functionally separate and independent. . . . Communications between the two organizations must be restricted to the following: (a) business proposed or consummated between the two organizations; (b) information, gossip, evaluation, etc. which any independent company might exchange with one another; (c) accounting and forwarding instructions and information relating to business done or contemplated through or with Tradax, Incorporated." Cargill, Incorporated, executives were not to give any "direction" to Tradax; dealings with the latter were to be as with an independent company. At the same time, the very reason for Tradax existence was to enhance the international trading of Cargill, Incorporated. There were going to be innumerable links between the two, advice, coordinated efforts, buying and selling arrangements, with each paying the other for services rendered on a regular commercial basis.

Problems about this concept now multiplied with the far more complex role assumed by Tradax Geneve (and Tradax New York). The knotty question of Tradax open positions and limits, already an irritant from the Montreal experience, continued as a sore spot. Earlier, Erv Kelm had stated the linked hedging policy of Geneva and Minneapolis in a memorandum to John Jr.: "Cargill Internacional is setting itself up to do a world trade in grains and commodities and should be able at a fee of about 1/4¢ per bushel to keep short 8–10 million dollars for the risk of Incorporated," to be established "at the instruction of Incorporated but after consultation with Cargill Internacional." In October 1956, Gage wrote Peterson that he was "long a fair amount of grain," suggesting that "practically speaking, no limit be placed on our position in those grains . . . this business is not and cannot be done as a continuing series of cross hedges but rather a continuing series of speculations . . . for the most part the cross hedges that are available through transactions and cash commodities in international trades, are not really cross hedges at all but two sided speculations." Kelm opposed Gage on this. While he agreed that "the only large-scale sensitive markets are world commodity markets," he worried about the open positions. "I think what Walter means by his talk of 'a series of speculations,' " Kelm hopefully stated, "is that he should take some unhedged position in cheaper grains in addition to a cross-hedged position and does not mean to infer that there is no alternative to wholesale speculation."

Gage did intend mainly speculation, however, and Peterson sided with him, not because of Gage's philosophy but because the amounts involved were small at this time. Nevertheless, he lectured Gage: "Human experience and the theory of capital conservation seem to be against open positions. Human experience seems to approve the observation that when crashes like that of February 1948 occur, cross hedges pay off, but in the interim, insurance against such a contingency may be costly. Capital . . . seems to be willing to bear such costs [but] unwilling to be engaged in excessive open positions."[7]

John Jr., eager to increase the throughput of Cargill, Incorporated, grain into international trading, worried that the amount of grain moving through the Company's Baton Rouge and Albany terminals was not what it should be, and he urged Gage to keep Minneapolis informed of all Tradax bids. Gage wrote a testy letter back, pointing out that it *was* in Tradax's interest to trade with Cargill but that "it requires not only complete co-operation between our two companies but also from European buyers and the last is beyond our ability to control. . . . We rarely offer at anything over Cargill's price to us and frequently at less simply because competition forces it." Nevertheless it was true that Gage was very profit-oriented—as one of the "English Mafia" put it, "he was extremely bloody minded." Gage constantly emphasized that Tradax had a number of customers and Cargill was only one of them.

One of the early members of the Geneva group put the tensions about sales between Tradax and the Minneapolis merchants this way: "It was almost worse than trading with third parties—you were afraid the other side was not telling you everything you needed to know. If you learned of a new bullish factor, you made the trades, *then* you told. There were many shouting matches and terrible telexes."

While the Gage notion of unlimited "limits" was anathema to the Cargill executives, the brightening, indeed buoyant conditions in the United States over the summer and fall of 1956 gave the Minneapolis group a more entrepreneurial approach. In the Finance Committee's report to the directors in May 1956, a special appendix had been attached concerning limits, and the Committee had concluded that the Grain Division and Vegetable Oil Division limits "could well be reviewed, and to good advantage." A "Special Committee" was established, with Kelm as chair and Fred Seed and Bob Diercks as members. The committee, rather than concentrating on the limits, recommended that it be given a "capital fund" for taking advantage of seasonal market trends. Even here "outright long or short positions are avoided," and the trading positions were to be "made on a statistical basis, rather than on a basis of human judgment." In other words, trading was to be by previously established formulas. These were to be mostly spreads; Kelm reported to John Jr. in February 1957 that the " 'S' Account should have a spread or two on its books at least most of the time." Thus, the Gage advocacy of speculative positions did not seem as far out of line with the Minneapolis beliefs as it might have been at an earlier period.[8]

By the end of the calendar year 1956, Tradax would have almost a full year of trading from Geneva; by November 30, 1956, they reported a profit of $877,000, with all of their subsidiaries in the black. John Jr., skeptical, wrote Peterson, who was vacationing in Jamaica in January 1957: "Kelm and I are not too sure that, in one sense, the figures are fictitious. We suspect that they may have brought some of their long freight to the market. In the case of open freight, I think the principle of cost or market (whichever is lower) should be applied."

It was true that the Tradax situation made for complicated accounting concerns. Tradax was trading in many currencies all over the world, was buying and selling short-term and long-term ocean freight, was even engaging in some barter. Therefore it was difficult to get a handle on just where Tradax stood at a particular moment. This seeming imprecision often led to disputes with Minneapolis, with the latter group believing on more than one occasion that Tradax was overstating its profits. This related directly to the issue of bonuses, a particularly sensitive issue. Tradax did not yet have a formalized executive compensation plan. Peterson, calling the Tradax group the "forgotten men," had been able to persuade Cargill MacMillan to authorize substantial bonuses, with both salaries and bonuses to be decided by Gage and Peterson. The Minneapolis group more than once was irritated by the size of these Tradax management bonuses.

Thus, there was a growing mistrust between Minneapolis and Geneva. Minneapolis traders seemed particularly exercised about the Tradax New York office, which they felt did not communicate openly about the state of the market in Europe and the Tradax plans there. John Peterson, embarrassed about this, wrote the Tradax representative in New York to "immediately investigate" the complaints. Finally, in August 1957, the Tradax New York office was closed. All of the people remained in place but became Cargill, Incorporated, personnel.

A considerable part of this friction between Geneva and Minneapolis was inevitable, given the strikingly different situations for the two offices. The Geneva ethos was highly entrepreneurial, and Gage and his young group saw themselves as being in a "fast track" business environment, one that begged for aggressive risk-taking and wide-ranging business contacts. The Geneva group worked very long hours (a pattern that worried the Minneapolis executives, who frequently commented on this). If Montreal seemed a grain trade backwater, Geneva was certainly not. The first year of Tradax Geneve had been a controversial but spectacular one.[9]

John Jr. made two long inspection trips to Europe, one in April–May 1956 and the other in April 1957. For both, the *Carmac* was deadheaded to Europe so that he and his party could visit the European ports where Tradax might want grain trading facilities (and, incidentally, have John Jr. served food of his own choice by his own steward). The 1956 trip was a euphoric one, taken just at the start of Tradax Geneve. Even though Dutch newspapers treated the *Carmac* stop there as a visit by a millionaire in his yacht ("the newspapers misrepresented our trip shamefully, it was a business trip and we are salaried employees of the company," John Jr. wrote a Dutch friend), the trip was a resounding success. John Jr. returned "highly pleased with our present European personnel" and full of new plans.

By the time of the spring 1957 visit, however, John Jr. was more critical of the Geneva group. The softening of time charter rates had caught Tradax with exposed long freight (ocean shipping) positions. There were also difficulties with grain trading that spring. John Jr. wrote Austen Cargill in April 1957: "The boys made some serious mistakes in that they did not give enough allowance for the impact of Southern Hemisphere grains and they took quite a trimming on the premiums of their long North American grains." Apparently John Jr. came over with a chip on his shoulder, believing that many of his views had been ignored by Geneva. He wrote in his diary, "Gage clearly doesn't want us in Europe!" Taking umbrage at this, he wrote Gage a waspish letter: "I think I have some very worth-while ideas in re the growth and development of Tradax, which is the basic reason for my making the trip—which is not easy for me to do. I think my trip would be wasted unless I can obtain the undivided attention of you and your staff . . . as you know, the family look to me as the Operating Head of our enterprises, and I simply have not been kept properly posted on what was going on."

On his return, John Jr. still seemed irascible. In a sharply worded memorandum he commented on Gage: "WALTER is overloading himself by not delegating enough. He is apparently his own BOSS TRADER. We never considered TRADING to be his forte . . . he should appoint a head merchant . . . and then make sure he does not exceed the limits assigned him." John Jr. wanted a full-blown freight department, worrying that the Tradax merchants were trading freight too much on a short-term basis. He complained once more of the long hours at the office (which he felt were ineffective); he wrote his brother: "Walter resents my accusation that he is running a sweat shop, and insists that everyone just loves working 14 hours a day." He also faulted the group for "a bad case of telephonitis," not taking full advantage of the wire system.

A European Port Terminal, Ocean Ships

From the 1956 trip, John Jr. pushed for Cargill's own port facilities in Europe and Cargill's own ships to reach them. "Grain is moved in small, inefficient sized vessels," he wrote on May 18, 1956, "in marked contrast to the movement of ore and petroleum. There are no storage facilities of consequence in European ports . . . discharge is slow and storage at destination frightfully expensive." Except for a "few vessels owned by Dreyfus, Continental, & Andre" none of the shippers had their own bottoms. In brief, he concluded, "THE FIELD IS WIDE OPEN."

On the basis of his judgments from this 1956 trip, John Jr. proposed that Cargill build storage and handling facilities "in 4 ports in the following order: (1) Rotterdam (2) Antwerp (3) Hamburg (4) Liverpool." Later, similar facilities could be obtained in London, Lisbon and Sicily. In turn, Tradax would begin aggressive ocean shipping chartering, including the encouraging of future time charters in ships built to Tradax specifications and then leased.

John Jr. had particularly pressed for the Rotterdam office and elevator. He felt that the Geneva group was "stalling" on both. In addition, he wanted Tradax to investigate the building of three 5,000-ton self-unloading coastal vessels and two or three small tugs, also for European ports. Cargill would also develop plans for three larger, 14-knot, oceangoing dry-cargo carriers, to operate out of Baie Comeau, Norfolk and Baton Rouge.

From 1957 through 1959, John Jr. went through several versions of plans relating to these oceangoing vessels. An oceangoing barge carrier still intrigued him very much, and a number of his plans were built around this notion. By September 1957, John Jr. proposed a trip to Asia to investigate further Tradax links there and, particularly, to discuss shipbuilding possibilities with Japanese shipbuilding companies.

Kelm had proposed feed mills abroad (he first suggested Mexico), and the Oil Division already had indicated interest in possible plants in Europe. Walter Gage and John Peterson seemed always lukewarm about such plans. Peterson put their joint views succinctly in a letter to John Jr.: "As to the investment in various types of property throughout the world, I have no doubt that if one had unlimited funds for investment one could make such suitable investments that would prove advantageous . . . however, we in Tradax are confronted with a proposition, namely we are a trading organization and as a trading organization we need immediate tools which I like to think of in terms of things that come first, namely money in the business to justify credit." Peterson did agree that Tradax needed "suitable ships . . . Tradax expects to own ships and perhaps many ships. The only thing uncertain about this bit of optimism is the time when these things shall occur. My theory, therefore, is to continue to do business with the tools we have, keep whatever money we make in the business and dream about the happier days to come to the poor Greeks and others engaged in shipping business."

There continued to be ambivalence from Minneapolis over just how much influence to exert on Geneva in terms of the latter's trades. In the spring of 1958, for example, Geneva had problems controlling some barley trades by Stuart Allan in Argentina, where he had been posted by Tradax as their manager. Gage, when queried by Kelm about the losses that had ensued, reacted with irritation, and Peterson defended him: "Alas, that we should be engaged in a trading business where margins to justify risk turn out to be crocodile tears and empty phraseology." Kelm wrote a diplomatic letter back to Peterson: "It appears to me that Walter has misinterpreted the purpose of my letter . . . regarding our unfortunate happenings in the Argentine. My letter was not to place the blame for the situation on any one. We fully realize the difficulties under which Stuart Allan has been operating . . . if anything, the blame for allowing him to take such a large position is squarely here." Once again, this seemed to beg the question about who was calling the shots—why should Minneapolis be held accountable for a Geneva decision?

John Jr.'s expansive plans brought concern to his colleagues in Minneapolis, especially regarding the financing of these ideas. By October 1956, the Finance Committee had decided that no major commitments for capital expenditures be made "beyond those reasonably necessary," and in a special board meeting the directors elected to vote a formal statement to that effect, which was not their usual approach. By early 1957, money was tightening, and Albert Egermayer, who had assumed John Peterson's role as Cargill's banking contact, reported that "there has been a certain amount of talk coming from our banking friends with respect to our bank balances. For the most part, it has been in the nature of hinting, but in two or three instances rather direct approaches have been made."

Egermayer then surprised everyone with an intriguing insight about John Peterson's long-standing arrangement with the Chase National Bank. Egermayer questioned its inflexibility: "The company has paid 1/4% over the prime rate throughout the long period of relatively plentiful money, recently ended, when banks were much more interested in loans than in balances." Egermayer implied that the payment of the 1/4 percent over prime could be justified as a policy only in times when money was tight.

For years, Peterson unwaveringly had paid this premium to the Chase. Some in the Company felt this was mostly Peterson's largess, tendered because of his cozy relationship with his old bank. There may have been some of this. Even after his retirement from Cargill, Peterson maintained his partly deferential, partly conspiratorial role with Hugo Scheuermann, writing him in January 1955: "It has always been a source of the greatest pleasure to go back into the Chase and always be treated as if I was a graduate in good standing. . . . I can conceive of nothing lacking in our combination that has been so productive for our mutual institutions." When Scheuermann died two years later, Peterson persuaded the Cargill Foundation to contribute $5,000 to a New Jersey hospital in his memory (a sum that Cargill MacMillan objected to).

With business both in Minneapolis and Geneva not as good in the spring of 1957 as the previous year, John Jr. agreed that "we have to pull in our horns and minimize our capital expenditures" and suggested that several projects be postponed. But, he maintained, "I do not think we should let anything interfere with the Seven Islands and Rotterdam plans."[10]

A Fresh Public Relations Approach

Cargill's Oats Case had caused bad publicity for the Company. The *Time* magazine article "Wild Oats" in May 1954 had talked of the Company's "shenanigans on the commodity exchanges." Senator Paul Douglas had identified Cargill as "the largest dealer and speculator in the world"; Senator William Jenner described the Company as an "international speculator who reaped millions of dollars of profits by forcing American oat prices down with Canadian oats." Further, all of the litigation and its attendant publicity in the 1952–1954 period had produced an unexpected fallout—a steady deterioration of the Company's influence in government, particularly with the Department of Agriculture.

Bob Woodworth, who had held the post of vice president in charge of public relations, urged the board in early 1956 to authorize a quite substantial sum of money to hire an outside public relations counsel, one of the outstanding firms in the country, Carl Byoir & Associates. John Jr. wrote John Peterson: "We did not feel it could wait . . . it is expensive but I think the only thing we could do . . . our Public Relations people estimate that the annual cost of this will be $150,000. This figure staggered me when first presented, but I am satisfied that we just cannot afford not to try it for a while at least." Peterson, still on the Cargill board at that time, opposed it, but the board finally voted the amount.

The responsibility at the Company for the new public affairs effort was given to a young Cargill lawyer, William R. Pearce. With the help of the Byoir organization, plans moved quickly and within weeks Pearce and his colleagues had the outlines of a comprehensive program. In the Byoir group's preliminary study, they had collected and photostated every reference to the Company that had appeared in three of the nation's leading newspapers over the entire period 1940–1956. As an internal memorandum put it, "of the many references turned up, only two were positive . . . all of the others . . . contributed to the notion that we were (1) a large speculator, (2) constantly involved in legal difficulties . . . and (3) making unconscionable profits at the expense of producers and consumers." The Byoir group emphasized that Cargill's dynamic, innovative nature was its greatest asset, "a paradox in view of the difficulty it has caused us with the trade." Soon news releases, picture features and other media contacts were put in the hands of the media emphasizing the set of strengths that Cargill brought to the marketplace.

It did not take long, however, for John Jr.'s instinctive secretiveness and desire to stay out of the limelight to reassert itself. Just after the first of the year, 1957, a Byoir-written news release reported that the Company had "handled a record volume of grain" since the previous June and that the total by the end of the crop year in May "may well exceed half a billion bushels." John Jr., in Jamaica for his winter vacation, wrote an irate letter to Cargill MacMillan, "This makes me see red. . . . If there is any more of this we will make an absolutely clean sweep in Public Relations. Please issue an *ultimatum*. . . . I am HOT." Cargill MacMillan wrote back: "I just don't know what to say about your letter of January tenth in which you nearly rupture a blood vessel over a January second press release. . . . I think Byoir is doing a very valuable job if only from the effect that it is having on the morale of our own organization. . . . It is helpful to our own people to feel that, for a change, they are getting good publicity instead of bad."

John Jr. not only failed to take this advice but continued sending critical missives to Minneapolis, not just about public relations but on other matters, too. Finally, in mid-February, Cargill MacMillan wrote his brother: "For heavens sake, stop needling everybody or we won't have any organization left. The best job ever turned in is simply being met by a stream of querulous letters from Jamaica. I am very serious—we very nearly lost Ray King and I am fearful of three others more important than King." John Jr. attached his brother's note to his diary page and penned a defiant comment: "Why my B.P. [blood pressure] is high." Once again, John Jr. seemed to be exhibiting a pattern of irritability and impatience, so much so that it was affecting the organization.

However, the public relations efforts continued as planned and soon contributed to a signal success story for the private grain trade in its relations with the U.S. Department of Agriculture. It began with two steps backward. In January 1956, the House Committee on Appropriations issued a preliminary report highly critical of the private-trade warehousemen about the deteriorating condition of government-held grain. Then, on April 6, 1956, the USDA issued an order limiting delivery of grain for Commodity Credit Corporation (CCC) export contracts only to seaboard points. This wiped out the flexibility that the private grain trade had had in delivering grain for export at inland points, important for companies like Cargill with facilities in many parts of the country. The *Northwestern Miller* commented about this controversial decision: "USDA officials agree that interior sales do not necessarily dislocate internal market price patterns . . . that any such dislocations . . . are quickly equalized. But they say . . . that the f.o.b. port sales decision will remove even any *trace* of such dislocation" (emphasis mine). The editors felt that this rigid CCC position was drawing a "deepening wedge" between the government and private industry; "the department [USDA] may be only a step away from a complete takeover of the entire trade in grains."

Cargill executives, with the help from the Byoir group, worked assiduously with many others in the industry to reverse this decision and had quick success. On July 17, 1956, the government, in a surprising turn-around, killed the plan altogether, in the process allowing grain traders to fill some of the requirements from open market purchases around the country. A payment-in-kind subsidy for exporters of wheat also was established. Certificates were issued at the applicable subsidy rate when exporters made private sales at the lower market rate, and these certificates were redeemable in wheat from CCC stocks.

The *Northwestern Miller* hailed a "return to free marketing," noting that the grain trade was "cautiously pinching itself to see if it's awake and not dreaming, that there is at long last a bend, if not a reverse turn, in the rough and narrow road of state trading. . . . The government does not, indeed, completely retire from the grain market, but at least it lifts one of its feet from it."

An outgrowth of the earlier decision of the government not to allow CCC deliveries other than at seaboard points had been a tightening of grain available for sale at interior points. Cargill had been quick to buy what was left, particularly grain from the Northwest, and a number of the commission men in Minneapolis felt their own interests were being damaged. Finally, John Jr. decided to enter the public relations fray himself. He wrote his daughter the next day: "Yesterday I had another very strenuous day when I was host at luncheon for the eight leading commission men in Minneapolis . . . our aggressive procurement program in the country has gotten them by the ears and it reached a point where I almost needed a bodyguard to go around town." John Jr. had been diplomatic at this meeting, and it seemed to alleviate much of the tension.

There also had been new contacts between Cargill and the Chicago Board of Trade. In August 1956, John Jr. received an invitation to lunch from Julius Mayer, his old friend from Continental Grain who had stood behind him in the Corn Case. On this occasion Mayer, now chairman of the board of the CBOT, posed the question of whether Cargill could be persuaded to return to the Exchange. John Jr.'s diary entry recorded the results: "Told him impossible until they get rid of limitation of lines" (i.e., limiting the amount of futures Cargill and other large traders could hold). The idea of return had taken root, however, and John Jr. wrote Robert Liebenow, the CBOT president, in December 1957, that he and his associates "have been giving serious thought to the matter of resolving our differences of opinion . . . and applying for clearing-membership . . . [in] reaching friendly ground, I sincerely hope that the following expression of our views will be helpful." John Jr. then proceeded to impose the condition that the CBOT must reconstitute its way of choosing directors so as to give explicit representation for the operating companies themselves. Apparently the CBOT board felt this to be too gratuitous, and the reconciliation fell through.[11]

The Research and Development Department

Cargill had been doing research for a good many years. Some had been of very high quality—the grain laboratory, where Julius Hendel had first worked, had done an outstanding job on grain grading, and Hendel also had interested himself in scientific feeds in the 1940s. However, most research had been done by individual divisions and, to use *Cargill News* words, "this resulted in an overlap of effort and facilities, and oftentimes a lack of qualified trained personnel to do the work." This slippage, a potential weakness of decentralization, now persuaded the Company that an outside consultant was needed, and the Midwest Research Institute was hired to study the Company's research function. Out of this came a suggestion that a Research and Development Department be formed. Dr. A. Richard Baldwin, who had headed the research department of Corn Products Company, was interviewed as a possible head. Even at this point, the Company executives seemed of two minds about just how much centralization could be accomplished. Pete McVay, for one, wanted to hire Baldwin but only for Oil Division research. Baldwin finally refused to come unless there was a truly centralized research effort. The dissenters grudgingly gave in, and he agreed to come as Cargill's first director of research.

With a large room at the Minneapolis Grain Exchange, he began what first seemed a rather ambiguous assignment—"John Jr. felt that I was there to help him get his own ideas further advanced; Cargill MacMillan thought I was there to keep John Jr. under control." Cargill MacMillan's concern was probably well considered, for John Jr.'s inventive mind was still actively producing a stream of new ideas. Some of these provided "leading edge" technology for the industry. Others had less direct application to Cargill business, and some were even outright failures. In the sweep of John Jr.'s inventions, the success rate was comfortably high, but a substantial percentage of failures was also to be expected.

John Jr.'s innovational thrust seemed to increase in the 1950s. Despite a demanding personal calendar cluttered with both internal problems and outside distractions, especially the Oats Case and the Seed Adulteration Case, he attempted to maintain a schedule that allowed a day a week at home, where he pored over piles of data and reduced his fresh ideas to hundreds of sheets of note paper. He instigated some major breakthroughs in grain trade technology. In 1957, he obtained an important patent on water craft propulsion. The notion had been tried on the two Cargill towboats, the *Carpolis* and the *Carpaul*, and involved a horizontal groove on each side of the vessel's stern that would channel water toward the propeller to take advantage of the jetlike force from the channeling through the groove (not unlike the pinching of a watermelon seed between two fin-

Schematic diagram of the "bubbler" ship propulsion design by John MacMillan, Jr., 1957.

gers). Nicknamed "the Bubbler," it worked very well and gave substantially increased efficiency to a ship's propulsion (*Cargill News* estimated some 20 percent). It had wide application, too, much beyond just Mississippi River towboats.

He also developed a heated tank for barging molasses, and new materials-handling notions were tried for unloading bulk aggregates. An air-inflated plastic cover for barges was also given a number of trials, and there were several rudimentary storage facilities on land using a polyethylene covering (Company personnel gave the name "Chloe" to these "stepchildren" after the poor girl lost in the swamplands, popularized at this time by bandleader Spike Jones).

The idea of using air actually to *hold up* a roof had intrigued John Jr. since the 1930s. At that time, he had applied for and obtained a patent on a form of air-inflated roof. There were several other related ideas patented by others, so it was not a singular invention. At the time, it was not clear whether this was a practical idea. In 1943, a Los Angeles construction company had put up such a building, an "igloo" form using a canvas roof. It was to become a laundry supply service's sorting station. Cargill's Fred

Drum was living at that time in California, and he kept John Jr. informed about it. John Jr. wrote: "I am quite sure he is infringing on my patent and we will wait until the building is up (or perhaps until he has a few more built) and then move in on him." Things were not right, however, and the entire edifice ignominiously collapsed shortly after it had been inflated. John Jr. wrote Drum: "I cannot help but think if they had consulted us first it could have been avoided," and he bemoaned the fact that "there are no prospects of my collecting any royalties."

But John Jr. still wanted to try it himself. A mockup was constructed at Port Cargill and seemed to work well. Then the decision was made to put up a full-scale grain storage elevator in Fort Worth, Texas, built on a modified igloo configuration, with square ends. It was a huge building, covering almost 2.3 acres—550 feet long and 158 feet wide; at inflation it was to be 38 feet high. The fabric was an aluminized steel sheet; this was to be held up by forced air. After many false starts, the "blow-up party" (John Jr.'s words) took place in July 1958. After five hours of inflation (John Jr. called it his "huff and puff"), the entire structure was in place. Even after the elevator was filled to capacity (with 1.8 million bushels of grain), the air pressure would continue to be used.

Unfortunately, the entrances and exits for loading and unloading drew away too much air pressure. Once again there was an equally ignominious collapse, and the Fort Worth project had to be abandoned. Company gossip sometimes attributed the collapse to the accuracy of the Fort Worth schoolboys with BB guns, but the truth was that a structure using the then-existing technology was not readily adapted to entrance-egress needs. This problem, of course, has been solved in more recent years; the Minneapolis Metrodome and others are good examples. Later, a circular variation was tried by the Company in Maumee, Ohio, with success.

Fort Worth elevator with air-inflated roof, before inflation and after inflation, June 1958.

There were other John Jr. innovations in the 1950s that had little or nothing to do with the grain trade. He had continued his interest in the helicopter and suggested to the air force an application of the same propulsion notion that he had developed for shipping. There were exchanges of letters and some model building, providing once again a distraction from regular duties. A good deal of time also was spent on an electrical amplifying device, and there was an exchange of correspondence with the Air Force Research and Development Command concerning his thoughts on guided missiles.

John Jr. also had become quite intrigued by the unidentified flying objects (UFO) phenomenon. He and Cargill MacMillan believed that they had seen one in March 1953 while vacationing at the latter's Spooner, Wisconsin, property. Once again, John Jr. made contact with the air force concerning this, as well as maintaining contacts with fellow UFO aficionados. He also continued his longtime interest in weather, keeping up his links with officials at the Air Force Cambridge Research Center and in 1957 appearing as a discussant at a conference on the "Present Position and Future Outlook for Applied Meteorology" (writing in his diary at that time, "My weather studies becoming increasingly interesting. My understanding of the mechanism increases year by year. For a week now have concentrated on the solar-lunar series").

In the mid-1950s, John Jr. had another idea that was before its time. This was the use of sails as auxillary power for large-scale shipping. He had several tall masts erected at Port Cargill in order to experiment with the extent of wind power at various mast heights. He wrote Austen Cargill in March 1955: "We should build ourselves an Inspection Vessel which is a combination sail and power. We can test out our sailing ship ideas at little or no risk ... the attraction of sail is that it would simplify our long voyages ... particularly to Europe and the Philippines. Fuel capacity becomes a minor item with sail." He drew plans for a 10-masted ship and estimated that it could make an Albany–Antwerp trip at about two-thirds the cost for a diesel ship. Nothing much happened to these ideas, and the notion faded away, accompanied by some derision on the part of Cargill employees. By the 1980s this idea had become a reality, with applications both to large cruise ships and commercial vessels.

Yet from a company viewpoint, Cargill MacMillan's and others' concern that Cargill's research capability not be dissipated by extraneous effort was well placed. Recent writers analyzing the innovation process have pointed to the need for an open, informal administrative structure for research and access on a wide basis for new ideas. Having as strong and dominating a force as John Jr. fueling the research effort at Cargill could tend to channel new ideas too narrowly.

In August 1955, the Company announced that it was going to construct a major Research Department facility, two stories in height and costing approximately $350,000, to be located across the road from the Lake Office, in Minnetonka. The family corporation, Cargill Securities Company, provided the original financing. In 1958 it sold the building to the Cargill Pension Trust and the Cargill Foundation. The building opened in March 1956 and was dedicated to Austen Cargill.

Now Baldwin was able to pull nearly all of Cargill research into the department's orbit (although, at a later point, this high degree of centralization began to erode under renewed division pressure to "do our own research"). He supervised hybrid seed corn research, which continued at St. Peter, Minnesota, and Grinnell, Iowa, with new personnel added. The Oil Division laboratory was now brought into the Research Department, with a special oils and resins section and with several new people. The grain research laboratory at Elevator T, which had been under control of the terminal group, also was absorbed and continued its work on grain cleaning, separation and drying. This group also had done industry-leading work in explosion control.

It took several months to persuade the Nutrena group to become involved in the Research Department. It had an experimental farm at Pleasant Hill, Missouri; this seemed too far away to Baldwin, so he searched for a site in Minnesota, finding the right location at Elk River, some 30 minutes from Minneapolis; and Nutrena Research moved there under Baldwin.

One of the most important dimensions of feed research was the development of a proper scientific balance of ingredients. In the earlier days, feed mixing was a "rough-and-ready" task, but by the 1950s, feed companies competed vigorously on the basis of better scientific mixes. This now led the Company into another new technological field, the use of the computer.[12]

The IBM 650

By the early 1950s, a frontier in applied science, Operations Research, or OR, had found its way into the public press. In a significant *Fortune* magazine article in April 1951, what was called "this infant craft" was described in some detail. Up to this time the applications of OR had been primarily military. Its name had been coined by military scientists at the outset of World War II. "Now," *Fortune* said, it "may have a great future in the U.S. private economy." OR concepts involved complex mathematical calculations, using particularly the esoteric mathematics of linear programming (LP) models. LP was a method of solving a large array of simultaneous linear equations to provide a single "best" solution. As applied to business problems, it was highly effective in leading to a "least cost" solution. Given the complexity involved, it took a giant innovation to make OR a reality. This was the electronic computer. International Business Machines (IBM) was the pioneer here and in the early 1950s had developed an impressive machine they labeled the 650.

The Company first had installed IBM tabulating equipment back in 1927 under the aegis of John Jr. In August 1954, John Jr. requested Bob Harrigan, the Company's comptroller, to study the possible use of computers by Cargill. Calvin Smith was given the assignment to determine whether a computer could be economically justified to process normal accounting, financial and operating data.

As an interim step in October 1954, the Company ordered two IBM 604 electronic calculators. In the words of the IBM salesman, "the 604's were algebraically sound, could handle 100 cards a minute, and all you had to do was plug it in the wall." In May 1955, IBM announced the advanced IBM 650 magnetic tape system. Smith obtained approval to order the system, and on February 12, 1957, this computer became the second 650 tape system to be installed commercially in the United States.

Yet the power of this new instrument extended far beyond the mundane tasks of data processing, for with LP and other sophisticated mathematical techniques, a computer programmer could solve heretofore unsolvable problems. One of the first units of Cargill to begin to recognize this was the Feed Division. The missionary there, the person who initiated the thought and then pushed, persuaded and cajoled the division management to consider using a computer to try to rationalize some of the basic feed pricing problems was James R. Cargill, the son of Austen Cargill. The younger Cargill had been in the Feed Division for almost a decade, taking a wide range of responsibilities. In 1953 he was administrative assistant to J. D. Armstrong and had the responsibility for publishing Nutrena's weekly feed price lists, based on a set of costs calculated locally and sent in by each of the 10 Nutrena mills. Cargill, noting the lack of price consistency among the Company's geographically continguous mills and a rigidity in the feed formulas of several of these, suggested to James North (who had succeeded R. E. Whitworth when Whitworth died) and to other key Nutrena executives that Nutrena investigate using the IBM 650 to calculate feed formulas. There was only grudging backing of him at the start, for the existing way of calculating the formulas had become quite ingrained.

Despite the fact that proceeding on this would challenge some vested interests of plant managers, North allowed Cargill to proceed. Jim Cargill became a one-man committee, using a long series of memoranda from May 1955 to October 1956. His opening memorandum began: "The Age of Electronics has come to the feed business. We have arrived at the point where we must make a decision on how to apply the fantastic capabilities of an

ELECTRONIC DIGITAL COMPUTER to our business." The new computer, he vowed, readily could be adapted to calculating formulas, one of the most critically important decisions in the feed industry, with tremendous competitive implications. "Let's DON'T use it for checking our present method as that would be a waste of the computer's uncanny ability for volume and speed," he concluded; "let's put this thing to work where it will do us and our customers the most good."

Peat, Marwick, Mitchell & Co., Cargill's outside auditor (now named KPMG Peat Marwick), had a new OR department. So the Company requested it to recommend several possible OR firms for professional advice and help in writing LP programs for the Nutrena group. Caywood-Schiller Associates was selected and at one of the early sessions presented some very complex concepts. After the session there was some timidity and concern from the Nutrena group as to whether it could master the techniques. At a subsequent review session, Caywood told some of the disbelievers, "You have to have faith in God and chemistry." Jim Cargill wrote another persuading memorandum: "Is this the point to give up, or should we go ahead?" He urged a program for applying the LP techniques to one of Nutrena's most important products, Chick Starter.

Cargill and his programming colleague, Joe Clements, worked on the Caywood program under the direction of Caywood partner Don Schiller, and after a visit to the IBM home office to modify the Company's 650, the program was successfully run on this computer.

In September 1957, Nutrena went on-line with its major volume product called All-Mash Egg Feed, formulated by the sophisticated mathematics of LP, figured by the computer. All of this was accompanied by advertising that featured the computer, with a large full-page picture of Cargill's IBM 650 along with a poultry farmer and his wife. The lead for the advertisement trumpeted: "We saw Nutrena's electronic brain analyze 4 million ways to make egg feed." Nutrena was first in the industry to use a computer for scientific feed formulation, and this gave it an enormous competitive advantage. Other companies had to try to follow, but because of the complexity of the techniques, Nutrena had gained a quantum jump.

Shortly after Nutrena came on-line, Pfizer Corporation developed a new feed additive specifically designed to reduce costs for producers of broiler chicken feed. In order to promote this, Pfizer established a national competition, with the winner to be the person who could formulate the lowest-cost feed using Pfizer's additive. This was a natural application for LP, so Jim Cargill decided to enter Nutrena in the competition, using Nutrena's sophisticated computer program as a starting point. He drew on the 650 to compute the first 10 decimal places of the Pfizer-specified feed formula and, still not certain that only 10 decimal places would win, used a hand calculator to add 10 additional places. He submitted three entries, assigning the best of the three to his colleague, Clements, the next best to Warren Armstrong and the third best to himself. When the national results were in, Pfizer announced that Cargill had taken the first three places, just as Jim Cargill had planned. A three-wheeled Italian automobile was the prize, and Clements was awarded it.

The stunningly successful Nutrena use of the computer opened the eyes of the rest of the Cargill people. In April 1957, Jim Cargill was named staff assistant to Erv Kelm, "responsible for the application of Operations Research techniques in both the analysis of Company problems and in the development of long-range plans." John Jr. wrote a relative in December 1958: "Jimmie Cargill . . . is responsible for some accounting changes through the use of the I.B.M. electronic computers which have resulted in some spectacular progress." In 1959, plans went forward for use in the rest of the Cargill divisions, and John Jr. wrote his brother: "The most exciting thing we have had around here in a long time has been Jimmie Cargill's contention that we can add at least a cent a bushel to our terminal elevator margins by using the IBM computer. I must say that all the trial runs to date seem to confirm his contention. We are also getting pretty broad experience from the results of Nutrena's use of the machine, and everyone insists that the net gain is at the very least $2.00 per ton. So Jimmie's stock is going up daily."[13]

If linear programming could work for Nutrena feed formulas, it seemed to its boosters also to be applicable to the Grain Division, where grain mixing to grade was a key function. Once again, however, there was resistance from its line executives, who prided themselves on their ability to mix by drawing on their extensive past experience (in other words, by "feel").

A telling experiment was tried in 1963, when Cargill participated (with several other grain companies) in an extensive grain sale to the Soviet Union, the first that had been made to that country since the cold war began in the late 1940s. Part of Cargill's commitment was for 200,000 tons of durum. Durum grading was complicated; there were five grades, each with additional measures (density, moisture content, percentage of foreign material, etc.). LP seemed ideally fitted to the complicated matrix that would be involved here.

But serious logistics problems surfaced. The Albany terminal was to be the exporting elevator, as there was an adequate number of bins there to store the different lots. But the incoming rail cars could not be scheduled accurately enough to provide the various needed lots at the right time. The CCC was releasing some of the stored durum for part of the sale but was not willing to coordinate this with Cargill's dictated blending needs. Some incoming cars were misgraded, and other logistic complications multiplied. Finally, the Grain Division management fell back on traditional methods depending on human skill, and the Russians received their order on schedule. But it was a disappointing development for the LP enthusiasts. As Jim Cargill put it, in a later speech on the Russian sale at an Operations Research Institute convention, "Our computer will serve us mightily and well, but in the clutch, men will continue to serve themselves."

Farmers and Farm Policy, 1956–1959

The Soil Bank legislation in 1956 and the constant pressure by the USDA on the farmer to cut production had led to a substantial decline in acreage for many crops as the 1950s progressed. Wheat acreage, at almost 62 million in 1951, had dropped to 43.7 million in 1957; corn acreage had stood at 80.7 million in 1951 and had dropped to 71.9 million in 1957. Yet the incredible productivity of the farmer from better equipment, wider use of fertilizers, more productive seeds and advanced cropping techniques overpowered all of this, with output staying at high levels all through the decade. The trend toward increasingly large farms had continued, and farm productivity, expressed as output per unit of input, using a baseline of 100 for the year 1951, skyrocketed to 122 in 1958 and to 128 in 1960. Wheat yields per acre stood at 15.7 bushels in 1950, rose to 19.4 in 1955 and to 24 in 1960. For corn, the same figures were 37.8, 42.9 and 56.5 bushels per acre. With generally dropping prices on the six "basic" commodities and with the parity concept essentially held in place (with only Secretary Benson's small downward calibration), it was inevitable that the government would be buying, storing and making attempts to sell huge amounts of storable commodities.

The value of the United States private sector's agricultural exports had been declining through the early 1950s, from a high of $3.4 billion at the end of the Korean War to a low of $2.2 billion in 1956, while the trend line of government export amounts was upward in this same period. With the new arrangements instituted in July 1956—the payment-in-kind and related programs—private grain trade exports totals jumped to $2.8 billion in 1957 and remained just below this figure in 1958.[14]

Cargill, in part because of its new posture in public relations, now became more vocal concerning national farm policy. In May 1957, *Cargill News* reported on a company proposal concerning a wheat subsidy (to eliminate a CCC regional differential between the East and the West coasts) and in August 1957 noted that Senator Hubert Humphrey had read into the *Congressional Record* the Company's views supporting renewal of P.L. 480. In March 1958, Cargill MacMillan made the unusual decision (for him) to write a letter on Cargill stationery to all of the congressmen in the United States. The Reciprocal Trade Agreements Act was being considered for extension by the House Ways and Means Committee at this time, and it seemed to Cargill MacMillan that protectionist elements were

Cargill MacMillan after his election as president of Cargill, 1957.

constraining the international trading of grain. The example he used was Japan's decision to turn to China for soybeans, rather than trading with the United States, where prices were too high because of "unrealistic" support prices. A copy of his letter was also printed in the April 1958 *Cargill News* under the title "Going on the Record in Congress."

Personal replies came from a number of congressmen, exhibiting a wide gamut of opinion. The farm policy debate had become increasingly acrimonious, witnessed by a widening breach between congressmen from the farm states and those with more urban and consumer bases. In the process, new coalitions between Republicans and Democrats were beginning to surface. Cargill MacMillan was the recipient of more hostility than one might have expected. As one could guess, the farm-based congressmen were less than enthusiastic about anything attacking supports. But even industry-oriented members criticized him. One, a representative from West Virginia, wrote: "It is plain from the tenor of your letter that you belong to the Long-haired internationalist group . . . because of your interest in the exportation of surplus American wheat to foreign markets. . . . Why should this continue when hundreds of small American industries are not getting government subsidies and are being forced to liquidate because they cannot meet the prices of foreign-made goods that are gradually taking over the American consumer market." It was probably the first time that Cargill MacMillan had ever been called "long-haired."[15]

John Jr. also entered the argument, making several major speeches on why there was "too much government in the grain trade." The editor of an Indiana University publication, *Business Horizons*, persuaded John Jr. to contribute an article on his views. John Jr. agreed, and "Farm Surpluses: How to End Them" came out in the spring of 1959. It ranged over many issues. Population increases were analyzed and even dietary changes in India were mentioned. Central to the piece, however, was John Jr.'s desire for a free enterprise rationale for the farmer. The larger farmers would "utilize all of their tillable land, boost their total production, and lower their per-unit costs still further." The less efficient, "who have been willing to receive smaller margins in order to ride the gravy train in comfort," would have to "go back to work" and learn the new, efficient techniques.

The argument that skilled farmers would not be hurt by the elimination of support prices was widely debated in this period. Two economists, Willard Cochrane and Mary Ryan, in a 1976 book, analyzed this senstive issue and concluded that if supports had been taken off in the late 1950s, "the index of prices received would fall between 10 to 20 percent . . . the studies consistently indicated that the price of wheat would fall by nearly 50 percent, feed grains by 20 to 30 percent." Over the longer run, so other studies posited, the laws of supply and demand would stabilize farm prices and farm income. But Cochrane and Ryan disputed even this conclusion: "The elimination of government programs in the agricultural sector in the decades of the 1950s and 1960s would have resulted in extended periods of severely depressed farm prices and incomes . . . government programs did support farm prices and incomes significantly above equilibrium levels in the short and intermediate runs." Over the "very long run there is still some question," but Cochrane and Ryan concluded that few could have held on for that long. Only "some commercial farmers—the fittest" would have survived and grown.[16]

The Death of Austen Cargill

On May 24, 1957, Austen Cargill died. He had just turned 69 years of age. He had had the longest service in senior management of anyone in the Company at this point, joining Cargill in 1909 and becoming a director in 1911. After working with Ed Grimes in Milwaukee, he left for service in World War I, returning first to the La Crosse & Southeastern Railroad and then to the family's Cargill Securities Company lumbering operation in British Columbia. In 1926, he returned to the parent company, after a short stint with the La Crosse & Southeastern bus operation. He had concentrated on the country elevator system, but his interests were varied, and he

Austen S. Cargill,
mid-1950s.

made major contributions to the transportation side of the business, too. Elected executive vice president in 1944, he became Cargill's chairman of the board in 1950, a post he held until he retired in 1953. He remained on the board and its Salary Committee, however, and held these posts until his sudden death.

It was not just that Austen Cargill was a longtime member of top management. Whereas John Jr. and Cargill MacMillan were from the third generation of the family, he was second-generation, for he was the youngest son of the founder of the Company, W. W. Cargill. His position as the representative of the Cargill family interests was critically important. From time to time there had been tensions between the two families, the Cargills and the MacMillans, the most serious being the struggle for control in 1925. To the credit of the three family members—Austen Cargill, John Jr. and Cargill MacMillan—they had been able to move through these differences of opinion to a rapprochement that resulted in unified management—at least unified publicly. Some private reservations might have remained.

Yet there was more than just an accommodation among the three; there was friendship and goodwill, although one could not classify this as being 100 percent. John Jr.'s dominating personality had sometimes been less than fully attractive to Austen Cargill (as it had been equally unattractive to others). Austen's relationship to Cargill MacMillan seemed more straightforward. They appeared to think more nearly alike on many matters, and both men provided a steadying rein for John Jr.'s impulsivity. When one views Austen Cargill's role as a family balance wheel between the Cargills and the MacMillans, his loss becomes far more significant. Eras had passed with the deaths of W. W. Cargill, John MacMillan, Sr., and Ed Grimes. A similar milestone was reached with the death of Austen Cargill.

There was the usual eulogy in the minutes of the corporation, but this time it took a different path. The directors chose to reprint in full "as being the most fitting memorial" the speech that Austen Cargill had made at the commencement of the 1949 graduating class of Lake Forest Academy, from which he had graduated in 1908. He had asked the graduates for "your *whole* integrity and *absolute* honesty," rather than living in half-truths. One found what he called "the absolutes," not by intellect alone but by a personal God. "You don't have to go to church to find Him," he ended; "you can find Him anywhere. I found Him in the forests of British Columbia when I came up against a major crisis [his relation there with John Jr.]. I find Him when I am aboard ship at sea, when I am hunting or fishing. In fact, I feel closest to Him when I am close to nature." He exhorted the graduates to find "these great spiritual overtones" and to live by them. The sincerity of his words did seem to exemplify the man himself—he had been a very large moral force on the Company, and this legacy was probably his most important.[17]

Austen Cargill's death changed the ownership holdings equations in the Company, particularly so because his executors needed to sell Cargill stock in order to pay the estate taxes. To see this in perspective, some other issues related to stock holdings first need to be introduced.

Common Stock, Management Stock

In the late 1940s and early 1950s, John Jr., Cargill MacMillan and Austen Cargill had become aware again of the relationship between family holdings and outsiders' holdings of common stock and of the related issue of building an incentive system for senior management that would retain key people in the Company. They had come to believe that there was too much regular common stock being held by non-family members. Cargill MacMillan expressed this in one of his private memoranda as follows: "More & more Cargill stock falling into hands of trustees—we may wake up to find owner management a myth." John Jr. explained to the Executive Committee in the early summer of 1954 his goal of (1) reducing the number of common stockholders to 20, (2) exploring the possibility of changing the stock base of the four senior management people who had ordinary common stock (John Peterson, Fred Seed, Erv Kelm and Julius Hendel) and (3) developing a plan of reorganization of the corporate structure that would create a new class of stock, to be called management stock. It is not clear what was motivating John Jr. on this, but it seems likely from subsequent events that it was not just the desire for a management incentive program but also a strong personal desire to narrow the control of the Company into the hands of only the three families.

John Peterson prepared a long memorandum to the Executive Committee in August 1954, analyzing the stock holdings. He saw the 48 non-family shareholders as representing four different categories. First, there were the old employees and their heirs, who had been sold stock in 1916 by John MacMillan, Sr., at the time of reorganization. Second, there were the collateral relatives of W. W. Cargill, their heirs, trusts, and so on. Third, there was a set of shares owned by the John D. McMillan family, the Edward Osborne family, and James Taylor. And fourth, there were the four officers (Peterson, Hendel, Seed and Kelm) who owned what Peterson called "incentive stock." These four groups comprised 28 individuals. The remaining 20 common stockholders were the direct descendants of W. W. Cargill and John MacMillan, Sr., their trusts and members of their families. On July 31, 1954, there was a total of 236,614 shares of common stock.

Peterson further classified these according to the difficulty there might be in regaining control of the shares: All of the old employees, holding 7,645 shares, had at the start agreed to the Company's having a unilateral repurchase option; several of the collateral family (the Barkers, the Wisners, the Allers), holding a total of 7,850 shares, had given similar options. Likewise, the four officers had tendered options for repurchase—a total of 30,500 shares. Then there was a set of collateral family who had given no options: James B. Taylor, Ed Osborne and George Hoffman and his relatives, with a total of 19,234 shares. Last, there was the John D. McMillan "clan" (Peterson's word), who also had given no option and who held 2,775 shares. The total of all of these was 68,004 shares, leaving the three direct families holding 168,610 shares.

John Peterson saw some problems here. "The really troublesome stock," he wrote, "is likely to be that of Ed Osborne, Jim Taylor—each for his own special reason—and the heirs and their trusts of John D. McMillan." Further, the terms of any repurchase of the stock owned by the four management men had not been reduced to a formal option agreement. However, Peterson continued, "we all know what the intention was." The provisions that applied with the purchase of the Dwayne Andreas stock could apply here. This management stock, Peterson pointed out, was "not in the nature of remuneration in the sense of ordinary income . . . it was a stock transaction"; so if this stock were changed over to another form of management stock, it should not be taxable in any way as remuneration. Peterson also discussed the retirement of the minority block of Nutrena shares, still held by the R. E. Whitworth estate and other original Nutrena stockholders.

Cargill MacMillan, with the help of H. B. Juneau, now proposed a new "management stock" plan, one that would require a major reorganization of the capital structure of the Company. This came into being in August 1956, and in the process the capital structure was redefined. The common stock was split three-for-one, and additional shares of preferred stock and special preferred stock were authorized. In addition, a new form of stock ownership, "management stock," was established. The effect of these changes can be seen as follows:

As of June 30, 1956, *before* reorganization:

	Shares authorized	Shares outstanding
Preferred stock—$50 par value	120,000	101,945
Special preferred stock—$50 par value	6,000	6,000
Common stock—$10 par value	370,000	231,889

As of August 14, 1956, the date the reorganization was voted:

	Shares authorized	Shares outstanding
Preferred stock—$50 par value	400,000	101,945
Special preferred stock—$50 par value	10,000	6,000
Common stock—$5 par value	1,000,000	695,667
Management stock—$5 par value	165,000	—

The new management stock was to be issued by the board selectively to individuals in senior management on an individual-by-individual basis. The total number of shares could not exceed one-sixth of the number of shares of common stock outstanding. At any time the individual could convert his management stock to preferred stock. The Company, in turn, had the right to do the same unilaterally at its discretion. An "adjusted book value" would be determined at the end of each calendar year, which would be the actual book value at the time after the elimination of any value for patents, trademarks and goodwill and also would show the result of depreciation and amortization in reduction of book values. This up-to-date book value would then apply for any repurchase, required at an individual holder's retirement or death.

The establishment of the management stock also changed the way directors were elected. The special preferred stock would continue to elect the largest minority of directors, but now the management stockholders would have the right independently to elect one director. Then the remaining directors would be elected by a combination of the preferred, common and management stockholders, voting together share and share alike. To authorize any sale, lease or mortgage of assets of the corporation, consolidation or merger, decision to liquidate or dissolve or any decision to increase or decrease the amounts of stock authorized, it would take an affirmative vote of a majority of all of the holders of the various shares of stock (without distinction between the classes) and also a separate affirmative vote of a majority of the special preferred stock.

Thus, the directors had incorporated a top management incentive plan directly into the corporate structure of the Company. The opening paragraph of the plan stated this well. The Company "has grown and prospered under a regime . . . of management . . . by stockholders. . . . The incentive of a proprietary interest in the corporation is the best method of securing and maintaining executive talent of a high order. Competition of other companies for the men in policy making positions in this organization is extremely keen. . . . The offer of a stock interest in the corporation will be of great value in inducing good men to remain in the employ of the corporation."[18]

Before the plan went into effect, the Company exercised its option to eliminate the common stock holdings of those old employees, heirs and collateral family who had earlier given such options. Some of this common stock was purchased outright from them, and in other cases the employee or collateral family member chose to convert to preferred stock.

Allocating the Management Stock

Establishing the management stock was one thing; allocating it, quite another—not at all a routine matter. John Jr., Cargill MacMillan and Austen Cargill first wanted to eliminate the common stock holdings earlier sold to Julius Hendel, John Peterson, Fred Seed and Erv Kelm. These holdings originally had been acquired by the four on a different basis from the proposed management stock. They had actually purchased the stock by borrowing the money with which to buy it and with the Company guaranteeing their loans. These loans varied in amount and were made at different points for each of the four. Therefore, the Company's option to buy, using a formula based on book value, varied substantially among the four. Cargill MacMillan, in a private memorandum, called this "very embarrassing . . . if we exercise option some stock is called at 130, some at 115 and some at 80."

When Dwayne Andreas, one of the original holders of common stock given to management, cashed his holdings when he left the Company in 1952, the calculation allowed him just over 93 percent of the book value. Essentially this same valuation was now used for the four remaining. Hendel and Peterson were not in management by this time, so their common stock was converted to preferred stock. Seed and Kelm had theirs converted to management stock. The formula produced slightly varying effects—Peterson and Seed received just over 90 percent of book value; Hendel, 87.8 percent; and Kelm, 82 percent.

Next there was the question of how to allocate stock to other senior members of management. As the three family members talked over how many people to include, a substantial difference of opinion surfaced. John Jr. wrote in his diary for August 1, 1956: "I am for the least in number, about 9. C Mac & ASC for the most, about 22." A working formula was needed, and the decision was made to use job levels as the starting criteria—so much for the chief executive officer, a somewhat smaller amount for the executive vice president and so on down the management ladder. Titles did not signify the same responsibility across divisions, and there needed to be balance between those management members who were also directors, some of whom were on the Executive Committee, and those who were not. Further, there were to be limits set in terms of total holdings of management stock. Therefore, when the actual decisions were made for allocating stock, it was not an automatic exercise; the board discussed each person and decided each year whether he or she should be included.

Further, under the new plan, the employees would not be able to buy the stock outright, using loans guaranteed by the Company, as with the earlier plan. Rather, each person would have a "participation allocation," a fictitious sum of shares he was entitled to hold. Each year the earnings per share was calculated; this figure were then split in half, with one half used to purchase stock for each executive holding an allocation of management stock and the other half put into a "deferred bonus" non-interest-bearing account, also in the executive's name. The number of fictitious shares in the allocation for the next year was reconciled with the actual shares purchased. A cash sum was also paid to cover taxes. When a holder of management stock left Cargill at his retirement date, or if he died prior to that date, his two accounts would be automatically cashed out, using a Company-defined updated book value calculation for the management stock. If he resigned before retirement, at the Company's discretion he would be able to cash out at that point (there were no women holders of management stock at this time).

It was an ingenious system, giving the executive portions of his stock each year but holding out the carrot of the much larger holding if he stayed with the Company and continued to perform (the allotment could be increased or reduced at the discretion of the board). Senior management jokingly called this the "golden handcuff." Further, as compensation was tied directly to the growth in net worth of the Company, there was more incentive for management shareholders to promote its growth. Dividend policy had always been set by the family members as owners, and over the years, including the days of John Sr., their philosophy had been to pay substantial salaries and only moderate dividends and retain most of the earnings to build up net worth. Now, by the nature of the calculation of the value of management stock, paying only nominal dividends was in the management stockholders' interests, too.

By the end of the first year of the plan's operation—the end of the crop year 1956–1957—there were only five holders of management stock (and one of these was John Peterson, just phasing out due to his retirement). By the end of the next crop year, eight more people were added, with six more in the crop year 1958–1959. The numbers added slowed for a while after this.[19]

Buying Out Relatives

Not so easy, however, were those situations where the nonoption collateral family and the John D. McMillan group were involved. Here the purchase of the shares became a matter for negotiation. Had the Company been publicly held, with its shares fully distributed and with good market liquidity and with dividends comparable to that of similar companies, there would have been a market price that could have been readily determined. Cargill, Incorporated, was a private company, however, with its stock closely held, no foreseeable public market and a nominal dividend. Thus, the stock would logically carry an "illiquid price," somewhat below the liquid price. Just exactly what this amount was would be determined on the basis of the situation of the Company at the time the sale was proposed. Not only would the then-existing book value be an important determinant but also the relative desires of the Company and the stockholder as to whether each wished the sale to occur. If the holder wanted the sale more than the Company did, the price might be lower than if the opposite were true. Two examples will illustrate this problem.

The first case occurred just before World War II and involved Roy Hoople, one of the Company's long-service employees. Hoople, fearing that federal capital gains taxes would be raised in 1942 and nearing the end of his working career, asked John Sr. about disposing of some of his regular common stock. John Sr. referred the request to Cargill MacMillan, who proposed a price of $18 per share to Hoople. "This not only gave me a decided jolt," Hoople wrote John Jr., "but was not particularly conducive to my physical well being." Hoople added that he understood that Cargill was a closely held corporation and was not required to buy at all, "but to say that a stock that has a book value of over $55 per share is worth only $18 per share is absurd." Hoople ended: "I had hoped to round out a half century with the Company before retiring, but it is perhaps apropos that I do so at this time and I therefore hereby tender my resignation."

Hoople's action was an unexpected development. John Jr. subsequently penned on the letter: "Resignation not accepted and pay went on whether he came to work or not." Finally, Hoople was persuaded to reconsider, and he stayed active with the Company until December 1946. By then he had compiled over 53 years of service. He kept his stock until his sudden death in 1949 (he was an avid duck hunter and died near a duck blind, going to pick up a duck he had just shot).

The second case involved Howard McMillan. On August 2, 1955, he submitted his resignation as a director of Cargill, Incorporated, Erv Kelm replacing him. He had been on the board since the Company had been reorganized in 1936. Some remember certain ill feeling connected with this resignation, but the remaining record does not authenticate this. Howard McMillan had been elected president of the Minneapolis Grain Exchange and apparently felt that it would be a potential conflict of interest were he to stay on the Cargill Board. There also had been some competitive disagreements between Cargill and Osborne-McMillan.

There *was* animosity, however, just one year later, when Howard McMillan decided to sell his Cargill regular common stock back to the Company. This was in the period when John Jr. was urging such sales, so the motivation came from both parties. There was no option extant, and therefore the price was to be bargained. The Company offered McMillan $100 per share, just under 60 percent of the book value at that moment. The offer was accepted. It was a grudging acceptance, however, for John Jr. noted in his diary on the day of the sale: "We bought Howard's & Katherine's C. Inc. stock for 100 but Howard is intensely annoyed at our bid." John Jr. rationalized his offer by comparing it to an offer Howard McMillan was making in his own company: "Our stock has $84 per share of wkg. capital & book value of about 170. Howard is bidding 1st Nat Bank for Jim Taylor's O&M [the Osborne & McMillan Company] stock only 175 whereas it has book value of 400 & net current of 170."

Perhaps Howard McMillan was antagonized not so much about the sale price being 60 percent of book—Cargill *was* a prime example of an illiquid company—but by the way John Jr. did the bargaining. John Jr.'s diary gives some further clues in its next sentence: "Trouble was we would bid only 80 for 1/2 the bloc or 100 for the whole." Apparently the irritation did not fade away in a few days, for John Jr. recorded in his diary entry of September 18, 1956: "Dorsey phoned in p.m. to say Howard still very peeved at his sale of C. Inc. stock." There seems no doubt that the McMillan family did hold some residual resentment about this event. The John MacMillans, father and son, and the Howard McMillans continued to be friends, however. John Jr.'s diary entry for July 6, 1958, notes: "To the Howard McM's for cocktails & dinner. Home by 10 p.m. & in bed."

At this same time, Edward Osborne sold his block of 1,960 shares of common stock. There was no option here, either, and substantial bargaining was involved. The offering price was the same as Howard McMillan's, but Osborne could have sold all or some at the $100 figure. He chose to sell all.

The other "really troublesome stock" (John Peterson's words) was that held by James B. Taylor. He was a relative of the MacMillans, and his wife was related to the Osbornes. He had been on the other side and perhaps led the insurgency in the family stockholder battle of 1925. He was asked to resign then but continued to hold his stock and to come to stockholder meetings over the ensuing 29 years. This was a substantial block of some 10,430 shares. Taylor died on January 21, 1955, and in July 1955 (a year before the Howard McMillan negotiations), John Jr. initiated bargaining with Taylor's son. There is no record of just how these negotiations were conducted, but the result was a sale of all of the Taylor stock: his holdings of common stock in Cargill as well as his stock in the Minnesota River Company and the Minnesota Western Company and some shares in the Cargill Securities timber company in Canada. The Taylor estate received 47 percent of book for its sale at $78.50. While this was smaller than that received by Howard McMillan a year later, the two instances are not comparable, inasmuch as Taylor's son made a "package deal" with Cargill for the sale of all of the stock, the total to be adjusted to come out to exactly $1 million.[20]

Two Estate Common Stock Problems

Settling the estates of Ed Grimes and Austen Cargill caused difficulty concerning their respective common stock holdings. The two situations were quite different.

Before Ed Grimes died in 1953, he had been given an option to buy 2,500 shares of common stock. After he died, as part of the settlement of the common stock holdings in his estate, his son, Weston Grimes, asked that the option be given to him. The request was granted, and Weston bought the shares in July 1954 at a figure just over 47 percent of book value at that time. The younger Grimes then resigned his post as Washington representative for Cargill and director of its Office of Government Relations, to go into private legal practice in Washington. He held the common stock that was in his own name until April 1956, when he sold it back to the Company for a per-share amount just under 68 percent of book value per share. The additional substantial holdings of Ed Grimes were sold back to the Company between 1953 and 1963 at a fixed per-share amount, and thus the percentage of the book value dropped each year with the rise in book value. The first year's sale (1953) brought 52 percent of book value; the last sale (1963), just under 28 percent. In effect, the Ed Grimes stock had been cashed out at a frozen figure, with no account taken of the growth of net worth over the 10-year payout time.

In the case of the Austen Cargill estate, a more significant question of equity was at stake. It was learned that Austen Cargill had not left enough ready cash to pay the substantial estate taxes due. The extent of this tax liability finally became known in 1960, and the executors decided that they needed to sell enough shares to realize about $700,000. Once again, this was a matter for bargaining—there was no formula or option in place for any of the three family members. John Jr. handled the negotiations for the Company, and when the figure was finally set, it was 48.67 percent of the net worth per share. Austen Cargill was not just an employee shareholder nor even a "collateral family" holder, he was one of the triumvirate of three family members who had built the Company over a great many years. In his case, he had been centrally involved in the Company since 1909. His estate was in the position of being a suppliant—it had to have the money for the taxes. The conservative figure established by the Company seemed to Austen Cargill's heirs short of giving full credit for his major contributions, and this belief has persisted.[21]

Expansion—with Caution

The bolder public relations program now encouraged the Company to be publicly proud of its accomplishments. In the January 1958 edition of *Cargill News*, Cargill MacMillan, in his new role as president (he was elected on August 13, 1957), wrote a two-page letter to the employees on the Company's "record volume" and "coast-to-coast expansion." The Company had had its first billion-dollar sales year, handling over 14 million tons of agricultural commodities. He even made a general statement about profitability: "Cargill's profit margin was within the one percent level we believe to be best." It would have been unheard of to publicize the profit figure itself. Indeed, the quote was misleading, for, with sales of 1.02 billion and profits of $4.2 million, the figure was substantially less— about 0.4 percent.

The Grain Division had now expanded. There were 48 terminal and subterminal elevators, "on all coasts and in the interior," and 50 country elevators. The Norfolk terminal had been completed and was in operation; there were new grain-storage tanks at Sacramento and a large addition at Maumee, Ohio; a new elevator at Perry, Georgia, serving the north Georgia poultry industry; and the a large elevator leased at Plainview, Texas, in the center of the country's leading grain sorghum-producing area. The Oil Division had completed its new facility at Memphis, Tennessee, the Company's ninth soybean processing plant. During the year, Cargill had processed 35 million bushels of soybeans and flaxseed, the production of approximately 2.5 million acres of farmers' crops. The Feed Division had finished its 840-acre research farm near Elk River, Minnesota; the Research and Development Department had moved into its new building in Minnetonka. The overall tone of the report was upbeat, a well-deserved paean to the 4,313 employees.[22]

To John Jr., it seemed an expansive period. He wrote in his diary: "Never in my experience have I seen so many attractive opportunities for profitable investment. They exist in grain storage, bulk feeds, veg oil & transportation, singly & in combinations." As usual, he was keen on expanding ocean transportation, to be able to ship grain from Cargill's new terminals on the East Coast—Norfolk and Baie Comeau (when completed)—across the Atlantic to Rotterdam and elsewhere. Further, he wanted to have the Company's own facility at Rotterdam and to have the coastal and inland barges redeliver grain and other commodities to various other ports and towns in Europe.

The European part was going to be difficult, for, as John Jr. put it in his diary, "Tradax will have nothing to do with facilities of any kind. . . . Cross, J.G.P. & Gage are against adding any facilities to their responsibilities." Because of this, John Jr.'s plans began to center more directly on tugs and barges for the ocean voyages. Leasing of tugs was investigated, but as John Jr. put it to Kelm, "Your most interesting letter, with the high quotation for TUG HIRE from Merritt Chapman came yesterday. What it boils down to is that there is no surplus of powerful tugs, and that they want salvage rates for their hire. There can be only one answer: WE MUST BUILD OUR OWN."

Kelm suggested that with Liberty ships now obsolete and cheap to buy, towing two of them without power as "barges" might work. However, this appeared to be navigationally tricky. It might be successful in good weather "but never in winter in the North Atlantic." John Jr. now intensified his belief that Cargill should build and own an oceangoing tug and barges. A number of alternative plans were drawn by John Jr. during this year of 1958, both on a barge carrier configuration and a *Carport*-type tug-barge combination (an unconventional pattern, where the tug fitted into a V in the stern of the barge and pushed it).

John Jr. also wanted to expand the number of domestic inland waterways barges owned by the Company and began experimenting in early 1958 with a potentially cheaper version, a wooden barge. In September 1958, a wooden mockup barge was constructed of plaster lath at the Minnetonka offices, one-eighth the width of a full-size barge (about 4 feet) but only 8 feet long. There was a large concrete-bottomed pond at the Lake Office, which had been installed by the Rand family when they owned the property (they had called the estate "Still Pond"). John Jr. decided to put the mockup filled with sand into the pool for testing. His diary entry of September 4 commented: "My wooden barge looks good. Model put in swimming pool."

The next day the diary had a second entry: "My wooden barge tested to destruction; failed on deck." The water had soaked the wooden lath, pulling the staples out and creating leaks. It had been tied to the shoreline with a rope, and now all that was visible was the length of rope extending down into the swimming pool—the model had sunk. The pool had to be drained completely before the model could be recovered for salvage.

In spite of the demise of the model, it was decided to build a full-scale version of the wooden barge, to be called the *W1*. When finished by a Cargill crew, it was used for three or four trips but was not built strongly enough to stand the constant wear and tear. Most captains who had anything to do with the *W1* hated it, saying they were ashamed to be seen with a wooden barge, so they always put it on the outside and therefore it got hit an inordinate number of times. Further, it was a fire hazard, particularly when being repaired, and was leaky. John Jr. asked the builder what was wrong with the *W1*, and he replied, "If you nail a million boards together with a million nails you've got two million leaks." Another version of the wooden barge, the *W2*, was built by an outside contractor, but it too proved to be marginally useful. Finally, John Jr. became convinced that wooden barges were not viable.[23]

In the midst of this flurry of ideas and plans going back and forth between John Jr. and his design and engineering team, he left in March 1958 for a long trip to Asia, his first time there. Earlier in the year, while on vacation in Jamaica, a potential boatbuilder had appeared. John Jr. also found "a dream of a site" for shipbuilding, a piece of property in Jamaica that "belongs to the BOY SCOUTS . . . just East of the Insane Asylum." Nothing came of this, so he wrote John Peterson just before he left for Japan: "I intend to ask for quotations on the cost of tugs and barges with a view to letting a contract, if possible, in June." The trip was made with Walter Gage, and they visited Japan, Hong Kong, the Philippines, Singapore, Thailand, India and Pakistan. Tradax had a representative in Japan, and Cargill, Incorporated had a man in the Philippines. John Jr. and Gage planned to investigate additional trade possibilities, and consider a more formal Far Eastern Division office in one of the countries.

As John Jr.'s letters and cables came back to Minneapolis, the rest of the

"A million nails, two million leaks"; Cargill's wooden barge, 1958.

board members, particularly Cargill MacMillan, began to worry that he might make financial commitments that would exceed the board's approval. Finally, on April 4, 1958, Cargill MacMillan sent a sharply worded cable: "Will greatly appreciate your compliance with own policy of not making commitments when away from home office and without possession of all facts. Matter in question exceedingly complex and even we here still do not have all details." He followed this with another cable on the same day, "Add . . . my cable . . . highly important no statement public or private be made by yourself or anyone connected with company." John Jr., unfazed, wrote in his diary that day: "A weird cable from Cargill."

When John Jr. returned, he made a lengthy report to the board. He had been impressed with the Tradax group in Japan and also liked Hong Kong as a possible site for a headquarters. He was particularly excited by the Philippines and told the board: "Opportunities here are simply limitless . . . we have an immediate opportunity in copra, on which something should be done 'at once.' " (Later, the Company did develop its own collecting facilities there, including an intercoastal vessel system.)

The board, apparently relieved that John Jr. had not made any vessel commitments in Japan, now seemed a bit more receptive to his ocean transport ideas. John Jr. wrote in his diary: "My barge carrier very well received [by the Board] but they are not ready for the 18 . . . barges & tugs."[24]

The board's hesitancy about John Jr.'s plans stemmed in part from its concern about his rampant enthusiasms and quirky designs and in part from some heightening worry about the Company's financing, particularly because of the heavy cash drain for the Baie Comeau terminal. In June 1958, Cargill MacMillan wrote about this to Charles Cain, Jr., the executive vice president at Chase Manhattan Bank, who had become Cargill's senior contact after Hugo Scheuermann's death. Because of upcoming capital needs and concern about further working capital, "we feel the need of additional permanent or semi-permanent funds in our business [because of] our desire not to diminish the rate of our historical growth . . . at the same time . . . to avoid solicitation of outside equity capital." The government was stepping out of its warehousing of grain, so "we will be called upon to warehouse and handle more of our own grain [with] more and more funds tied up in commodities and positions that are not available for collateral purposes." He added, "We realize, only too well, that we must clean up our unsecured borrowings periodically or our banking friends will very correctly assume that we are trying to use bank credit in lieu of working capital."

Out of these conversations with Cain and collateral research by Albert Egermayer, the Company's senior financial officer (replacing John Peterson), a plan evolved that led, in December 1958, to a major new financing arrangement: two long-term loan agreements, one for $10 million from the Northwestern Mutual Life Insurance Company and another for $5 million from the Prudential Insurance Company of America. The agreements for both loans contained some stringent constraints on the Company. The Company could incur no additional debt except current secured borrowings not to exceed 300 percent of the net worth, current unsecured borrowings were not to exceed 100 percent of the net worth, and other purchased money obligations and additional secured or unsecured indebtedness were not to exceed a maximum of $3 million at any one time. Further, the Company was not to incur rental obligations to exceed 15 percent of the beginning working capital of a given year, and the Company's net working capital was required to be maintained at a figure not less than $30 million. Indeed, the Company had no intention of letting its net worth decline below that figure. Cargill MacMillan wrote in his private notebook in March 1958: "In 1965 Cargill will celebrate its 100th anniversary. I am extremely anxious that when that year comes we will be able to exhibit a net worth of a hundred million dollars." Additional provisions also put constraints on the ability of the Company to sell plant or equipment.

These were not onerous limitations—the then-existing Company financial policies already meshed well with them. In the normal course of business the insurance company restraints would pose no problem. Nevertheless, the message was implanted—there should not be any crash programs of capital expenditures nor sudden, huge spurts in expansion plans. The allusion to John Jr. was unmistakable.

John Jr. was not enthusiastic about the insurance companies' proposals, believing they had too high a cost. In his diary he commented, "If we borrow the $15 × 10⁶ from N.W. Life Ins. will have to pay 5¾% for 20 years. A better idea would be to buy out Peavey [the competitor grain company]." In that same diary entry, he laid out the Peavey company balance sheet figures; he estimated its net worth to be $43.1 million. Aside from the fact that Cargill's net worth was just $55 million, and the absorption of Peavey would be an enormous financial challenge, it also was not evident how John Jr. expected the acquisition of Peavey assets to fit what he perceived as Cargill's objectives.

John Peterson, looking at the insurance company agreements from the perspective of Tradax (and perhaps angry because of not being directly involved and not being able to bring in his old Chase friends) was not pleased. John Jr. wrote Kelm: "Pete is really annoyed at our not sending him a copy of our borrowing agreement with the N.W. Mutual. He has a point when he contends that our agreeing to maximum borrowings of 3 ×

Net Worth is most embarrassing to him, as the Chase regularly lends Tradax 12 million on a net worth of only 3. He thinks the rate is too high, etc., etc." Tradax was totally separate from the standpoint of financing, so the insurance constraints did not apply, but it did seem to be an anomaly that the parent company had such tight constraints and that Tradax, the independent arm, had less strict limits.[25]

Tradax Success—Independently

In April 1959, John Jr. made another inspection trip to Europe, again sending the *Carmac* ahead so that he could use it for investigating new sites. Before boarding, he stopped in Geneva and wrote Kelm on his arrival: "The boys here, and especially Walter & Pete are terribly disturbed. . . . I am increasingly convinced that we simply have to appoint a liaison man who does nothing else but smooth over the relations with Tradax." He also found Geneva still less than enthusiastic about visits from the Minneapolis group: "They resent very much our sending over personnel. They insist that they absorb an immense amount of time and no constructive results ensue. However, I attach increasing importance to frequent visits by you, brother Cargill and myself . . . also frequent visits by the members of our family [mentioning also Jim Cargill] . . . let's keep all others at home."

After completing the Geneva part of the trip, John Jr. seemed to have second thoughts about Tradax, faulting in a letter to Kelm "their organization set-up" and disapproving of Tradax "making far-flung investments like Johannesburg and Djibouti." He was particularly exercised that "they simply won't develop a training program . . . instead, they are hiring young men *trained by others* [his emphasis], some 5 to 10 years older." If, instead, Tradax took people "right out of college . . . there would never be any doubts lurking in our minds as to the loyalty of our organization." The Tradax approach "is a terrible mistake and I don't like any part of it." Nevertheless, his conclusion was that "their results are so good that it is hard to criticize or even suggest. We must not discourage them."

The remainder of John Jr.'s spring 1959 trip was taken up with planning physical facilities for Europe. Already new contacts had been made in the Netherlands. The thought of a Rotterdam terminal had been supplanted by a Peterson/Gage proposal for a facility at Amsterdam. For many years this port had been overshadowed in the grain business by its neighbor, Rotterdam. Now the town fathers proposed to build a grain transfer and storage facility, in the process working exclusively with Tradax. Tradax would need only to make a commitment to furnish a specified minimum amount of tonnage and would not be called upon to invest any capital.

John Jr. saw the plans on his trip and approved, "except [there were] no large bins." Later in the trip he visited a number of North Sea ports and crossed to England with stops at several ports.

The voyage ended in London, where the press visited the *Carmac*. In one paper, a picture of John Jr. on the aft deck was accompanied by a caption that read: "Here is Mr. John H. MacMillan, grain tycoon and 100 per cent, 22 carats, genuine multi-millionaire. Beneath him his 300-ton fantabulous diesel yacht, *Carmac*. And what is the background? It's another Riches to Rags story. . . . Mr. MacMillan has chosen to chug his vision of floating richness right into raggety old Chadwell Basin in East End Dockland. And, of course, it's a happy ending. MacMillan is here for a 7-day . . . business trip."

This was the end of the trip, and John Jr. wrote Kelm on May 16 of his evolving plans. First, he now had decided that the coastal shipping could be handled by buying the surplus Liberty ships, either towed or self-propelled. There would be need for coastal port facilities, both in England and along the North Sea and Atlantic coast and, foremost, a large ocean-going ship to connect Baie Comeau with Europe. "We can beat existing (very low) rates by at least a dollar a ton provided we are willing to move it in equipment of our own design in units not less than 40,000 long tons."

In his report to the board on June 1, 1959, after returning, he put this belief even more strongly, attaching the following "urgent agenda" at the beginning, putting it in all-capital letters: "THE PICTURE HEREIN PRESENTED IS VERY PLAIN. THE FIRM WHO FIRST WORKS OUT A SCHEME FOR TAKING ADVANTAGE OF LARGE TRANS-ATLANTIC CARRIERS WILL BE IN THE DRIVER'S SEAT. BUNGE HAVE NOW UNDER CHARTER A 45,000 D.W.T. CARRIER, AND ALSO A 35,000 D.W.T. IN BRIEF THEY ARE FARTHER ALONG IN DEVELOPING THIS PICTURE THAN IS CARGILL OR TRADAX. SPEED IN DEVELOPING THIS PROGRAM IS OF THE UTMOST LONG-RANGE IMPORTANCE." In late June, he wrote his younger son, Duncan, still in Geneva with Tradax: "I have been struggling unbelievably with my boat program but just do not seem to be able to get anywhere. It is not that anyone is against me, it is just that it takes an infernal amount of time and I am losing patience."

On August 3, 1959, he drew up a "Marine Program, 1959–1964" to present to the board. It included purchase of the Liberty ships, larger barges for the *Carport*, construction of a barge carrier, several oceangoing ships and a North Sea program, and a proposal for a 12,000-horsepower Mississippi River towboat as well as a smaller towboat and 100 new jumbo barges. The total for the whole "program" came to $63,525,000. Meeting with the board in September 1959, he allowed that this was an "appalling" figure "but necessary."[26]

Good Year, Great Year

The excitement and preoccupation with the interaction of Tradax and the Minneapolis export business tended to overshadow solid domestic performance in those last two years of the decade, the crop years 1957–1958 and 1958–1959. Profits in the first of these had been almost $5 million, although the sales had dipped back below $1 billion, at $959,000,000. The crop year 1958–1959, the one used for the *"Fortune 500"* comparisons at the beginning of this chapter had been a spectacular one by all measures. Sales once again jumped beyond $1 billion, and earnings were far above any previous year, at $9.1 million. Net worth was up almost 15 percent, to end the year at $66.8 million. The Grain Division's profitability was high, at $3.7 million; the Feed Division did well, too, with a contribution of $1.3 million. It was the Vegetable Oil Division that was the star, however, posting a figure well over double that of the previous year and ending with a contribution to the total of $4.7 million.

There was significant domestic expansion throughout the three divisions. Terminal capacity was now up to over 151 million bushels. The Baton Rouge terminal, first opened in July 1955, had had its capacity boosted by almost 4.5 million bushels, to a total of 7.7 million; there were significant additions at a number of other locations, old and new, and by the end of the decade, total capacity had been raised more than 15 percent over that of 1955. The total volume of grain going through the elevators had increased in this period by more than 75 percent. Virtually every plant in Nutrena had been upgraded and one major new mill constructed at Peoria, Illinois. The total feed tonnage had gone up about 12 percent in this five-year period, but the even greater increase in dollar sales and profitability was a tribute to the division's overall efficiency. The Vegetable Oil Division had added two major plants, at Memphis and at Norfolk, and a smaller company, Sioux Industries, had been purchased, with plants in Sioux Falls and Sioux City, Iowa. The total volume of oil-bearing materials processed by the division (soybeans, flaxseed, copra) had climbed over 38.7 percent in the five-year period. The inland waterway fleet of CCI had added capacity. In 1956, the new towboat *Carcrosse* (Cargill and La Crosse), a 2,400-horsepower twin screw vessel, was added. Then, in late 1958, the *Claude Tully* was added, an eight-year-old boat built by the same company that built the *Carcrosse*. The *Tully* had a much larger capacity, however, with two 1600-horsepower engines, the most powerful towboat in the Cargill fleet. Meanwhile, the *Carpolis* and the *Carpaul* had been cut apart and combined as the *Carcities* (a not-too-effective vessel, called by many the "Cartrocities"). Almost a hundred barges of various sizes complemented the towboat equipment. Two of the Company's lakers also remained in operation, the *Calumet* and the *Hemlock*. There was still a piece missing in the equation, however, one that was needed both for domestic and for international use—the terminal at Baie Comeau. Here things were far from right.

Slow Completions: The Seaway, Baie Comeau

When the Eisenhower-backed Wiley-Dondero Act establishing the St. Lawrence Seaway Development Corporation was passed in May 1954, it was believed that the Seaway might open for traffic in 1958, and indeed there was some traffic through it that year. Even that limited use had shown that ships could be handled faster in the locks than expected, and already there were estimates that the annual capacity of the Seaway might reach 75 million tons, instead of the 50 million originally estimated. Obviously, there would be some real battles for traffic, with the railroads rushing to cut rates and increase service to compete. As one newspaper writer put it in January 1959, "Opportunity isn't knocking—it's breaking down the door." Weston Grimes, hired by Cargill as a representative for the Company with the St. Lawrence Seaway Development Corporation, put the whole situation well with one word—"mercurial."

John Jr. had taken a fresh look at the Seaway in a position paper in August 1957 and once again estimated that costs would decline about 5 cents per bushel between Western lake ports and tidewater. It was this differential that had led Cargill to conclude that Albany would be at a

Queen Elizabeth II speaks at the dedication of the St. Lawrence Seaway, with President Dwight D. Eisenhower seated at right, June 26, 1959 (The Bettmann Archive).

competitive disadvantage and brought the decision to build the Baie Comeau terminal. The Company was now eager to proceed with extensive use of the Seaway. However, on April 25, 1959, when Queen Elizabeth II and President Eisenhower jointly dedicated the Waterway, the Cargill link was still uncompleted.

When the Finance Committee had authorized over $13 million for construction of the Baie Comeau terminal, it had seemed a huge sum, far and away the largest the Company had ever committed. Construction had begun in late 1958 under trying conditions, in terms of both weather and logistics. In April 1959, John Jr. wrote his brother some disturbing news: "We had a real blow today as it develops we cannot possibly get Baie Comeau ready to ship grain before December 1st, and a more realistic date probably is January 1st. . . . The trouble came in the foundation problem on the shipping pier. This pier will take eight months to build instead of the two and a half." One consolation was that they likely would be able to receive grain by about September 1, he added.

By September it looked as if costs were likely to be far greater than the estimates, and Cargill's tax analyst, Al James, sent a memorandum to all concerned requesting that "Cargill people visiting Baie Comeau and other Canadian offices refrain from discussing the cost of the construction program with anyone outside of the Cargill organization." By the first of the year 1959, it still had not been possible to unload any grain there, and John Jr. wrote John Peterson: "We are trying to untangle the Baie Comeau mess, but still do not know enough to make any intelligent comments. . . . It now turns out that no concrete floor was laid in the first big bin; one was laid in the second big bin. They won't be able to lay the floor in the first big bin until the frost is completely out of the ground, which is usually the first part of June." A wire from Cargill's man in charge in late December put the problem graphically: "Already too late, with continually below freezing weather, to pour thin slab on ground already frozen, considering that this area is mostly solid rock and rock fill . . . also on a slope."[27]

The French Barges

When John Jr. told the board in September 1959 that the cost of his $63 million "Marine Program" was "appalling" but "necessary," the board agreed with him on only the first of these two words. Although John Jr. had made several specific proposals for oceangoing vessels in 1958 and 1959, and despite the outstanding performance of the Company in the 1958–1959 crop season (with its 15 percent jump in net worth), the board did not approve a single proposal for a Cargill ocean vessel. This led to tension between John Jr. and board members. As a result, John Jr. now chose to "go it alone" on a major oceangoing vessel. This is an important story, not just for its transportation implications but also because of subsequent problems that led finally to a protracted interfamily argument between the John Jr. family on the one hand and the Cargill MacMillan and Austen Cargill families on the other.

This project had its impetus from Cuban sugar. Since the early 1950s, John Jr. had followed the fortunes of Caribbean sugarcane, both in Jamaica, where he was growing cane on his own properties, and in the great sugar producer of the area, Cuba. The latter had the greatest economic potential, and in the mid-1950s John Jr. had sent his own men there several times to investigate sources. Later, in 1956, he asked Dick Baldwin, Cargill's new director of research to study the problem of drying and pelletizing sugarcane bagasse, the residue of the cane stalk after crushing, which John Jr. proposed to mix 50-50 with molasses for animal feed. Baldwin decided to conduct an experiment at a Company alfalfa-drying site and, after searching the Southeast, found a farmer in Florida with enough sugarcane in his field to yield two truckloads of bagasse. The tests were not promising—drying the molasses in the bagasse mixture was difficult, and the pellets picked up moisture from the air and turned into solid blocks. The costs were beyond original expectations, too.

Despite the question of whether effective pellets could be produced, John Jr. persisted in wanting to develop the marine equipment for handling sugarcane operations between Cuba and the United States (the *Carport* had carried some of this already). For his expanded plans, he wanted to use the *Carport* towboat (with its notch configuration) but with two new 6,000-ton barges, some 350 feet long, 50 feet wide and 27 feet deep (or, alternatively, adopt a barge carrier configuration). As he put it to Cargill MacMillan in an early letter on the project in March 1956, "we simply have to order two barges at once."

There were serious design problems to be worked out, however, stemming particularly from American Bureau of Shipping concerns about the seaworthiness of such a vessel. In 1956, when the *Carport* was caught in the hurricane, the Bureau raised a number of questions about the notch concept (although eventually letting the vessel continue its intercoastal work). So in these various proposals in late 1958 and early 1959, John Jr. found the board unwilling to commit Cargill funds.

At this point, he decided to establish his own separate company for the construction and ownership of the vessels, whichever configuration, and formed the Havana Company, a shell entity incorporated in Liberia but with offices in Minneapolis. Then he himself would build the equipment and develop lease arrangements with the Company for its use. In other words, the sugarcane project would become a Cargill operation but with vessels from John Jr.'s new corporation.

The final project now was set. Hopefully, it was to involve the three

Carport barges so that there could be one at each port loading/unloading and one in transit. John Jr.'s earlier visit to Japan had impressed him with the shipbuilders there, and he hoped to have them do the construction. Failing this, Germany was his second choice. Bids on the barges from Japan, Germany and several other European countries were higher than he had expected. Finally, a French shipbuilder came in with a low enough bid. John Jr. wrote Duncan Watson, now his chief of engineering, in November 1959: "We have covered the world . . . for offers on these barges and the French company is definitely low. . . . If we make a counter bid we run a grave risk of losing the offer and furthermore Tradax is very anxious for a working arrangement with them. . . . If we lose this offer, we would have to trade with the Orient which would not pls me at all."

In these negotiations, John Jr. soon involved Company lawyers, both from Minneapolis and from Geneva. He visited the French firm in November 1959, at its shipyard in Dunkerque, and found he needed considerable help from the Minneapolis legal department concerning details. The lawyers were helpful but insisted that John Jr. make it clear that it was a project of the Havana Company, not Cargill. John F. McGrory, a young lawyer at the Company (and subsequently Cargill's general counsel), wired one of the Company's lawyers in Europe: "Cargill does not, repeat not, guarantee

John MacMillan, Jr.,
late 1950s.

performance. . . . Mr. MacMillan willing to personally guarantee performance of Liberian corp. . . . Mr. MacMillan authorizes commitment on behalf of Havana Co., not, repeat not, Cargill."

One of the key questions here was the number of barges to be ordered. In his early discussions with the French firm, John Jr. had expanded the number to four. The price if four were purchased would be $341,000 per barge. If only three were built, the price increased to $345,000. If only two, the amount would be $349,000.

John Jr. intended from the start to offer shares in the Havana Company to the rest of the family and to senior management, similar to the mechanism that had been used so many times in the past (for example, with the Minnesota Company, Wesota, etc.). However, he now found little enthusiasm among this group for the prospect of joining with him. His brother was strongly opposed. A Company legend handed down from this period recounts that as John Jr. toured the offices to persuade executives to accept, Cargill MacMillan followed 10 minutes later to tell each one, "Don't do it!" Cargill MacMillan wrote John Jr. in mid-January 1960: "In re your Havana Company, Fred Seed is the only one so far who has definitely asked to be counted in. I think the others are waiting for me to let them know how much it would cost. For most of them, it is simply out of the question as they can't raise the money." Whatever the true story, the fact was that no one joined with John Jr. in the project, and he decided to go ahead on his own. He finally chose to build two barges, rather than four, with the total commitment at just $700,000.

Meanwhile, an unexpected event occurred that was to be devastating for the project. In January 1959, Fidel Castro had overthrown the regime of the Cuban dictator, President Fulgencio Batista. Castro took office as premier in February and in June promulgated an agrarian reform law calling for appropriation of large land holdings. Under this law, the United States sugar companies were to lose their land. Castro then signed an agreement with the Soviet Union in February 1960 for purchase of sugar. In July, President Eisenhower cut Cuba's sugar sales quota to the United States by 95 percent. In October the United States imposed an embargo on *all* trade with Cuba. Thus, the producer of the greatest supply of bulk semirefined sugar in the Caribbean was excluded as a potential source.

John Jr., although warned earlier by Company lawyers about this eventuality, was taken aback but, with his ever-present ability to justify what he wanted to do, had an alternative:

We are quite embarrassed over the developments in the Cuban situation and I am very doubtful if we will be able to use [the barges] in the Cuban trade—which means we would have to switch either to Barranquilla or Vera Cruz, [also] with a strong possibility they would have to remain in Europe and we would have to use them in the cross channel trade from London to Holland and Denmark. She [the towboat-barge unit] should be profitable in any one of these runs but she will be able to carry such a staggeringly large tonnage that we have to be sure we can dig up business enough to keep her busy.

Thus, the raison d'être of the Havana Company project—trade between the United States and Cuba—was now extinct. Further, because the two barges were being built in France, not the United States, they were not "U.S. bottoms" and so could not by law be used in intercoastal shipping like the old *Carport*. As the barges moved to completion in late 1960, there were serious questions about their usefulness.[28]

Calendar 1960, Tragic Year

It would have been wonderful to top the record profitability of the crop year 1958–1959, but the remainder of calendar year 1959 brought substantially lessened performance. The Feed Division profits were substantially lower; the Vegetable Oil group also reported lower earnings. Although the volume of grain acquisition and sales moved well through the season, the lucrative carrying charges from CCC grain were down considerably, as the many congressional inquiries had made the CCC cautious and it had begun using more of its own storage facilities. There was yet another such inquiry in the early months of 1960, a special investigating subcommittee of the Senate Committee on Agriculture and Forestry, to probe once again into "the policies, activities, operations and management" of the CCC. The chairman was Senator Stuart Symington. Some 57 warehouse companies, including Cargill, were studied. The General Accounting Office reported on these companies' net profits from CCC storage and showed a wide variance among them. A large Cargill CCC storage at Port Cargill came under scrutiny in the process. John Jr. wrote John Peterson: "What makes one so mad [is] that everyone knows that it is nothing but an attempt on the part of Symington to get some publicity." The furor died away by late summer.

The Company ended the 1959–1960 crop year with record sales, which were up to almost 1.3 billion. There were record tonnages for grains and soybean products and for copra and coconut products, with somewhat lower feed tonnage. It was not the total volume that hurt—it was the high operating ratios (operating income/operating expense). The Grain Division had had an operating ratio of 82.1 percent in 1958–1959; this rose to 95.7 percent in 1959–1960. The Feed Division was up from 80.3 percent to 96.2 percent; Vegetable Oil, from 57.4 percent to 74.2 percent. The total Company operating ratio was up from 75.9 percent to 89.5 percent. Inexorably, as expenses rose, profitability fell. The 1959–1960 crop year ended with a $4.3 million profit, well below the figures for three of the four previous years. Costs were up almost across the board, with salaries, interest paid and rentals especially prominent. John Jr. summed up the situation in a letter to John Peterson in February 1960: "We are still doing a good volume of business, but with no carrying charges in sight, there is nothing to do but start liquidating, as our expenses . . . are eating us up. This is not a very happy picture" (once again, though, his natural ebullience dominated; he wrote his son Duncan in August: "All in all, I am not nearly depressed about last year as I might be").

In the planning were some substantial new projects. In early January 1960, a new office complex was announced for downtown Minneapolis, to be called the Cargill Building, a 16-story building that would house the Company on four of its floors and other tenants on the rest. Also contemplated in the project was a large motel, an above-street plaza, a 700-seat restaurant, rooftop garden and swimming pool, a shopping arcade and a 1,000-car parking ramp. The $20 million project, hailed by Twin City civic leaders as being of "tremendous importance," was to be a joint project of Cargill, Northwestern National Bank and Baker Properties, Inc. The Baker group would be principal owners, the bank would lease the property, and Cargill would lease its floors to provide quarters for approximately 650 people (but would have no financial responsibility for the building itself). Cargill's part of the project had been planned by John Savage, Cargill MacMillan, Jr., and E. T. Pettersen. After making every conceivable study of location factors, Cargill Jr. told the newspapers, "We found that downtown Minneapolis is by far the best answer, all factors considered." The executive group would remain at the Lake Office, but now Cargill had a more permanent arrangement for most of the rest of its Twin Cities office employees.

The other major project involved a transportation vessel, not the oceangoing variety so favored by John Jr. but one from his domestic wish list— a major new towboat. Early in 1960, it had appeared as if Cargill might be able to purchase a 6,000-horsepower towboat and 60 barges from the aluminum subsidiary of Olin Matheson Corporation. John Jr. wrote to John Peterson in February: "Hughie [John H. MacMillan III] is disgusted at this because he wants a new 6,000 h.p. towboat of his own."

The Olin deal fell through and the Company decided to contract for its own towboat, built to its own specifications. In April, a 6,150-horsepower vessel, triple-screw and capable of towing up to 32 jumbo barges was ordered from the St. Louis Ship Building & Steel Company. The total cost was estimated to be $1.5 million, but it came in at $1,382,850. It was to be a Cargo Carriers (CCI) boat—in other words, owned by Cargill, Incorporated, and therefore not using the outside-ownership basis of several of the earlier vessels. Clearly to be the flagship of Cargill's entire fleet, it was named the *Austen S. Cargill*.[29]

In the international sphere, Tradax grew rapidly in importance. Erv Kelm reported in April 1959: "It has developed the best grain trading organization in Europe, according to several independent observers." Beyond grain, oil and proteins, its traders had moved into a wide range of other commodities—phosphates, coal, nitrogen fertilizers, potash, silica sand, salt, rice, pumice, molasses, sugar, gypsum, cement, steel and even wine. The Amsterdam terminal facility had opened in 1960, built not quite to Cargill specifications but still promising to be an important end-of-the-line for Atlantic grain shipping. For the time being, the commodities would be transported in other peoples' ships, "even though the separable tug and barge could perform the trans-Atlantic grain transportation cheapest under ideal conditions," so reported Kelm in a late 1960 report to the board. Kelm's conclusions stressed the importance of Tradax: "All in all, Cargill, Incorporated has in Tradax an incomparable facility to increase its export volume. If one would examine our direct sales for export in 1954–55 and compare them to 1959–60, it will show what Tradax means to Cargill. . . . Tradax was started to extend the effectiveness of Cargill—it is fulfilling our fondest dreams, and it must be maintained and extended."

John Peterson was blunt, however, in a letter to John Jr. in March 1960, in picturing the adverse effects on Tradax of some of Cargill's decisions: "Our policy ties to your wishes. You need volume for your seaboard plants as well as plants on the waterways. In order to achieve this volume, we have to sell when buyers want to buy and at prices at which our competitors are both willing and perhaps eager to sell. Your FOB prices reflect everything being squeezed out at seaboard, leaving us with a shell of risks—FOB prices, freight, exchange and subsidies. It is no comfort to have to make a choice between going 'busted' by expense or by risk taking."

Peterson and Gage constantly pushed for better margins and more preferences from Cargill trades, in the process also pressing the case for high bonuses for the Tradax group. The Geneva people thought very short-term, traders always. A high short-term bonus for high performance fit this ethos very well. Their profitability had risen steadily every year through 1959, with a commensurate rise in the book value of Tradax common stock. In 1960, however, the organization did take a substantial loss, their first.[30]

The delayed start of the Baie Comeau terminal had something to do with this. It had continued to be plagued with construction problems, some of which seemed to be caused by chicanery on the part of certain vendors to the project. On July 27, 1960, the terminal finally was finished, and John Jr. and the directors made a trip on the *Carmac* to dedicate "perhaps the most momentous event in the 95-year history of our company." The newspapers, writing of the plant, estimated that the facility would export annually 60 million bushels of grain. "That could mean as many as 250 ships coming and going each year," John Jr. stated. "It will become, as your late Prime Minister predicted, one of the most important shipping centers in the world." Montreal must have thought so—one of their newspapers headlined: "Elevator Threat to City Port." No longer would export by lake be unavailable during the winter months due to ice in the lakes and on the St. Lawrence Seaway. Baie Comeau could be filled to capacity before the freeze, but shipments overseas could be accomplished at *any* time during the year. Protocols were worked out with the United States government to store American grain and Canadian grain separately, "identity-preserved," so that the American grain would be certificated as such, not subject to duty. Federal inspection officials would be posted to the Canadian port as a permanent cadre.

Right away, John Jr. wanted to expand it. "We immediately came to another conclusion . . . that Baie Comeau simply was not large enough and we would have to enlarge it immediately . . . increasing the total capacity to 33 million bushels instead of the 11.5 million we have today . . . in time for the next crop. It looks like the added space will cost around 19¢ per bushel—which will give us a staggering total investment there."

Unfortunately, the chicanery soon became apparent. In August 1960, there was a collapse of the concrete in part of the terminal (due, as a later lawsuit brought by Cargill showed, to poor construction). John Jr. wrote in mid-September: "Our Baie Comeau mess is slowly drifting to a climax and I rather think we will ask for an indictment against the crooks who tried to 'take us.' " He wrote his son Duncan: "That plant seems to be hoodoo'ed."

Baie Comeau was on a restricted basis for a number of months. It was a disappointing first year, but John Jr.'s vision had been essentially right— it did become a world-class port, fulfilling the Company's expectations.[31]

In May 1960, Continental Grain moved into a major terminal in the Minneapolis area on the Minnesota River upstream from Port Cargill. John Jr. wrote John Peterson: "Quite frankly I do not see how they are able to do the things they are doing with such limited working capital and net worth" (he estimated these at $31 million and $14 million, respectively). John Jr. noted Continental's New Orleans elevator and their lease of a huge elevator in Kansas City and puzzled as to "how they can do the enormous volume of business they are doing." It was even rumored in the trade that Continental was going to build a towboat of the size of Cargill's, to cost about $1.8 million. "They are about as annoying competition as I think we have ever had." Fortunately, Cargill also had been able to obtain two export-oriented terminals (albeit elderly ones) from Norris Grain Company, at Duluth and Toledo. John Jr.'s concluding paragraph was revealing as to Cargill's strength: "We got the actual figures by exporters from the United States for last year. Cargill led the field with 28.6% and

Continental was second with 25.4, Dreyfus and Bunge had 17 and 10, respectively. Our work is cut out for us."[32]

Personal Losses

These many plans, successes and progress, slips and steps backward were trivial in comparison to a set of human tragedies that occurred in the year 1960. The effects of these on the fortunes of the Company were profound.

Cargill MacMillan had been taken ill just after Christmas 1959 and had gone into the hospital. He had had pneumonia, and this had caused some severe cardiac damage along with various infections. He left the hospital in mid-March and had been home only one night when he had a stroke caused by an embolism. It was a severe one, which left him completely paralyzed on the right side of his body and with no power of speech whatever. John Jr. reported to his cousin, William Cargill, in August 1960: "His mental powers were seriously impaired but somehow I do not think that will necessarily be permanent. At any rate it was very evident that he could not carry on, so the Directors gave him a 12-months leave of absence. . . . However, we simply had to have a President in the meantime so we promoted our Executive Vice President [Erv Kelm] to be President . . . with the understanding that if, as and when, Cargill is able to come back to the business, he will come back as Chairman and I will retire, which I am anxious to do."

"We are fortunate in one respect," he continued;

both Cargill and I have four very able sons. . . . Cargill Junior has been made a vice-president and is in charge of the administrative side of the business. Cargill's other son, Whitney, is in charge of all of our branch offices in the Grain Division—which is a most responsible position. . . . Hugh, my oldest, is in charge of our river operations and Duncan lives in Geneva and is active in commodity trading other than grain. Jimmie Cargill is also with us . . . and has been developing magnificently. He is the assistant head of our Research and Development Division and is really contributing heavily . . . while my son-in-law Hubert Sontheim, is the head of a Legal and Finance Department for Tradax in Geneva. It is really hard to picture how fortunate both Cargill and I are in that we have genuine talent and character in this next generation.

Through the fall of 1960, John Jr. continued to worry about expenses; he wrote his son Duncan in late September: "We have been putting on an extensive drive to cut costs. [Robert] Harrigan has estimated that the Grain Division alone can reduce their expenses by no less than 3½ million dollars a year without in any way impairing the efficiency and volume of their division. He has made such a profound impression on us that we are all doing our best to implement his program." But John Jr.'s "always move ahead" mentality showed through: "I have made another stipulation . . .

Right, one of the "big bins" of the Baie Comeau terminal elevator, 1960.

Above and below, dedication of the Baie Comeau terminal elevator, July 1960.

the reduction in expenses is to be accomplished by an intensive drive to increase our through-put in our plants. Our real objective is not to just cut expenses but to cut costs per bushel of sales . . . we have a lot of fat which must be gotten rid of." And there were new John Jr. projects—he was keen on a Tradax notion for trading canned goods from the United States and also was immersed in a project to buy a salt mine in Louisiana.

On November 23, 1960, John Jr. wrote another letter to William Cargill (the son of W. W.'s first son, Will) about a loss: "I am terribly distressed to have to tell you that Howard McMillan died last night of a heart attack. . . . It is most distressing as he was in seemingly good health and about to leave for his annual holiday in Santa Barbara." This was a particular shock to John Jr. because he apparently felt (as he told his wife, Marion) that he had not been able to make amends with McMillan over the issue of the latter's sale of Cargill stock, and "now I will never be able to."

The next day, John Jr. was back in the office; the last letter he dictated that day was the one to William Cargill about Howard McMillan's death. That evening at the dinner table, he suddenly became ill and lapsed into unconsciousness. He was rushed to the hospital, and the early diagnosis attributed the illness to a heart attack. After many tests, the doctors diagnosed it as a cerebral hemorrhage. There were moments when he seemed not to recognize anyone, and in mid-December he was moved to the Duke Hospital, to be under the supervision of Dr. Kempner. Leo Sheehan, John Jr.'s secretary, reported to William Cargill: "Mr. McMillan's letter to you on the occasion of Howard McMillan's death was one of the last he dictated . . . he was terribly distressed over Howard's passing."

On the morning of December 23, 1960, John Jr. died. Cargill MacMillan did not have the expected recovery from his stroke and remained permanently disabled. With John Jr.'s passing, the last two of the three family members who (along with Austen Cargill) had held the top positions in the Company for many years now had been taken completely out of the orbit of the Company. The Cargill of 1961 would be a very different institution.[33]

CHAPTER NINETEEN

Cargill's Culture

In the nineteenth century the dominant forces of growth and expansionism and the spirit of transcendentalism were often characterized as intensely individualistic. When Ralph Waldo Emerson wrote in "Self-Reliance" in 1841, "An institution is the lengthened shadow of one man," he captured the era's principal concept of a leader. Nowhere has it persisted to this day with more validity than in the tightly held family company. Cargill has been an excellent example for much of its history.

In this chapter we will see how the Company's dominant values were shaped and expressed over its first hundred years by Cargill's family presidents, not always intentionally or even visibly at the time. By 1961, size and complexity teamed with vastly different external forces to produce a more complicated cultural pattern, as described later in the chapter. Thoughtful observers of the corporate scene generally support the notion that there is an identifiable uniqueness in many organizations. In not a few business corporations, the specialness of the group makes a statement. The organization's features can readily be identified, and one can realistically assume certain behaviors and outcomes. The term "corporate culture" has been applied to this phenomenon in recent years .

The Cargill of 1961 fit this definition well. There *was* a unique Cargill culture that had been generated over the years by its chief executive officers. It provided both a rallying point for people within the organization and also a clearly identifiable set of expected behaviors for those viewing the Company from the outside. This Cargill culture provides the central theme for this chapter.

W. W. Cargill, the Company's first leader, was not an introspective person and most likely did not give much thought to a corporate purpose. That post–Civil War age in which he first put together his small organization was a fluid, fast-paced environment that allowed little time for considering the future. The farming frontier of those days was rugged and demanding, with primitive accounting and financial controls and a widely fluctuating business cycle that often brought severe depressions but also provided periods of rapid expansion and unusual opportunities. Businessmen's ethics were often uncertain. The local, state and even federal laws to constrain excesses were, at best, rudimentary. The frontier provided its own definition of the Gilded Age, a period of tremendous growth for American business—and countless examples of double-dealing, bad faith and roguery.

W. W. was a product of all of this. His was one of the era's business success stories. He had amassed a far-flung organization and a considerable personal fortune by the turn of the century. His management skills were diffuse, and his approach was often haphazard. Disorganized and forgetful, he never knew exactly where he had been or exactly where he was going. Yet he was honest and stood by his word. His ebullience and enthusiasm seemed to affect a great many people positively, among them important businessmen who were willing to join with him in his various enterprises. He was not a complex man. Newly prosperous, he enjoyed his accomplishments but was ready to forge ahead to new endeavors. However, his grasp of the essentials of the grain trade was certainly present. His acquisitions of facilities from southern Minnesota to La Crosse and then eastward to Green Bay, Wisconsin, evidenced a keen sense of the natural flow of the grain trade. Early on, he integrated vertically into simple feed mixing and flour milling. Later he pursued many interests in transportation and established Lake Michigan and Lake Superior terminal hubs. His brothers Sam, Sylvester and Jim helped him measurably, particularly Sam, who developed the Minneapolis and Duluth operations so well.

At other times there was less logic to W. W.'s new endeavors—the Pine Bluff, Arkansas, lumbering operation and the later purchases of timberland in Mexico and British Columbia seemed almost random acquisitions. The La Crosse & Southeastern railway project demanded huge funds. The Valier, Montana, enterprise was a unique high-risk endeavor.

Generous and sympathetic with both friends and family, W. W. pampered his wife, Ellen. Both, in turn, were supportive and indulgent with their eldest son Will, and so the son developed an overweening personal ego. He too would go like a whirlwind into a situation but did not seem to have sustained interest for routine work. Will had a creative mind but not much financial sense, and he lacked his father's ability to empathize with people and make friends. W. W. Cargill's ability to establish and articulate a coherent vision for the Company was incomplete, while the early patterns of his son Will's efforts in the same vein were even less successful.

The crisis in the W. W. Cargill empire, already building due to Will Cargill's unwise investments in Montana, was brought to a head by the sudden death of the patriarch. But the organization was saved by the business acumen of his son-in-law John MacMillan, Sr. Already John Sr. had been tempered in business, first by an abject failure of his own family's attempt in the grain business in Texas and then in a demanding and difficult role as the head of the Pine Bluff lumber operation. Taking over the northern grain operation, John Sr. had proceeded to consolidate the Cargill Elevator Company sufficiently to survive the financial debacle that the W. W. Cargill estate faced.

John Sr., suddenly taking command of a many-faceted organization, was able to create a sense of purpose and generate a move toward specific goals. He inherited a group of able executives (hired originally by Sam Cargill, not W. W.), then molded them to his own resolutely held and ethically oriented definition of the corporation. He gave them a vision. His own life was rooted in facts; he expected just this from others. Frankness and honesty were cardinal virtues to him, from others no less than from himself. He had a sense of order about business, which he needed to pull together the threads of disarray in W. W. Cargill's companies. His keen appreciation and understanding of accounting, advanced for his times, was eminently practical in that the bottom line was the profitability and financial stability of the enterprise. In an industry characterized by tremendous swings in credit needs, accompanied by wild fluctuations in working capital, he strove constantly to rationalize the system and hold it on course. His accounting skills were extraordinary, and his grasp of finance in the occasional times of great danger for the business provides one of the explanations for the signal success of the Cargill Elevator Company during his tenure.

John Sr. was often cautious to a fault. John Jr. in later years sometimes spoke about the "terrific desire—an overwhelming anxiety for security" that the previous generation held (his words from a speech in 1953). John Sr. wanted to be fully hedged. He disliked spending any money for fixed assets, never feeling comfortable with paying high salaries or large dividends.* His heavy red pencil on expenditures was well known in the Company. A vignette will illustrate: In the 1928 move to the new downtown Minneapolis office, the decorator added some color and decoration to the conference room, but everyone was "scared of Father's reaction," wrote Cargill MacMillan, who was "wishing that Mother were there . . . she dared do anything."[1]

Financial acumen alone would not have produced his successes, however, for the human relations stresses in these years were uncommon. John

---

*Dividends had not been picayune under John Sr., however; in the board meeting of August 10, 1926, probably because of the stockholder revolt the previous year, he summarized the dividend record since July 1916, when the employees first held stock; in that 11-year period there had been $1,198,000 in cash dividends, another $800,000 in a stock dividend. With the earned surplus, the total applicable to common stock was over $3.6 million, "an average of 22.7% per annum on original shares," he concluded.

Sr.'s human relations skills were considerable. He had a well-defined ego—he knew that he was the head of the organization and was able right from the start to make decisions, to say no, to discipline and to exhort. More important, he knew how to say yes in a positive, motivating affirmation of support, where the person involved believed himself or herself a part of a team effort. In a meeting with such an individual, he would often use the expression, "Let's think aloud." His integrity and openness to his employees gave the work force of the Cargill Elevator Company a sense of belonging and of comradeship. The men of the Company were expected to be gentlemen, and John Sr.'s leadership gave them that desire. He had an ability to inspire trust, both within the organization and externally. This trust, especially from the banking community, really saved the whole organization in the time of financial trouble after W. W. Cargill's death. John Sr.'s charisma did not lie in a powerful and overbearing personality but was built on fairness, honesty and, to use a now-outmoded term, "courtliness."

The reasons why this last word is so appropriate were aptly illustrated in a 1932 memorandum John Sr. sent to all employees. Apparently the wire system (from the Taylor & Bournique acquisition in 1923) had begun to be used sarcastically by a few employees: some messages from the field were "put down" and summarily dismissed by home office personnel. John Sr. wrote:

Our branch offices have felt many times very much hurt by the tenor of messages from this office, and we cannot get best results from those whose feelings have been hurt. It destroys their initiative and self-respect. These branch offices are just as enthusiastic as any of us [but] may make suggestions that may seem unnecessary, or even foolish, because we cannot see the factors that prompted these suggestions. [These] suggestions from subordinates always should be encouraged and not discouraged . . . courtesy is the lubricant of personal contact and with its proper use we will be able to acquire smooth and harmonious results.[2]

John Sr. had weaknesses. His perspective was that of a regional small-company owner. His decisions were made in the context of Minneapolis, and his view of the grain trade itself was that of a burgher of this lively but still quite provincial city. He had traveled widely, to be sure, and had taken a national role for his industry during World War I. Yet not only his roots but also his outlook seemed inextricably tied to the Upper Midwest. It had been the younger executives, led by John Jr. and Ed Grimes, who had encouraged the purchase of Taylor & Bournique, which allowed the first move eastward.

Further, his caution made him uneasy about looking too far ahead, taking too many chances. To use the economist's terms, he was more oriented toward historical cost than to "opportunity" cost. In other words, he seemed at times overly concerned about money already expended in a particular facility or operation or tract of land. He was unwilling to consider selling it until "the Company could get its money out of it," forgetting the carrying costs and the need to have money available to finance new opportunities, let alone the worry that management assumed. In this sense at least, one could argue that John Sr. was too "tight" with money, too unwilling to spend to make more money, too unwilling to cut losses.

As he grew older, John Sr. tended increasingly to look backward, often worrying over or being unable to forget past setbacks. This trait is illustrated by the extended saga concerning Guaranty Trust's rejection of credit for the Company in the early 1930s. John Sr. continued to nurse what he felt was a slight and perseverated about the issue over and over, even as late as 1940. At that time nephew Morris Barker had met E. H. Rawls, John Sr.'s adversary, at the annual meeting of the Guaranty Trust and reported: "He said you were one of the finest and best friends he had . . . a grand fellow but of all the stubborn Scotchmen he ever met, you were the most stubborn . . . it was impossible to convince you in an argument and what was worse you were generally right." John Sr. (mistakenly) took this as an apology: "He has evidently had a complete change of heart. . . . He was absolutely wrong . . . and never has given me the satisfaction of admitting he was wrong—and it is a great satisfaction to hear in this way that he is now convinced of it." Whether this was an olive branch or not, John Sr. remained unforgiving. He continued: "We have done no business whatever with him or his bank during all that time . . . he boasted to me at the time that if I did not do as he wanted that we would not have any credit left to run the business on, and it has been one of the most complete satisfactions I have ever had in my life to prove to him that even in his own field he did not know what he was talking about."[3]

The Corn Case provided another telling example of John Sr.'s hindsightedness. While he supported John Jr. throughout the battle, it also was evident that his thoughts centered on the decisions that already had been made and had boomeranged and on damaging testimony. John Sr. seemed to emphasize all of the negatives of the case.

John Sr. defined details very well indeed. He knew exactly where he was; he knew how to live within the context of his society. During his earlier days with Cargill Elevator Company, from 1903 through World War I and into the early 1920s, this perspective probably was all that was required. The Company begged for rationalization. It needed to be departmentalized, to have its management structure better organized, to bring in good new men and give them effective management training and development and to become a strong, well-managed organization. This John MacMillan, Sr., did with great success. In the process, however, he did not have a sense of the larger world, a vista of growth and expansion. He had a general management point of view but not a grasp of the strategic demands. If an analogy can be drawn from the days of W. W. Cargill and his son Will, there was nothing of their "frontier" mentality about John Sr. He did not have a vision of the world as it was going to become, and thus he could not position his company within that vision.

Fortuitously, the transition in the 1920s within the industry, where past patterns of regionalization were rapidly changing to a national perspective, coincided with the time when John MacMillan, Jr., joined the company, bringing with him innovative ways of thinking about business and technological innovation. Some of these stemmed from John Sr. Indeed, throughout this story there are rich examples of fathers passing along to their sons whole sets of strictures concerning family standards and personal qualities. John Sr.'s banker father not only exhorted his son about the virtues of careful, meticulous work but even specified the best writing instrument for good penmanship. John Jr. had absorbed his father's excitement about and preoccupation with business. Although at several points John Jr. had expressed interest in other professions (forestry, engineering), there really was not much doubt that he would end up at Cargill Elevator Company. John Jr.'s Yale training had given him a good grounding in economics. His understanding of the fundamentals of the business, the physical more than the financial, was quite well developed.

Right from the start, in John Jr.'s early days with the Company, he seemed to have his father's ability to view the organization as a whole, with all of its complexities and details. A *New York Times* analyst in 1984 called this quality "cognitive complexity"; he wrote: "Recent research suggests that the most successful corporate leaders [have this] ability to plan strategically without being rigidly locked in to one course of events, the capacity to acquire ample information for decision-making without being overwhelmed and . . . able to grasp relationships between rapidly changing events." John Jr. had this synthesizing sense about business, for he could see components in their individual niches, then put them together in the overall picture. He could see threats and negative changes as opportunities. The remarkable assignment given to him at such an early age, when he was made an adjutant in a United States Army brigade, was based on a recognition of this organizing and conceptualizing ability. But, unlike his father, occasionally he seemed *not* to want the facts—lawyers' admonitions, for example—unless they fit into his view of the whole. Sumner "Ted" Young, a senior Company lawyer, commented: "When you had to tell John no on the subject of law, you had to have two or three Supreme Court decisions of the United States going your way . . . it was good training for the Law Department because we got pretty used to being loaded for bear when we'd go to tell him no." And when financial advisors warned him regarding the expense involved in a new strategic or technological idea, he also did not wish to hear.

The very time that John Jr. was joining the Company was a period of great change in the grain trade. He sensed this from the start. His concept of the "endless belt," whereby a grain company would benefit if it were to control every stage of the process, was a perceptive insight for that time. He understood that the industry was going to move East, and then on across the waters. More important, he knew that *Cargill* would have to do so. Perhaps it was that Yale training, combined with his experience during World War I that gave him more of an international perspective than his father had. If so, it was serendipitous for the Company that John Jr. was able to urge these changes just at a time when they were going to be most important.

By the end of the 1920s, a decade that had finished with the great market crash and the Company's need for innovative corporate planning, John Jr. had already begun to assume the role of chief executive officer for the organization. Two years later, in 1932, he was named formally as the Company's general manager. John Sr. was still reasonably active in the business, although illness was beginning to intrude. However, his interests turned toward other members of the family and relatives outside the Company and to national political questions, particularly government control of commodities, with which he had been so involved during and just after World War I. He still was titular head of Cargill Elevator, but John Jr. was already its general manager in fact. There was no question by this time who was the heir apparent. It was John MacMillan, Jr.

Significant differences distinguished father and son. Their personalities were developed out of divergent experiences, made further evident by the patterns of living that the two men experienced. John Jr.'s emotional makeup was considerably more volatile than that of his father, although John Sr. *had* had "several nervous breakdowns" (his doctor's words) during the Texas grain company mishap before the turn of the century. In particular, John Jr.'s not-infrequent attacks of nerves seemed to give him some unease about his relationships with others and caused him momentarily to lose his self-confidence. Indeed, there was one long bout with this, early in the 1920s, when John Jr. banished himself to the woods of British Columbia after raising the ire of his fellow executives. At certain times, he had a need to cut down on input from the outside. He seemed to sense at these more fragile moments that he could not handle dissonance, for he appeared sometimes not to have inner abilities to screen out conflicting inputs from others. He worked only with Austen Cargill there, but even with him he was tendentious. John Jr.'s illness at the beginning of World War II shocked his brother, who felt unequal to being left with all of the responsibility. John Jr. did not recuperate very well, and Cargill MacMillan wrote his mother and father: "John is not in good shape and I do not know what to do about it. All he needs is a vacation for it is entirely a matter of nerves, and the nervousness is entirely mental. Yet there is nothing that he seems to be able to do about it. He throws up regularly every morning after he comes into the office, and unless he leaves the office right after lunch he is sick again." The rice diet from Kempner after the war seemed to restore John Jr.'s vigor, but until his death he remained inordinately concerned about his health. He more than once disconcerted Wayzata dinner hostesses when he brought along his spirit lamp and cooking pot and set them right on the dining table to cook his own rice.

John Jr.'s interpersonal skills, although not inconsequential, were not of as high a level as his father's. He was not intuitive in relationships with others—at Yale he had had to self-consciously practice this ability. A senior manager in the terminal side of the business commented shortly after John Jr.'s death, "He never fraternized with the superintendents very much. I think he would have liked to, but I don't think he knew how." Yet John Jr. was able to elicit great loyalty from people he worked with, both as equals and as subordinates. This loyalty was mixed with fear on the part of many people beholden to him for employment or contracts, for John Jr. could be intolerant of any deviation from unfettered loyalty. Often when he met someone, particularly someone he considered a social and intellectual equal, sparks of mutual excitement and interest brought great friendship, and one quality of these several friendships did seem to be a mutual loyalty. But he had less empathy for ordinary human beings and did not think their needs important. John Jr. might sometimes be difficult to deal with, but he generally commanded the respect of others. His cerebral, wide-ranging mind moved fast, just as did his speech, and new ideas came from this like sparks shooting out in all directions. He had a verve about him that often put him on the bull side of the market and into major expansion. John Jr. was not as much interested in the details—he wanted to see where the project was going, what might be done beyond it. He, more than his father, was opportunity-cost oriented—if a new idea would not work, he was prepared to give it up and move on.

In his first decade with the Company he made many unilateral decisions—altering the ways of purchasing insurance and chartering lake freight, changing office procedures and shifting responsibilities. These changes were made quickly and decisively, in a manner often bordering on the autocratic. Generally, though, John Jr. seemed willing to listen (if the speaker could talk quickly), if most of the time only to take the other person's idea and incorporate it into his own tenacious vision. He thrived on intellectual combat, often reiterating that he did not want to hire people "just like himself." However, in such situations he often would reply, "You're absolutely right, *but* . . ." He could be, and often was, a spark plug for others—but he also could come down very hard on viewpoints with which he did not agree. Mistakes were not tolerated with much compassion by John Jr. In this he differed from his father, who was willing to accept a mistake if openly reported, provided the person learned from the mistake and could go on from there. John Jr. had an essential sense of his rightness about decisions and was perfectly willing to state these bluntly, decisively—and irrevocably. In a posthumous article about him in *Cargill News*, he was quoted as earlier admitting to a reporter, "Either way you like it—a man of strong opinions or an opinionated man, I see things in black and white. If there are shades of grey, I have no time for them."[4]

Overt hostility came out many times about some of these strongly articulated decisions by John Jr.—the revolt in 1925 was the clearest example, but there were other such antagonisms. John Sr. backed his son throughout, as if saying, "it is my son's company, his decision holds sway." Earlier in this book it was suggested that perhaps John Sr. was even a bit dazzled by his intelligent and voluble son—almost overpowered by him in some instances. He seemed to take pleasure in seeing things happen that circumstances and his own caution had not allowed earlier.

The dozen years from the Great Crash of 1929 to Pearl Harbor in late 1941 transformed Cargill from a medium-size regional grain company to a large national corporation with fresh links abroad. Cargill had changed from a little-known midwestern company in the early 1920s to a respected but often feared major national force. Indeed, particularly because of the inglorious Corn Case, the name Cargill and that of its chief executive officer, John MacMillan, Jr., became well known much beyond the confines of the grain trade itself. Company officials savored the recognition garnered by their innovations, although often feeling that John Jr. took the lion's share of the credit. But they disliked intensely the notoriety stemming from that case.

John Jr. dominated this period. Even taking into account the Company's able cadre of senior executives, John Jr. was the chief executive officer in its most literal sense. Few decisions were made without his imprint; few deviations were allowed without his prior approval. John Jr.'s philosophy of management had persuaded him to centralize authority largely in his own hands. The endless-belt concept that John Jr. held so tenaciously tended to encourage this centralization. The automaticity of a belt going endlessly took away considerably from individuality within the system. No longer could Lindahl and his successors in Duluth and others like them throughout the divisions have the autonomy and the individual credit for profitability of the old days under John Sr. The advantages of the endless belt were many, but this was one of its disadvantageous features, only partially addressed in the decentralization efforts after World War II.

John Jr.'s predilections for dominating the decision-making process sometimes exacerbated this problem. Yet this was not a single-dimensional autocrat. When retired employees who had worked with him talk about him, it is with a wry smile, a story of one of his "crazy ideas," a testimony to the excitement he generated, followed by a statement that while he "was often eccentric," he was the smartest man they ever met.

It had been a period of extraordinary innovation by John Jr. himself, pushed along by his eclectic interests, his wide-ranging mind and his abilities as an amateur engineer and helped also by Frank Neilson's equally amateur technical expertise. Together they had fostered many new ideas for the grain trade, widely publicized and widely although not universally acclaimed. The Omaha/Albany "tent" roof configuration and the "big bin" system of storage at those terminals had worked well for the Company (large bulk storage for small cost) despite misgivings by bankers and insurance companies about the explosion hazard in light of the one severe explosion at Omaha in 1934. Even as late as December 1940, the USDA official in charge of the federal government's Warehouse Act was asking about the Company's new St. Louis terminal: "How you are going to handle these many different classes with their many different grades in an elevator with so few containers?" The answer, Ed Grimes stated, was to use it in tandem with the older St. Louis terminal—but this response really did not speak to the questions about the "big bin" itself.[5]

The inland-waterway visions of John Jr. in the 1930s with respect to the Erie Canal also were strikingly successful. The single-skin steel barges and the *Carneida*-type towboats with the V notch greatly increased the efficiency and capacity of the Company's grain transportation. To be sure, this was on the Erie; when John Jr. later took them to the Mississippi, they were not up to the task. John Jr.'s ocean transport concepts, used in the construction of the *Carlantic/Victoria* were not as unequivocally successful. Nevertheless, the welded plates in this vessel and the simplified Cargill method of construction garnered considerable interest in the industry, although initially there were many skeptics about the durability of both the knuckle joints and the welding. The ship's miraculous survival after several direct torpedo hits gained some believers.

The tent-roof plan, first used at Omaha, led John Jr. to design the roofing of other structures. Right after World War II, John Jr. anticipated some of the modern fabric dome roofs of sports palaces around the United States when he experimented with a similar air-pressure-supported system with a metal roof for a large grain elevator ("the perfect application for this is for sport events, armories, garages," he wrote in July 1946).[6] The fact that later his full-scale version ignominiously collapsed is often cited as an example of John Jr.'s "harebrained side," that many of his innovations proved to be unworkable. But in this case he was just ahead of the necessary technology for entrance and egress. He did misfire on some plans but seemed to be able quickly to forget about a failure and ebulliently go on to his next new idea. He communicated a conviction that he was always right—a supreme, egotistical confidence, even though he was wrong many times.

Innovations for the grain trade were not the only things that intrigued John Jr. He evidenced ever deeper interests in weather patterns as he continued interacting with his mathematician uncle, Will. During World War II he began writing a book on the subject and was in contact with and giving advice to the Weather Bureau of the United States government (his advice was ignored, however). John Jr. also continued his interests in ocean transportation. Among his personal files are huge notebooks of drawings of various vessel configurations, with detailed analyses of shipping times and sailing distances all over the world. Finding little financial support from his colleagues at Cargill for oceangoing barges, he made the ill-conceived decision to form his own company to build them. They were just being completed at his death. He was interested in navigational equipment and had personal designs, for example, for gyrocompasses. His files contain drawings for an "electric still for home use" (to purify water), for a low-heat cooker, for a new type of tennis court and for other projects unrelated to the grain trade. He also had corresponded with his Uncle Will for years on their mutual interest in astronomy. In the World War II period, John Jr. developed a theory of a tenth planet in the solar system.[7]

John Jr.'s focus always was on winning and in the process positioning Cargill for the future. His almost-frenzied buying in his challenge of the Call Rule after the Company's expulsion at the time of the Corn Case was as much an emotional response as it was a business decision. Once again it was the dominance of the trading mentality, always so very strong in the Company (thus, the conventional wisdom that only a successful trader was capable of taking upper-level line responsibility). It was a merchant mentality, a transactional "win-lose" viewpoint (as with Julius Hendel's maxim, "you're mine for 1/4th"), rather than a customer-related "win-win" relational basis. Yet John Jr.'s thinking ahead tended to reach beyond the trader's horizon to true long-range planning.

The Corn Case was decided, both in the courts and at the bar of public opinion, as much by the values and ethics of the individuals involved as by the specifics of marketing corn and the mechanics of trading. John Jr. and Julius Hendel had aggressively, indeed unrelentingly, pursued their goal of domination of the corn futures contract at the Chicago Board of Trade and had used some competitive tactics bordering on subterfuge. So too had the other side, but it was Cargill and John Jr. that were censured by the government's Commodity Exchange Authority.

Looking over the sweep of management decision making carried through by John Sr. through his years of stewardship in the Company, there are significant contrasts in values between his approach and that of John Jr., although one must avoid oversimplifying and stereotyping these.

John Sr.'s high level of personal ethics and consistent application of these in the business stand out among his many virtues. John Jr. competed vigorously, sought every legitimate advantage possible, often proceeded secretively. Were one to look at the Corn Case alone as a microcosm of John Jr.'s values, one is tempted to make some sharply negative judgments. As one family member put it, "Instead of running down the center of the field he skirted the sidelines and sometimes stepped out of bounds" (and if the football analogy is pursued, he had a number of spectacular touchdowns!). He held strong views about politics, indeed about the whole human race, and stated these opinions vocally and bluntly, in the process often appearing arrogant, stubborn and elitist. John Sr. was equally stubborn but certainly would eschew much of John Jr.'s aggressiveness and embroilment in public controversy. Yet John Jr. rigidly stressed "playing by the rules" (but *his* rules, defined by him) and always keeping one's word. His standards of ethics were articulated differently from his father's but had many (but not all) of the same features.

Where John Sr. and John Jr. parted was on the extent of risk taking. John Jr.'s innovativeness, drive and aggressiveness constantly carried him into new projects, always searching for a better way, a larger piece, a greater involvement, a cheaper cost. He consistently sought to be ahead of everyone, what today's economists call exploiting "first mover" advantages. He told successive trainee classes after World War II that Cargill's market share should be "60% or above." While both men were conservatives in a political sense, John Sr. was a conservative almost across the board. His constant concern about spending money, his need for precise accounting, his worry about holding down costs and his caution about taking a chance on a new idea stand in stark contrast to the attitudes of his son.

It is interesting to speculate on the interaction and differing personalities of John MacMillan, Sr., and John MacMillan, Jr. These two intelligent men had been the driving force for the Company since almost the turn of the century. One wonders what the Company might have been had their roles been reversed—if John Jr., with his charge-ahead philosophy and risk-taking mentality had been the chief executive at the time of the crisis of W. W. Cargill's death and John Sr. in charge during the rapidly moving, complex challenges of the 1930s. In this situation, it is probable that the Company still would have been a small regional force, if indeed it had not gone under altogether because the wrong mentality was present at the time for caution and an equally wrong mentality at the time for growth and opportunity. Such "counterfactual" history can only be hypothesis and supposition; the succession from John Sr. to John Jr. is the reality. That this was an efficacious combination seems validated by the success of the Company by 1960.

Cargill MacMillan was more like his father than was his brother. A family man, he was characterized widely as loving and gentle. He was a true intellectual, had attended Cambridge University after Yale, was an avid collector of books over a whole spectrum of interests, and was an artist of some ability. He had a pervasive preoccupation with conserving family assets over the long run and a strong belief that governments squander money. He felt that the business corporation was a better steward than government but worried about the corporation staying strong over generations. He often cited the Hudson's Bay Company and Harvard University as examples of self-perpetuating institutions that had dealt well with the issue of longevity. He continued to search for a vehicle to allow the positioning of some Company assets outside the country, not because he believed this would be operationally more sound but because it would conserve assets. The Company's outside counsel warned him at one point, in May 1937, that the Bureau of Internal Revenue was watching with a jaundiced eye the formation of offshore corporations "in small and obscure islands" and that it would "resist to the utmost any such schemes."[8] But Cargill MacMillan's interest continued unabated.

He was the inside man, immersed, perhaps overly so, in details of all sorts, concerned about taxes and the bottom line of profitability and always deferring to his older brother. John Jr. must have been an awesome role model for a brother five years younger. Often, Cargill MacMillan was put in the position of making John Jr.'s ideas happen—he had responsibility but little authority. Yet he was always willing to speak his mind to his respected and beloved older brother. For example, at a height of tension in World War II, when John Jr. wanted to build another oceangoing version of the *Victoria*, Cargill wired his brother: "Just received your proposed memo. . . . I like it but still wish caution. Impression one gets when too radical ideas are too hurriedly presented." In the late 1950s, when John Jr. vehemently urged the building of oceangoing barges, it was his brother who kept the project from being Company-sponsored. Thus, in the final analysis, Cargill MacMillan consistently acted as a balance wheel of prudence for John Jr.'s adventuresomeness.[9]

Cargill MacMillan also became the watchdog for executive salaries. There had been an early bonus system, one not formalized but applied selectively by John Sr., Austen Cargill, John Jr. and Cargill MacMillan upon recommendation of a senior executive or branch office manager. However, it seemed that most requests initiated by a senior executive demanding more money would be looked at by the four with considerable outrage. Julius Hendel, for example, had asked for a raise in June 1940, and Cargill MacMillan's draft reply stated: "I have talked with Father and John Jr. We are all sorry you felt it was necessary to approach us on various occasions for what might be termed a raise, for we have prided ourselves in our policy of seeing to it that our key executives were paid enough so that there could be no question of their satisfaction and loyalty, and the fact that you are the only one who has pushed or prodded us in this regard has caused us grave concern." (Times did change after World War II, however, and more and more key executives pressed for increases.) John Jr.'s friendship with Julius Hendel seemed to cool at about this time. For example, he wrote Cargill MacMillan in February 1941: "Julius's predeliction for being a good fellow when out of town [referring to expense accounts] has always exasperated me, just as it does you." Yet this relationship between John Jr. and Hendel should not be downgraded, either. Hendel had been one of the premier innovators, both in his early work in grain analysis in the Grain Laboratory in the 1920s and in his efforts for scientific feeds in the 1940s. Hendel long had been John Jr.'s mentor on grain trading— they had pulled off many of the early coups together. But now John Jr. was fascinated by shipping; Hendel had become more interested in feed and oil, and they had begun to drift apart.[10]

Cargill MacMillan did have the special quality of being able to look at himself objectively and introspectively, to analyze his own strengths and weaknesses. In early 1944, he wrote his older brother an insightful letter in which he compared himself to John Jr. The subject happened to be the management role of Austen Cargill, the third member of the family triad that had led Cargill all through this period. The key sections read as follows:

Austen is adding, I think, the ingredient that you and I have been looking for. I think we have found our general manager. He has a great deal of the personality that you and I lack and as you say is a horse for work. I also have a feeling that Austen has finally come to the point of view that he is perfectly willing to defer to our judgment. I don't think he has been able to put this thought into words, but I am sure he feels it. Namely, that your extraordinary faculty of synthesis is a rare and valuable one, something that has long been a mystery to him but which he is now ready to appreciate.

I rather have the feeling that this ability to synthesize is a Cargill trait and I am sure Austen has it to a much greater degree than I. On the other hand, I think I have father's ability of analysis, a MacMillan trait. Give either father or me a problem, mathematical or otherwise, and we'll come out with a nearer correct answer than you or any other Cargill.

In other words, I feel very happy in thinking as you do that Austen has found his place in the business. He no longer distrusts you and me and I think he will supply the complement of energy and personality that we lack.

Cargill MacMillan may have assumed too much here, for these comments had not had the benefit of a personal discussion with Austen about his presumed newly discovered feelings of trust toward the two Mac-Millans. Indeed, the tinge of superiority in this letter may have reflected an attitude that would be communicated to Austen. It was on the basis explored in this letter, however, that Austen Cargill then assumed the position of executive vice president of the Company in August 1944 (positioned above all of the other vice presidents, including Cargill MacMillan). However, this balance of skills of the three still was not all that was needed, Cargill MacMillan felt: "I think we still have need of a fourth wheel. One thing all three of us have in common is courage. Another thing we all lack is psychological ability. Our immediate friends understand us but all of us shock what might be termed the general public and we hate to be brought into direct contact therewith. Perhaps Bob Woodworth or Ralph Golseth can help us out here."[11]

It was true that none of the three (nor John Sr. in his day, for that matter) felt comfortable with public relations, and as a result the Company had not been good at it. Ed Grimes had served well with many sensitive industry relationships, but he, like his contemporary, John Sr., was pulling back from major involvement at that time. As valid as Cargill MacMillan's suggestion of involving Golseth or Woodworth was at this time, it was not until the late 1950s that Woodworth was given this assignment. The legacy of secrecy held so strongly by John Sr. died hard.

The role of Austen Cargill was more important than Company oral or written history accords him. Cargill MacMillan's perceptive linking of Austen with John Jr. in respect to synthesizing (or, to put it another way, to see the broader perspective and not be a prisoner of details) captures Austen's key ability very well. Austen Cargill was *not* a detail man, although he knew accounting exceptionally well. He was able to delegate and yet keep track of what was going on in his own country elevator organization. Here he was probably a better management man than John Jr., for John Jr. had so highly centralized the Company in his own hands by Pearl Harbor that it was remarkable that he did not *over*dominate his executive colleagues (a testimony, incidentally, to the strengths of these two other family men). For this reason, John Jr. was not as good a mentor for younger people as he might have been. He did have the ability, by his charisma, to excite and intrigue people, and in this sense his leadership was quite positive. But his instinct for domination soon would take over, often with critical comments that would negate the positive. John Jr. did not suffer fools readily, and he did not recognize or value the need to nurture, to shape growth. John Sr. always commented on good things and coated his criticism. Austen Cargill had this same quality. But neither John Jr. nor Cargill MacMillan did—they tended often to skirt over or skip the positive and to emphasize the negative. John Jr. and Cargill seemed to have forgotten John Sr.'s example.

Austen was independent, personally detached, in his own milieu of country elevator managers and friends out in the field. Yet his ideas, too, had significant impact on John Jr. and on the Company as well. Austen was an innovator in his own right. Indeed, more than one Company innovation during this period was his, not John Jr.'s. For example, one of the problems with the *Carneida*-type barge arrangement was steering; something needed to be done to better control the front end. In July 1941, John Jr. wrote Neilson: "Austen suggested that we steer the barge with Sperry automatic steering mechanism actuated by relay from the tug. This would enable us to pull instead of push. He also suggested we might use Diesel electric propulsion with the Diesels on the tug and a motor on the barge, but I am afraid this would run afoul of the Maritime laws. Don't you consider the first suggestion entirely practicable?"[12] Frank Neilson certainly did, and this bow steering device became a hallmark of the Cargill barge units, subsequently to be adopted widely by the industry.

Thus, the triumvirate of Austen Cargill, John Jr. and Cargill MacMillan was a felicitous one most of the time—more so, again, than oral history accords it. None of them ever completely forgot the stockholder battle in 1925, despite Cargill MacMillan's roseate words in his 1944 letter. But any differences had long since been papered over, and the three men presented a unified view to their colleagues. Whether they believed it privately is less clear.

What Role for the Next Generation?

The death of Austen Cargill in 1957, the permanently damaging stroke of Cargill MacMillan in early 1960 and, finally, the death of John Jr. at the end of that same year left a huge void in the families' role in Cargill top management. Given the dominant position John Jr. had assumed as chief executive officer, his sudden unexpected demise left a gaping vacuum. How was this to be filled?

Members of the next generation of Cargills and MacMillans were already in the business—Jim Cargill (born 1923), son of Austen Cargill; Cargill MacMillan, Jr., (1927) and Whitney (1929), sons of Cargill MacMillan; Hugh (1928) and Duncan MacMillan (1930), sons of John Jr. All were in their 30s; all had assignments in middle management (some in staff positions, others with line responsibilities). None had had general management responsibility, and none had yet been elected to the Cargill board.

Management vacuums more than infrequently tend to go through a competitive winnowing before final resolution. Given the absence here of specific succession plans, it was to be expected that several alternatives could be envisioned. An early question related to the role of these five young men in the next generation of management. Senior management was predominantly professional from outside the family (from the family, only Cargill MacMillan, Sr., remained on the board of directors, but he was inoperative as a decision maker due to his stroke). This management team now speculated what would be the new relationship of these five younger family members to the Company—and, specifically, to the senior managers. Would the five assert their ownership prerogatives in some unforeseen way?

But the five quickly resolved any concern that senior management might have held. Several of the senior group had been helpful with advice, particularly Erv Kelm, then Cargill's president; H. T. "Terry" Morrison, vice chairman under John Jr.; Sumner B. "Ted" Young and Joseph H. Colman (a member of Cargill's outside counsel). The five family members, however, decided in the spring of 1961 to meet on their own to discuss their upcoming responsibilities to the Company. This was the first such meeting for what became an ongoing use of the "family meeting" by these five over the succeeding years, down to the present.

Shortly before this first meeting in April 1961, two of the five, Jim Cargill and Whitney MacMillan, had attended a middle-management training session, a first involvement with Ben Tregoe from the firm of Kepner Tregoe,

The second of the Kepner, Tregoe senior management sessions, February 1962. Seated, left to right, Charles Mooers, Barney Saunders, Erv Kelm, Pete McVay, Dick Baldwin, Bob Diercks, Bert Egermayer, Herb Juneau; standing, Ben Tregoe, Sid Burkett, Bob Harrigan, Cargill MacMillan, Jr., Bob Burkey, Don Levin, Fred Seed, Hap Wyard, John Savage.

an outside consultant. Tregoe had developed a unique problem-solving concept, and Cargill was trying it out for the first time. It involved an ordering of objectives on a "must/want" hierarchy and, by the use of a common language developed by Tregoe, the application of a rational thought process to decision making. (The Tregoe method was a signal success in the Company, and its use has extended down to the present.) The two family members described this process to the other three, and a modification was then constructed for that first "family meeting" that produced a collectively generated list of family objectives. A lengthy list of possible objectives was elaborated. Some were oriented toward the Company, others to the individual family. Then each member of the group applied the Tregoe concepts for his own ordering process, and these were then cumulated for a "collective wisdom." The top five of all of the objectives were (1) "best management to the top," (2) maintaining a fiduciary responsibility to employees, (3) preserving control by the families, (4) continuing the retention of earnings, and (5) making capital grow.

The objective of having the best-qualified management leadership possible was picked as the top objective by all five young men. Further, the group defined this as keeping in place in the Company the best-qualified management team, whether or not from the family. Over the succeeding years, other objectives rose strongly in their hierarchy at these family meetings, but "best management to the top" has remained a paramount objective of this generation of owners down to the present.

And so over a number of meetings with the management group in that critical transition year of 1961, the five family members made it clear that they believed themselves not yet ready for senior management responsibility and not yet ready to assume positions on the board of directors. Ted Young took John Jr.'s vacant board post, and the remainder of the board stayed the same as it had been the previous year (Kelm and Morrison, together with Fred M. Seed, Albert G. Egermayer, James C. North, Robert C. Woodworth, H. Robert Diercks and the nonoperative Cargill Mac-Millan, Sr.). Kelm became chief executive officer in addition to president; Morrison took the position of chairman, and when he retired in August 1962, Jim Cargill became the first of the five younger family members to join the board (Cargill MacMillan, Jr., followed in 1963, Whitney and Duncan MacMillan in 1966).

There was not always unanimity in subsequent family meetings over the years. For example, in the early 1960s, the group (soon expanded to six with the addition of Hubert F. Sontheim, the husband of Marion Mac-Millan, daughter of John Jr.) had had to deal with an acrimonious issue relating to John Jr.'s French-built oceangoing barges. Although John Jr. initially owned these barges, they were sold after his death to Cargo Carriers, Incorporated (CCI), the inland waters transportation arm of Cargill.

The new leadership of Cargill, 1961: left to right, Fred Seed, Bob Diercks and Erv Kelm.

The terms of this sale favored the John MacMillan, Jr., estate and family more than the Cargill MacMillan family and the Austen Cargill estate as represented by Jim Cargill and his sister. As long as the barges were on the CCI books, all of the families were sharing the losses, even though it was a project only of John Jr. The issue was finally resolved by the John MacMillan, Jr., estate reimbursing the other families, utlizing in part notes from John Jr.'s widow, Marion, at nominal rates. But the entire process had eroded some of the goodwill in the family group. There have been only a few further examples of such tensions. One of the high-ranking objectives in that first 1961 accord and one that has remained important over the years was "avoid family feuds."[13]

Cargill, 1961

The resolution of this potentially knotty management succession issue gave further texture to the overall picture of Cargill as a company.

Two concepts—independence and control—underlie Cargill beliefs. The first of these, independence, was not a particularly strong goal of W. W. Cargill. He was a consensus-builder, joining with a wide group of other people in various combinations of partnerships, joint ventures and so forth. This was not so, however, for John Sr. The onerous task of settling the W. W. Cargill estate and the feeling of being at the mercy of creditors and others truly upset him, as it had back in his own family's Texas grain business. This fear of being deprived of power was transmitted intact to the next generation, so throughout the officerships of both John Sr. and John Jr. the Company chose always to "go it alone." In the highly competitive industry in which they lived, the ability to move quickly and decisively on the basis of one's own information and analysis without giving up any independence to another company was viewed as a cardinal virtue. Joint ventures or any other kind of shared ownership were instinctively mistrusted. The industry was one of secrecy to begin with, and Cargill carried this to its logical end and sometimes beyond.

Juxtaposed to independence was a second, sometimes quite antithetical goal—control. One would gain more independence over a particular function if full control was held and, in this sense, the concepts were congruent. The two families wanted complete control of "their" company. While John Sr. had allowed about one-third ownership by employees and outsiders in the settlement of the W. W. Cargill estate in 1916, later the family (led by John Jr.) pushed hard to return all of the voting control to the two families. The desire for family control was strong among the five young members of the next generation in that 1961 discovery of their own objectives.

Ownership control through shareholding is not, of course, the same thing as control of the people of the organization, and here the Cargill chief executive officer and other senior officers consistently had difficulty in defining just how much centralized control of management could and should be used. John Sr., a strong and decisive chief executive officer, believed strongly in vesting responsibility and authority down into the organization. Indeed, one of the tenets strongly held by Cargill people down to the present is the belief that people should be given as much responsibility as possible as early as possible in their corporate careers. On the other hand, John Jr. paid much lip service to this concept over his years of leadership but frequently seemed to have difficulty in allowing others to make decisions that he thought he could make better. His supreme self-confidence generally convinced him that he was right—the arrogance of a very intelligent person with a keenly tuned strategic view of the world.

Manifestations of this tension between independence and control, between centralization and decentralization, were seen readily in the issue of management recruiting. Since the days of John Sr., the Company had paid great attention to recruiting management trainees. During the time of John Jr., this became a rigorous and highly credible process that brought to the Company a set of outstanding new people. These people received a short but well-defined training and were given significant responsibilities quite early in their career. The training program first initiated by Julius Hendel in 1930, reinstituted strongly after World War II and continued with equal fervor after his retirement in 1955, became an outstanding model for the industry. Out in the field, in the terminals and branch offices, these young management people obtained a practical education of great value, with considerable independence vested in them. This testing experience bred many outstanding leaders. Yet the reality of decentralization under John Jr. was frequently less than was professed. In certain key respects, John Jr. did not allow Cargill people to grow and seemed not to have full respect for the organization. He bragged about the Company's fast promotional track to responsibility, but it was a Cargill dominated by his own vision.

The recruiting process was highly stylized. The trainees were generally college graduates out of midwestern schools, generally with agricultural and business management undergraduate majors (although there were significant numbers of eastern candidates, too). There came to be, for example, an almost intractable bias against the master of business administration graduate being hired for a line position. All were white males with only modestly diverse religions. The apparent sameness of this recruiting was replicated more strongly in the training and subsequent promotion patterns for these people. Individuals stayed almost universally within their own initial functions. One was a grain trader or a member of the oilseed group or part of the feed group, but hardly ever did anyone move from one to another. One of the strongest elements of Cargill culture throughout its recent history has been this identification with a particular division, and stereotypes grew about people in each of these divisions being different from the others. Territorial battles were frequent and often surprisingly acrimonious. The system bred insularity, which, repeated throughout the Company, produced a further corporate insularity. Cargill thought its own way was best, seemed often to have a sublime arrogance about Company abilities and a scorn for any other way of doing things. Cargill truly had constructed an organizational mind-set that seemed to tell its people that they didn't need any help from anyone—they were doing things the best way, and the system could not be improved. The pervasive disdain for consultants in the Company during this period was an apt example of this hubris.

There was a sharp difference also between the days of John Sr. and those of John Jr. in regard to innovation. John Sr. wanted steady growth and no swings; caution and conservatism were his bywords. Conservatism was certainly a favorite word in the days of John Jr., too, but it was a very different form of conservatism, applied particularly to national affairs and political philosophy. John Jr. was not a conservative in terms of the business (even though Cargill MacMillan, Austen Cargill and John Peterson strove to control him in regard to financing expansion). John Jr. had an idea a minute, and many of these were very good indeed. Some of the significant and lasting innovations of the industry came directly from his aegis.

But it always was *his* agenda, and innovations always had to be fitted to his own concepts of the business. Good as these often were, his vision of innovation, as with other aspects of the organization, tended often to encompass the whole field—John Jr.'s dominance sometimes stifled other innovation in the organization. Cargill MacMillan sensed this early on; he wrote John Jr. in 1937: "All the boys have the idea . . . that whenever you are on a vacation you come back all full of new ideas and you might be very much annoyed if we spent any money which you might want for your ideas . . . they are undoubtedly right." However, this did not seem to change John Jr. one iota—he thought this was the way things should be.

Throughout the eras of both John Sr. and John Jr., loyalty to the Company was highly valued, "disloyalty" highly denigrated. It was a telling comment that John Jr. made in the late 1950s about the new, independent Tradax group in Geneva, that it should not hire people with extensive outside experience but rather fresh college graduates, for then there would "never be any doubts lurking in our minds as to the loyalty of our organization." Often the term paternalistic has been applied to Cargill, perhaps more so during the years of John Sr. than John Jr. Both of these men were compelling chief executive officers who believed they knew what was best for their employees. In this sense, the word paternalism seems apt. Yet it oversimplifies, in the sense that there was a verve and excitement to the Company all through this period, a reciprocal enthusiasm on the part of the people about what Cargill was doing and where it was going that made the sum of management-employee relations so effective. There was a powerful set of shared values, unreservedly reciprocated between and among people all through the organization, that gave Cargill a particularly strong combination of employee beliefs and faithfulness. One younger executive left the Company in 1947 but wrote Ed Grimes: "There is something about a spirit in Cargill that exists in few other firms . . . several people told me that they thought I had Cargill stamped all over me and could never rub it off. I am finding that it is very difficult to make the change." In some complex way, Cargill meant a great deal to its employees. Being a Cargill person was a matter of pride within the Company and envy from those on the outside. That this was true despite a modest salary and compensation structure is all the more remarkable.[14]

Some significant part of this stemmed from the values and ethics of one person, John MacMillan, Sr. His honesty, his sense of fairness and propriety, his frank and straightforward manner (which he expected others to reciprocate) cumulated as a set of personal characteristics that served as an extremely potent role model for people with whom he worked. He strove to pass these qualities on to John Jr., but they never quite took. Perhaps his esteem for and immoderate pride in his brilliant son got in his way.

Again, caution about stereotyping is in order, for it was not that John Jr. was the antithesis of these qualities. Rather, John Jr. came up through a different set of experiences in the business, a trading mentality, that gave him a combative, argumentative, bargaining basis for his business life: "Weren't we clever, wasn't it exciting that we were able to outwit them." John Sr. never wanted to fool people, but this quality is often part and parcel of trading and bargaining. John Jr. always hewed strictly to his own definition of honesty and had an unwavering view of this. He never knowingly told a falsehood himself, nor would he allow this within the Company. At the same time, he was always pushing at the margins, always wanting the next and best tactical step, willing to test both industry and government if he believed that the vigors of competition were being meddled with by anyone. The Company, too, in his time was more willing to risk than under John Sr.

Thus, this bedrock Cargill value of integrity and honesty was particularly the product of those complex, believable convictions of John Sr., represented personally in his lifetime and recalled after it. Austen Cargill also provided a singular moral force at several critical testing times. For example, his insistence in the mid-1930s on Cargill giving a lifeline to a whole set of failing country elevators rather than picking up their properties after a bankruptcy, a decision that countered John Jr.'s original plan, gained the Company wide approbation and loyalty among its customers. Cargill MacMillan and Terry Morrison, too, spoke frankly, representing the John Sr. viewpoint, at a few key junctures in the later periods of John Jr.'s time. Ed Grimes' relations with older employees also were a bridge back to John Sr..

The sum of all of these Cargill attributes gave a uniqueness to the Company that for years had been widely recognized in American industry. When the word "Cargill" was mentioned, in 1961 and earlier, it conjured up to the person hearing it a cohort of individuals thinking alike, unpretentious people believing strongly in and representing very well their Company and industry. Cargill had been able to institutionalize excellence, a precious and elusive quality. By 1961, Cargill was *the* leader of the world grain trade, respected, envied and even feared by those who had to deal with it. For its employees it was a company that could be believed in and trusted and one in which they could hold much pride. Cargill people typically were strongly committed to a work ethic, had accepted their organization's goals as their own and pursued these in a persistent and often self-sacrificing manner.

So many of these qualities accurately describe the Cargill of today that one would not be far off the mark in saying that the modern Cargill already had been established at the end of 1960—that the present Cargill belief system is a direct extension of the set of values put in place by these pioneers, W. W. Cargill, John MacMillan, Sr., John MacMillan, Jr., Cargill MacMillan and Austen Cargill (and with a few significant additions from other family members, Daniel MacMillan in particular, and their senior colleagues throughout this period). That this is so is ample testimony to the robustness of that historic vision.

The Chase Looks at Cargill

Many features of the Company's culture were put in sharp focus in the fall of 1963, when the Chase Manhattan Bank was asked by Cargill top management to evaluate the organization's overall performance. The occasion for the study stemmed from the Company's consideration earlier that year of possibly forming a wholly owned finance subsidiary to hold portions of the Company's receivables and from the additional notion of borrowing a sum of up to $40 million in the commercial paper market in lieu of that amount of bank borrowings. Management's reasons for raising these two possibilities originated in some weak performance in the period immediately after John Jr.'s death. The causes of this mostly lay within specific Company businesses, but they also were influenced by the transition problems themselves. Earnings, which had averaged $5.5 million in the preceding six years, dropped to $3.5 million in 1962, with only a moderate increase to $4.3 million in 1963. The first of these figures was the lowest since the unfortunate 1955 experience.[15]

The Chase consulting group was urged by Cargill management to look at all aspects of the business and to be frank in its analysis. Because of this wide-ranging scope, it was a "first" for this proud Cargill management team, so wary of outside advice, so mistrustful of "management consultants." Chase had been Cargill's lead bank for many decades; its senior officers, old trusted friends. They probably were in the best position of any group of people to command management's attention—and they got it. The resulting report was painfully honest, and quite critical of Cargill in a number of respects.

First, the team constructed a credible set of industry figures for comparison, cumulating the figures of 11 outside companies for a composite to test against Cargill's overall performance. Subgroup composites were used to highlight individual Cargill divisions. This approach led to some telling comments about these individual divisions. The analysts were equally trenchant in their generalizations about the Company as a whole, for they went beyond quantitative comparisons alone to speak to the Cargill culture itself.

The Chase team found what they considered to be disturbing comparisons. Net profit had declined in an absolute amount, in relation to sales and as return on both net worth and total capital. Working capital had moved irregularly downward over the preceding five years and, in comparison with the industry composite, appeared to be substandard. Cargill was more highly leveraged than the composite, with heavy debt concentrated in current borrowings (a pattern, of course, common to the grain trade). However, although Cargill's capital and debt seemed clearly out of line, this was "more effect than cause of the poor earnings." Indeed, said the authors, there were significant problems in a number of the individual operations. "A major part of the Company's trouble," said the authors, was in the Grain Division, which since 1958 had had a substantially lower return on investment than the Company as a whole. The division's trading had been "competent and successful," but storage revenues had been increasingly disappointing. Because of heavy political pressure, the Commodity Credit Corporation, which had taken on the "mountains" of surplus commodities, had begun to eschew private warehousing and had relied more on its own storage. An industry problem of grain storage overcapacity ensued, with sagging storage rates as its inevitable end product. The division had attempted to increase storage for its own account, but this effort had fallen short. So the analysts urged Cargill to make a careful study, elevator by elevator, to determine which locations were bleeding the Company the most. The Company's own elevators should be shut down first, but even leased space (some considerable part of which was tied up in longer-term, expensive leases) should be considered for subleasing to others.

The Feed Division had been experiencing a revolutionary change in the market. A pronounced trend toward fewer and larger farms made farmers more sophisticated in keeping records of feed consumption, weight gain, and the like. Under the old system, radio had been used as the prime marketing device for advertising. Orders originated from just the dealer network. This gave way to a much more complex form of marketing, in which dealers now had to be intelligent salesman, much better educated and trained. Cargill was in the process of upgrading its entire marketing arm in the Feed Division. The leading competitor, Ralston Purina, already had moved aggressively in this direction; Cargill should too. The Chase analysts were particularly concerned about the Feed Division's poultry feed business. Poultry industry performance had been spectacularly poor for several years, and Cargill had become deeply involved in the production side of the business, with contract production of turkey and eggs that had been unprofitable. The Company also had begun to extend credit to farmer customers, especially poultry growers, to allow them to buy grain locally for mixing with Cargill's feed and sometimes to finance farmers' fixed assets. "The results have been unfortunate; Cargill has charged off $1,967,000 of uncollectable receivables . . . over the past five years—more than the division's entire net profit for the period." The Company, said the analysts, should either pull back from the business or be prepared to spend large sums of money to make the poultry business stand on its own feet. It should not be considered a poor relation of the feed business and should not try to do the job with half-hearted allocations of money and manpower.

In either case, the division needed to develop much better records, for the lack of accurate individual product-line figures "reveal very little as to the reason for this sudden drop and the disappointing record." The Chase report even quoted an embarrassingly naive statement from the 1963 report of the division: "This is the first year that we have attempted to run on a tight, detailed budget at all offices and plants. It is the first time we used it as a management tool and we can't help but believe it had a beneficial effect on our operations."

The Oil Division record was excellent. Cargill led the industry, its return on average net worth and return on average capital much higher than the Chase's industry composite. The soybean was the star, but flax also had been highly profitable, and the copra business had been reasonably successful.

In the Special Products Division, the Chase analysts advised against continuing with hybrid seed corn. There had been losses in this operation in 11 of the previous 14 years. The resin business, on the other hand, had been profitable. The analysts counseled moving slowly in new directions, with more exhaustive product and market research. Similarly in the commodities department, molasses and salt backhauls had been increased over the recent period; a large salt mine had just been constructed on Belle Isle in Louisiana. Production here was promising, but there would be much increased marketing demands on the operation. In this division there was also a new fishmeal operation in Peru, just purchased, with its potential still to be determined.

Cargo Carriers Incorporated (CCI), the Company's inland-water transportation arm, was still a subsidiary, wholly owned by Cargill but its stock remaining in a voting trust for legal reasons arising out of Cargill's secured bank borrowings. Its inland-waterways barge operations had provided CCI's major profitability, although, the analysts pointed out, the "Erie Canal business is dead" with the opening of the St. Lawrence Seaway, and

Cargill's equipment was for sale. Similarly, the French barges ordered by John Jr. had proved to this point to be almost unusable and certainly unsalable. The analysts urged the Company to resist the temptation to expand into other types of shipping in the future; the idea had been given a fair trial and found to be a costly mistake. (Here the Chase group was proved wrong by later events, for Cargill expanded its ocean shipping with success, especially in the 1970s.) Further, the Company should not feel obliged to continue CCI forever; it did not appear necessary in order to conduct Cargill's principal business successfully. When Cargill's return on investment was greater than CCI's, then disposal of that branch might be considered, putting the money realized to work in Cargill, where it would bring a greater return.

Tradax had been a completely separate company from Cargill since its institution in the mid-1950s, but in 1962 this changed. Cargill's wholly owned Canadian subsidiary purchased newly issued Tradax stock in an amount sufficient to give the Canadian company a 55 percent holding, and for the first time Tradax was consolidated in Cargill's 1963 statements. The Chase group had no specific recommendations here.

The Chase analysts felt that certain aspects of the special Cargill culture were at the root of some of the Company's malaise at this time. Cargill's management "gives the impression of being grain-oriented . . . both a strength and a weakness." There had been real synergy between the Grain Division's trading over the years and the subsequent success of similar soybean trading in the Oil Division. Yet this bias toward grain included a reporting and accounting method that did not provide a breakout between trading and storage and led to feed and oil not having adequate bases of comparison. It was necessary for profit-and-loss figures to include cost of goods sold, margins, expense, and so on, with ratios to sales computed for major categories. In sum, the Company needed to employ more of the tools of financial analysis that by this point were in widespread use in American industry. These techniques would expose for each product and function the strengths and weaknesses and ultimately the underlying as-sumptions that to some extent had been hidden by the method Cargill had been using for many years to present financial information.

"Great emphasis is placed throughout the Company on sales growth and expansion of activities, geographically and into new product areas," the analysts continued, but "any worth-while ambition can be carried to extremes . . . this preoccupation with growth and expansion has been more of a factor in management thinking than have considerations of profits." In a speech to a Company management conference in 1953, John Jr. had summarized this corporate emphasis on growth in sales: "We have an ab-normally rapid growth factor . . . there's nothing, if you want opportunity, like going with a growing concern . . . pass that on everytime you see any of these kids; just pound it home to them. Its a terrific selling point. Every youngster knows what he wants; he wants opportunity!"[16]

However, said the Chase analysts, the preoccupation with sales had not been followed by an equal concern for profitability. Rather than profits-to-sales ratios, the Company had given major focus to Cargill's net worth, and it was always absolute size, rather than a concentration on percentage figures of return on net worth. Cargill MacMillan had signaled this preoccupation once again, in March 1958, when he wrote: "In 1965 Cargill will celebrate its 100th anniversary. I am extremely anxious that when that year comes we will be able to exhibit a net worth of a hundred million dollars." (Though disabled, he did live to see this wish come true, for the net worth at the end of the 100th year, the crop year 1965–1966, was $109,982,000.)

John Jr. had often stated that the family wanted to "double the company every seven years." However, only in various combinations of years during and immediately after World War II had the doubling of net worth in a seven-year span occurred. The average return on net worth during the 1950s was 12.2, but this had dropped to an average of 6.4 for the years 1960–1962, the three years just prior to the Chase study. Their report concluded, "this industry is not doing as well as American industry generally, and Cargill is not doing as well as its industry." Inasmuch as dividends of the Company over the years were uniformly low, the net worth percentages were not strikingly good even in the excellent years, and the Chase analysts felt that this reinforced the view that Cargill's profitability was being submerged by the lack of good accounting and control mechanisms and the longstanding focus on absolute size of net worth as a criterion for rating performance. Being privately held, with no public focus on "the next quarter's results," the Company had been able to take a long-term view on profit maximization. What concerned the Chase group was whether hewing to such a net worth criterion might be a rationalization for poor short-term performance.

Management thinking still was bulk-commodity oriented, as it was here that management felt it had its core competencies. Some people in the Company characterized this as "a futures market mentality not in touch with the realities of consumer attitudes." But the situation was beginning to shift to a "market-served" basis, rather than a narrower "division-served" basis, with its pervasive "my division" autonomy (this shift has become increasingly apparent in more recent periods). In more and more of the Company's efforts sophisticated marketing was required. Yet Cargill was slow to fill this need, and some senior managers even seemed to resist help on occasion. The Chase analysts advocated more careful planning and market research before new ventures were started and "more willingness to stop or curtail a losing operation" if profitability did not result.

The report also contained a set of finance-oriented suggestions. The authors advocated giving up the idea of a captive finance company, as they believed that the paper provided by Cargill would not be attractive and Cargill already enjoyed a leverage with its current bank borrowings equal to or better than that possible with a finance company (a self-serving recommendation, as Chase would lose business if Cargill did this). The finance subsidiary idea had come about because of the Company's desire to eliminate unsecured current borrowings at the end of the crop year, an unwavering conviction of John MacMillan, Sr., and a continuing article of faith in the period of John Jr.'s leadership, particularly pushed by John Peterson. The Chase analysts disagreed: "While this clean-up of unsecured debt once had meaning, it no longer does, and we consider that no stigma whatever attaches to the showing of this debt at fiscal year-end. The public . . . never sees Cargill's figures; there is nothing to be gained by removing the receivables and corresponding debt from Cargill's balance sheet for the benefit of the public or security analysts." They also recommended against borrowings by use of commercial paper, in effect saying, "stay with the banks, they are Cargill's best friend in times of stress." Actually, said the analysts, the finance company and the commercial paper proposals were really peripheral—they failed to strike at the heart of Cargill's real problem—greater profitability.

Perhaps the most controversial of the Chase recommendations was their suggestion that Cargill might consider a public offering of either common or preferred stock or convertible debentures. They believed "it should be possible to go public without causing the family to lose control." A collateral benefit would be the ability of the families to "possibly liquidate some of their own holdings, if they chose to, and diversify their investment portfolios." The analysts continued with a seminal thought: "There is also something to be said for the whetstone effect of having public ownership. A company and its management can be sharpened by being exposed to the criticisms of sophisticated stockholders, enduring the scrutiny of professional security analysts, and submitting to public appraisal in comparison with its competitors and peers."

The Chase Manhattan Bank analysis of Cargill was categorically a defining moment, not because management rushed to meet all of the specific recommendations—actually, only a few were accepted. Rather, the value of the report was in what the Chase analysts had dubbed "the whetstone effect," the submission to outside scrutiny and challenge. In essence, Chase had momentarily assumed the role of a surrogate outside director, a post that Cargill had avoided throughout most of its history. John Jr. was enthusiastic about the advantages of Cargill's wholly inside board of directors, especially its ability to meet "on five minutes' notice." The disadvantage of not allowing independent scrutiny by an able outside peer was dismissed. John Jr., in particular, tended to mistrust outsiders and would not have relished such a criticism or challenge, either.

The Chase report forced Cargill management to be more introspective than it had been in a good many years of self-satisfaction under John Jr. A whetstone "sharpens or makes keen"; to whet is to "goad, incite." That is what happened here.

Cargill 1963–1991: A Synopsis

The histories of the grain-trading industry and of Cargill from the death of John Jr. to the present are both very complex; neither can be summarized in a few pages. There *is* no definitive chronicle of the industry in this period, nor of Cargill, and both will be addressed in books to follow this study.[17]

Many notable events have occurred in the industry during these three decades. Perhaps most striking were the first grain sales to Russia in 1963, followed by Russia's buying again during the 1970s and the embargo by President Jimmy Carter of further American sales to that country in 1980 because of its invasion of Afghanistan. There was another controversial embargo, promulgated in 1973 by President Richard Nixon, when soybean exports were totally banned. Grain inspection continued to be a major problem. In 1976 the government brought suit against 16 firms ("including all the Big League companies with the exception of Cargill," noted Richard Gilmore in his book *A Poor Harvest*) for violations of inspection on $13 billion worth of grain exports. The basic federal law on agriculture had been amended in 1968 and was once again rewritten by Congress in 1977. The world's agricultural production during the three decades 1960–1990 continued to be characterized by recurring surpluses (although a few periods of shortages because of climate, Middle Eastern clashes and other unexpected events brought back once again the controversial pattern of rapid swings in prices). The protectionism in the "Common Agricultural Policy" of the European Economic Community and similar beliefs in Japan clashed with the free trade beliefs of the United States. Domestic U.S. farm policy went through continued iterations, almost always concentrating on oversupply and subsidies. A vocal public often took the farmers to task and just as often expressed skepticism about "the middlemen," the grain-trading companies.[18]

At Cargill, Chase Manhattan Bank's 1963 consulting report, which had been blunt and highly credible because of its quality, made quite an impact on Company top management and likely marked the pivotal point in the transition from John Jr.'s era. Erv Kelm and his colleagues needed just two more years to turn the Company's performance around. In the crop year

1965–1966, Cargill had record profits of $16.7 million, and the following two years were equally good. Kelm believed in becoming more solidly positioned in the Company's most singular skills and abilities, its core competencies. "Don't drop a going boat," he exhorted. Kelm's instinct was expansionist about the international grain trade, a view reinforced by his visit to Russia in 1963. So (for example) export capacity was expanded in the Gulf of Mexico and elsewhere, and oilseed crushing was extended to Europe. The oilseed group also moved into corn milling, a decision that proved very fortuitous. A striking new idea, the "rent-a-train," also was instituted: the Company took long-term leases on entire trains and kept them moving back and forth between central Illinois and the Gulf of Mexico on a turnaround schedule (a project particularly associated with Cargill's Jim Springrose). The Chase report to the contrary, the Company also entered ocean shipping in a significant way.

After a sharp downward step in 1968–1969, when the Grain Division alone lost $3.2 million (longshoremen's strikes at Gulf and Atlantic ports and two similar strikes on the Great Lakes were the most prominent of a number of problems behind this), the Company entered a period of unprecedented growth and profitability over the next seven years. The huge grain sales to Russia beginning in 1972 provided a base, but outstanding performance marked most of the Company's operations. There were record profits all through this period, the $218.4 million of the crop year 1974–1975 being the largest. By 1977, the end of this unprecedented seven-year period, net worth had increased to over $1 billion. That perennial goal of hoping to double the size of net worth every seven years had been greatly exceeded.

The Cargill of 1977 was a vastly different Company from that at the end of the 1960s. The three families, the descendants of Austen Cargill, John Jr. and Cargill MacMillan, had kept ownership of the Company, choosing in the process to continue the policy of small dividends, with most profits funneled back to invested capital. Its huge jump in that seven-year period had made possible both substantial additions in existing businesses (deepening domestic holdings and expanding overseas) and the purchase of new businesses, most in basic commodities but some in other fields (mini-steel plants and the financial markets division are notable examples). Several of these—the new steel plants, meatpacking and expanded poultry production in particular, had relatively large numbers of employees, posing new challenges to a corporate culture that had been built on the closeness of small, tightly knit groups of people.

A new generation of management now took over, as Fred Seed retired in 1974 (he had been president under Kelm from 1969), and Kelm himself retired in 1977. Whitney MacMillan became president in 1976, then chairman and chief executive officer in 1977. In his place, M. D. "Pete" McVay was elected president, and when McVay retired in 1984, James R. Spicola assumed the presidency. Spicola died in 1991, and Heinz F. Hutter was elected president. Both Jim Cargill and Cargill MacMillan, Jr., were in senior management, Hugh MacMillan continued his interest in shipping during some of this period and Duncan MacMillan headed Waycrosse, the family holding company successor to Cargill Securities Company.

Over the years 1960–1991, a number of nonfamily professional management served on the board. The post of vice chairman, first assumed by Terry Morrison at the start of this period, was later held successively by Bob Diercks, Walter B. "Barney" Saunders and William R. Pearce. Other board members, in order of their election, were R. J. Harrigan, W. F. Gage, D. C. Levin, C. L. Smith, B. B. Hanson, B. S. Jaffray, J. P. Cole, J. A. Howard and G. M. Mitchell. Cargill continued through 1991 with a wholly inside board of directors.

The years 1977–1990 had been steady growth years in both sales and net worth. Profitability was more modest in the earlier years of this period— several of Cargill's longer-term industries were in a mature, less robust phase, with some retrenchments—but profits picked up measurably in the more recent years. In the crop year 1989–1990, the Company had record earnings of $372.4 million on sales of $44.1 billion, with year-end net worth standing at almost $3.7 billion. The Company continued to move out ahead of its traditional rivals in the grain trade (Continental, Dreyfus, Bunge), but there was no resting on laurels as newer rivals, such as Archer-Daniels-Midland and ConAgra began catching up fast.

At this point the Company was once again facing the challenge of a major transition. In several important respects the situation in 1991 had direct parallels to the 1961 transition, in that there were no family members of the next generation yet in senior management. But there were further complications in 1991 in that such a large portion of senior professional management was reaching the compulsory retirement age at the same time that the senior management family members also were to retire from the board. This time, however, Whitney MacMillan and his colleagues chose to draw on new outside "whetstones" before the transition was thrust upon them. Two separate prestigious national management consulting firms and an able individual consultant were involved with management in assessing key questions concerning the new, more complex marketing role the Company had assumed, the North American organizational structure to effect this, and the overall strategic concerns that would underlie the organization.

Throughout these three decades, that culture put in place so definitively by the three previous generations continued to set the agenda for the Company. The Cargill of 1991 would not be a carbon copy of the Cargill of 1961—too much had happened in those 30 years. Yet, as the Company celebrated its 125th anniversary in an 18-month set of events in 1990 and 1991, and as the new transition loomed ever closer, the motto chosen for the anniversary seemed as appropriate for this moment as it would have been in 1961—"building on tradition."

Cargill Elevator Company/ Cargill, Incorporated, and Subsidiaries

Net Earnings and Net Worth, 1915–1961 ($000 omitted)

	1915–1934			1935–1954			1955–1961	
Crop year	Net earnings $	Net worth $	Crop year	Net earnings $	Net worth $	Crop year	Net earnings $	Net worth $
1915–16	n.a.	2,400	1935–36	(972)	8,094	1955–56	5,510	46,517
1916–17	1,024	2,668	1936–37	2,194	9,311	1956–57	4,218	50,096
1917–18	85	2,606	1937–38	(1,136)	8,544	1957–58	4,979	55,486
1918–19	578	3,051	1938–39	211	8,601	1958–59	9,121	63,682
1919–20	431	3,221	1939–40	1,117	9,263	1959–60	4,282	66,781
1920–21	(116)	3,093	1940–41	105	9,340	1960–61	5,088	70,716
1921–22	442	3,210	1941–42	2,749	11,620			
1922–23	34	3,244	1942–43	2,044	13,669			
1923–24	325	3,407	1943–44	973	15,480			
1924–25	859	3,840	1944–45	681	16,644			
1925–26	549	4,068	1945–46	1,537	17,643			
1926–27	433	4,265	1946–47	4,484	20,407			
1927–28	609	4,574	1947–48	3,008	23,722			
1928–29	531	4,871	1948–49	2,348	25,706			
1929–30	1,236	5,665	1949–50	5,292	27,973			
1930–31	1,302	6,392	1950–51	5,877	33,988			
1931–32	482	6,533	1951–52	673	34,202			
1932–33	1,156	6,977	1952–53	4,437	37,331			
1933–34	1,995	8,209	1953–54	3,972	39,844			
1934–35	944	8,592	1954–55	2,506	42,098			

A Glossary of Common Grain Merchandising Terms

The language of the marketplace is often as distinctive as the practices conducted there. Commodity trading has its own lexicon, and in fact, the same word may have distinctly differing meanings from one area of commodity trading to another. This glossary comprises terminology and definitions that relate more or less specifically to the grain trade (CMD Merchandising Training Manual, Cargill, Incorporated).

ACREAGE ALLOTMENT   The limitation on planted acreage established by the government for each farmer for some basic crops.

ACREAGE RESERVE   A part of the farm program that applies to basic commodities, under which the farmer receives payment from the government for not planting part or all of his acreage allotment.

ACTUALS   Physical commodities, especially as distinguished from *Futures Contracts*.

AERATION   Movement of outside air through grain, one of the most effective methods of conditioning grain; the system usually consists of a fan to move air and ducting to direct air movement.

AFLOAT   Grain that is loaded in barges or vessels, in harbor or in transit, but has not reached its destination and been unloaded.

AMBIENT TEMPERATURE   Temperature of the atmosphere surrounding the grain.

ARBITRAGE   Simultaneous purchase of cash commodities or futures in one market against the sale of cash commodities or futures in the same or a different market in order to profit from a discrepancy in prices; also includes some aspects of hedging. See *Spreads*.

BACK LEG   Condition that occurs when a leg is carrying an excessive amount of grain or the discharge spout is plugged, causing grain to fall back in the *Leg*.

BASIS   Usually the spread or difference between the spot or "cash" price and the price of the nearby future. Basis may also be used to designate price differentials between "cash" and more distant futures, as well as different locations as specified.

BEAR   One who believes prices are too high and will decline.

BEAR MARKET   One in which large supplies and/or poor demand cause a decline in price.

BEARISH AND BULLISH   When conditions suggest lower prices, a bearish situation is said to exist. If higher prices appear warranted, the situation is said to be bullish.

BID   A price offered by a prospective buyer or his agent, subject, unless otherwise stated, to immediate acceptance for a specific amount of commodity; the expression of a firm interest in buying at a specified price.

BIN   Storage room for grain, flat-bottomed or hoppered, constructed of steel, cement or wood.

BIN BOARD   A board or electronic graphics CRT with bin layout superimposed upon it, used to record daily changes in stocks of grain in elevator; references grain by lot, grade factors, date and amount.

BINDICATOR   A device that indicates grain level in a bin, scale or spout.

BLENDING   Mixing together two or more grains of different grade factors to attain a desired product.

BOARD APPEAL   Step above *Federal Appeal* in the appeal process. The U.S. Department of Agriculture reviews the inspection and can overrule a federal appeal.

BOARD ORDER or MARKET IF TOUCHED (MIT) ORDER   An order to buy or sell when the market reaches a specific point. A board order to buy becomes a market order when the commodity sells (or is offered) at or below the order price. A board order to sell becomes a market order when the commodity sells (or is bid) at or above the order price.

BOARD OF TRADE, CHICAGO   A licensed contract commodity exchange located in Chicago; affords facilities for both cash and futures trading in grains.

BOERNER DIVIDER   A device that reduces the size of a sample of grain while maintaining the representatives of the original sample; used to cut the required size portion from the original sample.

BOP   Branch office position; tells company what commodity-by-commodity and total position is—long/short/even.

BOT   Abbreviation for "bought."

BREAK   A sharp price decline.

BROAD TAPE   A teletype reporting system that automatically prints out news, weather, markets, etc., as furnished from professional and government reporting services.

BROKER   An agent entrusted with the execution of an order. He or she may be employed in the office of the commmission house that carries the account or may be a floor broker or pit broker who actually executes the order on the trading floor. See *Customer's Man*.

BROKERAGE   The fee charged by a broker for execution of a transaction; may be a flat amount or a percentage.

BUCKET, BUCKETING   The illegal practice of some brokers in accepting orders to buy or sell without executing such orders. Such a broker hopes to profit by pocketing the loss a customer may experience upon closing out the transaction. If the customer closes out at a profit, the broker pays that profit. The illegality lies in an agent's direct dealing with his principal without disclosing that fact.

BUHLER   Type of conveyor, utilizing steel flighting on a chain to push grain through an enclosed housing; a relatively dust-free method of conveying grain.

BULGE   A sharp price advance.

BULL   One who believes prices are too low and will advance.

BULL MARKET   A market in which small supplies and/or strong demand causes prices to rise.

BUTTERFLY SPREAD   A spread involving purchases or sales of one futures contract month occurring between the offsetting sales or purchases of two other futures contract months.

BUYING HEDGE   Buying futures to hedge cash sales in the present or future. See *Hedging*.

BUYER'S MARKET   A condition of the market in which there is an abundance of goods available, and hence buyers can afford to be selective and may be able to buy at less than the price that had previously prevailed.

BUY IN   To cover or liquidate a sale.

CALL   A period in which trading is conducted to establish the price for each futures month at a particular time (i.e., an opening or closing call).

Buyer's Call   Purchase of a specified quantity of a specific grade of a commodity at a fixed number of points above or below a specified delivery month in futures, with the buyer being allowed a certain period of time within which to fix the price by either purchasing a future for the account of the seller or indicating to the seller when he wishes to price-fix.

Seller's Call   The same as *Buyer's Call*, with the difference that the seller has the right of determining the time to price-fix. See *Futures Contracts*.

CALLS AND PUTS   "Call," an option permitting its holder (who has paid a fee for the option) to call for a certain commodity or security at a fixed price in a stated quantity within a stated period. The broker is paid to bring the buyer and seller together. The buyer of this right to call expects the price of the commodity or security to rise so that he can call for it at a profit. If the price falls, the option will not be exercised. The reverse transaction is a "Put."

CARLOAD   For grains, rail cars hold about 3,300 bushels.

CAR MOVER   A hydraulic mechanism that moves rail cars into position for unloading or loading.

CARRYING CHARGES, CHARGING COSTS   (1) Those costs incurred in warehousing the physical commodity generally including interest, insurance and storage; (2) full carrying charge market: a situation in the futures market when the price difference between delivery months reflects the full costs of interest, insurance and storage.

CARRYOVER   That part of current supplies of a commodity composed of stocks from previous production/marketing seasons.

CARTER DOCKAGE TESTER   A machine that runs samples of grain over a series of sieves, removing the collecting dockage for grade determination. Sieves are interchangeable, and the machine may be adjusted to perform for most grains.

CASH COMMODITY   Physical merchandise; goods available for delivery immediately or within a designated period following sale; includes a commodity bought or sold "to arrive."

CASH TRANSACTION   Purchase or sale of physical merchandise; can involve futures contracts; however, term is commonly used to differentiate between cash and futures transactions.

CCC   Commodity Credit Corporation.

CEC   Commodity Exchange Commission.

C. & F. (COST AND FREIGHT)   Cost and freight paid to port of destination.

CFTC   Commodity Futures Trading Commission (replaced CEA, 1975).

CERTIFIED STOCKS   Stocks of a commodity that have been graded, have passed various tests and found to be of deliverable quality against *Futures Contracts*, which are stored at the delivery points and in warehouses designated regular for delivery by the exchange.

CHARTER   A contract governing the engagement of a vessel, usually to a given destination at a fixed rate.

CHARTING   The use of graphs and charts in the technical analysis of futures markets to plot trends of price movements, average movements of price, and volume and open interest. See *Technical Analysis*.

CIF   Cost, insurance and freight paid (or included) to a port of destination.

CLASS 2, GROUP G Designates electrical equipment that is certified by underwriter laboratories as explosion-proof.

CLEANING The act of removing foreign material and "fines" from grain. Usually done just prior to loading out, accomplished by running the grain over screens. See *Fines*.

CLEARING CONTRACTS The process of substituting principals to transactions through the operation of clearing associations, in order to simplify the settlement of accounts.

CLEARING HOUSE, CLEARING ASSOCIATION The separate agency associated with a futures exchange through which *Futures Contracts* are offset or fulfilled and through which financial settlement is made.

CLEARING MEMBER A member of a *Clearing House* or association. Each clearing member must also be a member of the exchange. Each member of the exchange, however, need not be a member of the clearing association; if not, his trades must be registered and settled through a clearing member.

CLOSE The period at the end of the trading session during which all trades are officially declared as having been executed "at or on the close." The closing range is the range of prices on trades made during this designated period.

CLOSE or OPENING ORDER An order that specifies buying or selling at the end or beginning of the session at a price within the closing or opening range.

C.O.F.O. Commercially objectionable foreign odor.

COMMISSION Fee charged by a broker for performance of specified market functions.

COMMISSION HOUSE, BROKERAGE HOUSE A concern that buys or sells for the accounts of customers.

COMMISSION MERCHANT One who makes a trade, either for another member of the exchange or for a nonmember client, but who makes the trade in his own name and becomes liable as principal to the other party to the transaction.

COMMITMENT OF TRADERS REPORT A report issued by the Chicago Board of Trade at the end of each month that defines the futures market positions of various classes of traders.

CONDITION Refers to the quality of the grain with respect to temperature, moisture, mold and insect infestations.

CONSIGNMENT An unsold shipment of grain placed with a commission man who will offer it for sale.

CONTRACT (1) The bilateral obligations of buyer and seller in a transaction; (2) a unit of the commodity being traded. Orders must specify the number of bushels to be bought and sold. Also see *Round Lot*.

CONTRACT GRADES, DELIVERABLE GRADES The grades of a commodity listed in the rules of an exchange as those that can be used to deliver against a *Futures Contract*.

CONTRACT MARKET An organized commodity futures market that qualifies under the Commodity Exchange Act.

CONSERVATION RESERVE The section of the *Soil Bank* program calling for long-term contracts for the conversion of crop land into grasses, trees and water conservation uses.

CONTROLLED COMMODITY Commodities subject to Commodity Exchange Authority regulation, listed in the Commodity Exchange Act. The list is composed of domestically produced agricultural products.

CORNER (1) To secure such relative control of a commodity or security that its price can be manipulated; (2) in the extreme situation, obtaining more contracts requiring the delivery of commodities or securities than the quantity of such commodities or securities actually in existence.

COUNTRY ELEVATOR A grain elevator located in the immediate farming community to which farmers bring their grain for sale or storage, as distinct from a terminal elevator, which is located at a major marketing center.

COVER The purchase of futures and/or cash to offset a previously established short position.

CROP YEAR Period used for statistical purposes, from the harvest of a crop to the corresponding period in following year. U.S. wheat crop year begins June 1 and ends May 31; cotton, August 1–July 31; varying dates for other commodities. Also, some agribusiness firms often refer to their corporate fiscal year as their crop year.

C.R.P. Conservation Reserve Program, a 10-year government set-aside program that pays producers an annual payment if they agree to idle erodible land.

CRUDE OIL Oil that has undergone the first stage(s) of refinement.

CRUSH (Soybeans) The process that converts soybeans into meal and oil; also, a term used to describe a particular spreading posture between soybeans and products.

CURRENT DELIVERY Delivery during the present month.

CUSTOMER'S MAN, FUTURES COMMISSIONS BROKER, REGISTERED REPRESENTATIVE An employee of a commission house (also called a broker, account executive, solicitor, or registered representative) who engages in soliciting or accepting and handling orders for the purchase or sale of any commodity for future delivery on or subject to the rules of any contract market and who, in or in connection with such solicitations or acceptance of orders, accepts any money, securities, or property (or extends credit in lieu thereof) to margin any trades or contracts that result or may result therefrom. They must be licensed under the Commodity Exchange Act when handling business in commodities covered thereby.

CUT A portion of a sample drawn by a manual or automatic sampling device.

CYCLONE A machine for removing dust from dust-laden air. It blows air into a chamber where the dust-laden air moves in a circular path. Centrifugal force is used to separate out the dust, which collects at the hoppered bottom of the chamber.

DATE GAME A practice followed by some futures longs during delivery months that is aimed at the avoidance or stopping of taking physical deliveries of commodities unless carrying charges are relatively attractive or close to full.

DAY ORDERS Limited orders that are to be executed the day for which they are effective and are automatically canceled at the close of that day.

DAY TRADERS Commodity traders, generally members of the exchange active on the trading floor, who take positions in commodities and then liquidate them prior to the close of the same trading day.

DEFAULT (1) In reference to the federal farm loan program, the decision on the part of a producer of commodities not to repay the government loan but instead to surrender his crops; (2) in futures markets, the theoretical failure of a party to a *Futures Contract* to either make or take delivery of the physical commodity as required under the contract.

DEFICIENCY PAYMENT Difference between target price and loan rate or market price; payment to producer for complying with program set-aside requirements, providing the producer income protection without supporting prices directly.

DELIVERY MARKET STOCKS, VISIBLE Grain stocks physically located in the delivery marketplace and theoretically available for delivery in satisfaction of *Futures Contracts*.

DELIVERY MONTH   The calendar month during which a *Futures Contract* matures.

DELIVERY NOTICE   The notification of delivery of the actual commodity on the contract issued by the seller of the futures to the *Clearing House*.

DELIVERY POINTS   Those locations designated by commodity exchanges at which a commodity covered by a *Futures Contract* may be delivered in fulfillment of the contract.

DELIVERY PRICE   The price fixed by the *Clearing House* at which deliveries on futures are invoiced; also the price at which the *Futures Contract* is settled when deliveries are made.

DEMURRAGE   Fees charged to shippers/receivers who fail to load/unload transportation equipment in the allowed free time.

DIFFERENTIALS   The price differences between classes, grades and locations of a given commodity.

DISCOUNT   Applied to cash grain prices that are below the future, to deliveries at a lesser price than others (May at a discount under July) or to lesser prices caused by quality differences.

DISCRETIONARY ACCOUNT   An account for which buying and selling orders can be placed by a broker or other person without the prior consent of the account owner for each such individual order, specific authorization having been previously granted by the account owner.

DISTANT or DEFERRED DELIVERY   Usually means one of the more distant months in which futures or cash trading is taking place.

D.L.Q.   Distinctly Low Quality. Grain that is obviously of inferior quality because it contains foreign substances or because it is in an unusual state or condition and cannot be graded properly by use of the other grading factors provided in the standards. D.L.Q. includes any objects too large to enter the sampling device.

DIVERSION PAYMENT   Per acre payment producer receives for idling land in addition to the unpaid acreage reduction program; optional.

DOCKAGE   Essentially consists of grain of nonstandard size and other nongrain matter that can be readily removed from grain samples by the use of appropriate sieves and cleaning devices, including those employing air currents. Dockage normally is free of cost to the buyer, deducted from the gross weight of the shipment.

DRYER   A unit that provides the conditions for removing moisture from a product.

DRYERATION   A modified drying process involving the portable batch or continuous-flow dryer. In this process the product is dried with heated air to a moisture level of 16%–18%, wet basis. The product is transferred immediately without cooling to a temporary storage (dryeration) bin equipped for aeration. The product is allowed to set for a few hours to become tempered before aeration is started. Cooling is accomplished in about 12 hours with airflow rates of about 0.007 $m^3 m^3 s$ (1/2 cfm/bu.). At this low airflow rate, nearly all of the heat in the product is utilized to further dry it. The moisture content may be further reduced 3% to 4% during the 12 hours of cooling.

DRYING   The removal of moisture from a substance, involving the simultaneous transfer of heat *to* the substance and moisture *from* the substance, known as unit operation. The heat for evaporation of the moisture in the material is transferred by conduction, convection, radiation and internal heating, such as by respiration and dielectric heating. The vapor mass is transferred by diffusion or capillary flow to the surface, from which the vapor is carried by a gas. As a result of drying, the biological and chemical activity of the product is decreased.

ELASTICITY   A characteristic of commodities that describes the interaction of the supply, demand, and price of a commodity. A commodity is said to be elastic in demand when a price change creates an increase or decrease in consumption. The supply of a commodity is said to be elastic when a change in price creates change in the production of the commodity. Inelasticity of supply or of demand exists in either of the reverse situations, when either supply or demand is relatively unresponsive to changes in price.

ELEVATIONS   Profits taken on a sale contract that is recognized as the grain is loaded out of an elevator.

ELLISCUP   Manual sampling device, designed to draw a sample from grain moving to a conveyor belt.

ENSILAGE   Chopped animal feed that is stored in bulk, usually in a moist condition.

EVEN   No position or no net position, as in the case where purchases of cash grain or futures contracts are offset by sales of cash grain or futures contracts.

EXCHANGE OF SPOT or CASH COMMODITY FOR FUTURES   The simultaneous exchange of a specified quantity of a cash commodity for the equivalent quantity in futures; usually instituted between parties carrying opposite hedges in the same delivery month. Also known as "exchange for physical," "against actuals," or "giving up futures for cash." In grain, the exchange is made outside the *Pit*.

EX-PIT TRANSACTION   A trade made outside the exchange trading ring or pit, which is legal in certain instances. It is primarily used in price fixing transactions involving the purchase of cash commodities at a specified basis.

FARMER OWNED RESERVE   A U.S. Department of Agriculture program that enables the farmer to store "loan" grain for 3 years in return for storage payments from the government. The FOR provides a government incentive to store grain when prices are relatively low.

FARM PRICES   The prices received by farmers for their products, as published by the U.S. Department of Agriculture; determined as of the 15th of each month.

F.A.Q.   Fair average quality.

FEDERAL APPEAL   May be called for at any time, but must be preceded by an official inspection, a reinspection, or appeal. It is usually called when either buyer or seller believes the original inspection to be in error because of the original inspector's interpretation of his findings. See *Board Appeal*.

FEED RATIOS   The variable relationships of the cost of feeding animals to market-weight sales prices, expressed as ratios, such as the hog/corn ratio. These serve as indicators of the profit return or lack of it in feeding animals to market weight.

F.G.I.S.   Federal Grain Inspection Service.

FILL OR KILL ORDER   A commodity order that demands immediate execution or cancellation.

FINES   Small-diameter particles such as those that form from larger particles during handling and drying.

FIRST NOTICE DAY   The first day on which notices of intentions to deliver actual commodities against futures market positions can be made or received. First notice day will vary with each commodity and exchange. It usually precedes the beginning of the delivery period.

FIXING THE PRICE   The determination of the exact price at which a cash commodity will be invoiced after a "call sale" has previously been made based on a specific number of points "on or off" a specified futures month.

FLAKE   A soybean morsel from which the oil has been extracted.

FLASH Hand signals used by *Pit Brokers*.

FLAT PRICES TRADES Trades in which the actual flat price is established at the time of the trade—no exchange of futures.

FLOOR BROKER Any person who, in or surrounding any *Pit, Ring*, post, or other place provided by a contract market for the meeting of persons similarly engaged, executes for others any order for the purchase or sale of any commodity for future delivery on or subject to the rules of any contract market and who for such services receives or accepts a prescribed fee or brokerage.

FLOOR PHONE MAN An employee of a brokerage house who serves as the communication link between his firm's office and the brokers in the pits.

FLOOR TRADER An exchange member who executes his own trades by being personally present in the place provided for futures trading.

F.O.B. Free on board. Usually covers all delivery, inspection and elevation costs involved in putting commodities on board whatever shipment conveyance is being used.

FORAGE Natural pasture for livestock.

FREE SUPPLY The quantity of a commodity available for commercial sale; does not include government-held stocks.

FUMIGANT A chemical used to destroy insects in grain; may come in solid, liquid or gaseous form. Active form is gaseous, poison; may be toxic to humans also.

FUNDAMENTAL ANALYSIS An approach to analysis of futures markets and commodity futures price trends that examines the underlying factors affecting the supply and demand of the commodity being traded in *Futures Contracts*. For contrast, see *Technical Analysis*.

FUNGIBILITY The characteristic of total interchangeability. *Futures Contracts* for the same commodity and delivery month are fungible due to their standardized specifications for quality, quantity, delivery date and delivery locations.

FUTURES CONTRACT Agreement to buy and receive or to sell and deliver a commodity at a future date, with the following distinguishing characteristics:

    1. All trades in the same contract, such as a 5,000-bushel *Round Lot* of grain, have the same unit of trading.

    2. The terms of all trades are standardized.

    3. A position may be offset later by an opposite trade in the same contract.

    4. Prices are determined by trades made by open outcry in the *Pit* within the hours prescribed.

    5. The contract has a basic grade, but more than one grade may be deliverable.

    6. Delivery is required during designated periods.

    7. The trades are cleared through a *Clearing House* daily. (Traders in cash or spot goods usually refer to sales for shipment or delivery in the future as "deferred" or "forward" sales. Such sales, however, are not standardized as are futures contracts described above.)

GENERIC CERTIFICATE A form of currency backed by CCC-owned commodities and issued by the U.S. Department of Agriculture primarily to producers as payment for participation in various farm programs.

GIVE-UP A contract executed by one broker for the client of another broker, which the client orders turned over to the latter broker. Generally speaking, the order is sent over the leased wires of the first broker, who collects a wire toll from the other broker for the use of his facilities.

GOOD-TIL-CANCELLED (G.T.C.), OPEN ORDER An order that will remain open for execution at any time in the future until the customer cancels it.

GRAIN FUTURES ACT A federal statute that regulates trading in grain futures.

GRAINS For purposes of the Chicago Board of Trade: wheat, oats, rye, corn and soybeans.

GROSS PROCESSING MARGIN (GPM) In the case of soybeans, GPM refers to the difference between the price paid for soybeans and the sum of prices received from the sale of oil and meal products after processing.

HARD SPOT An interval of strength in the market, usually resulting from considerable buying.

HEAVY Applied to a market with an apparent number of selling orders overhanging the market without a corresponding number of buying orders.

HEDGING Briefly stated, hedging is the sale of futures against the physical commodity or its equivalent, as protection against a price decline, or the purchase of futures against forward sales or anticipated requirements of the physical commodity as protection against a price advance. Hedging on futures markets consists in buying (or selling) *Futures Contracts* in the amount to which one is long (or short) on the actual commodity. Usually, the futures transaction is nearly simultaneous with the spot transaction. Hedgers thereby fix or protect a *Carrying Charge*, a processing margin, etc. The futures hedge is thus a temporary substitute for an ordinary transaction that will occur later. Hedging also provides opportunities for added profit.

HOT SPOT Grain that has become hot as a result of excessive respiration or insect activity.

I.C.C. Interstate Commerce Commission.

IN BOND An inspected, sealed and cleared shipment, actually in transit or scheduled for export.

INDICATION, INTIMATION A tentative or subject bid; a less-than-firm expression of willingness to buy at a specified price.

INSPECTION, OFFICIAL INSPECTION In commodity marketing, an official evaluation procedure that results in a grade or class designation being assigned. Supplied by the Federal Grain Inspection Service (FGIS).

INVERSES, INVERTED MARKET A futures market in which the nearer months are selling at premiums to the more distant months, hence, a market displaying "inverse carrying charges." These price relationships are characteristic of situations in which supplies are currently in shortage.

INVISIBLE SUPPLY Uncounted stocks in the hands of wholesalers, manufacturers and producers that cannot be identified accurately; stocks outside commercial channels but available for commerce.

JOB LOT A unit of trading smaller than the regular *Round Lot*, usually, in grains, 1,000 or 2,000 bushels. No job lots are traded on the Chicago Board of Trade.

LAST TRADING DAY The day on which trading ceases for a particular delivery month. All contracts that have not been offset by the end of trading on that day must thereafter be settled by delivery of the actual physical commodity or by agreement in the form of *Wash Sales*.

LEG A vertical, enclosed conveyor belt that has buckets attached to the belt that elevates grain. The grain is discharged by centrifugal force at the top of the enclosure.

LETTER OF WARNING A written notice issued by the CEA to an individual or firm, advising of an improper practice or specific violation of law, trading regulations, etc.

LIFE OF DELIVERY or CONTRACT The period between the beginning of trading in a particular future to the expiration of that future.

LIMIT ONLY   In trading, the definite price stated by a customer to a broker restricting the execution of an order to buy for not more than or to sell for not less than the stated price.

LIMIT (UP or DOWN)   The maximum price advance or decline from the previous day's settlement price permitted in one trading session by the rules of the exchange.

LIMITED ORDER   One in which the client sets a limit on the price, as contrasted with a *Market Order*.

LIQUIDATION   The closing out of a long position. It is also sometimes used to denote closing out a short position, but this is more often referred to as "covering."

LIQUIDATING MARKET   One in which the predominant feature is longs selling their holdings.

LOAD ORDER   Identify grain to be shipped, specify grade factors to be met and give all information necessary for shipping grain in terms of quality and quantity. It gives the superintendent authority to load grain out of the elevator.

LOAN PRICE   The statutory price at which growers may obtain crop loans from the government.

LOAN PROGRAM   The primary means of government price support, in which the government lends money to the farmer at a preannounced price schedule with the farmer's crop as collateral; The primary method by which the government acquires stocks of agricultural commodities.

LOAN RATE   Government support price; price at which government agrees to lend producers money on eligible bushels; price at which government agrees to purchase grain.

LONG   One who has bought grain; also one who is on the buying side of an open (unhedged) futures contract.

LONG THE BASIS   This is said of one who has bought cash or spot goods and has hedged them with sales of the futures. He has therefore bought at a certain *Basis* on or off futures and hopes to sell at a better basis in the future for a profit.

LOTTING SYSTEM   Used to identify the kind and quality of the various types and varieties of grain as grouped in the bins in an elevator.

MARGIN   The amount deposited by buyers and sellers of futures to insure performance on contract commitments, serving as a performance bond rather than a down payment; established by the respective exchanges.

MARGIN CALL   A request to deposit either the original margin at the time of the transaction or to restore the guarantee to "maintenance margin" levels required for the duration of the time the contract is held.

MARKET ORDER, BOARD ORDER   An order to buy or sell when the market reaches a specified point. A board order to buy becomes a market order when the commodity sells (or is bid) at or above the order price.

MARKETING LOAN   The Secretary of Agriculture is required to lower the repayment level for loans when prices drop below the loan rate for certain crops. Most common repayment level is the "World Market Price."

MARKETING QUOTA   A federally enforced restriction on the amount of a commodity that a producer is permitted to sell. Usually conforms to the quantity of wheat, cotton, etc., the farmer can grow on his acreage allotment.

MATURITY   The period within which a futures contract can be settled by delivery of the actual commodity; the period between *First Notice Day* and *Last Trading Day*.

MEMBERS' RATE   The commission charge for the execution of an order for a person who is a member of and thereby has a seat on the exchange. It is less than the commission charged to a customer who does not have a seat on the exchange.

NEGOTIABLE WAREHOUSE RECEIPT Document issued by a "regular" warehouse, which guarantees existence and grade of commodity held in store. Transfer of ownership can be accomplished by endorsement of the *Warehouse Receipt*.

NOMINAL PRICE A declared price for a futures month. Used at times to designate a closing price when no trading has taken place in that particular contract during the final few minutes of the trading session. It is usually the average between the bid and asked prices.

NONRESOURCE LOAN A loan under the U.S. agricultural program to farmers on the security of surplus crops that are delivered to the government and held off the market. The loan must be liquidated as provided by the government's program, but the government has no recourse against the farmer for a deficiency if the security fails to bring the amount of the loan.

NO PRICE ESTABLISHED (N.P.E.) A form of cash grain contracting which, while initially establishing neither an unpriced basis nor a fixed flat price, does transfer title and risk of loss to the buyer upon delivery and provides the seller with the option of subsequently fixing a price related to bids made by the buyer for nearby delivery to the same location as that at which the contracted grain was originally received. This form of trading is sometimes referred to as deferred price contracting.

NOTICE DAY Any day on which notices of intent to deliver on *Futures Contracts* may be issued.

O.C.O. One cancels other, in which filling of one order cancels customer's alternative order.

OFFER A firm expression of willingness to sell at a given price.

OFF-GRADE A grade different from the grade of grain in the major portion of the lot.

OFFICIAL INSPECTION See *Inspection*.

OFFSET Usually the liquidation of a long or short futures position by an equal and opposite futures transaction.

OFF-UNDER In quoting the *Basis*, the number of points the cash price will be off or under a specified futures price.

OILS In commodity trading usually includes soybean oil, cottonseed oil, olive oil and other edible fats that are broadly substitutive.

OMNIBUS ACCOUNT An account carried by one futures commission merchant with another, in which the transactions of two or more persons are combined rather than designated separately, and the identity of individual accounts is not disclosed.

ON-OVER In quoting the *Basis*, the number of points the cash commodity is above or over a specified futures month.

ON CONSIGNMENT GRAIN Usually refers to grain conveyed to a broker for sale in the cash market.

OPEN CONTRACTS Contracts that have been bought or sold without the transaction having been completed by subsequent sale or repurchase or actual delivery or receipt of commodity.

OPEN INTEREST The total of unfilled or unsatisfied contracts on one side of the market. In any one delivery month the short interest always equals the long interest, since the total number of contracts sold must equal the total number bought.

OPEN OUTCRY Required method of registering all bids and offers in the *Pits*.

OPENING RANGE, CLOSING RANGE In open auction with many buyers and sellers, commodities are often traded at several prices at the opening or close of the market. Buying or selling orders at the opening or closing might be filled at any point within such a price range.

OPTION A term sometimes erroneously applied to a futures contract. It may refer to a specific delivery month, as "the July option." Puts and *Calls* or privileges are true options entailing no delivery obligation. Futures contracts are not options.

ORIGINAL MARGIN The margin needed to cover a specific new position.

OUT-OF-CONDITION Grain that has deteriorated in soundness (e.g., heating, sour or musty grain).

OVERSOLD or OVERBOUGHT MARKETS When the speculative long interest has been drastically reduced and the speculative short interest increases, actually or relatively, a market is said to be oversold. At such times, sharp rallies often materialize. On the other hand, when the speculative short interest decreases sharply, a market is said to be overbought. At such times, the market is often in a position to decline sharply.

OVERSUPPLY A market situation in which available commodities exceed demonstrated demand; the result is usually seen in lower prices.

PAPER PROFIT The profit that might be realized if the open contract were liquidated as of a certain time or at a certain price. Margin requirements are adjusted according to paper profits; hence, they are to some extent "real."

PARITY A theoretically equal relationship between commodity prices and all other prices; equality of relationship. Specifically, in farm program legislation, parity is defined in such a manner that the purchasing power of a unit of the commodity is maintained at the level prevailing during some earlier historical base period.

PELICAN A device used for cutting across a flowing stream of grain in order to obtain a representative sample for grading purposes.

PIK Payment in kind; government payment for participating in various farm programs is in commodities versus cash.

PIK & ROLL Term used to describe the procedure a producer follows in redeeming government commodities with generic certificates.

PIT BROKER A broker who works in the *Pit* filling *Futures Contract* orders for customers.

PIT, RINGS Designated locations on the trading floor where futures trading takes place in particular commodities.

PLACEMENT DATE Constructive placement occurs when a railroad is unable to place cars on elevator tracks for loading or unloading due to the elevator's inability to accept the units when they arrive; *demurrage* begins at first 7:00 A.M. thereafter. Actual placement is when the cars are placed on the elevator's tracks.

PLIMSOLL MARK A load line or set load-line markings on an oceangoing cargo ship.

PLUGGED LEG A *Leg* in which the boot has become filled with grain and stopped the belt.

POINT The minimum price fluctuation in futures. It is equal to 1/100 of one cent in most futures traded in decimal units. In grains it is 1/8 of one cent.

POSITION LIMIT The maximum number of contracts one can hold "open" under the rules of the CEA.

POSITION TRADER A commodity trader who either buys or sells contracts and holds them for an extended period of time, as distinguished from the day trader, who will normally initiate and liquidate a futures position within a single trading session.

PREMIUM   The excess in price at which one delivery or quality of grain is selling over the value of another delivery or quality, or the price relationship between cash and future.

PRIMARY MARKET, COUNTRY MARKET   The centers to which the farmers bring their crops for sale, such as country grain elevators.

PRIVATE WIRE   A leased or owned communication link for the exclusive use of a single individual or brokerage house.

PROBE (Trier)   A double-tube compartmented device of varying standard lengths made from brass or aluminum and used to sample grain.

PUBLIC ELEVATORS   Grain storage facilities in which space is rented out to whoever wishes to pay for it; where grain is stored in bulk. These are licensed and regulated by the state and/or federal government and may also be approved as regular for delivery on an organized commodity exchange.

PURCHASE AGREEMENT   A form of government price support in which the government agrees to buy commodities from a farmer at a specified time at a designated loan price.

PURCHASE AND SALES STATEMENT (P & S)   A statement sent by a *Commission Merchant* to a customer when his futures position has changed. It shows the amount involved, the prices at which the position was acquired and closed out, the gross profit or loss, the commission charges and the net profit or loss on the transactions.

PUT THRU   Elevator loads plus unloads divided by two.

PYRAMIDING   Using the profits on previously established positions as margin for adding to that position.

QUOTATIONS   The changing prices on cash grains and futures.

QUOTE   A tentative or subject offer; a less-than-firm expression of willingness to sell at a specified price.

RANGE   The difference between the highest and lowest prices recorded during a specified trading period.

REACTION   Downward tendency in prices following an advance.

REALIZING   Taking profits.

RECOVERY   Advance after a decline.

REGULATED COMMODITIES   Those commodities over which the Commodity Exchange Authority has supervision are known as "regulated." This does not mean that the prices are controlled. The CEA simply concerns itself with the orderly operation of the futures market and at times, investigates abnormal price movements. Under the Commodity Exchange Act, approved June 15, 1936, definite regulations were established providing for the safeguarding of customers' money deposited as margin.

REPORTING LIMIT   Sizes of positions set by the exchanges and/or by the Commodity Exchange Authority at or above which commodity traders must make daily reports to either or both the exchange and the Commodity Exchange Authority as to the size of the position by commodity, by delivery month, and according to the purpose of trading (i.e., speculative or *Hedging*).

REPRESENTATIVE SAMPLE   A sample obtained by *Official Inspection* that is of the proper size (approximately 2½ quarts) and handled in a secure manner.

RESTING ORDER   Instructions to buy at a figure below the present market price or sell at a figure above it.

RESTRICTED STOCKS   Loan stocks, etc.; a separate segregation that, during recent years of control, has been applied to supplies officially off the market for a definite or indefinite period.

RETENDER   The right of holders of *Futures Contracts* who have been tendered a

Delivery Notice through the *Clearing House* to offer the notice for sale on the open market, liquidating their obligation to take delivery under the contract; applicable only to certain commodities and only within a specified period of time.

REX Refers to a reinspection, may be called for by a shipper when he thinks the official grade is too low. A rex may be called by the buyer when he thinks the grade may be too high. Ordinarily, the last official grade applies on the sale whether it is fixed after or before the sale is made.

RIVER HOUSE *Terminal Elevator* located on an inland waterway; barge load primary function, may be capable also of shipping by rail/truck.

ROUND LOT A contract trading unit. Round lots of grain are 5,000 bushels.

ROUND TURN The completion of both a purchase and an offsetting sale of futures or vice versa.

SAMPLE In marketing, one or more units of a product given free (or sold at a price far below market) in order to induce prospective buyers to give it a trial or to enable them to determine its characteristics by inspection or analysis.

SAMPLE GRADE In commodities, usually the lowest-quality grade designation, one that normally is not acceptable for delivery in settlement of a *Futures Contract*.

SCALPER A speculator operating on the trading floor who provides market liquidity by buying and selling rapidly, with small profits or losses, and who holds his position for a short time. Typically, a scalper stands ready to buy at a fraction below the last transaction price and to sell at a fraction above.

SELLER'S MARKET A condition of the market in which there is a scarcity of goods available, and hence sellers can obtain better conditions of sale or higher prices.

SELLER'S OPTION The right of a seller to select, within the limits prescribed by a contract, the quality of the commodity delivered and/or the time and/or place of delivery.

SELLING HEDGE Selling futures to hedge cash purchases in present or future. See *Hedging*.

SETTLEMENT PRICE The daily price at which the *Clearing House* clears all of the day's trades; also a price that may be established by the Exchange to settle contracts unliquidated because of acts of God, such as floods, market congestion or other causes.

SHORT The selling side of an open futures contract; also refers to a trader whose net position shows an excess of open sales over open purchases.

SHORT THE BASIS This is said of a person or firm who has sold cash or spot goods and has hedged them with purchases of futures. He has therefore sold at a certain *Basis* and expects to buy back at a lower basis for a profit.

SHRINKAGE Grain shrinks in both weight and volume when dried. The volume of shrinkage for shelled corn is relatively high compared to other grains, figured using table for varying amounts of moisture removal.

SLATE POSITION, FLAT PRICE POSITION The net exposed or unhedged position in a given commodity. The net difference between total sales of futures and/or cash and total purchases of futures and/or cash.

SOIL BANK A government program designated to take farmland out of productive use. The government pays the farmer to not plant crops; instead, to plant the land in grass or trees.

SOLICITOR A member or nonmember who solicits business for a member.

SPECULATOR One who attempts to anticipate price changes and through market activities make profits and who is not hedging or spreading.

SPOT COMMODITY Physical goods available for immediate delivery following sale;

improperly used to include a commodity bought or sold "to arrive"; also called *Actuals*.

SPOT PRICE   The current or nearby price at which a physical commodity is selling at a designated place.

SPREADING, SPREADS, STRADDLES   These terms mean the same thing, but in practice the grain trade uses the term "spread," whereas other commodity interests use the term "straddle." A spread may be defined as the purchase of one future against the sale of another future of the same commodity or a different commodity in the same or different markets. CEA defines spreading only in terms of the same commodity, whereas exchanges define it to also include different but related commodities. The term "spread" is also used to refer to the difference between the price of one futures month and the price of another month of the same commodity.

SQUEEZE   A manipulative attempt by one principal or company or a small group of traders to influence market prices in a certain direction.

STIPULATION OF COMPLIANCE   In commodity usage, formal assurance on the part of an individual or firm that an administrative request or order from CEA or other regulative body will be followed.

STOP ORDER, STOP LOSS ORDER   An order entered to buy or sell when the market reaches a specified point. A stop order to buy becomes a *Market Order* when the commodity sells (or is bid) at or above the stop price. A stop order to sell becomes a *Market Order* when the commodity sells (or is offered) at or below the stop price. The purpose of a stop loss order is to limit losses or protect a profit.

SUBSIDY   A sum of money offered by government to assist in the establishment or support of an enterprise or program that is considered to be in the public interest.

SWAPS   Switching one cash position for another—same quantity, same price, different position.

SWEATING   Accumulation of free moisture on the surface of the kernels.

SWITCH   The liquidation of a position in one future of a commodity and the simultaneous reinstatement of such position in another future of the same commodity. It may be done "at market" or at a specified difference. When done by hedgers, this tactic is referred to as "rolling forward" the hedge.

TARGET PRICE   Used to calculate *Deficiency Payment*.

TARIFF   (1) Rail grain rates apply equally to all shippers and are filed with the regulatory bodies in schedules called tariffs; (2) a published schedule of charges for handling and storing grain for the account of others at licensed public grain *Terminal Elevators*.

TECHNICAL ANALYSIS   An approach to analysis of futures markets and likely future trends of commodity prices that examines the technical factors of market activity. Technical analysts normally examine patterns of price change, rates of change, and changes in volume of trading and open interest. This data is often charted to show trends and formations that will in turn serve as indicators of likely future price movements.

TECHNICAL RALLY (or DECLINE)   A price movement resulting from conditions developing within the futures market itself and not dependent on outside supply and demand factors. These conditions would include changes in the *Open Interest* volume, degree or recent price movement and approach of *First Notice Day*.

TENDER   (1) Delivery against a futures position; (2) an announcement that expresses the terms under which a principal has interest in either buying or selling commodities.

TERMINAL ELEVATOR A grain storage facility at one of the major centers of agricultural product marketing, such as Kansas City or Chicago.

TEST WEIGHT (TW) A factor in grading of grain. TW is the weight of the quantity of grain required to fill completely a Winchester bushel. Minimum pounds per bushel are established in the U.S. grain standards for the various numerical sample grades.

TICKER TAPE A stock or commodity quotation system.

TO ARRIVE (1) Price is based on delivery at the destination point, and the seller pays the freight in shipping it to that point; (2) grain contracted for delivery to a designated destination that is either in transit or not yet shipped.

TRACK, TRACK COUNTRY STATION Usually involves a price designation; indicates the cost of a given commodity loaded in rail car and ready for shipment from an interior location.

TRADING LIMIT In virtually all North American commodity contract markets there is a maximum price change permitted for a single session. These limits vary in the different markets. After prices have advanced or declined to the permissible daily limits, the trading automatically ceases unless, of course, offers appear at the permissible upper trading limit or bids appear at the permissible lower limit.

TRANSFER To move grain from one location in an elevator to another, also called turning; will blend off uneven areas, disperse hot spots, and insect activity, dispel areas of high humidity and accumulated odors.

TRANSFERABLE NOTICE or DELIVERY NOTICE A written announcement issued by a seller signifying his intention of making delivery in fulfillment of a *Futures Contract*. The recipient of the notice may make a sale of the future and transfer the notice within a specified time to another party, on some exchanges directly and on others through the clearing association.

TRANSIT Application of through-freight rates to a shipment stopped at a point intermediate to final destination for storage and/or milling and processing.

TRANSLOCATION Movement of moisture through grain.

UNDERSUPPLY A situation in which demand for a commodity exceeds physical stocks offered for sale in the market; result is usually seen in rising prices. See *Oversupply*.

UNPRICED TRADES No flat price is established at the time of the trade—only the basis level is agreed to by the buyer and seller.

USDA United States Department of Agriculture.

UNPRICED TRADES No flat price is established at the time of the trade—only the basis level is agreed to by the buyer and seller.

VARIATION MARGIN CALL A request for additional margin funds as collateral, occasioned by negative price movement against the held position.

VISIBLE SUPPLY The amount of a particular commodity in store at loading centers; in the grain markets, the total stock of grain in store, in public and some private elevators, in the principal primary markets, plus certain stock *Afloat*.

VOLUME OF TRADING The purchases and sales of a commodity during a specified period. Inasmuch as purchases equal sales, only one side is shown in published reports.

WAREHOUSE RECEIPT A document evidencing possession by a warehouseman (licensed under the U.S. Warehouse Act or under the laws of a state) of the commodity named in the receipt. Warehouse receipts, to be tenderable on future contracts, must be negotiable receipts covering commodities in warehouses recognized for delivery purposes by the exchange on which such futures contracts are traded.

WASH SALES Fictitious transactions contrived by two or more brokers in order to create a market price for a security or for tax evasion. It may also consist of two or more outside operators who match their orders for purchase and sale so that a seeming market activity is given to stock. Illegal and prohibited by law and by the exchanges. Tax law usually considers a repurchase within 30 days at a loss to be a wash sale. In commodity futures, contracts left open after the last day of trading may be settled by wash sales in lieu of delivery.

WIRE HOUSE Refers to a *Commission House* with branch offices connected by telephone, teletype, telegraph or cable.

Notes

1. Frontier Entrepreneur (pp. 3–64)

1. "Life . . . roseate," Edwin C. Bailey, *Past and Present of Winneshiek County, Iowa* (Chicago: S. J. Clarke Publishing Co., 1913), p. 203. There is no documentation of the precise date of W. W. Cargill's arrival in Conover; a lengthy article in the *La Crosse Republican & Leader*, October 23, 1880, on the "Past and Present of the Cargill Brothers," which presumably was written from personal information supplied by W. W., confirms the 1865 date and his location in Conover.

2. For pre–Civil War history of the McGregor railroad efforts, see Realto E. Price (ed.), *History of Clayton County Iowa* (Chicago: Robert O. Law Company, 1916), vol. 1, pp. 176–77. The Minnesota Western Rail Road Company became part of the Milwaukee & St. Paul Railway Co. in 1867, the latter later to be part of the Chicago, Milwaukee, St. Paul and Pacific Railroad (the "Milwaukee" line). See especially August W. Derleth, *The Milwaukee Road: Its First Hundred Years* (New York: Creative Press, 1948); Appendix A gives a complete history of the Milwaukee's name changes. See also Herbert William Rice, "Early History of the Chicago, Milwaukee and St. Paul Railway Company," Ph.D. dissertation, State University of Iowa, 1938; John W. Cary, *The Organization and History of the Chicago, Milwaukee & St. Paul Railway Company* (Milwaukee: Cramer, Aikens & Cramer, 1892). For the Iowa extensions, see Frank P. Donovan, "The Milwaukee in Iowa," *The Palimpsest* 45 (1964): 177; "Guide to Iowa Railroads, 1850–1872," mimeograph, 1984, State Historical Society of Iowa. On land grant use by railroads, see Robert L. Frey (ed.), "Railroads in the Nineteenth Century," *Encyclopedia of American Business History and Biography* (New York: Facts on File, 1988), p. 369; Richard C. Overton, *Burlington West: A Colonization History of the Burlington Railroad* (Cambridge, Mass.: Harvard University Press, 1941), passim. Quotation on "two fights," *McGregor North Iowa Times*, November 5, 1865; "gridded the midwestern states," Allen G. Bogue, *From Prairie to Corn Belt: Farming on the Illinois and Iowa Prairies in the Nineteenth Century* (Chicago: University of Chicago Press, 1963), p. 281.

3. John L. Work, *Cargill Beginnings . . . an Account of Early Years* (privately printed, n.d. [ca. 1965], pp. 61–62; "far . . . from tidewater," *The History of Cargill, Incorporated, 1865–1945* (Minneapolis: privately printed, 1945), p. 12; D. I. Nelke, *The Columbian Biographical Dictionary and Portrait Gallery of the Representative Men of the United States, Wisconsin Volume* (Chicago: Lewis Publishing Company, 1895), pp. 125–26. For example of advertisements about land in Wisconsin, see *New York Daily Tribune*, May 23, September 22, October 10 and 22, and December 17, 1855. A formal search for a Union army record for William Wallace Cargill was carried through in 1990 with the Military Service Branch (NNMS) of the National Archives and Records Administration, with no positive identification.

4. "Did not shell out," *Decorah (Iowa) Republic*, January 19, 1865; "boss town," Charles H. Sparks, *History of Winneshiek County, with Biographical Sketches of Its Eminent Men* (Decorah, Iowa: Jas. Alex. Leonard, 1877), p. 138; quotations from *McGregor North Iowa Times*, vol. 10, as follows: "Dan Kirwan," September 20, 1865; "young town," October 11; "lots

change hands," October 18; "Sam Counover," October 25; advertisement of "Proprietors" and "Nile" quotation, December 13; Calmar "left out," *Decorah Republic*, June 29, 1865; "on the brain," ibid., November 30, 1865.

5. Discussion of Midwest varieties of wheat, Charles Byron Kuhlmann, *The Development of the Flour-Milling Industry of the United States, with Special Reference to the Industry in Minneapolis* (Boston: Houghton Mifflin, 1929), pp. 73–78; Gilbert Fite, *The Farmers' Frontier, 1865–1900* (New York: Holt, Rinehart and Winston, 1966), pp. 48–49. Varietal names from Bogue, op. cit., p. 127. For Chicago Board of Trade grading efforts of the 1850s, see William Cronon, *Nature's Metropolis: Chicago and the Great West* (New York: W. W. Norton & Company, 1991), pp. 104–19. The original credit ledgers of the Mercantile Agency and its successor, R. G. Dun & Co., ca. 1840–1890, are in the R. G. Dun & Co. Collection in Baker Library, Harvard Business School. For a history of credit agencies in this period, see James Madison, "The Evolution of Commercial Credit Reporting in Nineteenth Century America," *Business History Review* 48 (1974): 167. For the early history of the agency itself, see Bertram Wyatt-Brown, "God and Dun & Bradstreet, 1841–1951," ibid., 40 (1966): 432. See also James D. Norris, *R. G. Dun & Co., 1841–1900": The Development of Credit-Reporting in the Nineteenth Century* (Westport, Conn.: Greenwood Press, 1978). For Marsh & Lambert, Howard County, 261; for Marsh and Knowlton, ibid., 277; comments on Bassett & Huntting, Clayton County, 259 e; Dun's comments on Joseph Reynolds, ibid., 238 p. See also William J. Peterson, "The Diamond Jo Line," *The Palimpsest* 51 (April 1970): 169; Lena Meyers, "McGregor Notable, 'Diamond Jo,' " *North Iowa Times* (McGregor), May 31, 1951; quotation on "whole street of warehouses," ibid., December 13, 1865; wheelbarrow story, *Cargill News*, June 1951. For selling alternatives for farmers, see Henrietta M. Larson, "The Wheat Market and the Farmer in Minnesota, 1858–1900," *Studies in History, Economics and Public Law*, 122, (2, Whole No. 269) 1926 (reprinted New York: Ams Press, 1969), p. 184; Morton Rothstein, untitled history of the grain trade in the 19th century, unpublished MS, chaps. 6, 10; G. W. Schatzel, "Among the Wheat-Fields of Minnesota," *Harper's New Monthly Magazine* 36 (1868): 190; for early hedging, "The Rejection and Acceptance of a Marketing Innovation: Hedging in the Late 19th Century," *Review of Research in Futures Markets* 2 (1983): 201; "hedge or sell all," Kenneth D. Ruble, *The Peavey Story* (Minneapolis: Peavey Co., 1963), p. 18.

6. For credit correspondent entries on Conover, see R. G. Dun & Co., op. cit., Winneshiek County, 16, 17, 18, 32, 71, 79, 80, 85, 86, 89, 111, 146, 203. For entries on W. A. Stowell and his partnerships, ibid., 21, 79, 120. Biographical information on Stowell from John Work, *Cargill Beginnings*, op. cit., pp. 84–85. Quotation on Ossian from James T. Hair (ed.), *Iowa State Gazetteer* (Chicago: Bailey & Hair, 1865), p. 391. See also C. C. Cornell, *The History of Ossian and Military Township*, 1858–1974: a chronological account of the first hundred years of this town's existence interspersed with tales of its people (Decorah, Iowa: Anundsen Publishing Co., 1984).

7. The story of Conover's demise is told variously in John Clifford Eichorn, *Calmar: Cradled by the Gods!, 1850–1950*, Decorah, Iowa: Posten Press, 1950; "Calmar Is Winner," *Telegraph-Herald* (Dubuque, Iowa), December 5, 1943; for early history of Cresco, see *Cresco Times*, January 19, 1949; for City Hotel fire, *Decorah Republic[an]*, December 20, 1867; for Lime Springs history, see ibid., October 1, 1912, and the *Courier* (Waterloo, Iowa), May 28, 1953. Construction costs from Cecil Cook, *Marquette: The Biography of an Iowa Railroad Town* (Des Moines, Iowa: Waukon & Mississippi Press, 1975), p. 28; on land grant requirements, ibid., p. 29; "sleeping on cots," John Work, Cargill Beginnings . . . , op. cit., p. 79. The sale of the Stowell business to H. C. Marsh later became the subject of a court case in the District Court of Winnesheik County (W326:453, October 1867).

8. Credit correspondent entries on Cresco, R. G. Dun & Co., op. cit., Howard County, 242, 244, 245, 250, 255–58, 260, 262, 264, 268, 269, 270, 300, 311. Entries on Purdy & Hanchette, ibid., 252–60; *Cresco Times*, January 30 and May 14, 1868.

9. "Three . . . businessmen," *Cresco Times*, April 30, 1868; "target shooters," ibid., July 23, 1868; "skedaddled," ibid., December 19, 1867; baseball game, ibid., April 23, 1868; Conover trip, ibid., July 11 and 18, September 21, 1867.

10. Population migration figures from U.S. Bureau of the Census, *Historical Statistics of the United States, Colonial Times to 1970*, Part 1, chaps. A and C (Washington, D.C.: U.S. Government Printing Office, 1975); growth of "West North Central" states, Fred A. Shannon, *The Farmer's Last Frontier: Agriculture, 1860–1897* (New York: Rinehart & Co., 1945), pp. 36–

39; on Iowa migration, William L. Harter and R. E. Stewart, *The Population of Iowa: Its Composition and Changes*, Iowa State College of Agriculture and Mechanical Arts Bulletin 275, Ames, Iowa, 1930; description of barging across Mississippi River, August Derleth, *The Milwaukee Road*, op. cit., p. 113.

11. "Hop, step and jump," *Iowa State Agriculture Society Report*, 1865 (Des Moines, 1866), p. 413; on agricultural technology, see Wayne G. Broehl, Jr., *John Deere's Company: A History of Deere & Company and Its Times* (New York: Doubleday & Co., 1984); Robert L. Ardrey, *American Agricultural Implements: A Review of Invention and Development in the Agricultural Implement Industry of the United States*, 1894 (reprinted, New York: Arno Press, 1972; Leo Rogin, *The Introduction of Farm Machinery in Its Relation to the Productivity of Labor in the Agriculture of the United States During the Nineteenth Century*, 1931 (reprinted New York: Johnson Reprint Corp., 1966; Clarence H. Danhof, *Change in Agriculture: The Northern United States, 1820–1870* (Cambridge, Mass: Harvard University Press, 1969).

12. United States wheat production from U.S. Bureau of the Census, *Historical Statistics of the United States*, op. cit., pp. 512–13; Beadle and Slee warehouse description, *Cresco Times*, March 6, 1867; "trust in Providence," ibid., May 30, 1867; "ahead of all," ibid., February 20, 1868; for agricultural conditions in Iowa and southern Minnesota during the decade after the Civil War, see Mildred Throne, "'Book Farming' in Iowa, 1840–1870," *Iowa Journal of History* 49 (1951): 117, and ibid., "A History of Agriculture in Southern Iowa, 1833–1890," unpublished Ph.D. dissertation, State University of Iowa, 1946; Edward Van Dyke Robinson, "Early Economic Conditions and the Development of Agriculture in Minnesota," University of Minnesota, *Studies in the Social Sciences 3*, (March 1915); Beadle & Slee warehouse, *Cresco Times*, October 6, 1867; "the North Pole," ibid., October 10, 1867; on marriage of Will Cargill and Ellen Stowell, news article on "death of Mrs. Ella T. Cargill," Cargill Archives (CA) 34-04; grain shipments, ibid., October 6, 1867, and February 20, 1868; Marsh & Cargill warehouse at Lime Springs, ibid., September 5 and November 14, 1867; Lime Springs lumber business, ibid., March 20, October 17, and November 21, 1867; railroad construction data, August Derleth, *The Milwaukee Road*, op. cit., pp. 288–90; "lots of lumber," *Cresco Times*, April 2, 1868; Dun's report on B. J. Van Valkenburgh, Mower County 231; origin of Cresco name, *Cresco Times*, November 30, 1937; "blind horse," Diedrick Jenk to H. Robert Diercks, undated (ca. February 1965), John Work MS.

13. Biography of Sylvester Smith Cargill in R. I. Holcombe, and William H. Bingham, *Compendium of History and Biography of Minneapolis and Hennepin County, Minnesota*, (Chicago: Henry Taylor & Co., 1914), vol. 2, pp. 335–36; Account Book, W. W. Cargill, 1875–1884, CA Oversize.

14. "Have not seen Sam," W. W. Cargill to "my dear parents," n.d. (ca. 1871), CA, John Work MS (W. D. MacMillan); for the Minnesota railroad construction, see John C. Luecke, *Dreams, Disasters and Demise: The Milwaukee Road in Minnesota* (Egan, Minn.: Grenadier Publications, 1988); "Freeborn County coroner," L. W. Spicer to Cargill MacMillan, October 27, 1945, CA 54-03 (reprinted in *Cargill News*, November 1945); "all over the baby," W. A. Stowell to W. W. Cargill, October 3, 1871, CA 34-04; "since burned," Charles S. Bryant, *History of Freeborn County, Minnesota, Including Explorers and Pioneers of Minnesota and Outline History of the State of Minnesota by Reverend Edward D. Neill* (Minneapolis: Minnesota Historical Company, 1882), p. 369; on W. W. Cargill well, ibid., p. 270.

15. Bassett & Huntting office property in Albert Lea, lease agreement, August 15, 1873, CA W. W. Cargill I, Leases and Deeds; in *Hyde, Cargill & Co. v. Foster O. Hagen*, Case #305, Freeborn County District Court, April 19, 1877, the complaint lists William T. Huntting, J. T. Bassett, Joseph Reynolds, and B. J. Van Valkenburgh as co-partners with S. G. Hyde and W. W. Cargill; example of letterhead, "Articles of Agreement" with P. C. Johnson, March 23, 1874, CA "Exhibit"; for example of W. W. and S. D. Cargill relationship, see "Whalen Mill" contract, W. W. Cargill II, Leases and Deeds; ibid. I and II for other property deeds; "all excepting $200," agreement with B. J. McGinnis, October 26, 1871, CA Leases and Deeds I; agreement with Duzella M. Flowers, n.d. (ca. 1872), ibid.;"fat cattle" story in *Freeborn County Standard* (Albert Lea), April 30, 1874; "good nature," ibid., May 14, 1874; remarks on J. M. Flowers, R. G. Dun & Co., Mower County, 231; on Hyde, Cargill & Co., ibid. 48; on W. W. Cargill, ibid., 37; on the hog butchering contract with J. Edward, n.d., March 1874, CA Leases and Deeds I; Mankato Operations, *Freeborn County Standard* (Albert Lea), June 15, 1876.

16. Jason Clark Easton papers, Library and Archives Division, Minnesota Historical So-

ciety; biography of Easton in *United States Biographical Dictionary and Portrait Gallery of Eminent and Self-Made Men*, Minnesota volume (New York: American Biographical Publishing Company, 1879), pp. 326–31; the key case against Easton was *Louis Grieser* v. *Charles McIlrath*, Receiver of the Southern Minnesota Railroad, Minnesota Executive Documents, 1877, ii, 340; see also *La Crosse Republican and Leader*, March 14 and 28 and April 11, 1874; "money Lord," ibid., February 10, 1877; "eligible as director," J. C. Easton to W. W. Cargill, November 1, 1875, Easton papers, Box 83, 6.A.9. 3B; "lambs to slaughter," Easton to Cargill, July 15, 1876, CA Leases and Deeds I; Robert Eliot papers, Archives Division, State Historical Society of Wisconsin, Milwaukee; for biography of Eliot, see James S. Buck, *Pioneer History of Milwaukee from the First American Settlement in 1833, to 1841*, vol. 1 (Milwaukee: Milwaukee News Company, 1876), pp. 96–98, 1154; *The History of Cargill, Incorporated, 1865–1945*, op. cit., p. 14; Dun credit correspondent comments on Eliot, R. G. Dun & Co., op. cit., Wisconsin 36:145 and 38:158; "Cost of Cresco Elevator," Leases and Deeds II; on Jason Easton overcharges and B. J. Van Valkenburgh suit, *Freeborn County Standard* (Albert Lea), March 26, 1874; W. W. Cargill suit, ibid., September 10, 1874; Minnesota Senate Journal, 1874, pp. 553–65; the case was tried in Freeborn County District Court, Nos. 737 and 740, April 1874, Minnesota Historical Society, 62B, 63B.

17. For "Balance, W. D. Cargill," see CA, WWC III; W. W. Cargill note to W. D. Cargill, September 1, 1877, ibid.; on W. D. Cargill contribution to Janesville church, John Work, *Cargill Beginnings*, op. cit., p. 90; insurance agreement, W. W. Cargill and Josiah Thompson, Jr., June 26, 1873, CA W. W. Cargill I, Leases and Agreements.

18. Josephine Barry Donovan, "Grasshopper Times," *Palimpsest* 4:194 (reprinted in Annette Atkins, *Harvest of Grief: Grasshopper Plagues and Public Assistance in Minnesota 1873–78* [St. Paul: Minnesota Historical Society Press, 1984]), p. 17; Edward Van Dyke Robinson, "Early Economic Conditions and the Development of Agriculture in Minnesota," op. cit. pp. 75–77; on wagon trains, *Freeborn County Standard* (Albert Lea), June 5, 1873, and June 4, 1874; on collecting grasshoppers, ibid. June 10, 1875; on natural enemies, see "The Grasshopper Scourge of the 70's," scrapbook, "Minutes of the Pioneer Society," Freeborn County Historical Society, Albert Lea, Minnesota.

19. Henrietta Larson, *The Wheat Market and the Farmer in Minnesota*, op. cit., pp. 84–85, 111; "on the square," *Cresco Times*, October 24, 1867; "oppression and greedy gain," *Freeborn County Standard*, July 24, 1873; on development of the Grange, Edward W. Martin (James D. McCabe, Jr.), *The History of the Grange Movement* (Chicago: National Publishing Company, 1874); Solon Justus Buck, *The Granger Movement: A Study of Agricultural Organization and Its Political Economic and Social Manifestations, 1870–1880* (Cambridge, Mass.: Harvard University Press, 1913); "Granger tornado," testimony of Robert Eliot before Cullom Committee, *Report of the Senate Select Committee on Interstate Commerce*, Senate Report 46 (49th Cong., 1st Sess.; 1886), Part 2, p. 695; testimony on the "wheat ring," *Report of the Special Joint Railroad Investigating Committee to the Legislature of the State of Minnesota*, Thirteenth Session (St. Paul, Minn.: Press Printing Company, 1871), pp. 118, 144–47, 151, 167, 171; on "brass kettle," Martin W. Odland, "The History of the Minnesota Railroad and Warehouse Commission," typescript, Minnesota Historical Society, 1944, pp. 17–20; "lying little kettle," Martin Ridge, *Ignatius Donnelly: The Portrait of a Politician* (Chicago: University of Chicago Press, 1962), p. 183; "dangerous . . . as a porcupine," *Litchfield News-Ledger*, quoted in the *Anti-Monopolist* (St. Paul), September 13, 1874.

20. For early history of Wisconsin railroad legislation, see Herbert William Rice, "Early History of the Chicago, Milwaukee and St. Paul Railway Company," op. cit., chap. 9; the Potter Law is discussed here, and in Auguest Derleth, the *Milwaukee Road* . . . , op. cit., chap. 5. See also John W. Cary, *The Organization and History of the Chicago, Milwaukee and St. Paul Railway Company*, op. cit. pp. 200–207. "Considerable excitement," *New York Times*, April 28, 1874; see also ibid., April 30 and May 4, 1874. The Wisconsin Supreme Court case, ibid., September 16, 1874. La Crosse letter-writer reactions, *Republican and Leader* (La Crosse), May 2, 1874; *Munn* v. *Illinois*, 94 U.S. 113 (1877); the long haul–short haul case was *Wabash, St. Louis & Pacific Railroad Company* v. *Illinois*, 118 U.S. 57 (1806); see also *Dartmouth College* v. *Woodward*, 4 Wheat. 518 (1819). For railroad legal efforts in Wisconsin, Robert S. Hunt, *Law and Locomotives: The Impact of the Railroad on Wisconsin Law in the Nineteenth Century* (Madison: State Historical Society of Wisconsin, 1958); Stanley P. Caine, *The Myth of a Progressive Reform: Railroad Regulation in Wisconsin, 1903–1910*, ibid., 1970.

21. Martin W. Odland, "The History of the Minnesota Railroad and Warehouse Commission," op. cit., pp. 28–33 (quotation from p. 32).

22. "Sorry to lose," *Freeborn County Standard* (Albert Lea), April 17, 1875; "men of pluck," W. Duncan MacMillan, with Patricia Condon Johnston, *MacGhillemhaoil* (Wayzata, Minn: privately printed, 1990), p. 145; on Cargill Science Hall at Albert Lea College, see *Bulletin of The Albert Lea College* 8 (December 1914), pp. 9–10; census figures, *Republican and Leader* (La Crosse), July 10, 1875; "largest cities," ibid., June 12, 1875; on grain trade of La Crosse, ibid., October 14, 1876; for "local" items, ibid., August 12, 19, 26, and September 2, 9, 16, and 23, 1876.

23. The R. G. Dun & Co. opened a branch office in La Crosse in 1876; this is described in *Republican and Leader* (La Crosse), February 12 and 26, 1876; Credit correspondent on Hodges & Hyde, R. G. Dun & Co., op. cit., Wisconsin 29: 238.53 and 255; on W. W. Cargill & Bro., ibid., Wisconsin 30:546; "did not seriously compete," Henrietta Larson, *The Wheat Market and the Farmer in Minnesota,* op. cit., p. 140; "hot wheat," *Republican and Leader,* June 17 and July 1, 1876; "buy Chicago," W. Duncan MacMillan, *MacGhillemhaoil,* op. cit., p. 150; partnership percentages, J. H. Ellsworth memorandum, November 15, 1878, CA Leases and Deeds I; "would have done it," H. D. Brown to W. W. Cargill, June 28, 1876, ibid.; "fault I found," John Kaercher to Hyde, Cargill, January 28, 1877, ibid.; "poorly drawn," S. D. Abbott to Hyde, Cargill, November 16, 1876, Leases and Deeds II; "heard nothing from you," E. N. Oshman to G. W. Sawyer, September 9, 1874, Easton papers, op. cit., Letterbook 14, 6.A.2.4F; "neglected to leave," ibid.; "except on orders," J. C. Easton to "G.W.S." [George W. Sawyer], September 8, 1874, ibid.; "insist," Easton to his Lanesboro bank, August 22, 1874, ibid.; on handwriting, *Cargill News*, February 1944.

24. "Make reports," contract with Downing Bros., July 7, 1875, CA Leases and Deeds II; another partnership, Cargill & King, dealt in cattle, hogs, wool, and hops, *La Crosse Chronicle*, September 25, 1879; "not make more favorable," C. M. Lovell to Hyde, Cargill, January 2, 1875, Leases and Deeds I; on rebates, unsigned memorandum, Southern Minnesota Railroad, April 25, 1875, ibid.; Liverpool wheat sale, Henrietta Larson, *The Wheat Market and the Farmer,* op. cit., p. 141, quoting *Preston* (Minn) *Republican,* June 22, 1878; on New York City terminals, *Frank Leslie's Illustrated Newspaper* 45 (November 10, 1875): 153; 48 (April 5, 1878): 76; and 50 (April 24, 1880): 121; "wealthy . . . dealers," testimony of Robert Eliot before Cullom Committee, *Report of the Senate Committee on Interstate Commerce,* op. cit., p. 692; "law, loan & collection," Eugene E. Snow to Hyde, Cargill, December 13, 1876, Leases and Deeds I; "no stone unturned," Hyde, Cargill to T. Eaton, September 9, 1876, ibid.; "two spring colts," John R. D——[handwriting unclear], n.d. (ca. April 1874), ibid.

25. "Deadbeat," R. T. Glover to W. W. Cargill & Bro., January 26, 1880, CA, Leases and Deeds I; "sue him," W. W. Cargill to C. R. Tubbs, December 31, 1879, ibid.; "skipped the country," C. E. Wenzel to Cargill & Van, February 19, 1880, ibid.; "dishonest wife," E. B. Clark to "Friend Cargill," March 6, 1882, Leases and Deeds II.

26. Cleaning elevator, Chicago, Milwaukee & St. Paul Railway to W. W. Cargill & Bro., August 28, September 10, and December 8, 1880, CA Leases and Deeds I; patent right on "cockle machine," agreement of Edward P. Allis and Hyde, Cargill, May 6, 1876, ibid.; for grain distributor, agreement of Charles S. Hamilton and "Cargill & Brother," October 4, 1880, ibid., II; on seed experimentation, W. Duncan MacMillan, *MacGhillemhaoil,* op. cit., p. 151; "contrary to our understanding," Southern Minnesota Railroad to "W. W. Cargill & Co.," October 18, 1876, Hyde, Cargill Railroad Rebates, ibid.; rebates listed, Cargill & Van, Green Bay office, October 31, 1880, ibid.

27. "Milled at Hokah," W. W. Cargill & Bro. to W. F. Davidson, May 7, 1882, Davidson (William Fuson and Family) papers, Minnesota Historical Society A.D253; Don Gregg papers, Alpha 23, 29.H.8.3B, Crescent, Minn.; Minnesota Historical Society; Edward D. Neill, *History of Houston County, including: Explorers and pioneers of Minnesota, and outline history of the state of Minnesota* (Minneapolis: Minnesota Historical Company, 1882); on Whalan fire, *Northwestern Miller*, December 26, 1884, June 5, 1885; the Whalan mill had another partner, a Mr. Williams; "Salt Fish Stock on Hand," n.d. (ca. 1881), CA Leases and Deeds I; for history of the Green Bay and Minnesota Railroad Company, its predecessors and successors, see Stan Mailer, *Green Bay & Western: The First 111 Years* (Edmonds, Wash.: Hundman Publishing Inc., 1989); the history of the Cargill home in La Crosse is described in *La Crosse Sunday Tribune*, February 1, 1959; see also "W. W. Cargill," box 303, Freeborn County Historical

Society, Albert Lea; "quiet enjoyment," *Republican and Leader* (La Crosse), October 23, 1880; "out of health," *La Crosse Chronicle*, August 18, 1881. For quotation on Green Bay terminal and tug, A. T. Andreas (prop.) *History of Northern Wisconsin* (Chicago: Western Historical Company, 1881), p. 120; on telephone, *La Crosse Chronicle*, July 31, 1879.

28. On "Mule Farm," see *Martin County Sentinel* (Minnesota), June 27, October 24, November 14, 1879; fire, ibid., November 21, 1879; "lavish hand," ibid., July 10, 1885; "hard on 'old Harv,' " ibid., July 17, 1885; on sale of farm, ibid., April 9 and 30, May 14, 1886; "the more money they lost," Anna J. Larson, *Jay Township, Martin County, Minnesota: An Historical Narrative Prepared for Martin County Historical Society* (Fairmont, Minn.: Sentinel Publishing Company, 1931), p. 7; termination of Cargill & Van partnership, agreement of June 9, 1882, between W. W. Cargill and B. J. Van Valkenburgh, Leases and Deeds II; see also John Work, *Cargill Beginnings*, op. cit., pp. 96–100.

29. "What to do with oats," L. W. Eckert to W. W. Cargill, January 6, 1879, CA Leases and Deeds I; "took advantage," ibid., March 26, 1879; letters on Charles City farm, W. A. Stowell to W. W. Cargill, December 19, 1880, and September 6, 1882, Leases and Deeds II.

30. "Millers' world," see Henrietta Larson, *The Wheat Market and the Farmer in Minnesota*, op. cit., pp. 91–92, 155–56; Martin Odland, "History of Minnesota Railroad and Warehouse Commission," op. cit., pp. 18–25; for early development of the Minneapolis Chamber of Commerce [grain exchange], see Horace B. Hudson, *A Half Century of Minneapolis* (Minneapolis: Hudson Publishing Company, 1908), pp. 353–61; Joseph Stipanovich, *City of Lakes: An Illustrated History of Minneapolis* (Woodland Hills, Calif., Windsor Publishing, 1982), pp. 89–92; on "new process" milling, Charles Byron Kuhlmann, *The Development of the Flour Milling Industry in the United States*, op. cit., pp. 115–20.

31. Obituary, James Flett Cargill, unnamed newspaper, ca. 1917, CA 34-04; J. F. Cargill organization, General Ledgers A (1883) and B (1884), CA Oversize; "Wheat Ledger Balances," Wahpeton, Dak., August 20, 1884, CA ibid. on cribbed elevators, Milo S. Ketchum, *The Design of Walls, Bins and Grain Elevators* (New York: Engineering News Publishing Co., 1907), pp. 227–28; on simultaneous "invention of the steel plow," Wayne G. Broehl, Jr., *John Deere's Company*, op. cit., pp. 44–46; *Annual Report of the Railroad and Warehouse Commissioners of Minnesota, for the Year Ending June 30, 1886* (St. Paul: Pioneer Press Company, 1886); listing also in *Saint Paul and Minneapolis Pioneer Press* (St. Paul), December 12, 1885.

32. "Biography sketch by George Colt Bagley," n.d. (ca. 1945), MS collection Ralph Bagley, pp. 9, 15–16, 19, 24, 29; see also Horace B. Hudson, *A Half Century of Minneapolis*, op. cit., p. 364; John Work, *Cargill Beginnings*, op. cit., p. 95; Marion Daniel Shutter, *History of Minneapolis* (Minneapolis: S. J. Clarke, 1923). On George W. Van Dusen history, see Henrietta M. Larson, *The Wheat Market and the Farmer in Minnesota, 1858–1900*, op. cit., pp. 86–87, 136–41; "History of Van Dusen-Harrington Company," Peavey Company MS collection, Minnesota Historical Society, 15 E 2 4 F (Box 50).

33. Termination of J. F. Cargill role in agreement with W. W. Cargill & Bro., June 17, 1887, CA, Law Department.

34. Cargill Brothers, General Ledger, August 15, 1885, to August 15, 1886, CA V4; ibid., August 15, 1886, to August 15, 1887, V7; W. W. Cargill to S. D. Cargill, June 24, 1889, CA, WWC Leases and Deeds III, #11; "Statement of Permanent Account, Without Encumbrances," October 5, 1889, ibid.

2. Two Families Link (pp. 70–129)

1. The definitive history of the MacMillan family is W. Duncan MacMillan's, *MacGhillemhaoil*, op. cit.; see also *The Industries of LaCrosse, Wis.* (LaCrosse, Wisc.: Spicer & Bushman, 1888), p. 26; *History of LaCrosse County, Wisconsin* (Chicago: Western Historical Company, 1881), pp. 462–63; for Dun correspondent quotations, R. G. Dun & Co. Collection, op. cit, Wisconsin 29:236 7/8, 238–48; 30:488,549. The establishment of the "gas works" by Alexander and Duncan MacMillan is discussed *History of La Crosse County, Wisconsin*, op. cit, p. 630. This also lists the Holley & Borreson banking firm, which in 1883 was incorporated as the State Bank of La Crosse, with Daniel D. MacMillan as president. The latter was also president of the Black River Improvement Company, an organization of loggers and sawmill owners in the La Crosse lumbering industry. See Albert H. Sanford and H. J. Hirshheimer,

A History of La Crosse, Wisconsin 1841–1900 (La Crosse, Wisc.: La Crosse County Historical Society, 1951), pp. 160, 211.

2. The two letters to John MacMillan, Sr., from his father, dated August 10 and September 3, 1888, are in family papers under custody of W. Duncan MacMillan; on West Texas development, Jeffrey Barton, "Economic Development of the Texas Panhandle," unpublished master's thesis, North Texas State College, 1950; Frances Phillips, "Development of Agriculture in the Panhandle–Plains Region of Texas to 1920," unpublished master's thesis, West Texas State College, 1946. Additional information on the Texas business from La Crosse newspapers, 1891–1896, and from the Hixon papers, Area Research Center, University of Wisconsin, La Crosse branch.

3. For Texas story, see W. Duncan MacMillan, *MacGhillemhaoil*, op. cit., pp. 216–18, 223–25, 236–37, 239–40, 242. The definitive analysis of the railroads' efforts in the Panhandle is Richard C. Overton, *Gulf to Rockies: The Heritage of the Fort Worth and Denver-Colorado and Southern Railways, 1861–1898* (Austin: University of Texas Press, 1953); quotations from railroads, ibid., pp. 212–13. See also S. G. Reed, *A History of the Texas Railroads, and of the Transportation Conditions Under Spain and Mexico and the Republic and the State* (Houston: St. Clair Publishing Co., 1941), chaps. 30, 31; Frederick W. Rathjen, *The Texas Panhandle Frontier* (Austin: University of Texas Press, 1973), chap. 8; Donna A. Barnes, *Farmers in Rebellion: The Rise and Fall of the Southern Farmers Alliance and People's Party in Texas* (Austin: University of Texas Press, 1984), pp. 148–50. B. B. Paddock biography: Patricia Lenora Duncan, "Enterprise: B. B. Paddock and Ft. Worth—a Case Study of Late Nineteenth Century American Boosterism," unpublished master's thesis, University of Texas, Arlington, 1982. For Paddock relationships to W. W. Cargill: B. B. Paddock MS, Box GA 194, year 1898, ibid. his letters to both W. W. Cargill and John MacMillan, 1900–1902, CA John Work #1.

4. "Fellahs of Egypt," Henrietta Larson, *The Wheat Market and the Farmer in Minnesota, 1858–1900*, op. cit., p. 168, and *Great West*, March 14, 1890; for rate differentials from Crookston to Liverpool, ibid., pp. 198–203, and *Great West*, April 11 and May 2, 1890; for mention of "Chili but not Argentina," "Message from President," Senate Ex. Doc. 161, 48th Congress, 1st Session (1884), pp. 16–17; the entry of Argentina into world markets is described in James R. Scobie, *Revolution on the Pampas: A Social History of Argentine Wheat, 1860–1910* (Austin: University of Texas Press, Institute of Latin American Studies, 1964), chap. 6; see also Carl E. Solberg, *The Prairies and the Pampas: Agrarian Policy in Canada and Argentina, 1880–1930* (Stanford, Calif.: Stanford University Press, 1987), chaps. 1, 2; for Ignatius Donnelly view, see Martin Ridge, *Ignatius Donnelly: The Portrait of a Politician*, op. cit., chap. 17. Wheat prices in second half of 19th century: Thorstein B. Veblen, "The Price of Wheat since 1867," *Journal of Political Economy* 1 (1893): 68.

5. Comments by W. W. Cargill in "Testimony Taken by Interstate Commerce Commission October 15–November 23, 1906 in Matter of Relations of Common Carriers to the Grain Trade," Senate Doc. 278, 59th Congress, 2nd Session, pp. 800–806; "highly selected," Henrietta Larson, *The Wheat Market . . .* , op. cit., p. 204.

6. On Peavey concrete elevator see Kenneth D. Ruble, *The Peavey Story*, op. cit., pp. 41–42; Frank Peavey description in his letter to John G. Massie, November 3, 1899, Peavey Company MS, Minnesota Historical Society 15.D.6.10F; on margins, Peavey to George E. Roberts, October 22, 1901, ibid.; see also Morton Rothstein, "Anglo-American Wheat Trade," unpublished manuscript, University of California, Davis, chap. 10; C. A. Pillsbury letter, Henrietta Larson, *The Wheat Market . . .* , op. cit., pp. 203–4. The Crédit Lyonais letters are printed in full in *Great West*, January 23 and February 13, 1891; the mention of Cargill, ibid., February 6, 1891; "options gambling," ibid., March 8, July 31, and August 7, 1891. The two cases on "gambling" at the Chicago Board of Trade are *Kinsey v. Board of Trade*, 198 US 236 (1905), and *Board of Trade v. Christie Grain and Stock Company*, also 198 US 236 (1905). See Jonathan Lurie, *The Chicago Board of Trade, 1859–1905: The Dynamics of Self-Regulation* (Urbana: University of Illinois Press, 1979), pp. 185–98; and William G. Ferris, *The Grain Traders: The Story of the Chicago Board of Trade* (East Lansing: Michigan State University Press, 1988), pp. 117–30.

7. The Cargill Elevator Company charter was granted by the secretary of state for Minnesota, H. Hallsom, March 18, 1890; the commencement of the corporate business was stated there to be April 1, 1890, with the duration of the corporation 30 years. In the minutes of the corporation for its first meeting, April 1, 1890, the 71 country terminals and 28 coal sheds

were listed. The W. W. Cargill Company charter was granted by the secretary of state for Wisconsin, T. D. Cunningham, July 28, 1892; its first meeting was held July 30, 1892. See *The History of Cargill, Inc., 1865–1945,* op. cit. p. 18, and Cargill Elevator Co. 1890 *Minute Book,* pp. 11–14. The *LaCrosse Chronicle,* December 11, 1899, notes the formation of both companies and lists their capital. An enigmatic comment ends this article: "An option is out on the Minneapolis line but it will soon expire and Mr. Cargill does not expect or desire to hear from it again." Building of Duluth terminal, ibid., p. 25; hedging, S. D. Cargill to Jones & Brinker, October 28, 1891, CA Deeds and Documents 1; on blockade, ibid., October 19, 1891; for Soo land project, see particularly, "Articles of Association of the Soo Land Company, Ltd.," 1895, CA Deeds and Documents III; J. M. Burton to John MacMillan, Sr., December 23, 1926, CA 35-10; C. A. Wheelock to Cargill MacMillan, September 23, 1929, ibid.

8. "Self-delusive as to the profits," Robert Eliot to W. W. Cargill, December 26, 1894. CA 34-03; quotations from *Fort Worth Gazette,* W. Duncan MacMillan, *MacGhillemhaoil,* op. cit.

9. The five letters of John MacMillan, Sr. to Edna MacMillan, dated December 19, 1893, January 14 and 16, 1895, and September 7 and 9, 1896, are all in the family papers under custody of W. Duncan MacMillan; Panhandle agriculture in the drought, Garry L. Nall, "The Farmers' Frontier in the Texas Panhandle," *Panhandle-Plains Historical Review* 45 (1972): 1; Roy Sylvan Dunn, "Drouth in West Texas, 1890–1894," *West Texas Historical Association Year Book,* 37 (October 1961): 121; grasshoppers, Frances Phillips, "Development of Agriculture in the Panhandle . . . ," op. cit., p. 20; on nervous breakdowns, Dr. W. W. Young file 21283 BUI, January 22, 1932, CA 34-05.

10. Original document in Register of Deeds Office, La Crosse County Courthouse, dated December 1, 1896 (Book 95, pp. 224–29); "dry, hot winds," Richard Overton, *Gulf to Rockies* . . . , op. cit., p. 347.

11. Quotations from *Leslie's Illustrated Weekly,* issue of January 6, 1898. The classic analysis of P. D. Armour is in Harper Leech and John Charles Carroll, *Armour and His Times* (New York: D. Appleton-Century Company, 1938). The story of the Hutchinson corner of the wheat market in 1888 is contained in chap. 14; the quotation here is from p. 262. The "Leiter Corner" is in Chapter 17, appropriately titled "Lochinvar Ensnared." Morton Rothstein quotation from "Frank Norris and Popular Perceptions of the Market," *Agricultural History* 56 (January 1982): p. 58. William Cronon quotation from *Nature's Metropolis,* op. cit., p. 125. The William Jennings Bryan story is recounted in James E. Boyle, *Speculation and the Board of Trade* (New York: Macmillan, 1921), p. 69. "Faithful in discharging . . . duty," Daniel MacMillan to John MacMillan, March 22, 1899; on "banker's pitiless stare," ibid., March 28, 1903; Lubbock, Texas, farm, W. D. MacMillan to John MacMillan, Sr., January 14, February 1, March 2, and September 26, 1900; May 30, 1901; January 1 and 14, February 6, 1902; April 3, 1903; CA, John Work box, Sawyer & Austin files. Quotation on William D. MacMillan graduation in his letter to John Sr., dated August 2, 1908, CA 35-03. Fort Worth University was later amalgamated with an Oklahoma institution, Methodist Episcopal University.

12. The 1893 "country warehouse" statute was Minn. Gen. Laws 1893, ch. 28; the 1895 statute was ibid., 1895, ch. 148. The State of Minnesota Supreme Court decision was 77 Minn. 223 (79 N.W. 962); the U.S. Supreme Court case was 180 U.S. 452, decided March 5, 1901. "Cleveland luck," Ralph Whelan to Sam Cargill, July 12, 1899, CA Law Department, McGrory papers. See also Martin W. Odland, "The History of the Minnesota Railroad and Warehouse Commission," op. cit., pp. 43–45.

13. W. W. Cargill on crop prospects, *Republican and Leader* (LaCrosse), June 13, 1898; sale of *Morning Chronicle,* "Articles of Incorporation, Chronicle Publishing Company," October 6, 1899, CA, W. W. Cargill I, *Morning Chronicle;* Ellis B. Usher to Chronicle Publishing Company, ibid; E. H. Hoffman, "Curbstone Pickings," March 21, 1938, newspaper file, La Crosse Public Library.

14. Quotation on wall eye, *The History of Cargill, Incorporated,* op. cit., pp. 23–24; salaries from Cargill Elevator Company General Ledger, August 15, 1899–August 15, 1900, CA Oversize Shelf; quotation on Sam Cargill from *History of Cargill, Incorporated,* 1865–1945, op. cit., p. 23; "cost us $50,000," *Minneapolis Journal,* June 27, 1900. On Leiter corner, S. D. Cargill to B. L. Jones, January 7, 1899, CA John Work 1; on barley dispute, S. D. Cargill to I. Blumenthal, September 11, 1897, Chicago Board of Trade Archives, University of Illinois, Chicago campus, AAA, folder 22; Morton Rothstein, "Anglo-American Wheat Trade," op. cit., p. 459.

15. See, especially, Sawyer & Austin stock certificate book, Corporate Secretary Office, Cargill, Incorporated; *History of Cargill, Incorporated, 1865–1945*, pp. 30–31.

16. John MacMillan, Sr., to Edna MacMillan, July 15, 1900, family papers in custody of W. Duncan MacMillan.

17. W. W. Cargill plans for Pine Bluff, his letter to S. W. Anderson, June 11, 1901, CA John Work 1; "stuff at Green Bay," ibid., June 4, 1900; "one horse," ibid., June 5, 1900; "scary time," ibid., August 6, 1900; "will all work out," ibid., September 21, 1900; "banks that won't interfere," ibid., September 22, 1900; "will show up," ibid., February 9, 1901; "turned down," ibid; "on velvet," ibid., February 27, 1901; warnings from Sam Cargill in his letters of December 12 and 16, 1901, ibid; "Sam and Mr. Eliot . . . opposed," ibid., September 25, 1900; "divided up," ibid., September 26, 1901; "whisky," ibid., December 7, 1900; "niggers," ibid., September 22, 1900; examples of forgetfulness, September 25, 1900, and June 15, September 12 and 30, 1901; Robert Eliot comment in his letter to W. W. Cargill, December 7, 1902; incident of safe, W. W. Cargill to John MacMillan, Sr., December 3 and 7, 1900, ibid.; on gold mining stock, September 21 and 25, 1902, ibid; rebate, see D. H. Kendall to W. S. Cargill and John MacMillan, Sr., March 24, 1908. CA 76-001 (temp).

18. S. D. Cargill death, *La Crosse Daily Press*, March 16, 1903; the development of the gas and electric companies of La Crosse is summarized in La Crosse Public Library Archives, memorandum of May 17, 1948, and in "Change of Rates for Electric Current, as Ordered for the La Crosse Gas and Electric Co. by the Railroad Commission of Wisconsin," September 19, 1907, ibid; accident with bicycle, *La Crosse Tribune*, June 29, July 1 and 2, 1904; see also August 23 and 24 and August 31, 1904, for other incidents involving Will Cargill's automobile; "weatherbrained snobs," ibid., September 1, 1904; "W. W. Cargill was an esteemed man," ibid., July 10, 1905. Quotations on Will Cargill from *History of Cargill, Incorporated, 1865–1965*, op. cit., pp. 41, 43; for W. W. Cargill stroke, see ibid., p. 41; Ellen Cargill to John and Edna MacMillan, March 23, 1904, and Ellen Cargill to Edna MacMillan, ca. April 1904, manuscript collection, W. Duncan MacMillan.

19. On Hoople, *History of Cargill, Incorporated 1865–1945*, p. 35; *Cargill News*, December 1935 and June 1943.

20. Precise financial details of the Thorpe Elevator Company acquisition are no longer extant. The Thorpe corporate minute book does not record the sale per se; at the meeting of September 20, 1904, two Thorpes, Garret L. and Charles, went off the board of directors, and John MacMillan, Sr., became president; E. L. Matthews, vice president; and D. D. MacMillan, secretary-treasurer (at the meeting of November 2, 1904). The Thorpe minutes apparently continue only to the meeting of October 19, 1906; the organization became a subsidiary of Cargill Elevator Company at this time.

21. For Spencer dispute, see *Cargill Elevator Company* v. *Spencer Grain Company*, Hennepin County District Court, case 99030, filed August 27, 1906; on Elevator T in early days, anonymous chronology, ca. 1937. CA 38-04.

22. The Superior Terminal Elevator Company was incorporated on February 20, 1893, with its legal office at Superior, Wisconsin; W. W. Cargill held 3,330 shares; S. D. Cargill, 1,660. The early records of the Cargill Commission Company of Duluth are no longer extant. There is a short biographical sketch of Frederick E. Lindahl in *Cargill News*, July 1940; his obituary is given in the March 1945 issue. See *Cargill News*, January 1938, for obituary of Arthur M. Prime.

23. Henrietta M. Larson, *The Wheat Market and the Farmer in Minnesota, 1858–1900*, op. cit, chaps. 7, 8. For relationship to Peavey, see *Commercial West*, July 20, 1901, p. 25; Interstate Commerce Commission, "Testimony on the Grain Trade," 59th Congress, 2nd Sess., Senate Document No. 278, p. 848. For the early advantages held by Milwaukee and Chicago in the flour milling industry, see Charles Byron Kuhlmann, *The Development of the Flour-Milling Industry in the United States, with Special Reference to the Industry in Minneapolis*, op. cit., pp. 88ff.

24. Quid pro quo, MacMillan to Lindahl, November 8, 1908, August 6, 1909, CA 12-01.

25. On competition, Lindahl to MacMillan, October 12, 1908; MacMillan to Lindahl, October 1, 1908, CA 12-01; price changes, MacMillan to H. F. Douglas, November 29, 1907, CA 21-02, on "hoggish," W. W. Cargill to MacMillan, October 1, 1909, CA 12-02.

26. Motivation of customers, Lindahl to MacMillan, August 13, 1909, and MacMillan to Lindahl, August 14, 1909, CA 12-01.

27. *History of Cargill, Incorporated, 1865–1945,* op. cit., pp. 36–37; the merchant mentality, MacMillan to A. M. Prime, January 10, 1908; Prime to MacMillan, September 16, 1907, CA 21-02; "pulled out," MacMillan to W. W. Cargill, September 19, 1908, CA 12-02; "only way . . . is to sell," Prime to MacMillan, February 3, 1927, CA 28-05; on speculative trading, T. F. Baxter to MacMillan, September 2, 1911; MacMillan to Baxter, September 12, 1911, CA 20-01, "B."; see also James S. Schonberg, *The Grain Trade: How It Works* (New York: Exposition Press, 1956), p. 72.

28. Lindahl to MacMillan, November 23, 1908, CA 12-01. MacMillan to Lindahl, January 6, 1909, CA 12-01. The History of the Duluth–Superior grain market is described in some detail in *Report of the Federal Trade Commission on the Grain Trade* 2 (September 15, 1920): 153–58.

29. Disappointment, MacMillan to Lindahl, March 6, 1909, ibid.

30. Declining market, Lindahl to MacMillan, February 4, 1909, CA, ibid.

31. Hedge against durum, MacMillan to Lindahl, February 6, 1909, CA, ibid.; "wiggle," Lindahl to MacMillan, October 23, 1908; "be a hog," ibid, November 10, 1908, CA, ibid.

32. Office procedures in regard to mail, Lindahl to MacMillan, September 25, 1908, ibid.

33. MacMillan to Lindahl, November 5, 1908, CA 12-01, and Lindahl's replies on November 6, 1908, and November 24, 1908, ibid. See also MacMillan to Lindahl, November 24, 1908, ibid.

34. MacMillan to Lindahl, January 9 and February 5, 1909, ibid.

35. Lindahl to MacMillan, January 7, 1909; MacMillan to Lindahl, December 5, 1908, and March 3, 1909, ibid.

36. *United States* v. *Patten,* 226 U.S. 525 (1913); see also Jerry W. Markham, *The History of Commodity Futures Trading and Its Regulation* (New York: Praeger, 1987), pp. 6, 26; *Fortune,* August 1949, pp. 81–83, 106–14; on corners, see Jonathan Lurie, *The Chicago Board of Trade, 1859–1905: The Dynamics of Self-Regulation,* op. cit., pp. 46–49, 51–55, 67–69.

37. Business to Armour, MacMillan to Lindahl, August 3, 1909, ibid.

38. "Stringing us," Prime to MacMillan, November 5, 1908, CA, ibid.; "sounds very nice," ibid., November 23, 1908; on raise, ibid., November 2, 1907, CA 21-02.

39. Tissue copies, MacMillan to N. C. Clark, September 22, 1908, CA 12-01. Clark's reply of September 23 notes a problem with the ink and assures MacMillan that the copies from that time forward would be "perfectly plain." Clark to MacMillan, September 23, 1908, CA 12-01; on "importance of time," MacMillan to J. C. Spencer, July 3, 1907, CA Palmer file.

40. Comparability of data, John MacMillan, Sr., to W. S. Cargill, November 20, 1908, CA 12-02.

41. Country elevator purchases, MacMillan to George Edwards, Kempton, N. Dak., October 26, 1907, CA 21-02, "E."

42. Seed loss and record keeping, John MacMillan, Sr., to W. W. Cargill, July 16 and 17, 1909, CA 12-02; "strongly prejudiced," ibid., November 5, 1908; "flatfooted," MacMillan to W. S. Cargill, February 18, 1908, CA 21-02.

43. Motivation of elevator employee, Lindahl to MacMillan, November 5, 1909, CA 12-01. Layoffs, Lindahl to MacMillan, May 26, 1909, and MacMillan to Lindahl, May 27, ibid.; homesick employee, John MacMillan to W. S. Cargill, April 8, 1908, CA 21-02, La Crosse; "square deal," MacMillan to W. W. Cargill, September 19, 1908, CA 12-02, La Crosse.

44. Letters about loan and pen, W. E. Burnett, Pine Bluff, Ark., to John MacMillan, Sr., "July, 1911"; MacMillan to Burnett, July 31, 1911; Burnett to MacMillan, August 3 and August 8, 1911, CA 20-01, "B."

45. Exchange of correspondence over several weeks between W. T. Radford and MacMillan, August 16, 1909, October 21, 1909, CA 13-01, "R."

46. "Ashamed," John MacMillan, Sr. to W. W. Cargill, December 10, 1907, CA 21-02, La Crosse; employee paying back losses, MacMillan to F. C. Thomas, Stewartville, Minn., November 3, 1906, ibid.; disloyalty, MacMillan to W. W. Cargill, February 3, 1908, ibid.

47. Secrecy, MacMillan to Taylor, July 10, 1911, CA 12-02.

48. On recommendation, MacMillan to York Lumber & Mfg. Co., January 14, 1911, CA 13-01, "XYZ."

49. MacMillan to Miss Phillips (otherwise unidentified), care of Sawyer & Austin Lumber Company, Pine Bluff, Ark., August 12, 1909, CA 13-01.

50. Members of the Jewish faith, John MacMillan, Sr., to James A. Walker, January 23, 1922, CA 24-01, "C"; James Taylor to MacMillan, September 2, 1911, CA 12-02; James Taylor to George Erickson, May 14, 1915, CA 32-10, "E"; labor union, MacMillan to D. A. Kendall, October 13, 1906, CA 21-01.

51. Incident of wife's affections, MacMillan to —— (I have omitted the name), January 21, 1910, CA 13-1, file "O."

52. Donation for high school, MacMillan to Charles Nelson, Hatton, N. Dak., March 16, 1908, CA 21-02, "N."

53. The Ada, Minn., editorial, "Grain Producers Get Short End," was in the Ada *Herald* of January 19, 1908; John MacMillan, Sr., reply, to D. H. Fulton, was dated January 10, 1908, CA 21-02, F.

54. Coming to Minneapolis, MacMillan to C. H. Quackenbush, July 30, 1908, CA 12-02; moving Cargill operation from LaCrosse to Minneapolis, MacMillan to W. W. Cargill, September 17, 1908, ibid.; open positions, MacMillan to Lindahl, October 26, 1908, CA 12-01; giving initiative, MacMillan to Taylor, September 5, 1911, 12–02 La Crosse; Clark as a trader, MacMillan to W.S. Cargill, February 19, 1908, 21-02 La Crosse.

55. For profitability, 1903–1910, see John MacMillan, Sr., to Gilbert G. Thorne, September 3, 1910, CA 13-01.

3. *A Panic and Its Aftermath (pp. 131–58)*

1. Quotations on W. W. Cargill personality from *History of Cargill, Incorporated, 1865–1945*, op. cit., p. 13; "aged so this winter," Ellen Cargill to Edna MacMillan, May 8, 1907, MS collection, W. Duncan MacMillan.

2. The Pillsbury receivership of 1908 is described in detail in William J. Powell, *Pillsbury's Best: A Company History from 1869* (Minneapolis: The Pillsbury Company, 1985), pp. 41–94; for bankruptcy laws at the end of the 19th century, see Peter J. Coleman, *Debtors and Creditors in America: Insolvency, Imprisonment for Debt, and Bankruptcy, 1607–1900* (Madison: State Historical Society of Wisconsin, 1974;) see also Don W. Larson, *Land of the Giants* (Minneapolis: Dorn Books, 1979), p. 71; "general gossip," MacMillan to Fogg Bros. & Co., August 17, 1908, CA 21-02.

3. Duluth salaries, Lindahl to John MacMillan, Sr., September 25, 1907; MacMillan to Lindahl, September 26; MacMillan to Lindahl, December 9; Lindahl to MacMillan, December 13, 1907, CA 21-02, "Duluth."

4. Weak concerns, MacMillan to W. W. Cargill, September 9, 1907; efforts to obtain credit, MacMillan to A. G. Becker & Co., September 26, 1907; "things . . . too hot," Cargill to MacMillan, September 18, 1907; worries about obtaining funds, MacMillan to Cargill, October 18, 1907; Cargill's walk down the La Crosse street, October 18, 1907; the worsening money situation, MacMillan to Cargill, October 21, 1907; Batavian bank cancelation, Cargill to MacMillan, October 25, 1907; the scare in New York, Cargill to MacMillan, October 23 and 29, 1907; concerted effort of the Duluth grain operators not to buy, MacMillan to Cargill, October 29, 1907; CA 21-02.

5. Belen copper mine proposal, MacMillan to Cargill October 9, 1907, ibid.

6. "Work very closely," MacMillan to Walter B. Gueinzius, December 31, 1906, CA 21-01; countermanding hedging decision; Gueinzius to MacMillan, June 17 and August 27, 1907, ibid., "hind teat," Dudley M. Irwin to MacMillan, December 26, 1907, CA 21-02; selling problem in Green Bay, MacMillan to W. W. Cargill, November 13, 1907; problems of control at the country elevators, Cargill to MacMillan, October 29 and MacMillan to Cargill, October 30, 1907; CA, ibid.

7. About timberland holdings, J. B. Taylor to J. H. MacMillan, March 14, 1908, CA, ibid.; "only that I own," Cargill to MacMillan, March 4, 1909, CA 12-02; change of name for seed company, MacMillan to W. W. Cargill, November 5, 1908, ibid.

8. Son's difficulties, MacMillan to Harry T. Kendall, September 4, 1907. Audit of books, ibid., August 29, 1907. Accounting lacks in St. Louis, MacMillan to W. W. Cargill, September 12, 1907, CA, ibid.

9. "Acting for the President," Cargill to MacMillan September 20, 1907; MacMillan re-

ply, September 19, 1907. Accounting system at Banner Lumber, Cargill to George W. Funck, September 20, 1907, CA 21-02; objections, Cargill to MacMillan, ibid.

10. Promptness, MacMillan to J. W. Spencer, November 22, 1908, CA 21-02, "S." "Lame" woods, MacMillan to Cargill, September 19, 1907, CA 21-02.

11. "Old type of businessman," MacMillan to W. W. Cargill, December 6, 1907, CA, ibid.

12. W. W. Cargill view of accounting, his letter to MacMillan of October 8, 1907; MacMillan concept of accounting, October 8, 1907, CA, ibid.; accounting practices in the first decade of the 20th century, see H. Thomas Johnson and Robert S. Kaplan, *Relevance Lost: The Rise and Fall of Management Accounting* (Boston: Harvard Business School Press, 1987), chaps. 2, 3; Michael Chatfield, *A History of Accounting Thought*, revised edition (Huntington, N.Y.: Robert E. Krieger Publishing Co., 1977), chaps. 6, 8, 9. See also JoAnne Yates, *Control through Communication: The Rise of System in American Management* (Baltimore: Johns Hopkins University Press, 1989).

13. Bookkeeper in St. Louis, W. W. Cargill to MacMillan, October 9, 1907, CA, ibid.

14. Funck to MacMillan, November 26, 1907, CA, ibid.; "up and dressed," D. A. Kendall to John Sr., November 24, 1906, CA 21-01; instructions to collectors, under Banner Lumber Co. letterhead dated October 14, 1907.

15. Comments on office stenographer, H. R. Hayden to MacMillan, October 20, 1907; information on Funck son's competitive company, ibid. November 10, 1907, CA 21-02.

16. Hayden to MacMillan, January 7, 1908; on effects of panic, MacMillan to Hayden, October 23, 1907; fire, W. W. Cargill to MacMillan, January 7, 1908; MacMillan to Cargill, January 13, 1908, CA, ibid.

17. MacMillan to George W. Funck, February 18, 1908, CA, ibid. H. R. Hayden's new assignment was with Stout-Greer Lumber Company in Thornton, Ark.; see Hayden to MacMillan, February 23, 1908, CA 21-02.

18. "Jacking a good man up," W. S. Cargill to J. H. MacMillan, March 13, 1908; CA, ibid.

19. Brewer association pressure, Harry W. Rickel, president, Manufacturers and Dealers Association (Detroit), to Cargill Elevator Company, May 11, 1908, CA 21-02, M. See also MacMillan to Dudley M. Irwin, March 14, 1908, ibid., MacMillan to A. M. Prime, March 19, 1908, and MacMillan to W. S. Cargill, March 14, 1908, ibid., Duluth.

20. "Talk with . . . crowd," MacMillan to W. S. Cargill, March 14, 1908; W. S. Cargill report to MacMillan on his visit, "without losing temper," April 7, 1908; MacMillan on the need to gain "practical knowledge," in his letter to W. S. Cargill, June 9, 1908; W. W. Cargill, "You sort of figure it out," in his letter to MacMillan, May 25, 1908; MacMillan strategy in the negotiations for the stock, in his letter to W. W. Cargill, May 26, 1908; exhortation to W. S. Cargill about "stay right there," MacMillan to W. S. Cargill, June 9, 1908; details of sale of stock, W. W. Cargill to MacMillan, August 29, 1908. All in CA 21-02, La Crosse.

21. Laying men off, MacMillan to R. M. Johnston, March 14, 1908, CA 21-02, "Johnston."

22. MacMillan to T. F. Doyle, Lowell, Mich., November 5, 1907, CA 21-02.

23. "Eastern Dutchmen" quotation, A. M. Prime to MacMillan, October 30, 1908, CA 12-01; for the effects of the German brewers on prohibition, see Richard B. Morris, *Encyclopedia of American History* (New York: Harper & Brothers, 1953), p. 278.

24. Caution, MacMillan to Prime, September 4, 8, and 14, 1908; Prime to MacMillan, September 15, 1908, CA 12-01.

25. Prime sells at cost, Prime to MacMillan, September 28, 1908; MacMillan to Prime, September 29, MacMillan to Lindahl, September 29, CA, ibid.

26. Terminal at Buffalo, MacMillan to Lindahl, January 30 and February 1, 1909, CA, ibid.

27. Concerns about Armour, MacMillan to Prime, November 16, 1908; Green Bay sales and sharp letter to Irwin, Prime to MacMillan, November 19, 1908; Irwin advising low bids, Prime to MacMillan, September 12, 1908, CA, ibid.

28. Quotations on "Hoodoo," Prime to MacMillan, September 30, 1908; MacMillan to Prime, October 1, 1908, CA, ibid.

29. Irwin to Cargill Commission Company, September 28, 1908, CA, ibid.

30. Prime on needling machine, October 21 and October 22, 1908; MacMillan urgings

for inspection, October 21 and October 23, Prime letter to W. W. Cargill, October 16, 1908, CA, ibid.

31. MacMillan support, October 19, 1908, CA, 12-02; purchase of "two or three" needling machines, Prime to MacMillan, October 24 and October 27, 1908, CA, 12-01.

32. Prime to MacMillan on the warehouse difficulties, November 8, 1909, CA, ibid.

33. Change to Gibbs, Prime to MacMillan, October 23, 1908; "so sick" of Buffalo, October 21; "pressing effect on Irwin," October 29; difficulties in following year and continuing Irwin complaint, Prime to MacMillan, August 23 and August 25, 1909, and MacMillan to Prime, August 26 and September 10, 1909, CA, ibid.

34. Irwin abilities, Walter Gueinzius to W. W. Cargill, November 19, 1908; termination of Irwin, W. W. Cargill to MacMillan, December 2, 1908; Cargill slippage and Irwin, MacMillan to W. W. Cargill, December 6, 1908, CA 12-02.

35. Bills payable, J. B. Taylor to MacMillan, September 17, 1908; "5 o'clock and . . . go home," Cargill to MacMillan, November 11, 1908; results for the year 1908, see Lindahl to MacMillan, December 19, 1908, CA 12-01.

36. MacMillan's wish for Cargill to move to Minneapolis, September 17, 1908; Cargill equivocation, his letter to MacMillan, September 22; Security Bank relationships, Cargill to MacMillan, January 9, 1909; financial statements, J. B. Taylor to MacMillan, January 28, 1909; MacMillan to Taylor, January 29, 1909; promising Cargill Elevator banking account, Cargill to MacMillan, June 6, 1909, CA 12-02.

37. Bauxite deposits, MacMillan to Cargill, February 27, 1909; Cargill to F. W. Child, New York City, March 3, 1909, CA 12-02.

38. Lacey proposed visit to Mexico, W. W. Cargill to MacMillan, September 28, 1908; MacMillan to Cargill, November 10, 1908, CA, ibid.

39. Mexican land, W. W. Cargill to John MacMillan, January 30, 1908, CA 21-02.

40. "Ranch proposition," MacMillan to Cargill, March 5, 1909, CA 12–02. Quotation on copper mine, MacMillan to Cargill, May 26, 1909; see also his letter of July 14, 1909, and Cargill reply on January 15, 1909, ibid.

41. "Rosy" Montana project, E. S. Bristol to W. W. Cargill, January 23, 1909, and Cargill to Bristol, January 25, 1909, CA 35-03; "enormous" shipments, MacMillan to Lindahl, October 12, 1908, CA 12-01; draft of bankers' letter in Will Cargill's handwriting, CA 35-03; Will Cargill plans in Montana, William S. Cargill to MacMillan, November 17, 1908; Will Cargill return to La Crosse in December, W. W. Cargill to MacMillan, December 21, 1908; MacMillan view on Montana, MacMillan to W. S. Cargill, November 18, 1908.

42. "All velvet," W. W. Cargill to James F. Cargill, April 5, 1909, Hixon and Company MS, Associated Companies, B-73, Area Research Center, University of Wisconsin, La Crosse; spring work in Montana, W. W. Cargill to MacMillan, May 4, 1909; W. W. Cargill enthusiasm, Cargill to MacMillan, August 14, 1909; C. T. Jaffray financing, MacMillan to W. W. Cargill, August 13, 1909, CA 12-02.

43. Incorporating in Montana, MacMillan to W. W. Cargill, August 13 and September 3, 1909, CA 12-02. See also Ralph W. Hidy et al., *The Great Northern Railway: A History* (Boston: Harvard Business School Press, 1988).

44. "Considerable more money," W. W. Cargill to A. G. Becker & Co., August 5, 1909, CA 35-03; "contract large liabilities," Fogg Bros. & Co. to W. W. Cargill, July 22, 1909, ibid.; firing of Gueinzius, W. W. Cargill to W. S. Cargill, July 31, 1909, CA Deeds and Documents 2; John MacMillan to W. S. Cargill, August 7, 1909, CA 12-02; playing golf in Madison, W. W. Cargill to MacMillan, August 25, 1909, ibid. Elevator Company capital needs, MacMillan to W. W. Cargill, June 4, 1909; bills payable, J. B. Taylor to MacMillan, September 17, 1908; on W. W. Cargill assurances, his letter to MacMillan, November 11, 1908, ibid. William D. MacMillan to John H. MacMillan, August 2, 1908, CA 35-03.

45. Word as good as our bond, MacMillan to Prime September 10, 1909, CA 12-01.

46. Prime to MacMillan on the cold elevator, September 11, 1909, CA 12-01.

47. Treating customers courteously, MacMillan to Prime, September 18, 1909; compliments to Prime, September 18, 1909. Prime mistrust of Irwin, Prime to MacMillan, September 20, 1909, CA 12-01.

48. Irwin sample received, MacMillan to Prime, September 20, 1909; two samples requested, MacMillan to Prime, September 21, 1909, CA 12-01.

49. Stiff letter, MacMillan to Lindahl, September 24, 1909; on difficulties in Duluth, MacMillan to W. W. Cargill, July 1, 1909, CA 12-02. "Friction," MacMillan to Dudley Irwin, July 1, 1909, CA 29-01.

50. Prime is ill, Lindahl to MacMillan, September 27, CA 12-01; "lost confidence," Lindahl to MacMillan, October 1, 1909; Prime resignation, MacMillan to Prime, September 30; save Prime, MacMillan to Lindahl, ibid., CA 12-01.

51. Prime meeting in letter of MacMillan to W. W. Cargill, October 12, 1909, CA, 12-02; tightening up, Lindahl to MacMillan, October 9, 1909, CA 12-01.

4. *W. W.'s Business Collapses (pp. 163–94)*

1. See Marwick, Mitchell & Co. audit statement, dated November 1, 1909, for initial balance sheet figures; these were expanded in detail in balance sheet and supporting text, dated April 30, 1910, "Petition of Administrators for Settlement of Estate and Distribtion of Assets," County Court for La Crosse, State of Wisconsin, February 29, 1912; on "sympathy . . . for Mrs. Cargill," John H. MacMillan to Fred Hanchette, February 29, 1912, CA 24-01; MacMillan note re Mrs. Cargill's negative statement in his diary, January 6, 1910, CA 41-12; see Margaret Barker to J. F. Cargill, undated (ca. January 1910), CA 35-03 for actual statement; on "heart is breaking," Ella Cargill to Edna MacMillan, December 9, 1909, MS collection, W. Duncan MacMillan. On Mexican unrest, John P. Harper to D. A. Kendall, July 3, 1908; Creditors' Committee (S&E, Cargill Lumber and Mexican lands) CA; "knew nothing," MacMillan to R. M. Johnston, November 11, 1909, CA 29-01.

2. New York banking, MacMillan to Gilbert C. Thorne, August 5, 1909; Thorne to MacMillan, August 9, 1909, CA 13-01; "affairs somewhat involved," MacMillan to B. F. Edwards, November 3, 1909, ibid. Running conservatively, MacMillan to Lindahl, October 26, 1909, CA 12-01; instructions to Prime, October 26, 1909, CA, ibid. Pushing the business along, Lindahl to MacMillan, October 16; "keep your nerve," Prime to MacMillan, January 14, 1910, CA, ibid.; Clive T. Jaffray "Reminiscences," 1956, Minnesota Historical Society, CCT, J23.

3. Cargill estate and New York bank, MacMillan to Gilbert G. Thorne, November 5; Thorne to MacMillan, November 8, 1909, CA, ibid. 4. Account "cleaned up," MacMillan to M. T. Shepherdson, Sioux City, Iowa, October 28, 1909, CA 12-01.

5. Undocumented news clipping of December 24, 1909, CA 35-03. The article noted that a similar policy had been written a few weeks earlier for A. C. Loring, president of the Pillsbury Flour Mills Company. The MacMillan policy was "the fourth big deal of its kind" in the city. Quotation on "butt in," Leonard K. Thompson, president, Northwestern National Life Insurance Company, to MacMillan, February 14, 1910, CA 13-02.

6. Peavey insurance plan, Don W. Larson, *Land of the Giants* op. cit., p. 71.

7. Assurances to Lindahl, MacMillan to Lindahl, November 5, 1909, CA 12-01.

8. Prime cutting loose, Lindahl to MacMillan, November 6, 1909; Prime responses to MacMillan, November 22 and November 29, 1909, CA, 12-01. "Stiff upper lip," Lindahl to MacMillan, November 11, 1909, ibid.

9. Employee loan, N. C. Clark to MacMillan, January 2, 1910; MacMillan to Clark, January 4, 1910; payment noted, ibid., January 6, 1910, CA, 12-01.

10. "Other fellow take the loss," MacMillan to Prime, January 19, 1910. Completing treatment, MacMillan to Prime, December 22, 1909. Assurances from Prime, December 23, 1909; Buffalo temptations, MacMillan to Prime, December 24, CA, 12-01.

11. E. Naumburg & Co. to Cargill Elevator Company, February 25, 1910; the latter's reply, February 28, 1910, CA 13-01.

12. See Corporate Minute Book, Cargill Elevator Company, Vol. 1, meeting of August 9, 1910. The option date of November 1, 1909, is enumerated here; the transfers of the elevators, warehouses coal sheds, and other property were made on this latter date. The total amount of indebtedness was $234,879.89.

13. See James Taylor to Long-Bell Lumber Co., June 2, 1911, CA 20-01; John MacMillan to Fred Hanchette, July 31, 1911, CA 24-01; MacMillan to Baxter, July 26, 1913, ibid.

14. "Land hunger," W. M. Wayman to MacMillan, December 14, 1909, CA 13-01; "getting to the bottom," MacMillan to Henry C. Wood, December 4, 1909, ibid; financial situation at Conrad Land & Water Co., W. C. Winton to C. T. Jaffray, May 28, 1910, CA 29-06;

Trowbridge & Niver bonds, J. W. Goldsbury to MacMillan, May 31, 1910, CA 13-01; progress of land sales, W. M. Wayman to MacMillan, April 6, 1910, ibid; "dividend," MacMillan to W. M. Wayman, February 28, 1910, and MacMillan to Ralph Whelan, March 3, 1911, ibid.; Chicago meeting, John MacMillan diary, March 3, 1910, ibid.; "bad, getting worse," telegram from Wayman to MacMillan, July 9, 1910, and letter of July 13, 1910, ibid.; receivership, MacMillan to Whelan, July 13, 1910, ibid.; text of agreement, March 3, 1910, in Hixon and Company MS, Associated Companies, B-73, Area Research Center, University of Wisconsin, La Crosse; "money . . . not considered," James T. Stanford to Ralph Whelan, February 14, 1910, ibid.

15. "At least $1,000,000 profit," MacMillan to W. C. Winton, May 24, 1910, ibid.; shaking hands with Will Cargill, John MacMillan to Edna MacMillan, July 20, 1910, MS collection, W. Duncan MacMillan; Receivers' Certificates, Winton to MacMillan, July 25, 1910; Carey Board extension, John W. Wade (chairman) to Messrs. Stanford and Winton (receivers), July 27, 1910, ibid.; "easing settlers' minds," Winton to MacMillan, July 28, 1910, ibid.; "putting his teams . . . down there," Winton to MacMillan, August 7, 1910, ibid.; independent engineering analysis, "Large Report to Knauth, Nachod & Kuhne by Ford, Bacon & Davis and J. C. Holcombe," December 15, 1910, CA, 29-07; syndicate, passim CA 13-01, July 1910–June 1911 (see, particularly, MacMillan to Henry C. Wood, October 7 and 17, 1910; Ralph Whelan to C. T. Jaffray, October 7 and 12, 1910); "doubtful value," MacMillan to C. T. Jaffray, et al., June 17, 1910, CA Deeds and Documents #30.

16. Cargill & Withee claim, MacMillan to Jaffray, March 2, 1911, CA 13-01; MacMillan to Ralph Whelan, March 3, 1911, ibid.; issue of W. W. Withee share in Cargill & Withee, W. W. Cargill to E. S. Bristol, January 25, 1909, CA 35-03, and Fred Hanchette to John and Edna MacMillan, December 22, 1909, ibid.; "would not tolerate," MacMillan letter to Whelan, March 3, 1911, ibid.; "foolish to shower sympathy" in Hanchette letter to John and Edna MacMillan, December 22, 1909, ibid.; for comments on Will Cargill "blemishes in personal life," see Clarence Stowell to MacMillan, December 6, 1910, CA 35-03; MacMillan to Fred Hanchette, July 8 and July 28, 1911, CA 24-01; MacMillan to T. F. Baxter, October 24, 1911, CA 20-01; "devil," Hanchette to MacMillan, July 20, 1910, CA 35-03; signing of releases by Cargill & Withee, MacMillan to W. C. Winton, June 8 and July 8, 1911, CA 13-01; Valier and Williams elevators, ibid., June 28, 1911; reprieve of rain, Winton to MacMillan, June 28, 1911, ibid. There were further claims by Cargill & Withee in the following year—see MacMillan to W. A. Lancaster, February 26, 1913, CA 20-01.

17. Frank Hixon plan, his letter to Judge W. A. Lancaster of August 10, 1911, and attached "To Creditors of W. W. Cargill Company and of Estate of W. W. Cargill," CA 24-01; "whipping . . . into . . . shape," James Taylor to MacMillan, August 11, 1911, CA 12-02; "strongly biased in their feelings," MacMillan to Hixon, September 6 and 11, 1911, CA 24-01; "clearly appeal to the creditors," Hixon to MacMillan, September 12, 1911, ibid.; "not offer to shake hands," MacMillan to Fred and Emma Hanchette, September 22, 1911, ibid.; Will Cargill agenda, MacMillan to T. F. Baxter, September 22 and October 6, 1911; Hixon to MacMillan, September 7, 1911; MacMillan to the Hanchettes, September 23 and 25, 1911; MacMillan to Hixon, September 25 and October 20, 1911; MacMillan to J. B. Taylor, September 27, 1911, ibid.; arbitration agreement draft is dated October 9, 1911, CA 12-02; final signing was August 28, 1912; "painfully shy," MacMillan to Fred Hanchette, February 20, 1912, CA 24-01; "the woman," draft letter, MacMillan to T. F. Baxter, CA 20-01; small creditors, undated newspaper article, "Small Creditors May Block Plan," ibid.; an overview of all relations with Will Cargill is in John Sr. to Mrs. W. S. Cargill, August 4, 1911, CA 28-03.

18. Administrators' fee, MacMillan to Fred Hanchette, February 8, 24 and 29, April 3 and 24, May 1, 1912; Hanchette to MacMillan, March 3, 1912; MacMillan to Hixon, February 23, March 1 and 19, April 2, 1912; Hixon to MacMillan, March 14 and 19, 1912; MacMillan to T. F. Baxter, March 8 and 11, April 3, 1912; Baxter to MacMillan, March 11, 1912, all in CA 24-01.

19. See Cargill Elevator Company *Minute Book* for special meeting of the shareholders on July 26, 1910, changing the nature of the statement on purposes. The election of M. B. Kuhn, F. B. Hixon and C. T. Jaffray (along with J. B. Cooper, J. D. McMillan and J. H. MacMillan) in the minutes of August 9, 1910. Cargill Securities Company corporate minute book, May 8, 1912, discusses trusteeship of the Minneapolis Trust Company; the minute book also contains

a balance sheet as of September 30, 1912, showing that 8,362 shares of Cargill Elevator stock appear as an asset, and $2,525,000 of bonds appear as a liability. *Titanic* disaster in MacMillan to C. T. Jaffray, April 22, 1912, CA 29-07.

20. "Perfect right," MacMillan to Mary R. Barker, August 6, 1912; "instead of pulling," ibid., August 1, 1913, CA 24-01, B; "man in New York," Lindahl to MacMillan, February 2, 1909, CA 12-01; ocean freight costs, A. D. Thompson Co. to Cargill Commission Co., June 17, 1913, CA 28-04; the Audit Company of New York audit, covering the crop year ending July 16, 1910, was dated August 15, 1910, CA 13-01; the first Marwick Mitchell & Co. audit was dated August 21, 1911, ibid.; "not clean up," MacMillan to G. W. Turner, April 26, 1911, CA 13-01; "not . . . banking business," MacMillan to Nelson Bros., April 26, 1911, ibid.; "purely banking," MacMillan to Robert H. Rippe, October 3, 1911, CA 20-01; Peavey difficulties, MacMillan to T. F. Baxter, July 13, 21 and 27, 1911, and Baxter to MacMillan, July 18 and 24, 1911, CA 20-01.

21. "Not germinating," Dudley M. Irwin to John MacMillan, September 8, 1911; MacMillan to Irwin, September 12, 1911, CA 12-02; MacMillan to Irwin, September 23 and 25, 1911, CA, ibid.

22. See Irwin to MacMillan, October 31, 1911, CA 12-02.

23. "Don't say anything to Prime," MacMillan to Irwin, November 2, 1911; "kindergarten learning," Irwin to Cargill Commission Company, Duluth, December 15, 1911, CA 12-02.

24. "An old game," MacMillan to Irwin, December 18, 1911; chemical analysis, Irwin to MacMillan, December 21, 1911; "not a pound of Canadian," MacMillan to Irwin, December 26, 1911, CA 12-02.

25. Impossibility of chemical analysis, MacMillan to Irwin, December 26 and 30, 1911; Irwin's dilemma, his letter to MacMillan, December 28, 1911, ibid.; federal grain standards, see "National Inspection and Grading of Grain," hearings on Senate bills 151 and 3685, Senate Committee on Agriculture and Forestry, 59-1, February 26 and March 1, 1906; "Grain Inspection and Grading Bills," House Committee on Interstate and Foreign Commerce," 61-2, May 20, 1910; "Inspection and Grading of Grain," hearings on S. 223, Senate Committee on Agriculture and Forestry, 62-2, May 27, 1912; "Warehouse and Grain Standards Legislation," hearings on H.R. 8040 and H.R. 4646, House Committee on Agriculture, 64-1, January 13, 1916; "Agriculture Appropriation Bill, 1917," hearings on H.R. 12717, Senate Committee on Agriculture and Forestry, May 19, 20, 1916. Quotation by Carl L. Alsberg, chief of the Bureau of Chemistry, U.S. Department of Agriculture, "Uniform Grading of Grain," hearings on H.R. 14493, House Committee on Agriculture, 63-1, 2 and 3, April 27, 28, 29 and 30, May 1, 2, 7 and 11 and June 1, 1914, p. 55.

26. "Patience . . . exhausted," Irwin to MacMillan, February 20, 1912; "Quackenbush correct," MacMillan to Irwin, February 29, 1912; "utterly vicious," MacMillan to Irwin, March 5, 1912, CA 12-02.

27. Competition between offices, MacMillan to Irwin, March 22, 1912; "worked hard to avoid," Irwin to MacMillan, March 25, 1912; CA 12-02.

28. "Different point of view," MacMillan to Irwin, March 28, 1912, CA 12-02.

29. Prime's department, MacMillan to Irwin, October 14, 1912, CA 12-02.

30. Obituary of Dudley Irwin, *Buffalo Evening News*, March 1, 1945.

31. "Fourth Annual Outing of the Cargill Elevator Company at St. Alban's Bay Hotel," July 10, 1915, and attached materials, CA John Work 1.

32. Austen Cargill wedding, James Taylor to W. E. Olson, September 18, 1913, CA 35-10, "O."

33. Firing the Green Bay manager, W. S. Cargill to John MacMillan, August 5, 1909; MacMillan to W. S. Cargill August 7, 1909, CA 12-02. See also MacMillan to Lindahl, September 1, 1909, CA 12-01; "develop . . . in an executive way," MacMillan to Austen Cargill, April 21, 1913; "in charge of . . . seeds," Cargill to MacMillan, July 26, 1913; "make a showing," MacMillan to Cargill, July 30, 1913.

34. Advantages of Milwaukee, MacMillan to Robert Eliot, CA 28-03, E.

35. "Showed his teeth," Edward J. Grimes to MacMillan, June 27, 1914, CA 24-04, Milwaukee; "sorry for the trouble," Grimes to MacMillan, June 30, 1914, ibid.; "duly suggested," MacMillan to Fred Hanchette, June 10, 1914, CA 24-02.

36. Commission business, Austen Cargill to James Taylor, November 4, 1915, CA 36-02, C.

37. Quotations and story from an anonymous chronology, assembled at the time of the "Corn case" of 1937, CA 38-04.

38. "Wonderful strides," Grimes to MacMillan, July 19, 1915; "train your customers," MacMillan to Grimes, July 20, 1915, CA 24-04, Milwaukee.

39. "Surprised . . . about your clover," MacMillan to Grimes, April 9, 1915, CA 24-04.

40. "Dislike to complain," Grimes to MacMillan, October 26, 1915; "up to you," MacMillan to Grimes, October 27, 1915, CA 24-04.

41. "Mailing . . . straightened out," MacMillan to Grimes, September 30, 1914; "have been caught," ibid., March 6 and 8, 1916, CA, ibid.

42. Tuition charges, John MacMillan to Phillips Academy, Andover, Mass., September 9, 1910; Alfred Stearns to MacMillan, September 9, 1910; MacMillan to Stearns, September 19, 1910, CA 13-01, "PQ." Baggage check, R. E. Hoadley to C. L. Kimball, assistant general passenger agent, Pennsylvania Lines, Minneapolis, June 10, 1911; F. J. McWade, Pennsylvania Railroad Company, Philadelphia, to MacMillan, July 17, 1911, ibid.

43. Lack of information, MacMillan to Grimes, May 8, 11 and 14; Grimes to MacMillan, May 10 and 12, 1915, CA 24-04.

44. Osseo, Austen Cargill to MacMillan, October 7, 1915, CA, ibid.

45. Defalcation at Bear Creek, Grimes to MacMillan, May 26, 1915, CA, ibid.

46. A register of the Austen Cargill purchases in Arkansas, together with a plat map of all of these, is located in CA 36-02; on Cargill Securities Company purchasing Arkansas land in name of Austen Cargill, James Taylor to M. Danaher, June 3, 1924, CA 42-01.

47. The story of the original building of Elevators K and M from the 1945 *History*, op. cit., p. 25; the purchase of the Peavey elevator, known as the Belt Line elevator, was authorized in a special meeting of the directors of the Superior Terminal Elevator Company on January 26, 1914; special meeting of the directors of the Cargill Elevator Company, reporting on the fire and authorizing rebuilding, is in their minutes of May 6, 1914. Details of the Frank Peavey purchase of the Belt Line elevator from Kenneth D. Ruble, *The Peavey Story, a History of Pioneering Achievement in the Grain Industry since* 1874 (Minneapolis: Peavey Company, 1963) p. 41. The 1914 capacity figures at Superior from the 1945 *History*, pp. 33, 35, 37.

48. One of the best sources for the experience just before and during World War I for the world's grain trade is M. K. Bennett, "Wheat and War, 1914–18 and Now," *Wheat Studies* 16 (1939), pp. 67–112. Quoted statistics, ibid., p. 82.

49. Comments on year 1915, MacMillan to Grimes, April 8, 1915, and MacMillan to Cargill, January 25, 1915, CA 24-04; MacMillan to F. M. Hanchette, March 15, 1915, CA 24-02, HI.

50. Wheat corner, MacMillan to Grimes, April 6, 1915, CA, 24-04, Milwaukee.

51. James E. Boyle, *Speculation and the Chicago Board of Trade* (New York: Macmillan, 1920) pp. 71ff.; the quotation on "the three big corners," p. 67; on May wheat corner see *Report of the Federal Commission on the Grain Trade: Vol. 7, Effects of Future Trading*, June 25, 1926 (Washington, DC: Government Printing Office, 1926), p. 243.

5. Reorganization, the Great War (pp. 200–245)

1. "Won't use a pony," and football, John MacMillan, Jr., to John Sr., September 24, 1910; accounting system, ibid., MS collection, W. Duncan MacMillan.

2. "Get ahead," John MacMillan, Sr., to John Jr., October 20, 1912, ibid.

3. "Not living within . . . income," John Sr. to John Jr., January 10, 1913; "own way in the world," February 26, 1913, ibid.

4. "Playing the baby," John Sr. to John Jr., December 13, 1912, ibid; "a roughhouse," John Jr. to W. Duncan MacMillan, May 1, 1947, CA 47-11.

5. Discipline of John Jr., Charles H. Forbes to John Sr., December 20, 1912, CA 28-04. Vacation absence penalty, MacMillan to Forbes, January 14 and 20, 1913; Forbes to MacMillan, January 17 and 27, 1913; CA 24-01, F.; John Jr. "insubordination," John Sr. to John Jr., February 11, 1913, MS collection, W. Duncan MacMillan.

6. "Be a leader," John Sr. to John Jr., January 10, 1913, ibid.

7. "Know the big men," John Sr. to John Jr., April 11, 1913, ibid.

8. "Differences in social strata," John Sr. to John Jr., October 20, 1912, ibid.

9. Farmer's life, John Jr. to Edna MacMillan, n.d., (ca. summer 1914), ibid.

10. Yale professors, John Jr. to John Sr., November 14, 1914; discussion of Irving Fisher course, John Jr. to Edna MacMillan, February 15, 1915; the Irish visitor, June 7, 1915, ibid. See also Sumner B. Young interview, ca. 1964, John Work MS.

11. John Jr.'s 21st birthday, John Sr. to John Jr., November 28, 1916, CA, John Work box 5. "Poor physical condition," John Sr. to John Jr., April 21, 1913; smoking at Andover, ibid., November 2, 1916; smoking as a vice, ibid, March 18, 1917. First letter in MS collection, W. Duncan MacMillan, second and third in CA, John Work MS box, CA.

12. Quotation on "aggressive merchandising" from *History*, op. cit. p. 53; concern about default, John Sr. to Bond & Goodwin, Boston, April 27, 1916, and Bond & Goodwin to John Sr., May 1, 1916, CA 24-01, B.

13. Not disclosing profits, John Sr. to T. F. Baxter, Boston, July 2 and July 7, 1915, CA 24-01, B; telephone call to Boston, John Sr. to Baxter, December 28, 1915, ibid.

14. John Jr. quotation on Valier from extant partial transcript of the original thesis, MS collection, W. Duncan MacMillan (see also Work, *Cargill Beginnings . . .* , op. cit., p. 141).

15. Austen Cargill "shrinking," MacMillan to Fred M. Hanchette, Pasadena, Calif., March 14, 1916, CA 24-02, HI.

16. Possible voting trust, John Sr. to Hanchette, April 14, 1916, ibid.

17. Will Cargill "threatened . . . trouble," John Sr. to Hanchette, May 11, 1916; basic plan, John Sr. to F. P. Hixon, May 29, 1916, CA, ibid.

18. Increase in authorized capital stock and establishment of preferred stock, Corporate Minute Book of Cargill Elevator Company, June 28, 1916 (meeting of Board of Directors), and subsequent stockholder meeting (July 1, 1916); reorganization plan, Noteholders Protective Committee memorandum of June 15, 1916, CA 35-03; "heartiest congratulations," John Sr. to Mrs. George R. Barker, July 3, 1916, CA 24-01, B; "not . . . borrow a dollar," John Sr. to T. F. Baxter, July 5, 1916.

19. "Taking in the boys," W. W. Cargill to John MacMillan, October 4, 1906, CA 36-07; C. T. Jaffray misgivings, John Sr. to F. P. Hixon, May 29, 1916, CA 24-02, HI; allocations of stock, John Sr. to R. E. Wisner, July 3, 1916, CA 24-03, UVW; the Noteholders Protective Committee summation on their report of June 15, 1916, CA 35-03.

20. "Fearful of Will," John Sr. to Hixon, June 7, 1916, CA 24-02, HI. Purchase of shares from William S. Cargill, John Sr. to Baxter, June 13–16, 1916, CA 24-01, B. The John Work book describes this arrangement in slightly different form:

> In the Summer of 1915, when Austen was sent down from Minneapolis with a proposed settlement for my father's one-fourth interest, my father was hungry. Austen had with him an appraisal of the total business in which the Mexican property had been written off entirely, and so had the property in British Columbia. The total value of the estate, as shown in the appraisal, was $2 million. Austen was empowered to offer my father notes totaling $250,000 and the balance, except for a cash payment of $25,000 in gold bonds on the La Crosse and Southeastern Railway. The bonds were paying interest, and later they were redeemed for full value. In any case, my father took the offer. (pp. 151–52)

For details on arrangements between John MacMillan, Sr., and Austen Cargill re the W. S. Cargill stock, see August 11, 1916, CA 28-03. Will's recalcitrance, Austen Cargill to John Sr., August 5, 1916, CA, ibid.; "put the plan thru rough shod," John Sr. to T. F. Baxter, June 7, 1916, CA 24-01, B.

21. The provisions for the sale of "employee stock" is spelled out in the Corporate Minute Book of Cargill Elevator Company, in the meeting of July 16, 1916; the "Contract of Purchase and Repurchase . . . ," form is attached to these minutes. For full list of stockholdings after this 1916 sale to employees and outsiders, see Marwick, Mitchell, Peat & Co. audit statement for the Company for the year 1916–1917, Schedule 8.

22. "Splendid shape," F. P. Hixon to Emma Hanchette, June 14, 1916, CA 35-03; Emma's "funny ideas," Austen Cargill to J. B. Taylor, July 28, 1916, CA 28-03; "secure for you an income," Cargill to Emma Hanchette, July 29, 1916, ibid.; John Sr. explanation of 1912 fees and his first plan of reorganization in his letter to Fred and Emma Hanchette, September 5, 1916, ibid.; Emma Hanchette response in her undated letter, ca. September 10 to John Sr., CA 35-03; John Sr. response in his letter to the Hanchettes, September 18, 1916, ibid.; "no fair" comment by Fred Hanchette in his letter to John Sr., October 3, 1916, CA 35-03; "favored and

carried along," John Sr. to Fred Hanchette, October 13, 1916, CA 28-03; reply from Hanchette dated October 17, 1916, ibid.

23. World War I grain problems, M. K. Bennett, "Wheat and War, 1914–18 and Now," in Food Research Institute, Stanford University *Wheat Studies*, Vol. 16, No. 3 (November 1939): 67–112. See also Tom Gibson Hall, Jr., "Cheap Bread from Dear Wheat: Herbert Hoover, the Wilson Administration, and the Management of Wheat Prices, 1916–1920," Ph.D. dissertation, University of California, Davis, 1970.

24. Bennett, op. cit, p. 93; he quotes here from *Royal Commission on Wheat Supplies, First Report* (Cmd. 1544, London, 1921).

25. Frank M. Surface, *The Grain Trade During the World War, Being a History of the Food Administration Grain Corporation and the United States Grain Corporation* (New York: MacMillan, 1928), p. 28; *Northwestern Miller*, May 16, 1917, p. 465.

26. See Bruno Lasker, "The Food Riots," in *The Survey*, March 3, 1917, p. 638; *New York Times*, February 22, 1917; *Minneapolis Morning Tribune*, February 20, 1917.

27. Lasker, op. cit., p. 638; statement of St. Louis chairman in *New York Times*, February 23, 1917.

28. Henrietta M. Larson, *The Wheat Market and the Farmer in Minnesota, 1858–1900*, op. cit., p. 303.

29. See, especially, Frank M. Surface, op. cit.

30. Meeting of the Committee of Grain Exchanges in Aid of National Defense with Herbert Hoover, see Surface, op. cit., pp. 37–38. The text of their reply is on pp. 573–76. John MacMillan, Sr., letter to Hoover, May 21, 1917, CA, 24-02, HI; comments on Hoover, John Sr. to T. F. Baxter, May 19, 1917, CA 24-01, B; John Sr. on patriotism in his letter to John Jr., February 23, 1917, CA, John Work box. Telegram recommending status quo, W. O. Timmerman to John Sr., May 15, 1917, CA 28-04, T.

31. Wheat ceiling prices, MacMillan to Julius H. Barnes, June 8, 1917; CA 24-01, B.

32. Congress setting of maximum prices, John Sr. to J. Ralph Pickell, June 8, 1917, CA 28-04, PQ.

33. "Fair" price determination of 1917, Surface, op. cit., chap. 4. The price structure is enumerated at p. 72. For the politics evolving around this, see Hall, op. cit., chap. 2. Stephen Leacock quotation reprinted in Carl E. Solberg, *The Prairies and the Pampas: Agrarian Policy in Canada and Argentina*, 1880–1930, op. cit., p. 173.

34. Surface, op. cit., pp. 28–29.

35. Speculation, John Sr. to Knute Nelson, May 23 and 31, 1917; Nelson to John Sr., May 26, 1917; CA 24-02, N.

36. "Wheat and War, 1914–18 and Now," op. cit., p. 69. Bread quality, "Wanted, a New Bread," *Bulletin of the Pan American Union* 45 (1917): 188; Committee on Public Information, U.S. Government, Vol. 2, No. 248 (March 4, 1918) pp. 1, 5; barley bread, James Taylor to F. E. Lindahl, April 10, 1918; CA 32-01, Duluth.

37. Declaration of dividend, John Sr. to Fred Hanchette, June 15, 1917, CA 28-03.

38. Article in Dawson, N. Dak., *Press*, June 7, 1917; Company reply, June 9 and June 12, 1917; promise of retraction, B. G. McElroy to Cargill Elevator Co., June 23, 1917; CA 28-03, D.

39. "Don't Destroy the Wheat Market of the Farmer by Means of Vicious Legislation," speech of Hon. Knute Nelson, Minnesota, July 9, 1917, pp. 6–8 (Washington, D.C.: U.S. Government Printing Office, 1917); CA 24-02, W.

40. Hoover agreement with the millers, see Surface, op. cit., 91–112; Hall, op. cit., 85–88. Arrangements with the elevator companies, Surface, pp. 79–82.

41. Canadian negotiations, Surface, op. cit., 273–89 and in Hall, 106–13. For the Australian and Argentine developments, see Surface, op. cit., pp. 289–98.

42. Personal animosity between Herbert Hoover and William G. McAdoo concerning rail embargoes of 1917–1918 is described in Hall, op. cit., pp. 113–19.

43. Election of John Sr. to the presidency of the Council of Grain Exchanges, *Proceedings of the Ninth Annual Meeting*, Chicago, January 17, 1918; CA 41-12. Query to Fred Hanchette re dividends, John Sr. to Hanchette, June 20, 1918, CA 28-03; proposal to Austen Cargill, John Sr. to Cargill, July 3, 1918, ibid.

44. Connecticut National Guard in Mexican border service, John Sr. to T. F. Baxter, June

23, 1916, CA 24-01, B; John Sr. to Fred Hanchette, July 6, 1916, CA 24-02, HI; John Jr. desire to go to Mexico, his letter to John Sr., April 21, 1915, MS collection, W. Duncan MacMillan. John Jr.'s promotion to corporal, see letter of confirmation, dated June 28, 1916, ibid.

45. Green Bay elevator, John Sr. to John Jr., November 13, 1916; CA, John Work box; report on fire, John Gruber, "On Green Bay Skyline Since the Civil War," *Voyageur* 8 (Summer, Fall, 1991), p. 46; "the President did the right thing," ibid., February 5, 1917; officer training corps at Yale, ibid., February 14, 1917; efforts by John Sr. in regard to appointment, ibid., April 23, 24, 25 and 26, 1917 (quotation from letter of April 24); mathematics of artillery shelling, William D. MacMillan to John MacMillan, Jr., February 12, 1918; CA, John Work box.

46. Austen Cargill enlistment, F. E. Lindahl to J. B. Taylor, April 11, 1918, CA 32-07, JBT.

47. Authority for John Jr. being the youngest major in the army is his father (in a letter to Austen Cargill, dated September 9, 1918, CA 24-01, C). A copy of the recommendation for promotion, dated August 17, 1918, is in CA, John Work box; on colonel's files, John Jr. to John Sr. and Edna, ca. August 1918, W. Duncan MacMillan MS collection.

48. The originals of the John Jr. correspondence from France are in the W. Duncan MacMillan manuscript collection; typescripts are in CA 41-11. The trip over is described in Letter #4 (undated) and Letter #5, September 10, 1918; description of London, ibid.; the chateaus are described in Letter #9, September 23, 1918; week schedule from Letter #13, October 6, 1918; action at front and comments on officers, John Jr. to Daniel MacMillan, October 26, 1918.

49. For an excellent review of the literature on eugenics, see Daniel J. Kevles, *In the Name of Eugenics: Genetics and the Uses of Human Heredity* (New York: Alfred A. Knopf, 1985); quotation on use of armed services IQ tests on pp. 80–81; rankings re intelligence tests, John Jr. to John and Edna MacMillan, June 14, 1918, CA 34-05.

50. Three categories of headquarters officers, John Jr. to John Sr., November 8, 1918, CA 41-11; on being a field grade officer, Letter 17, November 5, 1912; the "MacMillan conceit," Letter 10, September 24, 1918.

51. Lowered morale, John Sr. to John Jr., January 14, 1919; CA, John Work box.

52. John Jr.'s promotion, Austen Cargill to John Jr., October 6, 1918, ibid.; visit to Bordeaux, Anne Cargill to J. B. Taylor, June 25, 1918, CA 40-03; difficulties on Austen Cargill's discharge, CA 24-01, C.

53. Cargill MacMillan at Andover, his letters of October 22, November 2 and 23, 1916, and January 6 and 31, May 9 and 23, 1917, W. Duncan MacMillan MS collection; school newspaper, John Jr. to Cargill MacMillan, October 14, 1917, and to Edna MacMillan, December 12, 1917; Cargill MacMillan service at Yale, his letter to John Jr., October 5, 1918; CA, John Work box; "enthusiasm," John Sr. to John Jr., October 15, 1918, ibid.

54. John Maynard Keynes, *Two Memoirs* (London: Rupert Hart-Davis, 1949), p. 26. Herbert Hoover's "war bread," Hall, op. cit., p. 181.

6. Farmer Discontent, Regulatory Concerns (pp. 247–79)

1. For data on 1919 crop and on the establishment of the post of Wheat Director, see Frank M. Surface, *The Grain Trade during the World War* . . . , op. cit., pp. 146–57; Tom Gibson Hall, Jr., *Cheap Bread from Dear Wheat* . . . , op. cit., pp. 213–30. The legislation establishing the United States Grain Corporation was the Wheat Guarantee Act (March, 1919); see U.S. Statues at Large, 40:1384–1353; Executive Order 3087, May 14, 1919.

2. "Low price on bread," John MacMillan to Julius H. Barnes, April 22, 1919, CA 24-03, UVW. See also Harry Fornari, *Bread upon the Water* (Nashville, Tenn.: Aurora Publishers, 1973), pp. 74–79.

3. *New York Times*, July 30, 1919.

4. "Mr. Hoover's deceit," *Wallace's Farmer*, March 5, 1920, p. 763. Farmer "false optimism," Tom Gibson Hall, Jr., *Cheap Bread from Dear Wheat*, op. cit., p. 255; George N. Peek and Hugh S. Johnson, *Equality for Agriculture* (Moline, Ill.: H. W. Harrington, 1922).

5. John C. Hudson, *Plains Country Towns* (Minneapolis: University of Minnesota Press, 1985), p. 5; bread and Bolshevism, *Northwestern Miller*, April 9, 1919; headline and article on

Winnipeg strike, ibid., July 2, 1919; "neurasthenic women," Lois and Alan Gordon, *American Chronicle* (New York: Atheneum, 1987), p. 7.

6. Socialists as "free lovers," *Grand Forks Herald*, April 6, 1916, reprinted in Robert L. Morlan, *Political Prairie Fire: The Nonpartisan League, 1915–1922* (St. Paul: Minnesota Historical Society Press, 1955, 1985), p. 61. "Led by an anarchist," quotation from Willis Williams in *St. Paul Dispatch*, September 22, 1917.

7. Alarm about Nonpartisan League, John MacMillan, Sr., to L. F. Gates, September 22, 1919, CA 24-01; union relations in Duluth, F. E. Lindahl to MacMillan, August 22, 25, 26 and 29, 1919; "riots in any city," MacMillan to Lindahl, November 24, 1919, CA 24-04. Early Duluth labor relations, Curtis S. Miller, "Organized Labor: A Look Back" in Ryck Lydecker and Lawrence J. Sommer, eds., *Duluth: Sketches of the Past* (Duluth: American Revolution Bicentennial Commission, 1976); material on grain handlers union, pp. 212–13.

8. "Three or four months rest," John MacMillan, Sr., to Fred and Emma Hanchette, December 30, 1918, CA 24-02; trip with Hub Owen, John Sr. to Fred Hanchette, May 15, 1919, ibid.; "wreck," ibid., July 2, 1919; rye account, John Sr. to F. E. Lindahl, September 23, 1919, ibid.; John Sr. to A. M. Prime, same date, ibid.; "doing allright," Lindahl to John Sr., November 6, 1919, CA 24-04; "startled to read," John Sr. to John MacMillan, Jr., November 17, 1919, ibid.; Argentine and Winnipeg offices, Lindahl to John Sr., December 20, 1919, ibid.; "a little early yet," John Sr. to Lindahl, January 24, 1920, ibid.; John Jr. illness, John Sr. to Lindahl, January 29 and 31, February 3, 6, 10, 11, 14, 25, March 5, 1920, ibid.; nurses in Duluth, Lindahl to John Sr., February 4, 1920, ibid.; quotation on Minneapolis doctor re influenza, Richard Collier, *The Plague of the Spanish Lady: the Influenza Pandemic of 1918–1919* (New York: Atheneum, 1974), p. 179; statistics on 1918–1919 epidemic, ibid., p. 306.

9. "After-effect," John Sr. to Fred Hanchette, February 20, 1920, CA 24-02; trip to Seattle and Vancouver, ibid., June 14, 1920; "meals in his room," ibid., June 14 and 19, 1920; John Sr. visit to Will Cargill, his letter to F. E. Lindahl, June 25, 1920, ibid.; "feeling pretty well," John Sr. to Austen Cargill, September 20, 1920, CA 21-02; problem with manager, John Sr. to Fred Hanchette, October 12, 1920, CA 24-02; another year for responsibility, John Sr. to Austen Cargill, September 28, 1920, CA 21-04; "life agrees," John Sr. to Fred Hanchette, December 1, 1920, CA 24-02; "little fearful of your condition," John Sr. to John MacMillan, Jr., December 23, 1920, ibid.

10. Hedges and speculation, John Sr. to A. M. Prime, January 2 and February 11, 1920, CA 24-04; Chicago Board of Trade, L. F. Gates to MacMillan, October 10, 1919, CA 24-01; John Sr. to Prime, August 2, 1919, CA 24-04; John Sr. to John MacMillan, Jr., January 16, 1920, ibid.; high cost of living, John Sr. to Managing Editor, *New York World*, August 5, 1919, CA 24-02.

11. "Business panic," John MacMillan, Sr., to John Jr., November 9, 1920, CA 24-02; "watch out for doubtful customers," John Sr. to A. L. Jacobs, March 15, 1921, CA 24-04; banks worried, July 17, 1921, CA 29-03; "professional agitators," John Sr. to Knute Nelson, July 26, 1921, CA 28-05; for effects on farmers, see James Shideler, *Farm Crisis, 1919–1923* (Berkeley: University of California Press, 1957).

12. Austen "living on float," John Sr. to Fred Hanchette, October 1, 1921, CA 28-04; "played pinochle," Julius Hendel and Austen Cargill, "The Human Side of Business," May 16, 1946, in Gerald A. Joines, ed., *Cargill's Business: A General Information Manual of the Grain, Feed, Seed and Vegetable Oil Business of Cargill, Incorporated*. Training Department, various dates, January, 1945-January, 1949.

13. "Abnormal times," John Sr. to Fred Hanchette, February 1, 1922, CA 29-03.

14. The nine volumes of the *Report of the Federal Trade Commission on the Grain Trade* (Washington, D.C.: Government Printing Office, 1920–1926) are as follows:

Vol. 1: *Country Grain Marketing*, September 15, 1920
Vol. 2: *Terminal Grain Markets and Exchanges*, ibid.
Vol. 3: *Terminal Grain Marketing*, December 21, 1921
Vol. 4: *Middlemen's Profits and Margins*, September 26, 1923
Vol. 5: *Future Trading Operations in Grain*, September 15, 1920
Vol. 6: *Prices of Grain and Grain Futures*, September 10, 1924
Vol. 7: *Effects of Future Trading*, June 25, 1926
Report of the Federal Trade Commission on the Methods and Operations of Grain Exporters:

Vol 1: *Interrelations and Profits*, May 16, 1922
Vol 2: *Speculation, Competition and Prices*, June 18, 1923
Initiation of the study, Tom Gibson Hall, Jr., *Cheap Bread from Dear Wheat* . . . , op. cit.,
pp. 25–30; "manipulations, controls," Woodrow Wilson to William J. Harris, chairman of
the Federal Trade Commission, February 7, 1917, cited in Henry Miller, *World War Activities
by the Federal Trade Commission, 1917–1918* (Washington, D.C.: Government Printing Office,
1940), pp. 66–69; "corrupt individual," Hall, op. cit., p. 27; William Edgar quotation on
"bread trust," *Northwestern Miller*, February 28, 1917.

15. Federal Trade Commission, Vol. 1, op. cit., pp. 35, 64.
16. Ibid., p. 195.
17. "Coming down to list," ibid., p. 252; "no storage . . . charged," ibid., p. 256; "when
. . . a drop," ibid., p. 259; cooperative competition, ibid., p. 267; confining aggression, ibid.,
p. 280; farmers farming the buyer, ibid., p. 301.
18. Ibid., pp. 244–45.
19. Ibid., Vol. 4, pp. 81–82.
20. "Highly controversial state," ibid., Vol. 2, pp. 52–53; proportional rates, ibid., pp.
43–44.
21. "Litchfield list," ibid., Vol. 3, p. 224; Stirum and Dresden examples, Vol. 3, pp. 202–3.
22. FTC quotation on wire services, ibid., Vol. 7, p. 306; John MacMillan, Sr., view in his
letter to F. A. Chamberlain, February 21, 1921, CA 24-01; "government control," his letter to
Horace C. Klein, November 13, 1923, CA 28-05.
23. Futures trading, Henrietta M. Larson, *The Wheat Market and the Farmer in Minnesota, 1858–1900*, op. cit., p. 206; Samuel Untermyer, "Speculation on the Stock Exchanges
and Public Regulation of the Exchanges," *American Economic Review* (Supplement), 5 (1915):
24–68.
24. Corners, Federal Trade Commission, Vol. 5, pp. 322–46; Vol. 7, pp. 242–74, op. cit.
25. Ibid., Vol. 5, p. 21; the attempt by Arthur Cutten to corner the May 1922 wheat
contract on the Chicago Board of Trade is discussed in William G. Ferris, *The Grain Traders
. . .* , op. cit., pp. 166–73; *Northwestern Miller*, April 19 and June 7, 1922.
26. Capper-Tincher bill, John MacMillan, Sr., to John Jr., June 7, 1921, CA 29-03; statement on unconstitutionality of the Act, *Northwestern Miller*, May 17, 1922; advice to Representative Tincher, John Sr. to J. M. Tincher, May 20, 1921, CA 28-04; news release of Secretary
of Agriculture concerning revised version, Division of Publications, Press Service, USDA,
December 10, 1921 (copy in CA 24-03); statement by Chicago Board of Trade, *Northwestern
Miller*, April 18, 1923.
27. For "grain futures trading" laws, George Wright Hoffman, *Future Trading upon Organized Commodity Markets in the United States* (Philadelphia: University of Pennsylvania
Press, 1932), pp. 363–75; Cedric B. Cowing, *Populists, Plungers and Progressives: A Social History
of Stock and Commodity Speculation, 1890–1936* (Princeton, N.J.: Princeton University Press,
1965), pp. 92–95; Donald L. Winters, *Henry Cantwell Wallace as Secretary of Agriculture, 1921–
1924* (Urbana: University of Illinois Press, 1970), p. 199; barring Soviet futures purchases,
Northwestern Miller, October 1, 1930; *Wheat Studies*, 7 (February 1931): 262.
28. National Association of Grain Dealers meetings in 1923, *Northwestern Miller*, October
3, 1923; MS of John MacMillan, Sr., speech, "Grain Financing in the Northwest," dated
February 1922, is at CA 40-08 (excerpted version reprinted in *Cargill News*), March 1931; for
Wheat Conference, see *Northwestern Miller*, June 20 and 27, 1923; John Sr. comments on this
meeting in his letter to John Jr., June 23, 1923, CA 28-03; "wheat problem" commission, see
Wall Street Journal, October 30, 1923; John H. Rich, "The Economic Position of Agriculture
in the Northwestern Grain Raising Areas," Federal Reserve Board and Conference of Federal
Reserve Agents, November 12, 1923, CA 31-01; Publicity Committee, Minneapolis Chamber
of Commerce, "Orderly Marketing," ca. September 1923, ibid.; Eugene Meyer, Jr., and Frank
W. Mondell, *Report to the President on the Wheat Situation* (Washington, D.C.: Government
Printing Office, 1923); Cargill Elevator Company to Walter H. Newton, November 7, 1923,
ibid. McNary-Haugen bills, Gilbert C. Fite, *George N. Peek and the Fight for Farm Parity*
(Norman: University of Oklahoma Press, 1954).
29. Art Museum, *Minneapolis Morning Tribune*, January 11, 1911. Donations, Sheltering
Arms, September 30, 1915; infant welfare, September 21, 1914; Bureau of Legal Aid, May 3,

1913; Animal Rescue League, June 1, 1917; Anti-Mosquito Committee, June 1, 1916, CA 24-01; YMCA donations, June 28, 1909, October 5, 1910, CA 13-01; 1915 YMCA donation, October 8, 1915, CA 24-01; Belgian Relief, November 13, 1914, CA 28-01; American Red Cross "War Fund," June 14, 1917, CA 24-01; Minneapolis Society of Fine Arts, October 1, 1913, ibid.; MacMillan letter to American Defense Society, July 7, 1920; donation to American Committee of Minneapolis, August 26, 1919, ibid.; "desecration," John Sr. to Minneapolis Committee, National Memorial on Rushmore Mountain, January 3, 1928, CA 28-04; MacMillan quotation on solicitation of employees in letter to F. H. Carpenter, December 8, 1913, ibid.; publicizing philanthropy, John MacMillan to George W. Harsh, November 8, 1922, CA 24-01; graduate student project, R. S. Possinger to MacMillan, January 5, 1924, and MacMillan to Possinger, January 9, 1924, ibid.

30. November 1915 Cargill response to Federal Trade Commission request for data on foreign trade, see CA, 24-01; the two FTC reports are *Methods and Operations of Grain Exporters*, Vol. 1, *Interrelations and Profits*, May 16, 1922, and Vol. 2, *Speculation, Competition and Prices*, June 18, 1923.

7. Expanding Eastward, a Revolt (pp. 280–314)

1. Telegraph and telephone, F. E. Lindahl to MacMillan, September 12, 1907, CA 21-02, Duluth. Buffalo problems, MacMillan to Fred Hanchette, October 25, 1922, CA 28-04, HJ. For the Canadian "pool" experience, see Carl E. Solberg, *The Prairies and the Pampas: Agrarian Policy in Canada and Argentina, 1880–1930*, op. cit., pp. 188–211; Allan Levine, "Open Market or 'Orderly Marketing': The Winnipeg Grain Exchange and the Wheat Pools, 1923–1929, *Agricultural History* 61 (Spring, 1987): 50.

2. Poor prospects for year, John MacMillan to Austen Cargill, April 17, 1923, CA 24-01, C.

3. "Comments by J. H. MacMillan, Stillwater Meeting," November 13–15, 1953; CA 63-05. On European firms in New York City, see Morton Rothstein, "Multinationals in the Grain Trade, 1850–1914," *Business and Economic History*, 2nd ser., 12 (1983): 85; Mira Wilkins, *The History of Foreign Investment in the United States to 1914* (Cambridge, Mass.: Harvard University Press, 1989), pp. 316–20.

4. 1920 arbitration cases, A. L. Jacobs to MacMillan, October 29, 1920, CA 24-04, Milwaukee; the Armour difficulties and effect on Taylor & Bournique, John MacMillan to Austen Cargill, May 31, 1923, CA 24-01, C.

5. Erie Railroad proposal, John MacMillan to John W. Adams, November 13, 1922, CA 28-03, E.; speculative accounts, MacMillan to A. L. Jacobs, May 12, 1921, CA 24-04, Milwaukee.

6. Negotiations on Taylor & Bournique acquisition, A. L. Taylor to MacMillan, April 24; Lyman Bournique to MacMillan, May 17 and 18; MacMillan to Lyman Bournique, May 21, CA 28-04, T. Contract for transfer in letter, Bournique to MacMillan, June 4, 1923, ibid.

7. Private wire system described in MacMillan to Austen Cargill, May 31 and July 6, 1923, CA 24-01, C; the name "Clement-Curtis" came from the company of the same name, the supplier of the system. Earlier wire services by T&B to Iowa, A. L. Jacobs to MacMillan, February 23, 1921, CA 24-04, Milwaukee.

8. John MacMillan opposition earlier to private wire services, his letter to J. P. Griffin, president, Chicago Board of Trade, March 11, 1921, CA 24-01, C; "keeps us posted," MacMillan to Austen Cargill, July 6, 1923, CA, ibid.

9. Austen Cargill view of Taylor & Bournique, in his letter to John MacMillan, May 26, 1923, CA 24-01, A.

10. Prospects for Taylor & Bournique, MacMillan to Fred Hanchette, June 4, 1923, CA 28-04, HI.

11. Grimes on Milwaukee office, letter to MacMillan, May 27, 1923, CA 28-04, G; issue of T&B secretary, MacMillan to Lyman Bournique, May 21, 1923; Bournique reply, May 22, and MacMillan decision on May 23, 1923, CA 28-04, T.

12. Buffalo arrangements, Dudley Irwin to John MacMillan, Sr., May 5, 1923, and MacMillan to Irwin, May 21 and 23, 1923, CA, ibid. Trip of Grimes and John MacMillan, Jr., John Sr. to Austen Cargill, June 15, 1923, CA 24-01, C.

13. Statement on Cargill ethics, MacMillan to A. R. Taylor, June 25, 1923, CA 24-04, Milwaukee.

14. "Hard [time] with Taylor," MacMillan to Fred Hanchette, November 8, 1923, CA 28-04; Taylor's "bad deals," MacMillan to Austen Cargill, November 14, 1923, CA 21-06; firing of Taylor, MacMillan to Taylor, May 9, 1924, 31-02, Milwaukee.

15. Milwaukee fire insurance loss, John MacMillan, Sr., to John MacMillan, Jr., June 24, 1924, CA 29-03; John Sr. to John Jr. and Cargill MacMillan, August 1, 1924, CA 28-03. See also MacMillan to F. P. Hixon, September 4, 1924, CA 28-04, HI. Unwillingness of railroad to rebuild, MacMillan to L. G. Bournique, September 8, 1924, CA 28-03 B; H. E. Byram, president, Chicago Milwaukee & St. Paul Railroad to MacMillan, July 2, 1924, CA 24-01, C; final settlement of the insurance claim, MacMillan to Austen Cargill, August 28, 1924, 24-01.

16. Armour mill, H. G. Atwood to MacMillan, April 29, 1927; Philip D. Armour, May 10, May 12 and July 11, 1927; MacMillan to Armour, May 11, May 13, July 13, 1927, CA 28-03, A. The lease for Elevator E in Milwaukee from the Milwaukee Railroad is noted in Cargill Elevator Company Minute Book, June 29, 1927. See also correspondence between Philip D. Armour and John MacMillan in letters of May 10, 11, 12 and 13 and July 11 and 13, 1927, CA 28-03, A, for unwillingness to rebuild, see John MacMillan to R. M. Calkins, chief traffic officer, Chicago, Milwaukee & St. Paul Railroad, November 27, 1925, CA 28-03, C.

17. The "proportional rate" case of 1922 is discussed in an extensive set of correspondence between John MacMillan, Sr., and various elevator company executives and Interstate Commerce Commission officers in CA 41-12; the results of the I.C.C. decision (I&S Docket 1725) are summarized in a letter and attached analysis from J. G. Woodworth, vice president, Northern Pacific Railway Company, dated May 22, 1923, CA 28-05, N. For a discussion of how this case affected Milwaukee, see MacMillan to A. L. Jacobs, April 6, 1923, CA 24-04, Milwaukee.

18. The *Cargill Chaff*, published by the Cargill Commission Company (Minneapolis), began publication in August 1919; 27 extant copies remain in the Cargill Archives, covering the period December 1919–January 1923; no information is available as to when the publication was taken out of circulation.

19. For Hendel biographical data, see *Cargill News*, May 1965; Robert Diercks comments, ca. 1983, Marvin Borman MS collection; Marvin Borman comments, March 22, 1983, ibid. Articles on the Cargill Laboratory and Julius Hendel role, *Cargill Chaff*, August, September, October, 1922. Hendel article entitled "The Mill Mixture" is in *Northwestern Miller*, December 26, 1923. Parody on wheat testing, ibid., November 29, 1922.

20. John Jr.'s health, John MacMillan, Sr., to Fred Hanchette, August 25, 1921; CA 28-03, Estate; on Cargill MacMillan "keeping the books," ibid., October 3, 1922; CA 29-03, JHM Personal.

21. Hendel weather correlations, John Sr. to John Jr., April 23, 1923; CA 28-03, M; John H. MacMillan, Jr., "Federal Spring Wheat Grades," *Cereal Chemistry* 1 (March 1924): 65.

22. Injury to hand, John Sr. to Emma Hanchette, May 6, 1924, CA 28-03, Estate.

23. Assignment of Flood and Hendel, John Sr. to John Jr., June 24, 1924, CA 29-03, loose folder. Difficulties with floor membership, ibid., July 19, August 12, 1924; CA 28-03, JHM Personal.

24. *Cargill News*, May 1965.

25. For an excellent discussion of anti-Semitism in Minneapolis, see Herbert Samuel Rutman, "Defense and Development: A History of Minneapolis Jewry, 1920–1950," Ph.D. dissertation, University of Minnesota, June 1970. See also John Higham, *Send These to Me: Jews and Other Immigrants in Urban America* (New York: Atheneum, 1975), pp. 163–65; Charles I. Cooper, "The Jews of Minneapolis and Their Christian Neighbors," *Jewish Social Studies* 8 (1946): 32. See also "35 Years in Minneapolis," *The American Jewish World*, September 12, 1947. A full text of the Carey McWilliams article, "Minneapolis Called Anti-Semitic Capital of U.S.," is found in *Minneapolis Star-Tribune*, October 18, 1946. Mayor Hubert Humphrey's Mayor's Committee on Human Relations is analyzed in a *Christian Science Monitor* article, also reprinted in the *Star Tribune*, March 29, 1947. The 11 Cargill members of the Minneapolis Chamber of Commerce in 1924 were A. L. Ashenden (Cargill Commission), George H. Fulton (Cargill Elevator), Fred W. Drum (Cargill Commission), Geo. H. Feetham (Cargill Elevator), Julius Hendel (Cargill Elevator), Cargill MacMillan (Cargill Commission), D. D.

MacMillan (Minneapolis Seed), J. H. MacMillan, Sr. (Cargill Elevator), J. H. MacMillan, Jr. (Cargill Commission), A. I. Owen (Cargill Commission), John Tresise (Cargill Commission).

26. British Columbia logging operation, Frank Hixon to John MacMillan, Sr., January 24, 1924; CA 28-04, H-I. Differences on railroad, Austen Cargill to J. B. Taylor, April 19, 1924, CA 29-06. Austen Cargill abilities, John Sr. to Hixon, January 18, 1924, ibid.; "standard ideas," John Jr. to John Sr., April 20, 1924, MS collection, W. Duncan MacMillan; "petty," Austen Cargill to J. B. Taylor, June 11, 1924, CA 29-06.

27. "Feeling safe," John MacMillan, Sr., to Austen Cargill, August 28, 1924, CA 24-01, C.

28. Buffalo terminals and elevation charges, John MacMillan, Jr., to John Sr., January 13, 1925, CA 28-03, JHM Personal. Hedges, John Sr. to John Jr., January 20, 1925, ibid.

29. John Jr. "tired out," John Sr. to "Arthur" (unidentified), December 11, 1924, CA 28-03, JHM Personal.

30. For Goldman Sachs relationship, see Goldman Sachs to E. S. Mooers, December 20, 1924, and John Sr. to Goldman Sachs, December 22, 1924; CA 28-04, G.

31. John Jr. illness, John Hawley, Jr., to John MacMillan, Sr., February 24, 1925; John Sr. to John Jr., February 19, 1925; CA 28-03, JHM Personal.

32. John Jr. complete rest, John Sr. to John Jr., February 28, 1925; on Hendel correlations, ibid., February 27, 1925; CA, ibid.

33. European trip, John Sr. to F. E. Lindahl (and others), March 23, 1925; CA, wine cellar box. John Sr., to A. L. Wheeler, March 25, 1925, CA, ibid.

34. Meeting with Austen Cargill, John B. Hawley, Jr., to John MacMillan, Sr., July 24, 1925, CA 35-03.

35. John MacMillan, Jr., meeting with Austen Cargill, John Jr. to John Sr., July 26, 1925, CA, ibid.

36. For proposed change in insurance brokers, see John MacMillan, Sr., to F. E. Lindahl, January 31, 1925, CA, wine cellar box.

37. Telegram via Western Union, dated July 26, 1925, 11:12 P.M., to Cargill MacMillan from "Junior," CA 35-03; blood pressure, John MacMillan, Sr., diary, August 12, 1925, CA 36-07; John Sr. letter to 11 banks, August 1, 1925; probing bank reply in D. B. Stern to E. S. Mooers, September 5, 1925, CA 28-03.

38. "Principal complaint," Austen Cargill to Frank Hixon, August 7, 1925, CA John Work; the voting trust was effective as of August 20, 1925; its terms are elaborated in the Cargill Elevator Company Corporate Minute Book, pp. 170A–170G. Inasmuch as Cargill Elevator proxies were limited by bylaws to a one-year period, the bylaws were amended at a special meeting of the stockholders on September 3, 1925, to make proxies valid for ten years; see Lancaster, Simpson Junnell & Dorsey to F. P. Hixon, August 1925, and John MacMillan, Sr., to Hixon, August 15, 1925; CA 28-04, HI.

39. Report on meeting re voting trust, John MacMillan, Sr., to Fred Hanchette, August 18, 1925, CA 28-04, HI; Hanchette reply, August 28, 1925 (actually an incorrect dating; letter postmarked August 24), ibid. John Jr. appears to confirm the role of the bankers in his letter to Emma Hanchette of September 10, 1925, CA 35-03.

40. Events, MacMillan to Hanchette, August 29, 1925, ibid.

41. The Hanchette role in the stockholder challenge, Emma Hanchette to John MacMillan, Sr., "Fri. p.m." (N.B., September 18, 1925), ibid.

42. John MacMillan, Jr., business abilities, John Sr. to Emma Hanchette, September 24, 1925, CA 28-04, HI; MacMillan to Fred Hanchette, October 27, 1925, ibid.

43. The exchange of letters with Margaret Barker and her daughter: John MacMillan, Sr., to Mrs. Geo. R. Barker, September 16 and 23, 1925, CA 28-03, B.; Mary R. Barker to MacMillan, September 23, 1925, CA 28-03, Personal; MacMillan to Mary Barker, September 29, 1925, CA 28-03, B.

44. Alleged statements, see notarized statement, dated October 18, 1925, and signed by John B. Hawley, Jr.; attached to this in the CA file, is a typed, unsigned page, undated, with additional statements, CA 35-03.

45. Mention of stock sale, Hanchette to John Sr., November 20, 1925, CA 28-04, HI.

46. Possible sale of Hanchette stock, John B. Hawley, Jr., to "Uncle Fred," September

30, 1925, CA 35-03; Fred Hanchette to John MacMillan, December 5, 1925, CA 28-04, HI.; for details of one of the proposed plans, see "Tentative Plan No. 2, Purchase of Hanchette Interest, Cargill Companies," undated (ca. July 1925), author identified only as "F" but speaks of "Father's estate" re W. W. Cargill estate.

47. The authority for this dating (and for the amount) is found in a major document, "Historical Outline, of the Estate of W. W. Cargill," undated but with internal evidence suggesting that it was written by "Scott" (otherwise unidentified) and dated October 7, 1935. Internal evidence in this document suggests that it had been prepared for estate purposes among the Cargill heirs. The document is held in the manuscript collection of James F. Cargill.

48. Hanchette to John Sr., December 5, 1925, op. cit.; Hanchette to Austen Cargill, ibid.

49. Loan to the Hanchettes, John Sr. to Fred Hanchette, July 27, 1921, CA 29-03; John Sr. view of the Hawley option and the subsequent purchase, his letter to Fred Hanchette of December 14, 1925, CA 28-04, HI.

50. "Historical Outline of the Estate of W. W. Cargill," op. cit.

51. James Taylor role, Emma Hanchette to Edna MacMillan, November 5, 1925; John MacMillan, Sr., extract from this, dated November 20, 1925; statement of John H. MacMillan, dated November 23, 1925; in regard to statement of John D. McMillan, signed by the former on November 23 and by the latter on November 24, 1925; CA 35-03.

52. Austen Cargill role, Frank Hixon to John MacMillan, Sr., November 24 and 28, 1925, CA 35-03.

53. Letter concerning Austen Cargill, Hixon to MacMillan, January 28, 1926, ibid.

54. For Austen Cargill role in Commission Department, see "Report Commission Department, July 1, 1926, to June 30, 1933," CA, Special. "Family viewpoint," John MacMillan, Sr., to John Jr., February 1, 1926, CA 28-03, M. For reasons bus operation initiated, see John MacMillan, Sr., to H. E. Pierpont, Chicago, Milwaukee & St. Paul Railway Co., April 22, 1926, CA 28-03, C.

55. "Paving the way," Hixon to MacMillan, August 16, 1926, ibid.

8. Centralization and the "Endless Belt" (pp. 316–36)

1. Military forms of organization, John MacMillan, Jr., "Theory and Practice of Organization," printed speech, May 10, 1946, CA, Special.

2. For earlier Chandler concepts on organization, see especially Alfred D. Chandler, Jr., *Strategy and Structure: Chapters in the History of the Industrial Enterprise* (Cambridge, Mass.: MIT Press, 1962); I have also drawn from Thomas K. McCraw, ed., *The Essential Alfred Chandler: Essays Toward a Historical Theory of Big Business* (Boston: Harvard Business School Press, 1988), pp. 1–21, 472–504, and Professor Chandler's *Scale and Scope: the Dynamics of Industrial Capitalism* (Cambridge, Mass.: Belknap Press of Harvard University Press, 1990).

3. "Marine department," John MacMillan, Sr., to R. M. Knox, January 31, 1925; Knox to MacMillan, February 2, 1925; John MacMillan, Jr., to Knox, March 11, 1925; CA, 28-04, K.

4. Centralizing brokerage and insurance, John Jr. to John Sr., August 22, 1925, CA 28-03, M; for later developments, see John Jr. to F. J. Hays, December 18, 1929, CA Whitney MacMillan MS 5; see also John Jr. testimony on this in the Chicago Board of Trade "corn case," CBOT Archives, University of Illinois, Chicago, AAA 6062-5, 553.

5. Disobeying orders, John MacMillan, Sr. to A. M. Prime and to F. E. Lindahl, both letters dated August 27, 1925; Lindahl to MacMillan, August 28, 1925; MacMillan to Lindahl and to Prime, September 1, 1925; CA, wine cellar box. New office accounting, MacMillan to R. N. Hoople, August 31, 1927, CA 28-04, M.

6. Effect of stock dividend on employee notes to the widows, John MacMillan, Sr., to Fred Hanchette, June 14, 1922; MacMillan to Margaret F. Barker, October 27, 1922; R. E. Wisner to MacMillan, October 31, 1922; Wisner to MacMillan, November 3 and 9, 1922; CA 28-03, Estate. Lindahl's desire to sell stock, his letter to MacMillan, August 17, 1922; MacMillan to Austen Cargill, same date; CA, ibid. Cargill's attitude toward Lindahl, his letter to MacMillan, June 19, 1923, CA 24-01, C.

7. "Organization as a whole," John MacMillan, Sr., to Lindahl, February 13, 1925, CA, wine cellar box; new accounting allocations, MacMillan to Lindahl, September 10 and 14,

1926, CA 28-05, Duluth; "exceedingly fond," ibid., January 3, 1927. "Bad egg," Lindahl to MacMillan, June 2, 1926; screenings inspection issue, MacMillan to Lindahl, September 29 and November 24, 1926; MacMillan to E. McManus, November 24, 1926; Lindahl to MacMillan, November 26, 1926; screenings belonging to elevators, Lindahl to MacMillan, September 13, 1926; CA 28-05, Duluth.

8. Curt letter, MacMillan to L. N. Cote, November 9 and 23, 1927; employee stock, MacMillan to W. R. Paul, September 22, 1925; raise in Milwaukee, MacMillan to A. Jacobs, January 22, 1927; CA 28-04. Pleasure about reports, MacMillan to R. J. Semsch, October 23 and November 4, 1925; MacMillan to R. R. Valier, November 3, 1925; CA 28-05, L.

9. See, particularly, *Report of the Federal Trade Commission on the Methods and Operations of Grain Exporters*, Vol. 1, pp. 1–62; Vol. 2, pp. 52–123, op. cit.

10. "Deep-Waterway-to-the-Sea," John MacMillan, Sr., to J. L. Record, Tidewater Subcommittee, Minneapolis Civic & Commerce Association, October 21, 1920; CA 24-02, M; Welland Canal, Lindahl to John Sr., June 9, 1926; John Sr. to Lindahl, June 10, 1926; John Jr. to John Sr., January 12, 1925; John Sr. to John Jr., January 16, 1925; CA, 28-05, Duluth, 28-03, Personal; Chicago elevator, John Sr. to F. W. Sargent, May 3, 1927, CA 28-03, C., on Ogdensburg losses, John Sr. to H. E. Tweeden, August 24, 1928, CA 31-04, Buffalo; "end of Buffalo," John Jr. to John Sr., February 18, 1929, CA 30-01, JHM, Jr. Personal; Churchill, Canada route, John Jr. to John Sr., February 15 and March 29, 1929, ibid; see also *Northwestern Miller*, May 16, 1923, p. 712.

11. Exchanging oats, John MacMillan, Sr., to Lindahl, May 10, 1926; Lindahl to MacMillan, May 13, 1926; CA 28-05, Duluth.

12. Oats price differentials, John Sr. to Lindahl, June 25, 1926; Lindahl to MacMillan, June 26, 1926; CA, ibid.

13. Sale of oats to Grimes, John Sr. to Lindahl, October 26 and 27, 1926, CA, ibid.

14. About F. J. Hays, John MacMillan, Jr., to H. E. Tweeden, April 12, 1929, CA, ibid.

15. Cleaning machinery, Lindahl to John Sr., May 13, 1926; John Sr. to Lindahl, May 15, 1926; CA, ibid.

16. Excessive charges, Lindahl to John Sr., July 1, 1926; John Sr. to Lindahl, July 2, 1926; CA, ibid.

17. Lindahl illness, Mrs. F. E. Lindahl to John Sr., January 19, 1927; John Sr. to Lindahl, January 20, 1927, CA, ibid.

18. Volume statistics are summarized in a set of handwritten tables, CA 54-12. See also charts at 56-10.

19. Misapprehension by Buffalo manager, John Sr. to H. E. Tweeden, October 1, 1927; slowness of Duluth bids, Tweeden to John Sr., September 24, 1927; CA 28-03, Buffalo.

20. Election of Tweeden as vice president, John Sr. to Tweeden, April 5, 1926; Lockport mistake, Daniel D. MacMillan to Tweeden, April 6, 1925; CA 28-05, B.

21. Agricultural progress in the second half of the 1920s, see especially the year-end reviews of world wheat in *Wheat Studies of the Food Research Institute*, Vols. 2–6 (Stanford, Calif.: Stanford University, 1926–1929). For an excellent summary of national legislation in this period, see Chester C. Davis, "The Development of Agricultural Policy since the End of the World War," in *Farmers in a Changing World: The Yearbook of Agriculture, 1940* (Washington, D.C.: U.S. Department of Agriculture, 1940), pp. 297–326. Quotation on "striking upbuilding," *Wheat Studies*, Vol. 6, p. 55.

22. Credit statistics, CA 41-12.

23. Hawley work with Superior terminal, F. E. Lindahl to John Sr., March 9, 1928, CA 28-02, Duluth; break with Hawley, diary entries, John MacMillan, Sr., November 9 and 27 and December 8, 1928, CA 36-07; Hawley to John Sr., September 8, 1928, CA 34-05; memorandum to executives concerning Hawley, December 8, 1928, CA 33-02, Personal; see also John Work interview with Julius Hendel, ca. 1964, John Work MS CA.

24. A. M. Prime hearing, John MacMillan, Sr., to Prime, June 25, 1929, CA 31-02; board of directors resolution, ibid., June 29, 1929.

25. Frank Neilson shift to Cargill organization, see John MacMillan, Sr., to John Jr., July 1, 1926; John Sr. to Fred Hanchette, December 7, 1926; CA 28-04.

26. Fobbing, John Sr. to Lindahl, October 11, 1927; Lindahl to John Sr., October 22, 1927; A. M. Prime to John Sr., ibid., CA 28-05, Duluth; John Jr. to F. J. Hays, December 18, 1929,

CA Whitney MacMillan MS 5. Lindahl willingness, John Jr. to John Sr., February 23, 1929, CA, 30-01, JHM, Jr. Personal. Paraphrased quotation on effect of World War I on CIF trading from Charles B. Kuhlmann, *The Development of the Flour Milling Industry in the United States*, op. cit., pp. 311–12.

27. Inroads of Continental, Dreyfus and Bunge, John MacMillan, Jr., to John Sr., March 20, 1929, CA 30-01, JHM Jr. Personal.

28. "Raced," John Sr. to John Jr., July 9, 1929, CA 33-02.

9. Hoover's Farm Board (pp. 340–74)

1. Agriculture in 1920s, Ross M. Robertson, *History of the American Economy*, 3rd ed. (New York: Harcourt Brace Jovanovich, 1973), p. 515; Chester C. Davis, "The Development of Agricultural Policy since the End of the World War," op. cit., pp. 297–341; M. K. Bennett, Helen C. Farnsworth and Alonzo E. Taylor, "The World Wheat Situation, 1929–30," *Wheat Studies* 7 (1930–31): 89–164; Gilbert C. Fite, *George N. Peek and the Fight for Farm Parity*, op. cit., chaps. 6–14. For agricultural views of Herbert Hoover, see especially David E. Hamilton, "From New Day to New Deal: American Agriculture in the Hoover Years, 1928–1933," Ph.D. dissertation, University of Iowa, 1985, chap. 2; David Bruce Miller, "Origins and Functions of the Federal Farm Board," Ph.D. dissertation, University of Kansas, 1973, chap. 2; Hoover's overall views on associational activities, Evan B. Metcalf, "Secretary Hoover and the Emergence of Macroeconomic Management," *Business History Review* 49 (Spring 1975): . 60–80. See also Ellis W. Hawley, *The Great War and the Search for a Modern Order: A History of the American People and Their Institutions, 1917–1933* (New York: St. Martin's Press, 1979), pp. 104–7; Murray R. Benedict, *Farm Policies of the United States, 1790–1950: A Study of Their Origins and Development* (New York: The Twentieth Century Fund, 1953), pp. 239–41.

2. Fite, *George N. Peek . . .*, op. cit., p. 225.

3. Secretary Hyde, *Northwestern Miller*, March 6, 1929; John MacMillan, Jr., to John Sr., March 20, 1929; CA 30-01, Personal.

4. John Sr. to J. M. Barker, April 29, 1929; Barker to John Sr., June 24, 1929; CA 31-01, B; "Anglo-Saxon code of law," Cargill MacMillan to Sumner B. Young, December 21, 1929, CA 41-12.

5. Buyers backing away, John Sr. to George E. Roberts, May 20, 1929, CA 31-02, R; enormous inventory and notes payable, John Sr. to T. F. Baxter, May 20, 1929, CA 31-01, B; reserve, John Sr. to John Jr., June 27, 1929, CA 33-02, Personal; fobbing vs. CIF, ibid., August 3, 1929; "wonderful" carrying charge, John Sr. to A. M. Prime, November 4, 1929, CA 31-02, PQ.

6. Alexander Legge meeting with cooperatives, John Sr. to John Jr., July 30, 1929, CA 33-02, Personal; Minneapolis Grain Commission Merchants Association to Legge, November 21, 1929, CA 31-01, F; reply, ibid., November 22; John Sr. meeting with Legge, telegram from John Sr. to John Jr., November 21, 1929; Gerald Nye quotation in *St. Paul Pioneer Press*, December 10, 1929; *Nation's Business* quotation, November 9, 1929, CA 32-03, Misc.; John Sr. newspaper statement in *Minneapolis Sunday Journal*, November 17, 1929; Legge on "special right or franchise," in his letter to Walter Newton, February 17, 1930, Herbert Hoover Papers, Herbert Hoover Presidential Library, West Branch, Iowa; on efficiency, John Sr. to Curtis L. Mosher, January 3, 1930, CA 31-01, N; farm machinery comparisons, John Sr. to S. D. Gaugher, December 18, 1929, CA 31-01G; *Wheat Studies*, 7:155.

7. For an excellent analysis of the early experience of the federal Farm Board, see "Wheat in the First Year of the Agricultural Marketing Act," *Wheat Studies* 7 (1930–31):145–64; press release on Alexander Legge remarks, federal Farm Board, December 19, 1929, CA 31-01, F; "grain men . . . alone," Sumner B. Young to Cargill MacMillan, December 20, 23, 1929, CA 41-12; "radical farm bunch," J. M. Barker to John Sr., December 18, 1929, CA 31-02, B.

8. Query on Cargill note, unidentified writer to Jeffrey C. Pick, Goldman, Sachs & Company, December 27, 1929; John Sr. to Messrs. Goldman, Sachs & Company, December 30, 1929, CA 31-02, G.

9. The proposal to sell country elevators is in letter to Alexander Legge of January 15, 1930, signed by J. H. MacMillan, B. H. Woodworth and F. B. Wells, CA 31-02, Personal; the Legge reply to them is dated January 25, 1930, CA 41-12; "anything to come of this," John Sr. to J. M. Barker, January 17, 1930, CA 31-02, B. The offer to the American Farm Bureau Fed-

eration is dated July 12, 1924, and signed by Cargill and 32 other companies, CA 41-12; see also *Minneapolis Journal*, July 21, 1924; "war," Miller, op. cit., p. 178.

10. The "carrying charge" issue is discussed in detail in *Wheat Studies* 7:158–64, and in John Sr. to Bert H. Lang, April 12, 1930, CA 31-01, Z.

11. "Stiffen up," John Jr. to John Sr., telegram, February 3, 1930, CA 30-01, Personal; "Publicity Committee," John Jr. to John Sr., ibid; for exchanges with the Farm Board, see John Sr. to Alexander Legge, March 1, 1930, and telegram, ibid., March 3, 1930; Cargill Elevator Company to Arthur M. Hyde, March 1, 1930; on Legge's "a new crop month," his letter to MacMillan of March 7, 1930; "Armour Grain Co.," John Jr. to Walter H. Newton, March 3, 1930; "our advice . . . to wire Mr. Barnes," John Jr. to Legge, March 14, 1930; "always glad to have the opinion," Alexander Legge to John Sr., March 22, 1930, CA 31-01.

12. For Chamber of Commerce meetings, April 30 through May 2, 1930, see Hamilton, op. cit., pp. 173–75; and Miller, op. cit., pp. 217–20. Quotations from federal Farm Board, press release, May 2, 1930; a copy of the Chamber resolution is in CA, 31-02, Public Relations Reprints.

13. John Sr.'s solution for the May contract, his letter to Lang, March 14 and April 3, 1930; resolution of issue, John Sr. to Lang, May 1, 1930, and John Sr. to George Roberts, May 1, 1930, CA 31-01. Barker to John Sr., July 2, 1930, CA 31-01, B.

14. The delivery rule amendments, to Rules 282 and 292, were proposed by the CBOT board of directors in their meeting of September 16, 1930, and posted for vote on September 24, 1930, CA 31-01, Chicago Delivery Rule. John Sr.'s letter to J. W. T. Duvel is dated September 11, 1930; his letter to Arthur M. Hyde, September 24, ibid. Duvel's reply was sent through his assistant, J. M. Mehl, September 19, 1930; Hyde's reply is dated September 30; the several letters of John Sr. to bank presidents were dated September 24, ibid. The letter to J. M. Barker after the vote is dated October 7, 1930, ibid. See also *Business Week*, September 17, 1930, and John Sr.'s letter to them, dated September 20, 1930, ibid.

15. Effects in Europe, John Sr. to George E. Roberts, March 28, 1930, CA 31-01, R; "Russian business is paralyzing," John Jr. to Julius Hendel, February 10, 1938, CA 30-01. Quotations on Russian trading on Chicago Board of Trade, *Northwestern Miller*, October 1 and 15, 1930. For comments on Secretary Arthur Hyde's attitudes on Soviet trading, *Northwestern Miller*, October 1, 1930; see also Hamilton, op. cit., pp. 208–9; Josef Stalin quotation from *New York Times*, November 26, 1930.

16. Drought of 1930, David E. Hamilton, "Herbert Hoover and the Great Drought of 1930," *Journal of American History* 68 (March 1930): 850; quotation on Hoover, p. 875; see also Hamilton's book, *American Farm Policy from Hoover to Roosevelt* (Chapel Hill: University of North Carolina Press, 1991).

17. Alexander Legge to George Milnor, December 31, 1930, Legge file, Grain Stabilization Corporation Papers, RG 103, National Archives.

18. John MacMillan, Jr., "Prospective Grain Prices for the New Crop Year and Their Effect on the General Economic Situation," February 9, 1931 (updated November 12, 1932), CA 41-12; on millers' reluctance, John Jr. to John Sr., February 2, 1931, CA 32-03.

19. Legge "isolated," Morris Barker to John Sr., January 24, 1931, CA 31-02; Legge "broken," Forrest Crissey, *Alexander Legge, 1866–1933* (Chicago: Alexander Legge Memorial Committee, 1936), p. 206; "smash the grain trade," John Sr. to Morris Barker, August 7, 1931, CA 31-02, B; Arthur Hyde statement on Hoover's "childlike faith," entry of November 10, 1930, Niles A. Olsen Papers, Iowa State University, Ames.

20. Cargill handling Farm Board sales, John Jr. to John Sr., February 11, 1931, and February 27, 1931, CA 32-03.

21. For analysis of the crop year 1930–1931, see "The World Wheat Situation, 1930–31," *Wheat Studies* 8 (December 1931): 67–186; private grain trade policies, p. 155; for problems of "out of position" grain and bargaining sessions on rates, see especially John Sr. to Bert H. Lang, March 30 and April 4, 1931, and Lang to John Sr., April 2, 1931, CA 31-01; John Jr. to George Milnor, April 10, 1931, CA 32-03; Grain Stabilization Corporation to Cargill Elevator Company, April 21, 1931; John Jr. to W. C. Engel, April 23, 1931, ibid.; diplomacy of John Sr. and John Jr., see John Sr. letter to C. V. Essroger, April 10, 1931, CA 31-01. Quotation on "most vilified . . . since the Freedman's Bureau," Hamilton, op. cit., p. 232.

22. "Grain paper . . . in east," Frank D. Hixon to John Sr., July 1, 1930, CA 31-02; the year-end review is in John Sr. to Hixon, July 16, 1931, CA 33-02.

23. John Sr.'s description of new corporation in his letter to Hixon, June 27, 1930, CA 31-02, H. The certificate of incorporation for Cargill, Incorporated, is dated July 18, 1930; the exchange of stock with the Cargill Securities Company is noted in its meeting of July 13, 1931. For analysis of the effects on stockholdings of the establishment of Cargill, Incorporated, and this subsequent stock exchange, see unsigned memorandum of Cargill MacMillan, June 11, 1947, CA 36-05; on "women members," see "Historical Outline of the Estate of W. W. Cargill," ca. October 7, 1935, CA.

24. The details of the new second preferred stock are elaborated in the Cargill Elevator Company shareholder meetings of August 11 and 20, 1931. The internal memorandum "Outline of Proposed Plan to Be Presented to Cargill Elevator Co. Stockholders at Annual Meeting for Discussion" is undated and unsigned, CA 33-02; John Sr.'s letter to Frank Hixon is dated August 17, 1931, ibid; the *Cargill News* article is in its August 1931 issue. The results of the first year of exchange of stock is noted in John Sr. to Goldman, Sachs & Company, July 28, 1932, ibid.; these figures also in Cargill Elevator Company minutes of annual shareholder meeting, August 9, 1932; nonemployee transfers, Cargill MacMillan to James B. Taylor, September 25, 1931, and July 5, 1932, CA 45-03.

25. Oswego negotiations, series of telexes between John Jr. and Harold Tweeden, late October 1929, CA 30-01, Personal. Hotel bill problem, John Jr. to John Sr., February 20, 1930, ibid. The Cargill training program is first mentioned in *Cargill News*, July 1930; "opportunity," ibid., November 1931; the "kindergarten," John Jr. to L. L. Crosby, July 24, 1931, CA 32-03; recruiting policy, Maurice R. Smith to John Jr., January 10, 1934, and John Jr. to Smith, January 23, 1934, CA 35-06, S.

26. Hiring friends, John Jr. to Ed Grimes, April 16, 1935, CA 36-04; pirating of employee, John Jr. to Carlos Falk, May 1, 1936; R. F. Straub to John Jr., May 7, 1936, CA 36-04, B; "approximately six Yale men," John Jr. to Stuart H. Clement, March 25, 1936, CA 36-04; "avoid the diamond in the rough," in John Jr. speech, May 10, 1946, "Theory and Practice of Organization," in *Cargill's Business*, corporate training manual, Gerald A. Joines, general editor.

27. "Marked preference for . . . Yale," John Jr. to Delano DeWindt, January 3, 1946, CA 46-08; "salaries . . . low," undated memorandum, ca. February 1933, CA 35-07.

28. Julius Hendel injury in train crash, John Jr. to John Sr., February 28 and March 3, 1931, CA 32-03; friction, John Sr. to J. Hendel and E. J. Grimes, May 12, 1931, CA 33-02; Lindahl response on centralization of rye in his letter to John Sr., July 29, 1931, ibid.; buying wheat in Omaha, John Sr. to L. L. Crosby, August 12, 1931, CA 33-03, O.; petitions for signatures, memorandum of September 2, 1931, under signature of John Sr., CA 33-02; "I am tired," John Sr. to J. M. Barker, January 26, 1931, CA 31-02, B; John Sr. medical problems in early 1932, see J. A. C. Colston to Cargill MacMillan, February 9, 1932, and attached medical report; John Sr. describes his recovery in a letter to Edna MacMillan, June 20, 1932, CA 34-04; "cured," John Jr. to John Sr., February 29, 1932, CA 32-03.

29. Shifting Boden and Flood, John Jr. to John Sr., March 4, 1932, CA 32-02; advertising, John Sr. to "All Department Managers," July 23, 1931, CA 32-06; "signed by the dictator," H. B. Juneau and Eileen Lewis to "All Stenographers," August 6, 1931, CA 32-07; proposed feed project, Oscar O. Opsal to E. J. Grimes, August 28, 1931, Grimes to Opsal, September 1, 1931, CA 32-06; for discussion of relation between centralization and diversification, see Thomas K. McCraw, ed., *The Essential Alfred Chandler: Essays Toward a Historical Theory of Big Business*, op. cit., pp. 114, 126–29; chastisement of Harold Tweeden, John Sr. to Tweeden, May 27, 1931, CA 33-02; molasses project, Grimes to P. C. Sayles, October 27, 1931; Sayles to Grimes, January 15, 1932, CA 33-01; proposed molasses project, A. L. Kefer to John Jr., with attachment, January 4, 1932, CA 32-03; A. L. Kaplan to John Jr., April 13, 1932, and John Jr. to Kaplan, April 18 and July 1, 1932, ibid.; Walter Stanger to R. W. Carmichel, January 14, 1932, and Carmichael to Stanger, January 20, 1932, CA 32-06; Tweeden's merchandising changes, John Jr. to Tweeden, May 3, 1932, ibid.; Harold Tweeden's role, John Sr. to D. L. Norby, C. Costenbader, C. C. Boden and B. J. Bolan, July 5, 1932, CA 33-02; John Sr. to Harold Tweeden, May 25, 1932, ibid. Memorandum on secrecy, September 7, 1932, CA 33-02; two representative manager responses are L. N. Cote to John Sr., September 9, 1932, and L. L. McCulloch to John Sr., same date, both in CA 33-03.

10. New Elevators, Cargill's Bank Crisis (pp. 378–418)

1. Quotation on Omaha as feeder for Duluth, John MacMillan, Jr., testimony, *Cargill, Incorporated, Complainant v. the Board of Trade of the City of Chicago*, CEA Docket #6, testimony, p. 559; on initiation of Omaha terminal, John Jr. to John Sr., telegram December 5, 1929, CA 30-01, Personal; bargaining with Omaha Grain Exchange, John Jr. to John Sr., March 1, 1930, ibid.; effort to persuade Farm Board on Omaha elevator, John Sr. to Alexander Legge, March 1, 1930; the text was written by John Jr., as described in his letter of March 1 to John Sr., CA 31-01 and 30-01; Frank Neilson role, *Cargill News*, April 1933.

2. Omaha plans, John Jr. to Rodger R. Kauffman, July 31, 1930, CA 30-02, T; configuration of terminal, Original Inspection Report No. 232, Nebraska Inspection Bureau, August 13, 1930; see also *Cargill News* July and August 1930; *Engineering News-Record*, October 1, 1931, and August 3, 1933; costs, John Sr. to Frank Hixon, July 2, 1930, CA 31-02, H; questions about bin moisture, Bert H. Lang to John Jr., September 29, 1930, CA 30-01, F; "most economical," John Jr. to Lang, September 25, 1930, ibid.; "wonderful day," John Sr. to Cargill MacMillan, August 22, 1930, CA 33-02; constraints regarding visits, John Sr. to L. L. Crosby, September 5, 1930, CA 31-02; "vats," John Sr. to John Jr., Julius Hendel, Frank Neilson, Louis Crosby and Frank Hays, May 15, 1931, CA 33-02.

3. Report to Russian government, John Jr. to B. M. Mishin, May 22, 1936, with attachment, "The Cargill Design for Elevator Construction," CA 36-04; railroad use of Cargill design, John Jr. to Ralph Budd, December 10, 1935, CA 39-02; the 10,000-bushel comparison was made, for example, in "History of the Cargill Organization," a proposal to the Soviet Union in 1936, CA 36-04.

4. "Best year," John Sr. to Frank Hixon, July 11, 1930, CA 31-02, H; capacity figures from "Estimated Earnings for Crop Year 1930–31," July 2, 1930, CA 41-11 and 30-01; see also "Terminal Elevator Capacities—12 Year Figures" in *Financial and Statistical Statements*, Cargill Elevator Company and Subsidiaries, December 31, 1935.

5. Albany plans, John Jr. to Port of Albany Commission, August 18, 1931, CA 35-07; shortage of canal shipping, John Jr. to Peter Ten Eyck, August 5, 1932, ibid.; safety of Albany terminal, C. V. Essroger to John Sr., July 14, 1932, and John Sr. to Essroger, July 15, 1932; CA 33-02.

6. For details of grain bin accident, see Omaha *World-Herald*, February 17, 1931; John Jr. to John Sr., February 24, 1931, CA 32-03; the 1931 Omaha terminal explosion is described in *Milwaukee Journal*, August 4, 1931; a picture of it was published widely, for example, in *New York News*, August 4, 1931, ibid.; *Grain & Feed Journal*, August 12, 1931; discipline of employee, Frank Neilson to P. G. Ossuscik, October 11, 1932, CA 33-03; exchanges between Bert Lang and John Sr., August 6, 8, 22 and 24, 1932, CA 33-02.

7. The terminal operation costs for Chicago and Albany and several selected other Cargill terminals for this period showed the following:

Average Costs per 1000 Bu.

	Chicago		Albany		K–L (Superior)		T (Minneapolis)		Omaha	
	34*	35**	34	35	34	35	34	35	34	35
Unloading	1.96	1.62	2.56	2.60	1.19	1.48	.83	1.08	.58	.50
Transferring	2.07	3.25	.36	.33	.58	1.96	.60	.68	.49	.53
Direct transfer	1.07	2.10	—	—	—	—	—	—	—	—
Loading	1.14	1.88	.76	.76	.29	.65	.63	.66	.45	.60

*July 1, 1933–June 30, 1934.
**July 1, 1934–June 30, 1935.
Source: "Cost of Elevator Operations," consolidated working paper for final closing figures, 1933–34 and 1934–35.

The Chicago transfer terminal is described in the *Daily Calumet*, July 23, 1932, and *Cargill News*, August 1932; "anticipated war" quotation, ibid., May 1932; "dodging gangster bullets," ibid., November 1932. The developing relationship with the Chicago and North Western Railroad is described in an undated "Memorandum for Mr. Sargent," ca. July 1932 and John MacMillan, Jr., to Fred W. Sargent, November 1, 1932, CA 32-03; John Jr.'s discussion of a possible board of director's post with the railroad in his letter to Sargent of June 30, 1932, ibid. Development of Chicago as a grain market, see Edward A. Duddy and David A. Revzan, "The Distribution of Grain and Grain Products from the Chicago Market," *Journal of Business* 8 (January 1935): 65, and ibid. "The Shipment of Grain and Grain Products from Chicago, 1924–25—1932-33," ibid., 8 (April 1935): 150; Guy A. Lee, "The Historical Significance of the Chicago Grain Elevator System," *Agricultural History* 11 (January 1937): 16. John MacMillan, Jr.'s comments on Chicago Board of Trade hostility on the Company's Grain Laboratory in his testimony in *Cargill, Incorporated, Complainant v. the Board of Trade of the City of Chicago, respondent,* CEA Docket #6, testimony, p. 545.

8. Minneapolis Industrial Committee letter on unemployment, over signature of A. R. Rogers, chairman, undated, ca. September 1931, CA 33-03, M; unemployment plan in *Minneapolis Journal,* December 23, 1931, John Sr. to C. A. Prosser, December 28, 1931, and Prosser to MacMillan, January 5, 1932, CA 33-03; employee pension plan, John Sr. to F. E. Lindahl, August 14, 1931, CA 33-02; Lindahl layoff plans, his letters to John Sr., October 8, November 25 and 27, 1931, ibid.; employee wage study is dated October 1, 1931, CA 41-11.

9. For John Sr.'s handwritten draft of the Christmas message in the December 1931 issue of *Cargill News,* see CA 33-02; for general employee letter on the wage cuts, dated April 29, 1932, ibid. The July 1, 1932, letter to stockholders is in Cargill Elevator Company corporate minutes, meeting of July 1, 1932; restoring cuts, see John Sr. to Harold Tweeden, July 18, 1932, CA 32-03; passing of dividend, Robert Hixon to John Sr., July 8, 1932, and John Sr. to Hixon, July 11, 1932, CA 33-02.

10. For the University of Chicago economists' paper, "A Memorandum Presented to a Member of the House Committee on Military Affairs, April 26, 1932," see CA 32-03, M; John Jr. letter to Robert Maynard Hutchins, May 25, 1932, and Hutchins reply of June 2, 1932, CA 32-03, GH; John Sr.'s view in his letter to William D. MacMillan, May 24, 1932, CA 33-02; Will's reply of May 27, 1932, CA 32-03; Will's letter to Daniel MacMillan, June 3, 1932, CA 39-11; Daniel to Will, June 1, 1932, ibid.; John Jr.'s response to Will, June 10, 1932, CA 32-03; Civil War gold contracts, John Jr. to John Sr., March 15, 1932, CA 32-02; gold as legal tender with CBOT, ibid., March 17, 1932, CA 32-02.

11. Sets of dossiers on the "Argentine peso" matter, containing the complete set of correspondence among Cargill personnel and to and from the National City Bank were prepared in November 1932 and sent to a number of Cargill's other banks. Several of these sets are extant in CA 33-03, National City Bank. The original contract is elaborated in telegrams and memoranda, March 8–24, 1932; the difficulties are first described in correspondence of July 12–13, 1932; quotation on "your people must have known," W. A. Simonson to John Jr., August 11, 1932; John Jr. reply, ibid., August 15, 1932; "I did not wish to argue," Cargill MacMillan to J. A. Jackson, September 3, 1932; John Jr. offer of "informal arbitration," his letter to Jackson, September 22, 1932; refusal by bank, Jackson to John Jr., September 26, 1932; "blundered," John Sr. to Jackson, September 30, 1932; reply to this letter by L. N. Shaw, October 6, 1936; cancellation of Cargill contract, Shaw to John Sr., October 14, 1932; termination of Cargill banking relationship with bank, Jackson to John Sr., October 20, 1932; "exceedingly sharp practice," John Sr. to Jackson, October 31, 1932; "I cannot help but resent," Jackson to John Sr., November 4, 1932. For treatment of dossier by First National Bank of St. Louis, John Sr. to Bert H. Lang, November 29, 1932, and Lang to John Sr., December 2, 1932. Quotation on selecting "our Vice President, Mr. J. G. Byam," n.d., see CA 33-02, Personal.

12. William E. Leuchtenburg, *Franklin D. Roosevelt and the New Deal, 1932–1940* (New York: Harper & Row, 1963), pp. 2, 3.

13. "The World Wheat Situation, 1931–32," *Wheat Studies* 9 (1932): 63; Edwin G. Nourse, Joseph S. Davis and John D. Black, *Three Years of the Agricultural Adjustment Act* (Washington: Brookings Institution, 1937), pp. 21–22; Joseph S. Davis, *Wheat and the AAA,* ibid., 1935, pp. 24–25.

14. "Farm holiday" quotations from John D. Hicks, *Republican Ascendancy, 1921–1933* (New York: Harper & Row, 1960), pp. 266–67.

15. For Franklin D. Roosevelt's preelection agricultural positions, see Gertrude A. Slichter, "Franklin D. Roosevelt and the Farm Problem, 1929–1932," *Mississippi Valley Historical Review* 43 (1956–1957): 238; "fighting grain man," C. C. Lewis to Ed Grimes, June 23, 1932, CA 32-06, L; John Sr. views on the election in his letter to J. M. Barker, September 1, 1932, and to F. E. Lindahl, October 25, 1932, CA 33-02; on FDR at Albany, Grimes to T. Y. Wickham, August 26, 1932, CA 32-06.

16. Cargill Elevator Company, "Economic Situation as of November, 1932," November 12, 1932; see also ibid., "Prospective Grain Prices for the Crop Year and Their Effect on the General Economic Situation," February 1931; these positions were stated publicly by Austen Cargill in his speech "A 'Thought' to Think About," address, "Farm and Home Hour," National Broadcasting System, December 14, 1932, CA 35-07, and "Austen Cargill" files, James F. Cargill; on Austen Cargill speech, John Sr. to Emma Hanchette, December 30, 1932, CA 33-02, H; on terminal superintendents' comments, *Cargill News*, December 1932.

17. John Jr. to "Mother and Father," January 5, 1933, CA 33-06; ibid. to W. B. Allen, January 7, 1933, ibid.

18 These notes are listed on memorandum dated January 7, 1933, CA 35-07; on bankers acceptances, John Sr. to John Jr., November 12, 1930, Whitney MacMillan archives, II. A. Matthews to John Sr., August 23, 1932, and John Sr. to Matthews, August 25, 1932, CA 33-02.

19. John Jr. to John Sr., January 31, 1933, CA 32-03; John Jr. to C. V. Essroger, February 1, 1933, CA 33-06; John Jr. to John Sr., February 7, 1933, CA 32-03; Daniel MacMillan to John Sr., March 14, 1933, CA 39-11.

20. Cargill MacMillan to "Mother and Father," February 1, 1933, CA 34-04; John Jr. to John Sr., February 7, 1933, ibid.

21. Austen Cargill to John Sr., February 8, 1933, CA 34-04; William Feick to John Sr., February 8, 1933, CA 35-06.

22. John Jr. to John Sr., February 14, 15, 18, 21, 1933, CA 35-07, and February 20, CA 34-04; C. T. Jaffray to John Sr., April 26, 1933, CA 41-11; John Jr. to John Sr., February 25, 28 and March 1, CA 35-07; ibid., February 27, CA 34-04; William A. McGregor to Cargill Grain Company, February 21, 1933, CA 35-06.

23. John Jr. to John Sr., March 1, 1933, CA 35-07; ibid., March 7, 1933, CA 34-04.

24. John Jr. to John Sr., March 3, 1933 (with attachments), CA 34-04; John Jr. to E. H. Rawls, March 4, 1933, CA 35-06; Rawls to John Jr., wire, March 6, 1933, ibid; John Sr. to John Jr., wire, March 6, 1933, CA 35-07; John Jr. to John Sr., March 7 and 11, 1933, CA 34-04; John Jr. to "Mother and Father," ca. March 8, 1933, ibid.; Daniel MacMillan to John Sr., March 14, 1933, CA 39-11; John Jr. to John Sr., March 13, 1933, CA 35-07; see also telegrams of July 7, 8 and 11, 1933, CA 43-03.

25. "Summary of Syndicated Secured Credit for Cargill Elevator Company," undated, ca. May 1933; CA 43-03; "Cargill Elevator Company and the Chase National Bank of the City of New York, as managers, and others," agreement dated May 1, 1933, ibid.; John Peterson MS, "The Cargill story as I met it and helped it," CA; the commitment fee and custodian fee are specified in H. E. Scheuermann to Cargill Elevator Company, April 29, 1933, CA Lake 14; constraints of upper limit, John Jr. to Bert H. Lang, July 31, 1933, CA 33-06; the voting trust arrangements are documented in the Cargill Elevator Company minutes of May 1, 1933; see also John G. Peterson telegram to Chase National Bank, July 6, 1933, CA 43-03; J. E. Dorsey telex to New York office, July 8, 1933, ibid.

26. See "Report, Commission Department, July 1, 1926, to June 30, 1933," ca. 1934, CA; "Suggested Reorganization, Cash Grain Department, Cargill Commission Company," n.d. (ca. May 31, 1933), CA 41-11, Company Organization; *Cargill News*, November 1933.

27. John Jr. to Charles S. McCain, August 3, 1933, CA 43-03; McCain to John Jr., August 7, 1933, ibid.; John Peterson to John Jr., August 7 and 21, 1933, ibid.; John Jr. to E. H. Rawls, August 24, 1933, CA 33-06; Peterson to J. C. Rovensky, September 20, 1933, and to H. E. Scheuermann, September 29, 1933, CA 43-03.

28. John Jr. to Bert H. Lang, July 31, 1933, CA 33-06; "Coming to Cargill of John G. Peterson," John Work interview of Julius Hendel, n.d. (ca. 1959), CA.

29. Cargill MacMillan to John Jr., June 13 and 14, 1933, CA 43-03; "rumblings," Charles S. McCain to John G. Peterson, September 23, 1933, ibid.

30. John Jr. to James M. Sutherland, April 18, 1949, CA Lake 2.

11. *International Interests: Poland, Argentina, Russia (pp. 419–55)*

1. Samuel Rosenman, ed., *The Public Papers and Addresses of Franklin D. Roosevelt*, Vol. 2 (New York: Russell & Russell, 1969), pp. 11–15; William E. Leuchtenburg, *Franklin D. Roosevelt and the New Deal*, op. cit., p. 46.

2. George N. Peek and Hugh S. Johnson, *Equality for Agriculture* (Moline, Ill.: H. W. Harrington, 1922).

3. For details of the four AAA commodity programs, see Edwin G. Nourse, Joseph S. Davis and John D. Black, *Three Years of the Agricultural Adjustment Administration* (Washington: Brookings Institution, 1937); Henry I. Richards, *Cotton under the Agricultural Adjustment Act*, ibid., 1934; Joseph S. Davis, *Wheat and the AAA*, ibid., 1935; D. A. Fitzgerald, *Corn and Hogs under the AAA*, ibid., 1934. For an excellent discussion of the politics of the early days of the AAA, see Theodore Saloutos, *The American Farmer and the New Deal* (Ames: Iowa State University, 1982), pp. 34–97). Quotation on "piglets overran the stockyards," Leuchtenburg, *Franklin D. Roosevelt and the New Deal*, op. cit., p. 73; Henry Wallace on "full pigginess," *New Frontiers* (New York: Reynal & Hitchcock, 1934), p. 180.

4. For an excellent description of the July 19–20 wheat futures price break, see Joseph S. Davis, *Wheat and the AAA*, op. cit., pp. 205–19; the Henry Wallace statement on wheat supplies is in USDA Press Release No. 96–34, July 18, 1933; George Peek quotation from AAA Press Release No. 283–34, August 9, 1933; for comparison of industry attitudes before and after the price break, see Grain Committee on National Affairs newsletters of July 1, 15 and 22, 1933, CA 35-09; see also "A Message from President Booth to All Direct and Affiliated Members!" Grain and Feed Dealers National Association, July 27, 1933, ibid.; *Northwestern Miller*, July 19 and 26, 1933. For Grain Exchange Code, see AAA Press Release No. 2169–34, March 20, 1934; *Northwestern Miller*, September 13, 1933; wages and hour provisions of code, Grimes to C. F. McDonald, August 23, 1933, CA 35-09; "further delay a serious mistake," John Jr. to Grimes, telegram, September 6, 1933, ibid.; Kansas City Exchange objections, unnamed executive of Exchange to Grimes, telegram, September 7, 1933, ibid., and Grimes to Thomas K. Martin, telegram, September 8, 1933, ibid.; "unjust to Chicago," Grimes to Edgar Markham, October 5, 1933, ibid.; for quotation by Peter B. Carey, president of the CBOT, see 73rd Cong. 2nd sess., Hearing before House Committee on Agriculture on H.R. 8829, April 11, 1934, p. 86.

5. E. J. Grimes, "Which Way for Wheat Prices?", *The Magazine of Wall Street*, December 9, 1933, CA 35-07; John Sr. to Grimes, December 18, 1933, ibid.

6. "Executives . . . tired," John Sr. to John Jr., January 24, 1934, CA 34-04; lack of coordination among executives, Cargill MacMillan to John and Edna MacMillan, January 20, 1934, CA 36-01; appointment of sales manager, John Jr. to Grimes, January 20, 1934, CA 35-07; lunch room, John Sr. to John Jr., January 24, 1934, CA 34-04. For general discussion of employee welfare programs in the country, see Stuart D. Brandes, *American Welfare Capitalism, 1880–1940* (Chicago: University of Chicago Press, 1976).

7. Kidnapping menace, John Jr. to John and Edna MacMillan, February 5, 1934, CA 35-07.

8. Citizens Alliance of Minneapolis, *Special Weekly Bulletin No. 815*, August 31, 1934, CA 35-09.

9. John Sr. on Roosevelt, his letter to A. B. Dickinson, October 25, 1934, CA 33-06 DE.

10. Never engaging in export, John Sr. to David Block, July 15, 1927, CA 28-03, B; John Jr. views on opportunities in Europe and not "stirring up" competition, his letter to John Sr., June 17, 1929, CA 33-02; ethics abroad, John Jr. to C. C. Boden, June 9, 1930, CA 30-01; "perfect your Italian," John Jr. to Leonard Corlett, November 25, 1929, ibid.; "gradual" approach in Europe, John Jr. to Sir Herbert Robson, February 13, 1931, CA 32-02, S; "hazardous operation," John Sr. to E. H. Rawls, September 3, 1932, CA 33-02, G. For Bunge and Dreyfus competition, Horace J. W. Phillips to John Jr., April 12, 1932; John Jr. to Phillips, April 18, 1932; CA 32-02.

11. "Can you intimate to me," Siebel C. Harris to Ed Grimes, telegram, October 26, 1933; Grimes to Harris, October 26 and 27, 1933, CA 37-03; "trade likes our foreign rye," John Jr. to Grimes, January 30, 1934, ibid.; 5-cent profit, John Jr. to John and Edna MacMillan, February 5, 1934, ibid.; "encountered competition," John Jr. to John Sr., February 20, 1934, ibid. Alleged contamination of rye stored in Albany, see C. C. Boden to John Jr., wire, April 14,

1934, ibid.; proving malice, John Junell to James E. Dorsey, telegram, ibid.; on *New York Herald Tribune* action, C. Norman Stabler to C. C. Boden, telegrams, April 14 and 16, 1934, CA 35-06; decision by Secretary Henry Morgenthau, *Chicago Tribune*, April 13, 1934, CA 35-07; Cargill position on rye tariff, E. J. Grimes, "Brief Opposing the Increase in the Tariff on Rye," November 23, 1933, CA 35-07. "$10 million loss," *Northwestern Miller*, June 6, 1934; see also ibid., June 13, 1934, April 17, October 23 and 30, 1935.

12. "Personal liberty," John Sr. to H. S. Abbott, July 23, 1934, CA 33-06; "outlook . . . dark," John Jr. to P. S. Bush, September 19, 1934, CA 35-07.

13. 1934 drought effects, see Davis, *Wheat and the AAA*, op. cit., pp. 111–17; Leuchtenburg, *Franklin D. Roosevelt and the New Deal*, op. cit., pp. 172–73; R. Douglas Hurt, *Dust Bowl: The Southern Plains in the 1930s* (New York: Oxford University Press, 1979); ibid., *The Dust Bowl: An Agricultural and Social History* (Chicago: Nelson-Hall, 1981); Matthew Paul Bonnifield, *The Dust Bowl: Men, Dirt, and Depression* (Albuquerque: University of New Mexico Press, 1979). For description of Henry Wallace speech on "ever-normal granary," Saloutos, *The American Farmer and the New Deal*, op. cit., p. 203. See also Fitzgerald, *Livestock under the AAA*, op. cit., chap. 10. The overall agricultural results in this period are summarized in "The World Wheat Situation, 1934–35," *Wheat Studies* 12 (1935) 101; *New Yorker* quotation from March 6, 1989, issue; see also Michael Parfit, "The Dust Bowl," *Smithsonian*, June 1989.

14. Soil conservation efforts of the mid-1930s, Saloutos, *The American Farmer and the New Deal*, op. cit., pp. 192–207; "rattle-brained theorists," p. 199. Brookings Institution study's views on the "ever-normal granary," Nourse, Davis and Black, *Three Years of the Agricultural Adjustment Administration*, op. cit., chap. 15 and supplementary statement by Black.

15. Proposal for building Argentine elevators, John Jr. to Grimes, March 1, 1934, CA 35-07; plans for Argentina, England, Holland and Italy, ibid., May 4, 1934; no bribery, John Jr. to James W. Ringwald, June 4, 1934 (with attachments), CA 35-06; "tightening up regulations," Grimes to John Jr., July 14, 1934, ibid.; Hitler, June 28, 1934, ibid.

16. Criticism of Omaha terminal safety, John Jr. to Victor B. Smith, June 26, 1933, CA 35-06; John Jr. to Bert H. Lang, July 31, 1933, CA 33-06; Lang to John Jr., telegram, June 12, 1933, CA 43-03. Minneapolis dust explosion of June 8, 1934, *Cargill News*, July 1934; confirmation of Omaha explosion, Bert Lang to John Sr., telegram, and John Peterson to Lang, November 23, 1934, CA 43-03; "sympathy to you," Thomas W. Bowers to John Jr., December 1, 1934, and John Jr. to Bowers, December 3, 1934, CA 35-07; causes of explosion, Frank L. Neilson, "The Omaha Explosion," n.d., CA 35-11; the insurance report, by W. H. Laird of Marsh & McLennan, is dated December 10, 1934, ibid.; remedial suggestions, W. H. Laird to James Hayhoe, May 18, 1935, ibid.

17. Cargill MacMillan to John Jr., January 16, 1935, CA 45-02; ibid., January 19, 1935, CA 36-04; Cargill MacMillan to John Sr. and Edna MacMillan, January 26, February 9 and 19, 1935, CA 36-01; ibid., February 26, 1935, CA 34-04; John Jr. to John Sr., March 4, 1935, CA 36-04.

18. John Jr. insurance, Cargill MacMillan to John Jr., January 12, 1935, CA 35-07; ibid., January 23, 1935, CA 36-04; ibid., January 30, 1935, CA 45-02; Cargill MacMillan to John Sr. and Edna, February 19, 1935, CA 36-01; John Peterson to Cargill MacMillan, February 20, 1935, CA 40-03.

19. John Sr. illness, John Jr. to Cargill MacMillan, June 10, July 16 and 31, 1935, CA 36-04.

20. John Sr. to E. H. Rawls, September 26 and October 29, 1935, CA 39-02; ibid., to W. P. Conway, same date, ibid.; this archives file also contains the handwritten manuscripts; E. H. Rawls to John Sr., October 23, 1935, ibid.; W. P. Conway to John Sr., November 1, 1935, ibid.; John Jr. to H. M. Giles, July 15, 1935, CA 39-02, M; John Sr.'s diary confirms the relevant dates, CA 34-04; Rawls had advocated bankers' acceptances in November 1930, John Sr. to John Jr., November 18, 1930, CA Whitney MacMillan MS 7; John Peterson quotation on Guaranty Trust in "Banks, Men and Business," *Cargill's Business, A General Information Manual* . . . , Training Department (Gerald A. Joines, general editor), January 20, 1949, p. 474.

21. For an excellent analysis of the Soil Conservation and Domestic Allotment Act, see Theodore Saloutos, *The American Farmer and the New Deal*, op. cit., pp. 236–45.

22. Negotiations in Argentina, John Jr. to Cargill MacMillan, ca. February 1 and June 10,

1935, CA 45-02; Maxwell Upson to John Jr., February 26 and June 10, 1935, CA 36-03; J. W. Ringwald to John Jr., April 19 and May 22, 1935, ibid.; John Jr. to Upson, April 5, 1935, ibid.; John Jr. to Ringwald, May 13, 1935, ibid.; John Jr. to Ed Grimes, June 10, 1935, CA 36-04. Negotiations with Bunge North American Grain Corporation, John Jr. to Carlos Falk, July 17, 1935, ibid.; John Jr. to Ed Grimes, July 18, 1935, ibid.; "cut wide open," C. C. Boden to John Jr., wire, July 12, 1935, CA 36-03; termination of elevator project, Upson to John Jr., October 1, 1935, ibid.; John Jr. to Ringwald, October 29, 1935, ibid.; John Jr. to James C. Stewart, November 12, 1935, ibid.; John Jr. to Cargill MacMillan, January 25, 1936, CA 36-04; Ringwald to Frank Neilson, January 31, 1936, CA 35-12; Ringwald to John Jr. April 20, 1936, CA 36-03; John Jr. to D. L. Williams, September 23, 1936, ibid; Williams to John Jr., November 24, 1936, ibid. "Bring them to time," John Jr. to Grimes, July 18, 1935, CA 36-04. Statistics on Bunge y Born in Argentina from Carl E. Solberg, *The Prairies and the Pampas*, op. cit., pp. 67, 143; "sells . . . rope," Nick Butler, *The International Grain Trade: Problems and Prospects* (New York: St. Martin's Press, 1986), p. 104; on overall United States private investment in Argentina, Mira Wilkins, *The Maturing of Multinational Enterprise: American Business Abroad from 1914 to 1970* (Cambridge: Harvard University Press, 1974), passim.

23. The Russian proposal was outlined in John Jr. to B. M. Mishin, May 22, 1936; attached was memorandum on "The Cargill Design for Elevator Construction," CA 36-04. The country elevator proposal was elaborated in John Jr. to A. Y. Sokolov, July 9, 1936, ibid.; "tremendous strength," John Jr. to John Sr., March 24, 1937, CA 38-04.

24. John Jr.'s alfalfa feed project was first mentioned in his letter to Cargill MacMillan, January 25, 1936, CA 36-04. See also John Jr. to John Sr., February 18, 1936, ibid. For the early development of the Valier operation, see various letters between John Jr., Frank Neilson, R. W. Speer and Blaine Ferguson, February 24, 1936–July 31, 1937, CA 39-01.

25. Development of soybean futures contract, Chicago Board of Trade, *Report of the President, Seventy-Ninth Annual Report of the Trade and Commerce of Chicago* (Chicago: Lincoln Printing Company, 1937); *Northwestern Miller*, February 26, 1936. Cargill's role, John Peterson to Charles McCain, Jr., October 27, 1936, CA 43-03. See also Paul F. Larris, Richard T. Crowder, Reynold P. Dahl and Sarahelen Thompson, "Economics of Grain and Soybean Processing in the United States," in Chester O. McCorkle, Jr., ed., *Economics of Food Processing in the United States* (San Diego, Calif.: Academic Press, 1988), pp. 341–47.

26. "Humility," John Peterson to H. E. Scheuermann, April 28, 1936, CA 43-03; Bert Lang to Peterson, August 7, 1936, ibid.; closing Montreal office, John Jr. to B. J. Bolan, July 18, 1936, CA 36-03.

27. Quotation on drought, *Wheat Studies* 13 (December 1936): 108. Telegrams from Daniel MacMillan to the Company, July 17–August 18, 1936, are in CA 36-04. See also note 13.

28. Feed wheat issue, Cargill MacMillan to Ed Grimes, January 22, 1935, CA 37-03; Cargill MacMillan to John Sr. and Edna, January 26, 1935, CA 36-01; Herman Lakler to Commissioner of Customs, February 21, 1936, CA 37-03; Ed Grimes to Henry A. Wallace, September 3, 1936, ibid.; Wallace to Grimes, September 15, 1936, ibid.; Grimes to Lawrence Myers, October 26, 1936, ibid.; Grimes to G. W. Ashworth, October 26 and November 18, 1936, ibid.; J. H. Moyle to Grimes, November 27, 1936, ibid. See also *Northwestern Miller*, July 24 and October 30, 1935.

29. Private-trade dimensions of seed grain program, see Grain Committee on National Affairs memoranda of August 20 and 26, 1936, CA 37-02; Frank A. Theis to Grimes, August 22, 1936, CA 37-01. Formal announcement by Henry Wallace in press release, Office of Information, United States Department of Agriculture, September 16, 1936, ibid. See also *Northwestern Miller*, August 5, and 26 and November 26, 1936.

30. John Peterson to Scheuermann, September 4, 1936, CA 43-03; Peterson to J. N. Maxwell, September 23, 1936, ibid.; Peterson to Elliot T. Cooper, February 13, 1937, ibid.

31. "Mudraking," John Jr. to John Sr., February 24, 1936, CA 36-04. Federal Trade Commission query, Cargill MacMillan to Charles M. March, February 28, 1936, CA 45-02; Dutch company, see its first annual meeting minutes, July 15, 1936, CA 40-03 (this file also documents the establishment of the firm); for Guernsey trip, see Cargill MacMillan to John and Edna MacMillan, November 12, 1936, CA 34-04; "forced to move," Cargill MacMillan to James E. Dorsey, March 13, 1937, MS collection, Cargill MacMillan. The materials on the 1936 reorganization are voluminous; see, particularly, "Plan of Reorganization of Cargill Companies,"

October 2, 1936, CA 39-02 (a copy is in Cargill Elevator Company corporate minutes). The announcement to the stockholders is dated December 1, 1936, CA 39-11. John Sr. quotation on John Jr. assuming presidency in his letter to Harry M. Giles, December 7, 1936, CA 39-02.

12. The Great Battle with the Chicago Board of Trade (pp. 457–535)

1. Disclosing Albany stocks, William B. Bosworth to E. J. Grimes, July 19, 1932; Grimes to Bosworth, July 23, 1932; CA 33-08; distinguishing spreading from hedging, Fred Clutton to CBOT membership, November 2, 1932; Bosworth to Cargill Grain Company, November 12, 1932; Grimes to Bosworth, November 23 and December 21, 1932; ibid.; wires, John Jr. to Grimes (2), December 20, 1932, CA 33-01.

2. The membership provision of the CBOT is in its "Rules and Regulations," chap. 11, paragraph 313; this read as follows in the *Seventy-Seventh Annual Report of the Trade and Commerce of Chicago for the Year Ended December 31, 1934* (the 1934 CBOT annual report):

> *313. MEMBERSHIP IN CLEARING HOUSE.—The Clearing House may prescribe the qualifications of its own members. Corporations registered under Rule 226, which were members of the Clearing House on April 2, 1929, may be members of the Clearing House for the purpose of clearing commodities only. No partnership may be a member of the Clearing House unless it is registered under Rule 226, and unless two of its general partners are members of the Association. No person or firm shall become a member of the Clearing House until approved by the Board.

> *Amended November 7, 1929; to become effective January 1, 1930; postponed to April 1, 1930; postponed to October 1, 1930; amended September 22, 1930.

Cargill had not been a member on April 2, 1929, and therefore was excluded.

For the history of Cargill's efforts to obtain a Clearing House membership, see "Brief and Argument for and on Behalf of Cargill Elevator Company and Subsidiaries, including Cargill Grain Company and Cargill Warehouse Company," before the Secretary of Agriculture of the United States of America, Agricultural Adjustment Administration, National Recovery Administration, Docket No. C-298, June 1, 1935, CA 36-04; "Ed confident," John Jr. to John and Edna MacMillan, January 29, 1934, CA 35-07; "things look brighter" and "nobody working the other side," Philip Sayles to Grimes, wires, September 21, 1934; "out with an ax" and "its Cargill all over" and "rotten talk," wires, ibid., September 26, 1934, CA 35-08; "stirred up ill feeling," *Chicago Daily Tribune*, September 27, 1934, CA 37-03.

3. "Personal interest," Secretary's Correspondence, CBOT, AAA 5380, 261-10, CBOT Archives, Special Collections, University of Illinois, Chicago Library; 4–3 vote of the Code Authority, Edgar Markham to Fred Clutton, March 12, 1935, AAA 2506-233, ibid.; the testimony of the meeting of March 6, 1935, is in this same file.

4. For C. E. Huff quotation, *Northwestern Miller*, May 22, 1935; see also *Chicago Tribune*, May 16, 1935; *Chicago Journal of Commerce and LaSalle Street Journal*, May 17, 1935; "Code Body Finds Against Chicago Board of Trade," *The Co-op Kick-back*, Farmers National Grain Corporation, May 1935. The Cargill brief for the Code hearings (AAA Docket C-298) is dated June 1, 1935, CA 40-08; William E. Leuchtenburg, *Franklin D. Roosevelt and the New Deal*, op. cit., pp. 145, 170; Schechter Poultry Corp. v. U.S., 295 US 495.

5. Not advisable "to make any threats," undated letter (ca. July 7), CA 36-04; estimate of votes needed in undated telegram from "B.MP" to Grimes, ibid.; holding in abeyance FTC case, telex Grimes to John Jr., July 9, ibid. The amended Rule 313 now read: "A corporation may be a member of the Clearing House if two of its bona fide and active executive officers are members of the Board of Trade." Philip Sayles and John MacMillan, Sr., were such members; on October 4, 1935, John Sr.'s membership was transferred to John Jr., CA 40-05, CBT.

6. The Edward J. Grimes testimony in the hearings on the Grain Futures Act, April 20, 1935, was given on behalf of the Minneapolis Chamber of Commerce; see Law Dept. 190, "Commodity Exchange Act" file. "Horse racing," John Jr. to J. M. Mehl, June 4, 1935, CA 36-04. See also Ed Grimes to John Sr., June 15 and July 3, 1935, CA 36-04; John Sr. to Carl W. Jones, September 20, 1935, CA 39-02. For a brief description of the Cutten and Howell cases, see *Report of the Chief of the Grain Futures Administration, 1935*, August 31, 1935; William G.

Ferris, *The Grain Traders: The Story of the Chicago Board of Trade* (East Lansing: Michigan State University Press, 1988), pp. 166–98. The attitude of the grain trade industry is summarized in *Northwestern Miller*, February 13, 1935, p. 339.

7. Press release of Secretary of Agriculture Henry A. Wallace, August 17, 1935, ibid.

8. C. D. Sturtevant to Executive Committee, Grain Committee on National Affairs, September 3, 1935, CA 37-01; Minneapolis "extremely reluctant to relax," Grimes to Sturtevant, September 26, 1935, ibid.; "Chicago should be permitted," Sturtevant to Grimes, October 11, 1935, ibid.; "refuse representation," Grimes to Sturtevant, October 14, 1935, ibid.; "be advised," ibid., October 17, 1935; argument over CBOT hours, John Jr. to John Sr., February 28 and March 3, 1936, CA 36-03.

9. The new Commodity Exchange Act, signed by President Roosevelt on June 15, 1936, was implemented by the Secretary of Agriculture on June 27, 1936; see "Commodity Exchange Control Set in Motion," Office of Information, U.S. Department of Agriculture, June 27, 1936.

10. Grimes to John Jr., June 1, 1936, wire, CA 36-04.

11. "Chicago chairmanship," Edgar Markham to Grimes, May 27, 1936, CA 36-05; "incorporation should not be put off," Grimes to W. B. Lathrop, September 4, 1936, CA 37-01; "non-assessment organization," Grimes to J. V. Lauer, August 14, 1936, CA 37-02.

12. Rye to Rosenbaum, John MacMillan, Jr., to John Sr., April 23 and April 30, 1935, CA 36-04, Personal; *Northwestern Miller*, May 1, 1935.

13. "Dummy for Continental," John MacMillan, Jr., to Grimes, June 4, 1935, ibid.; Grimes to John Jr., June 12, 1935, CA 36-04, Grimes; negotiations on Rosenbaum terminal, John MacMillan, Jr., to Fred W. Sargent, June 7, 1935, CA 39-02, C; John Sr. to Cargill MacMillan, June 28, 1935, CA 39-02, Personal; John MacMillan, Jr., to Cargill MacMillan, July 24, 1935, CA 36-04, Personal. Arbitration case, Grimes to John MacMillan, Jr., August 30, 1935, ibid. For transferrence of CBOT membership, see John Jr. to Philip Sayles, August 22, 1935, ibid., and William B. Bosworth, Assistant Secretary, Chicago Board of Trade, to Weston B. Grimes, August 19, 1935, and Bosworth to John Jr., October 4, 1935; CA 40-05, CBT.

14. For earlier Daniel F. Rice relations, see E. J. Grimes to Rice, September 17, 1931, CA 32-06, R; on the warehouse grading difficulties, see Philip Sayles to John MacMillan, Jr., October 24, 1935, CA 36-04, Chicago; John Sr. to John Jr., January 3 and 10, 1936, CA 39-02. The Daniel Rice difficulties in loading out wheat are described in Directors Regular Meeting, CBOT, September 6, 1938, and letter from Rice to Kenneth Templeton, September 1, 1938, CBOT Archives, op. cit., 143 AAA 3527. See also correspondence between F. S. Lewis Company and Cargill, December 23, 24, 25, 1936, CA 36-05.

15. See "The World Wheat Situation, 1936–37," *Wheat Studies* 14 (December 1937): 103–157.

16. The first evidence of Cargill difficulty in the September 1936 corn futures contract is in John MacMillan, Jr., to Philip Sayles, August 10, 1936, CA 36-04, Chicago. The query from the Business Conduct Committee (BCC) on "speculative nature" is in D. B. Bagnell to John Jr., August 11, 1936, CA 40-05; John Jr. reply, ibid., August 13, 1936. The chronology of the September 1936 events are covered in detail in the subsequent CEA case (the case itself ruled on issues relating to the September 1937 corn futures contract but included extensive analyses of Cargill's role in the September and December 1936 corn contracts, as well as the December 1936 wheat contract): *Cargill, Incorporated, Complainant v. the Board of Trade of the City of Chicago, respondent,* CEA Docket No. 6, August 16, 1940. In the CEA's "Tentative Proposed Findings of Fact, Conclusions of Law and Order," April 3, 1940, there were additional CEA proposed findings of fact that were deleted by the Commission issuing the final decision and order (this commission was composed of the Secretary of Agriculture, the Secretary of Commerce and the Attorney General); all of these deletions were exceptions of Cargill, sustained by the Commission. See also the internal memorandum by Cargill lawyers entitled "The September, 1936 Corn Incident," n.d., CA 56-03. For minutes of Business Conduct Committee, September 25, 1936, see CBOT Archives, Archives Department, University of Illinois, Chicago campus, AAA 6076-3.

17. John MacMillan Jr. to J. W. T. Duvel, October 8, 1936, CA 36-04, G; on Argentine corn, Daniel F. Rice to Board of Directors, Board of Trade of the City of Chicago, November

26, 1936, CA 37-02; see also Rice concerns about wheat grading in William H. McDonald to "President and Directors" of the CBOT, August 24, 1936, CA 40-05.

18. Statistics on 1936 United States corn crop and chronology of the December corn and wheat futures contracts from *Cargill, Incorporated, Complainant...*, CEA Docket No. 6, op. cit. See paragraph 84, c, for John MacMillan, Jr., "declined to state." The order of the Business Conduct Committee is reprinted in 84, g; Cargill letter of December 12, 1937, is at 84, j; "willing seller [at] 9¢," paragraph 94. Cargill statements on case from internal memorandum, "The December, 1936 Corn Incident," op. cit., pp. 54ff. See also second memorandum, "The December, 1936 Wheat Incident," op. cit. There is also a detailed chronology of both December incidents by Weston B. Grimes, "Memorandum, Re: Chicago December (1936) Wheat and Corn Futures," December 18, 1936, CA 38-04, Chicago office; Weston B. Grimes memorandum, "Points to Be Considered Re Withdrawal from the Board of Trade of the City of Chicago," December 18, 1936, is in CA, 38-04, Chicago office. Quotation on "moral support" of Dr. Duvel, John Jr. to John Sr., telex, December 10, 1936, CA 36-04, Chicago; on withdrawing from CBOT, ibid., December 11, 1936; "tense situation," *Chicago Tribune*, December 19, 1936.

19. Cargill wires re election campaign, Philip Sayles to Grimes, December 26 and 31, 1936, CA 37-02, Chicago; comments on results and influence of "the machine" in two wires, Sayles to Grimes, on January 5, 1937, ibid. The results were reported to the CBOT membership in its "Monthly Letter," January 15, 1937; quotation on "explicable" from "Proposed Findings of Fact and Conclusions of Law Submitted by Respondent," *Cargill, Incorporated v. the Board of Trade of the City of Chicago*, CEA Docket No. 6, p. 37.

20. Oats position discussed in Cargill MacMillan to John Sr., January 21, 1937, and J. W. T. Duvel to Grimes, January 19, 1937; CA 38-04, Personal. The Cargill MacMillan decisions discussed in his letter to John Jr., January 29, 1937, ibid.

21. Cargill MacMillan to John Jr., February 13, 1937, ibid.

22. For Daniel Rice side of oats controversy, Board of Directors Regular Meeting, September 9, 1938 (attached letter from Rice to Kenneth Templeton, dated September 1, 1938), CBOT Archives, 143 AAA 3527, op. cit. Quotation on shipping, Daniel F. Rice to Board of Directors, CBOT, September 17, 1937, CBOT Archives, AAA 5380, 261-5. The Cargill charge and its withdrawal in Secretary's Correspondence, Chicago Board of Trade, CBOT Archives, AAA 5380, 261-5. Letter concerning rumors, John Jr. to Kenneth Templeton, May 7, 1937, CA 40-05, CBT. On conference with Dr. Duvel, John Jr. to John Sr., April 2, 1937, CA 38-05, Personal.

23. Statistics on 1937 corn crop, *Cargill, Incorporated, Complainant...*, CEA Docket No. 6, op. cit., paragraphs 121–31. See also *Wheat Studies* 14 (December 1937): 103–13.

24. Rice does not "expect to cover," telex from "FV UJ" to Julius Hendel, May 28, 1937, CA 38-07, U. "Beating down... price," Cargill internal memorandum, "The September 1937 Corn Incident," n.d., Law Department 207, p. 64; "clever, though unscrupulous," ibid., p. 72; syndicated Associated Press article from *Minneapolis Tribune*, August 21, 1937.

25. Telex examples from "The September 1937 Corn Incident," op. cit., pp. 39–43. The entire McDonald Committee testimony has been preserved verbatim in CBOT Archives, AAA 6061, 6071, 6073, 6074, 6076, 6078, 6080, 6081, op. cit; Albert Williams testimony, AAA 6073-3; Alex Moore, AAA 6076-6; Harold Spinney, AAA 6073-7; "idle gossip and rumor," AAA 6076-10.

26. The Uhlmann and Continental contracts are elaborated in detail in *Cargill, Incorporated, Complainant...*, CEA Docket No. 6, op. cit., paragraphs 117–20.

27. The minutes of the Business Conduct Committee for this period have been preserved verbatim in CBOT Archives, AAA 6061-5 (second copy at AAA 5855-8). The Cargill brief sent to the Business Conduct Committee, dated September 4, 1937, and signed by John MacMillan, Jr., apparently did not have a title page; it was mimeographed and contained 47 pages, with additional charts; see Law Department 206. The subsequent action of the Committee is recorded in "Decision of the Business Conduct Committee of the Chicago Board of Trade on the September Corn Situation," September 16, 1937, CA, 38-04. John MacMillan, Jr., testimony before Business Conduct Committee on September 2, 1937, CBOT Archives, op. cit.

28. Wire messages in *Cargill, Incorporated, Complainant...*, CEA Docket #6, op. cit.,

paragraphs 133, 135. Quotations on Cargill strategy in paragraph 134. Frank Jost testimony, CBOT Archives, AAA 6073–6. See also 6074–2 and 6076–4 for Daniel Rice research file on crop conditions in the summer of 1937 and the field reports of Frank Jost.

29. For chronology of events in this period, September 1–22, see *Cargill, Incorporated, Complainant . . .* , CEA Docket No. 6, op. cit., paragraph 158; for Cargill's percentage of open interest, see paragraph 119; the Business Conduct Committee decision of September 16, 1937, is in 158, l; their September 21 letter is in 158, p; Cargill's reply is in this section; the September 22 late-night meeting is in 158, q. The Cargill comments on the reported Duvel call on September 18 are in "The September 1937 Corn Incident," op. cit., p. 161. The Sayles account of the late-night meeting is in CA, Law Department 207. See also *Wall Street Journal* comments from its issue of September 20, 1937. Sayles comments on September 23 meetings in internal memorandum of that date; see CA, Law Department 207. For the September 20, 1937, meeting between Ed Grimes and Dr. Duvel, see "The September 1937 Corn Incident," op. cit., pp. 165–73; Richard Uhlmann comments on BCC membership in his letter to Kenneth Templeton, November 18, 1937, in Directors Meeting of November 23, 1937, CBOT Archives, AAA 3591; the BCC version of the September 22 meeting with Ellis and Sayles, CBOT Archives, AAA 6061–5; see also quotation about shorts "being babied," *Chicago Daily News*, September 18, 1937. The CBOT notice about the shorts was in a memorandum from William B. Bosworth to the CBOT membership, dated September 15, 1937, CA 40-05.

30. On Uhlmann Grain Company decision to terminate arrangements with Cargill, see McDonald Committee report of January 31, 1938, op. cit., and the Grimes memorandum on his testimony before them, "Memorandum of Meeting with the McDonald Committee of the Chicago Board of Trade, held in Chicago at 2 o'clock P.M. Thursday, January 6, 1938," CA 38-04, CBOT. Quotation from internal memorandum, CA Law Department 206. Fred Uhlmann quotation from CBOT Archives, AAA 6061–5. For question of whether Duvel ordered this market closed, see "Notes of Meeting of February 18, 1938," CBOT Archives, AAA 6061–9.

31. Quotation on enabling shorts to buy in corn pit in Cargill's brief, "Suggestions and Exceptions of Complainant to Tentative Proposed Findings of Fact and Conclusions of Law of the Referee" in *Cargill, Incorporated Complainant . . .* , CEA Docket No. 6, op. cit., p. 136. Quotation on Cargill's strategy from McDonald Committee report, January 31, 1938, op. cit.; on "loading newspaper," Weston Grimes to John Jr., telex, September 29, 1937, CA 40-03; on members "indignant," Philip Sayles to John Jr., telex, September 27, 1937, CA 45-02.

32. "Immensely puzzled," John MacMillan, Jr., to Charles T. Peavey, September 29, 1937, CA 38-05, P; memorandum on proposed investigation, n.d., is at CA 38-05, L; John Jr. comments on Thomas Howell from the trial record in CEA No. 6, 3561; his comments on Chinese and British role in his handwritten manuscript, ca. December 1938, W. Duncan MacMillan MS collection.

33. Philip Sayles comments on the appointment of the McDonald Committee in his letter to E. J. Grimes, October 15, 1937, CA 38-06, Chicago office. The Wood Committee was constituted on October 14, 1937, and its final report was dated November 16, 1937, CA 38-04, CBT correspondence. A draft of the Cargill brief to the Committee, dated October 27, 1937, is in CA, Law Department 206. The McDonald Committee was constituted October 15, 1937; its final report was dated March 25, 1938. The exchange of telegrams between W. H. McDonald and John MacMillan, Jr., is in CA 38-07, CBT correspondence. Dow Jones ticker announcement in CA 38-06, Chicago office. Report on Earle English visit to Minneapolis in CBOT Archives, AAA 6076–11 and AAA 6080–4.

34. Commodity Exchange Authority, "Matter of Limits on Position and Daily Trading in Grain for Future Delivery, Hearing Docket CEA #3," Chicago, December 1, 1937. John MacMillan, Jr., quotations, Vol. 1, pp. 41, 58–59; C. D. Sturtevant quotation, ibid., Vol. 2, pp. 22–23. The "proposed order," under signature of Henry A. Wallace, is dated June 13, 1938; Cargill filed exceptions to this order, "Suggestions of Cargill, Incorporated regarding 'Proposed Order in the Matter of Limits . . . ,' " taking issue particularly with the proposed exemption to manufacturers and processors. John MacMillan, Jr.'s testimony was reprinted in full in the *Cargill Crop Bulletin*, December 23, 1937, pp. 12–16. Weston Grimes telegram to Sayles is dated November 15, 1937, CA 38-06, Chicago office. John Jr. telegram to Sayles, November 18, 1937, CA 38-04; comments on limits, J. W. T. Duvel to John Jr., December 3,

1936, CA 36-04; John Jr. to Duvel, ibid; Chicago symposium citation in chapter 17, note 16.

35. "Avoid compounding the offense," telex, John Peterson to John Jr., November 19, 1937, CA 39-02; "cite Call Rule," telex, John Jr. to Weston Grimes, December 9, 1937, CA 38-04; Fred and Richard Uhlmann testimony to McDonald Committee re John Jr., CBOT Archives, AAA 6073-1.

36. Cargill's version of the meeting is described in "The September 1937 Corn Incident," op. cit., pp. 89–94, and in Ed Grimes, "Memorandum of Meeting with the McDonald Committee of the Chicago Board of Trade, Held in Chicago at 2 o'clock P.M. Thursday, January 6, 1938," January 11, 1938, CA 38-04, CBOT correspondence. The "McDonald Committee" report was to the CBOT, dated January 31, 1938, and transmitted to Cargill on February 1, 1938, CA, ibid. The J. W. T. Duvel letter to the McDonald Committee was dated January 24, 1938, CBOT Archives AAA 6062-9; a copy was also sent to Grimes, "The September 1937 Corn Incident," op. cit., p. 92; Duvel telephone call of September 18, Kenneth S. Templeton to officers and directors of the CBOT, ca. December 1938, CBOT Archives, AAA 6086-24.

37. The Committee charges, addressed to the board of directors of the CBOT on January 31, 1938, were forwarded to Cargill on February 1, 1938, CA 38-04, CBOT correspondence. On conciliation, John Peterson to Kenneth Templeton, January 31, 1938, and attached memorandum re "olive branch," CA 43-03. Cargill press release on McDonald Committee charges in Cargill MacMillan to John Jr., February 2, 1938, CA 38-04; public announcement of the institution of Cargill's CEA charge, dated February 26, 1938, is in CA 38-06, Chicago office. The text of this charge can be found in *Cargill, Incorporated Complainant . . .*, CEA Docket No. 6, op. cit., p. 1; "pussy-footing," John Jr. to Cargill MacMillan, "Feb. 38," MS collection, Cargill MacMillan; "horror," John Sr. to Cargill MacMillan, February 10, 1938, ibid.; "fight to the finish," ibid., February 5, 1938, "despondency," John Jr. to Cargill MacMillan, February 11, 1938, ibid.

38. Income tax audit, Cargill MacMillan to Irving Goldsmith, February 15, 1938, CA 43-05; Cargill's financial strength, John Peterson to Business Conduct Committee, February 28, 1938, CA 43-03-21. Letter on arbitration, E. L. Rickel Grain Company to Cargill Grain Company, February 8, 1938, CA 45-03.

39. Cargill's refusal to testify before the board of directors of the CBOT in John MacMillan, Jr., to Kenneth S. Templeton, March 1, 1938, CA 38-04, CBOT; quotations on the issue in "Address of Retiring President Kenneth S. Templeton," *Eighty-First Annual Report of the Trade and Commerce of Chicago for the Year Ended December 31, 1938*, Chicago Board of Trade, 1939, pp. xx–xxi; quotation on "Richard Whitney scandal," John MacMillan, Jr., to John Sr., March 18, 1938, CA 38-04, Personal; on Duvel "escape," Howard W. Vesey to Howard Ellis, March 10, 1938, CBOT Archives, AAA 6077-19; *Chicago Daily News* quotation from its issue of June 8, 1938; *Time* magazine article in its issue of April 4, 1938. Cargill statement on expulsion is reprinted in full in *Cargill News*, March 1938, pp. 2–3; on worries about credit, John MacMillan, Jr., to John Peterson, March 28 and April 1, 1938, CA 38-04, Personal; map of new transportation routes, dated March 30, 1938, in CA 38-07, Traffic Department.

40. The so-called call rule provisions read as follows, from Eightieth Annual Report . . . Chicago Board of Trade, 1937 (Chicago: Lincoln Printing Company, 1932), pp. 316–17:

    331. GRAIN TO ARRIVE.—The Board shall maintain a desk in the Exchange Hall in charge of a reporter, to whom, during regular trading hours, bids may be submitted to buy grain to arrive. Members desiring to buy grain to arrive during such hours must submit bids to the reporter, who shall immediately post on a blackboard the highest bids submitted. All bids shall specify the kind of grain, the billing, the grade, the price, and the time of shipment. The posting of a higher bid cancels all lower bids for the same grade of the same grain for the same shipment. Unaccepted bids may be withdrawn by notice to the reporter and shall promptly be erased from the blackboard. The highest unwithdrawn bid constitutes an open offer to buy, which may be accepted by any other member who may compel the bidder to take at least one carload. The last posted and unwithdrawn bids at the close of the regular market shall constitute the closing prices of the day for the particular grades, billing, and shipments specified in such bids.

    332. BIDS DURING THE SESSION.—During the session, members are prohibited from bidding the country for wheat, corn, rye, oats and soy beans to arrive at prices in excess of

the last posted prices less the following minimum charges; on purchases from non-members, 1% with minimum charges of 1½¢ per bushel on wheat, 1¢ per bushel on corn, rye and soy beans, ¾¢ per bushel on oats: on purchases from members ¾ of one per cent, with minimum charges of 1¢ per bushel on wheat, ¾¢ per bushel on corn, rye, and soy beans, and ½¢ per bushel on oats.

333. BIDS AFTER SESSION.—After the session, members are prohibited from bidding the country for grain to arrive at prices in excess of the closing price of the day less the minimum charges above specified, except as follows: a member having a bona fide bid from a buyer in Chicago in excess of any closing price may bid the country such bid price less the regular charges. A member who has made bona fide bids to not less than five members in the cash grain business in excess of any closing price may bid the country the price named in such bids less the regular charges. Members thus bidding in excess of any closing price must file with the Secretary before 8:00 A.M. of the following day, a statement showing the prices at which they bid the country and the facts justifying such bids under this Rule.

The "call rule" of the Chicago Board of Trade was validated in the Supreme Court case, *Board of Trade of City of Chicago, et al. v. United States,* March 4, 1918, 246 U.S. 231; Justice Louis D. Brandeis wrote the majority opinion; quotation on "traders . . . at a loss," *Chicago Herald and Examiner,* April 2, 1938, CA, Law Department 206; telexes on rate, July 7, 8, 1938, CA 39-03, Chicago office; "hoodoo," John Jr. to John Sr., April 1, 1938, CA 34-04.

41. *Time* magazine articles on Farmers National Grain Corporation in the issues of October 4, 1937, and February 7, 1938.

42. Quotation on Secretary Roper's comments, J. M. Barker to John MacMillan, Sr., June 9, 1938, CA 39-02, B.

43. John MacMillan, Jr., to Henry A. Wallace, May 17, 1938; Wallace to John Jr., June 4, 1938; CA 38-05, VW; John MacMillan, Sr., to J. W. T. Duvel, August 22, 1938, CA 38-04, CBT; *Time* article on "tipsters," August 15, 1938; John Jr. to John Sr., ca. November 28, 1938, CA 39-02; "Getting all the breaks," John Jr. to Mrs. John MacMillan, Jr., November 29, 1938, CA 39-02; John Jr.'s stamina, John Sr. to John Jr., November 30 and December 1, 1938, ibid.; "front page of the *Wall Street Journal*," John Sr. to Sumner B. Young, December 2, 1938, ibid.; John Jr.'s testimony, Young to John Sr., December 8, 1938, ibid.; "magnificent performance," Young to Leo Sheehan, December 13, 1938, ibid.; "ruff treatment," John Jr. to John Sr., telex, December 13, 1938, ibid.; "fear and trepidation" and "constant slurs," trial testimony, CEA Docket No. 6, 567, 573, 589. Testimony on "logical" hedging, CEA No. 6, op. cit., 3297–3302; on corners and squeezes, 3365–3384.

44. "Cargill are through," Sayles to Grimes, telex, December 27, 1938, ibid.; Dow Jones announcement, ibid.; earlier CEA inquiry, John Jr. to J. W. T. Duvel, October 28, 1938, CA 38-04. Pencil comment on *Chicago Daily News* article of December 28, 1938, CBOT Archives, AAA 6071–8; "behind the 8-ball," ibid, AAA 6034–1.

45. Sumner B. Young to John Sr., January 7, 1939.

46. Dow Jones ticker tape on Templeton statement, dated January 16, 1939, is in CA 38-04; John Peterson on "short jabs" in his letter to John Jr., January 18, 1939, ibid.; John Sr. concern, his letter to John Jr., January 16, 1939, CA 45-08; John Jr. preoccupation, Cargill MacMillan to John and Edna MacMillan, February 27, 1939, CA 45-01; *Cargill Crop Bulletin* article, "Trial of the Board of Trade of the City of Chicago," February 8, 1939, CA 38-05; on testimony re *Crop Bulletin,* Hayes Miller to John Sr., March 2, 1939, ibid.

47. Legislative efforts, John Jr. to Weston Grimes, January 30 and to Irving Goldsmith, January 31, 1939; Weston Grimes telex to John Jr., February 2, 1939; CA 38-04. The representative was Usher Lloyd Burdick of North Dakota; the bill was H.R. 25, on investigating short selling.

48. "Precarious condition" of CBOT, John Jr. to John Sr., February 17, 1939; "Wallace . . . Presidential Bee," ibid., February 20, 1939; CA 38-04.

49. "Risks involved," Cargill MacMillan to John and Edna MacMillan, March 22, 1939, CA 45-01; "apt to disturb," John Sr. to Cargill MacMillan, March 24, 1939, MS collection Cargill MacMillan.

50. Duvel testimony, John Jr. to John Sr., April 1 and 4, 1939, CA 38-04. Headline on Duvel from *Chicago Daily News,* March 30, 1939.

51. "Drama of Corn" quotations from unnamed Chicago newspaper, May 3,-1939, clippings in CA 38-05; Professor Roland Vaile testimony, John Jr. to Cargill MacMillan, April 10, 1939, CA 38-04; see also clippings file for April 26, 1939, CA 38-05; *Chicago American*, May 15, 1939; the CEA ruling on inclusion of the Vaile testimony is in *Cargill, Incorporated, Complainant* . . . , CEA Docket No. 6, op. cit., and in "Tentative Proposed Findings of Fact, Conclusions of Law and Order," p. 7.

52. Wheat "squeeze" of May 1939, clippings file, CA 38-05; *Business Week* quotation from its issue of May 27, 1939; John Jr. memorandum on publicity, June 5, 1939, CA 40-06; turning down article, Leo Sheehan to Philip Sayles, June 7, 1939, CA 38-04; on gift of stock, John Sr. to Sumner B. Young, June 30, 1939, CA 45-08.

53. Daniel Rice complaint on Cargill's Northwestern terminal in letter to John G. McCarthy, president of the CBOT, June 20, 1939, CBOT Archives, AAA 3584–16; dismissal of case, *Minneapolis Star*, June 1, 1939; *Chicago Daily News*, June 6, 1939; *Chicago Tribune*, August 10, 1939; Hayes Miller to John Sr., August 9, 1939, CA 40-06. Statement on condition of Cargill corn in the Chicago elevator, H. S. Yohe to Fred H. Clutton, July 6, 1939, CA 40-06; on "capitalizing," John Jr. to Sumner B. Young, June 30, 1939, CA 40-03.

54. The record of testimony in CEA Docket No. 11 can be found in CBOT Archives, AAA 5960, 5970–5973; quotation on stipulation from "Re Requested Stipulation that Cargill's December Corn Transactions Occurred Mainly in the Pit," February 12, 1940, Law Department 158; quotation on wash sales, Julius Hendel to L. R. Barker, August 14, 1939, CA 40-06; on "no barbs," Fred Clutton to Earle English, January 11, 1940, ibid., AAA 5407. The final order on *Secretary of Agriculture, Complainant vs. Cargill, Inc., Cargill Grain Company of Illinois, John H. MacMillan, Jr., E. J. Grimes, Julius Hendel and Philip C. Sayles, Respondents*, CEA Docket No. 11, i, dated March 7, 1940; see James E. Dorsey to John Sr., March 7, 1940, CA 40-06; the *Chicago Tribune* article mentioning John Jr. is of the same date; for Cargill decision to forgo trial, see Cargill MacMillan to John Jr., cablegrams, February 12, 15, 16 and 20 and March 1, 1940, CA 40-06. The Minneapolis Chamber of Commerce decision to bar John Jr. is dated March 12, 1940; "singled out . . . honor of family . . . to bitter end," John Sr. to Cargill MacMillan, February 2, 5 and 9, 1940, MS collection, Cargill MacMillan; "goat . . . peace of mind," John Jr. to Cargill MacMillan, January 31 and February 12, 1940, ibid.

55. Return to CBOT, Kenneth S. Templeton to John Jr., November 4, 1940, CA 40-06; "get out of jail," telex, John Jr. to Weston Grimes, December 10, 1941, and letter of March 31, 1941, CA 43-05; the CEA order reinstating John Jr. is dated June 25, 1942; the Weston Grimes comments are in his letter to Cargill MacMillan, June 24, 1942, W. Duncan MacMillan manuscript collection; refusal to accept CEA order, John Jr. to Secretary of Agriculture, July 9, 1942, CA 43-04.

56. Quotations on John MacMillan, Jr., and Daniel Rice from "The Grain Traders," *Fortune*, August 1949. Testimony by Fred and Richard Uhlmann in McDonald Committee hearings in CBOT Archives, AAA 6073–1; on Daniel Rice, Jonathan R. Laing, "Still Full of Beans," *Barron's*, April 30, 1990.

57. Alonzo Taylor, "Speculation, Short Selling, and the Price of Wheat," *Wheat Studies* 7 (1930–31): 231; for stereotypes of the "bull" and the "bear," see Cedric B. Cowing, "Market Speculation in the Muckraker Era: The Popular Reaction," *Business History Review* 31 (1957): 403; *Business Week* quotation from its issue of April 16, 1949; Minneapolis Chamber of Commerce open interest figures from Thomas Totushek memorandum, August 21, 1939, Law Dept. 158; daily closing prices on corn futures in the Minneapolis Exchange in *Fifty-sixth Annual Report of the Chamber of Commerce, Minneapolis, Minn.*, December 1938; on bigness, Ed Grimes to John Jr., May 24, 1939, CA 40-06; on bigness, Ed Grimes to John Jr., May 24, 1939, CA 40-06.

58. "Combined Expense, Board of Trade and CEA Cases, to June 30, 1940, CA 45-03; poem excerpt from manuscript collection, John MacMillan, Jr., December 1, 1945.

13. *Transportation in the 1930s (pp. 536–71)*

1. Dedication of Albany deep-water port, see "The Port of Albany, Dedicated June 6 and 7, 1932," Commercial Bank of Albany, CA 35-07; quotations from Franklin D. Roosevelt speech, *New York Times*, June 8 and 9, 1932.

2. *Montreal Gazette*, June 13, 1932, CA 35-07.

3. Corps of Engineers, U.S. Army, War Department, *Transportation on the Great Lakes*, rev. ed. (Washington, D.C.: Government Printing Office, 1937), pp. 92–93, 183; Charles Hadfield, *World Canals: Inland Navigation Past and Present* (New York: Facts on File Publications, 1986), pp. 357–58.

4. "Trihey Denies Albany Threat," undated newspaper fragment, ca. June 14, 1932, CA 35-07.

5. Ed Grimes speech at Twenty-third Annual Convention, New York State Waterways Association, Buffalo, N.Y., September 19, 1932, CA 33-01; John Sr. to C. T. Jaffray, August 15, 1932, CA 33-03; for West Coast shipping, see D. W. Meinig, *The Great Columbia Plain: A Historical Geography, 1805–1910* (Seattle: University of Washington Press, 1968); ibid., *On the Margins of the Good Earth: The South Australian Wheat Frontier, 1869–1884* (Adelaide: Rigby, 1970); Albro Martin, *James J. Hill and the Opening of the Northwest* (St. Paul: Minnesota Historical Society Press, 1991).

6. *Report of the Federal Trade Commission on the Grain Trade*, Vol. 4, op. cit., September 26, 1923, pp. 81–82.

7. For an excellent summary of the ten-month rule, see Ed Grimes to Thomas W. Page (who was chairman of the Committee for Reciprocity, U.S. Tariff Commission), April 10, 1935, CA 36-04.

8. "Projected Waterways in North America as Related to Export of Wheat," *Wheat Studies* 8 (August 1932): 452.

9. The Commonwealth preference is discussed in D. A. MacGibbon, *The Canadian Grain Trade, 1931–1951* (Toronto: University of Toronto Press, 1952), pp. 17–32; "British Preference for Empire Wheat," *Wheat Studies* 10 (October 1933): 1–33. See also V. D. Wickizer, "Shipping and Freight Rates in the Overseas Grain Trade," ibid., 15 (October 1938): 49–120; "Canadian Wheat Stabilization Operations, 1929–1935," ibid., 12 (March 1936): 249–72.

10. "Ex-Lake Grain to North Atlantic Ports," 235 I.C.C. 415, *Decisions* Docket 4618 (November 25, 1939), p. 418.

11. On 1¾-cent rate, Grimes to D. Sullivan & Co., May 26, 1932, CA 35-08; 235 I.C.C. 415, op. cit, p. 420; J. L. Bolus to Ed Grimes (with attachment), December 21, 1932, CA 33-08; John Jr. to B. J. Bolan, February 21, 1933, CA 35-06.

12. "Hudson River . . . boom," John Jr. to R. G. Narelle, April 30, 1932 CA 32-02; "outrageous . . . proposal," John Jr. to Peter G. Ten Eyck, December 9, 1931, CA 32-03; comparison of trucks, E. J. Grimes to J. P. Dervin, April 28, 1933, CA 33-01; "discouraged about . . . rates," Grimes to F. B. McGrath, February 11, 1933, CA 33-01.

13. John Jr. to John Sr., March 10, 1933, CA 34-04.

14. *Albany Evening News*, February 3, 1933; M. V. Beckstedt to Grimes, February 7, 1933; Grimes to Beckstedt, February 11, 1933; CA 33-07; Grimes to Dervin, June 22, 1933, CA 33-07.

15. Grimes to Beckstedt, June 1, 1933, ibid.

16. "Ex-Lake Grain from Ogdensburg to New England," 208 I.C.C. 385, Docket 4017 (March 28, 1935); *City of Oswego, N.Y. v. Baltimore & Ohio Railroad Co., et al.*, 146 I.C.C. 293, Docket 17837 (July 3, 1928).

17. 209 I.C.C. 500, Docket 4017 (June 25, 1935).

18. John MacMillan, Sr., to J. L. Record, October 21, 1920, CA 24-02; John Jr. to Peter G. Ten Eyck, May 23, 1932, CA 35-07; John Jr. to Sen. Hiram Bingham, August 3, 1932, CA 32-03; John Sr. to J. Adam Bede, November 25, 1930, CA 33-02; John Sr. to Sen. William E. Borah, November 10, 1932, CA 35-07; on saving ¼ cent, Corps of Engineers, *Transportation on the Great Lakes*, op. cit., p. 115. See also *Cargill News*, November 1932; "conscientiously opposed," John Jr. to Marcus Marshall, March 24, 1936, CA 36-05.

19. Ed Grimes to Harold O. Hunt, May 28, 1932, CA 32-06.

20. Trucking effects on country elevators, *Minneapolis Journal*, November 7, 1932; John Jr. to John E. Bierwirth, October 17, 1935, CA 36-03.

21. J. J. Shonhart to Grimes, January 31, 1935, CA 35-09, Grimes to Mark Marshall, May 27, 1936, CA 36-05.

22. "Unable to build," John Jr. to Peter G. Ten Eyck, March 21 and 24, 1932, CA 32-03; "competitor elevator," John Jr. to John Sr., April 4, 1932, ibid.; "block expansion," John Jr. to D. D. LaDu, April 10, 1935, CA 36-04.

23. "Very inexpensive house," John Jr. to Ed Grimes, April 15, 1935, CA 36-04; "18 plants," John Jr. to John Sr., ibid.; "larger than a country elevator," John Jr. to John E. Bierwirth, October 17, 1935, CA 36-03.

24. Corps of Engineers, U.S. Army, *Transportation on the Great Lakes*, op. cit., p. 183.

25. Ibid., pp. 181–82.

26. John Jr. to Bierwirth, October 17, 1935, op. cit.

27. Boston terminal project, John Sr. to Harvey C. Miller, August 7, 1934, and Frank Neilson correspondence with Miller and Arthur B. Hayward, CA 35-13; see also Commonwealth of Massachusetts, "Special Report of the Department of Public Works and the Boston Port Authority Relative to the Adequacy of Terminal Facilities and to the Construction of a Modern Grain Elevator," December 3, 1930, House of Representatives Document 171 (1931). The Boston *Evening Transcript*, October 4, 1934, comments on the project. Newark proposal, Weston Grimes to John Jr., September 24, 1935, CA 36-04; Ed Grimes to John Jr., September 24, 1935, CA 36-05; various undated memoranda regarding negotiations with Horace K. Corbin, conducted by Grimes and Frank Neilson, CA 35-13 and 37-01; John Jr. to John Sr., February 24, 1936, CA 36-04. Providence proposal, John Jr. to Mayor S. Frank Nolan, November 15, 1935; and reply by telegram, December 4, 1935, CA 36-03. Philadelphia proposal, correspondence between Frank Neilson and Messrs. C. C. Boden, Weston Grimes and Fred Drum, CA 35-13.

28. Negotiations on the Great Eastern (and also the Dakota) Elevator, Ed Grimes to John Jr., October 10, 1936, CA 37-01; John Jr. to Cargill MacMillan, November 30, 1936, CA 36-04; George R. Basler to Frank Neilson, December 14, 1936, CA 35-12; A. F. Benny to Cargill Grain Company, November 27, 1936, CA 37-02. *Cargill News*, April 1933 for Saskatchewan Pool lease; ibid., August and November 1937, for Great Eastern.

29. Early negotiations on St. Louis, W. T. Brooking to John Jr., telegram, March 15, 1935, CA 36-04; John Jr. to Bernard F. Dickmann, May 29, 1935, CA 36-03; John Jr. to Bert H. Lang, June 3, 1935, ibid.; John Jr. to Cargill MacMillan, June 10, 1935, CA 36-04; Lang to John Sr., June 21, 1935, CA 39-02; William M. Spann to John Jr., October 2, 1935, ibid.; John Jr. to P. G. Palmer, October 4, 1935, ibid. Memphis terminal, see Frank Neilson–Memphis Harbor Commission correspondence, July 11, 1935–May 12, 1937, CA 35-11. Backhaul problem, Grimes to J. E. Zednicheck, August 21, 1936, CA 37-02.

30. Paul E. Sweeney, "Locational Economics and the Grain Trade and Flour Milling Industry of Buffalo," Ph.D. dissertation, University of Buffalo, 1942, p. 371.

31. "Cheap way," John Jr. to E. T. Pettersen, April 17, 1935, CA 36-03; Pettersen to John Jr., April 22, July 24 and October 17, 1935, ibid.; on Japanese, John Peterson to Pettersen, August 14, 1936, CA 43-03.

32. John Sr. to Edna MacMillan, May 18 and 21, June 5, 1907, MS collection, W. Duncan MacMillan.

33. Availability of lake steamers, John Jr. to John Sr., March 25, 1935, CA 36-04; John Sr. to O. L. Carlton, June 26, 1935, CA 39-02; renovation costs discussed in John Jr. to John Sr., April 30, 1935, CA 36-04. On purchase of SS *Mayan*, John Jr. to Cargill MacMillan, September 25, 1935, CA 40-03; difficulties with harbor drafts, Weston Grimes to John Jr., November 4, 1935, CA 36-04. See also *Cargill News*, December 1935, January and March 1936; "crucified," Cargill MacMillan to John Jr., February 13, 1937, CA 45-02.

34. "Travel on the Erie Canal," *Cargill News*, June 1937; see also "Fifteen Miles on the Erie Canal," ibid., July 1937.

35. "Cargill Grain Barges," *Cargill News*, December 1939; "'Carneida' type Erie Canal Equipment," internal memorandum (John Jr.?), November 28, 1940, CA 43-05; "sardine fleet," John Jr. to Ed Grimes, May 26, 1939, CA 38-04.

36. Towboat decision, John Sr. to John Jr., January 16, 1939, CA 45-08; cost figures on the tug/barge units from "closing statements," December 31, 1940, pp. 61–62.

37. Financing towboat/barge units, John Jr. to John Peterson, December 14, 1939, CA 40-06.

38. Delivery of tugs and barges, John Jr. to John Sr., March 27, 1940, CA 40-06; Frank Neilson reservations concerning Great Lakes trip, his wire to John Jr., March 27, 1980, ibid.; wires on Carneida trip through the river system, ibid; John Jr. weather prediction, Philip Sayles to Cargill MacMillan, July 31, 1940, CA 45-02; sinking reported in *Cargill News*, August

1940; *Chicago Tribune*, August 24, 1940; *Minneapolis Star-Journal and Tribune*, August 23, 1940; telegrams on diver at wreck, ibid.; telegram from Neilson to John Jr. on condition of tug when raised, May 12, 1941, CA 43-05; see also *Cargill News*, May 1941.

39. Rate case, "Grain Proportionals, Ex-Barge to Official Territory," 246 ICC 353 (July 31, 1941); reconsideration, 248 ICC 307 (December 1, 1941); the Eastman quotation, p. 321. See also Flagler F. Flinchbaugh to Ed Grimes, November 4, 1940; *Chicago Tribune*, January 1, 1946; Chicago Journal of Commerce, August 16, 1940; "Grain and Grain Products Within the Western District and For Export," Docket 17000, 243 I.C.C. 83 (December 7, 1940).

14. The Late 1930s (pp. 573–613)

1. Wheat price data from "The World Wheat Situation, 1937–38," *Wheat Studies* 15 (December 1938): 200; "unconscious conspiracy" from *The Secret Diary of Harold L. Ickes* Vol. 2 (New York: Simon and Schuster, 1953), p. 241; quotations by Robert Jackson and Ickes, William E. Leuchtenburg, *Franklin D. Roosevelt and the New Deal*, op. cit., p. 247.

2. "The World Wheat Situation, 1937–38," op. cit., pp. 214, 234; Leuchtenburg, op. cit., p. 255; Henry A. Wallace, "The Joseph Idea, the Drought and the American Consumer," speech at Great Lakes Exposition, Cleveland, Ohio, August 19, 1936, CA 37-02; James E. Boyle, "That Ever-Normal Granary," *Saturday Evening Post*, May 8, 1937. Antecedents of the 1938 AAA legislation, Theodore Saloutos, *The American Farmer and the New Deal*, op. cit., pp. 242–44; an excellent description of the Act itself is in Chester C. Davis, "The Development of Agricultural Policy since the End of the World War," in *Farmers in a Changing World*, op. cit, pp. 317–23; 1938–39 export subsidies, Gilbert C. Fite, *George N. Peek and the Fight for Farm Parity*, op. cit., p. 300; removal of the Canadian preference, Kelvin Gary Grant, "The Canadian Wheat Trade During the Inter-War Years," Ph.D. dissertation, University of Western Ontario, 1984, pp. 28–40.

3. For full list of TNEC publications, see 76th Congress, 3rd Session, Senate Committee Print, "Investigation of Concentration of Economic Power," Temporary National Economic Committee, *Description of Hearings and Monographs* (Washington, D.C.: Government Printing Office, 1941).

4. John Jr. to John Sr., March 24, 1938, CA 38-04.

5. Closing of offices reported in *Cargill News*, August 1938; St. Louis plans, ibid., September 1938. Wage cuts, John Sr. to John Jr., December 6, 1938, CA 39-02. Dividend policy, R. S. Wisner to Austen Cargill, May 2, 1938; John Sr. to Wisner, telegram, May 6, 1938, and letter of same date; CA 39-01; Wisner to John Sr., October 8, 1938; John Sr. to Wisner, October 10, 1938; John Sr. to J. M. Barker, ibid.; CA 39-02; "defer to Julius," John Jr. to Cargill MacMillan, April 21, 1937, CA 40-03; chart on possible salary cut in John Sr.'s file, CA 41-12.

6. Internal audit report on insider trading, R. J. Semsch to E. J. Grimes, August 8, 1938, CA 45-03; John Sr. editorial, *Cargill News*, December 1938. Speculating in Canadian grain, A. C. Greenman to Cargill MacMillan, February 18, 1939; MacMillan to Greenman, March 2, 1939; Greenman to MacMillan, February 18, 1939; CA 40-03.

7. "Cut . . . dead wood," John Sr. to John Jr., January 5, 1939, CA 45-08; "cutting . . . to bone," John Sr. to Cargill MacMillan, January 4, 1939, ibid.; "little dissatisfied," Ed Grimes to John Sr., May 2, 1939, ibid.; handwritten memorandum on individual cuts, n.d., ibid.

8. "The World Wheat Situation, 1938–39," *Wheat Studies* 16 (December, 1939): 113, 183ff.; "war excitement," John Sr. to Cargill MacMillan, August 25, 1939, CA 45-08.

9. Walter W. Wilcox, *The Farmer in the Second World War* (Ames: Iowa State College Press, 1947), pp. 7–19, 35–47; "no new goals," ibid., p. 36; Willard W. Cochrane and Mary E. Ryan, *American Farm Policy, 1948–1973* (Minneapolis: University of Minnesota Press, 1975), pp. 3–23; "The World Wheat Situation, 1939–40," *Wheat Studies* 17 op. cit.; ibid., 1940–41, 18; "Wheat in the Third War Year: Major Developments, 1941–42," ibid., 19 (December 1942, pp. 85–120.

10. Parity, Chester C. Davis, "The Development of Agricultural Policy since the End of the World War" in *Yearbook of Agriculture, 1940*, op. cit. pp. 316–20; Wilcox, op. cit., pp. 9–11; "mechanical use," ibid., p. 41; "party regulars . . . aghast," William E. Leuchtenberg, *Franklin D. Roosevelt and the New Deal*, op. cit., p. 317.

11. Government storage plans, Ed Grimes to A. B. Gunnarson, October 18, 1939; National

Grain Trade Council *Newsletter*, August 24 and September 7, 1940, April 29, 1941; wires, passim, Ed Grimes, CA 40-02; terminal elevator capacities, *Closing Statements*, May 31, 1941, p. 101; *Cargill News*, August 1940.

12. "To All Branch Managers," May 28, 1940, CA 40-06; reorganization of country terminals, Austen Cargill to Commitment Committee, March 29, 1940, CA 40-06; *Cargill News*, September 1939.

13. College trainees, Cargill MacMillan to Stuart H. Clement, January 16, 1936, CA 45-02; John MacMillan, Jr., to James F. Bell, November 29, 1940, CA 40-06.

14. "The World Wheat Situation, 1939–40," *Wheat Studies 17*, op. cit., p. 145; Michael R. Cross to Cargill MacMillan, December 14, 1937, January 11, 1938, CA 45-02; Norris collaboration, MacMillan to Cross, June 14, 1939, ibid.; E. J. Grimes to MacMillan, June 18, 1939, CA 46-03; James Norris to Grimes, July 27, 1939 CA 40-01.

15. "Ocean Transportation and Its Relation to Cargill, Inc.," handwritten and typed copy, unsigned, John MacMillan, Jr., n.d. (ca. September 1939), CA 40-06.

16. John Jr. to F. L. Neilson, October 9, 1939 CA 40-06.

17. Cargill MacMillan on horsepower in his letter to E. J. Grimes, December 2, 1939, CA 40-03.

18. Transshipping, John Jr. to Grimes, December 1, 1939, CA 40-03; specifications on initial proposal, John Jr. "personal" file, CA 40-06.

19. Lisbon transshipping, Michael R. Cross to E. J. Grimes, December 19, 1939, CA 40-01; negotiations with British, series of cables between Frank Neilson and Cargill/Minneapolis, February 27–March 21, 1940, CA 40-02; British offer, John Jr. to Neilson, March 21, April 3 and 6, 1940, CA 40-06; "design . . . unusual," Cross to Cargill MacMillan, March 26, 1940, CA 45-03.

20. Caution of naval architects, John Jr. to John Sr., March 27, 1940, CA 40-06; interior shipyards, Cargill MacMillan to Cross, October 24, 1940, CA 45-03; "build ourselves," Cargill MacMillan to Neilson, May 9, 1940, CA 40-03; "war risk" insurance, John Jr. to John Sr., March 21, 1940, CA 45-08.

21. "Not be willing commit ourselves," Cargill MacMillan to John Jr., June 19, 1940, CA 40-03.

22. John Jr., "Memorandum for Mr. Moore," June 24, 1940, CA 43-04; John Jr. to Maurice Moore, July 8, 1941 (and attached drawing for "ocean going barge carrier"), CA 43-04.

23. Testing Cargill's hull at David Taylor Model Basin of the Bureau of Ships, Navy Department, Capt. H. E. Saunders to Cargill, Inc., January 19, 1942, CA 43-05; "New Shipbuilding Method a Success," *F-M News* (Fairbanks-Morse & Co.) 18 (January–February 1942): 2.

24. Steamer *Rees* as oceangoing vessel, John Jr. to John Sr., March 27, 1940, CA 40-06; moving Rees "on her side," John Jr. to Neilson, March 29, 1940, ibid.; costs of refurbishing the *Rees*, Neilson to John Jr., April 3, 1940, ibid; on "high prices," John Jr. to H. E. Scheuermann, December 11, 1940, CA 40-05; "upset price," John Jr., "Memorandum on Plant Operation and New Construction," December 26, 1940, CA 41-11; subsidy, J. J. Hays to John Jr., October 30, 1940, CA 40-06.

25. "Spent so much money," John Sr. to John Jr., January 14, 1941, CA 43-04; financial situation, Cargill MacMillan to John Jr., February 4 and 18, 1931, CA 41-04; "error was mine," John Jr. to Cargill MacMillan, n.d. (ca. February 20, 1941), ibid. East St. Louis pilings problem, Cargill MacMillan to John Jr., March 4, 1941; John Jr. to John Sr., March 7, 1941; Bert H. Lang to John G. Peterson, May 14, 1941, Peterson to Lang, May 16, 1941; ibid.

26. "Old iron flew," Cross to Cargill MacMillan, October 8, 1940, CA 45-03; sale of barges for Europe, MacMillan to Cross, November 28, 1940, CA 30-04; "destroyers for convoy," John Jr. to Frank Neilson, November 28, 1940, and Neilson to MacMillan, November 29, 1940; CA 40-06; losses to U-boats, *New York Herald*, December 3, 1940; visit to British Purchasing Commission, John Jr. to Cyril Thompson, December 2, 1940, ibid.; "coldest reception," Cargill MacMillan to Cross, December 4, 1940, ibid.; "would not dicker," John Jr. to Weston Grimes, December 11, 1940, ibid.; "get terrific propaganda," John Jr. to Weston Grimes, March 31, 1941, CA 43-05; "play us for suckers," John Jr. to Weston Grimes, March 31, 1940, CA 43-05; "anxious to agree," John Jr. to George G. Sharp, December 11, 1940, CA 40-05.

27. Navy interested, John Jr. to John Sr., January 24, 1941, CA 41-04; Cargill proposal, Weston B. Grimes to Lieutenant H. P. Bearce, January 24, 1941, CA 30-03; "knuckle form," Cargill MacMillan to John Jr., February 7, 1941, CA 41-04; tuna boats, ibid., January 21, 1941, CA 43-04.

28. Great Lakes preference, Weston B. Grimes to Cargill MacMillan, CA 30-03; "could easily move," Neilson to Weston Grimes, January 23, 1941, ibid.; Midwest sites, Neilson to Cargill MacMillan, January 28, 1941, and MacMillan to Neilson, ibid.; La Crosse and Buffalo, Weston Grimes to MacMillan, and MacMillan to Weston Grimes, January 29, 1941, CA 43-05; "any stone unturned," MacMillan to Neilson, February 1, 1941, ibid.; Duluth shipbuilding, Julius H. Barnes to John Sr., April 23, 1940, and John Sr. to Barnes, May 2, 1940, CA 45-08.

29. "The Shipbuilding Problem," Business Executive Publications, June 12, 1941, CA 43-05; see also *Wall Street Journal*, June 3 and 11, 1941; appropriation for "Emergency Cargo Ship Construction," U.S. House of Representatives, 77th Congress, 1st Session, Report No. 10, January 22, 1941; "will not tolerate," John Jr. to Weston Grimes, July 9, 1941, CA 30-03; "arbitrary position," in "Excerpt from Letter of Weston B. Grimes," July 8, 1941, ibid. Ocean-going barge carrier, George G. Sharp memorandum, May 1941, CA, John Jr. MS collection; vessel design, Neilson to Chris Jensen, September 17, 1941, ibid.

30. "Not . . . freakish," John Jr. to Cargill MacMillan, April 14, 1941, CA 43-04; Portugese negotiations, ibid.; April 8, 1941, ibid; oil company negotiations, see extensive correspondence in CA 43-05; ibid. for Argentine negotiations; "thinks he can scalp," C. C. Boden to John Jr., August 22, 1941, ibid.; Trinidad charter, Cargill MacMillan to Weston Grimes, June 12, 1941, CA 45-02; inspection and trials of *Carlantic/Victoria*, see CA 43-05; formal approval, Stanley S. Hall, American Shipping Bureau, November 18, 1941, CA 30-05.

31. "Pioneer spirit" quotation in "The 'Victoria,' The First Ocean-Going Vessel Ever Built in Albany, New York Inaugurates Career," undated manuscript, ca. November 10, 1941, ibid.

32. Compensation plan, Cargill MacMillan to Herbert W. Warden, Jr., August 21, 1939, CA 45-03; "trading center" plan for distribution center, Warden to MacMillan, September 21, 1939, ibid.; arrangements with Chase National Bank, MacMillan to Hugo E. Scheuermann, September 22, 1939, ibid.; map of proposed land, Warden to MacMillan, September 26, 1939, ibid.; "up to the point [of] . . . money," MacMillan to Warden, October 10, 1939, ibid. See also "Outline for Report of Plans for Future Operations to Directors of Minnesota Western Company," draft memorandum, Cargill MacMillan, February 7, 1951, MS collection, Whitney MacMillan.

33. Lennox feed plant, Austen Cargill to Commitment Committee, June 12, 1939 (two memoranda), CA 45-03.

34. Minneapolis feed mill project, Cargill MacMillan to John Jr., January 28, 1941, CA 41-04; Willard C. Lighter to International Sugar Feed Corporation, March 18, 1941, CA 45-02; *Cargill News*, November 1939, April 1942 and November 1944; sugar bag and chromium nickel steel proposals, Julius Hendel to Cargill MacMillan, three wires, February 19, 1940, Archives 40-02.

35. Cargill cooperation with Federal Trade Commission, Cargill MacMillan to Col. Charles H. March, February 24, 1936, CA 45-02; grain trade references in Temporary National Economic Committee hearings, *Verbatim Record of the Proceedings* . . . , Vol. 2 (January 21, 1939–March 24, 1939), pp. 282–87, and Vol. 3 (March 24, 1939–May 29, 1939), pp. 45–47. Terminal markets, "Agriculture and the National Economy," TNEC Monograph 23 (Washington, D.C.: Government Printing Office, 1940), pp. 33–34; "Large-Scale Organization in the Food Industry," ibid., Monograph 35; "yield . . . disappointing," Leuchtenberg, op. cit., p. 259. See also the comments of Robert Sobel in *The Age of Giant Corporations: A Microeconomic History of American Business 1914–1970* (Westport, Conn.: Greenwood Press, 1972), pp. 115–121.

36. Almon Greenman evacuation from Europe, *Cargill News*, July 1940; L. L. Corlett evacuation, *Cargill News*, July 1940.

37. Memorandum on married women, n.d. (ca. late June 1941), CA 43-04.

38. Charles A. Lindbergh visit, John Jr. to Cargill MacMillan, April 29, 1941, ibid.; "doubtful . . . ever support," John Sr. to Richard C. Gale, August 13, 1941, CA 45-08; "feels

strongly," John Jr. to John D. M. Hamilton, June 21, 1946, ibid.; John Jr., "Strictly Confidential—A National Program to Ensure the Defense of the Nation, the Improvement of the Race, and Maintenance of Liberty and a Higher Standard of Living," July 6, 1940, CA 40-05; "defeat of Hitler," John Jr. to Weston Grimes, November 27, 1941, CA 43-05. For an excellent review of the literature on eugenics, see David J. Kevles, *In the Name of Eugenics: Genetics and the Uses of Human Heredity* (New York: Alfred A. Knopf, 1985), pp. 64, 80–81; reply to "National Program," Loring M. Staples to John Jr., July 29, 1940, CA 47-10; two-ocean navy, Staples to John Jr., October 10, 1940, and John Jr. to Staples, October 23, 1940; CA 40-05.

15. *Cargill in World War II (pp. 618–83)*

1. Farm legislation and price control mechanisms in the early part of World War II, "Wheat in the Fourth War Year: Major Developments, 1942–43," *Wheat Studies 20* (November 1943): 37–66; see also Walter W. Wilcox, *The Farmer in the Second World War*, op. cit, pp. 51–52; quotation on p. 243.

2. Limitations on futures trading in World War I, *Northwestern Miller*, May 16, 1917; effects of OPA price controls on wheat and flour in October 1942, ibid., October 28, 1942; Cargill "apathetic," Loren W. Johnson to Ed Grimes, November 9, 1942, CA 43-06; Julius Hendel statement reprinted in its entirety in *Northwestern Miller*, October 21, 1942; Leon Henderson statement, Weston Grimes to Ed Grimes, November 14, 1943, CA 43-06.

3. For text of the Office of Defense Transportation Executive Order 6989, December 18, 1941, amended May 6, 1942, see *Chicago Journal of Commerce*, May 7, 1942, CA 43-04; permit system described in a series of memoranda January 2–August 4, 1942, Ed Grimes correspondence, CA 43-06; *Time* story, May 4, 1942.

4. Sidney Anderson to Ed Grimes, June 1, 1942, CA 43-06.

5. Sea Otter proposal, Weston B. Grimes to Joe Gardner, December 10, 1941, CA 47-01; eight-month deadline, John MacMillan, Jr., to Grimes, December 10, 1941, CA 43-05; "fantastic premiums," John Jr. to George Basler, December 24, 1941, ibid.; "not a luxury liner," John Jr. to Chris Jensen, December 26, 1941, ibid.

6. Cargill MacMillan reports on telephone call from Commander Phillip Lemler, his diary of shipbuilding project, January 8–June 17, 1942, CA 47-01; John Jr. letter to Lemler, January 21, 1942, CA 43-05; Cargill proposal, "Tank Carriers and Facilities for the Production Thereof," dated January 16, 1942, CA 44-01; Brooklyn shipyard, "Memorandum for Mr. R. J. Semsch," John Jr., December 21, 1942, CA 47-01.

7. "Nine-foot channel" project, Raymond H. Merritt, *Creativity, Conflict & Controversy: A History of the St. Paul District, U.S. Army Corps of Engineers* (Washington, D.C.: U.S. Government Printing Office, 1979), pp. 187–214; Minnesota River proposal, Philip B. Fleming to John Jr., October 4, 1938, CA 38-04; John Jr. letter to John Sr., January 21, 1942, CA 43-04.

8. "Counted out" and "sit tight," *Cargill MacMillan Port Cargill Diary*, January 30, 1942, CA 47-01; "lose our crew," John Jr. to Weston Grimes, February 4, 1942, ibid.; AOG specifications, *Diary*, op. cit., February 9–10, 1942; see also "Cost Data—6 AOGs," n.d., CA 47-01; misgivings of J. K. Welding Co., *Diary*, op. cit., February 11, 1942; "picayunish contract," John Jr. to Weston Grimes, February 4, 1942; Albany wage scales, ibid.; Cargill MacMillan to John Sr., February 4, 1942; CA 47-01; "pig-headed," John Jr. to John Sr., February 20, 1942, CA 43-04.

9. Problems of Minnesota River draft, Cargill MacMillan *Diary*, op. cit., February 18, 19, 1942; propulsion at New Orleans, ibid., March 2, 1942; "completely disgusted," John Jr. to John Sr., February 25, 1942; CA 43-04; "without 'crutches,' " *Diary*, op. cit., February 21, 1942; fixed price for two boats, John Jr. to Weston Grimes, February 10, 1942, CA 47-01; letter of intent, *Diary*, op. cit., March 19, 1942; postwar shipyard and "pain in the neck," Cargill MacMillan to Weston Grimes, May 22, 1942, CA 45-02; agreement on dredging, Cargill MacMillan to Lt. Col. J. W. Moreland, May 28, 1942, CA 43-04; rock ledge described, John Jr. to John and Edna MacMillan, March 30, 1942, CA 43-04; comments to board of directors in their meeting of June 1, 1942.

10. The key critical articles on Savage project, *Saint Paul Pioneer Press*, April 1942. See also *Diary*, op. cit., April 18, 1942; Weston Grimes to Cargill MacMillan, April 20 and 22, 1942, CA 44-05.

11. Minnesota Western Railway Company project described in John Jr.'s letters to John and Edna MacMillan, March 4, 5, 10, 12 and 16, 1942, CA 43-04; "fearful of tying up assets," John Sr. to John Jr., March 7, 1942, CA 41-03.

12. "Fun with . . . railroad," John Jr. to Frank Neilson, August 6, 1942, CA 43-05; ore project described, John Jr. to J. D. Beeler, October 16, 1942, ibid.; Beeler to John Jr., October 20, 1942, ibid; see also extensive set of wires between Weston Grimes and John Jr., October 19–November 1, ibid.; Granite City project, Weston Grimes to John Jr., October 24, 1942, ibid.; "Report on Movement of Iron Ore from Minnesota Ranges to Granite City, Illinois," ibid.; on rail opposition, John Jr. to Grimes, October 20, 1942, ibid.; see also John B. Keeler to J. D. Beeler, November 14, 1942, ibid.; John Jr. as "syndicate manager," A. M. Thompson to John Jr., December 18, 1942, ibid.; John Jr. to Keeler, December 14, 1942, ibid.; key articles in the *Saint Paul Pioneer Press*, October 23 and 25, November 12, 25, 26 and 28 and December 1 and 4, 1942; *Mac Weekly* article, December 11, 1942; see also John Jr. to Charles J. Turck, January 16, 1943, CA 43-04; Turck to John Jr., January 19, 1943, ibid.; "stick to this," Weston Grimes to John Jr., January 8, 1943; CA 44-08; Drew Pearson interest, Weston Grimes to Ed Grimes, December 3, 1942, CA 43-06; decision against project, Office of War Information, Office of Defense Transportation, news release of March 31, 1943, CA 44-08.

13. Savage shipyard description, *Cargill News*, July and September 1942, and Alan Clegg, "Shipyard Obituary—Without Crepe," undated internal MS, ca. 1945, CA 47-01. Cargill MacMillan health problem, John Jr. to Edna and John MacMillan, February 26 and 27, 1942. Storekeeper job, Cargill MacMillan to Marcus Marshall, April 4 and 8, 1942; Marshall to James Hayhoe, April 7, 1942; CA 45-02. Arthur Wheeler relations with John Sr., September 12, 1940–January 9, 1942, CA 45-08; and John Sr. letter to Wheeler, March 17 and 30, 1942, CA 43-04; movement of Albany stores, Cargill Shipbuilding Division to Lieutenant Commander Stolz and Lieutenant Commander C. L. Seveney, December 9, 1942, CA 47-06.

14. First leg of trip, C. C. Boden to John Jr., January 2, 1942, CA 43-05; Fairbanks-Morse engineer, Fred K. Troughton, on voyage, December 26, 1941, ca. March 31, 1942; quotation on owners March 1, 1942; on unwillingness of crew, undated letter (ca. March 1, CA 43-05 and 30–03; *Cargill News* story on torpedoes, April 1942; *Time* articles, May 4 and June 22, 1942; damage, C. C. Boden to Weston Grimes and Chris Jensen, May 5, 1942, CA 45-02; "made up for our feelings," Cargill MacMillan to Michael R. Cross, May 5, 1942, CA 45-03; U.S. government reclaiming *Victoria*, see *Minneapolis Tribune*, July 22, 1942; later voyage in North Atlantic, John Jr. to John Sr., January 25, 1943, CA 44-08.

15. "Familiar with the work," Cargill MacMillan to Sumner B. Young, November 10, 1942, CA 47-01; Cargill MacMillan to Weston Grimes, November 13, 1942, ibid.; Weston Grimes to John Jr., December 2, 1942, ibid.; barge carrier proposal, John Jr. to Grimes, January 5, 1943 (and attached memorandum), CA 44-09 and 43-05; towboat proposal, Grimes to John Jr., January 12, 1943; use of steamer *Rees*, John Jr. to Chris Jensen, February 17, 1942; CA 43-05; John Jr. to John Sr., February 20, 1942, CA 43-04; Jensen to Cargill MacMillan, March 2, 1942, CA 47-01; Jensen to John Jr., March 3, 1942, CA 43-04; Weston Grimes to John Jr., January 28, 1943, CA 44-08; "[don't] let BC interfere," Grimes to John Jr., February 1, 1943, ibid.; flood, John Jr. to John and Edna MacMillan, April 1, 1943; *Agawam* launching, "Shipyard Obituary—Without Crepe," op. cit., p. 10; quotation from *Minneapolis Tribune* on launching, April 16, 1943; *Time* on Cargill, September 13, 1943; Mickey Rooney quotation from *Minneapolis Tribune*, September 18, 1943; contract for 12 additional AOGs, N. W. Gokey to Cargill, Incorporated, August 13, 1943, CA 44-08.

16. Minnesota River log, George Van Den Houten, 1943–1947, n.d., CA, Port Cargill Shipbuilding Division files; *Agawam* article, *St. Paul Pioneer Press*, November 6, 1943; *Agawam* trip downriver, John Jr. to John MacMillan III, November 5, 19 and 23, 1943, CA 44-08; *Chehalis* reunion, *Amarillo* (Texas) *News*, October 21, 1989; service records of the 18 AOGs, A. E. Becker to Sen. David Durenberger (with attachments), November 29, 1989, CA; sea trials, F. R. Stolz to "All Cargill Shipyard Workers," April 10, 1944, CA, John MacMillan Jr. MS collection; strike in February 1944, G. J. O'Donnell to John Jr., February 20, 1944, CA 45-07; October 1944 strike, *Minneapolis Morning Tribune*, October 26, 1944, ibid.

17. Letter of termination of Green Bay lease, Homer E. McGee to John MacMillan, Sr., May 21, 1942; "peremptory treatment," Ed Grimes to McGee, April 24, 1942, CA 43-06; McGee to Grimes, April 27, 1942, ibid.; on disrepair of Chicago and North Western terminal, Lt. Com. A. F. Glaza to Grimes, May 2, 1942, CA 43-07.

18. On status of Farmers National Grain Corporation, Weston Grimes to Leavitt R. Barker, August 29, 1940, CA 40-05; institution of suit, *New York Times*, October 25, 1940; the *Chicago Tribune*, October 26, 1940, stated amount as $2 million; the *Journal of Commerce* called it $1,890,000. Publicity to banks, John Jr. to John Peterson, September 3 and 4, 1940, and Peterson to John Jr., August 29 and September 4, 1940, ibid.; "arbitrate a loss," E. L. Rickel to Cargill Grain Company, February 8, 1938, CA 45-03; "drafted into Navy production," Weston Grimes to Cargill MacMillan, January 8, 1942, CA 47-01.

19. On lost Form 1099, Hayes Miller to John Jr., July 31, 1941, CA 43-04; difficulties with broker records, Leavitt R. Barker to Douglas Bagnell, September 19, 1941, CA 45-02; Barker automobile accident, Clark R. Fletcher to Cargill MacMillan (and attachment), November 13, 1944, ibid.; Fletcher pretrial memoranda are dated November 2 and 26 and December 9 and 17, 1942, CA 45-02 and 43-04; board of directors decision on trial by jury, December 30, 1942; private settlement, Austen Cargill to John Jr., February 4, 1943, CA 44-09; Farmers National agreement on no announcement, Howard Ellis to Leo F. Tierney, February 10, 1943, ibid.; "ashamed," John Jr. to Sumner B. Young, February 5, 1943, CA 44-08; Young reply, February 12, 1943, CA 44-09.

20. Overall rye production, James S. Schonberg, *The Grain Trade: How It Works* (New York: Exposition Press, 1956), pp. 78-80; "clubby traders," Jerry W. Markham, *The History of Commodity Futures Trading and Its Regulation*, op. cit., p. 45; rye at "even money," John Jr. to New York Office, November 13, 1942, CA 43-04; "first rate 'corner,' " John Peterson to John Sr., February 8, 1944, CA 44-08; Cargill losses on hedges in May 1944 rye futures, John Jr. to Cargill MacMillan, May 5, 1944, CA 44-08; CEA Complaint, Docket No. 34, dated May 26, 1945, names as respondents General Foods Corporation, Charles W. Metcalf, Daniel F. Rice and Company, Daniel F. Rice, Lawrence J. Ryan and Philip R. O'Brien, Archives Law Department No. 608; the Referee's Report by Jack W. Bain dated September 10, 1946; final CEA decision against protestants dated April 28, 1947; circuit court case, *General Foods Corporation v. Brannan, Secretary of Agriculture*, October 9, 1948, 170 F. 2nd 220; quotations by Rep. Frank B. Keefe from *New York Times*, July 4, 1945; Drew Pearson quotation from his column "Senators Linked to Rye Speculation," July 18, 1945; *Fortune* quotation from its article "The Grain Traders," August 1949; *Business Week* article, "Mystery in Rye," November 4, 1944; "punch in the nose," from "Answer of Rice Respondents, CEA No. 34, July 27, 1945, CA Law Department 608P; plans and memoranda re potential Cargill testimony, see ibid.; Cargill's relations with Collector of Customs, Austen Cargill to Collector of Customs, April 28, 1944; Austen Cargill to Ford Ferguson, April 29, 1944, CA 44-08; CBOT decision on import duty, Joseph R. Rice to directors, May 29, 1944, CBOT Archives AAA 3826-10; Law Committee to Philip R. O'Brien and board of directors, June 12, 1944, ibid.; mixing wires, Hayes Miller to Sumner B. Young, October 7, 1946, CA Law Department 608P.

21. *Board of Trade of City of Chicago v. Illinois Commerce Commission et al.; Great Lakes Elevator Corporation et al. v. Same*, June 7, 1946, 156 F. 2nd 33; *Rice et al. v. Santa Fe Elevator Corporation et al.; Illinois Commerce Commission et al. v. Same*, May 5, 1947, 331 U.S. 218. See also *Volkart Brothers, Inc., Volkart Brothers Company, Alfred Boedtker and Kurt Muller v. Orville L. Freeman, Secretary of Agriculture*, December 5, 1962, 331 F. 2nd 52.

22. The list of the 711 "large traders," *New York Times*, December 23, 1947; on political implications, Arthur Krock, "In the Nation," *New York Times*, December 19, 1947; "deprive markets," Chicago *Journal of Commerce*, December 24, 1947; Senate Committee report, *New York Times* December 28, 1947; concern about bank reaction, John Jr. to Hugo Scheuermann, December 22, 1947, CA Lake 23; Scheuermann to John Jr., December 29, 1947, ibid.

23. Criticisms by Julius Hendel, John Jr. to Weston Grimes, January 26, 1943, CA 44-08; "if the two . . . agreed," ibid., January 23, 1943, ibid.; "If good men agree," ibid., March 16, 1943, ibid.; bulletin to farmers, "WFA Urges Farmers to Market Corn," Office of War Information, Department of Agriculture, June 30, 1943; the WFA seizure, *Northwestern Miller*, June 30, 1943; Cargill grain seized, John Jr. to Ed and Weston Grimes, July 6, 1943, CA 44-03; Hermitage Mills problem, Weston Grimes to Ed Grimes, July 13, 1943; Hermitage Feed Mills to William McArthur July 16, 1943; McArthur to Weston Grimes, July 23, 1943; Weston Grimes to McArthur, August 5, 1943; all in CA 44-08; Senator Bridges accusation, Weston Grimes to Ed Grimes, June 29, 1943; empty terminals, John Jr. to Frank Neilson, January 11, 1944; CA 44-09; John Jr. to John and Edna MacMillan, January 18, 1944, CA 44-08; "OPA . . . driving us all crazy," ibid., January 21, 1944, ibid.; "go around us," ibid., February 25,

1944, ibid.; appointment of Woodworth, Austen Cargill to Weston Grimes, March 30, 1944, CA 45-06; Austen Cargill to John Jr., March 31, 1944, ibid.; corn and meat black markets, Wilcox, *The Farmer in the Second World War*, op. cit., pp. 175–81.

24. On original dog food proposal, Newell H. Schooley to Cargill MacMillan, July 22 and 31, 1941, and Cargill MacMillan to Schooley, July 29 and August 18, 1941; CA 45-03; Cargill project in Cargill MacMillan to Schooley May 6, 1942, ibid.; John Jr. interest, Cargill MacMillan to Schooley, October 28, 1942, and Schooley to MacMillan, October 29, 1942, ibid.; see John Jr. to Schooley, February 8 ("any reasonable . . . expense"), and September 27, 1943, CA 45-07; Julius Hendel/Fred Seed trip, John Jr. to Schooley, January 14, 1944, ibid.; in 1944, the Federal Trade Commission issued a cease and desist order to Schooley and Cargill for implying a meat content in the dogfood, file No. 1–18866, April 11, 1944.

25. For Iowa Milling Company, see Cargill MacMillan to F. E. Lindahl, January 19, 1943, CA 45-02; Illinois Soy Products project, *Illinois State Journal*, October 27, 1943, and in the Cargill, Incorporated, board of directors meeting, November 4, 1943; Plymouth Processing Company purchase, *Cargill News*, November 1943; "bought it himself," John Jr. to John and Edna MacMillan, February 27, 1943, CA 44-08.

26. Cargill broadcasting, *Cargill News*, September 1942; John Jr. comments, his letter to John and Edna MacMillan, March 2, 1944, CA 44-08.

27. *Cargill, Inc. et al. v. United States et al., Inland Waterways Corporation v. Same* (April 16, 1942), 44 F. Supp 368; *Interstate Commerce Commission et al. v. Inland Waterways et al.* (June 14, 1943), 319 U.S. 671; *Interstate Commerce Commission v. Mechling et al.* (March 31, 1947), 330 U.S. 567. See also "Grain Proportionals, Ex. Barge to Official Territory," 262 I.C.C. 7, Docket 4718 (February 13, 1945).

28. Tennessee River trip, John Jr. to A. L. Mechling, June 15, 1943, CA 44-09; comparison to 1923 trip, John Jr. to Frank Neilson, June 14, 1943, ibid.; Guntersville elevator project, *Cargill News*, August 1943; towboat/barge length, C. T. Barker to John Jr., July 27 and December 27, 1943, ibid.; see also John Jr. to David E. Lilienthal, January 17, 1944, ibid.; use of *Sea Mule* concept, John Jr. to Frank Neilson, December 21, 1943, ibid.; correspondence with R. I. Ingalls, Ingalls Shipbuilding Corporation, August 2 and 21 and November 28, 1944, CA 45-07; Chaska shipbuilding unit, *Cargill News*, May 1944; maiden voyage of *Cartasca*, John Jr. to John MacMillan III, November 24, 1944, CA 45-06; damage to *Cartasca*, John Jr. to Frank Neilson, February 7, 1945, ibid.

29. "Pick up suitable boat," John Jr. to C. C. Boden, April 17, 1944, CA 44-09; specifications for proposed boat, "Proposed Specifications for an Inspection Vessel," n.d., ca. November 1948, MS collection, John MacMillan Jr.; *Carmac* purchase is noted in Cargill, Incorporated, closing statements, December 31, 1945, p. 150; "not . . . a yacht," John Jr. to Charles T. Pichel, August 4, 1958, CA 59-10.

30. *Cargill News*, March 1943, July 1945. "Putting a girl on," Robert Parrott to Ed Grimes, February 13, 1942, CA 43-06; redefining job titles for draft boards, John Jr. to John and Edna MacMillan, March 7, 1944, CA 44-08.

31. Employment figures from "Allocation of Employees, September 1944," CA 45-06.

32. Frank Neilson health, John Jr. to George B. Bickelhaupt, March 23, 1942, CA 43-05; Arthur Wheeler's death, John Jr. to Malcolm M. Rowles, November 24, 1942, CA 45-08; death of Ross B. Wilson, *Cargill News*, February 1943; "shocking state," John Jr. to John and Edna MacMillan, January 27, 1944, CA 44-08; "enjoyed . . . Austen," ibid., March 10, 1944, ibid.

33. The "Employees' Profit Sharing–Stock Bonus Trust" is described in the Cargill, Incorporated, board of directors meeting of December 31, 1942; public announcement in December 1942 *Cargill News*.

34. January 1942, storm, John Jr. to John and Edna MacMillan, January 6, 1942, CA 44-01; ibid., January 21, 1942, ibid., 43–04; "Turkestan driest," ibid., February 10, 1942, ibid.; meeting with Weather Bureau, John Jr. to John Sr., September 28, 1942, ibid., 43–05; John Jr. to Commander F. W. Reichelderfer, October 13, 1942, ibid., CA 44-09; patenting weather theory, Maurice M. Moore to John Jr., June 8, 1944, ibid. CA 45-07; second visit to Weather Bureau, John Jr. to Reichelderfer, June 5, 1944, ibid., CA 44-09; Reichelderfer to John Jr., August 4, 1944, ibid. CA 45-07; C.N. Touart to John Jr., April 21 and 30, 1953, ibid.

35. "Burden on the rest of us," John Jr. to Allan S. Phillips, May 21, 1943, CA 44-09; John

Sr. statement on friction, draft, May 14, 1942; final copy, May 18, 1942, CA 45-08; "not . . . co-operators," John Jr. to Weston Grimes, June 29, 1943, CA 44-08; reorganization of August 31, 1943, CA 44-08; traffic study, John Jr. to John Peterson, Ed Grimes and F. W. Hays, January 25, 1944, CA 45-06; merchandising study, Ralph Golseth to John Jr., February 4, 1944; press releases, John Jr. to Department Managers, November 1, 1944, ibid., quotation on functional system, *Cargill News*, January 1945; conflict of interest, John Jr. draft and memorandum "to all officers," December 31, 1943, CA 44-08; new budget, see Cargill MacMillan to E. J. Grimes, July 12, 1944, CA 44-03.

36. "Few months to live," John Jr. to Howard A. MacMillan, November 10, 1944, CA 45-07.

37. Negotiations for Cargill's Rand house purchase, John Jr. to Mrs. R. R. Rand, August 30, 1944, CA 45-07; Albert Egermayer to Austen Cargill, September 12, 1944, ibid. Cedric Adams article, *Minneapolis Sunday Tribune*, June 14, 1945; *Business Week* article, January 6, 1945; *Northwestern Miller* quotation, January 24, 1945.

38. Julius Hendel speech, "Cargill Incorporated and Postwar Plans," October 16, 1943, CA 46-08; quotation by John Jr., "Report on Cedar Rapids Visit," June 8, 1945, CA 45-03; for terms, Julius Hendel to Sumner Young, February 26, 1945, CA 45-06; "Summary of Terms of Purchase by Cargill, Incorporated of Honeymead Products Company Plant at Cedar Rapids, Iowa," March 15, 1945, CA 45-06; Port Cargill postwar development, *Minneapolis Daily Times*, October 6, 1944; "Port Cargill Development," n.d. (ca. early 1945), CA 47-01; Hendel comment on training own men, his wire to John Jr., December 23, 1943, CA 44-08.

16. Rocky Reconversion (pp. 686–734)

1. Byrnes quotations from "War's End in Europe Will Create Large Food Surplus," *Northwestern Miller*, September 13, 1944; see also A. C. Greenman, "Europlan Food Situation," February 21, 1946, *Cargill's Business*, op. cit.

2. Hugo E. Scheuermann to John G. Peterson, April 20, 1945, MS collection, John MacMillan, Jr.; Bunge and Dreyfus competition, *Cargill News*, January 1945; "efficient production" quotation, ibid., August 1945.

3. Quotation by John Jr., "Report on Cedar Rapids Visit," June 8, 1945, CA 45-03; for terms, see Julius Hendel to Sumner Young, February 26, 1945, CA 45-06; "Summary of Terms of Purchase by Cargill, Incorporated of Honeymead Products Company plant at Cedar Rapids, Iowa," March 15, 1945, CA 45-06; Andreas family background, E. J. Kahn, Jr., "The Absolute Beginning," *The New Yorker*, February 16, 1987, pp. 63–64; on assistant vice president assignment, John Jr. to Dwayne Andreas, August 14, 1945, CA 46-07; description of functional organization, Austen Cargill to Andreas, November 26, 1945; ibid.; on "entirely destroy," Austen Cargill to Fred Seed, January 20, 1946, CA Austen Cargill MS, Oil.

4. Nutrena purchase, minutes of the board of directors, September 28, 1945; *Cargill News*, October 1945.

5. Postwar Port Cargill, *Minneapolis Daily Times*, October 6, 1944; "Port Cargill Development," n.d. (ca. July 1945), CA 47-01; concerns by Commitment Committee in "Memorandum from Commitment Committee of Cargill, Incorporated to Commitment Committee of Shipbuilding Division," n.d. (ca. January 1944), CA 45-08; on purchase of *Victoria*, Weston Grimes to John Jr., August 20, 1945; John Jr. to Grimes, ibid., CA 46-07; J. L. Pimper to Austen Cargill, March 4, 1947, and reply, CA Austen Cargill MS.

6. Unsatisfactory voyage on Mississippi, John Jr. to C. C. Burger, Jr., January 15, 1945, CA 45-06; Burger to John Jr., January 20, 1945, CA 45-07; George R. Goethals to John Jr., February 10, 1945, ibid.; on interest in the Southeast, John Jr. to Freder R. Harris, July 30, 1945, CA 46-08; quotations on wheat in the Southwest, Harold Johnson, "A Study of Wheat," May 2, 1946, *Cargill's Business*, op. cit.; use of Sea Mule concept, John Jr. to Frank Neilson, August 27, 1943, CA 44-09; Neilson to John Jr., September 24, 1943, ibid.; Chaska barges, *Cargill News*, May 1944; "three . . . for price of one," John Jr. to Neilson, December 21, 1943, ibid.; test voyage described in wire messages, and final report in CA 46-07; gasoline leak, Austen Cargill to Duncan Watson, December 6, 1944, ibid.; sinking of *Cartasca*, *Saint Paul Pioneer Press*, December 11, 1945; decision to send barges to Erie Canal, John Jr. to George Basler, April 26, 1945, ibid.; on bow steering, John Jr. to Edna MacMillan, October 21, 1946,

CA 47-11; John Jr. to Hugh and Duncan MacMillan, ibid.; Federal Barge "integrated tow," John Jr. to A. C. Ingersoll, Jr., April 23, 1948, CA Lake 23.

7. Wartime agricultural production figures from U.S. Bureau of the Census, *Historical Statistics of the United States, Colonial Times to 1957* (Washington, D.C., 1960), pp. 290–304; "watershed," Gilbert C. Fite, *American Farmers, The New Minority* (Bloomington: Indiana University Press, 1981), p. 88; Truman address on hunger, *Minneapolis Morning Tribune*, April 20, 1946; Herbert Hoover quotation, Fite, op. cit., p. 89; LaGuardia quotation, *Tribune*, op. cit.

8. Rye statistics from Commodity Research Bureau, Inc., *Commodity Yearbook 1948*, pp. 413–18; "personal contacts" in "Feed and Oil Division Meeting of Plant Managers," December 15, 1945, CA 54-03; nylon stocking trades, John Peterson to John Jr., January 31, 1946, CA 46-07; quotations from John Jr., "Plain Talk," February 23, 1946, CA 46-07; for "cure for high prices," see draft, n.d., ibid.

9. "No stone unturned," John Jr. to Ed Grimes, February 21, 1946, ibid.; grain ceiling hike analyzed in Special Press Bulletin, *Northwestern Miller*, May 9, 1946.

10. For separate actions of the three exchanges, see *Northwestern Miller*, May 14, 1946, p. 10; *Minneapolis Tribune*, May 13, 1946; "Save . . . Shorts," Chicago *Journal of Commerce*, May 14, 1946; "this bunch of cookies," John Jr. to Ed Grimes, February 21, 1946 (second wire), CA 46-07; "nick us," John Jr. to Cargill MacMillan, May 14, 1946, ibid.; "red flag," Julius Hendel to John Jr., May 11, 1946, ibid.; telegram to Secretary of Agriculture Clinton P. Anderson, May 10, 1946, ibid.; *New York Times* quotation on Cargill antitrust suit, May 22, 1946; contested regulation 1899, adopted by CBOT on June 13, 1946, reprinted in Chicago *Journal of Commerce*, June 14, 1956; amended figure for treble damages noted in Hayes Miller to Austen Cargill and Ed Grimes, March 6, 1947; *New York Times*, March 18, 1947; rationale behind total figure described in Leavitt R. Barker to John Jr., April 2, 1947, Law Department, CA Box 3; "please don't ever sue me," F. Peavey Heffelfinger to John Jr., June 2, 1946, CA 46-07; "defeated by a wide margin," Julius Hendel to John Jr., May 11, 1946, ibid.; quotation of Circuit Court Justice Sherman Minton from *Cargill, Inc. v. Board of Trade of City of Chicago, et al.*, 164 Federal Reporter, 2nd ser., December 23, 1947; Supreme Court citations, 333 U.S. 880, April 26, 1948, and 334 U.S. 835, June 1, 1948; comparison of Minneapolis and Chicago exchanges, "Report of the Federal Trade Commission on Economic Effects of Grain Exchange Actions Affecting Futures Trading During the First Six Months of 1946," February 4, 1947, p. 70; see also Production and Marketing Administration, USDA, "Effect on Futures Trading in Grains of Changes in Price Ceilings of May 3, 1946," August 12, 1946; hearings before the House Committee on Agriculture, 80th Cong., 1st sess., *Long-Range Agricultural Policy*, (part 4), 1947, pp. 578, 581, 582; "B.O. trade," John Jr. to Cargill MacMillan, June 21, 1946, CA 53-04; accounting for losses, F. J. Hays to Cargill MacMillan, November 28, 1947, CA 53-01.

11. Effects on shorts, *New York Times*, May 22 and June 1, 1946; ibid., June 14, 1946, for structure of price control bill of Senate; veto of final bill, ibid., June 30; new OPA legislation was agreed to on July 25; "reluctantly" quotation from President Truman's Message to Congress, *New York Times*, July 26; grain trade campaign against price controls, see ibid., August 3, 1946; Price Recontrol Board controls, ibid., August 21; "blackest markets," ibid., May 10, 1946. Prices for individual grains in 1946 from Commodity Yearbook, 1948, op. cit.

12. Port Cargill flax plant, *Cargill News*, September 1946; sale of flax, see Dorsey, Colman, et al. to Albert G. Egermayer, August 28, 1946, CA 47-11; bonus, Fred Seed memorandum, September 24, 1946, Whitney MacMillan MS, No. 1; "remarkable support," identical letters to E. E. Kelm, Ford Ferguson and L. L. Crosby from John Jr., September 10, 1946, CA 47-11.

13. Cargill quotation on high flax prices, *Minneapolis Morning Tribune*, October 29, 1946; *St. Paul Pioneer Press* on "flax scandal," October 26, 1946; see also ibid., October 29 and November 4 and 13; probe, ibid. January 7, 1947; government pledge, ibid., February 18, 1947.

14. Move to Rand house ("Lake Office"), H. B. Juneau, June 3, 1946, CA 47-11; "none . . . deal with the public," memorandum of John Jr., October 10, 1952, CA Lake 20; John Jr.'s "Cargill House," in his wire to Cargill MacMillan, June 5, 1946, CA 53-04; the "Anonymous" article, *Cargill News*, June 1946. The records in the CA on the Kempner Foundation are voluminous; see CA 47-10 and 47-11, 59–10 and Lake 3 and 5; first contact by John Jr. in his

telegram to Dr. Kempner, May 28, 1946, CA 46-08; "plunger," John Jr. to John and Edna MacMillan, n.d., CA 34-04; "greatest in the 81-year history," John Jr. to Hugh and Duncan MacMillan, November 1, 1946, CA 47-11; "relatively new field," John Jr. to Edna MacMillan, ibid.; ulcers, John Jr. to Cargill MacMillan, January 11, 1947, CA 53-04; "memory goes back," John Peterson to John Jr., October 30, 1946, CA 47-11.

15. John Jr., "Theory and Practice of Organization," May 10, 1946, CA 46-07; Nutrena move to Minneapolis, *Cargill News*, January and July 1947; consolidation of all feeds into Nutrena, ibid., January 1947 and February 1948; A. J. James to Mrs. F. B. Nelson, February 6, 1948, CA Law 3; R. E. Whitworth to Julius Hendel et al., August 12, 1947, ibid.; "evacuation" quotation, ibid., January 1947; "good manners," R. E. Whitworth to John Jr., June 14, 1946, CA 47-10; "employee" common stock, Dwayne Andreas to Austen Cargill, November 10, 1947, CA Austen Cargill MS, Salary Committee; bean buying policy, in "Meeting of Division Heads," October 14, 1947, CA Lake 22; sale of stock is described in Minutes of Board of Directors, November 17, December 5, 1947; J. G. Peterson, Annual Report, April 20, 1948, CA Whitney MacMillan MS 5.

16. Julius Hendel on decentralization, memorandum to John Jr., Austen Cargill and Cargill MacMillan, July 23, 1947, CA Austen Cargill MS; accounting decentralization, Booz, Allen & Hamilton, "Interim Program Report, Accounting System Installation," September 30, 1948, CA 56-05; "prevent a fiasco," R. J. Harrigan to E. E. Kelm, April 12, 1949, CA 53-01; Kelm response in his letter to Cargill MacMillan, May 25, 1949, ibid.; "superbly done," Clyde Hegman to Cargill MacMillan, August 20, 1949, CA Whitney MacMillan MS 5; "present personnel is not ready," Hendel and Fred Seed to Austen Cargill, December 31, 1947, ibid.; "Meeting of Division Heads," January 20, 1948, CA Lake 22; Morrison hiring, Cargill MacMillan to John Jr., August 13, 1946, CA 53-04; promotion from within, *Cargill News*, January 1948; memorandum on decentralization, John Jr., to 15 senior executives, May 6, 1949; Peterson opposition discussed in Austen Cargill to John Jr., May 2, 1949, CA 34-04.

17. Teacher training program, *Cargill News*, February 1945; Austen Cargill on history of training program, October 4, 1945, CA Austen Cargill MS; "Report on General Training Program," John Savage, n.d., ibid.; prewar experience, H. B. Juneau to Cargill MacMillan, November 15, 1945, CA Whitney MacMillan MS 3; postwar record, "Present Job Assignments of Men Recently Hired Through the College Graduate Recruiting Program," January 1, 1954, ibid.; "intense competitive spirit," John Jr. to Delano DeWindt, January 3, 1948, CA 47-11; advantage of eastern schools, John Jr. to Duncan MacMillan, March 13, 1947, ibid.; Yale men disappointing, John Jr. to Donald S. Funk, July 13, 1956, CA 59-11; self-discipline, John Jr. to Dr. Clarence Danhof, October 20, 1956, CA Lake 3; stability of Cargill, John Jr., "Facts about Cargill," February 5, 1946, CA 46-07; first Stillwater "management conference," *Cargill News*, March 1949; vote on *Carmac* is recounted in Albert J. James, "Memories, Memories," October 25, 1982, CA.

18. "Without . . . the courtesy," John Jr. to Dwight P. Joyce, March 9, 1953, CA Lake 20; not "chattels," Joyce to John Jr., March 16, 1953, ibid.; "*very large* investment," John Jr. to A. E. Staley, June 14, 1955, CA Lake 3; "young organization," Cargill MacMillan to Cargill MacMillan, Jr., October 20, 1952, CA Whitney MacMillan MS 7.

19. Establishment of Salary Committee, Austen Cargill, et al. to John Jr., August 26, 1946, CA 47-11; see Annual Reports, 1947–1949 (Corporate Minute Book); "Incentive Pay Plan," see Minutes of Board of Directors, December 13, 1948; initial division minimums, ibid., August 12, 1948, August 9, 1949, and August 8, 1950.

20. "Little property," John Jr. to James Gould, December 3, 1947, CA Lake 23; "anything but poor," John Jr. to Edna MacMillan, October 10, 1946, CA 47-11; on "saved gutting the company," John Jr. to Duncan M. Rowles, October 23, 1947, CA 53-04.

21. Initial purchase of Falk & Company, board of directors, June 2, 1947; purchase of the remainder in "President's Report to the Stockholders," August 4, 1950, CA Lake 21; Peterson opposition, memorandum of May 9, 1947, to John Jr. and Cargill MacMillan, CA 53-09; first three years of the Falk operation, Sumner B. Young, "S.B.Y.'s Final Chronological Narrative, Re the Linseed-Oil Incidents Which Occurred at Two Falk Plants During the Years 1949 and 1951," CA Law Department #5 (quotation from p. 5); John Peterson quotation, memorandum to John Jr. and Cargill MacMillan, April 29, 1949, CA 53-09.

22. Opening of copra operation in San Francisco, see *Cargill News*, September 1947; Howard Boone article, ibid., December 1948. Prospectus on the West Coast crushing project, Cargill MacMillan to John Jr., August 12, 1946, CA 34-04.

23. Sunflower project, Claude S. Halderman to Agricultural Services Department, May 28, 1947, CA Lake 24; Halderman to John Jr., et al., December 17, 1948, CA Lake 21; on safflower, report of David F. MacKnight, March 12, 1946, CA 46-08; Halderman to L. L. Crosby, May 2, 1947, CA 47-10. *Cargill News* articles, September 1947 (sunflower) and December 1947 (safflower).

24. "Look into South America," Cargill MacMillan to Michael R. Cross, July 22, 1947, CA 56-05; announcement of Puerto Rico project, *Cargill News*, January 1948; its abandonment, ibid., December 1948; Argentine hybrid corn, J. G. Peterson to Commitment Committee, August 29, 1949, CA 53-09; fobbing, Al Greenman, "Cargill in Argentina," August 21, 1950, CA Lake 21; initial contact with Nelson Rockefeller, wires March 13, 1947, CA 47-11; initial skepticism by John Jr., letter to Cargill MacMillan, March 31, 1947, ibid., and his letters to Rockefeller, July 14 and August 6, 1947; memorandum of agreement, John Jr. to Rockefeller, May 28 and August 6, 1947 CA Lake 23; project announced in Cargill *News Bulletin*, April 7, 1948, CA Lake 1; description of projects, Wayne G. Broehl, Jr., *The International Basic Economy Corporation* (Washington D.C.: National Planning Association, 1968), pp. 58–62; Venezuela grain elevators, John Jr. to Cargill MacMillan, March 1, 1949, CA Lake 5. Panama project, Cargill MacMillan, "Report on Darien Survey Made Feb. 25, 1949," CA Lake 1, Panama; "Report of Latin American Section of Trip of Messrs. John J. MacMillan, Jr. and Ricardo Robles, June 1949," ibid.; John Jr. to Austen Cargill and Cargill MacMillan, February 1, 1949, ibid.

25. "Costly errors," John Jr. to Hendel, June 24, 1948, CA Lake 21; "wicked decline," J. G. Peterson, Annual Report, April 20, 1948, CA Whitney MacMillan MS 5.

26. Issues of strike, *New York Times*, September 24 and 27, 1947; Company's response, series of wires from J. A. Brooks to Austen Cargill, October 3–7, 1947, CA Austen Cargill MS; withdrawal of injunction, *New York Times*, October 22, 1947; *Job Policies* pamphlet, ibid.

27. Representation election, Labor Relations Department, Annual Report, December 31, 1946, CA 47-10; "heavy circuits," John B. Alcorn to James A. Brooks, March 22, 1947, and Brooks to Alcorn, March 27, 1947, CA Austen Cargill MS; union's side of negotiations, Frank M. Dinghofer, "Minneapolis Is In!", CA 47-04; "torn tape" system described, *Cargill News*, February 1949.

28. Resignation from Chicago and North Western Railway board, John Jr. to R. L. Williams, February 19, 1948, CA Lake 23; Williams to John Jr., March 8, 1948, ibid; "pitchfork in . . . back," Gilbert Fite, *American Farmers, the New Minority*, op. cit., p. 97; "hogs . . . to three cents," Harry S. Truman speech, Dexter, Iowa, *New York Times*, September 19, 1948; against managed economy, John Jr. to Alfred D. Lindley, June 4, 1948, CA Lake 4; on Committee for Economic Development, M.B. Folsom to John Jr., October 12, 1951, CA Lake 4.

29. Brannan plan, "like a bomb," Willard W. Cochrane and Mary E. Ryan, *American Farm Policy, 1948–1973*. (Minneapolis: University of Minnesota Press, 1976), p. 87; terms of International Wheat Agreement, ibid., P.L. 421, 63 Stat. 945, October 27, 1949; on 1948 elections, John Jr. memorandum, November 8, 1948, W. Duncan MacMillan MS; view on Brannan plan, John Jr. to Vernon Mund, April 25, 1949, CA Lake 5.

30. U.S. Senate Committee on Agriculture and Forestry, *Investigation of Storage and Processing Activities of the Commodity Credit Corporation*, Part 1 (January 18–April 29, 1952), Senate Report 82–2048; quotation of Erwin E. Kelm, ibid., p. 33; *Fortune* quotation on 1949 May wheat contract in August 1949 issue, p. 110; *Business Week* article, "Cargill Reaps New Harvest," April 16, 1949; futures trading policy, John Jr. to Julius Hendel, September 2, 1949, CA Lake 21; "change it around," John Jr. to James M. Sutherland, April 18, 1949, CA Lake 2; "Excessive Profits," *Minneapolis Tribune*, May 8, 1952.

17. Korean War, Tradax Beginnings (pp. 737–85)

1. "Over in two weeks," John Jr. to H. T. Morrison, July 31, 1950, CA Lake 21.

2. John MacMillan, Jr. on effects of Korean War on employment, *Cargill News*, Septem-

ber 1950; "seen everything," Cargill MacMillan to John Jr. January 21, 1950, CA 53-05; Mexia terminal described, *Cargill News*, July 1950; big-bin storage, President's Report to the Stockholders, August 4, 1950, in Minutes of Board of Directors, August 8, 1950; dredging at Corpus Christi, George Basler to Erwin E. Kelm, April 9, 1951, CA Lake 1; floating elevator, John Jr. to Capt. A. C. Ingersoll, Jr., March 13, 1951; Ingersoll to John Jr., March 20, 1951, CA Lake 21.

3. Development of *Carport*, see John Jr. to Lorentz Hansen, c/o George G. Sharp, and attached memorandum, September 22, 1949, CA Lake 1.

4. Carpeake Corporation incorporation, December 21, 1951; construction of intercoastal tug-barge described in Minutes of the Board of Directors, December 27, 1951, Corporate Secretary 85-49; Bethlehem Steel Company Shipbuilding Division, Beaumont, Texas, to H. Duncan Watson, November 5, 1951, CA Lake 19; Minnesota Western Railway Company "disliked by Cargill top executives," Cargill MacMillan, December 25, 1950, Whitney MacMillan MS 5; establishing a separate transportation unit, ibid., March 4, 1951; Cargill owning two transportation carriers, Oliver E. Sweet (ICC) to James E. Dorsey, April 30, 1942, CA 56-05; formation of Minnesota Western Company, Dorsey to John Jr., June 23 and July 14, 1948, CA Lake 21; Dorsey to Cargill MacMillan, September 20, 1949, CA 56-05; construction of towboats and barges, Albert G. Egermayer to Sumner B. Young, March 15, 1955, Corporate Secretary 85-08; "Report of the President to the Stockholders of the Minnesota River Company," October 13, 1953, ibid., 85-62; relationship between Minnesota River Company and other Company corporate entities, "Re: Capital Structure and Ownership," January 10, 1957, ibid., 85-08; Wesota Company was incorporated January 7, 1950; leases for elevators, Minutes of Board of Directors, January 26, 1950, Corporate Secretary 85-60; Port Cargill loading facilities described, *Cargill News*, July 1950.

5. Royal Feed and Milling Company acquisition, Cargill *News Bulletin*, May 31, 1951; *Cargill News*, November 1957 and May 1952; "Memo re Proposed Nutrena—Royal Merger," May 10, 1951, CA 53-06; see also John Jr. to Marion MacMillan, May 28, 1951, CA Lake 5; Kansas City flood, *Cargill News*, August 1951.

6. New Chicago plants, *Annual Report of the Commitment Committee*, May 31, 1950, CA Whitney MacMillan MS 4; solvent plant, "Memorandum re Proposal to Build Solvent Extraction Plant in Chicago," December 29, 1948, CA Lake Office 4; bank caution, Hugo Scheuermann to John Jr., March 3, 1949, ibid., 2; *Cargill News*, June 1950.

7. *Cargill News* on Minneapolis Seed Company, September 1931; development of Cargill hybrid corn, February 1944, August 1946 and July 1948 issues. Discontinuance of Farm Supply Department, ibid., January 1950. Introduction of "Miracle Green," memorandum to all employees, March 14, 1951, CA Whitney MacMillan MS 4; FTC query in Charles E. Grandey to Cargill, Inc., June 11, 1951, Law Department 5. "All boasting will be limited," T. T. Hale to John Jr., July 30, 1951, CA Lake Office 21.

8. Cargill Foundation proposal, "To the Preferred and Common Stockholders of Cargill, Incorporated," August 31, 1950, and board of directors meetings of May 31 and September 12 and 15, 1950, *Corporate Minute Book*; "proliferation," Albert G. Egermayer to Calvin J. Anderson, October 24, 1975, Perth Corporation file, William A. Pearce. See also "Memorandum: Suggestions with Respect to Proposed Reorganization of Cargill, Incorporated," September 21, 1948; "Report of the Special Committee on Reorganization of Cargill Corporate Structure," July 25, 1949, ibid.

9. Alfalfa seed case, Federal Seed Case No. 681, U.S. District Court for the District of Minnesota, Fourth Division, *Information*, n.d., Law Department 7, B7-101.1; hearing record, ibid., Case No. 8280 Criminal, March 16, 1953, ibid.; "moral turpitude," p. 15; Judge Nordbye's statements, p. 7; subsequent criminal cases against four former Cargill employees, *Minneapolis Morning Tribune*, November 25, 1953; Cargill Hotel story, *Des Moines Register*, October 16, 1951; quotation on "front page," CA 57-02.

10. Senator Allan J. Ellender hearings, *New York Times* May 7, 1952; "conversions," ibid., February 5, 1952; charge against Cargill in Clayton M. Nickolson, Chief, Fiscal Division, Production and Marketing Division, U.S. Department of Agriculture, March 6, 1952, CA Lake 21; Weston Grimes quotation, *New York Times*, May 7, 1952; "settle . . . or else," John Peterson memorandum, March 14, 1952, CA 53-09; M. D. Wyard as coordinator, April 7, 1952, ibid.; "thou shalt not be," John Peterson to Erv Kelm, April 8, 1952, ibid.; "picture as the

management sees it," May 8, 1952, CA Whitney MacMillan MS 3; Cargill MacMillan description in his letter to Cargill, Jr., October 20, 1952, ibid., 7; "not guilty" verdict, R. C. Woodworth to John Jr., November 9, 1954, CA Lake 19; quotations from Judge Stephen W. Brennan in *Cargill, Incorporated v. Commodity Credit Corporation*, U.S. District Court, Northern District of New York, Civil Suit 6207, September 3, 1958.

11. Charges of Senator William F. Jenner, *New York Times*, May 2, 1953; *Wall Street Journal*, May 4, 1953; Cargill MacMillan description of case, letter to Cargill Jr., November 4, 1952, CA Whitney MacMillan MS 7; Senator Milton R. Young comments, undated newspaper story (ca. May 2, 1953), CA Lake 3; CEA complaint, *In re Cargill, Incorporated and Erwin E. Kelm*, Docket No. 58 June 11, 1953, CA Law B-12, 514.1; Austen Cargill statement, *Cargill News*, June 1953; John Jr. memorandum, "Reasons for Large Scale Importations of Canadian Oats during 1951, 1952 and 1953," dated August 5, 1953, CA Whitney MacMillan MS 3; Julius Hendel memorandum, "A Short Story of the Grain Market," CA John Peterson MS; "largely beneficial," Winnipeg Grain Exchange, "The Trade of Canada and the United States of America and Imports of Canadian Grain by the United States of America," November 2, 1953, CA Whitney MacMillan MS 3; "halt record-breaking imports," *Wall Street Journal*, November 4, 1953; Senator Paul Douglas allegation of cost to farmers of $600,000,000, *New York Times*, September 25, 1954.

12. Meeting with Secretary of Agriculture Ezra T. Benson, his letters to F. Peavey Heffelfinger, November 30, 1953, and John Jr. to Benson, December 14, 1953, CA Lake 20; complaint, George E. MacKinnon, U.S. Attorney, District Court, District of Minnesota, Fourth Division, *United States of America v. Cargill, Incorporated and Cargill Grain Company, Limited*, Civil 4849, February 20, 1954.

13. "Put not faith in Princes," Cargill MacMillan to John Jr., February 9, 1954, CA 56-03; "interfering with the plans," John Jr. to Austen Cargill and Cargill MacMillan, March 8, 1954, ibid.; hedging policy, John Jr. to "all Merchandising Personnel," March 22, 1954, CA Lake 9; Austen Cargill concern in Cargill MacMillan to John Jr., February 19, 1954, ibid.; "the very devil," John Jr. to Cargill MacMillan, February 18, 1954, ibid.

14. Stipulation for case, Civil 4849, op. cit., is dated May 3, 1954; "write the language . . . ourselves," John Jr. to Cargill MacMillan, April 30, 1954, CA 56-03; notice to employees, *The Green Wave*, May 4, 1954, Law B12, 514.1; "great victory," John Jr. to Alan S. Phillips, May 7, 1954, CA Lake 2; story in *Minneapolis Star*, John Jr. to Gideon Seymour, May 6, 1954; John Cowles to John Jr., May 29, 1954, ibid; antitrust case, brought by F. Arthur Jost and Aaron B. Weiner, was filed on November 5, 1953, and dismissed on May 27, 1954, *New York Times*, November 6, 1953, and May 27, 1954.

15. To "our banking friends," memorandum of John Peterson, n.d. (ca. May 1954), Law B12, 514.1; *Time* article, "Wild Oats," May 17, 1954; Pillsbury charges, unnamed newspaper, November 6, 1954, CA Lake 3; Archer-Daniels-Midland suit, *Saint Paul Pioneer Press*, October 9, 1954; "Cargill's aggressiveness," *Fortune*, December 1965.

16. The CBOT symposium paper of John Jr., "Grain Futures Trading—Steps Necessary for Its Successful Continuation," is dated September 8, 1955, Law Department, A4, 503,2.

17. Hedging of oats, H. Robert Diercks, "As I Recall It," MS collection of Diercks; "constructive," John Jr. to Austen Cargill and Cargill MacMillan, March 8, 1954, CA 56-03.

18. Quotations from Dwayne Andreas from my interview, January 29, 1990, and E. J. Kahn, Jr., "Profiles: The Absolute Beginning," *The New Yorker*, February 16, 1987; "deeply shocked," John Peterson to John Jr., March 24, 1952, CA 56-03; on tighter limits, Albert G. Egermayer to Finance Committee, May 20, 1954, CA Whitney MacMillan MS 3; "Position and Trading Limits, Grain Division . . . ," September 30, 1954, ibid.; "Position and Trading Limits, Oil Division," October 21, 1954, CA Lake 19.

19. "A Godsend," Cargill MacMillan to Austen Cargill, April 7, 1952, CA 56-03; John Jr. memorandum "To All Division Heads," June 10, 1952, CA Lake 21; appointment of M. D. McVay, *Cargill News*, June 1952; Oil Division–Grain Division arrangements, John Jr. to John Peterson, November 9, 1951, ibid.; new arrangements between divisions, E. E. Kelm and M. D. McVay to Cargill MacMillan, July 17, 1952, CA Whitney MacMillan MS 3.

20. John Jr. address to Cargill Management Conference Series, March 27, 1953, CA Lake 14; see also John Jr.'s memorandum to division heads, September 28, 1951; *Cargill News* editorial, June 1951.

21. Dan Morgan, *Merchants of Grain* (New York: Viking Press, 1979), pp. 96–97; Guernsey in Channel Islands as location, Cargill MacMillan to John Jr., February 19, 1937, CA 38-04; "breakers ahead," in "Memorandum for A.S.C. and C. Mac, Exclusively," February 26, 1949, CA Lake 21; Don Levin, "Memorandum Re Proposed Foreign Trading and Shipping Operations," December 27, 1951, CA 53-01; "endless belt theory," Erwin E. Kelm, "Relationship of Incorporated to Tradax," April 16, 1959, CA Whitney MacMillan MS 3; "*intra* national business," Cargill MacMillan to Whitney MacMillan, December 31, 1954, ibid., No. 5; Lord, Day & Taylor, "Memorandum re Proposed Foreign Operations of Cargill Internacional, CA Don Levin MS; ownership structure, Cargill MacMillan, "Outline for Plan in re Panamanian Corporation," November 26, 1951, CA John MacMillan, Jr. MS; copra, Donald C. Levin to Cargill MacMillan, December 28, 1951, CA 53-01; Coprax, Levin to George Burton, June 26, 1952, ibid.; Canadian grain, Levin to Kelm, February 19, 1954, Corporate Secretary, Tradax Internacional No. 1; organizational structure, Erwin E. Kelm, "Prospectus of Cargill, International [*sic*] and Its Subsidiaries and Agents, March 15, 1954, CA Don Levin MS; choice of "Kerrgill," Levin to C. C. Boden, July 13, 1954, Corporate Secretary, Tradax Internacional 1; use of Handel Maatschappij, Sumner B. Young to Peterson, September 24, 1946, CA 53-01.

22. Purchase of Kerr-Gifford, Corporate Minutes, Cargill, Incorporated, June 9, 1953; announcement, J. G. Peterson to "Our Banking Friends," June 9, 1953, Lake 20; "carry . . . our own trades," Peterson to John Jr., June 15, 1953, ibid.; structure of Kerr-Gifford, A. J. James to Peterson, October 19, 1953, CA Whitney MacMillan MS 3.

23. Early results, Cargill MacMillan to Austen Cargill, December 20, 1954, CA 56-03; organization in Montreal, Kelm to Cargill MacMillan, August 13, 1954, CA Whitney MacMillan MS 3; first year of Tradax, "Analysis and Observations," C. J. Stuart Allan report, May 31, 1955, CA Lake 20; "almost completely . . . in Wayzata," Don Levin to Cargill MacMillan, November 11, 1954, Corporate Secretary, Tradax Internacional 1; conflicts between Cargill Internacional offices, Cargill MacMillan memorandum, December 24, 1954, CA Whitney MacMillan MS 5; futures trading, "Cargill Internacional, S.A.—Futures Trading," n.d. (ca. March 1955), CA Don Levin MS; Montreal limits problem, John Jr. to John Peterson, Austen Cargill and Cargill MacMillan, March 21, 1955, CA Lake 20.

24. Harry A. Bullis, "Agricultural Policies," *New York Times*, July 19, 1953; John Jr. to Bullis, August 17, 1953, CA Lake 2; John Jr. to Arthur F. Burns, October 16, 1953, CA Lake 20; John Jr. to Sherman Adams, ibid.; Gabriel Hauge to John Jr., December 21, 1953, ibid.; on CED, John Jr. to Paul S. Gerot, May 6, 1954, ibid.

25. $800,000 a day in storage charges, Gilbert C. Fite, *American Farmers: The New Minority*, op. cit., p. 105; Public Law 480, Willard W. Cochrane and Mary E. Ryan, *American Farm Policy, 1948–1973*, op. cit., pp. 31–32, 144–145; backhaul problem at Port Cargill, Robert B. Parrott to Cargill MacMillan, February 23, 1951, CA Lake 21; coal backhaul, *Cargill News*, December 1952; molasses project, *Cargill News*, August 1953.

26. Flax plant explosion, Cargill MacMillan to Whitney MacMillan, February 18, 1955, CA Whitney MacMillan MS 6; John Jr. to Cargill MacMillan, March 10, 1955, CA Lake 20; *Cargill News*, March 1955; crowded port at New Orleans, Kelm to John Jr., February 11, 1953, CA Lake 20.

27. Sinking of *Carmac I*, exchange of wires, September 22, 1953, CA Lake 19; San Francisco crash, clipping, unnamed San Francisco newspaper, November 21, 1955, CA Lake 20.

28. CEA concerning "big bin," memorandum of Weston Grimes, October 6, 1953, CA 53-09; John Jr. to Ezra Taft Benson, August 3 and September 16, 1954, CA Lake 20; L. A. Hoopes to John Jr., September 2, 1954, ibid.

29. "Run-in with J.G.P.," John Jr., 1955 diary, July 27, 1955; "new low in weight," ibid., July 14 and 15; indoctrination program on "vital trading information," John C. Savage to John Jr., February 14, 1955, CA Lake 19; "complacency," John Jr. to Cargill MacMillan, March 3, 1955, CA Lake 20; time to "cry 'wolf,' " John Jr. to Austen Cargill, March 4, 1953, ibid.; "unsolicited advice is unwelcome," Julius Hendel to John Jr., August 6, 1953, CA Lake 19; request for retirement, ibid., n.d. (ca. August 1955), CA Lake 19; "real contribution," Oliver S. Powell to John Jr., September 5, 1955, ibid.; "friendly customer," John Jr. to Hendel, August 6, 1956, CA 59-10; " 'Jewish' gentleman," letter to John Jr., September 3, 1947, CA Lake 24; "run on the Hollywood style," John Peterson to Austen Cargill, February 16, 1955, CA 53-09.

18. Corporate Leadership, Management Losses (pp. 786–844)

1. "Mormon zeal," Ross M. Robertson, *History of the American Economy*, op. cit., p. 529; on Soil Bank program, Willard W. Cochran and Mary E. Ryan, *American Farm Policy, 1948–1973*, op. cit., pp. 33, 147.

2. *Fortune*, "The 500 Largest Industrials," July 1960; ibid., "Merchandising Firms," August 1960; "Fat on dole," Gilbert C. Fite, *American Farmers, The New Minority*, op. cit., p. 108; statistics on Commodity Credit Corporation, U.S. Bureau of the Census, *Historical Statistics of the United States Colonial Times to 1970* (Washington, D.C.: 1975), p. 488.

3. "Missing out," John Jr. to John III and W. Duncan MacMillan, April 9, 1956, CA Lake 3; sugarcane in Cuba, ibid., March 16, 1956; Jamaican sugar cane, John Jr. to Cargill MacMillan, January 25, 1957, CA Whitney MacMillan MS 6; *Carport* disaster, Cargill MacMillan to John Peterson, September 24, 1956, CA 59-10; John Jr., 1956 *Diary*, ibid.; barges for Cuban trade, John Jr. to John III and W. Duncan MacMillan, April 20, 1956, CA Lake 3; dedication of Norfolk terminal and speech, John Jr., 1957 diary, July 29 and August 3, 1957; *Congressional Record* reprint, ibid., August 26, 1957; Albany through, memorandum to John Jr. and Cargill MacMillan, April 5, 1956, CA Whitney MacMillan MS 4; John Jr. unhappiness with Norfolk project in his letter to Austen Cargill, December 2, 1955, CA Lake 2; plans for Norfolk, Erwin E. Kelm to John Jr., March 22, 1956, CA Lake 19.

4. Purchase of three lakers, *Cargill News*, March 1956; Quebec North Shore, John Jr., to Frank A. Augsbury, Jr. August 28, 1953, CA Lake 20; first contact with Hanna, John Jr. to J. H. Thompson, December 11, 1953, ibid.; Hanna link proposal, Cargill MacMillan to John Jr., July 3, 1956, CA 59-10; John Jr. quotation on "5¢ a bushel," handwritten notes of Cargill MacMillan, July 27–August 2, 1956, CA Whitney MacMillan MS 7; location of terminal at Seven Islands, John Jr. to G. W. Humphrey, August 6, 1956, CA 59-08; draft "Seven Islands" proposal, Don Levin MS CA; purchase of land, Donald C. Levin to John Jr. and others, October 3, 1956; alternative site at Baie Comeau, Levin to Earle H. Greene, with attachment, June 5, 1958, CA Whitney MacMillan MS 4.

5. Subterminal project, unsigned memorandum to Cargill MacMillan and John Jr., April 5, 1956, CA Whitney MacMillan MS 4; Michigan City, Indiana—Chicago warehouse link, E. E. Kelm to John Jr., et al., September 16, 1957, ibid.

6. Swiss tax, Don Levin to Cargill MacMillan, February 5, 1956, CA Whitney MacMillan MS 6; tax implications of transit grain, Walter Gage to John Peterson, October 12, 1956, CA 53-09; "ridiculously small," Peterson to C. J. S. Allan, July 17, 1956, CA 53-09; early conception of the Geneva organization, "a plan for the reorganization of Cargill, Internacional and subsidiaries," n.d. (ca. summer 1954), CA Don Levin MS; plans for move in "Time Schedule," April 1, 1956, CA 59-10; German office, Levin to A. C. Greenman and Charles E. Bachman, May 25, 1955, CA Whitney MacMillan MS 4; "repercussions . . . among our banking friends," Peterson to Austen Cargill, May 17, 1956, CA 53-09; Peterson retirement, John Jr. to Peterson, June 21, 1956, CA Lake 20; effect of Peterson retirement on his officerships, James E. Dorsey to Cargill MacMillan, December 21, 1956, CA Whitney MacMillan MS 6; long position on Suez War, John Jr. to Austen Cargill, December 11, 1956, CA 59-10.

7. "Too near together," Peterson to Allan, July 17, 1956, op. cit.; memorandum on "separate and independent," H. B. Juneau, May 16, 1956, CA Whitney MacMillan MS 4; earned "at the instruction of," Kelm to John Jr., December 15, 1955, CA Lake 19; "no limit be placed," Walter Gage to Peterson, October 15, 1956, CA 53-09; "does not mean to infer," Kelm to Peterson, October 22, 1959, ibid.; "human experience . . . against," Peterson to Gage, October 23, 1959, ibid.

8. Throughput, John Jr. to Gage, August 24, 1956, CA 53-09; Gage reply, August 29, 1956, CA 59-09; special "Report on Control of Risks and Use of Funds," May 31, 1956, Section B of *Annual Report of the Finance Committee*, Cargill, Incorporated Corporate Minutes, May 31, 1956; "capital fund," memorandum of Special Committee, September 18, 1956, CA Whitney MacMillan MS 4; "spread or two," T. J. Totushek to John Jr., February 19, 1957, CA Lake 17.

9. "Figures are fictitious," John Jr. to John Peterson, January 25, 1957, CA Whitney MacMillan MS 6; "forgotten men," Peterson to Gage, December 7, 1956, CA 53-09; New York office, Peterson to W. W. Hyde, November 27, 1956, ibid; Kelm to Peterson, May 29, 1957, Don Levin MS CA; coordination between Minneapolis and Geneva, Kelm to Peterson, December 10, 1957, ibid.

10. "Newspapers misrepresented," John Jr. to K. F. J. Poolen, June 19, 1956, CA 59-10; report on trip by John Jr., Hamburg, Germany, May 18, 1956, CA *1956 Diary*; no major commitments, Albert G. Egermayer to A. S. Cargill, et al., October 8, 1956, CA Lake 19; tightening money, Egermayer to Finance Committee, January 31, 1957, CA Whitney Mac-Millan MS 4; John Jr. to Kelm, March 19, 1957, ibid.; postpone all except Rotterdam and Seven Islands, John Jr. to Kelm, March 6, 1957, CA 59-10; on priorities, John Jr. to Cargill MacMillan, February 8, 1957, CA Whitney MacMillan MS 6; "Gage . . . doesn't want us," John Jr. diary entry, March 21, 1957, CA 1957 Diary; "Walter resents," John Jr. to Cargill MacMillan, May 6, 1957, CA Whitney MacMillan MS 6; Northern Europe plans, John Jr. memorandum, May 31, 1957, CA Whitney MacMillan MS 4; "boss trader," John Jr. report, Messina, Italy, April 29, 1957, ibid.; shipbuilding in Japan, John Jr. to T. H. G. Huxley, September 24, 1957, CA 59-09; time charters, John Jr. to Kelm, March 19, 1957, CA 59-10; "serious mistakes," John Jr. to Austen Cargill, April 5, 1957, ibid.; feed mills abroad, Kelm to John Jr., May 15, 1957, CA 59-09; "if . . . unlimited funds," John Peterson to John Jr., March 13, 1958, CA Lake 15; problems in Argentina, Kelm to Peterson, February 27, 1958; Walter F. Gage to Peterson, March 11 and 13, 1958; Kelm to Peterson, March 18, 1958; CA John Mac-Millan, Jr. MS. "Graduate in good standing," John Peterson to Hugo S. Scheuermann, January 4, 1955, CA 53-08; gift for estate, Peterson to John Jr., June 17, 1956, CA 59-10.

11. "Wild Oats" article, *Time*, May 17, 1954; "only two . . . positive," William R. Pearce, Colorado Springs speech, April 1959, John Work MS; "figure staggered me," John Jr. to John Peterson, April 24, 1956; appointment of Carl Byoir & Associates, *Green Wave*, April 23, 1956; Byoir program, Del Beman to John G. Peterson, et al., May 11, 1956, CA 59-08; "Cargill Blasts Grain Export Policy of CCC," *Minneapolis Star*, May 4, 1956, CA Lake 3; "see red," John Jr. to Cargill MacMillan, January 10, 1957, CA Whitney MacMillan MS 6; reply, January 15, 1957, ibid.; on lowest possible weight, Walter Kempner to John Jr., December 27, 1957, CA 59-10; "stop needling," Cargill MacMillan to John Jr., February 15, 1957, CA John Jr. Diary 1957; reply, ibid.; USDA position on shipment of inland grain, *Northwestern Miller*, April 10, 1956; USDA news release, April 6, 1956; "deepening wedge," *Northwestern Miller*, May 1, 1956; reversal of CCC policy, *Northwestern Miller*, July 17, 1956; "return to free marketing," ibid.; "gotten them by the ears," John Jr. to Marion H. MacMillan, December 21, 1956, CA 59-10; "Resume of Meeting with . . . Commission Merchants Association," December 20, 1956, ibid,; meeting with CBOT, Julius Mayer to John Jr., August 24, 1956, ibid.; "impossible," John Jr. diary entry, November 21, 1955, CA; reentry to CBOT, John Jr. to Robert C. Liebenow, December 6, 1957, and reply, December 11, 1957, CA 59-09; Senator Hubert Humphrey remarks on amendment of the Agricultural Trade Development and Assistance Act of 1954, see *Congressional Record*, Senate (1956), pp. 10585–10604, CA 59-09.

12. Research building, Corporate Minute Book, November 10, 1956, and March 4, 1958; *Cargill News*, August 1955 and February 1957; transfer of Nutrena Research Center, *Green Wave*, January 4, 1957; "keep John Jr. under control," interview Richard Baldwin, February 3, 1987, CA; propulsion design (U.S. patent 2,784, 691, March 12, 1957), *Cargill News*, May 1957; CA Lake 3, 59-11; British patent 796,307, October 1, 1958; "infringing on my patent," John Jr. to Fred W. Drum, November 19 and December 17, 1943, CA 44-09; "blow-up party," Kelm to John Jr., April 11, 1958, CA Lake 13; H. D. Watson to John Jr., n.d. (ca. spring 1958, CA 59-10; "huff and puff," John Jr. entry, November 2, 1958, CA *1958 Diary*; "Chloe" form, *Cargill News*, October and November 1958, April 1959; pipeline conveyor, CA Lake 3; electric amplifier, ibid.; for guided missile, John Jr. to David M. Schlatter, September 28, 1950, and reply, January 6, 1951, CA Lake 4; Department of the Air Force, "Memorandum for General Schlatter: Comments on Cargill, Inc. Letter of 28 September 1950," November 1, 1950, ibid.; sighting a "flying saucer," John Jr. to Marion MacMillan, March 30, 1953, CA Lake 20; Thomas C. Darcy to John Jr., April 2, 1953, CA Lake 2; helicopter, John Jr. to Arthur S. Caine, November 21, 1952, CA Lake 3; Darcy to John Jr., June 1, 1953, CA Lake 2; conference on meteorology, John Jr. diary entry, October 29, 1957, CA *1957 Diary*; weather consultations with Air Force Cambridge Research Center, exchange of correspondence between John Jr. and C. N. Touart, March–May, 1953, CA Lake 2; U.S. Naval Observatory, correspondence between John Jr. and Edgar W. Woolard, December 1953, CA Lake 3; Krick Weather Forecasting Service, correspondence between John Jr. and Irving P. Krick, November–December 1957, CA 59–10; Cargill, Incorporated, contract with Krick, Cameron B. Newell to Regional Managers, November 17, 1958, CA Whitney MacMillan MS 3; "Charting Weather Years

Ahead," *Business Week*, October 11, 1958; sailing ship, John Jr. memorandum and drawings, November 18, 1954, CA Lake 3; John Jr. to Austen Cargill, March 11, 1955, CA Lake 20; Cargill MacMillan to John Jr., January 14, 1955, CA 56-03.

13. Herbert Solow, "Operations Research," *Fortune*, April 1951; "fantastic capabilities," James R. Cargill to J. C. North, et al., May 19, 1955, CA James R. Cargill MS; "we arrive at the point," ibid., November 11, 1955; "All-Mash Egg Feed" project, ibid., May 25 and 31, June 19 and 25, 1956; analysis of computer costs, C. L. Smith report, June 26, 1958, CA 59-08; *Business Week*, June 21, 1958; IBM 650 at the company, *Cargill News*, February and November 1956 and April 1957; Nutrena applications, ibid., April 1957; "We saw . . . 4 million ways," Nutrena advertisement, ca. 1958, CA James R. Cargill MS; "most exciting thing," John Jr. to Cargill MacMillan, April 9, 1959, CA Lake 13.

14. Basic agricultural statistics from Bureau of the Census, *Historical Statistics of the United States: Colonial Times to 1970*, Part 1, op. cit., K.496-537; on yields, Willard W. Cochrane and Mary E. Ryan, *American Farm Policy, 1948-1973*, op. cit., pp. 280-374; Cochrane, *The Development of American Agriculture: A Historical Analysis*, op. cit., p. 128.

15. "Single Wheat Subsidy Suggested by Cargill," *Cargill News*, May 1957; "Cargill Urges Senate to Liberalize Export," ibid., August 1957; Cargill MacMillan letter to Congressmen reprinted in *Cargill News*, April 1958; "long haired," Joseph P. O'Hara to MacMillan, April 1, 1958.

16. John Jr. speech, National Soybean Processors Association, August 10, 1959, CA John MacMillan Jr. MS; ibid. to First Bank Stock Corporation, November 20, 1959, CA Lake 14; speech before Grain & Feed Dealers, *Feeds Illustrated*, ca. October 1958, CA 59-08; John Jr., "Farm Surpluses: How to End Them," *Business Horizons*, Spring 1959; Cochrane and Ryan, *American Farm Policy, 1948-1973*, op. cit., 360, 363.

17. Austen Cargill death, *Cargill News*, June 1957; board of directors resolution in its meeting of July 30, 1957.

18. Early plans for corporate reorganization, "Preliminary and Tentative Memorandum to Executive Committee," John Peterson, August 31, 1954, CA John MacMillan Jr. MS; Cargill MacMillan memorandum, August 7, 1956, CA 56-05; the plan is summarized in three memoranda to stockholders, dated July 25, 1956, CA 59-08; "participation allotment plan" described in Fred Seed memorandum (as chairman of the Salary Committee), November 19, 1957; Cargill, Inc. common stock, Nelson M. Hagen file, Office of Corporate Secretary; tax complications, H. T. Swartz to Joseph H. Coleman, January 23, 1956; Whitney MacMillan MS 1.

19. "Very embarrassing," Cargill MacMillan private memorandum, August 7, 1956, CA 56-05; "I am for the least," John Jr. diary entry of August 1, 1956, CA 1956 *Diary*; determination of levels of management, Cargill MacMillan private memorandum, July 25, 1956, CA 56-03; holdings of "restricted common stockholders," A. J. James to Leland Scott, July 18, 1956 (with attachment), ibid.; initial allotments, Herbert B. Juneau to Salary Committee, November 19, 1957, CA Whitney MacMillan MS 1; calculation of individual amounts, see, as example, Fred M. Seed to Juneau, November 19, 1957, Juneau MS.

20. Discussion of "illiquid price" concept, George B. Weiksner to Calvin J. Anderson, February 12, 1980; Roy Hoople proposed sale, his letter to John Jr., December 2, 1941, Pauline MacMillan MS., CA; resignation, Howard I. McMillan to John Jr., August 2, 1955, CA Lake 3; sale of stock, John Jr. diary entry, August 13 and September 18, 1956, CA 1956 *Diary*; sale of Osborne stock, Cargill MacMillan to E. N. Osborne, August 16, 1956 (with attachment), CA Lake 20; negotiations on Taylor stock, John Jr. to Cargill MacMillan, April 28, 1955; A. J. James to Joseph Coleman, July 19, 1955; Lew Wallace to Cargill MacMillan, July 20, 1955, CA Corporate Secretary, Waycrosse, Inc.

21. Austen Cargill estate sale of common stock, John Jr. to W. Duncan MacMillan and Marion MacMillan, June 10, 1960, W. Duncan MacMillan MS; Weston Grimes negotiations, A. J. James to John Jr., October 3, 1952, CA Lake 19; Weston Grimes to John Jr., September 30, 1952, CA Lake 19; John Jr. to Grimes, October 2, 1952, ibid.; relative stock prices, Joyce Keskitalo to James R. Cargill, et al., April 20, 1990 (with attachment), CA Wayne Broehl MS.

22. "Record Volume, Expansion Marks Company's '57 Year," *Cargill News*, January 1958.

23. "So many . . . opportunities," John Jr. diary entry, October 28, 1958, CA 1958 *Diary*; "must build our own," John Jr. to Kelm, January 22, 1958, CA 59-10; Kelm to John Jr., January 9, 1958, ibid.; "never in winter," wire of January 10, 1958, ibid.; wooden barge, Duncan Watson

to John Jr., March 25, 1960, CA Lake 15; "tested to destruction," John Jr. diary entries September 4 and 5, 1958, CA *1958 Diary*.

24. Jamaica property, John Jr. to H. Duncan Watson, February 14, 1958, CA 59-10; quotations on Japanese ships, John Jr. to John Peterson, March 7, 1958, CA Lake 15; "should have been here," John Jr. to Kelm, April 7, 1958, CA 59-09; "appreciate your compliance," Cargill MacMillan to John Jr., April 4, 1958 (two wires), and reply, John Jr. diary entry, CA *1958 Diary*; "very well received," ibid., May 2, 1958; copra project "at once," John Jr. report to board of directors, May 19, 1958, CA Lake 13.

25. Cargill MacMillan to Charles Cain, Jr., June 16, 1958, CA Whitney MacMillan MS 3; insurance loans, see Corporate Minutes, December 9, 1958, and attached "Memorandum Re Cargill, Incorporated Proposed Term Loan," December 1, 1958; "buy out Peavey," John Jr. diary entry, October 29, 1958, CA *1958 Diary*; "Pete is . . . annoyed," John Jr. to Kelm, April 22, 1959, CA Lake 16.

26. "Boys . . . disturbed," John Jr. to Kelm, April 22, 1959, CA Lake 13; "far flung investments," John Jr. to Kelm, May 6, 1959, CA Lake 18; "multi-millionaire," *Daily Express* (London), May 25, 1959; "urgent agenda," John Jr. "Report on the North Sea Survey," June 1, 1959, CA Lake 14; "Marine Program, 1959–1964," John Jr. report, August 3, 1959, CA Lake 14; "appalling," Corporate Minutes, September 22, 1959; lack of training program at Tradax, John Jr. to Cargill MacMillan, April 5, 1959, MS collection Pauline MacMillan, CA.

27. "Breaking down the door," *Chicago American*, January 20, 1959; rate issues, *Wall Street Journal*, February 9, March 3 and 9, 1959; "mercurial," Weston B. Grimes to J. L. Hazard, July 18, 1957, CA 59-08; "the St. Lawrence Seaway and Its Effect on the North American Grain Trade," John Jr. memorandum, August 7, 1957, ibid.; Akhilesh Dubey, "The Effects of the St. Lawrence Seaway on Ohio Wheat Marketing," Ph.D. dissertation, Ohio State University, 1958; Joseph R. Hartley, *The Effect of the St. Lawrence Seaway on Grain Movements, Business Report* 24 (1957) (Indiana University School of Business); "real blow today," John Jr. to Cargill MacMillan, April 9, 1959, CA Lake 13; "refrain from discussing," A. J. James memorandum, September 15, 1959, CA Lake 15; "untangle the . . . mess," John Jr. to John Peterson, January 4, 1960, CA Whitney MacMillan MS 6; "too late . . . to pour," H. Duncan Watson to John Jr., wire, December 19, 1959, CA Lake 19.

28. Cuban sugar prospects, John Jr. to Cargill MacMillan, March 24, 1956, CA Lake 19; research project, interview with Richard Baldwin, February 3, 1987, CA; on American Bureau of Shipping, Watson to John Jr., April 15, 1958, CA Lake 13; specifications for oceangoing barge, September 1, 1959, CA Lake 14; "counter bid," John Jr. to W. Duncan MacMillan, November 17, 1959, CA, ibid.; "not . . . guarantee," John C. McGrory to Hubert Sontheim, wire, November 15, 1959; ibid.; "re your Havana Company," Cargill MacMillan to John Jr., January 15, 1960, Whitney MacMillan MS 6; "we are quite embarrassed," John Jr. to W. Duncan MacMillan, September 2, 1960, W. Duncan MacMillan MS.

29. Special Investigating Subcommittee of the Senate Committee on Agriculture and Forestry, *Investigation of Grain Storage Operations of the Commodity Credit Corporation,* 82nd Cong., 2nd sess., January 12–May 26, 1960; "not a very happy picture," John Jr. to John Peterson, February 5, 1960, CA Whitney MacMillan MS 6; "not nearly depressed," John Jr. to W. Duncan MacMillan, August 1, 1960, W. Duncan MacMillan MS; "found that downtown," Minneapolis *Star Journal*, January 4, 1960; "Hughie . . . disgusted," Cargill MacMillan to John Jr., February 12, 1960, CA Whitney MacMillan MS 6.

30. "Best grain trading," Erwin Kelm memorandum, April 16, 1959, CA Whitney MacMillan MS 3; Tradax nongrain commodities, "Report of Meetings, April 4–8, 1960 by Tradax Internacional S.A. Commodity Department," CA Lake 15; "perform . . . cheapest," Erwin Kelm memorandum, November 16, 1960, ibid.; "you need volume," John Peterson to John Jr., March 30, 1960, ibid.

31. Baie Comeau dedication by John Jr., July 27, 1960, CA John MacMillan, Jr. MS; "Elevator Threat," July 28, 1960, unidentified newspaper clipping, CA Lake 15; "capacity to 33 million," John Jr. to W. Duncan MacMillan, August 25, 1960, W. Duncan MacMillan MS; "to a climax," ibid., September 16, 1960; "hoodoo'ed," ibid., March 18, 1960.

32. Comparison with Continental Grain Company, John Jr. to John Peterson, May 13, 1960, CA Lake 16.

33. Cargill MacMillan stroke, John Jr. to William W. Cargill, August 9, 1960, CA Lake

16; "drive to cut costs," John Jr. to W. Duncan MacMillan, September 23, 1960, W. Duncan MacMillan MS; Howard McMillan death, John Jr. to Cargill, November 23, 1960, CA Lake 16; Leo Sheehan to Cargill, December 2, 1960, ibid.

19. Cargill's Culture (pp. 847–74)

1. "Overwhelming desire for security," typescript of speech by John MacMillan, Jr., Stillwater conference, November 13, 1953, CA 63-05; decoration of office, Cargill MacMillan to Edna MacMillan, June 20, 1928, CA John Work 1.

2. "Think aloud," Julius Hendel and Austen Cargill, "The Human Side of Business," May 16, 1946, *Cargill Business*, op. cit.; abuses of wire system, memorandum "To all employees using our wire system," John H. MacMillan, Sr., August 8, 1932, CA 33-02, JHM Personal.

3. E. H. Rawls, Morris Barker to John Sr., January 2, 1940, CA 45-08; John Sr. to Barker, January 3, 1940, ibid.

4. "Cognitive complexity," Daniel Goleman, "Successful Executives Rely on Own Kind of Intelligence," *New York Times*, July 31, 1984; "strong opinions," *Cargill News*, October–November, 1965. John Jr. health, Cargill MacMillan to Clark R. Fletcher, April 14, 1942, CA 45-02; Cargill MacMillan to Weston Grimes, January 21, 1942, ibid.; nervous nausea, Cargill MacMillan to John and Edna MacMillan, March 31, 1942, CA 43-04; "don't think he knew how," John Work interview of Joe Bailey, ca. 1964; "loaded for bear," ibid., Sumner B. Young.

5. Query on "big bin" at St. Louis terminal, H. S. Yohe to Ed Grimes, December 28, 1940; Grimes to Yohe, January 2, 1941, CA 41-06.

6. Inflatable roofs for "sport events," John Jr. to Herbert H. Stephens, Jr., July 5, 1946, CA 47-10.

7. Materials on John MacMillan, Jr., inventions are voluminous; see, particularly, his personal MS file in custody of W. Duncan MacMillan and CA 36-04 and 43–04, passim.

8. "First mover" advantages, Alfred D. Chandler, Jr., *Scale and Scope: The Dynamics of Industrial Enterprise* (Cambridge, Mass.: Harvard University Press, 1990), chap. 1; "fusible link" plan, Cargill MacMillan to James E. Dorsey, September 21, 1938, CA 45-02; IRS views on tax avoidance, Leland W. —— [signature not clear] to Cargill MacMillan, May 4, 1937, CA 45-02.

9. "Too radical ideas," Cargill MacMillan to John Jr., June 20, 1941, CA 40-03.

10. Hendel salary request, draft letter, Cargill MacMillan to Julius Hendel, June 21, 1940, Whitney MacMillan MS collection; "good fellow," John Jr. to Cargill MacMillan, February 10, 1941; CA 43-04.

11. Austen Cargill as general manager, Cargill MacMillan to John Jr., March 24, 1944, CA 47-01.

12. Sperry steering mechanism, John Jr. to Frank Neilson, July 15, 1941, CA 43-05.

13. The first Kepner Tregoe "Apex" meeting was held at Stillwater, Minnesota, April 3–7, 1961. The first of the extensive and long-standing "family meetings" of the next generation was April 11, 1961; family objectives rating scale in the meeting of May 18, 1961 (see also meeting of July 17, 1963). The process was repeated at a number of successive meetings; see September 28, 1964, March 11, 1969, November 11, 1971. The concept has continued in modified form to the present. See also meetings of family with Erwin Kelm (April 21, 1961) and his memorandum of that date and meeting with H. T. Morrison of April 27, 1961, with his letter to Kelm of April 25, 1961 (with two separate attached memoranda). Early thinking of family group in an internal memorandum, "A Timely Statement from Ownership to Management," dated May 18, 1961, and discussed orally with senior management. See also "Family Statement to Morrison and Kelm," n.d. (ca. May 1961. Family discussions concerning the sale of the French barges to Cargo Carriers, Incorporated, and impact on the three sets of family members extended over a number of meetings in the period 1961–1965; see, particularly, A. J. James memorandum of January 8, 1962, James to Whitney MacMillan, June 21, 1963, the latter's memoranda of July 9 and October 14, 1963, and "Varden West Report, G-2 and G-3 Barges," February 24, 1964. The barges were the subject of a number of family meetings; see, for example, July 17, 1963.

14. "Cargill stamped," Loren W. Johnson to Ed Grimes, August 2, 1947, CA 47–04; "might be . . . annoyed," Cargill MacMillan to John Jr., February 13, 1947, ibid., 45-02.

15. Alex H. Ardrey, Jr., "Report on Cargill, Incorporated to Mr. Charles Cain, Jr., Executive Vice President," October 18, 1963, John Peterson MS collection, CA; Robert J. Harrigan, "Chase Manhattan Report on Cargill: Highlights," November 5, 1963, ibid. Cargill Mac-Millan, Sr., memorandum on "net worth of a hundred million dollars," dated March 11, 1958, Whitney MacMillan MS collection, CA; the Company's recent "Cargill's Mission: Where We Are Going" (1990), phrases the performance goal "to double the size of Cargill's business every five to seven years."

16. John Jr., "Summary of Cargill Management Conference Series," March 27, 1953, CA Lake 14.

17. There are a number of books on the grain trade in the period 1960–1990; none can be considered comprehensive. See, for example, Nick Butler, *The International Grain Trade: Problems and Prospects* (New York: St. Martins Press, 1986); William G. Ferris, *The Grain Traders: The Story of the Chicago Board of Trade* (East Lansing: Michigan State University Press, 1988); Harry Fornari, *Bread upon the Waters: A History of United States Grain Exports* (Nashville, Tenn.: Aurora Publishers, 1973); John Freivalds, *Grain Trade: The Key to World Power and Human Survival* (New York: Stein and Day, 1976); Richard Gilmore, *A Poor Harvest: The Clash of Policies and Interests in the Grain Trade* (New York: Longman, 1982); Francis Moore Lappe, *Food First: Beyond the Myth of Scarcity* (Boston: Houghton Mifflin, 1977); Jerry W. Markham, *The History of Commodity Futures Trading and Its Regulation* (New York: Praeger, 1987); Dan Morgan, *Merchants of Grain* (New York: Viking Press, 1979); Alex F. McCalla and Timothy E. Josling, *Agricultural Policies and World Markets* (New York: Macmillan, 1985); James Trager, *Amber Waves of Grain* (New York: Arthur Fields Books), 1973.

Similarly, the writings on Cargill in the period 1960–1990 are sketchy. See Sally Apgar, "Cargill's New President Calculates Risk," *Minneapolis Star Tribune*, February 18, 1991; Marcia Berss, "End of an Era," *Forbes*, April 29, 1991 (and May 13, 1991); Eric Black, "Cargill's Whitney MacMillan Gaining Fame after Fortune," *Minneapolis Star and Tribune*, October 11, 1987; Steve Brandt, "Cargill's Pretax Profits Rise Sharply," *Minneapolis Star and Tribune*, February 27, 1987; Terry Brown, "The Cargill Combination—The World's Largest Grain Trader Plays for Huge Stakes, but Rarely Gambles," *Corporate Report*, May 1983; Harlan S. Byrne, "Cargill Inc., A Giant in Troubled Industry Keeps Reaping Riches," *Wall Street Journal*, November 7, 1975; "Cargill: Preparing the Next Boom in Worldwide Grain Trading," *Business Week*, April 16, 1979; Christine Donahue, "Revenge of the Frostbelt," *Forbes*, November 5, 1984; Lee Egerstrom, "MacMillan Sees Cargill Economic Development Role," *Saint Paul Pioneer Press Dispatch*, May 9, 1988; "The Free World of Private Companies," *Dun's Review*, September 1978; Richard Gibson, "Cargill Discloses Fiscal '85 Earnings Were Among the Lowest in Recent Years," *Wall Street Journal*, November 20, 1985; ibid., "Cargill Thrives Despite Farming's Ills, Plans Expansion, Filing in U.K. Shows," *Wall Street Journal*, February 27, 1987; Stanley Ginsberg, "The Singles Hitter," *Forbes*, February 16, 1981; Andrew Gowers, "How the Merchants of Grain Are Riding Out the Storm," *Financial Times*, November 28, 1986; Steven Greenhouse, "Talking Business with W. B. Saunders of Cargill," *New York Times*, September 25, 1984; ibid., "For a Grain Giant, No Farm Crisis," *New York Times*, March 30, 1986; ibid., "Slowly But Surely, Cargill Expands," *International Herald Tribune*, April 7, 1986; William A. Haffert, Jr., "Cargill: The Reluctant Integrator," *Feed Management*, October 1969; Hubert Kay, "The Two-Billion-Dollar Company That Lives by the Cent," *Fortune*, December 1965; Seth King, "It's Said, 'The Sun Never Sets on Cargill,' " *New York Times*, September 25, 1972; Dale Kurschner, "Pending Exits by Top Brass Send Cargill into a Quandary," *City Business*, October 15–21, 1990; Bonnie Leslie, "Cargill: All in the Family," *Minneapolis*, September 1976; Tina Russo McCarthy, "The Very Private Sector," *Forbes*, December 10, 1990; Lisa Miller Mesdag, "The 50 Largest Private Industrial Companies," *Fortune*, May 31, 1982; Mike Meyers, "Profits Slim, but Cargill Plows Patiently Through Crisis," *Minneapolis Star and Tribune*, May 18, 1986; Lawrence Minard, "In Privacy They Thrive," *Forbes*, November 1, 1976; Barbara Minor, "The Corporate Report Private 100," *Corporate Report*, December 1988; Lisa Mirabile (ed.), "Cargill, Inc.," *International Directory of Company Histories II* (Chicago: St. James Press, 1990); Dan Morgan, *Merchants of Grain*, op. cit.; Ralph Nader and William Taylor, *The Big Boys: Power and Position in American Business* (New

York: Pantheon Books, 1986); Leslie Pittel, "Behind the Paper Curtain: The Largest Private Companies in the U.S.," *Forbes*, November 18, 1985; "Private Lives," *Forbes*, June 23, 1980; Dan Rottenberg, "All in the Family, Inc.—The Top Privately Held Companies in America," *Town & Country*, August 1984; Walter B. Saunders, "Testimony before the Multinational Corporations Subcommittee of the Senate Committee on Foreign Relations," Washington, D.C., June 24, 1976; Sue Schellenbarger, "Bigness Counts in Agribusiness, and Cargill Inc. Is Fast Becoming a Commodities Conglomerate," *Wall Street Journal*, May 7, 1982; Barry Stavro, "Quit? Hell, No," *Forbes*, August 26, 1985; Bob Tamarkin, "What and Who Makes Cargill So Powerful," *Forbes*, September 18, 1978; Jack Willoughby, "More Fun Than Flogging Frosting," *Forbes*, November 17, 1986.

18. "All the Big League" from Richard Gilmore, *A Poor Harvest: The Clash of Policies and Interests in the Grain Trade*, op. cit., p. 124.

Illustrations

Index

DOCUMENTOS RELATIVOS

A LA

INDEPENDENCIA DE NORTEAMÉRICA

EXISTENTES EN ARCHIVOS ESPAÑOLES

DOCUMENTOS RELATIVOS A LA INDEPENDENCIA DE NORTEAMÉRICA EXISTENTES EN ARCHIVOS ESPAÑOLES

I. Archivo General de Indias. Sección de Gobierno (Años 1752-1822).

II. Archivo General de Indias. Sección Papeles de Cuba. Correspondencia y documentación oficial de los Gobernadores de Luisiana (Años 1777-1803).

III. Archivo Histórico Nacional. Correspondencia diplomática de la Embajada en Washington (Años 1801-1820).

IV. Archivo Histórico Nacional. Embajada en Washington. Expedientes (Años 1801-1820).

V. Archivo General de Simancas. Secretaría de Estado: Inglaterra (Años 1750-1820).

VI. Archivo General de Simancas. Secretaría de Estado: Francia (1774-1786).

VII. Archivo General de Indias. Sección Papeles de Cuba. Correspondencia y documentación oficial de varias autoridades de Luisiana y de las dos Floridas (Años 1778-1817).

VIII. Archivo Histórico Nacional. Embajada en Washington. Correspondencia diplomática (Años 1821-1833).

IX. Archivo General de Indias. Sección Papeles de Cuba. Correspondencia y documentación oficial de los Intendentes de Luisiana (Años 1765-1827).

X. Archivo Histórico Nacional. Estado. Embajada de Washington. Expedientes (Años 1821-1850).

XI. Archivo General de Simancas. Secretaría de Guerra: Guerra Moderna (Años 1779-1807).

«Los trabajos de recogida de datos para la redacción de estos inventarios, así como la edición de los mismos, han sido realizados bajo los auspicios del Comité Conjunto Hispano-Norteamericano para Asuntos Educativos y Culturales del Tratado de Amistad y Cooperación entre España y los Estados Unidos de América de 24 de enero de 1976.»

A LA

INDEPENDENCIA DE NORTEAMÉRICA

EXISTENTES EN ARCHIVOS ESPAÑOLES

VIII

ARCHIVO HISTÓRICO NACIONAL
CORRESPONDENCIA DIPLOMÁTICA (AÑOS 1821 - 1833)

POR
PILAR LEÓN TELLO

CON LA COLABORACIÓN DE
CONCEPCIÓN MENÉNDEZ Y CARMEN TORROJA

MINISTERIO DE ASUNTOS EXTERIORES
DIRECCIÓN GENERAL DE RELACIONES CULTURALES
MADRID

Ministerio de Asuntos Exteriores, Madrid, 1982.

Depósito Legal: M. 22006 - 1976.

ISBN 84-500-1410-7. Obra completa.
ISBN 84-85290-35-6. Tomo VIII.

Impreso en España. Printed in Spain.
Gráficas Cóndor, S. A., Sánchez Pacheco, 81, Madrid, 1982. — 5416.

INTRODUCCIÓN

Continuamos en este volumen la catalogación de los despachos oficiales que los representantes de España en Estados Unidos enviaban con toda asiduidad a la corte desde 1821 hasta 1833, en que termina esta serie de *Correspondencia diplomática* que conservamos en el Archivo Histórico Nacional.

En ese período fueron ministros plenipotenciarios en Estados Unidos, Francisco Dionisio Vives, que había sido enviado allí anteriormente, para gestionar la ratificación del tratado del 22 de febrero de 1819; Joaquín Anduaga que ocupó luego el cargo durante dos años escasos, y hasta mediados de 1827, en que llegó a Filadelfia el nuevo ministro Francisco Tacón, estuvo resolviendo los asuntos de la embajada, el encargado de negocios, Hilario Rivas Salmón.

Muy lejanos ya los días de la independencia, y tras el desmoronamiento de nuestro imperio colonial y el traspaso de las Floridas que España había cedido a Estados Unidos, los temas que se trataban entre ambas naciones, carecen de relieve político. La correspondencia de nuestros enviados se nutría en especial, de las noticias referentes a Hispanoamérica, sus guerras civiles o entre distintos países, de las anteriores posesiones españolas a las que Estados Unidos prestaban ayuda y enviaban, los primeros, sus agentes.

La expansión estadounidense se verificaba en esta época a costa de las tribus indias que cedían inmensos territorios a cambio de convenios e indemnizaciones anuales; al mismo tiempo se consolidaba la preponderancia de los Estados de la Unión, mediante ventajosos tratados con las principales naciones europeas y con los nuevos gobiernos de América del Sur.

La documentación que reseñamos está comprendida en los legajos 5.647 a 5.659 de la Sección de Estado.

LEGAJO 5.647

AÑO 1821

CORRESPONDENCIA DE FRANCISCO DIONISIO VIVES, MINISTRO PLENIPOTENCIARIO DE ESPAÑA EN ESTADOS UNIDOS, CON EVARISTO PÉREZ DE CASTRO, SECRETARIO DE ESTADO

1

N.º 97. — 10 de enero, Washington.

Acusa recibo de dos oficios sobre el artículo 8.º del tratado con Estados Unidos y espera los documentos e instrucciones necesarios para llevar a cabo la ratificación del mismo. En sus conversaciones con Forsyth, ministro americano en Madrid, habría podido observar que el gobierno estadounidense no quería llegar a ningún acuerdo sobre ese artículo, sino que insistía en que debían anularse las concesiones de tierras que estaban en litigio y que quedaran a favor de Estados Unidos (Principal y duplicado).

2

N.º 98. — 10 de enero, Washington.

Expresa su satisfacción por la mejoría del infante don Carlos Luis María.

3

N.º 99. — 10 de enero, Washington.

Acusa recibo de una comunicación en la que le manifestaban que había salido de Madrid Juan Manuel de Barros, portador de la ratificación y de otros documentos concernientes a la conclusión del tratado pendiente con Estados Unidos; este gobierno creía que la ratificación se haría sin nueva propuesta que alterase la anulación de las concesiones de tierras y la cesión de ellas a su favor (Principal y duplicado).

4

N.º 101. — 9 de enero, Washington.

Comunica las noticias que le había enviado Pablo Morillo acerca del armisticio que había firmado con Bolívar el 26 de noviembre último, por tiempo de seis meses, a fin de tratar de la reconciliación de las provincias disidentes.

Adjunto:

— Traducción de dos párrafos de la gaceta de Washington del 4 de enero 1821, sobre el tratado de las Floridas y la toma de Santa Marta por los patriotas. Otro párrafo de la gaceta nacional del 29 de diciembre 1820 daba cuenta del apresamiento por lord Cochrane de un barco procedente de Manila que se dirigía a Valparaíso con medio millón de pesos a bordo. Como en Manila no había fuerza militar, en caso de no recibir tropas, el gobernador pensaba poner la plaza bajo la protección de los ingleses.
— Minutas dirigidas a Vives anunciándole correspondencia de Ultramar y recepción de sus oficios (7 de enero a 29 de marzo 1821).
— Oficio de Ramón Feliú, de Gobernación de Ultramar, al encargado del despacho de Estado, devolviendo un pliego con noticias publicadas en los periódicos de Estados Unidos (25 de marzo 1821).

5

N.º 102. — 11 de enero, Washington.

Remite los documentos relativos a la reclamación del comerciante de Matanzas, Jaime Badía, por el apresamiento en las costas de África de su goleta Esperanza por la corbeta de guerra de los Estados Unidos, Cyane.

Adjunto:

— Copia de la representación de Jaime Badía a Vives, como representante de España, a fin de que interviniera para acelerar la conclusión del juicio que se seguía contra la Esperanza en Nueva York, a cuyo puerto había sido conducida, y explicando los detalles de su apresamiento basado en que se dedicaba al tráfico de negros, que estaba prohibido por las leyes americanas (Nueva York, 25 de agosto 1820).

— Copia de la reclamación que había hecho Vives al secretario de Estado John Quincy Adams, contra el apresamiento de la Esperanza, y anunciando la presentación de una serie de documentos legalizados en debida forma, que demostraban el insultante comportamiento del comandante del Cyane; pedía que se abonaran los perjuicios causados al propietario del barco español (Nueva York, 7 de septiembre 1820).

— Copia de la sentencia pronunciada en la corte del distrito de los Estados Unidos, condenando a la Esperanza por haber infringido las leyes americanas enrolando marineros de dicho país en lugar de los que, según había declarado el capitán del buque, habían desertado en el puerto de Charleston, donde había entrado de arribada forzosa para reparar averías (Nueva York, 8 de noviembre 1820).

— Copia de una carta de Vives a Badía extrañando que le hubiera silenciado la arribada de su buque a Charleston; como el principal fundamento sobre el que se apoyaba la sentencia era el haber aumentado la tripulación en esa ciudad, pedía le informara si este cambio de gente fue anotado en el roll por el cónsul del puerto (Washington, 27 de noviembre 1820).

— Copia de la respuesta de Badía a Vives manifestando que la goleta Esperanza había entrado de arribada forzosa en Charleston, donde tuvieron que desembarcar el cargamento, y en todo tiempo estuvo a bordo un oficial del resguardo; los marineros americanos que embarcaron no pudieron hacerlo sin conocimiento de los de la aduana que sabían el objeto de su viaje; por su parte el capitán ignoraba que al admitir a los marineros estaba infrigiendo las leyes americanas (Washington, 7 de diciembre 1820).

6

N.º 104. — 12 de enero, Washington.

Da cuenta de que había hecho toda clase de diligencias para adquirir los reglamentos militares que le había solicitado, pero no se vendían al público sino que circulaban entre el ejército cuando se publicaban; sólo había podido comprar dos ejemplares del almanaque nacional que trataba algo de la organización de pequeños cuerpos de tropas, aunque creía que no se podría aplicar a nuestro ejército.

7

N.º 105. — 12 de enero, Washington.

Queda enterado de que las tropas de guarnición en Lisboa habían seguido el ejemplo de las de Oporto y habían reiterado el juramento de fidelidad al rey Juan VI, procediendo a la formación de una junta interina de gobierno.

8

N.º 106. — 12 de enero, Washington.

Da cuenta de que en los periódicos americanos se hablaba de los movimientos de Oporto y Lisboa, pero ninguno había cometido la injusticia de suponer la menor influencia en ellos del gobierno español.

9

N.º 107. — 18 de enero, Washington.

Remite copia de varios documentos que le había enviado el gobernador de San Agustín de la Florida, José Coppinger, referentes a la entrada en el puerto de San José de la fragata francesa la Eugenia; Anselmo Gay, que se titulaba consignatario de la fragata, de acuerdo con los interesados en la carga del buque, había comprometido al gobernador, haciéndole ver las ventajas que resultarían al habilitar el puerto de San José, al que acudirían muchos barcos franceses.

Adjunto:

— Copia de la comunicación dirigida por José Coppinger a Vives, quejándose de los atropellos cometidos en el caso de las fragatas francesas Eugenia y Apolo (San Agustín de la Florida, 22 de diciembre 1820).

— Respuesta de Vives manifestando que ya se había enterado por el embajador francés en Estados Unidos, de lo ocurrido a la fragata Eugenia desde su entrada en las aguas del Bell; le advertía que si seguía admitiendo buques franceses en el puerto de San José se expondría a nuevos desaires e incidentes. Se había ratificado el tratado de cesión de las Floridas (Washington, 18 de enero 1821).

— Cuadernillo con copia del memorial presentado ante el gobernador de San Agustín de la Florida por Anselmo Gay, consignatario de la fragata Eugenia, exponiendo que había llegado al puerto de San José amparada en la protección legítima del territorio español, y después de depositar el capitán los papeles correspondientes en la aduana había sido sorprendida por fuerzas de Estados Unidos que, violando los derechos más sagrados, se introdujeron en los dominios de España y le conminaron a que llevara a descargar su buque al puerto americano de Santa María de Georgia, poniéndolo mientras arreglaba la documentación bajo la batería del pueblo de Fernandina. Sigue traducción de documentos, decretos, declaraciones del capitán del barco Eloy Cantín y otras diligencias de protesta por el atropello cometido por los americanos (4 a 22 de diciembre 1820).

10

N.º 108. — 18 de enero, Washington.

Remite traducción de la carta que el ministro de Hacienda norteamericano había dirigido al presidente de la cámara de representantes con motivo de la habilitación del puerto de San José en el río Bell, por el gobernador de San Agustín de la Florida; considera posible que el gobierno adopte las medidas que propone el ministro de Hacienda para impedir el comercio que llaman clandestino, si por parte española se establecieran los puertos de depósito a que se refiere el ministro, y podrían surgir nuevos problemas si con ese pretexto, quisieran establecer algún fuerte en el territorio de Tejas, cuya feracidad ambicionaban los habitantes de Kentucky y demás estados colindantes; hacía días que los periódicos difundían la idea de que no debía admitirse la ratificación del tratado pendiente, porque no compensaba la adquisición de las Floridas a la renuncia a los derechos sobre Tejas. Comunicaría en cuanto lo supiera, la resolución que sobre ello adoptara el congreso (Principal y duplicado).

Adjunto:

— Traducción de la carta del ministro de Hacienda Crawford al presidente de la cámara de representantes, Taylor, manifestando que en cumplimiento de una resolución de dicha cámara que pedía información sobre el tonelaje de los buques franceses que habían llegado al río de Santa María y sobre las medidas convenientes para la mejor recaudación de las rentas en la frontera del sur, daba cuenta de la entrada de dos buques con carga de vinos y frutas que sin duda intentarían introducir en los Estados Unidos. Se habían recibido noticias de que se trataba de establecer en varios puntos de las Floridas depósitos de géneros y esclavos, para introducirlos subrepticiamente en Estados Unidos y extraer del mismo modo sus productos para aprovisionar las islas, estableciendo depósitos al oeste de la frontera, en las costas desiertas de Méjico, si se verificaba la cesión de las Floridas. Al congreso correspondía determinar el derecho que tenía un gobierno extranjero para habilitar en su territorio dichos establecimientos, con el objeto de eludir las leyes de la Unión respecto al contrabando, y tomar medidas para evitarlo, dado que se convertiría aquella zona en un nido de piratas. Estimaba conveniente establecer fuertes en el Sabina y el río Rojo, y algunos guardacostas en el golfo de Méjico, para impedir el tráfico ilegal; una nueva aduana vigilaría todos los ríos, bahías y costas del oeste de Luisiana (17 de enero 1821). Duplicado.

11

N.º 109. — 24 de enero, Washington.

Da cuenta de que el cónsul en Nueva York le había comunicado que el juez del tribunal del almirantazgo de dicha ciudad había declarado buena presa la goleta española María Gertrudis, que la corbeta de Estados Unidos Cyane había apresado en las costas de África cuando se dedicaba al tráfico de negros bozales, fundándose en que era propiedad americana y que la expedición se había proyectado en Estados Unidos; lo mismo había ocurrido con la goleta española Dichosa, basándose también en que el buque y la carga pertenecían a un comerciante americano. Los interesados no tenían más recurso que apelar al tribunal supremo de los Estados Unidos. La participación de ciudadanos americanos era muy frecuente en los buques que se dedicaban a tráfico de negros, sin duda porque tenían parte en su cargamento.

12

N.º 113. — 16 de febrero, Washington.

Queda enterado del nombramiento de Manuel González Salmón para enviado extraordinario y ministro plenipotenciario de España en Rusia.

13

N.º 114. — 16 de febrero, Washington.

Acusa recibo de un oficio al que acompañaban cuatro ejemplares de la constitución política de la monarquía.

14

N.º 115. — 16 de febrero, Washington.

Por un oficio de octubre último quedaba enterado de la concesión a Juan Manuel de Barros, agregado a la legación, de un sueldo anual de doce mil reales de vellón, que le serían satisfechos de los fondos de la misma.

15

N.º 116. — 19 de febrero, Washington.

Remite copia de la respuesta que había recibido del gobernador de San Agustín de la Florida, en la que daba cuenta de que, para evitar que la admisión de buques franceses en las aguas del río Bell produjese fricciones con las autoridades de Santa María de

Georgia, había ordenado que los que no pudiesen entrar en el puerto de San Juan se dirigieran al de San Agustín, desde cuyo fondeadero se transportaría la carga en embarcaciones menores, ingresándose el numerario en las cajas nacionales. Comunica que la fragata Apolo había entrado de buena fe en el río Bell, porque aún no habían expuesto los Estados Unidos sus pretensiones, y el admitir en el despoblado puerto de San José a la fragata Eugenia había sido cumpliendo órdenes de la Habana, de buscar el medio de paliar los prejuicios provenientes de la injusta usurpación por los Estados Unidos del puerto de Fernandina, que impedía aprovechar las ventajas del comercio francés para fomentar la población y el comercio en la provincia. Los estados de la Unión habían impuesto un crecido derecho de tonelaje a los buques franceses en réciprocidad, pero el gobierno español era ajeno a ello totalmente y no tenía por qué negar la entrada en sus puertos a ningún buque; lo mismo que los buques americanos se acogían a puertos cercanos a Francia para eximirse del pago del derecho de tonelaje impuesto por el gobierno francés, podían los de este país entrar en los puertos cercanos a Estados Unidos con el mismo fin; siendo por tanto una violación del territorio lo acaecido en el río Bell.

Adjunto:

— Copia del despacho del gobernador de San Agustín de la Florida con la detallada explicación del incidente (San Agustín de la Florida, 3 de febrero 1821).

16

N.º 117. — 19 de febrero, Washington.

Da cuenta de la publicación en el «National Intelligencer» de 26 de enero último de una carta escrita por un tal Robinson, que había sido aprisionado con los insurgentes de Terán en Méjico y conducido a Cádiz de donde se había fugado; en ella ponderaba las grandes ventajas que resultarían para Estados Unidos de continuar explorando las costas del noroeste y pasar después a las de Asia, con objeto de extender su comercio, de peletería principalmente. Incluía copia de un importante manuscrito que los insurgentes habían interceptado en Méjico, que era el relato de dos misioneros que por los años 1810 y 1811 habían subido por el río Colorado de las Californias, para explorarlo hasta su nacimiento;

por los indios conocieron la existencia al oeste del citado río, de otros dos muy grandes y siguiendo el cauce de uno de ellos que era profundo y como de una milla de ancho llegaron a la costa de California sobre los 43 grados y 30 minutos y desde allí fueron por la costa hasta Monterrey, hallando a su paso hermosas bahías.

Poco después se había publicado el informe de una comisión del congreso sobre las ventajas del comercio de peletería y pesca de la ballena en las costas del noroeste, refiriéndose al que hacen los ingleses en la misma costa y a los nuevos establecimientos de los rusos. La comisión había propuesto la expulsión de los territorios de Estados Unidos, de los extranjeros que comerciaban en aquellas regiones y que se estableciera un centro militar y comercial a la entrada del río Columbia.

Además de las copias de los mencionados documentos remite la traducción de un artículo, procedente con toda probabilidad de la legación inglesa, rectificando algunos datos del informe de la comisión mencionada, referentes al establecimiento de los ingleses en Nootka.

Adjunto:

— Traducción del informe de la comisión encargada de estudiar la conveniencia de ocupar el río Columbia, en el Pacífico, y establecer allí un centro comercial de donde salieran expediciones con pieles para Cantón y donde tuvieran su base para la pesca de la ballena.

— Traducción de una nota publicada en el «National Intelligencer» de 10 de febrero 1821, rectificando algunos puntos del informe de dicha comisión referentes al establecimiento de puertos ingleses en la costa del Pacífico; concretándose al de Nootka, refería que, sometido por un buque español, había sido devuelto a los súbditos británicos por una orden de Floridablanca en 1791 (10 de febrero 1821).

— Nota informativa (1 de mayo 1821).

— Minuta a Francisco Dionisio Vives acusando recibo del despacho en el que había comunicado el proyecto del gobierno americano de establecer un puesto militar y comercial en el río Columbia, pudiendo fundar en el mismo los establecimientos que desearan sin perjuicio para nuestros intereses. En cuanto a la expulsión de aquellos territorios de ingleses y rusos era cuestión que no atañía a España. Eran poco de fiar las noticias transmitidas por Robinson, que se caracterizaba por su poca veracidad (7 de mayo 1821).

17

N.º 118. — 19 de febrero, Washington.

Anuncia remisión de dos ejemplares del almanaque nacional de los Estados Unidos, con algunas noticias sobre la organización de su ejército.

18

N.º 119. — 19 de febrero, Washington.

Comunica la reelección de James Monroe como presidente de Estados Unidos por absoluta unanimidad, y de Daniel D. Tompkins como vicepresidente para los cuatro próximos años. Al hacer el recuento de votos se había suscitado la cuestión de si debían incluirse los de Missouri, por considerarse estado adherido a la Unión, o si era solamente un territorio; el problema dimanaba de la rivalidad de los estados del norte que querían imponer a los de Missouri la condición de que renunciaran a la esclavitud, a lo que se habían negado amenazando con dejar la Unión. Se consiguió llegar al compromiso de que, exceptuado el Missouri, quedaba abolida la esclavitud en todo el territorio de los Estados Unidos. Missouri había pasado en consecuencia a ser un estado de la Unión con su propia constitución; el congreso hallaba que una de sus cláusulas estaba en contradicción con los principios generales de que todos los ciudadanos debían gozar los mismos derechos y prerrogativas en todos los estados de la Unión. Era probable sin embargo, que se solucionase pacíficamente esta cuestión.

19

N.º 120. — 21 de febrero, Washington.

Acusa recibo del oficio en el que le comunicaba el regreso de los reyes a la corte donde habían sido recibidos con gran entusiasmo, noticia que contradecía las que habían publicado en las gacetas los periodistas franceses e ingleses, que cargaban las tintas al describir los infaustos sucesos ocurridos en Madrid.

20

N.º 121. — 21 de febrero, Washington.

Se muestra enterado por un oficio de 27 de noviembre último, y por las gacetas que le habían remitido, de los sucesos ocurridos con la tropa en dicho mes en Lisboa, acerca de lo cual ya había recibido noticia por vía de Inglaterra.

21

N.º 122. — 22 de febrero, Washington.

Da cuenta de que había trasladado al cónsul general en Estados Unidos la real orden sobre pasaportes de 20 de noviembre, para que la hiciera llegar a los demás cónsules.

22

N.º 123. — 23 de febrero, Washington.

Remite la traducción del tratado que el gobierno de los Estados Unidos había firmado recientemente con los indios choctaws, por el cual les cedían un territorio comprendido dentro de los límites de los de España; aunque podía tratarse de un error había enviado la nota de protesta cuyo copia adjunta; envía también dos periódicos que daban la noticia, y la traducción de un artículo de un periodista que se distinguía siempre por defender los derechos de España, por lo cual propone que se le recompense de alguna manera.

Adjunto:

— Traducción del tratado de amistad y límites entre los Estados Unidos de América y la nación de los indios choctaws, por el que se anexiona al estado de Mississipi una pequeña porción de terreno que pertenecía a los indios, cediéndoles en cambio un territorio al oeste del Mississipi, entregándoles armas y víveres y prestándoles otras ayudas (Washington, 8 de enero 1821).

— Ejemplar del «Daily National Intelligencer» de Washington (13 de enero 1821).

— Ejemplar del «The National Gazette» de Filadelfia (24 de enero 1821).

— Traducción de un artículo de la última gaceta en el que un periodista denuncia el fallo existente en el tratado con los indios choctaws al cedérseles territorios incluidos en los límites de las posesiones de España, advirtiendo que estaban equivocados los mapas de estas tierra existentes en los Estados Unidos.

— Copia de la nota que Vives había enviado al secretario de Estado pidiendo una explicación a dicho punto del tratado, que en su opinión se debía a un error de los comisionados y que no dudaba sería subsanado para atender a los límites fijados en el tratado con España (Washington, 23 de febrero 1821).

— Minuta informativa (28 de abril 1821).

— Minuta a Vives: aunque al firmarse el tratado con los indios choctaws aún podía aquel gobierno permutar un territorio que había cedido anteriormente, como el principal comisionado para efectuar la permuta con los indios era el general Jackson, conocedor del territorio en cuestión y constante enemigo de España, era verosímil que se tratara de mala fe más que de un error geográfico. Se le ordena insistir enérgicamente en sus reclamaciones. Respecto a la recompensa para el periodista aludido se había resuelto ya en marzo último (9 de mayo 1821).

23

N.º 127. — 7 de marzo, Washington.

Remite copia y traducción de la respuesta del secretario de Estado sobre la transacción de las grandes concesiones de tierras que le había propuesto. Por haberla recibido con bastante retraso no había podido enviarla con el teniente de zapadores Antonio Donis, que había salido con el tratado ratificado por el presidente. Principal y duplicado.

Adjunto:

— Dos copias de la carta de Adams a Vives.

— Dos traducciones de dicha carta en la que respondía a la petición que Vives le había hecho de que se indemnizara a los españoles demandantes por las tierras que habían perdido por el tratado de 1819; decía que el tratado había sido muy beneficioso para España y que no debía indemnizarse a los dueños de tierras que habían sido reconocidas por las dos partes como malas y sin valor; este punto había sido detalladamente discutido entre Forsyth y el ministro español de Relaciones Exteriores y no valía la pena volver sobre ello. Manifestaba su satisfacción por la ratificación del tratado, que esperaba aumentaría la armonía entre los dos países (Washington, 28 de febrero 1821).

24

N.º 128. — 7 de marzo, Washington.

Acusa recibo de una comunicación relativa a varias medidas adoptadas por las cortes: sobre un empréstito de 200 millones, la libertad de imprenta, restricción de licencia de sociedades patrióticas, supresión de mayorazgos y concesión de asilo en España a las personas y bienes de extranjeros.

25

N.º 129. — 7 de marzo, Washington.

Acusa recibo del oficio en el que le comunicaba que se habían cerrado las cortes en el día previsto por la constitución, no habiendo asistido el rey por estar indispuesto. Con el oficio había recibido los ejemplares del discurso del rey, que había leído el presidente del congreso.

26

N.º 130. — 7 de marzo, Washington.

Participa que había hecho llegar al cónsul general el oficio que había recibido del 18 de noviembre.

27

N.º 131. — 6 de marzo, Washington.

Acababa de recibir el oficio en el que le comunicaba el traslado de los reyes a San Lorenzo para pasar unos días. En cumplimiento de sus órdenes haría publicar en los periódicos la nueva ley de asilo.

28

N.º 132. — 7 de marzo, Washington.

Comunica que el 4 de marzo se había disuelto el congreso por haberse cumplido el tiempo reglamentario, siendo reelegido el presidente por otros cuatro años, con cuyo motivo había pronunciado un discurso que se había publicado en el «National Intelligencer», del cual remite dos ejemplares. Adjunta también la traducción de los párrafos que se referían a España y un extracto del resto. Había terminado pacíficamente la cuestión del Missouri, siendo admitido en la Unión con tal de que su legislación no impidiera a los ciudadanos de los demás estados establecerse allí, pero quedaba sin solucionar la cuestión de si los negros o mulatos libres eran ciudadanos.

Adjunto:

— Dos ejemplares del «National Intelligencer» de Washington (6 de marzo 1821).
— Extracto del discurso del presidente pronunciado con motivo de su reelección por cuatro años (5 de marzo 1821).
— Minuta a Vives acusando recibo de sus últimas comunicaciones (8 de abril 1821).

29

N.º 133. — 13 de marzo, Washington.

Da cuenta de lo tratado en una entrevista mantenida por iniciativa del secretario de Estado Adams: éste le había comunicado que su gobierno había designado el comisario y el geómetra que, en unión de los que nombraran por parte española, debían proceder a la demarcación de límites; él había respondido que tras la ratificación del tratado recibiría instrucciones sobre el particular. Acto seguido Adams había leído el artículo 7.º del tratado y le había preguntado si estaba autorizado para ordenar a los gobernadores de San Agustín y Panzacola que entregaran las Floridas a los comisionados que el gobierno federal nombrase para recibirlas; le había manifestado que dependiendo dichos jefes del capitán general de la isla de Cuba, sólo de él podían recibir dicha orden; que era necesario que el gobierno de Estados Unidos preparara los buques, víveres y escolta que trasladaran a la Habana a todos los empleados y guarniciones de las Floridas, a lo que contestó Adams que una corbeta de guerra estaba dispuesta por su gobierno para llevar a la Habana la real cédula de entrega de las Floridas, y que se proporcionaría los buques, víveres y escolta necesarios. Principal y duplicado.

Adjunto:

— Copia y traducción de una nota de Adams a Vives urgiéndole el envío de la orden del gobierno español al capitán general de Cuba para la entrega a los Estados Unidos del territorio de las Floridas (Washington, 10 de marzo 1821).
— Copia de la carta de Vives al capitán general de Cuba remitiéndole la real cédula para la entrega de las Floridas; una vez señalada la fecha de su ejecución, debería dar al comisionado una relación de todas las personas que debían trasladarse a la Habana, indicando los puntos de sus residencias. Había pedido a Adams que para evitar posibles fricciones no entraran las tropas americanas en las Floridas hasta que las hubiesen abandonado las españolas, y aunque no se había llegado a un acuerdo completo, le había prometido adoptar todas las precauciones necesarias. Los dos adjuntos están duplicados (Washington, 11 de marzo 1821).
— Minuta a Vives acusando recibo de su comunicación referente al envío al capitán general de Cuba de la real cédula; se estudiaba el nombramiento de los comisionados que en unión con los designados por los Estados Unidos, debían proceder a la demarcación de límites (28 de junio 1821).

30

N.º 134. — 13 de marzo, Washington.

Comunica que había mantenido con Adams una entrevista para tratar de la cuestión de límites y evacuación de las Floridas; le había preguntado ante qué organismo debían presentar sus reclamaciones los españoles que habían sufrido perjuicio por las operaciones del ejército americano en las Floridas para que, según lo estipulado en el artículo 9.º del tratado, obtuvieran la debida indemnización. Adams había respondido que su gobierno ignoraba que se hubieran producido tales perjuicios, pero lo consultaría con el presidente. En vista de ello le había enviado la nota cuya copia remite. Principal y duplicado.

Adjunto:

— Nota de Vives a Adams señalando que en el artículo 9.º del tratado se ofrecía por parte de los Estados Unidos indemnizar los perjuicios que los españoles de las Floridas justificaran legalmente haber sufrido durante las operaciones del ejército americano en dicho territorio; preguntaba ante qué tribunal y en qué forma tenían que acudir los perjudicados en demanda de compensación (Washington, 9 de marzo 1821). Duplicado.
— Minuta a Vives aprobando el contenido de la nota a Adams y ordenándole apoyar las reclamaciones que se presentaren (8 de junio 1821).

31

N.º 137. — 17 de marzo, Washington.

Remite las certificaciones del juramento que habían prestado a la constitución los vicecónsules en Nueva Orleans y Natchez, Nicolás José de Villavaso y Diego Morphy.

Adjunto:

— Testimonio del juramento de Villavaso (Nueva Orleans, 7 de febrero 1821).
— Testimonio del juramento de Diego Morphy (Nueva Orleans, 7 de febrero 1821).

32

N.º 139. — 19 de marzo, Washington.

Acusa recibo de un ejemplar del suplemento de la «Gaceta del Gobierno» del 23 de noviembre último, en el que se trataba de la violenta interpretación que el cuerpo diplomático había dado a un párrafo de la exposición que el inspector general de milicias, Francisco Ballesteros, había hecho a la diputación permanente de las cortes, así como copia de las notas que en nombre de sus colegas había enviado el nuncio y contestación a la misma, de Pérez de Castro.

33

N.º 140. — 19 de marzo, Washington.

Acusa recibo de una comunicación referente a la deserción de varios soldados que, con su cabecilla Gregorio Morales, se habían dirigido de Talavera de la Reina hacia Ávila con ánimo belicoso, de los cuales algunos habían sido apresados y otros habían pasado a Portugal; también quedaba enterado de lo ocurrido en Burgos con una partida capitaneada por un sastre.

34

N.º 141. — 23 de marzo, Washington.

Remite copia de una serie de notas y documentos que había recibido del ministro de Estado; por ellos podía ver la justificación que trataba de hacer Adams de la violación del territorio, fundándose en razones que ya le había expuesto verbalmente en varias ocasiones, a lo cual había respondido con la nota cuya copia envía.

Adjunto:

— Copia y traducción de una carta del secretario de Hacienda Crawford al colector de Santa María de Georgia, Archibald Clarke, en la que manifestaba que se había dado cuenta al presidente de la denuncia de que había buques británicos en la parte meridional de la ría de Santa María dispuestos a burlar las leyes de los Estados Unidos y hacer contrabando en la orilla septentrional, puesto que al no existir ningún poblado en la parte española su intención no podía ser la de comerciar normalmente; si su deseo era traficar con los Estados Unidos debían someterse a sus leyes y el presidente había ordenado que se aplicaran las mismas a todos los buques, fuera cual fuese la orilla en la que se detuvieran. Sólo se exceptuarían los buques españoles, pero no debía hacerse pública esta excepción para evitar que se utilizara la bandera española para eludir el pago de los derechos (6 de mayo 1818).

— Traducción de la carta de Archibald Clarke al secretario del despacho de Hacienda Crawford, dando cuenta de la entrada de un buque francés con carga de vino y champagne, que había anclado frente a la población de Fernandina. Hechas las averiguaciones resultaba que procedía de la Rochela y su destino era Charleston, pero alertado de la nueva ley restrictiva del congreso se había dirigido a la isla Amalia, permaneciendo el buque anclado frente a Fernandina mientras su capitán se había dirigido a San Agustín para llevar allí su cargamento. Por considerarlo asunto importante para las relaciones comerciales con Francia, preguntaba si dichos buques estaban incluidos en las instrucciones de 6 de mayo de 1818 (25 de agosto 1820).

— Copia y traducción de una nota de Eduardo Jones, oficial mayor de Hacienda a Archibald Clarke, comunicando que consultado con el secretario de Estado el caso que había expuesto de un barco francés, consideraba que estaba comprendido en las referidas instrucciones (9 de septiembre 1820).

— Copia y traducción de una carta de J. F. Clarke, vicecónsul de España en Santa María, a James E. Forbes Escudero, comunicándole el establecimiento de un nuevo puerto llamado de San José en la frontera de la Florida oriental, en el río Bell a media distancia entre la ciudad de Fernandina y Santa María; en él se podían obtener fácilmente víveres frescos, leña y un agua excelente. Los derechos de aduana eran limitados y los gastos de puerto moderados; allí estaba anclada la fragata francesa Apolo y consideraba un punto interesante para el comercio con este país así como con las islas. No creía que Estados Unidos adoptase medidas en contra, puesto que obraban según el tratado (Santa María, 15 de septiembre 1820).

— Copia y traducción de una nota de J. F. Clarke a James G. Forbes Escudero pidiendo que hiciera insertar en algunas gacetas la noticia sobre la habilitación del nuevo puerto de San José en la frontera de Florida oriental, para que llegara a conocimiento de los americanos y sobre todo de los franceses. Lo había comunicado ya al colector de Santa María para prevenir posibles incidentes (Santa María, 17 de septiembre 1820).

— Copia y traducción del interrogatorio a que se había sometido a Juan Santiago Edón, capitán del buque Apolo, en el almirantazgo del distrito de Georgia (26 de enero 1821).

— Copia y traducción de una comunicación de Adams a Vives; disculpa su tardanza en responderle en lo referente a la fragata Apolo pues esperaba la decisión del tribunal que entendía en dicha causa. Ya desde 1818 se planteaba el problema de que buques que trataban de vender sus mercancías en Estados Unidos los introducían fraudulentamente, evitando el pago de los derechos al acogerse a la protección española, por lo que se habían cursado las instrucciones cuya copia remitía, y que habían sido eficaces hasta la llegada del Apolo. Por copias que adjuntaba de cartas de I. F. Clarke, podía ver que el puerto de San José no había sido habilitado por el gobernador de Florida oriental sino por el mismo Clarke, a quien se reconocía como vicecónsul de España en Santa María. El tribunal decidiría si el Apolo había transgredido las leyes americanas, pero entre tanto el presidente requería que dicho Clarke cesara como agente consular en los Estados Unidos (20 de marzo 1821).

— Nota de Vives a Adams acusando recibo de su comunicación y los documentos que adjuntaba, todo lo cual remitiría a su gobierno (23 de marzo 1821).

35

N.º 142. — 26 de marzo, Washington.

Remite certificado del juramento que habían prestado a la constitución los españoles residentes en Nueva Orleans.

Adjunto:

— Certificación del juramento prestado ante Nicolás José de Villavaso, vicecónsul en Luisiana por los españoles Antonio Sedella, Pablo Rodón, Juan Rodón, Ignacio Ayguanegra y Juan Bartolomé Jiménez (Nueva Orleans, 21 de noviembre 1820).

36

N.º 143. — 26 de marzo, Washington.

Anuncia remisión de unos periódicos y un extracto de las noticias más importantes.

Adjunto:

— Extracto de unas noticias publicadas en la «National Gazette» del 5 al 16 de marzo de 1821. Se refieren a la lucha contra la subversión en Buenos Aires y a la formación de un cuerpo de milicias; que Guayaquil se había unido a la república de Columbia (Colombia); la escuadra independiente, bajo las órdenes

de lord Cochrane, había sacado del puerto de Callao una fragata española. Un despacho del general Trujillo anunciaba la ocupación de Mérida y Trujillo por fuerzas de los independientes. Bolívar no había aceptado la firma de un armisticio que le proponía Morillo dado que la acción era favorable para los independientes con la ocupación de Venezuela y Quito, y Morillo había tenido que reconocer tácitamente la independencia de Colombia. Relación de las fuerzas de mar y tierra que componían la expedición contra Lima que mandaba San Martín, a la cual el virrey no podía oponer más que tres mil cien hombres. Parecía que en Santo Domingo, Boyer estaba preparando una expedición contra la parte española de la isla. En Méjico había una insurrección dirigida por un descendiente de Moctezuma. Robinson decía en una carta que cerca de Santo Domingo había una isleta despoblada llamada Gonave y que allí se podría establecer la gente de color libre que quisiera emigrar de los Estados Unidos, en vez de ir hasta la costa de África; en caso de que necesitaran extenderse podrían hacerlo hacia la parte española de Santo Domingo, que España no podría conservar por mucho tiempo.
— Minuta a Vives acusando recibo de algunos despachos (28 de mayo 1821).

37

N.º 146. — 5 de abril, Washington.

Remite copia y traducción de la respuesta del secretario de Estado a la nota que había enviado sobre el tratado que el gobierno de Estados Unidos había hecho con los indios choctaws. Principal y duplicado.

Adjunto:
— Copia y traducción de la respuesta de Adams en la que manifestaba que había sido revisada la línea divisoria con España convenida en el tratado de 1819 y la que se había concertado con los indios choctaws, no hallando ninguna incompatibilidad entre las dos.

38

N.º 147. — 5 de abril, Washington.

Envía la respuesta de Adams a la pregunta que le había formulado acerca de cuál era el tribunal designado para atender las reclamaciones de los españoles de las Floridas, por los perjuicios que había sufrido al ocupar aquellas provincias el ejército americano.

Adjunto:

— Copia y traducción de la respuesta de Adams participándole que no podía designar el tribunal que solicitaba, hasta que los Estados Unidos estuvieran en posesión de las Floridas y el sistema judicial debidamente organizado en aquellos territorios (Washington, 3 de abril 1821).

39

N.º 148. — 12 de abril, Washington.

Acusa recibo de dos oficios en los que le comunicaba la reforma que se había hecho en la carrera diplomática y el nombramiento de algunos ministros, así como la provisión de la secretaría del despacho de la Gobernación de Ultramar, y nombramiento de jefe político de Madrid, capitán general de Castilla la Nueva e inspector de caballería.

40

N.º 149. — 14 de abril, Washington.

Se da por enterado de la resolución adoptada respecto a algunos empleados de la legación que habían sido trasladados.

41

N.º 150. — 16 de abril, Washington.

Acusa recibo de la copia de un oficio que se había enviado al cónsul general en Estados Unidos sobre la reforma de consulados.

42

N.º 152. — 16 de abril, Washington.

Participa la recepción de un oficio cifrado a cuyo contenido daría cumplimiento. Desde Filadelfia indicaría los libros que le gustaría le enviaran de Madrid.

Las noticias publicadas en las gacetas eran en general imparciales y más bien alababan al nuevo gobierno de España, incluso las que eran contrarias como «La Aurora»; sólo criticaban la política que se seguía respecto a las colonias, porque la consideraban contraria a sus intereses, opinión que había contrarrestado en cierto modo el editor del «National Gazette». Recientemente se habían publicado artículos contra España que también se habían refutado; sería más difícil contradecirlos en lo sucesivo porque el nuevo arancel era contrario a los intereses americanos y procurarían desahogarse con invectivas.

43

N.º 153. — 16 de abril, Washington.

Incluye un extracto de noticias publicadas en los periódicos así como copia de una carta de una persona fidedigna establecida en Caracas, por la que podía ver que se habían renovado las hostilidades y se confirmaba la noticia de que los insurgentes se habían apoderado de Maracaibo.

Adjunto:

— Extracto de las noticias referentes a que el cólera había hecho estragos en Manila, y el pueblo, inducido por personas que achacaban la causa a los extranjeros, había dado muerte a treinta de ellos pudiendo escapar a duras penas el cónsul americano. En Buenos Aires algunos de los diputados elegidos por el congreso que debía reunirse en Córdoba, no se atrevían a ir por temor a ser insultados por el pueblo. Artigas, batido por los portugueses, se había refugiado en Paraguay, que se mantenía aislado. Rodríguez, gobernador de Buenos Aires, había ido a contener a los indios del interior, que le atacaban instigados por Carrera. En Buenos Aires se había detenido a muchas personas por sospechar que tramaban algo contra el gobierno.

San Martín estaba en Ancón, un poco al norte de Lima e intentaba atacar por tierra mientras lord Cochrane la bloqueaba por mar; este último había sacado de Callao la fragata Esmeralda con la sola pérdida de quince hombres. El pueblo de Lima había asesinado a parte de la tripulación de la fragata americana Macedonia por sospechar que había cooperado con Cochrane, el cual había resultado herido. Guayaquil se había revolucionado con la noticia del desembarco de San Martín en Lima. Se creía que Bolívar, a petición del general la Torre, había enviado comisionados a España para tratar de la pacificación completa.

La legación de España que había ido a Buenos Aires no había logrado nada porque el gobernador exigía el reconocimiento previo de su independencia antes de entrar en negociaciones.

En Brasil se había establecido un gobierno constitucional después de una breve lucha entre las tropas y el pueblo; habían ofrecido la presidencia al gobernador, pero éste la había rechazado alegando su juramento de obediencia al rey; a las tropas europeas que estaban en Río Janeiro les habían ofrecido incorporarlas a su ejército pero con excepción de doce hombres, habían preferido volver a Portugal.

En Méjico, según noticias procedentes de Veracruz, el virrey había sido depuesto y se había formado una junta que había nombrado unos diputados para que fueran a España a pedir a las cortes un rey, escogido entre las personas de la familia real, para que residiera en aquel país, o de lo contrario, que reconocieran la independencia de aquel reino.

Refuta unas noticias procedentes de una carta escrita desde Gibraltar, que describía con negras tintas la situación española y lo inadecuado de algunos decretos de las cortes (21 de marzo a 16 de abril 1821).

— Copia de una proclama de Miguel de la Torre a los habitantes de las provincias de Venezuela dándoles cuenta de que, existiendo un armisticio con el general Bolívar, éste había intimado su suspensión sin atenerse a razones, por lo que participaba que nuevamente estaban en guerra (Caracas, 23 de marzo 1821).

— Copia de una carta explicando los hechos llevados a cabo por Bolívar que había provocado la sublevación de Maracaibo, ocupando luego Ocaña y Barinas y afirmando que quería la independencia o la guerra (Sin fecha).

— Minuta a Vives acusando recibo de algunos despachos (6 de julio 1821).

44

N.º 155. — 2 de mayo, Camden.

Comunica su traslado al pueblo de Camden (Nueva Jersey), siguiendo la costumbre de los diplomáticos extranjeros en Estados Unidos.

45

N.º 156. — 2 de mayo, Camden.

Acusa recibo de las órdenes que se le habían comunicado en oficio muy reservado del 4 de enero.

46

N.º 157. — 2 de mayo, Camden.

Queda enterado de que el rey había accedido a sus deseos de volver a España en cuanto se concluyeran los principales asuntos pendientes, a causa de su delicada salud que no le permitiría permanecer otro invierno en un clima tan duro.

CORRESPONDENCIA DE FRANCISCO DIONISIO VIVES, MINISTRO PLENIPOTENCIARIO DE ESPAÑA EN ESTADOS UNIDOS, CON FRANCISCO DE PAULA ESCUDERO, SECRETARIO DE ESTADO

47

N.º 158. — 2 de mayo, Camden.

Queda enterado de que, una vez que se examinen sus cuentas, se le comunicaría las resoluciones que se adoptaran sobre las mismas.

48

N.º 159. — 8 de mayo, Camden.

Había comunicado al cónsul general, para que lo hiciera llegar al de Filadelfia, la determinación de que debía continuar pagando los treinta duros anuales por los tres bancos que tenía España en la iglesia de Santa María de Filadelfia.

49

N.º 161. — 8 de mayo, Camden.

Participa que había llegado la contestación a la solicitud de Antonio Mendieta, pero no había podido comunicarla al interesado por encontrarse en España.

50

N.º 162. — 8 de mayo, Camden.

Despacho cifrado en parte, participando que había recibido copia de la correspondencia cruzada entre Evaristo San Miguel y el secretario de Gobernación de Ultramar.

Adjunto:

— Minuta a Vives acusando recibo de varios despachos (20 de junio 1821).

51

N.º 163. — 2 de mayo, Camden.

Anuncia el envío de una carta dirigida a la casa de David Deforest, de Baltimore, en la que se confirmaba el apresamiento por lord Cochrane de la fragata Esmeralda en el puerto de Callao, la insurrección de Guayaquil y la deserción del batallón Numancia, que se había unido al ejército de San Martín. Respecto a la revolución de Méjico, se decía que el brigadier Iturbide había enarbolado el estandarte de la rebelión y el virrey había despachado contra él seis mil hombres.

VIII. — 3

Por carta de un comerciante de la Habana sabía que se había suspendido allí la puesta en vigor del nuevo arancel establecido por las cortes, y que probablemente no se aceptaría ninguno que restringiera el comercio de aquella isla, por temor a la ruina.

52

N.º 164. — 10 de mayo, Camden.

Auncia remisión de unas gacetas y del resumen de su contenido.

53

N.º 165. — 12 de mayo, Camden.

Da cuenta de que los periódicos americanos habían rectificado las noticias que exageraban los sucesos ocurridos en España los días 4 a 7 de febrero último.

Adjunto:

— Minuta a Vives acusando resibo de varios despachos (25 de junio 1821).

54

N.º 168. — 21 de mayo, Camden.

Remite extracto de las noticias publicadas en los periódicos.

Adjunto:

— Extracto de noticias aparecidas del 6 de marzo al 24 de abril, dando cuenta de la pacificación del virreinato de Méjico, donde se había rendido el coronel Iturbide; de la dimisión del virrey de Lima, Pezuela, en favor de José de la Serna; en Brasil, la guarnición de Bahía había pedido al infante don Pedro que les concediera la constitución de Portugal; a instancias del intendente el rey accedió a ello, comunicando al mismo tiempo, que había determinado transferir su corte a Portugal.

55

N.º 169. — 1 de junio, Camden.

Había recibido el oficio referente al cambio del ministerio efectuado por el rey, en uso de las facultades que le concedía la constitución.

56

N.º 170. — 1 de junio, Camden.

Anteriormente había dado cuenta de la equivocación en que había incurrido el cónsul en Nueva Orleans al decir que había sido rechazada la demanda de Luis Seri; no había obtenido respuesta la nota que a consecuencia de aquello había enviado al secretario de Estado en noviembre último, pero el hecho de que no se hubiera procedido contra Villavaso inducía a pensar que no se cometería ningún atropello.

Se afirma en su creencia, ya manifestada en anterior despacho, de que no se podría recobrar nada de los 44.000 pesos que habían gastado Fatio y Renovales.

57

N.º 172. — 1 de junio, Camden.

Queda enterado de que habían sido aprobadas las cuentas relativas a la asignación de Casta M.ª de Zires; las del viaje que él había efectuado de Londres a Nueva York, y la gratificación para alimentos del teniente de zapadores Antonio Donis.

58

N.º 173. — 1 de junio, Camden.

Acusa recibo de la comunicación con las instrucciones sobre la cuantía que le correspondía percibir de los fondos de la legación, por su viaje de Londres a Nueva York, computándose noventa reales de vellón por legua de mar, siendo la distancia entre las dos ciudades, de mil ciento cincuenta y tres leguas.

59

N.º 174. — 1 de junio, Camden.

Despacho, cifrado en parte, en el que participa que había llegado a su conocimiento la respuesta del secretario del despacho de Gobernación de Ultramar, sobre los auxilios que se prestarían a los habitantes de las Floridas que quisieran trasladarse a las provincias internas y posiciones españolas en aquel continente.

60

N.º 175. — 1 de junio, Camden.

Queda enterado de que se habían recibido varios oficios suyos.

61

N.º 176. — 8 de junio, Camden.

Manifiesta su satisfacción por la noticia de que en cumplimiento de la constitución, se había celebrado la primera junta preparatoria de las cortes.

62

N.º 178. — 8 de junio, Camden.

Responde al oficio de Joaquín de Anduaga en el que le había comunicado los ceses como secretarios de despacho de Evaristo Pérez de Castro, Agustín Argüelles, Ramón Gil de la Quadra, Manuel García Herreros, José Canga Argüelles y Cayetano Valdés, y los nombramientos para desempeñarlos interinamente del mariscal de campo Ignacio Balanzat, para Guerra, Joaquín de Anduaga para Estado, Ignacio Baeza para Gobernación de la península, Antonio Guilleman para Ultramar, Manuel Encina para Gracia y Justicia y Luis Sorela para Hacienda.

63

N.º 179. — 8 de junio, Camden.

Manifiesta su satisfacción por la noticia de que el día primero de marzo el rey había renovado el pacto que le unía a la nación.

64

N.º 180. — 8 de junio, Camden.

Queda enterado de que tras haber consultado el rey al Consejo de Estado, había procedido a los siguientes nombramientos: Eusebio Bardají y Azara para el desempeño de la secretaría de Estado; para Gobernación de la península, Mateo Valdemoro; Gobernación de Ultramar, Ramón de Feliú; secretario de Gracia y Justicia, Vicente Cano Manuel; para Hacienda, Antonio Barata; para el despacho de Guerra, el teniente general Tomás Moreno, y de Marina, Francisco de Paula Escudero.

65

N.º 181. — 8 de junio, Camden.

Ha recibido la comunicación relativa a que, por ausencia de los nombrados para las secretarías de Estado, Gracia y Justicia y Guerra, continuaban desempeñándolas los anteriores titulares.

66

N.º 182. — 11 de junio, Camden.

Transmite las malas noticias que habían llegado referentes a la apurada situación de Lima, la nueva insurrección de Méjico, los sucesos de la Costa Firme donde parecía que se había perdido Coro, Caracas y La Guayra, y sobre la anarquía reinante en Buenos Aires. Noticias posteriores decían que San Martín se había retirado de Lima y que los insurgentes habían sido batidos en Puebla, y bloqueado cerca de Acapulco, Iturbide.

Acababa de enterarse de que Mier, que estaba preso en la Habana, liberado por el populacho, había llegado a Nueva York en la fragata Fulton.

Tiene noticias de que Forsyth proyectaba salir de Nueva York con su familia, en la fragata Fabius.

Adjunto:

— Extracto de noticias publicadas en los periódicos de 26 de mayo a 11 de junio.
— Minuta a Vives acusando recibo de varios oficios.

67

N.º 183. — 30 de junio, Camden.

Comunica que el país estaba libre de toda enfermedad contagiosa.

68

N.º 184. — 1 de julio, Camden.

Incluye copia de un oficio que había recibido del capitán general de Cuba, en el que acusaba recibo de su comunicación referente a la entrega de las Floridas en virtud del tratado de 1819 que había sido ratificado, y de la real cédula que ordenaba llevarlo a efecto, así como lo estipulado respecto a los buques, víveres y escolta que debía proporcionar el gobierno americano para que se trasladaran a la Habana todos los españoles que debían evacuar el territorio. Estaban preparadas las comunicaciones para la entrega, destinadas a los gobernadores de las Floridas, las cuales serían conducidas por la corbeta de guerra de Estados Unidos Hornet, dispuesta a salir para Panzacola.

Aunque no había recibido la confirmación, creía que el general Jackson había tomado ya posesión como gobernador de las Floridas.

Adjunto:

— Copia del oficio del capitán general de Cuba, Nicolás Mahy (Habana, 18 de mayo 1821).

69

N.º 185. — 4 de julio, Camden.

(Dirigido a Bardají aunque el secretario de Estado era Escudero).

Participa que pese a sus reiteradas reclamaciones al intendente de la isla de Cuba, no había recibido ninguna cantidad a cuenta del situado del año en curso; como por un oficio del virrey de Nueva España comprendía que no podría recibir nada de las cajas de la Habana y Méjico, dadas las dificultades ya existentes y las que representaba el nuevo levantamiento de los disidentes en Nueva España, que habían cortado las comunicaciones entre la capital y Veracruz, solicitaba que se le proveyera de los fondos necesarios para pagar los sueldos de todos los empleados, en la forma que se estimara conveniente.

Adjunto:

— Copia de un oficio del virrey de Méjico, conde de Venadito, a Vives comunicando que, pese a las graves obligaciones que tenía de socorrer a Santo Domingo, Puerto Rico, tropas expedicionarias de Tierra Firme y el apostadero de Maracaibo, haciendo un gran esfuerzo había logrado enviar cincuenta mil pesos al intendente de la Habana con destino a la legación de Estados Unidos, pero le era imposible repetirlo por las graves obligaciones de la tesorería y los escasos fondos con que contaba (Méjico, 29 de enero 1821).

— Copia de un oficio de Vives al intendente de la Habana manifestando la situación crítica que atravesaba al no poder pagar a los empleados de la legación y consulados por carecer de fondos, y rogando, que de la manera que pudiera le remitiese alguna suma para satisfacer las cantidades adeudadas (Filadelfia, 20 de mayo 1821).

— Minuta a Vives acusando recibo del despacho 185; ya se le habían comunicado las disposiciones adoptadas para el pago de los sueldos de los empleados en Estados Unidos desde primero de julio; en cuanto a las cantidades que se adeudaban con anterioridad, se había dado orden al intendente de la Habana para que enviara sin demora los dos tercios del situado del año en curso, con cuyo importe podría satisfacerlas (17 de noviembre 1821).

70

N.º 186. — 16 de julio, Camden.

Anuncia remisión de unas gacetas por las que se podría ver que las tropas habían recobrado Caracas y la Guayra; se incrementaba la insurrección de Méjico y Lima; se aseguraba que el 25 de junio se había verificado la entrega de las Floridas a los agentes del gobierno americano. Pese a la reciente llegada de varios buques de Europa, hacía cuatro meses que no había recibido ningún despacho de España.

Adjunto:

— Minuta a Vives acusando recibo de varios oficios y la cuenta de gastos correspondientes al primer tercio del año (30 de octubre 1821).

71

N.º 192. — 7 de septiembre, Camden.

Da cuenta de que el intendente de Venezuela, Diego de Alegría, le había escrito manifestando los apuros de los defensores de Puerto Cabello y Cumaná por falta de numerario y de víveres, y pedía que le auxiliara a través de algún comerciante americano. Por mediación del vicecónsul en Filadelfia, Juan Leamy, persona de toda confianza, había gestionado dicha ayuda sin conseguirlo, por considerar los comerciantes muy incierto el cobro de las cantidades que adelantaran; tampoco él había podido hacerlo por carecer de fondos incluso para pagar a sus empleados.

Adjunto:

— Nota informativa de Narciso de Heredia (2 de enero 1821).

72

N.º 194. — 12 de septiembre, Camden.

Comunica la llegada del coronel de ingenieros Félix Lemaur y del capitán de infantería Domingo Aristizábal, que le habían entregado un oficio del capitán general de Cuba en el que los nombraba comisionados para fijar los límites de demarcación acordados por el tratado de 22 de febrero de 1819; tenían también las instrucciones sobre ciertos puntos que debían aclarar con los comisionados americanos. Pero antes de que empezaran a actuar había él recibido un despacho del secretario de Estado comunicándole que el rey se ocupaba en el nombramiento de los comisionados que debían proceder a la demarcación de límites; ante la duda de si serían las mismas o diferentes personas que las designadas por el capitán general de Cuba, había ordenado a Lemaur y Aristizábal que esperaran hasta recibir la confirmación de su nombramiento.

73

N.º 196. — 12 de septiembre, Camden.

Transmite a Eusebio Bardají, las noticias llegadas de Veracruz sobre la unión a los disidentes de todo el reino de Méjico, excepto de la capital; que el virrey Apodaca había dimitido de su cargo a petición de sus tropas, sucediéndole el teniente general Francisco Novella y que los generales Cruz y Negrete se habían unido a Iturbide. Eran igualmente descorazonadoras las noticias de Tierra Firme: los restos del ejército derrotado en Carabobo y perseguido, se habían refugiado en Puerto Cabello donde el vómito negro estaba haciendo estragos; había muerto el cónsul Pereira y se hallaban enfermos los generales Torres y Morales. Los únicos puntos fieles que quedaban en aquel continente eran Puerto Cabello y Cumaná, que estaban faltos de víveres y cercados por los disidentes.

La fiebre amarilla, se había extendido a Nueva York, además de los otros puertos de Estados Unidos donde ya la había.

74

N.º 197. — 12 de septiembre, Camden.

(Dirigido a Bardají aunque el secretario de Estado era Escudero). Acusa recibo del oficio de junio último con instrucciones para el pago de ciertas partidas; por las cuentas había visto que había abonado catorce meses a Casta María de Zires; y como por falta de fondos del ministerio no podía él cobrar el viaje que había hecho de Londres a Nueva York, había decidido percibir una parte de las mensualidades excedentes de dicha señora.

75

N.º 198. — 14 de septiembre, Camden.

Acusa recibo a Francisco de Paula Escudero del oficio en el que le había participado su nombramiento como secretario de Estado y el de Joaquín de Anduaga, oficial mayor más antiguo de la secretaría de Estado, como enviado extraordinario y ministro plenipotenciario en Washington.

76

N.º 199. — 16 de septiembre, Camden.

Participa que había recibido la aprobación de la cuenta de gastos ordinarios y extraordinarios de la legación, por lo que había cargado las partidas con arreglo a las instrucciones que había recibido sobre el particular; había pasado al cónsul general la orden de que los cónsules en Estados Unidos limitaran sus gastos extraordinarios.

Adjunto:
— Minuta a Vives acusando recibo de varios oficios (20 de noviembre 1821).

77

N.º 201. — 21 de septiembre, Camden.

Muestra su satisfacción por las noticias recibidas sobre la tranquilidad que reinaba en Madrid, las medidas que se habían tomado para mantenerla, y que carecían de importancia los sucesos que habían ocurrido en la corte, pese a la exageración de las notas que habían publicado los periódicos franceses.

78

N.º 202. — 21 de septiembre, Camden.

Participa que comunicará cuantas noticias se conozcan referentes a la resolución que pueda adoptar el congreso, sobre el proyecto del gobierno americano de ubicar un establecimiento militar y comercial en el río Columbia, del cual había informado con anterioridad.

79

N.º 204. — 21 de septiembre, Camden.

Comunica a Bardají que había recibido la aprobación de la nota enviada al gobierno de Estados Unidos sobre el tribunal que debería entender de las reclamaciones por los perjuicios que habían sufrido los habitantes de las Floridas a consecuencia de la ocupación del territorio por el ejército americano.

80

N.º 205. — 22 de septiembre, Camden.

Acusa recibo de varios oficios con resoluciones sobre los cónsules, que había trasladado al cónsul general.

81

N.º 206. — 21 de septiembre, Camden.

Transmite a Bardají la respuesta del secretario de Estado americano a la nota que le había enviado, pidiendo aclaración sobre la línea divisoria estipulada en el tratado con los indios choctaws, que en opinión de Vives entraba dentro de los límites españoles; decía Adams en su respuesta que revisadas las demarcaciones no existía incompatibilidad entre ellas, y que tomaría todas las medidas para que fueran respetados los límites con España.

82

N.º 207. — 21 de septiembre, Camden.

Queda enterado de que se iba a proceder a la publicación en Madrid del tratado de 22 de febrero de 1819 con los Estados Unidos; y de que se estaban eligiendo comisionados para que, en unión con los americanos, establecieran la línea divisoria entre las dos potencias; agradecía el propósito de tener presente la recomendación que había hecho del agregado cesante de la legación, Francisco Pizarro Martínez, para secretario de dicha comisión.

83

N.º 208. — 30 de septiembre, Camden.

Había ido a Washington con el secretario de la legación, Hilario de Rivas Salmón, a fin de presentarlo al gobierno como encargado de negocios, a su marcha; pero estando ausente el presidente y el secretario de Estado lo había efectuado al oficial mayor del departamento, Daniel Brent, que tenía autorización para ello. En la misma fecha lo había comunicado al cónsul general de Estados Unidos, a los virreyes de Perú y Méjico, capitán general e intendente de Cuba y al capitán general de Venezuela, para que hasta la llegada de su sucesor Joaquín de Anduaga, trataran todos los negocios con Hilario de Rivas.

En breve emprendería el viaje a España por lo delicado de su salud y lo avanzado de la estación.

Adjunto:

— Minuta a Vives acusando recibo de varios oficios (26 de diciembre 1821).

CORRESPONDENCIA DE HILARIO DE RIVAS Y SALMÓN, ENCARGADO DE NEGOCIOS EN ESTADOS UNIDOS, CON EL SECRETARIO DE ESTADO FRANCISCO DE PAULA ESCUDERO

84

N.º 1. — 30 de septiembre, Filadelfia.

(Los tres primeros despachos van dirigidos a Bardají).

Da cuenta de que el general Vives, próximo a regresar a España, le había presentado en Washington al gobierno federal como encargado de negocios de España y le había entregado los papeles de la legación. Promete desvelarse en el desempeño de su cargo, haciéndose acreedor a la confianza que se le había dispensado.

85

N.º 2. — 1 de octubre, Filadelfia.

Manifiesta el estado en que había encontrado la legación al encargarse de ella: había una falta absoluta de fondos y un retraso de muchos meses en el pago de los sueldos a los empleados y cónsules. Pese a las diligencias que había realizado con ayuda de Vives, no había logrado que los bancos le prestaran dinero para atender a lo más urgente; enterado de que el vicecónsul en Charleston tenía en su poder un depósito de seis mil duros, procedentes del bergantín Ceres, por ignorar su destinatario, había librado contra él por 5.800 duros. Para reponer este depósito pensaba librar dicha cantidad contra las cajas de la Habana. Era tan angustiosa la situación que ignoraba la solución que podría adoptar si alguno de estos trámites fallaba.

86

N.º 3. — 8 de octubre, Filadelfia.

Despacho reservado dando cuenta de la llegada del coronel José Callava, comisario para la entrega de la Florida occidental, acompañado del secretario, subteniente José Cruzat, para dar cuenta de lo que había ocurrido en Panzacola el 22 de agosto último. Por la copia que remite de la protesta presentada por Callava se podía enterar del ultraje que el general Jackson había inferido a su persona, propiedades y los papeles de gobierno, excepto los reservados que eran los únicos que había podido salvar, así como del pretexto para tal atropello. La celebridad de Jackson, debida a la victoria de Nueva Orleans contra los ingleses, que se había logrado por otras causas más que por su talento, le había proporcionado el mando de los ejércitos, aunque el gobierno le temía y por mantenerlo a distancia lo había enviado a las Floridas; allí dejando de lado la constitución, gobernaba despóticamente con pretexto de la guerra, mermando su popularidad, y dejando la impresión de su dureza y despotismo. Había pasado a Adams una nota de protesta por el trato que se había infligido al comisario, publicando varios artículos en las gacetas a favor de España. Sospechaba que el gobierno federal se negaría a dar ninguna satisfacción si no era a cambio de alguna ventaja; alaba la actuación de Callava que había trabajado ímprobamente para preparar la entrega de las Floridas, en tratos con un hombre tan brutal como Jackson.

Adjunto:

— Protesta del coronel José Callava, gobernador cesante en la Florida occidental y comisario para llevar a efecto el tratado ratificado en 22 de febrero de 1819, por las acciones que contra su persona, casa y papeles había ejecutado Andrés Jackson, comisario en Florida por los Estados Unidos. El día 17 de julio, en un acto público celebrado en la casa del gobierno, le había entregado la Florida occidental que estaba a su cargo, con todos los archivos y documentos protocolizados relativos a la propiedad y soberanía de aquella provincia. Del alcalde constitucional español había recibido también inventario de todas las causas criminales y civiles, el alcalde que Jackson había nombrado. Quedaron a cargo del secretario del gobierno los papeles de la correspondencia oficial pertenecientes a la secretaría, los del escribano de Guerra y Hacienda, los militares, procedimientos judiciales de la Hacienda Nacional y arribadas, que debían trasladarse a la Habana. Respecto a personal habían quedado algunos soldados enfermos y varios trabajadores, pendientes de la resolución de una consulta que ambos comisarios, de común acuerdo, habían elevado al presidente de los Estados Unidos y al ministro plenipotenciario de España. Unos individuos se habían presentado en casa del escribano Sousa pretendiendo llevarse por la fuerza unos papeles que querían revisar, por lo que el escribano los había depositado para su custodia en casa de Callava; Jackson había ordenado detener a Sousa y luego al mismo Callava, a quien había tomado declaración sin intérprete eficaz, por lo que ni Callava había sabido de qué se le acusaba, ni Jackson las respuestas que Callava había dado en su descargo, reteniéndolo en la cárcel hasta el día siguiente (3 de octubre 1821).

— Copia de una carta de Rivas y Salmón al secretario de Estado, Adams, manifestando que el coronel Callava, gobernador de Florida occidental y comisario nombrado para realizar la entrega de las Floridas, había permanecido allí después del día señalado para ultimar asuntos que no se habían podido concluir antes y en espera de la resolución de ambos gobiernos acerca de si la artillería debía estar incluida en la entrega, conservando por tanto su carácter oficial de comisario; por la adjunta protesta podía enterarse de los acontecimientos que habían ocurrido en Panzacola; se habían entregado todos los papeles excepto los que tenían que ser trasladados a la Habana. Jackson no había solicitado oficialmente ningún documento, sino que había enviado a casa de Callava unos hombres para que los tomasen por la fuerza de las armas, asaltando y allanando su casa y haciéndolo salir de la cama donde se encontraba enfermo, lo habían sometido a un simulacro de juicio sin intérprete y encarcelado después hasta el día siguiente. Su casa y sus papeles habían quedado a merced de los soldados, que violaron y revisaron la correspondencia oficial. Lo mismo la constitución americana que la española rechazaban los hechos que constituían una gran ofensa para el gobierno español. Esperaba que la conducta de Jackson fuera reprobada y que se diera la debida explicación a su gobierno, máxime cuando éste acababa de conceder un permiso para establecer en Mahón un depósito donde poder introducir víveres y pertrechos navales libres de derechos (Filadelfia, 6 de octubre 1821).

— Copia del testimonio firmado por seis testigos conocedores de los idiomas inglés y español, de que durante el interrogatorio que Jackson había hecho a Callava la noche de su detención, los intérpretes habían hecho una traducción tan mala de lo hablado por ambas partes, por impedirles Jackson actuar de otra manera, que ni el comisario español supo las razones que aducía Jackson ni éste había permitido traducir las declaraciones de Callava (Panzacola, 24 de agosto 1821).

— Copia de la declaración de varios testigos sobre los hechos ocurridos: apresamiento de Callava, simulacro de proceso e injurias infligidas por Jackson.

— Copia del sumario relativo al arresto de Domingo Sousa, José Callava y Antonio Fullarat (Panzacola, 21 y 22 de agosto 1821).

— Copia del testimonio firmado por varios testigos, del estado en que había encontrado su casa el coronel Callava al regresar de la prisión (Panzacola, 24 de agosto 1821).

— Copia de un oficio de José Coppinger a Francisco Dionisio Vives mostrando su extrañeza por la interpretación que los americanos daban a un punto del tratado, pretendiendo incluir en las fortificaciones toda la artillería y municiones; mostraba su vacilación respecto a si debían entregarse los documentos del archivo público que permanecía a cargo del escribano público Juan de Entralgo, y aunque el gobernador americano exigía que se entregaran a una persona determinada, estaba resuelto a no hacerlo hasta que resolvieran sobre ello ambos gobiernos. Exponía su opinión de que, conteniendo dicho archivo todos los justificantes de las propiedades de los habitantes de la provincia, sería más beneficioso que permanecieran allí que trasladarlo a la Habana, adonde tendrían que recurrir con motivo de cualquier pleito o justificación, además de exponer a los peligros de un viaje por mar una carga tan preciosa. Aunque Vives le había recomendado que no demorara su salida de dicha plaza, pensaba permanecer hasta recibir la contestación del capitán general de Cuba relativa a las familias que quisieran emigrar a la Habana (San Agustín de la Florida, 12 de septiembre 1821).

— Copia de la protesta que había formulado el comisario José Callava, aclarando lo ocurrido con los papeles del archivo que conservaba Sousa (Filadelfia, 3 de octubre 1821).

87

N.º 4. — 8 de octubre, Filadelfia.

Remite traducción de la respuesta de Adams al oficio que le había enviado Vives relativo a la permuta de la artillería por los víveres.

Adjunto:

— Respuesta de Adams manifestando que había expuesto al presidente el asunto de la interpretación de los artículos 2 y 7 del tratado de 1819; y consideraba que si por parte española se consideraba que los víveres iban incluidos en los transportes, que según lo estipulado, tenían que proporcionarse a las tropas españolas que abandonaran las Floridas, de igual modo se debía interpretar el artículo que establecía la entrega de las fortificaciones, que debían incluir la artillería y el armamento que contenían. En cuanto a la conducta del capitán general de Cuba sobre la ejecución del tratado, se harían las reclamaciones por medio del ministro de Estados Unidos en Madrid (Washington, 25 de septiembre 1821).

88

N.º 5. — 8 de octubre, Filadelfia.

Anuncia remisión de unas gacetas con noticias muy importantes: el general O'Donojú había reconocido la independencia de Méjico en nombre del rey, quedando federado con España con un Borbón como emperador; que el nuevo virrey de Lima había derrotado a San Martín; que en Chile había síntomas de una guerra civil; que el comandante inglés Hardy desaprobaba el bloqueo de Cochrane y había salido hacia Lima para obligarle a revocarlo. El vicecónsul en Nueva Orleans le había comunicado la estancia en Tejas del general Long, Trespalacios y Morillo. Por el cónsul general sabía que se estaba armando en Baltimore un corsario insurgente llamado José y que el vicecónsul en aquel puerto había pedido al administrador de la aduana que lo detuviera.

Adjunto:

— Minuta a Rivas acusando recibo de varios oficios (26 de diciembre 1821).

CORRESPONDENCIA DE JOAQUÍN DE ANDUAGA, MINISTRO PLENIPOTENCIARIO EN ESTADOS UNIDOS, CON EL SECRETARIO DE ESTADO FRANCISCO DE PAULA ESCUDERO

89

N.º 2. — 7 de noviembre, Filadelfia.

(Dirigido a Bardají aunque el secretario de Estado era Escudero).

Da cuenta de la precaria situación en que había encontrado a los secretarios de la legación y empleados del consulado que llevaban cinco meses sin cobrar, lo que había obligado a Rivas y Salmón a servirse de un depósito perteneciente a particulares para obtener fondos; era preferible prescindir de representantes en países extranjeros, mientras no fuera posible mantenerlos. Había sido protestada una letra que había girado contra el intendente de la Habana; tampoco el banquero de Londres había enviado ninguna orden para el pago de los sueldos, como debía haber hecho, y por su parte casi había consumido ya la cantidad que había percibido para el viaje. Ante la perspectiva de tener que cerrar la legación y volver a España, había resuelto enviar a la Habana a Francisco Martínez Pizarro para que expusiera al intendente la situación en que se hallaban; la legación no podría subsistir más que hasta el 10 de enero, siendo imposible obtener préstamo ni ayuda en los Estados Unidos. Duplicado.

Adjunto:

— Minuta al tesorero real participándole que, vista la imposibilidad de que las cajas de Méjico y la Habana proporcionaran el situado asignado al ministerio en los Estados Unidos, se había ordenado que desde primero de julio último se efectuara dicho pago por cuenta del giro nacional. Ante la situación que había expuesto el ministro en Washington, se le prevenía la urgencia de dictar las órdenes necesarias para que inmediatamente se abonaran los sueldos que se adeudaban (29 de diciembre 1821).

— Minuta al ministro en Estados Unidos Joaquín de Aduaga anunciando remisión de la real orden para que el capitán general de Cuba organizara la comisión de límites, que junto con la nombrada por el gobierno federal, debía entender en la demarcación de la Luisiana, con arreglo al artículo 4.º del tratado; debería comunicar el nombramiento de los comisarios al gobierno de Estados Unidos y trasladar copia de dicha real orden al coronel de ingenieros Félix Lemaur, nombrado comisario principal de límites y jefe de la expedición, así como el nombramiento de comandante de la escolta al capitán Domingo Aristizábal. Debería avisar al comisario Lemaur la urgencia de cumplir el encargo, y la conveniencia de que se trasladaran a Nueva Orleans a esperar las órdenes del capitán general de la isla de Cuba (30 de diciembre 1821).

90

N.º 4. — (Falta el despacho).

Llevaba adjunto la traducción de una proclama del general Jackson por la que conminaba a salir del territorio de las Floridas a ocho oficiales españoles, que habían permanecido allí sin licencia tras la salida de las tropas del rey, y después de los seis meses que era el límite admitido para su permanencia; además habían publicado una nota en defensa del coronel Callava, resaltando la injusticia del trato que le había infligido Jackson sometiéndolo a un interrogatorio judicial sin proporcionarle un intérprete adecuado (Panzacola, 29 de septiembre 1821).

91

N.º 5. — 19 de noviembre, Filadelfia.

Remite copia de una nota que había enviado al secretario de Estado, Adams, protestando por la nueva arbitrariedad de Jackson al expulsar de las Floridas a los oficiales españoles, aunque éstos habían sido imprudentes con la publicación de aquella nota, en la que trataban de justificar a su jefe Callava ante la opinión americana; después de su salida habían publicado en las gacetas un artículo cuya copia también adjuntaba. Respecto a las posibles satisfacciones del gobierno de Estados Unidos no abrigaba grandes esperanzas.

Adjunto:

— Copia de la nota que había enviado Anduaga a Adams, manifestando su disconformidad con la proclama que había publicado Jackson; alegaba que puesto que se basaba en que tenían que haber salido todos los oficiales españoles, no debía haberse dirigido solamente a los ocho mencionados, sino a todos los que aún permanecían en dicho territorio. Por otra parte, lo que denunciaban en su nota era del dominio público, puesto que había ocurrido ante muchas personas y el mismo intérprete había admitido en un artículo publicado en las gacetas, que ni las preguntas del interrogatorio ni las respuestas habían sido traducidas más que en una mínima parte (Filadelfia, 18 de noviembre 1821).

— Copia de una nota que dichos oficiales habían enviado para su publicación en una gaceta, reiterando sus acusaciones contra Jackson y despidiéndose de sus amigos floridanos.

92

N.º 9. — 28 de noviembre, Filadelfia.

Anuncia remisión del extracto de las noticias relativas a América contenidas en las gacetas.

93

N.º 11. — 5 de diciembre, Filadelfia.

(Dirigido a Bardají).

Remite copia de una carta referente al estado de Costa Firme, dado que su contenido podía interesar al gobierno.

Adjunto:

— Copia de una carta de Gerardo Patrulló a Juan Leamy, en la que trataba varios asuntos: enviaba una relación de las fuerzas existentes en Venezuela, que ascendían a cuatro mil setecientos hombres; daba cuenta de algunos movimientos de Bolívar, de las capitulaciones de Cumaná y Cartagena y otros sucesos de Costa Firme; preguntaba si podía reclamar del gobierno español el pago de treinta y ocho mil pesos que le debía el americano, por el valor de un buque con su carga de que lo había despojado el corsario Saratoga. En su opinión la guerra entre Rusia y Turquía podía acarrear graves consecuencias (Curaçao, 1 de noviembre 1821).

— Oficio de Ramón López Pelegrín, de Gobernación de Ultramar, al secretario de Estado Marqués de Santa Cruz, devolviendo la carta relativa a los sucesos de Costa Firme (6 de febrero 1822).

94

N.º 13. — 5 de diciembre, Filadelfia.

Remite a Escudero extractos de noticias aparecidas en las gacetas.

Adjunto:

— Extracto de varias noticias relativas a la América española.
«La Aurora» del 26 de noviembre, daba cuenta de la rendición

de Cumaná a los insurgentes bajo las órdenes de Bermúdez; de que el congreso de Colombia había elegido presidente a Bolívar y vicepresidente a Santander y que el cabildo de Lima había declarado la independencia del Perú el 15 de julio.

La gaceta de Filadelfia de la misma fecha, decía que todo el reino de Nueva España, desde el Orinoco hasta el golfo de Méjico, con excepción de Veracruz, se había declarado independiente; que Puerto Cabello en Venezuela y San Juan de Ulúa eran las únicas fortalezas en poder de los realistas; que Méjico se había rendido y Veracruz había sido abandonada.

«La Aurora» de 28 de noviembre publicaba que se había confirmado la toma de Lima; que el general San Martín había entrado en Lima el día 22 de julio, encontrando que el gobernador de la plaza había huido al interior con dos mil quinientos hombres y una gran suma de dinero. Tras el ataque a Callao de la escuadra chilena al mando de Cochrane, se había rendido la ciudad resultando apresadas tres fragatas, dos bergantines y varios mercantes españoles.

El 30 de noviembre transmitía la noticia, procedente de la Habana, sobre el nombramiento de una regencia en Méjico formada por Juan O'Donojú, primer regente y capitán general interino; Pérez, obispo de Puebla, segundo regente, e Iturbide tercero y comandante general del ejército; y los siguientes ministros: Almara, de Relaciones Exteriores; Cruz, de Guerra, y de Hacienda, el fiscal de la Audiencia; de Marina, Apodaca; de Gracia y Justicia, el arzobispo de Méjico, y superintendente general de la moneda, Fagoaga.

La gaceta de Filadelfia de 30 de noviembre: por conducto de la Habana había llegado la noticia de la muerte del general O'Donojú, se creía que envenenado. El 1 de diciembre anunciaba la llegada de los generales Apodaca y Novella; que Veracruz estaba independiente y que no se había confirmado la muerte de O'Donojú.

«National Gazette» de 3 de diciembre, comunicaba la entrada en Méjico del ejército imperial el 27 de septiembre y el nombramiento de una regencia presidida por Iturbide y con O'Donojú como uno de sus miembros.

95

N.º 14. — 5 de diciembre, Filadelfia.

(Dirigido a Bardají).

El día anterior se habían reunido las dos cámaras en el capitolio de Washington, según establecía la constitución, y una delegación compuesta por varios representantes de ambas cámaras debía anunciar al presidente la inauguración de este congreso. Se había procedido a la votación para elegir presidente sin conseguir el número necesario de votos tras siete votaciones. Duplicado.

96

N.º 15. — 7 de diciembre, Filadelfia.

Participa que el día 4, después de doce votaciones, los representantes habían elegido por su presidente a P. P. Barbour, del estado de Virginia, lo que probaba la mayoría que tenían en el congreso los estados del sur. Remite el mensaje que había pronunciado James Monroe, presidente de los Estados Unidos. Había sido aceptada la dimisión de su cargo, que había presentado el general Jackson, gobernador de las Floridas. Duplicado.

Adjunto:

— Traducción duplicada del mensaje del presidente de los Estados Unidos de América, James Monroe, al congreso, dando cuenta de su gestión. Se refería al comercio exterior, nulo con Gran Bretaña, casi nulo con Francia, por exigir ambos países ventajas que no se había considerado conveniente conceder, y normales con los restantes países europeos. Se refería a los casos del Apolo y Eugenia, buques franceses que habían pretendido eludir las leyes arancelarias.

Aún no se sabía la decisión del emperador de Rusia, a cuyo criterio se había sometido la cuestión de límites. Respecto a España se había cumplido en parte el tratado de 22 de febrero de 1819; se habían entregado las Floridas a los Estados Unidos, pero no así los archivos y papeles que tenían relación con ellas. Daba cuenta de los nombramientos que se habían producido en dichas provincias y las divisiones territoriales que se habían efectuado, así como de algunas fricciones que habían surgido entre el gobernador del territorio y el juez de la provincia occidental por cuestión de competencias. Aludía a los esfuerzos de las colonias españolas para independizarse y esperaba que España acogiera el hecho con magnanimidad; trataba de las cuentas de la tesorería y manifestaba su esperanza de que se lograra la industrialización del país, tan bien provisto de materias primas. Se vigilaban las costas y se construían buques para proteger el comercio, manteniendo una escuadrilla en el Mediterráneo para salvaguardar la paz con los países berberiscos (Washington, 3 de diciembre 1821).

97

N.º 16. — 14 de diciembre, Filadelfia.

Despacho, cifrado en parte, comentando el discurso del presidente Monroe, que no se mostraba muy partidario de Francia tergiversando el asunto del Apolo, por el cual dicha potencia pensaba exigir completa satisfacción; también era partidista al decir que España no había cumplido lo estipulado en el tratado y era evidente que apoyaba en todo a Jackson. Las notas que había enviado no recibían respuesta del gobierno de la Habana para resolver lo de los archivos.

Nada más incorporarse a su destino se había informado del carácter del gobierno y especialmente del de Adams; el presidente era honrado, instruido y de mucho mérito. El ministerio de Estado estaba dividido, siendo pública la oposición entre Crawford y Adams, ambos aspirantes a la presidencia.

Hay una nota que dice que no era posible descifrar este despacho, pues no servían las cifras que se habían utilizado anteriormente; que se le advirtiera la equivocación en que había incurrido y que remitiera nuevamente las noticias. Duplicado.

Adjunto:

— Copia de una nota que había enviado Anduaga al secretario de Estado americano, reiterando la petición de que se le entregara la relación de los daños que los americanos habían sufrido de Francia, en las costas y puertos de España, con el nombre de las presas y su verdadero valor para que el gobierno español pudiera resarcir dichos perjuicios, como se estipulaba en el artículo 14 del tratado de 1819 (Filadelfia, 13 de diciembre 1821).

98

N.º 17. — 14 de diciembre, Filadelfia.

Comunica que en la cámara de representantes se había propuesto pedir al secretario de Estado copia de todos los informes que había en su despacho relativos a las discusiones del general Jackson con el juez Fromentin, así como las referentes a la dilación de los jefes españoles para entregar a los comisionados de Estados Unidos los archivos y documentos relacionados con la propiedad y soberanía de las Floridas, y de las medidas adoptadas para obtener dichos fondos. Duplicado.

99

N.º 19. — 17 de diciembre, Filadelfia.

Transmite la noticia recibida por carta de Santo Tomás, de que el general Morales había salido de aquel puerto con mil hombres el día 10 de noviembre con destino desconocido. Duplicado.

100

N.º 20. — 26 de diciembre, Filadelfia.

Da cuenta de que se había rechazado la propuesta que se había presentado al congreso, de que se pidieran copias de todos los informes relativos a los asuntos de las Floridas existentes en la secretaría de Estado. Pese a los rumores que se habían difundido en las gacetas sobre el regreso de Morales a Puerto Cabello sin haber logrado su objetivo, no se sabía nada con certeza. Una hija de José Bonaparte había llegado a Filadelfia para vivir con su padre.

101

N.º 21. — 26 de diciembre, Filadelfia.

Remite el informe que el ministro de Hacienda había dado en el congreso, sobre el estado de la economía. Duplicado.

Adjunto:

— Copia del informe dado al congreso en cumplimiento de las instrucciones del acta adicional a la de la formación del departamento de Hacienda, por el secretario de dicho departamento W. H. Crawford.

LEGAJO 5.648

CORRESPONDENCIA DEL MINISTRO PLENIPOTENCIARIO DON JOAQUÍN
DE ANDUAGA CON LOS SECRETARIOS DE ESTADO ESPAÑOLES

AÑO 1822

102

N.º 22. — 4 de enero, Filadelfia.

A Francisco de Paula Escudero, remite copia de la nota enviada
por Erving a favor de Ricardo Meade.

Adjunto:
— En la citada nota de Erving a Casa Irujo, se refería a dos me-
moriales de Meade al rey, en el primero pedía una comisión
para liquidar los anticipos que le habían concedido para la armada en la última guerra, así como una compensación para él
por sus sufrimientos pasados en el último consejo de guerra.
En la segunda petición, hecha a nombre de John Dickson se
refiere a una carga de tabaco vendida y entregada al gobierno
español en 1815; reclama por la injusticia de una decisión del
consejo de guerra y ruega al rey que ordene el envío de todos
los antecedentes sobre el asunto para que fuesen examinados
por el Supremo Consejo de Hacienda de Indias. A continuación
Erving defiende las peticiones de Meade como razonables y hace
una larga loa de los valiosos servicios prestados por éste al gobierno español.

103

N.º 24. — 7 de enero, Filadelfia.

Anuncia a Escudero remisión de un artículo de gaceta con noticias del reconocimiento por el rey de Portugal de la independencia de Buenos Aires.

104

N.º 25. — 7 de enero, Filadelfia.

Comunica a Escudero que la expedición que salió de Puerto Cabello al mando de Morales, había regresado a dicho puerto sin haber hecho nada y con alguna pérdida.

105

N.º 26. — 7 de enero, Filadelfia.

A Francisco de Paula Escudero, anuncia remisión de un artículo con noticias de algunas victorias de los insurgentes.

106

N.º 27. — 10 de enero, Filadelfia.

A Eusebio Bardají, remite copia y traducción de una carta de Ricardo Meade, que había sido vicecónsul de Estados Unidos en Cádiz.

Adjunto:

— Carta en la que Meade expone las gestiones hechas para obtener el pago de un crédito que tenía contra la Hacienda española (Filadelfia, 2 de enero 1822).
— Respuesta de Anduaga manifestando que cuando el gobierno español hizo la cesión de las Floridas, por el tratado de 1819, quedaron cancelados todos los créditos que pudiesen tener los ciudadanos americanos contra España (Filadelfia, 11 de enero 1822).

107

N.º 28. — 10 de enero, Filadelfia.

Anuncia a Bardají remisión de noticias sobre América española, contenidas en varias gacetas.

108

N.º 29. — 20 de enero, Filadelfia.

A Ramón López Pelegrín, anuncia remisión del censo de la población de Estados Unidos.

109

N.º 31. — 24 de enero, Filadelfia.

Comunica al marqués de Santa Cruz su salida para Washington y expone la imposibilidad de subsistir con un descuento del 30 % en su sueldo.

110

N.º 32. — 21 de enero, Filadelfia.

Remite a López Pelegrín la traducción de una propuesta hecha al congreso para que se tomasen las medidas oportunas por los abusos cometidos contra los barcos americanos en la Habana y otros puertos de América española.

COMUNICACIONES DE ANDUAGA AL MARQUÉS DE SANTA CRUZ

111

N.º 35. — 6 de febrero, Washington.

Anuncia su llegada a Washington acompañado de su secretario Manuel de Barros.

112

N.º 38. — 14 de febrero, Washington.

Comunica que no había recibido respuesta de Adams a sus notas de protesta sobre la conducta del general Jackson en las Floridas.

113

N.º 43. — 14 de febrero, Washington.

Anuncia remisión del informe de la comisión del congreso sobre la ocupación del río Columbia.

114

N.º 44. — 14 de febrero, Washington.

Comunica que se ocuparía de hacer cumplir las obligaciones contraídas con las casas que negociaron el empréstito de doscientos millones.

115

N.º 45. — 14 de febrero, Washington.

Quedaba enterado del oficio relativo al comportamiento del cuerpo diplomático cuando el rey asistía a las cortes.

116

Quedaba enterado de la moderada respuesta que había dado a Estados Unidos en relación con la acusación hecha al capitán general de la Habana por Mr. Forbes, de mezclar intereses económicos en el desempeño de sus obligaciones, sin acompañar ninguna prueba. En opinión de Anduaga la poca energía ante una acusación de esta naturaleza se debía sin duda a la difícil situación de España.

117

N.º 49. — 14 de febrero, Washington.

Acusa recibo de varios oficios informándole de la absoluta normalidad que había en España. Anduaga, al agradecer estas noticias pide que se le tenga al corriente de la realidad, ya que, por otras vías había tenido conocimiento de los disturbios ocurridos en varias provincias españolas, y consideraba que un ministro del rey en el extranjero debía ser merecedor de confianza y estar informado de los sucesos de su patria.

118

N.º 50. — 15 de febrero, Washington.

Remite las mociones que Nelson y Trimble presentaron en el congreso americano dirigidas al reconocimiento de los nuevos gobiernos de América.

Adjunto:

— Copia de las citadas mociones, la de Mr. Trimble más explícita decía que todas las posesiones de América española que hubieran establecido su independencia debían ser reconocidas por Estados Unidos. Se hacía expresa mención de Colombia (29 y 31 de enero 1822).

— Copia del oficio enviado a Luis Calvo para encargarle de llevar a España estos documentos para mayor seguridad y rapidez (Washington, 15 de febrero 1822).

119

N.º 52. — 26 de febrero, Washington.

Trata del regreso a Estados Unidos de Mr. Forsyth quien probablemente, no sería sustituido, sirviendo su sueldo para pagar al ministro que se enviase a la llamada república de Colombia.

120

N.º 53. — 26 de febrero, Washington.

Anuncia remisión del mensaje del presidente americano al congreso, relativo a la conducta de Jackson.

121

N.º 54. — 26 de febrero, Washington.

Comunica que en adelante enviará sus notas oficiales en francés por encontrar dificultades en la traducción del inglés.

122

N.º 55. — 26 de febrero, Washington.

Informa de que Luis Calvo, comisionado para llevar a España unos documentos oficiales, había embarcado para Cádiz.

COMUNICACIONES DE ANDUAGA A MARTÍNEZ DE LA ROSA

123

N.º 57. — 6 de marzo, Washington.

Remite copiado un párrafo de gaceta donde se ponían de manifiesto los deseos del gobierno americano en relación con los territorios al oeste del Mississipi.

(Hay dos ejemplares).

124

N.º 58. — 6 de marzo, Washington.

Avisa de que el gobierno americano estaba armando barcos con objeto de desembarcar en Cuba para perseguir a los piratas.

125

N.º 59. — 6 de marzo, Washington.

Da cuenta del mal efecto que había producido en Estados Unidos una publicación reciente del emperador de Rusia, estableciendo las reglas de navegación a lo largo de la costa noroeste de América; disponía que ninguna nación, excepto la rusa, podría comerciar, pescar, ni tener industria alguna de toda esta costa, así como desde las islas Aleutianas a la costa oriental de Siberia.

126

N.º 60. — 6 de marzo, Washington.

Da cuenta del resultado en la cámara de representantes de la polémica sobre las acusaciones contra Jackson, que había quedado definitivamente disculpado gracias a los muchos amigos que tenía en esta cámara. En opinión de Anduaga se trataba de un nuevo insulto para el gobierno español, y aconsejaba que si el gobierno americano no daba por fin la satisfacción pedida por el asunto de Jackson debía retirarse la legación española de este país.

127

N.º 61. — 6 de marzo, Washington.

Informa que había sido deshechada en el congreso otra proposición contra Jackson.

128

N.º 62. — 6 de marzo, Washington.

Acusa recibo de varios oficios.

129

N.º 67. — 12 de marzo, Washington.

Remite copia de una nota que había mandado a Adams pidiendo el cumplimiento de parte del artículo 9.º del tratado de 1819.

VIII. — 5

Adjunto:

— Nota en la que solicitaba a Adams que fueran examinadas las reclamaciones de los habitantes y oficiales españoles que hubiesen sufrido perjuicios por las operaciones del ejército americano en las Floridas (Washington, 8 de marzo 1822).

130

N.º 68. — 12 de marzo, Washington.

Participa que no traducía sus notas al francés, como había prometido, porque pensaba que permanecería poco tiempo en este destino y temía que su sucesor no conociese bien esta lengua.

131

N.º 70. — 13 de marzo, Washington.

Notifica la próxima partida de los ministros francés y ruso y dice que a su marcha no quedarían en Estados Unidos más representantes extranjeros que el de Inglaterra.

132

N.º 71. — 13 de marzo, Washington.

Envía una serie de cartas duplicadas en distintos correos, por considerar las noticias que contenían de la mayor importancia.

133

N.º 72. — 13 de marzo, Washington.

Da cuenta del mensaje presentado por el presidente a la cámara de representantes proponiendo el reconocimiento de los gobiernos insurgentes de la América española.

134

N.º 76. — 22 de marzo, Filadelfia.

Comunica distintas noticias de las gacetas de Caracas diciendo que Bolívar había vuelto de Quito después de haber asegurado su independencia y que se preparaba una expedición a Puerto Cabello.

135

N.ᵒˢ 82 y 83. — 13 de abril, Filadelfia.

Remite una carta que le había escrito el astrónomo Lambert, con dos ejemplares del mensaje del presidente, relativo a la altitud del Capitolio de Washington, al norte del Ecuador y a su longitud occidental de París y Greenwich.

Adjunto:

— Carta citada, que Anduaga debía trasmitir a los astrónomos de Madrid y Cádiz (Washington, 15 de marzo 1822).

136

N.º 86. — 17 de abril, Filadelfia.

Acusa recibo de varios oficios a los que promete dar cumplimiento (Hay dos ejemplares).

137

N.º 87. — 17 de abril, Filadelfia.

Anuncia remisión de varias gacetas con noticias sobre América española.

138

N.º 88. — 18 de abril, Filadelfia.

Anuncia remisión del mensaje del presidente relativo a las discusiones entre Estados Unidos y Rusia.

139

N.º 90. — 29 de abril, Filadelfia.

Remite copia y traducción de la respuesta que el secretario de Estado americano Adams, daba en relación con las reclamaciones sobre la conducta del general Jackson en las Floridas. En ella decía que el presidente americano no daría una satisfacción al gobierno español porque aprobaba completamente la actuación de Jackson. Anduaga no parecía sorprendido por la reacción del gobierno americano, puesto que, en su opinión, este gobierno había mantenido siempre el mismo tipo de relaciones con España.

Adjunto:

— Nota citada en la que Adams decía que el presidente después de reflexionar todas las circunstancias de las transgresiones de Jackson, atribuía al capitán general de Cuba, a los gobernadores de ambas Floridas y a algunos oficiales españoles, el incumplimiento de lo acordado en el tratado, al no haber evacuado las provincias dentro de los seis meses estipulados y entregado dentro de estos mismos plazos, los archivos y documentos que tuviesen relación con la propiedad y soberanía de esas provincias. Desde Panzacola se habían enviado a la Habana veinte cajones con documentos que contenían todos los registros de la propiedad más importantes de la Florida occidental; su gobernador Callava a quien debía sustituir Jackson una vez finalizados los seis meses de plazo establecidos entre ambos gobiernos, se negaba a entregar los documentos y a manifestar a Jackson su paradero por lo que fue conducido a prisión, pero se le dejó en libertad al siguiente día, a la entrega de la documentación. El mismo problema había surgido con el gobernador de la Florida oriental, Coppinger, que dilataba la entrega de los papeles existentes en su provincia, de los que debía hacerse entrega al coronel Butler designado para sustituirlo (Washington, 15 de abril 1822).

— Copia del nombramiento de los comisarios Forbes, Bell y Law encargados por el gobierno americano de tomar posesión de los registros y archivos existentes en la Florida oriental, de los que harían un inventario separando los que tuviesen relación con la propiedad y soberanía de la provincia, de los de asuntos privados. Correspondencia cruzada entre aquéllos y el gobernador interino de la Florida oriental, W. G. Wosthington, quien les decía que si hubiera alguna resistencia para entregar estos archivos estaban autorizados a tomarlos por la fuerza (San Agustín, 1 de octubre a 14 de enero 1822).

— Extracto de una carta del general Jackson a Adams, justificativa de su actuación. Manifestaba que el anterior gobernador de San Agustín de la Florida, Coppinger, había violado el tratado al negarse a entregar los archivos en el tiempo estipulado y que uno de los motivos de esta negativa era para esquivar los títulos de las cesiones subreticias de grandes cantidades de tierra hechas en la Florida oriental; éstos serían sin duda, los documentos que se transportaron a la Habana en evitación de que se descubriera el fraude si se entregaban a las autoridades americanas. Otro tanto podía decirse de Florida occidental. En su opinión se trataba de una combinación de las autoridades españolas para privar a los ciudadanos americanos de sus derechos de propiedad que les aseguraba el tratado cuando se acordó que los archivos y documentos referentes a la propiedad y soberanía de las Floridas se debían transferir a la entrega de estas provincias (Nashville, 22 de enero 1822).

— Copia de una nota de Joaquín de Anduaga a Adams; acusa recibo a su nota del 15 de abril, en la que lejos de dar ninguna satisfacción al gobierno español por la conducta de Jackson, la justificaba plenamente, y aunque Anduaga esperaba instrucciones de su gobierno, hacía algunas observaciones personales entre las que cabía destacar una rotunda defensa del capitán general de Cuba, Mahy, a quien se había acusado de deshonrosas miras pecuniarias (24 de abril 1822).

Hay algunos documentos repetidos.

140

N.º 92. — 29 de abril, Filadelfia.

Acusa recibo de varios oficios.

Hay dos ejemplares.

141

N.º 93. — 29 de abril, Filadelfia.

Informa en relación con el nombramiento de los comisarios para la demarcación de límites, de las provincias españolas en América, uno de los cuales debía marchar inmediatamente a Nueva Orleans para comenzar su operación. Dice que no podía ejecutarse esta orden porque desde hacía tiempo Estados Unidos ponía impedimentos para que se hiciese.

Hay dos ejemplares.

142

N.º 94. — 29 de abril, Filadelfia.

Pide instrucciones sobre la artillería que había quedado depositada en las Floridas.

Hay dos ejemplares.

143

N.º 95. — 29 de abril, Filadelfia.

Acusa recibo del oficio del 1 de marzo donde le comunicaba su reciente nombramiento para la secretaría de Estado, felicitándolo por ello.

144

N.º 96. — 9 de mayo, Filadelfia.

Notifica que el senado americano había aprobado el presupuesto de cien mil duros para el envío de ministros a los gobiernos insurgentes de América española.

145

N.º 99. — 8 de mayo, Filadelfia.

Comunica la renuncia de Hilario de Rivas Salmón al consulado general en Estados Unidos, por hallarse falto de recursos para hacer frente a los gastos extraordinarios que pudieran ocasionarse. En opinión de Anduaga este consulado debía extinguirse y resolverse en el ministerio de su cargo los asuntos relacionados con los cónsules particulares, que por otra parte no eran demasiado numerosos, y con ello se ahorraría al presupuesto del estado español de seis a siete mil duros al año.

Hay dos ejemplares.

Adjunto:

— Copia de la carta de Hilario Rivas comunicando su renuncia. Hacía presente la difícil situación económica de los empleados en América desde que faltaban los auxilios de la Habana (Filadelfia, 6 de mayo 1822).

— Incluye copia de la correspondencia entre Anduaga e Hilario Rivas sostenida con este motivo (Filadelfia, 30 de abril a 4 de mayo 1822).

146

N.º 100. — 8 de mayo, Filadelfia.

Participa la partida de Mateo de la Serna, que había sido cónsul general en Estados Unidos.

147

N.º 101. — 8 de mayo, Filadelfia.

Remite copia de los oficios de los cónsules de Baltimore y Filadelfia relativos a marineros que se hallaban sin auxilios y de las disposiciones que se habían tomado para solucionar este problema. Pide instrucciones para que sirviesen de norma en adelante.

Adjunto:

— Oficios de Manuel Valdor y Juan Leamy, cónsules de Baltimore y Filadelfia, a Anduaga, dando cuenta de que habían llegado a cada uno de estos puertos las tripulaciones de dos buques españoles procedentes de la Habana, pidiendo asistencia por haber naufragado sus respectivos barcos. Ambos cónsules solicitaban ayuda económica por carecer ellos completamente de medios. Respuestas de Anduaga disponiendo que dichas tripulaciones debían volver a la Habana, pero que se les pagase la manutención mientras permanecieran en sus respectivas ciudades, quedando Anduaga encargado de sufragar estos gastos (29 de abril a 6 de mayo 1822).

Hay dos ejemplares.

148

N.º 102. — 16 de mayo, Nueva York.

Da cuenta de varios asuntos tratados en el último congreso: la conclusión de un tratado de comercio con Francia, el nombramiento de nuevos secretarios de legación para Madrid y Lisboa, y la partida del ministro de Rusia.

Hay dos ejemplares.

149

N.º 104. — 25 de mayo, Nueva York.

Acusa recibo de su oficio del 11 de marzo con noticias satisfactorias de los reyes.

150

N.º 106. — 1 de junio, Nueva York.

Remite una representación de Narciso Noeli en la que pedía un aumento de sueldo; Anduaga apoya esta solicitud por considerarla justa.

Adjunto:

— Representación de Noeli manifestando que venía desempeñando el cargo de secretario del consulado general en Estados Unidos con un sueldo mitad o tercera parte del que gozaban otros empleados españoles en estas provincias, y que no le permitía subsistir. Solicitaba un aumento o su regreso a España (Filadelfia, 28 de mayo 1822).

151

N.º 109. — 23 de junio, Nueva York.

Anuncia remisión de una carta del cónsul de Baltimore con órdenes del ministerio de Hacienda español, lo que en opinión de Anduaga era antirreglamentario.

152

N.º 110. — 21 de junio, Nueva York.

Notifica la presentación de Manuel de Torres al presidente americano, como encargado de negocios de Colombia.

153

N.º 117. — 24 de julio, Nueva York.

A Santiago Usoz, participa algunas noticias: la llegada de Juan Jabat a la Habana; la salida para su país del ministro de Francia Mr. Neuville; la epidemia existente en Washington que había obligado a salir a todos los ministros; la muerte en Filadelfia del encargado de negocios en Colombia, Manuel de Torres y otros asuntos.

COMUNICACIONES DE ANDUAGA A EVARISTO SAN MIGUEL

154

N.º 119. — 1 de agosto, Nueva York.

Acusa recibo de su oficio de 13 de mayo.

155

N.º 122. — 5 de agosto, Nueva York.

Comunica haberse declarado la fiebre amarilla en Nueva York, lo que le obligaba a partir para el campo. Indica la conveniencia de que los buques que llegasen de América a España, guardasen rigurosa cuarentena.

156

N.º 123. — 31 de agosto, Ballston Spa.

Da cuenta de que la epidemia seguía aumentando en Nueva York. Hay dos ejemplares.

157

N.º 128. — 15 de septiembre, Boston.

Avisa su llegada a Boston y dice que la epidemia se había extendido a Filadelfia y Baltimore.

158

N.º 130. — Acusa recibo de varios oficios llegados con mucho retraso.

Hay dos ejemplares.

159

N.º 131. — 15 de septiembre, Boston.

Acusa recibo del oficio relativo a un decreto sobre empleados españoles en países extranjeros.

Hay dos ejemplares.

160

N.º 132. — 15 de septiembre, Boston.

Había recibido un oficio donde se le comunicaba la resolución de las cortes relativa a los socorros que los ministros y cónsules españoles en países extranjeros debían de dar a los súbditos de su país.

Hay dos ejemplares.

161

N.º 134. — 15 de septiembre, Boston.

Notifica haber trasladado a Francisco Pizarro la comunicación del 22 de marzo último.

Hay dos ejemplares.

162

N.º 135. — 15 de septiembre, Boston.

Había recibido el oficio aprobando la conducta de Miguel Valdor.

Hay dos ejemplares.

163

N.º 138. — 19 de septiembre, Boston.

Da cuenta del estado de la opinión pública contra España e informa de varias noticias: que el buque de guerra de Estados Unidos, Grampus, había apresado en Puerto Rico al corsario español Panchita alegando que éste hizo la primera descarga; que el comandante general de Puerto Rico había puesto un embargo en todos los buques angloamericanos; horrores que seguían cometiendo los piratas en Cuba, y otros.

164

N.º 140. — 8 de octubre, Filadelfia.

Avisa de la llegada a Norfolk de dos comisionados franceses para los gobiernos insurgentes de América, también portadores de la ratificación del tratado de comercio entre Estados Unidos y Francia.

Hay dos ejemplares.

165

N.º 143. — 20 de octubre, Filadelfia.

Felicita a Evaristo San Miguel por su elevación al ministerio en el pasado agosto.

166

N.º 147. — 20 de octubre, Filadelfia.

Remite copia de la nota que había dirigido al secretario de Estado americano, Adams, pidiendo que según el artículo 9.º del Tratado de 1819 se designase el tribunal o autoridad a que debían recurrir los españoles que habían padecido perjuicios por las operaciones del ejército americano en las Floridas.

Adjunto:

— Nota a Adams al que pedía una pronta contestación (Filadelfia, 20 de octubre 1822).

167

N.º 148. — 20 de octubre, Filadelfia.

Comunica que se había declarado la fiebre amarilla en Nueva Orleans y Panzacola.

168

N.º 152. — 1 de noviembre, Filadelfia.

Avisa que Mr. Forsith, ministro de Estados Unidos en España, había sido nombrado del congreso americano.

169

N.º 153. — 20 de noviembre, Filadelfia.

Remite copia y traducción, de la contestación de Adams relativa al artículo 9.º del tratado de 1819.

Adjunto:

— Nota de Adams manifestando que se llevaría el asunto a la próxima sesión del congreso.
Hay dos ejemplares.

170

S/n.º — 29 de noviembre, Nueva York.

Anuncia remisión de una gaceta con noticias del ejército expedicionario de Costa Firme.

171

N.º 154. — 7 de diciembre, Nueva York.

Anuncia remisión del mensaje del presidente americano al congreso, en el que se notaba poca indignación contra los piratas, y la falta de medidas para contenerlos.

172

N.º 155. — 7 de diciembre, Filadelfia.

Avisa la llegada a Filadelfia del ministro de negocios, José Manuel de Loizaga, acompañado de varias personas.
Hay dos ejemplares.

173

N.º 159. — 11 de diciembre, Nueva York.

Remite la correspondencia sostenida con el cónsul de Baltimore, Juan Bernabéu, con motivo del desembolso efectuado por la llegada de varios marineros españoles a aquel puerto.

Adjunto:

— Correspondencia en la que Bernabéu exponía a Anduaga el naufragio y pérdida total de la goleta española la Plata, a la entrada de Baltimore. Acompaña nota en la que figuraban los gastos ocasionados para auxiliar a la tripulación, que ascendían a más de 51 duros. En su respuesta Anduaga aprueba las citadas partidas, autorizándolo a incluir estas cantidades en la cuenta de gastos extraordinarios para su abono por el ministerio correspondiente (Baltimore, Nueva York, octubre, a 11 de diciembre 1822).

— Oficio a Anduaga aprobando de parte del rey su actuación en este asunto (Madrid, 26 de febrero 1823).

174

N.º 160. — 11 de diciembre, Nueva York.

Remite copias de su correspondencia con el encargado del consulado de Norfolk, Antonio Pomar, y con el cónsul de Nueva York, Tomás Stoughton, en relación con la arribada a Newbern de la fragata española Gacela, que transportaba desde la Habana a España, a varios oficiales y soldados españoles, y de los desembolsos hechos con este motivo.

Adjunto:

— Copia de las cartas de Pomar a Anduaga notificando que la Gacela, que transportaba un rico cargamento, procedente de la Habana y con destino a Cádiz, se había visto obligada a refugiarse en Newbern donde había sido auxiliada. Incluye una lista de los oficiales y tropas, algunos de los cuales se encontraban sin ropa. En su respuesta Anduaga manifiesta a Pomar la obligación del capitán de la Gacela de mantener a su tripulación durante el tiempo que permaneciese en Newbern como lo hubiera hecho

en el mar si su viaje por vientos contrarios hubiera durado muchos meses. En cuanto a la ropa le autorizaba a emplear cincuenta duros en ella, remitiendo recibos por triplicado y firmados por los interesados. Solicitaba ser informado inmediatamente del estado de la corbeta y cuándo podría hacerse a la vela. Pomar acusa recibo de lo anterior, y expone las dificultades para dar inmediato cumplimiento a sus órdenes por las 190 millas que le separaban de Newbern. Le notificaba que se había trasladado a Filadelfia el capitán de la Gacela, quedando al cargo de la tropa un solo oficial y todos en un estado miserable por lo que insistía en sus anteriores peticiones, a las que Anduaga respondía que por carecer de fondos debería atenerse a lo prevenido en este punto (Norfolk y Nueva York, 28 de octubre a 12 de diciembre 1822).
— El cónsul de Nueva York, Tomás Stoughton, comunica a Anduaga que un oficial de la goleta Gacela, con su asistente llegaron a esa ciudad y, faltos de medios, pidieron ser restituidos a la Habana, lo que costaría unos 90 pesos. Se podría conseguir esta suma en la Habana con un oficio de Anduaga al capitán general de esta plaza.
— Oficio de Anduaga al capitán general de Cuba solicitando la suma requerida (Nueva York y Filadelfia, 26 de octubre a 21 de noviembre 1822).

175

N.º 161. — 11 de diciembre, Nueva York.

Remite copia de su correspondencia con el vicecónsul español en Charleston, Diego Williams, relativo al desembolso que hizo para auxiliar al capitán Escandell y sus marineros.

Adjunto:
— Correspondencia de Williams informando del proceso seguido contra Escandell y sus marineros, por cómplices de piratería, cuya causa se había visto recientemente, y puestos en libertad, se hallaban totalmente faltos de recursos y casi sin ropa. Solicitaba algún tipo de ayuda económica para ellos. Anduaga respondía que los gastos ocasionados por el proceso debían ser abonados por el dueño del buque corsario a que pertenecían, y que él podía dedicar sesenta pesos para ropa y girar con cargo a su ministerio su importe, debiendo acompañar seis reci-

bos firmados por Escandell (Charleston y Filadelfia, 4 a 28 de noviembre 1822).

176

N.º 162. — 11 de diciembre, Nueva York.

Remite copia de su correspondencia con el cónsul de España en Nueva Orleans, Antonio Argote Villalobos, en relación con la llegada a este puerto de varios buques españoles y de los gastos ocasionados.

Adjunto:

— Argote anuncia remisión de una cuenta con los desembolsos hechos para auxiliar a ocho prisioneros españoles que condujo a Nueva Orleans un bergantín inglés. Seis de los siete marineros socorridos huyeron al tiempo de ser embarcados para la Habana. Incluye asimismo cuenta de los gastos de Manuel Barros, que formaba parte de esta expedición, y por tratarse de un particular había girado contra el intendente de la Habana. Anduaga aprueba todas estas gestiones (Nueva Orleans y Nueva York, 30 de octubre a 11 de diciembre 1822).

177

N.º 164. — 11 de diciembre, Nueva York.

Remite copia de la contestación de Francisco Martínez Pizarro al oficio donde se le pedía la devolución de los doce mil reales que había recibido para regresar a España, en vista de que no se realizaba este viaje.

Adjunto:

— Carta de Pizarro dando cuenta de sus preparativos para regresar a la península, pasando por la Habana, pero que por circunstancias familiares y económicas, tenía que solicitar permiso para residir en esta isla en vez de volver a España (Nueva Orleans, 4 de octubre 1822). En la portadilla dice que se lo había concedido el consulado de Panzacola.

178

N.º 165. — 11 de diciembre, Nueva York.

Remite copia de una carta del intendente de la Habana sobre el pago de una letra de 301 pesos a Diego Morphy, ex vicecónsul de Luisiana, que había adelantado este dinero para defender las propiedades españolas de los insurgentes (Habana, 20 de agosto 1822).

179

N.º 167. — 16 de diciembre, Nueva York.

Comunica la entrega de credenciales al presidente americano, del ministro de Méjico, José Manuel Loizaga.

180

N.º 170. — 17 de diciembre, Nueva York.

Anuncia remisión de los artículos publicados en Nueva York por el vicecónsul español en la misma, Francisco Stoughton, sobre las operaciones de Morales y la expedición contra Puerto Rico. Hace un gran elogio de los méritos de Stoughton y de su padre, a quienes recomienda.

181

N.º 171. — 17 de diciembre, Nueva York.

Expone la deplorable situación económica de Narciso Noeli quien le venía ayudando con gran dedicación, en las tareas de su ministerio, pero con una asignación tan corta que apenas podía cubrir sus necesidades. Por ello y en vista de que no obtenía contestación a sus anteriores reclamaciones, Anduaga había decidido concederle un suplemento de un duro diario con cargo a gastos extraordinarios.

En la portadilla, nota diciendo que cesase la asignación extraordinaria cuando recibiere el nombramiento para el consulado de Washington.

LEGAJO 5.649

AÑO 1823

CORRESPONDENCIA DEL MINISTRO EN ESTADOS UNIDOS DON
JOAQUÍN DE ANDUAGA AL SECRETARIO DE ESTADO,
EVARISTO SAN MIGUEL

182

N.º 174. — 1 de enero, Nueva York.

Remite copia de la correspondencia que había cruzado con el
vicecónsul en Charleston Diego Williams, sobre la llegada a aquel
puerto del capitán Meñaca.

Adjunto:

— Carta de Diego Williams dando cuenta de la llegada a Charleston en un bergantín francés, procedente de Campeche y con
destino a Burdeos, del teniente coronel Juan Manuel Meñaca
con su familia. Cerca de Campeche unos piratas que habían
saqueado el buque lo habían despojado de todo; preguntaba
hasta qué cuantía podía ayudarle (Charleston, 13 de diciembre
1822).

— En su respuesta, Anduaga había ordenado a Williams que hiciera embarcar inmediatamente a Meñaca y los suyos para la
Habana y Puerto Rico, previniendo al capitán general de alguna
de dichas islas para que abonara los pasajes; podía proveerle
de cincuenta pesos mensuales hasta el momento del embarque,
cesando todo socorro en caso de que se negara a marcharse
(Nueva York, 25 de diciembre 1822).

— Carta de Meñaca, capitán de infantería, dando cuenta a Anduaga de sus vicisitudes y solicitando una nueva ayuda, por no bastar para cubrir sus necesidades más perentorias los cincuenta pesos que había recibido de Williams (Carleston, 14 dediciembre 1822).

— Carta de Anduaga a Williams corrigiendo una inexactitud de su informe sobre Meñaca, pues sabía por la carta de dicho sujeto que después de sufrir el saqueo, el buque había ido a la Habana, desde donde había partido para Burdeos, viéndose obligado a entrar en Charleston de arribada, a causa de una vía de agua. Una vez iniciado el viaje de la Habana para Burdeos era el capitán del buque el que tenía que correr con los gastos de su estancia en Charleston, por lo que tenía que forzarle a que lo cumpliera o a que devolviese el medio flete. El socorro para vestidos tenía que haberlo solicitado al capitán general de Cuba, haciéndole comprender que Anduaga carecía de fondos y sólo podría facilitarle cincuenta duros, en el caso de que no pudiera embarcar para Cuba antes de un mes (Nueva York, 26 de diciembre 1822).

183

N.º 180. — 1 de enero, Nueva York.

Remite traducción de la nota que había enviado a Francisco Tomás Morales, general en jefe de las tropas españolas en el continente, el comandante de la fragata americana Cyane y oficial de Marina más antiguo de las Indias occidentales, Robert Treal Spence; en el escrito protestaba de forma insolente contra el decreto de 15 de septiembre último, relativo a los extranjeros que se hallaban en Venezuela; le conminaba a no ejecutar las penas y castigos contenidos en el decreto, contra los ciudadanos americanos establecidos en aquellos territorios. Consideraba el bloqueo que había decretado el general Morillo como un pretexto para interrumpir el comercio de Estados Unidos, secuestrar las propiedades y maltratar a los tripulantes; respecto a las expoliaciones se pediría la restitución, aunque magnánimamente no se tomarían represalias; en todos los lugares donde comerciasen los ciudadanos de la Unión debían ser considerados neutrales.

Anduaga hace notar que en el escrito se aludía a los americanos que buscaban la gloria entre los ejércitos de los insurgentes. No había recibido ninguna comunicación de Morales al respecto, por lo que no había enviado ninguna protesta sobre este nuevo insulto.

Adjunto:

— Traducción de la protesta de Robert Treat Spence al general Francisco Tomás Morales (Curaçao, 10 de noviembre 1822).

184

N.º 181. — 1 de enero, Nueva York.

Remite copia de una carta del vicecónsul en Charleston Williams, en la que comunicaba que Escandel, capitán de un corsario español y sus marineros, habían embarcado en la Palmira para Puerto Rico, gracias a la cantidad que les había él proporcionado y que esperaba le fuera restituida por Anduaga. Una balandra que Escandel había apresado, había sido restituida a sus oficiales bajo la fianza que había dado el cónsul americano en Curaçao; como no era justo que Escandel perdiera su presa, esperaba conseguirlo mediante una orden del secretario de Estado que Anduaga debería solicitar.

En la respuesta de Anduaga al vicecónsul le comunicaba que había recibido una carta de Escandel pidiendo que, en nombre del gobierno, reclamara por los daños y perjuicios que le había producido el incidente; pero como su corsario era propiedad de particulares, eran éstos los llamados a presentar la reclamación; y en caso de que dicho capitán careciera de fondos, debería embarcarlo inmediatamente, junto con sus marineros, para la Habana.

Adjunto:

— Carta de Williams a Anduaga comunicándole el embarque para la Habana de Escandel y sus marineros (Charleston, 13 de diciembre 1822).
— De Anduaga a Williams, comunicándole la petición de Escandel para que hiciera una reclamación oficial y su respuesta de que eran los dueños del corsario los que tenían que hacerlo (Nueva York, 21 de diciembre 1822).

185

N.º 183. — 6 de enero, Nueva York.

Anduaga se muestra dolido por una represión recibida del anterior secretario de Estado, Francisco Martínez de la Rosa, a causa de no haber dado cuenta de si el senado había autorizado o no el reconocimiento de la independencia de las provincias disidentes, otorgado por la cámara de representantes. Este paso debería haber precedido a la resolución, de que se entregaran cien mil duros al poder ejecutivo para que enviara ministros a los gobiernos insurgentes. Las discusiones sobre la conveniencia de aceptar a estos gobiernos se habían desarrollado en el congreso, que había concedido al poder ejecutivo la facultad de reconocerlos cuando lo juzgara oportuno; en el senado sólo se había tratado lo que había comunicado en un despacho suyo anterior.

186

N.º 186. — 8 de enero, Nueva York.

Acusa recibo de los duplicados de varias comunicaciones llegadas con mucho retraso, a la vez que lamenta la prolongada enfermedad de la reina.

187

N.º 188. — 8 de enero, Nueva York.

Acusa recibo del duplicado de un oficio de septiembre último, en cumplimiento de cuyas instrucciones había enviado una nota al secretario de Estado John Quincy Adams; en ella aludía a la que Evaristo San Miguel había remitido al ministro de Estados Unidos en Madrid, sobre la negativa del rey a aceptar la interpretación dada por el presidente de Estados Unidos a los artículos 2 y 7 del tratado de 1819, referentes a la artillería y pertrechos de guerra existentes en las Floridas al tiempo de su entrega. Tal interpretación perjudicaba a España ya que exigía la entrega de la artillería y demás efectos, sin reconocer el derecho a que el gobierno americano facilitara los víveres para las tropas españolas que salían de dicha provincia; esperaba que atendida la justicia de las razones expuestas, daría las órdenes para la entrega del armamento, así como la cuenta de las raciones suministradas a las tropas. Por otra parte, si el gobierno americano estaba interesado en comprar parte de los efectos de guerra, estaba autorizado para transmitir sus proposiciones al gobierno español, pudiéndose nombrar peritos por ambas partes para la valoración.

Adjunto:

— Copia de la nota de Anduaga a Adams comunicando la negativa a aceptar la interpretación americana de los artículos del tratado referentes al armamento que había en las Floridas y a la provisión de víveres para las tropas. Todos los documentos están duplicados (Nueva York, 6 de enero 1823).

188

N.º 189. — 8 de enero, Nueva York.

Acusa recibo de un oficio de 28 de agosto último relativo a las reclamaciones de Meade y se muestra satisfecho por el beneplácito que había merecido su actuación.

189

N.º 190. — 8 de enero, Nueva York.

Comunica la recepción, de un oficio de septiembre último que incluía copia de la nota que Evaristo San Miguel había pasado al ministro de Estados Unidos, relativa a la entrega de los papeles de las Floridas, y quedaba enterado de que debería oponerse a que el gobierno americano tratara de enviar a la Habana otro comisionado para el mismo asunto.

190

N.º 192. — 8 de enero, Nueva York.

Anuncia el envío de los documentos relativos al mensaje del presidente del 3 de diciembre, el informe sobre el estado de la Hacienda americana y las cuentas de lo que el gobierno de Estados Unidos había gastado en el año último.

Adjunto:

— Minuta al ministro en Estados Unidos acusando recibo de sus despachos 173 a 192 inclusive y comunicando que continuaba la indisposición de la reina (28 de febrero 1823).

191

N.º 193. — 15 de enero, Nueva York.

Da cuenta de que no se habían recibido instrucciones sobre el asunto de los pleitos de consolidación, pese a haberlas solicitado reiteradamente su antecesor en el cargo, Mateo de la Serna. Acababa de recibir una carta del abogado Ingersoll en la que le comunicaba que se podría decidir el asunto en la corte suprema en el próximo mes de febrero, por lo que pedía instrucciones sobre si debía sostener la apelación. Anduaga acusa de desidia al ministerio de Hacienda y expone que, para luchar por un éxito incierto, habrían de realizarse cuantiosos gastos en prosecución de la causa, pero no quería cargar él con la responsabilidad de abandonarla. Como no podría continuarse sin los documentos repetidamente solicitados por Mateo de la Serna, había optado por decir a Ingersoll que tratara de posponer la vista de la apelación hasta la corte suprema del próximo año 1824. Esperaba que se aprobase su resolución y hacía presente que, si se conseguía la dilación pedida y continuaba sin instrucciones para la apertura de la sesión del año próximo, consideraría el silencio como prueba de que debía abandonar el asunto.

Adjunto:

— Copia y traducción de la carta del Ingersoll a Anduaga pidiendo instrucciones sobre la prosecución o abandono de la apelación ante la corte suprema de los pleitos pendientes de la Caja de Consolidación (Filadelfia, 10 de diciembre 1822. Por error pone 1823).

— Carta de Anduaga a Ingersoll ordenándole solicitar una dilación de la vista de dichos pleitos (Nueva York, 10 de enero 1823).

192

N.º 195. — 15 de enero, Nueva York.

Comunicaba que el comodoro Porter preparaba activamente una flotilla para perseguir a los piratas de la isla de Cuba, noticia que había hecho llegar también al capitán general de la Habana.

Adjunto:

— Nota para redactar la comunicación de dicho despacho a Ultramar, advirtiendo que existían fundadas sospechas de que con el pretexto de perseguir a los piratas de Cuba, tratarían de realizar desembarcos de tropas americanas en aquellas costas; era de suma urgencia avisar a aquellas autoridades para que se preparasen a impedir cualquier intento en dicho sentido, evitando a la vez cualquier violencia. Debería dar cuenta igualmente al ministro de Marina y a Jabat, para que con discreción, aprovechara la rivalidad existente entre Inglaterra y los Estados Unidos, a fin de que aquel gobierno impidiera por su propio interés la agresión de los americanos contra nuestras islas (17 de mayo 1823).

193

N.º 196. — 26 de enero, Nueva York.

Da cuenta de una serie de nombramientos que había efectuado el presidente: de Nelson, miembro de la cámara de representantes del congreso, para suceder a Forsyth en Madrid; el general Jackson, enviado extraordinario y ministro plenipotenciario en Méjico; Prodney ministro plenipotenciario en Buenos Aires; Anderson ministro plenipotenciario en Columbia (Colombia) y Allen ministro plenipotenciario para Chile. El nombramiento de Nelson, que había sido el que propuso en la cámara que se llevase a efecto el reconocimiento de los gobiernos insurgentes, y el de Jackson, probaban la animosidad del gobierno americano hacia España.

194

N.º 198. — 6 de febrero, Nueva York.

Remite copia de la correspondencia que había cruzado con Ingersoll sobre los pleitos de la Caja de Consolidación.

Adjunto:

— Carta de Ingersoll a Anduaga manifestando que como se habían demorado tres años los pleitos pendientes de Consolidación, por carecer de instrucciones del gobierno español al respecto, dudaba que se consiguiera un nuevo aplazamiento; pero trataría de obtenerlo, para lo cual convendría que Anduaga enviara una petición en tal sentido, como autoridad competente (Filadelfia, 30 de enero 1823).

— Anduaga en su respuesta pedía que le enviara un modelo de la representación que debería enviar a la corte suprema (Nueva York, 4 de febrero 1823).

— Remisión por Ingersoll a Anduaga del modelo solicitado, que éste mandaba ya redactado (Filadelfia, 5 de febrero 1823).

— Representación de Anduaga exponiendo que las gestiones para recuperar los créditos de la tesorería los había llevado el coronel Francisco Caballero Sarmiento, muerto en Madrid hacía poco; que dichos pleitos se habían empezado antes de su venida como ministro a Estados Unidos, por lo que no conocía todas sus circunstancias; que las alteraciones políticas en España habían interrumpido el curso de las negociaciones, pero no dudaba que los documentos necesarios, así como las instrucciones terminantes, llegarían antes de la sesión de la corte suprema de 1824, en cuyo momento se proseguiría la apelación de la sentencia del tribunal del distrito de Pensilvania en el pleito contra Roberto y Juan Oliver, o se abandonaría definitivamente (Nueva York, 6 de febrero 1823).

El despacho y todos los documentos están duplicados.

195

N.º 200. — 1 de marzo, Nueva York.

Remite copia de su correspondencia con el cónsul en Boston, Raimundo Chacón.

Adjunto:

— Carta de Chacón a Anduaga dando cuenta de que se habían presentado en el consulado seis españoles de la tripulación de la goleta Josefa, de la matrícula de la Habana, naufragada en la costa de África; se encontraban en la miseria y le habían pedido ayuda para regresar a Cuba, pero le había sido imposible auxiliarlos por falta de medios, por lo que solicitaba autorización para girar una letra por la cantidad que juzgara conveniente (Boston, 13 de enero 1823).

— En su respuesta Anduaga autorizaba a Chacón a librar contra él el importe del socorro (Nueva York, 16 de enero 1823).

— Nota de Chacón a Anduaga remitiendo los recibos y participándole que libraba por el importe de cuarenta y un pesos fuertes, a su orden (Boston, 21 de febrero 1823).

— Minuta a Anduaga comunicando la aprobación de su gestión en favor de los náufragos de la Josefa y que se había dado parte de ello al secretario de Ultramar (Sevilla, 10 de mayo 1823).

196

N.º 201.—1 de marzo, Nueva York.

Remite copia de la correspondencia cruzada con el cónsul en Norfolk Pablo Chacón, referente al socorro prestado a los marineros de la goleta la Plata.

Adjunto:

— Carta de Pablo Chacón a Anduaga dando cuenta de que, hallándose ausente de Norfolk, Alberto Allmand, que estaba al frente del consulado, había tenido que socorrer a los marineros de la goleta la Plata, naufragada cerca de los cabos de Virginia, invirtiendo en ello once pesos con ochenta y tres centavos, que esperaba que le fueran reembolsados (Norfolk, 9 de enero 1823).

— Minuta a Anduaga comunicando que se aprobaba la entrega del socorro a los náufragos de la Plata (Sevilla, 10 de mayo 1823).

— Minuta al secretario de Gobernación de Ultramar dando cuenta de que se le enviarían los recibos de la cantidad entregada a los marineros, para que ordenara su abono (Sevilla, 10 de mayo 1823).

197

N.º 203.—1 de marzo, Nueva York.

Notificando que el presidente había nombrado varios cónsules para los puertos de Méjico.

Adjunto:

— Minuta al secretario de Gobernación de Ultramar dándole cuenta de dicha comunicación (Sevilla, 2 de mayo 1823).

198

N.º 204. — 1 de marzo, Nueva York.

Notifica que la cámara de representantes había solicitado del presidente un informe sobre los progresos que se habían realizado en la demarcación de límites, especificada en el artículo 4.º del tratado con España de 1819.

199

N.º 205. — 1 de marzo, Nueva York.

Comunica que la cámara de representantes había pedido al presidente que informara sobre las medidas que se habían adoptado para contrarrestar el bloqueo de Costa Firme, y para obtener la restitución de los buques americanos apresados por corsarios de Puerto Rico y de otras islas españolas, bajo pretexto del citado bloqueo, e impedir que se repitieran en lo sucesivo dichos apresamientos.

200

N.º 206. — 1 de marzo, Nueva York.

Participa que la cámara de representantes había resuelto solicitar al presidente que iniciara las negociaciones que estimara convenientes con las potencias marítimas de Europa y América para extinguir por completo el tráfico de negros, declarándolo piratería entre las naciones civilizadas.

Adjunto:

— Minuta trasladando la anterior comunicación probablemente a Gobernación de Ultramar (Sevilla 10 de mayo 1823).
— Minuta al encargado de negocios en Estados Unidos acusando recibo de varios despachos (Sevilla, 14 de mayo 1823).

201

N.º 208. — 14 de marzo, Nueva York.

Remite un memorial de Juan Leamy, cuyos méritos recomienda.

Adjunto:

— Memorial de Juan Leamy, natural de Irlanda, vicecónsul de España en Pensilvania, en el que solicitaba que le fuera compensada una crecida suma que había invertido en 1818 en una expedición de ayuda a la provincia de Yucatán, con la adjudicación de una cantidad proporcionada de tierras útiles en la isla de Puerto Rico donde, para ejercer el comercio sin trabas, pedía que se le concediera carta de naturaleza (Filadelfia, 28 de febrero 1823).

— Minuta al encargado de negocios en Estados Unidos dando cuenta de que, respecto a la concesión de tierras en Puerto Rico, se había pedido información; y en cuanto a la concesión de carta de naturaleza tenía que hacer la solicitud en debida forma (Sevilla, 11 de mayo 1823).

202

N.º 209. — 14 de marzo, Nueva York.

Anduaga da cuenta a Evaristo San Miguel de que, no siéndole posible continuar desempeñando el ministerio en Estados Unidos, se proponía partir para Inglaterra el día primero del próximo mes, dejando como encargado de negocios a Hilario de Rivas. Debido a los peligros que corría la correspondencia no exponía los poderosos motivos que le habían movido a tomar esta resolución, lo que haría personalmente al llegar a Madrid. Había creído conveniente enviar a Narciso Noely como correo extraordinario para llevar el presente despacho.

CORRESPONDENCIA DEL ENCARGADO DE NEGOCIOS EN LOS ESTADOS UNIDOS, HILARIO DE RIVAS Y SALMÓN A LOS SECRETARIOS DE ESTADO

203

N.º 4. — 9 de abril, Filadelfia.

Remite al secretario de Estado, Álvaro Flórez Estrada, copia y traducción de una nota de Adams, en la que le anunciaba que se había establecido en las Floridas un tribunal para dar cumplimiento al artículo 9 del último tratado, que se refería al traspaso al gobierno de Estados Unidos de las reclamaciones que hubiera pendientes contra el de España. En igual fecha lo comunicaba al capitán general de Cuba, para que lo hiciera llegar a conocimiento de los interesados.

Adjunto:

— Nota de John Quincy Adams con la que remitía una copia del decreto del congreso sobre el cumplimiento del artículo 9.º del tratado de 22 de febrero de 1819, por el cual se establecía que los jueces de los tribunales superiores de San Agustín y Panzacola podían admitir las reclamaciones de los habitantes de los respectivos territorios; en los casos en que las resoluciones fuesen a favor de los reclamantes, deberían elevar estas declaraciones, y los testimonios en que se fundaran, a la secretaría del despacho de Hacienda la cual, una vez hechas las necesarias comprobaciones, satisfaría su importe de los fondos de la tesorería que no se destinaran a otro objeto. Firman Felipe P. Barbour, presidente de la cámara de representantes, y Juan Gaillart, presidente interino del senado, con el visto bueno de Diego Monroe (Washington, 5 de abril 1823).

204

N.º 6. — 20 de abril, Filadelfia.

Comunica a Álvaro Flórez Estrada que Ricardo Meade le había escrito la carta cuya copia adjunta, por la cual y en vista de las instrucciones que había recibido por diversos conductos, había resuelto enviar a Adams una nota de la que igualmente enviaba copia. Su antecesor Anduaga le había ordenado mostrar a Meade, sin reserva alguna, todo lo que existiera en la legación relativo a sus reclamaciones; pero como esta orden contradecía las instrucciones posteriores, sólo le había enseñado las órdenes más recientes, ocultando las reservadas; consideraba probable que por otro conducto llegara a conocimiento de Meade el contenido de dichos oficios reservados.

Adjunto:

— Copia de la carta de Meade a Rivas y Salmón anunciando el envío de un ejemplar de la reclamación que había presentado contra el gobierno español a los comisionados, y del memorial que sobre el mismo asunto había presentado al presidente. Enterado por Anduaga de que el asunto debía decidirse pronto y que los comisionados persistían en desechar la liquidación, reclamaba el apoyo del gobierno español para impedir la injusticia que pretendían hacer los comisionados, por lo que le rogaba el envío a Adams de un oficio en tal sentido (Filadelfia, 10 de abril 1823).

— Oficio de Anduaga a Rivas y Salmón manifestándole que por ser del mayor interés que el gobierno de Estados Unidos satisficiera a Ricardo Meade la reclamación que tenía contra España, según lo estipulado en el tratado, debería facilitarle sin reserva ni demora alguna, cuantas noticias sobre dicho asunto hubiera en el archivo de la legación, siendo responsable de un posible fracaso en el asunto si incumplía dicha orden (Nueva York, 14 de marzo 1823).

— Nota de Rivas y Salmón a Meade remitiéndole la que había enviado a Adams (Filadelfia, 17 de abril 1823).

— Carta de Rivas y Salmón a Adams en apoyo de las reclamaciones de Meade y rechazando con firmeza la negativa a satisfacer el crédito que éste tenía contra la nación española y que, en virtud del último tratado, había tomado sobre sí los Estados Unidos. Posiblemente fuera éste el único crédito que había reconocido el rey, a instancias del ministro de Estados Unidos en Madrid, y su reconocimiento se había hecho en circunstancias que no admitían duda respecto a su legitimidad e importe, habiendo sido presentado a ambos gobiernos durante la negociación. Las complicadas cuentas habían pasado varias revisiones hasta ser finalmente sancionadas por el rey. La nación española era responsable del total del crédito, pero en virtud de la ratificación del tratado, el gobierno americano había tomado la deuda sobre sí conociendo su importe exacto, y era inadmisible que los comisionados rehusaran satisfacerla negando que estuviera comprendida en el tratado; protestaba contra cualquier decisión de los comisionados que invalidara el reconocimiento de la deuda (Filadelfia, 15 de abril 1823).

205

N.º 8. — 5 de mayo, Filadelfia.

Acusa recibo al secretario de Estado Manuel Vadillo, de varios despachos de los meses de febrero y marzo, que incluían algunas gacetas.

206

N.º 15. — 20 de mayo, Filadelfia.

Acusa recibo a José María Pando de un oficio de enero referente al sueldo y asignaciones para gastos de secretaría y correo de la legación y consulados.

207

N.º 16. — 20 de mayo, Filadelfia.

Da cuenta al secretario de Estado José María Pando, de que había recibido quince oficios del mes de febrero, cuyos duplicados habían llegado también ya; adjunta la cubierta o sobre que los contenía, cuya letra y sello parecían ser de Joaquín de Anguaga, de lo cual deducía que había llegado felizmente a Inglaterra, donde había abierto los pliegos destinados a la legación de Estados Unidos, remitiéndolos posteriormente.

208

N.º 17. — 20 de mayo, Filadelfia.

Da cuenta a José M.ª Pando de que, aunque en una comunicación anterior le había anunciado la llegada a Nueva York del segundo secretario de la legación Manuel Barros, el cual desde allí le había escrito que había salvado los pliegos que traía de España, sólo le había entregado uno que contenía varios oficios, y le había dicho que otros tres que tenían gacetas, los había quemado en Vizcaya por salvar el que había considerado más importante que logró esconder de los facciosos.

Adjunto:

— Copia del oficio de Rivas y Salmón a Manuel Barros pidiendo que firmara la declaración, que había hecho verbalmente, sobre la imposibilidad en que se había visto de salvar de los facciosos más que un pliego, de los cuatro que traía para la legación (Filadelfia, 20 de mayo 1823).

— Oficio a Barros comunicándole que por las dificultades existentes para endosar letras de cambio, no podía darle los cuatro mil reales que debía entregarle a la recepción de los pliegos ni pasarle la pensión alimentaria y que, incluso los sueldos, le serían abonados con mucho retraso (Filadelfia, 20 de mayo 1823).

209

N.º 18. — 20 de mayo, Filadelfia.

Comunica a José M.ª Pando la reciente llegada de Antonio Figueroa, teniente coronel del regimiento de Burgos, que regresaba con licencia a España procedente del alto Perú; había llegado enfermo y en situación extremadamente precaria, pero por fortuna se encontraba en el puerto de Filadelfia un buque americano presto a hacerse a la mar, cuyo capitán, por gestión del vicecónsul Juan Leamy, se había comprometido a llevarlo a la Habana, donde recibiría del intendente los gastos del pasaje y manutención.

210

N.º 19. — 20 de mayo, Filadelfia.

Acusa recibo a José M.ª Pando de varios oficios relativos a la comisión de límites, de cuya disolución se congratulaba, porque opinaba que eran insignificantes las ventajas que se derivaban para España de la señalización práctica de los límites que establecía el tratado, en comparación con los enormes gastos que supondría la expedición; en cambio interesaba a los Estados Unidos que se llevara a efecto la demarcación de aquellos extensos territorios; se podía excusar tal dispendio, entre otras razones por haber reconocido los Estados Unidos la independencia de las provincias americanas.

211

N.º 21. — 21 de mayo, Filadelfia.

Se refiere a los motivos, de los que ya anteriormente había dado cuenta a Pando, que le habían impulsado a enviar a Adams la nota cuya copia había remitido, en apoyo de las justas reclamaciones de Meade y para evitar el desaire que según las apariencias, intentaban hacer los comisionados de reclamaciones. Por la rápida respuesta de Adams había que descartar cualquier injuria, pues aunque era cierto que la comisión no admitía la liquidación hecha en España, tenía fundadas razones para llevarla a cabo. Estando la reclamación de Meade comprendida en el tratado, se le podía culpar por haber solicitado la intervención de ambos gobiernos durante la negociación; y si sufría pérdidas en lo que le correspondiera en el prorrateo, bien porque no alcanzara la suma que se le asignase o porque no pudiera presentar todos los justificantes exigidos ante la comisión americana que debía liquidar la reclamación, no podría imputar culpa a España, que había hecho cuanto había podido en su favor. Se había logrado exonerar a España de esta importante reclamación, pasando al gobierno americano la obligación de pagar a Meade y demás reclamantes, y Adams aseguraba en su nota que no existía el menor intento de desairar a las autoridades españolas; le había contestado que el rey se daba por satisfecho con su explicación.

Adjunto:
— Copia de una nota de Rivas y Salmón en respuesta a otra de Adams en la que explicaba que el hecho de que los comisionados de reclamaciones hubieran rechazado la liquidación hecha en España, no se debía a que dudaran de la integridad de los tribunales, sino porque en virtud de los términos del tratado, debían prescindir de toda liquidación que no hubieran realizado ellos mismos (Filadelfia, 12 de mayo 1823).
— Copia y traducción de una detallada exposición de Adams, en respuesta a una nota de Hilario Rivas, de las especiales condiciones de la reclamación de Ricardo Meade, que si consideraba inclusa en el artículo 9.º del tratado, tenía que ser en las mismas condiciones que las de los otros reclamantes (Washington, 29 de abril 1823).

212

N.º 23. — 30 de mayo, Filadelfia.

Anuncia al secretario de Estado José Vargas el envío de una gaceta con la noticia de la importante victoria que el comandante Laborde había obtenido contra Daniels, que bloqueaba con una flotilla Puerto Cabello y que no se sabía con certeza si había muerto o había sido herido y apresado. Parecía que la relación de los hechos era un poco exagerada, pues no podía Laborde contar con tantas fuerzas como se le atribuían y tampoco eran cuatro sino dos, los buques apresados: el María Francisca y el Carabobo. Anuncia la llegada a Nueva York del ministro y cónsul general de Colombia que se esperaba.

213

N.º 30. — 1 de julio, Filadelfia.

Anuncia a José Vargas el envío de unas gacetas que, debido a una indisposición y al escaso personal de la legación y los consulados que tenía a su cargo, no le había sido posible extractar ni traducir.

214

N.º 34. — 23 de julio, Filadelfia.

Da cuenta a José Vargas de que había tenido que abonar al cónsul en Baltimore Juan Bautista Bernabéu, cierta cantidad que había entregado a unos marineros.

Adjunto:
— Copia de una carta de dicho cónsul en la que le comunicaba que había tenido que prestar ayuda a cinco marineros de un falucho español que procedía de Cádiz y había sido apresado cerca de Puerto Rico por el bergantín colombiano el Vencedor, que los había abandonado en tierra desnudos y desprovistos de todo. Había dispuesto que se corriera con su manutención hasta que pudieran embarcar para Cuba y Puerto Rico (Baltimore, 25 de junio 1823).

— Carta de Bernabéu comunicando la salida hacia Puerto Rico de los cinco españoles, cuyos gastos habían ascendido a poco más de diez y ocho pesos (Baltimore, 21 de julio 1823).

215

N.º 35. — 30 de julio, Filadelfia.

Comunica a José Vargas que el pasaje y manutención de Antonio Figueroa, que por instancias de Leamy había sido admitido en un buque que se dirigía a la Habana por encontrarse gravemente enfermo, no había sido satisfecho por el intendente de aquel puerto, por lo que Leamy había tenido que abonar al capitán del barco los setenta duros que habían acordado.

Adjunto:

— Carta de Juan Leamy pidiendo instrucciones para resolver una solicitud de Antonio de Figueroa, teniente coronel graduado del regimiento de Burgos, procedente del puerto de Arequipa, en el Perú, y con destino a la península, que deseaba ayuda para ir a la Habana (Filadelfia, 21 de abril 1823).
— Leamy comunicaba que por no haber sido satisfecho por el intendente de la Habana el pasaje y manutención de Figueroa, había tenido que pagar al capitán del Hamlet los setenta duros en que lo habían ajustado, cantidad que esperaba le fuera reembolsada (Filadelfia, 25 de julio 1823).

216

N.º 38. — 20 de agosto, Filadelfia.

Da cuenta al secretario de Estado, Víctor Sáez, de su negativa a conceder la ayuda que había solicitado un grupo de tres sargentos y diez y siete soldados, basándose en que ya Anduaga les había socorrido en otra ocasión, que la ayuda no era de absoluta necesidad y que por ser ellos muchos y los socorros escasos, apenas les representaría alivio.

Adjunto:

— Carta de Pablo Chacón, cónsul en Norfolk, a Rivas y Salmón participando que por causa de la guerra no habían salido para

España los soldados que, procedentes de la Habana y con destino a Cádiz, habían llegado a Newbern en octubre pasado a bordo de la corbeta Gacela; por orden de Anduaga les había socorrido con cincuenta pesos y nuevamente solicitaban ayuda (Norfolk, 11 de agosto 1823).

— Representación de los soldados al cónsul de España exponiendo la situación en que se encontraban, con la manutención solucionada pero sin ropa ni calzado, por lo que solicitaban ser enviados a España o a Cuba y si esto no era posible que se les prestara alguna ayuda (Portsmouth, 23 de julio 1823).

217

N.º 39. — 30 de agosto, Filadelfia.

Remite al secretario de Estado, Luis María Salazar, copia de la correspondencia relativa al teniente Francisco del Puerto, cuya llegada le había comunicado Tomás Sotughton, cónsul en Nueva York; procedía de la Habana y marchaba hacia la península en la corbeta española la Gacela, pero por temor a la guerra con Francia el capitán se había negado a partir hasta recibir nuevas instrucciones de los dueños del buque; en vista de ello Francisco del Puerto había solicitado ayuda por encontrarse sin medios, y estando próximo a partir para Gibraltar el bergantín americano Marcellus, Stoughton había conseguido, tras vencer muchas dificultades, que su capitán aceptara conducirlo a aquel puerto, donde el cónsul de España le abonaría el importe del pasaje. Stoughton había solicitado que le enviara un oficio para dicho cónsul a fin de que cumpliera lo acordado y exponía la difícil situación en que se encontraba por falta de fondos, pues eran muchos los marineros y náufragos enfermos realmente necesitados, a quienes había podido embarcar por su amistad con los capitanes de buques, pero empezaban a cansarse de estos favores y podía llegar a ser dramática la situación de muchos españoles. Da cuenta por último de que como el cónsul en Gibraltar no había podido abonar el pasaje, había tenido que pagarlo él mismo.

Adjunto:

— Carta de Tomás Stoughton a Rivas y Salmón comunicándole la llegada de Francisco del Puerto, teniente del regimiento de caballería del ejército expedicionario de Costa Firme, con pasa-

porte en regla del capitán general de la Habana, en cuyo puerto
había embarcado en la corbeta Gacela con destino a la península, pero había tocado en Newbern para hacer reparaciones, ne-
gándose el capitán a seguir sin instrucciones concretas de los
dueños; había tratado de disuadir a del Puerto de que pidiera
ayuda a Rivas y Salmón, por saberle falto de medios; tras vencer muchas dificultades había conseguido que Guillet, capitán
del bergantín americano Marcellus, aceptara conducirlo a Gibraltar, que era su punto de destino, donde el cónsul de España
le abonaría el pasaje (Nueva York, 10 de junio 1823).
— Tomás Sotughton acusa recibo a Hilario Rivas, del oficio que
había solicitado para el cónsul de Gibraltar a fin de que abonara
el importe del pasaje; pero los dueños del bergantín se habían
opuesto al traslado del pasajero si el mismo Stoughton no se
comprometía a satisfacer el importe de la travesía, en caso de
no hacerlo la persona designada (Nueva York, 15 de junio 1823).
— Carta de Joseph Shee a Rivas y Salmón comunicando la feliz
llegada a Gibraltar de Francisco del Puerto, pero careciendo de
fondos para abonar su pasaje le había aconsejado dirigirse al
comandante militar de Algeciras (Gibraltar, 24 de julio 1823).

218

N.º 45. — 9 de octubre, Filadelfia.

Remite al secretario de Estado José Luyando, relación de los
gastos ocasionados con ocasión de la llegada de dos funcionarios,
que por su adhesión a España habían sido expulsados de Santo Domingo, así como correspondencia cruzada sobre el mismo asunto.

Adjunto:

— Carta de Diego Williams, cónsul de Charleston, comunicando
la llegada a dicha ciudad de José R. Cabral, oficial de milicias,
y de Antonio R. Sarmiento, guarda mayor y vista de la aduana
de Santo Domingo, que por su adhesión a España habían sido
encarcelados y luego forzados a embarcar en un bergantín ruso
que los había dejado en tierra en un estado miserable, por lo
que había tenido que proveer a su manutención hasta la salida
de uno para la Habana y otro para Santo Tomás; esperaba que
le fueran reembolsados los cuarenta y seis pesos que había invertido en ellos (Charleston, 2 de junio 1823).
— Carta de Diego Williams dando cuenta de que los dos sujetos

mencionados habían sido acusados de conspirar contra el actual gobierno por oponerse a los negros de Santo Domingo, y tras sufrir tres meses de prisión los habían conducido a Puerto Príncipe, embarcándolos en el bergantín ruso Alexandre le Grand. A su llegada a Charleston, sin pasaportes ni despachos, había tenido que comprobar la veracidad de sus declaraciones por medio de personas que los conocían y era de opinión que se les debería ayudar (Charleston, 10 de julio 1823).

219

N.º 50. — 15 de octubre, Filadelfia.

Acusa recibo a José Luyando, de una comunicación sobre la cuarentena que tenían que hacer en Mahón los buques americanos que arribaran antes del 30 de noviembre próximo, pero no había considerado oportuno publicarla por la demora con que se había recibido. En su opinión convendría que dicha medida sanitaria tuviera vigencia permanente por la abundancia de casos de fiebre amarilla, respecto a cuya naturaleza había diferentes opiniones, sobre si era endémica o contagiosa. También causaban estragos desde hacía tres años unas calenturas que llamaban «temblonas», principalmente en el campo. Habían estado enfermos el cónsul en Baltimore, el vicecónsul Leamy y toda su familia, habiendo muerto el jardinero. Estaba todavía en cama, aunque muy mejorado, el secretario de la legación Manuel Barros.

220

N.º 51. — 16 de octubre, Filadelfia.

Anuncia a José Luyando remisión de una gaceta que insertaba el desmentido que había hecho de la noticia difundida sobre la supuesta cesión a los ingleses de la isla de Cuba.

221

N.º 53. — 18 de octubre, Filadelfia.

Comunica a José Luyando que no había recibido dos mesadas que le habían dicho que estaban en poder del pagador del ministerio Vicente Herreros, ni tenía la menor noticia sobre ello.

222

N.º 54. — 19 de octubre, Filadelfia.

Anuncia a Luyando remisión de una gaceta con tres noticias importantes: que el congreso había ratificado en Buenos Aires la convención hecha con España, accediendo a ello la provincia de Tucumán; que en Veracruz había embarcado para Inglaterra, tras hacer un convenio con el gobierno de Méjico, un probable agente secreto inglés, y que el gobierno de Buenos Aires estaba en situación tirante con el emperador de Brasil.

223

N.º 56. —

Recibos de varias cantidades que iban adjuntos, como justificantes, al n.º 56. Falta el despacho.

Adjunto:

— James Welater declara haber recibido del cónsul de España en Nueva York Tomás Stoughton, por orden de Rivas y Salmón, cien pesos fuertes por el pasaje y manutención hasta Gibraltar del oficial español Francisco del Puerto, por no haberlo pagado el cónsul español en aquella plaza (Nueva York, 19 de septiembre 1823).

— Carta de pago de Tomás Stoughton de la cantidad que había recibido de Hilario de Rivas a cuenta de lo que había pagado al abogado del pirata Taylor por las costas de los tres procesos que había entablado contra él (Nueva York, 11 de octubre 1823).

— Recibo duplicado de Antonio Rendon Sarmiento de veintiséis pesos que le había entregado Diego Williams, cónsul de España en Charleston, para su manutención, por haber sido expulsado de Santo Domingo por el gobierno de negros, acusado de conspirar a favor de España (Charleston, 23 de mayo 1823).

— Otro recibo en inglés firmado por Thomas Monroe de una cantidad percibida por el porte de una carta de la delegación de España en Estados Unidos (10 de octubre 1823).

224

N.º 57. — 21 de octubre, Filadelfia.

Remite a Luyando unos documentos sobre los pleitos que Tomás Stoughton había seguido contra el pirata Taylor, con resultado adverso para el primero, de cuya resolución pensaba reclamar al gobierno americano, por la injusticia de tal decisión.

Adjunto:

— Carta de Tomás Stoughton acusando recibo a Rivas y Salmón del oficio en que le daba cuenta de la negativa del intendente de la Habana a enviarle cierta cantidad y le rogaba el envío del sobrante que obraba en su poder, por necesitarlo para pagar a los cónsules. Acababa de recibir de Aarón Palmer, abogado de Taylor, la cuenta de lo que tenía que abonar a éste por las costas de los pleitos que había seguido contra él, apreciadas en una cantidad mucho menor de la que había reclamado Palmer. Aún tenía que pagar Stoughton la cuenta del abogado Wells, que había defendido su derecho. Por todo ello había dispuesto de la cantidad que obraba en su poder para efectuar dichos pagos (Nueva York, 4 de octubre 1823).
— Notas de Rivas y Salmón a Stoughton aprobando el empleo que había hecho de dichos fondos y prometiendo enviarle el resto en cuanto pudiera (Filadelfia, 7 de octubre 1823).
— Carta de Stoughton a Rivas haciéndole una reclamación del desarrollo de los pleitos contra Taylor. Enterado de la llegada de éste a Nueva York con el título de «almirante del gobierno de Buenos Aires» para asistir a Aguirre, representante del mismo gobierno, en la habilitación de las fragatas de guerra Curiacio y Horacio que se estaban construyendo allí, le había arrestado el 28 de agosto de 1818, reclamándole cien mil duros que era el valor de las presas españolas que había hecho: la faluca General Morales y los bergantines Tenerife y Gacela. Luego se había iniciado otro pleito por la captura de la fragata General Terán, pero se había dejado en suspenso. El resultado había sido que el tribunal le había puesto en libertad con el pretexto de que no tenía facultad para declarar responsable a Taylor. Las elevadas costas del proceso habían sido satisfechas por Onís. Se habían hecho las reclamaciones ante el tribunal de los Estados Unidos, probándose por muchos testigos que Taylor había salido de Bal-

timore sin tocar en ningún puerto insurgente, pese a lo cual no se le había encausado por delito de piratería.

También en Baltimore se había gastado mucho en pleitos contra el pirata Almeida, que de todos había salido libre. Onís había presentado reclamaciones en todos los casos de piratería, sin haber obtenido jamás respuesta del secretario de Estado americano.

Le hace notar que por el artículo 9.º del tratado de 1819, España renunciaba a todas las reclamaciones de sus súbditos por presas y confiscaciones injustas anteriores a dicha fecha, pero en su opinión había que representar al gobierno de Estados Unidos la injusticia de que recayeran sobre España los costos de los pleitos contra los que infrigían el tratado vigente (Nueva York, 19 de octubre 1823).

225

N.º 60. — 26 de octubre, Filadelfia.

Rivas anuncia a José Luyando el envío de un memorial del cónsul de España en San Agustín de la Florida, en el que suplicaba al rey que le removiera de aquel destino por las razones que exponía y por ser inútil un cónsul en aquel puerto.

226

N.º 62. — 5 de noviembre, Filadelfia.

Anuncia remisión a José Luyando de una gaceta que contenía la noticia de que las tropas realistas habían vuelto a evacuar Lima en agosto, y se retiraban al alto Perú después de haber conseguido una contribución de trescientos mil duros y quemado algunos edificios.

LEGAJO 5.650

AÑO 1824

CORRESPONDENCIA DE HILARIO DE RIVAS Y SALMÓN AL SECRETARIO DE ESTADO ESPAÑOL, CONDE DE OFALIA

227

N.º 71. — 1 de enero, Filadelfia.

Se queja por falta de noticias desde hacía seis meses y felicita a los reyes por los últimos acontecimientos de Cádiz.

Hay dos ejemplares.

228

N.º 72. — 4 de enero, Filadelfia.

Da cuenta de la enfermedad de Manuel Barros y de los auxilios económicos que le había proporcionado.

229

N.º 74. — 11 de enero, Filadelfia.

Informa de la situación en Grecia y dice que la causa griega era mirada con tanta simpatía en Estados Unidos, que había llevado a los particulares y corporaciones a promover una suscripción en su favor.

230

N.º 76. — 15 de enero, Filadelfia.

Remite copia de una nota pasada a Mr. Adams, secretario de Estado americano, con motivo de la injusta prisión de dos marineros españoles en el arsenal de Norfolk.

Adjunto:

— Nota con un informe del cónsul de esa ciudad, Pablo Chacón, en el que decía que los citados marineros viajaban en un pequeño barco, propiedad de uno de ellos y cuando iban de Puerto Rico a San Juan de los Remedios fueron despojados de su barco por dos goletas de guerra de Estados Unidos; habían permanecido en Norfolk encarcelados durante catorce meses acusados de piratería pero sin ser juzgados, y solicitaba su puesta en libertad y una indemnización por todas sus pérdidas (Filadelfia, 10 de enero 1824).

— Minuta a Rivas acusando recibo de los anteriores oficios (Aranjuez, 31 de marzo 1824).

231

N.º 77. — 30 de enero, Filadelfia.

Informa de la proposición hecha en el congreso para reconocer la independencia de los griegos, que no llegó a aceptarse por el temor del gobierno a comprometerse nacionalmente y enfrentarse con la Santa Alianza, si bien individualmente se seguía prestando ayudas.

232

N.º 85. — 15 de febrero, Filadelfia.

Da cuenta de haberse concedido la libertad a los dos marineros españoles presos en Norfolk.

Adjunto:

— Copia del oficio de Pablo Chacón informando de lo anterior y de los auxilios que les había prestado (Norfolk, 19 de enero 1824).

233

N.º 86. — 18 de febrero, Filadelfia.

Remite copia de un oficio que había mandado al capitán general de Cuba, pidiendo el castigo del capitán de la goleta española Primera Ligera, por haber dejado a su tripulación abandonada en Estados Unidos, lo que había causado una serie de gastos.

Adjunto:
— Oficio citado que incluía otros de Stoughton, cónsul de España en Nueva York, a Rivas y al capitán de la Primera Ligera, Jaime Roca, diciendo que era obligación de éste, como representante de los dueños del barco, sufragar los gastos ocasionados (Filadelfia y Nueva York, 13 de febrero y 14 de enero 1824).
— Carta del capitán Roca a Rivas prometiendo que se haría cargo de los gastos de la tripulación de su buque así como de conseguir embarcarla para territorios españoles; respuesta de Rivas insistiendo en la total responsabilidad que tenía de cumplir sus promesas (Nueva York, 24 y 25 de enero 1824).
— Oficios de Stoughton a Hilario Rivas diciendo que había decidido enviar a la tripulación de la Primera Ligera a la Habana, pagando diez pesos por persona, en vista de que el capitán Roca se negaba a prestarles ningún auxilio (Nueva York, 29 de enero 1824).

234

N.º 87. — 18 de febrero, Filadelfia.

Anuncia la llegada a Baltimore, fugados de Tenerife, de unos individuos llamados, Mejía, Zeruti y Pérez y del teniente coronel Spínola. Llegaron en la mayor miseria y pidiendo socorros y pasajes al gobierno mejicano.

235

N.º 88. — 18 de febrero, Filadelfia.

Remite copia del oficio de Francisco Martínez Pizarro, diciendo que no había podido hacerse cargo del consulado de Panzacola por falta de recursos para trasladarse.

Adjunto:

— Oficio en el que Pizarro se quejaba de su penosa situación económica, pues hacía dos años que no percibía su sueldo (Nueva Orleans, 15 de enero 1824).

236

N.º 89. — 19 de febrero, Filadelfia.

Pone de manifiesto la miseria en que se hallaba el cónsul español en Savannah a quien el gobierno debía más de 9.000 duros.

237

N.º 90. — 20 de febrero, Filadelfia.

Dice que desde hacía ocho meses no recibía oficios ni gacetas de España.

238

N.º 91. — 22 de febrero, Filadelfia.

Da cuenta de un caucus o junta particular de los miembros del congreso donde se decidió recomendar a Mr. Crawford, ministro de Hacienda, para suceder al presidente americano. Con este motivo hace un análisis de los restantes candidatos a la presidencia.

239

N.º 92. — 25 de febrero, Filadelfia.

Anuncia remisión del mensaje del presidente de Estados Unidos relativo al tratado de 22 de febrero, donde se ponía de manifiesto la política del gobierno americano que aprovechaba los desgraciados acontecimientos de la península no sólo para conseguir la ratificación del tratado, sino además para obtener un ventajoso convenio de comercio.

240

N.º 96. — 18 de marzo, Filadelfia.

Remite recorte de gaceta y su traducción relativo a las concesiones de tierra en las Floridas.

Adjunto:

— Artículo del «National Intelligencer» haciendo referencia a los decretos españoles que declaraban enajenables las concesiones de tierras hechas al duque de Alagón (Washington, 15 de marzo 1824).

241

N.º 99. — 30 de marzo, Filadelfia.

Desde hacía nueve meses estaba sin noticias. Sospechaba que estaba siendo interceptado el correo y propone un medio para solucionar esta incomunicación.

242

N.º 100. — 10 de abril, Filadelfia.

Anuncia remisión de dos ejemplares de una publicación de Mexía, el autor del Zurriago.

243

N.º 102. — 25 de abril, Filadelfia.

Avisa nuevamente del acuerdo tomado por los gobiernos de Colombia y Méjico para enviar una expedición contra Cuba.

Adjunto:

— Minuta al capitán general de Cuba diciendo que se activaban las disposiciones para mandarle los refuerzos que tenía solicitados.

En relación con los jefes militares emigrados a Cuba después de la participación en la insurrección de la Isla de León que fueron separados del ejército por este motivo, el rey dejaba a su criterio concederles un indulto especial (Madrid, 2 de julio 1824).

244

N.º 103. — 6 de mayo, Filadelfia.

Remite un memorial del cónsul de Baltimore, Juan Bautista Bernabéu, solicitando ser restituido en su consulado y pidiendo ayuda económica. Rivas apoyaba esta petición por considerar a Bernabéu el mejor y más antiguo de los empleados españoles en Estados Unidos.

Adjunto:

— Carta al secretario de Estado con el mencionado memorial al rey, donde Bernabéu exponía los motivos de su precaria situación económica después de treinta años de servicios (Baltimore, 27 de abril 1824).

245

N.º 105. — 9 de mayo, Filadelfia.

Da cuenta de haber conseguido la libertad de un español de Cádiz llamado Francisco García, condenado en Charleston hacía dos años, a siete de cárcel por haber pagado alguna mercancía con pesos que resultaron ser falsos.

Adjunto:

— Aprobación de la gestión de Rivas y petición de un estado de cuentas de su legación desde 1820 (Madrid, 2 de julio 1824).

246

N.º 109. — 20 de mayo, Filadelfia.

Anuncia remisión de varias gacetas con noticias importantes de las dos Américas:

De Méjico, que se había descubierto una conspiración contra el gobierno, a favor de Iturbide y el congreso mejicano había determinado nombrar un dictador supremo. En Perú estaba dividido tanto el ejército español como el llamado patriota; los realistas habían derrotado a los constitucionales quienes habían intentado acercarse a Bolívar. En Chile, Quintanilla se había apoderado de Valdivia; el gobierno había hecho un ventajoso concordato con el Papa. De Buenos Aires, que dos indios habían atacado y derrotado al gobernador de Santa Fe. En Montevideo, el general Lecor se había apoderado de esta plaza y había embarcado las tropas portuguesas para Europa. Varias piraterías en el Pacífico, noticias del congreso, y otras.

247

N.º 112. — 25 de mayo, Filadelfia.

Remite copia de una nota pasada al gobierno federal pidiendo la corbeta española La Ceres apresada por los colombianos y conducida al puerto de Panzacola.

Adjunto:

— Nota de Rivas al secretario de Estado Adams, apoyando su reclamación de La Ceres en el tratado de 1795 por el que Estados Unidos y España prometían proteger y defender todos los buques que se hallasen en su jurisdicción, además de mencionar los establecidos por el derecho de gentes, que una presa no se consideraba propiedad del enemigo hasta que hubiese sido conducida al país del apresador. Hay dos ejemplares (Filadelfia, 24 de mayo 1824).

248

N.º 114. — 26 de mayo, Filadelfia.

Remite copia de la respuesta de Adams a su queja por la comisión de reclamaciones relacionadas con el tratado de 1819.

Adjunto:

— Nota de Adams a Rivas en la que decía que se había estipulado en el tratado de 22 de febrero de 1819 que el importe y reconocimiento de todas las reclamaciones que en él se tratasen, se sometería a la decisión de los comisionados sin autorizar la intervención de uno u otro gobierno. Hay dos ejemplares Washington, 22 de mayo 1824).

249

N.º 115. — 27 de mayo, Filadelfia.

Informa de que se había introducido en Filadelfia una sociedad secreta, contra la familia de los Borbones, con el título de los Carbonarios. Anuncia remisión de un discurso, que sospechaba sería de Mexía el editor del Zurriago, con el fin de atacar a esta familia.

250

N.º 116. — 26 de mayo, Filadelfia.

Comunica la muerte del cónsul español en Savannah, Carlos Mulvey.

251

N.º 119. — 31 de mayo, Filadelfia.

Dice que el congreso americano había autorizado a su gobierno para crear un fondo de cinco millones de pesos que pagarían lo estipulado en el artículo 11 del tratado de 22 de febrero.

252

N.º 120. — 31 de mayo, Filadelfia.

Informa de varias noticias: insurrección de la guarnición de Callao formada por gente de color que llevó Bolívar; en un congreso de Colombia el gobierno había manifestado su decisión de no tratar con España mientras no le reconociese su independencia; motivos por los que no había sido reconocido el encargado de negocios del Brasil.

253

N.º 122. — 5 de junio, Filadelfia.

Da cuenta de que había proporcionado 200 pesos, al encargado de negocios Manuel Barros con cargo a sus atrasos. Anteriormente se le había proporcionado otra cantidad por parte de sus mensualidades adeudadas.

Adjunto:

— Nota de Barros a Rivas solicitando esta ayuda (Filadelfia, 1 de junio 1824). Oficio pidiendo la aprobación real.

254

N.º 125. — 20 de junio, Filadelfia.

Había mandado 100 pesos a la viuda de Mulvey, cónsul de Savannah, a cuenta de los atrasos que se adeudaban a su marido, que ascendían a cerca de diez mil duros.

Adjunto:

— Carta de la citada viuda exponiendo su difícil situación y solicitando alguna ayuda (Filadelfia, 18 de junio 1824).

255

N.º 129. — 6 de julio, Filadelfia.

Da cuenta de que había pedido al gobierno americano un préstamo de seis mil duros, contra el ministerio de Estado en Madrid. Había pedido este préstamo por el gran número de atrasos que tenía su legación y sin esperanza de recibir más dinero de la Habana.

Adjunto:

— Copia de la carta de Adams a Rivas para que interviniese cerca de su gobierno para el pronto pago de las letras citadas, y la respuesta de Rivas que creía estarían ya satisfechas, pero que insistiría hasta asegurarse (Washington y Filadelfia, 29 de junio y 6 de julio 1824).

256

N.º 130. — 1 de julio, Filadelfia.

Informa de que había pagado con cargo a su legación la cantidad de 90 pesos por los gastos de dos empleados del gobierno español que naufragaron cuando se dirigían desde la Habana a su destino de Puerto Rico, habiéndose refugiado en Charleston.

Adjunto:

— Copias de cartas del vicecónsul español en Charleston, Juan Gualberto de Ortega a Rivas, avisándole de que había librado contra las cajas de Puerto Rico los 90 pesos adelantados para pagar los gastos de dichos empleados, cuyas letras habían sido protestadas (Charleston, 4 de junio 1824).

Respuesta de Rivas que se haría cargo de estos pagos, pero que en adelante debía seguirse una rigurosa economía y no librar letras contra las cajas de Méjico y Cuba (Filadelfia, 14 de junio 1824).

Ortega acusa recibo a Rivas y agradece la gestión (Charleston, 23 de junio 1824).

257

N.º 131. — 2 de julio, Filadelfia.

Avisa la llegada del teniente coronel Rossi y del comisario de guerra Manuel Martínez, procedentes de Colombia, que habían sido apresados en Guayaquil por los insurgentes de este país, faltando a la capitulación acordada, y consiguiendo escapar más tarde. Quedaban en Guayaquil presos, unos cien españoles más. Rivas había auxiliado con doce pesos a cada uno de estos dos empleados que procuraría enviar a Cuba.

258

N.º 132. — 2 de julio, Filadelfia.

Da cuenta de la arribada forzosa a Charleston de la fragata mercante española Tarántula y del socorro que pedía su tripulación.

Adjunto:

— Oficios del vicecónsul español en Charleston, Gualberto Ortega informando de lo anterior y solicitando ayuda para la tripulación de la Tarántula (Charleston, 24 a 29 de junio 1824).

259

N.º 135. — 9 de julio, Filadelfia.

Dice que en vista de la falta de recursos en que se encontraba su legación había pasado circulares al capitán general de Cuba, a los cónsules españoles en Estados Unidos y al de Nueva York, Stoughton, en particular, solicitando ayuda económica, especialmente para atender a los centenares de españoles expulsados de Colombia, que probablemente se dirigirían a puertos americanos en lugar de hacerlo a Cuba.

Adjunto:

— Oficios de Rivas al capitán general de Cuba solicitando un crédito para aplicarlo únicamente al socorro de los españoles que pudiesen llegar a Estados Unidos expulsados por los colombianos. A los cónsules les decía que había sido nombrado José de Iznardi para sustituirlo en el ministerio y traería fondos consigo, pero mientras tanto no podría él hacerse cargo de los gastos extraordinarios de los cónsules, como venía haciendo. A Stoughton, solicitando el envío de unas cantidades que le había anunciado hacía más de tres meses (Filadelfia, 5 a 8 de julio 1824).

260

N.º 136. — 10 de julio, Filadelfia.

Remite copia de una nota pasada a Adams en relación con los artículos 11 y 14 del tratado de 22 de febrero de 1819.

Adjunto:

— Nota de Rivas pidiendo el resultado de las liquidaciones hechas por la comisión de reclamaciones del tratado (Filadelfia, 8 de julio 1824).

261

N.º 137. — 10 de julio, Filadelfia.

Informa del cisma ocurrido en la iglesia de Santa María de Filadelfia y pregunta si debería abandonar o vender los bancos de la legación española, que costaban 30 pesos anuales.

CORRESPONDENCIA DE HILARIO RIVAS A CEA BERMÚDEZ, SECRETARIO DE ESTADO

262

N.º 145. — 31 de julio, Filadelfia.

Remite un memorial al rey de la viuda del cónsul Mulvey pidiendo los atrasos que se debían a su marido.

Adjunto:

— Memorial citado exponiendo los méritos de Mulvey que estuvo al servicio real durante más de veinte años y a quien se debían algunas cantidades atrasadas (Filadelfia, 25 de julio 1824).

263

N.º 148. — 2 de agosto, Filadelfia.

Acusa recibo de varios oficios.

264

N.º 149. — 3 de agosto, Filadelfia.

Se daba por enterado de que quedaban confirmados en sus consulados de Nueva York y Baltimore, Tomás Stoughton y Juan Bautista de Bernabéu, pero reduciendo sus sueldos de cuarenta a treinta mil reales por las apuradas circunstancias del erario. Lo comunicaría a los interesados.

Adjunto:

— Acuse de recibo de Bernabéu (Baltimore, 5 de agosto 1824).

265

N.º 151. — 5 de agosto, Filadelfia.

Remite una solicitud de Manuel Barros, agregado en su legación, pidiendo una pensión alimenticia, de la que le debían trece mensualidades.

Adjunto:

— Solicitud en la que Barros decía que esta pensión se concedía a los de su clase, como un socorro en atención al corto sueldo de que disponían (Filadelfia, 1 de agosto 1824).

266

N.º 153. — 12 de agosto, Filadelfia.

Remite memorial del teniente de fragata Juan José de la Serna, solicitando prórroga de su licencia.

Adjunto:

— Memorial citado (Nueva York, 10 de agosto 1824).

267

N.º 155. — 12 de agosto, Filadelfia.

Anuncia remisión de gaceta con un extracto de la convención que había hecho con Rusia el gobierno americano, y que parecía muy ventajosa para Estados Unidos, puesto que Rusia renunciaba al ucase que excluía a los extranjeros del norte del Pacífico, fijaba sus límites en el grado 54 y concedía la libertad de comercio y de pesca a los Estados Unidos.

268

N.º 156. — 15 de agosto, Filadelfia.

Acusa recibo de varios oficios.

269

N.º 159. — 21 de agosto, Filadelfia.

Pone de manifiesto la necesidad de personas que le ayudasen en las funciones de su ministerio, muy atrasadas por la larga enfermedad de Manuel Barros. Proponía a Narciso Noeli, secretario del consulado general, y a Francisco Martínez Pizarro, agregado a la legación, como personas competentes.

270

N.º 161. — 18 de agosto, Filadelfia.

Da cuenta de los armamentos de barcos que se venían haciendo en Estados Unidos en favor de los insurgentes. Se habilitaban los buques y aumentaban su fuerza sin faltar a las leyes, llevando su artillería como lastre cuando no era permitido llevarla sobre cubierta y aumentando el número de su tripulación como si fueran pasajeros. Da algunos detalles más, relacionados con este asunto como las contratas para la construcción de varios buques de vapor para la navegación y defensa de los ríos y lagos de Costa Firme. Se habían construido diez lanchas cañoneras por cuenta del gobierno de Méjico y se estaban fabricando doce más por el de Colombia; además este gobierno proyectaba la construcción de tres o cuatro buques mayores. Según las gacetas, Bolívar había comprado en Guayaquil una fragata grande del comercio de esta ciudad y la estaba armando para enviarla contra los españoles; da noticias de más barcos.

Las presas españolas eran conducidas por los insurgentes a puertos americanos, donde se les facilitaba la venta de sus cargamentos tan ilegales como lucrativos. Los insurgentes les ofrecían ventajas prohibidas por el derecho de gentes que exigía que los comandantes y las dos terceras partes o más de la tripulación de los buques nacionales y corsarios fuesen naturales del país o al menos naturalizados. Los colombianos ofrecían su pabellón a todo buque y capitán extranjero que llegase, sin restricción alguna, ofreciéndoles legalizar las presas de propiedad española. No sería fácil enumerar los corsarios sacados de América por los insurgentes.

Adjunto:
— Oficio del cónsul de Nueva York, Tomás Stoughton a Rivas, diciendo que no estaba confirmada la noticia de que Holstein fuese perseguido por haber habilitado una expedición contra Puerto Rico. Daba también noticias del corsario de Colombia, general Santander, que había apresado varias goletas americanas en Nueva York, apoderándose de sus cargamentos pertenecientes en su mayor parte a súbditos españoles y estaban asegurados en compañías americanas que habían elevado una reclamación por estos sucesos (Nueva York, 12 de agosto 1824).
Nota de Rivas al secretario de Estado americano, Adams, po-

niendo de manifiesto la responsabilidad del gobierno de Estados Unidos por la ayuda que prestaban a las provincias de Ultramar sublevadas, principalmente en lo que se refería al armamento de barcos. Estos armamentos así como la expedición que Holstein habilitó contra Puerto Rico se formaban y salían de los puertos de Estados Unidos. Muchos de los corsarios que entorpecían el comercio español se construían y armaban en puertos americanos y eran también mandados por ciudadanos de esta Unión; no teniendo de las provincias disidentes españolas más que el pabellón con que navegaban, atacando igualmente las propiedades y derechos de ambas naciones como verdaderos piratas; citaba varios casos como el del corsario colombiano, general Santander, que después de haber aumentado ilegalmente su armamento sobre el río Mississipi, apresó en el golfo de Méjico varios buques de Estados Unidos, con el pretexto de que conducían propiedades españolas. En opinión de Rivas estos armamentos eran contrarios al derecho de gentes y a la neutralidad que debían mantener los dos países, y el escrupuloso cumplimiento de los tratados interesaba a ambos (Filadelfia, 15 de agosto 1824).

271

N.º 162. — 25 de agosto, Filadelfia.

Dice que el atraso en el envío del correo se debía al vicecónsul en esta ciudad, Juan Leamy, encargado de este servicio y que últimamente lo demoraba intencionadamente por estar descontento con sus retribuciones.

272

N.º 164. — 25 de agosto, Filadelfia.

Comunica varias noticias: la vuelta de Bolívar al Callao y Lima; que el general Olañeta con su ejército se había pasado a los insurgentes, proclamando la independencia del Perú; llegada de Iturbide al Soto de la Marina en Méjico; y que el general Lafayette había llegado a Nueva York y Boston siendo muy obsequiado.

273

N.º 167. — 2 de septiembre, Filadelfia.

Anuncia el arresto y ejecución de Iturbide, poco después de su llegada a Méjico.

274

N.º 168. — 5 de septiembre, Filadelfia.

Comunica que Juan Bautista Bernabéu aceptaba el cargo interino de cónsul general en Estados Unidos con ciertas condiciones.

Adjunto:

— Oficio de Bernabéu a Rivas diciendo que mientras durase la interinidad desempeñaría el consulado general desde Baltimore (Baltimore, 26 y 27 de agosto 1824).

275

N.º 170. — 9 de septiembre, Filadelfia.

Comunica varias noticias importantes: Que un coronel llamado Rodríguez había intentado proclamar la constitución en Cuba, lo que, en opinión de Rivas, podría ser un paso hacia la independencia. Se había confirmado oficialmente la deserción del general Olañeta en Perú, lo que haría difícil a las tropas españolas sostenerse en Lima. El Callao continuaba bloqueado por buques colombianos y peruanos. Bolívar había recibido numerosos refuerzos desde Costa Firme. Las piraterías seguían en aumento y también los insurgentes continuaban llevando sus presas a puertos de Estados Unidos.

276

N.º 174. — 21 de septiembre, Filadelfia.

Se interesa vivamente por el pago definitivo de la letra de 6.000 duros que se debía al gobierno americano.

277

N.º 183. — 21 de octubre, Filadelfia.

Da cuenta de los gastos causados por Nicolás Galiano; en una riña entre españoles y otros que se decían colombianos que estaban pescando en Cayo-Bacas (Estados Unidos) resultó uno muerto y Galindo fue acusado de homicidio.

Adjunto:

— Minuta a Rivas acusando recibo (Madrid, 25 de diciembre 1824).

278

N.º 184. — 21 de octubre, Filadelfia.

Informa de varias noticias importantes: Se confirmaba la conspiración en Callao en favor de los insurgentes. El almirante Cochrane además de bloquear a Pernambuco por mar, había desembarcado 5.000 hombres. Los insurgentes habían apresado dos buques más americanos porque conducían propiedad española y que un corsario de Maracaibo acababa de hacer tres presas españolas.

Adjunto:

— Minuta a Rivas acusando recibo y diciendo que debían trasladarse estas noticias a los capitanes generales de Cuba y Puerto Rico (Palacio, 25 de diciembre 1824).

279

N.º 186. — 24 de octubre, Filadelfia.

Comunica que había socorrido e intentaba enviar a la Habana a unos soldados y marineros españoles prisioneros de los insurgentes, que consiguieron escapar y llegar a Filadelfia.

Adjunto:

— Minuta aprobando la conducta de Rivas y que en adelante procediese de la misma manera (Palacio, 25 de diciembre 1824).

280

N.º 189. — 9 de noviembre, Filadelfia.

Comunica que el cónsul español en San Agustín había tenido que abandonar su puesto por falta de recursos, ya que se le debía el sueldo correspondiente a su cargo.

Adjunto:

— Oficio de A. de Letamendía, cónsul de San Agustín, a Rivas, diciendo que por no haber recibido sus haberes desde su instalación en el consulado, se veía precisado a abandonarlo (San Agustín, 19 de octubre 1824).

281

N.º 190. — 9 de noviembre, Filadelfia.

Remite copia de una carta de Pizarro que pretendía ocupar nuevamente su puesto como agregado en el ministerio.

Adjunto:

— Carta de Pizarro diciendo que se incorporaría al ministerio, cosa que no había hecho antes por falta de medios (Nueva Orleans, 8 de octubre 1824).

— Respuesta de Rivas que antes de volver debía esperar la resolución del rey pues de lo contrario el desplazamiento y el resto de los gastos correría de su cuenta, dado que su ministro carecía de todo recurso (Filadelfia, 5 de noviembre 1824).

282

N.º 191. — 10 de noviembre, Filadelfia.

Comunica varias noticias: rumores de una nueva intervención de Bolívar en Perú, en la que había perdido unos 6.000 hombres; en Guatemala había empezado una guerra civil; el general Alvear, ministro argentino iba a cooperar con los insurgentes de Chile contra las tropas españolas de Perú. Continuaban los armamentos de buques en Estados Unidos para los insurgentes.

283

N.º 193.— 19 de noviembre, Filadelfia.

Sigue dando noticias importantes; los generales Valdés y Carratalá habían sido derrotados en Potosí por los insurgentes; los colombianos continuaban haciendo innumerables presas y seguían las piraterías en la costa de Cuba; lord Cochrane se había apoderado de Pernambuco. Preparativos para la reñida elección del nuevo presidente de Estados Unidos, que estaría entre Adams y Crawford.

Adjunto:

— Extracto del «Filadelfia Gazette» dando detalles de algunas de estas noticias (16 de noviembre 1824).

284

N.º 194.— 22 de noviembre, Filadelfia.

Remite extracto del «National Gazette» donde se hablaba del rápido avance de Bolívar sobre la antigua capital del Perú.

Adjunto:

— «Gaceta» dando noticias también de Panamá y de Chile (20 de noviembre 1824).

285

N.º 197.— 27 de noviembre, Filadelfia.

Le daba la enhorabuena por su nombramiento como secretario de Estado del que había tenido conocimiento el pasado 15 de septiembre.

286

N.º 202.— 9 de diciembre, Filadelfia.

Remite traducido extracto del mensaje del presidente americano al congreso.

Adjunto:

— Mensaje en el que hablaba el presidente de los cambios ocurridos en España y Portugal en los dos últimos años y del reconocimiento por Estados Unidos de los gobiernos independientes de América meridional, como los de Colombia, Chile, Guatemala, Buenos Aires y Méjico; con Colombia se había terminado un tratado de comercio y se esperaba hacer otro parecido con Buenos Aires; que a consecuencia del tratado de cesión de las Floridas se había autorizado un empréstito de cinco millones de dólares a favor del gobierno español; con esta medida los ciudadanos españoles que habían perdido tierras en esta cesión se verían compensados. Seguía la lucha para suprimir la piratería, aunque con dudosos resultados. Refuerzo de la escuadra americana en el Mediterráneo para evitar posibles conflictos con Argel. Los nuevos Estados en lucha con España habían consolidado su independencia antes de que fuera reconocido por el gobierno americano y se iban estableciendo en gobiernos electivos y representativos parecidos en todo al de Estados Unidos. Hacía también referencia el presidente, al convenio con Gran Bretaña sobre el comercio de esclavos que no estaba definitivamente arreglado (7 de diciembre 1824).

287

N.º 205. — 17 de diciembre, Filadelfia.

Remite copia de nota pasada por el cónsul de San Agustín A. de Letamendía, pidiendo ayuda económica para un cabo procedente del ejército de Cuba que se encontraba en esta ciudad en la mayor miseria y a quien Letamendía había adelantado algún dinero.

Adjunto:

— Nota fechada en San Agustín el 25 de noviembre de 1824 y respuesta de Rivas de que los fondos de su legación estaban agotados de tal manera que él mismo no sabría cómo podría subsistir (Filadelfia, 17 de diciembre 1824).

DESPACHOS DE LOS REPRESENTANTES DE ESPAÑA EN PARÍS

288

9 de febrero 1824.

Despacho del duque de San Carlos al secretario de Estado, conde de Ofalia, anunciando remisión de la copia de una carta del ministro de Marina de Francia, marqués de Clermont Tonnerre, con la cual le había enviado un despacho del general La Torre para el ministro de la Guerra español, dando cuenta de que la isla de Puerto Rico estaba bajo su autoridad.

289

15 de febrero 1824.

El duque de San Carlos acusa recibo al conde de Ofalia de un oficio en el que le comunicaba las prevenciones que se habían tomado en vista de una carta del antiguo cónsul Francisco Stoughton, y del intento de los gobiernos insurgentes para unirse a los angloamericanos. También había recibido otro oficio con una carta del rey para el de Francia que entregaría inmediatamente; otra, de la reina para el ministro de Sajonia y una cédula del Consejo de Indias.

290

22 de septiembre 1824.

El marqués de Casa Irujo encargado de negocios en París da cuenta al secretario de Estado, Cea Bermúdez, de la noticia recientemente propalada en Londres de que había desembarcado en Méjico, Agustín de Iturbide, y que había sido ejecutado por los republicanos de San Antonio de Padilla; dos gacetas inglesas, cuya remisión anuncia, parecían confirmar esta importante noticia.

291

1 de septiembre 1824.

Irujo comunica a Cea Bermúdez que, después de las noticias enviadas anteriormente, había llegado entre la correspondencia de Londres una carta de Cea Bermúdez, en la que daba cuenta de que Chile se había declarado en favor del rey, lo que había sembrado la consternación en el gobierno revolucionario, cuyos fondos habían bajado notablemente. Reitera, por encargo de los agentes de la Santa Alianza, la importancia de acelerar la salida de alguna expedición.

292

6 de octubre 1824.

El marqués de Casa Irujo, encargado de negocios en París, comunica a Cea Bermúdez que por conducto fidedigno había sabido la llegada a Roma del agente colombiano N. Tejada, que había salido de Londres para París con pasaporte del príncipe de Polignac, embajador de Francia en Inglaterra, y en París había mantenido una conferencia con el nuncio, de quien había obtenido el visado. Su misión parecía ser la obtención de bulas del papa para varios obispos de la llamada república colombiana.

El rey Carlos X de Francia había recibido la víspera al cuerpo diplomático. Se había suprimido la censura de los periódicos que, en su opinión se restablecería si se renovaban los agrios ataques al ministerio.

Adjunto:

— Minuta al encargado de negocios de París, marqués de Casa Irujo, comunicándole que ya el ministro de Roma, marqués de la Constancia, había participado la llegada de Tejada; en cuanto tuvo conocimiento de ello había reiterado al Santo Padre y a su ministro de Estado lo que anteriormente había dicho sobre este sujeto, pidiendo su expulsión de Roma y los estados pontificios, lo que se había llevado a efecto (San Lorenzo, 20 de octubre 1824).

— Minuta al marqués de la Constancia acusando recibo de un oficio reservado en el que participaba que, atendiendo a su solicitud, el santo padre había ordenado la salida de los estados pontificios de Ignacio Tejada, nombrado ministro por la rebelde república de Colombia; a la vez que aprueba su actuación quiere el rey que manifieste su gratitud al Santo Padre por esta disposición que patentiza su interés por los asuntos de España.

Aprovecha la salida de un correo extraordinario para el príncipe Maximiliano de Sajonia, padre de la reina, para enviar el presente aviso (San Lorenzo, 16 de octubre 1824).

LEGAJO 5.651

AÑO 1825

CORRESPONDENCIA DE HILARIO DE RIVAS Y SALMÓN, ENCARGADO
DE NEGOCIOS EN ESTADOS UNIDOS, CON EL SECRETARIO
DE ESTADO FRANCISCO CEA BERMÚDEZ

293

N.º 209. — 1 de enero, Filadelfia.

Remite copia de un oficio que había enviado el agregado a la
legación Manuel Barros, para prevenir la situación, que parecía
inminente, de que se encontrara sin medios para sobrevivir en Estados Unidos ni para volver a España (por error dice en la fecha
1824).

Adjunto:

— Oficio de Rivas a Manuel Barros advirtiéndole que ese trimestre
sería el último en que podría pagarle la pensión alimenticia,
para que si quería volver a España, en caso de no poder sobrevivir sin ella, lo manifestara a fin de pagarle el pasaje con
el importe de los bancos de la iglesia de Santa María, que había
puesto en venta (Filadelfia, 1 de enero 1825).

294

N.º 211. — 3 de enero, Filadelfia.

Transmite la información que el gobierno federal había dado
al congreso sobre el establecimiento de fanales en algunos de los

islotes del canal de la Bahama. El gobierno federal había encargado al comandante Porter averiguar si alguno de los islotes de este canal estaba sin dueño, especialmente los de Abaco y los llamados Double headed Shot Keys, que parecían los más convenientes para ello; el capitán general de Cuba había informado al comandante Porter que los Double headed Shot Keys, pertenecían a España, pero que procuraría que se cediera alguno a los Estados Unidos en caso de que su gobierno no quisiera encargarse de poner los fanales. El gobernador inglés de las Bahamas pretendía que todos los islotes o cayos que se hallaban inmediatos a aquellas islas pertenecían a Gran Bretaña y sería preciso negociar con su gobierno la posible cesión de alguno de ellos. El ministro americano en Londres había entablado la negociación, pero el gabinete británico se negaba a cederlos alegando que se encargaría del establecimiento de dichos fanales, siempre que los buques americanos pagasen al gobierno inglés un derecho proporcionado a las ventajas que ello les reportara.

295

N.º 212. — 5 de enero, Filadelfia.

Remite copia de la nota que había redactado en apoyo de las reclamaciones de Valverde y del teniente coronel Nicolás Desiniers.

Adjunto:

— Copia de la nota que Rivas y Salmón había enviado al secretario de Estado Juan Quincy Adams, en la que anunciaba remisión de un memorial que había presentado al congreso, el apoderado de Isabel Osorno de Valverde, y otros que le había dirigido el teniente coronel de ingenieros Nicolás Desiniers. Se referían ambos a las reclamaciones contra los Estados Unidos en virtud del tratado de 1819, por los daños y perjuicios que les habían resultado al ocupar las Floridas las tropas americanas. Aunque sólo tenía instrucciones concretas de apoyar la de Valverde, hacía lo mismo con la de Desiniers por considerarla igualmente justa (Filadelfia, 31 de diciembre 1824).

296

N.º 216. — 9 de enero, Filadelfia.

Adjunta un memorial del agregado de la legación Manuel Barros en el que pide que le sean devengados sus atrasos.

Adjunto:

— Memorial de Manuel Barros en el que exponía que se le adeudaban los sueldos desde 1.º de diciembre de 1823, hasta aquel momento, pese a haber sido el único empleado de la legación y el consulado general durante bastantes meses, a las órdenes del encargado de negocios Hilario de Rivas y Salmón, y se hallaba en trance de que le fuera suprimida la pensión alimenticia que disfrutaban los de su clase; durante muchos años había trabajado sin sueldo, con lo que había consumido sus bienes, cerca del rey de Sicilia, en la primera secretaría de Estado, en la última época del general Vives y con el actual encargado de negocios. Por todo lo cual esperaba que, le fueran devengados los trece mil reales que se le adeudaban por encontrarse con absoluta falta de medios (Filadelfia, 31 de diciembre 1824).

297

N.º 220. — 15 de enero, Filadelfia.

Envía traducción de un artículo publicado en el «National Journal» que contenía el mensaje del presidente de los Estados Unidos, James Monroe, en el que respondía a la pregunta que le había formulado el senado sobre las medidas que consideraba necesarias para suplir la piratería. Proponía que se le autorizara a hacer desembarcos en Cuba y Puerto Rico, tomar represalias y bloquear los puertos que tuviera por conveniente; y como toda la nación estaba dispuesta a cooperar con el gobierno para extirpar los actos de piratería, se podían considerar que estas medidas estarían pronto en vigor. Lo que era dudoso es que algunas potencias como Inglaterra y Francia reconocieran el bloqueo, en tiempo de paz, de los principales puertos de Cuba o Puerto Rico; pero podría tratarse de un bloqueo parcial impidiendo solamente la entrada y salida de buques españoles, lo cual favorecería a aquellas naciones que podrían hacer el comercio que a ellos se les impidiera.

Adjunto:

— Traducción de un artículo del «National Journal» del 14 de enero 1825, que contenía el mensaje del presidente Monroe en el que se incluían las exposiciones de los secretarios de Estado y de Marina; las medidas que propugnaba eran: la persecución de los reos en los lugares donde se refugiaran, tomar represalias y bloquear los puertos de aquellas islas. Tales medidas, que podrían suponer una intromisión en los asuntos de España y de las islas, no serían rechazadas por no poder ni el gobierno español ni las autoridades locales luchar por sus medios contra la piratería, y era de esperar que cooperaran con los americanos en la extirpación de aquellos mares de tan peligroso comercio (Washington, 13 de enero 1825).

298

N.º 223. — 22 de enero, Filadelfia.

Comunica que la cámara de representantes tenía como norma permitir al presidente de los Estados Unidos que reservara la documentación que considerase conveniente cuando se le pedía informe sobre algún asunto. Recientemente le habían pedido aclarase los motivos que habían existido para hacer un consejo de guerra al comodoro Stewart y otros oficiales que habían vuelto con él del Pacífico, a lo que había respondido el presidente que era asunto que convenía reservarlo. El año anterior, a la información solicitada sobre la repercusión que había tenido en las relaciones con España el reconocimiento de la independencia de la América disidente por los Estados Unidos, había contestado que por ser tan voluminosa la correspondencia no podía dar la información solicitada hasta la próxima sesión; y cumpliendo dicho ofrecimiento había entregado al congreso sólo los documentos en los que hacía aparecer como mucho más importantes los motivos de queja de los Estados Unidos, que los que tenía España contra los americanos. Silenciaba la injustísima prisión de Pedro Castro y de Isidoro Romero poniendo en cambio de relieve el caso de Pereyra. Llama Rivas la atención sobre las instrucciones que Adams había dado a mister Nelson, en las que rebatía las reclamaciones que la legación española había formulado con motivo de los buques que los marinos americanos habían apresado; presentaba hábilmente como ilegales nuestros bloqueos, se quejaba de la conducta del último ministro Joaquín de Anduaga, e insistía en que debíamos suprimir las piraterías dando pronta satisfacción a las reclamaciones de los ciudadanos de Estados Unidos contra España; finalmente trataba de las desavenencias surgidas con motivo de la artillería y los archivos de las Floridas, que debíamos de entregar y daba cuenta de que el nuevo gobierno de Méjico había reconocido los límites estipulados en el tratado de 1819. En una carta de Mr. Nelson, a ejemplo de su predecesor Forsyth, aconsejaba a su gobierno que amenazara y tomara fuertes medidas para imponerse al gobierno español y vencer su natural apatía.

299

N.º 224. — 23 de enero, Filadelfia.

Anuncia remisión de los informes que el presidente había dado al congreso sobre las piraterías en Cuba y Puerto Rico.

300

N.º 225. — 24 de enero, Filadelfia.

Comunica el regreso de Eugenio Cortés, capitán de fragata español y jefe de la marina de Méjico, que acompañado de otros dos oficiales había vuelto a Estados Unidos, probablemente para dirigir la construcción de varias fragatas de guerra. Cortés había dado noticias sobre la guerra del Perú relativas a la derrota del general Canterac, en Huamanga, las cuales se habían confirmado por vía de Caracas. Otras noticias más recientes del Perú, sin negar la victoria de Bolívar, aseguraban que el virrey La Serna estaba a treinta leguas de Cuzco esperando que se le reuniera el general Valdés. El navío Asia estaba bloqueado en el Callao, donde todavía había guarnición española, aunque Lima había sido evacuada.

Los colombianos hacían cada día presas y se aseguraba que el castillo de San Juan de Ulúa estaba bloqueado por los mejicanos.

Se decía que un ministro estaba próximo a salir de Méjico para Roma a fin de negociar un concordato y que el congreso de Estados

Unidos había votado quinientos mil duros para la construcción de una fragata de vapor, con muchos botes y gente a bordo, para perseguir a los piratas.

Tiene adjunto un recorte de gaceta con las noticias a que se refiere.

Adjunto:

— Traducción de un artículo del «Philadelphia Gazette» de 19 de enero 1825, sobre las noticias de Cortés: el cuartel general de Bolívar estaba en Andahuaylas, camino de Cuzco, después de haber derrotado a Canterac en Huamanga sobre el río Pampas; el resto del ejército de Canterac se retiraba hacia Cuzco a reunirse con las fuerzas de La Serna que habían sido derrotadas cerca de Charcas por el ejército de Buenos Aires. Estas fuerzas habían tomado posesión de las provincias de Potosí, Cochabamba, Orudo, Puno y Santa Cruz de la Sierra. Bolívar aseguraba la próxima conclusión de la campaña puesto que un ejército chileno iba de Arica para unirse a los de Perú y Buenos Aires; habían llegado los refuerzos de Cartagena, Santa Marta, y Puerto Cabello a Huancho de Panamá, donde también se había embarcado un millón y medio de pesos para el ejército que estaba en el Perú. Lima había sido tomada por los patriotas y el Callao estaba bloqueado por tierra y mar, por fuerzas del comodoro Blanco al servicio de Chile. Los navíos españoles Asia y Aquiles habían tratado de escapar de Callao volviendo al puerto al verse perseguidos por la escuadra peruana y chilena.

Noticias procedentes de Curaçao anunciaban que se preparaba en la Habana una expedición para algún puerto de Colombia; habían llegado a Puerto Cabello varios buques españoles apresados por los colombianos. El bergantín Tampico, procedente de la Guayra, había sido abordado por el bergantín de guerra español Roma Libre, que iba a entregarse al gobierno de Colombia por decisión unánime de todos sus tripulantes.

El almirante patriota Guise, desde la isla de San Lorenzo, bloqueaba el puerto del Callao donde había varios barcos españoles que no tardarían en caer en su poder. Noticias procedentes de Lima anunciaban la llegada a Huanchaco de mil quinientos colombianos procedentes de Panamá; Bolívar, según las últimas noticias, estaba en Huamango marchando hacia Cuzco. Los realistas, mandados por el virrey La Serna, treinta leguas más allá de Cuzco, esperaban que se les reuniera Valdés y se creía que

Bolívar entraría pronto en Cuzco la antigua capital del Perú (19 y 20 de enero 1825).

301

N.º 226. — 24 de enero, Filadelfia.

Anuncia remisión de unas gacetas que contenían la discusión que se había mantenido sobre las medidas propuestas para reprimir las piraterías, de resultas del dictamen que había dado la comisión diplomática al senado. Aunque la discusión no se había concluido y no se había tomado ningún acuerdo, había aprovechado la salida de un buque hacia Gibraltar para adelantarle la noticia.

302

N.º 228. — 11 de febrero, Filadelfia.

Comunica que, con arreglo a la constitución, el congreso había procedido al recuento de los votos de los colegios electorales, resultando elegido vicepresidente de los Estados Unidos para los cuatro próximos años mister Calhoun, secretario de Guerra; pero ninguno de los cuatro candidatos para la presidencia había obtenido la mayoría requerida, y la constitución prevenía que en estos casos recayera la elección en la cámara de representantes, haciéndose la votación por estados y que la elección había de ser entre uno de los tres candidatos que hubieran obtenido más votos en los colegios electorales; así que se había efectuado la votación entre el general Jackson, mister Adams y mister Crawford, ministro de Hacienda, quedando excluido por ocupar el cuarto lugar mister Clay. En la primera votación había sido elegido presidente de los Estados Unidos mister John Quincy Adams. Hay dos ejemplares.

303

N.º 230. — 12 de febrero, Filadelfia.

Acusa recibo de un oficio de 17 de octubre último, referente al sueldo de los secretarios de legación interinos que accidentalmente ejerzan las funciones de encargado de negocios.

304

N.º 232. — 13 de febrero, Filadelfia.

Manifiesta que eran muy contradictorias las noticias que llegaban sobre la guerra en Chile y Perú y que algunas batallas minuciosamente descritas no habían existido en la realidad. Lo único que consideraba cierto es que Bolívar se había detenido en Huamanga a esperar los refuerzos de Colombia y que Canterac se había retirado a Cuzco para unirse al virrey y al general Valdés, dispuestos a rechazar a Bolívar.

El comandante americano Hull estaba bloqueando el Callao; poco antes habían salido los navíos Asia y Aquiles ahuyentando al colombiano Guise. Creía cierta la noticia de que el gobierno inglés estaba dispuesto a reconocer la independencia de Méjico y Buenos Aires, e incluso la de Colombia si Bolívar concluía favorablemente la campaña en el Perú, aunque no se le había notificado oficialmente al gobierno de Estados Unidos. Decían que el nuncio había salido de Chile disgustado por las reformas radicales que se habían hecho en el clero, a ejemplo de las cortes de España.

El gobierno federal y los estados particulares estaban dando un gran incremento a la construcción de caminos y canales en todas direcciones, lo que reportaría grandes ventajas a su comercio; entre otros, trataban de abrir un camino de San Agustín a Panzacola, lo que proporcionaría a los Estados Unidos el comercio exclusivo de las provincias internas y las Californias. También se proponían establecer un arsenal en Panzacola o sus cercanías. Hay dos ejemplares.

Adjunto:

— Traducción duplicada de varias noticias que habían aparecido en las gacetas dando cuenta de que Bolívar estaba en posesión de Lima y que el comodoro Hull bloqueaba el puerto del Callao de resultas del apresamiento de la corbeta americana China por el general realista Rodil; que los tripulantes del bergantín Betsey, naufragado a principio de enero, habían sido asesinados en una rada cerca de Matanzas, salvándose solamente dos hombres; que el Callao y Lima estaban en poder de los realistas pero pronto caerían en manos de los patriotas, cuyo general Bolívar iba en seguimiento del general realista Canterac y probablemente llegaría hasta Cuzco y podía darse como seguro el triunfo de la causa de la independencia en el Perú. Noticias procedentes de Salta aseguraban que Olañeta tenía las provincias de Potosí y Cochabamba, pero con muy pocas fuerzas y armamento; por último, se aseguraba que el gobierno de Londres estaba presto a reconocer la independencia de Méjico y Buenos Aires e incluso la de Colombia, si se decidía definitivamente la guerra del Perú (17 de noviembre 1824 a 8 de febrero 1825).

305

N.º 233. — 14 de febrero, Filadelfia.

Anuncia la recepción de un oficio del capitán general de Puerto Rico, copia del que había dirigido al secretario de Estado, dando cuenta de la ocurrencia de Fajardo, del que ya tenía conocimiento por haberse publicado en las gacetas hacía unos meses. En su opinión había pasado la ocasión de reclamar ante el gobierno por dicha causa y era preferible esperar la llegada del comodoro Porter, por si daba alguna satisfacción, o la incorporación del nuevo ministro.

306

N.º 235. — 18 de febrero, Filadelfia.

Envía traducción de las noticias que habían aparecido en varias gacetas que confirmaban la profecía de Bolívar: el ejército realista había sido vencido el 9 de diciembre pasado en los Campos de Huamanguilla, siendo herido y aprisionado el virrey; Canterac había capitulado incluyendo el Callao en la rendición, con lo que era probable que los navíos Asia y Aquiles sirviesen a los insurgentes para volver las tropas colombianas a Panamá y no tardarían en atacar Cuba y Puerto Rico. Hay dos ejemplares.

Adjunto:

— Traducción de varias noticias insertas en las gacetas: el ejército libertador a las órdenes del general Sucre, había derrotado al español el 9 de diciembre en los llanos de Huamanguilla; su general en jefe La Serna había sido herido y hecho prisionero, igual que los generales Canterac, Valdés, Carratalá y otros jefes. Había dirigido las operaciones sobre el campo de batalla el teniente coronel y edecán del Libertador, Medina, que había sido asesinado después por los rebeldes del pueblo de Perando. Canterac, que había tomado el mando al ser herido la Serna, había capitulado ante Sucre con la expresa condición de entregar la fortaleza del Callao.

Una noticia procedente de Cartagena añadía que se había dado orden de que se detuvieran los refuerzos que se dirigían al Perú por no haber ya necesidad de ellos. Inmediatamente saldría una goleta americana para llevar la noticia a Inglaterra (18 de diciembre 1824 a 16 de febrero 1825). Hay dos ejemplares.

307

N.º 236. — 19 de febrero, Filadelfia.

Anuncia remisión de unas gacetas que contenían la interesante discusión que se había mantenido en el senado sobre la supresión de las piraterías en la isla de Cuba, así como el bill que había resultado de la discusión, en el que se había suprimido la parte relativa al bloqueo.

Adjunto:

— Minuta a Rivas y Salmón acusando recibo de varios oficios y participando la llegada a Aranjuez de los reyes e infantes con sus huéspedes; al día siguiente habían salido para una estancia de tres días en Toledo los reyes con el príncipe Maximiliano y su hija la princesa Amalia, regresando seguidamente a Aranjuez (Aranjuez, 16 de abril 1825).

308

N.º 237. — 6 de marzo, Filadelfia.

Da cuenta de la discusión en el senado sobre el bill propuesto para la supresión de las piraterías. Por último se habían eliminado las medidas de rigor, reduciéndose únicamente a autorizar al gobierno para construir diez corbetas de guerra para la persecución de los piratas.

Adjunto:

— Oficio al rey dando cuenta de lo anterior (Palacio, 9 de julio 1815).

— Minuta a Rivas acusando recibo (Madrid, 12 de julio 1825).

309

N.º 240. — 8 de marzo, Filadelfia.

Comunica que John Quincy Adams había sido designado para la presidencia de Estados Unidos y daba la lista del nuevo ministerio que se había formado y de otros nombramientos como el del nuevo ministro plenipotenciario para España, Alexander Everett; para ministro de Méjico, Poinsett, que era un gran defensor de la independencia de América, y Forbes, encargado de negocios para Buenos Aires.

310

N.º 242. — 12 de marzo, Filadelfia.

Anuncia remisión de varias gacetas de Estados Unidos y Méjico que informaban de un supuesto embargo de los buques que se hallaban en el puerto de Alvarado, con intención de enviar una expedición contra el general Santa Ana que se había rebelado en Campeche; pero se había abandonado el proyecto y levantado el embargo con motivo de la llegada al castillo de San Juan de Ulúa de un fuerte refuerzo de tropas de la Habana. Los franceses tenían bloqueado Puerto Cabello, lo que producía mucho recelo en Méjico porque sospechaban que España y Francia intentaban corromper a Bolívar con el ofrecimiento de coronarlo en América.

Tiene adjunto un recorte de periódico.

311

N.º 244. — 14 de marzo, Filadelfia.

Acusa recibo de varios oficios y como en uno de ellos se le reiteraba la orden de informar puntualmente a los capitanes generales de Cuba y Puerto Rico de cuantas noticias pudieran interesarles, da cuenta de que lo había cumplido puntualmente, remitiéndoles a cuenta de los fondos de la legación, las gacetas de los Estados Unidos. Otro de los oficios recibidos hacía referencia a una nota del ministro americano en Madrid, con motivo de la protección que el cónsul de su país en Tánger dispensaba a algunos revolucionarios. Hay dos ejemplares.

312

N.º 245. — 15 de marzo, Filadelfia.

Comunica que había revocado el nombramiento de cónsul interino en Alejandría en favor de mister Neale, cumpliendo una real orden de 19 de diciembre último.

313

N.º 250. — 24 de marzo, Filadelfia.

Avisa la próxima salida para Cádiz de mister Everet, que sustituía a mister Nelson como ministro en España.

314

N.º 251. — 12 de abril, Filadelfia.

Acusa recibo de varios oficios que adjuntaban algunas gacetas.

315

N.º 252. — 12 de abril, Filadelfia.

Acusa recibo de un oficio en el que se ordenaba, en virtud de real decreto, que se diera un certificado de conducta política a los españoles que regresaran a España. Había dado traslado de esta orden a los cónsules.

316

N.º 253. — 12 de abril, Filadelfia.

Se justifica ante la amonestación contenida en un oficio de que en lo sucesivo procurara que las noticias que comunicara fueran fidedignas, que en todas las ocasiones, había dado como ciertas las noticias que sabía ciertas y como dudosas las que no habían tenido confirmación; las enviadas en el despacho 194, a que aludía, y que no eran ciertamente muy halagüeñas, se habían confirmado con posterioridad. Hay dos ejemplares.

317

N.º 254. — 13 de abril, Filadelfia.

Acusa recibo de la comunicación relativa a la permanencia de las tropas francesas en España.

318

N.º 256. — 30 de abril, Filadelfia.

Anuncia remisión de varias gacetas y amplía algunas noticias que había enviado referentes a la batalla de Ayacucho. Según el general Sucre las fuerzas españolas ascendían a nueve mil hombres, pero haciendo el recuento de muertos, heridos y prisioneros después de la capitulación firmada en el mismo campo de batalla, no resultaban más que cinco mil. En una proclama de Olañeta, decía que unidos a sus hombres los cinco mil del mariscal de campo Pío Tristán, podrían salvar el Perú; y si Pío Tristán estuvo en Ayacucho podrían ser éstos los hombres cuyo paradero se desconocía. El comandante de la plaza del Callao no se había entregado a Bolívar contraviniendo las capitulaciones del general Canterac, por lo que el libertador le había puesto sitio y esperaba rendirla con refuerzos llegados de Guayaquil.

Eran contradictorias las noticias llegadas sobre el navío Asia, pues unas decían que había salido para Manila, otras que se encontraba cruzando contra los insurgentes y otras que se había destinado a la conducción de prisioneros. Parecía que algunos generales, oficiales y jefes se habían embarcado en buques franceses para España.

Los rumores de que Francia había tratado de seducir a Bolívar para que abandonara la causa de la independencia parecían ciertos; y el congreso extraordinario reunido en Bogotá no había admitido la dimisión de Bolívar, que antes de la batalla de Ayacucho había prometido rehusar el mando de la república.

En octubre próximo debía reunirse en Panamá el congreso, y uno de los principales asuntos que trataría sería el modo de atacar a Cuba y Puerto Rico.

Las últimas noticias de Buenos Aires decían: que el representante inglés había concluido con aquel gobierno un tratado ventajoso y que estaba muy adelantado otro con Méjico, y que el gobierno de Colombia había rehusado negociar un tratado con el presidente de Haití para no indisponerse con Francia. Por las gacetas que adjuntaba, podía ver que los angloamericanos habían sido afortunados en la persecución de los piratas y lo mismo las autoridades de Puerto Rico. Estaban nombrados los miembros del consejo de guerra que tenían que investigar la conducta del comandante Porter en Fajardo; incluye la correspondencia que se había publicado de este oficial con el ministro de Marina.

319

N.º 259. — 8 de mayo, Filadelfia.

Anuncia remisión de unas gacetas que contenían noticias del general Olañeta y del navío Asia y una relación de las fuerzas marítimas de los insurgentes en el Pacífico.

Adjunto:

— Varios recortes de gacetas unidos al despacho (26 de diciembre 1824 a 5 de mayo 1825).
— Traducción de noticias importantes del «National Journal» de Washington. El general Sucre había comunicado a Bolívar la sumisión del general Olañeta, por lo que estaba en manos de los patriotas todo el Perú, a excepción del castillo del Callao; si el general Rodil se obstinaba en sostenerse en él mientras tuviera víveres, el cerco podría prolongarse dos o tres meses, pero estaba bloqueado por mar y por tierra y en cualquier momento podría rendirse. La escuadra española había salido para Manila nada más recibir la noticia de la batalla de Ayacucho (Lima, 29 de enero 1825).

320

N.º 264. — 31 de mayo, Filadelfia.

Remite copia de la correspondencia que había mantenido con el vicecónsul en Charleston acerca del corsario colombiano Polly

Hampton y de la nota que sobre ello había enviado al gobierno de Estados Unidos.

Adjunto:

— Copia de una carta del vicecónsul en Charleston, Joseph Mulvey, al encargado de negocios enviándole copia de la que había recibido de Morris Goldsmith, diputado del distrito, sobre ciertas presas que el corsario colombiano Polly Hampton había hecho en la costa de Cuba y se habían vendido ilegalmente en Key West. Mulvey pedía instrucciones porque estimaba que sería posible recuperar muchas propiedades de españoles (Charleston, 21 de mayo 1825).

— Copia y traducción de la carta de Goldsmith a Mulvey dando cuenta de la llegada a Key West (Cayo Hueso) de la goleta Polly Hampton con una presa de mucho valor; había sido multada por el gobierno de Estados Unidos, lo mismo que se había hecho en ocasiones análogas. Explicaba que algunos buques tenían la costumbre de cruzar sobre la costa de Cuba y llevar las presas a tierra americana; en Key West, se reunía un jurado que concedía un derecho de salvamento muy considerable, y la mayor parte de la carga pasaba a poder de los apresadores. Goldsmith podría llevar ante la justicia de Estados Unidos a los oficiales de la Polly Hampton y poner fin a un trato tan ilícito, ofreciéndose a activar el asunto, siempre que lo remuneraran en la Habana con la cantidad que se juzgara conveniente (Charleston, 20 de mayo 1825).

— Respuesta de Rivas al vicecónsul en Charleston lamentando no poder sufragar con los fondos de la legación la gestión que proponía realizar Goldsmith; podría recomendarlo a las autoridades de Cuba para que le abonaran los gastos y le recompensaran, aunque sin salir personalmente garante de ello (Filadelfia, 29 de mayo 1825).

— Copia de la nota enviada por Rivas y Salmón al secretario de Estado americano, reiterándole las quejas contra los buques que se armaban en puertos de Estados Unidos y cubriéndose con las banderas de los gobiernos disidentes, hacían el corso contra los buques españoles, lo que se veía confirmado por la carta de Goldsmith relativa a la acogida que se ofrecía en Key West a tales corsarios (Filadelfia, 30 de mayo 1825).

— Minuta a Rivas aprobando la nota que había enviado al secretario de Estado y pidiendo que informe sobre la respuesta que recibiera así como de si había avisado al capitán general de Cuba para que pagara a Goldsmith (San Ildefonso, 29 de julio 1825).

321

N.º 266. — 8 de junio, Filadelfia.

Alude a la petición que había hecho al capitán general de Cuba, de la que había dado cuenta en el momento oportuno, para que debido a varias razones, una de las cuales era la escasez de fondos, suspendiera de momento la correspondencia indirecta que mantenía con él, por resultar muy costosa. A pesar de esto le había avisado el administrador de Correos de Washington que tenía a su disposición un pliego de dicho capitán general, cuyo importe ascendía a quince duros. En su respuesta, cuya copia adjunta, le había rogado que lo guardase hasta que él o alguno de sus sucesores lo pidiera y si eso no fuera posible, le autorizaría a quemarlo para no tener que realizar dicho desembolso.

Adjunto:
— Copia de una carta de Thomas Monroe, administrador de Correos de Washington, a Rivas y Salmón, comunicándole la llegada del pliego del capitán general de Cuba y la respuesta de Rivas en el sentido indicado (6 y 8 de junio 1825).
— Minuta a Rivas y Salmón acusando recibo de un oficio y participándole el traslado de los reyes a San Ildefonso (San Ildefonso, 29 de junio 1825).

322

N.º 271. — 16 de junio, Filadelfia.

Da cuenta de que Francisco Hernández Nogués le había mostrado una real patente de 9 de septiembre de 1824, por la que se le nombraba cónsul del rey en Filadelfia, nombramiento que había sido confirmado por el mismo Cea Bermúdez. Aunque no tenía noticia oficial directa de dicho nombramiento, en vista de la patente y de un oficio y varias cartas que atestiguaban su cargo, había ordenado a Juan Leamy, que lo desempeñaba interinamente, que le hiciera entrega del consulado.

Adjunto:

— Minuta a Rivas y Salmón notificándole que efectivamente, Francisco Hernández Nogués había sido nombrado cónsul en Filadelfia el 4 de septiembre anterior y confirmado dicho nombramiento el 19 de enero último (San Ildefonso, 17 de agosto 1825).

323

N.º 272. — 23 de junio, Filadelfia.

Participa que por medio del cónsul en Gibraltar había recibido el oficio relativo a la obligación de proveer de un certificado de su conducta política a los españoles que regresaren a España; ya anteriormente había recibido la misma notificación, pero aún no había llegado el real decreto de 8 de enero a que se refería.

324

N.º 275. — 14 de julio, Filadelfia.

Acusa recibo de varios oficios llegados por vía de Gibraltar y de varias gacetas.

325

N.º 276. — 14 de julio, Filadelfia.

Da cuenta de que había remitido al cónsul de San Agustín, Letamendía, un pliego dirigido a él que había llegado entre la correspondencia oficial, y a la vez le había enviado el oficio del 2 de mayo sobre la nulidad de su nombramiento, lo cual había comunicado igualmente al gobierno federal.

326

N.º 283. — 9 de agosto, Filadelfia.

Informa de que estando cerca de Manila los navíos Asia y Aquiles se había sublevado la tripulación del primero, y dejando en la isla de Guajan (Guam) a su comandante Guruceta y algunos oficiales, llevaron el buque a Monterrey y lo entregaron junto con el bergantín Constante al gobierno de Méjico, en las condiciones descritas en una gaceta adjunta; el Aquiles había seguido a Manila. Se había confirmado la derrota y muerte del general Olañeta. Se estaban reuniendo los ministros para el congreso de Panamá, que debía abrirse pronto. El gobierno francés había vendido la libertad que deseaban los negros de Haití o Santo Domingo por ciento cincuenta millones y algunos privilegios mercantiles. Bolívar había ido al alto Perú a organizar un gobierno; el Callao, que se mantenía firme, tendría que rendirse de un momento a otro. Tenía noticias de que el gobierno colombiano había preparado una expedición de varios buques al mando del almirante Padilla, para auxiliar a los mejicanos contra el castillo de San Juan de Ulúa; había llegado a Nueva York, con el fin de estudiar las instituciones de los Estados Unidos, el duque de Saxe Weimar; también habían llegado, de arribada, José Carro, Miguel Llaner y Manuel M. Frigor, agentes de Colombia, camino de Londres. Duraba todavía el consejo de guerra contra el comandante Porter; remite una gaceta que contenía la primera parte de su defensa, que era la que más podía interesar por referirse al asunto de Fajardo.

327

N.º 284. — 1 de agosto, Filadelfia.

Comunica que, cerciorado de que Francisco Hernández Nogués había sido nombrado cónsul en Filadelfia, había pedido al presidente el correspondiente «exequatur». Una vez posesionado de su cargo había pedido autorización para trasladarse a los baños de Saratoga por motivos de salud, a lo que había accedido, continuando Leamy en el desempeño del consulado.

328

N.º 286. — 13 de agosto, Filadelfia.

Acusa recibo de un pliego que contenía el traslado de un oficio del superintendente general de policía, al que daría cumplimiento, y unas gacetas.

329

N.º 290. — 27 de agosto, Filadelfia.

Extracta las noticias contenidas en unas gacetas que adjuntaba: que se iba estrechando por mar y tierra el cerco del Callao; que el comandante de las fuerzas francesas en el Pacífico había mantenido una conferencia con Bolívar de la cual ambos habían quedado satisfechos; que igual que Colombia y Méjico, Perú había prohibido la importación de mercancías españolas bajo cualquier bandera y que un nuncio apostólico, con poderes especiales de León XIII, estaba autorizando algunas reformas eclesiásticas en Chile.

330

N.º 293. — 24 de septiembre, Filadelfia.

Acusa recibo de varios oficios y gacetas; entre aquellos uno cerrado para el agregado Manuel Barros.

331

N.º 295. — 25 de septiembre, Filadelfia.

Da cuenta de la llegada de mister Nelson, ministro cesante en Madrid, sin que le acompañara Heredia como le había asegurado. Como no creía probable que llegara un nuevo ministro para Estados Unidos ni que le remitieran fondos para mantener la legación, había pasado a los cónsules una circular, cuya copia incluye, y al agregado Manuel Barros un oficio que también remite. Este último carecía de recursos y no tenía quien le pudiera prestar ayuda.

Adjunto:

— Circular de Rivas y Salmón a los cónsules ordenándoles que suspendieran la correspondencia que mantenían con él por la absoluta falta de recursos en que se encontraba; sólo podrían comunicarle algo si se trataba de un asunto de mucha importancia y sin ocasionar ningún gasto (Filadelfia, 25 de septiembre 1825).

— Nota de Rivas a Manuel Barros comunicándole que, hasta recibir nuevos fondos, se veía obligado a retirarle la pensión alimenticia que le correspondía como agregado a la legación.

332

N.º 297. — 26 de septiembre, Filadelfia.

Da cuenta de que el comandante Stewart, acusado en consejo de guerra de haber faltado a la neutralidad debida favoreciendo a los realistas en contra de los insurgentes, había sido declarado inocente.

333

N.º 299. — 30 de septiembre, Filadelfia.

Anuncia remisión del tratado de alianza ofensiva y defensiva entre la república de Colombia y la de Guatemala o estados de América central, que se había publicado en las gacetas. Por el artículo 18 se estipula que ambas partes se obligan a rechazar cualquier demanda de indemnización que les hiciera el gobierno español, directamente o por medio de tercero, por la pérdida de su soberanía sobre aquellos países.

334

N.º 300. — 2 de octubre, Filadelfia.

Informa de que el nuevo cónsul Francisco Hernández Nogués había quedado en escribirle desde Saratoga, a donde había ido a tomar baños, pero no lo había hecho; por medio de Manuel Barros había recibido una carta que aquél había entregado a Juan Leamy.

Adjunto:
— Copia de la carta de Francisco Hernández a Rivas participándole que salía hacia la Habana para buscar a su familia; continuando Leamy encargado del consulado (Filadelfia, 28 de septiembre 1825).
— Minuta a Rivas y Salmón acusando recibo de varios oficios (Madrid, 23 de diciembre 1825).

CORRESPONDENCIA DE HILARIO DE RIVAS Y SALMÓN
CON EL DUQUE DEL INFANTADO

335

N.º 305. — 6 de diciembre, Filadelfia.

Acusa recibo de un oficio en el que se le notificaba el nombramiento de Francisco Tacón para ministro residente en Estados Unidos; también habían llegado varias gacetas. El mejor conducto para enviarle la correspondencia era por el puerto de El Havre, en Francia, desde donde salían buques con regularidad con destino a Estados Unidos.

336

N.º 307. — 8 de diciembre, Filadelfia.

Anuncia el envío del mensaje que el presidente había remitido al congreso el día siguiente a su apertura; en él había señalado lo que hacía relación con España y sus posesiones. Resalta la diferencia con los discursos de años anteriores, llenos de insultos y amenazas si el gobierno español no accedía a las reclamaciones del ministro americano en Madrid y no se reprimían las piraterías; en el presente se hablaba poco de las relaciones entre los dos países y lo que se decía era en tono mesurado. Confirma la noticia enviada anteriormente, de que el gobierno de Estados Unidos pensaba enviar un representante al congreso de Panamá.

Adjunto:

— Minuta a Rivas acusando recibo de varios oficios (El Pardo, 22 de febrero 1826).

337

N.º 310. — 19 de diciembre, Filadelfia.

De Nueva York había llegado la noticia de que el capitán de un buque de Nueva Orleans había encontrado cerca de la Habana al bergantín de guerra mejicano La Victoria que conducía al comandante y guarnición del castillo de San Juan de Ulúa, que se había rendido el 22 de noviembre. También eran malas las noticias del Callao, como podía ver por las gacetas que adjuntaba.

CORRESPONDENCIA DE LOS MINISTROS ESPAÑOLES EN PARÍS Y LONDRES, CON EL SECRETARIO DE ESTADO FRANCISCO CEA BERMÚDEZ, SOBRE ASUNTOS DE AMÉRICA

338

10 de enero 1825, París.

El marqués de Casa Irujo da cuenta a Francisco Cea Bermúdez de una comunicación que había remitido mister Canning a los agentes de la Alianza en Londres, sobre la nota que había enviado al gobierno de España comunicando la resolución de Inglaterra de establecer tratados comerciales con Méjico, Colombia y Buenos Aires; lo mismo había comunicado el embajador inglés en París al gobierno francés. La noticia había causado gran conmoción por fomentar los principios revolucionarios en América, que algún día podrían repercutir en Europa. A consecuencia de éstos se habían reunido los embajadores y ministros de las cortes aliadas con el ministro de Negocios Extranjeros, y habían manifestado que sus respectivos soberanos verían con desagrado esta medida porque reconocían el derecho de España a someter sus colonias insurreccionadas; de resultas de esta conferencia se había acordado que el gobierno francés enviaría una comunicación que manifestara al secretario de Estado español su actitud ante la resolución de Gran Bretaña. La misma orden iban a dar a sus representantes en Madrid, el embajador de Rusia y los demás miembros de la Santa Alianza. Todos coincidían en que, dada la situación de España, debían protestar por esta resolución de Inglaterra, reiterando su reconocimiento al derecho que tenía de restablecer su dominio en sus posesiones ultramarinas; procurarían recursos para organizar una expedición de cinco o seis mil hombres que desembarcarían en el reino de Méjico, y otros, para que ayudaran a las fuerzas españolas en el Perú.

Camilo Gutiérrez de los Ríos, nombrado ministro en Londres, le había rogado que expusiera al secretario de Estado la situación embarazosa en que se encontraría de llegar a su puesto tras el paso dado por el gabinete británico, por lo que pensaba que debía presentarse con la protesta del gobierno español en este delicado asunto.

El gobierno francés reiteraba sus ofrecimientos de hacer lo que permitieran las circunstancias en favor de España. Esperaba que los ánimos se encresparían aún más en París cuando los agentes de la Alianza recibieran instrucciones de sus respectivos gobiernos.

339

18 de junio 1825.

El conde de la Puebla del Maestre anuncia remisión a Francisco Cea Bermúdez de dos pliegos: uno del ministro español en Londres y otro del encargado de negocios en los Países Bajos. Habían alarmado a los agentes de la Alianza y a los miembros del gabinete las últimas noticias llegadas de Cuba; todos opinaban que se debían enviar urgentemente socorros a aquella isla para calmar los ánimos y evitar los males que pudieran suceder en aquella colonia. Les había respondido que su gobierno procuraba tomar las medidas requeridas por las circunstancias para conservar aquella parte de la monarquía española.

Adjunto:

— Minuta al conde de la Puebla, en París, aprobando su respuesta y ordenándole que, reservadamente, comunicara a los representantes de la Alianza la próxima salida de otra expedición para Cuba y Puerto Rico, compuesta de tres mil hombres (Madrid, 4 de julio 1825).

340

N.º 1. — 3 de agosto, Londres.

Francisco Tacón manifiesta a Francisco Cea Bermúdez que en cuanto llegara a Estados Unidos estudiaría las circunstancias y los méritos del agregado de aquella legación Francisco Pizarro Martínez, y le daría cuenta de todo ello en cumplimiento de la real orden que había recibido en tal sentido.

341

N.º 3. — 19 de agosto, Londres.

Francisco Tacón acusa recibo de la real orden por la cual se nombraba a Miguel Tacón agregado diplomático de la legación en Estados Unidos.

342

N.º 4. — 16 de septiembre, Londres.

Tacón comunica que tiene en su poder la representación de la viuda de Carlos Mulvey, vicecónsul que fue en Savannah, que le había sido remitida y que enviaría desde Estados Unidos el informe solicitado sobre su contenido.

LEGAJO 5.652

AÑO 1826

CORRESPONDENCIA DE HILARIO RIVAS SALMÓN CON EL DUQUE
DEL INFANTADO, SECRETARIO DE ESTADO

343

N.º 313. — 3 de enero, Filadelfia.

Dice que el gobierno de Buenos Aires había incorporado a su
república la banda oriental y que amenazaba con la guerra al emperador del Brasil si se oponía a este decreto; que Bolívar había
circulado una proclama declarando libres y llamando a las armas
a los esclavos criollos del Brasil. Anuncia remisión del tratado de
alianza entre Méjico y Colombia. Trata también de la expedición
que se preparaba en la Costa Firme para provocar una revolución
en Cuba, que no sería difícil de conseguir dada la desunión de
los cubanos.

344

N.º 314 .— 12 de enero, Filadelfia.

Da cuenta de haber librado mil duros contra esa secretaría de
Estado, por la difícil situación económica en que se encontraba.

345

N.º 316. — 18 de enero, Filadelfia.

Acusa recibo de varios oficios y lo felicita por el nombramiento
para la secretaría de Estado.

346

N.º 317. — 20 de enero, Filadelfia.

Había trasladado al gobierno americano la política amistosa que quería seguir España con la Unión.

347

N.º 320. — 12 de febrero, Filadelfia.

Da cuenta de varias noticias: la rendición de Callao; formación de la expedición contra Cuba, que Estados Unidos no apoyaría por temor a que cayese en poder de los negros, como pasó en Santo Domingo; en relación con el congreso de Panamá dice que Estados Unidos no debían tomar parte en sus discusiones de las que podrían surgir medidas contra España y Europa, incompatibles con la neutralidad a que se habían comprometido los Estados de la Unión, aunque por otra parte España había aceptado anteriormente que el gobierno americano reconociese la independencia de sus colonias.

El presidente de Méjico había alardeado en el congreso de que casi todas las potencias de Europa habían reconocido la independencia de esta nación y que parecía inevitable la guerra entre Buenos Aires y Brasil.

348

N.º 321. — 13 de febrero, Filadelfia.

Continúa dando noticias: se confirmaba la guerra entre Brasil y Buenos Aires, habiendo gran descontento en el Brasil por el reclutamiento para el servicio de mar y tierra que hacía su emperador. En Río de Janeiro se esperaba el ataque de Bolívar, que también operaría en Panamá y Perú por contar con un ejército de más de diez mil hombres, bien equipados y disciplinados. Estas actuaciones de Bolívar repercutirían también en Cuba.

349

N.º 322. — 4 de marzo, Filadelfia.

Notifica que Callao seguía sin rendirse; el gobierno de Chile preparaba una expedición contra Chiloé; por el tratado de alianza contra Colombia y centroamérica se obligaban a no acceder a las demandas de indemnizaciones que el gobierno español pudiese pedir por la supremacía que tuvo sobre aquellos países. En el congreso de Panamá se trataría de que las nuevas repúblicas ayudasen con los medios a su alcance a conseguir la independencia a Cuba y Puerto Rico.

350

N.º 324. — 10 de marzo, Filadelfia.

Dice que había recibido un pequeño socorro de la intendencia de la Habana y también que había vendido algunos objetos de plata pertenecientes a su legación. Estas cantidades las emplearía en costear los atrasos existentes.

Adjunto:

— Oficio al secretario del despacho de Hacienda comunicando lo anterior (Sacedón, 11 de julio 1826).

351

N.º 327. — 26 de marzo, Filadelfia.

Anuncia remisión de gacetas de Colombia y Méjico con extracto de las memorias de los diferentes ministros a los congresos de estas repúblicas.

352

N.º 328. — 30 de marzo, Filadelfia.

El Callao se mantenía firme; había salido de Valparaíso la expedición contra Chiloé con 3.500 hombres al mando de Freyre; en relación con Cuba decía que había un depósito de armas en

Cartagena destinado a la proyectada expedición para llevar la revolución a esta isla; empezaría el ataque por el sur, Santiago, Guantánamo, etc., donde se esperaba encontrar poca resistencia; pero la verdadera expedición se concertaría en Panamá adonde iban llegando tropas del Perú; el ministro de la Guerra mejicano aconsejaba la intervención de Bolívar para obtener un resultado seguro. Se decía, que el gobierno americano había buscado la mediación de varias potencias de Europa para inducir a España a reconocer la independencia de sus posesiones en América.

353

N.º 332. — 10 de abril, Filadelfia.

Informa que el 23 de enero último se había rendido Callao; Rodil no teniendo ya más que 500 hombres, había capitulado con el general Salon.

354

N.º 334. — 20 de abril, Filadelfia.

Hacía referencia a las rendiciones de Callao y Chiloé. Inglaterra y Francia habían enviado agentes al congreso de Panamá, donde hasta ahora no había sino representantes americanos. El coronel van Halen se ofrecía para ayudar a Mina a efectuar una contrarrevolución en España.

355

N.º 336. — 10 de mayo, Filadelfia.

Remite recorte de gaceta diciendo que el Tribunal Supremo había fallado en contra de Gualberto Ortega.

356

N.º 337. — 15 de mayo, Filadelfia.

Remite estado de las fuerzas marítimas de Colombia y Méjico. Cuba había adquirido mayor seguridad por refuerzos recibidos últimamente, lo que había hecho a los insurgentes desistir de su proyecto de invasión.

Adjunto:

— Relación de las fuerzas y recursos de los colombianos y mejicanos a principios de 1826.

357

N.º 340. — 30 de mayo, Filadelfia.

Da cuenta del peligro en que se encontraba Colombia por una insurrección que se proyectaba contra ella.

358

N.º 349. — 13 de julio, Filadelfia.

Informa que el emperador del Brasil había abdicado la corona de Portugal en favor de su hija María, y del discurso del presidente de Méjico al clausurarse el congreso.

Adjunto:

— Minuta a Rivas acusando recibo de varios despachos (Aranjuez, 31 de mayo 1826).

359

N.º 351. — 24 de julio, Filadelfia.

Anuncia remisión de un documento con los reglamentos comerciales de Colombia y sus relaciones con Estados Unidos.

360

N.º 353. — 29 de julio, Filadelfia.

Habían llegado algunos prisioneros procedentes de Chile y Perú pidiendo ayuda para regresar a España. Rivas se queja una vez más de la falta de recursos de su legación y por tanto de la imposibilidad de atender estos gastos.

Adjunto:

— Minuta al secretario de Hacienda diciendo de parte del rey que no se retrasasen los pagos a la legación española en Estados Unidos (Palacio, 8 de octubre 1826).

361

N.º 356. — 15 de agosto, Filadelfia.

Da varias noticias: que el comandante Porter, americano, había entrado al servicio de Méjico, quien en opinión de Rivas, podría perjudicar los intereses españoles. Varios buques sueco-colombianos estaban embargados en Nueva York. El ministro inglés para Colombia, Alexander Corburn, se había vuelto desde la Costa Firme cuando supo la insurreción del general Páez en aquel país.

362

N.º 357. — 18 de agosto, Filadelfia.

Da las gracias por el pago de las letras que había librado a principios de año.

CORRESPONDENCIA DE RIVAS CON MANUEL GONZÁLEZ SALMÓN

363

N.º 358. — 28 de agosto, Filadelfia.

Informa sobre: el congreso de Panamá; llegada de Bolívar a Bogotá y venta en pública subasta de los buques sueco-colombianos detenidos en Nueva York.

364

N.º 360. — 4 de septiembre, Filadelfia.

Comunica varias noticias: venta de dos buques sueco-colombianos; disputas que Bolívar había tenido en Lima con el congreso; en Puerto Rico se había descubierto una conspiración bastante seria de los negros, probablemente tramada por los agentes de Santo Domingo o Haití.

365

N.º 361. — 9 de septiembre, Filadelfia.

Anuncia remisión del dictamen pronunciado por Vidaurre en la inauguración del congreso de Panamá, que más adelante se había trasladado a Méjico por ser Panamá poco saludable. Hay dos ejemplares.

366

N.º 363. — 20 de septiembre, Filadelfia.

Da cuenta de los preparativos de una expedición secreta que proyectaban los insurgentes en el Pacífico. La escuadra de Laborde había sido destrozada por un temporal entre la Habana y la Costa Firme.

367

N.º 364. — 22 de septiembre, Filadelfia.

Anuncia remisión de una gaceta que hablaba de los tratados públicos y secretos que los representantes en el congreso de Panamá habían firmado el 15 de julio antes de separarse para volverse a reunir en Tacubaya, junto a Méjico. Da noticias de la escuadra de Laborde.

Adjunto:
— Nota informativa al rey notificando lo anterior.

368

N.º 370. — 11 de octubre, Filadelfia.

Sigue dando noticias de la Costa Firme. Maracaibo había declarado que se mantenía neutral en la contienda entre Páez y el gobierno de Bogotá. El comandante Porter tomaría el mando de las fuerzas marítimas combinadas de Méjico y Colombia.

369

N.º 371. — 21 de octubre, Filadelfia.

Dice que había vuelto a la Habana el cónsul Francisco Hernández Nogués.

370

N.º 372. — 22 de octubre, Filadelfia.

Informa de los socorros que había proporcionado a dos oficiales del bergantín español General Eustaquio, arribado a Norfolk por temporal.

371

N.º 373. — 23 de octubre, Filadelfia.

Acusa recibo de los oficios relativos a los gastos de cada ministerio, nombramiento de Francisco Stoughton para suceder a su padre, y otros.

372

N.º 375. — 24 de octubre, Filadelfia.

Anuncia remisión de la convención de comercio y navegación de Estados Unidos con Dinamarca, ventajosa para la Unión.

373

N.º 382. — 15 de noviembre, Filadelfia.

Acusa recibo al secretario de Estado Manuel González Salmón, del oficio en el que le comunicaba su nombramiento como secretario de Estado y del despacho interinamente; y de otro relativo al pago de sueldos por el real giro a los representantes en Estados Unidos, del cual daría traslado a los cónsules.

374

N.º 384. — 19 de noviembre, Filadelfia.

Anuncia remisión de varias gacetas de Caracas y Guayaquil; una de ellas contenía una proclama del general Páez en la que decía que había tomado el mando a instancia del pueblo que deseaba reformas en la constitución, y para que se restableciera el orden y la tranquilidad en la república, el pueblo debía manifestar sus deseos con toda libertad; reunido acto seguido el cabildo de Caracas había declarado que la voluntad popular era que se representara al congreso y gobierno de Bogotá el deseo de que una gran convención decidiera las reformas más convenientes. Esto parecía indicar que Páez y los jefes que le habían seguido trataban de volver a la obediencia del gobierno de Bogotá sin efusión de sangre. Personas conocedoras de aquel país opinaba que Bolívar se había valido de Briceño, el intendente Mendoza y una hermana del mismo Bolívar, residente en Caracas, para inducir a Páez a abandonar su empresa; también habría influido en su decisión el deseo de evitar una guerra civil de consecuencias desastrosas. No era cierto que, como decían las gacetas, Páez hubiera licenciado sus tropas ni que el general Marcero hubiera arreglado con él sus diferencias. Se decía que Bermúdez había vuelto a Cumaná; que la isla de Margarita se había insurreccionado y separándose del departamento de Maturín, al que pertenecía, se había unido al de Venezuela; el cabildo de Puerto Cabello había disentido de los de Valencia y Caracas; el de Guayaquil había propuesto que se le diera a Bolívar la dictadura perpetua, a lo que se había adherido el de Quito y probablemente también el de Cartagena. Las gacetas afirmaban que se había descubierto en Lima una seria conspiración contra Bolívar. Según decían algunos testigos, el comandante Laborde había regresado a la isla de Cuba, quedando su navío desmantelado enfrente de Baracoa; los demás buques de su escuadra habían llegado a buen puerto y reparadas las averías estarían listos para volver a cruzar, según había comunicado el general Vives. Estaba próximo para salir para el congreso de Tacubaya, mister Sergeant. El gobierno americano estaba molesto con el de Méjico porque sus cruceros habían detenido varios de sus buques apoderándose de la correspondencia que conducían, y no se había vuelto a hablar del tratado que se decía que tenían concluido en Méjico.

375

N.º 386. — 3 de diciembre, Filadelfia.

En las gacetas que adjuntaba había detalles muy interesantes acerca de la conspiración contra Bolívar descubierta en el Perú de la que había dado cuenta; había sido elegido presidente de la república de su nombre, cuya constitución había forjado a su gusto; pero su ambición lo empujaba a intervenir también en las de Perú, Colombia y Chile; en Perú se había insurreccionado un cuerpo de tropa apostado en las cercanías de Huamanga y se había tramado una conspiración cuyo objeto era desarmar a los colombianos y asesinar o al menos expulsar del Perú a Bolívar; pero descubierta por éste la conspiración, había arrestado a los principales jefes del Perú y de Buenos Aires acusándolos de alta traición, y estaba remitiendo a Colombia toda la artillería peruana; entre los arrestados estaban el almirante Guise y el general peruano Nicochea. Había que esperar el efecto que producirían estas noticias en la Costa Firme y en el congreso de Tacubaya, pues era probable que los gobiernos de Buenos Aires y Chile no aprobasen la conducta de Bolívar, que era el promotor de dicho congreso. Había embarcado para Veracruz mister Sergeant y su secretario de legación. Estaba próximo a partir para el Brasil donde iba en calidad de encargado de negocios el coronel Palacios, primo de Bolívar. El navío Asia había entrado en la isla de Puna a reparar, para poder doblar el cabo de Hornos.

376

N.º 387. — 6 de diciembre, Filadelfia.

El día cuatro de diciembre había iniciado sus sesiones el congreso y el presidente había presentado su mensaje; refiriéndose a la muerte del emperador Alejandro de Rusia, decía que tuvo con él una comunicación franca y confidencial acerca de los asuntos de América meridional.

377

N.º 389. — 12 de diciembre, Filadelfia.

Informa de la desintegración de la república de Colombia a consecuencia de la insurrección del general Páez; el 28 de agosto Guayaquil se había separado del gobierno de Bogotá, adoptando la constitución dada por Bolívar y declarándolo dictador; Quito y Panamá habían seguido el mismo ejemplo de Guayaquil. Venezuela y el Apure se declararon independientes, continuando Páez con el mando civil y militar y convocando un congreso constituyente, al tiempo que se prevenía contra Mendoza que se declaraba en favor del gobierno de Bogotá y contra Páez; el general Bermúdez había sitiado Cumaná por mar y tierra, quedando así iniciada una verdadera guerra civil. Hay tres ejemplares iguales.

378

N.º 390. — 13 de diciembre, Filadelfia.

Por una carta de Lima había conocido más detalles de la conspiración que se había tramado contra Bolívar y de la situación en que se hallaba aquel país; estaban arrinconadas las fuerzas navales y se habían marchado muchos extranjeros que se habían alistado en ellas y lo mismo había ocurrido en Colombia, donde apenas había medios para mantener la marina. Se decía que Páez había hecho desmantelar todos los buques que había en Cartagena. Iguales dificultades padecían los mejicanos para mantener su marina con lo que quedaban en suspenso todos sus proyectos de invadir Cuba. Hay dos ejemplares.

379

N.º 391. — 18 de diciembre, Filadelfia.

Acusa recibo de varios oficios y agradece la gestión realizada acerca del secretario del despacho de Hacienda para el pago de sus sueldos. Hay dos ejemplares.

380

N.º 392. — 18 de diciembre, Filadelfia.

Anuncia remisión de unas gacetas que insertaban la vuelta de Bolívar a Colombia y la proclama que había pronunciado en Guayaquil; probablemente su presencia calmaría las luchas que había en la república, al menos de momento. Hay dos ejemplares.

381

N.º 393. — 24 de diciembre, Filadelfia.

Inserta un oficio que había enviado a las autoridades de las islas de Cuba y Puerto Rico, en el que les comunicaba que el día 5 del presente mes pensaba salir al mar el comandante Porter con varios buques, con intención, según parecía, de hacer una incursión en las costas sur de Puerto Rico. Anuncia remisión de unas gacetas de Méjico en las que ni siquiera se mencionaba el congreso de Tacubaya, del que opinaban en Veracruz que no llegaría a celebrarse. Hay dos ejemplares.

382

N.º 394. — 26 de diciembre, Filadelfia.

Noticias de Guatemala, donde reinaba la mayor anarquía y confusión; se confirmaba la guerra civil. Trata también del congreso de Panamá. Hay dos ejemplares.

383

N.º 395. — 31 de diciembre, Filadelfia.

Anuncia remisión de las cuentas de gastos ordinarios y extraordinarios de su legación, correspondientes al último trimestre del año, que ascendían a 1.397 pesos, así como la cuenta general de todo el año, de la que resultaba un saldo a favor de Rivas de 7.044 pesos.

LEGAJO 5.653

AÑO 1827

CORRESPONDENCIA DEL ENCARGADO DE NEGOCIOS ESPAÑOL EN
ESTADOS UNIDOS, HILARIO RIVAS Y SALMÓN CON EL SECRETARIO
DE ESTADO, MANUEL GONZALEZ SALMÓN

384

N.º 396. — 1 de enero, Filadelfia.

A pesar de varias reales órdenes disponiendo que le fueran devengados los gastos de la legación, había concluido el año sin
recibir cantidad alguna con lo que sus atrasos ascendían ya a siete
mil duros. Como no le era posible continuar así, se había visto
obligado a librar contra el mismo secretario de Estado una letra
a treinta días vista por la cantidad de cinco mil duros, que esperaba fuera aceptada como en otras ocasiones.

385

N.º 399. — 5 de enero, Filadelfia.

Remite los estados de cuentas que los ministros de Marina y
Hacienda habían presentado al congreso de los Estados Unidos,
relativos a sus respectivos departamentos.

Adjunto:

— Folleto del Departamento del Tesoro americano con los mencionados estados de las finanzas durante 1825 y 1826 (13 de diciembre 1826).

386

N.º 400. — 6 de enero, Filadelfia.

Anuncia remisión de gaceta con noticias relativas a la guerra civil entre Guatemala y Colombia, así como el nuevo arancel de la república de Perú.

387

N.º 401. — 10 de enero, Filadelfia.

Comunica que Bolívar había llegado a Bogotá el día 14 de noviembre y había disuelto el congreso tomando el mando absoluto de la república; había decretado la reducción del ejército y el aumento de los sueldos en la marina y parecía que pensaba trasladar el gobierno a Cartagena, donde iría a mediados de enero.

388

N.º 402. — 20 de enero, Filadelfia.

Acusa recibo de varios oficios relativos a la viuda de Mulvey y su hijo José; éste se hallaba ausente, la viuda y una hija habían fallecido y otro hijo se estaba muriendo. La miseria y la pesadumbre habían acabado con la familia. El agregado de la legación Manuel Barros le había entregado varios oficios que había recibido por medio del cónsul en El Havre, procedentes del secretario de Estado. Acusa recibo de otros oficios y recuerda que hacía seis meses que no recibía gacetas de la corte.

389

N.º 403. — 30 de enero, Filadelfia.

Comunica que el comandante Porter se había hecho a la vela, el 8 de diciembre con cuatro buques, había apresado el bergantín

Hércules, que procedente de Cádiz se dirigía a la Habana, y según decían, había enviado recado al comandante Laborde para que fuera al cabo San Antonio si quería batirse; éste había aceptado el reto saliendo en su busca con tres fragatas y algunos buques menores, y mantenía a Porter bloqueado en Cayo Hueso, donde se había refugiado.

Anuncia remisión de varias gacetas con interesantes noticias: continuaba la guerra civil en Guatemala y la de Colombia había amainado con la llegada de Bolívar, estando Páez, que la había iniciado, completamente sometido al Libertador. Hay dos ejemplares.

390

N.º 404. — 4 de febrero, Filadelfia.

Por vía de la Guayra había recibido noticias de la llegada de Bolívar a Maracaibo, Puerto Cabello y Valencia, debiendo hacer su triunfal entrada en Caracas el día 9 ó 10; se había hecho con el mando absoluto, logrando pacificar el país sin derramar una gota de sangre; había prometido olvidar lo pasado y lejos de desaprobar la insurrección de Páez le había confirmado en el mando civil y militar de Venezuela. Anuncia remisión de las últimas proclamas de Bolívar y unas gacetas con noticias de Méjico, entre ellas el discurso de su presidente al cerrar el congreso. Había concluido un tratado de amistad y comercio con los Estados Unidos.

Habían llegado a Veracruz dos presas españolas que había hecho Porter; según noticias procedentes de Cartagena se estaba preparando la escuadra colombiana para unirse a la de Méjico y el famoso Pioli, fugado de la isla de Cuba, se ocupaba de recluir en Nueva York marineros para Cartagena, y hacer venir por Panamá los que tenían en el Pacífico los colombianos y peruanos. Probablemente Bolívar y los suyos pondrían todo su interés en crear una marina según las recomendaciones del congreso de Panamá.

391

N.º 405. — 24 de febrero, Filadelfia.

Noticias de Méjico aseguraban que se habían sublevado los indios de la Sonora y algunos indios y colonos en la provincia de

Tejas, y además se había descubierto una conspiración en la capital en favor del rey de España; el gobierno mejicano aprovechaba estos incidentes para deshacerse de algunas personas. Discurso del presidente mejicano sobre el estado del país.

392

N.º 408. — 26 de marzo, Filadelfia.

Acusa recibo de varios oficios y comunica que hacía ocho meses que no recibía gacetas de la corte.

393

N.º 409. — 27 de enero, Filadelfia.

En cumplimiento de la real orden de 7 de enero último había pasado una nota al secretario de Estado pidiendo respuesta a las que había enviado anteriormente relativas a la reclamación de Juan Miguel Losada.

394

N.º 410. — 28 de marzo, Filadelfia.

Anuncia el envío, con especial recomendación, de un memorial del antiguo cónsul Pablo Chacón.

395

N.º 411. — 28 de marzo, Filadelfia.

Da cuenta de que había participado al agregado de la legación Manuel Barros, la real orden de 26 de diciembre último, y justifica la decisión que había tomado de suspenderlo en su destino por razones de conveniencia para el real servicio, medida que no había sido aprobada; había basado su resolución, sin mala fe, en la práctica observada con los cónsules en Estados Unidos por sus inmediatos antecesores Joaquín de Anduaga y Mateo de la Serna.

396

N.º 412. — 28 de marzo, Filadelfia.

Da cuenta del tratado de comercio y navegación concluido entre Estados Unidos y Méjico, al que el senado americano intentaba hacer algunas modificaciones favorables a su gobierno. Volvía a hablarse de una expedición contra Cuba y Puerto Rico, a pesar de que Cuba había sido reforzada tanto en el interior como en sus costas. Se anunciaba en Méjico la instalación de un congreso en Tacubaya. Bolívar había dimitido de su presidencia absoluta en Colombia, pero parecía una maniobra política para aumentar su poder erigiéndose presidente vitalicio de Colombia, Perú y Bolivia, formando una federación entre ellas.

397

N.º 413. — 3 de abril, Filadelfia.

Amplía las noticias sobre la proyectada expedición contra Cuba diciendo que Bolívar había enviado a Páez a los Llanos a recoger tropas con este objeto, al mismo tiempo que hizo marchar a Cartagena el célebre batallón del Apure y otras fuerzas más, con un total de cuatro a cinco mil hombres, contando además con recursos de Inglaterra, cuya guerra con España creía inevitable y próxima. Confirma el nombramiento de Bolívar como presidente de Perú y lo mismo sucedería en Colombia. Hay dos ejemplares.

398

N.º 414. — 26 de abril, Filadelfia.

Anuncia una nueva revolución en Perú en la que había participado activamente el general Santa Cruz, a quien Bolívar confió este gobierno en su ausencia y que había declarado forzada la constitución boliviana y convocado un congreso nacional para que adoptase otra más conveniente. Esta revolución podría estropear los planes ambiciosos de Bolívar en Colombia, donde el general Santander pretendía hacerse con el poder. Guayaquil, Quito, Cartagena y Caracas seguían favorables a la constitución de Bolívar.

Adjunto:

— Oficio al secretario del despacho de Guerra informando de lo anterior (Palacio, 6 de junio 1827).

399

N.º 415. — 1 de mayo, Filadelfia.

Noticias de Méjico y Colombia. En Méjico la conspiración del padre Arenas, así como las del padre Martínez, brigadier Arana y generales Echéverri y Negrete, ponían esta república en una delicada situación. Lo mismo ocurría con Colombia donde se estaba llegando a un lastimoso estado de miseria. Bolívar había abandonado su proyectada expedición contra Cuba no sólo por falta de medios sino porque no se había declarado la guerra en Europa contra España.

400

N.º 418. — 20 de mayo, Filadelfia.

Acusa recibo de varios oficios y manifiesta que hacía ya diez meses que no recibía gacetas de la corte.

401

N.º 427. — 27 de junio, Filadelfia.

Anuncia remisión de varias gacetas que contenían el discurso del emperador del Brasil a la apertura del congreso. Da cuenta de que el encargado de negocios de Estados Unidos en Brasil, irritado por la poca consideración con que trataban allí a los buques de su país acusados de violar el bloqueo contra Buenos Aires, había amenazado con marcharse si el emperador no le daba una satisfacción completa, actitud que adoptaba siempre que presentaba alguna queja; esta vez su amenaza no había surtido efecto y el emperador le había concedido el pasaporte, llegando a Washington hacía un par de semanas. El representante en Estados Unidos del emperador del Brasil había mantenido varias conferencias con el secretario de Estado sobre aquellas desavenencias, arreglando amigablemente el asunto.

Las tropas colombianas que habían causado la última revolución en el Perú se habían embarcado hacia Colombia y marchaban contra Guayaquil que se había unido a Bolívar; probablemente las habría llamado el general Santander para defender al gobierno de Bogotá, a donde intentaba pasar el Libertador. Aseguraban que el congreso había admitido su renuncia y que el general Sucre había determinado defenderlo y mantener la constitución boliviana en el alto Perú.

402

N.º 430. — 9 de julio, Filadelfia.

Acusa recibo de varios oficios, y pide se le remita la guía del año.

403

N.º 431. — 13 de julio, Filadelfia.

Avisa la llegada a Nueva York del nuevo ministro Francisco Tacón.

404

N.º 432. — 29 de julio, Filadelfia.

Anuncia remisión de gacetas con noticias de Colombia donde se había vuelto a encender la guerra civil.

405

N.º 433. — 9 de julio, Filadelfia.

Avisa que Francisco Tacón, ministro español, había sido presentado y reconocido por el gobierno americano.

406

N.º 435. — 30 de julio, Filadelfia.

Dice que habiendo cesado como encargado de negocios y dado que le debían cantidades, por más de 4.700 pesos, se le librasen al menos 4.000 pesos, quedando el resto para cobrar por la intendencia de la Habana.

CORRESPONDENCIA DE FRANCISCO TACÓN, MINISTRO ESPAÑOL
EN ESTADOS UNIDOS, CON EL SECRETARIO DE ESTADO
MANUEL GONZÁLEZ SALMÓN

407

N.º 10. — 26 de mayo, Havre.

Comunica que se encontraba en este puerto esperando su salida para Nueva York.

408

N.º 11. — 12 de julio, Nueva York.

Participa su llegada a Nueva York después de treinta y ocho días de navegación.

409

N.º 12. — 25 de julio, Filadelfia.

Da cuenta de que había presentado sus credenciales al presidente americano y había establecido contacto con los encargados de negocios de Rusia y Suecia. Hay dos ejemplares.

Adjunto:

— Extracto de una carta del corresponsal español en la Habana con diversas noticias. Dice que había prosperidad y tranquilidad bajo el mando del general Vives y que se proyectaba establecer un Banco con la protección del gobierno (Habana, 30 de julio 1827).

410

N.º 13. — 1 de agosto, Filadelfia.

Dice que se había hecho cargo del archivo de la legación y que estaba en perfecto orden a partir de la llegada de Vives, pero lo correspondiente a la época anterior necesitaba una metódica clasificación. En cuanto al material e instalaciones de despacho necesitaban también una renovación. Hay dos ejemplares.

411

N.º 14. — 1 de agosto, Filadelfia.

Comunica que había participado su nombramiento como ministro español en Estados Unidos, a los embajadores y ministros de las cortes de Europa así como a los capitanes generales de Cuba y Puerto Rico.

412

N.º 17. — 10 de agosto, Filadelfia.

Remite una instancia de la viuda de Carlos Mulvey, que fue vicecónsul de Savannah, solicitando los sueldos que se debían a su marido.

Adjunto:

— La citada instancia donde exponía la precaria situación de su familia (Filadelfia, 25 de julio 1824).

413

N.º 19. — 11 de agosto, Filadelfia.

Da cuenta del debate entre la legislatura de Veracruz y el ministro de Estados Unidos Poinsett, a quien se acusaba de intervenir en los negocios internos de Méjico. Se había reunido en la Habana un consejo de guerra para discutir la posibilidad de atacar la escuadrilla mejicana en Cayo Hueso. Llegada de Bolívar a Cartagena donde se preparaba con 12.000 hombres para dirigirse a Bogotá. Hay dos ejemplares.

414

N.º 20. — 11 de agosto, Filadelfia.

Daría cumplimiento a la real orden que prohibía a los empleados diplomáticos y cónsules españoles librar contra el tesoro real sin previa autorización y rogaba que se estableciese algún medio seguro para que los funcionarios españoles en Estados Unidos recibieran con regularidad sus sueldos. Hay dos ejemplares.

415

N.º 21. — 24 de agosto, Filadelfia.

Avisa de varias noticias transmitidas por el oficial español José Llorente, que había estado prisionero en Colombia; la llegada de Bolívar a Cartagena procedente de Caracas, quien quería dirigirse con tropas a Bogotá para reducir al vicepresidente Santander y su partido, que tenían sometido al pueblo a una gran penuria. Hay dos ejemplares.

416

N.º 22. — 24 de agosto, Filadelfia.

En contestación a la real orden de 27 de abril último dice no haberse encontrado noticias acerca de la reclamación de Roberto Oliver.

417

N.º 23. — 24 de agosto, Filadelfia.

Da cuenta de que habían sido ahorcados en Richmond tres españoles por haber cooperado con el francés Tardy a asesinar a la tripulación y pasajeros del bergantín de Nueva York, Crawford, con el objeto de robar el buque y su cargamento y conducirlo todo a Hamburgo. Por tratarse de un crimen de esta naturaleza Tacón no había intervenido en favor de los españoles.

Adjunto:

— Un párrafo del Herald, con su traducción explicando extensamente las circunstancias del atentado (15 de junio 1827). Hay dos ejemplares.

418

N.º 24. — 25 de agosto, Filadelfia.

Propone que pasen a depender de su legación los archivos y sellos de los viceconsulados vacantes por no estar debidamente custodiados.

Adjunto:

— Relación de los archivos existentes en Charleston, Savannah, Panzacola, Alejandría, etc. con noticias de su paradero.

419

N.º 25. — 25 de agosto, Filadelfia.

Remite traducido un artículo de la gaceta de Nueva York hablando de la feliz situación en Cuba bajo el general Vives.

Adjunto:

— Traducción del artículo en el que se decía que entre otras mejoras, estaba el proyecto de establecer un banco bien constituido patrocinado por el gobierno (14 de agosto 1827).

420

N.º 27. — 28 de agosto, Filadelfia.

Enviaba noticias de Méjico, donde aumentaba la inquietud; los masones estaban decididos a quitar la presidencia a Vitoria. Parecía confirmarse que el gobierno americano había sustituido a su ministro, Poisett, por un encargado de negocios, en vista de los fuertes enfrentamientos de éste con la legislatura de Veracruz. El comodoro Porter regresó de Veracruz a Cayo Hueso con un pequeño refuerzo para repetir sus incursiones sobre las costas de Cuba. Se esperaban noticias del resultado del viaje de Bolívar a Bogotá. Acuerdo de paz entre Brasil y Buenos Aires.

Adjunto:

— Minuta al presidente de la Junta Suprema de Sanidad comunicándole que en Charleston se habían registrado algunos casos de fiebre amarilla. Sin fecha.

421

N.º 30. — 30 de agosto, Filadelfia.

Anuncia remisión de un extracto de gaceta diciendo que las autoridades de Cuba se habían quejado de que las fuerzas de Méjico, bajo el mando de Porter, habían violado la neutralidad de Cayo Hueso, y que se había encargado al comandante Ridgely, jefe de la escuadra americana en el golfo de Méjico, de hacer las indagaciones necesarias.

Adjunto:

— Copias traducidas de dos cartas de Porter: una al editor de la «Louisiana Advertiser» donde le negaba los cargos que hacían contra él, diciendo que el colectivo del puerto y todos sus habitantes lo habían defendido (Nueva Orleans, 31 de julio 1827); en la segunda carta, dirigida al comandante Ridgely, Porter decía que carecía de fundamento la acusación de haber violado la neutralidad de Estados Unidos; pedía que se le avisase de oficio cuando al gobierno americano le desagradase que las fuerzas navales de Méjico disfrutaran de la hospitalidad de Cayo Hueso (Panzacola, 13 de julio 1827). Hay dos ejemplares.

422

N.º 32. — 12 de febrero, Filadelfia.

Quedaba enterado del asesinato perpetrado por los tripulantes del corsario Palmira, del que había sido informado anteriormente.

423

N.º 33. — 12 de septiembre, Filadelfia.

Dice que daría cumplimiento a la orden relacionada con el esclavo a quien se refería el capitán general de Puerto Rico.

424

N.º 34. — 12 de septiembre, Filadelfia.

Quedaba enterado y daría cumplimiento a la propuesta de que Antonio Pomar quedara encargado interinamente del consulado de Norfolk.

425

N.º 36. — 13 de septiembre, Filadelfia.

Anuncia remisión de un manifiesto del general Santander, vicepresidente de Colombia, justificándose de las acusaciones que se le habían hecho de entorpecer los planes de Bolívar. La guerra y la miseria continuaban en Perú, Guatemala y Méjico, y en San Salvador seguía la guerra civil.

426

N.º 37. — 20 de septiembre, Filadelfia.

Participa que había dado pasaporte para España a Pablo Chacón que venía desempeñando el consulado de Norfolk.

427

N.º 39. — 28 de septiembre, Filadelfia.

Remite traducido el tratado de paz concluido entre el emperador del Brasil y el representante de Buenos Aires, que no había sido ratificado porque el representante argentino se había excedido en sus atribuciones.

Adjunto:

— El mencionado tratado, publicado en la gaceta de Baltimore de 19 de septiembre 1827. Extracto de otra gaceta donde se daban las razones por las que el gobierno de Buenos Aires había desaprobado el tratado, pero que estaba dispuesto a llegar a un arreglo y fijar los límites territoriales de ambos Estados y establecer las relaciones comerciales (Baltimore, 20 de septiembre 1827).

428

N.º 41. — 29 de septiembre, Filadelfia.

Da cuenta de un informe del cónsul de Baltimore acerca de los corsarios que se estaban armando en aquel puerto. En él se mencionaba a dos en concreto que decían se estaban habilitando para el transporte de negros aunque su verdadero destino parecía dirigirse contra el comercio español.

429

N.º 45. — 30 de septiembre, Filadelfia.

Anuncia remisión de gacetas de Colombia y Méjico. El mensaje del vicepresidente de Colombia al congreso ponía de manifiesto las dificultades para conseguir su emancipación. Anunciaba la llegada de Bolívar a Mompós para preparar un ataque contra Bogotá.

Continuaba la guerra civil en Guatemala y había peligro de que se emprendiera en Méjico ya que se habían sublevado en Veracruz parte de la guarnición.

430

N.º 46. — 13 de octubre, Filadelfia.

Comunica la información que había recibido de los distintos cónsules en relación con los emigrados de América, de los que dicen no hallarse apenas en sus distritos. Hay dos ejemplares.

431

N.º 47. — 14 de octubre, Filadelfia.

Había tenido noticias de que el gobierno revolucionario de Chile proyectaba una expedición contra Manila, para lo que estaba habilitando varios buques, algunos desde Holanda, que debían reunirse en Valparaíso con este fin. Tacón había pasado aviso al capitán general de Filipinas a fin de que estuviera prevenido.

432

N.º 48. — 14 de octubre, Filadelfia.

Da cuenta de su viaje a Washington, donde había ido para presentar una reclamación al gobierno americano sobre la conducta del aventurero Porter y más concretamente, sobre la construcción y armamento de la corbeta mejicana Kensington.

433

N.º 49. — 14 de octubre, Filadelfia.

Anuncia remisión de una gaceta de Buenos Aires con las negociaciones de paz entre esta república y Brasil: el emperador de esta nación abandonaba el derecho que creía tener a la banda oriental. Hay dos ejemplares.

434

N.º 50. — 14 de octubre, Filadelfia.

En relación con el robo cometido en la goleta española Dolores por un corsario insurgente, decía no tener noticias concretas.

435

N.º 51. — 14 de agosto, Filadelfia.

Daría cumplimiento a la orden de 19 de agosto último relativa a Wallenstein.

436

N.º 52. — 14 de octubre, Filadelfia.

Haría las pertinentes gestiones con el gobernador americano para conseguir le fuesen devueltas al marqués de Casa Irujo las tierras que compró en Florida occidental. Hay dos ejemplares.

VIII. — 12

437

N.º 53. — 14 de agosto, Filadelfia.

Informa de varias noticias: decreto del congreso de Méjico expulsando a los españoles que hubieran venido de la península a partir de 1824; parece que este decreto era efecto de la conspiración del padre Arenas, que había inspirado desconfianza en los naturales del país, quienes temían una invasión desde Cuba. En la Costa Firme triunfaba el partido de Bolívar contra Santander. Hay dos ejemplares.

438

N.º 56. — 28 de octubre, Filadelfia.

Avisa la llegada a Nueva York de Francisco Armenteros, procedente de París y Londres y de su salida para la Habana. En todos estos viajes no tenía sus pasaportes debidamente autorizados. Hay dos ejemplares.

439

N.º 59. — 30 de octubre, Filadelfia.

Daría cumplimiento a la real orden por la que se había dispuesto que los cónsules remitiesen las cuentas de los gastos de sus respectivos consulados. Hay dos ejemplares.

440

N.º 60. — 30 de octubre, Filadelfia.

Las últimas noticias de Buenos Aires decían que no se terminaba el acuerdo de paz con Brasil sino que por el contrario, había nuevos preparativos para continuar la guerra. Hay dos ejemplares.

441

N.º 61. — 30 de octubre, Filadelfia.

Anuncia remisión de gacetas de Colombia diciendo que Bolívar había llegado a Bogotá y que fue bien recibido en Guayaquil. Creían que el general Sucre volvería a Colombia. Había sido decretada la expulsión de todos los españoles de Méjico y en Guatemala seguían este ejemplo. Hay dos ejemplares.

442

N.º 64. — 14 de noviembre, Filadelfia.

Avisa de que se habían establecido en Nueva York paquetes para Gibraltar debiendo salir uno cada mes desde ambos puertos.

443

N.º 65. — 14 de noviembre, Filadelfia.

Remite copia de algunos párrafos de la gaceta de Colombia.
Adjunto:
— Extracto de la Gaceta de Colombia con un decreto especificando la fuerza efectiva del ejército de esta república. Francia y las ciudades Hanseáticas habían reconocido la independencia y soberanía de Colombia. Nombramiento de obispos y juramento del de Andalucía, promociones eclesiásticas, y otros asuntos.

444

N.º 66. — 14 de noviembre, Filadelfia.

Da cuenta del oficio que había pasado al capitán general de Filipinas sobre un proyecto de expedición contra estas islas.

445

N.º 67. — 14 de noviembre, Filadelfia.

Anuncia remisión de varias gacetas de Méjico conteniendo las discusiones que se habían suscitado en el congreso de esta república por haberse decretado la expulsión de los españoles, medida considerada por el senado como anticonstitucional. Esta disposición había ocasionado muchos atropellos, robos e incluso muertes a los españoles establecidos en Méjico, y algunos abandonaban el país voluntariamente. Continuaba la guerra entre Buenos Aires y Brasil.

446

N.º 68. — 28 de noviembre, Filadelfia.

Daría cumplimiento a la orden por la que debía pedir al cónsul de Nueva Orleans copia del expediente seguido en Yucatán por el atropello del vicecónsul Villavaso.

447

N.º 71. — 28 de noviembre, Filadelfia.

Da cuenta de haberse publicado en casi todas las gacetas de Estados Unidos el resultado de la balanza general del comercio de Cuba, lo que sería un estímulo para emprender operaciones mercantiles que aumentasen el progreso del comercio y agricultura en aquella isla.

Adjunto:

— Extracto de gaceta traducido con las consideraciones arriba indicadas (Habana, 28 de octubre 1827).

448

N.º 73. — 28 de noviembre, Filadelfia.

Parecía que Porter tenía el plan de apoderarse de la fragata Perla, que iba desde la Habana a Cádiz con un importante botín; se lo había comunicado al capitán general de Cuba para que tomase medidas. Los agentes de Francia en Bogotá habían tomado ya el título de cónsules.

449

N.º 74. — 30 de noviembre, Filadelfia.

Da cuenta de los libramientos hechos contra las cajas de la intendencia de la Habana a favor de los empleados de la legación y cónsules españoles.

Adjunto:

— Copia del oficio de Claudio Martínez de Pinillos, intendente de la Habana, a Francisco Tacón, felicitándolo por su nombramiento para ministro residente español en Estados Unidos y le avisa que podían pagarse con cargo a las intendencias de la Habana, los atrasos de los empleados españoles (Habana, 4 de octubre 1827).

— Respuesta de Tacón acusando recibo y acompañando una lista particular de dichos libramientos (Filadelfia, 30 de noviembre 1827).

450

N.º 75. — 2 de diciembre, Filadelfia.

Acusa recibo de varias reales órdenes.

451

N.º 76. — 26 de diciembre, Filadelfia.

Dice que daría cumplimiento a la real orden de 13 de septiembre último relativa a los españoles que llegaron a Estados Unidos emigrados de las posesiones españolas en América.

452

N.º 77. — 2 de diciembre, Filadelfia.

Acusa recibo del oficio por el que se ordenaba no librar letras contra esa secretaría de Estado.

453

N.ºˢ 79, 80. — 2 de diciembre, Filadelfia.

Acusa recibo de varios oficios con noticias de los reyes. Hay dos ejemplares.

454

N.º 82. — 6 de diciembre, Filadelfia.

Remite el mensaje del presidente americano al congreso, correspondiente al 4 de diciembre. Hay dos ejemplares.

Adjunto:

— Mensaje incluido en un recorte del «National Intelligencer», y la traducción. Ponía de manifiesto las dificultades en el desarrollo del tratado de 1782 y 1783 entre Estados Unidos y Gran Bretaña, principalmente en la cuestión de límites y comercio, y las medidas adoptadas para mantener una relación amistosa entre ambos países. No había novedades en las relaciones con el resto de las naciones europeas. Proyecto de un tratado de comercio con Suecia. Disposiciones amistosas de Estados Unidos hacia las repúblicas del sur como lo demostraban al apoyar el tratado de Panamá, así como el tratado de paz firmado entre Buenos Aires y Brasil. Conflictos con los indios en distintos puntos de la Unión. Mejora gradual de la marina y puesta en marcha del proyecto de defensa nacional (Washington, 4 de diciembre 1827). Hay dos ejemplares.

455

N.º 84. — 13 de diciembre, Filadelfia.

Informa de la elección de Stevenson para presidente de la cámara de diputados. Hay dos ejemplares.

456

N.º 85. — 13 de diciembre, Filadelfia.

Anuncia remisión de periódicos de Méjico y Veracruz y participa que estaban próximas a salir de la Habana las principales fuerzas marítimas.

457

N.º 86. — 13 de diciembre, Filadelfia.

Quedaba enterado de la real orden disponiendo, que sólo podía incluirse en gastos extraordinarios el coste de los armarios necesarios para guardar los papeles del archivo de su legación, pero no el resto de los efectos de la secretaría.

458

N.º 87. — 24 de diciembre, Filadelfia.

Remite copia relativa a la reclamación que Losada había enviado al gobierno americano.

Adjunto:

— El ministro contador de Hacienda, Juan Miguel de Losada pedía a Clay, secretario de Estado americano, que le fuera devuelto un terreno de su propiedad (Filadelfia, 20 de diciembre 1827).

459

N.º 88. — 24 de diciembre, Filadelfia.

Remite copia de la nota que había pasado al gobierno reclamando el esclavo sustraído en Puerto Rico en la corbeta americana Mary.

Adjunto:

—Nota de Tacón al secretario de Estado americano Enrique Clay (Filadelfia, 21 de diciembre 1827).

460

N.º 91. — 29 de diciembre, Filadelfia.

Anuncia remisión de un folleto de Feliciano Montenegro.

461

N.º 92. — 29 de diciembre, Filadelfia.

Anuncia su próximo viaje a Washington. Hay dos ejemplares.

462

N.º 94. — 29 de diciembre, Filadelfia.

Avisa que un hijo de Luciano Bonaparte, casado con una hija de José, que residía en Estados Unidos desde hacía algunos años, iba a establecerse con su familia en Italia. Hay dos ejemplares.

Adjunto:

— Carta de José Bonaparte a su hermano Napoleón, dando noticias de distintos miembros de la familia (Filadelfia, 25 de enero 1818).

463

N.º 95. — 29 de diciembre, Filadelfia.

Comunica diferentes noticias: había calma en el Perú; el nuevo presidente general Lamar inspiraba confianza; en Chile se preparaba una expedición contra Filipinas; el ministro de Rusia, barón Grudner había sido reconocido por el gobierno americano. Hay dos ejemplares.

464

N.º 96. — 30 de diciembre, Filadelfia.

Anuncia remisión de varios periódicos de Veracruz con noticias del aventurero Porter.

465

N.º 97. — 31 de diciembre, Filadelfia.

Comunica la salida desde la Habana para Costa Firme de varios buques con víveres y dinero efectivo y en letras.

LEGAJO 5.654

AÑO 1828

CORRESPONDENCIA DEL MINISTRO EN ESTADOS UNIDOS, FRANCISCO TACÓN, CON EL SECRETARIO DE ESTADO MANUEL GONZALEZ SALMÓN

466

N.º 99. — 11 de enero, Washington.

Comunica que el ministro plenipotenciario de las ciudades Hanseáticas, mister Rumpf, había concluido un acuerdo comercial con los Estados Unidos por el cual se concedían recíprocamente el privilegio de importar los productos de los países firmantes, con las mismas ventajas que los nacionales. El gobierno de Brasil había reducido de veinticuatro a quince, los derechos de importación respecto a Inglaterra, Francia y las ciudades Hanseáticas.

Adjunto:

— Nota informativa (Madrid, 13 de marzo 1828).

467

N.º 100. — 12 de enero, Washington.

Da cuenta de la cuestión que se había suscitado en la cámara de representantes sobre si los esclavos eran propiedad, motivada por la petición de un ciudadano de Luisiana de ser indemnizado por uno de ellos; había respondido el diputado de Virginia, mister Randolph, poniendo de relieve los temores que debían causar los negros y presentando como inevitable la disolución de la unión federal, si el congreso se apropiaba la facultad de decidir algo en perjuicio de los derechos de propiedad de los dueños de esclavos, que aumentaría la rivalidad entre los estados del norte y los del sur. En el mensaje que mister Clinton, gobernador del de Nueva York, había dirigido a la asamblea de su propio estado con motivo de su apertura, se había referido a la agitación e inquietud que reinaba en todas partes, achacándolo a las intrigas producidas por las frecuentes elecciones de presidente y al privilegio reservado a la cámara de efectuar la elección entre un corto número de candidatos, si en la elección no se llegaba a un acuerdo. Clinton era uno de los más fervorosos partidarios del general Jackson y se creía que ocuparía alguno de los ministerios del gobierno federal, si aquél llegaba a la presidencia del mismo.

468

N.º 101. — 12 de enero, Washington.

Anuncia el envío por el cónsul en Nueva York, de un folleto publicado por el secretario de Estado, Henry Clay, con motivo de la próxima elección de presidente, en el que exponía la opinión desfavorable que le merecía Bolívar; también acompañaba una gaceta de Lima redactada por José María Pando, antes ferviente admirador de Bolívar y ahora enemigo suyo. Había tenido lugar un espantoso terremoto en Bogotá a consecuencia del cual se habían desplomado la mayoría de los edificios de la capital. La legislatura del estado de Veracruz había decretado la expulsión de los españoles europeos. La corbeta colombiana de guerra Bolívar, que había llegado a Nueva York para su reparo, había tenido que venderse por falta de fondos. Estaba próximo para embarcar para su destino, mister Rochester, nombrado representante de Estados Unidos para Guatemala. Dos bergantines y una corbeta españoles estaban cruzando sobre la costa de Veracruz y parecía que habían hecho varias presas.

Adjunto:
— Declaración pública de Henry Clay, refutando los cargos que había presentado contra él el general Andrés Jackson, referentes

a la última elección presidencial. Folleto impreso de 61 páginas, en inglés (Washington, 1827).

— Copia de la orden de Manuel Barragán, gobernador del estado de Veracruz, por la que se expulsaba del territorio a los españoles, medida que debía permanecer en vigor hasta que España reconociera expresamente la independencia de la república de Méjico (Jalapa, 4 de diciembre 1827).

469

N.º 104. — 24 de enero, Washington.

Remite copia de la nota que había pasado al gobierno federal solicitando el reconocimiento y confirmación de las tierras del marqués de Casa Irujo, que se hallaban en territorios que habían estado en litigio antes de la cesión de las Floridas, lo que había puesto en duda el derecho de las autoridades españolas para concederlas. Había pendientes de los tribunales varios pleitos análogos, cuya resolución tendría que ser la misma y aunque aún tardarían dos años en verse, opina que su gestión podía contribuir a que se solucionaran favorablemente.

Adjunto:

— Copia de la carta de Francisco Tacón al secretario de Estado Enrique Clay, exponiendo los antecedentes de dichas tierras, que habían sido concedidas por el intendente de Florida occidental Juan Ventura Morales, en 1804, a Beverley Checo y Ricardo Relf, comerciantes americanos de Nueva Orleans; las tierras estaban situadas en el nuevo establecimiento de Santa Elena, en la margen oeste del río San Vicente, diez y seis millas al sur de la línea divisoria con los Estados Unidos, según constaba en los títulos expedidos por el intendente Morales; los propietarios las habían vendido en enero de 1805 a Daniel Clark, quien en febrero del mismo año las había traspasado al difunto marqués de Casa Irujo, oficial de la primera secretaría del despacho de Estado, por lo que solicitaba que fuera reconocida y confirmada la referida propiedad, en virtud del artículo 8.º del tratado de 22 de febrero.

470

N.º 107. — 27 de marzo, Washington.

Remite un ejemplar del tratado de comercio que acababa de ratificarse entre Suecia y Estados Unidos.

Adjunto:

— Ejemplar impreso del tratado entre Estados Unidos y Suecia firmado en Estocolmo el 4 de julio de 1827, en inglés y francés.

471

N.º 109. — 28 de enero, Washington.

Anuncia remisión de unas gacetas de Méjico donde continuaba el desorden producido por la expulsión de los españoles; en Colombia había producido descontento el intento de Bolívar de hacerse con el mando absoluto y no se habían ajustado a sus deseos el resultado de las elecciones para el congreso extraordinario; un corsario español había apresado y conducido a Puerto Rico un buque colombiano cuyo cargamento se estimaba en cien mil pesos; en Buenos Aires continuaban los preparativos para proseguir la guerra con Brasil.

472

N.º 110. — 10 de febrero, Washington.

Acusa recibo de la correspondencia que había llegado por el correo del El Havre que contenía, entre otras reales órdenes, una para que se publicara en los periódicos de Estados Unidos la noticia de que el día de San Fernando se celebraría la segunda exposición pública de la industria española; otra para que averiguara la importancia de los archivos de los consulados que quedaban vacantes y lo que costaría su conservación y traslado al lugar de su residencia; y otra autorizándolo a residir en cualquier ciudad que no fuera Washington.

473

N.º 112. — 10 de febrero, Washington.

Dispuesto a regresar a Filadelfia en virtud de la real orden de 28 de octubre que había recibido, había ido a despedirse del secretario de Estado, Clay, acompañado del secretario de la legación; le había suplicado que se resolviera satisfactoriamente la reclamación de Losada así como el expediente relativo a la infracción de la neutralidad por el aventurero Porter y por otros ciudadanos americanos; Clay había respondido que, pese a su deseo de mantener la mejor armonía con el rey, las leyes y la constitución de su país coartaban la libertad del gobierno federal que se veía en la imposibilidad de contentar ni al gobierno español ni a los disidentes, aunque procuraba observar la neutralidad más perfecta. A esto había respondido Tacón que un decreto recientemente publicado por Porter demostraba el abuso de los insurgentes que ofrecían patentes de corso mejicanas a cualquier aventurero y mandaban detener cualquier buque americano que llevara pertrechos de guerra dedicados a posesiones españolas, lo que constituía un ultraje para el pabellón de Estados Unidos. Clay había reconocido la justeza de sus aseveraciones y había concluido reiterando sus deseos de mantener la armonía entre los dos gobiernos.

474

N.º 113. — 11 de febrero, Washington.

Comunica la llegada a Nueva Orleans, a bordo del bergantín Rose, de cincuenta pasajeros españoles procedentes de Veracruz, casi todos comerciantes excepto tres o cuatro militares capitulados; probablemente irían a la Habana donde se les había asegurado un buen recibimiento, pero los militares serían vigilados por los cónsules en la Habana. Hacía tiempo que el conde de Moctezuma residía en Nueva Orleans; había ido a Méjico para ocuparse de la administración de su hacienda, pero habiéndolo considerado peligroso aquel gobierno, le había ordenado salir de su territorio y permanecer en Estados Unidos si quería gozar de sus rentas.

475

N.º 114. — 14 de febrero, Filadelfia.

Remite un oficio del cónsul en Nueva Orleans en el que comunicaba noticias de Méjico y la llegada de cuarenta españoles expulsados de allí. Residía en Filadelfia un individuo llamado Cajigao, procedente también de Nueva España, que dice haber sido oficial de la real armada y que pretendía mantenerse en Estados Unidos dando lecciones de dibujo y de español. No se había presentado en la legación ni el consulado y se le consideraba fugitivo por haber pertenecido al partido constitucional. Noticias de Caracas daban cuenta del deplorable estado de aquel país por la mala administración de Bolívar; que los jefes realistas Cisneros y Centeno unidos, habían derrotado al revolucionario apodado «Burronegro» y que había numerosas partidas hostigando en los Llanos al actual gobierno de aquella república. Principal y duplicado.

Adjunto:

— Copia del oficio del cónsul en Nueva Orleans Antonio Argote Villalobos a Francisco Tacón dando cuenta de la llegada de un barco procedente de Veracruz con españoles expulsados de allí, y anunciando la salida de un barco francés para la Habana con más exilados. Daba noticias de la anarquía existente en Méjico donde parecía que se había iniciado una insurrección, cuya cabeza era un tal Montano (Nueva Orleans, 19 de enero 1828). Principal y duplicado.

476

N.º 115. — 15 de febrero, Filadelfia.

Remite traducción de la respuesta sobre la reclamación del ministro de la Real Hacienda Juan Miguel de Losada; por ella se podía ver que el gobierno federal trataba de dar un corte al asunto, con lo que quedaba en pie la pretensión de que eran sus tribunales la autoridad más competente en dichas causas. Había respondido conforme a la real orden de que no admitiese de ningún modo los principios que quisiera establecer el gobierno americano en este asunto, aprovechando también la ocasión para recordar el caso parecido del vicecónsul de Nueva Orleans, Villavaso, que todavía estaba pendiente.

Adjunto:

— Copia y traducción de la carta de Clay a Francisco Tacón en la que manifestaba que, el presidente de los Estados Unidos había hecho llegar a Salmón su consideración de que no tenía bases sólidas la reclamación que había presentado el anterior ministro en Estados Unidos, a favor de Juan Miguel de Losada, por lo que consideraba inútil prolongar la discusión; el presidente persistía en su creencia de que la reclamación de Losada contra el gobierno americano debía de haber seguido los trámites ordinarios, presentando su defensa ante el tribunal de Escambia que era donde el demandante, Caro, había promovido el juicio; luego hubiera podido recurrir a tribunales superiores hasta llegar al Supremo y solamente después de la sentencia que éste hubiera emitido, podría haber presentado una reclamación el gobierno español al americano (Washington, 5 de febrero 1828).

— Respuesta de Francisco Tacón a Enrique Clay, acusando recibo de su comunicación. Tenía que tener en cuenta el presidente que Losada había contratado con Caro como agente público o ministro en nombre de la Real Hacienda de España y así lo había considerado el mismo Caro puesto que no había apelado contra Losada en la Florida sino después de haberlo hecho infructuosamente contra la Real Hacienda de la Habana, y el tribunal de Escambia había fallado contra Losada sabiendo que no era el verdadero deudor; y lo que Tacón trataba de defender era el principio de que los tribunales americanos no eran competentes para juzgar la conducta oficial de un agente del rey en causas puramente españolas. Un caso análogo había ocurrido al vicecónsul en Nueva Orleans, Villavaso, amenazado de cárcel por las autoridades americanas, por un aviso oficial y reservado que, como cónsul, había dado al capitán general de Yucatán. Concluía rogando que el presidente de Estados Unidos tomara de nuevo en consideración la reclamación de Losada para ser indemnizado o repuesto en la posesión de sus bienes (Washington, 9 de febrero 1828).

477

N.º 118. — 19 de febrero, Filadelfia.

Acusa recibo de una real orden disponiendo que no se cubrieran los viceconsulados vacantes, por considerarse innecesarios dadas las escasas relaciones comerciales existentes con los puertos americanos, y que se investigara la importancia de los documentos de sus archivos y el coste que podría ocasionar su traslado, por si el interés de su conservación lo requería.

478

N.º 120. — 21 de febrero, Filadelfia.

Comunica que había desembarcado en Baltimore un agente del gobierno de Chile llamado Joaquín Campino, que decía poseer, credenciales de ministro plenipotenciario en Estados Unidos; había traído con él a José Joaquín Pérez como secretario de la legación. Mister Herman Allen, ministro de Estados Unidos en Chile, había llegado a Nueva York con su esposa, dejando allí un encargado de negocios.

479

N.º 121. — 21 de febrero, Filadelfia.

Remite la cuenta de gastos extraordinarios del cónsul en Baltimore, que ignoraba la anulación de una orden del tiempo constitucional que concedía a los consulados cargar la suma de ciento cincuenta pesos anuales por gastos de secretaría y correo.

Adjunto:
— Cuentas de cantidades empleadas en auxiliar a españoles prisioneros de los insurgentes; diligencias practicadas ante los tribunales o asistencia a españoles durante los años 1823-1827.
— Cuenta de la asignación de tres mil reales de vellón anuales para gastos del consulado, según real orden de 26 de julio 1822, y que no se habían cobrado en los años 1822-1827.
— Copia del oficio de Juan Bautista Bernabéu a Francisco Tacón acusando recibo de su notificación sobre haberse anulado la orden citada. Como ignoraba la cancelación de dicha orden y se le adeudaban seis años de la asignación, había efectuado unos gastos que esperaba le fueran reembolsados (Baltimore, 22 de enero 1828).

480

N.º 122. — 21 de febrero, Filadelfia.

Remite la cuenta de gastos extraordinarios del cónsul en Boston y copia del oficio que la acompañaba; parecía que estaba enterado de la anulación de la orden del gobierno constitucional por la cual se concedía una cantidad fija para gastos de correos y escritorio.

Adjunto:

— Cuenta de gastos extraordinarios del consulado de España en Boston en el año 1827 (Boston, 31 de diciembre 1827).
— Copia del oficio de remisión de las cuentas del cónsul en Boston Raimundo Chacón (Boston, 5 de enero 1828).

481

N.º 123. — 22 de febrero, Filadelfia.

Da cuenta de haberse publicado en la gaceta de Filadelfia los nombramientos de Samson C. Russell, Guillermo H. Tracy y Tomás Davidson para cónsules de Estados Unidos en los tres puertos de la isla de Puerto Rico: Mayagüez Guyamas y Ponce.

482

N.º 124. — 22 de febrero, Filadelfia.

Acusa recibo de una real orden y un real decreto que debería publicarse en las gacetas, referente a la segunda exposición pública de la industria española que se celebraría el día de San Fernando.

483

N.º 127. — 25 de febrero, Filadelfia.

Inserta un artículo que se había publicado en un periódico de Filadelfia con noticias de América central; según el cual, conti-

VIII. — 13

nuaba la guerra civil destruyendo las provincias de Nicaragua, San Salvador y Guatemala; los del partido del gobierno de Nicaragua habían tomado la fortaleza de San Carlos a la entrada del lago de Nicaragua, cortando de este modo toda comunicación con el interior; las tropas del presidente Arce habían obtenido victorias contra los de Granada, el comercio estaba aniquilado, destruidos los ganados y haciendas y no se podía esperar un pronto fin de la guerra por ser muy escasos los recursos por ambas partes.

484

N.º 128. — 26 de febrero, Filadelfia.

Remite un ejemplar de la «Gaceta del Gobierno» de Caracas, que contenía la correspondencia entre el comandante general del apostadero de la Habana, Ángel Laborde, y el general Páez, sobre el canje de prisioneros. También insertaba la noticia de la hostilidad de las tropas peruanas que parecía querían apoderarse de las provincias que había usurpado Colombia durante el mandato de Bolívar, en Lima.

Adjunto:
— Ejemplar de la «Gaceta del Gobierno» de Caracas del 6 de febrero 1828.

485

N.º 129. — 27 de febrero, Filadelfia.

Anuncia remisión de varios impresos de Méjico que contenían noticias sobre una insurrección producida por el encono de los partidos de masones llamados escoceses y yorkinos y las violentas medidas que se habían tomado contra los españoles; al frente de la insurrección se hallaba el general Bravo, vicepresidente de la república, siendo el teniente coronel Montaño el primero que se había levantado en los llanos de Apam y participando también los generales Santana y Barragán, muchos coroneles y oficiales e incluso la guarnición de la capital; pero el general Guerrero, la había sofocado capturando a Bravo con varios oficiales en Tulancingo. Noticias posteriores indicaban que continuaba la rebelión pese al arresto del general Bravo. Con este motivo se habían acelerado las causas pendientes de los implicados en la conspiración del padre Arenas; se creía que se había ejecutado al brigadier Arana y que le seguirían pronto los generales Negrete y Echéverri. Cartas de Veracruz anunciaban la llegada del navío Asia, procedente de Valparaíso; en un buque procedente de Tampico habían llegado a Nueva Orleans veinticinco españoles expulsados de Méjico.

486

N.º 130. — 28 de febrero, Filadelfia.

Da cuenta de que se había confirmado la noticia de que la fragata española La Lealtad había apresado al bergantín Guerrero de los rebeldes mejicanos; era el mejor que se conocía en su clase, construido en Nueva York bajo la dirección del comodoro Porter, que había confiado el mando a un sobrino suyo, oficial de la marina de los Estados Unidos al que consideraban muerto en la acción. Según noticias de la Habana la lucha había empezado con dos buques pequeños llamados Marte y Amalia, acudiendo después la fragata Lealtad. Las bajas de los mejicanos habían sido más de setenta entre muertos y heridos de una tripulación de doscientos veinte hombres. Duplicado.

487

N.º 131. — 11 de marzo, Filadelfia.

Acusa recibo de varios despachos sobre asuntos de trámite y otro comunicando la salida de los reyes de Valencia para Barcelona, tras haber sido evacuada esta plaza por las tropas francesas.

488

N.º 132. — 11 de marzo, Filadelfia.

Anuncia remisión de una gaceta y envía la traducción de un artículo sobre el convite que había dado Bolívar a los nuevos obispos de Bogotá, Santa Marta, Antioquía y Guayana, y sobre el contenido de una bula del papa León XII nombrando a Fernando Caicedo de Flores, arzobispo de Santa Fe.

Adjunto:

— Traducción de unas noticias publicadas en Nueva York, en el periódico «New York Daily Advertiser», sobre el reconocimiento por parte de la Santa Sede de los obispos que había nombrado Bolívar y que habían sido revestidos de su autoridad: Fernando Caicedo, obispo de Santa Fe de Bogotá; José María Esteves obispo de Santa Marta; fray Mariano Garnica, de Antioquía, y Mariano Talavera, obispo de Guayana. Se habían recibido en Bogotá las bulas para los obispos y Bolívar los había invitado a su mesa con los oficiales de los diferentes departamentos y los cónsules y agentes diplomáticos. Se inserta traducción de la bula de León XII, de 21 de mayo 1827, por la que se nombraba a Fernando Caicedo de Flores, arzobispo de Santa Fe de Bogotá (Filadelfia, 7 de marzo 1828).

489

N.º 133. — 11 de marzo, Filadelfia.

En cumplimiento de la real orden que había recibido, aprovecharía la primera oportunidad para presentar la reclamación sobre el robo cometido en la goleta española Dolores.

490

N.º 134. — 11 de marzo, Filadelfia.

Acusa recibo de una real orden disponiendo conservase unas circulares que se le indicaban.

491

N.º 135. — 11 de marzo, Filadelfia.

Remite un folleto que acababa de publicar J. M. Salazar, que había sido ministro del gobierno de Colombia en Estados Unidos, sobre el estado de aquella república y la clase de gobierno que le convendría. Anuncia remisión también de un periódico de Méjico que contenía un artículo sobre las intenciones de Bolívar.

Adjunto:

— Folleto de J. M. Salazar titulado «Observaciones sobre las reformas políticas de Colombia», impreso en Filadelfia en 1828, en español y en inglés.

492

N.º 136. — 11 de marzo, Filadelfia.

Anuncia remisión de los últimos periódicos de Méjico que habían llegado a Estados Unidos con las declaraciones del vicepresidente de aquella república y de varios oficiales arrestados por la insurrección de Montaño; parecía que con la prisión del general Bravo y del teniente coronel Montaño se habían tranquilizado las autoridades de Méjico, pero por diferentes conductos habían llegado noticias de que amenazaba a la capital una tremenda crisis por la exaltación que se había producido entre los diversos partidos. Principal y duplicado.

493

N.º 138. — 14 de marzo, Filadelfia.

Da cuenta de que Joaquín Campino había sido recibido por el presidente como ministro plenipotenciario y enviado extraordinario del gobierno de Chile.

494

N.º 139. — 14 de marzo, Filadelfia.

Comunica que había salido del puerto de Hampton el navío Delaware, de la marina de los Estados Unidos, en dirección al Mediterráneo, conduciendo a un hijo de Luciano Bonaparte con su esposa y dos hijos, que iban a fijar su residencia en Italia.

495

N.º 140. — 14 de marzo, Filadelfia.

Participa la muerte de dos americanos distinguidos por sus servicios y talento: el mayor general Brown, general en jefe del ejército de los Estados Unidos, y mister Clinton, gobernador del estado de Nueva York.

496

N.º 141. — 14 de marzo, Filadelfia.

Remite la relación de los españoles que acababan de llegar a Nueva York expulsados de Méjico. Había llegado en el mismo buque J. M. Gutiérrez, secretario de la legación mejicana en Londres, que decía ser portador de un tratado con Holanda, ratificado por el gobierno de Méjico.

Adjunto:

— Relación de los españoles que habían llegado a Nueva York, procedentes de Veracruz: presbíteros y laicos del hospital de San Nicolás y del hospicio de Santo Tomás, todos de la misión de Filipinas que residían en Méjico; comerciantes, cultivadores, un médico y un marino (Filadelfia, 12 de marzo 1828).

497

N.º 142. — 14 de marzo, Filadelfia.

Por el capitán de la goleta Messenger, que había llegado a Baltimore procedente de Trujillo, tenía noticias del desorden que reinaba en el puerto de Omoa a causa de la guerra civil entre los seguidores del vicepresidente y los del presidente; de otros puntos de América llegaban noticias de continuos desórdenes; en Guadalajara había tales alborotos que se aprestaban a abandonarla los extranjeros residentes en ella; el cónsul general de Inglaterra en Guatemala había sido asesinado por un criado, movido por la codicia que habían despertado en él las joyas que muchas personas habían entregado al cónsul para que las custodiara, por considerar su casa más segura. Muchos comerciantes de Estados Unidos habían quebrado al no poder cobrar los productos que habían enviado a las antiguas colonias españolas.

498

N.º 143. — 21 de marzo, Filadelfia.

Acusa recibo de dos pliegos que había recibido por medio del cónsul en El Havre, que contenían quince despachos.

499

N.º 145. — 21 de marzo, Filadelfia.

Agradece el envío de tres ejemplares de la «Guía de forasteros» del año en curso, uno de los cuales había entregado al secretario de la legación.

500

N.º 148. — 22 de marzo, Filadelfia.

Remite copia del oficio que había enviado al capitán general de la isla de Cuba, con motivo del crecido número de soldados españoles que se habían reunido en Nueva Orleans al ser expulsados de Méjico. No había querido que pasaran a la Habana sin el expreso consentimiento de dicho capitán general, por si consideraba que podría perjudicar a la disciplina de la tropa a sus órdenes, el contacto con unos militares que la habían quebrantado de manera tan palmaria.

Adjunto:
— Copia del oficio de Francisco Tacón a Francisco Dionisio Vives, en el que insertaba el que había recibido del cónsul en Nueva Orleans, acerca de la llegada a dicho puerto de más de cien soldados que habían abandonado sus banderas pasándose a los rebeldes de Méjico, pero habían sido expulsados de allí y enviados a Nueva Orleans donde se encontraban en la mayor indigencia. También habían llegado a Nueva York algunos procedentes de Tampico y aún era probable que se produjeran nuevas llegadas (Filadelfia, 20 de marzo 1828).

501

N.º 150. — 23 de marzo, Filadelfia.

Remite un memorial de Francisco Hernández Nogués, cónsul de Filadelfia, solicitando que se le concediera un sueldo de dos mil duros anuales, como disfrutaban casi todos los otros cónsules en Estados Unidos. Tacón aclara que la dotación de mil doscientos duros que recibía, era una cantidad realmente exigua para poder vivir con decencia.

Adjunto:

— Memorial de Francisco Hernández Nogués solicitando el aumento de la retribución que estaba asignada al consulado de Filadelfia que se le había concedido (Filadelfia, 16 de febrero 1828).

502

N.º 151. — 23 de marzo, Filadelfia.

Acusa recibo de la real aprobación de un oficio que había remitido al capitán general de Filipinas.

503

N.º 159. — 29 de marzo, Filadelfia.

Envía una relación de los españoles procedentes de Méjico que habían salido para la Habana, que le había mandado el cónsul en Nueva Orleans, comunicándole que ascendía a doscientos el número de soldados procedentes de Méjico que se hallaban concentrados en aquella ciudad; le habían presentado un memorial para el capitán general de Cuba, que había remitido con una carta del corregidor, correspondencia de la cual enviaba copias.

Adjunto:

— Lista de los españoles emigrados de Méjico a quienes se había dado pasaporte para la Habana (Nueva Orleans, 27 de febrero 1828).
— Traducción de una carta de J. Roffignac, corregidor de Nueva Orleans, al cónsul español en la misma ciudad Antonio Argote Villalobos, dándole cuenta de que había llegado un crecido número de españoles, que siguiendo a sus jefes se habían pasado al servicio del nuevo gobierno de Méjico, habiéndose decretado posteriormente la expulsión de los mismos; si se les daban seguridades de obtener una buena acogida, casi todos regresarían a su país (Nueva Orleans, 26 de febrero 1828).
— Respuesta de Antonio Argote Villalobos, cónsul en Nueva Orleans, al corregidor Roffignac manifestando que había enviado al capitán general de Cuba copia de su carta, junto con el me-

morial que había firmado un crecido número de estos españoles (Nueva Orleans, 27 de febrero 1828).

— Oficio reservado de Francisco Tacón al secretario de Estado Manuel González Salmón, participándole que era mister Everett, ministro de Estados Unidos en Madrid, el autor de una carta inserta en un artículo publicado en la gaceta de Nueva York, cuya remisión anunciaba (Filadelfia, 29 de marzo 1828).

504

N.º 161. — 30 de marzo, Filadelfia.

Por varios conductos se habían recibido noticias de la insurrección general de los negros de Omoa; habiendo llegado tropas de San Salvador hasta San Pedro Sula, a diez leguas de Omoa, el gobierno de esta ciudad había formado una partida de negros que saliese contra ellos; pero los de San Salvador incitaron a los negros, los cuales vueltos a Omoa, habían amenazado de muerte a los blancos obligándolos a marcharse; las pocas fuerzas que quedaban en la plaza, viéndose sin posibilidad de restablecer la paz, la habían abandonado también. Las últimas noticias de Veracruz confirmaban la expulsión de los españoles de Méjico. El aventurero Porter permanecía en aquel puerto y sus oficiales querían equipar un buque para salir a vengar el apresamiento del bergantín Guerrero y la muerte de su capitán. Remite copia de dos cartas con noticias de Cartagena y Sisal.

Adjunto:

— Copia de unas noticias procedentes de Cartagena de Indias, dando cuenta de la intranquilidad reinante en el país; el partido de Santander contaba con los clérigos y abogados y el de Bolívar con el ejército, lo que podía dar lugar a una guerra civil y se temía una invasión española; los ingleses eran los dueños del comercio porque tenían mucho dinero; Francia, que no había reconocido a la república, parecía que se entendía con España (3 de febrero 1828).

— Copia de una carta procedente de Sisal, poniendo de relieve el deplorable estado en que había quedado el comercio tras la expulsión de los españoles (28 de febrero 1828).

505

N.º 163. — 11 de abril, Filadelfia.

Participa que había socorrido a la viuda de Wiseman con cien pesos y que habiendo examinado el libro de cuentas de la legación, había comprobado que hasta 1821 sus antecesores cargaban regularmente dicha cantidad cada semestre, lo que hacía doscientos pesos al año. Como la interesada creía, equivocadamente, que era una pensión fija asignada por el rey, le había hecho entender que se trataba de un socorro extraordinario que se le concedía.

506

N.º 164. — 11 de abril, Filadelfia.

Da cuenta de la llegada, en un buque procedente de la Guayra, de un tal Michilena, de la familia de este nombre en Caracas, que había sido secretario particular de Bolívar en Perú y temía ser atropellado por haberse indispuesto con él; eso les había ocurrido a algunos diputados nombrados para la convención de Ocaña cuyas conclusiones diferían de los proyectos del Libertador, que aspiraba a constituirse en dictador perpetuo. Las autoridades de Puerto Cabello no reconocían los decretos de la convención de Ocaña y querían nombrar a Bolívar dictador, lo que quizá costara una guerra civil; se decía, que los de Guayaquil le habían declarado la guerra y que las tropas peruanas les ayudarían para vengarse de las tropelías que los colombianos habían cometido en Perú; el general había abandonado Bolivia, en el alto Perú, y volvía a Colombia con sus tropas. Había tal temor en Caracas y la Guayra que algunas personas no se atrevían ni a escribir porque abrían todas las cartas.

Según noticias de Michilena cuando Bolívar estaba en Perú había mantenido correspondencia con el emperador de Brasil con objeto de pedirle una princesa de la casa de Braganza, y para gestionar esta alianza había enviado como ministro a Río Janeiro a su primo el coronel Palacios.

507

N.º 166. — 14 de abril, Filadelfia.

Comunica la llegada al puerto de la Habana el 24 de marzo, del comandante Laborde, con los tres buques con los que había salido a principios de diciembre. Remite el extracto de una carta que daba cuenta de la llegada a la Habana del navío Soberano.

Adjunto:

— Extracto de una carta de la Habana participando la llegada del navío Soberano, procedente de Cádiz, y el próximo arribo de otro buque de cincuenta cañones, también de aquel departamento, con lo que quedaría Cuba completamente protegida y con posibilidad de bloquear los puertos de Méjico y Veracruz. Se estaba arreglando el bergantín Guerrero que había sido apresado por la Lealtad, cuyo comandante había demostrado el sentimiento que le había producido la desgraciada suerte del capitán Porter por el aprecio que le merecía un oficial tan distinguido.

Había llegado a Jamaica la goleta inglesa Espiegle, con el encargo, según se creía de agitar la cuestión del tráfico de negros, que tanto inquietaba a Cuba. Se hacían grandes preparativos para celebrar el cumpleaños de la reina, bajo la inspección del capitán general Vives, persona muy competente bajo cuya administración había mejorado mucho la isla de Cuba, lo mismo respecto a fortificaciones, que a las fuerzas del ejército y marina, disciplinadas y puntualmente pagadas. La tesorería, hábilmente llevada por el intendente Pinillos, había producido un saldo a favor de un millón de duros. Todos los residentes en Cuba reconocían unánimemente que la prosperidad de que gozaba la isla, antes desconocida, se debía a sus excelentes dotes de mando, unidas a la formidable preparación del intendente Pinillos, no habiendo una queja respecto al desempeño de la autoridad. No ocurría lo mismo respecto a la administración de justicia que daba lugar a muchas quejas; pero su adecuación no dependía del gobierno colonial siguiéndose las costumbres y prácticas antiguas, cuya interrupción podría dar lugar a mayores males. Había que exceptuar el tribunal del consulado, exclusivamente comercial, al cual podía acudir cualquier extranjero, y que administraba la justicia sin demora (La Habana, 9 de marzo 1828).

— Ejemplar de «The National Gazette» de Filadelfia que contiene la carta anteriormente extractada (Filadelfia, 7 de abril 1828).

508

N.º 167. — 14 de abril, Filadelfia.

Da cuenta de la llegada a Nueva Orleans de treinta españoles, en su mayoría dependientes de casas de comercio, procedentes de Méjico que pretendían pasar en seguida a la Habana. Habían llegado también al mismo punto Narciso Amitua y Pascual Prieto, procedentes de Río Grande, que pensaban hacer el viaje por Inglaterra y Francia para recoger parte de su capital que habían remitido a los referidos países; su proyecto era dedicarse a la explotación de minas por la experiencia que había adquirido trabajando como minero en Méjico; con estos conocimientos y su capital creía que podría emprender algo ventajoso para él y para su patria.

509

N.º 168. — 14 de abril, Filadelfia.

Anuncia remisión de unas gacetas de Méjico que contenían las declaraciones de varios testigos y del vicepresidente, el general Bravo, sobre la última insurrección ocurrida en aquel país donde parece que continuaba el desorden y la efervescencia que amenazaba la vida de aquella república.

510

N.º 169. — 25 de abril, Filadelfia.

Anuncia remisión de varias gacetas de Méjico que manifiestan el deplorable estado de aquel país, donde parecía que la desolación iría en aumento. Duplicado.

Adjunto:

— Nota informativa (6 de junio 1828).

511

N.º 171. — 27 de abril, Filadelfia.

Comunica la llegada al puerto de Norfolk, en el buque Savannah, de cuarenta y tres pasajeros procedentes de Veracruz, que habían seguido hacia Nueva York para de allí pasar a Europa que era su destino. Habían dado noticias del deplorable estado de Méjico dominado por completo por el partido llamado de York, integrado por la peor gente, que se dedicaba a robar y atacar a los ricos y sus propiedades. Aseguraban que protegía y apoyaba este partido el ministro de Estados Unidos de Méjico, que era el principal agente de los desórdenes, por cuya razón lo detestaban los del bando contrario.

Adjunto:

— Relación de los españoles que habían llegado en el Savannah, indicando su lugar de nacimiento, familia y acompañantes, profesión y punto de destino.

512

N.º 173. — 27 de abril, Filadelfia.

Por un buque procedente de Cartagena se había recibido la noticia de que el general Padilla había intentado oponerse al general Montilla, el cual había recibido una orden reservada de Bolívar para tomar el mando de aquel departamento, y había tratado de sorprenderlo con mil hombres armados cuando se hallaba en Turbaco, cerca de la capital; pero lejos de conseguirlo se había visto él mismo sitiado en Cartagena. El cónsul inglés había estado desde el principio en favor de Montilla amenazando con retirarse de la ciudad si Padilla continuaba excitando al pueblo contra las autoridades del llamado Libertador. Padilla se había visto obligado a huir entrando Montilla triunfalmente en la ciudad. En el mismo buque había llegado el encargado de negocios de los Estados Unidos mister Watts.

Había visto gacetas de Bogotá y de Venezuela con una proclama de Bolívar despidiéndose de la capital para acudir a los departamentos de Maturín, Venezuela, Orinoco y el Zulia donde consideraba necesaria su presencia, y al mismo tiempo declaraba que conservaría la autoridad extraordinaria con la cual se hallaba investido como jefe de la república. Parecía que serían escasos los diputados asistentes a la convención de Ocaña porque los enemigos del Libertador estaban intimidados o apresados por los gobernadores de las diferentes provincias, a quienes Bolívar había facultado para este objeto.

El estado mayor y varios cuerpos y oficiales de la tropa y milicias de Venezuela, habían pedido a Bolívar que no dejara el mando y que no se obedecieran los decretos de la convención de Ocaña, que consideraban anticonstitucionales de una facción dirigida por el general Santander, vicepresidente de la república, a quien trataban de usurpador y malversador de los públicos. Todo esto concordaba con las noticias que había dado Michilena. Creía probable que Bolívar lograra afirmarse en el mando absoluto de la república que era la meta de su ambición y sus intrigas.

Adjunto:
— Ejemplar del «Mercurio Peruano» con la proclama de Bolívar (Lima, 18 de septiembre 1827).

513

N.º 174. — 28 de abril, **Filadelfia.**

Participa la llegada de tres españoles procedentes de la Guayra, naturales de Vizcaya y llamados Bernardo Domenzain, y Miguel y Vicente Artaza; llevaban más de diez años trabajando en casas comerciales de dicha ciudad y se dirigían a la Habana con sus escasos caudales, para continuar allí con la misma profesión. Se habían presentado en la legación y habían dicho que quedaban muy pocos españoles en la Costa Firme, donde reinaba gran intranquilidad, que el comercio se había arruinado, y que apenas se veía más que gente de color. Habían salido para Gibraltar desde Nueva York, ocho soldados españoles que habían sido expulsados de Méjico.

514

N.º 177. — 29 de abril, **Filadelfia.**

Comunica que el barón de Krudner, ministro de Rusia, que se había detenido algunas horas en Filadelfia en su viaje de Washington a Nueva York, había tenido la amabilidad de visitarlo. Le había dicho que sabía por el secretario de Estado mister Clay que el encargado de negocios de Estados Unidos en Colombia, mister Watts, recién llegado de Cartagena, había informado del mal estado en que se encontraba aquel país y de la imposibilidad de que subsistiera el gobierno de Colombia, seguramente porque Bolívar trataba de apoderarse del mando absoluto por la fuerza armada, violencia que disgustaría mucho al gobierno de la Unión. El referido barón, que hacía muy pocos días que había abierto su casa en Washington, había dado ya una comida al cuerpo diplomático y un lucido baile.

515

N.º 178. — 2 de mayo, Filadelfia.

Acusa recibo de un pliego llegado por conducto del cónsul en Gibraltar, que contenía tres reales órdenes que menciona.

516

N.º 179. — 2 de mayo, Filadelfia.

Había recibido un oficio en el que se manifestaba que el rey había aprobado la comunicación que había enviado a los capitanes generales de las islas de Cuba y Puerto Rico, acerca del coronel Feliciano Montenegro.

517

N.º 180. — 3 de mayo, Filadelfia.

Participa la llegada de un oficio ordenando reiterar a los capitanes generales de Cuba y Puerto Rico el cumplimiento de la real orden de 25 de enero de 1802 añadiendo que evitaran que ningún joven de dichas islas fuera a educarse a los colegios de Estados Unidos y que se tomaran las medidas necesarias para establecer colegios en las mismas.

518

N.º 181. — 3 de mayo, Filadelfia.

Remite unos recibos del pago de suscripciones a varios periódicos como justificantes de la cuenta de gastos que se le habían solicitado para proceder o no, a su aprobación; de algunas partidas no podría conseguir recibos como ocurría con las gacetas de Méjico que se tomaban de segunda mano, con los gastos de su viaje a Washington y otros de correo y secretaría, por ser imposible obtener justificantes de cantidades pequeñas.

Adjunto:

— Cuatro recibos de suscripciones al «The Daily National Intelligencer», «National Journal» y «National Intelligencer».

519

N.º 183. — 3 de mayo, Filadelfia.

Anuncia remisión de unos ejemplares del periódico «Correo de la Federación» del 14 de febrero al 15 de marzo, que ponían de manifiesto el deplorable estado en que se encontraba Méjico desde el punto de vista del partido yorkino al que dicho periódico apoyaba, mientras que «El Sol» ayudaba a los escoceses. Hay dos ejemplares.

520

N.º 184. — 3 de mayo, Filadelfia.

Remite extracto de una carta del Callao que había publicado una gaceta de Filadelfia. Por diversos conductos sabía que el gobierno del Perú se había unido a las demás provincias para resistir a los colombianos, seguros de que Bolívar se proponía volver a Lima con fuerzas respetables y que varios buques al mando del capitán inglés Guise iban a cruzar a la costa de Guayaquil, para evitar que las tropas de Colombia llegasen por mar al Perú.

Adjunto:

— Extracto de una carta del Callao en la que se manifestaban las sospechas de que los colombianos preparaban un ataque, por lo que todo el ejército peruano se había dirigido a la frontera del norte; sus hombres no sobrepasaban los tres mil, pese a haberse alistado todos los artesanos y labradores. Se refería a la lentitud con que se iba redactando la constitución por perder el tiempo en discusiones superfluas, y a la probable caída del congreso y gobierno por un movimiento popular. El entonces

presidente del congreso, que se elegía mensualmente, era el ex-
jesuita Luna de Pizarro, del partido opuesto a Bolívar, que había propuesto que se volviera a llamar a los españoles expulsados, medida que unida a la destrucción del poder de Bolívar,
podría dar lugar al reconocimiento de Fernando VII. En su opinión los hombres sensatos del Perú adoptarían cualquier otro
sistema de gobierno que ofreciera más firmeza y mayor seguridad personal (El Callao, 13 de diciembre 1827).

521

N.º 185. — 5 de mayo, Filadelfia.

Acusa recibo de once comunicaciones llegadas a Nueva York
por la vía del Havre.

522

N.º 186. — 6 de mayo, Filadelfia.

Agradece en nombre propio y de todos los empleados de la legación y consulados, la real orden al secretario del despacho de Hacienda relativa al pago por la intendencia de la Habana de sus
sueldos y demás haberes.

523

N.º 187. — 6 de mayo, Filadelfia.

Acusa recibo de un oficio que respondía a dos despachos suyos,
con uno de los cuales había remitido el folleto publicado por el
coronel Feliciano Montenegro.

524

N.º 189. — 7 de mayo, Filadelfia.

Acusa recibo a un oficio en respuesta de dos suyos.

525

N.º 190. — 7 de mayo, Filadelfia.

Muestra su satisfacción por haberse aprobado su conducta al
disculparse para no concurrir a un banquete.

VIII. — 14

526

N.º 191. — 7 de mayo, Filadelfia.

Da cuenta de los pasos que había dado en apoyo de la reclamación de Juan Miguel Losada, asunto en el que ya no le quedaba nada por hacer.

527

N.º 192. — 8 de mayo, Filadelfia.

Queda enterado de la estancia de los reyes en Barcelona, así como de que habían llegado varios despachos suyos.

528

N.º 193. — 8 de mayo, Filadelfia.

Acusa recibo de una gaceta de España que contenía el arancel provisional de los derechos que se tenían que cobrar en el comercio de importación y exportación de América, arancel que procuraría que se publicara en los periódicos de los Estados Unidos.

529

N.º 194. — 8 de mayo, Filadelfia.
Acusa recibo de su oficio.

530

N.º 195. — 8 de mayo, Filadelfia.

Queda enterado de que continuaba la estancia de los reyes en Barcelona.

531

N.º 196. — 9 de mayo, Filadelfia.

Había recibido la orden propuesta por el consejo de ministros de que se facilitara pasaporte a los españoles que hubieran sido expulsados de América y se les protegiera, siempre que no estuvieran comprendidos en las excepciones del indulto del 1 de mayo de 1824. Había trasladado dicha orden a los cónsules para su debido cumplimiento.

532

N.º 197. — 10 de mayo, Filadelfia.

Comunica que había llegado al puerto de Norfolk la goleta mercante española Princesa, para reparar las averías que había sufrido en un temporal. Procedente de la Habana se dirigía a Santo Tomé, en la costa de África, para donde proseguiría el viaje una vez realizadas las reparaciones. Aunque el encargado del consulado de Norfolk había encontrado todos sus papeles en regla, el crecido número de gente que llevaba en proporción con su aparejo, hacía sospechar que su principal objeto fuera el tráfico de negros.

533

N.º 200. — 12 de mayo, Filadelfia.

Remite traducción de un artículo que había aparecido en la gaceta del gobierno del Brasil; las últimas noticias de aquel país aseguraban que estaban próximos a batirse en las inmediaciones de San Pedro de Río Grande los ejércitos del emperador y de Buenos Aires, al mando del general Lecor y de Lavalleja respectivamente.

Adjunto:

— Ejemplar del periódico «The Philadelphia Gazette» con noticias de Bolívar tomadas de una gaceta brasileña (3 de mayo 1828).

— Traducción del artículo mencionado en el que se aseguraba que Bolívar había reunido en Cartagena siete mil hombres con los cuales pensaba marchar contra Colombia, país que se encontraría en la ruina si Bolívar no tomaba el poder coronándose rey. América había sacudido el yugo español y su independencia era ya indestructible, pero para que pudiera desenvolverse con tranquilidad era necesario que su forma de gobierno se adaptara a sus costumbres con la monarquía. No se admitiría a Fernando VII, pero la paz empezaría cuando príncipes de su familia reinaran en las nuevas naciones. El infante don Sebastián, que además de poseer sangre real era un príncipe americano, estaba llamado a gobernar en una gran parte de las antiguas posesiones españolas. También podrían ocupar tronos el infante don Francisco de Paula y el príncipe de Luca, apoyados no sólo por los realistas sino por la inmensa mayoría de los habitantes, que aunque no querían al rey Fernando VII, tampoco deseaban una forma de gobierno tan distinta como la republicana; para ello sería necesario que el gobierno de Madrid renunciara a un dominio inmediato en América, y estableciera un plan de negociación con Bolívar («Gaceta de Filadelfia», 3 de mayo 1828).

534

N.º 201.—13 de mayo, Filadelfia.

Queda enterado de la real orden que se había enviado a los capitanes generales de Cuba y Puerto Rico para que no permitieran que ningún joven de aquellas islas fuera a educarse a Estados Unidos y que propusieran los medios a adoptar para establecer colegios en aquellas islas.

535

N.º 204.—21 de mayo, Filadelfia.

Acusa recibo de un oficio en el que se le comunicaba la aprobación por la conducta que había observado en Washington, declinando una invitación.

536

N.º 205.—22 de mayo, Filadelfia.

Remite un ejemplar del tratado de comercio entre Suecia y Estados Unidos con la ratificación de ambos gobiernos; requisito del que carecía el que había enviado anteriormente.

Adjunto:

— Mensaje del presidente de Estados Unidos Adams, dando a conocer el «Tratado de Comercio y Navegación» entre dicho país y el rey de Suecia y Noruega, firmado en Estocolmo en 4 de julio de 1827 y ratificado en Washington el 18 de enero 1828. Cuadernillo impreso de 20 páginas, en inglés (Washington, 7 de febrero 1828).

537

N.º 209. — 28 de mayo, Filadelfia.

Participa que había llegado al puerto de Nueva York, con objeto de aprovisionarse, un bergantín francés que hacía el viaje de Veracruz a Burdeos, permaneciendo tres días en el fondeadero de la cuarentena. Entre los pasajeros había veinticinco comerciantes españoles acaudalados, que volvían a sus pueblos de origen; también iban el marqués de Vivanco, general de brigada y natural de Méjico, que emigraba voluntariamente, en desacuerdo con los acontecimientos de su país, para fijar su residencia en Francia o Italia; varios oficiales españoles de los capitulados; los coroneles Blanco y Mingo y el licenciado Francisco Barreda, autor de la defensa del general Arana, que se dirigía a Madrid. Todos viajaban con sus familias y reunían capital de seiscientos mil pesos fuertes. El marqués de Vivanco había solicitado embarcar en un buque que saldría inmediatamente para El Havre.

538

N.º 210. — 28 de mayo, Filadelfia.

Remite las últimas gacetas llegadas de Caracas, que daban cuenta del triste estado de Venezuela y de la acusación que se hacía al general Santander de que trataba de enriquecerse por todos los medios. Hay dos ejemplares.

Adjunto:

— Dos ejemplares de «El Voto de Venezuela» (Caracas, 11 y 29 de marzo 1828).

— 5 ejemplares de la «Gaceta del Gobierno» (Caracas, 5, 9, 12, 19 y 23 de abril 1828).

— Nota informativa (2 de agosto 1828).

539

N.º 211. — 29 de mayo, Filadelfia.

Participa la llegada a Nueva York del buque Virginia, procedente de Veracruz, con los pasajeros españoles que se citan en una relación adjunta; todos eran ricos y se proponían volver a España por la vía del Havre. Habían confirmado las noticias sobre la anarquía que reinaba en Méjico, y opinaban que sería fácil su reconquista por España; habían producido gran alarma en Méjico y Veracruz las noticias llegadas por los prisioneros del bergantín Guerrero, de que iban a ser bloqueadas sus costas por buques españoles y contaban que el padre Martínez había causado admiración por su firmeza ante la muerte y que los mejicanos no creían que fuera eclesiástico sino algún general español disfrazado.

Adjunto:

— Relación de los comerciantes españoles, que habían llegado a Nueva York en el buque americano La Virginidad, procedentes de Veracruz y con destino a España.

540

N.º 212. — 29 de mayo, Filadelfia.

Da cuenta del fin de la primera sesión del congreso, de cuya actividad se quejaba el pueblo por considerar que había empleado mucho tiempo en intrigas de elecciones y negocios de escasa importancia o de interés local.

541

N.º 213. — 29 de mayo, Filadelfia.

Comunica los nombramientos del secretario de Guerra, mister James Barbour, como ministro plenipotenciario de Estados Unidos en Inglaterra, ocupando su puesto actual el general Pedro B. Porter; para ministro en Colombia, el general William H. Harrison, elección que algunos consideraban como un deseo de adular a Bolívar, por ser puramente militar el gobierno de aquel país.

542

N.º 214. — 29 de mayo, Filadelfia.

Acusa recibo de un oficio.

543

N.º 215. — 30 de mayo, Filadelfia.

Transmite las últimas noticias recibidas de Cartagena que aseguraban que el general Padilla había sido arrestado en Mompós y se le juzgaría en la capital; de Montevideo decían que aún no se habían batido los ejércitos de Brasil y Buenos Aires, aunque estaban acampados a corta distancia; en Lima se trabajaba en redactar una nueva constitución y Chile solicitaba el privilegio exclusivo del comercio de granos; en Lima se habían aumentado hasta el noventa por ciento los derechos de importación sobre muebles, tejidos de algodón y otros artículos de Estados Unidos; por último que el corsario español llamado el Griego había hecho varias presas en el Pacífico y las había remitido a Manila, donde había sido armado.

544

N.º 216. — 30 de mayo, Filadelfia.

Remite una gaceta que contiene las actas del congreso relativas al nuevo arancel que se había aprobado, aumentando los derechos de importación de tal manera que haría casi prohibitiva la introducción de miel, lana, hierro y plomo. También se había aprobado un bill referente a los vinos, que en unos casos aumenta y en otros reduce los derechos de arancel. Acompaña traducción de las actas referidas.

Adjunto:

— Ejemplar del «National Gazette» que contiene un artículo sobre los cambios en el arancel (Filadelfia, 24 de mayo 1828).
— Traducción del acta del congreso por la que se modificaban los derechos sobre importaciones (19 de mayo 1828).

545

N.º 217. — 30 de mayo, Filadelfia.

Anuncia remisión, en paquete separado y por vía de Gibraltar, de varios periódicos de Méjico. Por ellos podría ver el estado de anarquía que reinaba en aquel país; que el padre Martínez había sido ejecutado como complicado en la conspiración del padre Arenas; que los generales Bravo, Barragán y otros oficiales de aquel gobierno rebelde habían sido sentenciados a un destierro de siete años, con media paga, y aunque no se había dicho adonde los mandaban, se sabía que iban a embarcarse para Chile o Lima; que se había concedido una pensión de ciento ochenta duros mensuales a la viuda y sucesores del comandante del bergantín Guerrero; las sumas que se reunían para reemplazar dicho bergantín, que se había perdido, por la corbeta Kensington a la que se había puesto el nombre que aquel llevaba.

El gobierno mejicano había concedido un terreno muy extenso en la provincia de Tejas, cerca de Arkansas, a la casa de Baring y Cía., de Londres, para explorar y colonizar el país.

546

N.º 218. — 30 de mayo, Filadelfia.

Enterado por los periódicos de Méjico y noticias de Veracruz de que el gobierno mejicano conseguiría mediante donativos los fondos necesarios para reemplazar la pérdida del bergantín Guerrero por la corbeta Kensington, existente en el puerto de Filadelfia, había pasado aviso al capitán general de la isla de Cuba. Conserva varios números del periódico «Correo de la Federación Mejicana» con noticias relativas a dichos donativos y a la aplicación que se les daría, para probar la falta de neutralidad que representaría por parte del gobierno de Estados Unidos dejarlo salir de dicho puerto.

Adjunto:
— Copia del oficio que Francisco Tacón había enviado al capitán general de la isla de Cuba, dándole cuenta de que la corbeta Kensington, que había sido construida y armada en Filadelfia por el gobierno de Méjico, se hallaba puesta en venta por no

haberse pagado todo su importe; pero las últimas noticias indicaban que aquel gobierno estaba recaudando donativos para completar el pago, basándose en la valiente defensa que había sostenido el bergantín Guerrero frente al barco español Lealtad. Los mejicanos querían reemplazar dicha pérdida con la corbeta Kensington, a la que habían puesto el nombre del General Guerrero. Los periódicos americanos, decían que el capitán Hayes, que debía conducirlo a Veracruz con pabellón americano, saldría dentro de unas semanas; pese a las representaciones que sobre ello había hecho el gobierno, no tenía esperanzas de que surtieran efecto para impedir su salida de Filadelfia.

Una goleta armada en Baltimore, de la cual había hablado anteriormente, estaba ya despachada por la aduana para San Bartolomé donde su capitán, Chase, simularía la venta del buque y entregaría la patente americana al cónsul de Estados Unidos, y seguidamente saldría con la bandera de Buenos Aires a cruzar contra el comercio español y brasileño (Filadelfia, 30 de mayo 1828).

547

N.º 219. — 30 de mayo, Filadelfia.

Anuncia remisión de varios números del periódico mejicano «El Sol», así como de un suplemento del «Correo de la Federación» que publicaba un dictamen relativo a los misioneros de California. Hay dos ejemplares.

548

N.º 220. — 4 de junio, Filadelfia.

Anuncia remisión, por medio del cónsul de España en Gibraltar, de varios ejemplares del periódico «Correo de la Federación». Hay dos ejemplares.

549

N.º 221. — 4 de junio, Filadelfia.

Acusa recibo de diez reales órdenes que relaciona.

550

N.º 222. — 5 de junio, Filadelfia.

Queda enterado de un oficio relativo al corsario John and Joseph; pondría todo su celo en averiguar el destino de los buques que se alistan y preparan en los puertos de Estados Unidos.

551

N.º 223. — 6 de junio, Filadelfia.

Cumpliendo las órdenes recibidas, había escrito al cónsul en Nueva Orleans para que vigilara la conducta del conde de Moctezuma.

552

N.º 224. — 6 de junio, Filadelfia.

Manifiesta su satisfacción por haberse aprobado los términos en que había sostenido los derechos de España en la conferencia mantenida con el secretario de Estado mister Clay.

553

N.º 228. — 9 de junio, Filadelfia.

Remite una relación de todas las actas del congreso en la sesión que había concluido el 26 de mayo último; también remitiría los impresos de las que tuvieran relación con España o considerara dignas de interés.

Adjunto:
— Relación de todas las actas decretadas por el congreso de los Estados Unidos de América en la sesión concluida el 26 de mayo último.

554

N.º 229. — 9 de junio, Filadelfia.

No había terminado aún la impresión del nuevo arancel de derechos de importación, pero podía informar de la alteración que se hacía en él de los vinos, según un acta del congreso.

555

N.º 230. — 9 de junio, Filadelfia.

Anuncia remisión de un diario de Washington que publica la convención de amistad, comercio y navegación entre los Estados Unidos y las ciudades Hanseáticas, ratificada por los respectivos gobiernos; una vez que se imprimiera dicho tratado enviaría un ejemplar.

Adjunto:

— Ejemplar del «National Journal» que contiene el referido tratado (Washington, 4 de junio 1828).

556

N.º 232. — 10 de junio, Filadelfia.

Comunica que como consecuencia de la información que habían dado los prisioneros del bergantín Guerrero sobre los preparativos de la escuadra de la Habana para salir a bloquear el puerto de Veracruz y hostilizar a los mejicanos, los cincuenta mil duros que éstos habían recaudado para terminar de pagar la corbeta Kensington, anclada en Filadelfia, los habían invertido en proveer de víveres el castillo de Ulúa y varios de sus buques de guerra, así como en trasladar tropas para organizar la defensa de las costas.

También como consecuencia de dicha alarma habían internado a muchos españoles que esperaban en Veracruz y en Tampico la llegada de buques para trasladarse a Europa, haciéndoles objeto de insultos y malos tratos.

Antes de estos sucesos habían remitido al comerciante Chew, de Baltimore, diez mil pesos para pagar a los acreedores de la corbeta

Kensington, asegurándole la próxima llegada de lo que faltaba para terminar su pago; pero Chew y el titulado ministro de Méjico, Obregón, acordaron apropiarse de ellos a cuenta de lo que les pertenecía por su comisión el primero, y por los atrasos que sufría en la percepción de sus sueldos, el segundo.

Trataría de impedir la salida de la Kensington aunque no esperaba que el gobierno le prestase oídos.

557

N.º 234. — 14 de junio, Filadelfia.

Anuncia remisión de varios números del periódico de Méjico «El Sol» y de unos impresos muy interesantes por las personas que los firmaban y que describían la crítica posición en que se encontraba aquel país.

Adjunto:

— Ejemplar del «Mercurio de Nueva York» (Nueva York, 9 de agosto 1828).
— Ejemplar de «A Aurora Fluminense» (Río de Janeiro, 16 de junio 1828).

558

N.º 237. — 20 de junio, Filadelfia.

Anuncia remisión de un ejemplar impreso de la tarifa de derechos de importación, con las alteraciones que en ellos se habían producido.

559

N.º 238. — 20 de junio, Filadelfia.

Participa que, habiendo tenido que abandonar Washington por motivos de salud el secretario de Estados Unidos mister Clay, había quedado encargado de sustituirlo durante su ausencia, el oficial mayor de su secretaría, mister Daniel Brent.

560

N.º 240. — 24 de junio, Filadelfia.

Comunica que el ministro de Rusia en Estados Unidos, barón de Krudner, le había manifestado el deseo de tener una nota confidencial de los principales buques armados que habían salido de los puertos americanos para ayuda de los insurgentes, como ocurría con la goleta de guerra Kensington construida expresamente para los rebeldes mejicanos; el objeto era su propia información y poder exponerlo en los casos que se le presentaran como acciones opuestas al derecho de gentes. Como consideraba que no había inconveniente en acceder a su petición y podía ser valiosa su opinión, contraria a la tolerancia del gobierno americano, le había entregado la nota cuya copia adjuntaba.

Adjunto:
— Traducción de la nota referente a los buques que se habían armado en Estados Unidos, especialmente en Baltimore, con tripulación igualmente americana; también en sus puertos se habían construido verdaderas flotas para las repúblicas de Colombia y Méjico, que salían con pabellón de Estados Unidos y nada más llegar a sus destinos enarbolaban los pabellones insurgentes, dedicándose a hacer el corso contra el comercio español (Sin fecha).
— Nota informativa (15 de agosto 1828).

561

N.º 242. — 26 de junio, Filadelfia.

Comunica el nombramiento de mister Carlos S. Walsh para secretario de la legación de Estados Unidos en Madrid, en sustitución de Juan A. Smith que debía pasar a París con igual destino. Walsh era hermano del editor del periódico «The National Gazette and Literary register», que le había ponderado mucho el talento y cultura del nuevo secretario de la legación de Madrid.

562

N.º 243. — 27 de junio, Filadelfia.

Remite una relación de los españoles procedentes de Méjico que habían salido de Nueva York en el presente mes para Burdeos, Havre, Gibraltar y Vigo.

Adjunto:

— Relación de los españoles que habían salido de Nueva York con pasaporte del cónsul de España en dicho puerto, con destino a Europa (Filadelfia, 27 de junio 1828).

563

N.º 244. — 28 de junio, Filadelfia.

En cumplimiento de órdenes recibidas había enviado al gobierno federal una nota cuya copia remite.

Adjunto:

— Traducción de la nota de Francisco Tacón al secretario de Estado Henry Clay, manifestando que enterado su gobierno de que el comodoro Porter, al servicio de Méjico, había publicado un decreto ordenando detener cualquier buque neutral que condujese géneros de propiedad española o efectos conocidos como contrabando de guerra, tenía orden de manifestar que el gobierno español tendría que dar un trato recíproco a los buques de Estados Unidos, si se permitiera a los insurgentes de Méjico llevar a efecto el referido decreto (Filadelfia, 28 de junio 1828).

564

N.º 245. — 28 de junio, Filadelfia.

Anuncia remisión de un periódico que contiene un artículo relativo a las reclamaciones del gobierno americano contra varias naciones europeas; hace notar que aunque algunas de dichas reclamaciones eran de gran importancia y antigüedad, de ningún país había obtenido satisfacción tan generosa como lo que había otorgado España con la cesión de las Floridas, pese a tratarse en algunos casos de potencias tan poco relevantes como Nápoles o Dinamarca; incluso el emperador del Brasil, cuyo poder aún no estaba consolidado, despreciaba las reclamaciones y quejas de este gobierno, que lo soportaba sin proferir amenazas como hacía en el caso de España, sin duda para no poner en peligro su extensísimo comercio.

565

N.º 246. — 29 de junio, Filadelfia.

Remite un recorte de una gaceta con su correspondiente traducción, que contiene el discurso del emperador del Brasil al congreso sobre sus relaciones con todas las potencias. Se creía que después tuvo lugar una batalla entre el ejército brasileño y el de Buenos Aires en la que venció el primero.

Adjunto:

— Recorte del periódico, unido a su traducción, con la exposición que había hecho el emperador del Brasil ante el congreso en la sesión de apertura, en la que tras referirse a las relaciones con las distintas cortes europeas, todas las cuales excepto la de Madrid, habían reconocido su imperio, y con varias de las cuales habían concluido tratados de amistad y comercio, analizaba rápidamente los principales negocios internos del país (3 de mayo 1828).

566

N.º 247. — 30 de junio, Filadelfia.

Participa que el cónsul en Nueva Orleans le había comunicado que el vicecónsul, Nicolás José Villavaso, obligado a tomar los baños termales de San Diego, había recibido pasaporte para la Habana; y que acababa de llegar a aquella ciudad, procedente de Veracruz, el coronel caraqueño Montenegro, de cuya conducta avisaría a los capitanes generales de Cuba y Puerto Rico.

567

N.º 248. — 30 de junio, Filadelfia.

Comunica que el encargado de negocios de Estados Unidos para Guatemala, mister Rochester, se había vuelto desde Omoa antes de llegar a su destino, en vista de que se había disuelto el gobierno cerca del cual iba acreditado y dado lo peligroso que hacía el viaje la guerra existente; las noticias de los periódicos referentes a ello aseguraban que San Salvador había sido pasado a sangre y fuego y el comercio con esos países había disminuido mucho a consecuencia de dichos acontecimientos.

568

N.º 249. — 30 de junio, Filadelfia.

Acusa recibo de las reales órdenes siguientes: mandando declarar al gobierno federal que se obraría con reciprocidad si por su parte no hacía respetar su bandera por los rebeldes mejicanos; disponiendo que no se formara la cuenta de los gastos extraordinarios, por haberse designado una cuota fija para cada uno de los consulados y legaciones; manifestando el desagrado por la conducta negligente del cónsul en Boston al no reclamar a tiempo el esclavo sustraído de Puerto Rico en un buque americano; participando el nombramiento de cónsul general en Estados Unidos a favor de Francisco Hernández Nogués.

569

N.º 250. — 1 de julio, Filadelfia.

Había hecho saber a los cónsules en Estados Unidos el nombramiento de Francisco Hernández Nogués como cónsul general, con residencia en Filadelfia.

570

N.º 251. — 3 de julio, Filadelfia.

Remite relación de los tres españoles procedentes de Méjico que habían salido de Nueva York para la península.

Adjunto:

— Nota de los españoles que habían salido para la península con pasaporte del cónsul en Nueva York, Francisco Stoughton.

571

N.º 252. — 4 de julio, Filadelfia.

Da cuenta de la llegada a Filadelfia de la viuda de Iturbide con una de sus hijas enferma para someterla a tratamiento médico; dicha señora residía con todas sus hijas en el convento católico de monjas establecido en Georgetown; estaba obligada, lo mismo que su hijo mayor, a obtener el consentimiento del representante de los rebeldes mejicanos para cambiar de residencia, a fin de seguir disfrutando la pensión que tenían asignada. El joven Iturbide se había decidido por seguir la misma carrera de su padre en la escuela militar de mister Patridge, en Connecticut.

572

N.º 254. — 12 de julio, Filadelfia.

Había transmitido al cónsul en Boston la disconformidad por su negligencia en no reclamar a tiempo ante los tribunales locales el esclavo sustraído de Puerto Rico por un buque americano.

573

N.º 255. — 13 de julio, Filadelfia.

Da cuenta de las últimas noticias llegadas de Méjico que se referían a las luchas entre yorkinos y escoceses; se dice que habían sido arrestadas allí varias personas complicadas en una conspiración para expulsar a todos los españoles que aún quedaban en aquel reino; los amigos de Bravo seguían publicando escritos declarando su inocencia y criticando la injusticia de su destierro; noticias de Chester, donde residía parte de la familia de Porter, daban cuenta de que éste había escrito comunicando su próxima llegada, provisto de los fondos necesarios para concluir el pago de la fragata construida en Filadelfia para la marina mejicana. Ya anteriormente había tenido noticias de su próxima venida y lo había comunicado al cónsul en Nueva Orleans Antonio Argote Villalobos, para que avisase si llegaba y lo mantuviera vigilado. Acababa de morir en Veracruz el hijo de Foster, que junto con su sobrino se habían unido también a los enemigos de España.

Adjunto:

— Traducción de un recorte de gaceta que lleva anejo, comunicando el anuncio de la próxima salida de Porter para Estados Unidos, con fondos suficientes para terminar de pagar la fragata construida para la marina mejicana y que estaba anclada en Filadelfia.

574

N.º 256. — 14 de julio, Filadelfia.

Da cuenta de que el día nueve de abril último se había inaugurado la convención de Ocaña, pese a que sólo asistieron sesenta y cuatro de los ciento ocho representantes nombrados; se había declarado necesaria y urgente la reforma de la contribución, de lo que se ocuparían seguidamente. Remite copia del mensaje de Bolívar a la convención en el que se notaba que le contrariaba la oposición a sus planes, que empezaba a manifestarse; las noticias llegadas de Colombia pronosticaban que, atropellando la convención, se apoderaría del mando absoluto aunque fuera exponiéndose a un final trágico. De Buenos Aires aseguraban que se habían desvanecido las esperanzas de paz después de la llegada de un buque inglés procedente de Río Janeiro. La situación en Perú era muy confusa por sucederse continuamente en el mando diversas personas.

Adjunto:

— Copia del mensaje del Libertador a los representantes reunidos en la convención nacional de Colombia, en el que tras declarar que ponía en sus manos, como representantes del pueblo, la autoridad y el mando que había recibido, exponía la triste situación en que se encontraba la república, analizando los fallos en su sistema de gobierno y estimulando a los legisladores a proporcionar al país leyes justas e inexorables.

575

N.º 258. — 20 de julio, Burlington.

Anuncia remisión de los últimos números del periódico de Méjico «El Sol» y promete enviar, por la vía del Havre, el que contiene el discurso que había pronunciado el general Victoria en la sesión de clausura del congreso de la Unión. Hay dos ejemplares.

576

N.º 259. — 24 de julio, Burlington.

Acusa recibo de varios despachos.

577

N.º 260. — 24 de julio, Burlington.

Participa que había dado cuenta a Manuel Barros de la autorización recibida para abonarle la cantidad que se había fijado a cuenta de sus atrasos para que pudiera volver a España, suma que se le entregaría a la vez que el pasaporte.

578

N.º 262. — 25 de julio, Burlington.

Había trasladado al cónsul general la orden relativa al crédito que reclamaba la viuda de Bartolomé Renguenet y remitiría las cuentas en cuanto dicho cónsul se las enviase.

579

N.º 263. — 26 de julio, Burlington.

Aproximándose la elección de nuevo presidente de la república, consulta si debería cumplimentar personalmente en Washington al elegido, como era costumbre del cuerpo diplomático, o limitarse a hacerlo por escrito desde Filadelfia. Estaban muy equilibradas las fuerzas de los dos candidatos que eran el general Jackson y el presidente Adams, que podría ser reelegido por otros cuatro años.

Adjunto:

— Nota informativa (22 de septiembre 1828).

580

N.º 264. — 26 de julio, Burlington.

Anuncia remisión de un ejemplar del periódico de Méjico «El Sol», que contenía el discurso del general Victoria al llamado congreso de la Unión al cerrar sus sesiones; se decía en él que el ministro de Estados Unidos no había podido concluir el tratado de comercio y navegación, pero sí el de límites, en el que se fijaban los mismos que España había estipulado en el 22 de febrero de 1819.

581

N.º 265. — 27 de julio, Burlington.

Comunica que se había declarado en Charleston una epidemia de la enfermedad conocida en la Habana con el nombre de «dengue», que aunque tenía los mismos síntomas que la fiebre amarilla era más benigna; casi toda la población la padecía y era probable que se extendiera a otros puntos dado las escasas precauciones que se adoptaban para evitarlo.

582

N.º 267. — 29 de julio, Burlington.

Remite una gaceta de Filadelfia y la traducción de una noticia que contenía sobre una sublevación de las tropas extranjeras en Río Janeiro.

Adjunto:
— Ejemplar del «The National Gazette» (Filadelfia, 28 de julio 1828).
— Traducción de unas noticias del Brasil insertas en dicho periódico, dando cuenta de que se había producido una insurrección de las tropas irlandesas y alemanas contra las brasileñas a consecuencia del castigo que se había infligido a un soldado alemán.

583

N.º 268. — 30 de julio, Burlington.

Sus indagaciones sobre la estancia del coronel Montenegro en Estados Unidos habían obtenido la siguiente información: que recibía un sueldo de noventa duros mensuales de una casa de comercio, y por cuenta del gobierno rebelde de Méjico, y otros ciento cincuenta duros para gastos extraordinarios. Su misión era, mediante una correspondencia secreta con Cuba, mantener a los mejicanos al tanto de cualquier movimiento de las tropas y fuerzas navales de la Habana. Había dado aviso a los capitanes generales de dicha isla y de la de Puerto Rico. Acababan de llegar de Nueva York, procedentes de Veracruz, dos coroneles al servicio de aquel gobierno llamado Facio y Thoabet de Beauchasse; éste, natural de Francia con el encargo de imprimir la biografía de los hombres ilustres de la revolución mejicana. Decían que ambos militares y otros mejicanos que les acompañaban, eran contrarios al partido yorkino en el poder y habían tenido que abandonar el país.

584

N.º 269. — 8 de agosto, Burlington.

Acusa recibo de varios despachos.

585

N.º 272. — 9 de agosto, Burlington.

Queda enterado de la asignación concedida al cónsul general en Estados Unidos, Francisco Hernández Nogués, de un sueldo anual de cuarenta mil reales de vellón.

586

N.º 274. — 10 de agosto, Burlington.

Acusa recibo de una circular relativa a la restructuración del cuerpo diplomático.

587

N.º 275. — 10 de agosto, Burlington.

Inserta un oficio que había recibido del cónsul en Nueva Orleans, en respuesta al que le había dirigido inquiriendo noticias sobre el conde de Moctezuma; parecía indudable que su viaje a Méjico desde Europa era para reclamar el cobro de la pensión de veinticinco mil pesos anuales que le había asignado el gobierno español en Méjico y que había recibido hasta que los revolucionarios se habían hecho con el poder. Careciendo de noticias del agente a quien había encargado la administración de su hacienda se había trasladado a Méjico de donde había sido invitado a salir; estaba en tan penosa situación que había podido subsistir gracias a la ayuda que le prestaba un hombre adinerado llamado Nicolás Girod. Las gestiones hechas por medio de un agente para proseguir sus reclamaciones parecía llevar buen camino; la marquesa de la Cortina, que administraba su hacienda, le había propuesto comprársela. Por lo demás su conducta era normal, llevaba una vida modesta y no parecía ser partidario de los independientes de Méjico.

588

N.º 277. — 11 de agosto, Burlington.

Remite una nota sobre los tres españoles procedentes de California que habían salido hacía poco de Boston para la península.

Adjunto:
— Nota de los españoles que con pasaporte del cónsul en Boston habían salido para la península, vía Gibraltar; eran dos franciscanos, expulsados de la alta California, y su asistente (Burlington, 11 de agosto 1828).

589

N.º 278. — 12 de agosto, Burlington.

Da cuenta de que el presidente de la república se encontraba viajando por los estados del este mientras el secretario de Estado

Clay recorría los del oeste. También estaban viajando varios altos empleados del gobierno, el ministro de Rusia y otros individuos del cuerpo diplomático, por razones de las que anteriormente había informado.

590

N.º 279. — 12 de agosto, Burlington.

Remite copia de dos oficios del cónsul en Nueva York referentes al atrevimiento que había tenido el español José Quintana de citarle, sin su conocimiento, como posible informante, en el prospecto de una academia de español que se proponía establecer en Tompkinsville, cerca de Nueva York y manifiesta la celeridad con que el referido cónsul lo había desmentido en todas las gacetas de la ciudad. La explicación del cónsul Stoughton coincidía con las noticias llegadas por otros conductos sobre la relajada conducta de Quintana.

Adjunto:

— Copia del oficio de Francisco Stoughton a Francisco Tacón anunciando remisión de un número de «El Mercurio de Nueva York» con el anuncio de la academia de español de José Quintana, en el que le citaba como persona que podía informar respecto a dicho establecimiento. Inmediatamente lo había desmentido públicamente en todas las gacetas mediante una nota que remite, junto con su traducción. Lo mismo que su nombre, había usado los de otras personas sin conocimiento de los interesados. En todas sus actuaciones era Quintana persona inmoral y sin escrúpulos: había llegado a Nueva York huyendo de la Habana, donde iban a encerrarlo en un castillo por sus trampas y enredos, y se había dedicado a escribir cartas denigrando a las autoridades de Cuba por su rectitud en aplicar las leyes; había vivido disolutamente en la cuarentena (Nueva York, 4 de agosto 1828).

— Ejemplar del «Mercurio de Nueva York» (2 de agosto 1828).

— Recorte del periódico con la nota que Stoughton había hecho publicar en todas las gacetas de Nueva York aclarando que Quintana había usado su nombre sin su consentimiento, y traducción del texto.

— Copia de un oficio de Stoughton a Francisco Tacón dándole cuenta de que Quintana lo había visitado y pedido explicaciones por la nota que había publicado y que, según él, atentaba contra su honor y buen nombre y requería una rectificación pública en la misma forma. A su respuesta de que él era el ofendido y a quien correspondía recibir satisfacción, Quintana había contestado que escribiría en las gacetas sobre las injusticias que le habían hecho las autoriades de la Habana en el pleito que había mantenido con el conde de la Reunión. Stoughton le había advertido que lo perseguiría ante los tribunales por cualquier libelo que publicara en ese sentido (Nueva York, 8 de agosto 1828).

— Recorte de una gaceta con la traducción de una nota que había insertado José Quintana Warnes exponiendo el resultado de la conversación que había mantenido con el cónsul Stoughton (Staten Island, 7 de agosto 1828).

— Nota informativa (26 de octubre 1828).

591

N.º 282. — 14 de agosto, Burlington.

Aparte de las noticias contenidas en un periódico cuya remisión anunciaba, las más recientes procedentes de la Guayra decían que las autoridades de dicha ciudad habían declarado a Bolívar jefe supremo de toda Colombia. Entre los editores de dicho periódico en Nueva York se contaban un español llamado Lanuza, que había sido médico en Córdoba, y José Lerena, llegado de Cádiz hacía cinco años. Trataba de conseguir un ejemplar de la nueva constitución del Perú para enviarlo en la primera ocasión.

Adjunto:

— Nota informativa (15 de noviembre 1828).

592

N.º 283. — 14 de agosto, Burlington.

Remite un recorte del periódico «Journal of Commerce», con su traducción, conteniendo la proclama de Bolívar que equivalía a una declaración de guerra contra el Perú; creía posible que la dictadura de Bolívar diera lugar a graves acontecimientos en Costa Firme, pues aunque contaba con el apoyo de la tropa, se le oponían casi todos los pueblos.

Habían llegado tres representantes de la llamada convención de Ocaña: Fernando Peñalver, diputado por Cumaná, y Santiago Rodríguez y Valentín Ocio por Carabobo, los cuales habían emigrado de Colombia por ser contrarios a Bolívar y no encontrarse seguros allí, después de disolverse la citada convención.

Adjunto:

— Recorte del «Journal of Commerce» (Nueva York, 13 de agosto 1828).
— Recorte de un periódico con su traducción. Noticias de Caracas daban cuenta de que Bolívar había sido nombrado dictador de Colombia y no tardaría en proclamarse Simón I como rey; ya se habían nombrado pares, duques y caballeros. Un reciente terremoto había producido considerables daños.
— Traducción de noticias importantes de Colombia, que daban como próxima la guerra entre Colombia y Perú, según se deducía de las noticias aparecidas en la «Gaceta de Cartagena». El comandante en jefe de Guayaquil decía al comandante en jefe del ejército del sur que los peruanos estaban decididos a marchar contra Colombia, habiendo salido de Callao varios transportes de tropas en dirección a Patra; se habían concedido empréstitos para las necesidades bélicas.
El comandante en jefe del ejército del sur daba cuenta al secretario de Estado y ministro de la Guerra de las consecuencias de la sublevación de Chuquisaca y de la desgracia del presidente de Bolivia; del ataque del ejército peruano mandado por el general Lamar, y de la defensa que se aprestaba a hacer Colombia contra los agresores.
Una proclama de Simón Bolívar al pueblo del sur manifestaba que las tropas peruanas habían entrado hasta el centro de Bolivia sin previa declaración de guerra, por lo que animaba a colombianos y bolivianos a aprestarse para defender su patria (Bogotá, 3 de julio 1828).

593

N.º 287. — 20 de agosto, Burlington.

Remite una relación de los españoles procedentes de Méjico que habían obtenido pasaporte del cónsul en Nueva Orleans para volver a la península.

Adjunto:

— Lista de los pasaportes concedidos en el consulado de Nueva Orleans a españoles procedentes de Nueva España, desde el 12 de marzo al 16 de julio 1828.

594

N.º 288. — 28 de agosto, Burlington.

Remite un recorte de gaceta con noticias sobre el armamento que se proyectaba hacer para el aventurero Porter; había avisado al cónsul general para que alertara a los demás cónsules a fin de que indagaran la posible construcción o armamento de buques con el mismo fin.

Adjunto:

— Recorte de un periódico que insertaba un artículo referente a la preparación de veinte buques con su armamento, provisiones y tripulación que, bajo el mando del comodoro Porter, pudieran proteger la independencia y el comercio de Méjico, su patria de adopción. Traducción del mismo.

595

N.º 290. — 29 de agosto, Burlington.

Anuncia remisión de una gaceta del Brasil que trataba de la sublevación de las tropas extranjeras que había comunicado anteriormente; noticias posteriores informaban de que en Bahía se había descubierto una conspiración contra el gobierno imperial, que se habían reanudado las negociaciones de paz con Buenos Aires y que la reina de Portugal, María de la Gloria, había salido de Río Janeiro para completar su educación en Viena. Noticias de Lima daban cuenta de que había sido depuesto el general Lamar y habían vuelto a tomar el mando los partidarios de Bolívar, a cuya cabeza estaba el general Santa Cruz, siendo probable que esta nueva revolución se extendiera hasta el alto Perú.

596

N.º 293. — 5 de septiembre, Filadelfia.

Acusa recibo de varios despachos llegados a Nueva York en un buque procedente del Havre.

597

N.º 298. — 12 de septiembre, Filadelfia.

Inserta un oficio que había recibido de Francisco Stoughton, en el que le comunicaba que la composición de la escuadra del gobierno de Buenos Aires, de cuya llegada le había avisado, era la corbeta Bolívar, un bergantín y una goleta que estaban fondeados en Long Pond, a veinte millas de Nueva York; procedían de la isla dinamarquesa de Santo Tomás y su comandante era el mismo Fournier que había preparado la referida corbeta Bolívar y ahora estaba reclutando la marinería; había mantenido también conferencias con el propietario de un navío sueco y con el constructor naval Eckford, y les había hecho proposiciones de compra.

Como corría el rumor de que el destino de esta escuadra podría ser Cuba o Puerto Rico, lo había comunicado a los respectivos capitanes generales a la vez que manifestaba al administrador de la aduana de Nueva York la grave infracción de la neutralidad que supondría si llegara a realizarse.

Por otro conducto había recibido también noticias de dichos buques; el bergantín se estaba preparando por cuenta del capitán Cotherell, que probablemente intentaría hacer el corso con la bandera de los rebeldes americanos.

Adjunto:

— Carta de Manuel Valdor a Francisco Tacón comunicándole que un capitán recién llegado de Santo Tomás le había dicho que la corbeta Bolívar, con el Juncal y otro bergantín goleta, habían llegado allí el 6 de agosto para alistar gente, pero el 8 se había recibido una orden del capitán general de las islas dinamarquesas prohibiendo la estancia en sus puertos, por más de cuarenta y ocho horas, a los corsarios y buques de guerra de Colombia y Buenos Aires, por lo que habían tenido que salir a cruzar con tripulaciones malas y escasas. Respecto a la corbeta Bolívar dice que era un buque malo y anticuado, con más de catorce años, y en cuanto a un nuevo bergantín que se estaba armando, por haberlo llevado a la punta del muelle no lo había visto en los últimos días, pero haría una visita para ver el estado en que se hallaba (Baltimore, 7 de septiembre 1828).

— Copia de la misma carta.

598

N.º 299. — 12 de septiembre, Filadelfia.

Da cuenta de la llegada de Jacobo Talard de Arambuja para relevar al encargado de negocios de Portugal cerca de Estados Unidos, pero como sus credenciales procedían del anterior gobierno, cesado hacía cerca de cuatro años y no del vigente, era probable que encontrara dificultades para ser reconocido. El encargado de negocios de Brasil no había querido devolverle la visita protocolaria que le había hecho a su llegada y actuaba para que no se reconociera ningún representante del rey don Miguel; como el gobierno americano esperaba concluir un tratado comercial ventajoso con Brasil, guardaba muchas consideraciones al emperador don Pedro, lo que inducía a pensar que diferiría el reconocimiento del nuevo representante de Portugal.

599

N.º 300. — 12 de septiembre, Filadelfia.

Comunica el regreso, después de tres años de licencia en su país, del ministro de Dinamarca en Estados Unidos, Pedersen, que era probable fijase su residencia en Filadelfia como anteriormente. Mister Walsh, nombrado secretario de la legación americana en Madrid, había embarcado en Nueva York con dirección al Havre.

600

N.º 301. — 12 de septiembre, Filadelfia.

Participa que el día anterior había llegado a Filadelfia el presidente de la república y en la mañana del presente había salido para Washington. Aunque su proyecto era viajar hasta mediados de octubre, una grave enfermedad de su esposa lo había obligado a regresar.

601

N.º 302. — 13 de septiembre, Filadelfia.

Anuncia remisión de cincuenta y dos números del periódico de Méjico «El Sol», carentes de noticias de interés. Los masones, yorkinos y escoceses se ocupaban preferentemente en que la elección del nuevo presidente de aquella república recayera en alguno de los suyos y parecía que los primeros tenían más probabilidades de ganar por lo que saldría el general Guerrero. Hay dos ejemplares.

602

N.º 303. — 13 de septiembre, Filadelfia.

Comunica el suicidio, por causas que se ignoraban, del ministro de Méjico en Estados Unidos, que estaba próximo a regresar a su país.

Las últimas noticias de Veracruz decían que el aventurero Porter, no pudiendo pagar a los tripulantes de la escuadrilla mejicana, los había despedido y pensaba regresar a Estados Unidos para recuperar la salud y reponerse de sus desgracias. Los agentes de los mejicanos y de los colombianos en los Estados Unidos sufrían tales retrasos en el cobro de sus sueldos que les era muy difícil subsistir, y el encargo de negocios de Colombia estaba a punto de volver a su país. No se había ratificado el tratado de paz negociado entre Guatemala y El Salvador, por lo que se había recrudecido la guerra civil que asolaba aquellos territorios.

Adjunto:

— Traducción de una nota publicada en el «Diario Nacional» de Washington, en la que se daba cuenta del suicidio del ministro de Méjico, Pablo Obregón (Washington, 11 de septiembre 1828).

603

N.º 304. — 24 de septiembre, Filadelfia.

Acusa recibo de varios despachos.

604

N.º 306. — 25 de septiembre, Filadelfia.

Queda enterado de que habían sido aprobadas las cuentas extraordinarias de la legación, correspondientes al primer trimestre de 1828.

605

N.º 307. — 25 de septiembre, Filadelfia.

Había recibido el oficio de 14 de julio, con un decreto al margen escrito y rubricado por el propio rey, acerca de la admisión en Cuba de los españoles, militares y paisanos expulsados de Nueva España.

606

N.º 308. — 25 de septiembre, Filadelfia.

Acusa recibo de un oficio.

607

309. — 26 de septiembre, Filadelfia.

Remite la traducción de un artículo publicado en la «Gaceta de Nueva York», que insertaba una carta de la Habana en la que se describía el estado de prosperidad de la isla de Cuba.

Adjunto:
— Traducción de una carta del corresponsal en la Habana de la «Gaceta de Nueva York», publicada el 11 de septiembre. Presentaba la situación de Cuba como muy floreciente en cuanto a la agricultura, con cafetales inmensos y nuevas haciendas de azúcar, que habían elevado mucho el valor de las tierras. Se había aumentado enormemente el volumen de las importaciones y exportaciones. El trabajo de los habitantes de la isla era compensado con una gran riqueza que les permitía disfrutar en una paz nunca perturbada.
Eran muy buenas las fuerzas navales y disciplinado el ejército. Los gastos públicos que necesariamente eran inmensos se llevaban con una habilidad sorprendente por el intendente Pinillos que, sin imponer ninguna contribución directa y con una inteligente distribución de las indirectas, conseguía satisfacer los crecidos gastos de una marina y un ejército brillantes y aún quedaban fondos para mejoras internas. A su extraordinaria inteligencia y penetración se debía tal estado de prosperidad

y riqueza; con rigor y energía había terminado con la venalidad de algunos funcionarios y abolido el contrabando, que se aceptaba como un mal necesario, favoreciendo a los negociantes honrados. Bajo su administración habían prosperado las rentas, la agricultura y el comercio; se mantenían con holgura el ejército y la marina, extinguiéndose los derechos de exportación del café, a pesar de lo cual las rentas habían aumentado notablemente sobre el año anterior. Cuba era ahora un país próspero donde la pobreza era desconocida (La Habana, 17 de agosto 1828).

608

N.º 310. — 26 de septiembre, Filadelfia.

Anuncia remisión de dos cartas para Manuel de Barros, llegadas con el último correo, por haber salido el destinatario hacía más de un mes del puerto de Nueva York con destino al Havre.

609

N.º 311. — 27 de septiembre, Filadelfia.

Comunica que había llegado a Nueva York el general holandés Verveer que, según se creía, traía credencial del rey de Países Bajos cerca de la república de América Central o Guatemala. Dicho general había asistido comisionado por su gobierno al congreso de Panamá y Tacubaya, regresando a Europa el año pasado. Un tal Alvarado, que había sido agente de Guatemala en Londres y ahora se encontraba en Nueva York, había dicho que esperaba al general Verveer para acompañarle a su país y que traía consigo un proyecto para abrir un canal al mar Pacífico.

610

N.º 312. — 27 de septiembre, Filadelfia.

Agradece la comunicación que había recibido participándole que, por el nuevo arreglo adoptado en el cuerpo diplomático, debería continuar como ministro residente en Estados Unidos.

611

N.º 314. — 28 de septiembre, Filadelfia.

Anuncia remisión de un memorial de la viuda de Bouligny, que le había entregado su hijo, uno de los senadores más respetables de la Unión.

Adjunto:

— Nota informativa.

612

N.º 317. — 28 de septiembre, Filadelfia.

Comunica que había llegado a Nueva York, procedente de Liverpool, un antiguo empleado de la legación francesa en Estados Unidos llamado Bresson. Regresado a París hacía dos años, venía ahora con comisión de su gobierno para Méjico y otros puntos de América española. Próximamente embarcaría en Norfolk, en un buque francés que le llevaría a Veracruz. Según el mismo Bresson había dicho a Francisco Stoughton, tenía plan de permanecer tres meses en Méjico y luego pasar a Guatemala, Caracas, Bogotá, Guayaquil y Lima, teniendo a su disposición dicho buque para los puertos del Atlántico; le acompañan mister Terreau, sobrino del comerciante de Lion del mismo nombre, y el duque de Montebello. El primero, que va como secretario de la comisión, era un joven de veinticinco años educado en una universidad alemana y con fama de literato; el duque había conseguido el nombramiento de agregado a la comisión por su afición a los viajes. Se ignoraba el verdadero objeto de la misión de Bresson, pero parecía que era presentar a su gobierno un informe exacto del estado de dichas provincias.

Adjunto:

— Despacho reservado y cifrado en parte, del secretario de la embajada de España en París, Andrés Villalba, al secretario de Estado Manuel González Salmón, dando cuenta de que se había anunciado en algunos periódicos de París el nombramiento de varios comisarios para que examinaran el estado de los países de América, a fin de ver el enfoque que podría dar el gabinete francés a sus relaciones comerciales con ellos y con objeto de reconocer lo antes posible la independencia de los nuevos estados. En su opinión, con el envío de estos comisarios el gobierno francés pretendía ganar tiempo ante los clamores de los que deseaban el inmediato reconocimiento de estas repúblicas. Por otra parte, se sabía la anarquía y miseria que reinaba en varios puntos de América española; un enviado de Guatemala, había hecho fijar un aviso en la bolsa de Londres, declarando la imposibilidad de pagar el dividendo del empréstito contraído por dicha república con la casa de Barclay Norrino y Compañía. Esto, unido a casos análogos en Colombia y otros puntos, habían desvanecido las ilusiones que se habían hecho los comerciantes sobre la emancipación de América.

Tenía motivos para pensar que España encontraría apoyo en el gabinete francés para recuperar sus antiguas colonias o al menos las principales. Por su extraordinario interés comunicaba estas noticias al enviado en Londres, conde de Ofalia (París, 27 de julio 1828).

613

N.º 319. — 30 de septiembre, Filadelfia.

No había apenas noticias interesantes de las provincias de América, siendo únicamente de reseñar una procedente de Caracas, que decía que Bolívar había hecho arrestar a su rival, el general Santander. Anuncia remisión de periódico con un artículo referente a Madrid. Respecto a Estados Unidos tampoco había novedad importante, ocupándose toda la atención en la próxima elección de presidente.

Adjunto:

— Ejemplar del «Mercurio de Nueva York» (27 de septiembre 1828).

614

N.º 320. — 7 de octubre, Filadelfia.

Acusa recibo de varios oficios.

615

N.º 321. — 7 de octubre, Filadelfia.

Remite una nota de Antonio Pomar, encargado del consulado de Norfolk durante la ausencia del titular Pablo Chacón y que había cesado al suprimirse dicho consulado, en la que solicitaba que le fueran concedidos los ciento cincuenta pesos anuales que le estaban asignados para gastos de correo, secretaría e impresos. Tacón apoyaba su solicitud por parecerle tanto más justa cuanto que había desempeñado el consulado sin sueldo ni apenas obvenciones.

Adjunto:

— Solicitud de Antonio Pomar de que le fueran concedidos ciento cincuenta pesos para los gastos del consulado de Norfolk (Norfolk, 1 de septiembre 1828).
— Nota informativa (15 de diciembre 1828).
— Minuta al director del Real Giro ordenándole abonar la cuenta que había presentado Antonio Pomar de la suma asignada para gastos eventuales en el presupuesto de su ministerio. Se comunica también a Tacón para conocimiento del interesado.

616

N.º 322. — 8 de octubre, Filadelfia.

Comunica que Raimundo Chacón, cónsul en Boston, había embarcado en Nueva York con pasaporte para Riga y le había enviado un oficio, cuya copia adjunta, declarando la persona a quien había autorizado para que percibiera sus sueldos atrasados; el correspondiente al año 27 y primer semestre del 28 lo había cobrado por libramientos contra las Reales Cajas de la intendencia de la Habana, y esperaba que Pinillos admitiera también que se dieran libranzas a los cónsules suprimidos, por el tiempo que se les debía. Hay dos ejemplares.

Adjunto:

— Copia del oficio de Raimundo Chacón participando a Tacón que había recibido el pasaporte por mano de Stoughton y quedaban como representantes suyos con poderes para cobrar las cantidades que se le debían, los señores William Swett y Cía. del comercio de Boston (Nueva York, 1 de octubre 1828). Hay dos ejemplares.
— Nota informativa (14 de enero 1828).

617

N.º 323. — 9 de octubre, Filadelfia.

Explica el motivo de que hubieran ido en el mismo buque el principal y el duplicado de un oficio; se debía a que habiéndose retrasado el correo de tierra en que los remitía al cónsul en Nueva York para que los enviara en distintos paquetes a Gibraltar y el Havre, cuando llegaron sólo pudo alcanzar el de Gibraltar a cuyo capitán los había entregado creyendo que eran pliegos de diferente contenido.

618

N.º 324. — 9 de octubre, Filadelfia.

Había recibido el oficio relativo a la cuenta de gastos extraordinarios del cónsul en Nueva Orleans y lo había trasladado al cónsul general Francisco Hernández Nogués para que lo comunicara al interesado.

619

N.º 325. — 9 de octubre, Filadelfia.

Había comunicado al cónsul general la real orden relativa a la clasificación de cesantes y jubilados para que la hiciera llegar a los demás cónsules.

620

N.º 326. — 10 de octubre, Filadelfia.

Comunica que habían salido para Cádiz en la fragata mercante americana Fabius los españoles que se citan en una relación adjunta, que habían llegado a Nueva York procedentes de Méjico.

Adjunto:

— Relación de los españoles que habían salido de Nueva York para Cádiz en la fragata Fabius; se trataba de siete religiosos, del Hospicio de San Nicolás varios de ellos, y de dos comerciantes (Filadelfia, 10 de octubre 1828).

621

N.º 328. — 12 de octubre, Filadelfia.

Remite las últimas gacetas que habían llegado de Colombia y una de Nueva York, con noticias de la guerra civil en el alto Perú y de la que se había recrudecido entre El Salvador y Guatemala. No había llegado ninguna de Méjico debido al mal tiempo. Las elecciones para nuevo presidente de Estados Unidos estaban bastante equilibradas y no se podía saber cuál saldría elegido.

Adjunto:

— Ejemplar de la «Gaceta de Colombia» (Bogotá, 20 de julio 1828).
— Tres ejemplares de la «Gaceta de Gobierno» (Caracas, 27 y 30 de agosto y 6 de septiembre 1828).
— Ejemplar del «Mercurio de Nueva York» (Nueva York, 11 de octubre 1828).
— Ejemplar impreso de una «Representación de Martín Tovar a S. E. el general J. A. Páez, jefe superior de Venezuela» en la que exponía que a la vuelta de la gran convención de Ocaña, adonde había ido como diputado designado por la provincia de Caracas, le había sido negado el permiso para entrar en su patria sin darle ninguna explicación, por lo que pedía que le fuera permitido volver o en caso de que un tribunal decidiera que era reo de alguna culpa que se lo impidiera, que se permitiera salir a su familia para trasladarse con ella a algún país que los acogiera (La Guayra, 25 de agosto 1828).

622

N.º 329. — 13 de octubre, Filadelfia.

Da cuenta de que había entrado en el puerto de Filadelfia la goleta americana llamada Maryland, que había salido de la Habana para la Coruña con el correo de aquella isla. Se habían arreglado las averías rápidamente y se había dado de nuevo a la vela para su destino. Hay dos ejemplares.

623

N.º 330. — 13 de octubre, Filadelfia.

Queda enterado de que en lo sucesivo no debería efectuar ciertos pagos sin obtener previamente la autorización del gobierno; el que había hecho había sido inducido por la certidumbre del crédito que reclamaba el obispo de Charleston y la dignidad de aquel prelado, la pequeñez de la suma y la gran distancia que lo separaba de la metrópoli.

624

N.º 331. — 13 de octubre, Filadelfia.

Amplía las noticias sobre el hijo mayor de Iturbide, cuyos movimientos había vigilado; se encontraba en Nueva York pronto a embarcarse para Cartagena de Indias ocultamente, después de haber estudiado algún tiempo en el colegio militar de Middleton, en Connecticut, bajo la dirección del capitán Partridge; decían que dicho joven, que tenía veintiún años, era de gran viveza y genio militar y tenía muchísima ambición, sin recatarse de decir que su difunto padre había perdido la corona y la fortuna por indecisión y pusilanimidad y que él en su caso obraría de otro modo; debía tener algún partido en Méjico y la legación de aquel país en Estados Unidos tenía orden de celar estrechamente su conducta y movimientos. El gobierno mejicano tenía tal temor de que se presentase allí que había amenazado con retirar la pensión que gozaba su madre si se ausentaba de Washington más de veinticuatro horas sin licencia, condición de la que muchas veces se le había oído quejarse. Si se arriesgaba a perder dicha pensión partiendo para Cartagena había que pensar que iría con la anuencia de Bolívar, que probablemente tendría el proyecto de establecer en Méjico un gobierno más conforme a sus miras que el que existía y contra el cual intrigaba, según decían, el ministro colombiano en Méjico. Hay dos ejemplares.

625

N.º 332. — 25 de octubre, Filadelfia.

Acusa recibo de varios oficios llegados por la vía del Havre.

626

N.º 333. — 25 de octubre, Filadelfia.

Comunica que el día anterior se había incorporado a su puesto de secretario de la legación Francisco de Paula Quadrado, que había llegado a Nueva York procedente de Gibraltar; su antecesor Hilario de Rivas y Salmón esperaba la ayuda de costas para el largo viaje que debía emprender.

627

N.º 335. — 27 de octubre, Filadelfia.

Participa que efectivamente el joven Iturbide había salido de Nueva York para Cartagena en el buque americano Medina. El cónsul en Nueva York Francisco Stoughton, le había comunicado que el ex-ministro del gobierno de Colombia, Salazar, afirmaba que Bolívar mantenía correspondencia desde hacía mucho tiempo con el joven Iturbide. Hay dos ejemplares.

628

N.º 336. — 28 de octubre, Filadelfia.

Había recibido de Washington los impresos correspondientes a las actas del congreso de la Unión desde el 14 de diciembre de 1827 al 28 de marzo del presente año y anuncia remisión de las más interesantes, advirtiendo que quedaba en la legación una colección completa de dichas actas. Hay dos ejemplares.

629

N.º 337. — 28 de octubre, Filadelfia.

Da cuenta de que el secretario de la legación, Francisco de Paula Quadrado, le había hecho entrega de un tomo que comprendía las gacetas de Madrid del año 1827 y un legajo de las del año en curso hasta finales de agosto, con lo cual había cumplido el encargo recibido. Hay dos ejemplares.

630

N.º 338. — 30 de octubre, Filadelfia.

Queda enterado de la real orden relativa al expediente de Nicolás Villavaso, en el sentido de que quedara la causa sobreseída si éste no era molestado por los tribunales; pero en el caso de que se tratase de ejecutar la sentencia del juez de paz de Nueva Orleans, presentara una enérgica reclamación al gobierno federal, informando inmediatamente al secretario de Estado, González Salmón, para recibir las oportunas instrucciones. Hay dos ejemplares.

631

N.º 339. — 30 de octubre, Filadelfia.

Incluye copia de un oficio del cónsul general en Estados Unidos, que insertaba el que había recibido del de Nueva Orleans participando la llegada de un tal Valle como vicecónsul de los rebeldes mejicanos y las últimas noticias de Nueva España.

Por cartas recientes de Veracruz se sabía que aunque el general Santa Ana había sido suspendido de su cargo de vicegobernador por el congreso del estado, según informaba una gaceta que remitía, y posteriormente había sido arrestado, había logrado hacerse con ochocientos hombres y treinta mil duros del erario público, dejando en Jalapa al general Mora sin pertrechos de guerra ni fondos para adquirirlos; a sus fuerzas se había unido la guarnición del castillo de Perote y se había declarado dispuesto a mantener con sus hombres la elección de Guerrero como presidente, pese a que sólo tres estados habían votado a su favor, haciéndolo nueve a favor de Pedraza; Guerrero había salido de Méjico con Bustamante y otros oficiales sin conocimiento del gobierno, que estaba consternado, y el país consideraba inevitable la guerra civil. Estaban próximas a llegar nuevas noticias de Veracruz.

Adjunto:

— Copia del oficio del cónsul general Francisco Hernández Nogués a Francisco Tacón, insertando el que había recibido del de Nueva Orleans, participando que acababa de llegar de Veracruz Manuel Valle como vicecónsul de la república mejicana; había ido

a parar a la casa que habitaba el cónsul Montenegro, que ya
había dicho que la tomaba para residir en ella el cónsul mejicano. Las noticias de Nueva España se referían a las elecciones
de nuevo presidente, en las que llevaba mucha ventaja Gómez
Pedraza a Guerrero. En Veracruz Antonio López de Santa Ana
había querido sublevar al pueblo contra la voluntad del congreso
y éste le había destituido y hecho arrestar. En Oaxaca había
habido refriegas con varios muertos y heridos, y en todo el país
había tal agitación que se temía una guerra civil (Filadelfia, 25
de octubre 1828).
— Ejemplar del «Noticioso comercial y científico» (Veracruz, 9
de septiembre 1828).

632

N.º 341. — 30 de octubre, Filadelfia.

Las últimas noticias recibidas de Costa Firme decían que Bolívar
había movilizado a todos los hombres útiles de los 15 a los 45 años,
pero como carecía de recursos para pagarlos, muchos se negaban
a alistarse ocultándose en los montes, lo que había producido la
destrucción de la agricultura. También había pretendido armar dos
fragatas para que pasaran al Pacífico, pero como llevaban cuatro
años en el puerto y necesitaban muchos reparos y no había ni dinero ni marineros, se hacía difícil su habilitación. Eran grandes las
miserias y el descontento general.

Los jefes de las partidas se aprovechaban de estas circunstancias: Centeno se había apoderado de los fondos destinados a la
siembra del tabaco en Orituco; Cisneros, sorprendiendo a la guarnición de Ocumare, se había apoderado de las armas y municiones,
retirándose posteriormente a las montañas donde había sido reforzado por Arizalbo. En Caracas continuaba la proscripción de los
descontentos. Bolívar había ordenado recoger las patentes de los
corsarios para conseguir marinería para las fragatas anteriormente
citadas; su objetivo era la guerra del Perú a cuya posesión aspiraba
por considerar próxima la disolución de su gobierno en Costa
Firme. Trataba de asustar al gobierno con decretos como el del
alistamiento de cuarenta mil hombres, cuando no tenía gente para
dominar a las partidas que aumentaban cada día en el interior.
Falto de fondos para sostenerlas, había tenido que retirar todas las
legaciones en el extranjero.

633

N.º 342. — 30 de octubre, Filadelfia.

Comunica la llegada a Filadelfia, procedentes de Washington, del ministro de los Países Bajos en Estados Unidos caballero Huygens, del general holandés Veveer y un hijo del ministro como secretario de la misión de dicho general. Los dos últimos habían salido para Nueva York a fin de embarcar en la corbeta de guerra americana Erie para Curaçao, en el mismo viaje en que mister Harrison, nombrado ministro del gobierno federal de Colombia, se dirigía a Costa Firme. Los dos ingenieros elegidos para la obra del canal de que ya había informado anteriormente, saldrían de Holanda para la Costa Firme directamente. Al quedarse solo el ministro Huygens lo había invitado a una comida, correspondiendo a la que él había dado en Washington; asistieron también el ministro de Dinamarca y los diplomáticos residentes en Filadelfia, además de varias personas de relieve, y había procurado actuar con esplendidez para demostrar que los representantes de España estaban en condiciones de devolver los obsequios que recibían. Huygens había ido luego a Nueva York a disfrutar de la compañía de su hijo y a llevar luego a Washington a una hija del general Veveer. Hay dos ejemplares.

634

N.º 344. — 13 de noviembre, Filadelfia.

El comandante de la fragata americana Macedonia, que había llegado a Norfolk procedente del Río Janeiro, había portado unos despachos de mister Tudor, encargado de negocios de Estados Unidos en Brasil, con los que había una copia del tratado de paz concluido entre el emperador de aquel país y los comisionados de Buenos Aires. Aunque no se había publicado su contenido, se sabía que el Brasil entregaba la banda oriental al gobierno de Buenos Aires y éste se comprometía a pagar una indemnización.

635

N.º 345. — 13 de noviembre, Filadelfia.

Comunica que el cónsul general le había dado cuenta de que se le habían presentado dos marineros procedentes de Lisboa y pertenecientes a la matrícula de la Habana, que habían sido apresados por un corsario colombiano a la altura de las islas Terceras; se hallaban sin ropas y en la mayor miseria, sin posibilidad de regresar a la Habana por tener que hacerlo en buques americanos que exigían que el pago se hiciera en el lugar de embarque. Como ignoraba de qué fondos podría disponer para solucionar este problema y otros análogos que le había consultado el cónsul de Nueva York Stoughton, pedía instrucciones al respecto considerando probable que se volviera a repetir el caso, así como los posibles apresamientos que hicieran los corsarios de Buenos Aires que libres ya de la guerra con Brasil, se dedicarían con toda seguridad a perseguir a los buques españoles.

636

N.º 347. — 14 de noviembre, Filadelfia.

Anuncia remisión de un fragmento de una gaceta de Nueva York, cuya traducción incluye, relativo a la conspiración que se había formado en Bogotá con resultado favorable a Bolívar, pese a que su viaje había corrido serio peligro. Las últimas noticias añadían que la ejecución de Horment y Padilla habría sido el día nueve del mes pasado, no ocurriendo lo mismo con Santander por ser indispensable terminar su causa por haber estado también complicado en la anterior conspiración de Cartagena.

Adjunto:

— Traducción de una carta de Cartagena que contenía noticias sobre la revolución de Bogotá, en la que se habían sublevado todos los cuerpos de artillería con intención de dar muerte al Libertador y sus seguidores; una parte había marchado hacia palacio sorprendiendo a la guardia y Bolívar había tenido que escapar por una ventana y después permanecer escondido bajo un puente, con el agua hasta la cintura, para burlar la persecución de sus enemigos. Posteriormente pudo unirse en la plaza a sus amigos del cuartel de Vargas, que habían recibido una recompensa por la ayuda prestada. Habían sido fusilados seis de los principales conspiradores.

Sigue una proclama del intendente de Bogotá a los habitantes de Cundinamarca, dándoles cuenta de la sublevación que se había producido en la que la artillería se había levantado intentando matar a Bolívar, que había sido apoyado y defendido por el batallón de granaderos y el de Vargas. Bolívar había conseguido huir y reunirse luego con sus amigos y seguidores. Firma la proclama el intendente Pedro A. Herrán.

Noticias posteriores decían que habían sido fusilados al día siguiente el general Padilla, el francés Horment y el coronel Huerta; otros conspiradores seguirían la misma suerte en cuanto se concluyeran sus causas. Sigue la lista de las personas que habían sido arrestadas (Cartagena, 14 de octubre).

637

N.º 348. — 14 de noviembre, Filadelfia.

Sin noticias directas de Veracruz se había sabido por otros conductos que el general Santa Ana, después de haberse apoderado del castillo de Perote, se había adueñado del paso del Puente del Rey; que depuesto en el mando de Veracruz el general Mora, había sido relevado por el coronel Rincón que había salido con cuatro mil hombres contra Santa Ana; que la presidencia había recaído en el general Gómez Pedraza, permaneciendo el general Guerrero inactivo. Remite copia de la proclama de Santa Ana en la que manifestaba el estado en que se hallaba el país y varias gacetas con noticias de los sucesos de Oaxaca en el acto de la votación de presidente.

Adjunto:

— Copia del «Manifiesto que el ejército libertador hace a los pueblos del Anahuac», en el que Santa Ana y sus colaboradores exponían a los mejicanos la situación en que se hallaban en su lucha por la libertad y proponían varios puntos que deberían cumplirse inexorablemente: anular las elecciones en las que había salido presidente el ministro de la Guerra, Manuel Gómez Pedraza, a quien de ninguna manera se admitía como presidente ni vicepresidente, por considerarlo enemigo de las instituciones mejicanas; la total expulsión de todos los españoles del territorio; que se eligiera como presidente de la república a Vicente Guerrero; que se repitieran las elecciones en las legislaturas que habían contrariado el voto de los pueblos; para evitar una guerra civil y que el ejército evitara el derramamiento de sangre defendiendo el presente pronunciamiento, debían prestar obediencia a la constitución de los Estados Unidos Mejicanos y al

presidente de la república Guadalupe Victoria (Perote, 16 de septiembre 1828).
— Fragmento del «Mercurio de Nueva York» (1 de noviembre 1828).
— Nota informativa (23 de diciembre 1828).

638

N.º 349. — 14 de noviembre, Filadelfia.

Da cuenta de que habían salido de Nueva York en la corbeta de guerra Eire el general holandés Veveer y mister Harrison, nombrado ministro de Estados Unidos en Colombia.

639

N.º 351. — 14 de noviembre, Filadelfia.

Noticias de Valparaíso aseguraban que el gobernador insurgente de Perú había ordenado el alistamiento, en el término de tres días, de todos los hombres comprendidos entre los quince y los cincuenta años; que se iba a disolver el llamado congreso constituyente; que se había levantado la orden de destierro a Manuel Lorenzo Vidaurre, ordenándole regresar a la capital, y que quizá por efecto del terremoto de marzo, se había comprobado que el canal de la isla de San Lorenzo era navegable para buques de 600 toneladas. Por conducto de Panamá se había sabido que las tropas de Colombia y Perú se habían enfrentado en Bolivia, por lo que parecía inevitable la guerra. Posteriormente se había sabido que Sucre había capitulado con Gamarra, comandante de las tropas peruanas.

640

N.º 352. — 26 de noviembre, Filadelfia.

Acusa recibo de varias reales órdenes.

641

N.º 353. — 26 de noviembre, Filadelfia.

Queda enterado de que debe evitar el envío de la correspondencia por la vía de Inglaterra y por conducto del ministro de España en Londres, a no ser en caso de urgencia.

642

N.º 354. — 26 de noviembre, Filadelfia.

Acusa recibo de una circular del ministerio de Hacienda referente al fomento de la agricultura, artes y comercio de España, al pago de los cáñamos extranjeros y su introducción en la península, lo que había trasladado al cónsul general para que lo comunicara a los demás residentes en los puertos de Estados Unidos.

643

N.º 355. — 27 de noviembre, Filadelfia.

Había comunicado a Juan Leamy la resolución que se había adoptado de pasar al ministerio de Hacienda la exposición que había remitido.

644

N.º 356. — 27 de noviembre, Filadelfia.

Había entregado a Juan Leamy, vicecónsul que había sido en Filadelfia, la cantidad que había reclamado por el alquiler del cuarto en el que tuvo custodiado el archivo de la legación, cantidad que cargaría en la cuenta de gastos imprevistos. Y había comunicado al mismo Leamy que el abono de la asignación de gastos extraordinarios, que también reclamaba, se haría cuando se determinara en general el pago de atrasos.

645

N.º 357. — 27 de noviembre, Filadelfia.

Comunica la imposibilidad de enviar un ejemplar del tratado de límites entre los gobiernos de Estados Unidos y Méjico, pues el americano mantenía en el mayor sigilo todos los convenios hasta que pasaran al senado para su ratificación; pero creía que no tardaría en verificarlo por estar próxima la apertura de las sesiones del congreso y del senado y ser éste uno de los primeros asuntos que se tratarían. Hay dos ejemplares.

646

N.º 358. — 27 de noviembre, Filadelfia.

Acusa recibo de un oficio relativo a los dos meses que se le adeudaban como perteneciente a la comisión de reclamaciones en Londres; y había comunicado a Miguel Tacón, lo concerniente a la reclamación que él había presentado.

647

N.º 359. — 27 de noviembre, Filadelfia.

Queda enterado de lo que se le había prevenido tocante al alquiler de la casa de campo para la legación y respecto a la solicitud de Luis Potestad.

648

N.º 361. — 28 de noviembre, Filadelfia.

Comunica las últimas noticias que habían llegado de Cartagena de Indias y de Bogotá: el gobierno de Bolívar había indultado de la pena capital y desterrado del país a Wilthen, Arnero, Parada, Vallarino, Carrasquillo, Gaitán, Merizalde, Dievano, Barquisimeto, Aldana, Plata, Guzmán y al general José María Obando, todos complicados en la rebelión de que ya había informado. No se habían publicado los cargos pues el gobierno tenía interés en ocultar que los colombianos habían sido capaces de atentar contra su libertador. Habían sido decapitados Ramón Guerra, el general Padilla, Horment, Zulayban, Silva, Galindo y López y proseguía viéndose en secreto la causa de los demás encartados, pero parecía que ninguno de ellos sería condenado a la última pena, incluso ni el general Santander, por haberse visto Bolívar empujado a la indulgencia por el gran número de implicados. En Caracas y demás pueblos de la provincia se habían extinguido los ayuntamientos restableciéndose los antiguos corregidores que prescribían las leyes de Indias; se había obligado a la milicia y a todos los habitantes a prestar un nuevo juramento de obediencia a Bolívar y probablemente se organizaría la oposición y podrían repetirse en este país las sangrientas escenas que se habían desarrollado en Méjico.

649

N.º 362. — 28 de noviembre, Filadelfia.

Las últimas noticias de Bogotá habían confirmado la capitulación de Gamarra, comandante de las tropas peruanas con Sucre, jefe de las de Bolivia. Se habían firmado los preliminares del tratado en Piquiza entre Gamarra y Urdinea, comisionado por Sucre para ello. Los principales puntos del tratado eran los siguientes: que en el término de quince días ambos generales evacuarían el país y permanecerían a la espectativa, hasta que se reuniera la asamblea nacional y determinara si las tropas deberían permanecer o no sobre las armas; que los escuadrones de húsares y granaderos de Colombia pasarían a Arica y de allí a su patria por cuenta de Bolivia; que el congreso constituyente de Bolivia debería convocarse en Chuquisaca para recibir la dimisión de Sucre y nombrar un gobierno provisional, reunir la asamblea nacional y revisar la vigente constitución; que este congreso debería nombrar un presidente y determinar cuándo evacuarían los dos ejércitos los territorios ocupados; que las dos repúblicas restablecerían las comunicaciones diplomáticas, que ambas partes contratantes se comprometían a no hacer ningún convenio con Brasil hasta que se normalizaran sus relaciones con el Río de la Plata y que se olvidaría todo lo pasado impidiendo cualquier persecución de los oficiales y soldados por lo pasado.

650

N.º 363. — 29 de noviembre, Filadelfia.

Comunica las noticias más recientes sobre la elección del nuevo presidente de la república, que parecía iba a recaer sobre el general Jackson, puesto que había obtenido noventa y cinco votos más de los necesarios; sus partidarios se habían valido de todas las intrigas para obtener la presidencia, aunque la mayoría de los ciudadanos preferían a Adams conociendo los buenos resultados de su administración y el próspero estado en que había puesto la hacienda pública. En Nueva Orleans había sido mal recibida su elección, que consideraban como una calamidad pública para los estados del sur; algunos componentes del cuerpo diplomático temían que surgieran disgustos y problemas dado su carácter orgulloso, cosa que probablemente sucedería en el caso de España a quien Jackson profesaba profundo odio, evidenciado en la toma de posesión de las Floridas. Manifiesta estos temores por si se estimaba conveniente enviarle instrucciones al respecto. Hay dos ejemplares.

Adjunto:
— Minuta al ministro de Estados Unidos acusando recibo del anterior despacho; no se le enviaban instrucciones especiales, solamente el encargo de que prestase gran atención a los proyectos del nuevo presidente con respecto a España.

651

N.º 364. — 29 de noviembre, Filadelfia.

Expone la desagradable situación en que se encontraba el secretario de la legación, Hilario de Rivas y Salmón, por la animadversión de un vecino que habitaba una casa colindante con la suya, llamado William Kirk, cuyos hijos y criados le molestaban constantemente de palabra y de obra, llegando incluso a irrumpir en su casa en diversas ocasiones; había enviado al secretario de Estado mister Clay una nota de protesta, cuya copia adjunta, así como de la respuesta que había recibido de Clay. Interpuesta una acción judicial por Rivas, el vecino había resultado absuelto con lo que quedaba otra vez a merced de sus insultos, intrigas y molestias. Dado el carácter diplomático que ostentaba Rivas, había consultado el caso con los representantes de Holanda, Dinamarca y Portugal que unánimemente habían opinado que debía instarse al gobierno federal para que hiciera más eficaz la protección de los miembros del cuerpo diplomático, por lo que había presentado una nueva nota, de la cual remitía también copia, solicitando una garantía de que en lo sucesivo no se repetirían los hechos denunciados.

Adjunto:

— Copia de la nota de Francisco Tacón al secretario de Estado Henry Clay denunciando los insultos y molestias a que sometía a Rivas y Salmón su vecino William Kirk, por medio de sus hijos y criadas (Filadelfia, 29 de agosto 1828).
— Copia y traducción de la respuesta de Daniel Brent, en ausencia de Clay, manifestando que había informado a Carlos Ingersoll, fiscal de los Estados Unidos en Filadelfia, de las quejas que Rivas había presentado contra su vecino Guillermo Kirk y no dudaba de que adoptaría las medidas necesarias para evitar su repetición.
— Carta de Tacón a Henry Clay insistiendo en las quejas por la falta de protección en que se encontraba Rivas, componente del cuerpo diplomático, que pese a ser el agraviado, había estado a punto de ser encarcelado por la tergiversación de los hechos que había presentado Kirk, con lo que quedaba sin efecto el derecho de gentes, reconocido en la constitución de los Estados Unidos (Filadelfia, 19 de noviembre 1828).

652

N.º 365. — 29 de noviembre, Filadelfia.

Había mantenido una conversación con el ministro de Holanda que había pasado por Filadelfia camino de Washington, y éste le había dicho que no eran ciertas las noticias que se habían publicado en las gacetas, referentes a que el general Veveer tenía credenciales para representar al rey de Holanda cerca del gobierno de Guatemala; su soberano no había reconocido tal gobierno y la misión del general era únicamente estudiar el terreno para el proyectado canal al mar Pacífico. Hay dos ejemplares.

653

N.º 366. — 29 de noviembre, Filadelfia.

Remite un fragmento de una gaceta, con su traducción, en el que había denunciado las intenciones de los mejicanos de destruir la escuadra española fondeada en la Habana, intenciones que ya habían sido descubiertas por las autoridades de dicha isla y las había declarado en un periódico de la ciudad para hacerlas saber a todo el mundo; con la misma intención él las había hecho publicar en una gaceta de Nueva York a la que corresponde el fragmento y la traducción que remite.

Adjunto:

— Fragmento de la gaceta mencionada con la traducción, en la que manifestaba que había ofrecido al comodoro Porter el mando de una escuadra de veinte buques, con sus tripulaciones, provisiones y armamento, para proteger el comercio de su patria de adopción. Noticias de Veracruz aseguraban que había un acuerdo entre el gobierno mejicano y Porter, por el que aquél pagaría una crecida cantidad al autor del proyecto de volar, dentro del puerto de la Habana, dos navíos y una fragata de guerra, pero solamente se pagaría cuando el asunto se hubiera concluido y se pudiera acreditar que los buques se habían hundido. Laborde y demás autoridades de la Habana estaban sobre aviso y no se dejarían sorprender.

654

N.º 368. — 29 de noviembre, Filadelfia.

Despacho cifrado en su mayor parte, por lo que no se extrae nada de su contenido.

655

N.º 369. — 30 de noviembre, Filadelfia.

Comunica las últimas noticias recibidas de Veracruz que daban cuenta de que Santa Ana había sido cercado por las tropas de Rincón teniendo que escapar él solo a caballo y habiendo sido prendidos todos sus oficiales y tropa; aunque Rincón había enviado en su persecución 400 caballos, se creía que lograría evadirse pasando a Guatemala.

656

N.º 370. — 10 de diciembre, Filadelfia.

Anuncia remisión de un oficio de Antonio Argote Villalobos, cónsul en Nueva Orleans, para el presidente de la junta de cesantes y jubilados, a fin de que se le tramitara el expediente respectivo; aunque no acompañaba toda la documentación necesaria lo había enviado para que no se le produjese ningún perjuicio por la demora en solicitarlo, pero le había prevenido que debía enviar una relación de todas sus circunstancias acompañada de copias de todos los documentos que se refieren a ellas.

657

N.º 372. — 10 de diciembre, Filadelfia.

Anuncia remisión de un ejemplar del discurso del presidente del gobierno federal en la apertura de las cámaras para la legislatura del año, con su correspondiente traducción. No aludía directamente a sus relaciones con el gobierno español y, sólo al hablar de América española, dice que las turbulencias interiores habían sido más frecuentes de lo que desearían los amigos de su emancipación; que algunas dificultades habían impedido la conclusión del tratado con los rebeldes mejicanos; al referirse al tratado entre el gobierno del Brasil y los rebeldes de Buenos Aires, dice que los ciudadanos de Estados Unidos habían obtenido algunas indemnizaciones por pérdidas sufridas en sus relaciones con el imperio. Por lo demás el discurso se refería al estado interno de la Unión, y la prosperidad a que había llegado durante su administración.

Incluía la relación de los individuos que componían las diversas comisiones para instruir los negocios sometidos al examen del congreso; continuaba como presidente de la comisión diplomática mister Everett, hermano del ministro en Madrid. El congreso no había tratado cosas de importancia; sólo había presentado una petición J. Leander Cathcart, cónsul en Argel, para el pago de sus reclamaciones comprendidas en el artículo 11 del tratado de la

Florida, por haber facilitado tres buques de guerra, y se habían remitido a las comisiones otros artículos de escaso interés. Resultando ya seguro que el general Jackson sería elegido presidente y que tomaría posesión de su cargo el día 4 de marzo próximo, se decía que residiría en Filadelfia hasta el momento de trasladarse a Washington, para evitar un viaje largo y penoso en el rigor del invierno. Por otra parte se decía que el actual presidente tenía alquilada una casa en las inmediaciones de Washington para retirarse a ella en el momento en que cesara en sus funciones.

Adjunto:

— Traducción del discurso del presidente de los Estados Unidos John Quincy Adams, al senado y a la cámara de representantes (Washington, 2 de diciembre 1828).

658

N.º 373. — 10 de diciembre, Filadelfia.

Remite fragmento de una gaceta de Filadelfia que había publicado el tratado concluido entre el gobierno del Brasil y el llamado de Buenos Aires, junto con su traducción. A consecuencia de la ratificación de dicho tratado el almirante brasileño había levantado el bloqueo de Buenos Aires, con lo que habían entrado en dicho puerto veinticuatro buques que estaban al ancla en el de Montevideo.

Adjunto:

— Recorte de una gaceta de Filadelfia con el tratado suscrito entre Brasil y las Provincias Unidas del Río de la Plata (Río de Janeiro, 27 de agosto 1828).
— Traducción de dicho tratado.

659

N.º 374. — 11 de diciembre, Filadelfia.

Da cuenta de que se habían presentado algunos obstáculos para la aprobación del tratado de límites y comercio entre los Estados Unidos y el gobierno de Méjico, por lo que se había remitido a dicha república para que, obviadas dichas dificultades, pudiera presentarse al senado para su ratificación. Por ello era probable que no pudiera presentarse en esta legislatura, lo que impediría seguramente conseguir una copia. Hay dos ejemplares.

660

N.º 375. — 11 de diciembre, Filadelfia.

Da cuenta de que el encargado de negocios y cónsul general de Portugal, Joaquín Barroso Pereyra, había publicado un artículo en las gacetas de Filadelfia invitando a todos los portugueses residentes en dicha ciudad a prestar juramento de fidelidad a la hija del emperador del Brasil, doña María de la Gloria, como reina de Portugal y lo mismo había hecho el cónsul en Nueva York en los diarios de aquella ciudad.

También había difundido Barroso un folleto en el que se trataba de hacer ver cuál era el legítimo rey de Portugal. El representante de esta nación que había llegado a Washington, continuaba sin ser reconocido como tal.

661

N.º 377. — 12 de diciembre, Filadelfia.

Las últimas noticias recibidas del Perú decían que las fuerzas peruanas que mandaba Gamarra habían eliminado de la presidencia de Bolivia al general Sucre, que había llegado al Callao en un bergantín inglés, saliendo seguidamente para Guayaquil; y que las tropas colombianas se habían embarcado en Arica también para Guayaquil. El congreso constituyente de Bolivia, reunido en Chuquisaca, había elegido presidente al general Santa Cruz y vicepresidente al general Velasco. El gobierno del Perú había declarado bloqueados los puertos de Colombia entre los grados que indica. El presidente Lamar debía tomar el mando del ejército del norte y se temía que de un momento a otro empezaran las hostilidades entre los colombianos y los peruanos.

662

N.º 378. — 12 de diciembre, Filadelfia.

Da cuenta de que un decreto del gobierno de la república de América Central establecería la prohibición del comercio desde sus puertos con España y sus colonias, impidiéndose también la introducción de mercancías de esa procedencia, aunque fueran para territorios neutrales.

663

N.º 383. — 14 de diciembre, Filadelfia.

Las escasas noticias de Costa Firme decían que para asegurar la tranquilidad se trataba de revestir a Bolívar con la corona imperial, dudándose si darle el nombre de Imperio de Bolívar o de los Andes; reinaba en el país un gran desorden. Parecía que Bolívar había ordenado aumentar el ejército hasta cuarenta mil hombres para luchar contra el Perú uniéndose al ejército de Sucre y se preparaban varios buques con el mismo objeto; se hacían grandes esfuerzos para pagar la deuda pública.

664

N.º 384. — 14 de diciembre, Filadelfia.

Las últimas noticias de Veracruz daban cuenta de que Santa Ana continuaba perseguido por las tropas mejicanas, que no habían podido alcanzarlo y que había muchos complicados en la rebelión de este caudillo contra los que se tomaría severas medidas en cuanto fuera capturado.

665

N.º 385. — 14 de diciembre, Filadelfia.

Anuncia remisión de algunos duplicados de correspondencia y tres números del periódico mejicano «El Sol». Hay dos ejemplares.

666

N.º 386. — 20 de diciembre, Filadelfia.

Anuncia remisión, por vía de Gibraltar, de varios números del periódico mejicano «El Sol», con noticias interesantes sobre el general Santa Ana. Hay dos ejemplares.

667

N.º 387. — 25 de diciembre, Filadelfia.

Remite copia y traducción de la nota que había recibido del gobierno federal en respuesta a la que él había enviado protestando por los insultos y molestias inferidos a Rivas y Salmón, antiguo secretario de la legación, por un vecino de su casa; de la exposición que éste había presentado de los hechos, desfigurándolos completamente, y por último de la nueva nota que había enviado al secretario de Estado rebatiendo las falsedades del vecino con las declaraciones del propio Rivas, sus criados y varios testigos. No esperaba que el gobierno tomara en consideración estos comprobantes, pues siempre defendían a ultranza a sus ciudadanos.

Adjunto:

— Copia y traducción de la respuesta del secretario de Estado Clay, a la nota en la que Tacón le había dado cuenta de las molestias y vejaciones a que había estado sometido Rivas y Salmón por la familia y criados de su vecino Kirk; había solicitado del fiscal de los Estados Unidos, Ingersoll, que hiciera las indagaciones pertinentes y de ellas había resultado que era precisamente Kirk el ofendido al haber agredido Rivas a uno de sus hijos y una criada en su propio domicilio, por lo que debería el secretario de la legación dar una satisfacción plena y satisfactoria. Por otra parte la causa de tales actos residía, en parte, en el hecho de que la legación de España estuviera en Filadelfia, a una gran distancia de la capital del gobierno federal de los Estados Unidos; si estuviera en Washington los hechos ocurridos hubieran podido ser atajados desde el principio (Washington, 10 de diciembre 1828).

— Copia y traducción de la exposición del caso por Guillermo Kirk, nacido en el estado de Delaware y de profesión fabricante de ladrillos; presentaba los hechos como una serie de provocaciones y ataques por parte de Rivas sin que nadie de su casa hubiera dado lugar a ello, y seguían las declaraciones del hijo de Kirk, de once años, y de dos criadas (Filadelfia, 19 de noviembre 1828).

— Copia y traducción de la declaración de Juan Topham, que enviado por un corregidor había ido a casa del señor Salmón con una orden de arresto por la denuncia que había presentado contra él su vecino Kirk; pero tras aclarar un mal entendido que se había producido y enterado del carácter diplomático de Rivas, no había ejecutado la citada orden (Filadelfia, 15 de diciembre 1828).

— Copia y traducción de la declaración que había prestado Rivas y Salmón ante William Wilmor, comisario de cuartel, sobre los hechos acaecidos con su vecino mister Kirk (Filadelfia, 19 de diciembre 1828).

— Copia y traducción de la declaración que había prestado Rebeca Russell, amiga del ama de llaves de Rivas, de molestias verbales que les habían infligido los familiares de Kirk en una visita que les había hecho (Filadelfia, 18 de diciembre 1828).

— Nota de Francisco Tacón al secretario de Estado Clay, refutando las acusaciones que se habían hecho a Rivas Salmón con la declaración de los testigos de su casa y las de varias personas que habían testificado en favor de Salmón (Filadelfia, 20 de diciembre 1828).

— Copia y traducción de la declaración que en favor de Rivas había hecho Nathan Thomas, antiguo criado de dicho señor (Filadelfia, 16 de diciembre 1828).

— Copia y traducción de la declaración que había hecho en favor de Rivas, Hannah Bowers Wright, que había sido su cocinera y ama de llaves (Filadelfia, 18 de diciembre 1828).

— Copia y traducción de la declaración que había prestado a favor de Rivas Joseph Wright, que había estado anteriormente a su servicio (Filadelfia, 18 de diciembre 1828).

— Copia y traducción de la declaración prestada por Samuel Price, hijo del dueño de la casa en la que vivía Rivas (Filadelfia, 18 de diciembre 1828).

668

N.º 389. — 25 de diciembre, Filadelfia.

Da cuenta de que había enviado a Ángel Laborde, comandante general de la escuadra española en la Habana, una obra impresa titulada «Tablas que demuestran los palos, vergas, jarcias y provisiones de toda especie que corresponde a las diferentes clases de buques pertenecientes a la marina de los Estados Unidos, hechas por una junta encargada de dichos trabajos y aprobadas por el ministerio de la Marina». Le había costado mucho la obtención del ejemplar porque el gobierno los reservaba solamente para los comandantes de los buques de guerra. Creía que contenía algunos errores dada la magnitud del proyecto, que probablemente se subsanarían en posteriores ediciones, por lo que estaría atento a procurarse un ejemplar en cuanto viera la luz.

669

N.º 391. — 26 de diciembre, Filadelfia.

Continuaban las sesiones del congreso sin asuntos de importancia; solamente había una proposición de mister White para que la comisión de comercio examinara las ventajas que se seguirían de extender el privilegio concedido a los buques españoles por el artículo 15 del tratado de la Florida a todos los puertos situados en el territorio de dichas Floridas.

670

N.º 392. — 27 de diciembre, Filadelfia.

Por noticias posteriores se habían confirmado las que había remitido referentes al bloqueo de los puertos colombianos que había decretado el gobierno del Perú por medio de su vicepresidente Salazar, como consecuencia de la proclama del 3 de julio del general Bolívar, en la que declaraba la guerra al Perú. Se consideraban incluidos en el bloqueo todos los puertos y bahías desde Tumbes hasta Panamá inclusive. Se fijaban plazos comprendidos entre los dos meses para Chile y América Central y un año para los establecimientos europeos en Asia y la costa oriental de África, al término de los cuales se considerarían notificadas todas las naciones y cualquier buque que fuera apresado en dichos puertos sería conducido al Callao para ser juzgado.

Parece que se habían fletado barcos para Arica, donde debía embarcarse el ejército al mando de Gamarra y en cualquier momento se esperaba un choque entre las fuerzas peruanas y colombianas, cuyas fuerzas calculaban en unos seis mil hombres por cada parte.

671

N.º 393. — 28 de diciembre, Filadelfia.

Según las últimas noticias de Costa Firme se esperaba en Bogotá la llegada del general Harrison, ministro del gobierno federal de Estados Unidos, con cuya presencia suponían que concluirían los malos tratos que recibían en los puertos de dichas provincias los ciudadanos americanos.

Continuaban las causas por la conspiración del 23 de septiembre y aunque los periódicos no publicaban nada sobre el general Santander, parecía que el consejo de guerra lo había condenado a muerte, pero que sería indultado y desterrado a los Estados Unidos. Los periódicos de Cartagena publicaban sobre todo pastorales de los obispos, decretos nombrando nuevos ministros y uno sobre la dirección que debía imprimirse a la educación de la juventud, redactado con tal ignorancia y estupidez que ordenaba suspender las cátedras de Legislación Universal, Derecho Público y Ciencia Administrativa. Parecía que los coroneles Obando e Hilario Gómez iban a reclutar gente en Pasto para un levantamiento y se temía que pudieran pasar a Popayán y se apoderaran de 500 fusiles para armar a la gente. Bravo y varios de los desterrados habían sido bien recibidos en Guayaquil.

672

N.º 394. — 30 de diciembre, Filadelfia.

Por un buque llegado de Veracruz se había recibido información sobre el estado de la república de Méjico donde, lejos de haberse calmado las inquietudes causadas por la rebelión de Santa Ana, se producían nuevas tentativas contra el gobierno, y las autoridades seguían desunidas. Santa Ana, reforzado con los caballos que había robado en Oaxaca, había ido a cortar el paso a Rincón en la cuesta de San Juan del Estado, y en el camino había dispersado las tropas de Miranda que desde Tehuacán había ido a reforzar a Reyes, cuya caballería estaba agotada tras muchos días de continuas marchas. Santa Ana había atacado a Rincón pero al ver vacilar a sus tropas había pedido suspensión de las hostilidades para hacer propuestas al gobierno y había vuelto a Oaxaca donde ocupó el convento de Santo Domingo. Se habían reunido a Rincón los generales Calderón y Valdivieso con algunos refuerzos, pero no parecía probable que pudieran coger a Santa Ana, que lograría internarse en Guatemala con lo que se prolongaría la guerra civil. En Iguala se había preparado una conspiración acaudillada por Andrés María Nieto, español fugado de una prisión de Méjico, que debía estallar en Tepecoacuilco, cuyo ayuntamiento había pedido refuerzos para sofocarla. En Oaxaca habían sido ajusticiados los españoles fray Domingo de San José, carmelita y fray Mateo Morán, franciscano, acusados de haber tratado de que, por medio de una revolución, volvieran a la autoridad del rey los dominios emancipados de América.

673

N.º 395. — 29 de diciembre, Filadelfia.

Muestra su extrañeza por el ofrecimiento que habían hecho al gobierno de Méjico los cónsules extranjeros residentes en la capital y en Veracruz, para subvenir a las necesidades urgentes de su erario y recuperar la paz alterada por los movimientos de Santa Ana, noticias que insertaban unas gacetas cuya remisión anuncia.

674

N.º 396. — 30 de diciembre, Filadelfia.

Participa que hacía algún tiempo que carecía de noticias de la corte, llegando sólo hasta el 3 de octubre las últimas que había recibido.

LEGAJO 5.655

AÑO 1829

CORRESPONDENCIA DEL MINISTRO EN ESTADOS UNIDOS, FRANCISCO TACÓN, CON EL SECRETARIO DE ESTADO, MANUEL GONZÁLEZ SALMÓN

675

N.º 397. — 2 de enero, Filadelfia.

Informa que había sido suspendida la comisión de Mr. Bresson a las Américas españolas hasta que se apaciguase el reino de Méjico; entretanto había pasado por tierra desde Washington a Panzacola.

676

N.º 398. — 10 de enero, Filadelfia.

Anuncia remisión de un impreso redactado por Montenegro, ridiculizando la expedición que se preparaba en España contra Méjico, y que intentaban hacer circular en la isla de Cuba.

677

N.º 400. — 12 de enero, Filadelfia.

Acusa recibo de la correspondencia oficial duplicada, en un buque procedente de Gibraltar.

678

N.º 402. — 13 de enero, Filadelfia.

Promete ajustar su conducta en el caso de Ricardo Meade, a las instrucciones que le había dado de limitarse a observar el giro que tomaban sus reclamaciones.

679

N.º 404. — 13 de enero, Filadelfia.

Comunica que el 12 de noviembre del año anterior 1828, Obando, uno de los enemigos de Bolívar, se había dirigido a Popayán apoderándose de la plaza de acuerdo con el comandante López que se pasó a su bando con la mayor parte de la guarnición; Bolívar había partido para esa ciudad con el fin de dominar a los rebeldes. En la gaceta había salido un decreto de Bolívar del 12 de noviembre relativo al comercio de géneros españoles en Tierra Firme. Al general Santander le habían conmutado la pena de muerte y quedaba preso en Bocachica. Hasta la isla Margarita que no producía más que sal y pescado, se había declarado independiente.

680

N.º 407. — 25 de enero, Filadelfia.

Acusa recibo de varias reales órdenes remitidas por vía del Havre y de Gibraltar.

681

N.º 408. — 25 de enero, Filadelfia.

Queda enterado de la real resolución decidiendo que en la legación y consulados de Norteamérica no se autorizasen los documentos que presentaran los españoles firmados por las autoridades insurgentes, limitándose a dar nuevos pasaportes a los que quisieran pasar a la península.

682

N.º 409. — 25 de enero, Filadelfia.

Comunica que ha recibido oficio con la aprobación del nombramiento que hizo para vicecónsul de Cayo Hueso a favor de don Juan Notlit; la patente del título se la había dirigido al interesado.

683

N.º 410. — 25 de enero, Filadelfia.

En las notas del congreso de Estados Unidos, en la parte relacionada con España, no se hacía mención de las reclamaciones de los ciudadanos americanos contra nuestro gobierno, pero estaba él haciendo toda clase de diligencias para adquirir un conocimiento exacto de las mismas.

684

N.º 412. — 26 de enero, Filadelfia.

Cumpliendo sus órdenes, se trasladaría a Washington con motivo de la elección del nuevo presidente; aparte de él, sólo el ministro de Dinamarca y los encargados de negocios de Prusia y Portugal, residían en Filadelfia, y el resto del cuerpo diplomático, en Washington.

685

N.º 413. — 26 de enero, Filadelfia.

Agradece la aprobación a los gastos que había realizado para la conducción a la Habana del español Felipe Vicente que había obtenido el perdón después de haber sido condenado a encierro perpetuo.

686

N.º 414. — 26 de enero, Filadelfia.

Había comunicado al cónsul en Baltimore la real resolución sobre su solicitud para el abono de las partidas que le fueron deducidas en su última cuenta.

687

N.º 415.— 27 de enero, Filadelfia.

Comunica que había llegado a Nueva York en barco procedente del Havre, un sujeto llamado Raynal, natural de Baltimore, que en la época constitucional se llamaba coronel español y que estuvo encarcelado en la Habana y después pasó a Madrid, en donde la policía le obligó a salir de allí y de todos los dominios reales; lo considera autor de un artículo contra España inserto en el periódico llamado «Enquirer».

Adjunto:
— Ejemplar del «New York Enquirer» en el que se inserta un artículo contra España y con referencias al general Jackson (20 de enero 1829).
— Traducción del artículo citado del «Enquirer».

688

N.º 417.— 27 de enero, Filadelfia.

Avisa que habían enviado a la Habana un bergantín de guerra construido en los astilleros de Nueva York para venderlo a los insurgentes de Buenos Aires, pero al concluir éstos la paz con el Brasil, intentaban enajenarlo en cualquier otro sitio; a pesar del hermoso aspecto de la embarcación, le habían asegurado que no estaba hecho con buenas maderas, advirtiéndolo así al capitán general de Cuba para que procurase hacer un buen reconocimiento del mismo en caso de pensar en su adquisición.

689

N.º 419.— 28 de enero, Filadelfia.

Comunica que se había presentado al congreso un proyecto de ley para autorizar al presidente la construcción de fortalezas en la embocadura del río Oregón. El ministro de Inglaterra interpuso una queja formal contra este proyecto que al fin fue rechazado por el congreso.

690

N.º 423. — 29 de enero, Filadelfia.

Anuncia remisión del expediente de don Antonio Argote Villa-lobos, cónsul en Nueva Orleans, para que lo entreguen al presidente de la junta de clasificación de cesantes y jubilados.

691

N.º 425. — 7 de febrero, Filadelfia.

Comunica su satisfacción por el feliz alumbramiento de la infanta Luisa Carlota.

692

N.º 426. — 7 de febrero, Filadelfia.

Anticipándose a sus órdenes, había comunicado ya cuantas noticias sabía referentes a la comisión de Mr. Bresson para América del Sur. Había dado encargo al cónsul de Nueva Orleans, para que lo tuviera al tanto de lo que pudiera averiguar sobre esta residencia. Principal y duplicado.

693

N.º 427. — 7 de febrero, Filadelfia.

Había comunicado al cónsul de Nueva York la aprobación a su conducta con motivo de haber sido citado en el prospecto de la Academia del español José Quintana Warnes.

694

N.º 428. — 7 de febrero, Filadelfia.

Había sabido que mr. Tudor, encargado de negocios americanos en Río de Janeiro, había concluido un tratado de comercio entre Estados Unidos y el Brasil.

VIII. — 18

695

N.º 429. — 7 de febrero, Filadelfia.

Los empresarios de las líneas de paquetes del Havre y Nueva York habían modificado la salida de sus barcos disponiéndola cada diez días en lugar de cada 15.

696

N.º 430. — 8 de febrero, Filadelfia.

Traslada un acuerdo tomado por la legislación de Nueva Orleans escargando al gobernador del estado que entre en correspondencia con el capitán general de Cuba a fin de obtener la entrega de los títulos y otros documentos depositados en la Habana, que tuvieren relación con propiedades de tierras y otros de la Luisiana.

697

N.º 432. — 8 de febrero, Filadelfia.

Había sabido por vía de Curaçao que Centeno con 300 caballos había ocupado el pueblo de Cumalagua, apoderándose de su guarnición, y que Cisneros continuaba en la montaña obrando de acuerdo con Centeno.

698

N.º 434. — 9 de febrero, Filadelfia.

Anuncia remisión de un ejemplar del «Mercurio» de Nueva York sobre los sucesos ocurridos en Méjico. Seguía el gobierno de Guerrero y sus partidarios mandando en la capital, sin que las otras ciudades reconociesen ese gobierno.

699

N.º 435. — 16 de febrero, Filadelfia.

Queda enterado de la real resolución disponiendo que continuara como cónsul de Nueva York don Francisco Stoughton y que se nombrasen dos vicecónsules para los puertos de Nueva Orleans y de Baltimore.

700

N.º 437. — 17 de febrero, Filadelfia.

Había recibido la comunicación sobre la solicitud de Juan Bautista Bernabéu nombrado cónsul en Kronstadt que había pedido su traslado a otro clima más benigno.

701

N.º 438. — 17 de febrero, Filadelfia.

Acusa recibo de varias reales órdenes.

702

N.º 439. — 17 de febrero, Filadelfia.

Anuncia remisión de un impreso, que no figura, relatando que de los puertos de Santa Catalina, San Bartolomé y San Eustaquio, salían los piratas armados que infestaban los mares. Añadía que los rebeldes de Buenos Aires no autorizaban a sus corsarios a hostilizar a buques españoles. En un corsario de esa nación llamado Patriot, se amotinó la tripulación y condujo el barco a Puerto Rico, donde fue apresado en el Morro su capitán Almeyda.

703

N.º 440. — 17 de febrero, Filadelfia.

Remite copia de la correspondencia intercambiada con el capitán general de la isla de Cuba, acerca del proyecto que le habían denunciado para destruir los buques españoles surtos en la Habana. Había hecho diligencias para descubrir al autor del proyecto que se llamaba J. L. Ripaud o J. L. Daupré, que debía estar avecindado en Nueva York, pero no se habían encontrado huellas del mismo.

Adjunto:

— Copia de la comunicación dirigida por el jefe de la escuadrilla de la república mejicana y departamento de Marina de Veracruz al ministro de Guerra y Marina sobre propuesta para destruir dos navíos españoles y una fragata fondeados en la Habana, por una cantidad que debía de entregarse al autor del proyecto después de realizada la empresa. En el mismo cuadernillo se copia también la aceptación de la propuesta por el gobierno mejicano, comunicación de la misma por el comandante David Porter, al ingeniero Ripaud, donde se insertan las condiciones que había presentado este ingeniero, como autor del proyecto (Veracruz, 18 de junio y 19 de julio 1828).

— Copia de los oficios dirigidos por el capitán general de la isla de Cuba, Francisco Dionisio Vives, al ministro de España en Estados Unidos, transmitiéndole el informe dado por el jefe de las fuerzas navales de la Habana, acerca de unas conversaciones que había tenido algún tiempo antes con una persona identificable con el ingeniero Ripaud, acerca de su proyecto; según el intendente de la misma ciudad, había motivos para sospechar de la sinceridad del autor del proyecto y no se debía de adelantar ninguna cantidad para evitar el daño posible, sino tomar las providencias oportunas de defensa. Anuncia remisión de copia de los documentos reseñados en el primer apartado (Habana, 24 y 28 de diciembre 1828).

704

N.º 441. — 17 de febrero, Filadelfia.

Comunica que había facilitado pasaporte para la Habana, al teniente de fragata Juan José Lerena que deseaba incorporarse al real servicio, después de haber permanecido durante algún tiempo en Nueva York como periodista.

705

N.º 442. — 17 de febrero, Filadelfia.

Comunica la propuesta presentada al congreso de Estados Unidos para ampliar el privilegio concedido a los buques españoles por el artículo 15 del tratado de la Florida, a todos los puertos situados en el territorio de dichas Floridas; de momento, el congreso había resuelto que se quedara el proyecto sobre la mesa.

Adjunto:

— Dictamen de la comisión de Comercio sobre ampliación del privilegio que tenían los buques españoles, cargados con productos y manufacturas españolas y procedentes de España o de sus colonias, para que durante 12 años pudieran ser admitidos en los puertos de Panzacola y de San Agustín, si pagaran más derechos que los buques de Estados Unidos sobre sus cargamentos y tonelaje; opinaba la comisión que extender ese privilegio a otros puertos, perjudicaría a los americanos. Es una nota impresa a la que acompaña su traducción (30 de diciembre 1828).
— Nota del asesor de la secretaría de Estado sobre este asunto y resolución marginal (18 de abril y 3 de mayo 1829).
— Minuta en cifra al ministro de España en Estados Unidos disponiendo que indagase con toda exactitud, si el gobierno de Estados Unidos hacía cumplir lo estipulado por el artículo 15 del tratado con las Floridas (Madrid, 8 de mayo 1829).

706

N.º 443. — 18 de febrero, Filadelfia.

Transmite algunas noticias recibidas de Buenos Aires: el día 1 de diciembre (1828) había estallado en la ciudad una revolución promovida por la primera división del ejército dirigida por el coronel Olazábal y por sus compañeros Olavarría y Correa. El gobierno llamó al general Juan Lavalle, pero cuando llegó a la capital se encontró que las autoridades habían huido; reunido el pueblo eligieron a Lavalle por gobernador, el cual derrotó a las tropas de su antecesor en el cargo, coronel Dorrego. Hay principal y duplicado.

707

N.º 444. — 18 de febrero, Filadelfia.

Comunica que en el senado, en presencia de la cámara de representantes, se había hecho el día 11 de ese mes, la apertura de votos de las elecciones para nombrar presidente y vicepresidente, resultando elegidos Andrés Jackson y Juan C. Calhoun para cada uno de los cargos.

708

N.º 445. — 18 de febrero, Filadelfia.

Remite copia de la nota que le había pasado el secretario de Estado Mr. H. Clay relativa a su protesta por los insultos inferidos por un vecino al secretario de la legación don Hilario de Rivas, y sobre la cuestión de la residencia del ministro español en Washington.

Adjunto:

— Oficio del secretario de Estado americano, H. Clay, a Tacón; sobre los cargos producidos por la familia de William Kirk contra el secretario de la legación española, había que cargar a este último la violencia ejercida contra Thomas Kirk y Ann Shivery y el haberse apoderado de las alfombras de Mr. Kirk; aunque las molestias que experimentaba el Sr. Rivas Salmón eran bastante desagradables, no estaban tipificadas en las leyes. Insiste en las ventajas que supondría el establecimiento de la legación española en Washington. Traducción de esta nota (7 de febrero, 1829).

— Acuse de recibo de Tacón a la nota que le había enviado Henry Clay (Filadelfia, 16 de febrero 1829).

709

N.º 446. — 18 de febrero, Filadelfia.

Remite noticias sobre la Guayra y Cartagena. De la primera sólo se sabía que se había dado orden para que toda la fuerza armada disponible, pasase a Santa Fe. De Cartagena decían había salido el general Córdoba hacia Popayán, de donde había partido Ovando por no haberse incorporado la provincia de San Buenaventura a su partido. Los valles de Cauca se habían declarado a favor del libertador. Santander seguía preso en Bocachica. Bolívar se había dirigido a Bojacá y después a Neiva; estaban organizando una expedición de la que iba a formar parte un hijo de Iturbide a quien

Bolívar había hecho capitán de sus ejércitos. El general Montilla había desterrado a Costa Firme a las familias de Posada, León y Narváez. Principal y duplicado.

710

N.º 447. — 18 de febrero, Filadelfia.

Relata los sucesos ocurridos últimamente en Méjico. Se habían inaugurado las sesiones del nuevo congreso con un discurso del presidente Victoria; declaradas nulas las elecciones de Pedraza, habían elegido a Vicente Guerrero como presidente y a Anastasio Bustamante como vicepresidente renunciando Pedraza a disputar la presidencia y pidiendo pasaporte para salir de Nueva España; el general Santa Ana que había tomado el nombre de Moctezuma, había sido nombrado ministro de la Guerra; Lobato, comandante de Valladolid y Zabala, gobernador de Méjico; todos los jefes de la última revolución habían sacado buen empleo. Guadalajara y Zacatecas eran los estados que no reconocían al gobierno de Guerrero.

El paquete Virginia se había fletado en Veracruz para llevar emigrados a Burdeos.

Adjunto:

— Lista de los pasajeros llegados a Nueva York el 8 de febrero 1829, en el paquete Virginia.

— Periódico de Veracruz llamado «Noticioso comercial y científico» con noticias de los sucesos de Méjico (8 de enero 1829).

711

N.º 448. — 20 de febrero, Filadelfia.

Anuncia remisión de unos libros de la Sociedad Filosófica de Filadelfia que había recogido el secretario de la legación y académico Francisco de Paula Quadrado, para la Academia de la Historia.

712

N.º 449. — 26 de febrero, Filadelfia.

Remite una exposición sobre el estado del archivo de la legación, que había sido ordenado por Francisco de Paula Quadrado con la ayuda de Miguel Tacón y Luis Potestad.

Adjunto:

— Oficio de Quadrado a su jefe Francisco Tacón manifestando el estado confuso en que había encontrado el archivo de la legación, y dando idea de su contenido, después de haberlo ordenado. Lo había clasificado en 6 secciones: despachos de los secretarios de Estado a los representantes del rey en Estados Unidos; correspondencia de éstos con el gobierno de Madrid; notas de la legación al gobierno americano y sus contestaciones; cuentas, correspondencia de y con los cónsules españoles en los puertos de Estados Unidos; y por último un apartado de varios en el que se reúne la correspondencia con los ministros y cónsules reales en Europa, con las autoridades españolas en América, con los ministerios de Hacienda y de Indias y con particulares y extranjeros que tuvieron asuntos con la legación (24 de febrero 1829).

713

N.º 451. — 26 de febrero, Filadelfia.

Había tenido noticias de que O'Leary, ayudante de Bolívar estaba comisionado para concluir una amnistía con el Perú; de que la provincia de la Concepción estaba amenazada por los indios; que en Bolivia habían elegido a Loaysa por presidente, quien tuvo que pedir auxilio al general peruano Aparicio para restablecer el orden, pero éste se había negado a prestarle ayuda.

714

N.º 452. — 26 de febrero, Filadelfia.

Por no haber llegado a Filadelfia, ningún barco de Veracruz, no sabía nada del estado del reino de Méjico, que estaba a merced de partidas de ladrones reunidas con el achaque de hostilizar a los empleados.

715

N.º 453. — 26 de febrero, Filadelfia.

En cumplimiento de las órdenes recibidas, pasaba a Washington, como la mayoría del cuerpo diplomático, para cumplimentar al nuevo presidente.

716

N.º 454. — 5 de marzo, Washington.

Trata de la ceremonia de la proclamación y juramento del nuevo presidente, que se había celebrado en medio de un gran tumulto y desorden.

717

N.º 455. — 5 de marzo, Washington.

Remite el discurso que había pronunciado el nuevo presidente Andrew Jackson, tras haber prestado juramento.

Adjunto:
— Recorte de gaceta con el discurso inaugural del presidente, y su traducción manuscrita (4 de marzo 1829).

718

N.º 456. — 6 de marzo, Washington.

Notifica que se había disuelto la cámara de diputados, pero el senado seguía reunido para aprobar los nuevos nombramientos y resolver los asuntos pendientes, como el tratado con el Brasil. Se esperaba fuera también sancionado un nuevo tratado de comercio y navegación, basado en la reciprocidad, con el rey de Prusia.

719

N.º 457. — 6 de marzo, Washington.

Habiendo presentado dimisión de su cargo como secretario de negocios extranjeros, Mr. Clay, había nombrado el presidente para su desempeño, a Mr. James Hamilton, interinamente.

720

N.º 458. — 8 de marzo, Washington.

El senado había sancionado el nombramiento efectivo de Martín van-Buren, gobernador del estado de Nueva York, para ministro de Relaciones Exteriores.

721

N.º 459. — 8 de marzo, Washington.

Había dilatado su estancia en Washington para conocer y felicitar a van-Buren.

722

N.º 460. — 8 de marzo, Washington.

Transmite las noticias recibidas del capitán general de Cuba acerca del incidente ocurrido con la goleta americana Widowison, cuyo capitán José Moris, por un mal entendido, fue castigado cuando entró en su bote al castillo del Morro. Principal y duplicado.

Adjunto:

— Copia del oficio de Francisco Dionisio Vives a Tacón con la relación de lo sucedido a la goleta americana Widowison. Hay dos ejemplares (Habana, 26 de enero 1829).

723

N.º 461. — 10 de marzo, Washington.

Comunica que había accedido a la petición de pasaporte a favor de José María Bustamante, natural de Méjico que quería pasar a Cádiz en la fragata Leónidas que debía conducir a varias familias expulsadas de Nueva España.

Da informes de Bustamante y de sus antepasados y ocupaciones. Principal y duplicado.

724

N.º 462. — 10 de marzo, Washington.

Sobre la comisión de Bresson a las Américas españolas, le habían informado que el hijo del general inglés sir Roberto Wilson, edecán de Bolívar, fue a visitar a Bresson a Nueva Orleans, y lo indujo a que en vez de pasar a Méjico, fuera a Santa Fe a entrevistarse con Bolívar, así es que marchó a la Guayra y después a

Caracas. El hijo de Wilson y uno de los miembros de la llamada gran convención de Ocaña, Ignacio Rodríguez, se hallaban en Filadelfia con alguna comisión desconocida. Principal y duplicado.

725

N.º 463. — 10 de marzo, Washington.

Comunica que Juan Bautista Bernabéu, cónsul en Baltimore, que había sido destinado a Kronstadt, había preferido quedar cesante y volver a España con su familia.

726

N.º 464. — 11 de marzo, Washington.

El senado había sancionado los nombramientos de Samuel Ingham para ministro de Hacienda; el de Juan H. Eaton, para Guerra; a Juan Branch para Marina; a Juan Mc Pherson Berrien para fiscal general y a W. F. Barry para director general de Correos. Principal y duplicado.

727

N.º 465. — 11 de marzo, Washington.

Según las últimas noticias, resulta: en la provincia de Nicaragua había estallado una contrarrevolución, habiendo sido arrestado y pasado por las armas el general Serdá y otros oficiales; los de Nueva Granada habían marchado contra Nicaragua que tuvo que entregárselas sin disparar un tiro; los guatemaltecos habían conseguido algunas ventajas sobre los de San Salvador; los de la ciudad de León se habían separado de la liga de Granada, por la gran cantidad de vejaciones e impuestos que sufrían sus habitantes.

728

N.º 466. — 11 de marzo, Washington.

Remite recorte de la gaceta de Nueva York que inserta las actas de la villa de Araure y ciudad de Angostura en la Costa Firme manifestando los males que padecía el país, y basándose en ellos, para que dominase el partido de Bolívar.

Adjunto:

— Parte del periódico «Mercurio de Nueva York» (1829).

729

N.º 467. — 11 de marzo, Washington.

En Méjico, según decían, no deseaban que fuese Guerrero presidente, sino que siguiera Victoria en el cargo.

730

N.º 468. — 12 de marzo, Washington.

Remite impreso y traducción de un discurso pronunciado por Mr. Clay, ex-ministro de negocios extranjeros, en el convite de despedida de su cargo. Principal y duplicado.

Adjunto:

— Recorte de periódico dando noticia de la comida ofrecida a Mr. Clay, e insertando el discurso del mismo. Manifestaba que aunque aceptaba al supremo magistrado que se había elegido para el gobierno de Estados Unidos, se había opuesto a su elección porque, aparte de una ofensa personal que le había hecho, temía el acceso al poder de los militares; a la cabeza de 8 de los 9 gobiernos independientes establecidos en ambas Américas, se hallaban establecidos generales: Lavalle en la república del Plata; Santa Cruz en Bolivia; el coronel Pinto en Chile; el general Lamar en Perú y Bolívar en Colombia. Casi toda América central estaba desgarrada por las facciones militares que se disputaban el mando (Washington, 7 de marzo 1829).

— Traducción del discurso.

731

N.º 469. — 14 de marzo, Washington.

Acerca de las reclamaciones de ciudadanos americanos contra España, sólo había encontrado las que habían hecho los propietarios del bergantín James Lawrence dirigidas al senado y cámara de representantes, que habían resuelto pedir al presidente toda la documentación sobre las mismas.

732

N.º 471. — 17 de marzo, Washington.

Las últimas noticias de Zacatecas recibidas en Tampico anunciaban que en Sombrerete había habido los mismos robos y saqueos que en Méjico, habiendo perdido la compañía inglesa de minas todo su numerario y ganado. La cámara de diputados de Méjico había propuesto la expulsión de todos los españoles, del reino.

733

N.º 472. — 17 de marzo, Washington.

No había recibido despachos de España en el último paquete del Havre.

734

N.º 478. — 28 de marzo, Washington.

Remite «El Redactor», periódico que se publicaba en castellano en Nueva York, y que traía noticias de Méjico.

Adjunto:

— Noticias de Méjico aparecidas en «El Redactor»: los angloamericanos se habían apoderado del presidio de San Francisco situado en los 38º 45·· latitud norte de la alta California, bajo pretexto de que estaba comprendido en la última demarcación de límites entre el gobierno de Estados Unidos y el de Méjico; también habían invadido la provincia de Tejas. El general (Carlos María de) Bustamante que mandaba en aquella provincia se batía en retirada y pedía refuerzos, habiéndole enviado algunas tropas de Tampico. La emigración del país, era horrorosa, no sólo de españoles sino también de los naturales más acomodados. Se esperaba saliera muy en breve la ley de expulsión general de los españoles que se discutía en el senado. En Sombrerete había habido una sublevación y habían saqueado todas las casas de los europeos, así como las minas de Zacatecas (Nueva York, 20 de marzo 1829).

— Resumen de estas noticias redactado por el asesor jurídico de la secretaría de Estado (Aranjuez, 16 de mayo 1829).

735

N.º 479. — 6 de abril, Filadelfia.

Tras haber felicitado a van Buren por su nuevo destino, había abandonado Washington. Principal y duplicado.

736

N.º 480. — 6 de abril, Filadelfia.

Acusa recibo de las reales órdenes que relaciona, prometiendo irlas contestando por separado.

737

N.º 481. — 6 de abril, Filadelfia.

Ha trasladado a Juan de Leamy la resolución del ministro de Hacienda de que se le hiciera efectiva una letra de 687 libras esterlinas que tomó al ministro de España en Estados Unidos don Joaquín de Anduaga, y que no había sido pagada por la casa de Bernales de Londres.

738

N.º 482. — 6 de abril, Filadelfia.

Había comunicado a madame d'Auberville, viuda de Bouligny, la orden relativa al pase de su solicitud al ministerio de la Guerra.

739

N.º 483. — 6 de abril, Filadelfia.

Se había clausurado el senado por decisión del presidente; había éste publicado otros dos nombramientos para empleos del interior.

En las sesiones secretas, sólo se había tratado de sancionar los nombramientos y de discutir sobre la publicación del mensaje relativo a las instrucciones para los plenipotenciarios enviados a Panamá. Principal y duplicado.

740

N.º 484. — 7 de abril, Filadelfia.

Comunica que había sancionado el senado el nombramiento de Thomas P. Moore diputado del estado de Kentucky, como ministro plenipotenciario del llamado gobierno de Colombia en reemplazo del general Harrison. Principal y duplicado.

741

N.º 485. — 7 de abril, Filadelfia.

Informe sobre los antecedentes políticos, formación y carácter del nuevo secretario de Estado Martín van Buren, antes, gobernador del estado de Nueva York. Principal y duplicado.

742

N.º 486. — 7 de abril, Filadelfia.

Manifiesta que había pasado al comandante general de Marina de la Habana, una obra que le había solicitado.
Adjunto:

— Copia de la comunicación de Ángel Laborde a Tacón, agradeciéndole el envío de las Tablas o Reglamentos de dimensiones de arboladura, aparejo, etc. que el gobierno de los Estados Unidos había señalado para régimen de su Marina en 1826, y que por su utilidad, estaba traduciendo (Habana, 3 de febrero 1829).

743

N.º 490. — 8 de abril, Filadelfia.

Agradece la aprobación a su conducta por haber delatado el proyecto que habían formado para quemar la escuadra real en la

Habana. Promete proceder con cautela en la cuestión de hacer ofertas de recompensas. Principal y duplicado.

744

N.º 491. — 8 de abril, Filadelfia.

Agradece en su nombre y en el del interesado, la concesión de la cruz de comendador de la real orden americana de Isabel la Católica, a don Hilario Rivas Salmón.

745

N.º 493. — 8 de abril, Filadelfia.

Había comunicado a don Antonio Pomar, encargado que fue del consulado de España en Norfolk, la aprobación a las cuentas de ese consulado. Como tenía autorización del intendente de la Habana, iba a facilitarle los correspondientes libramientos para que percibiera de las reales cajas las correspondientes cantidades.

746

N.º 494. — 8 de abril, Filadelfia.

Promete avisar de los proyectos del nuevo presidente respecto a España. Hasta entonces sólo se había preocupado de renovar a los empleados y poner los afectos a su causa; toda la capital estaba llena de pretendientes a cargos. Cifrada, con la traducción al margen.

747

N.º 495. — 8 de abril, Filadelfia.

Remite un ejemplar del tratado celebrado entre Estados Unidos y el rey de Prusia, ratificado en Washington el 14 de marzo 1829.

Adjunto:

— «Convention between the United States of America, and His Majesty, the king of Prussia. Concluded may 1, 1928». Consta de 16 artículos en dos columnas en inglés y en francés, acordado por los plenipotenciarios Luswig Niedersletter y H. Clay. La ratificación, por Andrew Jackson con el refrendo del secretario de Estado, James A. Hamilton (Impreso, 7 págs.).

748

N.º 496. — 8 de abril, Filadelfia.

Remite copia de un oficio que le había remitido el cónsul de Nueva Orleans con la lista de emigrados que habían llegado a ese puerto. Le había comunicado que podría dar pasaporte para la península a los que no habían servido a los rebeldes; otros, como Juan Antonio Ozta y Francisco de Paula Tamariz, si querían ser indultados, tenían que solicitarlo al rey.

Adjunto:

— Copia del oficio del cónsul de Nueva Orleans, Antonio Argote Villalobos, a Tacón, expresando los nombres de algunas personas de categoría que habían llegado a la ciudad, procedentes de Méjico. Informa también sobre el carácter y situación de algunos de ellos (Nueva Orleans, 26 de febrero 1829).

749

N.º 497. — 8 de abril, Filadelfia.

El cónsul de Nueva Orleans le había comunicado que don Joaquín Haro y Tamariz gobernador de la Puebla y natural de Nueva España, le había visitado y hecho confidencias sobre los desórdenes del partido que se había apoderado del gobierno de Méjico. Le había contestado al cónsul que si Haro iba buscando el indulto, debería formalizar su instancia al rey.

750

N.º 498. — 8 de abril, Filadelfia.

Le había participado el cónsul de Nueva Orleans que el coronel Montenegro vivía en esa ciudad, probablemente comisionado por los revolucionarios de Méjico para tramar la insurrección de la isla de Cuba; se dedicaba también a observar la conducta y conexiones de los emigrados de Méjico, españoles y criollos. Principal y duplicado.

751

N.º 499. — 8 de abril, Filadelfia.

Con Antonio Argote, cónsul, le comunica que el conde de Moctezuma se hallaba en Nueva Orleans, ocupado en reclamar el pago de las grandes cantidades que le adeudaba el gobierno rebelde de Nueva España, sin que hasta entonces hubiera conseguido nada. Principal y duplicado.

752

N.º 501. — 8 de abril, Filadelfia.

El capitán general de la isla de Cuba le había remitido copia autorizada por el capitán don Vicente Sebastián Pintado, agrimensor que fue de la Florida occidental, de la relación que se hizo en los años 1823 y 1824, de todas las donaciones de tierras, solares y aguas que se habían hecho en ambas Floridas por las autoridades españolas. Abarca las ventas, concesiones y repartos de tierras desde 1801 a 1818. Dado lo voluminoso del expediente, había mandado copiar el índice para entregarlo al gobierno de Estados Unidos que lo había reclamado. Principal y duplicado.

753

N.º 510. — 15 de abril, Filadelfia.

Sobre la orden que le obligaba a reclamar del gobierno americano la deuda que Tomás Brent, encargado de negocios en la corte de Lisboa, contrajo con la viuda de Larrard y Sarmiento, había convenido con mr. Brent, oficial mayor de la secretaría de Negocios Extranjeros, y pariente de Thomas, en que se le iría descontando de su sueldo, ya que se encontraba en quiebra.

Adjunto:

— Copia y traducción de una carta de Daniel Brent a Tacón exponiendo las circunstancias económicas por las que había pasado su pariente y comprometiéndose a que éste separara una parte de sus emolumentos para liquidar la deuda que tenía pendiente con la casa Larrad y Compañía de Barcelona (Washington, 8 de abril 1829).

754

N.º 516. — 17 de abril, Filadelfia.

Había salido de Washington nada más saludar al secretario de Estado van Buren, por no tener que asistir al convite que daría el presidente Jackson al cuerpo diplomático, en el que tendría que relacionarse con el plenipotenciario Joaquín Campino, representante de Chile. Principal y duplicado.

Adjunto:

— Copia y traducción del discurso que había pronunciado el presidente en la comida y recepción del cuerpo diplomático (Washington, 6 de abril 1829).

755

N.º 520. — 24 de abril, Filadelfia.

Da cuenta de que ha recibido la relación de donaciones en las Floridas, que había redactado el Tribunal de Cuentas de la Habana, más 11 documentos sobre lo mismo, todo lo cual debía pasar al gobierno americano después de tomar nota de lo que juzgara interesante; por otra parte, ya había remitido a ese gobierno federal el índice de otra relación que le había enviado el capitán general de la isla de Cuba.

Adjunto:

— Copia y traducción de una nota del secretario de Estado americano van Buren acusando recibo de la lista que le había enviado Tacón, de las concesiones de tierras hechas en las Floridas por el rey de España.

756

N.º 522. — 25 de abril, Filadelfia.

Comunica que el gobierno de Estados Unidos había nombrado a Luis Mc Lane, senador por Delaware, ministro para la corte de Londres, y a Enrique Lee de Virginia, para cónsul general en Argel.

757

N.º 523. — 25 de abril, Filadelfia.

Había recibido dos oficios acusando recibo de sus anteriores despachos.

758

N.º 524. — 26 de abril, Filadelfia.

Remite la lista de españoles a los que se ha concedido pasaporte en el consulado de Nueva Orleans.

Adjunto:
— Copia de la lista de pasaportes otorgados en Nueva Orleans en el mes de marzo de 1829 (Filadelfia, 26 de abril 1829).

759

N.º 528. — 28 de abril, Filadelfia.

Anuncia remisión de unos impresos de documentos del senado y cámara de representantes. Principal y duplicado.

760

N.º 530. — 29 de abril, Filadelfia.

Por una gaceta de Nueva Orleans que daba noticia de un convite celebrado a bordo del buque de guerra mejicano, Morelos, para celebrar la elección de nuevo presidente Vicente Guerrero, se veía que el canónigo Monteagudo era partidario de los revolucionarios; también el conde Moctezuma había tomado parte en los festejos. Principal y duplicado.

Adjunto:

— Fragmento de gaceta del 2 de abril 1829.

761

N.º 531. — 29 de abril, Filadelfia.

Acusa recibo de oficios duplicados de la corte y uno principal noticiando el traslado de los reyes al Pardo.

762

N.º 532. — 30 de abril, Filadelfia.

Trata de un pleito fallado por el Tribunal Supremo sobre concesiones de tierras en la Florida occidental. Fue promovido por el marqués de Casa Irujo y otros propietarios que habían recurrido contra la ocupación de terrenos suyos por el americano Neilson. El tribunal de 1.ª instancia había fallado a favor del nuevo dueño y el Supremo había confirmado la sentencia; lo cuestionable era si esos territorios pertenecían a Florida occidental como habían declarado España y Francia siempre, o si formaban parte de la Luisiana como pretendían los Estados Unidos, extendiendo los límites de esta provincia hasta el Río Perdido, en lugar del Iberville. Esto era considerado por el Supremo como asunto político que debía resolver el congreso, y no judicial.

763

N.º 533. — 30 de abril, Filadelfia.

La nueva administración continuaba ocupándose de la renovación de empleados sustituyéndolos con sujetos inmorales, amigos del presidente. Despacho cifrado con la transcripción al margen.

764

N.º 535. — 6 de mayo, Filadelfia.

Queda enterado de la resolución disponiendo que se pasara al secretario de Hacienda la instancia de Francisco Hernández Nogués, cónsul general en Estados Unidos, solicitando la remoción de su destino.

765

N.º 536. — 6 de mayo, Filadelfia.

Había recibido 8 reales órdenes, que se disponía a contestar.

766

N.ª 538. — 7 de mayo, Filadelfia.

Remite el n.º 1 de un periódico llamado «El Español» que trataba de publicar don Tiburcio Campa en Nueva Orleans.

Adjunto:
— Ejemplar de «El Español» (6 de abril 1829).

767

N.º 539. — 7 de mayo, Filadelfia.

Comunica que había expedido pasaporte para España a don Juan Bautista Bernabéu, que había sido cónsul de Baltimore; manifiesta los pagos que se le habían hecho. Principal y duplicado.

768

N.º 540. — 7 de mayo, Filadelfia.

Remite la traducción del impreso con el fallo del Tribunal Supremo sobre las tierras concedidas por el rey en Florida occidental.

Adjunto:

— Traducción de la sentencia del Tribunal Supremo pronunciada por mr. Marshall en 9 de marzo 1829.

769

N.º 542. — 8 de mayo, Filadelfia.

Comunica que el general dinamarqués mr. Scholten, gobernador de la isla de Santo Tomás, había llegado a Nueva York para proseguir viaje a Europa. El ministro de esa potencia se proponía pasar a Washington para tratar con el gobierno americano de los apresamientos hechos en aquellas islas por piratas de Estados Unidos. Principal y duplicado.

770

N.º 543. — 8 de mayo, Filadelfia.

Refiere que en una travesía de Providencia a Nueva York, se había tirado al agua el hijo mayor del ex-presidente, mr. Jorge Washington Adams. Principal y duplicado.

771

N.º 546. — 8 de mayo, Filadelfia.

Había naufragado cerca de Cayo Hueso, el correo español que hacía el viaje entre Habana y Cádiz, aunque buques americanos, habían logrado salvar la tripulación y cargamento. Principal y duplicado.

772

N.º 548. — 16 de mayo, Filadelfia.

Había recibido autorización del intendente de las reales cajas de la Habana, para librar contra ellas los 20.000 reales de vellón que se le había ordenado entregar a don Hilario Rivas Salmón, que pasaba a la península a ocupar su nuevo cargo en la Primera Secretaría.

773

N.º 549. — 16 de mayo, Filadelfia.

La continua remoción de empleados públicos estaba originando el descontento entre los ciudadanos; últimamente la deposición de mr. Slade, oficial de la secretaría de Negocios Extranjeros, había producido una correspondencia muy viva a través de las gacetas entre él y su jefe. Despacho cifrado con traducción al margen.

774

N.º 553. — 17 de mayo, Filadelfia.

Había sido muy bien acogido en Estados Unidos el decreto del 21 de febrero declarando a Cádiz puerto franco. Principal y duplicado.

775

N.º 554. — 18 de mayo, Filadelfia.

Cumpliendo órdenes, iba a procurar enviar una copia del Reglamento consular.

776

N.º 556. — 18 de mayo, Filadelfia.

Habiendo presentado su dimisión mr. J. Brown, plenipotenciario de la Unión en Francia, al enterarse del nombramiento de Jackson como presidente, se había elegido para ocupar aquel cargo a M. C. Rives. Principal y duplicado.

777

N.º 557. — 20 de mayo, Filadelfia.

Anuncia remisión de un pliego vía Burdeos. Principal y duplicado.

778

N.º 558. — 26 de mayo, Filadelfia.

Continúa haciendo diligencias para cumplimentar una real orden sobre asunto que no especifica.

779

N.º 559. — 26 de mayo, Filadelfia.

Remite un decreto del presidente concediendo a Austria que sus buques no paguen más derechos de tonelaje en los puertos de la Unión, que los propios del país.

Adjunto:

— Edicto impreso y su traducción manuscrita, con la proclama de Andrew Jackson declarando que en virtud del acta del congreso del 7 de enero 1824, titulado «An act concerning discriminating duties and impost», que disponía que las naciones extranjeras que no exigiesen más impuestos de toneladas a los buques americanos que los que pagaban los de la nación, tendrían reciprocidad en los puertos de Estados Unidos, concedía este derecho a los navíos austriacos, según convenio del emperador de Austria con el presidente de Estados Unidos.

780

N.º 562. — 27 de mayo, Filadelfia.

Promete cumplir las instrucciones recibidas sobre el traslado de su residencia a Washington. Principal y duplicado.

781

N.º 565. — 28 de mayo, Filadelfia.

Noticias recibidas de Argentina manifestaban el estado de confusión en que se hallaba; los monteros o capataces del campo, acaudillados por el general Rosas, tenían cercada la capital y asesinaban a todos los partidarios de Lavalle; compañías de ladrones de a 300 guachos recorrían las orillas del Salado y aunque fueron obligados a retirarse al otro lado del río por el general Rauch, fue éste atacado y destruido su ejército por los indios; la ciudad de Buenos Aires se encontraba sometida a saqueos y asesinatos aunque la llegada de Lavalle había suspendido momentáneamente tanto desorden. También se decía que Blanco, titulado presidente de Bolivia, había muerto en una revolución que estalló en la capital.

782

N.º 566. — 28 de marzo, Filadelfia.

Anuncia remisión de los números 2 a 5 del periódico titulado «El Español», publicado en Nueva Orleans por don Tiburcio Campe; aunque las noticias que publicaba sobre Nueva España eran atrasadas, eran interesantes sus propósitos de quitar la máscara al traidor Montenegro y de descubrir todas sus maquinaciones.

Adjunto:

— Resumen de las noticias contenidas en «El Español», por el asesor de Secretaría (sin fecha).

783

N.º 567. — 28 de mayo, Filadelfia.

Acusa recibo de las órdenes recibidas vía el Havre y Gibraltar. Se alegra de que la familia real siguiera bien en el Pardo.

784

N.º 568. — 29 de mayo, Filadelfia.

Remite gacetas en las que se inserta la carta que mr. Wythe había dirigido a Jackson sobre su administración y un artículo de la oposición formada en Baltimore para ir contra las decisiones del gobierno. Principal y duplicado.

Adjunto:

— Recorte de la gaceta llamada «National Journal» (20 de mayo 1829).
— Recorte de «United States Telegraph» (21 de mayo 1829).

785

N.º 569. — 29 de mayo, Filadelfia.

Don Antonio Argote Villalobos le había comunicado desde Nueva Orleans, que el titulado coronel Montenegro y su partido trabajaban para hacer cesar la publicación de «El Español», amenazando al editor con persecuciones judiciales.

786

N.º 570. — 29 de mayo, Filadelfia.

Informa acerca del gobernador del estado de Vermont, van Ness, que según las gacetas había sido nombrado plenipotenciario de la Unión, cerca del gobierno de España.

787

N.º 573. — 4 de junio, Filadelfia.

Comunica que había salido para Nueva York, con intención de embarcarse en el paquete de Liverpool, don Hilario Rivas Salmón, a quien había entregado ayuda de costa para el viaje; aprovecha para remitir algunos pliegos.

788

N.º 576. — 7 de junio, Filadelfia.

Anuncia remisión de una solicitud de Toribio Segura, profesor de música de Valencia del que conocía su habilidad en el violín.

789

N.º 578. — 7 de junio, Filadelfia.

Confirma el nombramiento de Cornelio van Ness, del estado de Vermont para ministro de la Unión en la corte española.

Adjunto:

— Minuta a Tacón pidiendo dé noticias del carácter, opiniones políticas y crédito de la persona de van Ness (Madrid, 9 de septiembre 1829).

790

N.º 579. — 7 de junio, Filadelfia.

Continuaba el nuevo gobierno haciendo nombramientos de representantes de la Unión en naciones extranjeras. A Willian Pitt Preble lo habían destinado como plenipotenciario, cerca de los Países Bajos; a Washington Irving que había residido durante algunos años en España para recoger material para la publicación de una obra sobre Colón, lo habían nombrado secretario de la legación de Gran Bretaña; y a Carlos Carroll Harper, le habían dado igual destino en París. Principal y duplicado.

791

N.º 584. — 16 de junio, Filadelfia.

Comunica que el presidente había nombrado a mr. Caleb Atwater de Ohio y a los coroneles Mc Neil y Menard, para que hicieran tratados con varias tribus indias establecidas en las inmediaciones del Mississipi, a fin de evitar desavenencias sobre límites del río y su navegación, y para comprar a los indios el territorio situado al sur del río Wisconsin y el de Lead Mines. Principal y duplicado.

792

N.º 585. — 16 de junio, Filadelfia.

Anuncia remisión de un decreto del presidente, corrigiendo otro suyo anterior y autorizando al presidente a no exigir de los buques extranjeros más derechos que los que pagasen los americanos en las naciones respectivas.

793

N.º 586. — 16 de junio, Filadelfia.

Había llegado a Filadelfia J. Capece Galeota, cónsul general de Sicilia, que se titulaba duque de Regina; había pasado luego a Washington con el fin de pedir el exequatur.

794

N.º 587. — 17 de junio, Filadelfia.

Da noticias del encargado de negocios del rebelde gobierno de Colombia en Méjico, llamado Santa María, el cual había pasado a Londres a solicitar ayuda para derribar a Guerrero de la presidencia de Méjico, y colocar a Bravo.

795

N.º 588. — 17 de junio, Filadelfia.

Había gran descontento por la política del presidente de renovar los antiguos cargos; últimamente, el bibliotecario de las cámaras, mr. Watterston había sido reemplazado por Meehan, lo que había sido considerado como un ultraje al congreso.

796

N.º 590. — 18 de junio, Filadelfia.

Remite lista de pasaportes dados por el cónsul de Nueva York desde el 1 de abril al 15 de junio del año en curso.

Adjunto:

— Relación de los pasaportes expedidos por el cónsul de Nueva York a los españoles procedentes de Méjico que pasaban a la península (Nueva York, 15 de junio 1829).

797

N.º 594. — 28 de junio, Filadelfia.

Acusa recibo de varias reales órdenes.

798

N.º 595. — 29 de junio, Filadelfia.

Da cuenta de las cantidades que habían reunido para contribuir a remediar las necesidades producidas por el terremoto.

799

N.º 599. — 1 de julio, Filadelfia.

Habían llegado a Filadelfia los hijos del virrey de Méjico, Iturrigaray, y estaban solicitando cartas de introducción para hablar con José Bonaparte que vivía en una casa de campo de Bordentown.

800

N.º 600. — 2 de julio, Filadelfia.

Remite lista de pasaportes concedidos por el vicecónsul de Nueva Orleans.

Adjunto:

— Relación de los españoles procedentes de Nueva España, que habían salido de Nueva Orleans para la península y la Habana en el mes de mayo (sin fecha).

801

N.º 602. — 4 de julio, Filadelfia.

Remite el discurso pronunciado por mr. Clay, ex secretario de Estado, en la comida homenaje que le dieron sus partidarios en su país natal, Lexington Ky, del estado de Kentucky.

Adjunto:

— Discurso de Mr. Clay en el que critica las operaciones de la nueva administración, fundando su manera de obrar en lo que hizo Jefferson; considera poco oportuna la renovación de algunos empleados sustituidos por otros cuyos defectos detalla. Declara que no admitiría ser elegido para representante de su país ni para el congreso ni para su estado. Inserto en el «Daily National Journal» (13 de junio 1829).

— Traducción del discurso.

802

N.º 604. — 5 de julio, Filadelfia.

Participa que había sido asesinado Mc Crea, fiscal del distrito del sur de la Florida, por el americano Hawkins, que había estado sirviendo en la marina de los rebeldes de Méjico; achacaban la causa del homicidio a tratos ilícitos de Mc. Crea con la mujer del asesino.

803

N.º 608. — 8 de julio, Filadelfia.

Continuaban las críticas contra el gobierno por la renovación de cargos. En la fragata Natchez había salido el comodoro Cassim para relevar del mando de la escuadra en los mares del Brasil a mr. Creighton; y en la Ontario iría mr. Biddle que iba a relevar a mr. Crane en la escuadra del Mediterráneo.

804

N.º 610. — 16 de julio, Filadelfia.

Había recibido las reglas dictadas para evitar los abusos que cometían los correos de gabinete españoles y extranjeros, conduciendo en sus valijas efectos de comercio ilícito. Principal y duplicado.

805

N.º 611. — 16 de julio, Filadelfia.

Había trasladado a don Antonio Argote Villalobos, cónsul en Nueva Orleans, la aprobación a sus cuentas de gastos extraordinarios anteriores al 1 de junio de 1823.

806

N.º 612. — 16 de julio, Filadelfia.

Se había celebrado en Washington el aniversario de la independencia, habiendo asistido a la ceremonia los representantes del cuerpo diplomático establecidos en la capital. Principal y duplicado.

807

N.º 613. — 16 de julio, Filadelfia.

El gobierno rebelde de Colombia había adquirido en Baltimore los víveres y efectos que necesitaba para abastecer dos fragatas que habilitaban en Puerto Cabello para ir al Pacífico a hostilizar a los peruanos.

808

N.º 614. — 17 de julio, Nueva York.

Habían llegado a Nueva York los generales insurgentes Bravo y Barragán; era probable que hubieran cambiado de parecer sobre su idea de derribar a Guerrero de la presidencia del llamado gobierno mejicano, ante la noticia de la expedición que iba a salir de la Habana hacia Méjico, según se aseguraba en una proclama del general Vives; por su parte permanecería en Nueva York para averiguar los propósitos de ambos rebeldes.

809

N.º 619. — 18 de julio, Nueva York.

Da cuenta del armamento de un barco llamado la Concepción preparado en Baltimore por un americano residente en la Habana y que con bandera española pensaba dirigir a la costa de África. Los cuáqueros de Baltimore lo habían denunciado como pirata y como buque destinado al comercio de negros, pero el tribunal lo había declarado libre. Principal y duplicado.

810

N.º 620. — 18 de julio, Nueva York.

Tanto Tacón como los otros funcionarios de la legación habían sentido mucho la muerte de la reina acaecida el 17 de mayo último.

811

N.º 621. — 19 de julio, Nueva York.

Mr. Bresson se había anunciado al titulado secretario de Relaciones Exteriores del rebelde Bolívar, como comisionado del rey de Francia.

Adjunto:

— Copia de las credenciales presentadas ante los miembros del Consejo del Gobierno de Colombia (sin fecha).

— Contestación del presidente del Consejo, en ausencia del Libertador, agradeciendo el reconocimiento de Francia y de su monarca Carlos X (sin fecha).

812

N.º 622. — 19 de julio, Nueva York.

Participa que había repartido ciertas cantidades entre las personas de la legación con motivo del luto por la reina.

813

N.º 623. — 19 de julio, Nueva York.

Comunica que ha abonado también 100 pesos por lutos a don Luis Potestad, que trabajaba sin sueldo alguno como agregado de la legación.

814

N.º 624. — 20 de julio, Nueva York.

Comunica que habían salido de la Habana varios navíos con más de 4.000 soldados para realizar una expedición cuyo fin no se especifica.

815

N.º 625. — 26 de julio, Nueva York.

Ha recibido las reales órdenes que menciona.

816

N.º 626. — 26 de julio, Nueva York.

Comunica que había dado por concluso el desagradable suceso ocurrido con don Hilario Rivas, que no se especifica.

817

N.º 627. — 26 de julio, Nueva York.

Queda enterado de la licencia que había concedido el rey al guarda almacén Benito Romero, para pasar por asuntos propios a París, Londres y Filadelfia. Principal y duplicado.

818

N.º 629. — 27 de julio, Nueva York.

Comunica que el portugués Da Costa acababa de publicar en Nueva York el n.º 1 de un periódico titulado «El ciudadano del mundo» con el que se proponía dar a conocer los sucesos de su época, preferentemente los de Portugal y Brasil; le había pedido ayuda pecuniaria, pero se la había negado por no considerarse con facultades para intervenir en ese asunto.

Adjunto:

— Ejemplares números 1 y 2 de «El ciudadano del mundo», impreso en español (varias fechas).

819

N.º 633. — 29 de julio, Nueva York.

Describe el viaje del presidente a la fortaleza de Monroe y a Norfolk, recibiendo en ambos lugares honores inusitados, más propios de un emperador que de un republicano.

820

N.º 634. — 29 de julio, Nueva York.

Trata de la posibilidad de ayuda al periódico de Nueva York «El Redactor» expresando el deseo de los editores de que se les tomase un crecido número de ejemplares que ellos se obligarían a distribuir en varios puntos de América española.

821

N.º 638. — 6 de agosto, Nueva York.

Comunica que viajaba a la península don Antonio Paúl, emigrado de Méjico, donde había desempeñado el cargo de administrador de la renta de tabacos, y aunque había estado algún tiempo con el gobierno rebelde, se había limitado a ejercer su profesión.

822

N.º 641. — 8 de agosto, Nueva York.

Manifiesta la decadencia en que se encontraban el comercio y fábricas de Estados Unidos, debido en parte al sistema de restricciones adoptado por el gobierno federal respecto a la introducción de géneros extranjeros, que se vendían a menor costo por la baratura de la mano de obra europea; la medida había desarrollado el contrabando y la bancarrota de gran número de fabricantes.

823

N.º 645. — 9 de agosto, Nueva York.

Comunica el nombramiento de cónsules para diversos puertos; la llegada del fiscal general a Nueva York con las instrucciones para los ministros que habían de pasar a Francia y Gran Bretaña; la conducta del conde de Menou, encargado de negocios francés en la Unión, que estaba más ligado a la administración y presidente de Estados Unidos que a sus colegas diplomáticos; el ministro de Inglaterra había pasado al Canadá para informarse de algunos puntos relativos a la cuestión de límites.

824

N.º 647. — 9 de agosto, Nueva York.

El portugués Da Costa, editor del periódico «El ciudadano del mundo» había publicado el número 2; había recibido ayuda entre otras personas, del cónsul de Nueva York Francisco Stouhgton; en realidad éste le había pagado una corta cantidad para que pudiera pagar el pasaje y su manutención durante una semana.

825

N.º 651. — 10 de agosto, Nueva York.

Extrañado de no haber recibido órdenes en el último paquete llegado del Havre, se lo comunicaba por si se hubiesen extraviado.

826

N.º 653. — 15 de agosto, Filadelfia.

Informe sobre el colegio de cadetes llamado Academia Militar de West-Point, detallando las asignaturas que estudiaban y el grado de formación de los alumnos en cada una de ellas.

827

N.º 654. — 16 de agosto, Filadelfia.

Comunica que se estaban publicando en las gacetas del gobierno unos artículos denominados Política y diplomacia que tenían en realidad por objeto criticar la presidencia de mr. Adams y elogiar la del general Jackson; el estado de salud de este último, dada su edad y sus achaques, tenía alarmados a sus partidarios. Se estaba haciendo una reforma en el ejército para promover a los más adictos al gobierno. Principal y duplicado.

Adjunto:

— Extracto de artículos de gaceta refiriendo varios cargos contra la política seguida por Adams y extendiéndose en reseñar los principales aciertos de la administración de Jackson. Principal y duplicado.

828

N.º 656. — 17 de agosto, Filadelfia.

Continuaban saliendo de Nueva York españoles procedentes de Méjico. Anuncia remisión de listas.

829

N.º 657. — 17 de agosto, Filadelfia.

Anuncia remisión de un tercer número de los folletos que publicaba el portugués Da Costa; probablemente sería el último porque se hallaba preso por deudas; por no haberle ayudado, hablaba mal del capitán general Francisco Tomás Morales y de otras autoridades de las islas Canarias.

830

N.º 662. — 24 de agosto, Filadelfia.

Anuncia remisión de despachos duplicados, en un buque que salía de Nueva York para Cádiz. Principal y duplicado.

831

N.º 663. — 26 de agosto, Filadelfia.

Hace una relación de las reales órdenes que había recibido.

832

N.º 664. — 26 de agosto, Filadelfia.

Había comunicado a doña María Luisa de Senechal d'Auberville, viuda del brigadier don Francisco Bouligny, la resolución del consejo de guerra respecto a su viudedad. Principal y duplicado.

833

N.º 665. — 27 de agosto, Filadelfia.

Había pasado a los cónsules de Estados Unidos, la orden de que se remitiera al gobierno noticias circunstanciadas de los españoles emigrados en países extranjeros, y sobre los motivos de sus salidas de España. Principal y duplicado.

834

N.º 666. — 27 de agosto, Filadelfia.

Cumpliendo sus órdenes remitiría el ejemplar de la suscripción que había hecho al periódico que se publicaba en castellano en Nueva Orleans. Principal y duplicado.

835

N.º 668. — 27 de agosto, Filadelfia.

Remite una relación de los españoles emigrados de Méjico que habían salido de Nueva Orleans para la península e isla de Cuba. Principal y duplicado.

Adjunto:

— Lista de los pasaportes que se habían entregado en Nueva Orleans a españoles, durante el mes de junio. Principal y duplicado.

836

N.º 669. — 28 de agosto, Filadelfia.

Aclara que el primer apellido del Sr. Rivello que había llegado como encargado de negocios del Brasil, en la Unión, era Araujo.

837

N.º 672. — 29 de agosto, Filadelfia.

Anuncia remisión de copia de un oficio del cónsul de Nueva Orleans sobre la arribada de la fragata Bingham a ese puerto y las disposiciones que había tomado para el desembarco y auxilio de la tropa.

838

N.º 674. — 30 de agosto, Filadelfia.

Había recibido la real orden sobre el arreglo del archivo de la legación, lo cual había sido ejecutado por el secretario Francisco de Paula Quadrado y los auxiliares Miguel Tacón y Luis Potestad. Principal y duplicado.

839

N.º 675. — 30 de agosto, Filadelfia.

Agradece la aprobación a su conducta respecto a las prevenciones dadas al cónsul de Nueva Orleans sobre la llegada a ese puerto de varios mejicanos. Principal y duplicado.

840

N.º 676. — 30 de agosto, Filadelfia.

Promete dar cumplimiento a la orden de que se abonase a un ejemplar del periódico que publicaba en Nueva Orleans el Sr. Campe. Principal y duplicado.

841

N.º 677. — 30 de agosto, Filadelfia.

Continuaba practicando diligencias para informarse de la comisión del coronel Montenegro en Nueva Orleans; hasta entonces se estaba dedicando a espiar las fuerzas de la Habana para comunicarlas a los mejicanos, observando al mismo tiempo la conducta de españoles o criollos llegados de Méjico a Nueva Orleans. Principal y duplicado.

842

N.º 678. — 30 de agosto, Filadelfia.

Queda enterado de la R. O. disponiendo no se diera pasaporte al canónigo Monteagudo ni a los otros individuos que asistieron al convite dado el 29 de abril para celebrar la elección del presidente mejicano Vicente Guerrero. Principal y duplicado.

843

N.º 679. — 30 de agosto, Filadelfia.

Trata de la misión del gobierno americano a las tribus indias y de los proyectos hostiles de éstas; en el distrito de Randolf tuvieron un encuentro conflictivo que obligó a los americanos a dejar cien hombres de guardia en la parte más avanzada de la frontera; los creeks manifestaban deseos de paz con tal de que no los obligasen a dejar un palmo de su territorio. Principal y duplicado.

844

N.º 680. — 30 de agosto, Filadelfia.

Comunica que el presidente había salido de Washington para reponer su salud en la isla de Rip Raps, situada a la entrada de Hampton Roads; la oposición pedía que gobernara en su lugar el vicepresidente mr. Calhoum. Los partidarios de la administración elogiaban al secretario de Estado van Buren como futuro candidato a la presidencia; se hallaba éste preparando las instrucciones que había de llevar van Ness a España. Principal y duplicado.

845

N.º 681. — 30 de agosto, Filadelfia.

Comunica algunas noticias poco interesantes de Costa Firme; aún no había llegado a Puerto Cabello la fragata Colombiana que conducía preso al llamado general Santander; a Arequipa habían ido ocho comisionados de Bolivia para persuadir al general Santa Cruz a aceptar la presidencia de la república de América Central. En Lima estaban dispuestos a continuar la guerra con Colombia habiendo enviado socorros a Guayaquil para que no se rindiese; Lamar había resuelto anular la convención de Tarqui con la fuerza de las armas.

846

N.º 682. — 30 de agosto, Filadelfia.

Trata de la llegada a Nueva Orleans de la goleta Eclipse, procedente de Tampico hacia donde decían se dirigía una escuadra que sería la real que había partido de la Habana. Las tropas españolas arribadas a Nueva Orleans desembarcaron en English Turn y seguían en un campamento que les había asignado. Corría el rumor de que había sido asesinado en Méjico el ministro de Estados Unidos mr. Poinsett.

847

N.º 683. — 30 de agosto, Filadelfia.

Había estado en Filadelfia el rebelde Barragán que se había dirigido a Nueva York sin duda para entrevistarse con Bravo y más tarde con Echéverri y Negrete que residían en New Brunswich. Anuncia el envío de un recorte de gaceta que inserta una disertación de don Tiburcio Campa sobre el ofrecimiento de varios mejicanos para incorporarse en las filas de los españoles leales. Bravo y sus compañeros dilataban embarcarse para Nueva España, temiendo probablemente que la expedición real empezase a obrar en Méjico; en realidad a lo que aspiraban era a posesionarse del puesto de Guerrero.

848

N.º 684. — 6 de septiembre, Filadelfia.

Comunica que los Estados Unidos habían logrado un convenio con las tribus indias de los creeks, los winnebagoes, los potawatamies y los chippewas. Mediante dinero, la Unión había adquirido todo el terreno situado al sur de Wisconsin entre la orilla superior del Mississipi y el lago Michigán. Principal y duplicado.

849

N.º 685. — 6 de septiembre, Filadelfia.

Manifiesta que en el pueblo de Georgetown, del estado de Carolina del sur, se había descubierto una conspiración que trataba de prender fuego a la ciudad y aprovechar la alarma para asesinar a los blancos; se había desarmado a todos los esclavos. Principal y duplicado.

850

N.º 687. — 7 de septiembre, Filadelfia.

Seguían los negros cometiendo excesos y manifestando su desprecio hacia los blancos. En la isla de San Bartolomé habían rodeado la casa del mayor Pelluson, comandante de la milicia, la cual por exigencia de los negros, tuvo que ser retirada antes de dispersarse ellos. Principal y duplicado.

851

N.º 688. — 7 de septiembre, Filadelfia.

En Nueva Orleans estaba haciendo muchos estragos la fiebre amarilla, habiendo atacado a algunos españoles y mejicanos de los expulsados de Nueva España.

852

N.º 690. — 8 de septiembre, Filadelfia.

Trata de la misión de don Gregorio Tagle y de la retirada del ejército federal mandado por Rosas hacia el interior, estableciendo su campamento en Chasomus, debido a la seguridad que había dado Lavalle de que retirado el ejército nombraría comisionados para empezar una negociación en favor de la paz; tanto los jefes citados como los cabecillas de los monteros e indios, aspiraban a ponerse al frente del gobierno.

853

N.º 691. — 8 de septiembre, Filadelfia.

Corrían noticias de que los peruanos habían abandonado Guayaquil llevándose las municiones e inutilizando la artillería, sin duda por temor a Bolívar que entró a continuación en la ciudad.

854

N.º 692. — 8 de septiembre, Filadelfia.

Comunica el retorno del presidente americano a Washington y que van Ness, nombrado ministro para España, se disponía a partir en el próximo octubre hacia Cádiz. Principal y duplicado.

855

N.º 693. — 8 de septiembre, Filadelfia.

Remite la traducción de una proclama que habían publicado los periódicos americanos con la alocución que el comandante don Manuel de los Santos había dirigido a sus soldados al tener que desembarcar en Nueva Orleans.

Adjunto:

— Proclama exponiendo Manuel de los Santos los peligros que habían pasado por la tempestad y exhortando a los soldados a que observasen subordinación y disciplina mientras estuvieren en tierra extranjera (English Turn, 31 de julio 1839).

856

N.º 694. — 9 de septiembre, Filadelfia.

Trata de la llegada a la Habana de los buques de guerra españoles, después de haber desembarcado la mitad de las tropas en Tampico y la otra mitad a 6 millas de aquel pueblo; la guarnición de Tampico y muchos de caballería de los rebeldes de Méjico se habían incorporado a las filas de los leales. Se había desmentido el asesinato de Poinsett.

Adjunto:

— Despacho del conde de Ofalia a González Salmón anunciando remisión de artículos de periódicos en los que se notaba una tendencia más templada hacia España y más despectiva con los insurgentes de Méjico. No se había confirmado la noticia de que Ruis-Effendi hubiera ido a avistarse con el general ruso Diebith (París, 15 de septiembre 1829).

857

N.º 706. — 26 de septiembre, Filadelfia.

Quedaba enterado de la real orden concediendo permiso a don Antonio Romero teniente de caballería impurificado, para que acompañase a su padre don Benito en su viaje a París, Londres y Filadelfia.

858

N.º 707. — 26 de septiembre, Filadelfia.

Anuncia remisión de una lista de los pasaportes dados por el cónsul de Nueva York a los expulsados de Méjico que iban a regresar a la península, vía Santander.

859

N.º 711. — 28 de septiembre, Filadelfia.

Comunica que se había nombrado a Sidney Mason de Virginia, para cónsul de Estados Unidos en San Juan de Puerto Rico, en reemplazo de Robert Jacques, y el de William Shaler de Massachusetts, con igual destino para la Habana, en lugar de Tomás Rodney; consideraba inútiles los pasos que pudiera dar para anular los nombramientos puestos que iban a relevar a otros que habían ejercido el mismo cargo; proporciona algunos informes sobre los recién nombrados.

860

N.º 713. — 29 de septiembre, Filadelfia.

Trata de la llegada a Filadelfia de Bravo y su contacto con dos negociantes americanos y con el secretario de la misión que envió el gobierno de Estados Unidos al congreso de Panamá, para solicitar fondos para acudir a la defensa de su patria; esos tres individuos se los ofrecieron a cambio de la enajenación de las provincias internas, lo que rehusó Bravo. Montoya el encargado de negocios de los rebeldes de Méjico, había ofrecido algunas tierras en Tejas, a los que equipasen y armaran la corbeta Kensington, pero por falta de garantías no había encontrado aceptadores. Remite copia de algunas noticias recibidas del cónsul de Nueva York.

Adjunto:
— Copia de carta de Francisco Stoughton, cónsul de Nueva York a Tacón, dándole cuenta de una reunión que habían tenido Bravo, Cañas, Ruiz Armero y otros en Brooklyn para celebrar el aniversario de la rebelión en Nueva España; Bravo había propuesto un plan para alarmar a España respecto a la isla de Cuba con el fin de evitar que desplazara parte de sus fuerzas a Nueva España (Nueva York, 18 de septiembre 1829).
— Traducción de los brindis que pronunciaron los patriotas mejicanos durante la fiesta (sin fecha).
— Copia de carta dirigida por Tacón al capitán general de la isla de Cuba, Francisco Dionisio Vives, sobre los proyectos de Bravo y los otros rebeldes.

861

N.º 717. — 6 de octubre, Filadelfia.

Remite copia y traducción de un memorial de ciudadanos de la Luisiana reclamando sus derechos a la posesión de los terrenos que habían adquirido de España en los años 1803 a 1805.

Adjunto:

— Exposición de Félix y Octavio de Armas, de J. B. de Grand Pré y otros, manifestando que habían comprado terrenos en Luisiana con garantía de las leyes españolas y pidiendo a Tacón entablara una negociación amistosa para que el gobierno americano reconociera sus derechos. Copia y traducción (sin fecha).

— Instancia de James Foster y Pleasants Clam pidiendo a Tacón les diera indemnización por unos territorios que habían comprado a Jaime Jordá, con intervención del intendente Juan Ventura Morales, en la Luisiana, y que el gobierno de Estados Unidos había declarado nula la compra por no pertenecer, según decían, aquellos territorios a España. Copia y traducción (sin fecha).

862

N.º 718. — 7 de octubre, Filadelfia.

Había llegado a Filadelfia mr. Gattin de Crapong que había llegado de Francia en 1825 y había residido en Santo Domingo, Estados Unidos y Méjico; antes de volver a Europa quiso entrevistarse con Tacón para darle noticias de Nueva España, y le había manifestado sus deseos de comunicar al gobierno español noticias del país rebelde, a su paso por Cádiz. Tacón le había facilitado una carta de presentación para González Salmón.

Adjunto:

— Copia de una carta de presentación facilitada por Tacón a Gattin de Grapong y dirigida al secretario de Estado (Filadelfia, 7 de octubre 1829). Original y dos copias.

— Minuta al conde de Ofalia presentándole a Gattin de Grapong (4 de febrero 1830).

863

N.º 722. — 8 de octubre, Filadelfia.

Comunica que el presidente de Estados Unidos había concedido el «exequatur» para que residiera en Nueva York, al cónsul general de Francia, Durant de Saint Andrés. Principal y duplicado.

864

N.º 725. — 8 de octubre, Filadelfia.

Había recibido la comunicación del rey manifestando al presidente de Estados Unidos el fallecimiento de su augusta esposa. Siguiendo la costumbre, se disponía a ir a Washington a entregarla en mano.

865

N.º 726. — 10 de octubre, Filadelfia.

Quedaba enterado de la designación de cónsul general de Estados Unidos, a favor de Juan Bautista Bernabéu.

866

N.º 727. — 10 de octubre, Filadelfia.

Había recibido el oficio relativo al decreto del aventurero Porter sobre detención de buques con efectos de pertenencia española; daría cumplimiento a la resolución real.

867

N.º 728. — 11 de octubre, Filadelfia.

Anuncia remisión de lista de los pasaportes expedidos en Nueva Orleans a los expulsados de Méjico para pasar a la Habana.

868

N.º 732. — 12 de octubre, Filadelfia.

El plenipotenciario de Estados Unidos, C. N. van Ness, había pasado por Filadelfia camino de Nueva York donde embarcaría con destino a Cádiz.

869

N.º 734. — 14 de octubre, Filadelfia.

Remite copias del oficio que le había dirigido el cónsul de Nueva Orleans y de la nota que había pasado al gobierno de Estados Unidos, sobre la entrega de un desertor de la expedición salida de la Habana para las costas de Nueva España.

Adjunto:

— Cuadernillo con copia de cartas dirigidas por el cónsul de Nueva Orleans Antonio Argote Villalobos, a Tacón y a Pedro Derbigny, gobernador del estado de Luisiana, dando noticias de la deserción y reclamaciones efectuadas para que fuese reintegrado a las tropas, el soldado Juan Sánchez. Se copia también la sentencia del juez Gallent Tobar decretando se pusiera en libertad a Sánchez y condenado al cónsul al pago de las costas (Nueva Orleans, 5 de septiembre a 24 de agosto 1829).

— Nota dirigida por Tacón al secretario de Estado americano Martín van Buren dando cuenta de la arribada forzosa a Nueva Orleans de la fragata americana Bingham conduciendo a cerca de 500 soldados españoles embarcados en la Habana, a los que se había concedido hospitalidad en un campamento próximo al Mississipi llamado Torno del Inglés, donde permanecieron hasta que fueron recogidos por buques de la armada española mandados por el comandante Ángel Laborde. El caso de uno de los pocos soldados que habían desertado de aquel campamento José Sánchez, fue llevado a un tribunal americano, que llegando a la inaudita investigación de los requisitos que se necesitaban para los alistamientos según las ordenanzas militares españolas, decidió dejar libre a Sánchez y condenar en costas al cónsul de Nueva Orleans que había presentado las oportunas reclamaciones del reo. Según el tratado del 22 de febrero de 1819, recurría Tacón al presidente de Estados Unidos, para que anulase el fallo del tribunal de Nueva Orleans (Filadelfia, 14 de octubre 1829).

870

N.º 735. — 14 de octubre, Filadelfia.

Remite copias del oficio y documentos remitidos por el cónsul de Nueva Orleans sobre las disposiciones tomadas por el comandante Ángel Laborde y todo lo ocurrido con las tropas arribadas a Nueva Orleans.

Adjunto:

— Dos cuadernillos con copia de varias comunicaciones referentes al arribo y estancia en Nueva Orleans de las tropas expedicionarias conducidas en la fragata mercante Bingham; son cartas de Argote Villalobos, del comandante Manuel de los Santos Guzmán y certificado de Ángel Laborde de las buenas disposiciones de Argote para el establecimiento de las tropas en el Torno inglés (20 de agosto a 17 de septiembre 1829).

871

N.º 740.— 27 de octubre, Filadelfia.

Sobre una propuesta que había hecho don Manuel Agustín de Heredia para el establecimiento de una línea de paquetes de Málaga a Nueva York, informa Tacón exponiendo las normas que se observaban en esta última ciudad, para recibir y entregar correspondencia de los diferentes puntos de Europa; generalmente se encargaban de ello empresas mercantiles en las que no intervenía la renta de correos.

872

N.º 743.— 27 de octubre, Filadelfia.

Comunica que por falta de fondos, don Tiburcio Campé, editor del periódico titulado el Español, había tenido que cesar en su empresa; había pedido pasaporte para Tampico, adonde trasladaría su imprenta.

873

N.º 747.— 28 de octubre, Filadelfia.

Comunica su visita al presidente de Estados Unidos para comunicarle la noticia del fallecimiento de la reina.

Adjunto:

— Cuenta del gasto producido por Tacón en el viaje de ida y vuelta a Washington.

VIII.— 21

874

N.º 748. — 28 de octubre, Filadelfia.

En su viaje a Washington había visitado al secretario van Buren para tratar de la reclamación de Juan Miguel Losada; sobre el desertor de las tropas arribadas a Nueva Orleans, y acerca de la protesta que tenía que remitirle por la venta de tierras del coronel Muñiz. Van Buren le comunicó que España había reconocido por rey de Portugal a Miguel I. Principal y duplicado.

875

N.º 750. — 29 de octubre, Filadelfia.

Respecto a la nota pasada al secretario de Estado americano sobre el desertor José Sánchez, le habían contestado que el presidente tomaría informes.

Adjunto:

— Copia traducida de la nota del departamento de Estado comunicando la decisión del presidente de que se indagaran los procedimientos seguidos en el tribunal de Nueva Orleans en el caso de José Sánchez (Washington, 21 de octubre 1829).

876

N.º 752. — 31 de octubre, Filadelfia.

Remite ejemplares del periódico «Muerte política de la república mexicana».

Adjunto:

— Ejemplares números 1 a 33 del periódico citado. Méjico, 1829.

877

N.º 753. — 31 de octubre, Filadelfia.

Anuncia remisión de varios impresos del senado y cámara de representantes de la legislatura que terminó el 4 de marzo del año en curso, y que había recogido en su viaje a Washington. En nota aparte dice que los impresos se enviaron por separado dado su mucho volumen.

878

N.º 756. — 6 de noviembre, Filadelfia.

Habiendo recibido tarde la orden disponiendo que a los representantes en el extranjero no se les diera ninguna cantidad para lutos, le habían suplicado el secretario y agregados de la legación, que no les hicieran devolver el dinero que habían recibido y gastado con ocasión del fallecimiento de la reina.

Adjunto:

— Copia de una real orden que transmitió el marqués de Casa Irujo al representante en Estados Unidos, manifestando las cantidades que debían asignarse a cada uno de los empleados en las cortes extranjeras, por razón de lutos (Madrid, 1 de marzo 1819).

879

N.º 757. — 7 de noviembre, Filadelfia.

Comunica el cambio de cónsules de Estados Unidos en puertos rebeldes de Méjico, Panamá y Perú, así como el nombramiento de encargado de negocios cerca de los rebeldes de Perú, a favor de J. West.

880

N.º 760. — 8 de noviembre, Filadelfia.

Anuncia remisión de un cuarto número del periódico que publicaba el portugués Da Costa, que ya había salido de la prisión en la que se hallaba por deudas.

881

N.º 763. — 8 de noviembre, Filadelfia.

Anuncia remisión de un sobre cerrado dirigido al rey que le había entregado Manuel Sáinz, a quien no conocía.

Adjunto:

— Comunicación de Manuel Sáinz a Tacón suplicándole remitiera los pliegos que había escrito al rey (Nueva Orleans, 10 de octubre 1829).

— Copia de la respuesta de Tacón prometiendo enviar a España los pliegos que le había entregado Sáinz (Filadelfia, 6 de noviembre 1829).

882

N.º 765. — 16 de noviembre, Filadelfia.

El cónsul de Nueva Orleans le había comunicado que el coronel comisionado Manuel García Muñiz, estaba practicando diligencias para proveer al brigadier Barradas de los víveres y transportes que necesitaba para la conducción de tropas de Tampico a la Habana.

883

N.º 766. — 16 de noviembre, Filadelfia.

Remite copia del oficio que le había enviado don Antonio Argote Villalobos sobre una declaración que solicitaban tres españoles expulsados de Méjico.

Adjunto:

— Copia del oficio de Argote Villalobos insertando una nota aparecida en el periódico la «Abeja», firmada por Diego Argüelles, Cayetano Herrera y Velarde y Antonio de Flores, en la que pedían se publicase que jefes y oficiales españoles expulsados de la república mejicana, se habían presentado a aquel gobierno. Sin duda estos españoles habían querido aparecer como rebeldes, después del desgraciado suceso del ejército de Barradas (Nueva Orleans, 21 de octubre 1829).

— Borrador de minuta pasada a los secretarios del despacho, relativa al aviso del cónsul de Nueva Orleans (25 de enero 1830).

884

N.º 769. — 18 de noviembre, Filadelfia.

El secretario de Estado van Buren había pasado a Richmond para ir preparando la opinión pública para las próximas elecciones; habían acudido a Filadelfia mr. Brown, plenipotenciario de Estados Unidos en Francia, y le iban a ofrecer una comida pública; aunque habían invitado a Tacón, había rehusado la asistencia.

885

N.º 773. — 27 de noviembre, Filadelfia.

Informa sobre el carácter de van Ness, nombrado ministro de Estados Unidos en España. Era abogado de reputación y tenía considerable fortuna, lo que le había servido para ser nombrado gobernador de Vermont. En Washington había trabajado para que saliera elegido Jackson. En cifra y descifrado interlineal.

886

N.º 775. — 28 de noviembre, Filadelfia.

Habían vuelto a manifestarse los deseos de que la Unión tratara de apoderarse de las provincias de Tejas, aunque el gobierno no había dado ningún paso sobre este asunto. Van Buren había regresado a Washington, acompañado del plenipotenciario de Países Bajos mr. Huyguens. Habían nombrado a mr. Moore, plenipotenciario de Estados Unidos cerca de los rebeldes de Colombia, habiendo manifestado Jackson que se abstendrían de toda intervención en los negocios interiores del país. Principal y duplicado.

887

N.º 776. — 28 de noviembre, Filadelfia.

Trata del banquete que había ofrecido mr. Brown en Filadelfia; del cuerpo diplomático, sólo asistió el encargado de negocios de Prusia, mr. Niedersletter y varios cónsules extranjeros.

888

N.º 779. — 28 de noviembre, Filadelfia.

Los acreedores de la corbeta Kensington habían propuesto la venta del buque al plenipotenciario de Rusia en Estados Unidos;

habían llegado a Nueva York varios comisionados rusos para inspeccionarla.

889

N.º 780. — 7 de diciembre, Filadelfia.

Remite copia del oficio pasado por el departamento de Estado, relativo a la reclamación de la casa comercial representada por doña María Larrard contra Tomás Brent, encargado de negocios de Estados Unidos en Lisboa, por cuestión de deudas. Tacón creía que el gobierno americano no se mezclaría en asunto que competía a los tribunales.

Adjunto:

— Copia y traducción del oficio de van Buren prometiendo trasladar a Brent la nota que le había enviado Tacón, para que explicara su actitud (Washington, 30 de noviembre 1829).

890

N.º 782. — 8 de diciembre, Filadelfia.

Comunica que, conforme a las reglas de la constitución de los Estados Unidos, se había abierto el congreso el primer lunes de diciembre.

891

N.º 785. — 9 de diciembre, Filadelfia.

Remite recorte de gaceta con el discurso del presidente pronunciado en la apertura del congreso; se autorizaba al ministro de Estados Unidos en España a procurar una convención de comercio y a la aceptación de los beneficios mutuos del acta de navegación; se le encargaba que pidiera indemnización por las pérdidas sufridas por algunos ciudadanos de Estados Unidos que habían sido despojados de sus propiedades; en Méjico, a petición de los rebeldes, se había retirado a Poinsett como encargado de negocios.

Adjunto:

— Recorte del periódico «Aurora» con el discurso de Andrew Jackson (Filadelfia, 9 de diciembre).

892

N.º 786. — 17 de diciembre, Filadelfia.

Remite la traducción del discurso del presidente que por estar escrito en estilo metafísico resultaba poco inteligible aún para los americanos.

No había tratado de la misión enviada a Colombia; llamaba la atención las reformas que pensaba introducir en la constitución, especialmente, las relativas a la elección y permanencia del presidente, y la de los funcionarios en sus destinos. Trataba del adelanto en las fábricas y manufacturas y de las trabas del comercio. No se hacía mención en el discurso de la cesión del territorio de Tejas y de las Floridas.

Adjunto:

— Traducción del mensaje pronunciado por el presidente el 7 de diciembre.

893

N.º 788. — 17 de diciembre, Filadelfia.

Agradece la aprobación real a su conducta con el portugués Da Costa.

894

N.º 789. — 17 de diciembre, Filadelfia.

Promete dar cumplimiento a la orden de que no debía satisfacer cosa alguna a un gacetero de Nueva York.

895

N.º 790. — 17 de diciembre, Filadelfia.

Da las gracias por la aprobación a la respuesta que dio al cónsul de Nueva Orleans, respecto al arribo a ese puerto de la fragata Bingham.

896

N.º 794. — 18 de diciembre, Filadelfia.

Había desembarcado en Nueva York el coronel mejicano Basadre, comisionado por el gobierno rebelde para hacer ver a los gobiernos de Estados Unidos, Francia e Inglaterra, que Méjico contaba con recursos suficientes para mantener su independencia y para mostrarles unos documentos que el cónsul mejicano Torres había cogido en Bogotá al duque de Montebello, referentes a la coronación de Bolívar.

897

N.º 795. — 18 de diciembre, Filadelfia.

Mr. Hugues había renunciado a su posible nombramiento como encargado de negocios de Estados Unidos en Méjico, siendo designado para este destino Antonio Butler que parecía persona insignificante.

898

N.º 797. — 18 de diciembre, Filadelfia.

Se habían presentado en el congreso las memorias de los secretarios del gobierno. El de Guerra trataba de la disciplina en el ejército, aunque se experimentasen algunas deserciones; proponía arreglos para los ascensos y para que se fijara por ley los sueldos de los militares, aumento de fuerzas en las fronteras con los indios, ampliación del cuerpo de ingenieros y mejoras en la academia militar. Principal y duplicado.

899

N.º 799. — 27 de diciembre, Filadelfia.

Trata algunos puntos de la memoria presentada por el ministro de Marina al congreso: de la escuadra del Mediterráneo y de la insubordinación de algunos de sus oficiales, aunque habían observado buena conducta con las potencias berberiscas; de la fuerza naval en los mares de la India; de la que protegía el comercio americano en el golfo de Méjico; de la que cruzaba en las costas del Brasil y Buenos Aires; de la situada en el mar Pacífico; del corte de maderas para la construcción de buques; de los arsenales; de la contratación de la marinería; de la utilidad de establecer un depósito de efectos navales en el Cayo de las Tortugas; y de las escuelas de guardias marinas. Finaliza la memoria exponiendo que el cuerpo naval era superior a las necesidades de la Unión federal.

900

N.º 800. — 28 de diciembre, Filadelfia.

Acerca de la reclamación que había hecho al gobierno americano sobre un desertor de las tropas españolas arribadas a Nueva Orleans, había recibido una comunicación del departamento de Estado desentendiéndose del asunto por haber huido el desertor en cuanto le dieron libertad. Tacón había insistido en la entrega del mismo en cuanto volviera a Estados Unidos, la devolución de las costas exigidas al cónsul de Nueva Orleans y satisfacción por la violación cometida por el tribunal, contra los tratados vigentes.

Adjunto:

— Copia y traducción, de una carta de John Slider a van Buren comunicándole que el desertor José Sánchez había salido de Nueva Orleans y también probablemente, de Estados Unidos (Nueva Orleans, 23 de noviembre 1829).
— Comunicación de van Buren a Tacón manifestándole que Juan Slidell, fiscal de Estados Unidos en el distrito meridional de Luisiana, había averiguado que el desertor José Sánchez se hallaba fuera de la jurisdicción de Estados Unidos, y el gobierno consideraba ya inútil tomar medidas en este asunto (Washington, 16 de diciembre 1829). Copia y traducción de la misma.
— Respuesta de Tacón reclamando la devolución de las costas que se había obligado a pagar al cónsul de Nueva Orleans, y una satisfacción contra la violación manifiesta de los tratados, por el tribunal de esa ciudad (Filadelfia, 21 de diciembre 1829).

901

N.º 803. — 29 de diciembre, Filadelfia.

Se había propuesto en el congreso la conveniencia de separar los poderes delegados al gobierno, de los que conservaba el pueblo. Ayudaba a Jackson, mr. Hamilton, fiscal del distrito de Nueva York, al que probablemente nombrarían subsecretario de Estado o ministro del Interior si se conseguía del congreso la creación de este ministerio.

LEGAJO 5.656

AÑO 1830

CORRESPONDENCIA DE FRANCISCO TACÓN, MINISTRO ESPAÑOL
EN ESTADOS UNIDOS, CON EL SECRETARIO DE ESTADO,
MANUEL GONZÁLEZ SALMÓN

902

N.º 807. — 6 de enero, Filadelfia.

Comunica varias noticias de lo aprobado en el senado: ratificación de nombramientos hechos por el presidente y de los tratados hechos con los indios limítrofes; arreglo de los derechos consulares; posible naufragio de la corbeta americana Hornet, y otros.

903

N.º 814. — 16 de enero, Filadelfia.

Avisa de la reaparición en Nueva Orleans de «El Español» que había dejado de publicarse, y remite un prospecto de dicho periódico.

Adjunto:

— Prospecto con la distribución que tendría «El Español». Se darían noticias de Méjico, Guatemala y de España. Se trataría del comercio en Nueva Orleans y Cuba, y se insertaría toda clase de artículos de interés general siempre que no atacasen a España.

904

N.º 820. — 17 de enero, Filadelfia.

Informa de haberse aprobado una proposición para que pudiesen usar los libros de la biblioteca del congreso, los ex-presidentes de Estados Unidos, los secretarios de Estado, y los ministros extranjeros residentes en Washington.

905

N.º 821. — 18 de enero, Filadelfia.

Dice no haber recibido noticias en los tres últimos barcos llegados de España.

906

N.º 823. — 18 de enero, Filadelfia.

Participa que había llegado a Nueva York, procedente de Veracruz, un nuevo plenipotenciario representante de los rebeldes de Méjico cerca del gobierno de Estados Unidos.

907

N.º 825. — 18 de enero, Filadelfia.

Anuncia remisión de un libro, recién publicado, con los retratos y biografías del presidente americano y las personas que componían su gabinete.

908

N.º 826. — 27 de enero, Filadelfia.

Comunica la presentación al congreso de los tratados con algunas tribus indias relativos a la cesión de tierras a cambio de una indemnización del gobierno de la Unión. Remite traducida parte del mensaje del presidente americano al congreso informando que el gobierno de Colombia había enviado una medalla de oro que había sido presentada por el llamado gobierno de Colombia en conmemoración de la libertad de Bolívar. Trata también del proyecto de nueva constitución para Virginia.

Adjunto:

— Extracto del mensaje citado. Hay dos ejemplares.

909

N.º 833. — 7 de febrero, Filadelfia.

Anuncia remisión de un memorial de José Quintero Castro en el que solicitaba ser repuesto en su destino de capitán de infantería.

910

N.º 835. — 8 de febrero, Filadelfia.

Da cuenta del mensaje del presidente americano al congreso recomendando la revisión de la ley que fijaba los emolumentos de los diplomáticos de la Unión.

911

N.º 839. — 8 de febrero, Filadelfia.

Acusa recibo del nuevo código de comercio por el que debían regirse en las posesiones españolas en adelante.

912

N.º 840. — 16 de febrero, Filadelfia.

Informa de varios acuerdos tomados en el congreso americano: modificación de los aranceles por los encontrados intereses entre los estados del norte y del sur, principalmente en los derechos de los algodones, café y te. Bolívar había enviado una medalla al presidente, y se había propuesto que se depositase en la secretaría de Estado. Aprobación por el senado de los nombramientos hechos por el presidente para los destinos diplomáticos de la Unión, entre ellos el ministro para España, van Ness.

913

N.º 842. — 17 de febrero, Filadelfia.

Participa que los individuos que componían la llamada legación de los rebeldes de Méjico, se habían entrevistado con el presidente americano.

914

N.º 845. — 25 de febrero, Filadelfia.

Acusa recibo de varias reales órdenes entre las que destacaba la referente al código de comercio.

915

N.º 847. — 26 de febrero, Filadelfia.

Felicita a González Salmón por haberle sido concedida la gran cruz de Carlos III.

916

N.º 848. — 26 de febrero, Filadelfia.

Anuncia remisión de varios números de «El Español» que se publicaba en Nueva Orleans.

917

N.º 852. — 6 de marzo, Filadelfia.

Daría cumplimiento a la real orden relativa a la cuenta mensual de todos los pasaportes que se expidiesen por los diferentes cónsules españoles en Estados Unidos. Hay dos ejemplares.

918

N.º 853. — 6 de marzo, Filadelfia.

Quedaba enterado del matrimonio real por lo que, enviaba su felicitación y promete comunicarlo al presidente de Estados Unidos.

919

N.º 859. — 8 de marzo, Filadelfia.

Seguían las sesiones del congreso con discusiones sobre las tarifas y las cuestiones con los indios. Dictamen acerca de los sueldos de los ministros y cónsules americanos en el extranjero. Hay dos ejemplares.

920

N.º 862. — 12 de marzo, Filadelfia.

Avisa de la llegada a Washington, de paso para Nueva York, del coronel rebelde Basadre, que estaba muy desprestigiado tanto en estas ciudades como entre su partido de Méjico. Los corsaristas de Baltimore trataban de reclutar marineros españoles en los puertos de Cuba.

Adjunto:

— Oficio de Tacón a Francisco Dionisio Vives, capitán general de Cuba para que evitase el reclutamiento (Filadelfia, 13 de febrero 1830).

921

N.º 864. — 13 de marzo, Filadelfia.

Anuncia remisión de varios números de «El Español».

922

N.º 870. — 23 de marzo, Washington.

Anuncia su llegada a la capital y dice que había remitido al secretario de Estado americano la copia de la carta real donde se notificaba al gobierno americano el matrimonio del rey.

923

N.º 871. — 23 de marzo, Filadelfia.

Acusa recibo de varias reales órdenes.

924

N.º 873. — 24 de marzo, Washington.

Remite copia de la lista de pasaportes dados en el consulado español en Nueva Orleans durante el mes de febrero de 1830.

Adjunto:
— La lista citada (Washington, 24 de marzo 1830).

925

N.º 874. — 25 de marzo, Washington.

Acusa recibo de un oficio aprobando su conducta por la reclamación que había hecho al gobierno americano de un desertor de la tropa española que había llegado a Nueva Orleans.

926

N.º 875. — 25 de marzo, Washington.

Acusa recibo del real decreto que trataba del modo con que se habían de solicitar privilegios exclusivos para asegurar la propiedad de cualquier invento.

927

N.º 880. — 29 de marzo, Washington.

Remite varios números de «El Español», periódico que continuaba publicándose en Nueva Orleans y que entre otras cosas trataban de los desórdenes de Nueva España.

Adjunto:

— Números de «El Español» del 54 al 58. Figura una exposición del nuevo ministro de Hacienda mejicano, Rafael Mangino, al congreso de la república, haciendo destacar el estado lamentable en que se encontraba Méjico, en gran parte por la carencia de recursos. En general dedica bastantes espacios a esta república, y también da noticias de Brasil, Centroamérica, España y resto de Europa.

928

N.º 881. — 29 de marzo, Washington.

Comunica algunos nombramientos aprobados por el senado americano, el de Porter para cónsul general en Argel; el de Butler como encargado de negocios para Méjico, y a West, para el Perú.

929

N.º 883. — 3 de abril, Filadelfia.

Avisa de su regreso a Filadelfia. Durante su estancia en Washington había sido invitado a una comida oficial por el secretario de Estado.

930

N.º 887. — 6 de abril, Filadelfia.

A la orden disponiendo que la correspondencia cifrada debía reducirse a lo muy preciso, Tacón dice que así lo venía haciendo.

Adjunto:

— Nota informativa exponiendo lo anterior, y minuta a Tacón diciendo que no debía cifrar de más ni de menos (24 y 30 de julio 1830).

931

N.º 888. — 7 de abril, Filadelfia.

Anuncia remisión de los impresos del congreso publicados hasta el momento.

VIII. — 22

932

N.º 892. — 16 de abril, Filadelfia.

Remite un número de «El Redactor», de Nueva York, donde se inserta la proclama del comandante general de la escuadra española en Cuba, Ángel Laborde Navarro, imponiendo la pena capital a los marineros que se pasasen al servicio de los rebeldes de Méjico.

Adjunto:

— Número del «El Redactor» donde figura la proclama (Nueva York, 10 de abril 1830).
— Nota informativa al rey comunicando lo anterior (Palacio, 1 de junio 1830).
— Minutas a Tacón y al secretario de Marina con la aprobación real en este asunto (16 de junio 1830).

933

N.º 893. — 16 de abril, Filadelfia.

Remite una lista de los pasaportes expedidos en los consulados españoles durante el mes de marzo, todos con destino a Cuba.

Adjunto:

— La lista citada.

934

N.º 898. — 18 de abril, Filadelfia.

Participa la venta de la corbeta Kensington para el gobierno de Rusia.

935

N.º 899. — 26 de abril, Filadelfia.

Hace una recapitulación de las reales órdenes recibidas a lo largo del mes. Entre ellas figuraba la que disponía que continuase dando noticias sobre Tejas.

936

N.º 901. — 26 de abril, Filadelfia.

Acusa recibo de la circular ordenando que no diera curso a las cartas de Manuel Sáinz, desde Nueva Orleans, por estar llenas de faltas de respeto a la autoridad real.

937

N.º 904. — 27 de abril, Filadelfia.

Remite una lista de los pasaportes expedidos en el consulado español en Nueva Orleans en el pasado mes de marzo, todos con destino a Cuba.

Adjunto:

— La lista citada (Filadelfia, 27 de abril 1830).

938

N.º 906. — 28 de abril, Filadelfia.

Anuncia remisión de un estado completo de las rentas y gastos de Estados Unidos desde el 4 de marzo de 1789 hasta el 31 de diciembre 1829.

939

N.º 909. — 28 de abril, Filadelfia.

Informa de varias noticias. Muerte del senador Smith; disminución de las tarifas del te y el café, y oposición del estado de Georgia a dar cumplimiento a los tratados concluidos con los indios. Hay dos ejemplares.

940

N.º 915. — 7 de mayo, Filadelfia.

Propuesta para que se autorizase al presidente americano a nombrar un subsecretario de Estado, que probablemente recaería en Hamilton. Aprobada la introducción de productos y frutos de un país extranjero con el derecho del 30 % únicamente. Fallecimiento de Mr. West, encargado de negocios americanos en Perú.

941

N.º 917. — 8 de mayo, Filadelfia.

Se había concedido permiso a Venezuela para introducir frutos naturales y manufacturados de España, con tal de que esta importación se hiciese con buques neutrales.

942

N.º 919. — 8 de mayo, Filadelfia.

Comunica el regreso a Estados Unidos de Poinsett, a quien se había dado una comida pública, a la que no asistió ninguno de los representantes extranjeros residentes en el país. Se confirmaba la mala situación de Méjico.

Adjunto:
— Copia del discurso de Poinsett con ocasión de la comida que se le había ofrecido a su regreso de Méjico, donde había estado como ministro americano. Decía eran falsas las acusaciones que le habían hecho, de que él, valido de la amistad que tenía con algunos dirigentes mejicanos, había abusado de su ministerio, mezclándose en los negocios internos de este país, y que tenía una especial adversión a Inglaterra, Francia y España. Poinsett aseguraba que no había hecho más que aconsejar que las instituciones republicanas eran preferibles a las monárquicas.
— Nota informativa con las anteriores noticias (29 de junio 1830).

943

N.º 921. — 16 de mayo, Filadelfia.

Acompaña una lista de los pasaportes expedidos en los consulados de Filadelfia y Boston durante el mes de abril.

Adjunto:
— Copia de la lista citada.

944

N.º 922. — 16 de mayo, Filadelfia.

Envía noticias del congreso donde se había presentado una petición de los indios cherokees, quejándose de los atropellos que sufrían por parte de las autoridades del este de Georgia. Nombramiento del doctor Hamm de Zanesville, como encargado de negocios cerca de los rebeldes de Guatemala.

945

N.º 923. — 17 de mayo, Filadelfia.

Anuncia remisión de varios números de «El Español» con noticias de Nueva España.

946

N.º 926. — 19 de mayo, Filadelfia.

Informa de la salida para Madrid de Rowan, con la misión de activar la petición y entrega de los títulos de las dotaciones de tierras en las Floridas.

947

N.º 927. — 19 de mayo, Filadelfia.

Participa la salida para Europa de Niedersletter, encargado de negocios de Rusia, con licencia de su gobierno. Hay dos ejemplares.

948

N.º 928. — 19 de mayo, Filadelfia.

Da cuenta de la posibilidad de que se hiciese un tratado de comercio entre Estados Unidos y Portugal. Hay dos ejemplares.

949

N.º 929. — 23 de mayo, Filadelfia.

Acusa recibo de varias reales órdenes.

950

N.º 930. — 24 de mayo, Filadelfia.

Comunica varias noticias de Haití: el tratado de comercio con Francia había quedado sin firmar; llegada de un comisionado de la isla para fijar los preliminares de un tratado comercial entre Estados Unidos y Haití.

951

N.º 934. — 26 de mayo, Filadelfia.

Remite copia de la lista de pasaportes expedidos en el mes de abril por los consulados de Nueva York y Nueva Orleans.

Adjunto:
— Copia de la citada lista (Filadelfia, 26 de mayo 1830).

952

N.º 935. — 26 de mayo, Filadelfia.

Comunica que los colonos franceses que habían llegado a Nicaragua para establecerse en este país, tenían pocas posibilidades de sobrevivir.

953

N.º 936. — 27 de mayo, Filadelfia.

Informa de la venta en pública subasta del navío sueco Japperheten, por 15.000 pesos. Había sido adquirido por un comerciante de Nueva York.

954

N.º 942. — 29 de mayo, Filadelfia.

Dice que continuaban las sesiones del congreso. Se estaba terminando la discusión sobre el decreto de los indios aprobado en el senado.

955

N.º 945. — 6 de junio, Filadelfia.

Da cuenta del nombramiento de Randolph para ministro plenipotenciario en Rusia; del doctor Hamm como encargado de negocios cerca de los rebeldes de Chile y de E. Brown para el mismo cargo en el Brasil.

956

N.º 948. — 7 de junio, Filadelfia.

Remite copia de la lista de los pasaportes expedida por los cónsules de Filadelfia y Nueva York en el mes de mayo.

Adjunto:
— La lista citada (Filadelfia, 17 de junio 1830).

957

N.º 950. — 8 de junio, Filadelfia.

Anuncia remisión de varios números de «El Español» de Nueva Orleans.

Adjunto:
— Dos despachos, que había recibido de Stoughton con noticias de diferentes puntos de América (Nueva York, 10 y 20 de junio 1830).
— Nota al secretario de Estado indicándole que dijese a los representantes españoles en América que se abstuviesen de remitir periódicos sin noticias de interés y siempre acompañados con una reseña de su contenido.

— Minuta a Tacón con estas mismas instrucciones (Madrid, 5 y 6 de agosto 1830).

958

N.º 953. — 8 de junio, Filadelfia.

Avisa de la terminación de las sesiones del congreso. Entre otros acuerdos se había tomado el de disminuir los derechos sobre el te y café, sal, melaza y ron, se había aprobado la asignación de fondos para carreteras, formación de canales, limpieza y alumbrado de puertos y otros. El conflicto con los indios cuyo territorio era fronterizo con el estado de Georgia, se había solucionado llevándolos más allá del Mississipi, mediante una indemnización.

959

N.º 954. — 8 de junio, Filadelfia.

Da cuenta del tratado concluido entre Estados Unidos y Dinamarca para liquidar las reclamaciones de ciudadanos americanos contra el gobierno danés.

960

N.º 959. — 17 de junio, Filadelfia.

Incluye lista de los pasaportes expedidos en mayo por los cónsules de Baltimore y Boston.

Adjunto:

— Copia de la lista citada (Filadelfia, 7 de junio 1830).

961

N.º 960. — 17 de junio, Filadelfia.

Da cuenta de la petición de fondos que habían hecho los editores del «Redactor» de Nueva York, por la penuria en que se encontraban debido al atraso sufrido en percibir las pocas suscripciones con que contaban fuera de este país. Se había hecho responsable de alguna de sus deudas el cónsul español en Nueva York. En opinión de Tacón debería auxiliárseles con quinientos pesos, en tanto llegaba una respuesta oficial a sus pretensiones.

962

N.º 961. — 18 de junio, Filadelfia.

Avisa la llegada a Nueva York de dos oficiales y varios soldados españoles de los desertores que pasaron a Portugal en 1826 y desde allí a Londres. No tenían otro objeto que el de buscar su subsistencia, lo que no sería fácil por falta de conocimiento del idioma, por lo que trataría de conseguir que fuesen enviados a Cuba.

Adjunto:

— Nota al secretario de Estado anunciando lo anterior (Filadelfia, 11 de junio 1830).

963

N.º 965. — 26 de junio, Filadelfia.

Acusa recibo de varias reales órdenes.

964

N.º 966. — 27 de junio, Filadelfia.

Remite lista de los pasaportes expedidos en el consulado de Nueva Orleans en el pasado mayo.

Adjunto:

— Copia de la lista citada, la mayoría con destino a la Habana (Filadelfia, 27 de junio 1830).

965

N.º 968. — 27 de junio, Filadelfia.

Participa la salida de Washington del presidente americano, en dirección a Tennessee, no sólo para pasar el verano, sino para conseguir que los indios cumpliesen lo decretado por el congreso, sobre el territorio que debían desocupar, mediante las indemnizaciones contratadas.

966

N.º 969. — 28 de junio, Filadelfia.

Remite una relación de los militares españoles llegados a Nueva York desde Londres.

Adjunto:
— Lista mencionada donde figuraban los nombres y circunstancias de cada uno (Filadelfia, 28 de junio 1830).

967

N.º 972. — 28 de junio, Filadelfia.

Comunica varias noticias de Méjico: toma de Acapulco por el general de los rebeldes, Bravo, lo que suponía una derrota para el partido de Guerrero, y una nueva conspiración en la capital.

968

N.º 973. — 5 de julio, Filadelfia.

En relación con el informe que se le había solicitado, sobre si el derecho de extranjería o de aubaine debía aplicarse en Estados Unidos para facilitar la libre sucesión de los españoles en la herencias, dice que según lo estipulado en el tratado de 1795 con el gobierno americano, se concedía a los ciudadanos de ambos estados la libertad de disponer de sus bienes personales por testamento o donación.

969

N.º 974. — 5 de julio, Filadelfia.

Acusa recibo de la real pragmática que establecía la sucesión regular en la corona de España, por lo que envía su felicitación. Hay dos ejemplares.

970

N.º 976. — 6 de julio, Filadelfia.

Remite varios números de «El Español», que se publicaba en Nueva Orleans, con noticias de Méjico y la llegada a este puerto de los rebeldes Lorenzo Zavala y Ramón Ceruti, expulsados de Méjico.

Adjunto:

— Números 87 y 93 de «El Español» con las noticias de Méjico, de España, Francia y Colombia (Nueva Orleans, 28 de mayo a 12 de junio 1830).

971

N.º 978. — 7 de julio, Filadelfia.

Comunica varias noticias de Estados Unidos. Regreso a Washington del secretario de Estado. El jefe de los indios Choctaws, residente en el Estado de Mississippi, se había presentado como candidato al congreso, por gozar el derecho de ciudadanos los indios de este estado. En el caso probable de salir elegido, sería el primer indio que ocuparía un asiento en el congreso. Hay dos ejemplares.

972

N.º 979. — 8 de julio, Filadelfia.

Comunica noticias de Bogotá: la parte del sur se había separado del gobierno de Caicedo, acaudillada por el general Flores; Bolívar estaba en Turbaco, alentando todavía a los partidarios que lo rodeaban. En Veracruz había también un desorden general; Bustillo e Infantes se habían unido contra Páez.

973

N.º 980. — 8 de julio, Filadelfia.

Sigue dando noticias de los militares españoles que habían desertado a Portugal en 1826 y llegaban a Estados Unidos para organizar su vida. Hay dos ejemplares.

974

N.º 981. — 8 de julio, Filadelfia.

Remite una lista de los pasaportes expedidos durante el mes de junio en los consulados españoles de Filadelfia, Nueva York y Boston.

Adjunto:

— Lista con los nombres de los citados pasaportes (Filadelfia, 8 de julio 1830).

975

N.º 982. — 8 de julio, Filadelfia.

Da cuenta de la llegada a Nueva York de un hijo del desaparecido general rebelde, Miranda, que debía ir a Londres como secretario de la legación de Bogotá, pero que no se incorporaría a su destino mientras no se aclarase la situación en su país. Hay dos ejemplares.

976

Hace un comentario al discurso pronunciado por el ministro nombrado por Estados Unidos para Rusia, antes de marcharse a ocupar su destino. Hay dos ejemplares.

Adjunto:

— Carta de Francisco Stoughton a Hilario Rivas y Salmón, anunciando remisión de gacetas con noticias sobre Bogotá y otras relativas a los progresos de los colonos negros que emigraron de Estados Unidos a Liberia (Nueva York, 30 de junio 1830).

977

N.º 985. — 11 de julio, Filadelfia.

Anuncia remisión del manuscrito del padre Gaspar Hernández, titulado «Revista político religiosa de las Américas españolas bajo la Independencia». En él se manifestaban las causas, orígenes y consecuencias de la revolución en las posesiones españolas de América. Estaba escrito en forma de cartas de un independiente a un anti-independiente.

Adjunto:

— Copia de carta de Gaspar Hernández a Tacón, adjuntando el manuscrito para que lo enviase al rey y solicitase su impresión (Nueva York, 11 de junio 1830).

— Nota informativa dando cuenta de lo anterior (9 de marzo 1831).

— Minuta a Tacón diciendo de parte del rey que no parecía conveniente consentir en la impresión de la obra de Gaspar Hernández, pues aunque en ella se rebatían las falsas doctrinas de los insurgentes de América, al ponerse de manifiesto estas mismas doctrinas, podrían producirse mayores daños que beneficios (Aranjuez, 16 de abril 1831).

978

N.º 986. — 12 de julio, Filadelfia.

Participa la llegada a Nueva York del nuevo ministro plenipotenciario de Francia, Jean Baptiste Roux de Rochelle. Hay dos ejemplares.

979

N.º 987. — 12 de julio, Filadelfia.

Dice que había pasado por Nueva York el ministro de los rebeldes de Méjico, que viajaba hacia el Norte.

980

N.º 992. — 16 de julio, Filadelfia.

Hace un detallado análisis de la situación en Méjico desde su independencia, bajo el riguroso sistema establecido por el gobierno de Bustamante quien tenía confiados los principales cargos a personas muy adictas a su causa para sostenerse en el mando. El llamado ejército permanente de la federación mejicana no excedía de 12.000 hombres y los fondos eran tan escasos que apenas bastaban para atender a la tropa y a los empleados civiles. Las relaciones diplomáticas de esta nueva república con las potencias extranjeras parecían satisfactorias a su gobierno, quien creía que eso influiría en el rey de España para que reconociese su independencia. Según sus noticias este nuevo gobierno mejicano trataría por todos los medios de excitar la independencia de Cuba.

981

N.º 993. — 17 de julio, Filadelfia.

Carta cifrada sin traducción.

982

N.º 999. — 26 de julio, Filadelfia.

Acusa recibo de varias reales órdenes.

983

N.º 998. — 26 de julio, Filadelfia.

Manifiesta su satisfacción por hallarse la reina en el quinto mes de su embarazo.

984

N.º 999. — 27 de julio, Filadelfia.

Anuncia remisión de varios números de «El Español», con noticias de Nueva España.

985

N.º 1.000. — 27 de julio, Filadelfia.

Remite lista de los pasaportes expedidos en Nueva Orleans durante el mes de junio pasado.

Adjunto:

— Copia de la citada lista, cuyos pasaportes eran todos para la Habana (Filadelfia, 27 de julio 1830).

986

N.º 1.001. — 28 de julio, Filadelfia.

Participa la llegada a Filadelfia del general Scholten, procedente de Dinamarca y la próxima partida del ministro de esta nación para su país.

987

N.º 1.002. — 28 de julio, Filadelfia.

Da cuenta de las diferencias existentes entre los diversos estados de la Unión, provocadas principalmente porque las disposiciones mercantiles favorecían a unos y eran perjudiciales a los otros. Este descontento se manifestaba especialmente en Carolina del Sur, por ser uno de los estados más necesitados y causaba a sus habitantes indignación la indiferencia con que el congreso acogía sus peticiones.

988

N.º 1.005. — 5 de agosto, Filadelfia.

Acusa recibo de la real orden en la que se le prevenía que evitase los viajes a Washington.

989

N.º 1.006. — 6 de agosto, Filadelfia.

Remite lista de los pasaportes expedidos en julio por los cónsules de Filadelfia y Nueva York y por los vicecónsules de Baltimore y Boston.

Adjunto:

— Copia de la lista de pasaportes casi todos con destino a Cuba (Filadelfia, 6 de agosto 1830).

990

N.º 1.007. — 6 de agosto, Filadelfia.

Anuncia remisión de varios números de «El Español», en que se trataba de la expedición española a Méjico.

991

N.º 1.008. — 6 de agosto, Filadelfia.

Informa de la reclamación del vicecónsul de Nueva Orleans para el pago de gastos a este consulado; había pasado a Cuba para que fuese satisfecho por aquella intendencia.

Adjunto:

— Copia del informe del intendente de la Habana, conde de Villanueva, diciendo que no tenía atribuciones para atender a estos gastos (Habana, 3 de julio 1830).

992

N.º 1.009. — 7 de agosto, Filadelfia.

Da cuenta del paso por Filadelfia, con dirección a Baltimore del ministro de los rebeldes de Méjico, Jornel.

993

N.º 1.011. — 8 de agosto, Filadelfia.

Acusa recibo de la orden indicando que le proporcionara una entrevista con cierto individuo, a lo que daría cumplimiento. Hay dos ejemplares.

994

N.º 1.014. — 16 de agosto, Filadelfia.

Anuncia la firma de un tratado entre Estados Unidos y el gobierno turco, por el que se aseguraba a la Unión el libre paso por el mar Negro.

995

N.º 1.015. — 17 de agosto, Filadelfia.

Da cuenta del apresamiento de la goleta española, Fénix, por la de guerra de Estados Unidos, Grampus, que la condujo a Nueva Orleans para ser juzgada por sospecha de piratería. El capitán y tripulación de la Fénix, que habían sido apresados, fueron puestos en libertad rápidamente por no haber encontrado el fiscal de Estados Unidos en qué fundar la acusación.

Adjunto:

— Nota de Antonio Argote Villalobos, vicecónsul español en Nueva Orleans, a Tacón, incluyendo copia de la carta que había recibido, del teniente de la marina americana, Wilson, avisando de la llegada a Nueva Orleans, de la Fénix a la que se había imputado tentativa de piratería contra un buque americano. Le comunicaba también que el buque Fénix llevaba a su bordo ochenta y dos esclavos negros de la costa de África (Nueva Orleans, 20 de julio 1830).

— Respuesta de Argote a Wilson diciendo que una vez probado que la imputación de piratería no tenía ningún fundamento, el capitán y tripulación del Fénix, debían ser juzgados por un tribunal español por tráfico de esclavos (Nueva Orleans, 22 de julio 1830).

— Copia del oficio de Tacón a Argote diciendo que en su respuesta al teniente Wilson se debía haber limitado a decir que daba conocimiento de todo al capitán general de Cuba y al ministro español en Estados Unidos, sin tomar ninguna otra iniciativa. Hay dos ejemplares, uno en inglés (Filadelfia, 15 de agosto 1830).

996

N.º 1.018. — 26 de agosto, Filadelfia.

Acusa recibo de las reales órdenes recibidas durante el mes de agosto, con fechas a partir de mayo.

997

N.º 1.019. — 26 de agosto, Filadelfia.

Acompaña copia de la lista de pasaportes concedidos por el vicecónsul español en Nueva Orleans en el pasado julio.

Adjunto:

— Lista de los citados pasaportes. Hay dos ejemplares (Filadelfia, 20 de agosto 1830).

998

N.º 1.021. — 27 de agosto, Filadelfia.

Remite copia de la nota que había dirigido al secretario de Estado americano para que tomase las medidas convenientes para averiguar la verdad sobre la muerte del español José de la Luz Machado, acaecida en la balandra americana Hudson, en su travesía de la Habana a Nueva Orleans.

Adjunto:

— Copia del oficio de Francisco Tacón a Martín van Buren, secretario de Estado americano, exponiendo las circunstancias en que había muerto José de la Luz y pidiendo se esclarecieran los hechos (Filadelfia, 19 de agosto 1830).

999

N.º 1.022. — 28 de agosto, Filadelfia.

Comunica la salida de Estados Unidos del encargado de negocios, ruso, barón de Krudner, y la venida del representante de Dinamarca, S. Bille.

1.000

N.º 1.026. — 29 de agosto, Filadelfia.

Remite un proyecto para la reconquista y posesión del reino de Nueva España, hecho por una persona que ocultaba su nombre, pero sin duda muy interesado en esta empresa.

Adjunto:

— Proyecto conteniendo una serie de puntos, entre los que cabía destacar que se reunirían en la Habana ocho mil hombres para embarcarse hacia las costas de Nueva España, que con los seis mil del país, que era los que juzgaba el autor poder reunir a sus órdenes, se haría posible obtener la sumisión de este reino. Debería contarse también con un fondo de cien mil pesos fuertes para el mantenimiento de los hombres hasta su definitiva incorporación al ejército real. Se exigiría también una amplia garantía para los que siguiesen la causa y aun la concesión de ascensos a aquellos que fuesen más necesarios. Y, de adoptarse este plan, convendría aprovecharse de los disturbios internos para ganar partidarios entre los descontentos con Bustamante (Filadelfia, 29 de agosto 1830).

— Modificaciones sobre el plan presentado; es una serie de observaciones hechas por Tacón sobre las dificultades de reunir tanto número de hombres y de llevar a cabo el desembarco de los mismos, pareciéndole asimismo excesivo el riesgo de que fuese descubierto el plan con las consiguientes pérdidas y otros perjuicios (Filadelfia, 29 de agosto 1830).

1.001

N.º 1.027. — 7 de septiembre, Filadelfia.

Acusa recibo de varios oficios.

1.002

N.º 1.028. — 7 de septiembre, Filadelfia.

Quedaba enterado del desestanco del tabaco en el puerto franco de Cádiz.

1.003

N.º 1.031. — 9 de septiembre, Filadelfia.

Avisa de la arribada forzosa a Nueva York de la corbeta Kensington, habiendo perdido todo su velamen y parte de su arboladura y haciendo cinco pies de agua.

1.004

N.º 1.033. — 11 de septiembre, Filadelfia.

Hace referencia a la incertidumbre del estado de seguridad en Francia, debido a los últimos acontecimientos ocurridos, lo que le inclinaba a suspender la correspondencia por el Havre.

1.005

N.º 1.034. — 21 de septiembre, Filadelfia.

Recapitula las reales órdenes recibidas durante el presente mes.

1.006

N.º 1.035. — 21 de septiembre, Filadelfia.

Remite copia de la lista de pasaportes expedidos en el mes de agosto último, por los cónsules de Filadelfia, Nueva York y Boston.

Adjunto:

— Lista citada.

1.007

N.º 1.037. — 23 de septiembre, Filadelfia.

En cifra, traducida, remite una carta que había recibido Mexía de un tal Joaquín Posada dando noticias de Méjico donde seguía el mayor desorden y persecuciones. Se hablaba de mandar tropas a Cuba, desde Méjico, para favorecer su independencia (Jalapa, 6 de agosto 1830).

Adjunto:

— Copia del oficio de Tacón al capitán general de Cuba insertando varios párrafos de la anterior carta, para que estuviese prevenido (Filadelfia, 21 de septiembre 1830).

1.008

N.º 1.038. — 2 de octubre, Filadelfia.

Informa de la entrevista que había celebrado el presidente americano con los jefes de los indios en la que les había propuesto un cambio de territorios. Trata también del reconocimiento por Estados Unidos de los encargados de negocios de Prusia y Dinamarca.

1.009

N.º 1.039. — 2 de octubre, Filadelfia.

Remite copia y traducción de la respuesta del gobierno americano a la nota sobre el presunto asesinato del español José de la Luz Machado, a bordo de la balandra americana Hudson, en la que se decía que esta comunicación se había trasladado al fiscal de la Luisiana, para que procediese según la ley.

Adjunto:

— Oficio y traducción, del Departamento de Estado a Francisco Tacón con los anteriores informes.

1.010

N.º 1.043. — 8 de octubre, Filadelfia.

Remite lista de los pasaportes concedidos por los cónsules españoles durante el mes de septiembre pasado.

Adjunto:

— Relación de pasaportes, casi todos para Cuba. Hay dos ejemplares (Filadelfia, 8 de octubre 1830).

1.011

N.º 1.044. — 9 de octubre, Filadelfia.

Comunica que el gobierno de Gran Bretaña había abierto por un tiempo indefinido a los buques de los Estados Unidos los puertos de sus posesiones coloniales en América del Sur e islas de Bahama y Bermudas, pagando los mismos derechos que los ingleses; y que por lo tanto los puertos de Estados Unidos quedaban abiertos para todos los buques ingleses, con el mismo cargo de derechos que los naturales del país. Hay dos ejemplares.

1.012

N.º 1.045. — 10 de octubre, Filadelfia.

Continúa dando noticias de los últimos sucesos de Francia, que se celebraban en Nueva York con diferentes comidas dadas por los emigrados franceses e italianos y los rebeldes mejicanos, felicitándose por la salida de Francia de Carlos X y su familia. Estaba sin confirmar la noticia de que José Bonaparte se disponía a trasladarse a Europa.

Adjunto:

— Recorte de gaceta y su traducción con una carta de José Bonaparte, probablemente al general francés Lallemand, donde descartaba la posibilidad de dirigirse a Europa en un plazo inmediato (Point Breeze, 14 de septiembre 1830).

1.013

N.º 1.046. — 15 de octubre, Filadelfia.

Envía noticias que trataban de la uniformidad de los planes de los emigrados revolucionarios españoles y mejicanos existentes en Estados Unidos y Londres. Se había hecho una suscripción en Nueva York, Boston y Filadelfia para costear el transporte a Francia de los españoles emigrados reunidos en Nueva York, que tenían el plan de revolucionar la península.

Adjunto:

— Varios documentos que le había enviado el confidente del que había hablado en anteriores despachos y que eran: carta a Ramón Ceruti, uno de los principales implicados, que había llegado a Filadelfia para comprar buques y armamentos para la república mejicana, de uno que se firmaba F. H. S. y escribía desde Gibraltar, proporcionándole algunos nombres de personas que pudieran ayudarle en su comisión (Gibraltar, 7 de mayo 1825).

— Carta con asuntos personales de G. de Gorostiza a Ceruti (2 de septiembre sin año).

— Copia de apuntaciones particulares de Ceruti, llenas de cifras y correcciones y que en opinión de Tacón, demostraban la iniquidad de sus proyectos.

— Copia de otra comunicación recibida por Tacón donde se informaba de los contactos establecidos entre los emigrados españoles y Díaz Morales, el general Torrijos y el coronel Grases para llevar adelante la revolución en España y arrojar a la familia real (s. l. ni fecha).

— Nota de los revolucionarios que se habían reunido en Nueva York disponiéndose para pasar a Francia (Filadelfia, 15 de octubre 1830).

1.014

N.º 1.047. — 31 de octubre, Filadelfia.

Da cuenta de los revolucionarios españoles que estaban preparados para salir hacia el Havre próximamente. Informa también de la salida para Liverpool, del general Lallemand.

1.015

N.º 1.048. — 31 de octubre, Filadelfia.

Comunica que Pedro Pablo Cagigao había tomado pasaje para marchar al Havre, con objeto de reunirse a los revolucionarios españoles que estaban en Francia.

1.016

N.º 1.051. — 5 de noviembre, Filadelfia.

Acusa recibo de las reales órdenes recibidas en el mes último. Hay dos ejemplares.

1.017

N.º 1.053. — 5 de noviembre, Filadelfia.

Da cuenta del tratado concluido entre los indios choctaws y el gobierno americano, por el cual los indios cedían el país que ocupaban, obligándose a evacuarlo en el término de tres años, pasados los cuales se situarían al otro lado del Mississippi, corriendo Estados Unidos con los gastos de traslado y mantenimiento de los indios durante un año y a pagarles una renta de veinte mil duros por espacio de veinte años.

1.018

N.º 1.056. — 6 de noviembre, Filadelfia.

Remite copia y traducción de la nota del ministro de negocios extranjeros americano, sobre la muerte del español José de la Luz Machado, ocurrida a bordo de la goleta Hudson en su travesía de la Habana a Nueva Orleans.

Adjunto:

— Oficio de van Buren, secretario de Estado americano, a Tacón, Washington, 8 de octubre de 1830, incluyendo una carta del fiscal de Estados Unidos para el distrito de Luisiana, Slidell, en relación con la muerte de Machado. En ella se descartaba el asesinato de Machado, pareciendo más bien que se trataba de un suicidio; después de su muerte se había sabido que Machado había estado complicado en alguna conspiración contra el gobierno de España (Nueva Orleans, 27 de septiembre 1830).

— Respuesta de Tacón a van Buren agradeciendo su gestión (Filadelfia, 14 de octubre 1830).

1.019

N.º 1.057. — 6 de noviembre, Filadelfia.

Seguía haciendo averiguaciones sobre los rebeldes en Estados Unidos. Un tal La Torre, empleado en alguna oficina de la Habana, era uno de los que tenía correspondencia con los agentes rebeldes en Estados Unidos. Y un oficial llamado Segura, se comunicaba con Montenegro. Hay dos ejemplares.

Adjunto:

— Minuta al rey informando de lo anterior (12 de enero 1831).

1.020

N.º 1.058. — 6 de noviembre, Filadelfia.

Comunica que se seguían celebrando en Estados Unidos, los últimos sucesos de Francia, habiendo asistido a algunos de estos actos el mismo presidente y otras autoridades del país.

1.021

N.º 1.060. — 6 de noviembre, Filadelfia.

Anuncia remisión de los reglamentos de las academias de música de Nueva York y Filadelfia.

1.022

N.º 1.063. — 11 de noviembre, Filadelfia.

Dice que no se había accedido a las solicitudes de Antonio Pomar y Manuel Valdor, vicecónsules de Norfolk y Baltimore, de que se les concediese alguna asignación para gastos de escritores y de correo.

1.023

N.º 1.064. — 12 de noviembre, Filadelfia.

Remite la lista de los pasaportes expedidos por los cónsules españoles en el mes de octubre.

Adjunto:
— Relación de pasaportes en la que constaba que todos los individuos pasaban a Cuba. Hay dos ejemplares.

1.024

N.º 1.065. — 12 de noviembre, Filadelfia.

Manifiesta que el llamado ministro de Méjico, había anunciado al público la nulidad de los contratos de ventas de tierras a ciudadanos de esta Unión para establecerse en las provincias de Coahuila y Tejas.

1.025

N.º 1.066. — 13 de noviembre, Filadelfia.

Daría cumplimiento a la real orden de 11 de septiembre último, por la que se había determinado que cesasen las pensiones alimenticias que percibían los empleados españoles en su legación, debiendo ser por cuenta de Tacón el alojamiento y manutención de dichos empleados. Se quejaba de las dificultades que tendría para subvenir a estos gastos.

1.026

N.º 1.067. — 13 de noviembre, Filadelfia.

Participa la elección de Adams, anterior presidente, para diputado del congreso. El ministro de Francia en Estados Unidos había presentado al presidente una carta del duque de Orleans anunciándole su acceso al trono de Francia. Hay dos ejemplares.

1.027

N.º 1.071. — 22 de noviembre, Filadelfia.

Anuncia remisión de impresos del congreso americano.

1.028

N.º 1.072. — 25 de noviembre, Filadelfia.

Acusa recibo de varias reales órdenes.

1.029

N.º 1.073. — 25 de noviembre, Filadelfia.

Remite copia de nota que había enviado al gobierno americano en relación con la detención en Nueva Orleans de la goleta española Fénix.

Adjunto:

— Copia de nota de Tacón a van Buren, secretario de Estado americano, protestando contra toda intervención de los tribunales americanos, pidiendo la inmediata puesta en libertad de la Fénix y su cargamento, a disposición del cónsul español en Nueva Orleans (Filadelfia, 23 de noviembre 1830).

1.030

N.º 1.076. — 10 de diciembre, Filadelfia.

Participa la salida para el Havre del emigrado español Joaquín Carrasco, con el pasaporte francés que sacó de la península como prisionero constitucional.

1.031

N.º 1.079. — 12 de diciembre, Filadelfia.

Remite el discurso del presidente de Estados Unidos, Andrés Jackson, al comienzo de la segunda sesión del 21 congreso.

Adjunto:
— El discurso, con su traducción, en el que apenas se habla de España; sólo decía que se tomarían medidas para remediar las diferencias entre los dos países. Se manifestaba favorable al cambio de gobierno en Francia, con el que tenía fundadas esperanzas de llegar a acuerdos comerciales. Exponía la conclusión del convenio con Gran Bretaña relativo al comercio entre Estados Unidos y las colonias inglesas en las Antillas y América del norte. Con Rusia se conservaban las más amistosas relaciones, así como con Dinamarca. De los robos cometidos por los buques de guerra portugueses, esperaba informes. De las pretendidas repúblicas de la América española, sólo hablaba de Méjico, con el que esperaba llegar a un acuerdo en el establecimiento de las líneas fronterizas. Al hablar de los asuntos anteriores se refería al aumento de la navegación y caminos. Anuncia haber llegado a un término feliz la política del gobierno con los indios. Presenta el estado de las rentas públicas. Hay dos ejemplares (Filadelfia, 12 de diciembre 1830).

1.032

N.º 1.080. — 12 de diciembre, Filadelfia.

Remite la lista de los pasaportes expedidos por los cónsules españoles en Estados Unidos.

Adjunto:

— Relación de pasaportes correspondiente al mes de noviembre (Filadelfia, 10 de noviembre 1830).

1.033

N.º 1.081. — 17 de diciembre, Filadelfia.

Participa la salida para el Havre de tres soldados españoles que llegaron a Estados Unidos procedentes de Londres.

1.034

N.º 1.082. — 18 de diciembre, Filadelfia.

Expone lo más esencial de las memorias presentadas en el congreso por los secretarios de Guerra, Hacienda y director de Correos. El de Guerra decía el mal resultado obtenido con la abolición de la pena de muerte por delitos de deserción, que habían aumentado considerablemente.

1.035

N.º 1.083. — 18 de diciembre, Filadelfia.

Hace un extracto de la memoria presentada por el ministro de Marina en el congreso. Dice que la marina no había sufrido más pérdida que la de la corbeta Hornet, ocurrida en las costas de Nueva España, que las fuerzas se hallaban distribuidas en los mares del Sur y Mediterráneo, siendo esta escuadra la mayor que continuaba gozando del privilegio concedido por el gobierno español en Mahón. Proponía que se aumentase el presupuesto para construir escuelas náuticas y mejores hospitales, y que se aumentase la graduación de los oficiales de marina, cuyo rango mayor era el de capitán. Dice que estaban disminuyendo las enfermedades de los barcos gracias al uso de las fumigaciones de clórido, cal y sosa, recientemente introducidas.

Adjunto:

— Nota informativa exponiendo lo anterior (22 de febrero 1831).

1.036

N.º 1.084. — 19 de diciembre, Filadelfia.

Por una circular del ministerio de Hacienda de Estados Unidos había visto confirmada la continuación de la franquicia concedida a los buques españoles en los puertos de Panzacola y San Agustín, según el tratado de la Florida.

1.037

N.º 1.086. — 28 de diciembre, Filadelfia.

Remite copias de la nota del secretario de Estado americano, y de la protesta del capitán del bergantín americano, Elisabeth, quejándose de que habían hecho fuego a dicho buque desde el fuerte de Matanzas, a su salida del puerto, hiriendo al piloto y a dos marineros.

Adjunto:

— Copia y traducción de la protesta del capitán Daniel Sainborn, contra el comandante del puerto español de Matanzas, por la agresión que sufrió su barco, sin ninguna justificación, en la que resultaron varios heridos (Matanzas, 12 de noviembre 1830).
— Oficio del secretario de Estado van Buren a Tacón, quejándose de estas irregularidades y pidiendo se indemnizase por los daños causados (Washington, 23 de diciembre 1830).
— Respuesta de Tacón lamentando lo ocurrido, y prometiendo que lo notificaría a su gobierno para una pronta resolución (Filadelfia, 27 de diciembre 1830).

1.038

N.ᵒˢ 1.087 y 1.088. — 28 de diciembre, Filadelfia.

Acusa recibo del oficio por el que se le informaba del nacimiento de la infanta María Isabel Luisa; enviaba su felicitación, y prometía comunicarlo al gobierno americano.

1.039

N.º 1.089. — 29 de diciembre, Filadelfia.

Quedaba enterado del real decreto por el que se disponía que la infanta María Isabel Luisa recibiría los honores de Príncipe de Asturias, por ser la heredera y legítima sucesora de la corona, mientras el rey no tuviese un hijo varón.

1.040

N.º 1.090. — 29 de diciembre, Filadelfia.

Acusa recibo del real decreto estableciendo reglas para evitar las maquinaciones de los rebeldes, asegurando la tranquilidad del Estado.

1.041

N.º 1.091. — 30 de diciembre, Filadelfia.

Había dado cumplimiento a la real orden de que reclamase la devolución de la goleta Fénix; avisaría de su resultado.

1.042

N.º 1.092. — 30 de diciembre, Filadelfia.

Manifiesta su satisfacción por la derrota de los revolucionarios españoles que trataban de perturbar el orden en Guipúzcoa y Navarra.

1.043

N.º 1.093. — 30 de diciembre, Filadelfia.

Felicita a Salmón por su nombramiento para secretario de Estado que venía desempeñando interinamente y en difíciles circunstancias.

LEGAJO 5.657

CORRESPONDENCIA DE DON FRANCISCO TACÓN, MINISTRO
EN ESTADOS UNIDOS, CON EL SECRETARIO DE ESTADO,
DON MANUEL GONZALEZ SALMÓN

1.044

N.º 1.094. — 6 de enero, Filadelfia.

Acusa recibo de reales órdenes y expresa sus deseos de bienestar para la regia familia.

1.045

N.º 1.105. — 24 de enero, Filadelfia.

Comunica que las sesiones del congreso no aportaban gran interés. Habían aprobado en el senado la concesión al presidente de la Unión de una cantidad para que fletase dos buques destinados a prestar auxilios a las embarcaciones de las costas que habían sido dañadas por un temporal terrible; todos los ríos estaban helados y apenas se podía transitar por las calles con trineos.

1.046

N.º 1.106. — 14 de febrero, Filadelfia.

Remite lista de pasaportes expedidos por los distintos consulados en la Unión durante el mes de enero, y por el viceconsulado de Nueva Orleans del mes de diciembre anterior.

Adjunto:

— Relación de los pasaportes expedidos por los cónsules y vice-cónsules españoles (Filadelfia, 31 de enero 1831).

1.047

N.º 1.107. — 14 de febrero, Filadelfia.

Había regresado a Nueva Orleans el príncipe Pablo Guillermo de Witemberg que había hecho una expedición por una parte de la América septentrional para adquirir conocimientos topográficos y físicos de aquellas regiones, y deshacer algunos errores descubiertos en los mapas publicados hasta el día; se proponía pasar luego a Nueva España con el mismo objeto.

1.048

N.º 1.111. — 16 de febrero, Filadelfia.

Expresa su satisfacción por las medidas adoptadas por el rey para contrarrestar los ataques intentados por los revolucionarios españoles refugiados en Francia.

1.049

N.º 1.112. — 16 de febrero, Filadelfia.

Promete cumplir la orden que disponía remitiera la correspondencia por la vía del Havre.

1.050

N.º 1.113. — 28 de febrero, Filadelfia.

Acusa recepción de algunas reales órdenes.

1.051

N.º 1.117. — 2 de marzo, Filadelfia.

Había llegado a Nueva York Mr. Serurier, plenipotenciario de Francia en Estados Unidos, y Mr. Rowan que regresaba de Madrid con pliegos del ministro americano en la corte.

1.052

N.º 1.118. — 2 de marzo, Filadelfia.

Habían publicado las gacetas que el vicecónsul francés en Montevideo había pasado nota a ese gobierno reconociendo su independencia y proponiendo la formación de un tratado de navegación y comercio.

1.053

N.º 1.119. — 3 de marzo, Filadelfia.

Remite folleto con la correspondencia entre el general Jackson y J. Calhoun ministro de la Guerra durante el gobierno de Monroe, con motivo de las luchas con los indios seminoles; trata de la ocupación indebida de las Floridas por Jackson quien tenía órdenes de respetar el territorio español, y en la publicación se descubre el secreto de las deliberaciones del gabinete de Washington en 1818, apareciendo las autoridades encubiertas en mutuas acusaciones.

Adjunto:

— «Correspondence between gen. Andrew Jackson and John C. Calhoun, president and vice-president of the Unitet States, on the subject of the course of the letter, in the deliberatios of the cabinet of Mr. Monroe, on the ocurrences in the seminoles war». Impreso en Washington, 1831, 52 págs.

1.054

N.º 1.120. — 3 de marzo, Filadelfia.

Comunica algunas de las decisiones adoptadas en el congreso: había ratificado el tratado de navegación y comercio con Turquía menos el artículo secreto sobre construcción de buques; había sido sancionado el convenio con los indios choctaws; un proyecto que había presentado el estado de Virginia sobre castigar a las personas que proporcionasen instrucción a los negros libres, había sido desechado.

Trata también del incendio ocurrido en el fuerte de Delaware, a la entrada del río de ese nombre.

1.055

N.º 1.126. — 12 de marzo, Filadelfia.

Remite listas de pasaportes expedidos por el cónsul en Nueva Orleans, en el mes de enero. Principal y duplicado.

Adjunto:

— Relación nominal de las personas a quienes se había concedido pasaporte, expresando sus lugares de destino (5 de marzo 1831).

1.056

N.º 1.128. — 13 de marzo, Filadelfia.

Refiere las principales cuestiones tratadas en el 21 congreso, la mayoría de interés local y casi ninguna relacionada con potencias extranjeras. Había designado a George Erving como encargado de negocios en Constantinopla. Se había notado en las sesiones un gran aumento de la oposición contra el gobierno, y desunión entre las autoridades.

1.057

N.º 1.129. — 14 de marzo, Filadelfia.

Había presentado sus credenciales el nuevo plenipotenciario de Francia, habiendo sido recibido en audiencia, como despedida, su antecesor, Mr. Roux de Rochelle.

1.058

N.º 1.131. — 25 de marzo, Filadelfia.

Había trasladado al cónsul general en Estados Unidos la orden dirigida al director del Real Giro, sobre la clasificación del cónsul cesante en Nueva Orleans, don Antonio Argote Villalobos.

1.059

N.º 1.134. — 26 de marzo, Filadelfia.

Comunica la llegada a Filadelfia del teniente de navío Juan José Martínez, comisionado por las autoridades de la Habana para contratar en Estados Unidos un pontón de vapor, útil para la limpieza de la bahía de aquel puerto. También de Puerto Rico le habían anunciado la llegada del teniente de navío Antonio Aubarede con un encargo similar.

1.060

N.º 1.136. — 28 de marzo, Filadelfia.

Una delegación de los indios cherokees había ido a Washington para presentar ante el tribunal supremo de justicia, una reclamación contra el estado de Georgia. El tribunal se había declarado incompetente para intervenir en esas contiendas.

1.061

N.º 1.140. — 30 de marzo, Filadelfia.

Acusa recibo de reales órdenes y celebra la buena salud de los reyes y de la infanta recién nacida.

1.062

N.º 1.141. — 7 de abril, Filadelfia.

Remite un oficio que el capitán general de Filipinas don Mariano Ricafort había enviado junto con un pliego dirigido al secretario de Guerra, a Francisco Ezequiel de las Bárcenas, administrador de Correos que había fallecido hacía poco.

1.063

N.º 1.143. — 8 de abril, Filadelfia.

Se estaba generalizando la oposición contra el gobierno de Jackson, y en Filadelfia se había celebrado una concentración de partidarios de Mr. Clay para promover su nombramiento para la presidencia; otras reuniones análogas habían tenido lugar en distintos estados.

1.064

N.º 1.144. — 8 de abril, Filadelfia.

Había llegado a Méjico el príncipe Pablo Guillermo de Wirtemberg; también publicaban las gacetas de aquel país que se había presentado Mr. Grothe, encargado de negocios en Países Bajos, a Bustamante, para entregarle carta de su soberano participándole el matrimonio de su hija la princesa Guillermina con el príncipe Alberto de Rusia.

1.065

N.º 1.147. — 16 de abril, Filadelfia.

Remite lista de pasaportes.

Adjunto:
— Relación de los pasaportes expedidos por los cónsules de Filadelfia, Nueva York, Boston, Baltimore y Charleston, durante el mes de marzo, y por el vicecónsul de Nueva Orleans en el mes de febrero.

1.066

N.º 1.148. — 16 de abril, Filadelfia.

Trata de la cuestión del arbitraje del rey Guillermo de los Países Bajos, en el litigio sobre los límites del noroeste del territorio de la Unión que confinaba por el estado de Maine con las posesiones británicas.

1.067

N.º 1.151. — 20 de abril, Filadelfia.

Transmite el agradecimiento de don Francisco de Paula Quadrado, secretario de la legación, por el aprecio que había manifestado el rey por sus trabajos en la ordenación del archivo. Principal y duplicado.

1.068

N.º 1.152. — 20 de abril, Filadelfia.

Transmite el agradecimiento de don Luis Potestad, agregado a la legación de Estados Unidos, por la satisfacción real debida a sus trabajos en el archivo. Principal y duplicado.

1.069

N.º 1.153. — 20 de abril, Filadelfia.

Acusa recibo de una copia de la nota que se había entregado al ministro de Estados Unidos en Madrid, en contestación a la propuesta que hizo de un tratado de comercio con España al mismo tiempo que reclamaba contra los derechos de tonelada que se exigían a los buques de su nación en Cádiz. Principal y duplicado.

1.070

N.º 1.154. — 23 de abril, Filadelfia.

Había recibido la orden circulada a los empleados de las carreras diplomática y consular, disponiendo que no se librara cantidad alguna contra la secretaría de Estado, sin estar expresamente autorizado.

1.071

N.º 1.155. — 23 de abril, Filadelfia.

Quedaba enterado de la orden encargándole insistiera en la reclamación pendiente de Juan Miguel de Losada.

1.072

N.º 1.158. — 27 de abril, Filadelfia.

Expresa la satisfacción suya y de los empleados en la legación, por el triunfo contra las tentativas de los revolucionarios y la lealtad de los españoles a su soberano. Principal y duplicado.

Adjunto:

— Minuta anunciando remisión de gaceta con noticias del triunfo contra los que amenazaban la tranquilidad de los españoles, y con las muestras de adhesión al rey (8 de marzo 1831).

1.073

N.º 1.159. — 27 de abril, Filadelfia.

Anuncia remisión de unos periódicos de Nueva York en los que se insertaban las declaraciones del pirata Carlos Gibbs, que había sido condenado a muerte en un islote de la bahía de Nueva York por sus actos de piratería; estas confesiones desvanecerían la leyenda de muchos robos atribuidos a españoles.

1.074

N.º 1.160. — 27 de abril, Filadelfia.

Da gracias por la aprobación de la cuenta de suscripción al periódico «El Redactor» de Nueva York, que los editores se encargaban de pasar a Costa Firme y a otros puntos disidentes de América.

Adjunto:

— Oficio de Francisco Stoughton, cónsul en Nueva York, asegurando que con su intervención, los editores remitían los ejemplares de su periódico suscritos por el gobierno, a Nueva España, Nuevo Reino de Granada, la Guayra, Río de la Plata, Montevideo y otros puntos (Nueva York, 24 de abril 1831).

1.075

N.º 1.164. — 29 de abril, Filadelfia.

La desunión entre los diversos ministros había dado lugar a que presentaran su dimisión antes de que terminara el período de gobierno del presidente Jackson, caso no ocurrido hasta entonces en la república. Tacón expresa las causas que cada uno había manifestado para dejar el cargo, y las contestaciones de Jackson, el cual tenía bastantes dificultades para formar nuevo gabinete. Nombra Tacón a algunos que se consideraban sucederían a los dimisionarios. Principal y duplicado.

1.076

N.º 1.165. — 30 de abril, Filadelfia.

Habiendo dimitido George Erving como encargado de negocios de Turquía, se había elegido para el mismo cargo, a David Porter, cónsul en las potencias berberiscas. Principal y duplicado.

1.077

N.º 1.166. — 30 de abril, Filadelfia.

Acusa recibo de reales órdenes. Principal y duplicado.

1.078

N.º 1.167. — 8 de mayo, Filadelfia.

Remite lista de pasaportes. Principal y duplicado.

Adjunto:
— Relación de pasaportes expedidos por los cónsules en el mes de abril y por el vicecónsul de Nueva Orleans en el mes de marzo. Dos copias (Filadelfia, 5 de mayo 1831).

1.079

N.º 1.169. — 9 de mayo, Filadelfia.

No se había publicado aún el nombramiento de los nuevos ministros por lo que estaba paralizada la administración pública. Principal y duplicado.

1.080

N.º 1.171. — 23 de mayo, Filadelfia.

Noticias de Río de Janeiro aseguraban que había estallado una revolución en el Brasil por las diferencias entre los republicanos y los portugueses europeos residentes en el país. El emperador Pedro había abdicado en su hijo, pero como esta decisión no había aquietado los ánimos, se había tenido que refugiar en una fragata inglesa que estaba en el puerto.

1.081

N.º 1.172. — 27 de mayo, Filadelfia.

Promete Tacón enviar en cuanto pudiera tres ejemplares de la obra «La correspondencia diplomática de la revolución americana», que le habían pedido.

1.082

N.º 1.177. — 29 de mayo, Filadelfia.

Comunica que había regresado a Nueva York el español Juan Pablo Cagigao, que había salido del país para Francia.

1.083

N.º 1.178. — 29 de mayo, Filadelfia.

Mr. Vaughan, plenipotenciario inglés, había salido con licencia para su país, quedando como encargado de negocios Mr. Bankhead, secretario de la legación. Habían llegado a Filadelfia los magistrados franceses De Beaumont y De Tonqueville, comisionados por el ministro del Interior para observar las cárceles de Estados Unidos e informar de ello a Francia. Principal y duplicado.

1.084

N.º 1.179. — 30 de mayo, Filadelfia.

Comunica el nombramiento de Eduardo Livingston como secretario de Estado. Tacón informa sobre sus cualidades y sobre otros nombramientos de ministros. Principal y duplicado.

1.085

N.º 1.180. — 30 de mayo, Filadelfia.

Remite cuenta de gastos eventuales de la legación. Principal y duplicado.

Adjunto:

— Recibo de 450 pesos fuertes que había pagado don Francisco Tacón por la suscripción de 150 ejemplares de «El Redactor» (Nueva York, 31 de mayo 1831).

1.086

N.º 1.181. — 30 de mayo, Filadelfia.

Cuenta detalles de la revolución de Río de Janeiro del 15 de marzo al 7 de abril, día en que el emperador Pedro, después de haber abdicado en su hijo, tuvo que refugiarse en el buque inglés Warspite; vencidos los portugueses, muchos abandonaron la ciudad temiendo por sus vidas; el ejército se había pasado casi totalmente, al partido de los brasileños independentistas.

1.087

N.º 1.182. — 30 de mayo, Filadelfia.

Acusa recibo de varias reales órdenes.

1.088

N.º 1.184. — 8 de junio, Filadelfia.

Comunica la llegada a Filadelfia con dirección a Washington del príncipe Pablo Guillermo de Wirtemberg, debiendo regresar a Baltimore para descansar de sus expediciones científicas. Principal y duplicado.

1.089

N.º 1.186. — 9 de junio, Filadelfia.

Remite lista mensual de pasaportes.

Adjunto:

— Relación de los pasaportes expedidos por los cónsules del rey en Estados Unidos. Firmada por el cónsul general Juan Bautista Bernabéu (Filadelfia, 6 de junio 1831).

1.090

N.º 1.188. — 12 de junio, Filadelfia.

Participa que el príncipe Pablo Guillermo de Wirtemberg había salido para el puerto del Havre. Principal y duplicado.

1.091

N.º 1.190. — 18 de junio, Filadelfia.

Remite copia de la nota que había mandado a Mr. Livingston para reclamar de nuevo por el apresamiento de la goleta española Fénix por la de Estados Unidos, Grampus; pedía que se entregara el buque y su cargamento, al cónsul del rey en Nueva Orleans, donde se hallaba el barco detenido.

Adjunto:

— Copia del oficio que Tacón había dirigido al secretario de Estado de la Unión, Eduardo Livingston, en protesta por el embargo de la goleta Fénix (Filadelfia, 6 de junio 1831).
— Copia y traducción de la contestación de Livingston manifestando que el buque había sido condenado en virtud de un acta para proteger el comercio de Estados Unidos y castigar el crimen de piratería que imponía la confiscación del buque por tentativa a cometer piratería, pero si el acto no se había llevado a cabo, la tripulación debía de quedar libre, que es lo que se había concedido. Podía apelar al Tribunal Supremo (Washington, 11 de junio 1831).

1.092

N.º 1.191. — 18 de junio, Filadelfia.

Le había participado el cónsul general que al llegar el nuevo vicecónsul don Antonio Larrañaga a Charleston, no pudo hacerse cargo de los archivos del consulado, por negarse a su entrega los herederos del último cónsul don José Mulvey, pretextando que el gobierno debía grandes cantidades al difunto Mulvey; aunque Larrañaga había acudido al gobernador del estado y al fiscal general del distrito, no habían querido éstos mezclarse en esas cuestiones. Había Tacón dirigido una nota al secretario de Estado para que el presidente tomara las providencias convenientes, pero se le había contestado que no era este asunto atribución del presidente, sino que debía de acudir a los tribunales de justicia.

Adjunto:
— Copia del oficio enviado por Tacón al secretario de Estado, Livingston, para que interesara al presidente en la devolución de los archivos del consulado de Charleston, que estaban en poder de Jane Muir (Filadelfia, 4 de junio 1831).
— Copia y traducción de la respuesta de Livingston manifestando que según sus facultades constitucionales, no podía acceder a lo que había pedido Tacón (Washington, 8 de junio 1831).
— Copia de oficio de Tacón a Livingston solicitando nuevamente la ayuda que dentro de sus facultades constitucionales acostumbraba a prestar el gobierno federal a los representantes extranjeros que no podían presentarse ante los tribunales de la Unión ni someterse a sus decisiones; los archivos del consulado del rey en Charleston eran propiedad de España y pedía ayuda para obligar a su entrega al nuevo cónsul (Filadelfia, 13 de junio 1831).

1.093

N.º 1.195. — 24 de junio, Filadelfia.

Comunica de la isla de Santo Domingo que las negociaciones entabladas entre el cónsul francés y el gobierno de Haití no habían tenido resultado favorable, por lo que el cónsul había resuelto salir de la isla y aconsejaba a todos los franceses que siguieran su ejemplo.

1.094

N.º 1.196. — 24 de junio, Filadelfia.

Se había encargado de los ministerios de Guerra y de Hacienda al doctor Randolph y a Mr. Dickens respectivamente. El presidente se disponía a pasar algunos días en Rip-Raps, y Poinsett pensaba embarcarse en Nueva York para Liverpool, tal vez con alguna comisión del gobierno. Principal y duplicado.

1.095

N.º 1.197. — 24 de junio, Filadelfia.

Remite copia de la contestación que le había dado el secretario de Estado respecto a la entrega del archivo del consulado de Charleston, con una carta del presidente solicitando de la señora Muir que entregara los papeles al cónsul Larrañaga.

Adjunto:

— Copia y traducción de oficio del secretario de Estado a Tacón remitiendo copia de la carta enviada por el presidente a la señora Muir para obtener la entrega de los archivos al cónsul Larrañaga; traducción de la misma (Washington, 16 de junio 1831).

1.096

N.º 1.198. — 27 de junio, Filadelfia.

Anuncia remisión de un pliego que le había dirigido el capitán general de Filipinas para el secretario de Marina. Principal y duplicado.

1.097

N.º 1.199. — 28 de junio, Filadelfia.

Acusa recepción de reales órdenes. Principal y duplicado.

1.098

N.º 1.200. — 7 de julio, Filadelfia.

Remite copia y traducción de la nota que le había dirigido el secretario de Negocios Extranjeros, sobre la fianza que debían presentar las personas que desembarcasen en el puerto de Cádiz. Principal y duplicado.

Adjunto:

— Copia y traducción del oficio enviado por Livingston a Tacón incluyendo el traslado de una comunicación que el secretario de Estado, González Salmón, había pasado al ministro de Estados Unidos en Madrid, van Ness. Quería saber Livingston el objeto y consecuencias de la orden sobre fianzas personales en el puerto de Cádiz, la cual parecía contraria al tratado existente entre ambas naciones (Washington, 2 de julio 1831).

— Copia de comunicación de González Salmón manifestando que para conservar el buen orden en Cádiz el rey había decidido que las personas que desembarcaran en ese puerto debían presentar la fianza de un sujeto abonado que respondiera de su conducta (Aranjuez, 10 de abril 1831).

— Respuesta de Tacón a Livingston manifestando que no tenía orden dada por el gobierno español respecto al puerto de Cádiz, pero consideraba que las precauciones que se adoptaban por circunstancias especiales, eran semejantes a las que se observaban en Gibraltar, en la Habana y en otros puntos, sin que afectasen a las estipulaciones de los tratados (Filadelfia, 5 de julio 1831).

Todos los documentos adjuntos están duplicados.

1.099

N.º 1.201. — 7 de julio, Filadelfia.

Remite un periódico que contiene la correspondencia que había mediado entre el cónsul de Francia y el gobierno de Haití.

Adjunto:

— Gaceta «El «Redactor», con la correspondencia seguida por el presidente de Haití, Juan Pedro Boyer y el cónsul de Francia, sobre la falta de pago de la cantidad de 150 millones de francos, convenida para la cesión de esa parte de la isla por los franceses (Nueva York, 2 de julio 1831).

1.100

N.º 1.202. — 8 de julio, Filadelfia.

Había llegado a Estados Unidos el general mejicano Barragán que pensaba embarcarse para el Havre; se creía que abandonaba Méjico por desavenencias con Bustamante.

1.101

N.º 1.203. — 8 de julio, Filadelfia.

Remite lista de pasaportes. Principal y duplicado.
Adjunto:
— Relación de los pasaportes expedidos por los cónsules en el mes de junio, firmada por Juan Bautista Bernabéu (Filadelfia, 6 de julio 1831).

1.102

N.º 1.206. — 17 de julio, Filadelfia.

Había sido nombrado Mr. Luisbass, secretario de la Guerra, y Mr. R. B. Taney, fiscal general. El ex-presidente Monroe había muerto el 4 de julio, aniversario de la independencia; en el mismo día fallecieron sus antecesores Adams y Jefferson. Principal y duplicado.

1.103

N.º 1.208. — 20 de julio, Filadelfia.

Anuncia remisión de los impresos de la segunda sesión del 21 congreso de la Unión. Principal y duplicado.

1.104

N.º 1.209. — 27 de julio, Filadelfia.

Comunica la salida de Nueva York para Portsmouth de la corbeta rusa Kensington.

1.105

N.º 1.213. — 29 de julio, Filadelfia.

Participa las causas que habían obligado a varios ministros del gobierno a presentar la dimisión; según un artículo que había publicado en las gacetas de Washington el ex-fiscal general del reino, Mr. Berrien, el motivo había sido porque no querían esos ministros que sus familias tuvieran trato con la mujer del ministro de la Guerra, Eaton, amigo del presidente. Entre las señoras que habían conspirado contra la de Eaton, estaba la del embajador de Holanda.

1.106

N.º 1.214. — 31 de julio, Filadelfia.

Acusa recibo de reales órdenes.

1.107

N.º 1.215. — 31 de julio, Filadelfia.

Comunica que se habían encontrado en una casa de Nueva York algunas de las joyas que hacía dos años habían sido robadas a la princesa de Orange y cuyo valor se estimaba en cien mil duros; aunque el ministro de Holanda las había reclamado, las autoridades creían que por haber sido introducidas de contrabando, correspondía decomisarlas.

1.108

N.º 1.216. — 19 de agosto, Filadelfia.

Remite lista de pasaportes.

Adjunto:

— Estado mensual de los pasaportes expedidos por los cónsules y vicecónsules del rey en Estados Unidos, durante el mes de julio. Firmado por Juan Bautista Bernabéu (Filadelfia, 5 de agosto 1831).

1.109

N.º 1.217. — 15 de agosto, Filadelfia.

Participa que el teniente de navío Juan José Martínez había contratado con Andrés Patrulló, comerciante español nacionalizado en Estados Unidos, la construcción de un pontón a vapor y cuatro goletas ganguiles, para la limpieza del puerto de la Habana.

1.110

N.º 1.218. — 15 de agosto, Filadelfia.

Había llegado a Nueva York, Luis MacLane, plenipotenciario en Londres a quien se había nombrado ministro de Hacienda y a Mr. Cass, ministro de la Guerra. Van Buren iría a Inglaterra como embajador, llevando como secretario de la legación a Aarón Vail que reemplazaba a Washington Irving.

1.111

N.º 1.219. — 16 de agosto, Filadelfia.

El presidente de Bogotá había restituido en el cargo y honores, según los tenía en 1823, a Francisco de Paula Santander.

1.112

N.º 1.220. — 16 de agosto, Filadelfia.

Seguía la causa referente a las joyas de la princesa de Orange; se había detenido cerca de Nueva York a un individuo Constant Polari quien aseguraba las había comprado en Argel. Las leyes del estado de Nueva York de 1830 autorizaban a los jueces a tomar conocimiento de todos los robos cometidos en la Unión, o en otros países, siempre que la propiedad robada se encontrara en Estados Unidos y aunque este robo había sido anterior, pretendía el procurador que se hiciera el juicio por el delito de haber sido introducida la cosa robada.

1.113

N.º 1.221. — 20 de agosto, Filadelfia.

Anuncia remisión de dos «Cuadernos de las Transacciones de la Sociedad Filosófica Americana», que le había entregado don Francisco de Paula Quadrado para que se hicieran llegar a la Academia de la Historia.

1.114

N.º 1.222. — 31 de agosto, Filadelfia.

El 21 de agosto se habían sublevado unos 200 esclavos negros de Cayo Cruz en el territorio de Southampton en el estado de Virginia, saqueando las casas de las familias pudientes y matando a bastantes blancos; al pasar el río fueron rechazados por la tropa de línea y la milicia que acudió a batirlos. Principal y duplicado.

1.115

N.º 1.224. — 1 de septiembre, Filadelfia.

Acusa recepción de reales órdenes. Principal y duplicado.

1.116

N.º 1.225. — 2 de septiembre, Filadelfia.

Quedaba enterado Tacón de que el rey había accedido a la solicitud de muchos particulares pidiendo poder continuar la correspondencia de intereses y de familia con españoles residentes en el extranjero, a pesar del decreto sobre emigrados del 1 de octubre 1830. Principal y duplicado.

1.117

N.º 1.227. — 15 de septiembre, Filadelfia.

Remite lista de pasaportes. Principal y duplicado.

VIII. — 25

Adjunto:

— Estado mensual de los pasaportes expedidos por los cónsules y vicecónsules del rey en Estados Unidos. Firmado por Juan Bautista Bernabéu (Filadelfia, 5 de septiembre 1831).

1.118

N.º 1.228. — 15 de septiembre, Filadelfia.

Había llegado a Filadelfia Mr. Draper con pliegos del plenipotenciario de Estados Unidos en París, Mr. Rives, que contenían el tratado concluido entre ambas naciones relativo a la reclamación que desde 1810 tenía pendiente la federación por las pérdidas sufridas por su comercio en virtud de los decretos de Berlín y Milán en el último período de mando de Napoleón. Parecía seguro que Francia se comprometía a pagar unos 28 millones de francos y se conseguía rebaja de derechos de vinos franceses que se importasen en Estados Unidos, y del algodón americano que se introdujere en Francia.

1.119

N.º 1.229. — 16 de septiembre, Filadelfia.

Trata de los desastres producidos por un huracán en la isla de la Barbada, la más oriental de las Antillas de Barlovento, donde habían muerto la mayor parte de la población; en Bridgetow apenas se había librado una casa de la avería; los buques fondeados en la bahía de Carlisle, habían encallado en la costa, inutilizándose además en tierra, todas las cosechas. También se habían producido daños en la Martinica, la Antigua, Santa Lucía y otras de las Antillas; la ciudad de Nueva Orleans estaba en parte, navegable. En la isla de Cuba sólo había sufrido el puerto de Santiago, y en Puerto Rico, los perjuicios eran de escasa consideración.

1.120

N.º 1.231. — 17 de septiembre, Filadelfia.

La sublevación de los negros en Southampton había puesto de manifiesto que había un plan mucho más ambicioso y extensivo a todos los negros del país que aspiraban a obtener los derechos de ciudadanos con las mismas prerrogativas que los blancos. En Washington se habían publicado órdenes muy severas para formar un empadronamiento de los negros con el fin de someterlos a vigilancia. Principal y duplicado.

1.121

N.º 1.232. — 22 de septiembre, Filadelfia.

Renueva la reclamación sobre la devolución de la goleta Fénix con su cargamento, después de haber reunido la documentación pertinente, considerando injusta la sentencia de los tribunales americanos por sospecha de infracción a las leyes de España por súbditos españoles.

Adjunto:

— Copia y traducción del decreto del juez del almirantazgo de Nueva Orleans condenando a la goleta Fénix por tentativa de piratería, la cual había sido apresada cerca de Haití por la goleta Grampus de Estados Unidos; alegaban también los acusadores que llevaba a bordo 82 negros, tráfico entonces prohibido por las leyes de España; muchos de los negros, que estaban de momento a cargo del gobierno de los Estados Unidos, habían muerto, decidiendo el fiscal que podían entregarse, bajo fianza a personas que los mantuvieran a cambio de su trabajo. Sigue la reclamación de los africanos por parte de Pablo de la Torre en nombre del propietario de los mismos, José Givert, residente en la Habana. El tribunal había desechado la reclamación (sin fecha).

— Copia de carta de Joaquín Roig a Francisco Pablo de la Torre, sobre movimiento de barcos y de un poder dado a José Givert dueño del pailebot Fénix a Serafín Cucullu, para que representase y defendiera sus derechos en Nueva Orlenas (Habana, 31 de mayo 1831).

— Copia de los dos decretos del juez del almirantazgo de Nueva Orleans mandando vender la goleta Fénix y distribuir su producto conforme a las leyes, y negando el derecho del reclamante español a la devolución de los negros (Nueva Orleans, 5 de julio 1831).

1.122

N.º 1.235. — 25 de septiembre, Filadelfia.

Acusa recibo de reales órdenes.

1.123

N.º 1.236. — 7 de octubre, Filadelfia.

Comunica que el presidente había estado gravemente enfermo; que en el mes anterior había habido una reunión en Baltimore, de comisionados de la mayor parte de los estados, decidiendo excluir de los destinos públicos a los que pertenecieren a la masonería; se propuso para candidatos a la presidencia y vicepresidencia, respectivamente, a W. Wirt de Maryland y a Amos Ellmaker; otra reunión se había celebrado en Filadelfia, llamada del comercio libre, para representar al congreso la necesidad de alterar los aranceles. Principal y duplicado.

1.124

N.º 1.237. — 8 de octubre, Filadelfia.

Se tenía noticias de que en Méjico dos coroneles habían enviado una representación al congreso sobre los españoles que sin permiso se introducían en el país; con este motivo había habido alguna alteración en la capital. Una casa alemana y otra inglesa habían suspendido pagos, alarmando al comercio y aumentando la desconfianza de los vecinos.

1.125

N.º 1.238. — 8 de octubre, Filadelfia.

Había llegado a Nueva York Juan de Dios Cañedo que se dirigía con el carácter de plenipotenciario de Méjico a las distintas repúblicas de América del sur, y al Brasil, acompañado de Morales como secretario de su misión. El general Negrete que residía en Estados Unidos, se disponía a marchar a Burdeos, a reunirse con su familia.

1.126

N.º 1.239. — 14 de octubre, Filadelfia.

El vicecónsul del rey en Nueva Orleans, Antonio Argote Villalobos, le había comunicado que el intendente de la Habana no podía dar cumplimiento a la orden disponiendo que le pagasen una determinada cantidad por gastos extraordinarios. Argote debía de cobrar 20.000 reales de vellón anuales.

1.127

N.º 1.240. — 16 de octubre, Filadelfia.

Remite lista de pasaportes. Principal y duplicado.

Adjunto:

— Estado mensual de los pasaportes expedidos por cónsules y vicecónsules durante el mes de septiembre, y por el vicecónsul de Nueva Orleans, en el mes de agosto. Remitido por Juan Bautista Bernabéu (Filadelfia, 6 de octubre 1831).

1.128

N.º 1.241. — 17 de octubre, Filadelfia.

Los negros de la isla de la Tórtola se habían sublevado pidiendo la libertad y negándose a trabajar en los plantíos; afortunadamente se había descubierto antes la conspiración que habían tomado para degollar a los blancos y atacar la ciudad; el gobierno de Santo Tomás había enviado un buque dinamarqués con cuyo apoyo habían apresado a muchos revoltosos, entre ellos al cabecilla Romney.

1.129

N.º 1.242. — 17 de octubre, Filadelfia.

En Río de Janeiro se había descubierto una conspiración de negros y mulatos para acabar con los blancos, en un plan muy extenso que difundían las asociaciones secretas. También llegaban noticias alarmantes de Bahía y Pernambuco, por los movimientos de los partidos. Las tropas de línea se inclinaban a proclamar una república en el país.

1.130

N.º 1.243. — 18 de octubre, Filadelfia.

Participa que J. Randolph de Roanoke, plenipotenciario de Estados Unidos en San Petersburgo, había regresado a la Unión a causa de su estado de salud. Se planeaba celebrar en Nueva York una reunión de los contrarios a que se hicieran innovaciones en los aranceles, formando comisiones que rebatieran los argumentos de la reunión del comercio libre. En el sur continuaban las rebeliones de la gente de color. Principal y duplicado.

1.131

N.º 1.244. — 18 de octubre, Filadelfia.

En Filadelfia y Nueva York se habían celebrado varias reuniones para excitar a los jóvenes a que se alistasen y dispusieran a pasar a Polonia para contribuir a su defensa, pero el presidente había dado orden a los fiscales para que se opusiesen a esos planes, conforme al acta del congreso del 20 de abril de 1818 que prohibía a los ciudadanos de Estados Unidos formar en su país un cuerpo militar con objeto de servir a una potencia extranjera. Principal y duplicado.

1.132

N.º 1.246. — 28 de octubre, Filadelfia.

El presidente después de su restablecimiento, pasaba de nuevo a Washington; Tacón se disponía también a marchar a ese punto para entrevistarse con el secretario de Estado.

1.133

N.º 1.247. — 15 de noviembre, Filadelfia.

Trata de las entrevistas mantenidas en Washington con el secretario de Estado, Livingston, al que había reclamado de nuevo la devolución de la goleta Fénix y su cargamento de negros, y la entrega de los archivos de Charleston, retenidos por la señora Muir.

Adjunto:
— Notas de la legación de España dirigidas a la secretaría de Estado sobre asuntos pendientes (sin fecha).
— Copia de la comunicación dirigida a Livingston por Tacón, contra el proceder de la señora Muir que se negaba a entregar los papeles del archivo del consulado de Charleston, y pidiendo la ayuda del presidente, dado que los representantes extranjeros no podían presentarse ante los tribunales de la Unión (Washington, 1 de noviembre 1831).
— Copia y traducción de la nota enviada por Livingston a Tacón manifestándole que el presidente había dado orden para que los documentos oficiales de España fuesen devueltos al cónsul de Nueva Orleans (Washington, 7 de noviembre 1831).

1.134

N.º 1.249. — 16 de noviembre, Filadelfia.

Participa que se había verificado en Nueva York la reunión de los contrarios a que se hicieran innovaciones en los aranceles; se había nombrado una comisión para que informara al pueblo sobre sus verdaderos intereses, y otra, para que preparara la redacción de un informe al congreso haciendo conocer la urgencia de proteger la industria americana y de rebajar los derechos de todos los artículos que no entraran en concurrencia con las industrias del país; se estaban recogiendo datos de todos los estados, sobre agricultura, fábricas, artes mecánicas y comercio. Era probable que se obtuviera una disminución de derechos en artículos de importación, alcanzando a los vinos de Cataluña, Málaga y Jerez, cuyo consumo se iba generalizando. Había salido para Nápoles Juan Nelson, comisionado por el gobierno para exigir contestación a varias reclamaciones de americanos por pérdidas en su comercio. Principal y duplicado.

1.135

N.º 1.250. — 16 de noviembre, Filadelfia.

El gobierno de Portugal había solicitado a Estados Unidos que nombrase un agente con instrucciones competentes para concluir un tratado de comercio en Lisboa; se había encargado de este asunto al doctor Randolph, que había sido oficial mayor de la secretaría de guerra. Principal y duplicado.

1.136

N.º 1.252. — 17 de noviembre, Filadelfia.

Expresa su satisfacción por la noticia publicada en las gacetas, de hallarse la reina en quinto mes de embarazo; por si el rey con motivo del alumbramiento, tuviera a bien agraciar a sus vasallos, proponía se recordaran los méritos del secretario y agregado de la legación. Principal y duplicado.

1.137

N.º 1.253. — 20 de noviembre, Filadelfia.

Anuncia remisión de la lista de pasaportes expedidos. Principal y duplicado.

1.138

N.º 1.255. — 22 de noviembre, Filadelfia.

Transmite noticias de Venezuela y Santa Fe. Después del armisticio entre Monagas y Páez, se había retirado el primero a Barcelona, sucediéndole otro titulado general llamado José Gregorio Monagas; las partidas de Rojas, Zamora, Sotillo, Torres y Centeno, mantenían sus posesiones sin entregar las armas y amenazando siempre al gobierno. Bermúdez propugnaba una separación de las provincias del este. Páez se había encargado del gobierno pero los partidos estaban decididos a dejarle sólo el mando militar. En Panamá había gran desorden y habían sido pasados por las armas, el general Luis Urdaneta, coronel Alzuru, capitán Araujo y el paisano Estrada.

1.139

N.º 1.256. — 23 de noviembre, Filadelfia.

Se había renovado en Méjico la ley del 20 de marzo de 1829 relativa a la expulsión de españoles.

1.140

N.º 1.257. — 23 de noviembre, Filadelfia.

Agradecía la aprobación de la cuenta que había enviado, importe de la suscripción durante unos meses, al periódico «El Redactor»; al mismo tiempo comunicaba al cónsul de Nueva York, que según órdenes recibidas, debía suspender dicha suscripción en adelante. Principal y duplicado.

1.141

N.º 1.258. — 23 de noviembre, Filadelfia.

Ya había comunicado sus gestiones para conseguir fuesen devueltos los archivos del consulado de España en Charleston; sólo restaba esperar el resultado de lo que decidiera el fiscal de aquella ciudad.

1.142

N.º 1.259. — 24 de noviembre, Filadelfia.

Había enviado ya los documentos que se le pedían referentes a la reclamación de la goleta Fénix.

1.143

N.º 1.260. — 25 de noviembre, Filadelfia.

Había trasladado al cónsul general la orden emanada de Guerra sobre el modo de socorrer los cónsules a los oficiales del ejército que se hallaren en tránsito por los lugares de su residencia. Principal y duplicado.

1.144

N.º 1.261. — 26 de noviembre, Filadelfia.

Quedaba enterado de la orden pasada por Guerra al capitán general de Cuba, disponiendo que los individuos que se expatriaron cuando se proclamó la constitución del emperador don Pedro de Portugal, no debían ser admitidos en territorio español. Principal y duplicado.

1.145

N.º 1.261. — 28 de noviembre, Filadelfia.

Con motivo del próximo congreso, estaban llegando personajes a Washington, entre ellos, el ex-presidente Adams y el ex-secretario de Estado, Enrique Clay que había sido elegido senador por Kentucky. Principal y duplicado.

1.146

N.º 1.263. — 29 de noviembre, Filadelfia.

Acusa recepción de reales órdenes.

1.147

N.º 1.264. — 2 de diciembre, Filadelfia.

La señora Muir que tan ilegalmente retenía los archivos del vice-consulado de Charleston, los había entregado ya, movida por las gestiones que Tacón había realizado; había dado las gracias al presidente.

1.148

N.º 1.265. — 3 de diciembre, Filadelfia.

Anuncia remisión de una instancia de Jerónimo Stagno residente en la Habana, que estuvo complicado en la causa de Porlier y pretendía regresar libremente a los dominios reales.

Adjunto:

— Informe de Juan Bautista Bernabéu a Francisco Tacón sobre Jerónimo Stagno; había llegado a Estados Unidos en 1815 huyendo de España como uno de los conspiradores de Porlier y se mantenía fabricando cigarros hasta la revolución de 1820, en que se trasladó a la Habana; al extinguirse el gobierno constitucional, regresó a Estados Unidos ocupándose en Nueva York como maestro de lengua castellana y observando buena conducta (Filadelfia, 26 de noviembre 1831).

1.149

N.º 1.266. — 6 de diciembre, Filadelfia.

Anuncia remisión de un pliego que le había enviado el teniente de navío Juan José Martínez, para su entrega al conde de Salazar, secretario de Marina; comprendía un tratado sobre las máquinas de vapor y sus aplicaciones, recogiendo todos los inventos que sobre el tema se habían hecho en otras naciones para simplificar los costes de la construcción de buques y sus carenas, y las fábricas de jarcias, lonas, cañones y diques; consideraba Tacón que se podía asignar a este oficial una dotación para que desde la Habana remitiese planos e informase de los nuevos inventos; Martínez había desempeñado muy bien el encargo de adquirir una máquina de vapor en Estados Unidos, para limpiar el puerto de la Habana.

1.150

N.º 1.267. — 9 de diciembre, Filadelfia.

Habían comenzado las sesiones del 22 congreso de Estados Unidos; se había elegido como presidente de la cámara de representantes a A. Stevenson, diputado de Virginia. Inserta Tacón la traducción del párrafo del discurso del presidente, relativo a España en el que manifestaba que las relaciones entre ambos países, estaban arregladas por el tratado del 22 de febrero de 1819; pero el comercio americano con las antiguas colonias españolas, se veía molestado por buques de guerra y de corso, con el pretexto de que como España no había reconocido la independencia de esos territorios, tenía derecho a prohibir el tráfico con dichos estados en virtud de las leyes coloniales. Para arreglar este asunto había enviado un comisionado a Madrid con instrucciones para que el ministro americano tratara de resolverlo con el gobierno, o en caso contrario, el congreso como juez constitucional adoptaría las medidas pertinentes. Trata también el discurso de las mejoras que experimentaban en la agricultura, fábricas y medios de comunicación interior, y del comercio y relaciones de Estados Unidos con otras naciones. Principal y duplicado.

Adjunto:

— Ejemplar del periódico «The United States Telegraph», con el discurso del presidente (Washington, 7 de diciembre 1831).

1.151

N.º 1.268. — 17 de diciembre, Filadelfia.

Remite la traducción íntegra del mensaje del presidente. Principal y duplicado.

Adjunto:

— Dos ejemplares de gaceta con el discurso del presidente (6 de diciembre 1831).
— Dos traducciones al castellano del mismo discurso.

1.152

N.º 1.269. — 22 de diciembre, Filadelfia.

Remite lista mensual de pasaportes. Principal y duplicado.

Adjunto:

— Estado de los pasaportes expedidos por los cónsules y vicecónsules en Estados Unidos durante el mes de noviembre, excepto del cónsul de Nueva Orleans, que eran las del mes de octubre. Firmado por Juan Bautista Bernabéu (Filadelfia, 8 de diciembre 1831).

1.153

N.º 1.270. — 23 de diciembre, Filadelfia.

Hace un resumen de las Memorias que los ministros de Hacienda, Guerra y Marina, y la del director general de Correos, habían presentado al congreso. El de Hacienda exponía las existencias en tesorería, gastos, cuentas de la deuda pública y presupuestos; tanto los productos de aduanas como de las tierras públicas, habían superado los cálculos previstos; consideraba que debían de dedicarse algunas sumas a aumentar los recursos navales y militares, extender las fábricas de armas y fortificar las fronteras. El secretario de Guerra creía satisfactorio el estado del ejército; expone el número de oficiales y existencias de armas. El de Marina manifiesta el número y distribución de las fuerzas navales; recomendaba la construcción de dos baterías flotantes de vapor, medio de defensa que habían adoptado Francia e Inglaterra. El director general de Correos decía que había un saldo favorable de estas rentas. Principal y duplicado.

1.154

N.º 1.271. — 25 de diciembre, Filadelfia.

Trata de las propuestas presentadas al congreso, entre ellas; disminución de derechos de aranceles; que la comisión de negocios extranjeros informase sobre la conveniencia de dar una ley en que se determinase la indemnización debida a los que se les hubieran destruido sus propiedades, de resultas de las operaciones militares del ejército americano en la Florida oriental, en 1812 y 1814, y sobre títulos de tierras; reclamaciones de los comerciantes por daños sufridos por los franceses antes de 1800; que se remunerase a don Bernardo de Soto capitán del bergantín León y a su tripulación, por haber librado a más de sesenta ciudadanos que se hallaban a bordo de la fragata Minerva, incendiada en las costas de Cuba.

1.155

N.º 1.274. — 27 de diciembre, Filadelfia.

A la pregunta que había hecho Tacón al capitán general de Cuba sobre la manutención y pago de transporte de los negros hallados en la goleta Fénix, en caso de que los devolviera el gobierno americano, había contestado al capitán general que los negros libres que había en la isla estaban haciendo tales estragos que el ayuntamiento de la Habana había conseguido autorización real para expuīsarlos de allí; había decidido Tacón no reclamar a los de la Fénix si no se hacía al mismo tiempo devolución de la goleta.

1.156

N.º 1.275. — 29 de diciembre, Filadelfia.

Participa que por la crudeza del invierno se hallaba interrumpida la navegación y helados los ríos, y que se había extendido una enfermedad llamada influenza, especie de catarro inflamatorio.

LEGAJO 5.658

AÑO 1832

CORRESPONDENCIA DEL MINISTRO EN ESTADOS UNIDOS, FRANCISCO TACÓN, CON EL SECRETARIO DE ESTADO, MANUEL GONZÁLEZ SALMÓN

1.157

N.º 1.277. — 7 de enero, Filadelfia.

Remite la lista de los pasaportes expedidos en el mes de diciembre último, a excepción de los de Charleston y Nueva Orleans que son de noviembre. Hay dos ejemplares.

Adjunto:

— Relación de los pasaportes expedidos por los cónsules y vicecónsules de Filadelfia, Nueva York, Boston, Charleston, Norfolk, Panzacola, Baltimore y Nueva Orleans.

1.158

N.º 1.278. — 10 de enero, Filadelfia.

El presidente había aludido en su discurso de apertura de la sesión del congreso, a las desavenencias que habían surgido con el gobierno de Buenos Aires por el apresamiento de tres buques americanos en las islas Malvinas, pero era de presumir que se solucionarían con facilidad, porque se debía únicamente a la violación de las leyes de pesquerías establecidas respecto a aquellas islas.

1.159

N.º 1.279. — 16 de enero, Filadelfia.

Comunica que continuaban las sesiones del congreso sin más novedad que la de haberse aprobado los nombramientos de los secretarios de Guerra y Marina y de fiscal general; los de Estado y Hacienda se habían diferido por las discusiones que habían surgido al proponerse el nombramiento de van Buren para ministro plenipotenciario en Londres, y no se sancionarían más nombramientos hasta que éste se resolviera. Se habían ratificado por el senado los nombramientos de Francis Baylies para encargado de negocios en Buenos Aires, de Juan Nelson con el mismo cargo en Nápoles, de Davezac para Países Bajos y de James Buchanan como ministro plenipotenciario en San Petersburgo. Se había rechazado la proposición de Wilkins, acordando no invertir más que la suma anual asignada en los presupuestos ordinarios para fortificar las costas; el presidente había dirigido al congreso un informe del secretario de Estado relativo a un tratado comercial con Colombia, que precisaba una autorización de la cámara de diputados para acordar los derechos y toneladas. La comisión encargada de informar sobre la recompensa al capitán y propietarios del bergantín español León por haber salvado a la tripulación de una fragata americana, había propuesto que se distribuyeran tres mil pesos fuertes. Había obtenido autorización para regresar a Europa el ministro de los Países Bajos, que había presentado a su hijo, mister Huygens, como encargado de negocios y estaba próximo a embarcar para Inglaterra. Domingo Acosta había sido reconocido como encargado de negocios y cónsul general de la república de Colombia, y un cónsul para Nueva York del gobierno de Bélgica. El presidente de la república había sufrido una operación para extraerle una bala que conservaba desde la batalla de Nueva Orleans, con resultado plenamente satisfactorio.

1.160

N.º 1.280. — 17 de enero, Filadelfia.

Las últimas noticias de Buenos Aires daban cuenta de que al haber sido asesinado un capitán que llevaba despachos para el jefe en Madrid, se había renovado la guerra civil entre los unitarios y los federalistas, siendo vencedor el partido del gobierno. Hay dos ejemplares.

1.161

N.º 1.281. — 17 de enero, Filadelfia.

Comunica que había salido para Guatemala el ministro plenipotenciario de Méjico Juan de Dios Cañedo, que había estado en Filadelfia con objeto de contraer matrimonio con una hermana del vicecónsul de Méjico en esa ciudad. Hay dos ejemplares.

1.162

N.º 1.282. — 22 de enero, Filadelfia.

Anuncia el envío de una traducción de la memoria que el secretario de Marina americano había presentado al congreso.

1.163

N.º 1.283. — 26 de enero, Filadelfia.

Noticias de Santo Tomás daban cuenta de que se había producido un fuego tan devastador que había arruinado a casi todos los comerciantes; aunque no se conocían detalles, parecía deberse a un gran descuido en la casa comercial de Gil, que era donde había empezado. Por los periódicos de Jamaica se sabía que había ocurrido un levantamiento de negros en una hacienda de Cornwall, donde habían prendido fuego a las casas negándose a trabajar, por lo que se había declarado la ley marcial y partido el general Coton con cuatrocientos hombres para Montego, que era donde estaban los sublevados. Hay dos ejemplares.

1.164

N.º 1.284. — 27 de enero, Filadelfia.

Por cartas de Guatemala se sabía que de nuevo se había encendido la guerra civil, pues la plaza de Omoa había depuesto a las

VIII. — 26

autoridades que gobernaban en nombre del gobierno de Morazán y encargado el mando al capitán Tadeo Martínez; pero no contentándoles tampoco éste habían llamado al coronel Domínguez, declarado enemigo de Morazán, quien había tomado el mando de Omoa y preparado una expedición contra el castillo de San Felipe, en el que sin disparar un solo tiro, se habían apoderado de la fortaleza y de los víveres y armamento que contenía; la ciudad de Trujillo había seguido el ejemplo de Omoa y parecía probable que hicieran los mismo Usula y Olancho. Todos los partidarios de Morazán habían sido detenidos. El anterior presidente depuesto, Arce, amenazaba a Morazán desde la fronteras de Nueva España y también el Salvador disentía políticamente de Guatemala. Hay dos ejemplares.

1.165

N.º 1.285. — 27 de enero, Filadelfia.

El capitán de la goleta Splendid, llegado de Puerto Cabello, había comunicado la muerte del general Bermúdez, no se sabía si asesinado por el coronel Correa o de resultas de una herida producida en duelo con el mismo. De Bogotá se sabía que la llamada convención o congreso había decidido reconocer la separación de Venezuela de la república de Colombia, quedando las provincias del centro bajo la denominación de república de Nueva Granada, con el mismo territorio que tenía la capitanía del mismo nombre en 1810.

Noticias de Santa Marta recibidas en Jamaica decían que los pardos de aquella ciudad, Cartagena y Mompós, habían tramado una conspiración para asesinar a todos los blancos; que se había descubierto por la delación de uno de los complicados y aunque se había apresado a los principales cabecillas estaban sobre las armas todos los habitantes de aquel país. Hay dos ejemplares.

1.166

N.º 1.286. — 28 de enero, Filadelfia.

Comunica noticias sobre una nueva revolución que amenazaba al reino de Méjico. La guarnición de Veracruz se había reunido para declarar la renovación del plan de Jalapa y sostener la constución federal, pidiendo al vicepresidente la remoción de su ministro, acusado de promover el centralismo y tolerar que se atacasen los derechos civiles e individuales; habían redactado un acta de cuatro artículos en la que pedían al general Antonio López de Santa Ana que fuese a tomar el mando de la ciudad y le facultaban para que adoptase las disposiciones que creyera convenientes. Llegado a Veracruz Santa Ana había sido muy bien recibido y al día siguiente había despachado al capitán Vega con cartas para Bustamante, en Méjico, y copia del acta de la guarnición, documentos que deberían ser enviados a todas las autoridades de la federación. También en Jalisco se habían producido alborotos y era de temer que se renovaran los hechos sangrientos de la época de Guerrero. Hay dos ejemplares.

1.167

N.º 1.287. — 29 de enero, Filadelfia.

Se había tratado en el congreso la conveniencia de hacer algunas alteraciones en los aranceles; el senado había aprobado el nombramiento de Livingston como secretario de Estado y el del ministro de Hacienda, quedando pendiente el de van Buren como ministro en Inglaterra; se habían producido otros nombramientos, entre ellos el del marino Porter como encargado de negocios en Constantinopla. Procedente de Smirna había llegado a Boston W. B. Hodgcon con la ratificación del tratado de comercio concluido entre el gobierno americano y Turquía. Se aseguraba que también había llegado ratificado por Bustamante y su congreso el tratado concluido con los disidentes de Nueva España. Remitiría ambos en cuanto se publicaran. Principal y duplicado.

1.168

N.º 1.288. — 30 de enero, Filadelfia.

En los dos últimos meses no había recibido correo de la península. Había disminuido la epidemia de influenza a pesar de ser lo más riguroso del invierno. Se sabía extraoficialmente que el senado había desaprobado en sesión secreta el nombramiento de van Buren como ministro en Londres, pero la noticia no estaba confirmada. Principal y duplicado.

1.169

N.º 1.289. — 7 de febrero, Filadelfia.

Amplía las noticias que había enviado sobre la guerra civil en las repúblicas de Centroamérica, dando cuenta de que en octubre del pasado 1831, se había producido en Quito una revolución provocada por el sargento Miguel Arboleda, sentenciado a muerte por insubordinación, pero que pudo escapar de la cárcel, sublevar a la guarnición, apoderándose del cuartel de artillería, y detener a todos los oficiales junto con el comandante general Diego Whittle. El presidente de dicho estado, Juan J. Flores, había tratado de dominar la tropa sin conseguirlo. Quito había sido escenario de actos vandálicos hasta que el ejército, temiendo la reacción del vecindario, había dejado la ciudad. El general Whittle había salido con una partida detrás de los rebeldes, quienes lo sorprendieron en una emboscada y lo hicieron fusilar. Habían surgido desavenencias entre los estados de Ecuador y Nueva Granada por la posesión del departamento de Cauca. Al renunciar Caicedo a la vicepresidencia de Nueva Granada, le había sustituido el general Obando. En la convención de dicho estado se había acordado reunir toda la documentación relativa a la primera junta de los plenipotenciarios americanos, para proponer a su vista las medidas que debían adoptarse en el nuevo congreso que pedían los mejicanos. Principal y duplicado.

1.170

N.º 1.290. — 8 de febrero, Filadelfia.

Confirma la información enviada anteriormente relativa al rechazo por el senado del nombramiento del ex secretario de Estado van Buren, como ministro en Londres. El principal motivo para desaprobarlo eran las instrucciones que dio a mister Mac Lane cuando fue a Londres en 1829, en las que reconocía la justicia de las razones que habían impedido a Inglaterra acceder a lo que solicitaba la administración de mister Adams respecto a negociaciones comerciales. Los periódicos habían publicado muchos comentarios, según la tendencia a la que pertenecían, y los de la administración habían propuesto a van Buren para candidato a la vicepresidencia. Seguían las especulaciones respecto al que resultaría elegido para ir a Londres. El presidente había propuesto al senado el nombramiento de un encargado de negocios para Bélgica, que algunos consideraban prematuro. Principal y duplicado.

1.171

N.º 1.291. — 12 de febrero, Filadelfia.

Remite la relación de los pasaportes expedidos en los meses de diciembre y enero últimos. Principal y duplicado.

Adjunto:
— Lista de los pasaportes expedidos por los cónsules y vicecónsules de Filadelfia, Nueva York, Boston, Charleston, Nueva Orleans y Panzacola (Filadelfia, 7 de febrero 1832). Hay dos ejemplares.

1.172

N.º 1.292. — 12 de febrero, Filadelfia.

Comunica que había salido de Nueva York, con destino a Londres, el ministro de Holanda en Estados Unidos mister Huygens con su familia; llevaba las alhajas pertenecientes a la princesa de Orange, que se habían hallado en manos del italiano Constant Polari; como ya había informado anteriormente, había conseguido su entrega al haberse retirado la pretensión de que las declarasen decomisadas. Estaba pendiente la entrega del reo, solicitada por el mismo ministro. Principal y duplicado.

1.173

N.º 1.293. — 14 de febrero, Filadelfia.

Las últimas noticias de Veracruz daban cuenta de que se había levantado la guarnición del puerto encabezada por Santa Ana, pidiendo la destitución del vicepresidente. Bustamante que no estaba dispuesto a acceder a dicha petición, había ordenado el envío de tropas contra Veracruz, estando expuesto Santa Ana a ser pasado por las armas si lo cogían. Se había adherido a Santa Ana la guarnición de Alvarado, poniéndose la de Jalisco al lado del gobierno. El objeto de todo el plan era poner a Santa Ana al frente de la república. Principal y duplicado.

1.174

N.º 1.294. — 15 de febrero, Filadelfia.

Los periódicos de Jamaica daban cuenta de que había sido dominada la insurrección de los negros mediante la publicación de la ley marcial, la pena capital impuesta a sesenta de los conspiradores y los castigos infligidos a más de cien culpados; las pérdidas que habían experimentado las plantaciones eran cuantiosas; se esperaba que los rebeldes que aún estaban ocultos en los bosques se acogerían al indulto que se les había ofrecido. Principal y duplicado.

1.175

N.º 1.295. — 17 de febrero, Filadelfia.

Da cuenta del incidente que había surgido en una comida a la que el presidente había invitado al cuerpo diplomático acreditado en Filadelfia; al sentirse relegado el ministro de Francia Serurier, había manifestado su desaprobación en términos poco correctos. En una reunión del gabinete al día siguiente, habían acordado que todos los secretarios de Estado tendrían preferencia en el protocolo sobre los ministros extranjeros, resolución por la que Serurier también había protestado. Principal y duplicado.

1.176

N.º 1.296. — 24 de febrero, Filadelfia.

Remite copia de la nota que había enviado al secretario de Estado en respuesta a la que éste le había mandado acompañando la protesta del capitán del bergantín americano Elisabeth, en la que se quejaba de que al salir del puerto le habían hecho fuego desde el fuerte de Matanzas.

Adjunto:

— Copia de la carta de Francisco Tacón al secretario de Estado Eduardo Livingston, en respuesta a su nota que acompañaba la protesta de Daniel Sainborn, capitán del bergantín americano Elisabeth, de Boston, contra el comandante del fuerte de Matanzas, en la isla de Cuba, y contra los que cumplieron sus órdenes la noche del 10 al 11 del mes de noviembre de 1830. De las averiguaciones realizadas había resultado que dicho capitán había despreciado las leyes de Indias y las ordenanzas de la real armada, que prohiben la entrada o salida de todo buque desde la hora de retreta hasta la de diana y autoriza a los comandantes del puerto a impedirlo, batiéndoles si fuera necesario; como él había intentado salir entre las doce y la una de la noche desatendiendo las órdenanzas el comandante del fuerte, se había visto en la necesidad de hacer fuego, que por otra parte no había producido heridos. Además dicho buque estaba anclado en el puerto junto a un bergantín español que había tratado de fugarse la noche precedente y se parecía mucho en su aparejo, lo que pudo aumentar la confusión. Aunque suponía que el presidente estaría enterado de todos estos datos por la correspondencia que había mediado entre el capitán general de Cuba y el comodoro Elliott, comandante de las fuerzas navales de los Estados Unidos en las Indias Occidentales, tenía orden de comunicárselo (Filadelfia, 24 de febrero 1832).

1.177

N.º 1.298. — 25 de febrero, Filadelfia.

Quedaba enterado de las medidas que se habían tomado con motivo de la llegada a Cádiz de varios buques procedentes de Manila y el norte de Europa para evitar la propagación de enfermedades, principalmente del cólera morbo extendido en todos los países; lo había hecho saber al gobierno de Estados Unidos a fin de que no adoptara con los procedentes de España más que las medidas indispensables para preservarse del mal. En Estados Unidos las medidas sanitarias se adoptaban por los gobiernos de cada Estado estableciendo, según lo habían creído oportuno, cuarentenas de observación para las procedencias de los puntos infestados.

1.178

N.º 1.299. — 25 de febrero, Filadelfia.

Da cuenta de que había comunicado a mister Walsh la resolución afirmativa respecto a su proposición sobre el intercambio de semillas con el Real Jardín Botánico de Madrid; cuando recibiera el catálogo de las plantas y semillas que pudiera proporcionar así como la lista de las que necesitara, los enviaría para su estudio y resolución. Principal y duplicado.

1.179

N.º 1.300. — 26 de febrero, Filadelfia.

Anuncia remisión de una nueva solicitud de José Bellido, que había sido tesorero de Valladolid de Michoacan, del cual ya había enviado otra anteriormente en el mismo sentido; lo mismo el cónsul general como el vicecónsul en Panzacola lo recomendaban por su buena conducta y desgraciada situación, por lo que adjuntaba copia de sus cartas para apoyar la petición.

1.180

N.º 1.301. — 27 de febrero, Filadelfia.

Comunica que en las sesiones del congreso se seguía discutiendo la conveniencia de alterar los aranceles, debate que parecía sería largo; los partidarios de la reforma sostenían que el gobierno de la Unión era despótico y arbitrario, que no tenía facultad para imponer contribuciones y que los estados del sur estaban más oprimidos que cualquier colonia, por lo que si en la presente legislación no se abandonaba el plan de aranceles, el sur tendría que separarse forzosamente de la Unión. Los que se oponen a las innovaciones aseguraban que la decadencia de los estados del sur se debía a las costumbres de los habitantes, la falta de industria y sobre todo a la emigración hacia el oeste, en cuyas provincias se habían aumentado las plantaciones de algodón, que por la naturaleza del terreno y el modo de cultivarlo se producía con menos costos que en las Carolinas y la Luisiana.

Con motivo de celebrarse el centenario del nacimiento de Jorge Washington el 22 del corriente, se había propuesto el traslado de sus restos y los de su mujer, que reposaban en su pueblo natal de Virginia, para depositarlos en un monumento que se erigiera a su memoria en el capitolio; pero sus herederos se habían opuesto y la legislatura de Virginia había protestado y no dejaba que salieran de su estado los restos de un hijo benemérito. En consecuencia había quedado sin efecto el decreto del congreso, acordándose elevar una estatua de mármol a Washington en el gran salón de entrada del capitolio para perpetuar la memoria de su fundador.

En Filadelfia se había celebrado dicho día un acto solemne consistente en una procesión a la que habían concurrido todas las autoridades. Había recibido invitación para el acto, pero se había excusado con su precario estado de salud casi todos los cónsules habían hecho lo mismo, excepto los de Francia y Suecia, que eran los únicos que habían concurrido.

El estado sanitario del país era bueno. Principal y duplicado.

1.181

N.º 1.302. — 28 de febrero, Filadelfia.

Acusa recibo de varios despachos por vía de Gibraltar, todos del año precedente. Principal y duplicado.

1.182

N.º 1.303. — 6 de marzo, Filadelfia.

Remite copias de los oficios que había cruzado con el secretario de Estado relativos a la protesta de éste por haberse hecho fuego en varias ocasiones, desde el fuerte de Tarifa, contra dos buques americanos que llevaban arbolada la bandera. Como carecía de noticias al respecto había sugerido la conveniencia de suspender el juicio sobre dicho suceso hasta estar convenientemente informado.

Adjunto:

— Copia y traducción de la relación de W. B. Hodgson al secretario de Estado Eduardo Livingston, dando cuenta de lo que el capitán Gale, del bergantín americano Carolina, había publicado en las gacetas de Boston acerca de lo ocurrido en su travesía por el estrecho de Gibraltar al hacerse fuego contra él desde el fuerte español de Tarifa, ignorando la causa de dicho acto de hostilidad por parte de la guarnición española. Un hecho parecido había pasado en noviembre último al bergantín Angelina, donde el mismo Hodgson iba como agente público conduciendo el tratado ratificado entre Estados Unidos y Turquía; al rebasar la Punta de Europa habían recibido una bala de cañón, lo que les había obligado a pararse, y mientras estaban detenidos, con la bandera desplegada, otro cañonazo les había sido lanzado, pudiendo posteriormente proseguir la navegación. Ignoraba si podía deberse al incumplimiento de algún uso marítimo al paso por el fuerte de Tarifa, y pedía se aclarase para evitar la repetición de tales actos (Washington, 27 de febrero 1832).

— Copia y traducción de la nota con la que el secretario de Estado Livingston acompañaba la anterior declaración a Francisco Tacón, para que le informara acerca de los hechos relatados (Washington, 3 de marzo 1832).

— Carta de Francisco Tacón al secretario de Estado Eduardo Livingston, acusando recibo de la nota que acompañaba a la exposición de mister Hodgson relativa a los hechos ocurridos a dos buques americanos que habían recibido fuego desde el fuerte de Tarifa, llevando su pabellón enarbolado; como el suceso era muy extraño debían suspenderse los juicios sobre él hasta conocer los detalles del hecho (Filadelfia, 6 de marzo 1832).

1.183

N.º 1.305. — 8 de marzo, Filadelfia.

Comunica que se había producido el relevo del comodoro Biddle, que habiendo cumplido los tres años de su comisión en el Mediterráneo, había sido sustituido por el comodoro Patterson, el cual con el navío de cien cañones Delaware y la fragata Constellation, reemplazaría a dos fragatas que deberían regresar a su país. Principal y duplicado.

1.184

N.º 1.306. — 12 de marzo, Filadelfia.

Remite la lista mensual de pasaportes. Principal y duplicado.

Adjunto:

— Relación de los pasaportes expedidos durante el mes de febrero por los cónsules y vicecónsules de Filadelfia, Nueva York, Baltimore, Norfolk, Charleston y Nueva Orleans.

1.185

N.º 1.308. — 14 de marzo, Filadelfia.

Noticias de Costa Firme decían que continuaba la división en aquella provincia, principalmente desde la muerte de Bermúdez; todos los ciudadanos estaban sobre las armas y se temía un motín militar en la Guayra. No había podido reunirse el congreso de Caracas por no haberse presentado más que diez y seis diputados, excusándose el resto por motivos de enfermedad, lo que había obligado a conducirlos con escolta. Páez continuaba en Apure, en espera de la decisión del congreso acerca de la facción que le era contraria. Reinaba un gran desorden y se temía una revolución de los negros. De Bogotá sólo se sabía que Obando había sido elegido vicepresidente. Principal y duplicado.

1.186

N.º 1.309. — 15 de marzo, Filadelfia.

Las últimas noticias de Nueva España daban cuenta de que Santa Ana continuaba cercado en Veracruz y dispuesto a mantener la plaza contra el ataque de Bustamante; aunque las fuerzas de éste eran superiores a las sitiadas, no se podía predecir cuál sería el final. Casi toda la población había abandonado la ciudad. Principal y duplicado.

1.187

N.º 1.310. — 16 de marzo, Filadelfia.

A las noticias enviadas sobre las discusiones que tenían lugar en el congreso acerca de la conveniencia de alterar los aranceles, cuya resolución era de gran importancia para los estados del sur, había que añadir un nuevo incidente provocado por las autoridades del estado de Georgia que habían hecho prender a unos misioneros que predicaban en el territorio de los indios cherokees; éstos recurrieron contra Georgia ante el Tribunal Supremo de Washington por haberse violado su territorio, cuya independencia estaba garantizada por los tratados concluidos con los Estados Unidos; su derecho había sido reconocido en la sentencia del Tribunal, que había autorizado al presidente de la Unión a enviar tropas que hicieran respetar el territorio de los indios, si el estado de Georgia no acataba la sentencia.

1.188

N.º 1.311. — 31 de marzo, Filadelfia.

Acusa recibo de varias reales órdenes. Principal y duplicado.

1.189

N.º 1.313. — 6 de abril, Filadelfia.

Por noticias de la Costa Firme se sabía que se había constituido el congreso de Venezuela con los suplentes, y aunque se habían nombrado comisiones no se esperaba que pudieran hacer cosa de importancia. Continuaban las luchas entre los paisanos armados y los militares; habían desertado varios negros de las haciendas de Toro, y Guayabita, que interceptando la comunicación entre Valencia y Maracaibo habían asesinado a los blancos que encontraban. En la Serranía los tenientes Chirinos y Carnicero, pardos libres, habían sublevado a la gente de color que incendiaron las haciendas de Ocina y San Diego enarbolando la bandera de Haití; la milicia de Carora había sorprendido a un grupo en la sierra entre los cuales estaba Chirinos, a quien se había encontrado la constitución de Haití y la proclama de Boyer llamándolos a la Unión. Principal y duplicado.

1.190

N.º 1.314. — 7 de abril, Filadelfia.

Por el bergantín Gasden, que había llegado a Nueva York procedente de Veracruz, se sabía que continuaba la guerra civil en

Méjico siendo inútiles las tentativas del gobierno de Bustamante para llegar a un acuerdo con Santa Ana, que continuaba defendiendo Veracruz; había hecho una salida con sus hombres apresando un convoy con treinta mil pesos, municiones y provisiones de boca. Principal y duplicado.

1.191

N.º 1.315. — 8 de abril, Filadelfia.

Remite la lista mensual de pasaportes.

Adjunto:

— Relación de los pasaportes expedidos por los cónsules y vicecónsules durante los meses de febrero y marzo (Filadelfia, 5 de abril 1832).

1.192

N.º 1.316. — 14 de abril, Filadelfia.

Acusa recibo de un despacho.

1.193

N.º 1.317. — 15 de abril, Filadelfia.

Da cuenta de que Santa Ana, alentado por el feliz resultado de su primera salida, había efectuado otra con mil de sus hombres encontrando las tropas de Bustamante, mandadas por Calderón, en las llanuras de Solome, donde había sostenido una sangrienta batalla en la que habían muerto trescientos de los suyos, siendo apresados otros trescientos y teniendo que retirarse con el resto nuevamente a Veracruz. Las guarniciones de Tampico y Pueblo Viejo se habían declarado a su favor. Principal y duplicado.

1.194

N.º 1.318. — 16 de abril, Filadelfia.

Remite original y traducción de la resolución del tribunal supremo de Washington en la causa seguida por el gobierno español contra la casa de Roberto y Juan Oliver; por ella se declaraba anulada la apelación que se había elevado al supremo desde el tribunal del distrito de Pensilvania, pues habiendo sido presentada por parte española hacía siete años no había sido proseguida.

Adjunto:

— Certificación del Tribunal Supremo de los Estados Unidos declarando anulada la apelación presentada por parte española (7 de abril 1832).
— Traducción de la anterior certificación.

1.195

N.º 1.320. — 21 de abril, Filadelfia.

Anuncia remisión de un ejemplar del convenio de límites entre Estados Unidos y Méjico, firmado en dicha ciudad el 12 de enero de 1828 y ratificado en Washington, el 5 de abril de 1832. En él se declara haberse admitido la misma línea divisoria que se había adoptado en el tratado concluido con España el 22 de febrero de 1819.

1.196

N.º 1.321. — 24 de abril, Filadelfia.

Tras la revisión de los papeles existentes en el archivo del viceconsulado en Boston no se había hallado más que la pequeña relación que adjunta sobre los permisos que se habían concedido de 1804 a 1808 para expediciones realizadas a los dominios del rey de América.

Adjunto:

— Relación de los privilegios existentes en el viceconsulado de Boston, que se habían concedido por el ministerio de Hacienda a comerciantes de la Unión, para hacer expediciones a Veracruz y otros puertos de América española (Boston, 10 de abril 1832).

1.197

N.º 1.322. — 26 de abril, Filadelfia.

Había salido de Norfolk la fragata Constellation con destino a las islas Terceras a observar la expedición de Pedro IV, y de allí pasaría al Mediterráneo a reunirse con la escuadra americana que cruzaba en aquel punto, en sustitución de otro buque que, como había anunciado anteriormente, volvería a los Estados Unidos. El senado había aprobado la propuesta de nombramiento de un encargado de negocios para Bélgica, sancionando el de mister Hugh S. Legare, de Carolina del Sur. Principal y duplicado.

1.198

N.º 1.323. — 29 de abril, Filadelfia.

Comunica que había salido de Baltimore para la Habana el teniente de navío de la real armada Juan José Martínez, una vez cumplido el encargo que había motivado su estanco de la adquisición de un pailebote construido en aquel puerto y un pontón con máquina de vapor destinado a limpiar el puerto de la Habana, donde ya había cuatro goletas gánguiles. Dichos buques llevaban bandera americana y suponía que merecerían la aprobación de las autoridades de la Habana, pues habían sido construidos con la mayor exactitud, bajo la estrecha vigilancia de Martínez que había demostrado sus conocimientos de la materia. Principal y duplicado.

1.199

N.º 1.324. — 1 de mayo, Filadelfia.

Remite un ejemplar de «El Redactor», de Nueva York, con los documentos oficiales publicados por los disidentes de Buenos Aires relativos a las represalias que el comandante de la corbeta de Estados Unidos, Lexington, había tomado por las desavenencias surgidas entre los dos países en las islas Malvinas. Principal y duplicado.

Adjunto:

— Dos ejemplares de «El Redactor» de Nueva York (28 de abril 1828).

1.200

N.º 1.325. — 7 de mayo, Filadelfia.

Anuncia remisión de Memorias de una sociedad americana, que a petición del secretario de la legación Francisco de Paula Quadrado, enviaba con destino a la Real Academia de la Historia, a la que aquél pertenecía. Principal y duplicado.

1.201

N.º 1.326. — 6 de mayo, Filadelfia.

Enterado por una gaceta de Nueva York de que había muerto en Cartagena de Indias Juan Andrés Bird, natural de Cádiz, sin hacer testamento, había ordenado al cónsul en Nueva York que hiciera las gestiones necesarias para averiguar todos los bienes que le pertenecían en aquella plaza, a fin de adoptar las medidas convenientes para que pasara su propiedad a los herederos, según las leyes de aquel estado.

1.202

N.º 1.327. — 6 de mayo, Filadelfia.

Remite la lista mensual de los pasaportes expedidos en Estados Unidos. Principal y duplicado.

Adjunto:

— Relación de los pasaportes expedidos por los cónsules y vicecónsules en Filadelfia, Nueva York, Boston, Norfolk, Charleston y Nueva Orleans en marzo y abril (Filadelfia, 5 de mayo 1832).

1.203

N.º 1.328. — 15 de mayo, Filadelfia.

En respuesta a la orden que había dado al cónsul en Nueva York relativa a la indagación sobre los fondos que hubieran quedado a la muerte de Juan Andrés Bird en Cartagena de Indias, aquél había comunicado que en una compañía de seguros existían a su nombre una cantidad, que había dado aviso para que no se dispusiera de ella sin su orden y a la vez había escrito a la madre del difunto, residente en Cádiz, explicándole los documentos que debía enviar para acreditar que le correspondía dicha suma.

1.204

N.ᵒ 1.329. — 16 de mayo, Filadelfia.

Da cuenta de que continuaban las sesiones del congreso, que había empleado varias semanas en juzgar la conducta de Samuel Houston, ex-gobernador del estado de Tennessee y ex-diputado, por haber apaleado en la calle a un diputado que había puesto en entredicho su conducta. Finalmente se había sentenciado a Houston a recibir una reprensión pública del presidente de la cámara de diputados por el desprecio y violación que había supuesto su agresión. Principal y duplicado.

1.205

N.ᵒ 1.330. — 16 de mayo, Filadelfia.

Comunica que a mediados de abril aún continuaba Santa Ana defendiendo Veracruz de las tropas de Bustamante, que habían empezado a bombardear la ciudad; había varios rumores pero no se sabía con certeza si alguna otra plaza había seguido el ejemplo de Tampico de adherirse al partido de Santa Ana. Principal y duplicado.

1.206

N.ᵒ 1.331. — 17 de mayo, Filadelfia.

El gobierno de Colombia había enviado dos oficiales con despachos para el general Santander, anunciándole que había sido elegido presidente de Nueva Granada e invitándole a regresar para tomar posesión de su cargo, lo que probablemente haría en la primera ocasión. Por el mismo conducto se había sabido que en Nueva Granada se había reconocido la separación del estado formado por los departamentos de Ecuador, Arucú y Guayaquil, y que se trataba de reunir una convención de sus representantes con los de Venezuela para evitar la guerra con la que amenazaba el general Flores desde Quito, de resultas de la rebelión militar que había encabezado el comandante del Cauca en Popayán. Principal y duplicado.

1.207

N.º 1.332. — 18 de mayo, Filadelfia.

El mismo día que había tenido lugar la represión pública a que había sido condenado el ex-gobernador de Houston, el diputado Cook se había quejado a la cámara de que a consecuencia de las opiniones que había expuesto sobre el caso, le había desafiado un tal doctor Davis; y concluida la sesión se había producido un caso aún más escandaloso al ser atacado el diputado Arnald en las mismas escaleras del capitolio por el mayor Morgan A. Heard, reyerta que había concluido con el descalabro de Heard. Estos sucesos desacreditaban al gobierno del presidente Jackson, a quien el partido de la oposición acusaba de protegerlos; así el diputado Stamberg, el apaleado por Houston, había dicho al congreso que los ataques cometidos contra los individuos de la cámara por sus opiniones, eran alentados por el lenguaje del presidente, lo que podría probar con evidencia. Nunca se había manifestado tal encono entre los partidos del congreso principalmente por dos cuestiones: la forma de algunos artículos de la tarifa vigente y la prórroga solicitada para la subsistencia del Banco de los Estados Unidos, sobre los cuales eran encontrados los intereses de estados y ciudadanos. Principal y duplicado.

1.208

N.º 1.333. — 18 de mayo, Filadelfia.

Remite copia de la correspondencia cruzada entre el cónsul de Nueva Orleans y el fiscal de los Estados Unidos, que él había apoyado con una reclamación al secretario de Estado, para que se pusiera en libertad el bergantín español Dos Amigos, detenido en Nueva Orleans por llevar a su bordo un negro, esclavo del dueño del buque, que se trataba de confiscar en cumplimiento de la ley que prohibía la introducción de esclavos.

Adjunto:

— Traducción de la carta del cónsul en Nueva Orleans, Antonio Argote Villalobos, al fiscal de Estados Unidos Juan Slidell, exponiendo la reclamación que le había presentado el capitán del buque español Dos Amigos, Francisco Casanovas, del embargo que se había hecho de su buque sin que él supiera qué ley de este país había contravenido. Al leer la acusación había visto que se le acusaba de haber introducido un esclavo negro, cosa que no era cierta puesto que la persona a que se refería, un moreno llamado Francisco, esclavo del dueño del buque, formaba parte de su tripulación como cocinero (Nueva Orleans, 2 de abril 1832).

— Respuesta de Juan Slidell a Argote Villalobos insertando el acta del congreso que prohibía la introducción de esclavos negros o mulatos, exponiéndose a ser confiscado el buque que lo hiciera. El buque Dos Amigos había transgredido indudablemente la legislación, que por otra parte no preveía el caso presente de que un esclavo negro formara parte de alguna tripulación; tendría que legislar sobre dicho punto, aunque existía la posibilidad de que, amparándose en ello, se tratara de introducir esclavos de otras repúblicas, donde su precio era sólo un tercio del que se pagaba en Estados Unidos. Estimaba el fiscal Slidell que enterado el ejecutivo de las circunstancias del caso, levantaría el embargo del bergantín y devolvería el negro (Nueva Orleans, 3 de abril 1832).

— Traducción de la carta de Argote Villalobos al fiscal Slidell acusando recibo de su respuesta y agradeciendo sus buenos oficios, para que el ejecutivo, una vez consideradas las circunstancias del caso, levantara el embargo del Dos Amigos; enteraba del asunto al ministro de España cerca del gobierno americano, puesto que a él correspondía llevar estas gestiones (Nueva Orleans, 4 de abril 1832).

— Copia de la carta de Francisco Tacón al secretario de Estado Livingston, con la que le remitía las de la correspondencia que habían mantenido el cónsul de España en Nueva Orleans y el fiscal de los Estados Unidos en aquel distrito acerca de la detención impuesta en aquel puerto al bergantín Dos Amigos, por llevar entre sus tripulantes un esclavo negro; como la intención no había sido introducirlo como tal en los Estados Unidos esperaba que, con la mediación que había ofrecido el mismo fiscal Slidell, se resolviera el asunto levantando el embargo del buque (Filadelfia, 30 de abril 1832).

1.209

N.º 1.334. — 31 de mayo, Filadelfia.

Da cuenta de que en Pernambuco se había producido una sublevación capitaneada por Francisco José Martínez, que se había apoderado de la fortaleza de Brun con el objetivo de restablecer en el trono al emperador don Pedro, pero el movimiento había sido sofocado por el gobernador de la ciudad. Los periódicos culpaban del suceso a los portugueses, por lo que habían sido perseguidos y asesinados por los brasileños, tratando de huir todos los que podían. También se habían producido insurrecciones en otros puntos del país y los buques anclados en Pernambuco estaban llenos de refugiados portugueses y extranjeros.

1.210

N.º 1.335. — 31 de mayo, Filadelfia.

Amplía noticias sobre los altercados que se habían producido entre miembros del congreso, a consecuencia de los cuales estaba preso el mayor Heard para ser juzgado por el tribunal civil, igual que el ex-gobernador Houston. Continuaban las sesiones del congreso y en ellas se debatía la conveniencia de renovar la patente del Banco de los Estados Unidos. Principal y duplicado.

1.211

N.º 1.336. — 31 de mayo, Filadelfia.

La Gaceta de Washington había publicado una comunicación del cónsul de Estados Unidos en la isla de Madera, en la que iba inserta la que le había dirigido F. Sertorius, vicealmirante de las fuerzas navales de doña María Gloria de Portugal, comunicándole que la isla y el puerto de Funchal quedaban bloqueados, permitiéndose solamente el comercio neutral e impidiendo la introducción de provisiones y efectos de guerra. Principal y duplicado.

1.212

N.º 1.337. — 31 de mayo, Filadelfia.

Un joven americano, teniente de marina llamado Slidell, había publicado a fines de 1830 una obra titulada «Un año en España», de la que algunas gacetas habían hecho elogios, pero habiéndola leído había comprobado que contenía un gran número de inexactitudes y calumnias por lo que se había apresurado a refutarlo consiguiendo su descrédito. Tenía noticias de que el mismo sujeto pensaba volver a España para continuar escribiendo en el mismo sentido, por lo que se creía en la obligación de avisar su próxima salida en un buque con destino a Gibraltar; anuncia remisión de un ejemplar de la mencionada obra para que puedan comprobarse las infames calumnias que había propalado. Principal y duplicado.

Adjunto:

— Nota confidencial de Francisco Tacón al conde de la Alcudia haciéndole saber que en la obra titulada «Un año en España», de cuyo contenido había dado cuenta al secretario de Estado, se calumniaba atrozmente a la familia real, extremo del cual no había dado cuenta en su despacho para evitar que quedara constancia en el archivo, en el caso de que la publicación no llegara a manos del secretario de Estado (Filadelfia, 31 de mayo 1832).

— Minutas al ministro en Filadelfia acusando recibo de su comunicación sobre el libro «Un año en España» publicado en Estados Unidos; al secretario de Gracia y Justicia dándole cuenta de ello y de que, por orden del rey, debía impedirse la introducción en España del libro y de su autor si, como parecía, intentaba hacerlo; al cónsul en Gibraltar advirtiéndole que, si dicho sujeto intentaba obtener el visado para pasar a España, le fuera negado (San Ildefonso, 26 de julio 1832).

1.213

N.º 1.338. — 6 de junio, Filadelfia.

Tras las noticias sobre la sublevación de Pernambuco se había sabido que también en Río de Janeiro se habían producido disturbios, al levantarse contra el gobierno el partido de los republicanos y apoderarse de los dos fuertes que dominan la capital, pero la guardia nacional los había derrotado en el campo de Santa Ana obligándolos a capitular sin conseguir su intento de cambiar la regencia. Ésta había conseguido que el joven emperador fuese trasladado de San Cristóbal al palacio de la capital. Unos días después se habían levantado los de otra facción marchando desde San Cristóbal a la ciudad proclamando a Pedro I; también habían sido derrotados pero se temía que si llegaban a unirse los republicanos y los del ex-emperador podrían destruir el gobierno existente y encender de nuevo la guerra civil.

1.214

N.º 1.338. — 6 de junio, Filadelfia.

Da cuenta de que el gobierno insurgente de Venezuela, deseoso de favorecer en su territorio la emigración de los naturales de las Canarias, había insertado en la gaceta un aviso del secretario del Interior, en el que se disponía que en virtud del decreto de 11 de junio de 1831, por el que se protegía la emigración de dichas islas, se diera carta de naturaleza a dos canarios que habían llegado al país, y se les concedieran las tierras que pudiesen cultivar, exentas de contribución durante diez años, estando los colonos por igual tiempo libres del servicio de las armas. Principal y duplicado.

1.215

N.º 1.340. — 7 de junio, Filadelfia.

Continuaban las sesiones del congreso ocupándose preferentemente de la modificación de los aranceles y de la conveniencia de renovar la patente del Banco de los Estados Unidos.

El gobierno se había visto obligado a enviar la milicia de San Luis a la frontera con los indios del Missouri, obligado por las frecuentes incursiones que éstos realizaban; en un ataque los indios habían forzado a las milicias a retroceder a sus límites, que habían sobrepasado en Dixon. El general Atkinson se disponía a acudir en socorro de aquel puesto. También los indios de Sac y Fox se disponían a atacar Chicago, tras cometer varios asesinatos, pero se esperaba que las milicias de Michigán, a cuya cabeza se había puesto el gobierno del estado, terminarían con estas depredaciones. Principal y duplicado.

1.216

N.º 1.341. — 8 de junio, Filadelfia.

Da cuenta de que había partido de Norfolk, en dirección a El Havre, el español Agustín de Letamendi, con el objeto, según parecía, de esperar en Bruselas la llegada del nuevo encargado de negocios de Estados Unidos, que le había prometido darle una colocación por haber sido Letamendi su maestro de castellano.

1.217

N.º 1.342. — 8 de junio, Filadelfia.

Remite la lista mensual de los pasaportes expedidos en Estados Unidos. Principal y duplicado.

Adjunto:

— Relación de los pasaportes concedidos por los cónsules y vicecónsules de Filadelfia, Nueva York, Baltimore, Charleston y Nueva Orleans, en el mes de mayo.

1.218

N.º 1.344. — 16 de junio, Filadelfia.

Da cuenta de que había presentado sus cartas credenciales al presidente de la república el nuevo ministro de Bélgica, barón Desiré Behr. El antiguo cónsul de Francia en la Habana, marqués de Nins de Peyrae, había llegado a Nueva York con el nombramiento de cónsul general de su país en Estados Unidos.

1.219

N.º 1.345. — 17 de junio, Filadelfia.

Continuaba Santa Ana defendiendo Veracruz del sitio a que lo tenía sometido Bustamante; contaba con una fuerza de unos mil hombres. Noticias posteriores llegadas de Tampico indicaban que la noche del 12 al 13 de mayo anterior, la tropa mandada por Calderón, había levantado sitio de Veracruz retirándose hacia el interior, según unos por las continuas deserciones que se producían y según otros por evitar las enfermedades propias de la estación.

Uno de los más allegados a Santa Ana era el coronel Mexía, anterior secretario de la legación mejicana en Estados Unidos. Principal y duplicado.

1.220

N.º 1.347. — 19 de junio, Filadelfia.

Por los documentos que acompañaban a la real orden del 11 de febrero último, quedaba enterado de las razones que aducía el gobierno de España para rechazar las injustas pretensiones de la Unión y en ese sentido respondería en caso de que el gobierno federal le planteara el asunto. Consciente de la gran importancia que tenía avisar rápidamente cualquier reacción que provocara el discurso del presidente al comenzar la presente legislatura, había ordenado a uno de los agregados de la legación que residiera en Washington y asistiera diariamente a las sesiones del congreso, para dar aviso rápidamente de cualquier debate que se relacionara con las reclamaciones del gobierno contra España. Procedente de Washington había pasado para embarcar en Nueva York con destino a Gibraltar mister Siliman, con despachos del gobierno para el ministro americano en Madrid.

1.221

N.º 1.348. — 20 de junio, Filadelfia.

Envía su felicitación y la de todo el personal a sus órdenes al conde de la Alcudia por su nombramiento para secretario interino del despacho de Estado, que le había comunicado Francisco Tadeo Calomarde. Principal y duplicado.

1.222

N.º 1.349. — 21 de junio, Filadelfia.

Queda enterado de que había sido aprobada la cuenta de los gastos extraordinarios que había enviado.

1.223

N.º 1.350. — 22 de junio, Filadelfia.

Comunica que había trasladado al antiguo alférez de navío Pedro Pablo Cagigao, por conducto del vicecónsul en Nueva Orleans, la real orden que el secretario del despacho de Marina había dirigido al director general de la Real Armada.

1.224

N.º 1.351. — 25 de junio, Filadelfia.

Había remitido al secretario de Estado la comunicación en la que el rey anunciaba el feliz alumbramiento de la reina y avisa remisión de la respuesta del presidente, congratulándose por el suceso.

1.225

N.º 1.352. — 26 de junio, Filadelfia.

Da cuenta de que había sido ahorcado en el pueblo de Doylestown un individuo llamado Mina, que de las indagaciones practicadas resultaba ser hijo de un tal Entralvo, capitán de Correos jubilado y residente en Trinidad de Cuba. Estaba acusado de haber causado la muerte por envenenamiento con arsénico a un ciudadano de Estados Unidos llamado Chapman, con cuya viuda se había casado a los diez días de la muerte del marido. En un largo proceso la mujer había resultado absuelta y él condenado a la horca como culpable, aunque en el patíbulo había declarado su inocencia. Había dejado escrito un folleto con el título de «Vida de Mina», impreso en Filadelfia. Principal y duplicado.

1.226

N.º 1.353. — 27 de junio, Filadelfia.

Como ampliación de las noticias que había enviado sobre enfrentamientos con los indios, comunica que el secretario de Guerra había ordenado reunir en Chicago unos mil hombres sacados de las guarniciones de la costa, bajo el mando del general Scott, que estaba autorizado para reunir a sus órdenes a la milicia de los estados inmediatos que pudiera necesitar. El plan de operaciones consistía en un movimiento combinado de las fuerzas de Scott con las del general Atkinson desde Chicago y el Mississipi, para atacar por ambos flancos a los indios mandados por el famoso Black Hawk, conocido por sus depredaciones; las gacetas de Washington indicaban que se había logrado el plan previsto, aunque con pérdida de cien hombres y de trescientos indios muertos. De resultas de estas hostilidades se podría producir la internación de los indios y que los Estados Unidos se apoderaran del territorio. Principal y duplicado.

1.227

N.º 1.354. — 27 de junio, Filadelfia.

Remite copia de las notas que había cruzado con el secretario de Estado Eduardo Livingston, acerca del armamento de la goleta mercante mejicana llamada Veracruzano en el puerto de Nueva Orleans, que había sido autorizada a hacerse a la mar pese a las reclamaciones del cónsul de España, por suponer que se proponía hostilizar el comercio español. El secretario de Estado había respondido que se indagaría el caso procediéndose a la formación de una causa, si fueran ciertas sus sospechas. Por su parte había advertido al cónsul que colaborara para el esclarecimiento del asunto y que comunicara la salida del Veracruzano al comandante general de apostadero de marina de la Habana. Principal y duplicado.

Adjunto:
— Copia de la carta de Francisco Tacón a Livingston dando cuenta de que el cónsul en Nueva Orleans le había notificado la salida de aquel puerto del buque mercante Veracruzano, después de ser armado al menos con un cañón, según declaración de un testigo; por otra parte tres tripulantes que se habían enrolado para hacer un crucero contra Santa Ana en las costas de Méjico, dijeron que después de embarcar, el contramaestre había manifestado que iban al mar a buscar su suerte. Tales hechos habían quebrantado la neutralidad que debían observar los Estados Unidos (Filadelfia, 18 de junio 1832). Hay dos ejemplares.

— Copia y traducción de la respuesta del secretario de Estado a Tacón, participándole que se habían dado instrucciones a las autoridades de Nueva Orleans para que averiguaran si eran ciertas las suposiciones que había expuesto el cónsul de España (Washington, 22 de junio 1832). Hay dos ejemplares de la copia y dos de la traducción.

1.228

N.º 1.355. — 28 de junio, Filadelfia.

Acusa recibo de varios despachos llegados en el mes de junio. Principal y duplicado.

1.229

N.º 1.356. — 28 de junio, Filadelfia.

Enterado de que el cónsul general en Estados Unidos había notificado a la secretaría de Estado todo lo que el cónsul en Nueva York le había informado sobre la epidemia de cólera que se había introducido en América, se limita a manifestar que las gacetas de Quebec y Montreal decían que había disminuido mucho la enfermedad degenerando en tifus, y que no había adelantado en el estado de Nueva York.

1.230

N.º 1.359. — 15 de julio, Filadelfia.

El general Santander había salido de Nueva York con destino a Cartagena, después de haber sido elegido presidente de la república de Nueva Granada; antes de su salida había publicado una despedida del pueblo de Nueva York por la buena acogida que le habían dispensado durante su estancia entre ellos. El congreso de aquella república había concluido una nueva constitución que había sido adoptada por todos sin oposición. En Venezuela se habían revocado las órdenes de Bolívar que prohibían la inmigración de españoles permitiéndose ya la entrada a los que quisieran hacerlo y asimismo la introducción de frutos, efectos y manufacturas españoles. Principal y duplicado.

1.231

N.º 1.360. — 15 de julio, Filadelfia.

Remite la lista mensual de los pasaportes expedidos en Estados Unidos. Principal y duplicado.

Adjunto:

— Relación de los pasaportes despachados por los cónsules y vice-cónsules de Filadelfia, Baltimore, Boston, Charleston y Nueva Orleans en el mes de junio (Filadelfia, 7 de julio 1832).

1.232

N.º 1.361. — 17 de julio, Filadelfia.

Había llegado a Filadelfia un individuo llamado Castillo que se titulaba secretario de Santa Ana; venía de Veracruz comisionado para proponer al general Gómez Pedraza que fuera a ocupar la presidencia de Méjico, para la que había sido elegido en 1828, y destinado poco después. Pedraza había declinado la invitación ne-gándose a secundar los designios del mismo que había contribuido a hacerle salir de su patria; tampoco había aceptado una cantidad que le había traído Castillo para el viaje. Santa Ana se había apo-derado de Jalapa y quería seguir hacia Méjico, lo que no presen-taría grandes dificultades dado el mal estado de la fuerza que man-daba Calderón. Principal y duplicado.

1.233

N.º 1.362. — 18 de julio, Filadelfia.

Participa que había terminado las sesiones del congreso, que se habían prolongado mucho y en las que el partido de la oposición había querido dejar sin resolver la mayoría de las propuestas del gobierno a que Jackson había aludido en el discurso de apertura. Se había aceptado por ambas cámaras la prórroga de quince años de la patente del Banco de los Estados Unidos, pero el presidente, usando la facultad que le concedía la constitución, se había negado a promulgarlo como ley. Próximamente se publicarían las variaciones de los aranceles que se habían aprobado en el congreso, pero ya se sabía que quedaban libres de todo derecho el te y el café y se habían disminuido los del azúcar. Principal y duplicado.

1.234

N.º 1.364. — 18 de julio, Filadelfia.

Comunica que José Bonaparte había tomado pasaje para Liverpool en la fragata mercante Alejandro, que iba a salir de Filadelfia. Había preparado el viaje con gran reserva, favorecida por residir en su casa de campo a cuarenta Kms. de esa ciudad. A finales de junio había estado en Washington con el pretexto de hacer una visita de amistad al presidente, pero en realidad el objeto había sido despedirse del general Jackson. Con igual fecha comunicaba la noticia al embajador español en París y al ministro en Londres.

1.235

N.º 1.365. — 18 de julio, Filadelfia.

Da cuenta de que continuaba el cólera extendiéndose en Nueva York, donde la Junta de Sanidad había declarado que se habían producido ciento cuarenta y tres casos nuevos y sesenta muertos. En Filadelfia se habían producido diez y seis casos y se temía que aumentaran.

1.236

N.º 1.366. — 22 de julio, Filadelfia.

José Bonaparte había salido ya para Liverpool, bajo el título con el que había sido conocido en Estados Unidos de conde Survilliers; le acompañaban su secretario mister Maillard, el coronel Collins, mister Lacoste y su hijo, cinco criados y el llamado capitán Sary, su esposa y tres hijos. Este capitán era el que había sacado a Napoleón de la isla de Elba en el buque que mandaba, por lo que José Bonaparte le había dispensado la mayor protección. Las gacetas de Filadelfia habían tratado poco de la marcha, pero algunas decían que Bonaparte había partido presionado por personas que le instaban a que se presentase en Europa. La explicación que había dado Bonaparte de su viaje era que quería ver a su sobrino el duque de Reichstadt, suponiéndose que desde Inglaterra iba a solicitar al emperador de Austria dicha gracia, permitiéndole pasar al punto que le fuera indicado.

Las noticias del cólera en Nueva York indicaban que se habían producido trescientos quince casos nuevos y ciento cuatro muertos en las últimas veinticuatro horas; en Filadelfia no se había producido ningún nuevo caso en los últimos cuatro días.

1.237

N.º 1.367. — 25 de julio, Filadelfia.

Habiendo solicitado el clero de Caracas que el gobierno de aquel país expidiese el correspondiente pasaporte a los obispos que había en Curaçao, se les había enviado y el 19 de abril habían desembarcado en la Guayra el arzobispo de Caracas, Méndez, y el vicario apostólico de Guayana, Talavera, que habían llegado a Caracas el 21 y prestado el juramento a la constitución de Venezuela sin ninguna condición, volviendo a entrar en funciones de sus cargos.

Noticias de Río Janeiro decían que en aquel país reinaba el mayor desorden, habiendo entrado el populacho en el salón del congreso con pretexto de apaciguar a los diputados, y cometido allí grandes excesos. De Méjico se sabía que el vicepresidente Bustamante no había aprobado el armisticio que se había hecho para terminar la guerra civil y, habiendo vuelto Santa Ana a Veracruz, se proponía salir con todas sus fuerzas para llevar adelante sus planes. En Lima el presidente Gamarra había conseguido abortar una revolución que se dirigía contra su persona, habiendo hecho ajusticiar al capitán Felipe Rosel, que la dirigía. También en aquel país reinaba la misma miseria e intranquilidad que en las demás repúblicas. Principal y duplicado.

1.238

N.º 1.368. — 26 de julio, Filadelfia.

Comunica que la cámara del congreso había aprobado la disminución de derechos en la importación de los vinos franceses, según se había estipulado en el artículo 7.º del tratado concluido con Francia.

1.239

N.º 1.369. — 26 de julio, Filadelfia.

Participa que el presidente de la república había salido, acompañado por mister G. Breathitt, para pasar una temporada en su casa «The Hermitage», en el estado de Tennessee, como solía hacer otros años.

1.240

N.º 1.371. — 29 de julio, Filadelfia.

Había disminuido la epidemia de cólera en Nueva York, dando el último parte ciento cuarenta y cinco enfermos y sesenta y ocho muertos. En Filadelfia, tras una pausa de seis días, habían enfermado ocho individuos, de los cuales siete habían muerto. La enfermedad se iba extendiendo por las inmediaciones de Nueva York y por el estado de Nueva Jersey. El cónsul de España en Nueva York, que había sido atacado por la enfermedad, estaba ya fuera de peligro.

1.241

N.º 1.372. — 31 de julio, Filadelfia.

Continuaban los casos de cólera en Filadelfia, donde seguramente seguiría el mismo curso que en Nueva York.

1.242

N.º 1.373. — 6 de agosto, Filadelfia.

Da cuenta de que había llegado a Filadelfia, comisionado por el superintendente general de la Real Hacienda de la isla de Cuba, Nicolás Campos, segundo director de los trabajos de la conducción que se iba a establecer para el abastecimiento de agua de la Habana, a fin de formalizar las contratas de los tubos que fueran necesarios para dicha obra. Recibida la conveniente información y estudiadas las propuestas de las fundiciones establecidas en los alrededores, el comisionado había concluido, con la anuencia de

Tacón, el contrato más favorable, del cual resultaría un gran servicio para la ciudad de la Habana. Principal y duplicado.

1.243

N.º 1.374. — 7 de agosto, Filadelfia.

Remite la lista mensual de los pasaportes expedidos. Principal y duplicado.

Adjunto:

— Relación de los pasaportes despachados por los cónsules y vicecónsules en Filadelfia, Baltimore, Nueva York y Nueva Orleans durante el mes de julio.

1.244

N.º 1.375. — 8 de agosto, Filadelfia.

Comunica que el 8 de julio último se había producido un incendio en Puerto Príncipe, en una casa frente al cuartel de la guardia del presidente y que a causa del gran viento que soplaba había tomado gran incremento quedando destruidas las casas de diez y seis calles, pese a los esfuerzos hechos para detenerlo. A los pocos días se había producido otro fuego en el centro de la ciudad, pero había sido extinguido rápidamente. Según ciertas estimaciones parecía que más de mil personas habían quedado sin hogar y la ciudad como una plaza tomada por asalto. Principal y duplicado.

1.245

N.º 1.376. — 8 de agosto, Filadelfia.

Sigue aumentando el cólera en Filadelfia habiéndose dado en las últimas veinticuatro horas sesenta y seis casos de los que habían muerto veintiséis; la epidemia se extendía por los lugares inmediatos, aumentando en Virginia y disminuyendo lentamente en Nueva York. Los periódicos daban cuenta de que se había producido una enfermedad parecida en Santiago de Chile, donde en ocho días habían muerto quinientos noventa y una personas.

1.246

N.º 1.378. — 18 de agosto, Linnoan Hill (Linnaean Hill).

Acusa recibo de una comunicación en la que se ordenaba desestimar la solicitud de Segundo Correa Bottino para volver el servicio del rey y que no se le permitiera regresar a España si no era para someterse a juicio con arreglo a las leyes. Aunque dicho individuo no residía ya en el país, lo tendría en cuenta por si regresaba a él.

1.247

N.º 1.379. — 15 de agosto, Linnoan Hill.

Había transmitido al secretario de la legación, Francisco de Paula Quadrado, la real orden que le concernía, y se había mostrado muy satisfecho de que el rey hubiera sido informado del elogio que de su persona había hecho Jaime Monroe, así como por la resolución de que se tuviera en cuenta su conducta para sus ascensos en la carrera.

1.248

N.º 1.381. — 17 de agosto, Linnoan Hill.

Participa que tras la salida de la capital del presidente, para su acostumbrado viaje de verano, y del secretario de Estado para unos baños en el estado de Virginia, había quedado encargado del despacho de los asuntos, el oficial mayor de dicha secretaría Daniel Brent. También había salido para su pueblo en el estado de Michigán el secretario de Guerra. Principal y duplicado.

1.249

N.º 1.383. — 18 de agosto, Linnoa Hill.

Las últimas noticias de Veracruz decían que no parecía próximo el fin de la guerra civil a causa de las peticiones de Santa Ana, que llegaba a exigir la deposición del vicepresidente Bustamante. También se sabía que había aparecido muerto el general

Terán, según unos por suicidio y otra opinión más probable, decía que asesinado por sus contrarios. Principal y duplicado.

1.250

N.º 1.384. — 18 de agosto, Linnoan Hill.

Continuaba haciendo estragos el cólera en Filadelfia, no siendo excesivo el número de nuevos casos por haber salido de la ciudad gran parte de la población; en Canadá y estado de Nueva York continuaba disminuyendo, aumentaba en Norfolk y Virginia y habían aparecido algunos casos en Baltimore y Washington.

1.251

N.º 1.385. — 31 de agosto, Linnoan Hill.

Acusa recibo de varios despachos recibidos en el mes de agosto. Principal y duplicado.

1.252

N.º 1.386. — 3 de septiembre, Linnoan Hill.

Participa que había sido declarado libre de delito de contrabando por la introducción de joyas el italiano Carrara, conocido por el nombre de Constant Polari, en cuyo poder habían sido halladas algunas de las joyas que en 1829 habían sido robadas a la princesa de Orange; se había puesto a disposición del encargado de negocios de Holanda, que lo había embarcado en un pailebot con destino a uno de los puertos de su nación. Principal y duplicado.

1.253

N.º 1.387. — 5 de septiembre, Linnoan Hill.

Da cuenta de que continuaban fuera de Washington el presidente y todos los secretarios de despacho excepto el de Marina, que era el único que continuaba en la ciudad. La epidemia de cólera iba en aumento.

1.254

N.º 1.388. — 5 de septiembre, Linnoan Hill.

Las últimas noticias llegadas de Méjico indicaban que aumentaba el partido de Santa Ana mientras bajaba el del gobierno de Bustamante. Unos buques enviados por éste a atacar el fuerte de Tabasco, que defendía Pedraza, partidario de Santa Ana, tras una reñida lucha habían tenido que entregarse después de haber resultado muertos ochenta y siete hombres y treinta y cinco heridos. El ayuntamiento de Tamaulipas había declarado al general Gómez Pedraza presidente de la república y declarado usurpador a Bustamante; lo mismo había hecho la provincia de Zacatecas, poniendo a disposición de Santa Ana seis mil hombres armados. Todo el reino de Méjico continuaba en el mayor desorden, lleno de luchas internas. Principal y duplicado.

1.255

N.º 1.389. — 16 de septiembre, Linnoan Hill.

Remite la lista de los pasaportes que se habían expedido durante el mes de agosto pasado. Principal y duplicado.

Adjunto:

— Relación de los pasaportes concedidos por los cónsules y vicecónsules de Filadelfia, Nueva York, Norfolk, Charleston y Nueva Orleans. Hay dos ejemplares.

1.256

N.º 1.391. — 22 de septiembre, Linnoan Hill.

Las noticias de Nueva España decían que el vicepresidente Bustamante había obtenido permiso del congreso para ponerse al frente del ejército que debía combatir a Santa Ana, por lo que había salido de Méjico con tres mil hombres. El congreso había nombrado a Múzquiz gobernador del estado de Méjico para desempeñar el poder ejecutivo y éste había formado un nuevo gobierno con Fagoaga para Estado, Irriberri para Guerra, Alas para Justicia y

Mangino para Hacienda. Varios estados querían que Gómez Pedraza se hiciera cargo de la presidencia, para la que había sido elegido en 1828, y habían enviado a Nueva Orleans a los comisionados Cerecero y Soto para que le instaran a regresar; aunque no se sabía con certeza, era muy probable que aceptara la proposición. El 20 de agosto estaba Santa Ana en Orizaba enfermo, pero dispuesto a resistir el ataque de Facio. Había tenido lugar en Tejas una batalla entre las tropas de Bustamante y los colonos de Estados Unidos, partidarios de Santa Ana, que habían vencido haciendo prisionero al coronel Piedras y resultando varios muertos y heridos por ambas partes.

1.257

N.º 1.392. — 23 de septiembre, Linnoan Hill.

Da cuenta de que había entrado en el puerto de Nueva Orleans la goleta de guerra americana Grampus, que había apresado a la entrada de Tampico a la mejicana Moctezuma, perteneciente a la escuadra de Santa Ana, por sospecha de que había abordado y saqueado un buque mercante americano; en los tribunales competentes se debatiría el derecho a apresar el Moctezuma considerándolo pirata.

1.258

N.º 1.394. — 6 de octubre, Filadelfia.

Debido a las circunstancias de haber cesado los fuertes calores y haberse extinguido casi totalmente la epidemia del cólera, había regresado a Filadelfia con todos los componentes de la legación. La enfermedad disminuía progresivamente en casi todo el país, siendo Richmond la ciudad donde aún persistía con fuerza.

1.259

N.º 1.395. — 6 de octubre, Filadelfia.

Acusa recibo de la comunicación participándole el matrimonio del infante don Sebastián con la princesa María Amalia de Nápoles, noticia que había transmitido al encargado de la secretaría de Estado para que la hiciera llegar al presidente. Envía su felicitación y la del personal de la legación por el enlace. Principal y duplicado.

1.260

N.º 1.396. — 7 de octubre, Filadelfia.

Había transmitido al interesado la resolución real acerca de la solicitud de Manuel Peláez, que había sido subdelegado de justicia mayor de las cuatro villas de Oaxaca, denegando su solicitud de que se le reconociera el grado de capitán. Principal y duplicado.

1.261

N.º 1.397. — 7 de octubre, Filadelfia.

Queda enterado de que se habían aprobado las diligencias que había practicado para averiguar los fondos que existían en el país pertenecientes al difunto Juan Bird, gestión a la que ya había respondido el cónsul en Nueva York; también había obtenido respuesta la carta que había dirigido al comerciante Francisco Jimeno Harmony, de Cádiz, el cual le había notificado que había insertado una nota en el diario y realizado otras gestiones para encontrar a la madre o herederos del difunto Bird.

1.262

N.º 1.398. — 8 de octubre, Filadelfia.

Muestra su satisfacción por haberse aprobado la forma de llevar las gestiones relativas a la reclamación del bergantín español Dos Amigos, detenido en Nueva Orleans por llevar a bordo como cocinero un esclavo negro; ya había comunicado la favorable terminación de dicho asunto con la libertad del buque y del esclavo, por lo que no había tenido que insistir sobre ello.

1.263

N.º 1.399. — 8 de octubre, Filadelfia.

Remite copia de un oficio del cónsul general en Estados Unidos Juan Bautista Bernabéu, que acompañaba una instancia de Francisco Preto y Neto, natural de Mahón, que en 1821 había sido nombrado oficial de la dirección de Fomento General del reino y solicitaba permiso para regresar a Mahón acogiéndose el último indulto. Principal y duplicado.

Adjunto:

— Copia del oficio de Juan Bautista Bernabéu a Francisco Tacón, recomendándole la instancia que adjuntaba por ser Francisco Preto persona de buena conducta y encontrarse en lastimoso estado (Filadelfia, 28 de septiembre 1832).

1.264

N.º 1.400. — 12 de octubre, Filadelfia.

Remite la lista mensual de los pasaportes concedidos. Principal y duplicado.

Adjunto:

— Relación de los pasaportes expedidos por los cónsules y vice-cónsules de Filadelfia, Boston, Charleston, Baltimore y Nueva Orleans, durante el mes de septiembre (Filadelfia, 6 de octubre 1832). Hay dos ejemplares.

1.265

N.º 1.401. — 15 de octubre, Filadelfia.

Cumpliendo las órdenes recibidas había enviado al secretario de Estado, junto con una nota cuya copia adjunta, el traslado de las dos sumarias que se habían practicado relativas a la queja del gobierno americano por el ataque que se había producido desde el fuerte de Tarifa contra dos bergantines de la Unión, a las que acompañaba el informe del gobernador de la mencionada plaza. Tratarían de desmentir las falsedades y calumnias que se había propalado sobre dicho asunto.

Adjunto:

— Copia de la nota que Francisco Tacón había enviado al encargado de la secretaría de Estado Daniel Brent, en contestación a la nota de su antecesor en el cargo Livingston, sobre el ataque

que se había efectuado desde el fuerte de Tarifa contra dos
buques americanos. El gobernador de la plaza había remitido,
con un informe, las dos sumarias que se habían practicado con
dicho motivo, y de todo ello resultaba que se había hecho fuego
contra los buques Caroline y Angeline por haberse aproximado
a medio tiro de cañón de las baterías de Tarifa, sin mostrar su
pabellón ni contestar las señales acostumbradas de noche, lo
que demostraba la inexactitud de la relación que mister Hodgson
había hecho del suceso (Filadelfia, 15 de octubre 1832).

1.266

N.º 1.402. — 16 de octubre, Filadelfia.

Comunica que habían dado comienzo las elecciones para los
cargos de los diferentes estados, que habían sido muy acaloradas.
En Filadelfia la oposición había movilizado todos los recursos para
conseguir la elección de sus partidarios, lo que había dado lugar
a algunos excesos. Se ignoraba cuál sería el resultado de las próximas elecciones para presidente de la república, pues los defensores de Clay interesados en el Banco de los Estados Unidos, no
perdonaban la fatiga para salir victoriosos y los de Jackson se
valían de todos los recursos que les proporcionaba el gobierno para
conseguir la reelección del actual presidente. Principal y duplicado.

1.267

N.º 1.403. — 17 de octubre, Filadelfia.

Avisa que se había declarado en Nueva Orleans una epidemia
de fiebre amarilla, con la fuerza acostumbrada de otros años, por
lo que se había prevenido a los habitantes ausentes para que no
regresaran de momento; no parecía probable que durara mucho
tiempo por estar muy adelantada la estación calurosa. Principal
y duplicado.

1.268

N.º 1.404. — 18 de octubre, Filadelfia.

Aumenta el cólera morbo en Richmond, Cincinnati y Missouri,
habiendo disminuido notablemente en las cercanías de Filadelfia,

donde la última semana no había muerto nadie de dicho mal; en Nueva York aún tenía cierta fuerza. Principal y duplicado.

1.269

N.º 1.405. — 22 de octubre, Filadelfia.

Participa que habían regresado a Washington el presidente de la república y el secretario de Estado. El resultado de los encuentros con los indios fronterizos, después de varios choques con las milicias reunidas en Chicago, había sido que los indios habían accedido a llegar a un acuerdo con los comisionados del gobierno, general Scott y gobernador Reynolds, por el cual la tribu de los winnebagoes había cedido unos cuatro millones de acres de tierra situada al sur de Wisconsin y al este del Mississipi; la de los Sacs y Foxes cerca de seis millones de acres entre los mismos paralelos, obligándose los Estados Unidos a indemnizarlos con una anualidad de veinte mil duros por treinta años, a saldarles sus deudas y a proporcionarles ciertas provisiones. Jefferson tenía como rehenes, por el tiempo que el presidente considerara necesario para el cumplimiento de dichos convenios, al principal caudillo de los indios llamado Black-Hawk, sus dos hijos y otros cinco de los principales guerreros. Para concluir las diferencias con todas las tribus de indios sólo faltaba el arreglo con la de los chickasaws, que parecía haberse concluido según anunciaban los diarios de Nashville; los Estados Unidos habían conseguido las tierras que aquellos poseían en el estado del Mississipi, con lo que internados los indios, se había producido el engrandecimiento de la república.

1.270

N.º 1.406. — 23 de octubre, Filadelfia.

Recomienda nuevamente la instancia que había enviado con anterioridad, en la que el cónsul en Nueva York, Francisco Stoughton, había solicitado la concesión de la cruz de comendador de la Real Orden Americana de Isabel la Católica, de la que era caballero desde 1819, en reconocimiento a sus méritos y servicios en la carrera diplomática y consular, y al desempeño de su cometido en los últimos tiempos con la constante vigilancia de la conducta de los emigrados y la comunicación a las autoridades de la isla de Cuba de las noticias relativas al cólera morbo y a los métodos de curación, incluso estando él atacado del mismo mal.

1.271

N.º 1.407. — 25 de octubre, Filadelfia.

Remite traducción de una carta autógrafa del presidente de la república, que le había enviado el secretario de Estado, en la que Jackson respondía a su anuncio de la boda del infante don Sebastián.

Adjunto:

— Traducción de la respuesta de Andrés Jackson dando la enhorabuena al rey por la boda de su sobrino el infante don Sebastián, que se había celebrado el 25 de mayo pasado (Washington, 23 de octubre 1832).

1.272

N.º 1.408. — 28 de octubre, Filadelfia.

Había remitido al secretario de Estado, para que la hiciera llegar al presidente, la participación del nacimiento del infante don Fernando María Mariano; envía su felicitación y la de todos los empleados de la legación por tan fausto motivo.

1.273

N.º 1.409. — 29 de octubre, Filadelfia.

El cónsul de Estados Unidos en Tampico había comunicado a su gobierno que se había reñido una dura batalla entre las tropas de Moctezuma, partidario de Santa Ana, y las del vicepresidente Bustamante que había resultado vencedor, perdiendo los vencidos unos mil quinientos hombres; esta acción prolongaría la guerra civil de aquel país. Principal y duplicado.

1.274

N.º 1.410. — 30 de octubre, Filadelfia.

Envía la relación de las reales órdenes que había recibido desde primero de septiembre pasado. Principal y duplicado.

1.275

N.º 1.411. — 6 de noviembre, Filadelfia.

Remite traducción de una carta del presidente de la república recibida por medio del secretario de Estado, en la que enviaba su felicitación por el feliz alumbramiento de la infanta Luisa Carlota que le había sido participado.

Adjunto:

— Traducción de la carta en la que Andrés Jackson felicitaba a Fernando VII por el niño que había dado a luz la infanta Luisa Carlota, esposa de su hermano el infante don Francisco de Paula, a quien había puesto el nombre de Fernando María Mariano (Washington, 31 de octubre 1831).

1.276

N.º 1.412. — 11 de noviembre, Filadelfia.

Anuncia remisión de un ejemplar del «Mercurio de Nueva York» del 27 de octubre último, que contenía el manifiesto del vicepresidente de Méjico, Anastasio Bustamante, al hacerse cargo del mando de las tropas que iban a luchar contra Santa Ana, dejando el poder ejecutivo a su sucesor Melchor Múzquiz, así como el discurso de éste al tomar posesión interinamente de la presidencia. También contiene el tratado de paz entre Bolivia y Perú concluido el 8 de noviembre de 1831, en el cual se establecía una concordia permanente y duradera.

1.277

N.º 1.413. — 14 de noviembre, Filadelfia.

Remite la lista mensual de pasaportes. Principal y duplicado.

Adjunto:

— Relación de los pasaportes expedidos por los cónsules y vice-cónsules de Filadelfia, Nueva York, Boston y Nueva Orleans en los meses de septiembre y octubre pasados. Hay dos ejemplares.

1.278

N.º 1.414. — 15 de noviembre, Filadelfia.

Queda enterado de la real orden relativa a las colecciones de todas las clases de tabaco de polvo español, que debían remitirse a los puntos que se designaban según despacho del secretario de Hacienda.

1.279

N.º 1.415. — 16 de noviembre, Filadelfia.

Empezaba a disminuir el cólera en Richmond, Cincinnati y Missouri; en Nueva York no había concluido completamente y se había propagado a Charleston y Nueva Orleans, donde aún no se había extinguido la fiebre amarilla y donde se temía que hiciera los mismos o mayores estragos que en otros estados. Principal y duplicado.

1.280

N.º 1.416. — 23 de noviembre, Filadelfia.

Las últimas noticias de Costa Firme, llegadas en cartas particulares, indicaban que el país continuaba dividido: el oriente no quería seguir unido a Venezuela y a Mariño se le había negado el paso a Cumaná por haberse evidenciado que iba a sublevar aquel pueblo y efectuar la separación. Monagas gobernaba a su antojo la provincia de Barcelona sin someterse a Venezuela; Mérida se hallaba en completo desorden, con las cárceles llenas de malhechores guardados por paisanos, por no haber un solo soldado. Páez intrigaba para que resultara elegido vicepresidente su amigo el doctor Peña. En Cartagena se había descubierto otra conspiración del batallón Pichinche en favor de Flores, y había varios oficiales en capilla para ser pasados por las armas. Flores se preparaba a atacar Nueva Granada para lo cual replegaba sus fuerzas en la ciudad de Pasto, habiendo ocupado el pueblo llamado Tablón de los Gómez. Anunciaban de Quito que no podría continuar mucho tiempo Flores en la presidencia por tener muchos enemigos y haberse declarado en su contra el batallón que llevaba su nombre. El general José María Obando había salido de Popayán para Juanambú al frente de la primera división que debía oponerse a Flores, esperando que se le uniesen otros cuerpos, algunos de los cuales habían entrado en Popayán con la oficialidad solamente, por haber desertado todos los soldados. Santander permanecía en Cúcuta y temía ir a Bogotá a hacerse cargo de un país en tan espantoso desorden. Principal y duplicado.

1.281

N.º 1.417. — 24 de noviembre, Filadelfia.

Sin haberse publicado aún el resultado de las elecciones ya parecía seguro que Jackson saldría elegido por otros cuatro años, pese a los esfuerzos realizados por los partidarios de mister Clay e interesados en el Banco de los Estados Unidos. Respecto a la vicepresidencia no se sabía sobre quién recaería la designación. Empezaban a llegar a Washington los representantes que deberían abrir las sesiones del congreso dentro de breves días. Habían salido de Norfolk las corbetas Saint Louis, mandada por Zantzinger, Vandalia, por Bood y la goleta Porpoise, por Mac Kintosh para reforzar las fuerzas navales que protegían el comercio de la Unión en el golfo de Méjico y Costa Firme, bajo el mando del comodoro Stenly. Principal y duplicado.

1.282

N.º 1.418. — 26 de noviembre, Filadelfia.

Las alteraciones introducidas en los aranceles en el último congreso habían exasperado a los estados del sur que se consideraban perjudicados en sus intereses, por lo que habían obligado a las respectivas legislaturas a convocar una reunión de diputados de todos ellos con el nombre de Convención en Columbia, capital de Carolina del Sur, el 19 del corriente. Esta asamblea debería proponer las medidas adecuadas para libertarse de la opresión federal y como sus resoluciones estarían en oposición con lo acordado en el congreso de la Unión, podían seguirse resultados funestos al no poder combinarse los intereses de los estados del norte con los del sur, con lo que peligraría la tranquilidad del país. Principal y duplicado.

1.283

N.º 1.419. — 28 de noviembre, Filadelfia.

Acusa recibo de cuatro reales órdenes recibidas en el mes de noviembre.

1.284

N.º 1.420. — 28 de noviembre, Filadelfia.

Noticias de Veracruz informaban de que había tenido lugar un enfrentamiento en San Agustín del Palmar entre las tropas de Santa Ana y las de Facio resultando vencedor el primero, que tras superar también la oposición de Andrade había podido seguir hacia la Puebla. Al aproximarse Santa Ana a Méjico se temían grandes desórdenes en la ciudad y el gobernador había pedido a los habitantes que ayudaran a las tropas haciendo fuego contra los que intentasen cualquier acto de pillaje en tiendas o viviendas.

1.285

N.º 1.421. — 28 de noviembre, Filadelfia.

Había empezado a disminuir el cólera morbo en Richmond, Cincinnati y Missouri, habiéndose extinguido totalmente en Nueva York. En Charleston aún se daban algunos casos; donde estaba en su apogeo era en Nueva Orleans donde coincidiendo con la fiebre amarilla se habían enterrado en un sólo día ciento veintisiete personas. Según las últimas noticias había cedido algo. Principal y duplicado.

1.286

N.º 1.422. — 6 de diciembre, Filadelfia.

Remite el discurso que el presidente de la república había pronunciado en la sesión de apertura del congreso; por falta de tiempo había sido imposible concluir su traducción, por lo que insertaba los párrafos relacionados con España.

Refiriéndose en primer lugar a las reclamaciones de los ciudadanos americanos contra el gobierno español, se había comprobado que algunas eran de tal naturaleza que no justificaban la intervención del estado, por lo que se habían enviado nuevas instrucciones para que sólo se presentaran las que se podían exigir con toda justicia según el derecho de gentes. Las gestiones habían sufrido retraso por la demora en conseguir la documentación necesaria y por la enfermedad del rey; pero superados ya estos obstáculos era de esperar su pronta resolución. La reclamación presentada para la entrega de los archivos de las Floridas, que habían sido trasladados a la Habana, había dado lugar a una real orden al efecto. El ministro de Estados Unidos en Madrid había obtenido la reducción del derecho de toneladas que pagaban los buques americanos en los puertos españoles, consiguiendo fuesen iguales a los que pagaban los súbditos de España.

Respecto a otros asuntos mostraba su satisfacción por el estado de los negocios públicos y comerciales, así como por las amistosas relaciones que se mantenían con Francia e Inglaterra, aunque con esta última quedaba pendiente la cuestión de los límites de la frontera del nordeste.

De Portugal se había recibido parte de la indemnización estipulada por las pérdidas que el comercio americano había sufrido en el bloqueo de las islas Terceras, y debido a la guerra civil que sufría aquel país no había podido abonar el resto. Dinamarca había pagado lo estipulado en su convención; no así Nápoles, que había demorado la satisfacción debida a los americanos. Con Rusia se trataba de fundar un comercio con bases permanentes, como se hacía con el gobierno austríaco. Los Estados Unidos disfrutaban de libre comercio y navegación en el mar Negro y todos los puertos pertenecientes al imperio turco. Respecto a las provincias disidentes de América continuaba la amistad y el comercio, que era obstaculizado en Méjico por la guerra civil que padecía; en América Central no se había conseguido establecer relaciones diplomáticas por la muerte del individuo nombrado para ello; el ministro americano en Nueva Granada tenía orden de procurar la reunión de los tres estados que formaban la república llamada de Colombia; con relación a Buenos Aires, las desavenencias en las Malvinas continuaban como había expuesto en su último discurso; se había establecido con Chile un tratado de amistad y comercio; había disminuido notablemente el tráfico con los estados inmediatos al Perú, por los enormes derechos impuestos sobre las exportaciones americanas y no se había podido nombrar un agente diplomático para Bolivia y Perú por las continuas desavenencias existentes entre ambos países. En Brasil los continuos disturbios aumentaban los perjuicios causados al comercio, por lo que no se habían tomado en consideración las reclamaciones. Manifiesta que era excelente el estado de la hacienda pública, que los fondos de tesorería aumentarían con los ingresos de las aduanas, a cuyas leyes se habían opuesto algunos estados poniendo en peligro la Unión, pero esperaba que las autoridades del gobierno general podrían vencer estas dificultades. Se refiere a la gestión del Banco de los Estados Unidos con parte de los accionistas, perjudicial al gobierno; proponía la inmediata venta de las tierras públicas; refiere el fin de las desavenencias con los indios debida a la buena organización del ejército, no habiéndose conseguido nada con los cherokees, que vivían en el estado de Georgia. Concluye exponiendo la protección que la Marina había prestado al comercio de la Unión, lo próspero de la renta de Correos; llama la atención sobre las ideas manifestadas anteriormente sobre la elección de presidente y vicepresidente de la república; indica los defectos de la ley que castiga los fraudes de los empleados y recuerda la imperfección del sistema judicial vigente. Este era el contenido del discurso del presidente, al cual seguirían las memorias de los respectivos secretarios del despacho. Principal y duplicado.

Adjunto:

— Folleto impreso con el mensaje del presidente pronunciado en la sesión de apertura del congreso de la Unión (4 de diciembre 1832).

— Fragmento del periódico «The Globe» con el discurso completo del presidente Jackson en la apertura del congreso (Washington, 5 de diciembre 1832).

1.287

N.º 1.423. — 6 de diciembre, Filadelfia.

Da cuenta de que la convención que se había reunido en Columbia estaba compuesta solamente por diputados de todos los distritos del estado de Carolina del Sur y había acordado que su presidente, que era el gobernador del mismo estado, nombrase una comisión que informara sobre las medidas que deberían adoptarse respecto a la violación de la constitución de los Estados Unidos, en las disposiciones del congreso relativas a los derechos e impuestos decretados para proteger las manufacturas nacionales. La comisión había propuesto y se había aprobado, que se publicara una ley para contener los efectos de aquellas disposiciones del congreso de la federación, declarándose dispuestos a resistir con la fuerza si el gobierno general trataba de obligarlos a aceptar los aranceles vigentes. Había sorprendido tal actitud que amenazaba la existencia misma de la Unión, y aunque el presidente se había referido a ellos en su discurso, se creía que hablaría más extensamente de un asunto que podía involucrar a otros varios estados del sur. Principal y duplicado.

Adjunto:
— Fragmento del periódico «The National Gazette» con la relación de lo que se había tratado en la convención de Carolina del Sur (Filadelfia, 29 de noviembre 1832). Hay dos ejemplares.
— Traducción de lo tratado en la convención de Carolina del Sur para suspender la acción de ciertas actas del congreso de los Estados Unidos que imponían derechos e impuestos sobre la importación de géneros extranjeros. En dicha convención se rechazaba, como anticonstitucionales, las actas del congreso de los Estados Unidos aprobadas el 19 de mayo de 1828 y 14 de julio de 1832, referentes a la imposición de impuestos que en realidad favorecían a ciertos individuos en detrimento de otros; las declaraba de ningún valor y amenazaban con retirarse de la Unión y constituirse en estado independiente si se trataba de obligarlos por la fuerza a aceptar dichas actas. Hay dos ejemplares.

1.288

N.º 1.424. — 13 de diciembre, Filadelfia.

Remite la traducción completa del discurso del presidente Jackson. Principal y duplicado.

Adjunto:

— Traducción del discurso del presidente Andrés Jackson en la sesión de apertura del congreso de los Estados Unidos (4 de diciembre 1832).
— Ejemplar de «El Redactor» con el discurso completo del presidente en lengua española (Nueva York, 8 de diciembre 1832).

1.289

N.º 1.425. — 13 de diciembre, Filadelfia.

Remite la lista mensual de pasaportes. Principal y duplicado.

Adjunto:
— Relación de los pasaportes expedidos por los cónsules y vice-cónsules de Filadelfia, Nueva York, Baltimore, Norfolk y Nueva Orleans en los meses de octubre y noviembre. Hay dos ejemplares.

1.290

N.º 1.426. — 14 de diciembre, Filadelfia.

Participa que a pesar de que la Junta de Sanidad de Nueva Orleans había dado por desaparecido el cólera en aquella ciudad el 13 de noviembre, dándose sólo algún caso aislado en los arrabales, noticias posteriores afirmaban que, si bien había disminuido notablemente, ya que a principios de noviembre la mortalidad era de unos trescientos diarios, aún existían bastantes casos de la enfermedad; tampoco en Boston y otros puntos se había extinguido totalmente. Principal y duplicado.

1.291

N.º 1.427. — 14 de diciembre, Filadelfia.

Las últimas noticias llegadas de Veracruz decían que Santa Ana, que estaba sitiando Méjico, había levantado el cerco para luchar

VIII. — 29

contra Bustamante y evitar los males de un asalto a la capital si salía vencedor, como esperaba. Pedraza había llegado a Veracruz siendo recibido con los mayores honores y repuesto en su cargo de gobernador, exonerando del mismo a Zabala, que había sido expatriado por el gobierno de Bustamante. Principal y duplicado.

1.292

N.º 1.428. — 20 de diciembre, Filadelfia.

Había llegado a Filadelfia, procedente de la Habana, el teniente de navío Juan José Martínez con el encargo de la junta superior directiva de Real Hacienda de aquella isla, de comprar cuatro buques bateas y uno pequeño de vapor para reemplazar a los cuatro gánguiles del pontón Cristina como menos adecuados para ese fin. Le había pedido que lo auxiliara e interviniera en los contratos que hiciera dicho oficial, que ya anteriormente había sido comisionado para hacer construir el pontón de vapor para la limpieza del puerto de la Habana, encargo que había desempeñado a completa satisfacción de las autoridades de Cuba. Principal y duplicado.

1.293

N.º 1.429. — 20 de diciembre, Filadelfia.

Participa la llega a Portsmouth, en el estado de New Hampshire, de mister J. Nelson, encargado de negocios de Estados Unidos cerca del rey de las Dos Sicilias, que parecía ser portador de un tratado concluido en Nápoles en el que se estipulaba el pago de las indemnizaciones. Principal y duplicado.

1.294

N.º 1.430. — 22 de diciembre, Filadelfia.

Una vez que la convención de Carolina del Sur había adoptado los acuerdos de los que anteriormente había dado cuenta, dieron por terminadas sus sesiones; el 27 de noviembre había iniciado las suyas la legislatura de aquel estado con la lectura por su gobernador, mister J. Hamilton, de un discurso en el cual pedía la cooperación del poder ejecutivo para poder llevar a cabo lo acordado por la convención e impedir que se cumplieran las actas del congreso general de la Unión que dicha convención había anulado. Se había propuesto que, en caso de que los administradores de aduanas se negaran a despachar la documentación con arreglo a las decisiones de la convención, se autorizara al gobernador del estado a hacerlo él mismo; que se aceptase el servicio de diez mil voluntarios para la defensa de todo el estado; que se asignara una cantidad para comprar armas, municiones y víveres; que se pidiera al presidente de los Estados Unidos que ordenase desocupar la ciudadela de Charleston para que la defendieran dos mil voluntarios de los anteriores citados; y que manifestara el deseo de que el congreso y el gobierno general accedieran a convocar una convención de todos los estados, para que resolviera los problemas surgidos. Estas propuestas estaban siendo estudiadas por varias comisiones que aún no se habían pronunciado al respecto.

El presidente de la república había publicado una proclama dando cuenta de la reunión de la convención de Carolina del Sur, su objetivo y conclusiones, que consideraba ilegales por carecer de derecho cualquier estado para anular sus leyes, pues en caso de parecerles contrarias a sus intereses podían haber apelado al poder judicial y a los demás estados, como había ocurrido en ocasiones semejantes en que las dificultades se habían solventado en unión con el gobierno general. Enumera las ventajas de pertenecer a una nación que procura sus intereses y el temor de que pudiera desatarse una guerra civil, pues como primer magistrado no podía permitir que se incumplieran las leyes; y si los de Carolina del Sur pretendían hacerlo por la fuerza, usaría el poder para hacer cumplir la constitución. Se había elogiado mucho esta proclama aunque se dudaba de que surtiera el efecto buscado; se creía que una tropa de dos mil hombres estaba dispuesta a obrar a las órdenes del mayor general Scott y que la corbeta de guerra Natchez estaba preparada por si era necesario que actuara. Principal y duplicado.

1.295

N.º 1.431. — 22 de diciembre, Filadelfia.

Da cuenta de que continuaban las sesiones del congreso de la Unión, habiéndose pasado a las correspondientes comisiones una serie de asuntos de interés local. También se habían presentado las memorias de los secretarios de los respectivos despachos. El de Hacienda había dado cuenta de los ingresos y gastos en el año en curso en el que se había reducido algo la deuda pública; el saldo de las importaciones y exportaciones, a lo que había que añadir la indemnización de Dinamarca pagadera en el mismo año; como resultaba un superavit en las rentas de seis millones, proponía reducir éstas disminuyendo los derechos de importación; concluía la memoria con una acusación contra el Banco de los Estados Unidos por la transacción que había hecho con los tenedores del tres por ciento. El ministro de la Guerra había expuesto las operaciones contra los indios Sac y Fox que terminaron con la sumisión de dichas tribus; recomendaba la creación de un regimiento de dragones como el más idóneo para luchar con ellos y que se aumentara el cuerpo de ingenieros; manifestaba el floreciente estado de la academia militar, cuyo edificio convenía ampliar. Recomendaba que se trasladase a los indios al este del Mississipi; se refería al tratado concluido con los creeks y los seminoles de la Florida y a los convenios terminados con las tribus de shawnees, delawares, peorias y kaskaskias en los que éstas cedían sus derechos territoriales en Missouri e Illinois y terminaba exponiendo la cesión de vastos territorios en Illinois e Indiana hecha por los potawatomies. El director general de Correos, tras exponer el número de millas andadas para facilitar las comunicaciones, los nuevos caminos trazados y mejora de los mal conservados, manifestaba que el déficit que se había producido se debía al aumento del número de administraciones de correos que se habían multiplicado en el año en curso. Principal y duplicado.

1.296

N.º 1.432. — 24 de diciembre, Filadelfia.

La memoria del secretario de Marina presentada al congreso empezaba manifestando la importancia de las fuerzas navales y de la acción que habían llevado a cabo auxiliando al comercio, evitando agresiones y amenazas. Refiriéndose a la escuadra del Mediterráneo decía que al llegar la fragata Constellation, a la isla de Madera, su comandante había observado que las fuerzas que llevaban a cabo el bloqueo eran escasas y condescendientes con las banderas de otras naciones; en consecuencia, aunque tenía órdenes de observar neutralidad respetando el gobierno existente, como debía proteger el comercio de su país había proporcionado la entrada en el puerto a los cargamentos expuestos a pederse. Se habían incorporado a dicha escuadra las fragatas Constellation y United States y había regresado la Ontario; el navío Delaware estaba siendo examinado en los diques antes de que se incorporara a aquel punto para reemplazar a las corbetas Boston y Concord y a la fragata Brandwine. Respecto a la escuadra del Pacífico el único hecho notable había sido el castigo infligido por la fragata Potomac a los piratas malayos. El resultado del viaje del Potomac a Sumatra había sido acallar las amenazas de aquellos piratas; para evitar posteriores ataques había seguido al Potomac un destacamento de la misma escuadra para que tocase en Sumatra y los puntos de la costa oriental de África, de India y China que conviniera, para proteger el comercio de aquella región. Una corbeta de la escuadra destinada en Brasil había puesto término al apresamiento de algunos buques americanos en las islas Malvinas. La goleta Boxer después de tocar en Liberia, en la costa de África, había extendido la protección a las inmediaciones de Para. En los últimos disturbios de Montevideo la goleta Enterprize que se había encontrado en situación difícil, había podido auxiliar no sólo a los americanos sino también a las autoridades constituidas del país. Dada la situación de América del Sur y la necesidad de proteger el comercio de la India se habían añadido a la escuadra del Brasil la corbeta Peacock y las goletas Boxer y Enterprize. Las fuerzas empleadas en el golfo de Méjico durante las conmociones de aquel país, habían protegido no sólo a los americanos sino también a los de otros países. El apresamiento de la goleta Moctezuma, del partido de Santa Ana, se había hecho por la goleta Grampus sin órdenes del gobierno, pero su comandante lo había estimado necesario para defender la bandera americana de posibles agresiones. Se había destacado parte de esta escuadra a las islas de Cabo Verde y a la costa de África en persecución de un pirata que, cerca de las Azores, había apresado un mercante mejicano que llevaba un cargamento muy valioso. Las corbetas Fairfield, Vincennes y Eris, que necesitaban reparos, habían sido sustituidas por las San Luis y Vandalia.

Un buque había cruzado constantemente sobre la costa del país y otros tres, que se destinaban a impedir los robos de arbolados, se habían retirado por no responder su gasto al beneficio que producían. Se habían empezado a cumplir las disposiciones del congreso sobre la reparación de las fragatas Macedonia, Java y Cyane;

se precisaba una asignación para la construcción de unas baterías de vapor muy útiles para facilitar la entrada y salida de los buques con cualquier viento y marea; aumentaban los acopios en los arsenales no sólo con lo necesario para la construcción de buques sino ligaduras, hierro, cobre y plomo en cantidad, así como cañones, fusiles y otras armas, y pólvora, azufre y nitro cuidadosamente conservados; se habían cuidado convenientemente el hospital y los pensionistas del ramo; no se habían concluido los diques por un accidente en uno de ellos, la existencia del cólera en las inmediaciones de otro y la crudeza del último invierno; era necesario un ingeniero para vigilar estos diques, cuyo gasto se podía compensar con la supresión de dos de los constructores navales, que no eran necesarios. Respecto al personal convenía aumentar el número de comandantes, reduciendo un poco los capitanes y guardias marinas.

Anuncia remisión con este despacho de trece documentos que comprendían la lista de los buques armados, estado de las provisiones, informe sobre los adelantos hechos en los diques, presupuesto general, orden para examinar los buques después de un crucero, gastos para la revisión del código naval y otros varios que remitiría con los impresos del congreso. Principal y duplicado.

LEGAJO 5.659

AÑO 1833

CORRESPONDENCIA DEL MINISTRO ESPAÑOL EN ESTADOS UNIDOS, FRANCISCO TACÓN, CON LOS SECRETARIOS DE ESTADO, JOSÉ CAFRANGA Y FRANCISCO CEA BERMÚDEZ SUCESIVAMENTE

1.297

N.º 1.434. — 2 de enero Filadelfia.

Comunica el descontento que había causado en Carolina del Sur, la proclama del presidente relativa a la llamada «nulificación», o sea la anulación de los aranceles, decretada por el congreso americano. Hay dos ejemplares.

1.298

N.º 1.435. — 8 de enero, Filadelfia.

Acusa recibo del oficio del pasado 2 de octubre, donde se le comunicaba el nombramiento de Cea Bermúdez como ministro secretario de Estado, desempeñando Cafranga este cargo interinamente. Hay dos ejemplares.

1.299

N.º 1.436. — 8 de enero, Filadelfia.

Quedaba enterado del oficio donde se le comunicaba que la reina se haría cargo de los asuntos del Estado durante la enfermedad del rey. Hay dos ejemplares.

1.300

N.º 1.438. — 12 de enero, Filadelfia.

Recapitula varias reales órdenes recibidas durante el mes de enero. Hay dos ejemplares.

1.301

N.º 1.439. — 14 de enero, Filadelfia.

Participa el regreso a la Habana desde Filadelfia de Nicolás de Campos, comisionado para comprar tubos de hierro y otros efectos para construir cañones. Hay dos ejemplares.

1.302

N.º 1.440. — 14 de enero, Filadelfia.

Remite la lista mensual de los pasaportes expedidos por los cónsules españoles en Estados Unidos. Hay dos ejemplares.

Adjunto:
— Copia de la citada lista (Filadelfia, 8 de enero 1833).

1.303

N.º 1.441. — 24 de enero, Filadelfia.

Continúa hablando de la repercusión que había tenido en Carolina del Sur la ley de «nulificación», que este estado se negaba a cumplir, preparándose militarmente para el caso de tener que usar la fuerza. El presidente americano había tomado medidas para que se cumpliese esta ley, y el vicepresidente, que era el de Carolina del Sur, había presentado la dimisión, para demostrar su disconformidad. Se esperaba que el congreso concediese al presidente las más amplias facultades para que se respetasen las leyes y para impedir la disolución de la Unión. Hay dos ejemplares.

1.304

N.º 1.442. — 27 de enero, Filadelfia.

Acusa recibo de la resolución de la reina por la que se le autorizaba a cargar en las cuentas de la legación el importe de su casa de campo. Hay dos ejemplares.

1.305

N.º 1.444. — 31 de enero, Filadelfia.

Acusa recibo de varias reales órdenes.

1.306

N.º 1.445. — 6 de febrero, Filadelfia.

Comunica de Méjico el armisticio convenido entre las tropas de Santa Ana y Bustamante, mediante el cual parecía terminada la contienda de estos dos caudillos acordándose que Pedraza ocupase la presidencia. Hay dos ejemplares.

1.307

N.º 1.446. — 7 de febrero, Filadelfia.

Da cuenta de haberse empezado en el senado una serie de debates en relación con los sucesos de Carolina del Sur. Hay dos ejemplares.

1.308

N.º 1.447. — 8 de febrero, Filadelfia.

Informa que había sido acordado un tratado entre el rey de las Dos Sicilias y el presidente de Estados Unidos, por el que se estipulaba el pago de más de dos millones de ducados napolitanos al gobierno americano, por las pérdidas que tuvieron en este lugar los comerciantes americanos, durante los años 1809 a 1812. Hay dos ejemplares.

1.309

N.º 1.448. — 18 de febrero, Filadelfia.

Francisco Tacón a Cea Bermúdez, dice haberse enterado por un diario de Cádiz de que estaba ya desempeñando la secretaría de Estado, por lo que le felicita y se pone a su disposición. Hay dos ejemplares.

1.310

N.º 1.449. — 21 de febrero, Filadelfia.

Continuaba dando noticias relativas a Carolina del Sur. La comisión nombrada para este asunto se negaba a conceder al presidente las facultades extraordinarias para hacer uso de la fuerza a fin de que se obedeciesen las leyes. Los senadores Clay y Calhoum, principales caudillos de la oposición, formaron un proyecto para disminuir progresivamente los aranceles, de modo que quedasen combinados los intereses de los estados del Norte y del Sur, con el objeto de terminar de este modo la cuestión de la Carolina. Hay dos ejemplares.

1.311

N.º 1.450. — 22 de febrero, Filadelfia.

Comunica la reelección de Andrés Jackson, y la elección de Martin van Buren como vicepresidente. Hay dos ejemplares.

1.312

N.º 1.451. — 13 de marzo, Filadelfia.

Da cuenta de su desplazamiento a Washington para asistir a la toma de posesión del presidente y vicepresidente. Remite varios documentos relativos a este asunto.

Adjunto:

— Copia y traducción de la nota del secretario de Estado, Eduardo Livinston, a Tacón, invitándole a las ceremonias de la elección (Washington, 27 de febrero 1833).
— Copia de nota describiendo el acto de elección del presidente y vicepresidente.
— Copia del discurso, pronunciado por el presidente con motivo de su reelección, el 4 de marzo de 1833, en el cual encarecía la conservación de la Unión.
— Copia del discurso pronunciado por el ministro de Francia, como miembro más caracterizado del cuerpo diplomático para felicitar al presidente por su reelección (5 de marzo 1833).
— Copia de la contestación del presidente al ministro francés. Hay dos ejemplares (sin fecha).

1.313

N.º 1.452. — 13 de marzo, Filadelfia.

Daría cumplimiento a la real orden relativa a la rectificación de cualquier posible error que tuviese el gobierno americano acerca de la verdadera situación de España y miras de su gobierno. Hay dos ejemplares.

1.314

N.º 1.453. — 14 de marzo, Filadelfia.

Acusa recibo de la real orden y gaceta en que se inserta la declaración hecha por el rey, anulando un decreto donde derogaba la pragmática sanción de 29 de marzo de 1830. Este decreto lo había firmado el rey por sorpresa durante su enfermedad.

1.315

N.º 1.454. — 14 de marzo, Filadelfia.

Comunica haber terminado sus sesiones el congreso y las leyes que había decretado. Hay dos ejemplares.

1.316

N.º 1.455. — 14 de marzo, Filadelfia.

Da cuenta del resultado favorable que había tenido en el congreso el proyecto de los senadores Clay y Calhoun, para disminuir progresivamente los aranceles de estos Estados hasta 1842, a partir de cuya fecha quedarían limitados los derechos al 20 %. La aprobación de esta ley podría dar fin a la cuestión promovida en Carolina. Hay dos ejemplares.

1.317

N.º 1.456. — 14 de marzo, Filadelfia.

Remite cuenta de los gastos eventuales producidos por su desplazamiento a Washington el pasado 26 de febrero, para que le fuese abonado su importe.

Adjunto:

— Copia de la citada cuenta, que ascendía a 260 pesos (Filadelfia, 14 de marzo 1833).

1.318

N.º 1.457. — 27 de marzo, Filadelfia.

Remite «The National Gazette», de Filadelfia, con la noticia de haberse apoderado los ingleses de las islas Malvinas.

Adjunto:

— La mencionada gaceta decía, que la goleta Sun, de New London, había llegado a Montevideo, expulsada por los ingleses de las Malvinas, donde habían puesto la bandera británica (Filadelfia, 22 de marzo 1833).

1.319

N.º 1.458. — 28 de marzo, Filadelfia.

Da cuenta de haberse reunido una convención en Carolina del Sur que había anulado la ley de aranceles decretada por el gobierno general, también se dejaba sin efecto la ley que autorizaba al presidente americano a usar de facultades ordinarias para este objeto. Hay dos ejemplares.

1.320

N.º 1.459. — 29 de marzo, Filadelfia.

Recapitula varias reales órdenes. Hay dos ejemplares.

1.321

N.º 1.460. — 29 de marzo, Filadelfia.

Comunica el regreso a Nueva York de Mr. Vaughan ministro plenipotenciario de Inglaterra.

1.322

N.º 1.461. — 22 de marzo, Filadelfia.

Informa del tratado acordado entre el reino de Nueva Granada y el Ecuador, en el que se reconocían recíprocamente como estados independientes. Hay dos ejemplares.

1.323

N.º 1.462. — 29 de marzo, Filadelfia.

Remite una solicitud de Francisco de Paula Escudero, secretario de su legación, pidiendo algún ascenso en su carrera.

Adjunto:

— Instancia de Escudero al rey exponiendo su antigüedad y otros méritos, por lo que pedía ser ascendido (Filadelfia, 29 de marzo 1833).

1.324

N.º 1.463. — 2 de abril, Filadelfia.

Anuncia remisión de impresos relativos a los acuerdos tomados durante el pasado año en el congreso americano.

Adjunto:

— Oficio de Tacón al administrador de correos de Cádiz encargándole que hiciese llegar al secretario de Estado los mencionados impresos (Filadelfia, 2 de abril 1833).

— Oficio del administrador de correos de Cádiz al secretario de Estado español, diciendo que los impresos procedentes de América, iban en dirección a Marsella, por no haberse dado entrada en Cádiz al buque que los transportaba (Cádiz, 28 de junio 1833).

— Nota informativa al cónsul español en Marsella para que se hiciese cargo de los citados impresos (6 de julio 1833).

1.325

N.º 1.464. — 4 de abril, Filadelfia.

Expresa su satisfacción por el feliz restablecimiento del rey, que había vuelto a hacerse cargo de su despacho. Hay dos ejemplares.

1.326

N.º 1.465. — 4 de abril, Filadelfia.

Da cuenta del incendio ocurrido en la secretaría de Hacienda, situada a cien metros de la casa del presidente, salvándose la mayor parte de los papeles. Hay dos ejemplares.

1.327

N.º 1.466. — 6 de abril, Filadelfia.

Remite un párrafo de la gaceta de Bogotá, donde se publicaba la obligación de pagar doce reales por tonelada a los buques de todas las naciones que comerciaren con las costas de la Guajira, Darien y Mosquitos.

Adjunto:

— Recorte de la Gaceta de Nueva Granada, con los citados arreglos comerciales (Bogotá, 20 de enero 1833). Hay dos ejemplares.

1.328

N.º 1.467. — 12 de abril, Filadelfia.

Comunica haber sido designado Agustín de Iturbide como encargado de negocios de la república de Méjico cerca del gobierno americano. Presentación de credenciales del ministro francés, barón Deffaudis, al gobierno mejicano. Pedraza había asumido la presidencia de este país.

Adjunto:

— Copia del discurso del barón Deffaudis, ministro plenipotenciario francés, al presidente de la república mejicana, con ocasión de la presentación de credenciales, deseando que las relaciones entre ambos países se estrechasen cada vez más, llegando a acuerdos comerciales y de todo tipo (sin fecha).

— Respuesta del presidente mejicano expresando su satisfacción por ser el primero en recibir un plenipotenciario del gobierno francés poniendo de manifiesto las analogías existentes entre ambos países (sin fecha). Hay dos ejemplares.

1.329

N.º 1.468. — 16 de abril, Filadelfia.

Da cuenta de la designación para secretario de la legación americana en España de Carlos S. Walsh. Dice también que el fuego que destruyó la secretaría de Hacienda no había sido casual. Hay dos ejemplares.

1.330

N.º 1.469. — 20 de abril, Filadelfia.

Confirma la noticia, ya remitida, de haberse posesionado de las Malvinas las fuerzas marítimas de Gran Bretaña. Hay dos ejemplares.

1.331

N.º 1.470. — 21 de abril, Filadelfia.

Acusa recibo de varias reales órdenes. Hay dos ejemplares.

1.332

N.º 1.471. — 23 de abril, Filadelfia.

Remite un número de «El Redactor», publicado en Nueva York, donde se insertan noticias de Buenos Aires, en relación con la toma de las islas Malvinas por la corbeta Elio de Gran Bretaña.

Adjunto:

— Recorte de «El Redactor» con detalles de la operación llevada a efecto por la corbeta Elio para poner el pabellón inglés alegando el derecho de soberanía que sobre estas islas tenía su gobierno; en las Malvinas, que pertenecían hasta ese momento a la república Argentina, había tenido lugar recientemente una insurrección militar (Nueva York, 20 de abril 1833). Hay dos ejemplares.

— Extracto de un oficio del secretario de Estado de los Estados Unidos a su ministro en Madrid, pidiendo le informase con la mayor exactitud de la extensión que tenía el gobierno de Buenos Aires mientras se hallaba bajo el dominio de España (sin fecha).

1.333

N.º 1.474. — 27 de abril, Filadelfia.

Da cuenta de haber dado publicidad a la real orden expedida para el establecimiento de cuarentenas a los buques procedentes de Oporto y otros puntos de Portugal.

1.334

N.º 1.475. — 28 de abril, Filadelfia.

Acusa recibo del oficio de 21 de febrero relativo al real decreto de amnistía, al que daría cumplimiento.

1.335

N.º 1.476. — 28 de abril, Filadelfia.

Participa el nombramiento para cónsul de Estados Unidos en la Habana a Nicolás Felipe Frist de Virginia. Hay dos ejemplares.

1.336

1.477. — 30 de abril, Filadelfia.

Acusa recibo de varias reales órdenes. Hay dos ejemplares.

1.337

N.º 1.478. — 4 de mayo, Filadelfia.

Avisa de que habían llegado a la Guayra ciento cuatro emigrados de Canarias. Informa asimismo del tratado de comercio firmado entre el cónsul de Francia y la república de Venezuela.

1.338

N.º 1.479. — 10 de mayo, Filadelfia.

Da cuenta del agravio cometido contra el presidente americano, y de la protesta de las letras giradas contra el gobierno de Francia por el ministerio de Hacienda de Washington, con ocasión del tratado firmado entre ambos países. Trata de los fuegos ocurridos en Nueva York. Hay dos ejemplares.

1.339

N.º 1.480. — 11 de mayo, Filadelfia.

Comunica varias noticias de Nueva España: que el general Santa Ana había sido elegido presidente de esta república; la evasión de Méjico del encargado de negocios de Holanda, F. Grothe, para evitar el pago de treinta mil duros que debía a varias personas. Hay dos ejemplares.

1.340

N.º 1.481. — 27 de mayo, Filadelfia.

Anuncia remisión de una gaceta con el tratado de comercio y navegación concluido en 1832 entre Rusia y Estados Unidos. En él se establecía la libertad y reciprocidad de comercio y navegación que disfrutaban las naciones más favorecidas; la facultad del nombramiento de cónsules; el permiso de poder disponer los individuos de ambos países de sus bienes personales, y otros.

1.341

N.º 1.482. — 27 de mayo, Filadelfia.

Sigue dando noticias de Nueva España: nombramiento de vicepresidente; principios de desavenencias con Bravo, que mandaba una división en el sur; Máximo Garro había sido nombrado ministro plenipotenciario de esta república en Londres. Hay dos ejemplares.

1.342

N.º 1.483. — 27 de mayo, Filadelfia.

Informa del proyecto de viaje del presidente a diferentes estados del norte y del oeste y de que el navío Delaware, se destinaría a reforzar la escuadra del Mediterráneo. Hay dos ejemplares.

1.343

N.º 1484. — 31 de mayo, Filadelfia.

Participa los nombramientos, de los ministros de Estado y Hacienda de Estados Unidos, y el de Mr. Livingston para plenipotenciario en Francia. Hay dos ejemplares.

1.344

N.º 1.485. — 10 de junio, Filadelfia.

Acusa recibo al oficio donde se le comunicaba los cambios de ministerio ocurridos en España, así como de la circular dirigida a los capitanes generales recomendándoles la represión de todo espíritu de partido. Hay dos ejemplares.

1.345

N.º 1.486. — 10 de junio, Filadelfia.

Quedaba enterado del decreto por el que se establecían las reglas para el cumplimiento de la amnistía.

1.346

N.º 1.487. — 12 de junio, Filadelfia.

Comunica la salida de Washington del presidente americano, con objeto de visitar diferentes estados del Norte. Hay dos ejemplares.

1.347

N.º 1.488. — 12 de junio, Filadelfia.

Da cuenta del accidente ocurrido en el vapor Lioness, que navegaba por el Mississipi, donde perdieron la vida diez y seis personas, entre ellas el senador de la Luisiana Josiah Johnston. Hay dos ejemplares.

1.348

N.º 1.489. — 13 de junio, Filadelfia.

Contesta a la real orden que le prolongaba su misión diplomática en Estados Unidos. Hay dos ejemplares.

1.349

N.º 1.490. — 27 de junio, Filadelfia.

Dice que continuaba su viaje el presidente americano y le informa de algunos nombramientos. Hay dos ejemplares.

1.350

N.º 1.491. — 28 de junio, Filadelfia.

Acusa recibo del oficio donde se le comunicaban las medidas sanitarias que se habían adoptado para evitar la propagación en la península de la epidemia ocurrida en Lisboa. Hay dos ejemplares.

1.351

N.º 1.492. — 28 de junio, Filadelfia.

Dice que daría la mayor difusión a la real orden para la disminución de cuarentenas y precauciones sanitarias vigentes. Hay dos ejemplares.

1.352

N.º 1.493. — 29 de junio, Filadelfia.

Manifiesta que informaría a José Miguel Bellido la resolución a la instancia que había dirigido.

1.353

N.º 1.494. — 29 de junio, Filadelfia.

Acusa recibo de la comunicación donde se le informaba de la aparición del cólera en Oporto. Hay dos ejemplares.

1.354

N.º 1.495. — 22 de junio, Filadelfia.

Recapitula las reales órdenes recibidas durante el mes de febrero. Hay dos ejemplares.

1.355

N.º 1.496. — 3 de julio, Filadelfia.

Anuncia remisión de la instancia del coronel de infantería Gilberto Andry, pidiendo ser trasladado de Nueva Orleans al estado mayor de la Habana. Hay dos ejemplares.

1.356

N.º 1.497. — 3 de julio, Filadelfia.

Informa de la llegada a Estados Unidos del nuevo encargado de negocios de los Países Bajos A. Martini. Hay dos ejemplares.

1.357

N.º 1.498. — 4 de julio, Filadelfia.

Participa que se había declarado el cólera en Tampico, con una mortandad de 80 a 90 personas por día, en una población de tres mil almas. Hay dos ejemplares.

1.358

N.º 1.499. — 7 de julio, Filadelfia.

Da cuenta del inesperado regreso del presidente a Washington, al parecer por su delicado estado de salud. Hay dos ejemplares.

1.359

N.º 1.500. — 15 de julio, Filadelfia.

Sigue dando noticias de Nueva España, donde Santa Ana ocupaba la presidencia y trataba de contener las nuevas rebeliones. Había empezado a ceder el cólera en Tampico. Hay dos ejemplares.

1.360

N.º 1.501. — 15 de julio, Filadelfia.

Notifica haberse mejorado la salud del presidente. Hay dos ejemplares.

1.361

N.º 1.502. — 23 de julio, Filadelfia.

Remite copia y traducción de la circular que había recibido del departamento de Estado americano indicándole la conveniencia de que trasladase su residencia oficial a Washington. En opinión de Tacón, este traslado haría la vida mucho más costosa e incómoda, por carecer la ciudad de Washington de comercio, agricultura y fábricas y por su enorme extensión, que hacía de ella la ciudad más grande del mundo, con las consiguientes dificultades de comunicación.

Adjunto:

— Copia y traducción de la circular de Louis Mac Lane, secretario de Estado americano, recomendándole el traslado de su legación a Washington, para facilitar las comunicaciones con el resto de los ministros extranjeros (Washington, 13 de julio 1833).
— Copia de la respuesta de Tacón a Mac Lane, diciendo que no se consideraba autorizado para variar su residencia sin el previo conocimiento de su soberano (Filadelfia, 13 de junio 1833). Hay dos ejemplares.

1.362

N.º 1.503. — 29 de julio, Filadelfia.

Remite una instancia de Antonio Pomar, vicecónsul español en Norfolk, donde solicitaba se le abonasen los tres mil reales anuales asignados para gastos de correo y escritorio.

Adjunto:

— Instancia de Pomar al rey con la petición mencionada (Norfolk, 29 de junio 1833).

1.363

N.º 1.504. — 29 de julio, Filadelfia.

Comunica que el presidente americano se había trasladado desde la capital a la fortaleza de Rip-Raps cerca de Chesapeake. Hay dos ejemplares.

1.364

N.º 1.505. — 30 de julio, Filadelfia.

Comunica las últimas noticias de Nueva España: el regreso de Santa Ana a la capital, y el desorden de las tropas de Escalada que se habían rebelado anteriormente. Hay dos ejemplares.

1.365

N.º 1.506. — 5 de agosto, Filadelfia.

Informa acerca de la utilidad del nombramiento de un vicecónsul para el puerto de Mobila, por la importancia que había adquirido este puerto.

1.366

N.º 1.507. — 5 de agosto, Filadelfia.

Acusa recibo de la real orden relativa a las medidas adoptadas para suavizar el rigor de las disposiciones sanitarias con respecto a los países situados al norte de los Pirineos. Hay dos ejemplares.

1.367

N.º 1.508. — 5 de agosto, Filadelfia.

Daría cumplimiento a la real orden que le decía trasladase la residencia de su legación a Washington y pedía ayuda para llevar a cabo este nuevo establecimiento, que ocasionaría numerosos gastos. Hay dos ejemplares.

Adjunto:
— Nota informativa a la reina comunicando lo anterior y pidiendo se concediese a Tacón algún auxilio para hacer frente a los crecidos gastos que le ocasionaría su traslado (8 de octubre 1833).
— Nota a José Heredia pidiendo su dictamen (15 de octubre 1833).
— Informe de José Heredia a Cea Bermúdez diciendo que podría aumentarse el sueldo de Tacón a nueve mil duros, en vez de ocho

que disfrutaba en aquel momento (Madrid, 10 de noviembre 1833).

1.368

N.º 1.509. — 11 de agosto, Filadelfia.

Comunica que el presidente continuaba en Rip-Raps, y la salida del navío Delaware hacia el Havre, donde iba Livingston, nombrado ministro plenipotenciario para Francia. Hay dos ejemplares.

1.369

N.º 1.510. — 13 de agosto, Filadelfia.

Remite una gaceta de Washington anunciando la impresión de los documentos públicos comunicados al congreso, y los resultados del mismo, desde el principio del gobierno hasta el día.

Adjunto:
— «Daily National Intelligencer» con el aviso de la recopilación e impresión de los citados documentos (Washington, 5 de agosto 1833). Se inserta también una carta de Luis de Onís al capitán general de Caracas destacando lo poco que favorecía la administración americana a España y el apoyo que prestaba a Napoleón en la guerra de la independencia española. Analizaba la situación y aconsejaba una gran vigilancia en las colonias españolas porque tenía noticias de que además los franceses e ingleses habían enviado varios agentes para fomentar la revolución (Filadelfia, 2 de febrero 1810).
Acompaña una nota del presidente Madison enviando esta carta al congreso para poner de manifiesto la severidad con que Onís juzgaba la política de su gobierno (10 de enero 1811). Hay dos ejemplares.
— Minuta a José de Heredia diciéndole si tenía noticia de las circunstancias que hicieron llegar al gobierno americano la carta de Onís (Madrid, 15 de octubre 1833).
— Extracto de José de Heredia a Cea Bermúdez, informando de lo anterior y diciendo que el gobierno disidente establecido en Caracas, que se apoderó de los archivos de la capitanía general, había dado conocimiento de esta carta al gobierno americano,

para indisponerlo con España, dando como resultado que dicho gobierno no reconociese por entonces a Onís como ministro de España (Madrid, 1 de enero 1834).

1.370

N.º 1.512. — 21 de agosto, Filadelfia.

Participa haber llegado a Montevideo ciento ochenta emigrados de las islas Canarias para establecerse como colonos.

1.371

N.º 1.513. — 21 de agosto, Filadelfia.

Dice que había llegado a Nueva York un ministro de Francia, con destino posterior a la república de Colombia. Hay dos ejemplares.

1.372

N.º 1.514. — 25 de agosto, Filadelfia.

Acusa recibo de la carta que le participaba el alumbramiento de la infanta María Luisa Carlota. Hay dos ejemplares.

1.373

N.º 1.515. — 26 de agosto, Filadelfia.

Daría cumplimiento a la real orden que le pedía todas las noticias de que tuviese conocimiento sobre las islas Malvinas.

1.374

N.º 1.516. — 29 de agosto, Filadelfia.

Acusa recibo de varias reales órdenes. Hay dos ejemplares.

1.375

N.º 1.517. — 2 de septiembre, Filadelfia.

Anuncia remisión de una carta autógrafa del presidente americano, congratulándose por el feliz alumbramiento de la infanta Luisa Carlota.

1.376

N.º 1.518. — 2 de septiembre, Filadelfia.

Anuncia remisión de una gaceta de Washington donde se inserta el tratado concluido y ratificado entre el rey de las Dos Sicilias y el gobierno americano.

1.377

N.º 1.519. — 3 de septiembre, Filadelfia.

Daría cumplimiento a la orden, que le decía manifestase al gobierno americano el sentimiento del rey por el ultraje cometido contra su presidente. Hay dos ejemplares.

1.378

N.º 1.520. — 3 de septiembre, Filadelfia.

Da cuenta del regreso del presidente de Estados Unidos a Washington. Hay dos ejemplares.

1.379

N.º 1.521. — 4 de septiembre, Filadelfia.

Comunica las últimas noticias de Nueva España, que continuaba con guerra civil, habiéndose visto obligado Santa Ana a salir de la capital al frente de una división, para someter a las partidas mandadas por Arista. Hay dos ejemplares.

1.380

N.º 1.522. — 4 de septiembre, Filadelfia.

Da cuenta de que el gobierno de Buenos Aires había encargado a su ministro en Londres, que hiciese una enérgica reclamación al gobierno británico por la violación que suponía la toma de las islas Malvinas, exigiendo su restitución y la satisfacción correspondiente. Hay dos ejemplares.

1.381

N.º 1.523. — 5 de septiembre, Filadelfia.

Acusa recibo de su nombramiento como ministro plenipotenciario, por lo que expresa su agradecimiento. Quedaba enterado asimismo, del juramento, como princesa heredera de la primogénita infanta Isabel Luisa. Hay dos ejemplares.

1.382

N.º 1.524. — 18 de septiembre, Filadelfia.

Anuncia remisión de un pliego del encargado de negocios de Portugal en Estados Unidos para el ministro de su gobierno en España. Hay dos ejemplares.

1.383

N.º 1.525. — 19 de septiembre, Filadelfia.

Envía noticias de América del Sur: en Bogotá se había descubierto una conspiración que trataba de asesinar al presidente Santander; en Cartagena hubo desavenencias muy serias con el cónsul de Francia; en Venezuela el congreso había expedido una serie de decretos, siendo los más notables, abolición de los diezmos, concesión de tierras y ciertos derechos a los extranjeros que se situasen en la Guayana, y el principio de un tratado de comercio con Francia; en Buenos Aires y Chile se seguía la guerra contra los indios. Hay dos ejemplares.

1.384

N.º 1.527. — 28 de septiembre, Filadelfia.

Participa el nombramiento de un nuevo secretario de Hacienda para el gobierno americano, por haberse negado su antecesor a cumplir lo que le mandaba el presidente de que no continuase depositando en el banco de los Estados Unidos los ingresos de las aduanas y otras rentas del Estado. Hay dos ejemplares.

1.385

N.º 1.528. — 28 de septiembre, Filadelfia.

Participa que el cólera estaba haciendo grandes estragos en Nueva España y especialmente entre las tropas que peleaban a las órdenes de Santa Ana y de Arista, habiendo perdido cerca de dos mil hombres cada uno de los bandos contendientes. Hay dos ejemplares.

1.386

N.º 1.529. — 29 de septiembre, Filadelfia.

Acusa recibo de varias reales cédulas. Hay dos ejemplares.

1.387

N.º 1.530. — 12 de octubre, Filadelfia.

Anuncia remisión de dos pliegos del encargado de negocios de Portugal. Hay dos ejemplares.

1.388

N.º 1.531. — 13 de octubre, Filadelfia.

Quedaba enterado de la orden relativa a la manutención de los correos de gabinete y daría cumplimiento. Hay dos ejemplares.

1.389

N.º 1.532. — 13 de octubre, Filadelfia.

Dice que el cólera seguía en Nueva España, donde se suponía habían muerto más de diez y seis mil personas, habiendo llegado a suspenderse las operaciones militares por falta de tropa.

1.390

N.º 1.533. — 14 de octubre, Filadelfia.

Participa que la atención pública continuaba ocupada en los negocios del banco de Estados Unidos. Hay dos ejemplares.

1.391

N.º 1.534. — 25 de octubre, Filadelfia.

Dice que había comunicado a los jefes de las legaciones las medidas que debían observar con los buques procedentes de los **Países Bajos** en donde se había producido el cólera.

1.392

N.º 1.535. — 26 de octubre, Filadelfia.

Acusa recibo de su oficio donde le hablaba de la aparición de enfermedades sospechosas en la villa de Huelva. Hay dos ejemplares.

1.393

N.º 1.536. — 26 de octubre, Filadelfia.

Acusa recibo de la orden relativa a lo dispuesto acerca de los individuos que solicitaran pasaporte para el Brasil. Hay dos ejemplares.

1.394

N.º 1.537. — 27 de octubre, Filadelfia.

Informa de que las gacetas de Bogotá habían publicado el tratado acordado entre su gobierno y Francia, en el que se estipulaba que los agentes diplomáticos de ambos países gozarían de los mismos privilegios que los de cualquier otra nación. En Nueva España había disminuido la epidemia y las tropas de Santa Ana y Arista, renovaron sus hostilidades. Hay dos ejemplares.

1.395

N.º 1.538. — 27 de octubre, Filadelfia.

Da parte del nombramiento de Daniel de Richmond, para fiscal general de Estados Unidos. Hay dos ejemplares.

1.396

N.º 1.539. — 29 de octubre, Filadelfia.

Acusa recibo de la carta credencial que le acreditaba cerca del gobierno americano como enviado extraordinario y ministro plenipotenciario de España, la que presentaría próximamente. Hay dos ejemplares.

1.397

N.º 1.540. — 29 de octubre, Filadelfia.

Acusa recibo de varias reales órdenes.

1.398

N.º 1.541. — 11 de noviembre, Washington.

Da cuenta de haberse trasladado con la legación a Washington y de haber presentado sus credenciales. Hay dos ejemplares.

1.399

N.º 1.542. — 18 de noviembre, Washington.

Remite un número de «El Redactor», donde se inserta la correspondencia entablada entre el jefe del apostadero de la Martinica, el comandante de dos corbetas francesas y el gobernador de Cartagena, relativo a la satisfacción que piden los primeros por el arresto del cónsul de su nación. Hay dos ejemplares.

Adjunto:

— «El Redactor» (Nueva York, 9 de noviembre 1833).

1.400

N.º 1.543. — 20 de noviembre, Washington.

Dice que había trasladado al cónsul general español en Estados Unidos, la orden disponiendo que ninguno de los cónsules españoles en el extranjero pudiese hacer ningún nombramiento sin autorización del rey. Hay dos ejemplares.

1.401

N.º 1.544. — 20 de noviembre, Washington.

Da cuenta de que los comerciantes españoles residentes en Estados Unidos, ya establecidos o solo temporalmente, no gozaban de ningún fuero particular en las causas civiles o criminales.

1.402

N.º 1.545. — 21 de noviembre, Washington.

Comunica el nombramiento del nuevo fiscal general, y que continuaban experimentándose desgracias en los buques de vapor, habiéndose incendiado dos últimamente. Hay dos ejemplares.

1.403

N.º 1.546. — 30 de noviembre, Washington.

Acusa recibo de varias reales órdenes.

1.404

N.º 1.547. — 1 de diciembre, Washington.

Da cuenta de haber llegado a Buenos Aires más de cuatrocientos emigrados de las islas Canarias, para establecerse en este país.

1.405

N.º 1.548. — 1 de diciembre, Washington.

Dice que se había arrestado a la persona que insultó al presidente de Estados Unidos. Hay dos ejemplares.

1.406

N.º 1.549. — 1 de diciembre, Washington.

Sigue dando noticias de Nueva España donde Santa Ana había obligado a rendirse a Arista después de un reñido encuentro. Hay dos ejemplares.

1.407

N.º 1.550. — 4 de diciembre, Washington.

Manifiesta su sentimiento por el fallecimiento del rey, rogándole lo transmitiera a la reina gobernadora.

1.408

N.ºs 1.551-1.552. — 4 de diciembre, Washington.

Informa de que había entregado al presidente de la Unión la noticia oficial del fallecimiento del rey de España, así como de haber presentado sus credenciales como ministro plenipotenciario de la reina Isabel II, representada por su madre como regente.

1.409

N.º 1.553. — 5 de diciembre, Washington.

Acusa recibo del oficio que le incluía las cláusulas del testamento de Fernando VII en virtud de las cuales instituía a la reina regente y gobernadora durante la menor edad de su hija primogénita Isabel II, todo lo cual lo comunicaría al gobierno de estos Estados.

1.410

N.º 1.554. — 5 de diciembre, Washington.

Promete comunicar al gobierno americano los principios que seguiría la regencia de España durante la menor edad de la reina Isabel II. Hay dos ejemplares.

1.411

N.º 1.556. — 5 de diciembre, Washington.

Remite el mensaje del presidente americano al empezar las sesiones del congreso, donde había procedido a la aprobación de los poderes de los nuevos senadores y diputados. En relación con los asuntos de España ponía de manifiesto el deseo de su gobierno de que se igualasen los derechos de tonelaje en los puertos de Estados Unidos y en los de España en los buques de ambas naciones haciendo una especial mención a Cuba y Puerto Rico. Hacía referencia también a las medidas adoptadas para acelerar la entrega a Estados Unidos de los archivos de las Floridas. El resto del discurso estaba dedicado a tratar del estado de las relaciones con otras potencias extranjeras y a asuntos internos del país como el próspero estado de la Hacienda pública, lo que permitiría en un plazo corto la extinción de la deuda nacional; las negociaciones con las tribus de los indios; las propuestas de los secretarios de Guerra y Marina para mejorar sus respectivos departamentos, etc.

Adjunto:
— Recorte de gaceta con el mensaje de Jackson (Washington, 3 de diciembre 1833).

1.412

N.º 1.557. — 10 de diciembre, Washington.

Remite la traducción completa del discurso del presidente americano.

Adjunto:
— «The Globe», con el mensaje de Jackson completo (Washington, 3 de diciembre 1833). Hay dos ejemplares.

1.413

N.º 1.558. — 10 de diciembre, Washington.

Remite la carta del presidente americano en contestación a la de la reina participando a los Estados Unidos el fallecimiento del rey y la accesión al trono de su hija doña Isabel.

1.414

N.º 1.559. — 21 de diciembre, Washington.

Acusa recibo del oficio en que le comunicaba el fallecimiento de Fernando VII, así como la carta credencial que le acreditaba cerca del gobierno americano. Hay dos ejemplares.

1.415

N.º 1.560. — 21 de diciembre, Washington.

Hace un extracto de las memorias de los secretarios de Guerra, Marina y Hacienda presentadas en el congreso de la Unión. El de Guerra manifestaba una disminución en las deserciones y mayor facilidad para los alistamientos, anunciaba la formación de un regimiento de dragones, que sería de gran utilidad en el servicio contra los indios. El secretario de Marina hacía una enumeración de los barcos, soldados, oficiales y la suma de gastos generales de la armada, recomendando la construcción de algunos buques más. El secretario de Hacienda presentaba las cuentas correspondientes al año con un balance positivo y decía que el presupuesto para 1834 comprendía el pago total de la deuda pública. Hay dos ejemplares.

1.416

N.º 1.561. — 22 de diciembre, Washington.

Comunica que Santa Ana había vuelto a encargarse de la presidencia en Méjico y que había expedido un decreto reconociendo al difunto Agustín Iturbide como uno de los principales autores de la independencia mejicana. Hay dos ejemplares.

1.417

N.º 1.562. — 31 de diciembre, Washington.

Anuncia remisión de la exposición de Manuel Martínez de Morentin, comandante de tiradores, ofreciendo sus servicios desde Connecticut, al gobierno de la reina.

1.418

N.º 1.563. — 31 de diciembre, Washington.

Participa que continuaban las sesiones del congreso en la Unión, siendo de destacar lo relativo a los depósitos que se hacían en el banco de los Estados Unidos y que por disposición del presidente se habían trasladado a otros bancos de los diferentes estados. Hay dos ejemplares.

1.419

N.º 1.564. — 31 de diciembre, Washington.

Acusa recibo de varias reales órdenes.

S U M A R I O

entrega de Florida occidental. — Transporte de las tropas españolas que abandonaban las Floridas. — Noticias sobre los insurgentes de la América española, aparecidas en las gacetas estado-unidenses.

Correspondencia de Joaquín Anduaga, ministro plenipotenciario en Estados Unidos, con el secretario de Estado, Escudero.

Arbitrariedades de Jackson en las Floridas; expulsión de oficiales españoles. — Relación de las fuerzas existentes en Venezuela, movimientos de Bolívar, capitulaciones de Cumaná y Cartagena. — Mensaje de Monroe al congreso. — El general Morales había salido del puerto de Santo Tomás con mil hombres.

LEGAJO 5.648

Año 1822

Correspondencia del ministro plenipotenciario Joaquín Anduaga con sucesivos secretarios de Estado.

Reconocimiento por el rey de Portugal de la independencia de Buenos Aires. — Reclamaciones de Ricardo Meade, vicecónsul de Estados Unidos en Cádiz. — Mociones presentadas en el congreso para el reconocimiento de los nuevos gobiernos de América. — El emperador de Rusia había tomado disposiciones para que sólo a su nación se permitiera comerciar y pescar en la costa noroeste de América. — Desechadas por el congreso las acusaciones españolas contra Jackson. — El astrónomo Lambert fija la altitud del capitolio de Washington. — El senado había aprobado un presupuesto para el envío de ministros a los gobiernos insurgentes de la América española. — Epidemia en Washington y Nueva York. — Ratificación del tratado de comercio entre Estados Unidos y Francia.

LEGAJO 5.649

Año 1823

Correspondencia de Joaquín de Anduaga con la secretaría de Estado.

Protesta de Robert Treal Spence, oficial de Marina, contra el decreto relativo a los extranjeros que se hallasen en Venezuela y contra el bloqueo que había impuesto el general Morillo. — Interpretaciones sobre la entrega del armamento que había en las Floridas y la provisión de víveres para las tropas. — Pleitos de consolidación. — Intentos de desembarcos americanos en las costas de Cuba, con el pretexto de perseguir a los piratas. — Nombramientos que había efectuado el presidente americano. — Auxilios a náufragos y prisioneros. — Petición de la cámara de representantes para extinguir el tráfico de negros.

Correspondencia del encargado de negocios en Estados Unidos, Hilario Rivas y Salmón.

Establecimiento en las Floridas de un tribunal que decidiera las causas referentes al traspaso al gobierno de Estados Unidos de las reclamaciones que hubiera pendientes contra el de España. — Disolución de la comisión de límites entre las tierras españolas y las de Estados Unidos. — Ayudas a náufragos y prisioneros. — Epidemias en Norteamérica; cuarentena que tenían que hacer los buques de Estados Unidos en Mahón. — Pleitos contra piratas americanos.

LEGAJO 5.650

Año 1824

Correspondencia del encargado de negocios en Estados Unidos, Hilario Rivas Salmón, con el conde de Ofalia y Cea Bermúdez, secretarios de Estado.

En Estados Unidos se había promovido una suscripción a favor de Grecia. — Informe sobre candidatos a la presidencia. — Los gobiernos de Colombia y Méjico habían acordado enviar una expedición contra Cuba. — Noticias de los insurgentes en las provincias de la América española. — En Filadelfia se había introducido una sociedad secreta llamada de los Carbonarios, contra la familia de los Borbones. — Necesidad de ayuda económica para atender a los españoles expulsados de Colombia. — Convenio de Estados Unidos con Rusia por el que renunciaba esta potencia al ucase que excluía a los extranjeros, del norte del Pacífico. — Armamento de barcos en Estados Unidos a favor de los insurgentes. — Vuelta de Bolívar a Lima; el general Olañeta se había pasado a los insurgentes proclamando la independencia del Perú; llegada de Iturbide al Soto de la Marina. — El general Lafayette estaba siendo muy obsequiado en Nueva York y Boston. — Bloqueo de Callao por buques colombianos y peruanos; conspiración en la ciudad a favor de los insurgentes. — Lord Cochrane se había apoderado de Pernambuco. — Despachos del duque de San Carlos y del marqués de Casa Irujo, representantes de España en París, con noticias de los gobiernos insurgentes de América.

LEGAJO 5.651

Año 1825

Correspondencia del encargado de negocios en Estados Unidos, Hilario Rivas Salmón, con los secretarios de Estado Francisco Cea Bermúdez y el duque del Infantado.

Establecimiento de fanales en algunos islotes de las Bahamas. — Reclamaciones por los perjuicios causados a españoles al ocupar las Floridas las tropas americanas. — Propuesta de Monroe para acabar con la piratería pidiendo se le autorizara para hacer desembarcos en Cuba y Puerto Rico y para bloquear los puertos que creyera convenientes, lo que supondría una intervención en los asuntos de España y sus islas. — Noticias sobre la guerra del Perú. — Elección de John Quincy Adams para presidente de Estados Unidos. — El ejército realista había sido vencido el 9 de diciembre en Huamanguilla y se había tenido que entregar la fortaleza del Callao; noticias de la batalla de Ayacucho. — El gobierno francés había dado libertad a los negros de Haití por una suma de dinero y privilegios mercantiles. — Tratado de alianza entre la república de Colombia y la de Guatemala obligándose a rechazar cualquier demanda de indemnización que le pudiera hacer el gobierno español por la pérdida de su soberanía sobre aquellos países. — Nombramiento de Francisco Tacón para ministro residente en Estados Unidos. — Rendición del castillo de San Juan de Ulúa. — Correspondencia de los ministros españoles en París y Londres con Cea Bermúdez, sobre asuntos de América.

LEGAJO 5.652

Año 1826

Correspondencia de Hilario Rivas Salmón con el duque del Infantado y con Manuel González Salmón, secretarios de Estado.

El gobierno de Buenos Aires había incorporado a su república, la banda oriental y amenazaba con la guerra al emperador del Brasil; Bolívar había llamado a las armas a los esclavos criollos de esta última nación; tratado de alianza entre Méjico y Colombia. — Rendición de Callao; expedición contra Cuba. — Reconocimiento del congreso mejicano por algunas potencias europeas. — Expedición chilena contra Chiloé. — Estado de las fuerzas marítimas de Colombia y Méjico. — El emperador del Brasil había abdicado la corona de Portugal en su hija María. — El comandante americano Poter había entrado al servicio de Méjico y podría perjudicar los intereses españoles. — Insurrección de Páez en Colombia. — Congreso de Panamá. — Conspiración de negros en Puerto Rico. — La escuadra del general Laborde había sido destrozada entre la Habana y Costa Firme. — Convención de comercio y navegación entre Estados Unidos y Dinamarca. — Conspiración contra Bolívar en el Perú. — Muerte del emperador Alejandro de Rusia. — Noticias sobre la anarquía reinante en Guatemala.

LEGAJO 5.653

Año 1827

Correspondencia de Hilario Rivas y del ministro en Estados Unidos, Francisco Tacón, con Manuel González Salmón.

Noticias relativas a la guerra entre Guatemala y Colombia. — Bolívar había disuelto el congreso y tomado el mando absoluto de la república; Páez se había sometido al libertador. — Tratado de comercio y navegación entre Estados Unidos y Méjico. — Proyecto de expedición contra Cuba y Puerto Rico. — Se acusa a Poinsett, ministro de Estados Unidos en Méjico, de intervenir en los asuntos internos del país. — Bolívar pensaba dirigirse desde Cartagena a Bogotá, para reducir al vicepresidente Santander. — La gaceta de Nueva York trata de la feliz actuación en Cuba del general Vives. — Decreto del congreso de Méjico expulsando a los españoles que estuvieran residiendo en el país desde 1824. — Francia y las provincias Hanseáticas habían reconocido la independencia de Colombia. — Balanza del comercio de Cuba. — Los agentes de Francia en Colombia habían tomado ya el título de cónsules. — Conflictos con los indios en distintos puntos de la Unión.

LEGAJO 5.654

Año 1828

Correspondencia de Francisco Tacón con González Salmón.

Acuerdo comercial entre Estados Unidos y las provincias Hanseáticas. — Cuestiones sobre propiedad de los esclavos. — Terremoto en Bogotá. — Reconocimiento de las posesiones del marqués de Casa Irujo en las Floridas. — Infracción de la neutralidad por el aventurero Porter y por otros americanos. — La guerra civil seguía destruyendo las provincias de Nicaragua, San Salvador y Guatemala. — Insurrecciones en Méjico. — Reconocimiento por la S. S. de los obispos que había nombrado Bolívar. — Un hijo de Luciano Bonaparte y su familia, que durante varios años habían residido en Estados Unidos, pasaban a fijar su domicilio en Italia. — Insurrección de los negros de Omoa. —

Elogios del general Vives en el desempeño de su cargo de capitán general de Cuba. — Se acentúa el número de pasajeros que procedentes de Méjico pretendían pasar a Europa. — Convención de Ocaña. — El gobierno de Perú toma precauciones contra los colombianos. — Cerca de San Pedro de Río Grande, se esperaba tuvieran un encuentro las tropas del emperador del Brasil y el ejército de Buenos Aires. — Tratado de navegación y comercio entre Estados Unidos y los gobiernos de Suecia y Noruega. — Arancel aumentando los derechos de importación en Estados Unidos. — Estado de anarquía en Méjico. — Preparativos de la escuadra de la Habana para bloquear el puerto de Veracruz. — Epidemia en Charleston. — Noticias sobre el conde Moctezuma. — Las autoridades de la Guayra declaran a Bolívar jefe supremo de Colombia. — Composición de la escuadra del gobierno de Buenos Aires. — El general holandés Verveer había asistido, comisionado por su gobierno, al congreso de Panamá y Tacubaya. — Comisión al francés Bresson para visitar Méjico y otros puntos de América española, con el fin de dar a su gobierno un informe del estado de esas provincias. — Informes sobre el hijo de Iturbide, que ambicionaba establecer en Méjico un gobierno favorable a sus proyectos; se había embarcado para Cartagena de Indias y mantenía correspondencia con Bolívar. — El general Santa Ana que había sido suspendido en su cargo de vicegobernador, se había levantado en armas dispuesto a mantener la elección de Guerrero como presidente de Méjico, a pesar de que había resultado Pedraza vencedor. — Bolívar había ordenado un alistamiento para la guerra del Perú. — Proyectos de abrir un canal en el mar Pacífico. — Tratado de paz entre el emperador del Brasil y el gobierno de Buenos Aires. — Conspiración en Bogotá con resultado favorable a Bolívar. — Se confirma la presidencia de Méjico al general Gómez Pedraza. — El gobierno insurgente del Perú se prepara para la guerra, habiendo levantado la orden de destierro a Manuel Lorenzo Vidaurre. — Bloqueo de los puertos colombianos, decretado por el gobierno del Perú.

LEGAJO 5.655

Año 1829

Correspondencia del ministro en Estados Unidos, Francisco Tacón, con el secretario de Estado, Manuel González Salmón.

En noviembre anterior Obando se había apoderado de la plaza de Popayán. — Suspensión de la comisión de Mr. Bresson a las Américas españolas. — Proyecto presentado al congreso para autorizar al presidente a la construcción de las fortalezas en la embocadura del río Oregón. — Tratado de comercio entre Estados Unidos y el Brasil. — El gobernador de Nueva Orleans debía de entrar en correspondencia con el capitán general de Cuba a fin de obtener la entrega de títulos y documentos depositados en la Habana, relacionados con propiedades en las Floridas. — Ocupación de Cumalagua por las tropas de Centeno. — Revolución en Buenos Aires y elección de Lavalle como gobernador. — Elección de Andrés Jackson como presidente de Estados Unidos. — Los valles de Cauca se habían declarado a favor de Bolívar, quien había nombrado capitán de sus ejércitos a un hijo de Iturbide. — Se reconoce de nuevo a Vicente Guerrero como presidente de Méjico, menos las provincias de Guadalajara y Zacatecas. — Arreglo del archivo de la legación por Francisco de Paula Quadrado. — Elección de Loaysa por presidente de Bolivia. — Contrarrevolución en Nicaragua. — Robos y saqueos en Sombrerete. — Se apoderan los norteamericanos del presidio de San Francisco. — El coronel Montenegro residente en Nueva Orleans, se dedicaba a observar la conducta de los emigrados de Méjico y también probablemente, a preparar la insurrección de Cuba. — Relación de las donaciones de tierras que se hicieron entre 1823 y 1824, y las ventas y repartos verificados entre 1801 a 1818. — Convenio de Estados Unidos con el emperador de Austria sobre impuestos de toneladas a los buques. — Críticas contra el nuevo gobierno de Estados Unidos por la renovación de cargos. — Convenios de Estados Unidos con las tribus indias. — Entrada de Bolívar en Guayaquil. — Planes de Bravo y otros insurgentes de Méjico para alarmar a España respecto a la isla de Cuba. — Arribada forzosa en Nueva Orleans de la fragata Bingham que conducía 500 soldados españoles salidos de la Habana; reclamación de un desertor. — Nombramiento de van Ness para ministro de Estados Unidos en España.

LEGAJO 5.656

Año 1830

Correspondencia de Francisco Tacón, ministro español en Estados Unidos con el secretario de Estado, Manuel González Salmón.

Reaparición en Nueva Orleans del periódico «El Español». — Aprobación de una propuesta para que pudiesen usar los libros de la biblioteca del congreso, los ex-presidentes de Estados Unidos, los secretarios de Estado y los ministros extranjeros residentes en Washington. — Llegada a Nueva York de un nuevo representante de Méjico. — Tratados con algunas tribus indias sobre cesión de tierras. — Modificación de aranceles. — Medalla de oro enviada por el gobierno de Colombia en conmemoración de la libertad de Bolívar. — Sueldos a los ministros y cónsules americanos en el extranjero. — Proclama de Ángel Laborde imponiendo la pena capital a los marineros que se pasaran al servicio de Méjico. — Oposición del estado de Georgia a dar cumplimiento a los tratados acordados con los indios. — Se aprueba la introducción de frutos de un país extranjero con el 3 % de impuestos. — Regreso de Poinsett a Estados Unidos; se confirma la mala situación de Méjico. — Preliminares de un tratado comercial entre Estados Unidos y Haití. — Los colonos franceses tenían poca posibilidad de subsistir en Nicaragua. — Nombramientos. — Los indios fronterizos con el estado de Georgia, se habían establecido más allá del Mississipi, mediante una indemnización. — Tratado entre Estados Unidos y Dinamarca para liquidar las reclamaciones de los americanos. — Llegada a Nueva York de soldados desertores españoles de los que pasaron a Portugal en 1826. — El jefe de los indios choctaws se había presentado como candidato al congreso. — Disturbios en Bogotá y en Veracruz. — Llega a Nueva York un hijo del general rebelde Miranda, destinado a Londres como secretario de la legación de Bogotá. — Análisis del estado de Méjico desde su independencia. — Descontento en Carolina del Sur y otros estados, provocado por las disposiciones mercantiles. — Tratado entre Estados Unidos y el gobierno turco, por el que se aseguraba a la Unión el libre paso por el mar Negro. — Apresamiento de la goleta Fénix por la de Estados Unidos, Grampus. — Proyecto para la reconquista de Nueva España. — Presunto asesinato de José de la Luz Machado a bordo de una balandra americana. — Gran Bretaña abre los puertos de sus posesiones coloniales a los buques de Estados Unidos en reciprocidad con esta nación. — Los emigrados franceses e italianos celebran en Nueva York la salida de Francia del rey Carlos X. — Suscripción en Nueva York para costear el transporte a Francia a los revolucionarios españoles residentes en esta ciudad con el fin de sublevar la península. — Discurso del presidente Jackson y memorias de los ministros de Guerra, Marina y Hacienda, y del director de Correos. — Protesta del capitán del bergantín americano Elisabeth por agresión a su barco desde Matanzas.

LEGAJO 5.657

Año 1831

Correspondencia de don Francisco Tacón, ministro en Estados Unidos, con el secretario de Estado don Manuel González Salmón.

El senado aprueba la concesión de una cantidad para fletar dos buques destinados a prestar auxilio a las embarcaciones de las costas, dañadas por un terrible temporal. — Expedición científica del príncipe Pablo Guillermo de Witemberg por América septentrional. — El gobierno francés reconoce la independencia del Uruguay. — Folleto sobre las luchas con los indios seminoles durante el gobierno de Monroe, y la ocupación de las Floridas por Jackson. — El congreso ratifica el tratado de navegación y comercio con Turquía y el convenio con los indios choctaws. — Designación de George Erving como encargado de negocios en Constantinopla. — Las autoridades de la Habana y de Puerto Rico contratan en Estados Unidos la fabricación de un pontón de vapor para la limpieza de los puertos. — Reclamación de los indios cherokees contra el estado de Georgia. — Oposición al gobierno de Jackson. — Arbitraje del rey Guillermo de los Países Bajos, en el litigio entre Estados Unidos e Inglaterra por cuestión de límites en el estado de Maine. — Varios ministros presentan su dimisión al presidente Jackson. — David Porter sucede a Erving como encargado de negocios en Turquía. — Revolución en el Brasil. — Inspección de las cárceles de Estados Unidos por magistrados franceses. — Nombramiento de Eduardo Livingston para secretario de Estado. — Apresamiento de la goleta española Fénix por la de Estados Unidos, Grampus. — Los herederos del cónsul José Mulvey se niegan a entregar los archivos del consulado de Charleston, al sucesor en el cargo. — Fracaso de las negociaciones entabladas entre el cónsul francés y el gobierno de Haití. — Desavenencias del general mejicano Barragán con Bustamente. — Fallecimiento del ex-presidente Monroe. — Recuperación de joyas robadas a la princesa de Orange. — Sublevación de negros en Southampton. — Convenio comercial de Francia con Estados Unidos. — Huracán en la isla Barbada. — Propuesta para excluir de los destinos públicos a los masones. — Sublevación de negros en la isla de la Tórtola. — Estudios sobre aplicación de nuevos aranceles en Estados Unidos. — Proyecto de tratado de Estados Unidos con Portugal. — Noticias de Venezuela y Santa Fe. — Los individuos expatriados cuando se proclamó la constitución del emperador don Pedro de Portugal, no podían ser admitidos en territorio español. — Tratado sobre máquinas de vapor y sus aplicaciones, por Juan José Martínez. — Corsarios y buques de guerra dificultan el comercio americano con las antiguas colonias españolas. — Memorias y propuestas presentadas en el congreso de Estados Unidos por los ministros de Hacienda, Guerra y Marina, y el director general de Correos. — Autorización real para expulsar a los negros de la Habana.

LEGAJO 5.658

Año 1832

Correspondencia del ministro en Estados Unidos Francisco Tacón, con los secretarios de Estado, conde de la Alcudia y José Cafranga.

Nombramientos de altos cargos y de plenipotenciarios y encargados de negocios en el extranjero. — Renovación de la guerra entre unitarios y federalistas, en Buenos Aires. — Incendio desvastador en Santo Tomás. — Sublevación de negros en Cornwall. — Se renueva la guerra civil en Guatemala. — La convención de Bogotá había decidido la separación de Colombia de la república de Venezuela. — Conspiración de los pardos de Santa Marta, Cartagena y Mompós, contra los blancos. — Amenazas de revoluciones en Méjico. — Noticias de guerras en las repúblicas de Centroamérica. — Levantamiento de la guarnición de Veracruz para poner al general Santa Ana al frente de la república. — Protesta contra el comandante del fuerte de Matanzas por haber abierto fuego contra un bergantín americano. — Medidas sanitarias en Cádiz para evitar la propagación del cólera morbo. — Intercambio de semillas de

Estados Unidos con el Jardín Botánico de Madrid. — Festejos en el centenario del nacimiento de Jorge Washington. — Protesta por haberse hecho fuego desde el fuerte de Tarifa contra buques americanos. — Disturbios en Costa Firme. — Combates en Méjico entre las tropas de Santa Ana y las del general Santander. — Convenio entre Estados Unidos y Méjico sobre límites. — El general Santander es elegido presidente de Nueva Granada. — Apresamiento en Nueva Orleans del buque español Dos Amigos, por llevar a bordo un negro, esclavo del dueño del barco. — Sublevación en Pernambuco y Río de Janeiro a favor del restablecimiento en el trono del rey Pedro. — Bloqueo de la isla y puerto de Funchal. — Intentos del gobierno de Venezuela para atraer la emigración de las islas Canarias. — Enfrentamientos de los norteamericanos con los indios de Missouri. — Protesta por el armamento en Nueva Orleans de la goleta mejicana Veracruzana, que pretendía hostilizar el comercio español. — El general Gómez Pedraza rechaza la presidencia de Méjico. — Salida de Estados Unidos de José Bonaparte. — Epidemia de cólera en Nueva York. — Noticias de disturbios en Brasil, Méjico y Perú. — Obras para el abastecimiento de agua a la Habana. — Graves incendios en Puerto Príncipe. — Alteraciones producidas por la modificación de aranceles. — Discurso del presidente en la sesión de apertura del congreso dando cuenta de las relaciones de Estados Unidos con distintas naciones, y del estado satisfactorio de la hacienda pública. — Convención en Columbia para estudiar los derechos e impuestos decretados para proteger las manufacturas nacionales. — Memorias presentadas al congreso por los secretarios de Hacienda y Marina.

LEGAJO 5.659

Año 1833

Correspondencia del ministro en Estados Unidos, Francisco Tacón, con los secretarios de Estado, José Cafranga y Francisco Cea Bermúdez.

Proclama del presidente de Estados Unidos relativa a la nulificación o anulación de los aranceles. — Armisticio celebrado en Méjico entre las tropas de Santa Ana y las de Bustamante. — Tratado entre el rey de las Dos Sicilias y el presidente de Estados Unidos, sobre pago de deudas por daños, a los comerciantes americanos. — Reelección de Jackson para presidente de Estados Unidos y de Martín van Buren, como vicepresidente. — Los ingleses se apoderan de las Malvinas. — Tratado entre el reino de Nueva Granada y El Ecuador, reconociéndose recíprocamente como estados independientes. — Designación de Agustín de Iturbide como encargado de negocios de Méjico en Estados Unidos. — Llegada de emigrados de Canarias a la Guaira. — Tratado de comercio entre Francia y Venezuela. — Elección del general Santa Ana como presidente de Méjico. — Tratado de comercio entre Rusia y Estados Unidos. — Traslado de la residencia de la legación de España, a Washington. — Emigrados de las islas Canarias llegan a Montevideo y a Buenos Aires, para establecerse como colonos. — Noticias de conspiraciones y disturbios en varios países de América del Sur. — Fallecimiento de Fernando VII. — Mensaje del presidente aludiendo al deseo de Estados Unidos de convenir con España en igualar los derechos de tonelaje en los puertos. — Extracto de las memorias presentadas al congreso por los secretarios de Guerra, Marina y Hacienda. — Agustín Iturbide es reconocido como uno de los principales autores de la independencia mejicana.

ÍNDICE ALFABÉTICO